THE EUROPEAN FOOTBALL YEARBOOK 96/97

OVER 1200 PAGES

General Editor **MIKE HAMMOND** Published by **SPORTS PROJECTS LTD**

ICELAND
Arctic Circle
NORWAY
FAROE ISLANDS
SWEDEN
Baltic Sea
NORTHERN IRELAND
SCOTLAND
North Sea
DENMARK
REPUBLIC OF IRELAND
WALES
ENGLAND
LITHUAN
RUSSIA
HOLLAND
BELGIUM
GERMANY
POLAND
LUXEMBOURG
CZECH REPUBLIC
Bay of Biscay
FRANCE
SLOVAKIA
LIECHTENSTEIN
SWITZER-LAND
AUSTRIA
HUNGARY
SLOVENIA
CROATIA
YUGOSLAVIA
BOSNIA-HERZEGOVINA
PORTUGAL
SPAIN
ANDORRA
MONACO
ITALY
SAN MARINO
CORSICA (Fr)
VATICAN CITY
ALBANIA
MA
DO
SARDINIA (It)
GREEC
Mediterranean
SICILY
MALTA

THE EUROPEAN FOOTBALL YEARBOOK 1996/97

ACKNOWLEDGEMENTS

The European Football Yearbook 1996/97
First Published in Great Britain by Sports Projects Ltd
November 1996

188 Lightwoods Hill, Smethwick, Warley, West Midlands,
B67 5EH, England

ISBN 0 946866 37 6 (paperback)
ISBN 0 946866 38 4 (hardback)

Printed in Great Britain

General Editor
Mike Hammond

Editorial and Research Co-ordinators
Lakis Avramides, Mert Aydin, José Del Olmo, András Dénes, Tamás Dénes, Dimcho Dimitrov Ivanov, Marshall Gillespie, Michael Hansen, Peter Hekkema, Gevorg Hovhannisyan, Romeo Ionescu, Valery Karpoushkin, Skifter Këlliçi, Amiran Kharatishvili, Daniel Kolbusch, Jean-Paul Kolbusch, Dragan Krstic, Zdenek Kucera, Esko S. Lahtinen, Dag Lindholm, Margus Luik, Robert McElroy, Kevin McNamara, Theodore Mantzouranis, Francesco Mascalchi, Kazimierz Oleszek, Barbara Ospelt, Alexander Pauk, Humberto M. Pereira Silva, Zdravko Reic, Mike Ritter, Revaz Shenguelia, Vídir Sigurdsson, Andrej Stare, Janne Stark, Algimantas Staskevicius, Edouard Stutz, Matej Széher, Mel ap ior Thomas, Serge Van Hoof, Victor Vassallo, Stefan Welte, Rufat Zeynalov, Luciano Zinelli, Jacob Ziv.

Special thanks to
Steven Bergström, Susan Hammond, Jeanine Rohner, June Smallbone.

Photographs:
Empics Ltd, Sports Projects Ltd and courtesy of featured clubs

Design, layout and graphics:
Nadine Goldingay, Phil Lees and Vic Millward

Cover design:
Bernard Gallagher

COMMENT BY MIKE HAMMOND 6
EUROPEAN CHAMPIONSHIPS 1996
FINALS 8
QUALIFYING GROUPS 32
WORLD CUP 1998
FINALS SCHEDULE 48
EUROPEAN QUALIFYING FIXTURES 49
EUROPEAN CUPS 1995/96
UEFA CHAMPIONS' LEAGUE 54
CUP-WINNERS' CUP 68
UEFA CUP 76
QUALIFIERS 96/97 88
MISCELLANEOUS 90
INTRODUCTION TO NATIONS/CLUBS 92
ALBANIA 93
ARMENIA 117
AUSTRIA 120
AZERBAIJAN 138
BELARUS 142
BELGIUM 164
BOSNIA-HERZEGOVINA 190
BULGARIA 192
CROATIA 216
CYPRUS 238
CZECH REPUBLIC 258
DENMARK 283
ENGLAND 303
ESTONIA 334
FAROE ISLANDS 348
FINLAND 363
FRANCE 384
GEORGIA 415
GERMANY 437
GREECE 467
HOLLAND 493
HUNGARY 521
ICELAND 545
ISRAEL 561
TEAM STRIPS/CLUB & NATIONAL EMBLEMS
96-PAGE COLOUR SECTION
ITALY 584
LATVIA 614
LIECHTENSTEIN 630
LITHUANIA 633
LUXEMBOURG 654
MACEDONIA 672
MALTA 675
MOLDOVA 691
NORTHERN IRELAND 712
NORWAY 726
POLAND 747
PORTUGAL 773
REPUBLIC OF IRELAND 802
ROMANIA 821
RUSSIA 847
SAN MARINO 871
SCOTLAND 881
SLOVAKIA 899
SLOVENIA 918
SPAIN 935
SWEDEN 969
SWITZERLAND 991
TURKEY 1012
UKRAINE 1038
WALES 1063
YUGOSLAVIA 1091
CLOSE-SEASON TRANSFERS 1113

INTRODUCTION

Welcome to the 7th edition of the European Football Yearbook.

As the game continues to expand world-wide so does interest in our comprehensive publication.

At the last count the European Football Yearbook was circulating in almost 80 countries around the globe. Here's the full list:

Algeria, Andorra, Argentina, Australia, Austria, Belgium, Bolivia, Bosnia, Brazil, Bulgaria, Canada, Canary Islands, Chile, China, Colombia, Costa Rica, Croatia, Cyprus, Czech Republic, Denmark, Dubai, England, Equador, Estonia, Faroe Islands, Finland, France, Germany, Gibraltar, Greece, Guernsey, Holland, Honduras, Hong Kong, Hungary, Iceland, Indonesia, Iran, Ireland, Israel, Italy, Jamaica, Japan, Korea, Kuwait, Latvia, Lebanon, Lithuania, Luxembourg, Malaysia, Malta, Mexico, Monaco, New Zealand, Norway, Peru, Poland, Portugal, Qatar, Russia, Saudi Arabia, Scotland, Singapore, Slovenia, South Africa, Spain, Sweden, Switzerland, Taiwan, Turkey, Ukraine, United Arab Emirates, Uruguay, USA, Venezuela and Wales.

This year a new feature has been added to the book – maps of each country showing club locations. I hope you like the idea, which is one that has been suggested by many of our readers over the years.

As always your comments and suggestions, even criticisms, are welcome.

If any reader would like to become a contributor to this publication then please make contact at the publisher's address on the facing page, or at our new email address which is:

101320.3216@compuserve.com

BERNARD GALLAGHER
Publisher

COMMENT

An end, please, to this po-faced pragmatism

One of the most pleasing spectacles of Euro '96 occurred at half-time in the final. There was no football involved. The entertainment was provided by 'Half a Pint of Lager', one of those brass bands without whose jaunty melodies and rhythms no match involving the Dutch national team would be complete.

Yet Holland were not playing. This was the final between Germany and the Czech Republic at Wembley. Perhaps the band were appearing by public request. They certainly merited an encore. Their two familiar catchy numbers rang out to an ecstatic, flag-waving response from all those who had spurned the dubious pleasures of an over-priced sausage roll or fizzy drink and remained in their seats. It was a sound and sight to behold - fans from Germany, the Czech Republic, England and wherever else Euro '96 final tickets had been acquired simply joining together to lap up the atmosphere and have a good time. A last public-address airing of the unofficial Euro '96 theme "Three Lions" elicited the same enthusiastic reaction. It was audience participation at its most joyful.

Not very long ago, such a scene would have been impossible in an English football stadium. Any kind of common revelry with opposing fans would have been a non-starter. The men in orange would have been booed off the pitch before they had completed the first bar.

Euro '96 was glorious proof that things have changed,. that the angry young men who once bathed in the vainglorious title of 'English Football Hooligan' have been ostracised from the game. So many tales of impending doom were reported before the finals got underway. But the reality was a tournament in which the people of 16 nations came simply to have fun and enjoy themselves, and were allowed to do just that. Jovial fraternisation was plain to see at every Euro '96 venue. There was no hint that trouble would break out. The media heavy artillery were out in force waiting (hoping?) for something to happen, but they were wasting their time. The atmosphere was just as it should be for any major international sporting event - colourful, varied and good-humoured.

What a pity, then, that many of those fans were provided with so little by way of entertainment on the football field.

In terms of crowd involvement, security, policing and general organisation, everything ran as smoothly as could be imagined, and, in that respect, Euro '96 was a great success. But, in terms of the product itself - the football - the tournament was a disappointment.

With 16 finalists included for the first time, Euro '96 promised to be the greatest footballing extravaganza Europe had ever witnessed. The structure of the event itself was fine. And there was nothing inherently wrong with UEFA's decision to double the number of participating teams. It was the negative attitude of the coaches and the players that left so much to be desired. Unlike that Dutch brass band, the desire to entertain is not, apparently, a top priority for national football teams these days. It is often said - and understandably so - that the result is everything. But when winning ranks a distant second behind not losing, the time has come to look closely at what can be done to reverse the trend.

At Euro '96, only England, Portugal and, perhaps, Italy came out for every match with the overriding intention of taking the game to their opponents and beating them. The other teams were largely content to indulge in tactical warfare, favouring caution over endeavour and pragmatism over ingenuity. It was football with a frown. The licence to entertain had been withdrawn.

Too many players were slaves to the unadventurous, safety-first systems of their coach. Free spirits such as Rui Costa, Davor Suker and Paul Gascoigne were in all too short supply among the automatons. In a sport which permits a team of 11 players, why do so many coaches deploy just one of those players in a uniquely attacking rôle? The whole essence of football is scoring goals. If fewer players are sent onto the field for that purpose, fewer chances will be created and fewer goals will be scored. That is straightforward logic. So, why do so many teams play so defensively? It is not naïve to play gung-ho fantasy football and win 4-3. It's just fashionable to say that it is.

The players themselves must also take their share of the blame. At Euro '96 the general standard of football in the attacking third of the field was lamentable. One of the reasons why England's 4-1 victory over Holland was so thrilling was that the quality of England's attacking play was so much better than anything seen in the other matches. The final balls were accurate, the finishing was ruthless.

Overall, the shooting, especially from outside the penalty area, was extremely poor. The number of times that players sent the ball soaring into the crowd from an unchallenged position 20-25 yards out was as astonishing as it was depressing. The set-pieces were even worse. Hristo Stoichkov, of Bulgaria, was the only player in the entire

COMMENT

Football was finally handed back to the true fans during Euro '96

31-match tournament to score direct from a free-kick. There was very little artistry or invention from inviting dead-ball positions. On the evidence of Euro '96, the free-kick specialist is a dying breed; or maybe it was just that players such as Baggio, Cantona and Le Tissier were not brought to the tournament - three classic victims of the current preference for strategies over stars.

Whatever the systems analysts purporting to be coaches might argue, it is originality and flair rather than discipline and tactical awareness which will always appeal to the committed football spectator. By the same token, attackers will always be revered and idolised more than defenders. One day, maybe, the penny will drop.

The most exciting phase of Euro '96 was at the end of the first round, when teams had to come out of their shells and win matches in order to stay in the competition. The three-points-for-a-win formula once again proved its worth in a major tournament. Spain, for example, would not have been obliged to win their final match against Romania under the old two-point system. Three draws would have put them through ahead of Bulgaria on goal difference.

Because of this positive format, the opening round of the tournament was largely enjoyable and entertaining. There were some excellent matches - Denmark v Portugal, Italy v Czech Republic, England v Holland - and only two (out of a possible 24) goalless draws. The big let-down was the knock-out phase, where, once again, the penalty shoot-out dominated thoughts and priorities in its usual negative way.

Maybe it should be renamed the penalty cop-out, because, as was proved only too often at Euro '96, that is what it has now become. There is no denying that the drama of the shoot-out itself produces a riveting spectacle. It is exciting, nerve-wracking and makes the heart pound and flutter. But its looming presence at the end of a game presents teams with the opportunity to defend their way to victory. It goes against the basic sporting principle that the best team wins.

As for the newly-introduced 'Golden Goal', that will never work as long as the penalty shoot-out is written in as a get-out clause. If one accepts that in a major tournament it is not feasible for extra-time to be played *ad infinitum*, then the 'Golden Goal' serves no positive purpose. Given the prevailing attitudes witnessed at Euro '96, both teams will still defend rather than attack for the extra 30 minutes.

However, there would be a place for the 'Golden Goal' if the penalty shoot-out were staged at the end of 90 minutes, i.e. *before* extra-time.

Such a system would guarantee at least one team having to attack in the extra 30 minutes. If the loser of the shoot-out failed to score the 'Golden Goal', they would be eliminated. Knowing that victory could only be achieved by scoring a goal, they would have no option but to 'go for it'.

The winner of the shoot-out, on the other hand, would probably try to defend. Or would they? It would be a risky policy, because with the 'Golden Goal' in force - rather than the standard 30-minute extra-time period - there would be no way back if they made one defensive error and conceded a goal.

There is another point worth considering - one to which Gareth Southgate, Reynald Pedros, Clarence Seedorf and Miguel Angel Nadal will surely raise an arm. With the shoot-out being staged before extra-time, the pain of the unfortunate player who missed the vital penalty would be alleviated, because he would have a chance to redeem himself in the extra 30 minutes.

Admittedly, the shoot-out would not be so dramatic if it were not seen to be the 'final solution'. But surely that would be a price worth paying if it meant another 30 minutes ('Golden Goal' permitting) of genuine, crowd-pleasing football.

MIKE HAMMOND

EURO 96 FINALS Group A

England treat Wembley to a Dutch destruction

Euro '96, the third largest sporting event in the world and the biggest in England since the 1966 World Cup, got underway at Wembley stadium on June 8 with the Opening Match between England and Switzerland.

After two and a half years of shadow boxing, it was time for Terry Venables and his team to show what they were made of. The pre-tournament build-up had been soured by tales of drunkenness and debauchery on an ill-conceived trip to the Far East. But the message from the England headquarters at Bisham Abbey was that the team were fit and ready for the challenge.

Of all the countries participating at Euro '96, England would probably have selected Switzerland as their ideal opening opponents. They had beaten them 3-1 at Wembley in a friendly the previous November. And since qualifying in style under English coach Roy Hodgson, the Swiss had suffered declining fortunes under their new boss, Artur Jorge.

For both Artur Jorge and Terry Venables, it was the first competitive international in charge of their respective sides. The pressure was intense. A full house at Wembley greeted the two teams after a colourful and theatrical opening ceremony, during which the 76,567 spectators were fed a mixed selection of *hors d'oeuvres*, including St. George and the Dragon, Sir Stanley Matthews, and the Red Arrows.

England seized the initiative from the first minute and might even have scored with their first attack. The hosts looked the livelier, more inventive team. Midway through the half, and just a minute after full-back Gary Neville had burned Marco Pascolo's fingers with a long-range pile-driver, England took the lead. The scorer was Alan Shearer,

GROUP A MATCH DETAILS

08/06/96, Wembley
ENGLAND 1 Shearer (23)
SWITZERLAND 1 Türkyilmaz (82p)
referee - Díaz Vega (ESP)
ENGLAND - Seaman; Neville G., Adams, Southgate, Pearce; Anderton, Ince, Gascoigne (Platt 77), McManaman (Stone 69); Sheringham, Shearer.
SWITZERLAND - Pascolo; Jeanneret, Vega, Henchoz, Quentin; Vogel, Geiger (Koller 67), Sforza, Bonvin (Chapuisat 69); Grassi, Türkyilmaz.

11/06/96, Birmingham
HOLLAND 0
SCOTLAND 0
referee - Sundell (SWE)
HOLLAND - Van der Sar; Reiziger, Blind, Bogarde; De Boer R. (Winter 68), Davids, Seedorf, Witschge (Cocu 78); Taument (Kluivert 63), Bergkamp, Cruijff.
SCOTLAND - Goram; McKimmie (Burley 85), Calderwood, Hendry, Boyd; Gallacher (McKinlay B. 56), McCall, McAllister, Collins; Booth (Spencer 46), Durie.

13/06/96, Birmingham
SWITZERLAND 0
HOLLAND 2 Cruijff (66), Bergkamp (79)
referee - Ouzounov (BUL)
SWITZERLAND - Pascolo; Jeanneret (Comisetti 68), Vega, Henchoz, Quentin; Hottiger, Sforza, Vogel; Türkyilmaz, Grassi, Chapuisat.
HOLLAND - Van der Sar; Reiziger, Blind, Bogarde; De Boer R. (Davids 80), Winter, Seedorf (De Kock 26), Witschge; Cruijff (Kluivert 84), Bergkamp, Hoekstra.

15/06/96, Wembley
SCOTLAND 0
ENGLAND 2 Shearer (52), Gascoigne (79)
referee - Pairetto (ITA)
SCOTLAND - Goram; McKimmie, Calderwood, Hendry, Boyd; Collins, McCall, McAllister, McKinlay T. (Burley 82); Spencer (McCoist 67), Durie (Jess 87).
ENGLAND - Seaman; Neville G., Adams, Southgate, Pearce (Redknapp 46; Campbell 85); Anderton, Ince (Stone 80), Gascoigne, McManaman; Sheringham, Shearer.

18/06/96, Birmingham
SCOTLAND 1 McCoist (36)
SWITZERLAND 0
referee - Krondl (TCH)
SCOTLAND - Goram; Burley, Calderwood, Hendry, Boyd; Collins, McCall, McAllister, McKinlay T. (Booth 60); McCoist (Spencer 84), Durie.
SWITZERLAND - Pascolo; Hottiger, Vega, Henchoz, Quentin (Comisetti 80); Vogel, Koller (Wicky 46), Sforza; Türkyilmaz, Bonvin, Chapuisat.

18/06/96, Wembley
HOLLAND 1 Kluivert (78)
ENGLAND 4 Shearer (23p, 57), Sheringham (51, 62)
referee - Grabher (AUT)
HOLLAND - Van der Sar; Reiziger, Blind, Bogarde; Winter, Seedorf, De Boer R. (Kluivert 72), Witschge (De Kock 46); Cruijff, Bergkamp, Hoekstra (Cocu 72).
ENGLAND - Seaman; Neville G., Adams, Southgate, Pearce; McManaman, Ince (Platt 68), Gascoigne, Anderton; Sheringham (Barmby 76), Shearer (Fowler 76).

EURO 96 FINALS Group A

who latched on to a gentle rolling through-ball from Paul Ince and lashed the ball home off the inside of the near post with his right foot. It was Shearer's first goal for his country in almost two years. The relief and joy was evident as his team-mates mobbed him in celebration.

England were still 1-0 up at half-time, and with the pacy Steve McManaman and the skilful Paul Gascoigne calling the tune in midfield, the home side looked to be well in control. Nevertheless, the Swiss spurned the best chance of the game after 41 minutes when Grassi, somehow, struck the crossbar from just a couple of yards out after excellent work from Türkyilmaz.

It was a warning shot, because in the second half England completely lost their rhythm and the Swiss began to dominate. It seemed as if the English players had been instructed simply to hold onto the 1-0 lead, but they were unable to keep the ball, and the Swiss midfield pair of Sforza and Vogel started to orchestrate the game. For all the Swiss possession, however, England 'keeper David Seaman was not called into serious action... until, with just eight minutes left, Switzerland were awarded a penalty.

It was a hugely controversial decision. Grassi flicked the ball into the penalty area and it struck Stuart Pearce's raised arm. There was clearly no deliberate intention to handle, but, as every football fan knows, incidents such as those are entirely down to the interpretation of the referee. In this case, Spanish official Díaz Vega pointed to the spot, and Türkyilmaz calmly slotted the penalty into the corner to bring Switzerland level. Irrespective of the rights and wrongs of that decision, England could not complain about the justice of the scoreline. They had taken their foot off the throttle in the second half and had paid the price. It served them right. The Swiss deserved the draw.

Two days later, Holland and Scotland got their campaigns underway at Villa Park in Birmingham. The ground was full of noise and colour; bagpipes and tartan at one end, trumpets and orange at the other. The Dutch, without suspended skipper Danny Blind, made their presence felt early on with a succession of raids on the Scottish goal. Andy Goram, preferred to veteran Jim Leighton, made one brilliant save from Clarence Seedorf, and a minute later he had his outfield colleague John Collins to thank for palming the ball off the goal-line following a goalmouth scramble. Luckily for the Scots, the Swedish referee did not see the incident. Had he been better positioned, he would surely have awarded a penalty and sent Collins off.

But the Scots survived and gradually came back into the game. Holland's early fury fizzled out. Dennis Bergkamp, playing in an unfamiliar centre-forward rôle, missed two chances before the break. And eight minutes into the

Holland's Ronald de Boer fends off Swiss defender Ramon Vega

second half Seedorf made poor contact with a great cross from Gaston Taument, his free header bouncing down and over the crossbar. The Scots, defending well as a unit, held out happily for a goalless draw. As for the Dutch, they came off the field disappointed. Despite a massive terriorial dominance, they did not show enough flair or imagination to turn their pressure into clear-cut openings.

Holland returned to Villa Park three days later to take on Switzerland, and for the first 45 minutes there was no significant improvement from Guus Hiddink's team. Edgar Davids had been dropped in favour of Aron Winter, and 20 minutes into the game, Davids' pal, Clarence Seedorf, was fortunate still to be on the pitch after committing what appeared to be a second yellow-card offence. The Bulgarian referee let him off, but Hiddink withdrew him before any further damage was done.

An even first half turned in Holland's favour after the interval. Switzerland's Marc Hottiger, suspended for the opening game against England, ballooned a great chance into the crowd. The Dutch came back and, with 66 minutes on the clock, scored their first goal of the tournament. Jordi Cruijff - son of the great Johan - was the scorer, gathering a loose ball on the edge of the area and driving it low and hard inside Pascolo's near post. The Swiss then began to press forward, but Holland were canny enough to exploit the unguarded territory at the other end and sealed the game with a second goal from Dennis Bergkamp 12 minutes from time.

The match every English and Scottish fan had been looking forward to for months took place at Wembley tw

EURO 96 FINALS Group A

days later on a baking hot Saturday afternoon. For 45 minutes, nerves got the better of the two teams, and there was pitifully little to entertain the tournament's biggest crowd (76,864). The football was dire, with England, in particular, looking static and uninspired. Scotland were marginally better, but only because there was a more orderly pattern to their play.

Mercifully, the action livened up dramatically in the second half. With Redknapp on for Pearce, England suddenly looked a completely different team. Steve McManaman began to run at the Scottish defence, and for the first time the crowd were up off their seats. After 52 minutes, England's pressure was rewarded with a goal. A measured build-up down the right ended with Gary Neville floating in a perfect centre which Shearer met with his forehead at the far post. Eight minutes later Teddy Sheringham should have put England 2-0 up, but from an unmarked position he headed straight at Goram.

That was the signal for Scotland to respond, and at a stroke the action swung to the other end. David Seaman made a brilliant one-handed save to claw back a header from Gordon Durie that seemed destined for the back of the net. Then, with just 12 minutes to go, the Arsenal goalkeeper earned his place in history by saving a penalty. For the second match in succession, England had been victims of a harsh decision, Tony Adams appearing to nick the ball away from Durie just before he fell. But Scottish captain Gary McAllister opted to fire his spot-kick with power into the middle of the goal. Seaman, going to his right, stretched back an arm and the ball cannoned to safety off his elbow.

The Scots in the crowd were crestfallen, but their torture was not over yet. Just as they were lifting their heads out of their hands, they saw England break forward down the left. Anderton fed the ball through to Paul Gascoigne, and the rest was sheer genius by the Glasgow-based Englishman. Racing towards the area, Gascoigne clipped the ball over Colin Hendry with his left foot and, in the same action, rifled it past Goram with his right. Wembley erupted. The match was won. The Auld Enemy had been slain. And for the home fans, Euro '96 was up and running.

There was more to come. Next up were the Dutch. As things stood, both teams could afford to share a draw and still go through. But if Holland were ready to settle for such an outcome, England certainly weren't. Their tails were up, and with the country now well and truly behind them, they had a duty to entertain, and to win.

The result of their refreshing, positive approach was one of the most thrilling England performances in years. It was a game for the purist as well as the partisan. Alan Shearer maintained his goal-a-game sequence by putting England ahead from the penalty spot after Paul Ince was upended by Danny Blind. Then, in a dazzling 17-minute period after the interval, England tore the Dutch defence to shreds, adding three further goals - a well-placed header from Teddy Sheringham, a crashing right-foot shot from Shearer after a magnificent build-up involving McManaman, Gascoigne and Sheringham, and, to finish, a precise right-footer from Sheringham after an Anderton shot had rebounded back into his path.

Alan Shearer reels away after giving England the lead over Scotland

With Scotland leading Switzerland 1-0 at Villa Park thanks to a superb Ally McCoist goal, Holland were now seriously endangered with elimination. They needed a goal to put themselves back ahead of the Scots, and as England eased off in the final 15 minutes, with goal heroes Shearer and Sheringham both being substituted to rapturous acclaim, it was a Dutch substitute, Patrick Kluivert, who stole in to grab Holland's lifeline.

Scotland could not add to their tally, so Holland were safe. But they weren't celebrating. Guss Hiddink's team had been given a good hiding by a magnificent England side. The 4-1 win was undoubtedly one of the greatest results in England's history. And the ecstatic singing, dancing, flag-waving fans were eager for more...

GROUP A FINAL TABLE

		Pd	W	D	L	F	A	Pt	GD
1	England	3	2	1	0	7	2	7	+5
2	Holland	3	1	1	1	3	4	4	-1
3	Scotland	3	1	1	1	1	2	4	-1
4	Switzerland	3	0	1	2	1	4	1	-3

TOP SCORERS

4 Alan SHEARER (England)
2 Teddy SHERINGHAM (England)

EURO 96 FINALS Group B

France and Spain oust Eastern Europeans

After the Opening Match at Wembley, Euro '96 took to the provinces, with Bulgaria and Spain the first into action at Elland Road, Leeds. There was very little form guide to the match. The teams had only ever faced each other twice before, the last time in December 1985.

An even encounter was anticipated, and that was what transpired. There was a jaunty pace to proceedings early on, and Spain should have taken the lead when Julen Guerrero, clean through in the penalty area with just the goalkeeper to beat, sliced wildly into the crowd. No other such opportunities were created in the first half, although Bulgarian defender Trifon Ivanov went close with two spectacular and beautifully-struck 30-yard drives.

Three minutes into the second half Bulgaria had the ball in the net when Hristo Stoichkov slipped unnoticed behind the Spanish defence and latched onto Kiriakov's through-ball with a glorious volleyed finish. But a late flag from the Italian linesman cut his celebrations short. It was a tight decision, but a faulty one. Still, Stoichkov got his own back later on in the half when he put Bulgaria into the lead from the penalty spot. The decision was questionable, Emil Kostadinov appearing to take a dive as Sergi tried to dispossess him from behind, but Stoichkov clipped the spot-kick in via the foot of the post after sending his ex-Barcelona team-mate Andoni Zubizarreta the wrong way.

Controversy also surrounded Spain's equaliser nine minutes later. Sweeper Hubchev was caught out of position by a long ball and tangled with the goal-bound Caminero on the edge of the area. The Italian referee again failed to spot the dive - this time by Caminero - and Hubchev was sent off. A couple of minutes elapsed before the ensuing free-kick could be taken. Hierro's shot was blocked, Sergi

GROUP B MATCH DETAILS

09/06/96, Leeds
SPAIN 1 Alfonso (74)
BULGARIA 1 Stoichkov (65p)
referee - Ceccarini (ITA)
SPAIN - Zubizarreta; Belsué, Alkorta, Abelardo, Sergi; Caminero (Donato 82), Hierro, Guerrero (Amavisca 52), Amor (Alfonso 73), Luis Enrique; Pizzi.
BULGARIA - Mikhailov; Kishishev, Hubchev, Ivanov, Kiriakov (Tsvetanov 70); Lechkov, Yankov, Balakov; Kostadinov (Yordanov 71), Penev (Borimirov 77), Stoichkov.

10/06/96, Newcastle
ROMANIA 0
FRANCE 1 Dugarry (25)
referee - Krug (GER)
ROMANIA - Stelea; Petrescu (Filipescu 77), Mihali, Belodedici, Selymes; Lupescu, Popescu, Hagi, Munteanu; Lacatus (Ilie 56), Raducioiu (Moldovan 46).
FRANCE - Lama; Thuram, Blanc, Desailly, Di Meco (Lizarazu 68); Karembeu, Djorkaeff, Deschamps, Zidane (Roche 80), Guérin; Dugarry (Loko 68).

13/06/96, Newcastle
BULGARIA 1 Stoichkov (3)
ROMANIA 0
referee - Mikkelsen (DEN)
BULGARIA - Mikhailov; Kishishev, Yankov, Ivanov, Tsvetanov; Lechkov (Genchev 90), Yordanov, Balakov; Kostadinov (Borimirov 32), Penev (Sirakov 72), Stoichkov.
ROMANIA - Stelea; Petrescu, Belodedici, Prodan, Selymes; Lupescu (Gâlca 46), Popescu (Ilie 78), Hagi, Munteanu; Lacatus (Moldovan 29), Raducioiu.

15/06/96, Leeds
FRANCE 1 Djorkaeff (48)
SPAIN 1 Caminero (85)
referee - Zhuk (BLS)
FRANCE - Lama; Angloma (Roche 65), Blanc, Desailly, Lizarazu; Karembeu, Djorkaeff, Deschamps, Zidane, Guérin (Thuram 81); Loko (Dugarry 74).
SPAIN - Zubizarreta; Otero (Kiko 59), Alkorta, López, Abelardo, Sergi; Amavisca, Hierro, Caminero, Luis Enrique (Manjarín 55); Alfonso (Salinas 83).

18/06/96, Newcastle
FRANCE 3 Blanc (20), Penev (62og), Loko (90)
BULGARIA 1 Stoichkov (68)
referee - Gallagher /Durkin (ENG)
FRANCE - Lama; Thuram, Blanc, Desailly, Lizarazu; Karembeu, Djorkaeff, Deschamps, Zidane (Pedros 62), Guérin; Dugarry (Loko 70).
BULGARIA - Mikhailov; Kremenliev, Hubchev, Ivanov, Tsvetanov, Lechkov, Yankov (Borimirov 78), Balakov (Donkov 82), Yordanov; Penev, Stoichkov.

18/06/96, Leeds
ROMANIA 1 Raducioiu (29)
SPAIN 2 Manjarín (11), Amor (84)
referee - Çakar (TUR)
ROMANIA - Prunea; Petrescu, Dobos, Prodan (Lupescu 86), Selymes; Gâlca, Popescu, Ilie (Munteanu 66), Sfînga; Raducioiu (Vladoiu 78), Hagi.
SPAIN - Zubizarreta; López, Alkorta, Abelardo (Amor 64), Sergi; Amavisca (Guerrero 72), Nadal, Hierro, Manjarín; Pizzi (Alfonso 57), Kiko.

EURO 96 FINALS Group B

fired the ball back into the danger zone and Alfonso, who had just come on as a substitute, was perfectly placed to deflect the ball into the net with his very first touch. At one goal apiece, both teams seemed happy with their lot. Spanish striker Pizzi wasn't, though. He was sent off 15 minutes from time for a reckless tackle on Kishishev. Given that the offence took place far away from either goal, he was unlucky to go. But if referee Ceccarini was wrong again, at least he had been consistently wrong throughout the match.

The following day it was the turn of France and Romania to revive a contest that had begun in the qualifying competition. The 3-1 victory by Aimé Jacquet's team in Bucharest the previous October had been arguably France's most impressive performance in the 23-match unbeaten run which they brought to the finals. But during the early stages of the rematch in Newcastle the French seemed short of confidence and somewhat nervous going forward. Luckily for them, Romania were in a generous mood, and after 25 minutes goalkeeper Bogdan Stelea gifted the French the lead. For some unexplained reason he ventured all the way to the edge of the area to claim a harmless cross from the right, then collided with his team-mate Gheorghe Mihali and watched disconsolately as the ball bounced its way into the unguarded net after Christophe Dugarry had beaten both Romanians in the aerial challenge.

The French improved after that goal, but the Romanians continued to make unforced errors, and despite the best efforts of skipper Gheorghe Hagi to put the well-organised French defence under pressure, there was no way back. Substitute Moldovan worked his way into a good shooting position late on, but then proceeded to fire his team's best chance horribly over the bar. It was a poor finish to a poor match. Neither team looked impressive. Romania were incapable of varying their play and chasing the game, while France, though deservedly victorious, did little to threaten a second goal and looked bereft of adventure up front.

Romania's defeat left them propping up the group and requiring a victory in their next game, also in Newcastle, against Bulgaria, to retain their hopes of qualification. The 'Battle of the Balkans' was a potentially intriguing encounter, with the Stoichkov v Hagi sideshow holding the key to the outcome. Surprisingly, less than 20,000 turned up to watch in supposedly football-mad Tyneside. But those who did come along were treated to a match of high technique and sumptuous ball skills, if not much goalmouth action.

Stoichkov opened up the game by netting his second goal of the competition after just three minutes. It was a fine solo effort. He seized possession 30 yards out, saw a gap in the Romanian defence and went for it. His shot, though lacking force, was accurate enough to find its way into the corner of the net via Stelea's fingertips.

Romania responded well to that early setback, and veteran forward Marius Lacatus should have equalised just five minutes later when fed beautifully by Popescu on the edge of the area. After 31 minutes the Romanians were up in arms. A thunderous shot from Dorinel Munteanu crashed against the underside of the crossbar and bounced down a foot over the goal-line. It was a clear goal, but the Danish officials refused to acknowledge it. Referee Peter Mikkelsen did not even consult his linesman. Later, on seeing the proof on television, he no doubt wished that he had.

Screaming for vengeance, Romania had the vast majority of play in the second half. But luck was not with them. The best two chances fell to defender Prodan, but he failed to find the target on both occasions. It was Romania's second defeat, and that meant they were the first team to be eliminated from the competition.

Both France and Spain came to Euro '96 bolstered by long unbeaten runs. A draw was therefore the obvious tip for their direct confrontation in Leeds. And so it proved. There was a tremendous atmosphere at Elland Road, but the quality of the game itself did not match the carnival spirit in evidence in the stands. The two teams paid each other too much respect. Goalscoring chances were few and far between - indeed, there was only one in the first half, when Zubizarreta pulled off a brilliant one-handed save from Vincent Guérin. The entertainment quality improved in the second period thanks to Youri Djorkaeff, who tucked away Christian Karembeu's chipped pass with the skill and

Frenchman Didier Deschamps outpaces Spain's Caminero

EURO 96 FINALS Group B

composure of the great finisher that he is. Spain had to respond, and were assisted by some personnel changes in the French defence. Amavisca forced a good save from Lama, then Alfonso just failed to make contact with a cross-shot from substitute Kiko. Time was running out for Spain, but they did not give up, and with five minutes left their perseverence paid off when Caminero mishit Salinas's pull-back and saw the ball bounce past the wrong-footed Lama into the corner.

Spain could breathe again, but they knew that another draw in their final match, against eliminated Romania, would not be enough to keep them in the competition. And if France and Bulgaria decided to share a high-scoring draw (2-2 or greater) in Newcastle, nothing, not even a 10-0 victory over Romania, could prevent the Spaniards from going out.

The return of Nadal, suspended for the first two games, beefed up Spain's midfield. Another newcomer to the team was winger Javier Manjarín, and he gave Spain the perfect start with a goal after just 11 minutes, converting with precision after the ball fortuitously landed in his path on the edge of the area. A much-changed Romanian side, in which Hagi was earning his 100th cap, passed tha ball around prettily in the first half and grabbed a deserved equaliser when Spanish-based striker Florin Raducioiu, who had been invisible in the earlier games, raced onto Hagi's pass and shot past Zubizarreta for Romania's first goal of the tournament.

The second half saw Spain up the tempo a notch. The news from St. James' Park favoured them, if only they could find another goal. For half an hour, they huffed and puffed, but could not make the beakthrough. But as the Romanian resistance weakened late on, Spain pounced. Man-of-the-match Sergi crossed into the area, Alfonso knocked the ball back across goal and, with the Romanian central defenders conspicuous by their absence, Amor stooped forward to head in Spain's winner.

It was the goal that sent Javier Clemente's team through to the quarter-finals. In Newcastle, Bulgaria faded after a promising start and were soundly beaten by a French team on a mission of revenge after their World Cup qualifying nightmare against the Bulgarians two and a half years earlier.

Two Bulgarians - Yordan Lechkov and Borislav Mikhailov - were in outstanding form, but that was not enough. France were much the better team. They went ahead after 20 minutes when defender Laurent Blanc timed his run perfectly to head Djorkaeff's corner down and over the line. In the second half Blanc again came forward for a free-kick, and his presence led to Bulgarian centre-forward Liuboslav Penev heading into his own net.

Romania's Constantin Gâlca and Kiko of Spain tussle for a high ball

Hristo Stoichkov, who had been having a running battle with Marcel Desailly throughout the game, put his team back in contention six minutes later when he curled in the only direct free-kick goal of the tournament. But that was Bulgaria's only threatening moment of the entire second half. Even when the message filtered through that Spain were winning, they had no more to give, and it was France who rounded off the scoring, in the final minute, when Patrice Loko beat the Bulgarian offside trap, skipped past Mikhailov and fired a left-foot shot into the corner of the net.

GROUP B FINAL TABLE

		Pd	W	D	L	F	A	Pt	GD
1	France	3	2	1	0	5	2	7	+3
2	Spain	3	1	2	0	4	3	5	+1
3	Bulgaria	3	1	1	1	3	4	4	-1
4	Romania	3	0	0	3	1	4	0	-3

TOP SCORER

3 Hristo STOICHKOV (Bulgaria)

EURO 96 FINALS Group C

Italy sent crashing as Germany hold firm

Every major tournament, it seems, has a 'Group of Death', and this one was to live up to its billing. Between them, Germany, Italy, Russia and the Czech Republic fought out a marvellous opening round, with excitement, drama and controversy colouring every game. There was no shortage of top-quality football, either, and some of the 17 goals scored were among the best seen in the entire tournament.

Germany and the Czech Republic set the ball rolling at Old Trafford. The Germans, billed as the tournament favourites, gave every encouragement to those who had backed them with a convincing and controlled opening performance. The Czechs, on the other hand, gave no hint of what was to come. Once Berti Vogts' team got into their stride - and the loss of Jürgen Kohler through injury early on delayed them in that respect - there was only one likely winner.

The match was settled by two excellent carbon-copy goals in the second quarter. The first came from Christian Ziege on his major tournament début. After an exchange of passes with striker Fredi Bobic, deputising for the suspended Jürgen Klinsmann, the Bayern Munich left-back cut inside and beat Petr Kouba with a perfectly placed low right-foot shot. Six minutes later, Andreas Möller converted a replica goal after a neat one-two with Stefan Kuntz. That was game over as far as the Germans were concerned. In the second half they were content to control the game without adding to the scoreline, and the Czechs could not gain sufficient possession to pose a threat.

Italy kicked off their campaign at Anfield against a Russian team which, as is their custom, came into the

GROUP C MATCH DETAILS

09/06/96, Manchester
GERMANY 2 Ziege (26), Möller (32)
CZECH REPUBLIC 0
referee - Elleray (ENG)
GERMANY - Köpke; Kohler (Babbel 14), Sammer, Helmer; Reuter, Hässler, Eilts, Möller, Ziege; Bobic (Strunz 65), Kuntz (Bierhoff 83).
CZECH REPUBLIC - Kouba; Hornak, Kadlec, Suchoparek; Latal, Frydek (Berger 46), Bejbl, Nedved, Nemec; Poborsky (Drulak 46), Kuka.

11/06/96, Liverpool
ITALY 2 Casiraghi (5, 52)
RUSSIA 1 Tsymbalar (20)
referee - Mottram (SCO)
ITALY - Peruzzi; Mussi, Apolloni, Costacurta, Maldini; Di Livio (Fuser 62), Di Matteo, Albertini, Del Piero (Donadoni 46); Zola, Casiraghi (Ravanelli 80).
RUSSIA - Cherchesov; Tetradze, Bushmanov (Yanovski 46), Onopko, Kovtun; Kanchelskis, Karpin (Kiryakov 63), Radimov, Mostovoi, Tsymbalar (Dobrovolski 71); Kolyvanov.

14/06/96, Liverpool
CZECH REPUBLIC 2 Nedved (5), Bejbl (36)
ITALY 1 Chiesa (18)
referee - López Nieto (ESP)
CZECH REPUBLIC - Kouba; Hornak, Kadlec, Suchoparek; Latal (Nemecek 88), Nedved, Bejbl, Berger (Smicer 64), Nemec; Poborsky, Kuka.
ITALY - Peruzzi; Mussi, Apolloni, Costacurta, Maldini; Fuser, Albertini, Baggio D. (Carboni 39), Donadoni; Chiesa (Zola 78), Ravanelli (Casiraghi 58).

16/06/96, Manchester
RUSSIA 0
GERMANY 3 Sammer (56), Klinsmann (77, 90)
referee - Nielsen (DEN)
RUSSIA - Kharin; Kovtun, Nikiforov, Onopko; Tetradze, Kanchelskis, Radimov (Karpin 46), Mostovoi, Khokhlov (Simutenkov 66), Tsymbalar; Kolyvanov.
GERMANY - Köpke; Babbel, Sammer, Helmer; Reuter, Hässler (Freund 67), Eilts, Möller (Strunz 87), Ziege; Klinsmann, Bierhoff (Kuntz 85).

19/06/96, Liverpool
CZECH REPUBLIC 3 Suchoparek (7), Kuka (19), Smicer (89)
RUSSIA 3 Mostovoi (49), Tetradze (54), Beschastnykh (85)
referee - Frisk (SWE)
CZECH REPUBLIC - Kouba; Hornak, Kubik, Suchoparek; Latal, Nedved, Bejbl, Berger (Nemecek 90), Nemec; Poborsky, Kuka (Smicer 64).
RUSSIA - Cherchesov; Gorlukovich, Nikiforov, Tetradze; Karpin, Radimov, Yanovski, Khokhlov, Tsymbalar (Shalimov 67); Kolyvanov (Mostovoi 46), Simutenkov (Beschastnykh 46).

19/06/96, Manchester
ITALY 0
GERMANY 0
referee - Goethals (BEL)
ITALY - Peruzzi; Mussi, Costacurta, Maldini, Carboni (Torricelli 78); Fuser (Di Livio 81), Albertini, Di Matteo (Chiesa 68), Donadoni; Zola, Casiraghi.
GERMANY - Köpke; Freund, Sammer, Helmer; Strunz, Hässler, Eilts, Möller (Bode 89), Ziege; Klinsmann, Bobic.

EURO 96 FINALS Group C

Pierluigi Casiraghi milks the applause after firing Italy into a 2-1 lead against Russia at Anfield

tournament as dark horses after a strong series of qualifying results. Arrigo Sacchi, the Italian coach, selected Pierluigi Casiraghi ahead of Juventus's Fabrizio Ravanelli as the partner up front for Gianfranco Zola. Within just five minutes his choice was vindicated when a poor clearance by Russian goalkeeper Stanislav Cherchesov was fed back by Angelo Di Livio to an unmarked Casiraghi on the edge of the penalty area. Without hesitation the Lazio striker swung his right foot at the ball and buried it in the corner.

It was just the start the Italians had hoped for, but they were unable to build on it. It shook the Russians into action, and for the remainder of the first half Oleg Romantsev's team called the tune. Two half-chances for Igor Kolyvanov went begging before Ilya Tsymbalar rewarded Russian pressure by firing in a left-footer at the near post.

Russia were now the team in the ascendancy, but after the interval, with veteran Roberto Donadoni replacing the ineffective Alessandro Del Piero, Italy soon rediscovered their early poise. Demetrio Albertini, especially, seemed transformed by his former club colleague's presence and began to boss the midfield with tremendous authority. Within seven minutes of the restart Italy were back in front, and Casiraghi was again the scorer. It was a marvellously worked goal, created by Zola and finished by Casiraghi with such speed and precision that the Russian defence could do nothing to prevent it. This time Italy held on to their lead. They should have added to it late on when substitute Ravanelli uncharacteristically made a hash of two clear openings. But with Russian substitute Igor Dobrovolski proving equally profligate with a late chance at the other end, Italy's three points were safe.

There was much for the Italians to be pleased about. The first match was the one they feared most. But the feel-good factor generated by the victory was to work against them as they prepared for their next, equally important, match against the Czech Republic. Instead of sticking with the team that had defeated Russia, Arrigo Sacchi decided to make unnecessary changes. His argument was that he wanted his first-choice forwards and midfielders to conserve their energy for later games. He appeared to forget one thing. Italy were not yet through to the next round.

The Czech Republic's poor opening performance against Germany appeared to bamboozle Sacchi into thinking that they had already given up on the tournament. Not a bit of it. With a surprisingly large contingent of Czech fans to offer support, Dusan Uhrin's team went for the Italians from the start. Karel Poborsky caught the Italian defence cold, marching to the byline and whipping over a cross which found Pavel Nedved unmarked on the penalty spot. The Sparta Prague midfielder coolly tucked the ball past Peruzzi for his first international goal.

In the 18th minute Poborsky caused more panic in the Italian defence, and defender Apolloni appeared to handle as he slipped, but the referee signalled play on and, with the Czechs caught unawares, Italy broke quickly up the right flank. Diego Fuser slipped the ball into Enrico Chiesa and he turned it expertly past Kouba.

A classic encounter was fast developing, but on 28 minutes Apolloni sent Italy spinning out of control when he stupidly got himself sent off - and rightly so - for a second bad foul on Pavel Kuka. Surprisingly, Sacchi failed to respond with an immediate substitution, and within eight minutes the Italians were behind again. Once more it was a cross from the right - this time from Kuka - that penetrated the Italian defence. Radek Bejbl, who had earlier left the field on a stretcher, proved that he was fully recovered by sweeping the ball first-time into the corner on the volley.

A thoroughly absorbing first half ended, but there was plenty more excitement to come in the second half.

EURO 96 FINALS Group C

The Czechs played shrewdly and skilfully, but Italy showed tremendous spirit and continued to press forward in search of an equaliser. It was riveting entertainment. Three minutes into stoppage time, Italy got their golden chance to equalise. With the Czech fans screaming for the final whistle, Zola found his fellow substitute Casiraghi in the area. The two-goal hero of the opening match set himself up perfectly, but whacked the ball over the bar.

Germany and Russia were hard pressed to follow that a couple of days later at Old Trafford. The first half began with chances created at both ends. Russia matched the Germans step for step, and Aleksandr Mostovoi was guilty of a bad miss when he failed to control the ball after being sent clean through by Khokhlov. Having competed on equal terms for 45 minutes, the Russians slackened in the second half and paid the penalty when Matthias Sammer raced on to a brilliant Möller through-ball and scored at the second attempt to give Germany the lead. When Yuri Kovtun was sent off 15 minutes later, Russia were finished. It was time for Jürgen Klinsmann to take over.

Back in the team after his controversial suspension from the first match against the Czechs, the German skipper proved his class with two late goals to wrap up a 3-0 victory. His first, in the 77th minute, was sheer brilliance. Having killed Russian sweeper Yuri Nikiforov for pace with a sharp turn, he cut inside towards the goal and unleashed a magnificent shot with the outside of his right foot which sailed into the far corner of the net.

Despite winning their first two matches with convincing scorelines, Germany were not yet officially qualified for the second round.

Even so, it was Italy who felt the pressure going into their final game at Old Trafford. Unless they defeated their old foes, they would have to rely on Russia beating the Czech Republic at Anfield. Given the circumstances, it was hardly surprising that Italy should force the pace of the game, but that they should outplay Germany so completely was astonishing. And yet, despite dominating possession for the entire 90 minutes the Italians could not score. Their big chance came early on when Gianfranco Zola's timid penalty was saved by Andreas Köpke. The German goalkeeper should not have been there to make the save. His deliberate foul on a goal-bound Casiraghi warranted immediate dismissal, but referee Goethals did not even administer a yellow card.

The Germans, led by the immaculate Dieter Eilts, defended with iron resolve and were content merely to protect their own penalty area. Even when Thomas Strunz was sent off after an hour, the German defence still held firm. Italy, becoming more frustrated and less potent as the match went on, began to rely increasingly on the extraordinary goings-on in Liverpool.

There were no goals at Old Trafford, but the Czech Republic and Russia were to share half a dozen in an amazing ding-dong contest at Anfield. The Czechs, still on a high after beating Italy, grabbed two quick goals through Suchoparek and Kuka and hit the woodwork twice before the interval. But Russia, still not mathematically eliminated, came back brilliantly in the second half, drawing level with goals from Mostovoi and Tetradze and then, with just five minutes remaining, taking the lead with a spectacular shot from substitute Beschastnykh.

That goal was what Italy desired and the Czechs feared. But it was not yet over. Lubos Kubik, selected in place of the suspended Miroslav Kadlec, played a marvellous through-ball in for Vladimir Smicer, and the Slavia Prague striker shot low and accurately into the corner past a stunned and motionless Cherchesov. A minute later the final whistle sounded.

The Czechs were jubilant. They had the same number of points as Italy and an inferior goal-difference, but because they had won the head-to-head encounter, they were through, and Italy, despite playing some marvellous football, were out.

Christian Ziege and Roberto Di Matteo in action at Old Trafford

GROUP C FINAL TABLE

		Pd	W	D	L	F	A	Pt	GD
1	Germany	3	2	1	0	5	0	7	+5
2	Czech Republic	3	1	1	1	5	6	4	-1
3	Italy	3	1	1	1	3	3	4	=
4	Russia	3	0	1	2	4	8	1	-4

TOP SCORERS

2 Jürgen KLINSMANN (Germany)
Pierluigi CASIRAGHI (Italy)

EURO 96 FINALS Group D

Sweet-passing Portugal turn on the style

After opening games of varying quality in the other three groups, Euro '96 really came to life as Portugal and Denmark concluded the first weekend of competition with a thrilling, high-quality encounter at Hillsborough.

Denmark, the European Championship holders, were not expected to achieve much in England, but that did not prevent their marvellous fans from turning up in vast numbers in Sheffield, their first-round home. The Kop end at Hillsborough was a seething mass of red and white, with an estimated 15,000 Danes having made the trip to South Yorkshire. By comparison, the Portuguese following was small, but that was no reflection on the team they had come to support. Against the Danes, António Oliveira's side were a sheer joy to watch. Their opening performance lit up the tournament.

Nevertheless, it was Denmark who opened the scoring - with their first and only chance of the first half. It came in the 22nd minute, and was the result of a hurried clearance by Portuguese goalkeeper Vítor Baía. His kick rebounded into the path of Brian Laudrup, who cut inside and smashed an unstoppable right-foot shot into the net.

For the remainder of the opening period, Portugal were in complete control. They mesmerised the Danes - and the crowd - with the intricacy and accuracy of their midfield passing and movement. Rui Costa, the playmaking number ten, was at the heart of most things, ably suported by João Pinto and Figo. But there was nothing at the end of this marvellous build-up play, and that was due to poor finishing and some outstanding goalkeeping from Peter Schmeichel. Two misses by Figo were followed by a brilliant Schmeichel save from a Rui Costa free-kick. Then the Manchester United custodian athletically saved

GROUP D MATCH DETAILS

09/06/96, Sheffield
DENMARK 1 Laudrup B. (22)
PORTUGAL 1 Sá Pinto (53)
referee - Van der Ende (HOL)
DENMARK - Schmeichel; Helveg, Høgh, Rieper, Risager; Larsen (Vilfort 90), Thomsen (Piechnik 83), Laudrup M., Nielsen B.S.; Laudrup B., Beck.
PORTUGAL - Vítor Baía; Paulinho Santos, Fernando Couto, Hélder, Dimas; Oceano (Folha 37), Paulo Sousa (Tavares 79), Rui Costa, Figo (Domingos 63); Sá Pinto, João Pinto.

11/06/96, Nottingham
TURKEY 0
CROATIA 1 Vlaovic (85)
referee - Muhmenthaler (SUI)
TURKEY - Rüstü; Vedat, Rahim, Alpay; Ogün, Tolunay (Saffet 88), Sergen, Tugay, Abdullah; Arif (Hami 82), Hakan.
CROATIA - Ladic; Bilic, Jerkan, Stimac; Stanic, Prosinecki, Boban (Soldo 48), Asanovic, Jarni; Boksic (Vlaovic 72), Suker (Pavlicic 89).

13/06/96, Nottingham
PORTUGAL 1 Fernando Couto (66)
TURKEY 0
referee - Puhl (HUN)
PORTUGAL - Vítor Baía; Paulinho Santos, Fernando Couto, Hélder, Dimas; Figo, Paulo Sousa, Rui Costa, Folha (Tavares 46); Sá Pinto (Cadete 65), João Pinto (Porfírio 77).
TURKEY - Rüstü; Recep, Vedat, Ogün (Rahim 46), Alpay; Oguz (Arif 69), Sergen, Tugay, Abdullah; Saffet (Tolunay 62), Hakan.

16/06/96, Sheffield
CROATIA 3 Suker (53p, 89), Boban (80)
DENMARK 0
referee - Batta (FRA)
CROATIA - Ladic; Bilic, Jerkan, Stimac; Stanic, Prosinecki (Mladenovic 88), Boban (Soldo 82), Asanovic, Jarni; Vlaovic (Jurcevic 82), Suker.
DENMARK - Schmeichel; Helveg (Laursen 46), Thomsen, Høgh, Rieper; Larsen (Tøfting 69), Vilfort (Beck 58), Laudrup M., Schjønberg, Nielsen B.S.; Laudrup B..

19/06/96, Nottingham
CROATIA 0
PORTUGAL 3 Figo (4), João Pinto (33), Domingos (83)
referee - Heynemann (GER)
CROATIA - Mrmic; Simic, Bilic, Pavlicic, Soldo; Jurcevic, Mladenovic (Boban 46), Prosinecki (Asanovic 46), Jarni; Vlaovic, Pamic (Suker 46).
PORTUGAL - Vítor Baía; Secretário, Fernando Couto, Hélder, Dimas; Oceano, Paulo Sousa (Tavares 70), Rui Costa (Pedro Barbosa 61), Figo; Sá Pinto (Domingos 46), João Pinto.

19/06/96, Sheffield
TURKEY 0
DENMARK 3 Laudrup B. (50, 84), Nielsen A. (69)
referee - Levnikov (RUS)
TURKEY - Rüstü; Recep (Bülent K. 68), Vedat, Ogün, Alpay; Tayfun, Tugay, Orhan (Saffet 68), Abdullah; Hami, Hakan (Arif 46).
DENMARK - Schmeichel; Helveg, Høgh, Thomsen, Rieper; Nielsen A., Laudrup M., Schjønberg (Larsen 46), Nielsen B.S.; Laudrup B., Andersen E.B. (Andersen S. 89).

EURO 96 FINALS — Group D

at the feet of João Pinto, who had squirmed his way into a shooting position.

Grossly unfortunate to be a goal down at the interval, Portugal did not let their heads drop, and eight minutes into the second half they were rewarded with an equaliser. Paulo Sousa made a brilliant tackle on Brian Laudrup, the ball was fed on to substitute Folha, and he swung over a teasing cross which Sá Pinto coolly headed in on the bounce at the far post for his first international goal.

After the Portuguese equaliser, there was more of an even flow to the game, but the artistry from the men in red and green did not disappear. Schmeichel made another fine save, with his legs, to deny João Pinto. Then Vítor Baía was called into action to save with his foot from Brian Laudrup. Along with great saves there were bad misses - from Claus Thomsen with a free header for the Danes, and then, in the last minute, from Portuguese substitute Tavares, who hooked his shot wide of an empty goal with Schmeichel stranded. The Danes could argue that they deserved a draw for their solid defending and willingness to compete, but Portugal were clearly the better team and could take enormous encouragement from their first match in a major finals for a decade.

Relative to the sumptuous fare on offer at Hillsborough, the other Group D opener, between Turkey and Croatia at the City Ground, was dreadfully sub-standard. It started brightly enough, but on a grey, wet night in Nottingham, inspiration was clearly lacking, and nothing developed from the opening exchanges. The Turks could not find an accurate final ball to attach to their midfield interpassing, and Croatia, curiously, just did not look interested.

The first half was devoid of clear-cut chances. In fact, Turkey, despite the encouragement of their huge, vocal support, did not create anything worthwhile all game. Nevertheless, with Croatia drawing blanks at the other end, they seemed set to hang on for a draw until, with five minutes left, the match was lifted from its mediocrity by a flash of genius. A Turkish corner came to nothing, and as Aljosa Asanovic took possession midway inside his own half, he caught sight of substitute striker Goran Vlaovic making a dash through the centre circle. With one glorious reverse pass, Asanovic sent Vlaovic on his way. He ran half the length of the field before veering right beyond the goalkeeper and shooting into the empty net. The pursuing defender, Alpay, deserved credit for not bringing Vlaovic down, and he duly received it when UEFA gave him their Euro '96 Fair Play prize.

But Turkey had still lost, and they knew they would be out of the tournament unless they could get something from their next game, also in Nottingham, against the dynamic Portuguese.

Once again, Turkey began well. But their lack of sharpness and subtlety in the final third appeared to be a chronic ailment, and even when a chance was created, Hakan Sükür, the goalscoring hero of the qualifying tournament, was so surprised to find the ball at his feet that he hastily shot wide. Portugal showed less all-round glamour than in their opening match, but Rui Costa was still in ebullient form. One glorious run from him set up Sá Pinto, but he wasted the opportunity, clipping wide with the goal at his mercy.

With Turkey wilting in the second half, Portugal seized the initiative and began to increase the pressure. But, for the second match running, their poor finishing betrayed some quite wonderful approach play. It was a defender who eventually saved the forwards' blushes. Fernando Couto, outstanding at the back, came upfield for a corner, and as the ball deflected to him 18 yards out, he volleyed the ball hard and low with his left-foot through a crowd of players into the net. That was all Portugal were to get for their second-half domination. Turkey, with their second successive defeat, were out, their mood summed up by Sergen's embarrassingly bad free-kick in the last minute, which, before the new stand was built, would have ended up in the River Trent.

With Portugal going strongly, the pressure was on Denmark and Croatia to add to their points tally in their second game, at Hillsborough. Denmark coach Richard Møller-Nielsen made no secret of his intention to gain a second successive draw. He dropped striker Mikkel Beck and left winger Brian Laudrup on his own up front. It was a craven policy, but for 45 minutes it worked. The Danes successfully stifled a Croatian team whose own commitment to winning the game also appeared questionable.

The picture changed completely in the second half. Davor Suker, who had been the liveliest player on view

GROUP D FINAL TABLE

		Pd	W	D	L	F	A	Pt	GD
1	Portugal	3	2	1	0	5	1	7	+4
2	Croatia	3	2	0	1	4	3	6	+1
3	Denmark	3	1	1	1	4	4	4	=
4	Turkey	3	0	0	3	0	5	0	-5

TOP SCORER

3 Brian LAUDRUP (Denmark)

2 Davor SUKER (Croatia)

EURO 96 FINALS Group D

Croatia's Davor Suker and Zvonimir Boban celebrate after their goals had defeated Denmark 3-0

in the opening period, moved up another couple of gears and produced the most enthralling individual display of the whole tournament. His was the glorious through-ball which fed Mario Stanic after 53 minutes and which resulted in the contested award of a penalty. Stanic appeared to run straight into a hesitant Peter Schmeichel before falling to the ground, but the French referee, perhaps influenced by two earlier Croatian penalty claims, pointed to the spot. Schmeichel was visibly enraged but could do nothing as Suker sent him the wrong way from the ensuing penalty.

The Danes then introduced Beck for Vilfort in an attempt to save the game, but their negative approach seemed set in the players' minds, and they were unable to create anything other than one chance, which Brian Laudrup clipped against the post. That apart, the remainder of the game was all Croatia's, in particular Suker's. Igor Stimac crashed a shot against the Danish crossbar, then Suker's excellent left-wing cross was converted at the far post by skipper Boban to make it 2-0.

The game's two most memorable moments were reserved for the last five minutes. The first saw Suker attempt an amazingly audacious lob from 45 yards. The shot was going in, but Schmeichel managed to trackback just in time and keep the ball out. A few minutes later, however, the Danish 'keeper was well and truly embarrassed by the Croatian number nine. As Schmeichel raced back to his area after a vain sortie upfield, Suker, just onside, gathered a long pass upfield, controlled it masterfully and galloped towards the Danish penalty area. Once there, he delicately chipped the ball over Schmiechel's head and into the net with the outside of his left foot.

With that 3-0 victory, Croatia were confirmed as the only team after two matches to be certain of a place in the quarter-finals. But coach Miroslav Blazevic reacted negatively to the achievement by fielding a team of reserves for the final group game against Portugal. Most of Croatia's best players were rested, including the rampant Suker. The decision was a slur on the tournament. In particular, it reduced Denmark's chances of survival to a minimum. The holders could still reach the quarter-finals if they beat Turkey and Croatia beat Portugal, but Blazevic's decision made it easy for the Portuguese, who were to have little difficulty in overcoming Croatia's second XI and finishing on top of the group.

For the first time in the tournament, Portugal applied some clever finishing to their fancy touches in midfield. Figo opened the scoring early on with a neat sidefoot from Secretário's excellent right-wing cross. And João Pinto showed similar composure to double Portugal's lead after an attempted bicycle-kick by Sá Pinto fell at his feet.

With Blazevic apparently seeing the error of his ways and introducing Suker, Asanovic and Boban at half-time, Croatia had much more of the game in the second half, but it was a Portuguese half-time substitute, Domingos, who scored the only additional goal, steering in a fine low shot after a Croatian defensive mix-up had left him with a clear run on goal.

The 3-0 scoreline at the City Ground was matched at Hillsborough, where Denmark simultaneously defeated the already eliminated Turks thanks to two more goals from Brian Laudrup - easily Denmark's player of the tournament - and another from Allan Nielsen. Turkey had one goal cruelly and debatably disallowed, from Saffet, which meant that they departed Euro '96 without a point or a goal. Denmark, too, were out, but at least they had ended their four-year reign with a resounding victory. The 'Roligans' would go home disappointed but not disheartened.

Seaman's heroics save England

Goalkeeper David Seaman is mobbed by his team-mates after seeing England through their penalty shoot-out with Spain

England went into their quarter-final with the euphoria of their brilliant victory over Holland still dominating everybody's thoughts. A nation had suddenly fallen in love with its national football team. The opening round had been successfully negotiated, and the possibility that Terry Venables' team might actually go on and lift the Henri Delaunay trophy had now become very real.

Spain, though, had other ideas. Just 25 seconds had elapsed when Abelardo received his second yellow card of the tournament for a tackle from behind on Alan Shearer. The tournament's leading scorer was clearly a marked man, but he managed to escape in the fourth minute, lashing in a fierce left-foot shot which Zubizarreta turned away for a corner. That was to be a rare English assault in a first half which Spain dominated. Clemente was proving to be a shrewder tactician than Venables. Spain refused to allow England to settle on the ball, they defended in numbers and showed much more cut and thrust in attack, especially down the left side, where England were slow to cover Sergi's dynamic bursts.

Twice in the opening period Spain put the ball in the net, but on both occasions French referee Batta ruled out the goals. The first, from Kiko, was clearly offside, but the second, from Julio Salinas, was perfectly legal, Tony Adams stepping forward a fraction too late, to put Salinas in the clear. Just before half-time Spain had a glorious opportunity to make up for that injustice when Manjarín was sent sprinting clear. But the Spaniard was completely unnerved when David Seaman came out to meet him and his feeble effort enabled the England 'keeper to avert the danger with his legs.

England made moves to counter the Sergi threat at half-time, and slowly but surely they began to take the game to their opponents for the first time - not, however, before the Spaniards had again been denied by Batta, who ruled that Alfonso, a second-half substitute, had dived for a penalty when Gascoigne's outstretched foot clearly seemed to impede him. Chances suddenly came thick and fast for England, with McManaman and Gascoigne beginning to work the openings denied to them earlier. In the 73rd minute, just after Spain had had another penalty claim turned down, England created the best opportunity of the game, Gascoigne chipping to the far post, where Shearer, incredibly, blasted over from two yards out.

Spain then had the better of the closing exchanges before the whistle sounded and the match went into sudden-death extra-time. For the first time in a senior international competition, the 'Golden Goal' was in play. The tension was unbearable. Both teams pressed for the winner, but the two defences held out bravely for the full 30 minutes, and Euro '96 had its first penalty shoot-out.

England went first, and Shearer blasted his spot-kick past Zubizarreta. Then it was Hierro's turn, and to the delight of most of the 75,447 in the crowd, he crashed his shot against the crossbar. Platt and Amor then put their shots comfortably away. Nervelessly, Stuart Pearce, England's penalty villain in the 1990 World Cup semi-final, stepped forward and buried his shot to put England 3-1 up. The crowd were as ecstatic as the scorer. Belsué and Gascoigne also converted. Now it was up to Nadal. He had to score to keep Spain alive, but Seaman turned to his left and fisted his shot to safety. England were through to the semi-finals. Spain, dogged by bad luck throughout, were on their way home.

MATCH DETAILS

22/06/96, Wembley

SPAIN 0 ENGLAND 0

(aet; 2-4 on pens.)

referee - Batta (FRA)

SPAIN - Zubizarreta; Belsué, Alkorta (López 74), Abelardo, Sergi; Manjarín (Caminero 46), Hierro, Nadal, Amor; Kiko, Salinas (Alfonso 46).

ENGLAND - Seaman; Neville G., Adams, Southgate, Pearce; McManaman (Stone 109), Platt, Gascoigne, Anderton (Barmby 109); Sheringham (Fowler 109), Shearer.

EURO 96 FINALS Quarter-Finals

Penalty fortune favours the French

Holland returned to the scene of their magnificent qualifying play-off victory over the Republic of Ireland. But as they arrived at Anfield, they were still trying to come to terms with the thrashing they had received from England at Wembley. France, on the other hand, could not have been more confident. They had won a difficult opening group without over-exerting themselves and were still unbeaten under Aimé Jacquet after 26 matches.

Patrick Kluivert, Holland's hero last time out at Anfield and also their saviour at Wembley, earned himself a first Euro '96 start, although questions remained as to whether the youngster was fully fit. France, too, made a change in attack, bringing in the more technical Loko for the more diligent Dugarry.

Predictably, the two teams spent the opening phase of the game fencing with each other, searching for weaknesses and exploring avenues of attack. No damage was inflicted, however, and although there was plenty to appreciate from a tactical point of view, there was disappointingly little goalmouth action. The best two chances of the first half arrived within a minute of each other, and there was one for either side. Firstly, Ronald de Boer was presented with a free header at the back post from a right-wing corner, but he headed it down and wide without troubling the goalkeeper. Moments later Christian Karembeu had two shots at goal, but sent his second effort wastefully over the bar.

The stalemate continued in the first 15 minutes of the second half, so both coaches tried to liven things up by making substitutions. Clarence Seedorf came on for the injured Bergkamp, who, despite being restored to his familiar support-striker rôle, could not form any understanding with an equally uninspired Kluivert. France replaced Loko with Dugarry, but, with ten minutes to go, the Bordeaux striker was also forced out of the action with an injury.

MATCH DETAILS

22/06/96, Liverpool
FRANCE 0 HOLLAND 0
(aet; 5-4 on pens.)
referee - López Nieto (ESP)
FRANCE - Lama; Thuram, Blanc, Desailly, Lizarazu; Karembeu, Djorkaeff, Deschamps, Zidane, Guérin; Loko (Dugarry 62; Pedros 80).
HOLLAND - Van der Sar; Reiziger, Blind, De Kock, Bogarde; De Boer R., Witschge (Mulder 80); Cruijff (Winter 69), Bergkamp (Seedorf 60), Kluivert, Cocu.

It was only then, with extra-time in view, that the excitement began to mount. And it was Holland who pressed for victory. In the 84th minute French defender Marcel Desailly clearly handled the ball inside the penalty area, but the Spanish referee timidly awarded a free-kick on the edge of the area. Justice was almost done when, from the resulting free-kick, Philip Cocu's shot was deflected towards the French goal. But as time, and goalkeeper Lama, stood still for a moment, the ball span just wide after brushing the post. With just one minute left, Holland came forward again. A lovely pass from substitute Youri Mulder presented Seedorf with a marvellous opportunity to put his name up in lights, but the young midfielder could not get sufficient lift on his shot and Lama saved brilliantly with his legs to send the ball arching over the top of the goal.

If Holland had the best of the closing stages in normal time, it was France who seemed more committed to grab the 'Golden Goal' in extra-time. They created one clear opportunity at the end of the first period when Youri Djorkaeff was astutely played in by Zidane. But Van der Sar was up to the challenge and brilliantly kept his team in the tournament with a smothering save. Djorkaeff then tried his luck on three more occasions, but the goal of deliverance would not come. The second goalless quarter-final was to be concluded in the same manner as the first - on penalties.

The first six kicks all found their target - De Kock, De Boer and Kluivert for Holland, Zidane, Djorkaeff and Lizarazu for France. But then it was Seedorf's turn. He looked nervous enough as he walked up for his kick, but when the referee told him to replace the ball, the outcome was inevitable. He hit a tame shot straight at Lama, and Holland were in serious trouble. Guérin then scored for France, and Blind did the same for Holland. The moment of truth rested with Laurent Blanc. He fell over as he struck the shot, but it was firm and accurate and found the bottom corner. France were through to the semi-finals.

Germans come through bruising encounter

Croatian coach Miroslav Blazevic had said prior to his team's final group match with Portugal that he fancied playing against the Germans in the quarter-final. Well, he got his wish, and, in hindsight, perhaps his words were not quite so tongue-in-cheek as initially intended. The Germans had looked poor against Italy, and there was a mounting injury crisis within the squad. It was a good time to play them.

Blazevic, of course, dispensed with the patchwork team he had fielded against Portugal, and restored his first-choice XI. Boksic was unavailable through injury, and the only slight surprise was the exclusion of Prosinecki in favour of Jurcevic, Croatia's best player against the Portuguese. German boss Berti Vogts selected Mehmet Scholl in place of the out-of-form Hässler, but he also included Reuter and Helmer, who were both carrying injuries.

From the first whistle the match looked as if it was going to be a physical one. Matthias Sammer was booked early on for a foul on Stanic, and a minute later Jürgen Klinsmann was lucky to see yellow not red after a hack at Vlaovic's ankle. Vlaovic should have extracted his revenge soon afterwards when put clean through by Asanovic, but his finish was woeful. It was the first of many times the Germans would be let off the hook.

With Germany sitting back soaking up pressure as they had done against the Italians, Croatia held the early initiative. But in the Germans' first attack of any note, they scored. Libero Sammer burst forward down the right, and as he entered the penalty area, for no apparent reason his Croatian counterpart Nikola Jerkan stuck out a hand and conceded a penalty. Jürgen Klinsmann clipped the spot-kick unerringly into the corner.

Ten minutes later, Klinsmann left the field clutching an injured calf muscle that threatened his presence in the rest of the competition. It was the only slice of good fortune that came Croatia's way. Just after the German captain went off, Davor Suker should have been given a penalty - or at the very least an indirect free-kick - when Helmer blocked him in the area as he skilfully shaped to get the ball onto his favoured left foot. But the Swedish referee, Leif Sundell, gave nothing. It was not the first, or the last, bad decision from the referee. Just before half-time Croatian defender Slaven Bilic had a rush of blood and kicked the grounded Christian Ziege just a yard away from where the referee was standing. Again, no punishment.

With Suker looking dangerous, the Croatian players were evidently instructed at half-time to give him more of the ball. Six minutes after the interval he got the goal Croatia deserved. The opportunity arose from a sloppy pass by Sammer. Steffen Freund, Klinsmann's replacement, was dispossessed by Jurcevic, who fed Suker in the inside-right channel. He bore down on Köpke, and as the goalkeeper and everybody else expected him to shoot with his left, Suker rolled the ball brilliantly on to his other foot and stroked it impudently into the net.

It was time now for Croatia to turn the screw. But, inexcusably, just five minutes after getting on level terms, defender Igor Stimac got himself sent off for a stupid tackle on Scholl - his second yellow-card offence. It was unproffesionalism of the first order, and within two minutes Stimac's abandoned colleagues had fallen behind again.

Sammer, the most influential German on the pitch, scored the goal, tucking it away with calm authority after the ball broke kindly for him following an aerial challenge. But it should not have been allowed. Markus Babbel clearly pushed Jerkan off the ball before setting up the chance. Croatia tried to come back, and Suker should have done better than send two headers straight at Köpke. But the Croatians' earlier authority had gone. They had not punished their opponents when the chance had beckoned. A wonderful opportunity had gone begging and the Germans had escaped. They, not Croatia, would go on to face England in the Wembley semi-final.

MATCH DETAILS

23/06/96, Manchester

GERMANY 2 Klinsmann (21p), Sammer (59)

CROATIA 1 Suker (51)

referee - Sundell (SWE)

GERMANY - Köpke; Babbel, Sammer, Helmer; Reuter, Scholl (Hässler 88), Eilts, Möller, Ziege; Klinsmann (Freund 39), Bobic (Kuntz 46).

CROATIA - Ladic; Stimac, Jerkan, Bilic; Stanic, Jurcevic (Mladenovic 78), Boban, Asanovic, Jarni; Vlaovic, Suker.

EURO 96 FINALS Quarter-Finals

Poborsky punishes Portuguese

With England, France and Germany already through to the semi-finals, the pressure was on Portugal to complete a successful weekend for all four first-round group winners.

The Czech Republic created the first half-chance of the match when defender Michal Hornak headed Karel Poborsky's flick just over the bar. But Portugal were in control for the remainder of the first half. As in previous matches, the Portuguese midfielders were excellent at retaining possession under pressure, moving the ball swiftly to feet, and creating room to build attacks. But the Czechs were superbly marshalled in defence.

Nevertheless, chances were created, and it was thanks to the excellent goalkeeping of Petr Kouba, who denied both Fernando Couto and Sá Pinto midway through the half, that the Czechs reached half-time with the scores still level at 0-0. On the balance of play, Portugal deserved to be in front, but to cement their superiority with a goal, they needed to show more variety, increase their mobility and get round the back of the Czech defence.

But in the second half Portugal did none of those things. And after just eight minutes they fell behind. The Czechs had not looked much of a threat in attack, but they began the second half with frenzied commitment and were rewarded with a quite extraordinary goal from Poborsky. The little winger was favoured by the bounce of the ball as he burst through a couple of Portuguese defenders. But with the goal in sight and the goalkeeper coming out to meet him, he concocted the most extravagant finish, lifting the ball almost vertically from the turf and sending it looping over Vítor Baía's head into the goal.

Once ahead, the Czechs were rarely threatened. Portugal became increasingly leg-weary and bereft of forward movement, and the Czechs began to take control, without actually creating any chances to increase their lead. The chief concern for coach Dusan Uhrin was an unbelievably card-happy German referee. Four Czech players received their second yellow cards of the tournament, all of them important members of the team - Suchoparek, Latal, Kuka and Bejbl. The cards picked up by Suchoparek and Kuka were extremely harsh, but Latal could not really complain when he was sent off for an agricultural lunge on Dimas eight minutes from time.

Karel Poborsky takes off on his celebratory run after scoring against Portugal

Down to ten men, the Czechs suddenly looked vulnerable, and Portugal created their only genuine chance of the half shortly after the sending-off when, from the area Latal would normally have occupied, Folha sent over an excellent cross, which Cadete, on as a substitute for Figo, headed badly wide.

That was Portugal's last chance to save themselves. It was not their day, and they could have no complaints about the result after such a disappointing second half. As for the Czechs, they had kept their shape and their discipline magnificently - despite the handicap of the referee, who did his best to ruin their chances of making further progress with his overfussy officiating.

The four quarter-finals had produced just four goals in seven hours of football. The matches had all been tight and tense, but the entertainment value had been low. The tournament had not taken off as everybody had hoped. But, with the Czechs still in there, at least the neutrals had an unlikely underdog to root for.

MATCH DETAILS

23/06/96, Birmingham

PORTUGAL 0

CZECH REPUBLIC 1 Poborsky (53)

referee - Krug (GER)

PORTUGAL - Vítor Baía; Secretário, Fernando Couto, Hélder, Dimas; Figo (Cadete 83), Oceano (Folha 65), Paulo Sousa, Rui Costa; Sá Pinto (Domingos 46), João Pinto.

CZECH REPUBLIC - Kouba; Hornak, Kadlec, Suchoparek; Latal, Poborsky, Bejbl, Nemecek (Berger 90), Nemec; Smicer (Kubik 85), Kuka.

Penalties decide drab encounter

After a series of unimpressive quarter-finals, Euro '96 was in desperate need of a lift. But the first of the semi-finals, between France and the Czech Republic at Old Trafford, was not about to provide it. The Czechs, decimated with suspensions, were always going to count their losses and consolidate the excellent defensive display they had produced against Portugal. As for the French, with captain Deschamps injured and Karembeu suspended, they too had their selection problems, but the dice still seemed heavily loaded in their favour. And yet, right from the outset, it was clear that the French intended to be every bit as cagey and as cautious as the Czechs. With two teams committed only to protecting their goal, a drab stalemate was inevitable.

It was a truly awful match, lacking in eveything that one would expect from a European Championship semi-final. There was no sense of occasion in the stands - the official attendance figure of 43,877 must have been plucked out of thin air - and this affected the players, who acted as if entering their opponents' penalty area was a sin. In the first 45 minutes there was barely a single moment of excitement. The first meaningful shot on goal did not come until five minutes before the interval.

It took an hour for the first sign of urgency to be brought to the proceedings. Frenchman Youri Djorkaeff was unlucky not to give his side the lead twice in as many minutes. With his first effort, from 25 yards out, he rattled the crossbar; a minute later he tried a spectacular scissors-kick, but the shot was just too high. This sparked the Czechs into life, and a good run from half-time substitute Patrik Berger threatened to open up the French defence, but it came to nothing.

MATCH DETAILS

26/06/96, Manchester

FRANCE 0 CZECH REPUBLIC 0

(aet; 5-6 on pens.)

FRANCE - Lama; Thuram (Angloma 83), Blanc, Roche, Lizarazu; Lamouchi (Pedros 62), Djorkaeff, Desailly, Zidane, Guérin; Loko.

CZECH REPUBLIC - Kouba; Hornak, Kadlec, Rada; Poborsky, Novotny, Nemecek, Nedved, Nemec (Kubik 84); Smicer (Berger 46), Drulak (Kotulek 70).

France's Bixente Lizarazu takes on the Czech defence

Both teams were desperately short of a decent striker. Aimé Jacquet and Dusan Uhrin had both opted to use just one man up front, but Patrice Loko and Radek Drulak might as well have been on the bench for all the threat they posed. The game was crying out for a goal, but there was no one to provide it. Poborsky and Berger tried to inject some pace and mobility for the Czechs, but they were too often isolated and crowded out. The Czechs finished normal time the stronger but without seriously threatening to score.

Not a lot changed in extra-time. The prospect of the 'Golden Goal' simply intensified the desire of both teams to batten up their hatches at the back. Throwing caution to the wind and going all out for glory seemed to be an alien concept. France had the better efforts, with Kouba being forced into saves from Pedros and Loko, but a penalty shoot-out had long seemed the only way of separating these two negative teams. After two hours of turgid football, this artificial tie-breaker, for once, came as a huge relief.

Referee Mottram, who had been the most impressive individual on the pitch, called the two teams to the centre circle. France were the first to go, and Zidane finally raised a cheer by giving his team the lead. It was the first of ten successful spot-kicks. Kubik, Nedved, Berger, Poborsky and Rada found the target for the Czechs, and, as against Holland, Djorkaeff, Lizarazu, Guérin and Blanc joined Zidane in converting for the French.

But when it came to sudden-death, Reynald Pedros, arguably the most adventurous Frenchman on the day, shot weakly and Kouba saved. The Czechs just needed to score their next penalty to win. The only problem was that nobody was willing to come forward and take it. Kubik offered his services, but as he had already taken the first penalty, the referee sent him back. The responsibility eventually fell to Miroslav Kadlec. If the Czech captain was nervous, he didn't show it. His shot was perfect. Lama was beaten, so were the French, and the pre-tournament 80-1 outsiders marched on to Wembley for the final.

EURO 96 FINALS Semi-Finals

History repeats itself for unlucky England

MATCH DETAILS

26/06/96, Wembley
GERMANY 1 Kuntz (16)
ENGLAND 1 Shearer (3)
(aet; 6-5 on pens.)
referee - Puhl (HUN)
GERMANY - Köpke; Babbel, Sammer, Helmer (Bode 110); Reuter, Scholl (Hässler 77), Freund (Strunz 118), Eilts, Möller, Ziege; Kuntz.
ENGLAND - Seaman; Southgate, Adams, Pearce; Anderton, Platt, Ince, Gascoigne, McManaman; Sheringham, Shearer.

England went into their most important match for six years wearing all grey. At the end of an evening of incredible drama and emotion, they could have been forgiven for leaving Wembley dressed all in black. Just as in the 1990 World Cup, England played their best match of the tournament, drew it 1-1, and then lost in a penalty shoot-out. Now, as then, their opponents were arch-rivals Germany.

A nation mourned England's passing. Some even took to the streets in drunken rage. But beneath the sadness there was immense pride. In two and a half weeks Terry Venables' team had restored English football to a place of prominence in the world game. The lengthy standing ovation the coach and his players received from the Wembley crowd after it was all over was a testament to what they had accomplished.

But it was Germany, not England, who went on to the final. Berti Vogts' team won a tight, epic encounter through courage, hard work, a bit of luck and a timeless ability to hold their nerve under pressure.

The match began just as every England fan had dreamed it would. A powerful long-range strike from Ince was punched away by Köpke, and from the corner, taken by Gascoigne, Alan Shearer charged in to head in from Adams' flick-on. It was the England number nine's fifth goal in five games. Never had he scored a more important one for his country.

But Germany were unflustered by this early setback and on 16 minutes they drew level. Möller fed Helmer, and his cross was angled perfectly behind the England defence for Stefan Kuntz to get ahead of Pearce and force the ball past Seaman. The rest of the first-half was even, but England had the better chances, Sheringham forcing a goal-line save from Reuter and Shearer heading fractionally wide from an Anderton cross.

In the second-half the high quality of play from both teams continued. Helmer wasted a glorious chance for Germany when he clipped the ball over the bar from an Eilts pass, but ten minutes later he was back in defence to make a brilliant saving tackle from a goal-bound Gascoigne.

Into extra-time and the action boiled to a crescendo. After just three minutes England were cruelly denied when Anderton connected with McManaman's cross and watched the ball thud against the post and back into Köpke's arms. Then the Germans piled on the pressure. Möller crashed in a tremendous shot which Seaman tipped over, and from the corner Kuntz headed in - only for referee Puhl, excellent throughout, to rule out the goal for pushing. Then it was back to the other end where Gascoigne arrived a fraction of a second too late to connect with Shearer's volleyed pass across the face of an open German goal. The crowd were off their seats. The tension was unbearable. But despite the best efforts of two wonderfully positive teams, the 'Golden Goal' would not come. As in Turin six years earlier, England and Germany were forced to settle their combat from the penalty spot.

There was so much at stake. Both teams fancied their chances against the Czech Republic in the final. And for England, the moment was perfect to erase the nightmare of Italia '90. It all hinged on the courage and ability of the penalty-takers. The chosen five from each team struck their kicks with amazing composure and accuracy. Shearer, Platt, Pearce, Gascoigne and Sheringham all converted for England. Hässler, Strunz, Reuter, Ziege and Kuntz did likewise for Germany. Every time England scored, the sense of expectation grew. But the Germans immediately crushed the crowd's hopes. Gareth Southgate was next up for England. Everybody else had struck their kicks hard; he shot weakly and Köpke saved low to his right. Andreas Möller, who knew he would be suspended for the final, now had the chance to put Germany through. Like all the previous German penalties, his shot was struck with awesome power and precision. Seaman had no chance. Germany were jubilant, England griefstricken.

Controversial 'Golden Goal' gives Germany third title

Euro '96 ended in major controversy. German substitute Oliver Bierhoff's second goal of the game - the extra-time 'Golden Goal' that decided the final and brought Germany their third European Championship triumph - was only allowed to stand because the Italian referee, Pierluigi Pairetto, failed to respond to a flag raised by his linesman for offside.

As the ball bobbled into the corner of the Czech net, via two deflections, the linesman clearly signalled that another German striker, Stefan Kuntz, was standing in an offside position. Whether he was interfering with play or not was down to the interpretation of the referee. But Pairetto was too busy watching the German players and coaching staff indulge in their celebrations to notice. As the seconds ticked away without a response, the linesman lowered his flag. But he raised it again when Czech officials approached him, and it was only then that Pairetto came over to seek his advice. By then, however, the moment had passed. There were jubilant Germans all over the pitch. It would have taken a referee of considerably greater courage than Pairetto to have cancelled the goal and restarted the match.

That the final should be concluded in such an unworthy and farcical fashion was a great pity, because it had been a largely enjoyable match. Despite the elimination of England, there was a great sense of occasion at a packed-out Wembley. German and Czech fans were there in large numbers, and the two teams responded positively to the favourable atmosphere.

The Czechs lined up with seven home-based players and included Suchoparek, Bejbl and Kuka, all back from suspension. Germany had skipper Jürgen Klinsmann available again despite doubts that the calf strain which excluded him from the semi-final had fully healed. So bad was the German injury crisis that UEFA, outrageously, had allowed them to call up two extra players. But, sensibly, in view of the criticism that greeted this decision, Berti Vogts did not even put the one player he had brought in - Jens Todt - on the substitutes' bench.

The early passage of play saw the Germans probing for openings and the Czechs defending tightly and in large numbers. When the opportunity arose, however, the Czechs broke quickly and skilfully, and two minutes before half-time they should have gone ahead when the impressive Kuka broke clear after dispossessing Eilts but could only direct his shot straight at Köpke. Germany's best two chances of the half fell to Stefan Kuntz, but he was denied on both occasions by last-ditch saves, first from defender Rada, then from goalkeeper Kouba.

The Czechs worked a couple of good openings early in the second half, and after 58 minutes they were awarded a penalty. Sammer felled Poborsky just outside the area, but the referee got everything wrong. He failed to send Sammer off and awarded a penalty. Patrik Berger rammed home the spot-kick and the Czech Republic were ahead. A couple of minutes later another German player should have been expelled when Helmer deliberately bodychecked a goalbound Kuka, but Pairetto's nightmare performance continued as Helmer escaped with a yellow card.

That was the turning point of the match. Germany brought Oliver Bierhoff on for Scholl, and within four minutes of his arrival he had headed Christian Ziege's superb free-kick down and in past a strangely hesitant Kouba. Back on level terms, the Germans then began to dominate, creating a cluster of chances in the last 15 minutes, the best of them for Klinsmann, whose shot was brilliantly blocked by Rada. With one minute to go, Czech substitute Vladimir Smicer, back from his wedding two days earlier, nearly scored a goal more important even than his first-round strike against Russia, forcing a fingertip save from Köpke after a wonderful Czech move.

Extra-time arrived, but no sooner had it started than Germany had won the game, and the tournament, with Bierhoff's second goal of the evening. For the first time in five attempts at Euro '96 somebody had finally struck gold. But what a flawed gem it turned out to be.

MATCH DETAILS

30/06/96, Wembley

CZECH REPUBLIC 1 Berger (58p)

GERMANY 2 Bierhoff (73, 95)

(golden goal)

referee - Pairetto (ITA)

CZECH REPUBLIC - Kouba; Hornak, Rada, Kadlec, Suchoparek; Poborsky (Smicer 88), Nedved, Bejbl, Berger, Nemec; Kuka.

GERMANY - Köpke; Babbel, Sammer, Helmer; Strunz, Hässler, Eilts (Bode 46), Scholl (Bierhoff 69), Ziege; Klinsmann, Kuntz.

EURO 96 FINALS Miscellaneous

TOP SCORERS

5	Alan SHEARER	(England)
3	Hristo STOICHKOV	(Bulgaria)
	Brian LAUDRUP	(Denmark)
	Jürgen KLINSMANN	(Germany)
	Davor SUKER	(Croatia)
2	Pierluigi CASIRAGHI	(Italy)
	Teddy SHERINGHAM	(England)
	Matthias SAMMER	(Germany)
	Oliver BIERHOFF	(Germany)

YELLOW & RED CARDS

ENGLAND	(9 yellow/0 red)
SWITZERLAND	(12 yellow/0 red)
SCOTLAND	(8 yellow/0 red)
HOLLAND	(9 yellow/0 red)
SPAIN	(12 yellow/1 red)
BULGARIA	(7 yellow/1 red)
FRANCE	(11 yellow/0 red)
ROMANIA	(7 yellow/0 red)
GERMANY	(16 yellow/1 red)
CZECH REPUBLIC	(18 yellow/1 red)
RUSSIA	(9 yellow/1 red)
ITALY	(5 yellow/1 red)
DENMARK	(4 yellow/0 red)
PORTUGAL	(12 yellow/0 red)
TURKEY	(8 yellow/0 red)
CROATIA	(10 yellow/1 red)
TOTALS	**(157 yellow/7 red)**

SENDINGS-OFF

Petar HUBCHEV	(Bulgaria v Spain)
Juan Antonio PIZZI	(Spain v Bulgaria)
Luigi APOLLONI	(Italy v Czech Republic)
Yuri KOVTUN	(Russia v Germany)
Thomas STRUNZ	(Germany v Italy)
Igor STIMAC	(Croatia v Germany)
Radoslav LATAL	(Czech Republic v Portugal)

'THE EUROPEAN FOOTBALL YEARBOOK' EURO '96 ALL-STAR TEAM

David SEAMAN
(England)

Matthias SAMMER
(Germany)

Laurent BLANC (France) **FERNANDO COUTO** (Portugal)

Dieter EILTS
(Germany)

Karel POBORSKY (Czech Republic) **Radek BEJBL** (Czech Republic) **Steve McMANAMAN** (England)

RUI COSTA
(Portugal)

Alan SHEARER (England) **Davor SUKER** (Croatia)

SUBSTITUTES

Andreas KÖPKE (Germany) Marcel DESAILLY (France) Aljosa ASANOVIC (Croatia)
Paul GASCOIGNE (England) Hristo STOICHKOV (Bulgaria)

Captain Jürgen Klinsmann hoists aloft the trophy (above) followed by the German side acknowledging their tournament triumph (below)

EURO 96 FINALS Squads/Appearances

GROUP A

ENGLAND

No.	Player	P	Ap	(s)	Gls
1	David SEAMAN	G	5		
2	Gary NEVILLE	D	4		
3	Stuart PEARCE	D	5		
4	Paul INCE	M	4		
5	Tony ADAMS	D	5		
6	Gareth SOUTHGATE	D	5		
7	David PLATT	M	2	(2)	
8	Paul GASCOIGNE	M	5		1
9	Alan SHEARER	A	5		5
10	Teddy SHERINGHAM	A	5		2
11	Darren ANDERTON	M	5		
12	Steve HOWEY	D			
13	Tim FLOWERS	G			
14	Nick BARMBY	A		(3)	
15	Jamie REDKNAPP	M		(1)	
16	Sol CAMPBELL	D		(1)	
17	Steve McMANAMAN	M	5		
18	Les FERDINAND	A			
19	Philip NEVILLE	D			
20	Steve STONE	M		(3)	
21	Robbie FOWLER	A		(2)	
22	Ian WALKER	G			

Coach - Terry VENABLES

SWITZERLAND

No.	Player	P	Ap	(s)	Gls
1	Marco PASCOLO	G	3		
2	Marc HOTTIGER	D	2		
3	Yvan QUENTIN	D	3		
4	Stéphane HENCHOZ	D	3		
5	Alain GEIGER	M	1		
6	Raphaël WICKY	D		(1)	
7	Sébastien FOURNIER	M		(1)	
8	Patrick SYLVESTRE	M			
9	Marco GRASSI	A	2		
10	Ciriaco SFORZA	M	3		
11	Stéphane CHAPUISAT	A	2	(1)	
12	Stephan LEHMANN	G			
13	Sébastien JEANNERET	D	2		
14	Kubilay TÜRKYILMAZ	A	3		1
15	Ramon VEGA	D	3		
16	Marcel KOLLER	M	1	(1)	
17	Johann VOGEL	M	3		
18	Régis ROTHENBÜHLER	D			
19	David SESA	A			
20	Alexandre COMISETTI	M		(2)	
21	Christophe BONVIN	A	2		
22	Joël CORMINBOEUF	G			

Coach - ARTUR JORGE

SCOTLAND

No.	Player	P	Ap	(s)	Gls
1	Jim LEIGHTON	G			
2	Stewart McKIMMIE	D	2		
3	Tom BOYD	D	3		
4	Colin CALDERWOOD	D	3		
5	Colin HENDRY	D	3		
6	Derek WHYTE	D			
7	John SPENCER	A	1	(2)	
8	Stuart McCALL	M	3		
9	Ally McCOIST	A	1	(1)	1
10	Gary McALLISTER	M	3		
11	John COLLINS	M	3		
12	Andy GORAM	G	3		
13	Tosh McKINLAY	M	2		
14	Gordon DURIE	A	3		
15	Eoin JESS	M		(1)	
16	Craig BURLEY	D	1	(2)	
17	Billy McKINLAY	M		(1)	
18	Kevin GALLACHER	M	1		
19	Darren JACKSON	M			
20	Scott BOOTH	A	1	(1)	
21	Scot GEMMILL	M			
22	Nicky WALKER	G			

Coach - Craig BROWN

HOLLAND

No.	Player	P	Ap	(s)	Gls
1	Edwin VAN DER SAR	G	4		
2	Michael REIZIGER	D	4		
3	Danny BLIND	D	3		
4	Clarence SEEDORF	M	3	(1)	
5	Jaap STAM	D			
6	Ronald DE BOER	M	4		
7	Gaston TAUMENT	A	1		
8	Edgar DAVIDS	M	1	(1)	
9	Patrick KLUIVERT	A	1	(3)	1
10	Dennis BERGKAMP	A	4		1
11	Peter HOEKSTRA	A	2		
12	Aron WINTER	M	2	(2)	
13	Arthur NUMAN	D			
14	Richard WITSCHGE	M	4		
15	Winston BOGARDE	D	4		
16	Ed DE GOEY	G			
17	Jordi CRUIJFF	A	4		1
18	Johan DE KOCK	D	2	(2)	
19	Youri MULDER	A		(1)	
20	Philip COCU	M	1	(2)	
21	Ruud HESP	G			
22	John VELDMAN	D			

Coach - Guus HIDDINK

EURO 96 FINALS Squads/Appearances

GROUP B

SPAIN

No.	Player	P	Ap	(s)	Gls
1	Andoni ZUBIZARRETA	G	4		
2	Juan Manuel LOPEZ	D	2	(1)	
3	Alberto BELSUE	D	2		
4	Rafael ALKORTA	D	4		
5	ABELARDO Fernández	D	4		
6	Fernando HIERRO	M	4		
7	José Emilio AMAVISCA	M	2	(1)	
8	Julen GUERRERO	M	1	(1)	
9	Juan Antonio PIZZI	A	2		
10	DONATO Gama da Silva	M		(1)	
11	ALFONSO Pérez	A	1	(3)	1
12	SERGI Barjuán	D	4		
13	Santiago CAÑIZARES	G			
14	Francisco Narváez "KIKO"	A	2	(1)	
15	José Luis CAMINERO	M	2	(1)	1
16	Jorge OTERO	D	1		
17	Javier MANJARIN	M	2	(1)	1
18	Guillermo AMOR	M	2	(1)	1
19	Julio SALINAS	A	1	(1)	
20	Miguel Angel NADAL	M	2		
21	LUIS ENRIQUE Martínez	M	2		
22	José Francisco MOLINA	G			

Coach - Javier CLEMENTE

BULGARIA

No.	Player	P	Ap	(s)	Gls
1	Borislav MIKHAILOV	G	3		
2	Radostin KISHISHEV	D	2		
3	Trifon IVANOV	D	3		
4	Ilian KIRIAKOV	D	1		
5	Petar HUBCHEV	D	2		
6	Zlatko YANKOV	M	3		
7	Emil KOSTADINOV	A	2		
8	Hristo STOICHKOV	A	3		3
9	Liuboslav PENEV	A	3		
10	Krasimir BALAKOV	M	3		
11	Yordan LECHKOV	M	3		
12	Dimitar POPOV	G			
13	Boncho GENCHEV	M		(1)	
14	Nasko SIRAKOV	M		(1)	
15	Ivailo YORDANOV	M	2	(1)	
16	Daniel BORIMIROV	M		(3)	
17	Emil KREMENLIEV	D	1		
18	Tsanko TSVETANOV	D	2	(1)	
19	Gosho GINCHEV	D			
20	Georgi DONKOV	A		(1)	
21	Ivo GEORGIEV	A			
22	Zdravko ZDRAVKOV	G			

Coach - Dimitar PENEV

FRANCE

No.	Player	P	Ap	(s)	Gls
1	Bernard LAMA	G	5		
2	Jocelyn ANGLOMA	D	1	(1)	
3	Eric DI MECO	D	1		
4	Franck LEBOEUF	D			
5	Laurent BLANC	D	5		1
6	Vincent GUERIN	M	5		
7	Didier DESCHAMPS	M	4		
8	Marcel DESAILLY	D	5		
9	Youri DJORKAEFF	M	5		1
10	Zinedine ZIDANE	M	5		
11	Patrice LOKO	A	3	(2)	1
12	Bixente LIZARAZU	D	4	(1)	
13	Christophe DUGARRY	A	2	(2)	1
14	Sabri LAMOUCHI	M	1		
15	Lilian THURAM	D	4	(1)	
16	Fabien BARTHEZ	G			
17	Michaël MADAR	A			
18	Reynald PEDROS	M		(3)	
19	Christian KAREMBEU	M	4		
20	Alain ROCHE	D	1	(2)	
21	Corentin MARTINS	M			
22	Bruno MARTINI	G			

Coach - Aimé JACQUET

ROMANIA

No.	Player	P	Ap	(s)	Gls
1	Bogdan STELEA	G	2		
2	Dan PETRESCU	D	3		
3	Daniel Claudiu PRODAN	D	2		
4	Miodrag BELODEDICI	D	2		
5	Ioan LUPESCU	M	2	(1)	
6	Gheorghe POPESCU	M	3		
7	Marius LACATUS	A	2		
8	Ioan Ovidiu SABAU	M			
9	Florin RADUCIOIU	A	3		1
10	Gheorghe HAGI	M	3		
11	Dorinel MUNTEANU	M	2	(1)	
12	Florian PRUNEA	G	1		
13	Tibor SELYMES	D	3		
14	Constantin GÂLCA	M	1	(1)	
15	Anton DOBOS	D	1		
16	Gheorghe MIHALI	D	1		
17	Iulian FILIPESCU	D		(1)	
18	Ovidiu STÎNGA	M	1		
19	Adrian ILIE	M	1	(2)	
20	Dinu Viorel MOLDOVAN	A		(2)	
21	Ion VLADOIU	A		(1)	
22	Florin Alexandru TENE	G			

Coach - Anghel IORDANESCU

EURO 96 FINALS Squads/Appearances

GROUP C

GERMANY

No.	Player	P	Ap	(s)	Gls
1	Andreas KÖPKE	G	6		
2	Stefan REUTER	M	4		
3	Marco BODE	M		(3)	
4	Steffen FREUND	M	2	(2)	
5	Thomas HELMER	D	6		
6	Matthias SAMMER	D	6		2
7	Andreas MÖLLER	M	5		1
8	Mehmet SCHOLL	M	3		
9	Fredi BOBIC	A	3		
10	Thomas HÄSSLER	M	4	(2)	
11	Stefan KUNTZ	A	3	(2)	1
12	Oliver KAHN	G			
13	Mario BASLER	M			
14	Markus BABBEL	D	4	(1)	
15	Jürgen KOHLER	D	1		
16	René SCHNEIDER	D			
17	Christian ZIEGE	M	6		1
18	Jürgen KLINSMANN	A	4		3
19	Thomas STRUNZ	M	2	(3)	
20	Oliver BIERHOFF	A	1	(2)	2
21	Dieter EILTS	M	6		
22	Oliver RECK	G			

Coach - Berti VOGTS

CZECH REPUBLIC

No.	Player	P	Ap	(s)	Gls
1	Petr KOUBA	G	6		
2	Radoslav LATAL	M	4		
3	Jan SUCHOPAREK	D	5		1
4	Pavel NEDVED	M	5		1
5	Miroslav KADLEC	D	5		
6	Vaclav NEMECEK	M	2	(2)	
7	Jiri NEMEC	M	6		
8	Karel POBORSKY	M	6		1
9	Pavel KUKA	A	5		1
10	Radek DRULAK	A	1	(1)	
11	Martin FRYDEK	M	1		
12	Lubos KUBIK	D	1	(2)	
13	Radek BEJBL	M	5		1
14	Patrik BERGER	M	3	(3)	1
15	Michal HORNAK	D	6		
16	Pavel SRNICEK	G			
17	Vladimir SMICER	A	2	(3)	1
18	Martin KOTULEK	D		(1)	
19	Karel RADA	D	2		
20	Pavel NOVOTNY	M	1		
21	Milan KERBR	A			
22	Ladislav MAIER	G			

Coach - Dusan UHRIN

RUSSIA

No.	Player	P	Ap	(s)	Gls
1	Dmitri KHARIN	G	1		
2	Omari TETRADZE	D	3		1
3	Yuri NIKIFOROV	D	2		
4	Ilya TSYMBALAR	M	3		1
5	Yuri KOVTUN	D	2		
6	Valeri KARPIN	M	2	(1)	
7	Viktor ONOPKO	M	2		
8	Andrei KANCHELSKIS	M	2		
9	Igor KOLYVANOV	A	3		
10	Aleksandr MOSTOVOI	M	2	(1)	1
11	Sergei KIRYAKOV	A		(1)	
12	Stanislav CHERCHESOV	G	2		
13	Yevgeni BUSHMANOV	D	1		
14	Igor DOBROVOLSKI	M		(1)	
15	Igor SHALIMOV	M		(1)	
16	Igor SIMUTENKOV	A		(1)	
17	Vladimir BESCHASTNYKH	A		(1)	1
18	Igor YANOVSKI	M	1	(1)	
19	Vladislav RADIMOV	M	3		
20	Sergei GORLUKOVICH	D	1		
21	Dmitri KHOKHLOV	M	2		
22	Sergei OVCHINNIKOV	G			

Coach - Oleg ROMANTSEV

ITALY

No.	Player	P	Ap	(s)	Gls
1	Angelo PERUZZI	G	3		
2	Luigi APOLLONI	D	2		
3	Paolo MALDINI	D	3		
4	Amedeo CARBONI	D	1	(1)	
5	Alessandro COSTACURTA	D	3		
6	Alessandro NESTA	D	1		
7	Roberto DONADONI	M	2	(1)	
8	Roberto MUSSI	D	3		
9	Moreno TORRICELLI	D		(1)	
10	Demetrio ALBERTINI	M	3		
11	Dino BAGGIO	M	1		
12	Francesco TOLDO	G			
13	Fabio ROSSITTO	M			
14	Alessandro DEL PIERO	M	1		
15	Angelo DI LIVIO	M	1	(1)	
16	Roberto DI MATTEO	M	2		
17	Diego FUSER	M	2	(1)	
18	Pierluigi CASIRAGHI	A	2	(1)	2
19	Enrico CHIESA	A	1	(1)	1
20	Fabrizio RAVANELLI	A	1	(1)	
21	Gianfranco ZOLA	A	2	(1)	
22	Luca BUCCI	G			

Coach - Arrigo SACCHI

EURO 96 FINALS Squads/Appearances

GROUP D

DENMARK

No.	Player	P	Ap	(s)	Gls
1	Peter SCHMEICHEL	G	3		
2	Thomas HELVEG	D	3		
3	Marc RIEPER	D	3		
4	Lars OLSEN	D			
5	Jes HØGH	D	3		
6	Michael SCHJØNBERG	M	2		
7	Brian Steen NIELSEN	M	3		
8	Claus THOMSEN	M	3		
9	Mikkel BECK	A	1	(1)	
10	Michael LAUDRUP	M	3		
11	Brian LAUDRUP	A	3		3
12	Torben PIECHNIK	D		(1)	
13	Henrik LARSEN	M	1	(1)	
14	Jens RISAGER	D	1		
15	Erik Bo ANDERSEN	A	1		
16	Lars HØGH	G			
17	Allan NIELSEN	M	1		1
18	Kim VILFORT	M	1	(1)	
19	Stig TØFTING	M		(1)	
20	Jacob LAURSEN	D	1	(1)	
21	Søren ANDERSEN	A		(1)	
22	Mogens KROGH	G			

Coach - Richard MØLLER-NIELSEN

PORTUGAL

No.	Player	P	Ap	(s)	Gls
1	VÍTOR BAÍA	G	4		
2	SECRETÁRIO	D	2		
3	PAULINHO SANTOS	D	2		
4	OCEANO	M	3		
5	FERNANDO COUTO	D	4		1
6	TAVARES	M		(3)	
7	VÍTOR PANEIRA	M			
8	JOÃO PINTO	A	4		1
9	SÁ PINTO	A	4		1
10	RUI COSTA	M	4		
11	CADETE	A		(2)	
12	ALFREDO	G			
13	DIMAS	D	4		
14	PEDRO BARBOSA	M		(1)	
15	DOMINGOS	A		(3)	
16	HÉLDER	D	4		
17	PORFÍRIO	A		(1)	
18	FOLHA	M	1	(2)	
19	PAULO SOUSA	M	4		
20	FIGO	M	4		1
21	PAULO MADEIRA	D			
22	RUI CORREIA	G			

Coach - ANTÓNIO OLIVEIRA

TURKEY

No.	Player	P	Ap	(s)	Gls
1	ADNAN Erkan	G			
2	RECEP Çetin	D	2		
3	ALPAY Özalan	D	3		
4	VEDAT Inceefe	D	3		
5	TUGAY Kerimoglu	M	3		
6	ERTUGRUL Saglam	A			
7	HAMI Mandirali	A	1	(1)	
8	OGÜN Temizkanoglu	D	3		
9	HAKAN Sükür	A	3		
10	OGUZ Çetin	M	1		
11	ORHAN Çikrikçi	A	1		
12	FARUK Yigit	A			
13	RAHIM Zafer	D	1	(1)	
14	SAFFET Sancakli	A	1	(2)	
15	TAYFUN Korkut	M	1		
16	SERGEN Yalçin	M	2		
17	ABDULLAH Ercan	M	3		
18	ARIF Erdem	A	1	(2)	
19	TOLUNAY Kafkas	M	1	(1)	
20	BÜLENT Korkmaz	D		(1)	
21	SANVER Göymen	G			
22	RÜSTÜ Reber	G	3		

Coach - FATIH Terim

CROATIA

No.	Player	P	Ap	(s)	Gls
1	Drazen LADIC	G	3		
2	Nikola JURCEVIC	M	2	(1)	
3	Robert JARNI	M	4		
4	Igor STIMAC	D	3		
5	Nikola JERKAN	D	3		
6	Slaven BILIC	D	4		
7	Aljosa ASANOVIC	M	3	(1)	
8	Robert PROSINECKI	M	3		
9	Davor SUKER	A	3	(1)	3
10	Zvonimir BOBAN	M	3	(1)	1
11	Alen BOKSIC	A	1		
12	Marijan MRMIC	G	1		
13	Mario STANIC	M	3		
14	Zvonimir SOLDO	D	1	(2)	
15	Mladen MLADENOVIC	M	1	(2)	
16	Dubravko PAVLICIC	D	1	(1)	
17	Igor PAMIC	A	1		
18	Elvis BRAJKOVIC	D			
19	Goran VLAOVIC	A	3	(1)	1
20	Dario SIMIC	D	1		
21	Igor CVITANOVIC	A			
22	Tonci GABRIC	G			

Coach - Miroslav BLAZEVIC

QUALIFYING GROUP 1

Victory in Bucharest sees France through

GROUP 1 RESULTS - 1994/95

ISRAEL 2, POLAND 1
ROMANIA 3, AZERBAIJAN 0
SLOVAKIA 0, FRANCE 0
FRANCE 0, ROMANIA 0
ISRAEL 2, SLOVAKIA 2
POLAND 1, AZERBAIJAN 0
ROMANIA 3, SLOVAKIA 2
POLAND 0, FRANCE 0
AZERBAIJAN 0, ISRAEL 2
AZERBAIJAN 0, FRANCE 2
ISRAEL 1, ROMANIA 1
ISRAEL 0, FRANCE 0
ROMANIA 2, POLAND 1
SLOVAKIA 4, AZERBAIJAN 1
POLAND 4, ISRAEL 3
FRANCE 4, SLOVAKIA 0
AZERBAIJAN 1, ROMANIA 4
POLAND 5, SLOVAKIA 0
ROMANIA 2, ISRAEL 1

France, the 1998 World Cup hosts, were desperate to get to England. But they made life extremely difficult for themselves when they could only draw 1-1 against Poland on a balmy August night in the Parc des Princes. It was the fifth draw in seven matches for Aimé Jacquet's team, but it could so easily have been their first defeat.

After Polish striker Andrzej Juskowiak had given the visitors a flattering half-time lead with his sixth goal of the qualifying competition (and the first conceded by France), the home side came storming back, creating chance upon chance in a pulsating second period. Assisted by the sending-off of Polish defender Tomasz Lapinski, France bombarded their opponents' goal incessantly for 45 minutes. Youri Djorkaeff had a goal disallowed, Bixente Lizarazu had a penalty saved, and then, just when all hope seemed lost, Djorkaeff finally beat the brilliant Polish goalkeeper Andrzej Wozniak with a clever free-kick.

The result gave the French some breathing space, but they now needed three wins to stand a realistic chance of automatic qualification. Azerbaijan were easy meat in Auxerre. The French registered a record 10-0 scoreline, with local boy Christophe Cocard, fittingly, netting the tenth goal in the final minute.

The tough one was Romania in Bucharest. The Romanians had already guaranteed themselves one of the two top places by holding Poland to a goalless draw in Zabrze. Perhaps that was why they looked out of sorts against a superbly committed French team, who won the match with three fine goals from Christian Karembeu, Youri Djorkaeff and Zinedine Zidane. Romania's only response was a single strike from veteran striker Marius Lacatus that should have been ruled out for offside.

Romania still held a one-point lead going into the final match, and they succeeded in holding onto it with a fine Gheorghe Hagi-inspired 2-0 win away to a Slovakian team that had won their previous three matches. France, meanwhile, had to erase the memory of their World Cup disaster two years earlier and beat Israel. They did so thanks to the excellence of goalkeeper Bernard Lama, who kept his eighth clean sheet of the competition, and the opportunism of Djorkaeff, who struck his fifth goal in four matches to give France the lead midway through the second half. Full-back Lizarazu made up for his penalty miss against Poland with a late second and France were through - just - as the sixth best placed of the eight runners-up.

TOP SCORERS

7	Andrzej JUSKOWIAK (Poland)
6	Ronen HARAZI (Israel)
5	Florin RADUCOUIU (Romania)
	Youri DJORKAEFF (France)

GROUP 1 FINAL TABLE

			Home					Away					Total						
		Pd	W	D	L	F	A	W	D	L	F	A	W	D	L	F	A	Pt	GD
1	Romania	10	4	0	1	11	7	2	3	0	7	2	6	3	1	18	9	21	+9
2	France	10	3	2	0	17	1	2	3	0	5	1	5	5	0	22	2	20	+20
3	Slovakia	10	3	1	1	9	4	1	1	3	5	14	4	2	4	14	18	14	-4
4	Poland	10	3	2	0	10	3	0	2	3	4	9	3	4	3	14	12	13	+2
5	Israel	10	2	3	0	7	4	1	0	4	6	9	3	3	4	13	13	12	=
6	Azerbaijan	10	0	1	4	1	9	0	0	5	1	20	0	1	9	2	29	1	-27

QUALIFYING GROUP 1

GROUP 1 MATCH DETAILS 1995/96

16/08/95, Paris
FRANCE 1 Djorkaeff (85)
POLAND 1 Juskowiak (35)
referee - Díaz Vega (ESP)
FRANCE - Lama; Angloma (Karembeu 66), Lizarazu, Thuram, Leboeuf (Djorkaeff 69), Guérin, Deschamps, Desailly, Dugarry, Zidane, Ginola (Pedros 64).
POLAND - Wozniak; Lapinski, Zielinski, Kozminski, Waldoch, Iwan, Swierczewski P., Nowak (Czerwiec 57), Juskowiak, Kosecki (Wojtala 72), Kowalczyk (Bukalski 61).

16/08/95, Trabzon
AZERBAIJAN 0
SLOVAKIA 1 Jancula (60)
referee - Hamer (LUX)
AZERBAIJAN - Sadikov; Getman, Nosenko, Ahmedov, Agayev (Asadov 71), Abusov, Huseynov Y., Diniyev (Kurbanov M. 46), Kadirov, Lichkin, Alekberov.
SLOVAKIA - Molnar; Balis (Prazenica 89), Sobona, Tomaschek, Kinder, Tittel, Pecko, Simon, Rusnak (Jancula 58), Dubovsky, Moravcik (Faktor 78).

06/09/95, Auxerre
FRANCE 10 Desailly (13), Djorkaeff (17, 78), Guérin (33), Pedros (49), Leboeuf (54, 74), Dugarry (65), Zidane (72), Cocard (90)
AZERBAIJAN 0
referee - Micallef (MLT)
FRANCE - Lama; Angloma (Thuram 57), Lizarazu, Desailly, Leboeuf, Djorkaeff, Deschamps, Guérin, Dugarry (Cocard 68), Zidane, Pedros (Ginola 65).
AZERBAIJAN - Hasanov (Sadikov 36); Asadov, Getman, Ahmedov, Agayev, Abusov, Huseynov Y., Diniyev, Kadirov (Huseynov M. 74), Kurbanov M. (Alekberov 46), Lichkin.

06/09/95, Zabrze
POLAND 0
ROMANIA 0
referee - Gallagher (ENG)
POLAND - Wozniak; Jaskulski, Zielinski, Kozminski, Waldoch, Bednarz (Bukalski 63), Swierczewski P., Iwan (Czerwiec 76), Juskowiak, Kosecki, Wieszczycki (Podbrozny 70).
ROMANIA - Stelea; Petrescu, Prodan, Mihali, Lupescu, Popescu, Lacatus (Timofte I. 84), Sabau, Vladoiu (Panduru 64), Munteanu (Gâlca 75), Selymes.

06/09/95, Kosice
SLOVAKIA 1 Jancula (55)
ISRAEL 0
referee - Sandra (BEL)
SLOVAKIA - Molnar; Balis (Kostka 89), Karhan, Juriga, Kinder, Tittel, Pecko, Simon (Faktor 80), Jancula (Rusnak 61), Dubovsky, Moravcik.
ISRAEL - Cohen; Brumer G., Glam, Hazan, Harazi A., Klinger (Rosenthal 46), Banin, Mizrahi, Berkovitch (Driks 66), Revivo, Shelach.

11/10/95, Ramat-Gan
ISRAEL 2 Harazi R. (31, 51)
AZERBAIJAN 0
referee - Detruche (SUI)
ISRAEL - Ginzburg; Halfon, Amsalem, Hazan, Shelach, Brumer G., Banin, Revivo (Klinger 87), Berkovitch (Zohar 71), Harazi R. (Atar 79), Rosenthal.
AZERBAIJAN - Jidkov; Asadov, Khairrov (Agayev 58), Ahmedov, Vahabzade, Abusov, Lichkin (Mamedov 79), Rzayev (Kurbanov K. 70), Kadirov, Suleymanov, Kasumov.

11/10/95, Bucharest
ROMANIA 1 Lacatus (51)
FRANCE 3 Karembeu (29), Djorkaeff (41), Zidane (72)
referee - Pairetto (ITA)
ROMANIA - Stelea; Petrescu, Prodan, Mihali (Lupu 46), Lupescu, Popescu, Lacatus, Dumitrescu (Vladoiu 46), Selymes, Hagi (Panduru 63), Munteanu.
FRANCE - Barthez; Angloma, Di Meco, Karembeu, Leboeuf, Guérin, Deschamps, Desailly, Djorkaeff (Lizarazu 73), Zidane (Thuram 84), Dugarry (Madar 62).

11/10/95, Bratislava
SLOVAKIA 4 Dubovsky (32p), Jancula (68), Ujlaky (77), Simon (83)
POLAND 1 Juskowiak (19)
referee - Monteiro Coroado (POR)
SLOVAKIA - Molnar; Balis, Karhan, Zeman, Kinder, Tittel, Juriga (Ujlaky 71), Simon, Jancula (Bochnovic 87), Dubovsky, Moravcik.
POLAND - Wozniak; Lapinski, Zielinski, Bukalski, Waldoch, Kozminski (Bednarz 59), Swierczewski P., Iwan, Juskowiak, Kosecki, Baluszynski (Czereszewski 80).

15/11/96, Caen
FRANCE 2 Djorkaeff (69), Lizarazu (89)
ISRAEL 0
referee - Grabher (AUT)
FRANCE - Lama; Angloma, Di Meco (Lizarazu 63), Karembeu (Keller 90), Leboeuf, Guérin, Deschamps, Desailly, Djorkaeff, Zidane, Madar (Loko 63).
ISRAEL - Cohen; Halfon, Glam, Hazan, Brumer G., Klinger (Zohar 78), Banin, Shelach, Berkovitch (Atar 69), Harazi R. (Mizrahi 84), Rosenthal.

15/11/95, Trabzon
AZERBAIJAN 0
POLAND 0
referee - Mottram (SCO)
AZERBAIJAN - Jidkov; Getman, Gaisumov, Ahmedov, Vahabzade, Abusov, Agayev, Rzayev (Kurbanov K. 69), Kadirov (Kurbanov M. 65), Suleymanov (Lichkin 86), Kasumov.
POLAND - Wozniak; Jaskulski, Swierczewski M., Sokolowski, Waldoch, Czereszewski, Wojtala, Bukalski (Lenart 71), Baluszynski (Kuzba 65), Czerwiec, Majak (Siadaczka 46).

15/11/95, Kosice
SLOVAKIA 0
ROMANIA 2 Hagi (68), Munteanu (82)
referee - Uilenberg (HOL)
SLOVAKIA - Molnar; Balis, Karhan, Tomaschek, Kinder, Tittel, Pecko (Juriga 46), Simon (Semenik 78), Jancula (Ujlaky 69), Dubovsky, Moravcik.
ROMANIA - Stelea; Petrescu, Prodan, Dobos, Lupescu, Popescu, Lacatus (Dumitrescu 72), Selymes, Moldovan (Timofte I. 87), Hagi (Panduru 84), Munteanu.

QUALIFYING GROUP 2

Danes safely through to defend their trophy

GROUP 2 RESULTS - 1994/95

BELGIUM 2, ARMENIA 0
CYPRUS 1, SPAIN 2
FYR MACEDONIA 1, DENMARK 1
ARMENIA 0, CYPRUS 0
DENMARK 3, BELGIUM 1
FYR MACEDONIA 0, SPAIN 2
BELGIUM 1, FYR MACEDONIA 1
CYPRUS 2, ARMENIA 0
SPAIN 3, DENMARK 0
BELGIUM 1, SPAIN 4
FYR MACEDONIA 3, CYPRUS 0
CYPRUS 1, DENMARK 1
SPAIN 1, BELGIUM 1
BELGIUM 2, CYPRUS 0
DENMARK 1, FYR MACEDONIA 0
ARMENIA 0, SPAIN 2
ARMENIA 2, FYR MACEDONIA 2
DENMARK 4, CYPRUS 0
SPAIN 1, ARMENIA 0
FYR MACEDONIA 0, BELGIUM 5

At the outset, Group Two looked to be the toughest and the tightest of the eight qualifying sections. But in the end it was all fairly simple and straightforward for Spain and Denmark.

The Spaniards were sure-fire certainties to qualify right from an early stage. Their big wins over Denmark and Belgium had left them in a comfortable position, and they made certain of a place in the finals with a 1-1 draw in Copenhagen, becoming one of only two teams - Russia were the others - to seal their qualification before their final match. With a 3-0 victory at home to Macedonia to complete their programme, Spain finished clear group winners with eight wins and two draws from their ten games.

The main interest centred on the meeting between Belgium and Denmark in Brussels on September 6. The Danes had rarely been lucky in major tournament qualifiers before, but they certainly had more than their fair share in this encounter. They were outplayed by the Belgians for most of the match, but were gifted three goals. Michael Laudrup skilfully tucked away the first after a bad goalkeeping error from Gilbert Bodart. Then, two minutes later, Mikkel Beck didn't know what hit him as Kim Vilfort seized upon another defensive aberration and saw his shot deflect in off the young forward's head. Belgian defender Georges Grün pulled a goal back shortly afterwards with a powerful header from a Luc Nilis corner, but the match was decided in Denmark's favour midway through the second half when a header from Vilfort was adjudged marginally, but contestably, to have crossed the line before being headed clear.

With that victory, Denmark assured themselves of a place in the top two and also confirmed Belgium's failure to qualify for three European Championship finals in succession. The 1-1 draw with Spain, in which Vilfort, with his fifth goal of the competition, became the group's leading scorer, delayed certain qualification, but the chances of the Danes missing out on one of the best runners-up spots were so remote that they could take it easy in their final match at home to Armenia - so easy, in fact, that coach Richard Møller-Nielsen did not even feel the need to put on any substitutes. With their 21 points, the 1992 champions had room to spare and rightfully took their place in England to defend their trophy.

TOP SCORERS

5 Kim VILFORT (Denmark)
4 Fernando HIERRO (Spain)
Michael LAUDRUP (Denmark)
Marc DEGRYSE (Belgium)

GROUP 2 FINAL TABLE

			Home					Away					Total						
		Pd	W	D	L	F	A	W	D	L	F	A	W	D	L	F	A	Pt	GD
1	Spain	10	4	1	0	14	1	4	1	0	11	3	8	2	0	25	4	26	+21
2	Denmark	10	4	1	0	12	3	2	2	1	7	6	6	3	1	19	9	21	+10
3	Belgium	10	2	1	2	7	8	2	2	1	10	5	4	3	3	17	13	15	+4
4	FYR Macedonia	10	1	1	3	5	10	0	3	2	4	8	1	4	5	9	18	7	-9
5	Cyprus	10	1	3	1	6	5	0	1	4	0	15	1	4	5	6	20	7	-14
6	Armenia	10	0	2	3	2	8	1	0	4	3	9	1	2	7	5	17	5	-12

QUALIFYING GROUP 2

GROUP 2 MATCH DETAILS 1995/96

16/08/95, Yerevan
ARMENIA 0
DENMARK 2 Laudrup M. (33), Nielsen A. (46)
referee - Dardenne (GER)
ARMENIA - Petrosyan Arm.; Hovsepyan, Khachatryan V., Khachatryan A., Hovhannisyan, Tonoyan, Petrosyan Art., Grigoryan, Tahmazyan (Ter-Petrosyan 41), Shahgeldyan, Avetisyan A. (Avetisyan V. 80).
DENMARK - Schmeichel; Laursen, Rieper, Høgh, Risager (Schjønberg 85), Thomsen, Jensen (Nielsen A. 46), Nielsen B.S., Beck, Laudrup M., Rasmussen.

06/09/95, Brussels
BELGIUM 1 Grün (25)
DENMARK 3 Laudrup M. (20), Beck (22), Vilfort (66)
referee - Zhuk (BLS)
BELGIUM - Bodart; Genaux, Grün, Medved, Smidts (Renier 77), Staelens (Nilis 14), Karagiannis, De Bilde, Degryse, Scifo, Schepens (Foguenne 54).
DENMARK - Schmeichel; Laursen, Rieper, Høgh, Risager, Thomsen, Nielsen B.S., Vilfort, Beck (Rasmussen 70), Laudrup M. (Schjønberg 90), Laudrup B. (Andersen E.B. 76).

06/09/95, Granada
SPAIN 6 Guerrero (45), Alfonso (60), Pizzi (74, 79), Hierro (78), Caminero (83)
CYPRUS 0
referee - Jol (HOL)
SPAIN - Zubizarreta; Beslué, Aranzábal, Alkorta, Nadal, Hierro, Luis Enrique, Guerrero (Manjarín 77), Alfonso (Pizzi 61), Caminero, Amavisca (Fran 53).
CYPRUS - Panayiotou; Andreou S., Pittas, Christodoulou, Panayi, Charalambous N., Ashiotis, Andoniou (Andreou P. 80), Gogic, Malekkos (Sotiriou 57), Hadjilucas (Ioannou Y. 68).

06/09/95, Skopje
FYR MACEDNIA 1 Micevski (10)
ARMENIA 2 Grigoryan (61), Shahgeldyan (78)
referee - Melo Pereira (POR)
FYR MACEDONIA - Celeski; Nikolovski, Stojkovski, Markovski, Babunski, Jovanovski, Serafimovski (Karadzov 46), Memed (Veselinoski 65), Hristov, Savevski, Micevski.
ARMENIA - Petrosyan Arm.; Gspeyan, Khachatryan V., Soukiasyan, Hovhannisyan, Stepanyan (Ter-Petrosyan 75), Petrosyan Art. (Khachatryan A. 84), Grigoryan (Avetisyan V. 68), Mkhitaryan, Shahgeldyan, Hovsepyan.

07/10/95, Yerevan
ARMENIA 0
BELGIUM 2 Nilis (28, 38)
referee - Mitrev (BUL)
ARMENIA - Abrahamyan; Soukiasyan, Khachatryan V., Khachatryan A., Hovsepyan, Gspeyan, Petrosyan Art., Grigoryan (Avetisyan V. 46), Mkhitaryan (Margaryan 71), Shahgeldyan, Avetisyan A..
BELGIUM - De Wilde; Genaux, Crasson, De Boeck, Smidts, Staelens, Karagiannis (Vermant 81), Schepens, Nilis, Scifo, De Bilde (Goossens 63).

11/10/95, Limassol
CYPRUS 1 Agathocleous (90)
FYR MACEDONIA 1 Jovanovski (31)
referee - Irvine (NIR)
CYPRUS - Petrides; Costa, Pittas, Christodoulou, Charalambous M., Kalotheou (Agathocleous 63), Engomitis (Papavassiliou 46), Sotiriou (Larkou 80), Gogic, Malekkos, Savvides.
FYR MACEDONIA - Celeski; Jovanovski, Karadzov, Markovski, Nikolovski, Jovanovski, Veselinoski (Hristov 84), Savevski, Memed, Ciric, Serafimovski (Karanfilovski 77).

11/10/95, Copenhagen
DENMARK 1 Vilfort (47)
SPAIN 1 Hierro (17p)
referee - Krondl (TCH)
DENMARK - Schmeichel; Laursen, Rieper, Høgh, Risager, Piechnik, Nielsen B.S. (Wieghorst 67), Vilfort, Beck, Laudrup M., Rasmussen.
SPAIN - Zubizarreta; Belsué, Sergi, Alkorta, Abelardo, Hierro, Manjarín (Donato 61), Nadal, Pizzi (Alfonso 46), Caminero (Fran 29), Luis Enrique.

15/11/95, Limassol
CYPRUS 1 Agathocleous (15)
BELGIUM 1 De Bilde (68)
referee - Cesari (ITA)
CYPRUS - Panayiotou; Costa, Pittas, Christodoulou, Charalambous M., Andreou A., Engomitis, Gogic (Elia 80), Malekkos (Larkou 50), Papavassiliou, Agathocleous (Zembashis 75).
BELGIUM - De Wilde; Genaux, Grün, De Boeck, Smidts (Schepens 80), Staelens, Karagiannis (Goossens 46), Boffin (Huysmans 60), Degryse, Nilis, De Bilde.

15/11/95, Copenhagen
DENMARK 3 Schjønberg (20), Beck (36), Laudrup M. (58)
ARMENIA 1 Petrosyan Art. (47)
referee - Veissière (FRA)
DENMARK - Schmeichel; Helveg, Rieper, Høgh, Risager, Schjønberg, Nielsen B.S., Vilfort, Beck, Laudrup M., Rasmussen.
ARMENIA - Abrahamyan; Artoyan, Khatcharyan V., Hovsepyan, Vardanyan, Gsepyan (Krbashyan 74), Petrosyan Art., Avetisyan V. (Margaryan 70), Mkhitaryan, Nikolyan, Avetisyan A..

15/11/95, Elche
SPAIN 3 Kiko (17), Manjarín (72), Amavisca (79)
FYR MACEDONIA 0
referee - Steinborn (GER)
SPAIN - Zubizarreta; Belsué, Sergi, Alkorta, Nadal, Donato, Manjarín, Kiko (Goicoechea 74), Pizzi (Alfonso 46), Amavisca (Ferrer 46), Luis Enrique.
FYR MACEDONIA - Celeski; Jovanovski, Stojkovski, Serafimovski (Veselinoski 52; Hristov 78), Babunski, Jovanovski (Nikolovski 72), Karadzov, Memed, Boskovski, Ciric, Micevski.

QUALIFYING GROUP 3

Draws in Sweden do for Swiss and Turks

GROUP 3 RESULTS - 1994/95

HUNGARY 2, TURKEY 2
ICELAND 0, SWEDEN 1
SWITZERLAND 4, SWEDEN 2
TURKEY 5, ICELAND 0
SWEDEN 2, HUNGARY 0
SWITZERLAND 1, ICELAND 0
TURKEY 1, SWITZERLAND 2
HUNGARY 2, SWITZERLAND 2
TURKEY 2, SWEDEN 1
HUNGARY 1, SWEDEN 0
SWITZERLAND 1, TURKEY 2
SWEDEN 1, ICELAND 1
ICELAND 2, HUNGARY 1

Turkey and Switzerland, level at the top of the table going into the final phase of the qualifying competition, had identical fixtures to close their campaign - visits to Iceland and Sweden and a home fixture against Hungary.

Sweden were the only team who could prevent the Turks and the Swiss from filling the top two places, but Tommy Svensson's World Cup semi-finalists appeared to have already abandoned hope when they faced Roy Hodgson's Switzerland in September.

The Swiss had got their show back on the road with an important 2-0 win in Iceland three weeks earlier, and they had the better of a rather dull encounter watched by only 18,500 in the Nya Ullevi stadium. Christophe Ohrel and Kubilay Türkyilmaz both went close for the away team, and although Sweden's Martin Dahlin got the ball in the net in the second half, it was correctly ruled out for a push.

That decison, and the subsequent 0-0 draw, confirmed Sweden's absence from the finals. It also meant that with Turkey defeating Hungary 2-0 on the same night thanks to a brace of headers from top-scoring striker Hakan Sükür, the two front-runners were certain to finish in the top two places. The race was now on to see which team could win the group.

Switzerland's final match was on October 11 in Zürich against a Hungarian side that had long since come to terms with another qualifying failure. With coach Roy Hodgson set to move to Italian club Inter, there was added purpose about the Swiss players. They wanted to give their boss a perfect send-off, and they did so with a convincing 3-0 victory. All three goals resulted from free-

Turkish striker Hakan Sükür topped the Group Three scoring charts with seven goals

GROUP 3 FINAL TABLE

			Home					Away					Total						
		Pd	W	D	L	F	A	W	D	L	F	A	W	D	L	F	A	Pt	GD
1	Switzerland	8	3	0	1	9	4	2	2	0	6	3	5	2	1	15	7	17	+8
2	Turkey	8	3	0	1	10	3	1	3	0	6	5	4	3	1	16	8	15	+8
3	Sweden	8	1	3	0	5	3	1	0	3	4	7	2	3	3	9	10	9	-1
4	Hungary	8	2	2	0	6	4	0	0	4	1	9	2	2	4	7	13	8	-6
5	Iceland	8	1	1	2	2	4	0	1	3	1	8	1	2	5	3	12	5	-9

QUALIFYING GROUP 3

kicks, the best of them being Ciriaco Sforza's chip into the top corner for the decisive second goal.

On the same day, Turkey could only manage a draw with Iceland, but, with an identical goal-difference to the Swiss (the two teams had cancelled each other out in their direct confrontations), they could still top the group by winning their final game against Sweden.

To the Swiss, it was neither here nor there how the Turks performed against the Swedes. By calculating all the various permutations from the other groups, they knew that they had already done enough to qualify. UEFA would not confirm this fact until several weeks later, but the mathematics, although complex, were conclusive: if Switzerland did not win the group, they would definitely be one of the six best runners-up.

In the event, the Swiss did win the group. Turkey, in their 299th official international, could only draw against the Swedes, but they, too, were delighted with the outcome. The 2-2 draw, a thrilling match in which they worked themselves into the ground and twice came from behind, secured the country's first ever qualification for the European Championship. Switzerland, too, were into the finals for the very first time.

TOP SCORERS

7 HAKAN Sükür (Turkey)
3 Kubilay TÜRKYILMAZ (Switzerland)

GROUP 3 MATCH DETAILS 1995/96

16/08/95, Reykjavík
ICELAND 0
SWITZERLAND 2 Knup (4), Türkyilmaz (18)
referee - Wojcik (POL)
ICELAND - Kristinsson B.; Adolfsson, Jónsson K. (Dervic 88), Jónsson S., Gunnlaugsson B., Kristinsson R., Bergsson, Örlygsson, Gunnlaugsson A., Thórdarson, Sverrisson (Ingólfsson 67).
SWITZERLAND - Pascolo; Hottiger, Quentin, Henchoz, Geiger, Fournier, Sutter (Bickel 79), Ohrel, Knup, Sforza, Türkyilmaz (Bonvin 85).

06/09/95, Gothenburg
SWEDEN 0
SWITZERLAND 0
referee - Ceccarini (ITA)
SWEDEN - Andersson B.; Kåmark, Andersson P., Björklund, Nilsson, Schwarz (Erlingmark 90), Alexandersson, Andersson K., Thern, Dahlin, Brolin (Larsson 78).
SWITZERLAND - Pascolo; Hottiger, Quentin, Henchoz, Geiger, Fournier, Sutter (Herr 46), Ohrel, Knup, Sforza, Türkyilmaz (Grassi 90).

06/09/95, Istanbul
TURKEY 2 Hakan (9, 32)
HUNGARY 0
referee - Krondl (TCH)
TURKEY - Rüstü; Recep, Ogün, Osman, Tugay, Alpay, Abdullah, Sergen (Tolunay 46), Hakan (Bülent U. 89), Oguz, Hami (Bülent K. 86).
HUNGARY - Petry; Nagy N. (Sallói 46), Telek, Mészöly, Kozma, Lipcsei, Kiprich, Halmai, Arany, Illés (Klausz 46), Farkasházy.

11/10/95, Reykjavík
ICELAND 0
TURKEY 0
referee - Strampe (GER)
ICELAND - Kristinsson B.; Gíslason, Ingólfsson (Stefánsson 71), Jónsson (Grétarsson 43), Adolfsson, Kristinsson R., Bergsson, Örlygsson, Gunnlaugsson A., Gudjohnsen, Sverrisson (Gunnlaugsson B. 80).
TURKEY - Rüstü; Recep, Ogün, Osman, Tugay, Alpay, Hami, Abdullah, Ertugrul, Oguz, Sergen (Tolunay 74).

11/10/95, Zürich
SWITZERLAND 3 Türkyilmaz (23), Sforza (56), Ohrel (89)
HUNGARY 0
referee - Agius (MLT)
SWITZERLAND - Pascolo; Hottiger, Quentin, Henchoz, Geiger, Fournier (Bickel 81), Yakin, Ohrel, Knup (Bonvin 89), Sforza, Türkyilmaz (Sutter 85).
HUNGARY - Hajdu; Mracskó, Telek, Simon (Jagodics 24), Urban, Lipcsei, Halmai, Nyilas (Mónos 64), Jován, Illés (Arany 64), Vincze.

11/11/95, Budapest
HUNGARY 1 Illés (11p)
ICELAND 0
referee - Bikas (GRE)
HUNGARY - Hajdu; Mónos, Csábi, Szlezák, Illés (Zombori 89), Bánfi, Bükszegi, Nyilas, Orosz (Farkasházy 75), Duró, Vincze (Nagy T. 88).
ICELAND - Kristinsson B.; Gíslason, Jónsson K., Grétarsson (Stefánsson 79), Adolfsson, Kristinsson R. (Danielsson 83), Bergsson, Örlygsson, Gunnlaugsson A., Gudjohnsen, Sverrisson.

15/11/95, Solna
SWEDEN 2 Alexandersson (25), Pettersson (64)
TURKEY 2 Hakan (63), Andersson P. (72og)
referee - Wojcik (POL)
SWEDEN - Ravelli; Lucic, Andersson P., Björklund, Alexandersson, Schwarz, Mild, Fursth, Pettersson (Sahlin 83), Dahlin, Brolin (Zetterberg 70).
TURKEY - Rüstü; Alpay, Ogün (Kemalettin 46), Osman, Tugay, Halil Ibrahim, Tolunay, Tayfun, Hakan, Oguz (Ertugrul 68), Oktay (Arif 46).

QUALIFYING GROUP 4

Croatia and Italy unchallenged at the top

GROUP 4 RESULTS - 1994/95

ESTONIA 0, CROATIA 2	CROATIA 4, UKRAINE 0
SLOVENIA 1, ITALY 1	LITHUANIA 0, CROATIA 0
UKRAINE 0, LITHUANIA 2	SLOVENIA 3, ESTONIA 0
ESTONIA 0, ITALY 2	UKRAINE 0, ITALY 2
CROATIA 2, LITHUANIA 0	CROATIA 2, SLOVENIA 0
UKRAINE 0, SLOVENIA 0	ESTONIA 0, UKRAINE 1
UKRAINE 3, ESTONIA 0	LITHUANIA 0, ITALY 1
ITALY 1, CROATIA 2	LITHUANIA 2, SLOVENIA 1
SLOVENIA 1, LITHUANIA 2	ESTONIA 1, SLOVENIA 3
ITALY 4, ESTONIA 1	UKRAINE 1, CROATIA 0

As expected, Croatia and Italy confirmed their superiority over the other teams in the group and strode through to England in convincing style. If there was a surprise, it was that Italy did not top the group. But after their defeat at home to the Croatians in Palermo, achieving that objective was always an uphill struggle for Arrigo Sacchi and his team.

The Italians could just be thankful that at Euro '96, unlike previous tournaments, there was enough room to accommodate seven runners-up as well as the eight group winners. Italy had the best record in the runners-up 'table', with 13 points from the six games that counted, against Croatia, Lithuania and Ukraine.

The big match between the two group front-runners took place in Split on October 8. The Croatians had warmed up for it with a resounding 7-1 thrashing of Estonia in Zagreb, while the Italians, as is their custom, had settled for a single goal to defeat Slovenia. All of coach Sacchi's best-laid plans went out of the window after nine minutes when goalkeeper Bucci was red carded for handling outside his area. Gianfranco Zola was withdrawn, and substitute goalkeeper Francesco Toldo came on for his first cap. The advantage should have been Croatia's, but a firmly drilled free-kick by Demetrio Albertini gave the vistors the lead, and it was only after half-time that the big crowd had something to cheer. Toldo brought down Alen Boksic, and Davor Suker stroked home the penalty.

The 1-1 draw was a satisfactory result for both teams - as the sterile last 30 minutes proved - but Italy still had some work to do against Ukraine and Lithuania. After poor starts in both matches - the *Azzurri* were a goal down early on to Ukraine and stood 0-0 at half-time against Lithuania - they came through impressively in the second half on each occasion. A magnificent solo goal from Paolo Maldini, added to a couple of Ravanelli tap-ins, secured three points in the first match, and Zola came off the bench to inspire Italy to a four-goal romp in the second. Zola was credited with two goals. He would have had a hat-trick - the first for an

TOP SCORERS

12	Davor SUKER (Croatia)
6	Gianfranco ZOLA (Italy)
5	Timerlan GUSEINOV (Ukraine)
4	Fabrizio RAVANELLI (Italy)
	Zlatko ZAHOVIC (Slovenia)
3	Arunas SUIKA (Lithuania)
	Darius MACIULEVICIUS (Lithuania)
	Primoz GLIHA (Slovenia)
	Saso UDOVIC (Slovenia)
	Martin REIM (Estonia)

GROUP 4 FINAL TABLE

		Home						Away					Total						
		Pd	W	D	L	F	A	W	D	L	F	A	W	D	L	F	A	Pt	GD
1	Croatia	10	4	1	0	16	2	3	1	1	6	3	7	2	1	22	5	23	+17
2	Italy	10	4	0	1	13	4	3	2	0	7	2	7	2	1	20	6	23	+14
3	Lithuania	10	2	1	2	8	5	3	0	2	5	7	5	1	4	13	12	16	+1
4	Ukraine	10	2	1	2	4	4	2	0	3	7	11	4	1	5	11	15	13	-4
5	Slovenia	10	2	1	2	9	7	1	1	3	4	6	3	2	5	13	13	11	=
6	Estonia	10	0	0	5	1	9	0	0	5	2	22	0	0	10	3	31	0	-28

QUALIFYING GROUP 4

GROUP 4 MATCH DETAILS 1995/96

16/08/95, Tallinn
ESTONIA 0
LITHUANIA 1 Maciulevicius (48)
referee - Nilsson (SWE)
ESTONIA - Poom; Lemsalu, Kirs, Kiisman (Kraam 46), Lell, Kallaste R., Lindmaa, Lepa, Kristal, Reim, O'Konnel-Bronin (Olesk 73).
LITHUANIA - Stauce; Ziukas, Sukristovas, Tereskinas, Vainoras, Suika, Maciulevicius, Ivanauskas, Stonkus, Skarbalius (Kancelskis 75), Slekys (Zuta 65).

03/09/95, Zagreb
CROATIA 7 Mladenovic (3), Suker (19p, 58, 89), Boksic (29), Boban (42), Stimac (82)
ESTONIA 1 Reim (17)
referee - Huzu (ROM)
CROATIA - Ladic (Mrmic 30); Mladenovic, Jarni, Stimac (Turkovic 83), Jerkan, Bilic (Pralija 75), Stanic, Prosinecki, Suker, Boban, Boksic.
ESTONIA - Poom; Lemsalu, Kirs, Kallaste T., Kallaste R., Kiisman (Lell 43), Lindmaa (Olumets 76), Lepa (Linnumäe 46), Kristal, Reim, Rajala.

06/09/95, Udine
ITALY 1 Ravanelli (13)
SLOVENIA 0
referee - Gadosi (SVK)
ITALY - Peruzzi; Ferrara, Carboni, Di Matteo, Costacurta, Tacchinardi, Di Livio, Albertini, Del Piero (Signori 46), Zola (Baggio R. 61), Ravanelli (Baggio D. 81).
SLOVENIA - Zupan; Galic, Milanic, Poljsak, Jermanis, Ceh, Kokol (Binkovski 46), Cvikl (Valentincic 78), Zahovic (Becaj 58), Udovic, Gliha.

06/09/95, Vilnius
LITHUANIA 1 Maciulevicius (17)
UKRAINE 3 Guseinov (62, 72), Gusin (83)
referee - Shorte (IRL)
LITHUANIA - Stauce; Ziukas, Sukristovas, Tereskinas (Preiksaitis 68), Vainoras, Suika, Maciulevicius, Ivanauskas, Stonkus, Skarbalius (Zvingilas 77), Slekys.
UKRAINE - Suslov; Luzhnyi, Skrypnyk, Holovko, Zhabchenko (Pokhlebayev 68), Horilyi, Orbu, Kalitvintsev, Bezhenar, Gusin, Guseinov (Yevtushok 86).

08/10/95, Split
CROATIA 1 Suker (49p)
ITALY 1 Albertini (29)
referee - Uilenberg (HOL)
CROATIA - Ladic; Jurcevic (Kozniku 46), Mladenovic, Stimac, Jerkan, Pavlicic, Asanovic, Stanic, Suker, Boban, Boksic.
ITALY - Bucci; Ferrara (Benarrivo 84), Maldini, Di Matteo, Apolloni, Costacurta, Di Livio, Albertini, Del Piero (Crippa 86), Zola (Toldo 9), Ravanelli.

11/10/95, Vilnius
LITHUANIA 5 Maciulevicius (8), Suika (13, 39), Slekys (44), Ivanauskas (62)
ESTONIA 0
referee - Pauchard (FRA)
LITHUANIA - Stauce (Martinkenas 46); Kancelskis, Rimkus, Stonkus, Vainoras, Suika (Zvingilas 74), Maciulevicius, Ivanauskas, Baltusnikas, Vencevicius, Slekys (Jankauskas 46).
ESTONIA - Poom; Olesk, Lepa (Reim 46), Kallaste T., Lell (Kristal 46; Krõm 79), Zelinski, Lindmaa, Kallaste R., Linnumäe, Rajala, Oper.

11/10/95, Ljubljana
SLOVENIA 3 Udovic (53, 89), Zahovic (73)
UKRAINE 2 Skrypnyk (24), Guseinov (44)
referee - Hamer (LUX)
SLOVENIA - Zupan; Galic, Englaro, Milanic, Rudonja, Ceh, Novak, Udovic, Zahovic, Florjancic (Cvikl 71), Gliha.
UKRAINE - Suslov; Luzhnyi, Skrypnyk, Holovko, Zhabchenko, Shmatovalenko (Polunin 89), Orbu, Kalitvintsev (Yevtushok 71), Bezhenar, Gusin (Nahornyak 46), Guseinov.

11/11/96, Bari
ITALY 3 Ravanelli (21, 49), Maldini (54)
UKRAINE 1 Polunin (19)
referee - Muhmenthaler (SUI)
ITALY - Peruzzi; Benarrivo, Maldini, Di Matteo, Ferrara, Costacurta, Baggio D. (Crippa 46), Albertini, Del Piero (Carboni 87), Zola (Simone 67), Ravanelli.
UKRAINE - Suslov; Luzhnyi, Skrypnyk, Bezhenar, Horilyi (Yevtushok 15), Polunin, Orbu, Kalitvintsev, Nahornyak (Pokhlebayev 70), Sharan (Popov 51), Guseinov.

15/11/95, Reggio Emilia
ITALY 4 Suika (52og), Zola (65, 81), Vainoras (82og)
LITHUANIA 0
referee - Díaz Vega (ESP)
ITALY - Peruzzi; Mussi, Maldini (Carboni 72), Di Matteo, Ferrara, Costacurta, Statuto (Zola 46), Albertini, Casiraghi (Ravanelli 46), Del Piero, Simone.
LITHUANIA - Stauce; Ziukas, Tereskinas, Stonkus, Vainoras, Suika (Vencevicius 79), Maciulevicius (Zvingilas 46), Ivanauskas (Zutautas 59), Preiksaitis, Skarbalius, Rimkus.

15/11/95, Ljubljana
SLOVENIA 1 Gliha (36)
CROATIA 2 Suker (40p), Jurcevic (55)
referee - Goethals (BEL)
SLOVENIA - Zupan; Galic, Krizan, Englaro, Jermanis, Zulic (Rudonja 62), Novak, Udovic, Ceh, Gliha, Florjancic (Cvikl 62).
CROATIA - Ladic; Jurcevic, Jarni, Soldo, Jerkan, Bilic, Pralija (Mladenovic 65), Prosinecki, Suker, Stanic, Mornar.

Italian international since Paolo Rossi in 1984 - but for the Italians' insistence that deflected shots count as own-goals. Alessandro Del Piero was denied his début international goal for the same reason. Italy's strong finish could not, however, deny Croatia a deserved first place. They rounded off a superb first major championship qualifying campaign by beating neighbours Slovenia 2-1 in Ljubljana. There was another penalty for Suker, who, with a grand total of 12 goals, finished as the competition's top scorer.

QUALIFYING GROUP 5

Czechs and Dutch cash in on Norway's decline

GROUP 5 RESULTS - 1994/95

CZECH REPUBLIC 6, MALTA 1
LUXEMBOURG 0, HOLLAND 4
NORWAY 1, BELARUS 0
MALTA 0, CZECH REPUBLIC 0
NORWAY 1, HOLLAND 1
BELARUS 2, LUXEMBOURG 0
HOLLAND 0, CZECH REPUBLIC 0
BELARUS 0, NORWAY 4
MALTA 0, NORWAY 1
HOLLAND 5, LUXEMBOURG 0
MALTA 0, LUXEMBOURG 1
LUXEMBOURG 0, NORWAY 2
HOLLAND 4, MALTA 0
CZECH REPUBLIC 4, BELARUS 2
NORWAY 5, LUXEMBOURG 0
BELARUS 1, MALTA 1
CZECH REPUBLIC 3, HOLLAND 1
LUXEMBOURG 1, CZECH REPUBLIC 0
NORWAY 2, MALTA 0
BELARUS 1, HOLLAND 0

Norway were within six minutes of becoming the first team to qualify for Euro '96. In the end they failed to make it at all. Their desire to get the easy games out of the way first failed to pay off. Once Jan Suchoparek's header crashed into Erik Thorstvedt's net in the 84th minute of the all-important Norway-Czech Republic clash in August, the Norwegian challenge began to slip away.

Egil Olsen's team should have wrapped it all up in Oslo. They had plenty of chances to increase the lead given to them by Henning Berg's first-half goal, but a couple of bad misses and a header against the post by Jostein Flo proved to be early warning signs that fate was against them.

A month later, in Prague, the Czechs consolidated their position, defeating the Norwegians fair and square with an early penalty and a delightful late second goal from veteran substitute Radek Drulak. With Holland also rising again from the ashes with a late winner at home to Belarus, the three-way battle for qualification was well and truly joined.

The key match for the Czech Repuublic was away to Belarus in Minsk . It was a difficult place to win - the Dutch could tell them that - but they played splendidly and came away with a vital 2-0 victory. After that, all Dusan Uhrin's team needed was a revenge victory over Luxembourg and first place in the group would be theirs. No problem. Another brace of goals from Drulak added to Berger's strike equalled five home wins out of five and a qualifying ticket for England.

While the Czechs were completing their own formalities, Holland and Norway were battling it out in Rotterdam. One of the teams was sure to go out. Norway could afford to draw. The Dutch had no option but to win. After 45 minutes of stout Norwegian defending, things looked bleak for the men in orange, but a freak goal from Clarence Seedorf just after half-time turned the tide in the home side's favour. Norway had one great chance to equalise, but Jan Åge Fjørtoft squandered it, and late breakaway goals from Youri Mulder and Marc Overmars settled the match for Holland.

The Dutch were not out of the woods yet. They still had to negotiate a tricky play-off against the Republic of Ireland at Anfield. But, in the event, they produced their finest performance in years to dismiss the Irish 2-0 with Patrick Kluivert coolly despatching both goals. The Ajax striker was one of a number of Dutch heroes on the night. Reiziger, Seedorf, Davids and début boy Bogarde were all outstanding, but man of the match was midfielder Ronald de Boer, who was absolutely faultless throughout.

TOP SCORERS

6 Patrik BERGER (Czech Rep.)
5 Sergei GERASIMETS (Belarus)
4 Marc OVERMARS (Holland)
Clarence SEEDORF (Holland)

GROUP 5 FINAL TABLE

			Home					Away					Total						
		Pd	W	D	L	F	A	W	D	L	F	A	W	D	L	F	A	Pt	GD
1	Czech Republic	10	5	0	0	18	4	1	3	1	3	2	6	3	1	21	6	21	+15
2	Holland	10	4	1	0	13	0	2	1	2	10	5	6	2	2	23	5	20	+18
3	Norway	10	3	2	0	10	2	3	0	2	7	5	6	2	2	17	7	20	+10
4	Belarus	10	2	1	2	4	7	1	1	3	4	6	3	2	5	8	13	11	-5
5	Luxembourg	10	2	1	2	2	6	1	0	4	1	15	3	1	6	3	21	10	-18
6	Malta	10	0	1	4	0	8	0	1	4	2	14	0	2	8	2	22	2	-20

QUALIFYING GROUP 5

GROUP 5 MATCH DETAILS 1995/96

16/08/95, Oslo
NORWAY 1 Berg H. (27)
CZECH REPUBLIC 1 Suchoparek (84)
referee - Khusainov (RUS)
NORWAY - Thorstvedt; Håland, Johnsen R., Berg H., Løken, Flo J., Bohinen, Leonhardsen, Fjørtfot (Brattbakk 80), Solbakken, Jakobsen (Brendesaether 64).
CZECH REPUBLIC - Kouba; Latal (Poborsky 78), Suchoparek, Hapal, Kadlec, Repka, Nemec, Berger (Nedved 46), Kuka, Drulak (Samec 78), Frydek.

06/09/95, Luxembourg
LUXEMBOURG 1 Holtz (45)
MALTA 0
referee - Dubinskas (LIT)
LUXEMBOURG - Koch; Vanek, Deville, Birsens, Strasser, Saibene, Hellers, Weis, Holtz (Cardoni 84), Langers, Groff (Theis 68).
MALTA - Cluett; Delia (Agius 27; Gregory 89), Buhagiar, Galea, Woods, Buttigieg, Busuttil, Saliba, Sant Fournier, Laferla, Carabott (Attard 46).

06/09/95, Rotterdam
HOLLAND 1 Mulder (83)
BELARUS 0
referee - Sedlacek (AUT)
HOLLAND - Van der Sar; Reiziger (Trustfull 70), Blind, De Kock, De Boer F., Witschge (Numan 86), Winter, De Boer R., Eykelkamp (Mulder 65), Bergkamp, Overmars.
BELARUS - Satsunkevich; Gurenko, Dovnar, Rodnenok, Taikov, Zygmantovich, Gerasimets, Zhuravel (Vekhtev 89), Romashchenko (Vergeichik 86), Yusipets (Kashentsev 69), Kachuro.

06/09/95, Prague
CZECH REPUBLIC 2 Skuhravy (6p), Drulak (86)
NORWAY 0
referee - Röthlisberger (SUI)
CZECH REPUBLIC - Kouba; Latal, Suchoparek, Nedved, Kadlec, Nemecek, Nemec, Repka, Kuka (Drulak 19), Skuhravy (Lokvenc 80), Frydek (Poborsky 70).
NORWAY - Thorstvedt; Løken, Johnsen R., Berg H., Johnsen E., Flo J., Bohinen (Rekdal 75), Leonhardsen, Fjørtoft (Brattbakk 71), Solbakken, Jakobsen.

07/10/95, Minsk
BELARUS 0
CZECH REPUBLIC 2 Frydek (25), Berger (84)
referee - Frisk (SWE)
BELARUS - Shantalosov; Gurenko, Dovnar, Rodnenok, Taikov, Yusipets (Baranov 74), Gerasimets, Zhuravel, Belkevich, Kashentsev, Kachuro.
CZECH REPUBLIC - Kouba; Latal, Nedved (Berger 74), Hapal, Kadlec, Nemecek (Hornak 15), Nemec, Repka, Kuka, Drulak, Frydek (Poborsky 87).

11/10/95, Luxembourg
LUXEMBOURG 0
BELARUS 0
referee - Durkin (ENG)
LUXEMBOURG - Koch; Vanek, Deville, Birsens, Strasser, Saibene, Hellers, Weis, Holtz (Lamborelle 90), Langers (Theis 81), Morocutti (Cardoni 72).
BELARUS - Shantalosov; Gurenko, Dovnar, Rodnenok, Taikov, Yusipets, Zhuravel, Baranov, Belkevich, Kashentsev (Vergeichik 88), Kachuro.

11/10/95, Ta' Qali
MALTA 0
HOLLAND 4 Overmars (53, 60, 85), Seedorf (82)
referee - Nielsen (DEN)
MALTA - Cluett; Attard (Galea 70), Buhagiar, Brincat, Woods, Zammit, Busuttil, Saliba, Agius (Sant Fournier 6), Laferla, Carabott.
HOLLAND - Van der Sar; Reiziger, Blind (Trustfull 71), De Boer F., Numan, Witschge, De Boer R., Seedorf, Mulder (Helder 64), Kluivert, Overmars.

12/11/95, Ta' Qali
MALTA 0
BELARUS 2 Gerasimets (78, 82)
referee - Tokat (TUR)
MALTA - Cluett; Vella, Attard, Brincat (Sant Fournier 50), Woods, Zammit, Busuttil, Saliba, Agius (Carabott 63), Laferla, Buhagiar.
BELARUS - Shantalosov; Gurenko, Dovnar, Khmelnitski (Belkevich 44), Taikov, Zygmantovich (Yusipets 59), Gerasimets, Baranov, Maleyev (Makovski 75), Metlitski, Kachuro.

15/11/95, Rotterdam
HOLLAND 3 Seedorf (49), Mulder (87), Overmars (88)
NORWAY 0
referee - Gallagher (ENG)
HOLLAND - Van der Sar; Reiziger, Blind, De Boer F., Numan, Witschge (Davids 56), Overmars, Seedorf, De Boer R., Bergkamp (Mulder 79), Helder (De Kock 86).
NORWAY - Grodås; Løken (Håland 62), Johnsen E., Berg H., Bjørnebye, Mykland (Leonhardsen 59), Bohinen (Solbakken 81), Flo T-A., Fjørtoft, Rekdal, Jakobsen.

15/11/95, Prague
CZECH REPUBLIC 3 Drulak (37, 46), Berger (57)
LUXEMBOURG 0
referee - Wieser (AUT)
CZECH REPUBLIC - Kouba; Latal, Suchoparek, Hapal, Kadlec, Nemecek (Poborsky 72), Nedved, Berger (Smicer 84), Kuka (Lokvenc 87), Drulak, Frydek.
LUXEMBOURG - Koch; Ferron, Vanek, Deville (Theis 59), Strasser, Holtz (Ganser 76), Hellers, Weis, Saibene (Cardoni 90), Langers, Groff.

PLAY-OFF MATCH

13/12/95, Liverpool
HOLLAND 2 Kluivert (29, 88)
REPUBLIC OF IRELAND 0
referee - Zhuk (BLS)
HOLLAND - Van der Sar; Reiziger, Blind, Seedorf, Bogarde, De Boer R., Overmars, Davids, Kluivert, Bergkamp (De Kock 57), Helder (Winter 80).
REPUBLIC OF IRELAND - Kelly A.; Kelly G., Irwin, Babb, McGrath, Kenna, Townsend (McAteer 50), Aldridge (Kernaghan 72), Cascarino, Sheridan, Phelan.

QUALIFYING GROUP 6

Portugal stretch away from the pack

GROUP 6 RESULTS - 1994/95

NORTHERN IRELAND 4, LIECHTENSTEIN 1
NORTHERN IRELAND 1, PORTUGAL 2
LIECHTENSTEIN 0, AUSTRIA 4
LATVIA 0, REPUBLIC OF IRELAND 3
LATVIA 1, PORTUGAL 3
AUSTRIA 1, NORTHERN IRELAND 2
REPUBLIC OF IRELAND 4, LIECHTENSTEIN 0
PORTUGAL 1, AUSTRIA 0
LIECHTENSTEIN 0, LATVIA 1
N. IRELAND 0, REPUBLIC OF IRELAND 4
PORTUGAL 8, LIECHTENSTEIN 0
AUSTRIA 5, LATVIA 0
REPUBLIC OF IRELAND 1, N. IRELAND 1
AUSTRIA 7, LIECHTENSTEIN 0
REPUBLIC OF IRELAND 1, PORTUGAL 0
LATVIA 0, NORTHERN IRELAND 1
LIECHTENSTEIN 0, REPUBLIC OF IRELAND 0
PORTUGAL 3, LATVIA 2
NORTHERN IRELAND 1, LATVIA 2
REPUBLIC OF IRELAND 1, AUSTRIA 3

With Portugal maintaining a steady hand at the top of the table, Austria and the Republic of Ireland began to shake nervously as the day of judgment drew closer. The Austrians, back in the qualifying race following a handsome 3-1 victory over the Irish in Dublin, undid all that good work with a lazy 2-3 defeat in Riga. But just when the door had been opened to them, the Republic were unable to step through it. Their visit to Vienna brought another 3-1 defeat, and suddenly their horizon was clouded once again.

The Austrians played very well against the Irish, especially midfielder Peter Stöger, who hit a hat-trick of exceptional quality - two perfectly struck volleys sandwiching a superbly worked second goal set up by midfield partner Andreas Herzog, now back in the team after his controversial absence from the first fixture at Lansdowne Road.

Stöger put his name on the scoresheet again in Austria's next game, at home to Portugal, but a magnificent equaliser from Portuguese full-back Paulinho Santos just after half-time gave the visitors a deserved point. That was enough to guarantee Portugal one of the top two places in the group. They celebrated at the final whistle as if they were already through.

António Oliveira's team were evidently aware of Ireland's declining fortunes and felt confident that they would overcome them in Lisbon. Portugal had slipped up a couple of months earlier against a Northern Ireland team undefeated on their travels. But against Jack Charlton's Republic the Portuguese completed their qualification with a scintillating second-half display, rubbing Irish noses into the mud on a damp, dark night in the Stadium of Light. The first of the home side's three goals, from Rui Costa, was arguably the best of the qualifying tournament - a succulent chip from all of 35 yards after an exquisite build-up.

The 3-0 victory gave Portugal first place and the biggest winning margin in any group. The Republic were not yet dead and buried, however. A dreadful display by Austria in equally murky Belfast resulted in a 3-5 defeat. That spelt the end for them, while Jack Charlton's demoralised troops were handed one last chance, in the play-off against Holland in home-from-home Liverpool. The Irish support at Anfield was huge, but the team were a spent force and no match for the Dutch, who won more comfortably than the 2-0 scoreline suggested. It was a tough way for Charlton to bow out, but the fact was that his team did not do nearly enough to justify a place in the finals.

TOP SCORERS

11 Toni POLSTER (Austria)
6 DOMINGOS (Portugal)
5 PAULO ALVES (Potugal)
John ALDRIDGE (Rep. of Ireland)
Iain DOWIE (Northern Ireland)
Vitas RIMKUS (Latvia)

GROUP 6 FINAL TABLE

			Home					Away					Total						
		Pd	W	D	L	F	A	W	D	L	F	A	W	D	L	F	A	Pt	GD
1	Portugal	10	4	1	0	16	3	3	1	1	13	4	7	2	1	29	7	23	+22
2	Republic of Ireland	10	3	1	1	9	5	2	1	2	8	6	5	2	3	17	11	17	+6
3	Northern Ireland	10	2	0	3	11	12	3	2	0	9	3	5	2	3	20	15	17	+5
4	Austria	10	3	1	1	17	4	2	0	3	12	10	5	1	4	29	14	16	+15
5	Latvia	10	2	0	3	5	9	2	0	3	6	11	4	0	6	11	20	12	-9
6	Liechtenstein	10	0	1	4	0	16	0	0	5	1	24	0	1	9	1	40	1	-39

QUALIFYING GROUP 6

GROUP 6 MATCH DETAILS 1995/96

15/08/95, Eschen/Mauren
LIECHTENSTEIN 0
PORTUGAL 7 Domingos (25), Paulinho Santos (33), Rui Costa (41, 71p), Paulo Alves (67, 73, 90)
referee - Poljak (CRO)
LIECHTENSTEIN - Heeb; Hanselmann, Zech J., Moser, Hasler, Telser (Oehri 67), Stocker (Marxer 46), Hilti, Frick M., Zech H., Klaunzer (Frick C. 46).
PORTUGAL - Alfredo (Rui Correia 82); Dimas (Paulo Alves 55), Jorge Costa, Oceano (Sá Pinto 46), Fernando Couto, Paulinho Santos, Secretário, Rui Barros, Domingos, Rui Costa, Folha.

16/08/95, Riga
LATVIA 3 Rimkus (11, 59), Zeiberlinsh (88)
AUSTRIA 2 Polster (69), Ramusch (78)
referee - Koho (FIN)
LATVIA - Laizans; Troitsky, Astafyev, Zemlinsky, Shevlyakov, Bleidelis, Ivanov, Zeiberlinsh, Rimkus, Babichev (Yeliseyev 75), Zakreshevsky (Monyak 82).
AUSTRIA - Konrad; Pfeffer, Schöttel, Kogler J. (Schopp 46), Kogler W., Marasek, Ogris (Stöger 64), Prosenik (Ramusch 64), Polster, Feiersinger, Pfeifenberger.

03/09/95, Oporto
PORTUGAL 1 Domingos (47)
NORTHERN IRELAND 1 Hughes (67)
referee - Harrel (FRA)
PORTUGAL - Vítor Baía; Secretário, Jorge Costa (Rui Barros 74), Oceano, Fernando Couto, Paulo Sousa, Figo, Paulinho Santos, Domingos, Rui Costa (Paulo Alves 82), Folha.
NORTHERN IRELAND - Fettis; Morrow, Worthington, Hill, Hunter, Lomas, Gillespie, Magilton (Rowland 79), Dowie (Gray 76), Lennon, Hughes.

06/09/95, Vienna
AUSTRIA 3 Stöger (3, 64, 77)
REPUBLIC OF IRELAND 1 McGrath (74)
referee - Cakar (TUR)
AUSTRIA - Konsel; Schopp, Schöttel, Pfeffer, Fürstaller, Marasek, Pfeifenberger, Kühbauer, Polster (Cerny 79), Herzog, Stöger.
REPUBLIC OF IRELAND - Kelly A.; Kelly G., Irwin, Kernaghan, McGrath, Keane, Townsend, Houghton (Cascarino 67), Quinn, Sheridan, Kennedy.

06/09/95, Riga
LATVIA 1 Zeiberlinsh (83)
LIECHTENSTEIN 0
referee - Ovrebo (NOR)
LATVIA - Karavayev; Troitsky, Astafyev, Zemlinsky, Shevlyakov, Bleidelis (Boulders 28), Ivanov, Zeiberlinsh, Rimkus, Babichev (Karashauskas 75), Monyak.
LIECHTENSTEIN - Heeb; Frick C., Zech J., Oehri (Bicker 63), Hasler, Telser, Stocker (Klaunzer 85), Hilti, Schädler, Frick M., Marxer (Frick D. 73).

11/10/95, Vienna
AUSTRIA 1 Stöger (21)
PORTUGAL 1 Paulinho Santos (49)
referee - Levnikov (RUS)
AUSTRIA - Konsel; Schopp, Schöttel, Pfeffer, Feiersinger, Marasek, Pfeifenberger, Kühbauer, Polster (Cerny 83), Herzog, Stöger.
PORTUGAL - Vítor Baía; Nélson, Hélder, Oceano, Jorge Costa, Paulo Sousa, Secretário (Sá Pinto 59), João Pinto (Folha 46), Domingos (Dominguez 72), Rui Costa, Paulinho Santos.

11/10/95, Dublin
REPUBLIC OF IRELAND 2 Aldridge (61p, 64)
LATVIA 1 Rimkus (78)
referee - Fernández Marín (ESP)
REPUBLIC OF IRELAND - Kelly A.; Kelly G., Phelan, Babb, McGrath, Kenna, Townsend, McAteer, Quinn, Aldridge (Kelly D. 79; Kennedy 84), Staunton.
LATVIA - Karavayev; Troitsky, Astafyev, Zemlinsky, Shevlyakov, Stepanov I.N., Ivanov, Zeiberlinsh, Rimkus, Babichev (Yeliseyev 73), Zakreshevsky.

11/10/95, Eschen/Mauren
LIECHTENSTEIN 0
NORTHERN IRELAND 4 O'Neill (36), McMahon (49), Quinn Ji. (55p), Gray (72)
referee - Michel (SVK)
LIECHTENSTEIN - Oehry; Hefti, Frick C. (Hanselmann 78), Hilti (Ospelt J. 66), Hasler, Klaunzer, Telser, Stocker (Sele 46), Schädler, Zech H., Oehri.
NORTHERN IRELAND - Fettis (Wood 75); Lomas, Worthington, Hill, Hunter, Lennon, McMahon (McGibbon 80), O'Neill, Quinn Ji., Gray, Hughes (Rowland 90).

15/11/95, Belfast
NORTHERN IRELAND 5
O'Neill (27, 78), Dowie (32p), Hunter (53), Gray (64)
AUSTRIA 3 Schopp (56), Stumpf (70), Wetl (801
referee - Sundell (SWE)
NORTHERN IRELAND - Fettis; Lomas, Worthington, Hunter, Hill, Lennon, Gillespie, O'Neill, Dowie (Quinn Ji. 81), Gray (McDonald 78), Hughes.
AUSTRIA - Konsel; Schopp, Kogler W., Pfeffer, Feiersinger, Marasek, Pfeifenberger, Herzog (Wetl 46), Polster, Kühbauer (Stumpf 46), Stöger.

15/11/95, Lisbon
PORTUGAL 3 Rui Costa (59), Hélder (74), Cadete (89)
REPUBLIC OF IRELAND 0
referee - Ceccarini (ITA)
PORTUGAL - Vítor Baía (Neno 85); Secretário, Hélder, Oceano, Fernando Couto, Paulo Sousa, Figo, João Pinto (Cadete 68), Domingos (Folha 72), Rui Costa, Paulinho Santos.
REPUBLIC OF IRELAND - Kelly A.; Kelly G., Irwin, Babb, McGrath, McAteer, Kennedy (Cascarino 75), Kenna, Quinn, Aldridge, Staunton (Kernaghan 78).

QUALIFYING GROUP 7

Four straight wins lift Germany to the top

GROUP 7 RESULTS - 1994/95

WALES 2, ALBANIA 0
GEORGIA 0, MOLDOVA 1
BULGARIA 2, GREECE 0
MOLDOVA 3, WALES 2
ALBANIA 1, GERMANY 2
BULGARIA 4, MOLDOVA 1
GEORGIA 5, WALES 0
ALBANIA 0, GEORGIA 1
WALES 0, BULGARIA 3
MOLDOVA 0, GERMANY 3
GERMANY 2, ALBANIA 1
ALBANIA 3, MOLDOVA 0
BULGARIA 3, WALES 1
GEORGIA 0, GERMANY 2
GERMANY 1, WALES 1
GEORGIA 2, ALBANIA 0
MOLDOVA 0, BULGARIA 3
BULGARIA 3, GERMANY 2
WALES 0, GEORGIA 1
MOLDOVA 2, ALBANIA 3

Those who thought Germany's place in the Euro '96 finals might be under threat following their 2-3 reverse in Sofia were made to think again as Berti Vogts' team returned from their summer break to win all four of their remaining matches and overtake long-time front-runners Bulgaria at the top of the group table.

The Germans began as they meant to go on, destroying a Georgian side who had had the audacity to take the lead midway through the first half in Nuremberg. Andreas Möller quickly restored parity, and from then on the Germans were at full throttle, adding three further second-half goals to seal an important and an impressive 4-1 win.

Möller scored two more goals in a five-star display the following month against Moldova in Leverkusen. His Borussia Dortmund team-mate Matthias Sammer also struck twice in a 6-1 victory that could have been heavier had Jürgen Klinsmann been wearing his shooting boots. In the last five minutes the Bayern Munich striker had no fewer than four clear chances to score, including one from the penalty shot, but he spurned them all.

But when Germany really needed a goal from their captain, three days later in Cardiff, Klinsmann responded like a true champion, netting a crucial late winner against Wales to round off a crazy six-minute sequence that featured an own-goal at each end as a prelude to Klinsmann's decisive blow.

While Germany gathered a maximum nine points, leaders Bulgaria were struggling to pick up just four over the same stretch. They completed a perfect home record with a 3-0 victory over Albania. But a draw in Tirana and a defeat in Tbilisi left Dimitar Penev's World Cup semi-finalists vulnerable to German attack in the last game.

When the two teams kicked off their final match before a sell-out crowd in Berlin, there was nothing at stake except the group leadership. Other results earlier that night had ensured that both Germany and Bulgaria would be going to England. With the pressure off, an enjoyable game ensued. Bulgaria drew first blood - a fine tenth goal of the competition for Hristo Stoichkov - but,

TOP SCORERS

Goals	Player
10	Hristo STOICHKOV (Bulgaria)
9	Jürgen KLINSMANN (Germany)
7	Emil KOSTADINOV (Bulgaria)
4	Temur KETSBAIA (Georgia)
	Sokol KUSHTA (Albania)
	Shota ARVELADZE (Georgia)
3	Andreas MÖLLER (Germany)
	Ulf KIRSTEN (Germany)
	Krasimir BALAKOV (Bulgaria)
	Giorgi KINKLADZE (Georgia)

GROUP 7 FINAL TABLE

			Home					Away					Total						
		Pd	W	D	L	F	A	W	D	L	F	A	W	D	L	F	A	Pt	GD
1	Germany	10	4	1	0	16	5	4	0	1	11	5	8	1	1	27	10	25	+17
2	Bulgaria	10	5	0	0	15	4	2	1	2	9	6	7	1	2	24	10	22	+14
3	Georgia	10	3	0	2	9	4	2	0	3	5	9	5	0	5	14	13	15	+1
4	Moldova	10	2	0	3	8	13	1	0	4	3	14	3	0	7	11	27	9	-16
5	Wales	10	2	0	3	4	6	0	2	3	5	13	2	2	6	9	19	8	-10
6	Albania	10	1	2	2	6	5	1	0	4	4	11	2	2	6	10	16	8	-6

QUALIFYING GROUP 7

as against Georgia, Germany were quick to retaliate. Klinsmann levelled three minutes later after some suicidal Bulgarian defending, then Thomas Hässler added a second from a free-kick before Klinsmann - with his ninth Euro '96 qualifying goal - completed a revenge 3-1 victory from the penalty spot. As if the Germans would have settled for anything other than first place...

GROUP 7 MATCH DETAILS 1995/96

06/09/95, Tirana
ALBANIA 1 Rraklli (15)
BULGARIA 1 Stoichkov (8)
referee - Agius (MLT)
ALBANIA - Strakosha; Abazi, Shulku, Xhumba, Vata, Lekbello, Kushta, Bellai, Kola (Shehu 65; Pano 88), Rraklli, Bozgo (Demollari 86).
BULGARIA - Mikhailov; Kremenliev, Ivanov, Tsvetanov, Hubchev, Borimirov, Kostadinov, Stoichkov, Penev (Sirakov 75), Balakov, Lechkov (Chomakov 75).

06/09/95, Nuremberg
GERMANY 4 Möller (38), Ziege (56), Kirsten (62), Babbel (72)
GEORGIA 1 Ketsbaia (28)
referee - McCluskey (SCO)
GERMANY - Kahn; Babbel, Ziege, Kohler, Helmer, Freund, Möller, Strunz, Klinsmann, Hässler, Kirsten.
GEORGIA - Devadze; Gujabidze, Kudinov, Shelia, Chikhradze, Gogichaishvili (Arveladze A. 68), Nemsadze, Kavelashvili (Kilasonia 46), Ketsbaia, Kinkladze, Arveladze S..

06/09/95, Cardiff
WALES 1 Speed (55)
MOLDOVA 0
referee - Orrason (ISL)
WALES - Southall; Bowen, Coleman, Williams A., Symons, Pembridge, Horne, Nogan (Phillips 46), Rush (Hartson 69), Hughes M., Speed.
MOLDOVA - Ivanov; Fistican, Testimitanu, Culibaba, Rebeja (Gavriliuc 84), Stroenco S., Oprea, Belous, Nani (Suharev 76), Cebotar, Clescenco.

07/10/95, Sofia
BULGARIA 3 Lechkov (13), Kostadinov (82, 84)
ALBANIA 0
referee - Hirviniemi (FIN)
BULGARIA - Mikhailov; Kremenliev, Ivanov, Tsvetanov, Yankov, Kiriakov (Borimirov 88), Kostadinov (Sirakov 86), Stoichkov, Penev, Balakov, Lechkov.
ALBANIA - Strakosha; Zmijani, Malko, Xhumba, Shulku, Dema, Kushta, Bellai, Kola, Rraklli, Abazi (Demollari 85).

08/10/95, Leverkusen
GERMANY 6 Stroenco S. (16og), Helmer (18), Sammer (24, 72), Möller (47, 61)
MOLDOVA 1 Rebeja (80)
referee - Ziober (POL)
GERMANY - Köpke; Babbel, Ziege, Freund, Helmer, Sammer (Wörns 83), Möller (Scholl 78), Eilts, Klinsmann, Hässler, Herrlich (Bobic 74).
MOLDOVA - Ivanov; Secu, Testimitanu, Culibaba, Rebeja, Stroenco S., Oprea (Gavriliuc 86), Belous, Nani (Miterev 60), Curtianu, Clescenco.

11/10/95, Cardiff
WALES 1 Helmer (78og)
GERMANY 2 Melville (75og), Klinsmann (81)
referee - Craciunescu (ROM)
WALES - Southall; Jenkins (Mardon 71), Bowen, Symons, Melville, Pembridge (Williams G. 82), Horne, Saunders, Blake (Hodges 82), Speed, Giggs.
GERMANY - Köpke; Babbel (Wörns 46), Ziege, Freund, Helmer, Sammer, Möller, Eilts, Klinsmann, Hässler, Herrlich (Kuntz 74).

11/10/95, Tbilisi
GEORGIA 2 Arveladze S. (1), Kinkladze (47p)
BULGARIA 1 Stoichkov (87)
referee - Meier (SUI)
GEORGIA - Zoidze; Gudushauri (Beradze 82), Kudinov, Shelia, Chikhradze, Gogichaishvili, Nemsadze, Jamarauli (Kilasonia 74), Arveladze A. (Kavelashvili 46), Kinkladze, Arveladze S..
BULGARIA - Mikhailov; Kiriakov, Ivanov (Chomakov 58), Tsvetanov, Yankov, Sirakov (Borimirov 58), Kostadinov, Stoichkov, Penev, Balakov, Lechkov.

15/11/95, Tirana
ALBANIA 1 Kushta (3p)
WALES 1 Pembridge (43)
referee - Suheil (ISR)
ALBANIA - Strakosha; Zmijani, Shulku, Dema (Milori 83), Vata, Lekbello, Kushta (Bushi 57), Malko, Bozgo (Zalla 78), Rraklli, Pano.
WALES - Southall; Jenkins, Bowen, Phillips, Young, Melville, Taylor (Robinson 84), Hughes C. (Savage 63), Saunders, Pembridge, Giggs.

15/11/95, Berlin
GERMANY 3 Klinsmann (50, 77p), Hässler (56)
BULGARIA 1 Stoichkov (47)
referee - Nikakis (GRE)
GERMANY - Köpke; Babbel, Freund, Kohler (Strunz 46), Helmer, Sammer, Eilts, Basler, Klinsmann, Hässler (Reuter 88), Kuntz (Bobic 82).
BULGARIA - Popov; Kremenliev, Dartilov, Tsvetanov, Ginchev, Yankov, Kostadinov, Stoichkov, Penev (Sirakov 79), Balakov (Borimirov 82), Lechkov (Kiriakov 62).

15/11/95, Chisinau
MOLDOVA 3 Testtmitanu (5p), Miterev (17, 68)
GEORGIA 2 Janashia (68), Culibaba (81og)
referee - Van der Ende (HOL)
MOLDOVA - Coselev; Secu, Testimitanu, Culibaba, Belous, Nani, Oprea (Suharev 52), Kirilov, Miterev, Curtianu (Cebotar 72), Clescenco.
GEORGIA - Zoidze; Gudushauri (Janashia 58), Kudinov, Beradze, Chikhradze, Gogichaishvili, Tskitishvili, Jamarauli (Machavariani 62), Ketsbaia, Kinkladze, Arveladze S..

QUALIFYING GROUP 8

Russians and Scots finish in faultless style

GROUP 8 RESULTS - 1994/95

FINLAND 0, SCOTLAND 2
FAROE ISLANDS 1, GREECE 5
GREECE 4, FINLAND 0
SCOTLAND 5, FAROE ISLANDS 1
RUSSIA 4, SAN MARINO 0
FINLAND 5, FAROE ISLANDS 0
GREECE 2, SAN MARINO 0
SCOTLAND 1, RUSSIA 1
FINLAND 4, SAN MARINO 1
GREECE 1, SCOTLAND 0
SAN MARINO 0, FINLAND 2
RUSSIA 0, SCOTLAND 0
GREECE 0, RUSSIA 3
SAN MARINO 0, SCOTLAND 2
FAROE ISLANDS 0, FINLAND 4
RUSSIA 3, FAROE ISLANDS 0
FAROE ISLANDS 3, SAN MARINO 0
SAN MARINO 0, RUSSIA 7
FAROE ISLANDS 0, SCOTLAND 2
FINLAND 2, GREECE 1

Maybe Finland were lulled into a false sense of security by their position at the top of the Group Eight table. But in their first match back after a two-month gap, they lacked any of the fighting qualities normally associated with a potential qualifier and were pummeled into submission by a rampant Russian side in Helsinki. 0-6 was the final result. The Finns were lucky to keep the scoreline in single figures.

On the same mid-August evening that Finland were being eliminated from the running, Scotland were doing their best to put distance between themselves and Greece at Hampden Park. It was a match of huge importance for both sides. Scotland knew that a place in England would be theirs if they won their final three matches, and this was their toughest assignment. For most of the 90 minutes the two teams were evenly matched. A moment's inspiration was required to break the deadlock and it was provided by veteran goalgrabber Ally McCoist. Within a minute of coming off the bench for his first taste of international football for almost two and a half years, the Rangers striker glanced in the winner.

The following month Scotland added victory number two, against Finland. Again it was a tight affair, with 1-0 the final result. Scotland did not have so long to wait for their goal this time, Scott Booth heading them into a tenth-minute lead. But it was a struggle to hold on, and Hjelm and Suominen both missed clear chances to equalise in the second half.

If Scotland's qualification was all over bar the calculating after that win, so, too, was Russia's. They ran up another big score away to the Faroe Islands, leaving themselves with the formality of taking three points from their final two matches to confirm their presence in England.

Everything was resolved - both for Russia and Scotland - when Oleg Romantsev's team beat Greece 2-1 in Moscow on October 11. The Russians became the first team to book their qualifying place (Spain joined them later that day) and Scotland knew that their second place was secure - win, lose, or draw against San Marino in a meaningless final game. Of course, Scotland did win, 5-0, but more important were the results coming in from other groups that enabled Craig Brown's team to start the match knowing that they were certain of qualifying as one of the best six runners-up.

TOP SCORERS

7 Mika-Matti PAATELAINEN (Finland)
5 Igor KOLYVANOV (Russia)
4 Dmitri RADCHENKO (Russia)
John COLLINS (Scotland)
Scott BOOTH (Scotland)
Nikos MAHLAS (Greece)
Panayotis TSALOUHIDIS (Greece)
Alexandros ALEXANDRIS (Greece)
Jari LITMANEN (Finland)
Todi JONSSON (Faroe Islands)

GROUP 8 FINAL TABLE

			Home					Away					Total						
		Pd	W	D	L	F	A	W	D	L	F	A	W	D	L	F	A	Pt	GD
1	Russia	10	4	1	0	12	2	4	1	0	22	3	8	2	0	34	5	26	+29
2	Scotland	10	4	1	0	13	2	3	1	1	6	1	7	2	1	19	3	23	+16
3	Greece	10	4	0	1	12	3	2	0	3	11	6	6	0	4	23	9	18	+14
4	Finland	10	3	0	2	11	10	2	0	3	7	8	5	0	5	18	18	15	=
5	Faroe Islands	10	1	0	4	6	16	1	0	4	4	19	2	0	8	10	35	6	-25
6	San Marino	10	0	0	5	1	18	0	0	5	1	18	0	0	10	2	36	0	-34

QUALIFYING GROUP 8

GROUP 8 MATCH DETAILS 1995/96

16/08/95, Helsinki
FINLAND 0
RUSSIA 6 Kulkov (32, 49), Karpin (39), Radchenko (42), Kolyvanov (67, 69)
referee - Puhl (HUN)
FINLAND - Laukkanen; Mäkelä (Suominen 46), Kanerva, Holmgren, Nieminen, Lindberg, Sumiala, Rantanen (Grönlund 65), Hjelm, Tiainen, Paatelainen (Järvinen 46).
RUSSIA - Kharin (Cherchesov 82); Kovtun, Nikiforov, Tsymbalar, Khlestov, Karpin (Kanchelskis 61), Onopko, Kulkov, Mostovoi, Radchenko (Kiryakov 68), Kolyvanov,

16/08/95, Glasgow
SCOTLAND 1 McCoist (72)
GREECE 0
referee - Mikkelsen (DEN)
SCOTLAND - Leighton; McKimmie, Boyd, McCall, Calderwood, McKinlay T., Shearer (McCoist 71), Burley, Jackson (Robertson 73), McAllister, Collins.
GREECE - Atmatsidis; Apostolakis, Karataidis, Kalllitzakis, Dabizas, Tsalouhidis, Zagorakis (Yoryadis Y.H. 79), Batista (Alexandris 49), Vrizas (Mahlas 30), Tsartas, Kassapis.

06/09/95, Glasgow
SCOTLAND 1 Booth (10)
FINLAND 0
referee - Melnichuk (UKR)
SCOTLAND - Leighton; McKimmie (McKinlay B. 88), Boyd, Calderwood, Hendry, McKinlay T., Spencer (McCoist 75), McLaren, Booth (Jackson 80), McAllister, Collins.
FINLAND - Laukkanen; Rissanen, Kanerva, Holmgren, Suominen, Lindberg, Nieminen (Grönlund 64), Myyry, Hjelm, Litmanen, Järvinen.

06/09/95, Serravalle
SAN MARINO 0
GREECE 4 Tsalouhidis (6), Yoryadis Y.H. (31), Alexandris (59), Donis (80)
referee - Mitrovic (SLO)
SAN MARINO - Muccioli; Gobbi, Gennari, Mazza M., Matteoni, Guerra, Manzaroli (Peverani 89), Della Valle, Bacciocchi, Mularoni (Montagna 79), Francini (Canti 76).
GREECE - Atmatsidis; Apostolakis, Karataidis, Ouzounidis, Dabizas, Tsalouhidis, Zagorakis, Nikolaidis (Alexandris 46), Mahlas (Batista 79), Yoryadis Y.H. (Yorgatos 58), Donis.

06/09/95, Toftir
FAROE ISLANDS 2 Jarnskor H. (12), Jonsson (55)
RUSSIA 5 Mostovoi (10p), Kiryakov (60), Kolyvanov (65), Tsymbalar (83), Shalimov (88)
referee - Snoddy (NIR)
FAROE ISLANDS - Knudsen; Johannesen, Hansen T.E. (Joensen A. 81), Rasmussen Ja., Hansen J.C., Hansen Ø., Mørkøre K., Johnsson, Müller (Rasmussen J.E. 72), Jonsson, Jarnskor H..
RUSSIA - Cherchesov; Kovtun, Nikiforov, Tsymbalar, Shalimov, Kanchelskis (Beschastnykh 58), Onopko, Kulkov (Mamedov 65), Mostovoi, Radchenko (Kiryakov 46), Kolyvanov.

11/10/95, Serravalle
SAN MARINO 1 Valentini M. (55)
FAROE ISLANDS 3 Jonsson (42, 44, 59)
referee - Beck (LIE)
SAN MARINO - Muccioli; Valentini V., Gennari, Matteoni (Peverani 75), Valentini M., Guerra, Manzaroli, Mazza M. (Mularoni 57), Bacciocchi, Francini, Montagna (Gasperoni 81).
FAROE ISLANDS - Knudsen; Hansen A.F., Hansen J.C., Rasmussen Ja., Jarnskor H. (Bertholdsen 88), Mørkøre A., Jarnskor M., Hansen Ø. (Reynheim 81), Müller, Jonsson (Petersen 75), Dam.

11/10/95, Moscow
RUSSIA 2 Ouzounidis (38og), Onopko (72)
GREECE 1 Tsalouhidis (64)
referee - Grabher (AUT)
RUSSIA - Kharin; Kovtun, Nikiforov, Tsymbalar (Radchenko 61), Khlestov, Karpin (Shalimov 76), Onopko, Kulkov, Mostovoi, Yuran (Kiryakov 46), Kolyvanov.
GREECE - Mihopoulos; Apostolakis, Kassapis, Ouzounidis, Kallitzakis (Dabizas 46), Tsalouhidis, Zagorakis, Alexandris, Batista (Mahlas 66), Tsartas (Yorgatos 46), Donis.

15/11/95, Iraklion
GREECE 5 Alexandris (59), Nikolaidis (62), Mahlas (66), Donis (76), Tsartas (80)
FAROE ISLANDS 0
referee - Mitrev (BUL)
GREECE - Atmatsidis; Apostolakis, Kassapis, Ouzounidis, Dabizas, Tsalouhidis (Nikolaidis 46), Zagorakis (Konstantinidis 70), Alexandris (Yoryadis Y.H. 75), Mahlas, Tsartas, Donis.
FAROE ISLANDS - Mikkelsen; Johannesen, Hansen T.E., Hansen J.C., Hansen Ø. (Bertholdsen 90), Mørkøre A., Jarnskor M., Jarnskor H., Müller (Petersen 83), Reynheim (Johnsson 55), Dam.

15/11/95, Glasgow
SCOTLAND 5 Jess (30), Booth (45), McCoist (49), Nevin (71), Francini (90og)
SAN MARINO 0
referee - Bohunek (TCH)
SCOTLAND - Leighton; McLaren, Boyd, Calderwood, Hendry, Gemmill, Nevin, Booth (Jackson 66), Jess, McAllister (McCoist 48), Collins (McKinlay B. 59).
SAN MARINO - Muccioli; Moroni, Gennari, Mazza M. (Della Valle 82), Valentini M., Guerra (Montagna 71), Manzaroli, Matteoni, Bacciocchi, Mularoni (Canti 52), Francini.

15/11/95, Moscow
RUSSIA 3 Radchenko (40), Kulkov (55), Kiryakov (71)
FINLAND 1 Suominen (44)
referee - Merk (GER)
RUSSIA - Cherchesov; Mamedov (Dobrovolski 46), Nikiforov, Tsymbalar, Khlestov, Karpin (Kanchelskis 75), Onopko, Kulkov, Mostovoi, Yuran, Radchenko (Kiryakov 62).
FINLAND - Niemi; Rissanen, Nuorela, Hyryläinen, Nieminen, Lindberg, Sumiala (Kangaskorpi 76), Suominen (Ylönen 88), Hjelm, Myyry, Grönlund (Koskinen 70).

FINALS SCHEDULE - WORLD CUP 1998

QUALIFYING PROCESS (EUROPE)

The nine group winners qualify automatically for the finals together with the best runner-up. The other eight runners-up will be drawn in pairs and play off against each other on a home-and-away basis. The four winners will also qualify for the finals. France qualify automatically as hosts.

THE VENUES

Town	Stadium	No. matches
PARIS SAINT-DENIS	Stade de France	9
PARIS	Parc des Princes	6
BORDEAUX	Stade Lescure	6
LENS	Stade Félix-Bollaert	6
LYON	Stade de Gerland	6
MARSEILLE	Stade Vélodrome	7
MONTPELLIER	Stade de la Mosson	6
NANTES	Stade de la Beaujoire	6
SAINT-ETIENNE	Stade Geoffroy-Guichard	6
TOULOUSE	Stadium Municipal	6

PREVIOUS WINNERS

1930 URUGUAY
1934 ITALY
1938 ITALY
1950 URUGUAY
1954 WEST GERMANY
1958 BRAZIL
1962 BRAZIL
1966 ENGLAND
1970 BRAZIL
1974 WEST GERMANY
1978 ARGENTINA
1982 ITALY
1986 ARGENTINA
1990 WEST GERMANY
1994 BRAZIL

FIXTURES & VENUES

• FIRST ROUND

GROUP A

Date	Venue	Teams
Wed, 10 June	Paris Saint-Denis	A1 v A2
Wed, 10 June	Montpellier	A3 v A4
Tue, 16 June	Nantes	A1 v A3
Tue, 16 June	Bordeaux	A2 v A4
Tue, 23 June	Marseille	A1 v A4
Tue, 23 June	Saint-Etienne	A2 v A3

GROUP B

Date	Venue	Teams
Thu, 11 June	Bordeaux	B1 v B2
Thu, 11 June	Toulouse	B3 v B4
Wed, 17 June	Montpellier	B1 v B3
Wed, 17 June	Saint-Etienne	B2 v B4
Tue, 23 June	Paris Saint-Denis	B1 v B4
Tue, 23 June	Nantes	B2 v B3

GROUP C

Date	Venue	Teams
Fri, 12 June	Marseille	C1 v C2
Fri, 12 June	Lens	C3 v C4
Thu, 18 June	Paris Saint-Denis	C1 v C3
Thu, 18 June	Toulouse	C2 v C4
Wed, 24 June	Lyon	C1 v C4
Wed, 24 June	Bordeaux	C2 v C3

GROUP D

Date	Venue	Teams
Fri, 12 June	Montpellier	D3 v D4
Sat, 13 June	Nantes	D1 v D2
Fri, 19 June	Saint-Etienne	D1 v D3
Fri, 19 June	Paris	D2 v D4
Wed, 24 June	Lens	D1 v D4
Wed, 24 June	Toulouse	D2 v D3

GROUP E

Date	Venue	Teams
Sat, 13 June	Paris Saint-Denis	E1 v E2
Sat, 13 June	Lyon	E3 v E4
Sat, 20 June	Marseille	E1 v E3
Sat, 20 June	Bordeaux	E2 v E4
Thu, 25 June	Saint-Etienne	E1 v E4
Thu, 25 June	Paris	E2 v E3

GROUP F

Date	Venue	Teams
Sun, 14 June	Saint-Etienne	F3 v F4
Mon, 15 June	Paris	F1 v F2
Sun, 21 June	Lens	F1 v F3
Sun, 21 June	Lyon	F2 v F4
Thu, 25 June	Montpellier	F1 v F4
Thu, 25 June	Nantes	F2 v F3

GROUP G

Date	Venue	Teams
Mon, 15 June	Lyon	G1 v G2
Mon, 15 June	Marseille	G3 v G4
Mon, 22 June	Toulouse	G1 v G3
Mon, 22 June	Montpellier	G2 v G4
Fri, 26 June	Paris Saint-Denis	G1 v G4
Fri, 26 June	Lens	G2 v G3

GROUP H

Date	Venue	Teams
Sun, 14 June	Toulouse	H1 v H2
Sun, 14 June	Lens	H3 v H4
Sat, 20 June	Nantes	H2 v H4
Sun, 21 June	Paris	H1 v H3
Fri, 26 June	Bordeaux	H1 v H4
Fri, 26 June	Lyon	H2 v H3

• SECOND ROUND

Group Winners (1) and Runners-up (2) qualify.

Date	Venue	Teams	Game
Sat, 27 June	Paris	1A v 2B	1
Sat, 27 June	Marseille	1B v 2A	2
Sun, 28 June	Lens	1C v 2D	3
Sun, 28 June	Paris Saint-Denis	1D v 2C	4
Mon, 29 June	Toulouse	1E v 2F	5
Mon, 29 June	Montpellier	1F v 2E	6
Tue, 30 June	Bordeaux	1G v 2H	7
Tue, 30 June	Saint-Etienne	1H v 2G	8

• QUARTER-FINALS

Date	Venue	Teams	Game
Fri, 3 July	Nantes	Winners 1v Winners 4	A
Fri, 3 July	Paris Saint-Denis	Winners 2 v Winners 3	B
Sat, 4 July	Marseille	Winners 5 v Winners 8	C
Sat, 4 July	Lyon	Winners 6 v Winners 7	D

• SEMI-FINALS

Date	Venue	Teams
Tue, 7 July	Marseille	Winners A v Winners C
Wed, 8 July	Paris Saint-Denis	Winners B v Winners D

• THIRD-PLACE PLAY-OFF

Sat, 11 July Paris

• FINAL

Sun, 12 July Paris Saint-Denis

EUROPEAN QUALIFYING GROUPS

GROUP ONE

DENMARK, GREECE, CROATIA, SLOVENIA, BOSNIA-HERZEGOVINA

1995/96 MATCH DETAILS

24/04/96, Athens
GREECE 2 Batista (55), Nikolaidis (65)
SLOVENIA 0
referee - Pedersen (DEN)
GREECE - Atmatsidis; Apostolakis, Kassapis, Ouzounidis, Kallitzakis, Konstantinidis (Alexandris 46), Zagorakis, Vrizas, Batista, Tsartas (Frantzeskos 82), Donis (Nikolaidis 61).
SLOVENIA - Boskovic; Galic, Englaro, Milanic, Jermanis, Ceh, Novak, Zidan (Gajser 37), Udovic (Gliha 70), Zahovic, Florjancic.

1996/97 FIXTURES

01/09/96	Greece v Bosnia-Herzegovina
	Slovenia v Denmark
09/10/96	Denmark v Greece
	Bosnia-Herzegovina v Croatia
09 or 10/11/96	Slovenia v Bosnia-Herzegovina
10/11/96	Croatia v Greece
29/03/97	Croatia v Denmark
02/04/97	Croatia v Slovenia
	Bosnia-Herzegovina v Greece
30/04/97	Denmark v Slovenia
	Greece v Croatia
08/06/97	Denmark v Bosnia-Herzegovina

1997/98 FIXTURES

20/08/97	Bosnia-Herzegovina v Denmark
06/09/97	Croatia v Bosnia-Herzegovina
06 or 07/09/97	Slovenia v Greece
10/09/97	Denmark v Croatia
	Bosnia-Herzegovina v Slovenia
11/10/97	Greece v Denmark
	Slovenia v Croatia

GROUP TWO

ITALY, ENGLAND, POLAND, GEORGIA, MOLDOVA

1996/97 FIXTURES

01/09/96	Moldova v England
05/10/96	Moldova v Italy
09/10/96	England v Poland
	Italy v Georgia
09/11/96	Georgia v England
10/11/96	Poland v Moldova
12/02/97	England v Italy
29/03/97	Italy v Moldova
02/04/97	Poland v Italy
30/04/97	England v Georgia
	Italy v Poland
31/05/97	Poland v England
07/06/97	Georgia v Moldova
14/06/97	Poland v Georgia

1997/98 FIXTURES

10/09/97	England v Moldova
	Georgia v Italy
24/09/97	Moldova v Georgia
07/10/97	Moldova v Poland
11/10/97	Italy v England
	Georgia v Poland

Parc des Princes, Paris - one of the venues for the 1998 World Cup Finals in France

EUROPEAN QUALIFYING GROUPS

GROUP THREE

NORWAY, SWITZERLAND, FINLAND, HUNGARY, AZERBAIJAN

1995/96 MATCH DETAILS

02/06/96, Oslo
NORWAY 5 Solbakken (8, 46), Soljskjaer (37, 90), Strandli (60)
AZERBAIJAN 0
referee - Snoddy (NIR)
NORWAY - Grodås; Håland, Berg, Johnsen R., Bjørnebye, Rudi, Solbakken (Larsen 80), Rekdal, Leonhardsen (Flo T-A. 46), Solskjaer, Strandli.
AZERBAIJAN - Jidkov; Gaisumov, Getman, Ahmedov, Agayev (Nosenko 40), Idigov, Abusov (Asadov 79), Rzayev (Kurbanov K. 46), Huseynov, Lichkin, Suleymanov.

1996/97 FIXTURES

31/08/96	Azerbaijan v Switzerland
01/09/96	Hungary v Finland
06/10/96	Finland v Switzerland
09/10/96	Norway v Hungary
10/11/96	Switzerland v Norway
	Azerbaijan v Hungary
02/04/97	Azerbaijan v Finland
30/04/97	Norway v Finland
	Switzerland v Hungary
08/06/97	Finland v Azerbaijan
	Hungary v Norway

1997/98 FIXTURES

20/08/97	Finland v Norway
	Hungary v Switzerland
06/09/97	Switzerland v Finland
	Azerbaijan v Norway
10/09/97	Hungary v Azerbaijan
	Norway v Switzerland
11/10/97	Finland v Hungary
	Switzerland v Azerbaijan

GROUP FOUR

SWEDEN, SCOTLAND, AUSTRIA, LATVIA, BELARUS, ESTONIA

1995/96 MATCH DETAILS

01/06/96, Solna
SWEDEN 5
Andersson K. (20p, 62), Dahlin (30), Andersson P. (77), Larsson (87)
BELARUS 1 Belkevich (75)
referee - Harrel (FRA)
SWEDEN - Andersson B.; Nilsson, Andersson P., Björklund, Sundgren, Ingesson (Mild 85), Thern, Zetterberg, Limpar, Dahlin (Larsson 77), Andersson K..
BELARUS - Satsunkhevich; Gurenko, Khatskevich, Shtanyuk, Kashentsev (Kulchi 63), Vergeichik, Belkevich, Maleyev, Romashchenko (Kachuro 57), Makovski, Baranov.

1996/97 FIXTURES

31/08/96	Austria v Scotland
	Belarus v Estonia
01/09/96	Latvia v Sweden
05/10/96	Estonia v Belarus
	Latvia v Scotland
09/10/96	Sweden v Austria
	Estonia v Scotland
	Belarus v Latvia
09/11/96	Austriav Latvia
10/11/96	Scotland v Sweden
29/03/97	Scotland v Estonia
02/04/97	Scotland v Austria
30/04/97	Austria v Estonia
	Sweden v Scotland
	Latvia v Belarus
18/05/97	Estonia v Latvia
08/06/97	Estonia v Sweden
	Latvia v Austria
	Belarus v Scotland

1997/98 FIXTURES

20/08/97	Estonia v Austria
	Belarus v Sweden
06/09/97	Austria v Sweden
	Scotland v Belarus
	Latvia v Estonia
10/09/97	Sweden v Latvia
	Belarus v Austria
11/10/97	Austria v Belarus
	Scotland v Latvia
	Sweden v Estonia

EUROPEAN QUALIFYING GROUPS

GROUP FIVE

RUSSIA, BULGARIA, ISRAEL, CYPRUS, LUXEMBOURG

1996/97 FIXTURES

01/09/96	Israel v Bulgaria
	Russia v Cyprus
08/10/96	Luxembourg v Bulgaria
09/10/96	Israel v Russia
10/11/96	Cyprus v Israel
	Luxembourg v Russia
14/12/96	Cyprus v Bulgaria
15/12/96	Israel v Luxembourg
29/03/97	Cyprus v Russia
30/03/97	Luxembourg v Israel
02/04/97	Bulgaria v Cyprus
03/04/97	Israel v Cyprus
30/04/97	Russia v Luxembourg
08/06/97	Bulgaria v Luxembourg
	Russia v Israel

1997/98 FIXTURES

20/08/97	Bulgaria v Israel
07/09/97	Luxembourg v Cyprus
10/09/97	Bulgaria v Russia
11/10/97	Cyprus v Luxembourg
	Russia v Bulgaria

GROUP SIX

SPAIN, CZECH REPUBLIC, SLOVAKIA, YUGOSLAVIA, MALTA, FAROE ISLANDS

1995/96 MATCH DETAILS

24/04/96, Belgrade
YUGOSLAVIA 3 Savicevic (3, 29), Milosevic (38)
FAROE ISLANDS 1 Petersen (53)
referee - Beck (LIE)
YUGOSLAVIA - Kocic; Curcic (Mirkovic 61), Djorovic, Jokanovic, Brnovic, Mihajlovic (Pantic 40), Jugovic, Savicevic, Mijatovic, Stojkovic, Milosevic (Nadj 86).
FAROE ISLANDS - Knudsen; Johannesen, Hansen J.C., Hansen A., Johnsson, Mørkøre A., Jarnskor H., Dam, Müller, Petersen, Rasmussen J.E. (Jarnskor M. 75).

GROUP SIX (CONTINUED)

02/06/96, Belgrade
YUGOSLAVIA 6 Zammit (2og), Mijatovic (38), Stojkovic (45), Milosevic (68), Savicevic (70p, 71)
MALTA 0
referee - Albrecht (GER)
YUGOSLAVIA - Kocic; Mirkovic, Djorovic (Saveljic 86), Jokanovic, Djukic, Mihajlovic, Jugovic (Nadj 50), Savicevic, Mijatovic, Stojkovic, Milosevic (Kovacevic 79).
MALTA - Cluett; Attard (Woods 46), Buhagiar, Vella, Debono, Zammit (Camilleri J. 75), Busuttil, Turner, Brincat, Chetcuti, Agius.

1996/97 FIXTURES

31/08/96	Faroe Islands v Slovakia
04/09/96	Faroe Islands v Spain
18/09/96	Czech Republic v Malta
22/09/96	Slovakia v Malta
06/10/96	Faroe Islands v Yugoslavia
09/10/96	Czech Republic v Spain
23/10/96	Slovakia v Faroe Islands
10/11/96	Yugoslavia v Czech Republic
13/11/96	Spain v Slovakia
14/12/96	Spain v Yugoslavia
18/12/96	Malta v Spain
12/02/97	Spain v Malta
31/03/97	Malta v Slovakia
02/04/97	Czech Republic v Yugoslavia
30/04/97	Yugoslavia v Spain
	Malta v Faroe Islands
21/05/97	Slovakia v Czech Republic
08/06/97	Yugoslavia v Slovakia
	Faroe Islands v Malta
	Spain v Czech Republic

1997/98 FIXTURES

20/08/97	Czech Republic v Faroe Islands
06/09/97	Faroe Islands v Czech Republic
10/09/97	Slovakia v Yugoslavia
24/09/97	Malta v Czech Republic
	Slovakia v Spain
11/10/97	Malta v Yugoslavia
	Czech Republic v Slovakia
	Spain v Faroe Islands

EUROPEAN QUALIFYING GROUPS

GROUP SEVEN

HOLLAND, BELGIUM, TURKEY, WALES, SAN MARINO

1995/96 MATCH DETAILS

02/06/96, Serravalle
SAN MARINO 0
WALES 5 Melville (20), Hughes (32, 43), Giggs (50), Pembridge (85)
referee - Lubos (SVK)
SAN MARINO - Muccioli S.; Gasperoni, Valentini M., Guerra, Gobbi, Manzaroli, Pasolini (Muccioli R 71), Mazza, Casadei (Peverani 75), Mularoni (Valentini V. 46), Montagna.
WALES - Southall; Bowen, Melville, Coleman, Pembridge, Browning (Goss 70), Horne (Savage 81), Robinson (Legg 80), Hughes M., Saunders, Giggs.

1996/97 FIXTURES

31/08/96	Belgium v Turkey
	Wales v San Marino
05/10/96	Wales v Holland
09/10/96	San Marino v Belgium
09/11/96	Holland v Wales
10/11/96	Turkey v San Marino
14/12/96	Belgium v Holland
14 or 15/12/96	Wales v Turkey
20/03/97	Holland v San Marino
29/03/97	Wales v Belgium
02/04/97	Turkey v Holland
30/04/97	San Marino v Holland
	Turkey v Belgium
07/06/97	Belgium v San Marino

1997/98 FIXTURES

20/08/97	Turkey v Wales
06/09/97	Holland v Belgium
10/09/97	San Marino v Turkey
11/10/97	Belgium v Wales
	Holland v Turkey

GROUP EIGHT

ROMANIA, REPUBLIC OF IRELAND, LITHUANIA, ICELAND, FYR MACEDONIA, LIECHTENSTEIN

1995/96 MATCH DETAILS

24/04/96, Skopje
FYR MACEDONIA 3 Milosevski (5), Babunski (49p), Zaharievski (80)
LIECHTENSTEIN 0
referee - Loizou (CYP)

GROUP EIGHT (CONTINUED)

FYR MACEDONIA - Celeski; Babunski, Markovski (Nikolovski 60), Jovanovski, Stojkovski, Milosevski, Milosavov, Gosev (Zaharievski 75), Ciric, Boskovski, Hristov (Naumovski 71).
LIECHTENSTEIN - Heeb; Hanselmann, Hasler, Stocker (Quaderer 46), Zech, Frick C., Frick D., Frick M., Hilti, Oehri, Telser (Sele 60).

01/06/96, Reykjavík
ICELAND 1 Gudjohnsen A. (63)
FYR MACEDONIA 1 Memed (51)
referee - Luinge (HOL)
ICELAND - Kristinsson B.; Adolfsson, Sigurdsson, Grétarsson , Jónsson S., Kristinsson R., Bergsson, Gudjohnsen A., Thórdarson (Stefánsson 67), Gudjónsson T. (Benediktsson 80), Gunnlaugsson B. (Gylfason 28).
FYR MACEDONIA - Celeski; Milosavov, Markovski, Nikolovski, Stojkovski, Sedloski, Memed, Gosev, Ciric (Saciri 36), Hristov (Borov 84), Milosevski.

1996/97 FIXTURES

31/08/96	Liechtenstein v Republic of Ireland
	Romania v Lithuania
05/10/96	Lithuania v Iceland
09/10/96	Iceland v Romania
	Republic of Ireland v FYR Macedonia
	Lithuania v Liechtenstein
09/11/96	Liechtenstein v FYR Macedonia
10/11/96	Republic of Ireland v Iceland
14/12/96	FYR Macedonia v Romania
29/03/97	Romania v Liechtenstein
02/04/97	Lithuania v Romania
	FYR Macedonia v Republic of Ireland
30/04/97	Liechtenstein v Lithuania
	Romania v Republic of Ireland
07/06/97	Republic of Ireland v Liechtenstein
	FYR Macedonia v Iceland
11/06/97	Iceland v Lithuania

1997/98 FIXTURES

19/08/97	Liechtenstein v Iceland
20/08/97	Republic of Ireland v Lithuania
	Romania v FYR Macedonia
06/09/97	Iceland v Republic of Ireland
	Liechtenstein v Romania
	Lithuania v FYR Macedonia
10/09/97	Romania v Iceland
	Lithuania v Republic of Ireland
11/10/97	Iceland v Liechtenstein
	Republic of Ireland v Romania
	FYR Macedonia v Lithuania

EUROPEAN QUALIFYING GROUPS

GROUP NINE

ALBANIA, ARMENIA, GERMANY, NORTHERN IRELAND, PORTUGAL, UKRAINE

1996/97 FIXTURES

31/08/96	Northern Ireland v Ukraine
	Armenia v Portugal
05/10/96	Northern Ireland v Armenia
	Ukraine v Portugal
09/10/96	Albania v Portugal
	Armenia v Germany
09/11/96	Albania v Armenia
	Germany v Northern Ireland
	Portugal v Ukraine
14/12/96	Northern Ireland v Albania
	Portugal v Germany
29/03/97	Albania v Ukraine
	Northern Ireland v Portugal
02/04/97	Albania v Germany
	Ukraine v Northern Ireland
30/04/97	Germany v Ukraine
	Armenia v Northern Ireland
07/05/97	Ukraine v Armenia
07/06/97	Portugal v Albania
	Ukraine v Germany

1997/98 FIXTURES

20/08/97	Northern Ireland v Germany
	Portugal v Armenia
	Ukraine v Albania
06/09/97	Germany v Portugal
	Armenia v Albania
10/09/97	Albania v Northern Ireland
	Germany v Armenia
11/10/97	Germany v Albania
	Portugal v Northern Ireland
	Armenia v Ukraine

Savo Milosevic (above) on the mark for Yugoslavia in their resounding 6-0 World Cup qualifying victory against Malta

Martin Dahlin (below) was another to make an early mark on the qualifiers, scoring for Sweden as they beat Belarus 5-1

UEFA CHAMPIONS' CUP

PRELIMINARY ROUND

While the champions of Italy, Germany, Spain, Holland, Portugal, England, France and Russia sat it out until September, 16 other national title holders entered the mid-summer scramble for a place in the lucrative UEFA Champions' League.

The action got underway on Wednesday August 8 at a time when most clubs were still in pre-season training. Not so Sweden's IFK Gothenburg, who were in the middle of their domestic championship as they lined up to face Legia Warsaw of Poland. Both teams had been involved in the previous season's Champions' League preliminaries, but while the Swedes had gone through, the Poles had been eliminated. So there was a surprising reversal of fortune when Legia won both matches to take the tie 3-1 on aggregate.

Two other 1994/95 Champions' League participants failed to make the grade a year later. Casino Salzburg, of Austria, were defeated 1-0 by Steaua Bucharest, and Hajduk Split, forced by UEFA to play their home leg up the coast in Rijeka, lost out on the away-goals rule to Panathinaikos. Steaua's victory bought them a return ticket to the Champions' League, and for the second year running Dynamo Kiev made it beyond the preliminary round at the expense of the champions of Denmark.

The biggest surprise of the round was the elimination of Anderlecht, the ninth seeds in the competition, by unfancied Ferencváros. The Belgian champions had made a bad start in their domestic league, but few expected them to struggle against the Hungarians. A breakaway goal from one of Ferencváros's two new Yugoslavs, Zoran Kuntic, gave them a shock 1-0 victory in Brussels, and an opening goal in the home leg from Kuntic's fellow countryman, Goran Kopunovic, ensured further progress.

A 0-1 home defeat was costly also for Maccabi Tel-Aviv. The Israelis set them themselves up for an historic qualification by drawing their first leg 1-1 away to Grasshoppers in Zürich, but a goal conceded in the fourth minute of the return leg undid their confidence and they were unable to get back into the tie. Anorthosis Famagusta also made a brave effort to put Cypriot football on the map in their tie with perennial Scottish champions Rangers, but Gordon Durie's goal in the first leg at Ibrox proved sufficient for Walter Smith's men to squeeze through to their promised land after two seasons of early-round failures.

Most of the ties were low-scoring, with the importance of victory forcing teams to be over-cautious and negative in their approach. One team which bucked the trend were Rosenborg of Norway, They went for the jugular in their home leg against Besiktas and were rewarded with an excellent 3-0 win. Another entertaining game took place a fortnight later in Istanbul, but Harald Brattbakk's second goal of the tie proved decisive in sending the Norwegians through. Brattbakk was the only player to score in both preliminary-round games, but two others managed to get on the scoresheet twice in the same match - Stefan Kuntz of Besiktas and Sergiy Shevchenko of Dynamo Kiev.

PRELIMINARY ROUND RESULTS

GRASSHOPPER-CLUB ZÜRICH 1 Yakin (50)
MACCABI TEL-AVIV 1 Kashentsev (55)
MACCABI TEL-AVIV 0
GRASSHOPPER-CLUB ZÜRICH 1 Comisetti (4)
(GRASSHOPPER-CLUB ZÜRICH 2-1)

RANGERS 1 Durie (68) **ANORTHOSIS FAMAGUSTA 0**
ANORTHOSIS FAMAGUSTA 0 RANGERS 0
(RANGERS 1-0)

LEGIA WARSZAWA 1 Podbrozny (49p) **IFK GÖTEBORG 0**
IFK GÖTEBORG 1 Blomqvist (25)
LEGIA WARSZAWA 2 Pisz (73), Bednarz (90)
(LEGIA WARSZAWA 3-1)

SV CASINO SALZBURG 0 STEAUA BUCURESTI 0
STEAUA BUCURESTI 1 Ilie A. (32) **SV CASINO SALZBURG 0**
(STEAUA BUCURESTI 1-0)

DYNAMO KYIV 1 Pokhlebayev (82p) **AAB 0**
AAB 1 Rasmussen P. (86)
DYNAMO KYIV 3 Kalitvintsev (37), Shevchenko (50, 77)
(DYNAMO KYIV 4-1)

ROSENBORG BK 3 Hoftun (21), Strand (26), Brattbakk (75)
BESIKTAS 0
BESIKTAS 3 Kuntz (9, 85p), Mehmet (88)
ROSENBORG BK 1 Brattbakk (68)
(ROSENBORG BK 4-3)

RSC ANDERLECHT 0 FERENCVÁROS 1 Kuntic (58)
FERENCVÁROS 1 Kopunovic (50) **RSC ANDERLECHT 1** De Bilde (64)
(FERENCVÁROS 2-1)

PANATHINAIKOS 0 HAJDUK SPLIT 0
HAJDUK SPLIT 1 Stimac (4) **PANATHINAIKOS 1** Borelli (53)
(1-1; PANATHINAIKOS on away goal)

UEFA CHAMPIONS' LEAGUE GROUP A

Joining automatic qualifiers FC Porto and Nantes in a very evenly balanced Group A were preliminary-round survivors Panathinaikos and Dynamo Kiev. The Ukrainians

UEFA CHAMPIONS' CUP

had run up the most convincing aggregate scoreline in the preliminary round, but their participation in the Champions' League was to last just one match.

85,000 people turned up to see Kiev's opening game at home to Panathinaikos, but they were all unaware that their team's future participation in the competition was already under threat. The Spanish referee Antonio López Nieto and his two linesman had allegedly been offered money and fur coats by Dynamo directors on the eve of the game in an attempt to secure a Kiev victory. The news became public a few days later when UEFA's disciplinary committee announced that the Ukrainian champions had been ejected from the Champions' League with immediate effect and banned from Europe for a further two years. It was one of the biggest bribery scandals in European Cup history.

Two teams benefitted from the decision - Panathinaikos, who had lost the match 1-0, were allowed to wipe the slate clean and start again, and AaB, the Danish champions eliminated by Kiev in the preliminary round, were handed the Champions' League place vacated by the Ukrainians.

The whole affair overshadowed everything else in Group A. The goalless draw with which Nantes and Porto had opened their campaign seemed a trifle irrelevant, and there was a distorted look to the group table until AaB and Panathinaikos finally found time to play their 'match in hand' on October 25. It was only three days before their first match, away to FC Porto, that AaB learned of their

Roman Kosecki netted FC Nantes' third goal as the French side overcame AaB 3-1

CHAMPIONS' LEAGUE GROUP A RESULTS & FINAL TABLE

FC NANTES 0 FC PORTO 0

DYNAMO KYIV 1 Kosovskyi (60) **PANATHINAIKOS 0**
(result later annulled)

FC PORTO 2 Rui Barros (40, 63) **AAB 0**

PANATHINAIKOS 3 Yoryadis Y.H. (17), Warzycha (30, 46)
FC NANTES 1 N'Doram (87)

FC PORTO 0 PANATHINAIKOS 1 Markos (39)

FC NANTES 3 Ouédec (5), Pedros (55), Kosecki (74) **AAB 1** Andersen (46)

AAB 2 Andersen (42), Madsen (90) **PANATHINAIKOS 1** Warzycha (41)

AAB 0 FC NANTES 2 Guyot (10), Ouédec (69)

PANATHINAIKOS 0 FC PORTO 0

FC PORTO 2 Drulovic (10), José Carlos (55) **FC NANTES 2** Pedros (3, 34)

PANATHINAIKOS 2 Alexoudis (1), Yoryadis Y.S. (38) **AAB 0**

FC NANTES 0 PANATHINAIKOS 0

AAB 2 Andersen (11), Madsen (69) **FC PORTO 2** Emerson (63, 75)

FINAL TABLE			Home					Away					Total						
		Pd	W	D	L	F	A	W	D	L	F	A	W	D	L	F	A	Pt	GD
1	Panathinaikos	6	2	1	0	5	1	1	1	1	2	2	3	2	1	7	3	11	+4
2	FC Nantes	6	1	2	0	3	1	1	1	1	5	5	2	3	1	8	6	9	+2
3	FC Porto	6	1	1	1	4	3	0	3	0	2	2	1	4	1	6	5	7	+1
4	AaB	6	1	1	1	4	5	0	0	3	1	7	1	1	4	5	12	4	-7

UEFA CHAMPIONS' CUP

confirmed Champions' League participation. So, it was no surprise that they lost the match, with Porto substitute Rui Barros scoring both goals in a 2-0 victory for the Portuguese champions. On the same night, Panathinaikos also made good use of home advantage, treating a 60,000 crowd in Athens to an excellent and thoroughly deserved 3-1 victory over Nantes. The Greeks also had a two-goal hero - Polish striker Krzysztof Warzycha.

Panathinaikos's next match was away to Porto. It was the first major confrontation of the group. Porto welcomed back their coach, Bobby Robson, who had been back in England recovering from facial cancer surgery, but the night was one to forget for his team. They were the dominant side throughout, but even though they had a one-man advantage for most of the game (after Alexoudis's first-half sending-off), Porto just could not score the goal they deserved. For the entire second half they were forced to chase the game, but it was still 0-1 at the final whistle, Panathinaikos having scored from one of only two chances they created all evening.

The Greeks now led the group with a maximum six points from two games, and they were expected to maintain their 100% record as they travelled to Denmark to face AaB, who looked anything but Champions' League material in their 1-3 defeat away to Nantes. But Juan Ramón Rocha's side could not seize the opportunity and were surprisingly beaten by a last-minute goal from Jens Christian Madsen.

AaB's credentials were put to the test again at home just one week later, when Nantes were the visitors. Another victory would have put Sepp Piontek's team right back in contention. But on an evening when English referee David Elleray did them no favours whatsoever, AaB succumbed to their second defeat by the Frenchmen. A goal in each half, the first a scrappy effort from close range by Laurent Guyot, the second a deflected free-kick by Nicolas Ouédec, put Nantes on top of the Group A table, thanks to the simultaneous 0-0 draw between Panathinaikos and Porto in Athens.

The key match of the group took place on November 22 in Oporto. It was a match the home side had to win. The visitors, Nantes, could afford a draw, but a victory would assure them of a place in the quarter-finals. It was Nantes who opened the scoring after just three minutes when Reynald Pedros raced clear and lobbed Porto 'keeper Vítor Baía from 25 yards. It was the first of two spectacular counter-attacking goals from the French international midfielder. His second, on 34 minutes, regained the lead for Nantes after Ljubinko Drulovic had earlier equalised for Porto. Bobby Robson's team drew level again ten minutes into the second half when defender José Carlos shot home after a free-kick rebounded to him on the edge of the area, and with just 15 minutes to go, Porto had the perfect opportunity to win the match and put their Champions' League destiny in their own hands when they were awarded a debatable penalty. But Domingos, the club's top scorer in the league, blasted the ball into the evening sky, and Porto's quarter-final hopes followed it into the darkness.

On the same night, Panathinaikos confirmed their qualification for the last eight by comfortably beating AaB 2-0 at home. The Greeks' first goal arrived after just 26 seconds, with Alexoudis, back from suspension, poking in a left-wing cross with his first touch to mark an impressive return.

Porto travelled to Denmark for their final match with qualification out of their hands. A draw between Nantes and Panathinaikos was sure to condemn them to third place, and that is precisely what happened. On a snow-covered pitch in the Beaujoire, the French champions made no significant attempt to secure the victory that would have taken them to the top of the group. They, like their opponents, were perfectly content with a draw. In the event, the result in France was irrelevant because Porto did not gain the victory they required against AaB. The best

Spartak Moscow's Andrei Pyatnitski in Group B action against Blackburn Rovers

UEFA CHAMPIONS' CUP

CHAMPIONS' LEAGUE GROUP B RESULTS & FINAL TABLE

LEGIA WARSZAWA 3 Pisz (65, 74), Staniek (69)
ROSENBORG BK 1 Jakobsen (63p)

BLACKBURN ROVERS 0 SPARTAK MOSKVA 1 Yuran (41)

ROSENBORG BK 2 Løken (30), Stensaas (86)
BLACKBURN ROVERS 1 Newell (62)

SPARTAK MOSKVA 2 Nikiforov (13p), Yuran (52)
LEGIA WARSZAWA 1 Jozwiak (82)

LEGIA WARSZAWA 1 Podbrozny (26) **BLACKBURN ROVERS 0**

ROSENBORG BK 2 Løken (2), Brattbakk (45)
SPARTAK MOSKVA 4 Alenichev (59), Nikiforov (66), Kechinov (75, 82)

SPARTAK MOSKVA 4 Shmarov (1), Yuran (6), Tsymbalar (19), Tikhonov (80)
ROSENBORG BK 1 Løken (90)

BLACKBURN ROVERS 0 LEGIA WARSZAWA 0

ROSENBORG BK 4 Strand (17), Brattbakk (44), Jakobsen (65), Heggem (89)
LEGIA WARSZAWA 0

SPARTAK MOSKVA 3 Alenichev (28), Nikiforov (47), Mamedov (54)
BLACKBURN ROVERS 0

LEGIA WARSZAWA 0 SPARTAK MOSKVA 1 Mamedov (41)

BLACKBURN ROVERS 4 Shearer (16p), Newell (31, 38, 40)
ROSENBORG BK 1 Iversen (30)

FINAL TABLE

			Home					Away					Total						
		Pd	W	D	L	F	A	W	D	L	F	A	W	D	L	F	A	Pt	GD
1	Spartak Moscow	6	3	0	0	9	2	3	0	0	6	2	6	0	0	15	4	18	+11
2	Legia Warszawa	6	2	0	1	4	2	0	1	2	1	6	2	1	3	5	8	7	-3
3	Rosenborg BK	6	2	0	1	8	5	0	0	3	3	11	2	0	4	11	16	6	-5
4	Blackburn Rovers	6	1	1	1	4	2	0	0	3	1	6	1	1	4	5	8	4	-3

they could manage was a 2-2 draw, with Brazilian midfielder Emerson scoring both goals as the Portuguese twice came from behind to equalise.

GROUP B

The anomalies and injustices of UEFA's Champions' League seeding system were thrown into light by the appearance of Blackburn Rovers as one of the two automatic qualifiers in Group B. The English champions had only ever played in one European tie before, and they had lost it, the season before, to Swedish part-timers Trelleborg. Spartak Moscow, on the other hand, fully deserved their privileged status. This was their third successive participation in the Champions' League, and their seasoned European credentials made them the favourites to progress in a none-too-difficult section which also featured Legia Warsaw and Rosenborg.

Spartak's first fixture was ostensibly their most difficult - away to Blackburn at Ewood Park. But history spoke for the Russian champions. They had never previously lost a European tie to a team from England. Indeed, three seasons earlier they had beaten Liverpool both home and away in the UEFA Cup. The portents were good, and they were realised by an exceptional Spartak performance, in which they outpassed and outplayed Blackburn and took the three points thanks to a single goal from Russian international striker Sergei Yuran, who took advantage of a monstrous blunder by Blackburn goalkeeper Tim Flowers to slide the ball into an empty net four minutes before half-time. Beaten by a technically and tactically more proficient team, the future did not look good for Blackburn, whose only decent chance of the came when defender Colin Hendry headed straight at the goalkeeper midway through the second half.

The early group leaders were not Spartak, but Legia Warsaw, who came from a goal behind to beat Rosenborg 3-1. Skipper Leszek Pisz was their inspiration, although they were helped by a poor performance betwen the posts from Rosenborg's stand-in goalkeeper Jørn Jamtfall.

Rosenborg bounced back from that defeat with a 2-1 home win over Blackburn in their next match, defender Ståle Stensaas firing in a powerful winning goal four minutes from time to leave the English Premiership champions bottom of the table without a point. Leading the group with a maximum six points were Spartak Moscow, 2-1 victors at home to Legia thanks to another decisive goal from Yuran.

The Russians' next two matches were both against Rosenborg. In the first encounter, in Trondheim, Oleg Romantsev's team looked to be really struggling against a rampant, in-form home side, and at the interval they found themselves two goals down. But the picture changed completely in the second period. Spartak moved up a

UEFA CHAMPIONS' CUP

couple of gears and silenced the home crowd with four goals. The 4-2 victory in Trondheim was followed by an even more decisive 4-1 triumph in Moscow. Spartak simply carried on where they had left off, scoring twice, through Shmarov and Yuran, in the opening minutes and then adding a fabulous third from Ilya Tsymbalar. Andrei Tikhonov scored the fourth late on, but Rosenborg did not go home entirely empty-handed. Karl-Petter Løken's last-minute goal - his third in successive Champions' League games - maintained their long domestic and European run of scoring in every game.

While Spartak Moscow ensured their quarter-final qualification with the two victories over Rosenborg, Blackburn Rovers disappeared out of contention after picking up just one point in their two confrontations with Legia Warsaw. A single goal from Legia striker Jerzy Podbrozny was enough to give the Poles victory in the home leg. But at Ewood Park, where Blackburn had to win to survive, there was an improved performance from the English side, only for wasted chances in front of goal to leave them with nothing better than a 0-0 draw. The best chance of all arrived in the final minute, and it fell to England striker Alan Shearer. But the player who had scored in every one of Blackburn's home games in the Premiership could not open his European account and fired the shot straight at goalkeeper Szcesny. That miss spelt elimination for Blackburn and prolonged the sorry tale of English teams in the Champions' League.

Blackburn's next match, in Moscow, was an opportunity to recover some lost pride. But, despite the encouragement of a 7-0 victory over Nottingham Forest the previous weekend, things went from bad to worse for Ray Harford's team in Europe. There was an extraordinary incident in the fifth minute when Blackburn's two England internationals, Graeme Le Saux and David Batty, actually came to blows after a harmless dispute over a throw-in. A diabolical miss by Henning Berg a couple of minutes later did nothing to restore the team's morale, and for the rest of the match Blackburn were once again taught a footballing lesson by the Russians. Spartak's quick passing and movement was too much for the Rovers defence and it brought three fine goals, two of them from defenders, Nikiforov and Mamedov, who were free to join in up front, so little were they given to do at the back. Blackburn's night of shame was complete when Colin Hendry was sent off (harshly) for pushing Tikhonov.

With Rosenborg thrashing Legia Warsaw 4-0 at home in their penultimate match, there was plenty to play for on the final day of Champions' League action in Group B. Rosenborg arrived at bottom-placed Blackburn needing to gain a better result than Legia, who were at home to already-qualified Spartak. But the Norwegians picked the wrong night. Blackburn, despite the suspensions of Moscow bad boys Hendry, Le Saux and Batty, at last came out of their shell and won the match 4-1, with Mike Newell scoring a magnificent nine-minute hat-trick in the first half. An equally impressive goal from Rosenborg's Steffen Iversen was only relevant in extending the club's record of scoring in every game to 77 matches. After Newell's goal-blitz there was no way back - even after Blackburn's Paul Warhurst was sent off for his second bookable offence early in the second half.

In the event, a draw would have been enough for Rosenborg to progress. On an evening of sub-zero temperatures in Warsaw, Legia were beaten 1-0 by Spartak. The Poles had only acquired seven points, but, thanks to Blackburn, they were through to the quarter-finals. So, too, were Spartak, highly impressive group winners with a maximum haul of 18 points from their six matches.

GROUP C

The toughest of the Champions' League groups by far was Group C. Preliminary-round qualifiers Rangers and Steaua Bucharest knew that they would have to play beyond themselves if they were to make further progress from a section that contained the champions of Italy and Germany.

Juventus and Borussia Dortmund, the group heavyweights, were drawn to face each other in the opening match. The two sides had become regular foes in Europe, contesting the UEFA Cup final in 1993 and the semi-final of the same competition two years later. Within the context of the opening match in the Champions' League, the pressure was not quite so intense, but with four ex-Juventus players in the Dortmund line-up - Kohler, Júlio César, Reuter and Möller - there were still plenty of old scores to settle.

Dortmund must have thought they were dreaming when, after just 31 seconds, they grabbed the lead. Andy Möller, one of the Juve old boys, flashed in a glorious first-time left-footer to give the Germans the perfect start on their Champions' League début. But it was a false dawn. Juventus, despite the absence through suspension of their two attacking spearheads Ravanelli and Vialli, were soon on level terms, with a headed goal from replacement striker Michele Padovano. And nine minutes before half-time a magnificent curling shot from Alessandro Del Piero gave the Italians the lead. Dortmund created a number of chances to draw level, but expensive new signing Heiko

UEFA CHAMPIONS' CUP

Alessandro Del Piero - star of the show for Juventus

Herrlich was too nervous in front of goal and they all missed the target. The match was decided midway through the second half with a brilliant third goal for Juventus. Man of the match Del Piero clipped in a beautiful cross and Antonio Conte despatched it into the net with a powerful and accurate diving header. 3-1 should have been 4-1 in the final minute, but Fortunato had his second goal of the evening ruled out for an imaginary offside.

The other three points at stake on opening night went to Steaua Bucharest. Rangers held the Romanians for 85 minutes with a strong defensive performance led by goalkeeper Andy Goram. But with just five minutes left a thunderous left-foot volley, direct from a corner, by Romanian international defender Daniel Prodan found Goram's net and gave Steaua the victory.

In round two, the opening-match winners came face to face in Turin. It was clear from the outset that Juventus would have little difficulty in seeing off Steaua. Vialli and Ravanelli were both back in the team, but it was once again Del Piero who stole the show, scoring the second of Juventus's three goals with a carbon copy of the strike he had netted against Dortmund, curling in a fabulous right-foot shot from the corner of the penalty area right into the far stanchion of the goal. Meanwhile, in Glasgow, Rangers and Borussia Dortmund claimed their first point in a competitive and entertaining, if error-strewn, 2-2 draw. All four goals came from headers, with Rangers twice being required to come from behind to avoid a second successive defeat.

With just one point from their opening two games, Rangers now faced a double date with Juventus. In theory, they had to get something from the two matches against the Italian champions in order to mainatin their interest in the competition. In practice, they never looked likely to get anything except a hard and painful lesson in

CHAMPIONS' LEAGUE GROUP C RESULTS & FINAL TABLE

BORUSSIA DORTMUND 1 Möller (1)
JUVENTUS 3 Padovano (12), Del Piero (36), Conte (68)

STEAUA BUCURESTI 1 Prodan (85) **RANGERS 0**

JUVENTUS 3 Di Livio (34), Del Piero (39), Ravanelli (49)
STEAUA BUCURESTI 0

RANGERS 2 Gough (62), Ferguson (72)
BORUSSIA DORTMUND 2 Herrlich (19), Kree (69)

JUVENTUS 4 Moore (15og), Conte (23), Del Piero (30), Ravanelli (75)
RANGERS 1 Gough (77)

BORUSSIA DORTMUND 1 Ricken (58) **STEAUA BUCURESTI 0**

RANGERS 0
JUVENTUS 4 Del Piero (11), Torricelli (65), Ravanelli (88), Marocchi (90)

STEAUA BUCURESTI 0 BORUSSIA DORTMUND 0

JUVENTUS 1 Del Piero (90) **BORUSSIA DORTMUND 2** Zorc (29), Ricken (65)

RANGERS 1 Gascoigne (39) **STEAUA BUCURESTI 1** Ilie A. (55)

BORUSSIA DORTMUND 2 Möller (17), Riedle (48)
RANGERS 2 Laudrup (11), Durie (85)

STEAUA BUCURESTI 0 JUVENTUS 0

FINAL TABLE			Home					Away					Total						
		Pd	W	D	L	F	A	W	D	L	F	A	W	D	L	F	A	Pt	GD
1	Juventus	6	2	0	1	8	3	2	1	0	7	1	4	1	1	15	4	13	+11
2	Borussia Dortmund	6	1	1	1	4	5	1	2	0	4	3	2	3	1	8	8	9	=
3	Steaua Bucuresti	6	1	2	0	1	0	0	1	2	1	5	1	3	2	2	5	6	-3
4	Rangers	6	0	2	1	3	7	0	1	2	3	7	0	3	3	6	14	3	-8

UEFA CHAMPIONS' CUP

the finer arts of the game. Quite simply, Juventus destroyed Rangers. Not just in Turin, but at Ibrox too.

Both matches resulted in four-goal victories for the Italian champions, and in each game the team in the black and white stripes were completely dominant. In Turin, Rangers were missing both of their creative stars, Paul Gascoigne and Brian Laudrup, but such was Alessandro Del Piero's breathtaking form on the night that no other player on earth would have been able to upstage the brilliant youngster. Juventus were already 2-0 up when, on 30 minutes, he produced another of his trademark masterpieces, curling in a free-kick from 25 yards out near the left touchline. But even that was capped by a piece of sheer sorcery from the little number ten at the start of the second half. He so bemused Rangers full-back Alex Cleland with an ingenious party-piece over on the left touchline that when he next received possession a moment later and threatened to make a fool of his opponent again, Cleland just clattered into Del Piero and was rightly sent off.

Richard Gough managed to score a late deflected goal in the Stadio delle Alpi, but at Ibrox, a fortnight later, Rangers fans had nothing to console them. A couple of headed efforts against the Juventus post were as near as they got to scoring. The Italians, on the other hand, showed Rangers how to finish. Del Piero, again, scored the first goal, and that was followed in the second half by three more from Torricelli, Ravanelli and Marocchi.

The two victories over Rangers confirmed both Juventus's presence in the quarter-finals and their leadership of the group. After four games Borussia Dortmund were up into second place - seven points behind the Italians - having beaten Steaua Bucharest 1-0 at home and then settled for a laborious 0-0 draw against the same opponents in Romania.

Given the situation in the group, Juventus were able to rest six first-choice players when Dortmund came to visit them in the penultimate game. It was hardly fair on Rangers and Steaua, who still hoped to unseat the Germans from second spot. But Juventus had an important Serie A game against Parma coming up, so Torricelli, Ravanelli, Deschamps, Ferrara, Paulo Sousa and Del Piero were all missing from the starting line-up. At first it seemed that Juventus were as hungry as Dortmund for victory, but once the Germans went ahead with a strong left-foot shot from captain Michael Zorc after 29 minutes, there was little resistance from the home side. The longer the match went on, the more dominant Dortmund became, and when Lars Ricken exploited an error from Carrera to make it 2-0, Juve were finished. All that remained was for Alessandro Del Piero to come on as a substitute and score a free-kick with the last kick of the game, enabling him to set a new Italian record with his fifth goal in successive Champions' Cup/League matches.

The victory was enough to see Dortmund safely through to the next round. That was because Rangers and Steaua shared a 1-1 draw at Ibrox, the highlight of which was a stunning solo goal from Paul Gascoigne.

The last two games were irrelevant, and both were played in very wintry conditions. With ice and snow on the pitch and in the stands, Juventus's match in Bucharest would surely not have been staged had there been something more important than financial bonuses at stake. A 0-0 draw was inevitable in the impossible conditions. In Dortmund, Borussia and Rangers repeated the 2-2 scoreline of their previous encounter, with Gordon Durie, on his 30th birthday, scoring Rangers' late equaliser after Gascoigne had been red-carded for swearing at the referee.

GROUP D

Group D was heavily weighted in favour of the two seeded teams. Ajax and Real Madrid had won ten Champions' Cups between them. Grasshopper-Club of Zürich and Ferencváros of Budapest were surprise qualifiers from

Real Madrid's Raúl bagged himself a hat-trick against Ferencváros

UEFA CHAMPIONS' CUP

countries which had never previously risen to the lofty heights of the Champions' League.

The two Group D favourites came face to face immediately, in Amsterdam. Ajax, the Champions' Cup holders, were without their goalscoring hero of the 1995 final, Patrick Kluivert, who withdrew his services after being involved in a fatal car accident a few days before the game. And Real Madrid, on their first appearance in the Champions' League, had to make do without midfield orchestrator Michael Laudrup. It was not the classic encounter many people had forecast, but the 40,000 crowd went home happy thanks to an early goal from winger Marc Overmars, which brought Ajax a deserved 1-0 victory.

The early group leaders, surprisingly, were Ferencváros, who, having eliminated Anderlecht in the preliminary round, raced to the top of the table with a remarkable 3-0 victory away to Grasshoppers. All three of the Hungarians' goals came in the second half as the Swiss were caught out chasing the game.

Ferencváros's bid for glory did not last long. In their next game, at home to the holders, they held Ajax for almost an hour. But once Jari Litmanen scored the first goal, the floodgates opened. Four further Ajax goals followed, including two more for Litmanen, in a brilliant second-half display that provided the perfect retort to the racist chants directed at Ajax's black players from certain sections of the Hungarian crowd.

Real got their campaign into gear with a 2-0 victory at home to Grasshoppers. It was not a vintage performance from the team, but such were Real's problems in the domestic league, with a big game against Barcelona looming three days later, that they were happy just to get the three points. Chilean striker Iván Zamorano eased their fears with two opportunistic strikes in the second half.

After the third round of matches, it was as clear as daylight how the group was going to finish up. Ajax inflicted a third successive defeat on Grasshoppers with a 3-0 victory in Amsterdam, while Real hammered a weakened Ferencváros 6-1 in Madrid. It was a night for the teenagers, with 19-year-old Kluivert scoring two excellent goals for Ajax and 18-year-old Raúl going one better with the first hat-trick of his career for Real.

In the return matches two weeks later, Ajax and Real were both expected to settle the issue of qualification by repeating their victories. But, surprisingly, both teams were held to draws. Real even fell a goal behind to Ferencváros when Flórián Albert scored via the underside of the bar after 36 minutes. But Raúl rescued the Spaniards with a fine left-foot volley from Alkorta's right-wing cross 14 minutes from time. Had Real lost the game, Ferencváros would have drawn level on points with them, so it was a crucial goal from the young striker.

Ajax's 0-0 draw away to Grasshoppers was even more of a turn-up. It was the first time the Dutch champions had failed to win in 16 league and Cup games. Nevertheless,

CHAMPIONS' LEAGUE GROUP D RESULTS & FINAL TABLE

AJAX 1 Overmars (14) **REAL MADRID 0**

GRASSHOPPER-CLUB ZÜRICH 0
FERENCVÁROS 3 Lisztes (61), Vincze (82, 90)

FERENCVÁROS 1 Nyilas (59p)
AJAX 5 Litmanen (57, 80p, 85), Kluivert (67), De Boer F. (85)

REAL MADRID 2 Zamorano (69, 89) **GRASSHOPPER-CLUB ZÜRICH 0**

AJAX 3 Kluivert (10, 68), George (87) **GRASSHOPPER-CLUB ZÜRICH 0**

REAL MADRID 6 Raúl (23, 25, 84), Zamorano (33, 46), Hierro (54)
FERENCVÁROS 1 Kopunovic (63)

GRASSHOPPER-CLUB ZÜRICH 0 AJAX 0

FERENCVÁROS 1 Albert (36) **REAL MADRID 1** Raúl (74)

REAL MADRID 0 AJAX 2 Litmanen (63), Kluivert (76)

FERENCVÁROS 3 Albert (20), Lisztes (24), Nyilas (85p)
GRASSHOPPER-CLUB ZÜRICH 3 Subiat (22), Comisetti (48), Ibrahim (64)

AJAX 4 Overmars (16), De Boer R. (21), Litmanen (61, 65) **FERENCVÁROS 0**

GRASSHOPPER-CLUB ZÜRICH 0
REAL MADRID 2 Raúl (55), Míchel (66)

FINAL TABLE			Home					Away					Total						
		Pd	W	D	L	F	A	W	D	L	F	A	W	D	L	F	A	Pt	GD
1	Ajax	6	3	0	0	8	0	2	1	0	7	1	5	1	0	15	1	16	+14
2	Real Madrid	6	2	0	1	8	3	1	1	1	3	2	3	1	2	11	5	10	+6
3	Ferencváros	6	0	2	1	5	9	1	0	2	4	10	1	2	3	9	19	5	-10
4	Grasshopper-Club Zürich	6	0	1	2	0	5	0	1	2	3	8	0	2	4	3	13	2	-10

UEFA CHAMPIONS' CUP

the draw enabled Ajax to set a new Champions' Cup/League record. It was their 15th successive match without defeat in the competition, beating the old record held jointly by Liverpool (1984-85) and Ajax themselves (1971-73). Grasshoppers might have felt proud to hold Ajax to a goalless stalemate, especially with raw reserve goalkeeper Foletti between the posts, but the result still meant elimination for the Swiss champions.

Ajax had strolled their way through their first four matches, but in their fifth game, away to Real Madrid in the Bernabéu, they put on their party suits and delivered a performance to remember. There were over 100,000 people in the stadium to witness one of the great Champions' Cup/League displays. Not even the most ardent Real Madrid diehard could fail to be impressed with what he saw. The Spaniards were simply spellbound by football from another galaxy.

Ajax turned it on right from the start. In the first half alone they had two goals wrongly disallowed and struck the frame of the Real goal three times. First of all, Kluivert had a perfectly good goal annulled for a non-existent offside. Then the same player volleyed a Finidi George cross against the crossbar. Next to hit the woodwork was Jari Litmanen. His free-kick bounced down at least a foot over the line, but again the goal was incorrectly chalked off by the German officials. Marc Overmars then took his turn at testing the strength of the Real crossbar with a blistering shot, which rebounded to Litmanen, who headed over.

How Real escaped into the dressing-rooms at half-time with 0-0 still flashing on the scoreboard was a miracle. But justice was done in the second half, as Ajax continued to press and were rewarded with goals from the two players who had been cruelly denied in the first half. Litmanen was the first to get his name on the scoresheet, skilfully beating the offside trap and shooting through Buyo's legs. 13 minutes later Kluivert joined him with a beautiful finish to Overmars' cross. It was an awesome display from the holders. Real were nowhere. The victory took Ajax through to the last eight as group winners, happy in the knowledge that their quarter-final opponents would not be Juventus.

While Ajax were raising the game of football to a higher plane in Madrid, Ferencváros and Grasshoppers were slugging out a 3-3 draw in Budapest. There was controversy in that match, too, as the Swiss side were denied their first victory of the competition by a scandalous late penalty decision in favour of the Hungarians. Elek Nyilas dived to get the penalty, then picked himself up to fire home the equaliser from the spot.

That goal still, theoretically, kept Ferencváros's hopes alive, but with a visit to Amsterdam to complete their programme, they were never likely to get the victory they required to pip Real Madrid for the runners-up spot. Sure enough, Ajax blitzed them as they had done in Budapest. 4-0 was the final score, Ajax comfortably securing their third successive home win, all of them obtained without conceding a goal. Two second-half goals from Jari Litmanen brought his total against Ferencváros to five and his total for the Champions' League to six - the best of the competition, one better than Raúl, who scored the first of Real's goals in the 2-0 victory away to Grasshoppers that confirmed their date with Juventus in the quarter-finals.

QUARTER-FINALS

The pre-programmed structure of the Champions' League resulted in a very bottom-heavy quarter-final draw. Real Madrid v Juventus and Borussia Dortmund v Ajax were the ties everybody wanted to see. Legia Warsaw v Panathinaikos might have been a pairing in the preliminary round, and Nantes v Spartak Moscow had lost much of its gloss in the three months since the Champions' League because of a mass exodus of players from the Russian club.

Had Spartak been able to hold onto the likes of Yuran, Kulkov and Cherchesov, not to mention coach Romantsev, who had thrown in his lot full-time with the Russian national team, they might have been one of the favourites to lift the trophy. But against Nantes, the Russians were desperately under strength, and it was no big surprise that they failed to make any futher progress in the competition.

The French champions had got lucky again. The withdrawal of Dynamo Kiev in their Champions' League

QUARTER-FINAL RESULTS

LEGIA WARSZAWA 0 PANATHINAIKOS 0
PANATHINAIKOS 3 Warzycha (34, 58), Borelli (72)
LEGIA WARSZAWA 0
(PANATHINAIKOS 3-0)

FC NANTES 2 N'Doram (28), Ouédec (68) **SPARTAK MOSKVA 0**
SPARTAK MOSKVA 2 Nikiforov (32, 38)
FC NANTES 2 Ouédec (63, 86)
(FC NANTES 4-2)

REAL MADRID 1 Raúl (21) **JUVENTUS 0**
JUVENTUS 2 Del Piero (16), Padovano (53) **REAL MADRID 0**
(JUVENTUS 2-1)

BORUSSIA DORTMUND 0 AJAX 2 Davids (8), Kluivert (83)
AJAX 1 Musampa (75) **BORUSSIA DORTMUND 0**
(AJAX 3-0)

UEFA CHAMPIONS' CUP

Juventus's Jugovic and Quique of Real Madrid tussle for the ball during the battle of the giants in the quarter-finals

group had opened up Nantes' path to the quarter-finals. Now, again, Spartak made life easier for Jean-Claude Suaudeau's modest team by pressing the self-destruct button. The first leg in Nantes was decided in the home side's favour by two headed goals, one in either half, from Japhet N'Doram and Nicolas Ouédec. The only disappointment of the evening for the home fans was the sending-off of Reynald Pedros, who had supplied the crosses for both of the goals.

Spartak were forced to stage the second leg of the quarter-final in the home of their city rivals Lokomotiv rather than in their own Luzhniki stadium, which was undergoing repair. So only 30,000 spectators were present to see whether the 'new Spartak' could recover from their first defeat of the competition and still make the semi-finals. At half-time there was genuine hope that they could. Yuri Nikiforov led a one-man salvage operation, scoring twice within six minutes to draw Spartak level on aggregate. But while Nikiforov proved to be the goalscoring hero for Spartak, Nantes had a hit-man of their own who was familiar with the experience of putting goals past Russian goalkeepers. In the previous season's UEFA Cup campaign Nicolas Ouédec had scored three goals against Rotor Volgograd and four against Tekstilschik Kamyshin. Now he made it three against Spartak as well, adding two classy second-half strikes to his first-leg header to take Nantes into the semi-finals.

Despite freezing conditions, the first leg of the Legia Warsaw-Panathinaikos tie was allowed to go ahead. The decision did the home side no favours and the result was a predictable goalless draw. For the return leg in Athens, the temperature was considerably warmer, and Panathinaikos's Polish striker Krzysztof Warzycha proved why he is happily settled in Greece by scoring twice against his fellow countrymen and setting Panathinaikos on their way into a first European semi-final for 26 years. Legia, only just back in domestic league action after a long winter break, offered nothing at all. Panathinaikos simply swamped them, and the 3-0 scoreline, completed by Argentinian midfielder Borelli's sumptuous curling shot, was an accurate reflection of the Greek side's dominance.

Ajax went into the first leg of their quarter-final with Borussia Dortmund without several first-choice players, including winger Marc Overmars and leading scorer Jari Litmanen. They had also suffered a lapse in form in domestic competition. But if Dortmund, themselves without the injured Andy Möller, thought that they were facing the holders at the right time, they were quickly led to believe otherwise as Ajax came at them strongly from the start. After just eight minutes they were ahead, Edgar Davids collecting a one-two from Patrick Kluivert and shooting past Klos with his left foot after a neat piece of control with his right.

Davids was to be the dominant personality of the evening as Ajax controlled the game for long periods, not allowing Dortmund to settle into any sort of pattern. Evidence of Dortmund's discomfiture came 21 minutes into the second half when sweeper Matthias Sammer was sent off for his second yellow-card offence. Ajax took full advantage of his absence. With seven minutes left they conjured up a quite breathtaking goal. It was the reverse of the opening strike. This time Davids made it, and Kluivert scored it. Both the creation and the execution were stunning.

Two weeks later, in front of a sell-out 43,000 crowd in Amsterdam, Ajax had the straightforward task of holding on to their 2-0 lead. German opposition should never be underestimated, but a Dortmund side missing the suspended Sammer and Reuter and the injured Möller and Herrlich were no match for the Dutchmen. No matter that Dortmund had not lost away from home since the

UEFA CHAMPIONS' CUP

previous August, or that they had won 5-0 in Stuttgart the previous weekend. Ajax were in a different class; they had shown that in the first leg. The match was a mere formality for the holders. Perhaps it was a lack of urgency that made Litmanen and Kanu both miss easy chances to increase Ajax's lead. But with 15 minutes left, one of the Ajax new breed, Kiki Musampa, showed them how to finish, tucking in a superb pass from Kanu.

For all the style and panache of Louis van Gaal's Ajax, Real Madrid v Juventus was unquestionably the glamour tie of the round. Whatever Barcelona and Milan might claim, these two clubs remain the traditional giants of Spanish and Italian football. Both were desperate for Champions' Cup success in a way, perhaps, that no other club could possibly imagine. Real had gone 30 years without a Champions' Cup triumph; Juventus needed to erase the black memory of Heysel.

Real had won the two previous meetings between the clubs, and there was a magical atmosphere in the Bernabéu, full to its capacity, as the two teams took the field. Both captains were injured - Sanchis for Real, Vialli for Juventus - but for most of the first half neither were missed as the action took place predominantly in the Juventus half. After 21 minutes Real took a deserved lead, Zamorano and Laudrup working a delightful opening for Raúl, who finished like a veteran, guiding the ball into the corner of the net with his trusty left foot. Throughout the opening period Real played fluid and confident football, with Laudrup running the show in midfield against his former club, and they might have gone a further goal ahead but for confident work in the Juventus goal by Angelo Peruzzi.

Juve coach Marcello Lippi strengthened his midfield after the interval, withdrawing Alessandro Del Piero from attack, and there was more of an even balance to the play. After Zamorano had missed an easy chance for Real, Juventus thought they might have been awarded a penalty, but Ravanelli clearly dived after being fed in the area by Del Piero. New Real Madrid coach Arsenio Iglesias made a very strange move midway through the half when he brought off the influential Laudrup. The fizz suddenly disappeared from Real's play, and by the final whistle, with the Italians beginning to get back into the game, the crowd were happy with the 1-0 scoreline.

There was a big responsibility on Juventus's shoulders two weeks later. The night before, both Milan and Roma had gone out of the UEFA Cup, leaving Juve as the sole remaining Italian representatives in Europe. Not that they didn't feel the pressure sufficiently from within. Vialli was back to lead Juve on their night of destiny, but Ravanelli was suspended. Zamorano was also missing from the Real attack, and Iglesias decided to leave Raúl up front on his own. His intentions were clear. He felt Real were good enough to defend their 1-0 lead.

Kluivert, Kanu and Davids celebrate during Ajax's triumph over Borussia Dortmund

Only 16 minutes into the game, however, the Juventus fans were up on their feet acclaiming another wonder goal from their hero Alessandro Del Piero. His free-kick actually went through the Real wall and still found its way into the corner of the net to bring the tie all-square. Surprisingly, the goal did not alter Real's defensive approach, and they continued to absorb Juventus pressure through to the half-time interval without further addition to the scoreline.

Juventus entered the second half with all guns blazing. The crowd could sense a goal and they got one after just eight minutes when poor defending by Real defender Alkorta allowed Juventus to break the offside trap. Porrini fed Padovano, and the replacement for Ravanelli rifled a superb left-foot shot into the far corner. Juventus continued to press for the third goal that would kill the tie, and Vialli twice went close. But gradually, the game began to deteriorate into a series of petty fouls, and Dutch referee Mario van der Ende began to lose control, sending off Alkorta and Juventus defender Moreno Torricelli for what were no more than good, honest challenges.

The situation was very tight. Real just needed to score

UEFA CHAMPIONS' CUP

once to go ahead on the away-goals rule, and in the 83rd minute they came desperately close to doing just that when Luis Milla received possession following a free-kick and rolled the ball inches wide of the target with Peruzzi stranded. But that was Real's only chance. Juventus held on for a deserved victory. It had been a dramatic game, a classic reminder of why two-legged knock-out football is still the best type of European football there is.

SEMI-FINALS

The Stadio delle Alpi is not a venue for which Juventus fans have any dying affection, but for the semi-final visit of Nantes, the *Bianconeri* diehards did their best to fill it. The atmosphere was tremendous as Juventus entered the arena buoyed by their quarter-final comeback against Real Madrid and confident of seeing off a team that was only halfway up the French First Division table.

The first half did not run according to plan for Juve. Nantes defended their goal well and might even have had an early penalty when Ouédec was blocked in the area by Pessotto. The only genuine chance of the first 45 minutes was created out of nothing by Gianluca Vialli, who forced a brilliant save from Nantes goalkeeper Casagrande with an audacious overhead kick. The turning point of the match arrived right on half-time when Nantes midfielder Bruno Carotti was sent off - and rightly so - for his second yellow-card offence.

It was one-way traffic after the interval. Only four minutes had passed when Vialli put Juventus in front with his first goal of the competition, knocking the ball into the net from close range with his knee after Del Piero had flicked on a corner. Padovano and Del Piero had further good chances to increase the Italians' lead before the second goal arrived - a tremendous rising right-foot drive from Vladimir Jugovic, which nestled spectacularly in the top corner of Casagrande's net. That second goal was the security Juventus needed for the return leg in Nantes.

Just 17 minutes into the match in the Beaujoire, the tie was all over. With an immaculate flick off the outside of his right boot, Vialli put Juventus 3-0 up in the tie. Nantes now required four goals. Their task should have been made even more difficult when Casagrande handled outside his penalty area, but referee Puhl displayed only a yellow card when most officials would have sent him off.

A header from Capron, which only just crossed the line, restored parity just before half-time, but five minutes after the interval Juventus were back in charge, Vialli feeding Paulo Sousa for a rare goal from the Portuguese midfielder. With their place in the final secure, Juventus relinquished their hold of the game and allowed a spirited Nantes to score two further goals, through N'Doram and substitute Renou. The result went down as a 3-2 victory for Nantes, and the home fans were evidently delighted with their team's efforts, but the reality was that Juventus were always fully in control of their destiny from the moment that man of the match Vialli opened the scoring. 11 years after Heysel, Juve were back in the Champions' Cup final, and nobody could dispute their right to be there.

Ajax were fully expected to join Juventus in Rome, but they received a massive jolt in the first leg of their semi-final, at home to Panathinaikos. It was Ajax's last big fixture in the Olympic stadium before decamping to

Ajax coach Louis van Gaal in thoughtful mood

SEMI-FINAL RESULTS

JUVENTUS 2 Vialli (49), Jugovic (65) **FC NANTES 0**

FC NANTES 3 Decroix (43), N'Doram (69), Renou (82)
JUVENTUS 2 Vialli (17), Paulo Sousa (50)
(JUVENTUS 4-3)

AJAX 0 PANATHINAIKOS 1 Warzycha (87)

PANATHINAIKOS 0 AJAX 3 Litmanen (4, 77), Wooter (85)
(AJAX 3-1)

UEFA CHAMPIONS' CUP

their flashy new Amsterdam Arena home. Apart from long-term injury victim Marc Overmars, they were at full strength. Panathinaikos were clearly taking the tie seriously despite all the silly predictions which suggested that they might care to forfeit the tie in advance.

Panathinaikos boss Juan Ramón Rocha massed his troops in defence, and from the first minute the pattern of the match was set. Ajax were free to have as much possession as they liked, but as soon as they approached the danger zone, several green shirts would appear to block their route to goal. Ajax created only three chances in the first half, but Kanu (twice) and Litmanen were inches wide of the target on each occasion. In the second half, Panathinaikos's defensive discipline began to get to the Ajax players, and suddenly all their invention disappeared. Finidi George had an especially poor game on the right wing, and Kluivert could hardly get a kick.

Ajax were given a real scare after 71 minutes when the Greeks broke from the back and substitute Yoryadis was sent clean through from Borelli's pass, only for his shot to be saved by the long legs of Ajax 'keeper Edwin van der Sar. But the warning went unheeded. With just three minutes left and the home side having apparently given up hope of ever breaking down the magnificent Panathinaikos rearguard, they were caught by the classic sucker punch. The speedy Donis darted forward athletically through the centre and fed Krzysztof Warzycha. His finish was that of a seasoned goalscorer, precise and deadly.

Panathinaikos had won 1-0. It was a sensational result. Rocha's tactics had worked perfectly. His team had defended with discipline, not with violence, and had squeezed the creative juices out of Ajax to the point where their gifted players began to misplace passes and commit unforced errors. Then the Greeks had delivered the telling blow. Ajax's first defeat in 20 European matches was hard for the holders to bear, but it was no miscarriage of justice; they had been beaten fair and square.

But of course the tie was not yet over. In Greece the victory was received as if the country had won the World Cup. In reality, the job was only half done.

The Olympic stadium in Athens was full for the first time in nine years for the return leg. It was a grand setting. The pitch was in immaculate condition. Every seat in the stadium was taken. And two teams, each containing 11 full internationals, prepared to do battle for a place in the European Champions' Cup final.

Pre-match debate over whether Panathinaikos would defend their lead or go for more goals was rendered irrelevant after just four minutes when Jari Litmanen, with his seventh goal of the competition, coolly slotted Ajax into the lead. It was a wish come true for Ajax, and for the remainder of the first half they completely dominated possession, just as they had done in the first leg. The Greeks just could not get hold of the ball. Ajax were the masters again, but the second goal they needed to assume complete control did not come. Litmanen and Kanu both missed chances in the first half, and then the two of them combined to waste an easy opportunity early in the second. But finally, with 13 minutes left on the clock, the second goal finally arrived, Litmanen tucking away Kanu's cross neatly with his left foot after the ball had sailed over the Greek defenders' heads. Five minutes from the end substitute Nordin Wooter completed a tremendous Ajax comeback with a third goal, tapping in from close range following Ronald de Boer's diving header.

Ajax were through. The holders had shown that they possessed resilience and staying power as well as abundant skill. Europe now had the final it wanted. The Dream Final - Ajax v Juventus.

FINAL

For the second year in a row Ajax took on the might of Italy. The previous season Louis van Gaal's team had defeated Milan in Vienna. Now they had to beat Juventus ... in Rome.

It was virtually a home fixture for Juventus. Although the club is based up in the north-west of the country, Juventus are essentially the team of all Italy. They have just as many fans in Milan and Rome as they do in Turin. No doubt about it, this was a match Juventus simply could not lose. History beckoned them. The horror of Heysel was still with them. They had to beat Ajax and bury the demon forever.

Free of suspensions and injuries, Juventus had everything in their favour. Ajax were without right-back Michael Reiziger, who was suspended. Patrick Kluivert was only fit enough to claim a place on the bench after being out with injury for the previous five weeks. And Frank de Boer, though selected, was not fully fit.

Juventus made a bright, positive start. They were clearly in the mood. Ajax, however, looked shaky in defence, and after 12 minutes Frank de Boer and goalkeeper Van der Sar were caught in a terrible mix-up just inside the penalty area. De Boer's loose header was drifting out for a corner. But Fabrizio Ravanelli was lurking, and before Sonny Silooy could get back to cover the goal-line, the silver-haired striker had squeezed the ball into the net from the tightest of angles with his weaker right foot. It was a tremendous finish, and it sent the crowd into ecstasy.

UEFA CHAMPIONS' CUP

TOP SCORERS

9 Jari LITMANEN (Ajax)
6 Alessandro DEL PIERO (Juventus)
RAUL González (Real Madrid)
Krzysztof WARZYCHA (Panathinaikos)
5 Patrick KLUIVERT (Ajax)
Nicolas OUEDEC (FC Nantes)
Yuri NIKIFOROV (Spartak Moskva)
4 Iván ZAMORANO (Real Madrid)
Fabrizio RAVANELLI (Juventus)
Mike NEWELL (Blackburn Rovers)

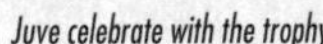

Juve celebrate with the trophy

Juventus continued to force the pace. Their tactics were spot-on. Ajax were not allowed to settle. Every time a player in red and white received possession, he was hounded by an opponent in blue. But Ajax were experienced enough to keep their cool, and with the first half ebbing to a close, they suddenly drew level. It was poor defending from goalkeeper Peruzzi and Vierchowod which allowed Jari Litmanen to stab home his ninth goal of the competition from close range.

There was a scrappy start to the second half, for which Ajax brought on Kluivert for Musampa and Kanu slipped back into midfield. Neither team created a clear chance for half an hour, but with the 90 minutes drawing to a close, Juventus once again picked up the tempo, driven on by man of the match Moreno Torricelli. Juve skipper Gianluca Vialli had a glorious opportunity to claim the winner three minutes from time, but after creeping in to a good position behind the goalkeeper he just could not wrap his left leg around the ball and direct it to goal.

Like so many major finals in recent years, the match went into extra-time. Still Juventus were the stronger side. Silooy nearly scored an own-goal after Del Piero clipped the ball in from the left. Then Jugovic had a free-kick deflected narrowly wide off Kanu's head. Kluivert had a chance to steal victory for Ajax and write the Champions' Cup final headlines for the second year in a row, but he fluffed his near-post effort completely. And on the final whistle, Italy's golden boy, Alessandro Del Piero, was presented with a clear chance, but could only direct his shot straight at Van der Sar.

To penalties. Ajax went first, but Edgar Davids shot weakly and Peruzzi made an easy save. Ferrara was first to shoot for Juventus. He scored. Then Litmanen, Pessotto, Scholten and Padovano (just) all found the target. It was Silooy's turn, but Peruzzi moved to his left and saved again. A roar went up in the stadium. Then quiet. Vladimir Jugovic, a penalty shoot-out winner with Red Star Belgrade in 1991, stepped up for the decisive kick. He was the man chosen to lead Juventus into paradise. He struck his shot sweetly and decisively into the net.

Juventus had done it. Their moment of deliverance had arrived amidst unbearable tension. But they were the right winners. They had been the better team on the night. And when skipper Gianluca Vialli hoisted the trophy into the Roman sky, eveyrbody knew that Juventus's long crusade for European Champions' Cup glory was finally over.

FINAL

22/05/96, Rome
JUVENTUS 1 Ravanelli (12)
AJAX 1 Litmanen (41)
(aet; 4-2 on pens.)
referee - Díaz Vega (ESP)
JUVENTUS - Peruzzi; Ferrara, Pessotto, Torricelli, Vierchowod, Paulo Sousa (Di Livio 57), Deschamps, Conte (Jugovic 43), Vialli, Del Piero, Ravanelli (Padovano 77).
AJAX - Van der Sar; Silooy, Blind, De Boer F. (Scholten 69), Bogarde, De Boer R. (Wooter 91), George, Davids, Kanu, Litmanen, Musampa (Kluivert 46).

CUP-WINNERS' CUP

PRELIMINARY ROUND

For the third year in succession the European Cup-winners' Cup boasted a record entry. 48 teams were included, with exactly two-thirds of them forced into early-season action in the preliminary round. Every UEFA member bar two entered a team. San Marino do not participate in the European club competitions, and Croatia could not take part because their representative, Croatia Zagreb, were banned for a year because of crowd trouble. There was, however, a place for reinstated Yugoslavia - taken by a Second Division club, Obilic Belgrade, runners-up in the Yugoslav Cup to 'double'-winners Red Star Belgrade. And, for the first time, four new UEFA nations, Armenia, Azerbaijan, Georgia and Macedonia, were permitted to enter the competition.

Only Azerbaijan, of the new quartet, failed to get their team through the preliminary round, Neftchi Baku falling to APOEL Nicosia after a 0-3 defeat in Cyprus and a 0-0 draw at home. The most impressive of the newcomers were Macedonia's Sileks Kartovo and Armenia's Ararat Yerevan. Sileks were comfortable 4-2 aggregate winners over Hungarian side Vác FC-Samsung, and Ararat ended Polish team GKS Katowice's tenth successive season of European football with a penalty shoot-out victory after coming back from a 0-2 deficit in the first leg.

PRELIMINARY ROUND RESULTS

TILIGUL TIRASPOL 0 FC SION 0
FC SION 3 Moser (23), Herr (29), Bonvin (45)
TILIGUL TITASPOL 2 Oprea (79), Popovici (90)
(FC SION 3-2)

VÁC FC-SAMSUNG 1 Romanek (90) **SILEKS KRATOVO 1** Micevski (58)
SILEKS KRATOVO 3 Memed (15), Borov (36, 67)
VÁC FC-SAMSUNG 1 Borgulja (21)
(SILEKS KRATOVO 4-2)

TPS 1 Wallden (29p) **TEUTA DURRËS 0**
TEUTA DURRËS 3 Vila (9), Koça (20), Bushi (55) **TPS 0**
(TEUTA DURRËS 3-1)

FC VADUZ 0
SK HRADEC KRALOVE 5 Cerny (15), Samec (32, 50, 58), Ptacek (37)
SK HRADEC KRALOVE 9 Samec (4, 9, 30, 53), Urban (14, 83p), Vrabel (37), Smarda (50p) , Ptacek (63)
FC VADUZ 1 Ritter (28)
(SK HRADEC KRALOVE 14-1)

APOEL NICOSIA 3 Andoniou (18), Ioannou (43, 65) **NEFTCHI BAKU 0**
NEFTCHI BAKU 0 APOEL NICOSIA 0
(APOEL NICOSIA 3-0)

WREXHAM 0 PETROLUL PLOIESTI 0
PETROLUL PLOIESTI 1 Pirlog (59) **WREXHAM 0**
(PETROLUL PLOIESTI 1-0)

VALLETTA 0 INTER BRATISLAVA 0
INTER BRATISLAVA 5 Rupec (10), Tomko (15, 58), Gregusko (79), Landerl (85)
VALLETTA 2 Doncic (60), Zarb (85)
(INTER BRATISLAVA 5-2)

SHAKHTAR DONETSK 4 Atelkin (9), Matveyev (18), Orbu (28, 90)
LINFIELD 1 Ewing (47)
LINFIELD 0 SHAKHTAR DONETSK 1 Voskoboinik (87)
(SHAKHTAR DONETSK 5-1)

ZALGIRIS VILNIUS 2 Baltusnikas (53), Tereskinas (67)
MURA MURSKA SOBOTA 0
MURA MURSKA SOBOTA 2 Kokol (11), Alihodzic (89)
ZALGIRIS VILNIUS 1 Vencevicius (73)
(ZALGIRIS VILNIUS 3-2)

GKS KATOWICE 2 Bilski (27), Karwan (29) **ARARAT YEREVAN 0**
ARARAT YEREVAN 2 Gspeyan (23), Tonoyan (26p) **GKS KATOWICE 0** (aet)
(2-2; ARARAT YEREVAN 5-4 on pens.)

OBILIC BEOGRAD 0 DINAMO BATUMI 1 Machutadze (71)
DINAMO BATUMI 2 Machutadze (65), Mujiri (82p)
OBILIC BEOGRAD 2 Sarac (8), Popovic (35)
(DINAMO BATUMI 3-2)

DERRY CITY 1 McCourt (44) **LOKOMOTIV SOFIA 0**
LOKOMOTIV SOFIA 2 Slavchev (6), Khvoinev (29) **DERRY CITY 0**
(LOKOMOTIV SOFIA 2-1)

MACCABI HAIFA 4 Mizrahi (9, 36, 84p), Shitrit (66) **KÍ 0**
KÍ 3 Danielsen (54, 65, 72)
MACCABI HAIFA 2 Revivo (32), Shitrit (82)
(MACCABI HAIFA 6-3)

DINAMO-93 MINSK 1 Lobanov (37) **MOLDE FK 1** Solskjaer (85)
MOLDE FK 2 Solskjaer (4), Stavrum A. (67)
DINAMO-93 MINSK 1 Skripchenko (19)
(MOLDE FK 3-2)

CS GREVENMACHER 3 Jungblut (8, 52), Alves Silva (58)
KR 2 Bibercic (50), Egilsson (80)
KR 2 Bibercic (45), Porca (67) **CS GREVENMACHER 0**
(KR 4-3)

DAG-LIEPAYA 1 Dobretsov (5)
FC LANTANA TALLINN 2 Lapsa (17), Borissov (75) (later awarded as 3-0)
FC LANTANA TALLINN 0 DAG-LIEPAYA 0
(DAG-LIEPAYA 3-0)

CUP-WINNERS' CUP

Most of the ties were closely fought. There were only two in which one team won both matches. One of those was Shakhtar Donetsk of Ukraine against Northern Ireland's Linfield. Shakhtar won the first leg 4-1 in front of the biggest attendance of the round (31,000) and ensured a second victory with a late goal in Belfast. The other one-sided tie amounted to an annihilation as Hradec Kralove of the Czech Republic slaughtered Liechtenstein's FC Vaduz, winning 5-0 away and then 9-1 at home. Czech international striker Petr Samec had a field day, scoring half of his team's 14 goals - three in the first leg, four in the second.

There was major controversy in the Baltic derby between Latvia's DAG-Liepaya and Estonia's Lantana Tallinn. Lantana won the first leg away from home 2-1, but the scorer of their winning goal, midfielder Andrei Borissov, played despite being under suspension. The match was awarded 3-0 to the Latvians, and they qualified for the first round after a goalless draw in the second leg.

FIRST ROUND

16 teams came through from the preliminary round to face 16 automatically-qualified teams from Europe's major footballing nations, and only one of the pre-qualifiers survived - Hradec Kralove.

The Czechs' confidence was evidently boosted by the 14-goal rout of Vaduz in the first round, because in their opening first-round match at home to Danish Cup winners FC Copenhagen, Hradec Kralove hit the goal trail again, winning 5-0, with star striker Samec again grabbing a couple of goals to take his total to nine in three games. He was unable to reach double figures for the tournament in the second leg, but his team scored two quick goals and were never in the slightest danger of a Danish comeback.

Two other preliminary-round qualifiers came close to joining Hradec Kralove in round two. Lokomotiv Sofia looked set to make further progress after beating Sweden's Halmstads BK 3-1 in the Bulgarian capital. But a 0-2 away defeat eliminated them on the away-goals rule. Shakhtar Donetsk gave the Belgians of Club Bruges a mighty fright, but despite registering the largest home attendance for the second round in succession (39,000), they could not come back from an unfortunate late goal conceded in the first leg in Bruges.

In the other ties, the favourites all went through without difficulty. Parma were grateful for two late Gianfranco Zola goals in the first leg of their 4-0 aggregate victory over Albanian side Teuta Durrës. Paris Saint-Germain also got off the mark late away to the Norwegians of Molde before sailing comfortably through. And Borussia Mönchangladbach convincingly ended the hopes of Sileks Kratovo, scoring three times in each leg to match PSG's 6-2 aggregate scoreline.

The two Spanish entries, holders Real Zaragoza and Copa del Rey winners Deportivo La Coruña, eased themselves into round two. Zaragoza had five different goalscorers in their 5-1 triumph against Slovakia's Inter Bratislava, while Deportivo left all their goalscoring against APOEL Nicosia until the second leg at home in the Riazor, with Brazilian striker Bebeto netting three of their goals in an 8-0 victory. Three days later Bebeto was to complete an amazing week by netting all five of his team's goals in a Spanish league victory at home to Albacete.

There were three other hat-tricks, both scored in the first leg. Sporting Portugal's new signing from Vitória Guimarães, midfielder Pedro Barbosa, made a glorious European début with three excellent goals in a 4-0 win at home to Maccabi Haifa. Feyenoord's Regi Blinker bagged his three goals away from home. They all came in a 15 minute-period at the start of the second half of his team's 7-0 demolition of DAG-Liepaya in Latvia. The Dutch Cup holders dished out similar treatment back in Rotterdam, where Nigerian striker Mike Obiku outdid Blinker's achievement by scoring a hat-trick within just eight minutes in a 6-0 romp. Having also found the target once in the first leg, Obiku became the first round's joint leading scorer on four goals. The other player to match his tally was Celtic's German striker Andreas Thom, who scored twice in each game as the Scots eliminated Dinamo Batumi of Georgia 7-2 on aggregate.

The other British team, FA Cup winners Everton, were back in this competition for the first time since winning the trophy in 1985. The Merseysiders had not been able to defend their title because of the ban on English clubs following the Heysel disaster. But Joe Royle's team made light work of the club's belated re-introduction to the European scene, defeating Iceland's KR with a pair of three-goal victories.

Feyenoord hat-trick man Regi Blinker

CUP-WINNERS' CUP

FIRST ROUND RESULTS

DAG-LIEPAYA 0 FEYENOORD 7 Larsson (2, 61), Blinker (47, 58, 62), Koeman (78), Obiku (88)
FEYENOORD 6 Heus (37p), Trustfull (43), Obiku (57, 63, 65), Gláucio (61) **DAG-LIEPAYA 0**
(FEYENOORD 13-0)

CLUB BRUGGE KV 1 Spehar (88) **SHAKHTAR DONETSK 0**
SHAKHTAR DONETSK 1 Voskoboinik (61)
CLUB BRUGGE KV 1 Stanic (60)
(CLUB BRUGGE KV 2-1)

DINAMO BATUMI 2 Machutadze (11), Tugushi (68)
CELTIC 3 Thom (21, 87), Donnelly (39)
CELTIC 4 Thom (18, 20), Donnelly (46), Walker (90) **DINAMO BATUMI 0**
(CELTIC 7-2)

SK HRADEC KRALOVE 5 Samec (32, 75), Hynek (39), Cerny (52), Ptacek (90)
FC KØBENHAVN 0
FC KØBENHAVN 2 Tengstedt (27), Tur (72)
SK HRADEC KRALOVE 2 Urbanek (10), Rehak (12)
(SK HRADEC KRALOVE 7-2)

LOKOMOTIV SOFIA 3 Marinov (41), Petkov (43p), Donev (57)
HALMSTADS BK 1 Svensson M. (33)
HALMSTADS BK 2 Andersson R. (22), Andersson T. (75)
LOKOMOTIV SOFIA 0
(3-3; HALMSTADS BK on away goal)

KR 2 Bibercic (37, 68p)
EVERTON 3 Ebbrell (22), Unsworth (57p), Amokachi (88)
EVERTON 3 Stuart (56), Grant (65), Rideout (87) **KR 1** Daníelsson (22)
(EVERTON 6-3)

INTER BRATISLAVA 0 REAL ZARAGOZA 2 Morientes (43), Oscar (61)
REAL ZARAGOZA 3 Poyet (12), Nayim (64), Dani (72)
INTER BRATISLAVA 1 Obsitnik (76)
(REAL ZARAGOZA 5-1)

SK RAPID WIEN 3 Barisic (45, 90p), Ivanov (59)
PETROLUL PLOIESTI 1 Toader (65)
PETROLUL PLOIESTI 0 SK RAPID WIEN 0
(SK RAPID WIEN 3-1)

MOLDE FK 2 Solskjaer (55), Stavrum A. (81)
PARIS SAINT-GERMAIN FC 3 Le Guen (76), Djorkaeff (78p), Dely Valdes (84)
PARIS SAINT-GERMAIN 3 Nouma (7, 13), Djorkaeff (77) **MOLDE FK 0**
(PARIS SAINT-GERMAIN 6-2)

DINAMO MOSKVA 3 Teryokhin (45, 90), Safronov (73)
ARARAT YEREVAN 1 Stepanyan (70)
ARARAT YEREVAN 0 DINAMO MOSKVA 1 Teryokhin (65)
(DINAMO MOSKVA 4-1)

AEK 2 Vlahos (45), Borbokis (69) **FC SION 0**
FC SION 2 Bonvin (20), Giallanza (85) **AEK 2** Ketsbaia (82), Batista (87)
(AEK 4-2)

BORUSSIA MÖNCHENGLADBACH 3 Pflipsen (6), Effenberg (19), Klinkert (88)
SILEKS KRATOVO 0
SILEKS KRATOVO 2 Memed (51), Boskovski (62)
BORUSSIA MÖNCHENGLADBACH 3 Effenberg (29), Dahlin (54), Nielsen (80)
(BORUSSIA MÖNCHENGLADBACH 6-2)

TEUTA DURRËS 0 PARMA 2 Zola (82, 85)
PARMA 2 Melli (8), Inzaghi (90) **TEUTA DURRËS 0**
(PARMA 4-0)

ZALGIRIS VILNIUS 2 Tereskinas (7), Mikulenas (67)
TRABZONSPOR 2 Arveladze S. (25), Abdullah (54)
TRABZONSPOR 1 Hami (37) **ZALGIRIS VILNIUS 0**
(TRABZONSPOR 3-2)

SPORTING CP 4 Pedro Barbosa (7, 10, 47), Sá Pinto (88)
MACCABI HAIFA 0
MACCABI HAIFA 0 SPORTING CP 0
(SPORTING CP 4-0)

APOEL NICOSIA 0 RC DEPORTIVO 0
RC DEPORTIVO 8 Bebeto (17, 22, 45), Radchenko (28, 67), Beguiristáin (43), Donato (60), Aldana (79)
APOEL NICOSIA 0
(RC DEPORTIVO 8-0)

SECOND ROUND

The second-round stage of all three competitions was to prove fatal for British hopes in Europe. In the Cup-winners' Cup, Everton and Celtic completed a miserable first week of November for England and Scotland by exiting the competition without managing a single goal between them in their two ties.

Everton had happy memories of Rotterdam. It was in the Feyenoord stadium that they had lifted the Cup-winners' Cup in 1985, beating Rapid Vienna 3-1 in the final. But on their return visit a little over a decade later, they were to have no luck at all. The first leg, at Goodison Park, showed up Everton's deficiencies in front of goal and finished 0-0. In Rotterdam, the English Cup winners had more of the game than Feyenoord but went out to a single Regi Blinker goal scored late in the first half. Everton did everything in their power to score the all-important away goal in the second half, but efforts from Short,

CUP-WINNERS' CUP

Rideout, Hinchcliffe and Stuart all failed to beat in-form Feyenoord goalkeeper Ed de Goey. Everton's frustration was complete when Short was sent off in stoppage-time for elbowing Ronald Koeman.

Celtic played some impressive football in their away leg against Paris Saint-Germain before Youri Djorkaeff grabbed a late goal to give the French side a fortunate 1-0 advantage. But at Parkhead, Tommy Burns' team were comprehensively outplayed by a rampant PSG side. Patrice Loko, who had not made the best of starts after his summer move from Nantes, finished off two excellent Paris counter-attacks to put his team 2-0 up at the interval, and his replacement, Pascal Nouma, added a third midway through the second half to tie up an impressive 3-0 win.

German Cup winners Borussia Mönchengladbach also made it through to the quarter-finals with room to spare, humbling AEK of Greece 5-1 over the two legs. All six of the goals in the tie came in the second half, five of them in the first leg in Germany, where, bizarrely, the Portuguese referee blew his whistle for half-time after just 42 minutes and then had to call the players back on to the pitch after realising his error.

There were no problems either for the Spanish pair of Zaragoza and Deportivo. The Cup holders seemed in danger of going out when they conceded a second-half penalty to Belgian league leaders Club Bruges and only won the home leg 2-1. But a fine defensive performance in Bruges kept their slender lead intact for 90 minutes before young striker Dani settled Spanish nerves with a winning goal in the last minute. Deportivo also won their away leg 1-0, beating Trabzonspor with a second-half strike from Spanish international midfielder Donato. Back home in Galicia, Deportivo turned on the style, with Donato opening the scoring again and Bebeto adding two more goals to the three he had scored in the first round to make himself the leading scorer in the competition.

The other three ties were rich in drama. Hradec Kralove's run from the preliminary round came to an end in a penalty shoot-out at home to Dinamo Moscow after two 1-0 home wins. The Czechs missed all of their spot-kicks to give the Russians an easy ride into the quarter-finals. Rapid Vienna were within a few seconds of elimination when striker Christian Stumpf scored a last-gasp goal in the second leg of the Austrians' tie with Sporting Portugal. Just as Casino Salzburg had done to the Portuguese side in the third round of the UEFA Cup a couple of years earlier, Rapid finished them off in extra-time, with Stumpf and his German strike partner Carsten Jancker adding two further goals to complete a brilliant comeback and give Rapid a 4-2 aggregate victory.

The most sensational tie of the round, however, was between UEFA Cup holders Parma and Swedish part-timers Halmstad. The Swedes hosted the first leg in Gothenburg's Gamla Ullevi stadium due to the high demand for tickets. It was expected that this move to alien territory might harm their chances. On the contrary, they played out of their skins. The very windy conditions did not help the Italians, and when local hero Niklas Gudmundsson fired a crafty left-foot shot into the corner of the Parma net after just seven minutes, they knew they were in for a difficult night. It was to get worse. Gudmundsson's second delightful finish of the match, after 31 minutes, put Halmstad 2-0 up, and as Parma tried desperately to get back into the game in the second half,

SECOND ROUND RESULTS

SPORTING CP 2 Sá Pinto (12), Paulo Alves (23) **SK RAPID WIEN 0**
SK RAPID WIEN 4 Kühbauer (25), Stumpf (90, 105), Jancker (110)
SPORTING CP 0 (aet)
(SK RAPID WIEN 4-2)

DINAMO MOSKVA 1 Kuznetsov (58) **SK HRADEC KRALOVE 0**
SK HRADEC KRALOVE 1 Kaplan (15) **DINAMO MOSKVA 0** (aet)
(1-1; DINAMO MOSKVA 3-0 on pens.)

HALMSTADS BK 3 Gudmundsson (7, 31), Andersson R. (75) **PARMA 0**
PARMA 4 Inzaghi (1), Baggio (28), Stoichkov (53), Andersson T. (59og)
HALMSTADS BK 0
(PARMA 4-3)

PARIS SAINT-GERMAIN FC 1 Djorkaeff (76) **CELTIC 0**
CELTIC 0 **PARIS SAINT-GERMAIN FC 3** Loko (36, 43), Nouma (68)
(PARIS SAINT-GERMAIN FC 4-0)

REAL ZARAGOZA 2 Aragón (28p), Dani (34)
CLUB BRUGGE KV 1 Staelens (74p)
CLUB BRUGGE KV 0 **REAL ZARAGOZA 1** Dani (90)
(REAL ZARAGOZA 3-1)

BORUSSIA MÖNCHENGLADBACH 4 Dahlin (51, 90), Pflipsen (55), Wynhoff (67) **AEK 1** Maladenis (78)
AEK 0 **BORUSSIA MÖNCHENGLADBACH 1** Effenberg (71)
(BORUSSIA MÖNCHENGLADBACH 5-1)

EVERTON 0 **FEYENOORD 0**
FEYENOORD 1 Blinker (39) **EVERTON 0**
(FEYENOORD 1-0)

TRABZONSPOR 0 **RC DEPORTIVO 1** Donato (61)
RC DEPORTIVO 3 Donato (22), Bebeto (39, 80) **TRABZONSPOR 0**
(RC DEPORTIVO 4-0)

CUP-WINNERS' CUP

Gudmundsson punished them again, charging down the left and delivering the perfect cross for his forward partner Robert Andersson to blast the Swedes into a 3-0 lead.

It was Parma's first defeat in ten European games, but they had won all of their previous eight home matches in Europe, so they knew they still had a chance. Nevio Scala's team got off to the ideal start in the return leg when Inzaghi crashed in a left-foot shot in the first minute. And for the rest of the opening period they attacked incessantly, gaining their reward with a second goal from Dino Baggio, who latched on to an excellent Stoichkov through-ball and fired a raking left-foot shot in off the upright. When Stoichkov himself curled in a free-kick to level the tie up at 3-3 shortly after the interval, the Swedes looked dead and buried. But they did create one golden chance when Vougt twisted in the area and forced a brilliant save from goalkeeper Bucci. Soon afterwards, though, Parma got their fourth goal - a shot from Benarrivo which deflected off Halmstad defender Tommy Andersson - and that was the comeback complete. From that moment on, Parma simply defended their lead, which they accomplished without further threat.

There was much sympathy for the Swedes after their storming first-leg performance, but Parma's fightback was phenomenal. It made them only the second Italian team ever to come back from a 0-3 first-leg deficit in Europe.

QUARTER-FINAL RESULTS

DINAMO MOSKVA 0 SK RAPID WIEN 1 Stumpf (34)
SK RAPID WIEN 3 Jancker (48, 74), Stöger (62p)
DINAMO MOSKVA 0
(SK RAPID WIEN 4-0)

PARMA 1 Stoichkov (58) **PARIS SAINT-GERMAIN FC 0**
PARIS SAINT-GERMAIN FC 3 Raí (9p, 69p), Loko (38)
PARMA 1 Melli (26)
(PARIS SAINT-GERMAIN 3-2)

RC DEPORTIVO 1 David (70) **REAL ZARAGOZA 0**
REAL ZARAGOZA 1 Morientes (37) **RC DEPORTIVO 1** Bebeto (63)
(RC DEPORTIVO 2-1)

BORUSSIA MÖNCHENGLADBACH 2 Wynhoff (4), Kastenmaier (43p)
FEYENOORD 2 Van Gastel (33), Koeman (45p)
FEYENOORD 1 Trustfull (85)
BORUSSIA MÖNCHENGLADBACH 0
(FEYENOORD 3-2)

QUARTER-FINALS

There was little doubt about the pick of the quarter-final ties. Parma against Paris Saint-Germain. The Italians had reached European finals in each of the past three seasons; the French side had been a semi-final ever-present over the same stretch. Something had to give.

There was very little to choose between the two teams in the first leg, in Parma. The French team came into the game boosted by a couple of defeats for their French league rivals Auxerre and Metz two days earlier, but they were without their influential skipper Vincent Guérin, and after 42 minutes he was joined on the treatment table by Youri Djorkaeff, substituted because of a cut to his right knee. Parma also lost their playmaker, Gianfranco Zola, in the first half. He had not looked fully fit from the start.

13 minutes after the interval Parma went ahead when Hristo Stoichkov, who had squandered an easy chance in the first half, broke down the left and drilled a cross-shot past goalkeeper Lama. PSG were unlucky not to get straight back on level terms when Patrice Loko struck the inside of the post, but they subsequently had Lama to thank when he made an excellent save from Inzaghi to keep the score down to 1-0. The Parisians barely attacked at all in Italy, but back at the Parc des Princes they had no option but to go for an all-out assault on the Parma goal. A crowd of 43,686 came to watch what turned out to be another of PSG's classic European comebacks. Just nine minutes had elapsed when the home side drew level on aggregate, Raí converting from the penalty spot after Cannavaro had clumsily fouled Nouma. But midway through the first half they had it all to do again when Parma equalised. The goal was entirely Lama's fault. Melli shot from the edge of the area, but the PSG 'keeper allowed the ball to squirm through his arms and under his body. He endeavoured to make up for his blunder with a great save from Pin at the end of the first half, by which stage PSG were back in the lead on the night thanks to a second goal from Loko.

The game's big talking point came midway through the second half when the Swedish referee, Leif Sundell, awarded the home side a second penalty. Fournier was clearly chopped down by Apolloni after a goalmouth scramble, but there had been several PSG players in an offside position leading up to the incident. Italian protests forced a long delay before Raí stepped up to bury the spot-kick low in the corner for the second time. PSG coach Luis Fernandez could not bear to watch the penalty, and he was up and down off the bench in agitation for the last 20 minutes as his team hung tenaciously onto their lead. After Lazio and Milan, Parma were the third Italian team to be eliminated from Europe by a French side in 1995/96. PSG kept their annual semi-final date, but Parma would not be going through to their fourth successive European final.

While most of Europe viewed Parma v PSG as the quarter-final bill-topper, everyone in Spain focussed their

CUP-WINNERS' CUP

attention on the all-Primera Division clash between Deportivo and Zaragoza. It was only the second time ever that two Spanish teams had come face to face in the Cup-winners' Cup. Much was riding on the tie as neither team was going well in the domestic league. Deportivo coach John Toshack had even fallen out with his star man Bebeto, who did not feature in the first leg in La Coruña.

Nevertheless, even without the Brazilian, Deportivo dominated the first leg and should have won by more than the eventual 1-0 victory margin. The scorer of the only goal was supersub David, a youngster who had never started a match for Deportivo but who put his team ahead with a glorious finish in the 70th minute.

For the second leg, David was back on the bench, and Bebeto was back in the team. Deportivo were again the more constructive of the two sides, but after a bad miss by Fran, who sliced wide with the goal at his mercy, Zaragoza were allowed to get back into the game and they took advantage by grabbing an equaliser through Morientes. Bebeto then had a goal disallowed for a very contestable offside decision, but the Brazilian was clearly out to impress, and early in the second half, just after he had had a free-kick deflected onto a post, he slid in for Deportivo's equaliser. There was no way back for Zaragoza. Like UEFA Cup holders Parma, the Cup-winners' Cup holders had been knocked out by a World Cup-winning Brazilian.

Borussia Mönchengladbach against Feyenoord was one of those ties that UEFA describe as 'high-risk'. The German leg was switched from 'Gladbach's Bökelberg stadium to Düsseldorf, and there was a blow for the home team when Swedish striker Martin Dahlin hobbled off after just two minutes with a leg injury. Peter Wynhoff immediately cheered the Borussia fans up with a magnificent strike from the edge of the area, but the Germans were unable to control the game against a committed Dutch side, who deservedly drew level after 33 minutes when Jean-Paul van Gastel drove in a free-kick which the 'Gladbach defence clearly expected Ronald Koeman to take. A first half littered with poor passing and defensive errors ended, fittingly, with a penalty-kick awarded for each side. Kastenmeier converted Mönchengladbach's after Maas's foul on Sternkopf, and Koeman did the honours for Feyenoord after goalkeeper Kamps had jumped all over Taument. With no further scoring in a dull second half, everything was to play for in Rotterdam.

Alas, the quality did not improve despite a big crowd in "De Kuip". Chances were few and far between. Feyenoord, with two goals, did not need to score, and 'Gladbach badly missed Dahlin, who was still injured. The tie was settled by a goal for the home side five minutes from time. It was credited to substitute Orlando Trustfull, but his shot clearly benefitted from a deflection off his team-mate Giovanni van Bronckorst's leg.

The fourth quarter-final saw a rematch between Dinamo Moscow and Rapid Vienna, who had faced each other 11 years earlier at the semi-final stage. Now, as then, the Austrians were to emerge triumphant. They were in superb form in the first leg in Moscow and should have won by more than the single goal which Christian Stumpf scored, after a great solo run, in the 34th minute. Dinamo only came close once to equalising, when Kobelev struck a free-kick against a post. Rapid struggled to impose themselves in a similar fashion in the first half of the return leg, but once tall German striker Carsten Jancker had opened the scoring just after the interval, Rapid were able to freewheel to a comfortable 3-0 victory and join Paris Saint-Germain, Deportivo and Feyenoord in the semi-finals.

SEMI-FINALS

Unlike Feyenoord and Rapid Vienna, neither Deportivo La Coruña nor Paris Saint-Germain had ever reached a European final. Yet it was the semi-final confrontation between the Cup winners of Spain and France that did more to capture the imagination of the European football-watching public at large. PSG were under particular pressure. They had been knocked out in the semi-finals of European competition three years in a row. They knew that another defeat at this stage would be impossible for their supporters to bear.

But the Parisians did not go into the tie in the best of form. They had lost their last two French league games and were almost out of the domestic title hunt. Their quarter-final hero Raí was injured, and French international Youri Djorkaeff was not fit enough to start the match.

For the first 45 minutes, PSG, wearing an Ajax-style kit, set out their stall in defence. It proved very effective. Deportivo, despite the backing of a big crowd, could do nothing to penetrate, and their best effort of the half was a 40-yard shot from defender Paco. The second half was much more entertaining. Lama was forced into his first serious save of the evening when he dived at Manjarín's feet after PSG's offside trap had been broken by Aldana's shrewd pass. Liaño, the Deportivo goalkeeper, then pulled off an even more impressive save to tip over a close-range Dely Valdes header. In time the Spaniards began to find more and more holes in the French defence, and substitute Aitor Beguiristáin was guilty of an horrendous miss when, from barely a yard out, he could only clip the bar after Lama parried a Fran free-kick into his path. Three minutes from time PSG also survived a penalty appeal

CUP-WINNERS' CUP

when Alfredo lost his footing in the area. The Parisians were hanging on for dear life when, totally out of the blue, in the very last minute, they stunned the home crowd into silence with a goal. It was no ordinary goal, either. Djorkaeff, who had come on as a late substitute, evaded the challenge of three Spainsh defenders before cutting inside and unleashing a tremendous right-foot shot into the far corner. Liaño could only stand and watch as the ball soared past him into the net.

After that smash-and-grab victory, the advantage was clearly with the French Cup holders. Fernandez had a full squad to choose from for the return in the Parc des Princes, but defending the lead was clearly his priority as he left both Dely Valdes and Raí on the bench. This time Djorkaeff was on active service from the start. Deportivo, on the other hand, were without three key players - Djukic, Mauro Silva and Fran. They were to miss them badly.

With a place in the final so close, PSG might have been expected to show some nerves. But Deportivo made it easy for them. The Spaniards hardly ever broke into the PSG half. Apart from a header in the first half which Manjarín looped onto the top of the crossbar after a swift counter-attack, Deportivo were anonymous in attack. PSG did not take too many risks, but they created the better chances. The best of all fell in the first half to Pascal Nouma, but he shot badly wide of the target after being set up by a wonderful cross-field pass from Fournier.

The goal PSG required to complete their task arrived just before the hour when Djorkaeff fed Patrice Loko, who drilled a low right-foot shot into the corner past Liaño. After that the Spaniards appeared to give up and did not make any further impression. It was a poor game, but the big crowd in the Parc des Princes were not too concerned. They were just delighted that their team had ended their jinx and were finally through to a first European final.

Like Everton a couple of rounds earlier, Rapid Vienna returned to Rotterdam, where they had made their only previous European final appearance, 11 years earlier. Now the Austrians' task was to continue the form they had shown all season both in Europe and in domestic competition and reach the Cup-winners' Cup final again. Feyenoord had not reached a European final for twice as long as Rapid. Their supporters had to stretch their memories back to 1974 when Feyenoord beat Tottenham Hotspur over two legs to win the UEFA Cup.

The first leg was just as cagey as the other semi-final in La Coruña, with both teams marking tightly in defence and few chances being created. The 1-1 result was a fair reflection of the play, with on-loan German striker Carsten Jancker tipping the tie in Rapid's favour after equalising a Ronald Koeman penalty midway through the second half.

Encouraged by their team's display in Rotterdam, the Viennese came out in force for the return leg, filling the Ernst Happel stadium to its capacity on a warm April evening. For security reasons no tickets were sold to Feyenoord fans, so the Dutch side were really up against it from the start - even more so when, after just two minutes, they fell behind. Jancker, who injured his head in the opening seconds, was in the right place to prod the ball home after Marasek flicked on Heraf's corner-kick.

Backed by fervent support, Rapid continued to go at Feyenoord like a whirlwind. After 32 minutes they grabbed a second goal, Christian Stumpf taking full advantage of a slip by Feyenoord defender Boateng to lob Jancker's knock-on over the advancing De Goey. Three minutes later goal number three arrived, and what a goal it was! Marasek initiated a fast breakout from his own half. He fed Heraf, who in turn swung over a magnificent cross which Jancker hooked in spectacularly on the volley for his sixth goal of the competition. The crowd, understandably, went wild with delight.

By half-time the contest was effectively over. Feyenoord had been blitzed. The Dutch brought on an extra striker, Mike Obiku, at half-time to try to turn the tide. But although they dominated the second half in terms of possession, they created very little, and Rapid 'keeper Michael Konsel was only twice called into serious action, first from Ronald Koeman's subtle first-time chip, then, late in the game, from a low shot by Obiku. Rapid did not need to develop further attacks. They had done all that was necessary in the first half. Their place in Brussels was safe. For coach Ernst Dokupil and his players, it was a night they would never forget.

SEMI-FINAL RESULTS

FEYENOORD 1 Koeman (53p) **SK RAPID WIEN 1** Jancker (67)
SK RAPID WIEN 3 Jancker (2, 35), Stumpf (32) **FEYENOORD 0**
(SK RAPID WIEN 4-1)

RC DEPORTIVO 0 PARIS SAINT-GERMAIN FC 1 Djorkaeff (90)
PARIS SAINT-GERMAIN 1 Loko (59) **RC DEPORTIVO 0**
(PARIS SAINT-GERMAIN FC 2-0)

TOP SCORERS

6	Carsten JANCKER (SK Rapid Wien)
	BEBETO (RC Deportivo)
4	Youri DJORKAEFF (Paris Saint-Germain FC)
	Patrice LOKO (Paris Saint-Germain FC)
	Mike OBIKU (Feyenoord)
	Andreas THOM (Celtic)
	Regi BLINKER (Feyenoord)

CUP-WINNERS' CUP

FINAL

The first European final in Brussels since the Heysel disaster in 1985 welcomed two teams, Paris Saint-Germain and Rapid Vienna, who had never previously won a European trophy. The new King Baudouin stadium, built on the same site as the former Heysel, was not full, but 36,000 spectators, more than half of them having made the short trip from Paris, ensured a vibrant and good-humoured atmosphere.

Both teams were able to field full-strength sides, although Paris Saint-Germain suffered a major blow after just 12 minutes when Brazilian midfielder Raí was fouled by Rapid defender Peter Schöttel and had to make way for Panamanian striker Julio César Dely Valdes.

As in most one-off European finals, there was a very slow, ponderous start to the action, with both teams struggling to find their rhythm amidst a flurry of fouls and misplaced passes. PSG playmaker Youri Djorkaeff offered the first notable piece of excitement when he hooked in a shot from a tight angle, forcing Rapid goalkeeper Michael Konsel, a survivor from Rapid's last Cup-winners' Cup final appearance 11 years earlier, to tip the ball behind for a corner.

Djorkaeff was instrumental in most things PSG did. On 29 minutes he touched a free-kick to his right, and PSG defender Bruno Ngotty let fly from 30 yards out. His low right-foot shot was struck well, but it was a deflection off Schöttel's knee which enabled the ball to elude the diving hands of Konsel and give PSG the lead.

The match needed a goal, and Ngotty had provided it, to the rapturous approval of the red-and-blue clad hordes in the stands. A goal to the good, PSG upped the tempo and dominated the remainder of the half. Dely Valdes and Bravo both wasted half-chances before Djorkaeff worked a clear opening for Loko, but his cross failed to find Dely Valdes and the opportunity was squandered.

Rapid were barely recognisable from the team that had destroyed Feyenoord in the semi-final. They were incapable of sustaining any attacking momentum, and it was not until the 64th minute that they created anything worthwhile up front - a far-post effort from Heraf which was blocked for the Austrians' first corner. The better chances continued to come Paris Saint-Germain's way, with Djorkaeff creating endless problems for the Rapid defence. On one occasion he slipped past the sweeper Ivanov and shot against the outside of the post. Then he set up Dely Valdes, whose miserable evening in front of goal continued as he mis-controlled and fell over just at the crucial moment.

As the match wore on, it seemed inevitable that PSG would seal their victory with a second goal. But they just could not kill Rapid off. Twice in a minute late on Vincent Guérin broke clear on the left, but his composure failed him on both occasions and Rapid were let off the hook again.

The misses nearly became so costly when, on the stroke of 90 minutes, Rapid created their best chance of the game. But, fortunately for the French, goalkeeper Bernard Lama was alert enough to tip Ivanov's header over for a corner. It was a moment of great danger for PSG, but they survived it, and deservedly so. They had dominated the match completely and were worth at least another couple of goals against the modest Austrians.

The final whistle was greeted with intense relief and jubilation by the PSG players and coaching staff. Luis Fernandez, who had announced his imminent departure from the club just a few days earlier, became the first French coach in 40 years to lift a European trophy - at the age of only 36. And Paris Saint-Germain followed Marseille into the record books as only the second French club ever to win a European Cup. Marseille's Champions' Cup victory over Milan in 1993 had been achieved with a single goal from a defender of African origin - Basile Boli. Now another, Bruno Ngotty, was the unlikely hero of the hour as Paris and the whole of France celebrated a deserved and historic Cup-winners' Cup triumph.

Party time for PSG

FINAL

08/05/96, Brussels

PARIS SAINT-GERMAIN FC 1 Ngotty (29)

SK RAPID WIEN 0

referee - Pairetto (ITA)

PARIS SAINT-GERMAIN FC - Lama; Le Guen, Colleter, Ngotty, Roche, Djorkaeff, Bravo, Guérin, Fournier (Llacer 76), Raí (Dely Valdes 11), Loko.

SK RAPID WIEN - Konsel; Hatz, Guggi, Ivanov, Schöttel, Stöger, Stumpf (Barisic 46), Marasek, Jancker, Kühbauer, Heraf.

UEFA CUP

PRELIMINARY ROUND

The UEFA Cup preliminary round, packed full of national champions not considered good enough to have a crack at the Champions' League, also contained, for the first time, the four qualifiers from UEFA's new brainchild, the InterToto Cup. With these summer survivors added to the other 64 teams involved, there were more ties in the preliminary round than in the first round proper.

No seeding structure was applied at this stage of the competition, which gave it a mismatched look, with top ties such as Sparta Prague v Galatasaray and Red Star Belgrade v Neuchâtel Xamax running in tandem with much less glamorous offerings like Afan Lido v RAF Yelgava and FH v Glenavon.

Czech champions Sparta Prague, unfortunate to be denied a place in the Champions' League preliminary round due to an anomaly in UEFA's co-efficient structure, did extremely well to get past a Galatasaray side which had beaten Barcelona in the Champions' League the previous season. Czech international Pavel Nedved guided Sparta through, scoring three goals in the tie - an individual total matched, in other ties, by Stefan Rusnak (Slovan Bratislava), Tomislav Erceg (Lugano) and Mons Ivar Mjelde (FK Austria).

Sparta's city rivals Slavia also drew the short straw when they were paired with Austrian side Sturm Graz. But a late penalty converted by Radek Bejbl in the first leg, away from home, was the key to Slavia's 2-1 aggregate victory.

The three Bulgarian teams were not favoured, either. Slavia Sofia were knocked out by Olympiakos of Greece, while Levski Sofia and Botev Plovdiv did well to survive equally tricky ties against the Dinamos of Tbilisi and Bucharest, respectively. Levski avoided a second successive UEFA Cup preliminary-round elimination with an extra-time winner in the home leg.

Like Dinamo Tbilisi, another former European trophy winner, Red Star Belgrade, went out after failing to score in both matches. This was Red Star's big return to the European scene after an enforced three-year absence. But although 19,000 fans turned up for the first leg at home to Neuchâtel Xamax, they were hugely disappointed when Red Star conceded a late goal and lost the match. The Yugoslav champions were unable to recover the deficit in Switzerland and departed the competition knowing that they faced a long road to recovery from the three wasted years they had spent on the outside looking in.

PRELIMINARY ROUND RESULTS

ÖREBRO SK 0 AVENIR BEGGEN 0
AVENIR BEGGEN 1 Holtz (21) **ÖREBRO SK 1** Birgisson (88)
(later awarded as 3-0)
(AVENIR BEGGEN 3-0)

TPV 0 VIKING FK 4
Gawara (48og), Østenstad (58), Medalen (73), Sørloth (87)
VIKING FK 3 Bergersen (4, 41), Sørloth (64) **TPV 1** Wiss (88)
(VIKING FK 7-1)

BANGOR CITY 0 WIDZEW LODZ 4 Czerwiec (25, 42), Koniarek (51, 90)
WIDZEW LODZ 1 Pikuta (83) **BANGOR CITY 0**
(WIDZEW LODZ 5-0)

SHELBOURNE 0
ÍA 3 Gunnlaugsson B. (19), Gunnlaugsson A. (83), Reynisson (84)
ÍA 3 Jónsson S. (45), Thórdarson Ó. (59), Pétursson (90) **SHELBOURNE 0**
(ÍA 6-0)

GLENAVON 0 FH 0
FH 0 GLENAVON 1 Johnston (65)
(GLENAVON 1-0)

BRØNDBY IF 3 Hansen (13), Bjur (45), Sand (82)
INKARAS-GRIFAS KAUNAS 0
INKARAS-GRIFAS KAUNAS 0
BRØNDBY IF 3 Møller (53, 65), Risager (62)
(BRØNDBY IF 6-0)

LILLESTRØM SK 4 Ingelstad (43), Ingebrigtsen (60), Gulbrandsen (68, 87)
FC FLORA TALLINN 0
FC FLORA TALLINN 1 Korgalidze (54) **LILLESTRØM SK 0**
(LILLESTRØM SK 4-1)

MOTHERWELL 1 McSkimming (9)
MYPA 3 Grönholm (13), Tiainen (31), Mahlio (55)
MYPA 0 MOTHERWELL 2 Burns (28), Arnott (69)
(3-3; MYPA on away goals)

SKONTO RIGA 1 Babichev (11) **MARIBOR BRANIK 0**
MARIBOR BRANIK 2 Sterbal (17), Fricelj (20) **SKONTO RIGA 0**
(MARIBOR BRANIK 2-1)

SK STURM GRAZ 0 SLAVIA PRAHA 1 Bejbl (83p)
SLAVIA PRAHA 1 Hysky (45) **SK STURM GRAZ 1** Haas (55)
(SLAVIA PRAHA 2-1)

JEUNESSE ESCH 0 FC LUGANO 0
FC LUGANO 4 Erceg (18, 46, 54), Esposito (35) **JEUNESSE ESCH 0**
(FC LUGANO 4-0)

UEFA CUP

PRELIMINARY ROUND RESULTS (CONTINUED)

SLOVAN BRATISLAVA 4 Tittel (8), Rusnak (15, 41), Faktor (90) **OSIJEK 0**
OSIJEK 0 SLOVAN BRATISLAVA 2 Rusnak (55), Gomes (86)
(SLOVAN BRATISLAVA 6-0)

DUNDALK 0 MALMÖ FF 2 Pettersson (1), Andersson A. (11)
MALMÖ FF 2 Andersson A. (22), Fjellström (50) **DUNDALK 0**
(MALMÖ FF 4-0)

CRUSADERS 1 Hunter G. (67)
SILKEBORG IF 2 Fernandez (15), Larsen (47p)
SILKEBORG IF 4 Larsen (10), Fernandez (61), Sommer (68, 84)
CRUSADERS 0
(SILKEBORG IF 6-1)

AFAN LIDO 1 Moore (30)
RAF YELGAVA 2 Karashauskas (20), Bogdan (68)
RAF YELGAVA 0 AFAN LIDO 0
(RAF YELGAVA 2-1)

RAITH ROVERS 4 Dair (40), Rougier (47), McAnespie (78), Cameron (80)
GÍ 0
GÍ 2 Jarnskor H. (77), Jarnskor M. (87)
RAITH ROVERS 2 Lennon (30), Crawford (81)
(RAITH ROVERS 6-2)

SLAVIA SOFIA 0 OLYMPIAKOS 2 Ivic (80), Juskowiak (90)
OLYMPIAKOS 1 Ivic (10) **SLAVIA SOFIA 0**
(OLYMPIAKOS 3-0)

ZIMBRU CHISINAU 2 Gavriliuc (27), Rebeja (71) **HAPOEL TEL-AVIV 0**
HAPOEL TEL-AVIV 0 ZIMBRU CHISINAU 0
(ZIMBRU CHISINAU 2-0)

SPARTA PRAHA 3 Nedved (18, 73), Lokvenc (23)
GALATASARAY 1 Saunders (57)
GALATASARAY 1 Saunders (3) **SPARTA PRAHA 1** Nedved (23)
(SPARTA PRAHA 4-2)

OMONIA NICOSIA 3 Stefan (40p, 52), Malekkos (75)
SLIEMA WANDERERS 0
SLIEMA WANDERERS 1 Suda (43)
OMONIA NICOSIA 2 Stefan (70), Xiourouppas (86)
(OMONIA NICOSIA 5-1)

1.FC KOSICE 0 ÚJPESTI TE 1 Tiefenbach (40)
ÚJPESTI TE 2 Bérczy (56), Szanyó (81p) **1.FC KOSICE 1** Weiss (85)
(ÚJPESTI TE 3-1)

UNIVERSITATEA CRAIOVA 0 DINAMO MINSK 0
DINAMO MINSK 0 UNIVERSITATEA CRAIOVA 0 (aet)
(0-0; DINAMO MINSK 3-1 on pens.)

FENERBAHÇE 2 Bolic (71), Bülent (87) **PARTIZANI TIRANË 0**
PARTIZANI TIRANË 0
FENERBAHÇE 4 Bülent (15), Kemalettin (23), Bolic (59), Aygün (86)
(FENERBAHÇE 6-0)

VARDAR SKOPJE 1 Nikolovski (9) **SAMTREDIA 0**
SAMTREIA 0 VARDAR SKOPJE 2 Serafimovski (19), Petreski (39)
(VARDAR SKOPJE 3-0)

BOTEV PLOVDIV 1 Gerov (45) **DINAMO TBILISI 0**
DINAMO TBILISI 0 BOTEV PLOVDIV 1 Vidolov (90)
(BOTEV PLOVDIV 2-0)

APOLLON 1 Kola (42) **SCT OLIMPIJA LJUBLJANA 0**
SCT OLIMPIJA LJUBLJANA 3 Bozgo (11, 66), Zulic (81)
APOLLON 1 Kola (2)
(SCT OLIMPIJA LJUBLJANA 3-2)

CRVENA ZVEZDA BEOGRAD 0 NEUCHATEL XAMAX FC 1 Wittl (86)
NEUCHATEL XAMAX 0 CRVENA ZVEZDA BEOGRAD 0
(NEUCHATEL XAMAX FC 1-0)

HIBERNIANS 2 Lawrence (28), Sultana (87) **CHORNOMORETS ODESA 5**
Guseinov (14), Gashkin (22), Musolitin (39, 53), Kardash (48)
CHORNOMORETS ODESA 2 Kozakevych (34), Masolitin (76)
HIBERNIANS 0
(CHORNOMORETS ODESA 7-2)

KEPEZ 0
FK AUSTRIA WIEN 4 Mjelde (30), Belajic (38), Flögel (49), Pacult (86)
FK AUSTRIA WIEN 5 Mjelde (10, 29), Ogris (18, 42), Glatzer (64)
KEPEZ 1 Suleymanov (26)
(FK AUSTRIA WIEN 9-1)

TIRANA 0 HAPOEL BEER SHEVA 1 Zeiberlinsh (1)
HAPOEL BEER SHEVA 2 Gusev (19), Avigdor (22) **TIRANA 0**
(HAPOEL BEER SHEVA 3-0)

DINAMO BUCURESTI 0 LEVSKI SOFIA 1 Ivanov (30)
LEVSKI SOFIA 1 Vasilev (110) **DINAMO BUCURESTI 1** Lupu (70) (aet)
(LEVSKI SOFIA 2-1)

ZAGLEBIE LUBIN 0 SHIRAK GYUMRI 0
SHIRAK GYUMRI 0 ZAGLEBIE LUBIN 1 Machaj (23)
(ZAGLEBIE LUBIN 1-0)

InterToto semi-finals

KARLSRUHER SC 0
GIRONDINS DE BORDEAUX 2 Dugarry (40), Dutuel (87)
GIRONDINS DE BORDEAUX 2 Lizarazu (2p, 11)
KARLSRUHER SC 2 Fink (40), Schmitt (88)
(GIRONDINS DE BORDEAUX 4-2)

FC TIROL INNSBRUCK 1 Schiener (63) **RC STRASBOURG 1** Sauzée (26)
RC STRASBOURG 6 Sauzée (16, 54), Mostovoi (65), Keller (67, 70, 89)
FC TIROL INNSBRUCK 1 Kirchler (51)
(RC STRASBOURG 7-2)

UEFA CUP

FIRST ROUND

France entered the first round with a record entry of six teams. Joining the four seeded sides were Bordeaux and Strasbourg, who claimed the two InterToto berths. Next in the seeding hierarchy were Italy, Germany and England, all with four teams, followed by Spain, Portugal, Russia and Belgium (three each) and Holland (two).

The first-round line-up was as strong as any previously seen in the UEFA Cup. There were no fewer than nine European Champions' Cup winners included. Milan, Bayern Munich, Manchester United, Benfica and Nottingham Forest were all aiming to win the UEFA Cup for the first time. Liverpool, Barcelona, Inter and PSV were all out to regain it.

Of the six-strong French contingent - none of them former European trophy-winners - only Monaco, the 1992 European Cup-winners' Cup runners-up, went out. French teams have never performed well against English opposition, and Jean Tigana's team were stunned into a 0-3 home defeat by Leeds United in their home leg. Ghanaian striker Tony Yeboah grabbed a brilliant hat-trick for the Yorkshire club, but there was grave concern over the welfare of two Monaco players, defender Basile Boli and Marc Delaroche, who collided horrifically as Yeboah went through for his third goal and were both knocked unconscious. Fortunately, after a few hours in hospital, they were back to full health, suffering only from concussion.

Leeds lost the return match at Elland Road but survived. Manchester United were not so lucky. They believed they had done the hard part by drawing 0-0 away to Rotor Vologograd in the first leg, but at Old Trafford they conceded two first-half goals to the Russians, and only

FIRST ROUND RESULTS

OLYMPIAKOS 2 Juskowiak (32), Skartados (68p) **MARIBOR BRANIK 0**
MARIBOR BRANIK 1 Karic (70)
OLYMPIAKOS 3 Ivic (38), Skartados (64), Hantzidis (82)
(OLYMPIAKOS 5-1)

HAPOEL BEER SHEVA 0
FC BARCELONA 7 De la Peña (5), Roger (45, 68, 78), Oscar (63), Figo (66, 82)
FC BARCELONA 5 Guardiola (12), Hagi (27), Toni (52), Carreras (62), Amor (66)
HAPOEL BEER SHEVA 0
(FC BARCELONA 12-0)

LAZIO 5 Casiraghi (11, 16, 88), Rambaudi (52), Signori (55p)
OMONIA NICOSIA 0
OMONIA NICOSIA 1 Xiourouppas (68) **LAZIO 2** Casiraghi (15), Di Vaio (75)
(LAZIO 7-1)

RC STRASBOURG 3 Zitelli (7), Leboeuf (72p), Baticle (74) **ÚJPESTI TE 0**
ÚJPESTI TE 0 RC STRASBOURG 2 Mostovoi (9), Zitelli (77)
(RC STRASBOURG 5-0)

MILAN 4 Savicevic (11), Machaj (47og), Weah (67), Boban (71)
ZAGLEBIE LUBIN 0
ZAGLEBIE LUBIN 1 Krzyzanowski (72)
MILAN 4 Eranio (53), Simone (63), Boban (86, 90)
(MILAN 8-1)

VARDAR SKOPJE 0 GIRONDINS DE BORDEAUX 2 Bancarel (25, 75)
GIRONDINS DE BORDEAUX 1 Lizarazu (61p)
VARDAR SKOPJE 1 Serafimovski (58)
(GIRONDINS DE BORDEAUX 3-1)

VITÓRIA GUIMARÃES 3 Gilmar (22, 89), Edinho (69)
R STANDARD LIEGE 1 Schepens (32)
R STANDARD LIEGE 0 VITÓRIA GUIMARÃES 0
(VITÓRIA GUIMARÃES 3-1)

FENERBAHÇE 1 Aykut (73) **REAL BETIS 2** Pier (27), Sabas (80)
REAL BETIS 2 Alexis (21p), Cañas (38) **FENERBAHÇE 0**
(REAL BETIS 4-1)

ROTOR VOLGOGRAD 0 MANCHESTER UNITED 0
MANCHESTER UNITED 2 Scholes (59), Schmeichel (89)
ROTOR VOLGOGRAD 2 Nidergaus (18), Veretennikov (25)
(2-2; ROTOR VOLGOGRAD on away goals)

MYPA 1 Mahlio (29) **PSV 1** Ronaldo (50)
PSV 7 Ronaldo (14, 45, 73, 83), Jonk (57, 71), Hoekstra (65)
MYPA 1 Keskitalo (15)
(PSV 8-2)

RC LENS 6 Camara (11, 49), Meyrieu (33), Tiéhi (62, 74), Boli (70)
AVENIR BEGGEN 0
AVENIR BEGGEN 0 RC LENS 7 Camara (20), Meyrieu (25), Boli (40), Delmotte (55, 73), Tiéhi (57, 72)
(RC LENS 13-0)

SPARTA PRAHA 0 SILKEBORG IF 1 Fernandez (6)
SILKEBORG IF 1 Petersen (51)
SPARTA PRAHA 2 Lokvenc (21), Nemec (51)
(2-2; SPARTA PRAHA on away goals)

K LIERSE SK 1 Huysmans (39p)
SL BENFICA 3 Valdo (25p), Marcelo (51), Paulo Bento (62)
SL BENFICA 2 João Pinto (25), Kenedy (60)
K LIERSE SK 1 Van Kerckhoven (35)
(SL BENFICA 5-2)

NEUCHATEL XAMAX FC 1 Jeanneret (14) **ROMA 1** Moriero (19)
ROMA 4 Balbo (25, 35), Fonseca (32), Rueda (58og)
NEUCHATEL XAMAX FC 0
(ROMA 5-1)

UEFA CUP

salvaged their unbeaten home record in Europe thanks to goalkeeper Peter Schmeichel, who joined the attack and scored United's late equaliser with his head. Heroic though the Dane's enterprise was, it could not save United from an away-goals elimination. Liverpool also drew at home to Russian opposition, but they came through on the strength of an excellent 2-1 away win against Russian champions-elect Spartak Vladikavkaz. The only English team to win at home was Nottingham Forest. Dutchman Bryan Roy smashed in a ferocious left-foot shot to put Forest through on away goals against Malmö of Sweden, 2-1 winners in the first leg.

Like England, Italy had to bid farewell to one of their quartet. Milan, Lazio and Roma all came through their ties convincingly, but Inter crashed out to modest Swiss side Lugano. After a 1-1 draw in Switzerland and a poor start in the Italian league, Inter coach Ottavio Bianchi was sacked. His temporary replacement, Luis Suárez, had only been in charge of team affairs for 24 hours when the second leg came around in the San Siro. It was to be a nightmare début for the Spaniard as Inter succumbed to a late free-kick goal from José Carrasco, the son of a Chilean political refugee, who had also scored in the first leg.

FIRST ROUND RESULTS (CONTINUED)

SEVILLA FC 2 Suker (29, 34) **BOTEV PLOVDIV 0**
BOTEV PLOVDIV 1 Ivanov (69) **SEVILLA FC 1** Monchu (57)
(SEVILLA FC 3-1)

RODA JC 5
Van Galen (2), Roelofsen (23), Babangida (34), Graef (44), De Kock (88p)
SCT OLIMPIJA LJUBLJANA 0
SCT OLIMPIJA LJUBLJANA 2 Bozgo (38), Zulic (78) **RODA JC 0**
(RODA JC 5-2)

FC BAYERN MÜNCHEN 0 LOKOMOTIV MOSKVA 1 Kharlachov (71)
LOKOMOTIV MOSKVA 0 FC BAYERN MÜNCHEN 5 Klinsmann (26, 34), Herzog (39), Scholl (45), Strunz (78)
(FC BAYERN MÜNCHEN 5-1)

FK AUSTRIA WIEN 1 Kogler (84)
DINAMO MINSK 2 Zhuravel (26), Shukanov (40)
DINAMO MINSK 1 Belkevich (90) **FK AUSTRIA WIEN 0**
(DINAMO MINSK 3-1)

MALMÖ FF 2 Persson J. (59), Andersson A. (72)
NOTTINGHAM FOREST 1 Woan (38)
NOTTINGHAM FOREST 1 Roy (69) **MALMÖ FF 0**
(2-2; NOTTINGHAM FOREST on away goal)

CHORNOMORETS ODESA 1 Kozakevych (84) **WIDZEW LODZ 0**
WIDZEW LODZ 1 Mikhalchuk (81) **CHORNOMORETS ODESA 0** (aet)
(1-1; CHORNOMORETS ODESA 6-5 on pens.)

AS MONACO 0 LEEDS UNITED 3 Yeboah (2, 65, 81)
LEEDS UNITED 0 AS MONACO 1 Anderson (22)
(LEEDS UNITED 3-1)

BRØNDBY IF 3 Hansen (38), Eggen (57), Bjur (88p) **LILLESTRØM SK 0**
LILLESTRØM SK 0 BRØNDBY IF 0
(BRØNDBY IF 3-0)

RAITH ROVERS 3 Lennon (14, 66), Wilson (79) **ÍA 1** Thórdarson Ó. (45)
ÍA 1 Gunnlaugsson A. (52) **RAITH ROVERS 0**
(RAITH ROVERS 3-2)

SC FREIBURG 1 Todt (78) **SLAVIA PRAHA 2** Novotny (22), Penicka (75)
SLAVIA PRAHA 0 SC FREIBURG 0
(SLAVIA PRAHA 2-1)

SLOVAN BRATISLAVA 2 Tittel (28), Sobona (74)
1.FC KAISERSLAUTERN 1 Hollerbach (64)
1.FC KAISERSLAUTERN 3 Wegmann (27, 56), Wollitz (38) **SLOVAN BRATISLAVA 0**
(1.FC KAISERSLAUTERN 4-2)

FC LUGANO 1 Carrasco (67) **INTER 1** Roberto Carlos (13)
INTER 0 FC LUGANO 1 Carrasco (86)
(FC LUGANO 2-1)

SC FARENSE 0 OLYMPIQUE LYONNAIS 1 Giuly (5)
OLYMPIQUE LYONNAIS 1 Sassus (47) **SC FARENSE 0**
(OLYMPIQUE LYONNAIS 2-0)

LEVSKI SOFIA 1 Vasilev (68)
KSC EENDRACHT AALST 2 Markov (57og), Paas (78)
KSC EENDRACHT AALST 1 Lamberg (57) **LEVSKI SOFIA 0**
(KSC EENDRACHT AALST 3-1)

GLENAVON 0 SV WERDER BREMEN 2 Cardoso (60), Vier (80)
SV WERDER BREMEN 5 Hobsch (26, 36, 39), Basler (37p), Borowka (66)
GLENAVON 0
(SV WERDER BREMEN 7-0)

VIKING FK 1 Ulfstein (55) **AJ AUXERRE 1** West (14)
AJ AUXERRE 1 Silvestre (47) **VIKING FK 0**
(AJ AUXERRE 2-1)

SPARTAK VLADIKAVKAZ 1 Kasymov (21)
LIVERPOOL 2 McManaman (33), Redknapp (52)
LIVERPOOL 0 SPARTAK VLADIKAVKAZ 0
(LIVERPOOL 2-1)

ZIMBRU CHISINAU 1 Testimitanu (40) **RAF YELGAVA 0**
RAF YELGAVA 1 Zuyev (77) **ZIMBRU CHISINAU 2** Gavriliuc (5, 25)
(ZIMBRU CHISINAU 3-1)

UEFA CUP

Germany, too, failed to take their full four-team complement through, losing European débutants Freiburg, beaten by Slavia Prague, who, like their fellow Czechs Sparta Prague, came through with an impressive 2-1 victory away from home. Bayern Munich were another side in apparent danger of going out after losing their home leg 0-1 to Lokomotiv Moscow, but in the Russian capital the Bundesliga leaders stormed back to win 5-0.

Spain were the only nation with three representatives or more to survive the first round intact. Barcelona, one of the tournament favourites, destroyed Israeli side Hapoel Beer Sheva 12-0 on aggregate, with youngster Roger García scoring a hat-trick on his first European appearance in the 7-0 first-leg win in Israel. Barcelona's was not the biggest aggregate victory of the round, however. That honour went to French side Lens, who blitzed Luxembourg's Avenir Beggen 13-0, with Ivory Coast striker Joël Tiéhi scoring four goals, one fewer than the leading scorer of the round, Brazilian teenager Ronaldo, who netted five of PSV's eight goals against Finnish side MyPa.

SECOND ROUND

Getting through the second round proved to be routine business for most of the fancied teams. Barcelona, Milan, Roma, Bayern Munich and PSV were all untroubled as they eased themselves through to the last 16.

SECOND ROUND RESULTS

AJ AUXERRE 0 NOTTINGHAM FOREST 1 Stone (23)
NOTTINGHAM FOREST 0 AJ AUXERRE 0
(NOTTINGHAM FOREST 1-0)

FC BARCELONA 3 Kodro (45, 67), Celades (76) **VITÓRIA GUIMARÃES 0**
VITÓRIA GUIMARÃES 0
FC BARCELONA 4 Kodro (19), Oscar (62), Celades (67), Sergi (77)
(FC BARCELONA 7-0)

ROMA 4 Vanderhaeghe (6og), Van der Hoorn (51og), Balbo (70), Totti (77)
KSC EENDRACHT AALST 0
KSC EENDRACHT AALST 0 ROMA 0
(ROMA 4-0)

FC LUGANO 1 Shalimov (84) **SLAVIA PRAHA 2** Vagner (20), Penicka (26)
SLAVIA PRAHA 1 Smicer (62) **FC LUGANO 0**
(SLAVIA PRAHA 3-1)

CHORNOMORETS ODESA 0 RC LENS 0
RC LENS 4 Meyrieu (14), Vairelles (20), Dehu (26), Foé (77)
CHORNOMORETS ODESA 0
(RC LENS 4-0)

BRØNDBY IF 0 LIVERPOOL 0
LIVERPOOL 0 BRØNDBY IF 1 Eggen (78)
(BRØNDBY IF 1-0)

SV WERDER BREMEN 5
Shtanyuk (53og), Basler (63, 83), Hobsch (72), Bode (88)
DINAMO MINSK 0
DINAMO MINSK 2 Khatskevich (76p), Shukanov (90)
SV WERDER BREMEN 1 Bode (25)
(SV WERDER BREMEN 6-2)

RC STRASBOURG 0 MILAN 1 Simone (80)
MILAN 2 Baggio (29, 44p) **RC STRASBOURG 1** Sauzée (45)
(MILAN 3-1)

SL BENFICA 1 Panduru (79) **RODA JC 0**
RODA JC 2 Hesp D. (61), Trost (74) **SL BENFICA 2** Hassan (86, 90)
(SL BENFICA 3-2)

SPARTA PRAHA 4 Frydek (23), Nedved (44p, 56), Budka (57)
ZIMBRU CHISINAU 3 Suharev (56), Testimitanu (62, 90p)
ZIMBRU CHISINAU 0 SPARTA PRAHA 2 Koller (45), Vonasek (64)
(SPARTA PRAHA 6-3)

GIRONDINS DE BORDEAUX 2 Histilloles (47), Witschge (90p)
ROTOR VOLGOGRAD 1 Nidergaus (40)
ROTOR VOLGOGRAD 0 GIRONDINS DE BORDEAUX 1 Bancarel (83)
(GIRONDINS DE BORDEAUX 3-1)

1.FC KAISERSLAUTERN 1 Koch (46)
REAL BETIS 3 Alfonso (45, 73), Alexis (54)
REAL BETIS 1 Jarni (55) **1.FC KAISERSLAUTERN 0**
(REAL BETIS 4-1)

LEEDS UNITED 3 Speed (6), Palmer (48), McAllister (72)
PSV 5 Eykelkamp (11), Vink (36), Jonk (39), Nilis (84, 89)
PSV 3 Cocu (12, 73), Pemberton (42og) **LEEDS UNITED 0**
(PSV 8-3)

SEVILLA FC 1 Juanito (90) **OLYMPIAKOS 0**
OLYMPIAKOS 2 Sapanis (72), Juskowiak (93p)
SEVILLA FC 1 Suker (110) (aet)
(2-2; SEVILLA FC on away goal)

OLYMPIQUE LYONNAIS 2 Devaux (15), Deplace (64)
LAZIO 1 Winter (23)
LAZIO 0 OLYMPIQUE LYONNAIS 2 Maurice (22), Assadourian (59)
(OLYMPIQUE LYONNAIS 4-1)

RAITH ROVERS 0 FC BAYERN MÜNCHEN 2 Klinsmann (6, 73)
FC BAYERN MÜNCHEN 2 Klinsmann (52), Babbel (64)
RAITH ROVERS 1 Herzog (42og)
(FC BAYERN MÜNCHEN 4-1)

UEFA CUP

Barcelona's shooting practice continued with a 7-0 aggregate dstruction of Vitória Guimarães, who had been impressive in knocking out Standard Liège in the opening round. After four games Barça had run up 20 goals and conceded none. Their principal marksman on this occasion was Bosnian centre-forward Meho Kodro, a new signing from Real Sociedad, who scored three goals. Milan also won both of their games against InterToto qualifiers Strasbourg. A wonderful George Weah-assisted goal by Marco Simone gave the Italians a 1-0 win in Strasbourg, and with those two players unavailable for the second leg, Roberto Baggio took centre stage with both goals in the 2-1 win in the San Siro. Roma did all their goal-scoring in the home leg, registering their second successive 4-0 home win of the competition to eliminate Belgium's last remaining representatives, Eendracht Aalst.

Bayern Munich and PSV both prevailed against British opposition. While there was nothing surprising about Bayern's 4-1 aggregate win over Scotland's European first-timers Raith Rovers (with three of the four goals going to Jürgen Klinsmann), PSV could not have expected such an easy ride against Leeds United. An extraordinary first leg at Elland Road ended 5-3 to the visitors from Holland, with Belgian striker Luc Nilis netting two late goals to swing the tie irretrievably in PSV's favour. A 0-3 defeat in Eindhoven completed Leeds' humiliation.

Even more of a blow to English pride was the shock elimination of Liverpool, beaten 1-0 by Brøndby in the one-time European stronghold of Anfield. Like Manchester United in the previous round, Roy Evans' team made the fatal error of believing that a 0-0 draw in the away leg would be sufficient to see them through. At Anfield the Liverpool attack was frustrated by a Brøndby defence that achieved its sixth straight clean sheet of the competition. The Danes' dramatic winner came from their Norwegian libero Dan Eggen, who punished some slack Liverpool defending by heading in direct from a corner 12 minutes from time.

Another major surprise was the elimination of Lazio by French mid-table side Lyon. The Roman side were lucky to lose the first leg in France by only a 2-1 margin, but in the return leg they were unable to repair the damage. Just two days after demolishing Italian champions Juventus 4-0 in Serie A, Lazio went down 0-2 to Lyon in the same Stadio Olimpico. Giuseppe Signori's missed penalty when the score was 0-1 finished off their challenge.

Portuguese giants Benfica came within four minutes of going out to Roda JC of Holland. The Lisbon Eagles won the home leg 1-0, but when Roda took a 2-0 lead midway through the second half of the second leg, they looked doomed. But luck was on their side. New Moroccan striker Hassan Nader, the Portuguese league's top scorer the previous season, scored two late goals, but both were tainted with controversy. The first appeared to be scored from an offside position, and the second was allowed to stand even though the free-kick which led up to it was taken before the referee had blown his whistle.

The giant-killers of the first round, Lugano and Rotor Volgograd, were brought back down to earth in the second. Their respective conquerors, Slavia Prague and Bordeaux, both came through with their third successive away wins of the competition. Sparta Prague made it a Czech double for the third round in a row, dismissing the most surprising second-round suvivors, Moldova's Zimbru Chisinau, 6-3 on aggregate.

Spain's triumvirate also progressed *en bloc.* Joining Barcelona in round three were the Seville pair of Sevilla and Real Betis. Sevilla required a wonderful Davor Suker free-kick in extra-time to dispose of a very unfortunate Olympiakos on the away-goals rule, while Betis were highly impressive winners against German side Kaiserslautern. Their 3-1 victory in the Betzenberg was the result of a tremendous tactical display, with Spanish international striker Alfonso Pérez scoring two of the goals.

Nottingham Forest became the sole British survivors in the two European knockout competitions when they edged past Auxerre with a single away goal scored by in-form midfielder Steve Stone. Forest were extremely fortunate to survive. Auxerre out-passed them and generally outplayed them for the full three hours' play, but thanks to some wasteful finishing by the French and some staunch defending from the English, Frank Clark's team made it into round three.

THIRD ROUND

Bayern Munich against Benfica was the pick of several intriguing third-round ties. The record champions of Germany and Portugal promised to provide an enthralling contest. It was a surprise that one team - and one player - should be so dominant.

The first leg in Munich was played in freezing temperatures, with most of the players electing to wear gloves. Bayern skipper Lothar Matthäus was back for only his second game after a ten-month injury lay-off. But it was the other world-class player in the red and blue stripes, Jürgen Klinsmann, who was to capture the headlines with a quite stunning individual performance. The German international striker sent three early chances wide of the target before he opened the scoring on 27 minutes by stabbing in Mehmet Scholl's perfect through-ball. Three minutes later Dimas equalised for Benfica with a fulminating shot into the roof of the Bayern net, but it was to be

UEFA CUP

THIRD ROUND RESULTS

FC BAYERN MÜNCHEN 4 Klinsmann (27, 32, 43, 46)
SL BENFICA 1 Dimas (30)
SL BENFICA 1 Valdo (14)
FC BAYERN MÜNCHEN 3 Klinsmann (32, 67), Herzog (84)
(FC BAYERN MÜNCHEN 7-2)

PSV 2 Ronaldo (9p), Nilis (83) **SV WERDER BREMEN 1** Bode (55)
SV WERDER BREMEN 0 PSV 0
(PSV 2-1)

NOTTINGHAM FOREST 1 McGregor (84)
OLYMPIQUE LYONNAIS 0
OLYMPIQUE LYONNAIS 0 NOTTINGHAM FOREST 0
(NOTTINGHAM FOREST 1-0)

BRØNDBY IF 2 Møller (47), Bjur (77) **ROMA 1** Fonseca (17)
ROMA 3 Totti (23), Balbo (72), Carboni (89)
BRØNDBY IF 1 Møller (85)
(ROMA 4-3)

MILAN 2 Weah (33, 77) **SPARTA PRAHA 0**
SPARTA PRAHA 0 MILAN 0
(MILAN 2-0)

GIRONDINS DE BORDEAUX 2 Dutuel (25), Croci (80)
REAL BETIS 0
REAL BETIS 2 Alexis (30), Stosic (45)
GIRONDINS DE BORDEAUX 1 Zidane (4)
(GIRONDINS DE BORDEAUX 3-2)

SEVILLA FC 1 Suker (45) **FC BARCELONA 1** Hagi (65)
FC BARCELONA 3 Bakero (61), Popescu (79), Roger (81)
SEVILLA FC 1 Moya (80)
(FC BARCELONA 4-2)

SLAVIA PRAHA 0 RC LENS 0
RC LENS 0 SLAVIA PRAHA 1 Poborsky (95) (aet)
(SLAVIA PRAHA 1-0)

Klinsmann's night. He headed in a second Bayern goal a couple of minutes later, then made it 3-1 with his hat-trick strike just before half-time. After Portuguese international João Pinto had wasted a simple chance for Bayern on the stroke of half-time, Klinsmann grabbed his fourth goal just a minute into the second period, heading in after some brilliant approach work from Scholl. From that moment on, Benfica were really struggling. The action faded in the last half-hour, but there was still time for Emil Kostadinov to strike the underside of the Benfica crossbar with two minutes remaining.

Bayern travelled to Lisbon full of confidence. They had won their previous two away matches and did not intend to allow Benfica to chip away their lead by playing all-out defensive football in the Stadium of Light. Valdo gave the home side something to cheer with a nicely worked goal in the 14th minute, but when Klinsmann grabbed his fifth goal of the tite - and tenth of the competition - in the 32nd minute, the tie was over. In the second half Klinsmann added yet another goal before Austrian midfielder Andreas Herzog finally proved that there was somebody else in the Bayern side capable of scoring when he crashed home a left-foot volley to complete a 3-1 victory and a magnificent 7-2 aggregate triumph.

While Bayern sounded out a warning to the other teams in the competition, the other remaining German side, Werder Bremen, were eliminated. The 2-1 aggregate defeat by PSV proved to be very costly for Werder coach Aad de Mos, who was sacked soon afterwards. But the Dutchman deserved better luck against his former club. PSV won the first leg 2-1 in Eindhoven, Luc Nilis scoring his 30th goal in European competition to settle the outcome late on. But Bremen dominated the second leg and were twice cruelly denied the one goal they needed by harsh refereeing decisions. The first moment of controversy came when a header from Dietmar Beiersdorfer appeared to be saved by Stanley Menzo just over the goal-line, but the referee refused to award the goal. Then, with just two minutes left, PSV defender Stan Valckx kicked Angelo Vier in the head in the penalty area, but, incredibly, the referee awarded a free-kick to PSV. Bremen still had a great chance to take the tie, but, with the goal at his mercy, Beiersdorfer blasted a half-volley straight at Menzo.

Milan put on a spectacular performance at home to Sparta Prague, with George Weah scoring two brilliant goals, the second - a ferocious volley on the turn - stamped with genuine master-class. They would have run up at least half a dozen goals had it not been for Petr Kouba, who produced one of the most brilliant goalkeeping displays of the European season to keep the score down to 2-0. That allowed Sparta a modicum of hope for the return, but on a snow-covered pitch in Prague the Italians defended their lead with typical discipline and professionalism. It was certainly very different from the one-sided first leg. Indeed, Sparta had more of the play. But they could not get the orange ball into the Milan net despite an encouraging wave of attacking play in the second half.

Roma ensured a two-pronged Italian challenge in the quarter-finals by defeating Liverpool's conquerors Brøndby. But they did not make things easy for themselves and eventually prevailed only on the strength of a last-minute goal in the Stadio Olimpico from Italian international full-back Amedeo Carboni. It was cruel luck on the Danes, who recovered from conceding their first goal of the

UEFA CUP

competition to win the home leg 2-1 and then levelled the scores late on in Rome with a second goal of the tie from striker Peter Møller. Five seasons earlier, in the semi-finals, Brøndby had also had their UEFA Cup hopes shattered by a late Roma strike.

The winning goal came even later in the Lens-Slavia Prague tie. After three hours of goalless but not uneventful football, the two teams went into extra-time in the Félix Bollaert stadium. A moment of inspiration was required to break the deadlock, and it was provided five minutes into the extra period by Czech international Karel Poborsky. Breaking through the Lens offside trap, the diminutive winger tore through the middle, waltzed round the goalkeeper and just gave himself time to select his target before shooting accurately into the net. It gave Slavia their fourth away victory on the trot.

Another French side to fall were Lyon. Like Auxerre before them, they could not penetrate Nottingham Forest's well-organised defence and fell to a solitary goal, scored late in the first leg in Nottingham by substitute Paul McGregor, who followed up after Stuart Pearce's penalty had been saved by Pascal Olmeta. Lyon piled continuous pressure on the Forest backline in the second half of the second leg in the Stade Gerland, but the sole remaining English team hung on for glory and a place in the last eight. Lyon's frustrations were summed up when their top striker Florian Maurice was sent off late in the game for elbowing Forest's outstanding performer on the night, centre-back Colin Cooper.

Bordeaux, the InterToto qualifiers, spared further French blushes by continuing their remarkable run with a 3-2 aggregate victory over Real Betis. A 2-0 home win gave the Girondins a sound platform for the second leg, but it was a glorious early goal in Spain which sealed the tie in their favour. French international midfielder Zinedine Zidane was the scorer, lobbing the Betis 'keeper from all of 40 yards '*à la* Nayim'. Betis were joined on the third-round scrapheap by their city neighbours Sevilla, who were soundly beaten 4-2 on aggregate in their all-Spanish tie with Barcelona. The Catalans were made to work for their victory, but after Gheorghe Hagi had equalised Suker's opener in the first leg, they were always in control of the tie.

QUARTER-FINALS

The pairing of Italian league leaders Milan with InterToto qualifiers and French league strugglers Bordeaux looked to be something of a mismatch for a UEFA Cup quarter-final. In fact, it proved to be a tie to remember, the French side causing one of the biggest upsets seen in the competition for years.

There was nothing in the first leg, in the San Siro, to suggest that Milan's progress to the semi-final would be at risk. Even without the suspended George Weah and injured midfield duo Demetrio Albertini and Zvonimir Boban, Milan's formidable strength in depth enabled Fabio Capello to field an impressive-looking team. Bordeaux's struggles in domestic football, where they had not won away all season, had prompted the dismissal of coach Slavo Muslin. In his place was the German, Gernot Rohr, appointed as caretaker coach until the end of the season.

Rohr's strategy in the San Siro was risk-free, all-out defence. Roberto Baggio threatened several times to find a way through in the first half before Stefano Eranio shot the home side in front with a powerful drive from Dejan Savicevic's touch-back. Savicevic was in his most exuberant form and was the object of incessant fouling. It was as a result of one of those fouls on the elusive Montenegrin that Milan scored their second goal, Baggio curling a classic free-kick into the top corner for his 26th goal in Europe. After going two-up Milan noticeably relaxed their grip, seemingly content in the knowledge that 2-0 would be a sufficient lead to take to Bordeaux.

But at the Parc Lescure, Milan were to crash to one of their worst defeats in years. Cheered on by a sell-out 32,500 crowd, Bordeaux played with extraordinary spirit and gusto. They took the lead on the night after just 15 minutes when full-back Bixente Lizarazu burst down the left and fired in a low cross which Didier Tholot, from two yards out, bundled inelegantly into the net. Milan searched

QUARTER-FINAL RESULTS

FC BARCELONA 2 Bakero (20), Abelardo (70) **PSV 2** Nilis (5, 50)
PSV 2 Zenden (44), Eykelkamp (65)
FC BARCELONA 3 Bakero (3), Figo (22), Sergi (78)
(FC BARCELONA 5-4)

SLAVIA PRAHA 2 Poborsky (10), Vagner (50) **ROMA 0**
ROMA 3 Moriero (60, 99), Giannini (82)
SLAVIA PRAHA 1 Vavra (112) (aet)
(3-3; SLAVIA PRAHA on away goal)

MILAN 2 Eranio (29), Baggio (74) **GIRONDINS DE BORDEAUX 0**
GIRONDINS DE BORDEAUX 3 Tholot (15), Dugarry (64, 70)
MILAN 0
(GIRONDINS DE BORDEAUX 3-2)

FC BAYERN MÜNCHEN 2 Klinsmann (16), Scholl (45)
NOTTINGHAM FOREST 1 Chettle (17)
NOTTINGHAM FOREST 1 Stone (84) **FC BAYERN MÜNCHEN 5**
Ziege (30), Strunz (45), Klinsmann (65, 80), Papin (74)
(FC BAYERN MÜNCHEN 7-2)

UEFA CUP

for the away goal that would kill the tie, but only the restored Weah, who injured his hand early on, seemed up for the fight. Roberto Baggio was anonymous and was substituted at half-time.

The second half produced a match-winning hero in French international striker Christophe Dugarry. In the 64th minute he brought Bordeaux level on aggregate, shooting powerfully into the corner after a free-kick from Zidane was kindly diverted into his path by the referee. Six minutes later Dugarry nearly ripped the Milan net off its hinges with a magnificent right-foot drive. It was a goal fit for the occasion, and it won Bordeaux the tie.

Nottingham Forest's Steve Chettle reels away after scoring against Bayern at the Olympic Stadium

Roma, the other Italian quarter-final survivors, were drawn away from home in their first leg, and they were also vanquished on foreign soil by a survivor from the preliminary round. Slavia Prague, going well in their domestic championship, adapted much better to the rock-hard pitch and falling snow. The Czechs took the lead after just ten minutes when Poborsky swung in a free-kick from the left. It was either a fantastic shot or a cross that went wrong, but, either way, it deceived the Roma goalkeeper Cervone and entered the net in the top corner.

Roma came close to equalising when Abel Balbo smashed a shot against the crossbar. But further attempts by the Italians to pilfer an away goal were foiled by ex-Czech international Jan Stejskal, a goalkeeper clearly at the top of his form. Not so Cervone, who was at fault for Slavia's second goal, early in the second half, as he failed to hold Lerch's cross and Varga tapped in the loose ball. Slavia might have extended their lead late in the game. Roma defender Petruzzi was rightly sent off ten minutes from time for a disgraceful 'professional foul' on goal-bound substitute Vavra. And with the very last kick of the game Hysky smashed a beautiful shot against the top of the Roma crossbar.

Back in Rome, where the snow had turned to rain, Slavia faced a real test of their character in front of 60,000 noisy Italians. For an hour there was little to choose between the two teams. It was only after Roma opened the scoring - an excellent first-time shot from Francesco Moriero - that the Italians began to raise their game. All of a sudden Stejskal's goal was under constant siege. Another goal seemed inevitable, and it arrived when an unmarked Giuseppe Giannini flicked in a header from Carboni's free-kick.

The match went into extra-time, and after just nine minutes Roma appeared to have won the tie when Moriero ran on to Totti's magnificent long pass, beat Novotny for pace and shot violently into the corner. The crowd were going crazy, especially as news filtered through of Milan's demise in Brodeaux. A place in the last four looked certain. But Slavia wouldn't give up. They launched one more attack, and substitute Jiri Vavra sent a deafening silence all round the Olimpico with a fabulous drive past Cervone. It was the all-important away goal. Slavia were through. Roma, like Milan, were out. Having provided both finalists the previous season, Italy now had no team in the semi-finals.

With the two Serie A sides eliminated, the way was clear for the other two big favourites - Barcelona and Bayern Munich. Barcelona struggled badly at home to PSV in the first leg. Luc Nilis continued his extraordinary goalscoring record in Europe by netting both of his team's goals in a 2-2 draw in the Nou Camp, with Bakero and Abelardo replying for the Catalans. In Eindhoven, however, it was Barcelona who struck first, through Bakero and Figo, and a happy return to his homeland looked on the cards for Barcelona coach Johan Cruijff. But goals from Zenden and Eykelkamp restored parity. An exciting match seemed to be heading for extra-time when Barcelona won the tie with an extraordinary goal from Sergi, who ran half the length of the pitch before rounding the goalkeeper and slotting the ball home.

Bayern Munich also struggled to impose themselves at home against Nottingham Forest. The English side had happy memories of the Olympiastadion, having won the European Champions' Cup there in 1978. And they did well to restrict Bayern to a 2-1 first-leg lead. After a dull opening 15 minutes Jürgen Klinsmann put Bayern ahead

UEFA CUP

with the first chance of the game, heading in Mehmet Scholl's right-wing cross. Almost immediately Forest were back on level terms, defender Steve Chettle nodding the ball in at the far post after the Bayern defence had failed to cut out a free-kick. But just before the interval a rare error from the otherwise impressive Forest goalkeeper, Mark Crossley, upset his team's concentration, and man of the match Scholl converted Sforza's pass to restore Bayern's lead. In the second half Forest gave as good as they got and restricted the Germans to very few openings.

The return, at the City Ground, was a different story altogether. Once Bayern, playing all in white, had opened the scoring with a Christian Ziege free-kick, Forest were forced to chase the game. Their defence was left exposed and Bayern ran riot, adding another four goals, two of them to the irrepressible Klinsmann, who thus brought his total to a record-equalling 14, matching the previous best individual goals-total for a season in Europe, jointly held by José Altafini, Lothar Emmerich and John Wark. The 5-1 victory was also Bayern's fourth away win in a row. They looked to be in unstoppable form.

SEMI-FINALS

There was a lop-sided look to the semi-finals, with the two giants, Barcelona and Bayern Munich, being drawn together, while the two preliminary-round qualifiers, Bordeaux and Slavia Prague, did battle in the other tie.

As against Roma, Slavia switched their home tie to the national stadium, the Strahov. And once again, despite the advent of spring, it was a cold, chilly evening in Prague. The difference was that on this occasion the visitors, not Slavia, took the early lead. It was a soft goal to concede. Zinedine Zidane pulled the Slavia defence apart with some excellent work on the left before crossing for Christophe Dugarry in the centre. The conqueror of Milan shot weakly, but somehow the ball found its way via Stejskal's body into the net.

It was the perfect start for Bordeaux. For the rest of the first half they controlled the game. Dugarry struck the foot of the post and then forced a good save from Stejskal, while Zidane bamboozled the Slavia defence with some wonderful skills and twice curled shots just wide of the target. There was very little from the home side. Bordeaux pressed their opponents brilliantly, denying them any room for manoeuvre, and were dominant in every facet of the play. It was not until late in the game that the Czech side made any impression on the Bordeaux defence, one Poborsky run and a strong left-foot shot from Bejbl being the sum total of their worthwhile efforts.

Bordeaux deserved their win, but there was some disappointment in the French ranks that they had not killed off the tie there and then. All of the team's key players - Zidane, Dugarry, Witschge and Lizarau - had performed well, and a bigger margin of victory was certainly within their grasp against a disappointing Slavia team missing only defender Suchoparek from their first-choice side.

Back in Bordeaux a fortnight later, the Girondins struggled to impose themselves as they had done in Prague. They knew that Slavia had eliminated another French team, Lens, earlier in the competition with a victory on Gallic soil, and for the first 45 minutes they played tentatively in defence of their one-goal lead. Deliverance was provided, however, shortly after the restart when Didier Tholot scored a tremendous solo goal. Receiving the ball 40 yards out, the Bordeaux striker headed for goal, skilfully slipped his marker and then beat Stejskal at the second attempt after his first shot was parried back to him. 31,500 fans rared their approval. Slavia were finished.

By beating Slavia and reaching the UEFA Cup final, Bordeaux not only proved to be the perfect advertisement for the InterToto Cup (after 18 European games during the season, they were still going strong). The team also erased the bitter memory of European semi-final defeats in 1985 and 1987. Their victory made them only the sixth French team - after Reims, Saint-Etienne, Bastia, Monaco and Marseille - to reach a European final (Paris Saint-Germain would become number seven a couple of days later).

All 63,000 tickets for the first leg of the Bayern Munich-Barcelona semi-final were sold out within 24 hours. It was a classic confrontation, and yet the teams had never previously met in Europe. Johan Cruijff and Franz Beckenbauer had, of course, and this was the Dutchman's first return to the Olympiastadion in an official capacity since the 1974 World Cup final.

Barcelona were without three key defenders in Nadal, Abelardo and Sergi, all suspended, and in the opening minutes there was a distinct lack of harmony in the Barça rearguard. Christian Nerlinger broke through after just two minutes and wasted a glorious chance to give Bayern an early lead. He was left to regret it when, on 14 minutes,

SEMI-FINAL RESULTS

FC BAYERN MÜNCHEN 2 Witeczek (52), Scholl (57)
FC BARCELONA 2 Oscar (14), Hagi (76)
FC BARCELONA 1 De la Peña (88),
FC BAYERN MÜNCHEN 2 Babbel (39), Witeczek (84)
(FC BAYERN MÜNCHEN 4-3)

SLAVIA PRAHA 0 GIRONDINS DE BORDEAUX 1 Dugarry (8)
GIRONDINS DE BORDEAUX 1 Tholot (47) **SLAVIA PRAHA 0**
(GIRONDINS DE BORDEAUX 2-0)

UEFA CUP

the Spaniards went ahead, Oscar chipping into the corner of Oliver Kahn's net after a one-two with Bakero had dissected the centre of the Bayern defence. The young striker was free again five minutes later after a magnificent pass from Figo, but he stubbed his foot against the ball and the chance went begging. Bayern began to get round the back of the Barcelona defence on both sides towards the end of the first half, but only created one clear-cut chance, which Scholl pulled wide of the goal.

In Bayern's first genuine attack of the second half, however, they equalised, substitute Marcel Witeczek firing in a left-foot shot with only his second touch of the ball. In the next two minutes Barcelona had two great chances to restore their lead, but Kahn denied both Bakero and Jordi Cruijff with two good blocks, and before the Spaniards had got over the disappointment, they found themselves 2-1 down, Scholl scoring at the second attempt after the Barça defence was opened up again down the left flank. The rest of the game saw Bayern intensify their assault on Barcelona's fragile defence, but in this ever-changing match it was no real surprise when the visitors, totally against the run of play, got back on level terms. The goal was a result of a disastrous back-pass from defender Markus Babbel. Gheorghe Hagi, anjoying a rare outing in the Barcelona starting XI, pounced on the loose ball and drove it firmly into the corner. Before the final whistle the Spaniards created another chance, through substitute Iván de la Peña, but after nutmegging Lothar Matthäus the youngster shot straight at Kahn. It could have been 3-2, but Barcelona went back to Spain happy enough with a 2-2 draw.

Yet, as the Germans had shown in every previous round, they were stronger away from home than in the Olympiastadion. A six-figure crowd filled the Nou Camp to see if Barcelona could end Bayern's run. Barcelona had lost the Spanish Cup final a week earlier and were eager to atone by reaching their first UEFA Cup final since 1966 (when the competition was known as the Fairs' Cup).

But it was to be another disappointing night for the Catalan faithful. Barcelona were incoherent and disconnected in a first half dominated by the Germans. A 39th-minute goal from Markus Babbel, Bayern's first-leg sinner, was no more than Otto Rehhagel's team deserved. In the second period, Barcelona finally began to get their act together, but skipper Bakero was gulity of a dreadful miss, skying over Figo's perfect cut-back with the goal gaping. Bayern continued to look the more composed unit, with Mehmet Scholl showing some particularly impressive form. After 84 minutes, with Barcelona's adrenalin beginning to sag as the Bayern defence held firm, Figo lost possession and Marcel Witeczek bore down on the Barcelona goal. As he approached the area, he shot, and the ball deflected into the net off Nadal. That appeared to be that. But in the 88th minute De la Peña pulled a goal back for Barça, his free-kick deflecting in off Thomas Strunz's heel. The crowd bayed frantically for more, but Bayern held out. They had won away from home yet again and were in their first European final for nine years.

FINAL

Otto Rehhagel had taken Bayern Munich into the UEFA Cup final, but he was not around to see his work fulfilled. Just four days before the first leg of the final against Bordeaux, Rehhagel was sacked. The team's poor performances in the Bundesliga and a growing mood of discontent among the players had led to his dismissal. His temporary successor was none other than club president Franz Beckenbauer. The first match against Bordeaux, in the Olympiastadion, was the 'Kaiser''s first match back on the Bayern bench.

Bordeaux were not without their own problems. They too had changed their coach midway through the season, but Gernot Rohr - a former Bayern player, no less - was long settled in the post, even if, like Beckenbauer, he was only ever intended as a temporary solution. Bordeaux's concern was their players, and with their two attacking stars, Zidane and Dugarry, both suspended, they were expected to keep it tight at the back and try to give themselves something to defend back at the Parc Lescure.

After half an hour of fairly nondescript football, it was Bordeaux, surprisingly, who created the first chance of the match. Tholot attempted a reprisal of his semi-final goal, seizing on an error by Sforza and running half the length of the pitch alone. But just as he prepared to shoot, the ball got caught under his feet and he allowed Oliver Kahn to save. Within seconds the ball was up at the other end and Bayern were ahead, Thomas Helmer sending a powerful and unstoppable header past Huard from Matthäus's right-wing corner. It remained 1-0 at half-time but only because of a truly world-class point-blank save that Kahn made from Bancarel just before the break.

Kahn was at it again early in the second half, saving again from Lizarazu. The big blond 'keeper was undoubtedly the man of the match.

TOP SCORERS

15	Jürgen KLINSMANN (FC Bayern München)
6	RONALDO (PSV)
5	Luc NILIS (PSV)
	Mehmet SCHOLL (FC Bayern München)
4	ROGER (FC Barcelona)
	Davor SUKER (Sevilla FC)
	Joël TIEHI (RC Lens)
	Bernd HOBSCH (SV Werder Bremen)
	Pierluigi CASIRAGHI (Lazio)

UEFA CUP

FINAL

01/05/96, Munich
FC BAYERN MÜNCHEN 2 Helmer (34), Scholl (60)
GIRONDINS DE BORDEAUX 0
referee - Muhmenthaler (SUI)
FC BAYERN MÜNCHEN - Kahn; Babbel, Ziege, Kreuzer, Helmer, Hamann, Scholl, Sforza, Klinsmann, Matthäus (Frey 54), Papin (Witeczek 70).
GIRONDINS DE BORDEAUX - Huard; Grenet, Lizarazu, Friis-Hansen, Dogon, Lucas, Croci, Dutuel, Tholot (Anselin 89), Witschge, Bancarel.

15/05/96, Bordeaux
GIRONDINS DE BORDEAUX 1 Dutuel (75)
FC BAYERN MÜNCHEN 3 Scholl (54), Kostadinov (65), Klinsmann (78)
referee - Zhuk (BLS)
GIRONDINS DE BORDEAUX - Huard; Bancarel, Lizarazu (Anselin 30), Friis-Hansen, Dogon, Lucas (Grenet 80), Zidane, Croci (Dutuel 58), Tholot, Witschge, Dugarry.
FC BAYERN MÜNCHEN - Kahn; Babbel, Ziege, Strunz, Helmer, Frey (Zickler 60), Scholl, Sforza, Klinsmann, Mathäus, Kostadinov (Witeczek 75).

(FC BAYERN MÜNCHEN 5-1)

Jürgen Klinsmann lifts the trophy

Bayern's best outfield player, not for the first time in the tournament, was Mehmet Scholl, and it was his excellent solo goal, on the hour mark, that put the Germans a flattering two goals in front. Jürgen Klinsmann, seeking the one goal that would earn him a place alone in the European Cup history books, was denied a look-in for most of the game, but in the 89th minute he wasted a glorious opportunity to score his 15th goal of the competition - and kill the tie - when he side-footed embarrassingly over an open goal after the ball rebounded to him off the crossbar.

With Bayern's staggering away form to take into account, Bordeaux were under no illusions about the size of their task in the return leg a fortnight later. They had to attack Bayern from the first minute to have a chance of picking up their first European trophy and emulating Paris Saint-Germain's achievement in the Cup-winners' Cup. The return of Zidane and Dugarry helped their cause, and these two were the most prominent individuals during a first half in which the home side dominated but failed to score.

There was a strange inevitability about the goal with which Bayern opened the scoring and ended Bordeaux's hopes six minutes into the second half. It came from the Germans' first genuine attack of the match, and was scored by Scholl, who netted his fifth goal of the competition via a deflection after Bulgarian striker Emil Kostadinov had cleverly back-heeled the ball into his path. Two minutes later it was obvious that this was just not going to be Bordeaux's night when Tholot crashed a shot against the foot of the Bayern post. And, sure enough, in Bayern's next attack, they scored again, Kostadinov, Bayern's best player on the night, heading in unmarked at the near post from a corner. Daniel Dutuel, a second-half substitute, seemed to have a point to prove when he scored ten minutes later for Bordeaux with a free-kick that Kahn uncharacteristically mishandled into the net. The midfielder raced to the bench pointing to the number 14 on his back. Evidently he believed he should have been on from the start.

By then, of course, the contest was already over and the UEFA Cup safely in Bayern's hands. What the Germans really wanted to crown their triumph was a goal for Klinsmann. He had gone three games without scoring, and it looked as if he would miss out on setting a new European goalscoring record. But, with 12 minutes to go, Strunz fired in a shot and Klinsmann deflected it into the net. It was irrelevant to the match, but it was an historical moment and the perfect end to Bayern's triumph.

With the 3-1 victory in Bordeaux, Bayern also completed an unprecedented clean sweep of six away wins. The UEFA Cup triumph also placed the German giants in the illustrious company of Juventus, Ajax and Barcelona - the only other teams to have won all three European trophies.

EUROPEAN CUP QUALIFIERS 1996/97

COUNTRY	CHAMPIONS' CUP	CUP-WINNERS' CUP	UEFA CUP
ALBANIA		Flamurtari Vlorë	Tirana *, Teuta Durrës
ARMENIA		Kotayk Abovyan	Pyunik Yerevan *, Shirak Gyumri
AUSTRIA	SK Rapid Wien	SK Sturm Graz	FC Tirol Innsbruck, Grazer AK
AZERBAIJAN		Karabag	Neftchi *, Khazri
BELARUS		MPKC Mozyr	Dinamo Minsk *, Dinamo-93 Minsk
BELGIUM	Club Brugge KV	KSV Cercle Brugge	RSC Anderlecht, KFC Germinal Ekeren, RWD Molenbeek
BULGARIA		Levski Sofia	Slavia Sofia *, Lokomotiv Sofia
CROATIA		Varteks Varazdin	Croatia Zagreb *, Hajduk Split
CYPRUS		AEK Larnaca	APOEL Nicosia *, Anorthosis Famagusta
CZECH REPUBLIC	Slavia Praha	Sparta Praha	Sigma Olomouc
DENMARK	Brøndby IF	AGF	OB, Lyngby FC
ENGLAND	Manchester United	Liverpool	Aston Villa, Newcastle United, Arsenal
ESTONIA		Tallinna Sadam	FC Lantana Tallinn *, FC Flora Tallinn
FAROE ISLANDS		HB	GÍ *, B68
FINLAND		MyPa	FC Haka *, HJK, FC Jazz
FRANCE	AJ Auxerre	Paris Saint-Germain FC Olympique Nîmes	FC Metz, AS Monaco, RC Lens, Montpellier HSC, En Avant Guingamp **
GEORGIA		Dinamo Batumi	Dinamo Tbilisi *, Margveti Zestafoni
GERMANY	Borussia Dortmund	1.FC Kaiserslautern	FC Bayern München, FC Schalke 04, Borussia Mönchengladbach, Hamburger SV, Karlsruher SC **
GREECE	Panathinaikos	AEK	Olympiakos, Iraklis
HOLLAND	Ajax	PSV	Feyenoord, Roda JC
HUNGARY	Ferencváros	Kispest-Honvéd FC	BVSC-Dreher
ICELAND		KR	ÍA *, ÍBV
ISRAEL	Maccabi Tel-Aviv	Hapoel Irony Rishon Lezion	Beitar Jerusalem, Maccabi Haifa
ITALY	Juventus, Milan	Fiorentina	Lazio, Parma, Roma, Inter
LATVIA		RAF Yelgava	Skonto Riga *, Dinaburg Daugavpils

EUROPEAN CUP QUALIFIERS 1996/97

COUNTRY	CHAMPIONS' CUP	CUP-WINNERS' CUP	UEFA CUP
LIECHTENSTEIN		FC Vaduz	
LITHUANIA		Kareda Siauliai	Inkaras-Grifas Kaunas *, Zalgiris Vilnius
LUXEMBOURG		Union Luxembourg	Jeunesse Esch *, CS Grevenmacher
MACEDONIA		Sloga Jugomagnat Skopje	Sileks Kratovo *, Vardar Skopje
MALTA		Valletta	Sliema Wanderers *, Floriana
MOLDOVA		Constructorul Chisinau	Zimbru Chisinau *, Tiligul Tiraspol
N. IRELAND		Glentoran	Portadown *, Crusaders
NORWAY	Rosenborg BK	SK Brann	Molde FK, FK Bodø/Glimt
POLAND	Widzew Lodz	Ruch Chorzow	Legia Warszawa, Hutnik Krakow
PORTUGAL	FC Porto	SL Benfica	Sporting CP, Boavista FC, Vitória Guimarães
REP. IRELAND		Shelbourne	St. Patrick's Athletic *, Bohemians
ROMANIA	Steaua Bucuresti	Gloria Bistrita	FC National Bucuresti, Rapid Bucuresti
RUSSIA	Alania Vladikavkaz	Lokomotiv Moskva	Spartak Moskva, Torpedo Moskva, Dinamo Moskva, CSKA Moskva
SCOTLAND	Rangers	Heart of Midlothian	Aberdeen, Celtic
SLOVAKIA		Chemlon Humenne	Slovan Bratislava *, 1.FC Kosice
SLOVENIA		SCT Olimpija Ljubljana	HIT Gorica *, Mura Murska sobota
SPAIN	Atlético Madrid	FC Barcelona	Valencia CF, RCD Espanyol, CD Tenerife
SWEDEN	IFK Göteborg	AIK	Helsingborgs IF, Halmstads BK, Malmö FF
SWITZERLAND	Grasshopper-Club Zürich	FC Sion	Neuchâtel Xamax FC, FC Aarau
TURKEY	Fenerbahçe	Galatasaray	Trabzonspor, Besiktas
UKRAINE	Dynamo Kyiv	Nyva Vynnytsya	Chornomorets Odesa
WALES		Llansantffraid	Barry Town *, Newtown
YUGOSLAVIA		Crvena zvezda Beograd	Partizan Beograd *, Vojvodina Novi Sad, FK Becej

*N.B. * = National champions competing in UEFA Cup; ** = InterToto qualifiers.*

MISCELLANEOUS

Ronald de Boer proudly holds up the Toyota Cup after Ajax's victory in Tokyo

WORLD CLUB CUP 1995

28/11/95, Tokyo
AJAX 0
GRÊMIO 0
(aet; 4-3 on pens.)
referee - Elleray (ENG)
AJAX - Van der Sar; Reiziger, Blind, De Boer F., Bogarde, De Boer R., Litmanen (Reuser 93), Davids, George, Kluivert, Overmars (Kanu 69).
GRÊMIO - Danrlei; Arce, Rivarola, Adilson, Roger, Goiano, Dinho, Arilson (Luciano 61), Carlos Miguel (Gelson 95), Paulo Nunes, Jardel (Magno 78).

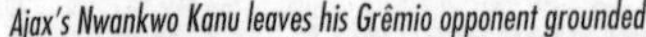
Ajax's Nwankwo Kanu leaves his Grêmio opponent grounded

European Footballer of the Year, George Weah

EUROPEAN SUPER CUP 1996

06/02/96, Zaragoza
REAL ZARAGOZA 1 Aguado (28)
AJAX 1 Kluivert (71)
referee - Harrel (FRA)
REAL ZARAGOZA - Juanmi; Belsué, Cuartero, Oscar, Aguado, Solana, López (Berti 76), Nayim, Higuera, Morientes, Dani (Pardeza 76).
AJAX - Van der Sar; Reiziger, Blind, De Boer F., Bogarde, Scholten, Litmanen (Wooter 66), Musampa (Van den Bergh 56), George, Kluivert, De Boer R..

28/02/96, Amsterdam
AJAX 4 Bogarde (41), George (55), Blind (66p, 69p)
REAL ZARAGOZA 0
referee - Mottram (SCO)
AJAX - Van der Sar; Reiziger, Blind, De Boer F., Silooy, Scholten (Van den Bergh 79), Kluivert (Demchenko 71), Davids, George (Gehring 71), Kanu, Bogarde.
REAL ZARAGOZA - Cedrún; Belsué, Aguado, García Sanjuán, Oscar, Cáceres, Aragón, López (Gay 62), Higuera (Belman 64), Dani, Morientes (Cuartero 80).

(AJAX 5-1)

MISCELLANEOUS

EUROPEAN FOOTBALLER OF THE YEAR 1995

Pts	Player/Club(s)/Nationality
144	George WEAH (Milan/LIBERIA)
108	Jürgen KLINSMANN (Tottenham Hotspur/ FC Bayern München/GERMANY)
67	Jari LITMANEN (Ajax/FINLAND)
57	Alessandro DEL PIERO (Juventus/ITALY)
47	Patrick KLUIVERT (Ajax/HOLLAND)
41	Gianfranco ZOLA (Parma/ITALY)
36	Paolo MALDINI (Milan/ITALY)
33	Marc OVERMARS (Ajax/HOLLAND)
18	Matthias SAMMER (Borussia Dortmund/GERMANY)
17	Michael LAUDRUP (Real Madrid/DENMARK)
16	Marcel DESAILLY (Milan/FRANCE)
15	Frank RIJKAARD (Ajax/HOLLAND)
	Fabrizio RAVANELLI (Juventus/ITALY)
14	Hristo STOICHKOV (FC Barcelona/Parma/BULGARIA)
	PAULO SOUSA (Juventus/PORTUGAL)
12	Dejan SAVICEVIC (Milan/YUGOSLAVIA)
10	Davor SUKER (Sevilla FC/CROATIA)
9	Fernando HIERRO (Real Madrid/SPAIN)
8	Gianluca VIALLI (Juventus/ITALY)
7	Gabriel BATISTUTA (Fiorentina/ARGENTINA)
6	Finidi GEORGE (Ajax/NIGERIA)
	Franco BARESI (Milan/ITALY)
5	Anthony YEBOAH (Leeds United/GHANA)
	Roberto BAGGIO (Juventus/Milan/ITALY)
	Zvonimir BOBAN (Milan/CROATIA)
4	RONALDO (PSV/BRAZIL)
3	Juan Eduardo ESNAIDER (Real Zaragoza/Real Madrid/ARGENTINA)
	Iván ZAMORANO (Real Madrid/CHILE)
	Andreas MÖLLER (Borussia Dortmund/GERMANY)
2	BEBETO (RC Deportivo/BRAZIL)
	VÍTOR BAÍA (FC Porto/PORTUGAL)
1	FIGO (Sporting CP/FC Barcelona/PORTUGAL)
	Alan SHEARER (Blackburn Rovers/ENGLAND)
	Ian WRIGHT (Arsenal/ENGLAND)

TOP EUROPEAN LEAGUE SCORERS 1995/96

Pts	Player/Club/Nationality
40	Zviad ENDELADZE (Margveti Zestafoni)
38	Ken McKENNA (Conwy United)
34	Vladimir GAVRILIUC (Zimbru Chisinau)
32	Vladimir KOSSE (Tiligul Tiraspol)
31	Alan SHEARER (Blackburn Rovers)
	Mikheil ASHVETIA (Torpedo Kutaisi)
	Juan Antonio PIZZI (CD Tenerife)
29	Marek KONIAREK (Widzew Lodz)
	Robert SEMENIK (1.FC Kosice)
	Eifion WILLIAMS (Caernarfon Town)
28	Ara ADAMYAN (Shirak Gyumri)
	Robbie FOWLER (Liverpool)
	Ermin SILJAK (SCT Olimpija Ljubljana)
	Predrag MIJATOVIC (Valencia CF)
26	Alexandre IASHVILI (Dinamo Tbilisi)
	Vassilis TSARTAS (AEK)
	Haim REVIVO (Maccabi Haifa)
	Harald BRATTBAKK (Rosenborg BK)
	Ion VLADOIU (Steaua Bucuresti)
	Pierre VAN HOOIJDONK (Celtic)
25	József KIPRICH (APOEL Nicosia)
	Les FERDINAND (Newcastle United)
	Edgardas JANKAUSKAS (Zalgiris Vilnius)
	Serghei ROGACIOV (Olimpia Balti)
	DOMINGOS (FC Porto)
	Oleg VERETENNIKOV (Rotor Volgograd)
	BEBETO (RC Deportivo)
	Shota ARVELADZE (Trabzonspor)
	Frank MOTTRAM (Bangor City)
24	Hovhannes TOUMBARYAN (Tsement Ararat)
	Suni Fridi JOHANNESEN (B68)
	Igor PROTTI (Bari)
	Giuseppe SIGNORI (Lazio)
	Zoran BOSKOVSKI (Sileks Kratovo)
	Faik KAMBEROVIC (Publikum Celje)

INTRODUCTION TO NATIONS/CLUBS

The following pages contain individual reviews of each of the UEFA nations, including Statistics, a General Review, Photographs, Profiles, Players of the Season and, in a separate section, Colour Team Strips and Emblems.

As a general guide, all Clubs are referred to by the names of their original language in statistical tables and headings. In narrative text, however, some will be referred to by their English names (e.g. Crvena zvezda Beograd = Red Star Belgrade; 1.FC Köln = Cologne)

The abbreviations and explanations below should act as a guide to assist the reader in understanding and appreciating the various items of information.

NATIONAL SECTION

LEAGUE CHAMPIONSHIP RESULTS

Home teams are listed, together with numbers, in the left-hand column. Away teams are ranged horizontally across the top of the table, with the team's corresponding number as reference. Teams are listed alphabetically.

LEAGUE CHAMPIONSHIP FINAL TABLE

This is the final table of the country's First, or Premier, Division championship, with clubs listed in official classification order. Home, Away and Total performance records are shown in separate columns.

KEY:
Pd = Played W = Won
D = Drawn L = Lost
F = Goals for A = Goals against
Pt = Points GD = Goal Difference

An unbroken line (———) indicates the relegation zone.

A dotted line (................) indicates the play-off zone.

Any irregularities from the standard formula of 3 points for a win, 1 point for a draw and 0 points for a defeat are stipulated at the foot of the table.

TOP SCORERS

These refer to league goals only.

DOMESTIC CUP

The rounds included are those in which the First, or Premier, Division clubs are involved.
For two-legged ties, the aggregate scores and qualifiers are shown in brackets.
(aet) = after extra-time
(asd) = after sudden-death

NATIONAL TEAM RESULTS

This covers all the official full international matches played by the country's national team from July 1995 to June 1996.

KEY:
(ECQ) = European Championship Qualifier
(ECF) = European Championship Finals
(WCQ) = World Cup Qualifier
H = Home A = Away
N = Neutral p = penalty
og = own-goal

NATIONAL TEAM APPEARANCES

This lists all the players who have appeared in their national team during the 1995/96 season, together with date of birth, club(s), match-by-match appearances and all-time appearance and goal totals.

KEY:
G = Goalkeeper D = Defender
M = Midfielder A = Attacker
s = substitute

The number after the letter indicates the time of substitution.

Cps = Total full international caps gained at the end of the season.

Gls = Total full international goals scored at the end of the season.

Three-letter codes have been used as column headings to indicate opponents. These are as follows:

EUROPE
ALB = Albania
AUT = Austria
BLS = Belarus
BOS = Bosnia-Hercegovina
CRO = Croatia
TCH = Czech Republic
ENG = England
FAR = Faroe Islands
FRA = France
GER = Germany
HOL = Holland
ISL = Iceland
ITA = Italy
LIE = Liechtenstein
LUX = Luxembourg
MLT = Malta
NIR = Northern Ireland
POL = Poland
IRL = Republic of Ireland
RUS = Russia
SCO = Scotland
SLO = Slovenia
SWE = Sweden
TUR = Turkey
WAL = Wales
ARM = Armenia
AZB = Azerbaijan
BEL = Belgium
BUL = Bulgaria
CYP = Cyprus
DEN = Denmark
EST = Estonia
FIN = Finland
GEO = Georgia
GRE = Greece
HUN = Hungary
ISR = Israel
LAT = Latvia
LIT = Lithuania
MAC = Macedonia
MOL = Moldova
NOR = Norway
POR = Portugal
ROM = Romania
SMR = San Marino
SVK = Slovakia
ESP = Spain
SUI = Switzerland
UKR = Ukraine
YUG = Yugoslavia

NON-EUROPE
ALG = Algeria
AUS = Australia
BRA = Brazil
CMR = Cameroon
CAY = Cayman Islands
CHI = Chile
COL = Colombia
ECU = Ecuador
SAL = El Salvador
GUI = Guinea
HON = Honduras
INA = Indonesia
CIV = Ivory Coast
JPN = Japan
KAZ = Kazakhstan
KGZ = Kirghistan
LBN = Lebanon
LBY = Libya
MAU = Mauritius
MAR = Morocco
NIG = Nigeria
PAR = Paraguay
QTR = Qatar
SEN = Senegal
SAF = South Africa
ARG = Argentina
BOL = Bolivia
BUR = Burundi
CAN = Canada
CHD = Chad
CHN = China
CON = Congo
EGY = Egypt
GHA = Ghana
HAI = Haiti
HKG = Hong Kong
IRQ = Iraq
JAM = Jamaica
JOR = Jordan
KEN = Kenya
KUW = Kuwait
LIB = Liberia
MLI = Mali
MEX = Mexico
NZL = New Zealand
PAN = Panama
PER = Peru
SAU = Saudi Arabia
SRL = Sierra Leone
KOR = South Korea
SUR = Surinam
TAD = Tadjikistan
TOG = Togo
TUN = Tunisia
UAE = United Arab Emirates
URU = Uruguay
VIE = Vietnam
ZAM = Zambia
SYR = Syria
THA = Thailand
TRI = Trinidad & Tobago
UGA = Uganda
USA = United States
UZB = Uzbekistan
ZAI = Zaire
ZIM = Zimbabwe

EUROPEAN CUPS RESULTS

Results, goalscorers, goal-times and full line-ups are included
KEY: H = Home A = Away

The three-letter country codes used are the ame as those shown above.

CLUB SECTION

LEAGUE RESULTS

This lists each club's league matches in chronological order, giving Date, Opponent, Venue, Result and Goalscorer(s)

KEY: H = Home A = Away
p = penalty og = own-goal

APPEARANCES

The figures refer to league games only.

KEY:
P = Position
Ap = Number of appearances in starting line-up
(s) = Number of appearances as a substitute
Gls = Number of goals scored
G = Goalkeeper D = Defender
M = Midfielder A = Attacker

Foreign players are indicated using the same three-letter codes as shown above.

When there is no separate '(s)' column (Moldova), substitute appearances have been included in the 'Ap' column.

DIRECTORIES

Where more than one Coach/Manager has been used during the course of the season, these are all indicated. New Coaches/Managers for the 1996/97 season have been added where known at the time of going to press. Club Secretaries have been included where provided.

PROMOTED CLUBS

The clubs promoted to the First, or Premier, Division at the end of the 1995/96 season are presented at the back of each national section, together with Second, or First, Division tables and Promotion/Relegation Play-off details. These tables use the same abbreviations as the LEAGUE CHAMPIONSHIP FINAL TABLE (see above), except that no Home and Away performance records are shown.

An unbroken line (———) at the top of the table indicates the promotion zone.
A dotted line (..........) at the top of the table indicates the promotion play-off zone
An unbroken line (———) at the bottom of the table indicates the relegation zone
A dotted line (..........) at the bottom of the table indicates the relegation play-off zone.

N.B. Where reference is made to the 1995/96 domestic season, this should be understood as the 1995 season for Belarus, the Faroe Islands, Finland, Iceland, Latvia, Norway, Russia and Sweden.

ALBANIA

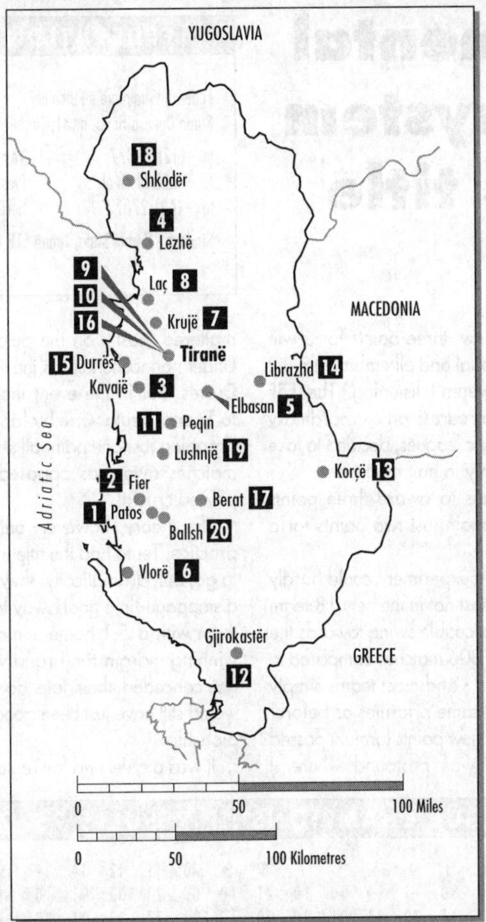

1	ALBPETROL PATOS	98
2	APOLONIA FIER	99
3	BESA KAVAJË	100
4	BESËLIDHJA LEZHË	101
5	ELBASANI	102
6	FLAMURTARI VLORË	103
7	KASTRIOTI KRUJË	104
8	LAÇI	105
9	OLIMPIK TIRANË	106
10	PARTIZANI TIRANË	107
11	SHKUMBINI PEQIN	108
12	SHQIPONJA GJIROKASTËR	109
13	SKËNDERBEU KORÇË	110
14	SOPOTI LIBRAZHD	111
15	TEUTA DURRËS	112
16	TIRANA	113
17	TOMORI BERAT	114
18	VLLAZNIA SHKODËR	115
19	LUSHNJË	116
20	BYLIS BALLSHI	116

'DOUBLE' DELIGHT FOR TIRANA

Experimental points system decides title

FEDERATION DIRECTORY

Federata Shqiptarë e Futbollit
Rruga Dervish Hima, nr.31, Tiranë

tel - (42) 27877
tlx - 2228 bfssh ab
fax - (42) 27877

Year of Formation - 1930
President - Edmond Spaho
Secretary - Eduard Dervishi

Stadium - Qemal Stafa, Tiranë (18,000)

FIFA's directive over the new three-points-for-a-win system was supposed to be global and all-embracing. But in Albania they obviously weren't listening. The FSF (Albanian FA), determined to redress an extraordinary home-team bias in their domestic leagues, decided to take on board the new rule, but only in half measures.

Their go-it-alone policy was to award three points for an away win, but to maintain just two points for a victory at home.

At the end of the season the experiment could hardly be regarded as a success, at least not in the new 18-team First Division. There was no noticeable swing towards the away team - 44 away wins in 306 matches compared to 29 in 240 the previous season - and most teams simply treated their matches with the same priorities as before.

But that is not to say that the new points formula passed without notice. Its influence was profound where it mattered most - on the outcome of the championship. Under normal conditions the title would have gone to Teuta Durrës. But in the event they missed out by one point to Tirana. Teuta were by far the stronger team at home, dropping just one point all season. But Tirana won seven matches away, as opposed to Teuta's four, and that proved crucial.

The theory, however, only came after the event. In practice, Teuta had the title in their grasp with one game to go, but, dramatically, they let it slip. While they lost to a stoppage-time goal away to Partizani, Tirana overtook them with a 5-1 home win against Albpetrol. The final winning margin for Tirana was a point, but had Teuta not conceded their late goal Tirana's goal difference would still have just been good enough to claim the championship.

It was a cruel end for Teuta, the 1993/94 champions,

LEAGUE CHAMPIONSHIP RESULTS 95/96

		1	2	3	4	5	6	7	8	9	10	11	12	13	14	15	16	17	18
1	Albpetrol Patos		0-0	3-0	1-1	1-0	0-0	1-0	2-1	1-0	0-0	2-1	0-2	5-1	1-0	2-1	0-0	2-1	2-1
2	Apolonia Fier	0-0		1-1	3-0	3-1	0-1	2-0	0-0	1-0	0-1	7-1	2-1	0-1	3-2	1-1	2-1	1-1	2-2
3	Besa Kavajë	1-0	2-2		4-0	2-1	1-0	2-0	1-0	0-1	2-0	1-0	0-1	0-1	0-0	0-0	1-0	2-1	2-2
4	Besëlidhja Lezhë	2-0	0-2	3-1		1-0	0-0	1-0	0-1	0-1	1-0	5-4	0-1	2-0	1-1	1-0	0-1	1-0	0-0
5	Elbasani	1-0	2-1	1-0	2-0		3-0	1-0	6-5	2-2	0-0	0-0	2-0	1-0	1-1	0-0	0-0	2-2	0-1
6	Flamurtari Vlorë	1-0	3-0	3-2	1-0	2-1		0-1	3-1	0-0	0-0	1-0	3-0	5-1	1-2	0-1	2-0	1-0	3-0
7	Kastrioti Krujë	2-1	0-2	2-0	1-0	1-1	1-0		2-0	1-1	0-1	0-0	1-0	1-0	0-2	2-1	0-0	2-1	2-2
8	Laçi	0-0	3-2	0-1	1-1	4-1	4-0	2-1		2-0	3-0	5-3	1-0	1-0	2-0	3-3	2-3	3-1	2-0
9	Olimpik Tiranë	5-1	2-0	2-1	1-1	3-0	2-0	1-0	4-0		2-1	1-0	0-0	4-2	5-0	0-0	0-1	1-0	0-0
10	Partizani Tiranë	6-0	6-1	0-0	0-0	0-2	0-0	4-2	3-0	1-0		3-1	3-1	3-0	3-1	1-0	0-2	2-1	0-0
11	Shkumbini Peqin	4-0	3-0	2-0	0-0	1-0	2-2	2-1	2-1	3-0	0-1		3-1	4-1	2-1	0-0	0-0	2-0	1-0
12	Shqiponja Gjirokastër	4-1	1-3	0-0	1-0	0-0	0-1	0-1	1-0	0-2	1-2	1-0		2-1	5-0	0-0	0-1	3-0	2-0
13	Skënderbeu Korçë	3-1	2-1	0-1	2-1	2-0	0-1	1-0	2-1	3-0	1-0	2-0	4-1		0-1	0-1	1-1	0-0	1-0
14	Sopoti Librazhd	1-0	1-0	1-1	1-0	1-1	4-5	2-1	2-0	0-0	0-0	0-0	4-2	1-0		0-1	0-1	4-1	0-0
15	Teuta Durrës	1-0	1-1	2-0	1-0	2-1	3-1	4-2	3-0	3-0	1-0	2-1	3-1	3-1	3-1		2-0	1-0	3-1
16	Tirana	5-1	2-0	1-0	4-0	2-1	3-0	1-1	2-0	3-1	1-2	1-0	1-1	3-1	4-1	1-1		1-1	4-1
17	Tomori Berat	2-0	1-3	1-0	1-1	2-0	2-0	2-1	2-0	2-1	1-0	1-1	2-1	1-1	1-0	1-2	0-0		1-0
18	Vllaznia Shkodër	1-2	1-0	0-0	4-1	2-1	1-2	2-1	2-1	1-0	0-0	0-0	0-0	3-0	2-0	0-0	0-2	1-1	

LEAGUE CHAMPIONSHIP FINAL TABLE 95/96

			Home					Away					Total						
		Pd	W	D	L	F	A	W	D	L	F	A	W	D	L	F	A	Pt	GD
1	Tirana	34	12	4	1	39	12	7	6	4	13	10	19	10	5	52	22	55	+30
2	Teuta Durrës	34	16	1	0	38	10	4	9	4	12	12	20	10	4	50	22	54	+28
3	Partizani Tiranë	34	11	4	2	35	11	5	5	7	8	13	16	9	9	43	24	46	+19
4	Flamurtari Vlorë	34	12	2	3	29	9	5	4	8	13	26	17	6	11	42	35	45	+7
5	Olimpik Tiranë	34	12	4	1	33	7	3	4	10	9	23	15	8	11	42	30	41	+12
6	Apolonia Fier	34	8	6	3	28	14	4	3	10	18	30	12	9	13	46	44	37	+2
7	Besa Kavajë	34	10	4	3	21	9	2	5	10	8	22	12	9	13	29	31	35	-2
8	Sopoti Librazhd	34	8	6	3	22	13	3	3	11	13	34	11	9	14	35	47	34	-12
9	Shkumbini Peqin	34	12	4	1	31	8	0	5	12	12	32	12	9	13	43	40	33	+3
10	Vllaznia Shkodër	34	8	6	3	20	11	1	7	9	10	25	9	13	12	30	36	32	-6
11	Albpetrol Patos	34	11	5	1	23	9	1	2	14	7	39	12	7	15	30	48	32	-18
12	Laçi	34	12	3	2	38	16	1	1	15	11	37	13	4	17	49	53	31	-4
13	Elbasani	34	9	7	1	24	12	1	3	13	11	29	9	10	15	35	41	31	-6
14	Tomori Berat	34	11	4	2	23	11	0	5	12	11	29	11	9	14	34	40	31	-6
15	Shqiponja Gjirokastër	34	8	3	6	21	12	3	3	11	13	29	11	6	17	34	41	31	-7
16	Skënderbeu Korçë	34	11	2	4	24	10	2	1	14	11	39	13	3	18	35	49	31	-14
17	Kastrioti Krujë	34	9	5	3	18	12	2	1	14	12	28	11	6	17	30	40	30	-10
18	Besëlidhja Lezhë	34	9	3	5	18	12	0	6	11	6	28	9	9	16	24	40	27	-16

N.B. 2 pts for a home win.

who had gone 12 games unbeaten prior to that traumatic last fixture. But for Tirana it was a day to remember. The victory over Albpetrol not only enabled them to defend their title. It also took the club's all-time total to 16 championship wins, thereby making Tirana the record champions of Albania. Before the season they had been tied with the other two Tirana clubs, Partizani and Olimpik (formerly Dinamo), on 15 wins each.

The last day of the championship was particularly memorable for Tirana striker Indrit Fortuzi, back at the club after an unsatisfactory spell in Austria, who scored a hat-trick in the team's 5-1 win. But while Fortuzi's exploit seemed to be above board, there was plenty of odd goalscoring activity elsewhere.

Laçi striker Altin Çuko struck all five of his team's goals in a 5-6 defeat by Elbasani. Surprise, surprise, he was going for the league top scorer

DOMESTIC CUP RESULTS

1/8 FINALS

Kastrioti Krujë v Tirana 0-1; 1-3
(Tirana 4-1)
Besa Kavajë v Teuta Durrës 0-0; 0-3
(Teuta Durrës 3-0)
Laçi v Partizani Tiranë 3-1; 0-3
(Partizani Tiranë 4-3)
Besëlidhja Lezhë v Flamurtari Vlorë 1-0; 0-1
(1-1; Flamurtari Vlorë 4-3 on pens.)
Elbasani v Shqiponja Gjirokastër 2-0; 1-2
(Elbasani 3-2)
Vllaznia Shkodër v Albpetrol Patos 4-0; 1-1
(Vllaznia Shkodër 5-1)
Apolonia Fier v Shkumbini Peqin 0-0; 0-2
(Shkumbini Peqin 2-0)
Tomori Berat v Olimpik Tiranë 1-2; 0-5
(Olimpik Tiranë 7-1)

QUARTER-FINALS

Elbasani v Tirana 0-1; 0-2
(Tirana 3-0)
Vllaznia Shkodër v Teuta Durrës 0-1; 1-1
(Teuta Durrës 2-1)
Shkumbini Peqin v Flamurtari Vlorë 1-0; 0-4
(Flamurtari Vlorë 4-1)
Olimpik Tiranë v Partizani Tiranë 2-1; 1-0
(Olimpik Tiranë 3-1)

SEMI-FINALS

Olimpik Tiranë v Tirana 1-3; 0-2
(Tirana 5-1)
Flamurtari Vlorë v Teuta Durrës 1-1; 2-1
(Flamurtari Vlorë 3-2)

FINAL

15/05/96, Tirana
TIRANA 1 Dede (72)
FLAMURTARI VLORË 1 Daullja (70)
(aet; 4-3 on pens.)

TOP SCORERS

21	Altin ÇUKO (Tomori Berat/Laçi)
19	Shpetim KATESHI (Shkumbini Peqin)
16	Arben SHEHU (Shqiponja Gjirokastër)
	Alket ZEQO (Apolonia Fier)
14	Luan BRASHA (Sopoti Librazhd)
	Elton KOÇA (Teuta Durrës)
13	Hekuran JAKUPI (Elbasani)
12	Artan ÇIÇIKU (Laçi)
11	Roland ZAJMI (Olimpik Tiranë/ Partizan Tiranë)
9	Artan BARE (Apolonia Fier)
	Saimir MALKO (Tirana)

crown, as was Shkumbini striker Shpetim Kateshi, whose last-day hat-trick followed a four-goal jaunt in Shkumbini's 4-5 defeat by Besëlidhja four days earlier. Other multiple goalscorers on the final day included Zeqo of Apolonia, Jakupi of Elbasani, Shehu of Shqiponja and Brasha of Sopoti, all of whom were jostling for position at the head of the top scorer table. Remarkably, the FSF took no disciplinary action against the players or the clubs for these comic capers, so five-goal Çuko, who had started the season with Tomori, ended it as the league's top marksman, having scored 16 goals in as many games for his new club Laçi.

A week after the drama and farce of the league's conclusion, Tirana faced Flamurtari in the final of the Albanian Cup. No Tirana team had ever previously won the domestic 'double', so a place in the history books beckoned coach Sulejman Mema and his players. As in the previous season, the final went to a penalty shoot-out. A year earlier the Tirana players had been denied that first 'double' with a shoout-out defeat by Teuta, but on this occasion they held their nerve, and a 4-3 victory was secured when goalkeeper Blendi Nallbani made the crucial last save.

The 'double'-winning squad was a young one, with the veteran Arben Minga, at 37, failing to make too much impression on the average age. The best players were mostly in defence. Goalkeeper Nallbani had an excellent

NATIONAL TEAM APPEARANCES 95/96

Coach - Neptun BAJKO	MLT	BUL	BUL	WAL	BOS	BOS	Cps	Gls
Blendi NALLBANI (30/05/71) - Tirana	G				G46	G67	10	-
Ilir ALLIU (14/03/73) - Teuta Durrës	D				D66		2	-
Saimir MALKO (17/03/70) - Tirana	D		D	D	D	D	11	-
Përparim DAIU (21/04/70) - Besa Kavajë	D35						1	-
Ilir SHULKU (02/01/69) - Partizani Tiranë	D	D	D	D	D57		19	-
Alban BUSHI (24/08/73) - Tirana/Flamurtari Vlorë	M			s57		M80	3	1
Edi MARTINI (02/01/73) - SAK Klagenfurt (AUT)	M						2	-
Adrian MEMA (16/02/70) - Tirana	M					s43	2	-
Artan PALI (18/03/73) - Hamburg 93 (GER)	M						2	-
Sokol PRENGA (24/05/71) - Tirana	A67				A70	A63	5	-
Ervin LAMÇE (1972) - Hamburg 93 (GER)	A67						1	-
Ervin FAKAJ (15/07/76) - Flamurtari Vlorë	s35						1	-
Auron MILOTI (04/08/73) - Tirana	s67				s65		2	-
Redi JUPI (31/08/74) - Partizani Tiranë	s67				M68		2	-
Foto STRAKOSHA (29/03/65) - Olympiakos (GRE)		G	G	G			19	-
Artur LEKBELLO (19/02/66) - Aris (GRE)		D		D			28	-
Rudi VATA (13/02/69) - Celtic (SCO)		D		D			21	1
Artan XHUMBA (20/10/69) - PAS Yannina (GRE)		D	D			M	9	-
Edmond ABAZI (10/06/63) - Boavista FC (POR)		M	M85				14	2
Arian BELLAI (05/02/71) - PAS Yannina (GRE)		M	M				8	1
Bledar KOLA (01/08/72) - Apollon (GRE)		M65	M				6	-
Sokol KUSHTA (17/04/64) - Ethnikos Akhnas (CYP)		A	A	A57			30	10
Altin RRAKLLI (17/07/70) - SC Freiburg (GER)		A	A	A			18	5
Kliton BOZGO (15/07/69) - SCT Olimpija Ljubljana (SLO)		A86		M78		M78	6	-
Ylli SHEHU (18/03/66) - KSV Cercle Brugge (BEL)		s65/88					9	1
Sulejman DEMOLLARI (15/05/64) - Panionios (GRE)		s86	s85				45	1
Ledio PANO (23/05/68) - Xanthi (GRE)		s88		M			8	-
Gjergji DEMA (17/08/71) - Vevce Donit Filtri (SLO)			D	D83			8	-
Hysen ZMIJANI (29/04/63) - Al Hasir (SAU)			D	D			36	2
Alvaro ZALLA (23/11/72) - Teuta Durrës				s78			5	-
Arben MILORI (22/11/69) - Partizani Tiranë				s83			10	-
Afrim TOLE (13/04/70) - Partizani Tiranë					D		1	-
Altin HAXHI (17/06/75) - Shqiponja Gjirokastër					M55		1	-
Nesti QENDRO (22/12/73) - Teuta Durrës					M		3	1
Elton KOÇA (05/08/73) - Teuta Durrës					A65	s46	2	-
Roland ZAJMI (06/11/73) - Olimpik Tiranë					A77		1	-
Xhevair KAPLLANI (21/06/74) - Teuta Durrës					s46	s67	5	-
Enkelejd DOBI (27/05/75) - Teuta Durrës					s55		1	1
Nevil DEDE (10/01/75) - Tirana					s57	D	2	-
Geri ÇIPI (28/02/76) - Flamurtari Vlorë					s66		1	-
Nordik RUHI (24/08/70) - Tirana					s68		1	-
Alpin GALLO (03/03/74) - Tirana					s70		2	-
Gentjan ÇOÇJA (18/03/74) - Vllaznia Shkodër					s77		1	-
Ardian BEHARI (12/08/73) - Flamurtari Vlorë						D86	1	-
Artan MERGJYSHI (06/05/68) - Olimpik Tiranë						D	1	-
Fatmir VATA (1976) - Samobor (CRO)						D43	1	-
Dashnor KASTRIOTI (1975) - FSG Schiffweiler (GER)						A46	1	-
Arjan PEÇO (26/04/75) - Olimpik Tiranë						s63	1	-
Dritan BAHOLLI (23/08/74) - Partizani Tiranë						s78	1	-
Mahir HALILI (1977) - Kastrioti Krujë						s80	1	-
Erion BOGDANI (1976) - Partizani Tiranë						s86	1	-

EUROPEAN CUPS RESULTS 95/96

CUP-WINNERS' CUP

● TEUTA DURRËS

Preliminary round TPS (FIN)

A 0-1
Kapllani; Abazi, Xhai, Qendro, Koka, Furrxhi, Alliu, Vila, Dobi (Mehmeti 71), Koça, Bushi.

H 3-0 Vila (9), Koça (20), Bushi (55)
Kapllani; Koka, Abazi, Furrxhi, Qendro, Alliu, Dobi (Begeja 86), Dashi (Mehmeti 83), Vila, Koça, Bushi (Çanaku 83).

1st round PARMA (ITA)

H 0-2
Kapllani; Xhai, Abazi, Furrxhi, Qendro, Alliu (Istrefi 83), Mehmeti, Koka, Vila, Begeja (Dashi 43), Koça.

A 0-2
Kapllani; Vila, Abazi, Furrxhi, Alliu, Qendro, Mehmeti, Koka (Bushi 88), Dobi, Xhai, Koça.

UEFA CUP

● TIRANA

Preliminary round HAPOEL BEER SHEVA (ISR)

H 0-1
Nallbani; Dede, Minga, Gallo (Markoçi 46), Kukli, Prenga,vMema, Baholli, Miloti, Ruhi, Riza.

A 0-2
Nallbani; Baholli, Minga, Dede, Gallo (Markoçi 46), Kukli, Ruhi (Hyka 64), Mema, Prenga, Miloti, Riza.

● PARTIZANI TIRANË

Preliminary round FENERBAHÇE (TUR)

A 0-2
Musta; Tole, Gega (Zere 46), Damo, Yzeiri, Shulku (Bogolani 75), Nikolla, Ymeri, Tafaj, Haxhiaj, Kodra (Ndoci 67).

H 0-4
Musta; Tole (Ymeri 71), Gega, Shulku, Yzeiri, Nikolla (Ndoci 46), Xheka (Damo 56), Milori, Tafai, Marini, Kodra.

NATIONAL TEAM RESULTS 95/96

10/08/95	Malta	A	Ta' Qali	1-2	Bushi (72)
06/09/95	Bulgaria (ECQ)	H	Tirana	1-1	Rrakli (15)
07/10/95	Bulgaria (ECQ)	A	Sofia	0-3	
15/11/95	Wales (ECQ)	H	Tirana	1-1	Kushta (3p)
30/11/95	Bosnia-Herzegovina	H	Tirana	2-0	Qendro (30)), Dobi (50)
24/04/96	Bosnia-Herzegovina	A	Zenica	0-0	

season, as did youngsters Nevil Dede and Alpin Gallo. The real star of the side, however, was national team regular Saimir Malko, who was also Tirana's top goalscorer.

With his tenth international goal - a penalty against Wales - Sokol Kushta became the first Albanian to reach double figures at national team level. Unfortunately, the goal was not enough to take Albania away from bottom place in their European Championship group. But that 1-1 draw against Wales, plus another 1-1 draw two months earlier at home to Bulgaria, offered some encouragement for the future. Coach Neptun Bajko used the remainder of the season casting his net far and wide for new talent. In the two friendlies against Bosnia-Herzegovina he awarded no fewer than 17 new caps, 15 of them to home-based players.

INTERNATIONAL HONOURS

None

PLAYERS OF THE SEASON

SAIMIR MALKO

Along with Partizani defender Ilir Shulku, Tirana's Saimir Malko was the only home-based player to earn a regular place in Albania's European Championship XI. The 26-year-old centre-back also appeared in all three friendlies played by Albania during the season, and it was not difficult to see why coach Neptun Bajko placed so much faith in him. Malko was the outstanding player in Tirana's league and Cup 'double' triumph. He was the only ever-present in the team and, although a defender, he was the club's top goalscorer in the league with nine goals. In the previous season he had not scored at all.

BLENDI NALLBANI

Blendi Nallbani made big headlines as a 17-year-old when he made his international début for Albania at Wembley in a World Cup qualifier against England. Now, eight years older, he is at last ready to claim a permanent place in the team. Greek-based Foto Strakosha was still the man in possession at the end of the Euro '96 qualifiers, but Nallbani is becoming a stronger challenger every year. In 95/96 he was in outstanding form for Tirana, earning himself a second title in less than two seasons with the club and proving himself to be the match-winning hero in the Cup final, where his penalty sealed Tirana's historic 'double'.

ALBPETROL PATOS

CLUB DIRECTORY

Klubi sportiv Albpetrol
Stadiumin Patosi
Patos
tel - 34964
fax - 34964
Year of Formation - 1947
President - Sokol Bejleri
Secretary - Roland Mehmeti
Coach - Vangjel Capo
Stadium - Patosi (5,000)

APPEARANCES 95/96

	P	Ap	(s)	Gls
Ilir ABAZI	D	30	(1)	2
Edmond AHMETAJ	M	4		
Eduard AHMETAJ	M	3	(8)	
Altin BEGA	A	17	(5)	
Artan BREGU	G	8	(2)	
Mihail ÇOBA	A	22	(1)	2
Arian HASA	D	32		5
Altin HOXHA	A	8	(4)	2
Altin JAUPI	A	6	(10)	1
Ermion KAPAJ	M	5	(4)	
Gentian KRIPA	M	11	(5)	
Altin LISI	D	32		2
Elton MARKU	M	13	(5)	
Artjan PAPA	A	23		5
Altin POÇI	A	2	(3)	
Arben POÇI	D	34		
Dashnor POÇI	A	26		8
Ardian PRIFTI	D	31		1
Flamar SHEHU	M	13	(1)	
Fatos SULA	D	28	(2)	1
Durim VELÇANI	G	26	(2)	

LEAGUE RESULTS 1995/96

02/09/95	Teuta Durrës	H	2-1	Jaupi, Papa
09/09/95	Sopoti Librazhd	A	0-1	
16/09/95	Apolonia Fier	A	0-0	
23/09/95	Shkumbini Peqin	H	2-1	Poçi D., Prifti
30/09/95	Elbasani	A	0-1	
11/10/95	Laçi	H	2-1	Lisi, Hasa (p)
14/10/95	Flamurtari Vlorë	A	0-1	
21/10/95	Partizani Tiranë	H	0-0	
28/10/95	Besëlidhja Lezhë	H	1-1	Hoxha
04/11/95	Olimpik Tiranë	A	1-5	Hasa
11/11/95	Shqiponja Gjirokastër	H	0-2	
18/11/95	Besa Kavajë	A	0-1	
25/11/95	Kastrioti	H	1-0	Poçi D.
02/12/95	Vllaznia Shkodër	A	2-1	Papa, Lisi
09/12/95	Skënderbeu Korçë	H	5-1	Abazi, Papa, Poçi D. 2, Hasa
16/12/95	Tomori Berat	A	0-2	
23/12/95	Tirana	H	0-0	
03/02/96	Teuta Durrës	A	0-1	
10/02/96	Sopoti Librazhd	H	1-0	Papa
17/02/96	Apolonia Fier	H	0-0	
24/02/96	Shkumbini Peqin	A	0-4	
02/03/96	Elbasani	H	1-0	Poçi D.
09/03/96	Laçi	A	0-0	
16/03/96	Flamurtari Vlorë	H	0-0	
23/03/96	Partizani Tiranë	A	0-6	
27/03/96	Besëlidhja Lezhë	A	0-2	
30/03/96	Olimpik Tiranë	H	1-0	og
06/04/96	Shqiponja Gjirokastër	A	4-1	Papa
13/04/96	Besa Kavajë	H	3-0	Poçi D. (p), Sula, Çoba
17/04/96	Kastrioti	A	1-2	Abazi
20/04/96	Vllaznia Shkodër	H	2-1	Poçi D. 2 (1p)
27/04/96	Skënderbeu Korçë	A	1-3	Hoxha
04/05/96	Tomori Berat	H	2-1	Çoba, Hasa (p)
08/05/96	Tirana	A	1-5	Hasa

APOLONIA FIER

CLUB DIRECTORY

Klubi sportiv Apolonia
Rruga 1 Maji, nr.73
Fier
tel - 393
Year of Formation - 1925
President - Fatmir Kajolli
Secretary - Besnik Veliu
Coach - Thanas Tupe
Stadium - Apolonia (10,000)

APPEARANCES 95/96

	P	Ap	(s)	Gls
Dritan ALIAJ	M	6		
Artan BARE	D	26		9
Agron BASHOLLI	M	28	(2)	3
Dashnor BITA	D	28	(1)	1
Gezim BUZIU	D	22	(1)	
Oltion ÇANOLE	M	14	(1)	
Ledio CAPO	G	5		
Helidon ÇOBANI	A	8	(2)	
Jeton ÇUBRELI	A	12	(1)	3
Leonard FEJZULLAHU	M	12	(18)	1
Arben JAHIQI	M	24	(4)	3
Julian KOLIÇI	D	19	(3)	
Ardian MUÇA	D	17	(1)	
Taulant MUHAJ	M	15	(8)	1
Robert NUREDINI	D	20		
POÇI	D	12	(10)	
Spartak RESULI	A	7		
Vaske RUKO	M	15	(12)	5
Arben SINANI	G	28		1
Kujtim ZENA	A	18	(5)	
Alket ZEQO	A	27	(1)	16

LEAGUE RESULTS 1995/96

02/09/95	Besëlidhja Lezhë	H	3-0	Basholli, Bare, Fejzullahu
09/09/95	Olimpik Tiranë	A	0-2	
16/09/95	Albpetrol Patos	H	0-0	
23/09/95	Besa Kavajë	A	2-2	Zeqo, Jahiqi
30/09/95	Vllaznia Shkodër	A	0-1	
11/10/95	Flamurtari Vlorë	H	0-1	
14/10/95	Teuta Durrës	A	1-1	Bare
21/10/95	Laçi	H	0-0	
28/10/95	Partizani Tiranë	A	1-6	Bare
04/11/95	Elbasani	H	3-1	Bare 2, Basholli
11/11/95	Sopoti Librazhd	A	0-1	
18/11/95	Shqiponja Gjirokastër	H	2-1	Zeqo 2
25/11/95	Tirana	H	2-1	Bare, Zeqo
02/12/95	Skënderbeu Korçë	A	1-2	Zeqo
09/12/95	Shkumbini Peqin	H	7-1	Jahiqi, Zeqo 2, Basholli, Ruko 2, Bare
16/12/95	Kastrioti	A	2-0	(w/o)
23/12/95	Tomori Berat	H	1-1	Zeqo
03/02/96	Besëlidhja Lezhë	A	2-0	Çubreli, Jahiqi
10/02/96	Olimpik Tiranë	H	1-0	Ruko
17/02/96	Albpetrol Patos	A	0-0	
24/02/96	Besa Kavajë	H	1-1	Ruko
02/03/96	Vllaznia Shkodër	H	2-2	Bita (p), Zeqo
09/03/96	Flamurtari Vlorë	A	0-3	
16/03/96	Teuta Durrës	H	1-1	Çubreli
25/03/96	Laçi	A	2-3	Muhaj, Sinani (p)
27/03/96	Partizani Tiranë	H	0-1	
30/03/96	Elbasani	A	1-2	Çubreli
06/04/96	Sopoti Librazhd	H	3-2	Ruko, Bare, Zeqo
13/04/96	Shqiponja Gjirokastër	A	3-1	Zeqo, Bare, og
17/04/96	Tirana	A	0-2	
20/04/96	Skënderbeu Korçë	H	0-1	
27/04/96	Shkumbini Peqin	A	0-3	
04/05/96	Kastrioti	H	2-0	Zeqo 2
08/05/96	Tomori Berat	A	3-1	Zeqo 3

BESA KAVAJË

CLUB DIRECTORY

Klubi sportiv Besa
Rruga Vangjel Thanasi, nr.7
Kavajë
tel - 341
Year of Formation - 1925
President - Taip Dedej
Secretary - Bujar Pagria
Coach - Azem Mullaliu
Stadium - Besa (10,000)

APPEARANCES 95/96

	P	Ap	(s)	Gls
Neritan BAJAZITI	A		(3)	
Ilir BITURKU	M	19	(6)	1
Hasan ÇIKALLESHI	A	10	(2)	
Perparim DAIU	D	29		5
Mirazh DEKAVELLI	M	3	(7)	
Ilir DOKA	A		(5)	
Artan DUKA	M	9	(15)	
Bajram FRAHOLLI	M	32		3
Romeo HAXHIAJ	M	23	(2)	3
Elvis HUSHI	D	18	(3)	
Lulzim HUSHI	D	30		
Gentjan KAJA	M	4	(2)	
Dritan KAPIDANI	D	30		2
Gazmend KARRIQI	G	16		
Abdyl KURIU	M	30	(1)	7
Sokol PRENGA	M	14		2
Artur QERROLLI	D	33		
Altin RRICA	A	26	(4)	4
Arben TELAKU	G	17	(2)	
Elvis XHAFA	M	19	(4)	1
Elorenc XHINANI	A	1	(2)	
Shkelzen YPI	A		(13)	

LEAGUE RESULTS 1995/96

02/09/95	Flamurtari Vlorë	H	1-0	Biturku
09/09/95	Tirana	A	0-1	
16/09/95	Shqiponja Gjirokastër	A	0-0	
23/09/95	Apolonia Fier	H	2-2	og, Fraholli
30/09/95	Laçi	A	1-0	Prenga
11/10/95	Shkumbini Peqin	H	1-0	Rrica
14/10/95	Vllaznia Shkodër	A	0-0	
21/10/95	Tomori Berat	H	2-1	Xhafa, Daiu
28/10/95	Elbasani	A	0-1	
04/11/95	Partizani Tiranë	H	2-0	Prenga (p), Kuriu
11/11/95	Teuta Durrës	A	0-2	
18/11/95	Albpetrol Patos	H	1-0	Daiu
25/11/95	Olimpik Tiranë	A	1-2	Daiu (p)
02/12/95	Besëlidhja Lezhë	H	4-0	Kuriu 3, Kapidani
09/12/95	Sopoti Librazhd	H	0-0	
16/12/95	Skënderbeu Korçë	A	1-0	Haxhiaj
23/12/95	Kastrioti	H	2-0	Rrica, Haxhiaj
03/02/96	Flamurtari Vlorë	A	2-3	Kuriu, Haxhiaj
10/02/96	Tirana	H	1-0	Kapidani
17/02/96	Shqiponja Gjirokastër	H	0-1	
24/02/96	Apolonia Fier	A	1-1	Daiu
02/03/96	Laçi	H	1-0	Rrica
09/03/96	Shkumbini Peqin	A	0-2	
16/03/96	Vllaznia Shkodër	H	2-2	Fraholli 2
23/03/96	Tomori Berat	A	0-1	
27/03/96	Elbasani	H	2-1	Daiu, Kuriu
30/03/96	Partizani Tiranë	A	0-0	
06/04/96	Teuta Durrës	H	0-0	
13/04/96	Albpetrol Patos	A	0-3	
17/04/96	Olimpik Tiranë	H	0-1	
20/04/96	Besëlidhja Lezhë	A	1-3	Rrica
27/04/96	Sopoti Librazhd	A	1-1	Kuriu
04/05/96	Skënderbeu Korçë	H	0-1	
08/05/96	Kastrioti	A	0-2	(w/o)

BESËLIDHJA LEZHË

CLUB DIRECTORY

Klubi sportiv Besëlidhja
Lagjja Besëlidhja, nr.54
Lezhë
tel - 255
Year of Formation - 1936
President - Leke Miraj
Secretary - Nikolin Lorenci
Coach - Paulin Deda; Taip Piraniqi
Stadium - Besëlidhja (5,000)

APPEARANCES 95/96

	P	Ap	(s)	Gls
Toulant BRAHMI	A	11	(6)	
Kliton ÇAÇI	M	17	(3)	3
Shkelqim FRASHERI	D	10	(3)	
Juljan GJELOSHI	G	28		3
Ardian GJERGJI	D	9	(2)	3
Valentin GJETJA	D	30		
Vladimir GJUZI	D	11	(3)	
Gentian HASA	D	31		2
Gezim HASKU	G	6		
Bujar HAXHIA	M	4	(4)	
Hasan HOXHA	M	24	(8)	5
Agim IBRO	M	10	(3)	1
Shkelqim JUSHI	M	3	(12)	2
Behar KALAJ	M	13		
Eduard KASTRATI	A	17	(5)	1
Ilir KEÇI	A	11		
Shkelzen KEÇI	M	15	(15)	
Saimir KOLA	A	13		
Bernard PALOKA	D	22		
Edi PERLOSHI	A	12	(11)	
Julian PERLOSHI	A		(1)	
Leonand PERLOSHI	M	7	(2)	
Lulzim PJETRUSHI	A	2	(10)	
Taulant SALIU	M	20		1
Refail SULA	M	21	(4)	3
Atin VESELI	M	8	(2)	
Roland ZEQIRI	A	19	(4)	

LEAGUE RESULTS 1995/96

Date	Opponent	H/A	Score	Scorers
03/09/95	Apolonia Fier	A	0-3	
09/09/95	Partizani Tiranë	H	1-0	Gjeloshi
16/09/95	Skënderbeu Korçë	A	1-2	Saliu
23/09/95	Shqiponja Gjirokastër	H	0-1	
30/09/95	Kastrioti	A	0-1	
11/10/95	Tomori Berat	H	1-0	Çaçi
14/10/95	Tirana	A	0-4	
21/10/95	Teuta Durrës	H	1-0	Sula
28/10/95	Albpetrol Patos	A	1-1	Hoxha
04/11/95	Flamurtari Vlorë	H	0-0	
11/11/95	Olimpik Tiranë	H	0-1	
18/11/95	Laçi	A	1-1	Hoxha
25/11/95	Sopoti Librazhd	H	1-1	Hoxha
02/12/95	Besa Kavajë	A	0-4	
09/12/95	Elbasani	H	1-0	Hasa
16/12/95	Shkumbini Peqin	A	0-0	
23/12/95	Vllaznia Shkodër	H	0-0	
03/02/96	Apolonia Fier	H	0-2	
10/02/96	Partizani Tiranë	A	0-0	
17/02/96	Skënderbeu Korçë	H	2-0	Çaçi, Gjeloshi (p)
24/02/96	Shqiponja Gjirokastër	A	0-1	
02/03/96	Kastrioti	H	1-0	Hoxha
09/03/96	Tomori Berat	A	1-1	Gjergji
16/03/96	Tirana	H	0-1	
23/03/96	Teuta Durrës	A	0-1	
27/03/96	Albpetrol Patos	H	2-0	Gjergji, Çaçi
30/03/96	Flamurtari Vlorë	A	0-1	
06/04/96	Olimpik Tiranë	A	1-1	Sula
13/04/96	Laçi	H	0-1	
17/04/96	Sopoti Librazhd	A	0-1	
20/04/96	Besa Kavajë	H	3-1	Kastrati, Gjergji, Jushi
27/04/96	Elbasani	A	0-2	
04/05/96	Shkumbini Peqin	H	5-4	Hoxha, Jushi, Gjeloshi (p), Hasa, Sula
08/05/96	Vllaznia Shkodër	A	1-4	Ibro (p)

ELBASANI

CLUB DIRECTORY

Klubi sportiv Elbasani
Rruga Qemal Stafa, nr. 25
Elbasan
tel - (545) 2146
Year of Formation - 1924
President - vacant
Secretary - Xhevahir Taushani
Coach - Dashamir Stringa; Astrit Sejdini
Stadium - Elbasani (11,000)

MAJOR HONOURS
League Championship - (1) 1984.
Domestic Cup - (2) 1975, 1992.

APPEARANCES 95/96

	P	Ap	(s)	Gls
Taulant BAKIU	D	18	(3)	
Alban BALLIU	D	14	(5)	
Elton CENA	M	23	(1)	3
Klevis DALIPI	M	26	(1)	3
Bardhyl DOSKU	G	27		
Ilirjan FILJA	M	33		1
Isuf IBERSHIMI	M	27	(4)	5
Hekuran JAKUPI	A	32		13
Klevis JANI	M	2	(7)	
Ilirjan LUTAJ	D	22	(4)	
Bujar MUÇA	M	11		1
Aurel MUKA	M	18	(8)	2
Oltion OSMANI	A	30		5
Arjan PISHA	D	32		
Ilir QORRI	M	28	(1)	1
Armand SHUTERIQI	A	13	(9)	1
Blendi SUVARIA	G	7	(2)	
Vladimir TAFANI	A	8	(5)	
Florind VATA	M	2	(1)	
Elton VERÇANI	A	1	(5)	

LEAGUE RESULTS 1995/96

02/09/95	Shqiponja Gjirokastër	A	0-0	
09/09/95	Shkumbini Peqin	H	0-0	
16/09/95	Partizani Tiranë	A	2-0	Cena, Jakupi
23/09/95	Vllaznia Shkodër	H	0-1	
30/09/95	Albpetrol Patos	H	1-0	Osmani (p)
11/10/95	Skënderbeu Korçë	A	0-2	
14/10/95	Sopoti Librazhd	H	1-1	Ibershimi
21/10/95	Olimpik Tiranë	A	0-3	
28/10/95	Besa Kavajë	H	1-0	Muka
04/11/95	Apolonia Fier	A	1-3	Muka
11/11/95	Kastrioti	H	1-0	Shuteriqi
18/11/95	Tirana	A	1-2	Dalipi
25/11/95	Flamurtari Vlorë	A	1-2	Osmani
02/12/95	Tomori Berat	H	2-2	Osmani (p), Jakupi
09/12/95	Besëlidhja Lezhë	A	0-1	
16/12/95	Teuta Durrës	H	0-0	
23/12/95	Laçi	A	1-4	Ibershimi
03/02/96	Shqiponja Gjirokastër	H	2-0	Jakupi, Ibershimi
10/02/96	Shkumbini Peqin	A	0-1	
17/02/96	Partizani Tiranë	H	0-0	
24/02/96	Vllaznia Shkodër	A	1-2	Ibershimi
02/03/96	Albpetrol Patos	A	0-1	
09/03/96	Skënderbeu Korçë	H	1-0	Dalipi
16/03/96	Sopoti Librazhd	A	1-1	Jakupi
23/03/96	Olimpik Tiranë	H	2-2	Cena, Ibershimi
27/03/96	Besa Kavajë	A	1-2	Jakupi
30/03/96	Apolonia Fier	H	2-1	Osmani (p), Cena
06/04/96	Kastrioti	A	1-1	Dalipi
13/04/96	Tirana	H	0-0	
17/04/96	Flamurtari Vlorë	H	3-0	Jakupi 3
20/04/96	Tomori Berat	A	0-2	
27/04/96	Besëlidhja Lezhë	H	2-0	Osmani (p), Jakupi
04/05/96	Teuta Durrës	A	1-2	Jakupi
08/05/96	Laçi	H	6-5	Jakupi 3, Qorri, Filja, Muça

FLAMURTARI VLORË

CLUB DIRECTORY

Klubi sportiv Flamurtari
Rruga Perlat Rexhëpi, nr.41
Vlorë
tel - (63) 25567
Year of Formation - 1923
President - Shkelqim Selami
Secretary - Skënder Ibrahimi
Coach - Bejkush Birçe
Stadium - Flamurtari (15,000)

MAJOR HONOURS

League Championship - (1) 1991.
Domestic Cup - (2) 1985, 1988.

APPEARANCES 95/96

	P	Ap	(s)	Gls
Dritan ALIAJ	A	7	(10)	2
Anesti ARAPI	G	34		
Roland BAJRAMI	M	9	(8)	
Ardian BEHARI	D	25	(2)	
Alban BUSHI	A	10		5
Geri ÇIPI	D	31		2
Viktor DAULLJA	M	31		4
Jorgaq DIAMANTI	A	7	(6)	1
Johan DRIZA	D	20	(3)	2
Artur DURO	D	9	(1)	
Ervin FAKAJ	M	26		4
Vasillaq GJONÇE	A	5	(4)	
Latif GJONDEDA	M	5		
Ferd HAXHIU	M	12	(2)	5
Ardian LIKA	M	4	(6)	1
Aurel LLANAJ	D		(2)	
Eqerem MEMUSHI	M	12		1
Sokol MUHO	M	3	(2)	
Devi MUKA	M	25	(1)	3
Erion PALI	M		(2)	
Leonard PERLOSHI	A	6		1
Dritan RESULI	A	13	(2)	1
Driner REXHEPI	M	6	(4)	
Dritan SADEDINI	D	15		1
Rrapo TANO	D	30		
Anesti VITO	A	28		7
Fjodor XHAFA	M	1	(5)	

LEAGUE RESULTS 1995/96

Date	Opponent	H/A	Score	Scorers
02/09/95	Besa Kavajë	A	0-1	
09/09/95	Vllaznia Shkodër	H	3-0	Haxhiu, Vito, Driza
16/09/95	Shkumbini Peqin	A	2-2	Haxhiu 2
23/09/95	Tomori Berat	H	1-0	Vito
30/09/95	Teuta Durrës	H	0-1	
11/10/95	Apolonia Fier	A	1-0	Çipi
14/10/95	Albpetrol Patos	H	1-0	Aliaj
21/10/95	Shqiponja Gjirokastër	A	1-0	Haxhiu
28/10/95	Laçi	H	3-1	Vito, Diamanti, Fakaj
04/11/95	Besëlidhja Lezhë	A	0-0	
11/11/95	Skënderbeu Korçë	H	5-1	Fakaj, og, Daullja, Aliaj, Çipi
18/11/95	Olimpik Tiranë	A	0-2	
25/11/95	Elbasani	H	2-1	Memushi, Lika
02/12/95	Tirana	A	0-3	
09/12/95	Kastrioti	H	0-1	
16/12/95	Partizani Tiranë	A	0-0	
23/12/95	Sopoti Librazhd	H	1-2	Haxhiu
03/02/96	Besa Kavajë	H	3-2	Perloshi, Daullja, Muka
10/02/96	Vllaznia Shkodër	A	2-1	Vito, Daullja
17/02/96	Shkumbini Peqin	H	1-0	Driza
24/02/96	Tomori Berat	A	0-2	
02/03/96	Teuta Durrës	A	1-3	Muka
09/03/96	Apolonia Fier	H	3-0	Fakaj (p), Resuli, Muka
16/03/96	Albpetrol Patos	A	0-0	
23/03/96	Shqiponja Gjirokastër	H	3-0	Bushi 2 (1p), Daullja
27/03/96	Laçi	A	0-4	
30/03/96	Besëlidhja Lezhë	H	1-0	Fakaj
06/04/96	Skënderbeu Korçë	A	1-0	Bushi
13/04/96	Olimpik Tiranë	H	0-0	
17/04/96	Elbasani	A	0-3	
20/04/96	Tirana	H	2-0	Bushi, Vito
27/04/96	Kastrioti	A	0-1	
04/05/96	Partizani Tiranë	H	0-0	
08/05/96	Sopoti Librazhd	A	5-4	Vito 2, Bushi, Sadedini, og

KASTRIOTI KRUJË

CLUB DIRECTORY

Klubi sportiv Kastrioti
Komiteti Ekzekutiv
Krujë
tel - 288
Year of Formation - 1946
Secretary - Astrit Merlika
Coach - Gjergj Mone; Spartak Qose
Stadium - Kastrioti (6,500)

APPEARANCES 95/96

	P	Ap	(s)	Gls
Armand AGAI	A	5	(10)	
Sinan BARDHI	M	5		2
Artan BELA	M	3	(3)	
Shyqyri BELTOJA	M	2	(3)	
Artan ÇOPANI	D	6	(7)	
Pellumb DEMIRI	A	24	(1)	3
Luan DOBROZI	A	5	(7)	
Shaban DOLLAKU	D	16	(1)	1
Mahir HALILI	M	15	(1)	4
Besnik HASA	D	29	(1)	2
Artan HOXHA	D	29		
Devis ISMAILI	M	16		
Shkelzen KEÇI	M	11	(2)	
Thoma KOKURI	G	32	(1)	
Saimir KOLA	D	14		1
Kujtim LEKA	G	1	(1)	
Ilir LIMANAJ	D	16	(7)	
Saimir MALOKU	M	18	(3)	6
Ramazan NDREU	D	14		
Xheladin NDREU	A	12	(2)	
Saimir PATUSHI	M	17	(2)	3
Spartak QOSJA	A	28	(1)	3
Shkelzen RUSTAMI	M	25		1
Ilir SEFERI	M	9	(4)	
Ilir TEMA	M	10	(3)	
Luljan THAÇI	M	1	(1)	

LEAGUE RESULTS 1995/96

Date	Opponent	H/A	Score	Scorers
02/09/95	Partizani Tiranë	A	2-4	Patushi, Bardhi
09/09/95	Laçi	H	2-0	Maloku, Dollaku (p)
16/09/95	Olimpik Tiranë	H	1-1	Maloku
23/09/95	Teuta Durrës	A	2-4	Demiri, Qosja
30/09/95	Besëlidhja Lezhë	H	1-0	Hasa
11/10/95	Sopoti Librazhd	A	1-2	Maloku
14/10/95	Shkumbini Peqin	H	0-0	
21/10/95	Skënderbeu Korçë	A	0-1	
28/10/95	Tirana	A	1-1	Maloku
04/11/95	Vllaznia Shkodër	H	2-2	Demiri, Qosja
11/11/95	Elbasani	A	0-1	
18/11/95	Tomori Berat	H	2-1	Patushi 2
25/11/95	Albpetrol Patos	A	0-1	
02/12/95	Shqiponja Gjirokastër	H	1-0	Bardhi
09/12/95	Flamurtari Vlorë	A	1-0	Qosja
16/12/95	Apolonia Fier	H	0-2	(w/o)
23/12/95	Besa Kavajë	A	0-2	
03/02/96	Partizani Tiranë	H	0-1	
10/02/96	Laçi	A	1-2	og
17/02/96	Olimpik Tiranë	A	0-1	
24/02/96	Teuta Durrës	H	2-1	Maloku, Halili
02/03/96	Besëlidhja Lezhë	A	0-1	
09/03/96	Sopoti Librazhd	H	0-2	
16/03/96	Shkumbini Peqin	A	1-2	Maloku
23/03/96	Skënderbeu Korçë	H	1-0	Demiri
27/03/96	Tirana	H	0-0	
30/03/96	Vllaznia Shkodër	A	2-1	Halili
06/04/96	Elbasani	H	1-1	Kola
13/04/96	Tomori Berat	A	1-2	Halili
17/04/96	Albpetrol Patos	H	2-1	og, Halili
20/04/96	Shqiponja Gjirokastër	A	1-0	Rustami
27/04/96	Flamurtari Vlorë	H	1-0	Hasa
04/05/96	Apolonia Fier	A	0-2	
08/05/96	Besa Kavajë	H	2-0	(w/o)

LAÇI

CLUB DIRECTORY

Klubi sportiv Laçi
Laç
tel - 312
Year of Formation - 1960
President - Ram Geci
Secretary - Shkelqim Hoxha
Coach - Astrit Maçi
Stadium - Laçi (4,000)

APPEARANCES 95/96

	P	Ap	(s)	Gls
Arian BASHA	G	18		
Artan ÇIÇIKU	M	30	(2)	12
Altin ÇUKO	A	15	(1)	16
Artan DELIU	M	24	(2)	1
Eriton KASMI	G	13		
Pjerin MARTINI	G	3		
Sabah MICI	A	31		2
Alfred MJEDA	M	22	(6)	7
Krenar MUÇA	M	1	(3)	
Alban NOGA	M	16		
Safet OSJA	D	31		
Artan PALOKA	D	12	(4)	
Kastriot RAMA	M	2	(2)	
Sokol SHLLAKU	D	31		1
Vladimir STANI	M	11	(1)	
Aleksander TARE	M	24		5
Bashkim TOSKA	A	16		
Ilir TUÇI	A	4	(6)	
Artur TUNA	A	1	(1)	
Roland TUNA	D	31	(1)	1
Saimir URETANI	A	6	(7)	
Astrit XHELA	M	16	(4)	3
Pellumb YZEIRI	A	16		1

LEAGUE RESULTS 1995/96

02/09/95	Tirana	H	2-3	Mjeda, Tare
09/09/95	Kastrioti	A	0-2	
16/09/95	Teuta Durrës	H	3-3	Shllaku, Mjeda, Çiçiku
23/09/95	Olimpik Tiranë	A	0-4	
30/09/95	Besa Kavajë	H	0-1	
11/10/95	Albpetrol Patos	A	1-2	Deliu
14/10/95	Shqiponja Gjirokastër	H	1-0	Xhela
21/10/95	Apolonia Fier	A	0-0	
28/10/95	Flamurtari Vlorë	A	1-3	Mici
04/11/95	Sopoti Librazhd	H	2-0	Çiçiku, Xhela (p)
11/11/95	Tomori Berat	A	0-2	
18/11/95	Besëlidhja Lezhë	H	1-1	Mici
25/11/95	Skënderbeu Korçë	H	1-0	Çiçiku (p)
02/12/95	Shkumbini Peqin	A	1-2	Mjeda
09/12/95	Partizani Tiranë	H	3-0	Çiçiku 2, Mjeda
12/12/95	Vllaznia Shkodër	A	1-2	Mjeda
23/12/95	Elbasani	H	4-1	Mjeda, Çiçiku, Tare 2
03/02/96	Tirana	A	0-2	
10/02/96	Kastrioti	H	2-1	Çuko 2
17/02/96	Teuta Durrës	A	0-3	
24/02/96	Olimpik Tiranë	H	2-0	Tare, Çuko
02/03/96	Besa Kavajë	A	0-1	
09/03/96	Albpetrol Patos	H	0-0	
16/03/96	Shqiponja Gjirokastër	A	0-1	
23/03/96	Apolonia Fier	H	3-2	Çiçiku, Tare, Çuko
27/03/96	Flamurtari Vlorë	H	4-0	Tuna R., Çiçiku, Çuko 2 (1p)
30/03/96	Sopoti Librazhd	A	0-2	
06/04/96	Tomori Berat	H	3-1	Çuko 2, Çiçiku
13/04/96	Besëlidhja Lezhë	A	1-0	Çuko
17/04/96	Skënderbeu Korçë	A	1-2	Çiçiku
20/04/96	Shkumbini Peqin	H	5-3	Çiçiku 2 (1p), Yzeiri, Mjeda, Xhela
27/04/96	Partizani Tiranë	A	0-3	
04/05/96	Vllaznia Shkodër	H	2-0	Çuko 2
08/05/96	Elbasani	A	5-6	Çuko 5

OLIMPIK TIRANË

CLUB DIRECTORY

Klubi sportiv Olimpik
Rruga Dervish Hima, nr.30
Tiranë
tel - (42) 23000
Year of Formation - 1950
President - Ferdinand Ibrahimi
Secretary - Gani Xhafa
Coach - Faruk Sejdini
Stadium - Olimpik (12,500)

MAJOR HONOURS

League Championship - (15) 1950, 1951, 1952, 1953, 1955, 1956, 1960, 1967, 1973, 1975, 1976, 1977, 1980, 1986, 1990.
Domestic Cup - (12)
1950, 1951, 1952, 1953, 1954, 1960, 1971, 1974, 1978, 1982, 1989, 1990.

APPEARANCES 95/96

	P	Ap	(s)	Gls
Edmond AHMETAJ	A	21	(2)	
Eduard AHMETAJ	M	10	(8)	4
Edmond DALIPI	M	12	(1)	
Gentian HAJDARI	M	1	(5)	
Blendi HAXHIA	M	31	(1)	
Ilir KURTI	D	30	(1)	
Genc MAHMUTAJ	A	17	(11)	4
Erion MATRAKU	M	14	(6)	
Artan MERGJYSHI	M	34		
Artan NIKA	G	30		
Arjan PEÇO	M	31		3
Luan PINARI	A	27	(2)	
Sokol RAMBI	M	11	(7)	4
Artan RREDHAJ	G	4	(4)	
Gazmend SALLAKU	D	26		2
Arben TOLE	D	17	(4)	3
Edmond VODA	M	6	(3)	
Artan VOKSHI	M	7	(5)	
Agron XHAFA	A	21	(3)	8
Fatjon YMERI	M	11	(6)	6
Roland ZAJMI	A	13	(1)	8

LEAGUE RESULTS 1995/96

Date	Opponent	H/A	Score	Scorers
02/09/95	Skënderbeu Korçë	A	0-3	
09/09/95	Apolonia Fier	H	2-0	Zajmi, Rambi
16/09/95	Kastrioti	A	1-1	Xhafa
23/09/95	Laçi	H	4-0	Xhafa, Zajmi, Sallaku, Rambi
30/09/95	Shqiponja Gjirokastër	A	2-0	Xhafa, Zajmi
11/10/95	Vllaznia Shkodër	H	0-0	
14/10/95	Tomori Berat	A	1-2	Zajmi
21/10/95	Elbasani	H	3-0	Xhafa 2, Zajmi
28/10/95	Teuta Durrës	A	0-3	
04/11/95	Albpetrol Patos	H	5-1	Rambi, Zajmi 2, Ymeri 2
11/11/95	Besëlidhja Lezhë	A	1-0	Zajmi
18/11/95	Flamurtari Vlorë	H	2-0	Ahmetaj Edu., Peço
25/11/95	Besa Kavajë	H	2-1	Ahmetaj Edu. 2
02/12/95	Partizani Tiranë	A	0-1	
09/12/95	Tirana	H	0-1	
16/12/95	Sopoti Librazhd	A	0-0	
23/12/95	Shkumbini Peqin	H	1-0	Xhafa
03/02/96	Skënderbeu Korçë	H	4-2	Ymeri, Xhafa 2, Mahmutaj
10/02/96	Apolonia Fier	A	0-1	
17/02/96	Kastrioti	H	1-0	Ymeri
24/02/96	Laçi	A	0-2	
02/03/96	Shqiponja Gjirokastër	H	0-0	
09/03/96	Vllaznia Shkodër	A	0-1	
16/03/96	Tomori Berat	H	1-0	Tole
23/03/96	Elbasani	A	2-2	Peço, Tole
27/03/96	Teuta Durrës	H	0-0	
30/03/96	Albpetrol Patos	A	0-1	
06/04/96	Besëlidhja Lezhë	H	1-1	Rambi
13/04/96	Flamurtari Vlorë	A	0-0	
17/04/96	Besa Kavajë	A	1-0	Peço
20/04/96	Partizani Tiranë	H	2-1	Ahmetaj Edu., Mahmutaj
27/04/96	Tirana	A	1-3	Mahmutaj
04/05/96	Sopoti Librazhd	H	5-0	Ymeri 2, Mahmutaj, Sallaku, Tole
08/05/96	Shkumbini Peqin	A	0-3	

PARTIZANI TIRANË

CLUB DIRECTORY

Klubi sportiv Partizani
Rruga Frosina Plaku, nr.31
Tiranë
tel - (42) 23933
Year of Formation - 1946
President - Antonio De Simone
Secretary - Bujar Labinoti
Coach - Hasan Lika; Ramadan Shehu; Sulejman Starova
Stadium - Qemal Stafa (20,000)

MAJOR HONOURS

League Championship - (15) 1947, 1948, 1949, 1954, 1957, 1958, 1959, 1961, 1963, 1964, 1971, 1979, 1981, 1987, 1993.
Domestic Cup - (13)
1948, 1949, 1957, 1958, 1961, 1964, 1966, 1968, 1970, 1973, 1980, 1991, 1993.

APPEARANCES 95/96

	P	Ap	(s)	Gls
Dritan BAHOLLI	M	30	(1)	3
Artan BANO	M	13		
Arjan BEQA	G	18		
Erion BOGDANI	A	15	(5)	2
Skerdilajd CURRI	A	18	(9)	6
Armand DAMO	D	9	(6)	1
Skender GEGA	D	3		1
Adriatik GJONI	M	20		2
Elton HASANI	A		(2)	
Redi JUPI	M	17		1
Edmond KODRA	M	13	(10)	4
Elton MARINI	M	13	(10)	5
Arben MILORI	M	29		5
Perlat MUSTA	G	16		
Denis NDOCI	M	9	(7)	
Andrea NIKOLLA	M	9	(1)	5
Ilir SHULKU	D	22		1
Alban TAFAJ	D	20	(6)	1
Afrim TOLE	D	29		
Amarildo XHEKA	M	12	(1)	
Arben YMERI	D	17	(6)	2
Pellumb YZEIRI	D	16		
Roland ZAJMI	A	16		3
Kreshnik ZHEGA	A	10	(4)	1

LEAGUE RESULTS 1995/96

02/09/95	Kastrioti	H	4-2	Kodra 2, Damo, Baholli
09/09/95	Besëlidhja Lezhë	A	0-1	
16/09/95	Elbasani	H	0-2	
23/09/95	Tirana	A	2-1	Milori 2
30/09/95	Sopoti Librazhd	H	3-1	Gega, Baholli, Shulku (p)
11/10/95	Shqiponja Gjirokastër	A	2-1	Nikolla, Ymeri
14/10/95	Skënderbeu Korçë	H	3-0	Nikolla, Milori, Marini
21/10/95	Albpetrol Patos	A	0-0	
28/10/95	Apolonia Fier	H	6-1	Nikolla 3, Milori, Kodra, Curri
04/11/95	Besa Kavajë	A	0-2	
11/11/95	Vllaznia Shkodër	H	0-0	
18/11/95	Shkumbini Peqin	A	1-0	Kodra
25/11/95	Tomori Berat	A	0-1	
02/12/95	Olimpik Tiranë	H	1-0	Zhega
09/12/95	Laçi	A	0-3	
16/12/95	Flamurtari Vlorë	H	0-0	
23/12/95	Teuta Durrës	A	0-1	
03/02/96	Kastrioti	A	1-0	Zajmi
10/02/96	Besëlidhja Lezhë	H	0-0	
17/02/96	Elbasani	A	0-0	
24/02/96	Tirana	H	0-2	
02/03/96	Sopoti Librazhd	A	0-0	
09/03/96	Shqiponja Gjirokastër	H	3-1	Milori, Zajmi, Curri
16/03/96	Skënderbeu Korçë	A	0-1	
23/03/96	Albpetrol Patos	H	6-0	Baholli, Ymeri, Gjoni, Marini, Curri, Jupi
27/03/96	Apolonia Fier	A	1-0	Zajmi
30/03/96	Besa Kavajë	H	0-0	
06/04/96	Vllaznia Shkodër	A	0-0	
13/04/96	Shkumbini Peqin	H	3-1	Bogdani, Gjoni, Marini
17/04/96	Tomori Berat	H	2-1	Curri, Marini
20/04/96	Olimpik Tiranë	A	1-2	Marini
27/04/96	Laçi	H	3-0	Bogdani, Tafaj, Curri
04/05/96	Flamurtari Vlorë	A	0-0	
08/05/96	Teuta Durrës	H	1-0	Curri

SHKUMBINI PEQIN

CLUB DIRECTORY

Klubi sportiv Shkumbini
Pranë Bashkisë
Peqin
tel - 301
Year of Formation - 1951
Presient - vacant
Sercretary - Hasan Mezja
Coach - Shyqyri Rreli; Vasil Bici
Stadium - Peqin (4,000)

APPEARANCES 95/96

	P	Ap	(s)	Gls
Adnan BELBA	D	3	(2)	
Bujar BIBA	A	1	(2)	
Ferdinand BILALI	M	28		3
Sokol BRANICA	A	9	(1)	1
Madrid ÇANAKU	M	13	(1)	1
Klodian DERVISHI	D	27		1
Drinush ELEZI	D	26	(1)	5
Klodian ELEZI	G	19		
Gerti HAXHIU	M	9		2
Astrit ISAI	D	7	(5)	
Maksim KAJA	A	9	(3)	
Shpetim KATESHI	M	31	(1)	19
Kujtim KRYEMADHI	G	14	(4)	
Florian LLUCA	M	9	(4)	
Bukurosh MAÇI	M	9	(6)	
Gugash MAGANI	M	32		3
Ferdinand MINOLI	D	2	(8)	
Bujar MUÇA	M	10	(3)	1
Afrim MYFTARI	A	24	(2)	1
Elton NAÇI	M	2	(3)	
Astrit NEXHA	A	27	(1)	3
Gentian STOJKU	A	14	(1)	3
Kastriot TOSKU	D	30		1
Shkelzen XHIHANI	D	8	(4)	

LEAGUE RESULTS 1995/96

02/09/95	Sopoti Librazhd	H	2-1	Kateshi, Stojku
09/09/95	Elbasani	A	0-0	
16/09/95	Flamurtari Vlorë	H	2-2	Stojku, Magani
23/09/95	Albpetrol Patos	A	2-1	Kateshi, Elezi D.
30/09/95	Skënderbeu Korçë	H	4-1	Nexha, Kateshi 2, Tosku
11/10/95	Besa Kavajë	A	0-1	
14/10/95	Kastrioti	A	0-0	
21/10/95	Vllaznia Shkodër	H	1-0	Elezi D.
28/10/95	Tomori Berat	A	1-1	Muça
04/11/95	Teuta Durrës	H	0-0	
11/11/95	Tirana	A	0-1	
18/11/95	Partizani Tiranë	H	0-1	
25/11/95	Shqiponja Gjirokastër	A	0-1	
02/12/95	Laçi	H	2-1	Kateshi 2
09/12/95	Apolonia Fier	A	1-7	Stojku
16/12/95	Besëlidhja Lezhë	H	0-0	
23/12/95	Olimpik Tiranë	A	0-1	
03/02/96	Sopoti Librazhd	A	0-0	
10/02/96	Elbasani	H	1-0	Nexha
17/02/96	Flamurtari Vlorë	A	0-1	
24/02/96	Albpetrol Patos	H	4-0	Elezi D. 2, Nexha, Haxhiu
02/03/96	Skënderbeu Korçë	A	0-2	(w/o)
09/03/96	Besa Kavajë	H	2-0	Bilali, Haxhiu (p)
16/03/96	Kastrioti	H	2-1	Myftari, Bilali (p)
23/03/96	Vllaznia Shkodër	A	0-0	
27/03/96	Tomori Berat	H	2-0	Elezi D., Branica
30/03/96	Teuta Durrës	A	1-2	Kateshi
06/04/96	Tirana	H	0-0	
13/04/96	Partizani Tiranë	A	1-3	Çanaku
17/04/96	Shqiponja Gjirokastër	H	3-1	Kateshi, Bilali, Magani
20/04/96	Laçi	A	3-5	Kateshi 2, Magani
27/04/96	Apolonia Fier	H	3-0	Kateshi 2 (1p), Dervishi
04/04/96	Besëlidhja Lezhë	A	4-5	Kateshi 4 (1p)
08/05/96	Olimpik Tiranë	H	3-0	Kateshi 3

SHQIPONJA GJIROKASTËR

CLUB DIRECTORY

Klubi sportiv Shqiponja
Rruga Çerçiz Topulli 17
Gjirokastër
tel - 213
Year of Formation - 1929
Secretary - Hito Hitaj
Coach - Mustafa Hysi
Stadium - Subi Bakiri (8,000)

APPEARANCES 95/96

	P	Ap	(s)	Gls
Aleko BURDHIMA	D	2	(2)	1
Arben ÇONI	D	23	(4)	1
Odise GRABOVA	D	29	(1)	1
Thanas GUXHO	M	4		
Altin HAXHI	D	28		7
Gentian HITAJ	M	14	(9)	3
Aurel KACI	A	31	(2)	1
Dritan KRISTIDHI	G	32		
Roland MIHO	M	28		
Nalton MUSTA	M	23	(3)	2
Neritan NOVI	M	21	(3)	2
Arian PUTO	G	2	(1)	
Lorenc RUSTI	A	1	(9)	
Kastriot SALARIA	M	25	(1)	
Melsi SEJDO	D	13	(8)	
Ilir SELIMI	M	27	(1)	
Admir SHEHU	M	1	(1)	
Arben SHEHU	A	28	(1)	16
Elton SINO	D	2	(4)	1
Altin XHUMBA	M	32		1
Andrea ZHDAVO	D	8	(9)	

LEAGUE RESULTS 1995/96

02/09/95	Elbasani	H	0-0	
09/09/95	Teuta Durrës	A	1-3	Haxhi
16/09/95	Besa Kavajë	H	0-0	
23/09/95	Besëlidhja Lezhë	A	1-0	Shehu Ar.
30/09/95	Olimpik Tiranë	H	0-2	
11/10/95	Partizani Tiranë	H	1-2	Shehu Ar.
14/10/95	Laçi	A	0-1	
21/10/95	Flamurtari Vlorë	H	0-1	
28/10/95	Sopoti Librazhd	A	2-4	Novi 2
04/11/95	Tomori Berat	H	3-0	Grabova, Shehu Ar. (p), Haxhi
11/11/95	Albpetrol Patos	A	2-0	Shehu Ar., Haxhi
18/11/95	Apolonia Fier	A	1-2	Hitaj
25/11/95	Shkumbini Peqin	H	1-0	Hitaj
02/12/95	Kastrioti	A	0-1	
09/12/95	Vllaznia Shkodër	H	2-0	Xhumba, Haxhi
16/12/95	Tirana	A	1-1	Haxhi
23/12/95	Skënderbeu Korçë	H	2-1	Kaci, Musta
03/02/96	Elbasani	A	0-2	
10/02/96	Teuta Durrës	H	0-0	
17/02/96	Besa Kavajë	A	1-0	Çoni
24/02/96	Besëlidhja Lezhë	H	1-0	Hitaj
02/03/96	Olimpik Tiranë	A	0-0	
09/03/96	Partizani Tiranë	A	1-3	Shehu Ar.
16/03/96	Laçi	H	1-0	Shehu Ar.
23/03/96	Flamurtari Vlorë	A	0-3	
27/03/96	Sopoti Librazhd	H	5-0	Musta, Shehu Ar. 4
30/03/96	Tomori Berat	A	1-2	Burdhima
06/04/96	Albpetrol Patos	H	4-1	Haxhi 2, Shehu Ar. 2
13/04/96	Apolonia Fier	H	1-3	Shehu Ar.
17/04/96	Shkumbini Peqin	A	1-3	Shehu Ar.
20/04/96	Kastrioti	H	0-1	
27/04/96	Vllaznia Shkodër	A	0-0	
04/05/96	Tirana	H	0-1	
08/05/96	Skënderbeu Korçë	A	3-5	Shehu Ar. 2, Sino

SKËNDERBEU KORÇË

CLUB DIRECTORY

Klubi sportiv Skënderbeu
Bardhyl Pojani L2 No.7
Korçë
tel - 2241
Year of Formation - 1926
President - Servet Peka
Secretary - Jani Kaçi
Coach - Edmond Gezdari
Stadium - Skënderbeu (10,000)

MAJOR HONOURS
League Championship - (1) 1933.

APPEARANCES 95/96

	P	Ap	(s)	Gls
Roland DEMBO	D	13	(8)	
Altin DRITA	D	31		
Festim FETOLLARI	M	29		1
Gentian GJERGO	G	4	(2)	
Olsi GJOKA	D	24	(2)	
Gazmend HOXHA	D	5	(4)	
KOLECI	M	6	(4)	
Gentian LIÇI	M	15		2
Ermal MERGJYSHI	G	14		
META	M		(2)	
Rigers QOSE	A	25	(5)	4
Devis RUÇO	D	23	(3)	1
Kastriot RUSTEMI	D	30		
Edvin SHAHOLLARI	M	22	(14)	
Roland SHEHU	D	30		6
Hektor SHKURTI	G	15		
Eltion SIMAKU	M	14		3
TIKO	M	5	(1)	1
Bledar VILA	A	26	(1)	3
Artan XHEDIKU	M	12	(9)	5
XHEKA	M	3	(2)	
Enkeleid ZYLO	A	17	(5)	8

LEAGUE RESULTS 1995/96

Date	Opponent	H/A	Score	Scorers
02/09/95	Olimpik Tiranë	H	3-0	Zylo, Liçi, Vila
09/09/95	Tomori Berat	A	1-1	Shehu
16/09/95	Besëlidhja Lezhë	H	2-1	Xhediku, Ruço
23/09/95	Sopoti Librazhd	A	0-1	
30/09/95	Shkumbini Peqin	A	1-4	Xhediku
11/10/95	Elbasani	H	2-0	Vila, Liçi
14/10/95	Partizani Tiranë	A	0-3	
21/10/95	Kastrioti	H	1-0	Vila
28/10/95	Vllaznia Shkodër	A	0-3	
04/11/95	Tirana	H	1-1	Qose
11/11/95	Flamurtari Vlorë	A	1-5	Qose
18/11/95	Teuta Durrës	H	0-1	
25/11/95	Laçi	A	0-1	
02/12/95	Apolonia Fier	H	2-1	Xhediku, Shehu
09/12/95	Albpetrol Patos	A	1-5	Simaku
16/12/95	Besa Kavajë	H	0-1	
23/12/95	Shqiponja Gjirokastër	A	1-2	Fetollari
03/02/96	Olimpik Tiranë	A	2-4	Simaku (p), Tiko
10/02/96	Tomori Berat	H	0-0	
17/02/96	Besëlidhja Lezhë	A	0-2	
24/02/96	Sopoti Librazhd	H	0-1	
02/03/96	Shkumbini Peqin	H	2-0	(w/o)
09/03/96	Elbasani	A	0-1	
16/03/96	Partizani Tiranë	H	1-0	Qose
23/03/96	Kastrioti	A	0-1	
27/03/96	Vllaznia Shkodër	H	1-0	Zylo
30/03/96	Tirana	A	1-3	Shehu (p)
06/04/96	Flamurtari Vlorë	H	0-1	
13/04/96	Teuta Durrës	A	1-3	Xhediku
17/04/96	Laçi	H	2-1	Shehu (p), Simaku
20/04/96	Apolonia Fier	A	1-0	Xhediku
27/04/96	Albpetrol Patos	H	3-1	Zylo, Qose, Shehu
04/05/96	Besa Kavajë	A	1-0	Zylo
08/05/96	Shqiponja Gjirokastër	H	5-3	Zylo 4, Shehu

SOPOTI LIBRAZHD

CLUB DIRECTORY

Klubi sportiv Sopoti
Prane Bashkirë
Librazhd
tel - 254
Year of Formation - 1948
President - Jovan Gugu
Coach - Luan Deliu
Stadium - Sopoti (3,000)

APPEARANCES 95/96

	P	Ap	(s)	Gls
Ferit ALLKJA	M	15		1
Erget BAKALLI	M	10	(7)	1
Bujar BORIÇI	D	23	(1)	
Luan BRASHA	M	30	(4)	14
Besnik ÇOTA	A	33		3
Besnik FACJA	A	3	(2)	
Gentian GRABOCKA	M	22		6
Elton HASANI	A	3	(6)	2
Albert HAXHIA	D	24		1
Besnik KOLA	D	32		2
Ardian KRYEMADHI	M	13	(14)	
MERAKU	G	2		
Erjon NOVAKU	M	22		1
Besnik POÇI	D	34		3
Arben RIRA	D	4	(4)	
Gezim RROCA	D	27	(4)	1
Kastriot SHAHINI	D	27		
Sajmir SHENGJERGJI	M	18	(8)	
Romeo VILA	G	32		

LEAGUE RESULTS 1995/96

02/09/95	Shkumbini Peqin	A	1-2	Grabocka
09/09/95	Albpetrol Patos	H	1-0	Kola (p)
16/09/95	Tomori Berat	A	0-1	
23/09/95	Skënderbeu Korçë	H	1-0	Çota (p)
30/09/95	Partizani Tiranë	A	1-3	Çota
11/10/95	Kastrioti	H	2-1	Brasha 2
14/10/95	Elbasani	A	1-1	Novaku
21/10/95	Tirana	H	0-1	
28/10/95	Shqiponja Gjirokastër	H	4-2	Allkja, Rroca, Çota, Brasha
04/11/95	Laçi	A	0-2	
11/11/95	Apolonia Fier	H	1-0	Brasha
18/11/95	Vllaznia Shkodër	A	0-2	
25/11/95	Besëlidhja Lezhë	A	1-1	Grabocka
02/12/95	Teuta Durrës	H	0-1	
09/12/95	Besa Kavajë	A	0-0	
16/12/95	Olimpik Tiranë	H	0-0	
23/12/95	Flamurtari Vlorë	A	2-1	Grabocka, Brasha
03/02/96	Shkumbini Peqin	H	0-0	
10/02/96	Albpetrol Patos	A	0-1	
17/02/96	Tomori Berat	H	4-1	Brasha 2, Grabocka, Poçi
24/02/96	Skënderbeu Korçë	A	1-0	Grabocka
02/03/96	Partizani Tiranë	H	0-0	
09/03/96	Kastrioti	A	2-0	Brasha, Grabocka
16/03/96	Elbasani	H	1-1	Brasha
23/03/96	Tirana	A	1-4	Poçi
27/03/96	Shqiponja Gjirokastër	A	0-5	
30/03/96	Laçi	H	2-0	Bakalli, Hasani
06/04/96	Apolonia Fier	A	2-3	Brasha, Hasani
13/04/96	Vllaznia Shkodër	H	0-0	
17/04/96	Besëlidhja Lezhë	H	1-0	Poçi
20/04/96	Teuta Durrës	A	1-3	Kola
27/04/96	Besa Kavajë	H	1-1	Haxhia
04/05/96	Olimpik Tiranë	A	0-5	
08/05/96	Flamurtari Vlorë	H	4-5	Brasha 4

TEUTA DURRËS

CLUB DIRECTORY

Klubi sportiv Teuta
Rruga Mujo Ulqinaku, nr.19
Durrës
tel - 2215
Year of Formation - 1925
President - Abdurrahim Sulimani
Secretary - Hektor Dervishi
Coach - Bashkim Koka
Stadium - Teuta (10,000)

MAJOR HONOURS
League Championship - (1) 1994.
Domestic Cup - (1) 1995.

APPEARANCES 95/96

	P	Ap	(s)	Gls
Ardian ABAZI	D	31		1
Ilir ALLIU	D	28	(1)	2
Gentjan BEGEJA	M	22	(4)	6
Ardian BUSHI	A	10	(18)	7
Gazmend ÇANAKU	M	1	(4)	
Ardian DASHI	A	25	(4)	4
Enkelejd DOBI	M	25	(2)	7
Indrit ESTREFI	M		(5)	
Mikel FURRXHI	D	30		3
Ardit GJONI	M		(1)	
Xhevair KAPLLANI	G	33		
Elton KOÇA	A	34		14
Artan KOKA	A	26	(1)	2
Fatos KUÇI	M	4	(5)	
Geg LLESHI	M	1		
Alban MEHMETI	M	23	(4)	
Nesti QENDRO	D	29	(3)	2
Kujtim SHTAMA	G	1	(1)	
Artan VILA	D	29	(1)	
Maringlen XHAI	M	22	(5)	1

LEAGUE RESULTS 1995/96

Date	Opponent	H/A	Score	Scorers
02/09/95	Albpetrol Patos	A	1-2	Abazi
09/09/95	Shqiponja Gjirokastër	H	3-1	Dobi, Koça, Bushi
16/09/95	Laçi	A	3-3	Dobi, Begeja 2
23/09/95	Kastrioti	H	4-2	Alliu, Begeja, Koça 2
30/09/95	Flamurtari Vlorë	A	1-0	Begeja
11/10/95	Tirana	H	2-0	Dobi, Bushi
14/10/95	Apolonia Fier	A	1-1	Dobi
21/10/95	Besëlidhja Lezhë	A	0-1	
28/10/95	Olimpik Tiranë	H	3-0	Dashi 2, Dobi
04/11/95	Shkumbini Peqin	H	0-0	
11/11/95	Besa Kavajë	H	2-0	Dobi, Bushi
18/11/95	Skënderbeu Korçë	A	1-0	Qendro
25/11/95	Vllaznia Shkodër	H	3-1	Koça 2, Bushi
02/12/95	Sopoti Librazhd	A	1-0	Bushi
09/12/95	Tomori Berat	H	1-0	Koka (p)
16/12/95	Elbasani	A	0-0	
23/12/95	Partizani Tiranë	H	1-0	og
03/02/96	Albpetrol Patos	H	1-0	Begeja
10/02/96	Shqiponja Gjirokastër	A	0-0	
17/02/96	Laçi	H	3-0	Koça 2, Qendro
24/02/96	Kastrioti	A	1-2	Bushi
02/03/96	Flamurtari Vlorë	H	3-1	Dashi, Koça 2 (1p)
09/03/96	Tirana	A	1-1	Furrxhi
16/03/96	Apolonia Fier	H	1-1	Furrxhi
23/03/96	Besëlidhja Lezhë	H	1-0	Furrxhi
27/03/96	Olimpik Tiranë	A	0-0	
30/03/96	Shkumbini Peqin	A	2-1	Koça (p), Bushi
06/04/96	Besa Kavajë	A	0-0	
13/04/96	Skënderbeu Korçë	H	3-1	Dashi, Alliu, Begeja
17/04/96	Vllaznia Shkodër	A	0-0	
20/04/96	Sopoti Librazhd	H	3-0	Koka, Koça 2
27/04/96	Tomori Berat	A	2-1	Koça 2
04/05/96	Elbasani	H	2-1	Xhai, Dobi
08/05/96	Partizani Tiranë	A	0-1	

TIRANA

CLUB DIRECTORY

Klubi sportiv Tirana
Rruga e Kavajes nr. 71
Tiranë
tel - (42) 27006
Year of Formation - 1920
President - Metush Seferi
Secretary - Millan Baçi
Coach - Sulejman Mema
Stadium - Qemal Stafa (20,000)

MAJOR HONOURS

League Championship - (16) 1930, 1931, 1932, 1934, 1936, 1965, 1966, 1967, 1968, 1970, 1982, 1985, 1988, 1989, 1995, 1996.
Domestic Cup - (8) 1963, 1976, 1977, 1983, 1984, 1986, 1994, 1996.

APPEARANCES 95/96

	P	Ap	(s)	Gls
Krenar ALIMEHMETI	D	17	(2)	1
Sokol BULKU	M	1	(7)	
Asllan BUSHI	A	2		3
Ervin CASLLI	A		(1)	
Nikolin ÇOÇLLI	M	22	(9)	3
Nevil DEDE	D	28	(2)	5
Indrit FORTUZI	A	5	(1)	4
Alpin GALLO	D	27	(4)	2
Endi HYKA	M		(6)	
Devis ISMAILI	M	8	(6)	1
Eriton KASMI	G	1		
Agustin KOLA	M	1	(3)	
Artan KUKLI	M	19	(11)	1
Saimir MALKO	D	34		9
Eldorado MARKOÇI	M	23	(9)	2
Adrian MEMA	M	31		1
Skender MERGJYSHI	G	2		
Auron MILOTI	A	30	(1)	7
Arben MINGA	D	18	(13)	1
Lulian MULLETI	M		(1)	
Blendi NALLBANI	G	31		1
Sokol PRENGA	M	16	(2)	2
Florian RIZA	A	26	(7)	8
Nordik RUHI	D	31	(2)	1
Taulant STERMASI	M		(4)	
Edmond SULA	M	1	(2)	

LEAGUE RESULTS 1995/96

Date	Opponent	H/A	Score	Scorers
02/09/95	Laçi	A	3-2	Dede, Bushi 2
09/09/95	Besa Kavajë	H	1-0	Bushi
16/09/95	Vllaznia Shkodër	H	2-0	Riza, Markoçi
23/09/95	Partizani Tiranë	H	1-2	Riza
30/09/95	Tomori Berat	A	0-0	
11/10/95	Teuta Durrës	A	0-2	
14/10/95	Besëlidhja Lezhë	H	4-0	Miloti 2, Alimehmeti, Çoçlli
21/10/95	Sopoti Librazhd	A	1-0	Miloti
28/10/95	Kastrioti	H	1-1	Çoçlli
04/11/95	Skënderbeu Korçë	A	1-1	Riza
11/11/95	Shkumbini Peqin	H	1-0	Miloti
18/11/95	Elbasani	H	2-1	Riza, Dede
25/11/95	Apolonia Fier	A	1-2	Gallo
02/12/95	Flamurtari Vlorë	H	3-0	Malko (p), Riza, Nallbani (p)
09/12/95	Olimpik Tiranë	A	1-0	Ruhi
16/12/95	Shqiponja Gjirokastër	H	1-1	Çoçlli
23/12/95	Albpetrol Patos	A	0-0	
03/02/96	Laçi	H	2-0	Riza, Miloti
10/02/96	Besa Kavajë	A	0-1	
17/02/96	Vllaznia Shkodër	H	4-1	Riza, Gallo, Mema, Prenga
24/02/96	Partizani Tiranë	A	2-0	Minga, Malko
02/03/96	Tomori Berat	H	1-1	Riza
09/03/96	Teuta Durrës	H	1-1	Miloti
16/03/96	Besëlidhja Lezhë	A	1-0	Malko
23/03/96	Sopoti Librazhd	H	4-1	Malko 3 (2p), Kukli
27/03/96	Kastrioti	A	0-0	
30/03/96	Skënderbeu Korçë	H	3-1	Dede, Ismaili, Prenga
06/04/96	Shkumbini Peqin	A	0-0	
13/04/96	Elbasani	A	0-0	
17/04/96	Apolonia Fier	H	2-0	Miloti, Malko (p)
20/04/96	Flamurtari Vlorë	A	0-2	
27/04/96	Olimpik Tiranë	H	3-1	Malko, Fortuzi, Markoçi
04/05/96	Shqiponja Gjirokastër	A	1-0	Dede
08/05/96	Albpetrol Patos	H	5-1	Fortuzi 3, Dede, Malko

TOMORI BERAT

CLUB DIRECTORY

Klubi sportiv Tomori
Rruga Skapari 21
Berat
tel - 627
Year of Formation - 1923
President - Gezim Hyskja
Secretary - Ismet Ajazi
Coach - Kiço Mile; Fatos Karkanjozi
Stadium - Tomori (13,000)

LEAGUE RESULTS 1995/96

02/09/95	Vllaznia Shkodër	A	1-1	Çuko
09/09/95	Skënderbeu Korçë	H	1-1	Gjata
16/09/95	Sopoti Librazhd	H	1-0	Çuko
23/09/95	Flamurtari Vlorë	A	0-1	
30/09/95	Tirana	H	0-0	
11/10/95	Besëlidhja Lezhë	A	0-1	
14/10/95	Olimpik Tiranë	H	2-1	Gjata, Lako
21/10/95	Besa Kavajë	A	1-2	Elezi
28/10/95	Shkumbini Peqin	H	1-1	Çuko
04/11/95	Shqiponja Gjirokastër	A	0-3	
11/11/95	Laçi	H	2-0	Gjata, Elezi
18/11/95	Kastrioti	A	1-2	Çuko
25/11/95	Partizani Tiranë	H	1-0	Mile
02/12/95	Elbasani	A	2-2	Elezi, Çuko
09/12/95	Teuta Durrës	A	0-1	
16/12/95	Albpetrol Patos	H	2-0	Zere, Elezi
23/12/95	Apolonia Fier	A	1-1	Lako
03/02/96	Vllaznia Shkodër	H	1-0	Mile
10/02/96	Skënderbeu Korçë	A	0-0	
17/02/96	Sopoti Librazhd	A	1-4	Cjapi
24/02/96	Flamurtari Vlorë	H	2-0	Gjata 2 (1p)
02/03/96	Tirana	A	1-1	Elezi
09/03/96	Besëlidhja Lezhë	H	1-1	Elezi
16/03/96	Olimpik Tiranë	A	0-1	
23/03/96	Besa Kavajë	H	1-0	Dino
27/03/96	Shkumbini Peqin	A	0-2	
30/03/96	Shqiponja Gjirokastër	H	2-1	Zere, Xheka
06/04/96	Laçi	A	1-3	Xheka
13/04/96	Kastrioti	H	2-1	Xheka, Gjata
17/04/96	Partizani Tiranë	A	1-2	Elezi
20/04/96	Elbasani	H	2-0	og, Çobani
27/04/96	Teuta Durrës	H	1-2	Lako
04/05/96	Albpetrol Patos	A	1-2	og
08/05/96	Apolonia Fier	H	1-3	Kona

APPEARANCES 95/96

	P	Ap	(s)	Gls
Eduart ALIAJ	D	30		
Shkelqim CJAPI	A	10	(15)	1
Arian ÇOBANI	A	24		1
Altin ÇUKO	A	13	(1)	5
Klodian DINO	M	23	(3)	1
Bardhyl ELEZI	A	31	(1)	7
Elton FANI	M	10	(17)	
Edmond GJATA	M	21	(7)	6
Nurjan KANANI	M	31		
Thimi KONA	D	26	(1)	1
Gentian LAKO	D	24	(1)	3
Madrid MEXHAJ	G	20	(2)	
Arben MILE	M	31		2
Altin SEVO	M	13		
Klodian SHEHU	D	21	(3)	
Xhevahir SULA	G	14	(1)	
Amarildo XHEKA	A	10	(15)	3
Gentian ZERE	M	22	(1)	2

VLLAZNIA SHKODËR

CLUB DIRECTORY

Klubi sportiv Vllaznia
Prane stadiumit
Vojo Kushi
Shkodër
tel - 2045
Year of Formation - 1919
President - Azem Hajdari
Secretary - Ramazan Rragami
Coach - Sahba Bizi; Hysen Dedja
Stadium - Vllaznia (16,000)

MAJOR HONOURS

League Championship - (7) 1945, 1946, 1972, 1974, 1978, 1983, 1992.
Domestic Cup - (5)
1965, 1972, 1979, 1981, 1987.

APPEARANCES 95/96

	P	Ap	(s)	Gls
Briken BIZI	M	13	(1)	2
Endri ÇAKU	A	8	(6)	
Gentjan ÇOÇJA	M	24		7
Armando CUNGU	D	28		2
Hektor DANI	G	3		
Ilir DIBRA	M	13	(6)	
Ardit DUKA	M	1		
Gjergj FISHTA	A	24		1
Vladimir GJUZI	A	14	(6)	
Shpetim GRUDA	A	19	(2)	2
Blendi HOXHA	M	24	(4)	
Luan JAHJA	A	1	(9)	
Ibrahim KALAJ	A	5	(14)	2
Suad LIÇI	D	31		7
Petrit MUHARREMI	A	5	(4)	
Gentian MUHJA	M		(1)	
Alban NOGA	D	14	(7)	
Astrit PREMÇI	D	26		2
Admir QRIMA	G	31		
Gjergj SHLLAKU	M	6	(3)	2
Vorosin SINANI	M	9	(7)	
Altin XHANHYSA	D	26	(4)	
Ilir YMERI	D	21	(4)	
Luan ZMIJANI	M	28	(2)	2

LEAGUE RESULTS 1995/96

02/09/95	Tomori Berat	H	1-1	Zmijani
09/09/95	Flamurtari Vlorë	A	0-3	
16/09/95	Tirana	H	0-2	
23/09/95	Elbasani	A	1-0	Lici
30/09/95	Apolonia Fier	H	1-0	Bizi (p)
11/10/95	Olimpik Tiranë	A	0-0	
14/10/95	Besa Kavajë	H	0-0	
21/10/95	Shkumbini Peqin	A	0-1	
28/10/95	Skënderbeu Korçë	H	3-0	Cungu, Çoçja 2
04/11/95	Kastrioti	A	2-2	Cungu, Lici
11/11/95	Partizani Tiranë	A	0-0	
18/11/95	Sopoti Librazhd	H	2-0	Shllaku, Kalaj
25/11/95	Teuta Durrës	A	1-3	Lici
02/12/95	Albpetrol Patos	H	1-2	Premçi
09/12/95	Shqiponja Gjirokastër	A	0-2	
16/12/95	Laçi	H	2-1	Premçi, Coçja
23/12/95	Besëlidhja Lezhë	A	0-0	
03/02/96	Tomori Berat	A	0-1	
10/02/96	Flamurtari Vlorë	H	1-2	Gruda
17/02/96	Tirana	A	1-4	Kalaj
24/02/96	Elbasani	H	2-1	Zmijani (p), Lici
02/03/96	Apolonia Fier	A	2-2	og, Gruda
09/03/96	Olimpik Tiranë	H	1-0	Çoçja
1/03/96	Besa Kavajë	A	2-2	Bizi, Lici
23/03/96	Shkumbini Peqin	H	0-0	
27/03/96	Skënderbeu Korçë	A	0-1	
30/03/96	Kastrioti	H	2-1	Çoçja 2
06/04/96	Partizani Tiranë	H	0-0	
13/04/96	Sopoti Librazhd	A	0-0	
17/04/96	Teuta Durrës	H	0-0	
20/04/96	Albpetrol Patos	A	1-2	Lici
27/04/96	Shqiponja Gjirokastër	H	0-0	
04/05/96	Laçi	A	0-2	
08/05/96	Besëlidhja Lezhë	H	4-1	Çoçja, Fishta, Shllaku, Lici

PROMOTED CLUBS

SECOND DIVISION FINAL TABLES 95/96

GROUP A

		Pd	W	D	L	F	A	Pt	GD
1	**Bylis Ballshi**	**30**	**26**	**4**	**0**	**121**	**14**	**72**	**+107**
2	Memaliaj	30	18	6	6	60	26	52	+34
3	Tepelena	30	14	3	13	64	63	40	+1
4	Selenica	30	13	3	14	54	63	35	-9
5	Erseka	30	11	6	13	48	60	33	-12
6	Pogradeci	30	13	1	16	58	62	32	-4
7	Delvina	30	12	2	16	52	60	30	-8
8	Kuçova	30	10	4	16	37	60	27	-23
9	Permeti	30	9	5	16	26	60	26	-34
10	Cerriku	30	9	5	16	50	70	25	-20
11	Saranda	30	9	3	18	38	70	25	-32

GROUP B

		Pd	W	D	L	F	A	Pt	GD
1	**Lushnja**	**27**	**21**	**4**	**2**	**81**	**8**	**58**	**+73**
2	Burreli	27	21	1	5	80	24	55	+56
3	Rrogoghina	27	19	4	4	51	19	50	+32
4	Durrësi	27	14	4	9	44	29	39	+15
5	Korabi	27	10	7	10	35	32	33	+3
6	Albanët	27	9	5	13	36	41	28	-5
7	Shijorku	27	8	5	14	39	46	25	-7
8	Ilirija	27	6	3	18	20	65	17	-45
9	Romët	27	3	4	20	26	79	12	-53
10	Kamza	27	2	5	20	27	96	11	-69

CLUB DIRECTORY

Klubi sportiv Bylis Ballshi
Ballsh
Year of Formation - 1976
President - Shkëlqim Jahjai
Secretary - Agron Murati
Coach - Migjen Skënderi
Stadium - Ballshi (3,000)

CLUB DIRECTORY

Klubi sportiv Lushnja
Lagjja e Re 15
Lushnja
tel - 300
Year of Formation - 1926
President - Pellumb Xhaferi
Secretary - Genc Tufa
Coach - Adnan Haxhiu
Stadium - Lushnja (8,000)

ARMENIA

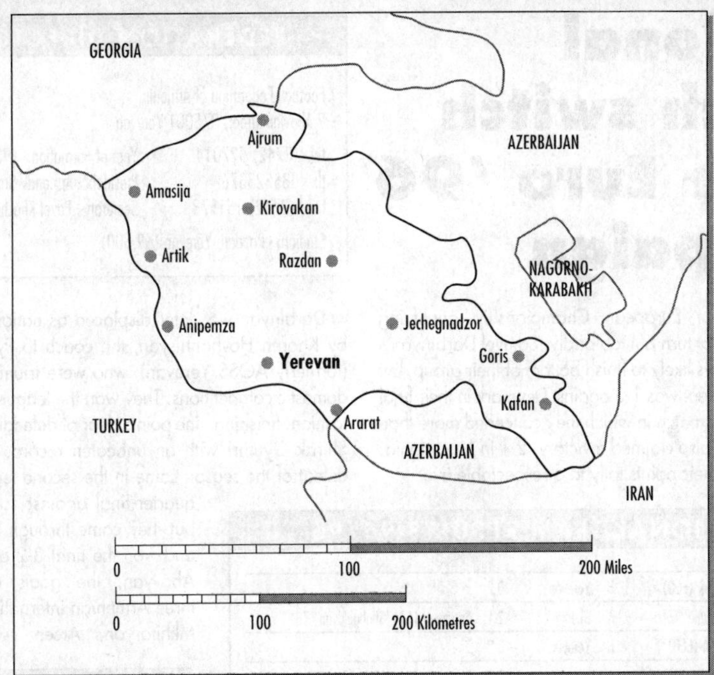
GEORGIA
AZERBAIJAN
Ajrum
Amasija
Kirovakan
Artik
Razdan
NAGORNO-KARABAKH
Anipemza
Jechegnadzor
Yerevan
Goris
Kafan
Ararat
TURKEY
AZERBAIJAN
IRAN
0
100
200 Miles
0
100
200 Kilometres

'DOUBLE' FOR PYUNIK YEREVAN

National coach switch after Euro '96 campaign

FEDERATION DIRECTORY

Football Federation of Armenia
9 Abovian street, 375001 Yerevan

tel - (3742) 527014 — Year of Formation - 1934
tlx - 885523376 — Presidebt - Armenak Sarkisyan
fax - (3742) 151573 — Secretary - Pavel Khachatryan

Stadium - Razdan, Yerevan (69,500)

Armenia's début European Championship qualifying campaign did not turn out too badly. Samvel Darbinyan's team were always likely to finish bottom of their group, but their heaviest defeat was 1-3 against Denmark in their final fixture - the only match in which they conceded more than two goals. They also claimed a victory, 2-1 in Macedonia, which boosted their points tally to a respectable five.

Darbinyan was later displaced as national team boss by Khoren Hovhannisyan, the coach to Pyunik Yerevan (formerly AOSS Yerevan), who were triumphant in both domestic competitions. They won the league in handsome fashion, finishing nine points clear of defending champions Shirak Gyumri with an unbeaten record. Pyunik's only defeat of the season came in the second leg of their Cup quarter-final against Tsement Ararat, but they came through on aggregate and won the final 3-2 against Kotayk Abovyan, the goals coming from three Armenian internationals, Hamlet Mkhitaryan, Arsen Avetisyan and

NATIONAL TEAM RESULTS 95/96

Date	Opponent		Venue	Score	Scorers
16/08/95	Denmark (ECQ)	H	Yerevan	0-2	
06/09/95	Macedonia (ECQ)	A	Skopje	2-1	Grigoryan (61), Shahgeldyan (78)
07/10/95	Belgium (ECQ)	H	Yerevan	0-2	
15/11/95	Denmark (ECQ)	A	Copenhagen	1-3	Petrosyan Art. (47)
17/01/96	Morocco	N	Vitrolles	0-6	
05/06/96	France	A	Lille	0-2	
20/06/96	Peru	A	Lima	0-4	
25/06/96	Paraguay	A	Asuncion	2-1	Avetisyan V. (33), Yessayan (56)
30/06/96	Ecuador	A	Portoviejo	0-3	

TOP SCORERS

28 Ara ADAMYAN (Shirak Gyumri)
24 Hovhanness TOUMBARYAN (Tsement Ararat)
20 Tigran ESSAYAN (Yerevan)
13 Artour PETROSYAN (Shirak Gyumri)
Artour MANOUTSYAN (Zangezour Goris)

EUROPEAN CUPS RESULTS 95/96

CUP-WINNERS' CUP

● ARARAT YEREVAN

Preliminary round GKS KATOWICE (POL)

A 0-2
Abrahamyan (Petrosyan 58); Shahgeldyan, Gspeyan, Tonoyan, Stepanyan, Nigoyan (Barsegyan 82), Mkryan, Ter-Petrosyan, Mkhitaryan, Arzumanyan, Mikaelyan (Kotcharyan 46)

H 2-0 Gspeyan (23), Tonoyan (26p) (aet; 5-4 on pens)
Petrosyan; Shahgeldyan, Gspeyan, Tonoyan, Stepanyan, Nigoyan, Ayrapetyan, Ter-Petrosyan (Kotcharyan 61), Mkhitaryan, Arzumanyan (Harutyunyan 26), Voskanyan.

1st round DINAMO MOSKVA (RUS)

A 1-3 Stepanyan (70)
Petrosyan; Shahgeldyan, Gspeyan, Tonoyan, Stepanyan, Harutyunyan, Mkryan, Ter-Petrosyan (Nazaryan 83), Mkhitaryan, Kotcharyan, Voskanyan.

H 0-1
Petrosyan; Shahgeldyan, Gspeyan, Tonoyan, Stepanyan (Harutyunyan 65), Nigoyan, Mkryan, Ter-Petrosyan, Mkhitaryan, Ayrapetyan, Voskanyan (Kotcharyan 46).

UEFA CUP

● SHIRAK GYUMRI

Preliminary round ZAGLEBIE LUBIN (POL)

A 0-0
Novhannisyan; Khodgoyan (Bernetsyan 46), Karapetyan, Yepranosyan (Tumasyan 73), Adamyan, Nikolyan (Avetisyan 77), Petrosyan, Tahmazyan, Artoyan, Grigoryan, Margaryan.

H 0-1
Novhannisyan; Margaryan, Karapetyan, Vardanyan, Adamyan, Nikolyan, Petrosyan, Tahmazyan, Yepranosyan (Tumasyan 69), Grigoryan (Khodgoyan 75), Bernetsyan (Avetisyan 66).

LEAGUE CHAMPIONSHIP FINAL TABLE 95/96

		Pd	W	D	L	F	A	Pt	GD
1	Pyunik Yerevan	22	19	3	0	71	14	60	+57
2	Shirak Gyumri	22	16	3	3	67	23	51	+44
3	Yerevan	22	13	5	4	43	24	44	+19
4	Tsement Ararat	22	12	3	7	57	33	39	+24
5	Ararat Yerevan	22	12	3	7	58	28	39	+30
6	Kotayk Abovyan	22	11	3	8	31	33	36	-2
7	Kharabagh Yerevan	22	8	5	9	29	28	29	+1
8	Van Yerevan	22	7	3	12	42	42	24	=
9	HMM Yerevan	22	6	3	13	30	52	21	-22
10	Zangezour Goris	22	5	2	15	26	60	17	-34
11	Aragats Gyumri	22	4	3	15	35	89	15	-54
12	Aznavour Noyemberyan	22	0	2	19	19	82	2	-63

N.B. Promoted - CSCA Yerevan, Arabkir Yerevan

DOMESTIC CUP FINAL

28/05/96, Yerevan
PYUNIK YEREVAN 3 Mkhitaryan (45), Avetisyan A. (54), Khachatryan (58)
KOTAYK ABOVYAN 2 Mirzoyan (84), Sargsyan (85)

Vardan Khachatryan. Mkhitaryan joined Pyunik in mid-season from Ararat, for whom he had played four games in the European Cup-winners' Cup earlier in the campaign. Ararat knocked out perennial European qualifiers GKS Katowice of Poland before falling to Dinamo Moscow. In the UEFA Cup, Shirak Gyumri were also paired initially with Polish opposition, but, having held Zaglebie Lubin 0-0 away, were eliminated after losing 0-1 at home.

NATIONAL TEAM APPEARANCES 95/96

Coach - Samvel DARBINYAN; Khoren HOVHANNISYAN	DEN	MAC	BEL	DEN	MAR	FRA	PER	PAR	ECU	Cps	Gls
Armenak PETROSYAN (13/11/73) - Ararat Yerevan	G	G								5	-
Sarkis HOVSEPYAN (02/11/72) - Pyunik Yerevan	D	M	D	D	D	D	D	D	D	17	-
Vardan KHACHATRYAN (12/10/68) - Pyunik Yerevan	D	D	D	D	sii	D	D	D	D69	11	-
Ashot KHACHATRYAN (03/08/59) - Ysse-les-Moulineaux (FRA)	D	s84	D							5	-
Sarkis HOVHANNISYAN (17/08/68) - Lokomotiv Moskva (RUS)	D	D				D				8	-
Aramayis TONOYAN (26/10/69) - Ararat Yerevan/Pyunik Yerevan	D					M58	Di	D	D	14	-
Artour PETROSYAN (06/08/71) - Shirak Gyumri	M	M84	M	M	M	M	M	M89	M	18	1
Razmik GRIGORYAN (11/10/71) - CSKA Sofia (BUL)/Ararat Yerevan	M	M68	M46		M	M65				12	2
Hovhanness TAHMAZYAN (11/01/70) - Shirak Gyumri	M41									5	-
Armen SHAHGELDYAN (28/08/73) - Ararat Yerevan	A	A	A		A		Av			12	2
Arsen AVETISYAN (08/10/73) - Pyunik Yerevan	A80		A	A		s65	Aiii	s73	s53	15	1
Hakob TER-PETROSYAN (31/08/71) - Ararat Yerevan	s41	s75			Miii	M		M73	M54	8	-
Varazdat AVETISYAN (05/01/72) - Pyunik Yerevan	s80	s68	s46	A70	siii	A	Aiv	A84	A	12	1
Tigran GSEPYAN (17/10/69) - Ararat Yerevan		D	D	D74	Di					8	-
Haroutyun VARDANYAN (05/12/70) - Shirak Gyumri		D		D	Dii	s58	Dii	D78	D53	14	-
Levon STEPANYAN (22/04/71) - Ararat Yerevan		M75								1	-
Hamlet MKHITARYAN (24/11/73) - Ararat Yerevan/Pyunik Yerevan		M	M71	M	M	M	M	M	M	15	-
Haroutyun ABRAHAMYAN (28/08/71) - Ararat Yerevan			G	G	G	G	G	G	G	13	-
Yervan SOUKIASYAN (20/01/67) - FC Tirol Innsbruck (AUT)			D			D				9	-
Hayk MARGARYAN (16/09/69) - Pyunik Yerevan			s71	s70						2	-
Hakob ARTOYAN (08/05/70) - Shirak Gyumri				D	D					2	-
Samvel NIKOLYAN (11/09/64) - Shirak Gyumri				A						1	-
Yervand KRBASHYAN (01/10/71) - Yerevan				s74	si		si	s78	s69	9	-
Artour KOCHARYAN (14/09/74) - Ararat Yerevan					D					1	-
Artour MKRTCHYAN - Pyunik Yerevan							D	s89		2	-
Vardan MINASYAN - Pyunik Yerevan							sii	M	M80	3	-
Tigran YESSAYAN - Yerevan							siii	A	A	3	1
Arayik ADAMYAN - Shirak Gyumri							siv	s84	s54	3	-
Andranik HOVSEPYAN - Van Yerevan							sv		s80	4	-

AUSTRIA

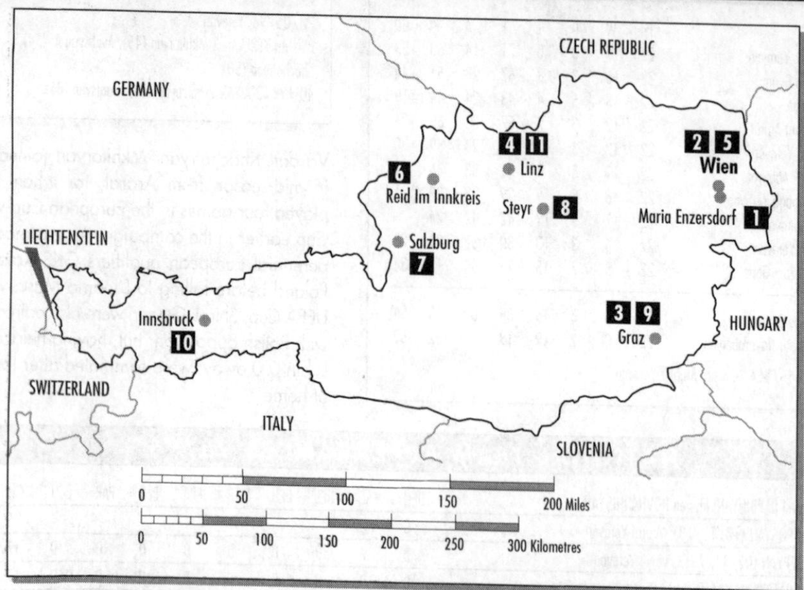

1	FC ADMIRA WACKER	127
2	FK AUSTRIA WIEN	128
3	GRAZER AK	129
4	LASK LINZ	130
5	SK RAPID WIEN	131
6	SV RIED	132
7	SV CASINO SALZBURG	133
8	SK VORWÄRTS STEYR	134
9	SK STURM GRAZ	135
10	FC TIROL INNSBRUCK	136
11	FC LINZ	137

FIRST TROPHY FOR STURM GRAZ

Resurgent Rapid back in business

FEDERATION DIRECTORY

Österreichischer Fussball-Bund
Ernst Happel Stadion, Sektor A/F, Meiereistrasse 7
Postfach 340, A-1021 Wien

tel - (0222) 72718-0
tlx - 111919 oefb a
fax - (0222) 72816-32

Year of Formation - 1904
President - Beppo Mauhart
Secretary - Alfred Ludwig

Stadium - Ernst Happel,-Stadion, Wien (47,500)

Threatened with bankruptcy and possible extinction just two years earlier, Austria's most famous club Rapid Vienna were once again basking in long-lost on-field glory at the end of the 1995/96 season. The Green-and-Whites gave their loyal fans cause for extensive celebrations both at home and abroad, clinching their first Austrian title since 1988 and reaching the final of the European Cup-winners' Cup.

Like the three Austrian finalists in European competition before them, Rapid were unable to claim the ultimate prize, going down 0-1 in the Brussels showdown to French side Paris Saint-Germain. But along the way they provided just as much heart-stopping entertainment as Salzburg had done during their fairytale journey to the UEFA Cup final two years previously.

After a shaky start against Romania's Petrolul Ploiesti, Rapid were on the brink of elimination in their second-round tie with Sporting Portugal. But in another parallel with Salzburg's Euro adventure, the Viennese came back from a first-leg defeat to equalise in the last minute and then eliminate the Portuguese side in extra-time. Into 1996 and Rapid kept the momentum going with a convincing win over Dinamo Moscow and then an amazing semi-final triumph over Feyenoord. The twin strikeforce of Christian Stumpf and towering German Carsten Jancker struck top form, and in the second leg against Feyenoord, they thrilled a packed-out Ernst Happel stadium with three memorable goals in the first 35 minutes.

When Rapid went down to PSG in the final, the thought suddenly occurred that, for all the enjoyment

LEAGUE CHAMPIONSHIP RESULTS 95/96

		1	2	3	4	5	6	7	8	9	10
1	FC Admira Wacker		1-1	0-2	0-1	1-1	3-2	1-2	4-1	1-5	0-0
			0-3	1-1	0-1	0-0	1-3	2-2	3-0	0-2	1-4
2	FK Austria Wien	3-1		3-2	0-1	4-1	0-0	3-0	4-0	0-3	1-0
		0-1		0-1	3-0	0-2	2-0	2-0	2-0	0-1	1-0
3	Grazer AK	1-1	0-0		1-0	1-2	4-2	0-0	1-1	3-2	3-0
		2-0	2-2		1-0	1-1	1-1	2-1	3-2	1-0	1-3
4	LASK Linz	2-0	0-1	0-0		2-0	1-1	0-0	1-0	2-1	1-2
		0-0	2-0	1-1		0-2	0-0	3-0	3-1	2-1	1-1
5	SK Rapid Wien	1-1	1-0	3-1	1-1		4-1	3-1	4-3	0-2	3-1
		6-0	0-1	1-0	2-1		4-2	3-1	2-0	2-0	3-1
6	SV Ried	2-2	0-0	0-0	1-0	2-1		0-0	3-1	2-4	2-1
		2-3	1-0	2-2	1-0	1-1		1-1	1-1	2-2	0-6
7	SV Casino Salzburg	2-2	2-2	2-1	1-1	0-3	1-1		4-0	1-1	3-1
		2-2	1-1	0-0	3-0	4-2	0-3		4-0	1-2	0-2
8	SK Vorwärts Steyr	0-1	0-0	1-2	0-3	0-2	0-2	0-6		1-3	2-2
		0-2	2-2	0-1	1-2	2-3	1-2	1-3		1-3	0-3
9	SK Sturm Graz	0-0	2-0	1-1	3-1	0-1	1-0	0-2	4-2		2-0
		2-0	3-0	0-2	2-1	1-0	3-1	2-1	0-0		0-1
10	FC Tirol Innsbruck	3-0	3-1	1-1	2-1	1-2	2-0	1-1	5-1	2-2	
		2-0	2-0	2-0	2-1	1-1	0-3	3-1	3-0	1-1	

TOP SCORERS

20	Ivica VASTIC (SK Sturm Graz)
15	Christian STUMPF (SK Rapid Wien)
14	Gernot KRINNER (SK Vorwärts Steyr/ FC Tirol Innsbruck)
	Heimo PFEIFENBERGER (SV Casino Salzburg)
12	Mario HAAS (SK Sturm Graz)
11	Mons Ivar MJELDE (FK Austria Wien)
10	Arnold WETL (SK Sturm Graz)
9	Herfried SABITZER (Grazer AK)
	Jerzy BRZECZEK (FC Tirol Innsbruck)
	Thomas JANESCHITZ (FC Tirol Innsbruck)
	Christoph WESTERTHALER (SK Vorwärts Steyr/LASK Linz)

LEAGUE CHAMPIONSHIP FINAL TABLE 95/96

		Home						Away					Total						
		Pd	W	D	L	F	A	W	D	L	F	A	W	D	L	F	A	Pt	GD
1	SK Rapid Wien	36	14	2	2	43	17	8	5	5	25	21	22	7	7	68	38	73	+30
2	SK Sturm Graz	36	11	3	4	26	13	9	4	5	35	22	20	7	9	61	35	67	+26
3	FC Tirol Innsbruck	36	11	5	2	36	16	7	3	8	28	24	18	8	10	64	40	62	+24
4	Grazer AK	36	9	7	2	28	18	5	8	5	18	18	14	15	7	46	36	57	+10
5	FK Austria Wien	36	11	1	6	28	13	3	8	7	14	22	14	9	13	42	35	51	+7
6	LASK Linz	36	8	7	3	21	11	5	2	11	15	24	13	9	14	36	35	48	+1
7	SV Ried	36	6	9	3	23	25	5	5	8	24	28	11	14	11	47	53	47	-6
8	SV Casino Salzburg	36	6	8	4	31	24	4	6	8	22	27	10	14	12	53	51	44	+2
9	FC Admira Wacker	36	3	6	9	19	31	4	7	7	16	30	7	13	16	35	61	34	-26
10	SK Vorwärts Steyr	36	0	3	15	12	42	0	3	15	13	51	0	6	30	25	93	6	-68

and excitement the team had brought to their long-suffering fans, they might still end the season with nothing to show for their endeavour. It was time to knuckle down to their domestic chores. They still had six matches left in the Austrian championship, their one-time 11-point lead had evaporated, and Sturm Graz and Tirol-Innsbruck were now both breathing heavily down their neck.

To their enormous credit, the Rapid players responded with the traditional fighting qualities for which the club has become famous. They won four and drew one of their next five matches to set up a last-match June 1 showdown with Sturm in the Ernst Happel stadium.

Rapid went into the match three points clear of their rivals, but as the two teams had an identical goal-difference, a Sturm victory would give the club from Styria their first ever national title. All was to play for, and a record Austrian league attendance of 48,000 turned up to witness the event. The atmosphere was clearly more suited to Rapid. Their players had grown accustomed to such nail-biting occasions during their European run, and they duly dominated the game, scoring two goals, one early and one late, to complete a memorable season in fitting style.

The title was the first for coach Ernst Dokupil, whose best previous achievement had been an Austrian Cup-winners medal as a player with Rapid back in 1975. He made the most of his resources, using only 19 players throughout the 36-match campaign and resisting the temptation to recruit any newcomers during the mid-season break. There was a strong backbone to the team. Goalkeeper Michael Konsel was the only player in the league to be present on the field for every minute of every game, and he rarely let the side down. Bulgarian crowd favourite Trifon Ivanov was another key component, as were Austrian international midfielders Dietmar Kühbauer and Peter Stöger and forward revelation Christian Stumpf. Others such as Heraf, Hatz and Marasek could also claim to have enjoyed the best season of their careers.

Second-placed Sturm Graz were inevitably disappointed to come so close to a first championship for the second year running. But just four days after their title-deciding defeat by Rapid, they returned to Vienna to lift the Austrian Cup, beating relegation-threatened Admira Wacker 3-1.

It was the club's first major honour after a wait of 87 years. Celebrations were predictably manic, and coach Ivica Osim was hailed as a saint by the Sturm fans. Just as sweet as the final victory was the semi-final win over city rivals Grazer AK, who had single-handedly destroyed Sturm's championship ambitions by beating

NATIONAL TEAM RESULTS 95/96

Date	Opponent		Venue	Score	Scorers
16/08/95	Latvia (ECQ)	A	Riga	2-3	Polster (69), Ramusch (78)
06/09/95	Rep. Ireland (ECQ)	H	Vienna	3-1	Stöger (3, 64, 77)
11/10/95	Portugal (ECQ)	H	Vienna	1-1	Stöger (21)
15/11/95	Northern Ireland (ECQ)	A	Belfast	3-5	Schopp (56), Stumpf (70), Wetl (81)
27/03/96	Switzerland	H	Vienna	1-0	Ogris (73)
24/04/96	Hungary	A	Budapest	2-0	Polster (12), Marasek (68)
29/05/96	Czech Republic	H	Salzburg	1-0	Wetl (86)

them three times and drawing with them once in their four league meetings.

Ivica Vastic, Sturm's Croatian/Austrian forward, claimed the Bundesliga's top scorer prize with 20 goals. He was well backed up in the goalscoring department by team skipper Arnold Wetl, promising youngster Mario Haas and classy midfielder Markus Schopp. All four of these players appear to have a bright future together in the national team. Schopp quit Sturm for German club Hamburg at the end of the season, but the gap he left looked to be more than adequately filled by the ambitious acquisition of ex-Italian international playmaker Giuseppe Giannini from Roma. With Osim also staying on, Sturm's upwardly mobile trend looks safe for at least another season.

GAK turned out to be the most impressive newly-promoted team in the Austrian Bundesliga for many a year. As well as reaching the Cup semi-finals they finished fourth in the league, high enough to earn themselves an

NATIONAL TEAM APPEARANCES 95/96

Coach - Herbert PROHASKA	LAT	IRL	POR	NIR	SUI	HUN	TCH	Cps	Gls
Otto KONRAD (01/11/64) - SV Casino Salzburg	G							12	-
Peter SCHÖTTEL (26/03/67) - SK Rapid Wien	D	D	D			s69	D	40	-
Walter KOGLER (12/12/67) - FK Austria Wien	D			D			s63	16	1
Anton PFEFFER (17/08/65) - FK Austria Wien	D	D	D	D	D	D	D	41	1
Johann KOGLER (12/05/68) - FC Admira Wacker	M46							7	-
Christian PROSENIK (07/06/68) - SV Casino Salzburg	M64							20	1
Wolfgang FEIERSINGER (30/01/65) - SV Casino Salzburg	M		D	D	M	D		27	-
Heimo PFEIFENBERGER (29/12/66) - SV Casino Salzburg	M	M	M	M	M			28	8
Stefan MARASEK (04/01/70) - SK Rapid Wien	M	M	M	M	D	M	M46	10	1
Andreas OGRIS (07/10/64) - FK Austria Wien	A64				s58	s75		61	11
Toni POLSTER (10/03/64) - 1.FC Köln (GER)	A	A79	A83	A	A58	A75	A72	76	34
Markus SCHOPP (22/02/74) - SK Sturm Graz	s46	M	M	M	D	M	M63	7	1
Peter STÖGER (11/04/66) - SK Rapid Wien	s64	M	M	M		M46	M46	46	9
Dieter RAMUSCH (31/10/69) - Grazer AK	s64						s63	5	1
Michael KONSEL (06/03/62) - SK Rapid Wien		G	G	G	G	G46	G46	26	-
Christian FÜRSTALLER (30/12/64) - SV Casino Salzburg		D						5	-
Dietmar KÜHBAUER (04/04/71) - SK Rapid Wien		M	M	M46				18	3
Andreas HERZOG (10/09/68) - FC Bayern München (GER)		M	M	M46		s46	M	53	10
Harald CERNY (13/09/73) - FC Tirol Innsbruck/TSV 1860 München (GER)		s79	s83				s72	13	-
Christian STUMPF (24/12/66) - SK Rapid Wien				s46	A58			2	1
Arnold WETL (02/02/70) - SK Sturm Graz				s46	M	M69	s46	7	3
Goran KARTALIJA (17/01/66) - LASK Linz					D		D	2	-
Ivica VASTIC (29/09/69) - SK Sturm Graz					M	A46	A46	3	-
Mario HAAS (16/09/74) - SK Sturm Graz					s58			1	-
Michael HATZ (17/11/70) - SK Rapid Wien						D		1	-
Andreas HERAF (10/09/67) - SK Rapid Wien						M46	s46	2	-
Franz WOHLFAHRT (01/07/64) - FK Austria Wien						s46		31	-
Peter ARTNER (20/05/66) - SV Casino Salzburg						s46	M63	55	1
Richard KITZBICHLER (12/01/74) - FC Tirol Innsbruck						s46		1	-
Wolfgang KNALLER (09/10/61) - FC Admira Wacker							s46	4	-
Roland KIRCHLER (29/09/70) - FC Tirol Innsbruck							s46	2	-

The Austrian national squad

96/97 in an attempt to drum up greater supprt from fans and the local community.

Another German coach, Horst Hrubesch, packed his bags at the end of the season after a disappointing year with FK Austria. Rapid's traditional rivals could only finish fifth, which meant missing out on European football for the first time since 1975. The big German did, however, leave behind him a nucleus of promising youngsters at the club, and there is every chance that FK Austria will be back challenging for honours before too long.

unexpected UEFA Cup spot (thanks to Sturm's Cup win). German coach Hans-Ulrich Thomale did a splendid job for the club, but he failed to settle in Austria and went home at the end of the season to take over at KFC Uerdingen. Another interesting postscript to GAK's season was the announcement that they would play their home games 50km away from Graz in Kapfenberg in

Casino Salzburg were the other major disappointments of the season. They made the worst title defence of any Austrian champion for 26 years, finishing one position above the relegation play-off zone in eighth place. And this from a team tipped pre-season by nine out of the ten Bundesliga coaches to retain their title. The bell tolled for

DOMESTIC CUP RESULTS

SECOND ROUND

Mattersburg 0, FK Austria Wien 1 (aet)
ASK Baumgarten 1, SK Rapid Wien 6
SC Zwettl 0, FC Admira Wacker 3
SV Marchtrenk 0, SK Sturm Graz 5
Wacker Innsbruck 0, SV Casino Salzburg 5
Feldkirchen 0, SV Ried 1
SV Traun 1, SK Vorwärts Steyr 3
Leibnitz 1, LASK Linz 2
SV Lendorf 1, Grazer AK 3 (aet)
ATSV Trimmelkam 1, FC Tirol Innsbruck 8
SV Schwechat 0, SG SV Gerasdorf/Wiener Sport-Club 2
SV Stockerau 0, First Vienna FC 3
TSV Hartberg 0, Flavia Solva 1
ASK Voitsberg 3, SAK Klagenfurt 0
Villach 1, SV Spittal an der Drau 2 (aet)
Wiener Neudorf 1, SV Oberwart 4
FC Deutschkreutz 0, VfB Mödling 2
SR Donaufeld 0, ASK Klingenbach 0 (aet; 3-5 on pens.)
Eibiswald 0, FC Linz 5
ESV Saalfelden 0, FC Kufstein 2 (aet)
FC Hard 2, SV Braunau 1
FC Puch 1, SC Austria Lustenau 2
Esternberg 0, DSV Leoben 3
SC Kundl 2, SV Wörgl 0
Waidhofen an der Ybbs 2, Kottingbrunn 0 (aet)
SV Fügen 2, VfB Hohenems 5
Parndorf 1, Bruck an der Leitha 0
SC Untersiebenbrunn 3, Admira Landhaus 1 (aet)
Köflach 1, Vöcklamarkt 0 (aet)
SW Bregenz 7, Henndorf 1
Austria Klagenfurt 2, Donau Linz 2 (aet; 4-3 on pens.)
Gersthofer SC 1, SV Essling 0

THIRD ROUND

FC Admira Wacker 4, SK Rapid Wien 1
FC Tirol Innsbruck 2, SK Sturm Graz 5
SV Ried 2, SV Casino Salzburg 3
SV Oberwart 0, LASK Linz 1
SW Bregenz 2, Grazer AK 7
Waidhofen an der Ybbs 2, FK Austria Wien 6
SC Untersiebenbrunn 0, SK Vorwärts Steyr 1
SC Austria Lustenau 0, FC Linz 2
ASK Voitsberg 1, VfB Mödling 3
VfB Hohenems 2, SV Flavia Solva 5
FC Hard 2, SV Spittal an der Drau 1
Köflach 2, ASK Klingenbach 3
Gersthofer SC 0, First Vienna FC 6
Parndorf 0, SG SV Gerasdorf/Wiener Sport-Club 3
Austria Klagenfurt 1, DSV Leoben 3
SC Kundl 2, FC Kufstein 0

FOURTH ROUND

Grazer AK 2, SV Casino Salzburg 0
SV Flavia Solva 1, LASK Linz 0
FC Hard 1, VfB Mödling 0
FK Austria Wien 0, SK Sturm Graz 1
FC Linz 1, SK Vorwärts Steyr 2
SC Kundl 4, DSV Leoben 3
First Vienna FC 0, FC Admira Wacker 3
SG SV Gerasdorf/Wiener Sport-Club 1, ASK Klingenbach 0

QUARTER-FINALS

SG SV Gerasdorf/Wiener Sport-Club 1, SK Sturm Graz 2
SV Flavia Solva 0, FC Admira Wacker 3 (aet)
FC Hard 0, SK Vorwärts Steyr 1 (aet)
SC Kundl 0, Grazer AK 1

SEMI-FINALS

SK Sturm Graz 3, Grazer AK 1
FC Admira Wacker 2, SK Vorwärts Steyr 0

FINAL

05/06/96, Vienna
SK STURM GRAZ 3 Milanic (31), Wetl (59, 67)
FC ADMIRA WACKER 1 Ogris (74)
referee - Plautz
SK STURM GRAZ - Gill; Neukirchner, Milanic (Prilasnig 46), Posch; Schopp, Hörmann, Swierczewski, Hörtnagl (Haas 63; Gruber 88), Reinmayr, Wetl; Vastic.
FC ADMIRA WACKER - Knaller; Graf, Müller (Ogris 54), Kogler; Binder, Rosenegger, Gager, Panis (Scharrer 71), Moros; Rodax, Mayrleb (Klausz 63).

EUROPEAN CUPS RESULTS 95/96

CHAMPIONS' CUP

● SV CASINO SALZBURG

Preliminary round STEAUA BUCURESTI (ROM)

H 0-0
Konrad; Mladenovic; Fürstaller, Lainer; Winklhofer, Prosenik, Feiersinger, Pfeifenberger, Hütter; Jancula (Stadler 66), Hasenhüttl.

A 0-1
Konrad; Mladenovic; Fürstaller, Lainer (Stadler 69); Winklhofer, Prosenik (Hiden 58), Feiersinger, Pfeifenberger, Hütter, Aigner F.; Hasenhüttl (Racunica 58).

CUP-WINNERS' CUP

● SK RAPID WIEN

1st round PETROLUL PLOIESTI (ROM)

H 3-1 Barisic (45, 90p), Ivanov (59)
Konsel; Ivanov; Schöttel, Hatz; Pivarnik (Jovanovic 77), Stöger, Barisic, Guggi, Heraf, Marasek; Stumpf (Jancker 70).

A 0-0
Konsel; Ivanov; Schöttel, Hatz; Pivarnik, Heraf, Stöger (Barisic 88), Guggi (Jovanovic 62), Kühbauer, Marasek; Stumpf (Haller 90).

2nd round SPORTING CP (POR)

A 0-2
Konsel; Ivanov; Hatz, Pivarnik; Stöger (Guggi 74), Barisic, Jovanovic, Kühbauer, Heraf, Marasek; Stumpf (Mandreko 52).

H 4-0 (aet) Kühbauer (25), Stumpf (90, 105), Jancker (110)
Konsel; Ivanov; Schöttel, Pivarnik; Heraf (Barisic 59), Jovanovic (Haller 65), Kühbauer, Stöger, Guggi; Stumpf, Jancker.

Quarter-final DINAMO MOSKVA (RUS)

A 1-0 Stumpf (34)
Konsel; Ivanov; Schöttel, Hatz; Guggi, Heraf, Jovanovic, Stöger, Marasek; Stumpf, Jancker.

H 3-0 Jancker (48, 74), Stöger (62p)
Konsel; Ivanov; Schöttel, Hatz; Guggi, Heraf, Jovanovic, Stöger, Marasek; Stumpf, Jancker.

Semi-final FEYENOORD (HOL)

A 1-1 Jancker (67)
Konsel; Ivanov; Pivarnik, Hatz, Guggi; Heraf, Schöttel, Stöger (Barisic 79), Marasek; Stumpf, Jancker (Haller 87).

H 3-0 Jancker (2, 35), Stumpf (32)
Konsel; Ivanov; Hatz, Schöttel, Guggi; Heraf, Kühbauer (Haller 86), Stöger (Mandreko 86), Marasek; Stumpf, Jancker.

Final PARIS SAINT-GERMAIN FC (FRA)

Brussels

0-1
Konsel; Ivanov; Hatz, Schöttel; Guggi, Stöger, Heraf, Kühbauer, Marasek; Stumpf (Barisic 46), Jancker.

UEFA CUP

● FK AUSTRIA WIEN

Preliminary round KEPEZ (AZB)

A 4-0 Mjelde (30), Belajic (38), Flögel (49), Pacult (86)
Wohlfahrt; Belajic; Kogler, Pfeffer; Schmid, Rakhimov, Flögel, Leitner, Pacult; Ogris (Nastl 70), Mjelde (Glatzer 76).

H 5-1 Mjelde (10, 29), Ogris (18, 42), Glatzer (64)
Wohlfahrt; Kogler, Pfeffer, Leitner; Schmid (Zechner 46), Rakhimov, Glatzer, Narbekovas (Schiesswald 61), Wagner; Ogris (Nastl 46), Mjelde.

1st round DINAMO MINSK (BLS)

H 1-2 Kogler (84)
Wohlfahrt; Glatzer (Pacult 65), Kogler, Pfeffer, Leitner; Flögel, Narbekovas, Rakhimov, Wagner; Ogris, Mjelde.

A 0-1
Wohlfahrt; Schmid, Kogler, Pfeffer, Leitner; Flögel (Nastl 59), Narbekovas, Rakhimov, Pacult; Ogris, Mjelde (Wagner 46).

● SK STURM GRAZ

Preliminary round SLAVIA PRAHA (TCH)

H 0-1
Goriupp; Chernyshov; Milanic, Posch; Schopp, Grassler, Hörmann (Reinmayr 69), Wetl, Prilasnig; Haas, Vastic.

A 1-1 Haas (55)
Goriupp; Milanic (Gruber 66); Neukirchner, Posch; Schopp, Grassler, Hörmann (Reinmayr 46), Wetl, Mählich; Haas (Prilasnig 75), Vastic.

● FC TIROL INNSBRUCK

Preliminary round/InterToto semi-final RC STRASBOURG (FRA)

H 1-1 Schiener (63)
Oraze; Sukiasyan, Baur, Streiter, Silberberger; Kitzbichler, Schiener, Brzeczek, Kirchler; Cerny, Sané (Grüner 53).

A 1-6 Kirchler (51)
Oraze; Streiter; Grüner, Baur, Prudlo; Janeschitz (Grabovac 58), Kitzbichler, Schiener, Brzeczek, Kirchler (Silberberger 68); Cerny (Gruber 80).

Salzburg early on. The catalyst was the Champions' League preliminary-round defeat by Steaua Bucharest. Coach Otto Baric began to fall out with his players, and after a 0-3 defeat away to FK Austria, the big Croatian handed in his notice. Ex-FK Austria coach Hermann Stessl took over, but he only lasted until Christmas. Former sweeper Heribert Weber was the next man in the hot seat, but he too struggled to put the team back on the right track.

The main western challenge to Vienna and Graz was provided by FC Tirol Innsbruck. An exhausting InterToto campaign left its scars on Didi Constantini's team in the autumn, but following a winter breather, the Tyroleans came back totally refreshed and reeled off eight straight victories to put themselves right back into title contention. Ultimately, however, they shot themselves in the foot when a pitch invasion prematurely ended their home match with

PLAYERS OF THE SEASON

IVICA VASTIC

He could have been included in the Croatian squad at Euro '96, but after taking out Austrian citizenship in December 1995, Ivica Vastic decided to throw in his lot with his adopted country. Austrian national coach Herbert Prohaska was clearly delighted and promptly gave the 26-year-old his début at the first opportunity - a friendly against neighbours Switzerland in Vienna. The Sturm Graz playmaker-cum-striker was not just the top scorer in the 95/96 Austrian Bundesliga. He was also the league's outstanding player, his exceptional ball skill echoing that of his father, who was once a goalscoring forward with Sarajevo, Hajduk Split and Varazdin in the former Yugoslavia.

ARNOLD WETL

If Vastic was Sturm Graz's star player in 95/96, 26-year-old local-born striker Arnold Wetl, now of FC Porto, ran him very close. Sturm coach Ivica Osim is not a man to offer faint praise, but he ranks his ex-team captain as a "player of extra quality". The former U-21 star has been on the fringes of the senior national team for some time (he made his début in April 1991), but proper recognition didn't come until the 95/96 season when he scored two goals, against Northern Ireland and Switzerland, and seemed set for an extended run in Herbert Prohaska's team.

MICHAEL HATZ

The Italians know a good defender when they see one, and 25-year-old Michael Hatz proved himself in 95/96 to be one of the very best man-to-man markers around. He shone for Rapid Vienna in both their domestic and European successes, and thoroughly earned his first national team call-up (v. Hungary), but he could still scarcely believe his luck when newly-promoted Serie A side Reggiana came in for his services at the season's end. Hatz leaves the club he first joined as a young boy, having played 137 games and scored eight goals in his six Bundesliga seasons.

SV Ried. The score was 2-2 at the time, but the ÖFB (Austrian FA) later awarded the match 3-0 to the visitors. Still, Tirol could feel very proud of their second half of the campaign, from which they earned a highly creditable 39 points. Their stars were Polish midfielder Jerzy Brzeczek, Russian goalkeeper Stanislav Cherchesov (signed mid-season from Spartak Moscow) and two new Austrian internationals Richard Kitzbichler and Roland Kirchler.

At the bottom of the Bundesliga table Vorwärts Steyr sank to unprecedented depths. No wins, six draws and 30 defeats told a bleak, bleak story. It was an extraordinary slide from a team which won its InterToto group at the start of the season and went on to reach the semi-finals of the Austrian Cup! Admira Wacker nearly joined Steyr in relegation, but they just managed to save themselves with a remarkable 6-0 away win in the second leg of the play-off with Gerasdorf, having lost the first leg at home 3-4. The decision to replace coach Walter Knaller with Peter Burgstaller after that first leg paid rich dividends.

INTERNATIONAL HONOURS

World Cup Finals appearances: 1934 (4th), 1954 (3rd), 1958, 1978 (2nd phase), 1982 (2nd phase), 1990

European Championship appearances (last 8): 1960.

Gerasdorf's demise meant that the only promoted team were FC Linz, who won the Second Division thanks in part to the goalscoring contributions of a certain 38-year-old Mexican by the name of Hugo Sánchez.

The Austrian national team also hoped to roll back the years as they strove to reach the latter stages of the European Championship for the first time since 1960. But their will-they-won't-they challenge ultimately ran aground on a soggy night in Balfast when they sank to an embarrassing 5-3 defeat. A draw would have earned Herbert Prohaska's side a place in the Anfield play-off against Holland, but losing away to both Latvia and Northern Ireland was hardly the stuff of deserving qualifiers.

More encouraging times lay ahead in the spring when Austria played three challenging World Cup warm-up games and won them all. Not with great panache, it has to be said, but a win is a win, and the third of them, 1-0 at home to eventual Euro '96 runners-up the Czech Republic, should in hindsight serve as a morale-booster for Prohaska and his team. New blood was successfully injected in that trio of friendlies, with the introduction of newly registered Austrian citizens Ivica Vastic and Goran Kartalija proving particularly beneficial, even if it was old warrior Toni Polster who grabbed most of the headlines when he joined Hans Krankl as the country's all-time top scorer by netting his 34th international goal in the 2-0 win against Hungary.

FC ADMIRA WACKER

CLUB DIRECTORY

FC Baumit Admira Wacker
(now - SC Niederösterreich FC Admira Wacker)
Johann-Steinböck-Strasse 1
2344 Maria Enzersdorf
tel - (02236) 23479
fax - (02236) 23479-12
Year of Formation - 1905
President - Erwin Proll
Secretary - Michaela Angeli
Coach - Walter Knaller (96/97 - Peter Burgstaller)
Stadium - Bundesstadion Südstadt (10,000)

MAJOR HONOURS
League Championship - (9) 1927, 1928, 1932, 1934, 1936, 1937, 1939, 1947, 1966.
Domestic Cup - (5)
1928, 1932, 1934, 1964, 1966.

APPEARANCES 95/96

	P	Ap	(s)	Gls
Helmuth ABERLE	A	1	(3)	
Gerald BACHER	D	25	(1)	3
Michael BINDER	M	11	(1)	
Ken BURWALL (SWE)	M	7	(3)	
Herbert GAGER	D	24	(8)	5
Helmut GRAF	D	27		
Franz GRUBER	G	4		
Wolfgang HACKER	M	7		2
HIBLINGER	M	1		
László KLAUSZ (HUN)	A	17	(12)	6
Wolfgang KNALLER	G	32		
Johann KOGLER	M	28		1
Christian MAYRLEB	A	31	(1)	8
Gabriel MENDEZ (AUS)	A	4	(8)	
Gennady MOROZ (UKR)	M	23	(6)	
Uwe MÜLLER	D	28	(6)	2
Igor OGRIS	D	5	(11)	
Alen ORMAN	M	9	(2)	
Jürgen PANIS	M	18		
Gerhard RODAX	A	8	(3)	
Markus SCHARRER	M	13	(13)	1
Manfred ROSENEGGER	M	29	(2)	2
Kim SUOMINEN (FIN)	M	6	(7)	
Jürgen WEBER	M	3	(1)	
Gerd WIMMER	A	5	(11)	1
Thomas ZINGLER	D	30	(1)	2

LEAGUE RESULTS 1995/96

Date	Opponent	H/A	Score	Scorers
02/08/95	SK Sturm Graz	H	1-5	Gager
05/08/95	FC Tirol Innsbruck	A	0-3	
12/08/95	SV Casino Salzburg	H	1-2	Zingler
18/08/95	SK Vorwärts Steyr	A	1-0	Mayrleb
25/08/95	SV Ried	H	3-2	Kogler, Bacher 2
30/08/95	SK Rapid Wien	A	1-1	Gager
16/09/95	FK Austria Wien	H	1-1	Mayrleb
20/09/95	LASK Linz	A	0-2	
23/09/95	Grazer AK	A	1-1	Mayrleb
03/10/95	Grazer AK	H	0-2	
06/10/95	SK Sturm Graz	A	0-0	
15/10/95	FC Tirol Innsbruck	H	0-0	
21/10/95	SV Casino Salzburg	A	2-2	Mayrleb, Hacker
28/10/95	SK Vorwärts Steyr	H	4-1	Zingler, Hacker, Müller, Mayrleb
04/11/95	SV Ried	A	2-2	Gager, og (Kramer)
08/11/95	SK Rapid Wien	H	1-1	Klausz
18/11/95	LASK Linz	H	0-1	
21/11/95	FK Austria Wien	A	1-3	Bacher
09/03/96	FC Tirol Innsbruck	H	1-4	Mayrleb
13/03/96	LASK Linz	A	0-0	
17/03/96	SK Rapid Wien	H	0-0	
20/03/96	SK Sturm Graz	A	0-2	
23/03/96	Grazer AK	A	0-2	
30/03/96	SV Casino Salzburg	H	2-2	Klausz 2
07/04/96	SK Vorwärts Steyr	H	3-0	Müller, Rosenegger 2
10/04/96	SV Ried	A	3-2	og (Stanisavljevic), Mayrleb, Klausz
13/04/96	FK Austria Wien	H	0-3	
16/04/96	FK Austria Wien	A	1-0	Mayrleb
20/04/96	SK Sturm Graz	H	0-2	
26/04/96	FC Tirol Innsbruck	A	0-2	
04/05/96	LASK Linz	H	0-1	
10/05/96	Grazer AK	H	1-1	Klausz
14/05/96	SK Rapid Wien	A	0-6	
18/05/96	SV Casino Salzburg	A	2-2	Gager, Klausz
25/05/96	SK Vorwärts Steyr	A	2-0	Scharrer, Wimmer
01/06/96	SV Ried	H	1-3	Gager (p)

FK AUSTRIA WIEN

CLUB DIRECTORY

FK Austria-Memphis
Ernst Happel Stadion
Meiereistrasse 7, Sektor D
1020 Wien
tel - (0222) 7286491/2
fax - (0222) 7283178
Year of Formation - 1911
President - vacant
Secretary - Werner Hebenstreir
Coach - Horst Hrubesch (96/97 - Walter Skocik)
Stadium - Horr (10,459)

MAJOR HONOURS
League Championship - (21)
1924, 1926, 1949, 1950, 1953, 1961, 1962, 1963, 1969, 1970, 1976, 1978, 1979, 1980, 1981, 1984, 1985, 1986, 1991, 1992, 1993.
Domestic Cup - (22) 1921, 1924, 1925, 1926, 1933, 1935, 1936, 1948, 1949, 1960, 1962, 1963, 1967, 1971, 1974, 1977, 1980, 1982, 1986, 1990, 1992, 1994.

APPEARANCES 95/96

	P	Ap	(s)	Gls
Stojan BELAIC (CRO)	D	19	(3)	1
Tomas DAUMANTAS (LIT)	M	12	(5)	
Ernst DOSPEL	D	18	(1)	
Thomas FLÖGEL	M	24	(5)	4
Rene GLATZER	M	6	(11)	
Wolfgang HACKER	M	3	(5)	
Christian KELLNER	A	7	(4)	2
Walter KOGLER	D	33		3
Jürgen LEITNER	D	34		
Mons Ivar MJELDE (NOR)	A	22	(7)	11
Arminas NARBEKOVAS (LIT)	M	9	(4)	2
Manfred NASTL	A	2	(4)	
Andreas OGRIS	A	30		7
Peter PACULT	A	15	(17)	3
Anton PFEFFER	D	31		1
Christoph POMPER	M	2	(1)	
Rashid RAKHIMOV (RUS)	D	30		2
Günter SCHIESSWALD	D	21	(5)	1
Manfred SCHMID	M	22		
Christian SCHMÖLZER	G	2	(1)	
Michael WAGNER	M	20	(2)	4
Franz WOHLFAHRT	G	34		
Michael ZECHNER	D		(5)	

LEAGUE RESULTS 1995/96

Date	Opponent	H/A	Score	Scorers
02/08/95	SK Vorwärts Steyr	H	4-0	Ogris 2 (2p), Mjelde 2
05/08/95	SK Rapid Wien	A	0-1	
11/08/95	LASK Linz	H	0-1	
19/08/95	SK Sturm Graz	A	0-2	
26/08/95	SV Casino Salzburg	H	3-0	Wagner, Ogris, Mjelde
30/08/95	SV Ried	A	0-0	
16/09/95	FC Admira Wacker	A	1-1	Narbekovas
20/09/95	Grazer AK	H	3-2	Narbekovas, Pfeffer, Kogler
23/09/95	FC Tirol Innsbruck	A	1-3	Flögel
03/10/95	FC Tirol Innsbruck	H	1-0	Kogler
06/10/95	SK Vorwärts Steyr	A	0-0	
14/10/95	SK Rapid Wien	H	4-1	Pacult, Kogler, Ogris 2
21/10/95	LASK Linz	A	1-0	Mjelde
28/10/95	SK Sturm Graz	H	0-3	
08/11/95	SV Ried	H	0-0	
18/11/95	Grazer AK	A	0-0	
21/11/95	FC Admira Wacker	H	3-1	Flögel, og (Rosenegger), Rakhimov
25/11/95	SV Casino Salzburg	A	2-2	Wagner, Mjelde
02/03/96	SK Vorwärts Steyr	H	2-0	Mjelde, Belaic
09/03/96	SV Ried	A	0-1	
13/03/96	SV Casino Salzburg	A	1-1	Ogris (p)
16/03/96	SK Sturm Graz	H	0-1	
23/03/96	FC Tirol Innsbruck	A	0-2	
29/03/96	LASK Linz	H	3-0	Wagner 2, Pacult
07/04/96	SK Rapid Wien	A	1-0	Schiesswald
10/04/96	Grazer AK	H	0-1	
13/04/96	FC Admira Wacker	A	3-0	Rakhimov, Ogris, Flögel
16/04/96	FC Admira Wacker	H	0-1	
20/04/96	SK Vorwärts Steyr	A	2-2	Pacult, Mjelde
27/04/96	SV Ried	H	2-0	Mjelde 2
04/05/96	SV Casino Salzburg	H	2-0	Mjelde 2
11/05/96	FC Tirol Innsbruck	H	1-0	Kellner
14/05/96	SK Sturm Graz	A	0-3	
18/05/96	LASK Linz	A	0-2	
25/05/96	SK Rapid Wien	H	0-2	
01/06/96	Grazer AK	A	2-2	Flögel, Kellner

GRAZER AK

CLUB DIRECTORY

Casino Graz-Grazer Athletik-Klub
Körösistrasse 57
8010 Graz
tel - (0316) 681201
fax - (0316) 6812019
Year of Formation - 1902
President - Harald Fischl
Secretary - Brigitta Birnstingl
Coach - Hans-Ulrich Thomale
(96/97 - Ljubomir Petrovic)
Stadium - Casino Stadion (10,000)

MAJOR HONOURS

Domestic Cup - (1) 1981.

APPEARANCES 95/96

	P	Ap	(s)	Gls
Franz ALMER	G	35		
Martin AMERHAUSER	A	21	(6)	3
Franz BLIZENEC	D	9	(14)	
Ales CEH (SLO)	M	31	(1)	
Klaus DIETRICH	D	4	(4)	
Eduard GLIEDER	A	24	(12)	7
Andreas KOCH	G	1		
Damir MUZEK (CRO)	M	20	(13)	
Marek PENKSA (SVK)	M	15		6
Gregor PÖTSCHER	M	26	(4)	
Martin PUZA	D	14	(12)	
Stojadin RAJKOVIC	D	27	(4)	1
Dieter RAMUSCH	M	34	(1)	4
Ludwig REINER	D		(1)	
Herfried SABITZER	A	17	(9)	9
Rudolf STEINBAUER	M	7	(6)	1
Gerald STRAFNER	A	12	(2)	2
Kurt TEMM	M	22	(4)	2
Zeljko VUKOVIC	D	35		6
Herbert WIEGER	A	15	(13)	
Michael ZISSER	D	27	(2)	2

LEAGUE RESULTS 1995/96

05/08/95	SK Vorwärts Steyr	A	2-1	Glieder, Sabitzer
12/08/95	SK Rapid Wien	H	1-2	Sabitzer (p)
19/08/95	LASK Linz	A	0-0	
26/08/95	SK Sturm Graz	H	3-2	Glieder, Sabitzer 2
30/08/95	SV Casino Salzburg	A	1-2	Vukovic
02/09/95	FC Tirol Innsbruck	H	3-0	Sabitzer, Temm, Vukovic
16/09/95	SV Ried	H	4-2	Sabitzer 2, Temm, Glieder
20/09/95	FK Austria Wien	A	2-3	Ramusch, Vukovic
23/09/95	FC Admira Wacker	H	1-1	Vukovic
03/10/95	FC Admira Wacker	A	2-0	Amerhauser 2
06/10/95	FC Tirol Innsbruck	A	1-1	Vukovic (p)
14/10/95	SK Vorwärts Steyr	H	1-1	Steinbauer
22/10/95	SK Rapid Wien	A	1-3	Vukovic
29/10/95	LASK Linz	H	1-0	Ramusch
04/11/95	SK Sturm Graz	A	1-1	Rajkovic
08/11/95	SV Casino Salzburg	H	0-0	
18/11/95	FK Austria Wien	H	0-0	
21/11/95	SV Ried	A	0-0	
28/02/96	SK Rapid Wien	A	0-1	
02/03/96	FC Tirol Innsbruck	A	0-2	
09/03/96	LASK Linz	H	1-0	Penksa
16/03/96	SV Casino Salzburg	H	2-1	Zisser, og (Hiden)
23/03/96	FC Admira Wacker	H	2-0	Penksa, Ramusch
30/03/96	SK Vorwärts Steyr	A	1-0	Strafner
06/04/96	SV Ried	H	1-1	Penksa
10/04/96	FK Austria Wien	A	1-0	og (Pfeffer)
13/04/96	SK Sturm Graz	H	1-0	Glieder
20/04/96	FC Tirol Innsbruck	H	1-3	Glieder
27/04/96	LASK Linz	A	1-1	og (Russ)
30/04/96	SK Sturm Graz	A	2-0	Penksa, Glieder
10/05/96	FC Admira Wacker	A	1-1	Sabitzer
14/05/96	SV Casino Salzburg	A	0-0	
18/05/96	SK Vorwärts Steyr	H	3-2	Sabitzer, Zisser, Glieder
21/05/96	SK Rapid Wien	H	1-1	Amerhauser
25/05/96	SV Ried	A	2-2	Strafner, Penksa
01/06/96	FK Austria Wien	H	2-2	Ramusch, Penksa

LASK LINZ

CLUB DIRECTORY

Linzer Athletik-Sport-Klub (LASK)
Daimlerstrasse 35
4030 Linz
tel - (0732) 3756660
fax - (0732) 3756669
Year of Formation - 1908
President - Wolfgang Rieger
Secretary - Christine Knaus
Coach - Günther Kronsteiner
(96/97 - Friedel Rausch)
Stadium - Linzer Stadion (27,000)

MAJOR HONOURS
League Championship - (1) 1965.
Domestic Cup - (1) 1965.

APPEARANCES 95/96

	P	Ap	(s)	Gls
Brendan AUGUSTINE (SAF)	A	7	(3)	
Dragoslav DUBAJIC (YUG)	A	14	(3)	
Ivica DUSPARA (CRO)	M	24		4
Gerhard ECKER	M	4	(5)	
Anton EHMANN	D	8	(5)	
Dietmar GRÜNEIS	D	9	(2)	
Rudolf GUSSNIG	A	4	(9)	
Anton HAIDEN	M	9	(7)	1
Walter HOCHMAIER	D	22	(1)	
Goran KARTALIJA	D	34		
Jürgen KAUZ	M	19	(3)	4
Mario KRASSNITZER	G	7	(1)	
Helmut LORENZ	M	14	(16)	
Aleksandr METLITSKI (BLS)	M	32		5
Klaus ROHSEANO	M	15	(12)	2
Kurt RUSS	D	30		1
Josef SCHICKLGRUBER	G	29		
Hannes STROMBERGER	M	21	(3)	
Manfred UNGER	D	30	(2)	2
Markus WEISSENBERGER	A	30	(3)	8
Thomas WEISSENBERGER	A	21	(9)	3
Christoph WESTERTHALER	A	13	(5)	6

LEAGUE RESULTS 1995/96

02/08/95	SV Casino Salzburg	A	1-1	Duspara
04/08/95	SV Ried	H	1-1	Kauz
11/08/95	FK Austria Wien	A	1-0	Weissenberger T.
19/08/95	Grazer AK	H	0-0	
26/08/95	FC Tirol Innsbruck	A	1-2	Russ
30/08/95	SK Vorwärts Steyr	H	1-0	Kauz
17/09/95	SK Rapid Wien	A	1-1	Weissenberger M.
20/09/95	FC Admira Wacker	H	2-0	Metlitski, Weissenberger M.
23/09/95	SK Sturm Graz	H	2-1	Weissenberger M., Metlitski
03/10/95	SK Sturm Graz	A	1-3	Haiden
06/10/95	SV Casino Salzburg	H	0-0	
14/10/95	SV Ried	A	0-1	
21/10/95	FK Austria Wien	H	0-1	
29/10/95	Grazer AK	A	0-1	
04/11/95	FC Tirol Innsbruck	H	1-2	Kauz
11/11/95	SK Vorwärts Steyr	A	2-0	Weissenberger M. 2 (match abandoned; later awarded as 3-0)
18/11/95	FC Admira Wacker	A	1-0	Unger
21/11/95	SK Rapid Wien	H	2-0	Metlitski, Weissenberger M.
02/03/96	SK Rapid Wien	H	0-2	
09/03/96	Grazer AK	A	0-1	
13/03/96	FC Admira Wacker	H	0-0	
16/03/96	SK Vorwärts Steyr	A	2-1	Weissenberger T., Metlitski
23/03/96	SV Ried	H	0-0	
29/03/96	FK Austria Wien	A	0-3	
07/04/96	SK Sturm Graz	H	2-1	Duspara, Unger
10/04/96	FC Tirol Innsbruck	A	1-2	Weissenberger M.
13/04/96	SV Casino Salzburg	H	3-0	Weissenberger M., Rohseano, Duspara
21/04/96	SK Rapid Wien	A	1-2	Westerthaler
27/04/96	Grazer AK	H	1-1	Westerthaler
30/04/96	SV Casino Salzburg	A	1-3	Duspara (later awarded as 0-3)
04/05/96	FC Admira Wacker	A	1-0	Westerthaler
11/05/96	SV Ried	A	0-1	
14/05/96	SK Vorwärts Steyr	H	3-1	Metlitski, Westerthaler 2
18/05/96	FK Austria Wien	H	2-0	Kauz, Weissenberger T.
25/05/96	SK Sturm Graz	A	1-2	Rohseano
01/06/96	FC Tirol Innsbruck	H	1-1	Westerthaler

SK RAPID WIEN

CLUB DIRECTORY

Sportklub Rapid Wien
Keisslergasse 6
1140 Wien
tel - (0222) 91001
fax - (0222) 9111906
Year of Formation - 1899
President - Günter Kaltenbrunner
Secretary - Werner Widhalm
Coach - Ernst Dokupil
Stadium - Gerhard-Hanappi (19,600)
League Championship - (30) 1912, 1913, 1916, 1917, 1919, 1920, 1921, 1923, 1929, 1930, 1935, 1938, 1940, 1941, 1946, 1948, 1951, 1952, 1954, 1956, 1957, 1960, 1964, 1967, 1968, 1982, 1983, 1987, 1988, 1996.
Domestic Cup - (14)
1919, 1920, 1927, 1946, 1961, 1968, 1969, 1972, 1976, 1983, 1984, 1985, 1987, 1995.

APPEARANCES 95/96

	P	Ap	(s)	Gls
Zoran BARISIC	M	18	(13)	8
Sascha BÜRRINGER	M		(2)	
Peter GUGGI	M	21	(8)	3
Rene HALLER	D	1	(5)	
Michael HATZ	D	30		1
Andreas HERAF	M	25	(7)	5
Trifon IVANOV (BUL)	D	30		7
Carsten JANCKER (GER)	A	18	(9)	7
Prvoslav JOVANOVIC	D	26	(8)	
Michael KONSEL	G	36		
Dietmar KÜHBAUER	M	24	(2)	6
Oliver LEDERER	M	1	(1)	
Sergei MANDREKO (TAD)	M	10	(8)	
Stefan MARASEK	M	32	(1)	2
Roman PIVARNIK (TCH)	D	19	(7)	2
Peter SCHÖTTEL	D	33	(2)	
Maciej SLIWOWSKI (POL)	A	8	(8)	5
Peter STÖGER	M	34	(1)	7
Christian STUMPF	A	30	(3)	15

LEAGUE RESULTS 1995/96

Date	Opponent	H/A	Score	Scorers
02/08/95	SV Ried	A	1-2	Stöger
05/08/95	FK Austria Wien	H	1-0	Stumpf
12/08/95	Grazer AK	A	2-1	Marasek, Barisic
19/08/95	FC Tirol Innsbruck	H	3-1	Stumpf 2, Heraf
26/08/95	SK Vorwärts Steyr	A	2-0	Stumpf, Marasek
30/08/95	FC Admira Wacker	H	1-1	Stöger
17/09/95	LASK Linz	H	1-1	Kühbauer
20/09/95	SK Sturm Graz	A	1-0	Kühbauer (p)
23/09/95	SV Casino Salzburg	H	3-1	Stöger 2, Ivanov
03/10/95	SV Casino Salzburg	A	3-0	Stumpf 2, Barisic
06/10/95	SV Ried	H	4-1	Stumpf, Pivarnik, Hatz, Barisic
14/10/95	FK Austria Wien	A	1-4	Barisic
22/10/95	Grazer AK	H	3-1	Stumpf 2, Jancker
28/10/95	FC Tirol Innsbruck	A	2-1	Jancker, Kühbauer (p)
05/11/95	SK Vorwärts Steyr	H	4-3	Kühbauer 2 (1p), Guggi, Ivanov
08/11/95	FC Admira Wacker	A	1-1	Ivanov
19/11/95	SK Sturm Graz	H	0-2	
21/11/95	LASK Linz	A	0-2	
28/02/96	Grazer AK	H	1-0	Jancker
02/03/96	LASK Linz	A	2-0	Stumpf, Jancker
10/03/96	SV Casino Salzburg	H	3-1	Stumpf 3
17/03/96	FC Admira Wacker	A	0-0	
24/03/96	SK Vorwärts Steyr	H	2-0	Jancker, Sliwowski
30/03/96	SV Ried	A	1-1	Heraf
07/04/96	FK Austria Wien	H	0-1	
10/04/96	SK Sturm Graz	A	0-1	
13/04/96	FC Tirol Innsbruck	H	3-1	Stumpf, Heraf, Jancker
21/04/96	LASK Linz	H	2-1	Guggi 2
27/04/96	SV Casino Salzburg	A	2-4	Jancker, Heraf
30/04/96	FC Tirol Innsbruck	A	1-1	Barisic
11/05/96	SK Vorwärts Steyr	A	3-2	Sliwowski 2, Ivanov
14/05/96	FC Admira Wacker	H	6-0	Stöger 3, Barisic, Ivanov, Sliwowski
18/05/96	SV Ried	H	4-2	Ivanov, Sliwowski, Barisic, Heraf
21/05/96	Grazer AK	A	1-1	Ivanov
25/05/96	FK Austria Wien	A	2-0	Barisic, Kühbauer
01/06/96	SK Sturm Graz	H	2-0	Pivarnik, Stumpf

SV RIED

CLUB DIRECTORY

SV Keli Ried im Innkreis
Bahnhofstrasse 19
4910 Ried/Innkreis
tel - (07752) 81100
fax - (07752) 81102
Year of Formation - 1912
President - Wenzel Schmidt
Secretary - Stefan Reiter
Coach - Klaus Roitinger
Stadium - Rieder Stadion (10,200)

APPEARANCES 95/96

	P	Ap	(s)	Gls
Michael ANGERSCHMID	M	28	(4)	2
Josef BÖGL	D		(7)	
Erwin DAMPFHOFER	A	27	(9)	8
Herwig DRECHSEL	M	19	(4)	2
Thomas EDER	D	30	(4)	3
Oliver GLASNER	M	25	(1)	4
Dirk HANNEMANN (GER)	M	7	(4)	2
Marinko IVSIC	M	31	(3)	
Leopold KIESENHOFER	D	28	(4)	1
Roland KRAMER	M	28	(1)	1
Andrzej LESIAK (POL)	D	30		6
Hubert MÖSENEDER	A	4	(24)	2
Pavel MRAZ (TCH)	A	25	(8)	3
Goran STANISAVLJEVIC (YUG)	M	32	(2)	7
Günter STEININGER	D	28	(3)	3
Alexander TREIBLMAIER	A		(6)	
Ronald UNGER	G	36		
Walter WALDHÖR	A	18		2
Hannes WEBER	A		(5)	
ZAUNER	M		(1)	

LEAGUE RESULTS 1995/96

Date	Opponent	H/A	Score	Scorers
02/08/95	SK Rapid Wien	H	2-1	Kramer, Mraz
04/08/95	LASK Linz	A	1-1	Dampfhofer
12/08/95	SK Sturm Graz	H	2-4	Stanisavljevic, Mraz
19/08/95	SV Casino Salzburg	A	1-1	Dampfhofer
25/08/95	FC Admira Wacker	A	2-3	Stanisavljevic , Glasner
30/08/95	FK Austria Wien	H	0-0	
16/09/95	Grazer AK	A	2-4	Dampfhofer, Glasner
20/09/95	FC Tirol Innsbruck	H	2-1	Lesiak, Dampfhofer
23/09/95	SK Vorwärts Steyr	A	2-0	Steininger, Stanisavljevic
03/10/95	SK Vorwärts Steyr	H	3-1	Dampfhofer, Möseneder, Drechsel
06/10/95	SK Rapid Wien	A	1-4	Angerschmid
14/10/95	LASK Linz	H	1-0	Lesiak
21/10/95	SK Sturm Graz	A	0-1	
28/10/95	SV Casino Salzburg	H	0-0	
04/11/95	FC Admira Wacker	H	2-2	Lesiak, Eder
08/11/95	FK Austria Wien	A	0-0	
18/11/95	FC Tirol Innsbruck	A	0-2	
21/11/95	Grazer AK	H	0-0	
02/03/96	SV Casino Salzburg	A	3-0	Lesiak, Stanisavljevic (p), Mraz
09/03/96	FK Austria Wien	H	1-0	Angerschmid
13/03/96	SK Sturm Graz	A	1-3	Glasner
16/03/96	FC Tirol Innsbruck	H	0-6	
23/03/96	LASK Linz	A	0-0	
30/03/96	SK Rapid Wien	H	1-1	Waldhör
06/04/96	Grazer AK	A	1-1	Steininger
10/04/96	FC Admira Wacker	H	2-3	Waldhör, Glasner
13/04/96	SK Vorwärts Steyr	A	2-1	Stanisavljevic (p), Drechsel
20/04/96	SV Casino Salzburg	H	1-1	Lesiak
27/04/96	FK Austria Wien	A	0-2	
30/04/96	SK Vorwärts Steyr	H	1-1	Dampfhofer
11/05/96	LASK Linz	H	1-0	Eder
14/05/96	FC Tirol Innsbruck	A	2-2	Hannemann 2 (match abandoned; later awarded as 3-0)
18/05/96	SK Rapid Wien	A	2-4	Stanisavljevic, Möseneder
22/05/96	SK Sturm Graz	H	2-2	Kiesenhofer, Lesiak
25/05/96	Grazer AK	H	2-2	Stanisavljevic, Steininger
01/06/96	FC Admira Wacker	A	3-1	Dampfhofer 2, Eder

SV CASINO SALZBURG

CLUB DIRECTORY

SV Casino Salzburg
Schumacherstrasse 14
5020 Salzburg
tel - (0662) 433332
fax - (0662) 430216
Year of Formation - 1933
President - Rudolf Quehenberger
Secretary - Iris Müller
Coach - Otto Baric; Hermann Stessl; Heribert Weber
Stadium - Lehen (14,457)

MAJOR HONOURS

League Championship - (2) 1994, 1995.

APPEARANCES 95/96

	P	Ap	(s)	Gls
Franz AIGNER	M	9	(4)	1
Peter ARTNER	M	25	(2)	1
Marcus di Giuseppe BICA (BRA)	A	3	(4)	3
Wolfgang FEIERSINGER	D	24		
Christian FÜRSTALLER	D	4		
Ralph HASENHÜTTL	A	23	(8)	5
Martin HIDEN	D	31		1
Adolf HÜTTER	M	28	(6)	1
Herbert ILSANKER	G	7	(1)	
Tibor JANCULA (SVK)	A	19	(7)	7
Nikola JURCEVIC (CRO)	A	1	(1)	
Tomislav KOCIJAN	M	25	(3)	4
Otto KONRAD	G	29		
Leo LAINER	D	30	(2)	1
Alexander MANNINGER	G		(1)	
Marco Antônio dos Santos "MARQUINHO" (BRA)	M	6	(4)	
Mladen MLADENOVIC (CRO)	M	15		7
PAMMINGER	A	3	(2)	
Heimo PFEIFENBERGER	A	30		14
Gernot PLASSNEGGER	A	1	(5)	
Christian PROSENIK	M	28	(7)	3
Dejan RACUNICA (CRO)	M	10	(8)	
Helmut ROTTENSTEINER	M		(1)	
Hermann STADLER	M	7	(20)	1
Gerhard STRUBER	A	8	(2)	1
Thomas WINKLHOFER	D	30	(3)	2

LEAGUE RESULTS 1995/96

02/08/95	LASK Linz	H	1-1	Hasenhüttl
05/08/95	SK Sturm Graz	A	2-0	Jancula 2
12/08/95	FC Admira Wacker	A	2-1	Mladenovic, Pfeifenberger
19/08/95	SV Ried	H	1-1	Pfeifenberger
26/08/95	FK Austria Wien	A	0-3	
30/08/95	Grazer AK	H	2-1	Jancula, Pfeifenberger
16/09/95	FC Tirol Innsbruck	A	1-1	Hasenhüttl
20/09/95	SK Vorwärts Steyr	H	4-0	Pfeifenberger 2, Mladenovic 2
23/09/95	SK Rapid Wien	A	1-3	Hütter
03/10/95	SK Rapid Wien	H	0-3	
06/10/95	LASK Linz	A	0-0	
14/10/95	SK Sturm Graz	H	1-1	Pfeifenberger (p)
21/10/95	FC Admira Wacker	H	2-2	Aigner, Pfeifenberger
28/10/95	SV Ried	A	0-0	
08/11/95	Grazer AK	A	0-0	
18/11/95	SK Vorwärts Steyr	A	6-0	Pfeifenberger (p), Mladenovic, Lainer, Jancula, Prosenik, Winklhofer
21/11/95	FC Tirol Innsbruck	H	3-1	Mladenovic 2, Artner
25/11/95	FK Austria Wien	H	2-2	Pfeifenberger (p), Mladenovic
02/03/96	SV Ried	H	0-3	
10/03/96	SK Rapid Wien	A	1-3	Kocijan
13/03/96	FK Austria Wien	H	1-1	Jancula
16/03/96	Grazer AK	A	1-2	Hasenhüttl
23/03/96	SK Sturm Graz	H	1-2	Prosenik
30/03/96	FC Admira Wacker	A	2-2	Pfeifenberger, Kocijan
06/04/96	FC Tirol Innsbruck	H	0-2	
10/04/96	SK Vorwärts Steyr	A	3-1	Hasenhüttl 2, Struber
13/04/96	LASK Linz	A	0-3	
20/04/96	SV Ried	A	1-1	Winklhofer
27/04/96	SK Rapid Wien	H	4-2	Hiden, Pfeifenberger, og (Heraf), Stadler
30/04/96	LASK Linz	H	3-1	Pfeifenberger 3 (later awarded as 3-0)
04/05/96	FK Austria Wien	A	0-2	
11/05/96	SK Sturm Graz	A	1-2	Prosenik
14/05/96	Grazer AK	H	0-0	
18/05/96	FC Admira Wacker	H	2-2	Kocijan 2
25/05/96	FC Tirol Innsbruck	A	1-3	Bica
01/06/96	SK Vorwärts Steyr	H	4-0	Bica 2, Jancula 2

SK VORWÄRTS STEYR

CLUB DIRECTORY

SK Vorwärts Steyr
Volksstrasse 3
4400 Steyr
tel - (07252) 54119
fax - (07252) 46195
Year of Formation - 1919
President - Alois Radelspäck
Secretary - Gerda Schwiegelhofer
Coach - Milan Djuricic; Radan Lukic & Kurt Hochedlinger; Marinko Kolgänin
Stadium - Steyr (9,900)

APPEARANCES 95/96

	P	Ap	(s)	Gls
Derek ARNDT (GER)	M		(1)	
Semida Mohamed AZIMA (EGY)	M	18		1
Peter BARAC	D	35		1
Dietmar BERCHTOLD	M	24	(6)	3
Edmond DOSTI (ALB)	A		(3)	
Thomas ENGELMAIER	G	10	(2)	
Marko FELBERMAYER	D	25	(3)	
Heinz FUCHSBICHLER	M	21	(5)	
Thomas GRÖBL	M	18	(5)	4
Amir GROSO (BOS)	M	3		
Eugen HABERFELLNER	A	3	(17)	1
Oliver HEIML	M	8	(10)	
Michael HELM	D	26		1
Ladislav HEVESSY	M		(4)	
Sinisa KONCALOVIC (CRO)	M	10	(2)	
Gernot KRINNER	A	11	(1)	5
Herbert LAUX	D	14	(2)	1
Manferd LINZMAIER	M	3		
Daniel MADLENER	M	17		
Alexander MANNINGER	G	5		
Henry McKOP (ZIM)	D	2		
Richard NAAWU (GHA)	A	6	(8)	
Günther OPEL	A	4	(9)	
Michael PAAL	G	4	(1)	
Zoran PETROVIC (CRO)	A	2		
Bernhard PFISTER	D	26		1
Rene RIEDL	A	1	(5)	
Edmond ROTTLER (GER)	G	10	(1)	
Niels SCHLOTTEBECK (GER)	D	2		
Christian SCHRAMMEL	M	26	(4)	1
Almir TURKOVIC (BOS)	A	7	(1)	1
Azrudin VALENTIC (BOS)	A	17		1
Mirza VARESANOVIC (BOS)	D	14		
Christoph WESTERTHALER	A	16	(1)	3
Bernhard ZOGLMEIER	G	7		

LEAGUE RESULTS 1995/96

02/08/95	FK Austria Wien	A	0-4	
05/08/95	Grazer AK	H	1-2	Barac
12/08/95	FC Tirol Innsbruck	A	1-5	Pfister
18/08/95	FC Admira Wacker	H	0-1	
26/08/95	SK Rapid Wien	H	0-2	
30/08/95	LASK Linz	A	0-1	
16/09/95	SK Sturm Graz	H	1-3	Krinner
20/09/95	SV Casino Salzburg	A	0-4	
23/09/95	SV Ried	H	0-2	
03/10/95	SV Ried	A	1-3	Westerthaler
06/10/95	FK Austria Wien	H	0-0	
14/10/95	Grazer AK	A	1-1	Gröbl
20/10/95	FC Tirol Innsbruck	H	2-2	Krinner 2
28/10/95	FC Admira Wacker	A	1-4	Turkovic
05/11/95	SK Rapid Wien	A	3-4	Krinner, Westerthaler 2
11/11/95	LASK Linz	H	0-2	(match abandoned; later awarded as 0-3)
18/11/95	SV Casino Salzburg	H	0-6	
22/11/95	SK Sturm Graz	A	2-4	Krinner, Azima
02/03/96	FK Austria Wien	A	0-2	
13/03/96	FC Tirol Innsbruck	A	0-3	
16/03/96	LASK Linz	H	1-2	Valentic
24/03/96	SK Rapid Wien	A	0-2	
30/03/96	Grazer AK	H	0-1	
07/04/96	FC Admira Wacker	A	0-3	
10/04/96	SV Casino Salzburg	H	1-3	og (Lainer)
13/04/96	SV Ried	H	1-2	Laux
16/04/96	SK Sturm Graz	H	1-3	Berchtold
20/04/96	FK Austria Wien	H	2-2	Gröbl 2
26/04/96	SK Sturm Graz	A	0-0	
30/04/96	SV Ried	A	1-1	Haberfellner
04/05/96	FC Tirol Innsbruck	H	0-3	
11/05/96	SK Rapid Wien	H	2-3	Berchtold 2
14/05/96	LASK Linz	A	1-3	Helm (p)
18/05/96	Grazer AK	A	2-3	Schrammel, Gröbl
25/05/96	FC Admira Wacker	H	0-2	
01/06/96	SV Casino Salzburg	A	0-4	

SK STURM GRAZ

CLUB DIRECTORY

SK Stabil Fenster Sturm Graz
Eggenbergergürtel 9
8020 Graz
tel - (0316) 975975-0
fax - (0316) 975975-8
Year of Formation - 1909
President - Hannes Kartnig
Secretary - Gerhard Stroicz
Coach - Ivica Osim
Stadium - Sturm-Platz (10,500)

MAJOR HONOURS
Domestic Cup - (1) 1996.

APPEARANCES 95/96

	P	Ap	(s)	Gls
Heinz ARZBERGER	G	3	(1)	
Andrei CHERNYSHOV (RUS)	D	29		
Thomas GILL (NOR)	G	18		
Roland GORIUPP	G	15		
Herbert GRASSLER	M	26	(5)	
Michael GRUBER	M	14	(14)	1
Mario HAAS	A	34	(1)	12
Wolfgang HOPFER	M		(1)	
Walter HÖRMANN	M	22		
Alfred HÖRTNAGL	M		(7)	
Roman MÄHLICH	M	22		2
Darko MILANIC (SLO)	D	30		3
Günther NEUKIRCHNER	D	17	(13)	
Zeljko PAKASIN (CRO)	D		(1)	
Mario POSCH	D	29	(2)	
Gilbert PRILASNIG	M	13	(15)	2
Hannes REINMAYR	M	9	(23)	2
Markus SCHOPP	M	33		6
Marek SWIERCZEWSKI (POL)	D	16	(2)	1
Hannes TOTH	A		(2)	
Ivica VASTIC	A	30	(1)	20
Arnold WETL	A	36		10

LEAGUE RESULTS 1995/96

02/08/95	FC Admira Wacker	A	5-1	Vastic 2 (1p), Haas, Schopp, Wetl
05/08/95	SV Casino Salzburg	H	0-2	
12/08/95	SV Ried	A	4-2	Haas, Wetl, Vastic 2
19/08/95	FK Austria Wien	H	2-0	Haas, Vastic
26/08/95	Grazer AK	A	2-3	Haas, Mählich
30/08/95	FC Tirol Innsbruck	H	2-0	og (Wazinger), Wetl
16/09/95	SK Vorwärts Steyr	A	3-1	Wetl 2, Schopp
20/09/95	SK Rapid Wien	H	0-1	
23/09/95	LASK Linz	A	1-2	Haas
03/10/95	LASK Linz	H	3-1	Milanic 2, Wetl
06/10/95	FC Admira Wacker	H	0-0	
14/10/95	SV Casino Salzburg	A	1-1	Wetl
21/10/95	SV Ried	H	1-0	Haas
28/10/95	FK Austria Wien	A	3-0	Haas, Prilasnig, Schopp
04/11/95	Grazer AK	H	1-1	Vastic
08/11/95	FC Tirol Innsbruck	A	2-2	Vastic, Milanic
19/11/95	SK Rapid Wien	A	2-0	Mählich, Vastic
22/11/95	SK Vorwärts Steyr	H	4-2	Vastic 2, Reinmayr 2
13/03/96	SV Ried	H	3-1	Vastic, og (Kramer), Haas
16/03/96	FK Austria Wien	A	1-0	Haas
20/03/96	FC Admira Wacker	H	2-0	Schopp, Vastic
23/03/96	SV Casino Salzburg	A	2-1	Vastic, Gruber
30/03/96	FC Tirol Innsbruck	H	0-1	
07/04/96	LASK Linz	A	1-2	Swierczewski
10/04/96	SK Rapid Wien	H	1-0	Vastic
13/04/96	Grazer AK	A	0-1	
16/04/96	SK Vorwärts Steyr	A	3-1	Vastic, Haas, Prilasnig
20/04/96	FC Admira Wacker	A	2-0	Wetl, Vastic (p)
26/04/96	SK Vorwärts Steyr	H	0-0	
30/04/96	Grazer AK	H	0-2	
11/05/96	SV Casino Salzburg	H	2-1	Haas, Schopp
14/05/96	FK Austria Wien	H	3-0	Schopp, Vastic (p), Haas
18/05/96	FC Tirol Innsbruck	A	1-1	Vastic
21/05/96	SV Ried	A	2-2	Wetl, Vastic
25/05/96	LASK Linz	H	2-1	Vastic, Wetl
01/06/96	SK Rapid Wien	A	0-2	

FC TIROL INNSBRUCK

CLUB DIRECTORY

FC Tirol Innsbruck
Resselstrasse 18/II
6020 Innsbruck
tel - (0512) 33432
fax - (0512) 393288
Year of Formation - 1913
President - Jürgen Bodenseer
Secretary - Siegmund Feistmantl
Coach - Dietmar Constantini
Stadium - Tivoli (17,532)

MAJOR HONOURS
League Championship - (7)
1971, 1972, 1973, 1975, 1977, 1989, 1990.
Domestic Cup - (7)
1970, 1973, 1975, 1978, 1979, 1989, 1993.

APPEARANCES 95/96

	P	Ap	(s)	Gls
Michael BAUR	M	33		1
Jerzy BRZECZEK (POL)	M	34		9
Harald CERNY	A	18		6
Stanislav CHERCHESOV (RUS)	G	17		
Walter DE VORA	G	13		
Damir GRABOVAC (CRO)	A	1	(5)	
Alexander GRUBER	A		(1)	
Theo GRÜNER	M	7	(20)	1
Jürgen HARTMANN	M	16		
Armin HOBEL	A		(1)	
Thomas JANESCHITZ	A	29	(6)	9
Roland KIRCHLER	M	27	(2)	7
Richard KITZBICHLER	M	31	(1)	7
Gernot KRINNER	A	18		9
Milan ORAZE	G	6	(1)	
Oliver PRUDLO	D	12	(7)	
Souleymane SANE (SEN)	A	5	(10)	3
Andreas SCHIENER	M	31	(1)	6
Christian SCHÖPF	A		(1)	
Florian SCHWARZ	A		(3)	
Attila SEKERLIOGLU	D	15	(1)	
Thomas SILBERBERGER	M	11	(17)	2
Michael STREITER	D	29	(2)	4
Yervand SUKIASYAN (ARM)	D	11	(5)	
Robert WAZINGER	M	32	(1)	1

LEAGUE RESULTS 1995/96

05/08/95	FC Admira Wacker	H	3-0	Streiter, Sané, Kirchler
12/08/95	SK Vorwärts Steyr	H	5-1	Cerny, Brzeczek, Streiter (p), Janeschitz, Silberberger
19/08/95	SK Rapid Wien	A	1-3	Cerny
26/08/95	LASK Linz	H	2-1	Janeschitz, Sané
30/08/95	SK Sturm Graz	A	0-2	
02/09/95	Grazer AK	A	0-3	
16/09/95	SV Casino Salzburg	H	1-1	Cerny
20/09/95	SV Ried	A	1-2	Cerny
23/09/95	FK Austria Wien	H	3-1	Silberberger, Schiener, Janeschitz
03/10/95	FK Austria Wien	A	0-1	
06/10/95	Grazer AK	H	1-1	Sané
15/10/95	FC Admira Wacker	A	0-0	
20/10/95	SK Vorwärts Steyr	A	2-2	Cerny, Schiener
28/10/95	SK Rapid Wien	H	1-2	Kirchler
04/11/95	LASK Linz	A	2-1	Schiener, Kitzbichler
08/11/95	SK Sturm Graz	H	2-2	Kirchler, Janeschitz
18/11/95	SV Ried	H	2-0	Schiener, Kitzbichler
21/11/95	SV Casino Salzburg	A	1-3	Cerny
02/03/96	Grazer AK	H	2-0	Brzeczek, Janeschitz
09/03/96	FC Admira Wacker	A	4-1	og (Zingler), Kitzbichler 2, Kirchler
13/03/96	SK Vorwärts Steyr	H	3-0	Brzeczek, Janeschitz, Schiener
16/03/96	SV Ried	A	6-0	Krinner 3, Brzeczek, Janeschitz, Kitzbichler
23/03/96	FK Austria Wien	H	2-0	Streiter (p), Kitzbichler
30/03/96	SK Sturm Graz	A	1-0	Brzeczek
06/04/96	SV Casino Salzburg	A	2-0	Kirchler, Janeschitz
10/04/96	LASK Linz	H	2-1	Krinner, Brzeczek
13/04/96	SK Rapid Wien	A	1-3	Brzeczek
20/04/96	Grazer AK	A	3-1	Kirchler, Baur (p), Grüner
26/04/96	FC Admira Wacker	H	2-0	Schiener, Kitzbichler
30/04/96	SK Rapid Wien	H	1-1	Janeschitz
04/05/96	SK Vorwärts Steyr	A	3-0	Krinner 3
11/05/96	FK Austria Wien	A	0-1	
14/05/96	SV Ried	H	2-2	Krinner, Wazinger (match abandoned; later awarded as 0-3)
18/05/96	SK Sturm Graz	H	1-1	Kirchler
25/05/96	SV Casino Salzburg	H	3-1	Brzeczek 2, Streiter (p)
01/06/96	LASK Linz	A	1-1	Krinner

PROMOTED CLUB

SECOND DIVISION FINAL TABLE 95/96

		Pd	W	D	L	F	A	Pt	GD
1	**FC Linz**	**30**	**21**	**5**	**4**	**62**	**27**	**68**	**+35**
2	SG SV Gerasdorf/Wiener Sport-Club	30	15	11	4	54	25	56	+29
3	First Vienna FC 1894	30	13	9	8	48	39	48	+9
4	VfB Mödling	30	13	7	10	45	33	46	+12
5	DSV Leoben	30	12	8	10	41	33	44	+8
6	Favoritner AC	30	10	14	6	38	31	44	+7
7	Austria Lustenau	30	9	13	8	34	24	40	+10
8	SV Braunau	30	9	11	10	39	40	38	-1
9	WSG Wattens	30	7	15	8	34	34	36	=
10	SV Flavia Solva	30	8	12	10	21	37	36	-16
11	SV Spittal an der Drau	30	9	8	13	35	42	35	-7
12	FC Kufstein	30	9	8	13	33	42	35	-9
13	VSE St. Pölten	30	8	10	12	36	51	34	-15
14	SAK Klagenfurt	30	8	8	14	30	50	32	-20
15	SV Oberwart	30	7	9	14	33	49	30	-16
16	ASK Klingenbach	30	4	8	18	28	54	20	-26

PROMOTION/RELEGATION PLAY-OFF
FC Admira Wacker 3, SG SV Gerasdorf/Wiener Sport-Club 4
SG SV Gerasdorf/Wiener Sport-Club 0, FC Admira Wacker 6
(FC Admira Wacker 9-4)

CLUB DIRECTORY

FC Linz
Ziegeleistrasse
Linzer Stadion
4020 Linz
tel - (0732) 610101
fax - (0732) 610101-72
Year of Formation - 1946
President - Karl Reisinger
Secretary - Tanja Draxler
Coach - Heinz Hochhauser
(96/97 - Zlatko Kranjcar)
Stadium - Linzer Stadion (25,000)

MAJOR HONOURS

League Championship - (1) 1974.

AZERBAIJAN

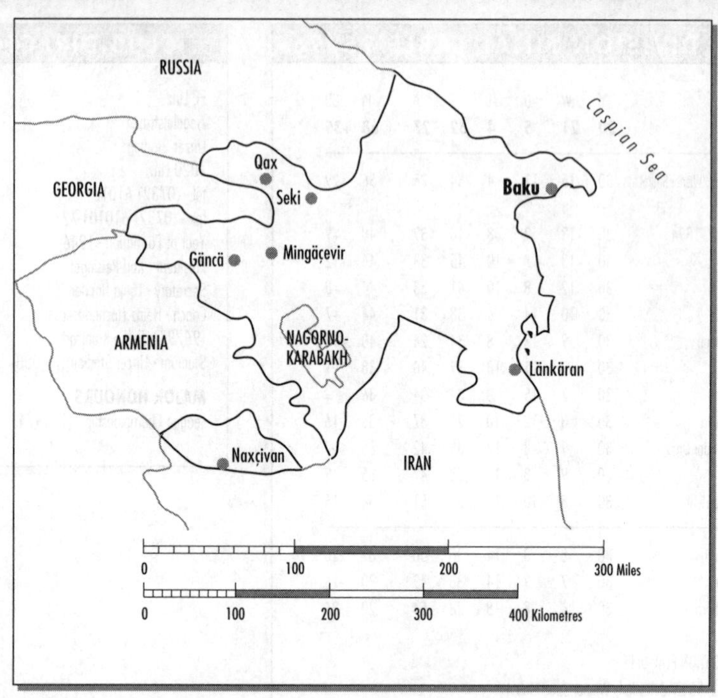
RUSSIA
Caspian Sea
GEORGIA
Qax
Seki
Baku
Gäncä
Mingäçevir
ARMENIA
NAGORNO-KARABAKH
Länkäran
Naxçivan
IRAN
0
100
200
300 Miles
0
100
200
300
400 Kilometres

BACK TO BAKU FOR NATIONAL TEAM

Neftchi use league format to their advantage

FEDERATION DIRECTORY

Azerbaycan Futbol Federasiyalari Assosiasiyasi
42 Husi Haciev, 370009 Baku

tel - (12) 940542
tlx - 142349 AFFA SU
fax - (12) 989393

Year of Formation - 1992
President - Fuad Musaev
Secretary - Cingiz Ismayilov

Stadium - Tofig Bahramov, Baku (54,000)

A rather strange new format was introduced to the 1995/96 national championship in Azerbaijan. 11 teams began the competition - an odd feature in itself - and the mid-season cut came after each team had played the others twice in traditional home-and-away fashion. The top six teams then went into a championship group, with the other five breaking off into a relegation group.

The novel ingredient was that instead of taking half their points totals from the first phase - a conventional format in similar systems around Europe - the teams only carried forward their records from the matches played against the other teams in their respective second-phase group.

This format proved heavily advantageous to the country's most powerful club, Neftchi Baku. They could only finish fifth in the first phase, but their 'head-to-head' results were good, and they began the play-offs well placed, just two points behind defending champions Kepez. Neftchi were the strongest side in the play-offs and went on to win the title for the second time, the first club to do so in the five years that the championship had been staged. They also completed the 'double' by successfully defending the national Cup, beating Karabag 3-0 in the final.

Most of the top Azerbaijani internationals still in the country were on Neftchi's books, including star midfield trio Yunis Huseynov, Vladislav Kadirov and Vyacheslav Lichkin. The latter was the player of the season and was rewarded with a transfer to Turkish club Trabzonspor. Curiously, at the same time that Lichkin packed his bags for

LEAGUE CHAMPIONSHIP RESULTS 95/96

FIRST PHASE

		1	2	3	4	5	6	7	8	9	10	11
1	Baki Fehlesi		1-0	2-3	2-4	1-0	2-1	0-2	1-1	0-2	1-2	0-2
2	Kepez	4-1		7-1	0-0	7-2	10-1	0-3	8-0	3-3	1-1	2-1
3	Kur-Nur	1-1	0-5		0-4	5-3	3-1	0-2	1-1	1-2	5-0	0-3
4	Neftchi	1-1	3-2	1-0		5-1	4-1	2-2	1-0	3-1	5-0	0-0
5	OIK	1-2	0-4	1-0	2-1		1-0	0-3	0-2	1-4	0-2	1-2
6	Pambykchy	0-1	2-10	3-5	0-0	2-0		0-7	0-0	1-4	0-2	0-1
7	Karabag	2-0	1-3	0-0	1-1	0-1	4-1		2-0	0-3	1-0	1-1
8	Shamkir	1-0	0-2	0-3	1-4	1-1	3-0	1-2		0-2	1-3	0-1
9	Turan	0-1	0-2	4-2	1-0	1-0	3-1	0-2	2-1		2-0	0-3
10	Vilyash	5-2	0-4	0-4	1-3	0-2	0-2	1-3	3-2	2-6		0-1
11	Khazri	3-1	0-0	1-1	1-0	2-0	3-0	1-0	3-0	1-1	1-0	

PLAY-OFFS

CHAMPIONSHIP GROUP		1	2	3	4	5	6
1	Kepez		0-1	3-2	0-0	0-1	0-0
2	Kur-Nur	0-2		1-2	2-2	0-1	0-1
3	Neftchi	1-2	3-1		2-1	3-1	0-0
4	Karabag	1-2	1-1	2-2		0-1	4-0
5	Turan	2-1	3-0	1-2	***		0-0
6	Khazri	1-0	2-1	0-1	2-2	4-1	

*** N.B. The Turan-Karabag match was awarded as a 0-3 defeat for both teams.

RELEGATION GROUP		1	2	3	4	5
1	Baki Fehlesi		0-0	6-3	1-2	1-0
2	OIK	0-2		3-0	0-1	0-2
3	Pambykchy	2-0	1-3		4-1	0-1
4	Vilyash	0-3	0-1	3-1		0-0
5	Shamkir	0-3	0-2	8-2	9-2	

INTERNATIONAL HONOURS

None

Trabzon, the national team were making plans to return to Baku for the World Cup qualifying campaign, having been exiled to the Turkish city for the European Championship qualifiers. It seems certain that Azerbaijan's results will improve now that FIFA have allowed them to stage matches once again on home soil.

LEAGUE CHAMPIONSHIP FINAL TABLES 95/96

FIRST PHASE

		Pd	W	D	L	F	A	Pt	GD
1	Khazri	20	14	5	1	31	7	47	+24
2	Kepez	20	13	4	3	74	20	43	+54
3	Turan	20	13	2	5	41	24	41	+17
4	Karabag	20	12	4	4	38	15	40	+23
5	Neftchi	20	11	6	3	42	17	39	+25
6	Kur-Nur	20	7	4	9	35	41	25	-6
7	Baki Fehlesi	20	6	3	11	20	35	21	-15
8	Vilyash	20	6	1	13	22	46	19	-24
9	OIK	20	5	1	14	16	43	16	-27
10	Shamkir	20	3	4	13	15	39	13	-24
11	Pambykchy	20	2	2	16	16	63	8	-47

PLAY-OFFS

Championship Group		First Phase Head-to-Head						Play-offs					Total						
		Pd	W	D	L	F	A	W	D	L	F	A	W	D	L	F	A	Pt	GD
1	Neftchi	20	4	4	2	14	8	6	2	2	18	12	10	6	4	32	20	36	+12
2	Khazri	20	4	5	1	12	5	4	4	2	10	9	8	9	3	22	14	33	+8
3	Kepez	20	5	3	2	24	12	4	2	4	10	9	9	5	6	34	21	32	+13
4	Turan	20	4	2	4	15	17	5	1	4	11	13	9	3	8	26	30	30	-4
5	Karabag	20	3	4	3	12	11	1	5	4	13	15	4	9	7	25	26	21	-1
6	Kur-Nur	20	0	2	8	5	29	1	2	7	7	17	1	4	15	12	46	7	-34

Relegation Group		First Phase Head-to-Head						Play-offs					Total						
		Pd	W	D	L	F	A	W	D	L	F	A	W	D	L	F	A	Pt	GD
7	Baki Fehlesi	16	4	1	3	10	11	5	1	2	16	7	9	2	5	26	18	29	+8
8	Vilyash	16	6	0	2	17	10	3	1	4	9	19	9	1	6	26	29	28	-3
9	Shamkir	16	3	3	2	11	8	4	1	3	20	10	7	4	5	31	18	25	+13
10	OIK	16	2	1	5	5	10	4	1	3	9	6	6	2	8	14	16	20	-2
11	Pambtkchy	16	2	1	5	5	9	2	0	6	13	25	4	1	11	18	34	13	-16

N.B. After the First Phase the top six teams qualify for the Championship play-off group and the bottom five go into a relegation play-off group. Each team carries forward its record from the First Phase 'head-to-head' matches played against the other teams in their respective play-off group.

EUROPEAN CUPS RESULTS 95/96

CUP-WINNERS' CUP

● NEFTCHI BAKU

Preliminary round APOEL NICOSIA (CYP)

A 0-3

Hasanov; Ismailov, Jounousov, Asadoullaev, Lichkin, Isaev (Azimov 41), Huseynov, Vahabzade, Moussaev, Aliev (Bairamov 75), Alekberov.

H 0-0

Hasanov; Ismailov, Jounousov, Asadov, Lichkin, Azimov, Huseynov, Vahabzade, Moussaev (Bairamov 61), Aliev (Isaev 46), Alekberov.

UEFA CUP

● KEPEZ

Preliminary round FK AUSTRIA WIEN (AUT)

H 0-4

Gafarov (Sukurov 46); Alahverdiev, Ahmedov J., Mammadov, Jabarov, Parvarov, Kurbanov, Mardanov, Tanriverdiyev, Ahmedov R., Suleymanov (Gulami 81).

A 1-5 Suleymanov (26)

Sukurov (Gafarov 46); Alahverdiev, Ahmedov J., Mammadov, Jabarov (Hajyev 46), Parvarov, Kurbanov, Mardanov, Tanriverdiyev, Ahmedov, Suleymanov.

DOMESTIC CUP RESULTS

SECOND ROUND

Kepez v LDU Khazar 12-1; 1-1 (Kepez 13-2)
Kafkaz v Pambykchy N 2-2; 0-3 (Pambykchy N 5-2)
Vilyash v Shirvan-Orkhan 0-1; 0-0 (Shirvan-Orkhan 1-0)
OIK-Goyazan v Neftchi 1-1; 0-3 (Neftchi 4-1)
Umud v Kobustan 8-0; 4-1 (Umud 12-1)
Shamkir v Kurmuk 6-2; 4-2 (Shamkir 10-4)
Nakhchivan v Baki Fehlesi 2-3; 1-0 (3-3; Baki Fehlesi on away goals)
Chinar PA v Pambychy B 2-0; 0-5 (Pambykchy B 5-2)
Kur-Nur v Goy-Gol 3-0; 3-0 (Kur-Nur 6-0)
Neftkaz v Khazri 2-0; 0-3 (Khazri 3-2)
OIK v Plastik 0-3; 2-1 (Plastik 4-2)
Azal v Karabag 0-2; 0-2 (Karabag 4-0)
Dinamo v Farid 1-1; 0-3 (Farid 4-1)
Tar-Tar v Ehtiyat Amak Kuvvelari 3-0; 3-0 (Tar-Tar 6-0)
Sumkayit v Ganclik 7-1; 3-0 (Sumkayit 10-1)
Turab v Kum Adasi 3-0; 3-0 (Turan 6-0)

THIRD ROUND

Kepez v Pambykchy N 7-1; 3-4 (Kepez 10-5)
Shirvan-Orkhan v Neftchi 0-3; 0-3 (Neftchi 6-0)
Umud v Shamkir 1-5; 1-5 (Shamkir 10-2)
Baki Fehlesi v Tar-Tar 3-0; 3-0 (Baki Fehlesi 6-0)
Turan v Pambykchy B 3-0; 3-0 (Turan 6-0)
Kur-Nur v Khazri 1-0; 0-5 (Khazri 5-1)
Sumkayit v Plastik 1-0; 1-2 (2-2; Sumkayit on away goal)
Karabag v Farid 2-0; 1-0 (Karabag 3-0)

QUARTER-FINALS

Kepez v Neftchi 1-0; 0-2 (Neftchi 2-1)
Shamkir v Baki Fehlesi 0-1; 0-2 (Baki Fehlesi 3-0)
Turan v Khazri 0-0; 0-1 (Khazri 1-0)
Sumkayit v Karabag 1-3; 0-0 (Karabag 3-1)

SEMI-FINALS

Neftchi v Baki Fehlesi 1-1; 3-0 (Neftchi 4-1)
Khazri v Karabag 1-0; 0-3 (Karabag 3-1)

FINAL

NEFTCHI 3
KARABAG 0

NATIONAL TEAM RESULTS 95/96

16/08/95	Slovakia (ECQ)	H	Trabzon	0-1	
06/09/95	France (ECQ)	A	Auxerre	0-10	
11/10/95	Israel (ECQ)	A	Tel-Aviv	0-2	
15/11/95	Poland (ECQ)	H	Trabzon	0-0	
09/04/96	Turkey	H	Baku	0-1	
27/05/96	Belarus	A	Molodecho	2-2	Kurbanov (53), Idigov (75)
02/06/96	Norway (WCQ)	A	Oslo	0-5	

NATIONAL TEAM APPEARANCES 95/96

Coach - Agasalim MIRDZHAVADOV; Kazbek TUAYEV	SVK	FRA	ISR	POL	TUR	BLS	NOR
Nizami SADIKOV - Turan Tovuz	G	s36					
Igor GETMAN - Anzhi Makhachkala (RUS)	D	D		D	D		D
Vladislav NOSENKO - Kryvbas Kryvyi Rih (UKR)	D				s46	D	s40
Tarlan AHMEDOV - Karabag Agdam	D	D	D	D	D	D	D
Emin AGAYEV - Anzhi Makhachkala (RUS)	D71	D	s58	M	M		M40
Rasim ABUSOV - Karabag Agdam	M	M	M	M	M46	M	M79
Yunis HUSEYNOV - Neftchi Baku	M	M			s83	M	M
Sahin DINIYEV - Beitar Tel-Aviv (ISR)	M46	M			M46	s66	
Vladislav KADIROV - Neftchi Baku	M	M74	M	M65	M		
Vyacheslav LICHKIN - Neftchi Baku	M	M	M79	s86	M	M	M
Samir ALEKBEROV - Neftchi Baku	A	s46					
Maxmud KURBANOV - Kepez Ganca	s46	A46		s65			
Arif ASADOV - Neftchi Baku	s71	D	D			D	s79
Elhan HASANOV - Neftchi Baku		G36			G		
Musvik HUSEYNOV - Karabag Agdam		s74					
Aleksander JIDKOV - Zafririm Holon (ISR)			G	G		G	G
Yashar VAHABZADE - Neftchi Baku			D	D			
Samir KHAIROV - Baki Fehlesi			D58				
Vidadi RZAYEV - Turan Tovuz			M70	M69	s46	M66	M46
Nazim SULEYMANOV - Spartak-Alania Vladikavkaz (RUS)			A	A86	A	A46	A
Veli KASUMOV - Albacete Balompié (ESP)			A	A	A83		
Kurban KURBANOV - Turan Tovuz			s70	s69		s46	s46
Elhan MAMEDOV - Turan Tovuz			s79				
Deni GAISUMOV - CSKA Moskva (RUS)/Sokol Saratov (RUS)				D	D	D	D
Ruslan IDIGOV - Spartak Nalchik (RUS)						M	M

BELARUS

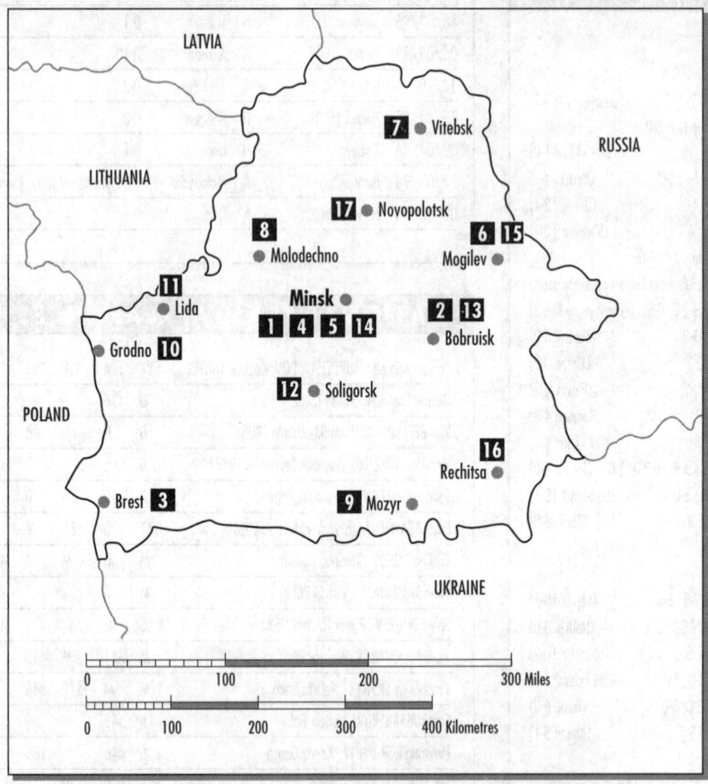

1	ATAKA-AURA MINSK	147	10	NEMAN GRODNO	156
2	FC BOBRUISK	148	11	OBUVSHCHIK LIDA	157
3	DINAMO BREST	149	12	SHAKHTER SOLIGORSK	158
4	DINAMO MINSK	150	13	SHINNIK BOBRUISK	159
5	DINAMO-93 MINSK	151	14	TORPEDO MINSK	160
6	DNEPR MOGILEV	152	15	TORPEDO MOGILEV	161
7	DVINA VITEBSK	153	16	VEDRICH RECHITSA	162
8	FC MOLODECHNO	154	17	NAFTAN-DEVON NOVOPOLOTSK	163
9	MPKC MOZYR	155			

MPKC MOZYR UP FOR THE CUP

Different championship, same winners

FEDERATION DIRECTORY

The Belarussian Football Federation
ul. Kirov 8/2, 220050 Minsk
tel - (0172) 272920/
272325/204540
tlx - 252175 athlet
fax - (0172) 272920
Stadium - Dinamo, Minsk (50,050)

Year of Formation - 1992
President - Yevgenyi Shuntov
Secretary - Vadim Zhuk

Having reached the conclusion that a five-month mid-season break was excessively long and bad for business, the Belarussian football authorities decided to switch the national championship to the Scandinavian/Russian spring-to-autumn format.

To do this, they introduced a mini-championship for the second half of 1995. There were still 16 teams involved as before, but they only played each other once. Other than that, it was a normal championship, with two UEFA Cup places up for grabs for the champions and runners-up.

The competition may have been nothing more than a filling-in exercise, but defending champions Dinamo Minsk took it very seriously. The team from the capital had won every previous national title since independence, and they made all but certain of taking their fifth in a row by winning all of their first ten matches.

Dinamo Minsk only had one challenger, ambitious newly-promoted club MPKC Mozyr, who also made a bold and confident start, scoring 16 goals without reply in their first three matches and maintaining an impressive sequence of results thanks to the prolific goalscoring of their striker Sergei Yaromko.

When the two leading teams came face to face for the one and only time at the beginning of November, Dinamo Minsk were five points clear. With only two games remaining they needed just a draw away to MPKC to seal the title. But the home side responded to the encouragement of the record 20,000 crowd by scoring twice in the first half and deservedly going on to win 2-1, thus handing Dinamo their first defeat in 33 matches.

The defeat, however, only delayed the inevitable. Three days later, back in their home stadium, Dinamo thrashed

INTERNATIONAL HONOURS

None

LEAGUE CHAMPIONSHIP RESULTS 1995

		1	2	3	4	5	6	7	8	9	10	11	12	13	14	15	16
1	Ataka-Aura Minsk		3-0	3-1						1-1			4-0	3-0		0-0	1-0
2	FC Bobruisk			1-4				0-0	0-7	0-5		0-2		0-4	0-0		
3	Dinamo Brest							1-1	3-2	0-3		1-1		4-2	1-2	3-0	
4	Dinamo Minsk	0-0	6-1	5-2				3-1	2-0			6-2	1-1		5-1		
5	Dinamo-93 Minsk	1-1	6-0	1-0	0-2				4-1			2-1	1-0		3-1		
6	Dnepr Mogilev	0-0	5-1	4-3	0-1	1-3						3-0	0-1		3-2		
7	Dvina Vitebsk	0-2				0-1	1-2			1-1	2-0			1-1		1-0	1-0
8	FC Molodechno	1-0					2-1	0-1		2-1	1-3			6-1		4-0	2-1
9	MPKC Mozyr				2-1	2-2	1-0				7-0			4-0		3-1	3-0
10	Neman Grodno	0-4	3-0	2-3	2-3	2-0	4-1					1-0	1-0				
11	Obuvshchik Lida	1-3						0-2	1-0	0-3				0-0	1-1	0-0	3-0
12	Shakhter Soligorsk		2-1	3-1				1-0	1-1	1-3		1-3			0-1		
13	Shinnik Bobruisk				0-3	0-1	1-2				3-1		3-1			0-2	1-1
14	Torpedo Minsk	2-1						0-0	0-4	0-5	1-0			0-1		0-3	1-0
15	Torpedo Mogilev		5-1		0-2	1-3	2-1				1-1		0-0				2-2
16	Vedrich Rechitsa		2-1	2-0	1-2	3-0	1-3				9-0		0-0				

LEAGUE CHAMPIONSHIP FINAL TABLE 1995

		Home						Away					Total						
		Pd	W	D	L	F	A	W	D	L	F	A	W	D	L	F	A	Pt	GD
1	Dinamo Minsk	15	6	2	0	28	8	6	0	1	14	5	12	2	1	42	13	38	+29
2	MPKC Mozyr	15	6	1	0	22	4	5	2	1	22	5	11	3	1	44	9	36	+35
3	Dinamo-93 Minsk	15	6	1	1	18	6	4	1	2	10	9	10	2	3	28	15	32	+13
4	Ataka-Aura Minsk	15	5	2	0	15	2	3	3	2	11	5	8	5	2	26	7	29	+19
5	FC Molodechno	15	6	0	2	18	8	2	1	4	15	11	8	1	6	33	19	25	+14
6	Dnepr Mogilev	15	4	1	3	16	11	3	0	4	10	12	7	1	7	26	23	22	+3
7	Dvina Vitebsk	15	3	2	3	7	7	2	3	2	5	5	5	5	5	12	12	20	=
8	Neman Grodno	15	5	0	3	15	11	1	1	5	5	24	6	1	8	20	35	19	-15
9	Torpedo Minsk	15	3	1	4	4	14	2	2	3	8	13	5	3	7	12	27	18	-15
10	Dinamo Brest	15	3	2	2	13	11	2	0	6	14	21	5	2	8	27	32	17	-5
11	Torpedo Mogilev	15	2	3	2	11	10	2	2	4	6	11	4	5	6	17	21	17	-4
12	Obuvshchik Lida	15	2	3	3	6	9	2	1	4	9	14	4	4	7	15	23	16	-8
13	Shakhter Soligorsk	15	3	1	3	9	10	1	3	4	3	10	4	4	7	12	20	16	-8
14	Vedrich Rechitsa	15	4	1	2	18	6	0	2	6	4	14	4	3	8	22	20	15	+2
15	Shinnik Bobruisk	15	2	1	4	8	11	2	2	4	9	18	4	3	8	17	29	15	-12
16	FC Bobruisk	15	0	2	5	1	22	0	0	8	5	32	0	2	13	6	54	2	-48

Obuvshchik Lida 6-2, with star striker Petr Kachuro completing a hat-trick with the last kick of the season to take his seasonal total to a goal-a-game 15, just one behind MPKC's Yaromko.

Hard-earned though their title triumph undoubtedly was, Dinamo Minsk were more pleased by the impressive form they showed in the UEFA Cup. They required penalty-kicks to get past Universitatea Craiova in the preliminary round, but against Austria Vienna, in round one, Ivan Shchekin's side won both matches in impressive style to earn a second-round date with Werder Bremen. The journey ended in Germany with a 0-5 defeat, but Dinamo were still able to rally themselves in the return leg and go ou on a high with a 2-1 victory.

With the league title in the bag once more, Dinamo had another six months to wait before they had a chance o completing the 'double'. The semi-finals of the nationa Cup brought together the league's top four teams, and the final welcomed the top two. Dinamo's home stadium wa the venue, but the visitors MPKC Mozyr were the team in

DOMESTIC CUP RESULTS

1/16 FINALS

Kommunalnik Pinsk 0, Dinamo Minsk 4
Fomalgaut Borisov 0, Neman Grodno 0 (6-5 on pens.)
Kimovets Vitebsk 0, Dinamo-93 Minsk 3
Brestbytkhim Brest 2, FC Molodechno 4
Transmash Mogilev 0, Dinamo Brest 1
Khimik Svetlogorsk 4, Torpedo Minsk 1
FC Gomel 2, Dvina Vitebsk 1
Kardan-Flaiyers Grodno 6, Obuvshchik Lida 2
Naftan-Devon Novopolotsk 1, Ataka-Aura Minsk 3
Dinamo-Yuni Minsk 4, Shinnik Bobruisk 0
KPF Slonim 3, Vedrich Rechitsa 0
Torpedo Zhodino 1, MPKC Mozyr 8
Grant Mikashevichi 1, Dnepr Mogilev 6
Stroitel Starye Dorogi 0, Torpedo Mogilev 3
Lokomotiv Vitebsk 0, Shakhter Soligorsk 1
Khimvolokno Grodno w/o FC Bobruisk

1/8 FINALS

Ataka-Aura Minsk 2, Dinamo-Yuni Minsk 0
MPKC Mozyr 2, Dnepr Mogilev 1
Dinamo Minsk 4, Khimik Svetlogorsk 0
Dinamo-93 Minsk 7, Khimvolokno Grodno 1
Dinamo Brest 1, FC Molodechno 4
Torpedo Mogilev 0, FC Gomel 1
Shakhter Soligorsk 2, Kardan-Flaiyers Grodno 1
KPF Slonim 1, Fomalgaut Borisov 4

QUARTER-FINALS

FC Molodechno 0, Dinamo-93 Minsk 1
Shakhter Soligorsk 2, MPKC Mozyr 3
FC Gomel 0, Ataka-Aura Minsk 4
Dinamo Minsk 3, Fomalgaut Borisov 1

SEMI-FINALS

MPKC Mozyr 5, Ataka-Aura Minsk 4
Dinamo-93 Minsk 0, Dinamo Minsk 4

FINAL

17/05/96, Minsk
MPKC MOZYR 4 Romashchenko (43), Yaromko (44, 79), Konovalov (89)
DINAMO MINSK 1 Chernyavski (65)
referee - Serezhkin
MPKC MOZYR - Svirkov; Sednev, Levchuk, Golmak, Skorobogatko (Denisyuk 74), Khripach (Sysoyev 34), Kulchi, Romashchenko (Konovalov 46), Gomonov, Gorovoi, Yaromko.
DINAMO MINSK - Varivonchik (Yevnevich 46); Yaskovich, Ostrovski, Lavrik, Khatskevich, Lukhvich, Chernyavski, Makovski M. (Mayorov 87), Belkevich, Makovski V. (Shavrov 74), Kachuro.

form and they cruised to an astonishingly easy 4-1 win, with the ever-reliable Yaromko scoring two of the goals.

A fortnight after the Cup final, Belarus began their World Cup campaign with a difficult match away to Sweden. It was to be a nightmare start. Despite the presence of seven foreign-based players in the starting line-up, the team crashed to a 5-1 defeat. A year earlier, Belarus had closed the international season with a famous 1-0 win against Holland. Now coach Borovski was forced to spend the summer reassessing his entire game plan.

NATIONAL TEAM APPEARANCES 95/96

Coach - Sergei BOROVSKI	LIT	HOL	TCH	LUX	MLT	TUR	SVK	POL	AZB	SWE	Cps	Gls
Andrei SATSUNKHEVICH (18/03/66) - Lokomotiv Nizhni Novgorod (RUS)	G	G				G		s46	G46	G	10	-
Sergei GURENKO (30/09/72) - Lokomotiv Moskva (RUS)	D	D	D	D	D	D	D		D	D	16	-
Alexander TAIKOV (23/06/70) - Maccabi Herzliya (ISR)	D	D	D	D	D		D		D46		14	1
Pavel RODNENOK (30/07/64) - Ataka-Aura Minsk	D	D	D	D		M	M	M			12	-
Andrei DOVNAR (29/01/73) - Dinamo-93 Minsk/Dinamo Minsk	D	D	D	D	D	D46	D46	D46			9	-
Konstantin KOVALENKO (02/05/75) - Kolos Krasnodar (RUS)	M										1	-
Alexander KHATSKEVICH (19/10/73) - Dinamo Minsk	M46					D		D	D	D	8	-
Alexander CHAIKA (27/01/76) - Dnepr Mogilev	M69							M54	s76		3	-
Yuri SHUKANOV (10/03/71) - Maccabi Tel-Aviv (ISR)	A67										6	-
Andrei KOVALENKO (20/03/70) - Kolos Krasnodar (RUS)	A87										1	-
Petr KACHURO (02/08/72) - Dinamo Minsk	A	A	A	A	A	A46	A	s46	s46	s57	15	3
Oleg KHMELNITSKI (25/10/67) - Ataka-Aura Minsk	s46				M44						3	-
Vladimir MAKOVSKI (23/04/77) - FC Molodechno/Dinamo Minsk	s67				s75	s78			A46	A	5	-
Pavel SHAVROV (29/01/71) - Dinamo-93 Minsk	s69										1	-
Sergei SHTANYUK (13/08/73) - Dinamo Minsk/Dinamo Moskva (RUS)	s87					D	D		D	D	5	1
Andrei ZYGMANTOVICH (02/12/62) - Racing Santander (ESP)		D			D59						9	-
Vladimir ZHURAVEL (09/06/71) - Dinamo Minsk		M89	M	M							8	-
Andrei YUSIPETS (16/04/67) - Alemannia Aachen (GER)		M69	M74	M	s59						10	-
Sergei GERASIMETS (13/10/65) - Bnei Yehuda (ISR)		M	M		M	M78					13	6
Myroslav ROMASHCHENKO (16/12/73) - Uralmash Yekaterinburg (RUS)		A86					A76	A	A76	A57	9	1
Yevgeni KASHENTSEV (12/03/71) - Maccabi Tel-Aviv (ISR)		s69	M	M88				M	s46	M63	10	-
Yuri VERGEICHIK (05/03/68) - RWD Molenbeek (BEL)		s86		s88					M46	M	5	1
Sergei VEKHTEV (08/05/71) - Borussia Dortmund (GER)		s89									3	-
Valeri SHANTALOSOV (15/03/66) -												
Lokomotiv Nizhni Novgorod (RUS)/Baltika Kaliningrad (RUS)			G	G	G		G	G46	s46		13	-
Valentin BELKEVICH (27/01/73) - Dinamo Minsk			A	A	s44	A	A	A	A	A	13	3
Vasili BARANOV (05/10/72) - Vedrich Rechitsa/Baltika Kaliningrad (RUS)			s74	M	M		M		M	M	6	-
Yuri MALEYEV (20/03/68) - Ataka-Aura Minsk					M75	M	s46	M86	M46	M	6	-
Alexander METLITSKI (22/04/64) - LASK Linz (AUT)					M						8	-
Alexander KULCHI (01/11/73) - MPKC Mozyr						M89	s76	s54	s46	s63	5	1
Valeri VELICHKO (12/09/66) - Lokomotiv Nizhni Novgorod (RUS)						s46					4	-
Andrei OSTROVSKI (23/06/70) - Dinamo Minsk						s46					2	-
Oleg AVGUL (07/03/72) - Dinamo-93 Minsk						s89					1	-
Erik YAKHIMOVICH (06/09/68) - Dinamo Moskva (RUS)							D		s46		9	-
Alexander ORESHNIKOV (25/05/73) - Krylya Sovetov Samara (RUS)								D			1	-
Andrei SINICHIN (01/06/72) - Stomil Olsztyn (POL)								M62			1	-
Andrei KHRIPACH (28/05/72) - Dnepr Mogilev								s62			3	-
Vladimir KLIMOVICH (24/10/74) - Dnepr Mogilev								s86			1	-

EUROPEAN CUPS RESULTS 95/96

CUP-WINNERS' CUP

● DINAMO-93 MINSK

Preliminary round MOLDE FK (NOR)

H 1-1 Lobanov (37)
Yevnevich; Pavlyuchuk, Lasovski (Avgul 68), Dovnar, Lavrik, Shilo (Tarlovski 57), Shushkevich, Gotsmanov (Sikorski 72), Skripchenko, Shavrov, Lobanov.

A 1-2 Skripchenko (19)
Yevnevich; Avgul, Gotsmanov, Dovnar, Pavlyuchuk, Sikorski, Shushkevich, Tarlovski (Bespanski 76), Skripchenko, Shavrov, Lobanov (Turchinovich 68).

UEFA CUP

● DINAMO MINSK

Preliminary round UNIVERSITATEA CRAIOVA (ROM)

A 0-0
Varivonchik; Taikov, Ostrovski, Shiroki, Shtanyuk, Khatskevich (Ostrikov 87), Mayorov, Volodenkov (Makarenko 73), Zhuravel, Shukanov, Kachuro.

H 0-0 (aet; 3-1 on pens.)
Varivonchik; Taikov, Shiroki, Shtanyuk, Ostrovski, Khatskevich, Zhuravel, Mayorov, Shukanov (Volodenkov 73), Borel (Putilo 46), Kachuro.

1st round FK AUSTRIA WIEN (AUT)

A 2-1 Zhuravel (26), Shukanov (40)
Varivonchik; Khatskevich, Ostrikov, Ostrovski, Shtanyuk, Mayorov (Lukhvich 89), Shiroki (Putilo 77), Shukanov, Zhuravel, Belkevich, Kachuro.

H 1-0 Belkevich (90)
Varivonchik; Khatskevich, Ostrikov, Shiroki, Shtanyuk, Ostrovski, Zhuravel, Chernyavski, Shukanov, Belkevich, Kachuro.

2nd round SV WERDER BREMEN (GER)

A 0-5
Varivonchik; Shtanyuk, Shiroki, Yaskovich, Ostrovski, Lukhvich (Ostrikov 64), Chernyavski, Zhuravel, Shukanov, Belkevich, Kachuro (Mayorov 73).

H 2-1 Khatskevich (76p), Shukanov (90)
Varivonchik; Khatskevich, Lukhvich, Shiroki, Shtanyuk, Zhuravel, Volodenkov (Makarenko 75), Mayorov (Chernyavski 51), Belkevich, Kachuro, Shukanov.

TOP SCORERS

16	Sergei YAROMKO (MPKC Mozyr)
15	Petr KACHURO (Dinamo Minsk)
11	Valentin BELKEVICH (Dinamo Minsk)
10	Maxim ROMASHCHENKO (MPKC Mozyr)
	Pavel SHAVROV (Dinamo-93 Minsk)
7	Alexander GAVLUSH (Ataka-Aura Minsk)
	Vladimir NEVINSKI (Dnepr Mogilev)

PLAYERS OF THE SEASON

SERGEI GURENKO

24-year-old right-back Sergei Gurenko has developed into one of the most dependable and consistent players in the Belarus national team. He played in all but one of the country's international matches in 1995/96 and by the end of the season had earned himself 16 caps - more than any other Belarussian footballer. A naturally gifted player, light on his feet and with plenty of pace, Gurenko has come on in leaps and bounds in recent seasons. In the summer of 1995 he left his hometown club Neman Grodno to play in the Russian championship with Lokomotiv Moscow. Less than a year later he was celebrating victory with his new club in the Russian Cup.

VLADIMIR MAKOVSKI

The discovery of the 1995 mini-championship was undoubtedly FC Molodechno teenager Vladimir Makovski. Or was it his twin brother Mikhail? Supporters and journalists found great difficulty in telling the two boys apart. The only visible difference on the football field was Vladimir's preference for his left foot while Mikhail favoured the right. Vladimir is 10 minutes younger than Mikhail, but it is he who has made the greater progress so far. He earned a first call-up for the Belarus national team against Lithuania in July 1995 at the age of 18 and he was in the starting line-up for the World Cup opener against Sweden the following June. By then both Vladimir and Mikhail had made the major career move from Molodechno to champions Dinamo Minsk.

NATIONAL TEAM RESULTS 95/96

29/07/95	Lithuania	A	Vilnius	1-1	Kachuro (73p)
06/09/95	Holland (ECQ)	A	Rotterdam	0-1	
07/10/95	Czech Republic (ECQ)	H	Minsk	0-2	
11/10/95	Luxembourg (ECQ)	A	Luxembourg	0-0	
12/11/95	Malta (ECQ)	A	Ta' Qali	2-0	Gerasimets (80, 85)
14/02/96	Turkey	A	Izmir	2-3	Belkevich (8), Shtanyuk (49)
27/03/96	Slovakia	A	Nitra	0-4	
01/05/96	Poland	A	Mielec	1-1	Kachuro (61)
27/05/96	Azerbaijan	H	Molodechno	2-2	Kachuro (49p), Kulchi (59)
01/06/96	Sweden (WCQ)	A	Solna	1-5	Belkevich (75)

ATAKA-AURA MINSK

CLUB DIRECTORY

FC Ataka-Aura Minsk
Avenue F. Skoriny 11/496
220050 Minsk
tel - (0172) 323939
Year of Formation - 1986
President - Leonid Stagonovich
Coach - Yakov Shapiro
Stadium - Orbita (1,000)

APPEARANCES 1995

	P	Ap	(s)	Gls
Alexander DANILENKO	A	8	(6)	5
Yuri DOROSHKEVICH	M	10	(4)	1
Andrei DROZD	G	14		
Alexander GAVLUSH	A	14		7
Igor GURINOVICH	A	10		5
Oleg KHMELNITSKI	D	14		
Sergei KOZLOVSKI	D	14		1
Leonid KUCHUK	D	13		
Alexander LISOVSKI	M	11	(2)	1
Yuri MALEYEV	M	5		
Sergei MAXIMOV	M	2	(5)	
Igor MYTNIK	M	3	(5)	1
Alexander NOVASH	M	6	(5)	
Andrei PYSHNIK	M	2	(5)	
Gennadi RABUSHKO	D		(2)	
Pavel RODNENOK	D	14		
Sergei SEMENOV	M		(1)	
Alexander YERMAKOVICH	M	14		1

LEAGUE RESULTS 1995

10/07/95	Torpedo Mogilev	H	0-0	
15/07/95	Torpedo Minsk	A	1-2	Gavlush (p)
20/07/95	Shakhter Soligorsk	H	4-0	Danilenko, Lisovski, Gavlush 2
25/07/95	Neman Grodno	A	4-0	Yermakovich, Gurinovich 2, Gavlush
01/08/95	Dvina Vitebsk	A	2-0	Danilenko 2
14/08/95	Shinnik Bobruisk	H	3-0	Gavlush, Danilenko, Gurinovich (p)
19/08/95	Vedrich Rechitsa	H	1-0	Mytnik
26/08/95	FC Molodechno	A	0-1	
17/09/95	Dinamo Brest	H	3-1	Kozlovski, Gurinovich, Gavlush
23/09/95	Dinamo-93 Minsk	A	1-1	Gurinovich (p)
30/09/95	MPKC Mozyr	H	1-1	Doroshkevich
14/10/95	Obuvshchik Lida	A	3-1	og (Romanovski), Gavlush, Danilenko
22/10/95	Dinamo Minsk	A	0-0	
27/10/95	Dnepr Mogilev	A	0-0	
06/11/95	FC Bobruisk	H	3-0	(w/o)

FC BOBRUISK

CLUB DIRECTORY

FC Bobruisk
ul. Octyabrskaya 117
213800 Bobruisk
tel - (02251) 26175/20962/26187
Year of Formation - 1984
President - Vladimir Taranov
Secretary - Konstantin Afanasiyev
Coach - Alexander Sabinin
Stadium - Spartak (3,500)

APPEARANCES 95

	P	Ap	(s)	Gls
Eduard APALKOV	M	4		
Yuri BOBRYSHEV	D	5		
Gennadi FEDOTOV	M	8	(1)	1
Sergei KHODUNOV	D	4	(1)	
Sergei KLIMENKO	M	3		
Alexander KUTSERO	A	8	(1)	
Sergei LOBAKH	A	4	(1)	
Valentin LYALIKOV	M	14		1
Vitali MATYUKHIN	A	7		1
Alexander PIKALOV	M	6	(1)	
Andrei PISKUN	G	1		
Andrei PISKUN (same player)	M	1		
Sergei RAZUMOVICH	D	14		
Alexander SABININ	D	8		
Vladimir SUSHI	A	2		1
Dmitri TRAVIN	D	5		
Oleg TROFIMIK	D	13		1
Sergei TRUNIN	M	7	(3)	1
Vyacheslav TSARYUK	D	8		
Andrei TURCHIN	M	8	(2)	
Viktor TYABUS	D	2		
Volodymyr VOROTELYAK (UKR)	D	4	(1)	
Sergei ZHEMCHUGOV	G	13		
Vladimir ZHURAVLEV	D	5		

LEAGUE RESULTS 1995

15/07/95	MPKC Mozyr	H	0-5	
21/07/95	Dinamo Minsk	A	1-6	Trofimik
26/07/95	Dvina Vitebsk	H	0-0	
01/08/95	Neman Grodno	A	0-3	
13/08/95	Shakhter Soligorsk	A	1-2	Fedotov (p)
18/08/95	Torpedo Minsk	H	0-0	
23/08/95	Dinamo Brest	H	1-4	Trunin
26/08/95	Torpedo Mogilev	A	1-5	Matyukhin
09/09/95	Dnepr Mogilev	A	1-5	Lyalikov
18/09/95	Obuvshchik Lida	H	0-2	
23/09/95	Vedrich Rechitsa	A	1-2	Sushi
02/10/95	Dinamo-93 Minsk	A	0-6	
15/10/95	FC Molodechno	H	0-7	
27/10/95	Shinnik Bobruisk	H	0-4	
06/10/95	Ataka-Aura Minsk	A	0-3	(w/o)

DINAMO BREST

CLUB DIRECTORY

Dinamo Brest
ul. Gogal 9
224000 Brest
tel - (01622) 67290
Year of Formation - 1960
President - Vladimir Gevorkian
Coach - Vladimir Gevorkyan
Stadium - Dinamo (10,500)

APPEARANCES 95

	P	Ap	(s)	Gls
Igor ASTAPCHIK	M	1	(2)	
Ruslan BELASH	A	10	(4)	4
Nikolai BRILEV	M	13	(2)	1
Andrei GORNOSTAYEV	A	13	(1)	4
Alexander GRISHCHENKO	M	12		
Andrei IGNATYUK	A		(2)	
Valeri KONDRATENKO	A	14		3
Valentin KOVALCHUK	M	1	(7)	
Yuri P. KOZLOV	D	13		
Oleg KRUCHOK	D	3	(4)	
Yuri LAGODICH	A	9	(5)	6
Nikolai LAZYUK	M	6	(1)	1
Andrei LYUBCHUK	D	14		
Oleg MANCHAK	M	11		3
Vadim SAVCHUK	M	15		4
Dmitri VIRKO	G	2	(1)	
Vladimir VORONOV	D	9		
Sergei VRUBLEVSKI	M	6	(2)	
Dmitri YEKIMOV	G	13	(1)	

LEAGUE RESULTS 1995/96

15/07/95	Dvina Vitebsk	H	1-1	Manchak (p)
21/07/95	Dinamo-93 Minsk	A	0-1	
26/07/95	FC Molodechno	H	3-2	Gornostayev, Lagodich, Manchak
01/08/95	Vedrich Rechitsa	A	0-2	
13/08/95	Dinamo Minsk	A	2-5	Lagodich, Savchuk
20/08/95	Obuvshchik Lida	H	1-1	Savchuk
23/08/95	FC Bobruisk	A	4-1	Belash 2, Lagodich 2
26/08/95	Shinnik Bobruisk	H	4-2	og (Avdeyenok), Belash, Savchuk, Lagodich
09/09/95	Neman Grodno	A	3-2	Kondratenko 2, Lazyuk
17/09/95	Ataka-Aura Minsk	A	1-3	Kondratenko
22/09/95	Torpedo Mogilev	H	3-0	Gornostayev 2, Manchak
01/10/95	Dnepr Mogilev	A	3-4	Belash, Brilev, Savchuk
14/10/95	Torpedo Minsk	H	1-2	Gornostayev
27/10/95	MPKC Mozyr	H	0-3	
06/11/95	Shakhter Soligorsk	A	1-3	Lagodich

DINAMO MINSK

CLUB DIRECTORY

Dinamo Minsk
ul. Kirov 8/2
220050 Minsk
tel - (0172) 270990/272321/275950
fax - (0172) 261694
Year of Formation - 1928
Secretary - Leonid Garai
Secretary - Leonid Vasilevski
Coach - Ivan Shchekin
Stadium - Dinamo (50,050)

MAJOR HONOURS
League Championship (USSR) - (1) 1982.
League Championship - (4) 1992, 1993, 1994, 1995, 1995 (autumn).
Domestic Cup - (1) 1992, 1994.

APPEARANCES 95

	P	Ap	(s)	Gls
Yuri AFANASENKO	G	1		
Valentin BELKEVICH	M	15		11
Viktor BOREL	A		(5)	1
Oleg CHERNYAVSKI	M	7	(2)	2
Petr KACHURO	A	15		15
Yevgeni KASHENTSEV	A	2		1
Alexander KHATSKEVICH	M	12	(1)	2
Alexander LUKHVICH	D	10	(1)	
Dmitri MAKARENKO	D		(8)	
Antuan MAYOROV	M	12	(2)	2
Alexander MISHCHISHIN	D	5	(1)	
Vladimir OSTRIKOV	M	5	(3)	
Andrei OSTROVSKI	D	13	(1)	1
Oleg PUTILO	A	1	(2)	
Sergei SHIROKI	M	15		
Sergei SHTANYUK	D	9	(2)	
Yuri SHUKANOV	M	14	(1)	5
Alexander TAIKOV	D	4		
Alexander TISHKOV	D		(1)	
Vitali VARIVONCHIK	G	14		
Vitali VOLODENKOV	M	1	(8)	
Sergei YASKOVICH	D	2	(3)	
Vladimir ZHURAVEL	M	8		2

LEAGUE RESULTS 1995

10/07/95	Torpedo Minsk	H	5-1	Belkevich, Kachuro 3 (1p), Mayorov
15/07/95	Torpedo Mogilev	A	2-0	Shukanov, Kashentsev
21/07/95	FC Bobruisk	H	6-1	Shukanov 2, Kachuro 2 (1p), Chernavski 2
25/07/95	Shinnik Bobruisk	A	3-0	Kachuro, Mayorov, Belkevich
01/08/95	Dinamo-93 Minsk	A	2-0	Kachuro, Belkevich
13/08/95	Dinamo Brest	H	5-2	Borel, Khatskevich, Kachuro, Belkevich 2
17/08/95	Dvina Vitebsk	H	3-1	Kachuro 2, Belkevich
27/08/95	Neman Grodno	A	3-2	Belkevich, Kachuro 2
17/09/95	FC Molodechno	H	2-0	Zhuravel, Belkevich
21/09/95	Dnepr Mogilev	A	1-0	Shukanov
01/10/95	Shakhter Soligorsk	H	1-1	Zhuravel
22/10/95	Ataka-Aura Minsk	H	0-0	
26/10/95	Vedrich Rechitsa	A	2-1	Belkevich, Shukanov
03/11/95	MPKC Mozyr	A	1-2	Belkevich
06/11/95	Obuvshchik Lida	H	6-2	Khatskevich (p), Kachuro 3, Ostrovski, Belkevich

DINAMO-93 MINSK

CLUB DIRECTORY

Dinamo-93 Minsk
ul. Kirov 8/2
220050 Minsk
tel - (0172) 270990/272321/275950
fax - (0172) 261694
Year of Formation - 1993
President - Leonid Garai
Secretary - Andrei Shalimo
Coach - Viktor Sokol
Stadium - Dinamo (50,050)

MAJOR HONOURS
Domestic Cup - (1) 1995.

APPEARANCES 95

	P	Ap	(s)	Gls
Vadim ARTAMONOV	D	6	(3)	
Oleg AVGUL	D	9	(2)	
Dmitri BESPANSKI	A	5	(3)	1
Vyacheslav DERBAN	M		(2)	
Andrei DOVNAR	D	11	(2)	
Sergei GOTSMANOV	M	3	(1)	
Vadim LASOVSKI	M	2	(2)	
Andrei LAVRIK	D	13	(1)	
Andrei LOBANOV	A	9	(6)	5
Radislav ORLOVSKI	D	9	(2)	2
Sergei PAVLYUCHUK	D	15		
Pavel SHAVROV	A	13	(1)	10
Andrei SHILO	M	6	(5)	
Sergei SHUSHKEVICH	A	11	(2)	1
Fedor SIKORSKI	M	12	(2)	1
Vadim SKRIPCHENKO	M	13		3
Igor TARLOVSKI	M	7	(2)	2
Andrei TURCHINOVICH	A	6	(5)	3
Alexander YEVNEVICH	G	15		

LEAGUE RESULTS 1995

11/07/95	FC Molodechno	H	4-1	Shavrov 3, Tarlovski
16/07/95	Vedrich Rechitsa	A	0-3	
21/07/95	Dinamo Brest	H	1-0	Turchinovich
25/07/95	Torpedo Mogilev	A	3-1	Shavrov, Shushkevich, Turchinovich
01/08/95	Dinamo Minsk	H	0-2	
15/08/95	Obuvshchik Lida	H	2-1	Tarlovski, Lobanov
19/08/95	MPKC Mozyr	A	2-2	Skripchenko, Shavrov
28/08/95	Dnepr Mogilev	A	3-1	Orlovski, Lobanov, Shavrov
09/09/95	Shakhter Soligorsk	H	1-0	Orlovski
18/09/95	Dvina Vitebsk	A	1-0	Skripchenko
23/09/95	Ataka-Aura Minsk	H	1-1	Skripchenko
02/10/95	FC Bobruisk	H	6-0	Lobanov 3, Shavrov, Sikorski, Bespanski
14/10/95	Shinnik Bobruisk	A	1-0	Shavrov
27/10/95	Neman Grodno	A	0-2	
05/11/95	Torpedo Minsk	H	3-1	Shavrov 2, Turchinovich

DNEPR MOGILEV

CLUB DIRECTORY

Dnepr Mogilev
Zadorozhnoye shosse 21
212026 Mogilev
tel - (0222) 263485/263009
Year of Formation - 1960
President - Valeri Streltsov
Secretary - Yuri Kolochinski
Coach - Vladimir Kostyukov
Stadium - Spartak (12,000)

APPEARANCES 95

	P	Ap	(s)	Gls
Vyacheslav BANUL	M	14	(1)	
Konstantin BELOUSOV	G		(2)	
Alexander CHAIKA	M	13		5
Igor CHUMACHENKO	M	11	(2)	2
Igor DOROSHENKO	D	11	(4)	1
Alexander FEDOROVICH	G	5	(1)	
Dmitri KALACHEV	M		(3)	
Yevgeni KAPOV	D		(2)	
Igor KHARLAN	G	10		
Viktor KLIMASHEVSKI	A	1	(4)	
Vladimir KLIMOVICH	D	3	(2)	
Dmitri LIKHTAROVICH	M	2	(7)	
Alexei LITVINKO	M	8	(6)	
Vladimir NEVINSKI	M	14	(1)	7
Dmitri OGORODNIK	A		(5)	
Oleg RADUSHKO	D	9	(1)	
Roman ROMANOV	M		(2)	
Vladimir SHUNEIKO	D	12		
Andrei SINICHIN	D	14		
Andrei SKOROBOGATKO	M	9	(2)	5
Vladimir SOLODUKHIN	A	15		6
Yaroslav SVERDLOV	M	14		

LEAGUE RESULTS 1995

26/07/95	Vedrich Rechitsa	A	3-1	Solodukhin 2, Chaika
01/08/95	Shakhter Soligorsk	H	0-1	
13/08/95	Torpedo Minsk	H	3-2	Skorobogatko (p), Nevinski, Solodukhin
19/08/95	Shinnik Bobruisk	A	2-1	Nevinski 2
23/08/95	Dvina Vitebsk	A	2-1	Solodukhin, Skorobogatko
28/08/95	Dinamo-93 Minsk	H	1-3	Skorobogatko
09/09/95	FC Bobruisk	H	5-1	Skorobogatko 2, Chaika 2, Nevinski
13/09/95	Neman Grodno	A	1-4	Solodukhin
17/09/95	MPKC Mozyr	A	0-1	
21/09/95	Dinamo Minsk	H	0-1	
27/09/95	Obuvshchik Lida	H	3-0	Nevinski 2 (1p), Chumachenko
01/10/95	Dinamo Brest	H	4-3	Solodukhin, Chaika 2, Doroshenko
14/10/95	Torpedo Mogilev	A	1-2	Chumachenko
27/10/95	Ataka-Aura Minsk	H	0-0	
06/11/95	FC Molodechno	A	1-2	Nevinski

DVINA VITEBSK

CLUB DIRECTORY

Dvina Vitebsk
ul.Akademik Pavlov 21
210015 Vitebsk
tel - (02122) 52040
Year of Formation - 1960
President - Vladimir Arestov
Secretary - Eduard Verkhovski
Coach - Vyacheslav Akshayev; Viktor Trubitsyn
Stadium - Dinamo (5,500)

APPEARANCES 95

	P	Ap	(s)	Gls
Viktor BEZMEN	D	12	(2)	
Eduard BOLTRUSHEVICH	D	13		
Igor FROLOV	A	2	(1)	
Vyacheslav GORMASH	A	4	(7)	1
Vadim KARTSEV	M	14		1
Alexander KHRAPSKI	M	4	(8)	
Yuri KONOPLEV	D	14		
Sergei KULANIN	M	14	(1)	3
Viktor MALYAVKO	D		(2)	
Viktor NAUMOV	A	2	(1)	
Mikhail PATSKO	M	4	(2)	
Igor POTAPOV	G	14		
Maxim RAZUMOV	A	9	(6)	2
Vitali ROGOZHKIN	M	12	(1)	1
Vladimir SELKIN	G	1		
Andrei SIVKOV	A	8	(5)	2
Andrei VASILIYEV	D	14		
Oleg VOROPAYEV	D	14		
Sergei YASINSKI	M	10	(4)	2

LEAGUE RESULTS 1995

15/07/95	Dinamo Brest	A	1-1	Razumov
20/07/95	Torpedo Mogilev	H	1-0	Kartsev
26/07/95	FC Bobruisk	A	0-0	
01/08/95	Ataka-Aura Minsk	H	0-2	
13/08/95	Vedrich Rechitsa	H	1-0	Kulanin (p)
17/08/95	Dinamo Minsk	A	1-3	Sivkov
23/08/95	Dnepr Mogilev	H	1-2	Sivkov
26/08/95	Torpedo Minsk	A	0-0	
09/09/95	MPKC Mozyr	H	1-1	Kulanin (p)
18/09/95	Dinamo-93 Minsk	H	0-1	
23/09/95	FC Molodechno	A	1-0	Yasinski
01/10/95	Shinnik Bobruisk	H	1-1	Rogozhkin
14/10/95	Shakhter Soligorsk	A	0-1	
27/10/95	Obuvshchik Lida	A	2-0	Kulanin, Gormash
06/11/95	Neman Grodno	H	2-0	Razumov, Yasinski

FC MOLODECHNO

CLUB DIRECTORY

FC Molodechno
ul. Masherov 6
223310 Molodechno
tel - (01773) 52444/54582
Year of Formation - 1989
President - Liudas Rumbutis
Coach - Liudas Rumbutis
Stadium - Metallurg (5,500)

APPEARANCES 95

	P	Ap	(s)	Gls
Nikolai ABRAMOVICH	G	3	(1)	
Dmitri AKULICH	M	5	(9)	1
Dmitri DROZHZHA	M	2	(8)	2
Sergei FEDOROVICH	D	1	(5)	
Alexander KLIMOVICH	D	15		1
Sergei KOBELSKI	D	8		
Sergei KOLTUNOVSKI	D	14		3
Vitali KOZYAK	A	14		6
Alexander LEBEDEV	D	15		
Fedor LUKASHENKO	M	8	(5)	
Ruslan LUKIN	A	10	(2)	5
Mikhail MAKOVSKI	M	7	(3)	3
Vladimir MAKOVSKI	M	14		6
Dmitri PODREZ	M	13		4
Sergei PONOMAREV	G	12	(1)	
Alexander SINKOVETS	D	11	(1)	1
Nikolai TARASEVICH	M	2	(6)	
Dmitri VYSHINSKI	M	11	(3)	1

LEAGUE RESULTS 1995

11/07/95	Dinamo-93 Minsk	A	1-4	Koltunovski (p)
16/07/95	Obuvshchik Lida	A	0-1	
21/07/95	Vedrich Rechitsa	H	2-1	Kozyak, Klimovich
26/07/95	Dinamo Brest	A	2-3	Makovski V., Vyshinski
01/08/95	MPKC Mozyr	H	2-1	Makovski V., Akulich
13/08/95	Neman Grodno	H	1-3	Podrez
18/08/95	Shakhter Soligorsk	A	1-1	Lukin
26/08/95	Ataka-Aura Minsk	H	1-0	Lukin
09/09/95	Shinnik Bobruisk	H	6-1	Podrez 3, Lukin 2, Kozyak
17/09/95	Dinamo Minsk	A	0-2	
23/09/95	Dvina Vitebsk	H	0-1	
01/09/95	Torpedo Mogilev	H	4-0	Sinkovets, Lukin, Makovski M., Drozhzha
15/10/95	FC Bobruisk	A	7-0	Kozyak 3 (1p), Makovski V. 3, Makovski M.
27/10/95	Torpedo Minsk	A	4-0	Koltunovski 2, Makovski V., Drozhzha
06/11/95	Dnepr Mogilev	H	2-1	Makovski M., Kozyak

MPKC MOZYR

CLUB DIRECTORY

FC MPKC Mozyr
V. Lenin square 9
247760 Mozyr
tel - (02351) 20207
Year of Formation - 1987
President - Nikolai Yashchenko
Coach - Anatoli Yurevich
Stadium - Spartak (5,000)

MAJOR HONOURS

Domestic Cup - (1) 1996.

APPEARANCES 95

	P	Ap	(s)	Gls
Alexander BOGAICHUK	M	11		2
Oleg CHEREPNEV	D	13	(1)	
Vasili DYATLOV	D	1	(1)	
Vadim GOLMAK	D	13	(1)	3
Sergei GOMONOV	D	6	(8)	2
Boris GOROVOI	M	9		1
Vladimir KONOVALOV	M	7	(2)	2
Viktor KUKAR	M	7	(4)	1
Alexander KULCHI	M	15		5
Vyacheslav LEVCHYK	D	13		
Yuri LUKASHOV	M		(4)	1
Alexander ORESHNIKOV	D		(3)	
Sergei POLYAKOV	M	1	(4)	
Maxim ROMASHCHENKO	M	12	(2)	10
Kirill SAVOSTIKOV	M	10	(1)	
Andrei SLUZHITELEV	M	7	(2)	1
Andrei SVIRKOV	G	9	(1)	
Yuri SVIRKOV	G	6	(1)	
Sergei TEREKHOV	M	2	(6)	
Yevgeni TIMOFEYEV	D	8	(3)	
Sergei YAROMKO	A	15		16

LEAGUE RESULTS 1995

10/07/95	Neman Grodno	H	7-0	Yaromko 3, Kulchi 2, Romashchenko, Lukashov
15/07/95	FC Bobruisk	A	5-0	Golmak, Yaromko, Romashchenko 3
20/07/95	Shinnik Bobruisk	H	4-0	Kulchi, Gomonov, Golmak, Yaromko
25/07/95	Shakhter Soligorsk	A	3-1	Golmak, Yaromko, Romashchenko
01/08/95	FC Molodechno	A	1-2	Bogaichuk
13/08/95	Torpedo Mogilev	H	3-1	Konovalov, Romashchenko (p), Yaromko (p)
19/08/95	Dinamo-93 Minsk	H	2-2	Gorovoi, Yaromko
26/08/95	Obuvshchik Lida	A	3-0	Romashchenko, Yaromko, Gomonov
09/09/95	Dvina Vitebsk	A	1-1	Yaromko
17/09/95	Dnepr Mogilev	H	1-0	Yaromko
22/09/95	Torpedo Minsk	A	5-0	Yaromko 3, Sluzhitelev, Bogaichuk
30/09/95	Ataka-Aura Minsk	A	1-1	Romashchenko
27/10/95	Dinamo Brest	A	3-0	Kukar, Kulchi (p), Yaromko
03/11/95	Dinamo Minsk	H	2-1	Yaromko, Romashchenko
06/11/95	Vedrich Rechitsa	H	3-0	Kulchi, Konovalov, Romashchenko

NEMAN GRODNO

CLUB DIRECTORY

Neman Grodno
ul. Kommunalnaya 3
230023 Grodno
tel - (0152) 453799/470971
Year of Formation - 1964
President - Iosif Shperling
Secretary - Stanislav Ulasevich
Coach - Ivan Letyago
Stadium - Krasnoye Znamya (14,000)

MAJOR HONOURS

Domestic Cup - (1) 1993

APPEARANCES 95

	P	Ap	(s)	Gls
Sergei ADAMOVICH	D	5	(5)	1
Alexander BALYUKHA	G	3		
Pavel BATYUTO	M	15		5
Marat BELEZYAKO	M	8	(3)	
Dmitri BORISEIKO	A	5	(9)	
Anatoli DRACHILOVSKI	M	12		
Artur KRIVONOS	M	15		1
Gennadi MARDAS	D	14		3
Sergei PARFEICHIK	G	1	(1)	
Pavel PUZYNA	A	8	(4)	1
Albert RYBAK	G	11		
Oleg SAVITSKI	A	7	(6)	1
Yevgeni SAVON	A	12	(3)	4
Vladimir SIDOROV	A	10	(1)	2
Vladimir SINYUK	M	2	(2)	
Oleg SYSOYEV	D	5	(2)	
Dmitri TROSKO	M	2	(2)	1
Alexander VERBITSKI	M	2		1
Oleg VERBITSKI	A		(1)	
Viktor YUIKO	M	15		
Alexander ZHILYUK	D	13		

LEAGUE RESULTS 1995

10/07/95	MPKC Mozyr	A	0-7	
20/07/95	Torpedo Minsk	A	0-1	
25/07/95	Ataka-Aura Minsk	H	0-4	
01/08/95	FC Bobruisk	H	3-0	Puzyna, Mardas (p), Batyuto
13/08/95	FC Molodechno	A	3-1	Batyuto, Trosko, Savon
18/08/95	Torpedo Mogilev	A	1-1	Mardas (p)
27/08/95	Dinamo Minsk	H	2-3	Batyuto, Savon
09/09/95	Dinamo Brest	H	2-3	Sidorov, Savon
13/09/95	Dnepr Mogilev	H	4-1	Krivonos, Batyuto, Savon, Savitski
17/09/95	Shinnik Bobruisk	A	1-3	Adamovich
22/09/95	Shakhter Soligorsk	H	1-0	Sidorov
01/10/95	Obuvshchik Lida	H	1-0	Batyuto
14/10/95	Vedrich Rechitsa	A	0-9	
27/10/95	Dinamo-93 Minsk	H	2-0	Verbitski A., Mardas (p)
06/11/95	Dvina Vitebsk	A	0-2	

OBUVSHCHIK LIDA

CLUB DIRECTORY

Obuvshchik Lida
ul. Kirov 32A
231300 Lida
tel - (015661) 29761
Year of Formation - 1962
President - Ivan Prokhorov
Coach - Andrei Petrov
Stadium - Obuvshchik (4,500)

APPEARANCES 95

	P	Ap	(s)	Gls
Anatoli AGEICHIK	G		(1)	
Valeri APANAS	D	15		
Zviad BURDZENIDZE (GEO)	A	11	(2)	1
Vitali DUSENOK	D		(1)	
Viktor KASHLEI	M	11		
Vitold KHOKHLACH	D	14		5
Valeri LYANTSEVICH	A		(1)	
Maxim LYCHEV	G	15		
Vladimir MIKHALTSOV	M	12		1
Viktor MIRON	D	13		1
Sergei PETRUSHEVSKI	M	15		
Vitali PIVOVARCHIK	A	2	(9)	
Alexander POZNYAK	A	8	(6)	1
Vitali RASHKEVICH	M	7		2
Genrikh ROMANOVSKI	M	11	(1)	
Yuri ROMANOVSKI	A	5	(2)	
Sergei SALYGO	D	12	(2)	3
Alexander YUREVICH	M	1	(4)	1
Stanislav ZINKOVICH	D	13		
Vyacheslav ZUIKO	D		(1)	

LEAGUE RESULTS 1995

10/07/95	Shakhter Soligorsk	A	3-1	Rashkevich 2, Salygo
16/07/95	FC Molodechno	H	1-0	Salygo
25/07/95	Torpedo Minsk	H	1-1	Burdzenidze
01/08/95	Torpedo Mogilev	H	0-0	
15/08/95	Dinamo-93 Minsk	A	1-2	Poznyak
20/08/95	Dinamo Brest	A	1-1	Miron
26/08/95	MPKC Mozyr	H	0-3	
09/09/95	Vedrich Rechitsa	H	3-0	Khokhlach 3
18/09/95	FC Bobruisk	A	2-0	Salygo, Khokhlach
23/09/95	Shinnik Bobruisk	H	0-0	
27/09/95	Dnepr Mogilev	A	0-3	
01/10/95	Neman Grodno	A	0-1	
14/10/95	Ataka-Aura Minsk	H	1-3	Khokhlach
27/10/95	Dvina Vitebsk	H	0-2	
06/11/95	Dinamo Minsk	A	2-6	Mikhaltsov, Yurevich

SHAKHTER SOLIGORSK

CLUB DIRECTORY

Shakhter Soligorsk
ul. M. Gorki
Sportkomplex
223710 Soligorsk
tel - (01710) 20621/25183
Year of Formation - 1963
President - Ivan Tupolski
Coach - Gennadi Plotnikov; Alexander Patsko
Stadium - Shakhter (5,000)

APPEARANCES 95

	P	Ap	(s)	Gls
Ivan ABRAMOV	M	14		1
Sergei ABRAMOV	D	15		
Vadim BRAZOVSKI	D	15		
Alexander CHISTYI	G	13	(1)	
Valentin CHUPRIS	D	8	(1)	
Alexander DASHKEVICH	A	2		
Viktor DENCHUK	M	12	(1)	2
Anatoli DOROSHKO	D	10		
Sergei DUDUKALOV	M	4	(1)	
Viktor FEDOROV	M	1	(3)	
Sergei FEDOROVICH	D	4	(1)	
Andrei GRIB	G	2		
Alexander KARPILENKO	M	1	(6)	1
Vladimir KAVALENYA	A	14		3
Vitali KIRIK	M	1	(6)	
Konstantin KOROLKOV	D	3	(2)	
Sergei MIROSHKIN	D	2		
Alexander PROTASENYA	D	14		1
Andrei RAPEIKO	M	13	(1)	3
Oleg SHATOV	A	15		1
Yuri ZENIN	D	2		

LEAGUE RESULTS 1995

10/07/95	Obuvshchik Lida	H	1-3	Kavalenya
16/07/95	Shinnik Bobruisk	A	1-3	Shatov
20/07/95	Ataka-Aura Minsk	A	0-4	
25/07/95	MPKC Mozyr	H	1-3	Kavalenya
01/08/95	Dnepr Mogilev	A	1-0	Denchuk
13/08/95	FC Bobruisk	H	2-1	Rapeiko 2
18/08/95	FC Molodechno	H	1-1	Rapeiko
26/08/95	Vedrich Rechitsa	A	0-0	
09/09/95	Dinamo-93 Minsk	A	0-1	
17/09/95	Torpedo Minsk	H	0-1	
22/09/95	Neman Grodno	A	0-1	
01/10/95	Dinamo Minsk	A	1-1	Abramov I.
14/10/95	Dvina Vitebsk	H	1-0	Denchuk
27/10/95	Torpedo Mogilev	A	0-0	
06/11/95	Dinamo Brest	H	3-1	Protasenya, Kavalenya (p), Karpilenko

SHINNIK BOBRUISK

CLUB DIRECTORY

Shinnik Bobruisk
ul. Uyanovskaya 94A
213800 Bobruisk
tel - (02251) 40056
Year of Formation - 1958
President - Gennadi Veraxa
Coach - Oleg Volokh
Stadium - Spartak (5,000)

APPEARANCES 95

	P	Ap	(s)	Gls
Alexander ARZAMASTSEV	D	10		1
Roman AVDEYENOK	D	9	(2)	
Sergei BALYKIN	D	5	(2)	
Alexander BORISIK	M	12	(2)	1
Oleg BULOICHIK	M	3	(5)	1
Eduard GRADOBOYEV	M	11	(1)	
Igor GRADOBOYEV	M	10	(1)	2
Ruslan KANANKOV	A		(1)	
Andrei KHMELEV	D	7	(3)	
Daniyar KIRICHENKO	G	12		
Dmitri KLYUIKO	A	11		3
Dmitri KURAKIN	M		(1)	
Igor PLETEZHOV	M	13	(1)	
Vladimir PUTRASH	A	12		6
Nikolai RYMPROV	M	2	(5)	
Vladimir RYZHCHENKO	G	3		
Igor SHUSTIKOV	D	10		
Alexander SOKOLOVSKI	M	11	(3)	1
Sergei ULEZLO	A	9	(5)	1
Andrei VIKHROV	M	15		1

LEAGUE RESULTS 1995

11/07/95	Vedrich Rechitsa	H	1-1	Borisik
16/07/95	Shakhter Soligorsk	H	3-1	Buloichik, Putrash, Klyuiko
20/07/95	MPKC Mozyr	A	0-4	
25/07/95	Dinamo Minsk	H	0-3	
01/08/95	Torpedo Minsk	A	1-0	Putrash
14/08/95	Ataka-Aura Minsk	A	0-3	
19/08/95	Dnepr Mogilev	H	1-2	Klyuiko
26/08/95	Dinamo Brest	A	2-4	Ulezlo, Putrash
09/09/95	FC Molodechno	A	1-6	Putrash
17/09/95	Neman Grodno	H	3-1	Putrash, Vikhrov, Gradoboyev I.
23/09/95	Obuvshchik Lida	A	0-0	
01/10/95	Dvina Vitebsk	A	1-1	Klyuiko
14/10/95	Dinamo-93 Minsk	H	0-1	
27/10/95	FC Bobruisk	A	4-0	Putrash (p), Sokolovski, Gradoboyev I., Arzamastsev
06/11/95	Torpedo Mogilev	H	0-2	

TORPEDO MINSK

CLUB DIRECTORY

FC Torpedo Minsk
ul. Sergei Lazo 10
220102 Minsk
tel - (0172) 429949/430771
Year of Formation - 1947
President - Viktor Bogmolov
Secretary - Gennadi Zverok
Coach - Vladimir Kosakovski
Stadium - Torpedo (5,000)

APPEARANCES 95

	P	Ap	(s)	Gls
Andrei ARKHANGELSKI	D	10		
Nikolai GLYANTSEVICH	M		(3)	
Alexander IGNATOV	A		(1)	
Alexander KACHANOVICH	D	4	(7)	
Boris KARASEV	D	15		3
Yuri KHOMKO	D	8		
Igor KOZA	M		(1)	
Dmitri KOZULIN	D	4	(1)	
Sergei LAGUN	M	2		
Vladimir LOMAKO	D	12		
Alexei MURAVEINIKOV	M	2	(1)	
Sergei PAVLYUKOVICH	M	14		3
Dmitri SAYENKO	M	13		
Andrei SELIVANOV	A	3	(6)	
Yuri SHAKUTA	A	7		
Vyacheslav SHPAKOVSKI	A	3	(6)	
Nikolai SMIRNOV	M		(2)	
Dmitri SOROKIN	A	6		
Andrei TSYBULKO	D	14		2
Valeri TYUNIS	A	4	(1)	
Andrei VASILENKO	M	2	(10)	1
Alexander VASILEVSKI	G	15		
Alexander VOLOVIK	A	14		3
Andrei YURKEVICH	D	13		

LEAGUE RESULTS 1995

10/07/95	Dinamo Minsk	A	1-5	Volovik
15/07/95	Ataka-Aura Minsk	H	2-1	Tsybulko, Karasev (p)
20/07/95	Neman Grodno	H	1-0	Karasev (p)
25/07/95	Obuvshchik Lida	A	1-1	Karasev (p)
01/08/95	Shinnik Bobruisk	H	0-1	
13/08/95	Dnepr Mogilev	A	2-3	Vasilenko, Pavlyukovich
18/08/95	FC Bobruisk	A	0-0	
26/08/95	Dvina Vitebsk	H	0-0	
10/09/95	Torpedo Mogilev	H	0-3	
17/09/95	Shakhter Soligorsk	A	1-0	Pavlyukovich (p)
22/09/95	MPKC Mozyr	H	0-5	
02/10/95	Vedrich Rechitsa	H	1-0	Tsybulko
14/10/95	Dinamo Brest	A	2-1	Volovik 2
27/10/95	FC Molodechno	H	0-4	
05/11/95	Dinamo-93 Minsk	A	1-3	Pavlyukovich

TORPEDO MOGILEV

CLUB DIRECTORY

Torpedo Mogilev
Avenue Vitebsk 43
212004 Mogilev
tel - (0222) 422447/422894
Year of Formation - 1974
President - Mikhail Bass
Secretary - Nikolai Nastashevski
Coach - Mikhail Bass
Stadium - Torpedo (7,000)

APPEARANCES 95

Player	Pos	Apps	Sub	Goals
Dmytro BARBASH (UKR)	A	12	(2)	
Igor BELYAI	M		(5)	
Dmitri BOROZNA	D	14		
Vyacheslav GERASHCHENKO	M	1		
Dmitri GITSELOV	M	3	(3)	
Dmitri GOLOVIN	M	15		5
Igor GORBACHEV	M	5	(4)	
Andrei GUZ	G	6		
Viktor IGNATIYEV	G	1		
Valeri KINASHENKO (UKR)	M	2		
Oleg KUZMENOK	M	15		3
Vitali LANKO	M		(2)	
Vladimir MIGURSKI	M	5	(2)	1
Nikolai NASTASHEVSKI	D	1		
Sergei OMELYUSIK	A	3		
Oleg PETRIKEVICH	M	2	(4)	
Viktor PINCHUK	M	5	(1)	
Alexander PRYKHODKO (UKR)	D	9		1
Viktor RUDOI (UKR)	M	14	(1)	2
Alexander RYABOKON (UKR)	D	8		1
Igor SAVELIYEV	M	14		1
Pavel SEDUN	M		(1)	
Sergei SINITSYN	G	8	(1)	
Sergei TEPLYAKOV	M	6	(1)	
Ernest TERNOVSKI	D	12	(1)	3
Yevgeni TSARKOV	A	4	(6)	

LEAGUE RESULTS 1995

Date	Opponent	H/A	Score	Scorers
10/07/95	Ataka-Aura Minsk	A	0-0	
15/07/95	Dinamo Minsk	H	0-2	
20/07/95	Dvina Vitebsk	A	0-1	
25/07/95	Dinamo-93 Minsk	H	1-3	Saveliyev
01/08/95	Obuvshchik Lida	A	0-0	
13/08/95	MPKC Mozyr	A	1-3	Ternovski
18/08/95	Neman Grodno	H	1-1	Ternovski
26/08/95	FC Bobruisk	H	5-1	Golovin (p), Migurski, Kuzmenok 2, Rudoi
10/09/95	Torpedo Minsk	A	3-0	Rudoi, Kuzmenok, Golovin (p)
17/09/95	Vedrich Rechitsa	H	2-2	Golovin, Ryabokon
22/09/95	Dinamo Brest	A	0-3	
01/10/95	FC Molodechno	A	0-4	
14/10/95	Dnepr Mogilev	H	2-1	Prykhodko, Ternovski
27/10/95	Shakhter Soligorsk	H	0-0	
06/11/95	Shinnik Bobruisk	A	2-0	Golovin 2 (2p)

VEDRICH RECHITSA

CLUB DIRECTORY

FC Vedrich Rechitsa
ul. 10 let Octyabrya 10
247500 Rechitsa
tel - (02340) 32315/34244/34259/32230
fax - (02340) 34259
Year of Formation - 1952
President - Konstantin Gorbunov
Coach - Vladimir Astratenko
Stadium - Rechitsadrev (5,500)

APPEARANCES 95

	P	Ap	(s)	Gls
Sergei ASTAPCHIK	G	12	(1)	
Andrei BARABASHIN	M	2	(4)	1
Vasili BARANOV	M	13		4
Igor BELKIN	D	13	(1)	
Sergei BYKOV	D	15		1
Roman DZHATAROV	D	14		1
Viktor IVANOV	A	4	(5)	2
Sergei KALASHNIKOV	D	15		
Dmitri KAPLENKO	D		(2)	
Gennadi KASHKAR	M	14		1
Oleg KOVTUN	M	13		2
Igor LOS	A		(5)	1
Fedor LUZAI	D	1		
Vyacheslav MARCHENKO	M	14		2
Igor MISOCHKA	G	3	(1)	
Igor MISOCHKA (same player)	A		(1)	
Andrei NIKITENKO	A	5	(5)	
Yuri NIKITOCHKIN	A	12	(2)	2
Vitali PAVLOV	A	1	(2)	
Konstantin PROKHORENKO	D	3		1
Alexander SAVELIYEV	M	1		
Igor SIMCHUK	M	10	(1)	4
Andrei YATSINOVICH	M		(2)	
Igor ZAITSEV	M		(1)	

LEAGUE RESULTS 1995

11/07/95	Shinnik Bobruisk	A	1-1	Baranov
16/07/95	Dinamo-93 Minsk	H	3-0	Prokhorenko (p), Baranov, Nikitochkin
21/07/95	FC Molodechno	A	1-2	Nikitochkin
26/07/95	Dnepr Mogilev	H	1-3	Marchenko
01/08/95	Dinamo Brest	H	2-0	Simchuk (p), Barabashin
13/08/95	Dvina Vitebsk	A	0-1	
19/08/95	Ataka-Aura Minsk	A	0-1	
26/08/95	Shakhter Soligorsk	H	0-0	
09/09/95	Obuvshchik Lida	A	0-3	
17/09/95	Torpedo Mogilev	A	2-2	Kovtun 2
23/09/95	FC Bobruisk	H	2-1	Simchuk (p), Bykov
02/10/95	Torpedo Minsk	A	0-1	
14/10/95	Neman Grodno	H	9-0	Baranov 2, Simchuk 2 (1p), Kashkar, Marchenko, Ivanov, Los, Dzhafarov
26/10/95	Dinamo Minsk	H	1-2	Ivanov
06/11/95	MPKC Mozyr	A	0-3	

PROMOTED CLUB

SECOND DIVISION FINAL TABLE 95

		Pd	W	D	L	F	A	Pt	GD
1	**Naftan-Devon Novopolotsk**	**14**	**10**	**2**	**2**	**29**	**14**	**32**	**+15**
2	Kommunalnik Pinsk	14	9	2	3	22	13	29	+9
3	Fomalgaut Borisov	14	8	4	2	24	13	28	+11
4	Kardan-Flayers Grodno	14	8	3	3	28	18	27	+10
5	KPF Slonim	14	7	5	2	25	15	26	+10
6	Brestbytkhim Brest	14	8	1	5	19	14	25	+5
7	Transmash Mogilev	14	6	4	4	20	16	22	+4
8	Khimik Svetlogorsk	14	5	2	7	19	17	17	+2
9	FC Gomel	14	5	2	7	19	17	17	+2
10	Lokomotiv Vitebsk	14	5	1	8	10	15	16	-5
11	Torpedo Zhodino	14	3	6	5	13	15	15	-2
12	Dinamo-Yuni Minsk	14	4	2	8	12	22	14	-10
13	Stroitel Starye-Dorogi	14	3	3	8	12	26	12	-14
14	Kimovets Vitebsk	14	2	3	9	9	28	9	-19
15	Khimvolokno Grodno	14	0	4	10	7	25	4	-18

PROMOTION/RELEGATION PLAY-OFF
Kommunalnik Pinsk 2, Shinnik Bobruisk 0
Shinnik Bobruisk 3, Kommunalnik Pinsk 0
(Shinnik Bobruisk 3-2)

CLUB DIRECTORY

Naftan-Devon Novopolotsk
ul. Molodezhnaya 49 A
211440 Novopolotsk
tel - (02144) 57740
Year of Formation - 1963
President - Anatoli Artyukh
Coach - Alexander Traiduk
Stadium - Atlanta (7,000)

BELGIUM

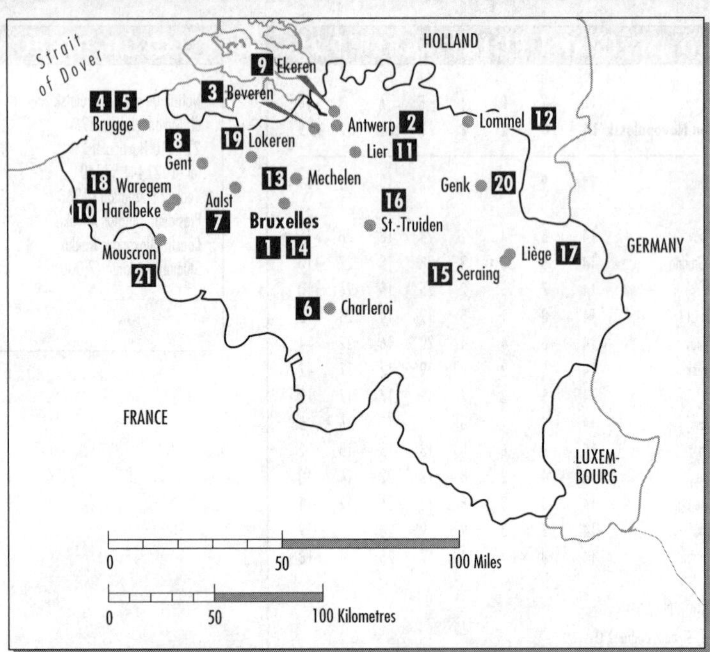

1	RSC ANDERLECHT	171	12	KFC LOMMELSE SK	182
2	ROYAL ANTWERP FC	172	13	KV MECHELEN	183
3	KSK BEVEREN	173	14	RWD MOLENBEEK	184
4	KSV CERCLE BRUGGE	174	15	RFC SERAING	185
5	CLUB BRUGGE KV	175	16	K ST.-TRUIDENSE VV	186
6	RSC CHARLEROI	176	17	R STANDARD LIEGE	187
7	KSC EENDRACHT AALST	177	18	KSV WAREGEM	188
8	KAA GENT	178	19	KSC LOKEREN	189
9	KFC GERMINAL EKEREN	179	20	KRC GENK	189
10	KRC HARELBEKE	180	21	R EXCELSIOR MOUSCRON	189
11	K LIERSE SK	181			

DOMESTIC 'DOUBLE' FOR CLUB BRUGES

'Annus horibilis' in the land of Bosman

FEDERATION DIRECTORY

Union Royale des Sociétés de Football Association
Houba de Strooperlaan 145, 1020 Bruxelles

tel - (02) 4771211 — Year of Formation - 1895
tlx - 23257 bvbfbf b — President - Michel D'Hooghe
fax - (02) 4782391 — Secretary - Alain Courtois

Stadium - Roi Baudoin, Bruxelles (40,000)

That old adage about being kicked when you're down certainly applied to Belgian football during the 1995/96 season. The previous 12 months had been bad enough. But even they were outdone by a long 'annus horibilis' that all Belgian fans will hurriedly wish to forget.

Perhaps the only Belgian footballer smiling at the end of it all was a certain Jean-Marc Bosman. His famous legal victory in the European Court of Justice struck a chord of consternation all over the Old Continent, shaking the very foundations of European football and thrusting it into a new-age revolution, the like of which has never been encountered before.

But while this one-time journeyman pro was making banner headlines all over the international press, Belgian football in general was cowering away somewhere in the smallprint. It was a truly awful season for the Belgian game, possibly the worst in the past 25 years. The national team failed miserably to make the short trip over the North Sea to Euro '96. Ambitious Anderlecht were not good enough to make it into the group stage of the Champions' League. And not one of the country's five-strong taskforce managed to remain in European club competition beyond November.

The crisis was particularly acute in the national team. The *Diables Rouges* began the season to the fanfare of the new King Baudouin stadium being unveiled on the site of the former Heysel stadium in Brussels. That day of supposed celebration turned sour when Belgium went down 1-2 to their invited guests Germany, whose followers added insult to injury by rioting in the city centre. It was symbolic of what was to come in the next few months.

LEAGUE CHAMPIONSHIP RESULTS 95/96

		1	2	3	4	5	6	7	8	9	10	11	12	13	14	15	16	17	18
1	RSC Anderlecht		1-1	1-0	3-0	2-1	0-2	4-0	3-0	4-2	1-3	3-1	3-2	3-1	1-0	7-0	4-0	2-1	2-0
2	Royal Antwerp FC	1-1		1-1	0-1	0-3	1-0	0-1	2-1	0-2	2-3	3-1	4-1	1-2	1-1	4-2	1-1	3-2	2-0
3	KSK Beveren	0-2	4-0		1-3	3-5	1-1	0-2	2-2	3-2	0-0	2-2	0-1	1-1	1-1	1-0	0-2	0-0	5-1
4	KSV Cercle Brugge	2-1	3-2	2-0		1-2	0-2	1-1	0-0	2-2	2-1	2-3	0-1	3-2	1-1	0-0	2-1	2-3	4-1
5	Club Brugge KV	2-1	2-0	3-1	2-2		0-0	1-3	3-0	3-1	2-0	2-1	2-0	6-0	3-0	3-1	2-0	6-1	3-1
6	RSC Charleroi	1-3	2-0	3-1	1-1	1-3		2-0	3-3	1-1	0-0	1-1	5-0	4-2	2-2	4-2	4-0	2-2	1-0
7	KSC Eendracht Aalst	3-1	0-0	5-1	4-3	0-2	3-4		2-2	2-0	2-0	1-2	4-1	3-2	1-1	5-0	0-0	1-1	1-1
8	KAA Gent	1-3	1-0	3-0	1-5	0-2	1-0	3-1		0-2	1-0	0-2	2-0	0-0	2-0	4-2	0-1	2-4	0-0
9	KFC Germinal Ekeren	2-2	2-0	1-0	1-0	1-2	3-1	5-1	2-0		1-1	1-1	1-2	1-0	1-0	5-0	3-1	2-0	2-0
10	KRC Harelbeke	0-4	3-1	1-0	0-2	0-2	4-0	2-1	0-1	1-2		2-3	0-3	0-0	4-2	2-1	3-0	2-3	2-1
11	K Lierse SK	3-2	1-2	3-1	0-1	2-2	2-1	3-1	2-3	2-1	0-1		3-1	0-3	1-1	4-0	3-0	0-0	1-1
12	KFC Lommelse SK	2-2	0-0	2-0	0-1	2-2	1-1	1-0	1-1	2-1	2-0	0-0		2-1	0-1	0-1	2-3	1-0	2-1
13	KV Mechelen	1-3	0-1	2-1	2-1	0-2	1-2	1-0	0-0	1-1	1-0	0-0	2-0		1-1	1-4	2-0	2-0	3-0
14	RWD Molenbeek	0-0	0-0	1-0	2-2	0-0	3-1	0-0	1-0	1-0	3-1	0-0	0-2	0-1		4-0	2-0	3-1	4-1
15	RFC Seraing	2-1	0-1	1-0	1-0	1-1	2-3	2-4	2-2	1-1	0-1	1-3	2-1	2-1	0-5		1-2	0-0	0-2
16	K St.-Truidense VV	0-5	2-3	0-2	1-1	2-4	4-1	2-2	1-0	2-1	2-0	3-1	0-2	2-2	0-1	4-1		3-1	1-1
17	R Standard Liège	2-4	1-0	2-2	4-0	1-0	2-2	2-1	1-1	0-0	2-1	2-0	1-0	2-1	1-1	3-0	1-1		1-1
18	KSV Waregem	1-4	1-1	1-4	1-1	2-5	4-1	0-0	2-2	1-0	1-2	1-3	1-3	0-1	0-1	0-3	2-1	0-4	

LEAGUE CHAMPIONSHIP FINAL TABLE 95/96

			Home					Away					Total						
		Pd	W	D	L	F	A	W	D	L	F	A	W	D	L	F	A	Pt	GD
1	Club Brugge KV	34	14	2	1	45	12	11	4	2	38	18	25	6	3	83	30	81	+53
2	RSC Anderlecht	34	14	1	2	44	14	8	4	5	39	23	22	5	7	83	37	71	+46
3	KFC Germinal Ekeren	34	12	3	2	34	11	3	5	9	19	26	15	8	11	53	37	53	+16
4	RWD Molenbeek	34	9	6	2	24	9	4	8	5	19	20	13	14	7	43	29	53	+14
5	K Lierse SK	34	8	4	5	30	21	6	6	5	24	24	14	10	10	54	45	52	+9
6	R Standard Liège	34	9	7	1	28	15	4	5	8	23	31	13	12	9	51	46	51	+5
7	RSC Charleroi	34	8	7	2	37	21	5	4	8	22	32	13	11	10	59	53	50	+6
8	KSV Cercle Brugge	34	7	5	5	27	23	6	5	6	24	24	13	10	11	51	47	49	+4
9	KFC Lommelse SK	34	7	6	4	20	15	7	0	10	20	30	14	6	14	40	45	48	-5
10	KSC Eendracht Aalst	34	8	6	3	37	21	4	4	9	18	29	12	10	12	55	50	46	+5
11	KV Mechelen	34	8	4	5	20	16	4	4	9	20	30	12	8	14	40	46	44	-6
12	KRC Harelbeke	34	8	1	8	26	26	5	3	9	14	22	13	4	17	40	48	43	-8
13	Royal Antwerp FC	34	7	4	6	26	23	4	5	8	12	23	11	9	14	38	46	42	-8
14	KAA Gent	34	8	2	7	21	22	2	9	6	18	27	10	11	13	39	49	41	-10
15	K St.-Truidense VV	34	7	4	6	29	28	4	3	10	13	32	11	7	16	42	60	40	-18
16	RFC Seraing	34	5	4	8	18	28	3	1	13	17	51	8	5	21	35	79	29	-44
17	KSK Beveren	34	4	7	6	24	25	2	2	13	14	32	6	9	19	38	57	27	-19
18	KSV Waregem	34	3	4	10	18	36	1	5	11	12	34	4	9	21	30	70	21	-40

N.B. When teams are level on points, classification is determined by the number of victories.

Paul Van Himst's team had set themselves up with a half-decent chance of qualifying for Euro '96 thanks to a trio of good results in the spring. But in the match that mattered, at home to Denmark, they blew it. Out of luck and short of ideas, they made two early blunders and never recovered. The 1-3 scoreline was harsh, but it signified the burial of their last hope of qualification. That left a couple of meaningless trips to Armenia and Cyprus, the latter of which yielded no more than a sterile 1-1 draw.

Dutifully, the Belgian FA decided to keep Paul Van Himst in the job. After all, this was a man who had just been honoured with official recognition as Belgium's greatest ever player. But when Belgium plumbed new depths in a friendly at home to France in March (just one shot at the French goal was registered in a 0-2 defeat), Van Himst simply had to go. His place was taken by another Belgian playing legend, Wilfried Van Moer, who had been Van Himst's assistant. He signed a one-year contract with the Federation and promptly led the side to two encouraging draws against Euro '96-bound Russia and Italy. The 2-2 draw against the Italians in Cremona certainly provided a shaft of light at the end of a long dark tunnel. Whether the new coach will be able to shed further illumination during the World Cup qualifiers, only time will tell. Still, at least Belgium know that they will soon end their depressing sequence of European Championship qualifying failures. They co-host the event with Holland in the year 2000.

An improvement in the international fortunes of Belgian clubs would also be welcome before the millenium is out. It seemed inconceivable that that the country's performances in the European Cups could be any worse in 95/96 than the season before. But they were. No team got further than the second round. 14 matches in all were played, of which only three ended with victory for the Belgian club.

INTERNATIONAL HONOURS

World Cup Finals appearances: 1930, 1934, 1938, 1954, 1970, 1982 (2nd phase), 1986 (4th), 1990 (2nd round), 1994 (2nd round)

European Championship appearances (last 8): 1972 (3rd), 1976, 1980 (runners-up), 1984

European Club Competitions

Cup-winners' Cup	RSC Anderlecht (1976, 1978)
	KV Mechelen (1988)
UEFA Cup	RSC Anderlecht (1983)
Super Cup	RSC Anderlecht (1976, 1978)

The big failure was that of Anderlecht, who prolonged a dreary sequence of results in the Champions' Cup/League by losing out to modest Ferencváros in the preliminary round after a stunning 0-1 reverse in the home leg. The timing of that first fixture could hardly have been worse. It came midway between two Belgian league defeats - Anderlecht's first two matches in defence of their title. And the inevitable outcome of that horrendous opening week of the season was the sacking of much-heralded new German coach Herbert Neumann, who had

NATIONAL TEAM APPEARANCES 95/96

Coach - Paul VAN HIMST; Wilfried VAN MOER	GER	DEN	ARM	CYP	FRA	RUS	ITA	Cps	Gls
Gilbert BODART (02/09/62) - R Standard Liège	G	G						12	-
Régis GENAUX (31/08/73) - R Standard Liège	D	D	D	D	D	D		14	-
Pascal RENIER (03/08/71) - Club Brugge KV	D	s77			D	D	D	10	-
Dirk MEDVED (15/09/68) - Club Brugge KV	D	D			D46	D	D	23	-
Rudy SMIDTS (12/08/63) - Royal Antwerp FC	D46	D77	D	D80	D			29	1
Alain BETTAGNO (09/11/68) - R Standard Liège	M							2	-
Lorenzo STAELENS (30/04/64) - Club Brugge KV	M	M14	M	M			M	37	1
Eric VAN MEIR (28/02/68) - RSC Charleroi	M46							4	-
Gunther SCHEPENS (04/05/73) - R Standard Liège	M	M54	M	s80		M		9	3
Luc NILIS (25/05/67) - PSV (HOL)	A	s14	A	A		A		36	4
Michael GOOSSENS (30/11/73) - R Standard Liège	A		s63	s46	s46			7	1
Philippe LEONARD (12/02/74) - R Standard Liège	s46					D	D	5	-
Ronald FOGUENNE (18/08/70) - R Standard Liège	s46	s54						2	-
Georges GRÜN (25/01/62) - RSC Anderlecht		D		D				77	6
Emmanuel KARAGIANNIS (22/11/66) - RSC Anderlecht		M	M81	M46				7	1
Enzo SCIFO (19/02/66) - AS Monaco (FRA)		M	M		M	M	M	74	17
Marc DEGRYSE (04/09/65) - Sheffield Wednesday (ENG)		A		A	A46			60	22
Gilles DE BILDE (09/06/71) - RSC Anderlecht		A	A63	A	s74			10	1
Filip DE WILDE (05/07/64) - RSC Anderlecht			G	G	G			7	-
Bertrand CRASSON (05/10/71) - RSC Anderlecht			D				D46	8	-
Glen DE BOECK (22/08/71) - RSC Anderlecht			D	D				3	-
Sven VERMANT (04/04/73) - Club Brugge KV			s81					1	-
Danny BOFFIN (10/07/65) - RSC Anderlecht				M60	M74			28	-
Dirk HUYSMANS (03/09/73) - K Lierse SK				s60				1	-
Philippe ALBERT (10/08/67) - Newcastle United (ENG)					D	D68		38	5
Frédéric PEIREMANS (03/09/73) - RSC Anderlecht					M	M		2	-
Luis OLIVEIRA (24/03/69) - Cagliari (ITA)					A		A	12	1
Günther VERJANS (06/10/73) - Club Brugge KV					s46	s68	s46	4	-
Philippe VANDE WALLE (22/12/61) - KFC Germinal Ekeren						G	G	2	-
Christophe LAUWERS (17/09/72) - KSV Cercle Brugge						A62	s77	2	-
Frédéric PIERRE (23/02/74) - RWD Molenbeek						s62		1	-
Geoffrey CLAEYS (05/10/74) - KSV Cercle Brugge							M	1	1
Gert VERHEYEN (20/09/70) - Club Brugge KV							M77	6	1
Nico VAN KERCKHOVEN (14/12/70) - K Lierse SK							A63	1	-
Karel SNOECKX (29/10/73) - K Lierse SK							s63	1	-

only been at the club for 52 days. Anderlecht installed a couple of caretakers, Jean Dockx and veteran Raymond Goethals, but there was to be no recovery in Europe as they drew the second leg 1-1 in Hungary and went out 2-1 on aggregate. By the end of an awful August, however, Anderlecht had a new coach, or rather an old one. Johan Boskamp had been persuaded to return - just a few months after the club had got rid of him following his third successive title win! In Boskamp's first game back he led his old troops to an important 2-1 victory over perennial rivals Club Bruges (a repeat of the SuperCup win a month earlier) and that, belatedly, got the club's season underway.

The early weeks of the championship belonged to Jan Ceulemans' Eendracht Aalst. Their opening-day 3-1 victory at home to Anderlecht sparked a run of five consecutive victories. But the joy didn't last. A defeat by Gent sent them spinning out of control and they rapidly disappeared from contention. Aalst did, however, provide the highlight of Belgium's European campaign by beating Bulgarian champions Levski Sofia home and away in the UEFA Cup... before Roma, predictably, thrashed them in round two.

Elsewhere in the UEFA Cup neither Standard Liège nor Lierse could get past their Portuguese first-round opponents. In the Cup-winners' Cup, Club Bruges edged past Shakhtar Donetsk of Ukraine 2-1 on aggregate and looked as if they might single-handedly keep Belgium's European interest alive beyond Christmas for the second year in a row. But the holders Real Zaragoza quickly wiped that thought from their minds, beating them convincingly in both matches in the second round.

At the time of their European exit Club Bruges had already made considerable strides towards regaining the domestic title they last won in 1992. By mid-September, after eight games, Hugo Broos's team had grappled to the top of the table, and with new Croatian striker Mario Stanic scoring goals from all angles (he bagged five in a 6-0 victory over Mechelen), they looked well set for a useful campaign.

With the season at its halfway point, Club Bruges held a two-point lead, their closest pursuers being Anderlecht, who had revived themselves remarkably since Boskamp's return. Everything was shaping up for another two-horse title race. The big match looming up on the fixture list was the direct confrontation in Bruges on February 11. Going into that game, both sides were on a roll. Anderlecht had won their previous six matches, Bruges their previous five. A capacity 18,000 crowd filled the Olympiastadion for what was

TOP SCORERS

20	Mario STANIC (Club Brugge KV)
19	Christophe LAUWERS (KSV Cercle Brugge)
15	John BOSMAN (RSC Anderlecht)
	Gilles DE BILDE (RSC Anderlecht)
14	Patrick GOOTS (KSK Beveren)
	Felix N'GONGE (KRC Harelbeke)
	Marc WILMOTS (R Standard Liège)
13	Francis SEVEREYNS (Royal Antwerp FC)
	Gunter HOFMANS (KFC Germinal Ekeren)
	Frédéric PIERRE (RWD Molenbeek)
	Michael GOOSSENS (R Standard Liège)

DOMESTIC CUP RESULTS

1/16 FINALS

KSC Lokeren 2, KAA Gent 1
Club Brugge KV 1, Poederlee 0
KFC Germinal Ekeren 1, KV Oostende 0
KV Mechelen 1, Royal Antwerp FC 3 (aet)
KSK Beveren 3, Excelsior Mouscron 1
K Beerschot VAV 3, KV Kortrijk 0
K St.-Truidense VV 3, RC Jet Wavre 0
KSV Cercle Brugge 2, KFC Lommelse SK 1
Westerlo 0, RTFC Liégeois 0 (aet; 0-3 on pens.)
RWD Molenbeek 2, Herentals 1
FC Boom 0, KSV Waregem 3
KRC Harelbeke 0, KSC Eendracht Aalst 1
FC Denderleeuw 1, KRC Genk 2
KSK Deinze 1, RFC Seraing 1 (aet; 4-5 on pens.)
RSC Charleroi 0, R Standard Liège 1
RSC Anderlecht 2, K Lierse SK 1 (aet)

1/8 FINALS

KSC Eendracht Aalst 0, K Beerschot VAV 0 (aet; 2-4 on pens.)
KSV Waregem 1, R Standard Liège 0
RFC Seraing 1, K St.-Truidense VV 4
RSC Anderlecht 3, KRC Genk 0 (aet)
Royal Antwerp FC 3, KFC Germinal Ekeren 2 (aet)
KSV Cercle Brugge 4, KSC Lokeren 1
KSK Beveren 1, Club Brugge KV 4
RTFC Liégeois 2, RWD Molenbeek 2 (aet; 5-4 on pens.)

QUARTER-FINALS

Club Brugge KV 2, RTFC Liégeois 1 (aet)
Royal Antwerp FC 3, KSV Waregem 0
KSV Cercle Brugge 2, K Beerschot VAV 1 (aet)
RSC Anderlecht 0, K St.-Truidense VV 1

SEMI-FINALS

Club Brugge KV v K St.-Truidense VV 3-1; 3-1 (Club Brugge KV 6-2)
Royal Antwerp FC v KSV Cercle Brugge 0-3; 3-3 (aet) (KSV Cercle Brugge 6-3)

FINAL

26/05/96, Brussels
CLUB BRUGGE KV 2 Stanic (24, 41)
KSV CERCLE BRUGGE 1 Torma (4)
referee - Jeurissen
CLUB BRUGGE KV - Verlinden; Verjans, Renier, Medved, Borkelmans, Vermant (De Brul 80), Van der Elst, Claessens (Lembi 75), Staelens, Verheyen (Plovie 88), Stanic.
KSV CERCLE BRUGGE - Henneman; Siquet, Camerman, Kooiman, Claeys, Selymes, Lamaire (Bwalya 65), Soenens, Renty (Beuken 55), Cooreman (Stan 82), Torma.

EUROPEAN CUPS RESULTS 95/96

CHAMPIONS' CUP

● RSC ANDERLECHT

Preliminary round FERENCVÁROS (HUN)

H 0-1
De Vlieger; Crasson (Haagdoren 50), Grün, Doll, Babayaro, Karagiannis, Walem, Preko, Boffin, Zetterberg (Versavel 64), De Bilde.

A 1-1 De Bilde (64)
De Wilde; Crasson (Haagdoren 58), Grün, Doll, Babayaro, Karagiannis (Bosman 86), Walem, Preko, Boffin, Versavel (Zetterberg 58), De Bilde.

CUP-WINNERS' CUP

● CLUB BRUGGE KV

1st round SHAKHTAR DONETSK (UKR)

H 1-0 Spehar (88)
Verlinden; De Brul, Renier, Medved, Borkelmans, Vermant, Van der Elst, Verjans (Verheyen 58), Claessens, Spehar, Stanic.

A 1-1 Stanic (60)
Verlinden; Medved, Renier, De Brul, Borkelmans, Van der Elst, Staelens, Claessens (Van der Heyden 80), Vermant, Verheyen (Lembi 87), Stanic.

2nd round REAL ZARAGOZA (ESP)

A 1-2 Staelens (74p)
Verlinden; Medved, Okon, Renier, Borkelmans, Van der Elst, Staelens, Van der Heyden, Vermant, Spehar, Stanic.

H 0-1
Verlinden; Medved (Verheyen 75), Okon, De Brul, Borkelmans, Van der Elst, Staelens, Vermant, Van der Heyden, Spehar, Stanic.

UEFA CUP

● R STANDARD LIEGE

1st round VITÓRIA GUIMARÃES (POR)

A 1-3 Schepens (32)
Bodart (Hubart 73); Genaux, Kimoni, Rednic, Léonard, Bettagno, Hellers, Ernst, Foguenne, Schepens, Goossens (Houlmont 63).

H 0-0
Bodart (Hubart 46); Genaux, Rednic, Dinga, Léonard, Bettagno (Foguenne 46), Hellers, De Condé (Ernst 70), Schepens, Goossens, Malbasa.

● KSC EENDRACHT AALST

1st round LEVSKI SOFIA (BUL)

A 2-1 Markov (57og), Paas (78)
Van Steenberghe; Van der Hoorn, De Vleeschauwer, Okpara, Van Riel, Temmerman, Lamberg, Van Wambeke, Meyssen (De Meersman 90), Van Ankeren, Paas (Kanu 88).

H 1-0 Lamberg (57)
Van Steenberghe; Van der Hoorn, De Vleeschauwer, Okpara, Lamberg, Van Riel, Temmerman (De Meyst 78), Van Wambeke (De Meersman 89), Meyssen, Van Ankeren (Benali 83), Paas.

2nd round ROMA (ITA)

A 0-4
Van Steenberghe; De Vleeschauwer, Van der Hoorn, Okpara, Van Riel, Temmerman, Lamberg (De Meyst 32), Vanderhaeghe (De Meersman 80), Meyssen, Paas (Benali 67), Van Ankeren,

H 0-0
Vaesen; Meyssen, De Vleeschauwer, Okpara, Van Riel, Van der Hoorn (Arnaud 89), Ebiede, Temmerman (De Meyst 68), Van Ankeren, Vanderhaeghe, Paas.

● K LIERSE SK

1st round SL BENFICA (POR)

H 1-3 Huysmans (39p)
Mampaey; Brocken, De Roover, Snelders, Van Kerckhoven, Snoeckx, Bovri (Goossens 54), Serneels, Rekdal, Huysmans, De Sousa (Peeters 60).

A 1-2 Van Kerckhoven (35)
Mampaey; Serneels (De Smet 79), De Roover, Snelders, Goossen, Pauwels, Snoeckx (Bovri 60), Rekdal, Van Kerckhoven, De Sousa (Peeters 70), Huysmans.

undoubtedly Belgium's 'match of the season'. Anderlecht drew first blood with a 13th-minute penalty from Belgian international Gilles De Bilde, and the scoreline remained unchanged until the same minute of the second half when the ever-dependable Lorenzo Staelens fired in the equaliser from Sven Vermant's cross. Once back on level terms Bruges began to up the tempo, and Anderlecht, skilful and confident in the first half under the orchestration of Swedish playmaker Zetterberg, found themselves pulling men back in a bid to hold onto the draw. 11 minutes from time, though, Stanic bamboozled two Anderlecht defenders with a wonderful run to the byline. His pull-back found Vermant, who slid forward to prod the ball into the net and send the local fans into unfettered jubilation.

If there was a moment when the championship changed hands, that was it. The victory put Club Bruges five points clear of the title holders. It was their sixth win on the trot, but the sequence did not stop there. Imbibed with confidence, the Blue-and-Blacks added eight more consecutive wins. The last of them, 2-1 at home to Lierse, confirmed what had long been inevitable. Club Bruges were Belgian champions for the tenth time in their history.

Hugo Broos's men eventually finished a full ten points above runners-up Anderlecht. The Brussels side had lost all chance of a comeback when they were sensationally beaten 1-3 at home by newly-promoted Harelbeke. And their woes continued with another shock home defeat in the quarter-finals of the Belgian Cup, 0-1 to St.-Truiden. Club Bruges found no such difficulty in eliminating Anderlecht's conquerors in the two-legged semi-final and went through to face city rivals and stadium-sharers Cercle in a repeat of the all-Bruges final of ten years earlier.

Club had won that 1986 encounter, and they completed a 'double' in two senses by triumphing 2-1 in the King Baudouin stadium thanks to two more crucial goals from the league's top scorer, Mario Stanic, who had only been allowed to play after gaining special dispensation from the Croatian national team, in training for Euro '96.

Club Bruges's second Cup and league 'double' (the first was in 1977) enabled Cercle to qualify for the Cup-winners' Cup. Alongside Anderlecht the other two UEFA Cup qualifiers were Germinal Ekeren, who had narrowly missed out on a place the previous season, and RWDM, back in Europe for the first time in 16 years thanks to a last-day goalless draw at home to Anderlecht which allowed them to pip early-season high-fliers Lierse.

Standard Liège had a very poor season, failing to challenge on any front. That prompted a mass exodus, with coach Robert Waseige leaving for Portugal and several leading players (Wilmots, Léonard, Genaux) all following him abroad. Standard's player pool was nevertheless increased by the club's end-of-season merger with Seraing, who, a year after RFC Liège, became the second club from the city to have their life-support machine switched off as a result of terminally ailing finances. Seraing's departure, along with that of relegated Beveren and Waregem, enabled three teams to be promoted. Lokeren and Genk came up automatically, with little Excelsior Mouscron battling their way up to previously unscaled heights through the play-offs.

NATIONAL TEAM RESULTS 95/96

Date	Opponent		Venue	Score	Scorers
23/08/95	Germany	H	Brussels	1-2	Goossens (17)
06/09/95	Denmark (ECQ)	H	Brussels	1-3	Grün (25)
07/10/95	Armenia (ECQ)	A	Yerevan	2-0	Nilis (28, 38)
15/11/95	Cyprus (ECQ)	A	Limassol	1-1	De Bilde (68)
27/03/96	France	H	Brussels	0-2	
24/04/96	Russia	H	Brussels	0-0	
29/05/96	Italy	A	Cremona	2-2	Claeys (5), Carboni (11og)

PLAYERS OF THE SEASON

PHILIPPE VANDE WALLE

Germinal Ekeren's veteran penalty-scoring goalkeeper had an outstanding season in 1995/96, earning himself a début call-up for Belgium at the ripe old age of 34. Vande Walle's brilliant displays were highly instrumental in taking Ekeren up into an unexpected third place. He even scored a last-minute equaliser in open play against Cercle Bruges as well as scoring at will from the penalty spot on numerous other occasions. With Gilbert Bodart at loggerheads with the national coach and Filip De Wilde injured, Vande Walle was handed his first two caps, against Russia and Italy, and excelled in both games. A former Club Bruges player, he is still a fan of the new Belgian 'double'-winners and never enters the field without a blue-and-black Club Bruges shirt tucked under his goalkeeper's jersey.

CHRISTOPHE LAUWERS

Like Vande Walle, Cercle Bruges striker Christophe Lauwers crowned the best season of his career with a national team call-up from new Belgian coach Wilfried Van Moer. The difference is that Lauwers is still only 24 and could be a long-term candidate for the national side if he can consolidate his 95/96 performances at his new club, the more ambitious Eendracht Aalst. The young striker scored 19 league goals for Cercle (one behind top marksman Stanic of Club Bruges) and his extra-time penalty in the Belgian Cup semi-final against Antwerp proved decisive in taking his club into Europe. Unfortunately, a booking in that game meant he was ineligible for the final, which, without him, Cercle lost 2-1 to Club Bruges.

LUC NILIS

During his many years at Anderlecht, Luc Nilis frequently seduced the crowds with his skill and daring, yet often came over as an underachiever because of his poor performances for the Belgian national team. But in his second season at PSV the man from Limburg set the Dutch league alight, even outshining all those fancy dans at Ajax to earn himself Holland's Player of the Year award. He also picked up the Eredivisie top scorer prize and supplemented his 21 league goals with another five in PSV's UEFA Cup run, including two special strikes against Barcelona in the Nou Camp. Nilis's goals are invariably spectacular, and it is his eye for the unexpected coupled with a masterful touch on the ball which have endeared him to the Dutch fans.

RSC ANDERLECHT

CLUB DIRECTORY

RSC Anderlecht
Avenue Theo Verbeeck 2
Anderlecht
1070 Bruxelles
tel - (02) 5221539/5229400
fax - (02) 5200740
Year of Formation - 1908
President - Constant Vanden Stock
Manager - Michel Verschueren
Coach - Herbert Neumann; Jean Dockx; Raymond Goethals; Johan Boskamp
Stadium - Constant Vanden Stock (28,063)

MAJOR HONOURS

League Championship - (24) 1947, 1949, 1950, 1951, 1954, 1955, 1956, 1959, 1962, 1964, 1965, 1966, 1967, 1968, 1972, 1974, 1981, 1985, 1986, 1987, 1991, 1993, 1994, 1995.
Domestic Cup - (8) 1965, 1972, 1973, 1975, 1976, 1988, 1989, 1994.
European Cup-winners' Cup - (2) 1976, 1978.
UEFA Cup - (1) 1983.
European Super Cup - (2) 1976, 1978.

APPEARANCES 95/96

	P	Ap	(s)	Gls
Isaac ASARE (GHA)	D	7	(3)	
Célestine BABAYARO (NIG)	D	28		5
Danny BOFFIN	M	32		5
John BOSMAN	A	21	(9)	15
Bertrand CRASSON	D	12		3
Gilles DE BILDE	A	26	(2)	15
Glen DE BOECK	D	20	(1)	2
Geert DE VLIEGER	G	4		
Filip DE WILDE	G	29		
Chris DEWITTE	A		(2)	
Olivier DOLL	D	17	(2)	
Olivier FIEUW	M		(1)	
Georges GRÜN	D	17	(1)	1
Filip HAAGDOREN	A	4	(5)	
Frédéric HERPOEL	G	1		
Nordin JBARI (MAR)	A	1		
Emmanuel KARAGIANNIS	M	16	(4)	
James OBIORAH (NIG)	A	6	(7)	4
Azubike OLISEH (NIG)	M		(1)	
Frédéric PEIREMANS	M	20		3
Yaw PREKO (GHA)	A	18	(2)	11
REINALDO Rosa dos Santos (BRA)	A		(2)	
Graeme RUTJES (HOL)	D	9	(3)	
Olivier SURAY	D	15	(5)	1
Bruno VERSAVEL	M	17	(9)	8
Johan WALEM	M	21	(4)	2
Josip WEBER	A	1	(1)	2
Pär ZETTERBERG (SWE)	M	32	(1)	5

LEAGUE RESULTS 1995/96

04/08/95	KSC Eendracht Aalst	A	1-3	Boffin
12/08/95	RSC Charleroi	H	0-2	
19/08/95	K St.-Truidense VV	H	4-0	Grün, Boffin, Preko, De Bilde (p)
26/08/95	RFC Seraing	A	1-2	Walem
29/08/95	Club Brugge KV	H	2-1	Preko 2
09/09/95	KV Mechelen	A	3-1	Crasson, Bosman, Zetterberg
16/09/95	KSV Waregem	H	2-0	De Bilde 2
20/09/95	KSK Beveren	H	1-0	De Bilde
24/09/95	KRC Harelbeke	A	4-0	Versavel, Preko, De Bilde (p), Boffin
30/09/95	Royal Antwerp FC	H	1-1	Weber
11/10/95	KFC Germinal Ekeren	A	2-2	Weber, Crasson
14/10/95	KFC Lommelse SK	A	2-2	Crasson, Preko
21/10/95	KAA Gent	H	3-0	Peiremans 2, Bosman
27/10/95	R Standard Liège	A	4-2	Babayaro, De Bilde, Preko 2
04/11/95	KSV Cercle Brugge	H	3-0	Babayaro, Zetterberg, Preko
18/11/95	K Lierse SK	A	2-3	Preko 2
25/11/95	RWD Molenbeek	H	1-0	Bosman
01/12/95	KSC Eendracht Aalst	H	4-0	Zetterberg, Bosman, Babayaro, Boffin
15/12/95	RSC Charleroi	A	3-1	Bosman 2, Preko
23/12/95	KFC Germinal Ekeren	H	4-2	Versavel, De Boeck, Zetterberg, De Bilde (p)
27/01/96	K St.-Truidense VV	A	5-0	Boffin, De Bilde, De Boeck, Versavel 2
03/02/96	RFC Seraing	H	7-0	og (Pagal), Babayaro, De Bilde 3, Versavel, Bosman
11/02/96	Club Brugge KV	A	1-2	De Bilde (p)
17/02/96	KV Mechelen	H	3-1	Versavel, Walem, Obiorah
01/03/96	KSK Beveren	A	2-0	Bosman 2
09/03/96	KRC Harelbeke	H	1-3	Versavel
17/03/96	Royal Antwerp FC	A	1-1	Peiremans
24/03/96	KSV Waregem	A	4-1	Bosman 2, De Bilde 2
30/03/96	KFC Lommelse SK	H	3-2	De Bilde, Bosman 2
06/04/96	KAA Gent	A	3-1	Obiorah 2, Bosman
12/04/96	R Standard Liège	H	2-1	Obiorah, Zetterberg
21/04/96	KSV Cercle Brugge	A	1-2	Suray
05/05/96	K Lierse SK	H	3-1	Versavel, Babayaro, Bosman (p)
12/05/96	RWD Molenbeek	A	0-0	

ROYAL ANTWERP FC

CLUB DIRECTORY

Royal Antwerp FC
Oude Bosuilbaan 54 A
2100 Deurne-Antwerpen
tel - (03) 3246406/3246270
fax - (03) 3260970
Year of Formation - 1880
President - Eddy Wauters
Secretary - Paul Bistiaux
Coach - László Fazekas; Ratko Svilar (96/97 - Georg Kessler)
Stadium - Bosuil (20,000)

MAJOR HONOURS
League Championship - (4)
1929, 1931, 1944, 1957.
Domestic Cup - (2) 1955, 1992.

APPEARANCES 95/96

	P	Ap	(s)	Gls
John ALOISI (AUS)	A	6	(6)	2
Nico BROECKAERT	D	22		
Petar CESTIC (YUG)	A	3	(1)	1
Geert EMMERECHTS	D	19	(1)	
Lamre Bimbo FATOKUM (NIG)	M		(2)	
Manuel GODFROID	M	23	(5)	2
Samuel GREVEN	D	3	(1)	
Dragan JAKOVLJEVIC (YUG)	M		(4)	
Nica JOZIC (YUG)	D		(2)	
Wim KIEKENS	D	28		2
George KULCSAR (AUS)	D	10	(2)	
Carlo LAVIGNE	M	12	(4)	
Sasha LENHART (GER)	A	6	(4)	
Cvijan MILOSEVIC (BOS)	M	23	(1)	1
Johan MUCHER	M	2	(1)	
Ossomo Alain MVIENA (CMR)	D	5	(5)	
Saniyu OWOLABI (NIG)	A	18	(2)	4
Krist PORTE	M	33		7
RUBENILSON Monteiro	A	4	(6)	2
Francis SEVEREYNS	A	27		13
Rudy SMIDTS	D	33		1
Ranko STOJIC (YUG)	G	14	(1)	
Milos SVILAR (YUG)	M	1		
Rudy TAEYMANS	D	16	(5)	
Ronny VAN RETHY	D	31		1
Yves VANDERSTRAETEN	G	20		
William VERBEECK	M	13	(13)	1
Willy VINCENT (MAU)	A	2	(4)	

LEAGUE RESULTS 1995/96

05/08/95	KSV Cercle Brugge	A	2-3	Severeyns 2
12/08/95	K Lierse SK	H	3-1	Rubenilson 2 (2p), Severeyns
16/08/95	RWD Molenbeek	A	0-0	
19/08/95	KSC Eendracht Aalst	H	0-1	
26/08/95	RSC Charleroi	A	0-2	
09/09/95	K St.-Truidense VV	A	3-2	Severeyns 2, Godfroid
16/09/95	RFC Seraing	H	4-2	og (Teppers), Owolabi, Severeyns 2
20/09/95	Club Brugge KV	A	0-2	
23/09/95	KV Mechelen	H	1-2	Kiekens (p)
30/09/95	RSC Anderlecht	A	1-1	Porte
15/10/95	KSK Beveren	H	1-1	Smidts
22/10/95	KRC Harelbeke	A	1-3	Godfroid
29/10/95	KSV Waregem	H	2-0	Aloisi, Severeyns
04/11/95	KFC Lommelse SK	H	4-1	Aloisi, Severeyns 3
11/11/95	KFC Germinal Ekeren	H	0-2	
18/11/95	KAA Gent	A	0-1	
26/11/95	R Standard Liège	H	3-2	Van Rethy, Porte 2
02/12/95	KSV Cercle Brugge	H	0-1	
16/12/95	K Lierse SK	A	2-1	Porte, Milosevic
23/12/95	RWD Molenbeek	H	1-1	Porte
27/01/96	KSC Eendracht Aalst	A	0-0	
03/02/96	RSC Charleroi	H	1-0	Owolabi
11/02/96	KFC Germinal Ekeren	A	0-2	
17/02/96	K St.-Truidense VV	H	1-1	Owolabi
03/03/96	Club Brugge KV	H	0-3	
09/03/96	KV Mechelen	A	1-0	Severeyns
17/03/96	RSC Anderlecht	H	1-1	Porte
23/03/96	RFC Seraing	A	1-0	Owolabi
30/03/96	KSK Beveren	A	0-4	
06/04/96	KRC Harelbeke	H	2-3	Porte, Kiekens (p)
14/04/96	KSV Waregem	A	1-1	Severeyns
20/04/96	KFC Lommelse SK	A	0-0	
05/05/96	KAA Gent	H	2-1	Verbeeck, Cestic
12/05/96	R Standard Liège	A	0-1	

KSK BEVEREN

CLUB DIRECTORY

KSK Beveren
Klapperstraat 151 bis
9120 Beveren
tel - (03) 7759000/7759697
fax - (03) 7550800
Year of Formation - 1935
President - Gerry Smet
Secretary - Karel Rotthier
Coach - René Desaeyere; Dimitri Davidovic; Barry Hulshoff
Stadium - Freethiel (15,400)

MAJOR HONOURS
League Championship - (2) 1979, 1984.
Domestic Cup - (2) 1978, 1983.

APPEARANCES 95/96

	P	Ap	(s)	Gls
Hans BELLIGH	M	20		
Marnik BOGAERTS	M	19	(8)	
Wesley DESMET	M	1	(8)	
Patrick GOOTS	A	30	(1)	14
Filip HAAGDOREN	A	12		2
Andy JANSSENS	D	10	(6)	
Krunoslav JURCIC (YUG)	D	20		
József KELLER (HUN)	M	7	(2)	
Igor KOZLOV (RUS)	M	1	(2)	
Erwin LEMMENS	G		(2)	
Julien LODDERS	D	22	(3)	
Peter MAES	G	34		
Frank MAGERMAN	M		(1)	
Carl MASSAGIE	D	31		
Peter MEEUSEN	M	17	(9)	1
Lambert SMID (TCH)	M	26	(4)	3
Dirk THOELEN	D	28	(3)	
Saso UDOVIC (SLO)	A	23	(4)	10
Bart VAN DEN EEDE	M	5	(7)	2
Steven VAN HERREWEGHEN	A	3		
David VAN HOYWEGHEN	D	21	(5)	2
Dominique VAN MAELE	M	9		1
Hervé VAN OVERTVELT	A	27	(4)	3
Stijn VLAEMINCK	A		(1)	
Dirk VOLKERICK	D	8	(4)	

LEAGUE RESULTS 1995/96

06/08/95	RWD Molenbeek	A	0-1	
12/08/95	KSC Eendracht Aalst	H	0-2	
16/08/95	RSC Charleroi	A	1-3	Goots
19/08/95	KFC Germinal Ekeren	H	3-2	Van Overtvelt, Goots, Udovic
26/08/95	K St.-Truidense VV	A	2-0	Goots 2
30/08/95	RFC Seraing	H	1-0	Udovic
10/09/95	Club Brugge KV	A	1-3	Goots
16/09/95	KV Mechelen	H	1-1	Smid
20/09/95	RSC Anderlecht	A	0-1	
23/09/95	KSV Waregem	H	5-1	Udovic 2, Meeussen, Goots, Van Overtvelt
30/09/95	KRC Harelbeke	H	0-0	
15/10/95	Royal Antwerp FC	A	1-1	Goots
21/10/95	KFC Lommelse SK	H	0-1	
28/10/95	KAA Gent	A	0-3	
04/11/95	R Standard Liège	H	0-0	
19/11/95	KSV Cercle Brugge	A	0-2	
25/11/95	K Lierse SK	H	2-2	Goots, Smid
02/12/95	RWD Molenbeek	H	1-1	Udovic
17/12/95	KSC Eendracht Aalst	A	1-5	Van Overtvelt (p)
23/12/95	RSC Charleroi	H	1-1	Udovic
28/01/96	KFC Germinal Ekeren	A	0-1	
03/02/96	K St.-Truidense VV	H	0-2	
10/02/96	RFC Seraing	A	0-1	
17/02/96	Club Brugge KV	H	3-5	Goots 2, Van Maele
01/03/96	RSC Anderlecht	H	0-2	
10/03/96	KSV Waregem	A	4-1	Udovic 2, Goots, Smid
17/03/96	KRC Harelbeke	A	0-1	
23/03/96	KV Mechelen	A	1-2	Udovic
30/03/96	Royal Antwerp FC	H	4-0	Udovic, Goots 2 (1p), Van den Eede
06/04/96	KFC Lommelse SK	A	0-2	
13/04/96	KAA Gent	H	2-2	Haagdoren, Van Hoyweghen
20/04/96	R Standard Liège	A	2-2	Van den Eede, Van Hoyweghen
05/05/96	KSV Cercle Brugge	H	1-3	Goots
12/05/96	K Lierse SK	A	1-3	Haagdoren

KSV CERCLE BRUGGE

CLUB DIRECTORY

KSV Cercle Brugge
Olympialaan 74
8200 Brugge
tel - (050) 389193
fax - (050) 391141
Year of Formation - 1899
President - Paul Duchêyne
Secretary - Hans Dewachtere
Coach - Jerko Tipuric
Stadium - Olympiastadion (18,021)

MAJOR HONOURS

League Championship - (3) 1911, 1927, 1930.
Domestic Cup - (2) 1927, 1985.

APPEARANCES 95/96

	P	Ap	(s)	Gls
Anthony ANNICAERT	A	11	(6)	1
Bernard BEUKEN	D	21	(5)	1
Joel BWALYA (ZAM)	M	6	(2)	
Alex CAMERMAN	D	25	(1)	1
Geoffrey CLAEYS	D	31		3
Davy COOREMAN	M	17	(10)	4
Dimitri DELPORTE	D	3	(4)	1
Yves FEYS	G	31		
Wim HENNEMAN	G	3	(1)	
Wim KOOIMAN (HOL)	D	29		3
Bert LAMAIRE	M	25		
Christophe LAUWERS	A	33		19
Kofi MBEAH (GHA)	A	1	(4)	
William OSEI-BERKOE (GHA)	M	1	(10)	
Björn RENTY	M	27	(1)	3
Joeri SABBE	D		(1)	
Tibor SELYMES (ROM)	D	31		3
Ylli SHEHU (ALB)	A	9	(15)	5
Thierry SIQUET	D	26		
Kurt SOENENS	M	25	(3)	
Fabrice STAELENS	M		(1)	
Ilie STAN (ROM)	M	12	(6)	
Gábor TORMA (HUN)	A	7	(13)	6

LEAGUE RESULTS 1995/96

05/08/95	Royal Antwerp FC	H	3-2	Lauwers 2, Shehu
12/08/95	KFC Lommelse SK	A	1-0	Lauwers
16/08/95	KAA Gent	H	0-0	
19/08/95	R Standard Liège	A	0-4	
27/08/95	KSV Waregem	A	1-1	Lauwers
30/08/95	K Lierse SK	H	2-3	Delporte, Lauwers (p)
09/09/95	RWD Molenbeek	A	2-2	Selymes, Claeys
16/09/95	KSC Eendracht Aalst	H	1-1	Claeys
20/09/95	RSC Charleroi	A	1-1	Kooiman
23/09/95	KFC Germinal Ekeren	H	2-2	Shehu, Kooiman
30/09/95	K St.-Truidense VV	A	1-1	Lauwers
14/10/95	RFC Seraing	H	0-0	
22/10/95	Club Brugge KV	A	2-2	Selymes, Lauwers
28/10/95	KV Mechelen	H	3-2	Cooreman, Renty, Lauwers
04/11/95	RSC Anderlecht	A	0-3	
19/11/95	KSK Beveren	H	2-0	Selymes, Annicaert
26/11/95	KRC Harelbeke	A	2-0	og (Vande Walle), Torma
02/12/95	Royal Antwerp FC	A	1-0	Lauwers
17/12/95	KFC Lommelse SK	H	0-1	
23/12/95	KAA Gent	A	5-1	Kooiman, Camerman, Shehu, Torma, Lauwers
25/01/96	R Standard Liège	H	2-3	Lauwers 2
04/02/96	KSV Waregem	H	4-1	Shehu 2, Lauwers 2
10/02/96	K Lierse SK	A	1-0	Claeys
18/02/96	RWD Molenbeek	H	1-1	Lauwers
02/03/96	RSC Charleroi	H	0-2	
10/03/96	KFC Germinal Ekeren	A	0-1	
17/03/96	K St.-Truidense VV	H	2-1	Torma, Cooreman
24/03/96	KSC Eendracht Aalst	A	3-4	Cooreman, Lauwers, Torma
30/03/96	RFC Seraing	A	0-1	
05/04/96	Club Brugge KV	H	1-2	Beuken
13/04/96	KV Mechelen	A	1-2	Torma
21/04/96	RSC Anderlecht	H	2-1	Lauwers 2
05/05/96	KSK Beveren	A	3-1	Renty, Torma, Cooreman
12/05/96	KRC Harelbeke	H	2-1	Lauwers, Renty

CLUB BRUGGE KV

CLUB DIRECTORY

Club Brugge KV
Olympialaan 74
8200 Brugge
tel - (050) 387155/402121
fax - (050) 381023
Year of Formation - 1891
President - Fernand de Clerck
Secretary - Jacques De Nolf
Coach - Hugo Broos
Stadium - Olympiastadion (18,021)

MAJOR HONOURS

League Championship - (10) 1920, 1973, 1976, 1977, 1978, 1980, 1988, 1990, 1992, 1996.
Domestic Cup - (7)
1968, 1970, 1977, 1986, 1991, 1995, 1996.

APPEARANCES 95/96

	P	Ap	(s)	Gls
Jürgen BELPAIRE	G	3		
Vital BORKELMANS	D	28	(1)	1
Yves BUELINCKX	M		(4)	
Gert CLAESSENS	M	26		6
Tjörven DE BRUL	D	18	(4)	2
René EYKELKAMP (HOL)	A	2		1
Nzelo LEMBI (ZAI)	D	12	(8)	4
Dirk MEDVED	D	27		
Erwin NIES	M		(1)	
Paul OKON (AUS)	D	14		1
Pascal PLOVIE	D		(5)	
Pascal RENIER	D	30	(1)	2
Robert SPEHAR (CRO)	M	18	(4)	11
Lorenzo STAELENS	M	30		12
Mario STANIC (CRO)	A	30		20
Franky VAN DER ELST	M	30		1
Stéphane VAN DER HEYDEN	M	11	(6)	3
Gert VERHEYEN	A	22	(3)	11
Günther VERJANS	M	15	(3)	1
Danny VERLINDEN	G	31		
Sven VERMANT	M	27	(3)	6

LEAGUE RESULTS 1995/96

Date	Opponent	H/A	Score	Scorers
06/08/95	KFC Germinal Ekeren	A	2-1	Staelens (p), Borkelmans
11/08/95	K St.-Truidense VV	H	2-0	Eijkelkamp, Claessens
16/08/95	RFC Seraing	A	1-1	Claessens
20/08/95	KSV Waregem	H	3-1	Spehar 2, Stanic
26/08/95	KV Mechelen	H	6-0	Spehar, Stanic 5
29/08/95	RSC Anderlecht	A	1-2	Stanic
10/09/95	KSK Beveren	H	3-1	Stanic 2, Vermant
17/09/95	KRC Harelbeke	A	2-0	Stanic, Spehar
20/09/95	Royal Antwerp FC	H	2-0	Claessens, Stanic
23/09/95	KFC Lommelse SK	A	2-2	Van der Elst, Vermant
01/10/95	KAA Gent	H	3-0	Stanic, Spehar, Lembi
13/10/95	R Standard Liège	A	0-1	
22/10/95	KSV Cercle Brugge	H	2-2	Stanic, Van der Heyden
28/10/95	K Lierse SK	A	2-2	Spehar, Okon
05/11/95	RWD Molenbeek	H	3-0	Lembi, Van der Heyden, Verjans
19/11/95	KSC Eendracht Aalst	A	2-0	Staelens 2
24/11/95	RSC Charleroi	H	0-0	
03/12/95	KFC Germinal Ekeren	H	3-1	Renier, Van der Heyden, Stanic
16/12/95	K St.-Truidense VV	A	4-2	Verheyen, Staelens, Stanic 2
23/12/95	RFC Seraing	H	3-1	Staelens, Renier, Lembi
28/01/96	KSV Waregem	A	5-2	Claessens, Verheyen 2, Staelens, De Brul
03/02/96	KV Mechelen	A	2-0	Staelens, Verheyen
11/02/96	RSC Anderlecht	H	2-1	Staelens, Vermant
17/02/96	KSK Beveren	A	5-3	Verheyen, De Brul, Staelens (p), Spehar, Stanic
03/03/96	Royal Antwerp FC	A	3-0	Verheyen, Spehar, Staelens (p)
10/03/96	KFC Lommelse SK	H	2-0	Verheyen, Spehar
17/03/96	KAA Gent	A	2-0	Vermant, Stanic
24/03/96	KRC Harelbeke	H	2-0	Stanic, og (Hameg)
31/03/96	R Standard Liège	H	6-1	Vermant 2, Staelens, Lembi, Verheyen, Claessens
05/04/96	KSV Cercle Brugge	A	2-1	Staelens (p), Spehar
14/04/96	K Lierse SK	H	2-1	Claessens, Spehar
19/04/96	RWD Molenbeek	A	0-0	
05/05/96	KSC Eendracht Aalst	H	1-3	Verheyen
12/05/96	RSC Charleroi	A	3-1	Verheyen 2, Stanic

RSC CHARLEROI

CLUB DIRECTORY

Royal Charleroi Sporting Club
Boulevard Zoë Drion 19
6000 Charleroi
tel - (071) 328734
fax - (071) 327514
Year of Formation - 1904
President - Jean-Paul Spaute
Manager - Gaston Colson
Coach - Luka Peruzovic
Stadium - Mambour (18,593)

APPEARANCES 95/96

	P	Ap	(s)	Gls
Tibor BALOG (HUN)	M	23		4
Drazan BRNCIC (YUG)	M	10	(10)	1
Dante BROGNO	A	32		8
Christ BRUNO	D	1		
Gábor BUKRAN	M	7	(17)	
Marco CASTO	M	32		5
Ivan DESLOOVER	D	6	(7)	
Lars ERIKSSON (SWE)	G	9		
Filip FIERS	A	4	(11)	2
Franky FRANS	G	15		
Roch GERARD	D	27	(1)	4
István GULYÁS (HUN)	G	10		
Edi KRNCEVIC (AUS)	A	14	(3)	4
Jean-Jacques MISSE-MISSE (CMR)	A	26	(3)	12
Raymond MOMMENS	M	28	(3)	1
Rudy MOURY	D	21		
Sergei OMELIANOVICH (RUS)	M	1	(6)	
Anthony PETACCIA	M		(1)	1
Michel RASQUIN	D	30		1
Samuel REMY	M	16	(13)	6
Fabrice SILVAGNI	D	31		1
Alexandre TEKLAK	M		(2)	
Eric VAN MEIR	D	28		5
Laurent WUILLOT	M	3	(10)	1

LEAGUE RESULTS 1995/96

Date	Opponent	H/A	Score	Scorers
05/08/95	KV Mechelen	H	4-2	Van Meir, Mommens, Missé-Missé, Krncevic
12/08/95	RSC Anderlecht	A	2-0	Gérard, Krncevic
16/08/95	KSK Beveren	H	3-1	Van Meir, Remy, Rasquin
20/08/95	KRC Harelbeke	A	0-4	
26/08/95	Royal Antwerp FC	H	2-0	Missé-Missé, Brogno
30/08/95	KFC Lommelse SK	A	1-1	Missé-Missé
09/09/95	KAA Gent	H	3-3	Missé-Missé, Brogno, Remy
15/09/95	R Standard Liège	A	2-2	Casto, Missé-Missé
20/09/95	KSV Cercle Brugge	H	1-1	Gérard
23/09/95	K Lierse SK	A	1-2	Remy
30/09/95	RWD Molenbeek	H	2-2	Van Meir, Remy
15/10/95	KSC Eendracht Aalst	A	4-3	Casto, Remy, Missé-Missé, Brncic
21/10/95	KSV Waregem	A	1-4	Petaccia
28/10/95	KFC Germinal Ekeren	H	1-1	Wuillot
04/11/95	K St.-Truidense VV	A	1-4	og (Nwanu)
18/11/95	RFC Seraing	H	4-2	og (Ducoulombier), Brogno, Van Meir, Missé-Missé
24/11/95	Club Brugge KV	A	0-0	
02/12/95	KV Mechelen	A	2-1	Balog, Missé-Missé
15/12/95	RSC Anderlecht	H	1-3	Krncevic
23/12/95	KSK Beveren	A	1-1	Missé-Missé
27/01/96	KRC Harelbeke	H	0-0	
03/02/96	Royal Antwerp FC	A	0-1	
10/02/96	KFC Lommelse SK	H	5-0	Krncevic, Casto, Gérard (p), Brogno 2
17/02/96	KAA Gent	A	0-1	
03/03/96	KSV Cercle Brugge	A	2-0	Fiers, Gérard (p)
09/03/96	K Lierse SK	H	1-1	og (Goossen)
14/03/96	RWD Molenbeek	A	1-3	Sabbadini
22/03/96	R Standard Liège	H	2-2	Brogno 2
30/03/96	KSC Eendracht Aalst	H	2-0	Balog, Brogno
05/04/96	KSV Waregem	H	1-0	Balog
14/04/96	KFC Germinal Ekeren	A	1-3	Fiers
20/04/96	K St.-Truidense VV	H	4-0	Missé-Missé, Casto, Silvagni, Balog
05/05/96	RFC Seraing	A	3-2	Casto, Missé-Missé 2
12/05/96	Club Brugge KV	H	1-3	Remy

KSC EENDRACHT AALST

CLUB DIRECTORY

KSC Eendracht Aalst
Bredestraat 10
9300 Aalst
tel - (053) 781177
fax - (053) 779878
Year of Formation - 1919
President - Erik Goethals
Secretary - Jean-Pierre Van Drogenbroeck
Coach - Jan Ceulemans
Stadium - Pierre Cornelis (10,000)

APPEARANCES 95/96

	P	Ap	(s)	Gls
János BÁNFI (HUN)	D	10		
Houssine BENALI (MAR)	A	8	(10)	
CARLOS de Jesus Júnior José (BRA)	M	10	(3)	5
Sébastien DE MEERSMAN	M	5	(4)	
Michael DE MEYST	M	6	(10)	1
Rickie DE SLOOVER	D		(2)	
Koen DE VLEESCHAUWER	D	27	(3)	
Emmanuel EBIEDE (NIG)	A	16	(10)	4
Mohammed KANU (SRL)	M	4	(7)	
Olivier LAMBERG	M	20	(8)	1
Harold MEYSSEN	M	30	(2)	9
Godwin OKPARA (NIG)	D	32		
David PAAS	A	24	(6)	12
Andy PELEMAN	M		(1)	
Chris TEMMERMAN	M	31	(1)	3
Peter THIJS	G	1		
Nico VAESEN	G	20		
Edwin VAN ANKEREN (HOL)	A	18		10
Fred VAN DER HOORN (HOL)	D	29		
Toon VAN DER KELEN	D		(1)	1
Stefan VAN RIEL	D	28	(3)	2
Jan VAN STEENBERGHE	G	13		
Peter VAN WAMBEKE	M	17	(4)	2
Sammy VANDENBOSSCHE	A	3	(4)	1
Yves VANDERHAEGHE	M	22		3

LEAGUE RESULTS 1995/96

04/08/95	RSC Anderlecht	H	3-1	Van Ankeren 3
12/08/95	KSK Beveren	A	2-0	Temmerman, Van Ankeren
16/08/95	KRC Harelbeke	H	2-0	Meyssen 2
19/08/95	Royal Antwerp FC	A	1-0	Meyssen
27/08/95	KFC Lommelse SK	H	4-1	Van Riel, Van Ankeren, Paas, Lamberg
30/08/95	KAA Gent	A	1-3	og (Ramcic)
09/09/95	R Standard Liège	H	1-1	Van Ankeren
16/09/95	KSV Cercle Brugge	A	1-1	Paas
20/09/95	K Lierse SK	H	1-2	Paas
23/09/95	RWD Molenbeek	A	0-0	
30/09/95	KSV Waregem	A	0-0	
14/10/95	RSC Charleroi	H	3-4	Paas, Meyssen, Van Ankeren
22/10/95	KFC Germinal Ekeren	A	1-5	Temmerman
28/10/95	K St.-Truidense VV	H	0-0	
03/11/95	RFC Seraing	A	4-2	Van Ankeren, Ebiede, Temmerman, Paas
19/11/95	Club Brugge KV	H	0-2	
25/11/95	KV Mechelen	A	0-1	
01/12/95	RSC Anderlecht	A	0-4	
17/12/95	KSK Beveren	H	5-1	De Meyst, Ebiede (p), Van Ankeren, Paas 2
20/12/95	KRC Harelbeke	A	1-2	Van Ankeren
27/01/96	Royal Antwerp FC	H	0-0	
03/02/96	KFC Lommelse SK	A	0-1	
11/02/96	KAA Gent	H	2-2	Van Wambeke, Paas
17/02/96	R Standard Liège	A	1-2	Vanderhaeghe
02/03/96	K Lierse SK	A	1-2	Ebiede (p)
10/03/96	RWD Molenbeek	H	1-1	Paas
17/03/96	KSV Waregem	H	1-1	Meyssen (p)
24/03/96	KSV Cercle Brugge	H	4-3	Vandenbossche, Carlos, Van Riel, Vanderhaeghe
30/03/96	RSC Charleroi	A	0-2	
06/04/96	KFC Germinal Ekeren	H	2-0	Meyssen, Carlos
13/04/96	K St.-Truidense VV	A	2-2	Carlos, Meyssen
20/04/96	RFC Seraing	H	5-0	Meyssen, Paas 2, Carlos, Van Wambeke
05/05/96	Club Brugge KV	A	3-1	Meyssen (p), Paas, Vanderhaeghe
12/05/96	KV Mechelen	H	3-2	Ebiede, Carlos, Van der Kelen

KAA GENT

CLUB DIRECTORY

KAA Gent
Bruiloftstraat 42
9050 Gentbrugge-Gent
tel - (09) 2306610
Year of Formation - 1898
President - Jean Van Milders
Manager - Michel Louwagie
Coach - Leo Clijsters
Stadium - Jules Ottenstadion (18,215)

MAJOR HONOURS
Domestic Cup - (2) 1964, 1984.

APPEARANCES 95/96

	P	Ap	(s)	Gls
Peter ANOSIKE (NIG)	A		(2)	
Mohammed BARKA	M	14	(13)	
Igor CALO (CRO)	A	19	(2)	7
Frank DAUWEN	D	31		3
Steve DE GROOTE	M	12	(6)	
Gunter DE MEYER	D	31	(1)	5
Pascal DE VREESE	M	26	(4)	4
Patrick DEMAN	G	34		
Sven GEERAERTS	M		(2)	
Tony HERREMAN	D	34		3
Suad KATANA (BOS)	D	34		2
Mohammed KURTULUS	D		(6)	
Sandy MARTENS	A	32		9
NIVALDO Vieira Lima (BRA)	A	1	(3)	1
Valery NTANAG (CMR)	M	2	(1)	1
Edin RAMCIC (BOS)	D	31		1
Axel SMEETS	D	20	(6)	
Dirk VAN GRONSVELD	D	3	(1)	
Nico VANDERDONCK	M	15	(5)	
Kenny VERHOENE	D	28	(2)	1
Sretko VUKSANOVIC (YUG)	A	4	(5)	
Mario WITVROUWEN	M	3	(19)	

LEAGUE RESULTS 1995/96

06/08/95	KSV Waregem	A	2-2	Martens, Dauwen
12/08/95	R Standard Liège	H	2-4	Calo 2
16/08/95	KSV Cercle Brugge	A	0-0	
19/08/95	K Lierse SK	H	0-2	
26/08/95	RWD Molenbeek	A	0-1	
30/08/95	KSC Eendracht Aalst	H	3-1	De Meyer, Calo, og (Van der Hoorn)
09/09/95	RSC Charleroi	A	3-3	Herreman, Martens, Calo
16/09/95	KFC Germinal Ekeren	H	0-2	
20/09/95	K St.-Truidense VV	A	0-1	
23/09/95	RFC Seraing	H	4-2	De Vreese, Dauwen, Calo, Martens
01/10/95	Club Brugge KV	A	0-3	
14/10/95	KV Mechelen	H	0-0	
21/10/95	RSC Anderlecht	A	0-1	
28/10/95	KSK Beveren	H	3-0	De Meyer, Verhoene, Calo
04/11/95	KRC Harelbeke	A	1-0	De Vreese
18/11/95	Royal Antwerp FC	H	1-0	Martens
25/11/95	KFC Lommelse SK	A	1-1	De Vreese
02/12/95	KSV Waregem	H	0-0	
16/12/95	R Standard Liège	A	1-1	Ntamag
23/12/95	KSV Cercle Brugge	H	1-5	Ramcic
27/01/96	K Lierse SK	A	3-2	Calo, De Meyer, Herreman
03/02/96	RWD Molenbeek	H	2-0	De Meyer, De Vreese
11/02/96	KSC Eendracht Aalst	A	2-2	Katana, De Meyer
17/02/96	RSC Charleroi	H	1-0	og (Gérard)
02/03/96	K St.-Truidense VV	H	0-1	
09/03/96	RFC Seraing	A	2-2	Dauwen, Martenss
17/03/96	Club Brugge KV	H	0-2	
24/03/96	KFC Germinal Ekeren	A	0-2	
30/03/96	KV Mechelen	A	0-0	
06/04/96	RSC Anderlecht	H	1-3	Martens
13/04/96	KSK Beveren	A	2-2	Nivaldo, Martens
20/04/96	KRC Harelbeke	H	1-0	Herreman (p)
05/05/96	Royal Antwerp FC	A	1-2	Katana
12/05/96	KFC Lommelse SK	H	2-0	Martens 2

KFC GERMINAL EKEREN

CLUB DIRECTORY

KFC Germinal Ekeren
Veltwijcklaan 33
2180 Ekeren
tel - (03) 5425565
fax - (03) 5414127
Year of Formation - 1920
President - Jos Verhaegen
Manager - Luc Verheyen
Coach - Herman Helleputte; Stanislas Gzil
Stadium - Veltwijckpark (17,500)

APPEARANCES 95/96

	P	Ap	(s)	Gls
Jean-Marie ABEELS	M	3	(1)	
Steve ADAM	M		(1)	
Björn DAELEMANS	A		(3)	
Eric DEFLANDRE	D	32		2
Alain DENIL	M	5	(10)	
Didier DHEEDENE	D	31	(1)	1
Gábor HALMAI (HUN)	D	21	(5)	2
Gunter HOFMANS	M	33		13
Rudy JANSSENS	M	30	(1)	1
Christophe KINET	D	3	(12)	1
Ervin KOVÁCS (HUN)	M	4		1
Roger Menema LUKAKU (ZAI)	A	28		9
Karim M'GOGHI	M	22	(5)	
Tomasz RADZINSKI (CAN)	A	22		9
ROGÉRIO Gonçalves (BRA)	A	1	(2)	
Marc SCHAESSENS	M	25		5
Simon TAHAMATA (HOL)	A	8	(15)	
Philippe VANDE WALLE	G	34		6
Stan VAN DEN BUYS	M	23		
Mike VERSTRAETEN	D	28		3
Bernard WEGRIA	D	21	(5)	

LEAGUE RESULTS 1995/96

06/08/95	Club Brugge KV	H	1-2	Vande Walle (p)
12/08/95	KV Mechelen	A	1-1	Radzinski
19/08/95	KSK Beveren	A	2-3	Vande Walle (p), Lukaku
27/08/95	KRC Harelbeke	H	1-1	Radzinski
10/09/95	KFC Lommelse SK	H	1-2	Hofmans
16/09/95	KAA Gent	A	2-0	Schaessens, Vande Walle (p)
20/09/95	R Standard Liège	H	2-0	Radzinski 2
23/09/95	KSV Cercle Brugge	A	2-2	Radzinski, Vande Walle
29/09/95	K Lierse SK	H	1-1	Hofmans
11/10/95	RSC Anderlecht	H	2-2	Lukaku, Deflandre
14/10/95	RWD Molenbeek	A	0-1	
22/10/95	KSC Eendracht Aalst	H	5-1	Hofmans 2, Halmai, Schaessens 2
28/10/95	RSC Charleroi	A	1-1	Lukaku
05/11/95	KSV Waregem	A	0-1	
11/11/95	Royal Antwerp FC	A	2-0	Lukaku, Verstraeten
19/11/95	K St.-Truidense VV	H	3-1	Kovács, Dheedene, Hofmans
25/11/95	RFC Seraing	A	1-1	Verstraeten
03/12/95	Club Brugge KV	A	1-3	Radzinski
17/12/95	KV Mechelen	H	1-0	Hofmans
23/12/95	RSC Anderlecht	A	2-4	Radzinski 2
28/01/96	KSK Beveren	H	1-0	Halmai
04/02/96	KRC Harelbeke	A	2-1	Lukaku, Hofmans
11/02/96	Royal Antwerp FC	H	2-0	Lukaku 2
17/02/96	KFC Lommelse SK	A	1-2	Radzinski
02/03/96	R Standard Liège	A	0-0	
10/03/96	KSV Cercle Brugge	H	1-0	Hofmans
16/03/96	K Lierse SK	A	1-2	Hofmans
24/03/96	KAA Gent	H	2-0	Schaessens, Deflandre
31/03/96	RWD Molenbeek	H	1-0	Verstraeten
07/04/96	KSC Eendracht Aalst	A	0-2	
14/04/96	RSC Charleroi	H	3-1	Hofmans 3
21/04/96	KSV Waregem	H	2-0	Lukaku, Vande Walle (p)
05/05/96	K St.-Truidense VV	A	1-2	Vande Walle (p)
12/05/96	RFC Seraing	H	5-0	Lukaku, Schaessens, Janssens, Hofmans, Kinet

KRC HARELBEKE

CLUB DIRECTORY

KRC Harelbeke
Stasegemsesteenweg 23
8530 Harelbeke
tel - (056) 718131
fax - (056) 718135
Year of Formation - 1930
President - Geert Sustronck
Secretary - Noël Ottevaere
Coach - Henk Houwaart
Stadium - Forestiersstadion (9,000)

APPEARANCES 95/96

	P	Ap	(s)	Gls
Benedict AKUWEGBU (NIG)	A	6	(17)	1
Eric AUFFRET (FRA)	D	7	(1)	
Francis COUVREUR	A	7	(2)	4
Joris DE TOLLENAERE	A	33		6
Ivan DE WILDE	G	31		
Alain DECLERCQ	D	27		1
Kurt DELTOUR	D	26	(4)	3
Florin Eugen FRUNZA (ROM)	M	29	(1)	6
Nordine HAMEG (ALG)	D	34		
Arkadiusz KUBIK (POL)	A	12		3
Felix Michael NGONGE (ZAI)	A	30	(1)	14
Bruno PARMENTIER	M	11	(1)	
Pascal PIETERS	M	1	(6)	
Koenraad SANDERS	D	22	(3)	
Chris SCHOUTTETENS	D		(1)	
Renzo TIELENS	M		(1)	
Hein VAN HAEZEBROUCK	D	32		
Tony VAN HOUTTEGHEM	M		(1)	
Jan VAN TIEGHEM	D	8	(17)	1
Franky VANDENBROUCKE	G	3	(1)	
Serge VANDEWALLE	D	14	(8)	
Steven WOSTIJN	A		(1)	
Steve YOUSFI	M	16	(5)	1
Patrice ZERE (FRA)	D	25		

LEAGUE RESULTS 1995/96

05/08/95	K Lierse SK	A	1-0	Ngonge (p)
13/08/95	RWD Molenbeek	H	4-2	Ngonge, Couvreur 2, Akuwegbu
16/08/95	KSC Eendracht Aalst	A	0-2	
20/08/95	RSC Charleroi	H	4-0	De Tollenaere 2, Ngonge (p), Couvreur
27/08/95	KFC Germinal Ekeren	A	1-1	Couvreur
30/08/95	K St.-Truidense VV	H	3-0	Ngonge 2, Frunza
09/09/95	RFC Seraing	A	1-0	Frunza (p)
17/09/95	Club Brugge KV	H	0-2	
20/09/95	KV Mechelen	A	0-1	
24/09/95	RSC Anderlecht	H	0-4	
30/09/95	KSK Beveren	A	0-0	
15/10/95	KSV Waregem	H	2-1	Frunza, Ngonge
22/10/95	Royal Antwerp FC	H	3-1	Frunza, De Tollenaere, Ngonge
28/10/95	KFC Lommelse SK	A	0-2	
05/11/95	KAA Gent	H	0-1	
18/11/95	R Standard Liège	A	1-2	Deltour
26/11/95	KSV Cercle Brugge	H	0-2	
03/12/95	K Lierse SK	H	2-3	Ngonge (p), Frunza
16/12/95	RWD Molenbeek	A	1-3	Yousfi
20/12/95	KSC Eendracht Aalst	H	2-1	Ngonge, Declercq
27/01/96	RSC Charleroi	A	0-0	
04/02/96	KFC Germinal Ekeren	H	1-2	Deltour
10/02/96	K St.-Truidense VV	A	0-2	
18/02/96	RFC Seraing	H	2-1	Ngonge, Kubik
03/03/96	KV Mechelen	H	0-0	
09/03/96	RSC Anderlecht	A	3-1	Ngonge 3 (1p)
17/03/96	KSK Beveren	H	1-0	De Tollenaere
24/03/96	Club Brugge KV	A	0-2	
31/03/96	KSV Waregem	A	2-1	De Tollenaere, Deltour (p)
06/04/96	Royal Antwerp FC	A	3-2	Frunza, Van Tieghem, Kubik
14/04/96	KFC Lommelse SK	H	0-3	
20/04/96	KAA Gent	A	0-1	
05/05/96	R Standard Liège	H	2-3	Ngonge, Kubik
12/05/96	KSV Cercle Brugge	A	1-2	De Tollenaere

K LIERSE SK

CLUB DIRECTORY

K Lierse SK
Voetbalstraat 4
2500 Lier
tel - (03) 4801370
fax - (03) 4880659
Year of Formation - 1906
President - Freddy Van Laer
Manager - Corneel De Ceulaer
Coach - Eric Gerets
Stadium - Herman Vanderpoortenstadion(14,000)

MAJOR HONOURS

League Championship - (3) 1932, 1942, 1960.
Domestic Cup - (1) 1969.

APPEARANCES 95/96

	P	Ap	(s)	Gls
Pascal BOVRI	D	18	(7)	
David BROCKEN	D	26	(4)	2
Jürgen CAVENS	M		(5)	
Bart DE ROOVER	D	29	(1)	
Stefaan DE SMET	M	6	(8)	
José Zefilho DE SOUSA (BRA)	A	22	(6)	12
Steven GOOSSEN (HOL)	D	32		
Dirk HUYSMANS	A	19		6
Dirk LEHMANN (GER)	A	12	(6)	7
Kris MAMPAEY	G	19	(1)	
Jan MOONS	G	15	(1)	
Raf PAUWELS	A	8	(16)	
Bob PEETERS	A	15	(14)	7
Jerry POORTERS	M		(1)	
Kjetil REKDAL (NOR)	M	34		12
Ives SERNEELS	D	31	(2)	1
Eddy SNELDERS	D	28	(2)	1
Karel SNOECKX	M	27	(5)	3
Nico VAN KERCKHOVEN	M	33		2
Frédéric WILKIN	D		(1)	

LEAGUE RESULTS 1995/96

05/08/95	KRC Harelbeke	H	0-1	
12/08/95	Royal Antwerp FC	A	1-3	Rekdal
16/08/95	KFC Lommelse SK	H	3-1	Serneels, Huysmans, Rekdal
19/08/95	KAA Gent	A	2-0	Rekdal, Snoeckx
26/08/95	R Standard Liège	H	0-0	
30/08/95	KSV Cercle Brugge	A	3-2	De Sousa 2, Brocken
09/09/95	KSV Waregem	A	3-1	De Sousa 2, Huysmans
16/09/95	RWD Molenbeek	H	1-1	De Sousa
20/09/95	KSC Eendracht Aalst	A	2-1	Snoeckx, Peeters
23/09/95	RSC Charleroi	H	2-1	Rekdal, De Sousa
29/09/95	KFC Germinal Ekeren	A	1-1	Huysmans
14/10/95	K St.-Truidense VV	H	3-0	De Sousa, Rekdal, Van Kerckhoven
21/10/95	RFC Seraing	A	3-1	Huysmans (p), Snelders, Pauwels
28/10/95	Club Brugge KV	H	2-2	De Sousa, Huysmans (p)
04/11/95	KV Mechelen	A	0-0	
18/11/95	RSC Anderlecht	H	3-2	Huysmans, De Sousa 2
25/11/95	KSK Beveren	A	2-2	Van Kerckhoven, Rekdal
03/12/95	KRC Harelbeke	A	3-2	Peeters 2, Snoeckx
16/12/95	Royal Antwerp FC	H	1-2	De Sousa
23/12/95	KFC Lommelse SK	A	0-0	
27/01/96	KAA Gent	H	2-3	Lehmann 2
03/02/96	R Standard Liège	A	0-2	
10/02/96	KSV Cercle Brugge	H	0-1	
17/02/96	KSV Waregem	H	1-1	Rekdal (p)
02/03/96	KSC Eendracht Aalst	H	3-1	Rekdal 2 (1p), Lehmann
09/03/96	RSC Charleroi	A	1-1	Lehmann
16/03/96	KFC Germinal Ekeren	H	2-1	Peeters 2
24/03/96	RWD Molenbeek	A	0-0	
30/03/96	K St.-Truidense VV	A	1-3	Lehmann
06/04/96	RFC Seraing	H	4-0	Brocken, Rekdal (p), Lehmann, De Sousa
14/04/96	Club Brugge KV	A	1-2	Rekdal (p)
20/04/96	KV Mechelen	H	0-3	
05/05/96	RSC Anderlecht	A	1-3	Peeters
12/05/96	KSK Beveren	H	3-1	Rekdal (p), Peeters, Lehmann

KFC LOMMELSE SK

CLUB DIRECTORY

KFC Lommelse SK
Gemeentelijk Sportcentrum
Speelpleinstraat 20
3920 Lommel
tel - (011) 546070
fax - (011) 552801
Year of Formation - 1932
President - Jan Vreys
Manager - Rik Lavreysen
Coach - Vic Hermans; Jos Daerden
(96/97 - Walter Meeuws)
Stadium - Gemeentelijk Sportcentrum (13,500)

APPEARANCES 95/96

	P	Ap	(s)	Gls
Hakan BAYRAKTAR	A		(1)	
Gert CANNAERTS	M	30		6
Kristof COOMANS	M		(1)	
Khalilou FADIGA (SEN)	A	17	(3)	
Eugène HANSSEN (HOL)	D	18	(2)	
Marc HENDRICKX	M	16	(9)	3
Jochen JANSSEN	M	8	(23)	3
Frank MACHIELS	D	26	(5)	2
Goram MAKAEV (BLS)	M	3	(4)	
Jacky MATTHIJSSEN	G	34		
Wim MENNES	A		(1)	
Jean-Claude MUKANYA (ZAI)	D	26	(2)	2
Daniel SCAVONE	D	32		3
Maarten SCHOPS	D	20	(4)	
Mohammed SILLAH (SRL)	D	5		
John VAN BROECKHOVEN	A	3	(5)	
Ronny VAN GENEUGDEN	M	33	(1)	9
Tom VAN MOL	D	32	(1)	1
Harm VAN VELDHOVEN (HOL)	M	25	(1)	3
Tom VANDERVEE	M	20	(3)	1
Miroslav WALIGORA (POL)	A	26	(7)	7

LEAGUE RESULTS 1995/96

Date	Opponent		Score	Scorers
05/08/95	R Standard Liège	A	0-1	
12/08/95	KSV Cercle Brugge	H	0-1	
16/08/95	K Lierse SK	A	1-3	Van Geneugden (p)
19/08/95	RWD Molenbeek	H	0-1	
27/08/95	KSC Eendracht Aalst	A	1-4	Waligora
30/08/95	RSC Charleroi	H	1-1	Cannaerts
10/09/95	KFC Germinal Ekeren	A	2-1	Janssen, Scavone
16/09/95	K St.-Truidense VV	H	2-3	Janssen, Van Veldhoven
20/09/95	RFC Seraing	A	1-2	Hendrickx
23/09/95	Club Brugge KV	H	2-2	Van Geneugden 2
30/09/95	KV Mechelen	A	0-2	
14/10/95	RSC Anderlecht	H	2-2	Machiels, Cannaerts
21/10/95	KSK Beveren	A	1-0	Van Mol
28/10/95	KRC Harelbeke	H	2-0	Cannaerts, Waligora
04/11/95	Royal Antwerp FC	A	1-4	Hendrickx
19/11/95	KSV Waregem	A	3-1	Van Geneugden 2, Van Veldhoven
25/11/95	KAA Gent	H	1-1	Van Geneugden
02/12/95	R Standard Liège	H	1-0	Cannaerts
17/12/95	KSV Cercle Brugge	A	1-0	Scavone
23/12/95	K Lierse SK	H	0-0	
28/01/96	RWD Molenbeek	A	2-0	Vandervee, Scavone
03/02/96	KSC Eendracht Aalst	H	1-0	Waligora
10/02/96	RSC Charleroi	A	0-5	
17/02/96	KFC Germinal Ekeren	H	2-1	Cannaerts, Waligora
02/03/96	RFC Seraing	H	0-1	
10/03/96	Club Brugge KV	A	0-2	
16/03/96	KV Mechelen	H	2-1	Van Veldhoven, Van Geneugden
23/03/96	K St.-Truidense VV	A	2-0	Waligora, Mukanya
30/03/96	RSC Anderlecht	A	2-3	Hendrickx, Mukanya
06/04/96	KSK Beveren	H	2-0	Machiels, Van Geneugden (p)
14/04/96	KRC Harelbeke	A	3-0	Waligora, Cannaerts, Van Geneugden
20/04/96	Royal Antwerp FC	H	0-0	
05/05/96	KSV Waregem	H	2-1	Janssen, Waligora
12/05/96	KAA Gent	A	0-2	

KV MECHELEN

CLUB DIRECTORY

KV Mechelen
Kleine Nieuwedijkstraat 62
2800 Mechelen
tel - (015) 218230
fax - (015) 219033
Year of Formation - 1904
President - Jef De Graef
Manager - Guido Mallants
Coach - Walter Meeuws; Willy Reynders
Stadium - Achter de Kazerne (14,131)

MAJOR HONOURS
League Championship - (4)
1943, 1946, 1948, 1989.
Domestic Cup - (1) 1987.
European Cup-winners' Cup - (1) 1988.
European Super Cup - (1) 1989.

APPEARANCES 95/96

	P	Ap	(s)	Gls
Johan BAL	M	9	(4)	
Carlo CAMILLERI	M	5	(11)	
Alex CZERNIATYNSKI	A	21	(4)	5
Jürgen DENEYS	A		(3)	
Marijo DODIK (CRO)	A	20	(7)	5
Pierre DROUGUET	G	34		
Davy GIJSBRECHTS	D	30		2
Koen KESSELAERS	M	2	(2)	
Frank LEEN	M	32		3
Jan-Pieter MARTENS	A	21	(9)	6
Bart MAUROO	D	18	(9)	
Desiré MBONABUCYA (BUR)	M	6		1
Michael MINKO (BUR)	A	6	(17)	3
Johnny MØLBY (DEN)	M	5		1
Alain PEETERMANS	M	17	(9)	2
Mathieu PEETERS	A	28	(2)	2
Marcos PEREIRA (BRA)	A	3	(4)	1
Patrick RONDAGS	G		(1)	
Didier SEGERS	M	27	(1)	
Joos VALGAEREN	D	30		4
Vital VANAKEN	D	33		3
Stijn VREVEN	D	27		1

LEAGUE RESULTS 1995/96

Date	Opponent	H/A	Score	Scorers
05/08/95	RSC Charleroi	A	2-4	og (Silvagni), Martens
12/08/95	KFC Germinal Ekeren	H	1-1	Vanaken
16/08/95	K St.-Truidense VV	A	2-2	Leen 2
19/08/95	RFC Seraing	H	1-4	Martens
26/08/95	Club Brugge KV	A	0-6	
30/08/95	KSV Waregem	H	3-0	Peeters, Mølby, Minko
09/09/95	RSC Anderlecht	H	1-3	Martens
16/09/95	KSK Beveren	A	1-1	Gijsbrechts
30/09/95	KRC Harelbeke	H	1-0	Martens
23/09/95	Royal Antwerp FC	A	2-1	Vreven, Martens
30/09/95	KFC Lommelse SK	H	2-0	Czerniatynski 2
14/10/95	KAA Gent	A	0-0	
21/10/95	R Standard Liège	H	2-0	Dodik, Peetermans
28/10/95	KSV Cercle Brugge	A	2-3	Peetermans, Czerniatynski
04/11/95	K Lierse SK	H	0-0	
18/11/95	RWD Molenbeek	A	1-0	Peeters
25/11/95	KSC Eendracht Aalst	H	1-0	Vanaken (p)
02/12/95	RSC Charleroi	H	1-2	Dodik
07/12/95	KFC Germinal Ekeren	A	0-1	
23/12/95	K St.-Truidense VV	H	2-0	Pereira, Dodik
27/01/96	RFC Seraing	A	1-2	Dodik
02/02/96	Club Brugge KV	H	0-2	
11/02/96	KSV Waregem	A	1-0	Dodik
17/02/96	RSC Anderlecht	A	1-3	Gijsbrechts
03/03/96	KRC Harelbeke	A	0-0	
09/03/96	Royal Antwerp FC	H	0-1	
16/03/96	KFC Lommelse SK	A	1-2	Valgaeren
23/03/96	KSK Beveren	H	2-1	Valgaeren, Martens
30/03/96	KAA Gent	H	0-0	
06/04/96	R Standard Liège	A	1-2	Minko
13/04/96	KSV Cercle Brugge	H	2-1	Czerniatynski, Valgaeren
20/04/96	K Lierse SK	A	3-0	Valgaeren, Czerniatynski, Minko
05/05/96	RWD Molenbeek	H	1-1	Vanaken
12/05/96	KSC Eendracht Aalst	A	2-3	Leen, Mbonabucya

RWD MOLENBEEK

CLUB DIRECTORY

RWD Molenbeek
Rue Charles Malis 61
1080 Bruxelles
tel - (02) 4119900
fax - (02) 4117797
Year of Formation - 1973
President - Serge Vilain
Secretary - Philippe Decleire
Coach - René Vandereycken
Stadium - Edmond Machtens (14,000)

MAJOR HONOURS
League Championship - (1) 1975.

APPEARANCES 95/96

	P	Ap	(s)	Gls
Adrian BAKALLI	A	10	(1)	
Rachid BAOUF	D	2		
Daniel CAMUS	D	28	(3)	2
Harold DEGLAS	A	2	(20)	4
Stéphane DEMETS	M	11	(11)	1
Wilfried GODART	G	2	(1)	
Spira GRUJCIC (MAC)	M	31		
Alan HAYDOCK	M	10	(11)	3
Gunter JACOB	M	31		
Peter JANSSEN	M		(2)	
Mike LAEREMANS	M		(1)	
Steve LAEREMANS	D	20		
Olivier MALCORPS	M	1	(16)	
Daniel NASSEN	D	32		
Kai NYYSSÖNEN (FIN)	A	12	(1)	3
Frédéric PIERRE	A	30	(2)	13
Dirk ROSEZ	G	32		
Thierry ROUYR	D	14	(1)	
Marino SABBADINI	M	25	(4)	4
Jürgen VAN DER VELDE	G		(1)	
Guy VANDERSMISSEN	D	33		
Yuri VERGEICHIK (BLS)	M	26	(1)	
Marc WUYTS	A	22	(3)	8

LEAGUE RESULTS 1995/96

06/08/95	KSK Beveren	H	1-0	Wuyts
13/08/95	KRC Harelbeke	A	2-4	Wuyts, Pierre
16/08/95	Royal Antwerp FC	H	0-0	
19/08/95	KFC Lommelse SK	A	1-0	Sabbadini
26/08/95	KAA Gent	H	1-0	Haydock
30/08/95	R Standard Liège	A	1-1	Sabbadini
09/09/95	KSV Cercle Brugge	H	2-2	Pierre 2
16/09/95	K Lierse SK	A	1-1	og (Huysmans)
20/09/95	KSV Waregem	A	1-0	Wuyts (p)
23/09/95	KSC Eendracht Aalst	H	0-0	
30/09/95	RSC Charleroi	A	2-2	Wuyts, Pierre
14/10/95	KFC Germinal Ekeren	H	1-0	Wuyts
21/10/95	K St.-Truidense VV	A	1-0	Pierre
28/10/95	RFC Seraing	H	4-0	Deglas 3, Pierre
05/11/95	Club Brugge KV	A	0-3	
18/11/95	KV Mechelen	H	0-1	
25/11/95	RSC Anderlecht	A	0-1	
02/12/95	KSK Beveren	A	1-1	Camus
16/12/95	KRC Harelbeke	H	3-1	Sabbadini, Wuyts, Pierre
23/12/95	Royal Antwerp FC	A	1-1	Deglas
28/01/96	KFC Lommelse SK	H	0-2	
03/02/96	KAA Gent	A	0-2	
11/02/96	R Standard Liège	H	3-1	Nyyssönen 2 (1p), Demets
18/02/96	KSV Cercle Brugge	A	1-1	Pierre
03/03/96	KSV Waregem	H	4-1	Nyyssönen, Camus, Pierre 2
10/03/96	KSC Eendracht Aalst	A	1-1	Haydock
15/03/96	RSC Charleroi	H	3-1	Pierre, Wuyts,Sabbadibi
24/03/96	K Lierse SK	H	0-0	
31/03/96	KFC Germinal Ekeren	A	0-1	
06/04/96	K St.-Truidense VV	H	2-0	Haydock, Pierre
13/04/96	RFC Seraing	A	1-0	Wuyts (match abandoned; later awarded as 5-0)
19/04/96	Club Brugge KV	H	0-0	
05/05/96	KV Mechelen	A	1-1	Pierre
12/05/96	RSC Anderlecht	H	0-0	

RFC SERAING

CLUB DIRECTORY

RFC Seraing (now defunct)
Rue de la Boverie 253
4100 Seraing
tel - (041) 372825
Year of Formation - 1900
President - Gérald Blaton
Manager - Francis Nicolay
Coach - Jean Thissen; Manu Fereira
Stadium - Stade du Pairay (14,389)

APPEARANCES 95/96

	P	Ap	(s)	Gls
Stéphane BARE	M		(1)	
Pascal BEEKEN	G	17		
Fabrice BELDE	M	2	(2)	
Roberto BISCONTI	M	17	(3)	2
Luciano CRAPA	D	22	(7)	
Frédéric CREMASCO	M		(2)	
David DASPREMONT	M		(1)	
Benjamin DEBUSSCHERE	D	30		1
Rudy DUCOULOMBIER	D	19	(1)	
EDMILSON Paulo da Silva (BRA)	A	27	(1)	12
EDSON Paulo da Silva (BRA)	D	6	(8)	1
Stéphane GUIDI	A		(3)	
Harald HEINEN	G	17		
Serge KIMONI	D	24	(1)	
Axel LAWAREE	A	24	(6)	8
Raphaël MICELI	A	12	(12)	2
Danny N'GOMBO (ZAI)	D	34		1
Jean-Claude PAGAL (CMR)	M	6	(1)	1
Didier QUAIN	D	26	(1)	
RIBEIRO PEREIRA Carlos (BRA)	D	9	(5)	
David SWERDTFEGERS	M	10	(3)	1
Patrick TEPPERS	M	33		3
Lilian THONET	M		(3)	
Christophe VAN DEN BERGH	D	15	(11)	
WAMBERTO de Jesus Sousa Campos (BRA)	A	24	(4)	2

LEAGUE RESULTS 1995/96

Date	Opponent	H/A	Score	Scorers
05/08/95	K St.-Truidense VV	A	1-4	Edmilson
12/08/95	KSV Waregem	H	0-2	
16/08/95	Club Brugge KV	H	1-1	Edmilson
19/08/95	KV Mechelen	A	4-1	Edmilson 2, Teppers, Wamberto
26/08/95	RSC Anderlecht	H	2-1	Wamberto, Miceli
30/08/95	KSK Beveren	A	0-1	
09/09/95	KRC Harelbeke	H	0-1	
16/09/95	Royal Antwerp FC	A	2-4	Lawaree, Edmilson
20/09/95	KFC Lommelse SK	H	2-1	Ngombo, Edmilson
23/09/95	KAA Gent	A	2-4	Lawaree, Edmilson
30/09/95	R Standard Liège	H	0-0	
14/10/95	KSV Cercle Brugge	A	0-0	
21/10/95	K Lierse SK	H	1-3	Edson
28/10/95	RWD Molenbeek	A	0-4	
03/11/95	KSC Eendracht Aalst	H	2-4	Lawaree, Teppers
18/11/95	RSC Charleroi	A	2-4	Teppers, Edmilson (p)
25/11/95	KFC Germinal Ekeren	H	1-1	Miceli
02/12/95	K St.-Truidense VV	H	1-2	Swerdtfegers
17/12/95	KSV Waregem	A	3-0	Bisconti, Edmilson, Lawaree
21/12/95	Club Brugge KV	A	1-3	Bisconti
27/01/96	KV Mechelen	H	2-1	Edmilson, Pagal
03/02/96	RSC Anderlecht	A	0-7	
10/02/96	KSK Beveren	H	1-0	og (Jurcic)
18/02/96	KRC Harelbeke	A	1-2	Debusschere
02/03/96	KFC Lommelse SK	A	1-0	Edmilson
09/03/96	KAA Gent	H	2-2	Lawaree 2
16/03/96	R Standard Liège	A	0-3	
23/03/96	Royal Antwerp FC	H	0-1	
30/03/96	KSV Cercle Brugge	H	1-0	Edmilson
06/04/96	K Lierse SK	A	0-4	
13/04/96	RWD Molenbeek	H	0-1	(match abandoned; later awarded as 0-5)
20/04/96	KSC Eendracht Aalst	A	0-5	
05/05/96	RSC Charleroi	H	2-3	Lawaree 2
12/05/96	KFC Germinal Ekeren	A	0-5	

K ST.-TRUIDENSE VV

CLUB DIRECTORY

K Sint-Truidense VV
Tiensesteenweg 223
3800 Sint-Truiden
tel - (011) 683219
fax - (011) 692380
Year of Formation - 1924
President - Henri Knapen
Secretary - Constant Peters
Coach - Guy Mangelschots; Wilfried Sleurs
Stadium - Staaien (14,800)

APPEARANCES 95/96

	P	Ap	(s)	Gls
Jean-Marie ABEELS	A	12		3
Tibor BALOG (HUN)	D	32		1
CALLEEUW	A		(2)	
Erwin COENEN	M	33		4
Sotiros COSTOULAS	D	7	(3)	
Nico CURTO	A	20	(9)	1
Patrick CYPERS	M	18	(5)	1
Dirk DAELMANS	D	17		2
Eddy DIERICKX	M	31		2
Johan DRIESEN	M	1		
GRAMMET	A		(3)	
Marc HOUDENAERT	G	8	(1)	
Lorenz KINDTNER	M	4	(11)	
Stefan MOLNAR	M	8	(4)	
Kurt MORHAYE	M	8	(7)	1
Anders NIELSEN (DEN)	A	24	(1)	9
Steven NIJS	M	2	(5)	
Chidi NWANU (NIG)	D	18		
Rene PETERSEN (DEN)	A	19		2
Wilfried SLEURS	D	10		
Stefaan TEUCHY	M	3	(4)	
Peter VAN HOUDT	A	24	(7)	8
Bart VAN MARSENILLE	A	13		8
Bart VANDERSMISSEN	A	3	(4)	
Roland VELKENEERS	G	26		
Peter VOETS	D	33		

LEAGUE RESULTS 1995/96

05/08/95	RFC Seraing	H	4-1	Van Houdt, Van Marsenille 3 (1p)
11/08/95	Club Brugge KV	A	0-2	
16/08/95	KV Mechelen	H	2-2	Nielsen 2
19/08/95	RSC Anderlecht	A	0-4	
26/08/95	KSK Beveren	H	0-2	
30/08/95	KRC Harelbeke	A	0-3	
09/09/95	Royal Antwerp FC	H	2-3	Balog, Van Houdt
16/09/95	KFC Lommelse SK	A	3-2	Van Marsenille, Nielsen, Van Houdt
20/09/95	KAA Gent	H	1-0	Van Marsenille
23/09/95	R Standard Liège	A	1-1	Abeels
30/09/95	KSV Cercle Brugge	H	1-1	Nielsen
14/10/95	K Lierse SK	A	0-3	
21/10/95	RWD Molenbeek	H	0-1	
28/10/95	KSC Eendracht Aalst	A	0-0	
04/11/95	RSC Charleroi	H	4-1	Nielsen 2, Abeels, Van Marsenille
19/11/95	KFC Germinal Ekeren	A	1-3	Van Marsenille (p)
25/11/95	KSV Waregem	H	1-1	Dierickx
02/12/95	RFC Seraing	A	2-1	Van Marsenille, Abeels
16/12/95	Club Brugge KV	H	2-4	Van Houdt, Coenen
23/12/95	KV Mechelen	A	0-2	
27/01/96	RSC Anderlecht	H	0-5	
03/02/96	KSK Beveren	A	2-0	Nielsen, Daelmans
10/02/96	KRC Harelbeke	H	2-0	Van Houdt, Curto
17/02/96	Royal Antwerp FC	A	1-1	Nielsen
02/03/96	KAA Gent	A	1-0	Coenen (p)
08/03/96	R Standard Liège	H	3-1	Van Houdt 2, Petersen
17/03/96	KSV Cercle Brugge	A	1-2	Van Houdt
23/03/96	KFC Lommelse SK	H	0-2	
30/03/96	K Lierse SK	H	3-1	Morhaye, Coenen, Dierickx
06/04/96	RWD Molenbeek	A	0-2	
13/04/96	KSC Eendracht Aalst	H	2-2	Cypers, Coenen
20/04/96	RSC Charleroi	A	0-4	
05/05/96	KFC Germinal Ekeren	H	2-1	Daelmans, Nielsen
12/05/96	KSV Waregem	A	1-2	Petersen

R STANDARD LIEGE

CLUB DIRECTORY

R Standard de Liège
Rue de la Centrale 2
4200 Liège
tel - (041) 522122/523287
fax - (041) 521469
Year of Formation - 1898
President - Jean Wauters
Manager - Roger Henrotay
Coach - Robert Waseige (96/97 - Jos Daerden)
Stadium - Sclessin (25,998)

MAJOR HONOURS
League Championship - (8) 1958, 1961, 1963, 1969, 1970, 1971, 1982, 1983.
Domestic Cup - (5)
1954, 1966, 1967, 1981, 1993.

APPEARANCES 95/96

	P	Ap	(s)	Gls
Alain BETTAGNO	M	21	(3)	5
Gilbert BODART	G	24		
Gheorghe BUTOIU (ROM)	A	9	(4)	2
Dimitri DE CONDE	M	25	(5)	2
Amilton DINGA (BRA)	D	14		
Didier ERNST	D	21	(8)	
Ronald FOGUENNE	M	19	(9)	4
Régis GENAUX	D	29		
Michael GOOSSENS	A	29		13
Guy HELLERS (LUX)	M	25		1
Steve HOSTE	M		(1)	
Hervé HOULMONT	M	2	(2)	
Guy HUBART	G	5	(2)	
Daniel KIMONI	M	12	(9)	
Philippe LEONARD	D	32		
Nebojsa MALBASA (YUG)	A	4	(12)	1
Tim NUYENS	G	3		
Didier PIOT	G	2		
Dario RAPPA	M		(3)	
Mircea REDNIC (ROM)	D	29		1
Sacha RYCHKOV (RUS)	M	8	(3)	1
Gunther SCHEPENS	M	30	(2)	5
Bernd THIJS	A	2	(12)	1
Shalom TIKVA (ISR)	M	3	(4)	1
Marc WILMOTS	A	26		14

LEAGUE RESULTS 1995/96

05/08/95	KFC Lommelse SK	H	1-0	Wilmots
12/08/95	KAA Gent	A	4-2	Goossens, Foguenne, Wilmots, De Conde
15/08/95	KSV Waregem	A	4-0	Foguenne, Wilmots 3
19/08/95	KSV Cercle Brugge	H	4-0	Bettagno, Schepens, Goossens, Foguenne
26/08/95	K Lierse SK	A	0-0	
30/08/95	RWD Molenbeek	H	1-1	Foguenne
09/09/95	KSC Eendracht Aalst	A	1-1	Thys
15/09/95	RSC Charleroi	H	2-2	Bettagno, Schepens
20/09/95	KFC Germinal Ekeren	A	0-2	
23/09/95	K St.-Truidense VV	H	1-1	Tikva
30/09/95	RFC Seraing	A	0-0	
13/10/95	Club Brugge KV	H	1-0	Schepens
21/10/95	KV Mechelen	A	0-2	
27/10/95	RSC Anderlecht	H	2-4	Goossens, Hellers
04/11/95	KSK Beveren	A	0-0	
18/11/95	KRC Harelbeke	H	2-1	De Conde, Bettagno
26/11/95	Royal Antwerp FC	A	2-3	Goossens, Malbasa
02/12/95	KFC Lommelse SK	A	0-1	
16/12/95	KAA Gent	H	1-1	Rychkov
21/12/95	KSV Waregem	H	1-1	Wilmots
25/01/96	KSV Cercle Brugge	A	3-2	Goossens 2, Butoiu
03/02/96	K Lierse SK	H	2-0	Wilmots 2 (1p)
11/02/96	RWD Molenbeek	A	1-3	Schepens
17/02/96	KSC Eendracht Aalst	H	2-1	Wilmots, Goossens
02/03/96	KFC Germinal Ekeren	H	0-0	
08/03/96	K St.-Truidense VV	A	1-3	Goossens
16/03/96	RFC Seraing	H	3-0	Goossens 2, Wilmots
22/03/96	RSC Charleroi	A	2-2	Goossens 2
31/03/96	Club Brugge KV	A	1-6	Wilmots
06/04/96	KV Mechelen	H	2-1	Bettagno, Butoiu
12/04/96	RSC Anderlechtl	A	1-2	Bettagno
20/04/96	KSK Beveren	H	2-2	Rednic, Wilmots
05/05/96	KRC Harelbeke	A	3-2	Wilmots 2, Goossens
12/05/96	Royal Antwerp FC	H	1-0	Schepens

KSV WAREGEM

CLUB DIRECTORY

KSV Waregem
Zuiderlaan 17
8790 Waregem
tel - (056) 600089
fax - (056) 600662
Year of Formation - 1946
President - Jean-Pierre Van Neder
Secretary - Rik Vererfven
Coach - Aimé Antheunis; André Van Maldeghem
Stadium - Regenboogstadion (14,815)

MAJOR HONOURS

Domestic Cup - (1) 1974.

APPEARANCES 95/96

	P	Ap	(s)	Gls
Marino BLANCKE	D	15	(4)	1
Frank BOSMANS	D	15	(7)	
David BOSSUYT	D	21	(8)	1
Hendrik BOSSUYT	M	2		
Fangio BUYSSE	D	32		1
Fode CAMARA	A	10	(13)	3
Rik CLAEYS	M	3	(6)	1
Danny D'HONDT	G	8	(1)	
Franky DEKENNE	D	7		
Nick DESCAMPS	D	15		
DESMET	A	1		
Bartel DEWAELE	M	31	(1)	1
Wouter HALSBERGHE	D		(1)	
Gideon IMAGBUDU (NIG)	A	12	(4)	1
Andrzej KUBICA (POL)	A	14	(1)	7
Kubu LEMBI (ZAI)	D	1	(3)	
Philippe LENGLOIS	D	14	(5)	
LOPES Rodrigues Ronaldo (BRA)	M	2	(4)	
Pieter MERLIER	M		(1)	
Zoran MILINKOVIC (YUG)	M	13		1
Souleymane OULARE (GUI)	A	13	(1)	3
Rodrigo PALOMINO (AUS)	A	4	(1)	1
Marcos ROCHA de Amorin (BRA)	M	13	(3)	1
Eddy SYX	M	20	(4)	
Flórián URBAN (HUN)	M	12	(1)	4
Chris VAN GEEM	D	26		1
Jude VANDELANNOITE	M	20	(1)	1
Franky VANDENDRIESSCHE	G	26		
Dirk VANDERBEKEN	D	24	(6)	1

LEAGUE RESULTS 1995/96

06/08/95	KAA Gent	H	2-2	Oulare 2
12/08/95	RFC Seraing	A	2-0	Claeys, Bossuyt D.
15/08/95	R Standard Liège	H	0-4	
20/08/95	Club Brugge KV	A	1-3	Vanderbeken
27/08/95	KSV Cercle Brugge	H	1-1	Palomino
30/08/95	KV Mechelen	A	0-3	
09/09/95	K Lierse SK	H	1-3	Urban
16/09/95	RSC Anderlecht	A	0-2	
20/09/95	RWD Molenbeek	H	0-1	
23/09/95	KSK Beveren	A	1-5	Buysse
30/09/95	KSC Eendracht Aalst	H	0-0	
15/10/95	KRC Harelbeke	A	1-2	Urban
21/10/95	RSC Charleroi	H	4-1	Imagbudu, Urban 2 (1p), Blancke
29/10/95	Royal Antwerp FC	A	0-2	
05/11/95	KFC Germinal Ekeren	H	1-0	Oulare
19/11/95	KFC Lommelse SK	H	1-3	Rocha
25/11/95	K St.-Truidense VV	A	1-1	Van Geem
02/12/95	KAA Gent	A	0-0	
17/12/95	RFC Seraing	H	0-3	
21/12/95	R Standard Liège	A	1-1	Vandelannoite
28/01/96	Club Brugge KV	H	2-5	Bossuyt, Kubica (p)
04/02/96	KSV Cercle Brugge	A	1-4	Kubica
11/02/96	KV Mechelen	H	0-1	
17/02/96	K Lierse SK	A	1-1	Kubica
03/03/96	RWD Molenbeek	A	1-4	Camara
10/03/96	KSK Beveren	H	1-4	Camara
17/03/96	KSC Eendracht Aalst	A	1-1	Kubica
24/03/96	RSC Anderlecht	H	1-4	Kubica (p)
31/03/96	KRC Harelbeke	H	1-2	Kubica (p)
05/04/96	RSC Charleroi	A	0-1	
14/04/96	Royal Antwerp FC	H	1-1	Camara
21/04/96	KFC Germinal Ekeren	A	0-2	
05/05/96	KFC Lommelse SK	A	1-2	Kubica
12/05/96	K St.-Truidense VV	H	2-1	Dewaele, Milinkovic

PROMOTED CLUBS

SECOND DIVISION FINAL TABLE 95/96

		Pd	W	D	L	F	A	Pt	GD
1	**KSC Lokeren**	**34**	**25**	**4**	**5**	**68**	**27**	**79**	**+41**
2	**KRC Genk**	**34**	**22**	**7**	**5**	**60**	**32**	**73**	**+28**
3	R Excelsior Mouscron	34	18	8	8	69	45	62	+24
4	KV Kortrijk	34	17	7	10	57	44	58	+13
5	KV Oostende	34	16	10	8	72	46	58	+26
6	K Beerschot VAV	34	15	10	9	52	51	55	+1
7	FC Verbroedering Geel	34	14	6	14	44	49	48	-5
8	FC Turnhout	34	11	14	9	39	41	47	-2
9	AA La Louvière	34	12	9	13	45	49	45	-4
10	KSK Deinze	34	9	15	10	36	47	42	-11
11	FC Tielen	34	11	8	15	55	53	41	+2
12	VC Westerlo	34	11	8	15	47	53	41	-6
13	Patro Eisden	34	10	11	13	45	36	41	+9
14	FC Kapellen	34	11	5	18	56	56	38	=
15	Overpelt VV	34	9	9	16	37	52	36	-15
16	SK St.-Niklaas	34	7	10	17	43	72	31	-29
17	SK Tongeren	34	7	8	19	33	59	29	-26
18	KTH Diest	34	3	7	24	38	84	16	-46

PROMOTION PLAY-OFFS FINAL TABLE

		Pd	W	D	L	F	A	Pt	GD
1	**R Excelsior Mouscron**	**6**	**4**	**1**	**1**	**14**	**7**	**13**	**+7**
2	K Beerschot VAV	6	3	0	3	10	13	9	-3
3	KV Oostende	6	2	1	3	13	10	7	+3
4	KV Kortrijk	6	2	0	4	6	13	6	-7

CLUB DIRECTORY

KSC Lokeren
Daknamstraat 91
9160 Lokeren
tel - (09) 2485305
Year of Formation - 1970
President - Roger Lambrecht
Secretary - André Verbraecken
Coach - Fi Van Hoof
Stadium - Daknam (12,000)

CLUB DIRECTORY

KRC Genk
Stadionplein 4
3600 Genk
tel - (011) 841608
Year of Formation - 1988
President - Remi Fagard
Secretary - Paul Baeten
Coach - Aimé Antheunis
Stadium - Thyl Gheyselinckstadium (16,000)

CLUB DIRECTORY

R Excelsior Mouscron
Rue du Stade au Canonnier 33
7700 Mouscron
Year of Formation - 1964
President - Filip Verbeke
Secretary - Jacques Vandewalle
Coach - Georges Leekens
Stadium - Canonnier (7,000)

BOSNIA-HERZEGOVINA

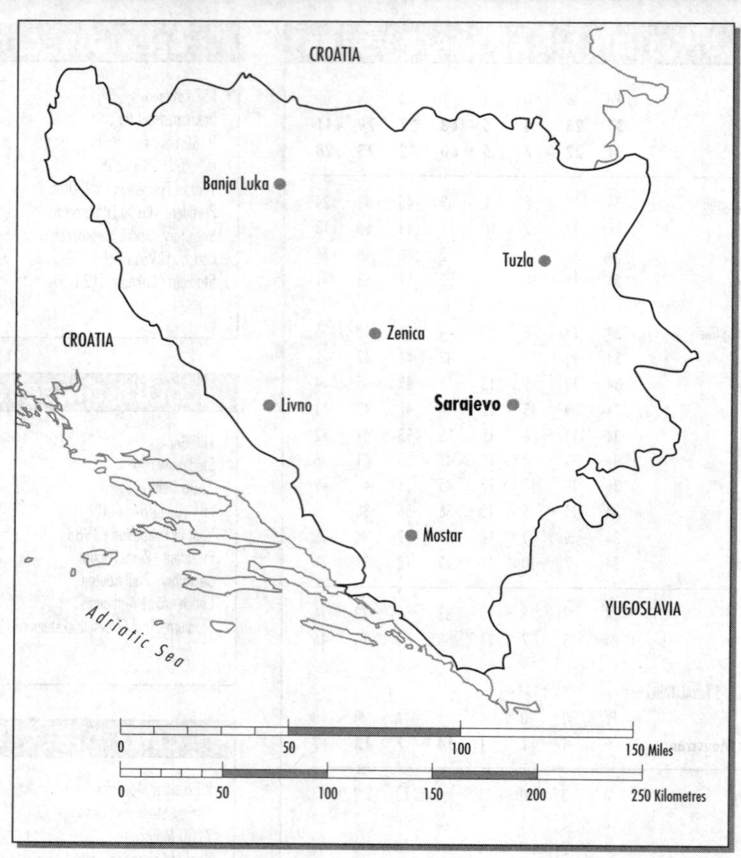

CELIK ZENICA ARE THE CHAMPIONS

World Cup place for FIFA's newest members

Out of the ashes of a decimated country, football has once again returned. Even after the civil war ceasefire and the Dayton agreement, Bosnia-Herzegovina remains a nation of conflict and confusion.

So it is in sport. A national football league was staged in 1995/96, but it was not a unified championship. Certain teams from the Muslim areas preferred to keep their distance and play amongst themselves. This disharmony left UEFA with no choice but to refuse admission to the European competitions for Bosnian clubs.

That meant no UEFA Cup or Cup-winners' Cup place for Celik Zenica, who won the 'double', beating Lukavac into second place in the league and defeating the league's third-placed team, Sloboda Tuzla, 2-1 after extra-time in the final of the Cup.

There is much better news, however, for the national team. FIFA's acceptance of Bosnia-Herzegovina as a full member enabled them to be placed in the qualifying competition for the 1998 World Cup - on the proviso that they stage their home matches outside the country.

Bosnia-Herzegovina will not qualify for France. That much was obvious from the team's two matches against Albania during the 1995/96 season. But some Bosnian players are already well known throughout Europe, notably strikers Meho Kodro (Spain) and Elvir Bolic (Turkey), and defender-cum-midfielder Refik Sabanadzovic (Greece).

FEDERATION DIRECTORY

Nogometni Savez Bosne i Hercegovine
Sirne Milutinovic - Sarajlije 10, Sarajevo

tel - (071) 670345/440644
fax - (071) 444332/447562

Year of Formation - 1921
President - Jusuf Pusina
Secretary - Savo Kosiric

Stadium - Kosevo, Sarajevo (20,000)

LEAGUE CHAMPIONSHIP FINAL TABLE 95/96

		Pd	W	D	L	F	A	Pt	GD
1	Celik Zenica	30	21	5	4	65	23	68	+42
2	Lukavac	30	20	4	6	69	22	64	+47
3	Sloboda Tuzla	30	19	6	5	59	29	63	+30
4	Zenica	30	15	8	7	45	22	53	+23
5	Jedinstvo Bihac	30	15	5	10	48	31	50	+17
6	Rudar Kakanja	30	14	5	11	46	35	47	+11
7	Sarajevo	30	12	7	11	38	29	43	+9
8	Rudar Breza	30	13	4	13	36	42	43	-6
9	Zeljeznicar Sarajevo	30	12	4	14	35	62	40	-27
10	Zmaj od Bosne Tuzla	30	11	6	13	52	37	39	+15
11	Travnik	30	10	7	13	40	43	37	-3
12	Gradina Srebrenik	30	9	6	15	35	54	33	-19
13	Turbina Jablonica	30	9	4	17	26	54	31	-28
14	Velez Mostar	30	8	3	19	30	61	27	-31
15	Olimpik Sarajevo	30	5	5	20	27	57	20	-30
16	Iskra Bugojno	30	4	7	19	16	66	19	-50

TOP SCORERS

27 Amir OSMANOVIC (Lukavac)
19 Halim STUPAC (Jedinstvo Bihac)
15 Nedim OMEROVIC (Sloboda Tuzla)

INTERNATIONAL HONOURS

None

DOMESTIC CUP FINAL

12/06/96, Sarajevo
CELIK ZENICA 2 Bujakovic (16), Tumbic (110)
SLOBODA TUZLA 1 Omerovic (28) (aet)

NATIONAL TEAM RESULTS 95/96

30/11/95	Albania	A	Tirana	0-2
24/04/96	Albania	H	Zenica	0-0

BULGARIA

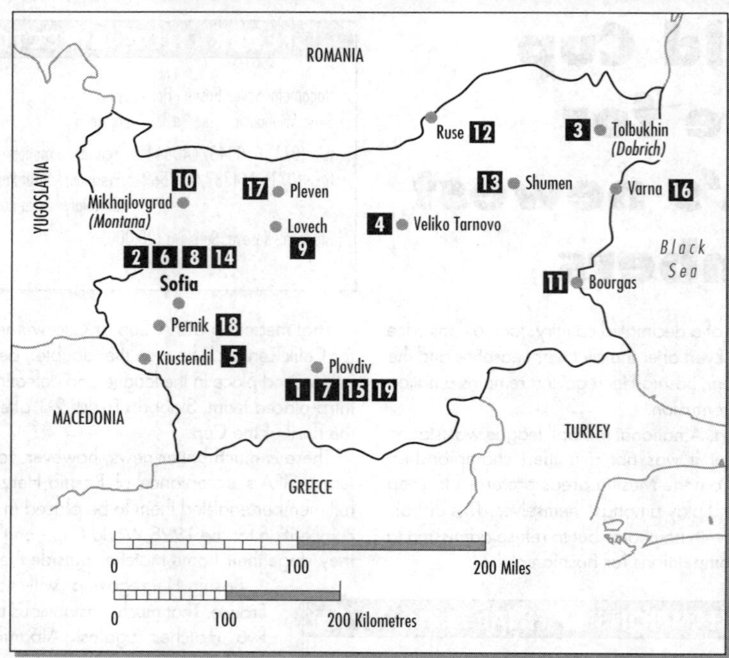

1	BOTEV PLOVDIV	199
2	CSKA SOFIA	200
3	DOBRUDZHA DOBRICH	201
4	ETAR VELIKO TARNOVO	202
5	LEVSKI KIUSTENDIL	203
6	LEVSKI SOFIA	204
7	LOKOMOTIV PLOVDIV	205
8	LOKOMOTIV SOFIA	206
9	LOVECH	207
10	MONTANA	208
11	NEFTOCHIMIK BOURGAS	209
12	RAKOVSKI RUSE	210
13	SHUMEN	211
14	SLAVIA SOFIA	212
15	SPARTAK PLOVDIV	213
16	SPARTAK VARNA	214
17	SPARTAK PLEVEN	215
18	MINIOR PERNIK	215
19	MARITSA PLOVDIV	215

SLAVIA 'DOUBLE' ENDS LONG DROUGHT

Stoichkov brilliance fails to turn the tide

In the build-up to Euro '96 there were indications that the Bulgarian national team was in decline. Although Stoichkov, Balakov and co. had reached the country's first European Championship finals in convincing fashion, their qualifying campaign had tapered off alarmingly towards the end with successive away defeats against Georgia and Germany. The final 1-3 loss in Berlin even allowed Germany to unseat Bulgaria from their place at the top of the Group Seven table which they had occupied throughout the qualifying campaign.

As the Euro '96 finals drew near, Dimitar Penev's team showed no clear sign of improvement. A trip to Wembley resulted in a flattering 0-1 defeat by England. And most of the team's leading players were struggling to impose themselves at club level.

Yordan Lechkov probably spent more time at the barber's than he did in the Hamburg first team. Emil Kostadinov couldn't make his mark alongside Jürgen Klinsmann at Bayern Munich. Goalkeeper and captain Borislav Mikhailov spent most of his first season at Reading on the treatment table. And, worst of all, the team's inspiration, Hristo Stoichkov, was enduring a nightmare first season in Italy with Parma.

But a couple of big wins in Sofia against Macedonia and the UAE clearly had a morale-boosting effect, because when Bulgaria came to England they suddenly looked ready, willing and able to turn the tide.

Perhaps the criticism that the team were too old got to the players. Or maybe it was the general prediction that they hadn't a prayer of qualifying from a group which contained France, Spain and Romania. But the fact is that Bulgaria began the tournament looking as fit and well-prepared as they had done two years earlier at the World Cup.

They deserved better than a 1-1 draw in their opening match against Spain. Hristo Stoichkov had a perfectly

FEDERATION DIRECTORY

Bulgarski Futbolen Soius
ul. Karnigradska 19, 1000 Sofia
tel - (02) 877490/874725
tlx - 23145 bfs bg
fax - (02) 803237
Stadium - Vasil Levski, Sofia (70,000)

Year of Formation - 1924
President - Ivan Slavkov
Secretary - Ivan Vutsov

LEAGUE CHAMPIONSHIP RESULTS 95/96

		1	2	3	4	5	6	7	8	9	10	11	12	13	14	15	16
1	Botev Plovdiv		0-4	1-0	1-0	3-0	1-1	5-0	3-0	1-0	0-0	2-1	1-1	0-1	0-1	2-0	1-3
2	CSKA Sofia	3-0		2-1	1-1	3-0	1-0	1-0	1-5	4-0	1-2	1-1	2-0	4-2	1-0	3-1	4-0
3	Dobrudzha Dobrich	1-0	2-0		0-2	2-1	2-1	2-0	0-1	1-2	1-0	1-3	2-0	1-0	1-0	1-0	3-2
4	Etar Veliko Tarnovo	1-2	0-0	2-2		1-0	0-1	3-0	0-1	1-0	4-0	0-2	1-0	1-0	0-2	1-0	2-1
5	Levski Kiustendil	2-1	0-0	2-0	2-0		2-0	0-0	2-1	0-0	1-1	1-0	3-0	2-0	0-0	3-0	1-0
6	Levski Sofia	2-1	3-1	2-0	2-0	3-0		4-0	0-1	4-0	2-1	1-2	1-0	2-1	0-0	3-0	4-1
7	Lokomotiv Plovdiv	0-0	2-1	3-1	2-0	2-2	0-1		1-0	2-1	0-4	2-0	2-0	2-0	2-4	1-0	2-1
8	Lokomotiv Sofia	2-1	0-0	2-0	3-0	3-0	0-2	4-0		3-1	3-0	3-1	4-1	1-1	2-2	4-0	5-0
9	Lovech	3-0	0-0	0-0	0-0	3-0	1-1	1-1	2-0		1-1	0-2	2-1	3-0	0-1	2-0	0-0
10	Montana	3-0	0-1	3-0	0-0	1-1	1-3	2-0	0-0	3-2		0-0	1-0	3-1	1-1	1-2	2-3
11	Neftochimik Bourgas	2-0	2-2	5-1	3-0	3-0	5-1	4-0	1-1	5-2	1-0		3-2	0-0	1-0	2-0	5-2
12	Rakovski Ruse	1-1	0-1	3-1	1-1	1-0	0-1	4-1	2-1	2-0	0-0	2-1		4-0	2-4	2-0	3-0
13	Shumen	1-1	1-0	1-0	3-0	3-1	0-2	1-0	0-0	1-1	0-1	2-3	2-0		0-1	3-1	2-0
14	Slavia Sofia	1-0	0-0	2-0	2-0	3-0	1-1	2-0	1-1	2-0	3-1	2-0	2-0	4-0		2-0	3-0
15	Spartak Plovdiv	2-4	2-4	1-1	3-0	1-0	0-1	0-0	1-2	2-1	2-1	0-0	0-0	4-2	1-3		0-1
16	Spartak Varna	2-1	1-3	2-3	3-0	2-1	0-0	2-0	1-2	2-1	2-0	3-0	3-1	2-0	0-2	8-1	

LEAGUE CHAMPIONSHIP FINAL TABLE 95/96

			Home					Away					Total						
		Pd	W	D	L	F	A	W	D	L	F	A	W	D	L	F	A	Pt	GD
1	Slavia Sofia	30	12	3	0	30	3	8	4	3	21	11	20	7	3	51	14	67	+37
2	Levski Sofia	30	12	1	2	33	8	7	4	4	16	14	19	5	6	49	22	62	+27
3	Lokomotiv Sofia	30	11	3	1	39	9	6	4	5	16	15	17	7	6	55	24	58	+31
4	Neftochimik Bourgas	30	12	3	0	42	11	5	3	7	16	20	17	6	7	58	31	57	+27
5	CSKA Sofia	30	11	2	2	32	13	5	6	4	17	13	16	8	6	49	26	56	+23
6	Spartak Varna	30	10	1	4	33	15	3	1	11	14	37	13	2	15	47	52	41	-5
7	Dobrudzha Dobrich	30	11	0	4	20	12	1	3	11	10	31	12	3	15	30	43	39	-13
8	Levski Kiustendil	30	10	5	0	21	3	0	2	13	6	34	10	7	13	27	37	37	-10
9	Montana	30	6	5	4	21	14	3	4	8	12	21	9	9	12	33	35	36	-2
10	Botev Plovdiv	30	8	3	4	21	12	2	3	10	12	26	10	6	14	33	38	36	-5
11	Lokomotiv Plovdiv	30	10	2	3	23	15	0	3	12	2	35	10	5	15	25	50	35	-25
12	Etar Veliko Tarnono	30	8	2	5	17	11	1	4	10	4	26	9	6	15	21	37	33	-16
13	Rakovski Ruse	30	9	3	3	27	12	0	2	13	6	29	9	5	16	33	41	32	-8
14	Shumen	30	8	3	4	20	11	1	2	12	8	33	9	5	16	28	44	32	-16
15	Lovech	30	6	7	2	18	7	1	2	12	11	33	7	9	14	29	40	30	-11
16	Spartak Plovdiv	30	5	4	6	19	20	1	0	14	5	38	6	4	20	24	58	22	-34

good goal ruled out for offside just after half-time, and although he later opened the scoring from a dodgy penalty, Bulgaria had enough of the game to end their opponents' long unbeaten run.

Up in Newcastle against Romania, Bulgaria recorded a famous 1-0 victory thanks to Stoichkov's outstanding early goal. But on this occasion the luck was with them as Romania had an even more obvious goal annulled through faulty officiating. Two down, one to go. Bulgaria stood on the brink of qualification. But against a French side seeking revenge for their late, late World Cup exit in November 1993, Penev's men dried up and were beaten 3-1. Complacency had set in, tempers began to fray, and they were punished with elimination when Spain struck a late winner against Romania down the A1 at Elland Road.

Bulgaria had set themselves up perfectly for a passage into the last eight but could not hold on to what they had. Recriminations inevitably followed, and a month after it was all over coach Penev - undeniably the

TOP SCORERS

21	Ivo GEORGIEV (Spartak Varna)
18	Vesko PETKOV (Neftochimik Bourgas)
16	Nasko SIRAKOV (Botev Plovdiv/Slavia Sofia)
12	Simeon CHILIBONOV (Lokomotiv Sofia)
11	Anatoli TONOV (Montana)
	Dimcho BELIAKOV (Lovech)
10	Hristo YOVOV (Levski Sofia)
	Marian HRISTOV (Levski Sofia)
9	Vladko SHALAMANOV (Slavia Sofia)
	Dimitar TOTEV (Rakovski Ruse/Slavia Sofia)
	Doncho DONEV (Lokomotiv Sofia/Levski Sofia)
	Petar ZHABOV (CSKA Sofia)
	Petar MIKHTARSKI (CSKA Sofia)

NATIONAL TEAM RESULTS 95/96

06/09/95	Albania (ECQ)	A	Tirana	1-1	Stoichkov (8)
07/10/95	Albania (ECQ)	H	Sofia	3-0	Lechkov (13), Kostadinov (82, 84)
11/10/95	Georgia (ECQ)	A	Tbilisi	1-2	Stoichkov (87)
15/11/95	Germany (ECQ)	A	Berlin	1-3	Stoichkov (47)
27/03/96	England	A	Wembley	0-1	
24/04/96	Slovakia	A	Trnava	0-0	
28/05/96	Macedonia	H	Sofia	3-0	Kostadinov (15), Stoichkov (67), Georgiev (77)
02/06/96	United Arab Emirates	H	Sofia	4-1	Yordanov (6), Stoichkov (28), Donkov (69), Sirakov (80)
09/06/96	Spain (ECF)	N	Leeds	1-1	Stoichkov (65p)
13/06/96	Romania (ECF)	N	Newcastle	1-0	Stoichkov (3)
18/06/96	France (ECF)	N	Newcastle	1-3	Stoichkov (68)

most successful Bulgarian coach of all time - discovered that his contract was not to be renewed. The players objected vehemently to the decision, but perhaps the BFS were right to instigate a change and set about building a new team for the World Cup qualifying campaign. Hristo Bonev, the man whose all-time Bulgarian record of 96 caps was overtaken by goalkeeper Mikhailov in England, is the man saddled with that task. He certainly has a hard act to follow.

Bulgarian fans were ultimately disappointed at their team's early exit from Euro '96, but on the whole the team did no more or less than was generally expected of them. As in America, Lechkov looked a class act, so clever and composed on the ball. And Mikhailov and Ivanov had their moments too. But the real star once again was Stoichkov.

In a tournament short of true individual genius, Stoichkov shone out. Nobody can condone his racist jibes against Frenchman Marcel Desailly, but as a footballer he is truly remarkable. He scored in each of Bulgaria's three matches (none of his teammates found the net once), and netted the only free-kick goal of the tournament. Despite a forgettable season in Italy, he scored in all but one of Bulgaria's matches over the course of the 95/96 campaign, taking his all-time total to 34 goals in 64 games. Only the aforementioned Bonev - with 47 international goals - has more. But the new coach cannot hold a candle to the worldwide achievements of Stoichkov. Without doubt he is the most brilliant and famous footballer Bulgaria has ever produced.

All but three of the Bulgarian players who took the field at Euro '96 were foreign 'exiles'. That says much about

NATIONAL TEAM APPEARANCES 95/96

Coach - Dimitar PENEV	ALB	ALB	GEO	GER	ENG	SVK	MAC	UAE	ESP	ROM	FRA	Cps	Gls
Borislav MIKHAILOV (12/02/62) - Reading (ENG)	G	G	G		G46	G46	G46	G46	G	G	G	97	-
Emil KREMENLIEV (13/08/69) - Levski Sofia/Olympiakos (GRE)	D	D		D	D85	D	D	D46			D	25	-
Trifon IVANOV (27/07/65) - SK Rapid Wien (AUT)	D	D	D58		D	D	D46		D	D	D	63	5
Petar HUBCHEV (26/02/64) - Hamburger SV (GER)	D				D		D46	D	D		D	34	-
Tsanko TSVETANOV (06/01/70) - SV Waldhof Mannheim (GER)	D	D	D	D			s46		s70	D	D	37	-
Yordan LECHKOV (09/07/67) - Hamburger SV (GER)	M75	M	M	M62	M	M63	M62	M	M	M90	M	38	4
Krasimir BALAKOV (29/03/66) - VfB Stuttgart (GER)	M	M	M	M82		M	M62	M	M	M	M82	56	7
Daniel BORIMIROV (15/01/70) - TSV 1860 München (GER)	M	s88	s58	s82	s46	M	s46	s46	s77	s32	s78	26	2
Emil KOSTADINOV (12/08/67) - FC Bayern München (GER)	A	A86	A	A	A	A	A46	A46	A71	A32		54	19
Liuboslav PENEV (31/08/66) - Atlético Madrid (ESP)	A75	A	A	A79	A85				A77	A72	A	52	11
Hristo STOICHKOV (08/02/66) - Parma (ITA)	A	A	A	A			A	A58	A	A	A	64	34
Krasimir CHOMAKOV (08/06/77) - Maritsa Plovdiv	s75		s58									2	-
Nasko SIRAKOV (26/04/62) - Botev Plovdiv/Slavia Sofia	s75	s86	M58	s79	s85	A73	A46	s58		s72		78	23
Ilian KIRIAKOV (04/08/67) - Anorthosis Famagusta (CYP)		M88	D	s62	M	M61	D46	M	D70			57	-
Zlatko YANKOV (07/06/66) - KFC Uerdingen 05 (GER)		M	D	M	M	D	M46	M	M	D	M78	54	4
Dimitar POPOV (27/02/70) - CSKA Sofia				G	s46		s73					10	-
Valentin DARTILOV (14/08/67) - Levski Sofia				D								1	-
Gosho GINCHEV (02/02/69) - Denizlispor (TUR)				D	D46		s46	D				5	-
Ivailo YORDANOV (12/01/66) - Sporting CP (POR)					M46	s63	s46	M58	s71	M	M	27	1
Boncho GENCHEV (07/07/64) - Luton Town (ENG)					s46	s61	s62			s90		12	-
Radostin KISHISHEV (30/07/74) - Neftochimik Bourgas					s85	D	s46	s46	D	D		6	-
Zdravko ZDRAVKOV (04/10/70) - Slavia Sofia						s46	s46	s46				3	-
							/73						
Marian HRISTOV (29/07/73) - Levski Sofia						s73						1	-
Georgi DONKOV (02/06/70) - CSKA Sofia							s46	s58			s82	4	1
Ivo GEORGIEV (12/05/72) - Spartak Varna							s62					1	1

EUROPEAN CUPS RESULTS 95/96

CUP-WINNERS' CUP

● LOKOMOTIV SOFIA

Preliminary round DERRY CITY (IRL)

A 0-1
Apostolov; Velkov, Yochev, Marinov, Zafirov, Koilov, Angelov, Donev, Radivojevic, Petkov, Khvoinev (Borisov 53).

H 2-0 Slavchev (6), Khvoinev (29)
Apostolov; Velkov, Koilov, Borisov (Marinov 84), Zafirov, Slavchev, Angelov, Khvoinev, Radivojevic, Petkov (Antonov 88), Donev.

1st round HALMSTADS BK (SWE)

H 3-1 Marinov (41), Petkov (43), Donev (57)
Manolkov; Velkov (Antonov 75), Marinov, Naidenov (Koilov 72), Zafirov, Slavchev, Donev, Khvoinev, Radivojevic, Petkov (Borisov 86), Chilibonov.

A 0-2
Apostolov; Velkov (Antonov 75), Marinov, Naidenov, Zafirov, Slavchev, Donev (Koilov 58), Chilibonov, Radivojevic, Petkov (Angelov 65), Petrov.

UEFA CUP

● LEVSKI SOFIA

Preliminary round DINAMO BUCURESTI (ROM)

A 1-0 Ivanov (30)
Nikolov; Kremenliev, Dartilov, Markov A., Vasilev, Yonkov, Penchev P., Hristov, Yankov (Simeonov 54), Velev, Ivanov.

H 1-1 (aet) Vasilev (110)
Nikolov; Kremenliev, Dartilov, Markov A. (Rusev 106), Vasilev, Yonkov, Penchev P. (Slavchev 65), Hristov, Simeonov (Yovov 75), Velev, Ivanov.

1st round KSC EENDRACHT AALST (BEL)

H 1-2 Vasilev (68)
Nikolov; Kremenliev, Dartilov, Markov A., Vasilev, Penchev P., Timnev (Yovov 57), Hristov (Yordanov 70), Simeonov, Velev, Ivanov (Slavchev 59).

A 0-1
Nikolov; Kremenliev, Dartilov, Slavchev (Zaitsev 74), Vasilev, Yonkov, Penchev P., Hristov, Yankov (Simeonov 67), Yordanov, Ivanov (Yovov 46).

● BOTEV PLOVDIV

Preliminary round DINAMO TBILISI (GEO)

H 1-0 Gerov (45)
Mikhailov; Lukov (Petrov A. 81), Petrov G., Dimitrov, Shopov, Sivinov, Kitanchev (Gemedzhiev 62), Markov, Gerov, Petrov P., Vidolov.

A 1-0 Vidolov (90)
Mikhailov; Lukov, Petrov G., Simeonov, Shopov, Petrov A., Markov, Petrov P. (Sivinov 86), Gerov (Ivanov 58), Sadakov (Gemedzhiev 66), Vidolov.

1st round SEVILLA FC (ESP)

A 0-2
Vasilev; Sivinov, Petrov G., Dimitrov, Simeonov, Markov, Shopov (Lukov 68), Ivanov (Gerov 85), Petrov A., Sadakov (Petrov P. 73), Vidolov.

H 1-1 Ivanov (69)
Vasilev; Sivinov, Petrov G., Shopov, Simeonov, Markov, Petrov A. (Petrov P. 58), Ivanov (Tsvetanov 85), Gerov, Sadakov, Vidolov.

● SLAVIA SOFIA

Preliminary round OLYMPIAKOS (GRE)

H 0-2
Zdravkov; Minchev (Dimitrov A. 58), Atsarov, Kolev, Kachamanov, Urukov, Ivanov, Dobrevski I. (Dafkov 80), Dobrevski G., Shalamanov, Kirov (Zheliazkov 78).

A 0-1
Zdravkov; Dafkov, Atsarov, Kolev, Kachamanov, Urukov, Tsvetanov, Dimitrov A., Ivanov (Minchev 64), Dobrevski G. (Zheliazkov 46), Kirov (Dobrevski I. 46).

the quality of the current generation of Bulgarian internationals. But it also throws a dim light on the domestic league, where money problems, poor attendances and low-quality football are sadly the order of the day.

Levski Sofia, the 1994/95 champions, were forced to sell off virtually all of their top players prior to the 95/96 season in a bid to survive. Amongst them were Yankov, Borimirov, Tsvetanov and Ginchev, all of whom appeared in Bulgaria's European Championship squad. Such is Levski's standing, however, that they were able to recruit from other Bulgarian clubs and remain competitive in the chase for domestic honours. Indeed, the new-look team, complete with new coach Ivan Kiuchukov, got off to a remarkably good start in the championship, conceding no goals in their first six away games and, thanks to a series of late winning goals, marching into a three-point lead at the winter break.

But Levski could not keep it up. They were forced to sell another international star - right-back Emil Kremenliev - at the end of the autumn season (he was sent off in his farewell match, a 2-0 victory over city rivals Lokomotiv, before joining Greek club Olympiakos). And on the championship resumption in the early spring the club fell to its heaviest league defeat for six years, crashing 5-1 to the surprise package of the season, Neftochimik Bourgas.

Before long Levski were joined at the top of the table by another Sofia club, Slavia. The all-whites had also made fundamental changes to their team in the summer, replacing promising youngsters such as Engibarov, Yonkov and Hristov with a cluster of ex-Levski and CSKA players such as goalkeeper Zdravko Zdravkov, libero Stefan Kolev, stoppers Kiril Kachamanov and Marius Urukov, playmaker Atanas Kirov and veteran international Nasko Sirakov.

Coached by former player Stoian Kotsev, Slavia were five points off the pace at the halfway point. But in the spring, despite the sale of top scorer Vladko Shalamanov to Turkey, they settled into a rich vein of form which put them firmly in contention for a first national title in 53 years. Sirakov was the goalscoring inspiration, finiding the net seven times in six games, all of which Slavia won by a two-goal margin.

That set them up for a crunch top-of-the-table encounter at home to Levski, with whom they were level on points. The 1-1 draw, in which Sirakov scored again, against his former club, gave Levski the league leadership by virtue of the away-goals rule (the first match, at Levski's ground, had ended 0-0). But it did not put Slavia out of their stride. They went on to win their next five matches as well, with Sirakov continuing to score at the rate of a goal per game.

With three games left, Slavia's lead over Levski was two points. With two to go, the lead was up to three. And with just one remaining, Slavia had gone four points clear. That was it. Slavia were the champions. While they could only draw their last three matches, Levski lost all of theirs. The Bulgarian title was back with Sofia's oldest football club for the first time since World War Two. And there was more...

The final of the Bulgarian Cup also brought together the top two teams in the league. The May Day showdown in Sofia attracted 20,000 fans, but they were all to be cheated by a remarkable incident in the 76th minute which forced the match to be abandoned.

Slavia were leading Levski 1-0 as the game entered the final quarter of an hour. Atanas Kirov's 35th-minute goal had put his team in sight of their first ever Bulgarian Cup victory when, quite without warning, Levski president Thomas Lavchis beckoned his players to leave the field. It was akin to the incident in the 1982 World Cup match between France and Kuwait, but on this occasion the teams did not return. Lavchis claimed he was making a stand against corruption. It was a bizarre ploy, and it certainly did no favours to his own team. A day after the abandoned match a special committe of the BFS awarded the victory to Slavia - by a 4-0 scoreline. Two days later Slavia would seal the championship with a 0-0 draw against CSKA. And a week after that they were presented with both league and Cup trophies. Quite an ending to the greatest season in the club's 83-year history.

For the first time in 18 years, both of Bulgarian football's traditional giants, Levski and CSKA Sofia, failed to win a trophy. The other domestic prize - the League Cup - went deservedly to Neftochimik. The Black Sea team,

DOMESTIC CUP RESULTS

1/16 FINALS
Spartak Pleven 2, Slavia Sofia 5
Gigant Belene 0, Lokomotiv Plovdiv 4
Etar Veliko Tarnovo 4, Lokomotiv Ruse 1
Spartak Varna 6, Chardafon Gabrovo 1
Benkovski Biala 0, Lokomotiv Sofia 7
Askent Gurkovo 1, CSKA Sofia 6
Atletik Velingrad 7, Rakovski Ruse 1
Shumen 1, Akademik Sofia 0
Vichren Sandanski 0, Neftochimik Bourgas 1
Metalurg Pernik 1, Botev Plovdiv 0
Ludogorets Razgrad 0, Spartak Plovdiv 1
Septemvri Sofia 3, Lovech 1
Storgozia Pleven 1, Levski Kiustendil 2
Levski Sofia 2, Cherno More Varna 0
Maritsa Plovdiv 3, Montana 2
Chirpan 2, Dobrudzha Dobrich 0

1/8 FINALS
Lokomotiv Sofia v Levski Kiustendil 5-1; 0-2
(Lokomotiv Sofia 5-3)
Spartak Varna v Levski Sofia 2-2; 1-4
(Levski Sofia 6-3)
Maritsa Plovdiv v Lokomotiv Plovdiv 2-1; 1-2
(3-3; Lokomotiv Plovdiv 7-6 on pens.)
Metalurg Pernik v Chirpan 2-0; 3-1
(Metalurg Pernik 5-1)
Spartak Plovdiv v Septemvri Sofia 3-0; 2-1
(Spartak Plovdiv 5-1)
Slavia Sofia v Shumen 4-0; 0-0
(Slavia Sofia 4-0)
CSKA Sofia v Etar Veliko Tarnovo 3-0; 3-0
(CSKA Sofia 6-0)
Atletik Velingrad v Neftochimik Bourgas 1-1; 0-3 (w/o)
(Neftochimik Bourgas 4-1)

QUARTER-FINALS
CSKA Sofia v Neftochimik Bourgas 3-0; 2-2
(CSKA Sofia 5-2)
Spartak Plovdiv v Lokomotiv Plovdiv 0-1; 1-1
(Lokomotiv Plovdiv 2-1)
Slavia Sofia v Metalurg Pernik 4-1; 0-0
(Slavia Sofia 4-1)
Levski Sofia v Lokomotiv Sofia 2-0; 5-2
(Levski Sofia 7-2)

SEMI-FINALS
Lokomotiv Plovdiv v Slavia Sofia 0-2; 1-2
(Slavia Sofia 4-1)
Levski Sofia v CSKA Sofia 1-0; 4-2
(Levski Sofia 5-2)

FINAL
01/05/96, Sofia
SLAVIA SOFIA 1 Kirov (35)
LEVSKI SOFIA 0
(match abandoned in 76th minute; later awarded 4-0 to Slavia Sofia)
referee - Mitrev
SLAVIA SOFIA - Zdravkov; Ivanov, Tsvetanov, Kolev, Kachamanov, Ristic, Angelov, Sirakov, Dimitrov A., Dermendzhiev (Zakhariev 63), Kirov.
LEVSKI SOFIA - Nikolov; Iliev, Dartilov, Ivanov, Vasilev, Yonkov, Timnev (Zaitsev 46), Hristov, Simeonov, Velev (Penchev P. 67), Yovov (Donev 62).

PLAYERS OF THE SEASON

LIUBOSLAV PENEV

Liuboslav Penev's European Championship was summed up by the own-goal he scored in the 1-3 defeat by France. The coach's nephew was expected to add presence and potency to the Bulgarian attack, but he provided neither. So who was this *Doppelgänger* in the Bulgaria number nine shirt? He certainly bore little resemblance to the Liuboslav Penev, nicknamed 'Lubo', who had enjoyed a marvellous first season for Spanish 'double'-winners Atlético Madrid, scoring 16 goals to become the club's top scorer in their historic championship triumph. Perhaps the marathon 42-match Liga campaign had simply taken its toll on the 30-year-old striker, who - lest it be forgotten - missed the 1994 World Cup because he was recovering from testicular cancer.

TRIFON IVANOV

If looks could kill... well, let's just say Trifon Ivanov would have a bit of explaining to do. The mean-eyed, semi-shaven, long-haired Bulgarian defender has been something of a wandering minstrel in recent years, but in 1995/96 he finally found a happy home. Austrian sleeping giants Rapid Vienna took on Ivanov at the start of the campaign, and by the end of it he had become a veritable cult hero amongst the Rapid fans. His solid presence at the back was one of the foundation stones on which the club rebuilt their fallen reputation, winning the Austrian title for the first time in eight years and reaching the final of the European Cup-winners' Cup. Ivanov also carried his good club form through to Euro '96, where his no-nonsense defending and long-distance free-kicks were a feature of the Bulgarian play.

Liuboslav Penev (above) and Trifon Ivanov (below).

NASKO SIRAKOV

Two years after skippering Levski Sofia to the Bulgarian league and Cup 'double', 34-year-old Nasko Sirakov did it again, this time for his new club Slavia Sofia, whom he had joined from Botev Plovdiv in the early weeks of the season. The veteran international was inspirational, his leadership and experience almost as crucial to Slavia's success as the 16 goals he scored in the league. Sirakov turned out once again for Bulgaria at Euro '96 - 10 years after his first major tournament, the 1986 World Cup, when he scored in the Opening Match against Italy. With 78 caps and 23 goals, his international playing career is now at an end, but he remains involved with Bulgaria - as assistant to new coach Hristo Bonev.

sponsored by the local oil refinery and featuring the revelation of the season in right-back Radostin Kishishev, had a tremendous run in the league, scoring more goals than any other to finish in fourth place.

That consistent ability to find the net was exposed in all its glory in the League Cup final when Neftochimik thrashed Montana 7-2 after extra-time, having been 0-2 down after 45 minutes. Two of those goals went to striker Vesko Petkov, second in the league scoring charts behind Spartak Varna's Ivo Georgiev, whose 21 goals included a rare double hat-trick against bottom club Spartak Plovdiv and led to a surprise call-up for Bulgaria's Euro '96 squad.

INTERNATIONAL HONOURS

World Cup Finals appearances: 1962, 1966, 1970, 1974, 1986 (2nd round), 1994 (4th)

European Championship appearances: 1968, 1996

BOTEV PLOVDIV

CLUB DIRECTORY

FC Botev Plovdiv
Bul. Iztochen 10
4000 Plovdiv
tel - (032) 226375/225736
fax - (032) 226388
Year of Formation - 1912
President - Mikhail Markochev
Coach - Atanas Dramov; Dinko Dermendzhiev; Kostadin Kostadinov
Stadium - Hristo Botev (21,000)

MAJOR HONOURS

League Championship - (2) 1929, 1967.

APPEARANCES 95/96

	P	Ap	(s)	Gls
Sasho ANGELOV	D	12	(1)	
Lilcho ARSOV	G	13		
Rumen DIMITROV	D	18	(1)	
Geno DOBREVSKI	M	9	(4)	2
Ivan DOBREVSKI	A	14		3
Ivan GEMEDZHIEV	A	4	(8)	
Veselin GEROV	A	5	(7)	1
Rumen IVANOV	A	21	(4)	5
Liubomir KITANCHEV	M	6	(8)	
Plamen LUKOV	M	9	(4)	
Georgi MARKOV	M	26		5
Borislav MIKHAILOV	G	2		
Aleksandar MILENKOV	M		(1)	
Esin MISHAOUI	M	1		
Anastas PETROV	A	15	(8)	5
Georgi PETROV	D	23		2
Plamen PETROV	A	14	(7)	1
Anio SADAKOV	M	8	(5)	
Petar SHOPOV	D	23	(1)	
Todor SIMEONOV	D	20	(1)	
Dimitar SIRAKOV	M		(1)	
Nasko SIRAKOV	A	5		
Anton SIVINOV	D	13	(5)	
Spas SPASOV	M	3	(4)	
Georgi TSVETANOV	A	16	(7)	2
Vasil VASILEV	G	15	(1)	
Kostadin VIDOLOV	M	25		7
Radoslav VIDOV	D	10	(1)	

LEAGUE RESULTS 1995/96

12/08/95	CSKA Sofia	A	0-3	
18/08/95	Lokomotiv Sofia	H	3-0	Petrov A., Petrov G., Gerov
26/08/95	Dobrudzha Dobrich	A	0-1	
02/09/95	Lokomotiv Plovdiv	H	5-0	Vidolov 3, Petrov A. 2
08/09/95	Neftochimik Bourgas	A	0-2	
16/09/95	Etar Veliko Tarnovo	H	1-0	Vidolov
22/09/95	Lovech	A	0-3	
30/09/95	Spartak Varna	H	1-3	Petrov A.
14/10/95	Levski Sofia	A	1-2	Tsvetanov
21/10/95	Slavia Sofia	H	0-1	
28/10/95	Shumen	A	1-1	Vidolov
04/11/95	Rakovski Ruse	A	1-1	Ivanov
18/11/95	Spartak Plovdiv	H	2-0	Ivanov, Petrov P.
25/11/95	Montana	A	0-3	
02/12/95	Levski Kiustendil	H	3-0	Ivanov 2, Vidolov
15/02/96	CSKA Sofia	H	0-4	
24/02/96	Lokomotiv Sofia	A	1-2	Markov
02/03/96	Dobrudzha Dobrich	H	1-0	Petrov G.
09/03/96	Lokomotiv Plovdiv	A	0-0	
13/03/96	Neftochimik Bourgas	H	2-1	Ivanov, Vidolov
16/03/96	Etar Veliko Tarnovo	A	2-1	Dobrevski G., Markov
22/03/96	Lovech	H	1-0	Petrov A.
30/03/96	Spartak Varna	A	1-2	Markov
06/04/96	Levski Sofia	H	1-1	Markov
10/04/96	Slavia Sofia	A	0-1	
13/04/96	Shumen	H	0-1	
20/04/96	Rakovski Ruse	H	1-1	Markov
27/04/96	Spartak Plovdiv	A	4-2	Dobrevski I. 2, Dobrevski G., Tsvetanov
04/05/96	Montana	H	0-0	
11/05/96	Levski Kiustendil	A	1-2	Dobrevski I. (p)

CSKA SOFIA

CLUB DIRECTORY

FC CSKA Sofia
Stadion Bulgarska Armia
Bul. Dragan Tsankov 3
Sofia
tel - (02) 656037/658200/566859
Year of Formation - 1948
President - Ilia Pavlov
Coach - Plamen Markov; Georgi Vasilev
Stadium - Bulgarska Armia (30,000)

MAJOR HONOURS
League Championship - (27)
1948, 1951, 1952, 1954, 1955, 1956, 1957, 1958, 1959, 1960, 1961, 1962, 1966, 1969, 1971, 1972, 1973, 1975, 1976, 1980, 1981, 1982, 1983, 1987, 1989, 1990, 1992.
Domestic Cup - (7)
1981, 1983, 1985, 1987, 1988, 1989, 1993.

APPEARANCES 95/96

	P	Ap	(s)	Gls
Georgi CHAKAROV	D	3	(3)	1
Metodi DEIANOV	M	1	(3)	1
Georgi DONKOV	A	19	(3)	5
Engibar ENGIBAROV	D	13	(2)	
Filip FILIPOV	D	13		
Georgi GEORGIEV	M	17	(1)	6
Marian GERMANOV	D	9		
Rumen HRISTOV	A	14	(8)	4
Galin IVANOV	D	13	(2)	1
Rosen KIRILOV	D	8		
Zdravko LAZAROV	M		(8)	
Stefan LULCHEV	D	3	(3)	
Hristo MARASHLIEV	A	3	(5)	
Petar MIKHTARSKI	A	13		9
Risto MILOSAVOV (MAC)	A	13	(1)	2
Dobromir MITOV	D	29		1
Ilija NAJDOSKI (MAC)	D	10		
Anatoli NANKOV	A	26	(1)	1
Viktorio PAVLOV	M		(1)	
Milen PETKOV	M	23	(5)	2
Petko PETKOV	G	4	(1)	
Dimitar POPOV	G	26	(1)	
Milen RADUKANOV	D	10	(3)	
Dimitar SIVOV	M	4	(1)	
Ilian STOIANOV	D	1	(2)	
Boiko VELICHKOV	M	6	(7)	
Hristo VOINOV	D		(2)	
Bozhidar YANKOV	M	18	(4)	2
Adalbert ZAFIROV	D	13		2
Martin ZAFIROV	A	2	(10)	1
Petar ZHABOV	A	16	(7)	9

LEAGUE RESULTS 1995/96

12/08/95	Botev Plovdiv	H	3-0	Hristov, Deianov, Mikhtarski
27/08/95	Montana	H	1-2	Zhabov
30/08/95	Levski Kiustendil	A	0-0	
09/09/95	Rakovski Ruse	H	2-0	Zhabov, Zafirov M.
13/09/95	Spartak Plovdiv	A	4-2	Donkov, Petkov, Zhabov, Nankov
17/09/95	Lokomotiv Sofia	H	1-5	Zhabov
23/09/95	Dobrudzha Dobrich	A	0-2	
30/09/95	Lokomotiv Plovdiv	H	1-0	Yankov
14/10/95	Neftochimik Bourgas	A	2-2	Zhabov, Yankov
21/10/95	Etar Veliko Tarnovo	H	1-1	Zhabov
28/10/95	Lovech	A	0-0	
04/11/95	Spartak Varna	H	4-0	og (Dimitrov Sl.), Hristov 2, Georgiev
18/11/95	Levski Sofia	A	1-3	og (Dartilov)
24/11/95	Slavia Sofia	H	1-0	Petkov
02/12/95	Shumen	A	0-1	
16/02/96	Botev Plovdiv	A	4-0	Zafirov A., Mitov, Donkov, Mikhtarski
24/02/96	Spartak Plovdiv	H	3-1	Mikhtarski 2, Georgiev (p)
02/03/96	Montana	A	1-0	Zafirov A.
09/03/96	Levski Kiustendil	H	3-0	Georgiev 2, Mikhtarski
13/03/96	Rakovski Ruse	A	1-0	Georgiev
16/03/96	Lokomotiv Sofia	A	0-0	
23/03/96	Dobrudzha Dobrich	H	2-1	Donkov (p), Mikhtarski
30/03/96	Lokomotiv Plovdiv	A	1-2	Georgiev
06/04/96	Neftochimik Bourgas	H	1-1	Ivanov
10/04/96	Etar Veliko Tarnovo	A	0-0	
13/04/96	Lovech	H	4-0	Zhabov 2, Hristov, Chakarov
20/04/96	Spartak Varna	A	3-1	Donkov 2, Mikhtarski
27/04/96	Levski Sofia	H	1-0	Mikhtarski
04/05/96	Slavia Sofia	A	0-0	
11/05/96	Shumen	H	4-2	Milosavov 2, Zhabov, Mikhtarski

DOBRUDZHA DOBRICH

CLUB DIRECTORY

FC Dobrudzha
ul. 25 Septemvri 10
Dobrich
tel - (058) 22591/28283
Year of Formation - 1919
President - Stefan Kolev
Coach - Yanko Dinkov
Stadium - Druzhba (20,000)

APPEARANCES 95/96

	P	Ap	(s)	Gls
Rumen BOEV	D	25		1
Georgi BONEV	D	3		
Dian BOZHILOV	A	29		8
Atanas GEORGIEV	M	14	(11)	
Svetoslav KRASTEV	D	30		
Petar KUSHEV	D	28	(1)	
Risto MILOSLAVOV	M	13		4
Emil MITSANSKI	M	22		1
Nedko NEDEV	G	27		
Nikolai PETRUNOV	A	22	(1)	3
Milen PEZKOV	A		(7)	
Venko POPOV	M	24		
Emil RAVNACHKI	D	23	(6)	
Svilen SIMEONOV	G	3	(1)	
Rumen SLAVOV	D	27		3
Stanislav SLAVOV	M	4	(7)	
Atanas STEFANOV	A	4	(2)	1
Rumen STOIANOV	A	6	(11)	3
Stoicho STOILOV	A	25		5
Tony ZLATKOV	M	1	(4)	1

LEAGUE RESULTS 1995/96

12/08/95	Slavia Sofia	H	1-0	Bozhilov (p)
19/08/95	Shumen	A	0-1	
26/08/95	Botev Plovdiv	H	1-0	Slavov
30/08/95	Spartak Plovdiv	A	1-1	Stefanov
09/09/95	Montana	H	1-0	Milosavov
16/09/95	Levski Kiustendil	A	0-2	
23/09/95	CSKA Sofia	H	2-0	Bozhilov, Milosavov
01/10/95	Lokomotiv Sofia	A	0-2	
14/10/95	Rakovski Ruse	H	2-0	Petrunov, Milosavov
21/10/95	Lokomotiv Plovdiv	H	2-0	Slavov, Stoianov
28/10/95	Neftochimik Bourgas	A	1-5	Bozhilov
04/11/95	Etar Veliko Tarnovo	H	0-2	
18/11/95	Lovech	A	0-0	
25/11/95	Spartak Varna	H	3-2	Milosavov, Bozhilov, Petrunov
02/12/95	Levski Sofia	A	0-2	
17/02/96	Slavia Sofia	A	0-2	
24/02/96	Shumen	H	1-0	Bozhilov
02/03/96	Botev Plovdiv	A	0-1	
09/03/96	Spartak Plovdiv	H	1-0	Petrunov
13/03/96	Montana	A	0-3	
16/03/96	Levski Kiustendil	H	2-1	Stoilov, Bozhilov
23/03/96	CSKA Sofia	A	1-2	Zlatkov
30/03/96	Lokomotiv Sofia	H	0-1	
06/04/96	Rakovski Ruse	A	1-3	Bozhilov (p)
10/04/96	Lokomotiv Plovdiv	A	1-3	Stoianov
13/04/96	Neftochimik Bourgas	H	1-3	Bozhilov
20/04/96	Etar Veliko Tarnovo	A	2-2	Stoilov, Slavov
27/04/96	Lovech	H	1-2	Stoilov
04/05/96	Spartak Varna	A	3-2	Mitsanski, Stoilov, Stoianov
11/05/96	Levski Sofia	H	2-1	Stoilov, Boev

ETAR VELIKO TARNOVO

CLUB DIRECTORY

FC Etar
Stadion Ivailo
5000 Veliko Tarnovo
tel - (062) 21907/36832
Year of Formation - 1924
President - Ivan Angelov
Coach - Georgi Tsingov; Stoian Petrov
Stadium - Ivailo (18,000)

MAJOR HONOURS
League Championship - (1) 1991.

APPEARANCES 95/96

	P	Ap	(s)	Gls
Daniel ANDREEV	D		(1)	
Stefan ATANASOV	M		(1)	
Dimitar BALABANOV	D	30		2
Kaloian CHAKAROV	G	1	(2)	
Ibriam DAIL	D	27		
Stefan DANAILOV	A	6	(9)	
Aleksandar DIMOV	M	6	(4)	
Georgi GEORGIEV	A	25		2
Plamen HADZHIISKI	M	10	(5)	
Velin KEFALOV	M	17		2
Igor KISLOV (UKR)	A	24		3
Vladimir KOLEV	A	27		3
Radoslav KOMITOV	A	2	(1)	
Stanimir LEFTEROV	M	8	(6)	
Emanuil LUKANOV	D	7	(12)	
Stoian MLADENOV	A	4	(2)	
Yordan NIKOLOV	A	18	(9)	5
Stanimir PALEV	G		(1)	
Yakov PAPARKOV	A	10		2
Tikhomir PETKOV	M	2	(1)	1
Igor SHELIST	G	29		
Martin STANKOV	D	29		
Stoian STOIANOV	D	23	(4)	
Martin TOPUZOV	D	17	(2)	
Boiko TSVETKOV	D	6	(3)	
Veselin VASILEV	M	1	(2)	
Manol ZAPRIANOV	M	1	(15)	1

LEAGUE RESULTS 1995/96

12/08/95	Lovech	H	1-0	Petkov
19/08/95	Spartak Varna	A	0-3	
27/08/95	Levski Sofia	H	0-1	
05/09/95	Slavia Sofia	A	0-2	
09/09/95	Shumen	H	1-0	Kefalov (p)
16/09/95	Botev Plovdiv	A	0-1	
23/09/95	Spartak Plovdiv	H	1-0	Kislov
30/09/95	Montana	A	0-0	
14/10/95	Levski Kiustendil	H	1-0	Kefalov
21/10/95	CSKA Sofia	A	1-1	Nikolov
28/10/95	Lokomotiv Sofia	H	0-1	
04/11/95	Dobrudzha Dobrich	A	2-0	Kolev, Balabanov
18/11/95	Lokomotiv Plovdiv	H	3-0	Kislov, Georgiev G., Zaprianov
25/11/95	Neftochimik Bourgas	A	0-3	
02/12/95	Rakovski Ruse	H	1-0	Nikolov
17/02/96	Lovech	A	0-0	
24/02/96	Spartak Varna	H	2-1	Kolev, Nikolov
02/03/96	Levski Sofia	A	0-2	
09/03/96	Slavia Sofia	H	0-2	
13/03/96	Shumen	A	0-3	
16/03/96	Botev Plovdiv	H	1-2	Kislov
23/03/96	Spartak Plovdiv	A	0-3	
30/03/96	Montana	H	4-0	Paparkov (p), Balabanov, Kolev, Georgiev G.
06/04/96	Levski Kiustendil	A	0-2	
10/04/96	CSKA Sofia	H	0-0	
13/04/96	Lokomotiv Sofia	A	0-3	
20/04/96	Dobrudzha Dobrich	H	2-2	Nikolov, Paparkov (p)
27/04/96	Lokomotiv Plovdiv	A	0-2	
04/05/96	Neftochimik Bourgas	H	0-2	
11/05/96	Rakovski Ruse	A	1-1	Nikolov

LEVSKI KIUSTENDIL

CLUB DIRECTORY

FC Levski
H-L Sport Palas
2500 Kiustendil
tel - (078) 43154
Year of Formation - 1920
President - Valeri Nenov
Coach - Stefan Grozdanov; Georgi Dimitrov
Stadium - Osogovo (11,000)

APPEARANCES 95/96

	P	Ap	(s)	Gls
Petar ADZHOV	A	14		2
Aleksandar ALEKSANDROV	A	6	(1)	1
Blagoi ALEKSANDROV	A	12	(2)	3
Dimitar CHOBANOV	M	3	(2)	
Dragomir DELEV	A	14	(3)	5
Zvetozar DERMENDZHIEV	M	13	(1)	3
Krasimir DIMITROV	G	3		
Rosen DIMITROV	D		(1)	
Nikolai GAVALIUGOV	D	2	(1)	
Martin GORANOV	D	7	(2)	
Daniel HRISTOV	D	23	(1)	
Ivailo ILARIONOV	A	8	(3)	1
Ivan IVANOV	M	27	(1)	1
Ivailo KIROV	M	6	(4)	
Rumen KOLEV	G	1		
Zarko MACHEV	D	11	(5)	
Ivan MARINOV	A	4	(2)	1
Ivan MIKHAILOV	A	13	(8)	
Mikhail MIKHAILOV	A	15	(2)	7
Dimitar NIKOV	A	6	(11)	
Krasimir PETKOV	G	26		
Rosen PETROV	A	5	(1)	
Georgi RUSIMOV	D	3		
Georgi STANISLAVOV	A	12	(4)	1
Asen STOIANOV	D	6	(3)	
Ivailo STRANDZHOV	A	5	(5)	
Nemetzhan TAKIROV (UZB)	D	29		
Stoimir UROSEVIC (MAC)	A	15	(5)	1
Ivo VELINOV	D	23	(2)	
Ivan VERGILOV	M		(1)	
Edson Silva VIEIRA (BRA)	A		(1)	
Krasimir VLADIMIROV	A	2	(9)	1
Evgeni YORDANOV	D		(1)	
Antoni ZDRAVKOV	D	16	(2)	

LEAGUE RESULTS 1995/96

12/08/95	Spartak Plovdiv	H	3-0	Dermendzhiev, Delev, Urosevic (p)
19/08/95	Montana	A	1-1	Dermendzhiev
26/08/95	Rakovski Ruse	H	3-0	Dermendzhiev, Mikhailov M. 2
30/08/95	CSKA Sofia	H	0-0	
09/09/95	Lokomotiv Sofia	A	0-3	
16/09/95	Dobrudzha Dobrich	H	2-0	Mikhailov M. 2 (1p)
23/09/95	Lokomotiv Plovdiv	A	2-2	Mikhailov M. (p), Delev
30/09/95	Neftochimik Bourgas	H	1-0	Delev
14/10/95	Etar Veliko Tarnovo	A	0-1	
21/10/95	Lovech	H	0-0	
28/10/95	Spartak Varna	A	1-2	Aleksandrov A.
04/11/95	Levski Sofia	H	2-0	Delev, Ilarionov
18/11/95	Slavia Sofia	A	0-3	
25/11/95	Shumen	H	2-0	Ivanov, Vladimirov
02/12/95	Botev Plovdiv	A	0-3	
17/02/96	Spartak Plovdiv	A	0-1	
24/02/96	Montana	H	1-1	Aleksandrov B. (p)
02/03/96	Rakovski Ruse	A	0-1	
09/03/96	CSKA Sofia	A	0-3	
13/03/96	Lokomotiv Sofia	H	2-1	Aleksandrov B.,Mikhailov M.
16/03/96	Dobrudzha Dobrich	A	1-2	Adzhov
23/03/96	Lokomotiv Plovdiv	H	0-0	
30/03/96	Neftochimik Bourgas	A	0-3	
06/04/96	Etar Veliko Tarnovo	H	2-0	Marinov, Mikhailov M.
10/04/96	Lovech	A	0-3	
13/04/96	Spartak Varna	H	1-0	Aleksandrov B. (p)
20/04/96	Levski Sofia	A	0-3	
27/04/96	Slavia Sofia	H	0-0	
04/05/96	Shumen	A	1-3	Stanislavov
11/05/96	Botev Plovdiv	H	2-1	Adzhov, Delev

LEVSKI SOFIA

CLUB DIRECTORY

FC Levski Sofia
ul. Todorini Kukli 47
kv. Poduiene
Sofia
tel - (02) 457013/476064/453071
Year of Formation - 1914
President - Tomas Lavchis
Coach - Ivan Kiuchiukov
(96/97 - Georgi Tsvetkov)
Stadium - Georgi Asparuchov (45,000)

MAJOR HONOURS
League Championship - (20)
1933, 1937, 1942. 1946, 1947, 1949, 1950, 1953, 1965, 1968, 1970, 1974, 1977, 1979, 1984, 1985, 1988, 1993, 1994, 1995.
Domestic Cup - (7)
1942, 1982, 1984, 1986, 1991, 1992, 1994.

APPEARANCES 95/96

	P	Ap	(s)	Gls
Valentin DARTILOV	D	26		
Doncho DONEV	A	11	(3)	5
Stanimir GOSPODINOV	D		(1)	
Marian HRISTOV	A	28		10
Borislav ILIEV	D	1	(2)	
Georgi IVANOV	A	11	(8)	
Krasimir KOLEV	G	4	(2)	
Plamen KOSTURKOV	A	8	(4)	
Emil KREMENLIEV	D	13		
Aleksandar MARKOV	D	7	(2)	
Dimcho MARKOV	D	9	(4)	
Plamen NIKOLOV	G	26		
Milen PENCHEV	M		(3)	
Petar PENCHEV	D	20	(3)	
Radostin RUSEV	D	16	(2)	
Veselin SARBAKOV	M	4	(2)	2
Ilian SIMEONOV	A	21	(4)	8
Georgi SLAVCHEV	D	8		
Plamen TIMNEV	A	10	(5)	2
Elin TOPUZAKOV	A		(2)	
Ivan VASILEV	D	28		1
Emil VELEV	M	24		3
Petar YANKOV	A	1	(6)	
Vladimir YONKOV	D	27	(2)	2
Kancho YORDANOV	A	9	(2)	1
Hristo YOVOV	A	11	(14)	10
Todor ZAITSEV	A	7	(13)	4

LEAGUE RESULTS 1995/96

Date	Opponent	H/A	Score	Scorers
12/08/95	Lokomotiv Plovdiv	A	1-0	Yordanov
18/08/95	Neftochimik Bourgas	H	1-2	og (Evtimov)
27/08/95	Etar Veliko Tarnovo	A	1-0	Simeonov
30/08/95	Lovech	H	4-0	Timnev 2, Yovov 2
08/09/95	Spartak Varna	A	0-0	
16/09/95	Rakovski Ruse	A	1-0	Yovov
22/09/95	Slavia Sofia	H	0-0	
30/09/95	Shumen	A	2-0	Hristov 2
14/10/95	Botev Plovdiv	H	2-1	Hristov, Zaitsev
22/10/95	Spartak Plovdiv	A	1-0	Yovov
28/10/95	Montana	H	2-1	Vasilev, Simeonov
04/11/95	Levski Kiustendil	A	0-2	
18/11/95	CSKA Sofia	H	3-1	Velev, Hristov, Simeonov
25/11/95	Lokomotiv Sofia	A	2-0	Hristov, Simeonov
02/12/95	Dobrudzha Dobrich	H	2-0	Zaitsev, Yonkov
17/02/96	Lokomotiv Plovdiv	H	4-0	Simeonov, Yovov 2, Donev
24/02/96	Neftochimik Bourgas	A	1-5	Donev
02/03/96	Etar Veliko Tarnovo	H	2-0	Simeonov, Sarbakov
09/03/96	Lovech	A	1-1	Zaitsev
13/03/96	Spartak Varna	H	4-1	Hristov 2, Yovov, Velev (p)
16/03/96	Rakovski Ruse	A	1-0	Donev
23/03/96	Slavia Sofia	A	1-1	Yovov
30/03/96	Shumen	H	2-1	Velev (p), Yonkov (p)
06/04/96	Botev Plovdiv	A	1-1	Zaitsev (p)
10/04/96	Spartak Plovdiv	H	3-0	Simeonov, Hristov, Sarbakov
13/04/96	Montana	A	3-1	Hristov, Donev, Yovov
20/04/96	Levski Kiustendil	H	3-0	Simeonov, Yovov, Hristov
27/04/96	CSKA Sofia	A	0-1	
04/05/96	Lokomotiv Sofia	H	0-1	
11/05/96	Dobrudzha Dobrich	A	1-2	Donev

LOKOMOTIV PLOVDIV

CLUB DIRECTORY

FC Lokomotiv
Sport komplex Lokomotiv
Park Lauta
4000 Plovdiv
tel - (032) 262511
Year of Formation - 1936
President - Nikola Popov
Coach - Gancho Peev; Vasil Ankov; Spas Garnevski; Ivan Glukhchev; Dinko Dermendzhiev
Stadium - Lokomotiv (25,000)

APPEARANCES 95/96

	P	Ap	(s)	Gls
Dimitar CHOBANOV	M	12	(2)	2
Georgi DIMITROV	A	17	(6)	3
Ivan DIMITROV	M		(5)	
Zheko DIMITROV	A	1	(3)	
Stefan DRAGONOV	A	15	(4)	2
Yulian DZHEVIZOV	M	13	(3)	1
Ivan GOVEDAROV	D	10	(4)	
Georgi IVANOV	A	12		3
Yovko IVANOV	A	12		3
Slavoljub JANKOVIC (YUG)	D	13		
Ilia KALINOV	A	24	(3)	1
Vasil KAMBUROV	G	18		
Dimitar KEKHAIOV	A	1	(6)	
Vasil KOLEV	A	11	(2)	
Krasimir KOSTOV	D	9	(3)	1
Vasil KRASTEV	M	27	(2)	4
Stefan LULCHEV	D	11		1
Plamen MADZHAROV	D	11	(1)	
Dimcho MARKOV	D	14		
Atanas PASHEV	A	3	(2)	
Petar PASHEV	M	20	(6)	2
Ivailo PETROV	M	5	(2)	
Milen RAIKOVSKI	G		(1)	
Radi RAIKOVSKI	D	24	(3)	
Muharem SAITI (YUG)	M	6	(2)	
Stefan SALAMANOV	D	5	(3)	
Stavri STAIKOV	G	12	(1)	
Ivan TANCHOVSKI	M		(6)	
Vasil USHEV	M	5	(3)	
Mikhail YUMERSKI	D	19		1
Georgi ZDRAVKOV	A		(6)	1

LEAGUE RESULTS 1995/96

Date	Opponent		Score	Scorers
12/08/95	Levski Sofia	H	0-1	
19/08/95	Slavia Sofia	A	0-2	
26/08/95	Shumen	H	2-0	Pashev P., Ivanov Y.
02/09/95	Botev Plovdiv	A	0-5	
09/09/95	Spartak Plovdiv	H	1-0	Ivanov Y.
16/09/95	Montana	A	0-2	
23/09/95	Levski Kiustendil	H	2-2	Draganov 2 (1p)
30/09/95	CSKA Sofia	A	0-1	
14/10/95	Lokomotiv Sofia	H	1-0	Lulchev
21/10/95	Dobrudzha Dobrich	A	0-2	
28/10/95	Rakovski Ruse	H	2-0	Ivanov Y. (p), Krastev
04/11/95	Neftochimik Bourgas	H	2-0	Chobanov, Dimitrov G.
18/11/95	Etar Veliko Tarnovo	A	0-3	
25/11/95	Lovech	H	2-1	Krastev, Chobanov
02/12/95	Spartak Varna	A	0-2	
17/02/96	Levski Sofia	A	0-4	
24/02/96	Slavia Sofia	H	2-4	Ivanov G., Dimitrov G.
02/03/96	Shumen	A	0-1	
09/03/96	Botev Plovdiv	H	0-0	
13/03/96	Spartak Plovdiv	A	0-0	
16/03/96	Montana	H	0-4	
23/03/96	Levski Kiustendil	A	0-0	
30/03/96	CSKA Sofia	H	2-1	Ivanov G., Kostov
06/04/96	Lokomotiv Sofia	A	0-4	
10/04/96	Dobrudzha Dobrich	H	3-1	Pashev P., Ivanov G., Dzhevizov
13/04/96	Rakovski Ruse	A	1-4	Zdravkov
20/04/96	Neftochimik Bourgas	A	0-4	
27/04/96	Etar Veliko Tarnovo	H	2-0	Kalinov, Yumerski
04/05/96	Lovech	A	1-1	Dimitrov G.
11/05/96	Spartak Varna	H	2-1	Krastev 2

LOKOMOTIV SOFIA

CLUB DIRECTORY

FC Lokomotiv
Bul. Rozhen 23
1220 Sofia
tel - (02) 384978/376406
fax - (02) 382887
Year of Formation - 1929
President - Nikolai Gigov
Coach - Grigor Petkov; Trendafil Terziiski
Stadium - Lokomotiv (25,000)

MAJOR HONOURS
League Championship - (4)
1940, 1945, 1964, 1978.
Domestic Cup - (1) 1995.

APPEARANCES 95/96

	P	Ap	(s)	Gls
Dian ANGELOV	M	5	(2)	
Georgi ANTONOV	D	10	(8)	1
Rumen APOSTOLOV	G	14		
Georgi BORISOV	A	17	(9)	5
Ivailo BRANKOV	A		(5)	1
Simeon CHILIBONOV	M	24	(3)	12
Sergei CHURADZE (GEO)	G		(1)	
Doncho DONEV	A	10	(3)	4
Veselin GEROV	A	8	(4)	3
Boris KHVOINEV	A	8		
Hristo KOILOV	M	24	(4)	1
Vladimir MANOLKOV	G	7		
Yordan MARINOV	M	27		7
Plamen MECHEV	D	4		
Aleksandar MINOVSKI	G	9	(6)	
Valentin NAIDENOV	D	24	(1)	
Dian PETKOV	M	18	(5)	8
Yasen PETROV	M	13	(8)	2
Ivan RADIVOJEVIC (YUG)	D	29		3
Ivo SLAVCHEV	M	28		4
Angel STOIKOV	D	4	(4)	1
Lazar VACHKOV	A		(10)	1
Yavor VALCHINOV	M	16	(1)	
Dimitar VASEV	D	8		
Anton VELKOV	D	13	(3)	1
Adalbert ZAFIROV	D	10	(2)	

LEAGUE RESULTS 1995/96

13/08/95	Shumen	H	1-1	Donev
18/08/95	Botev Plovdiv	A	0-3	
27/08/95	Spartak Plovdiv	H	4-0	Koilov, Borisov, Marinov 2
30/08/95	Montana	A	0-0	
09/09/95	Levski Kiustendil	H	3-0	Petkov, Antonov, Chilibonov
17/09/95	CSKA Sofia	A	5-1	Chilibonov 3, Slavchev, Borisov
23/09/95	Rakovski Ruse	H	4-1	Petkov 2, Chilibonov, Donev
01/10/95	Dobrudzha Dobrich	H	2-0	Petkov, Borisov
14/10/95	Lokomotiv Plovdiv	A	0-1	
21/10/95	Neftochimik Bourgas	H	3-1	Borisov, Chilibonov, Velkov
28/10/95	Etar Veliko Tarnovo	A	1-0	Donev
11/11/95	Lovech	H	3-1	Chilibonov 2, Vachkov
18/11/95	Spartak Varna	A	2-1	Donev, Petkov
25/11/95	Levski Sofia	H	0-2	
03/12/95	Slavia Sofia	A	1-1	Marinov
17/02/96	Shumen	A	0-0	
24/02/96	Botev Plovdiv	H	2-1	Slavchev, Chilibonov
02/03/96	Spartak Plovdiv	A	2-1	Gerov, Marinov
09/03/96	Montana	H	3-0	Borisov, Petkov 2
13/03/96	Levski Kiustendil	A	1-2	Chilibonov (p)
16/03/96	CSKA Sofia	H	0-0	
23/03/96	Rakovski Ruse	A	1-2	og (Tsochev)
30/03/96	Dobrudzha Dobrich	A	1-0	Gerov
06/04/96	Lokomotiv Plovdiv	H	4-0	Petrov, Radivojevic (p), Marinov, Petkov
10/04/96	Neftochimik Bourgas	A	1-1	Marinov
13/04/96	Etar Veliko Tarnovo	H	3-0	Radivojevic (p), Gerov, Brankov
20/04/96	Lovech	A	0-2	
27/04/96	Spartak Varna	H	5-0	Petrov, Radivojevic, Marinov, Chilibonov, Stoikov
04/05/96	Levski Sofia	A	1-0	Chilibonov
12/05/96	Slavia Sofia	H	2-2	Slavchev 2

LOVECH

CLUB DIRECTORY

FC Lovech
Stadion Lovech
5500 Lovech
tel - (068) 29091/24420
Year of Formation - 1921
President - Veselin Bogdanov
Coach - Georgi Denev; Radi Zdravkov
Stadium - Lovech (15,000)

APPEARANCES 95/96

	P	Ap	(s)	Gls
Kemuran AHMED	D	16	(2)	2
Tsvetan ANGELOV	M		(6)	
Ivan ARKHANGELOV	D	19	(6)	1
Chavdar ATANASOV	M	6	(6)	2
Dimcho BELIAKOV	A	28		11
Vasil BOEV	D	2	(8)	1
Dragomir DENEV	A	6	(2)	1
Marian DIMOV	A	1	(1)	
Biser DRAGOIEV	A	9	(7)	
Filip FILIPOV	D	11		
Valentin GEORGIEV	D	28		
Viktor GEORGIEV	G	4	(1)	
Radoi HRISTOV	D	8	(2)	
Ivailo ILARIONOV	A	5	(6)	2
Stanimir ILIEV	A	16	(1)	1
Radko KALAIDZHIEV	M	10		1
Rosen KIRILOV	D	12		
Evgeni MARINOV	D	26		
Vitali MUTAFCHIEV	M	27	(1)	2
Yonko PEIKOV	M	17	(8)	
Nikolai RAIKOVSKI	M	2	(1)	
Nikolai STEFANOV	D	7		1
Valentin STEFANOV	A	9	(1)	
Stoimen STOIKOV	A	4	(13)	
Valeri VALKOV	M	3	(4)	
Boiko VELICHKOV	M	14		4
Vitomir VUTOV	G	26	(1)	
Kostadin YANCHEV	M	14		

LEAGUE RESULTS 1995/96

Date	Opponent	H/A	Score	Scorers
12/08/95	Etar Veliko Tarnovo	A	0-1	
19/08/95	Rakovski Ruse	A	0-2	
26/08/95	Spartak Varna	H	0-0	
30/08/95	Levski Sofia	A	0-4	
09/09/95	Slavia Sofia	H	0-1	
16/09/95	Shumen	A	1-1	Kalaidzhiev
22/09/95	Botev Plovdiv	H	3-0	Beliakov 2 (1p), Ahmed
30/09/95	Spartak Plovdiv	A	1-2	Boev
14/10/95	Montana	H	1-1	Beliakov
21/10/95	Levski Kiustendil	A	0-0	
28/10/95	CSKA Sofia	H	0-0	
11/11/95	Lokomotiv Sofia	A	1-3	Beliakov
18/11/95	Dobrudzha Dobrich	H	0-0	
25/11/95	Lokomotiv Plovdiv	A	1-2	Stefanov N.
02/12/95	Neftochimik Bourgas	H	0-2	
17/02/96	Etar Veliko Tarnovo	H	0-0	
24/02/96	Rakovski Ruse	H	2-1	Arkhangelov, Velichkov
02/03/96	Spartak Varna	A	1-2	Denev
09/03/96	Levski Sofia	H	1-1	Iliev
13/03/96	Slavia Sofia	A	0-2	
16/03/96	Shumen	H	3-0	Atanasov, Ahmed, Beliakov (p)
22/03/96	Botev Plovdiv	A	0-1	
30/03/96	Spartak Plovdiv	H	2-0	Beliakov, Velichkov
06/04/96	Montana	A	2-3	Atanasov, Beliakov
10/04/96	Levski Kiustendil	H	3-0	Ilarionov, Mutafchiev, Beliakov
13/04/96	CSKA Sofia	A	0-4	
20/04/96	Lokomotiv Sofia	H	2-0	Beliakov, Ilarionov
27/04/96	Dobrudzha Dobrich	A	2-1	Mutafchiev, Beliakov
04/05/96	Lokomotiv Plovdiv	H	1-1	Velichkov (p)
11/05/96	Neftochimik Bourgas	A	2-5	Beliakov, Velichkov (p)

MONTANA

CLUB DIRECTORY

FC Montana
Stadion Ogosta
3400 Montana
tel - (096) 26768
Year of Formation - 1926
President - Ivo Georgiev
Coach - Dimitar Aleksiev; Boian Gergov
Stadium - Ogosta (10,000)

APPEARANCES 95/96

	P	Ap	(s)	Gls
Ilian ANTONOV	D	8	(13)	1
Atanas ATANASOV	A	27		2
Vasil BOTEV	D	8	(3)	
Angel CHERVENKOV	D	26	(1)	
Ilia GRUEV	M	12		
Said IBRAIMOV	M	30		1
Veselin IGNATOV	D	28		
Ventsislav ILIEV	D	25		
Dilian IVANOV	D	11	(9)	
Svetlin MATUSKI	A	2	(4)	
Rumen PANAYOTOV	A	27	(1)	6
Dimitar PEMPERSKI	M		(2)	
Stilian PETROV	M	1	(9)	1
Todor PRAMATAROV	A	28		8
Mikhail ROLEV	G	2	(3)	
Georgi SHEITANOV	G	28		
Anatoli TONOV	A	28	(1)	11
Venelin TSINTSARSKI	M	9	(6)	
Aleksandar YANAKIEV	A	2	(16)	3
Zdravko ZDRAVKOV	D	28		

LEAGUE RESULTS 1995/96

12/08/95	Rakovski Ruse	H	1-0	Pramatarov
19/08/95	Levski Kiustendil	H	1-1	Panayotov (p)
27/08/95	CSKA Sofia	A	2-1	Tonov, Panayotov
30/08/95	Lokomotiv Sofia	H	0-0	
09/09/95	Dobrudzha Dobrich	A	0-1	
16/09/95	Lokomotiv Plovdiv	H	2-0	Atanasov, Tonov
23/09/95	Neftochimik Bourgas	A	0-1	
30/09/95	Etar Veliko Tarnovo	H	0-0	
14/10/95	Lovech	A	1-1	Yanakiev
21/10/95	Spartak Varna	H	2-3	Panayotov 2
28/10/95	Levski Sofia	A	1-2	Tonov
04/11/95	Slavia Sofia	H	1-1	Tonov
18/11/95	Shumen	A	1-0	Pramatarov
25/11/95	Botev Plovdiv	H	3-0	Pramatarov 2, Tonov
03/12/95	Spartak Plovdiv	A	1-2	Tonov
17/02/96	Rakovski Ruse	A	0-0	
24/02/96	Levski Kiustendil	A	1-1	Tonov
02/03/96	CSKA Sofia	H	0-1	
09/03/96	Lokomotiv Sofia	A	0-3	
13/03/96	Dobrudzha Dobrich	H	3-0	Pramatarov, Tonov 2
16/03/96	Lokomotiv Plovdiv	A	4-0	Atanasov, Pramatarov 2, Antonov
23/03/96	Neftochimik Bourgas	H	0-0	
30/03/96	Etar Veliko Tarnovo	A	0-4	
06/04/96	Lovech	H	3-2	Ibraimov, Panayotov (p), Petrov
10/04/96	Spartak Varna	A	0-2	
13/04/96	Levski Sofia	H	1-3	Panayotov (p)
20/04/96	Slavia Sofia	A	1-3	Pramatarov
27/04/96	Shumen	H	3-1	Tonov 2, Yanakiev
04/05/96	Botev Plovdiv	A	0-0	
11/05/96	Spartak Plovdiv	H	1-2	Yanakiev

NEFTOCHIMIK BOURGAS

CLUB DIRECTORY

FC Neftochimik
Stadion Neftochimik
8000 Bourgas
tel - (056) 32023/39023/29741/38047
fax - (056) 24898
Year of Formation - 1932
President - Hristo Portochanov
Coach - Dimitar Dimitrov
Stadium - Neftochimik (22,000)

APPEARANCES 95/96

	P	Ap	(s)	Gls
Veselin BRANIMIROV	M		(2)	
Krasimir DENEV	D	8	(2)	
Krasimir DIMITROV	D	21	(2)	5
Stanimir DIMITROV	M	27		7
Gancho EVTIMOV	D	22	(1)	2
Hristo GEORGIEV	D	7	(8)	1
Milen GEORGIEV	A		(17)	2
Petko GINEV	D	2	(2)	
Ilia GRUEV	A	15		
Yovko IVANOV	A		(1)	
Ivan KANEV	G	5		
Todor KISELICHKOV	A	18	(7)	6
Radostin KISHISHEV	M	30		
Miroliub KOSEV	A	1	(5)	
Liubomir LIUBENOV	A		(3)	
Blagomir MITREV	M	12	(1)	1
Malin ORACHEV	M	11	(9)	
Velian PARUSHEV	D	14	(6)	4
Vesko PETKOV	A	24	(2)	18
Rosen PETROV	D	29		
Rumen PETROV	M	2	(3)	
Veselin SHULEV	G	20		
Ivan TENEV	D	17	(1)	2
Tikhomir TODOROV	G	5	(1)	
Mitko TRENDAFILOV	M	22	(2)	3
Stancho TSONEV	A	18	(11)	7

LEAGUE RESULTS 1995/96

Date	Opponent		Score	Scorers
12/08/95	Spartak Varna	H	5-2	Petkov 4, Tsonev
18/08/95	Levski Sofia	A	2-1	Petkov, Evtimov
26/08/95	Slavia Sofia	H	1-0	Dimitrov S.
02/09/95	Shumen	A	3-2	Petkov 2, Mitrev
08/09/95	Botev Plovdiv	H	2-0	Dimitrov S., Tsonev
16/09/95	Spartak Plovdiv	A	0-0	
23/09/95	Montana	H	1-0	Dimitrov S.
30/09/95	Levski Kiustendil	A	0-1	
14/10/95	CSKA Sofia	H	2-2	Tsonev, Dimitrov S.
21/10/95	Lokomotiv Sofia	A	1-3	Kiselichkov
28/10/95	Dobrudzha Dobrich	H	5-1	Dimitrov K. 2 (1p), Petkov 2, Georgiev H.
04/11/95	Lokomotiv Plovdiv	A	0-2	
18/11/95	Rakovski Ruse	H	3-2	Kiselichkov, Petkov, Georgiev M.
25/11/95	Etar Veliko Tarnovo	H	3-0	Tenev, Kiselichkov, Trendafilov
02/12/95	Lovech	A	2-0	Evtimov, Kiselichkov
17/02/96	Spartak Varna	A	0-3	
24/02/96	Levski Sofia	H	5-1	Tenev, Dimitrov K. 2 (2p), Dimitrov S., Petkov
02/03/96	Slavia Sofia	A	0-2	
09/03/96	Shumen	H	0-0	
13/03/96	Botev Plovdiv	A	1-2	Trendafilov
16/03/96	Spartak Plovdiv	H	2-0	Dimitrov K. (p), Kiselichkov
23/03/96	Montana	A	0-0	
30/03/96	Levski Kiustendil	H	3-0	Tsonev 2, Georgiev M.
06/04/96	CSKA Sofia	A	1-1	Tsonev
10/04/96	Lokomotiv Sofia	H	1-1	Parushev
13/04/96	Dobrudzha Dobrich	A	3-1	Parushev, Kiselichkov, Trendafilov
20/04/96	Lokomotiv Plovdiv	H	4-0	Petkov, Tsonev, Dimitrov S., Parushev (p)
27/04/96	Rakovski Ruse	A	1-2	Dimitrov S.
04/05/96	Etar Veliko Tarnovo	A	2-0	Petkov 2
11/05/96	Lovech	H	5-2	Petkov 4 (2p), Parushev

RAKOVSKI RUSE

CLUB DIRECTORY

FC Rakovski
ul Kinstantin Irechek 16
7000 Ruse
tel - (082) 233878
Year of Formation - 1992
President - Oscar Tsankov
Coach - Todor Todorov; Ilia Iliev
Stadium - Gradski (25,000)

APPEARANCES 95/96

	P	Ap	(s)	Gls
Viktor BANKOV	M		(1)	
Ivan BLIZNAKOV	D	26	(2)	
Yordan DZHENKOV	A	14	(5)	1
Krasimir GETSOV	M	6		
Dragomir GRIGOROV	D	29		
Kiril KIRILOV	M	17	(7)	3
Plamen KOVACHEV	M	2	(1)	
Simeon KRASTEV	A	19	(8)	5
Marin MARINOV	G	13	(1)	
Ventsislav MARINOV	M	13	(1)	
Ivan MILCHEV	G	17	(1)	
Marian OGNEANOV	D	2	(6)	
Plamen PETKOV	M	20	(1)	1
Yordan PETROV	M	10	(3)	
Georgi POPIVANOV	A	24	(2)	2
Plamen PRODANOV	M	12	(1)	2
Remzi SHENER	M	3	(10)	
Vanio SHISHKOV	A	13	(1)	6
Filip TEOFOOLU	A	23	(6)	5
Marian TODOROV	M	15		
Dimitar TOTEEV	A	12		8
Christopher TSOCHEV	M	13	(9)	
Mladen TSONEV	D	27		

LEAGUE RESULTS 1995/96

12/08/95	Montana	A	0-1	
19/08/95	Lovech	H	2-0	Teofoolu, Krastev
26/08/95	Levski Kiustendil	A	0-3	
30/08/95	Spartak Varna	H	3-0	Totev, Teofoolu, Prodanov
09/09/95	CSKA Sofia	A	0-2	
16/09/95	Levski Sofia	H	0-1	
23/09/95	Lokomotiv Sofia	A	1-4	Totev
30/09/95	Slavia Sofia	H	2-4	Totev, Krastev
14/10/95	Dobrudzha Dobrich	A	0-2	
21/10/95	Shumen	H	4-0	Totev 3, Prodanov
28/10/95	Lokomotiv Plovdiv	A	0-2	
04/11/95	Botev Plovdiv	H	1-1	Totev
18/11/95	Neftochimik Bourgas	A	2-3	Totev, Petkov
25/11/95	Spartak Plovdiv	H	2-0	Teofoolu, Krastev
02/12/95	Etar Veliko Tarnovo	A	0-1	
17/02/96	Montana	H	0-0	
24/02/96	Lovech	A	1-2	Kirilov (p)
02/03/96	Levski Kiustendil	H	1-0	Dzhenkov
09/03/96	Spartak Varna	A	1-3	Krastev
13/03/96	CSKA Sofia	H	0-1	
16/03/96	Levski Sofia	A	0-1	
23/03/96	Lokomotiv Sofia	H	2-1	Shishkov, Kirilov
30/03/96	Slavia Sofia	A	0-2	
06/04/96	Dobrudzha Dobrich	H	3-1	Popivanov 2, Kirilov (p)
10/04/96	Shumen	A	0-2	
13/04/96	Lokomotiv Plovdiv	H	4-1	Shishkov 2, Krastev, Teofoolu
20/04/96	Botev Plovdiv	A	1-1	Shishkov
27/04/96	Neftochimik Bourgas	H	2-1	Shishkov, Teofoolu
04/05/96	Spartak Plovdiv	A	0-0	
11/05/96	Etar Veliko Tarnovo	H	1-1	Shishkov (p)

SHUMEN

CLUB DIRECTORY

FC Shumen
ul Preslava 6
Shumen
tel - (054) 69894/66681/40175
Year of Formation - 1919
President - Hristo Hristov
Coach - Georgi Todorov; Yordan Stoikov; Dimitar Aleksiev
Stadium - Panaiot Volov (30,000)

APPEARANCES 95/96

	P	Ap	(s)	Gls
Angel ANGELOV	D	17	(3)	
Rumen BAIREV	D	6	(1)	
Genrich BERBERYAN (ARM)	M	2	(3)	1
Rumen CHAKAROV	A	9	(14)	1
Lachezar DAFKOV	M	6		
Stanislav DIMITROV	M		(1)	
Aleksei DIONISIEV	M	23	(1)	
Veselin DZHAMBOV	D	1	(4)	
Georgi GEORGIEV	D	9	(2)	2
Adrian ISAEV	M	4	(4)	
Srdjan KOCIC (YUG)	A	3	(9)	2
Nasko KOSTADINOV	M	18	(2)	2
Turgai KURDOV	A	4	(1)	
Plamen LALEV	M	9	(2)	
Ivan MILIEV	A		(2)	
Miroslav MIROSLAVOV	A	27	(1)	7
Sasa MRKIC (YUG)	D	14		
Viktorio PAVLOV	M	14		3
Rugério PEREIRA (BRA)	D	20		
Ivailo POPOV	G	6	(2)	
Shaban SHEVKED	M	26		
Ivelin SPASOV	A	17	(11)	8
Stoiko STOIKOV	D	16	(2)	
Ivan TANKOV	M	7	(2)	
Marian TODOROV	D	13		2
Ivan TRIFSKI	D	8	(2)	
Ilko VASILEV	G	24		
Daniel ZHELIAZKOV	A	19		
Nikolai ZHELIAZKOV	D	8	(4)	

LEAGUE RESULTS 1995/96

13/08/95	Lokomotiv Sofia	A	1-1	Miroslavov
19/08/95	Dobrudzha Dobrich	H	1-0	Miroslavov
26/08/95	Lokomotiv Plovdiv	A	0-2	
02/09/95	Neftochimik Bourgas	H	2-3	Miroslavov (p), Georgiev
09/09/95	Etar Veliko Tarnovo	A	0-1	
16/09/95	Lovech	H	1-1	Georgiev (p)
23/09/95	Spartak Varna	A	0-2	
30/09/95	Levski Sofia	H	0-2	
14/10/95	Slavia Sofia	A	0-4	
21/10/95	Rakovski Ruse	A	0-4	
28/10/95	Botev Plovdiv	H	1-1	Miroslavov
04/11/95	Spartak Plovdiv	A	2-4	Berberyan, Spasov
18/11/95	Montana	H	0-1	
25/11/95	Levski Kiustendil	A	0-2	
02/12/95	CSKA Sofia	H	1-0	Spasov
17/02/96	Lokomotiv Sofia	H	0-0	
24/02/96	Dobrudzha Dobrich	A	0-1	
02/03/96	Lokomotiv Plovdiv	H	1-0	Spasov
09/03/96	Neftochimik Bourgas	A	0-0	
13/03/96	Etar Veliko Tarnovo	H	3-0	Miroslavov, Spasov 2
16/03/96	Lovech	A	0-3	
23/03/96	Spartak Varna	H	2-0	Spasov (p), Kocic
30/03/96	Levski Sofia	A	1-2	Todorov
06/04/96	Slavia Sofia	H	0-1	
10/04/96	Rakovski Ruse	H	2-0	Chakarov, Miroslavov
13/04/96	Botev Plovdiv	A	1-0	Kostadinov
20/04/96	Spartak Plovdiv	H	3-1	Spasov, Miroslavov, Pavlov
27/04/96	Montana	A	1-3	Kostadinov
04/05/96	Levski Kiustendil	H	3-1	Todorov, Kocic, Pavlov
11/05/96	CSKA Sofia	A	2-4	Pavlov, Spasov (p)

SLAVIA SOFIA

CLUB DIRECTORY

FC Slavia
Bul. Koloman 1
1618 Sofia
tel - (02) 551137/550075
fax - (02) 555231
Year of Formation - 1913
President - Mladen Mikhalev
Coach - Stoian Kotsev (96/97 - Radoslav Zdravkav)
Stadium - Slavia (32,000)

MAJOR HONOURS
League Championship - (7)
1928, 1930, 1936, 1939, 1941, 1943, 1996.
Domestic Cup - (1) 1996.

APPEARANCES 95/96

	P	Ap	(s)	Gls
Dian ANGELOV	M	12		1
Stoian ATSAROV	D	28	(2)	1
Aleksandar BONCHEV	A		(3)	
Lachezar DAFKOV	M	4	(4)	1
Zvetozar DERMENDZHIEV	M	2	(5)	
Anton DIMITROV	A	17	(7)	1
Ivan DIMITROV	A	4	(2)	
Geno DOBREVSKI	A	12	(1)	2
Ivan DOBREVSKI	M		(9)	1
Stoicho DRAGOV	G	1	(1)	
Vladimir IVANOV	D	28		3
Kiril KACHAMANOV	D	27		1
Atanas KIROV	A	23	(4)	7
Stefan KOLEV	D	28		
Kiril METKOV	M	1	(3)	
Dobromir MINCHEV	M		(10)	
Aleksandar PANTALEEV	M		(1)	
Ivan PASKOV	M	1		
Nikola PRAMATAROV	M	2	(5)	
Zoran RISTIC (YUG)	A	10	(3)	
Vladko SHALAMANOV	M	13		9
Vanio SHISHKOV	A	3	(3)	
Nasko SIRAKOV	A	18	(2)	16
Dimitar TOTEV	A	12	(3)	1
Petar TSVETANOV	M	21	(2)	2
Marius URUKOV	D	27		4
Mikhail ZAKHARIEV	M	4	(7)	
Zdravko ZDRAVKOV	G	29		
Daniel ZHELIAZKOV	A	3		

LEAGUE RESULTS 1995/96

12/08/95	Dobrudzha Dobrich	A	0-1	
19/08/95	Lokomotiv Plovdiv	H	2-0	Dafkov, Tsvetanov
26/08/95	Neftochimik Bourgas	A	0-1	
05/09/95	Etar Veliko Tarnovo	H	2-0	Urukov, Dobrevski I.
09/09/95	Lovech	A	1-0	Kirov
16/09/95	Spartak Varna	H	3-0	Shalamanov 2, Kirov
22/09/95	Levski Sofia	A	0-0	
30/09/95	Rakovski Ruse	A	4-2	Shalamanov 3, Kirov
14/10/95	Shumen	H	4-0	Kachamanov, Shalamanov (p), Dobrevski G. 2
21/10/95	Botev Plovdiv	A	1-0	Shalamanov (p)
28/10/95	Spartak Plovdiv	H	2-0	og (Nenov), Sirakov
04/11/95	Montana	A	1-1	Atsarov
18/11/95	Levski Kiustendil	H	3-0	Urukov, Shalamanov 2
24/11/95	CSKA Sofia	A	0-1	
03/12/95	Lokomotiv Sofia	H	1-1	Ivanov
17/02/96	Dobrudzha Dobrich	H	2-0	Sirakov 2
24/02/96	Lokomotiv Plovdiv	A	4-2	Sirakov 2, Ivanov, Urukov
02/03/96	Neftochimik Bourgas	H	2-0	Tsvetanov, Sirakov
09/03/96	Etar Veliko Tarnovo	A	2-0	Sirakov, Totev
13/03/96	Lovech	H	2-0	Kirov, Sirakov (p)
16/03/96	Spartak Varna	A	2-0	Angelov, Kirov
23/03/96	Levski Sofia	H	1-1	Sirakov
30/03/96	Rakovski Ruse	H	2-0	Kirov, Sirakov
06/04/96	Shumen	A	1-0	Sirakov (p)
10/04/96	Botev Plovdiv	H	1-0	Urukov
13/04/96	Spartak Plovdiv	A	3-1	Kirov, Ivanov, Sirakov
20/04/96	Montana	H	3-1	Sirakov 2, Dimitrov A.
27/04/96	Levski Kiustendil	A	0-0	
04/05/96	CSKA Sofia	H	0-0	
12/05/96	Lokomotiv Sofia	A	2-2	Sirakov 2

SPARTAK PLOVDIV

CLUB DIRECTORY

FC Spartak
ul Makedonia 6
4000 Plovdiv
tel - (032) 767058/767060/767061
Year of Formation - 1947
President - Hristo Aleksandrov
Coach - Georgi Dermendzhiev
Stadium - Spartak (12,000)

MAJOR HONOURS
League Championship - (1) 1963.
Domestic Cup - (1) 1958.

APPEARANCES 95/96

	P	Ap	(s)	Gls
Ardashes ADAMYAN (ARM)	M	26		2
Kiril ANDONOV	D	5		
Georgi APOSTOLOV	A	1	(1)	
Marin BAKALOV	M	15		1
Atanas BALDZHIISKI	D	9	(3)	
Georgi CHAKAROV	D	11		1
Vladimir CHERNEV	G	10	(2)	
Stoian DELCHEV	A	13		1
Borislav DRAGOMIROV	G	20	(1)	
Tanio GANEV	D	23		1
Kostadin GERGANCHEV	A	10	(4)	2
Pavel HRISTOV	D	2		
Zvetan IVANOV	A	20	(5)	1
Dimitar KEKHAIOV	A	12	(1)	3
Ivan KOCHEV	D	21	(1)	
Valentin KUZMANOV	G		(3)	
Yonko NEDELCHEV	D	22	(1)	2
Neno NENOV	D	24	(1)	
Nikolai NIKOLOV	A	20	(5)	6
Dimitar ORMANOV	M		(7)	
Georgi PETKOV	A	11	(5)	1
Nikolai PRAMATAROV	A	11		2
Nouri RACHIM	M		(5)	
Dimitar RALCHEV	D	8	(2)	1
Stefan TENEV	D	7	(2)	
Ilia VAKLINOV	M	17	(5)	
Ivan VASILEV	D	3	(1)	
Radoslav VIDOV	D	9		
Zaprian YANKOV	M		(1)	

LEAGUE RESULTS 1995/96

12/08/95	Levski Kiustendil	A	0-3	
27/08/95	Lokomotiv Sofia	A	0-4	
30/08/95	Dobrudzha Dobrich	H	1-1	Bakalov
09/09/95	Lokomotiv Plovdiv	A	0-1	
13/09/95	CSKA Sofia	H	2-4	Ivanov, Pramatarov
16/09/95	Neftochimik Bourgas	H	0-0	
23/09/95	Etar Veliko Tarnovo	A	0-1	
30/09/95	Lovech	H	2-1	Chakarov (p), Nikolov
14/10/95	Spartak Varna	A	1-8	Ganev
22/10/95	Levski Sofia	H	0-1	
28/10/95	Slavia Sofia	A	0-2	
04/11/95	Shumen	H	4-2	Nedelchev, Nikolov, Gerganchev, Pramatarov
18/11/95	Botev Plovdiv	A	0-2	
25/11/95	Rakovski Ruse	A	0-2	
03/12/95	Montana	H	2-1	Nikolov, Gerganchev
17/02/96	Levski Kiustendil	H	1-0	Delchev
24/02/96	CSKA Sofia	A	1-3	Nikolov
02/03/96	Lokomotiv Sofia	H	1-2	Nedelchev
09/03/96	Dobrudzha Dobrich	A	0-1	
13/03/96	Lokomotiv Plovdiv	H	0-0	
16/03/96	Neftochimik Bourgas	A	0-2	
23/03/96	Etar Veliko Tarnovo	H	3-0	Kekhaiov, Nikolov, Adamyan
30/03/96	Lovech	A	0-2	
06/04/96	Spartak Varna	H	0-1	
10/04/96	Levski Sofia	A	0-3	
13/04/96	Slavia Sofia	H	1-3	Nikolov
20/04/96	Shumen	A	1-3	Adamyan
27/04/96	Botev Plovdiv	H	2-4	Ralchev, Kekhaiov
04/05/96	Rakovski Ruse	H	0-0	
11/05/96	Montana	A	2-1	Petkov, Kekhaiov

SPARTAK VARNA

CLUB DIRECTORY

FC Spartak
ul Seliolu 39
9000 Varna
tel - (052) 245020/225780/253090
fax - (052) 237541
Year of Formation - 1919
President - Nikolai Ishkov
Coach - Nikolai Hristov
Stadium - Spartak (12,000)

MAJOR HONOURS
League Championship - (1) 1932.

APPEARANCES 95/96

	P	Ap	(s)	Gls
Ivailo ANDEEV	D	2	(5)	
Rumen APOSTOLOV	G	12		
Georgi ARNAUDOV	G		(1)	
Ivan ATANASOV	G		(1)	
Mario DAVCHEV	M	24	(1)	4
Traian DIANKOV	A	3	(2)	
Ivailo DIMITROV	A	1	(6)	
Sergei DIMITROV	D	22	(3)	3
Slaveiko DIMITROV	D	29		
Dean DONCHEV	A	1	(6)	1
Dean GENCHEV	A	12	(9)	1
Borislav GEORGIEV	D	26	(1)	
Ivo GEORGIEV	A	27	(2)	21
Stancho GERDZHIKOV	D	1		
Mikhail HRISTOV	A	5	(4)	3
Zlatin MIKHAILOV	D	25		
Dimitar MITOV	D	15	(2)	
Zakharin SABLIOV	M	22	(1)	1
Nikola STANCHEV	A	29		2
Valentin STANCHEV	A	20	(1)	7
Radostin STANEV	G	12		
Todor STOIANOV	G	6		
Dimitar TRENDAFILOV	A	10	(3)	3
Krasimir VLAKHOV	D	24	(2)	
Yavor YORDANOV	A	2	(8)	

LEAGUE RESULTS 1995/96

12/08/95	Neftochimik Bourgas	A	2-5	Hristov, Georgiev I.
19/08/95	Etar Veliko Tarnovo	H	3-0	Georgiev I. 2, Hristov
26/08/95	Lovech	A	0-0	
30/08/95	Rakovski Ruse	A	0-3	
08/09/95	Levski Sofia	H	0-0	
16/09/95	Slavia Sofia	A	0-3	
23/09/95	Shumen	H	2-0	Stanchev N., Stanchev V.
30/09/95	Botev Plovdiv	A	3-1	Trendafilov 2, Dimitrov Se.
14/10/95	Spartak Plovdiv	H	8-1	Georgiev I. 6, Trendafilov, Stanchev V.
21/10/95	Montana	A	3-2	Stanchev V., Georgiev I. 2
28/10/95	Levski Kiustendil	H	2-1	Stanchev V., Georgiev I.
04/11/95	CSKA Sofia	A	0-4	
18/11/95	Lokomotiv Sofia	H	1-2	Davchev
25/11/95	Dobrudzha Dobrich	A	2-3	Georgiev I., Donchev
02/12/95	Lokomotiv Plovdiv	H	2-0	Georgiev I., Sabliov
17/02/96	Neftochimik Bourgas	H	3-0	og (Petrov Ro.), Georgiev I., Stanchev V.
24/02/96	Etar Veliko Tarnovo	A	1-2	Stanchev V.
02/03/96	Lovech	H	2-1	Davchev, Georgiev I.
09/03/96	Rakovski Ruse	H	3-1	Stanchev V. (p), Genchev, Georgiev I.
13/03/96	Levski Sofia	A	1-4	Dimitrov
16/03/96	Slavia Sofia	H	0-2	
23/03/96	Shumen	A	0-2	
30/03/96	Botev Plovdiv	H	2-1	Stanchev N., Davchev
06/04/96	Spartak Plovdiv	A	1-0	Dimitrov Se.
10/04/96	Montana	H	2-0	Georgiev I. (p), Davchev
13/04/96	Levski Kiustendil	A	0-1	
20/04/96	CSKA Sofia	H	1-3	Georgiev I.
27/04/96	Lokomotiv Sofia	A	0-5	
04/05/96	Dobrudzha Dobrich	H	2-3	Georgiev I. 2 (1p)
11/05/96	Lokomotiv Plovdiv	A	1-2	Hristov

PROMOTED CLUBS

SECOND DIVISION FINAL TABLE 95/96

		Pd	W	D	L	F	A	Pt	GD
1	**Maritsa Plovdiv**	**38**	**23**	**7**	**8**	**68**	**27**	**76**	**+41**
2	**Minior Pernik**	**38**	**24**	**3**	**11**	**60**	**31**	**75**	**+29**
3	**Spartak Pleven**	**38**	**21**	**5**	**12**	**59**	**39**	**68**	**+20**
4	Pirin Blagoevgrad	38	20	8	10	56	32	68	+24
5	Akademik Sofia	38	18	8	12	56	49	62	+7
6	Cherno More Varna	38	18	6	14	51	46	60	+5
7	Olimpik Galata	38	16	9	13	46	44	57	+2
8	Khaskovo	38	16	8	14	58	49	56	+9
9	Chardafon Gabrovo	38	17	5	16	40	34	56	+6
10	Septemvri Sofia	38	17	4	17	61	52	55	+9
11	Chirpan	38	16	7	15	41	38	55	+3
12	Lokomotiv Ruse	38	16	7	15	32	51	55	-19
13	Lokomotiv Gorna Oriahovitsa	38	16	6	16	49	46	54	+3
14	Chebar Pazardzhik	38	16	5	17	57	51	53	+6
15	Khan Asparuch Isperich	38	14	9	15	47	48	51	-1
16	Belasitsa Petrich	38	13	3	22	41	57	42	-16
17	Dunav Ruse	38	12	6	20	40	64	42	-24
18	Beroe Stara Zagora	38	10	6	22	38	67	36	-29
19	Storgozia Pleven	38	8	6	24	40	70	30	-30
20	Arda Kardzhalii	38	6	8	24	22	67	26	-45

CLUB DIRECTORY

Maritsa Plovdiv
ul. Pazardzhishko shose
Stadio Maritsa
Plovdiv
tel - (032) 455297
Year of Formation - 1921
President - Yuli Popov
Coach - Petar Zekhtinski
Stadium - Maritsa (8,000)

CLUB DIRECTORY

Minior Pernik
ul. Fizkulturna 1
Pernik
tel - (076) 23250/28306/23816
Year of Formation - 1919
Coach - Ventseslav Arsov; Dimitar Dimitrov; Evlogi Banchev
Stadium - Minior (20,000)

CLUB DIRECTORY

Spartak Pleven
ul. Kalatepe 3
Pleven
tel - (064) 38192
Year of Formation - 1919
President - Plamen Getov
Coach - Vachko Marinov
Stadium - Slavi Aleksiev (40,000)

CROATIA

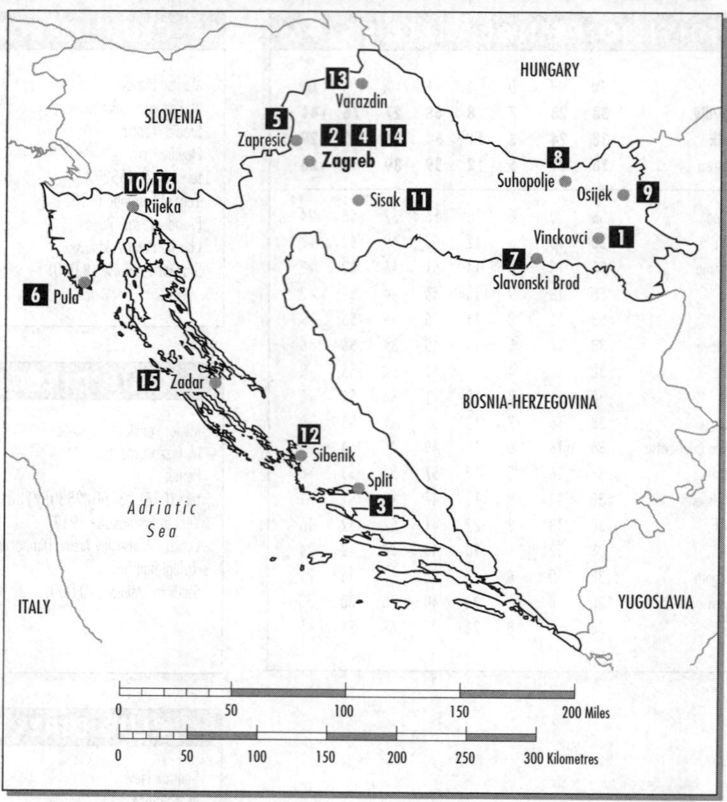

1	CIBALIA VINKOVCI	223
2	CROATIA ZAGREB	224
3	HAJDUK SPLIT	225
4	HRVATSKI DRAGOVOLJAC ZAGREB	226
5	INKER ZAPRESIC	227
6	ISTRA PULA	228
7	MARSONIA SLAVONSKI BROD	229
8	MLADOST 127 SUHOPOLJE	230
9	OSIJEK	231
10	RIJEKA	232
11	SEGESTA SISAK	233
12	SIBENIK	234
13	VARTEKS VARAZDIN	235
14	ZAGREB	236
15	ZADAR	237
16	ORIJENT RIJEKA	237

TAINTED 'DOUBLE' FOR CROATIA ZAGREB

Blazevic complacency proves costly

FEDERATION DIRECTORY

Croatian Football Federation
Ilica 31/II, 41 000 Zagreb
tel - (01) 4554100
fax - (01) 424639

Year of Formation - 1991
President - Nadan Vidosevic
Secretary - Josip Cop

Stadium - Maksimir, Zagreb (56,555)

The appearance of the Croatian national team at the 1996 European Championship finals was a matter of great pride and honour for the citizens of this beleaguered, war-torn country. Few Croatians could afford to travel to England to support their team (although those that did offered plenty of noise and colour), but back home, in Zagreb, Split and elsewhere, Euro '96 was unquestionably the televisual event of the decade.

Croatia arrived in England with high hopes. Having topped their qualifying group ahead of Italy, Miroslav Blazevic's team maintained their confidence level with a run of four successive home victories in the early spring. A couple of subsequent draws away to England and Ireland meant that when Croatia took the field against Turkey for their Euro '96 opener in Nottingham, they were unbeaten for precisely one year.

The "Firing Squad", as the Croatian fans nicknamed the team, looked to have only blanks in their ammunition as they struggled to impose themselves in a poor first performance against the Turks, but substitute Goran Vlaovic's magnificent late solo goal cancelled out all the disappintment and frustration of the previous 85 minutes, and Croatia were on their way. Against a doggedly defensive Denmark, Croatia looked similarly sterile for 45

LEAGUE CHAMPIONSHIP RESULTS 95/96

FIRST PHASE		1	2	3	4	5	6	7	8	9	10	11	12
1	Cibalia Vinkovci		2-2	2-4	2-2	1-1	0-0	2-0	1-1	2-1	2-1	1-0	2-1
2	Croatia Zagreb	3-0		1-0	5-1	4-0	5-0	2-0	2-0	4-0	2-1	2-0	2-0
3	Hajduk Split	4-1	2-1		3-1	5-0	3-0	2-0	1-0	3-1	0-0	0-0	2-1
4	Inker Zapresic	1-1	1-1	0-0		3-2	0-2	0-3	3-1	2-4	2-0	0-2	0-1
5	Istra Pula	0-0	1-0	3-1	0-1		0-0	0-0	0-1	1-3	2-2	1-1	1-1
6	Marsonia Slavonski Brod	2-1	0-3	0-0	0-1	0-3		0-2	0-1	3-1	2-0	1-2	1-2
7	Osijek	4-0	1-2	5-3	1-1	1-0	0-2		1-0	4-0	4-1	1-0	2-2
8	Rijeka	4-4	1-1	0-3	4-4	4-0	0-1	0-2		0-1	3-1	2-2	1-2
9	Segesta Sisak	3-1	1-0	1-1	0-1	3-0	2-0	0-4	6-0		2-2	1-2	2-2
10	Sibenik	0-1	0-0	0-0	3-1	2-0	4-0	1-1	2-1	2-0		1-0	1-0
11	Varteks Varazdin	3-0	1-1	0-3	3-1	2-0	2-0	1-0	2-1	1-0	3-1		0-0
12	Zagreb	0-0	1-3	2-1	0-2	1-1	1-0	0-2	3-0	0-0	2-0	2-2	

FINAL ROUND

CHAMPIONSHIP GROUP		1	2	3	4	5	6
1	Croatia Zagreb		4-1	6-0	2-1	3-4	5-1
2	Hajduk Split	3-2		5-1	2-0	1-0	2-1
3	Hrvatski dragovoljac Zagreb	0-1	2-2		2-1	0-1	1-2
4	Osijek	1-2	2-3	3-0		1-0	1-0
5	Varteks Varazdin	2-0	1-0	1-1	2-1		2-0
6	Zagreb	1-3	1-6	1-1	0-2	0-2	

RELEGATION GROUP		1	2	3	4	5	6	7	8
1	Cibalia Vinkovci		0-0	1-0	2-1	2-1	2-2	4-1	3-1
2	Inker Zapresic	3-0		1-1	1-2	1-1	2-0	0-0	0-1
3	Istra Pula	1-0	2-1		4-1	1-0	1-0	1-0	2-0
4	Marsonia Slavonski Brod	1-1	0-0	1-1		0-3	1-0	0-3	3-2
5	Mladost 127 Suhopolje	2-1	3-1	3-1	4-0		0-0	1-0	2-0
6	Rijeka	2-0	2-0	4-1	2-1	2-0		2-0	2-0
7	Segesta Sisak	2-1	1-0	4-1	2-1	1-1	3-3		2-1
8	Sibenik	1-0	2-0	1-0	1-0	4-1	3-0	2-0	

LEAGUE CHAMPIONSHIP FINAL TABLES 95/96

FIRST PHASE

			Home					Away					Total						
		Pd	W	D	L	F	A	W	D	L	F	A	W	D	L	F	A	Pt	GD
1	Croatia Zagreb	22	11	0	0	32	2	3	5	3	14	11	14	5	3	46	13	47	+33
2	Hajduk Split	22	9	2	0	25	5	3	4	4	16	14	12	6	4	41	19	42	+22
3	Osijek	22	7	2	2	24	11	5	2	4	14	8	12	4	6	38	19	40	+19
4	Varteks Varazdin	22	8	2	1	18	7	3	4	4	11	12	11	6	5	29	19	39	+10
5	Zagreb	22	4	4	3	12	11	3	4	4	12	14	7	8	7	24	25	29	-1
6	Segesta Sisak	22	5	3	3	21	13	3	1	7	11	22	8	4	10	32	35	28	-3
7	Cibalia Vinkovci	22	5	5	1	17	13	1	4	6	9	24	6	9	7	26	37	27	-11
8	Inker Zapresic	22	3	3	5	12	17	4	3	4	16	21	7	6	9	28	38	27	-10
9	Sibenik	22	7	3	1	16	4	0	3	8	9	24	7	6	9	25	28	27	-3
10	Marsonia Slavonski Brod	22	3	1	7	9	16	3	2	6	5	17	6	3	13	14	33	21	-19
11	Rijeka	22	2	4	5	19	21	2	1	8	6	21	4	5	13	25	42	17	-17
12	Istra Pula	22	2	6	3	9	10	1	2	8	7	26	3	8	11	16	36	17	-20

FINAL ROUND
CHAMPIONSHIP GROUP

			Home					Away					Total							
		Pd	W	D	L	F	A	W	D	L	F	A	W	D	L	F	A	Pt	GD	
1	Croatia Zagreb	10	4	0	1	20	7	3	0	2	8	7	7	0	3	28	14	26	+14	(5)
2	Hajduk Split	10	5	0	0	13	4	2	1	2	12	10	7	1	2	25	14	26	+11	(4)
3	Varteks Varazdin	10	4	1	0	8	2	3	0	2	7	5	7	1	2	15	7	24	+8	(2)
4	Osijek	10	3	0	2	8	5	1	0	4	5	8	4	0	6	13	13	15	=	(3)
5	Hrvatski dragovoljac Zagreb	10	1	1	3	5	7	0	2	3	3	16	1	3	6	8	23	7	-15	(1)
6	Zagreb	10	0	1	4	3	14	1	0	4	4	11	1	1	8	7	25	5	-18	(1)

RELEGATION GROUP

			Home					Away					Total							
		Pd	W	D	L	F	A	W	D	L	F	A	W	D	L	F	A	Pt	GD	
1	Sibenik	14	7	0	0	14	1	1	0	6	5	14	8	0	6	19	15	28	+4	(4)
2	Segesta Sisak	14	5	2	0	15	8	1	1	5	4	10	6	3	5	19	18	28	+1	(7)
3	Rijeka	14	7	0	0	16	2	0	3	4	5	12	7	3	4	21	14	26	+7	(2)
4	Mladost 127 Suhopolje	14	6	1	0	15	3	1	2	4	7	11	7	3	4	22	14	25	+8	(1)
5	Istra Pula	14	7	0	0	12	2	0	2	5	5	15	7	2	5	17	17	24	=	(1)
6	Cibalia Vinkovci	14	5	2	0	14	6	0	1	6	3	12	5	3	6	17	18	24	-1	(6)
7	Inker Zapresic	14	2	3	2	8	5	0	2	5	2	10	2	5	7	10	15	16	-5	(5)
8	Marsonia Slavonski Brod	14	2	3	2	6	10	1	0	6	6	16	3	3	8	12	26	15	-14	(3)

N.B. Where two or more teams are level on points, classification is determined by the results of the matches between them.
After 22 matches the top five teams play off for the title together with the Second Division champions. The other seven teams play off to avoid relegation together with the Second Division runners-up. Figures in brackets indicate points carried over from First Phase.

minutes, but in the second half, after taking the lead with a debatable penalty, they began to play to the gallery. Davor Suker, so ineffective against Turkey, suddenly looked like the world-class player who had top-scored in the qualifying competition. His audacious lob from the halfway line and brilliant late chip to make it 3-0 capped the individual performance of the tournament. With two wins, Croatia were the first team to reach the quarter-finals. But it was then that things began to go wrong.

Coach Blazevic, who had boldly proclaimed in the build-up to the tournament that Croatia had the best players in the world and would win Euro '96, suddenly found himself caught up in his own hype. In the last group match, against Portugal, he bizarrely chose to rest eight first-choice players, among them skipper Boban and crowd-pleaser Suker.

The decision blew up in his face. Portugal ran out easy 3-0 winners to take first place in the group, leaving Croatia to face favourites Germany, rather than the Czech Republic, in the quarter-final.

Blazevic maintained his stiff upper lip, claiming that Germany were the opponents he had wished for. In the event, Croatia did play well enough to defeat Berti Vogts' team, but two crucial individual errors (Jerkan's needless handball which presented Germany with a penalty; Stimac's rush of blood that brought him a red card) undid all the rest of the team's good work, and with their second defeat on the trot, Croatia went out.

The more level-headed of Croatian pundits had stated before the tournament that reaching the quarter-finals

NATIONAL TEAM APPEARANCES 95/96

Coach - Miroslav BLAZEVIC	EST	ITA	SLO	POL	KOR	ISR	HUN	ENG	IRL	TUR	DEN	POR	GER	Cps	Gls
Drazen LADIC (01/01/63) - Croatia Zagreb	G30	G	G	G46	G87				s46	G	G		G	26	-
Mladen MLADENOVIC (13/09/64) - SV Casino Salzburg (AUT)/Gamba Osaka (JPN)	D	D	s65					s76			s88	M46	s78	19	3
Igor STIMAC (06/09/67) - Hajduk Split/Derby County (ENG)	D83	D			D72	D77		D57	D	D	D		D	20	2
Nikola JERKAN (08/12/64) - Real Oviedo (ESP)	D	D	D	D46	D64		D	D	D	D	D		D	23	1
Slaven BILIC (11/09/68) - Karlsruher SC (GER)/West Ham (ENG)	D75		D		D	D	D46	D	D	D	D	D	D	25	-
Robert JARNI (26/10/68) - Real Betis (ESP)	D		D	D59	M			D	M	M	M	M	M	24	-
Mario STANIC (10/04/72) - Club Brugge KV (BEL)	M	M	M	A61	M79		M	s46	M80	M	M		M	11	1
Zvonimir BOBAN (08/10/68) - Milan (ITA)	M	M		M				M46	M	M48	M82	s46	M	21	4
Robert PROSINECKI (12/01/69) - FC Barcelona (ESP)	M		M	M		M65		M		M	M88	M46		16	3
Davor SUKER (01/01/68) - Sevilla FC (ESP)	A	A	A		A		A	A	A	A89	A	s46	A	23	21
Alen BOKSIC (21/01/70) - Lazio (ITA)	A	A						A71	A	A72				14	1
Marijan MRMIC (06/05/65) - Varteks Varazdin	s30						G	G	G46			G		6	-
Nenad PRALIJA (11/12/70) - Hajduk Split	s75		M65	s59	s64	s65								6	-
Dzevad TURKOVIC (17/08/72) - Croatia Zagreb	s83													6	-
Dubravko PAVLICIC (28/11/67) - Hércules CF (ESP)		D		s46		s46	D	D76		s89		D		18	-
Aljosa ASANOVIC (14/12/65) - Real Valladolid (ESP)/Hajduk Split		M		M81	M	M		M	M	M	M	s46	M	23	1
Nikola JURCEVIC (14/09/66) - SV Casino Salzburg (AUT)/SC Freiburg (GER)		D46	D	A46	M76	M74			s72		s82	M	M78	17	2
Ardijan KOZNIKU (27/10/67) - AS Cannes (FRA)		s46												4	1
Zvonimir SOLDO (02/11/67) - Croatia Zagreb			D	D	D	D		s57	s80	s48	s82	D		14	-
Ivica MOLNAR (12/01/74) - Eintracht Frankfurt (GER)			A		s76	s74	M							6	-
Danijel STEFULJ (02/06/73) - Croatia Zagreb				D			s76							2	-
Elvis BRAJKOVIC (12/06/69) - TSV 1860 München (GER)				D		D46	M							8	2
Tonci GABRIC (11/03/61) - Hajduk Split				s46	s87	G46								7	-
Goran VLAOVIC (07/08/72) - Padova (ITA)				s46	A83	A			A72	s72	A82	A	A	12	5
Igor CVITANOVIC (01/11/70) - Croatia Zagreb				s61	s79	s46	A71							10	3
Tomislav RUKAVINA (14/10/74) - Croatia Zagreb				s81										1	-
Dario SIMIC (12/11/75) - Croatia Zagreb					s72	s77						D		3	-
Milan RAPAIC (16/08/73) - Hajduk Split					s83	M46								3	-
Robert SPEHAR (13/05/70) - Club Brugge KV (BEL)						M46								6	-
Zeljko PAVLOVIC (02/03/71) - Zagreb						s46								1	-
Andrija BALAJIC (22/08/72) - Varteks Varazdin						s46	M							2	-
Igor PAMIC (19/11/69) - Osijek							A76	s71				A46		3	1
Miroslav BICANIC (29/10/69) - Osijek							s46							2	1
Davor VUGRINEC (24/03/75) - Varteks Varazdin							s71							1	-

would be considered a sound and satisfactory performance. But the afterthought was that the team had it in them to go further, perhaps even win the competition, as Blazevic had predicted.

Several Croatian players - notably Suker, Asanovic, Jarni and Jurcevic - emerged from the tournament with their reputations enhanced, but the coach himself returned home to a hailstorm of criticism. It was generally felt that his complacency against Portugal had needlessly undermined the team's confidence and stalled their challenge just as it had got going in the second half against Denmark. Blazevic looked set to quit, but having previously renewed his contract until 1998 and with his friends in high places - notably state president Franjo Tudjman - urging him to carry on, he remained in place as the new season approached.

It is said by some that nothing happens in Croatian football without the authorisation and approval of President Tudjman. The sacking of national team assistant Tomislav Ivic a few months before Euro '96 was viewed by many to be a 'decision from the very top' after Ivic had spoken out critically against Blazevic.

As well as projecting himself as the most ardent supporter of the national side, Tudjman is a keen follower of the club side Croatia Zagreb. Inevitably, in a country that is rife with chaos and corruption, this open favouritism by the man in power has led to accusations that Croatia Zagreb from time to time receive a helping hand from 'mysterious sources'.

With football widely recognised to be the drug of the masses in Croatia, many politicians have cottoned onto its appeal, using the game as a tool for wielding influence and boosting their own personal ambition. The constant manipulation of the domestic league structure is a case in point. Every year since the country became independent

INTERNATIONAL HONOURS

European Championship appearances: 1996 (qtr-finals)
Fairs' Cup - (1) Dinamo Zagreb (1967)

DOMESTIC CUP RESULTS

1/16 FINALS
Hrvatski dragovoljac Zagreb v Zadar 2-0; 0-3
(Zadar 3-2)
MIV Sracinec v Croatia Zagreb 0-11; 1-10
(Croatia Zagreb 21-1)
Cakovec Union v Cibalia Vinkovci 3-1; 0-2
(3-3; Cibalia Vinkovci on away goal)
Sibenik v Granicar Zupanja 6-1; 2-0
(Sibenik 8-1)
Marsonia Slavonski Brod v Istra Pula 3-0; 1-0
(Marsonia Slavonski Brod 4-0)
Neretva Metkovic v Bjelovar 4-1; 0-2
(Neretva Metkovic 4-3)
PIK Vrbovec v Inker Zapresic 0-3; 0-7
(Inker Zapresic 10-0)
Pomorac Kostrena v Hajduk Split 0-2; 1-1
(Hajduk Split 3-1)
Rovinj v Belisce 0-5; 0-7
(Belisce 12-0)
Slaven Belupo Koprivnica v Croatia Djakovo 1-0; 0-1
(1-1; Slaven Belupo Koprivnica 5-3 on pens.)
Varteks Varazdin v Jedinstvo Donji Miholjac 5-0; 4-0
(Varteks Varazdin 9-0)
Napredak Velika Mlaka v Zagreb 0-5; 0-9
(Zagreb 14-0)
Segesta Sisak v Karlovac 2-0; 7-0
(Segesta Sisak 9-0)
Nehaj Senj v Rijeka 1-5; 1-3
(Rijeka 8-2)
Djakovo v Dubrovnik 2-3; 0-5
(Dubrovnik 8-2)
Rastane v Osijek 1-7; 0-3
(Osijek 10-1)

1/8 FINALS
Dubrovnik v Zadar 1-2; 0-2
(Zadar 4-1)
Marsonia Slavonski Brod v Hajduk Split 1-0; 0-1
(1-1; Marsonia Slavonski Brod 4-2 on pens.)
Sibenik v Varteks Varazdin 1-1; 0-4
(Varteks Varazdin 5-1)
Neretva Metkovic v Inker Zapresic 1-1; 2-3
(Inker Zapresic 4-3)
Belisce v Croatia Zagreb 2-2; 1-6
(Croatia Zagreb 8-3)
Slaven Belupo Koprivnica v Rijeka 1-1; 0-1
(Rijeka 2-1)
Cibalia Vinkovci v Osijek 1-0; 0-4
(Osijek 4-1)
Segesta Sisak v Zagreb 2-0; 1-4
(Zagreb 4-3)

QUARTER-FINALS
Zagreb v Rijeka 5-0; 2-0
(Zagreb 7-0)
Zadar v Inker Zapresic 1-0; 0-0
(Zadar 1-0)
Varteks Varazdin v Osijek 4-1; 0-0
(Varteks Varazdin 4-1)
Marsonia Slavonski Brod v Croatia Zagreb 0-5; 0-5
(Croatia Zagreb 10-0)

SEMI-FINALS
Zadar v Croatia Zagreb 1-3; 1-2
(Croatia Zagreb 5-2)
Zagreb v Varteks Varazdin 1-2; 0-3
(Varteks Varazdin 5-1)

FINAL
01/05/96, Varazdin
VARTEKS VARAZDIN 0
CROATIA ZAGREB 2 Viduka (8), Cvitanovic I. (12)
referee - Kulusic
VARTEKS VARAZDIN - Mrmic; Toplak, Bancic (Mumlek 46), Madunovic (Paska 75), Kovac, Tezacki (Durakovic 46), Posavec, Besek, Vugrinec, Brlenic, Balajic.
CROATIA ZAGREB - Ladic; Stefulj, Krznar, Simic, Soldo, Mladinic, Cvitanovic I. (Maric 89), Viduka (Sliskovic 46), Mamic, Mlinaric (Saric 76), Rukavina.

16/05/96, Zagreb
CROATIA ZAGREB 1 Cvitanovic I. (60p)
VARTEKS VARAZDIN 0
referee - Kulusic
CROATIA ZAGREB - Ladic; Stefulj, Krznar, Simic, Soldo, Mamic (Petrovic 46), Gaspar, Rukavina, Viduka (Sliskovic 87), Mlinaric (Mujcin 27), Cvitanovic I..
VARTEKS VARAZDIN - Mrmic; Toplak, Madunovic (Bancic 76), Dalic (Tezacki 82), Kovac, Posavec, Gregoric, Mumlek (Ivankovic 64), Vugrinec, Brlenic, Balajic.
(CROATIA ZAGREB 3-0)

the format for the First Division has been modified. Political intervention and local vested interests are invariably the chief motivation behind this, with the effect the changes might have on the actual quality or appeal of the football ranking a distant second.

In 1995/96 a complicated new system was introduced in which the league was played in two separate halves. The top five from the original 12-team First Division were joined by the Second Division champions in a six-team play-off for the title, with bonus points being carried forward. The experiment lasted only one year. It was agreed by Croatian FA officials that starting in 1996/97, and lasting for at least four seasons, a new 10-team top division would be set up, with the teams each playing one another four times (as in Austria and Scotland).

But then in stepped the political movers and shakers. With just a few weeks to go before the 96/97 campaign got underway, the officials' hands were forced and Croatian football once again had a 16-team First Division, with the four 'relegated' teams plus the third and fourth-placed teams in the Second Division all being called back into the fray at the eleventh hour.

It has been proved in the past that a 16-team league is too big and unmanageable for a country as small and economically fragile as Croatia. Virtually all of the football clubs in the country have big financial problems. Attendances are poor and so is the general quality of the play. Every year, in summer and winter, scores of the country's best players quit Croatia for better deals abroad. In the 1996 close season another 31 players joined the exodus (eight to Germany, four to Spain, three to Israel and Austria, two to France, Portugal and Italy, one each to England, Turkey, Japan, China, Denmark, Switzerland and the Czech Republic). Croatia is proud that it consistently produces highly talented footballers, but there is little satisfaction gained by the fact that the country presently exports more players than any other nation in Europe.

Inevitably, the teams which do most of the foreign trading are Hajduk Split and Croatia Zagreb. Hajduk, the national champions in 93/94 and 94/95, were forced to offload several of their top players after failing to reach the group stages of the Champions' League. Their away-goals defeat by Panathinaikos was a real budget-wrecker, and in the weeks that followed three Croatian internationals - Aljosa Asanovic, Ivica Mornar and Igor Stimac - all left for foreign clubs.

In any normal season Hajduk's subsequent loss of form in the league (three defeats and two draws in a seven-game spell) would have seriously dented their title prospects. At the winter break they trailed leaders Croatia Zagreb by six points and at the 22-match cut-off point the deficit was five. But the new system meant that Hajduk

PLAYERS OF THE SEASON

NENAD PRALIJA

Despite being voted the best player in Croatia by the First Division coaches, Nenad Pralija did not make it into his country's European Championship squad. Most people found coach Blazevic's decision to exclude the Hajduk Split midfielder hard to believe. He had been involved in most of the build-up to the tournament and he had been in tremendous form for his club, scoring a career-best 17 goals, most of them decisive, to lift Hajduk into the championship frame. A tireless runner, good in one-to-one situations and with an instinctive eye for goal, the 26-year-old is a sound investment for Spanish side Espanyol, who bought him from Hajduk in the summer.

IGOR CVITANOVIC

The top scorer prize in the 1995/96 Croatian First Division went to Croatia Zagreb striker Igor Cvitanovic. In itself the award was not a surprise. After all, Cvitanovic had scored more goals in the Croatian league than any other player - 79 in five seasons. But the fact that he did not find the target until his club's 11th match of the season showed just how dramatically he discovered his shooting boots in the second half of the campaign. Ten goals came in Croatia Zagreb's last six games, and he also scored in both legs of the Cup final triumph against Varteks Varazdin. His form merited a place in Croatia's Euro '96 squad, allowing him to return to England where he had hoped, at the start of the season, to join Middlesbrough in a £1m deal.

MARIO STANIC

Fans of Belgian side Club Bruges must have found it bizarre to watch Croatia at Euro '96 and see their star striker playing at right-back. Considering that he was being played out of position, Mario Stanic had an impressive championship. The presence of Suker, Boksic and Vlaovic denied him a place up front, but he looked wholly at ease charging up and down the right touchline. He clearly came to England full of confidence after a brilliant first season in Belgium, where he helped Bruges to the 'double', top scoring with 20 goals in the league and striking both goals in the Cup final victory over Cercle Bruges. A predictable nickname it may be, but in Belgium they don't call him 'SuperMario' for nothing.

began the Final Round just a point behind the leaders. So, while the first phase of the season was rendered pretty academic, the final 10-match series, involving Croatia, Hajduk, Osijek, Varteks Varazdin, Zagreb and Division Two winners Hrvatski dragovljac, promised to be tight, competitive and eventful.

The race for the title soon developed into a three-way tussle between the Big Two and the surprise team of the season, Varteks. Inspired by the brilliant performances of their U-21 international striker Davor Vugrinec, Varteks looked poised to upset the established hierarchy and win a first major honour. They won both of their home games against Croatia and Hajduk and then really set the cat among the pigeons by beating Croatia 4-3 away (with a double from Vugrinec). An injury-time winner against Osijek in their next game put Varteks on top of the table, and they were still there a week later, with just one match to go - despite the setback of losing 0-2 at home to Croatia in the first leg of the Cup final.

It all came down to the final Sunday of the season. Varteks were a point ahead of both Croatia and Hajduk, but their last match was away to Hajduk, while Croatia had an easy match away to bottom club Zagreb. All three clubs were in a position to take the title.

That was the theory. In practice, however, there was an air of inevitability about the final outcome. Croatia were untroubled by their lame city rivals and won 3-1. Hajduk, allegedly offered a financial incentive from an unknown source to play 'clean' and with 'maximum effort', duly beat Varteks 1-0. The title, therefore, went to Croatia Zagreb.

They were level on points with Hajduk, but they had the better record in the matches between them (4-1; 2-3) and that proved decisive.

Four days later Croatia completed the 'double', beating Varteks 1-0 (and 3-0 on aggregate) in a Cup final second leg which was memorable only for some shameful officiating by referee Ante Kulusic, who had hardly distinguished himself in the first leg either. So, for Varteks, sadly, there was nothing to show for an exceptional season. The spoils had all gone to Zlatko Kranjcar's Croatia Zagreb. Neutrals everywhere were disappointed. But President Tudjman could not have been happier.

EUROPEAN CUPS RESULTS 95/96

CHAMPIONS' CUP

● HAJDUK SPLIT

Preliminary round PANATHINAIKOS (GRE)

A 0-0
Gabric; Butorovic, Jozinovic, Hibic, Stimac, Horvat, Vulic K., Pralija, Rapaic (Mestrovic 82), Asanovic, Mornar (Sarr 74).

H 1-1 Stimac (4)
Gabric; Butorovic, Jozinovic, Hibic, Stimac, Horvat, Vulic K. (Mestrovic 15), Pralija, Jurcec (Sarr 68), Asanovic, Mornar.

UEFA CUP

● OSIJEK

Preliminary round SLOVAN BRATISLAVA (SVK)

A 0-4
Zitnjak; Beljan (Popescu 74), Besirevic, Zgrablic, Lulic, Simunec, Osmanagic (Krpan 46), Bicanic, Labak, Pamic (Kulesevic 84), Vranjes.

H 0-2
Peric; Beljan, Besirevic, Vranjes (Plavsic 46), Lulic, Simunec, Osmanagic (Labak 46), Bicanic, Krpan, Pamic (Sunara 75), Popescu.

NATIONAL TEAM RESULTS 95/96

03/09/95	Estonia (ECQ)	H	Zagreb	7-1	Mladenovic (3), Suker (19p, 58, 89), Boksic (29), Boban (42), Stimac (82)
08/10/95	Italy (ECQ)	H	Split	1-1	Suker (49p)
15/11/95	Slovenia (ECQ)	A	Ljubljana	2-1	Suker (40p), Jurcevic (55)
28/02/96	Poland	H	Rijeka	2-1	Brajkovic (24), Cvitanovic (89)
13/03/96	South Korea	H	Zagreb	3-0	Vlaovic (23, 43, 63)
26/03/96	Israel	H	Varazdin	2-0	Stimac (74), Vlaovic (76)
10/04/96	Hungary	H	Osijek	4-1	Brajkovic (6), Suker (23), Pamic (65), Stanic (75)
24/04/96	England	A	Wembley	0-0	
02/06/96	Republic of Ireland	A	Dublin	2-2	Suker (4), Boban (45)
11/06/96	Turkey (ECF)	N	Nottingham	1-0	Vlaovic (85)
16/06/96	Denmark (ECF)	N	Sheffield	3-0	Suker (53p, 89), Boban (80)
19/06/96	Portugal (ECF)	N	Nottingham	0-3	
23/06/96	Germany (ECF)	N	Manchester	1-2	Suker (51)

TOP SCORERS

19	Igor CVITANOVIC (Croatia Zagreb)
17	Nenad PRALIJA (Hajduk Split)
	Igor PAMIC (Osijek)
	Davor VUGRINEC (Varteks Varazdin)
16	Hari VUKAS (Segesta Sisak)
15	Senad BRKIC (Rijeka)
12	Mark VIDUKA (Croatia Zagreb)
	Renato JURCEC (Hajduk Split)
	Vladimir PETROVIC (Segesta Sisak)
11	Elvis SCORIA (Istra Pula)
	Mate BATURINA (Sibenik)

CIBALIA VINKOVCI

CLUB DIRECTORY

HNK Cibalia Vinovci
Ruzina ulica 13
56 000 Vinkovci
tel - (032) 332364
fax - (032) 332364
Year of Formation - 1919
President - Bozo Galic
Director - Stjepan Bogdan
Coach - Tomislav Radic; Mile Petkovic
Stadium - Mladost (15,000)

APPEARANCES 95/96

	P	Ap	(s)	Gls
Ernad ADZULOVIC	M	1		
Antun ANDRICEVIC	D	11	(4)	
Dinko BESLIC	M	24	(6)	
Zlatko BIJELIC	D	5		1
Danijel BOGDAN	D	30		3
Miroslav BOJKO	M	14	(6)	1
Goran BRKIC	M	11		2
Darko CVIJANOVIC	M	9	(1)	2
Slaven DAMJANOVIC	A	23	(8)	5
Mirza GOLUBICA	A	11		5
Mirko GRABOVAC	A	10	(10)	1
Irfan ISLAMI	A	2	(7)	
Zeljko JURKOVIC	A		(9)	
Vladimir KLAIC	D	32		
Zeljko KOBAS	A	2	(10)	2
Drazenko KRMEK	M		(7)	
Rudolf MAJNOVIC	G	11	(2)	
Ivica MARIC	G	18		
Ivo MARINCIC	M	34		4
Goran MESTROVIC	A	30	(1)	6
Gojko MRCELA	G	7		
Drazen PERNAR	D	17	(1)	
Zlatko RAGUZ	D	20		2
Darko RAIC-SUDAR	M	25	(6)	4
Mehmed RIBIC	A	11	(17)	3
Sinisa SESAR	D	4		
Miljenko SEVELJ	M		(1)	
Nevres ZAHIROVIC	D	33		2

LEAGUE RESULTS 1995/96

Date	Opponent	H/A	Score	Scorers
13/08/95	Istra Pula	A	0-0	
20/08/95	Croatia Zagreb	A	0-3	
27/08/95	Rijeka	A	4-4	Raguz, Raic-Sudar 2, Marincic
10/09/95	Osijek	H	2-0	Bogdan, Ribic
13/09/95	Hajduk Split	A	1-4	Damjanovic
17/09/95	Inker Zapresic	H	2-2	Ribic, Zahirovic
20/09/95	Segesta Sisak	A	1-3	Bojko
24/09/95	Zagreb	H	2-1	Damjanovic, Grabovac
01/10/95	Marsonia Slavonski Brod	A	1-2	Raguz
15/10/95	Sibenik	A	1-0	Cvijanovic
22/10/95	Varteks Varazdin	H	1-0	Raic-Sudar
28/10/95	Istra Pula	H	1-1	Kobas
05/11/95	Croatia Zagreb	H	2-2	Bijelic, Kobas
11/11/95	Rijeka	H	1-1	Marincic
19/11/95	Osijek	A	0-4	
26/11/95	Hajduk Split	H	2-4	Cvijanovic (p), Ribic
02/12/95	Inker Zapresic	A	1-1	Mestrovic (p)
10/12/95	Segesta Sisak	H	2-1	Mestrovic, Damjanovic
17/12/95	Zagreb	A	0-0	
18/02/96	Marsonia Slavonski Brod	H	0-0	
24/02/96	Sibenik	H	2-1	Mestrovic 2 (1p)
02/03/96	Varteks Varazdin	A	0-3	
PLAY-OFFS				
09/03/96	Inker Zapresic	A	0-3	
17/03/96	Mladost 127 Suhopolje	A	1-2	Damjanovic
24/03/96	Rijeka	H	2-2	Bogdan, Raic-Sudar
31/03/96	Segesta Sisak	A	1-2	Golubica
08/04/96	Istra Pula	H	1-0	Mestrovic (p)
14/04/96	Sibenik	A	0-1	
21/04/96	Marsonia Slavonski Brod	H	2-1	Golubica, Bogdan
24/04/96	Inker Zapresic	H	0-0	
28/04/96	Mladost 127 Suhopolje	H	2-1	Golubica (p), Damjanovic
05/05/96	Rijeka	A	0-2	
12/05/96	Segesta Sisak	H	4-1	Marincic, Mestrovic, Brkic, Zahirovic (p)
19/05/96	Istra Pula	A	0-1	
22/05/96	Sibenik	H	3-1	Brkic, Golubica 2 (1p)
26/05/96	Marsonia Slavonski Brod	A	1-1	Marincic

CROATIA ZAGREB

CLUB DIRECTORY

NK Croatia Zagreb
Maksimirska 128
41 000 Zagreb
tel - (041) 2334111
fax - (041) 212316
Year of Formation - 1945
President - Martin Katicic
Director - Zdenko Mahmet
Coach - Zlatko Kranjcar (96/97 - Otto Baric)
Stadium - Maksimir (56,555)

MAJOR HONOURS
League Championship - (2) 1993, 1996.
Domestic Cup - (2) 1994, 1996.
League Championship (Yugoslavia) - (4) 1948, 1954, 1958, 1982.
Domestic Cup (Yugoslavia) - (8) 1951, 1960, 1963, 1965, 1969, 1973, 1980, 1983.
Fairs' Cup - (1) 1967.

APPEARANCES 95/96

	P	Ap	(s)	Gls
Igor CVITANOVIC	A	23		19
Mario CVITANOVIC	D	3	(1)	
Josip GASPAR	M	26	(2)	3
Mirza GOLUBICA	A		(1)	
Miralem IBRAHIMOVIC (BOS)	G	10		
Josko JELICIC	M	11		5
Domagoj KOSIC	M	2	(7)	1
Miljenko KOVACIC	A	4	(12)	4
Damir KRZNAR	D	27		2
Drazen LADIC	G	22		
Zoran MAMIC	M	20	(6)	5
Silvio MARIC	A	14	(7)	3
Srdjan MLADINIC	D	27		2
Marko MLINARIC	M	21	(2)	2
Edin MUJCIN	M	2	(8)	1
Alen PETROVIC	M	14	(10)	3
Dalibor POLDRUGAC	M		(1)	
Kresimir RADIC	M		(2)	
Tomislav RUKAVINA	M	11		
Danijel SARIC	M	3	(1)	
Dario SIMIC	D	25	(1)	2
Zoran SLISKOVIC	A	7	(13)	3
Zvonimir SOLDO	D	24		2
Danijel STEFULJ	D	11		2
Stjepan TOMAS	D	2	(5)	
Dzevad TURKOVIC	D	20	(4)	2
Mark VIDUKA (AUS)	A	23	(4)	12

LEAGUE RESULTS 1995/96

Date	Opponent	H/A	Score	Scorers
13/08/95	Marsonia Slavonski Brod	H	5-0	Kovacic, Petrovic 2, Turkovic, Maric
20/08/95	Cibalia Vinkovci	H	3-0	Turkovic, Simic, Kosic
27/08/95	Varteks Varazdin	H	2-0	Jelicic, Gaspar
10/09/95	Istra Pula	A	0-1	
13/09/95	Sibenik	H	2-1	Jelicic 2 (1p)
17/09/95	Rijeka	H	2-0	Maric, Kovacic
20/09/95	Osijek	A	2-1	Maric, Krznar
24/09/95	Hajduk Split	H	1-0	Viduka
30/09/95	Inker Zapresic	A	1-1	Kovacic
15/10/95	Segesta Sisak	H	4-0	Viduka 3 (1p), Sliskovic
22/10/95	Zagreb	A	3-1	Viduka, Sliskovic, Cvitanovic I.
28/10/95	Marsonia Slavonski Brod	A	3-0	Mamic, Jelicic, Cvitanovic I.
05/11/95	Cibalia Vinkovci	A	2-2	Mamic, Jelicic (p)
11/11/95	Varteks Varazdin	A	1-1	Cvitanovic I. (p)
19/11/95	Istra Pula	H	4-0	Cvitanovic I. 4 (1p)
26/11/95	Sibenik	A	0-0	
03/12/95	Rijeka	A	1-1	Soldo
10/12/95	Osijek	H	2-0	Viduka, Cvitanovic I.
17/12/95	Hajduk Split	A	1-2	Petrovic
18/02/96	Inker Zapresic	H	5-1	og (Ferencina), Viduka 2, Krznar, Kovacic
25/02/96	Segesta Sisak	A	0-1	
03/03/96	Zagreb	H	2-0	Stefulj, Cvitanovic I.
PLAY-OFFS				
10/03/96	Osijek	H	2-1	Sliskovic, Mujcin
16/03/96	Varteks Varazdin	A	0-2	
24/03/96	Hajduk Split	H	4-1	Gaspar, Mlinaric, Viduka, Mladinic
30/03/96	Hrvatski dragovoljac Zagreb	A	1-0	Mamic
07/04/96	Zagreb	H	5-1	Viduka, Mamic, Gaspar, Mlinaric, Cvitanovic I.
14/04/96	Osijek	A	2-1	Cvitanovic I. 2
21/04/96	Varteks Varazdin	H	3-4	Viduka 2 (1p), Cvitanovic I.
28/04/96	Hajduk Split	A	2-3	Cvitanovic I., Mladinic
05/05/96	Hrvatski dragovoljac Zagreb	H	6-0	Mamic, Soldo, Simic, Cvitanovic I. 3
12/05/96	Zagreb	A	3-1	Cvitanovic I. 2 (1p), Stefulj

HAJDUK SPLIT

CLUB DIRECTORY

HNK Hajduk Split
Poljudsko setaliste bb, 58 000 Split
tel - (021) 341755/355444
fax - (021) 585630
Year of Formation - 1911
President - Nadan Vidosevic
Director - Vedran Rozic
Coach - Ivan Katalinic; Mirko Jozic
(96/97 - Ivan Buljan)
Stadium - Poljud (50,000)

MAJOR HONOURS
League Championship - (3) 1992, 1994, 1995.
Domestic Cup - (2) 1993, 1995.
League Championship (Yugoslavia) - (9) 1927, 1929, 1950, 1952, 1955, 1971, 1974, 1975, 1979.
Domestic Cup (Yugoslavia) - (9) 1967, 1972, 1973, 1974, 1976, 1977, 1984, 1987, 1991.

APPEARANCES 95/96

	P	Ap	(s)	Gls
Aljosa ASANOVIC	M	12		3
Josko BILIC	D	7	(4)	
Marijo BOZIKOVIC	M	1	(4)	
Darko BUTOROVIC	D	16	(3)	2
Niko CEKO	D	11		3
Ivan CUBRETOVIC	D	1		
Ivo CUZZI	M	4	(2)	1
Tonci GABRIC	G	28		
Mirsad HIBIC	D	18		
Steven HORVAT (AUS)	D	29		
Darko JOZINOVIC	D	25	(1)	
Renato JURCEC	A	27	(5)	12
Ivan JURIC	M	17	(7)	2
Vik LALIC	M	7	(2)	1
Ivan LEKO	M	2	(1)	
Mario MESTROVIC	M	21	(7)	3
Ivica MORNAR	A	1		
Arben NUHIU (MAC)	A		(1)	
Nenad PRALIJA	M	25	(1)	17
Denis PUTNIK	D	3		
Milan RAPAIC	A	22	(3)	6
Mass SARR (LIB)	A	14	(10)	9
Josip SKOKO (AUS)	M	8	(6)	1
Igor STIMAC	D	6		
Dragan STOJKIC	G		(1)	
Anthony TOKPAH (LIB)	G	4	(3)	
Igor TUDOR	D	6	(3)	
Robert VLADISLAVIC	D	1		
Jurica VUCKO	A	5	(15)	3
Damir VUICA	D	22	(2)	2
Kazimir VULIC	M	9		

LEAGUE RESULTS 1995/96

13/08/95	Inker Zapresic	H	3-1	Pralija 2, Jurcec
18/08/95	Segesta Sisak	A	1-1	Pralija
27/08/95	Zagreb	H	2-1	Cuzzi, Sarr
10/09/95	Marsonia Slavonski Brod	A	0-0	
13/09/95	Cibalia Vinkovci	H	4-1	Jurcec, Pralija, Sarr 2
17/09/95	Varteks Varazdin	A	3-0	Skoko, Sarr, Vucko
20/09/95	Istra Pula	H	5-0	Jurcec 2, Juric, Sarr, Butorovic
24/09/95	Croatia Zagreb	A	0-1	
01/10/95	Rijeka	H	1-0	Pralija
15/10/95	Osijek	A	3-5	Pralija 2, Jurcec
22/10/95	Sibenik	H	0-0	
28/10/95	Inker Zapresic	A	0-0	
05/11/95	Segesta Sisak	H	3-1	Pralija, Jurcec, Lalic
11/11/95	Zagreb	A	1-2	Pralija
19/11/95	Marsonia Slavonski Brod	H	3-0	Sarr 2, Mestrovic
26/11/95	Cibalia Vinkovci	A	4-2	Sarr 2, Pralija, Rapaic
03/12/95	Varteks Varazdin	H	0-0	
10/12/95	Istra Pula	A	1-3	Vucko
17/12/95	Croatia Zagreb	H	2-1	Jurcec, Pralija
17/02/96	Rijeka	A	3-0	Jurcec, Rapaic 2
25/02/96	Osijek	H	2-0	Asanovic, Jurcec (p)
03/03/96	Sibenik	A	0-0	
PLAY-OFFS				
10/03/96	Zagreb	H	2-1	Jurcec, Rapaic
17/03/96	Hrvatski dragovoljac Zagreb	H	5-1	Asanovic, Pralija 2, Vuica, Ceko
24/03/96	Croatia Zagreb	A	1-4	Asanovic (p)
31/03/96	Osijek	H	2-0	Pralija, Mestrovic
07/04/96	Varteks Varazdin	A	0-1	
14/04/96	Zagreb	A	6-1	Rapaic, Butorovic, Jurcec 2, og (Zupanec), Vucko
20/04/96	Hrvatski dragovoljac Zagreb	A	2-2	Vuica, Ceko
28/04/96	Croatia Zagreb	H	3-2	Rapaic, Pralija, Ceko
05/05/96	Osijek	A	3-2	Pralija 2, Juric
12/05/96	Varteks Varazdin	H	1-0	Mestrovic

HRVATSKI DRAGOVOLJAC ZAGREB

CLUB DIRECTORY

Hrvatski dragovoljac Zagreb
Aleja pomoraca 17-19
10 000 Zagreb
tel - (01) 6553306
fax - (01) 526542
Year of Formation - 1975
President - Stjepan Spajic
Director - Ivica Perkovic
Coach - Rajko Magic; Branko Tucak
(96/97 - Ivo Susak)
Stadium - Siget (4,000)

APPEARANCES 95/96

	P	Ap	(s)	Gls
Zeljko ADZIC	M	3	(2)	1
Ivica ANTOLIC	D	3		
Mario BAZINA	M	1	(6)	
Bozidar CACIC	D	1	(2)	
Sladjan FILIPOVIC	A	4	(4)	
Ante HRGOVIC	M	3	(5)	
Anto JAKOVLJEVIC	G		(1)	
Goran JURIC	D	9		
Predrag JURIC	A	10		2
Neno KATULIC	A	8	(1)	1
Domagoj KOSIC	M	4	(1)	1
Zoran KUKOC	M	7	(1)	
Zvonko LIPOVAC	D	7		1
Elvis MARGETA	D	6		2
Mario MATAJA	M	10		
Igor MUSA	D	7	(1)	
Igor PANADIC	G	4		
Anton PRANJIC	M	1	(2)	
Denis SEDLAR	M	1		
Tomislav SITAR	A		(2)	
Blaz SLISKOVIC	M	5		
Stjepan TOMAS	D	10		
Vladimir VASILJ	G	6		

LEAGUE RESULTS 1995/96

PLAY-OFFS

Date	Opponent		Score	Scorers
17/03/96	Hajduk Split	A	1-5	Adzic
20/03/96	Varteks Varazdin	H	0-1	
23/03/96	Zagreb	H	1-2	Margeta
30/03/96	Croatia Zagreb	H	0-1	
07/04/96	Osijek	A	0-3	
13/04/96	Varteks Varazdin	A	1-1	Lipovac
20/04/96	Hajduk Split	H	2-2	Margeta, Katulic
28/04/96	Zagreb	A	1-1	Juric P. (p)
05/05/96	Croatia Zagreb	A	0-6	
12/05/96	Osijek	H	2-1	Juric P., Kosic

INKER ZAPRESIC

CLUB DIRECTORY

NK Inker Zapresic
Vladimira Novaka bb
41 211 Zapresic
tel - (01) 700290/703175/700922
fax - (041) 700466
Year of Formation - 1929
President - Dane Gudelj
Director - Stjepan Tomazin
Coach - Ante Cacic; Miroslav Orsag; Albert Pobor
Stadium - Inker (15,000)

MAJOR HONOURS
Domestic Cup - (1) 1992.

APPEARANCES 95/96

	P	Ap	(s)	Gls
Ivan ABAZA	M	2	(9)	
Sladjan ASANIN	D	33		
Drazen BOBINEC	A	6	(9)	
Zoran BOCH	D	1	(1)	
Mislav BRADVIC	D	2	(2)	
Zvjezdan BRLEK	D	26	(3)	2
Kresimir BRONIC	G	28		
Damir CACIC	D		(1)	
Roy FERENCINA	D	31	(1)	
Dalibor FILIPOVIC	A	10	(2)	4
Goran GERSAK	A	7	(8)	1
Darko HORVAT	G	7		
Davorin KABLAR	A		(2)	
Vjekoslav KNEZ	D	4	(2)	
Ninoslav KORDIC	D	5	(5)	
Mario KUS	M	17	(6)	
Marko LOVRIC	M		(2)	
Kresimir MARUSIC	M	9	(1)	
Darko NEKRET-KATIC	D	29		1
Sinisa ODORJAN	A	25	(2)	7
Mario OSIBOV	D	28	(1)	2
Boris PAVIC	D	26	(2)	1
Nikica PAVLEK	M	6	(4)	
Mico PERANOVIC	M	11	(12)	2
Samir PINJO (BOS)	D	17	(2)	3
Zeljko RUMBAK	G	1	(1)	
Nermin SABIC	M	17		
Ivan TOPIC	A		(2)	
Mario VRBANIC	M	18	(4)	7
Tvrtko VUKOVIC	M	4	(5)	
Tomislav ZITKOVIC	A	26	(6)	7

LEAGUE RESULTS 1995/96

13/08/95	Hajduk Split	A	1-3	Peranovic
20/08/95	Sibenik	A	1-3	Filipovic
26/08/95	Segesta Sisak	H	2-4	Filipovic, Peranovic
10/09/95	Zagreb	A	2-0	Vrbanic, Brlek (p)
13/09/95	Marsonia Slavonski Brod	H	0-2	
17/09/95	Cibalia Vinkovci	A	2-2	Filipovic, Pinjo
20/09/95	Varteks Varazdin	H	0-2	
24/09/95	Istra Pula	A	1-0	Nekret-Katic
30/09/95	Croatia Zagreb	H	1-1	Zitkovic
15/10/95	Rijeka	A	4-4	Odorjan 3, Gersak
21/10/95	Osijek	H	0-3	
28/10/95	Hajduk Split	H	0-0	
04/11/95	Sibenik	H	2-0	Osibov, Filipovic
11/11/95	Segesta Sisak	A	1-0	Odorjan
18/11/95	Zagreb	H	0-1	
26/11/95	Marsonia Slavonski Brod	A	1-0	Zitkovic
02/12/95	Cibalia Vinkovci	H	1-1	Pavic
09/12/95	Varteks Varazdin	A	1-3	Vrbanic
16/12/95	Istra Pula	H	3-2	Pinjo 2, Vrbanic
18/02/96	Croatia Zagreb	A	1-5	og (Simic)
24/02/96	Rijeka	H	3-1	Odorjan (p), Vrbanic 2
03/03/96	Osijek	A	1-1	Zitkovic
PLAY-OFFS				
09/03/96	Cibalia Vinkovci	H	3-0	Zitkovic 3
17/03/96	Rijeka	A	0-2	
23/03/96	Segesta Sisak	H	0-0	
31/03/96	Istra Pula	A	1-2	Vrbanic
07/04/96	Sibenik	H	0-1	
14/04/96	Marsonia Slavonski Brod	A	0-0	
20/04/96	Mladost 127 Suhopolje	H	1-1	Vrbanic
24/04/96	Cibalia Vinkovci	A	0-0	
27/04/96	Rijeka	H	2-0	Odorjan, Zitkovic
05/05/96	Segesta Sisak	A	0-1	
11/05/96	Istra Pula	H	1-1	Osibov
19/05/96	Sibenik	A	0-2	
22/05/96	Marsonia Slavonski Brod	H	1-2	Odorjan
26/05/96	Mladost 127 Suhopolje	A	1-3	Brlek

ISTRA PULA

CLUB DIRECTORY

NK Istra
Premanturska 20
52 000 Pula
tel - (052) 22751/34924
fax - (052) 214558
Year of Formation - 1961
President - Luciano Delbianco
Director - Marinko Sumic
Coach - Srecko Juricic; Ivica Kalinic; Milivoj Bracun
Stadium - Istra (12,000)

APPEARANCES 95/96

	P	Ap	(s)	Gls
Ibel ALEMPIC	D	15	(4)	1
Zaim ALIBASIC	A		(3)	
Stipe BALAJIC	M	31	(1)	2
Ivica BELJAN	D	9		
Hrvoje BISCAN	D	16	(3)	
Kristijan DADIC	D	30		4
Gordan DELUKA	M	5	(4)	
Nereo FATORIC	M	19	(8)	1
Zoran GOSPIC	G	5		
Sandi GUSIC	M	3	(5)	
Vanja IVESA	G	1		
Ilija KLJAJIC	A	2	(1)	
Ljupko KONTESIC	M	9	(7)	
Branko LADJEVIC	A	7	(25)	2
Davor LASIC	M	25		
Edin LOKVANCIC	G	4	(1)	
Tonci MARTIC	M	26	(1)	3
Hrvoje MESTROVIC	A	29		3
Damir PETRAVIC	A	1	(1)	
Sinisa PETROVIC	M	21	(3)	
Mauro PIUTTI	D	12		
Miodrag POPOVIC	D	28		3
Dragan RAKOVIC	M	6	(7)	
Elvis SCORIA	A	32		11
Zvonimir SUNJIC	D	2		
Sandro TOMIC	G	26		
Ognjen UGRCIC	D	24	(4)	
Danijel VIDAIC	A	1	(5)	
Goran VINCETIC	M	7	(13)	
Igor ZIKOVIC	M		(1)	

LEAGUE RESULTS 1995/96

13/08/95	Cibalia Vinkovci	H	0-0	
20/08/95	Varteks Varazdin	A	0-2	
27/08/95	Sibenik	H	2-2	Ladjevic, Alempic
10/09/95	Croatia Zagreb	H	1-0	Scoria
13/09/95	Rijeka	A	0-4	
17/09/95	Osijek	H	0-0	
20/09/95	Hajduk Split	A	0-5	
24/09/95	Inker Zapresic	H	0-1	
01/10/95	Segesta Sisak	A	0-3	
15/10/95	Zagreb	H	1-1	Scoria
22/10/95	Marsonia Slavonski Brod	A	3-0	(w/o)
28/10/95	Cibalia Vinkovci	A	1-1	Mestrovic
05/11/95	Varteks Varazdin	H	1-1	Scoria
11/11/95	Sibenik	A	0-2	
19/11/95	Croatia Zagreb	A	0-4	
26/11/95	Rijeka	H	0-1	
03/12/95	Osijek	A	0-1	
10/12/95	Hajduk Split	H	3-1	Popovic (p), Dadic, Martic
16/12/95	Inker Zapresic	A	2-3	Popovic, Dadic
18/02/96	Segesta Sisak	H	1-3	Balajic
25/02/96	Zagreb	A	1-1	Martic
03/03/96	Marsonia Slavonski Brod	H	0-0	
PLAY-OFFS				
17/03/96	Sibenik	H	2-0	Dadic, Scoria
20/03/96	Mladost 127 Suhopolje	H	1-0	Popovic (p)
24/03/96	Marsonia Slavonski Brod	A	1-1	Mestrovic
31/03/96	Inker Zapresic	H	2-1	Scoria 2
08/04/96	Cibalia Vinkovci	A	0-1	
14/04/96	Rijeka	H	1-0	Fatoric
21/04/96	Segesta Sisak	A	1-4	Mestrovic
24/04/96	Mladost 127 Suhopolje	A	1-3	Scoria
28/04/96	Sibenik	A	0-1	
05/05/96	Marsonia Slavonski Brod	H	4-1	Scoria 2, Dadic, Ladjevic
11/05/96	Inker Zapresic	A	1-1	Balajic
19/05/96	Cibalia Vinkovci	H	1-0	Martic
22/05/96	Rijeka	A	1-4	Scoria (p)
26/05/96	Segesta Sisak	H	1-0	Scoria

MARSONIA SLAVONSKI BROD

CLUB DIRECTORY

NK Marsonia Slavonski Brod
Brace Radica 26
55 000 Slavonski Brod
tel - (035) 231153
fax - (035) 231153
Year of Formation - 1909
President - Ivan Balen
Director - Tomislav Babic
Coach - Dragutin Krizmanic; Ivo Susak; Miroslav Buljan
Stadium - Marsonia (15,000)

APPEARANCES 95/96

	P	Ap	(s)	Gls
Ivica ANTOLIC	D	8		
Zeljko BOGADI	M	15	(8)	1
Damir BOGNAR	A	8		3
Zeljko BRKIC	D	18	(1)	
Mile BULE	D	1	(2)	
Kresimir CIVRAG	D		(2)	
Pavo CRNAC	D	28		2
Slaven CUCEK	A	12	(3)	1
Nenad DZIDIC (BOS)	G	27		
Mario JOZIC	G	2		
Veldin KARIC	A	11	(1)	6
Damir KASUMOVIC	D	33		2
Igor KOVACEVIC	A	5	(23)	1
Robert KOVACIC	M		(3)	
Josip LONCAREVIC	A	10	(13)	
Anto MAJSTORIC	M	27	(2)	2
Damir MATAJCIC	D		(1)	
Damir MATIJASEVIC	A	2	(5)	
Edin MUJCIN (BOS)	M	17		
Zemir MUJCIN (BOS)	M	28	(1)	
Emir MUSIC	A	1		
Zvonko NEDIC	A	3	(10)	
Tomislav PISACIC	D	7	(4)	
Anton PRANJIC	M	5		
Dinko ROSANDIC	D	2	(6)	
Mladen RUDONJA	A	13	(1)	1
Emanuele SACKEY (GHA)	A		(2)	
Mate SESTAN	A	15		3
Stjepan SIMIC	G	7		
Tomislav STEINBRÜCKNER	M	25	(1)	2
Boris ZIVKOVIC	D	31		1
Zoran ZIVKOVIC	D	10		
Nenad ZORIC	D	25		1

LEAGUE RESULTS 1995/96

13/08/95	Croatia Zagreb	A	0-5	
20/08/95	Rijeka	H	0-1	
27/08/95	Osijek	A	2-0	Karic 2 (1p)
10/09/95	Hajduk Split	H	0-0	
13/09/95	Inker Zapresic	A	2-0	Karic 2
17/09/95	Segesta Sisak	H	3-1	Kasumovic, Zivkovic B., Karic
20/09/95	Zagreb	A	0-1	
24/09/95	Sibenik	A	0-4	
01/10/95	Cibalia Vinkovci	H	2-1	Majstoric, Karic
15/10/95	Varteks Varazdin	A	0-2	
22/10/95	Istra Pula	H	0-3	(w/o)
28/10/95	Croatia Zagreb	H	0-3	
05/11/95	Rijeka	A	1-0	Kasumovic
11/11/95	Osijek	H	0-2	
19/11/95	Hajduk Split	A	0-3	
26/11/95	Inker Zapresic	H	0-1	
03/12/95	Segesta Sisak	A	0-2	
10/12/95	Zagreb	H	1-2	Majstoric
17/12/95	Sibenik	H	2-0	Steinbrückner 2 (1p)
18/02/96	Cibalia Vinkovci	A	0-0	
25/02/96	Varteks Varazdin	H	1-2	Rudonja
03/03/96	Istra Pula	A	0-0	
PLAY-OFFS				
10/03/96	Rijeka	H	1-0	Sestan
17/03/96	Segesta Sisak	A	1-2	Zoric
24/03/96	Istra Pula	H	1-1	Kovacevic
31/03/96	Sibenik	A	0-1	
08/04/96	Mladost 127 Suhopolje	H	0-3	(w/o)
14/04/96	Inker Zapresic	H	0-0	
21/04/96	Cibalia Vinkovci	A	1-2	Bognar
24/04/96	Rijeka	A	1-2	Bognar
28/04/96	Segesta Sisak	H	0-3	
05/05/96	Istra Pula	A	1-4	Sestan
12/05/96	Sibenik	H	3-2	Bogadi, Bognar, Sestan
19/05/96	Mladost 127 Suhopolje	A	0-4	
22/05/96	Inker Zapresic	A	2-1	Cucek, Crnac
26/05/96	Cibalia Vinkovci	H	1-1	Crnac

MLADOST 127 SUHOPOLJE

CLUB DIRECTORY

Mladost 127
Vukovarska ulica 6
33 410 Suhopolje
tel - (033) 771727
fax - (033) 771046
President - Djuro Decak
Director - Mijo Fett
Coach - Tonko Vukusic
Stadium - Mladost (5,500)

LEAGUE RESULTS 1995/96

PLAY-OFFS				
17/03/96	Cibalia Vinkovci	H	2-1	Bubek, Lalic
20/03/96	Istra Pula	A	0-1	
24/03/96	Sibenik	A	1-4	Harmat
31/03/96	Rijeka	H	0-0	
08/04/96	Marsonia Slavonski Brod	A	3-0	(w/o)
14/04/96	Segesta Sisak	H	1-0	Lalic
20/04/96	Inker Zapresic	A	1-1	og (Nekret-Katic)
24/04/96	Istra Pula	H	3-1	Juric (p), Harmat, Bubek
28/04/96	Cibalia Vinkovci	A	1-2	Islami
05/05/96	Sibenik	H	2-0	Mrzlecki, Lalic
12/05/96	Rijeka	A	0-2	
19/05/96	Marsonia Slavonski Brod	H	4-0	Loncarevic, Dittrich, Lalic (p), Djidic
22/05/96	Segesta Sisak	A	1-1	Lalic
26/05/96	Inker Zapresic	H	3-1	Bubek, Lalic (p), Matos

APPEARANCES 95/96

	P	Ap	(s)	Gls
Petar BOSNJAK	A	6	(4)	
Stipe BOSNJAK	D	12		
Mladen BUBEK	M	10	(2)	3
Damir DITTRICH	D	13		1
Jasmin DJIDIC	M	2	(3)	1
Ivica FERENCEVIC	D	13		
Mario HARMAT	A	11	(1)	1
Irfan ISLAMI	A	6	(6)	1
Dean JELIC	D	1		
Denis JELIC	D	1		
Jure JURIC	M	13		1
Marin LALIC	M	9	(1)	6
Mladen LONCAR	M		(1)	
Stjepan LONCAREVIC	M	11	(1)	1
Antun MATIJEK	G	12		
Goran MATOS	D	6	(3)	1
Alen MRZLECKI	D	13		1
Zvonko NEDIC	A	3	(3)	
Hrvoje PIPINCIC	M	10	(1)	
Zeljko PSIHISTAL	M		(2)	
Stipe REBIC	G	2		
Zeljko SOSTAR	A		(6)	

OSIJEK

CLUB DIRECTORY

NK Osijek
Wilsonova bb
31 000 Osijek
tel - (031) 141300/141400
fax - (031) 141500
Year of Formation - 1947
President - Antun Novalic
Director - Ante Vucemilovic-Simunovic
Coach - Ivica Matkovic; Ante Cacic; Ivan Katalinic
(96/97 - Goran Popovic)
Stadium - Gradski vrt (30,000)

APPEARANCES 95/96

	P	Ap	(s)	Gls
Davor BAJSIC	M		(1)	
Ivica BELJAN	D	16	(1)	1
Bakir BESIREVIC (BOS)	M	30	(1)	3
Miroslav BICANIC	M	27		4
Ivo ERGOVIC	D	20		1
Mario GALINOVIC	G		(1)	
Anel KARABEG	M	5	(2)	
Petar KRPAN	A	12	(14)	7
Ivica KULESEVIC	D	14	(4)	
Antun LABAK	A	4	(4)	
Mirko LULIC	D	10		
Domagoj MALOVAN	G	5	(2)	
Almin OSMANAGIC (BOS)	M	15	(6)	1
Igor PAMIC	A	25		17
Ilica PERIC	G	25		
Slavko PINTER	A	4	(7)	1
Lucian POPESCU (ROM)	A	23	(7)	2
Krunoslav RENDULIC	D	3	(3)	
Davor RUPNIK	M	19	(1)	1
Nermin SABIC	M	11		1
Ivica SIMUNEC	D	21	(2)	1
Kresimir SUNARA	M	3	(9)	1
Alen SUNDALIC	D		(2)	
Rudika VIDA	A	1	(4)	
Drazen VIDOVIC	D	3	(3)	
Stjepan VRANJES	D	18	(2)	1
Dragan VUKOJA	A	14	(2)	6
Luciano ZGRABLIC	D	22	(5)	
Miroslav ZITNJAK	G	2		

LEAGUE RESULTS 1995/96

Date	Opponent	H/A	Score	Scorers
13/08/95	Segesta Sisak	H	4-0	Pamic 3, Popescu
19/08/95	Zagreb	A	2-0	Krpan, Pamic
27/08/95	Marsonia Slavonski Brod	H	0-2	
10/09/95	Cibalia Vinkovci	A	0-2	
13/09/95	Varteks Varazdin	H	1-0	Pamic
17/09/95	Istra Pula	A	0-0	
20/09/95	Croatia Zagreb	H	1-2	Popescu
24/09/95	Rijeka	A	2-0	Bicanic, Krpan
01/10/95	Sibenik	H	4-1	og (Muriqi), Pamic, Bicanic, Krpan
15/10/95	Hajduk Split	H	5-3	Pamic 3, Vukoja, Vranjes
21/10/95	Inker Zapresic	A	3-0	Krpan, Vukoja, Besirevic
29/10/95	Segesta Sisak	A	4-0	Rupnik, Besirevic, Bicanic, Pamic
05/11/95	Zagreb	H	2-2	Pamic 2
11/11/95	Marsonia Slavonski Brod	A	2-0	Pamic, Vukoja
19/11/95	Cibalia Vinkovci	H	4-0	Vukoja, Simunec, Beljan, Krpan
25/11/95	Varteks Varazdin	A	0-1	
03/12/95	Istra Pula	H	1-0	Vukoja
10/12/95	Croatia Zagreb	A	0-2	
17/12/95	Rijeka	H	1-0	Bicanic
18/02/96	Sibenik	A	1-1	Ergovic
25/02/96	Hajduk Split	A	0-2	
03/03/96	Inker Zapresic	H	1-1	Pamic (p)
PLAY-OFFS				
10/03/96	Croatia Zagreb	A	1-2	Pinter
17/03/96	Zagreb	A	2-0	Pamic, Sunara
24/03/96	Varteks Varazdin	H	1-0	Pamic
31/03/96	Hajduk Split	A	0-2	
07/04/96	Hrvatski dragovoljac Zagreb	H	3-0	Krpan, Besirevic, Osmanagic
14/04/96	Croatia Zagreb	H	1-2	Pamic
21/04/96	Zagreb	H	1-0	og (Vukic)
28/04/96	Varteks Varazdin	A	1-2	Sabic
05/05/96	Hajduk Split	H	2-3	og (Vuica), Krpan
12/05/96	Hrvatski dragovoljac Zagreb	A	1-2	Vukoja

RIJEKA

CLUB DIRECTORY

NK Rijeka
Portic 3, 51 000 Rijeka
tel - (051) 261622/261626/261618
fax - (051) 261174
Year of Formation - 1946
President - Hrvoje Sarinic
Director - Niksa Grabovac
Coach - Marijan Jantoljak; Ranko Buketa; Josip Skoblar; Nenad Gracan (96/97 - Branko Wankovic)
Stadium - Kantrida (21,000)

MAJOR HONOURS

Domestic Cup (Yugoslavia) - (2) 1978, 1979.

APPEARANCES 95/96

	P	Ap	(s)	Gls
Bosko BALABAN	M	2		
Yves BELLE-BELLE (CMR)	A	1	(4)	
Igor BERNOBIC	D	10	(3)	
Ekrem BRADARIC (BOS)	D	5	(2)	
Senad BRKIC (BOS)	A	31		15
Davor DJELALIJA	A	29	(2)	7
Nenad GRACAN	M	9	(1)	1
Admir HASANCIC (BOS)	A	17	(10)	4
Almir HODZIC (BOS)	D	1	(4)	
Alen HORVAT	M	16	(3)	1
Mladen IVANCIC	D	19	(6)	
Irenko JURIC	D	11	(3)	
Renato MARKOVIC	M		(1)	
Damir MILINOVIC	D	31	(1)	3
Dean MLADENIC	G	8	(1)	
Stjepan OSTOJIC	M	15	(6)	
Robert PALISKA	D	1		
Borimir PERKOVIC	M	30		10
Renato PILIPOVIC	M	7	(7)	
Mladen ROMIC	D	9		
Senad ROZAJAC	M		(2)	
Robert RUBCIC	D	5		
Jasmin SAMARDZIC	A	5	(9)	2
Dragan SKOCIC	M	2		
Zoran SLAVICA	G	11		
Dario SMOJE	D	21		1
Mario TOKIC	M	34		1
Vlado TOMLJENOVIC	A	3	(2)	
Damir UREMOVIC	A	2	(6)	
Dalibor VISKOVIC	D	12	(2)	
Robert VLADISLAVIC	A	8		
Mladen ZGANJER	G	17	(1)	
Andrej ZIVKOVIC	M	24	(7)	1

LEAGUE RESULTS 1995/96

13/08/95	Zagreb	H	1-2	Brkic
20/08/95	Marsonia Slavonski Brod	A	1-0	Gracan
27/08/95	Cibalia Vinkovci	H	4-4	Horvat, Brkic 2, Perkovic
10/09/95	Varteks Varazdin	A	1-2	Brkic
13/09/95	Istra Pula	H	4-0	Dzelalija 2 (1p), Perkovic, Zivkovic
17/09/95	Croatia Zagreb	A	0-2	
20/09/95	Sibenik	H	3-1	Perkovic, Dzelalija, Brkic
24/09/95	Osijek	H	0-2	
01/10/95	Hajduk Split	A	0-1	
15/10/95	Inker Zapresic	H	4-4	Milinovic 2, Samardzic 2
22/10/95	Segesta Sisak	A	0-6	
29/10/95	Zagreb	A	0-3	
05/11/95	Marsonia Slavonski Brod	H	0-1	
11/11/95	Cibalia Vinkovci	A	1-1	Brkic
19/11/95	Varteks Varazdin	H	2-2	Dzelalija, Smoje
26/11/95	Istra Pula	A	1-0	Brkic
03/12/95	Croatia Zagreb	H	1-1	Perkovic
10/12/95	Sibenik	A	1-2	Brkic
17/12/95	Osijek	A	0-1	
17/02/96	Hajduk Split	H	0-3	
24/02/96	Inker Zapresic	A	1-3	Dzelalija
03/03/96	Segesta Sisak	H	0-1	
PLAY-OFFS				
10/03/96	Marsonia Slavonski Brod	A	0-1	
17/03/96	Inker Zapresic	H	2-0	Hasancic, Brkic
24/03/96	Cibalia Vinkovci	A	2-2	Brkic 2
31/03/96	Mladost 127 Suhopolje	A	0-0	
07/04/96	Segesta Sisak	H	2-0	Tokic (p), Dzelalija
14/04/96	Istra Pula	A	0-1	
21/04/96	Sibenik	H	2-0	Perkovic, Hasancic
24/04/96	Marsonia Slavonski Brod	H	2-1	Milinovic (p), Brkic
27/04/96	Inker Zapresic	A	0-2	
05/05/96	Cibalia Vinkovci	H	2-0	Hasancic, Perkovic
12/05/96	Mladost 127 Suhopolje	H	2-0	Perkovic, Hasancic
19/05/96	Segesta Sisak	A	3-3	Brkic 2, Dzelalija
22/05/96	Istra Pula	H	4-1	Perkovic 3, Brkic
26/05/96	Sibenik	A	0-3	

SEGESTA SISAK

CLUB DIRECTORY

NK Segesta Sisak
Borisa Brnada 56
44 000 Sisak
tel - (044) 47311/47108
fax - (044) 47311
Year of Formation - 1906
President - Branko Poljak
Director - Igor Sprajc
Coach - Milivoj Bracun; Branko Ivankovic; Ivica Vidovic
Stadium - Segesta (15,000)

APPEARANCES 95/96

	P	Ap	(s)	Gls
Bosko ANIC	D	15		1
Stipe BRNAS	M	33		
Mile BUINAC	D		(1)	
Zoran BUINAC	D	16	(3)	
Alen DAUTBEGOVIC	G	18		
Slavko ISTVANIC	D	10		
Zdenko JEDVAJ	D	3		
Damir JURKOVIC	D	29		
Matija KATALINIC	D		(2)	
Andjelko KVESIC	M	23	(7)	3
Hrvoje LONCAREVIC	D	16	(12)	
Josip MARKOVINOVIC	A	16	(11)	5
Armin MASIC	A	7	(3)	2
Anto PETROVIC	D	3	(18)	1
Vladimir PETROVIC	A	30		12
Krunoslav PINTURIC	M	5	(7)	
Tomislav PIPLICA	G	18		
Igor RADISIC	A	23	(6)	
Sinisa ROGULJIC	M	7	(4)	
Fuad SASIVAREVIC (BOS)	M	30		8
Niksa SKOKANDIC	D	3		
Dragan TADIC	M	29	(4)	3
Zoran TOMCIC	D	28		
Hari VUKAS	A	28	(1)	16
Zoran ZIVKOVIC	D	6		

LEAGUE RESULTS 1995/96

13/08/95	Osijek	A	0-4	
18/08/95	Hajduk Split	H	1-1	Vukas
26/08/95	Inker Zapresic	A	4-2	Sasivarevic, Markovinovic, Vukas 2
10/09/95	Sibenik	A	0-2	
13/09/95	Zagreb	H	2-2	Markovinovic, Vukas (p)
17/09/95	Marsonia Slavonski Brod	A	1-3	Vukas
20/09/95	Cibalia Vinkovci	H	3-1	Vukas 2, Kvesic
24/09/95	Varteks Varazdin	A	0-1	
01/10/95	Istra Pula	H	3-0	Vukas 2 (1p), Sasivarevic
15/10/95	Croatia Zagreb	A	0-4	
22/10/95	Rijeka	H	6-0	Tadic, Petrovic V. 3, Markovinovic, Sasivarevic
29/10/95	Osijek	H	0-4	
05/11/95	Hajduk Split	A	1-3	Sasivarevic
11/11/95	Inker Zapresic	H	0-1	
19/11/95	Sibenik	H	2-2	Tadic, Vukas
26/11/95	Zagreb	A	0-0	
03/12/95	Marsonia Slavonski Brod	H	2-0	Sasivarevic 2
10/12/95	Cibalia Vinkovci	A	1-2	Petrovic V.
17/12/95	Varteks Varazdin	H	1-2	Petrovic A.
18/02/96	Istra Pula	A	3-1	Anic, Vukas 2
25/02/96	Croatia Zagreb	H	1-0	Kvesic
03/03/96	Rijeka	A	1-0	Tadic
PLAY-OFFS				
10/03/96	Sibenik	A	0-2	
17/03/96	Marsonia Slavonski Brod	H	2-1	Petrovic V., Vukas (p)
23/03/96	Inker Zapresic	A	0-0	
31/03/96	Cibalia Vinkovci	H	2-1	Sasivarevic, Vukas
07/04/96	Rijeka	A	0-2	
14/04/96	Mladost 127 Suhopolje	A	0-1	
21/04/96	Istra Pula	H	4-1	Masic, Petrovic V. 2 (1p), Markovinovic
23/04/96	Sibenik	H	2-1	Markovinovic, Petrovic V.
28/04/96	Marsonia Slavonski Brod	A	3-0	Kvesic, Masic, Petrovic V.
05/05/96	Inker Zapresic	H	1-0	Petrovic V.
12/05/96	Cibalia Vinkovci	A	1-4	Vukas
19/05/96	Rijeka	H	3-3	Petrovic V. 2, Vukas (p)
22/05/96	Mladost 127 Suhopolje	H	1-1	Sasivarevic
26/05/96	Istra Pula	A	0-1	

SIBENIK

CLUB DIRECTORY

HNK Sibenik
Bana Jelacica bb
59 000 Sibenik
tel - (022) 22963/28163
fax - (022) 28161
Year of Formation - 1932
President - Ivo Baica
Director - Milivoj Boranic
Coach - Ivica Sangulin; Rajko Magic
(96/97 - Vinko Begovic)
Stadium - Subicevac (12,000)

APPEARANCES 95/96

	P	Ap	(s)	Gls
Zeljko ACKAR	M	28		4
Mate BATURINA	A	34		11
Denis BILUS	D		(1)	
Zoran BOBANOVIC	A	5	(9)	2
Ivan BULAT	M	26		2
Josip BULAT	D	31		1
Ibrahim DURO (BOS)	M	28	(2)	2
Andjelko GODINIC	M	16	(3)	
Antun GRDIC	D	10	(2)	
Ante IVICA	D	17	(9)	1
Toni JURJEV	G	36		
Anel KARABEG	M	18		1
Ivo MARICIC	D	3	(5)	
Sokol META (ALB)	M	23	(3)	2
Ivica MORIC	A		(5)	
Xhevdet MURIQI	D	31		3
Zoran NINIC	A	1	(7)	2
Mile PETKOVIC	D	30		2
Denis PUTNIK	D	15		
Goran TOMIC	M	5	(14)	
Klaudio VUKOVIC	A	13	(13)	6
Tonci ZILIC	D	26	(7)	5

LEAGUE RESULTS 1995/96

Date	Opponent		Score	Scorers
13/08/95	Varteks Varazdin	A	1-3	Baturina
20/08/95	Inker Zapresic	H	3-1	Muriqi (p), Baturina 2 (1p)
27/08/95	Istra Pula	A	2-2	Ackar, Vukovic
10/09/95	Segesta Sisak	H	2-0	Ackar, Baturina
13/09/95	Croatia Zagreb	A	1-2	Karabeg
17/09/95	Zagreb	H	1-0	Ninic
20/09/95	Rijeka	A	1-3	Vukovic (p)
24/09/95	Marsonia Slavonski Brod	H	4-0	Baturina 2, Vukovic, Duro
01/10/95	Osijek	A	1-4	Ackar
15/10/95	Cibalia Vinkovci	H	0-1	
22/10/95	Hajduk Split	A	0-0	
28/10/95	Varteks Varazdin	H	1-0	Baturina
04/11/95	Inker Zapresic	A	0-2	
11/11/95	Istra Pula	H	2-0	Baturina, Ninic
19/11/95	Segesta Sisak	A	2-2	Vukovic, Ivica
26/11/95	Croatia Zagreb	H	0-0	
03/12/95	Zagreb	A	0-2	
10/12/95	Rijeka	H	2-1	Meta, Bulat I.
17/12/95	Marsonia Slavonski Brod	A	0-2	
18/02/96	Osijek	H	1-1	Petkovic (p)
25/02/96	Cibalia Vinkovci	A	1-2	Zilic
03/03/96	Hajduk Split	H	0-0	
PLAY-OFFS				
10/03/96	Segesta Sisak	H	2-0	Duro, Vukovic
17/03/96	Istra Pula	A	0-2	
24/03/96	Mladost 127 Suhopolje	H	4-1	Baturina, Petkovic (p), Zilic, Muriqi
31/03/96	Marsonia Slavonski Brod	H	1-0	Bulat I.
07/04/96	Inker Zapresic	A	1-0	Ackar
14/04/96	Cibalia Vinkovci	H	1-0	Muriqi
21/04/96	Rijeka	A	0-2	
23/04/96	Segesta Sisak	A	1-2	Bobanovic
28/04/96	Istra Pula	H	1-0	Bobanovic
05/05/96	Mladost 127 Suhopolje	A	0-2	
12/05/96	Marsonia Slavonski Brod	A	2-3	Bulat J., Zilic
19/05/96	Inker Zapresic	H	2-0	Zilic 2
22/05/96	Cibalia Vinkovci	A	1-3	Vukovic
26/05/96	Rijeka	H	3-0	Baturina 2, Meta

VARTEKS VARAZDIN

CLUB DIRECTORY

NK Varteks Varazdin
Zagrebacka 94
42 000 Varazdin
tel - (042) 177095/212332
fax - (042) 55256
Year of Formation - 1931
President - Andjelko Herjavec
Director - Vladimir Knok
Coach - Luka Bonacic
(96/97 - Predrag Stilinovic)
Stadium - Varteks (12,000)

APPEARANCES 95/96

	P	Ap	(s)	Gls
Andrija BALAJIC	M	23	(1)	1
Ivica BANCIC	D	12		
Drazen BESEK	M	24	(2)	2
Goran BOROVIC	D	6		
Zoran BRLENIC	M	30	(1)	3
Damir CVETKO	A		(1)	
Zlatko DALIC	M	22	(5)	
Mensur DURAKOVIC (BOS)	D	18	(8)	
Diego GOYOAGA (ARG)	A	2	(4)	
Krunoslav GREGORIC	D	21	(8)	2
Mario IVANKOVIC	A	1	(13)	2
Grgica KOVAC	D	30		2
Drazen MADUNOVIC	D	7	(15)	
Marijan MRMIC	G	31		
Miljenko MUMLEK	M	16	(10)	4
Sasa PASKA	D	9	(2)	2
Mladen POSAVEC	M	28	(2)	5
Danijel STEFULJ	D	4		
Dzoni TAFRA	G	1		
Robert TEZACKI	M	12	(7)	1
Samir TOPLAK	D	21	(3)	
Igor TOTH	A	3	(8)	2
Davor VUGRINEC	A	31		17

LEAGUE RESULTS 1995/96

13/08/95	Sibenik	H	3-1	Paska, Kovac, Toth
20/08/95	Istra Pula	H	2-0	Vugrinec (p), Posavec
27/08/95	Croatia Zagreb	A	0-2	
10/09/95	Rijeka	H	2-1	Toth, Vugrinec (p)
13/09/95	Osijek	A	0-1	
17/09/95	Hajduk Split	H	0-3	
20/09/95	Inker Zapresic	A	2-0	Vugrinec, Posavec
24/09/95	Segesta Sisak	H	1-0	Posavec
01/10/95	Zagreb	A	2-2	Vugrinec, Ivankovic
15/10/95	Marsonia Slavonski Brod	H	2-0	Kovac, Vugrinec
22/10/95	Cibalia Vinkovci	A	0-1	
28/10/95	Sibenik	A	0-1	
05/11/95	Istra Pula	A	1-1	Mumlek
11/11/95	Croatia Zagreb	H	1-1	Besek
19/11/95	Rijeka	A	2-2	Vugrinec 2
25/11/95	Osijek	H	1-0	Vugrinec
03/12/95	Hajduk Split	A	0-0	
09/12/95	Inker Zapresic	H	3-1	Vugrinec 2, Posavec
17/12/95	Segesta Sisak	A	2-1	Vugrinec 2 (1p)
17/02/96	Zagreb	H	0-0	
25/02/96	Marsonia Slavonski Brod	A	2-1	Mumlek, Gregoric
02/03/96	Cibalia Vinkovci	H	3-0	Mumlek, Tezacki, Ivankovic
PLAY-OFFS				
16/03/96	Croatia Zagreb	H	2-0	Posavec, Brlenic
20/03/96	Hrvatski dragovoljac Zagreb	A	1-0	Mumlek
24/03/96	Osijek	A	0-1	
31/03/96	Zagreb	A	2-0	Besek, Gregoric
07/04/96	Hajduk Split	H	1-0	Brlenic
13/04/96	Hrvatski dragovoljac Zagreb	H	1-1	Vugrinec
21/04/96	Croatia Zagreb	A	4-3	Balajic, Vugrinec 2, Brlenic
28/04/96	Osijek	H	2-1	Vugrinec, Paska
05/05/96	Zagreb	H	2-0	og (Biskup), Vugrinec
12/05/96	Hajduk Split	A	0-1	

ZAGREB

CLUB DIRECTORY

NK Zagreb
Kranjceviceva 4
10 000 Zagreb
tel - (01) 334511
fax - (01) 338156
Year of Formation - 1945
President - Ante Vrdoljak
Director - Zlatko Dracic
Coach - Ilija Loncarevic; Ivica Matkovic
Stadium - NK Zagreb (12,000)

APPEARANCES 95/96

	P	Ap	(s)	Gls
Admir ADZEM	M		(1)	
Drazen BISKUP	D	28		2
Nino BULE	M	3	(1)	
Sandi CAVKIC	D	4	(1)	
Mario CIZMEK	M	18	(10)	2
Niko CEKO	D	14		1
Boris DRZANIC	G	3	(2)	
Asmir DZAFIC (BOS)	A	13	(14)	3
Sunaj KEQI	M	21	(5)	
Muhamed KONJIC (BOS)	D	14	(1)	1
Tomislav KRALJ	G	1		
Kresimir KRPAN	M	3	(4)	
Jaksa KRSTULOVIC	M	1	(4)	
Ivan KURTOVIC	D	11		1
Armin MASIC	A	1	(4)	
Ivo MILIC	D	1	(1)	
Dzelaludin MUHAREMOVIC	A	2	(4)	
Zeljko PAVLOVIC	G	28		
Vlado PEHAR	M	2		
Igor PETRCIC	A	1	(3)	
Hrvoje PIPINIC	M	3	(3)	
Josko POPOVIC	A	28		9
Robert REGVAR	A	17	(8)	1
Djovani ROSSO	M	20	(2)	4
Tomislav RUKAVINA	M	18		
Jasenko SABITOVIC	D	20	(4)	2
Zeljko SOIC	M	5		
Zeljko SOPIC	A	21	(5)	
Darko VUKIC	A	20	(2)	1
Goran ZUPANAC	D	2	(4)	
Zeljko ZUPETIC	M	29		2

LEAGUE RESULTS 1995/96

Date	Opponent		Score	Scorers
13/08/95	Rijeka	A	2-1	Rosso 2
19/08/95	Osijek	H	0-2	
27/08/95	Hajduk Split	A	1-2	Cizmek
10/09/95	Inker Zapresic	H	0-2	
13/09/95	Segesta Sisak	A	2-2	Dzafic, Popovic (p)
17/09/95	Sibenik	A	0-1	
20/09/95	Marsonia Slavonski Brod	H	1-0	Popovic
24/09/95	Cibalia Vinkovci	A	1-2	Popovic
01/10/95	Varteks Varazdin	H	2-2	Sabitovic, Popovic
15/10/95	Istra Pula	A	1-1	Popovic
22/10/95	Croatia Zagreb	H	1-3	Rosso
29/10/95	Rijeka	H	3-0	Sabitovic, Kurtovic, Regvar
05/11/95	Osijek	A	2-2	Popovic (p), Zupetic
11/11/95	Hajduk Split	H	2-1	og (Cubretovic), Dzafic
18/11/95	Inker Zapresic	A	1-0	Rosso
26/11/95	Segesta Sisak	H	0-0	
03/12/95	Sibenik	H	2-0	Vukic, Dzafic
10/12/95	Marsonia Slavonski Brod	A	2-1	Popovic, Ceko
17/12/95	Cibalia Vinkovci	H	0-0	
17/02/96	Varteks Varazdin	A	0-0	
25/02/96	Istra Pula	H	1-1	Konjic
03/03/96	Croatia Zagreb	A	0-2	
PLAY-OFFS				
10/03/96	Hajduk Split	A	1-2	Zupetic
17/03/96	Osijek	H	0-2	
23/03/96	Hrvatski dragovoljac Zagreb	A	2-1	og (Tomas), Popovic
31/03/96	Varteks Varazdin	H	0-2	
07/04/96	Croatia Zagreb	A	1-5	Cizmek
14/04/96	Hajduk Split	H	1-6	Popovic
21/04/96	Osijek	A	0-1	
28/04/96	Hrvatski dragovoljac Zagreb	H	1-1	Biskup (p)
05/05/96	Varteks Varazdin	A	0-2	
12/05/96	Croatia Zagreb	H	1-3	Biskup

PROMOTED CLUBS

SECOND DIVISION FINAL TABLE 95/96

		Pd	W	D	L	F	A	Pt	GD
1	Hrvatski dragovoljac Zagreb	18	13	2	3	30	11	41	+19
2	Mladost 127 Suhopolje	18	12	2	4	27	11	38	+16
3	**Zadar**	**18**	**9**	**5**	**4**	**24**	**13**	**32**	**+11**
4	**Orijent Rijeka**	**18**	**9**	**2**	**7**	**29**	**24**	**29**	**+5**
5	Neretva Metkovic	18	8	3	7	21	17	27	+4
6	Slavonija Pozega	18	6	4	8	26	26	22	=
7	Dubrovnik	18	6	4	8	15	15	22	=
8	Belisce	18	5	4	9	20	26	19	-6
9	Primorac Stobrec	18	5	2	11	14	33	17	-19
10	Uskok Klis	18	2	2	14	9	39	8	-30

CLUB DIRECTORY

Zadarkomerc Zadar
Stadionska 2
23000 Zadar
tel - (023) 314677/314124
fax - (023) 314124
Year of Formation - 1949
President - Ante Jurjevic
Director - Slavko Pernar
Coach - Stanko Mrsic
Stadium - Stanovi (15,000)

CLUB DIRECTORY

Orijent Rijeka
Kumiciceva bb (Krimeja)
51000 Rijeka
tel - (051) 218436/218090
fax - (051) 218282
Year of Formation - 1919
President - Milivoj Miletic
Director - Zeljko Lujanac
Coach - Boris Ticic
Stadium - Krimeja (5,300)

CYPRUS

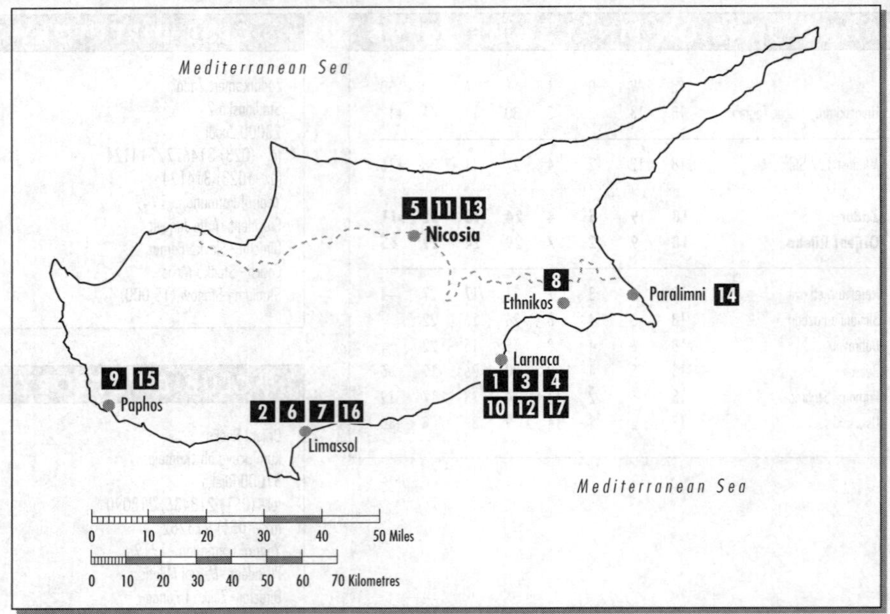

1	AEK LARNACA	243
2	AEL LIMASSOL	244
3	ALKI LARNACA	245
4	ANORTHOSIS FAMAGUSTA	246
5	APOEL NICOSIA	247
6	APOLLON LIMASSOL	248
7	ARIS LIMASSOL	249
8	ETHNIKOS AKHNAS	250
9	EVAGHORAS PAPHOS	251
10	NEA SALAMINA FAMAGUSTA	252
11	OLYMPIAKOS NICOSIA	253
12	OMONIA ARADIPPOU	254
13	OMONIA NICOSIA	255
14	PARALIMNI	256
15	APOP PAPHOS	257
16	APEP PITSILIAS	257
17	ANAGENNISIS DHERYNIA	257

CHAMPIONS' LEAGUE PLACE DISAPPEARS

Home ban can't stop unbeaten APOEL

FEDERATION DIRECTORY

Cyprus Football Association
Stasinos Street 1, Engomi 152, PO Box 5071, Nicosia

tel - (02) 325341/590342 — Year of Formation - 1934
tlx - 3880 football cy — President - Marios Lefkaritis
fax - (02) 590544 — Secretary - Lambros Adamou

Stadium - Makarion, Nicosia (20,000)

Of all the champions of Europe in 1995/96, none surely deserve higher praise than APOEL Nicosia. An undistinguished sixth the previous season, when they lost as many matches as they won, APOEL were suddenly transformed by new Bulgarian coach Hristo Bonev into a team of invincibles. They not only went through the entire league season without defeat. They did so despite the handicap of having five of their home games switched to neutral venues.

Incredibly, all five of those matches - against Apollon, AEK, AEL, Paralimni and Alki - resulted in victory. There was simply nothing that the other teams in the league could do to prevent APOEL's victory march. Six points clear at the halfway point, the Nicosians managed to keep their rivals at a safe distance and the destiny of the title was never in any doubt.

It was only when league points were not on the agenda that Bonev's men let their guard down. Anorthosis beat them on penalties in the pre-season SuperCup. Deportivo La Coruña thrashed them 8-0 in the European Cup-winners' Cup (after a goalless draw in Cyprus). And city rivals Omonia beat them 2-1 in the first leg of the domestic Cup semi-final.

But APOEL recovered from the third of those defeats, beating Omonia 2-0 in the return leg to reach the Cypriot Cup final for the second year running. The club's fourth 'double' was at stake as they took on the season's surprise package AEK Larnaca in Limassol. It was a tight encounter, with few chances created, until extra-time, when APOEL's superior confidence and mental strength enabled them to score twice and lift the trophy for a record 15th time.

The scorer of the decisive first goal, two minutes into the extra period, was veteran Hungarian striker József Kiprich. It capped a magnificent first season on the island for the ex-Feyenoord forward. He had arrived in the company of two other well-known Hungarians, István Kozma (ex-Liverpool) and Kálmán Kovács (ex-Auxerre), but Kiprich completely outshone his two compatriates, scoring 25 goals in 24 league games to take the league's top scorer crown. Two other players crucial to the team's success were goalkeeper Andros Petrides, a model of consistency all season long, and support strker Yiannos Ioanou who laid on a sizeable proportion of Kiprich's goals as well as scoring eight himself.

Sadly, APOEL's title win did not gain them access to the 1996/97 Champions' League. Juventus's penalty shoot-out victory against Ajax in the 95/96 Champions' Cup final meant that, with two Italian participants, the Cypriot champions,

LEAGUE CHAMPIONSHIP RESULTS 95/96

		1	2	3	4	5	6	7	8	9	10	11	12	13	14
1	AEK Larnaca		1-1	3-1	2-2	0-0	3-0	2-1	2-1	2-0	4-1	1-0	1-0	3-0	3-0
2	AEL Limassol	0-3		2-3	1-1	0-3	1-1	1-2	0-0	5-1	0-1	3-1	3-1	1-2	2-2
3	Alki Larnaca	1-3	2-4		0-3	1-2	2-2	0-2	3-3	1-0	5-0	1-0	5-1	2-0	0-0
4	Anorthosis Famagusta	2-1	2-2	2-2		3-3	1-0	4-2	2-0	2-0	3-2	1-0	6-0	1-0	5-0
5	APOEL Nicosia	1-0	3-0	2-1	3-0		1-0	2-2	3-2	5-1	4-1	1-0	5-0	1-1	3-2
6	Apollon Limassol	3-1	3-1	3-0	0-0	0-2		2-1	2-0	1-1	3-3	0-0	5-0	1-2	1-1
7	Aris Limassol	1-1	1-0	2-3	2-0	1-1	1-1		1-1	3-0	1-2	1-2	1-1	1-4	0-0
8	Ethnikos Akhnas	1-1	2-1	1-1	0-0	1-4	3-0	1-1		1-1	1-0	4-1	2-1	0-2	0-0
9	Evaghoras Paphos	0-1	0-2	2-2	0-2	1-1	0-5	1-2	0-0		1-2	0-2	5-0	0-2	2-2
10	Nea Salamina Famagusta	0-1	2-1	1-0	0-1	1-4	1-2	2-0	1-4	1-1		4-0	4-1	2-5	2-1
11	Olympiakos Nicosia	0-2	1-0	2-0	1-2	0-2	2-2	0-0	2-0	1-0	1-0		1-1	0-1	1-1
12	Omonia Aradippou	1-2	1-3	3-4	0-2	0-4	1-2	1-3	1-3	1-2	0-3	0-2		0-9	1-2
13	Omonia Nicosia	3-1	6-2	1-1	2-0	2-4	1-1	1-1	1-2	8-1	3-0	3-3	3-1		3-1
14	Paralimni	1-0	4-1	2-1	0-3	1-1	0-2	3-1	2-3	5-1	1-1	2-1	4-1	0-1	

LEAGUE CHAMPIONSHIP FINAL TABLE 95/96

			Home					Away					Total						
		Pd	W	D	L	F	A	W	D	L	F	A	W	D	L	F	A	Pt	GD
1	APOEL Nicosia	26	11	2	0	34	10	8	5	0	31	11	19	7	0	65	21	64	+44
2	Anorthosis Famagusta	26	10	3	0	34	12	6	4	3	16	11	16	7	3	50	23	55	+27
3	Omonia Nicosia	26	7	4	2	37	18	9	1	3	29	12	16	5	5	66	30	53	+36
4	AEK Larnaca	26	10	3	0	27	7	6	2	5	17	14	16	5	5	44	21	53	+23
5	Apollon Limassol	26	6	5	2	24	12	4	5	4	18	17	10	10	6	42	29	40	+13
6	Ethnikos Akhnas	26	5	6	2	17	13	4	4	5	19	20	9	10	7	36	33	37	+3
7	Paralimni	26	7	2	4	25	17	1	7	5	12	23	8	9	9	37	40	33	-3
8	Nea Salamina Famagusta	26	6	1	6	21	21	4	2	7	16	27	10	3	13	37	48	33	-11
9	Aris Limassol	26	3	6	4	16	16	4	4	5	18	20	7	10	9	34	36	31	-2
10	Alki Larnaca	26	5	3	5	23	20	3	4	6	19	26	8	7	11	42	46	31	-4
11	Olympiakos Nicosia	26	5	4	4	12	11	3	2	8	12	21	8	6	12	24	32	30	-8
12	AEL Limassol	26	3	4	6	19	21	3	2	8	18	28	6	6	14	37	49	24	-12
13	Evaghoras Paphos	26	1	4	8	12	23	1	3	9	9	36	2	7	17	21	59	13	-38
14	Omonia Aradippou	26	0	0	13	10	41	0	2	11	8	45	0	2	24	18	86	2	-68

placed 24th in the UEFA ranking, were 'relegated' to the UEFA Cup.

Anorthosis, who did make the Champions' League preliminaries in 95/96, served their country proudly with two fine performances against Rangers. The defending champions never subsequently looked like retaining their title (APOEL were simply too far ahead), but a strong burst in the second half of the season lifted them into the runners-up spot, which they snatched from Omonia Nicosia with a 1-0 victory over their direct rivals on the last day of the season.

At the other end of the table Omonia Aradippou, saved from the drop the previous season because of the league's expansion to 14 teams, could not be rescued a second time. While APOEL finished top of the league with no defeats, Aradippou ended up bottom with no wins, losing all 13 of their home matches. 13th-placed Evaghoras Paphos fared little better, but the big relegation shock was that of AEL, who had never previously dropped out of the

TOP SCORERS

25 József KIPRICH (APOEL Nicosia)
16 Boban KITANOV (AEL Limassol)
15 Costas MALEKKOS (Omonia Nicosia)
Slobodan KRCMAREVIC (Apollon Limassol)
Dragoslav MUSIC (Ethnikos Akhnas)
13 Pambis ANDREOU (Nea Salamina Famagusta)
Willy NWAKANMA (Paralimni)
12 Panikos XIOUROUPPAS (Omonia Nicosia)
Srboljub NIKOLIC (Aris Limassol)
Andreas AVLONITIS (Alki Larnaca)
Victor PAÇO (AEK Larnaca)

DOMESTIC CUP RESULTS

SECOND ROUND

Omonia Aradippou v Aris Limassol 2-1; 2-1
(Omonia Aradippou 4-2)
Paralimni v Apollon Limassol 0-1; 2-3
(Apollon Limassol 4-2)
Ethnikos Akhnas v Anorthosis Famagusta 3-1; 0-4
(Anorthosis Famagusta 5-3)
Olympiakos Nicosia v Evaghoras Paphos 2-1; 1-0
(Olympiakos Nicosia 3-1)
Ayia Napa v Omonia Nicosia 0-4; 2-2
(Omonia Nicosia 6-2)
AEK Larnaca v Alki Larnaca 1-0; 1-1
(AEK Larnaca 2-1)
PAEEK Kyrenia v Nea Salamina Famagusta 0-3; 0-1
(Nea Salamina Famagusta 4-0)
APOEL Nicosia v AEL Limassol 4-1; 4-3
(AEL Limassol 8-4)

QUARTER-FINALS

Olympiakos Nicosia v Omonia Nicosia 1-2; 2-2
(Omonia Nicosia 4-3)
AEK Larnaca v Omonia Aradippou 7-0; 0-1
(AEK Larnaca 7-1)
Apollon Limassol v Anorthosis Famagusta 1-0; 1-0
(Apollon Limassol 2-0)
Nea Salamina Famagusta v APOEL Nicosia 1-1; 1-2
(APOEL Nicosia 3-2)

SEMI-FINALS

APOEL Nicosia v Omonia Nicosia 1-2; 2-0
(APOEL Nicosia 3-2)
Apollon Limassol v AEK Larnaca 2-2; 1-1
(3-3; AEK Larnaca on away goals)

FINAL

29/05/96, Limassol
APOEL NICOSIA 2 Kiprich (92), Alexandrou (117)
AEK LARNACA 0
(aet)
referee - Ioannou
APOEL NICOSIA - Petrides; Costa, Aristotelous, Christodoulou, Sapuric, Kozma, Phasouliotis (Hadjilucas 104), Kovács (Alexandrou 100), Ioannou, Kiprich, Aristocleous (Timotheou 91).
AEK LARNACA - Mavris; Theodotou (Eleftheriou 85), Larkou, Constandinou, Misos, Stephani (Kysela 108), Pancho, Bakaris, Markou (Stylianides 108), Kovacevic, Alexandrou.

top division. Not even the 16 goals of imported striker Boban Kitanov could save them. Another AEL player who made positive news during the season was young forward Marios Agathocleous, but he saved his best for the Cyprus national team, scoring three important goals, two of them to earn 1-1 draws at home to Macedonia and Belgium in the Euro '96 qualifiers and the other to beat Latvia in a friendly. The Cypriots have been handed a tough World Cup group, but they will hope to take at least four points off Luxembourg and perhaps more than one from Israel.

NATIONAL TEAM APPEARANCES 95/96

Coach - Andreas MICHAELIDES	ESP	MAC	BEL	LBN	EST	LAT	GEO	ISL	Cps	Gls
Nicos PANAYIOTOU (06/12/70) - Anorthosis Famagusta	G		G	G78	G	G			15	-
Sozos ANDREOU (06/09/69) - Anorthosis Famagusta	D								1	-
George CHRISTODOULOU (22/08/65) - APOEL Nicosia	D	D	D	D	D	D46	D70	D	16	-
Nicos CHARALAMBOUS (03/11/66) - APOEL Nicosia	D								1	-
Pambos PITTAS (26/07/66) - Apollon Limassol	D	D	D			D	D	D46	56	6
George PANAYI (09/07/66) - Anorthosis Famagusta	M								17	-
Andonis ANDONIOU (25/07/70) - AEL Limassol	M80								3	-
Lucas HADJILUCAS (06/06/67) - APOEL Nicosia	M68								21	3
Dimitris ASHIOTIS (31/03/71) - Anorthosis Famagusta	A				A62	s62	s70		5	-
Costas MALEKKOS (09/04/71) - Omonia Nicosia	A57	A	A50	A77	A	A	A70		15	-
Sinisa GOGIC (20/10/63) - Anorthosis Famagusta	A	A	A80	A					16	3
Andros SOTIRIOU (07/06/68) - APOEL Nicosia	s57	A80							37	8
Yiannos IOANNOU (25/01/66) - APOEL Nicosia	s68			A75					28	3
Pambis ANDREOU (16/06/67) - Nea Salamina Famagusta	s80							s75	20	2
Andros PETRIDES (06/12/66) - APOEL Nicosia		G						G83	12	-
Costas COSTA (04/01/69) - APOEL Nicosia		D	D					D75	25	1
Yiannos KALOTHEOU (06/05/66) - Omonia Nicosia		D63							26	-
Marios CHARALAMBOUS (18/06/69) - Apollon Limassol		D	D						28	1
George SAVVIDES (08/02/61) - Omonia Nicosia		M							47	3
Yiotis ENGOMITIS (26/05/72) - Ethnikos Akhnas		A46	A		A62				11	2
Nicos PAPAVASSILIOU (31/08/70) - Apollon Limassol		s46	M	M	M62	A62	M	s46	25	1
Marios AGATHOCLEOUS (08/09/74) - AEL Limassol		s63	A75	s77		A	A		12	6
Neophytos LARKOU (08/03/66) - AEK Larnaca		s80	s50	D	D	M	M	s46	33	1
Andreas ANDREOU (02/02/66) - Omonia Nicosia			M	M58				M46	22	2
Andonis ZEMBASHIS (17/08/68) - Paralimni			s75	M	M	M	M		11	-
George ELIA (11/03/70) - Nea Salamina Famagusta			s80	s75				s75	12	1
Marios PEFKOS (19/08/71) - Aris Limassol				D58					2	-
Costas CONSTANDINOU (24/09/68) - Apollon Limassol				D	D46	s46	D61	D	38	1
Kyriakos PAPAKYRIAKOU (03/11/71) - Apollon Limassol				s58					1	-
Marios PASHIALIS (30/10/70) - Ethnikos Akhnas				s58	s62	s62	s61		5	-
Michalis CHRISTOPHI (24/07/69) - Apollon Limassol				s78			G46		19	-
George THEODOTOU (01/01/74) - AEK Larnaca					D	D	D		3	-
Marios CHRISTODOULOU (04/07/74) - Iraklis (GRE)					M		M54	M	4	-
Alexis ALEXANDROU (12/07/73) - APOEL Nicosia					s46			A75	2	-
Dimitris IOANNOU (08/12/68) - Anorthosis Famagusta					s62	D62	s54		28	2
Andreas MAVRIS (21/03/72) - AEK Larnaca					s62	s46	s46	s83	4	-
Charis NICOLAOU (31/03/74) - Alki Larnaca						M46	s70		2	-
George IOSIFIDES (08/01/68) - Apollon Limassol								M	2	-
Nicos TIMOTHEOU (04/11/73) - APOEL Nicosia								M	1	-
Klimis ALEXANDROU (01/09/74) - AEK Larnaca								A	1	1

EUROPEAN CUPS RESULTS 95/96

CHAMPIONS' CUP

● ANORTHOSIS FAMAGUSTA

Preliminary round RANGERS (SCO)

A 0-1

Panayiotou N.; Pounnas (Melanarkitis 82), Stavrou, Panayi, Kastanas, Andreou, Ashiotis, Kiriakov, Todorov, Ignatov (Christophorou 76), Gogic.

H 0-0

Panayiotou N.; Panayi, Panayiotou A., Stavrou, Kastanas, Andreou, Ashiotis (Pounnas 60), Kiriakov, Todorov, Gogic, Ignatov (Thoma 76).

CUP-WINNERS' CUP

● APOEL NICOSIA

Preliminary round NEFTCHI BAKU (AZB)

H 3-0 Andoniou (18), Ioannou (43, 65)

Petrides; Aristocleous, Charalambous, Christodoulou, Sapuric, Kozma, Andoniou, Kovács (Alexandrou 65), Sotiriou, Ioannou (Pounnas 82), Hadjilucas (Aristotelous 88).

A 0-0

Petrides; Aristocleous (Timotheou 70), Charalambous, Christodoulou, Sapuric, Kozma, Andoniou (Pounnas 62), Kovács, Sotiriou (Alexandrou 78), Ioannou, Hadjilucas.

1st round RC DEPORTIVO (ESP)

H 0-0

Petrides; Timotheou, Pounnas, Christodoulou, Alexandrou (Phasouliotis 62), Kozma, Andoniou, Sotiriou, Kovács (Skapoullis 87), Ioannou (Papadopoulos 85), Hadjilucas.

A 0-8

Petrides; Aristocleous, Timotheou (Phasouliotis 61), Pounnas, Christodoulou (Charalambous 24), Kozma, Ioannou, Hadjilucas, Kovács (Alexandrou 65), Kiprich, Sotiriou.

UEFA CUP

● OMONIA NICOSIA

Preliminary round SLIEMA WANDERERS (MLT)

H 3-0 Stefan (40p, 52), Malekkos (75)

Charitou; Ioakim, Christodoulou, Stefan, Christophi, Andreou S., Kantilos (Xiourouppas 46), Savvides, Djukanovic, Tutic (Kaiaphas 73), Malekkos.

A 2-1 Stefan (70), Xiourouppas (86)

Charitou; Kalotheou, Ioakim, Stefan, Christophi, Andreou S., Kantilos (Xiourouppas 44), Savvides (Kalotheou 82), Djukanovic, Tutic, Christodoulou.

1st round LAZIO (ITA)

A 0-5

Charitou; Kalotheou, Christodoulou, Stefan, Kalotheou, Andreou S., Kantilos (Andreou 69), Savvides, Malekkos (Constaninides 72), Tutic, Xiourouppas.

H 1-2 Xiourouppas (68)

Charitou; Kalotheou, Chrysanthou (Kaiaphas 46), Stefan (Kantilos 81), Ioakim, Andreou S. (Christodoulou 78), Panayiotou, Savvides, Malekkos, Tutic, Xiourouppas.

NATIONAL TEAM RESULTS 95/96

06/09/95	Spain (ECQ)	A	Granada	0-6	
11/10/95	Macedonia (ECQ)	H	Limassol	1-1	Agathocleous (90)
15/11/95	Belgium (ECQ)	H	Limassol	1-1	Agathocleous (15)
16/01/96	Lebanon	A	Beirut	0-1	
20/02/96	Estonia	H	Limassol	1-0	Constandinou (21)
12/03/96	Latvia	H	Larnaca	1-0	Agathocleous (46)
27/03/96	Georgia	H	Limassol	0-2	
05/06/96	Iceland	A	Reykjavík	1-2	Alexandrou K. (76)

INTERNATIONAL HONOURS

None

PLAYERS OF THE SEASON

ANDROS PETRIDES

A large slice of the credit for APOEL Nicosia's 'double' triumph has to go to the team's ever-present and ever-consistent goalkeeper, Andros Petrides. The 29-year-old bounced back brilliantly from the early-season shock of conceding eight goals in one match to Spanish side Deportivo. He played every single minute of all APOEL's league and Cup matches and was in top form for most of them. His only major slip-up came when he conceded a bad goal for Cyprus against Macedonia, which cost the APOEL 'keeper his national team place... until coach Michaelides felt duty-bound to recall him for the June friendly against Iceland.

NEOPHYTOS LARKOU

AEK Larnaca emerged from the fusion of Pezoporikos and EPA in 1994. The club's second season was a major triumph. They pressed hard for the league runners-up spot all season and qualified for Europe by virtue of their appearance in the Cypriot Cup final against champions APOEL. The club's impressive run had much to do with the sterling contributions of central defender Neophytos Larkou. The 30-year-old libero was the cool, composed leader AEK needed, and he carried that authority through to the Cypriot national team, where he was a regular choice throughout the season.

AEK LARNACA

CLUB DIRECTORY

AEK FC
PO Box 60
Larnaca
tel - (04) 655999/652464
fax - (04) 657173
Year of Formation - 1994
President - Dinos Lefkaritis
Secretary - Andreas Zachariou
Coach - Andreas Mouskalis
Stadium - Zenon (8,000)

APPEARANCES 95/96

	P	Ap	(s)	Gls
Andreas AFXENDIS	A		(2)	
Klimis ALEXANDROU	A	24		5
Lefteris ANDREOU	A	2		
Christos BAKARIS	M	21	(2)	2
George CONSTANDINOU	D	24		1
Michalis CONSTANDINOU	M	5	(8)	1
Lefteris ELEFTHERIOU	M	7	(9)	3
Milenko KOVACEVIC (YUG)	M	26		5
Stefan KYSELA (SVK)	A	10	(12)	3
Neophytos LARKOU	D	24	(1)	
Pavlos MARKOU	M	13	(4)	3
Andreas MAVRIS	G	26		
Angelos MISOS	D	26		1
Victor PAÇO (ALB)	A	20	(5)	12
Dimitris PANAYIOTOU	M		(5)	
Michalis PRODROMOU	D	3	(6)	1
Louis STEFANI	M	21	(1)	1
Stelios STYLIANIDES	M	10	(15)	4
George THEODOTOU	D	24		2

LEAGUE RESULTS 1995/96

24/09/95	Alki Larnaca	H	3-1	Paço, Constandinou M., Kysela
01/10/95	Nea Salamina Famagusta	H	4-1	Constandinou G., Alexandrou K., Prodromou, Kovacevic
15/10/95	Apollon Limassol	A	1-3	Alexandrou K.
22/10/95	Olympiakos Nicosia	H	1-0	Markou
28/10/95	Omonia Aradippou	A	2-1	Bakaris, Paço
05/11/95	Ethnikos Akhnas	H	2-1	Kovacevic, Bakaris
18/11/95	APOEL Nicosia	A	0-1	
25/11/95	Evaghoras Paphos	A	1-0	Paço
02/12/95	Anorthosis Famagusta	H	2-2	Kovacevic, Misos
09/12/95	AEL Limassol	A	3-0	Stylianides, Kovacevic, Markou
16/12/95	Aris Limassol	H	2-1	Markou, Paço
06/01/96	Paralimni	A	0-1	
13/01/96	Omonia Nicosia	H	3-0	Theodotou, Stylianides, Kysela
28/01/96	Nea Salamina Famagusta	A	1-0	Stylianides
11/02/96	Apollon Limassol	H	3-0	Theodotou, Stylianides, Paço
18/02/96	Olympiakos Nicosia	A	2-0	Paço 2
24/02/96	Omonia Aradippou	H	1-0	Eleftheriou
09/03/96	Ethnikos Akhnas	A	1-1	Stefani
24/03/96	APOEL Nicosia	H	0-0	
30/03/96	Evaghoras Paphos	H	2-0	Paço 2
06/04/96	Anorthosis Famagusta	A	1-2	Kovacevic
20/04/96	AEL Limassol	H	1-1	Paço
27/04/96	Aris Limassol	A	1-1	Eleftheriou
04/05/96	Paralimni	H	3-0	Paço, Alexandrou K. (p), Eleftheriou
11/05/96	Omonia Nicosia	A	1-3	Kysela
18/05/96	Alki Larnaca	A	3-1	Alexandrou K. 2, Paço

AEL LIMASSOL

CLUB DIRECTORY

AEL FC
PO Box 1606, Limassol
tel - (05) 362598
fax - (05) 373032
Year of Formation - 1930
President - Dimitris Solomonides
Secretary - Agis Agapiou
Coach - Andreas Kissonergis
(96/97 - Apostol Chetsevsky)
Stadium - Tsirion (22,000)

MAJOR HONOURS
League Championship - (5)
1941, 1953, 1955, 1956, 1968.
Domestic Cup - (6)
1939, 1940, 1948, 1985, 1987, 1989.

APPEARANCES 95/96

	P	Ap	(s)	Gls
Marios AGATHOCLEOUS	A	21	(2)	3
Andonis ANDONIOU	M	6	(5)	
Michalis ANDONIOU	D	10	(1)	
Andreas CHRISTODOULOU	A	1	(1)	
Ermogenis CHRISTOPHI	D	18	(3)	3
Christos CHRISTOU	G	11		
Andreas CHRISTOU	D	1		
Michalis CHRYSOSTOMOU	D	22		1
Marios DIMITRIOU	M	16	(8)	1
Marios GEORGIOU	M	9	(3)	
Christos IOANNOU	D	7	(8)	
Ioannis IOANNOU	D	18	(3)	1
Boban KITANOV (YUG)	A	20	(1)	16
Christos KOLIANDRIS	A	11		
Andonis KONNARIS	A	5	(2)	
Kyriakos KYRIAKOU	D	14		
Dimitris LEONIS	G	4		
Genadiy LITOVCHENKO (UKR)	M	4	(3)	
Mirko MIHIC (YUG)	A	21	(4)	8
Makis NEOPHYTOU	A	11	(6)	
Stelios NICOLAOU	D	1		
Christos PANAYIOTOU	G	11	(1)	
Andreas PATOUNAS	D	1	(2)	
Pavlos SAVVA	M	15	(7)	3
Makis SOCRATOUS	D	12	(6)	1
Telis TSINGIS	D	14	(2)	
Polykarpos VLAHOS	D	2	(3)	

LEAGUE RESULTS 1995/96

23/09/95	Paralimni	A	1-4	Agathocleous
01/10/95	Omonia Nicosia	H	1-2	Kitanov
15/10/95	Alki Larnaca	A	4-2	Kitanov 2, Mihic, Savva
22/10/95	Nea Salamina Famagusta	H	0-1	
28/10/95	Apollon Limassol	A	1-3	Mihic
04/11/95	Olympiakos Nicosia	H	3-1	Mihic 2, Agathocleous
19/11/95	Omonia Aradippou	A	3-1	Chrysostomou, Christophi 2
26/11/95	Ethnikos Akhnas	H	0-0	
02/12/95	APOEL Nicosia	A	0-3	
09/12/95	AEK Larnaca	H	0-3	
17/12/95	Anorthosis Famagusta	A	2-2	Kitanov, Savva
06/01/96	Evaghoras Paphos	A	2-0	Kitanov 2
13/01/96	Aris Limassol	H	1-2	Kitanov
28/01/96	Omonia Nicosia	A	2-6	Kitanov 2
11/02/96	Alki Larnaca	H	2-3	Mihic 2
17/02/96	Nea Salamina Famagusta	A	1-2	Mihic
24/02/96	Apollon Limassol	H	1-1	Kitanov (p)
10/03/96	Olympiakos Nicosia	A	0-1	
24/03/96	Omonia Aradippou	H	3-1	Kitanov 2, Mihic
30/03/96	Ethnikos Akhnas	A	1-2	Kitanov
06/04/96	APOEL Nicosia	H	0-3	
20/04/96	AEK Larnaca	A	1-1	Kitanov
28/04/96	Anorthosis Famagusta	H	1-1	Ioannou I.
04/05/96	Evaghoras Paphos	H	5-1	Christophi, Socratous (p), Agathocleous, Savva, Dimitriou
11/05/96	Aris Limassol	A	0-1	
18/05/96	Paralimni	H	2-2	Kitanov 2

ALKI LARNACA

CLUB DIRECTORY

Alki FC
Loukis Akritas
Larnaca
tel - (04) 54099
Year of Formation - 1948
President - Titos Christophides
Secretary - Stelios Stylianou
Coach - Angel Kolev; Ozak Kostel
Stadium - Zenon (8,000)

APPEARANCES 95/96

	P	Ap	(s)	Gls
Alexandros ALEXANDROU	G	14		
Michalis ANDREOU	G	11		
Andreas AVLONITIS	A	22	(2)	12
Charis CHARI	G	1		
George CONSTANDINOU	M		(1)	
Andreas EFTHYMIOU	D	20	(1)	2
Paraskevas ELIA	D	25	(1)	1
Christakis GEORGIOU	D	24		
Loizos HADJIANDONIS	M	9	(14)	2
Emilios LAZARIDIS	M	5	(10)	
Kyriakos MINA	M	8	(4)	1
Eugen NEAGOE (ROM)	M	24		4
Charis NICOLAOU	M	26		1
Nicos NICOLAOU	M	4	(10)	1
Janez PATE (SLO)	A	26		8
Yiannakis PONTIKOS	A	11	(15)	6
Andreas SARDALOS	D	1	(5)	
Savvas SAVVA	D	8	(4)	
Andreas YIATROU	A	21	(1)	2
Nicolae ZAMFIR (ROM)	M	26		2

LEAGUE RESULTS 1995/96

24/09/95	AEK Larnaca	A	1-3	Pate
30/09/95	Anorthosis Famagusta	A	2-2	Pontikos, Avlonitis
15/10/95	AEL Limassol	H	2-4	Pate, Avlonitis
21/10/95	Aris Limassol	A	3-2	Yiatrou, Pate, Pontikos
28/10/95	Paralimni	H	0-0	
04/11/95	Omonia Nicosia	A	1-1	Neagoe
19/11/95	Evaghoras Paphos	H	1-0	Yiatrou
26/11/95	Nea Salamina Famagusta	H	5-0	Avlonitis 3, Pate, Pontikos
02/12/95	Apollon Limassol	A	0-3	
10/12/95	Olympiakos Nicosia	H	1-0	Pate
16/12/95	Omonia Aradippou	A	4-3	Hadjiandonis 2, Pate, Elia
06/01/96	Ethnikos Akhnas	H	3-3	Pate (p), Nicolaou C., Neagoe
14/01/96	APOEL Nicosia	A	1-2	Neagoe
27/01/96	Anorthosis Famagusta	H	0-3	
11/02/96	AEL Limassol	A	3-2	Mina, Efthymiou, Avlonitis
17/02/96	Aris Limassol	H	0-2	
24/02/96	Paralimni	A	1-2	Zamfir
09/03/96	Omonia Nicosia	H	2-0	Pontikos, Pate
23/03/96	Evaghoras Paphos	A	2-2	Avlonitis 2
30/03/96	Nea Salamina Famagusta	A	0-1	
07/04/96	Apollon Limassol	H	2-2	Zamfir, Pontikos
21/04/96	Olympiakos Nicosia	A	0-2	
27/04/96	Omonia Aradippou	H	5-1	Avlonitis 2, Neagoe, Pontikos, Nicolaou N.
04/05/96	Ethnikos Akhnas	A	1-1	Avlonitis
12/05/96	APOEL Nicosia	H	1-2	Efthymiou
18/05/96	AEK Larnaca	H	1-3	Avlonitis

ANORTHOSIS FAMAGUSTA

CLUB DIRECTORY

Anorthosis FC of Famagusta
PO Box 756
Larnaca
tel - (04) 635833/4
fax - (04) 635833
Year of Formation - 1911
President - Kikis Constantinou
Secretary - Lucas Hadjilucas
Coach - Georgi Vasilev (96/97 - Dusan Vitosevic)
Stadium - Antonis Papadopoulos (8,000)

MAJOR HONOURS
League Championship - (7)
1950, 1957, 1958, 1960, 1962, 1963, 1995.
Domestic Cup - (4) 1949, 1962, 1971, 1975.

APPEARANCES 95/96

	P	Ap	(s)	Gls
Sozos ANDREOU	D	11	(7)	1
Dimitris ASHIOTIS	A	23	(1)	2
Zacharias CHARALAMBOUS	D	24		2
Stavros FOUKARIS	M		(1)	
Sinisa GOGIC	A	21		10
Valentin IGNATOV (BUL)	A	12	(9)	5
Dimitris IOANNOU	D	15		
Spyros KASTANAS	D	6	(1)	2
Ilian KIRIAKOV (BUL)	M	19		8
Andreas MELANARGITIS	D	14	(2)	
Vassos MELANARAGITIS	M	13	(11)	2
Panikos NEOCLEOUS	A	9	(15)	6
George PANAYI	D	14	(2)	
Andros PANAYIOTOU	D	11	(2)	1
Nicos PANAYIOTOU	G	26		
Panikos POUNNAS	M	20	(2)	1
Costas RIZOS	A	9	(13)	2
Costas STAVROU	D	20		1
Marios THOMA	M		(1)	
Nikolai TODOROV (BUL)	M	19	(3)	5

LEAGUE RESULTS 1995/96

23/09/95	Omonia Nicosia	A	0-2	
30/09/95	Alki Larnaca	H	2-2	Stavrou, Neocleous
15/10/95	Nea Salamina Famagusta	A	1-0	Gogic (p)
21/10/95	Apollon Limassol	H	1-0	Todorov
28/10/95	Olympiakos Nicosia	A	2-1	Todorov, Kiriakov
04/11/95	Omonia Aradippou	H	6-0	Kastanas 2, Gogic, Panayiotou A., Ignatov, Todorov
19/11/95	Ethnikos Akhnas	A	0-0	
26/11/95	APOEL Nicosia	H	3-3	Kiriakov 2, Melanargitis V.
02/12/95	AEK Larnaca	A	2-2	Gogic, Charalambous
09/12/95	Evaghoras Paphos	A	2-0	Todorov, Neocleous
17/12/95	AEL Limassol	H	2-2	Ignatov, Gogic
06/01/96	Aris Limassol	A	0-2	
14/01/96	Paralimni	H	5-0	Neocleous 2, Gogic, Ignatov, Kiriakov
27/01/96	Alki Larnaca	A	3-0	Kiriakov 2, Pounnas
10/02/96	Nea Salamina Famagusta	H	3-2	Kiriakov 2, Todorov
17/02/96	Apollon Limassol	A	0-0	
25/02/96	Olympiakos Nicosia	H	1-0	Rizos
09/03/96	Omonia Aradippou	A	2-0	Melanargitis V., Ignatov
23/03/96	Ethnikos Akhnas	H	2-0	Ashiotis ,Pizos
31/03/96	APOEL Nicosia	A	0-3	
06/04/96	AEK Larnaca	H	2-1	Ashiotis (p), Neocleous
21/04/96	Evaghoras Paphos	H	2-0	Gogic, Andreou S.
28/04/96	AEL Limassol	A	1-1	Gogic (p)
04/05/96	Aris Limassol	H	4-2	og (Loizou), og (Hailis), Gogic, Ignatov
11/05/96	Paralimni	A	3-0	Gogic 2 (1p), Charalambous
19/05/96	Omonia Nicosia	H	1-0	Neocleous

APOEL NICOSIA

CLUB DIRECTORY

APOEL FC
PO Box 1133
Nicosia
tel - (02) 495222/494994
fax - (02) 485517
Year of Formation - 1926
President - Ouranios Ioannides
Secretary - Gregoris Kazantzis
Coach - Hristo Bonev (96/97 - Jacek Gmoch)
Stadium - Makarion (20,000)

MAJOR HONOURS
League Championship - (16) 1936, 1937, 1938, 1939, 1940, 1947, 1948, 1949, 1952, 1965, 1973, 1980, 1986, 1990, 1992, 1996.
Domestic Cup - (15) 1937, 1941, 1947, 1951, 1963, 1968, 1969, 1973, 1976, 1978, 1979, 1984, 1993, 1995, 1996.

APPEARANCES 95/96

	P	Ap	(s)	Gls
Alexis ALEXANDROU	A	10	(12)	9
George ALONEFTIS	M		(2)	
Andonis ANDONIOU	A	5	(2)	
Aristos ARISTOCLEOUS	D	19	(6)	
Xenios ARISTOTELOUS	D	8	(1)	
Nicos CAHARALAMBOUS	D	5	(9)	
George CHRISTODOULOU	D	24	(1)	1
Costas COSTA	D	21		1
Lucas HADJILUCAS	A	18	(2)	2
Yiannos IOANNOU	A	21	(2)	8
József KIPRICH (HUN)	A	24		25
Christos KOUNTOURIS	D		(1)	
Kálmán KOVÁCS (HUN)	A	14	(8)	7
István KOZMA (HUN)	M	20		2
George PAPADOPOULOS	M	7	(1)	
Andros PETRIDES	G	26		
Costas PHASOULIOTIS	M	7	(13)	1
Christakis POUNNAS	M	13	(7)	
Toza SAPURIC	D	18		2
Nicos SATSIAS	M		(1)	
Costas SKAPOULIS	D		(1)	
Andros SOTIRIOU	A	7	(4)	4
Nicos TIMOTHEOU	D	19	(3)	1

LEAGUE RESULTS 1995/96

Date	Opponent		Score	Scorers
23/09/95	Nea Salamina Famagusta	A	4-1	Kiprich 2 (2p), Sotiriou 2
01/10/95	Apollon Limassol	H	1-0	Phasouliotis
14/10/95	Olympiakos Nicosia	A	2-0	Kiprich, Kozma
21/10/95	Omonia Aradippou	H	5-0	Kovács 2, Kiprich, Sotiriou, og (Yiorkas)
27/10/95	Ethnikos Akhnas	A	4-1	Alexandrou 3, Kiprich
04/11/95	Evaghoras Paphos	A	1-1	Alexandrou
18/11/95	AEK Larnaca	H	1-0	Costa
26/11/95	Anorthosis Famagusta	A	3-3	Alexandrou, Kiprich, Kovács
02/12/95	AEL Limassol	H	3-0	Timotheou, Kovács, Hadjilucas
10/12/95	Aris Limassol	A	1-1	Kiprich (p)
17/12/95	Paralimni	H	3-2	Kiprich 2 (1p), Ioannou
06/01/96	Omonia Nicosia	A	4-2	Alexandrou 2, Kiprich, Kozma
14/01/96	Alki Larnaca	H	2-1	Alexandrou, Kiprich
27/01/96	Apollon Limassol	A	2-0	Sapuric 2
10/02/96	Olympiakos Nicosia	H	1-0	Kovács
18/02/96	Omonia Aradippou	A	4-0	Kiprich 2 (1p), Ioannou, Christodoulou
24/02/96	Ethnikos Akhnas	H	3-2	Ioannou 2, Kovács
09/03/96	Evaghoras Paphos	H	5-0	Kiprich 4 (3p), Ioannou
24/03/96	AEK Larnaca	A	0-0	
31/03/96	Anorthosis Famagusta	H	3-0	Kiprich 3 (2p)
06/04/96	AEL Limassol	A	3-0	Kovács, Kiprich (p), Sotiriou
20/04/96	Aris Limassol	H	2-2	og (Tomic), Kiprich
27/04/96	Paralimni	A	1-1	Ioannou
05/05/96	Omonia Nicosia	H	1-1	Kiprich
12/05/96	Alki Larnaca	A	2-1	Hadjilucas, Ioannou
19/05/96	Nea Salamina Famagusta	H	4-1	Kiprich 2 (1p), Alexandrou, Ioannou

APOLLON LIMASSOL

CLUB DIRECTORY

Apollon FC
1 Mesolongiou Str.
PO Box 3206
Limassol
tel - (05) 363702/379082
fax - (05) 359116
Year of Formation - 1954
President - Dimis Kirzis
Secretary - George Papas
Coach - Martti Kuusela (96/97 - Moca Vukotic)
Stadium - Tsirion (22,000)

MAJOR HONOURS
League Championship - (2) 1991, 1994.
Domestic Cup - (4) 1966, 1967, 1986, 1992.

APPEARANCES 95/96

	P	Ap	(s)	Gls
Marios CHARALAMBOUS	D	23		
Michalis CHRISTOPHI	G	25		
Pambos CHRISTOPHI	D	10	(5)	
Costas CONSTANDINOU	D	19		
George EVRIPIDOU	M	1	(1)	
Christos GERMANOS	D	4	(7)	
Christos HADJICONSTANDIS	D	3		
George IOSIFIDES	M	24	(1)	2
Chrysostomos JURAS	D	11	(6)	1
George KAIS	D	3	(2)	
Slobodan KRCMAREVIC (YUG)	A	22		15
Marios MARNEROS	M	3	(3)	
George NICOLAOU	G	1		
Kakos PAPAKYRIAKOU	A	16	(4)	3
Nicos PAPAVASSILIOU	M	22		
Pambos PITTAS	D	22		2
Philippos PHILIPPOU	D	16	(1)	
Sladjan SCEPOVIC (YUG)	A	24	(1)	5
Andreas SOFOCLEOUS	D	4	(8)	
Stelios SOFOCLEOUS	M	4	(2)	
Milenko SPOLJARIC (YUG)	A	23		10
Angelos TSOLAKIS	A	6	(16)	4

LEAGUE RESULTS 1995/96

24/09/95	Ethnikos Akhnas	H	2-0	Spoljaric, Krcmarevic
01/10/95	APOEL Nicosia	A	0-1	
15/10/95	AEK Larnaca	H	3-1	Spoljaric, Krcmarevic, Tsolakis
21/10/95	Anorthosis Famagusta	A	0-1	
28/10/95	AEL Limassol	H	3-1	Spoljaric 2, Pittas
05/11/95	Aris Limassol	A	1-1	Papakyriakou
19/11/95	Paralimni	H	1-1	Spoljaric
25/11/95	Omonia Nicosia	A	1-1	Pittas
02/12/95	Alki Larnaca	H	3-0	Scepovic, Spoljaric, Papakyriakou
09/12/95	Nea Salamina Famagusta	A	2-1	Krcmarevic 2
16/12/95	Evaghoras Paphos	H	1-1	Scepovic
07/01/96	Olympiakos Nicosia	H	0-0	
13/01/96	Omonia Aradippou	A	2-1	Juras, Krcmarevic (p)
27/01/96	APOEL Nicosia	H	0-2	
11/02/96	AEK Larnaca	A	0-3	
17/02/96	Anorthosis Famagusta	H	0-0	
24/02/96	AEL Limassol	A	1-1	Tsolakis
09/03/96	Aris Limassol	H	2-1	Papakyriakou, Krcmarevic
23/03/96	Paralimni	A	2-0	Spoljaric, Krcmarevic
30/03/96	Omonia Nicosia	H	1-2	Krcmarevic
07/04/96	Alki Larnaca	A	2-2	Spoljaric 2
20/04/96	Nea Salamina Famagusta	H	3-3	Krcmarevic 3 (1p)
27/04/96	Evaghoras Paphos	A	5-0	Krcmarevic 3 (1p), Scepovic 2
04/05/96	Olympiakos Nicosia	A	2-2	Krcmarevic, Iosifides
12/05/96	Omonia Aradippou	H	5-0	Tsolakis 2, Iosifides, Scepovic, Spoljaric
18/05/96	Ethnikos Akhnas	A	0-3	

ARIS LIMASSOL

CLUB DIRECTORY

Aris FC
PO Box 579
Limassol
tel - (05) 382075/381076/360776
fax - (05) 379689
Year of Formation - 1930
President - Costakis Chrystophorou
Secretary - Nicos Georghiadis
Coach - Stavros Papadopoulos
(96/97 - Atanas Dramov)
Stadium - Tsirion (22,000)

APPEARANCES 95/96

	P	Ap	(s)	Gls
Andros CHRISTOPHI	G	17		
Pantelis DIMITRIADES	M	6		1
Kyriakos DIMOSTHENOUS	A	1	(1)	
Marios DIMOSTHENOUS	M	9	(12)	1
Kyriakos EVANGELOU	D	23		
George GEORGIOU	M	4	(2)	
Panikos HADJILOIZOU	A	1	(5)	1
Christakis HAILIS	M	23		
Christakis KASSIANOS	D	6	(9)	
Lambros LAMBROU	M		(2)	
Stelios LOGRAS	M	14	(4)	
Louis LOUIZOU	M	13	(2)	
Alkis MARKOU	G	9		
Jovo MISELJIC (YUG)	A	26		7
Nicos NICOLAOU	M	4	(2)	
Srboljub NIKOLIC (YUG)	A	24		12
Marios PEFKOS	A	11		1
Iosif PERATIKOS	A	2	(9)	
Achilleas SCHIZAS	M	17	(6)	3
George SOFOCLEOUS	A		(9)	
Vladan TOMIC (YUG)	M	26		7
Andreas TRATTOS	M	1	(1)	
Ioannis VASSILIOU	D	25		1
Christakis ZINONOS	D	24	(1)	

LEAGUE RESULTS 1995/96

23/09/95	Evaghoras Paphos	H	3-0	Nikolic 2, Schizas
30/09/95	Paralimni	H	0-0	
15/10/95	Omonia Nicosia	A	1-1	Nikolic
21/10/95	Alki Larnaca	H	2-3	Tomic, Nikolic
29/10/95	Nea Salamina Famagusta	A	0-2	
05/11/95	Apollon Limassol	H	1-1	Miseljic
19/11/95	Olympiakos Nicosia	A	0-0	
25/11/95	Omonia Aradippou	H	1-1	Hadjiloizou
02/12/95	Ethnikos Akhnas	A	1-1	Miseljic
10/12/95	APOEL Nicosia	H	1-1	Nikolic
16/12/95	AEK Larnaca	A	1-2	Miseljic
06/01/96	Anorthosis Famagusta	H	2-0	Tomic, Nikolic
13/01/96	AEL Limassol	A	2-1	Nikolic 2 (1p)
27/01/96	Paralimni	A	1-3	Nikolic
10/02/96	Omonia Nicosia	H	1-4	Miseljic
17/02/96	Alki Larnaca	A	2-0	Vassiliou, Schizas
28/02/96	Nea Salamina Famagusta	H	1-2	Nikolic (p)
09/03/96	Apollon Limassol	A	1-2	Nikolic
23/03/96	Olympiakos Nicosia	H	1-2	Tomic
31/03/96	Omonia Aradippou	A	3-1	Pefkos, Schizas, Tomic (p)
07/04/96	Ethnikos Akhnas	H	1-1	Dimosthenous
20/04/96	APOEL Nicosia	A	2-2	Miseljic, Tomic
27/04/96	AEK Larnaca	H	1-1	Tomic (p)
04/05/96	Anorthosis Famagusta	A	2-4	Miseljic 2
11/05/96	AEL Limassol	H	1-0	Nikolic
18/05/96	Evaghoras Paphos	A	2-1	Dimitriades, Tomic (p)

ETHNIKOS AKHNAS

CLUB DIRECTORY

Ethnikos FC of Akhna
Dhasaki Akhnas
tel - (04) 721302
fax - (04) 722060
Year of Formation - 1968
President - Kikis Philippou
Secretary - Theodosis Kontos
Coach - Takis Andoniou
(96/97 - Stavros Papadopoulos)
Stadium - Ethnikos (5,000)

APPEARANCES 95/96

	P	Ap	(s)	Gls
Pambos CHARALAMBOUS	D	9	(5)	
Christakis DAVID	D	4	(5)	
Dimitris DIMITRIOU	M	21		
Pambos ENGOMITIS	M	15	(2)	1
Yiotis ENGOMITIS	A	17	(1)	3
Christos FOULIS	D	21	(1)	1
Michalis GAVELIS	G	20	(1)	
Borce GJUREV (MAC)	A	25		4
George JAPOURAS	G	6		
Andreas KATZIS	D	10	(1)	
Sokol KUSHTA (ALB)	A	15	(4)	3
Lambros LAMBROU	A	10	(5)	2
Liasis LIASIS	D	7	(5)	1
Dragoslav MUSIC (YUG)	A	23	(3)	15
Floros NICOLAOU	D	20	(2)	1
Christos PASHIALIS	D	4	(14)	
Marios PASHIALIS	D	26		
Christos POYIATZIS	A		(1)	
Andonis SKAYIAS	A	11	(10)	2
Yiannos STAVRINOS	A	2	(9)	3
Lucas ZENIOU	A	20	(3)	

LEAGUE RESULTS 1995/96

Date	Opponent	H/A	Score	Scorers
24/09/95	Apollon Limassol	A	0-2	
30/09/95	Olympiakos Nicosia	H	4-1	Engomitis Y. 2, Music, Kushta
14/10/95	Omonia Aradippou	A	3-1	Skayias 2, Music
21/10/95	Evaghoras Paphos	A	0-0	
27/10/95	APOEL Nicosia	H	1-4	Kushta
05/11/95	AEK Larnaca	A	1-2	Music
19/11/95	Anorthosis Famagusta	H	0-0	
26/11/95	AEL Limassol	A	0-0	
02/12/95	Aris Limassol	H	1-1	Foulis
09/12/95	Paralimni	A	3-2	Music 2, Gjurev
16/12/95	Omonia Nicosia	H	0-2	
06/01/96	Alki Larnaca	A	3-3	Gjurev, Music (p), Engomitis Y.
13/01/96	Nea Salamina Famagusta	H	1-0	Music
27/01/96	Olympiakos Nicosia	A	0-2	
10/02/96	Omonia Aradippou	H	2-1	Music 2
17/02/96	Evaghoras Paphos	H	1-1	Stavrinos
24/02/96	APOEL Nicosia	A	2-3	Stavrinos, Liasis
09/03/96	AEK Larnaca	H	1-1	Lambrou
23/03/96	Anorthosis Famagusta	A	0-2	
30/03/96	AEL Limassol	H	2-1	Music 2
07/04/96	Aris Limassol	A	1-1	Music (p)
20/04/96	Paralimni	H	0-0	
27/04/96	Omonia Nicosia	A	2-1	Nicolaou., Lambrou
04/05/96	Alki Larnaca	H	1-1	Engomitis P.
11/05/96	Nea Salamina Famagusta	A	4-1	Music 2, Gjurev, Stavrinos
18/05/96	Apollon Limassol	H	3-0	Music, Gjurev, Kushta

EVAGHORAS PAPHOS

CLUB DIRECTORY

Evaghoras FC
P.O. Box 102
Paphos
tel - (06) 232550
fax - (06) 246301
Year of Formation - 1961
President - George Papaonisiforou
Secretary - George Hadjikyriakou
Coach - Aurel Ticleanu (96/97 - Fitos Neophytou)
Stadium - Paphiako (8,000)

APPEARANCES 95/96

	P	Ap	(s)	Gls
Andreas AGATHOCLEOUS	A	6	(2)	
Pambos CHARALAMBOUS	A	17	(2)	1
Costas CONSTANDINIDIS	M	3	(4)	
Tomis CHRYSOSTOMOU	A	2	(10)	
Dimos DIMOSTHENOUS	D	17	(4)	1
Ion DUDAN (ROM)	A	23		1
Efstathios EFSTATHIOU	D	6	(1)	
Marios GEORGIADIS	M		(1)	
Theodosis GEORGIADIS	D		(2)	
Gocha GOGRICHIANI (GEO)	A	15		2
Charis HADJIANDONIS	A		(2)	
Kyriakos IGNATIOU	A	6	(5)	
Marian IVAN (ROM)	M	12		3
Andreas KOMODROMOS	M	16	(2)	2
Petros MINA	M	11	(3)	
Michalis MICHAEL	D	24		
Dimitris NEOPHYTOU	D	4		
Andronikos NICOLAOU	D	4	(6)	
Marios ONISIFOROU	G	17	(1)	
Yiannis PAHTALIAS	M	21		3
Panayiotis PANAYIOTOU	D	10		1
Pambos PHILIOTIS	A	12	(1)	
Andreas POLYDOROU	M	11	(2)	
Nicos THEMISTOCLEOUS	D		(1)	
Andreas TSAPIS	A		(6)	
Marios TSIAKKAS	A	19	(2)	
Stephanos VOSKARIDIS	A	5	(4)	
Christos YIOUKVIET	G	9		
Savvas ZOITSAS	A	16	(7)	7

LEAGUE RESULTS 1995/96

23/09/95	Aris Limassol	A	0-3	
30/09/95	Omonia Aradippou	H	5-0	Ivan 2, Charalambous, Panayiotou, Dudan
15/10/95	Paralimni	A	1-5	Gogrichiani (p)
21/10/95	Ethnikos Akhnas	H	0-0	
29/10/95	Omonia Nicosia	A	1-8	Ivan
04/11/95	APOEL Nicosia	H	1-1	Zoitsas
19/11/95	Alki Larnaca	A	0-1	
25/11/95	AEK Larnaca	H	0-1	
03/12/95	Nea Salamina Famagusta	A	1-1	Komodromos
09/12/95	Anorthosis Famagusta	H	0-2	
16/12/95	Apollon Limassol	A	1-1	Komodromos
06/01/96	AEL Limassol	H	0-2	
13/01/96	Olympiakos Nicosia	A	0-1	
27/01/96	Omonia Aradippou	A	2-1	Zoitsas 2
10/02/96	Paralimni	H	2-2	Pahtalias (p), Dimosthenous
17/02/96	Ethnikos Akhnas	A	1-1	Zoitsas
24/02/96	Omonia Nicosia	H	0-2	
09/03/96	APOEL Nicosia	A	1-5	Pahtalias
23/03/96	Alki Larnaca	H	2-2	Pahtalias (p), Zoitsas
30/03/96	AEK Larnaca	A	0-2	
06/04/96	Nea Salamina Famagusta	H	1-2	Gogrichiani
21/04/96	Anorthosis Famagusta	A	0-2	
27/04/96	Apollon Limassol	H	0-5	
04/05/96	AEL Limassol	A	1-5	Zoitsas
11/05/96	Olympiakos Nicosia	H	0-2	
18/05/96	Aris Limassol	H	1-2	Zoitsas

NEA SALAMINA FAMAGUSTA

CLUB DIRECTORY

Nea Salamina FC of Famagusta
PO Box 345
Larnaca
tel - (04) 652317/654490
fax - (04) 626850
Year of Formation - 1948
President - Kikis Kazamias
Secretary - Nicos Charalambous
Coach - Boris Nikolov (96/97 - Slobodan Karalic)
Stadium - Ammohostos (8,000)

APPEARANCES 95/96

	P	Ap	(s)	Gls
Andreas ADAMOU	A	9	(4)	
Ardemis ANDREOU	M	8	(5)	
Pambis ANDREOU	A	26		13
Pantelis DIMITRIOU	D	23	(2)	
Elias ELIA	D	15	(4)	1
George ELIA	A	24	(1)	3
Andreas IOANNIDES	M	2	(9)	
Yiannakis IOANNOU	G	14		
Nebojsa JONTSEV (YUG)	M	24		6
Andonis LYSANDROU	G	12	(1)	
Vassos MAVROS	D	18	(4)	
Nicos NICOLAOU	A	19	(3)	2
Yiannakis OKKAS	A	5	(7)	3
Marios PAVLOU	D	2	(5)	
Tasos PORPHYRIOU	A	18	(5)	2
Elisseos PSARAS	D	25		
Sasa SKARA (YUG)	A	22		6
Milko TODOROVIC (YUG)	M	15	(3)	1
Kypros TSINGELIS	D	5	(9)	

LEAGUE RESULTS 1995/96

23/09/95	APOEL Nicosia	H	1-4	Andreou P.
01/10/95	AEK Larnaca	A	1-4	Todorovic
15/10/95	Anorthosis Famagusta	H	0-1	
22/10/95	AEL Limassol	A	1-0	Nicolaou
29/10/95	Aris Limassol	H	2-0	Skara, Elia G.
04/11/95	Paralimni	A	1-1	Elia G.
18/11/95	Omonia Nicosia	H	2-5	Andreou P. 2
26/11/95	Alki Larnaca	A	0-5	
03/12/95	Evaghoras Paphos	H	1-1	Jontsev
09/12/95	Apollon Limassol	H	1-2	Andreou P.
16/12/95	Olympiakos Nicosia	A	0-1	
07/01/96	Omonia Aradippou	H	4-1	Skara 2, Andreou P., Porphyriou
13/01/96	Ethnikos Akhnas	A	0-1	
28/01/96	AEK Larnaca	H	0-1	
10/02/96	Anorthosis Famagusta	A	2-3	Jontsev, Skara
17/02/96	AEL Limassol	H	2-1	Skara, Andreou P.
28/02/96	Aris Limassol	A	2-1	Elia E., Jontsev
10/03/96	Paralimni	H	2-1	Skara, Jontsev
23/03/96	Omonia Nicosia	A	0-3	
30/03/96	Alki Larnaca	H	1-0	Jontsev
06/04/96	Evaghoras Paphos	A	2-1	Andreou P. 2
20/04/96	Apollon Limassol	A	3-3	Andreou P. 3 (1p)
28/04/96	Olympiakos Nicosia	H	4-0	Okkas 2, Andreou P. (p), Jontsev
04/05/96	Omonia Aradippou	A	3-0	Porphyriou, Okkas, Andreou P.
11/05/96	Ethnikos Akhnas	H	1-4	Elia G.
18/05/96	APOEL Nicosia	A	1-4	Nicolaou

OLYMPIAKOS NICOSIA

CLUB DIRECTORY

Olympiakos FC
PO Box 2339
Nicosia
tel - (02) 430405/367170
fax - (02) 466292
Year of Formation - 1931
President - Nicos Hartziotis
Secretary - Andreas Tsangaris
Coach - Nicos Karoulias (96/97 - Andonis Natsis)
Stadium - Makarion (20,000)

MAJOR HONOURS
League Championship - (3) 1967, 1969, 1971.
Domestic Cup - (1) 1977.

APPEARANCES 95/96

	P	Ap	(s)	Gls
Iacovos APOSTOLOU	D	24		
Pambos CHARALAMBOUS	M	6	(6)	
Elias CHRYSOSTOMOU	D	6	(1)	
Renos DIMITRIADIS	D	3	(8)	1
Telis DRAKOPOULOS (GRE)	A	24		4
George GEORGIOU	A	6	(14)	3
Michalis JAPOURAS	M	11	(6)	
Dimitri KUDINOV (GEO)	D	23		
Andreas KOULOUMBRIS	A	4	(6)	
Nicos MAGNITIS	M	16	(4)	3
Marios MARKOU	D	11	(1)	
Vesko MIHAJLOVIC (YUG)	A	24		11
Nicos NEOCLEOUS	G	1		
George PANTELI	M	8	(4)	
Ara PETROSIAN	M	16	(5)	
Petros SAVVA	G	25		
Costas SERAFIM	D	24	(1)	
Nicos STAVROU	D	19	(2)	
Marios THEMISTOCLEOUS	M	24	(2)	2
Savvas TSIAKLIS	D	11	(3)	

LEAGUE RESULTS 1995/96

24/09/95	Omonia Aradippou	H	1-1	Mihajlovic
30/09/95	Ethnikos Akhnas	A	1-4	Magnitis
14/10/95	APOEL Nicosia	H	0-2	
22/10/95	AEK Larnaca	A	0-1	
28/10/95	Anorthosis Famagusta	H	1-2	Drakopoulos
04/11/95	AEL Limassol	A	1-3	Magnitis
19/11/95	Aris Limassol	H	0-0	
25/11/95	Paralimni	A	1-2	Mihajlovic
03/12/95	Omonia Nicosia	H	0-1	
10/12/95	Alki Larnaca	A	0-1	
16/12/95	Nea Salamina Famagusta	H	1-0	Drakopoulos
07/01/96	Apollon Limassol	A	0-0	
13/01/96	Evaghoras Paphos	H	1-0	Mihajlovic
27/01/96	Ethnikos Akhnas	H	2-0	Dimitriadis, Mihajlovic
10/02/96	APOEL Nicosia	A	0-1	
18/02/96	AEK Larnaca	H	0-2	
25/02/96	Anorthosis Famagusta	A	0-1	
10/03/96	AEL Limassol	H	1-0	Magnitis
23/03/96	Aris Limassol	A	2-1	Themistocleous, Mihajlovic
30/03/96	Paralimni	H	1-1	Mihajlovic
06/04/96	Omonia Nicosia	A	3-3	Drakopoulos, Mihajlovic, Georgiou
21/04/96	Alki Larnaca	H	2-0	Themistocleous, Georgiou
28/04/96	Nea Salamina Famagusta	A	0-4	
04/05/96	Apollon Limassol	H	2-2	Mihajlovic 2 (1p)
11/05/96	Evaghoras Paphos	A	2-0	Mihajlovic, Drakopoulos
18/05/96	Omonia Aradippou	A	2-0	Georgiou, Mihajlovic

OMONIA ARADIPPOU

CLUB DIRECTORY

Omonia FC
Aradippou
Larnaca
tel - (04) 625244
fax - (04) 636344
Year of Formation - 1929
President - Andreas Evangelides
Secretary - Lucas Michailas
Coach - Petar Slavkic (96/97 - Paris Rotoklis)
Stadium - Municipal (6,000)

APPEARANCES 95/96

	P	Ap	(s)	Gls
Tasos ALAMBRITIS	D	22		
Suad BESIREVIC (YUG)	A	10	(1)	1
Costas CHARALAMBOUS	A	17	(1)	2
George CONSTANDINOU	D	7	(6)	
Nicos ELIA	M	15	(3)	3
Iacovos IACOVOU	A	11	(6)	
Christos KITTOS	A	7	(4)	
Savvas KOLOS	D	11	(2)	
Andreas KOUNTOURIS	A	5	(2)	
George LIBERIS	D	13	(3)	
Andreas LIMBOURIS	G	17	(1)	
Lucas LUCA	A	7	(3)	
Mladen MILIKOVIC (YUG)	A	22		
George PANAYI	M	19	(2)	7
Lambros PANAYIOTOU	G	8	(2)	
Andreas PARTOS	G	1		
Dimitris SERGIOU	M	12	(12)	1
Nicos SHIKKIS	M	23		2
Damir SPICA (YUG)	A	14	(1)	1
Savvas THEODOROU	M	11	(4)	
George VASSILIOU	M	13	(10)	1
Petros YIORKAS	D	18	(2)	
Costas ZACHARIOU	D	3	(5)	

LEAGUE RESULTS 1995/96

24/09/95	Olympiakos Nicosia	A	1-1	Panayi
30/09/95	Evaghoras Paphos	A	0-5	
14/10/95	Ethnikos Akhnas	H	1-3	Vassiliou
21/10/95	APOEL Nicosia	A	0-5	
28/10/95	AEK Larnaca	H	1-2	Elia (p)
04/11/95	Anorthosis Famagusta	A	0-6	
19/11/95	AEL Limassol	H	1-3	Charalambous
25/11/95	Aris Limassol	A	1-1	Spica
02/12/95	Paralimni	H	1-2	Panayi
09/12/95	Omonia Nicosia	A	1-3	Elia
16/12/95	Alki Larnaca	H	3-4	Besirevic, Charalambous, Panayi
07/01/96	Nea Salamina Famagusta	A	1-4	Panayi
13/01/96	Apollon Limassol	H	1-2	Sergiou
27/01/96	Evaghoras Paphos	H	1-2	Shikkis
10/02/96	Ethnikos Akhnas	A	1-2	Panayi
18/02/96	APOEL Nicosia	H	0-4	
24/02/96	AEK Larnaca	A	0-1	
09/03/96	Anorthosis Famagusta	H	0-2	
24/03/96	AEL Limassol	A	1-3	Elia
31/03/96	Aris Limassol	H	1-3	Panayi
06/04/96	Paralimni	A	1-4	Shikkis
20/04/96	Omonia Nicosia	H	0-9	
27/04/96	Alki Larnaca	A	1-5	Panayi
04/05/96	Nea Salamina Famagusta	H	0-3	
11/05/96	Apollon Limassol	A	0-5	
18/05/96	Olympiakos Nicosia	H	0-2	

OMONIA NICOSIA

CLUB DIRECTORY

Omonia FC
PO Box 617
Nicosia
tel - (02) 441677
fax - (02) 437053
Year of Formation - 1948
President - Lakis Polykarpou
Secretary - Andros Hadjicharalambous
Coach - Gerd Prokop (96/97 - Angel Kolev)
Stadium - Makarion (20,000)

MAJOR HONOURS
League Championship - (17) 1961, 1966, 1972, 1974, 1975, 1976, 1977, 1978, 1979, 1981, 1982, 1983, 1984, 1985, 1987, 1989, 1993.
Domestic Cup - (10) 1965, 1972, 1974, 1980, 1981, 1982, 1983, 1988, 1991, 1994.

APPEARANCES 95/96

	P	Ap	(s)	Gls
Andreas ANDREOU	M	24		6
Kyriakos ANDREOU	A	12	(2)	5
Andreas CHARITOU	G	21		
George CONSTANTINIDES	M		(2)	
Christos CHRISTODOULOU	D	9	(6)	
Evaghoras CHRISTOPHI	D	25		2
George CHRISTOPHOROU	G	5	(2)	
Chrysanthos CHRYSANTHOU	D	2	(3)	
Dragan DJUKANOVIC (YUG)	A	16	(2)	8
Ioakim IOAKIM	D	11	(7)	
Costas KAIAFAS	A	18	(6)	3
Costas KALOTHEOU	M	8	(5)	1
Yiannos KALOTHEOU	D	15	(3)	
Andreas KANTILOS	A	7	(15)	1
Costas MALEKKOS	A	20	(1)	15
Panayiotis PANAYIOTOU	D	22		2
George SAVVIDES	A	23	(1)	1
Valentin STEFAN (ROM)	D	16	(3)	2
Nedim TUTIC (BOS)	M	18	(1)	6
Panikos XIOUROUPPAS	A	14	(7)	12

LEAGUE RESULTS 1995/96

23/09/95	Anorthosis Famagusta	H	2-0	Xiouruppas, Djukanovic
01/10/95	AEL Limassol	A	2-1	Malekkos, Christophi
15/10/95	Aris Limassol	H	1-1	Tutic
21/10/95	Paralimni	A	1-0	Malekkos
29/10/95	Evaghoras Paphos	H	8-1	Malekkos 3, Tutic, Kantilos, Djukanovic, Kaiafas, Xiovrouppas
04/11/95	Alki Larnaca	H	1-1	Kalotheou C.
18/11/95	Nea Salamina Famagusta	A	5-2	Malekkos 2, Christophi, Xiourouppas, Andreou A.
25/11/95	Apollon Limassol	H	1-1	Xiourouppas
02/12/95	Olympiakos Nicosia	A	1-0	Andreou A.
09/12/95	Omonia Aradippou	H	3-1	Xiourouppas 2, Tutic
16/12/95	Ethnikos Akhnas	A	2-0	Andreou K., Xiourouppas
06/01/96	APOEL Nicosia	H	2-4	Malekkos, Panayiotou
13/01/96	AEK Larnaca	A	0-3	
28/01/96	AEL Limassol	H	6-2	Xiourouppas 3, Djukanovic, Malekkos, Tutic
10/02/96	Aris Limassol	A	4-1	Xiourouppas 2 (1p), Malekkos, Djukanovic
17/02/96	Paralimni	H	3-1	Malekkos 2, Djukanovic
24/02/96	Evaghoras Paphos	A	2-0	og (Tsiakais), Djukanovic
09/03/96	Alki Larnaca	A	0-2	
23/03/96	Nea Salamina Famagusta	H	3-0	Stefan, Andreou K. 2
30/03/96	Apollon Limassol	A	2-1	Malekkos, Savvides
06/04/96	Olympiakos Nicosia	H	3-3	Andreou K., Kaiafas, Andreou A.
20/04/96	Omonia Aradippou	A	9-0	Malekkos 2, Djukanovic 2, Kaiafas, Andreou K., Tutic (p), Stefan, og (Milikovic)
27/04/96	Ethnikos Akhnas	H	1-2	Tutic (p)
05/05/96	APOEL Nicosia	A	1-1	Panayiotou
11/05/96	AEK Larnaca	H	3-1	Andreou A. 3
19/05/96	Anorthosis Famagusta	A	0-1	

PARALIMNI

CLUB DIRECTORY

Union of Paralimni
PO Box 20
Paralimni
tel - (03) 821352
fax - (03) 820514
Year of Formation - 1936
President - Costas Paphitis
Secretary - Marios Makronissos
Coach - Slobodan Vucekovic
(96/97 - Gerd Prokop)
Stadium - Paralimni (7,000)

APPEARANCES 95/96

	P	Ap	(s)	Gls
Afxendis AFXENDI	A	4	(5)	
Epaminondas CHRISTINAKIS	G	25		
Michalis CONSTANDINOU	A	11	(8)	6
Michalis ECONOMOU	A	22		1
George GAVRIEL	M	25		
Andonis IOANNOU	M		(5)	
Aristos KARAS	D	9	(10)	
Marios KARAS	D	17	(1)	1
George KIZAS	M	1	(7)	
George KOSMAS	D	12	(3)	
Radovan KRSTOVIC (YUG)	M	13	(2)	1
Kyriakos MASTROU	D	24		
George MERTAKAS	G	1	(1)	
Willy NWAKANMA	A	25		13
Christos PIERETIS	M		(1)	
Andreas PITIRIS	D		(1)	
Panayiotis SPYROU	M	16	(6)	
Nebojsa VELKOVIC (YUG)	M	25		
Nebojsa VIGNJEVIC (YUG)	A	23		6
Yiasemakis YIASOUMI	A	5	(16)	5
Dimos YOUMENOS	A	2	(2)	
Andonis ZEMBASHIS	M	26		4

LEAGUE RESULTS 1995/96

23/09/95	AEL Limassol	H	4-1	Zembashis 2, Krstovic, Nwakanma
30/09/95	Aris Limassol	A	0-0	
15/10/95	Evaghoras Paphos	H	5-1	Nwakanma 2, Vignjevic 2, Karas M.
21/10/95	Omonia Nicosia	H	0-1	
28/10/95	Alki Larnaca	A	0-0	
04/11/95	Nea Salamina Famagusta	H	1-1	Constandinou
19/11/95	Apollon Limassol	A	1-1	Zembashis
25/11/95	Olympiakos Nicosia	H	2-1	Zembashis, Nwakanma
02/12/95	Omonia Aradippou	A	2-1	Vignjevic, Nwakanma
09/12/95	Ethnikos Akhnas	H	2-3	Nwakanma 2
17/12/95	APOEL Nicosia	A	2-3	Vignjevic, Yiasoumi
06/01/96	AEK Larnaca	H	1-0	Nwakanma (p)
14/01/96	Anorthosis Famagusta	A	0-5	
27/01/96	Aris Limassol	H	3-1	Nwakanma 2, Constandinou
10/02/96	Evaghoras Paphos	A	2-2	Nwakanma, Yiasoumi
17/02/96	Omonia Nicosia	A	1-3	Constandinou
24/02/96	Alki Larnaca	H	2-1	Vignjevic, Nwakanma
10/03/96	Nea Salamina Famagusta	A	1-2	Yiasoumi
23/03/96	Apollon Limassol	H	0-2	
30/03/96	Olympiakos Nicosia	A	1-1	Yiasoumi
06/04/96	Omonia Aradippou	H	4-1	Economou, Constandinou, Vignjevic (p), Yiasoumi
20/04/96	Ethnikos Akhnas	A	0-0	
27/04/96	APOEL Nicosia	H	1-1	Constandinou
04/05/96	AEK Larnaca	A	0-3	
11/05/96	Anorthosis Famagusta	H	0-3	
18/05/96	AEL Limassol	A	2-2	Nwakanma, Constandinou

PROMOTED CLUBS

SECOND DIVISION FINAL TABLE 95/96

		Pd	W	D	L	F	A	Pt	GD
1	**APOP Paphos**	**26**	**16**	**7**	**3**	**56**	**26**	**55**	**+30**
2	**APEP Pitsilias**	**26**	**17**	**1**	**8**	**44**	**28**	**52**	**+16**
3	**Anagennisis Dherynia**	**26**	**13**	**10**	**3**	**49**	**20**	**49**	**+29**
4	Dighenis Morphou	26	14	3	9	49	24	45	+25
5	Halkanoras Dhali	26	12	5	9	47	38	41	+9
6	Onisillos Sotiras	26	12	5	9	40	38	41	+2
7	PAEEK Kyrenia	26	10	7	9	35	33	37	+2
8	Akritos Hloraka	26	10	6	10	41	42	36	-1
9	Ethnikos Ashia	26	10	5	11	50	55	35	-5
10	AEZ Zakaki	26	9	7	10	34	37	34	-3
11	Doxa Katokopias	26	8	9	9	34	35	33	-1
12	Ethnikos Latsia	26	6	5	15	36	56	23	-20
13	Othellos Athienou	26	6	4	16	29	67	22	-38
14	Ayia Napa	26	1	2	23	26	71	5	-45

CLUB DIRECTORY

APOP FC
PO Box 80
Paphos
tel - (06) 232004/235353
fax - (06) 232004
Year of Formation - 1953
President - Elias Eliades
Coach - Radmilo Ivanevic
Stadium - Paphiako (8,000)

CLUB DIRECTORY

APEP Pitsilias
PO Box 1451
Limassol
tel - (05) 532600
fax - (05) 532288
Year of Formation - 1979
President - Andreas Nicolaides
Coach - Akis Ayiomamitis
Stadium - Kyperounta (6,000)

CLUB DIRECTORY

Anagennisis Dherynia
6 Ammohostou Street
Dherynia
tel - (03) 821436
Year of Formation - 1920
Coach - Andreas Kissonergis
Stadium - Anagenissis (5,000)

CZECH REPUBLIC

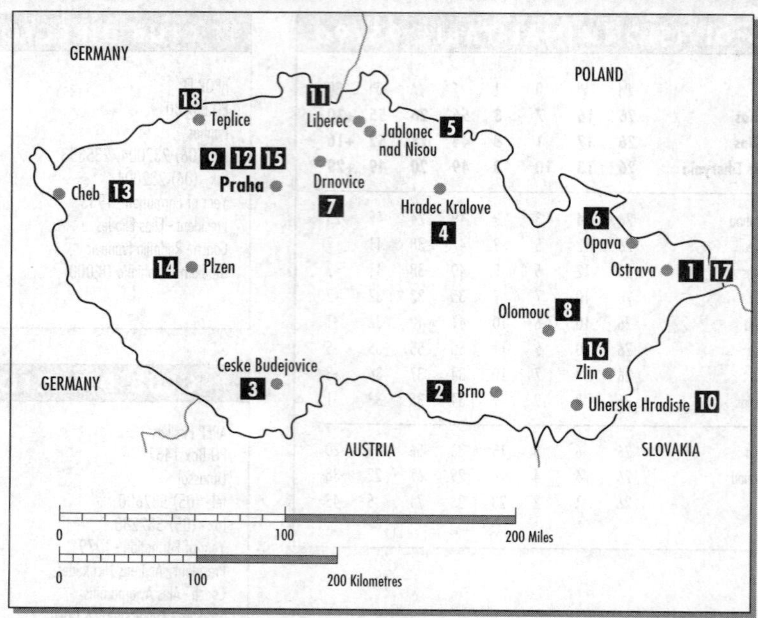

1	BANIK OSTRAVA	266
2	BOBY BRNO	267
3	SK CESKE BUDEJOVICE	268
4	SK HRADEC KRALOVE	269
5	JABLONEC NAD NISOU	270
6	KAUCUK OPAVA	271
7	PETRA DRNOVICE	272
8	SIGMA OLOMOUC	273
9	SLAVIA PRAHA	274
10	SLOVACKA SLAVIA UHERSKE HRADISTE	275
11	SLOVAN LIBEREC	276
12	SPARTA PRAHA	277
13	UNION CHEB	278
14	VIKTORIA PLZEN	279
15	VIKTORIA ZIZKOV	280
16	FC ZLIN	281
17	KARVINA VITKOVICE	282
18	FK TEPLICE	282

SLAVIA TASTE VICTORY AT LONG LAST

All praise for Uhrin's Euro heroes

FEDERATION DIRECTORY

Ceskomoravsky Fotbalovy Svaz
Diskarska 100, 169 00 Praha 6 - Strahov
tel - (02) 20513575/20513572/ 20513451/20513394
fax - (02) 352784
Stadium - Strahov, Prague (20,000)

Year of Formation - 1990
President - Frantisek Chvalovsky
Secretary - JUDr. Jan Obst

So, that 0-1 defeat in Luxembourg wasn't such a bad thing after all!

Just 12 months on from one of the most embarrassing results in Czech football history, Dusan Uhrin's team recovered sufficiently to become the vice-champions of Europe. It was an incredible transformation, and the Czech coach deserved high praise for skilfully guiding the team around a series of potential pitfalls and into the European Championship final.

At the start of the season, with the Luxembourg nightmare still weighing heavily on their conscience, the Czech players knew what they had do to qualify for England. They could not afford the slightest hiccup, or they would be out of the running. Jan Suchoparek's late saving header in Norway sparked the revival. Thereafter the Czechs did not put a foot wrong, comfortably beating Norway at home, driving themselves on to a brilliant win in Belarus, and, fittingly, confirming their qualification as Group Five winners with a revenge 3-0 triumph at home to Luxembourg.

A month later, at the Euro '96 Final Draw in Birmingham, the joy of qualification subsided when the Czech Republic found themselves thrown into the 'Group of Death' alongside Germany, Italy and Russia. Their task could not have been more daunting.

After a string of promising friendly results, the Czechs arrived in England high on confidence. But the bookmakers had them down as 80-1 outsiders for the title and at 20-1 just to get through their first-round group, and those odds lengthened after the Czechs' poor opening performance - a 0-2 defeat by Germany. It looked as if those of the team's many supporters who had only booked 10-day holidays had done the right thing.

But then came the tremendously exciting encounter with Italy at Anfield. Two excellent goals from Nedved and Bejbl, allied to a masterful tactical display, provided the upset of the tournament. From then on Euro '96 became a Czech fairytale - Smicer's memorable late equaliser against Russia; Poborsky's impudent lob against Portugal;

LEAGUE CHAMPIONSHIP RESULTS 95/96

		1	2	3	4	5	6	7	8	9	10	11	12	13	14	15	16
1	Banik Ostrava		0-2	0-1	2-0	1-1	1-2	5-3	3-1	1-2	2-1	1-0	4-1	3-0	3-2	2-2	3-1
2	Boby Brno	3-2		5-2	2-0	1-0	1-1	2-2	2-3	0-2	2-0	1-1	1-0	2-0	0-3	3-1	1-1
3	SK Ceske Budejovice	1-0	0-0		0-3	3-0	1-1	2-1	2-1	2-3	2-0	0-0	2-0	3-3	2-2	1-1	2-0
4	SK Hradec Kralove	2-1	1-0	1-2		2-2	0-1	1-0	1-3	0-3	2-0	0-0	0-2	0-1	0-0	2-0	0-2
5	Jablonec nad Nisou	3-0	3-0	2-1	4-2		2-1	0-1	4-2	2-1	4-0	1-0	1-0	0-0	1-0	5-0	1-0
6	Kaucuk Opava	3-0	0-2	3-1	2-1	0-1		1-2	1-1	1-1	2-0	0-0	2-0	4-1	2-0	1-0	3-2
7	Petra Drnovice	3-1	2-3	2-0	3-0	2-0	3-1		1-2	3-0	2-2	0-0	4-4	3-0	4-1	2-2	3-0
8	Sigma Olomouc	1-0	2-0	4-0	1-0	2-1	3-2	2-0		2-1	2-0	3-0	3-1	3-1	3-0	1-1	3-0
9	Slavia Praha	2-0	2-1	3-0	2-1	2-1	3-0	1-2	4-0		9-1	2-1	0-2	2-0	2-1	5-0	2-0
10	Slov. Slav. Uherske Hradiste	1-2	1-3	0-4	1-0	0-4	0-1	0-1	2-1	0-2		1-1	2-2	0-0	2-2	1-0	1-1
11	Slovan Liberec	3-0	1-0	2-1	3-2	1-0	1-0	4-0	2-0	2-3	4-0		1-0	2-3	1-0	0-0	1-2
12	Sparta Praha	1-1	4-0	3-0	5-0	1-1	1-1	2-1	0-2	3-1	4-0	3-1		3-0	1-0	1-0	3-0
13	Union Cheb	1-1	3-1	0-0	0-2	2-0	3-1	1-2	1-1	1-3	1-0	4-0	3-3		1-2	2-2	1-1
14	Viktoria Plzen	1-0	1-1	2-0	1-2	0-1	2-1	1-1	2-0	0-1	1-1	2-0	2-1	1-0		1-0	3-0
15	Viktoria Zizkov	2-1	4-0	4-0	2-2	1-0	1-1	1-0	1-2	1-3	2-2	1-1	1-4	2-0	2-0		3-0
16	FC Zlin	0-0	0-0	1-0	1-1	0-0	0-1	1-0	0-0	0-1	2-0	0-1	1-1	0-2	1-0	0-1	

LEAGUE CHAMPIONSHIP FINAL TABLE 95/96

			Home					Away					Total						
		Pd	W	D	L	F	A	W	D	L	F	A	W	D	L	F	A	Pt	GD
1	Slavia Praha	30	13	0	2	41	10	10	1	4	27	18	23	1	6	68	28	70	+40
2	Sigma Olomouc	30	14	1	0	35	7	5	3	7	19	26	19	4	7	54	33	61	+21
3	Jablonec nad Nisou	30	13	1	1	33	8	3	4	8	12	18	16	5	9	45	26	53	+19
4	Sparta Praha	30	11	3	1	35	8	3	4	8	21	27	14	7	9	56	35	49	+21
5	Petra Drnovice	30	9	4	2	37	16	5	2	8	16	24	14	6	10	53	40	48	+13
6	Kaucuk Opava	30	9	3	3	25	12	4	4	7	15	22	13	7	10	40	34	46	+6
7	Slovan Liberec	30	11	1	3	28	11	1	7	7	6	19	12	8	10	34	30	44	+4
8	Boby Brno	30	8	4	3	26	18	4	3	8	13	24	12	7	11	39	42	43	-3
9	Viktoria Plzen	30	9	3	3	20	9	2	3	10	13	25	11	6	13	33	34	39	-1
10	Viktoria Zizkov	30	8	4	3	28	16	1	6	8	10	27	9	10	11	38	43	37	-5
11	SK Ceske Budejovice	30	7	6	2	23	15	3	1	11	12	32	10	7	13	35	47	37	-12
12	Banik Ostrava	30	9	2	4	31	19	1	3	11	9	27	10	5	15	40	46	35	-6
13	Union Cheb	30	5	6	4	24	19	3	3	9	11	28	8	9	13	35	47	33	-12
14	SK Hradec Kralove	30	5	3	7	12	17	3	2	10	16	29	8	5	17	28	46	29	-18
15	FC Zlin	30	4	6	5	7	8	2	3	10	10	30	6	9	15	17	38	27	-21
16	Slov. Slav. Uherske Hradiste	30	3	5	7	12	24	0	3	12	7	41	3	8	19	19	65	17	-46

the shoot-out victory over long-unbeaten France. In their second meeting with Germany, at Wembley, the Czechs played some excellent football. But, although they took the lead with a non-existent penalty, luck and the officials were generally against them. The final, controversial 'golden goal' was a desperately unhappy ending to their magnificent adventure.

For a team competing in their first major tournament as an independent nation, the Czech Republic did extraordinarily well, surpassing everybody's expectations. The European Championship had long been a favoured tournament of the Czechs (and Slovaks, when the two were united), but even the victory of 1976, when the Germans were beaten on penalties in the final, seemed to pale in comparison with the exploits of the 1996 heroes. Certainly, the scenes of celebration in Prague and the rest of the country were unprecedented, and huge numbers of Czech fans came out onto the streets to welcome Uhrin and his players home.

One fact generally overlooked was that several of the Republic's leading players in England were relative

NATIONAL TEAM RESULTS 95/96

16/08/95	Norway (ECQ)	A	Oslo	1-1	Suchoparek (84)
06/09/95	Norway (ECQ)	H	Prague	2-0	Skuhravy (6p), Drulak (86)
07/10/95	Belarus (ECQ)	A	Minsk	2-0	Frydek (25), Berger (84)
15/11/95	Luxembourg (ECQ)	H	Prague	3-0	Drulak (37, 46), Berger (57)
13/12/95	Kuwait	A	Kuwait City	2-1	Gabriel (5), Drulak (30)
26/03/96	Turkey	H	Ostrava	3-0	Suchoparek (14), Kuka (59p, 90)
24/04/96	Republic of Ireland	H	Prague	2-0	Frydek (61), Kuka (68)
29/05/96	Austria	A	Salzburg	0-1	
01/06/96	Switzerland	A	Basle	2-1	Kuka (23, 84)
09/06/96	Germany (ECF)	N	Manchester	0-2	
14/06/96	Italy (ECF)	N	Liverpool	2-1	Nedved (5), Bejbl (36)
19/06/96	Russia (ECF)	N	Liverpool	3-3	Suchoparek (7), Kuka (19), Smicer (89)
23/06/96	Portugal (ECF)	N	Birmingham	1-0	Poborsky (53)
26/06/96	France (ECF)	N	Manchester	0-0	
30/06/96	Germany (ECF)	N	Wembley	1-2	Berger (58p)

TOP SCORERS

22 Radek DRULAK (Petra Drnovice)
14 Pavel NEDVED (Sparta Praha)
13 Miroslav BARANEK (Sigma Olomouc)
11 Robert VAGNER (Slavia Praha)
Rene WAGNER (Boby Brno)
Jiri BARTL (Kaucuk Opava)
Karel VACHA (SK Ceske Budejovice)
Jan SAIDL (SK Ceske Budejovice)
Karel POBORSKY (Slavia Praha)
10 Pavel CERNY (SK Hradec Kralove)
Radek ONDERKA (Sigma Olomouc)

NATIONAL TEAM APPEARANCES 95/96

Coach - Dusan UHRIN	NOR	NOR	BLS	LUX	KUW	TUR	IRL	AUT	SUI	GER	ITA	RUS	POR	FRA	GER	Cps	Gls
Petr KOUBA (28/01/69) - Sparta Praha	G	G	G	G		G	G		G	G	G	G	G	G	G	36	-
Pavel HAPAL (27/07/69) - CD Tenerife (ESP)	D		D	D		M	M									31	1
Jan SUCHOPAREK (23/09/69) - Slavia Praha	D	D		D		D		D	D	D	D	D	D		D	36	4
Miroslav KADLEC (22/06/64) - 1.FC Kaiserslautern (GER)	D	D	D	D		D	D46	D46	D	D	D		D	D	D	58	2
Tomas REPKA (02/01/74) - Sparta Praha	D	D	D				D									14	-
Radoslav LATAL (06/01/70) - FC Schalke 04 (GER)	M78	M	M	M		M	M59	M	M	M	M88	M	M			33	3
Martin FRYDEK (09/03/69) - Sparta Praha	M	M70	M87	M			M	M	M58	M46						25	3
Patrik BERGER (10/11/73) - Borussia Dortmund (GER)	M46		s74	M84			M	s46	s58	s46	M64	M90	s90	s46	M	21	9
Jiri NEMEC (15/05/66) - FC Schalke 04 (GER)	M	M	M					M46	M	M	M	M	M	M84	M	41	-
Radek DRULAK (12/01/62) - Petra Drnovice	A78	s19	A	A	A	A82	A		A46	s46				A70		15	4
Pavel KUKA (19/07/68) - 1.FC Kaiserslautern (GER)	A	A19	A	A87		A	A78	A64	A	A	A	A64	A		A	48	18
Pavel NEDVED (30/08/72) - Sparta Praha	s46	M	M74	M		M	s59	M	M	M	M	M		M	M	14	1
Karel POBORSKY (30/03/72) - Slavia Praha	s78	s70	s87	s72		M67		A77	s46	A46	A	A	M	M	M88	20	1
Petr SAMEC (14/02/64) - SK Hradec Kralove	s78															9	2
Vaclav NEMECEK (25/01/67) - Servette FC Genève (SUI)		M	M15	M72		M46	M46	D60			s88	s90	M90	M		60	6
Tomas SKUHRAVY (07/09/65) - Genoa (ITA)		A80														49	17
Vratislav LOKVENC (27/09/73) - Sparta Praha		s80		s87												2	-
Michal HORNAK (28/04/70) - Sparta Praha			s15			D70	D73	s60	D	D	D	D	D	D	D	12	-
Vladimir SMICER (24/05/73) - Slavia Praha				s84				s64			s64	s64	A85	A46	s88	8	1
Ladislav MAIER (04/01/66) - Slovan Liberec					G											1	-
Karel RADA (02/03/72) - Sigma Olomouc					D		s73							D	D	4	-
Lubos KOZEL (16/03/73) - Slavia Praha					D	s70										2	-
Petr GABRIEL (17/05/73) - Viktoria Zizkov					D											2	1
Radek BEJBL (29/08/72) - Slavia Praha					M	s46	s46	M	M	M	M	M	M		M	13	1
Jaromir NAVRATIL (20/02/63) - Jablonec nad Nisou					M	s67										2	-
Radim NECAS (26/08/69) - Union Cheb					M66											2	
Edvard LASOTA (07/03/71) - Petra Drnovice					M											1	-
Miroslav BARANEK (01/11/73) - Sigma Olomouc					M55											1	-
Josef OBAJDIN (07/11/70) - Slovan Liberec					A80											1	-
Robert VAGNER (15/05/74) - Slavia Praha					s55											1	-
Tomas GALASEK (15/01/73) - Banik Ostrava					s66											2	-
Radovan HROMADKO (16/05/69) - Jablonec nad Nisou					s80											1	-
Marek POSTULKA (21/06/70) - Banik Ostrava						s82										4	3
Lubos KUBIK (20/01/64) - Petra Drnovice							s46	s46				D	s85	s84		51	11
Milan KERBR (09/06/67) - Sigma Olomouc							s78	s77								2	-
Pavel SRNICEK (10/03/68) - Newcastle United (ENG)								G								4	-
Pavel NOVOTNY (14/09/73) - Slavia Praha														M		1	-
Martin KOTULEK (11/09/69) - Sigma Olomouc														s70		4	-

newcomers to the team. None of Poborsky, Bejbl, Nedved and Smicer had been regulars during the qualifying tournament. Indeed, the crucial goals scored by those players were all 'firsts' in international football. That magical foursome had another thing in common. They all came to Euro '96 as Czech league players, only to be sold off to different parts of Europe - respectively, England, Spain, Italy and France - after the tournament. Before departing the Czech club scene, however, the quartet also represented their country proudly on the European Cup front.

The 1995/96 season was a major success for Czech clubs in European competition. The performance of Hradec Kralove in reaching the Cup-winners' Cup second round earned many plaudits. But the UEFA Cup exploits of Prague's big two, Sparta and Slavia, dwarfed it.

A Nedved-inspired Sparta came through a very tough preliminary-round tie against Turkish side Galatasaray and lasted four rounds before succumbing to the might of Milan. As for Slavia, they were the revelation of the whole European season. Before Christmas they had already disposed of four distinguished opponents - Sturm Graz, Freiburg, Lugano and Lens - and this after winning all of their away games. Then, in the quarter-final, came a dramatic extra-time, away-goals victory over Italian side Roma. Bordeaux halted Slavia's run in the semi-finals, but not before the club in the distinctive red and white halves had made a whole continent sit up and take notice of them.

It was to be Slavia's year all round. Without a championship victory for almost half a century, the famous club finally ended that nightmare drought to bring huge relief and jubilation to their fans. During the early part of the season Slavia failed to make an impression. They lost three of their first six games, including 0-2 to arch-rivals Sparta, and it looked once again as if they would miss out on their long-cherished prize. But in the middle of the season, buoyed by their extended stay in Europe, Slavia got their act together. They put together a run of eight successive victories, one of which was awarded by default after their opponents, Kaucuk Opava, were caught in a snowstorm and failed to turn up in Prague. A second defeat by Sparta stalled the surge, but whereas the previous season Slavia had wilted in the closing stages under pressure from their arch-rivals, now they simply shrugged off the defeat and returned to their winning habit for another six games.

INTERNATIONAL HONOURS

World Cup Finals appearances: 1934 (runners-up), 1938 (qtr-finals), 1954, 1958, 1962 (runners-up), 1970, 1982, 1990 (qtr-finals)

European Championship appearances: 1960 (3rd), 1976 (Winners), 1980 (3rd), 1996 (runners-up)

DOMESTIC CUP RESULTS

SECOND ROUND

TJ Prestice 0, Slavia Praha 2
Horni Pocernice 0, Viktoria Zizkov 2
SK Trebon 1, Viktoria Plzen 6
SK Rakovnik 0, SK Ceske Budejovice 3
1.FC Brummer Ceska Lipa 1, Slovan Liberec 1 (4-5 on pens.)
SK Roudnice 0, Jablonec nad Nisou 7
FC Fomei Hradec Kralove 0, SK Hradec Kralove 6
Spolana Neratovice 0, Sparta Praha 2
ZETES Sveradice 0, Union Cheb 9
MSA Dolni Benesov 0, Banik Ostrava 5
KM Ratiskovice 2, Sigma Olomouc 4
PS Prerov 0, Svit Zlin 1
Novy Jicin 1, Kaucuk Opava 7
Synot Stare Mesto 0, JOKO Sl. Sl. Uherske Hradiste 5
VTJ Znojmo 2, Petra Drnovice 4
Unex Unicov 0, Boby Brno 0 (5-3 on pens.)
Admira/Slavoj Praha 2, GGS ARMA Usti nad Labem 1
Pelikan Decin 3, Chmel Blsany 2
Atlantic Lazne Bohdanec 2, SK Pardubice 0
NH Ostrava 3, Zelezarny Trinec 1
Motorpal Jihlava 1, ALFA Slusovice 0
Cesky Raj Turnov 0, SK Chrudim 2
Sparta Krc 0, Svarc Benesov 0 (0-3 on pens.)
PARES Prusanky 0, LeRK Brno 0 (6-7 on pens.)
VTJ Spartak Hulin 0, Tatran Postorna 5
Valasske Mezirici 1, FC Karvina Vitkovice 3
FK Krnov 1, VP Frydek-Mistek 5
EME Melnik 1, FK Teplice 2
SK Cesky Brod 1, Dukla Praha 4
CSK Uhersky Brod 0, Banik Havirov 2
Tatran VTJ Prachatice 1, FC Pribram 4
VT Chomutov 0, Bohemians Praha 1

THIRD ROUND

Dukla Praha 1, Viktoria Zizkov 1 (4-2 on pens.)
TK Teplice 4, Union Cheb 1
Pelikan Decin 2, Jablonec nad Nisou 6
Svarc Benesov 2, Slovan Liberec 0
FC Pribram 2, SK Ceske Budejovice 1
NH Ostrava 0, Banik Ostrava 4
FC Karvina Vitkovice 4, Svit Zlin 2
Tatran Postorna 0, Petra Drnovice 0 (1-4 on pens.)
VP Frydek-Mistek 0, Kaucuk Opava 1
LeRK Brno 2, JOKO Sl. Sl. Uherske Hradiste 2 (5-4 on pens.)
Unex Unicov 1, Motorpal Jihlava 1 (3-5 on pens.)
Banik Havirov 0, Sigma Olomouc 3
Admira/Slavoj Praha 2, Viktoria Plzen 1
Bohemians Praha 0, Slavia Praha 2
SK Chrudim 0, Sparta Praha 1
Atlantic Lazne Bohdanec 1, SK Hradec Kralove 1 (3-1 on pens.)

FOURTH ROUND

Dukla Praha 0, FK Teplice 1
Admira/Slavoj Praha 0, Jablonec nad Nisou 4
Svarc Benesov 0, FC Pribram 3
Motorpal Jihlava 1, LeRK Brno 1 (5-4 on pens.)
Banik Ostrava 1, Petra Drnovice 1 (3-5 on pens.)
Kaucuk Opava 3, Sigma Olomouc 0
FC Karvina Vitkovice 0, Slavia Praha 1
Atlantic Lazne Bohdanec 1, Sparta Praha 5

QUARTER-FINALS

Kaucuk Opava 0, Jablonec nad Nisou 0 (3-4 on pens.)
FK Teplice 0, Motorpal Jihlava 0 (5-4 on pens.)
Petra Drnovice 3, FC Pribram 0
Sparta Praha 2, Slavia Praha 0

SEMI-FINALS

Petra Drnovice 2, Jablonec nad Nisou 1
FK Teplice 1, Sparta Praha 4

FINAL

22/05/95, Prague
SPARTA PRAHA 4 Nedved (26, 55), Svoboda (45), Kouba (71p)
PETRA DRNOVICE 0
referee - Bohunek
SPARTA PRAHA - Kouba; Hornak, Novotny, Repka, Vonasek (Tyce 81), Mistr, Svoboda, Budka, Nedved, Frydek, Lokvenc (Obajdin 84).
PETRA DRNOVICE - Bernady; Slachta, Nesicky (Postulka 61), Silhavy, Vesely, Kafka, Baranek, Weber, Lasota, Timko (Rusnak 66), Drulak.

Ironically, the moment Slavia's triumph was sealed came after they had fallen to their heaviest defeat of the season, 0-3 at Drnovice. As the team stopped off at a hamburger restaurant on their way back to Prague, news came through that Sigma Olomouc, their closest pursuers, had sensationally been beaten by the league's bottom team Uherske Hradiste. That was it. 49 years of hurt had ended with a simple radio message. Champagne milk shakes all round!

Slavia won their title just in the nick of time. With the team's best players - Poborsky, Suchoparek, Bejbl, Smicer - all launching successful self-promotion campaigns at Euro '96, the team inevitably broke up during the summer, leaving coach Frantisek Cipro with the near impossible job of rebuilding a new side of equal stature.

Whether Slavia can remain at the top depends to a large extent on how Sparta deal with the wholescale reorganisation which took place at the club during the 95/96 season. Sparta came dangerously close to going out of business. An estimated £10 million in the red and with numerous bad debts, the club were in desperate financial straits. So desperate, in fact, that controversial young president Petr Mach was forced to accept a takeover bid from a Slovakian company, VSZ Kosice, the giant steelworks that also finance the Slovakian club 1.FC Kosice.

On the field Sparta's good run in Europe was not reflected by their league form. Apart from the two victories over Slavia they had a mediocre campaign and could only finish fourth, 21 points behind the champions. Not everything was bad news, however. Sparta completed a hat-trick of wins over Slavia in the Czech Cup and went on to win the trophy - and salvage a European place - by destroying Petra Drnovice 4-0 in the final.

That defeat completed a disastrous late run for Drnovice. Although the club finished in a best ever fifth place, they had expected at least a place in Europe. But five defeats in their last six league games, plus the Cup final débâcle, left that objective unfulfilled. The surprise achievements in the league were provided by second-placed Olomouc (14 wins and one draw at home), third-placed Jablonec (their best-ever placing) and sixth-placed Kaucuk Opava (in their first season at this level). The team that accompanied Opava up from the Second Division, Uherske Hradiste, went straight back down after a season of unending toil. They were joined by FC Zlin (Svit Zlin in the autumn) and, ultimately, by Union Cheb as well. Cheb's owner, Ivo Mlatilik, was unable to find sufficient sponsorship to keep the club afloat in the First Division, so their 96/97 place was withdrawn. This left an extra promotion spot. It should have gone to the third-placed team in Division Two, Tatran Postorna, but they declined the invitation, which then passed to Bohemians Prague, who duly accepted. So, just one year after their relegation, Bohemians were back among the big boys, climbing the ladder together with FC Karvina Vítkovice and FK Teplice.

PLAYERS OF THE SEASON

RADEK DRULAK

The Indian summer of 34-year-old striker Radek Drulak did not quite stretch through to Euro '96, where he only made a couple of brief appearances, but no one player was more instrumental in getting the Czechs to England in the first place. The balding marksman struck important goals against both Norway and Luxembourg to clinch his country's qualification ticket and earn himself the Czech Republic Player of the Year award for 1995. The Petra Drnovice forward also bagged the Czech league's top scorer prize for the second year running, increasing his winning total from 15 to 22 and bringing his all-time Czech/Czechoslovakian league total to 127 goals in 256 matches.

VLADIMIR SMICER

23-year-old Vladimir Smicer was good for a headline or two during Euro '96. His late equaliser against Russia took the Czechs into the quarter-finals and had Italians cursing his name from Udine to Palermo. It also nearly disrupted his wedding plans. In the end he went ahead with the nuptials despite the fact that they were scheduled for two days before the Euro '96 final. The newly-married man has now taken wife and football boots to French club Lens, one of the teams he helped to knock out of the UEFA Cup during his last, memorable season with Slavia Prague. A very clever, penetrative forward, he is poised for an outstanding career at the apex of the European game.

PAVEL NEDVED

But for Pavel Nedved, Sparta Prague would probably have sunk without trace in 1995/96. The midfield all-rounder plugged gaps, ran himself into the ground, and also managed to score 14 league goals - finishing second only to Drulak in the final listings. A technically accomplished player with exceptional fitness and a good turn of pace, he proved himself to be an indispensable element of the Czech Republic team at Euro '96. His goal against Italy was composure personified. It obviously impressed some of the watching scouts, because after Euro '96 Nedved became one of Europe's top transfer targets. He eventually chose to move to Lazio in a deal that was not without its financial complications.

EUROPEAN CUPS RESULTS 95/96

CUP-WINNERS' CUP

● SK HRADEC KRALOVE

Preliminary round FC VADUZ (LIE)

A 5-0 Cerny (15), Samec (32, 50, 58), Ptacek (37)
Vahala; Vrabel, Urban, Urbanek, Ulich, Ptacek, Hynek (Drozd 69), Cerny, Smarda, Samec (Masek 75), Kincl (Holub 58).

H 9-1 Samec (4, 9, 30, 53), Urban (14, 83p), Vrabel (37), Smarda (50p), Ptacek (63)
Postulka; Rehak, Urban, Vrabel (Pilny 64), Ulich, Dzubara, Ptacek, Cerny, Smarda (Drozd 58), Samec (Masek 71), Holub.

1st round FC KØBENHAVN (DEN)

H 5-0 Samec (32, 75), Hynek (39), Cerny (52), Ptacek (90)
Vahala; Rehak, Urban, Urbanek, Dzubara, Hynek, Cerny, Ulich (Ptacek 89), Smarda, Samec (Holub 90), Masek (Kaplan 86).

A 2-2 Urbanek (10), Rehak (12)
Vahala; Rehak, Urban, Vrabel, Dzubara, Ulich, Hynek, Cerny, Urbanek (Ptacek 82), Samec (Masek 40), Kaplan (Drozd 88).

2nd round DINAMO MOSKVA (RUS)

A 0-1
Vahala; Rehak (Vrabel 76), Urban, Urbanek, Dzubara, Hynek, Ptacek (Drozd 78), Cerny, Smarda, Masek, Kaplan (Holub 64).

H 1-0 Kaplan (15) (aet;1-3 on pens.)
Vahala; Rehak, Urban, Urbanek, Dzubara, Ulich, Hynek, Cerny, Drozd, Holub, Kaplan (Zoubek 73; Ptacek 117).

UEFA CUP

● SPARTA PRAHA

Preliminary round GALATASARAY (TUR)

H 3-1 Nedved (18, 73), Lokvenc (23)
Kouba; Hornak, Votava, Repka, Mistr (Svoboda 69), Budka, Frydek (Pozar 88), Nedved, Vonasek, Koller (Siegl 72), Lokvenc.

A 1-1 Nedved (23)
Kouba; Hornak, Votava, Repka, Vonasek, Mistr (Siegl 73), Budka (Pozar 85), Frydek, Nedved, Lokvenc, Koller (Svoboda 89).

1st round SILKEBORG IF (DEN)

H 0-1
Kouba; Hornak, Pozar, Repka, Vonasek, Svoboda (Mistr 46), Budka, Frydek, Nedved, Koller (Nemec 62), Lokvenc.

A 2-1 Lokvenc (21), Nemec (51)
Kouba; Pozar, Hornak, Repka, Vonasek, Mistr (Svoboda 72), Budka, Frydek (Tyce 87), Nedved, Nemec, Lokvenc.

2nd round ZIMBRU CHISINAU (MOL)

H 4-3 Frydek (23), Nedved (44p, 56), Budka (57)
Kouba; Hornak, Novotny, Pozar, Vonasek, Mistr (Kostelnik 89), Budka, Frydek (Svoboda 80), Nedved, Lokvenc, Koller (Nemec 46).

A 2-0 Koller (45), Vonasek (64)
Kostelnik; Vonasek, Novotny, Repka, Tyce, Mistr (Svoboda 74), Frydek, Pozar, Nedved, Lokvenc, Koller.

3rd round MILAN (ITA)

A 0-2
Kouba; Hornak, Novotny, Repka, Tyce, Mistr, Budka, Frydek, Nedved, Lokvenc, Koller (Svoboda 72).

H 0-0
Kouba; Pozar, Hornak, Repka, Vonasek, Mistr, Budka, Svoboda, Nedved, Lokvenc, Frydek (Koller 77).

● SLAVIA PRAHA

Preliminary round SK STURM GRAZ (AUT)

A 1-0 Bejbl (83p)
Stejskal; Suchoparek, Hysky, Penicka, Lerch, Poborsky, Bejbl, Smejkal (Kristofik 81), Novotny, Smicer (Vavra 67), Vagner (Novotny 86).

H 1-1 Hysky (45)
Stejskal; Penicka, Suchoparek, Hysky, Lerch, Poborsky, Bejbl, Smejkal (Kristofik 59), Novotny, Smicer (Vavra 62), Vagner (Hunal 84).

1st round SC FREIBURG (GER)

A 2-1 Novotny (22), Penicka (75)
Stejskal; Penicka, Suchoparek, Hysky, Vavra (Hogen 88), Lerch, Kristofik (Smejkal 31), Bejbl, Novotny, Smicer, Vagner (Hunal 62).

H 0-0
Stejskal; Penicka, Suchoparek, Jirasek, Vavra, Lerch (Pixa 62), Kristofik, Bejbl, Novotny, Smicer (Jarolim 83), Vagner (Hogen 87).

2nd round FC LUGANO (SUI)

A 2-1 Vagner (20), Penicka (26)
Stejskal; Hysky, Kozel, Novotny, Penicka, Poborsky (Jirasek 89), Kristofik (Lerch 56), Bejbl, Smejkal, Smicer (Jarolim 83), Vagner.

H 1-0 Smicer (62)
Stejskal; Penicka, Kozel, Suchoparek, Hunal (Jirasek 83), Hysky, Poborsky, Kristofik, Smejkal (Vavra 75), Smicer, Vagner (Jarolim 90).

3rd round RC LENS (FRA)

H 0-0
Stejskal; Penicka, Kozel, Hysky, Poborsky, Kristofik, Bejbl, Smejkal, Novotny, Smicer, Vagner (Vavra 60).

A 1-0 (aet) Poborsky (95)
Stejskal; Suchoparek, Kozel, Hysky (Hunal 46), Penicka (Vavra 114), Bejbl, Kristofik (Vagner 94), Smejkal, Novotny, Poborsky, Smicer.

Quarter-final ROMA (ITA)

H 2-0 Poborsky (10), Vagner (50)
Stejskal; Penicka, Kozel, Suchoparek, Novotny, Poborsky, Lerch, Bejbl, Kristofik (Hysky 66), Smicer (Hunal 88), Vagner (Vavra 74).

A 1-3 (aet) Vavra (112)
Stejskal; Hysky, Kozel, Suchoparek, Penicka, Poborsky, Lerch (Stajner 106), Bejbl, Kristofik (Vavra 68), Novotny, Smicer (Vagner 87).

Semi-final GIRONDINS DE BORDEAUX (FRA)

H 0-1
Stejskal; Hysky (Hunal 29), Kozel, Novotny, Lerch, Poborsky, Bejbl, Kristofik (Vavra 46), Smejkal (Stajner 77), Smicer, Vagner.

A 0-1
Stejskal; Penicka, Kozel, Hunal (Hysky 75), Suchoparek, Lerch, Bejbl, Poborsky, Kristofik (Stajner 74), Smicer, Vavra.

PROFILE
KAREL POBORSKY

If Karel Poborsky had been given one pound every time an onlooker at Euro '96 made reference to his extravagant hairstyle, he could probably have afforded to join Manchester United for nothing.

But even if it was the long unkempt tresses that first got him noticed, by the end of the tournament is was undoubtedly the player's exceptional footballing ability that had turned him into a household name around Europe (even if the TV captions did insist on mis-spelling his name as 'Poborski'). There was no official Player of the Tournament at Euro '96, but Poborsky would surely have picked up as many votes as the likes of Shearer, Sammer and Suker in any straw poll.

The remarkable thing about Poborsky's sudden claim to fame was that prior to the European Championship he was by no means a certainty in Dusan Uhrin's team. In the qualifying competition he only appearaed from the start in one match - away to Holland - and even then he did not complete 90 minutes. Latterly he had come to be used as a sort of 'supersub', his pace and trickery being employed to wreak havoc on tiring defences in the last 15 minutes.

In England, however, Poborsky was on the pitch from the start in all six of the Republic's matches, and he was the team's most prominent individual in at least half of those. The highpoint, of course, was his extra-ordinary scoop-shot which earned the Czechs their quarter-final victory over Portugal. It was Poborsky's first goal for his country.

Euro '96 capped a wonderful season for the quietly-spoken 24-year-old. He actually started it with Viktoria Zizkov. But after just one game, with Zizkov's finances in need of a short sharp shock, Poborsky was transferred across the capital to Slavia Prague. The move paid off handsomely for all concerned.

Poborsky rapidly developed into an inspirational string-puller in the Slavia midfield. In both the championship-winning campaign and the run to the UEFA Cup semi-finals the energetic young schemer sent the Slavia fans into raptures with his daring solo dribbles and spectacular goals. Two of his most memorable strikes were saved for Europe. The first came in the third round, away to Lens. The tie was all square, with extra-time just five minutes old, when Poborsky raced clear of the Lens offside trap, rounded the goalkeeper, paused to compose himself and then fired the ball home. The second was less elaborate, just a momentary show of genius as he curled the ball directly into the net from the touchline to open Slavia's account in the quarter-final against Roma.

A native of Trebon, a small town in Southern Bohemia, Poborsky received early encouragement in his footballing career from his father, himself an ex-professional, and joined the top local team Dynamo Ceske Budejovice when he was 12 years of age. At 18 Poborsky made his senior team début for the club and subsequently helped them into the Czechoslovakian First Division. Two years later, after the Czech Republic had set up its own independent national league, he left Ceske Budejovice for Prague, where one of the newly-admitted clubs, Viktoria Zizkov, were attempting to challenge the traditional giants of Prague football with money from the personal fortune of one-time expatriate millionaire Vratislav Cekan.

One of Poborsky's first games for Zizkov was in London, in a Cup-winners' Cup tie against Chelsea. He could hardly have imagined then that two years on he would be returning to the north-west of the city to play for his country in the European Championship final; even less that he would be making regular visits to the English capital in the red shirt of Manchester United.

But that is the reality. After his brilliant Euro '96, Slavia were never going to be able to hold on to their most prized asset. After a lot of to-ing and fro-ing United finally got their man for £3.5 million. He will be sorely missed in Prague. But in Manchester, Karel Poborsky has the talent and the temperament to become one of Old Trafford's finest.

BANIK OSTRAVA

CLUB DIRECTORY

FC Banik Ostrava
Stadion Bazaly
Bukovanskeho 4
710 00 Ostrava 2
tel - (069) 6214630/224129
fax - (069) 6233282
Year of Formation - 1922
President - Josef Burkovic
Secretary - Zdenek Rygel
Coach - Jan Zachar
Stadium - Bazaly (19,990)

MAJOR HONOURS
League Championship - (3) 1976, 1980, 1981.
Domestic Cup - (3) 1973, 1978, 1991.

APPEARANCES 95/96

	P	Ap	(s)	Gls
Vit BARANEK	G	9	(2)	
Rene BOLF	D	1	(2)	
Peter BUGAR (SVK)	M	9		2
Petr BYSTRON	M	6		1
Vladimir CAP	D	7	(2)	
Vaclav CINCALA	A	11	(9)	3
Martin CIZEK	M	27		9
Milan DUHAN	M	11	(9)	2
Tomas GALASEK	D	26		5
Pavel HARAZIM	D	14		
Richard HROTEK	D	6		
Marek JANKULOVSKI	M	3	(6)	1
Norbert JURACKA (SVK)	G	19		
Jakub KAFKA	G	2	(1)	
Roman KLIMES	D	16	(3)	
Lubomir KNOFLICEK	A	11	(2)	3
Pavel KUBANEK	M	6	(2)	
Karel KULA	M	1		
Karel KULYK	A	4	(4)	
Petr MASLEJ	M	18	(3)	3
Roman NOHAVICA	D	25		1
Michal ONDRACEK	D	13		
Michal PANCIK (SVK)	A	7	(2)	2
Ales PIKL	M	6	(1)	1
Marek POSTULKA	A	5	(2)	
Petr RUMAN	A	16	(7)	3
Radek SLONCIK	M	23		
David SOURADA	M	1	(12)	
Vitezslav TUMA	A	1	(4)	1
Petr VESELY	D	14		1
Ludek ZDRAHAL	D	12	(1)	1

LEAGUE RESULTS 1995/96

Date	Opponent	H/A	Score	Scorers
29/07/95	Viktoria Zizkov	A	1-2	Duhan
01/08/95	Union Cheb	H	3-0	Galasek, Bystron, Knoflicek
04/08/95	Sparta Praha	A	1-1	Galasek
20/08/95	Jablonec Nad Nisou	H	1-1	Ruman
27/08/95	Viktoria Plzen	A	0-1	
10/09/95	SK Ceske Budejovice	H	0-1	
17/09/95	Slovacka Slavia Uherske Hradiste	A	2-1	Vesely, Tuma
24/09/95	Boby Brno	A	2-3	Ruman, Knoflicek
29/09/95	Petra Drnovice	H	5-3	Cizek 3, Galasek (p), Maslej
15/10/95	SK Hradec Kralove	A	1-2	Nohavica
22/10/95	Slavia Praha	H	1-2	Cizek
29/10/95	Slovan Liberec	A	0-3	
03/11/95	Sigma Olomouc	H	3-1	Cizek 2, Cincala
19/11/95	Svit Zlin	A	0-0	
26/11/95	Kaucuk Opava	H	1-2	Cincala
25/02/96	Union Cheb	A	1-1	Pancik
01/03/96	Sparta Praha	H	4-1	Galasek 2 (1p), Bugar, og (Hornak)
09/03/96	Jablonec Nad Nisou	A	0-3	
23/03/96	SK Ceske Budejovice	A	0-1	
31/03/96	Slovacka Slavia Uherske Hradiste	H	2-1	Maslej, Duhan
02/04/96	Viktoria Zizkov	H	2-2	Cizek (p), Pancik
10/04/96	Viktoria Plzen	H	3-2	Cincala, Maslej, Cizek (p)
14/04/96	Petra Drnovice	A	1-3	Pikl
21/04/96	SK Hradec Kralove	H	2-0	Zdrahal, Knoflicek
28/04/96	Slavia Praha	A	0-2	
01/05/96	Slovan Liberec	H	1-0	Ruman
05/05/96	Sigma Olomouc	A	0-1	
08/05/96	Boby Brno	H	0-2	
12/05/96	FC Zlin	H	3-1	Bugar, Jankulovski, Cizek
18/05/96	Kaucuk Opava	A	0-3	

BOBY BRNO

CLUB DIRECTORY

FC Boby Sport Brno
Drobneho 45
602 00 Brno
tel - (05) 7272434/7272483/7272111
fax - (05) 42214415
Year of Formation - 1913
President - PaeDr. Lubomir Hrstka
Secretary - Radek Belak
Coach - Petr Ulicny
Stadium - Za Luzankami (35,600)

MAJOR HONOURS
League Championship - (1) 1978.

APPEARANCES 95/96

	P	Ap	(s)	Gls
Petr BASTAR	D	2	(3)	
Vladimir CHALOUPKA	A		(6)	
Marcel CUPAK	A	25	(3)	5
Richard DOSTALEK	M	27		7
Pavel HOLOMEK	A	28	(2)	5
Petr KOCMAN	M	22		1
Premsyl KOVAR	A		(2)	
Petr KRIVANEK	D	29		
Roman KUKLETA	A	5	(3)	3
Petr MALER	D	14	(3)	
Jan MAROSI	M	25	(2)	2
Milan PACANDA	A	3	(5)	
Jan PALINEK	D	27	(1)	1
Lubos PRIBYL	G	27		
Patrik SIEGL	A	7	(21)	1
Martin SPINAR	D		(5)	
Zdenek VALNOHA	M	23	(6)	2
Viliam VIDUMSKY (SVK)	D	24	(3)	
Radim VLASAK	G	3	(1)	
Rene WAGNER	A	24	(2)	11
Martin ZBONCAK	M	4	(5)	
Marek ZUBEK	M	11	(6)	1

LEAGUE RESULTS 1995/96

Date	Opponent	H/A	Score	Scorers
29/07/95	Slovan Liberec	A	0-1	
02/08/95	Viktoria Plzen	H	0-3	
06/08/95	Sigma Olomouc	A	0-2	
20/08/95	SK Ceske Budejovice	H	5-2	Cupak, Dostalek, Wagner, Holomek 2
27/08/95	Svit Zlin	A	0-0	
10/09/95	Slovacka Slavia Uherske Hradiste	H	2-0	Cupak (p), Wagner
17/09/95	Kaucuk Opava	A	2-0	Kukleta, Dostalek
24/09/95	Banik Ostrava	H	3-2	Zubek, Kukleta, Wagner
01/10/95	Viktoria Zizkov	A	0-4	
15/10/95	Petra Drnovice	H	2-2	Dostalek 2 (1p)
22/10/95	Union Cheb	A	1-3	Wagner
29/10/95	SK Hradec Kralove	H	2-0	Wagner, Kukleta
05/11/95	Sparta Praha	A	0-4	
17/11/95	Slavia Praha	H	0-2	
26/11/95	Jablonec Nad Nisou	A	0-3	
06/03/96	Viktoria Plzen	A	1-1	Dostalek
09/03/96	SK Ceske Budejovice	A	0-0	
19/03/96	Slovan Liberec	H	1-1	Holomek
23/03/96	Slovacka Slavia Uherske Hradiste	A	3-1	Valnoha, Marosi, Wagner
27/03/96	FC Zlin	H	1-1	Cupak
30/03/96	Kaucuk Opava	H	1-1	Palinek
03/04/96	Sigma Olomouc	H	2-3	Cupak 2
12/04/96	Viktoria Zizkov	H	3-1	Kocman, Wagner, Siegl
19/04/96	Petra Drnovice	A	3-2	Dostalek, Wagner, Valnoha
27/04/96	Union Cheb	H	2-0	Holomek, Wagner (p)
01/05/96	SK Hradec Kralove	A	0-1	
03/05/96	Sparta Praha	H	1-0	Dostalek
08/05/96	Banik Ostrava	A	2-0	Marosi, Wagner
12/05/96	Slavia Praha	A	1-2	Wagner
18/05/96	Jablonec Nad Nisou	H	1-0	Holomek

SK CESKE BUDEJOVICE

CLUB DIRECTORY

SK Ceske Budejovice
Strelecky ostrov 3
370 21 Ceske Budejovice
tel - (038) 7312504/7312502/7312503
fax - (038) 7312503
Year of Formation - 1905
President - Zdenek Cadek
Secretary - Emil Kus
Coach - Pavel Tobias
Stadium - Na Streleckem ostrove (12,000)

APPEARANCES 95/96

	P	Ap	(s)	Gls
Pavel BABKA	M	28		2
Milan BARTESKA	M	25	(1)	3
Josef BEJR	G	2	(2)	
Vladimir BLUML	D	2		
Erich BRABEC	D	2	(10)	
Michal BROZMAN	M	3	(1)	
Ladislav FUJDIAR	A	15	(12)	4
Martin HAVEL	A		(2)	
Peter HOLEC (SVK)	G	28		
Zdenek HRDINA	D	4	(8)	
Libor KOLLER	D	29		1
Jozef KOSTELNIK	M	4	(4)	
Petr KRISTUFEK	M	9	(6)	
Stanislav MAREK	D	27		
Pavel MEJDR	M	13	(1)	
Jiri NOVAK	A	5	(8)	
Tomas REHOR	M		(3)	
Jan SAIDL	A	30		11
Petr STRNADEL	A		(5)	
Radek TEJML	D	19	(2)	
Karel VACHA	A	23		11
Ivan VALACHOVIC (SVK)	D	25		1
Jiri VLCEK	M		(1)	
Stanislav VLCEK	A	12	(3)	
Martin WOHLGEMUTH	D	25	(1)	2

LEAGUE RESULTS 1995/96

Date	Opponent	H/A	Score	Scorers
29/07/95	Sparta Praha	A	0-3	
02/08/95	Jablonec Nad Nisou	H	3-0	Barteska, Vacha, Babka
06/08/95	Viktoria Plzen	A	0-2	
20/08/95	Boby Brno	A	2-5	Vacha, Saidl
27/08/95	Slovacka Slavia Uherske Hradiste	H	2-0	Vacha, Fujdiar
10/09/95	Banik Ostrava	A	1-0	Valachovic
15/09/95	Petra Drnovice	H	2-1	Fujdiar, Saidl
24/09/95	SK Hradec Kralove	A	2-1	Vacha, Wohlgemuth
01/10/95	Slavia Praha	H	2-3	Barteska, Vacha (p)
15/10/95	Slovan Liberec	A	1-2	Fujdiar
22/10/95	Sigma Olomouc	H	2-1	Barteska, Vacha
29/10/95	Svit Zlin	A	0-1	
05/11/95	Kaucuk Opava	H	1-1	Babka
19/11/95	Viktoria Zizkov	A	0-4	
24/11/95	Union Cheb	H	3-3	Saidl 3 (1p)
16/02/96	Sparta Praha	H	2-0	Vacha (p), Koller
25/02/96	Jablonec Nad Nisou	A	1-2	Vacha
03/03/96	Viktoria Plzen	H	2-2	Saidl, Vacha (p)
09/03/96	Boby Brno	H	0-0	
23/03/96	Banik Ostrava	H	1-0	Vacha
29/03/96	Petra Drnovice	A	0-2	
10/04/96	Slovacka Slavia Uherske Hradiste	A	4-0	Saidl 2, Vacha, Wohlgemuth
13/04/96	Slavia Praha	A	0-3	
17/04/96	SK Hradec Kralove	H	0-3	
21/04/96	Slovan Liberec	H	0-0	
28/04/96	Sigma Olomouc	A	0-4	
01/05/96	FC Zlin	H	2-0	Fujdiar, Saidl
05/05/96	Kaucuk Opava	A	1-3	Saidl
09/05/96	Viktoria Zizkov	H	1-1	Saidl (p)
18/05/96	Union Cheb	A	0-0	

SK HRADEC KRALOVE

CLUB DIRECTORY

SK Hradec Kralove
Vsesportovni stadion
500 09 Hradec Kralove 9
tel - (049) 5210819
fax - (049) 22730/22789
Year of Formation - 1905
President - MUDr. Jan Voda
Secretary - Ivan Cernik
Coach - Ludek Zajic; Dusan Radolsky
Stadium - Vsesportovni stadion (25,800)

MAJOR HONOURS
League Championship - (1) 1960.
Domestic Cup - (1) 1995.

APPEARANCES 95/96

	P	Ap	(s)	Gls
Ales BEDNAR	A		(2)	
Julius BIELIK	D	11		
Pavel CERNY	A	26		10
Petr DROZD	M	17	(7)	1
Josef DZUBARA	D	11	(2)	
Radim HOLUB	A	10	(12)	
Ales HYNEK	M	25		
Miroslav JIRKA	M	1	(2)	
Richard JUKL	M	1		
Daniel KAPLAN	M	7	(6)	2
Marek KINCL	A	1	(4)	
Michal LESAK	M	2	(2)	
Daniel MASEK	A	6	(1)	2
Jaroslav MICHALICKA (SVK)	D	7	(5)	
Michal PETROUS	M	1		
Bohuslav PILNY	D	4	(3)	
Petr POKORNY	D	2	(4)	
Tomas POSTULKA	G	14		
Milan PTACEK	D	8	(9)	
Rudolf REHAK (SVK)	D	11	(2)	
Petr SAMEC	A	19	(1)	5
Dalibor SLEZAK	A	12	(2)	3
Michal SMARDA	M	27		4
Jiri STUDENIK	M	7		
Dusan SUCHY	M		(3)	
Ivo ULICH	M	25	(2)	1
Tomas URBAN	D	14		
Karel URBANEK	D	20		
Stanislav VAHALA	G	16	(1)	
Jaroslav VRABEL	D	14	(1)	
Roman ZELENAY (SVK)	D	11	(2)	
Daniel ZOUBEK	A		(3)	

LEAGUE RESULTS 1995/96

Date	Opponent	H/A	Score	Scorers
29/07/95	Svit Zlin	A	1-1	Masek
01/08/95	Kaucuk Opava	H	0-1	
06/08/95	Viktoria Zizkov	A	2-2	Smarda 2 (2p)
20/08/95	Union Cheb	H	0-1	
28/08/95	Sparta Praha	A	0-5	
10/09/95	Jablonec Nad Nisou	H	2-2	Cerny, Masek
18/09/95	Viktoria Plzen	A	2-1	Cerny, Smarda
24/09/95	SK Ceske Budejovice	H	1-2	Kaplan
02/10/95	Slovacka Slavia Uherske Hradiste	A	0-1	
15/10/95	Banik Ostrava	H	2-1	Cerny, Smarda
23/10/95	Petra Drnovice	A	0-3	
29/10/95	Boby Brno	A	0-2	
19/11/95	Slovan Liberec	A	2-3	Cerny 2
26/11/95	Sigma Olomouc	H	1-3	Kaplan
30/11/95	Slavia Praha	H	0-3	
18/02/96	FC Zlin	H	0-2	
01/03/96	Viktoria Zizkov	H	2-0	Cerny 2
06/03/96	Kaucuk Opava	A	1-2	Slezak
09/03/96	Union Cheb	A	2-0	Cerny 2
17/03/96	Sparta Praha	H	0-2	
23/03/96	Jablonec Nad Nisou	A	2-4	Samec, Slezak
31/03/96	Viktoria Plzen	H	0-0	
14/04/96	Slovacka Slavia Uherske Hradiste	H	2-0	Samec, Cerny
17/04/96	SK Ceske Budejovice	A	3-0	Samec, Slezak, Drozd
21/04/96	Banik Ostrava	A	0-2	
27/04/96	Petra Drnovice	H	1-0	Samec
01/05/96	Boby Brno	H	1-0	Samec
05/05/96	Slavia Praha	A	1-2	Ulich
12/05/96	Slovan Liberec	H	0-0	
18/05/96	Sigma Olomouc	A	0-1	

JABLONEC NAD NISOU

CLUB DIRECTORY

FK Jablonec nad Nisou
U stadionu 5
466 01 Jablonec nad Nisou
tel - (0428) 21507/88042/88043
fax - (0428) 22947
Year of Formation - 1945
President - Miroslav Pelta
Secretary - Lubos Srejma
Coach - Jiri Kotrba
Stadium - Strelnice (14,620)

APPEARANCES 95/96

	P	Ap	(s)	Gls
David BREDA	A	18	(7)	2
Pavel HORVATH	M	19	(1)	3
Radovan HROMADKO	A	23	(1)	4
Zdenek JANOS	G	29		2
Jaroslav JENIK	M		(1)	
Pavel JIROUSEK	M	7	(2)	
Jiri KOBR	G	1	(1)	
David LUPA	M		(1)	
Pavel MEDYNSKY	M	27		1
Jaromir NAVRATIL	M	26	(2)	7
Tomas NEUMANN	M	25	(4)	3
Pavel PENICKA	D	23	(5)	3
Martin PROCHAZKA	A	10	(17)	5
Richard SITARCIK	A		(3)	
Roman SKUHRAVY	D	20	(5)	3
Roman SOKOL	D	20	(1)	2
Jan SOPKO	D	24	(1)	2
Vlastimil SVOBODA	M	19	(9)	
Ales VANECEK	D	1	(2)	
Martin VEJPRAVA	D	20	(5)	
Prokop VYRAVSKY	D	4		
Ludek ZELENKA	A	14	(15)	7

LEAGUE RESULTS 1995/96

Date	Opponent	H/A	Score	Scorers
30/07/95	Viktoria Plzen	H	1-0	Zelenka
02/08/95	SK Ceske Budejovice	A	0-3	
06/08/95	Slovacka Slavia Uherske Hradiste	H	4-0	Skuhravy, Zelenka, Neumann, Janos (p)
20/08/95	Banik Ostrava	A	1-1	Prochazka (p)
27/08/95	Petra Drnovice	H	0-1	
10/09/95	SK Hradec Kralove	A	2-2	Neumann, Sopko
17/09/95	Slavia Praha	H	2-1	Breda, Sokol (p)
24/09/95	Slovan Liberec	A	0-1	
01/10/95	Sigma Olomouc	H	4-2	Penicka, Horvath, Zelenka, Navratil
15/10/95	Svit Zlin	A	0-0	
20/10/95	Kaucuk Opava	H	2-1	Sopko, Sokol
29/10/95	Viktoria Zizkov	A	0-1	
05/11/95	Union Cheb	H	0-0	
19/11/95	Sparta Praha	A	1-1	Zelenka
26/11/95	Boby Brno	H	3-0	Hromadko, Prochazka, Breda
18/02/96	Viktoria Plzen	A	1-0	Medynsky
25/02/96	SK Ceske Budejovice	H	2-1	Horvath, Navratil
03/03/96	Slovacka Slavia Uherske Hradiste	A	4-0	Neumann, Zelenka, Navratil, Janos (p)
09/03/96	Banik Ostrava	H	3-0	Zelenka 2, Hromadko
17/03/96	Petra Drnovice	A	0-2	
23/03/96	SK Hradec Kralove	H	4-2	og (Bielik), Navratil 2, Prochazka
05/04/96	Slovan Liberec	H	1-0	Prochazka
14/04/96	Sigma Olomouc	A	1-2	Horvath
21/04/96	FC Zlin	H	1-0	Prochazka
25/04/96	Slavia Praha	A	1-2	Hromadko
28/04/96	Kaucuk Opava	A	1-0	Navratil
01/05/96	Viktoria Zizkov	H	5-0	Penicka 2, Skuhravy, Navratil, Hromadko
05/05/96	Union Cheb	A	0-2	
12/05/96	Sparta Praha	H	1-0	Skuhravy
18/05/96	Boby Brno	A	0-1	

KAUCUK OPAVA

CLUB DIRECTORY

FC Kaucuk Opava
Stadion v Mestskych sadech
746 01 Opava
tel - (0653) 213745/211246
fax - (0653) 215125
Year of Formation - 1901
President - Alois Sommer
Secretary - Ivan Bartosik
Coach - Petr Zemlik
Stadium - v Mestskych sadech (12,000)

APPEARANCES 95/96

	P	Ap	(s)	Gls
Vilem AXMANN	G	6	(2)	
Jiri BARTL	M	26	(1)	11
Ivo FARSKY	D	10	(4)	2
Alois GRUSSMANN	M	28		5
Michal HAMPEL	A	4	(7)	
Roman HENDRYCH	A	11	(15)	2
Roman JANOUSEK	A	6	(1)	2
Miroslav KAMAS	D	18	(5)	1
Pavel KOBYLKA	M	2	(3)	
Jaroslav KOLINEK	M	12	(4)	1
Radim KUCERA	M	25	(4)	1
Miroslav MENTEL (SVK)	G	23		
Martin MIKULA (SVK)	M	13	(7)	1
Miroslav ONUFER	D	15	(9)	1
Karel OREL	D	29		1
Jan PEJSA	D	14		1
Radomir PRASEK	A	15		4
Martin ROZHON	A	25	(2)	6
Ales ROZSYPAL	D	23		
Lumir SEDLACEK	M		(6)	
Ivan VACLAVIK (SVK)	M	12	(8)	
Dusko VICKOVIC (CRO)	M	2	(1)	

LEAGUE RESULTS 1995/96

29/07/95	Petra Drnovice	H	1-2	Prasek
01/08/95	SK Hradec Kralove	A	1-0	Rozhon
04/08/95	Slavia Praha	H	1-1	Bartl
18/08/95	Slovan Liberec	A	0-1	
27/08/95	Sigma Olomouc	H	1-1	Grussmann
10/09/95	Svit Zlin	A	1-0	Prasek
17/09/95	Boby Brno	H	0-2	
24/09/95	Viktoria Zizkov	H	1-0	Bartl
01/10/95	Union Cheb	A	1-3	Rozhon
14/10/95	Sparta Praha	H	2-0	Farsky, Rozhon
20/10/95	Jablonec Nad Nisou	A	1-2	Bartl (p)
29/10/95	Viktoria Plzen	H	2-0	og (Purkart), Onufer
05/11/95	SK Ceske Budejovice	A	1-1	Bartl
19/11/95	Slovacka Slavia Uherske Hradiste	H	2-0	Prasek, Bartl
26/11/95	Banik Ostrava	A	2-1	Farsky, Prasek
18/02/96	Petra Drnovice	A	1-3	Bartl (p)
01/03/96	Slavia Praha	A	0-3	(w/o)
06/03/96	SK Hradec Kralove	H	2-1	Rozhon, Bartl
15/03/96	Sigma Olomouc	A	2-3	Kolinek, Rozhon
22/03/96	FC Zlin	H	3-2	Bartl 2 (1p), Orel
26/03/96	Slovan Liberec	H	0-0	
30/03/96	Boby Brno	A	1-1	Janousek
07/04/96	Viktoria Zizkov	A	1-1	Grussmann
14/04/96	Union Cheb	H	4-1	Grussmann, Rozhon, Kucera, Bartl
21/04/96	Sparta Praha	A	1-1	Hendrych
28/04/96	Jablonec Nad Nisou	H	0-1	
01/05/96	Viktoria Plzen	A	1-2	Bartl (p)
05/05/96	SK Ceske Budejovice	H	3-1	Grussmann, Kamas, Hendrych
12/05/96	Slovacka Slavia Uherske Hradiste	A	1-0	Mikula
18/05/96	Banik Ostrava	H	3-0	Pejsa, Janousek, Grussmann

PETRA DRNOVICE

CLUB DIRECTORY

FC Petra Drnovice
Sportovni areal
683 04 Drnovice 704
tel - (0507) 55265/23847/55547
fax - (0507) 55265
Year of Formation - 1932
President - Vaclav Junek
Secretary - Vitezslav Zboril
Coach - Stanislav Jarabek
Stadium - Sportovni areal (7,500)

APPEARANCES 95/96

	P	Ap	(s)	Gls
Jan BARANEK	M	28	(1)	2
Pavel BARCUCH	G	10		
Tomas BERNADY	G	20		
Radek DRULAK	A	29		22
Pavel HARAZIM	D	15		1
Petr HRUSKA	M	12	(6)	1
Richard JUKL	M	14	(4)	1
Robert KAFKA (SVK)	M	28		1
Lubos KUBIK	D	13	(1)	2
Edvard LASOTA	M	29		7
Ales NESICKY	D	15	(5)	
Roman PAVELKA	M		(5)	
Milan POSTULKA	D	12	(2)	
Dusan RUPEC (SVK)	D	2	(7)	
Albert RUSNAK (SVK)	A	9	(13)	1
Jaroslav SCHINDLER	D	7	(1)	
Jaroslav SILHAVY	D	18		2
Michal SLACHTA	D	14	(9)	1
Lubos SMERDA	D		(1)	
Jaroslav TIMKO (SVK)	A	27		9
Pavol VASKOVIC (SVK)	D		(1)	
Petr VESELY	M	11	(4)	2
Jozef WEBER	M	17	(10)	1

LEAGUE RESULTS 1995/96

Date	Opponent	H/A	Score	Scorers
29/07/95	Kaucuk Opava	A	2-1	Lasota, Harazim
06/08/95	Union Cheb	A	2-1	Rusnak, Drulak
20/08/95	Viktoria Zizkov	H	2-2	Drulak 2 (1p)
27/08/95	Jablonec Nad Nisou	A	1-0	Drulak
10/09/95	Viktoria Plzen	H	4-1	Drulak 2, Timko 2
15/09/95	SK Ceske Budejovice	A	1-2	Lasota
24/09/95	Slovacka Slavia Uherske Hradiste	H	2-2	Drulak, Hruska
29/09/95	Banik Ostrava	A	3-5	Drulak 2 (1p), Lasota
15/10/95	Boby Brno	A	2-2	Baranek, Drulak (p)
23/10/95	SK Hradec Kralove	H	3-0	Drulak 2, Lasota
27/10/95	Slavia Praha	A	2-1	Timko, Drulak
05/11/95	Slovan Liberec	H	0-0	
08/11/95	Sparta Praha	H	4-4	Timko, Jukl, Drulak 2
19/11/95	Sigma Olomouc	A	0-2	
26/11/95	Svit Zlin	H	3-0	Drulak (p), Timko, Weber
18/02/96	Kaucuk Opava	H	3-1	Drulak 2, Lasota
25/02/96	Viktoria Zizkov	A	0-1	
03/03/96	Union Cheb	H	3-0	Timko, Kubik, Drulak
08/03/96	Sparta Praha	A	1-2	Kafka
17/03/96	Jablonec Nad Nisou	H	2-0	Slechta, Drulak
22/03/96	Viktoria Plzen	A	1-1	Baranek
29/03/96	SK Ceske Budejovice	H	2-0	Silhavy, Vesely
07/04/96	Slovacka Slavia Uherske Hradiste	A	1-0	Timko
14/04/96	Banik Ostrava	H	3-1	Kubik, Timko, Drulak
19/04/96	Boby Brno	H	2-3	Lasota, Timko
27/04/96	SK Hradec Kralove	A	0-1	
01/05/96	Slavia Praha	H	3-0	Drulak, Vesely, Lasota
05/05/96	Slovan Liberec	A	0-4	
10/05/96	Sigma Olomouc	H	1-2	Silhavy
18/05/96	FC Zlin	A	0-1	

SIGMA OLOMOUC

CLUB DIRECTORY

SK Sigma Olomouc MZ
Andruv Stadion
PS 145
Legionarska 12
771 00 Olomouc
tel - (068) 5222956/5220953/5223380
fax - (068) 5220953/5222656
Year of Formation - 1919
President - Ing. Jaromir Gajda
Secretary - Vlastimil Palicka
Coach - Karel Brückner
Stadium - Andruv (14,694)

APPEARANCES 95/96

	P	Ap	(s)	Gls
Jiri BALCAREK	A	8	(17)	5
Miroslav BARANEK	A	26		13
Jiri BARBORIK	M	19	(6)	3
Marek HOLLY (SVK)	M	22	(2)	1
Milan KERBR	A	27	(1)	6
Petr KIRSCHBAUM	M	1	(6)	
Radim KONIG	M		(15)	
Martin KOTULEK	D	11	(9)	1
Michal KOVAR	D	23		
Oldrich MACHALA	D	30		1
Josef MUCHA	M	26	(1)	6
Radek ONDERKA	A	25	(3)	10
Jiri POVISER	M	25	(3)	1
Karel RADA	D	29		4
Martin SAVRNAK	A		(1)	
Dalibor SLEZAK	A		(5)	1
Lubomir STRBIK	A		(1)	
Jiri VADURA	D	27		2
Martin VANIAK	G	30		
Petr VYBIRAL	M	1	(7)	

LEAGUE RESULTS 1995/96

28/07/95	Slavia Praha	H	2-1	Mucha, Rada
01/08/95	Slovan Liberec	A	0-2	
06/08/95	Boby Brno	H	2-0	Balcarek, Slezak
20/08/95	Svit Zlin	H	3-0	Baranek 2, Onderka
27/08/95	Kaucuk Opava	A	1-1	Onderka
10/09/95	Viktoria Zizkov	H	1-1	Baranek
17/09/95	Union Cheb	A	1-1	Mucha
22/09/95	Sparta Praha	H	3-1	Baranek, Rada, Onderka
01/10/95	Jablonec Nad Nisou	A	2-4	Machala, Holly
15/10/95	Viktoria Plzen	H	3-0	Kerbr, Balcarek, Barborik
22/10/95	SK Ceske Budejovice	A	1-2	Rada
29/10/95	Slovacka Slavia Uherske Hradiste	H	2-0	Vadura (p), Baranek
03/11/95	Banik Ostrava	A	1-3	Baranek
19/11/95	Petra Drnovice	H	2-0	Mucha, Baranek
26/11/95	SK Hradec Kralove	A	3-1	Onderka 2, Poviser
23/02/96	Slovan Liberec	H	3-0	Mucha, Onderka, Baranek
27/02/96	Slavia Praha	A	0-4	
09/03/96	FC Zlin	A	0-0	
15/03/96	Kaucuk Opava	H	3-2	Mucha, Kerbr, Onderka
23/03/96	Viktoria Zizkov	A	2-1	Kerbr 2
31/03/96	Union Cheb	H	3-1	Barborik, Vadura, Onderka
03/04/96	Boby Brno	A	3-2	Rada (p), Kerbr, Baranek
07/04/96	Sparta Praha	A	2-0	Baranek, Barborik
14/04/96	Jablonec Nad Nisou	H	2-1	Kotulek, Balcarek (p)
21/04/96	Viktoria Plzen	A	0-2	
28/04/96	SK Ceske Budejovice	H	4-0	Baranek 2, Onderka, Balcarek
01/05/96	Slovacka Slavia Uherske Hradiste	A	1-2	Balcarek (p)
05/05/96	Banik Ostrava	H	1-0	Onderka
10/05/96	Petra Drnovice	A	2-1	Baranek, Mucha
18/05/96	SK Hradec Kralove	H	1-0	Kerbr

SLAVIA PRAHA

CLUB DIRECTORY

SK Slavia Praha
Vladivostocka 1460/2
100 00 Praha 10
tel - (02) 67311102/67311070/67311071/749794/740523
fax - (02) 749794/748174
Year of Formation - 1893
President - Ing. Vladimir Leska
Secretary - Kamil Rehak
Coach - Frantisek Cipro; Josef Pesice
Stadium - Dr. Vacka "Eden" (16,320)

MAJOR HONOURS
League Championship - (10) 1925, 1929, 1930, 1931, 1933, 1934, 1935, 1937, 1947, 1996.

APPEARANCES 95/96

	P	Ap	(s)	Gls
Radek BEJBL	M	27	(1)	8
Jaromir BLAZEK	G	6	(1)	
Roman HOGEN	A	1	(4)	
Tomas HUNAL	D	11	(9)	
Martin HYSKY	D	17	(11)	2
Lukas JAROLIM	M		(11)	1
Jindrich JIRASEK	M	1	(2)	
Tomas KLINKA	A		(1)	
Lubos KOZEL	D	14		2
Ondrej KRISTOFIK (SVK)	M	19	(5)	1
Jiri LERCH	M	18	(1)	1
Dick LIDMAN (SWE)	A		(3)	1
Leos MITAS	M		(1)	
Pavel NOVOTNY	M	27		4
Martin PENICKA	D	24		3
Bohuslav PIXA	M		(2)	
Karel POBORSKY	M	26		11
Daniel SMEJKAL	M	20	(4)	3
Vladimir SMICER	A	27	(1)	9
Vaclav SPAL	M		(1)	
Jiri STAJNER	A		(3)	
Jan STEJSKAL	G	23		
Jan SUCHOPAREK	D	22		1
Robert VAGNER	A	22	(6)	11
Jiri VAVRA	A	14	(12)	3
Frantisek VESELY	M		(1)	
Ludek VYSKOCIL	A		(3)	1

LEAGUE RESULTS 1995/96

28/07/95	Sigma Olomouc	A	1-2	Vagner
01/08/95	Svit Zlin	H	2-0	Novotny, Hysky
04/08/95	Kaucuk Opava	A	1-1	Poborsky
27/08/95	Union Cheb	A	3-1	Vavra, Penicka, Poborsky (p)
09/09/95	Sparta Praha	H	0-2	
17/09/95	Jablonec Nad Nisou	A	1-2	Smicer
22/09/95	Viktoria Plzen	H	2-1	Bejbl, Hysky
01/10/95	SK Ceske Budejovice	A	3-2	Smejkal 2, Smicer
13/10/95	Slovacka Slavia Uherske Hradiste	H	9-1	Vagner 4, Smicer 2, Bejbl, Jarolim, og (Irovsky)
22/10/95	Banik Ostrava	A	2-1	Poborsky, Kozel
27/10/95	Petra Drnovice	H	1-2	Poborsky
10/11/95	Viktoria Zizkov	H	5-0	Bejbl 2, Poborsky, og (Casko), Vavra
17/11/95	Boby Brno	A	2-0	Smicer, Novotny
26/11/95	Slovan Liberec	H	2-1	Smicer, Vavra
30/11/95	SK Hradec Kralove	A	3-0	Kristofik, Lidman, Smejkal (p)
27/02/96	Sigma Olomouc	H	4-0	Bejbl, Penicka, Vagner, Smicer
01/03/96	Kaucuk Opava	H	3-0	(w/o)
09/03/96	Viktoria Zizkov	A	3-1	Bejbl, Penicka, Smicer
16/03/96	Union Cheb	H	2-0	Smicer, Vagner
23/03/96	Sparta Praha	A	1-3	Poborsky
06/04/96	Viktoria Plzen	A	1-0	Kozel
09/04/96	FC Zlin	A	1-0	Vagner
13/04/96	SK Ceske Budejovice	H	3-0	Poborsky 2, Novotny
21/04/96	Slovacka Slavia Uherske Hradiste	A	2-0	Vagner, Poborsky
25/04/96	Jablonec Nad Nisou	H	2-1	Bejbl 2
28/04/96	Banik Ostrava	H	2-0	og (Nohavica), Vyskocil
01/05/96	Petra Drnovice	A	0-3	
05/05/96	SK Hradec Kralove	H	2-1	Poborsky, Lerch
12/05/96	Boby Brno	H	2-1	Vagner 2
17/05/96	Slovan Liberec	A	3-2	Novotny, Suchoparek, Poborsky (p)

SLOVACKA SLAVIA UHERSKE HRADISTE

CLUB DIRECTORY

FC JOKO Slovacka Slavia Uherske Hradiste
Fotbalovy stadion
686 01 Uherske Hradiste
tel - (0632) 2110/2895
fax - (0632) 2110
Year of Formation - 1894
President - Pavel Velecky
Secretary - Jaroslav Bocek
Coach - Antonin Juran; Jiri Nevrly
Stadium - TIC Slovacka Slavia (10,500)

APPEARANCES 95/96

	P	Ap	(s)	Gls
Libor BUZEK	D	24		
Bronislav CERVENKA	M	17	(5)	
Vladimir CHALOUPKA	M	9	(1)	
Zdenek CIHLAR	D	2	(1)	
Vladimir HEKERLE	M	13	(2)	
Miroslav HLAHULEK	M	26		
Jiri HOMOLA	A	8	(6)	
Jaroslav IROVSKY	D	10		
Michal KOLOMAZNIK	M	10	(3)	3
Miloslav KUFA	M	9		4
Milan KULYK	M	1		
Andrei LUBCHENKO (BLS)	G	13		
Martin MADERA	A	1		
Stanislav MALUS	M		(1)	
Jaroslav MARX	M	20	(3)	
Igor MATUSEK	M	20	(7)	2
Vladimir MICHAL	D	5	(1)	
Pavel NEMCICKY	M	10	(1)	
Sergiy NIKITIN (UKR)	M	3	(4)	
Josef NOVAK	G	10		
Jiri PECHA	A	7	(14)	4
Niloslav PENNER	D	25	(1)	1
Petr PODANY	M	2	(4)	
Kasper Lensen SAABY (DEN)	A	2	(4)	2
Michael SIEGL	M	14	(1)	
Libor SOLDAN	A	30		3
Pavel SVOBODA	A	1		
Alexei TERESCHENKO (UKR)	D	24		
Vaclav UHLIR	D	5	(6)	
Jiri VOSYKA	G	7		
Petr VYBIRAL	M	2		

LEAGUE RESULTS 1995/96

29/07/95	Union Cheb	A	0-1	
01/08/95	Sparta Praha	H	2-2	Saaby, Kufa
06/08/95	Jablonec Nad Nisou	A	0-4	
20/08/95	Viktoria Plzen	H	2-2	Penner, Soldan
27/08/95	SK Ceske Budejovice	A	0-2	
10/09/95	Boby Brno	A	0-2	
17/09/95	Banik Ostrava	H	1-2	Kufa
24/09/95	Petra Drnovice	A	2-2	Kufa, Pecha
02/10/95	SK Hradec Kralove	H	1-0	Kufa (p)
13/10/95	Slavia Praha	A	1-9	Pecha
22/10/95	Slovan Liberec	H	1-1	Pecha
29/10/95	Sigma Olomouc	A	0-2	
05/11/95	Svit Zlin	H	1-1	Saaby
19/11/95	Kaucuk Opava	A	0-2	
26/11/95	Viktoria Zizkov	H	1-0	Matusek
18/02/96	Union Cheb	H	0-0	
25/02/96	Sparta Praha	A	0-4	
03/03/96	Jablonec Nad Nisou	H	0-4	
09/03/96	Viktoria Plzen	A	1-1	Matusek
23/03/96	Boby Brno	H	1-3	Soldan
31/03/96	Banik Ostrava	A	1-2	Soldan
07/04/96	Petra Drnovice	H	0-1	
10/04/96	SK Ceske Budejovice	H	0-4	
14/04/96	SK Hradec Kralove	A	0-2	
21/04/96	Slavia Praha	H	0-2	
28/04/96	Slovan Liberec	A	0-4	
01/05/96	Sigma Olomouc	H	2-1	Pecha, Kolomaznik
05/05/96	FC Zlin	A	0-2	
12/05/96	Kaucuk Opava	H	0-1	
18/05/96	Viktoria Zizkov	A	2-2	Kolomaznik 2

SLOVAN LIBEREC

CLUB DIRECTORY

FC Slovan Liberec
Na Hradbach 1300
460 01 Liberec
tel - (048) 27794/26390
fax - (048) 27794
Year of Formation - 1958
President - Ing. Jiri Drda
Secretary - Pavel Jirous
Coach - Jiri Stol
Stadium - U Nisy (7,000)

APPEARANCES 95/96

	P	Ap	(s)	Gls
Petr BULIR	A	13	(5)	2
Pavel CAPEK	M	2	(2)	
Martin CUPR	D	20	(5)	1
Karel DOBS	M		(2)	
Martin HASEK	M	25		4
Martin HRIDEL	A	14	(13)	1
Libor JANACEK	M	29		4
Pavel JANECEK	M	10	(8)	2
Jiri JESETA	M	3	(3)	
Josef JINOCH	M	26		3
Ludek KLUSACEK	D	24		1
Boris KOCI	M	5	(2)	
Josef LEXA	D	23	(1)	1
Oleg LIZOGUB	D	20	(1)	
Marcel MACHA	M	1		
Ladislav MAIER	G	30		
Josef NESVACIL	D	13	(1)	
Josef OBAJDIN	A	13	(1)	5
Zbynek RAMPACEK	D	24	(2)	2
Jiri STUDENIK	M	1		
Zdenek VACEK	A		(2)	
Pavol VASKOVIC (SVK)	M	1	(10)	
Jaroslav VODICKA	M	2	(2)	1
Benjamin VOMACKA	M	8	(4)	
Matt WINECKI (USA)	A		(3)	
Lubos ZAKOSTELSKY	A	23	(2)	4

LEAGUE RESULTS 1995/96

29/07/95	Boby Brno	H	1-0	og (Krivanek)
01/08/95	Sigma Olomouc	H	2-0	Zakostelsky, Janecek
06/08/95	Svit Zlin	A	1-0	Jinoch
18/08/95	Kaucuk Opava	H	1-0	Hasek
25/08/95	Viktoria Zizkov	A	1-1	Rampacek
10/09/95	Union Cheb	H	2-3	Janacek, Lexa
17/09/95	Sparta Praha	A	1-3	Zakostelsky
24/09/95	Jablonec Nad Nisou	H	1-0	Zakostelsky
01/10/95	Viktoria Plzen	A	0-2	
15/10/95	SK Ceske Budejovice	H	2-1	Obajdin, Rampacek
22/10/95	Slovacka Slavia Uherske Hradiste	A	1-1	og (Pecha)
29/10/95	Banik Ostrava	H	3-0	Hasek, Obajdin, Janacek
05/11/95	Petra Drnovice	A	0-0	
19/11/95	SK Hradec Kralove	H	3-2	Obajdin 2, Vodicka
26/11/95	Slavia Praha	A	1-2	Obajdin
23/02/96	Sigma Olomouc	A	0-3	
13/03/96	FC Zlin	H	1-2	Hasek (p)
19/03/96	Boby Brno	A	1-1	Zakostelsky
23/03/96	Union Cheb	A	0-4	
26/03/96	Kaucuk Opava	A	0-0	
31/03/96	Sparta Praha	H	1-0	og (Plachy)
05/04/96	Jablonec Nad Nisou	A	0-1	
17/04/96	Viktoria Zizkov	H	0-0	
21/04/96	SK Ceske Budejovice	A	0-0	
28/04/96	Slovacka Slavia Uherske Hradiste	H	4-0	Jinoch, Bulir, Cupr, Janecek
01/05/96	Banik Ostrava	A	0-1	
05/05/96	Petra Drnovice	H	4-0	Janacek 2, Hasek, Jinoch
08/05/96	Viktoria Plzen	H	1-0	Klusacek (p)
12/05/96	SK Hradec Kralove	A	0-0	
17/05/96	Slavia Praha	H	2-3	Bulir, Hridel

SPARTA PRAHA

CLUB DIRECTORY

AC Sparta Praha
Milady Horakove 98
170 82 Praha 7
tel - (02) 382441-8
fax - (02) 370207/379391
Year of Formation - 1893
President - Gejza Sestak
Manager - Frantisek Chovanec
Secretary - Josef Kopacka
Coach - Jozef Jarabinsky; Vlastimil Petrzela
Stadium - AC Sparta Praha (21,900)

MAJOR HONOURS
League Championship - (21)
1926, 1927, 1932, 1936, 1938, 1946, 1948, 1952, 1954, 1965, 1967, 1984, 1985, 1987, 1988, 1989, 1990, 1991, 1993, 1994, 1995.
Domestic Cup - (9) 1964, 1972, 1976, 1980, 1984, 1988, 1989, 1992, 1996.

APPEARANCES 95/96

	P	Ap	(s)	Gls
Vaclav BUDKA	M	19		2
Martin FRYDEK	M	28		4
Peter GUNDA (SVK)	D		(2)	
Michal HORNAK	D	25		1
Jan KOLLER	A	13	(10)	4
Petr KOSTELNIK	G	2		
Petr KOUBA	G	28		
Vratislav LOKVENC	A	28	(1)	9
Lumir MISTR	M	24	(2)	7
Pavel NEDVED	M	27		14
Josef NEMEC	M	5	(12)	1
Jiri NOVOTNY	D	13	(1)	
Josef OBAJDIN	A	9	(3)	1
Antonin PLACHY	M	6	(3)	
Tomas POZAR	D	9	(8)	
Miroslav RADA	D	3	(5)	
Tomas REPKA	D	29		3
Horst SIEGL	A		(2)	1
Ludek STRACENY	A	1	(2)	
Zdenek SVOBODA	M	17	(9)	4
Roman TYCE	M	14	(3)	
Roman VONASEK	M	22		4
Tomas VOTAVA	D	7		
Jan ZAKOPAL	D	1		

LEAGUE RESULTS 1995/96

29/07/95	SK Ceske Budejovice	H	3-0	Frydek, Vonasek, Svoboda (p)
01/08/95	Slovacka Slavia Uherske Hradiste	A	2-2	Koller, Nedved
04/08/95	Banik Ostrava	H	1-1	Budka
28/08/95	SK Hradec Kralove	H	5-0	Lokvenc 2, Mistr, Siegl, Frydek
09/09/95	Slavia Praha	A	2-0	og (Suchoparek), Lokvenc
17/09/95	Slovan Liberec	H	3-1	Lokvenc 2, Nedved
22/09/95	Sigma Olomouc	A	1-3	Svoboda
01/10/95	Svit Zlin	H	3-0	Nedved 2 (2p), Koller
14/10/95	Kaucuk Opava	A	0-2	
22/10/95	Viktoria Zizkov	H	1-0	Koller
27/10/95	Union Cheb	A	3-3	Koller, Budka, Frydek
05/11/95	Boby Brno	H	4-0	Lokvenc 2, Nedved, Mistr
08/11/95	Petra Drnovice	A	4-4	Nedved 2, Frydek, Nemec
19/11/95	Jablonec Nad Nisou	H	1-1	Lokvenc
02/12/95	Viktoria Plzen	A	1-2	Vonasek
16/02/96	SK Ceske Budejovice	A	0-2	
25/02/96	Slovacka Slavia Uherske Hradiste	H	4-0	Repka 2, Nedved, Obajdin
01/03/96	Banik Ostrava	A	1-4	Nedved
08/03/96	Petra Drnovice	H	2-1	Mistr 2
17/03/96	SK Hradec Kralove	A	2-0	Nedved, Mistr
23/03/96	Slavia Praha	H	3-1	Vonasek 2, Lokvenc
31/03/96	Slovan Liberec	A	0-1	
07/04/96	Sigma Olomouc	H	0-2	
14/04/96	FC Zlin	A	1-1	Nedved
21/04/96	Kaucuk Opava	H	1-1	Svoboda
26/04/96	Viktoria Zizkov	A	4-1	Nedved 2, Mistr, Svoboda
01/05/96	Union Cheb	H	3-0	Repka, Nedved, Hornak
03/05/96	Boby Brno	A	0-1	
12/05/96	Jablonec Nad Nisou	A	0-1	
18/05/96	Viktoria Plzen	H	1-0	Mistr

UNION CHEB

CLUB DIRECTORY

FC Union Cheb
Kozeluzska 28
postovni schranka 71
350 01 Cheb
tel - (0166) 22739/22357/22723
fax - (0166) 22357
Year of Formation - 1950
President - JUDr. Petr Nemec
Secretary - Ondrej Kozar
Coach - Frantisek Plass
Stadium - FK Chmel (10,000)

APPEARANCES 95/96

	P	Ap	(s)	Gls
Miroslav BACEK (SVK)	M	10	(8)	1
Julius BIELIK	D	8		
Radek CERNY	G	12		
Pavel DRSEK	M	3	(8)	
Roman FAIC	A	18	(5)	
Milan FORGAC (SVK)	M	3	(3)	
Roman GIBALA	A	28		3
Michal HRBEK	D	21		2
Lukas JAROLIM	M	1	(4)	
Jaromir JINDRACEK	A	29		8
Pavel JIROUSEK	M	4	(3)	
Marian KLAGO (SVK)	A	15	(10)	5
Jiri KRBECEK	G	2		
Michal KYCEK	G	2	(1)	
Robert MATEJICEK	D		(1)	
Martin MÜLLER	D	28		2
Viktor NAAR	D		(1)	
Radim NECAS	M	14		4
Michal PETROUS	D	9		
Frantisek SAMBERGR	A	9	(12)	2
Miroslav SEBESTA	A	4	(5)	1
Milan SEDIVY	D	18		1
Radek SINDELAR	A	20	(3)	2
Jaroslav SLAMA	D	29		1
Marcel SVEJDIK	A	11	(4)	2
Karel TICHOTA	M	6	(5)	
Frantisek VESELY	A	5	(4)	1
Pavel VELEMAN	D		(1)	
Jan VOJNAR	G	11		
Jiri VOSYKA	G	3	(1)	
Prokop VYRAVSKY	D	7		

LEAGUE RESULTS 1995/96

29/07/95	Slovacka Slavia Uherske Hradiste	H	1-0	Hrbek
01/08/95	Banik Ostrava	A	0-3	
06/08/95	Petra Drnovice	H	1-2	Sindelar
20/08/95	SK Hradec Kralove	A	1-0	Sambergr
27/08/95	Slavia Praha	H	1-3	Sindelar
10/09/95	Slovan Liberec	A	3-2	Sambergr, Necas, Svejdik
17/09/95	Sigma Olomouc	H	1-1	Necas
24/09/95	Svit Zlin	A	2-0	Svejdik, Jindracek
01/10/95	Kaucuk Opava	H	3-1	Sedivy, Müller, Necas
15/10/95	Viktoria Zizkov	A	0-2	
22/10/95	Boby Brno	H	3-1	Gibala, Klago 2
27/10/95	Sparta Praha	H	3-3	Klago 2, Jindracek
05/11/95	Jablonec Nad Nisou	A	0-0	
19/11/95	Viktoria Plzen	H	1-2	Müller
24/11/95	SK Ceske Budejovice	A	3-3	Jindracek 2, Necas (p)
18/02/96	Slovacka Slavia Uherske Hradiste	A	0-0	
25/02/96	Banik Ostrava	H	1-1	Slama
03/03/96	Petra Drnovice	A	0-3	
09/03/96	SK Hradec Kralove	H	0-2	
16/03/96	Slavia Praha	A	0-2	
23/03/96	Slovan Liberec	H	4-0	Gibala, Hrbek, Jindracek 2
31/03/96	Sigma Olomouc	A	1-3	Klago
06/04/96	FC Zlin	H	1-1	Vesely
14/04/96	Kaucuk Opava	A	1-4	Jindracek (p)
21/04/96	Viktoria Zizkov	H	2-2	Jindracek, Gibala
27/04/96	Boby Brno	A	0-2	
01/05/96	Sparta Praha	A	0-3	
05/05/96	Jablonec Nad Nisou	H	2-0	Bacek, Sebesta
12/05/96	Viktoria Plzen	A	0-1	
18/05/96	SK Ceske Budejovice	H	0-0	

VIKTORIA PLZEN

CLUB DIRECTORY

FC Viktoria Plzen
Struncovy sady 3
301 12 Plzen
tel - (019) 7235180/7236038
fax - (019) 7236520
Year of Formation - 1911
President - Milan Kosan
Secretary - Vaclav Korinek
Coach - Jaroslav Hrebik
Stadium - Struncovy sady (35,000)

APPEARANCES 95/96

	P	Ap	(s)	Gls
Zdenek BECKA	D	29		2
Michal CALOUN	G	29		
Libor CIHAK	D	3	(3)	
Michal DRAHORAD	D	2	(3)	
Radek HAVEL	G	1		
Tomas HERMAN	A	25	(5)	6
Miroslav JANOTA	D	28		
Roman JANOUSEK	A	19		6
Patrik JEZEK	A	12	(8)	
Petr KRALOVEC	D	1	(2)	
Martin KULHANEK	A	25	(2)	2
Miroslav MIKA	M	27		2
Vladimir MYSLIK	M		(1)	
Jaromir PLOCEK	M	12	(16)	
Stanislav PURKART	M	20	(7)	2
Jiri SANDA	M		(1)	
Jiri SKALA	M	28		2
Milos SLABY	D	25		4
Jiri STUDENIK	M	13	(4)	
Vaclav USAK	A	2	(3)	
Pavel VAIGL	D		(1)	
Jan VELKOBORSKY	D		(2)	
Petr VLCEK	M	29		6

LEAGUE RESULTS 1995/96

Date	Opponent	H/A	Score	Scorers
30/07/95	Jablonec Nad Nisou	A	0-1	
02/08/95	Boby Brno	A	3-0	Kulhanek, Janousek 2
06/08/95	SK Ceske Budejovice	H	2-0	Kulhanek, Janousek
20/08/95	Slovacka Slavia Uherske Hradiste	A	2-2	Herman, Slaby
27/08/95	Banik Ostrava	H	1-0	Slaby
10/09/95	Petra Drnovice	A	1-4	Janousek
18/09/95	SK Hradec Kralove	H	1-2	Vlcek
22/09/95	Slavia Praha	A	1-2	Herman
01/10/95	Slovan Liberec	H	2-0	Herman, og (Zakostelsky)
15/10/95	Sigma Olomouc	A	0-3	
22/10/95	Svit Zlin	H	3-0	Janousek, Slaby (p), Skala
29/10/95	Kaucuk Opava	A	0-2	
05/11/95	Viktoria Zizkov	H	1-0	Herman
19/11/95	Union Cheb	A	2-1	Herman, Purkart
02/12/95	Sparta Praha	H	2-1	Herman, Becka
18/02/96	Jablonec Nad Nisou	H	0-1	
03/03/96	SK Ceske Budejovice	A	2-2	Vlcek 2
06/03/96	Boby Brno	H	1-1	Slaby
09/03/96	Slovacka Slavia Uherske Hradiste	H	1-1	Vlcek
22/03/96	Petra Drnovice	H	1-1	Janousek
31/03/96	SK Hradec Kralove	A	0-0	
06/04/96	Slavia Praha	H	0-1	
10/04/96	Banik Ostrava	A	2-3	Skala, Vlcek
21/04/96	Sigma Olomouc	H	2-0	Vlcek, Mika
28/04/96	FC Zlin	A	0-1	
01/05/96	Kaucuk Opava	H	2-1	Mika, Becka
05/05/96	Viktoria Zizkov	A	0-2	
08/05/96	Slovan Liberec	A	0-1	
12/05/96	Union Cheb	H	1-0	Purkart
18/05/96	Sparta Praha	A	0-1	

VIKTORIA ZIZKOV

CLUB DIRECTORY

FK Viktoria Zizkov
Seifertova trida
130 00 Prague 3-Zizkov
tel - (02) 270785/272277
fax - (02) 272377
Year of Formation - 1903
President - Vratislav Cekan
Secretary - Jiri Jechoutek
Coach - Frantisek Kopac
Stadium - FK Viktoria (8,000)

MAJOR HONOURS
League Championship - (1) 1928.
Domestic Cup - (1) 1994.

APPEARANCES 95/96

	P	Ap	(s)	Gls
Michal BILEK	M	29		6
Jan BURYAN	D	1	(9)	
Jiri CASKO	D	29		
Petr GABRIEL	D	30		
Petr HOLOTA	M	21	(5)	2
Miloslav KORDULE	D	22	(2)	8
Frantisek KOUBEK	A	2	(10)	
Jozef KOZLEJ (SVK)	A	17	(3)	5
Tomas KREJCIK	A	6	(6)	1
Jaroslav LOZEK	M	26	(2)	
Jozef MAJOROS (SVK)	M	26	(2)	3
Daniel MASEK	A	12	(3)	4
Stefan MIHALIK	A		(1)	
Antonin MLEJNSKY	D	19	(2)	1
Michal NEHODA	A	9	(6)	1
Roman NOHAVICA	D		(1)	
Tibor NOTIN	D	18		1
Oldrich PARIZEK	G	19		
Michal PETROUS	D	15		1
Ivan PIHAVEK	M		(4)	
Karel POBORSKY	M	1		
Juraj SIMURKA	G	11	(2)	
Marek TRVAL	A	8	(10)	3
Tomas URBAN	D	9	(1)	1
Karel VALKOUN	M		(6)	

LEAGUE RESULTS 1995/96

29/07/95	Banik Ostrava	H	2-1	Notin, Kordule
06/08/95	SK Hradec Kralove	H	2-2	Kordule 2 (1p)
20/08/95	Petra Drnovice	A	2-2	Bilek, Petrous
25/08/95	Slovan Liberec	H	1-1	Trval
10/09/95	Sigma Olomouc	A	1-1	Majoros
17/09/95	Svit Zlin	H	3-0	Kozlej, Bilek, Majoros
24/09/95	Kaucuk Opava	A	0-1	
01/10/95	Boby Brno	H	4-0	Kordule 2, Krejcik, Holota
15/10/95	Union Cheb	H	2-0	Kozlej, Bilek
22/10/95	Sparta Praha	A	0-1	
29/10/95	Jablonec Nad Nisou	H	1-0	Kozlej
05/11/95	Viktoria Plzen	A	0-1	
10/11/95	Slavia Praha	A	0-5	
19/11/95	SK Ceske Budejovice	H	4-0	Masek, Majoros, Nehoda, Kozlej
26/11/95	Slovacka Slavia Uherske Hradiste	A	0-1	
25/02/96	Petra Drnovice	H	1-0	Bilek
03/03/96	SK Hradec Kralove	A	0-2	
09/03/96	Slavia Praha	H	1-3	Bilek
23/03/96	Sigma Olomouc	H	1-2	Kordule (p)
31/03/96	FC Zlin	A	1-0	Masek
02/04/96	Banik Ostrava	A	2-2	og (Klimes), Trval
07/04/96	Kaucuk Opava	H	1-1	Masek
12/04/96	Boby Brno	A	1-3	Holota
17/04/96	Slovan Liberec	A	0-0	
21/04/96	Union Cheb	A	2-2	Urban, Bilek
26/04/96	Sparta Praha	H	1-4	Trval
01/05/96	Jablonec Nad Nisou	A	0-5	
05/05/96	Viktoria Plzen	H	2-0	Masek, Kordule
09/05/96	SK Ceske Budejovice	A	1-1	Kozlej
18/05/96	Slovacka Slavia Uherske Hradiste	H	2-2	Kordule (p), Mlejnsky

FC ZLIN

CLUB DIRECTORY

FC Zlin
Tyrsovo nabrezi 4381
760 01 Zlin
tel - (067) 30023/7210506
fax - (067) 30023
Year of Formation - 1919
President - Jan Rehak
Secretary - Jan Somberg
Coach - Werner Licka
Stadium - Letna (11,000)

APPEARANCES 95/96

	P	Ap	(s)	Gls
Petr BRABEC	D	5	(4)	
Miroslav BREZIK	A	2	(2)	
Tomas CAPKA	A	4	(4)	2
Petr CERVENKA	D	3	(3)	
Marian CHLAD	A	5	(3)	
Karel DOBS	M	10	(1)	
Stanislav DOSTAL	M	8		
Josef DVORNIK	D		(1)	
Michal GOTTWALD	M	2		
Andriy GRISCHENKO (UKR)	A	7	(8)	
Milan HANKO	D		(4)	
Michal HLAVNOVSKY	M	5	(4)	1
Slavomir HODUL	D	18		1
Pavel HOFTYCH	D	11		
Miroslav HOLENAK	A	27	(2)	1
Tomas JANDA	A	12	(2)	3
Petr KLHUFEK	D	29		2
Radovan KRASA	G	1		
Marcel LITOS	D	20	(1)	
Tibor MICINEC	M	15	(1)	
Miroslav MIKULIK	M	12	(2)	2
Robert NOVAK (SVK)	M	17		1
Frantisek ONDRUSEK	G	29		
Sergei OSACHI (UKR)	A	1	(7)	
Rudolf OTEPKA	M	12	(3)	1
Roman SEDLACEK	A	1	(4)	
Dalibor SLEZAK	A	10		1
Ondrej SMELKO (SVK)	D	12	(1)	2
Roman STASTKA	D	6	(1)	
Jaroslav SVACH	M	7	(6)	
Marcel SVEJDIK	A	9	(4)	
Vladimir SYKORA	M	9	(2)	
Dusan TESARIK	M	20	(4)	
Vladimir VITEK	M	1	(7)	
Karel ZAMECNIK	M		(1)	

LEAGUE RESULTS 1995/96

Date	Opponent	H/A	Score	Scorers
29/07/95	SK Hradec Kralove	H	1-1	Smelko
01/08/95	Slavia Praha	A	0-2	
06/08/95	Slovan Liberec	H	0-1	
20/08/95	Sigma Olomouc	A	0-3	
27/08/95	Boby Brno	H	0-0	
10/09/95	Kaucuk Opava	H	0-1	
17/09/95	Viktoria Zizkov	A	0-3	
24/09/95	Union Cheb	H	0-2	
01/10/95	Sparta Praha	A	0-3	
15/10/95	Jablonec Nad Nisou	H	0-0	
22/10/95	Viktoria Plzen	A	0-3	
29/10/95	SK Ceske Budejovice	H	1-0	Hlavnovsky
05/11/95	Slovacka Slavia Uherske Hradiste	A	1-1	Slezak
19/11/95	Banik Ostrava	H	0-0	
26/11/95	Petra Drnovice	A	0-3	
18/02/96	SK Hradec Kralove	A	2-0	Klhufek, Janda
09/03/96	Sigma Olomouc	H	0-0	
13/03/96	Slovan Liberec	A	2-1	Mikulik, Holenak
22/03/96	Kaucuk Opava	A	2-3	Hodul, Mikulik
27/03/96	Boby Brno	A	1-1	Janda
31/03/96	Viktoria Zizkov	H	0-1	
06/04/96	Union Cheb	A	1-1	Janda
09/04/96	Slavia Praha	H	0-1	
14/04/96	Sparta Praha	H	1-1	Smelko
21/04/96	Jablonec Nad Nisou	A	0-1	
28/04/96	Viktoria Plzen	H	1-0	Klhufek
01/05/96	SK Ceske Budejovice	A	0-2	
05/05/96	Slovacka Slavia Uherske Hradiste	H	2-0	Capka, Otepka
12/05/96	Banik Ostrava	A	1-3	Novak
18/05/96	Petra Drnovice	H	1-0	Capka

PROMOTED CLUBS

SECOND DIVISION FINAL TABLE 95/96

		Pd	W	D	L	F	A	Pt	GD
1	**FC Karvina Vitkovice**	**30**	**17**	**6**	**7**	**36**	**18**	**57**	**+18**
2	**FK Teplice**	**30**	**16**	**8**	**6**	**41**	**23**	**56**	**+18**
3	Tatran Postorna	30	15	6	9	50	44	51	+6
4	**Bohemians Praha**	**30**	**13**	**9**	**8**	**48**	**32**	**48**	**+16**
5	Zelezarny Trinec	30	12	12	6	46	33	48	+13
6	FC Pribram	30	12	7	11	42	32	43	+10
7	ALFA Slusovice	30	11	9	10	44	38	42	+6
8	LeRK Brno	30	9	15	6	34	36	42	-2
9	SK Chrudim	30	11	7	12	40	38	40	+2
10	Valcovny Plechu Frydek-Mistek	30	10	8	12	34	36	38	-2
11	Chmel Blsany	30	8	13	9	28	31	37	-3
12	Banik Havirov	30	7	14	9	40	45	35	-5
13	GGS ARMA Usti nad Labem	30	7	12	11	39	43	33	-4
14	SK Pardubice	30	8	6	16	29	43	30	-14
15	Cesky Raj Turnov	30	5	10	15	23	45	25	-22
16	Svarc Benesov	30	5	6	19	25	62	21	-37

N.B. Tatran Postorna declined promotion place made available by Union Cheb's withdrawal from First Division. Bohemians Praha therefore promoted.

CLUB DIRECTORY

FC Karvina Vitkovice (now - FC Karvina)
Stadion Kovona Karvina
736 01 Karvina Nove Mesto
tel - (069) 6313674/6313675/9346627
fax - (069) 6313674
Year of Formation - 1922
President - Ing. Jaroslav Netolicka
Secretary - Ing. Vaclav Javorek
Coach - Lubomir Vasek
Stadium - Kovona Karvina (12,000)

MAJOR HONOURS
League Championship (1) 1986.

CLUB DIRECTORY

FK Teplice
Stadion Na Stinadlech 2796
415 01 Teplice
tel - (0417) 27612/23224/40543
fax - (0417) 27612/23224
Year of Formation - 1945
President - Frantisek Hrdlicka
Secretary - Frantisek Snobr
Coach - Frantisek Cerman
Stadium - Na Stinadlach (17,863)

CLUB DIRECTORY

FC Bohemians Praha
Vrsovicka 31
101 00 Praha 10
tel - (02) 723210/723398/722180
fax - (02) 722855
Year of Formation - 1905
President - Ales Zak
Secretary - Ludek Rychnovsky
Coach - Josef Hlousek
Stadium - V. Dolicku (16,000)

MAJOR HONOURS
League Championship - (1) 1983.

DENMARK

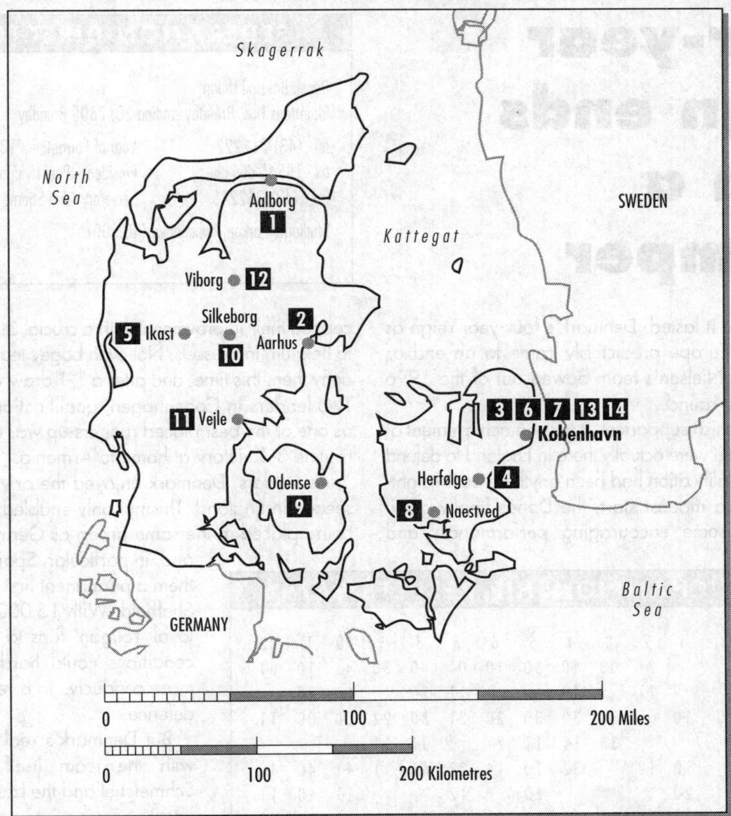

1	AAB	290	8	NAESTVED BK	297
2	AGF	291	9	OB	298
3	BRØNDBY IF	292	10	SILKEBORG IF	299
4	HERFØLGE BK	293	11	VEJLE BK	300
5	IKAST FS	294	12	VIBORG FF	301
6	FC KØBENHAVN	295	13	HVIDOVRE IF	302
7	LYNGBY FC	296	14	AB	302

BIG CROWDS BOOST DOMESTIC GAME

Four-year reign ends with a whimper

FEDERATION DIRECTORY

Dansk Boldspil Union
Idraettens Hus, Brøndby stadion 20, 2605 Brøndby

tel - (43) 262222	Year of Formation - 1889
tlx - 15545 dbu dk	President - Poul Hyldgaard
fax - (43) 262245	Secretary - Jim Stjerne Hansen

Stadium - Parken, København (40,300)

It was fun while it lasted. Denmark's four-year reign as champions of Europe predictably came to an end as Richard Møller-Nielsen's team bowed out of the 1996 finals in the first round.

For many Danish supporters, it was an achievement of sorts that the team were actually there in England to defend their crown. Qualification had been anything but straightforward. After a modest start, the Danes finally got it together with some encouraging performances and capped their improvement with a crucial 3-1 victory away to Belgium in Brussels. Not even bogey team Spain could deny them this time, and after a 1-1 draw with the Group Two leaders in Copenhagen, qualification for Euro '96 as one of the best-placed runners-up was assured with a routine 3-1 victory at home to Armenia.

As holders, Denmark enjoyed the privilege of being seeded in England. This not only enabled them to avoid being placed in the same group as Germany, England and, in particular, Spain. It also gave them a permanent first-round base in Sheffield. With 15,000 of their ever-loyal 'roligan' fans to support them, conditions could hardly have been more conducive to a respectable title defence.

But Denmark's real problems lay with the team itself. Goalkeeper Schmeichel and the Laudrup brothers apart, genuine international quality was sorely lacking. Møller-Nielsen all but acknowledged this by recalling

LEAGUE CHAMPIONSHIP RESULTS 95/96

		1	2	3	4	5	6	7	8	9	10	11	12
1	AaB		2-4	0-3	4-0	3-0	1-0	0-1	4-0	3-0	4-1	1-0	8-1
			2-1		4-0			1-1	2-0		0-1	2-0	
2	AGF	1-0		3-1	3-0	3-0	2-0	2-1	3-0	2-2	0-0	0-0	1-1
				3-3	1-1	1-1	2-1		3-1	1-1			
3	Brøndby IF	1-0	1-2		3-2	1-0	1-4	2-2	6-1	1-1	4-1	4-0	4-0
		2-0				2-0		1-2			1-1	6-0	1-1
4	Herfølge BK	1-1	1-5	0-1		1-0	0-3	2-2	2-0	1-2	5-2	2-4	3-3
				0-0		4-1		1-1				1-1	2-2
5	Ikast FS	0-3	2-2	1-2	1-0		4-2	0-4	1-2	1-3	1-0	2-1	1-1
		1-1					1-1	0-5			1-2		0-0
6	FC København	2-1	1-3	0-3	0-0	1-1		2-2	3-1	2-1	1-0	1-2	4-1
		3-1		0-4	2-1				1-1		1-0		2-0
7	Lyngby FC	0-0	0-1	1-3	2-0	3-2	2-2		1-1	0-2	1-2	3-0	4-0
			0-2				4-0		2-0	0-1	2-3	1-1	
8	Naestved BK	1-1	2-4	0-1	3-2	1-1	2-2	1-4		0-4	1-0	0-0	6-2
				0-1	0-4	0-2				1-1		1-0	
9	OB	1-1	1-0	0-3	0-2	2-0	0-0	2-2	5-0		1-0	1-0	3-1
		5-1		2-0	5-1	2-0	2-1						3-1
10	Silkeborg IF	2-1	0-3	2-0	1-0	1-1	3-1	1-1	5-0	2-1		1-2	0-2
			2-1		1-0				1-1	1-1		3-1	
11	Vejle BK	1-3	0-0	1-3	2-1	1-1	0-1	0-3	2-0	1-1	1-1		3-3
			0-1			5-0	1-2			2-0			0-1
12	Viborg FF	4-0	1-1	2-2	2-1	3-1	2-2	0-2	4-0	2-1	0-3	0-2	
		0-2	0-0					0-2	6-2		2-1		

TOP SCORERS

20	Thomas THORNINGER (AGF)
16	Per PEDERSEN (OB)
	Steffen HØJER (Viborg FF)
15	Peter MØLLER (Brøndby IF)
13	Erik Bo ANDERSEN (AaB)
12	Ebbe SAND (Brøndby IF)
11	Henrik LARSEN (Lyngby FC)
	Søren FREDERIKSEN (Viborg FF)
10	David NIELSEN (Lyngby FC)
	Miklos MOLNAR (Herfølge BK)
	Håvard FLO (AGF)

LEAGUE CHAMPIONSHIP FINAL TABLE 95/96

			Home					Away					Total						
		Pd	W	D	L	F	A	W	D	L	F	A	W	D	L	F	A	Pt	GD
1	Brøndby IF	33	10	4	3	41	17	10	3	3	30	15	20	7	6	71	32	67	+39
2	AGF	33	9	8	0	31	13	9	4	3	30	15	18	12	3	61	28	66	+33
3	OB	33	12	3	2	35	13	5	6	5	22	20	17	9	7	57	33	60	+24
4	Lyngby FC	33	6	4	7	26	20	8	7	1	35	15	14	11	8	61	35	53	+26
5	AaB	33	12	1	4	41	13	3	5	8	16	25	15	6	12	57	38	51	+19
6	Silkeborg IF	33	9	4	3	26	16	5	3	9	18	26	14	7	12	44	42	49	+2
7	FC København	33	9	4	4	26	22	4	5	7	22	27	13	9	11	48	49	48	-1
8	Viborg FF	33	7	4	5	28	22	2	7	8	20	45	9	11	13	48	67	38	-19
9	Vejle BK	33	4	5	7	20	21	4	4	9	14	29	8	9	16	34	50	33	-16
10	Herfølge BK	33	4	7	5	26	28	2	2	13	15	34	6	9	18	41	62	27	-21
11	Ikast FS	33	4	5	7	17	29	1	5	11	11	34	5	10	18	28	63	25	-35
12	Naestved BK	33	4	5	7	19	29	1	3	13	10	51	5	8	20	29	80	23	-51

several of his Old Guard, such as Lars Olsen, Torben Piechnik and Henrik Larsen, to the 22 in place of younger, fresher candidates like Christian Lønstrup and Thomas Thorninger.

Caution was the hallmark of Denmark's first two performances in the finals. They grabbed an ill-deserved draw against Portugal thanks to Schmeichel's resolute goalkeeping and a wonderful first-half screamer from Brian Laudrup. But against Croatia, in the next game, not even the stars could bale Denmark out. Møller-Nielsen cravenly opted for what could best be termed a 4-6-0 formation, hoping to crowd out the opposition midfield and snatch another point. But his plans evaporated after the interval, Davor Suker ripping gleefully into a Danish defence in which Schmeichel, astonishingly, was more at fault than any other.

Qualification was now out of Denmark's hands, and the subsequent 3-0 victory over Turkey, featuring two more fine Brian Laudrup goals, served merely as a pleasant parting gift to Møller-Nielsen. Croatia's unsporting decision to rest their best players for the match against Portugal killed off Denmark's last chances of hanging on to their crown (a Croatian win would have put the Danes through; they lost 0-3), and so the holders went home early - just as they, the media and most of their supporters had imagined they would.

INTERNATIONAL HONOURS

World Cup Finals appearances: 1986 (2nd round)

European Championship appearances: 1964 (4th), 1984 (semi-finals), 1988, 1992 (Winners), 1996

Thus ended Møller-Nielsen's six-year spell in charge of the team. Of his 73 matches Denmark won 43, drew 18 and lost 15. They also won the 1992 European Championship and the 1995 Intercontinental Cup. He may have lacked style and charisma, he may have received constant criticism for his team selections. But his record speaks for itself. He is unquestionably the most successful Danish national coach of all time.

Finland will now reap the benefits of Møller-Nielsen's experience as they seek to end their reputation as the poor relations of Nordic football. Travelling in the other direction is the Swede Bo Johansson, who has left Finnish club HJK to replace Møller-Nielsen as Danish coach. Johansson is familiar to Danish football having coached Silkeborg to their shock title triumph in 1994. His appointment - made public as early as September 1995 - was a surprise to many. His first task will be to take Denmark to the 1998 World Cup in France. With Croatia once again barring their route, it will not be easy.

If the national team seems set for a possible period of decline, the opposite is true for the Danish domestic game. Crowds are bigger than ever in the Superliga, and sponsors have not been slow to recognise this boom in public interest. Multinational giants Coca-Cola even ventured to sponsor the league in 95/96. Purists in the media initially objected to using the Coca-Cola prefix when referring to the national league, but eventually, reluctantly, they succumbed. Curiously, the 96/97 Superliga is being sponsored by a domestic soft drink, and as yet no one has shown similar opposition to what is now officially known as the Faxe Kondi Superligaen.

The 95/96 championship heralded a new format, with 14 teams each playing the others three times without

NATIONAL TEAM RESULTS 95/96

16/08/95	Armenia (ECQ)	A	Yerevan	2-0	Laudrup M. (33), Nielsen A. (46)
06/09/95	Belgium (ECQ)	A	Brussels	3-1	Laudrup M. (20), Beck (22), Vilfort (66)
11/10/95	Spain (ECQ)	H	Copenhagen	1-1	Vilfort (47)
15/11/95	Armenia (ECQ)	H	Copenhagen	3-1	Schjønberg (20), Beck (36), Laudrup M. (58)
27/03/96	Germany	A	Munich	0-2	
24/04/96	Scotland	H	Copenhagen	2-0	Laudrup M. (8), Laudrup B. (28)
02/06/96	Ghana	H	Copenhagen	1-0	Helveg (41)
09/06/96	Portugal (ECF)	N	Sheffield	1-1	Laudrup B. (22)
16/06/96	Croatia (ECF)	N	Sheffield	0-3	
19/06/96	Turkey (ECF)	N	Sheffield	3-0	Laudrup B. (50, 84), Nielsen A. (69)

recourse to play-offs. OB and Brøndby were the pre-season co-favourites, but it was AGF, from Aarhus, who set the pace early on and threatened to become the third different champion in as many seasons from the Jutland peninsula (after Silkeborg and AaB). AGF began with an undefeated 10-match run, and even after their first defeat (away to OB) they remained on course, winning six and drawing three of their nine matches before the winter break.

The only serious threat to AGF came from Brøndby. They toiled badly early on, taking just 18 points from their first 11 matches, but just as it seemed that this would be yet another season of unfulfilled expectations, they found form. Buoyed by a fine run in the UEFA Cup, they won seven games on the trot going into the winter break and trailed AGF by a mere three points.

One of Brøndby's earlier victories - away to reigning champions AaB in September - caused a major furore. Brøndby were leading 2-0 with 16 minutes to go when the home fans began to throw fireworks, clouding the pitch with thick smoke.

The referee was forced to abandon the game after appeals to the crowd went unheeded. Subsequently the Danish league authorities decided that the result would stand. AaB protested, however, that this was against the rules, and during the winter break it was agreed that the remaining 16 minutes would be replayed.

As it turned out, AaB and Brøndby were drawn to play each other in Aalborg in the quarter-final of the Danish Cup on April 6, so they agreed to play the remainder of the league fixture after the Cup match. The Danish FA had ruled that only players eligible to play the first game in September could take part, so after the Cup match (which Brøndby won 4-1) both clubs had to re-arrange their personnel.

Additionally, AaB, who had had a player sent off back in September, were only permitted to field 10 players. In the end, it was all a storm in a teacup. Brøndby added a further goal and went on to win the match 3-0 seven months after it had begun!

The result was not without its significance in the title race. As AGF struggled to rediscover their autumn form, Brøndby gradually seized control with five wins in nine games, one of them a spectacular 3-0 victory away to FC Copenhagen - a match watched by a Superliga record crowd of 39,640.

With four games remaining, Brøndby led by a point and travelled to Aarhus to face an AGF side which had beaten them in their two previous league meetings. It was

DOMESTIC CUP RESULTS

FOURTH ROUND
Esbjerg FB 5, Nørre Aaby IK 0
FC Fredericia 1, Viborg FF 3
BK Fremad Amager 2, Herfølge BK 3
Herning Fremad 2, B1919 3
HIK 0, AB 1
AC Horsens 1, Skive IK 3
Ikast FS 1, Vejle BK 4
Køge BK 2, Helsingør 0
Nykøbing Falster Alliancen 1, FC København 2
OB 1, Randers Freja FC 0
Skovshoved IF 1, Lyngby FC 7
Ølstykke FC 1, Naestved BK 1 (aet; 4-3 on pens.)
byes - AaB, AGF, Brøndby IF, Silkeborg IF

FIFTH ROUND
B1913 1, Herfølge BK 4
Brøndby IF 2, AB 1
Esbjerg FB 5, Køge BK 0
FC København 0, AGF 2
Silkeborg IF 4, Lyngby FC 2
Viborg FF 2, Skive IK 1
Ølstykke FC 2, OB 2 (aet; 3-4 on pens.)
AaB 4, Vejle BK 0

QUARTER-FINALS
Esbjerg FB 2, Herfølge BK 3
Silkeborg IF 1, AGF 2
Viborg FF 2, OB 2 (aet; 2-4 on pens.)
AaB 1, Brøndby IF 4

SEMI-FINALS
Brøndby IF v OB 1-0; 1-1
(Brøndby IF 2-1)
Herfølge BK v AGF 2-2; 1-1
(3-3; AGF on away goals)

FINAL
16/05/96, Copenhagen
AGF 2 Degn (32), Tøfting (44)
BRØNDBY IF 0
referee - Larsen J.W.
AGF - Windfeld; Nielsen, Lind, Piechnik, Bak, Degn (Siim 48), Vilstrup, Tøfting, Mortensen (Jokovic 54), Flo (Strück 72), Thorninger.
BRØNDBY IF - Krogh; Colding, Olsen, Nielsen P., Risager, Nielsen A. (Daugaard 63), Vilfort, Ravn (Bagger 74), Thøgersen (Bjur 59), Sand, Møller.

a classic encounter. A sell-out 19,500 crowd saw AGF recover from 0-1 down to sweep into a commanding 3-1 lead. The visitors pulled a goal back with 11 minutes to go, but all seemed lost until, in the final seconds, Brøndby goalkeeper Mogens Krogh, of all people, charged upfield *à la* Peter Schmeichel and headed in a last-gasp equaliser.

Four days later the two teams met again for the Cup final in Copenhagen. This time AGF ran out deserved winners before another record attendance (for a Danish Cup final) of 36,103. Three days after that the Aarhus side were back on top of the league and looking set for the 'double' as they won at Vejle and Brøndby were held at home by Silkeborg. But the position changed again within another four days as AGF slipped up at home to OB (1-1) and Brøndby thrashed FC Copenhagen once again in the Parken, 4-0 in front of another 30,000-plus crowd.

With one game left, the championship was back in Brøndby's sights. The biggest crowd ever seen at the Brøndby stadium (18,302) turned up to see if the yellow-and-blues could capture their first title since 1991. They did so without difficulty, beating a strangely disinterested AaB side 2-0 with goals from Kim Daugaard and Ruben Bagger. AGF's equally convincing 2-0 win at AaB's fellow UEFA Cup rivals Lyngby turned out to be all in vain.

Brøndby's success was particularly commendable given the injury problems that had gnawed away at Ebbe Skovdahl's squad throughout the season. Key players such as Eggen, Vilfort, Kristensen and Hansen were all laid low at one time or another, and, if midfielder Allan Nielsen was undoubtedly the star, it was the overall team effort above everything else which drove the club to its long-awaited success.

Such sturdy qualities were also in evidence as Brøndby sensationally knocked Liverpool out of the UEFA Cup,

NATIONAL TEAM APPEARANCES 95/96

Coach - Richard MØLLER-NIELSEN	ARM	BEL	ESP	ARM	GER	SCO	GHA	POR	CRO	TUR	Cps	Gls
Peter SCHMEICHEL (18/11/63) - Manchester United (ENG)	G	G	G	G	G	G46	G	G	G	G	87	-
Jacob LAURSEN (06/10/71) - Silkeborg IF	D	D	D			s81			s46		12	-
Jes HØGH (07/05/66) - Fenerbahçe (TUR)	D	D	D	D	D		D	D	D	D	25	1
Marc RIEPER (05/06/68) - West Ham United (ENG)	D	D	D	D	D	D	D	D	D	D	41	-
Jens RISAGER (09/04/71) - Brøndby IF	D85	D	D	D	D	D81	D46	D			13	-
Claus THOMSEN (31/05/70) - Ipswich Town (ENG)	M	D			M	M	s61	M83	D	D	9	-
John JENSEN (03/05/65) - Arsenal (ENG)	M46										69	4
Brian Steen NIELSEN (28/12/68) - OB	M	M	M67	M	s79	M	M	M	M	M	38	-
Michael LAUDRUP (15/06/64) - Real Madrid (ESP)	A	M90	M	M	M79	M86	M	M	M	M	91	35
Mikkel BECK (12/05/73) - Fortuna Köln (GER)	A	A70	A	A	A73	A	A	A	s58		11	3
Peter RASMUSSEN (16/05/67) - AaB	A	s70	M	A	M46						13	2
Allan NIELSEN (13/03/71) - Brøndby IF	s46				s46	s86				M	4	2
Michael SCHJØNBERG (19/01/67) - OB	s85	s90		M	M	M	M		M	M46	15	2
Kim VILFORT (15/11/62) - Brøndby IF		M	M	M			M61	s90	M58		77	14
Brian LAUDRUP (22/02/69) - Rangers (SCO)		A76			A	A	A77	A	A	A	66	14
Erik Bo ANDERSEN (14/11/70) - AaB/Rangers (SCO)		s76			s73					A89	6	-
Torben PIECHNIK (21/05/63) - AGF			M				s46	s83			15	-
Morten WIEGHORST (25/02/71) - Dundee (SCO)			s67								5	2
Thomas HELVEG (24/06/71) - Udinese (ITA)				D	M	M	D	D	D46	D	16	1
Lars OLSEN (02/02/61) - Brøndby IF						D					84	4
Mogens KROGH (31/10/63) - Brøndby IF						s46					5	-
Søren ANDERSEN (31/01/70) - AaB							s77			s89	3	-
Henrik LARSEN (17/05/66) - Lyngby FC								M90	M69	s46	39	5
Stig TØFTING (14/08/69) - AGF									s69		3	-

EUROPEAN CUPS RESULTS 95/96

CHAMPIONS' CUP

● AAB

Preliminary round DYNAMO KYIV (UKR)

A 0-1
Gill; Boye, Simonsen, Kristensen, Jessen, Thomsen L., Rasmussen H., Pedersen, Madsen (Thomasberg 85), Andersen (Grønkjaer 85), Rasmussen P..

H 1-3 Rasmussen P. (86)
Gill; Boye, Simonsen, Kristensen (Grønkjaer 46), Jessen, Thomsen L., Rasmussen H., Pedersen (Facius 46), Rasmussen P., Andersen, Madsen (Thomsen K. 74).

Champions' League

1st match FC PORTO (POR)

A 0-2
Gill; Simonsen, Boye, Kristensen, Jessen, Facius, Thomsen L. (Thomasberg 17), Rasmussen H., Pedersen (Madsen 63), Rasmussen P. (Grønkjaer 79), Andersen.

2nd match FC NANTES (FRA)

A 1-3 Andersen (46)
Gill; Simonsen, Boye, Thorst, Jessen (Krüger 87), Facius (Thomasberg 82), Rasmussen H., Pedersen, Rasmussen P., Madsen (Grønkjaer 70), Andersen.

3rd match PANATHINAIKOS (GRE)

H 2-1 Andersen (42), Madsen (90)
Gill; Boye, Simonsen, Thorst, Jessen, Thomasberg, Rasmussen H., Facius, Pedersen (Madsen 24), Rasmussen P. (Grønkjaer 85), Andersen.

4th match FC NANTES (FRA)

H 0-2
Gill; Boye, Simonsen, Thorst, Jessen, Thomasberg, Rasmussen H., Madsen (Hjermitslev 82), Facius (Thomsen K. 71), Rasmussen P., Andersen (Grønkjaer 46).

5th match PANATHINAIKOS (GRE)

A 0-2
Gill; Kristensen (Hjermitslev 82), Simonsen, Krüger, Facius, Rasmussen H., Madsen (Grønkjaer 60), Jessen, Rasmussen P., Andersen, Pedersen.

6th match FC PORTO (POR)

H 2-2 Andersen (11), Madsen (69)
Winde; Jessen, Kristensen, Krüger, Thomsen K., Thomasberg, Madsen (Pedersen Jari 82), Facius, Rasmussen P. (Hjermitslev 65), Grønkjaer (Nielsen 79), Andersen.

CUP-WINNERS' CUP

● FC KØBENHAVN

1st round SK HRADEC KRALOVE (TCH)

A 0-5
Bryaunis; Tobiasen, Tur, Jensen, Nielsen L-H. (Falch 45), Lønstrup (Johansen Ma. 59), Nielsen Mio, Uldbjerg, Nielsen Mo., Frandsen, Johansen Mi. (Schønnemann 59).

H 2-2 Tengstedt (27), Tur (72)
Zaza; Schønnemann, Tur, Frandsen (Sørensen 82), Nielsen L-H., Lønstrup, Nielsen Mio, Nielsen Mo. (Thorup 72), Tengstedt, Johannsen, Johansen Mi. (Jensen 45).

UEFA CUP

● BRØNDBY IF

Preliminary round INKARAS-GRIFAS KAUNAS (LIT)

H 3-0 Hansen (13), Bjur (45), Sand (82)
Krogh; Vilfort, Eggen, Nielsen P., Risager, Bjur, Daugaard (Ravn 63), Nielsen A., Kristensen (Rasmussen 77), Møller, Sand.

A 3-0 Møller (53, 65), Risager (62)
Krogh; Bjur (Colding), Eggen (Bjerregaard), Nielsen P., Risager, Daugaard, Nielsen A. (Sand), Ravn, Møller, Hansen, Vilfort.

1st round LILLESTRØM SK (NOR)

H 3-0 Hansen (38), Eggen (57), Bjur (88p)
Krogh; Colding, Eggen, Nielsen P., Bjerregaard (Sand 59), Bjur, Nielsen A., Ravn (Rasmussen 79), Daugaard (Jensen 81), Hansen, Møller.

A 0-0
Krogh; Colding, Eggen, Nielsen P., Risager, Bjur (Daugaard 67), Vilfort, Nielsen A., Ravn, Sand (Thøgersen 74), Hansen (Møller 76).

2nd round LIVERPOOL (ENG)

H 0-0
Krogh; Colding, Eggen, Nielsen P., Risager, Daugaard (Bagger 83), Vilfort, Ravn (Bjur 69), Nielsen A., Møller (Thøgersen 46), Sand.

A 1-0 Eggen (78)
Krogh; Colding, Eggen, Nielsen P., Risager, Bjur (Bagger 90), Vilfort, Ravn, Nielsen A., Thøgersen (Daugaard 69), Sand (Møller 78).

3rd round ROMA (ITA)

H 2-1 Møller (47), Bjur (77)
Krogh; Colding, Nielsen P., Eggen (Daugaard 16), Risager, Bjur, Vilfort, Ravn, Nielsen A., Møller (Sand 66), Thøgersen (Bagger 83).

A 1-3 Møller (85)
Krogh; Colding, Vilfort, Nielsen P., Risager, Bjur, Daugaard (Bagger 79), Ravn, Thøgersen, Sand, Møller.

● SILKEBORG IF

Preliminary round CRUSADERS (NIR)

A 2-1 Fernandez (15), Larsen (47p)
Kjaer; Kastbjerg, Laursen, Larsen, Petersen, Bruun, Thygesen (Knudsen 78), Sørensen, Bordinggaard, Reese (Hansen 90), Fernandez (Pedersen H. 60).

H 4-0 Larsen (10), Fernandez (61), Sommer (68, 84)
Kjaer; Knudsen, Larsen, Laursen, Petersen, Bruun, Thygesen, Sørensen (Møldrup 65), Bordinggaard, Reese (Sommer 63), Fernandez (Hansen 77).

1st round SPARTA PRAHA (TCH)

A 1-0 Fernandez (6)
Kjaer; Knudsen, Laursen, Sørensen, Petersen, Thygesen, Hansen, Bruun, Bordinggaard, Fernandez (Pedersen H. 75), Reese (Pedersen B. 71).

H 1-2 Petersen (51)
Kjaer; Knudsen, Laursen, Sørensen, Petersen, Thygesen, Bruun, Bordinggaard (Pedersen B. 78), Hansen (Zivkovic 82), Fernandez, Reese (Pedersen H. 60).

winning 1-0 in the once impenetrable fortress of Anfield. History repeated itself as Skovdahl's men lost out to a late goal by Roma in the next round (the same thing had occurred in the 1991 semi-final), but once again they had done Danish football proud with their European exploits.

Like Silkeborg the year before, AaB were knocked out of the Champions' League preliminaries by Dynamo Kiev, but this time the Danish champions lived to fight another day. The Ukrainians were thrown out of the competition for match-rigging, and AaB happily stepped into the breach to pick up their unbudgetted pile of Swiss francs.

On the field Sepp Piontek's team did little to earn their windfall, winning just one game, at home to eventual group winners Panathinaikos. Overall Piontek's was not a happy return to Danish football. Failure to take AaB back into Europe resulted in his end-of-season dismissal. The same fate was reserved for another under-achieving coach, Michael Schäfer of ambitious FC Copenhagen.

FC Copenhagen have the biggest turnover of all the Superliga clubs. They also have the biggest stadium. The previous occupants of the Parken, AB, returned to the top flight for the first time since 1973 when they won promotion alongside another team from the capital, Hvidovre, the traditional rivals of champions Brøndby. With these two esteemed newcomers on board, the Superliga can expect plenty of local rivalry and more big crowds in 1996/97.

PLAYERS OF THE SEASON

ALLAN NIELSEN

Nobody contributed more to Brøndby's sixth Danish title triumph than flamboyant 25-year-old midfielder Allan Nielsen. As positive going forward as he is resolute in defence, he appears to be the natural successor to his club colleague Kim Vilfort in the Danish national team. His international career certainly started with a bang as he scored a goal just 30 seconds into his début in the European Championship qualifier against Armenia. He also found the net on his one appearance at Euro '96 (against Turkey), prompting interest from a number of English Premiership clubs and resulting in a high-profile move to Tottenham Hotspur.

THOMAS THORNINGER

23-year-old Thomas Thorninger became the top scorer in the Superliga in only his second season with AGF. The young striker returned to Denmark in search of first-team football in 1994 after extensive trials with PSV Eindhoven's youth team, but because he was still contracted to the Dutch club he could only register in Denmark as an amateur. The Bosman case allowed the youngster to free himself from his PSV ties just in time to pocket 10,000 Danish Kroner for his top scorer prize. As an amateur, he would not have been entitled to claim the money.

MIKKEL BECK

Despite a dismal Euro '96, Mikkel Beck remains Denmark's best hope to succeed Preben Elkjaer and Flemming Povlsen as the team's goalscorer-in-chief. The blond youngster emerged from the obscurity of the German Second Division to cement his place in the European Championship team with a goal on his début against Finland and two more in the Euro '96 qualifiers against Belgium and Armenia. Much was expected of him in England, but he never got out of the starting blocks. Perhaps happier times await him in the Premiership with Bryan Robson's Middlesbrough, where he was set to continue his career after negotiating a major contractual hurdle with his German club Fortuna Cologne.

Mikkel Beck

AAB

CLUB DIRECTORY

Aalborg Boldspilklub A/S
Hornevej 2
9220 Aalborg Øst
Year of Formation - 1885
tel - (98) 153333/157222
fax - (98) 153334
Chairman - Poul Hedemann
Secretary - Birthe Jensen
Coach - Sepp Piontek (96/97 - Per Westergaard)
Stadium - Aalborg Stadion (13,600)

MAJOR HONOURS

League Championship - (1) 1995.
Domestic Cup - (2) 1966, 1970.

APPEARANCES 95/96

	P	Ap	(s)	Gls
Erik Bo ANDERSEN	A	20		13
Søren ANDERSEN	A	10	(1)	7
Jesper BORUP	A	1		
Torben BOYE	D	31		3
Calle FACIUS	M	28	(5)	1
Thomas GILL (NOR)	G	17		
Jesper GRØNKJAER	A	11	(18)	3
Torben HJERMITSLEV	M	1	(7)	
Jens JESSEN	D	31		3
Bjørn KRISTENSEN	D	16		1
Jacob KRÜGER	D	11	(7)	
Morten LAURITSEN	D		(1)	
Jens MADSEN	M	17	(13)	6
Johnny MØLBY	M	13	(1)	
Jimmy NIELSEN	G	1		
Johnny Helledie NIELSEN	D	3	(3)	
Thomas Buus NIELSEN	A		(1)	
Jan PEDERSEN	M	26	(1)	5
Jari PEDERSEN	M	1	(3)	
Henrik RASMUSSEN	M	29		2
Peter RASMUSSEN	A	29	(4)	8
Ib SIMONSEN	D	30		3
Thomas THOMASBERG	M	10	(19)	2
Kristian THOMSEN	M	3	(3)	
Lars THOMSEN	M	11		
Søren THORST	D	4	(2)	
Lars WINDE	G	16		

LEAGUE RESULTS 1995/96

Date	Opponent	H/A	Score	Scorers
30/07/95	Ikast FS	A	3-0	Madsen, Andersen E-B., Boye
02/08/95	FC København	H	1-0	Madsen
05/08/95	Viborg FF	H	8-1	Facius, Andersen E-B. 3, Rasmussen P., Pedersen Jan, Thomasberg 2
11/08/95	OB	A	1-1	Madsen
18/08/95	Silkeborg IF	H	4-1	Madsen, Boye, Andersen E-B. 2
27/08/95	Naestved BK	A	1-1	Andersen E-B.
01/09/95	Brøndby IF	H	0-3	
10/09/95	Vejle BK	A	3-1	Jessen, Simonsen (p), Andersen E-B.
17/09/95	Lyngby FC	H	0-1	
20/09/95	AGF	A	0-1	
24/09/95	Herfølge BK	H	4-0	Pedersen Jan, Rasmussen P., Boye, Grønkjaer
01/10/95	OB	H	3-0	Simonsen, Rasmussen P., Andersen E-B.
06/10/95	Viborg FF	A	0-4	
13/10/95	FC København	A	1-2	Kristensen
20/10/95	Ikast FS	H	3-0	Andersen E-B. 3
27/10/95	Herfølge BK	A	1-1	Madsen
05/11/95	AGF	H	2-4	Jessen, Rasmussen P.
10/11/95	Lyngby FC	A	0-0	
26/11/95	Brøndby IF	A	0-1	
29/11/95	Vejle BK	H	1-0	Andersen E-B.
31/03/96	Ikast FS	A	1-1	Pedersen Jan
04/04/96	Vejle BK	H	2-0	Rasmussen H., Rasmussen P.
08/04/96	Silkeborg IF	A	1-2	Rasmussen P.
14/04/96	Silkeborg IF	H	0-1	
17/04/96	Naestved BK	H	4-0	Pedersen Jan, Andersen S., Rasmussen P., Madsen
21/04/96	Viborg FF	A	2-0	Andersen S. 2
28/04/96	AGF	H	2-1	Andersen S., Simonsen (p)
05/05/96	OB	A	1-5	Grønkjaer
08/05/96	Naestved BK	H	2-0	Andersen S., Rasmussen H.
12/05/96	FC København	A	1-3	Andersen S.
19/05/96	Herfølge BK	H	4-0	Pedersen Jan, Andersen S., Jessen, Rasmussen P.
23/05/96	Lyngby FC	H	1-1	Grønkjaer
27/05/96	Brøndby IF	A	0-2	

AGF

CLUB DIRECTORY

Aarhus Gymnastik Forening
Terp Skovvej 16-18
8260 Viby J
tel - (86) 112733
fax - (86) 145779
Year of Formation - 1880
Chairman - Mogens Boyter
Secretary - Marianne Henriksen
Coach - Peter Rudbaek
Stadium - Aarhus Stadion (20,000)

MAJOR HONOURS
League Championship - (5)
1955, 1956, 1957, 1960, 1986.
Domestic Cup - (9) 1955, 1957, 1960, 1961, 1965, 1987, 1988, 1992, 1996.

APPEARANCES 95/96

	P	Ap	(s)	Gls
Lennart BAK	M	20	(8)	5
Jan BARTRAM	M	23	(1)	1
Peter DEGN	M	5	(4)	
Håvard FLO (NOR)	A	8	(15)	10
Arkadiusz GMUR (POL)	D	8	(1)	
Nocko JOKOVIC	A	20	(4)	6
Martin JØRGENSEN	M	23	(2)	1
Lars LAMBAEK	A	6	(14)	4
Henrik LARSEN	M	1	(1)	
Gunner LIND	D	28	(2)	2
Henrik MORTENSEN	M	8	(5)	3
Martin NIELSEN	D	33		
Torben PIECHNIK	D	31		3
Dennis SIIM	D	5	(5)	
Claus STEINLEIN	M		(4)	
Claus STRUCK	M	28	(2)	1
Palle SØRENSEN	M	14	(9)	1
Thomas THORNINGER	A	33		20
Stig TØFTING	M	24		3
Johnny VILSTRUP	M	12		
Lars WINDFELD	G	33		

LEAGUE RESULTS 1995/96

Date	Opponent		Score	Scorers
30/07/95	Silkeborg IF	H	0-0	
02/08/95	Naestved BK	A	4-2	Lind, Thorninger 2, Jokovic
04/08/95	Brøndby IF	H	3-1	Mortensen, Jokovic, Tøfting (p)
11/08/95	Vejle BK	A	0-0	
20/08/95	Lyngby FC	H	2-1	Lind, Jokovic
27/08/95	Viborg FF	A	1-1	Struck
03/09/95	Herfølge BK	A	5-1	Thorninger 3, Jokovic, Bak
10/09/95	Ikast FS	H	3-0	Thorninger, Piechnik, Bak
17/09/95	FC København	A	3-1	Tøfting, Thorninger, Lambaek
20/09/95	AaB	H	1-0	Jokovic
24/09/95	OB	A	0-1	
01/10/95	Vejle BK	H	0-0	
06/10/95	Brøndby IF	A	2-1	Thorninger, Piechnik
15/10/95	Naestved BK	H	3-0	Thorninger, Flo, Sørensen
22/10/95	Silkeborg IF	A	3-0	Thorninger 3
29/10/95	OB	H	2-2	Lambaek, Thorninger
05/11/95	AaB	A	4-2	Thorninger, Tøfting, Flo, Bartram
10/11/95	FC København	H	2-0	Jørgensen, Lambaek
26/11/95	Herfølge BK	H	3-0	Thorninger 2, Piechnik (p)
29/11/95	Ikast FS	A	2-2	og (Sørensen), Lambaek
31/03/96	Herfølge BK	H	1-1	Thorninger
04/04/96	Silkeborg IF	A	1-2	Bak
08/04/96	Lyngby FC	A	1-0	Flo
14/04/96	Naestved BK	H	3-1	Jokovic, Bak, Flo
17/04/96	Viborg FF	H	1-1	Bak
21/04/96	Ikast FS	H	1-1	Flo
28/04/96	AaB	A	1-2	Thorninger
05/05/96	FC København	H	2-1	Flo 2
08/05/96	Viborg FF	A	0-0	
12/05/96	Brøndby IF	H	3-3	Thorninger 2, Mortensen
19/05/96	Vejle BK	A	1-0	Mortensen
23/05/96	OB	H	1-1	Flo
27/05/96	Lyngby FC	A	2-0	Flo 2

BRØNDBY IF

CLUB DIRECTORY

Brøndbyernes Idraets Forening
Gildhøj 6
2605 Brøndby
tel - (43) 630810
fax - (43) 432627
Year of Formation - 1964
Chairman - Ole Borch
Secretary - Emil Bakkendorf
Coach - Ebbe Skovdahl
Stadium - Brøndby Stadion (22,600)

MAJOR HONOURS
League Championship - (6)
1985, 1987, 1988, 1990, 1991, 1996.
Domestic Cup - (2) 1989, 1994.

APPEARANCES 95/96

	P	Ap	(s)	Gls
Ruben BAGGER	A	6	(14)	7
Anders BJERREGAARD	D	6	(4)	
Ole BJUR	M	26	(6)	6
Søren COLDING	D	27	(2)	3
Kim DAUGAARD	M	21	(10)	3
Dan EGGEN (NOR)	D	18		
Bo HANSEN	A	9	(5)	4
John JENSEN	M	8	(2)	1
Jesper KRISTENSEN	M	3		
Mogens KROGH	G	33		1
Peter MØLLER	A	29	(4)	15
Allan NIELSEN	M	28		6
Morten B. NIELSEN	A		(1)	
Per NIELSEN	D	31		3
Lars OLSEN	D	13		1
Kenneth RASMUSSEN	D	3	(5)	
Allan RAVN	M	23	(7)	4
Jens RISAGER	D	30		
Ebbe SAND	A	15	(14)	12
Thomas THØGERSEN	M	11	(10)	1
Kim VILFORT	M	26	(1)	3

LEAGUE RESULTS 1995/96

30/07/95	Vejle BK	A	3-1	Bjur (p), Hansen, Nielsen A.
02/08/95	Lyngby FC	H	2-2	Hansen, Nielsen A.
04/08/95	AGF	A	1-3	Hansen
11/08/95	Herfølge BK	H	3-2	Sand 2, Møller
18/08/95	Ikast FS	A	2-1	Sand, Ravn
27/08/95	FC København	H	1-4	Daugaard
01/09/95	AaB	A	3-0	Nielsen P., Møller, Bagger
08/09/95	OB	H	1-1	Sand
17/09/95	Silkeborg IF	A	0-2	
20/09/95	Naestved BK	H	6-1	Møller 3, Sand 2, Ravn
22/09/95	Viborg FF	A	2-2	Nielsen A., Nielsen P.
01/10/95	Herfølge BK	A	1-0	Møller
06/10/95	AGF	H	1-2	Hansen
13/10/95	Lyngby FC	A	3-1	Sand, og (Christiansen), Vilfort
22/10/95	Vejle BK	H	4-0	Sand, Bagger, Colding, Bjur (p)
27/10/95	Viborg FF	H	4-0	Bagger, Vilfort, Bjur, Møller
05/11/95	Naestved BK	A	1-0	Møller
10/11/95	Silkeborg IF	H	4-1	Møller, Bjur 2, Ravn
17/11/95	OB	A	3-0	Thøgersen, Colding, Nielsen A.
26/11/95	AaB	H	1-0	Nielsen A.
24/03/96	FC København	A	3-0	Ravn, Nielsen A., Nielsen P.
31/03/96	Viborg FF	H	1-1	Møller
04/04/96	Herfølge BK	A	0-0	
08/04/96	Ikast FS	H	1-0	Jensen
14/04/96	Vejle BK	H	6-0	Bjur, Møller, Olsen, Sand, Bagger 2
21/04/96	Naestved BK	A	1-0	Vilfort
28/04/96	OB	A	0-2	
05/05/96	Lyngby FC	H	1-2	Sand
08/05/96	Ikast FS	H	2-0	Daugaard, Møller
12/05/96	AGF	A	3-3	Møller, Sand, Krogh
19/05/96	Silkeborg IF	H	1-1	Bagger
23/05/96	FC København	A	4-0	Møller 2, Colding, Sand
27/05/96	AaB	H	2-0	Daugaard, Bagger

HERFØLGE BK

CLUB DIRECTORY

Herfølge Boldklub
Vordingborgvej 124
Postbox 57
4681 Herfølge
tel - (56) 276021/56274230
fax - (56) 276141
Year of Formation - 1921
Chairman - Martin Juul
Secretary - Poul Erik Bermann
Coach - Ole Mørch
Stadium - Herfølge Stadion (6,000)

APPEARANCES 95/96

	P	Ap	(s)	Gls
Torben CHRISTIANSEN	M	22	(1)	2
Peter FRANK	D	13		
Michael GIOLBAS	M	28	(1)	
Jørgen HANSEN	M		(2)	
Tom JENSEN	D		(1)	
Martin JEPPESEN	M	4	(3)	
Danny JUNG	A	17	(6)	6
Henrik JØRGENSEN	M	2	(4)	
Jimmy KASTRUP	A	11	(11)	3
Kenneth KASTRUP	M	18	(9)	
Johnny KONGSBØG	M	3	(3)	
Brian KRISTENSEN	A	15	(8)	4
Kai LARSEN	G	18		
Henrik LYKKE	D	29		4
Søren LYNG	A	18	(9)	4
Steven ŁUSTÜ	D	26		
Thomas MATHIESEN	A		(3)	
Jakup MIKKELSEN (FAR)	G	15		
Kim MIKKELSEN	A	14	(11)	4
Miklos MOLNAR	A	21		10
Carsten NIELSEN	D	3	(5)	
Thomas NIELSEN	D	1	(2)	
Gert NODIN	D	19	(2)	1
Peter POULSEN	D	25	(5)	
Michael Beck RASMUSSEN	M	1		
Tommy SCHRAM	M	25	(3)	2
Kenneth WEGNER	D	15		1

LEAGUE RESULTS 1995/96

Date	Opponent	H/A	Score	Scorers
02/08/95	Silkeborg IF	A	0-1	
06/08/95	Naestved BK	H	2-0	Jung 2
09/08/95	OB	H	1-2	Mikkelsen K.
11/08/95	Brøndby IF	A	2-3	Mikkelsen K., Wegner (p)
20/08/95	Vejle BK	H	2-4	Nodin, Kastrup J.
27/08/95	Lyngby FC	A	0-2	
03/09/95	AGF	H	1-5	Lyng
10/09/95	Viborg FF	A	1-2	Lyng
17/09/95	Ikast FS	A	0-1	
20/09/95	FC København	H	0-3	
24/09/95	AaB	A	0-4	
01/10/95	Brøndby IF	H	0-1	
08/10/95	Naestved BK	A	2-3	Molnar, Schram
15/10/95	Silkeborg IF	H	5-2	Molnar 2, Lyng, Kastrup J., Lykke
22/10/95	OB	A	2-0	Kristensen, Molnar
27/10/95	AaB	H	1-1	Lyng
05/11/95	FC København	A	0-0	
12/11/95	Ikast FS	H	1-0	Kastrup J.
19/11/95	Viborg FF	H	3-3	Molnar 2, Mikkelsen K. (p)
26/11/95	AGF	A	0-3	
31/03/96	AGF	A	1-1	Kristensen
04/04/96	Brøndby IF	H	0-0	
08/04/96	Vejle BK	A	1-2	Lykke
14/04/96	OB	A	1-5	Schram
17/04/96	Lyngby FC	H	2-2	Molnar, Lykke (p)
21/04/96	FC København	A	1-2	Kristensen
28/04/96	Silkeborg IF	A	0-1	
05/05/96	Viborg FF	H	2-2	Jung, Mikkelsen K.
08/05/96	Lyngby FC	H	1-1	Christiansen
12/05/96	Ikast FS	H	4-1	Molnar, Lykke, Kristensen, Jung
19/05/96	AaB	A	0-4	
23/05/96	Naestved BK	A	4-0	Christiansen, Jung 2, Molnar
27/05/96	Vejle BK	H	1-1	Molnar

IKAST FS

CLUB DIRECTORY

Ikast Forenede Sportsklubber
Industrivej 15
7430 Ikast
tel - (97) 251211
fax - (97) 252330
Year of Formation - 1935
Chairman - Johnny Rune
Secretary - Kirsten Sørensen
Coach - Kim Brink (96/97 - Poul Hansen)
Stadium - Ikast Stadion (15,000)

APPEARANCES 95/96

	P	Ap	(s)	Gls
Søren AGGER	A	10	(6)	2
Rene S. ANDERSEN	M	23	(8)	1
Lars BRØGGER	A	27	(3)	4
Michael ELBAEK	M	23	(4)	
Kim ERIKSEN	D	13		
Ove HANSEN	A	14	(9)	2
Bo HARDER	M	17	(5)	2
Petri HELIN (FIN)	D	2		
Oleg IVANOV (RUS)	M	4	(2)	
Jacob H. JUHL	D	28		
Frode LANGAGERGAARD	D	7	(2)	
Jesper LARSEN	A		(1)	
Christian LUNDBERG	A	11	(2)	6
Kern LYHNE	M	22	(5)	5
Lars MEEDOM	M	8	(7)	
John NIELSEN	M	8	(11)	
Kent R. NIELSEN	M	12	(3)	
Chima OKORIE (NIG)	A	8	(1)	1
Markus PEDERSEN	A	4	(5)	1
Valeri POPOVITS (RUS)	A	6		3
Jan RINDOM	G	33		
Kenny SIVERTSEN	D	24	(4)	
Claus STEINLEIN	M	3	(3)	
Jan SØNKSEN	D	29		1
Dan SØRENSEN	D	27	(1)	
Jeppe TENGBJERG	A		(1)	

LEAGUE RESULTS 1995/96

30/07/95	AaB	H	0-3	
02/08/95	OB	A	0-2	
04/08/95	Silkeborg IF	H	1-0	Pedersen
13/08/95	Naestved BK	A	1-1	Lyhne
18/08/95	Brøndby IF	H	1-2	Andersen
27/08/95	Vejle BK	A	1-1	Hansen
03/09/95	Lyngby FC	H	0-4	
10/09/95	AGF	A	0-3	
17/09/95	Herfølge BK	H	1-0	Lyhne
20/09/95	Viborg FF	A	1-3	Brøgger
24/09/95	FC København	A	1-1	Hansen
01/10/95	Naestved BK	H	1-2	Agger
06/10/95	Silkeborg IF	A	1-1	Brøgger
15/10/95	OB	H	1-3	Agger
20/10/95	AaB	A	0-3	
29/10/95	FC København	H	4-2	Lyhne 2, Harder 2 (2p)
05/11/95	Viborg FF	H	1-1	Lyhne
12/11/95	Herfølge BK	A	0-1	
26/11/95	Lyngby FC	A	2-3	Popovits 2
29/11/95	AGF	H	2-2	Popovits, Sønksen
24/03/96	Vejle BK	H	2-1	Okorie, Lundberg
31/03/96	AaB	H	1-1	Lundberg
04/04/96	OB	A	0-2	
08/04/96	Brøndby IF	A	0-1	
14/04/96	Lyngby FC	H	0-5	
21/04/96	AGF	A	1-1	Lundberg
28/04/96	Naestved BK	A	2-0	Lundberg, Brøgger
05/05/96	Silkeborg IF	H	1-2	Lundberg
08/05/96	Brøndby IF	A	0-2	
12/05/96	Herfølge BK	A	1-4	Lundberg
19/05/96	FC København	H	1-1	Brøgger
23/05/96	Vejle BK	A	0-5	
27/05/96	Viborg FF	H	0-0	

FC KØBENHAVN

CLUB DIRECTORY

FC København
P.H Lings Allé 4
2100 København Ø
tel - (35) 437400
fax - (35) 437422
Year of Formation - 1992
Chairman - Harald Nielsen
Secretary - Charles Maskelyne
Coach - Michael Schäfer (96/97 - Kim Brink)
Stadium - Parken (40,300)

MAJOR HONOURS
League Championship - (1) 1993.
Domestic Cup - (1) 1995.

APPEARANCES 95/96

	P	Ap	(s)	Gls
Algimantas BRIAUNYS (LIT)	G	1		
Morten FALCH	M	15	(6)	2
Per FRANDSEN	A	25	(1)	7
Carsten HALLUM	A	9	(3)	2
Stefan K. HANSEN	M	4	(2)	
Carsten Vagn JENSEN	D	22	(9)	
Martin JOHANSEN	A	17	(7)	2
Michael JOHANSEN	M	27	(4)	8
Christian LØNSTRUP	M	27	(4)	4
Claus NIELSEN	M		(1)	
Lars Højer NIELSEN	M	13	(4)	8
Michael "Mio" NIELSEN	M	27	(5)	
Morten NIELSEN	D	22	(4)	4
Morten B. NIELSEN	A	4	(5)	2
Antti NIEMI (FIN)	G	17		
Kenneth PEREZ	A	1	(6)	
William PRUNIER (FRA)	D	11		
Thomas SCHØNNEMANN	D	10	(7)	
Jesper SØRENSEN	M	20	(1)	2
Rene TENGSTEDT	A	9	(2)	1
Kenny THORUP	A	1	(9)	
Ole TOBIASEN	D	13	(3)	
Diego TUR	D	24	(1)	3
Iørn ULDBJERG	D	29	(1)	3
Karim ZAZA	G	15		

LEAGUE RESULTS 1995/96

Date	Opponent	H/A	Score	Scorers
30/07/95	Viborg FF	H	4-1	Johansen Mi. 2, Nielsen L-H., Johansen Ma.
02/08/95	AaB	A	0-1	
06/08/95	OB	H	2-1	Nielsen L-H. (p), Frandsen
11/08/95	Silkeborg IF	A	1-3	Uldbjerg
20/08/95	Naestved BK	H	3-1	Tur, Johansen Mi., Nielsen L-H.
27/08/95	Brøndby IF	A	4-1	Tur, Nielsen L-H. (p), Johansen Mi., Lønstrup
01/09/95	Vejle BK	H	1-2	Frandsen
10/09/95	Lyngby FC	A	2-2	Johansen Mi., Nielsen Mo.
17/09/95	AGF	H	1-3	Nielsen Mo.
20/09/95	Herfølge BK	A	3-0	Nielsen Mo., Frandsen, Nielsen L-H.
24/09/95	Ikast FS	H	1-1	Nielsen Mo.
01/10/95	Silkeborg IF	H	1-0	Tengstedt
06/10/95	OB	A	0-0	
13/10/95	AaB	H	2-1	Frandsen 2
22/10/95	Viborg FF	A	2-2	Uldbjerg, Johansen Mi. (p)
29/10/95	Ikast FS	A	2-4	Falch, Uldbjerg
05/11/95	Herfølge BK	H	0-0	
10/11/95	AGF	A	0-2	
19/11/95	Lyngby FC	H	2-2	Falch, Sørensen
26/11/95	Vejle BK	A	1-0	Sørensen
24/03/96	Brøndby IF	H	0-3	
31/03/96	Vejle BK	A	2-1	Hallum, Nielsen M-B.
04/04/96	Naestved BK	H	1-1	Frandsen (p)
08/04/96	Naestved BK	A	2-2	Nielsen L-H. 2
14/04/96	Viborg FF	H	2-0	Lønstrup, Nielsen L-H.
21/04/96	Herfølge BK	H	2-1	Johansen Mi., Tur
28/04/96	Lyngby FC	A	0-4	
05/05/96	AGF	A	1-2	Nielsen M-B.
08/05/96	Silkeborg IF	H	1-0	Lønstrup
12/05/96	AaB	H	3-1	Johansen Ma., Frandsen, Hallum
19/05/96	Ikast FS	A	1-1	Johansen Mi.
23/05/96	Brøndby IF	H	0-4	
27/05/96	OB	A	1-2	Lønstrup

LYNGBY FC

CLUB DIRECTORY

Lyngby Fodbold Club
Lundtoftevej 61
2800 Lyngby
tel - (45) 884600
fax - (45) 874445
Year of Formation - 1921
Chairman - Michael Kjaer
Secretary - Poul-Erik Petersen
Coach - Benny Lennartsson
Stadium - Lyngby Stadion (15,000)

MAJOR HONOURS
League Championship - (2) 1983, 1992.
Domestic Cup - (3) 1984, 1985, 1990.

APPEARANCES 95/96

	P	Ap	(s)	Gls
Bo ANDERSEN	G	33		
Anders BJERRE	D	31		3
Bent CHRISTENSEN	M	13		1
Claus CHRISTIANSEN	D	18		
Denni CONTEH	A		(2)	
Ronnie EKELUND	A	3	(1)	
Peter FRANK	M	2	(4)	
Torben FRANK	A	3	(8)	
Carsten FREDGAARD	M	11	(13)	1
Michael GOTHENBORG	D	29		1
Piotr HAREN	A	1	(1)	
Thomas HØYER	M	2	(2)	
Erdin ILYAZOVSKI (MAC)	M		(1)	1
Jørgen Juul JENSEN	M	3	(1)	
Mikkel Bo JENSEN	D	1		
Niclas JENSEN	D	31	(1)	3
Todi JONSSON (FAR)	A	16		8
Brian KAUS	M	10	(4)	2
Christian KRONHOLM	M		(4)	
Allan KUHN	A	2	(5)	
Patrick KUKLINSKI	D	2		
Erik LARSEN	M	4	(10)	1
Henrik LARSEN	M	32		11
Jimmi LÜTHJE	M	18	(5)	4
Anders NIELSEN	M	24	(7)	2
David NIELSEN	A	13		10
Marino RAHMBERG (SWE)	A	5	(1)	1
Dennis ROMMEDAHL	A	2	(7)	
Thomas RYTTER	D	32		
Kenneth STORVIK (NOR)	A	4		
Arunas SUIKA (LIT)	A	10	(10)	4
Johnny VILSTRUP	M	8		7

LEAGUE RESULTS 1995/96

Date	Opponent	H/A	Score	Scorers
30/07/95	Naestved BK	H	1-1	Larsen H.
02/08/95	Brøndby IF	A	2-2	Larsen H., Vilstrup (p)
06/08/95	Vejle BK	H	3-0	Nielsen A., Vilstrup, Suika
13/08/95	Viborg FF	A	2-0	Vilstrup (p), Jonsson
20/08/95	AGF	A	1-2	Jonsson
27/08/95	Herfølge BK	H	2-0	Vilstrup, Suika
03/09/95	Ikast FS	A	4-0	Vilstrup 2, Suika, Jonsson
10/09/95	FC København	H	2-2	Vilstrup (p), Jonsson
17/09/95	AaB	A	1-0	Kaus
20/09/95	OB	H	0-2	
22/09/95	Silkeborg IF	A	1-1	Gothenborg
01/10/95	Viborg FF	H	4-0	Jonsson 2, Larsen H., Ilyazovski
08/10/95	Vejle BK	A	3-0	Lüthje, Larsen H., Jonsson
13/10/95	Brøndby IF	H	1-3	Kaus
22/10/95	Naestved BK	A	4-1	Nielsen A., Jonsson, Jensen N., Suika
29/10/95	Silkeborg IF	H	1-2	Larsen H.
05/11/95	OB	A	2-2	Rahmberg, Lüthje
10/11/95	AaB	H	0-0	
19/11/95	FC København	A	2-2	Bjerre, Larsen H.
26/11/95	Ikast FS	H	3-2	Bjerre, Lüthje, Jensen N.
04/04/96	Viborg FF	A	2-0	Larsen H. 2
08/04/96	AGF	H	0-1	
14/04/96	Ikast FS	A	5-0	Bjerre (p), Nielsen D., Larsen H., Lüthje, Jensen N.
17/04/96	Herfølge BK	A	2-2	Nielsen D., Christensen
21/04/96	Vejle BK	H	1-1	Larsen H.
28/04/96	FC København	H	4-0	Nielsen D. 2, Larsen E., Fredgaard
05/05/96	Brøndby IF	A	2-1	Nielsen D. 2
08/05/96	Herfølge BK	A	1-1	Nielsen D.
12/05/96	OB	H	0-1	
15/05/96	Silkeborg IF	H	2-3	Nielsen D., og (Sørensen)
19/05/96	Naestved BK	H	2-0	Larsen H., Nielsen D.
23/05/96	AaB	A	1-1	Nielsen D.
27/05/96	AGF	H	0-2	

NAESTVED BK

CLUB DIRECTORY

Naestved Boldklub A/S
Rolighedsvej 18
Postboks 51
4700 Naestved
tel - (55) 771012
fax - (55) 770510
Year of Formation - 1939
Chairman - Uffe Nielsen
Secretary - John Maagaard
Coach - Peter Bonde
Stadium - Naestved Stadion (20,000)

APPEARANCES 95/96

	P	Ap	(s)	Gls
Kenn ANDERSEN	G	9		
Christian BANK	D	10	(2)	
Peter BONDE	M		(1)	
Anders CHRISTENSEN	D	2	(2)	
Anders ERIKSEN	M		(1)	
Claus FALLENTIN	G	24		
Henrik FRIMANN	M	13	(5)	
Anders HANSEN	M		(2)	
Dennis HEINE	D	6		
Frank HOUGAARD	M	32	(1)	2
Henrik JACOBSEN	D		(1)	
Lars JAKOBSEN	M	14	(7)	1
Bjarne JENSEN	M	16	(4)	1
Claus JENSEN	A	3	(1)	
Steen JENSEN	A	7	(6)	2
Tom JENSEN	A	2	(3)	
Søren JUEL	A	13	(4)	
Henrik JØRGENSEN	D		(2)	
Gocha KOKOSHVILI (GEO)	D	12	(1)	
Søren Juul KRISTENSEN	M	10	(5)	
Thomas MATHIESEN	A	4	(3)	
Alex NIELSEN	A	28	(1)	8
Tommy NIELSEN	D	19	(6)	2
Michael NONBO	D	29	(3)	
Max PETERSEN	D	31		
John RUHE	D	3	(1)	
Morten SCHMIDT	M		(2)	
Mads SPUR-MORTENSEN	M	19	(8)	1
Mark STRUDAL	A	19	(4)	7
Søren SVENDSEN	M		(1)	
Rene TENGSTEDT	A	4	(7)	1
Kenny THORUP	M	7		
Nicolai WAEL	D	24	(3)	4
Tomas ZVIRGZDAUSKAS (LIT)	D	3	(1)	

LEAGUE RESULTS 1995/96

30/07/95	Lyngby FC	A	1-1	Nielsen A.
02/08/95	AGF	H	2-4	Nielsen A., Wael
06/08/95	Herfølge BK	A	0-2	
13/08/95	Ikast FS	H	1-1	Nielsen A.
20/08/95	FC København	A	1-3	Wael
27/08/95	AaB	H	1-1	Nielsen A.
01/09/95	OB	A	0-5	
08/09/95	Silkeborg IF	H	1-0	Hougaard (p)
17/09/95	Viborg FF	H	6-2	Nielsen A., Jakobsen, Jensen S., Jensen B., Strudal 2
20/09/95	Brøndby IF	A	1-6	Jensen S.
24/09/95	Vejle BK	H	0-0	
01/10/95	Ikast FS	A	2-1	Strudal, Nielsen A.
08/10/95	Herfølge BK	H	3-2	Nielsen T., Strudal 2
15/10/95	AGF	A	0-3	
22/10/95	Lyngby FC	H	1-4	Hougaard
29/10/95	Vejle BK	A	0-2	
05/11/95	Brøndby IF	H	0-1	
12/11/95	Viborg FF	A	0-4	
26/11/95	OB	H	0-4	
29/11/95	Silkeborg IF	A	0-5	
04/04/96	FC København	A	1-1	Wael
08/04/96	FC København	H	2-2	Nielsen A., Tengstedt
14/04/96	AGF	A	1-3	Spur-Mortensen
17/04/96	AaB	A	0-4	
21/04/96	Brøndby IF	H	0-1	
28/04/96	Ikast FS	H	0-2	
05/05/96	Vejle BK	H	1-0	Strudal
08/05/96	AaB	A	0-2	
12/05/96	Viborg FF	A	2-6	Nielsen T., Strudal
15/05/96	OB	H	1-1	Wael
19/05/96	Lyngby FC	A	0-2	
23/05/96	Herfølge BK	H	0-4	
27/05/96	Silkeborg IF	A	1-1	Nielsen A.

OB

CLUB DIRECTORY

Odense Boldklub
Box 344
Sdr. Boulevard 172
5100 Odense C
tel - (65) 912050
fax - (65) 912025
Year of Formation - 1887
Chairman - Fritz Bonde
Secretary - Doris Christensen
Coach - Viggo Jensen
Stadium - Odense Stadion (20,400)

MAJOR HONOURS
League Championship - (3) 1977, 1982, 1989.
Domestic Cup - (3) 1983, 1991, 1993.

APPEARANCES 95/96

	P	Ap	(s)	Gls
Morten BISGAARD	M	22	(3)	6
Carsten DETHLEFSEN	D	16	(4)	
Johnny HANSEN	D	12	(14)	
Carsten HEMMINGSEN	M	14		1
Michael HEMMINGSEN	D	32		1
Bo Bjørnholt HENRIKSEN	A	3	(7)	3
Jesper HJORTH	A	12	(4)	5
Lars HØGH	G	33		
Kenneth JENSEN	A	15	(9)	4
Ulrik Rosenløv LAURSEN	D	13		
Jens MELVANG	M	5	(6)	
Steen NEDERGAARD	M	24	(6)	1
Brian Steen NIELSEN	M	29		2
David NIELSEN	A		(1)	
Per PEDERSEN	A	31	(1)	16
Ulrik Baerholm PEDERSEN	M	20	(7)	5
Henrik RISOM	M		(6)	
Torben SANGILD	D	31		1
Michael SCHJØNBERG	M	32		5
Jesper STÜCKER	D		(2)	
Jess THORUP	A	19	(12)	6

LEAGUE RESULTS 1995/96

02/08/95	Ikast FS	H	2-0	Pedersen P., Pedersen U-B.
06/08/95	FC København	A	1-2	Thorup
09/08/95	Herfølge BK	A	2-1	Nielsen B-S., Hjorth
11/08/95	AaB	H	1-1	Hjorth
20/08/95	Viborg FF	H	3-1	Pedersen P. 2, Thorup
27/08/95	Silkeborg IF	A	1-2	Schjønberg (p)
01/09/95	Naestved BK	H	5-0	Henriksen 3, Jensen, Sangild
08/09/95	Brøndby IF	A	1-1	Pedersen P.
17/09/95	Vejle BK	H	1-0	Hemmingsen C.
20/09/95	Lyngby FC	A	2-0	Jensen, Pedersen P.
24/09/95	AGF	H	1-0	Jensen
01/10/95	AaB	A	0-3	
06/10/95	FC København	H	0-0	
15/10/95	Ikast FS	A	3-1	og (Meedom), Jensen, Pedersen P.
22/10/95	Herfølge BK	H	0-2	
29/10/95	AGF	A	2-2	Pedersen P., Pedersen U-B.
05/11/95	Lyngby FC	H	2-2	Pedersen P. 2
10/11/95	Vejle BK	A	1-1	Pedersen P.
17/11/95	Brøndby IF	H	0-3	
26/11/95	Naestved BK	A	4-0	Thorup, Schjønberg 2, Pedersen P.
04/04/96	Ikast FS	H	2-0	Schjønberg, Pedersen P.
08/04/96	Viborg FF	A	1-2	Thorup
14/04/96	Herfølge BK	H	5-1	Hemmingsen M., Bisgaard, Pedersen P., Pedersen U-B., Nielsen B-S.
17/04/96	Silkeborg IF	H	1-0	Pedersen U-B.
21/04/96	Silkeborg IF	A	1-1	Nedergaard
28/04/96	Brøndby IF	H	2-0	Bisgaard 2
05/05/96	AaB	H	5-1	Schjønberg (p), Bisgaard, Pedersen P. 2, Hjorth
08/05/96	Vejle BK	A	0-2	
12/05/96	Lyngby FC	A	1-0	Bisgaard
15/05/96	Naestved BK	A	1-1	Bisgaard
19/05/96	Viborg FF	H	3-1	Hjorth, Thorup 2
23/05/96	AGF	A	1-1	Pedersen P.
27/05/96	FC København	H	2-1	Hjorth, Pedersen U-B.

SILKEBORG IF

CLUB DIRECTORY

Silkeborg Idraets Forening
Ansvej 110
8600 Silkeborg
tel - (86) 804477
fax - (86) 804647
Year of Formation - 1917
Chairman - Steen Høholt
Secretary - Poul Erik Wilz Jensen
Coach - Preben Elkjaer
Stadium - Silkeborg Stadion (12,000)

MAJOR HONOURS
League Championship - (1) 1994.

APPEARANCES 95/96

	P	Ap	(s)	Gls
Keld BORDINGGAARD	M	18	(2)	3
Morten BRUUN	M	23		1
Heine FERNANDEZ	A	18		5
Michael HANSEN	M	23	(8)	5
Poul HENRIKSEN	D		(1)	
Henrik KASTBJERG	D	19	(1)	1
Peter KJAER	G	32		
Peder KNUDSEN	M	22	(6)	1
Michael LARSEN	D	8		
Thomas Røll LARSEN	A	1	(5)	1
Jacob LAURSEN	D	32		4
Martin LAURSEN	D	1		
Lars MELVANG	D	1	(5)	
Flemming MØLDRUP	D	5	(3)	
Brian PEDERSEN	M	6	(15)	1
Henrik PEDERSEN	A	2	(10)	4
Christian Duus PETERSEN	D	30		1
John RASMUSSEN	G	1	(1)	
Allan REESE	A	21	(2)	1
Henrik RISOM	M	14		3
Kenni SOMMER	A	9	(7)	5
Arunas SUIKA (LIT)	A	5		2
Peter SØRENSEN	M	29		
Jesper THYGESEN	M	28	(4)	6
Bora ZIVKOVIC (YUG)	D	15	(4)	

LEAGUE RESULTS 1995/96

Date	Opponent		Score	Scorers
30/07/95	AGF	A	0-0	
02/08/95	Herfølge BK	H	1-0	Fernandez
04/08/95	Ikast FS	A	0-1	
11/08/95	FC København	H	3-1	Thygesen, Kastbjerg, Pedersen H.
18/08/95	AaB	A	1-4	Laursen J.
27/08/95	OB	H	2-1	Bruun, Laursen J.
03/09/95	Viborg FF	H	0-2	
08/09/95	Naestved BK	A	0-1	
17/09/95	Brøndby IF	H	2-0	Bordinggaard, Pedersen H.
20/09/95	Vejle BK	A	1-1	Fernandez
22/09/95	Lyngby FC	H	1-1	Fernandez
01/10/95	FC København	A	0-1	
06/10/95	Ikast FS	H	1-1	Thygesen
15/10/95	Herfølge BK	A	2-5	Laursen J., Fernandez
22/10/95	AGF	H	0-3	
29/10/95	Lyngby FC	A	2-1	Hansen 2
05/11/95	Vejle BK	H	1-2	Thygesen
10/11/95	Brøndby IF	A	1-4	Hansen
26/11/95	Viborg FF	A	3-0	Risom, Bordinggaard, Pedersen H.
29/11/95	Naestved BK	H	5-0	Risom, Petersen, Fernandez, Bordinggaard, Pedersen H.
04/04/96	AGF	H	2-1	Suika, Thygesen
08/04/96	AaB	H	2-1	Suika, Hansen (p)
14/04/96	AaB	A	1-0	Knudsen
17/04/96	OB	A	0-1	
21/04/96	OB	H	1-1	Thygesen
28/04/96	Herfølge BK	H	1-0	Reese
05/05/96	Ikast FS	A	2-1	Sommer, Hansen
08/05/96	FC København	A	0-1	
12/05/96	Vejle BK	H	3-1	Sommer, Risom (p), Laursen J.
15/05/96	Lyngby FC	A	3-2	Thygesen, Sommer, Larsen T-R.
19/05/96	Brøndby IF	A	1-1	Sommer
23/05/96	Viborg FF	A	1-2	Sommer
27/05/96	Naestved BK	H	1-1	Pedersen B.

VEJLE BK

CLUB DIRECTORY

Vejle Boldklub
Helligkildevej 2
7100 Vejle
tel - (75) 727500
fax - (75) 833033
Year of Formation - 1891
Chairman - Ole Vedel
Secretary - Henrik Lund
Coach - Ole Fritsen
Stadium - Vejle Stadion (18,500)

MAJOR HONOURS
League Championship - (5)
1958, 1971, 1972, 1978, 1984.
Domestic Cup - (6)
1958, 1959, 1972, 1975, 1977, 1981.

APPEARANCES 95/96

	P	Ap	(s)	Gls
Erik BOYE	G	27		
Brian CHRISTENSEN	A	19	(8)	5
Finn CHRISTENSEN	M	27		1
Kenneth CHRISTIANSEN	A		(3)	
Peter CHRISTIANSEN	D	3	(1)	
Kaspar DALGAS	A	5	(3)	2
Eduard DEMENKOVETS (BLS)	M	10	(6)	3
Sob Evariste DIBO (CIV)	M	2	(3)	
Lars DØHR	D	32		
Klaus ESKILDSEN	D	19	(5)	
Kurt FRITSEN	D		(1)	
Niels Ejner GAMMELGAARD	A	1	(3)	
Dejvi GLAVEVSKI (MAC)	A	5		1
Peter GRAULUND	A	9	(10)	3
Thomas GRAVESEN	D	28		2
Carsten HOLM	A	2	(3)	
Henrik HOLM	M	12		
Lars JENSEN	D	1	(3)	
Jan LARSEN	D	7	(5)	
Jens MADSEN	M	28	(1)	4
Jesper MIKKELSEN	M	24	(6)	6
Kim NØRHOLT	A		(7)	
Alex NØRLUND	A	11	(1)	
Jacob OLSEN	M	7	(2)	
Lasse OTTESEN	M	13	(2)	
Benny POULSGAARD	D	10	(5)	
Brian RASMUSSEN	A		(2)	
John SIVEBAEK	M	27	(1)	
Jesper SØGAARD	A	28	(3)	7
Thomas SØRENSEN	G	6		

LEAGUE RESULTS 1995/96

30/07/95	Brøndby IF	H	1-3	Demenkovets
02/08/95	Viborg FF	A	2-0	Christensen B., Madsen
06/08/95	Lyngby FC	A	0-3	
11/08/95	AGF	H	0-0	
20/08/95	Herfølge BK	A	4-2	Søgaard 3, Mikkelsen
27/08/95	Ikast FS	H	1-1	Madsen
01/09/95	FC København	A	2-1	Søgaard, Mikkelsen
10/09/95	AaB	H	1-3	Graulund
17/09/95	OB	A	0-1	
20/09/95	Silkeborg IF	H	1-1	Graulund
24/09/95	Naestved BK	A	0-0	
01/10/95	AGF	A	0-0	
08/10/95	Lyngby FC	H	0-3	
15/10/95	Viborg FF	H	3-3	Mikkelsen 2, Graulund
22/10/95	Brøndby IF	A	0-4	
29/10/95	Naestved BK	H	2-0	Dalgas, Madsen
05/11/95	Silkeborg IF	A	2-1	Mikkelsen, Dalgas
10/11/95	OB	H	1-1	Mikkelsen
26/11/95	FC København	H	0-1	
29/11/95	AaB	A	0-1	
24/03/96	Ikast FS	A	1-2	Gravesen
31/03/96	FC København	H	1-2	Christensen B.
04/04/96	AaB	A	0-2	
08/04/96	Herfølge BK	H	2-1	Christensen F., Demenkovets
14/04/96	Brøndby IF	A	0-6	
21/04/96	Lyngby FC	A	1-1	Christensen B.
28/04/96	Viborg FF	H	0-1	
05/05/96	Naestved BK	A	0-1	
08/05/96	OB	H	2-0	Glavevski, Gravesen
12/05/96	Silkeborg IF	A	1-3	Søgaard
19/05/96	AGF	H	0-1	
23/05/96	Ikast FS	H	5-0	Demenkovets, Madsen, Søgaard (p), Christensen B. 2
27/05/96	Herfølge BK	A	1-1	Søgaard

VIBORG FF

CLUB DIRECTORY

Viborg Fodsports Forening
Postbox 214
8800 Viborg
tel - (86) 601066
fax - (86) 601066
Year of Formation - 1896
Chairman - Kurt Kvist
Secretary - Bjarne Vestdam
Coach - Ove Christensen
Stadium - Viborg Stadion (15,000)

APPEARANCES 95/96

	P	Ap	(s)	Gls
Søren BORUP	M	1	(3)	
Mike BURNS (USA)	D	15		
Graham EASTER (ENG)	A	4	(6)	
Thomas FRANDSEN	D	6	(5)	
Søren FREDERIKSEN	A	33		11
Jens Jørn GINNERUP	A	1	(8)	1
Dennis HANSEN	D	28	(1)	2
Peder HENRIKSEN	D	6	(5)	
Nichlas HINDSBERG	A	4	(8)	1
Steffen HØJER	A	32		16
Flemming JENSEN	M		(1)	
Morten JENSEN	D	25	(1)	
Risto KALLASTE (EST)	M	18	(5)	4
Roald KIILERICH	G	10		
Stephen LOWE (ENG)	G	23		
Bent NIELSEN	M		(2)	
Jakob Glerup NIELSEN	M	32		1
Leif NIELSEN	M	18	(7)	
Martin NIELSEN	D	28	(3)	
Ralf PEDERSEN	D	16	(2)	2
Thomas POULSEN	M	31		3
Jesper SCHAU	M	10	(13)	2
Jesper STÜCKER	D	14	(3)	2
Anders SØRENSEN	A	5	(1)	1
Per SØRENSEN	M		(2)	
Henrik TØNNESEN	D	3	(6)	
Anders WINTHER	M		(1)	

LEAGUE RESULTS 1995/96

30/07/95	FC København	A	1-4	Højer (p)
02/08/95	Vejle BK	H	0-2	
05/08/95	AaB	A	1-8	Sørensen A.
13/08/95	Lyngby FC	H	0-2	
20/08/95	OB	A	1-3	Højer (p)
27/08/95	AGF	H	1-1	Stücker
03/09/95	Silkeborg IF	A	2-0	Højer, Frederiksen
10/09/95	Herfølge BK	H	2-1	Højer, Stücker
17/09/95	Naestved BK	A	2-6	Højer, Poulsen
20/09/95	Ikast FS	H	3-1	Frederiksen, Højer, Hindsberg
22/09/95	Brøndby IF	H	2-2	Frederiksen, Kallaste
01/10/95	Lyngby FC	A	0-4	
06/10/95	AaB	H	4-0	Højer 2, Frederiksen, Kallaste
15/10/95	Vejle BK	A	3-3	Poulsen, Schau, Højer
22/10/95	FC København	H	2-2	Frederiksen, Kallaste
27/10/95	Brøndby IF	A	0-4	
05/11/95	Ikast FS	A	1-1	og (Silvertsen)
12/11/95	Naestved BK	H	4-0	Frederiksen, Højer, Poulsen, Ginnerup
19/11/95	Herfølge BK	A	3-3	Frederiksen 2, Schau
26/11/95	Silkeborg IF	H	0-3	
31/03/96	Brøndby IF	A	1-1	Frederiksen
04/04/96	Lyngby FC	H	0-2	
08/04/96	OB	H	2-1	Hansen, Højer
14/04/96	FC København	A	0-2	
17/04/96	AGF	A	1-1	Nielsen J-G.
21/04/96	AaB	H	0-2	
28/04/96	Vejle BK	A	1-0	Pedersen
05/05/96	Herfølge BK	A	2-2	Højer 2
08/05/96	AGF	H	0-0	
12/05/96	Naestved BK	H	6-2	Højer 2, Pedersen, Hansen, Kallaste, Frederiksen
19/05/96	OB	A	1-3	Frederiksen
23/05/96	Silkeborg IF	H	2-1	og (Zivkovic), Højer
27/05/96	Ikast FS	A	0-0	

PROMOTED CLUBS

SECOND DIVISION FINAL TABLE 95/96

		Pd	W	D	L	F	A	Pt	GD
1	**Hvidovre IF**	**30**	**18**	**10**	**2**	**57**	**32**	**64**	**+25**
2	**AB**	**30**	**18**	**7**	**5**	**72**	**24**	**61**	**+48**
3	Brønshøj BK	30	16	4	10	56	40	52	+16
4	Esbjerg FB	30	13	9	8	56	39	48	+17
5	Herning Fremad	30	14	6	10	51	35	48	+16
6	Svendborg FB	30	15	3	12	47	39	48	+8
7	BK Fremad Amager	30	10	10	10	40	40	40	=
8	B 93	30	9	10	11	40	47	37	-7
9	Ølstykke FC	30	9	9	12	49	58	36	-9
10	BK Avarta	30	9	9	12	37	47	36	-10
11	Køge BK	30	9	8	13	48	52	35	-4
12	FC Fredericia	30	9	8	13	51	59	35	-8
13	Holstebro BK	30	9	6	15	44	45	33	-1
14	HIK	30	7	12	11	34	51	33	-17
15	B 1909	30	5	12	13	36	53	27	-17
16	Nørre Aaby IK	30	6	5	19	30	87	23	-57

CLUB DIRECTORY

Hvidovre Idraets Forening
Sollentuna Allé 1-3
2650 Hvidovre
tel - (36) 781772
fax - (36) 781133
Year of Formation - 1925
Chairman - Frede Madsen
Secretary - Torben Lund
Coach - Jan Kalborg
Stadium - Hvidovre Stadion (15,000)

MAJOR HONOURS
League Championship - (3) 1966, 1973, 1981.
Domestic Cup - (1) 1980.

CLUB DIRECTORY

Akademisk Boldklub (AB)
Skovdiget 1
2880 Bagsvaerd
tel - (44) 987533
fax - (44) 441400
Year of Formation - 1889
Chairman - Henrik Mostrup
Secretary - Thomas Gram
Coach - Christian Andersen; Tonni Nielsen
Stadium - Gladsaxe Idraetspark (10,000)

ENGLAND

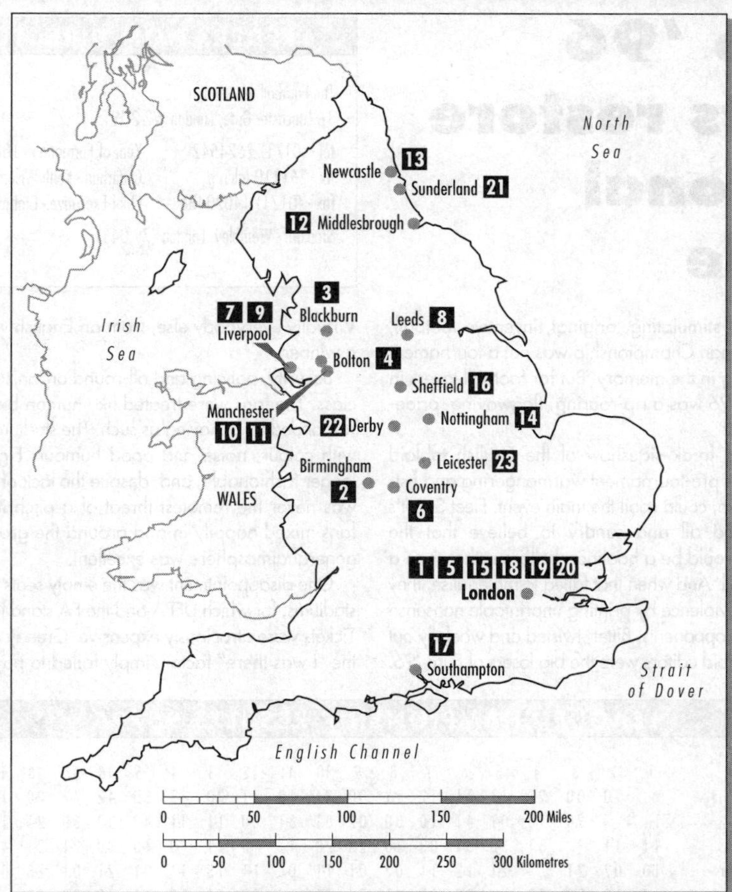

1	ARSENAL	313
2	ASTON VILLA	314
3	BLACKBURN ROVERS	315
4	BOLTON WANDERERS	316
5	CHELSEA	317
6	COVENTRY CITY	318
7	EVERTON	319
8	LEEDS UNITED	320
9	LIVERPOOL	321
10	MANCHESTER CITY	322
11	MANCHESTER UNITED	323
12	MIDDLESBROUGH	324
13	NEWCASTLE UNITED	325
14	NOTTINGHAM FOREST	326
15	QUEENS PARK RANGERS	327
16	SHEFFIELD WEDNESDAY	328
17	SOUTHAMPTON	329
18	TOTTENHAM HOTSPUR	330
19	WEST HAM UNITED	331
20	WIMBLEDON	332
21	SUNDERLAND	333
22	DERBY COUNTY	333
23	LEICESTER CITY	333

'DOUBLE DOUBLE' FOR MANCHESTER UNITED

Euro '96 hosts restore national pride

FEDERATION DIRECTORY

The Football Association
16 Lancaster Gate, London W2 3LW

tel - (0171) 2624542
tlx - 261110 faldn g
fax - (0171) 14020486
Stadium - Wembley, London (79,045)

Year of Formation - 1863
Chairman - Keith Wiseman
Chief Executive - Graham Kelly

For admirers of stimulating, original, inventive football, the 1996 European Championship was not a tournament that will live long in the memory. But for football lovers in England, Euro '96 was a rip-roaring, flagwaving, pride-restoring success.

Not even the freak sideshow of the English tabloid press, with all its pre-tournament warmongering and fist-in-the-face racism, could spoil the main event. Fleet Street's grimiest had led all and sundry to believe that the championship would be a hooligan hellfire rather than a festival of football. And when that failed to materialise, they tried to provoke violence by printing unprintable nonsense about England's opponents. Bitter, twisted and woefully out of touch, the tabloid editors were the big losers of Euro '96. Virtually everybody else, from an English viewpoint, was a winner.

Security, policing and all-round organisation was first-class. The fans were treated like human beings and they responded by behaving as such. The stadiums were awash with colour, noise and good humour. Fighting was no longer fashionable, and, despite the lack of fencing, there was never the remotest threat of a pitch invasion. Rival fans mixed happily in and around the grounds, and the general atmosphere was excellent.

One disappointment was the empty seats at many of the stadiums, for which UEFA and the FA stand jointly accused. Tickets were atrociously expensive. Greedy exploitation of the "I was there" factor simply failed to pay off.

LEAGUE CHAMPIONSHIP RESULTS 95/96

		1	2	3	4	5	6	7	8	9	10	11	12	13	14	15	16	17	18	19	20
1	Arsenal		2-0	0-0	2-1	1-1	1-1	1-2	2-1	0-0	3-1	1-0	1-1	2-0	1-1	3-0	4-2	4-2	0-0	1-0	1-3
2	Aston Villa	1-1		2-0	1-0	0-1	4-1	1-0	3-0	0-2	0-1	3-1	0-0	1-1	1-1	4-2	3-2	3-0	2-1	1-1	2-0
3	Blackburn Rovers	1-1	1-1		3-1	3-0	5-1	0-3	1-0	2-3	2-0	1-2	1-0	2-1	7-0	1-0	3-0	2-1	2-1	4-2	3-2
4	Bolton Wanderers	1-0	0-2	2-1		2-1	1-2	1-1	0-2	0-1	1-1	0-6	1-1	1-3	1-1	0-1	2-1	0-1	2-3	0-3	1-0
5	Chelsea	1-0	1-2	2-3	3-2		2-2	0-0	4-1	2-2	1-1	1-4	5-0	1-0	1-0	1-1	0-0	3-0	0-0	1-2	1-2
6	Coventry City	0-0	0-3	5-0	0-2	1-0		2-1	0-0	1-0	2-1	0-4	0-0	0-1	1-1	1-0	0-1	1-1	2-3	2-2	3-3
7	Everton	0-2	1-0	1-0	3-0	1-1	2-2		2-0	1-1	2-0	2-3	4-0	1-3	3-0	2-0	2-2	2-0	1-1	3-0	2-4
8	Leeds United	0-3	2-0	0-0	0-1	1-0	3-1	2-2		1-0	0-1	3-1	0-1	0-1	1-3	1-3	2-0	1-0	1-3	2-0	1-1
9	Liverpool	3-1	3-0	3-0	5-2	2-0	0-0	1-2	5-0		6-0	2-0	1-0	4-3	4-2	1-0	1-0	1-1	0-0	2-0	2-2
10	Manchester City	0-1	1-0	1-1	1-0	0-1	1-1	0-2	0-0	2-2		2-3	0-1	3-3	1-1	2-0	1-0	2-1	1-1	2-1	1-0
11	Manchester United	1-0	0-0	1-0	3-0	1-1	1-0	2-0	1-0	2-2	1-0		2-0	2-0	5-0	2-1	2-2	4-1	1-0	2-1	3-1
12	Middlesbrough	2-3	0-2	2-0	1-4	2-0	2-1	0-2	1-1	2-1	4-1	0-3		1-2	1-1	1-0	3-1	0-0	0-1	4-2	1-2
13	Newcastle United	2-0	1-0	1-0	2-1	2-0	3-0	1-0	2-1	2-1	3-1	0-1	1-0		3-1	2-1	2-0	1-0	1-1	3-0	6-1
14	Nottingham Forest	0-1	1-1	1-5	3-2	0-0	0-0	3-2	2-1	1-0	3-0	1-1	1-0	1-1		3-0	1-0	1-0	2-1	1-1	4-1
15	Queens Park Rangers	1-1	1-0	0-1	2-1	1-2	1-1	3-1	1-2	1-2	1-0	1-1	1-1	2-3	1-1		0-3	3-0	2-3	3-0	0-3
16	Sheffield Wednesday	1-0	2-0	2-1	4-2	0-0	4-3	2-5	6-2	1-1	1-1	0-0	0-1	0-2	1-3	1-3		2-2	1-3	0-1	2-1
17	Southampton	0-0	0-1	1-0	1-0	2-3	1-0	2-2	1-1	1-3	1-1	3-1	2-1	1-0	3-4	2-0	0-1		0-0	0-0	0-0
18	Tottenham Hotspur	2-1	0-1	2-3	2-2	1-1	3-1	0-0	2-1	1-3	1-0	4-1	1-1	1-1	0-1	1-0	1-0	1-0		0-1	3-1
19	West Ham United	0-1	1-4	1-1	1-0	1-3	3-2	2-1	1-2	0-0	4-2	0-1	2-0	2-0	1-0	1-0	1-1	2-1	1-1		1-1
20	Wimbledon	0-3	3-3	1-1	3-2	1-1	0-2	2-3	2-4	1-0	3-0	2-4	0-0	3-3	1-0	2-1	2-2	1-2	0-1	0-1	

LEAGUE CHAMPIONSHIP FINAL TABLE 95/96

			Home					Away					Total						
		Pd	W	D	L	F	A	W	D	L	F	A	W	D	L	F	A	Pt	GD
1	Manchester United	38	15	4	0	36	9	10	3	6	37	26	25	7	6	73	35	82	+38
2	Newcastle United	38	17	1	1	38	9	7	5	7	28	28	24	6	8	66	37	78	+29
3	Liverpool	38	14	4	1	46	13	6	7	6	24	21	20	11	7	70	34	71	+36
4	Aston Villa	38	11	5	3	32	15	7	4	8	20	20	18	9	11	52	35	63	+17
5	Arsenal	38	10	7	2	30	16	7	5	7	19	16	17	12	9	49	32	63	+17
6	Everton	38	10	5	4	35	19	7	5	7	29	25	17	10	11	64	44	61	+20
7	Blackburn Rovers	38	14	2	3	44	19	4	5	10	17	28	18	7	13	61	47	61	+14
8	Tottenham Hotspur	38	9	5	5	26	19	7	8	4	24	19	16	13	9	50	38	61	+12
9	Nottingham Forest	38	11	6	2	29	17	4	7	8	21	37	15	13	10	50	54	58	-4
10	West Ham United	38	9	5	5	25	21	5	4	10	18	31	14	9	15	43	52	51	-9
11	Chelsea	38	7	7	5	30	22	5	7	7	16	22	12	14	12	46	44	50	+2
12	Middlesbrough	38	8	3	8	27	27	3	7	9	8	23	11	10	17	35	50	43	-15
13	Leeds United	38	8	3	8	21	21	4	4	11	19	36	12	7	19	40	57	43	-17
14	Wimbledon	38	5	6	8	27	33	5	5	9	28	37	10	11	17	55	70	41	-15
15	Sheffield Wednesday	38	7	5	7	30	31	3	5	11	18	30	10	10	18	48	61	40	-13
16	Coventry City	38	6	7	6	21	23	2	7	10	21	37	8	14	16	42	60	38	-18
17	Southampton	38	7	7	5	21	18	2	4	13	13	34	9	11	18	34	52	38	-18
18	Manchester City	38	7	7	5	21	19	2	4	13	12	39	9	11	18	33	58	38	-25
19	Queens Park Rangers	38	6	5	8	25	26	3	1	15	13	31	9	6	23	38	57	33	-19
20	Bolton Wanderers	38	5	4	10	16	31	3	1	15	23	40	8	5	25	39	71	29	-32

Wembley was the one stadium that was always full to the brim. And understandably so, as that was where hosts England played all of their matches.

Euro '96 could not come soon enough for Terry Venables and his team. For two and a half years they had been fed an unappetising diet of friendlies, most of them at Wembley. When they jetted off to the Far East just before the finals, they did themselves more harm than good. An unruly incident involving some of the players on the flight home sent out all the wrong messages, and a weak final performance against a Hong Kong Select XI did little to engender confidence in the team's on-field capabalities.

But when the curtain rose on Euro '96, England came together in more ways than one. The opening 1-1 draw with Switzerland was panned by the critics, but the team played some delightful football in the first half, and but for a harsh penalty decision would have held on to the 1-0 win they had evidently settled for. Against Scotland the first-half performance was indeed miserable, but after the break England sparkled and deserved their 2-0 win. David Seaman's penalty save and Paul Gascoigne's brilliant individual goal not only turned the game. They ignited England's challenge.

England only needed a draw against Holland to be sure of winning the group and remaining at Wembley for the quarter-final. The Dutch also required just one point to qualify. Outsiders talked of a possible 'agreement', but English footballers, for all their other failings, have always been honest, committed competitors. Against Holland they were that and much, much more, producing one of England's greatest ever performances to win 4-1, thereby turning the tables on a country which had long snubbed their noses at what they regarded as a tactically and technically inferior footballing nation.

Into the last eight, and with confidence booming, England suddenly had everybody - the fans, the media, even the referee - on their side. Spain should have won. They were denied a clear goal and one, maybe two, decent penalty claims by the French officials. But England rode their luck and got through in a penalty shoot-out, giving the nation two new superheroes to acclaim - goalkeeper Seaman and lionheart defender Stuart Pearce.

The Big One was next. England v Germany. A chance to avenge the heartbreak of Italia '90. Alan Shearer, with his fifth goal of the competition, gave the hosts the perfect start. But Germany, as always, came back. The match was thrilling, tremendously nerve-wracking. And that was before the shoot-out. Twice in extra-time England were a hair's breadth away from netting the winning 'golden goal'. The stadium throbbed with anticipation. But the Germans were relentless. They blasted every penalty out of Seaman's reach. Then up stepped poor Gareth Southgate, his timid effort silencing the crowd and tragically bringing to an end England's Euro '96 dream.

The nation sank to its knees in despair. Some could not contain their rage and frustration at losing out again so bravely, so cruelly to the arch-enemy. At Trafalgar Square in central London alcohol-fuelled youths gave the attendant camera crews what they wanted, throwing stones, smashing cars and picking fights with men in uniform. At Wembley the dejected crowd gave the England players a long and moving ovation. Once again, it was not to be. But the team had done the nation proud. English football had shown that it could live with the best. Seaman, Shearer and Gascoigne had been world-class. McManaman, Neville and Southgate had provided real hope for the future. The glory of 1966 had not been repeated, but Terry Venables and his heroes could not have done much more to win the European Championship for the first time.

For the England players, Euro '96 was a career bench-mark. For the England coach, it was the final curtain. Terry Venables had announced six months before the event that he would not be staying on for the World Cup qualifying campaign. He had a number of court cases to fight, and that, he maintained, had to be his priority.

It took the FA a long time to find a replacement. Most of the chief candidates - Kevin Keegan, Bryan Robson, Gerry Francis - all publicly discounted themselves from the running early on. It was not until early May that Chelsea manager Glenn Hoddle was officially appointed. Clearly, he was not the FA's first choice, but he was an admirable one, a man who could plainly identify with what Terry Venables had built up and develop the team even further. Hoddle had no time at all to experiment before the World

DOMESTIC CUP RESULTS

THIRD ROUND
Arsenal 1, Sheffield United 1
(replay) Sheffield United 1, Arsenal 0
Barnsley 0, Oldham Athletic 0
(replay) Oldham Athletic 2, Barnsley 1
Birmingham City 1, Wolverhampton Wanderers 1
(replay) Wolverhampton Wanderers 2, Birmingham City 1
Bradford City 0, Bolton Wanderers 3
Crystal Palace 0, Port Vale 0
(replay) Port Vale 4, Crystal Palace 3 (aet)
Charlton Athletic 2, Sheffield Wednesday 0
Crewe Alexandra 4, West Bromwich Albion 3
Fulham 1, Shrewsbury Town 1
(replay) Shrewsbury Town 2, Fulham 1
Gravesend 0, Aston Villa 3
Grimsby Town 7, Luton Town 1
Hereford United 1, Tottenham Hotspur 1
(replay) Tottenham Hotspur 5, Hereford United 1
Huddersfield Town 2, Blackpool 1
Ipswich Town 0, Blackburn Rovers 0
(replay) Blackburn Rovers 0, Ipswich Town 1 (aet)
Leicester City 0, Manchester City 0
(replay) Manchester City 5, Leicester City 0
Liverpool 7, Rochdale 0
Manchester United 2, Sunderland 2
(replay) Sunderland 1, Manchester United 2
Millwall 3, Oxford United 3
(replay) Oxford United 1, Millwall 0
Norwich City 1, Brentford 2
Notts County 1, Middlesbrough 2
Peterborough 1, Wrexham 0
Plymouth Argyle 1, Coventry City 3
Reading 3, Gillingham 1
Stoke City 1, Nottingham Forest 1
(replay) Notingham Forest 2, Stoke City 0
Swindon Town 2, Woking 0
Tranmere Rovers 0, Queens Park Rangers 2
Walsall 1, Wigan Athletic 0
Watford 1, Wimbledon 1
(replay) Wimbledon 1, Watford 0
West Ham United 2, Southend United 0
Chelsea 1, Newcastle United 1
(replay) Newcastle United 2, Chelsea 2 (aet; 2-4 on pens.)
Derby County 2, Leeds United 4
Everton 2, Stockport County 2
(replay) Stockport County 2, Everton 3
Southampton 3, Portsmouth 0

FOURTH ROUND
Everton 2, Port Vale 2
(replay) Port Vale 2, Everton 1
Reading 0, Manchester United 3
Tottenham Hotspur 1, Wolverhampton Wanderers 1
(replay) Wolverhampton Wanderers 0, Tottenham Hotspur 2
Sheffield United 0, Aston Villa 1
Queens Park Rangers 1, Chelsea 2
Huddersfield Town 2, Peterborough 0
Charlton Athletic 3, Brentford 2
Coventry City 2, Manchester City 2
(replay) Manchester City 2, Coventry City 1
Middlesbrough 0, Wimbledon 0
(replay) Wimbledon 1, Middlesbrough 0
Nottingham Forest 1, Oxford United 1
(replay) Oxford United 0, Nottingham Forest 3
Southampton 1, Crewe Alexandra 1
(replay) Crewe Alexandra 2, Southampton 3
West Ham United 1, Grimsby Town 1
(replay) Grimsby Town 3, West Ham United 0
Swindon Town 1, Oldham Athletic 0
Ipswich Town 1, Walsall 0
Bolton Wanderers 0, Leeds United 1
Shrewsbury Town 0, Liverpool 4

FIFTH ROUND
Huddersfield Town 2, Wimbledon 2
(replay) Wimbledon 3, Huddersfield Town 1
Ipswich Town 1, Aston Villa 3
Swindon Town 1, Southampton 1
(replay) Southampton 2, Swindon Town 0
Manchester United 2, Manchester City 1
Grimsby Town 0, Chelsea 0
(replay) Chelsea 4, Grimsby Town 1
Leeds United 0, Port Vale 0
(replay) Port Vale 1, Leeds United 2
Liverpool 2, Charlton Athletic 1
Nottingham Forest 2, Tottenham Hotspur 2
(replay) Tottenham Hotspur 1, Nottingham Forest 1 (aet; 1-3 on pens.)

QUARTER-FINALS
Chelsea 2, Wimbledon 2
(replay) Wimbledon 1, Chelsea 3
Leeds United 0, Liverpool 0
(replay) Liverpool 3, Leeds United 0
Manchester United 2, Southampton 0
Nottingham Forest 0, Aston Villa 1

SEMI-FINALS
Manchester United 2, Chelsea 1
Liverpool 3, Aston Villa 0

FINAL
11/05/95, Wembley
MANCHESTER UNITED 1 Cantona (85)
LIVERPOOL 0
referee - Gallagher
MANCHESTER UNITED - Schmeichel; Irwin, May, Pallister, Neville P.; Beckham (Neville G. 89), Butt, Keane, Giggs; Cantona, Cole (Scholes 63).
LIVERPOOL - James; Babb, Wright, Scales; McAteer, Barnes, Redknapp, McManaman, Jones (Thomas 85); Collymore (Rush 74), Fowler.

NATIONAL TEAM APPEARANCES 95/96

Coach - Terry VENABLES	COL	NOR	SUI	POR	BUL	CRO	HUN	CHN	SUI	SCO	HOL	ESP	GER	Cps	Gls
David SEAMAN (19/09/63) - Arsenal	G	G	G	G	G	G	G65		G	G	G	G	G	29	-
Gary NEVILLE (18/02/75) - Manchester United	D	D	D	D	D	D	D	D	D	D	D	D		14	-
Tony ADAMS (10/10/66) - Arsenal	D	D	D	D				D76	D	D	D	D	D	45	4
Steve HOWEY (26/10/71) - Newcastle United	D			D	D									4	-
Graeme LE SAUX (17/10/68) - Blackburn Rovers	D			s80										12	1
Steve McMANAMAN (11/02/72) - Liverpool	M	M	M	s80	M	M		M76	M69	M	M	M109	M	15	-
Jamie REDKNAPP (25/06/73) - Liverpool	M74	M	M7					M		s46 /85				5	
Paul GASCOIGNE (27/05/67) - Rangers (SCO)	M74		M	M	M76	M		M	M77	M	M	M	M	43	8
Nick BARMBY (11/02/74) - Middlesbrough	M	M66		M80				A72	s69		s76	s109		9	2
Dennis WISE (15/12/66) - Chelsea	M	M66		M80			s65							12	1
Alan SHEARER (13/08/70) - Blackburn Rovers	A74	A	A	A			s77	A72	A	A	A76	A	A	28	10
John BARNES (07/11/63) - Liverpool	s74													79	11
Robert LEE (01/02/66) - Newcastle United	s74	M	M		s76		M							7	1
Teddy SHERINGHAM (02/04/66) - Tottenham Hotspur	s74	s66	A		A76	A	A		A69	A	A76	A109	A	20	4
Gary PALLISTER (30/06/65) - Manchester United		D	D											20	-
Stuart PEARCE (24/04/62) - Nottingham Forest		D	D	D80	D	D	D		D	D46	D	D	D	70	5
Steve STONE (20/08/71) - Nottingham Forest		s66	s7	M	M	M		s76	s69	s80		s109		9	2
Les FERDINAND (08/12/66) - Newcastle United				A68	A76		A77							10	4
Peter BEARDSLEY (18/01/61) - Newcastle United				s68				s72						59	9
Gareth SOUTHGATE (03/09/70) - Aston Villa				s80	D		s12	D	D	D	D	D	D	9	-
Paul INCE (21/10/67) - Inter (ITA)					M	M	M65		M	M80	M68		M	23	2
David PLATT (10/06/66) - Arsenal					s76	M	M65		s77		s68	M	M	62	27
Robbie FOWLER (09/04/75) - Liverpool					s76	A		s72			s76	s109		5	-
Mark WRIGHT (01/08/63) - Liverpool						D	D12							45	1
Darren ANDERTON (03/03/72) - Tottenham Hotspur							M	M	M	M	M	M109	M	16	5
Jason WILCOX (15/07/71) - Blackburn Rovers							M							1	-
Ian WALKER (31/10/71) - Tottenham Hotspur							s65	s64						2	-
Sol CAMPBELL (18/09/74) - Tottenham Hotspur							s65			s85				2	-
Tim FLOWERS (03/02/67) - Blackburn Rovers								G64						8	-
Philip NEVILLE (21/01/77) - Manchester United								D						1	-
Ugo EHIOGU (03/11/72) - Aston Villa								s76						1	-

Cup qualifiers, but he has inherited a very good team. All the Euro '96 players are still available for selection - even Stuart Pearce, who was persuaded by Hoddle to go back on his post-Euro '96 decision to quit the England team.

The veteran left-back is a player of huge international experience. He certainly picked up more of that than most of his England colleagues during the 1995/96 European club competitions. Pearce's Nottingham Forest were the only one of six English teams to progress beyond the second round. Forest went on to reach the UEFA Cup quarter-finals, but the Premiership élite of Blackburn Rovers, Everton, Liverpool, Manchester United and Leeds all departed early in what was one of the worst collective European performances ever by an English contingent. And this despite the flood of highly-paid top-class foreigners which arrived in the Premiership at the start of the season.

Perhaps the most depressing displays were that of Blackburn Rovers in the Champions' League. The Lancashire club were drawn in a weak group, but they were weak themselves. Only after they had been eliminated did they finally find form, hammering Rosenborg of Norway 4-1 in their final match. So, the English champions failed to reach the latter stages of Europe's premier club competition for the fifth year in succession.

EUROPEAN CUPS RESULTS 95/96

CHAMPIONS' CUP

● BLACKBURN ROVERS

Champions' League

1st match SPARTAK MOSKVA (RUS)

H 0-1

Flowers; Berg, Le Saux, Sherwood, Pearce, Hendry, Ripley (Makel 46), Batty, Shearer, Newell, Atkins (Sutton 73).

2nd match ROSENBORG BK (NOR)

A 1-2 Newell (62)

Flowers; Berg, Kenna, Sherwood (Warhurst 84), Hendry, Pearce, Batty, Sutton, Shearer, Newell, Makel (Ripley 46).

3rd match LEGIA WARSZAWA (POL)

A 0-1

Flowers; Berg, Pearce, Hendry, Kenna, Batty, Warhurst (Newell 81), Sherwood, Holmes, Shearer, Sutton.

4th match LEGIA WARSZAWA (POL)

H 0-0

Flowers; Berg, Pearce, Hendry, Kenna, Batty, Sherwood, Warhurst (Le Saux 61), Ripley, Shearer, Newell (Sutton 73).

5th match SPARTAK MOSKVA (RUS)

A 0-3

Flowers; Kenna, Le Saux (Holmes 56), Sherwood, Hendry, Berg, Ripley (Sutton 77), Batty, Shearer, Newell, Warhurst.

6th match ROSENBORG BK (NOR)

H 4-1 Shearer (16p), Newell (31, 38, 40)

Flowers; Berg, Kenna, Sherwood, Marker, Sutton, Ripley, Warhurst, Shearer, Newell, Holmes (Gallacher 72).

CUP-WINNERS' CUP

● EVERTON

1st round KR (ISL)

A 3-2 Ebbrell (22), Unsworth (57p), Amokachi (88)

Southall; Jackson (Holmes 61), Ablett, Unsworth, Watson, Hinchcliffe, Amokachi, Parkinson, Rideout, Ebbrell, Limpar (Grant 63).

H 3-1 Stuart (56), Grant (65), Rideout (87)

Southall; Barrett, Hinchcliffe, Unsworth, Short, Grant, Amokachi (Stuart 38), Parkinson, Ebbrell, Limpar, Rideout.

2nd round FEYENOORD (HOL)

H 0-0

Southall; Jackson (Barlow 81), Barrett, Short, Ablett, Unsworth, Samways, Horne, Limpar (Holmes 81), Rideout, Stuart.

A 0-1

Southall; Short, Watson, Ablett (Barlow 67), Jackson, Horne, Ebbrell (Grant 64), Stuart, Hinchcliffe, Rideout, Amokachi.

UEFA CUP

● LIVERPOOL

1st round SPARTAK VLADIKAVKAZ (RUS)

A 2-1 McManaman (33), Redknapp (52)

James; Jones, Harkness, Babb, Wright, Ruddock, McManaman, Collymore (Fowler 78), Thomas, Barnes, Redknapp.

H 0-0

James; Jones, Harkness, Babb, Wright, Ruddock, McManaman, Redknapp, Fowler (Rush 77), Barnes, Thomas.

2nd round BRØNDBY IF (DEN)

A 0-0

James; Jones, Harkness, Scales, Wright, Babb, McManaman, Redknapp, Rush, Barnes, Fowler (Thomas 83).

H 0-1

James; Jones (Collymore 80), Babb, Wright, Scales, Harkness (Kennedy 77), McManaman, Redknapp, Barnes, Fowler, Rush.

● MANCHESTER UNITED

1st round ROTOR VOLGOGRAD (RUS)

A 0-0

Schmeichel; Neville G., Bruce, Pallister, Irwin, Beckham, Butt, Keane (Davies 23), Sharpe, Giggs, Scholes (Parker 71).

H 2-2 Scholes (59), Schmeichel (89)

Schmeichel; O'Kane (Scholes 26), Neville P., Bruce, Sharpe, Pallister, Beckham (Cooke 83), Butt, Cole, Keane, Giggs.

● NOTTINGHAM FOREST

1st round MALMÖ FF (SWE)

A 1-2 Woan (38)

Crossley; Lyttle, Cooper, Chettle, Pearce (Bart-Williams 23), Stone, Phillips, Gemmill, Woan, Campbell (Lee 53), Roy.

H 1-0 Roy (69)

Crossley; Lyttle, Pearce, Cooper, Chettle, Bart-Williams, Stone, Bohinen (Gemmill 89), Lee, Roy (Silenzi 89), Woan.

Blackburn also made a poor fist of their title defence in the Premiership. The goals of Alan Shearer were not enough. And new manager Ray Harford looked ill at ease stepping into the shoes of Kenny Dalglish, who had decided to make a curious move 'upstairs' as the club's 'Director of Football'.

Manchester United went out of the UEFA Cup in the first round to Russian side Rotor Volgograd and they were also humiliated by Second Division York City in the Coca-Cola (League) Cup. But, other than that, it was to be a season of joy and jubilation for the Old Trafford club.

Manager Alex Ferguson came in for some stern criticism from the club's fans during the close season when he responded to the team's narrow failures in both Premiership and FA Cup by failing to buy in any replacements for the departed trio of Mark Hughes, Paul Ince and Andrei Kanchelskis. When a United team full of youngsters were beaten 3-1 by Aston Villa in their opening league game,

EUROPEAN CUPS RESULTS 95/96 (CONTINUED)

2nd round AJ AUXERRE (FRA)

A 1-0 Stone (23)
Crossley; Lyttle, Cooper, Chettle, Pearce, Stone, Håland, Bart-Williams, Gemmill, Woan, Lee (Silenzi 75).

H 0-0
Crossley; Lyttle, Pearce, Cooper, Chettle, Bart-Williams, Stone, Gemmill (Håland 67), Lee, Roy (McGregor 89), Woan.

3rd round OLYMPIQUE LYONNAIS (FRA)

H 1-0 McGregor (84)
Crossley; Lyttle, Pearce, Cooper, Chettle, Stone, Bart-Williams, Gemmill, Silenzi (McGregor 72), Roy (Howe 72), Woan.

A 0-0
Crossley; Lyttle, Pearce, Cooper, Chettle, Bart-Williams, Stone, Gemmill (Håland 72), Lee (Silenzi 85), Howe, Woan.

Quarter-final FC BAYERN MÜNCHEN (GER)

A 1-2 Chettle (17)
Crossley; Phillips, Pearce, Håland, Chettle, Gemmill, Stone, Bart-Williams, Woan, Campbell, Roy.

H 1-5 Stone (84)
Crossley; Lyttle (Håland 73), Pearce, Cooper, Chettle, Phillips, Stone, Bart-Williams (McGregor 64), Campbell (Lee 64), Woan, Roy.

● LEEDS UNITED

1st round AS MONACO (FRA)

A 3-0 Yeboah (2, 65, 81)
Lukic; Kelly, Wetherall, Pemberton, Dorigo (Beesley 46), Whelan, Palmer, McAllister, Speed, Deane, Yeboah.

H 0-1
Lukic; Kelly, Wetherall, Pemberton (Couzens 80), Beesley, White (Tinkler 53), Palmer, McAllister, Speed, Deane, Yeboah.

2nd round PSV (HOL)

H 3-5 Speed (6), Palmer (48), McAllister (72)
Lukic; Kelly, Pemberton, Wetherall, Dorigo (Beesley 78), Whelan (Wallace 79), Palmer, McAllister, Speed (Couzens 26), Yeboah, Deane.

A 0-3
Lukic; Kelly, Beesley (Ford 76), Palmer, Pemberton, Wetherall, Bowman, Yeboah, Whelan (White 59), McAllister, Speed (Sharp 54).

criticism turned to rage. But Ferguson remained faithful to his beliefs and before long - the two Cup exits notwithstanding - United were heading back on the right track, with young colts like Beckham, Butt, Scholes and the Neville brothers all revelling in their new high-profile rôles.

The moment all United fans had been waiting for arrived on the first day of October when 'The King' - otherwise known as Eric Cantona - returned from his nine-month suspension. The Frenchman marked his comeback with an assist and a penalty in a 2-2 draw against Liverpool. It was a sign of things to come. Because when Cantona fully recovered his form and fitness a couple of months later, United began to look invincible.

At the turn of the year, Ferguson's men were still some way behind the long-time leaders Newcastle United. For the second year in a row Kevin Keegan's team had been first out of the starting blocks, winning nine of their first ten matches and carving out a healthy lead at the top of the Premiership table. New signings Les Ferdinand and David Ginola had settled in brilliantly and a first championship title for the Magpies since 1927 looked a distinct possibility. A 0-2 defeat at Old Trafford two days after Christmas threatened to stall Newcastle's momentum, but they went on to win their next five matches, maintaining a nine-point gap between themselves and the other United.

In an attempt to bolster his squad for the championship run-in, Keegan splashed out £7.5 million to bring Colombian star Faustino Asprilla from Parma. Initially the Geordie fans were awestruck by the South American's sublime skills. But soon it became appparaent that, in attempting to accommodate Asprilla, Keegan had upset the balance of his team. Newcastle started to drop points at

INTERNATIONAL HONOURS

World Cup Finals appearances: 1950, 1954 (qtr-finals), 1958, 1962 (qtr-finals), 1966 (Winners), 1970 (qtr-finals), 1982 (2nd phase), 1986 (quarter-finals), 1990 (4th)

European Championship appearances: 1968 (3rd), 1972, 1980, 1988, 1992, 1996 (semi-finals)

European Club Competitions

Champions' Cup	Manchester United (1968) Liverpool (1977, 1978, 1981, 1984) Nottingham Forest (1979, 1980) Aston Villa (1982)
Cup-winners' Cup	Tottenham Hotspur (1963) West Ham United (1965) Manchester City (1970) Chelsea (1971) Everton (1985) Manchester United (1991) Arsenal (1994)
Fairs' Cup	Leeds United (1968, 1971) Newcastle United (1969) Arsenal (1970)
UEFA Cup	Tottenham Hotspur (1972, 1984) Liverpool (1973, 1976) Ipswich Town (1981)
Super Cup	Liverpool (1977) Nottingham Forest (1979) Aston Villa (1982)

an alarming rate. In a six-match period immediately after the Colombian's arrival the team lost four games. The most important of those was the head-to-head with Manchester United at St. James' Park. Newcastle had won all 13 of their previous home matches in the Premiership, but a single Cantona goal punctured that record, gave the visitors a crucial victory and blew the championship race wide open.

Suddenly 1-0 victories to Manchester United, with Cantona the scorer, became as commonplace as the sight of a Newcastle supporter with his head in his hands as he contemplated another costly defeat. Against Liverpool, at Anfield, Keegan's commitment to all-out attacking football produced one of the most exciting matches ever seen in England, but Newcastle's inadequate defence allowed Liverpool to come back from 1-3 down and steal a sensational 4-3 victory in the last minute.

The tide was turning against the Geordies. They courageously fought back, grabbing three successive 1-0 victories of their own, but Alex Ferguson's team were relentless, and when Newcastle could only draw their match in hand at Nottingham Forest, it meant that Manchester United, with a big goal-difference advantage, would be the champions if they could avoid defeat in their final match, away to a Middlesbrough side managed by former Old Trafford idol Bryan Robson and with nothing left to play for.

United won at a canter, 3-0. In the event, with Newcastle simultaneously failing to beat Tottenham at home, they could have lost by the same scoreline and still taken the title.

Alex Ferguson's third championship win was probably his most impressive. All the talk was about Newcastle throwing the title away, but just as their rivals had failed to handle the pressure, Manchester United, familiar with the experience, had thrived under it. Cantona, in particular.

With the Premiership sewn up, United now fixed their sights on the FA Cup. They had reached the final for the third year running, disposing of Glenn Hoddle's Chelsea (Newcastle's conquerors) 2-1 in the semi-final. Awaiting them beneath the Twin Towers were old adversaries Liverpool, who had beaten Coca-Cola Cup winners Aston Villa 3-0 in the semis and were hungry to crown a fine season by denying United a second 'double' in three years.

It was billed as the 'Dream Final', but it failed miserably to live up to expectations. Excitement and quality were sorely lacking. None of the many flair players on show performed. Except one.

With just five minutes left on the clock and the score still 0-0, Eric Cantona - who else? - broke the deadlock. A few days earlier the Frenchman had been named as the Football Writers' Player of the Year, becoming the first Manchester United player to win the prestigious award since George Best in 1969. Now he smashed a shot from the edge of the area through a crowd of Liverpool players. 1-0, Cantona. It was that old familiar scoreline again, and it meant that history had been made. United had done what no other club had ever achieved. They had won the league and FA Cup 'double' twice.

Praise and glory, then, for the red half of Manchester. But doom and gloom for the blue half as Manchester City were relegated from the Premiership to Division One - despite having arguably the most exciting player in the country in their ranks, Georgian midfielder Giorgi Kinkladze.

City were condemned on the final day of the season after a tense three-way struggle with Southampton and Coventry. They clawed their way back from 0-2 down to draw with Liverpool, but as both of their rivals also picked up a point at home, they went down on goal

NATIONAL TEAM RESULTS 95/96

06/09/95	Colombia	H	Wembley	0-0	
11/10/95	Norway	A	Oslo	0-0	
15/11/95	Switzerland	H	Wembley	3-1	Pearce (45), Sheringham (56), Stone (78)
12/12/95	Portugal	H	Wembley	1-1	Stone (44)
27/03/96	Bulgaria	H	Wembley	1-0	Ferdinand (7)
24/04/96	Croatia	H	Wembley	0-0	
18/05/96	Hungary	H	Wembley	3-0	Anderton (38, 62), Platt (52)
23/05/96	China	A	Beijing	3-0	Barmby (30, 53), Gascoigne (64)
08/06/96	Switzerland (ECF)	H	Wembley	1-1	Shearer (23)
15/06/96	Scotland (ECF)	H	Wembley	2-0	Shearer (52), Gascoigne (79)
18/06/96	Holland (ECF)	H	Wembley	4-1	Shearer (23p, 57), Sheringham (51, 62)
22/06/96	Spain (ECF)	H	Wembley	0-0	
26/06/96	Germany (ECF)	H	Wembley	1-1	Shearer (3)

TOP SCORERS

31	Alan SHEARER (Blackburn Rovers)
28	Robbie FOWLER (Liverpool)
25	Les FERDINAND (Newcastle United)
17	Dwight YORKE (Aston Villa)
16	Teddy SHERINGHAM (Tottenham Hotspur)
	Andrei KANCHELSKIS (Everton)
15	Ian WRIGHT (Arsenal)
	Chris ARMSTRONG (Tottenham Hotspur)
14	Stan COLLYMORE (Liverpool)
	Eric CANTONA (Manchester United)
	Dion DUBLIN (Coventry City)

PLAYERS OF THE SEASON

ALAN SHEARER
What a summer for England's deadliest striker! First he grabs the Premiership top scorer award for the second year in a row, becoming the first player since World War Two to score 30 goals or more in the top division three seasons running. Then he ends a 21-month goal drought at international level by becoming the leading scorer at Euro '96. A month later he is officially confirmed as the world's most expensive player after joining his hometown club Newcastle from Blackburn for £15 million. And, just to cap everything, Glenn Hoddle names the 26-year-old as the new England captain. What next? European Footballer of the Year? It is difficult to imagine a worthier candidate.

GARETH SOUTHGATE
It is not Gareth Southgate's fault that he will forever be remembered as the man who missed 'that penalty'. That is the nature of the shoot-out. It picks on one man and victimises him. But the Aston Villa defender is made of stern stuff, and he will surely bounce back from his personal nightmare. England colleague Stuart Pearce can tell him all about that. That fatal moment apart, Southgate was one of the best defenders on view at Euro '96. With only four caps to his name before the tournament, he played with the authority and coolness of a veteran. He had earned his place after a season of sustained excellence for his new club Aston Villa, where he operated as a continental-style libero in a three-man defence, helping the club to victory in the Coca-Cola Cup, a semi-final place in the FA Cup and fourth spot in the Premiership.

ROBBIE FOWLER
The Football Writers of England voted Eric Cantona as their Footballer of the Year for 1996. The runner-up was another European megastar, Ruud Gullit. How 21-year-old Robbie Fowler must have felt taking the other place on the podium behind this illustrious duo, only he can say. But 'proud' is the word that most readily springs to mind. Nobody can say the Liverpool striker didn't deserve his third place. He continued his meteoric progress of the past two seasons, scoring 28 goals in the Premiership and finding the net in every round of the FA Cup bar the final. A natural finisher with a venomous left foot, he is destined for a long international career with England. Alan Shearer will be a hard man to shift, but that shouldn't overworry the young Scouser, whose confidence apparently knows no bounds.

STEVE STONE
He was a bystander for most of Euro '96, but Steve Stone certainly left a huge impression on English football during the 95/96 season. The little winger was as influential as anybody in helping Nottingham Forest to their record Premiership run of 25 matches without defeat. And his contributions in the UEFA Cup - notably a crucial away goal against Auxerre - catapulted him into Terry Venables's national team. Goals and strong performances on each of his first two Wembley appearances - against Switzerland and Portugal - suggested that he would be a European Championship starter, but the return from injury of Darren Anderton denied him that honour. He probably deserved better.

difference. New manager Alan Ball surprisingly managed to remain in place for the duration of the season. Indeed, only one manager lost his job during the course of the Premiership campaign - Bolton's Roy McFarland. His successor Colin Todd could not, however, save the newly-promoted side from an immediate return to Division One, so they joined Manchester City and QPR in relegation.

Sunderland won the First Division title to give the North East three teams in the top flight for the first time in 20 years. They were accompanied up by two East Midland sides, Derby County and Leicester City. Leicester reached the First Division play-off final at Wembley for the fourth time in five seasons and deservedly won an absorbing match, beating Crystal Palace 2-1 with a dramatic winner from new signing Steve Claridge two seconds from the end of extra-time.

It was a goal worth millions. For in English football, increasingly, the Premiership is the only place to be. Attendances were up in the top division by another 13.5 per cent in 1995/96, with many clubs playing to sell-out crowds every week. Money is positively flowing through the coffers of the Premiership clubs. Sky television's new £743 million four-year deal promises even greater riches, with more and more big foreign superstars likely to be attracted to the increased glamour and wealth that the English league now provides. First there was Cantona and Klinsmann, then Gullit and Juninho, now Vialli and Ravanelli. Who next? What with Euro '96 and all that, it looks like football really has come home. To stay.

PROFILE
PAUL GASCOIGNE

If Euro '96 was Gazza's last stand, then he certainly went out with all guns blazing. His goal against Scotland was, for many, the outstanding moment of the entire tournament. But one suspects that the jovial Geordie will be back for more if England qualify for France '98. Certainly, there is no player who will be keener to get the team to the finals.

Paul Gascoigne knows all about the magic of the World Cup. It was the tournament that turned him into a global superstar. His brilliant performances at Italia '90 changed his life. Six eventful years later, he was back on the big stage again, at Euro '96. And once more England danced to his tune. His critics say that he is lazy, prone to crass errors and a threat to stability. Agreed. But he is also a diamond of a player, a true genius, blessed with gifts of nature that mere mortals can only worship or envy. Some despise the way he behaves, the way he looks, even the way he talks. Nobody ever said he was the model professional or the darling of the media. But when Paul Gascoigne lifted the ball over Colin Hendry and rifled it past Andy Goram on that baking Saturday afternoon in June, every Englishman adored him. Because, for all his faults, he was the only player on that Wembley pitch with the ability to score a goal of such beauty.

Gascoigne was born to be a star, but he has never had it easy. After a modest upbringing in the north-east, he quit school at 16 and joined his local club Newcastle United. His early prowess was evident to all who saw him kick a ball. Even Tyneside legend Jackie Milburn declared on television that Gascoigne would one day become the best player in the world.

He has never quite made it that far. But Gascoigne has not had luck on his side. Two career-threatening injuries - the first a torn cruciate knee ligament, the second a badly fractured leg - would have broken lesser men. But Gascoigne has come back from both of them and, although his fitness is not as sharp as other players, and some of his darting acceleration is no longer there, he has never lost his sublime artistry on the ball.

At the age of 21 Gascoigne left Newcastle for Tottenham. He stayed in London for three years, inspiring the club to an FA Cup triumph in 1991. Sadly, Gascoigne was not around to enjoy the celebrations. He was in hospital, his knee in tatters, after a rash challenge early in the final against Nottingham Forest. That was supposed to be his farewell appearance for Tottenham, as a deal had already been agreed to sell him to Italian club Lazio for £5 million. But for the next year and a half Gascoigne played no football. It was not until September 1992 that he returned... in the light-blue shirt of the Roman club, who, despite all the continuous setbacks to Gascoigne's rehabilitation, had gallantly stood by their man.

Gazza went on to spend three seasons in Italy, but injury problems continued to pursue him and he was never able to give Lazio their money's worth. The broken leg he incurred in a freak training accident towards the end of his second season, in April 1994, was a killer blow. Another year of Gascoigne's career was lost. But again he fought his way through the pain, the boredom and the frustration and bounced back. Not with Lazio, but with perennial Scottish champions Rangers.

Gascoigne was heavily criticised for choosing Rangers as his next club. He had long been earmarked for a return to the English Premiership. But the Scottish club made him the best offer. They also placed tremendous faith in him. And in his first season, Gascoigne delivered everything manager Walter Smith could have wished for and more. The Premier Division championship and Scottish Cup both came Rangers' way. And Gascoigne himself was voted Scotland's Player of the Year by both the national press and his fellow professionals.

It was an extraordinary comeback. But, then, as everybody should know by now, Paul Gascoigne is no ordinary footballer.

ARSENAL

CLUB DIRECTORY

Arsenal FC
Arsenal Stadium
Highbury
London N5 1BU
tel - (0171) 7044000
fax - (0171) 7044001
Year of Formation - 1886
Chairman - Peter Hill-Wood
Secretary - Ken Friar
Manager - Bruce Rioch (96/97 - Stewart Houston; Arsène Wenger)
Stadium - Highbury (38,500)

MAJOR HONOURS

League Championship - (10) 1931, 1933, 1934, 1935, 1938, 1948, 1953, 1971, 1989, 1991.
Domestic Cup - (6)
1930, 1936, 1950, 1971, 1979, 1993.
European Cup-winners' Cup - (1) 1994.
Fairs' Cup - (1) 1970.

APPEARANCES 95/96

	P	Ap	(s)	Gls
Tony ADAMS	D	21		1
Dennis BERGKAMP (HOL)	A	33		11
Steve BOULD	D	19		
Adrian CLARKE	A	4	(2)	
Paul DICKOV	A	1	(6)	1
Lee DIXON	D	38		2
John HARTSON (WAL)	A	15	(4)	4
Glenn HELDER (HOL)	M	15	(9)	1
David HILLIER	M	3	(2)	
Steve HUGHES	M		(1)	
John JENSEN (DEN)	M	13	(2)	
Martin KEOWN	M	34		
Andy LINIGHAN	D	17	(1)	
Eddie McGOLDRICK (IRL)	M		(1)	
Gavin McGOWAN	M	1		
Scott MARSHALL (SCO)	D	10	(1)	1
Paul MERSON	M	38		5
Steven MORROW (NIR)	M	3	(1)	
Ray PARLOUR	M	20	(2)	
David PLATT	M	27	(2)	6
Matthew ROSE	M	1	(3)	
David SEAMAN	G	38		
Paul SHAW	A		(3)	
Nigel WINTERBURN	D	36		2
Ian WRIGHT	A	31		15

LEAGUE RESULTS 1995/96

20/08/95	Middlesbrough	H	1-1	Wright
23/08/95	Everton	A	2-0	Platt, Wright
26/08/95	Coventry City	A	0-0	
29/08/95	Nottingham Forest	H	1-1	Platt
10/09/95	Manchester City	A	1-0	Wright
16/09/95	West Ham United	H	1-0	Wright (p)
23/09/95	Southampton	H	4-2	Bergkamp 2, Adams, Wright
30/09/95	Chelsea	A	0-1	
14/10/95	Leeds United	A	3-0	Merson, Bergkamp, Wright
21/10/95	Aston Villa	H	2-0	Merson, Wright
30/10/95	Bolton Wanderers	A	0-1	
04/11/95	Manchester United	H	1-0	Bergkamp
18/11/95	Tottenham Hotspur	A	1-2	Bergkamp
21/11/95	Sheffield Wednesday	H	4-2	Bergkamp, Winterburn, Dickov, Hartson
26/11/95	Blackburn Rovers	H	0-0	
02/12/95	Aston Villa	A	1-1	Platt
09/12/95	Southampton	A	0-0	
16/12/95	Chelsea	H	1-1	Dixon
23/12/95	Liverpool	A	1-3	Wright (p)
26/12/95	Queens Park Rangers	H	3-0	Wright, Merson 2
30/12/95	Wimbledon	H	1-3	Wright
02/01/96	Newcastle United	A	0-2	
13/01/96	Middlesbrough	A	3-2	Merson, Platt, Helder
20/01/96	Everton	H	1-2	Wright
03/02/96	Coventry City	H	1-1	Bergkamp
10/02/96	Nottingham Forest	A	1-0	Bergkamp
24/02/96	West Ham United	A	1-0	Hartson
02/03/96	Queens Park Rangers	A	1-1	Bergkamp
05/03/96	Manchester City	H	3-1	Hartson 2, Dixon
16/03/96	Wimbledon	A	3-0	Winterburn, Platt, Bergkamp
20/03/96	Manchester United	A	0-1	
23/03/96	Newcastle United	H	2-0	Marshall, Wright
06/04/96	Leeds United	H	2-1	Wright 2
08/04/96	Sheffield Wednesday	A	0-1	
15/04/96	Tottenham Hotspur	H	0-0	
27/04/96	Blackburn Rovers	A	1-1	Wright (p)
01/05/96	Liverpool	H	0-0	
05/05/96	Bolton Wanderers	H	2-1	Platt, Bergkamp

ASTON VILLA

CLUB DIRECTORY

Aston Villa FC
Villa Park
Trinity Road
Birmingham B6 6HE
tel - (0121) 3272299
fax - (0121) 3222107
Year of Formation - 1874
Chairman - Doug Ellis
Secretary - Steven Stride
Manager - Brian Little
Stadium - Villa Park (39,341)

MAJOR HONOURS
League Championship - (7)
1894, 1896, 1897, 1899, 1900, 1910, 1981.
Domestic Cup - (7)
1887, 1895, 1897, 1905, 1913, 1920, 1957.
European Champions' Cup - (1) 1982.
European Super Cup - (1) 1982.

APPEARANCES 95/96

	P	Ap	(s)	Gls
Mark BOSNICH (AUS)	G	38		
Paul BROWNE	D	2		
Franz CARR	A	1		
Gary CHARLES	D	34		1
Neil DAVIS	A		(2)	
Mark DRAPER	M	36		2
Ugo EHIOGU	D	36		1
Gareth FARRELLY	M	1	(4)	
Graham FENTON	A		(3)	
Lee HENDRIE	A	2	(1)	
Julian JOACHIM	A	4	(7)	1
Tommy JOHNSON	A	17	(6)	5
Paul McGRATH (IRL)	D	29	(1)	2
Savo MILOSEVIC (YUG)	A	36	(1)	12
Scott MURRAY (SCO)	A	3		
Ricardo SCIMECA	D	7	(10)	
Gareth SOUTHGATE	D	31		1
Nigel SPINK	G		(2)	
Steve STAUNTON (IRL)	D	11	(2)	
Ian TAYLOR	M	24	(1)	3
Carl TILER	D	1		
Andy TOWNSEND (IRL)	M	32	(1)	2
Alan WRIGHT	D	38		2
Dwight YORKE (TRI)	A	35		17

LEAGUE RESULTS 1995/96

19/08/95	Manchester United	H	3-1	Taylor, Draper, Yorke (p)
23/08/95	Tottenham Hotspur	A	1-0	Ehiogu
26/08/95	Leeds United	A	0-2	
30/08/95	Bolton Wanderers	H	1-0	Yorke
09/09/95	Blackburn Rovers	A	1-1	Milosevic
16/09/95	Wimbledon	H	2-0	Draper, Taylor
23/09/95	Nottingham Forest	H	1-1	Townsend
30/09/95	Coventry City	A	3-0	Yorke, Milosevic 2
14/10/95	Chelsea	H	0-1	
21/10/95	Arsenal	A	0-2	
28/10/95	Everton	H	1-0	Yorke
04/11/95	West Ham United	A	4-1	Milosevic 2, Johnson, Yorke
18/11/95	Newcastle United	H	1-1	Johnson
20/11/95	Southampton	A	1-0	Johnson
25/11/95	Manchester City	A	0-1	
02/12/95	Arsenal	H	1-1	Yorke
10/12/95	Nottingham Forest	A	1-1	Yorke
16/12/95	Coventry City	H	4-1	Johnson, Milosevic 3
23/12/95	Queens Park Rangers	A	0-1	
01/01/96	Middlesbrough	A	2-0	Wright, Johnson
13/01/96	Manchester United	A	0-0	
21/01/96	Tottenham Hotspur	H	2-1	McGrath, Yorke
31/01/96	Liverpool	H	0-2	
03/02/96	Leeds United	H	3-0	Yorke 2, Wright
10/02/96	Bolton Wanderers	A	2-0	Yorke 2
24/02/96	Wimbledon	A	3-3	og (Reeves), Yorke (p), og (Cunningham)
28/02/96	Blackburn Rovers	H	2-0	Joachim, Southgate
03/03/96	Liverpool	A	0-3	
06/03/96	Sheffield Wednesday	H	3-2	Milosevic 2, Townsend
09/03/96	Queens Park Rangers	H	4-2	Milosevic, Yorke 2, og (Yates)
16/03/96	Sheffield Wednesday	A	0-2	
19/03/96	Middlesbrough	H	0-0	
06/04/96	Chelsea	A	2-1	Milosevic, Yorke
08/04/96	Southampton	H	3-0	Taylor, Charles, Yorke
14/04/96	Newcastle United	A	0-1	
17/04/96	West Ham United	H	1-1	McGrath
27/04/96	Manchester City	H	0-1	
05/05/96	Everton	A	0-1	

BLACKBURN ROVERS

CLUB DIRECTORY

Blackburn Rovers FC
Ewood Park
Blackburn BB2 4JF
tel - (01254) 698888
fax - (01254) 671042
Year of Formation - 1875
Chairman - R.D. Coar
Secretary - John Howarth
Manager - Ray Harford
Stadium - Ewood Park (31,367)

MAJOR HONOURS

League Championship - (3) 1912, 1914, 1995.
Domestic Cup - (6)
1884, 1885, 1886, 1890, 1891, 1928.

APPEARANCES 95/96

	P	Ap	(s)	Gls
Mark ATKINS	M		(4)	
David BATTY	M	23		1
Henning BERG (NOR)	D	38		
Lars BOHINEN (NOR)	M	17	(2)	4
Chris COLEMAN (WAL)	D	19	(1)	
Graham FENTON	A	4	(10)	6
Gary FLITCROFT	M	3		
Tim FLOWERS	G	37		
Kevin GALLACHER (SCO)	A	14	(2)	2
Niklas GUDMUNDSSON (SWE)	A	1	(3)	
Colin HENDRY (SCO)	D	33		1
Matty HOLMES	M	8	(1)	1
Jeff KENNA (IRL)	D	32		
Graeme LE SAUX	D	13	(1)	1
Billy McKINLAY (SCO)	M	13	(6)	2
Nicky MARKER	D	8	(1)	1
Bobby MIMMS	G	1	(1)	
Mike NEWELL	A	26	(4)	3
Ian PEARCE	D	12		1
Stuart RIPLEY	M	28		
Alan SHEARER	A	35		31
Tim SHERWOOD	M	33		3
Chris SUTTON	A	9	(4)	
Paul WARHURST	M	1	(9)	
Jason WILCOX	M	10		3

LEAGUE RESULTS 1995/96

19/08/95	Queens Park Rangers	H	1-0	Shearer (p)
23/08/95	Sheffield Wednesday	A	1-2	Shearer
26/08/95	Bolton Wanderers	A	1-2	Holmes
28/08/95	Manchester United	H	1-2	Shearer
09/09/95	Aston Villa	H	1-1	Shearer
16/09/95	Liverpool	A	0-3	
23/09/95	Coventry City	H	5-1	Shearer 3, Hendry, Pearce
30/09/95	Middlesbrough	A	0-2	
14/10/95	Southampton	H	2-1	Bohinen, Shearer
21/10/95	West Ham United	A	1-1	Shearer
28/10/95	Chelsea	H	3-0	Sherwood, Shearer, Newell
05/11/95	Everton	A	0-1	
08/11/95	Newcastle United	A	0-1	
18/11/95	Nottingham Forest	H	7-0	Shearer 3, Bohinen 2, Newell, Le Saux
26/11/95	Arsenal	A	0-0	
02/12/95	West Ham United	H	4-2	Shearer 3 (1p), Newell
09/12/95	Coventry City	A	0-5	
16/12/95	Middlesbrough	H	1-0	Shearer
23/12/95	Wimbledon	A	1-1	og (Kimble)
26/12/95	Manchester City	H	2-0	Shearer, Batty
30/12/95	Tottenham Hotspur	H	2-1	Marker, Shearer
01/01/96	Leeds United	A	0-0	
13/01/96	Queens Park Rangers	A	1-0	Shearer
20/01/96	Sheffield Wednesday	H	3-0	Shearer, Bohinen, Gallacher
03/02/96	Bolton Wanderers	H	3-1	Shearer 3
10/02/96	Manchester United	A	0-1	
24/02/96	Liverpool	H	2-3	Wilcox, Sherwood
28/02/96	Aston Villa	A	0-2	
02/03/96	Manchester City	A	1-1	Shearer
13/03/96	Leeds United	H	1-0	Fenton
16/03/96	Tottenham Hotspur	A	3-2	Shearer 3 (1p)
30/03/96	Everton	H	0-3	
06/04/96	Southampton	A	0-1	
08/04/96	Newcastle United	H	2-1	Fenton 2
13/04/96	Nottingham Forest	A	5-1	Shearer, McKinlay, Wilcox 2, Fenton
17/04/96	Wimbledon	H	3-2	Shearer 2, Fenton
27/04/96	Arsenal	H	1-1	Gallacher
05/05/96	Chelsea	A	3-2	Sherwood, McKinlay, Fenton

BOLTON WANDERERS

CLUB DIRECTORY

Bolton Wanderers FC
Burnden Park
Bolton BL3 2QR
tel - (01204) 389200
fax - (01204) 382334
Year of Formation - 1874
Chairman - G. Hargreaves
Secretary - Des McBain
Manager - Roy McFarland; Colin Todd
Stadium - Burnden Park (20,500)

MAJOR HONOURS
Domestic Cup - (4) 1923, 1926, 1929, 1958.

APPEARANCES 95/96

	P	Ap	(s)	Gls
Gudni BERGSSON (ISL)	D	34		4
Nathan BLAKE (WAL)	M	14	(4)	1
Keith BRANAGAN	G	31		
Wayne BURNETT	M		(1)	
Simon COLEMAN	D	12		1
Owen COYLE (IRL)	A	2	(3)	
Sasa CURCIC (YUG)	M	28		4
Aidan DAVISON	G	2		
Fabian DE FREITAS (HOL)	A	17	(10)	5
Chris FAIRCLOUGH	D	33		
Scott GREEN	D	26	(5)	3
David LEE	M	9	(9)	1
Steve McANESPIE (SCO)	D	7	(2)	
Jason McATEER (IRL)	M	4		
John McGINLAY (SCO)	A	29	(3)	6
Mika-Matti PAATELAINEN (FIN)	A	12	(3)	1
Mark PATTERSON	M	12	(4)	1
Jimmy PHILLIPS	D	37		
Scott SELLARS	M	22		3
Bryan SMALL	D	1		
Richard SNEEKES (HOL)	M	14	(3)	1
Greg STRONG	D		(1)	
Alan STUBBS	D	24	(1)	4
Gerry TAGGART (NIR)	D	11		1
Scott TAYLOR	A		(1)	
Alan THOMPSON	M	23	(3)	1
Andrew TODD	D	9	(3)	2
Gavin WARD	G	5		

LEAGUE RESULTS 1995/96

Date	Opponent		Score	Scorers
19/08/95	Wimbledon	A	2-3	Thompson (p), De Freitas
22/08/95	Newcastle United	H	1-3	Bergsson
26/08/95	Blackburn Rovers	H	2-1	De Freitas, Stubbs
30/08/95	Aston Villa	A	0-1	
09/09/95	Middlesbrough	H	1-1	McGinlay
16/09/95	Manchester United	A	0-3	
23/09/95	Liverpool	A	2-5	Todd, Patterson (p)
30/09/95	Queens Park Rangers	H	0-1	
14/10/95	Everton	H	1-1	Paatelainen
21/10/95	Nottingham Forest	A	2-3	Sneekes, De Freitas
30/10/95	Arsenal	H	1-0	McGinlay
04/11/95	Manchester City	A	0-1	
18/11/95	West Ham United	H	0-3	
22/11/95	Chelsea	A	2-3	Curcic, Green
25/11/95	Southampton	A	0-1	
02/12/95	Nottingham Forest	H	1-1	De Freitas
09/12/95	Liverpool	H	0-1	
16/12/95	Queens Park Rangers	A	1-2	Sellars
23/12/95	Tottenham Hotspur	A	2-2	Green, Bergsson
27/12/95	Leeds United	H	0-2	
30/12/95	Coventry City	H	1-2	McGinlay
01/01/96	Sheffield Wednesday	A	2-4	Curcic, Taggart
13/01/96	Wimbledon	H	1-0	McGinlay (p)
20/01/96	Newcastle United	A	1-2	Bergsson
03/02/96	Blackburn Rovers	A	1-3	Green
10/02/96	Aston Villa	H	0-2	
17/02/96	Middlesbrough	A	4-1	Blake, Coleman, De Freitas, Lee
25/02/96	Manchester United	H	0-6	
02/03/96	Leeds United	A	1-0	Bergsson
16/03/96	Coventry City	A	2-0	Stubbs 2
20/03/96	Tottenham Hotspur	H	2-3	Stubbs, Sellars
23/03/96	Sheffield Wednesday	H	2-1	Sellars, Curcic
30/03/96	Manchester City	H	1-1	McGinlay
06/04/96	Everton	A	0-3	
08/04/96	Chelsea	H	2-1	McGinlay, Curcic
13/04/96	West Ham United	A	0-1	
27/04/96	Southampton	H	0-1	
05/05/96	Arsenal	A	1-2	Todd

CHELSEA

CLUB DIRECTORY

Chelsea FC
Stamford Bridge
London SW6 1HS
tel - (0171) 3855545
fax - (0171) 3814831
Year of Formation - 1905
Chairman - Ken Bates
Secretary - Yvonne Todd
Manager - Glenn Hoddle (96/97 - Ruud Gullit)
Stadium - Stamford Bridge (31,791)

MAJOR HONOURS

League Championship - (1) 1955.
Domestic Cup - (1) 1970.
European Cup-winners' Cup - (1) 1971.

APPEARANCES 95/96

	P	Ap	(s)	Gls
Craig BURLEY (SCO)	M	16	(6)	
Steve CLARKE (SCO)	D	21	(1)	
Andrew DOW	M	1		
Michael DUBERRY	D	22		
Paul FURLONG	A	14	(13)	3
Ruud GULLIT (HOL)	M	31		3
Gareth HALL (WAL)	M	5		1
Kevin HITCHCOCK	G	12		
Mark HUGHES (WAL)	A	31		8
Erland JOHNSEN (NOR)	D	18	(4)	
Dmitri KHARIN (RUS)	G	26		
David LEE	D	29	(2)	1
Scott MINTO	D	10		
Jody MORRIS	M		(1)	
Andy MYERS	D	20		
Eddie NEWTON	M	21	(3)	1
Gavin PEACOCK	M	17	(11)	5
Dan PETRESCU (ROM)	D	22	(2)	2
Terry PHELAN (IRL)	D	12		
David ROCASTLE	M	1		
Frank SINCLAIR	D	12	(1)	1
Nigel SPACKMAN	M	13	(3)	
John SPENCER (SCO)	A	23	(5)	13
Mark STEIN	A	7	(1)	
Dennis WISE	M	34	(1)	7

LEAGUE RESULTS 1995/96

19/08/95	Everton	H	0-0	
23/08/95	Nottingham Forest	A	0-0	
26/08/95	Middlesbrough	A	0-2	
30/08/95	Coventry City	H	2-2	Wise (p), Hughes
11/09/95	West Ham United	A	3-1	Wise, Spencer 2
16/09/95	Southampton	H	3-0	Sinclair, Gullit, Hughes
24/09/95	Newcastle United	A	0-2	
30/09/95	Arsenal	H	1-0	Hughes
14/10/95	Aston Villa	A	1-0	Wise
21/10/95	Manchester United	H	1-4	Hughes
28/10/95	Blackburn Rovers	A	0-3	
04/11/95	Sheffield Wednesday	H	0-0	
18/11/95	Leeds United	A	0-1	
22/11/95	Bolton Wanderers	H	3-2	Lee, Hall, Newton
25/11/95	Tottenham Hotspur	H	0-0	
02/12/95	Manchester United	A	1-1	Wise
09/12/95	Newcastle United	H	1-0	Petrescu
16/12/95	Arsenal	A	1-1	Spencer
23/12/95	Manchester City	A	1-0	Peacock
26/12/95	Wimbledon	H	1-2	Petrescu
30/12/95	Liverpool	H	2-2	Spencer 2
02/01/96	Queens Park Rangers	A	2-1	og (Brazier), Furlong
13/01/96	Everton	A	1-1	Spencer
20/01/96	Nottingham Forest	H	1-0	Spencer
04/02/96	Middlesbrough	H	5-0	Peacock 3, Spencer, Furlong
10/02/96	Coventry City	A	0-1	
17/02/96	West Ham United	H	1-2	Peacock
24/02/96	Southampton	A	3-2	Wise 2 (1p), Gullit
02/03/96	Wimbledon	A	1-1	Furlong
12/03/96	Manchester City	H	1-1	Gullit
16/03/96	Liverpool	A	0-2	
23/03/96	Queens Park Rangers	H	1-1	Spencer
06/04/96	Aston Villa	H	1-2	Spencer
08/04/96	Bolton Wanderers	A	1-2	Spencer
13/04/96	Leeds United	H	4-1	Hughes 3 (1p), Spencer
17/04/96	Sheffield Wednesday	A	0-0	
27/04/96	Tottenham Hotspur	A	1-1	Hughes
05/05/96	Blackburn Rovers	H	2-3	Wise, Spencer

COVENTRY CITY

CLUB DIRECTORY

Coventry City FC
Highfield Road Stadium
King Richard Street
Coventry CV2 4FW
tel - (01203) 234000
fax - (01203) 234099
Year of Formation - 1883
Chairman - Bryan Richardson
Secretary - Graham Hover
Manager - Ron Atkinson
Stadium - Highfield Road (23,500)

MAJOR HONOURS
Domestic Cup - (1) 1987.

APPEARANCES 95/96

	P	Ap	(s)	Gls
Jamie BARNWELL	A		(1)	
Willie BOLAND (IRL)	M	2	(1)	
Brian BORROWS	D	21		
David BURROWS	D	11		
David BUSST	D	16	(1)	2
Iyseden CHRISTIE	A		(1)	
Paul COOK	M	2	(1)	
Liam DAISH (IRL)	D	11		1
Dion DUBLIN	A	34		14
John FILAN (AUS)	G	13		
Marcus HALL	D	24	(1)	
ISAÍAS (BRA)	M	9	(2)	2
Eoin JESS (SCO)	A	9	(3)	1
Nii LAMPTEY (GHA)	A	3	(3)	
Peter NDLOVU (ZIM)	A	27	(5)	5
Steve OGRIZOVIC	G	25		
Ally PICKERING	D	26	(4)	
David RENNIE (SCO)	D	9	(2)	2
Kevin RICHARDSON	M	33		
John SALAKO	M	34	(3)	3
Richard SHAW	D	21		
Gordon STRACHAN (SCO)	M	5	(7)	
Paul TELFER	M	31		1
Noel WHELAN	A	21		8
Chris WHYTE	D	1		
Paul WILLIAMS	D	30	(2)	2

LEAGUE RESULTS 1995/96

Date	Opponent	H/A	Score	Scorers
19/08/95	Newcastle United	A	0-3	
23/08/95	Manchester City	H	2-1	Telfer, Dublin
26/08/95	Arsenal	H	0-0	
30/08/95	Chelsea	A	2-2	Isaías, Ndlovu
09/09/95	Nottingham Forest	H	1-1	Dublin
16/09/95	Middlesbrough	A	1-2	Isaías
23/09/95	Blackburn Rovers	A	1-5	Ndlovu
30/09/95	Aston Villa	H	0-3	
14/10/95	Liverpool	A	0-0	
21/10/95	Sheffield Wednesday	H	0-1	
28/10/95	Leeds United	A	1-3	Dublin
04/11/95	Tottenham Hotspur	H	2-3	Dublin, Williams
19/11/95	Queens Park Rangers	A	1-1	Dublin
22/11/95	Manchester United	H	0-4	
25/11/95	Wimbledon	H	3-3	og (Heald), Dublin, Rennie
04/12/95	Sheffield Wednesday	A	3-4	Dublin 3
09/12/95	Blackburn Rovers	H	5-0	Busst, Dublin, Rennie, Ndlovu, Salako
16/12/95	Aston Villa	A	1-4	Dublin
23/12/95	Everton	H	2-1	Busst, Whelan
30/12/95	Bolton Wanderers	A	2-1	Whelan, Salako (p)
01/01/96	Southampton	H	1-1	Whelan
14/01/96	Newcastle United	H	0-1	
20/01/96	Manchester City	A	1-1	Dublin
31/01/96	West Ham United	A	2-3	Dublin, Whelan
03/02/96	Arsenal	A	1-1	Whelan
10/02/96	Chelsea	H	1-0	Whelan
24/02/96	Middlesbrough	H	0-0	
02/03/96	West Ham United	H	2-2	Salenko, Whelan
09/03/96	Everton	A	2-2	Daish, Williams
16/03/96	Bolton Wanderers	H	0-2	
25/03/96	Southampton	A	0-1	
30/03/96	Tottenham Hotspur	A	1-3	Dublin
06/04/96	Liverpool	H	1-0	Whelan
08/04/96	Manchester United	A	0-1	
13/04/96	Queens Park Rangers	H	1-0	Jess
17/04/96	Nottingham Forest	A	0-0	
27/04/96	Wimbledon	A	2-0	Ndlovu 2
05/05/96	Leeds United	H	0-0	

EVERTON

CLUB DIRECTORY

Everton FC
Goodison Park
Liverpool L4 4EL
tel - (0151) 3302200
fax - (0151) 2869112
Year of Formation - 1878
Chairman - Peter Johnson
Secretary - Michael Dunford
Manager - Joe Royle
Stadium - Goodison Park (40,200)

MAJOR HONOURS
League Championship - (9) 1891, 1915, 1928, 1932, 1939, 1963, 1970, 1985, 1987.
Domestic Cup - (5)
1906, 1933, 1966, 1984, 1995.
European Cup-winners' Cup - (1) 1985.

APPEARANCES 95/96

	P	Ap	(s)	Gls
Gary ABLETT	D	13		
Daniel AMOKACHI (NIG)	A	17	(8)	6
Stuart BARLOW	A		(3)	
Earl BARRETT	D	8		
Graham BRANCH	A	1	(2)	
John EBBRELL	M	24	(1)	4
Duncan FERGUSON (SCO)	A	16	(2)	5
Tony GRANT	M	11	(2)	1
Andy HINCHCLIFFE	D	23	(5)	2
Paul HOLMES	D	1		
Barry HORNE (WAL)	M	25	(1)	1
Marc HOTTIGER (SUI)	D	9		1
Matthew JACKSON	D	14		
Andrei KANCHELSKIS (RUS)	M	32		16
Anders LIMPAR (SWE)	M	22	(6)	3
Jonathan O'CONNOR	M	3	(1)	
Joe PARKINSON	M	28		3
Paul RIDEOUT	A	19	(6)	6
Vinny SAMWAYS	M	3	(1)	1
Craig SHORT	D	22	(1)	2
Neville SOUTHALL (WAL)	G	38		
Graham STUART	M	27	(2)	9
David UNSWORTH	D	28	(3)	2
Dave WATSON	D	34		1

LEAGUE RESULTS 1995/96

Date	Opponent		Score	Scorers
19/08/95	Chelsea	A	0-0	
23/08/95	Arsenal	H	0-2	
26/08/95	Southampton	H	2-0	Limpar, Amokachi
30/08/95	Manchester City	A	2-0	Parkinson, Amokachi
09/09/95	Manchester United	H	2-3	Limpar, Rideout
17/09/95	Nottingham Forest	A	2-3	Rideout 2
23/09/95	West Ham United	A	1-2	Samways
01/10/95	Newcastle United	H	1-3	Limpar
14/10/95	Bolton Wanderers	A	1-1	Rideout
22/10/95	Tottenham Hotspur	H	1-1	Stuart
28/10/95	Aston Villa	A	0-1	
05/11/95	Blackburn Rovers	H	1-0	Stuart
18/11/95	Liverpool	A	2-1	Kanchelskis 2
22/11/95	Queens Park Rangers	H	2-0	Stuart, Rideout
25/11/95	Sheffield Wednesday	H	2-2	Kanchelskis, Amokachi
02/12/95	Tottenham Hotspur	A	0-0	
11/12/95	West Ham United	H	3-0	Stuart, Unsworth (p), Ebbrell
16/12/95	Newcastle United	A	0-1	
23/12/95	Coventry City	A	1-2	Rideout
26/12/95	Middlesbrough	H	4-0	Short, Stuart 2, Kanchelskis
30/12/95	Leeds United	H	2-0	og (Wetherall), Kanchelskis
01/01/96	Wimbledon	A	3-2	Ebbrell, Ferguson 2
13/01/96	Chelsea	H	1-1	Unsworth (p)
20/01/96	Arsenal	A	2-1	Stuart, Kanchelskis
03/02/96	Southampton	A	2-2	Stuart, Horne
10/02/96	Manchester City	H	2-0	Parkinson, Hinchcliffe (p)
21/02/96	Manchester United	A	0-2	
24/02/96	Nottingham Forest	H	3-0	Kanchelskis, Watson, Ferguson
02/03/96	Middlesbrough	A	2-0	Grant, Hinchcliffe (p)
09/03/96	Coventry City	H	2-2	Ferguson 2
17/03/96	Leeds United	A	2-2	Stuart, Kanchelskis
23/03/96	Wimbledon	H	2-4	Short, Kanchelskis
30/03/96	Blackburn Rovers	A	3-0	Amokachi, Kanchelskis 2
06/04/96	Bolton Wanderers	H	3-0	Hottiger, Kanchelskis, Amokachi
08/04/96	Queens Park Rangers	A	1-3	Ebbrell
16/04/96	Liverpool	H	1-1	Kanchelskis
27/04/96	Sheffield Wednesday	A	5-2	Amokachi, Ebbrell, Kanchelskis 3
05/05/96	Aston Villa	H	1-0	Parkinson

LEEDS UNITED

CLUB DIRECTORY

Leeds United AFC
Elland Road
Leeds LS11 OES
tel - (0113) 2716037
fax - (0113) 2720370
Year of Formation - 1919
Chairman - Bill Fotherby
Secretary - Nigel Pleasants
Manager - Howard Wilkinson
Stadium - Elland Road (39,775)

MAJOR HONOURS
League Championship - (3) 1969, 1974, 1992.
Domestic Cup - (1) 1972.
Fairs' Cup - (2) 1968, 1971.

APPEARANCES 95/96

	P	Ap	(s)	Gls
Mark BEENEY	G	10		
Paul BEESLEY	D	8	(2)	
Jason BLUNT	M	2	(1)	
Robert BOWMAN	D	1	(2)	
Tomas BROLIN (SWE)	A	17	(2)	4
Lee CHAPMAN	A	2		
Andrew COUZENS	D	8	(6)	
Brian DEANE	A	30	(4)	7
Tony DORIGO	D	17		1
Mark FORD	M	12		
Andy GRAY (SCO)	M	12	(3)	
Ian HARTE (IRL)	D	2	(2)	
Mark JACKSON	D		(1)	
Richard JOBSON	D	12		1
Gary KELLY (IRL)	D	34		
Harry KEWELL (AUS)	M	2		
John LUKIC	G	28		
Gary McALLISTER (SCO)	M	36		5
Philomen MASINGA (SAF)	A	5	(4)	
Alan MAYBURY (IRL)	M	1		
Carlton PALMER	M	35		2
John PEMBERTON	D	16	(1)	
Lucas RADEBE (SAF)	M	10	(3)	
Kevin SHARP	M		(1)	
Gary SPEED (WAL)	M	29		2
Mark TINKLER	M	5	(4)	
Rod WALLACE	M	12	(12)	1
David WETHERALL	D	34		4
Noel WHELAN	A	3	(5)	
David WHITE	M	1	(3)	1
Nigel WORTHINGTON (NIR)	D	12	(4)	
Tony YEBOAH (GHA)	A	22		12

LEAGUE RESULTS 1995/96

19/08/95	West Ham United	A	2-1	Yeboah 2
21/08/95	Liverpool	H	1-0	Yeboah
26/08/95	Aston Villa	H	2-0	Speed, White
30/08/95	Southampton	A	1-1	Dorigo
09/09/95	Tottenham Hotspur	A	1-2	Yeboah
16/09/95	Queens Park Rangers	H	1-3	Wetherall
23/09/95	Wimbledon	A	4-2	Palmer, Yeboah 3
30/09/95	Sheffield Wednesday	H	2-0	Yeboah, Speed
14/10/95	Arsenal	H	0-3	
21/10/95	Manchester City	A	0-0	
28/10/95	Coventry City	H	3-1	McAllister 3 (1p)
04/11/95	Middlesbrough	A	1-1	Deane
18/11/95	Chelsea	H	1-0	Yeboah
25/11/95	Newcastle United	A	1-2	Deane
02/12/95	Manchester City	H	0-1	
09/12/95	Wimbledon	H	1-1	Jobson
16/12/95	Sheffield Wednesday	A	2-6	Brolin, Wallace
24/12/95	Manchester United	H	3-1	McAllister (p), Yeboah, Deane
27/12/95	Bolton Wanderers	A	2-0	Brolin, Wetherall
30/12/95	Everton	A	0-2	
01/01/96	Blackburn Rovers	H	0-0	
13/01/96	West Ham United	H	2-0	Brolin 2
20/01/96	Liverpool	A	0-5	
31/01/96	Nottingham Forest	A	1-2	Palmer
03/02/96	Aston Villa	A	0-3	
02/03/96	Bolton Wanderers	H	0-1	
06/03/96	Queens Park Rangers	A	2-1	Yeboah 2
13/03/96	Blackburn Rovers	A	0-1	
17/03/96	Everton	H	2-2	Deane 2
30/03/96	Middlesbrough	H	0-1	
03/04/96	Southampton	H	1-0	Deane
06/04/96	Arsenal	A	1-2	Deane
08/04/96	Nottingham Forest	H	1-3	Wetherall
13/04/96	Chelsea	A	1-4	McAllister
17/04/96	Manchester United	A	0-1	
29/04/96	Newcastle United	H	0-1	
02/05/96	Tottenham Hotspur	H	1-3	Wetherall
05/05/96	Coventry City	A	0-0	

LIVERPOOL

CLUB DIRECTORY

Liverpool FC
Anfield Road
Liverpool L4 0TH
tel - (0151) 2632361
fax - (0151) 2608813
Year of Formation - 1892
Chairman - David Moores
Secretary - Peter Robinson
Manager - Roy Evans
Stadium - Anfield (41,210)

MAJOR HONOURS

League Championship - (18)
1901, 1906, 1922, 1923, 1947, 1964, 1966, 1973, 1976, 1977, 1979, 1980, 1982, 1983, 1984, 1986, 1988, 1990.
Domestic Cup - (5)
1965, 1974, 1986, 1989, 1992.
European Champions' Cup - (4)
1977, 1978, 1981, 1984.
UEFA Cup - (2) 1973, 1976.
European Super Cup - (1) 1977.

APPEARANCES 95/96

	P	Ap	(s)	Gls
Phil BABB (IRL)	D	28		
John BARNES	M	36		3
Stig Inge BJØRNEBYE (NOR)	D	2		
Nigel CLOUGH	A	1	(1)	
Stan COLLYMORE	A	30	(1)	14
Robbie FOWLER	A	36	(2)	28
Steve HARKNESS	D	23	(1)	1
David JAMES	G	38		
Rob JONES	D	33		
Mark KENNEDY (IRL)	M	1	(3)	
Jason McATEER (IRL)	M	27	(2)	
Steve McMANAMAN	M	38		6
Dominic MATTEO	D	5		
Jamie REDKNAPP	M	19	(4)	3
Neil RUDDOCK	D	18	(2)	5
Ian RUSH (WAL)	A	10	(10)	5
John SCALES	D	27		
Michael THOMAS	M	18	(9)	1
Mark WRIGHT	D	28		2

LEAGUE RESULTS 1995/96

Date	Opponent		Score	Scorers
19/08/95	Sheffield Wednesday	H	1-0	Collymore
21/08/95	Leeds United	A	0-1	
26/08/95	Tottenham Hotspur	A	3-1	Barnes 2, Fowler
30/08/95	Queens Park Rangers	H	1-0	Ruddock
09/09/95	Wimbledon	A	0-1	
16/09/95	Blackburn Rovers	H	3-0	Redknapp, Fowler, Collymore
23/09/95	Bolton Wanderers	H	5-2	Fowler 4, Harkness
01/10/95	Manchester United	A	2-2	Fowler 2
14/10/95	Coventry City	H	0-0	
22/10/95	Southampton	A	3-1	McManaman 2, Redknapp
28/10/95	Manchester City	H	6-0	Rush 2, Redknapp, Fowler 2, Ruddock
04/11/95	Newcastle United	A	1-2	Rush
18/11/95	Everton	H	1-2	Fowler
22/11/95	West Ham United	A	0-0	
25/11/95	Middlesbrough	A	1-2	Ruddock
02/12/95	Southampton	H	1-1	Collymore
09/12/95	Bolton Wanderers	A	1-0	Collymore
17/12/95	Manchester United	H	2-0	Fowler 2
23/12/95	Arsenal	H	3-1	Fowler 3
30/12/95	Chelsea	A	2-2	McManaman 2
01/01/96	Nottingham Forest	H	4-2	Fowler 2, Collymore, og (Cooper)
13/01/96	Sheffield Wednesday	A	1-1	Rush
20/01/96	Leeds United	H	5-0	Ruddock 2, Fowler 2 (1p), Collymore
31/01/96	Aston Villa	A	2-0	Collymore, Fowler
03/02/96	Tottenham Hotspur	H	0-0	
11/02/96	Queens Park Rangers	A	2-1	Wright, Fowler
24/02/96	Blackburn Rovers	A	3-2	Collymore 2, Thomas
03/03/96	Aston Villa	H	3-0	McManaman, Fowler 2
13/03/96	Wimbledon	H	2-2	McManaman, Collymore
16/03/96	Chelsea	H	2-0	Wright, Fowler
23/03/96	Nottingham Forest	A	0-1	
03/04/96	Newcastle United	H	4-3	Fowler 2, Collymore 2
06/04/96	Coventry City	A	0-1	
08/04/96	West Ham United	H	2-0	Collymore, Barnes
16/04/96	Everton	A	1-1	Fowler
27/04/96	Middlesbrough	H	1-0	Collymore
01/05/96	Arsenal	A	0-0	
05/05/96	Manchester City	A	2-2	og (Lomas), Rush

MANCHESTER CITY

CLUB DIRECTORY

Manchester City FC
Maine Road
Moss Side
Manchester M14 7WN
tel - (0161) 2245000
fax - (0161) 2488449
Year of Formation - 1887
Chairman - Francis Lee
Secretary - Bernard Halford
Manager - Alan Ball
Stadium - Maine Road (31,257)

MAJOR HONOURS
League Championship - (2) 1937, 1968.
Domestic Cup - (4) 1904, 1934, 1956, 1969.
European Cup-winners' Cup - (1) 1970.

APPEARANCES 95/96

	P	Ap	(s)	Gls
Peter BEAGRIE	M	4	(1)	
Ian BRIGHTWELL	D	26	(3)	
Michael BROWN	M	16	(5)	
Nigel CLOUGH	A	15		2
Gerry CREANEY (SCO)	A	6	(9)	3
Keith CURLE	D	32		
Richard EDGHILL	D	13		
Ronnie EKELUND (DEN)	A	2	(2)	
Gary FLITCROFT	M	25		
John FOSTER	D	4		
Michael FRONTZECK (GER)	D	11	(1)	
Scott HILEY	D	2	(4)	
Eike IMMEL (GER)	G	38		
Rae INGRAM	D	5		
Mikheil KAVELASHVILI (GEO)	A	3	(1)	1
Alan KERNAGHAN (IRL)	D	4	(2)	
David KERR	M		(1)	
Giorgi KINKLADZE (GEO)	M	37		4
Steve LOMAS (NIR)	M	32	(1)	3
Giuseppe MAZZARELLI (SUI)	M		(2)	
Terry PHELAN (IRL)	D	9		
Martin PHILLIPS	M	2	(9)	
Niall QUINN (IRL)	A	24	(8)	8
Uwe RÖSLER (GER)	A	34	(2)	9
Nicky SUMMERBEE	M	33	(4)	1
Kit SYMONS (WAL)	D	38		2
Paul WALSH	A	3		

LEAGUE RESULTS 1995/96

19/08/95	Tottenham Hotspur	H	1-1	Rösler
23/08/95	Coventry City	A	1-2	Rösler
26/08/95	Queens Park Rangers	A	0-1	
30/08/95	Everton	H	0-2	
10/09/95	Arsenal	H	0-1	
16/09/95	Newcastle United	A	1-3	Creaney
23/09/95	Middlesbrough	H	0-1	
30/09/95	Nottingham Forest	A	0-3	
14/10/95	Manchester United	A	0-1	
21/10/95	Leeds United	H	0-0	
28/10/95	Liverpool	A	0-6	
04/11/95	Bolton Wanderers	H	1-0	Summerbee
18/11/95	Sheffield Wednesday	A	1-1	Lomas
22/11/95	Wimbledon	H	1-0	Quinn
25/11/95	Aston Villa	H	1-0	Kinkladze
02/12/95	Leeds United	A	1-0	Creaney
09/12/95	Middlesbrough	A	1-4	Kinkladze
18/12/95	Nottingham Forest	H	1-1	Rösler
23/12/95	Chelsea	H	0-1	
26/12/95	Blackburn Rovers	A	0-2	
01/01/96	West Ham United	H	2-1	Quinn 2
13/01/96	Tottenham Hotspur	A	0-1	
20/01/96	Coventry City	H	1-1	Rösler
31/01/96	Southampton	A	1-1	Rösler
03/02/96	Queens Park Rangers	H	2-0	Clough, Symons
10/02/96	Everton	A	0-2	
24/02/96	Newcastle United	H	3-3	Quinn 2, Rösler
02/03/96	Blackburn Rovers	H	1-1	Lomas
05/03/96	Arsenal	A	1-3	Creaney
12/03/96	Chelsea	A	1-1	Clough
16/03/96	Southampton	H	2-1	Kinkladze 2
23/03/96	West Ham United	A	2-4	Quinn 2
30/03/96	Bolton Wanderers	A	1-1	Quinn
06/04/96	Manchester United	H	2-3	Kavelashvili, Rösler
08/04/96	Wimbledon	A	0-3	
13/04/96	Sheffield Wednesday	H	1-0	Rösler
27/04/96	Aston Villa	A	1-0	Lomas
05/05/96	Liverpool	H	2-2	Rösler (p), Symons

MANCHESTER UNITED

CLUB DIRECTORY

Manchester United FC
Sir Matt Busby Way
Old Trafford
Manchester M16 0RA
tel - (0161) 8721661/9301968
fax - (0161) 8765502
Year of Formation - 1878
Chairman - Martin Edwards
Secretary - Ken Merrett
Manager - Alex Ferguson
Stadium - Old Trafford (55,800)

MAJOR HONOURS
League Championship - (10) 1908, 1911, 1952, 1956, 1957, 1965, 1967, 1993, 1994, 1996.
Domestic Cup - (9) 1909, 1948, 1963, 1977, 1983, 1985, 1990, 1994, 1996.
European Champions' Cup - (1) 1968.
European Cup-winners' Cup - (1) 1991.
European Super Cup - (1) 1991.

APPEARANCES 95/96

	P	Ap	(s)	Gls
David BECKHAM	M	26	(7)	7
Steve BRUCE	D	30		1
Nicky BUTT	M	31	(1)	2
Eric CANTONA (FRA)	A	30		14
Andy COLE	A	32	(2)	11
Terry COOKE	A	1	(3)	
Simon DAVIES (WAL)	M	1	(5)	
Ryan GIGGS (WAL)	A	30	(3)	11
Denis IRWIN (IRL)	D	31		1
Roy KEANE (IRL)	M	29		6
Brian McCLAIR (SCO)	M	12	(10)	3
David MAY	D	11	(5)	1
Gary NEVILLE	D	30	(1)	
Philip NEVILLE	D	21	(3)	
John O'KANE	M		(1)	
Gary PALLISTER	D	21		1
Paul PARKER	D	5	(1)	
Kevin PILKINGTON	G	2	(1)	
William PRUNIER (FRA)	D	2		
Peter SCHMEICHEL (DEN)	G	36		
Paul SCHOLES	A	16	(10)	10
Lee SHARPE	M	21	(10)	4
Ben THORNLEY	A		(1)	

LEAGUE RESULTS 1995/96

Date	Opponent	H/A	Score	Scorers
19/08/95	Aston Villa	A	1-3	Beckham
23/08/95	West Ham United	H	2-1	Scholes, Keane
26/08/95	Wimbledon	H	3-1	Keane 2, Cole
28/08/95	Blackburn Rovers	A	2-1	Sharpe, Beckham
09/09/95	Everton	A	3-2	Sharpe 2, Giggs
16/09/95	Bolton Wanderers	H	3-0	Scholes 2, Giggs
23/09/95	Sheffield Wednesday	A	0-0	
01/10/95	Liverpool	H	2-2	Butt, Cantona (p)
14/10/95	Manchester City	H	1-0	Scholes
21/10/95	Chelsea	A	4-1	Scholes 2, Giggs, McClair
28/10/95	Middlesbrough	H	2-0	Pallister, Cole
04/11/95	Arsenal	A	0-1	
18/11/95	Southampton	H	4-1	Giggs 2, Scholes, Cole
22/11/95	Coventry City	A	4-0	Irwin, McClair 2, Beckham
27/11/95	Nottingham Forest	A	1-1	Cantona (p)
02/12/95	Chelsea	H	1-1	Beckham
09/12/95	Sheffield Wednesday	H	2-2	Cantona 2
17/12/95	Liverpool	A	0-2	
24/12/95	Leeds United	A	1-3	Cole
27/12/95	Newcastle United	H	2-0	Cole, Keane
30/12/95	Queens Park Rangers	H	2-1	Cole, Giggs
01/01/96	Tottenham Hotspur	A	1-4	Cole
13/01/96	Aston Villa	H	0-0	
22/01/96	West Ham United	A	1-0	Cantona
03/02/96	Wimbledon	A	4-2	Cole, og (Perry), Cantona 2 (1p)
10/02/96	Blackburn Rovers	H	1-0	Sharpe
21/02/96	Everton	H	2-0	Keane, Giggs
25/02/96	Bolton Wanderers	A	6-0	Beckham, Bruce, Cole, Scholes 2, Butt
04/03/96	Newcastle United	A	1-0	Cantona
16/03/96	Queens Park Rangers	A	1-1	Cantona
20/03/96	Arsenal	H	1-0	Cantona
24/03/96	Tottenham Hotspur	H	1-0	Cantona
06/04/96	Manchester City	A	3-2	Cantona (p), Cole, Giggs
08/04/96	Coventry City	H	1-0	Cantona
13/04/96	Southampton	A	1-3	Giggs
17/04/96	Leeds United	H	1-0	Keane
28/04/96	Nottingham Forest	H	5-0	Scholes, Beckham 2, Giggs, Cantona
05/05/96	Middlesbrough	A	3-0	May, Cole, Giggs

MIDDLESBROUGH

CLUB DIRECTORY

Middlesbrough FC
Cellnet Riverside Stadium
Middlesbrough
Cleveland
TS3 6RS
tel - (01642) 227227
fax - (01642) 248450
Year of Formation - 1876
Chairman - Steve Gibson
Chief Executive - Keith Lamb
Manager - Bryan Robson
Stadium - Riverside (30,500)

APPEARANCES 95/96

	P	Ap	(s)	Gls
Nick BARMBY	A	32		7
Michael BARRON	D	1		
Clayton BLACKMORE (WAL)	M	4	(1)	
BRANCO (BRA)	D	5	(2)	
Andrew CAMPBELL	A	1	(1)	
Neil COX	D	35		2
Jan Åge FJØRTOFT (NOR)	A	27	(1)	6
Curtis FLEMING (IRL)	D	13		1
Chris FREESTONE	A	2	(1)	1
John HENDRIE	A	7	(6)	1
Craig HIGNETT	M	17	(5)	5
JUNINHO (BRA)	M	20	(1)	2
Graham KAVANAGH	M	6	(1)	1
Craig LIDDLE	M	12	(1)	
Alan MILLER	G	6		
Alan MOORE	M	5	(7)	
Jaime MORENO (BOL)	M	2	(4)	
Chris MORRIS (IRL)	D	22	(1)	2
Robbie MUSTOE	M	21		1
Keith O'HALLORAN	D	2	(1)	
Nigel PEARSON	D	36		
Jamie POLLOCK	M	31		1
Bryan ROBSON	M	1	(1)	
Philip STAMP	M	11	(1)	2
Mark SUMMERBELL	M		(1)	
Steve VICKERS	D	32		1
Gary WALSH	G	32		
Phil WHELAN	D	9	(4)	1
Derek WHYTE (SCO)	D	24	(1)	
Paul WILKINSON	A	2	(1)	

LEAGUE RESULTS 1995/96

20/08/95	Arsenal	A	1-1	Barmby
26/08/95	Chelsea	H	2-0	Hignett, Fjørtoft
30/08/95	Newcastle United	A	0-1	
09/09/95	Bolton Wanderers	A	1-1	Hignett
12/09/95	Southampton	H	0-0	
16/09/95	Coventry City	H	2-1	Vickers, Fjørtoft
23/09/95	Manchester City	A	1-0	Barmby
30/09/95	Blackburn Rovers	H	2-0	Barmby, Hignett
15/10/95	Sheffield Wednesday	A	1-0	Hignett (p)
21/10/95	Queens Park Rangers	H	1-0	Hignett (p)
28/10/95	Manchester United	A	0-2	
04/11/95	Leeds United	H	1-1	Fjørtoft
18/11/95	Wimbledon	A	0-0	
21/11/95	Tottenham Hotspur	H	0-1	
25/11/95	Liverpool	H	2-1	Cox, Barmby
02/12/95	Queens Park Rangers	A	1-1	Morris
09/12/95	Manchester City	H	4-1	Barmby 2, Stamp, Juninho
16/12/95	Blackburn Rovers	A	0-1	
23/12/95	West Ham United	H	4-2	Fjørtoft, Cox, Morris, Hendrie
26/12/95	Everton	A	0-4	
30/12/95	Nottingham Forest	A	0-1	
01/01/96	Aston Villa	H	0-2	
13/01/96	Arsenal	H	2-3	Juninho, Stamp
20/01/96	Southampton	A	1-2	Barmby
04/02/96	Chelsea	A	0-5	
10/02/96	Newcastle United	H	1-2	og (Beresford)
17/02/96	Bolton Wanderers	H	1-2	Pollock
24/02/96	Coventry City	A	0-0	
02/03/96	Everton	H	0-2	
09/03/96	West Ham United	A	0-2	
16/03/96	Nottingham Forest	H	1-1	Mustoe
19/03/96	Aston Villa	A	0-0	
30/03/96	Leeds United	A	1-0	Kavanagh (p)
05/04/96	Sheffield Wednesday	H	3-1	Fjørtoft 2, Freestone
08/04/96	Tottenham Hotspur	A	1-1	Whelan
13/04/96	Wimbledon	H	1-2	Fleming
27/04/96	Liverpool	A	0-1	
05/05/96	Manchester United	H	0-3	

NEWCASTLE UNITED

CLUB DIRECTORY

Newcastle United FC
St. James' Park
Newcastle-upon-Tyne
NE1 4ST
tel - (0191) 2018400
fax - (0191) 2018600
Year of Formation - 1881
Chairman - Sir John Hall
Secretary - Russell Cushing
Manager - Kevin Keegan
Stadium - St. James' Park (36,610)

MAJOR HONOURS
League Championship - (4)
1905, 1907, 1909, 1927.
Domestic Cup - (6)
1910, 1924, 1932, 1951, 1952, 1955.
Fairs' Cup - (1) 1969.

APPEARANCES 95/96

	P	Ap	(s)	Gls
Philippe ALBERT (BEL)	D	19	(4)	4
Faustino ASPRILLA (COL)	A	11	(3)	3
Warren BARTON	D	30	(1)	
David BATTY	M	11		1
Peter BEARDSLEY	A	35		8
John BERESFORD	D	32	(1)	
Lee CLARK	M	22	(5)	2
Robbie ELLIOTT	D	5	(1)	
Les FERDINAND	A	37		25
Ruel FOX	M	2	(2)	
Keith GILLESPIE (NIR)	M	26	(2)	4
David GINOLA (FRA)	M	34		5
Shaka HISLOP	G	24		
Marc HOTTIGER (SUI)	D		(1)	
Steve HOWEY	D	28		1
Darren HUCKERBY	M		(1)	
Paul KITSON	A	2	(5)	2
Robert LEE	M	36		8
Darren PEACOCK	D	33	(1)	
Scott SELLARS	M	2	(3)	
Pavel SRNICEK (TCH)	G	14	(1)	
Steve WATSON	M	15	(8)	3

LEAGUE RESULTS 1995/96

19/08/95	Coventry City	H	3-0	Lee, Beardsley (p), Ferdinand
22/08/95	Bolton Wanderers	A	3-1	Ferdinand 2, Lee
27/08/95	Sheffield Wednesday	A	2-0	Ginola, Beardsley
30/08/95	Middlesbrough	H	1-0	Ferdinand
09/09/95	Southampton	A	0-1	
16/09/95	Manchester City	H	3-1	Beardsley (p), Ferdinand 2
24/09/95	Chelsea	H	2-0	Ferdinand 2
01/10/95	Everton	A	3-1	Ferdinand, Lee (p), Kitson
14/10/95	Queens Park Rangers	A	3-2	Gillespie 2, Ferdinand
21/10/95	Wimbledon	H	6-1	Howey, Ferdinand 3, Clark, Albert
29/10/95	Tottenham Hotspur	A	1-1	Ginola
04/11/95	Liverpool	H	2-1	Ferdinand, Watson
08/11/95	Blackburn Rovers	H	1-0	Lee
18/11/95	Aston Villa	A	1-1	Ferdinand
25/11/95	Leeds United	H	2-1	Lee, Beardsley
03/12/95	Wimbledon	A	3-3	Ferdinand 2, Gillespie
09/12/95	Chelsea	A	0-1	
16/12/95	Everton	H	1-0	Ferdinand
23/12/95	Nottingham Forest	H	3-1	Lee 2, Ginola
27/12/95	Manchester United	A	0-2	
02/01/96	Arsenal	H	2-0	Ginola, Ferdinand
14/01/96	Coventry City	A	1-0	Watson
20/01/96	Bolton Wanderers	H	2-1	Kitson, Beardsley
03/02/96	Sheffield Wednesday	H	2-0	Ferdinand, Clark
10/02/96	Middlesbrough	A	2-1	Watson, Ferdinand
21/02/96	West Ham United	A	0-2	
24/02/96	Manchester City	A	3-3	Albert 2, Asprilla
04/03/96	Manchester United	H	0-1	
18/03/96	West Ham United	H	3-0	Albert, Asprilla, Ferdinand
23/03/96	Arsenal	A	0-2	
03/04/96	Liverpool	A	3-4	Ferdinand, Ginola, Asprilla
06/04/96	Queens Park Rangers	H	2-1	Beardsley 2
08/04/96	Blackburn Rovers	A	1-2	Batty
14/04/96	Aston Villa	H	1-0	Ferdinand
17/04/96	Southampton	H	1-0	Lee
29/04/96	Leeds United	A	1-0	Gillespie
02/05/96	Nottingham Forest	A	1-1	Beardsley
05/05/96	Tottenham Hotspur	H	1-1	Ferdinand

NOTTINGHAM FOREST

CLUB DIRECTORY

Nottingham Forest FC
City Ground
Nottingham NG2 5FJ
tel - (0115) 9526000
fax - (0115) 9526003
Year of Formation - 1865
Chairman - Fred Reacher
Secretary - Paul White
Manager - Frank Clark
Stadium - City Ground (30,602)

MAJOR HONOURS

League Championship - (1) 1978.
Domestic Cup - (2) 1898, 1959.
European Champions' Cup - (2) 1979, 1980.
European Super Cup - (1) 1979.

APPEARANCES 95/96

	P	Ap	(s)	Gls
Chris ALLEN	A	1	(2)	1
Chris BART-WILLIAMS	M	33		
Kingsley BLACK (NIR)	M	1	(1)	
Lars BOHINEN (NOR)	M	7		
Kevin CAMPBELL	A	21		3
Steve CHETTLE	D	37		
Colin COOPER	D	37		5
Mark CROSSLEY	G	38		
Scot GEMMILL (SCO)	M	26	(5)	1
Stephen GUIVAN	A	1	(1)	
Alf Inge HÅLAND (NOR)	M	12	(5)	
Stephen HOWE	A	4	(5)	2
Richard IRVING	M		(1)	
Jason LEE	A	21	(7)	8
Des LYTTLE	D	32	(1)	1
Paul McGREGOR	A	7	(7)	2
Stuart PEARCE	D	31		3
David PHILLIPS (WAL)	M	14	(4)	
Bryan ROY (HOL)	A	25	(3)	8
Andrea SILENZI (ITA)	A	3	(7)	
Steve STONE	M	34		7
Ian WOAN	M	33		8

LEAGUE RESULTS 1995/96

19/08/95	Southampton	A	4-3	Cooper, Woan, Roy 2
23/08/95	Chelsea	H	0-0	
26/08/95	West Ham United	H	1-1	Pearce (p)
29/08/95	Arsenal	A	1-1	Campbell
09/09/95	Coventry City	A	1-1	Roy
17/09/95	Everton	H	3-2	og (Watson), Lee, Woan
23/09/95	Aston Villa	A	1-1	Lyttle
30/09/95	Manchester City	H	3-0	Lee 2, Stone
14/10/95	Tottenham Hotspur	A	1-0	Stone
21/10/95	Bolton Wanderers	H	3-2	Roy, Lee, Cooper
28/10/95	Queens Park Rangers	A	1-1	Lee
06/11/95	Wimbledon	H	4-1	Roy, Pearce, Lee, Gemmill
18/11/95	Blackburn Rovers	A	0-7	
27/11/95	Manchester United	H	1-1	McGregor
02/12/95	Bolton Wanderers	A	1-1	Cooper
10/12/95	Aston Villa	H	1-1	Stone
18/12/95	Manchester City	A	1-1	Campbell
23/12/95	Newcastle United	A	1-3	Woan
26/12/95	Sheffield Wednesday	H	1-0	Lee
30/12/95	Middlesbrough	H	1-0	Pearce (p)
01/01/96	Liverpool	A	2-4	Stone, Woan
13/01/96	Southampton	H	1-0	Cooper
20/01/96	Chelsea	A	0-1	
31/01/96	Leeds United	H	2-1	Campbell, Roy (p)
03/02/96	West Ham United	A	0-1	
10/02/96	Arsenal	H	0-1	
24/02/96	Everton	A	0-3	
02/03/96	Sheffield Wednesday	A	3-1	Howe, McGregor, Roy
16/03/96	Middlesbrough	A	1-1	Allen
23/03/96	Liverpool	H	1-0	Stone
30/03/96	Wimbledon	A	0-1	
06/04/96	Tottenham Hotspur	H	2-1	Stone, Woan
08/04/96	Leeds United	A	3-1	Cooper, Lee, Woan
13/04/96	Blackburn Rovers	H	1-5	Woan
17/04/96	Coventry City	H	0-0	
28/04/96	Manchester United	A	0-5	
02/05/96	Newcastle United	H	1-1	Woan
05/05/96	Queens Park Rangers	H	3-0	Stone, Roy, Howe

QUEENS PARK RANGERS

CLUB DIRECTORY

Queens Park Rangers FC
Rangers Stadium
South Africa Road
London W12 7PA
tel - (0181) 7430262
fax - (0181) 7490994
Year of Formation - 1885
Chairman - P.D. Ellis
Secretary - Miss S.F. Marson
Manager - Ray Wilkins
Stadium - Loftus Road (19,148)

APPEARANCES 95/96

	P	Ap	(s)	Gls
Bradley ALLEN	A	5	(3)	1
David BARDSLEY	D	28	(1)	
Simon BARKER	M	33		5
Matthew BRAZIER	M	6	(5)	
Rufus BREVETT	D	27		1
Trevor CHALLIS	D	10	(1)	
Lee CHARLES	A		(4)	
Daniele DICHIO	A	21	(8)	10
Kevin GALLEN	A	26	(3)	8
Gregory GOODRIDGE (BAR)	A		(7)	1
Mark HATELEY	A	10	(4)	2
Ian HOLLOWAY	M	26	(1)	1
Andy IMPEY	M	28	(1)	3
Alan McDONALD (NIR)	D	25	(1)	1
Danny MADDIX	D	20	(2)	
Paul MURRAY	M	1		
Simon OSBORN	M	6	(3)	1
Gary PENRICE	A		(3)	
Chris PLUMMER	D		(1)	
Nigel QUASHIE	M	11		
Karl READY (WAL)	D	16	(6)	1
Tony ROBERTS (WAL)	G	5		
Trevor SINCLAIR	A	37		2
Jurgen SOMMER (USA)	G	33		
Ray WILKINS	M	11	(4)	
Steve YATES	D	30		
Ned ZELIC (AUS)	M	3	(1)	

LEAGUE RESULTS 1995/96

Date	Opponent	H/A	Score	Scorers
19/08/95	Blackburn Rovers	A	0-1	
23/08/95	Wimbledon	H	0-3	
26/08/95	Manchester City	H	1-0	Barker
30/08/95	Liverpool	A	0-1	
09/09/95	Sheffield Wednesday	H	0-3	
16/09/95	Leeds United	A	3-1	Dichio 2, Sinclair
25/09/95	Tottenham Hotspur	H	2-3	Dichio, Impey
30/09/95	Bolton Wanderers	A	1-0	Dichio
14/10/95	Newcastle United	H	2-3	Dichio 2
21/10/95	Middlesbrough	A	0-1	
28/10/95	Nottingham Forest	H	1-1	Sinclair
04/11/95	Southampton	A	0-2	
19/11/95	Coventry City	H	1-1	Barker
22/11/95	Everton	A	0-2	
25/11/95	West Ham United	A	0-1	
02/12/95	Middlesbrough	H	1-1	McDonald
09/12/95	Tottenham Hotspur	A	0-1	
16/12/95	Bolton Wanderers	H	2-1	Osborn, Impey
23/12/95	Aston Villa	H	1-0	Gallen
26/12/95	Arsenal	A	0-3	
30/12/95	Manchester United	A	1-2	Dichio
02/01/96	Chelsea	H	1-2	Allen
13/01/96	Blackburn Rovers	H	0-1	
20/01/96	Wimbledon	A	1-2	Hateley
03/02/96	Manchester City	A	0-2	
11/02/96	Liverpool	H	1-2	Dichio
17/02/96	Sheffield Wednesday	A	3-1	Barker 2, Goodridge
02/03/96	Arsenal	H	1-1	Gallen
06/03/96	Leeds United	H	1-2	Gallen
09/03/96	Aston Villa	A	2-4	Dichio, Gallen
16/03/96	Manchester United	H	1-1	og (Irwin)
23/03/96	Chelsea	A	1-1	Barker
30/03/96	Southampton	H	3-0	Brevett, Dichio, Gallen
06/04/96	Newcastle United	A	1-2	Holloway
08/04/96	Everton	H	3-1	Gallen, Hateley, Impey
13/04/96	Coventry City	A	0-1	
27/04/96	West Ham United	H	3-0	Ready, Gallen 2
05/05/96	Nottingham Forest	A	0-3	

SHEFFIELD WEDNESDAY

CLUB DIRECTORY

Sheffield Wednesday FC
Hillsborough
Sheffield S6 1SW
tel - (0114) 2343122
fax - (0114) 2337145
Year of Formation - 1867
Chairman - David Richards
Secretary - Graham Mackrell
Manager - David Pleat
Stadium - Hillsborough (39,800)

MAJOR HONOURS
League Championship - (4)
1903, 1904, 1929, 1930.
Domestic Cup - (3) 1896, 1907, 1935.

APPEARANCES 95/96

	P	Ap	(s)	Gls
Peter ATHERTON	D	36		
Regi BLINKER (HOL)	M	9		2
Mark BRIGHT	A	15	(10)	7
Lee BRISCOE	D	22	(4)	
Marc DEGRYSE (BEL)	M	30	(4)	8
O'Neill DONALDSON	A	1	(2)	1
David HIRST	A	29	(1)	13
Ritchie HUMPHREYS	M	1	(4)	
Graham HYDE	M	14	(12)	1
Klas INGESSON (SWE)	M	3	(2)	
Darko KOVACEVIC (YUG)	A	8	(8)	4
Jon NEWSOME	D	8		1
Steve NICOL (SCO)	M	18	(1)	
Ian NOLAN	D	29		
Andy PEARCE	D	3		
Mark PEMBRIDGE (WAL)	M	24	(1)	1
Dan PETRESCU (ROM)	D	8		
Mark PLATTS	M		(2)	
Kevin PRESSMAN	G	30		
John SHERIDAN (IRL)	M	13	(4)	
Andy SINTON	M	7	(3)	
Dejan STEFANOVIC (YUG)	D	5	(1)	
Chris WADDLE	M	23	(9)	2
Des WALKER	D	36		
Julian WATTS	D	9	(2)	1
Guy WHITTINGHAM	A	27	(2)	6
Mike WILLIAMS	M	2	(3)	
Chris WOODS	G	8		

LEAGUE RESULTS 1995/96

19/08/95	Liverpool	A	0-1	
23/08/95	Blackburn Rovers	H	2-1	Waddle, Pembridge
27/08/95	Newcastle United	H	0-2	
30/08/95	Wimbledon	A	2-2	Degryse, Hirst
09/09/95	Queens Park Rangers	A	3-0	Bright 2, Donaldson
16/09/95	Tottenham Hotspur	H	1-3	Hirst
23/09/95	Manchester United	H	0-0	
30/09/95	Leeds United	A	0-2	
15/10/95	Middlesbrough	H	0-1	
21/10/95	Coventry City	A	1-0	Whittingham
28/10/95	West Ham United	H	0-1	
04/11/95	Chelsea	A	0-0	
18/11/95	Manchester City	H	1-1	Hirst (p)
21/11/95	Arsenal	A	2-4	Hirst, Waddle
25/11/95	Everton	A	2-2	Bright 2
04/12/95	Coventry City	H	4-3	Whittingham, Hirst, Degryse, Bright
09/12/95	Manchester United	A	2-2	Bright, Whittingham
16/12/95	Leeds United	H	6-2	Degryse 2, Whittingham, Bright, Hirst 2
23/12/95	Southampton	H	2-2	Hirst 2 (2p)
26/12/95	Nottingham Forest	A	0-1	
01/01/96	Bolton Wanderers	H	4-2	Kovacevic 2, Hirst 2 (1p)
13/01/96	Liverpool	H	1-1	Kovacevic
20/01/96	Blackburn Rovers	A	0-3	
03/02/96	Newcastle United	A	0-2	
10/02/96	Wimbledon	H	2-1	Degryse, Watts
17/02/96	Queens Park Rangers	H	1-3	Hyde
24/02/96	Tottenham Hotspur	A	0-1	
02/03/96	Nottingham Forest	H	1-3	Kovacevic
06/03/96	Aston Villa	A	2-3	Blinker 2
16/03/96	Aston Villa	H	2-0	Whittingham, Hirst
20/03/96	Southampton	A	1-0	Degryse
23/03/96	Bolton Wanderers	A	1-2	Whittingham
05/04/96	Middlesbrough	A	1-3	Pembridge
08/04/96	Arsenal	H	1-0	og (Whyte)
13/04/96	Manchester City	A	0-1	
17/04/96	Chelsea	H	0-0	
27/04/96	Everton	H	2-5	Hirst, Degryse
05/05/96	West Ham United	A	1-1	Newsome

SOUTHAMPTON

CLUB DIRECTORY

Southampton FC
The Dell
Milton Road
Southampton S015 2XH
tel - (01703) 220505
fax - (01703) 330360
Year of Formation - 1885
Chairman - Guy Askham
Secretary - Brian Truscott
Manager - Dave Merrington
(96/97 - Graeme Souness)
Stadium - The Dell (15,000)

MAJOR HONOURS
Domestic Cup - (1) 1976.

APPEARANCES 95/96

	P	Ap	(s)	Gls
Dave BEASANT	G	36		
Francis BENALI	D	28	(1)	
Frankie BENNETT	M	5	(6)	
Simon CHARLTON	D	24	(2)	
Jason DODD	D	37		2
Bruce GROBBELAAR (ZIM)	G	2		
Richard HALL	D	30		1
Neil HEANEY	M	15	(2)	2
David HUGHES	M	6	(5)	1
Matthew LE TISSIER	M	34		7
Paul McDONALD (SCO)	A		(1)	
Neil MADDISON	M	13	(2)	1
Jim MAGILTON (NIR)	M	31		3
Craig MASKELL	A		(1)	
Kenneth MONKOU (HOL)	D	31	(1)	2
Alan NEILSON (WAL)	D	15	(3)	
Matthew OAKLEY	A	5	(5)	
Matthew ROBINSON	M		(5)	
Neil SHIPPERLEY	A	37		7
Paul TISDALE	M	5	(4)	1
Barry VENISON	M	21	(1)	
Mark WALTERS	A	4	(1)	
Christer WARREN	M	1	(5)	
Gordon WATSON	A	18	(7)	3
Tommy WIDDRINGTON	M	20	(1)	2

LEAGUE RESULTS 1995/96

19/08/95	Nottingham Forest	H	3-4	Le Tissier 3 (2p)
26/08/95	Everton	A	0-2	
30/08/95	Leeds United	H	1-1	Widdrington
09/09/95	Newcastle United	H	1-0	Magilton
12/09/95	Middlesbrough	A	0-0	
16/09/95	Chelsea	A	0-3	
23/09/95	Arsenal	A	2-4	Watson, Monkou
02/10/95	West Ham United	H	0-0	
14/10/95	Blackburn Rovers	A	1-2	Maddison
22/10/95	Liverpool	H	1-3	Watson
28/10/95	Wimbledon	A	2-1	Shipperley 2
04/11/95	Queens Park Rangers	H	2-0	Dodd, Le Tissier
18/11/95	Manchester United	A	1-4	Shipperley
20/11/95	Aston Villa	H	0-1	
25/11/95	Bolton Wanderers	H	1-0	Hughes
02/12/95	Liverpool	A	1-1	Shipperley
09/12/95	Arsenal	H	0-0	
16/12/95	West Ham United	A	1-2	og (Bishop)
23/12/95	Sheffield Wednesday	A	2-2	Heaney, Magilton (p)
26/12/95	Tottenham Hotspur	H	0-0	
01/01/96	Coventry City	A	1-1	Heaney
13/01/96	Nottingham Forest	A	0-1	
20/01/96	Middlesbrough	H	2-1	Shipperley, Hall
31/01/96	Manchester City	H	1-1	Shipperley
03/02/96	Everton	H	2-2	Watson, Magilton
24/02/96	Chelsea	H	2-3	Widdrington, og (Clarke)
02/03/96	Tottenham Hotspur	A	0-1	
16/03/96	Manchester City	A	1-2	Tisdale
20/03/96	Sheffield Wednesday	H	0-1	
25/03/96	Coventry City	H	1-0	Dodd
30/03/96	Queens Park Rangers	A	0-3	
03/04/96	Leeds United	A	0-1	
06/04/96	Blackburn Rovers	H	1-0	Le Tissier (p)
08/04/96	Aston Villa	A	0-3	
13/04/96	Manchester United	H	3-1	Monkou, Shipperley, Le Tissier
17/04/96	Newcastle United	A	0-1	
27/04/96	Bolton Wanderers	A	1-0	Le Tissier
05/05/96	Wimbledon	H	0-0	

TOTTENHAM HOTSPUR

CLUB DIRECTORY

Tottenham Hotspur FC
748 High Road
Tottenham
London N17 0AP
tel - (0181) 3655000
fax - (0181) 3655005
Year of Formation - 1882
Chairman - Alan Sugar
Secretary - Peter Barnes
Manager - Gerry Francis
Stadium - White Hart Lane (33,083)

MAJOR HONOURS
League Championship - (2) 1951, 1961.
Domestic Cup - (8) 1901, 1921, 1961, 1962, 1967, 1981, 1982, 1991.
European Cup-winners' Cup - (1) 1963.
UEFA Cup - (2) 1972, 1984.

APPEARANCES 95/96

	P	Ap	(s)	Gls
Darren ANDERTON	M	6	(2)	2
Chris ARMSTRONG	A	36		15
Dean AUSTIN	D	28		
Colin CALDERWOOD (SCO)	D	26	(2)	
Sol CAMPBELL	D	31		1
Darren CASKEY	M	3		
Jason CUNDY	D		(1)	
Jason DOZZELL	M	24	(4)	3
Ilie DUMITRESCU (ROM)	M	5		
Justin EDINBURGH	D	15	(7)	
Ruel FOX	M	26		6
David HOWELLS	M	29		3
David KERSLAKE	D	2		
Gary MABBUTT	D	32		
Gerry McMAHON (NIR)	M	7	(7)	
Stuart NETHERCOTT	D	9	(4)	
Ronny ROSENTHAL (ISR)	A	26	(7)	1
Kevin SCOTT	D		(2)	
Teddy SHERINGHAM	A	38		16
Andy SINTON	M	8	(1)	
Steve SLADE	A	1	(4)	
Ian WALKER	G	38		
Clive WILSON	D	28		

LEAGUE RESULTS 1995/96

19/08/95	Manchester City	A	1-1	Sheringham
23/08/95	Aston Villa	H	0-1	
26/08/95	Liverpool	H	1-3	og (Barnes)
30/08/95	West Ham United	A	1-1	Rosenthal
09/09/95	Leeds United	H	2-1	Howells, Sheringham
16/09/95	Sheffield Wednesday	A	3-1	Sheringham 2 (1p), og (Walker)
25/09/95	Queens Park Rangers	A	3-2	Sheringham 2 (1p), Dozzell
30/09/95	Wimbledon	H	3-1	Sheringham 2, og (Elkins)
14/10/95	Nottingham Forest	H	0-1	
22/10/95	Everton	A	1-1	Armstrong
29/10/95	Newcastle United	H	1-1	Armstrong
04/11/95	Coventry City	A	3-2	Fox, Sheringham, Howells
18/11/95	Arsenal	H	2-1	Sheringham, Armstrong
21/11/95	Middlesbrough	A	1-0	Armstrong
25/11/95	Chelsea	A	0-0	
02/12/95	Everton	H	0-0	
09/12/95	Queens Park Rangers	H	1-0	Sheringham
16/12/95	Wimbledon	A	1-0	Fox
23/12/95	Bolton Wanderers	H	2-2	Sheringham, Armstrong
26/12/95	Southampton	A	0-0	
30/12/95	Blackburn Rovers	A	1-2	Sheringham
01/01/96	Manchester United	H	4-1	Sheringham, Campbell, Armstrong 2
13/01/96	Manchester City	H	1-0	Armstrong
21/01/96	Aston Villa	A	1-2	Fox
03/02/96	Liverpool	A	0-0	
12/02/96	West Ham United	H	0-1	
24/02/96	Sheffield Wednesday	H	1-0	Armstrong
02/03/96	Southampton	H	1-0	Dozzell
16/03/96	Blackburn Rovers	H	2-3	Sheringham, Armstrong
20/03/96	Bolton Wanderers	A	3-2	Howells, Fox, Armstrong
24/03/96	Manchester United	A	0-1	
30/03/96	Coventry City	H	3-1	Sheringham, Fox 2
06/04/96	Nottingham Forest	A	1-2	Armstrong
08/04/96	Middlesbrough	H	1-1	Armstrong
15/04/96	Arsenal	A	0-0	
27/04/96	Chelsea	H	1-1	Armstrong
02/05/96	Leeds United	A	3-1	Armstrong, Anderton 2
05/05/96	Newcastle United	A	1-1	Dozzell

WEST HAM UNITED

CLUB DIRECTORY

West Ham United FC
Boleyn Ground
Green Street
Upton Park
London E13 9AZ
tel - (0181) 5482748
fax - (0181) 5482758
Year of Formation - 1895
Chairman - Terence Brown
Secretary - Richard Skirrow
Manager - Harry Redknapp
Stadium - Upton Park (25,985)

MAJOR HONOURS

Domestic Cup - (3) 1964, 1975, 1980.
European Cup-winners' Cup - (1) 1965.

APPEARANCES 95/96

	P	Ap	(s)	Gls
Martin ALLEN	M	3		1
Slaven BILIC (CRO)	D	13		
Ian BISHOP	M	35		1
Jeroen BOERE (HOL)	A		(1)	
Marco BOOGERS (HOL)	A		(4)	
Tim BREACKER	D	19	(3)	
Kenny BROWN	D	3		
Tony COTTEE	A	30	(3)	10
DANI (POR)	M	3	(7)	2
Julian DICKS	D	34		10
Iain DOWIE (NIR)	A	33		8
Ilie DUMITRESCU (ROM)	M	2	(1)	
Rio FERDINAND	D		(1)	
Neil FINN	G	1		
Dale GORDON	A		(1)	
John HARKES (USA)	M	6	(4)	
Michael HUGHES (NIR)	M	28		
Don HUTCHISON (SCO)	M	8	(4)	2
Frank LAMPARD	M		(2)	
Stan LAZARIDIS (AUS)	M	2	(2)	
Alvin MARTIN	D	10	(3)	
Ludek MIKLOSKO (TCH)	G	36		
John MONCUR	M	19	(1)	
Steve POTTS	D	34		
Marc RIEPER (DEN)	D	35	(1)	2
Keith ROWLAND (NIR)	D	19	(4)	
Les SEALEY	G	1	(1)	
Robbie SLATER (AUS)	M	16	(6)	2
Mark WATSON	A		(1)	
Adrian WHITBREAD	D		(2)	
Danny WILLIAMSON	M	28	(1)	4

LEAGUE RESULTS 1995/96

Date	Opponent	H/A	Score	Scorers
19/08/95	Leeds United	H	1-2	Williamson
23/08/95	Manchester United	A	1-2	og (Bruce)
26/08/95	Nottingham Forest	A	1-1	Allen
30/08/95	Tottenham Hotspur	H	1-1	Hutchison
11/09/95	Chelsea	H	1-3	Hutchison
16/09/95	Arsenal	A	0-1	
23/09/95	Everton	H	2-1	Dicks 2 (2p)
02/10/95	Southampton	A	0-0	
16/10/95	Wimbledon	A	1-0	Cottee
21/10/95	Blackburn Rovers	H	1-1	Dowie
28/10/95	Sheffield Wednesday	A	1-0	Dowie
04/11/95	Aston Villa	H	1-4	Dicks (p)
18/11/95	Bolton Wanderers	A	3-0	Bishop, Cottee, Williamson
22/11/95	Liverpool	H	0-0	
25/11/95	Queens Park Rangers	H	1-0	Cottee
02/12/95	Blackburn Rovers	A	2-4	Dicks (p), Slater
11/12/95	Everton	A	0-3	
16/12/95	Southampton	H	2-1	Cottee, Dowie
23/12/95	Middlesbrough	A	2-4	Cottee, Dicks
01/01/96	Manchester City	A	1-2	Dowie
13/01/96	Leeds United	A	0-2	
22/01/96	Manchester United	H	0-1	
31/01/96	Coventry City	H	3-2	Rieper, Cottee, Dowie
03/02/96	Nottingham Forest	H	1-0	Slater
12/02/96	Tottenham Hotspur	A	1-0	Dani
17/02/96	Chelsea	A	2-1	Dicks, Williamson
21/02/96	Newcastle United	H	2-0	Williamson, Cottee
24/02/96	Arsenal	H	0-1	
02/03/96	Coventry City	A	2-2	Cottee, Rieper
09/03/96	Middlesbrough	H	2-0	Dowie, Dicks (p)
18/03/96	Newcastle United	A	0-3	
23/03/96	Manchester City	H	4-2	Dowie 2, Dicks, Dani
06/04/96	Wimbledon	H	1-1	Dicks
08/04/96	Liverpool	A	0-2	
13/04/96	Bolton Wanderers	H	1-0	Cottee
17/04/96	Aston Villa	A	1-1	Cottee
27/04/96	Queens Park Rangers	A	0-3	
05/05/96	Sheffield Wednesday	H	1-1	Dicks

WIMBLEDON

CLUB DIRECTORY

Wimbledon FC
Selhurst Park
London SE25 6PY
tel - (0181) 7712233
fax - (0181) 7680640
Year of Formation - 1889
Chairman - S.G. Reed
Secretary - Steve Rooke
Manager - Joe Kinnear
Stadium - Selhurst Park (26,309)

MAJOR HONOURS
Domestic Cup - (1) 1988.

APPEARANCES 95/96

	P	Ap	(s)	Gls
Neil ARDLEY	M	4	(2)	
Dean BLACKWELL	D	8		
Gary BLISSETT	A		(4)	
Stewart CASTLEDINE	M	2	(2)	1
Andy CLARKE	M	9	(9)	2
Kenny CUNNINGHAM (IRL)	D	32	(1)	
Robbie EARLE	M	37		11
Efan EKOKU (NIG)	A	28	(3)	7
Gary ELKINS	D	7	(3)	
Jason EUELL	A	4	(5)	2
Peter FEAR	M	4		
Scott FITZGERALD	D	2	(2)	
Marcus GAYLE	M	21	(13)	5
Jon GOODMAN	A	9	(18)	6
Mick HARFORD	A	17	(4)	2
Paul HEALD	G	18		
Dean HOLDSWORTH	A	31	(2)	10
Vinnie JONES (WAL)	M	27	(4)	3
Alan KIMBLE	D	31		
Øyvind LEONHARDSEN (NOR)	M	28	(1)	4
Brian McALLISTER	D	2		
Andy PEARCE	D	6	(1)	
Chris PERRY	D	35	(2)	
Alan REEVES	D	21	(3)	1
Hans SEGERS (HOL)	G	3	(1)	
Justin SKINNER	D	1		
Neil SULLIVAN	G	16		
Steve TALBOYS	M	3	(2)	
Andy THORN	D	11	(3)	
Simon TRACEY	G	1		

LEAGUE RESULTS 1995/96

Date	Opponent		Score	Scorers
19/08/95	Bolton Wanderers	H	3-2	Ekoku, Earle, Holdsworth
23/08/95	Queens Park Rangers	A	3-0	Leonhardsen, Holdsworth, Goodman
26/08/95	Manchester United	A	1-3	Earle
30/08/95	Sheffield Wednesday	H	2-2	Goodman, Holdsworth (p)
09/09/95	Liverpool	H	1-0	Harford
16/09/95	Aston Villa	A	0-2	
23/09/95	Leeds United	H	2-4	Holdsworth, Reeves
30/09/95	Tottenham Hotspur	A	1-3	Earle
16/10/95	West Ham United	H	0-1	
21/10/95	Newcastle United	A	1-6	Gayle
28/10/95	Southampton	H	1-2	Euell
06/11/95	Nottingham Forest	A	1-4	Jones
18/11/95	Middlesbrough	H	0-0	
22/11/95	Manchester City	A	0-1	
25/11/95	Coventry City	A	3-3	Jones (p), Goodman, Leonhardsen
03/12/95	Newcastle United	H	3-3	Holdsworth 2, Ekoku
09/12/95	Leeds United	A	1-1	Leonhardsen
16/12/95	Tottenham Hotspur	H	0-1	
23/12/95	Blackburn Rovers	H	1-1	Earle
26/12/95	Chelsea	A	2-1	Earle, Ekoku
30/12/95	Arsenal	A	3-1	Earle 2, Holdsworth
01/01/96	Everton	H	2-3	Holdsworth, Ekoku
13/01/96	Bolton Wanderers	A	0-1	
20/01/96	Queens Park Rangers	H	2-1	Leonhardsen, Clarke
03/02/96	Manchester United	H	2-4	Gayle, Euell
10/02/96	Sheffield Wednesday	A	1-2	Gayle
24/02/96	Aston Villa	H	3-3	Goodman 2, Harford
02/03/96	Chelsea	H	1-1	og (Clarke)
13/03/96	Liverpool	A	2-2	Ekoku, Holdsworth
16/03/96	Arsenal	H	0-3	
23/03/96	Everton	A	4-2	Gayle, Castledine, Clarke, Goodman
30/03/96	Nottingham Forest	H	1-0	Holdsworth
06/04/96	West Ham United	A	1-1	Jones
08/04/96	Manchester City	H	3-0	Earle 2, Ekoku
13/04/96	Middlesbrough	A	2-1	Earle, Ekoku
17/04/96	Blackburn Rovers	A	2-3	Earle, Gayle
27/04/96	Coventry City	H	0-2	
05/05/96	Southampton	A	0-0	

PROMOTED CLUBS

SECOND DIVISION FINAL TABLE 95/96

		Pd	W	D	L	F	A	Pt	GD
1	**Sunderland**	**46**	**22**	**17**	**7**	**59**	**33**	**83**	**+26**
2	**Derby County**	**46**	**21**	**16**	**9**	**71**	**51**	**79**	**+20**
3	Crystal Palace	46	20	15	11	67	48	75	+19
4	Stoke City	46	20	13	13	60	49	73	+11
5	**Leicester City**	**46**	**19**	**14**	**13**	**66**	**60**	**71**	**+6**
6	Charlton Athletic	46	17	20	9	57	45	71	+12
7	Ipswich Town	46	19	12	15	79	69	69	+10
8	Huddersfield Town	46	17	12	17	61	58	63	+3
9	Sheffield United	46	16	14	16	57	54	62	+3
10	Barnsley	46	14	18	14	60	66	60	-6
11	West Bromwich Albion	46	16	12	18	60	68	60	-8
12	Port Vale	46	15	15	16	59	66	60	-7
13	Tranmere Rovers	46	14	17	15	64	60	59	+4
14	Southend United	46	15	14	17	52	61	59	-9
15	Birmingham City	46	15	13	18	61	64	58	-3
16	Norwich City	46	14	15	17	59	55	57	+4
17	Grimsby Town	46	14	14	18	55	69	56	-14
18	Oldham Athletic	46	14	14	18	54	50	56	+4
19	Reading	46	13	17	16	54	63	56	-9
20	Wolverhampton Wanderers	46	13	16	17	56	62	55	-6
21	Portsmouth	46	13	13	20	61	69	52	-8
22	Millwall	46	13	13	20	43	63	52	-20
23	Watford	46	10	18	18	62	70	48	-8
24	Luton Town	46	11	12	23	40	64	45	-24

N.B. Teams level on points are classified by the number of goals scored.

PROMOTION PLAY-OFFS

Charlton Athletic 1, Crystal Palace 2
Crystal Palace 1, Charlton Athletic 0
(Crystal Palace 3-1)

Leicester City 0, Stoke City 0
Stoke City 0, Leicester City 1
(Leicester City 1-0)

Leicester City 2, Crystal Palace 1 (aet)

CLUB DIRECTORY

Sunderland AFC
Roker Park Ground
Sunderland
Tyne and Wear
SR6 9SW
tel - (0191) 5140332
fax - (0191) 5145854
Year of Formation - 1879
Chairman - R.S. Murray
Secretary - Mark Blackbourne
Manager - Peter Reid
Stadium - Roker Park (22,657)

MAJOR HONOURS

League Championship - (6)
1892, 1893, 1895, 1902, 1913, 1936.
Domestic Cup - (2) 1937, 1973.

CLUB DIRECTORY

Derby County FC
Baseball Ground
Shaftesbury Crescent
Derby DE23 8NB
tel - (01332) 340105
fax - (01332) 360988
Year of Formation - 1884
Chairman - Lionel Pickering
Secretary - Keith Pearson
Manager - Jim Smith
Stadium - Baseball Ground (18,000)

MAJOR HONOURS

League Championship - (2) 1972, 1975.
Domestic Cup - (1) 1946.

CLUB DIRECTORY

Leicester City FC
City Stadium
Filbert Street
Leicester LE2 7FL
tel - (0116) 2555000/2854000
fax - (0116) 2470585
Chairman - Tom Smeaton
Chief Executive - Barrie Pierpoint
Manager - Mark McGhee; Martin O'Neill
Stadium - Filbert Street (22,517)

ESTONIA

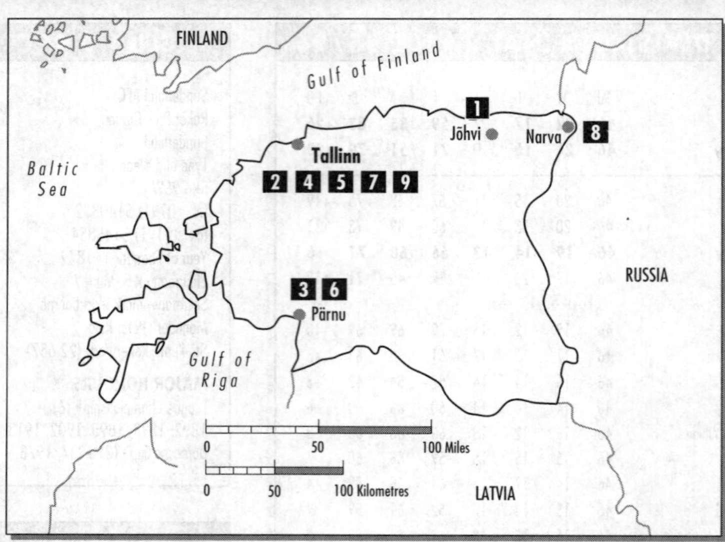

1	EP JÕHVI	339
2	FC FLORA TALLINN	340
3	JK/KALEV PÄRNU	341
4	FC LANTANA TALLINN	342
5	TALLINNA SADAM	343
6	TERVIS PÄRNU	344
7	FC TEVALTE-MARLEKOR TALLINN	345
8	TRANS NARVA	346
9	JK VALL TALLINN	347

FC LANTANA TAKE FIRST TITLE

Icelandic coach promises better times ahead

FEDERATION DIRECTORY

Eesti Jalgpalli Liit
Võidu 16, Tallinn EE 0012

tel - (6) 542715/6/7
fax - (6) 542719

Year of Formation - 1921
President - Peeter Küttis
Secretary - Ainar Leppänen

Stadium - Kadriorg (6,000)

The Estonian FA made a novel move in January 1996. They basically copied the actions of the country's leading club, FC Flora. The previous November, FC Flora had sacked their coach Roman Ubakivi, who also happened to be the coach of the Estonian national team, and replaced him with Teitur Thórdarson, an Icelander who had just a few months earlier knocked Flora out of the UEFA Cup as coach to Norwegian club Lillestrøm.

As Flora is the club which houses most of Estonia's international players, the Estonian FA asked Thórdarson if he would also do as Ubakivi did and coach the national team. He duly accepted, and a new era was about to begin.

Thórdarson immediately set about scrapping the old playing system used by his predecessor. Out went the sweeper formation. In came a four-man zonal defence. Training became much tougher, too. The disciplinarian Thórdarson adopted a much more professional approach than Ubakivi.

Some players did not take too kindly to the new régime. Regular internationals Indro Olumets, Tarma Linnumäe and Toomas Krõm were all kicked out of both the national squad and the FC Flora team for failing to toe the line.

Many Estonians considered that the new man was taking things too far in his determination to re-route the country's footballing destiny. But the national team's results told a different story.

Under Ubakivi, Estonia had gone from defeat to defeat. In Thórdarson's first seven games (including the Baltic tournament which Estonia hosted in July), there were five draws. Indeed, the 0-0 draw in Tallinn against Euro '96-bound Turkey was generally considered to be Estonia's best result for years. And, although there were no goals in that game, there were two against the Faroe Islands and one each against Latvia and Lithuania. Undoubtedly, Thórdarson was getting somewhere with his radical new methods.

At club level, however, the Icelander was unable to take Flora to a successful title defence. In fairness, the new coach had been left with a virtually impossible task.

INTERNATIONAL HONOURS

None

LEAGUE CHAMPIONSHIP RESULTS 95/96

AUTUMN (FIRST PHASE)

		1	2	3	4	5	6	7	8
1	EP Jõhvi		2-1	1-1	1-1	1-3	0-0	2-0	0-0
2	FC Flora Tallinn	2-2		5-0	1-5	3-0	7-0	2-1	0-1
3	JK/Kalev Pärnu	1-1	0-5		0-1	0-4	1-5	1-4	2-4
4	FC Lantana Tallinn	4-1	1-1	10-0		2-1	2-0	+++	1-0
5	Tallinna Sadam	0-0	2-2	7-1	0-2		0-1	1-0	1-0
6	Tervis Pärnu	0-2	2-6	5-0	2-4	1-2		3-1	2-2
7	FC Tevalte-Marlekor Tallinn	0-0	2-1	5-1	0-3	1-1	2-1		4-2
8	Trans Narva	4-0	1-1	4-0	1-1	2-1	0-3	1-0	

SPRING (FINAL ROUND)

		1	2	3	4	5	6
1	FC Flora Tallinn		0-0	1-0	2-0	0-1	0-1
2	FC Lantana Tallinn	0-1		3-4	3-0	2-0	4-2
3	Tallinna Sadam	0-0	0-3		2-5	1-3	3-2
4	Tervis Pärnu	1-5	0-3	0-5		+++	0-5
5	FC Tevalte-Marlekor Tallinn	0-4	0-3	2-0	2-0		2-0
6	Trans Narva	0-1	0-0	0-2	1-1	0-3	

+++ - match void; awarded as away win.

LEAGUE CHAMPIONSHIP FINAL TABLE 95/96

AUTUMN (FIRST PHASE)			Home					Away					Total						
		Pd	W	D	L	F	A	W	D	L	F	A	W	D	L	F	A	Pt	GD
1	FC Lantana Tallinn	14	5	1	1	20	3	5	2	0	17	5	10	3	1	37	8	33	+29
2	Trans Narva	14	4	2	1	13	6	2	2	3	9	10	6	4	4	22	16	22	+6
3	FC Flora Tallinn	14	4	1	2	20	9	2	3	2	17	10	6	4	4	37	19	22	+18
4	Tallinna Sadam	14	3	2	2	11	6	3	1	3	12	10	6	3	5	23	16	21	+7
5	FC Tevalte-Marlekor Tallinn	14	4	2	1	14	9	2	0	5	6	10	6	2	6	20	19	20	+1
6	Tervis Pärnu	14	2	1	4	15	17	3	1	3	10	12	5	2	7	25	29	17	-4
7	EP Jõhvi	14	2	4	1	7	6	1	4	2	6	11	3	8	3	13	17	17	-4
8	JK/Kalev Pärnu	14	0	1	6	5	24	0	1	6	3	37	0	2	12	8	61	2	-53

SPRING (FINAL ROUND)			Home					Away					Total						
		Pd	W	D	L	F	A	W	D	L	F	A	W	D	L	F	A	Pt	GD
1	FC Lantana Tallinn	10	3	0	2	12	7	3	2	0	9	0	6	2	2	21	7	37	+14 (17)
2	FC Flora Tallinn	10	2	1	2	3	2	4	1	0	11	1	6	2	2	14	3	31	+11 (11)
3	FC Tevalte-Marlekor Tallinn	10	3	0	2	6	7	4	0	1	7	3	7	0	3	13	10	31	+3 (10)
4	Tallinna Sadam	10	1	1	3	6	13	3	0	2	11	6	4	1	5	17	19	24	-2 (11)
5	Trans Narva	10	0	2	3	1	7	2	0	3	10	9	2	2	6	11	16	19	-5 (11)
6	Tervis Pärnu	10	0	0	5	1	18	1	1	3	6	10	1	1	8	7	28	13	-21 (9)

After 14 matches the top six play off for the title, taking half their points total (shown above in brackets). Half points are rounded upwards. The bottom two enter a promotion/relegation play-off with the top four from the Second Division.

When he arrived Flora were already some distance behind leaders FC Lantana. There was an 11-point gap at the end of the autumn season, and when the championship resumed in April for the play-offs Flora still had six points to make up in just ten games.

It was too much to ask. Flora's title hopes had been undone by three successive defeats at the end of the first phase, the most important of them being a 5-1 thrashing at home by Lantana on September 21 - the first time an Estonian league match had been played under floodlights.

Lantana were imperious during the autumn. The previous season's runners-up, coached by Anatoli Belov, closed the first part of the campaign with a big lead and what would have been an unbeaten record had it not been for a forfeited defeat by Tevalte-Marlekor after they were found guilty of fielding an ineligible player in their 2-0 win.

It was not the club's first offence. Three days before that Lantana were also deprived of a 2-1 victory over Latvian side DAG-Liepaya in the European Cup-winners' Cup after they had fielded midfield dynamo Andrei Borissov.

DOMESTIC CUP RESULTS

1/8 FINALS

Baltika Narva 0, EP Jõhvi 4
Devia Tallinn 0, FC Lantana Tallinn 9
Kompanii Märjamaa 0, Tallinna Sadam 11
Merkuur Tartu 0, Trans Narva 3
JK Dünamo Tallinn 0, Tervis Pärnu 2
Kalev Sillamäe 0, FC Flora Tallinn 6
Veteran Kohtla-Järve 2, JK/Kalev Pärnu 0
Kiviõli JK 2, FC Tevalte-Marlekor Tallinn 8

QUARTER-FINALS

Tervis Pärnu v FC Tevalte-Marlekor Tallinn 0-0; 0-2
(FC Tevalte-Marlekor Tallinn 2-0)
Tallinna Sadam v FC Flora Tallinn 2-0; 0-0
(Tallinna Sadam 2-0)
Trans Narva v FC Lantana Tallinn 0-2; 0-1
(FC Lantana Tallinn 3-0)
EP Jõhvi v Veteran Kohtla-Järve 3-0; 3-3
(EP Jõhvi 6-3)

SEMI-FINALS

FC Lantana Tallinn v Tallinna Sadam 0-1; 0-0
(Tallinna Sadam 1-0)
FC Tevalte-Marlekor Tallinn v EP Jõhvi 1-0; 0-2
(EP Jõhvi 2-1)

FINAL

21/06/96, Tallinn
TALLINA SADAM 2 Terehhov (27), Krõlov (60)
EP JÕHVI 0
referee - Timofejev
TALLINNA SADAM - Pareiko; Svets (Sarapik 88), Urjupin, Liivamaa, Rõtskov, Krõlov, Terehhov, Kaal, Ustritski, Kolbassenko, Slesarcuk (Pustov 89).
EP JÕHVI - Rjabstun; Voronin, Januskevits P., Sarajev, Varunov, Afanasjev, Braiko (Sõselov 46), Titov, Gromov, Kulikov, Melnikov.

Had they done their homework, they would have discovered that the player still had two matches to serve of a suspension dating back from a sending-off when he played for Norma Tallinn.

Still on the disciplinary front, Lantana were dealt a blow in the long mid-winter break when their right-back Igor Bahmatski was handed a two-and-a-half-year ban by the Estonian FA after assaulting a referee in an indoor event.

But Lantana had enough strength in depth to withstand all these off-field dramas. They could even afford to lose two matches in the spring, the first being at home to challengers Flora, and still romp home with the same six-point advantage they had enjoyed at the start of the play-offs.

Lantana owed their triumph to a strong defence and an inventive midfield. At the back the two key figures were ex-international captain Urmas Hepner and another former Estonian international Igor Prins. The midfield comprised the skilful Russian, Andrei Lapuskin, plus two more ethnic Russians, one-time prolific goalgetter Sergei Bragin and the best player in the country, Andrei Borissov. Up front the team's top scorer was Maksim Gruznov, but his 12-goal total could have been a lot higher had he shown a better goalscorer's instinct.

The top marksman of the campaign was Flora's Lembit Rajala. Elsewhere in the Flora team, neither Olumets nor Martin Reim lived up to expectations in midfield, but the new-look four-man defence was well marshalled by captain Marek Lemsalu, and in teenage brothers Meelis and Urmas Rooba, Flora looked to have found two real prospects for the future.

NATIONAL TEAM APPEARANCES 95/96

Coach - Roman UBAKIVI; Teitur THÓRDARSON	LIT	CRO	LIT	AZB	CYP	FAR	ISL	TUR	Cps	Gls
Mart POOM (03/02/72) - Portsmouth (ENG)/FC Flora Tallinn	G	G	G	G	G	G	G	G	39	-
Marek LEMSALU (24/11/72) - FC Flora Tallinn	D	D		D	D	D	D	D	31	-
Urmas KIRS (05/11/66) - FC Flora Tallinn	D	M		M90	M80	M	M	M	26	-
Janek KIISMAN (03/01/77) - FC Flora Tallinn	D46	D43							7	
Alari LELL (10/06/76) - FC Flora Tallinn	D	s43	D46						6	-
Risto KALLASTE (10/03/71) - Viborg FF (DEN)	M	M	M					M	36	-
Meelis LINDMAA (14/10/70) - FC Flora Tallinn	M	M76	M	D	D	D	D	D	24	-
Martin LEPA (28/10/76) - FC Flora Tallinn	M	D46	D46						5	-
Martin REIM (14/05/71) - FC Flora Tallinn	M	M	s46				M	M	36	5
Ivan O'KONNEL-BRONIN (10/02/73) - Tervis Pärnu	A73								3	
Marko KRISTAL (02/06/73) - FC Flora Tallinn	A	A	s46 /79	A72	A	M	A	M	41	1
Arvo KRAAM (23/02/71) - Tervis Pärnu	s46								3	-
Gert OLESK (08/08/73) - Tervis Pärnu	s73		D						7	-
Toomas KALLASTE (27/01/71) - FC Flora Tallinn		D	D	M	M	M	s58	D	37	-
Lembit RAJALA (01/12/70) - FC Flora Tallinn		A	A	s72	s55	A75	A	s90	24	2
Tarmo LINNUMÄE (11/11/71) - FC Flora Tallinn		s46	M	M	M55	s75	M58		29	-
Indro OLUMETS (10/04/71) - FC Flora Tallinn		s76		M	M	M	M		32	2
Indrek ZELINSKI (13/11/74) - Tervis Pärnu/FC Flora Tallinn			D	D	D	D	D79		10	-
Andres OPER (07/11/77) - FC Flora Tallinn			A					A90	4	-
Toomas KRÕM (22/09/71) - FC Flora Tallinn			s79	A	A	A	s79		11	-
Sergei HOHLOV-SIMSON (22/04/72) - FC Flora Tallinn				D	D	D	D	D	8	-
Argo ARBEITER (05/12/73) - Tervis Pärnu				s90	s80				6	-
Viktor ALONEN (23/03/69) - FC Flora Tallinn								M84	19	-
Liivo LEETMA (20/01/77) - Tervis Pärnu								s84	1	-

EUROPEAN CUPS RESULTS 95/96

CUP-WINNERS' CUP

● FC LANTANA TALLINN

Preliminary round DAG-LIEPAYA (LAT)

A 2-1 Lapsa (17), Borissov (75) (later awarded as 0-3)
Ussoltsev; Krasnopjorov, Bahmatski, Prins, Lebret, Hepner, Bragin (Tsurilkin 86), Lapsa, Borissov, Lapuskin, Leontjev (Gruznov 42; Nalivaiko 84).

H 0-0
Ussoltsev; Krasnopjorov, Bahmatski, Prins, Lebret, Hepner, Bragin, Lapsa, Gruznov (Gorjatsov 37), Lapuskin, Leontjev (Nalivaiko 66).

UEFA CUP

● FC FLORA TALLINN

Preliminary round LILLESTRØM SK (NOR)

A 0-4
Tohver; Lemsalu, Kirs, Kiisman, Lell, Alonen (Olumets 22; Oper 66), Lindmaa, Rajala, Korgalidze (Kristal 55), Reim, Jagmurjan.

H 1-0 Korgalidze (54)
Tohver; Lemsalu, Kirs, Kallaste, Kiisman (Lell 46), Lepa (Rajala 46), Lindmaa, Korgalidze, Kristal, Reim, Jagmurjan (Oper 76).

Another gifted youngster who made his name during the season was Tallinna Sadam goalkeeper Sergei Pareiko, who could soon challenge Mart Poom for the national team jersey. Pareiko did not concede a single goal throughout Sadam's triumphant run in the Estonian Cup.

Their victims in the final were EP Jõhvi, who were belatedly denied a place in the spring play-offs after the FA initially bungled over the criteria for qualification, but who returned to the top flight, along with newly-promoted JK Vall, at the end of the season.

PLAYERS OF THE SEASON

ANDREI BORISSOV

FC Lantana midfielder Andrei Borissov made headlines for all the wrong reasons at the start of the season when he played and scored his team's winning goal in the European Cup-winners' Cup tie against DAG-Liepaya...and then realised that he had not been eligible to play. But throughout the rest of the 95/96 league campaign Lantana were very pleased to have their gifted schemer on the pitch. He was the most attractive talent in the championship - a goalscorer, a dead-ball expert and an all-round free spirit in the Lantana midfield. Borissov's refusal to take out Estonian citizienship (despite his Estonian wife) precludes a selection for the Estonian national team. Thus deprived of international football, the 27-year-old needs to move to a foreign club if his talents are not to go to waste.

MAREK LEMSALU

The leader of the new-look Flora Tallinn and Estonia national team defence is 23-year-old Marek Lemsalu. A tall and powerful centre-back, he has been appointed skipper of both teams by coach Teitur Thórdarson. Apart from his leadership qualities, Lemsalu is strong in the air, shoots accurately from long distance and likes to break away at speed from defence, which can often catch opposing teams unawares. The player's progress over the past two seasons has been noted in Europe. Kaiserslautern and Manchester City both showed an interest in him before a contract was eventually signed with German Second Division side FSV Mainz.

TOP SCORERS

16	Lembit RAJALA (FC Flora Tallinn)
12	Maksim GRUZNOV (FC Lantana Tallinn)
8	Ivan O'KONNEL-BRONIN (Tervis Pärnu/ FC Flora Tallinn)
	Andrei BORISSOV (FC Lantana Tallinn)
	Aleksandr OLERSKI (FC Tevalte-Marlekor Tallinn)
	Boris NEJOLOV (Trans Narva)
	Dmitri USTRITSKI (Tallinna Sadam)
7	Olegas BOBRICKIS (FC Lantana Tallinn)
	Andrei LAPUSKIN (FC Lantana Tallinn)
	Sergei BRAGIN (FC Lantana Tallinn)

NATIONAL TEAM RESULTS 95/96

16/08/95	Lithuania (ECQ)	H	Tallinn	0-1	
03/09/95	Croatia (ECQ)	A	Zagreb	1-7	Reim (17)
11/10/95	Lithuania (ECQ)	A	Vilnius	0-5	
16/02/96	Azerbaijan	N	Larnaca	0-0	
20/02/96	Cyprus	A	Limassol	0-1	
24/02/96	Faroe Islands	N	Pyla	2-2	Kristal (13), Rajala (45)
24/04/96	Iceland	H	Tallinn	0-3	
29/05/96	Turkey	H	Tallinn	0-0	

EP JÕHVI

CLUB DIRECTORY

Jalgpalliklubi Eesti Põlevkivi Jõhvi
Jaama 10
Jõhvi EE 2045
tel - (33) 64427
fax - (33) 70054
Year of Formation - 1974
President - Väino Viilup
Secretary - Rudolf Varunov
Coach - Pavel Lukyanov
Stadium - Eesti Põlevkivi (2,000)

APPEARANCES 95/96

	P	Ap	(s)	Gls
Sergei AFANASJEV (RUS)	A	13		5
Juri BRAIKO	A	14		1
Andrei FROLOV	A	3	(9)	
Aleksandr GROMOV	M	9		1
Pjotr JANUSKEVITS	M	5	(1)	
Vladimir KULIKOV	M	13		1
Sergei MELNIKOV	M	9	(2)	1
Aleksandr RJABTSUN	G	14		
Eduard SARAJEV	M	14		
Nikolai SÕSELOV	M	9	(1)	
Aslan TEDTOV (RUS)	M	1		
Vladimir TIHHON	A		(4)	
German TITOV (RUS)	D	13		
Igor TSERKASSOV	M	7	(6)	1
Artur VARUNOV	A	7		
Vitali VASTSENKO	D		(11)	
Aleksandr VERGIN	D	12		1
Dmitri VORONIN	D	11		1

LEAGUE RESULTS 1995/96

16/07/95	JK/Kalev Pärnu	A	1-1	Afanasjev
19/07/95	Trans Narva	H	0-0	
23/07/95	FC Tevalte-Marlekor Tallinn	H	2-0	Melnikov, Tserkassov
26/07/95	Tervis Pärnu	A	2-0	Afanasjev, Kulikov
30/07/95	FC Flora Tallinn	A	2-2	Afanasjev 2
03/08/95	FC Lantana Tallinn	H	1-1	Gromov
11/08/95	Tallinna Sadam	H	1-3	Voronin
29/08/95	JK/Kalev Pärnu	H	1-1	Vergin
08/09/95	Trans Narva	A	0-4	
17/09/95	FC Tevalte-Marlekor Tallinn	A	0-0	
21/09/95	Tervis Pärnu	H	0-0	
01/10/95	FC Flora Tallinn	H	2-1	Braiko, Afanasjev
05/10/95	FC Lantana Tallinn	A	1-4	og (Hepner)
15/10/95	Tallinna Sadam	A	0-0	

FC FLORA TALLINN

CLUB DIRECTORY

Football Club Flora Tallinn
A. Kapi 9
Tallinn EE 0031
tel - (2) 451706/450875
fax - (2) 451706
Year of Formation - 1990
President - Aivar Pohlak
Secretary - Tõnu Kõiv
Coach - Roman Ubakivi; Teitur Thórdarson
Stadium - Kadriorg (6,000)

MAJOR HONOURS
League Championship - (2) 1994, 1995.
Domestic Cup - (1) 1995.

APPEARANCES 95/96

	P	Ap	(s)	Gls
Viktor ALONEN	D	3	(2)	
Algimantas BRIAUNYS (LIT)	G	3		
Marius DOVYDENAS (LIT)	M		(1)	
Sergei HOHLOV-SIMSON	D	10		
Vahe JAGMURJAN (ARM)	A	9	(2)	6
Toomas KALLASTE	D	18	(1)	2
Janek KIISMAN	D	10		
Urmas KIRS	M	15	(1)	3
Otar KORGALIDZE (GEO)	M	8		3
Marko KRISTAL	A	16	(5)	5
Toomas KRÕM	A	4	(5)	2
Alari LELL	D	4	(6)	
Marko LELOV	M	1	(2)	
Marek LEMSALU	D	24		3
Martin LEPA	D	3	(3)	
Meelis LINDMAA	M	17	(4)	2
Tarmo LIINUMÄE	M	12	(6)	2
Darius MAGDISAUSKAS (LIT)	D	6	(1)	
Remigijus MIKOCIONIS (LIT)	G	2		
Ivan O'KONNEL-BRONIN	A	1	(1)	
Indro OLUMETS	M	13	(5)	1
Andres OPER	A	6	(3)	2
Mati PARI	M	2	(2)	
Mart POOM	G	7		
Aivar PRIIDEL	M	2	(3)	
Lembit RAJALA	A	18	(2)	16
Martin REIM	A	23	(1)	2
Urmas ROOBA	D	5	(2)	
Toomas TOHVER	G	10		
Vahur VAHTRAMÄE	M	1		
Rain VESSENBERG	G	1		
Indrek ZELINSKI	A	9		1

LEAGUE RESULTS 1995/96

16/07/95	FC Tevalte-Marlekor Tallinn	A	1-2	Olumets
19/07/95	Tallinna Sadam	H	3-0	Lindmaa, Kristal, Kirs
23/07/95	Tervis Pärnu	H	7-0	Oper 2, Kristal 2, Reim, Jagmurjan, Rajala
26/07/95	FC Lantana Tallinn	A	1-1	Jagmurjan
30/07/95	EP Jõhvi	H	2-1	Lindmaa, Rajala
03/08/95	Trans Narva	A	1-1	Rajala
26/08/95	JK/Kalev Pärnu	A	5-0	Jagmurjan, Rajala, Lemsalu, Reim, Kallaste
29/08/95	FC Tevalte-Marlekor Tallinn	H	2-1	Jagmurjan, Korgalidze
08/09/95	Tallinna Sadam	A	2-2	Rajala, Korgalidze
17/09/95	Tervis Pärnu	A	6-2	Kirs 2, Jagmurjan 2, Rajala 2
21/09/95	FC Lantana Tallinn	H	1-5	Linnumäe
01/10/95	EP Jõhvi	A	1-2	Rajala
05/10/95	Trans Narva	H	0-1	
15/10/95	JK/Kalev Pärnu	H	5-0	Rajala 3, Korgalidze, Vahtramäe
PLAY-OFFS				
18/04/96	Tallinna Sadam	H	1-0	Lemsalu
27/04/96	Tervis Pärnu	A	5-1	Rajala 3, Kristal, Krõm
04/05/96	Trans Narva	H	0-1	
12/05/96	FC Tevalte-Marlekor Tallinn	H	0-1	
19/05/96	FC Lantana Tallinn	A	1-0	Lemsalu
23/05/96	Tallinna Sadam	A	0-0	
02/06/96	Tervis Pärnu	H	2-0	Linnumäe, Krõm
08/06/96	Trans Narva	A	1-0	Zelinski
12/06/96	FC Tevalte-Marlekor Tallinn	A	4-0	Rajala 2, Kallaste, Kristal
17/06/96	FC Lantana Tallinn	H	0-0	

JK/KALEV PÄRNU

CLUB DIRECTORY

Jalgpalliklubi Kalev Pärnu
Mai 59
Pärnu EE 3600
tel - (44) 24741
fax - (44) 24741
Year of Formation - 1989
President - Helmut Hunt
Coach - Ants Kommussaar
Stadium - Kalev (2,500)

APPEARANCES 95/96

	P	Ap	(s)	Gls
Teet ALLAS	M	13		2
Andrei DIVONIN	A	2	(8)	1
Vladimir DOLININ	D	13		1
Kalvi KAAS	A	7	(1)	
Andres KÕIV	D	13		
Erki KOMMUSSAAR	A	2	(2)	1
Marko LAPP	D	11	(1)	
Raino LAPP	M	13		
Tõnu MEETUA	G	9		
Kalev MITT	M	14		
Oleg MJASOJEDDOV	D	5	(5)	1
Kalev MOPPEL	G	5	(3)	
Heigo NIGULA	A	13		1
Raio PIIROJA	M	2	(6)	1
Rein RIISALU	M	14		
Risto TALV	D	13		
Seppo VILDERSON	A	5		

LEAGUE RESULTS 1995/96

16/07/95	EP Jõhvi	H	1-1	Dolinin
19/07/95	FC Lantana Tallinn	H	0-1	
23/07/95	Tallinna Sadam	A	1-7	Kommussaar
26/07/95	Trans Narva	H	2-4	Allas, Piiroja
30/07/95	Tervis Pärnu	A	0-5	
03/08/95	FC Tevalte-Marlekor Tallinn	A	1-5	Allas
26/08/95	FC Flora Tallinn	H	0-5	
29/08/95	EP Jõhvi	A	1-1	Nigula
08/09/95	FC Lantana Tallinn	A	0-10	
17/09/95	Tallinna Sadam	H	0-4	
21/09/95	Trans Narva	A	0-4	
01/10/95	Tervis Pärnu	H	1-5	Divonin
04/10/95	FC Tevalte-Marlekor Tallinn	H	1-4	Mjasojedov
15/10/95	FC Flora Tallinn	A	0-5	

FC LANTANA TALLINN

CLUB DIRECTORY

Football Club Lantana Tallinn
Kaupmehe 4-28
Tallinn EE 0001
tel - (2) 445549
fax - (2) 443738
Year of Formation - 1995
President - Sergei Olivson
Secretary - Juri Tsurilkin
Coach - Anatoli Belov
Stadium - Viimsi (3,000)

MAJOR HONOURS
League Championship - (1) 1996.
Domestic Cup - (1) 1993.

APPEARANCES 95/96

	P	Ap	(s)	Gls
Andrei AFANASOV	A		(9)	
Igor BAHMATSKI	D	8		
Olegas BOBRICKIS (LIT)	A	12	(1)	5
Andrei BORISSOV	M	21		8
Sergei BRAGIN	M	18		7
Oleg GORJATSOV	M	10	(7)	2
Maksim GRUZNOV	A	22		12
Urmas HEPNER	D	20		4
Oleg KOLOTSEI (RUS)	D		(3)	
Andrei KRASNOPJOROV	D	23		2
Andris LAPSA (LAT)	D	11		1
Andrei LAPUSKIN (RUS)	M	20		7
Juri LEBRET	A	23		1
Sergei LEONTJEV	A	4		1
Andrei MITJUNOV	D	3	(3)	
Dmitri NALIVAIKO (LAT)	A	5	(12)	6
Igor PRINS	D	22		
Stanislav SVETOGOR	A	2	(9)	
Artur SKETOV (LAT)	M	3		
Ain TAMMUS	G	5	(1)	
Andrei TJUNIN	M		(2)	
Juri TSURILKIN	D	3	(1)	1
Sergei USSOLTSEV	G	18	(1)	
Eduard USTINOV	M		(1)	

LEAGUE RESULTS 1995/96

19/07/95	JK/Kalev Pärnu	A	1-0	Gruznov
23/07/95	Trans Narva	A	1-1	Gruznov
26/07/95	FC Flora Tallinn	H	1-1	Gruznov
29/07/95	Tallinna Sadam	A	2-0	Bobrickis, Borissov
03/08/95	EP Jõhvi	A	1-1	Hepner
13/08/95	FC Tevalte-Marlekor Tallinn	H	0-0	(awarded as an away win)
19/08/95	Tervis Pärnu	H	2-0	Leontjev, Nalivaiko
28/08/95	Tervis Pärnu	A	4-2	Bragin 2, Lapuskin, Hepner
08/09/95	JK/Kalev Pärnu	H	10-0	Nalivaiko 4, Lapuskin 2, Bragin 2, Borissov, Gruznov
17/09/95	Trans Narva	H	1-0	Gruznov
21/09/95	FC Flora Tallinn	A	5-1	Borissov 3, Krasnopjorov, og (Tohver)
01/10/95	Tallinna Sadam	H	2-1	Lapsa, Lapuskin
05/10/95	EP Jõhvi	H	4-1	Gruznov 2, Nalivaiko, Borissov
15/10/95	FC Tevalte-Marlekor Tallinn	A	3-0	Lapuskin, Borissov, Bragin
PLAY-OFFS				
27/04/96	Trans Narva	A	0-0	
01/05/96	Tervis Pärnu	H	3-0	Hepner, Bragin, Gruznov
05/05/96	FC Tevalte-Marlekor Tallinn	A	3-0	Gruznov 2, Hepner
12/05/96	Tallinna Sadam	A	3-0	Bobrickis, Tsurikin, Bragin
19/05/96	FC Flora Tallinn	H	0-1	
24/05/96	Tervis Pärnu	A	3-0	Lebret, Gorjatsov, Bobrickis
01/06/96	Trans Narva	H	4-2	Lapuskin, Bobrickis, Borissov, Gorjatsov
06/06/96	FC Tevalte-Marlekor Tallinn	H	2-0	Gruznov, Lapuskin
11/06/96	Tallinna Sadam	H	3-4	Gruznov, Krasnopjorov, Bobrickis
17/06/96	FC Flora Tallinn	A	0-0	

TALLINNA SADAM

CLUB DIRECTORY

Tallinna Sadama Jalgpalliklubi
Sadama Str. 21
Tallinn EE 0100
tel - (6) 318374/318102
fax - (6) 318101
Year of Formation - 1992
President - Joel Tammeka
Secretary - Ivo Laino
Coach - Valeri Bondarenko; Uno Piir
Stadium - Kalev (12,000)

MAJOR HONOURS
Domestic Cup - (1) 1996.

APPEARANCES 95/96

	P	Ap	(s)	Gls
Vadim DOLININ	M,	6		1
Einars GNEDOI (LAT)	D	6	(3)	
Urmas KAAL	M	17	(1)	
Ain KARUTOOM	G	3		
Pavel KAZAKOV	D	2	(1)	
Paul KIRSIPUU	M	3	(1)	
Aleksei KLISIN (KAZ)	M	9		1
Konstantin KOLBASSENKO	M	20	(3)	5
Valentin KOMAROV	D	2		
Andrei KRÕLOV	D	17	(1)	3
Juri KUHTA	D		(2)	
Urmas LIIVAMAA	D	19		
Sergei MAKAROV	D	5	(4)	
Ernest MARTINSONS	G	4	(1)	
Sergei PAREIKO	G	17		
Aleksandr PUSTOV	A	15	(5)	4
Maksim RÕTSKOV	M	15	(6)	3
Risto SARAPIK	D	13	(1)	
Igor SLESARCUK (LAT)	A	8	(1)	1
Artur SKETOV (LAT)	M	14		1
Mark SVETS	M	13	(6)	6
Sergei TEREHHOV	M	17	(5)	6
Vladimir URJUPIN	D	19	(1)	
Dmitri USTRITSKI	A	19	(4)	8
Kristen VIIKMÄE	A	1	(2)	

LEAGUE RESULTS 1995/96

16/07/95	Trans Narva	A	1-2	Dolinin
19/07/95	FC Flora Tallinn	A	0-3	
23/07/95	JK/Kalev Pärnu	H	7-1	Svets 3, Kolbassenko 2, Terehhov, Klisin
26/07/95	FC Tevalte-Marlekor Tallinn	A	1-1	Terehhov
29/07/95	FC Lantana Tallinn	H	0-2	
03/08/95	Tervis Pärnu	H	0-1	
11/08/95	EP Jõhvi	A	3-1	Terehhov 2, Rõtskov
27/08/95	Trans Narva	H	1-0	Pustov
08/09/95	FC Flora Tallinn	H	2-2	Krõlov, Pustov
17/09/95	JK/Kalev Pärnu	A	4-0	Ustritski 2, Terehhov, Sketov
21/09/95	FC Tevalte-Marlekor Tallinn	H	1-0	Pustov
01/10/95	FC Lantana Tallinn	A	1-2	Ustritski
05/10/95	Tervis Pärnu	A	2-1	Pustov, Svets
15/10/95	EP Jõhvi	H	0-0	
PLAY-OFFS				
18/04/96	FC Flora Tallinn	A	0-1	
28/04/96	FC Tevalte-Marlekor Tallinn	A	0-2	
05/05/96	Tervis Pärnu	A	5-0	Ustritski 2, og (Rooba M.), Slesarchuk, Terehhov
12/05/96	FC Lantana Tallinn	H	0-3	
19/05/96	Trans Narva	A	2-0	Krõlov, Svets
23/05/96	FC Flora Tallinn	H	0-0	
01/06/96	FC Tevalte-Marlekor Tallinn	H	1-3	Ustritski
07/06/96	Tervis Pärnu	H	2-5	Krõlov, Kolbassenko
11/06/96	FC Lantana Tallinn	A	4-3	Ustritski 2, Kolbassenko 2
17/06/96	Trans Narva	H	3-2	Svets, Rõtskov 2

TERVIS PÄRNU

CLUB DIRECTORY

Tervis Pärnu (now - Lelle SK)
A. Kapi 9
Tallinn EE 0031
tel - (2) 451706/450875
fax - (2) 451706
Year of Formation - 1990
President - Aivar Pohlak
Secretary - Tõnu Kõiv
Coach - Sergei Ratnikov
Stadium - Kehtna Football School (1,500)

APPEARANCES 95/96

	P	Ap	(s)	Gls
Viktor ALONEN	M	7		1
Andre ANIS	M		(2)	
Argo ARBEITER	A	12	(1)	4
Andrius BORODULINAS (LIT)	M		(3)	
Vidas DANCENKA (LIT)	M	5		2
Marius DOVYDENAS (LIT)	M	2	(6)	2
Sergei HOHLOV-SIMSON	D	11	(1)	
Martin KAALMA	G	16	(1)	
Tõnis KALDE	A	6	(6)	
Janek KIISMAN	D	9		
Arvo KRAAM	D	12		
Liivo LEETMA	M	14	(3)	
Alari LELL	D	8		
Marko LELOV	M	7	(5)	1
Martin LEPA	D	3		
Janek MEET	D	18		
Raivo NÕMMIK	D	13	(2)	
Ivan O'KONNEL-BRONIN	A	14	(1)	8
Gert OLESK	D	14		2
Viktoras OLSANSKIS (LIT)	M	5		2
Andres OPER	A	8	(1)	3
Jan ÕUN	A	1	(1)	
Meelis ROOBA	M	19	(3)	1
Urmas ROOBA	D		(3)	
Tarmo SAKS	A	12	(8)	2
Dalius STALELIUNAS (LIT)	D	5	(1)	
Vahur VAHTRAMÄE	M	9		
Atko VÄIKMERI	D	1	(3)	
Rolandas VAINEIKIS (LIT)	A	5		3
Rain VESSENBERG	G	3	(3)	
Indrek ZELINSKI	M	10		
Vaidas ZUTAUTAS (LIT)	G	4		

LEAGUE RESULTS 1995/96

Date	Opponent	H/A	Score	Scorers
19/07/95	FC Tevalte-Marlekor Tallinn	A	1-2	O'Konnel-Bronin
23/07/95	FC Flora Tallinn	A	0-7	
26/07/95	EP Jõhvi	H	0-2	
30/07/95	JK/Kalev Pärnu	H	5-0	O'Konnel-Bronin, Saks, Olsanskis, Rooba M., Arbeiter
03/08/95	Tallinna Sadam	A	1-0	og (Kuhta)
11/08/95	Trans Narva	H	2-2	O'Konnel-Bronin, Olsanskis
19/08/95	FC Lantana Tallinn	A	0-2	
28/08/95	FC Lantana Tallinn	H	2-4	Arbeiter 2
08/09/95	FC Tevalte-Marlekor Tallinn	H	3-1	O'Konnel-Bronin, Vaineikis, Dancenka
17/09/95	FC Flora Tallinn	H	2-6	O'Konnel-Bronin, Olesk
21/09/95	EP Jõhvi	A	0-0	
01/10/95	JK/Kalev Pärnu	A	5-1	Dancenka, Arbeiter, O'Konnel-Bronin, Vaineikis, Lelov
05/10/95	Tallinna Sadam	H	1-2	Vaineikis
15/10/95	Trans Narva	A	3-0	Olesk, O'Konnel-Bronin 2
PLAY-OFFS				
27/04/96	FC Flora Tallinn	H	1-5	Dovydenas
01/05/96	FC Lantana Tallinn	A	0-3	
05/05/96	Tallinna Sadam	H	0-5	
11/05/96	Trans Narva	H	0-5	
19/05/96	FC Tevalte-Marlekor Tallinn	A	0-2	
24/05/96	FC Lantana Tallinn	H	0-3	
02/06/96	FC Flora Tallinn	A	0-2	
07/06/96	Tallinna Sadam	A	5-2	Oper 3, Dovydenas, Saks
11/06/96	Trans Narva	A	1-1	Alonen
17/06/96	FC Tevalte-Marlekor Tallinn	H	0-0	(awarded as away win)

FC TEVALTE-MARLEKOR TALLINN

CLUB DIRECTORY

Football Club Tevalte-Marlekor Tallinn
Pärnu mnt. 69-238
Tallinn EE 0001
tel - (6) 261616
fax - (6) 261622
Year of Formation - 1995
President - Peeter Sedin
Secretary - Vambola Tammiksaar
Coach - Vjatseslav Smirnov
Stadium - Kalev (12,000)

APPEARANCES 95/96

	P	Ap	(s)	Gls
Igor ANDREJEV	M	12		
Oleg ANDREJEV	G	22		
Andrei BELOHVOSTOV	D	5	(7)	
Olegas BOBRICKIS (LIT)	A	2		2
Jevgeni IVANOV	D	18	(4)	
Valeri JAKOVLEV (GEO)	M	4		
Denis JERSOV	M	1	(5)	
Aleksei KAPUSTIN	D	16	(1)	1
Paul KIRSIPUU	M	3		
Dmitri KURKA	A	2		
Sergei LEONTJEV	A	8		4
Viktor LOBANOV (RUS)	M		(1)	
Nikolai MIZEROV	M	1	(5)	
Anatoli NOVOZILOV	A	16		6
Aleksandr OLERSKI	A	17	(1)	8
Anton PAITSEV	A		(1)	
Viktor PASIKUTA	M	17	(5)	2
Arvidas RUKSENAS	M	12	(6)	2
Dmitri SKIPERSKI (RUS)	M	19	(1)	1
Maksim SMIRNOV	M		(1)	
Vjatseslav SMIRNOV	D	5	(1)	
Dalius STALELIUNAS (LIT)	D	7	(1)	
Andrei STEPANOV	D		(1)	
Andrei SAPOVALOV	M	9		1
Erik STEINBERG	A	1		
Aivar TRUBERG	A	3		
Eduard VINOGRADOV	D	21		
Juri VOLKOV	D	9		1
Aleksandr ZURKJIN	A	12		5

LEAGUE RESULTS 1995/96

16/07/95	FC Flora Tallinn	H	2-1	Olerski, Pasikuta
19/07/95	Tervis Pärnu	H	2-1	Novozilov 2
23/07/95	EP Jõhvi	A	0-2	
26/07/95	Tallinna Sadam	H	1-1	Novozilov
30/07/95	Trans Narva	A	0-1	
03/08/95	JK/Kalev Pärnu	H	5-1	Olerski 3, Ruksenas, Novozilov
13/08/95	FC Lantana Tallinn	A	0-0	(awarded as away win)
29/08/95	FC Flora Tallinn	A	1-2	Bobrickis
08/09/95	Tervis Pärnu	A	1-3	Bobrickis
17/09/95	EP Jõhvi	H	0-0	
21/09/95	Tallinna Sadam	A	0-1	
01/10/95	Trans Narva	H	4-2	Novozilov, Kapustin, Zurkin, Pasikuta
04/10/95	JK/Kalev Pärnu	A	4-1	Zurkin 2, Ruksenas, Olerski
15/10/95	FC Lantana Tallinn	H	0-3	
PLAY-OFFS				
20/04/96	Trans Narva	A	3-0	Volkov, Leontjev, Zurkin
28/04/96	Tallinna Sadam	H	2-0	Olerski, Leontjev
05/05/96	FC Lantana Tallinn	H	0-3	
12/05/96	FC Flora Tallinn	A	1-0	Sapovalov
19/05/96	Tervis Pärnu	H	2-0	Leontjev, Novozilov
25/05/96	Trans Narva	H	2-0	Zurkin, Leontjev
01/06/96	Tallinna Sadam	A	3-1	Olerski 2, Skiperski
06/06/96	FC Lantana Tallinn	A	0-2	
12/06/96	FC Flora Tallinn	H	0-4	
17/06/96	Tervis Pärnu	A	0-0	(awarded as away win)

TRANS NARVA

CLUB DIRECTORY

Jalgpalliklubi Trans Narva
Kangelaste 45-20
Narva EE 2000
tel - (35) 43696/43975
fax - (35) 44284
Year of Formation - 1979
President - Nikolai Burdakov
Coach - Nikolai Burdakov; Juri Salamov
Stadium - Kreenholm (2,000)

APPEARANCES 95/96

	P	Ap	(s)	Gls
Vitali BELÕI (RUS)	D	16	(1)	
Konstantin GOLITSÕN	A	11	(8)	3
Aleksandr IVARINEN	D		(2)	
Konstantin JAKUSEV	M		(3)	
Andrei JELISEJEV	D	7	(5)	
Konstantin KARIN	M	13	(8)	2
Vjatseslav KARIN	M	14	(1)	2
Sergei KAZAKOV	M		(1)	
Stanislav KITTO	D	21	(1)	3
Mihhail KOROTAJEV (RUS)	D	22		1
Oleg KUROTSKIN	D	18		1
Oleg KUROTSKIN (same player)	G	1		
Aleksandr MARASOV	M	19		1
Remigijus MIKOCIONIS (LIT)	G	8		
Boris NEJOLOV	A	21		8
Levani PARTSHIDZE	G		(2)	
Sergei SEREDNITSKI	D	4	(2)	
Aleksandr TARASSENKOV	M		(1)	
Nikolai TOSTSEV	M	20		4
Vladimir TROFIMOV	G	15		
Viktor VJALOV	D	24		3
Aleksandr VOLZINSKI	M		(1)	
Sergei ZAMORSKI	M	22		4
Azat ZIJAZOV (RUS)	M	8	(4)	

LEAGUE RESULTS 1995/96

16/07/95	Tallinna Sadam	H	2-1	Zamorski, Kitto
19/07/95	EP Jõhvi	A	0-0	
23/07/95	FC Lantana Tallinn	H	1-1	Vjalov
26/07/95	JK/Kalev Pärnu	A	4-2	Nejolov 2, Vjalov, Kitto
30/07/95	FC Tevalte-Marlekor Tallinn	H	1-0	Vjalov
03/08/95	FC Flora Tallinn	H	1-1	Kurotskin
11/08/95	Tervis Pärnu	A	2-2	Nejolov, Marasov
27/08/95	Tallinna Sadam	A	0-1	
08/09/95	EP Jõhvi	H	4-0	Karin V. 2, Nejolov, Tostsev
17/09/95	FC Lantana Tallinn	A	0-1	
21/09/95	JK/Kalev Pärnu	H	4-0	Nejolov, Zamorski, Tostsev, Korotajev
01/10/95	FC Tevalte-Marlekor Tallinn	A	2-4	Zamorski, Karin K.
05/10/95	FC Flora Tallinn	A	1-0	Tostsev
15/10/95	Tervis Pärnu	H	0-3	
PLAY-OFFS				
20/04/96	FC Tevalte-Marlekor Tallinn	H	0-3	
27/04/96	FC Lantana Tallinn	H	0-0	
04/05/96	FC Flora Tallinn	A	1-0	og (Hohlov-Simson)
11/05/96	Tervis Pärnu	A	5-0	Golitsõn 3, Karin K., Nejolov
19/05/96	Tallinna Sadam	H	0-2	
25/05/96	FC Tevalte-Marlekor Tallinn	A	0-2	
01/06/96	FC Lantana Tallinn	A	2-4	Tostsev, Nejolov
08/06/96	FC Flora Tallinn	H	0-1	
11/06/96	Tervis Pärnu	H	1-1	Kitto
17/06/96	Tallinna Sadam	A	2-3	Zamorski, Nejolov

PROMOTED CLUB

SECOND DIVISION FINAL TABLE 95/96

AUTUMN (FIRST PHASE)

		Pd	W	D	L	F	A	Pt	GD
1	FC Norma Tallinn	14	13	0	1	59	5	39	+54
2	JK Vall Tallinn	14	9	1	4	36	20	28	+16
3	Tallinna Jalgpallikool	14	7	1	6	19	30	22	-11
4	JK Dünamo Tallinn	14	7	1	6	35	30	22	+5
5	FC Lelle	14	6	2	6	32	30	20	+2
6	JK Tulevik Viljandi	14	6	0	8	28	34	18	-6
7	FC Arsenal Tallinn	14	5	0	9	26	31	15	-5
8	DAG Tartu	14	0	1	13	12	67	1	-55

PROMOTION/RELEGATION PLAY-OFF GROUP (SPRING)

		Pd	W	D	L	F	A	Pt	GD
1	EP Jõhvi	10	7	0	3	23	7	21	+16
2	**JK Vall Tallinn**	**10**	**7**	**0**	**3**	**18**	**9**	**21**	**+9**
3	FC Norma Tallinn	10	5	2	3	13	11	17	+2
4	Pärnu JK	10	4	2	4	12	20	14	-8
5	JK Dünamo Tallinn	10	2	2	6	8	14	8	-6
6	Tallinna Jalgpallikool	10	1	2	7	9	22	5	-13

CLUB DIRECTORY

Jalgpalliklubi Vall Tallinn
Wismari 15 A
Tallinn EE 0001
tel - (2) 439406
fax - (2) 439306
Year of Formation - 1993
President - Mati Kebina
Coach - Aivar Tiidus
(96/97 - Ants Kommussaar)

FAROE ISLANDS

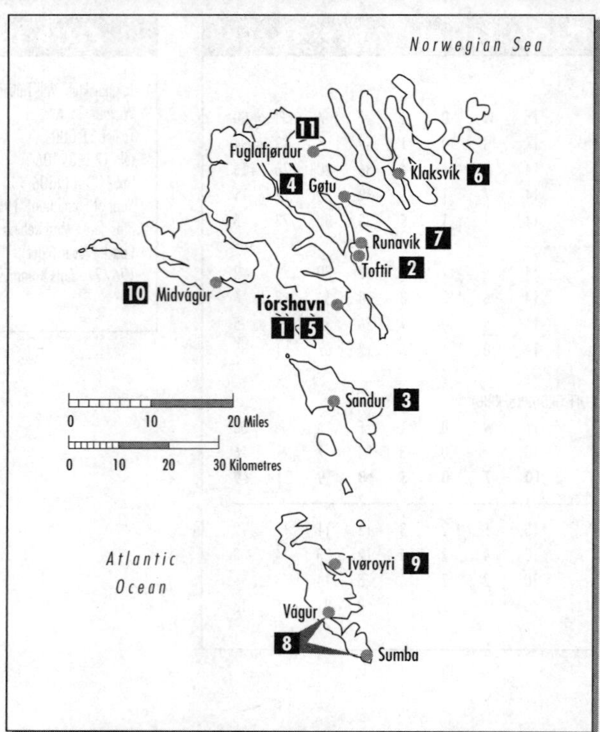

1	B 36	352
2	B 68	353
3	B 71	354
4	GÍ	355
5	HB	356
6	KÍ	357
7	NSÍ	358
8	SUMBA/VB	359
9	TB	360
10	FS VÁGAR	361
11	ÍF	362

JONSSON HAT-TRICK IN SAN MARINO

Gí fightback brings third title in a row

FEDERATION DIRECTORY

Fotboltssamband Føroya
Postboks 3028, FR-110 Tórshavn

tel - 16707	Year of Formation - 1979
tlx - 81332 itrott fa	President - Torleif Sigurdsson
fax - 19079	Secretary - Julian Eliasen

Stadium - Svangaskard, Toftir (6,000)

For the third season running GÍ from Gotu recovered from a poor start to storm home to the Faroe Isles First Division title. Victories in each of their last seven matches maintained a trend which they had set in both 1993 and 1994.

Perhaps HB, from Thorshavn, the other leading club on the islands, sensed that GÍ would produce one of their customary late-season bursts. Because they gave themselves a good head start in the early rounds of the campaign, winning six and drawing three of their first nine matches to build up a five-point lead over the defending champions at the halfway stage.

But the gap was not wide enough. In the head-to-head fixture in Gotu at the beginning of September GÍ grabbed all three points, the winning goal coming from the previous season's top scorer John Petersen, who had returned to the club in July after an unsatisfactory spell in the Danish Third Division. That victory closed the gap to two points. A fortnight later, when HB could only draw 1-1 away to lowly Sumba/VB, the two teams were level. And a week after that, GÍ were in front for the first time, thrashing KÍ 6-1 while HB went down 0-2 to B71.

The momentum was with GÍ, and the team led by national Under-18 coach Johan Nielsen duly made sure of a title hat-trick with a 2-0 away win against B36 in their penultimate match. Curiously, the match was decided by a pair of own-goals, one of them from goalkeeper Høgnesen, the other from international defender Tummas Eli Hansen.

HB's 0-2 defeat away to KÍ gave them the runners-up spot for the third year in succession. Once again, they had been overrun in the second half of the season

LEAGUE CHAMPIONSHIP RESULTS 1995

		1	2	3	4	5	6	7	8	9	10
1	B36		0-4	3-1	0-2	0-5	2-1	1-0	1-2	1-0	3-2
2	B68	2-0		1-1	1-1	1-2	2-1	4-1	3-0	1-2	5-0
3	B71	1-2	2-1		2-3	2-0	1-4	2-1	5-1	2-1	2-0
4	GÍ	2-0	0-2	3-2		2-1	5-1	5-1	3-0	2-0	2-1
5	HB	5-1	3-1	1-0	0-0		5-0	0-0	2-0	4-1	0-0
6	KÍ	2-2	4-3	1-3	1-6	2-0		2-1	1-2	2-2	0-0
7	NSÍ	1-2	0-5	0-2	0-1	0-0	1-2		0-3	2-3	1-2
8	Sumba/VB	1-2	2-1	2-6	0-2	1-1	1-2	1-3		4-1	2-2
9	TB	3-2	1-1	2-0	1-0	0-0	2-2	0-1	2-0		1-2
10	FS Vágar	1-1	1-5	1-1	3-2	3-5	5-3	2-0	2-4	3-1	

NATIONAL TEAM RESULTS 95/96

02/07/95	Iceland	A	Neskaupstadur	0-2	
06/09/95	Russia (ECQ)	H	Toftir	2-5	Jarnskor H. (12), Jonsson (55)
11/10/95	San Marino (ECQ)	A	Serravalle	3-1	Jonsson (42, 44, 59)
15/11/95	Greece (ECQ)	A	Iraklion	0-5	
24/02/96	Estonia	A	Pyla	2-2	Johannesen O. (30), Jarnskor H. (45)
24/04/96	Yugoslavia (WCQ)	A	Belgrade	1-3	Petersen (53)

TOP SCORERS

24	Suni Fridi JOHANNESEN (B68)
11	Jan Allan MÜLLER (Sumba/VB)
10	Eli HENTZE (B71)
	Magni JARNSKOR (GÍ)
	Kurt MØRKØRE (B68/KÍ)
9	Torbjørn JENSEN (B71)
8	Sigfridur CLEMENTSEN (HB)
	Olgar DANIELSEN (KÍ)
7	Kristjan a REYNATROD (B36)
	Henning JARNSKOR (GÍ)
	Uni ARGE (HB)

LEAGUE CHAMPIONSHIP FINAL TABLE 1995

			Home					Away					Total						
		Pd	W	D	L	F	A	W	D	L	F	A	W	D	L	F	A	Pt	GD
1	GÍ	18	8	0	1	24	8	5	2	2	17	8	13	2	3	41	16	41	+25
2	HB	18	6	3	0	20	3	3	3	3	14	11	9	6	3	34	14	33	+20
3	B68	18	5	2	2	20	8	4	1	4	23	13	9	3	6	43	21	30	+22
4	B71	18	6	0	3	19	13	3	2	4	16	14	9	2	7	35	27	29	+8
5	B36	18	5	0	4	11	17	3	2	4	12	18	8	2	8	23	35	26	-12
6	FS Vágar	18	4	2	3	21	22	2	3	4	9	16	6	5	7	30	38	23	-8
7	TB	18	4	3	2	12	8	2	1	6	11	21	6	4	8	23	29	22	-6
8	KÍ	18	3	3	3	15	19	3	1	5	16	24	6	4	8	31	43	22	-12
9	Sumba/VB	18	2	2	5	14	20	4	0	5	12	19	6	2	10	26	39	20	-13
10	NSÍ	18	0	1	8	5	20	2	1	6	8	17	2	2	14	13	37	8	-24

by GÍ. Fortunately for them, the Faroe Islands Cup was staged in the first half of the campaign, when HB were still stringing victories together. A new format to the competition, with the first phase being played in groups, favoured the top teams, and HB took advantage by reaching the final, against the team that would eventually finish third in the league, B68 from Toftir. A crowd of approximately 1,100 watched the game, staged in HB's own Gundadalur stadium, and the local side won comfortably, 3-1, taking the trophy for a record 24th time and booking themselves a place in Europe one year hence.

There was another success for HB at the end of the season when the club's reserve team won the Second Division. They could not be

DOMESTIC CUP RESULTS

1/8 FINALS
(Played in Groups)
Final Positions - top two teams qualify for quarter-finals
Group A - 1. NSÍ, 2. B71, 3. ÍF, 4. Fram
Group B - 1. HB, 2. Sumba/VB, 3. B36, 4. Skansin
Group C - 1. GÍ, 2. B68, 3. EB/Streymur, 4. LÍF
Group D - 1. KÍ, 2. TB, 3. FS Vágar, 4. SÍ

QUARTER-FINALS
B71 1, HB 2
B68 3, NSÍ 2
KÍ 2, Sumba/VB 1
TB 1, GÍ 0

SEMI-FINALS
KÍ v B68 0-3; 2-0 (B68 3-2)
TB v HB 2-1; 0-4 (HB 5-2)

FINAL
16/08/95, Torshavn
HB 3 Nolsø R. (24), Hansen A.F. (43), Samuelsen (75)
B68 1 Højgaard (76)
referee - Kjaerbo
HB - Johannesen; Johnsson, Lag, Dam Ja., Hansen A.F., Dam Jo. (Jakobsen 89), Arge, Nolsø R., Reynheim, Mohr (Hentze 85), Clementsen (Samuelsen 63).
B68 - Magnussen; Djurhuus, Jacobsen E., Olsen E. (Didriksen 68), Johannesen Si., Zachariassen (Petersen 46), Hansen A., Olsen J.E. (Højgaard 72), Hansen Ø., Johannesen S.F., Mørkøre.

INTERNATIONAL HONOURS

None

EUROPEAN CUPS RESULTS 95/96

CUP-WINNERS' CUP

● KÍ

Preliminary round MACCABI HAIFA (ISR)

A 0-4
Joensen Jo.; Poulsen, Joensen Ar., Andreasen, Høgnesen (Baldvinsson 65), Jacobsen, Danielsen (Steig 85), Joensen Ja., Mørkøre A., Hansen, Bertholdsen.

H 3-2 Danielsen (54, 65, 72)
Steig; Poulsen, Joensen Al., Bertholdsen, Andreassen, Hansen, Joensen Ja., Mørkøre A. (Eliasen 88), Høgnesen, Lutzen (Danielsen 46), Lakjuni He. (Joensen Ar. 46).

UEFA CUP

● GÍ

Preliminary round RAITH ROVERS (SCO)

A 0-4
Knudsen; Justinussen R. (Mikkelsen 86), Rasmussen, Justinussen S.P., Justinussen A., Jarnskor H., Olsen, Ennigard (Heinason 78), Jarnskor P. (Tvorfoss 72), Jarnskor M., Petersen.

H 2-2 Jarnskor H. (77), Jarnskor M. (87)
Knudsen; Justinussen R., Rasmussen, Justinussen S.P., Justinussen A., Jarnskor H., Olsen (Heinason 88), Jarnskor P. (Ennigard 12), Tvorfoss, Jarnskor M., Petersen.

PLAYERS OF THE SEASON

SUNI FRIDI JOHANNESEN

23-year-old B68 striker Suni Fridi Johannesen set a new record in 1995, netting 24 league goals to beat the previous mark set 12 months earlier bi GÍ's John Petersen. He needed eight goals in his last four games to do it, taking the record with a four-goal burst against his former club NSÍ in B68's penultimate match. Remarkably, Johannessen had only scored five goals the previous season, but his 1995 'explosion' earned him a first call up for the national team (against Iceland) and some keen interest from a couple of Danish Second Division clubs.

ALLAN MØRKØRE

He is still only 24, but KÍ midfielder Allan Mørkøre is one of the veterans in the Faroe Islands national team. He earned his 30th cap in the team's impressive opening World Cup performance away to Yugoslavia in Belgrade. A strong, agile midfielder, he is also powerful in the air and is frequently used in the centre of defence. His club KÍ had a poor season in the league in 1995, and that was primarily because of a knee injury which kept their star player out of action early in the season. He was back, however, for KÍ's historic 3-2 win over Maccabi Haifa in the European Cup-winners' Cup - the first victory ever for a Faroe Islands team in European club competition.

promoted, so the one automatic promotion spot went to runners-up ÍF. For the first time play-offs were introduced between the ninth-placed team in Division One and what, theoretically, should have been the second-placed in Division Two. Because of HB reserves' ineligibility for promotion, it was in fact the third-placed team, EB/Streymur, who had the honour of facing another recently-merged club, VB/Sumba. But there was no contest. Sumba/VB won the first leg 8-0, and that was that.

On the international front, there were a couple of satisfying results in European club competition and signs of improvement by Allan Simonsen's national team. Two hat-trick heroes made the biggest headlines. KÍ's Olgar Danielsen scored all three goals in his team's 3-2 victory over Maccabi Haifa in the Cup-winners' Cup. And Danish-based striker Todi Jonsson did likewise as the Faroe Islands completed a European Championship 'double' with a 3-1 victory over San Marino in Serravalle.

NATIONAL TEAM APPEARANCES 95/96

Coach - Allan SIMONSEN	ISL	RUS	SMR	GRE	EST	YUG	Cps	Gls
Jakup MIKKELSEN (14/08/70) - Herfølge BK (DEN)	G			G			2	-
Oli JOHANNESEN (06/05/72) - TB/B36	D	D		D	D	D	20	1
Janus RASMUSSEN (02/06/65) - GÍ	D	D	D		s66		10	-
Jens Christian HANSEN (03/09/71) - B36	D46	D	D	D	D66	D	12	1
Djoni N. JOENSEN (1972) - NSÍ	D						4	-
Tummas Eli HANSEN (11/02/66) - B36	M	M81		M			30	-
Øssur HANSEN (07/01/71) - B68	M	M	M81	M90	M		19	-
Harley BERTHOLDSEN (10/03/69) - KÍ	M78		s88	s90			3	-
Jan Allan MÜLLER (25/07/69) - AC Horsens (DEN)/ Sumba/VB/Esbjerg FB (DEN)	A	A72	A	A83	A	A	26	2
Suni Fridi JOHANNESEN (20/10/72) - B68	A63						1	-
Jens Erik RASMUSSEN (02/06/68) - TB/FS Vágar	A	s72			A72	M75	26	11
Henning JARNSKOR (15/11/72) - GÍ	s46	D	D88	D	D	D	13	2
Heri OLSEN (21/04/63) - FS Vágar	s63						3	-
Eydfinn DAVIDSEN (19/01/66) - FS Vágar	s78						3	-
Jens Martin KNUDSEN (11/06/67) - GÍ		G	G		G	G	45	-
Kurt MØRKØRE (20/02/69) - SIF (NOR)/KÍ		M			M		36	6
Julian JOHNSSON (24/02/75) - HB/B36		M		s55	s72	M	7	1
Todi JONSSON (02/02/72) - Lyngby FC (DEN)		A	A75				22	5
Allan JOENSEN (03/01/74) - KÍ		s81					4	-
Andreas F. HANSEN (1966) - HB			D			D	2	-
Jan DAM (07/09/68) - HB/Ølstykke FC (DEN)			D	D	D	D	34	3
Allan MØRKØRE (22/11/71) - KÍ			M	M	M	M	30	1
Magni JARNSKOR (16/11/68) - GÍ			M	M	M72	s75	28	1
John PETERSEN (1972) - GÍ			s75	s83		M	3	1
Kari REYNHEIM (15/02/64) - HB			s81	M55			47	5
Uni ARGE (21/01/71) - HB					s72		7	1

B 36

CLUB DIRECTORY

Boltfelagid 36 (B 36)
Postrum 1136
110 Tórshavn
tel - 11936
fax - 18036
Year of Formation - 1936
President - Kristjan A. Neystabo
Secretary - Gunnar Reynslag
Coach - Wieczek Zakrewski
Stadium - Gundadalur (8,000)

MAJOR HONOURS

League Championship - (5)
1936, 1948, 1950, 1959, 1962.
Domestic Cup - (1) 1991.

APPEARANCES 95

	P	Ap	(s)	Gls
Ken BAERENDSEN	D	3		
Zacharias BECH	D	2		
Sofus CLEMENTSEN	D	9	(2)	
Kari GULFOSS	M		(1)	
Jan GUTTESEN	M	5		
Joannes GUTTESEN	D	9	(1)	
Jakup W. HANSEN	A	11	(7)	3
Jens Christian HANSEN	M	17		3
Tummas Eli HANSEN	D	18		
John HARDLEY	A	4	(1)	
Hans Jakup HEINESEN	D	4	(2)	
Egin HØGNESEN	G	18		
Agnar HØJGAARD	D	16	(1)	
Sonni i INNISTOVU	A	1	(3)	
Danjal Petur JOHANSEN	D	3	(3)	
Hans Jakup JOHANSEN	M	8	(1)	
Magni a LAKJUNI	A	7		3
Finn MORK	M		(1)	
Jakup MORK	M	12	(1)	3
Gunnar NIELSEN	A	16	(2)	4
Kristjan a REYNATROD	M	14	(2)	7
Ronnie SAMUELSEN	M		(1)	
Rögvi THÓRSTEINSSON (ISL)	D	15		
Bogi VANG	D	6	(1)	

LEAGUE RESULTS 1995

14/05/95	HB	A	1-5	Hansen J.C. (p)
21/05/95	B71	H	3-1	Hansen J.C., Hansen J.W., Lakjuni
28/05/95	TB	A	2-3	Mork J., Nielsen
03/06/95	KÍ	H	2-1	Reynatrod, Nielsen
11/06/95	NSÍ	A	2-1	Lakjuni, Reynatrod
18/06/95	Sumba/VB	A	2-1	Reynatrod, Lakjuni
25/06/95	FS Vágar	H	3-2	Hansen J.C., Nielsen, Hansen J.W.
25/06/95	GÍ	A	0-2	
13/08/95	B68	H	0-4	
20/08/95	HB	H	0-5	
27/08/95	B71	A	2-1	Mork J., Reynatrod
02/09/95	TB	H	1-0	Reynatrod
10/09/95	KÍ	A	2-2	Reynatrod (p), Nielsen
17/09/95	NSÍ	H	1-0	Mork J.
24/09/95	Sumba/VB	H	1-2	Hansen J.W.
01/10/95	FS Vágar	A	1-1	Reynatrod
07/10/95	GÍ	H	0-2	
15/10/95	B68	A	0-2	

B 68

CLUB DIRECTORY

Tofta Ítrottarfelag B 68
650 Toftir
tel - 48068
fax - 49050
Year of Formation - 1962
President - Niclas Davidsen
Secretary - Janus Jensen
Coach - Petur Mohr
Stadium - Svangaskard (6,000)

MAJOR HONOURS

League Championship - (3) 1984, 1985, 1992.

APPEARANCES 95

	P	Ap	(s)	Gls
Frodi BENJAMINSEN	M	6	(1)	
Arnbjørn DANIELSEN	D	8	(3)	1
Johannes DANIELSEN	D	5		
Pall DIDRIKSEN	A	3	(2)	1
Jackup DJURHUUS	D	16		2
Abraham HANSEN	D	7	(1)	
Øssur HANSEN	M	18		4
Steinar HANSEN	D		(1)	
Aksel HØJGAARD	A	4	(8)	2
Edmund JACOBSEN	D	12	(1)	1
Øssur JACOBSEN	D	1	(4)	
Oleif JOENSEN	D	13	(3)	
Signar JOHANNESEN	M	12	(2)	
Suni Fridi JOHANNESEN	A	17		24
Olaf MAGNUSSEN	G	16		
Kurt MØRKØRE	M	8		7
Kjartan NESA	G	2		
Eydfinn OLSEN	M	17		1
Jakup Eli OLSEN	M	11	(1)	
Jan PETERSEN	D	12	(1)	
George POULSEN	D		(1)	
Finnbjørn ZACHARIASSEN	A	10	(7)	

LEAGUE RESULTS 1995

14/05/95	FS Vágar	H	5-0	Mørkøre 2, Johannesen S.F. 3
21/05/95	GÍ	A	2-0	Johannesen S.F. 2 (1p)
28/05/95	Sumba/VB	H	3-0	Mørkøre 2, Johannesen S.F.
03/06/95	HB	H	1-2	Mørkøre
11/06/95	B71	A	1-2	Johannesen S.F.
18/06/95	TB	H	1-2	Johannesen S.F.
25/06/95	KÍ	A	3-4	Djurhuus 2, Johannesen S.F.
06/08/95	NSÍ	H	4-1	Hansen Ø. 2, Højgaard 2
13/08/95	B36	A	4-0	Johannesen S.F. 3, Hansen Ø.
20/08/95	FS Vágar	A	5-1	Mørkøre 2, Johannesen S.F. 3
27/08/95	GÍ	H	1-1	Johannesen S.F. (p)
02/09/95	Sumba/VB	A	1-2	Jacobsen E.
10/09/95	HB	A	1-3	Hansen Ø.
17/09/95	B71	H	1-1	Olsen E.
24/09/95	TB	A	1-1	Johannesen S.F.
01/10/95	KÍ	H	2-1	Danielsen A., Johannesen S.F.
07/10/95	NSÍ	A	5-0	Johannesen S.F. 4, Didriksen
15/10/95	B36	H	2-0	Johannesen S.F. 2

B 71

CLUB DIRECTORY

Sandoyar Ítrottarfelag B 71
210 Sandur
tel - 61584
Year of Formation - 1970
President - Karl Vidfeldt
Secretary - Eli Hentze
Coach - Piotr Krakowski
Stadium - Sandur (2,000)

MAJOR HONOURS
League Championship - (1) 1989.
Domestic Cup - (1) 1983.

APPEARANCES 95

	P	Ap	(s)	Gls
Jonsvein BAERENTSEN	D		(1)	
Eydfinn CLEMENTSEN	M		(3)	
Eli HENTZE	A	17		10
Frankie JENSEN	D	2	(2)	
Tornbjørn JENSEN	A	17		9
Jakup JOENSEN	D		(1)	
Niclas JOENSEN	D	14	(1)	
Piotr KRAKOWSKI (POL)	M	6		1
Bjarki MOHR	D	18		1
Waldemar NOWICKI (POL)	G	18		
Ib Mohr OLSEN	M	17		2
Sorin OLSEN	D		(1)	
Jogvan Jon PETERSEN	M	4	(3)	
Pall a REYNATUGVU	M	16		4
Brandur SANDOY	A		(1)	
John SØRENSEN	D	11		
Kari SØRENSEN	D	3	(3)	1
Runi i SOYLU	D	18		
Jonsvein THOMSEN	A	2		
Julian THOMSEN	M	17	(1)	2
Mourits VIDERO	D		(1)	
Mrazek VIERZBICKI (POL)	M	18		4

LEAGUE RESULTS 1995

14/05/95	NSÍ	H	2-1	Vierzbicki, Hentze
21/05/95	B36	A	1-3	Hentze
28/05/95	FS Vágar	H	2-0	Hentze 2
03/06/95	GÍ	A	2-3	Vierzbicki, Hentze
11/09/95	B68	H	2-1	Hentze 2
18/06/95	HB	A	0-1	
25/06/95	Sumba/VB	H	5-1	Jensen T. 3, Hentze, Thomsen Ju.
06/08/95	TB	H	2-1	Jensen T. 2
13/08/95	KÍ	A	3-1	og (Bertholdsen), Jensen T. 2
20/08/95	NSÍ	A	2-0	Jensen T., Reynatugvu
27/08/95	B36	H	1-2	Vierzbicki (p)
02/09/95	FS Vágar	A	1-1	Thomsen Ju.
10/09/95	GÍ	H	2-3	Jensen T., Reynatugvu
17/09/95	B68	A	1-1	Olsen I.M.
24/09/95	HB	H	2-0	Olsen I.M., Mohr
01/10/95	Sumba/VB	A	6-2	Sørensen K., Reynatugvu 2, Hentze 2, Vierzbicki
07/10/95	TB	A	0-2	
15/10/95	KÍ	H	1-4	Krakowski

GÍ

CLUB DIRECTORY

Gotu Ítrottarfelag (GÍ)
510 Gotu
tel - 41022
fax - 41029
Year of Formation - 1926
President - Haldgrim Gregersen
Secretary - Magnus Gothe
Coach - Johan Nielsen
Stadium - Gotu (3,000)

MAJOR HONOURS
League Championship - (5)
1983, 1986, 1993, 1994, 1995.
Domestic Cup - (2) 1983, 1985.

APPEARANCES 95

	P	Ap	(s)	Gls
Pol ENNIGARD	D	12	(6)	
Ronnie HANSEN	A		(3)	
Heini HEINASON	A	3	(4)	
Jan JACOBSEN	M		(2)	
Henning JARNSKOR	D	18		7
Magni JARNSKOR	M	15	(2)	10
Pauli JARNSKOR	M	18		3
Samal JOENSEN	M	1	(4)	1
Sunvard JOENSEN	G	1		
Alvi JUSTINUSSEN	D	18		
Runi JUSTINUSSEN	D	17		2
Simun Petur JUSTINUSSEN	D	17		6
Jens Martin KNUDSEN	G	17		
Petur Pall MIKKELSEN	M	6	(1)	
Joan Petur OLSEN	M	17	(1)	4
John PETERSEN	A	12		4
Janus RASMUSSEN	D	17		
Erland TVORFOSS	M	9	(2)	2

LEAGUE RESULTS 1995

14/05/95	Sumba/VB	H	3-0	Jarnskor M. 2, Justinussen R.
21/05/95	B68	H	0-2	
28/05/95	HB	A	0-0	
03/06/95	B71	H	3-2	Jarnskor H. 2, Jarnskor P.
11/06/95	TB	A	0-1	
18/06/95	KÍ	H	5-1	Justinussen S.P. 2 (1p), Jarnskor P. (p), Jarnskor H. 2
25/06/95	NSÍ	A	1-0	Olsen
06/08/95	B36	H	2-0	Jarnskor M. 2
13/08/95	FS Vágar	A	2-3	Petersen, Jarnskor P. (p)
20/08/95	Sumba/VB	A	2-0	Jarnskor M., Olsen
27/08/95	B68	A	1-1	Tvorfoss
02/09/95	HB	H	2-1	Olsen, Petersen
10/09/95	B71	A	3-2	Justinussen S.P. 2, Jarnskor H.
17/09/95	TB	H	2-0	Joensen Sa., Jarnskor M.
24/09/95	KÍ	A	6-1	Jarnskor M., Jarnskor H. 2, Olsen, Tvorfoss, Justinussen R.
01/10/95	NSÍ	H	5-1	Jarnskor M. 2, Justinussen S.P., Petersen 2
07/10/95	B36	A	2-0	og (Høgnesen), og (Hansen T.E.)
15/10/95	FS Vágar	H	2-1	Justinussen S.P. (p), Jarnskor M.

HB

CLUB DIRECTORY

Havnar Boltfelag (HB)
Postrum 1333
110 Tórshavn
tel - 14046/17898
fax - 18502
Year of Formation - 1904
President - Sigrun Mikkelsen
Secretary - Oddmar Orvarodd
Coach - Joannes Jakobsen
Stadium - Gundadalur (8,000)

MAJOR HONOURS
League Championship - (14) 1955, 1960, 1963, 1964, 1965, 1971, 1973, 1974, 1975, 1978, 1981, 1982, 1988, 1990.
Domestic Cup - (24) 1955, 1957, 1959, 1962, 1963, 1964, 1968, 1969, 1971, 1972, 1973, 1975, 1976, 1978, 1979, 1980, 1981, 1982, 1984, 1987, 1988, 1989, 1992, 1995.

APPEARANCES 95

	P	Ap	(s)	Gls
Uni ARGE	A	13		7
Hans Petur i BREKKUNUM	M	1	(1)	
Sigfridur CLEMENTSEN	A	7	(9)	8
Jon DAHL	D	6		
Jan DAM	D	12		2
John Heri DAM	A	11	(2)	1
Hallur DANIELSEN	M	5		
Andreas F. HANSEN	D	17		1
Hogni HANSEN	D	2	(2)	1
Samal Erik HENTZE	M	10	(1)	1
Joannes JAKOBSEN	D	9		
Eydun JENSEN	M	1	(2)	
Kaj Leo JOHANNESEN	G	18		
Julian JOHNSSON	M	11	(1)	
Hans a LAG	D	8	(1)	2
Gunnar MOHR	A	16	(1)	5
Bjartur NOLSØ	D	6	(2)	
Runi NOLSØ	M	18		2
Regin REINERT	M	2		
Kari REYNHEIM	M	11		1
Eydun SAMUELSEN	A	4	(8)	2
Jonleif SOLSKER	M	6	(2)	1
Hans THOMASSEN	D	4	(1)	

LEAGUE RESULTS 1995

14/05/95	B36	H	5-1	Arge, Hansen A.F., Nolsø R., Mohr, Clementsen
21/05/95	FS Vágar	A	5-3	Nolsø R., Mohr 2, Arge, Clementsen
28/05/95	GÍ	H	0-0	
03/06/95	B68	A	2-1	Clementsen 2
11/06/95	Sumba/VB	H	2-0	Arge, Clementsen
18/06/95	B71	H	1-0	Mohr
25/06/95	TB	A	0-0	
06/08/95	KÍ	H	5-0	Clementsen, Arge 3, Reynheim
13/08/95	NSÍ	A	0-0	
20/08/95	B36	A	5-0	Dam Ja. 2, Hansen H., Dam J.H., Samuelsen
27/08/95	FS Vágar	H	0-0	
02/09/95	GÍ	A	1-2	Clementsen
10/09/95	B68	H	3-1	Clementsen, Lag 2
17/09/95	Sumba/VB	A	1-1	Samuelsen
24/09/95	B71	A	0-2	
01/10/95	TB	H	4-1	Mohr, Arge, Solsker, Hentze
07/10/95	KÍ	A	0-2	
15/10/95	NSÍ	H	0-0	

KÍ

CLUB DIRECTORY

Klaksvikar Ítrottarfelag (KÍ)
Postrum 204
700 Klaksvik
tel - 56184
fax - 57764
Year of Formation - 1904
President - Arni Joensen
Secretary - Hakun Dam
Coach - Sverri Jacobsen
Stadium - Klaksvik (4,000)

MAJOR HONOURS

League Championship - (16)
1942, 1945, 1952, 1953, 1954, 1956, 1957, 1958, 1961, 1966, 1967, 1968, 1969, 1970, 1972, 1991.
Domestic Cup - (4) 1966, 1967, 1990, 1994.

APPEARANCES 95

	P	Ap	(s)	Gls
Jan ANDREASSEN	D	15		
Finn BALDVINSSON	D	2	(6)	
Harley BERTHOLDSEN	D	18		
Olgar DANIELSEN	A	17	(1)	8
Simun ELIASEN	M	6	(2)	3
John HANSEN	M	16		1
Simun Waag HØGNESEN	M	7	(4)	1
Josvein JACOBSEN	D	6	(1)	1
Allan JOENSEN	D	16		1
Arnhold JOENSEN	M	16		5
Jan JOENSEN	M	16		1
Jon William JOENSEN	G	5		
Aksel JOHANNESEN	A		(2)	
Eydun KLAKKSTEIN	A	6		1
Hedin a LAKJUNI	A	2	(3)	3
Høgni a LAKJUNI	M		(1)	
Johan LUTZEN	D	3	(6)	
Allan MØRKØRE	D	10		3
Kurt MØRKØRE	A	1		3
Samal Eydfinn POULSEN	D	16		
Gunnar a STEIG	G	13	(1)	
Poul Juel VILHELMSEN	D	7		

LEAGUE RESULTS 1995

Date	Opponent	H/A	Score	Scorers
14/05/95	TB	A	2-2	Joensen Ar., Joensen Al. (p)
21/05/95	Sumba/VB	A	2-1	Jacobsen, Danielsen
28/05/95	NSÍ	H	2-1	Klakkstein, Danielsen
03/06/95	B36	A	1-2	Hansen
11/06/95	FS Vágar	H	0-0	
18/06/95	GÍ	A	1-5	Danielsen
25/06/95	B68	H	4-3	Danielsen 2, Mørkøre A., Lakjuni He.
06/08/95	HB	A	0-5	
13/08/95	B71	H	1-3	Joensen Ar.
20/08/95	TB	H	2-2	Joensen J., Mørkøre A.
27/08/95	Sumba/VB	H	1-2	Mørkøre A.
02/09/95	NSÍ	A	2-1	Danielsen, Eliasen
10/09/95	B36	H	2-2	Danielsen, Joensen Ar.
17/09/95	FS Vágar	A	3-5	Høgnesen, Lakjuni He. 2
24/09/95	GÍ	H	1-6	Danielsen
01/10/95	B68	A	1-2	Eliasen
07/10/95	HB	H	2-0	Eliasen, Joensen Ar.
15/10/95	B71	A	4-1	Mørkøre K. 3, Joensen Ar.

NSÍ

CLUB DIRECTORY

Nes Soknar Ítrottarfelag (NSÍ)
Postrum 173
620 Runavik
tel - 48100
Year of Formation - 1957
President - Jakup Egholm
Secretary - Magnus Rasmussen
Coach - Petur Simonsen
Stadium - Runavik (2,000)

MAJOR HONOURS
Domestic Cup - (1) 1986

APPEARANCES 95

	P	Ap	(s)	Gls
Simun DANIELSEN	A	5	(2)	1
Regin FREDERIKSBERG	A	9	(3)	
Eydun GAARDBO	D	18		
Oddfridur GAARDBO	D	18		
Danjal HANSEN	M	6	(1)	
Elian HANSEN	M	6	(2)	
Hallur HANSEN	G	2		
Kari HANSEN	D	10	(1)	
Magnus HANSEN	D	12		
Oli HANSEN	A	2	(5)	1
Anton HØJGAARD	A	1	(1)	
Sjurdur JACOBSEN	M	6	(5)	
John JAKOBSEN	A	3	(1)	
Djoni N. JOENSEN	M	16		2
Dan KNUDSEN	M		(1)	
Arnfinn LANGAARD	D	17	(1)	4
Tummas MAGNUSSEN	D	10	(3)	2
Arne MIDJORD	D	5		
Eddie MIKKELSEN	A		(2)	
Trugvy MORTENSEN	G	16		
Jonstein PETERSEN	A	18		1
Johnny SKIBENAES	A	1	(1)	
Eydstein SKIPANES	D		(1)	
Tummas Arne WINTHEREIG	A		(1)	
Egil ZACHARIASSEN	M	17		2

LEAGUE RESULTS 1995

14/05/95	B71	A	1-2	Petersen
21/05/95	TB	H	2-3	Danielsen, Langaard
28/05/95	KÍ	A	1-2	Joensen
03/06/95	Sumba/VB	A	3-1	Zachariassen 2, Magnussen
11/06/95	B36	H	1-2	Hansen O.
18/06/95	FS Vágar	A	0-2	
25/06/95	GÍ	H	0-1	
06/08/95	B68	A	1-4	Langaard
13/08/95	HB	H	0-0	
20/08/95	B71	H	0-2	
27/08/95	TB	A	1-0	Langaard
02/09/95	KÍ	H	1-2	Magnussen
10/09/95	Sumba/VB	H	0-3	
17/09/95	B36	A	0-1	
24/09/95	FS Vágar	H	1-2	Joensen
01/10/95	GÍ	A	1-5	Langaard
07/10/95	B68	H	0-5	
15/10/95	HB	A	0-0	

SUMBA/VB

CLUB DIRECTORY

Sumba/VB
Postrum 54
FR-900 Vagur
tel - 73679/70213
fax - 73679
Year of Formation - 1994
President - Poul Johannus Poulsen
Secretary - Yvonna Magnussen
Stadium - Vestri a Eidinum (3,000)

APPEARANCES 95

	P	Ap	(s)	Gls
Hans Pauli DAHL	M	1	(4)	
Jens Sivar DJURHUUS	D	1		
John EYSTBERG	A	8	(2)	1
Jon GAERDBO	D	6	(2)	
Bjarni HANSEN	M		(1)	
Eydun JACOBSEN	D	16		1
Magni JACOBSEN	M	5		
Danjal Johan JOENSEN	D	14	(4)	
Eirikur JOENSEN	A	11	(3)	2
Eydun JOENSEN	M	6		
Per JOENSEN	A	7	(1)	1
Bjarni JOHANSEN	G	18		
Pall Magnar KJAERBAECK	A	1	(1)	
Eydun KJAERBO	D	10	(1)	
Marlon KJAERBO	A	16	(2)	2
John Heri LARSEN	D	11		
Jon LISBERG	M	4	(5)	
Magni MAGNUSSEN	M	3	(2)	
Jan Allan MÜLLER	A	11		11
Magni MOHR	D	1		
Joan Pauli OLSEN	D	7		3
Trugvi NIELSEN	D	16	(1)	1
Egill STEINTORSSON (ISL)	A	5	(3)	1
René THOMSEN	A	2	(2)	
Pol THÓRSTEINSSON (ISL)	A	18		3

LEAGUE RESULTS 1995

14/05/95	GÍ	A	0-3	
21/05/95	KÍ	H	1-2	Joensen P.
28/05/95	B68	A	0-3	
03/06/95	NSÍ	H	1-3	Thorsteinsson
11/06/95	HB	A	0-2	
18/06/95	B36	H	1-2	Thorsteinsson
25/06/95	B71	A	1-5	Kjaerbo M.
06/08/95	FS Vágar	H	2-2	Müller, Steintorsson
13/08/95	TB	A	0-2	
20/08/95	GÍ	H	0-2	
27/08/95	KÍ	A	2-1	Müller, Joensen Ei.
02/09/95	B68	H	2-1	Müller 2
10/09/95	NSÍ	A	3-0	Thorsteinsson, Müller, Eystberg
17/09/95	HB	H	1-1	Olsen
24/09/95	B36	A	2-1	Olsen, Kjaerbo M.
01/10/95	B71	H	2-6	Müller, Jacobsen E.
07/10/95	FS Vágar	A	4-2	Müller 2, Olsen, Nielsen
15/10/95	TB	H	4-1	Müller 3, Joensen Ei.

TB

CLUB DIRECTORY

Tvoroyrar Boltfelag (TB)
Postrum 35
800 Tvoroyri
tel - 71570
fax - 72999
Year of Formation - 1892
President - Hans Pauli Holm
Secretary - Hentzar Hammer
Coach - Jacek Burkhardt
Stadium - Sevmyra (4,000)

MAJOR HONOURS
League Championship - (7)
1943, 1949, 1951, 1976, 1977, 1980, 1987.
Domestic Cup - (4) 1977, 1978, 1979, 1980.

APPEARANCES 95

	P	Ap	(s)	Gls
Bent ALBINUS	D	6		
Rolf CHRISTENSEN	G	18		
Birgir DIMON	D	17		
Hans HAMMER	M	3	(2)	
Jon Thordur HOLM	M	15	(1)	
Torur HOLM	M	18		3
Suni JACOBSEN	M	2	(1)	
Poul F. JOENSEN	M	15		
Bogi JOHANNESEN	A	9	(1)	4
John JOHANNESEN	A	3	(1)	
Oli JOHANNESEN	D	15		6
Birgir JØRGENSEN	A	4	(2)	3
Bjarni MORTENSEN	D	2	(2)	
Hermann MORTENSEN	A	12	(3)	2
Torfinnur MORTENSEN	D	12	(2)	
Peter NIELSEN	D	13		
Andreas NOLSØ	M	4	(1)	
Joan Petur OLGARSSON (ISL)	D	14	(1)	
Karl OSTER	A		(11)	
Dia PETERSEN	A		(1)	
Einar PETERSEN	D		(2)	
Magni PETERSEN	M	1	(1)	
Jens Erik RASMUSSEN	A	11		3
Eydun Gullok SVALBARD	M	4		2

LEAGUE RESULTS 1995

14/05/95	KÍ	H	2-2	Johannesen O. 2 (1p)
21/05/95	NSÍ	A	3-2	Holm T., Svalbard, Johannesen O.
28/05/95	B36	H	3-2	Holm T., Johannesen B. 2
03/06/95	FS Vágar	A	1-3	Johannesen B.
11/06/95	GÍ	H	1-0	Mortensen H.
18/06/95	B68	A	2-1	Jørgensen, Svalbard
25/06/95	HB	H	0-0	
06/08/95	B71	A	1-2	Johannesen B.
13/08/95	Sumba/VB	H	2-0	Johannesen O., Jørgensen
20/08/95	KÍ	A	2-2	Johannesen O., Rasmussen
27/08/95	NSÍ	H	0-1	
02/09/95	B36	A	0-1	
10/09/95	FS Vágar	H	1-2	Johannesen O.
17/09/95	GÍ	A	0-2	
24/09/95	B68	H	1-1	Holm T.
01/10/95	HB	A	1-4	Jørgensen
07/10/95	B71	H	2-0	Rasmussen, Mortensen H.
15/10/95	Sumba/VB	A	1-4	Rasmussen

FS VÁGAR

CLUB DIRECTORY

FS Vágar
FR-370 Midvagur
tel - 32806
Year of Formation - 1993
President - Sigfrid Olsen
Secretary - Neinbjørn Nattestad
Stadium - Midvagur (1,000) & Sandavagur (1,000)

APPEARANCES 95

	P	Ap	(s)	Gls
Mikkjal DANIELSEN	M		(2)	
Eydfinn DAVIDSEN	D	15	(1)	6
Erik HANSEN	M	8	(1)	
Emil HENTZE	M	16		1
Valbjørn Ole JACOBSEN	D	12		2
Bugvi JOENSEN	M	3	(6)	
Hedin JOENSEN	D		(1)	
Jogvan Pall JOENSEN	D	2	(4)	
Johannes JOENSEN	M	8	(1)	1
Jonhard JOENSEN	M	15	(1)	5
Petur Frank JOENSEN	M	1	(1)	
John JOHANSEN	A	1	(3)	
Valbjørn LAURITZEN	D	1		
Erik NIELSEN	D	7		1
Johan NIELSEN	D	2	(5)	1
Torkil NIELSEN	M	18		5
Hannus OLSEN	M	17		1
Heri OLSEN	A	16	(2)	6
Bjarni PRIOR	D	13	(1)	
Jens Erik RASMUSSEN	A	1		1
Johannus RASMUSSEN	M	5	(1)	
Alvur SAMUELSEN	G	18		
Hegga SAMUELSEN	A	18		
Eydstein SIMONSEN	A		(1)	
Magnus SIMONSEN	D	1		
Samal a VAGALID	A		(3)	

LEAGUE RESULTS 1995

14/05/95	B68	A	0-5	
21/05/95	HB	H	3-5	Rasmussen J.E., Nielsen T., Nielsen E.
28/05/95	B71	A	0-2	
03/06/95	TB	H	3-1	Olsen He., Davidsen 2
11/06/95	KÍ	A	0-0	
18/06/95	NSÍ	H	2-0	Jacobsen, Hentze
25/06/95	B36	A	2-3	Davidsen, Olsen He.
06/08/95	Sumba/VB	A	2-2	Nielsen J., Nielsen T.
13/08/95	GÍ	H	3-2	Jacobsen, Davidsen, Joensen Jon.
20/08/95	B68	H	1-5	Davidsen
27/08/95	HB	A	0-0	
02/09/95	B71	H	1-1	Olsen Ha.
10/09/95	TB	A	2-1	Davidsen, Olsen He.
17/09/95	KÍ	H	5-3	Joensen Jon., Nielsen T. 2, Olsen He., Joensen Joh.
24/09/95	NSÍ	A	2-1	Joensen Jon., Olsen He.
01/10/95	B36	H	1-1	Joensen Jon.
07/10/95	Sumba/VB	H	2-4	Olsen He., Nielsen T.
15/10/95	GÍ	A	1-2	Joensen Jon.

PROMOTED CLUB

SECOND DIVISION FINAL TABLE 95

		Pd	W	D	L	F	A	Pt	GD
1	HB II	18	11	3	4	56	32	36	+24
2	**ÍF**	**18**	**11**	**2**	**5**	**48**	**28**	**35**	**+20**
3	EB/Streymur	18	10	1	7	32	32	31	=
4	Sumba/VB II	18	9	2	7	34	29	29	+5
5	FS Vágar II	18	8	4	6	35	40	28	-5
6	LÍF	18	8	2	8	37	29	26	+8
7	KÍ II	18	6	6	6	44	36	24	+8
8	SÍ	18	5	4	9	34	47	19	-13
9	Royn	18	5	2	11	28	45	17	-17
10	GÍ II	18	2	4	12	20	50	10	-30

N.B. HB II, as a reserve team, are ineligible for promotion.

PROMOTION/RELEGATION PLAY-OFF
Sumba/VB 8, EB/Streymur 0
EB Streymur 0, Sumba/VB 0
(Sumba/VB 8-0)

CLUB DIRECTORY

Itrottarfelag Fuglafjardar (ÍF)
Postrum 96
530 Fuglafjordur
tel - 44636
fax - 44788
Year of Formation - 1946
President - Johan Joensen
Secretary - Rogvi Larsen
Stadium - Fuglafjordur (3,000)

MAJOR HONOURS
League Championship - (1) 1979.

FINLAND

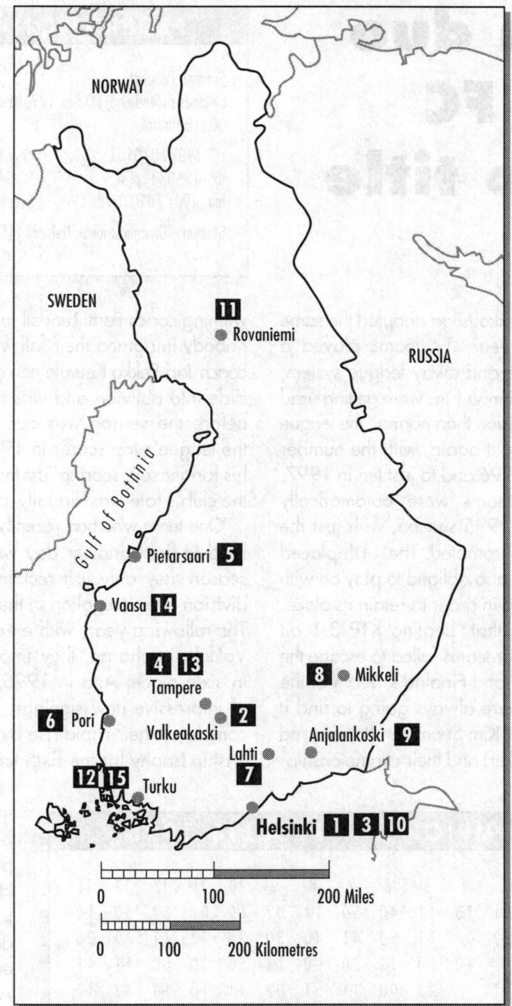

1	FINNPA	369	9	MYPA	377
2	FC HAKA	370	10	PONNISTUS	378
3	HJK	371	11	ROPS	379
4	FC ILVES	372	12	TPS	380
5	FF JARO	373	13	TPV	381
6	FC JAZZ	374	14	VPS	382
7	FC KUUSYSI	375	15	FC INTERTURKU	383
8	MP	376			

MØLLER-NIELSEN IS NEW NATIONAL COACH

Russian duo inspire FC Haka to title

FEDERATION DIRECTORY

Suomen Palloliitto
Finlands Bollförbund, PO Box 179, Läntinen Brahenkatu 2,
00510 Helsinki

tel - (90) 7010101
tlx - 126033 spl sf
fax - (90) 70101098

Year of Formation - 1907
President - Pentti Seppälä
Secretary - Pertti Alaja

Stadium - Olympiastadion, Helsinki (45,000)

For once the 1995 Finnish Veikkausliga adopted the same format as in the previous year. 14 teams played a conventional 26-game home-and-away league system, with no play-offs. But just as Finnish fans were getting used to the idea of a bigger top division than normal, the league organisers decided to reduce it again, with the number of teams being cut to 12 in 1996 and to just ten in 1997.

This meant that three teams were automatically relegated at the end of the 1995 season, with just the Second Division champions promoted. The 11th-placed team in the Veikkausliga was also obliged to play off with the Second Division runner-up in order to retain its place.

MP, of Mikkeli, duly did that, beating KTP 3-1 on aggregate. But two other major teams failed to escape the drop - 1994 champions TPV and Finalnd's 'Team of the Eighties', FC Kuusysi. TPV were always going to find it tough without their star player Kim Suominen (transferred to Austrian side Admira Wacker) and their championship-winning coach Pertti Lundell (prised away by FC Jazz). But nobody imagined their fall would be so emphatic. New coach Jari-Pekka Keurulainen could do nothing to halt their slide into oblivion and was replaced by Jussi Ristimäki before the season was out. Brazilian striker Dionísio, the league's top scorer in 1994, was a pale shadow of his former self, scoring just three goals, two of them after the club's fate was virtually sealed.

One team who had recently faced life at the bottom but lived to fight another day were FC Haka. In the 1993 season they only just reclaimed their place in the top division after struggling in the relegation play-off group. The following year, with ex-national team coach Jukka Vakkila in charge, they improved sufficiently to finish in sixth place. And in 1995, thanks to a steady influx of impressive new signings, the club from Valkeakoski completed their rapid rise by lifting the Finnish championship trophy for the sixth time in their history.

Backed by the local paper industry (United Paper Mills is one of the largest paper producers in the world), Haka had sufficient funds to meet coach Vakkila's demands and bring in several key players. Defenders Ari Heikkinen and Jari Kinnunen had arrived at the start of the 1994 campaign. Striker Jokke Kangaskorpi and another defender, Lasse Karjalainen came in at the beginning of 1995. But the most important two new recuits were the two Russians, Valeri Popovits and Oleg Ivanov, who joined Haka from hard-up FC Ilves

LEAGUE CHAMPIONSHIP RESULTS 1995

		1	2	3	4	5	6	7	8	9	10	11	12	13	14
1	FinnPa		1-3	0-1	1-3	1-1	4-0	5-0	1-1	0-2	6-0	0-1	3-2	3-0	1-0
2	FC Haka	0-0		2-2	0-1	1-1	5-0	4-1	4-0	3-0	3-0	4-2	1-1	1-0	2-0
3	HJK	2-0	2-0		4-0	0-0	1-2	2-0	0-0	1-1	5-0	1-0	0-0	1-1	4-1
4	FC Ilves	0-0	0-1	1-1		2-3	0-0	1-1	5-1	0-2	1-1	1-0	1-4	4-2	1-0
5	FF Jaro	3-1	1-3	1-2	1-2		0-2	3-0	4-0	1-3	3-0	0-1	4-2	4-2	1-0
6	FC Jazz	3-1	0-1	1-2	2-2	2-0		3-0	0-2	0-0	3-0	4-0	4-1	4-1	1-2
7	FC Kuusysi	3-1	0-1	1-1	3-2	1-1	0-3		2-1	1-3	3-1	0-1	0-1	0-0	0-1
8	MP	3-0	0-3	2-2	1-1	0-1	1-3	0-1		0-1	1-0	2-1	3-1	0-1	2-0
9	MyPa	1-2	3-1	1-0	4-0	2-0	1-1	3-2	1-0		5-0	0-0	3-0	1-1	3-1
10	Ponnistus	1-2	0-6	0-2	0-3	0-2	0-2	3-1	2-1	0-1		0-0	2-1	1-0	3-2
11	RoPS	0-0	0-1	2-3	3-2	1-1	1-1	1-1	0-0	3-1	4-1		0-1	3-4	2-0
12	TPS	5-1	1-3	0-0	2-1	3-0	2-1	0-1	0-0	1-3	0-0	1-0		3-0	2-1
13	TPV	4-3	0-2	2-4	1-2	0-1	1-1	4-1	1-1	1-0	4-1	1-3	1-1		0-1
14	VPS	1-3	1-1	0-1	1-0	1-0	1-0	4-0	0-1	1-0	2-3	0-0	1-0	2-1	

LEAGUE CHAMPIONSHIP FINAL TABLE 1995

			Home					Away					Total						
		Pd	W	D	L	F	A	W	D	L	F	A	W	D	L	F	A	Pt	GD
1	FC Haka	26	8	4	1	30	8	10	1	2	26	9	18	5	3	56	17	59	+39
2	MyPa	26	9	3	1	28	8	7	2	4	17	12	16	5	5	45	20	53	+25
3	HJK	26	7	5	1	23	5	7	5	1	21	13	14	10	2	44	18	52	+26
4	FC Jazz	26	7	2	4	27	12	5	4	4	16	17	12	6	8	43	29	42	+14
5	FF Jaro	26	7	0	6	26	18	4	5	4	11	14	11	5	10	37	32	38	+5
6	TPS	26	7	3	3	20	11	3	3	7	13	21	10	6	10	33	32	36	+1
7	FC Ilves	26	4	5	4	17	16	5	2	6	19	23	9	7	10	36	39	34	-3
8	FinnPa	26	6	2	5	26	14	3	3	7	14	26	9	5	12	40	40	32	=
9	RoPS	26	4	5	4	20	16	4	3	6	9	14	8	8	10	29	30	32	-1
10	VPS	26	7	2	4	15	10	3	0	10	11	24	10	2	14	26	34	32	-8
11	MP	26	5	2	6	15	15	2	5	6	8	20	7	7	12	23	35	28	-12
12	TPV	26	4	3	6	20	21	2	3	8	13	27	6	6	14	33	48	24	-15
13	FC Kuusysi	26	4	3	6	14	17	2	2	9	9	33	6	5	15	23	50	23	-27
14	Ponnistus	26	5	1	7	12	23	1	2	10	7	40	6	3	17	19	63	21	-44

midway through the 1994 campaign. Hopes were very high in Valkeakoski, and in the pre-season predictions Haka were ranked as serious championship contenders alongside HJK and MyPa. The first few weeks, however, did not bring the desired results - four draws and just one win, against newly-promoted strugglers Ponnistus, left Haka down in eighth place - and there was even talk that Vakkila would be sacked. But gradually the team picked themselves up, and after ten rounds they had lifted themselves to third, behind leaders MyPa and FC Jazz.

The real fuse to Haka's season was lit in the League Cup final against HJK on July 12. Haka won an exhilarating match 4-2, and from then on they began to turn on the style in every game. The Russian pair, Ivanov and Popovits, suddenly became irresistible, with the latter scoring goal after goal.

By the end of August, Haka had completed a fabulous run of nine successive league victories, with Popovits personally grabbing ten goals in the process. The ninth, and most important, win came at home to MyPa, whose long-time lead at the top of the table had been taken from them by Haka a couple of games earlier. With a rousing 3-0 win in Valkeakoski, Haka went five points clear of MyPa. It was the gateway to the title, and although Haka lost their unbeaten home record in their next match, against FC Ilves, it proved to be just a temporary hitch. Three impressive away wins followed - against TPS, FC Jazz and MP - and that wrapped up the title for Vakkila and his men with one match still left to play.

The final game, at home to RoPS, was an occasion for celebration - for goalkeeper and captain Olli Huttunen who marked his retirement by lifting the championship trophy; for Popovits, who netted another two goals in the 4-2 win to confirm himself as the league's top scorer; and for the other players, officials and fans of the club, which had not tasted such success for 18 years. Nobody could dispute their triumph. They had the best attack and the best defence in the league, and they generally played the most attractive football.

For MyPa, another small-town club with financial support from the local paper industry, there was only disappointment at finishing runners-up for the third season in succession. Harri Kampman's team led the way for most of the season, but the 0-3 defeat by Haka eroded their confidence, and they were unable to stage a fightback. However, a late salvo of three successive victories set them up nicely for the Finnish Cup final at the end of October, which they went on to win for the second time in four years, beating FC Jazz 1-0 with an early goal from young midfielder Sami Hyypiä in his last game before departing for a professional career in Holland with Willem II. MyPa's win enabled HJK to salvage something from a season of under-achievement by joining champions FC Haka in the UEFA Cup and returning to Europe after a rare year's absence.

INTERNATIONAL HONOURS

None

Of the three teams that did represent Finland in Europe in 1995/96, only MyPa achieved any degree of success. TPS and TPV were both eliminated without glory in the preliminary round, while MyPa came through their opening UEFA Cup tie on away goals after a stunning 3-1 victory in Scotland against Motherwell. They even held mighty PSV of Holland 1-1 at home in the first leg of their first-round tie, but there were no repeat away-day heroics in Eindhoven as the Dutchmen crushed them 7-1.

One MyPa player on duty in Eindhoven, midfielder Petri Tiainen, had also been on the receiving end of another, even more significant, thrashing a few weeks earlier when playing for Finland in the European Championship. The Finns were top of the Group Eight table when they took on Russia in Helsinki in the middle of August. But any hopes they had of qualifying for the finals in England were well and truly obliterated by the Russians, who toyed with Jukka Ikäläinen's side and ran out 6-0 winners.

Further defeats in Glasgow and Russia folowed, but some of the gloom surrounding the national team was lifted when it was announced that Richard Møller-Nielsen, the man who took Denmark to Euro '92 glory in Sweden, would be taking over as Finland coach on a four-year contract starting in July 1996. Ikäläinen, whose longer-than-expected stint as caretaker coach ended with a 1-2 home defeat by Turkey, stays on as Möller-Nielsen's assistant.

It was not a good year for the stand-in coach, the only highlight being a 1-0 win in Kuwait in March, a match which also brought veteran striker Ari Hjelm his 100th and last cap for Finland.

Jukka Ikäläinen - handed over the national side's reins to Richard Møller-Nielsen.

NATIONAL TEAM RESULTS 95/96

16/08/95	Russia (ECQ)	H	Helsinki	0-6	
06/09/95	Scotland (ECQ)	A	Glasgow	0-1	
04/10/95	Turkey	H	Helsinki	0-0	
15/11/95	Russia (ECQ)	A	Moscow	1-3	Suominen (44)
09/02/96	Thailand	A	Bangkok	0-1	
11/02/96	Denmark	N	Bangkok	0-0	
13/02/96	Romania	N	Bangkok	1-1	Koskinen (15)
16/02/96	Thailand	A	Bangkok	2-5	Ylönen (30), Rissanen (75)
16/03/96	Kuwait	A	Kuwait City	1-0	Johansson (89)
29/05/96	France	A	Strasbourg	0-2	
02/06/96	Turkey	H	Helsinki	1-2	Litmanen (25)

DOMESTIC CUP RESULTS

EIGHTH ROUND
FC Kontu 2, Reipas 2 (aet; 2-4 on pens.)
ÅIFK 3, Gnistan 2
Kultsu 0, RoPS 1
FC Ilves 1, FinnPa 0
Ponnistus 0, MP 1
EuPa 0, FC InterTurku 2
KajHa 5, PP-70 2
KTP 2, TPS 1
VaKP 1, FF Jaro 4
TP-Seinäjoki 2, VPS 1

NINTH ROUND
KTP 0, FC Ilves 4
ÅIFK 0, FF Jaro 9
HJK 2, RoPS 1
KajHa 0, FC Haka 3
FC InterTurku 1, TPV 1 (aet; 3-1 on pens.)
MyPa 2, FC Kuusysi 0
FC Jazz 2, MP 0
TP-Seinäjoki 2, Reipas 0

QUARTER-FINALS
HJK 4, FC Ilves 2
MyPa 2, FF Jaro 1
FC Jazz 2, FC Haka 1
TP-Seinäjoki 0, FC InterTurku 6

SEMI-FINALS
FC Jazz v HJK 2-0; 0-0
(FC Jazz 2-0)
MyPa v FC InterTurku 4-0; 1-2
(MyPa 5-2)

FINAL
28/10/95, Helsinki
MYPA 1 Hyypiä (7)
FC JAZZ 0
referee - Lehtiranta
MYPA - Jakonen; Viljanen, Hyypiä, Mahlio, Pohja, Tiainen, Roth, Keskitalo (Hernesniemi 65), Grönholm, Koskinen Ju., Huttunen.
FC JAZZ - Viitanen; Nieminen, Koskikangas (Rodrigo 46), Sulonen, Rantanen, Laaksonen (Alatensiö 56), Riippa, Piracaía, Puputti, Ruhanen, Luiz António.

NATIONAL TEAM APPEARANCES 95/96

Coach - Jukka IKÄLÄINEN	RUS	SCO	TUR	RUS	THA	DEN	ROM	THA	KUW	FRA	TUR	Cps	Gls
Kari LAUKKANEN (14/12/63) - FinnPa	G	G				G	G	G				47	-
Janne MÄKELÄ (23/07/71) - FinnPa	D46		D									18	-
Markku KANERVA (24/05/64) - HJK	D	D										59	1
Erik HOLMGREN (17/12/64) - FinnPa	D	D										60	2
Rami NIEMINEN (25/02/66) - FC Jazz	D	D64		D	D				D		s77	11	-
Janne LINDBERG (24/05/66) - Greenock Morton (SCO)	M	M	M	M								31	1
Rami RANTANEN (25/11/68) - Trelleborgs FF (SWE)	M65											14	-
Petri TIAINEN (26/09/66) - MyPa	M											15	2
Ari HJELM (24/02/62) - HJK	M	A	A85	A	M	M		M	M46			100	20
Antti SUMIALA (20/02/74) - NEC (HOL)	A			A76								15	3
Mika-Matti PAATELAINEN (03/02/67) - Bolton Wanderers (ENG)	A46											49	13
Kim SUOMINEN (20/10/69) - FC Admira Wacker (AUT)/ IFK Norrköping (SWE)	s46	M		M88	M	M	M	M	M	M	M	36	4
Petri JÄRVINEN (09/05/65) - FinnPa	s46				A	A	A20	A				35	4
Tommi GRÖNLUND (09/12/69) - HJK	s65	s64	M	M70	M66	M	M	M	M	M	M	11	-
Kari RISSANEN (29/08/66) - FinnPa		D	s85	D	D	D	D	D				10	1
Marko MYYRY (15/11/67) - SV Meppen (GER)		M	M	M								55	2
Jari LITMANEN (20/02/71) - Ajax (HOL)		M								M	M	43	8
Petri JAKONEN (09/06/67) - MyPa			G46						G			24	-
Jussi NUORELA (11/08/74) - FC Haka			D	D								5	-
Aki HYRYLÄINEN (17/04/68) - HJK			D	D		D	D	D	D	D	D	23	1
Antti HEINOLA (20/03/73) - HJK/Emmen (HOL)			D58							D	D	8	-
Sami HYYPIÄ (07/10/73) - MyPa/Willem II (HOL)			M71							M	M77	9	-
Jokke KANGASKORPI (02/03/72) - FC Haka			A58	s76	s46	M	s20	s46	A61			11	-
Antti NIEMI (31/05/72) - HJK/FC København (DEN)			s46	G	G					G	G	14	-
Sami VÄISÄNEN (09/05/73) - FC Haka			s58							A	A77	3	-
Jari JÄVÄJÄ (16/08/73) - VPS			s58		A46					s81	s77	4	-
Sami MAHLIO (12/01/72) - MyPa			s71		M	s82	s56	M57				5	-
Jarkko KOSKINEN (29/11/72) - MyPa				s70	s46	s61	D20					4	1
Harri YLÖNEN (21/12/71) - FC Haka				s88	D46	D	D	D	D	D	D	8	-
Lasse KARJALAINEN (22/10/74) - FC Haka					D	D		D46		D	D	7	-
Jasse JALONEN (18/07/73) - MyPa					s66	M82	M	M46	s66			6	-
Jarkko WISS (17/04/72) - FF Jaro						M61	s20	s46				3	-
Tom ENBERG (26/08/70) - MyPa							M56	s57	s46			5	-
Aarno TURPEINEN (21/03/71) - HJK									D			1	-
Kari UKKONEN (19/02/61) - LB Châteauroux (FRA)									D			59	4
Simo VALAKARI (28/04/73) - FinnPa									M66			1	-
Jonatan JOHANSSON (16/08/75) - TPS									s61			1	1
Joonas KOLKKA (28/09/74) - Willem II (HOL)										A81	A	6	2

FC Haka celebrate their Finnish championship triumph

TOP SCORERS

21	Valeri POPOVITS (FC Haka)
14	LUIZ ANTÓNIO (FC Jazz)
13	Miikka KAJANDER (FC Ilves)
12	Jari VANHALA (FF Jaro)
11	Ari HJELM (HJK)
	Kalle LEHTINEN (FinnPa)
10	Niclas GRÖNHOLM (MyPa)
9	Oleg IVANOV (FC Haka)
	RODRIGO (FC Jazz)
	Saku PUHAKAINEN (FC Kuusysi)
	Jari JÄVÄJÄ (VPS)

PLAYERS OF THE SEASON

OLLI HUTTUNEN

FC Haka's 36-year-old goalkeeper Olavi "Olli" Huttunen ended his 18-season-long career not only by capturing the league title for the first time but by setting a new Finnish league appearance record of 432 matches (all of them for Haka). He was given a rousing send-off by the home fans as he left the field early in the final match of the season against RoPS. It was a great season for Huttunen to go out on, conceding only 16 goals in his 25 and a half league games. Finland's most capped goalkeeper (60 full internationals between 1980 and 1992) is now employed as FC Haka's goalkeeping coach.

JARI LITMANEN

Nobody can be in any doubt that Jari Litmanen is Finland's finest footballer. But for him to take the overall 1995 Sportsman of the Year prize in a country full of world-class skiers, athletes, rally drivers and ice hockey players was nothing short of sensational. Litmanen can now claim to be the most famous Finnish footballer ever - and he is still only 25. In the 95/96 season he once again excelled himself for Ajax, especially in Europe where he was the Champions' League top scorer with nine goals, the last of them coming in the final against Juventus. Litmanen was on duty only three times for Finland during the season, but he will obviously be the first name on Richard Møller-Nielsen's teamsheet for the 1998 World Cup qualifiers.

EUROPEAN CUPS RESULTS 95/96

CUP-WINNERS' CUP

● TPS

Preliminary round TEUTA DURRËS (ALB)

H 1-0 Wallden (29p)
Toivonen; Casagrande, Keula, Sulonen, Oinas, Allen (Savolainen 88), Wallden, Jalonen, Enberg, Pylkäs, Johansson (Virtanen 79).

A 0-3
Toivonen; Casagrande, Keula, Sulonen, Miettinen, Allen, Savolainen (Jalonen 46), Wallden (Virtanen 69), Enberg, Pylkäs, Johansson (Peltola 84).

UEFA CUP

● TPV

Preliminary round VIKING FK (NOR)

H 0-4
Koivistoinen; Granholm, Gawara (Grandi 75), Mäkinen, Levola, Juntunen, Listenmaa (Karatayev 69), Wiss (Lindholm 46), Niemi, Aaltonen J., Dionísio.

A 1-3 Wiss (88)
Vahla; Lindholm, Mäkinen, Gawara, Levola (Listenmaa 76), Wiss, Tuomela, Juntunen, Niemi (Pellikka 46), Aaltonen J. (Kuula 68), Dionísio.

● MYPA

Preliminary round MOTHERWELL (SCO)

A 3-1 Grönholm (13), Tiainen (31), Mahlio (55)
Jakonen; Huttunen, Viljanen, Hyypiä, Koskinen Ju., Mahlio, Tiainen, Kautonen, Grönholm, Pohja (Keskitalo 46; Koskinen Ja. 87), Kolkka.

H 0-2
Jakonen; Huttunen, Viljanen, Hyypiä, Koskinen Ju., Mahlio, Kolkka, Kautonen, Tiainen (Koskinen Ja. 86), Keskitalo, Grönholm.

1st round PSV (HOL)

H 1-1 Mahlio (29)
Jakonen; Huttunen, Viljanen, Hyypiä, Koskinen Ju., Mahlio, Koskinen Ja., Kautonen, Tiainen (Pohja 85), Keskitalo (Kolkka 63), Grönholm.

A 1-7 Keskitalo (15)
Jakonen (Vuorinen 60); Huttunen, Viljanen, Hyypiä, Koskinen Ju., Mahlio, Kolkka, Kautonen, Tiainen, Keskitalo (Pohja 68), Grönholm.

FINNPA

CLUB DIRECTORY

Finnairin Palloilijat
Mannerheimintie 102 A
00250 Helsinki
tel - (90) 8188285
fax - (90) 8188286
Year of Formation - 1965
President - Claes Andersson
Secretary - Erkki Salo
Coach - Heikki Suhonen; Keijo Voutilainen
Stadium - Olympiastadion (45,000)

APPEARANCES 95

	P	Ap	(s)	Gls
Ville ANDERSEN	M	11	(5)	
Aly DIA (SEN)	A	2	(3)	
Tony ELOMAA	A	13	(7)	4
Petri HAAPIMAA	D	2	(3)	
Erik HOLMGREN	D	26		1
Petri JÄRVINEN	A	12		2
Mikael KAJANDER	M		(2)	1
Juha KARJALAINEN	G	1		
Sami KOSKINEN	M	6	(2)	
Kari LAUKKANEN	G	11		
Kalle LEHTINEN	M	13	(5)	11
Reijo LINNA	M	24	(1)	2
Pekka MATTILA	M	18	(6)	2
Janne MÄKELÄ	D	23		
Jari RANTANEN	A	15	(4)	3
Pasi RASIMUS	M	8		
Kari RISSANEN	D	25		2
Peter SAMPO	A	18	(7)	5
Petteri SCHUTSCHKOFF	D	15	(9)	2
Kimmo TARKKIO	A	7	(5)	2
Simo VALAKARI	M	22		3
Jani VIANDER	G	14		

LEAGUE RESULTS 1995

30/04/95	FC Haka	A	0-0	
02/05/95	MyPa	H	0-2	
11/05/95	RoPS	A	0-0	
15/05/95	FC Kuusysi	H	5-0	Rantanen, Schutschkoff, Holmgren, Lehtinen, Sampo
21/05/95	HJK	A	0-2	
25/05/95	VPS	A	3-1	Mattila, Rissanen, Elomaa
28/05/95	TPS	A	1-5	Rissanen
15/06/95	FC Ilves	H	1-3	Linna
18/06/95	FC Jazz	A	1-3	Lehtinen
21/06/95	FF Jaro	H	1-1	Rantanen
02/07/95	TPV	A	3-4	Mattila, Valakari, Lehtinen (p)
06/07/95	MP	A	0-3	
09/07/95	Ponnistus	H	6-0	Sampo 2, Lehtinen 2, Elomaa, Schutschkoff
15/07/95	FC Haka	H	1-3	Lehtinen
23/07/95	MyPa	A	2-1	Elomaa, Lehtinen
30/07/95	HJK	H	0-1	
07/08/95	VPS	H	3-2	Elomaa, Rantanen, Tarkkio
20/08/95	FF Jaro	A	1-3	Tarkkio
28/08/95	TPV	H	3-0	Järvinen, Sampo, Valakari
31/08/95	TPS	H	1-0	Kajander
10/09/95	FC Kuusysi	A	1-3	Linna
16/09/95	RoPS	H	0-1	
24/09/95	FC Ilves	A	0-0	
01/10/95	FC Jazz	H	4-0	Lehtinen 3, Järvinen
08/10/95	Ponnistus	A	2-1	Sampo, Valakari
15/10/95	MP	H	1-1	Lehtinen (p)

FC HAKA

CLUB DIRECTORY

FC Haka
Tehtaankatu 5 E 1
37600 Valkeakoski
tel - (937) 5845364
fax - (937) 5712290
Year of Formation - 1932
President - Jussi Sarvikas
Secretary - Anne Antti-Roiko
Coach - Jukka Vakkila
Stadium - Tehtaankenttä (6,000)

MAJOR HONOURS
League Championship - (5)
1960, 1962, 1965, 1977, 1995.
Domestic Cup - (9) 1955, 1959, 1960, 1963, 1969, 1977, 1982, 1985, 1988.

APPEARANCES 95

	P	Ap	(s)	Gls
Michael BELFIELD (ENG)	A	3	(10)	2
Ari HEIKKINEN	D	25		
Olli HUTTUNEN	G	26		
Janne HYÖKYVAARA	M	13	(7)	6
Oleg IVANOV (RUS)	M	24		9
Jari KAASALAINEN	M	16	(1)	3
Tommi KAINULAINEN	G		(1)	
Jokke KANGASKORPI	A	25	(1)	7
Miroslav KARAS (SVK)	D	14	(6)	
Lasse KARJALAINEN	D	23		
Jari KINNUNEN	D	23	(1)	
Pekka KUNNOLA	A		(1)	
Heikki LEINONEN	D		(6)	
Kari MARTONEN	D	7	(4)	
Jussi NUORELA	D	6	(1)	
Harri NYYSSÖNEN	M	1	(2)	
Kai NYYSSÖNEN	A	8	(14)	1
Valeri POPOVITS (RUS)	A	23	(1)	21
Sami RISTILÄ	A	12	(11)	2
Jari RÄSÄNEN	D	1		
Sami VÄISÄNEN	A	10	(1)	3
Harri YLÖNEN	D	26		2

LEAGUE RESULTS 1995

Date	Opponent	H/A	Score	Scorers
30/04/95	FinnPa	H	0-0	
07/05/95	VPS	A	1-1	Popovits
11/05/95	TPS	H	1-1	Hyökyvaara
22/05/95	Ponnistus	A	6-0	Kangaskorpi 2, Popovits 2, Kaasalainen, Ylönen
25/05/95	FF Jaro	H	1-1	Hyökyvaara
28/05/95	FC Ilves	A	1-0	Ivanov
04/06/95	FC Kuusysi	A	1-0	Kangaskorpi
15/06/95	FC Jazz	H	5-0	Kaasalainen 2 (1p), Ivanov, Ristilä, Belfield
18/06/95	HJK	A	0-2	
21/06/95	TPV	H	1-0	Popovits
02/07/95	MyPa	A	1-3	Ivanov
06/07/95	RoPS	A	1-0	Popovits
09/07/95	MP	H	4-0	Hyökyvaara, Ivanov, Kangaskorpi, Popovits
15/07/95	FinnPa	A	3-1	Ylönen, Popovits, Ivanov
23/07/95	VPS	H	2-0	Popovits 2
29/07/95	Ponnistus	H	3-0	Popovits, Kangaskorpi, Belfield
06/08/95	FF Jaro	A	3-1	Ivanov, Väisänen, Kangaskorpi
10/08/95	FC Kuusysi	H	4-1	Nyyssönen K., Popovits 2 (1p), Ivanov
19/08/95	TPV	A	2-0	Väisänen, Popovits
27/08/95	MyPa	H	3-0	Hyökyvaara 2, Popovits
10/09/95	FC Ilves	H	0-1	
17/09/95	TPS	A	3-1	Popovits, Kangaskorpi, Ristilä
23/09/95	FC Jazz	A	1-0	Popovits
30/09/95	HJK	H	2-2	Popovits, Ivanov
08/10/95	MP	A	3-0	Popovits 2, Väisänen
15/10/95	RoPS	H	4-2	Popovits 2, Hyökyvaara, Ivanov

HJK

CLUB DIRECTORY

Helsingin Jalkapalloklubi
Mannerheimintie 29
00250 Helsinki
tel - (90) 4774550
fax - (90) 47745510
Year of Formation - 1907
President - Olli-Pekka Lyytikäinen
Secretary - Tarja Pausso
Coach - Bo Johansson (96 - Tommy Lindholm)
Stadium - Olympiastadion (45,000)

MAJOR HONOURS
League Championship - (18)
1911, 1912, 1917, 1918, 1919, 1923, 1925, 1936, 1938, 1964, 1973, 1978, 1981, 1985, 1987, 1988, 1990, 1992.
Domestic Cup - (4) 1966, 1981, 1984, 1993.

APPEARANCES 95

	P	Ap	(s)	Gls
Obiora ANICHE (NIG)	A	6	(7)	7
Jari EUROPAEUS	D	25		1
Oscar GEAGEA	M		(3)	
Tommi GRÖNLUND	M	26		4
Antti HEINOLA	D	24		1
Marko HELIN	D	10		
Ari HJELM	A	25	(1)	11
Aki HYRYLÄINEN	D	12	(1)	
Markku KANERVA	D	23		
Mikaa KOTTILA	A	9	(12)	4
Mika LEHKOSUO	M	20	(4)	1
Ismo LIUS	A	13	(2)	7
Antti NIEMI	G	24		
Markku PALMROOS	G	2		
Aki RIIHILAHTI	M	1	(5)	
Heikki RITVANEN	A		(1)	
Janne SAARINEN	M	9	(5)	
Janne SUOKONAUTIO	M	9	(3)	3
Pasi TAURIAINEN	A	4	(6)	
Ari TEGELBERG	A	14	(9)	3
Aarno TURPEINEN	D	10	(1)	
Vesa VASARA	A	20	(4)	2
Kim WASSELL (ENG)	M		(1)	

LEAGUE RESULTS 1995

Date	Opponent	H/A	Score	Scorers
30/04/95	MP	H	0-0	
06/05/95	Ponnistus	A	2-0	Kottila, Hjelm
11/05/95	FC Jazz	H	1-2	Hjelm
14/05/95	TPS	A	0-0	
21/05/95	FinnPa	H	2-0	Hjelm, Lehkosuo
25/05/95	RoPS	H	1-0	Tegelberg
06/06/95	FF Jaro	A	2-1	Grönlund, Suokonautio
15/06/95	MyPa	A	0-1	
18/06/95	FC Haka	H	2-0	Grönlund, Suokonautio
21/06/95	FC Ilves	A	1-1	Hjelm
05/07/95	TPV	H	1-1	Aniche
16/07/95	MP	A	2-2	Kottila 2
26/07/95	Ponnistus	H	5-0	Aniche 3, Hjelm (p), Grönlund
30/07/95	FinnPa	A	1-0	Grönlund
03/08/95	VPS	H	4-1	Tegelberg 2, Vasara, Hjelm
06/08/95	RoPS	A	3-2	Suokonautio, Aniche, Hjelm
10/08/95	FF Jaro	H	0-0	
23/08/95	FC Kuusysi	A	1-1	Aniche
27/08/95	VPS	A	1-0	Hjelm
10/09/95	TPS	H	0-0	
14/09/95	FC Ilves	H	4-0	Lius 3, Europaeus
17/09/95	FC Jazz	A	2-1	Lius 2
20/09/95	MyPa	H	1-1	Kottila
30/09/95	FC Haka	A	2-2	Hjelm 2
10/10/95	FC Kuusysi	H	2-0	Lius, Aniche
15/10/95	TPV	A	4-2	Hjelm, Lius, Vasara, Heinola

FC ILVES

CLUB DIRECTORY

FC Ilves
Tursonkatu 3
33540 Tampere
tel - (931) 2559960
fax - (931) 2612614
Year of Formation - 1931
President - Reijo Runsas
Secretary - Mika Periviita
Coach - Esa Kuusisto
Stadium - Tammela (6,000)

MAJOR HONOURS
League Championship - (2) 1950, 1983.
Domestic Cup - (2) 1979, 1990.

APPEARANCES 95

	P	Ap	(s)	Gls
Jarkko ESKOLA	G	5		
Aleksandr HALZOV (RUS)	A	19	(3)	1
Petri HEINÄNEN	A	5	(10)	1
Sami HULKKONEN	A		(4)	
Seppo JOKISALO	A		(4)	
Mark JOSEPH (ENG)	D	23	(1)	
Tommi KAINULAINEN	G	15		
Miikka KAJANDER	M	25		13
Timo KORSUMÄKI	D	23	(1)	
Aleksandr KOSTIN (RUS)	M	24		2
Mikael KOTIRANTA	M	21	(2)	2
Toni KUIVASTO	D	20	(3)	1
Jussi KUOPPALA	D	12	(8)	
Kimmo KUULA	D	22	(1)	2
Joni LEHTONEN	M	25		3
Tomi LEPPINIEMI	A	5	(4)	
Jyri MÄKINEN	D	1		
Seppo NIKKILÄ	A	16	(4)	4
Arto PARTANEN	M	3	(4)	
Kimmo PIIRAINEN	A	16	(10)	6
Jani RIISSANEN	D		(1)	
Jani VIANDER	G	6		

LEAGUE RESULTS 1995

Date	Opponent	H/A	Score	Scorers
30/04/95	FC Jazz	H	0-0	
07/05/95	TPV	A	2-1	Kajander, Piirainen
11/05/95	FF Jaro	A	2-1	Kajander, og (Moilanen)
21/05/95	FC Kuusysi	A	2-3	Kajander 2
25/05/95	MP	H	5-1	Kajander 2, Kuula, Kotiranta, Kostin
28/05/95	FC Haka	H	0-1	
04/06/95	RoPS	A	2-3	Kuula, Piirainen
15/06/95	FinnPa	A	3-1	Nikkilä, Heinänen, Kajander
18/06/95	VPS	H	1-0	Kajander
21/06/95	HJK	H	1-1	Kajander (p)
02/07/95	Ponnistus	A	3-0	Kostin, Lehtonen 2
06/07/95	TPS	H	1-4	Halzov
09/07/95	MyPa	A	0-4	
16/07/95	FC Jazz	A	2-2	Piirainen, Kajander (p)
23/07/95	TPV	H	4-2	Kajander, Kuivasto, Nikkilä, Piirainen
30/07/95	FC Kuusysi	H	1-1	Piirainen
06/08/95	MP	A	1-1	Nikkilä
10/08/95	RoPS	H	1-0	Kajander (p)
27/08/95	Ponnistus	H	1-1	Kotiranta
10/09/95	FC Haka	A	1-0	Piirainen
14/09/95	HJK	A	0-4	
17/09/95	FF Jaro	H	2-3	Kajander (p), Lehtonen
24/09/95	FinnPa	H	0-0	
01/10/95	VPS	A	0-1	
08/10/95	MyPa	H	0-2	
15/10/95	TPS	A	1-2	Nikkilä

FF JARO

CLUB DIRECTORY

FF Jaro
Koulukatu 5
68600 Jakobstad
tel - (967) 7247936
fax - (967) 7230220
Year of Formation - 1965
President - Rainer Karvonen
Secretary - Rolf Ekstedt
Coach - Antti Muurinen
Stadium - Keskuskenttä (5,000)

APPEARANCES 95

	P	Ap	(s)	Gls
Arto HALONEN	M	17	(3)	
Thomas HONGELL	A	15	(8)	
Pasi KATAJAMÄKI	G		(1)	
Timo KIVILOMPOLO	M	20	(1)	4
Kari KORKEA-AHO	D	18	(5)	2
Ville LAAKKONEN	A	3	(15)	
Toni MENSAKOV	M		(1)	
Teuvo MOILANEN	G	26		
Tomas NYGÅRD	D	24	(1)	
Ville NYLUND	D	22	(1)	2
Daniel SNELLMAN	D	4	(10)	
Marko SORVISTO	M	10	(4)	1
Niklas STORBACKA	D		(2)	
Tero SUOMINEN	D	21	(3)	
Vesa TAURIAINEN	A	17	(1)	7
Jari VANHALA	A	21	(2)	12
Petteri VILJANEN	D	26		1
Jimmy WARGH	M		(1)	
Niklas WIDJESKOG	M	19	(4)	2
Aleksei YEREMENKO (RUS)	M	23		5

LEAGUE RESULTS 1995

30/04/95	Ponnistus	H	3-0	Tauriainen (p), Vanhala, Sorvisto
07/05/95	RoPS	A	1-1	Tauriainen
11/05/95	FC Ilves	H	1-2	Kivilomplo (p)
21/05/95	VPS	H	1-0	Tauriainen
25/05/95	FC Haka	A	1-1	Tauriainen
28/05/95	MP	A	1-0	Nylund
06/06/95	HJK	H	1-2	Vanhala
15/06/95	FC Kuusysi	A	1-1	Vanhala
18/06/95	TPS	H	4-2	Tauriainen 2, Widjeskog, Vanhala
21/06/95	FinnPa	A	1-1	Tauriainen (p)
02/07/95	FC Jazz	H	0-2	
06/07/95	MyPa	H	1-3	Yeremenko
09/07/95	TPV	A	1-0	Yeremenko
16/07/95	Ponnistus	A	2-0	Vanhala, Yeremenko
23/07/95	RoPS	H	0-1	
30/07/95	VPS	A	0-1	
06/08/95	FC Haka	H	1-3	Yeremenko
10/08/95	HJK	A	0-0	
20/08/95	FinnPa	H	3-1	Widjeskog, Viljanen, Korkea-aho
27/08/95	FC Jazz	A	0-2	
10/09/95	MP	H	4-0	Korkea-aho, Kivilompolo, Vanhala, Yeremenko
17/09/95	FC Ilves	A	3-2	Vanhala 2, Nylund
24/09/95	FC Kuusysi	H	3-0	Vanhala 2, Kivilompolo
01/10/95	TPS	A	0-3	
08/10/95	TPV	H	4-2	Vanhala 2, Kivilompolo, og (Gawara)
15/10/95	MyPa	A	0-2	

FC JAZZ

CLUB DIRECTORY

FC Jazz
Isolinnankatu 2
28 100 Pori
tel - (939) 6331999
fax - (939) 6331244
Year of Formation - 1934
President - Ilkka Huttunen
Secretary - Kari Annala
Coach - Pertti Lundell (96 - Jari Pyykölä)
Stadium - Porin (10,000)

MAJOR HONOURS
League Championship - (1) 1993.

APPEARANCES 95

	P	Ap	(s)	Gls
Jarmo ALATENSIÖ	M	18	(6)	5
Risto KOSKIKANGAS	D	21	(1)	1
Saku LAAKSONEN	A	13	(8)	1
Tomi LEIVO-JOKIMÄKI	M	5	(13)	
LUIZ ANTÓNIO Moraes (BRA)	A	24		14
Mikko NIEMINEN	D	1	(3)	
Rami NIEMINEN	D	23		4
PIRACAÍA (BRA)	M	24		3
Janne PUPUTTI	M	12	(6)	
Vesa RANTANEN	D	23	(1)	
RODRIGO Vaz (BRA)	M	23	(2)	9
Juha RIIPPA	M	24		3
Jukka RUHANEN	A	23		3
Jani SUIKKANEN	A	1	(9)	
Pasi SULONEN	D	25		
Jukka VANNINEN	M		(4)	
Esa VIITANEN	G	26		

LEAGUE RESULTS 1995

Date	Opponent		Score	Scorers
30/04/95	FC Ilves	A	0-0	
07/05/95	FC Kuusysi	H	3-0	Luiz António, Rodrigo 2
11/05/95	HJK	A	2-1	Rodrigo, Luiz António
21/05/95	TPV	A	1-1	Alatensiö (p)
25/05/95	Ponnistus	H	3-0	Luiz António 2, Rodrigo
04/06/95	MP	A	3-1	Piracaía, Alatensiö, Nieminen
15/06/95	FC Haka	A	0-5	
18/06/95	FinnPa	H	3-1	Luiz António, Laaksonen, Rodrigo
21/06/95	RoPS	H	4-0	Alatensiö 3 (1p), Ruhanen
28/06/95	MyPa	H	0-0	
02/07/95	FF Jaro	A	2-0	Ruhanen, Nieminen
06/07/95	VPS	H	1-2	Nieminen
09/07/95	TPS	A	1-2	Luiz António
16/07/95	FC Ilves	H	2-2	Rodrigo, Luiz António
23/07/95	FC Kuusysi	A	3-0	Riippa, Rodrigo, Luiz António
30/07/95	TPV	H	4-1	Rodrigo 2, Luiz António 2
06/08/95	Ponnistus	A	2-0	Koskikangas, Luiz António
10/08/95	MP	H	0-2	
20/08/95	RoPS	A	1-1	Nieminen
27/08/95	FF Jaro	H	2-0	Riippa, Piracaía
09/09/95	MyPa	A	1-1	Piracaía
17/09/95	HJK	H	1-2	Riippa
23/09/95	FC Haka	H	0-1	
01/10/95	FinnPa	A	0-4	
08/10/95	TPS	H	4-1	Luiz António 3, Ruhanen
15/10/95	VPS	A	0-1	

FC KUUSYSI

CLUB DIRECTORY

FC Kuusysi
Urheilukeskus
15110 Lahti
tel - (918) 7512505
fax - (918) 7516982
Year of Formation - 1934
President - Matti Viljanen
Secretary - Urpo Lampinen
Coach - Jorma Kallio (96 - Kari Kangasaho)
Stadium - Lahti (15,000)

MAJOR HONOURS
League Championship - (5)
1982, 1984, 1986, 1989, 1991.
Domestic Cup - (2) 1983, 1987.

APPEARANCES 95

	P	Ap	(s)	Gls
ANDERSON Menezen (BRA)	A	7	(2)	
Juha ANNUNEN	M	18	(2)	
Aleksei BURDMAN (RUS)	A	1	(1)	
Sasko GULEWSKI (GER)	M	7		
Jyrki HÄNNIKÄINEN	D	6	(2)	
Jani JOUKAINEN	M	1		
Kari KANKAHAINEN	D	9	(3)	
Kaarlo KANKKUNEN	M	4	(5)	1
Mikko KAVEN	G	18		
Tomi KINNUNEN	D	3	(2)	
Pteri KORHONEN	A	2	(3)	
Kari LAIHO	A	4	(7)	2
Sami LEHTINEN	A	1		
Miki LEHTONEN	G	1		
LUCIANO Martins (BRA)	A	11	(5)	2
Timo MARJAMAA	D	2		
Mika MOTTURI	D	26		
Jorma MÄKIPÄÄ	D	1	(1)	
Harri NYYSSÖNEN	M	7		
Esa PEKONEN	D	10		
Lasse PELTONEN	M	23		3
Robert PETRUS (SVK)	A	7		2
Saku PUHAKAINEN	A	15	(10)	9
Markku RAATIKAINEN	D	11		
Jukka RANTALA	M	17		
Tuomas SAARES	M	11		
Jami SIMANAINEN	A	4	(3)	
Niko SIMOLA	G	7	(1)	
Arto SIVONEN	D	13		1
Petri TUOVINEN	M		(2)	
Jari SULANDER	M	16	(4)	1
Sami VEHKAKOSKI	A	14	(5)	2
Anssi VIREN	D	9	(1)	

LEAGUE RESULTS 1995

Date	Opponent	H/A	Score	Scorers
30/04/95	TPV	H	0-0	
07/05/95	FC Jazz	A	0-3	
11/05/95	MP	H	2-1	Peltonen, Puhakainen
15/05/95	FinnPa	A	0-5	
21/05/95	FC Ilves	H	3-2	Luciano 2, Laiho
25/05/95	MyPa	A	2-3	Kankkunen, Puhakainen
04/06/95	FC Haka	H	0-1	
15/06/95	FF Jaro	H	1-1	Sivonen
18/06/95	RoPS	A	1-1	Puhakainen
21/06/95	VPS	A	0-4	
02/07/95	TPS	H	0-1	
05/07/95	Ponnistus	A	1-3	Puhakainen
18/07/95	TPV	A	1-4	Vehkakoski
23/07/95	FC Jazz	H	0-3	
30/07/95	FC Ilves	A	1-1	Puhakainen
03/08/95	MyPa	H	1-3	Peltonen (p)
10/08/95	FC Haka	A	1-4	Vehkakoski
20/08/95	VPS	H	0-1	
23/08/95	HJK	H	1-1	Petrus
27/08/95	TPS	A	1-0	Puhakainen
10/09/95	FinnPa	H	3-1	Puhakainen, Petrus (p), Sulander
17/09/95	MP	A	1-0	Puhakainen
24/09/95	FF Jaro	A	0-3	
01/10/95	RoPS	H	0-1	
10/10/95	HJK	A	0-2	
15/10/95	Ponnistus	H	3-1	Peltonen (p), Laiho, Puhakainen

MP

CLUB DIRECTORY

Mikkelin Palloilijat
PL 324
50101 Mikkeli
tel - (955) 161342
fax - (955) 365321
Year of Formation - 1929
President - Matti Vanhanen
Secretary - Arto Ollikainen
Coach - Hannu Touru; Kari Pasanen (96 - Tibor Gruborovics)
Stadium - Urheilupuisto (10,000)

MAJOR HONOURS
Domestic Cup - (2) 1970, 1971.

APPEARANCES 95

	P	Ap	(s)	Gls
Tibor GRUBOROVICS (HUN)	M	10	(2)	
Mika HAIKARAINEN	A		(2)	
Jari HUDD	D	20	(1)	1
Tero HULKKONEN	D		(3)	
Jussi JÄÄSKELÄINEN	G	26		
Juuso KANGASKORPI	A	26		5
Juha KARVINEN	M	25		6
Markku KESÄLAHTI	M	14	(10)	
Harri KORHONEN	M	15	(1)	1
Shefki KUQI (ALB)	A	14	(10)	3
Janne LAHTONEN	D	2	(4)	
Kim LEHTONEN	M	22	(1)	3
Jani LUUKKONEN	G		(1)	
Mikko MANNINEN	D	21	(2)	1
Ilkka MÄKELÄ	D	21		1
Jouni RÄSÄNEN	D	19	(4)	1
Jari SARIOLA	A	11	(10)	1
Tommi SARIOLA	A	1	(3)	
Niko TERÄSALMI	D	1	(1)	
Leo TUISKU	M	1		
Hannu VALTONEN	M	17	(1)	
Timo-Pekka VIITIKKO	D	20		

LEAGUE RESULTS 1995

30/04/95	HJK	A	0-0	
07/05/95	TPS	H	3-1	Kangaskorpi 2, Korhonen
11/05/95	FC Kuusysi	A	1-2	Karvinen
21/05/95	MyPa	H	0-1	
25/05/95	FC Ilves	A	1-5	Kuqi
28/05/95	FF Jaro	H	0-1	
04/06/95	FC Jazz	H	1-3	Kangaskorpi
14/06/95	VPS	A	1-0	Kangaskorpi
18/06/95	TPV	H	0-1	
21/06/95	Ponnistus	H	1-0	Karvinen
02/07/95	RoPS	A	0-0	
06/07/95	FinnPa	H	3-0	Karvinen, Kangaskorpi, Mäkelä (p)
09/07/95	FC Haka	A	0-4	
16/07/95	HJK	H	2-2	Karvinen 2
20/07/95	MyPa	A	0-1	
23/07/95	TPS	A	0-0	
06/08/95	FC Ilves	H	1-1	Lehtonen
10/08/95	FC Jazz	A	2-0	Karvinen, Manninen
20/08/95	Ponnistus	A	1-2	Räsänen
29/08/95	RoPS	H	2-1	Sariola J., Lehtonen
10/09/95	FF Jaro	A	0-4	
17/09/95	FC Kuusysi	H	0-1	
24/09/95	VPS	H	2-0	Kuqi 2
01/10/95	TPV	A	1-1	Hudd
08/10/95	FC Haka	H	0-3	
15/10/95	FinnPa	A	1-1	Lehtonen

MYPA

CLUB DIRECTORY

Myllykosken Pallo-47
Koulutie 1
46800 Anjalankoski
tel - (951) 3255292
fax - (951) 3255292
Year of Formation - 1947
President - Matti Tiihonen
Secretary - Paavo Oksanen
Coach - Harri Kampman
Stadium - Saviniemi (8,000)

MAJOR HONOURS
Domestic Cup - (2) 1992, 1995.

APPEARANCES 95

	P	Ap	(s)	Gls
Niclas GRÖNHOLM	A	22	(3)	10
Ilpo HELLSTEN	D	4	(7)	
Mika HERNESNIEMI	A	12	(8)	
Toni HUTTUNEN	D	26		2
Sami HYYPIÄ	D	26		3
Petri JAKONEN	G	25		
Tommi KAUTONEN	M	18	(2)	1
Mauri KESKITALO	A	17	(5)	5
Joonas KOLKKA	A	20	(2)	6
Jarkko KOSKINEN	D	8	(12)	
Jukka KOSKINEN	D	26		
Jukka LINDSTRÖM	D		(1)	
Sami MAHLIO	M	22	(2)	4
Antti POHJA	A	7	(11)	5
Anders ROTH	M	11	(4)	1
Petri TIAINEN	M	17	(2)	7
Mika VILJANEN	D	24		
Vesa VUORINEN	G	1		

LEAGUE RESULTS 1995

Date	Opponent	H/A	Score	Scorers
30/04/95	RoPS	H	0-0	
02/05/95	FinnPa	A	2-0	Huttunen, Grönholm
11/05/95	VPS	H	3-1	Kautonen, Mahlio 2
21/05/95	MP	A	1-0	Grönholm
25/05/95	FC Kuusysi	H	3-2	Tiainen 3 (1p)
04/06/95	TPV	A	0-1	
14/06/95	HJK	H	1-0	Kolkka
18/06/95	Ponnistus	A	1-0	Tiainen (p)
21/06/95	TPS	A	3-1	Keskitalo, Kolkka, Grönholm
28/06/95	FC Jazz	A	0-0	
02/07/95	FC Haka	H	3-1	Kolkka, Keskitalo, Grönholm
06/07/95	FF Jaro	A	3-1	Roth, Grönholm, Kolkka
09/07/95	FC Ilves	H	4-0	Pohja 2, Kolkka, Grönholm
16/07/95	RoPS	A	1-3	Hyypiä
20/07/95	MP	H	1-0	Hyypiä
23/07/95	FinnPa	H	1-2	Hyypiä (p)
03/08/95	FC Kuusysi	A	3-1	Tiainen 2 (2p), Keskitalo
19/08/95	TPS	H	3-0	Kolkka, Pohja, Keskitalo (p)
27/08/95	FC Haka	A	0-3	
02/09/95	TPV	H	1-1	Grönholm
09/09/95	FC Jazz	H	1-1	Tiainen (p)
16/09/95	VPS	A	0-1	
20/09/95	HJK	A	1-1	Keskitalo
01/10/95	Ponnistus	A	5-0	Grönholm 3, Mahlio, Pohja
08/10/95	FC Ilves	A	2-0	Huttunen, og (Kajander)
15/10/95	FF Jaro	H	2-0	Mahlio, Pohja

PONNISTUS

CLUB DIRECTORY

Ponnistus
Vallininkuja 2 C 40
00530 Helsinki
tel - (90) 736576
fax - (90) 61354250
Year of Formation - 1887
President - Jaakko Lempinen
Secretary - Mika Roos
Coach - Jari Niini; Anatoli Davydov (96 - Ari Aho)
Stadium - Olympiastadion (45,000) or
Velodrome (5,000)

APPEARANCES 95

	P	Ap	(s)	Gls
Moshood ABDUL'AZIZ (NIG)	A	3	(7)	
Anatoli DAVYDOV (RUS)	D	16	(4)	1
Keni HEIKKINEN	A		(3)	
Jarkko HÄIKIÖ	G	4	(1)	
Markus JUHOLA	G	1		
Olli KANGASLAHTI	A	21	(3)	7
Jukka KOIVURINTA	M		(1)	
Juha KOSKINEN	M	15	(3)	
Janne LAINE	D	23	(1)	
Matti LAITILA	D	6	(3)	
Jan LEINO	M	1	(3)	
Jani MYLLYNIEMI	A	17	(3)	1
Miikka NURMI	M	15	(6)	1
Jani NYHOLM	D	18	(3)	
Jukka OIKARINEN	G	19	(2)	
Tommi PAAVOLA	A	24	(1)	5
Reijo PAUKKU	D	10	(1)	
Pasi PIHAMAA	A	23	(2)	
Ari PYHÄLÄ	G	2		
Petteri SALONEN	D	11		
Janne SORSA	M	21	(2)	
Jari TAKATALO	M	6	(6)	1
Mika TETRI	M	10	(5)	
Sami YLÄ-JUSSILA	M	20	(4)	3

LEAGUE RESULTS 1995

30/04/95	FF Jaro	A	0-3	
06/05/95	HJK	H	0-2	
11/05/95	TPV	A	1-4	Kangaslahti
14/05/95	RoPS	H	0-0	
22/05/95	FC Haka	H	0-6	
25/05/95	FC Jazz	A	0-3	
05/06/95	VPS	H	3-2	Ylä-Jussila, Paavola, Takatalo
15/06/95	TPS	A	0-0	
18/06/95	MyPa	H	0-1	
21/06/95	MP	A	0-1	
02/07/95	FC Ilves	H	0-3	
05/07/95	FC Kuusysi	H	3-1	Paavola 2, Kangaslahti
09/07/95	FinnPa	A	0-6	
16/07/95	FF Jaro	H	0-2	
26/07/95	HJK	A	0-5	
29/07/95	FC Haka	A	0-3	
06/08/95	FC Jazz	H	0-2	
10/08/95	VPS	A	3-2	Paavola 2, Myllyniemi
20/08/95	MP	H	2-1	Kangaslahti 2
27/08/95	FC Ilves	A	1-1	Kangaslahti
10/09/95	RoPS	A	1-4	Ylä-Jussila
17/09/95	TPV	H	1-0	Kangaslahti
24/09/95	TPS	H	2-1	Davydov, Nurmi
01/10/95	MyPa	A	0-5	
08/10/95	FinnPa	H	1-2	Kangaslahti
15/10/95	FC Kuusysi	A	1-3	Ylä-Jussila

ROPS

CLUB DIRECTORY

Rovaniemen Palloseura
PL 2230
96201 Rovaniemi
tel - (960) 314977
fax - (960) 319837
Year of Formation - 1950
President - Matti Pelttari
Secretary - Markku Laines
Coach - Timo Salmi; Graham Williams; Ari Matinlassi (96 - Ari Rantamaa)
Stadium - Keskuskenttä (4,000)

MAJOR HONOURS
Domestic Cup - (1) 1986.

APPEARANCES 95

	P	Ap	(s)	Gls
Pekka AUTIO	A		(1)	
Arto AUTTI	D	22		
David ELLIOTT (ENG)	D	25		
Yrjö HAPPONEN	M	12	(1)	
Matti HIUKKA	A	4	(3)	3
Hannu HONKANEN	M	4	(8)	1
Mika HUIKARI	D	10	(4)	
Jari ILOLA	D		(2)	
Tero KEMPPAINEN	M	21	(2)	2
Marko KOIVURANTA	A	2	(5)	
Juha-Pekka NIVA	M		(1)	
Jacek PERZYK (POL)	D	25		4
Timo PIRILÄ	M	9	(3)	
Zeddy SAILETI (ZAM)	A	25		7
Pasi SALMELA	M	5	(5)	1
Kai SAVOLAINEN	A	18	(7)	1
Emmanuel SIWALE (ZAM)	M	21		4
Miika TOLVANEN	D	25		
Tuomas TUOMILEHTO	G	22		
Rami VEHMAS	M		(1)	
Matti VIKMAN	G	4		
Vesa WIMMER	D	11	(4)	2
Samuli YLIASKA	A	21	(2)	4

LEAGUE RESULTS 1995

Date	Opponent	H/A	Score	Scorers
30/04/95	MyPa	A	0-0	
07/05/95	FF Jaro	H	1-1	Saileti
11/05/95	FinnPa	H	0-0	
14/05/95	Ponnistus	A	0-0	
21/05/95	TPS	H	0-1	
25/05/95	HJK	A	0-1	
04/06/95	FC Ilves	H	3-2	Salmela, Siwale, Savolainen
15/06/95	TPV	A	3-1	Perzyk 2, Saileti
18/06/95	FC Kuusysi	H	1-1	Siwale
21/06/95	FC Jazz	A	0-4	
02/07/95	MP	H	0-0	
06/07/95	FC Haka	H	0-1	
09/07/95	VPS	A	0-0	
16/07/95	MyPa	H	3-1	Siwale, Yliaska, Kemppainen (p)
23/07/95	FF Jaro	A	1-0	Yliaska
30/07/95	TPS	A	0-1	
06/08/95	HJK	H	2-3	Perzyk, Siwale
10/08/95	FC Ilves	A	0-1	
20/08/95	FC Jazz	H	1-1	Saileti
29/08/95	MP	A	1-2	Hiukka
10/09/95	Ponnistus	H	4-1	Saileti 3, Perzyk
16/09/95	FinnPa	A	1-0	Yliaska
24/09/95	TPV	H	3-4	Yliaska, Honkanen, Kemppainen (p)
01/10/95	FC Kuusysi	A	1-0	Hiukka
08/10/95	VPS	H	2-0	Wimmer, Hiukka
15/10/95	FC Haka	A	2-4	Saileti, Wimmer

TPS

CLUB DIRECTORY

Jalkapallo TPS
Uudenmaankatu 19 B
20700 Turku
tel - (921) 2731140
fax - (921) 2731181
Year of Formation - 1922
President - Juhka Arnivaara
Secretary - Taina Sipilä
Coach - Juha Malinen
Stadium - Kupittaa (10,000)

MAJOR HONOURS
League Championship - (8) 1928, 1939, 1941, 1949, 1968, 1971, 1972, 1975.
Domestic Cup - (2) 1991, 1994.

APPEARANCES 95

	P	Ap	(s)	Gls
John ALLEN (WAL)	A	24	(2)	8
Marco CASAGRANDE	D	25		
Tom ENBERG	A	25	(1)	8
Peter ENCKELMAN	G	5	(1)	
Jasse JALONEN	M	22	(2)	1
Jonatan JOHANSSON	M	8	(1)	
Petteri KAIJASILTA	M		(2)	
Jani KEULA	D	25		
Petri KOKKO	M	11	(1)	4
Mark KULMALA	A		(1)	
Timo LAHTIVUORI	A	3	(4)	
Mikko LEHTOVAARA	M		(1)	
Kimmo MIETTINEN	D	5	(2)	
Johan NYLUND	M		(3)	
Janne OINAS	D	12	(2)	
Markus PAIJA	D		(2)	
Jani PELTOLA	A	8	(13)	2
Jani PYLKÄS	A	21	(4)	6
Janne SAVOLAINEN	M	17	(8)	1
Petri SULONEN	D	24		2
Panu TOIVONEN	G	20		
Jussi VILJANEN	M		(6)	
Petri VILJANEN	G	1		
Tommi VIRTANEN	M	7	(11)	
Mika WALLDEN	D	23	(1)	1

LEAGUE RESULTS 1995

Date	Opponent	H/A	Score	Scorers
30/04/95	VPS	H	2-1	Pylkäs, Allen
07/05/95	MP	A	1-3	Savolainen
11/05/95	FC Haka	A	1-1	Pylkäs
14/05/95	HJK	H	0-0	
21/05/95	RoPS	A	1-0	Kokko
25/05/95	TPV	H	3-0	Kokko, Allen 2
28/05/95	FinnPa	H	5-1	Enberg 4 (1p), Sulonen
15/06/95	Ponnistus	H	0-0	
18/06/95	FF Jaro	A	2-4	Kokko 2 (1p)
21/06/95	MyPa	H	1-3	Allen
02/07/95	FC Kuusysi	A	1-0	Sulonen
06/07/95	FC Ilves	A	4-1	Pylkäs 2, Allen, Enberg
09/07/95	FC Jazz	H	2-1	Pylkäs, Jalonen
16/07/95	VPS	A	0-1	
23/07/95	MP	H	0-0	
30/07/95	RoPS	H	1-0	Enberg
03/08/95	TPV	A	1-1	Wallden (p)
19/08/95	MyPa	A	0-3	
27/08/95	FC Kuusysi	H	0-1	
31/08/95	FinnPa	A	0-1	
10/09/95	HJK	A	0-0	
17/09/95	FC Haka	H	1-3	Peltola
24/09/95	Ponnistus	A	1-2	Allen
01/10/95	FF Jaro	H	3-0	Enberg, Peltola, Pylkäs
08/10/95	FC Jazz	A	1-4	Allen
15/10/95	FC Ilves	H	2-1	Enberg, Allen

TPV

CLUB DIRECTORY

Tampereen Pallo-Veikot (TPV)
Teiskontie 1A
33540 Tampere
tel - (931) 2617211
fax - (931) 2617241
Year of Formation - 1930
President - Jukka Gustafsson
Secretary - Jarmo Tuomiranta
Coach - Jari-Pekka Keurulainen; Jussi Ristimäki
(96 - Pertti Lundell)
Stadium - Tammela (6,000)

MAJOR HONOURS
League Championship - (1) 1994.

APPEARANCES 95

	P	Ap	(s)	Gls
Jari AALTONEN	A	17	(3)	6
Mika AALTONEN	M	20		1
DIONÍSIO (BRA)	A	19	(4)	3
Krzysztof GAWARA (POL)	D	12	(2)	
Marcelo GRANDI (BRA)	A	1	(9)	2
Marko GRANHOLM	D	24		
Miika JUNTUNEN	M	26		8
Vasili KARATAYEV (RUS)	M	11	(3)	1
Tommi KOIVISTOINEN	G	22		
Petri KUULA	A	2	(10)	1
Petri LEVOLA	D	19	(3)	
Timo LINDHOLM	D	11	(4)	
Jukka LISTENMAA	M	8	(6)	2
Juha-Pekka MÄKINEN	D	24		2
Jari NIEMI	M	10	(2)	
Anssi PELLIKKA	M	10	(8)	1
Jukka-Pekka PIETILÄ	D	4	(3)	
Marko TUOMELA	D	17	(6)	2
Ville VAHLA	G	4	(1)	
Jarkko WISS	M	25		3

LEAGUE RESULTS 1995

30/04/95	FC Kuusysi	A	0-0	
07/05/95	FC Ilves	H	1-2	Listenmaa
11/05/95	Ponnistus	H	4-1	Aaltonen M., Juntunen 2, Grandi
14/05/95	VPS	A	1-2	Mäkinen
21/05/95	FC Jazz	H	1-1	Grandi
25/05/95	TPS	A	0-3	
04/06/95	MyPa	H	1-0	Aaltonen J.
15/06/95	RoPS	H	1-3	Tuomela
18/06/95	MP	A	1-0	Aaltonen J.
21/06/95	FC Haka	A	0-1	
02/07/95	FinnPa	H	4-3	Juntunen 2, Aaltonen J., Karatayev
05/07/95	HJK	A	1-1	Aaltonen J.
09/07/95	FF Jaro	H	0-1	
18/07/95	FC Kuusysi	H	4-1	Wiss, Juntunen, Aaltonen J., Kuula
23/07/95	FC Ilves	A	2-4	Juntunen, Aaltonen J.
30/07/95	FC Jazz	A	1-4	Dionísio
03/08/95	TPS	H	1-1	Juntunen
19/08/95	FC Haka	H	0-2	
28/08/95	FinnPa	A	0-3	
02/09/95	MyPa	A	1-1	og (Hyypiä)
10/09/95	VPS	H	0-1	
17/09/95	Ponnistus	A	0-1	
24/09/95	RoPS	A	4-3	Mäkinen, Wiss 2, Dionísio
01/10/95	MP	H	1-1	Pellikka
08/10/95	FF Jaro	A	2-4	Dionísio, Tuomela
15/10/95	HJK	H	2-4	Juntunen, Listenmaa

VPS

CLUB DIRECTORY

Vasan Palloseura (VPS)
PL 454
65101 Vaasa
tel - (961) 3177884
Year of Formation - 1924
President - Eero Karhumäki
Secretary - Jukka Niemi
Coach - Boguslaw Hajdas (96 - Hannu Touru)
Stadium - Hietalahti (5,000)

MAJOR HONOURS

League Championship - (2) 1945, 1948.

APPEARANCES 95

	P	Ap	(s)	Gls
Tomasz ARCEUSZ (POL)	D	21		1
Kazimierz BUDA (POL)	D	23	(1)	
Jyrki HUHTAMÄKI	A	24		
Sasu IIVONEN	M	6	(10)	
Jari JÄVÄJÄ	A	24	(1)	9
Harri KEVARI	M	22		1
Christoffer KLOO	D	25		5
Jari KOLJONEN	A		(1)	
Ulf KORTESNIEMI	G	26		
Tomi KÄRKKÄINEN	M	6	(4)	1
Pasi NEVANPERÄ	A	2	(6)	1
Reijo PALOVUORI	D	19	(2)	
Mike PELTOLA	D	2	(13)	
Michael PUISTO	A	8	(4)	
Rami RINTANEN	M	24	(1)	2
Jari RÄSÄNEN	D	8		
Vladimir STROGANOV (RUS)	M	18		2
Marko SUOSTE	D	17		2
Leo TUISKU	M	3	(1)	
Peter WESTERSTEN	A	1		
Tommi VIRKAMA	M	7	(11)	

LEAGUE RESULTS 1995

30/04/95	TPS	A	1-2	Jäväjä
07/05/95	FC Haka	H	1-1	Kloo (p)
11/05/95	MyPa	A	1-3	Suoste
14/05/95	TPV	H	2-1	Jäväjä, Kloo (p)
21/05/95	FF Jaro	A	0-1	
25/05/95	FinnPa	H	1-3	Nevanperä
05/06/95	Ponnistus	A	2-3	Suoste, Jäväjä
14/06/95	MP	H	0-1	
18/06/95	FC Ilves	A	0-1	
21/06/95	FC Kuusysi	H	4-0	Stroganov, Jäväjä, Kärkkäinen, og (Motturi)
06/07/95	FC Jazz	A	2-1	Jäväjä 2
09/07/95	RoPS	H	0-0	
16/07/95	TPS	H	1-0	og (Casagrande)
23/07/95	FC Haka	A	0-2	
30/07/95	FF Jaro	H	1-0	Kloo (p)
03/08/95	HJK	A	1-4	Kloo (p)
07/08/95	FinnPa	A	2-3	Stroganov, Kloo (p)
10/08/95	Ponnistus	H	2-3	Jäväjä, Kevari
20/08/95	FC Kuusysi	A	1-0	Arceusz
27/08/95	HJK	H	0-1	
10/09/95	TPV	A	1-0	Jäväjä
16/09/95	MyPa	A	1-0	Rintanen
24/09/95	MP	A	0-2	
01/10/95	FC Ilves	H	1-0	Rintanen
08/10/95	RoPS	A	0-2	
15/10/95	FC Jazz	H	1-0	Jäväjä

PROMOTED CLUB

SECOND DIVISION FINAL TABLE 95

		Pd	W	D	L	F	A	Pt	GD
1	**FC InterTurku**	**26**	**17**	**5**	**4**	**63**	**20**	**56**	**+43**
2	KTP	26	11	9	6	45	37	42	+8
3	Kultsu	26	12	5	9	29	33	41	-4
4	Reipas	26	11	7	8	34	36	40	-2
5	KePS	26	9	11	6	48	35	38	+13
6	P-Iirot	26	11	5	10	44	48	38	-4
7	K-Team	26	8	10	8	42	37	34	+5
8	FC Kontu	26	7	13	6	39	38	34	+1
9	Gnistan	26	7	13	6	28	27	34	+1
10	GBK	26	8	10	8	36	44	34	-8
11	Rakuunat	26	8	7	11	34	38	31	-4
12	KuPS	26	6	7	13	27	36	25	-9
13	PV Kokkola	26	5	9	12	28	36	24	-8
14	PP-70	26	3	7	16	24	56	16	-32

PROMOTION/RELEGATION PLAY-OFF
KTP 0, MP 1
MP 2, KTP 1
(MP 3-1)

CLUB DIRECTORY

FC InterTurku
Maria Forss
Linnankatu 36 C
20100 Turku
tel - (921) 2312552
fax - (921) 2515873
Year of Formation - 1993
President - Stefan Håkans
Secretary - Maria Forss
Coach - Hannu Paatelo
Stadium - Kupittaa (10,000)

FRANCE

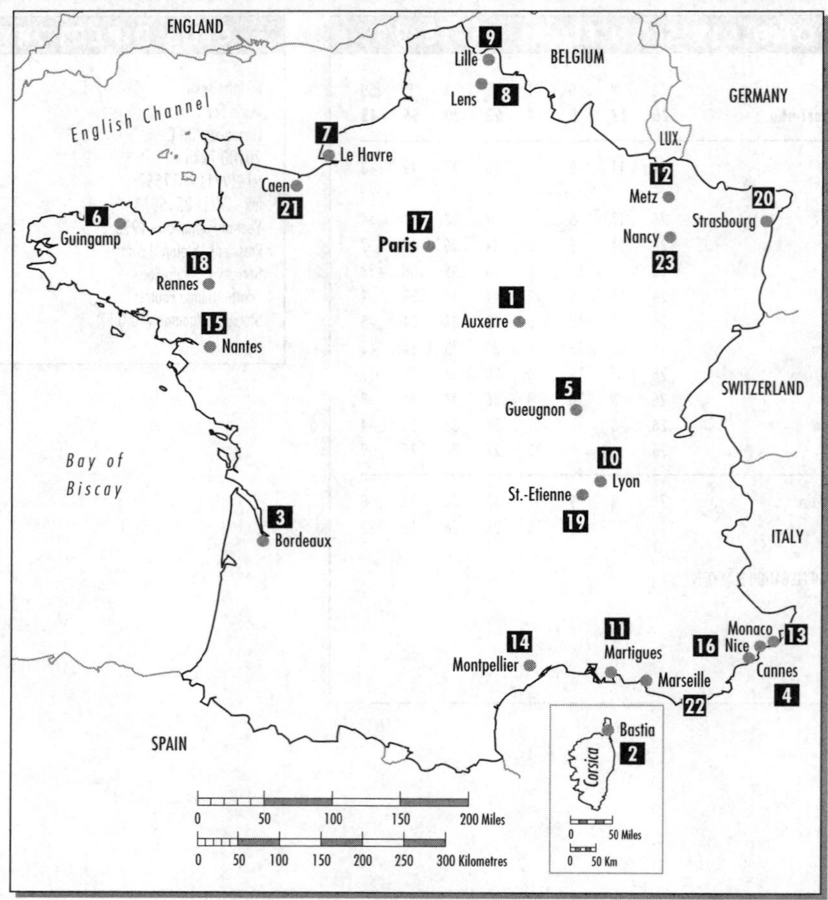

1	AJ AUXERRE	394
2	SC BASTIA	395
3	GIRONDINS DE BORDEAUX	396
4	AS CANNES	397
5	FC GUEUGNON	398
6	EN AVANT GUINGAMP	399
7	LE HAVRE AC	400
8	RC LENS	401
9	LILLE OSC	402
10	OLYMPIQUE LYONNAIS	403
11	FC MARTIGUES	404
12	FC METZ	405
13	AS MONACO	406
14	MONTPELLIER HSC	407
15	FC NANTES	408
16	OGC NICE	409
17	PARIS SAINT-GERMAIN FC	410
18	STADE RENNAIS FC	411
19	AS SAINT-ETIENNE	412
20	RC STRASBOURG	413
21	SM CAEN	414
22	OLYMPIQUE MARSEILLE	414
23	AS NANCY-LORRAINE	414

ROUX AND AUXERRE - A MAGIC 'DOUBLE' ACT

Unadventurous and unloved... but still unbeaten

FEDERATION DIRECTORY

Fédération Française de Football
60 bis Avenue d'Iena, 75783 Paris cedex 16

tel - (1 44) 317300
tlx - 620837 fedfoot f
fax - (1 47) 208296

Year of Formation - 1919
President - Claude Simonet
Secretary - Gérard Ernault

Stadium - Parc des Princes, Paris (48,712)

France at Euro '96 were everything that the pre-tournament soothsayers predicted they would be. Rock-solid in defence. Tactically well-organised. High on confidence and difficult to beat. They also possessed an impressive array of talented individuals, many of whom were on their way to some of European football's most revered clubs after the tournament.

In short, France had the look of champions. That they failed to regain the Henri Delaunay trophy they won on home soil 12 years earlier was ostensibly down to sheer bad luck. A penalty shoot-out defeat by the Czech Republic deprived Aimé Jacquet's team of a place in the Wembley final, where, possibly, they would have got the better of a German team they had already defeated a month earlier in Stuttgart.

But the truth of the matter is France did not do themselves justice. Not in the semi-final against a Czech team depleted by suspensions, and not in the tournament as a whole.

English fans were dismayed and bewildered by the non-selection of Premiership superstars Eric Cantona and David Ginola. France itself was split right down the middle as to whether Jacquet should have taken the pair to England. Ultimately, neither player was to make the squad, Jacquet insisting that although he admired the two players' individual talents, he did not want to disrupt the balance of a team that had not lost a single match in the two and a half years that he had been in charge. The coach had a point. After all, one of the longest-held maxims in football is that you don't change a winning team.

LEAGUE CHAMPIONSHIP RESULTS 95/96

		1	2	3	4	5	6	7	8	9	10	11	12	13	14	15	16	17	18	19	20
1	AJ Auxerre		3-0	2-0	5-1	4-0	1-2	1-0	0-1	1-2	2-0	4-0	0-0	1-2	1-0	2-1	2-1	3-0	2-1	2-0	1-0
2	SC Bastia	1-1		2-0	2-1	1-2	0-1	1-0	3-2	4-0	0-0	2-0	1-0	2-1	1-0	4-1	1-2	2-2	0-0	0-0	1-1
3	Girondins de Bordeaux	0-1	1-3		2-1	3-1	2-0	3-1	0-0	1-0	1-1	1-1	4-0	2-4	3-0	3-0	4-1	2-2	0-0	2-0	1-1
4	AS Cannes	0-1	1-0	1-1		2-0	3-0	0-0	5-2	2-1	3-0	2-1	1-2	1-1	2-1	0-2	1-3	0-2	3-0	2-0	0-3
5	FC Gueugnon	0-0	1-0	2-2	1-1		2-2	0-1	0-1	3-1	0-0	0-0	0-0	2-2	0-2	0-1	1-0	1-3	1-0	1-0	0-1
6	En Avant Guingamp	1-1	1-0	1-0	2-0	0-0		2-2	1-0	0-1	1-0	2-0	0-0	0-0	0-0	3-1	0-0	0-0	0-0	3-0	3-0
7	Le Havre AC	0-4	1-0	1-0	0-0	0-2	1-0		1-1	4-1	2-1	1-0	0-0	2-1	2-2	0-1	0-0	1-1	0-0	2-2	2-0
8	RC Lens	0-0	3-1	0-0	1-1	2-0	0-1	2-0		1-1	2-2	1-0	2-0	2-1	2-1	2-1	0-0	3-1	1-0	3-0	0-0
9	Lille OSC	0-4	0-2	0-2	0-2	2-0	0-3	2-0	1-3		2-1	0-0	0-0	0-0	1-1	0-0	1-0	0-0	0-0	1-1	2-0
10	Olympique Lyonnais	0-1	1-1	1-0	1-0	0-0	1-1	3-2	0-0	1-1		5-1	1-1	3-3	3-2	1-1	1-0	0-0	2-2	2-1	1-1
11	FC Martigues	1-2	3-1	3-1	2-1	3-0	2-1	0-1	0-1	1-0	1-2		0-1	0-4	0-1	0-4	0-0	2-4	1-2	1-1	2-0
12	FC Metz	3-1	2-0	2-0	0-0	1-2	3-0	2-1	2-0	2-0	0-1	2-0		0-3	1-0	0-0	4-0	0-3	0-0	1-2	3-2
13	AS Monaco	2-2	0-0	2-0	1-0	0-0	1-0	2-1	1-1	2-1	0-2	0-1	0-1		3-1	4-1	1-0	1-0	3-1	2-0	5-1
14	Montpellier HSC	3-1	4-3	3-0	3-1	2-2	2-1	2-0	0-0	0-0	2-1	2-0	1-2	0-0		1-0	0-1	1-0	3-1	1-0	2-2
15	FC Nantes	1-0	3-1	2-0	2-0	1-0	0-0	1-1	1-1	1-2	0-0	3-0	1-0	2-2	1-0		1-0	1-2	2-2	2-2	2-0
16	OGC Nice	1-3	3-1	1-0	1-2	3-1	2-1	1-2	1-1	2-1	1-0	1-0	0-1	1-2	1-2	1-0		1-2	0-0	2-0	2-2
17	Paris Saint-Germain FC	3-1	5-1	3-0	2-1	1-1	1-1	2-0	1-0	0-1	2-0	0-0	2-3	2-1	2-3	5-0	3-2		1-1	4-0	2-0
18	Stade Rennais FC	2-1	2-0	4-3	3-2	2-1	3-0	1-0	2-1	3-1	1-0	1-3	0-0	2-3	1-1	2-2	1-0	0-1		3-0	0-0
19	AS Saint-Etienne	0-5	3-0	2-0	2-2	2-0	4-0	1-1	1-1	1-1	1-1	2-2	1-1	2-4	0-2	0-0	1-1	1-1	0-0		2-0
20	RC Strasbourg	1-0	4-3	3-0	1-0	0-0	0-0	3-0	1-2	2-0	2-2	2-0	1-2	2-0	1-0	1-1	1-1	1-0	3-1	3-1	

LEAGUE CHAMPIONSHIP FINAL TABLE 95/96

			Home					Away					Total						
		Pd	W	D	L	F	A	W	D	L	F	A	W	D	L	F	A	Pt	GD
1	AJ Auxerre	38	14	1	4	37	11	8	5	6	29	19	22	6	10	56	30	72	+36
2	Paris Saint-Germain FC	38	12	4	3	41	16	7	7	5	24	20	19	11	8	65	36	68	+29
3	AS Monaco	38	12	4	3	30	13	7	7	5	34	26	19	11	8	64	39	68	+25
4	FC Metz	38	11	3	5	28	15	7	8	4	14	15	18	11	9	42	30	65	+12
5	RC Lens	38	11	7	1	27	10	5	8	6	18	21	16	15	7	45	31	63	+14
6	Montpellier HSC	38	12	5	2	32	15	5	4	10	19	25	17	9	12	51	40	60	+11
7	FC Nantes	38	10	7	2	27	13	4	6	9	17	29	14	13	11	44	42	55	+2
8	Stade Rennais FC	38	12	4	3	33	19	1	11	7	11	22	13	15	10	44	41	54	+3
9	RC Strasbourg	38	12	5	2	32	13	2	7	10	14	31	14	12	12	46	44	54	+2
10	En Avant Guingamp	38	9	9	1	20	5	4	5	10	14	28	13	14	11	34	33	53	+1
11	Olympique Lyonnais	38	7	11	1	27	18	3	7	9	14	23	10	18	10	41	41	48	=
12	OGC Nice	38	9	3	7	25	21	3	6	10	12	23	12	9	17	37	44	45	-7
13	Le Havre AC	38	8	8	3	20	16	3	4	12	13	29	11	12	15	33	45	45	-12
14	AS Cannes	38	10	3	6	29	20	2	5	12	16	31	12	8	18	45	51	44	-6
15	SC Bastia	38	10	6	3	28	14	2	2	15	17	41	12	8	18	45	55	44	-10
16	Girondins de Bordeaux	38	10	6	3	35	17	1	3	15	9	35	11	9	18	44	52	42	-8
17	Lille OSC	38	5	8	6	12	19	4	4	11	15	31	9	12	17	27	50	39	-23
18	FC Gueugnon	38	5	8	6	15	17	3	6	10	12	29	8	14	16	27	46	38	-19
19	AS Saint-Etienne	38	5	11	3	26	22	1	5	13	10	37	6	16	16	36	59	34	-23
20	FC Martigues	38	7	2	10	22	27	2	5	12	9	31	9	7	22	31	58	34	-27

But over the years France have built themselves a reputation as one of the most stylish and seductive teams in Europe. The French supporters have come to expect their national side to provide flair and ingenuity as well as discipline and commitment. In England, Youri Djorkaeff was the only French player who appeared to have any licence to entertain. While the rest of the players all diligently fulfilled their functions, the man in the number nine

TOP SCORERS

21	Sonny ANDERSON (AS Monaco)
20	Anto DROBNJAK (SC Bastia)
18	Florian MAURICE (Olympique Lyonnais)
15	Japhet N'DORAM (FC Nantes)
	Julio Cesar DELY VALDES (Paris Saint-Germain FC)
	Sylvain WILTORD (Stade Rennais FC)
14	RAÍ (Paris Saint-Germain FC)
13	Corentin MARTINS (AJ Auxerre)
	Youri DJORKAEFF (Paris Saint-Germain FC)

NATIONAL TEAM RESULTS 95/96

22/07/95	Norway	A	Oslo	0-0	
16/08/95	Poland (ECQ)	H	Paris	1-1	Djorkaeff (85)
06/09/95	Azerbaijan (ECQ)	H	Auxerre	10-0	Desailly (13), Djorkaeff (17, 78), Guérin (33), Pedros (49), Leboeuf (54, 74), Dugarry (65), Zidane (72), Cocard (90)
11/10/95	Romania (ECQ)	A	Bucharest	3-1	Karembeu (29), Djorkaeff (41), Zidane (72)
15/11/95	Israel (ECQ)	H	Caen	2-0	Djorkaeff (69), Lizarazu (89)
24/01/96	Portugal	H	Paris	3-2	Djorkaeff (24, 75), Pedros (77)
21/02/96	Greece	H	Nîmes	3-1	Loko (30, 46p), Zidane (49)
27/03/96	Belgium	A	Brussels	2-0	Albert (66og), Lamouchi (72)
29/05/96	Finland	H	Strasbourg	2-0	Loko (15), Pedros (18)
01/06/96	Germany	A	Stuttgart	1-0	Blanc (6)
05/06/96	Armenia	H	Villeneuve-d'Ascq	2-0	Angloma (15), Madar (70)
10/06/96	Romania (ECF)	N	Newcastle	1-0	Dugarry (25)
15/06/96	Spain (ECF)	N	Leeds	1-1	Djorkaeff (48)
18/06/96	Bulgaria (ECF)	N	Newcastle	3-1	Blanc (20), Penev (62og), Loko (90)
22/06/96	Holland (ECF)	N	Liverpool	0-0	
26/06/96	Czech Rep. (ECF)	N	Manchester	0-0	

NATIONAL TEAM APPEARANCES 95/96

Coach - Aimé JACQUET	NOR	POL	AZB	ROM	ISR	POR	GRE	BEL	FIN	GER	ARM	ROM	ESP	BUL	HOL	TCH	Cps	Gls
Bernard LAMA (07/04/63) - Paris Saint-Germain FC	G	G	G		G	G	G	G		G	G	G	G	G	G	G	33	-
Lilian THURAM (01/01/72) - AS Monaco	D	D	s57	s84			D	D46	D	D	s46	D	s81	D	D	D83	16	-
Alain ROCHE (14/10/67) - Paris Saint-Germain FC	D							D				s80	s65			D	25	1
Laurent BLANC (19/11/65) - AJ Auxerre	D							D		D	D	D	D	D	D	D	54	10
Bixente LIZARAZU (09/12/69) - Girondins de Bordeaux	D	D	D	s73	s63				s67	s66	D	s68	D	D	D	D	25	1
Claude MAKELELE (18/02/73) - FC Nantes	M																1	-
Vincent GUERIN (22/11/65) - Paris Saint-Germain FC	M	M	M	M	M	M46			M	M81	M46	M	M81	M	M	M	18	2
Paul LE GUEN (01/03/64) - Paris Saint-Germain FC	M68																17	-
Christophe COCARD (23/11/67) - AJ Auxerre	M73		s68														9	1
Zinedine ZIDANE (23/06/72) - Girondins de Bordeaux	M46	M	M	M84	M	M	s46			M46	M	M80	M	M62	M	M	17	5
Reynald PEDROS (10/10/71) - FC Nantes	A	s64	A65			s46	M	M73	M	s73				s62	s80	s62	22	3
Youri DJORKAEFF (09/03/68) - Paris Saint-Germain FC	s46	s69	M	M73	M	M	M46			M	M46	M	M	M	M	M	22	11
Franck LEBOEUF (22/01/68) - RC Strasbourg	s68	D69	D	D	D	D	s46		D								8	2
Corentin MARTINS (11/07/69) - AJ Auxerre	s73							M	M								13	1
Jocelyn ANGLOMA (07/08/65) - Torino (ITA)		D66	D57	D	D	D69	D46	s46	D	s84	D46		D65			s83	37	1
Didier DESCHAMPS (15/10/68) - Juventus (ITA)		M	M	M	M	M	M		M		M	M	M	M	M		54	3
Marcel DESAILLY (07/09/68) - Milan (ITA)		M	D	D	D	D	D		M		D	D	D	D	D	M	28	1
Christophe DUGARRY (24/03/72) - Girondins de Bordeaux		A	A68	A62				A80	s46	A73		A68	s74	A70	s62/80		15	2
David GINOLA (25/01/67) - Newcastle United (ENG)		A64	s65														17	3
Christian KAREMBEU (03/12/70) - Sampdoria (ITA)		s66		M	M90	M	M	M	s69	M84	s46	M	M	M	M		21	1
Fabien BARTHEZ (28/06/71) - AS Monaco				G													2	-
Eric DI MECO (07/09/63) - AS Monaco				D	D63	D		D	D67	D66		D68					23	-
Michaël MADAR (08/05/68) - AS Monaco				s62	A63						A						3	1
Patrice LOKO (06/02/70) - Paris Saint-Germain FC					s63	A78	A		A46	s46	s46	s68	A74	s70	A62	A	19	6
Marc KELLER (14/01/68) - RC Strasbourg					s90												1	-
Sabri LAMOUCHI (09/11/71) - AJ Auxerre						s69	M70	M	M69	s81	M					M62	7	1
Cyrille POUGET (06/12/72) - FC Metz						s78	s77	s80									3	-
Emmanuel PETIT (22/09/70) - AS Monaco							D77										15	-
Pierre LAIGLE (12/09/70) - RC Lens							s70	s73									2	-
Bruno MARTINI (25/01/62) - Montpellier HSC									G								31	-

shirt had to shoulder the creative, artistic burden alone. In attack, too, Patrice Loko was ill-equipped for the rôle assigned to him. Christophe Dugarry was more attuned to ploughing a lone furrow up front, but he was injured in the quarter-final against Holland, and with no deputy available, Loko simply worked himself to a standstill and was never an attacking threat.

The two goalless draws against Holland and the Czech Republic summed France up. Their defence, marshalled brilliantly by Laurent Blanc, Marcel Desailly and goalkeeper Bernard Lama, was the best in the tournament, rarely allowing the opposition a glimpse of goal. But in attack, despite Djorkaeff's best efforts, there was no cutting edge. After winning one penalty shoot-out, against the Dutch, it was only fair that they should lose the next one, against the Czechs. They deserved no more.

Whether the semi-final penalty loss actually counts as a defeat *per se* is one for the statisticians, but certainly Jacquet will claim that no team has ever beaten his during the course of a proper game of football, be it over 90 or 120 minutes.

28 matches without defeat is some record, and one the French coach will be determined to extend as he begins the team's build-up for the 1998 World Cup, hosted, of course, by France.

Jacquet is fortunate in that virtually all of the players he selected for Euro '96 will still be raring to go in two years' time. The Cantona/Ginola sideshow will not go away, but the coach is certain to make additions to his squad from the U-21 team, which reached the quarter-finals of the Olympic football tournament in Atlanta. Robert Pires, Patrick Vieira and Florian Maurice are the best of this latest generation.

Once upon a time in the not too distant past it was a rarity for a French international to play outside his own country. Nowadays they are all at it. If the trend continues - and the mass exodus in the summer of 1996 suggests it will - then the French squad chosen for the 1998 World Cup could be made up exclusively of expatriates. Of the 22 players Aimé Jacquet took to Euro '96, a mere nine are now domiciled in France.

A steady decline in the fortunes of French clubs in Europe appears to be an inevitable consequence of this disparity in pulling power between the French First Division and its equivalents in England, Italy and Spain. But in 1995/96, with most of the wantaways still on the leash, France enjoyed its best ever season in the European club competitions. With a record eight clubs entering the various first-round draws, thanks to the exploits of Bordeaux and Strasbourg in the InterToto Cup, France were dressed for success from the start. But the achievements of Paris Saint-Germain, Bordeaux and Nantes were none the less remarkable.

PSG followed in the footsteps of their great rivals Marseille by becoming only the second French club to lift a European trophy. After three successive seasons of semi-final failure, the Parisians were relieved to make it to the final of the Cup-winners' Cup. An impressive victory over Deportivo La Coruña ended the semi-final jinx, although once again PSG produced their most exciting performance in the quarter-final, defeating Parma 3-2 on aggregate after a typically belligerent second-leg fightback in the Parc des Princes.

In Brussels, Luis Fernandez's side were much superior to a drab, defensive Rapid Vienna. The 1-0 scoreline, earned by defender Bruno N'Gotty's deflected free-kick, flattered the Austrians, but PSG made life difficult for themselves by spurning chances, and the final whistle came as a huge reief, particularly for Fernandez, who thus became the first French coach to win a European trophy, just a few

DOMESTIC CUP RESULTS

1/32 FINALS

Olympique Lyonnais 0, AJ Auxerre 1
AS Monaco 1, RC Lens 0 (aet)
Stade Rennais FC 1, AS Nancy-Lorraine 2
FC Gueugnon 1, ASOA Valence 2
AS Cannes 5, Perpignan FC 1
Chamois Niortais 2, En Avant Guingamp 2 (aet; 7-6 on pens.)
Paris Saint-Germain FC 3, LB Châteauroux 1
Saint-Leu 0, Lille OSC 1
Valenciennes 1, RC Strasbourg 2 (aet)
Brest 1, OGC Nice 1 (aet; 3-4 on pens.)
Charnay 1, FC Metz 3
La Flèche 1, FC Martigues 3
Pont-de-Roide 1, Girondins de Bordeaux 4
Blénod 1, SC Bastia 0
Saint-Quentin 1, FC Nantes 7
Salbris 0, Le Havre AC 3
Pacy-sur-Eure 1, Montpellier HSC 2
AS Saint-Etienne 5, Saintes 0
USL Dunkerque 1, FC Sochaux 3
Stade Lavallois 4, Stade Poitiers 1
SM Caen 3, Amiens SCF 2 (aet)
Le Mans UC 72 1, Créteil 0
FC Mulhouse 3, Haguenau 2 (aet)
Saint-Lô 1, SCO Angers 3
Endoume Marseille 0, Olympique Marseille 2
Toulon 2, Pau 1
Pontivy 2, Trélissac 0
Nîmes Olympique 3, Saint-Priest 1
Toulouse-Fontaines 0, Istres 1
Nozay 0, Thouars 2
Marienau 1, Dijon 4
Raon-l'Etape 0, Poissy 1

1/16 FINALS

FC Nantes 2, AS Monaco 2 (aet; 4-5 on pens.)
Le Mans UC 72 0, AJ Auxerre 2
AS Nancy-Lorraine 0, Lille OSC 0 (aet; 2-4 on pens.)
FC Metz 0, SM Caen 1
AS Cannes 0, FC Sochaux 1
Paris Saint-Germain 2, SCO Angers 0
OGC Nice 0, Stade Lavallois 1
Montpellier HSC 2, Istres 1
Thouars 1, FC Martigues 0 (aet)
Toulon 3, Girondins de Bordeaux 2 (aet)
Nîmes Olympique 3, AS Saint-Etienne 1
Poissy 0, Strasbourg 0 (aet; 2-4 on pens.)
Blénod 1, Le Havre AC 1 (aet; 4-3 on pens.)
Chamois Niortais 1, FC Mulhouse 1 (aet; 4-3 on pens.)
ASOA Valence 3, Dijon 0
Pontivy 0, Olympique Marseille 2

1/8 FINALS

AJ Auxerre 3, Paris Saint-Germain FC 1
Lille OSC 1, AS Monaco 1 (aet; 5-4 on pens.)
Chamois Niortais 0, RC Strasbourg 1
Toulon 1, Montpellier HSC 1 (aet; 1-4 on pens.)
ASOA Valence 1, Stade Lavallois 0
SM Caen 5, FC Sochaux 0
Blénod 0, Olympique Marseille 2
Thouas 0, Nîmes Olympique 2

QUARTER-FINALS

Montpellier HSC 1, SM Caen 0
ASOA Valence 0, AJ Auxerre 2
Nîmes Olympique 3, RC Strasbourg 2 (aet)
Olympique Marseille 1, Lille OSC 0

SEMI-FINALS

Olympique Marseille 1, AJ Auxerre 1 (aet; 1-3 on pens.)
Nîmes Olympique 1, Montpellier HSC 0

FINAL

04/05/96, Paris
AJ AUXERRE 2 Blanc (53), Laslandes (88)
NIMES OLYMPIQUE 1 Belbey (26)
referee - Saules
AJ AUXERRE - Charbonnier; Goma, West, Blanc, Rabarivony, Violeau, Saib (Cocard 87), Martins, Lamouchi, Laslandes, Diomède.
NIMES OLYMPIQUE - Sence; Touron, Preget, Bochu, Ecker, Jeunechamp (Gros 90), Zugna (Vosalho 35), Belbey, Perez, Ramdane (Sabin 69), Marx.

PLAYERS OF THE SEASON

ERIC CANTONA
At the beginning of the 1995/96 season Eric Cantona was still under suspension. By the end of it he was collecting the English Football Writers' Player of the Year award and inspiring Manchester United to their historic 'double double'. No wonder the Frenchman is the king of Old Trafford. His goals were the key to United's success, none more so than the one he scored away to Newcastle in the league and his last of the season, in the FA Cup final, against Liverpool. That Cantona could not make it into the French European Championship squad appeared perverse to English fans, and there was no small irony in the fact that *Les Bleus* exited the competition on Cantona's home 'patch'. Nobody will ever know how France would have fared had 'Canto' been included, but the team's entertainment rating would certainly have soared in his presence.

ZINEDINE ZIDANE
Part of the reason for Cantona's Euro '96 non-appearance was the meteoric rise of Bordeaux midfielder and French Player of the Year Zinedine Zidane. The 24-year-old became a big favourite of Aimé Jacquet during the European Championship qualifying campaign, especially with his majestic goal that sealed France's momentous 3-1 victory in Bucharest. When Zidane came to England, however, he had run himself dry. For 12 months he had played non-stop football, helping Bordeaux from the InterToto Cup through to the UEFA Cup final and doing his best to keep the Girondins away from the relegation zone. And on top of that, he was involved in a car crash just before Euro '96. Luckily for 'Zizou', he had already signed a contract with Juventus prior to the finals. In Turin the pressure on him to rediscover his old form will be intense - especially with memories of the great Michel Platini still vivid in the minds of the local *tifosi*.

ROBERT PIRES
With so many of France's top names having left the country, there is ample room for Robert Pires to establish himself as the big star of the French league in 1996/97. Certainly, the young Metz forward will be doing all he can to earn himself a regular place in the senior French squad. Had he not been booked to play for France at the Atlanta Olympics, Pires might well have worn the blue shirt of his country at Euro '96. He was in brilliant form for Metz all season, helping the north-eastern club to victory in the League Cup and igniting an on-off championship challenge that really caught fire when Pires scored twice in a brilliant 3-2 victory over Paris Saint-Germain in the Parc des Princes.

SONNY ANDERSON
He is 26, he is Brazilian, and he is also one of the deadliest strikers in European football. So, how come the name Anderson da Silva is unfamiliar to most football followers outside France? Much of it has to do with the stiff competition for places in the Brazilian national team attack. Successive Brazilian coaches have ignored "Sonny" Anderson's claims, but it is difficult to see why. A striker of mobility and finesse, he has scored an abundance of goals for all three of his European clubs - first Servette, then Marseille, and now Monaco, for whom he struck 21 times in 1995/96 to earn himself the French First Division top scorer crown, overtaking Bastia's Montenegrin striker Anto Drobnjak with a brace of goals in the last game of the season against Rennes.

days after he had announced that he was leaving the club.

Fernandez felt drained by the pressure of coaching France's highest-profile club. There had been severe criticism of his failure to bring PSG the French title. For most of the 1995/96 campaign the club from the capital had looked odds-on favourites. But a sequence of awful results in the Parc des Princes late on destroyed their challenge.

Bordeaux, whose league form was disastrous, also redeemed themselves in Europe, reaching the final of the UEFA Cup in sensational fashion after a marathon trek from the early group phase of the InterToto competition. The bosses of UEFA, eager to deflect criticism of their sum-

INTERNATIONAL HONOURS

World Cup Finals appearances: 1930, 1938 (2nd round), 1954, 1958 (3rd), 1966, 1978, 1982 (4th), 1986 (3rd)

European Championship appearances: 1960 (4th), 1964, 1968, 1984 (Winners), 1992, 1996 (semi-finals)

European Club Competitions

Champions' Cup	Olympique Marseille (1993)
Cup-winners' Cup	Paris Saint-Germain FC (1996)

EUROPEAN CUPS RESULTS 95/96

CHAMPIONS' CUP

● FC NANTES

Champions' League

1st match FC PORTO (POR)
H 0-0
Marraud; Le Dizet, Guyot, Decroix, Pignol, Makélélé, Cauet, Carotti, N'Doram, Kosecki, Renou (Garcion 63).

2nd match PANATHINAIKOS (GRE)
A 1-2 N'Doram (87)
Marraud; Le Dizet, Guyot, Decroix (Chanelet 69), Pignol, Makélélé (Renou 76), Cauet, Carotti, N'Doram, Ouédec (Peyrelade 69), Kosecki.

3rd match AAB (DEN)
H 3-1 Ouédec (5), Pedros (55), Kosecki (74)
Casagrande; Chanelet, Guyot, Decroix, Pignol, Cauet, Makélélé, N'Doram, Pedros, Ouédec (Carotti 78), Kosecki (Da Rocha 90).

4th match AAB (DEN)
A 2-0 Guyot (10), Ouédec (69)
Casagrande; Cauet (Pignol 76), Decroix, Guyot, Carotti, Ferri, Makélélé (Chanelet 59), Pedros, N'Doram, Ouédec (Peyrelade 87), Kosecki.

5th match FC PORTO (POR)
A 2-2 Pedros (3, 34)
Casagrande; Chanelet, Guyot, Decroix, Le Dizet, Ferri, Carotti, Cauet, Makélélé, Kosecki (Renou 76; Savinaud 90), Pedros (Ouédec 70).

6th match PANATHINAIKOS (GRE)
H 0-0
Casagrande; Chanelet, Guyot, Decroix, Le Dizet, Makélélé, Ferri, Pedros, N'Doram, Kosecki (Renou 85), Ouédec.

Quarter-final SPARTAK MOSKVA (RUS)
H 2-0 N'Doram (28), Ouédec (68)
Casagrande; Le Dizet (Chanelet 70), Guyot, Decroix, Pignol, Cauet, Makélélé, N'Doram (Ferri 64), Pedros, Ouédec (Gourvennec 83), Kosecki.
A 2-2 Ouédec (63, 86)
Casagrande; Le Dizet, Carotti, Decroix, Capron, Pignol, Makélélé, Cauet, Gourvennec (Ferri 63), Kosecki (Chanelet 83), Ouédec.

Semi-final JUVENTUS (ITA)
A 0-2
Casagrande; Le Dizet, Decroix, Capron, Pignol, Cauet, Ferri, Carotti, Gourvennec (Chanelet 46), Kosecki (Guyot 68), Ouédec (Peyrelade 86).
H 3-2 Decroix (43), N'Doram (69), Renou (82)
Casagrande; Chanelet, Capron, Decroix, Pignol (Peyrelade 88), Makélélé, Ferri, Cauet, N'Doram, Kosecki (Renou 62), Ouédec (Gourvennec 38).

CUP-WINNERS' CUP

● PARIS SAINT-GERMAIN FC

1st round MOLDE FK (NOR)
A 3-2 Le Guen (76), Djorkaeff (78p), Dely Valdes (84)
Dutruel; Cobos (Llacer 68), N'Gotty, Dieng, Colleter, Fournier (Allou 80), Guérin, Djorkaeff, Le Guen, Dely Valdes, Gravelaine (Nouma 60).
H 3-0 Nouma (7, 13), Djorkaeff (77)
Dutruel; Llacer, N'Gotty, Dieng, Colleter (Mahé 56), Guérin (Fournier 46), Bravo (Allou 72), Djorkaeff, Le Guen, Nouma, Loko.

2nd round CELTIC (SCO)
H 1-0 Djorkaeff (76)
Lama; Cobos, Le Guen, Colleter, Bravo, Fournier (Llacer 80), Mahé, Guérin, Djorkaeff (Allou 89), Raí (Nouma 81), Loko.
A 3-0 Loko (36, 43), Nouma (68)
Lama; Cobos, Mahé (Dieng 28), Le Guen, Colleter, Bravo, Fournier (Llacer 68), Guérin, Djorkaeff, Raí, Loko (Nouma 59).

Quarter-final PARMA (ITA)
A 0-1
Lama; Cobos (Llacer 76), N'Gotty, Le Guen, Colleter, Bravo, Djorkaeff (Nouma 42), Raí, Mahé, Loko, Dely Valdes.
H 3-1 Raí (9p, 69p), Loko (38)
Lama; N'Gotty, Roche, Le Guen, Fournier (Mahé 75), Bravo, Colleter (Guérin 67), Nouma (Llacer 69), Raí, Loko, Dely Valdes.

Semi-final RC DEPORTIVO (ESP)
A 1-0 Djorkaeff (90)
Lama; N'Gotty, Le Guen, Roche, Fournier (Mahé 85), Bravo, Guérin, Colleter, Loko (Llacer 47), Dely Valdes (Djorkaeff 80), Nouma.
H 1-0 Loko (59)
Lama; N'Gotty, Le Guen, Roche, Fournier (Llacer 81), Bravo, Guérin, Colleter, Djorkaeff (Dely Valdes 79), Loko, Nouma (Raí 57).

Final SK RAPID WIEN (AUT)
Brussels
1-0 N'Gotty (29)
Lama; Roche, Le Guen, N'Gotty, Fournier (Llacer 77), Bravo, Guérin, Colleter, Loko, Raí (Dely Valdes 11), Djorkaeff.

UEFA CUP

● OLYMPIQUE LYONNAIS

1st round SC FARENSE (POR)
A 1-0 Giuly (5)
Olmeta; Deplace, Sassus, Marcelo, Laville, Deguerville, Roy, Giuly (Devaux 64), Rivenet, Maurice (Assadourian 84), Gava.
H 1-0 Sassus (47)
Olmeta; Devaux, Laville, Marcelo, Sassus, Deguerville, Roy, Deplace, Giuly (Patouillard 83), Assadourian (Rivenet 76), Bardon (Gava 68).

2nd round LAZIO (ITA)
H 2-1 Devaux (15), Deplace (64)
Olmeta; Anselmini (Chavrondier 51), Laville, Marcelo, Deguerville, Devaux, Roy, Deplace, Giuly, Assadourian (Bardon 82), Maurice.
A 2-0 Maurice (22), Assadourian (59)
Olmeta; Sassus, Laville, Marcelo, Devaux, Deguerville (Chavrondier 87), Roy, Deplace, Giuly (Roche 80), Maurice, Assadourian (Bardon 72).

EUROPEAN CUPS RESULTS 95/96 (CONTINUED)

3rd round NOTTINGHAM FOREST (ENG)
A 0-1
Olmeta; Moulin, Sassus, Marcelo, Laville, Devaux, Deplace, Roy, Roche (Deguerville 84), Giuly, Maurice.
H 0-0
Olmeta; Moulin, Sassus, Marcelo, Devaux, Roy, Deplace, Giuly (Roche 84), Rivenet (Chavrondier 76), Maurice, Bardon (Assadourian 76).

● AJ AUXERRE

1st round VIKING FK (NOR)
A 1-1 West (14)
Cool; West, Silvestre, Goma, Rabarivony (Rémy 51), Lamouchi, Saïb, Martins, Tasfaout, Laslandes, Diomède (Violeau 63).
H 1-0 Silvestre (47)
Cool; West, Goma, Silvestre, Rémy, Lamouchi, Saïb, Martins, Cocard, Laslandes, Diomède (Violeau 69).

2nd round NOTTINGHAM FOREST (ENG)
H 0-1
Cool; Goma, Silvestre, Blanc (Rabarivony 58), West, Lamouchi, Saïb, Martins, Cocard, Laslandes (Guivarc'h 77), Diomède (Tasfaout 67).
A 0-0
Cool; Violeau, West, Silvestre, Goma, Rabarivony, Lamouchi, Saïb, Martins, Cocard (Tasfaout 76), Laslandes (Guivarc'h 81).

● RC LENS

1st round AVENIR BEGGEN (LUX)
H 6-0 Camara (11, 49), Meyrieu (33), Tiéhi (62, 74), Boli (70)
Warmuz; Sikora, Magnier, Wallemme (Tiéhi 56), Adjovi-Boco, Dehu (Delmotte 76), Meyrieu, Laigle, Debève, Camara, Vairelles (Boli 68).
A 7-0 Camara (20), Meyrieu (25), Boli (40), Delmotte (55, 73), Tiéhi (57, 72)
Warmuz; Adjovi-Boco (Foé 72), Magnier (Sikora 57), Wallemme, Delmotte, Meyrieu, Oruma, Debève, Camara (Vairelles 57), Tiéhi, Boli.

2nd round CHORNOMORETS ODESA (UKR)
A 0-0
Warmuz; Sikora, Magnier, Wallemme, Adjovi-Boco, Dehu, Laigle, Delmotte (Vairelles 75), Debève, Camara, Meyrieu.
H 4-0 Meyrieu (14), Vairelles (20), Dehu (26), Foé (77)
Warmuz; Sikora, Magnier, Wallemme (Foé 62), Adjovi-Boco, Dehu, Laigle, Debève, Meyrieu (Boli 77), Camara (Delmotte 71), Vairelles.

3rd round SLAVIA PRAHA (TCH)
A 0-0
Warmuz; Sikora, Magnier, Wallemme, Adjovi-Boco, Dehu, Laigle, Delmotte, Debève, Meyrieu (Vairelles 76), Camara.
H 0-1
Warmuz; Sikora, Wallemme, Magnier, Adjovi-Boco (Boli 106), Debève (Arsène 106), Meyrieu, Foé, Laigle (Delmotte 46), Camara, Vairelles.

● AS MONACO

1st round LEEDS UNITED (ENG)
H 0-3
Piveteau (Delaroche 46; Puel 80); Valéry, Thuram, Boli, Di Meco, Dumas, Legwinski (Henry 71), Dos Santos, Scifo, Wreh, Anderson.
A 1-0 Anderson (22)
Barthez; Thuram, Boli, Dumas, Petit, Dos Santos (Wreh 82), Puel, Viaud (Petersen 62), Scifo, Madar, Anderson.

● GIRONDINS DE BORDEAUX

Preliminary round/InterToto semi-final KARLSRUHER SC (GER)
A 2-0 Dugarry (40), Dutuel (87)
Huard; Croci, Prunier, Dogon, Lizarazu, Lucas, Dutuel, Zidane, Witschge, Tholot, Dugarry.
H 2-2 Lizarazu (2p, 11)
Huard; Croci, Prunier, Dogon, Lizarazu, Lucas, Dutuel, Zidane, Witschge (Bancarel 55), Tholot (De Blasiis 45), Dugarry (Varesanovic 65).

1st round VARDAR SKOPJE (MAC)
A 2-0 Bancarel (25, 75)
Huard; Fischer, Prunier, Dogon, Lizarazu, Witschge, Lucas, Dutuel, Grenet, Bancarel, Dugarry (Croci 74).
H 1-1 Lizarazu (61p)
Huard; Fischer, Prunier, Dogon, Lizarazu, Lucas, De Blasiis (Toyes 74), Grenet, Histilloles (Castant 63), Witschge, Bancarel.

2nd round ROTOR VOLGOGRAD (RUS)
H 2-1 Histilloles (47), Witschge (90p)
Huard; Toyes (Grenet 83), Prunier, Dogon, Varesanovic, Lucas, Croci, Dutuel, Histilloles, Witschge, Bancarel.
A 1-0 Bancarel (83)
Huard; Lizarazu, Dogon, Toyes, Croci, Fischer, Witschge (Grenet 77), Zidane, Lucas, Dutuel, Bancarel.

3rd round REAL BETIS (ESP)
H 2-0 Dutuel (25), Croci (80)
Huard; Fischer (Toyes 68), Prunier, Dogon, Lizarazu, Lucas, Dutuel, Witschge, Zidane, Grenet (Croci 72), Bancarel.
A 1-2 Zidane (4)
Huard; Grenet, Fernandez, Prunier, Dogon, Toyes, Croci, Dutuel, Witschge (Histilloles 72), Zidane, Bancarel (De Blasiis 66).

Quarter-final MILAN (ITA)
A 0-2
Huard; Toyes, Dogon, Friis-Hansen, Lizarazu, Lucas (Dutuel 81), Croci, Bancarel, Witschge, Zidane, Dugarry (Tholot 88).
H 3-0 Tholot (15), Dugarry (64, 70)
Huard; Toyes, Friis-Hansen, Dogon, Lizarazu, Lucas, Dutuel (Grenet 60), Zidane, Witschge, Tholot (Fernandez 85), Dugarry.

Semi-final SLAVIA PRAHA (TCH)
A 1-0 Dugarry (8)
Huard; Toyes, Dogon, Friis-Hansen, Lizarazu, Bancarel (Fernandez 86), Croci, Lucas, Witschge, Zidane, Dugarry.
H 1-0 Tholot (47)
Huard; Toyes, Friis-Hansen, Dogon, Lizarazu, Lucas, Croci (Grenet 73), Zidane, Witschge, Tholot (Dutuel 81), Dugarry (Bancarel 87).

Continued Overleaf

EUROPEAN CUPS RESULTS 95/96 (CONTINUED)

Final FC BAYERN MÜNCHEN (GER)

A 0-2
Huard; Grenet, Dogon, Friis-Hansen, Lizarazu, Lucas, Croci, Dutuel, Witschge, Bancarel, Tholot (Anselin 89).

H 1-3 Dutuel (75)
Huard; Bancarel, Friis-Hansen, Dogon, Lizarazu (Anselin 30), Lucas (Grenet 80), Croci (Dutuel 58), Witschge, Zidane, Tholot, Dugarry.

● RC STRASBOURG

Preliminary round/InterToto semi-final FC TIROL INNSBRUCK (AUT)

A 1-1 Sauzée (26)
Vencel; Raschke, Leboeuf, Régis, Pouliquen, Djetou, Dacourt (Rott 66), Mostovoi, Sauzée, Keller, Zitelli (Frankowski 38; Thys 76).

H 6-1 Sauzée (16, 54), Mostovoi (65), Keller (67, 70, 89)
Vencel; Raschke, Leboeuf, Djetou, Régis, Pouliquen, Garde (Rott 83), Sauzée (Thys 80), Mostovoi, Keller, Baticle (Gohel 73).

1st round ÚJPESTI TE (HUN)

H 3-0 Zitelli (7), Leboeuf (72p), Baticle (74)
Vencel; Raschke, Régis, Leboeuf, Djetou, Pouliquen, Sauzée, Mostovoi, Keller, Baticle, Zitelli (Gohel 79).

A 2-0 Mostovoi (9), Zitelli (77)
Vencel; Raschke (Ismaël 64), Régis, Garde, Pouliquen, Djetou, Rott, Sauzée (Dacourt 46), Mostovoi, Keller, Baticle (Zitelli 58).

2nd round MILAN (ITA)

H 0-1
Vencel; Djetou, Leboeuf, Régis, Raschke, Dacourt (Pouliquen 72), Sauzée, Garde, Mostovoi, Keller, Zitelli.

A 1-2 Sauzée (45)
Vencel; Raschke, Régis (Ismaël 82), Leboeuf, Djetou, Garde (Pouliquen 82), Sauzée, Dacourt (Gohel 71), Mostovoi, Zitelli, Keller.

mertime Cup-without-a-trophy, were clearly delighted with Bordeaux's achievement. The quarter-final victory over Italian giants Milan was straight out of comic-book fiction. But Bayern Munich were too hot to handle in the final, and that was where the Girondins' dreams came to rest.

Nantes were another team who made up for domestic dalliance by surpassing themselves in Europe. With star players Karembeu and Loko sold in the summer, the 94/95 champions seemed unlikely to survive for very long in the intensity of Champions' League combat. But somehow they battled through to the semi-finals. Nantes were no match for Juventus, but they did bow out in style, defeating the Italians 3-2 at home after a 0-2 defeat in Turin.

Like Monaco and Lyon in the UEFA Cup, Auxerre's quest for European glory was sabotaged by an English club. They were eliminated in the second round by Nottingham Forest despite having roughly ninety per cent of the play and creating the better chances. But even in defeat the team from Burgundy gave evidence of an impressive collective ability that was to manifest itself much more effectively over the next six months in domestic competition.

Guy Roux, the Auxerre coach since 1961, saw his dream come true as the small-town club from the provinces did the impossible and won the French league and Cup 'double'.

Winning the French title had been Roux's lifelong ambition. Auxerre had long been known as one of the country's strongest, most consistent teams, but few pundits had them down as championship material. A long Cup run or a place in the UEFA Cup was all they were generally considered good for.

But in 1995/96 Auxerre carried all before them. The French Cup came first. After knocking out holders Paris Saint-Germain early on and then surviving in the boiling cauldron of the Stade Vélodrome to eliminate Marseille on penalties in the semi-final, Auxerre looked to have done the hard part. For their opponents in the final were modest National 1 side Nîmes, shock 1-0 victors over local rivals Montpellier in the semis. In the Parc des Princes the underdogs very nearly had their day. But Auxerre fought back from a 0-1 deficit and stole victory with a late winning goal from centre-forward Lilian Laslandes.

Broken-hearted in defeat, the Nîmes supporters were nevertheless on Auxerre's side as the championship boiled to its climax. They knew that if Auxerre added the league to their Cup triumph, a place in the European Cup-winners' Cup would be theirs.

Just one week after the Cup final, Nîmes and Auxerre both got what they wanted. With other results going in their favour, Guy Roux's team required only a point in Guingamp to clinch the championship. A 1-1 draw did the trick. The celebrations could begin in earnest for Roux and his players. They had held their nerve when others - notably Paris-Saint Germain and Metz - had lost theirs. With six wins and two draws from their last eight matches, Auxerre had proved their credentials when it mattered. Everybody in the team was a hero, from Laurent Blanc and Franck Sylvestre in defence, through Sabri Lamouchi and Corentin Martins in midfield to Lilian Laslandes and Bernard Diomède in attack.

The celebrations which took place in Burgundy were more than matched down in Provence, where Marseille ensured their promotion back to the élite after two years of purgatory in Division Two. 'OM' finished second and were promoted alongside Caen and Nancy. But as one of France's greatest clubs went up, another, Saint-Etienne, went down. Rescued from relegation the previous season by Marseille's financial ailments, *Les Verts* were offered no such safety net this time and crashed out of Division One in the company of two teams more familiar with life in the lower reaches of the French league, Gueugnon and Martigues.

PROFILE

YOURI DJORKAEFF

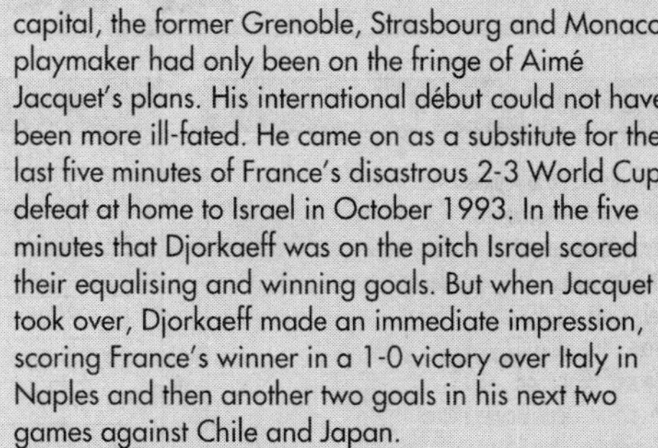

Youri Djorkaeff has a lot to live up to. His father, Jean, who now acts as his agent, was a highly successful international full-back in the 1960s, appearing 48 times for France and playing a starring rôle at the 1966 World Cup.

But if there is a pressure to emulate Dad's achievements, Djorkaeff junior is certainly on the right track. 30 years on from his father, Youri made the same hop across the Channel to England, and the impression he left was equally memorable.

For the French team in general, Euro '96 could only be considered a qualified success. But, for the 28-year-old midfield prober in the number nine shirt, it was a tournament to remember. France had lots of prominent individuals in defence, but only Djorkaeff looked sharp and dangerous in attack. At times he appeared to be carrying the fight to the opposition on his own, but he never tired and remained on the field for the full eight and a half hours of France's campaign. The highlight was his expertly taken goal against Spain, but he also provided the crosses for three other French goals and came closest to taking his country into the final when he struck the bar against the Czech Republic. In addition, Djorkaeff did his best to liven up the French play with a few party pieces. A back-heel here, a scissors-kick there. It all served to enhance a reputation that had been built up with a glut of goals during the latter stages of the qualifying competition.

Not that Djorkaeff was under any great obligation to sell himself at Euro '96. He had already agreed a deal to join Italian club Inter, thus becoming one of several players in Aimé Jacquet's squad to quit France for more fertile pastures abroad once the tournament was over. The offer from Inter was too good for Djorkaeff to refuse, but he would have happily stayed for another year or two at Paris Saint-Germain.

Djorkaeff had just one season in Paris, but it was a successful one - both for his club and for his coming of age in the national team. Before his move to the capital, the former Grenoble, Strasbourg and Monaco playmaker had only been on the fringe of Aimé Jacquet's plans. His international début could not have been more ill-fated. He came on as a substitute for the last five minutes of France's disastrous 2-3 World Cup defeat at home to Israel in October 1993. In the five minutes that Djorkaeff was on the pitch Israel scored their equalising and winning goals. But when Jacquet took over, Djorkaeff made an immediate impression, scoring France's winner in a 1-0 victory over Italy in Naples and then another two goals in his next two games against Chile and Japan.

The following season, however, Djorkaeff barely figured at all. It was not until his vital late free-kick against Poland in August 1995 that he finally cemented his place in the team. With goals in each of France's last four European Championship qualifiers, Djorkaeff suddenly became a figure of national worship. Another brace in a friendly against Portugal gave him a stunning record of 10 goals in his first 14 internationals - a better initial strike-rate than that of any other modern-day French international, Cantona, Papin and the great Platini included.

Djorkaeff was clearly revelling in the surroundings of his new club. After five seasons at Monaco, for whom he scored 60 goals in the French First Division, including a league-best 20 in 1993/94, Djorkaeff fancied a shot at the big time. There were no shortage of offers for his signature, but Paris Saint-Germain were always his first choice and he moved there in June 1995, joining Loko, Dely Valdes and Raí in a cosmopolitan and exciting four-man strikeforce.

The quartet hit it off immediately and the goals flowed. It looked as if PSG would sail to the title, but a poor run in the spring halted their progress and Auxerre sneaked in ahead of them. But ample consolation arrived in the shape of the European Cup-winners' Cup. For Djorkaeff, in particular, victory over Rapid Vienna in the final was sweet as it erased the memory of his losing final appearance for Monaco against Werder Bremen four years earlier. His magnificent late goal away to Deportivo La Coruña in the semi-final was the moment that PSG really believed the trophy could be theirs.

AJ AUXERRE

CLUB DIRECTORY

Association de la Jeunesse Auxerroise
Stade Abbé-Deschamps
Route de Vaux
89000 Auxerre
tel - (86) 723232
fax - (86) 522087
Year of Formation - 1905
President - Jean-Claude Hamel
Secretary - Jean Edy
Coach - Guy Roux
Stadium - Abbé-Deschamps (22,000)

MAJOR HONOURS

League Championship - (1) 1996.
Domestic Cup - (2) 1994, 1996.

APPEARANCES 95/96

	P	Ap	(s)	Gls
Laurent BLANC	D	23		2
Lionel CHARBONNIER	G	22	(1)	
Christophe COCARD	A	30	(2)	6
Fabien COOL	G	16		
Frédéric DANJOU	D	1	(6)	
Thomas DENIAUD	A		(4)	
Bernard DIOMEDE	A	29	(4)	9
Alain GOMA	D	32		
Arnaud GONZALES	M	1		
Stéphane GUIVARC'H	A	9	(14)	3
Christian HENNA	M		(4)	
Yann LACHUER	M		(1)	
Sabri LAMOUCHI	M	35	(1)	6
Lilian LASLANDES	A	31	(3)	12
Fabrice LEPAUL	A	1	(2)	1
Corentin MARTINS	M	35	(1)	13
Franck RABARIVONY	D	30	(2)	
Christophe REMY	D	11	(2)	
Moussa SAIB (ALG)	M	31	(2)	6
Franck SILVESTRE	D	37		1
Abdelhafid TASFAOUT (ALG)	M	3	(15)	5
Philippe VIOLEAU	M	24	(6)	
Taribo WEST (NIG)	D	17	(5)	

LEAGUE RESULTS 1995/96

Date	Opponent	H/A	Score	Scorers
19/07/95	FC Nantes	A	0-1	
26/07/95	FC Gueugnon	H	4-0	Silvestre, Guivarc'h, Martins, Tasfaout
05/08/95	AS Monaco	A	2-2	Guivarc'h, Saïb
09/08/95	RC Lens	H	0-1	
19/08/95	Montpellier HSC	A	1-3	Laslandes (p)
26/08/95	AS Cannes	H	5-1	Saïb, Laslandes 2, Cocard, Martins
29/08/95	Le Havre AC	A	4-0	Martins, Saïb, Laslandes, Cocard
09/09/95	RC Strasbourg	H	1-0	Tasfaout
16/09/95	Olympique Lyonnais	A	1-0	Diomède
22/09/95	Stade Rennais FC	H	2-1	Laslandes, Tasfaout
30/09/95	FC Metz	A	1-3	Martins
04/10/95	FC Martigues	A	2-1	Guivarc'h, Lamouchi
14/10/95	OGC Nice	H	2-1	Lamouchi, Tasfaout
22/10/95	Paris Saint-Germain FC	A	1-3	Cocard
27/10/95	Lille OSC	H	1-2	Tasfaout
04/11/95	Girondins de Bordeaux	A	1-0	Saïb
08/11/95	SC Bastia	H	3-0	Laslandes 2, Cocard
19/11/95	AS Saint-Etienne	A	5-0	Laslandes 2, Cocard, og (Billong), Martins
25/11/95	En Avant Guingamp	H	1-2	Diomède
30/11/95	FC Gueugnon	A	0-0	
09/12/95	AS Monaco	H	1-2	Lamouchi
16/12/95	RC Lens	A	0-0	
10/01/96	Montpellier HSC	H	1-0	Diomède
20/01/96	AS Cannes	A	1-0	Laslandes
27/01/96	Le Havre AC	H	1-0	Lamouchi
10/02/96	Olympique Lyonnais	H	2-0	Cocard, Diomède
17/02/96	Stade Rennais FC	A	1-2	Saïb
27/02/96	FC Metz	H	0-0	
02/03/96	FC Martigues	H	4-0	Martins 3, Lepaul
05/03/96	RC Strasbourg	A	0-1	
09/03/96	OGC Nice	A	3-1	Blanc, Laslandes, Diomède
24/03/96	Paris Saint-Germain FC	H	3-0	Diomède, Martins, og (Colleter)
30/03/96	Lille OSC	A	4-0	Martins 2, Lamouchi 2
09/04/96	Girondins de Bordeaux	H	2-0	Blanc (p), Martins
20/04/96	SC Bastia	A	1-1	Saïb
26/04/96	AS Saint-Etienne	H	2-0	Diomède, Laslandes
11/05/96	En Avant Guingamp	A	1-1	Diomède
18/05/96	FC Nantes	H	2-1	Diomède, Martins

SC BASTIA

CLUB DIRECTORY

Sporting Club de Bastia
Stade Armand-Cesari-Furiani
BP 640
20601 Bastia Cédex
tel - (95) 335654
fax - (95) 336774
Year of Formation - 1905
President - François Nicolaï
Secretary - Christian Villanova
Coach - Frédéric Antonetti
Stadium - Armand-Cesari-Furiani (7,800)

MAJOR HONOURS
Domestic Cup - (1) 1981.

APPEARANCES 95/96

	P	Ap	(s)	Gls
Sauveur AIELLO	M	1	(3)	
Bruno ALICARTE	D	16	(4)	
Hervé ANZIANI	A	6	(5)	
André BIANCARELLI	G	3	(1)	
François CAFFAREL	D	3	(2)	
Frédéric DARRAS	D	22	(1)	
Jean-Christophe DEBU	D	4	(5)	
Anto DROBNJAK (YUG)	A	36		20
Jean-Jacques EYDELIE	M	23		
Mamadou FAYE (SEN)	M	32	(5)	1
FRANCHI	G	1	(1)	
FRANGINI	A	1		
Pierre LAURENT	A	18	(8)	6
Rémy LORET	D	2	(24)	1
Pierre MAROSELLI	D	34		1
Laurent MORACCHINI	M	11	(7)	
Bruno RODRIGUEZ	A	34	(1)	11
Cyril ROOL	M	22	(5)	
Didier SANTINI	D	34	(2)	1
Morlaye SOUMAH (GUI)	D	31		
Piotr SWIERCZEWSKI (POL)	M	30	(5)	1
Bruno VALENCONY	G	34		
Franck VANDECASTEELE	A	2	(4)	
WILLIAM Andrade (BRA)	D	18	(3)	1

LEAGUE RESULTS 1995/96

18/07/95	Paris Saint-Germain FC	H	2-2	Laurent, Drobnjak
25/07/95	Lille OSC	A	2-0	Drobnjak, Rodriguez
05/08/95	Girondins de Bordeaux	H	2-0	Rodriguez 2
09/08/95	AS Monaco	H	2-1	Drobnjak, Faye
19/08/95	AS Saint-Etienne	A	0-3	
26/08/95	FC Gueugnon	H	1-2	Rodriguez
30/08/95	En Avant Guingamp	A	0-1	
09/09/95	FC Nantes	H	4-1	Rodriguez, Drobnjak 2, Loret
17/09/95	RC Lens	A	1-3	Drobnjak (p)
22/09/95	AS Cannes	H	2-1	og (Lambourde), Swierczewski
30/09/95	Stade Rennais FC	A	0-2	
04/10/95	Le Havre AC	H	1-0	Maroselli
14/10/95	Montpellier HSC	A	3-4	Laurent, Drobnjak 2
21/10/95	RC Strasbourg	H	1-1	Drobnjak
27/10/95	Olympique Lyonnais	A	1-1	Drobnjak
04/11/95	FC Metz	H	1-0	Drobnjak
08/11/95	AJ Auxerre	A	0-3	
18/11/95	FC Martigues	H	2-0	Laurent, Drobnjak
25/11/95	OGC Nice	A	1-3	Drobnjak
01/12/95	Lille OSC	H	4-0	Rodriguez 2, Drobnjak 2 (1p)
09/12/95	Girondins de Bordeaux	A	3-1	Rodriguez, Drobnjak, Laurent
16/12/95	AS Monaco	A	0-0	
10/01/96	AS Saint-Etienne	H	0-0	
20/01/96	FC Gueugnon	A	0-1	
27/01/96	En Avant Guingamp	H	0-1	
07/02/96	FC Nantes	A	1-3	Drobnjak
10/02/96	RC Lens	H	3-2	og (Dehu), Rodriguez 2
17/02/96	AS Cannes	A	0-1	
02/03/96	Le Havre AC	A	0-1	
09/03/96	Montpellier HSC	H	1-0	Drobnjak
23/03/96	RC Strasbourg	A	3-4	William, Laurent, Santini
30/03/96	Olympique Lyonnais	H	0-0	
05/04/96	Stade Rennais FC	H	0-0	
10/04/96	FC Metz	A	0-2	
20/04/96	AJ Auxerre	H	1-1	Rodriguez
27/04/96	FC Martigues	A	1-3	Drobnjak
11/05/96	OGC Nice	H	1-2	Drobnjak
18/05/96	Paris Saint-Germain FC	A	1-5	Laurent

GIRONDINS DE BORDEAUX

CLUB DIRECTORY

Football Club des Girondins de Bordeaux
Rue Juliot-Curie
BP 33
33186 Le Haillan Cedex
tel - (56) 161111
fax - (56) 575446
Year of Formation - 1881
President - Jean-Louis Triaud
Secretary - Charles Camporro
Coach - Slavo Muslin; Gernot Rohr (96/97 - Rolland Courbis)
Stadium - Parc Lescure (36,000)

MAJOR HONOURS
League Championship - (4)
1950, 1984, 1985, 1987.
Domestic Cup - (3) 1941, 1986, 1987.

APPEARANCES 95/96

	P	Ap	(s)	Gls
Kodjo AFANOU	D	1		
AMRANE	M		(1)	
Cédric ANSELIN	M	1	(2)	
Anthony BANCAREL	A	22	(10)	7
Raphaël CAMACHO	M		(1)	
Régis CASTANT	M	5	(7)	1
Laurent CROCI	D	26	(3)	
Jean-Yves DE BLASIIS	M	4	(12)	
Kaba DIAWARA	A	1		1
Jean-Luc DOGON	D	35		3
Christophe DUGARRY	A	22	(2)	4
Daniel DUTUEL	M	29	(3)	4
Joachim FERNANDEZ	D	4	(1)	
Yannick FISCHER	D	13	(6)	1
Franck FONTAN	G	3	(1)	
Jacob FRIIS-HANSEN (DEN)	D	18		2
GEOFFROY	M		(1)	
François GRENET	A	13	(13)	
Franck HISTILLOLES	A	9	(8)	
Gaétan HUARD	G	35		
Bixente LIZARAZU	D	23		3
Philippe LUCAS	M	27	(1)	
William PRUNIER	D	17		
Didier THOLOT	A	17	(2)	5
Geoffroy TOYES	D	23	(2)	
Mirza VARESANOVIC (BOS)	D	6	(6)	
Richard WITSCHGE (HOL)	M	33		7
Zinedine ZIDANE	M	31	(2)	6

LEAGUE RESULTS 1995/96

Date	Opponent	H/A	Score	Scorers
19/07/95	Lille OSC	H	1-0	Dutuel
26/07/95	AS Saint-Etienne	H	2-0	Lizarazu (p), Dogon
05/08/95	SC Bastia	A	0-2	
20/08/95	En Avant Guingamp	A	0-1	
26/08/95	AS Monaco	H	2-4	Bancarel, Tholot
29/08/95	FC Gueugnon	A	2-2	Witschge 2
01/09/95	FC Nantes	H	3-0	Zidane 2, Dugarry
09/09/95	AS Cannes	H	2-1	Fischer, Dugarry
17/09/95	Le Havre AC	A	0-1	
22/09/95	Montpellier HSC	H	3-0	Bancarel 2, Lizarazu
01/10/95	RC Strasbourg	A	0-3	
04/10/95	Olympique Lyonnais	H	1-1	Dogon
14/10/95	FC Metz	A	0-2	
21/10/95	Stade Rennais FC	H	0-0	
27/10/95	FC Martigues	A	1-3	Bancarel
04/11/95	AJ Auxerre	H	0-1	
08/11/95	RC Lens	A	0-0	
18/11/95	OGC Nice	H	4-1	Bancarel, Zidane, Dutuel 2
25/11/95	Paris Saint-Germain FC	A	0-3	
01/12/95	AS Saint-Etienne	A	0-2	
09/12/95	SC Bastia	H	1-3	Dutuel
16/12/95	FC Nantes	A	0-2	
10/01/96	En Avant Guingamp	H	2-0	Zidane, Witschge (p)
20/01/96	AS Monaco	A	0-2	
27/01/96	FC Gueugnon	H	3-1	Tholot 2, Friis-Hansen
07/02/96	AS Cannes	A	1-1	Witschge
10/02/96	Le Havre AC	H	3-1	Dogon, Witschge, Friis-Hansen
17/02/96	Montpellier HSC	A	0-3	
27/02/96	RC Strasbourg	H	1-1	Witschge
01/03/96	Olympique Lyonnais	A	0-1	
09/03/96	FC Metz	H	4-0	Zidane 2, Tholot, Dugarry
23/03/96	Stade Rennais FC	A	3-4	Witschge, Tholot, Dugarry
09/04/96	AJ Auxerre	A	0-2	
20/04/96	RC Lens	H	0-0	
26/04/96	OGC Nice	A	0-1	
05/05/96	FC Martigues	H	1-1	Lizarazu (p)
11/05/96	Paris Saint-Germain FC	H	2-2	Bancarel 2
18/05/96	Lille OSC	A	2-0	Castant, Diawara

AS CANNES

CLUB DIRECTORY

Association Sportive de Cannes
Stade Pierre de Coubertin
Avenue Pierre-Poési
06150 Cannes-La Bocca
tel - (93) 902420
fax - (93) 470713
Year of Formation - 1902
President - Yoackim Balicco
Secretary - Gilbert Chamonal
Coach - Safet Susic; William Ayache; Guy Lacombe
Stadium - Pierre de Coubertin (13,500)

MAJOR HONOURS
Domestic Cup - (1) 1932.

APPEARANCES 95/96

	P	Ap	(s)	Gls
Pascal BEDROSSIAN	M	7	(12)	1
Adel BOUTOBBA	M	2	(2)	
BRAIZAT	M		(1)	
Jean-Michel CAPOUE	M	28		3
Sébastien CHABAUD	M	3	(7)	
Laurent CHARVET	A	23	(8)	8
Lilian COMPAN	A	4	(6)	1
DA SILVA	M		(1)	
Michel DUSSUYER	G	11		
Jean-Jacques ETAME	M	18	(5)	2
Kader FERHAOUI (ALG)	M	27	(1)	2
Romain FERRIER	D	13	(6)	1
Fabrice GRONDIN	D	3	(3)	
Gilles HAMPARTZOUMIAN	D	18	(2)	
Kwami HODOUTO	D	17		
Christophe HORLAVILLE	A	31	(4)	12
Emmanuel HUTTEAU	D	9	(3)	
David JEMMALI	D	20		
Addick KOOT (HOL)	D	23		
Ardijan KOZNIKU (CRO)	A	19	(5)	7
Bernard LAMBOURDE	D	27	(1)	1
François LEMASSON	G	27		
Patrice MARQUET	M	8	(11)	1
Michaël MARSIGLIA	A	12	(9)	
Fernando MEIRELLES	D	7	(2)	
Johan MICOUD	M	31	(1)	5
Cédric MOURET	A		(3)	
Sacha OPINEL	D	1	(2)	
Sasa PERSON (CRO)	D	16	(2)	
Patrick VIEIRA	M	13		

LEAGUE RESULTS 1995/96

19/07/95	Olympique Lyonnais	H	3-0	Bedrossian, Horlaville, Kozniku
26/07/95	Stade Rennais FC	A	2-3	Horlaville 2
05/08/95	FC Metz	H	1-2	Micoud
09/08/95	FC Martigues	A	1-2	Kozniku
19/08/95	Lille OSC	H	2-1	Micoud, Horlaville
26/08/95	AJ Auxerre	A	1-5	Marquet
29/08/95	Paris Saint-Germain FC	H	0-2	
09/09/95	Girondins de Bordeaux	A	1-2	Micoud
16/09/95	AS Saint-Etienne	H	2-0	Kozniku 2
22/09/95	SC Bastia	A	1-2	Horlaville
30/09/95	OGC Nice	H	1-3	Kozniku
04/10/95	En Avant Guingamp	A	0-2	
14/10/95	FC Nantes	H	0-2	
21/10/95	FC Gueugnon	A	1-1	Horlaville (p)
27/10/95	AS Monaco	H	1-1	Kozniku
05/11/95	RC Strasbourg	H	0-3	
08/11/95	Montpellier HSC	A	1-3	Lambourde
18/11/95	Le Havre AC	H	0-0	
25/11/95	RC Lens	A	1-1	Kozniku
01/12/95	Stade Rennais FC	H	3-0	Ferhaoui, Charvet, Micoud
09/12/95	FC Metz	A	0-0	
16/12/95	FC Martigues	H	2-1	Charvet, Capoue
10/01/96	Lille OSC	A	2-0	Ferrier, Charvet
20/01/96	AJ Auxerre	H	0-1	
27/01/96	Paris Saint-Germain FC	A	1-2	Charvet
07/02/96	Girondins de Bordeaux	H	1-1	Ferhaoui
17/02/96	SC Bastia	H	1-0	Horlaville (p)
26/02/96	OGC Nice	A	2-1	Capoue, Horlaville
02/03/96	En Avant Guingamp	H	3-0	Horlaville, Capoue, Etamé
09/03/96	FC Nantes	A	0-2	
10/03/96	AS Saint-Etienne	A	2-2	Horlaville, og (Despeyroux)
23/03/96	FC Gueugnon	H	2-0	Horlaville, Charvet
30/03/96	AS Monaco	A	0-1	
09/04/96	RC Strasbourg	A	0-1	
20/04/96	Montpellier HSC	H	2-1	Micoud, Etamé
27/04/96	Le Havre AC	A	0-0	
11/05/96	RC Lens	H	5-2	Charvet 3 (1p), Compan, Horlaville
18/05/96	Olympique Lyonnais	A	0-1	

FC GUEUGNON

CLUB DIRECTORY

Football Club Gueugnonnais
2 rue de la Liberté
71130 Gueugnon
tel - (85) 851278
fax - (85) 851030
Year of Formation - 1940
President - Gilbert Pithioud
Secretary - Franck Sochan
Coach - Roland Gransart
Stadium - Jean-Laville (15,524)

APPEARANCES 95/96

	P	Ap	(s)	Gls
Jean ACEDO	D	36		
Christophe AJAS	A	2	(7)	
Ali BOUMNIJEL	G	37		
Philippe BRUNEL	A	29	(5)	4
Sylvain BUPTO	A	3	(6)	
Yannick CHANDIOUX	M	12	(3)	3
Laurent CIECHELSKI	D	6	(3)	1
Philippe CORREIA	M	31	(2)	1
Claude DAMBURY	D	18	(9)	1
Francis DICAN (ROM)	M	14	(5)	
Alain DURAND	A	2	(10)	
Nicolas ESCETH-N'ZI	M	11	(4)	
Patrice EYRAUD	M	7	(2)	
David FANZEL	D	32		1
Clément GARCIA	A	15	(9)	3
Franck GRANGER	D	22	(2)	
Franck JURIETTI	M	36		2
Mohammed LASHAF (MAR)	M	3	(4)	
Sylvain POINÇON	D	4	(3)	1
Stéphane POUNEWATCHY	M	28	(2)	
Fabien SAFANJON	D	25	(3)	
Jérôme SYKORA	G	1	(1)	
Amara TRAORE (SEN)	A	31	(2)	7
David TRIVINO	M	13	(2)	3

LEAGUE RESULTS 1995/96

Date	Opponent	H/A	Score	Scorers
19/07/95	FC Metz	H	0-0	
26/07/95	AJ Auxerre	A	0-4	
05/08/95	FC Martigues	H	0-0	
09/08/95	OGC Nice	A	1-3	Garcia
19/08/95	Paris Saint-Germain FC	H	1-3	Fanzel
26/08/95	SC Bastia	A	2-1	Ciechelski, Trivino
29/08/95	Girondins de Bordeaux	H	2-2	Trivino, Garcia
09/09/95	AS Saint-Etienne	A	0-2	
16/09/95	Lille OSC	H	3-1	Trivino, Traoré, Brunel
22/09/95	En Avant Guingamp	A	0-0	
30/09/95	FC Nantes	H	0-1	
04/10/95	RC Lens	H	0-1	
14/10/95	AS Monaco	A	0-0	
21/10/95	AS Cannes	H	1-1	Traoré (p)
27/10/95	Montpellier HSC	A	2-2	Traoré (p), Brunel
04/11/95	Le Havre AC	H	0-1	
08/11/95	Olympique Lyonnais	A	0-0	
18/11/95	RC Strasbourg	H	0-1	
25/11/95	Stade Rennais FC	A	1-2	Garcia
30/11/95	AJ Auxerre	H	0-0	
09/12/95	FC Martigues	A	0-3	
16/12/95	OGC Nice	H	1-0	Chandioux
10/01/96	Paris Saint-Germain FC	A	1-1	Brunel
20/01/96	SC Bastia	H	1-0	Traoré
27/01/96	Girondins de Bordeaux	A	1-3	Poinçon
10/02/96	Lille OSC	A	0-2	
17/02/96	En Avant Guingamp	H	2-2	Traoré, Dambury
23/02/96	AS Saint-Etienne	H	1-0	Chandioux
27/02/96	FC Nantes	A	0-1	
02/03/96	RC Lens	A	0-2	
09/03/96	AS Monaco	H	2-2	Traoré, Chandioux
23/03/96	AS Cannes	A	0-2	
30/03/96	Montpellier HSC	H	0-2	
09/04/96	Le Havre AC	A	2-0	Jurietti, Brunel
20/04/96	Olympique Lyonnais	H	0-0	
27/04/96	RC Strasbourg	A	0-0	
11/05/96	Stade Rennais FC	H	1-0	Traoré
18/05/96	FC Metz	A	2-1	Jurietti, Correia

EN AVANT GUINGAMP

CLUB DIRECTORY

En Avant Guingamp
15 boulevard Clémenceau
BP 66
22200 Guingamp
tel - (96) 401313
fax - (96) 210777
Year of Formation - 1912
President - Bertrand Salomon
Secretary - Aimé Dagorn
Coach - Francis Smerecki
Stadium - Roudourou (16,000)

APPEARANCES 95/96

	P	Ap	(s)	Gls
Yannick BARET	M	29	(4)	1
Vincent CANDELA	D	23	(4)	1
Stéphane CARNOT	M	38		6
Philippe CELDRAN	A	3	(6)	
Joël CLOAREC	A		(1)	
Charles-Edoard CORIDON	M	37		2
Sébastien DALLET	A	15	(17)	1
Fabrice DIVERT	A	4	(1)	2
Jérôme FOULON	D	32		
Hubert FOURNIER	D	36		1
Gilles GIULIANO	D		(10)	
Xavier GRAVELAINE	A	17		7
Laurent HERVE	M		(3)	
Jean-Jacques HOUZE	M	2	(5)	
Angelo HUGUES	G	38		
Nicolas LASPALLES	D	19	(1)	
Richard LECOMTE	D	24	(8)	
Claude MICHEL	M	32		
Gheorghe MIHALI (ROM)	D	30	(1)	2
Jérôme MOLINIER	A		(1)	
Réginald RAY	A	3	(13)	1
Lionel ROUXEL	A	30	(1)	9
Djordje TOMIC (YUG)	M	6	(6)	

LEAGUE RESULTS 1995/96

Date	Opponent	H/A	Score	Scorers
19/07/95	FC Martigues	H	2-0	Divert, Rouxel
26/07/95	Paris Saint-Germain FC	A	1-1	Divert
05/08/95	OGC Nice	H	0-0	
09/08/95	Lille OSC	A	3-0	Rouxel (p), Dallet, Carnot
20/08/95	Girondins de Bordeaux	H	1-0	Rouxel
26/08/95	AS Saint-Etienne	A	0-4	
30/08/95	SC Bastia	H	1-0	Carnot
09/09/95	Montpellier HSC	H	0-0	
16/09/95	FC Nantes	A	0-0	
22/09/95	FC Gueugnon	H	0-0	
30/09/95	AS Monaco	A	0-1	
04/10/95	AS Cannes	H	2-0	Candela, Rouxel (p)
14/10/95	RC Strasbourg	A	0-0	
21/10/95	Le Havre AC	H	2-2	Ray, Rouxel (p)
27/10/95	RC Lens	A	1-0	Baret
04/11/95	Olympique Lyonnais	H	1-0	Rouxel
07/11/95	Stade Rennais FC	A	0-3	
18/11/95	FC Metz	H	0-0	
25/11/95	AJ Auxerre	A	2-1	Carnot 2
01/12/95	Paris Saint-Germain FC	H	0-0	
09/12/95	OGC Nice	A	1-2	og (Fugen)
16/12/95	Lille OSC	H	0-1	
10/01/96	Girondins de Bordeaux	A	0-2	
20/01/96	AS Saint-Etienne	H	3-0	Coridon, Gravelaine (p), Mihali
27/01/96	SC Bastia	A	1-0	Gravelaine
10/02/96	FC Nantes	H	3-1	Carnot 2 (1p), Gravelaine
17/02/96	FC Gueugnon	A	2-2	Fournier, Gravelaine
27/02/96	AS Monaco	H	0-0	
02/03/96	AS Cannes	A	0-3	
09/03/96	RC Strasbourg	H	3-0	Gravelaine, Coridon, Rouxel
23/03/96	Le Havre AC	A	0-1	
31/03/96	RC Lens	H	1-0	Rouxel
05/04/96	Montpellier HSC	A	1-2	Rouxel
10/04/96	Olympique Lyonnais	A	1-1	Gravelaine (p)
20/04/96	Stade Rennais FC	H	0-0	
27/04/96	FC Metz	A	0-3	
11/05/96	AJ Auxerre	H	1-1	Mihali
18/05/96	FC Martigues	A	1-2	Gravelaine

LE HAVRE AC

CLUB DIRECTORY

Le Havre Athletic Club Football Association
32 rue de la Cavée-Verte
76620 Le Havre
tel - (35) 546262
fax - (35) 447272
Year of Formation - 1872
President - Jean-Pierre Hureau
Secretary - Alain Belsoeur
Coach - Guy David (96/97 - René Exbrayat)
Stadium - Jules-Deschaseaux (20,356)

MAJOR HONOURS
Domestic Cup - (1) 1959.

APPEARANCES 95/96

	P	Ap	(s)	Gls
Ibrahima BA	D	30	(3)	2
Teddy BERTIN	M	34	(1)	4
Frédéric BRANDO	M	27	(3)	1
Alain CAVEGLIA	A	35	(3)	11
Cédric DAURY	M	33	(3)	4
Olivier DEBERT	D		(3)	
Bertrand DELAS	D		(3)	
Jean-Pierre DELAUNAY	D	8		
Olivier DE LUCA	M	3	(1)	
Vikash DHORASOO	M	26	(4)	
Djibril DIAWARA (SEN)	M	20	(4)	
Iyambo ETSHELE	M	6	(2)	
Claude FICHAUX	D	12	(5)	
Vanja GRUBAC (YUG)	A	3	(5)	
Nicolas HUYSMAN	M	27	(2)	3
JEGOUZO	M		(1)	
Christophe LAGRANGE	A	26	(6)	3
Mathieu LOUIS-JEAN	D	12	(3)	
Bernard PASCUAL	D	33	(3)	
Ludovic POLLET	D	22	(4)	
Christophe REVAULT	G	38		
Stéphane SAMSON	A	7	(18)	4
Thierry UVENARD	D	15	(7)	1
ZOUAOUI	M	1		

LEAGUE RESULTS 1995/96

19/07/95	RC Lens	A	0-2	
26/07/95	RC Strasbourg	A	0-3	
05/08/95	Olympique Lyonnais	H	2-1	Daury, Caveglia
09/08/95	Stade Rennais FC	A	0-1	
19/08/95	FC Metz	H	0-0	
26/08/95	Paris Saint-Germain FC	A	0-2	
29/08/95	AJ Auxerre	H	0-4	
09/09/95	OGC Nice	A	2-1	Samson, Bertin
17/09/95	Girondins de Bordeaux	H	1-0	Daury
22/09/95	Lille OSC	A	0-2	
30/09/95	FC Martigues	H	1-0	Bertin
04/10/95	SC Bastia	A	0-1	
15/10/95	AS Saint-Etienne	H	2-2	Caveglia (p), Lagrange
21/10/95	En Avant Guingamp	A	2-2	Huysman (p), Samson
27/10/95	FC Nantes	H	0-1	
04/11/95	FC Gueugnon	A	1-0	Caveglia (p)
08/11/95	AS Monaco	H	2-1	Caveglia, Samson
18/11/95	AS Cannes	A	0-0	
25/11/95	Montpellier HSC	H	2-2	Lagrange, Caveglia
01/12/95	RC Strasbourg	H	2-0	Caveglia 2
09/12/95	Olympique Lyonnais	A	2-3	Bertin, Caveglia
16/12/95	Stade Rennais FC	H	0-0	
10/01/96	FC Metz	A	1-2	Huysman
19/01/96	Paris Saint-Germain FC	H	1-1	Caveglia
27/01/96	AJ Auxerre	A	0-1	
07/02/96	OGC Nice	H	0-0	
10/02/96	Girondins de Bordeaux	A	1-3	Daury
17/02/96	Lille OSC	H	4-1	Huysman, Daury, Caveglia 2
27/02/96	FC Martigues	A	1-0	Uvenard
02/03/96	SC Bastia	H	1-0	Bertin
09/03/96	AS Saint-Etienne	A	1-1	Ba
23/03/96	En Avant Guingamp	H	1-0	Ba
09/04/96	FC Gueugnon	H	0-2	
20/04/96	AS Monaco	A	1-2	Brando
27/04/96	AS Cannes	H	0-0	
02/05/96	FC Nantes	A	1-1	Samson
11/05/96	Montpellier HSC	A	0-2	
18/05/96	RC Lens	H	1-1	Lagrange

RC LENS

CLUB DIRECTORY

Racing Club de Lens
13 rue Souvraz
BP 236
62300 Lens
tel - (21) 692899
fax - (21) 692884
Year of Formation - 1906
President - Gervais Martel
Secretary - Louis Plet
Coach - Patrice Bergues (96/97 - Slavo Muslin)
Stadium - Félix-Bollaert (40,000)

APPEARANCES 95/96

	P	Ap	(s)	Gls
Jean-Marc ADJOVI-BOCO	D	24	(4)	
Pegguy ARPHEXAD	G	2	(1)	
Hervé ARSENE	M	9	(11)	
Roger BOLI	A	11	(17)	4
Aboubacar CAMARA (GUI)	A	29	(7)	9
Michaël DEBEVE	M	31	(5)	2
Frédéric DEHU	D	29	(6)	1
Christophe DELMOTTE	D	31	(7)	3
DUPONT	M		(1)	
Philippe DURPES	A	1		
Marc-Vivien FOE (CMR)	M	16	(3)	2
Pierre LAIGLE	M	33	(1)	1
Cyrille MAGNIER	D	26	(1)	
Frédéric MEYRIEU	M	30	(4)	7
Wilson ORUMA (NIG)	M	9	(5)	
Eric SIKORA	D	34		5
Joël TIEHI (CIV)	A	5	(7)	1
Tony VAIRELLES	A	30	(8)	9
Jean-Guy WALLEMME	D	32	(3)	1
Guillaume WARMUZ	G	36		

LEAGUE RESULTS 1995/96

19/07/95	Le Havre AC	H	2-0	Camara 2
26/07/95	FC Metz	A	0-2	
05/08/95	RC Strasbourg	H	0-0	
09/08/95	AJ Auxerre	A	1-0	Laigle
19/08/95	Olympique Lyonnais	H	2-2	Tiéhi, Camara
26/08/95	OGC Nice	A	1-1	Meyrieu
29/08/95	Stade Rennais FC	H	1-0	Vairelles
09/09/95	Lille OSC	A	3-1	Vairelles 2, Meyrieu
17/09/95	SC Bastia	H	3-1	Sikora (p), Boli, Meyrieu
22/09/95	FC Nantes	A	1-1	Camara
01/10/95	Paris Saint-Germain FC	H	3-1	Wallemme, Camara, Vairelles
04/10/95	FC Gueugnon	A	1-0	Camara
13/10/95	FC Martigues	H	1-0	Camara
21/10/95	AS Saint-Etienne	A	1-1	Delmotte
27/10/95	En Avant Guingamp	H	0-1	
04/11/95	AS Monaco	A	1-1	Debève (p)
08/11/95	Girondins de Bordeaux	H	0-0	
18/11/95	Montpellier HSC	A	0-0	
25/11/95	AS Cannes	H	1-1	Camara
01/12/95	FC Metz	H	2-0	Meyrieu, Foé
10/12/95	RC Strasbourg	A	2-1	Vairelles, Debève (p)
16/12/95	AJ Auxerre	H	0-0	
10/01/96	Olympique Lyonnais	A	0-0	
20/01/96	OGC Nice	H	0-0	
27/01/96	Stade Rennais FC	A	1-2	Vairelles
06/02/96	Lille OSC	H	1-1	Vairelles
10/02/96	SC Bastia	A	2-3	Camara, Sikora
16/02/96	FC Nantes	H	2-1	Sikora, Vairelles
27/02/96	Paris Saint-Germain FC	A	0-1	
02/03/96	FC Gueugnon	H	2-0	Delmotte, Sikora
09/03/96	FC Martigues	A	1-0	Vairelles
23/03/96	AS Saint-Etienne	H	3-0	Meyrieu, Foé, Boli
31/03/96	En Avant Guingamp	A	0-1	
08/04/96	AS Monaco	H	2-1	Meyrieu, Sikora (p)
20/04/96	Girondins de Bordeaux	A	0-0	
27/04/96	Montpellier HSC	H	2-1	Meyrieu, Delmotte
11/05/96	AS Cannes	A	2-5	Boli, Dehu
18/05/96	Le Havre AC	A	1-1	Boli

LILLE OSC

CLUB DIRECTORY

Lille Olympique Sporting Club
Stade Grimonprez-Jooris
allée du Petit-Paradis
59000 Lille
tel - (20) 128292
fax - (20) 420678
Year of Formation - 1944
President - Bernard Lecomte
Secretary - Loïc Chopinet
Coach - Jean Fernandez; Jean-Michel Cavalli
Stadium - Grimonprez-Jooris (24,000)

MAJOR HONOURS
League Championship - (2) 1946, 1954.
Domestic Cup - (5)
1946, 1947, 1948, 1953, 1955.

APPEARANCES 95/96

	P	Ap	(s)	Gls
Denis ABED	A	10	(4)	
Jean-Marie AUBRY	G	29		
Miladin BECANOVIC (YUG)	A	19	(7)	1
Djezon BOUTOILLE	A	18	(17)	5
Cédric CARREZ	D	21	(3)	1
Patrick COLLOT	A	30	(4)	3
David COULIBALY	M		(1)	
Pascal CYGAN	D	25	(2)	
Jérémy DENQUIN	D		(6)	
Frédéric DINDELEUX	D	25	(1)	1
Arnaud DUNCKER	M	25	(10)	1
Jacob FRIIS-HANSEN (DEN)	D	16		1
Joël GERMAIN	D	2	(9)	
Roger HITOTO	M	31	(1)	1
LAURICELLA	M		(1)	
Fabien LECLERCQ	D	16	(1)	
Philippe LEVENARD	D	26	(4)	
Frédéric MACHADO	M		(4)	
Géza MÉSZÖLY (HUN)	D	9	(7)	
Jean-Claude NADON	G	9		
Philippe PERILLEUX	M	18		
Frank PINGEL (DEN)	A	4	(1)	
Thierry RABAT	D	24		
Antoine SIBIERSKI	M	30	(3)	9
Amara SIMBA	A	30	(4)	4
Franck TURPIN	D	1	(1)	

LEAGUE RESULTS 1995/96

19/07/95	Girondins de Bordeaux	A	0-1	
26/07/95	SC Bastia	H	0-2	
05/08/95	AS Saint-Etienne	A	1-1	Sibierski
09/08/95	En Avant Guingamp	H	0-3	
19/08/95	AS Cannes	A	1-2	Sibierski (p)
25/08/95	FC Nantes	H	0-0	
29/08/95	AS Monaco	A	1-2	Duncker
09/09/95	RC Lens	H	1-3	Friis-Hansen (p)
16/09/95	FC Gueugnon	A	1-3	Sibierski
22/09/95	Le Havre AC	H	2-0	Sibierski, Becanovic
30/09/95	Montpellier HSC	A	0-0	
04/10/95	RC Strasbourg	H	2-0	Simba 2
14/10/95	Stade Rennais FC	A	1-3	Collot
21/10/95	FC Metz	H	0-0	
27/10/95	AJ Auxerre	A	2-1	Boutoille 2
04/11/95	FC Martigues	H	0-0	
08/11/95	OGC Nice	A	1-2	Sibierski
18/11/95	Paris Saint-Germain FC	H	0-0	
25/11/95	Olympique Lyonnais	A	1-1	Boutoille
01/12/95	SC Bastia	A	0-4	
09/12/95	AS Saint-Etienne	H	1-1	Boutoille
16/12/95	En Avant Guingamp	A	1-0	Collot
10/01/96	AS Cannes	H	0-2	
20/01/96	FC Nantes	A	2-1	Sibierski, Carrez
27/01/96	AS Monaco	H	0-0	
06/02/96	RC Lens	A	1-1	Sibierski
10/02/96	FC Gueugnon	H	2-0	Boutoille, Sibierski
17/02/96	Le Havre AC	A	1-4	Hitoto
27/02/96	Montpellier HSC	H	1-1	Dindeleux
02/03/96	RC Strasbourg	A	0-2	
09/03/96	Stade Rennais FC	H	0-0	
23/03/96	FC Metz	A	0-2	
30/03/96	AJ Auxerre	H	0-4	
09/04/96	FC Martigues	A	0-1	
20/04/96	OGC Nice	H	1-0	Simba
27/04/96	Paris Saint-Germain FC	A	1-0	Collot
11/05/96	Olympique Lyonnais	H	2-1	Sibierski, Simba
18/05/96	Girondins de Bordeaux	H	0-2	

OLYMPIQUE LYONNAIS

CLUB DIRECTORY

Olympique Lyonnais
350 avenue Jean-Jaurès
69007 Lyon
tel - (78) 767604
fax - (78) 720399
Year of Formation - 1950
President - Jean-Michel Aulas
Secretary - Marino Faccioli
Coach - Guy Stephan
Stadium - Gerland (43,000)

MAJOR HONOURS
Domestic Cup - (3) 1964, 1967, 1973.

APPEARANCES 95/96

	P	Ap	(s)	Gls
Samassi ABOU	A		(1)	
Ghislain ANSELMINI	D	19	(3)	
Eric ASSADOURIAN	A	24	(6)	2
Jacek BAK (POL)	D	12	(1)	
Cédric BARDON	A	7	(11)	1
Olivier BELLISI	M	2	(1)	
Christophe BRETON	G	2	(1)	
Laurent CASANOVA	D	14	(1)	1
Pierre CHAVRONDIER	M	4	(10)	2
Christophe DEGUERVILLE	D	21	(1)	
Sylvain DEPLACE	M	32	(1)	
Jean-Christophe DEVAUX	D	14	(3)	
Frédéric FOURET	A	3	(2)	1
Franck GAVA	M	11	(2)	2
Ludovic GIULY	M	25	(11)	4
Florent LAVILLE	D	26	(2)	
MARCELO Kiremitjian (BRA)	D	33		
Florian MAURICE	A	36		18
Jean-Marc MOULIN	D	4	(7)	
Pascal OLMETA	G	36		
Frédéric PATOUILLARD	M	3	(6)	1
Claude-Arnaud RIVENET	A	4	(9)	
Stéphane ROCHE	M	15	(9)	3
Eric ROY	M	37		3
Jean-Luc SASSUS	D	34		

LEAGUE RESULTS 1995/96

Date	Opponent	H/A	Score	Scorers
19/07/95	AS Cannes	A	0-3	
26/07/95	Montpellier HSC	H	3-2	Assadourian, og (Bonnissel), Gava
05/08/95	Le Havre AC	A	1-2	og (Fichaux)
19/08/95	RC Lens	A	2-2	Maurice 2 (1p)
26/08/95	Stade Rennais FC	A	0-1	
29/08/95	FC Metz	H	1-1	Maurice
01/09/95	RC Strasbourg	H	1-1	Maurice
09/09/95	FC Martigues	A	2-1	Maurice 2
16/09/95	AJ Auxerre	H	0-1	
22/09/95	OGC Nice	A	0-1	
30/09/95	AS Saint-Etienne	H	2-1	Assadourian, Maurice
04/10/95	Girondins de Bordeaux	A	1-1	Chavrondier
14/10/95	Paris Saint-Germain FC	H	0-0	
21/10/95	FC Nantes	A	0-0	
27/10/95	SC Bastia	H	1-1	Roy
04/11/95	En Avant Guingamp	A	0-1	
08/11/95	FC Gueugnon	H	0-0	
18/11/95	AS Monaco	A	2-0	Patouillard, Maurice
25/11/95	Lille OSC	H	1-1	Maurice (p)
01/12/95	Montpellier HSC	A	1-2	Chavrondier
09/12/95	Le Havre AC	H	3-2	og (Pascual), Roy, Roche
16/12/95	RC Strasbourg	A	2-2	Roche, Maurice
10/01/96	RC Lens	H	0-0	
20/01/96	Stade Rennais FC	H	2-2	Giuly 2
07/02/96	FC Martigues	H	5-1	Maurice 2 (1p), Roy, Gava, Roche
10/02/96	AJ Auxerre	A	0-2	
17/02/96	OGC Nice	H	1-0	Casanova
27/02/96	AS Saint-Etienne	A	1-1	Giuly
01/03/96	Girondins de Bordeaux	H	1-0	Maurice
05/03/96	FC Metz	A	1-0	Maurice
10/03/96	Paris Saint-Germain FC	A	0-2	
23/03/96	FC Nantes	H	1-1	Maurice
30/03/96	SC Bastia	A	0-0	
10/04/96	En Avant Guingamp	H	1-1	Maurice
20/04/96	FC Gueugnon	A	0-0	
27/04/96	AS Monaco	H	3-3	Maurice, Giuly, Fouret
11/05/96	Lille OSC	A	1-2	Maurice
18/05/96	AS Cannes	H	1-0	Bardon

FC MARTIGUES

CLUB DIRECTORY

Football Club de Martigues
31 chemin de Paradis
13500 Martigues
tel - (42) 421830
fax - (42) 802920
Year of Formation - 1921
President - Denis Lankar
Secretary - Jean-Michel Le Mons
Coach - René Exbrayat; Patrick Parizon
Stadium - Francis-Turcan (12,000)

APPEARANCES 95/96

	P	Ap	(s)	Gls
Abdoulkarim BANGOURA (GUI)	D	6	(7)	
Henrik BERTILSSON (SWE)	A	1	(1)	
Abassi BOINAHERI	A	5	(8)	1
Guillaume BOUISSET	D	20	(1)	
Laurent DAVID	M	2	(6)	
DJELLAL	M		(1)	
Didier DUBOIS	D	24		
Eric DURAND	G	37		
Maxence FLACHEZ	D	31		3
Gil FRECHINGUES	D	9		
Bruno GENESIO	M	21	(6)	1
Laurent GRIMAUD	D	4	(2)	
Olivier ICHOUA	M	26	(6)	3
David MAZZONCINI	M	35		4
Frédéric MENDY	M	27		
Stéphane ODET	M	23	(9)	
Gilles PETRUCCI	D	21	(1)	
Serge ROMANO	M	27	(1)	3
Franck SOLER	A	15	(10)	2
Abdelsalem SOW (GUI)	A	16	(7)	3
Mohamed SYLLA (GUI)	A	18	(5)	4
Abibou TCHAGNAO (TOG)	M	7	(2)	
Joël TIEHI (CIV)	A	20		5
Olivier VANDEVOORDE	A	9	(11)	1
Christophe VIALET	G	1		
Samir ZAMFIR (ROM)	M	13	(3)	1

LEAGUE RESULTS 1995/96

19/07/95	En Avant Guingamp	A	0-2	
26/07/95	FC Nantes	H	0-4	
05/08/95	FC Gueugnon	A	0-0	
09/08/95	AS Cannes	H	2-1	Sylla 2
19/08/95	AS Monaco	A	1-0	Sow
26/08/95	Montpellier HSC	H	0-1	
29/08/95	RC Strasbourg	A	0-2	
09/09/95	Olympique Lyonnais	H	1-2	Sylla
16/09/95	Stade Rennais FC	A	3-1	Romano, Soler, Mazzoncini
22/09/95	FC Metz	H	0-1	
30/09/95	Le Havre AC	A	0-1	
04/10/95	AJ Auxerre	H	1-2	Sow (p)
13/10/95	RC Lens	A	0-1	
21/10/95	OGC Nice	A	0-1	
27/10/95	Girondins de Bordeaux	H	3-1	Romano, Boinaheri, Sow
04/11/95	Lille OSC	A	0-0	
08/11/95	Paris Saint-Germain FC	H	2-4	Flachez, Ichoua (p)
18/11/95	SC Bastia	A	0-2	
25/11/95	AS Saint-Etienne	H	1-1	Zamfir
01/12/95	FC Nantes	A	0-3	
09/12/95	FC Gueugnon	H	3-0	Mazzoncini, Tiéhi, Vandevoorde
16/12/95	AS Cannes	A	1-2	Mazzoncini
09/01/96	AS Monaco	H	0-4	
20/01/96	Montpellier HSC	A	0-2	
27/01/96	RC Strasbourg	H	2-0	Soler, Tiéhi
07/02/96	Olympique Lyonnais	A	1-5	Tiéhi
10/02/96	Stade Rennais FC	H	1-2	Tiéhi (p)
17/02/96	FC Metz	A	0-2	
27/02/96	Le Havre AC	H	0-1	
02/03/96	AJ Auxerre	A	0-4	
09/03/96	RC Lens	H	0-1	
23/03/96	OGC Nice	H	0-0	
09/04/96	Lille OSC	H	1-0	Mazzoncini
23/04/96	Paris Saint-Germain FC	A	0-0	
27/04/96	SC Bastia	H	3-1	Romano, Ichoua, Sylla
05/05/96	Girondins de Bordeaux	A	1-1	Flachez
11/05/96	AS Saint-Etienne	A	2-2	Ichoua, Flachez
18/05/96	En Avant Guingamp	H	2-1	Génésio, Tiéhi

FC METZ

CLUB DIRECTORY

Football Club de Metz
Stade Saint-Symphorien
Nouvelle Tribune
57050 Longeville-lès-Metz
tel - (87) 667215
fax - (87) 561429
Year of Formation - 1932
President - Charles Molinari
Secretary - Patrick Razurel
Coach - Joël Muller
Stadium - Saint-Symphorien (27,000)

MAJOR HONOURS
Domestic Cup - (2) 1984, 1988.

APPEARANCES 95/96

	P	Ap	(s)	Gls
Stéphane ADAM	A	8	(11)	1
Frédéric ARPINON	M	18	(11)	2
Jocelyn BLANCHARD	M	34	(3)	3
D'ANGELO	G	1		
Philippe GAILLOT	D	38		
ISAÍAS Magalhães da Silva (BRA)	M	24	(80	2
Sylvain KASTENDEUCH	D	38		4
Didier LANG	D	19	(9)	
Patrick MBOMA	A	10	(7)	4
Franck MEYRIGNAC	D		(9)	
Samba N'DIAYE	A	6	(18)	2
Pascal PIERRE	D	35		1
Robert PIRES	A	38		11
Cyrille POUGET	A	35	(1)	11
Cyril SERREDSZUM	M	35	(1)	
Rigobert SONG (CMR)	D	33	(1)	
Jacques SONGO'O (CMR)	G	37		
Jeff STRASSER (LUX)	D		(5)	
David TERRIER	M	9	(11)	

LEAGUE RESULTS 1995/96

19/07/95	FC Gueugnon	A	0-0	
26/07/95	RC Lens	H	2-0	Pouget, N'Diaye
05/08/95	AS Cannes	A	2-1	Pires 2
09/08/95	Montpellier HSC	H	1-0	Isaías
19/08/95	Le Havre AC	A	0-0	
26/08/95	RC Strasbourg	H	3-2	Pouget, Isaías, Kastendeuch (p)
29/08/95	Olympique Lyonnais	A	1-1	Pouget
10/09/95	Stade Rennais FC	H	0-0	
16/09/95	AS Monaco	A	1-0	Pires
22/09/95	FC Martigues	A	1-0	Blanchard
30/09/95	AJ Auxerre	H	3-1	Kastendeuch, og (West), Adam
04/10/95	OGC Nice	A	1-0	Pires
14/10/95	Girondins de Bordeaux	H	2-0	Blanchard 2
21/10/95	Lille OSC	A	0-0	
26/10/95	Paris Saint-Germain FC	H	0-3	
04/11/95	SC Bastia	A	0-1	
08/11/95	AS Saint-Etienne	H	1-2	Arpinon
18/11/95	En Avant Guingamp	A	0-0	
25/11/95	FC Nantes	H	0-0	
01/12/95	RC Lens	A	0-2	
09/12/95	AS Cannes	H	0-0	
03/01/96	Montpellier HSC	A	2-1	Pouget, Pires
10/01/96	Le Havre AC	H	2-1	Pires, Pouget
20/01/96	RC Strasbourg	A	2-1	Pouget, N'Diaye
17/02/96	FC Martigues	H	2-0	Mboma 2
27/02/96	AJ Auxerre	A	0-0	
02/03/96	OGC Nice	H	4-0	Mboma 2, Arpinon, Pires
05/03/96	Olympique Lyonnais	H	0-1	
09/03/96	Girondins de Bordeaux	A	0-4	
16/03/96	Stade Rennais FC	A	0-0	
23/03/96	Lille OSC	H	2-0	Kastendeuch (p), Pires
30/03/96	Paris Saint-Germain FC	A	3-2	Pires 2, Pouget
10/04/96	SC Bastia	H	2-0	Pouget 2
14/04/96	AS Monaco	H	0-3	
20/04/96	AS Saint-Etienne	A	1-1	Kastendeuch (p)
27/04/96	En Avant Guingamp	H	3-0	Pierre, Pires, Pouget
11/05/96	FC Nantes	A	0-1	
18/05/96	FC Gueugnon	H	1-2	Pouget

AS MONACO

CLUB DIRECTORY

Association Sportive de Monaco
7 avenue des Castelans
98000 Monaco
tel - (92) 057473
fax - (92) 052454
Year of Formation - 1924
President - Jean-Louis Campora
Secretary - Pierre Liboldi
Coach - Jean Tigana
Stadium - Louis II (18,500)

MAJOR HONOURS
League Championship - (5)
1961, 1963, 1978, 1982, 1988.
Domestic Cup - (5)
1960, 1963, 1980, 1985, 1991.

APPEARANCES 95/96

	P	Ap	(s)	Gls
ANDERSON da Silva (BRA)	A	32	(2)	21
Fabien BARTHEZ	G	21		
Ali BENARBIA	M	20	(5)	4
Patrick BLONDEAU	D	24	(1)	1
Basile BOLI	D	11		
CLOTAIRE	M		(1)	
Marc DELAROCHE	G	5		
Eric DI MECO	D	30		
Manuel DOS SANTOS	D	12	(8)	
Franck DUMAS	D	33	(2)	
Gilles GRIMANDI	D	10	(15)	1
Thierry HENRY	A	5	(18)	3
Victor IKPEBA (NIG)	A	9	(7)	3
Bruno IRLES	D	4	(3)	
Sylvain LEGWINSKI	M	23	(6)	2
Michaël MADAR	A	22	(7)	8
Dan PETERSEN (DEN)	M	6	(4)	
Emmanuel PETIT	M	23		1
Fabien PIVETEAU	G	3		
Stéphane PORATO	G	9		
Claude PUEL	M	14	(10)	
Enzo SCIFO (BEL)	M	34		7
Lilian THURAM	D	36		5
Laurent TOMCZYK	A		(2)	
David TREZEGUET	A		(4)	
Patrick VALERY	D		(3)	
Laurent VIAUD	M	24	(1)	5
Christopher WREH (LIB)	A	8	(5)	3

LEAGUE RESULTS 1995/96

19/07/95	Stade Rennais FC	H	3-1	Anderson 2 (1p), Ikpeba
25/07/95	OGC Nice	A	2-1	Viaud, Madar
05/08/95	AJ Auxerre	H	2-2	Ikpeba, Thuram
09/08/95	SC Bastia	A	1-2	Anderson
19/08/95	FC Martigues	H	0-1	
26/08/95	Girondins de Bordeaux	A	4-2	Thuram, Wreh 2, Benarbia
29/08/95	Lille OSC	H	2-1	Henry, Anderson
09/09/95	Paris Saint-Germain FC	A	1-2	Anderson
16/09/95	FC Metz	H	0-1	
21/09/95	AS Saint-Etienne	A	4-2	Benarbia (p), Madar 2, Viaud
30/09/95	En Avant Guingamp	H	1-0	Madar
03/10/95	FC Nantes	A	2-2	Madar 2
14/10/95	FC Gueugnon	H	0-0	
21/10/95	Montpellier HSC	H	3-1	Scifo, Henry, Anderson
27/10/95	AS Cannes	A	1-1	Viaud
04/11/95	RC Lens	H	1-1	Anderson
08/11/95	Le Havre AC	A	1-2	Madar
18/11/95	Olympique Lyonnais	H	0-2	
24/11/95	RC Strasbourg	A	0-2	
01/12/95	OGC Nice	H	1-0	Anderson
09/12/95	AJ Auxerre	A	2-1	Anderson, Madar
16/12/95	SC Bastia	H	0-0	
09/01/96	FC Martigues	A	4-0	Scifo, Thuram, Anderson 2
20/01/96	Girondins de Bordeaux	H	2-0	Scifo, Viaud
27/01/96	Lille OSC	A	0-0	
07/02/96	Paris Saint-Germain FC	H	1-0	Petit
17/02/96	AS Saint-Etienne	H	2-0	Ikpeba, Viaud
27/02/96	En Avant Guingamp	A	0-0	
01/03/96	FC Nantes	H	4-1	Anderson 2, Thuram, Scifo (p)
09/03/96	FC Gueugnon	A	2-2	Anderson 2
23/03/96	Montpellier HSC	A	0-0	
30/03/96	AS Cannes	H	1-0	Legwinski
08/04/96	RC Lens	A	1-2	Anderson
14/04/96	FC Metz	A	3-0	Benarbia, Anderson, Scifo (p)
20/04/95	Le Havre AC	H	2-1	Blondeau, Grimandi
27/04/95	Olympique Lyonnais	A	3-3	Benarbia, Anderson, Scifo (p)
11/05/96	RC Strasbourg	H	5-1	Legwinski, Henry, Anderson, Wreh, Scifo
18/05/96	Stade Rennais FC	A	3-2	Anderson 2, Thuram

MONTPELLIER HSC

CLUB DIRECTORY

Montpellier Hérault Sports Club
Avenue Albert-Einstein
Domaine de Grammont
34000 Montpellier
tel - (67) 154600
fax - (67) 221273
Year of Formation - 1974
President - Louis Nicollin
Secretary - Philippe Peybernes
Coach - Michel Mézy
Stadium - La Mosson (22,000)

MAJOR HONOURS
Domestic Cup - (1) 1990.

APPEARANCES 95/96

	P	Ap	(s)	Gls
Hervé ALICARTE	D	7	(2)	2
Pascal BAILLS	D	34		
Ibrahim BAKAYOKO (CIV)	A	6	(8)	
BATHIE	M		(1)	
Wilfried BERTRAND	M		(1)	
Serge BLANC	D	22		
Jérôme BONNISSEL	M	32		
Philippe DELAYE	A	14	(13)	2
Michel DER ZAKARIAN	D	25	(1)	5
Philippe FLUCKLINGER	G	2		
Jean-Philippe JAVARY	A		(3)	
Thierry LAUREY	D	27		1
Fabien LEFEVRE	M	36	(1)	11
Gérald MARTIN	M		(1)	
Bruno MARTINI	G	36		
Michel PAVON	A	33	(2)	5
Vincent PETIT	A	4	(6)	1
Bertrand REUZEAU	D	8	(5)	
Franck RIZZETTO	M	28	(7)	2
Laurent ROBERT	A	7	(14)	5
Jean-Christophe ROUVIERE	M	27	(6)	
Christophe SANCHEZ	A	31	(2)	11
Manuel THETIS	D	22	(1)	1
José Luis VILLAREAL (ARG)	M	17	(3)	3

LEAGUE RESULTS 1995/96

Date	Opponent	H/A	Score	Scorers
19/07/95	RC Strasbourg	H	2-2	Lefèvre, Thétis
26/07/95	Olympique Lyonnais	A	2-3	Sanchez 2 (1p)
05/08/95	Stade Rennais FC	H	3-1	Villareal, Der Zakarian, Petit
09/08/95	FC Metz	A	0-1	
19/08/95	AJ Auxerre	H	3-1	Der Zakarian 2, Sanchez
26/08/95	FC Martigues	A	1-0	Villareal
29/08/95	OGC Nice	H	0-1	
09/09/95	En Avant Guingamp	A	0-0	
17/09/95	Paris Saint-Germain FC	H	1-0	og (N'Gotty)
22/09/95	Girondins de Bordeaux	A	0-3	
30/09/95	Lille OSC	H	0-0	
04/10/95	AS Saint-Etienne	A	2-0	Rizzetto, Laurey
14/10/95	SC Bastia	H	4-3	Lefèvre 3, Rizzetto
21/10/95	AS Monaco	A	1-3	Lefèvre
27/10/95	FC Gueugnon	H	2-2	Lefèvre, Sanchez
04/11/95	FC Nantes	A	0-1	
08/11/95	AS Cannes	H	3-1	Villareal, Sanchez 2
18/11/95	RC Lens	H	0-0	
25/11/95	Le Havre AC	A	2-2	Pavon 2
01/12/95	Olympique Lyonnais	H	2-1	Lefèvre, Sanchez
09/12/95	Stade Rennais FC	A	1-1	Lefèvre
03/01/96	FC Metz	H	1-2	Lefèvre
10/01/96	AJ Auxerre	A	0-1	
20/01/96	FC Martigues	H	2-0	Robert, Der Zakarian (p)
27/01/96	OGC Nice	A	2-1	Sanchez, Robert
11/02/96	Paris Saint-Germain FC	A	3-2	Sanchez, Lefèvre, Robert
17/02/96	Girondins de Bordeaux	H	3-0	Sanchez, Pavon, Delaye
27/02/96	Lille OSC	A	1-1	Der Zakarian
02/03/96	AS Saint-Etienne	H	1-0	Pavon
09/03/96	SC Bastia	A	0-1	
23/03/96	AS Monaco	H	0-0	
30/03/96	FC Gueugnon	A	2-0	Alicarte, og (Pounewatchy)
05/04/96	En Avant Guingamp	H	2-1	Pavon, Alicarte
09/04/96	FC Nantes	H	1-0	Robert
20/04/96	AS Cannes	A	1-2	Delaye
27/04/96	RC Lens	A	1-2	Sanchez
11/05/96	Le Havre AC	H	2-0	Robert, Lefèvre
18/05/96	RC Strasbourg	A	0-1	

FC NANTES

CLUB DIRECTORY

Football Club de Nantes Atlantique
BP 1124
44311 Nantes Cedex 03
tel - (40) 372929
fax - (40) 372921
Year of Formation - 1943
President - Guy Scherrer
Secretary - Alain Flores
Coach - Jean-Claude Suaudeau
Stadium - La Beaujoire-Louis-Fonteneau (34,647)

MAJOR HONOURS
League Championship - (7)
1965, 1966, 1973, 1977, 1980, 1983, 1995.
Domestic Cup - (1) 1979.

APPEARANCES 95/96

	P	Ap	(s)	Gls
Eddy CAPRON	D	9		
Bruno CAROTTI	M	27	(7)	1
Dominique CASAGRANDE	G	26		
Benoît CAUET	M	29	(2)	3
Jean-Marc CHANELET	D	22	(5)	1
Frédéric DA ROCHA	A	4	(7)	2
Eric DECROIX	D	31	(1)	1
Jean-Michel FERRI	M	24	(2)	
David GARCION	M	3	(11)	
Jocelyn GOURVENNEC	M	16	(3)	1
Laurent GUYOT	D	25	(6)	
Roman KOSECKI (POL)	A	23	(4)	2
Serge LE DIZET	D	27	(1)	
Sébastien LE PAIH	M		(3)	
Eric LOUSSOUARN	G	5		
Claude MAKELELE	M	31	(2)	
David MARRAUD	G	7		
Ludovic MARY	M		(1)	
Japhet N'DORAM (CHD)	M	22	(2)	15
Nicolas OUEDEC	A	15		4
Reynald PEDROS	M	34		7
Laurent PEYRELADE	A	2	(19)	1
Christophe PIGNOL	D	26	(1)	1
Franck RENOU	A	6	(16)	1
Nicolas SAVINAUD	D	4	(4)	1

LEAGUE RESULTS 1995/96

19/07/95	AJ Auxerre	H	1-0	Pedros
26/07/95	FC Martigues	A	4-0	Pedros, N'Doram 3 (1p)
04/08/95	Paris Saint-Germain FC	H	1-2	N'Doram
19/08/95	OGC Nice	H	1-0	N'Doram (p)
25/08/95	Lille OSC	A	0-0	
29/08/95	AS Saint-Etienne	H	2-2	N'Doram (p), Kosecki
01/09/95	Girondins de Bordeaux	A	0-3	
09/09/95	SC Bastia	A	1-4	N'Doram (p)
16/09/95	En Avant Guingamp	H	0-0	
22/09/95	RC Lens	H	1-1	N'Doram
30/09/95	FC Gueugnon	A	1-0	Pedros
03/10/95	AS Monaco	H	2-2	og (Thuram), N'Doram (p)
14/10/95	AS Cannes	A	2-0	Ouédec (p), Carotti
21/10/95	Olympique Lyonnais	H	0-0	
27/10/95	Le Havre AC	A	1-0	Ouédec
04/11/95	Montpellier HSC	H	1-0	og (Lefèvre)
08/11/95	RC Strasbourg	A	1-1	Cauet
18/11/95	Stade Rennais FC	H	2-2	N'Doram 2
25/11/95	FC Metz	A	0-0	
01/12/95	FC Martigues	H	3-0	Ouédec, Pedros, Cauet
09/12/95	Paris Saint-Germain FC	A	0-5	
16/12/95	Girondins de Bordeaux	H	2-0	N'Doram 2 (1p)
16/01/96	OGC Nice	A	0-1	
20/01/96	Lille OSC	H	1-2	Cauet
28/01/96	AS Saint-Etienne	A	0-0	
07/02/96	SC Bastia	H	3-1	Savinaud, Gourvennec, Da Rocha
10/02/96	En Avant Guingamp	A	1-3	og (Baret)
16/02/96	RC Lens	A	1-2	Chanelet
27/02/96	FC Gueugnon	H	1-0	Renou
01/03/96	AS Monaco	A	1-4	N'Doram
09/03/96	AS Cannes	H	2-0	Decroix, Ouédec
23/03/96	Olympique Lyonnais	A	1-1	Peyrelade
09/04/96	Montpellier HSC	A	0-1	
20/04/96	RC Strasbourg	H	2-0	Pignol, Pedros
27/04/96	Stade Rennais FC	A	2-2	N'Doram (p), Pedros
02/05/96	Le Havre AC	H	1-1	Pedros
11/05/96	FC Metz	H	1-0	Da Rocha
18/05/96	AJ Auxerre	A	1-2	Kosecki

OGC NICE

CLUB DIRECTORY

Olympique Gynamnaste Club de Nice Côte d'Azur
Parc des Sports Charles-Ehrmann
177 route de Grenoble
06200 Nice
tel - (93) 180727
fax - (93) 180679
Year of Formation - 1904
President - André Boïs
Secretary - Jean-Luc Bailet
Coach - Albert Emon
Stadium - Ray (15,000)

MAJOR HONOURS
League Championship - (4)
1951, 1952, 1956, 1959.
Domestic Cup - (2) 1952, 1954.

APPEARANCES 95/96

	P	Ap	(s)	Gls
Cyril ALOISIO	G	1		
Abdallah BAH (SEN)	G	3		
Bruno CALEGARI	D	16	(8)	
CASTILLA	G		(1)	
Mohamed CHAOUCH (MAR)	A	23	(13)	3
Stéphane COLLET	M	29		2
Thierry CRETIER	D	35		
Jean-François DANIEL	M	8	(3)	
James DEBBAH (LIB)	A	29	(1)	12
Thierry DE NEEF	M	35	(1)	
DOUCENDE	M		(2)	
Olivier FUGEN	D	27		
GALLO	M		(1)	
GENNARIELLI	M		(1)	
Frédéric GIORIA	M	3	(3)	
Jérôme GNAKO	M	23	(4)	2
Louis GOMIS	D	6	(4)	
HACHADI	M		(1)	
Samuel IPOUA (CMR)	A	13	(11)	9
Lionel LETIZI	G	34		
Yves MANGIONE	A	14	(16)	2
Frédéric MARTIN	D	29		
Jean-Philippe MATTIO	D	23	(2)	
Joe NAGBE (LIB)	A	27	(2)	4
RIGAUX	M		(1)	
Thierry ROSSI	D	4		
SAGNA	M		(2)	
Youssef SALIMI	D	12	(4)	
Henri SAVINI	M	11	(5)	
STEFANO	D	2	(3)	
Jean-Luc VANNUCHI	M	11	(9)	

LEAGUE RESULTS 1995/96

19/07/95	AS Saint-Etienne	A	1-1	Mangione
25/07/95	AS Monaco	H	1-2	Nagbe
05/08/95	En Avant Guingamp	A	0-0	
09/08/95	FC Gueugnon	H	3-1	Collet, Ipoua (p), Debbah
19/08/95	FC Nantes	A	0-1	
26/08/95	RC Lens	H	1-1	Nagbe
29/08/95	Montpellier HSC	A	1-0	Gnako
09/09/95	Le Havre AC	H	1-2	Debbah
16/09/95	RC Strasbourg	A	1-1	Chaouch
22/09/95	Olympique Lyonnais	H	1-0	Ipoua
30/09/95	AS Cannes	A	3-1	Gnako, Ipoua 2
04/10/95	FC Metz	H	0-1	
14/10/95	AJ Auxerre	A	1-2	Debbah
21/10/95	FC Martigues	H	1-0	og (Zamfir)
27/10/95	Stade Rennais FC	A	0-1	
05/11/95	Paris Saint-Germain FC	A	2-3	og (Le Guen), Debbah
08/11/95	Lille OSC	H	2-1	Ipoua, og (Dindeleux)
18/11/95	Girondins de Bordeaux	A	1-4	Debbah (p)
25/11/95	SC Bastia	H	3-1	Ipoua, Debbah 2
01/12/95	AS Monaco	A	0-1	
09/12/95	En Avant Guingamp	H	2-1	Debbah, Ipoua
16/12/95	FC Gueugnon	A	0-1	
16/01/96	FC Nantes	H	1-0	Mangione
20/01/96	RC Lens	A	0-0	
27/01/96	Montpellier HSC	H	1-2	Ipoua
07/02/96	Le Havre AC	A	0-0	
10/02/96	RC Strasbourg	H	2-2	Collet, Nagbe
17/02/96	Olympique Lyonnais	A	0-1	
26/02/96	AS Cannes	H	1-2	Debbah
02/03/96	FC Metz	A	0-4	
09/03/96	AJ Auxerre	H	1-3	Ipoua
23/03/96	FC Martigues	A	0-0	
30/03/96	Stade Rennais FC	H	0-0	
09/04/96	Paris Saint-Germain FC	H	1-2	Chaouch
20/04/96	Lille OSC	A	0-1	
26/04/96	Girondins de Bordeaux	H	1-0	Nagbe
11/05/96	SC Bastia	A	2-1	Debbah 2
18/05/96	AS Saint-Etienne	H	2-0	Chaouch, Debbah

PARIS SAINT-GERMAIN FC

CLUB DIRECTORY

Paris Saint-Germain Football Club
30 avenue du Parc des Princes
75016 Paris
tel - (40) 719191
fax - (40) 719397
Year of Formation - 1970
Presidents - Pierre Lescure & Michel Denisot
Secretary - Jean-François Domergue
Coach - Luis Fernandez (96/97 - Ricardo Gomes)
Stadium - Parc des Princes (48,712)

MAJOR HONOURS

League Championship - (2) 1986, 1994.
Domestic Cup - (4) 1982, 1983, 1993, 1995.
European Cup-winners' Cup - (1) 1996.

APPEARANCES 95/96

	P	Ap	(s)	Gls
Bernard ALLOU	M	2	(17)	
Nicolas ANELKA	A		(2)	
Djamel BELMADI	M		(1)	
Daniel BRAVO	M	30	(2)	
José COBOS	D	25	(3)	
Patrick COLLETER	D	32	(1)	
Júlio César DELY VALDES (PAN)	A	26	(7)	15
Oumar DIENG	D	8	(5)	1
Youri DJORKAEFF	M	33	(2)	13
Didier DOMI	D		(1)	
Pierre DUCROCQ	D		(1)	
Richard DUTRUEL	G	4	(2)	
Laurent FOURNIER	M	34		2
Xavier GRAVELAINE	A	2	(3)	1
Vincent GUERIN	M	29	(2)	1
Bernard LAMA	G	34		
Paul LE GUEN	D	31	(5)	2
Francis LLACER	D	13	(15)	1
Patrice LOKO	A	22	(5)	8
Stéphane MAHE	D	20	(3)	
Bruno N'GOTTY	D	23	(1)	1
Pascal NOUMA	A	8	(19)	5
Cédric PARDEILHAN	M	1		
RAÍ Souza de Oliveira (BRA)	M	27		14
Alain ROCHE	D	14		

LEAGUE RESULTS 1995/96

18/07/95	SC Bastia	A	2-2	Raí 2
26/07/95	En Avant Guingamp	H	1-1	Dely Valdes
04/08/95	FC Nantes	A	2-1	Raí, Nouma
09/08/95	AS Saint-Etienne	H	4-0	Djorkaeff 2, Dely Valdes, Raí
19/08/95	FC Gueugnon	A	3-1	Dely Valdes, Raí, Gravelaine
26/08/95	Le Havre AC	H	2-0	Dely Valdes, Djorkaeff
29/08/95	AS Cannes	A	2-0	Dely Valdes, Raí
09/09/95	AS Monaco	H	2-1	Dely Valdes, Fournier
17/09/95	Montpellier HSC	A	0-1	
22/09/95	RC Strasbourg	H	2-0	Dely Valdes 2
01/10/95	RC Lens	A	1-3	Nouma
04/10/95	Stade Rennais FC	H	1-1	Loko
14/10/95	Olympique Lyonnais	A	0-0	
22/10/95	AJ Auxerre	H	3-1	Djorkaeff, Raí, Nouma
26/10/95	FC Metz	A	3-0	Guérin, Raí 2
05/11/95	OGC Nice	H	3-2	Dely Valdes 2, Raí
08/11/95	FC Martigues	A	4-2	Djorkaeff 2, Dely Valdes, Nouma
18/11/95	Lille OSC	A	0-0	
25/11/95	Girondins de Bordeaux	H	3-0	Loko 2, Raí
01/12/95	En Avant Guingamp	A	0-0	
09/12/95	FC Nantes	H	5-0	Dely Valdes, Djorkaeff, Loko, Raí, Nouma
16/12/95	AS Saint-Etienne	A	1-1	Dely Valdes
10/01/96	FC Gueugnon	H	1-1	Djorkaeff
19/01/96	Le Havre AC	A	1-1	Raí
27/01/96	AS Cannes	H	2-1	Loko 2
07/02/96	AS Monaco	A	0-1	
11/02/96	Montpellier HSC	H	2-3	Dely Valdes, Llacer
17/02/96	RC Strasbourg	A	0-1	
27/02/96	RC Lens	H	1-0	Loko
02/03/96	Stade Rennais FC	A	1-0	Raí
10/03/96	Olympique Lyonnais	H	2-0	Loko, N'Gotty
24/03/96	AJ Auxerre	A	0-3	
30/03/96	FC Metz	H	2-3	Fournier, Le Guen
09/04/96	OGC Nice	A	2-1	Djorkaeff, Le Guen
23/04/96	FC Martigues	H	0-0	
27/04/96	Lille OSC	H	0-1	
11/05/96	Girondins de Bordeaux	A	2-2	Djorkaeff, Dieng
18/05/96	SC Bastia	H	5-1	Dely Valdes, Djorkaeff 3 (1p), og (Soumah)

STADE RENNAIS FC

CLUB DIRECTORY

Stade Rennais Football Club
111 route de Lorient
35000 Rennes
tel - (99) 330348
fax - (99) 332600
Year of Formation - 1901
President - René Ruello
Secretary - Yannick Boizard
Coach - Michel Le Milinaire (96/97 - Yves Colleu)
Stadium - Route de Lorient (19,000)

MAJOR HONOURS

Domestic Cup - (2) 1965, 1971.

APPEARANCES 95/96

	P	Ap	(s)	Gls
Pierre-Yves ANDRE	A	30	(6)	6
Patrice CARTERON	D	35		2
Gouanael CORBIN	D	1		
Jean-Pierre CYPRIEN	D	32		3
Qusmane DABO	M	2	(3)	
Olivier DALL'OGLIO	D	8	(8)	
Jean-Christophe DARCHEVILLE	A	3	(7)	1
François DENIS	D	30		1
Pascal FUGIER	D	36		
Marco GRASSI (SUI)	A	25	(2)	11
Tony HEURTEBIS	G	7	(1)	
Laurent HUARD	M	30	(3)	1
Brian JENSEN (DEN)	D	16	(9)	
Loïc LAMBERT	M	32		1
B. LE BRIS	M		(1)	
Régis LE BRIS	M	6	(9)	
Ulrich LE PEN	M	8	(23)	
David MERDY	A		(5)	
Goran PANDUROVIC (YUG)	G	31		
Mickaël SILVESTRE	D		(1)	
Jean-Christophe THOMAS	M	20	(7)	
David VOISIN	M	2	(1)	
Sylvain WILTORD	A	29	(8)	15
Stéphane ZIANI	M	35	(2)	1

LEAGUE RESULTS 1995/96

19/07/95	AS Monaco	A	1-3	Grassi (p)
26/07/95	AS Cannes	H	3-2	André, Huard, Cyprien
05/08/95	Montpellier HSC	A	1-3	Wiltord
09/08/95	Le Havre AC	H	1-0	Grassi (p)
19/08/95	RC Strasbourg	A	1-2	Wiltord
26/08/95	Olympique Lyonnais	H	1-0	Grassi
29/08/95	RC Lens	A	0-1	
10/09/95	FC Metz	A	0-0	
16/09/95	FC Martigues	H	1-3	Grassi
22/09/95	AJ Auxerre	A	1-2	Darcheville
30/09/95	SC Bastia	H	2-0	Wiltord, Lambert
04/10/95	Paris Saint-Germain FC	A	1-1	André
14/10/95	Lille OSC	H	3-1	Cyprien, Wiltord 2
21/10/95	Girondins de Bordeaux	A	0-0	
27/10/95	OGC Nice	H	1-0	André
04/11/95	AS Saint-Etienne	A	0-0	
07/11/95	En Avant Guingamp	H	3-0	Grassi 3
18/11/95	FC Nantes	A	2-2	Grassi 2
25/11/95	FC Gueugnon	H	2-1	André, Ziani
01/12/95	AS Cannes	A	0-3	
09/12/95	Montpellier HSC	H	1-1	Wiltord
16/12/95	Le Havre AC	A	0-0	
10/01/96	RC Strasbourg	H	0-0	
20/01/96	Olympique Lyonnais	A	2-2	og (Anselmini), André
27/01/96	RC Lens	H	2-1	Cyprien, André
10/02/96	FC Martigues	A	2-1	Wiltord 2
17/02/96	AJ Auxerre	H	2-1	Wiltord, Grassi (p)
02/03/96	Paris Saint-Germain FC	H	0-1	
09/03/96	Lille OSC	A	0-0	
16/03/96	FC Metz	H	0-0	
23/03/96	Girondins de Bordeaux	H	4-3	Carteron 2, Wiltord (p), og (Dogon)
30/03/96	OGC Nice	A	0-0	
05/04/96	SC Bastia	A	0-0	
09/04/96	AS Saint-Etienne	H	3-0	Wiltord 2, Grassi
20/04/96	En Avant Guingamp	A	0-0	
27/04/96	FC Nantes	H	2-2	Denis, Wiltord
11/05/96	FC Gueugnon	A	0-1	
18/05/96	AS Monaco	H	2-3	Wiltord 2 (1p)

AS SAINT-ETIENNE

CLUB DIRECTORY

SAEM Association Sportive de Saint-Etienne Loire
Stade Geoffroy-Guichard
32 rue Jean-Snella
42028 Saint-Etienne Cedex 01
tel - (77) 746355
fax - (77) 799522
Year of Formation - 1920
Presidents - Daniel Hurstel & Philippe Koehl
Coach - Elie Baup; Dominique Bathenay (96/97 - Pierre Mankowski)
Stadium - Geoffroy-Guichard (36,000)

MAJOR HONOURS
League Championship - (10) 1957, 1964, 1967, 1968, 1969, 1970, 1974, 1975, 1976, 1981.
Domestic Cup - (6)
1962, 1968, 1970, 1974, 1975, 1977.

APPEARANCES 95/96

	P	Ap	(s)	Gls
Dominique AULANIER	M	3	(17)	1
Pierre BASTOU	M	15	(4)	
Romarin BILLONG	D	12	(2)	1
Gilbert CECCARELLI	G	2		
Adel CHEDLI	A	3	(6)	1
COSTE	M		(1)	
Grégory COUPET	G	36		
Flavio CUCA (BRA)	A	9	(8)	3
Jean-Philippe DELPECH	M	4	(3)	
Pascal DESPEYROUX	M	12		1
Sylvain FLAUTO	A	4	(6)	1
Salem HARCHECHE	D	16	(6)	
Fabrice MANNUCCI	M	33	(2)	2
Lubomir MORAVCIK (SVK)	M	34		7
Patrick MOREAU	D	29	(2)	
Christophe OHREL (SUI)	M	34	(1)	
Sébastien PEREZ	D	12	(1)	
Lionel POTILLON	D	8	(1)	
Willy SAGNOL	D	10		
Liazid SANDJAK	A	32	(1)	8
Stéphane SANTINI	M	26	(6)	
Jean-Philippe SECHET	M	33	(1)	3
Jean-François SOUCASSE	D	22	(1)	
Yann SYNAEGHEL	M		(2)	
Didier THIMOTHEE	A	22	(5)	7
Jean-Luc VASSEUR	D	7	(2)	

LEAGUE RESULTS 1995/96

Date	Opponent		Score	Scorers
19/07/95	OGC Nice	H	1-1	Mannucci
26/07/95	Girondins de Bordeaux	A	0-2	
05/08/95	Lille OSC	H	1-1	Moravcik (p)
09/08/95	Paris Saint-Germain FC	A	0-4	
19/08/95	SC Bastia	H	3-0	Thimothée, Moravcik, Sandjak
26/08/95	En Avant Guingamp	H	4-0	Sandjak, Thimothée 2, Séchet
29/08/95	FC Nantes	A	2-2	Moravcik, og (Decroix)
09/09/95	FC Gueugnon	H	2-0	Moravcik (p), Thimothée
16/09/95	AS Cannes	A	0-2	
21/09/95	AS Monaco	H	2-4	Thimothée 2
30/09/95	Olympique Lyonnais	A	1-2	Sandjak
04/10/95	Montpellier HSC	H	0-2	
15/10/95	Le Havre AC	A	2-2	Cuca 2
21/10/95	RC Lens	H	1-1	Mannucci
27/10/95	RC Strasbourg	A	1-3	Cuca
04/11/95	Stade Rennais FC	H	0-0	
08/11/95	FC Metz	A	2-1	Sandjak, Moravcik
19/11/95	AJ Auxerre	H	0-5	
25/11/95	FC Martigues	A	1-1	Aulanier
01/12/95	Girondins de Bordeaux	H	2-0	Sandjak, Thimothée
09/12/95	Lille OSC	A	1-1	Moravcik (p)
16/12/95	Paris Saint-Germain FC	H	1-1	Séchet (p)
10/01/96	SC Bastia	A	0-0	
20/01/96	En Avant Guingamp	A	0-3	
28/01/96	FC Nantes	H	0-0	
17/02/96	AS Monaco	A	0-2	
23/02/96	FC Gueugnon	A	0-1	
27/02/96	Olympique Lyonnais	H	1-1	Séchet
02/03/96	Montpellier HSC	A	0-1	
09/03/96	Le Havre AC	H	1-1	Moravcik
16/03/96	AS Cannes	H	2-2	Despeyroux, Sandjak
23/03/96	RC Lens	A	0-3	
30/03/96	RC Strasbourg	H	2-0	Sandjak, Flauto
09/04/96	Stade Rennais FC	A	0-3	
20/04/96	FC Metz	H	1-1	Chedli
26/04/96	AJ Auxerre	A	0-2	
11/05/96	FC Martigues	H	2-2	Billong (p), Sandjak
18/05/96	OGC Nice	A	0-2	

RC STRASBOURG

CLUB DIRECTORY

Racing Club de Strasbourg
Stade de la Meinau
12 rue de l'Extenwoerth
67100 Strasbourg
tel - (88) 445500
fax - (88) 445501
Year of Formation - 1906
President - Roland Weller
Secretary - Jean-Michel Colin
Coach - Jacky Duguépéroux
Stadium - Meinau (41,223)

MAJOR HONOURS
League Championship - (1) 1979.
Domestic Cup - (2) 1951, 1966.

APPEARANCES 95/96

	P	Ap	(s)	Gls
Gérald BATICLE	A	29	(4)	6
Olivier DACOURT	M	30	(4)	
Martin DJETOU	D	28	(2)	1
Tomasz FRANKOWSKI (POL)	A	2	(9)	
Rémi GARDE	M	13	(3)	
Wilfrid GOHEL	A	6	(25)	3
Valérien ISMAËL	D	12	(7)	
Marc KELLER	A	31	(2)	8
David KLEIN	G		(1)	
Franck LEBOEUF	D	35		4
Aleksandr MOSTOVOI (RUS)	M	32		9
Yvan POULIQUEN	M	21	(9)	
Philippe RASCHKE	D	36		1
David REGIS	D	33	(2)	
Yannick ROTT	M	19	(10)	
Franck SAUZEE	M	27		5
Philippe THYS	D		(2)	
Alexander VENCEL (SVK)	G	38		
David ZITELLI	A	26	(5)	8

LEAGUE RESULTS 1995/96

19/07/95	Montpellier HSC	A	2-2	Baticle, Sauzée
26/07/95	Le Havre AC	H	3-0	Keller, Mostovoi, Gohel
05/08/95	RC Lens	A	0-0	
19/08/95	Stade Rennais FC	H	3-1	Keller 2, Mostovoi
26/08/95	FC Metz	A	2-3	Keller 2
29/08/95	FC Martigues	H	2-0	Baticle, Keller
01/09/95	Olympique Lyonnais	A	1-1	Mostovoi
09/09/95	AJ Auxerre	A	0-1	
16/09/95	OGC Nice	H	1-1	Baticle
22/09/95	Paris Saint-Germain FC	A	0-2	
01/10/95	Girondins de Bordeaux	H	3-0	Leboeuf (p), Mostovoi, Keller
04/10/95	Lille OSC	A	0-2	
14/10/95	En Avant Guingamp	H	0-0	
21/10/95	SC Bastia	A	1-1	Zitelli
27/10/95	AS Saint-Etienne	H	3-1	Zitelli, Sauzée, Mostovoi
05/11/95	AS Cannes	A	3-0	Sauzée, Leboeuf (p), Zitelli
08/11/95	FC Nantes	H	1-1	Keller
18/11/95	FC Gueugnon	A	1-0	Mostovoi
24/11/95	AS Monaco	H	2-0	Leboeuf, Zitelli
01/12/95	Le Havre AC	A	0-2	
10/12/95	RC Lens	H	1-2	Raschke
16/12/95	Olympique Lyonnais	H	2-2	Mostovoi, Gohel
10/01/96	Stade Rennais FC	A	0-0	
20/01/96	FC Metz	H	1-2	Sauzée
27/01/96	FC Martigues	A	0-2	
10/02/96	OGC Nice	A	2-2	Zitelli, Sauzée
17/02/96	Paris Saint-Germain FC	H	1-0	Leboeuf (p)
27/02/96	Girondins de Bordeaux	A	1-1	Baticle
02/03/96	Lille OSC	H	2-0	Zitelli, Mostovoi
05/03/96	AJ Auxerre	H	1-0	Baticle
09/03/96	En Avant Guingamp	A	0-3	
23/03/96	SC Bastia	H	4-3	Baticle, Mostovoi, Zitelli, og (Darras)
30/03/96	AS Saint-Etienne	A	0-2	
09/04/96	AS Cannes	H	1-0	Gohel
20/04/96	FC Nantes	A	0-2	
27/04/96	FC Gueugnon	H	0-0	
11/05/96	AS Monaco	A	1-5	Zitelli
18/05/96	Montpellier HSC	H	1-0	Djetou

PROMOTED CLUBS

SECOND DIVISION FINAL TABLE 95/96

		Pd	W	D	L	F	A	Pt	GD
1	**SM Caen**	**42**	**24**	**9**	**9**	**59**	**34**	**81**	**+25**
2	**Olympique Marseille**	**42**	**23**	**11**	**8**	**69**	**35**	**80**	**+34**
3	**AS Nancy-Lorraine**	**42**	**20**	**16**	**6**	**56**	**23**	**76**	**+33**
4	Stade Lavallois	42	21	9	12	52	46	72	+6
5	Toulouse FC	42	18	9	15	40	34	63	+6
6	Le Mans UC 72	42	15	17	10	37	36	62	+1
7	AS Red Star 93	42	16	13	13	56	38	61	+18
8	Perpignan FC	42	17	10	15	44	53	61	-9
9	LB Châteauroux	42	16	12	14	40	35	60	+5
10	FC Sochaux	42	15	14	13	49	40	59	+9
11	Louhans-Cuiseaux 71	42	16	10	16	57	49	58	+8
12	FC 56 Lorient	42	16	10	16	44	46	58	-2
13	Amiens SCF	42	13	15	14	43	49	54	-6
14	FC Mulhouse	42	13	12	17	44	45	51	-1
15	ASOA Valence	42	11	18	13	34	42	51	-8
16	Chamois Niortais	42	13	11	18	48	50	50	-2
17	Olympique Charleville-Mézières	42	11	15	16	34	54	48	-20
18	SA Epinal	42	9	18	15	41	46	45	-5
19	Stade Poitiers	42	9	18	15	36	50	45	-14
20	USL Dunkerque	42	9	16	17	30	43	43	-13
21	SCO Angers	42	7	16	19	31	53	37	-22
22	Olympique Alès	42	4	13	25	29	72	25	-43

CLUB DIRECTORY

Stade Malherbe Caen Calvados-Basse-Normandie
Boulevard Georges-Pompidou
BP 6138
14064 Caen
tel - (31) 291600
fax - (31) 736746
Year of Formation - 1913
President - Jean-François Fortin
Secretary - Francis Collado
Coach - Pierre Mankowski (96/97 - Guy David)
Stadium - Michel-d'Ornano (21,500)

CLUB DIRECTORY

Olympique de Marseille
25 rue Négresko
13008 Marseille
tel - (91) 765609
fax - (91) 760777
Year of Formation - 1899
President - Jean-Claude Gaudin
Secretary - Jean-Michel Roussier
Coach - Henri Stambouli; Gérard Gili
Stadium - Vélodrome (46,000)

MAJOR HONOURS

League Championship - (8) 1937, 1948, 1971, 1972, 1989, 1990, 1991, 1992.
Domestic Cup - (10) 1924, 1926, 1927, 1935, 1938, 1943, 1969, 1972, 1976, 1989.
European Champions' Cup - (1) 1993.

CLUB DIRECTORY

Association Sportive Nancy-Lorraine
Parc de Haye
54840 Velaine-en-Haye
tel - (83) 232822
fax - (83) 233034
Year of Formation - 1966
President - Gérard Parentin
Secretary - Pascal Rivière
Coach - Ladislau Bölöni
Stadium - Marcel-Picot (23,116)

MAJOR HONOURS

Domestic Cup - (1) 1978.

GEORGIA

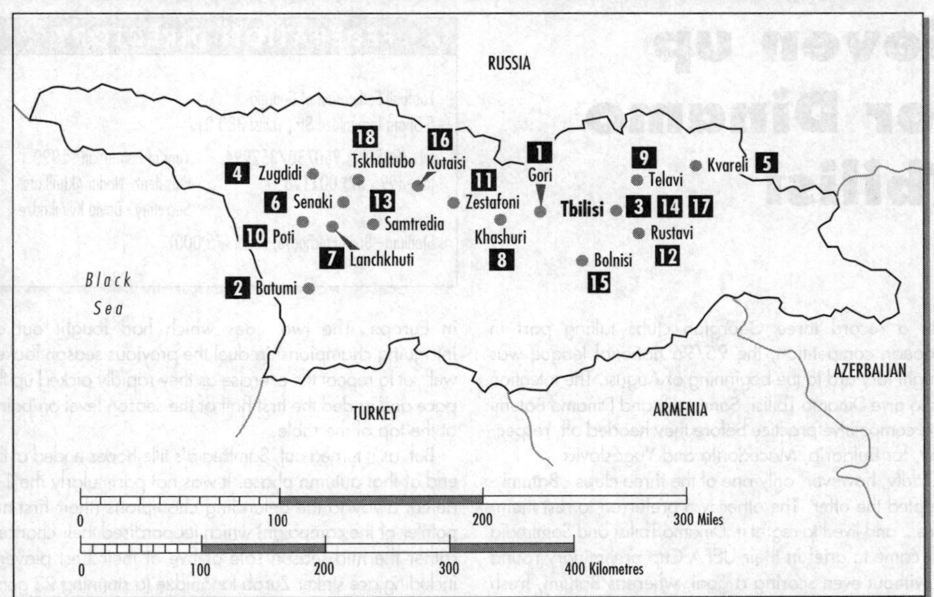

1	DILA GORI	420
2	DINAMO BATUMI	421
3	DINAMO TBILISI	422
4	DINAMO ZUGDIDI	423
5	DURUJI KVARELI	424
6	EGRISI SENAKI	425
7	GURIA LANCHKHUTI	426
8	IVERIA KHASHURI	427
9	KAKHETI TELAVI	428
10	KOLKHETI 1913 POTI	429
11	MARGVETI ZESTAFONI	430
12	METALURGI RUSTAVI	431
13	SAMTREDIA	432
14	SHEVARDENI 1906 TBILISI	433
15	SIONI BOLNISI	434
16	TORPEDO KUTAISI	435
17	MERANI 91 TBILISI	436
18	SAMGURALI TSKHALTUBO	436

WORLD CUP DEBUT BECKONS

Seven up for Dinamo Tbilisi

FEDERATION DIRECTORY

Football Federation of Georgia
5 Shota Iamanidze Str., Tbilisi 380 012
tel - (995 32) 960750/352994
fax - (995 32) 001128

Year of Formation - 1990
President - Nodar Akhalkatsi
Secretary - David Kvinikadze

Stadium - Boris Paichadze, Tbilisi (75,000)

With a record three Georgian clubs taking part in European competition, the 95/96 national league was brought forward to the beginning of August. The intention was to give Dinamo Tbilisi, Samtredia and Dinamo Batumi some competitive practice before they headed off, respectively, for Bulgaria, Macedonia and Yugoslavia.

Oddly, however, only one of the three clubs - Batumi - accepted the offer. The other two preferred to rest themselves... and lived to regret it. Dinamo Tbilisi and Samtredia both came to grief in their UEFA Cup preliminary round ties without even scoring a goal, whereas Batumi, fresh from an opening 3-0 win in the league, won the first leg of their Cup-winners' Cup tie 1-0 away to Obilic Belgrade and held onto their advantage in the return to earn themselves a first-round confrontation with Scottish giants Celtic.

The criticism levelled at Dinamo Tbilisi and Samtredia intensified when it became clear, through their early league results, that a bit more preparation would have considerably boosted their chances of negotiating the first hurdle in Europe. The two sides which had fought out an intriguing championship duel the previous season looked well set to repeat the exercise as they rapidly picked up the pace and ended the first half of the season level on points at the top of the table.

But, as it turned out, Samtredia's title hopes ended at the end of that autumn phase. It was not particularly the 1-3 defeat away to the defending champions (their first no-pointer of the campaign) which jeopardised their chances, rather the mid-season sale of five of their best players, including ace striker Zurab Ionanidze (a stunning 23 goals in 15 games) and Georgian internationals David Janashia and Besik Beradze. A spell of four games without a win

INTERNATIONAL HONOURS

European Club Competitions	
Cup-winners' Cup	Dinamo Tbilisi (1981).

LEAGUE CHAMPIONSHIP RESULTS 95/96

		1	2	3	4	5	6	7	8	9	10	11	12	13	14	15	16
1	Dila Gori		2-0	1-6	1-0	8-3	4-3	2-0	4-1	5-0	0-1	4-2	2-3	1-1	1-1	3-0	3-2
2	Dinamo Batumi	2-0		1-3	5-0	11-0	3-1	3-0	3-1	5-0	0-1	3-1	2-1	3-4	7-0	3-0	1-1
3	Dinamo Tbilisi	1-0	1-1		1-0	11-0	3-0	3-0	5-0	7-1	4-0	6-1	4-0	3-1	3-0	8-0	5-1
4	Dinamo Zugdidi	1-0	1-3	1-5		4-0	5-3	2-0	0-0	2-1	1-3	3-4	1-3	2-2	0-0	3-0	3-4
5	Duruji Kvareli	0-1	0-0	2-8	0-1		3-0	3-5	2-5	0-1	1-3	2-6	1-5	1-6	0-1	1-3	0-6
6	Egrisi Senaki	0-3	1-3	1-3	0-1	7-1		1-0	1-0	2-2	3-6	0-2	1-4	2-4	1-4	3-0	2-6
7	Guria Lanchkhuti	2-0	1-0	0-3	2-1	4-1	8-2		1-2	2-1	1-4	0-4	0-3	1-6	1-0	0-1	2-0
8	Iveria Khashuri	2-1	1-0	1-1	2-1	1-0	1-2	2-1		1-0	2-3	0-4	1-2	3-5	2-1	1-0	1-1
9	Kakheti Telavi	2-2	0-2	1-5	2-1	3-0	4-1	2-1	1-0		0-2	1-3	0-2	1-1	1-0	1-0	0-2
10	Kolkheti 1913 Poti	3-0	1-1	1-1	1-0	4-0	1-0	3-0	3-0	5-2		3-1	2-1	0-2	5-1	1-0	3-2
11	Margveti Zestafoni	1-1	2-0	1-0	4-0	7-0	5-1	3-0	3-0	3-0	4-2		3-0	0-0	4-0	5-2	5-3
12	Metalurgi Rustavi	5-1	1-0	0-2	3-1	4-0	4-1	3-0	2-1	3-0	3-1	0-1		2-1	3-2	5-0	4-3
13	Samtredia	4-1	2-2	0-0	5-2	3-0	3-1	8-3	4-1	4-1	4-0	3-1	3-0		4-2	5-0	2-2
14	Shevardeni 1906 Tbilisi	3-0	2-3	1-5	0-1	4-0	2-0	3-0	3-1	1-0	1-3	0-1	0-2	1-4		2-1	2-3
15	Sioni Bolnisi	4-2	0-1	0-1	5-2	4-2	3-0	3-0	2-0	3-0	0-2	1-3	0-2	0-3	3-1		3-1
16	Torpedo Kutaisi	2-0	0-0	0-1	4-2	1-0	2-2	5-0	1-0	3-1	3-2	2-1	2-0	2-2	2-2	3-0	

LEAGUE CHAMPIONSHIP FINAL TABLE 95/96

			Home					Away					Total						
		Pd	W	D	L	F	A	W	D	L	F	A	W	D	L	F	A	Pt	GD
1	Dinamo Tbilisi	30	14	1	0	65	5	11	3	1	44	11	25	4	1	109	16	79	+93
2	Margveti Zestafoni	30	13	2	0	50	9	9	0	6	35	28	22	2	6	85	37	68	+48
3	Kolkheti 1913 Poti	30	12	2	1	36	11	10	0	5	33	27	22	2	6	69	38	68	+31
4	Samtredia	30	12	3	0	54	16	8	5	2	42	22	20	8	2	96	38	68	+58
5	Metalurgi Rustavi	30	13	0	2	42	14	9	0	6	28	22	22	0	8	70	36	66	+34
6	Dinamo Batumi	30	11	1	3	52	13	5	5	5	16	15	16	6	8	68	28	54	+40
7	Torpedo Kutaisi	30	10	4	1	32	13	5	3	7	37	36	15	7	8	69	49	52	+20
8	Dila Gori	30	10	2	3	41	23	2	2	11	12	32	12	4	14	53	55	40	-2
9	Sioni Bolnisi	30	9	0	6	31	20	2	0	13	7	44	11	0	19	38	64	33	-26
10	Iveria Khashuri	30	8	2	5	21	22	2	1	12	12	35	10	3	17	33	57	33	-24
11	Dinamo Zugdidi	30	6	3	6	29	28	3	0	12	13	35	9	3	18	42	63	30	-21
12	Shevardeni 1906 Tbilisi	30	7	0	8	25	24	2	3	10	15	37	9	3	18	40	61	30	-21
13	Guria Lanchkhuti	30	8	0	7	25	28	1	0	14	10	46	9	0	21	35	74	27	-39
14	Kakheti Telavi	30	7	2	6	19	22	1	1	13	10	46	8	3	19	29	68	27	-39
15	Egrisi Senaki	30	4	1	10	25	39	1	1	13	17	51	5	2	23	42	90	17	-48
16	Duruji Kvareli	30	1	1	13	16	51	0	0	15	7	76	1	1	28	23	127	4	-104

in April finished off their challenge once and for all, and even, ultimately, denied them a return to Europe.

Dinamo Tbilisi, meanwhile, shot clear at the top with a procession of victories. Inspired by ex-Samtredia midfielder Kakhaber Gogichaishvili (signed as a replacement for Manchester-bound Giorgi Kinkladze) and leading scorer Aleksandre Iashvili, the team from the capital romped home to their seventh straight title, winning all of their last 13 games and chalking up 79 points - one better than their previous season's total. The only team to beat the champions were Margveti Zestafoni. A mere ninth in 94/95, Zaur Chibinidze's side improved beyond recognition and eventually clinched the runners-up spot, and with it a place alongside Dinamo Tbilisi in the UEFA Cup. It was a close run thing. With one game left, there were four teams - Margveti, Samtredia, Kolkheti 1913 Poti and Metalurgi Rustavi - all equal on 65 points and all gunning for second place.

With the number of victories counting as the deciding factor in case of equality, Metalurgi Rustavi, with one win more than Margveti and Kolkheti and three more than Samtredia, were the best placed. Plus, they entertained

DOMESTIC CUP RESULTS

SECOND ROUND

Dinamo Zugdidi v Margveti Zestafoni 4-4; 2-2
(6-6; Margveti Zestafoni on away goals)
Samtredia v Iveria Khashuri 2-0; 2-1
(Samtredia 4-1)
Metalurgi Rustavi v Dinamo Batumi 1-0; 0-2
(Dinamo Batumi 2-1)
Dila Gori v Egrisi Senaki 4-2; 3-0 (w/o)
(Dila Gori 7-2)
Torpedo Kutaisi v Dinamo-2 Tbilisi 4-1; 3-3
(Torpedo Kutaisi 7-4)
Kakheti Telavi v Kolkheti 1913 Poti 1-1; 1-3
(Kolkheti 1913 Poti 4-2)
Sh. SS Akademia Tbilisi v Sioni Bolnisi 1-0; 1-2
(2-2; Sh. SS Akademia Tbilisi on away goal)
Sh. SS Akademia Tbilisi v Dinamo Batumi 0-0; 0-4
(Dinamo Batumi 4-0)

QUARTER-FINALS

Torpedo Kutaisi v Samtredia 0-0; 0-2
(Samtredia 2-0)
Kolkheti 1913 Poti v Margveti Zestafoni 2-2; 0-1
(Margveti Zestafoni 3-2)
Dila Gori v Dinamo Tbilisi 0-3; 0-4
(Dinamo Tbilisi 7-0)

SEMI-FINALS

Dinamo Batumi v Margveti Zestafoni 1-0; 2-1
(Dinamo Batumi 3-1)
Samtredia v Dinamo Tbilisi 1-1; 0-3
(Dinamo Tbilisi 4-1)

FINAL

26/05/96, Tbilisi
DINAMO TBILISI 1 Inalishvili (96)
DINAMO BATUMI 0
(aet)
referee - Latsabidze
DINAMO TBILISI - Chanturia; Kobiashvili, Lobjanidze, Didava, Machavariani, Gogichaishvili, Kiknadze (Tskitishvili 105), Kizilashvili, Kerdzevadze, Anchabadze (Inalishvili 56), Iashvili (Demetradze 71).
DINAMO BATUMI - Togonidze; Shanidze, Chikovani, Makharadze I., Shekiladze, Torgashvili (Kantidze 73), Makharadze M., Glonti, Tugushi, Ujmajridze, Mujiri.

TOP SCORERS

40	Zviad ENDELADZE (Margveti Zestafoni)
31	Mikheil ASHVETIA (Torpedo Kutaisi)
26	Aleksandre IASHVILI (Dinamo Tbilisi)
23	Zurab IONANIDZE (Samtredia)
19	Kakhaber GOGICHAISHVILI (Dinamo Tbilisi)
18	David CHALADZE (Metalurgi Rustavi)
17	Giorgi DEMETRADZE (Dinamo Tbilisi)
16	Nugzar MIKABERIDZE (Kolkheti 1913 Poti)
	Kakhaber ALADASHVILI (Metalurgi Rustavi)

Margveti in the final match. Kolkheti and Samtredia both had easy home games, and if the two 'M's had drawn, Kolkheti, with a win, would have finished top of the quartet. That was indeed the situation with just six minutes of the season to play. But then, as if scripted, Margveti striker Zviad Endeladze stepped up to score his 40th league goal of the season and give his team the win they needed for that coveted European place. Kolkheti also won their match - 3-0 at home to lowly Guria Lanchkhuti - but Margveti had

NATIONAL TEAM RESULTS 95/96

Date	Opponent	Venue	City	Score	Scorers
06/09/95	Germany (ECQ)	A	Nuremberg	1-4	Ketsbaia (28)
11/10/95	Bulgaria (ECQ)	H	Tbilisi	2-1	Arveladze S. (1), Kinkladze (47p)
15/11/95	Moldova (ECQ)	A	Chisinau	2-3	Janashia (68), Culibaba (81og)
27/03/96	Cyprus	A	Limassol	2-0	Ketsbaia (53), Jamarauli (65)
24/04/96	Romania	A	Bucharest	0-5	
08/05/96	Greece	A	Ioannina	1-2	Gogrichiani (15)

NATIONAL TEAM APPEARANCES 95/96

Coach - Aleksandre CHIVADZE	GER	BUL	MOL	CYP	ROM	GRE	Cps	Gls
Akaki DEVADZE (28/11/71) - Rostselmash Rostov (RUS)	G				G		15	-
Gocha GUJABIDZE (07/07/71) - Rostselmash Rostov (RUS)	D						1	-
Murtaz SHELIA (25/03/69) - Spartak-Alania Vladikavkaz (RUS)	D	D		D			17	-
Dimitri KUDINOV (08/02/63) - Olympiakos Nicosia (CYP)	D	D	D	D	D	D	18	1
Giorgi CHIKHRADZE (01/10/67) - Shakhtar Donetsk (UKR)	D	D	D		D	D	11	-
Kakhaber GOGICHAISHVILI (31/10/68) - Dinamo Tbilisi	M68	M	M	M	M67	M	18	1
Giorgi NEMSADZE (10/05/72) - FC 08 Homburg (GER)	M	M		M	M46	M	19	-
Temur KETSBAIA (18/03/68) - AEK (GRE)	M		M	M	M	M	15	7
Giorgi KINKLADZE (06/07/73) - Manchester City (ENG)	M	M	M		M		17	3
Mikheil KAVELASHVILI (22/07/71) - Spartak-Alania Vladikavkaz (RUS)/Manchester City (ENG)	A46	s46		A72			14	2
Shota ARVELADZE (22/02/73) - Trabzonspor (TUR)	A	A	A	A	A46	A	17	6
Giorgi KILASONIA (09/09/68) - Lokomotiv Sankt-Peterburg (RUS)	s46	s74					4	-
Archil ARVELADZE (22/02/73) - Trabzonspor (TUR)	s68	A46					7	-
Irakli ZOIDZE (21/03/69) - Dinamo Tbilisi		G	G	G		G22	9	-
Gocha JAMARAULI (23/07/71) - Dinamo Tbilisi/Spartak-Alania Vladikavkaz (RUS)		M74	M62	M	M46		15	2
Giorgi GUDUSHAURI (18/02/73) - FSV Salmrohr (GER)		M82	M58	M84		M46	5	-
Besik BERADZE (20/02/68) - Samtredia		s82	D				8	-
Levan TSKITISHVILI (10/10/76) - Dinamo Tbilisi			M		s46		3	-
David JANASHIA (07/08/72) - Samtredia			s58				7	2
Mamuka MACHAVARIANI (27/11/70) - Dinamo Tbilisi			s62	s84			2	-
Kakhaber TSKHADADZE (07/09/68) - Eintracht Frankfurt (GER)				D	D77		14	-
Kakhi KALADZE (22/02/78) - Dinamo Tbilisi				s72			1	-
Zaza REVISHVILI (23/09/68) - Spartak-Alania Vladikavkaz (RUS)					D		12	-
Valter GUCHUA (06/07/75) - Samtredia					s46	s55	2	-
Gocha GOGRICHIANI (12/08/64) - Evaghoras Paphos (CYP)					s46	A55	6	2
Zurab IONANIDZE (02/12/71) - Zhemchuzhina Sochi (RUS)					s67		1	-
Vasil SEPASHVILI (17/02/69) - Lada Togliatti (RUS)					s77		3	-
Nugzar LOBJANIDZE (07/09/71) - Dinamo Tbilisi						D	5	-
Revaz ARVELADZE (15/09/69) - FC 08 Homburg (GER)						M	7	1
Nikoloz TOGONIDZE (24/04/71) - Dinamo Batumi						s22	1	-
Giorgi DEMETRADZE (26/09/76) - Dinamo Tblisi						s46	1	-

the superior goal difference and that proved decisive.

For the second year in a row the Georgian Cup final brought together the two 'Dinamos', Tbilisi and Batumi, the latter proving once again that they prefer the quick fix of Cup football to the more drawn-out slog of the league, in which they have never finished among the top three. Batumi knocked out both Metalurgi and Margveti en route to the final, thereby ensuring an immediate return to the Cup-winners' Cup. But as in 94/95, they were not good enough to prevent Tbilisi from securing another league and Cup 'double' - their fifth on the trot.

EUROPEAN CUPS RESULTS 95/96

CUP-WINNERS' CUP

● DINAMO BATUMI

Preliminary round OBILIC BEOGRAD (YUG)

A 1-0 Machutadze (71)
Baladze; Malania, Shanidze, Sichinava, Shekiladze, Torgashvili (Mujiri 65), Makharadze M., Machutadze, Ujmajuridze, Tugushi, Mindadze (Glonti 75).

H 2-2 Machutadze (60), Mujiri (82p)
Baladze; Malania (Glonti 46), Shanidze (Kantidze 78), Sichinava (Mujiri 46), Shekiladze, Torgashvili, Makharadze M., Machutadze, Tugushi, Ujmajuridze, Mindadze.

1st round CELTIC (SCO)

H 2-3 Machutadze (11), Tugushi (68)
Baladze; Malania (Kantidze 46), Shanidze (Putkaradze 86), Mujiri, Shekiladze, Torgashvili, Makharadze M., Machutadze, Tugushi, Ujmajuridze (Makharadze D. 46), Mindadze.

A 0-4
Togonidze; Shanidze, Putkaradze (Glonti 61), Mujiri, Shekiladze, Torgashvili, Makharadze M., Kantidze (Makharadze D. 46), Tugushi, Ujmajuridze, Mindadze.

UEFA CUP

● DINAMO TBILISI

Preliminary round BOTEV PLOVDIV (BUL)

A 0-1
Zoidze; Kobiashvili, Machavariani, Didava, Demetradze (Kaladze 67), Kiknadze, Gogichaishvili, Tskitishvili, Kacharava, Khomeriki, Gakhokidze (Tsaava 46).

H 0-1
Zoidze; Pirtskhalava, Lobjanidze, Didava, Machavariani, Gogichaishvili, Kobiashvili, Iashvili, Kacharava, Khomeriki (Demetradze 68), Tskitishvili (Kiknadze 70).

● SAMTREDIA

Preliminary round VARDAR SKOPJE (MAC)

A 0-1
Chanturia; Ionanidze, Guchua, Beradze, Jishkariani, Tsomaia, Tkavadze, Daraselia G., Janashia D., Janashia Z., Chkhaidze.

H 0-2
Chanturia; Ionanidze, Guchua, Beradze, Jishkariani (Jeladze 46), Tsomaia, Gogiashvili (Daraselia B. 46), Daraselia G., Janashia D. (Amashukeli 63), Janashia Z., Chkhaidze.

The underdogs stretched the champions all the way, but David Kipiani's team buttoned up another season of domestic omnipotence with an extra-time winner - the only goal of the game - from substitute Gela Inalishvili. For the first time ever, the Cup - a sparkling, new trophy - was presented by Georgian state president Edvard Shevardnadze.

Aleksander Chivadze's national team finished a creditable third (behind Germany and Bulgaria) in their European Championship group. The two defeats by Moldova were unsightly blemishes on the campaign, but they were erased somewhat by a splendid 2-1 victory over Bulgaria in Tbilisi - a match which Georgia dominated throughout the 90 minutes, rediscovering the form they had shown when thrashing Wales earlier in the competition.

On their day, Georgia are a match for anybody - especially at home in front of 70,000 passionate locals. In the World Cup qualifiers Italy and England will need to be very wary of a team that can count amongst its many exiles such talented individuals as Giorgi Kinkladze, Temur Ketsbaia and the Arveladze twins.

PLAYERS OF THE SEASON

GIORGI KINKLADZE

Not surprisingly, Giorgi Kinkladze was the runaway winner of the 1996 Georgian Player of the Year award. The dazzling Manchester City midfielder polled 177 points in the vote, leaving AEK's Temur Ketsbaia a distant runner-up with 98. Although his club were relegated from the English Premiership, 'Kinky', as the City fans adopted him, was an instant hit in the mother country of the game. The nonchalant ease of his ball control, his jinking forward bursts and his defence-splitting passes made him the envy of every other Premiership club. City bought him for £2 million. At current prices, he is now worth at least five times as much.

SHOTA ARVELADZE

In Turkey they call him 'Sota', and he is regarded as one of the finest foreign players ever to have played in the Turkish league. Having returned for a second spell with Trabzonspor midway through the 94/95 season, he really came alive in 95/96, appearing in all 34 league games and scoring 25 goals, a total which enabled him to become the first foreign player to win the Turkish First Division top scorer prize since Galatasaray's Yugoslav striker Tarik Hocic in 1983/84. Sadly, his efforts were not quite enough to give Trabzonspor the title, but in a season when his twin brother Archil was laid low with injury, Shota did enough on his own to promote the family name across Europe.

DILA GORI

CLUB DIRECTORY

Dila Gori
David Guramishvili street 5
Gori
tel - (270) 22107
Year of Formation - 1949
President - Nodar Dalakishvili
Coach - David Shavdatuashvili
Stadium - Central (10,000)

APPEARANCES 95/96

	P	Ap	(s)	Gls
Giorgi BALASHVILI	D	20		2
Jambul GAGNIDZE	D	25	(1)	5
Khvicha GAGNIDZE	M	17	(5)	
Bakur JALABADZE	A	1	(11)	1
Aleksandre KAIDARASHVILI	M	1	(8)	2
Revaz KHACHAPURIDZE	D	8	(7)	
Zurab KHORGUASHVILI	A	13	(1)	8
Giorgi LOMIDZE	D	28		4
Jimsher MAREKHASHVILI	M	27	(1)	7
Roin MARGISHVILI	A	25		12
David MDIVANI	G	5		
Paata PEZUASHVILI	D	2	(3)	
Giorgi REVAZISHVILI	A	23	(1)	3
Ramaz SOGOLASHVILI	G	23		
Shalva TABATADZE	M	16	(6)	1
Vaja TARKHNISHVILI	D	26		
Tamaz TSITSKISHVILI	M	24	(2)	3
Giorgi TSKRIALASHVILI	M	24	(3)	2

LEAGUE RESULTS 1995/96

Date	Opponent	H/A	Score	Scorers
02/08/95	Margveti Zestafoni	H	4-2	Marekhashvili 2, Gagnidze J., Khorguashvili
09/08/95	Shevardeni 1906 Tbilisi	A	0-3	
15/08/95	Iveria Khashuri	H	4-1	Khorguashvili 2, Marekashvili, Gagnidze J.
23/08/95	Kakheti Telavi	A	2-2	Khorguashvili, Lomidze
30/08/95	Guria Lanchkhuti	H	2-0	Tskrialashvili, Tsitskishvili
17/09/95	Duruji Kvareli	A	1-0	Margishvili
21/09/95	Sioni Bolnisi	H	3-0	Margishvili 2, Revazishvili
26/09/95	Dinamo Tbilisi	A	0-1	
04/10/95	Samtredia	H	1-1	Balashvili
18/10/95	Kolkheti 1913 Poti	A	0-3	(w/o)
23/10/95	Dinamo Batumi	H	2-0	Margishvili (p), Tsitskishvili
27/10/95	Dinamo Zugdidi	A	0-1	
31/10/95	Torpedo Kutaisi	H	3-2	Margishvili 2, Marekhashvili
09/11/95	Metalurgi Rustavi	A	1-5	Gagnidze J. (p)
23/11/95	Egrisi Senaki	H	4-3	Marekashvili, Margishvili, Balashvili, Lomidze
14/03/96	Margveti Zestafoni	A	1-1	Revazishvili
18/03/96	Shevardeni 1906 Tbilisi	H	1-1	Gagnidze J. (p)
22/03/96	Iveria Khashuri	A	1-2	Margishvili (p)
31/03/96	Kakheti Telavi	H	5-1	Khorguashvili 2, Tabatadze, Marekhashvili, Kaidarashvili
04/04/96	Guria Lanchkhuti	A	0-2	
08/04/96	Duruji Kvareli	H	8-3	Margishvili 3, Lomidze, Khorguashvili, Revazishvili, Kaidarashvili, Jalabadze
12/04/96	Sioni Bolnisi	A	2-4	Tskrialashvili, Tsitskishvili
19/04/96	Dinamo Tbilisi	H	1-6	Margishvili
28/04/96	Samtredia	A	1-4	Lomidze
01/05/96	Kolkheti 1913 Poti	H	0-1	
09/05/96	Dinamo Batumi	A	0-2	
13/05/96	Dinamo Zugdidi	H	1-0	Marekhashvili
17/05/96	Torpedo Kutaisi	A	0-2	
21/05/96	Metalurgi Rustavi	H	2-3	Khorguashvili, Gagnidze J. (p)
31/05/96	Egrisi Senaki	A	0-3	(w/o)

DINAMO BATUMI

CLUB DIRECTORY

Dinamo Batumi
H. Barbusse street 32
Batumi
tel - (88222) 72362/72369
Year of Formation - 1923
President - Revaz Chelebadze
Coach - Valerian Chkhartishvili
Stadium - Dinamo (25,000)

APPEARANCES 95/96

	P	Ap	(s)	Gls
Aslan BALADZE	G	4		
Gocha CHIKOVANI	D	23		
Vitali DARASELIA	M		(4)	2
Avtandil GLONTI	M	16	(8)	1
Aleksandre KANTIDZE	M	12	(6)	4
Paata MACHUTADZE	A	17	(1)	5
David MAKHARADZE	A	11	(4)	7
Ivane MAKHARADZE	D	13	(3)	2
Malkhaz MAKHARADZE	M	23		2
Mirian MALAKMADZE	G	11		
Soso MALANIA	D	3	(1)	
Zurab MINDADZE	D	16	(2)	3
Amiran MUJIRI	M	26	(1)	10
Badri PUTKARADZE	M	5	(5)	1
Valeri SHANIDZE	D	27		
Gela SHEKILADZE	D	29		
Tengiz SICHINAVA	D	5	(4)	1
Nikoloz TOGONIDZE	G	15		
Rostom TORGASHVILI	M	29		4
Temur TUGUSHI	M	21	(2)	13
David UJMAJURIDZE	A	24	(2)	13

LEAGUE RESULTS 1995/96

02/08/95	Guria Lanchkhuti	H	3-0	Machutadze (p), Tugushi, Mindadze
15/08/95	Sioni Bolnisi	H	3-0	Torgashvili, Tugushi, Ujmajuridze
19/08/95	Duruji Kvareli	A	0-0	
30/08/95	Samtredia	H	3-4	Tugushi 2, Torgashvili
18/09/95	Kolkheti 1913 Poti	A	1-1	Ujmajuridze
22/09/95	Egrisi Senaki	H	3-1	Ujmajuridze, Mujiri, Torgashvili
04/10/95	Torpedo Kutaisi	A	0-0	
14/10/95	Dinamo Zugdidi	H	5-0	Ujmajuridze 3, Makharadze M., Mindadze
18/10/95	Metalurgi Rustavi	H	2-1	Ujmajuridze, Makharadze D.
23/10/95	Dila Gori	A	0-2	
27/10/95	Margveti Zestafoni	H	3-1	Makharadze D. 2, Torgashvili
31/10/95	Shevardeni 1906 Tbilisi	A	3-2	Makharadze I. 2, Makharadze D.
09/11/95	Iveria Khashuri	H	3-1	Makharadze D., Mujiri, Kantidze
23/11/95	Kakheti Telavi	A	2-0	Ujmajuridze, Kantidze
27/11/95	Dinamo Tbilisi	A	1-1	Makharadze D.
14/03/96	Guria Lanchkhuti	A	0-1	
18/03/96	Duruji Kvareli	H	11-0	Tugushi 3, Machutadze 3, Mujiri, Glonti, Mindadze, Putkaradze, Makharadze D.
22/03/96	Sioni Bolnisi	A	1-0	Mujiri (p)
31/03/96	Dinamo Tbilisi	H	1-3	Ujmajuridze
04/04/96	Samtredia	A	2-2	Mujiri (p), Ujmajuridze
08/04/96	Kolkheti 1913 Poti	H	0-1	
12/04/96	Egrisi Senaki	A	3-1	Ujmajuridze, Kantidze, Makharadze M.
19/04/96	Dinamo Zugdidi	A	3-1	Machutadze, Mujiri, Tugushi
28/04/96	Torpedo Kutaisi	H	1-1	Mujiri (p)
01/05/96	Metalurgi Rustavi	A	0-1	
09/05/96	Dila Gori	H	2-0	Tugushi 2
13/05/96	Margveti Zestafoni	A	0-2	
17/05/96	Shevardeni 1906 Tbilisi	H	7-0	Ujmajuridze 2, Daraselia 2, Mujiri, Tugushi, Kantidze
21/05/96	Iveria Khashuri	A	0-1	
31/05/96	Kakheti Telavi	H	5-0	Mujiri 2, Tugushi 2, Sichinava

DINAMO TBILISI

CLUB DIRECTORY

Dinamo Tbilisi
Digomi Township
3rd Block
Tbilisi
tel - (8832) 984017/237023
Year of Formation - 1925
President - Merab Jordania
Coach - David Kipiani
Stadium - Boris Paichadze (75,000)

MAJOR HONOURS
League Championship (USSR) - (2) 1964, 1978.
League Championship - (7)
1990, 1991, 1992, 1993, 1994, 1995, 1996.
Domestic Cup (USSR) - (2) 1976, 1979.
Domestic Cup - (5)
1992, 1993, 1994, 1995, 1996.
European Cup-winners' Cup - (1) 1981.

APPEARANCES 95/96

	P	Ap	(s)	Gls
Giorgi ANCHABADZE	M	15	(2)	4
Gela CHANTURIA	G	8		
David CHICHVEISHVILI	D		(1)	
Jumber CHUKHUA	A		(1)	1
Giorgi DEMETRADZE	A	6	(18)	17
Givi DIDAVA	D	27	(1)	1
Temur GADELIA	M	1	(3)	
Paata GAMTSEMLIDZE	M		(5)	1
Kakhaber GOGICHAISHVILI	M	24		19
Aleksandre IASHVILI	A	23	(2)	26
Gela INALISHVILI	M	5	(1)	1
Gocha JAMARAULI	M	5	(2)	3
Gizo JELADZE	M		(1)	
Kakhi KACHARAVA	A	1		
Kakhi KALADZE	D	22	(1)	
Levan KHOMERIKI	A	7	(11)	8
Levan KHORKHELI	M	3	(7)	2
Roin KERDZEVADZE	M	24	(4)	8
Giorgi KIKNADZE	M	22	(3)	1
Levan KIPIANI	M	1		
David KIZILASHVILI	A	10	(1)	5
Levan KOBIASHVILI	D	27		
Nugzar LOBJANIDZE	D	19	(1)	
Mamuka MACHAVARIANI	D	28		2
David MUJIRI	M	4	(1)	1
Giorgi PIRTSKHALAVA	D	2		
Grigol TSAAVA	M	1		
Levan TSKITISHVILI	M	13	(6)	6
Irakli ZOIDZE	G	21		

LEAGUE RESULTS 1995/96

Date	Opponent	H/A	Score	Scorers
15/08/95	Kolkheti 1913 Poti	A	1-1	Didava
12/09/95	Egrisi Senaki	H	3-0	Gogichaishvili 2, Kerdzevadze
17/09/95	Torpedo Kutaisi	H	5-1	Demetradze 2, Gogichaishvili (p), Kerdzevadze, Mujiri
21/09/95	Metalurgi Rustavi	A	2-0	Kerdzevadze, Jamarauli
26/09/95	Dila Gori	H	1-0	Kerdzevadze
30/09/95	Dinamo Zugdidi	A	5-1	Iashvili 2, Kerdzevadze, Kiknadze, Chukhua (p)
04/10/95	Margveti Zestafoni	A	0-1	
18/10/95	Shevardeni 1906 Tbilisi	H	3-0	Khorkheli 2, Gamtsemlidze
22/10/95	Iveria Khashuri	A	1-1	Machavariani
26/10/95	Kakheti Telavi	H	7-1	Gogichaishvili 3 (1p), Iashvili 2, Tskitishvili, Jamarauli
31/10/95	Guria Lanchkhuti	A	3-0	Gogichaishvili 2, Iashvili
09/11/95	Duruji Kvareli	H	11-0	Iashvili 4, Gogichaishvili 2, Demetradze 2, Khomeriki, Jamarauli, Tskitishvili
23/11/95	Sioni Bolnisi	A	1-0	Gogichaishvili (p)
27/11/95	Dinamo Batumi	H	1-1	Khomeriki
01/12/95	Samtredia	H	3-1	Machavariani, Iashvili, Kerdzevadze
14/03/96	Egrisi Senaki	A	3-1	Kerdzevadze, Anchabadze, Iashvili
18/03/96	Samtredia	A	0-0	
22/03/96	Kolkheti 1913 Poti	H	4-0	Iashvili 2, Kizilashvili, Anchabadze
31/03/96	Dinamo Batumi	A	3-1	Kizilashvili 2, Gogichaishvili (p)
04/04/96	Dinamo Zugdidi	H	1-0	Gogichaishvili
08/04/96	Torpedo Kutaisi	A	1-0	Iashvili
12/04/96	Metalurgi Rustavi	H	4-0	Demetradze 2, Gogichaishvili (p), Khomeriki
19/04/96	Dila Gori	A	6-1	Gogichaishvili 3 (1p), Khomeriki, Iashvili, Inalishvili
28/04/96	Margveti Zestafoni	H	6-1	Iashvili 3, Kizilashvili 2, Gogichaishvili (p)
01/05/96	Shevardeni 1906 Tbilisi	A	5-1	Iashvili 2, Anchabadze, Kerdzevadze, Tskitishvili
13/05/96	Kakheti Telavi	A	5-1	Demetradze 3, Gogichaishvili, Khomeriki
15/05/96	Iveria Khashuri	H	5-0	Demetradze 2 (1p), Iashvili 2, Tskitishvili
17/05/96	Guria Lanchkhuti	H	3-0	(w/o)
21/05/96	Duruji Kvareli	A	8-2	Iashvili 3, Demetradze 2 (1p), Khomeriki 2, Anchabadze
31/05/96	Sioni Bolnisi	H	8-0	Demetradze 4 (1p), Tskitishvili 2, Iashvili, Khomeriki

DINAMO ZUGDIDI

CLUB DIRECTORY

Dinamo Zugdidi
David Agmashenebeli street 8
Zugdidi
tel - (215) 26157/26927
President - Bejan Gunava
Coach - Vladimir Tutberidze
Stadium - Central (7,500)

APPEARANCES 95/96

	P	Ap	(s)	Gls
Zurab AIANADI	D	5	(3)	
Badri AKHVLEDIANI	D	22		3
Zaza APAKIDZE	M	17	(1)	2
Gela ASLANISHVILI	D	6	(2)	
Ruslan BERANDZE	D	1		
Enriko BERISHVILI	D	10		
Levan BERISHVILI	A	12		5
Koba CHACHUA	M	11		1
Mamuka CHACHUA	M		(1)	
Levan CHITAIA	A	1	(2)	
Otar DZALAMIDZE	D	5		1
Zviad ERKVANIA	M	7	(5)	1
Vladimer GABEDAVA	M	23		4
Paata GIGIBERIA	A	4		
Roman GUGUCHIA	M	16	(3)	1
David IOSAVA	A	6		
Iago JABUA	D	1		
Lukhum JABUA	D	20	(4)	
Devi JAVASHVILI	D	10		
Gia JURKHANADZE	M	6	(5)	2
Zviad KADZANAIA	M	11		2
Beslan KARDAVA	M	1	(2)	
Tengiz KUKAVA	M	4	(2)	
Manuchar KUTALIA	M	26		5
Gocha KVARATSKHELIA	M	23		9
Manuchar KVARATSKHELIA	G	7		
Levan MIKADZE	D	21		2
Elguja MIKAIA	G	2	(1)	
David MIKAVA	G	3	(2)	
Mamuka NAKOPIA	G	17		
Kakha SICHINAVA	M		(2)	
Otar TUTBERIDZE	D	11		1
Ruslan VAKHANIA	D	10		
Koba VAZGANAVA	M		(2)	

LEAGUE RESULTS 1995/96

02/08/95	Kakheti Telavi	H	2-1	Dzalamidze, Kvaratskhelia G.
09/08/95	Guria Lanchkhuti	A	1-2	Berishvili L.
15/08/95	Duruji Kvareli	H	4-0	Berishvili L. 2, Kvaratskhelia G. (p), Akhvlediani
23/08/95	Sioni Bolnisi	A	2-5	Kvaratskhelia G. 2
17/09/95	Samtredia	A	2-5	Berishvili L. 2
22/09/95	Kolkheti 1913 Poti	H	1-3	Akhvlediani
30/09/95	Dinamo Tbilisi	H	1-5	Tutberidze
04/10/95	Egrisi Senaki	H	5-3	Chachua K., Gabedava, Kadzanaia, Kutalia, Akhvlediani
14/10/95	Dinamo Batumi	A	0-5	
22/10/95	Metalurgi Rustavi	A	1-3	Kadzanaia (p)
27/10/95	Dila Gori	H	1-0	Guguchia
31/10/95	Margveti Zestafoni	A	0-4	
23/11/95	Iveria Khashuri	A	1-2	Jurkhandze
27/11/95	Torpedo Kutaisi	H	3-4	Erkvania, Kutalia, Mikadze
30/11/95	Shevardeni 1906 Tbilisi	H	0-0	
14/03/96	Kakheti Telavi	A	1-2	Kvaratskhelia G. (p)
18/03/96	Guria Lanchkhuti	H	2-0	Gabedava, Kutalia
22/03/96	Duruji Kvareli	A	1-0	Apakidze (p)
31/03/96	Sioni Bolnisi	H	3-0	(w/o)
04/04/96	Dinamo Tbilisi	A	0-1	
08/04/96	Samtredia	H	2-2	Kvaratskhelia G. (p), Kutalia
12/04/96	Kolkheti 1913 Poti	A	0-1	
19/04/96	Dinamo Batumi	H	1-3	Kvaratskhelia G. (p)
28/04/96	Egrisi Senaki	A	1-0	Gabedava
04/05/96	Torpedo Kutaisi	A	2-4	Gabedava, Kvaratskhelia G.
09/05/96	Metalurgi Rustavi	H	1-3	Apakidze
13/05/96	Dila Gori	A	0-1	
17/05/96	Margveti Zestafoni	H	3-4	Kutalia, Mikadze, Kvaratskhelia G. (p)
21/05/96	Shevardeni 1906 Tbilisi	A	1-0	Jurkhandze
31/05/96	Iveria Khashuri	H	0-0	

DURUJI KVARELI

CLUB DIRECTORY

Duruji Kvareli
Kudigora street 2
Kvareli
tel - (253) 21070/22438
Year of Formation - 1953
President - Aleksandre Lapachishvili
Coach - Nikoloz Samitashvili
Stadium - Central (2,500)

APPEARANCES 95/96

	P	Ap	(s)	Gls
Aleksandre BOCHORISHVILI	D	27		1
Besik CHIKHRADZE	D	6	(2)	
Mikheil DARCHIASHVILI	A	14		
Gela DAVITASHVILI	M		(12)	
Valerian GEGESHIDZE	D	8		
Levan JIKURISHVILI	M	2	(12)	
Mamuka KANCHASHVILI	M	27	(1)	4
Gela KARENASHVILI	M	27		6
Valerian KIZILASHVILI	A	26	(1)	7
Shalva KOBIASHVILI	D	13	(7)	1
Niko KUPRASHVILI	M	8	(5)	
Vaja MAISURADZE	D	1		
Bejan MOSIASHVILI	D	21		
Otar OSADZE	D	14		
David OSEPASHVILI	M	24	(1)	1
David OSEPASHVILI (same player)	G	1		
Tamaz PAKSASHVILI	G	16		
Giorgi SOMKHISHVILI	G	10	(3)	
Mikheil SOMKHISHVILI	D	2	(5)	
Mikheil SOMKHISHVILI (same player)	G	1		
Grigol TSINTSADZE	D	19	(3)	
Ivane TSITSRIASHVILI	A	23	(4)	
Ioseb TUKHASHVILI	M		(4)	
Tedo VARDASHVILI	D	18		

LEAGUE RESULTS 1995/96

Date	Opponent	H/A	Score	Scorers
03/08/95	Kolkheti 1913 Poti	A	0-4	
15/08/95	Dinamo Zugdidi	A	0-4	
19/08/95	Dinamo Batumi	H	0-0	
23/08/95	Torpedo Kutaisi	H	0-6	
30/08/95	Metalurgi Rustavi	A	0-4	
17/09/95	Dila Gori	H	0-1	
21/09/95	Margveti Zestafoni	A	0-7	
27/09/95	Shevardeni 1906 Tbilisi	H	0-1	
04/10/95	Iveria Khashuri	A	0-1	
18/10/95	Kakheti Telavi	H	0-1	
22/10/95	Guria Lanchkhuti	A	1-4	Karenashvili
26/10/95	Egrisi Senaki	A	1-7	Karenashvili
31/10/95	Sioni Bolnisi	H	1-3	Kizilashvili
09/11/95	Dinamo Tbilisi	A	0-11	
23/11/95	Samtredia	H	1-6	Osepashvili
14/03/96	Kolkheti 1913 Poti	H	1-3	Kobiashvili
18/03/96	Dinamo Batumi	A	0-11	
22/03/96	Dinamo Zugdidi	H	0-1	
31/03/96	Torpedo Kutaisi	A	0-1	
04/04/96	Metalurgi Rustavi	H	1-5	Karenashvili (p)
08/04/96	Dila Gori	A	3-8	Kanchashvili 2, Kizilashvili
12/04/96	Margveti Zestafoni	H	2-6	Karenashvili (p), Kizilashvili
19/04/96	Shevardeni 1906 Tbilisi	A	0-4	
28/04/96	Iveria Khashuri	H	2-5	Bochorishvili (p), Karenashvili (p)
01/05/96	Kakheti Telavi	A	0-3	
09/05/96	Guria Lanchkhuti	H	3-5	Kizilashvili 2, Kanchashvili
13/05/96	Egrisi Senaki	H	3-0	(w/o)
17/05/96	Sioni Bolnisi	A	2-4	Kanchashvili, Kizilashvili
21/05/96	Dinamo Tbilisi	H	2-8	Karenashvili, Kizilashvili
31/05/96	Samtredia	A	0-3	(w/o)

EGRISI SENAKI

CLUB DIRECTORY

Egrisi Senaki
Mshvidoba street 168
Senaki
tel - (213) 21705
Year of Formation - 1936
President - Kakha Rusia
Coach - Nugzar Bojgua
Stadium - Egrisi (8,000)

APPEARANCES 95/96

	P	Ap	(s)	Gls
Merab AKHALAIA	D	14		1
Merab AKHALAIA (same player)	G	6		
Jemal BENDELIANI	D	24		2
Lasha BUKIA	M	6	(4)	
Zaal BULIA	G	19		
Zaal BULIA (same player)	A	1		1
Koba CHKHIKVADZE	D	8	(2)	
Shermadin DANELIA	M	15	(2)	1
Ioseb DZADZAMIA	D	5		
Manuchar GOGUA	D	11	(4)	
Revaz IOSELIANI	M	6	(5)	
Teimuraz JGARKAVA	D	12		1
Jumber KALANDADZE	A	12	(2)	8
Edisher KHEVSURIANI	D	3	(1)	
Vakhtang MIKADZE	M	3	(2)	
Amiran MIKAVA	A	8	(5)	
Grigol MIKAVA	M	9	(3)	1
Mikheil NACHKEBIA	D	16		
Nikoloz NODIA	M	26		2
Giorgi PIPIA	M	10		
Mamuka RUSIA	M	8		
Joni SHALAMBERIDZE	M	11	(1)	1
Kakhaber SIRIA	A	4	(3)	
Malkhaz TORIA	A	19	(4)	8
Besik TSULAIA	M	16	(1)	3
Nugzar TVARADZE	A	23		13
Zaza VAKHANIA	G	2	(1)	

LEAGUE RESULTS 1995/96

Date	Opponent	H/A	Score	Scorers
09/08/95	Margveti Zestafoni	H	0-2	
15/08/95	Samtredia	A	1-3	Tsulaia
23/08/95	Shevardeni 1906 Tbilisi	H	1-4	Tvaradze
30/08/95	Kolkheti 1913 Poti	A	0-1	
12/09/95	Dinamo Tbilisi	A	0-3	
17/09/95	Iveria Khashuri	H	1-0	Bendeliani
22/09/95	Dinamo Batumi	A	1-3	Tvaradze (p)
27/09/95	Kakheti Telavi	H	2-2	Shalamberidze, Tvaradze (p)
04/10/95	Dinamo Zugdidi	A	3-5	Kalandadze 3
18/10/95	Guria Lanchkhuti	H	1-0	Kalandadze
22/10/95	Torpedo Kutaisi	A	2-2	Nodia, Kalandadze
26/10/95	Duruji Kvareli	H	7-1	Tvaradze 3 (1p), Kalandadze 2, Nodia, Bendeliani
31/10/95	Metalurgi Rustavi	A	1-4	Tvaradze
10/11/95	Sioni Bolnisi	H	3-0	Tvaradze 2 (1p), Toria
23/11/95	Dila Gori	A	3-4	Kalandadze, Danelia, Toria
14/03/96	Dinamo Tbilisi	H	1-3	Akhalaia
18/03/96	Margveti Zestafoni	A	1-5	Toria
22/03/96	Samtredia	H	2-4	Tsulaia, Jgarkava
31/03/96	Shevardeni 1906 Tbilisi	A	0-2	
04/04/96	Kolkheti 1913 Poti	H	3-6	Tsulaia, Toria, Tvaradze
08/04/96	Iveria Khashuri	A	2-1	Tvaradze 2
12/04/96	Dinamo Batumi	H	1-3	Toria
19/04/96	Kakheti Telavi	A	1-4	Toria
28/04/96	Dinamo Zugdidi	H	0-1	
01/05/96	Guria Lanchkhuti	A	2-8	Mikava G., Bulia (p)
09/05/96	Torpedo Kutaisi	H	2-6	Toria 2 (1p)
13/05/96	Duruji Kvareli	A	0-3	(w/o)
17/05/96	Metalurgi Rustavi	H	1-4	Tvaradze (p)
21/05/96	Sioni Bolnisi	A	0-3	(w/o)
31/05/96	Dila Gori	H	0-3	(w/o)

GURIA LANCHKHUTI

CLUB DIRECTORY

Guria Lanchkhuti
Queen Tamar street 6
Lanchkhuti
tel - 4455/3657/3130
Year of Formation - 1952
President - Edisher Jordania
Coach - Boris Dudauri; Begi Sikharulidze
Stadium - Central (22,000)

MAJOR HONOURS
Domestic Cup - (1) 1990.

APPEARANCES 95/96

	P	Ap	(s)	Gls
Levan ABASHIDZE	G	14		
Malkhaz AKHVLEDIANI	M	11	(1)	2
Irakli BAKHTADZE	A	13	(1)	9
Gocha CHAFODZE	M	1		
Gela CHIGOGIDZE	M	10	(1)	3
Bidzina CHKONIA	A	6	(4)	2
Kakha CHUMBURIDZE	A	5		1
Sergo CHURADZE	G	10		
Giorgi DANIBEGASHVILI	A	4		
Kakhaber EBRALIDZE	M	18	(8)	1
Aleksandre GANIEV	M	24	(1)	1
Temur GOGICHAISHVILI	D	4	(6)	
Aleksandre GOGIBERISHVILI	A	11		1
Temur GURTSKAIA	D	25		2
David IMNADZE	D	8	(1)	
Kakhaber JANASHIA	M	4		
Iasha JIBUTI	D	8	(1)	
Zviad KIKAVA	M	24		2
Lasha KOLBAIA	M	24		2
Merab KUKULADZE	D	26		1
Aleksandre KUNCHULIA	G	2		
Aleksandre KUNCHULIA (same player)	A	1		
Teimuraz LORIA	M	16	(8)	1
Aleksandre MARGIANI	A	11	(1)	4
Murman MURMANISHVILI	M	1	(1)	
Avtandil NARIASHVILI	M	9	(2)	2
Nugzar NIKOLAISHVILI	D	3	(8)	
Giorgi OKROPIRIDZE	D	2		
Avtandil TSERTSVADZE	D	13		1
Amiran TSILOSANI	D	8	(5)	
Shalva TSULADZE	G	3		

LEAGUE RESULTS 1995/96

02/08/95	Dinamo Batumi	A	0-3	
09/08/95	Dinamo Zugdidi	H	2-1	Chumberidze, Kolbaia
15/08/95	Torpedo Kutaisi	A	0-5	
23/08/95	Metalurgi Rustavi	H	0-3	
30/08/95	Dila Gori	A	0-2	
17/09/95	Margveti Zestafoni	H	0-4	
21/09/95	Shevardeni 1906 Tbilisi	A	0-3	
27/09/95	Iveria Khashuri	H	1-2	Kolbaia
04/10/95	Kakheti Telavi	A	1-2	Akhvlediani
18/10/95	Egrisi Senaki	A	0-1	
22/10/95	Duruji Kvareli	H	4-1	Chkonia 2, Akhvlediani, Gogiberishvili
26/10/95	Sioni Bolnisi	A	0-3	
31/10/95	Dinamo Tbilisi	H	0-3	
17/11/95	Samtredia	A	3-8	Kikava, Loria, Kukuladze
23/11/95	Kolkheti 1913 Poti	H	1-4	Ganiev
14/03/96	Dinamo Batumi	H	1-0	Margiani
18/03/96	Dinamo Zugdidi	A	0-2	
22/03/96	Torpedo Kutaisi	H	2-0	Nariashvili (p), Margiani
31/03/96	Metalurgi Rustavi	A	0-3	
04/04/96	Dila Gori	H	2-0	Bakhtadze 2
08/04/96	Margveti Zestafoni	A	0-3	
12/04/96	Shevardeni 1906 Tbilisi	H	1-0	Bakhtadze
19/04/96	Iveria Khashuri	A	1-2	Margiani
28/04/96	Kakheti Telavi	H	2-1	Margiani, Nariashvili (p)
01/05/96	Egrisi Senaki	H	8-2	Bakhtadze 4, Chigogidze 3, Tsertsvadze
09/05/96	Duruji Kvareli	A	5-3	Bakhtadze 2, Gurtskaia 2, Kikava
13/05/96	Sioni Bolnisi	H	0-1	
17/05/96	Dinamo Tbilisi	A	0-3	(w/o)
21/05/96	Samtredia	H	1-6	Ebralidze
31/05/96	Kolkheti 1913 Poti	A	0-3	

IVERIA KHASHURI

CLUB DIRECTORY

Iveria Khashuri
Tabidze street 2
Khashuri
tel - (268) 22456
Year of Formation - 1936
President - Tamaz Beridze
Coach - Merab Kochlashvili; Malkhaz Latsabidze
Stadium - G. Jomartidze (8,000)

APPEARANCES 95/96

	P	Ap	(s)	Gls
Ivane BUKHRIKIDZE	M	16	(3)	
Vakhtang BUKHRIKIDZE	M	8	(4)	
Giorgi CHADUNELI	A	19		2
Gocha CHIBASHVILI	D	26	(1)	4
Mamuka GEGECHKORI	D	13		
Revaz GLUNCHADZE	A	7	(12)	5
Roin GOGALADZE	G		(3)	
David GVARAMADZE	G	30		
David IOBASHVILI	M	12		
Genadi KATSIASHVILI	A	28		6
Ivane KHARAZISHVILI	D	24		
Givi KOBELASHVILI	A	13		6
Malkhaz LATSABIDZE	D	11		2
Zaza LATSABIDZE	M	15		1
Guram LOMIDZE	M	18	(6)	2
Mikheil LOMIDZE	M		(1)	
Gela LURSMANASHVILI	D	15		3
David MAKATSARIA	M	9		
Paata MELADZE	M		(2)	
Nugzar NARMANIA	M		(5)	
Zaza NEKERASHVILI	D	30		
Paata NOZADZE	D		(2)	
Nodar PAPIDZE	M		(1)	
Badri TKEMALADZE	M	30		2
Besarion VESHAPIDZE	M	1	(7)	
Valeri ZIRAKADZE	A	5	(8)	

LEAGUE RESULTS 1995/96

Date	Opponent	H/A	Score	Scorers
02/08/95	Torpedo Kutaisi	A	0-1	
09/08/95	Metalurgi Rustavi	H	1-2	Latsabidze M.
15/08/95	Dila Gori	A	1-4	Katsiashvili
23/08/95	Margveti Zestafoni	H	0-4	
30/08/95	Shevardeni 1906 Tbilisi	A	1-3	Kobelashvili
17/09/95	Egrisi Senaki	A	0-1	
21/09/95	Kakheti Telavi	H	1-0	Kobelashvili
27/09/95	Guria Lanchkhuti	A	2-1	Kobelashvili, Chaduneli
04/09/95	Duruji Kvareli	H	1-0	Latsabidze M.
18/10/95	Sioni Bolnisi	A	0-2	
22/10/95	Dinamo Tbilisi	H	1-1	Kobelashvili
26/10/95	Samtredia	A	1-4	Chaduneli
31/10/95	Kolkheti 1913 Poti	H	2-3	Katsiashvili, Tkemaladze
09/11/95	Dinamo Batumi	A	1-3	Kobelashvili (p)
23/11/95	Dinamo Zugdidi	H	2-1	Kobelashvili, Katsiashvili
14/03/96	Torpedo Kutaisi	H	1-1	Katsiashvili
18/03/96	Metalurgi Rustavi	A	1-2	Glunchadze
22/03/96	Dila Gori	H	2-1	Lursmanashvili (p), Katsiashvili
31/03/96	Margveti Zestafoni	A	0-3	
04/04/96	Shevardeni 1906 Tbilisi	H	2-1	Lursmanashvili (p), Glunchadze
08/04/96	Egrisi Senaki	H	1-2	Lursmanashvili (p)
12/04/96	Kakheti Telavi	A	0-1	
19/04/96	Guria Lanchkhuti	H	2-1	Chibashvili 2 (1p)
28/04/96	Duruji Kvareli	A	5-2	Glunchadze 2, Katsiashvili, Latsabaidze Z., Lomidze G.
01/05/96	Sioni Bolnisi	H	1-0	Chibashvili
13/05/96	Samtredia	H	3-5	Lomidze G., Tkemaladze, Chibashvili
15/05/96	Dinamo Tbilisi	A	0-5	
17/05/96	Kolkheti 1913 Poti	A	0-3	
21/05/96	Dinamo Batumi	H	1-0	Glunchadze
31/05/96	Dinamo Zugdidi	A	0-0	

KAKHETI TELAVI

CLUB DIRECTORY

Kakheti Telavi
Leonidze street 13
Telavi
tel - (250) 31719
Year of Formation - 1936
President - Gocha Mamatsashvili
Coach - Gocha Rostomashvili; Jemal Makhashvili
Stadium - Givi Chokheli (17,000)

APPEARANCES 95/96

	P	Ap	(s)	Gls
Akaki ATUASHVILI	D	27		4
Soso BABULAIDZE	M	24	(1)	5
Badri BETSUKELI	G	1	(3)	
Badri BETSUKELI (same player)	M	1		
Guram CHIKVINIDZE	G	15		
Gocha CHVRITIDZE	A		(2)	1
Emzar GAGNASHVILI	M	7	(4)	
Zurab GOGIASHVILI	M	5	(9)	1
Giorgi GVINIASHVILI	A	22	(5)	2
Zaza JASHIASHVILI	M	25		2
Zurab KAADZE	M	11	(6)	
Kakha KAKHOIDZE	A	7	(5)	1
Merab KATSITADZE	D	13		3
Zviad KHACHIRASHVILI	G	14		
Gela LOBJANIDZE	M	26		1
Ioseb MAMISASHVILI	A	3	(9)	1
Revaz NAKUDAIDZE	D	26		2
Goderdzi NONIKASHVILI	M	11	(4)	
Evgeni SANADIRADZE	D	11	(1)	
Teimuraz SHALAMBERIDZE	D	13		
Emzar SHONIA	D	27	(1)	5
David SOLOGASHVILI	M	25		1
Vepkhia TARUGASHVILI	M	4	(5)	
Kakhaber TSIKLAURI	D	12		

LEAGUE RESULTS 1995/96

Date	Opponent	H/A	Score	Scorers
02/08/95	Dinamo Zugdidi	A	1-2	Chvritidze
09/08/95	Torpedo Kutaisi	H	0-2	
15/08/95	Metalurgi Rustavi	A	0-3	
23/08/95	Dila Gori	H	2-2	Gvinishvili, Nakudaidze
30/08/95	Margveti Zestafoni	A	0-3	
17/09/95	Shevardeni 1906 Tbilisi	H	1-0	Shonia
21/09/95	Iveria Khashuri	A	0-1	
27/09/95	Egrisi Senaki	A	2-2	Atuashvili (p), Katsitadze
04/10/95	Guria Lanchkhuti	H	2-1	Shonia, Atuashvili
18/10/95	Duruji Kvareli	A	1-0	Atuashvili
22/10/95	Sioni Bolnisi	H	1-0	Kakhoidze
26/10/95	Dinamo Tbilisi	A	1-7	Katsitadze
31/10/95	Samtredia	H	1-1	Katsitadze (p)
09/11/95	Kolkheti 1913 Poti	A	2-5	Sologashvili, Jashiashvili
23/11/95	Dinamo Batumi	H	0-2	
14/03/96	Dinamo Zugdidi	H	2-1	Jashiashvili (p), Shonia
18/03/96	Torpedo Kutaisi	A	1-3	Nakudaidze
22/03/96	Metalurgi Rustavi	H	0-2	
31/03/96	Dila Gori	A	0-5	
04/04/96	Margveti Zestafoni	H	1-3	Babulaidze
08/04/96	Shevardeni 1906 Tbilisi	A	0-1	
12/04/96	Iveria Khashuri	H	1-0	Atuashvili
19/04/96	Egrisi Senaki	H	4-1	Babulaidze 2, Shonia, Lobjanidze
28/04/96	Guria Lanchkhuti	A	1-2	Babulaidze
01/05/96	Duruji Kvareli	H	3-0	Gviniashvili, Shonia, Gogiashvili
09/05/96	Sioni Bolnisi	A	0-3	
13/05/96	Dinamo Tbilisi	H	1-5	Babulaidze
17/05/96	Samtredia	A	1-4	Mamisashvili
21/05/96	Kolkheti 1913 Poti	H	0-2	
31/05/96	Dinamo Batumi	A	0-5	

KOLKHETI 1913 POTI

CLUB DIRECTORY

Kolkheti 1913 Poti
Shevchenko street 17
Poti
tel - (293) 55886/55814
President - Valeri Gegidze
Coach - Soso Pilia
Stadium - Fazisi (10,000)

APPEARANCES 95/96

	P	Ap	(s)	Gls
Bakhva AMBIDZE	M	28	(1)	12
Malkhaz ARZIANI	D	8		1
Mamuka BULUKHIA	A	14	(11)	8
Gela GABISONIA	A	20		12
Zaveli GAGANIDZE	M	22	(6)	3
Gia GIGATADZE	D	19	(3)	
Gia GIORGADZE	M	23	(3)	1
Gia GOGUA	G	12	(1)	
Kakhaber GOROZIA	D	9		
Mamuka GVASALIA	G	17		
Zaza INIASHVILI	M	13	(3)	1
Baadur KAKACHIA	D	18	(1)	
Irakli KHUJADZE	M	2	(3)	
Shalva KHUJADZE	D	18	(2)	1
Tamaz KIKLIASHVILI	M	24		7
Mikheil KOBULADZE	D	15	(1)	
Gogita KUNTELIA	D	13	(6)	
Nugzar MIKABERIDZE	M	23		16
Otar TIBILASHVILI	D	7	(8)	
Valeri TORCHINAVA	M	14	(7)	4

LEAGUE RESULTS 1995/96

Date	Opponent		Score	Scorers
03/08/95	Duruji Kvareli	H	4-0	Bulukhia 2, Kikliashvili, Mikaberidze
09/08/95	Sioni Bolnisi	A	2-0	Gabisonia, Mikaberidze
15/08/95	Dinamo Tbilisi	H	1-1	Kikliashvili (p)
30/08/95	Egrisi Senaki	H	1-0	Ambidze
18/09/95	Dinamo Batumi	H	1-1	Ambidze
22/09/95	Dinamo Zugdidi	A	3-1	Mikaberidze 3
27/09/95	Torpedo Kutaisi	H	3-2	Mikaberidze 3
04/10/95	Metalurgi Rustavi	A	1-3	Mikaberidze
18/10/95	Dila Gori	H	3-0	(w/o)
22/10/95	Margveti Zestafoni	A	2-4	Ambidze, Torchinava
26/10/95	Shevardeni 1906 Tbilisi	H	5-1	Gabisonia 2, Ambidze, Torchinava, Bulukhia
31/10/95	Iveria Khashuri	A	3-2	Ambidze, Gabisonia, Bulukhia
09/11/95	Kakheti Telavi	H	5-2	Ambidze 2, Gaganidze, Gabisonia, Bulukhia
23/11/95	Guria Lanchkhuti	A	4-1	Mikaberidze, Gabisonia, Kikliashvili, Giorgadze
27/11/95	Samtredia	A	0-4	
14/03/96	Duruji Kvareli	A	3-1	Bulukhia, Gabisonia, Mikaberidze
18/03/96	Sioni Bolnisi	H	1-0	Mikaberidze
22/03/96	Dinamo Tbilisi	A	0-4	
31/03/96	Samtredia	H	0-2	
04/04/96	Egrisi Senaki	A	6-3	Mikaberidze 2, Kikliashvili, Ambidze, Gabisonia, Arziani
08/04/96	Dinamo Batumi	A	1-0	Gaganidze
12/04/96	Dinamo Zugdidi	H	1-0	Gabisonia
19/04/96	Torpedo Kutaisi	A	2-3	Bulukhia, Kikliashvili
28/04/96	Metalurgi Rustavi	H	2-1	Kikliashvili (p), Ambidze
01/05/96	Dila Gori	A	1-0	Mikaberidze
09/05/96	Margveti Zestafoni	H	3-1	Iniashvili, Kikliashvili, Mikaberidze
13/05/96	Shevardeni 1906 Tbilisi	A	3-1	Gabisonia 2, Ambidze
17/05/96	Iveria Khashuri	H	3-0	Torchinava 2, Gabisonia
21/05/96	Kakheti Telavi	A	2-0	Bulukhia, Khujadze S.
31/05/96	Guria Lanchkhuti	H	3-0	Ambidze 2, Gaganidze

MARGVETI ZESTAFONI

CLUB DIRECTORY

Margveti Zestafoni
Staroselski street 2
Zestafoni
tel - (292) 54567
Year of Formation - 1938
President - Vasil Khachapuridze
Coach - Zaur Chubinidze
Stadium - Central (10,000)

APPEARANCES 95/96

	P	Ap	(s)	Gls
David BEBIASHVILI	D	6	(6)	
David CHKHETIA	M	18	(10)	4
Zviad ENDELADZE	A	30		40
Tamaz GABRICHIDZE	M	24	(1)	
Mirian GETSADZE	D	12	(11)	2
Malkhaz GONGADZE	D	18		
Zaza GURIELIDZE	D	29		3
Vepkhia GVENTSADZE	G	28		
Malkhaz JVANIA	D	7	(3)	
Demur KAKUBAVA	M	26		4
Levan KEBADZE	A	14	(1)	10
Nodar KIKNADZE	M	23	(3)	5
Genadi LANCHAVA	D	7	(8)	
Irakli MAGLAKELIDZE	D	26	(1)	1
Temuri MORGOSHIA	M	12		2
Mamuka NIKABERIDZE	G	2	(2)	
Vladimer POTSKHVERASHVILI	M	5	(7)	1
Gocha SULAKADZE	A	8	(5)	3
Giorgi TKHELIDZE	M		(2)	
Jaba TSIKLAURI	A	19	(4)	7
Mamuka UKLEBA	M	16	(8)	2

LEAGUE RESULTS 1995/96

Date	Opponent	H/A	Score	Scorers
02/08/95	Dila Gori	A	2-4	Endeladze, Gurielidze
09/08/95	Egrisi Senaki	A	2-0	Endeladze 2 (1p)
15/08/95	Shevardeni 1906 Tbilisi	H	4-0	Endeladze 2 (1p), Kakubava, Sulakadze
23/08/95	Iveria Khashuri	A	4-0	Endeladze 2 (1p), Gurielidze, Tsiklauri
30/08/95	Kakheti Telavi	H	3-0	Tsiklauri 2, Endeladze
17/09/95	Guria Lanchkhuti	A	4-0	Endeladze 2, Kiknadze, Sulakadze
21/09/95	Duruji Kvareli	H	7-0	Endeladze 2, Chkhetia, Kiknadze, Potskhverashvili, Tsiklauri, og (Kuprashvili)
27/09/95	Sioni Bolnisi	A	3-1	Tsiklauri, Chkhetia, Kakubava
04/10/95	Dinamo Tbilisi	H	1-0	Kiknadze
18/10/95	Samtredia	A	1-3	Endeladze (p)
22/10/95	Kolkheti 1913 Poti	H	4-2	Endeladze 2 (1p), Sulakadze, Chkhetia
27/10/95	Dinamo Batumi	A	1-3	Kiknadze
31/10/95	Dinamo Zugdidi	H	4-0	Endeladze 2 (1p), Kakubava, Ukleba
09/11/95	Torpedo Kutaisi	A	1-2	Getsadze
23/11/95	Metalurgi Rustavi	H	3-0	Endeladze 2 (2p), Getsadze
14/03/96	Dila Gori	H	1-1	Kebadze
18/03/96	Egrisi Senaki	H	5-1	Endeladze 4 (1p), Kakubava
22/03/96	Shevardeni 1906 Tbilisi	A	1-0	Endeladze
31/03/96	Iveria Khashuri	H	3-0	Kebadze 2, Endeladze (p)
04/04/96	Kakheti Telavi	A	3-1	Endeladze 2 (2p), Kiknadze
08/04/96	Guria Lanchkhuti	H	3-0	Kebadze 2, Tsiklauri
12/04/96	Duruji Kvareli	A	6-2	Endeladze 2, Kebadze, Gurielidze, Maglakelidze, Morgoshia
19/04/96	Sioni Bolnisi	H	5-2	Endeladze 3 (1p), Kebadze, Tsiklauri
28/04/96	Dinamo Tbilisi	A	1-6	Morgoshia
01/05/96	Samtredia	H	0-0	
09/05/96	Kolkheti 1913 Poti	A	1-3	Endeladze
13/05/96	Dinamo Batumi	H	2-0	Endeladze 2
17/05/96	Dinamo Zugdidi	A	4-3	Endeladze, Ukleba, Chkhetia, Kebadze
21/05/96	Torpedo Kutaisi	H	5-3	Endeladze 3 (2p), Kebadze 2
31/05/96	Metalurgi Rustavi	A	1-0	Endeladze

METALURGI RUSTAVI

CLUB DIRECTORY

Metalurgi Rustavi
Nikoladze street 5
Rustavi
tel - 192010
Year of Formation - 1948
President - Guram Kashakashvili
Coach - Revaz Dzodzuashvili
Stadium - Poladi (10,719)

APPEARANCES 95/96

	P	Ap	(s)	Gls
Kakhaber ALADASHVILI	A	30		16
Lasha AMBIDZE	D	4	(3)	
Gela ARCHVADZE	D	17	(2)	2
Dimitri ARSOSHVILI	M	1		
Aleksandre BURNADZE	D	12	(1)	2
Mamuka BUTSUREISHVILI	M	11	(4)	1
David CHALADZE	A	29		18
Gubaz DOLIDZE	G	27	(1)	
Tengiz DOLIDZE	M		(7)	
Armaz JELADZE	A		(4)	1
Murad KAVELASHVILI	D	18	(1)	
Amiran KEDELASHVILI	D		(5)	1
Andro KOROSHINADZE	G	3	(2)	
Kakhaber KVINTRADZE	M		(4)	3
Zaza LOLASHVILI	G		(1)	
Mamuka MELADZE	M		(6)	1
Tamaz METREVELI	M	10	(1)	3
Zaza PATARIDZE	M	5	(6)	3
Tamaz PERTIA	A	22	(6)	1
Zurab POPKHADZE	D	27		5
Aleksandre REKHVIASHVILI	M	27		1
Levan SILAGADZE	D	15		
Normen TARTARASHVILI	M	20	(7)	1
Merab TEVZADZE	D	26	(1)	1
Robert ZIRAKISHVILI	A	26	(1)	10

LEAGUE RESULTS 1995/96

02/08/95	Shevardeni 1906 Tbilisi	H	3-2	Aladashvili (p), Popkhadze, Chaladze
09/08/95	Iveria Khashuri	A	2-1	Zirakishvili, Chaladze
15/08/95	Kakheti Telavi	H	3-0	Zirakishvili, Metreveli, Chaladze
23/08/95	Guria Lanchkhuti	A	3-0	Kvintradze 2, Popkhadze
30/08/95	Duruji Kvareli	H	4-0	Burnadze, Archvadze, Kvintradze, Aladashvili
17/09/95	Sioni Bolnisi	A	2-0	Burnadze, Chaladze
21/09/95	Dinamo Tbilisi	H	0-2	
27/09/95	Samtredia	A	0-3	
04/10/95	Kolkheti 1913 Poti	H	3-1	Aladashvili 3 (1p)
18/10/95	Dinamo Batumi	A	1-2	Aladashvili
22/10/95	Dinamo Zugdidi	H	3-1	Tartarashvili, Zirakishvili, Aladashvili
26/10/95	Torpedo Kutaisi	A	0-2	
31/10/95	Egrisi Senaki	H	4-1	Zirakishvili 2, Chaladze 2
09/11/95	Dila Gori	H	5-1	Chaladze 2, Butsureishvili, Aladashvili, Pertia
23/11/95	Margveti Zestafoni	A	0-3	
14/03/96	Shevardeni 1906 Tbilisi	A	2-0	Chaladze, Zirakishvili
18/03/96	Iveria Khashuri	H	2-1	Popkhadze, Aladashvili
22/03/96	Kakheti Telavi	A	2-0	Aladashvili, Zirakishvili
31/03/96	Guria Lanchkhuti	H	3-0	Zirakishvili, Pataridze, Aladashvili
04/04/96	Duruji Kvareli	A	5-1	Metreveli, Pataridze, Chaladze, Kedelashvili, Rekhviashvili
08/04/96	Sioni Bolnisi	H	5-0	Chaladze 2, Pataridze, Aladashvili, Metreveli
12/04/96	Dinamo Tbilisi	A	0-4	
19/04/96	Samtredia	H	2-1	Aladashvili (p), Chaladze
28/04/96	Kolkheti 1913 Poti	A	1-2	Archvadze
01/05/96	Dinamo Batumi	H	1-0	Aladashvili
09/05/96	Dinamo Zugdidi	A	3-1	Chaladze 2, Zirakishvili
13/05/96	Torpedo Kutaisi	H	4-3	Chaladze, Zirakishvili, Aladashvili, Jeladze
17/05/96	Egrisi Senaki	A	4-1	Chaladze, Popkhadze, Aladashvili, Meladze
21/05/96	Dila Gori	A	3-2	Chaladze, Popkhadze, Tevzadze (p)
31/05/96	Margveti Zestafoni	H	0-1	

SAMTREDIA

CLUB DIRECTORY

Samtredia
Javakhishvili street 10
Samtredia
tel - (211) 24988
Year of Formation - 1936
President - Tariel Chachua
Coach - Murtaz Khurtsilava; Juliver Elashvili
Stadium - Erosi Manjgaladze (15,000)

APPEARANCES 95/96

	P	Ap	(s)	Gls
Besik AMASHUKELI	M	22	(2)	6
Besik BERADZE	D	15		
Grigol CHANTURIA	G	19	(1)	
Grigol CHANTURIA (same player)	A	1		
Gia CHKHAIDZE	D	26	(1)	2
Shota CHOMAKHIDZE	M	9	(12)	3
Badri DARASELIA	M	6	(4)	2
Giorgi DARASELIA	M	26		13
Levan DOLABERIDZE	G	10	(3)	
Giorgi GOGIASHVILI	M	28	(1)	9
Valter GUCHUA	D	13		1
Eldar GVASALIA	A	11	(2)	8
Zurab IONANIDZE	A	15		23
David JANASHIA	M	15		8
Zaza JANASHIA	A	3	(1)	2
Zviad JELADZE	D	28		3
Gia JISHKARIANI	D	1		
David KHUCHUA	A	14		6
Vakhtang KHVADAGIANI	D	8		
Paata LURSMANASHVILI	D	14		
Gela PANCHULIDZE	M	24	(1)	4
Klementi RUKHADZE	M	5	(10)	
Giorgi TKAVADZE	A	4	(1)	2
David TSOMAIA	D	2		

LEAGUE RESULTS 1995/96

Date	Opponent	H/A	Score	Scorers
15/08/95	Egrisi Senaki	H	3-1	Ionanidze, Gogiashvili, Daraselia B.
26/08/95	Sioni Bolnisi	H	5-0	Ionanidze 4, Daraselia B. (p)
30/08/95	Dinamo Batumi	A	4-3	Gogiashvili 2, Janashia D., Ionanidze (p)
17/09/95	Dinamo Zugdidi	H	5-2	Ionanidze 4, Gogiashvili
21/09/95	Torpedo Kutaisi	A	2-2	Janashia D. 2
27/09/95	Metalurgi Rustavi	H	3-0	Ionanidze (p), Panchulidze, Janashia D.
04/10/95	Dila Gori	A	1-1	Ionanidze
18/10/95	Margveti Zestafoni	H	3-1	Daraselia G. 2, Ionanidze
22/10/95	Shevardeni 1906 Tbilisi	A	4-1	Daraselia G. 2 (1p), Ionanidze, Janashia D.
26/10/95	Iveria Khashuri	H	4-1	Ionanidze 2, Janashia D., Amashukeli
31/10/95	Kakheti Telavi	A	1-1	Janashia D.
17/11/95	Guria Lanchkhuti	H	8-3	Ionanidze 4, Janashia Z. 2, Daraselia G., Guchua
23/11/95	Duruji Kvareli	A	6-1	Ionanidze 3, Gogiashvili, Amashukeli, Daraselia G.
27/11/95	Kolkheti 1913 Poti	H	4-0	Gogiashvili, Amashukeli, Panchulidze, Janashia D.
01/12/95	Dinamo Tbilisi	A	1-3	Gogiashvili
14/03/96	Sioni Bolnisi	A	3-0	Tkavadze 2, Chkhaidze
18/03/96	Dinamo Tbilisi	H	0-0	
22/03/96	Egrisi Senaki	A	4-2	Daraselia G. 2, Chomakhidze, Gvasalia
31/03/96	Kolkheti 1913 Poti	A	2-0	Amashukeli 2 (1p)
04/04/96	Dinamo Batumi	H	2-2	Khuchua 2
08/04/96	Dinamo Zugdidi	A	2-2	Jeladze (p), Gvasalia
12/04/96	Torpedo Kutaisi	H	2-2	Gvasalia, Chomakhidze
19/04/96	Metalurgi Rustavi	A	1-2	Jeladze (p)
28/04/96	Dila Gori	H	4-1	Chkhaidze, Panchulidze, Gogiashvili, og (Tabatadze)
01/05/96	Margveti Zestafoni	A	0-0	
09/05/96	Shevardeni 1906 Tbilisi	H	4-2	Daraselia G. 3, Khuchua
13/05/96	Iveria Khashuri	A	5-3	Gvasalia 2, Amashukeli, Khuchua, Daraselia G.
17/05/96	Kakheti Telavi	H	4-1	Khuchua 2, Gogiashvili, Daraselia G.
21/05/96	Guria Lanchkhuti	A	6-1	Gvasalia 3, Jeladze (p), Chomakhidze, Panchulidze
31/05/96	Duruji Kvareli	H	3-0	(w/o)

SHEVARDENI 1906 TBILISI

CLUB DIRECTORY

Shevardeni 1906 Tbilisi
Bogdan Khmelnitsky street 40
Tbilisi
tel - (8832) 931921/719204
Year of Formation - 1906
President - Zurab Kitiashvili
Coach - Joni Janelidze; Murtaz Khurtsilava; Elguja Khutsishvili
Stadium - Shevardeni (10,000)

APPEARANCES 95/96

	P	Ap	(s)	Gls
Mamuka ABUSERIDZE	G	20		
Edisher ALADASHVILI	D	27	(1)	
Merab AMISULASHVILI	M	2	(6)	1
Ivane BERADZE	G	10	(1)	
David DATVADZE	M	17	(3)	4
David GODERDZISHVILI	A	16		9
Kakha GOGOLADZE	A	19	(2)	10
Gizo JELADZE	M	11		1
Mamia JIKIA	M	14		3
Koba JORJIKASHVILI	D	15		1
Irakli KALUJA	A	4	(1)	
Ilia KANKAVA	M	30		1
Gocha KANTARIA	A	2	(5)	
David KHETESHVILI	M	8	(8)	
Zurab KOIAVA	M	12	(7)	4
Gela KVITATIANI	D	13		
Givi KVELADZE	D	16	(1)	
Giorgi MAZANASHVILI	M	13	(1)	2
Giorgi MCHEDLISHVILI	D	10		
Konstantine MELKADZE	D	13		1
Nukri MINDIASHVILI	A	23	(5)	1
Giorgi MOSULISHVILI	D	9	(4)	
Kakhaber SVANIDZE	A	4	(2)	
Ioseb TAMAZASHVILI	D	12	(1)	
Klimenti TSITAISHVILI	A	10	(2)	2

LEAGUE RESULTS 1995/96

02/08/95	Metalurgi Rustavi	A	2-3	Goderdzishvili, Gogoladze
09/08/95	Dila Gori	H	3-0	Gogoladze 2, Goderdzishvili
15/08/95	Margveti Zestafoni	A	0-4	
23/08/95	Egrisi Senaki	A	4-1	Amisulashvili, Gogoladze, Jeladze, Kankava
30/08/95	Iveria Khashuri	H	3-1	Datvadze 2, Koiava
17/09/95	Kakheti Telavi	A	0-1	
21/09/95	Guria Lanchkhuti	H	3-0	Gogoladze 2, Mazanashvili
27/09/95	Duruji Kvareli	A	1-0	Jorjikashvili
04/10/95	Sioni Bolnisi	H	2-1	Gogoladze, Datvadze
18/10/95	Dinamo Tbilisi	A	0-3	
22/10/95	Samtredia	H	1-4	Mazanashvili
26/10/95	Kolkheti 1913 Poti	A	1-5	Gogoladze (p)
31/10/95	Dinamo Batumi	H	2-3	Koiava 2
23/11/95	Torpedo Kutaisi	H	2-3	Datvadze, Gogoladze
30/11/95	Dinamo Zugdidi	A	0-0	
14/03/96	Metalurgi Rustavi	H	0-2	
18/03/96	Dila Gori	A	1-1	Jikia
22/03/96	Margveti Zestafoni	H	0-1	
31/03/96	Egrisi Senaki	H	2-0	Goderdzishvili, Gogoladze
04/04/96	Iveria Khashuri	A	1-2	Melkadze
08/04/96	Kakheti Telavi	H	1-0	Mindiashvili
12/04/96	Guria Lanchkhuti	A	0-1	
19/04/96	Duruji Kvareli	H	4-0	Goderdzishvili 2, Jikia, Koiava
28/04/96	Sioni Bolnisi	A	1-3	Jikia
01/05/96	Dinamo Tbilisi	H	1-5	Goderdzishvili
09/05/96	Samtredia	A	2-4	Tsitaishvili, Goderdzishvili (p)
13/05/96	Kolkheti 1913 Poti	H	1-3	Goderdzishvili
17/05/96	Dinamo Batumi	A	0-7	
21/05/96	Dinamo Zugdidi	H	0-1	
31/05/96	Torpedo Kutaisi	A	2-2	Tsitaishvili, Goderdzishvili

SIONI BOLNISI

CLUB DIRECTORY

Sioni Bolnisi
Orbeliani street 106
Bolnisi
tel - (258) 22646
Year of Formation - 1936
President - Vaja Avkopashvili
Coach - Nodar Khizanishvili
Stadium - T. Stepania (3,000)

APPEARANCES 95/96

	P	Ap	(s)	Gls
Giorgi ANDGULADZE	A	17	(8)	7
Malkhaz BURDULI	D	9		1
Nugzar DALAKISHVILI	G	13	(1)	
Avtandil GABRICHIDZE	M	18	(2)	
Murman GOGOLADZE	M	26		5
Shalva ISIANI	M		(2)	
Joni JAGIDISI	A	9	(2)	4
Elguja JAPARIDZE	M	10	(3)	1
Giorgi KIPSHIDZE	D	26		
Iuza MEPARISHVILI	D	17	(4)	
Konstantine METREVELI	A	17	(3)	5
Bakhva MOSESHVILI	M	25	(2)	
Teimuraz PAIKIDZE	A	6	(9)	2
Zviad PAPIDZE	D	8		
David RUKHADZE	D	15		1
Mirza SAMKHARADZE	M	5	(2)	1
Vakhtang SAMKHARADZE	M	12	(11)	5
Archil SHAKIASHVILI	D	27		2
Nodar SIDAMONIDZE	G	14	(1)	
Gocha TOROSHELIDZE	M	26		1
Gagi TSOTADZE	G	1	(1)	
Giorgi VASHAKIDZE	D	7		

LEAGUE RESULTS 1995/96

09/08/95	Kolkheti 1913 Poti	H	0-2	
15/08/95	Dinamo Batumi	A	0-3	
23/08/95	Dinamo Zugdidi	H	5-2	Paikidze 2, Jagidisi, Rukhadze, Shakiashvili
26/08/95	Samtredia	A	0-5	
30/08/95	Torpedo Kutaisi	A	0-3	
17/09/95	Metalurgi Rustavi	H	0-2	
21/09/95	Dila Gori	A	0-3	
27/09/95	Margveti Zestafoni	H	1-3	Andguladze
04/10/95	Shevardeni 1906 Tbilisi	A	1-2	Gogoladze
18/10/95	Iveria Khashuri	H	2-0	Gogoladze, Jagidisi
22/10/95	Kakheti Telavi	A	0-1	
26/10/95	Guria Lanchkhuti	H	3-0	Andguladze, Jagidisi, Gogoladze
31/10/95	Duruji Kvareli	A	3-1	Andguladze, Jagidisi, Japaridze
10/11/95	Egrisi Senaki	A	0-3	
23/11/95	Dinamo Tbilisi	H	0-1	
14/03/96	Samtredia	H	0-3	
18/03/96	Kolkheti 1913 Poti	A	0-1	
22/03/96	Dinamo Batumi	H	0-1	
31/03/96	Dinamo Zugdidi	A	0-3	(w/o)
04/04/96	Torpedo Kutaisi	H	3-1	Toroshelidze, Samkharadze V. (p), Gogoladze
08/04/96	Metalurgi Rustavi	A	0-5	
12/04/96	Dila Gori	H	4-2	Metreveli 2, Samkharadze V. (p), Andguladze
19/04/96	Margveti Zestafoni	A	2-5	Metreveli, Samkharadze M.
28/04/96	Shevardeni 1906 Tbilisi	H	3-1	Andguladze, Samkharadze V., Metreveli
01/05/96	Iveria Khashuri	A	0-1	
09/05/96	Kakheti Telavi	H	3-0	Metreveli, Samkharadze V. (p), Andguladze
13/05/96	Guria Lanchkhuti	A	1-0	Shakiashvili
17/05/96	Duruji Kvareli	H	4-2	Burduli, Samkharadze V., Gogoladze, Andguladze
21/05/96	Egrisi Senaki	H	3-0	(w/o)
31/05/96	Dinamo Tbilisi	A	0-8	

TORPEDO KUTAISI

CLUB DIRECTORY

Torpedo Kutaisi
Akhalgazrdoba street Mesame Shesakhvevi 2
Kutaisi
tel - (231) 64678
Year of Formation - 1949
President - Murad Kutateladze
Coach - Revaz Burkadze; Jemal Kherkhadze
Stadium - Central (28,800)

APPEARANCES 95/96

	P	Ap	(s)	Gls
Mikheil ASHVETIA	A	27		31
Archil CHKHABERIDZE	D	25	(1)	
Kakha CHKHETIANI	M	23	(3)	2
Irakli GIORGOBIANI	M	14	(12)	2
Rati IOBIDZE	M		(4)	
Malkhaz JINCHARADZE	M	18		
Nikoloz KHELADZE	G	25		
Mamuka KHUNDADZE	M	15		9
Kakha KVETENADZE	M	23	(1)	4
David MAMARDASHVILI	G	5	(4)	
Gia MEGRELADZE	A	7	(10)	4
David NOZADZE	M	19	(3)	4
Koba SADILIANI	D	16	(1)	
Aleksandre SHEKRILADZE	D	28		
Giorgi SHENGELIA	A	12	(13)	6
Gela TSIKARISHVILI	M	12		
Vakhtang TURMANIDZE	D	28		
Zaza VACHIBERADZE	M	19	(5)	7
Malkhaz VOSKANOV	D	14	(2)	

LEAGUE RESULTS 1995/96

02/08/95	Iveria Khashuri	H	1-0	Vachiberadze
09/08/95	Kakheti Telavi	A	2-0	Ashvetia 2
15/08/95	Guria Lanchkhuti	H	5-0	Ashvetia 2, Kvetenadze, Khundadze, Vachiberadze
23/08/95	Duruji Kvareli	A	6-0	Ashvetia 3, Chkhetiani, Nozadze, Khundadze
30/08/95	Sioni Bolnisi	H	3-0	Khundadze, Nozadze, Ashvetia
17/09/95	Dinamo Tbilisi	A	1-5	Khundadze
21/09/95	Samtredia	H	2-2	Ashvetia 2
27/09/95	Kolkheti 1913 Poti	A	2-3	Khundadze, Ashvetia
04/10/95	Dinamo Batumi	H	0-0	
22/10/95	Egrisi Senaki	H	2-2	Vachiberadze, Megreladze
26/10/95	Metalurgi Rustavi	H	2-0	Ashvetia, Nozadze
31/10/95	Dila Gori	A	2-3	Kvetenadze, Ashvetia
09/11/95	Margveti Zestafoni	H	2-1	Khundadze 2
23/11/95	Shevardeni 1906 Tbilisi	A	3-2	Khundadze 2, Giorgobiani
27/11/95	Dinamo Zugdidi	A	4-3	Ashvetia 3, Shengelia
14/03/96	Iveria Khashuri	A	1-1	Ashvetia
18/03/96	Kakheti Telavi	H	3-1	Ashvetia 2, Vachiberadze
22/03/96	Guria Lanchkhuti	A	0-2	
31/03/96	Duruji Kvareli	H	1-0	Shengelia
04/04/96	Sioni Bolnisi	A	1-3	Shengelia
08/04/96	Dinamo Tbilisi	H	0-1	
12/04/96	Samtredia	A	2-2	Ashvetia 2
19/04/96	Kolkheti 1913 Poti	H	3-2	Kvetenadze, Shengelia, Megreladze
28/04/96	Dinamo Batumi	A	1-1	Megreladze
04/05/96	Dinamo Zugdidi	H	4-2	Ashvetia 2, Vachiberadze 2
09/05/96	Egrisi Senaki	A	6-2	Ashvetia 3, Shengelia, Chkhetiani, Giorgobiani
13/05/96	Metalurgi Rustavi	A	3-4	Ashvetia 2 (1p), Shengelia
17/05/96	Dila Gori	H	2-0	Vachiberadze, Ashvetia
21/05/96	Margveti Zestafoni	A	3-5	Ashvetia 2, Nozadze
31/05/96	Shevardeni 1906 Tbilisi	H	2-2	Kvetenadze, Megreladze

PROMOTED CLUBS

SECOND DIVISION FINAL TABLES 95/96

EASTERN ZONE

		Pd	W	D	L	F	A	Pt	GD
1	**Merani 91 Tbilisi**	**36**	**28**	**4**	**4**	**103**	**24**	**88**	**+79**
2	Dinamo-2 Tbilisi	36	26	3	7	99	27	81	+72
3	Morkinali Tbilisi	36	25	6	5	73	24	81	+49
4	Armazi Mtskheta	36	20	8	8	49	27	68	+22
5	Sh. SS Akademia Tbilisi	36	19	8	9	62	48	65	+14
6	ASC Tbilisi	36	19	5	12	71	45	62	+26
7	Azoti-Akademia Rustavi	36	18	8	10	64	40	62	+24
8	Universiteti Tbilisi	36	19	4	13	67	41	61	+26
9	Energetikosi Gardabani	36	14	7	15	54	61	49	-7
10	Algeti Marneuli	36	14	5	17	48	54	47	-6
11	Iberia Kareli	36	14	4	18	51	66	46	-15
12	Tskhinvali	36	12	7	17	48	43	43	+5
13	Chabukiani	36	12	7	17	58	59	43	-1
14	Shiraki Dedoplistskaro	36	9	8	19	48	79	35	-31
15	Mretebi Tbilisi	36	9	7	20	35	91	34	-56
16	Kodako Tbilisi	36	8	8	20	40	81	32	-41
17	Jineri Jinvali	36	7	8	21	38	89	29	-51
18	Meskheti Akhaltsikhe	36	6	5	25	39	101	23	-62
19	Tori Borjomi	36	5	4	27	31	78	19	-47

WESTERN ZONE

		Pd	W	D	L	F	A	Pt	GD
1	**Samgurali Tskhaltubo**	**38**	**33**	**3**	**2**	**132**	**28**	**102**	**+104**
2	Anjeli Abasha	38	33	2	3	96	27	101	+69
3	Magaroeli Chiatura	38	26	4	8	94	44	82	+50
4	Shukura Kobuleti	38	24	6	8	109	48	78	+61
5	Iaguari Khelvachauri	38	22	3	13	77	58	69	+19
6	Sulori Vani	38	19	6	13	68	54	63	+14
7	Mamisoni Oni	38	17	3	18	69	73	54	-4
8	Meshakhte Tkibuli	38	16	6	16	63	61	54	+2
9	Mertskhali Ozurgeti	38	15	9	14	51	57	54	-6
10	Rtsmena Kutaisi	38	16	4	18	68	58	52	+10
11	Imereti Khoni	38	15	7	16	56	53	52	+3
12	Dinamo-2 Zugdidi	38	13	7	18	65	74	46	-9
13	Kolkheti-2 Poti	38	13	6	19	48	59	45	-11
14	Skuri Tsalenjikha	38	12	5	21	50	67	41	-17
15	Samegrelo Chkhorotsku	38	11	8	19	61	80	41	-19
16	Sapovnela Terjola	38	10	11	17	51	80	41	-29
17	Margveti-2 Zestafoni	38	12	3	23	54	83	39	-29
18	Chkherimela Kharagauli	38	12	3	23	59	112	39	-53
19	Chikhura Sachkhere	38	10	3	25	62	124	33	-62
20	Bakhmaro Chokhatauri	38	0	3	35	40	133	3	-93

CLUB DIRECTORY

Merani 91 Tbilisi
Sarajishvili street 27
Tbilisi
tel - (8832) 626735
Year of Formation - 1991
President - Nugzar Navadze
Coach - Anzor Gdzelidze; Sergo Gabelaia
Stadium - Sinatle (2,500)

CLUB DIRECTORY

Samgurali Tskhaltubo
Chavchavadze street 1
Tskhaltubo
tel - (240) 24077/23615
Year of Formation - 1945
President - Grigol Katamadze
Coach - Samson Pruidze
Stadium - 26 Maisi (12,000)

GERMANY

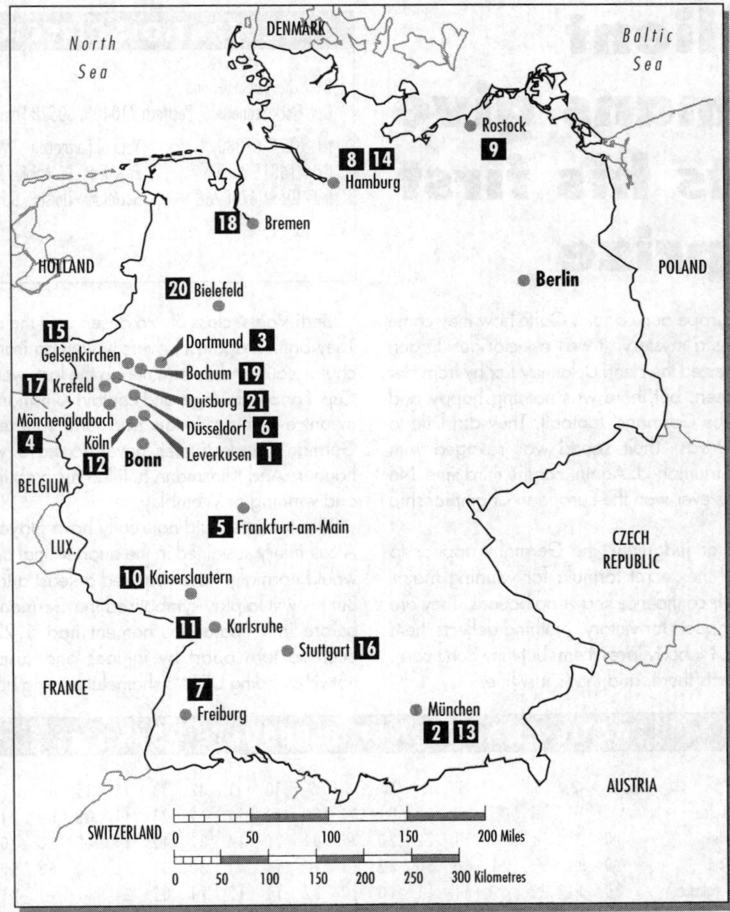

1	BAYER 04 LEVERKUSEN	448
2	FC BAYERN MÜNCHEN	449
3	BORUSSIA DORTMUND	450
4	BORUSSIA MÖNCHENGLADBACH	451
5	EINTRACHT FRANKFURT	452
6	FORTUNA DÜSSELDORF	453
7	SC FREIBURG	454
8	HAMBURGER SV	455
9	FC HANSA ROSTOCK	456
10	1.FC KAISERSLAUTERN	457
11	KARLSRUHER SC	458
12	1.FC KÖLN	459
13	TSV 1860 MÜNCHEN	460
14	FC ST. PAULI	461
15	FC SCHALKE 04	462
16	VFB STUTTGART	463
17	KFC UERDINGEN 05	464
18	SV WERDER BREMEN	465
19	VFL BOCHUM	466
20	ARMINIA BIELEFELD	466
21	MSV DUISBURG	466

KLINSMANN'S BAYERN LIFT UEFA CUP

Resilient Germans give Vogts his first big prize

FEDERATION DIRECTORY

Deutscher Fussball-Bund
Otto-Fleck-Schneise 6, Postfach 710405, 60528 Frankfurt am Main

tel - (069) 67880/1
tlx - 416815 dfb d
fax - (069) 6788266

Year of Formation - 1900
President - Dr. Egidius Braun
Secretary - Horst R. Schmidt

Germany rule Europe once again. Quite how they came to do so remains a mystery. It was a victorious Jürgen Klinsmann who seized the Henri Delaunay trophy from Her Majesty the Queen, but there was nothing happy and glorious about the Germans' football. They did little to entertain the crowds. Their squad was ravaged with injuries. Yet they triumphed. Again. For the third time. No other country has ever won the European Championship more than once.

Be it by luck or judgment, the Germans appear to have discovered the secret formula for winning major tournaments. Their confidence knows no bounds. They are relentless in their quest for victory. Nothing deflects them from their course. Nobody loves them, but they don't care. Everybody respects them, and that's just fine.

Berti Vogts' class of '96 deserve all the respect going. They battled against adversity with an iron resolve and, courageous and determined to the last, went on to lift the Cup. For coach Vogts and captain Klinsmann, the triumph meant eveything. Vogts had long suffered as the one German *Bundestrainer* never to have won a major honour. And Klinsmann fulfilled his ambition of playing and winning at Wembley.

Klinsmann should not really have played in the final. A calf injury sustained in the quarter-final against Croatia would normally have required at least a fortnight's rest. But his will to play symbolised the German effort. Never before in a major tournament had a 22-man squad been so torn apart by injuries and suspensions. But, notwithstanding UEFA's shameful helping hand before the

LEAGUE CHAMPIONSHIP RESULTS 95/96

		1	2	3	4	5	6	7	8	9	10	11	12	13	14	15	16	17	18
1	Bayer 04 Leverkusen		1-2	1-1	0-0	2-0	0-0	0-1	0-1	2-0	1-1	1-2	1-2	2-1	1-1	0-0	0-0	2-1	2-2
2	FC Bayern München	1-0		1-0	1-2	1-1	2-2	2-0	3-2	0-1	2-0	1-4	3-2	4-2	1-1	4-0	5-3	2-0	2-0
3	Borussia Dortmund	2-0	3-1		2-1	6-0	3-0	3-2	1-1	1-2	1-1	4-1	3-0	3-1	1-0	0-0	6-3	5-0	1-1
4	Borussia Mönchengladbach	0-0	3-1	2-2		4-1	1-1	1-0	1-2	3-2	1-1	1-2	2-1	0-2	2-4	4-1	1-1	2-1	1-0
5	Eintracht Frankfurt	1-1	4-1	3-4	0-2		3-0	0-1	1-4	1-3	3-1	2-2	1-0	4-2	2-2	0-3	2-2	1-0	1-0
6	Fortuna Düsseldorf	1-1	0-2	1-2	3-2	2-2		0-0	2-2	2-2	2-1	2-0	1-1	1-1	2-0	2-0	1-2	1-0	1-1
7	SC Freiburg	2-1	3-1	0-1	0-0	2-0	1-1		0-3	2-1	0-0	0-3	2-0	1-0	0-2	1-2	2-1	1-1	0-1
8	Hamburger SV	2-2	2-1	2-2	2-1	5-1	4-1	0-0		1-1	1-0	0-0	0-0	2-2	1-0	1-1	3-0	0-0	3-3
9	FC Hansa Rostock	1-2	0-0	3-2	2-3	1-1	0-0	1-0	2-0		3-0	1-1	0-1	0-3	2-0	1-2	3-3	1-0	2-1
10	1.FC Kaiserslautern	1-0	2-3	1-1	1-3	1-1	2-0	1-2	1-2	2-0		2-2	1-1	0-0	0-0	0-0	1-1	3-0	0-0
11	Karlsruher SC	1-4	2-6	5-0	4-0	1-1	3-1	1-1	3-1	0-2	0-0		1-0	1-1	2-2	0-1	1-2	2-0	1-1
12	1.FC Köln	2-2	0-0	0-0	0-2	3-0	0-0	1-1	3-2	3-0	0-1	0-1		2-0	1-0	0-1	2-2	0-0	1-2
13	TSV 1860 München	0-1	0-2	2-2	4-0	3-1	2-1	3-0	5-0	1-1	1-1	1-1	2-1		2-0	1-1	1-1	2-1	1-1
14	FC St. Pauli	2-1	0-1	0-3	0-2	2-1	2-1	1-1	1-1	3-2	1-2	1-1	3-3	4-2		2-0	1-3	0-2	1-2
15	FC Schalke 04	1-1	2-1	1-2	3-3	2-0	1-1	3-0	3-0	1-3	1-1	2-1	0-0	1-1	2-0		2-0	1-1	2-1
16	VfB Stuttgart	1-4	0-1	0-5	5-0	3-2	2-3	3-1	3-0	1-1	2-0	3-1	0-1	2-3	1-1	2-2		0-0	1-1
17	KFC Uerdingen 05	3-0	1-6	0-2	0-2	1-1	1-3	3-1	1-1	1-1	1-1	2-3	1-1	2-0	2-5	1-1	3-4		3-0
18	SV Werder Bremen	2-1	3-2	2-2	2-0	1-1	1-1	0-2	2-1	0-2	1-1	1-0	0-1	2-0	1-1	1-2	2-2	1-0	

LEAGUE CHAMPIONSHIP FINAL TABLE 95/96

			Home					Away					Total						
		Pd	W	D	L	F	A	W	D	L	F	A	W	D	L	F	A	Pt	GD
1	Borussia Dortmund	34	12	4	1	45	14	7	7	3	31	24	19	11	4	76	38	68	+38
2	FC Bayern München	34	11	3	3	35	20	8	2	7	31	26	19	5	10	66	46	62	+20
3	FC Schalke 04	34	8	7	2	28	16	6	7	4	17	20	14	14	6	45	36	56	+9
4	Borussia Mönchengladbach	34	8	5	4	29	22	7	3	7	23	29	15	8	11	52	51	53	+1
5	Hamburger SV	34	7	10	0	29	15	5	4	8	23	32	12	14	8	52	47	50	+5
6	FC Hansa Rostock	34	7	5	5	23	19	6	5	6	24	24	13	10	11	47	43	49	+4
7	Karlsruher SC	34	6	6	5	28	23	6	6	5	25	24	12	12	10	53	47	48	+6
8	TSV 1860 München	34	8	7	2	31	15	3	5	9	21	31	11	12	11	52	46	45	+6
9	SV Werder Bremen	34	7	6	4	22	19	3	8	6	17	23	10	14	10	39	42	44	-3
10	VfB Stuttgart	34	6	5	6	29	26	4	8	5	30	36	10	13	11	59	62	43	-3
11	SC Freiburg	34	7	4	6	17	18	4	5	8	13	23	11	9	14	30	41	42	-11
12	1.FC Köln	34	5	7	5	18	14	4	6	7	15	21	9	13	12	33	35	40	-2
13	Fortuna Düsseldorf	34	6	8	3	24	19	2	8	7	16	28	8	16	10	40	47	40	-7
14	Bayer 04 Leverkusen	34	4	8	5	16	15	4	6	7	21	23	8	14	12	37	38	38	-1
15	FC St. Pauli	34	6	4	7	24	28	3	7	7	19	23	9	11	14	43	51	38	-8
16	1.FC Kaiserslautern	34	4	9	4	19	16	2	9	6	12	21	6	18	10	31	37	36	-6
17	Eintracht Frankfurt	34	7	4	6	29	28	0	7	10	14	40	7	11	16	43	68	32	-25
18	KFC Uerdingen 05	34	4	6	7	26	32	1	5	11	7	24	5	11	18	33	56	26	-23

final, Vogts' troops, perfectly prepared as ever, withstood all the setbacks to come through and win.

Some will claim that Germany earned the luck that came their way, but they certainly had more than their fair share. There was nothing fortunate or untoward about their first two victories against the Czech Republic and Russia (although the Russians spurned several chances with the score at 0-0), but against Italy, in their final group game, goalkeeper Andreas Köpke should undoubtedly have been sent off.

Against Croatia the luck came Germany's way in barrel-loads - the fortuitous penalty, the non-expulsion of Klinsmann for a wild, uncharacteristic kick at an opponent, the unpunished push by Babbel on Jerkan before Sammer's winning goal. And at Wembley, too, against England and the Czechs, fortune favoured their brave efforts, not least with the hotly disputed golden goal from Bierhoff that won the final.

There was nothing lucky, of course, about the way Germany blasted home their six penalties in the semi-final shoot-out against England. That was an examination of their skill and nerve which they passed with merciless efficiency. Other plusses were the performances of Matthias Sammer at sweeper, Dieter Eilts in the anchor-man rôle and Köpke in goal. Andy Möller also had his moments, but most of the other players with an attacking bent were disappointing, especially Thomas Hässler and Fredi Bobic. Stefan Kuntz and Oliver Bierhoff were the goalscoring heroes, respectively, in the semi-final and final, but the question of who is best suited to partner Jürgen Klinsmann up front remained unanswered at the end of the tournament.

Kuntz and Bierhoff were the only two players in the Euro '96 squad not affiliated to German clubs. So, the victory of the *Nationalmannschaft* was also a triumph for the Bundesliga, which, despite the growing attractions of the English Premiership and the Spanish Liga, continued to go from strength to strength in 1995/96. Germany's Euro '96 victory can only maintain that trend.

For the second season in a row, the average Bundesliga attendance figure rose above the 30,000 mark. 30,892 was the precise 95/96 figure, with the best supported club being Bayern Munich, who drew a stunning average of 59,354 fans to the Olympiastadion and who also announced record season-ticket and merchandising sales.

The excitement in Munich was generated by the so-called 'Dream Team', constructed in the summer of 1995 by president Franz Beckenbauer with four new high-profile players - Strunz, Sforza, Herzog and Klinsmann - and a coach of equally impressive standing in Otto Rehhagel. After missing out on a trophy the previous season, the 'new Bayern' were desperate to restore the club's former glories. Priority number one was to wrest the Bundesliga title back from Borussia Dortmund.

Dortmund, however, had lofty ambitions of their own. A first national championship title for 32 years had whetted the club's appetite for more. They were certainly not prepared to reat on their laurels. Like Bayern, they spent heavily in the close season, recruiting Jürgen Kohler from Juventus, Rubén Sosa from Inter, Patrik Berger from Slavia Prague and, for a German domestic fee, Heiko Herrlich from Borussia Mönchengladbach.

The battle was on. Bayern and Dortmund dominated the pre-season predictions. And, sure enough, before the Bundesliga had even completed its second month, the two titans were way out in front, charging themselves up for a head-to-head fight to the finish.

Bayern made a formidable start, winning all of their first seven games to set a new Bundesliga record. That run ended when they travelled to Dortmund on the first day of October and were beaten 3-1. Another defeat two weeks later, 1-2 at home to Borussia Mönchengladbach, heralded the first signs of internal unrest, which was to haunt the club for the remainder of the season.

The problem at Bayern was the presence of too many outspoken personalities. From Beckenbauer in the boardroom to Rehhagel and Uli Hoeness on the bench to Matthäus, Papin, Klinsmann and Helmer on the pitch, everybody had strong opinions. And invariably they conflicted with those of somebody else. The internal warfare raged without end, and the local and national press were not slow to converge on the club and add their own flak to the proceedings.

Inevitably, all the off-field murmurings and mutinies were to have an adverse effect on Bayern's performances. The magnificent start was a false dawn. Two points behind Dortmund at the winter break (and ten points above the next best-paced team), Bayern were caught napping on the resumption in February, losing 1-2 away to Hamburg and then crashing 1-4 at home to a Karlsruhe side that they had annihilated 6-2 in the Wildparkstadion back in August.

Bayern recovered sufficiently from that double blow with five wins in their next six games to keep up the fight with Dortmund, but throughout the rest of the spring season they blew hot and cold. The fans were getting restless, but even

DOMESTIC CUP RESULTS

FIRST ROUND

TSG Pfeddersheim 1, Borussia Dortmund 1 (aet; 2-3 on pens.)
1.FC Nürnberg 2, FC Hansa Rostock 1
Arminia Bielefeld 2, Hamburger SV 1
MSV Duisburg 0, Bayer 04 Leverkusen 2
1.FC Nürnberg (amat.) 0, Borussia Mönchengladbach 3
FC Bayern München (amat.) 0, SV Werder Bremen 1
VfB Gaggenau 1, TSV 1860 München 6
1.FC Saarbrücken 1, Eintracht Frankfurt 2 (aet)
Heider SV 1, SC Freiburg 6
Tennis Borussia Berlin 1, Karlsruher SC 2
SpVgg Beckum 0, 1.FC Köln 0 (aet; 4-3 on pens.)
SSV Vorsfelde 0, FC Schalke 04 5
FC 08 Homburg 2, FC St. Pauli 1 (aet)
Dynamo Dresden 1, Fortuna Düsseldorf 3
FC Sachsen Leipzig 2, VfL Bochum 1
SV Mettlach 0, Hertha BSC Berlin 4
SV Werder Bremen (amat.) 0, SpVgg Unterhaching 2
FV Zeulenroda 0, FSV Zwickau 1
VfL Osnabrück 0, SV Waldhof Mannheim 1
FSV Salmrohr 0, VfB Leipzig 2
Greifswalder FC 4, VfB Lübeck 1
SC Neukirchen 2, FSV Mainz 05 2 (aet; 5-6 on pens.)
SC Norderstedt 0, SG Wattenscheid 09 1
Rot-Weiss Essen 2, Hannover 96 0
FSV Frankfurt 1, FC Carl Zeiss Jena 3
Fortuna Köln 3, 1.FC Kaiserslautern 4 (aet)
SV Sandhausen 2, VfB Stuttgart 2 (aet; 13-12 on pens.)
Stuttgarter Kickers 0, FC Bayern München 1
1.FC Köln (amat.) 0, KFC Uerdingen 05 2
Energie Cottbus 1, SV Meppen 2
SSV Ulm 46 2, Chemnitzer FC 3 (aet)
Lok Altmark Stendal 0, VfL Wolfsburg 0 (aet; 4-3 on pens.)

SECOND ROUND

Fortuna Düsseldorf 3, FC Bayern München 1
TSV 1860 München 5, Eintracht Frankfurt 1
Bayer 04 Leverkusen 2, Borussia Mönchengladbach 0
Borussia Dortmund 3, KFC Uerdingen 05 0
1.FC Kaiserslautern 3, SG Wattenscheid 09 0
FSV Mainz 05 2, SV Werder Bremen 3
SC Freiburg 1, Arminia Bielefeld 0
VfB Leipzig 0, FC Schalke 04 1
FC Carl Zeiss Jena 2, Chemnitzer FC 5
1.FC Nürnberg 2, SV Meppen 1
SV Waldhof Mannheim 2, FSV Zwickau 0
Lok Altmark Stendal 3, Hertha BSC Berlin 2 (aet)
FC Sachsen Leipzig 0, Karlsruher SC 2
SpVgg Beckum 2, SpVgg Unterhaching 3
Greifswalder FC 1, Rot-Weiss Essen 4
SV Sandhausen 1, FC 08 Homburg 2

THIRD ROUND

Lok Altmark Stendal 2, SV Waldhof Mannheim 2 (aet; 5-4 on pens.)
FC 08 Homburg 2, TSV 1860 München 1
1.FC Nürnberg 3, SV Werder Bremen 2
Rot-Weiss Essen 4, Bayer 04 Leverkusen 4 (aet; 1-4 on pens.)
Fortuna Düsseldorf 3, Chemnitzer FC 1
SpVgg Unterhaching 2, Karlsruher SC 3
1.FC Kaiserslautern 1, FC Schalke 04 0
SC Freiburg 0, Borussia Dortmund 1 (aet)

QUARTER-FINALS

Borussia Dortmund 1, Karlsruher SC 3
Fortuna Düsseldorf 1, 1.FC Nürnberg 0
FC 08 Homburg 3, 1.FC Kaiserslautern 4 (aet)
Lok Altmark Stendal 0, Bayer 04 Leverkusen 0 (aet; 4-5 on pens.)

SEMI-FINALS

Karlsruher SC 3, Fortuna Düsseldorf 1
1.FC Kaiserslautern 1, Bayer 04 Leverkusen 0

FINAL

25/05/96, Berlin
1.FC KAISERSLAUTERN 1 Wagner (42)
KARLSRUHER SC 0
referee - Krug
1.FC KAISERSLAUTERN - Reinke; Kadlec, Schäfer, Koch, Greiner, Roos (Wegmann 82), Hengen, Brehme, Wagner, Marschall (Lutz 75), Kuka (Wollitz 88).
KARLSRUHER SC - Reitmaier; Nowotny, Ritter (Carl 82), Schuster, Metz (Schmitt 73), Fink, Hässler, Bender, Tarnat, Knup, Dundee.

NATIONAL TEAM APPEARANCES 95/96

Coach - Berti VOGTS	BEL	GEO	MOL	WAL	BUL	SAF	POR	DEN	HOL	NIR	FRA	LIE	TCH	RUS	ITA	CRO	ENG	TCH	Cps	Gls
Andreas KÖPKE (12/03/62) - Eintracht Frankfurt	G		G	G	G	G	G	s18	G		G		G	G	G	G	G	G	39	-
Jürgen KOHLER (06/10/65) - Borussia Dortmund	D56	D			D46	D77	D	D46	D	D		D	D14						84	1
Thomas HELMER (21/04/65) - FC Bayern München	D	D	D	D	M	D	D	D	s46	D	M	M46	D	D	D	D	D110	D	54	2
Markus BABBEL (08/09/72) - FC Bayern München	D	D	D	D46	D		M	s46	s79		D		s14	D		D	D	D	19	1
Steffen FREUND (19/01/70) - Borussia Dortmund	M	M	M	M	M		M	M85	D		s46	s76		s67	D	s39	M118		19	-
Mehmet SCHOLL (16/10/70) - FC Bayern München	M		s78					M76	s84	M	s83	s64				M88	M77	M69	12	1
Mario BASLER (18/12/68) - SV Werder Bremen	M				M		s69	s76	M84	M	s46	s46							19	1
Thomas STRUNZ (25/04/68) - FC Bayern München	M46	M			s46					M		s46	s65	s87	M		s118	M	32	1
Jörg HEINRICH (06/12/69) - SC Freiburg	M																		2	-
Andreas MÖLLER (02/09/67) - Borussia Dortmund	A	M	M78	M		M	M			M	M	M64	M	M87	M89	M	M		66	25
Fredi BOBIC (30/10/71) - VfB Stuttgart	A		s74		s82	A				s46	A		A65		A	A46			11	1
Dieter EILTS (13/12/64) - SV Werder Bremen	s46		M	M	M			M	M79	M	M46	M46	M	M	M	M	M	M46	23	-
Marco HABER (21/09/71) - VfB Stuttgart	s56					D63													2	-
	/79																			
Bruno LABBADIA (08/02/66) - 1.FC Köln	s79																		2	-
Oliver KAHN (15/06/69) - FC Bayern München		G						G18		G									4	-
Thomas HÄSSLER (30/05/66) - Karlsruher SC		M	M	M	M88	M	M69	M	M90		M46	M46	M	M67	M	s88	s77	M	80	8
Christian ZIEGE (01/02/72) - FC Bayern München		M	M	M			M46	M	M	M46	M83	M76	M	M	M	M	M	M	25	3
Jürgen KLINSMANN (30/07/64) - FC Bayern München		A	A	A	A	A	A	A	A	A46	A	s76		A	A	A39		A	89	39
Ulf KIRSTEN (04/12/65) - Bayer 04 Leverkusen		A																	17	6
Matthias SAMMER (05/09/67) - Borussia Dortmund			D83	D	D		D		D46		D	D	D	D	D	D	D	D	47	8
Heiko HERRLICH (03/12/71) - Borussia Dortmund			A74	A74															5	1
Christian WÖRNS (10/05/72) - Bayer 04 Leverkusen			s83	s46		s63													8	-
Stefan KUNTZ (30/10/62) - Besiktas (TUR)				s74	A82	s77	A46		s90	s46		A	A83	s85		s46	A	A	23	5
Stefan REUTER (16/10/66) - Borussia Dortmund					s88	M		M	M		M	M76	M	M		M	M		57	2
René SCHNEIDER (01/02/73) - FC Hansa Rostock						D													1	-
Marco BODE (23/07/69) - SV Werder Bremen						M				s46		s46			s89		s110	s46	6	-
Jörg ALBERTZ (29/01/71) - Hamburger SV							s46	s85											2	-
Oliver BIERHOFF (01/05/68) - Udinese (ITA)							s46	A	A	A46		A	s83	A85				s69	8	5
Oliver RECK (27/02/65) - SV Werder Bremen												G							1	-

they were taken aback when, following a 0-1 home defeat by Hansa Rostock at the end of April, Bayern made the shock announcement that coach Rehhagel had been released with immediate effect.

Franz Beckenbauer took charge for the final four Bundesliga matches, but for once the 'Kaiser''s magic wand failed to function. Two back-to-back defeats in four days away to Werder Bremen and Schalke ended Bayern's title hopes, the final nail in their coffin coming with a last-minute goal from Schalke midfielder Andreas Müller in Gelsenkirchen.

Although the Bundesliga crown escaped them, Bayern still managed to finish the season on a high by winning the UEFA Cup. The victory enabled them to join Ajax, Juventus and Barcelona as the only teams to have won all three European trophies. It was the first victory for a German team in Europe for four seasons and Bayern's first major international prize since the third and last of their Champions' Cup wins in 1976.

Given all the problems at the club, Bayern deserved high praise for the manner of their victory. The campaign started with the embarrassment of a 0-1 home defeat by

EUROPEAN CUPS RESULTS 95/96

CHAMPIONS' CUP

● BORUSSIA DORTMUND

Champions' League

1st match JUVENTUS (ITA)

H 1-3 Möller (1)
Klos; Sammer, Kohler, Júlio César, Reuter, Freund, Möller, Zorc (Tanko 46), Reinhardt, Tretschok (Sosa 46), Herrlich (Ricken 72).

2nd match RANGERS (SCO)

A 2-2 Herrlich (19), Kree (69)
Klos; Sammer, Kohler, Júlio César (Schmidt 54), Reuter, Freund, Möller (Tretschok 85), Zorc, Kree, Ricken (Berger 80), Herrlich.

3rd match STEAUA BUCURESTI (ROM)

H 1-0 Ricken (58)
Klos; Sammer, Kohler, Júlio César, Reuter, Freund, Ricken, Berger (Tretschok 89), Reinhardt, Tanko (Zorc 46), Herrlich.

4th match STEAUA BUCURESTI (ROM)

A 0-0
Klos; Sammer, Kohler, Júlio César, Freund, Zorc, Möller, Ricken, Berger, Kree, Sosa (Tretschok 73).

5th match JUVENTUS (ITA)

A 2-1 Zorc (29), Ricken (65)
Klos; Sammer, Kohler, Schmidt, Reuter, Zorc, Freund, Möller (Sosa 89), Kree, Ricken (Berger 69), Herrlich (Riedle 76).

6th match RANGERS (SCO)

H 2-2 Möller (17), Riedle (48)
Klos; Franck, Freund, Kree, Wolters, Zorc, Möller, Berger, Reinhardt (Sosa 82), Herrlich, Riedle (Kutowski 66).

Quarter-final AJAX (HOL)

H 0-2
Klos; Sammer, Kohler, Júlio César, Schmidt (Herrlich 46), Reuter, Freund, Berger, Reinhardt, Ricken (Zorc 77), Riedle.

A 0-1
Klos; Júlio César, Kohler, Kree, Freund, Tretschok (Reinhardt 62), Wolters (Möller 61), Zorc, Ricken, Chapuisat (Sosa 79), Riedle.

CUP-WINNERS' CUP

● BORUSSIA MÖNCHENGLADBACH

1st round SILEKS KRATOVO (MAC)

H 3-0 Pflipsen (6), Effenberg (19), Klinkert (88)
Kässmann; Hoersen, Klinkert, Andersson, Neun, Hochstätter, Effenberg, Pflipsen (Frontzeck 90), Wynhoff (Huiberts 61), Dahlin, Sternkopf (Schneider 75).

A 3-2 Effenberg (29), Dahlin (54), Nielsen (80)
Kässmann; Kastenmaier, Klinkert, Andersson, Neun, Hochstätter, Nielsen, Effenberg, Wynhoff, Sternkopf, Dahlin.

2nd round AEK (GRE)

H 4-1 Dahlin (51, 90), Pflipsen (55), Wynhoff (67)
Kamps; Kastenmaier (Hoersen 76), Andersson, Klinkert, Neun, Schneider, Wynhoff, Pflipsen, Frontzeck, Dahlin, Effenberg.

A 1-0 Effenberg (71)
Kamps; Kastenmaier, Klinkert, Andersson, Neun, Schneider, Sternkopf, Pflipsen (Hochstätter 65), Wynhoff, Effenberg (Eichin 88), Dahlin (Wolf 72).

Quarter-final FEYENOORD (HOL)

H 2-2 Wynhoff (4), Kastenmaier (43p)
Kamps; Kastenmaier, Stadler, Andersson, Neun, Schneider (Eichin 61), Effenberg, Pflipsen, Wynhoff, Nielsen, Dahlin (Sternkopf 5).

A 0-1
Kamps; Eichin (Hochstätter 74), Klinkert, Andersson, Wolf (Huiberts 46), Schneider, Kastenmaier, Effenberg, Wynhoff, Nielsen (Pflipsen 64), Sternkopf.

UEFA CUP

● SV WERDER BREMEN

1st round GLENAVON (NIR)

A 2-0 Cardoso (60), Vier (80)
Reck; Scholz, Baiano, Borowka, Bode, Wiedener, Votava, Eilts, Cardoso, Hobsch (Neubarth 86), Beschastnykh (Vier 14).

H 5-0 Hobsch (26, 36, 39), Basler (37p), Borowka (66)
Reck; Scholz, Wolter, Borowka (Beiersdorfer 66), Bode, Basler (Vier 66), Wiedener, Eilts, Votava, Hobsch (Albayrak 66), Beschastnykh.

2nd round DINAMO MINSK (BLS)

H 5-0 Shtanyuk (53og), Basler (63, 83), Hobsch (72), Bode (88)
Reck; Wolter, Baiano, Wiedener, Bode, Scholz (Borowka 62), Basler, Votava, Eilta, Hobsch, Beschastnykh.

A 1-2 Bode (25)
Rost; Borowka, Baiano, Ramzy, Schulz (Neubarth 86), Wiedener, Votava (Unger 73), Cardoso, Bode, Basler, Hobsch (Vier 73).

3rd round PSV (HOL)

A 1-2 Bode (55)
Rost; Scholz (Basler 46), Baiano, Ramzy, Schulz, Wiedener, Votava, Eilts, Cardoso, Neubarth (Vier 68), Bode.

H 0-0
Rost; Eilts, Baiano, Ramzy (Beiersdorfer 55), Wiedener, Basler, Votava (Vier 81), Cardoso, Borowka, Neubarth, Bode.

● SC FREIBURG

1st round SPARTA PRAHA (TCH)

H 1-2 Todt (78)
Schmadtke; Sundermann, Vogel, Spanring, Kohl, Zeyer (Borodyuk 80), Heidenreich, Todt, Freund, Rath (Rraklli 46), Spies.

A 0-0
Schmadtke; Vogel, Sundermann (Buric 46), Spanring, Kohl (Seretis 55), Zeyer, Todt, Heidenreich, Heinrich, Wassmer, Spies (Rraklli 78).

EUROPEAN CUPS RESULTS 95/96 (CONTINUED)

● 1.FC KAISERSLAUTERN

1st round SLOVAN BRATISLAVA (SVK)

A 1-2 Hollerbach (64)
Reinke; Kadlec, Koch, Roos, Greiner (Flock 63), Hamann, Brehme, Wollitz (Schäfer 32), Hollerbach, Kuka, Wagner (Wegmann 81).

H 3-0 Wegmann (27, 56), Wollitz (38)
Reinke; Brehme, Roos (Schäfer 81), Koch, Wollitz, Kadlec, Hengen, Wagner (Hollerbach 15), Wegmann, Kuka, Marschall (Flock 76).

2nd round REAL BETIS (ESP)

H 1-3 Koch (46)
Reinke; Brehme, Roos (Lutz 27), Koch, Flock, Wollitz, Hengen (Anders 57), Wegmann (Hamann 86), Wagner, Kuka, Marschall.

A 0-1
Reinke; Brehme, Schäfer, Lutz, Greiner (Riedl 61), Wollitz, Hengen (Anders 64), Wegmann (Flock 67), Wagner, Hollerbach, Marschall.

● FC BAYERN MÜNCHEN

1st round LOKOMOTIV MOSKVA (RUS)

H 0-1
Kahn; Strunz (Nerlinger 15), Babbel, Helmer, Hamann, Scholl, Sforza, Herzog (Witeczek 72), Ziege, Klinsmann, Zickler (Sutter 46).

A 5-0 Klinsmann (26, 34), Herzog (39), Scholl (45), Strunz (78)
Kahn; Strunz (Frey 84), Helmer, Babbel, Hamann (Zickler 72), Scholl, Sforza, Herzog (Nerlinger 65), Ziege, Klinsmann, Kostadinov.

2nd round RAITH ROVERS (SCO)

A 2-0 Klinsmann (6, 73)
Kahn; Strunz, Kreuzer, Helmer, Zickler, Hamann, Sforza, Herzog (Nerlinger 63), Ziege, Klinsmann, Scholl (Papin 63).

H 2-1 Klinsmann (52), Babbel (64)
Kahn; Strunz, Babbel, Helmer, Zickler, Hamann, Sforza (Frey 78), Herzog (Witeczek 46), Nerlinger, Papin, Klinsmann.

3rd round SL BENFICA (POR)

H 4-1 Klinsmann (27, 32, 43, 46)
Kahn; Matthäus (Witeczek 69), Babbel (Kreuzer 46), Helmer, Hamann, Strunz, Sforza, Ziege, Scholl, Zickler (Kostadinov 84), Klinsmann.

A 3-1 Klinsmann (32, 67), Herzog (84)
Kahn; Matthäus (Kostadinov 55), Kreuzer, Helmer (Grill 87), Frey, Sforza, Nerlinger, Witeczek, Scholl (Herzog 75), Zickler, Klinsmann.

Quarter-final NOTTINGHAM FOREST (ENG)

H 2-1 Klinsmann (16), Scholl (45)
Kahn; Matthäus, Kreuzer, Helmer, Strunz, Sforza, Scholl, Nerlinger, Ziege, Zickler, Klinsmann.

A 5-1 Ziege (30), Strunz (45), Klinsmann (65, 80), Papin (74)
Kahn; Matthäus, Babbel, Helmer (Kreuzer 80), Strunz (Frey 61), Scholl, Sforza (Nerlinger 46), Herzog, Ziege, Klinsmann, Papin.

Semi-final FC BARCELONA (ESP)

H 2-2 Witeczek (52), Scholl (57)
Kahn; Matthäus, Helmer (Sforza 46), Helmer, Scholl, Babbel, Nerlinger, Herzog (Witeczek 46), Ziege, Papin, Klinsmann.

A 2-1 Babbel (19), Witeczek (84)
Kahn; Helmer, Babbel, Kreuzer, Nerlinger, Hamann (Strunz 74), Sforza, Scholl, Ziege, Klinsmann, Witeczek.

Final GIRONDINS DE BORDEAUX (FRA)

H 2-0 Helmer (34), Scholl (60)
Kahn; Helmer, Babbel, Kreuzer, Hamann, Sforza, Matthäus (Frey 54), Scholl, Ziege, Klinsmann, Papin (Witeczek 70).

A 3-1 Scholl (54), Kostadinov (65), Klinsmann (78)
Kahn; Matthäus, Babbel, Helmer, Strunz, Frey (Zickler 60), Sforza, Scholl, Ziege, Klinsmann, Kostadinov (Witeczek 75).

● KARLSRUHER SC

Preliminary round/InterToto semi-final GIRONDINS DE BORDEAUX (FRA)

H 0-2
Walte; Metz, Wittwer, Bilic, Schuster, Tarnat (Kiryakov 57), Bender (Wück 76), Fink, Hässler, Knup, Schmitt.

A 2-2 Fink (40), Schmitt (88)
Reitmeier; Metz (Wück 30), Reich (Carl 67), Bilic, Tarnat, Bender (Schmitt 7), Schuster, Fink, Hässler, Knup, Kiryakov.

Lokomotiv Moscow (this coming in the midst of their record-breaking winning run in the Bundesliga), but from then on Bayern remained undefeated. Indeed, they won ten of their next 11 games, including all six away from home. That was an unprecedented achievement. So, too, was that of Jürgen Klinsmann, who scored 15 goals in the competition, beating the previous record for the number of goals scored in a single European campaign.

It was rough justice that Otto Rehhagel should not be around to see his efforts rewarded. He it was who had guided the team past Lokomotiv Moscow, Raith Rovers, Benfica, Nottingham Forest and Barcelona only to be kicked out of office four days prior to the first leg of the final against Bordeaux. So, the man who will go down in the history books as Bayern's winning coach is Franz Beckenbauer, who watched from the bench as his team comfortably overran the InterToto qualifiers with a 2-0 victory in Munich and a 3-1 win in Bordeaux.

What Bayern accomplished in the UEFA Cup, Borussia Dortmund could not emulate in the Champions' League. They came comfortably through their group thanks to an improbable 2-1 win over already qualified Juventus in Turin, but were taught a lesson by Ajax in the quarter-finals, losing 0-2 at home and 0-1 in Amsterdam.

But at least Ottmar Hitzfeld's warriors earned themselves another tilt at the Champions' League by successfully defending their German title. Bayern Munich's squabbles undoubtedly helped Dortmund, but the *Schwarzgelben* were not without their own difficulties. The injury list from the previous season did not get any shorter. Key players such as Andreas Möller, Heiko Herrlich, Stéphane Chapuisat and Karlheinz Riedle were all laid low for lengthy periods. And there was a much-publicised set-to in the middle of the season between coach Hitzfeld and skipper Matthias Sammer.

But Dortmund had the necessary strength in depth to resist all setbacks. They also showed nerves of steel to get the right results when it mattered most - such as the 3-1 win at home to Bayern in October and the back-to-back victories over Uerdingen and Leverkusen which followed a shattering 0-5 defeat by Karlsruhe in the title run-in.

It was not quite as impressive as the previous season's triumph, but at least Dortmund did not have to wait until their final match before they could lift the trophy. Ironically, Dortmund completed their championship conquest in the home of their challengers after drawing 2-2 away to 1860 Munich in the Olympiastadion. The champagne flowed in Bayern's dressing-room after that match - but it was the intruders from the north in the yellow and black shirts who were doing all the celebrating.

For the second season running, Dortmund owed a huge debt to their local rivals Schalke. Their 2-1 victory over Bayern was just as crucial to Dortmund's success as the 4-2 defeat of Werder Bremen the previous season. But this time Schalke had everything to play for themselves. That last-minute goal from Müller also confirmed Schalke's return to European football after a 19-year absence. Schalke eventually took third place behind the 'Big Two' - a resounding triumph for coach Jörg Berger and his unheralded squad. They had the second-best defensive record in the league, and the man chiefly responsible for that was goalkeeper Jens Lehmann, who enjoyed a marvellous season and was unlucky not to be drafted into the Euro '96 squad.

Schalke's late run of five successive victories ousted Borussia Mönchengladbach from third place. The 'Gladbacher' were pleased to return to Europe, having lost out needlessly to Feyenoord in the quarter-finals of the Cup-winners' Cup, but overall their season was a disappointment. They had been expected to provide a greater challenge to Bayern and Dortmund, but despite the goals of Martin Dahlin and the artistry of national team outcast Stefan Effenberg they were too inconsistent to mount a serious assault on the title.

The fourth UEFA Cup place went to Hamburg, whose fortunes were transformed completely by a radical mid-season shake-up that saw two HSV legends, Uwe Seeler and Felix Magath, return to the club, respectively,

NATIONAL TEAM RESULTS 95/96

Date	Opponent		Venue	Score	Scorers
23/08/95	Belgium	A	Brussels	2-1	Möller (6), Bobic (83)
06/09/95	Georgia (ECQ)	H	Nuremberg	4-1	Möller (38), Ziege (56), Kirsten (62), Babbel (72)
08/10/95	Moldova (ECQ)	H	Leverkusen	6-1	Stroenco S. (16og), Helmer (18), Sammer (24, 72), Möller (47, 61)
11/10/95	Wales (ECQ)	A	Cardiff	2-1	Melville (75og), Klinsmann (81)
15/11/95	Bulgaria (ECQ)	H	Berlin	3-1	Klinsmann (50, 77p), Hässler (56)
15/12/95	South Africa	A	Johannesburg	0-0	
21/02/96	Portugal	A	Oporto	2-1	Möller (14, 65)
27/03/96	Denmark	H	Munich	2-0	Bierhoff (43, 60)
24/04/96	Holland	A	Rotterdam	1-0	Klinsmann (19p)
29/05/96	Northern Ireland	A	Belfast	1-1	Scholl (78)
01/06/96	France	H	Stuttgart	0-1	
04/06/96	Liechtenstein	H	Mannheim	9-1	Möller (4, 64), Kuntz (18, 90), Bierhoff (22), Ziege (38), Sammer (48), Kohler (53), Klinsmann (86)
09/06/96	Czech Republic (ECF)	N	Manchester	2-0	Ziege (26), Möller (32)
16/06/96	Russia (ECF)	N	Manchester	3-0	Sammer (56), Klinsmann (77, 90)
19/06/96	Italy (ECF)	N	Manchester	0-0	
23/06/96	Croatia (ECF)	N	Manchester	2-1	Klinsmann (21p), Sammer (59)
26/06/96	England (ECF)	A	Wembley	1-1	Kuntz (16)
30/06/96	Czech Republic (ECF)	N	Wembley	2-1	Bierhoff (73, 95)

TOP SCORERS

Goals	Player
17	Fredi BOBIC (VfB Stuttgart)
16	Sean DUNDEE (Karlsruher SC)
	Jürgen KLINSMANN (FC Bayern München)
	Giovane ELBER (VfB Stuttgart)
15	Martin DAHLIN (Borussia Mönchengladbach)
	Michael ZORC (Borussia Dortmund)
14	Olaf BODDEN (TSV 1860 München)
	Harald SPÖRL (Hamburger SV)
11	Mario BASLER (SV Werder Bremen)
	Stefan BEINLICH (FC Hansa Rostock)
	Martin MAX (FC Schalke 04)
	Erik MEIJER (KFC Uerdingen 05)
	Toni POLSTER (1.FC Köln)
	Harry DECHEIVER (SC Freiburg)

PLAYERS OF THE SEASON

JÜRGEN KLINSMANN
Tottenham Hotspur fans were immensely disappointed when Jürgen Klinsmann bade farewell to White Hart Lane after just one magnificent season. But the lure of Bayern Munich was strong, and the blond striker took to his new challenge with typical determination and commitment. In the UEFA Cup he was sensational. Four goals in one match against Benfica and six goals in the overall tie were impressive enough achievements on their own, but Klinsmann did not stop there. With the UEFA Cup already won, he crowned Bayern's triumph by scoring his record 15th goal of the competition late on in the second leg of the final against Bordeaux. Klinsmann was no slouch in the Bundesliga either, scoring 16 goals in his 32 appearances. And at Euro '96 he added three more goals to the nine he struck in the qualifying competition. Most important of all, he captained Germany to European Championship victory. Walking the famous Wembley steps and lifting the Henri Delaunay Cup will be a memory that this most personable and intelligent of footballers will cherish for the rest of his days.

OLIVER BIERHOFF
It was Berti Vogts' masterstroke to bring on Oliver Bierhoff as a substitute when Germany were 0-1 down to the Czech Republic in the Euro '96 final. But it was Bierhoff himself who struck the two championship-winning goals, and for that remarkable feat the big striker has already claimed his place in German football's Hall of Fame. Bierhoff's appearance at Wembley was only his eighth in the national team. Prior to 1996 he had never played for his country at senior level. He earned the call from Vogts with a number of fine performances in Italy for Udinese, where he was to become the club's top scorer with 17 goals. With two goals on his first start for Germany, he secured a place in the Euro '96 squad. But nobody could have predicted that he would turn out to be the match-winning hero of the final.

MEHMET SCHOLL
It was on the day that the Bosman verdict was passed that Mehmet Scholl announced his decision to remain at Bayern Munich until the year 2000. The Bayern fans were delighted and also extremely relieved, because for much of the early part of the season the little midfielder had been at loggerheads with coach Otto Rehhagel and had struggled to claim a regular place among the stars of the 'Dream Team'. When he did get a game, Scholl was outstanding, and even though Andy Herzog was Rehhagel's favourite, Scholl just kept delivering the goods and eventually forced his way into the team. He was an important contributor to the team's UEFA Cup success, scoring goals in the quarter-final, semi-final and both legs of the final. He also struck ten times in the Bundesliga, including the winner against Borussia Dortmund in the Olympiastadion. A member of the triumphant Euro '96 squad, Scholl is likely to be a major player for Germany at France '98.

FREDI BOBIC
Two goals in the last game of the season against Karlsruhe were enough to give Fredi Bobic the Bundesliga top scorer crown. The Slovenian-born youngster thus came out on top in his private duel with VfB Stuttgart team-mate Giovane Elber, who was also in the running for the *Torschützenkönig* prize. With 17 goals to Elber's 16, Bobic only just made it, but he certainly deserved the honour, having appeared in just 26 games to the Brazilian's 33. The 24-year-old's domestic proficiency was rewarded with regular invitations to the national squad. Indeed, Berti Vogts chose Bobic to play from the start in three Euro '96 matches, but by the end of the tournament, without a goal, the Stuttgart striker had fallen behind both Bierhoff and Kuntz in the pecking order to partner Jürgen Klinsmann.

SEAN DUNDEE
Rated alongside Bobic as the best young striker in Germany is South African-born Sean "Crocodile" Dundee of Karlsruher SC. The 23-year-old was unknown at the start of the season, but after initially creating ripples as a supersub for Winnie Schäfer's team in the autumn, he really made waves in the spring. Established internationals Knup and Kiryakov had to take a back seat as the younster time and again demonstrated the art of cool finishing under pressure. Two brilliant goals away to Bayern Munich in February were the perfect riposte to South African national coach Clive Barker, who had strangely ignored Dundee's claims for a place in the African Nations' Cup squad a few weeks earlier.

as president and coach. No sooner had the dynamic duo arrived than Hamburg began to shoot up the Bundesliga table, eventually lifting themselves from the relegation zone all the way to fifth place.

Hamburg's northern rivals, Werder Bremen, could not handle life without Otto Rehhagel. Replacing their coach of the past 15 seasons was a nigh-on impossible task. Dutchman Aad de Mos was clearly not up to it. He was sacked after just half a season, and new man "Dixie" Dörner, hired from the German Federation, could only steady the ship and guide Werder to mid-table.

Another new coach, Rolf Fringer, encountered problems he did not expect at VfB Stuutgart. The Swabians were sitting pretty in third place at the winter break, with their so-called 'magic triangle' of Fredi Bobic, Krasimir Balakov and Giovane Elber raising the temperature in every game they played. But in the spring Stuttgart nosedived into obscurity, winning just three of their 17 matches. With 62 goals conceded, it was obvious where the root of the team's problems lay.

Bremen and Stuttgart were not the only big clubs to suffer declining fortunes in 1995/96. Three Bundesliga ever-presents, Cologne, Kaiserslautern and Eintracht Frankfurt, were all involved in an intense struggle to avoid a first ever relegation.

In the final reckoning, only Cologne survived, and they did not secure a position of safety until the final day with a nerve-wracking 1-0 win away to Hansa Rostock. Eintracht Frankfurt brought back former coach Dragoslav Stepanovic in a bid to stave off the unthinkable, but the cigarillo-smoking Serb was powerless to stem the tide. Frankfurt conceded far too many cheap goals, 68 in total, which was a staggering statistic considering that their goalkeeper was none other than German number one Andy Köpke.

The final, most tortuous chapter in the relegation saga came on the last Saturday of the season in Leverkusen, where, with Cologne winning in Rostock, home side Bayer needed to avoid defeat against Kaiserslautern to remain in the Bundesliga, while their opponents could only survive with a victory. It was real heart-stopping do-or-die stuff. After a goalless first half Kaiserslautern struck first, in the 58th minute, through Pavel Kuka. The Czech striker then had another glorious opportunity to make the game safe for the visitors but missed it. And then, with just nine minutes left, Leverkusen sent their fans wild with an equaliser from defender Markus Münch - his first goal of the season.

Joy and relief for Leverkusen, but despair for Kaiserslautern, one of the great instutions of German football and - despite their relegation plight - the fourth-best supported team in the 95/96 Bundesliga with an average attendance at the Betzenberg of 36,699.

A week later many of those Kaiserslautern loyalists were able to wipe away their tears when the team travelled to Berlin and beat Karlsruhe 1-0 to win the German Cup. It was a drab final, decided by a deflected free-kick from former international Martin Wagner towards the end of the first half. But the result meant that in 1996/97 Kaiserslautern would have the pleasant distraction of European football to relieve the everyday mundanity of life in the German Second Division.

Strictly speaking, with Kaiserslautern already relegated to Division Two, the 1996 DFB-Pokal final was the fifth in succession to feature a non-Bundesliga side. Kaiserslautern, however, will be intent on making an immediate return to where they belong. It should not be too difficult for them or Frankfurt. After all, both VfL Bochum and MSV Duisburg managed it in 95/96. Bochum, the eternal yo-yo club, won the Second Division by a distance, finishing 12 points ahead of another famous name in German football, Arminia Bielefeld, whose gathering of golden oldies - Uli Stein, Fritz Walter, Thomas von Heesen etc. - returned the club to the top flight for the first time in 11 years.

INTERNATIONAL HONOURS

World Cup Finals appearances: 1934 (3rd), 1938, 1954 (Winners), 1958 (4th), 1962 (qtr-finals), 1966 (runners-up), 1970 (3rd), 1974 (Winners), 1978 (2nd phase), 1982 (runners-up), 1986 (runners-up), 1990 (Winners), 1994 (qtr-finals).

European Championship appearances: 1972 (Winners), 1976 (runners-up), 1980 (Winners), 1984, 1988 (semi-finals), 1992 (runners-up), 1996 (Winners)

European Club Competitions

Champions' Cup	FC Bayern München (1974, 1975, 1976)
	Hamburger SV (1983)
Cup-winners' Cup	Borussia Dortmund (1966)
	FC Bayern München (1967)
	Hamburger SV (1977)
	SV Werder Bremen (1992)
UEFA Cup	Borussia Mönchengladbach (1975, 1979)
	Eintracht Frankfurt (1980)
	Bayer 04 Leverkusen (1988)
	FC Bayern München (1996)
World Club Cup	FC Bayern München (1976)

PROFILE
MICHAEL ZORC

He was not included in the triumphant German squad at Euro '96. In fact, he has never represented his country at any major tournament. Just seven international caps have come his way during a 15-year Bundesliga career. He may not have gained the international recognition due to him, but in Germany itself, Michael Zorc is nothing short of a living legend.

No player has done more for Borussia Dortmund in the last decade and a half than their 34-year-old team captain. What Otto Rehhagel was as a coach to Werder Bremen, Zorc still is, as a player, to Dortmund. At the end of the 1995/96 season he had made a record 411 Bundesliga appearances for the club. His total of 123 goals was second only to another Dortmund legend Manfred Burgsmüller (135). And his remarkable tally of 46 successful penalty-kicks (as against just eight misses) is third in the all-time Bundesliga listings behind Hamburg's Manfred Kaltz (53) and Bayern Munich's Gerd Müller (51).

At the beginning of the 95/96 campaign, it looked as if Zorc's time at Dortmund might finally be up. The club had bought a number of new players, and places in the first team were at a premium. Coach Ottmar Hitzfeld made the bold but controversial move to leave his captain on the bench for some of the early matches. Many German players in such situations would have gone crying to the newspapers, but not Zorc. He simply knuckled down to the task of winning his place back, and his hard work paid off handsomely.

The turning point was when he came off the bench to score the third goal in Dortmund's all-important 3-1 victory at home to championship challengers Bayern Munich. After that Hitzfeld confessed the error of his ways and Zorc was back where he belonged, driving the team forward from midfield.

There would be many significant performers in the club's second successive championship win. German internationals Jürgen Kohler, Matthias Sammer, Steffen Freund and Andy Möller all played a fulsome part. But Zorc was the leader and the inspiration. He was also the team's leading goalscorer by some distance, matching his top-scoring total of 15 from the previous season. As proof of his consistency, all of Zorc's goals came in singles, with four of them arriving in the last four matches of the season when the title race was at its most competitive.

Zorc is a Dortmunder through and through. He was born in the city, joined the club at 16 and made his Bundesliga début at 18. His entire career has been spent with the *Schwarzgelben* in the top division, although he has been through many ups and downs with the club. He was on the field in 1986 when Dortmund only avoided relegation with a last-minute goal against Fortuna Cologne in the end-of-season play-offs. And in the last few years he has overseen the club's remarkable ascent to the very peak of German football. Second in 1992, fourth in both 1993 and 1994, and that first Bundesliga title in 1995, followed by another in 1996.

Zorc has fulfilled a dream in domestic football that has always been denied him on the international stage. All of his seven German caps came within the space of a year, from December 1992 to October 1993, but Zorc has long since given up hope of a recall from Berti Vogts. His sights are now fixed on captaining Borussia Dortmund to success in the UEFA Champions' League. Lifting the big silver trophy would certainly be the perfect end to a long and illustrious career for this most loyal, honest and professional of footballers.

BAYER 04 LEVERKUSEN

CLUB DIRECTORY

TSV Bayer 04 Leverkusen
Postfach 120140
51349 Leverkusen
tel - (0214) 86600
fax - (0214) 62709
Year of Formation - 1904
President - Rolf Büll
Manager - Reiner Calmund
Coach - Erich Ribbeck; Peter Hermann (96/97 - Christoph Daum)
Stadium - Ulrich-Haberland-Stadion (26,500)

MAJOR HONOURS
Domestic Cup - (1) 1993.
UEFA Cup - (1) 1988.

APPEARANCES 95/96

	P	Ap	(s)	Gls
Holger FACH	M	30	(1)	2
Markus FELDHOFF	A	5	(28)	3
Markus HAPPE	D	13	(1)	
Dirk HEINEN	G	34		
Sebastian HELBIG	M		(2)	
Ramon HUBNER (BRA)	M	5	(10)	1
Ulf KIRSTEN	A	29		8
Hans-Peter LEHNHOFF	M	23	(6)	1
Ioan LUPESCU (ROM)	D	29	(2)	
Markus MÜNCH	D	32		1
Josef NEHL	A	1		
Andreas NEUENDORF	M	16	(4)	1
PAULO SÉRGIO (BRA)	M	26	(2)	4
Carsten RAMELOW	M	13	(2)	2
Claudio REYNA (USA)	M	16	(5)	
Mike RIETPIETSCH	M	8	(9)	
José RODRIGO (BRA)	M	22	(5)	1
Bernd SCHUSTER	M	6	(2)	1
Mario TOLKMITT	M	9	(5)	
Rudi VÖLLER	A	32		10
Christian WÖRNS	D	25		2

LEAGUE RESULTS 1995/96

Date	Opponent	H/A	Score	Scorers
12/08/95	FC Hansa Rostock	A	2-1	Schuster, Feldhoff
19/08/95	Borussia Dortmund	H	1-1	Völler
29/08/95	Borussia Mönchengladbach	A	0-0	
02/09/95	FC St. Pauli	H	1-1	Kirsten
09/09/95	VfB Stuttgart	A	4-1	Völler, Kirsten 2, Hubner
16/09/95	Eintracht Frankfurt	H	2-0	Völler, Fach
23/09/95	FC Bayern München	A	0-1	
30/09/95	SV Werder Bremen	H	2-2	Paulo Sérgio, Völler
15/10/95	1.FC Köln	A	2-2	Feldhoff, Paulo Sérgio
20/10/95	FC Schalke 04	H	0-0	
28/10/95	Fortuna Düsseldorf	A	1-1	Völler
03/11/95	Hamburger SV	H	0-1	
11/11/95	Karlsruher SC	A	4-1	Völler 2, Kirsten, Feldhoff
18/11/95	KFC Uerdingen 05	H	2-1	Wörns, Kirsten
25/11/95	TSV 1860 München	A	1-0	Rodrigo
01/12/95	SC Freiburg	H	0-1	
09/12/95	1.FC Kaiserslautern	A	0-1	
23/02/96	Borussia Mönchengladbach	H	0-0	
08/03/96	VfB Stuttgart	H	0-0	
16/03/96	Eintracht Frankfurt	A	1-1	Fach
19/03/96	FC Hansa Rostock	H	2-0	Ramelow 2
23/03/96	FC Bayern München	H	1-2	Paulo Sérgio
30/03/96	SV Werder Bremen	A	1-2	Neuendorf
02/04/96	FC St. Pauli	A	1-2	Völler
06/04/96	1.FC Köln	H	1-2	Kirsten
09/04/96	FC Schalke 04	A	1-1	Kirsten
14/04/96	Fortuna Düsseldorf	H	0-0	
24/04/96	Hamburger SV	A	2-2	Völler, Wörns (p)
27/04/96	Karlsruher SC	H	1-2	Lehnhoff
30/04/96	KFC Uerdingen 05	A	0-3	
04/05/96	TSV 1860 München	H	2-1	Völler, Kirsten
07/05/96	Borussia Dortmund	A	0-2	
11/05/96	SC Freiburg	A	1-2	Paulo Sérgio
18/05/96	1.FC Kaiserslautern	H	1-1	Münch

FC BAYERN MÜNCHEN

CLUB DIRECTORY

FC Bayern München
Postfach 90 04 51
81504 München
tel - (089) 69931-0
fax - (089) 644165
Year of Formation - 1900
President - Franz Beckenbauer
Manager - Uli Hoeness
Coach - Otto Rehhagel; Franz Beckenbauer
(96/97 - Giovanni Trapattoni)
Stadium - Olympiastadion (64,000)

MAJOR HONOURS
League Championship - (13)
1932, 1969, 1972, 1973, 1974, 1980, 1981, 1985, 1986, 1987, 1989, 1990, 1994.
Domestic Cup - (8) 1957, 1966, 1967, 1969, 1971, 1982, 1984, 1986.
European Champions' Cup - (3)
1974, 1975, 1976.
European Cup-winners' Cup - (1) 1967.
UEFA Cup - (1) 1996.
World Club Cup - (1) 1976.

APPEARANCES 95/96

	P	Ap	(s)	Gls
Markus BABBEL	D	30		2
Dieter FREY	D	4	(4)	
Dietmar HAMANN	M	15	(5)	2
Thomas HELMER	D	32		4
Andreas HERZOG (AUT)	M	21	(7)	2
Oliver KAHN	G	32		
Jürgen KLINSMANN	A	32		16
Emil KOSTADINOV (BUL)	A	6	(12)	5
Oliver KREUZER	D	15	(4)	1
Lothar MATTHÄUS	D	19		1
Christian NERLINGER	M	22	(6)	4
Jean-Pierre PAPIN (FRA)	A	11	(9)	2
Michael PROBST	G	1	(1)	
Sven SCHEUER	G	1	(1)	
Mehmet SCHOLL	M	23	(7)	10
Ciriaco SFORZA (SUI)	M	30		2
Thomas STRUNZ	M	24		4
Marcel WITECZEK	A	4	(15)	
Alexander ZICKLER	A	19	(6)	8
Christian ZIEGE	M	33		3

LEAGUE RESULTS 1995/96

12/08/95	Hamburger SV	H	3-2	Herzog, Helmer, Scholl
19/08/95	Karlsruher SC	A	6-2	Ziege, Kreuzer, Zickler 2, Hamann, Scholl (p)
30/08/95	KFC Uerdingen 05	H	2-0	Papin, Helmer
02/09/95	TSV 1860 München	A	2-0	Ziege, Nerlinger
09/09/95	SC Freiburg	H	2-0	Klinsmann 2
16/09/95	1.FC Kaiserslautern	A	3-2	Babbel 2, Sforza
23/09/95	Bayer 04 Leverkusen	H	1-0	Klinsmann (p)
01/10/95	Borussia Dortmund	A	1-3	Nerlinger
14/10/95	Borussia Mönchengladbach	H	1-2	Papin
21/10/95	FC St. Pauli	A	1-0	Klinsmann
28/10/95	VfB Stuttgart	H	5-3	Strunz, Zickler 2, Scholl 2 (2p)
04/11/95	Eintracht Frankfurt	A	1-4	Helmer
10/11/95	FC Hansa Rostock	A	0-0	
18/11/95	SV Werder Bremen	H	2-0	Klinsmann, Zickler
26/11/95	1.FC Köln	A	0-0	
02/12/95	FC Schalke 04	H	4-0	Sforza, Scholl, Nerlinger, Kostadinov
09/12/95	Fortuna Düsseldorf	A	2-0	Hamann, Klinsmann (p)
11/02/96	Hamburger SV	A	1-2	Scholl
17/02/96	Karlsruher SC	H	1-4	Scholl
25/02/96	KFC Uerdingen 05	A	6-1	Helmer, Strunz 2, Klinsmann, Zickler, Scholl
02/03/96	TSV 1860 München	H	4-2	Klinsmann 2, Zickler 2
09/03/96	SC Freiburg	A	1-3	Klinsmann (p)
16/03/96	1.FC Kaiserslautern	H	2-0	Herzog, Ziege
23/03/96	Bayer 04 Leverkusen	A	2-1	Nerlinger, Matthäus
30/03/96	Borussia Dortmund	H	1-0	Scholl
07/04/96	Borussia Mönchengladbach	A	1-3	Klinsmann
10/04/96	FC St. Pauli	H	1-1	Klinsmann
13/04/96	VfB Stuttgart	A	1-0	Klinsmann
20/04/96	Eintracht Frankfurt	H	1-1	Scholl
27/04/96	FC Hansa Rostock	H	0-1	
04/05/96	1.FC Köln	H	3-2	Kostadinov 2, Klinsmann
07/05/96	SV Werder Bremen	A	2-3	Kostadinov 2
11/05/96	FC Schalke 04	A	1-2	Strunz
18/05/96	Fortuna Düsseldorf	H	2-2	Klinsmann 2

BORUSSIA DORTMUND

CLUB DIRECTORY

BV 09 Borussia Dortmund
Westfalenstadion
Strobelallee
Postfach 100509
44005 Dortmund
tel - (0231) 90200
fax - (0231) 9020105
Year of Formation - 1909
President - Dr. Gerd Niebaum
Manager - Michael Meier
Coach - Ottmar Hitzfeld
Stadium - Westfalenstadion (42,800)

MAJOR HONOURS

League Championship - (5)
1956, 1957, 1963, 1995, 1996.
Domestic Cup - (2) 1965, 1989.
European Cup-winners' Cup - (1) 1966.

APPEARANCES 95/96

	P	Ap	(s)	Gls
Patrik BERGER (TCH)	M	13	(12)	4
Stéphane CHAPUISAT (SUI)	A	16	(1)	3
Wolfgang DE BEER	G	1		
Thomas FRANCK	M	3	(2)	
Steffen FREUND	M	30		2
Jörg HEINRICH	M	17		2
Heiko HERRLICH	A	13	(3)	7
JÚLIO CÉSAR Silva (BRA)	D	23		2
Stefan KLOS	G	33		
Jürgen KOHLER	D	29		5
Martin KREE	D	15	(8)	
Günter KUTOWSKI	D	1	(2)	
Yahama MALLAM (GHA)	M		(1)	
Andreas MÖLLER	M	23		8
Lars MÜLLER	D		(5)	
Knut REINHARDT	M	16	(4)	
Stefan REUTER	M	26		6
Lars RICKEN	A	20	(6)	6
Karlheinz RIEDLE	A	14	(4)	7
Matthias SAMMER	D	22		3
Bodo SCHMIDT	D	9	(8)	
Harald SCHUMACHER	G		(1)	
Rubén SOSA (URU)	A	8	(9)	3
Ibrahim TANKO (GHA)	A	3		
René TRETSCHOK	M	8	(12)	2
Carsten WOLTERS	M	4	(6)	1
Michael ZORC	M	27	(3)	15

LEAGUE RESULTS 1995/96

Date	Opponent	H/A	Score	Scorers
11/08/95	1.FC Kaiserslautern	H	1-1	Herrlich
19/08/95	Bayer 04 Leverkusen	A	1-1	Möller (p)
29/08/95	FC Hansa Rostock	A	2-3	Sosa 2
01/09/95	Borussia Mönchengladbach	H	2-1	Reuter (p), Ricken
09/09/95	FC St. Pauli	A	3-0	Herrlich 2, Zorc
16/09/95	VfB Stuttgart	H	6-3	Júlio César, Sammer, Herrlich, Möller 2, Reuter (p)
22/09/95	Eintracht Frankfurt	A	4-3	Möller, Zorc, Herrlich, Ricken
01/10/95	FC Bayern München	H	3-1	Reuter (p), Sosa, Zorc
14/10/95	SV Werder Bremen	A	2-2	Möller, Berger
21/10/95	1.FC Köln	H	3-0	Kohler, Zorc, Herrlich
28/10/95	FC Schalke 04	A	2-1	Ricken, Zorc
04/11/95	Fortuna Düsseldorf	H	3-0	Wolters, Herrlich, Berger
10/11/95	Hamburger SV	A	2-2	Zorc, Möller
18/11/95	Karlsruher SC	H	4-1	Zorc, Kohler, Sammer, Riedle
25/11/95	KFC Uerdingen 05	A	2-0	Kohler, Zorc (p)
01/12/95	TSV 1860 München	H	3-1	Möller 2, Berger
09/12/95	SC Freiburg	A	1-0	Ricken
10/02/96	1.FC Kaiserslautern	A	1-1	Ricken
24/02/96	FC Hansa Rostock	H	1-2	Berger
02/03/96	Borussia Mönchengladbach	A	2-2	Riedle, Kohler
09/03/96	FC St. Pauli	H	1-0	Zorc
16/03/96	VfB Stuttgart	A	5-0	Riedle, Zorc, Chapuisat 2, Ricken
23/03/96	Eintracht Frankfurt	H	6-0	Riedle 2, Zorc, Freund, Heinrich, Chapuisat
30/03/96	FC Bayern München	A	0-1	
06/04/96	SV Werder Bremen	H	1-1	Tretschok
09/04/96	1.FC Köln	A	0-0	
13/04/96	FC Schalke 04	H	0-0	
20/04/96	Fortuna Düsseldorf	A	2-1	Freund, Sammer
27/04/96	Hamburger SV	H	1-1	Riedle
30/04/96	Karlsruher SC	A	0-5	
04/05/96	KFC Uerdingen 05	H	5-0	Kohler, Heinrich, Reuter 2, Zorc
07/05/96	Bayer 04 Leverkusen	H	2-0	Zorc, Júlio César
11/05/96	TSV 1860 München	A	2-2	Reuter, Zorc
18/05/96	SC Freiburg	H	3-2	Tretschok, Zorc, Riedle

BORUSSIA MÖNCHENGLADBACH

CLUB DIRECTORY

VfL 1900 Borussia Mönchengladbach
Bökelstrasse 165
41063 Mönchengladbach
tel - (02161) 92930
fax - (02161) 207778
Year of Formation - 1900
President - Karl-Heinz Drygalsky
Manager - Rolf Rüssmann
Coach - Bernd Krauss
Stadium - Bökelberg (34,500)

MAJOR HONOURS
League Championship - (5)
1970, 1971, 1975, 1976, 1977.
Domestic Cup - (3) 1960, 1973, 1995.
UEFA Cup - (2) 1975, 1979.

APPEARANCES 95/96

	P	Ap	(s)	Gls
Patrik ANDERSSON (SWE)	D	33		4
Martin DAHLIN (SWE)	A	23		15
Stefan EFFENBERG	M	31		7
Thomas EICHIN	D	3	(6)	
Michael FRONTZECK	M	2	(6)	
Markus HAUSWEILER	D	2	(1)	
Christian HOCHSTÄTTER	D	26		
Thomas HOERSEN	M	12	(7)	
Max HUIBERTS (HOL)	A	4	(6)	
Jörg KAESSMANN	G	5		
Uwe KAMPS	G	29		
Thomas KASTENMAIER	M	20	(4)	3
Marcel KETELAER	D		(1)	
Michael KLINKERT	D	27		1
Davor KRZNARIC (YUG)	M		(2)	
Jörg NEUN	D	31		
Peter NIELSEN (DEN)	M	12	(3)	
Jörgen PETTERSSON (SWE)	A	17	(5)	6
Karlheinz PFLIPSEN	M	18	(7)	4
Martin SCHNEIDER	M	21	(5)	
Stephan SCHULZ-WINGE	D		(1)	
Joachim STADLER	D	1	(5)	
Michael STERNKOPF	A	22	(10)	5
Dirk WOLF	D	4	(10)	
Peter WYNHOFF	M	31	(2)	5
Macchambes YOUNG MOUHONGA (CON)	M		(2)	

LEAGUE RESULTS 1995/96

Date	Opponent		Score	Scorers
13/08/95	SC Freiburg	H	1-0	Pflipsen
19/08/95	1.FC Kaiserslautern	A	3-1	Dahlin, Sternkopf, Wynhoff
29/08/95	Bayer 04 Leverkusen	H	0-0	
01/09/95	Borussia Dortmund	A	1-2	Dahlin
09/09/95	FC Hansa Rostock	A	3-2	Pflipsen, Dahlin 2
17/09/95	FC St. Pauli	H	2-4	Sternkopf, Dahlin
23/09/95	VfB Stuttgart	A	0-3	
01/10/95	Eintracht Frankfurt	H	4-1	Effenberg 2, Andersson, Dahlin
14/10/95	FC Bayern München	A	2-1	Effenberg, og (Herzog)
22/10/95	SV Werder Bremen	H	1-0	Effenberg
27/10/95	1.FC Köln	A	2-0	Pflipsen, Effenberg
05/11/95	FC Schalke 04	H	4-1	Dahlin 3, Pettersson
11/11/95	Fortuna Düsseldorf	A	2-3	Dahlin, og (Seeliger)
17/11/95	Hamburger SV	H	1-2	Dahlin
25/11/95	Karlsruher SC	A	0-4	
02/12/95	KFC Uerdingen 05	H	2-1	Meijer (p), Dahlin
09/12/95	TSV 1860 München	A	0-4	
09/02/96	SC Freiburg	A	0-0	
23/02/96	Bayer 04 Leverkusen	A	0-0	
02/03/96	Borussia Dortmund	H	2-2	Dahlin 2
10/03/96	FC Hansa Rostock	H	3-2	Effenberg, Pettersson, Kastenmaier (p)
16/03/96	FC St. Pauli	A	2-0	Kastenmaier, Effenberg
24/03/96	VfB Stuttgart	H	1-1	Pflipsen
30/03/96	Eintracht Frankfurt	A	2-0	Wynhoff, Pettersson
07/04/96	FC Bayern München	H	3-1	Pettersson 2, Wynhoff
10/04/96	SV Werder Bremen	A	0-2	
13/04/96	1.FC Köln	H	2-1	Wynhoff, Klinkert
16/04/96	1.FC Kaiserslautern	H	1-1	Dahlin
21/04/96	FC Schalke 04	A	3-3	Andersson, Sternkopf, Wynhoff
28/04/96	Fortuna Düsseldorf	H	1-1	Andersson
01/05/96	Hamburger SV	A	1-2	Andersson
04/05/96	Karlsruher SC	H	1-2	Pettersson
11/05/96	KFC Uerdingen 05	A	2-0	Sternkopf 2
18/05/96	TSV 1860 München	H	0-2	

EINTRACHT FRANKFURT

CLUB DIRECTORY

SG Eintracht Frankfurt
Sportplatz am Riederwald
Am Erlenbruch 25
60386 Frankfurt am Main
tel - (069) 4209700
fax - (069) 42097043
Year of Formation - 1899
President - Matthias Ohms
Manager - Bernd Hölzenbein
Coach - Karl-Heinz Körbel; Dragoslav Stepanovic
Stadium - Waldstadion (61,146)

MAJOR HONOURS
League Championship - (1) 1959.
Domestic Cup - (4)
1974, 1975, 1981, 1988.
UEFA Cup - (1) 1980.

APPEARANCES 95/96

	P	Ap	(s)	Gls
Michael ANICIC (YUG)	A	6	(6)	
Matthias BECKER	A	4	(19)	1
Rene BEUCHEL	D	7		
Uwe BINDEWALD	D	28	(1)	1
Manfred BINZ	D	25		4
Jörg BÖHNE	D	14	(4)	1
Rudi BOMMER	M	11		
Oliver BUNZENTHAL	M	8	(4)	
Mirko DICKHAUT	D	23	(5)	1
Thomas DOLL	A	9	(3)	2
Matthias DWORSCHAK	M	7	(1)	1
Johnny EKSTRÖM (SWE)	A	11	(5)	2
Ralf FALKENMAYER	M	10	(2)	
Thorsten FLICK	M		(2)	
Maurizio GAUDINO	M		(1)	
Matthias HAGNER	A	23	(3)	10
KAYMAN Burhanettin (TUR)	D	1	(1)	
Andreas KÖPKE	G	32		
Slobodan KOMLJENOVIC (YUG)	M	29	(2)	1
Ivica MORNAR (CRO)	A	16	(3)	1
Oka NIKOLOV	G	2	(2)	
Augustine OKOCHA (NIG)	M	23	(1)	7
Rainer RAUFFMANN	A	24	(2)	4
Dietmar ROTH	D	12	(5)	
Domenico SBORDONE	M	2	(5)	
Markus SCHUPP	M	29	(1)	4
Kakhaber TSKHADADZE (GEO)	D	2	(1)	
Ned ZELIC (AUS)	D	16	(1)	1

LEAGUE RESULTS 1995/96

Date	Opponent	H/A	Score	Scorers
12/08/95	Karlsruher SC	H	2-2	Rauffmann, Binz
19/08/95	KFC Uerdingen 05	A	1-1	Komljenovic
30/08/95	TSV 1860 München	H	4-2	Binz, Okocha, Böhme, Bindewald
02/09/95	SC Freiburg	A	0-2	
09/09/95	1.FC Kaiserslautern	H	3-1	Hagner, og (Kadlec), Okocha
16/09/95	Bayer 04 Leverkusen	A	0-2	
22/09/95	Borussia Dortmund	H	3-4	Schupp, Ekström, Rauffmann
01/10/95	Borussia Mönchengladbach	A	1-4	Hagner
14/10/95	FC St. Pauli	H	2-2	Okocha 2
21/10/95	VfB Stuttgart	A	2-3	Hagner, Mornar
28/10/95	FC Hansa Rostock	A	1-1	Okocha
04/11/95	FC Bayern München	H	4-1	Hagner 2, Binz 2
11/11/95	SV Werder Bremen	A	1-1	Hagner
18/11/95	1.FC Köln	H	1-0	Becker
25/11/95	FC Schalke 04	A	0-2	
02/12/95	Fortuna Düsseldorf	H	3-0	Schupp, Okocha, Hagner
08/12/95	Hamburger SV	A	1-5	Doll
10/02/96	Karlsruher SC	A	1-1	og (Ritter)
16/02/96	KFC Uerdingen 05	H	1-0	Rauffmann
24/02/96	TSV 1860 München	A	1-3	Hagner
02/03/96	SC Freiburg	H	0-1	
09/03/96	1.FC Kaiserslautern	A	1-1	Schupp
16/03/96	Bayer 04 Leverkusen	H	1-1	Doll (p)
23/03/96	Borussia Dortmund	A	0-6	
30/03/96	Borussia Mönchengladbach	H	0-2	
06/04/96	FC St. Pauli	A	1-2	Rauffmann
09/04/96	VfB Stuttgart	H	2-2	Ekström, Okocha
12/04/96	FC Hansa Rostock	H	1-3	Dickhaut
20/04/96	FC Bayern München	A	1-1	Hagner
27/04/96	SV Werder Bremen	H	1-0	Schupp
01/05/96	1.FC Köln	A	0-3	
04/05/96	FC Schalke 04	H	0-3	
11/05/96	Fortuna Düsseldorf	A	2-2	Dworschak, Zelic
18/05/96	Hamburger SV	H	1-4	Hagner

FORTUNA DÜSSELDORF

CLUB DIRECTORY

Fortuna Düsseldorf
Flinger Broich 87
40235 Düsseldorf
tel - (0211) 233059
fax - (0211) 232771
Year of Formation - 1895
President - Jürgen Hauswald
Secretary - Paul Jäger
Coach - Aleksandar Ristic
Stadium - Rheinstadion (55,850)

MAJOR HONOURS
League Championship - (1) 1933.
Domestic Cup - (2) 1979, 1980.

APPEARANCES 95/96

	P	Ap	(s)	Gls
Markus ANFANG	M	10	(1)	
Jörg BACH	D	25	(5)	3
Thomas BRDARIC	A	3	(7)	
Andrzej BUNCOL (POL)	M	19	(7)	2
Ryszard CYRON (POL)	A	20	(9)	9
Darko DRAZIC (CRO)	D	20		3
Vlatko GLAVAS (BOS)	M	24	(1)	2
Dennis IBRAHIM	D		(3)	
Rudi ISTENIC	M	6	(9)	
Thorsten JUDT	M	11	(6)	3
Harald KATEMANN	M	23	(1)	2
Georg KOCH	G	34		
Ben MANGA (SEN)	M	3		
Ulf MEHLHORN	M	27	(3)	
Frank MILL	A	19	(9)	2
Stefan MINKWITZ	M	5	(5)	
Darko PANCEV (MAC)	A	9	(5)	2
Zvezdan PEJOVIC (CRO)	D	4	(3)	
Jörn SCHWINKENDORF	D	11	(7)	
Thomas SEELIGER	M	28		4
Kujtim SHALA (CRO)	M	8	(7)	
Raffael TONELLO (ITA)	A	3	(7)	3
Karl WERNER	D	33		1
Andre WINKHOLD	M	29		3

LEAGUE RESULTS 1995/96

11/08/95	SV Werder Bremen	A	1-1	Cyron
20/08/95	1.FC Köln	H	1-1	Mill
30/08/95	FC Schalke 04	A	1-1	Mill
03/09/95	FC Hansa Rostock	H	2-2	Winkhold, Pancev
09/09/95	Hamburger SV	H	2-2	Seeliger, Cyron
15/09/95	Karlsruher SC	A	1-3	Drazic
22/09/95	KFC Uerdingen 05	H	1-0	Seeliger
30/09/95	TSV 1860 München	A	1-2	Drazic
14/10/95	SC Freiburg	H	0-0	
21/10/95	1.FC Kaiserslautern	A	0-2	
28/10/95	Bayer 04 Leverkusen	H	1-1	Buncol
04/11/95	Borussia Dortmund	A	0-3	
11/11/95	Borussia Mönchengladbach	H	3-2	Buncol, Winkhold 2
17/11/95	FC St. Pauli	A	1-2	Drazic
24/11/95	VfB Stuttgart	H	1-2	Katemann
02/12/95	Eintracht Frankfurt	A	0-3	
09/12/95	FC Bayern München	H	0-2	
14/02/96	1.FC Köln	A	0-0	
24/02/96	FC Schalke 04	H	2-0	Pancev, Seeliger
03/03/96	FC Hansa Rostock	A	0-0	
08/03/96	Hamburger SV	A	1-4	Tonello
12/03/96	SV Werder Bremen	H	1-1	Cyron
17/03/96	Karlsruher SC	H	2-0	Bach 2
23/03/96	KFC Uerdingen 05	A	3-1	Tonello, Seeliger, Glavas (p)
31/03/96	TSV 1860 München	H	1-1	Tonello
06/04/96	SC Freiburg	A	1-1	Cyron
10/04/96	1.FC Kaiserslautern	H	2-1	Werner (p), og (Brehme)
14/04/96	Bayer 04 Leverkusen	A	0-0	
20/04/96	Borussia Dortmund	H	1-2	Bach
28/04/96	Borussia Mönchengladbach	A	1-1	Cyron
01/05/96	FC St. Pauli	H	2-0	Cyron, Katemann
04/05/96	VfB Stuttgart	A	3-2	Cyron 2, Judt
11/05/96	Eintracht Frankfurt	H	2-2	Glavas, Judt
18/05/96	FC Bayern München	A	2-2	Judt, Cyron

SC FREIBURG

CLUB DIRECTORY

Sport-Club Freiburg
Schwarzwaldstrasse 193
79117 Freiburg
tel - (0761) 36261
fax - (0761) 23758
Year of Formation - 1904
President - Achim Stocker
Secretary - Bernd Ziegelbauer
Coach - Volker Finke
Stadium - Dreisamstadion (22,500)

APPEARANCES 95/96

	P	Ap	(s)	Gls
Stefan BENEKING	G		(2)	
Andreas BORNEMANN	M	2	(1)	
Alexander BORODYUK (RUS)	M	1	(2)	
Damir BURIC (CRO)	D	4	(11)	
Harry DECHEIVER (HOL)	A	22		11
Oliver FREUND	M	24	(3)	
Maximilian HEIDENREICH	M	26	(2)	
Jörg HEINRICH	M	8		
Nikola JURCEVIC (CRO)	M	18	(4)	2
Ralf KOHL	M	26	(3)	
Steffen KORELL	M	6	(9)	1
Stefan MÜLLER	D	12	(3)	
Karsten NEITZEL	M	4	(6)	
Thomas RATH	M	5	(12)	1
Altin RRAKLI (ALB)	A	5	(6)	
Jörg SCHMADTKE	G	34		
Paschalis SERETIS (GRE)	A	2	(6)	1
Martin SPANRING	D	32		1
Uwe SPIES	A	9	(1)	2
Axel SUNDERMANN	D	24	(3)	1
Alain SUTTER (SUI)	M	25		1
Jens TODT	M	29		4
Thomas VOGEL	D	16		
Uwe WASSMER	A	6	(12)	3
Andreas ZEYER	M	34		2

LEAGUE RESULTS 1995/96

13/08/95	Borussia Mönchengladbach	A	0-1	
19/08/95	FC St. Pauli	H	0-2	
30/08/95	VfB Stuttgart	A	1-3	Sundermann
02/09/95	Eintracht Frankfurt	H	2-0	Todt, Spies
09/09/95	FC Bayern München	A	0-2	
16/09/95	SV Werder Bremen	H	0-1	
23/09/95	1.FC Köln	A	1-1	Wassmer
30/09/95	FC Schalke 04	H	1-2	Spies
14/10/95	Fortuna Düsseldorf	A	0-0	
21/10/95	Hamburger SV	H	0-3	
27/10/95	Karlsruher SC	A	1-1	Zeyer
04/11/95	KFC Uerdingen 05	H	1-1	Sutter
11/11/95	TSV 1860 München	A	0-3	
18/11/95	FC Hansa Rostock	H	2-1	Jurcevic, Decheiver
25/11/95	1.FC Kaiserslautern	A	2-1	Spanring, Korell
01/12/95	Bayer 04 Leverkusen	A	1-0	Decheiver
09/12/95	Borussia Dortmund	H	0-1	
09/02/96	Borussia Mönchengladbach	H	0-0	
24/02/96	VfB Stuttgart	H	2-1	Todt, Decheiver
02/03/96	Eintracht Frankfurt	A	1-0	Rath
05/03/96	FC St. Pauli	A	1-1	Wassmer
09/03/96	FC Bayern München	H	3-1	Decheiver 2, Todt
15/03/96	SV Werder Bremen	A	2-0	Decheiver 2
23/03/96	1.FC Köln	H	2-0	Decheiver (p), Wassmer
30/03/96	FC Schalke 04	A	0-3	
06/04/96	Fortuna Düsseldorf	H	1-1	Decheiver
10/04/96	Hamburger SV	A	0-0	
13/04/96	Karlsruher SC	H	0-3	
19/04/96	KFC Uerdingen 05	A	1-3	Todt
27/04/96	TSV 1860 München	H	1-0	Decheiver
30/04/96	FC Hansa Rostock	A	0-1	
04/05/96	1.FC Kaiserslautern	H	0-0	
11/05/96	Bayer 04 Leverkusen	H	2-1	Jurcevic, Zeyer
18/05/96	Borussia Dortmund	A	2-3	Decheiver, Seretis

HAMBURGER SV

CLUB DIRECTORY

Hamburger Sport-Verein
Rothenbaumchaussee 125
20149 Hamburg
tel - (040) 4155-0
fax - (040) 4155109
Year of Formation - 1887
President - Uwe Seeler
Secretary - Hans Barske
Coach - Benno Möhlmann; Felix Magath
Stadium - Volksparkstadion (61,234)

MAJOR HONOURS
League Championship - (6)
1923, 1928, 1960, 1979, 1982, 1983.
Domestic Cup - (3) 1963, 1976, 1987.
European Champions' Cup - (1) 1983.
European Cup-winners' Cup - (1) 1977.

APPEARANCES 95/96

	P	Ap	(s)	Gls
Jörg ALBERTZ	M	34		9
Karsten BÄRON	A	18	(1)	7
André BREITENREITER	A	14	(11)	3
Christian CLAASSEN	A		(5)	
Francisco COPADO (ESP)	A	8	(2)	
Andreas FISCHER	M	29	(2)	4
Richard GOLZ	G	33		
Jürgen HARTMANN	M	31	(1)	1
Stéphane HENCHOZ (SUI)	D	31		2
Holger HIEMANN	G	1	(2)	
Bernd HOLLERBACH	M	14		
Petar HUBCHEV (BUL)	D	19	(4)	
Valdas IVANAUSKAS (LIT)	A	14	(3)	3
Uwe JÄHNIG	M	9	(4)	2
Niklas KINDVALL (SWE)	A		(3)	
Sven KMETSCH	M	26		
Carsten KOBER	D	2	(4)	
Marijan KOVACEVIC (CRO)	M	7	(10)	1
Yordan LECHKOV (BUL)	M	7	(2)	
Oliver LÜTTKENHAUS	D		(1)	
Michael MASON	A	3	(3)	
Frank ORDENEWITZ	A	2	(4)	1
Elard OSTERMANN	D	4	(5)	
Marko RIEGEL	M	3	(3)	
Matthias ROSE	D	3	(1)	
Hasan SALIHAMIDZIC (BOS)	A	7	(2)	2
Stefan SCHNOOR	D	19	(4)	2
Harald SPÖRL	M	31	(1)	14
Daniel STENDEL	M	5	(2)	
Marco WEISSHAUPT	M		(4)	
Dirk WOJEWSKY	A		(1)	

LEAGUE RESULTS 1995/96

Date	Opponent	H/A	Score	Scorers
12/08/95	FC Bayern München	A	2-3	Spörl, Fischer
18/08/95	SV Werder Bremen	H	3-3	Breitenreiter 2, Spörl
29/08/95	1.FC Köln	A	2-3	Henchoz, Albertz
02/09/95	FC Schalke 04	H	1-1	Ordenewitz
09/09/95	Fortuna Düsseldorf	A	2-2	Fischer, Albertz
17/09/95	FC Hansa Rostock	H	1-1	Albertz
23/09/95	Karlsruher SC	H	0-0	
29/09/95	KFC Uerdingen 05	A	1-1	Henchoz
14/10/95	TSV 1860 München	H	2-2	Hartmann, Albertz
21/10/95	SC Freiburg	A	3-0	Albertz 2, Spörl
28/10/95	1.FC Kaiserslautern	H	1-0	og (Wagner)
03/11/95	Bayer 04 Leverkusen	A	1-0	Ivanauskas
10/11/95	Borussia Dortmund	H	2-2	Fischer, Spörl
17/11/95	Borussia Mönchengladbach	A	2-1	Spörl 2
24/11/95	FC St. Pauli	H	1-0	Spörl (p)
02/12/95	VfB Stuttgart	A	0-3	
08/12/95	Eintracht Frankfurt	H	5-1	Ivanauskas, Bäron 2, Spörl, Kovacevic
11/02/96	FC Bayern München	H	2-1	Breitenreiter, Jähnig
02/03/96	FC Schalke 04	A	0-3	
05/03/96	SV Werder Bremen	A	1-2	Spörl
08/03/96	Fortuna Düsseldorf	H	4-1	Ivanauskas, Jähnig, Bäron, Albertz (p)
19/03/96	1.FC Köln	H	0-0	
22/03/96	Karlsruher SC	A	1-3	Spörl (p)
29/03/96	KFC Uerdingen 05	H	0-0	
06/04/96	TSV 1860 München	A	0-5	
10/04/96	SC Freiburg	H	0-0	
13/04/96	1.FC Kaiserslautern	A	2-1	Albertz, Spörl
17/04/96	FC Hansa Rostock	A	0-2	
24/04/96	Bayer 04 Leverkusen	H	2-2	Albertz, Spörl (p)
27/04/96	Borussia Dortmund	A	1-1	Spörl (p)
01/05/96	Borussia Mönchengladbach	H	2-1	Bäron, Schnoor
04/05/96	FC St. Pauli	A	1-1	Schnoor
11/05/96	VfB Stuttgart	H	3-0	Bäron, Fischer, Spörl
18/05/96	Eintracht Frankfurt	A	4-1	Bäron 2, Salihamidzic 2

FC HANSA ROSTOCK

CLUB DIRECTORY

FC Hansa Rostock
Kopernikusstrasse 17a
18057 Rostock
tel - (0381) 455517
fax - (0381) 455525
Year of Formation - 1965
President - Dr. Peter-Michael Diestel
Secretary - Dr. Helmut Hergesell
Coach - Frank Pagelsdorf
Stadium - Ostseestadion (25,600)

MAJOR HONOURS
League Championship (GDR) - (1) 1991.
Domestic Cup (GDR) - (1) 1991.

APPEARANCES 95/96

	P	Ap	(s)	Gls
Jonathan AKPOBORIE (NIG)	A	16		6
Steffen BAUMGART	A	26	(6)	10
Stefan BEINLICH	M	34		11
Christian BEECK	D	10	(4)	
Perry BRÄUTIGAM	G	34		
Matthias BREITKREUTZ	M	11	(7)	2
Slawomir CHALASKIEWICZ (POL)	A	7	(11)	1
Uwe EHLERS	D	4	(9)	
Martin GROTH	M	19	(5)	
André HOFSCHNEIDER	D	14	(1)	
Carsten KLEE	A	7	(7)	2
Timo LANGE	M	16	(5)	1
Heiko MÄRZ	D	28	(1)	
Goran MARKOV (MAC)	A	1	(6)	
Toni MICEVSKI (MAC)	A	3	(2)	1
Rocco MILDE	A	6	(10)	1
Dirk REHBEIN	M	11	(13)	
René SCHNEIDER	D	31		6
Stefan STUDER	M	32		1
Hilmar WEILANDT	M	34		3
Mike WERNER	D	1		
Marco ZALLMANN	D	29		1

LEAGUE RESULTS 1995/96

12/08/95	Bayer 04 Leverkusen	H	1-2	Baumgart
18/08/95	FC Schalke 04	A	3-1	Milde, Baumgart, Klee
29/08/95	Borussia Dortmund	H	3-2	Beinlich 2, Chalaszkiewicz
03/09/95	Fortuna Düsseldorf	A	2-2	Baumgart, Lange
09/09/95	Borussia Mönchengladbach	H	2-3	Baumgart, Breitkreutz
17/09/95	Hamburger SV	A	1-1	Baumgart
23/09/95	FC St. Pauli	H	2-0	Beinlich, Baumgart
30/09/95	Karlsruher SC	A	2-0	Baumgart, Beinlich
13/10/95	VfB Stuttgart	H	3-3	Weilandt, Schneider, og (Berthold)
20/10/95	KFC Uerdingen 05	A	1-1	Baumgart
28/10/95	Eintracht Frankfurt	H	1-1	Klee
04/11/95	TSV 1860 München	A	1-1	Studer
10/11/95	FC Bayern München	H	0-0	
18/11/95	SC Freiburg	A	1-2	Beinlich
25/11/95	SV Werder Bremen	A	2-0	Beinlich (p), Weilandt
02/12/95	1.FC Kaiserslautern	H	3-0	Weilandt, Schneider 2
10/12/95	1.FC Köln	A	0-3	
24/02/96	Borussia Dortmund	A	2-1	Baumgart, Akpoborie
03/03/96	Fortuna Düsseldorf	H	0-0	
10/03/96	Borussia Mönchengladbach	A	2-3	Beinlich (p), Micevski
19/03/96	Bayer 04 Leverkusen	A	0-2	
24/03/96	FC St. Pauli	A	2-3	Beinlich, Breitkreutz
30/03/96	Karlsruher SC	H	1-1	Beinlich (p)
04/04/96	VfB Stuttgart	A	1-1	Akpoborie
09/04/96	KFC Uerdingen 05	H	1-0	Beinlich (p)
12/04/96	Eintracht Frankfurt	A	3-1	Akpoborie, Zallmann, Schneider
17/04/96	Hamburger SV	H	2-0	Akpoborie, Beinlich
20/04/96	TSV 1860 München	H	0-3	
27/04/96	FC Bayern München	A	1-0	Akpoborie
30/04/96	SC Freiburg	H	1-0	Schneider
04/05/96	SV Werder Bremen	H	2-1	Baumgart, Akpoborie
07/05/96	FC Schalke 04	H	1-2	Schneider
11/05/96	1.FC Kaiserslautern	A	0-2	
18/05/96	1.FC Köln	H	0-1	

1.FC KAISERSLAUTERN

CLUB DIRECTORY

1.FC Kaiserslautern
Fritz-Walter-Stadion
67653 Kaiserslautern
tel - (0631) 31880
fax - (0631) 3188290
Year of Formation - 1900
President - Norbert Thines
Manager - Ignaz Good
Coach - Friedel Rausch; Eckhard Krautzun
(96/97 - Otto Rehhagel)
Stadium - Fritz-Walter-Stadion Betzenberg
(38,500)
League Championship - (3) 1951, 1953, 1991.
Domestic Cup - (2) 1990, 1996.

APPEARANCES 95/96

	P	Ap	(s)	Gls
Dirk ANDERS	M	2	(4)	
Gilberto ARILSON (BRA)	M	9	(1)	
Andreas BREHME	M	30		2
Christoph DENGEL	D	1	(1)	
Gerald EHRMANN	G	1		
Dirk FLOCK	M	5	(11)	
Frank GREINER	M	19	(2)	
Matthias HAMANN	D	2	(6)	
Thomas HENGEN	M	19	(6)	4
Bernd HOLLERBACH	M	7	(3)	
Miroslav KADLEC (TCH)	D	31		1
Mario KERN	D	2	(2)	
Harry KOCH	D	27	(3)	1
Pavel KUKA (TCH)	A	29	(1)	10
Roger LUTZ	D	10	(5)	
Olaf MARSCHALL	A	11	(8)	2
Andreas REINKE	G	29		
Thomas RIEDL	M	7	(6)	
Jürgen RISCHE	A	11	(6)	1
Thomas RITTER	D	3	(1)	
Axel ROOS	D	22	(2)	
Oliver SCHÄFER	D	22	(9)	
Marc SCHWARZER (AUS)	G	4		
Horst SIEGL (TCH)	A	10	(3)	
Martin WAGNER	M	24	(3)	6
Uwe WEGMANN	A	15	(11)	2
Claus-Dieter WOLLITZ	M	22	(4)	2

LEAGUE RESULTS 1995/96

11/08/95	Borussia Dortmund	A	1-1	Wagner
19/08/95	Borussia Mönchengladbach	H	1-3	Kadlec
29/08/95	FC St. Pauli	A	2-1	Kuka 2
02/09/95	VfB Stuttgart	H	1-1	Brehme (p)
09/09/95	Eintracht Frankfurt	A	1-3	Hengen
16/09/95	FC Bayern München	H	2-3	Brehme (p), Hengen
23/09/95	SV Werder Bremen	A	1-1	Hollerbach
30/09/95	1.FC Köln	H	1-1	Hengen
13/10/95	FC Schalke 04	A	1-1	Marschall
21/10/95	Fortuna Düsseldorf	H	2-0	Wagner, Wollitz
28/10/95	Hamburger SV	A	0-1	
04/11/95	Karlsruher SC	H	2-2	Kuka, Wollitz (p)
10/11/95	KFC Uerdingen 05	A	1-1	Wagner
18/11/95	TSV 1860 München	H	0-0	
25/11/95	SC Freiburg	H	1-2	Kuka
02/12/95	FC Hansa Rostock	A	0-3	
09/12/95	Bayer 04 Leverkusen	H	1-0	Rische
10/02/96	Borussia Dortmund	H	1-1	Kuka
23/02/96	FC St. Pauli	H	0-0	
02/03/96	VfB Stuttgart	A	0-2	
09/03/96	Eintracht Frankfurt	H	1-1	Wagner
12/03/96	FC Bayern München	A	0-2	
19/03/96	SV Werder Bremen	H	0-0	
29/03/96	1.FC Köln	A	1-0	Wagner
04/04/96	FC Schalke 04	H	0-0	
10/04/96	Fortuna Düsseldorf	A	1-2	Kuka
13/04/96	Hamburger SV	H	1-2	Hengen
16/04/96	Borussia Mönchengladbach	A	1-1	Wegmann
19/04/96	Karlsruher SC	A	0-0	
26/04/96	KFC Uerdingen 05	H	3-0	Kuka, Koch, Wegmann
04/05/96	SC Freiburg	A	0-0	
07/05/96	TSV 1860 München	A	1-1	Marschall
11/05/96	FC Hansa Rostock	H	2-0	Kuka 2 (1p)
18/05/96	Bayer 04 Leverkusen	A	1-1	Kuka

KARLSRUHER SC

CLUB DIRECTORY

Karlsruher Sport-Club
Adenauerring 17
76131 Karlsruhe
tel - (0721) 661091
fax - (0721) 661000
Year of Formation - 1894
President - Roland Schmider
Manager - Dieter Meinhold
Coach - Winfried Schäfer
Stadium - Wildparkstadion (33,000)

MAJOR HONOURS
League Championship - (1) 1909.
Domestic Cup - (2) 1955, 1956.

APPEARANCES 95/96

	P	Ap	(s)	Gls
Markus BÄHR	M	5	(7)	1
Manfred BENDER	M	27		7
Slaven BILIC (CRO)	D	11	(1)	
Eberhard CARL	A	5	(8)	
Sean DUNDEE (SAF)	A	24	(8)	16
Thorsten FINK	M	29		1
Thomas HÄSSLER	M	34		8
Sergei KIRYAKOV (RUS)	A	22	(7)	4
Adrian KNUP (SUI)	A	11	(12)	5
Raphael KRAUSS	D		(2)	
Gunther METZ	D	27	(3)	1
Jens NOWOTNY	D	24		1
Burkhard REICH	D	32	(1)	2
Claus REITMAIER	G	34		
Thomas RITTER	D	11		
Edgar SCHMITT	A	8	(16)	1
Markus SCHROTH	A		(4)	1
Dirk SCHUSTER	D	31		1
Michael TARNAT	M	27	(3)	2
Michael WITTWER	D	10	(12)	
Christian WÜCK	A	2	(1)	

LEAGUE RESULTS 1995/96

12/08/95	Eintracht Frankfurt	A	2-2	Schuster, Knup
19/08/95	FC Bayern München	H	2-6	Knup 2
29/08/95	SV Werder Bremen	A	0-1	
01/09/95	1.FC Köln	H	1-0	Hässler
10/09/95	FC Schalke 04	A	1-2	Hässler
15/09/95	Fortuna Düsseldorf	H	3-1	Bender 2, Schmitt
23/09/95	Hamburger SV	A	0-0	
30/09/95	FC Hansa Rostock	H	0-2	
14/10/95	KFC Uerdingen 05	H	2-0	Dundee 2
21/10/95	TSV 1860 München	A	1-1	Dundee
27/10/95	SC Freiburg	H	1-1	Dundee
04/11/95	1.FC Kaiserslautern	A	2-2	Dundee, Knup
11/11/95	Bayer 04 Leverkusen	H	1-4	Nowotny
18/11/95	Borussia Dortmund	A	1-4	Bender
25/11/95	Borussia Mönchengladbach	H	4-0	Bähr, Dundee 2, og (Klinkert)
02/12/95	FC St. Pauli	A	1-1	Kiryakov
09/12/95	VfB Stuttgart	H	1-2	Hässler (p)
10/02/96	Eintracht Frankfurt	H	1-1	og (Dickhaut)
17/02/96	FC Bayern München	A	4-1	Dundee 2, Bender 2
24/02/96	SV Werder Bremen	H	1-1	Metz
02/03/96	1.FC Köln	A	1-0	Kiryakov
09/03/96	FC Schalke 04	H	0-1	
17/03/96	Fortuna Düsseldorf	A	0-2	
22/03/96	Hamburger SV	H	3-1	Hässler (p), Dundee, Fink
30/03/96	FC Hansa Rostock	A	1-1	Knup
04/04/96	KFC Uerdingen 05	A	3-2	Reich, Hässler, Dundee
09/04/96	TSV 1860 München	H	1-1	Bender
13/04/96	SC Freiburg	A	3-0	Hässler, Reich, Schroth
19/04/96	1.FC Kaiserslautern	H	0-0	
27/04/96	Bayer 04 Leverkusen	A	2-1	Bender, Tarnat
30/04/96	Borussia Dortmund	H	5-0	Hässler (p), Kiryakov 2, Dundee, Tarnat
04/05/96	Borussia Mönchengladbach	A	2-1	Dundee 2
11/05/96	FC St. Pauli	H	2-2	Dundee, Hässler (p)
18/05/96	VfB Stuttgart	A	1-3	Dundee

1.FC KÖLN

CLUB DIRECTORY

1.FC Köln
Postfach 42 02 51
50896 Köln
tel - (0221) 9436430
fax - (0221) 4301851
Year of Formation - 1948
President - Klaus Hartmann
Manager - Bernd Cullmann
Coach - Morten Olsen; Stefan Engels; Peter Neururer
Stadium - Müngersdorfer Stadion (54,000)

MAJOR HONOURS
League Championship - (3) 1962, 1964, 1978.
Domestic Cup - (4) 1968, 1977, 1978, 1983.

APPEARANCES 95/96

	P	Ap	(s)	Gls
Henrik ANDERSEN (DEN)	M	5	(6)	
Karsten BAUMANN	D	27		1
Dietmar BEIERSDORFER	D	16		1
Martin BRAUN	D	14	(6)	
Thomas CICHON	M	12	(5)	
Christian DOLLBERG (ARG)	D	10	(1)	
Janosz DZIWIOR	M	18	(2)	1
Holger GAISSMAYER	A	8	(15)	4
Bjarne GOLDBAEK (DEN)	M	7	(9)	2
Ralf HAUPTMANN	D	25		1
Bodo ILLGNER	G	34		
Olaf JANSSEN	M	18	(3)	2
Stefan KOHN	A	20	(10)	4
Bruno LABBADIA	A	8		1
Dorinel MUNTEANU (ROM)	M	33		4
Sunday OLISEH (NIG)	M	24		
Toni POLSTER (AUT)	A	25	(3)	11
Michael RÖSELE	A		(7)	
Rico STEINMANN	M	11	(6)	
Reinhard STUMPF	D	11	(2)	
Pablo THIAM (GUI)	D	19	(4)	
Patrick WEISER	D	11	(1)	
Christian WOLSKI	M	3	(3)	
Thomas ZDEBEL	M	15	(8)	

LEAGUE RESULTS 1995/96

Date	Opponent		Score	Scorers
12/08/95	FC Schalke 04	H	0-1	
20/08/95	Fortuna Düsseldorf	A	1-1	Janssen
29/08/95	Hamburger SV	H	3-2	Polster 2, Labbadia
01/09/95	Karlsruher SC	A	0-1	
08/09/95	KFC Uerdingen 05	H	0-0	
16/09/95	TSV 1860 München	A	1-2	Baumann
23/09/95	SC Freiburg	H	1-1	Polster (p)
30/09/95	1.FC Kaiserslautern	A	1-1	Polster
15/10/95	Bayer 04 Leverkusen	H	2-2	Munteanu, Gaissmayer
21/10/95	Borussia Dortmund	A	0-3	
27/10/95	Borussia Mönchengladbach	H	0-2	
03/11/95	FC St. Pauli	A	3-3	Polster, Munteanu, Dziwior
11/11/95	VfB Stuttgart	H	2-2	Gaissmayer, Goldbaek
18/11/95	Eintracht Frankfurt	A	0-1	
26/11/95	FC Bayern München	H	0-0	
01/12/95	SV Werder Bremen	A	1-0	Kohn
10/12/95	FC Hansa Rostock	H	3-0	Kohn, Polster 2
14/02/96	Fortuna Düsseldorf	H	0-0	
02/03/96	Karlsruher SC	H	0-1	
05/03/96	FC Schalke 04	A	0-0	
09/03/96	KFC Uerdingen 05	A	1-1	Polster (p)
15/03/96	TSV 1860 München	H	2-0	Kohn, Goldbaek
19/03/96	Hamburger SV	A	0-0	
23/03/96	SC Freiburg	A	0-2	
29/03/96	1.FC Kaiserslautern	H	0-1	
06/04/96	Bayer 04 Leverkusen	A	2-1	Beiersdorfer, Polster
09/04/96	Borussia Dortmund	H	0-0	
13/04/96	Borussia Mönchengladbach	A	1-2	Janssen
20/04/96	FC St. Pauli	H	1-0	Gaissmayer
27/04/96	VfB Stuttgart	A	1-0	Polster
01/05/96	Eintracht Frankfurt	H	3-0	Kohn, Munteanu 2 (1p)
04/05/96	FC Bayern München	A	2-3	og (Matthäus), Polster (p)
11/05/96	SV Werder Bremen	H	1-2	Hauptmann
18/05/96	FC Hansa Rostock	A	1-0	Gaissmayer

TSV 1860 MÜNCHEN

CLUB DIRECTORY

TSV 1860 München
Grünwalder Strasse 114
81547 München
tel - (089) 64278560
fax - (089) 64278580
Year of Formation - 1860
President - Karl-Heinz Wildmoser
Secretary - Sven Jäger
Coach - Werner Lorant
Stadium - Olympiastadion (64,000)

MAJOR HONOURS
League Championship - (1) 1966.
Domestic Cup - (2) 1942, 1964.

APPEARANCES 95/96

	P	Ap	(s)	Gls
Rainer BERG	G	1	(1)	
Olaf BODDEN	A	24	(7)	14
Daniel BORIMIROV (BUL)	A	14	(11)	7
Elvis BRAJKOVIC (CRO)	D	8	(1)	
Harald CERNY (AUT)	M	12	(4)	2
Jens DOWE	M	14	(5)	
Holger GREILICH	D	19	(6)	1
Matthias HAMANN	D	13	(1)	
Horst HELDT	M	18	(10)	3
Jens JEREMIES	D	29		
Jens KELLER	M		(1)	
Alexander KUTSCHERA	D	10	(10)	
Marek LESNIAK (POL)	A	9	(5)	2
Bernd MEIER	G	33		
Thomas MILLER	D	26	(2)	
Piotr NOWAK (POL)	M	27		7
Rene RYDLEWICZ	M	19	(9)	
Thomas SCHMIDT	D	1	(1)	
Manfred SCHWABL	M	28		
Miroslav STEVIC (YUG)	M	14	(6)	2
Bernhard TRARES	D	32		4
Bernhard WINKLER	A	23	(1)	10

LEAGUE RESULTS 1995/96

12/08/95	FC St. Pauli	A	2-4	Borimirov 2
19/08/95	VfB Stuttgart	H	1-1	Borimirov
30/08/95	Eintracht Frankfurt	A	2-4	Borimirov (p), Lesniak
02/09/95	FC Bayern München	H	0-2	
08/09/95	SV Werder Bremen	A	0-2	
16/09/95	1.FC Köln	H	2-1	Winkler, Nowak
24/09/95	FC Schalke 04	A	1-1	Trares
30/09/95	Fortuna Düsseldorf	H	2-1	Winkler (p), Bodden
14/10/95	Hamburger SV	A	2-2	Bodden, Borimirov
21/10/95	Karlsruher SC	H	1-1	Borimirov
29/10/95	KFC Uerdingen 05	A	0-2	
04/11/95	FC Hansa Rostock	H	1-1	Bodden
11/11/95	SC Freiburg	H	3-0	Nowak, Stevic, Bodden
18/11/95	1.FC Kaiserslautern	A	0-0	
25/11/95	Bayer 04 Leverkusen	H	0-1	
01/12/95	Borussia Dortmund	A	1-3	Winkler
09/12/95	Borussia Mönchengladbach	H	4-0	Lesniak, Bodden, Winkler, Greilich
10/02/96	FC St. Pauli	H	2-0	Winkler (p), Nowak
17/02/96	VfB Stuttgart	A	3-2	Winkler, Bodden, Nowak
24/02/96	Eintracht Frankfurt	H	3-1	Trares 2, Cerny
02/03/96	FC Bayern München	A	2-4	Bodden, Winkler
09/03/96	SV Werder Bremen	H	1-1	Winkler (p)
15/03/96	1.FC Köln	A	0-2	
22/03/96	FC Schalke 04	H	1-1	Winkler
31/03/96	Fortuna Düsseldorf	A	1-1	Winkler
06/04/96	Hamburger SV	H	5-0	Heldt 2, Borimirov, Trares, Cerny
09/04/96	Karlsruher SC	A	1-1	Heldt
12/04/96	KFC Uerdingen 05	H	2-1	Bodden 2
20/04/96	FC Hansa Rostock	A	3-0	Bodden, Nowak 2
27/04/96	SC Freiburg	A	0-1	
04/05/96	Bayer 04 Leverkusen	A	1-2	Bodden
07/05/96	1.FC Kaiserslautern	H	1-1	Bodden
11/05/96	Borussia Dortmund	H	2-2	Bodden 2
18/05/96	Borussia Mönchengladbach	A	2-0	Nowak, Stevic

FC ST. PAULI

CLUB DIRECTORY

FC Sankt Pauli
Auf dem Heiligengeistfeld
20359 Hamburg
tel - (040) 3193103
fax - (040) 3191870
Year of Formation - 1910
President - Heinz Weisener
Manager - Helmut Schulte
Coach - Uli Maslo
Stadium - Wilhelm-Koch-Stadion (20,551)

APPEARANCES 95/96

	P	Ap	(s)	Gls
Ralf BECKER	M	8	(7)	1
Frank BÖSE	G		(1)	
Paul CALIGIURI (USA)	M	10	(5)	
Dirk DAMMANN	D	34		2
Michel DINZEY	M	29	(1)	
Martin DRILLER	A	22	(4)	6
Torsten FRÖHLING	D	1		
Jürgen GRONAU	M	11	(5)	1
Stefan HANKE	M	24	(6)	1
Leonardo MANZI (BRA)	D		(1)	
Tore PEDERSEN (NOR)	D	12		
Carsten PRÖPPER	M	31		5
Yuri SAVICHEV (RUS)	A	19	(1)	6
Jens SCHARPING	A	11	(13)	6
Dieter SCHLINDWEIN	D	6	(2)	
Oliver SCHWEISSING	M	9	(9)	1
Thomas SOBOTZIK	A	32	(1)	6
Christian SPRINGER	M	18	(9)	2
Holger STANISLAWSKI	M	15	(7)	2
Kay STISI	A	1	(6)	1
Dariusz SZUBERT (POL)	M	12	(11)	
Klaus THOMFORDE	G	34		
André TRULSEN	D	32		3
Hysen ZMIJANI (ALB)	D	3	(4)	

LEAGUE RESULTS 1995/96

Date	Opponent		Score	Scorers
12/08/95	TSV 1860 München	H	4-2	Pröpper, Scharping (p), Dammann, Savichev
19/08/95	SC Freiburg	A	2-0	Sobotzik, Scharping
29/08/95	1.FC Kaiserslautern	H	1-2	Savichev
02/09/95	Bayer 04 Leverkusen	A	1-1	Pröpper (p)
09/09/95	Borussia Dortmund	H	0-3	
17/09/95	Borussia Mönchengladbach	A	4-2	Savichev 2, Scharping, Becker
23/09/95	FC Hansa Rostock	A	0-2	
29/09/95	VfB Stuttgart	H	1-3	Driller
14/10/95	Eintracht Frankfurt	A	2-2	Savichev 2
21/10/95	FC Bayern München	H	0-1	
28/10/95	SV Werder Bremen	A	1-1	Hanke
03/11/95	1.FC Köln	H	3-3	Scharping (p), Pröpper, Trulsen
11/11/95	FC Schalke 04	A	0-2	
17/11/95	Fortuna Düsseldorf	H	2-1	Sobotzik, Driller
24/11/95	Hamburger SV	A	0-1	
02/12/95	Karlsruher SC	H	1-1	Driller
08/12/95	KFC Uerdingen 05	A	5-2	Trulsen, Sobotzik 3, Scharping
10/02/96	TSV 1860 München	A	0-2	
23/02/96	1.FC Kaiserslautern	A	0-0	
05/03/96	SC Freiburg	H	1-1	Sobotzik
09/03/96	Borussia Dortmund	A	0-1	
16/03/96	Borussia Mönchengladbach	H	0-2	
24/03/96	FC Hansa Rostock	H	3-2	Pröpper 2, Stisi
30/03/96	VfB Stuttgart	A	1-1	Driller
02/04/96	Bayer 04 Leverkusen	H	2-1	Driller, Scharping
06/04/96	Eintracht Frankfurt	H	2-1	Trulsen, Springer
10/04/96	FC Bayern München	A	1-1	Schweissing
13/04/96	SV Werder Bremen	H	1-2	Gronau
20/04/96	1.FC Köln	A	0-1	
26/04/96	FC Schalke 04	H	2-0	Driller, Dammann
01/05/96	Fortuna Düsseldorf	A	0-2	
04/05/96	Hamburger SV	H	1-1	Stanislawski
11/05/96	Karlsruher SC	A	2-2	Stanislawski, Springer
18/05/96	KFC Uerdingen 05	H	0-2	

FC SCHALKE 04

CLUB DIRECTORY

FC Schalke 04
Geschäftsstelle
Parkstadion
45891 Gelsenkirchen
tel - (0209) 700870
fax - (0209) 7008750
Year of Formation - 1904
President - Gerd Rehberg
Manager - Rudi Assauer
Coach - Jörg Berger
Stadium - Parkstadion (70,600)

MAJOR HONOURS
League Championship - (7)
1934, 1935, 1937, 1939, 1940, 1942, 1958.
Domestic Cup - (2) 1937, 1972.

APPEARANCES 95/96

	P	Ap	(s)	Gls
Jörg ALBRECHT	G	2		
Ingo ANDERBRÜGGE	M	24	(3)	9
Michael BÜSKENS	M	23	(4)	2
Sergei DIKHTIAR (UKR)	A		(1)	
Tom DOOLEY (USA)	M	13	(7)	1
Yves EIGENRAUCH	D	34		
Oliver HELD	M	7	(11)	
Waldemar KSIENZYK	M	1	(5)	1
Marco KURZ	M	18	(9)	
Radoslav LATAL (TCH)	M	26	(6)	1
Jens LEHMANN	G	32		
Thomas LINKE	D	26	(1)	3
Martin MAX	A	32		11
Youri MULDER (HOL)	A	33		10
Andreas MÜLLER	M	25	(3)	1
Jiri NEMEC (TCH)	M	28		
Michael PRUS	D	4	(9)	
Uwe SCHERR	M	6	(7)	
Frank SCHÖN	D	1	(8)	
Olaf THON	D	30		3
David WAGNER	A		(16)	2
Uwe WEIDEMANN	M	9	(4)	1

LEAGUE RESULTS 1995/96

Date	Opponent	H/A	Score	Scorers
12/08/95	1.FC Köln	A	1-0	Mulder
18/08/95	FC Hansa Rostock	H	1-3	Max
30/08/95	Fortuna Düsseldorf	H	1-1	Max
02/09/95	Hamburger SV	A	1-1	Max
10/09/95	Karlsruher SC	H	2-1	Mulder, Ksienzyk
16/09/95	KFC Uerdingen 05	A	1-1	Anderbrügge
24/09/95	TSV 1860 München	H	1-1	Mulder
30/09/95	SC Freiburg	A	2-1	Mulder, Latal
13/10/95	1.FC Kaiserslautern	H	1-1	Mulder
20/10/95	Bayer 04 Leverkusen	A	0-0	
28/10/95	Borussia Dortmund	H	1-2	Mulder
05/11/95	Borussia Mönchengladbach	A	1-4	Max
11/11/95	FC St. Pauli	H	2-0	Linke, Weidemann
19/11/95	VfB Stuttgart	A	2-2	Max, Thon
25/11/95	Eintracht Frankfurt	H	2-0	Büskens, Mulder
02/12/95	FC Bayern München	A	0-4	
09/12/95	SV Werder Bremen	H	2-1	Max, Anderbrügge
24/02/96	Fortuna Düsseldorf	A	0-2	
02/03/96	Hamburger SV	H	3-0	Anderbrügge, Max 2
05/03/96	1.FC Köln	H	0-0	
09/03/96	Karlsruher SC	A	1-0	Mulder
16/03/96	KFC Uerdingen 05	H	1-1	Linke
22/03/96	TSV 1860 München	A	1-1	Anderbrügge (p)
30/03/96	SC Freiburg	H	3-0	Anderbrügge (p), Dooley, Thon
04/04/96	1.FC Kaiserslautern	A	0-0	
09/04/96	Bayer 04 Leverkusen	H	1-1	Wagner
13/04/96	Borussia Dortmund	A	0-0	
21/04/96	Borussia Mönchengladbach	H	3-3	Mulder, Anderbrügge (p), Max
26/04/96	FC St. Pauli	A	0-2	
30/04/96	VfB Stuttgart	H	2-0	Mulder, Max
04/05/96	Eintracht Frankfurt	A	3-0	Linke, Anderbrügge, Max
07/05/96	FC Hansa Rostock	A	2-1	Büskens, Anderbrügge (p)
11/05/96	FC Bayern München	H	2-1	Thon, Müller
18/05/96	SV Werder Bremen	A	2-1	Wagner, Anderbrügge

VFB STUTTGART

CLUB DIRECTORY

VfB Stuttgart
Mercedesstrasse 109
70372 Stuttgart
tel - (0711) 55007-0
fax - (0711) 5500733
Year of Formation - 1893
President - Gerhard Mayer-Vorfelder
Secretary - Ulrich Schäfer
Coach - Rolf Fringer (96/97 - Joachim Löw)
Stadium - Gottlieb-Daimler-Stadion (53,218)

MAJOR HONOURS

League Championship - (4)
1950, 1952, 1984, 1992.
Domestic Cup - (2) 1954, 1958.

APPEARANCES 95/96

	P	Ap	(s)	Gls
Krasimir BALAKOV (BUL)	M	34		7
Thomas BERTHOLD	D	27		
Fredi BOBIC	A	24	(2)	17
Michael BOCHTLER	D	15	(2)	
Andreas BUCK	M	13	(6)	
Giovane ELBER (BRA)	A	33		16
Franco FODA	D	28		
Radoslaw GILEWICZ (POL)	M	4	(19)	5
Marco GRIMM	M	9	(12)	
Marco HABER	M	22	(3)	2
Hendrik HERZOG	D	29	(1)	2
Ludwig KÖGL	A	7	(4)	
Axel KRUSE	A	11	(16)	6
Thorsten LEGAT	D	12	(3)	
Michael OELKUCH	D	1	(9)	1
Gerhard POSCHNER	M	26	(2)	1
Günther SCHÄFER	D	6	(2)	
Thomas SCHNEIDER	D	14	(4)	
Danny SCHWARZ	M	7	(2)	
Eberhard TRAUTNER	G	5		
Frank VERLAAT (HOL)	D	17	(1)	1
Marc ZIEGLER	G	29		
Markus ZIEGLER	A	1	(1)	

LEAGUE RESULTS 1995/96

11/08/95	KFC Uerdingen 05	H	0-0	
19/08/95	TSV 1860 München	A	1-1	Balakov (p)
30/08/95	SC Freiburg	H	3-1	Elber 2, Balakov
02/09/95	1.FC Kaiserslautern	A	1-1	Bobic
09/09/95	Bayer 04 Leverkusen	H	1-4	Kruse
16/09/95	Borussia Dortmund	A	3-6	Elber, Gilewicz, Balakov
23/09/95	Borussia Mönchengladbach	H	5-0	Bobic 2, Elber 2, Balakov
29/09/95	FC St. Pauli	A	3-1	Elber, Bobic, Gilewicz
13/10/95	FC Hansa Rostock	A	3-3	Bobic, Verlaat, Elber
21/10/95	Eintracht Frankfurt	H	3-2	Balakov, Elber, Bobic
28/10/95	FC Bayern München	A	3-5	Kruse, Elber 2
04/11/95	SV Werder Bremen	H	1-1	Bobic
11/11/95	1.FC Köln	A	2-2	Bobic, Elber
19/11/95	FC Schalke 04	H	2-2	Balakov (p), Bobic
24/11/95	Fortuna Düsseldorf	A	2-1	Elber, Bobic
02/12/95	Hamburger SV	H	3-0	Bobic, Balakov (p), og (Schnoor)
09/12/95	Karlsruher SC	A	2-1	Bobic, Kruse
17/02/96	TSV 1860 München	H	2-3	Herzog, Bobic
24/02/96	SC Freiburg	A	1-2	Poschner
02/03/96	1.FC Kaiserslautern	H	2-0	Elber, Haber
08/03/96	Bayer 04 Leverkusen	A	0-0	
16/03/96	Borussia Dortmund	H	0-5	
19/03/96	KFC Uerdingen 05	A	4-3	Kruse, Herzog, Elber, Gilewicz
24/03/96	Borussia Mönchengladbach	A	1-1	Kruse
30/03/96	FC St. Pauli	H	1-1	Kruse
04/04/96	FC Hansa Rostock	H	1-1	Elber
09/04/96	Eintracht Frankfurt	A	2-2	Haber, Gilewicz
13/04/96	FC Bayern München	H	0-1	
20/04/96	SV Werder Bremen	A	2-2	Gilewicz, Oelkuch
27/04/96	1.FC Köln	H	0-1	
30/04/96	FC Schalke 04	A	0-2	
04/05/96	Fortuna Düsseldorf	H	2-3	Bobic 2
11/05/96	Hamburger SV	A	0-3	
18/05/96	Karlsruher SC	H	3-1	Bobic 2, Elber

KFC UERDINGEN 05

CLUB DIRECTORY

KFC Uerdingen 05
Postfach 110
47829 Krefeld
tel - (02151) 490505
fax - (02151) 471067
Year of Formation - 1905
President - Dr. Hermann Schulte-Wissermann
Secretary - Edgar Geenen
Coach - Friedhelm Funkel (96/97 - Hans-Ulrich Thomale)
Stadium - Grotenburg (34,500)

MAJOR HONOURS
Domestic Cup - (1) 1985.

APPEARANCES 95/96

	P	Ap	(s)	Gls
Alexander BADE	G	5		
Günter BITTENGEL (TCH)	M	15	(5)	2
John VAN BUSKIRK (HOL)	D		(1)	
Mustafa DOGAN	D	23	(5)	
Bernd DREHER	G	29		
Uwe GRAUER	D	19	(3)	
Sebastian HAHN	M	6	(9)	
Jan HEINTZE (DEN)	M	27		1
Axel JÜPTNER	M	17	(8)	
Rainer KRIEG	A	4	(4)	
Gerd KÜHN	D	10	(4)	
Heiko LAESSIG	A	27	(3)	4
Marek LESNIAK (POL)	A	16	(1)	3
Jos LUHUKAY (HOL)	M		(2)	
Michael LUSCH	M	16	(4)	
Erik MEIJER (HOL)	A	32		11
Jörg OBERLÄNDER	D	2		
Stephan PASSLACK	M	32		4
Heiko PESCHKE	D	11		2
Michal PROBIERZ (POL)	M		(3)	
Helmut RAHNER	D	25	(3)	
Horst STEFFEN	M	28		3
Marcus WEDAU	M	18	(14)	2
Zlatko YANKOV (BUL)	M	12	(3)	1

LEAGUE RESULTS 1995/96

Date	Opponent	H/A	Score	Scorers
11/08/95	VfB Stuttgart	A	0-0	
19/08/95	Eintracht Frankfurt	H	1-1	Peschke
30/08/95	FC Bayern München	A	0-2	
02/09/95	SV Werder Bremen	H	3-0	Meijer, Peschke (p), Wedau
08/09/95	1.FC Köln	A	0-0	
16/09/95	FC Schalke 04	H	1-1	Meijer
22/09/95	Fortuna Düsseldorf	A	0-1	
29/09/95	Hamburger SV	H	1-1	Laessig
14/10/95	Karlsruher SC	A	0-2	
20/10/95	FC Hansa Rostock	H	1-1	Meijer
29/10/95	TSV 1860 München	H	2-0	Passlack, Wedau
04/11/95	SC Freiburg	A	1-1	Yankov
10/11/95	1.FC Kaiserslautern	H	1-1	Bittengel
18/11/95	Bayer 04 Leverkusen	A	1-2	Meijer
25/11/95	Borussia Dortmund	H	0-2	
02/12/95	Borussia Mönchengladbach	A	1-2	Kastenmaier (p)
08/12/95	FC St. Pauli	H	2-5	Steffen, Heintze
16/02/96	Eintracht Frankfurt	A	0-1	
25/02/96	FC Bayern München	H	1-6	Meijer
01/03/96	SV Werder Bremen	A	0-1	
09/03/96	1.FC Köln	H	1-1	Lesniak
16/03/96	FC Schalke 04	A	1-1	Passlack
19/03/96	VfB Stuttgart	H	3-4	Meijer (p), Laessig, Bittengel
23/03/96	Fortuna Düsseldorf	H	1-3	Passlack
29/03/96	Hamburger SV	A	0-0	
04/04/96	Karlsruher SC	H	2-3	Lesniak, Passlack
09/04/96	FC Hansa Rostock	A	0-1	
12/04/96	TSV 1860 München	A	1-2	Meijer
19/04/96	SC Freiburg	H	3-1	Meijer, Steffen, Laessig
26/04/96	1.FC Kaiserslautern	A	0-3	
30/04/96	Bayer 04 Leverkusen	H	3-0	Lesniak, Steffen, Laessig
04/05/96	Borussia Dortmund	A	0-5	
11/05/96	Borussia Mönchengladbach	H	0-2	
18/05/96	FC St. Pauli	A	2-0	Meijer 2

SV WERDER BREMEN

CLUB DIRECTORY

SV Werder Bremen
Weserstadion
28205 Bremen
tel - (0421) 434500
fax - (0421) 493555
Year of Formation - 1899
President - Dr. Franz Böhmert
Manager - Willi Lemke
Coach - Aad de Mos; Hans-Jürgen Dörner
Stadium - Weserstadion (29,850)

MAJOR HONOURS
League Championship - (3) 1965, 1988, 1993.
Domestic Cup - (3) 1961, 1991, 1994.
European Cup-winners' Cup - (1) 1992.

APPEARANCES 95/96

	P	Ap	(s)	Gls
Erhan ALBAYRAK (TUR)	A		(2)	
Júnior BAIANO (BRA)	D	32		2
Mario BASLER	M	29	(1)	11
Dietmar BEIERSDORFER	D	1	(2)	
Vladimir BESCHASTNYKH (RUS)	A	16	(7)	1
Marco BODE	A	34		5
Uli BOROWKA	D	8	(2)	
Rodolfo Esteban CARDOSO (ARG)	A	24		2
Ersan DOGU (TUR)	D	1	(4)	
Dieter EILTS	M	32		
Bernd HOBSCH	A	27	(3)	9
Bruno LABBADIA	A	13		4
Arie VAN LENT (HOL)	A		(1)	
Frank NEUBARTH	A	3	(12)	1
Hany RAMZY (EGY)	D	21	(1)	
Oliver RECK	G	20		
Frank ROST	G	14	(1)	
Gunnar SAUER	D		(3)	1
Heiko SCHOLZ	M	26	(4)	1
Michael SCHULZ	D	6	(7)	
Lars UNGER	M		(3)	
Angelo VIER	A	2	(9)	1
Miroslav VOTAVA	M	27	(1)	
André WIEDENER	M	17	(8)	
Thomas WOLTER	M	21	(2)	

LEAGUE RESULTS 1995/96

11/08/95	Fortuna Düsseldorf	H	1-1	Hobsch
18/08/95	Hamburger SV	A	3-3	Hobsch 2, Basler
29/08/95	Karlsruher SC	H	1-0	Bode
02/09/95	KFC Uerdingen 05	A	0-3	
08/09/95	TSV 1860 München	H	2-0	Basler (p), Vier
16/09/95	SC Freiburg	A	1-0	Basler
23/09/95	1.FC Kaiserslautern	H	1-1	Basler
30/09/95	Bayer 04 Leverkusen	A	2-2	Basler, Neubarth
14/10/95	Borussia Dortmund	H	2-2	Bode, Hobsch
22/10/95	Borussia Mönchengladbach	A	0-1	
28/10/95	FC St. Pauli	H	1-1	Hobsch
04/11/95	VfB Stuttgart	A	1-1	Basler
11/11/95	Eintracht Frankfurt	H	1-1	Bode
18/11/95	FC Bayern München	A	0-2	
25/11/95	FC Hansa Rostock	H	0-2	
01/12/95	1.FC Köln	H	0-1	
09/12/95	FC Schalke 04	A	1-2	Baiano
24/02/96	Karlsruher SC	A	1-1	Hobsch
01/03/96	KFC Uerdingen 05	H	1-0	Basler
05/03/96	Hamburger SV	H	2-1	Scholz, Cardoso
09/03/96	TSV 1860 München	A	1-1	Cardoso (p)
12/03/96	Fortuna Düsseldorf	A	1-1	Labbadia
15/03/96	SC Freiburg	H	0-2	
23/03/96	1.FC Kaiserslautern	A	0-0	
30/03/96	Bayer 04 Leverkusen	H	2-1	Labbadia 2
06/04/96	Borussia Dortmund	A	1-1	Baiano
10/04/96	Borussia Mönchengladbach	H	2-0	Beschastnykh, Labbadia
13/04/96	FC St. Pauli	A	2-1	Hobsch, og (Trulsen)
20/04/96	VfB Stuttgart	H	2-2	Basler 2
27/04/96	Eintracht Frankfurt	A	0-1	
04/05/96	FC Hansa Rostock	A	1-2	Sauer
07/05/96	FC Bayern München	H	3-2	Hobsch, Bode 2
11/05/96	1.FC Köln	A	2-1	Basler 2 (1p)
18/05/96	FC Schalke 04	H	1-2	Hobsch

PROMOTED CLUBS

SECOND DIVISION FINAL TABLE 95/96

		Pd	W	D	L	F	A	Pt	GD
1	**VfL Bochum**	**34**	**21**	**6**	**7**	**68**	**30**	**69**	**+38**
2	**Arminia Bielefeld**	**34**	**16**	**9**	**9**	**55**	**45**	**57**	**+10**
3	**MSV Duisburg**	**34**	**15**	**11**	**8**	**55**	**37**	**56**	**+18**
4	SpVgg Unterhaching	34	14	10	10	52	38	52	+14
5	FSV Zwickau	34	15	4	15	39	48	49	-9
6	FC Carl Zeiss Jena	34	13	9	12	49	54	48	-5
7	SV Waldhof Mannheim	34	13	7	14	49	47	46	+2
8	Fortuna Köln	34	12	10	12	37	37	46	=
9	VfB Leipzig	34	13	6	15	35	49	45	-14
10	SV Meppen	34	10	14	10	45	43	44	+2
11	1.FSV Mainz 95	34	12	8	14	37	41	44	-4
12	VfL Wolfsburg	34	10	14	10	41	46	44	-5
13	VfB Lübeck	34	13	5	16	40	45	44	-5
14	Hertha BSC Berlin	34	11	12	11	37	35	42	+2
15	Chemnitzer FC	34	11	9	14	43	51	42	-8
16	Hannover 96	34	10	7	17	38	48	37	-10
17	1.FC Nürnberg	34	9	12	13	33	40	33	-7
18	SG Wattenscheid 09	34	8	7	19	38	57	31	-19

N.B. Hertha BSC Berlin deducted 3 pts; 1.FC Nürnberg deducted 6 pts.

CLUB DIRECTORY

VfL Bochum
Ruhrstadion
Gastroper Strasse 145
Postfach 10 28 22
44728 Bochum
tel - (0234) 592079/592084
fax - (0234) 592026
Year of Formation - 1848
President - Werner Altegoer
Manager - Klaus Hilpert
Coach - Klaus Toppmöller
Stadium - Ruhrstadion (42,000)

CLUB DIRECTORY

Arminia Bielefeld
Postafch 100 487
33504 Bielefeld
tel - (0521) 131415/133899
fax - (0521) 133003
Year of Formation - 1905
President - Hans-Hermann Schwick
Manager - Rüdiger Lamm
Coach - Ernst Middendorp
Stadium - Alm (22,000)

CLUB DIRECTORY

MSV Duisburg
Westender Strasse 36
47138 Duisburg
tel - (0203) 428577
fax - (0203) 423224
Year of Formation - 1902
President - Dieter Fischdick
Secretary - Dirk Keiper
Coach - Hannes Bongartz; Friedhelm Funkel
Stadium - Wedaustadion (30,128)

GREECE

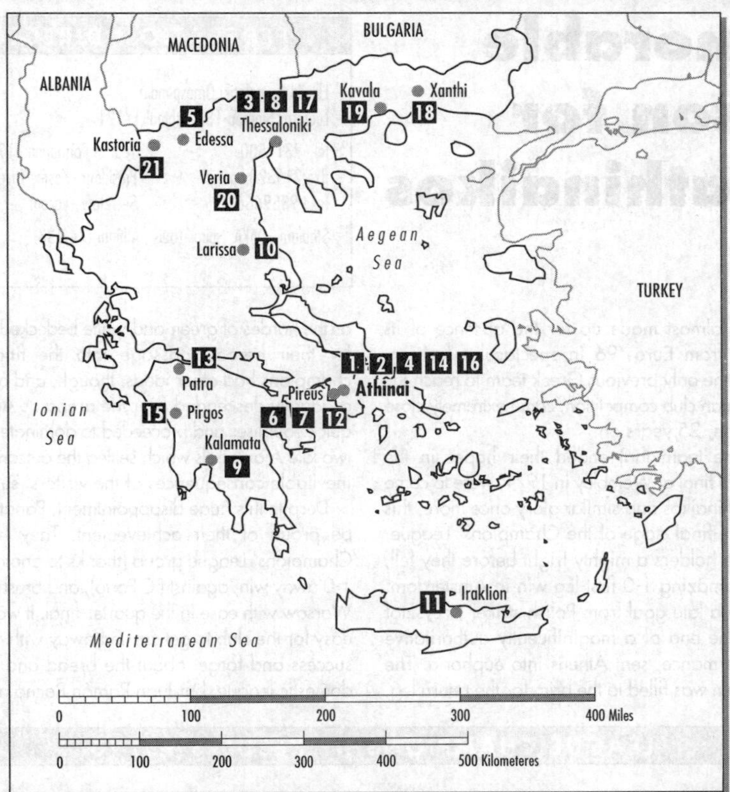

1	AEK	474	12	OLYMPIAKOS	485
2	APOLLON	475	13	PANAHAIKI	486
3	ARIS	476	14	PANATHINAIKOS	487
4	ATHINAIKOS	477	15	PANILIAKOS	488
5	EDESSAIKOS	478	16	PANIONIOS	489
6	ETHNIKOS	479	17	PAOK	490
7	IONIKOS	480	18	XANTHI	491
8	IRAKLIS	481	19	KAVALA	492
9	KALAMATA	482	20	VERIA	492
10	LARISSA	483	21	KASTORIA	492
11	OFI	484			

AEK IN RECORD CUP FINAL WIN

Memorable season for Panathinaikos

FEDERATION DIRECTORY

Elliniki Podosferiki Omospondia
Leoforos Singrou 137, Athinai 17121

tel - 9311500
tlx - 215328 epo gr
fax - 9359666

Year of Formation - 1926
President - Kostas Trivellas
Secretary - vacant

Stadium - OAKA 'Spiros Louis', Athinai (74,433)

Greek football almost made up for the absence of its national team from Euro '96 in spectacular fashion. Panathinaikos, the only previous Greek team to reach the final of a European club competition, came extremely close to doing it again, 25 years on.

But Ajax, the team that ended their hopes in the Champions' Cup final at Wembley in 1971, were to come between Panathinaikos and similar glory once more, this time at the semi-final stage of the Champions' League. 'Pana' gave the holders a mighty fright before they fell, however. The amazing 1-0 first-leg win in Amsterdam, concluded with a late goal from Polish striker Krzysztof Warzycha at the end of a maginificently authoritative defensive performance, sent Athens into euphoria. The Olympic Stadium was filled to the brim for the return leg, as the hordes of green-and-white bedecked fans prepared for their heroes' passage into the final. The Dutch champions had other ideas, though, and an eerie silence gradually descended over the arena as Ajax grabbed a quick equaliser and proceeded to dominate the game. The two late Ajax goals which settled the outcome were almost inevitable consequences of the visitors' superiority.

Despite this huge disappointment, Panathinaikos could be proud of their achievement. They had won their Champions' League group (thanks to another sensational 1-0 away win, against FC Porto), and brushed aside Legia Warsaw with ease in the quarter-final. It would have been easy for the club to get carried away with their European success and forget about the bread and butter of their domestic league, but Juan Ramón Rocha and his players

LEAGUE CHAMPIONSHIP RESULTS 95/96

		1	2	3	4	5	6	7	8	9	10	11	12	13	14	15	16	17	18
1	AEK		1-0	4-0	6-0	3-0	3-1	6-0	3-1	5-1	1-0	4-0	1-1	5-1	1-0	3-0	2-0	4-0	2-1
2	Apollon	0-3		4-1	0-0	1-1	3-1	4-1	2-1	2-1	4-0	0-1	3-4	2-0	2-3	2-1	0-1	0-1	3-1
3	Aris	2-1	2-0		1-1	2-0	4-1	2-0	0-0	1-1	6-0	2-1	0-0	1-0	1-1	3-1	4-2	0-0	2-2
4	Athinaikos	0-1	1-1	0-0		2-1	2-0	1-2	0-1	1-1	1-0	3-2	0-1	2-0	1-2	0-0	2-1	2-1	2-1
5	Edessaikos	2-5	0-0	1-1	5-2		6-2	0-1	2-0	1-0	3-1	3-2	2-5	2-0	1-3	1-3	2-1	3-3	1-1
6	Ethnikos	0-3	3-2	3-1	3-2	1-1		2-5	1-4	2-3	0-1	2-3	0-3	1-2	0-0	2-4	2-0	2-3	1-2
7	Ionikos	1-4	1-2	3-1	0-1	3-0	4-1		1-1	2-2	3-1	0-0	0-2	1-1	2-1	2-1	2-1	0-0	1-1
8	Iraklis	1-3	1-1	3-2	1-2	2-0	4-1	3-1		2-1	2-1	5-1	2-1	0-1	1-1	2-0	3-2	2-2	2-0
9	Kalamata	2-2	3-0	1-1	1-0	1-1	3-1	0-0	1-0		5-0	2-3	3-0	1-0	0-1	1-1	1-0	1-1	1-1
10	Larissa	1-0	1-1	1-0	1-1	0-2	0-1	1-0	0-1	1-1		2-6	3-2	4-1	0-1	1-0	0-0	2-1	1-2
11	OFI	1-1	2-1	2-0	0-1	4-1	3-2	3-1	0-0	3-0	0-0		2-1	1-0	2-1	2-2	2-2	2-1	3-0
12	Olympiakos	1-1	0-3	4-0	3-0	2-0	3-0	1-1	2-1	4-1	3-1	3-1		6-1	1-2	3-0	3-1	1-0	1-1
13	Panahaiki	1-1	2-1	0-1	2-0	1-0	1-0	1-2	1-0	1-0	1-1	0-1	1-1		0-1	0-0	1-0	3-2	1-2
14	Panathinaikos	1-0	3-1	3-1	0-0	3-1	3-0	3-0	4-0	4-0	6-1	4-0	1-0	1-0		4-1	5-3	2-0	2-0
15	Paniliakos	0-2	2-1	2-1	4-1	2-3	2-2	0-0	1-2	1-0	4-2	4-2	0-0	1-1	0-1		3-1	1-1	2-2
16	Panionios	1-2	2-2	0-2	1-2	1-2	2-1	1-3	0-0	2-1	0-0	1-0	1-2	1-0	1-3	1-0		2-1	3-0
17	PAOK	1-3	2-1	1-0	1-0	0-1	2-0	1-1	1-2	1-1	2-3	3-0	0-0	2-1	0-1	1-0	2-0		3-3
18	Xanthi	1-1	1-0	4-0	3-0	1-1	6-1	1-0	0-1	1-0	3-1	0-2	1-2	3-1	1-1	1-3	4-0	2-2	

LEAGUE CHAMPIONSHIP FINAL TABLE 95/96

			Home					Away					Total						
		Pd	W	D	L	F	A	W	D	L	F	A	W	D	L	F	A	Pt	GD
1	Panathinaikos	34	16	1	0	49	8	10	4	3	23	14	26	5	3	72	22	83	+50
2	AEK	34	16	1	0	54	6	9	5	3	33	16	25	6	3	87	22	81	+65
3	Olympiakos	34	12	3	2	41	14	7	5	5	25	20	19	8	7	66	34	65	+32
4	Iraklis	34	11	3	3	36	20	6	4	7	15	19	17	7	10	51	39	58	+12
5	OFI	34	11	5	1	32	14	6	1	10	25	38	17	6	11	57	52	57	+5
6	Xanthi	34	9	4	4	33	16	3	7	7	20	31	12	11	11	53	47	47	+6
7	Aris	34	10	7	0	33	11	2	3	12	12	36	12	10	12	45	47	46	-2
8	Ionikos	34	7	6	4	26	20	5	4	8	18	30	12	10	12	44	50	46	-6
9	Edessaikos	34	8	4	5	35	30	4	4	9	15	29	12	8	14	50	59	44	-9
10	Athinaikos	34	8	4	5	20	15	4	4	9	13	32	12	8	14	33	47	44	-14
11	Apollon	34	9	2	6	32	21	2	5	10	17	27	11	7	16	49	48	40	+1
12	Paniliakos	34	7	6	4	29	22	3	4	10	17	29	10	10	14	46	51	40	-5
13	Kalamata	34	8	7	2	27	12	1	5	11	14	34	9	12	13	41	46	39	-5
14	PAOK	34	8	4	5	23	17	2	7	8	19	29	10	11	13	42	46	38	-4
15	Panahaiki	34	8	4	5	17	13	2	2	13	10	34	10	6	18	27	47	36	-20
16	Larissa	34	7	4	6	19	20	2	3	12	13	44	9	7	18	32	64	34	-32
17	Panionios	34	7	3	7	20	21	1	2	14	15	38	8	5	21	35	59	29	-24
18	Ethnikos	34	4	2	11	25	39	1	1	15	15	51	5	3	26	40	90	18	-50

N.B. PAOK deducted 3 pts. Where two or more teams are level on points, classification is determined by the results of the matches between them.

were level-headed enough to conserve their energy and maintain their competitiveness on both fronts. The end-product was a second successive Greek title, won in style despite a strong challenge from city rivals AEK.

It was the first time ever that a Greek club had won the championship while simultaneously reaching the latter stages of a European Cup. For that reason many pundits claimed that 1995/96 was the best season in Panathinaikos's history. Coach Rocha certainly earned mountainous praise in the Greek press. Before the season there was criticism, especially from the club's fans, that no major signings had been made. But on Rocha's advice president Vardinoyannis kept his chequebook closed and the decision proved comprehensively to be the right one.

There was certainly no rush to replace the club's foreign contingent. Argentinian playmaker Juan Borelli and the two Poles, striker Warzycha and goalkeeper Jozef Wandzik, were all indispensable assets to the team, and the trio further enhanced their status in 95/96. Warzycha scored his usual glut of goals, including half a dozen in Europe; Borelli offered abundant skill and creativity; and Wandzik was as reliable as ever between the posts. The pick of the homegrown players was undoubtedly winger Yorgos Donis, who was in blistering form all season.

INTERNATIONAL HONOURS

World Cup Finals appearances: 1994

European Championship appearances: 1980

Donis left the club in the summer. But with plenty of savings and Champions' League funds in the kitty, Panathinaikos were able to treat themselves to a couple of useful new signings in Liberopoulos and Nassiopoulos. The building of a magnificent new training complex is likely to guarantee the development of the best local talent at Panathinaikos in the years to come.

AEK proved a stubborn rival to Panathinaikos in the title race. Even after their 0-1 defeat in the April head-to-head they refused to lie down, and it was not until the final game of the season that the outcome was finally settled. Once again AEK were the most attractive team to watch. They scored an all-time club record of 87 goals in the league and another 38 in the Greek Cup, which they won for the first time in 13 years, knocking out both Olympiakos and Panathinaikos before subjecting city rivals and Cup final débutants Apollon to a 7-1 demolition in the final - the biggest winning margin in the history of the fixture.

Hat-trick hero for AEK that day was star midfielder Vassilis Tsartas, who also earned the league's top scorer accolade with 26 goals. His departure to Sevilla at the end of the season left a bitter aftertaste to AEK's

NATIONAL TEAM RESULTS 95/96

Date	Opponent	Venue	City	Score	Scorers
16/08/95	Scotland (ECQ)	A	Glasgow	0-1	
06/09/95	San Marino (ECQ)	A	Serravalle	4-0	Tsalouhidis (6), Yoryadis Y.H. (31), Alexandris (59), Donis (80)
20/09/95	Yugoslavia	H	Salonika	0-2	
11/10/95	Russia (ECQ)	A	Moscow	1-2	Tsalouhidis (64)
15/11/95	Faroe Islands (ECQ)	H	Iraklion	5-0	Alexandris (58), Nikolaidis (62), Mahlas (66), Donis (75), Tsartas (80)
25/01/96	Israel	H	Halkida	2-1	Glam (27og), Tsartas (44p)
21/02/96	France	A	Nîmes	1-3	Alexandris (4)
27/03/96	Portugal	A	Lisbon	0-1	
24/04/96	Slovenia (WCQ)	H	Athens	2-0	Batista (55), Nikolaidis (65)
08/05/96	Georgia	H	Ioannina	2-1	Nikolaidis (58, 87)

TOP SCORERS

26	Vassilis TSARTAS (AEK)
19	Hristos KOSTIS (AEK)
	Krzysztof WARZYCHA (Panathinaikos)
	Vassilis KARAPIALIS (Olympiakos)
17	Nikos MAHLAS (OFI)
16	Themistoklis NIKOLAIDIS (Apollon)
	Yorgos NASSIOPOULOS (Edessaikos)
14	Temur KETSBAIA (AEK)
13	Bernard BARNJAK (Apollon)
	Nikos MIRTSEKIS (Iraklis)
	Ilija IVIC (Olympiakos)
	Paraskevas ZOUMBOULIS (PAOK)

campaign, but even more unpleasant for the club's followers was the loss of coach Dusan Bajevic to Olympiakos. Bajevic had extended his contract at the start of the season for another five years, but Olympiakos came up with an offer he could not refuse, so he left after eight years of magnificent service, which included four championship titles.

Olympiakos will certainly be hoping for some stability from their new coach. Once again in 95/96 they were overburdened with internal disputes and managerial changes. Dutchman Thijs Libregts did not even make it beyond pre-season, and Stavros Diamantopoulos, his successor, was dismissed before the season was half over. Olympiakos were unlucky in Europe, where, after cruising past Slavia Sofia and Maribor Branik in the UEFA Cup, they had the better of both of their second-round encounters with Sevilla, only to lose out on the away-goals rule in extra-time. In the league, though, the team could not find the consistency of their two great rivals and their faint hopes of a first title for nine years were finally laid to rest after a disastrous sequence of results (five defeats in eight games) during the final third of the campaign.

DOMESTIC CUP RESULTS

FIRST ROUND

Doxa Virona v Larissa 1-0; 2-1 (Doxa Virona 3-1)
Ionikos v Panelefsiniakos 4-0; 4-2 (Ionikos 8-2)
Apollon v Paniliakos 2-1; 3-3 (Apollon 5-4)
Athinaikos v Pontii Veria 4-0; 3-1 (Athinaikos 7-1)
Panahaiki v Panathinaikos 2-2; 0-3 (Panathinaikos 5-2)
Nigrita v Olympiakos 1-4; 1-3 (Olympiakos 7-2)
Niki Volos v OFI 1-3; 0-0 (OFI 3-1)
Agrotikos Asteras v Xanthi 1-1; 0-0 (1-1; Xanthi on away goal)
Fokikos v PAOK 0-1; 0-5 (PAOK 6-0)
Anayenissi Yanitsa v Aris 1-0; 1-3 (Aris 3-2)
Apollon Kalamarias v Kavala 3-0; 1-3 (Apollon Kalamarias 4-3)
Panetolikos v Varvasiakos 3-0; 1-0 (Panetolikos 4-0)
Hania v Trikala 2-0; 0-4 (aet) (Trikala 4-2)
Pirgos v Veria 0-0; 1-2 (Veria 2-1)
AEK v Iraklis 1-0; 2-0 (AEK 3-0)
Ialissos v Ayios Nikolaos 3-1; 2-3 (Ialissos 5-4)

SECOND ROUND

Doxa Virona v Panathinaikos 0-2; 1-3 (Panathinaikos 5-1)
PAOK v Ionikos 4-1; 1-0 (PAOK 5-1)
Athinaikos v Veria 5-2; 2-1 (Athinaikos 7-3)
Panetolikos v Apollon 1-2; 2-2 (Apollon 4-3)
Xanthi v Apollon Kalamarias 2-0; 3-0 (Xanthi 5-0)
Olympiakos v AEK 1-3; 1-1 (AEK 4-2)
OFI v Aris 1-0; 0-2 (Aris 2-1)
Trikala v Ialissos 2-0; 2-0 (Trikala 4-0)

QUARTER-FINALS

AEK v Panathinaikos 3-1; 2-2 (AEK 5-3)
Aris v Athinaikos 2-1; 0-2 (Athinaikos 3-2)
Apollon v Xanthi 4-0; 1-2 (Apollon 5-2)
PAOK v Trikala 3-0; 2-1 (PAOK 5-1)

SEMI-FINALS

AEK v Athinaikos 5-0; 1-0 (AEK 6-0)
Apollon v PAOK 1-1; 3-1 (Apollon 4-2)

FINAL

15/05/96, Athens
AEK 7 Batista (11, 33), Tsartas (22, 48p, 76), Ketsbaia (60), Kostis (89)
APOLLON 1 Barnjak (62)
referee - Sotiropoulos
AEK - Amatsidis; Borbokis, Kostenoglou (Maladenis 66), Manolas, Sabanadzovic, Vlahos, Ketsbaia (Kostis 65), Savevski, Batista, Tsartas (Karayannis 83), Kassapis.
APOLLON - Raptis; Ioannou, Mavridis (Lahanas 55), Theodoropoulos (Alexis 35), Apostolou (Kefalas 65), Tatsis, Velentzas, Erak, Barnjak, Kola, Nikolaidis.

Olympiakos were joined in the UEFA Cup frame by Iraklis, who earned their place by virtue of a last-minute header from defender Yorgos Papadopoulos on the final day of the season. This late late strike denied OFI, who had occupied fourth place for most of the season before losing out at the death.

Below OFI were Xanthi (in sixth place) and Ionikos (in eighth), who both celebrated the highest finishes in their history thanks to the input of their respective foreign coaches, Kurt Jara and Oleg Blokhin. Another team who would like to have kept hold of their foreign coach was PAOK, but Dutchman Arie Haan quit in controversial circumstances to join Feyenoord in October, and from that moment on the famous Salonika club began to slide precariously into the nether reaches of the league. At one point they were actually bottom of the table, but with the Swede Gunder Bengtsson belatedly installed in April, PAOK finally lifted themselves from danger.

NATIONAL TEAM APPEARANCES 95/96

Coach - Kostas POLIHRONIOU	SCO	SMR	YUG	RUS	FAR	ISR	FRA	POR	SLO	GEO	Cps	Gls
Ilias ATMATSIDIS (24/04/69) - AEK	G	G	s46		G	G	G	G	G	G46	20	-
Stratos APOSTOLAKIS (11/05/64) - Panathinaikos	D	D	D	D	D	D	D	D52	D	D46	81	4
Kiriakos KARATAIDIS (04/07/65) - Olympiakos	D	D	s46					D		s46	22	-
Yannis KALLITZAKIS (10/12/66) - Panathinaikos	D		D46	D46			D70	D	D	D	53	-
Nikos DABIZAS (03/08/73) - Olympiakos	D	D	s46	s46	D	D	D				15	-
Mihalis KASSAPIS (06/06/71) - AEK	D		D	D	D	D46	D	D	D	D	17	-
Panayotis TSALOUHIDIS (30/03/63) - PAOK	M	M	M62	M	M46						75	17
Theodoros ZAGORAKIS (17/10/71) - PAOK	M79	M	M72	M	M70	M	M78	M55	M	M	20	-
Vassilis TSARTAS (12/11/72) - AEK	M		s20 /76	M46	M	M61			M82	M46	19	3
Daniel BATISTA (09/09/64) - AEK	A49	s79	A46	A66				A77	A	s46 /56	11	2
Zissis VRIZAS (09/11/73) - Xanthi	A30					s46	A70	A	A	s46	13	2
Nikos MAHLAS (16/06/73) - OFI	s30	A79	s46	s66	A	s46	A70	s46			32	9
Alexandros ALEXANDRIS (21/10/68) - Olympiakos	s49	s46	A46	M	M75	M46	M	M	s46	A46	24	5
Yorgos H. YORYADIS (08/03/72) - Panathinaikos	s79	M58	M46		s75						6	2
Marinos OUZOUNIDIS (10/10/68) - Panathinaikos		D	D46	D	D	D	D		D	D46	8	-
Themistoklis NIKOLAIDIS (17/09/73) - Apollon		A46			s46	A46	s70	s77	s61	A	9	5
Yorgos DONIS (20/10/69) - Panathinaikos		A	s46	A	A	A46	A		A61	A46	17	4
Grigoris YORGATOS (31/10/72) - Panahaiki		s58	s46	s46							3	-
Nikos MIHOPOULOS (20/02/70) - PAOK			G46	G						s46	6	-
Yorgos KOUDAS (1946) - unattached			M20								43	4
Nikos SAKELLARIDIS (30/09/70) - Iraklis			s72			s46					5	-
Andreas NINIADIS (10/02/71) - Ethnikos			s76								1	-
Kostas KOSTANTINIDIS (31/08/72) - OFI			s62		s70	s61	s70	M	M46	s46	7	-
Nikos KOSTENOGLOU (03/10/70) - AEK						D24					1	-
Nikos LIBEROPOULOS (04/08/75) - Kalamata						s24	s78				2	-
Hristos KOSTIS (15/01/72) - AEK						s46	s70	A46			10	1
Kostas FRANTZESKOS (04/01/69) - OFI								s52	s82	s46	12	2
Yorgos ANATOLAKIS (16/03/74) - Iraklis								s55			1	-
Yorgos S. YORYADIS (30/01/71) - Panathinaikos										D	1	-
Yorgos NASSIOPOULOS (25/07/73) - Edessaikos										s56	1	-

EUROPEAN CUPS RESULTS 95/96

CHAMPIONS' CUP

● PANATHINAIKOS

Preliminary round HAJDUK SPLIT (CRO)

H 0-0
Nikopolidis; Apostolakis, Ouzounidis, Yoryadis Y.H., Kallitzakis, Yoryadis Y.S., Borelli (Hristodoulou 76), Markos, Warzycha, Maragos, Donis (Alexoudis 78).

A 1-1 Borelli (53)
Nikopolidis; Apostolakis, Ouzounidis, Yoryadis Y.H., Kallitzakis, Yoryadis Y.S., Borelli (Hristodoulou 70), Markos, Warzyvha (Lagonikakis 87), Maragos (Alexoudis 55), Donis.

Champions' League

1st match DYNAMO KYIV (UKR)

A 0-1 (match annulled)
Nikopolidis; Apostolakis, Ouzounidis, Markos, Kapouranis, Yoryadis Y.S., Borelli (Hristodoulou 70), Alexoudis, Warzycha, Maragos (Lagonikakis 81), Donis.

2nd match FC NANTES (FRA)

H 3-1 Yoryadis Y.H. (17), Warzycha (30, 46)
Wandzik; Borelli (Nioblias 79), Ouzounidis, Yoryadis Y.H., Kallitzakis, Yoryadis Y.S., Borelli, Alexoudis (Kapouranis 67), Warzycha, Maragos, Donis (Kolitsidakis 88).

3rd match FC PORTO (POR)

A 1-0 Markos (39)
Wandzik; Apostolakis, Ouzounidis, Yoryadis Y.H. (Lagonikakis 90), Kallitzakis, Yoryadis Y.S., Borelli (Kapouranis 67), Markos, Warzycha, Alexoudis, Donis (Kolitsidakis 81).

1st match (replacement fixture) AAB (DEN)

A 1-2 Warzycha (41)
Wandzik; Apostolakis, Ouzounidis, Yoryadis Y.H., Kallitzakis, Yoryadis Y.S., Borelli (Maragos 78), Markos, Warzycha, Kapouranis, Donis.

4th match FC PORTO (POR)

H 0-0
Wandzik; Apostolakis, Ouzounidis, Yoryadis Y.H., Kolitsidakis, Yoryadis Y.S., Borelli (Kapouranis 66), Markos, Warzycha (Lagonikakis 89), Maragos, Donis.

5th match AAB (DEN)

H 2-0 Alexoudis (1), Yoryadis Y.S. (38)
Wandzik; Apostolakis, Ouzounidis, Yoryadis Y.H., Alexoudis (Kapouranis 52), Yoryadis Y.S., Borelli, Markos, Warzycha, Maragos, Donis (Lagonikakis 89).

6th match FC NANTES (FRA)

A 0-0
Wandzik; Apostolakis, Ouzounidis, Hristodoulou, Kallitzakis, Yoryadis Y.S., Borelli (Goumas 90), Markos, Lagonikakis, Maragos, Kapouranis.

Quarter-final LEGIA WARSZAWA (POL)

A 0-0
Wandzik; Apostolakis, Markos, Yoryadis Y.H., Kallitzakis, Kolitsidakis, Borelli, Yoryadis Y.S., Warzycha, Maragos (Kapouranis 79), Alexoudis.

H 3-0 Warzycha (34, 58), Borelli (72)
Wandzik; Apostolakis, Ouzounidis, Yoryadis Y.S., Kallitzakis, Kolitsidakis, Borelli (Goumas 89), Kapouranis, Warzycha (Lagonikakis 89), Maragos (Nioblias 82), Donis.

Semi-final AJAX (HOL)

A 1-0 Warzycha (87)
Wandzik; Apostolakis, Ouzounidis, Yoryadis Y.H., Kallitzakis, Kolitsidakis, Borelli (Markos 83), Kapouranis, Warzycha (Nioblias 90), Maragos (Yoryadis Y.H. 60), Donis.

H 0-3
Wandzik; Apostolakis, Kolitsidakis, Yoryadis Y.H., Kallitzakis, Markos (Lagonikakis 85), Borelli, Kapouranis, Warzycha, Maragos (Nioblias 74), Donis.

CUP-WINNERS' CUP

● AEK

1st round FC SION (SUI)

H 2-0 Vlahos (45), Borbokis (69)
Atmatsidis; Borbokis (Kopitsis 85), Kostenoglou, Manolas, Maladenis, Vlahos, Ketsbaia, Savevski, Batista (Dimitriadis 90), Kostis (Tsartas 65), Kassapis.

A 2-2 Ketsbaia (82), Batista (87)
Atmatsidis; Borbokis (Kopitsis 77), Kostenoglou, Manolas, Maladenis, Vlahos, Ketsbaia, Sabanadzovic (Savevski 72), Batista, Tsartas (Saravakos 55), Kassapis.

2nd round BORUSSIA MÖNCHENGLADBACH (GER)

A 1-4 Maladenis (78)
Atmatsidis; Borbokis (Saravakos 60), Kostenoglou, Manolas, Sabanadzovic, Vlahos, Ketsbaia (Kopitsis 75), Savevski, Batista (Tsartas 68), Koutoulas, Kassapis.

H 0-1
Atmatsidis; Borbokis, Sabanadzovic, Manolas, Maladenis, Vlahos, Saravakos, Savevski (Ketsbaia 53), Kostis (Dimitriadis 53), Tsartas (Kopitsis 72), Kassapis.

UEFA CUP

● OLYMPIAKOS

Preliminary round SLAVIA SOFIA (BUL)

A 2-0 Ivic (80), Juskowiak (90)
Rantos; Karataidis, Pahatouridis, Dabizas, Passalis (Kallatzis 60), Skartados, Amanatidis, Alexandris (Marinakis 65), Sapanis (Juskowiak 78), Karapialis, Ivic.

H 1-0 Ivic (10)
Rantos; Hantzidis, Karataidis, Dabizas, Passalis, Skartados, Amanatidis (Kallatzis 69), Marinakis (Alexandris 83), Juskowiak (Sapanis 75), Karapialis, Ivic.

1st round MARIBOR BRANIK (SLO)

H 2-0 Juskowiak (32), Skartados (68p)
Rantos; Hantzidis (Pahatouridis 78), Karataidis, Dabizas, Passalis (Kallatzis 46), Skartados, Amanatidis, Marinakis, Juskowiak, Karapialis, Ivic (Alexandris 80).

A 3-1 Ivic (38), Skartados (64), Hantzidis (82)
Rantos; Hantzidis, Kallatzis, Dabizas, Passalis, Skartados, Amanatidis (Ioannidis 87), Marinakis, Juskowiak

EUROPEAN CUPS RESULTS 95/96 (CONTINUED)

2nd round SEVILLA FC (ESP)

A 0-1
Rantos; Hantzidis (Gonias 70), Karataidis, Dabizas, Passalis, Kallatzis, Amanatidis, Marinakis, Juskowiak (Sapanis 69), Karapialis, Ivic.

H 2-1 Sapanis (72), Juskowiak (93p)
(aet) Rantos; Karataidis, Pahatouridis (Alexoudis 55), Kallatzis, Passalis, Skartados, Sapanis (Ioannidis 106), Marinakis, Juskowiak, Karapialis (Gonias 98), Ivic.

● APOLLON

Preliminary round SCT OLIMPIJA LJUBLJANA (SLO)

H 1-0 Kola (42)
Minou; Lahanas (Theodoropoulos 89), Papadopoulos, Ioannou, Apostolou, Tatsis, Velentzas (Alexis 27; Kefalas 70), Erak, Barnjak, Kola, Nikolaidis T..

A 1-3 Kola (2)
Minou; Lahanas (Alexis 83), Papadopoulos (Lambriakos 90), Ioannou, Apostolou, Tatsis (Damigos 78), Velentzas, Erak, Barnjak, Kola, Nikolaidis T..

Nevertheless, finishing just four points above the relegation zone was too close for comfort, and with a new president and board of directors installed (Thomas Voulinos sold his majority of shares in January), a new beginning is anticipated in 96/97. Less fortunate than PAOK were 1988 champions Larissa, who could not recover from a disastrous start of seven straight defeats and went down to the Second Division along with Panionios and Ethnikos. Up to take their place came Kavala, Veria and Kastoria, the latter earning their promotion despite the distraction of changing coach five times.

It looked on the cards that the Greek national team would be changing their coach after the team failed to qualify for Euro '96 and Kostas Polihroniou's contract reached maturity in June. But the Federation decided to keep Polihroniou in place for the World Cup qualifying campaign, which got off to a promising start with a trouble-free 2-0 victory at home to Slovenia. Denmark and Croatia are sure to make a second successive World Cup qualification difficult, but Greece look to have a stronger team now than they have for some time.

The sudden interest in Greek players from abrod is evidence enough of this. Yorgos Donis, Vassilis Tsartas, Petros Marinakis and Nikos Mahlas have all been successfully courted by big foreign clubs. They are the first significant homegrown players to leave Greece since Nikos Anastopoulos quit Olympiakos for Italian side Avellino in 1987. The trend is promising. It may not please the fans of the clubs the players are abandoning. But for Greek football in general it has to be seen as a positive sign.

PLAYERS OF THE SEASON

VASSILIS TSARTAS

Having done as his supporters had hoped and added consistency and maturity to his game, AEK playmaker Vassilis Tsartas confirmed himself during the 95/96 season as the finest young player in Greece. He also demonstrated his budding prowess as a goalscorer, finishing as the league's top marksman with 26 goals and adding another six in AEK's successful Cup run, including a hat-trick in the final. His outstanding performances for AEK and Greece caught the eye of Spanish side Sevilla, who recruited him during the summer on a lucrative three-year contract.

YORGOS DONIS

Nicknamed "The Train", Yorgos Donis is undoubtedly one of the fastest wingers in Europe. He proved that much with several phenomenal performances during Panathinaikos's Champions' League run. A posse of European clubs were alerted to his awesome speed and effectiveness on the counter-attack, and Blackburn Rovers finally won the race for his signature. A natural athlete, Donis is rarely injured. He will be badly missed by Panathinaikos but Greek fans will still be able to see him go through his paces when the national team are in town. After several seasons on the fringes, the 27-year-old is now a permanent fixture in Kostas Polihroniou's team.

NIKOS LIBEROPOULOS

At 21 Nikos Liberopoulos is being tipped to become the new star of Greek football. He enjoyed a meteoric rise to prominence in 95/96, earning rave reviews with his superlative displays for unfashionable Kalamata. A creative attacking midfielder with an eye for goal, Liberopoulos found the net 11 times during the season and was rewarded with a call-up to the national team, making his début as a substitute in the January friendly against Israel. AEK and Panathinaikos subsequently duelled for his signature, and the youngster eventually plumped for the latter, who offered him abundant riches and a five-year contract.

AEK

CLUB DIRECTORY

AEK
Tritis Septemvriou 144
11251 Athinai
tel - 8224666
fax - 8234454
Year of Formation - 1924
President - Mihalis Trohanas
Coach - Dusan Bajevic (96/97 - Pertros Ravoussis)
Stadium - Nikos Goumas (33,494)

MAJOR HONOURS
League Championship - (11)
1939, 1940, 1963, 1968, 1971, 1978, 1979, 1989, 1992, 1993, 1994.
Domestic Cup - (9) 1932, 1939, 1949, 1950, 1956, 1966, 1978, 1983, 1996.

APPEARANCES 95/96

	P	Ap	(s)	Gls
Ilias ATMATSIDIS	G	30		
Daniel BATISTA	A	27		10
Vassilis BORBOKIS	D	20	(4)	2
Vassilis DIMITRIADIS	A	4	(17)	1
Vaios KARAYANNIS	D	9	(6)	
Vassilis KARAYANNIS	G	4		
Mihalis KASSAPIS	D	25	(3)	
Temur KETSBAIA (GEO)	M	31	(1)	14
Haralambos KOPITSIS	D	10	(9)	1
Nikos KOSTENOGLOU	D	28		
Hristos KOSTIS	A	31	(3)	19
Yorgos KOUTOULAS	D	2	(2)	
Hristos MALADENIS	M	20	(8)	1
Stelios MANOLAS	D	22		3
Kostas PAVLOPOULOS	D	6	(9)	1
Refik SABANADZOVIC (BOS)	D	27	(1)	3
Dimitris SARAVAKOS	A	2	(15)	1
Toni SAVEVSKI (MAC)	M	27	(3)	2
Stavros STAMATIS	M	1		
Vassilis TSARTAS	M	30	(3)	26
Mihalis VLAHOS	D	18	(6)	

LEAGUE RESULTS 1995/96

Date	Opponent		Score	Scorers
27/08/95	Paniliakos	H	3-0	Kostis, Batista, Sabanadzovic
10/09/95	Aris	A	1-2	Tsartas (p)
17/09/95	Panahaiki	H	5-1	Tsartas 2, Pavlopoulos, Ketsbaia, Kostis
24/09/95	Ethnikos	A	3-0	Sabanadzovic, Batista, Tsartas
02/10/95	Iraklis	H	3-1	Maladenis, Tsartas, Savevski
15/10/95	Kalamata	H	5-1	Ketsbaia, Kostis, Dimitriadis (p), Sabanadzovic, Tsartas
23/10/95	Ionikos	A	4-1	Tsartas 2, Manolas, Ketsbaia
28/10/95	Olympiakos	H	1-1	Kostis
06/11/95	PAOK	A	3-1	Tsartas, Ketsbaia, Kostis
18/11/95	Panathinaikos	H	1-0	Kostis
26/11/95	Apollon	A	3-0	Batista, Manolas, Ketsbaia
03/12/95	OFI	H	4-0	Ketsbaia, Tsartas, Kostis, Saravakos
09/12/95	Edessaikos	A	5-2	Ketsbaia, Batista 3, Kostis
17/12/95	Larissa	A	0-1	
07/01/96	Xanthi	H	2-1	Kostis, Tsartas
13/01/96	Athinaikos	A	1-0	Tsartas (p)
21/01/96	Panionios	H	2-0	Manolas, Tsartas
27/01/96	Paniliakos	A	2-0	Savevski, og (Lignous)
04/02/96	Aris	H	4-0	Tsartas 3, Kostis
11/02/96	Panahaiki	A	1-1	Borbokis
18/02/96	Ethnikos	H	3-1	Tsartas, Ketsbaia 2
25/02/96	Iraklis	A	3-1	Batista, Kostis, Ketsbaia
03/03/96	Kalamata	A	2-2	Ketsbaia 2
10/03/96	Ionikos	H	6-0	Batista 2, Tsartas 3 (1p), Kostis
17/03/96	Olympiakos	A	1-1	Tsartas
23/03/96	PAOK	H	4-0	Tsartas 2 (1p), Kostis 2
07/04/96	Apollon	H	1-0	Kostis
10/04/96	Panathinaikos	A	0-1	
28/04/96	OFI	A	1-1	Ketsbaia
05/05/96	Edessaikos	H	3-0	Borbokis, Ketsbaia, Batista
12/05/96	Larissa	H	1-0	Kostis
19/05/96	Xanthi	A	1-1	Kostis
26/05/96	Athinaikos	H	6-0	Kostis, og (Zotalis), Kopitsis, Tsartas 3 (1p)
29/05/96	Panionios	A	2-1	Kostis, og (Yannakouris)

APOLLON

CLUB DIRECTORY

Apollon
Antheon 45
Rizopolis
11143 Athinai
tel - 2514225
fax - 2517632
Year of Formation - 1891
President - Kostas Alamanos
Coach - Yannis Pathiakakis
(96/97 - Haralambos Tennes)
Stadium - Rizoupolis (16,000)

APPEARANCES 95/96

	P	Ap	(s)	Gls
Theodoros ALEXIS	M	21	(11)	5
Yannis APOSTOLOU	D	24	(1)	
Bernard BARNJAK (BOS)	A	29		13
Antonis DAMIGOS	D	9	(5)	
Vassilis DIMITROPOULOS	M		(1)	
Predrag ERAK (CRO)	D	24		
Kostas IOANNOU	D	23	(1)	
Vagelis KEFALAS	D	27	(2)	1
Bledar KOLA (ALB)	M	31		6
Panayotis LAHANAS	D	19	(3)	
Stavros LAMBRIAKOS	A	1	(20)	1
Kostas MAVRIDIS	D	10	(2)	1
Antonis MINOU	G	24		
Themistoklis NIKOLAIDIS	A	26	(3)	16
Yannis NIKOLAIDIS	A		(5)	
Manolis PAPADOPOULOS	D	24		
Apostolos PIKOULIDIS	M	2	(7)	
Dimitris RAPTIS	G	10	(1)	
Yannis TATSIS	M	28		1
Andreas THEODOROPOULOS	M	7	(12)	1
Lefteris VELENTZAS	M	28		2
Vagelis XANTHIS	M	7	(12)	2

LEAGUE RESULTS 1995/96

Date	Opponent		Score	Scorers
27/08/95	Edessaikos	A	0-0	
10/09/95	Larissa	H	4-0	Barnjak 3, Alexis
17/09/95	Xanthi	A	0-1	
24/09/95	Athinaikos	H	0-0	
01/10/95	Panionios	A	2-2	Barnjak, Velentzas
15/10/95	Paniliakos	H	2-1	Barnjak (p), Tatsis
22/10/95	Aris	A	0-2	
29/10/95	Panahaiki	A	1-2	Theodoropoulos
05/11/95	Ethnikos	H	3-1	Nikolaidis T. 2, Kola
19/11/95	Iraklis	A	1-1	Barnjak
26/11/95	AEK	H	0-3	
03/12/95	Ionikos	A	2-1	Barnjak 2 (1p)
10/12/95	Olympiakos	H	3-4	Barnjak 2 (2p), Xanthis
17/12/95	PAOK	A	1-2	Kola
06/01/96	Panathinaikos	H	2-3	Barnjak (p), Nikolaidis T.
14/01/96	Kalamata	H	2-1	Xanthis, Kola
21/01/96	OFI	A	1-2	Alexis
28/01/96	Edessaikos	H	1-1	Nikolaidis T.
04/02/96	Larissa	A	1-1	Nikolaidis T.
11/02/96	Xanthi	H	3-1	Nikolaidis T. 3 (1p)
18/02/96	Athinaikos	A	1-1	Alexis
25/02/96	Panionios	H	0-1	
03/03/96	Paniliakos	A	1-2	Nikolaidis T.
10/03/96	Aris	H	4-1	Alexis, Lambriakos, Kola, Nikolaidis T.
17/03/96	Panahaiki	H	2-0	Nikolaidis T. 2 (2p)
24/03/96	Ethnikos	A	2-3	Velentzas, Nikolaidis T.
31/03/96	Iraklis	H	2-1	Kefalas, Kola
07/04/96	AEK	A	0-1	
28/04/96	Ionikos	H	4-1	Mavridis, Nikolaidis T., Barnjak, Alexis
05/05/96	Olympiakos	A	3-0	Nikolaidis T., Barnjak, Kola
12/05/96	PAOK	H	0-1	
19/05/96	Panathinaikos	A	1-3	Nikolaidis T.
25/05/96	Kalamata	A	0-3	
29/05/96	OFI	H	0-1	

ARIS

CLUB DIRECTORY

Aris
Yeoryiou Angelou 14 B
54250 Thessaloniki
tel - (031) 307123
fax - (031) 423502
Year of Formation - 1914
President - Lambros Grantas
Coach - Yorgos Firos; Yannis Tzifopoulos; Jozef Jarabinsky (96/97 - Stavros Diamantopoulos)
Stadium - Harilaou (27,000)

MAJOR HONOURS
League Championship - (3) 1928, 1932, 1946.
Domestic Cup - (1) 1970.

APPEARANCES 95/96

	P	Ap	(s)	Gls
Dimitris ADAMIDIS	D		(1)	
Theodoros DALKIDIS	M	16	(7)	3
Yannis DIMITRIADIS	D	5	(9)	
Kostas IRIROTIS	D		(3)	
IVAN Silva Santos (BRA)	M	15	(2)	3
Hristos KARKAMANIS	G	24		
Theofanis KATERYANNAKIS	G	7	(1)	
Vagelis KOENTAS	G	3		
Savvas KOFIDIS	M	31		1
Yorgos KOLTSIDAS	D	14	(5)	
Vassilis KOUVALIS	D	15	(6)	
Artur LEKBELLO (ALB)	D	31		1
Apostolos LIOLIDIS	A	1	(2)	2
Zoran LONCAR (YUG)	A	15	(3)	4
Kostas LOUBOUTIS	M	4	(9)	
Dimitris MAVROYENIDIS	D	30	(1)	4
Ljubisa MILOJEVIC (YUG)	A	27	(4)	8
Manolis MITSOPOULOS	D	29	(1)	3
Mihalis PANOPOULOS	M	8	(1)	3
Kostas POZAPALIDIS	D	26		
Aleksandar SIMONOVIC (BOS)	M	15	(1)	4
Yorgos STRATILATIS	D	21	(1)	1
Theofanis TOUNTZIARIS	A	13	(9)	7
Nikos TSIANTAKIS	M	7	(1)	
Kosmas TZATZOS	M	10	(13)	1
Anastasios ZAHOPOULOS	D	7	(3)	

LEAGUE RESULTS 1995/96

Date	Opponent		Score	Scorers
27/08/95	Iraklis	A	2-3	Ivan, Stratilatis
10/09/95	AEK	H	2-1	Lekbello, Tountziaris
16/09/95	Ionikos	A	1-3	Loncar
23/09/95	Olympiakos	H	0-0	
01/10/95	PAOK	A	0-1	
14/10/95	Panathinaikos	H	1-1	Loncar
22/10/95	Apollon	H	2-0	Ivan, Loncar
29/10/95	OFI	A	0-2	
05/11/95	Edessaikos	H	2-0	Loncar (p), Milojevic
19/11/95	Larissa	A	0-1	
26/11/95	Xanthi	H	2-2	Milojevic, Dalkidis
03/12/95	Athinaikos	A	0-0	
10/12/95	Panionios	H	4-2	Dalkidis, Tountziaris 2 (1p), Ivan
17/12/95	Paniliakos	A	1-2	Tountziaris
07/01/96	Kalamata	A	1-1	Mavroyenidis
14/01/96	Panahaiki	H	1-0	Tountziaris
21/01/96	Ethnikos	A	1-3	Kofidis
28/01/96	Iraklis	H	0-0	
04/02/96	AEK	A	0-4	
11/02/96	Ionikos	H	2-0	Tzatzos, Mavroyenidis
18/02/96	Olympiakos	A	0-4	
25/02/96	PAOK	H	0-0	
02/03/96	Panathinaikos	A	1-3	Mavroyenidis
10/03/96	Apollon	A	1-4	Panopoulos
17/03/96	OFI	H	2-1	Dalkidis, Milojevic
24/03/96	Edessaikos	A	1-1	Mitsopoulos
31/03/96	Larissa	H	6-0	Mavroyenidis, Milojevic 3, Panopoulos, Simonovic (p)
07/04/96	Xanthi	A	0-4	
27/04/96	Athinaikos	H	1-1	Panopoulos
05/05/96	Panionios	A	2-0	Tountziaris, Simonovic
12/05/96	Paniliakos	H	3-1	Milojevic, Simonovic 2
19/05/96	Kalamata	H	1-1	Mitsopoulos
26/05/96	Panahaiki	A	1-0	Tountziaris (p)
29/05/96	Ethnikos	H	4-1	Milojevic, Liolidis 2, Mitsopoulos

ATHINAIKOS

CLUB DIRECTORY

Athinaikos
Neas Efessou 6
Vironas
16231 Athinai
tel - 7656200
fax - 7645500
Year of Formation - 1917
President - Spiros Kaloyannis
Coach - Haralambos Tennes
(96/97 - Yannis Pathiakakis)
Stadium - Virona (6,000)

APPEARANCES 95/96

	P	Ap	(s)	Gls
Mihalis ALVERTIS	M	29	(3)	5
Yorgos ANASTASIOU	M	16	(8)	1
Kiriakos ATHANASIOU	M	1	(2)	
Yannis BAKOPOULOS	G	8		
Theodoros BOUTZOUKAS	D	17	(4)	
Milan DABIC (YUG)	A	12	(15)	3
Pavlos DERMITZAKIS	A	4	(5)	1
Anastasios HATZIANGELIS	D	23		
Alexandros KAKLAMANOS	A	15		5
Nikos KEFALAS	G	5		
Yorgos KOLTZOS	D	21	(4)	1
Mariusz KURZEJA (POL)	M	11		
Nikos MAVROMATIS	D		(5)	
Tzanis MONOS	D	13	(3)	
Periklis PAPAPOSTOLOU	M	5	(7)	
Angelos PLIOTAS	G	21	(1)	
Efthimios SIDIROPOULOS	M	23	(4)	4
Antonis SPINOULAS	A	9	(15)	3
Anastasios TASSIOPOULOS	D	34		3
Milan TEBIC (YUG)	D	21	(5)	1
Kostas THEODORAKOS	D	19	(1)	
Kostas TSIRONIS	M	20	(8)	2
Hristos VASSIOS	A	1		
Hristos VELIS	M	27	(1)	3
Yorgos ZOTALIS	M	19	(4)	1

LEAGUE RESULTS 1995/96

27/08/95	Olympiakos	H	0-1	
10/09/95	PAOK	A	0-1	
17/09/95	Panathinaikos	H	1-2	Alvertis
24/09/95	Apollon	A	0-0	
01/10/95	OFI	H	3-2	Tebic, Velis, Dabic (p)
15/10/95	Edessaikos	A	2-5	Alvertis, Zotalis (p)
22/10/95	Larissa	H	1-0	Spinoulas
29/10/95	Xanthi	A	0-3	
05/11/95	Kalamata	A	0-1	
19/11/95	Panionios	H	2-1	Sidiropoulos, Tassiopoulos (p)
26/11/95	Paniliakos	A	1-4	Dermitzakis
03/12/95	Aris	H	0-0	
10/12/95	Panahaiki	A	0-2	
17/12/95	Ethnikos	H	2-0	Tassiopoulos, Sidiropoulos
07/01/96	Iraklis	A	2-1	Sidiropoulos 2
13/01/96	AEK	H	0-1	
21/01/96	Ionikos	A	1-0	Kaklamanos
28/01/96	Olympiakos	A	0-3	
04/02/96	PAOK	H	2-1	Alvertis, Kaklamanos
11/02/96	Panathinaikos	A	0-0	
18/02/96	Apollon	H	1-1	Dabic
25/02/96	OFI	A	1-0	Anastasiou
03/03/96	Edessaikos	H	2-1	Kaklamanos 2
10/03/96	Larissa	A	1-1	Tsironis
17/03/96	Xanthi	H	2-1	Kaklamanos, Alvertis
24/03/96	Kalamata	H	1-1	Dabic
06/04/96	Paniliakos	H	0-0	
27/04/96	Aris	A	1-1	Spinoulas
05/05/96	Panahaiki	H	2-0	Koltzos, Tassiopoulos
08/05/96*	Panionios	A	2-1	Velis, Tsironis
12/05/96	Ethnikos	A	2-3	Alvertis, Spinoulas
19/05/96	Iraklis	H	0-1	
26/05/96	AEK	A	0-6	
29/05/96	Ionikos	H	1-2	Velis

* 70 minutes played on 31/03/96.

EDESSAIKOS

CLUB DIRECTORY

Edessaikos
Filellinon 17
58200 Edessa
tel - (0381) 21050
fax - (0381) 23654
Year of Formation - 1939
President - Vangelis Konstantinidis
Coach - Angelos Anastassiadis
Stadium - Edessas (6,000)

APPEARANCES 95/96

	P	Ap	(s)	Gls
Yorgos ALAFOSTERYIOS	G	1	(1)	
Dimitris ALEXIADIS	A	1	(6)	
Vassilis ANDREADIS	A	19	(7)	7
Yorgos BETAS	D	14	(7)	1
Anastasios FEREKIDIS	M	12	(14)	2
Nikos HARALAMBOUS	D		(3)	
Kostas IKONOMIDIS	M	19	(4)	1
Yorgos KARAISARIDIS	D	19	(4)	1
Vassilis KASTANIOTIS	D	23	(5)	2
Zdrejan KOLAKOVIC (YUG)	A	13	(8)	5
Hristo KOLEV (BUL)	M	23	(3)	5
Savvas KOTSIFAS	D	13	(4)	1
Vassilis KOUTALIS	M		(2)	
Vassilis KOUTSOURES	M	24	(3)	2
Yorgos LADIAS	D	16	(3)	
Stavros MATZIOUNIS	D	5	(4)	2
Anastasios MAVRIDIS	G	1		
Yorgos NASSIOPOULOS	A	32	(1)	16
Anastasios PANAYOTIDIS	A	1	(9)	1
Savvas PAPADOPOULOS	D	12	(1)	1
Radek RABUCIC (YUG)	G	32		
Evripidis SAMOLIS	M	31		1
Dimitris STAFILIDIS	M	13	(5)	1
Nikos TELLIDIS	D	1	(2)	
Apostolos TSOPTSIS	D	25	(2)	
Alexandros TZIVENIS	M		(1)	
Vassilis VOUZAS	M	24	(2)	

LEAGUE RESULTS 1995/96

27/08/95	Apollon	H	0-0	
10/09/95	OFI	A	1-4	Kolev
17/09/95	Kalamata	A	1-1	Panayotidis
24/09/95	Larissa	H	3-1	Betas, Nassiopoulos, Andreadis
01/10/95	Xanthi	A	1-1	Kolev
15/10/95	Athinaikos	H	5-2	Ikonomidis, Samolis, Kolakovic, Nassiopoulos, Ferekidis
22/10/95	Panionios	A	2-1	Nassiopoulos, Kolakovic
29/10/95	Paniliakos	H	1-3	Kolakovic (p)
05/11/95	Aris	A	0-2	
19/11/95	Panahaiki	H	2-0	Andreadis (p), Nassiopoulos
26/11/95	Ethnikos	A	1-1	Matziounis
03/12/95	Iraklis	H	2-0	Kastaniotis, Nassiopoulos
09/12/95	AEK	H	2-5	Kotsifas, Kolakovic
17/12/95	Ionikos	A	0-3	
07/01/96	Olympiakos	H	2-5	Matziounis, Papadopoulos
14/01/96	PAOK	A	1-0	Kastaniotis
21/01/96	Panathinaikos	H	1-3	Koutsoures
28/01/96	Apollon	A	1-1	Nassiopoulos
04/02/96	OFI	H	3-2	Nassiopoulos 2, Kolev
11/02/96	Kalamata	H	1-0	Nassiopoulos
18/02/96	Larissa	A	2-0	Koutsoures, Nassiopoulos
25/02/96	Xanthi	H	1-1	Nassiopoulos
03/03/96	Athinaikos	A	1-2	Nassiopoulos (p)
10/03/96	Panionios	H	2-1	Kolakovic, Kolev
17/03/96	Paniliakos	A	3-2	Nassiopoulos, Andreadis, og
24/03/96	Aris	H	1-1	Nassiopoulos
31/03/96	Panahaiki	A	0-1	
07/04/96	Ethnikos	H	6-2	Nassiopoulos 2, Andreadis 2, Karaisaridis, Ferekidis
28/04/96	Iraklis	A	0-2	
05/05/96	AEK	A	0-3	
11/05/96	Ionikos	H	0-1	
19/05/96	Olympiakos	A	0-2	
26/05/96	PAOK	H	3-3	Kolev, Andreadis 2 (2p)
29/05/96	Panathinaikos	A	1-3	Stafilidis

ETHNIKOS

CLUB DIRECTORY

Ethnikos
Vassileos Yeoryiou B 5
18534 Piraeus
tel - 4111445
fax - 4112385
Year of Formation - 1925
President - Antonis Stelliatos
Coach - Kostas Tsangalidis; Jacek Gmoch; Hristos Hatziioannidis; Timo Tschanlighter
Stadium - Karaiskakis (34,023)

MAJOR HONOURS
Domestic Cup - (1) 1933.

APPEARANCES 95/96

	P	Ap	(s)	Gls
Yannis ANASTASIOU	A	24	(6)	9
Vagelis ANGELIS	D	16	(6)	
Anestis ATHANASSIADIS	A	19	(10)	5
Andreas BALOYANNIS	D	3	(1)	
Dimitris BOUGAS	D	25		3
Dimitris BOUYOUKLIS	M	9		1
Apostolos DIMOPOULOS	D	13	(4)	
Zoran DRASKOVIC (YUG)	A	2		
Mihalis GRIGORIOU	D	8	(8)	
Theodoros KANTAS	G	25		
Yannis KAMITSIS	A	25	(3)	2
Mihalis KAPSIS	D	17		
Vagelis KARASSAVAS	G	3		
Hristos KONTIS	M	18	(3)	2
Yannis MAKRAS	G	6	(2)	
Andreas NINIADIS	M	24	(2)	11
Bozidar PANTOVIC (YUG)	D	17		3
Periklis PAPAPANAYIS	M	3	(2)	
Goran PETKOVSKI (MAC)	M	13	(1)	
Vassilis STAVRAKAKIS	A	1	(4)	
Nikos TSIABIRAS	M	2	(2)	
Yannis TSIAMAKIS	M		(1)	
Dimitris TSIAOUSIS	M	20	(4)	2
Antonis TSIBAKIS	D	1	(4)	
Yorgos TSIOTRAS	D	13	(7)	
Yannis TSIPLAKIS	D	17		1
Roy WASSBERG (NOR)	D	27		
Vassilis XANTHIS	M	4	(1)	
Dimitris YELADARIS	D	14	(1)	1
Panayotis ZIAKKAS	A	5	(8)	

LEAGUE RESULTS 1995/96

27/08/95	Panahaiki	H	1-2	Athanassiadis
10/09/95	Kalamata	H	2-3	Niniadis 2 (1p)
17/09/95	Iraklis	A	1-4	Tsiaousis
24/09/95	AEK	H	0-3	
01/10/95	Ionikos	A	1-4	Pantovic
14/10/95	Olympiakos	H	0-3	
22/10/95	PAOK	A	0-2	
28/10/95	Panathinaikos	H	0-0	
05/11/95	Apollon	A	1-3	Anastasiou
19/11/95	OFI	A	2-3	Bouyouklis, Kamitsis
26/11/95	Edessaikos	H	1-1	Pantovic
03/12/95	Larissa	A	1-0	Bougas
10/12/95	Xanthi	H	1-2	Athanassiadis
17/12/95	Athinaikos	A	0-2	
07/01/96	Panionios	H	2-0	Tsiaousis, Niniadis
14/01/96	Paniliakos	A	2-2	Kamitsis, Tsiplakis
21/01/96	Aris	H	3-1	Pantovic, Yeladaris, Athanassiadis
28/01/96	Panahaiki	A	0-1	
04/02/96	Kalamata	A	1-3	Anastasiou
11/02/96	Iraklis	H	1-4	Niniadis
18/02/96	AEK	A	1-3	Niniadis (p)
25/02/96	Ionikos	H	2-5	Anastasiou, Niniadis (p)
03/03/96	Olympiakos	A	0-3	
10/03/96	PAOK	H	2-3	Anastasiou 2
16/03/96	Panathinaikos	A	0-3	
24/03/96	Apollon	H	3-2	Bougas, Niniadis 2
31/03/96	OFI	H	2-3	Anastasiou, Niniadis (p)
07/04/96	Edessaikos	A	2-6	Anastasiou, Athanassiadis
28/04/96	Larissa	H	0-1	
05/05/96	Xanthi	A	1-6	Anastasiou
12/05/96	Athinaikos	H	3-2	Kontis, Niniadis 2 (1p)
19/05/96	Panionios	A	1-2	Kontis
26/05/96	Paniliakos	H	2-4	Bougas, Anastasiou (p)
29/05/96	Aris	A	1-4	Athanassiadis

IONIKOS

CLUB DIRECTORY

Ionikos
Petrou Ralli 248
18451 Nikea Piraeus
tel - (01) 4964243
fax - (01) 4964502
Year of Formation - 1965
President - Nikos Kanellakis
Coach - Oleg Blokhin
Stadium - Neapolis (8,000)

APPEARANCES 95/96

	P	Ap	(s)	Gls
Thanassis BEKOS	D	7	(1)	
Yorgos DARAKLITSAS	M	25	(2)	1
Paolo DA SILVA (BRA)	M	10	(6)	
Vassilis FILIS	D	21	(5)	1
Nikos FROUSSOS	A	23	(8)	9
Mihalis GRIBILAS	A	15	(5)	3
Yannis HATZINIKOLAOU	D	12	(3)	
Mihalis IORDANIDIS	A	3	(10)	
Dimitris KALIKAS	M	22	(5)	3
Savvas KAPAYERIDIS	D	16	(2)	
Nikos KAROUSAKIS	M		(1)	
Miloje KLAEVIC (YUG)	D	20		2
Nikos KOURKOUNAS	G	11	(1)	
Mihalis LEONTIADIS	A		(1)	
Alexandros NIKOLAIDIS	G	2	(1)	
Vasyl NOVOHATSKI (UKR)	A	29	(2)	10
Amaeci OTIZI (NIG)	A	4	(13)	2
Nikos OUSTAMBASSIDIS	M	2	(5)	
Theodoros PAHATOURIDIS	D	17		
Theodoros PIETRIS	D	2	(1)	
Ilias SAVVIDIS	M	21	(7)	6
Panayotis SIDIROPOULOS	D	28	(1)	3
Stavros STAMATIS	M	19	(2)	1
Spiros STAMATOUKOS	D	10	(4)	
Yorgos STAMBOULIS	A		(1)	
Nikos TSIANTAKIS	M	14	(1)	
Yorgos TSITIRIDIS	M		(1)	
Antonis TZIKAS	A	2	(8)	
Yannis XANTHOPOULOS	D	18	(4)	2
Yorgos YORGOUSIS	G	21		

LEAGUE RESULTS 1995/96

Date	Opponent	H/A	Score	Scorers
27/08/95	Panionios	H	2-1	Gribilas, Kalikas
10/09/95	Paniliakos	A	0-0	
16/09/95	Aris	H	3-1	Gribilas, Savvidis, Kalikas
24/09/95	Panahaiki	A	2-1	Sidiropoulos, Otizi
01/10/95	Ethnikos	H	4-1	Gribilas (p), Sidiropoulos, Novohatski 2 (1p)
15/10/95	Iraklis	A	1-3	Novohatski
23/10/95	AEK	H	1-4	Novohatski
29/10/95	Kalamata	H	2-2	Froussos, Novohatski
05/11/95	Olympiakos	A	1-1	Savvidis
19/11/95	PAOK	H	0-0	
26/11/95	Panathinaikos	A	0-3	
03/12/95	Apollon	H	1-2	Novohatski
10/12/95	OFI	A	1-3	Xanthopoulos
17/12/95	Edessaikos	H	3-0	Kalikas, Daraklitsas, Novohatski
07/01/96	Larissa	A	0-1	
14/01/96	Xanthi	A	0-1	
21/01/96	Athinaikos	H	0-1	
28/01/96	Panionios	A	3-1	Klaevic 2 (2p), Novohatski
03/02/96	Paniliakos	H	2-1	Froussos, Stamatis
11/02/96	Aris	A	0-2	
17/02/96	Panahaiki	H	1-1	Froussos
25/02/96	Ethnikos	A	5-2	Savvidis 2, Froussos 3
03/03/96	Iraklis	H	1-1	Filis
10/03/96	AEK	A	0-6	
17/03/96	Kalamata	A	0-0	
24/03/96	Olympiakos	H	0-2	
31/03/96	PAOK	A	1-1	Xanthopoulos
07/04/96	Panathinaikos	H	2-1	Froussos 2
28/04/96	Apollon	A	1-4	Froussos (p)
05/05/96	OFI	H	0-0	
11/05/96	Edessaikos	A	1-0	Savvidis
18/05/96	Larissa	H	3-1	Savvidis, og (Nikolaou), Sidiropoulos
26/05/96	Xanthi	H	1-1	Novohatski
29/05/96	Athinaikos	A	2-1	Novohatski, Otizi

IRAKLIS

CLUB DIRECTORY

Iraklis
Vassileos Yeoryiou 33 A
54640 Thessaloniki
tel - (031) 834300
fax - (031) 836262
Year of Formation - 1908
President - Petros Theodoridis
Coach - Dusan Milosevic; Vassilis Antoniadis
Stadium - Kaftantzoglio (45,000)

MAJOR HONOURS
Domestic Cup - (1) 1976.

APPEARANCES 95/96

	P	Ap	(s)	Gls
Yorgos ANATOLAKIS	D	32		3
Stefanos BORBOKIS	A	31	(2)	5
Marios HRISTODOULOU (CYP)	M	22	(7)	1
Ivan JOVANOVIC (YUG)	M	20	(1)	3
Polihronis KALLIGAS	G	15	(1)	
Maximos KATIKARIDIS	M	2	(5)	
Sotiris KOSTANTINIDIS	M	17	(14)	7
Yorgos KOSTIS	A	24	(5)	1
Kostas LAGONIDIS	M	15		1
Alphonse MEBUNU (CMR)	A		(2)	
Nikos MIRTSEKIS	A	28	(1)	13
Anastasios MITROPOULOS	M	3	(5)	1
Yorgos MOURATIDIS	M		(4)	
Marko PANTELIC (YUG)	A	1	(7)	4
Daniil PAPADOPOULOS	D	27	(1)	3
Fotis PAPADOPOULOS	A		(1)	
Yorgos PAPADOPOULOS	D	15	(5)	1
Milan PAVLOVIC (YUG)	M	19	(5)	1
Yorgos PLITSIS	G	8		
Nikos SAKELLARIDIS	M	24	(6)	3
Periklis STOLTIDIS	M	24	(3)	
Ilias TALIKRIADIS	G	11	(1)	
Dimitris THODIS	M		(2)	
Yorgos XENIDIS	D	5	(11)	
Alexandros XENITOPOULOS	D	3	(4)	1
Lissandros YORGAMLIS	D	28		1

LEAGUE RESULTS 1995/96

27/08/95	Aris	H	3-2	Sakellaridis, Pavlovic, og (Mitsopoulos)
10/09/95	Panahaiki	A	0-1	
17/09/95	Ethnikos	H	4-1	Anatolakis, Kostantinidis, Borbokis, Pantelic
24/09/95	Kalamata	H	2-1	Mitropoulos, Anatolakis
02/10/95	AEK	A	1-3	Mirtsekis
15/10/95	Ionikos	H	3-1	Mirtsekis, Pantelic 2
22/10/95	Olympiakos	A	1-2	Jovanovic
29/10/95	PAOK	H	2-2	Borbokis, Jovanovic
05/11/95	Panathinaikos	A	0-4	
19/11/95	Apollon	H	1-1	Mirtsekis
25/11/95	OFI	A	0-0	
03/12/95	Edessaikos	A	0-2	
10/12/95	Larissa	H	2-1	Mirtsekis, Pantelic
17/12/95	Xanthi	A	1-0	Mirstekis
07/01/96	Athinaikos	H	1-2	Mirtsekis
14/01/96	Panionios	A	0-0	
21/01/96	Paniliakos	H	2-0	Kostantinidis, Papadopoulos D. (p)
28/01/96	Aris	A	0-0	
04/02/96	Panahaiki	H	0-1	
11/02/96	Ethnikos	A	4-1	Mirtsekis 2, Hristodoulou, Kostantinidis
18/02/96	Kalamata	A	0-1	
25/02/96	AEK	H	1-3	Kostis
03/03/96	Ionikos	A	1-1	Xenitopoulos
10/03/96	Olympiakos	H	2-1	Papadopoulos D. (p), Sakellaridis
16/03/96	PAOK	A	2-1	Mirtsekis, Lagonidis
24/03/96	Panathinaikos	H	1-1	Borbokis
31/03/96	Apollon	A	1-2	Borbokis
07/04/96	OFI	H	5-1	Papadopoulos D. (p), Mirtsekis 2, Kostantinidis, Sakellaridis
28/04/96	Edessaikos	H	2-0	Mirtsekis, Jovanovic
05/05/96	Larissa	A	1-0	Mirtsekis
12/05/96	Xanthi	H	2-0	Kostantinidis 2
19/05/96	Athinaikos	A	1-0	Kostantinidis
26/05/96	Panionios	H	3-2	Yorgamlis, Borbokis, og
29/05/96	Paniliakos	A	2-1	Anatolakis, Papadopoulos Y.

KALAMATA

CLUB DIRECTORY

Kalamata
Kapetan Kroba 5
22549 Kalamata
tel - (0721) 834130
fax - (0721) 225094
Year of Formation - 1967
President - Stavros Papadopoulos
Coach - Dragan Kokotovic; Elvio Mana; Bo Petersson
Stadium - Messiniakou (8,000)

APPEARANCES 95/96

	P	Ap	(s)	Gls
Panayotis BAHRAMIS	D	15	(3)	1
Arian BELA (ALB)	M	17	(4)	4
Vassilis BLETSAS	M	17		1
Alexandros DEDES	D	26	(6)	5
Pavlos DERMITZAKIS	A	7	(6)	2
Afo DODOO (GHA)	D	17		
Yannis DOUVIKAS	A	2	(3)	
Panayotis DROUGAS	M	1	(3)	
Arian DZOUBA (ALB)	D	30		1
Vassilis FOTINAKIS	A	1	(3)	
Efstratios GAROZIS	D	1	(2)	
Theodoros GOLIAS	D	8	(12)	
Ebenezer HAGAN (GHA)	M	14	(5)	1
Sam JOHNSON (GHA)	M	18	(2)	6
Yorgos KARATHANASIS	D	7	(3)	
Hristos KELPEKIS	G	7		
Sokratis KOPSAHILIS	G	26		
Panayotis KOSTANTINIDIS	D	23		1
Thanassis KOSTOULAS	D	20	(4)	
Nikos LIBEROPOULOS	M	29		11
Sotiris LIBEROPOULOS	G	1	(2)	
Vladan MILOJEVIC (YUG)	M	9		
Zdenko MUF (CRO)	A	9		3
Peter OFORLIKOUE (GHA)	A	2	(6)	1
Panayotis SAKELLAROPOULOS	D	13	(2)	
Thanasis SENTEMENTES	D	1	(1)	
Kostas STILIANOPOULOS	M	14	(4)	
Petros TENGELIDIS	M	27	(1)	3
Kostas TSANAS	M	9	(9)	1
Panayotis TZANAVARAS	D	1	(5)	
Nikos VAVILIS	D	2	(6)	

LEAGUE RESULTS 1995/96

Date	Opponent	H/A	Score	Scorers
26/08/95	OFI	H	2-3	Johnson 2
10/09/95	Ethnikos	A	3-2	Bela (p), Liberopoulos N., Muf
17/09/95	Edessaikos	H	1-1	Muf
24/09/95	Iraklis	A	1-2	Tsanas
30/09/95	Larissa	H	5-0	Dzouba, Liberopoulos N. 2, Muf (p), Bahramis
15/10/95	AEK	A	1-5	Bela
22/10/95	Xanthi	H	1-1	Liberopoulos N.
29/10/95	Ionikos	A	2-2	Johnson, Liberopoulos N.
05/11/95	Athinaikos	H	1-0	Dedes
19/11/95	Olympiakos	A	1-4	Dedes
26/11/95	Panionios	H	1-0	Kostantinidis
03/12/95	PAOK	A	1-1	Hagan
10/12/95	Paniliakos	H	1-1	Liberopoulos N.
17/12/95	Panathinaikos	A	0-4	
07/01/96	Aris	H	1-1	Tengelidis
14/01/96	Apollon	A	1-2	Dedes (p)
20/01/96	Panahaiki	H	1-0	Dermitzakis
28/01/96	OFI	A	0-3	
04/02/96	Ethnikos	H	3-1	Liberopoulos N. 2, Bela
11/02/96	Edessaikos	A	0-1	
18/02/96	Iraklis	H	1-0	Dermitzakis
25/02/96	Larissa	A	1-1	Liberopoulos N.
03/03/96	AEK	H	2-2	Johnson, Bela
09/03/96	Xanthi	A	0-1	
17/03/96	Ionikos	H	0-0	
24/03/96	Athinaikos	A	1-1	Tengelidis
31/03/96	Olympiakos	H	3-0	Liberopoulos N., Tengelidis, Dedes
07/04/96	Panionios	A	1-2	Johnson
28/04/96	PAOK	H	1-1	Johnson
04/05/96	Paniliakos	A	0-1	
12/05/96	Panathinaikos	H	0-1	
19/05/96	Aris	A	1-1	Liberopoulos N.
25/05/96	Apollon	H	3-0	Bletsas, Dedes, Oforlikoue
29/05/96	Panahaiki	A	0-1	

LARISSA

CLUB DIRECTORY

Larissa
Kiprou 72
41222 Larissa
tel - (041) 255095
fax - (041) 257960
Year of Formation - 1964
President - Nikos Papanikolaou
Coach - Yannis Mantzourakis; Sotiris Koukouthakis; Andreas Mihalopoulos (96/97 - Yorgos Firos)
Stadium - Alkazar (18,500)

MAJOR HONOURS
League Championship - (1) 1988.
Domestic Cup - (1) 1985.

APPEARANCES 95/96

	P	Ap	(s)	Gls
Thanassis DELOPOULOS	D	9	(2)	
Viktor DVIRNIK (UKR)	D	11	(2)	1
David EMBE (CMR)	A	24	(2)	7
Jean-Pierre FIALA (CMR)	D	6	(1)	
Fotis GOUZIOTIS	D	14	(3)	
Serge HONI	A	8	(1)	2
Kostas KOLOMITROUSIS	D	27		4
Hristos MIHAIL	G	5	(1)	
Slobodan MILETIC (YUG)	D	5	(4)	
Lefter MILLO (ALB)	M	2	(2)	1
Yorgos MITSIBONAS	D	27		3
Kostas MOURATIDIS	D	23	(3)	
Vagelis NASSIAKOS	D	18	(5)	
Kostas NEBEGLERAS	M	20	(9)	2
Haralambos NIKOLAOU	D	21	(6)	2
Yorgos PAPADOPOULOS	M	12	(6)	1
Hristos PAPAYANOPOULOS	G	3	(4)	
Dimitris PAPPAS	M	2	(3)	
Simeon PAVLIDIS	D	8	(4)	
Yannis PROVIDAS	A	4	(2)	
Stefan STOICA (ROM)	A	27	(1)	4
Kostas TAXIARHIS	M	21	(2)	1
Lefteris TIOUTIOS	M	4	(4)	
Dimitris TSAKMAKIDIS	A	2	(6)	1
Yannis TSAKMAKIDIS	M	11	(13)	3
Vassilis TSANAKIS	A	1		
Yorgos TSIBINIS	M	8	(2)	
Dimitris TZIOTZIOS	D	25	(2)	
Yannis VASSILIOU	A		(1)	
Hristos VELETANIS	D		(10)	
Angelos YEORYIOU	G	26		

LEAGUE RESULTS 1995/96

27/08/95	Panathinaikos	H	0-1	
10/09/95	Apollon	A	0-4	
17/09/95	OFI	H	2-6	Honi, Embé
24/09/95	Edessaikos	A	1-3	Nebegleras
30/09/95	Kalamata	A	0-5	
15/10/95	Xanthi	H	1-2	Honi
22/10/95	Athinaikos	A	0-1	
29/10/95	Panionios	H	0-0	
05/11/95	Paniliakos	A	2-4	Stoica 2
19/11/95	Aris	H	1-0	Mitsibonas
26/11/95	Panahaiki	A	1-1	Tsakmakidis Y.
03/12/95	Ethnikos	H	0-1	
10/12/95	Iraklis	A	1-2	Embé
17/12/95	AEK	H	1-0	Papadopoulos
07/01/96	Ionikos	H	1-0	Kolomitroussis
14/01/96	Olympiakos	A	1-3	Stoica
21/01/96	PAOK	H	2-1	Mitsibonas, Embé
28/01/96	Panathinaikos	A	1-6	Dvirnik
04/02/96	Apollon	H	1-1	Tsakmakidis Y.
11/02/96	OFI	A	0-0	
18/02/96	Edessaikos	H	0-2	
25/02/96	Kalamata	H	1-1	Embé
03/03/96	Xanthi	A	1-3	Kolomitrousis
10/03/96	Athinaikos	H	1-1	Taxiarhis
17/03/96	Panionios	A	0-0	
24/03/96	Paniliakos	H	1-0	Nikolaou
31/03/96	Aris	A	0-6	
07/04/96	Panahaiki	H	4-1	Kolomitrousis, Nikolaou, Embé, Nebegleras
28/04/96	Ethnikos	A	1-0	Stoica
05/05/96	Iraklis	H	0-1	
12/05/96	AEK	A	0-1	
18/05/96	Ionikos	A	1-3	Embé
26/05/96	Olympiakos	H	3-2	Millo, Kolomitrousis , Tsakmakidis Y.
29/05/96	PAOK	A	3-2	Embé, Mitsibonas (p), Tsakmakidis D.

OFI

CLUB DIRECTORY

Omilos Filathlon Irakliou (OFI)
Ikostis Pemptis Avgoustou 18
71202 Iraklion
Kriti
tel - (081) 243095
fax - (081) 288341
Year of Formation - 1925
President - Yannis Papamatheakis
Coach - Eugeniusz Gerard
Stadium - OFI (12,000)

MAJOR HONOURS

Domestic Cup - (1) 1987.

APPEARANCES 95/96

	P	Ap	(s)	Gls
Pavlos ADAMOS	D	15	(2)	
Manolis DERMITZAKIS	M		(6)	
Kostas FRANTZESKOS	M	26	(6)	12
Kostas HANIOTAKIS	G	32		
Kostas KIASSOS	D	23	(5)	2
Kostas KOSTANTINIDIS	M	24	(2)	2
Nikos KOUNENAKIS	M	1	(1)	
Yorgos KOUTSOUPIAS	D	9	(2)	
Stelios KOZANIDIS	M		(8)	
Nikos MAHLAS	A	33		17
Predrag MITIC (YUG)	A	27		5
Dimitris MOUTAS	D	23	(5)	3
Nikos PAPADOPOULOS	D	29		1
Manolis PATEMTZIS	D	20	(5)	1
Ilias POURSANIDIS	D	18	(11)	
Karol PRAZENICA (SVK)	D	29	(1)	
Zoran RIZNIC (YUG)	M	26	(3)	12
Yannis SAMARAS	M	1	(22)	
Andreas SKENTZOS	D	21	(1)	
Kostas STAVRAKAKIS	M		(4)	
Yannis THOMAIDIS	A		(4)	
Ilias TZIOKAS	M	5	(3)	
Stefanos VAVOULAS	D	10	(3)	2
Nikos YALAMAS	G	2		

LEAGUE RESULTS 1995/96

Date	Opponent	H/A	Score	Scorers
26/08/95	Kalamata	A	3-2	Mahlas, Vavoulas, Mitic
10/09/95	Edessaikos	H	4-1	Riznic, Mahlas, Mitic, Frantzeskos
17/09/95	Larissa	A	6-2	Mahlas, Riznic 2, Mitic, Moutas 2
24/09/95	Xanthi	H	3-0	Riznic 3 (1p)
01/10/95	Athinaikos	A	2-3	Frantzeskos, Mahlas
15/10/95	Panionios	H	2-2	Mahlas, Vavoulas
21/10/95	Paniliakos	A	2-4	Mitic, Riznic
29/10/95	Aris	H	2-0	Riznic (p), Mahlas
04/11/95	Panahaiki	A	1-0	Mahlas
19/11/95	Ethnikos	H	3-2	Frantzeskos (p), Mitic, Riznic
25/11/95	Iraklis	H	0-0	
03/12/95	AEK	A	0-4	
10/12/95	Ionikos	H	3-1	Frantzeskos, Riznic, Moutas
17/12/95	Olympiakos	A	1-3	Frantzeskos (p)
07/01/96	PAOK	H	2-1	Frantzeskos 2 (1p)
14/01/96	Panathinaikos	A	0-4	
21/01/96	Apollon	H	2-1	Kiassos, Mahlas
28/01/96	Kalamata	H	3-0	Mahlas 2, Frantzeskos
04/02/96	Edessaikos	A	2-3	Kostantinidis, Mahlas
11/02/96	Larissa	H	0-0	
18/02/96	Xanthi	A	2-0	Riznic, Papadopoulos
25/02/96	Athinaikos	H	0-1	
02/03/96	Panionios	A	0-1	
10/03/96	Paniliakos	H	2-2	Patemtzis, Mahlas
17/03/96	Aris	A	1-2	Mahlas
24/03/96	Panahaiki	H	1-0	Mahlas
31/03/96	Ethnikos	A	3-2	Frantzeskos, Mahlas, Riznic
07/04/96	Iraklis	A	1-5	Frantzeskos
28/04/96	AEK	H	1-1	Kostantinidis
05/05/96	Ionikos	A	0-0	
12/05/96	Olympiakos	H	2-1	Mahlas, Kiassos
19/05/96	PAOK	A	0-3	
26/05/96	Panathinaikos	H	2-1	Frantzeskos 2
29/05/96	Apollon	A	1-0	Mahlas

OLYMPIAKOS

CLUB DIRECTORY

Olympiakos
Ipsilantou 170
18535 Piraeus
tel - 4297225
fax - 4297228
Year of Formation - 1925
President - Sokratis Kokkalis
Coach - Stavros Diamantopoulos; Miletis Persias (96/97 - Dusan Bajevic)
Stadium - Karaiskakis (34,023)
League Championship - (25)
1931, 1933, 1934, 1936, 1937, 1938, 1947, 1948, 1951, 1954, 1955, 1956, 1957, 1958, 1959, 1966, 1967, 1973, 1974, 1975, 1980, 1981, 1982, 1983, 1987.
Domestic Cup - (19)
1947, 1951, 1952, 1953, 1954, 1957, 1958, 1959, 1960, 1961, 1963, 1965, 1968, 1971, 1973, 1975, 1981, 1990, 1992.

APPEARANCES 95/96

	P	Ap	(s)	Gls
Alexandros ALEXANDRIS	A	18	(7)	6
Yorgos AMANATIDIS	D	22	(5)	
Nikos DABIZAS	D	20	(7)	1
Panayotis GONIAS	M	6	(7)	
Minas HANTZIDIS	D	7	(1)	
Vassilis IOANNIDIS	D	8	(3)	2
Ilija IVIC (YUG)	A	26		13
Andrzej JUSKOWIAK (POL)	A	24	(1)	12
Alexandros KAKLAMANOS	A		(2)	
Hristos KALLATZIS	D	26	(4)	2
Vassilis KARAPIALIS	M	29	(2)	19
Theofilos KARASSAVIDIS	M	13	(6)	
Kiriakos KARATAIDIS	D	32	(1)	
Emil KREMENLIEV (BUL)	D	9	(5)	
Petros MARINAKIS	M	17	(11)	4
Theodoros PAHATOURIDIS	D		(5)	
Petros PASSALIS	M	28	(2)	
Alexandros RANTOS	G	22		
Ilias SAPANIS	A	8	(10)	2
Yorgos SKARTADOS	D	28	(1)	3
Foto STRAKOSHA (ALB)	G	12		
Grigoris TROUPKOS	D	6	(3)	
Grigoris YORGATOS	M	13	(4)	2

LEAGUE RESULTS 1995/96

Date	Opponent		Score	Scorers
27/08/95	Athinaikos	A	1-0	Sapanis
09/09/95	Panionios	A	2-1	Karapialis, Juskowiak
17/09/95	Paniliakos	H	3-0	Karapialis 2, Juskowiak
23/09/95	Aris	A	0-0	
01/10/95	Panahaiki	H	6-1	Juskowiak 2, Marinakis, Skartados, Karapialis, Alexandris
14/10/95	Ethnikos	A	3-0	Karapialis, Juskowiak, Marinakis
21/10/95	Iraklis	H	2-1	Juskowiak 2 (1p)
28/10/95	AEK	A	1-1	Kallatzis
05/11/95	Ionikos	H	1-1	Juskowiak
19/11/95	Kalamata	H	4-1	Marinakis, Juskowiak 2, Alexandris
26/11/95	PAOK	A	0-0	
02/12/95	Panathinaikos	H	1-2	Karapialis
10/12/95	Apollon	A	4-3	Ivic 4 (1p)
17/12/95	OFI	H	3-1	Dabizas, Alexandris, Ioannidis
07/01/96	Edessaikos	A	5-2	Ivic 3, Kallatzis, Yorgatos
14/01/96	Larissa	H	3-1	Alexandris, Karapialis 2
21/01/96	Xanthi	A	2-1	Karapialis, Juskowiak
28/01/96	Athinaikos	H	3-0	Ivic, Karapialis 2
04/02/96	Panionios	H	3-1	Ivic 2, Juskowiak
10/02/96	Paniliakos	A	0-0	
18/02/96	Aris	H	4-0	Ivic 2 (1p), Karapialis, Skartados
24/02/96	Panahaiki	A	1-1	Karapialis
03/03/96	Ethnikos	H	3-0	Yorgatos, Alexandris, Skartados
10/03/96	Iraklis	A	1-2	Karapialis
17/03/96	AEK	H	1-1	Karapialis
24/03/96	Ionikos	A	2-0	Ioannidis, Alexandris
31/03/96	Kalamata	A	0-3	
07/04/96	PAOK	H	1-0	Karapialis
28/04/96	Panathinaikos	A	0-1	
05/05/96	Apollon	H	0-3	
12/05/96	OFI	A	1-2	Karapialis
19/05/96	Edessaikos	H	2-0	Ivic (p), Karapialis
26/05/96	Larissa	A	2-3	Sapanis, Karapialis
29/05/96	Xanthi	H	1-1	Marinakis

PANAHAIKI

CLUB DIRECTORY

Panahaiki
Kiprou & Thrakis 36
26441 Patra
tel - (061) 434542
fax - (061) 434543
Year of Formation - 1924
President - Aristidis Loukopoulos
Coach - Hristos Arhontidis (96/97 - Nikos Anastopoulos; Andreas Mihalopoulos)
Stadium - Panahaiki (20,000)

APPEARANCES 95/96

	P	Ap	(s)	Gls
Iraklis ANASTASSAKIS	A	4	(14)	3
Andreas ANDROUTSOS	M		(14)	
Theodoros ANTONAKOS	A	13	(4)	
Dimitris ARYIROPOULOS	D	28	(2)	
Yannis BALTIMAS	G	1	(1)	
Zirgla CEROVIC (YUG)	M	9	(2)	
Yorgos DAFKOS	G	16		
Goran DJUROVIC (YUG)	A	5	(3)	
Mattheos GOTZIAS	M	24		
Raymond KALA (CMR)	D	19		
Napoleon KAMINIOTIS	D	21	(1)	
Vagelis KARASAVAS	G	16		
Valeri KARIPOV (RUS)	M	24	(5)	4
Yorgos KIRIAKOPOULOS	M	25	(4)	2
Igor KLEJCH (TCH)	A	33		8
Antonis KOMIANOS	D	4	(5)	
Panayotis MASOURAS	G	1		
Hristos MIKES	D	24		5
Krzysztof NOWAK (POL)	A	12	(1)	1
Thanassis PETOURIS	M	1	(3)	
Nikos PLITSIS	M	2	(6)	
Dimitris ROUSSOS	D	19	(7)	
Vassilis SAMARAS	D	18	(10)	
Stamatis SIRIGOS	M	16	(7)	
Yorgos VAITSIS	A	29		1
Grigoris YORGATOS	M	10		3

LEAGUE RESULTS 1995/96

Date	Opponent	H/A	Score	Scorers
27/08/95	Ethnikos	A	2-1	Yorgatos, Karipov
10/09/95	Iraklis	H	1-0	Yorgatos
17/09/95	AEK	A	1-5	Klejch
24/09/95	Ionikos	H	1-2	Klejch
01/10/95	Olympiakos	A	1-6	Karipov
15/10/95	PAOK	H	3-2	Karipov, Yorgatos, Kiriakopoulos
22/10/95	Panathinaikos	A	0-1	
29/10/95	Apollon	H	2-1	Mikes, Klejch
04/11/95	OFI	H	0-1	
19/11/95	Edessaikos	A	0-2	
26/11/95	Larissa	H	1-1	Klejch
03/12/95	Xanthi	A	1-3	Kiriakopoulos
10/12/95	Athinaikos	H	2-0	Mikes, Klejch
17/12/95	Panionios	A	0-1	
07/01/96	Paniliakos	H	0-0	
14/01/96	Aris	A	0-1	
20/01/96	Kalamata	A	0-1	
28/01/96	Ethnikos	H	1-0	Vaitsis
04/02/96	Iraklis	A	1-0	Mikes
11/02/96	AEK	H	1-1	Mikes
17/02/96	Ionikos	A	1-1	Klejch
24/02/96	Olympiakos	H	1-1	Mikes
03/03/96	PAOK	A	1-2	Klejch
10/03/96	Panathinaikos	H	0-1	
17/03/96	Apollon	A	0-2	
24/03/96	OFI	A	0-1	
31/03/96	Edessaikos	H	1-0	Anastassakis
07/04/96	Larissa	A	1-4	Klejch (p)
28/04/96	Xanthi	H	1-2	Anastassakis
05/05/96	Athinaikos	A	0-2	
12/05/96	Panionios	H	1-0	Anastassakis
19/05/96	Paniliakos	A	1-1	Nowak
26/05/96	Aris	H	0-1	
29/05/96	Kalamata	H	1-0	Karipov

PANATHINAIKOS

CLUB DIRECTORY

Panathinaikos
Athlitikes Egatastasis "Peania"
Karela Peanias
19002 Attiki
tel - 6029479
fax - 6029536
Year of Formation - 1908
President - Yorgos Vardinoyannis
Coach - Juan Ramón Rocha
Stadium - OAKA 'Spiros Louis' (74,433)

MAJOR HONOURS
League Championship - (18)
1930, 1949, 1953, 1960, 1961, 1962, 1964, 1965, 1969, 1970, 1972, 1977, 1984, 1986, 1990, 1991, 1995, 1996.
Domestic Cup - (15) 1940, 1948, 1955, 1967, 1969, 1977, 1982, 1984, 1986, 1988, 1989, 1991, 1993, 1994, 1995.

APPEARANCES 95/96

	P	Ap	(s)	Gls
Alexandros ALEXOUDIS	A	17	(1)	4
Efstratios APOSTOLAKIS	D	24	(2)	4
Angelos BASSINAS	D		(1)	
Juan BORELLI (ARG)	M	21	(3)	12
CARVALHO Eliomar (BRA)	A		(1)	
Yorgos DONIS	A	25	(4)	7
Yannis GOUMAS	M	1	(8)	
Leonidas HRISTODOULOU	M	14	(5)	2
Yorgos KAFFES	A		(1)	
Yannis KALLITZAKIS	D	25	(1)	2
Yorgos KAPOURANIS	D	23	(6)	1
Thanassis KOLITSIDAKIS	D	17	(2)	
Andreas LAGONIKAKIS	A	12	(15)	
Spiros MARAGOS	M	19	(7)	4
Dimitris MARKOS	M	25	(4)	3
Theofilakatos NIKOLAIDIS	D		(1)	
Antonis NIKOPOLIDIS	G	2	(1)	
Nikos NIOBLIAS	M	3	(10)	1
Marinos OUZOUNIDIS	D	27	(2)	2
Yannis THOMAIDIS	A		(10)	
Jozef WANDZIK (POL)	G	32		
Krzysztof WARZYCHA (POL)	A	32		19
Yorgos H. YORYADIS	M	29	(2)	10
Yorgos S. YORYADIS	D	26	(5)	1

LEAGUE RESULTS 1995/96

Date	Opponent	H/A	Score	Scorers
27/08/95	Larissa	A	1-0	Warzycha
09/09/95	Xanthi	H	2-0	Warzycha 2 (1p)
17/09/95	Athinaikos	A	2-1	Warzycha, Donis
23/09/95	Panionios	H	5-3	Warzycha 5 (1p)
01/10/95	Paniliakos	A	1-0	Borelli
14/10/95	Aris	A	1-1	Ouzounidis
22/10/95	Panahaiki	H	1-0	Markos
28/10/95	Ethnikos	A	0-0	
05/11/95	Iraklis	H	4-0	Warzycha, Ouzounidis, Maragos, Markos
18/11/95	AEK	A	0-1	
26/11/95	Ionikos	H	3-0	Hristodoulou, Donis, Borelli
02/12/95	Olympiakos	A	2-1	Borelli, Kapouranis
10/12/95	PAOK	H	2-0	Borelli, Yoryadis Y.H.
17/12/95	Kalamata	H	4-0	Yoryadis Y.H. 2, Borelli 2
06/01/96	Apollon	A	3-2	Borelli 2, Maragos
14/01/96	OFI	H	4-0	Maragos, Warzycha 2 (2p), Donis
21/01/96	Edessaikos	A	3-1	Warzycha 2 (1p), Yoryadis Y.H.
28/01/96	Larissa	H	6-1	Kallitzakis, Alexoudis 2, Maragos, Donis, Nioblias
04/02/96	Xanthi	A	1-1	Kallitzakis
11/02/96	Athinaikos	H	0-0	
18/02/96	Panionios	A	3-1	Apostolakis (p), Warzycha 2
25/02/96	Paniliakos	H	4-1	Alexoudis, Hristodoulou, Yoryadis Y.S., Yoryadis Y.H.
02/03/96	Aris	H	3-1	Yoryadis Y.H., Warzycha 2
10/03/96	Panahaiki	A	1-0	Alexoudis
16/03/96	Ethnikos	H	3-0	Donis 2 (1p), Yoryadis Y.H.
24/03/96	Iraklis	A	1-1	Markos
07/04/96	Ionikos	A	1-2	Yoryadis Y.H.
10/04/96	AEK	H	1-0	Borelli
28/04/96	Olympiakos	H	1-0	Apostolakis
05/05/96	PAOK	A	1-0	Borelli
12/05/96	Kalamata	A	1-0	Apostolakis (p)
19/05/96	Apollon	H	3-1	Borelli, Warzycha, Yoryadis Y.H.
26/05/96	OFI	A	1-2	Borelli
29/05/96	Edessaikos	H	3-1	Apostolakis (p), Donis, Yoryadis Y.H.

PANILIAKOS

CLUB DIRECTORY

Paniliakos
Miaouli 31
27100 Pirgos
tel - (0621) 25749
fax - (0621) 25749
Year of Formation - 1958
President - Dionissis Stavropoulos
Coach - Antonis Yoryadis; Nikos Aryiroulis; Yannis Kirastas (96/97 - Vassilis Daniil)
Stadium - Pirgos (12,000)

APPEARANCES 95/96

	P	Ap	(s)	Gls
Dimitris ALEMIS	D	12	(12)	
Theodoros ANDRIOPOULOS	D	24	(3)	2
Theodoros ARMILAGOS	A	18	(14)	11
Laurent BALLENGHIEN (BEL)	A	5	(3)	1
Predrag DJORDJEVIC (YUG)	M	31		2
Aleksandar ILIC (YUG)	D	30		1
Kostas KAKABAYAS	M		(1)	
Theodoros KIRIAKOULIS	G	25		
Nikos KIZERIDIS	A	21		3
Kostas KOLOSKOPIS	D	26	(1)	
Panayotis KOUMOULIDIS	D	9	(4)	
Vassilis LAKIS	M	9	(4)	
Mihalis LIGNOS	D	29		1
Vassilis LIRIS	D	2	(7)	
Sotiris MAVROMATIS	M	25	(1)	1
Miodrag MENTAN (YUG)	A	14	(5)	4
Dionissis PAPPAS	D	10	(10)	
Zuraba SANAYA (RUS)	G	9	(1)	
Yorgos STRANTZALIS	M	24	(1)	9
Hristos SOTIROPOULOS	D	10	(4)	
Zissis TSEKOS	M	10	(16)	2
Nikos TSOLERIDIS	A	2	(6)	1
Emil TSOUKANI	A	2	(3)	
Andreas VASILOPOULOS	D		(1)	
Stelios YANNAKOPOULOS	D	27		7

LEAGUE RESULTS 1995/96

27/08/95	AEK	A	0-3	
10/09/95	Ionikos	H	0-0	
17/09/95	Olympiakos	A	0-3	
24/09/95	PAOK	H	1-1	Armilagos
01/10/95	Panathinaikos	H	0-1	
15/10/95	Apollon	A	1-2	Kizeridis
21/10/95	OFI	H	4-2	Yannakopoulos 2, Armilagos 2
29/10/95	Edessaikos	A	3-1	Armilagos, Tsekos 2
05/11/95	Larissa	H	4-2	Armilagos 2, Mavromatis, Kizeridis
19/11/95	Xanthi	A	3-1	Djordjevic 2, Strantzalis (p)
26/11/95	Athinaikos	H	4-1	Lignos, Strantzalis 2 (2p), Yannakopoulos
03/12/95	Panionios	A	0-1	
10/12/95	Kalamata	A	1-1	Yannakopoulos
16/12/95	Aris	H	2-1	Kizeridis, Armilagos
07/01/96	Panahaiki	A	0-0	
14/01/96	Ethnikos	H	2-2	Strantzalis (p), Andriopoulos
21/01/96	Iraklis	A	0-2	
27/01/96	AEK	H	0-2	
03/02/96	Ionikos	A	1-2	Ballenghien
10/02/96	Olympiakos	H	0-0	
18/02/96	PAOK	A	0-1	
25/02/96	Panathinaikos	A	1-4	Andriopoulos
03/03/96	Apollon	H	2-1	Mentan, Yannakopoulos
10/03/96	OFI	A	2-2	Strantzalis, Tsoleridis
17/03/96	Edessaikos	H	2-3	Armilagos, Strantzalis
24/03/96	Larissa	A	0-1	
31/03/96	Xanthi	H	2-2	Stranzalis, Mentan
06/04/96	Athinaikos	A	0-0	
28/04/96	Panionios	H	3-1	og, Ilic, Mentan
05/05/96	Kalamata	H	1-0	Yannakopoulos
12/05/96	Aris	A	1-3	Armilagos
19/05/96	Panahaiki	H	1-1	Mentan
26/05/96	Ethnikos	A	4-2	Yannakopoulos, Stranzalis 2 (1p), Armilagos
29/05/96	Iraklis	H	1-2	Armilagos

PANIONIOS

CLUB DIRECTORY

Panionios
Ioannou Hrisostomou 1
Nea Smirni
17122 Athinai
tel - 9330096
fax - 9332036
Year of Formation - 1890
President - Yorgos Siotropos
Coach - Emerich Jenei; Nikos Alefantos; Hristos Emvioladis; Yannis Gounaris; Efstathios Haitas (96/97 -Yannis Kirastas)
Stadium - Neas Smirnis (22,500)

MAJOR HONOURS
Domestic Cup - (1) 1979.

APPEARANCES 95/96

	P	Ap	(s)	Gls
Yorgos ABADIOTAKIS	G	25		
Yorgos AGOROYANNIS	D	16		1
Stéphane DEMOL (BEL)	D	3		
Sulejman DEMOLLARI (ALB)	A	1	(4)	1
Yannis FAKIS	G	7	(1)	
Hristos FIGAS	M	4	(2)	
Panayotis FISSAS	M	32		3
Theodoros HRONOPOULOS	D	5	(1)	
Marian IVAN (ROM)	A	13	(3)	1
Kostas KATSAROS	A	6	(12)	1
Anastasios KATSIABIS	M	30		3
Kostas KLISARIS	A	1	(2)	
Nikos KOURBANAS	D	23	(2)	
Mihalis KOUSOULAS	D	17	(4)	
Apostolis MANTZIOS	D	20	(3)	
Vassilis MOURATIDIS	M	8	(9)	
Dimitris NALITZIS	A	4	(22)	1
Hristos PAPADOPOULOS	D	17	(4)	
Yorgos PAPATRIANTAFILOU	G	2		
Krzysztof POPCZYNSKI (POL)	A	5	(6)	
Marius PREDATU (ROM)	A	25	(3)	8
Antonis SAPOUNTZIS	M	28		4
Themistoklis TZANETIS	D	13	(8)	
Pantelis TZOULIS	A	24	(6)	7
Pagonis VAKALOPOULOS	D	14		1
Leonidas VOKOLOS	D	29		3
Andreas YANNAKOURIS	D	2	(1)	

LEAGUE RESULTS 1995/96

Date	Opponent		Score	Scorers
27/08/95	Ionikos	A	1-2	Demollari
09/09/95	Olympiakos	H	1-2	Predatu
17/09/95	PAOK	H	2-1	Predatu, Sapountzis
23/09/95	Panathinaikos	A	3-5	Tzoulis 3
01/10/95	Apollon	H	2-2	Katsiabis, Predatu
15/10/95	OFI	A	2-2	Katsiabis, Tzoulis
22/10/95	Edessaikos	H	1-2	Vokolos
29/10/95	Larissa	A	0-0	
05/11/95	Xanthi	H	3-0	Tzoulis, Predatu 2
19/11/95	Athinaikos	A	1-2	Vokolos
26/11/95	Kalamata	A	0-1	
03/12/95	Paniliakos	H	1-0	Fissas
10/12/95	Aris	A	2-4	Fissas, Katsiabis
17/12/95	Panahaiki	H	1-0	Predatu
07/01/96	Ethnikos	A	0-2	
14/01/96	Iraklis	H	0-0	
21/01/96	AEK	A	0-2	
28/01/96	Ionikos	H	1-3	Sapountzis
04/02/96	Olympiakos	A	1-3	Tzoulis
11/02/96	PAOK	A	0-2	
18/02/96	Panathinaikos	H	1-3	Sapountzis
25/02/96	Apollon	A	1-0	Fissas
02/03/96	OFI	H	1-0	Ivan
10/03/96	Edessaikos	A	1-2	Predatu
17/03/96	Larissa	H	0-0	
24/03/96	Xanthi	A	0-4	
07/04/96	Kalamata	H	2-1	Tzoulis, Agoroyannis (p)
28/04/96	Paniliakos	A	1-3	Vokolos
05/05/96	Aris	H	0-2	
08/05/96*	Athinaikos	H	1-2	og
12/05/96	Panahaiki	A	0-1	
19/05/96	Ethnikos	H	2-1	Nalitzis, Vakalopoulos
26/05/96	Iraklis	A	2-3	Katsaros, Predatu
29/05/96	AEK	H	1-2	Sapountzis (p)

* 70 minutes played on 31/03/96.

PAOK

CLUB DIRECTORY

PAOK
Lora Margariti 13
54622 Thessaloniki
tel - (031) 238560
fax - (031) 238557
Year of Formation - 1926
President - Yorgos Kalivas
Coach - Arie Haan; Stavros Sarafis; Dragan Kokotovic; Mihalis Bellis; Gunder Bengtsson
Stadium - Toumbas (41,000)

MAJOR HONOURS

League Championship - (2) 1976, 1985.
Domestic Cup - (2) 1972, 1974.

APPEARANCES 95/96

	P	Ap	(s)	Gls
Goran ALEKSIC (YUG)	A	1	(7)	
Alexandros ALEXIOU	D	27		1
Yannis ANASTASSIADIS	A	22	(8)	3
Yannis ANTONAS	A	6	(9)	1
Ioakim HAVOS	M	19	(10)	1
Jesper JOHANSEN (DEN)	A	4	(10)	
Miroslav JOVIC (YUG)	A	7	(4)	2
Dimitris KAPETANOPOULOS	D	27	(1)	3
Yorgos KOUMAROPOULOS	D	2	(1)	
Kostas LAGONIDIS	M	11		3
Nikos MIHOPOULOS	G	33	(1)	
Dimitris NOLIS	A	7	(12)	
Nikos PANAYOTIDIS	D	11	(4)	
Vagelis POURLIOTOPOULOS	G	1		
Mick QUINN (ENG)	A	5	(5)	1
Yorgos TOURSOUNIDIS	M	32	(1)	1
Panayotis TSALOUHIDIS	M	27	(1)	3
Maurice VAN HAM (BEL)	M	20	(3)	
Yannis VOLTEZOS	D	5	(2)	
Antonis YOUKOUDIS	D	26	(2)	9
Ahilleas ZAFIRIOU	D	27	(2)	
Theodoros ZAGORAKIS	M	27		
Paraskevas ZOUBOULIS	A	27	(4)	13

LEAGUE RESULTS 1995/96

27/08/95	Xanthi	A	2-2	Youkoudis, Lagonidis
10/09/95	Athinaikos	H	1-0	og
17/09/95	Panionios	A	1-2	Anastassiadis
24/09/95	Paniliakos	A	1-1	Lagonidis
01/10/95	Aris	H	1-0	Zouboulis
15/10/95	Panahaiki	A	2-3	Zouboulis 2
22/10/95	Ethnikos	H	2-0	Zouboulis, Tsalouhidis
29/10/95	Iraklis	A	2-2	Lagonidis, Quinn
06/11/95	AEK	H	1-3	Zouboulis
19/11/95	Ionikos	A	0-0	
26/11/95	Olympiakos	H	0-0	
03/12/95	Kalamata	H	1-1	Youkoudis (p)
10/12/95	Panathinaikos	A	0-2	
17/12/95	Apollon	H	2-1	Kapetanopoulos, Youkoudis (p)
07/01/96	OFI	A	1-2	Youkoudis
14/01/96	Edessaikos	H	0-1	
21/01/96	Larissa	A	1-2	Youkoudis (p)
28/01/96	Xanthi	H	3-3	Jovic, Youkoudis (p), Kapetanopoulos
04/02/96	Athinaikos	A	1-2	Tsalouhidis
11/02/96	Panionios	H	2-0	Zouboulis, Tsalouhidis
18/02/96	Paniliakos	H	1-0	Zouboulis
25/02/96	Aris	A	0-0	
03/03/96	Panahaiki	H	2-1	Anastassiadis, Youkoudis (p)
10/03/96	Ethnikos	A	3-2	Zouboulis, Youkoudis (p), Alexiou
16/03/96	Iraklis	H	1-2	Youkoudis (p)
23/03/96	AEK	A	0-4	
31/03/96	Ionikos	H	1-1	Zouboulis
07/04/96	Olympiakos	A	0-1	
28/04/96	Kalamata	A	1-1	Zouboulis
05/05/96	Panathinaikos	H	0-1	
12/05/96	Apollon	A	1-0	Zouboulis
19/05/96	OFI	H	3-0	Jovic, Anastassiadis, Havos
26/05/96	Edessaikos	A	3-3	Zouboulis 2, Antonas
29/05/96	Larissa	H	2-3	Toursounidis, Kapetanopoulos

XANTHI

CLUB DIRECTORY

Xanthi Skoda
Vassilissis Sofias 3
67100 Xanthi
tel - (0541) 24466
fax - (0541) 25852
Year of Formation - 1967
President - Aristidis Pialoglou
Coach - Vassilis Daniil; Yannis Ispirlidis; Kurt Jara
Stadium - Xanthis (15,000)

APPEARANCES 95/96

	P	Ap	(s)	Gls
Paraskevas ANTZAS	M	19	(7)	1
Pavlos FOURLAKIDIS	D	1		
Vagelis HOSADAS	G	23		
Yorgos IOSSIFIDIS	D	11	(9)	
Stefanos KARKANIS	G	11	(1)	
Nikos KARAYEORYIOU	D	31		
Nikos KEHAYAS	D	28		1
Yorgos KOYOGLOU	A	8	(3)	2
LUCIANO de Sousa (BRA)	M	8	(2)	
Triantafilos MAHERIDIS	D	19	(5)	1
MARCELO Verdiano (BRA)	A	29	(2)	7
Radim NECAS (TCH)	M	10		2
Ledio PANO (ALB)	M	10	(8)	8
Yannis PAPADIMITRIOU	D	11	(3)	2
Hristos SAMARAS	D	13	(5)	
Miltiadis TELIDIS	D	1	(5)	
Nikos TSIBLIDIS	A	4	(13)	1
Yorgos TSIFOUTIS	M	11	(9)	1
Stelios VENETIDIS	D	15	(1)	1
Angelos VILANAKIS	A	25	(1)	3
Zissis VRIZAS	A	26		12
Jiri ZALESKY (TCH)	D	25		3
Haralambos ZEKERIDIS	A	18	(8)	7
Andreas ZIKOS	D	17	(2)	

LEAGUE RESULTS 1995/96

27/08/95	PAOK	H	2-2	Zekeridis, Zalesky
09/09/95	Panathinaikos	A	0-2	
17/09/95	Apollon	H	1-0	Pano (p)
24/09/95	OFI	A	0-3	
01/10/95	Edessaikos	H	1-1	og (Samolis)
15/10/95	Larissa	A	2-1	Pano 2
22/10/95	Kalamata	A	1-1	Pano (p)
29/10/95	Athinaikos	H	3-0	Pano, Zalesky, Maheridis
05/11/95	Panionios	A	0-3	
19/11/95	Paniliakos	H	1-3	Pano
26/11/95	Aris	A	2-2	Zekeridis, Pano (p)
03/12/95	Panahaiki	H	3-1	Vrizas, Antzas, Zalesky
10/12/95	Ethnikos	A	2-1	Vrizas 2
17/12/95	Iraklis	H	0-1	
07/01/96	AEK	A	1-2	Necas
14/01/96	Ionikos	H	1-0	Vrizas
21/01/96	Olympiakos	H	1-2	Necas
28/01/96	PAOK	A	3-3	Vrizas (p), Vilanakis, Zekeridis
04/02/96	Panathinaikos	H	1-1	Vrizas
11/02/96	Apollon	A	1-3	Vrizas
18/02/96	OFI	H	0-2	
25/02/96	Edessaikos	A	1-1	Koyoglou
03/03/96	Larissa	H	3-1	Kehayas, Venetidis, Pano
09/03/96	Kalamata	H	1-0	Zekeridis
17/03/96	Athinaikos	A	1-2	Koyoglou
24/03/96	Panionios	H	4-0	Marcelo 3, Vrizas
31/03/96	Paniliakos	A	2-2	Zekeridis, Marcelo
07/04/96	Aris	H	4-0	Marcelo, Vrizas, Tsiblidis, Papadimitriou
28/04/96	Panahaiki	A	2-1	Vilanakis, Papadimitriou
05/05/96	Ethnikos	H	6-1	Marcelo 2, Zekeridis, Vrizas 2 (1p), Vilanakis
12/05/96	Iraklis	A	0-2	
19/05/96	AEK	H	1-1	Vrizas
26/05/96	Ionikos	A	1-1	Zekeridis
29/05/96	Olympiakos	A	1-1	Tsifoutis

PROMOTED CLUBS

SECOND DIVISION FINAL TABLE 95/96

		Pd	W	D	L	F	A	Pt	GD
1	**Kavala**	**34**	**21**	**7**	**6**	**58**	**18**	**70**	**+40**
2	**Veria**	**34**	**18**	**9**	**7**	**56**	**35**	**63**	**+21**
3	**Kastoria**	**34**	**16**	**7**	**11**	**44**	**38**	**55**	**+6**
4	Proodeftiki	34	15	9	10	50	34	54	+16
5	Levadiakos	34	14	10	10	36	33	52	+3
6	Doxa Drama	34	15	7	12	38	32	52	+6
7	Doxa Virona	34	14	7	13	45	47	49	-2
8	Apollon Kalamarias	34	13	8	13	42	38	47	+4
9	Trikala	34	12	11	11	40	39	47	+1
10	Naoussa	34	13	8	13	32	34	47	-2
11	EA Rethimniakos	34	13	8	13	34	32	47	+2
12	PAS Yannina	34	12	10	12	41	39	46	+2
13	Panelefsiniakos	34	11	13	10	39	36	46	+3
14	Panaryiakos	34	12	9	13	30	33	45	-3
15	Ialissos	34	12	8	14	46	50	44	-4
16	Anayenissi Kolindros	34	10	6	18	28	37	36	-9
17	Anayenissi Karditsa	34	6	6	22	30	73	24	-43
18	Pierikos	34	3	9	22	15	56	18	-41

CLUB DIRECTORY

Kavala
Filikis Eterias 7
65403 Kavala
tel - (051) 834130
fax - (051) 225094
Year of Formation - 1965
President - Yannis Papaioannou
Coach - Yorgos Parashos
Stadium - Kavalas (15,100)

CLUB DIRECTORY

Veria
Grammou 19A
59100 Veria
tel - (0331) 22959
fax - (0331) 22959
Year of Formation - 1960
President - Vassilis Tsiamitros
Coach - Thomas Katsavakis
Stadium - Veria (10,000)

CLUB DIRECTORY

Kastoria
Ptolemeon 1
52100 Kastoria
tel - (0467) 24880
fax - (0467) 26360
Year of Formation - 1963
President - Nikos Tsolakis
Coach - Miroslav Vukasinovic; Theodoros Pontikis; Yannis Gounaris; Stefanos Gaitanos; Spiros Livathinos; Yannis Gounaris
Stadium - Kastoria (10,000)

MAJOR HONOURS
Domestic Cup - (1) 1980.

HOLLAND

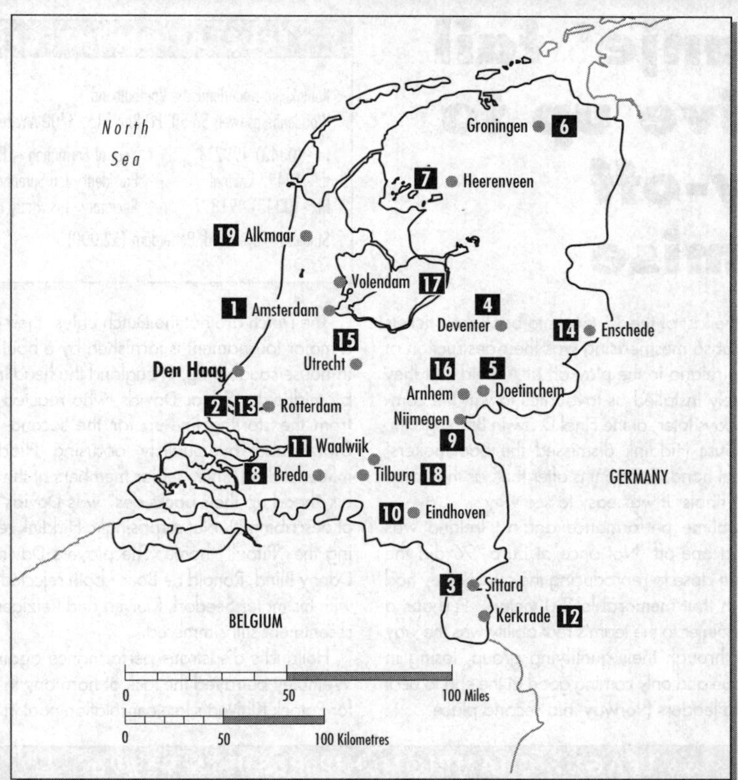

1	AJAX	502
2	FEYENOORD	503
3	FORTUNA SITTARD	504
4	GO AHEAD EAGLES	505
5	DE GRAAFSCHAP	506
6	FC GRONINGEN	507
7	SC HEERENVEEN	508
8	NAC	509
9	NEC	510
10	PSV	511
11	RKC	512
12	RODA JC	513
13	SPARTA	514
14	FC TWENTE	515
15	FC UTRECHT	516
16	VITESSE	517
17	FC VOLENDAM	518
18	WILLEM II	519
19	AZ	520

HAT-TRICK OF TITLES FOR AJAX

'Oranje' fail to live up to play-off promise

FEDERATION DIRECTORY

Koninklijke Nederlandsche Voetbalbond
Woudenbergseweg 56-58, PO Box 515, 3700 AM Zeist

tel - (0343) 499211
tlx - 40497 knvb nl
fax - (0343) 491397

Year of Formation - 1889
President - Jeu Sprengers
Secretary - Drs. Harry Been

Stadium - Feyenoord, Rotterdam (52,000)

Holland were the last of the 16 teams to book their tickets for Euro '96. But so mesmerising was their destruction of the Republic of Ireland in the play-off at Anfield that they were immediately installed as favourites to win the competition. A few days later, at the Final Draw in Birmingham, Dutch coach Guss Hiddink dismissed the bookmakers' predictions out of hand. Six months after that, as the action unfolded in the finals, it was easy to see why.

Holland's sublime performance against Ireland was no more than a one-off. Not once at Euro '96 did the Dutch come even close to reproducing the quality they had demonstrated in that memorable 2-0 victory. Perhaps a more accurate pointer to the team's real ability was the way they struggled through their qualifying group, losing in Minsk and Prague and only coming good at the end to beat long-time group leaders Norway into second place.

The Dutch are not the Dutch unless their appearance at a major tournament is tarnished by a bout of undignified in-house squabbling. In England the headlines were made by midfielder Edgar Davids, who reacted to his ejection from the starting line-up for the second match against Switzerland by publicly accusing Hiddink of being influenced by other, senior members of the squad (having his "head up their backsides" was Davids' colourful way of describing it). Not surprisingly, Hiddink reacted by sending the "Pitbull" home. The players Davids alluded to - Danny Blind, Ronald de Boer - both rejected the claims. But with his mates Seedorf, Kluivert and Reiziger still on board, resentment still simmered.

Holland's disastrous performance against England at Wembley betrayed the lack of harmony in the squad. But for Patrick Kluivert's late consolation goal in the 4-1 defeat,

LEAGUE CHAMPIONSHIP RESULTS 95/96

		1	2	3	4	5	6	7	8	9	10	11	12	13	14	15	16	17	18
1	Ajax		2-0	4-0	2-1	1-0	4-1	6-2	2-0	3-1	1-1	1-0	6-1	4-0	6-1	4-0	3-0	4-0	5-1
2	Feyenoord	2-4		1-0	2-2	2-0	4-1	4-1	2-2	2-1	0-0	4-2	2-0	1-1	1-0	3-0	5-2	5-1	2-0
3	Fortuna Sittard	1-2	1-0		2-2	1-0	0-0	1-2	2-2	1-1	1-3	0-0	1-1	0-1	1-1	2-1	0-0	2-2	0-0
4	Go Ahead Eagles	0-4	0-3	2-0		4-0	2-2	2-3	1-1	2-2	0-5	1-3	1-2	1-3	1-3	2-3	1-3	1-2	0-2
5	De Graafschap	0-0	1-1	1-1	3-2		3-1	2-2	1-1	2-3	1-2	1-1	0-2	5-2	0-3	3-0	2-3	1-0	1-2
6	FC Groningen	3-4	1-0	2-0	0-0	3-0		1-1	3-1	0-0	1-0	1-1	0-1	5-1	2-2	0-0	2-0	2-1	3-0
7	SC Heerenveen	0-4	0-1	5-1	2-1	2-2	1-0		1-1	4-1	1-3	2-1	3-2	4-0	1-1	4-2	1-2	4-3	2-2
8	NAC	0-1	0-3	2-0	2-0	2-1	1-1	5-1		2-1	3-0	0-1	0-0	0-0	4-1	3-0	2-2	4-0	0-1
9	NEC	0-6	1-3	0-2	0-2	1-1	0-2	1-3	1-3		0-5	2-1	1-4	2-2	1-4	2-0	0-1	2-1	1-1
10	PSV	1-1	3-0	3-0	3-1	8-0	7-1	5-1	4-1	1-0		4-0	3-0	1-2	3-0	0-0	1-0	7-0	2-0
11	RKC	0-3	1-1	1-1	1-1	5-0	1-3	2-3	2-2	4-0	1-3		2-0	0-0	1-0	1-0	0-2	2-0	3-2
12	Roda JC	2-0	1-1	1-1	5-0	3-1	0-0	2-2	5-1	1-0	1-1	2-2		1-0	0-0	3-1	0-1	2-0	1-1
13	Sparta	3-3	3-2	0-1	2-0	4-1	1-1	5-2	3-1	3-1	2-1	1-0	2-2		4-2	0-0	3-0	1-0	1-1
14	FC Twente	0-3	2-2	1-0	2-1	1-0	2-2	0-1	0-3	2-0	3-2	0-1	0-3	1-0		1-2	1-0	2-1	2-1
15	FC Utrecht	0-3	1-0	2-3	1-0	1-1	0-1	1-1	0-4	1-2	1-4	0-0	0-1	0-0	0-3		2-0	2-2	3-3
16	Vitesse	2-1	0-2	5-1	0-3	0-1	0-0	2-2	2-0	2-2	0-1	2-1	0-0	3-2	2-0	2-1		2-1	2-2
17	FC Volendam	0-0	0-3	2-0	2-1	1-1	2-1	1-1	1-2	1-0	0-5	1-1	1-0	1-1	1-3	0-1	1-1		0-0
18	Willem II	1-0	2-2	4-0	1-2	1-1	5-2	1-1	1-3	1-3	2-5	1-2	1-2	6-0	5-2	1-1	0-5	1-0	

LEAGUE CHAMPIONSHIP FINAL TABLE 95/96

		Home						Away					Total						
		Pd	W	D	L	F	A	W	D	L	F	A	W	D	L	F	A	Pt	GD
1	Ajax	34	16	1	0	58	9	10	4	3	39	15	26	5	3	97	24	83	+73
2	PSV	34	14	2	1	56	7	10	3	4	41	18	24	5	5	97	25	77	+72
3	Feyenoord	34	12	4	1	42	17	6	5	6	24	19	18	9	7	66	36	63	+30
4	Roda JC	34	8	8	1	30	12	7	4	6	21	23	15	12	7	51	35	57	+16
5	Vitesse	34	8	5	4	26	20	7	3	7	22	24	15	8	11	48	44	53	+4
6	Sparta	34	11	5	1	38	18	3	6	8	15	35	14	11	9	53	53	53	=
7	SC Heerenveen	34	9	4	4	37	27	5	7	5	29	41	14	11	9	66	68	53	-2
8	NAC	34	9	4	4	30	13	5	6	6	28	31	14	10	10	58	44	52	+14
9	FC Groningen	34	9	6	2	29	12	3	7	7	19	33	12	13	9	48	45	49	+3
10	FC Twente	34	9	2	6	20	22	5	4	8	26	33	14	6	14	46	55	48	-9
11	RKC	34	7	5	5	27	21	4	6	7	17	23	11	11	12	44	44	44	=
12	Willem II	34	6	4	7	34	31	3	8	6	19	28	9	12	13	53	59	39	-6
13	Fortuna Sittard	34	3	10	4	16	18	3	3	11	11	36	6	13	15	27	54	31	-27
14	De Graafschap	34	5	6	6	27	26	1	5	11	10	40	6	11	17	37	66	29	-29
15	FC Utrecht	34	3	6	8	15	28	3	4	10	12	31	6	10	18	27	59	28	-32
16	FC Volendam	34	5	7	5	15	21	1	2	14	14	44	6	9	19	29	65	27	-36
17	NEC	34	3	3	11	15	41	3	4	10	18	32	6	7	21	33	73	25	-40
18	Go Ahead Eagles	34	2	3	12	21	41	3	4	10	19	30	5	7	22	40	71	22	-31

Holland would have been out of the tournament there and then. Too many of Hiddink's players appeared to believe what had been pompously written in the Dutch press - that the hosts would settle for the draw because they feared Holland and one point was enough to keep them at Wembley for the next round.

Returning to Anfield for the quarter-final against France, the Dutch managed to rediscover some of the form they had shown in beating Switzerland 2-0 at Villa Park, but a penalty not awarded to them and a glorious late chance spurned by Seedorf resulted in a penalty shoot-out, in which the young Sampdoria player was once more to be cast as the unfortunate villain.

It was the second successive major tournament in which Holland had been eliminated at the quarter-final stage. They certainly deserved to go no further. There was none of the class and culture that Van Basten, Gullit, Rijkaard and co. had offered in the 1988 and 1992 tournaments. Ronald de Boer and Richard Witschge apart, it was difficult to find a player in an orange shirt who enhanced his status at Euro '96. The absence through injury of key players Marc Overmars and Frank de Boer clearly had a damaging effect, and Patrick Kluivert's lack of fitness deprived the team for much of the tournament of a ready-made goalscorer. But above all it was the age-old problem of internal feuding that did most to hamper Holland's chances.

Most Dutch supporters backed coach Hiddink's decision to stand firm against the criticism from within. Had the players in question been in top form, things might have been different. But the Davids and Seedorf of Euro '96 were pale shadows of the players who had illuminated Anfield six months earlier. Hiddink did, however, make mistakes of his own, and certain sections of the Dutch media felt justified in calling for him to resign. Whether he sees out his contract through to the 1998 World Cup finals remains a matter of conjecture. His record for the *Oranje* is far from impressive. And with big names such as Johan Cruijff and Louis van Gaal waiting in the wings, the pressure is certainly on Hiddink to return the team to their old swagger in double-quick time.

Now that Cruijff's golden reign at Barcelona has come to an end, he is once again a candidate for the top job in Dutch football. Relations between Holland's most famous footballer and the KNVB (Dutch FA) have improved considerably since December 1993, when Cruijff backed out of his original decision to take the *Oranje* to the 1994 World Cup after a dispute over money and sponsorship contracts. Proof that the damage has been repaired came in the summer when the KNVB announced that the Dutch SuperCup would from now on be known as the Johan Cruijff Shield.

As for Louis van Gaal, the Ajax coach's contract expires in 1997, and, even though Barcelona have eyes for him, Van Gaal has already declared a strong interest in taking charge of the national team some time in the future. Van Gaal is certainly one of the most respected coaches in

DOMESTIC CUP RESULTS

SECOND ROUND
TOP Oss 1, FC Zwolle 2
Sparta 3, FC Den Bosch 1
Go Ahead Eagles 1, Fortuna Sittard 1 (aet; Fortuna Sittard on pens.)
Roda JC 2, FC Groningen 1
SC Cambuur Leeuwarden 1, SC Heerenveen 0 (aet)
FC Den Haag 1, Vitesse 0 (aet)
Helmond Sport 3, Dordrecht '90 3 (aet; Helmond Sport on pens.)
NAC 4, SC Telstar 1
NEC 0, AZ 0 (aet; AZ on pens.)
FC Twente 2, Haarlem 0
FC Utrecht 0, PSV 2
VVV 2, RKC 0
Feyenoord 3, RBC 0
MVV 0, Willem II 0 (aet; MVV on pens.)
Sparta II 0, De Graafschap 2
SC Heracles 0, Ajax 3

THIRD ROUND
FC Den Haag 1, FC Twente 2
De Graafschap 1, PSV 3
Helmond Sport 1, MVV 2 (aet)
VVV 0, Fortuna Sittard 0 (aet; VVV on pens.)
Roda JC 1, FC Zwolle 1 (aet; Roda JC on pens.)
AZ 0, Sparta 1
Feyenoord 1, NAC 0
SC Cambuur Leeuwarden 2, Ajax 0

QUARTER-FINALS
VVV 0, Roda JC 2
FC Twente 1, PSV 3
MVV 1, Feyenoord 2
Sparta 1, SC Cambuur Leeuwarden 0

SEMI-FINALS
Sparta 1, Feyenoord 0 (asd)
PSV 3, Roda JC 1

FINAL
16/05/96, Rotterdam
PSV 5 Cocu (7), Vink (14), Veldman (65og), Jonk (87), Van der Doelen (90)
SPARTA 2 Van der Meer (45), De Nooijer D. (79p)
referee - Van der Ende
PSV - Waterreus; Van der Weerden, Valckx, Stam, Numan, Vink, Wouters (Van der Doelen 90), Jonk (Zenden 89), Cocu, Nilis (Ronaldo 75), Eykelkamp.
SPARTA - Metgod; Smith, Veldman, De Nooijer G., Van der Meer, Van der Laan, Jalink (Noorlander 83), Groenendijk, Krijgsman, De Nooijer D., Fortes (Renfurm 69).

Europe at the moment. In 1995/96 he led Ajax to their third Dutch title on the trot - and his 11th major honour in less than five years at the club. He also took them through to a second successive appearance in the European Champions' Cup final.

A successful defence of the Champions' Cup was always going to be a tough assignment, but Ajax came as close as they possibly could without actually completing their mission. Nobody could claim that they merited victory in the final against a hungrier, more committed Juventus, but losing on penalty-kicks was a cruel way for them to surrender their title. Along the road to Rome, Ajax won many new friends with a series of outstanding displays, especially away from home. The 2-0 victory in the Estadio Bernabéu against Real Madrid was one of the competition's truly great performances. Not far behind was the quarter-final victory away to Borussia Dortmund. And when Ajax looked to be in serious danger of going out after their shock home defeat by Panathinaikos, they were able to shift up a gear and demolish the Greeks with another sumptuous away performance in Athens.

Ajax may have been unlucky in the penalty shoot-out against Juventus in Rome. But fortune was on their side six months earlier when they won the World Club Cup by the same means against Brazilian side Gremio in Tokyo. Two hours of goalless football were succeeded by misses in the first three spot-kicks. Kluivert was the guilty party for Ajax, but subsequent conversions from the De Boer twins, Finidi George and, ultimately, captain Danny Blind gave Ajax the trophy for the second time.

NATIONAL TEAM RESULTS 95/96

06/09/95	Belarus (ECQ)	H	Rotterdam	1-0	Mulder (83)
11/10/95	Malta (ECQ)	A	Ta' Qali	4-0	Overmars (53, 60, 85), Seedorf (82)
15/11/95	Norway (ECQ)	H	Rotterdam	3-0	Seedorf (49), Mulder (87), Overmars (88)
13/12/95	Rep. Ireland (ECQ)	N	Liverpool	2-0	Kluivert (29, 88)
24/04/96	Germany	H	Rotterdam	0-1	
29/05/96	China	H	Tilburg	2-0	Winter (41), De Kock (89p)
04/06/96	Republic of Ireland	H	Rotterdam	3-1	Bergkamp (27), Seedorf (77), Cocu (88)
10/06/96	Scotland (ECF)	N	Birmingham	0-0	
13/06/96	Switzerland (ECF)	N	Birmingham	2-0	Cruijff (66), Bergkamp (79)
18/06/96	England (ECQ)	A	Wembley	1-4	Kluivert (78)
22/06/96	France (ECF)	N	Liverpool	0-0	

TOP SCORERS

21	Luc NILIS (PSV)
19	Mariano BOMBARDA (FC Groningen)
16	Graham ARNOLD (NAC)
	Dennis DE NOOIJER (Sparta)
15	Patrick KLUIVERT (Ajax)
14	Jon Dahl TOMASSON (SC Heerenveen)
13	Jari LITMANEN (Ajax)
	Nwankwo KANU (Ajax)
12	RONALDO (PSV)
	Philip COCU (PSV)
	Arnold BRUGGINK (FC Twente)

NATIONAL TEAM APPEARANCES 95/96

Coach - Guus HIDDINK	BLS	MLT	NOR	IRL	GER	CHN	IRL	SCO	SUI	ENG	FRA	Cps	Gls
Edwin VAN DER SAR (29/10/70) - Ajax	G	G	G	G	G		G	G	G	G	G	11	-
Michael REIZIGER (03/05/73) - Ajax	D70	D	D	D		D	D	D	D	D	D	12	-
Danny BLIND (01/08/61) - Ajax	D	D71	D	D	D	D72	D46		D	D	D	42	1
Johan DE KOCK (25/10/64) - Roda JC	D		s86	s57		s72	s46	D	s26	s46	D	12	1
Frank DE BOER (15/05/70) - Ajax	D	D	D		D							40	1
Ronald DE BOER (15/05/70) - Ajax	M	M	M	M		s57	M46	M68	M80	M72	M	28	6
Aron WINTER (01/03/67) - Lazio (ITA)	M			s80		M57	s46	s68	M	M	s69	58	5
Richard WITSCHGE (20/09/69) - Girondins de Bordeaux (FRA)	M86	M	M56		M56	M57	M	M78	M	M46	M80	29	1
René EYKELKAMP (06/04/64) - PSV	A65											6	-
Dennis BERGKAMP (10/05/69) - Arsenal (ENG)	A		M79	M57	M	M	M	A	A	A	M60	49	25
Marc OVERMARS (29/03/73) - Ajax	A	A	A	A								29	6
Youri MULDER (23/03/69) - FC Schalke 04 (GER)	s65	A64	s79		s56	A					s80	8	3
Orlando TRUSTFULL (04/08/70) - Feyenoord	s70	s71										2	-
Arthur NUMAN (14/12/69) - PSV	s86	D	D			D						14	-
Clarence SEEDORF (01/04/76) - Sampdoria (ITA)		M	M	M	M	M	M	M	M26	M	s60	15	5
Patrick KLUIVERT (01/07/76) - Ajax		A		A				s63	s84	s72	A	10	4
Glenn HELDER (28/10/68) - Arsenal (ENG)		s64	A86	A80								4	-
Edgar DAVIDS (13/03/73) - Ajax			s56	M		s57	M	M	s80			9	-
Winston BOGARDE (22/10/70) - Ajax				D	D		D	D	D	D	D	7	-
John VELDMAN (24/02/68) - Sparta					D78							1	-
Gaston TAUMENT (01/10/70) - Feyenoord					A56	A46	s27	A63				14	2
Jordi CRUIJFF (09/02/74) - FC Barcelona (ESP)					A	s46	A75	A	A84	A	A69	7	1
Peter HOEKSTRA (04/04/73) - Ajax					A	A72	A27		A	A72		5	-
Philip COCU (29/10/70) - PSV					s56	s72	s75	s78		s72	A	6	1
Jaap STAM (17/07/72) - PSV					s78							1	-
Ed DE GOEY (20/12/66) - Feyenoord						G						28	-

Blind was also on the spot twice in the European Super Cup as Ajax convincingly beat European Cup-winners' Cup holders Real Zaragoza 5-1 on aggregate. It was an important morale-boosting victory for the club, because at the time they were undergoing a mini-crisis in domestic competition. Ajax had begun the season in exhilarating fashion. A third successive Dutch title appeared to be a formality as they raced away to an unprecedented 12 successive victories, the first nine of them without conceding a single goal. It was blistering stuff. By the halfway mark the Amsterdammers had dropped just two points out of a possible 51, drawing 1-1 at home to their closest pursuers PSV at the beginning of November.

But after Christmas the bubble burst. A serious knee injury sustained by in-form winger Marc Overmars (11 goals in 15 games) in a routine league win over De Graafschap heralded the start of Ajax's troubles. Peter Hoekstra was immedietely snapped up from PSV as Overmars' replacement, but with subsequent injuries robbing the team of, among others, Jari Litmanen, Patrick Kluivert and new Brazilian defender Márcio Santos, Ajax were thrown out of kilter. On January 14 they were beaten for the first time in 52 Eredivisie matches. After a run of 44 wins and eight draws, they finally went down 0-2 in Tilburg to Willem II - the team that had last defeated them back in May 1994. The next blow to morale was a sensational 0-2 defeat by Eerste Divisie side Cambuur Leeuwarden in the Dutch Cup. A glut of postponements due to bad weather - including one match in Sittard that was called off just 30 minutes before kick-off - upset the team's rhythm, and when they were

EUROPEAN CUPS RESULTS 95/96

CHAMPIONS' CUP

● AJAX

Champions' League

1st match REAL MADRID (ESP)

H 1-0 Overmars (14)
Van der Sar; Reiziger, De Boer F., Litmanen, Bogarde, De Boer R. (Tutuheru 87), Reuser (Wooter 46), Davids, George, Kanu (Musampa 69), Overmars.

2nd match FERENCVÁROS (HUN)

A 5-1 Litmanen (57, 80p, 85), Kluivert (67), De Boer F. (85)
Van der Sar; Reiziger, Blind, De Boer F., Bogarde, De Boer R., Litmanen, Davids, George, Kanu (Kluivert 60), Overmars.

3rd match GRASSHOPPER-CLUB ZÜRICH (SUI)

H 3-0 Kluivert (10, 68), George (87)
Van der Sar; Reiziger, Blind (Scholten 73), De Boer F., Bogarde, De Boer R. (Kanu 62), Litmanen, Davids, George, Kluivert, Overmars.

4th match GRASSHOPPER-CLUB ZÜRICH (SUI)

A 0-0
Van der Sar; Reiziger, Blind, De Boer F., Bogarde, De Boer R., Litmanen (Kanu 59), Davids, George, Kluivert, Overmars (Reuser 75).

5th match REAL MADRID (ESP)

A 2-0 Litmanen (63), Kluivert (76)
Van der Sar; Reiziger, Blind, Davids, Bogarde, De Boer R., Litmanen, Musampa (Reuser 88), George, Kluivert, Overmars.

6th match FERENCVÁROS (HUN)

H 4-0 Overmars (16), De Boer R. (21), Litmanen (61, 65)
Van der Sar; Reiziger, De Boer F., Scholten, Bogarde, De Boer R., Litmanen (Reuser 76), Davids (Musampa 46), George (Wooter 76), Kluivert, Overmars.

Quarter-final BORUSSIA DORTMUND (GER)

A 2-0 Davids (8), Kluivert (83)
Van der Sar; Reiziger (Scholten 85), Blind, Davids, Silooy, George, Kluivert, De Boer R., Wooter (Musampa 46), Kanu, Bogarde.

H 1-0 Musampa (75)
Van der Sar; Silooy, De Boer F., Davids, Bogarde, Scholten, Litmanen (Landzaat 88), Musampa, Wooter, Kanu, De Boer R..

Semi-final PANATHINAIKOS (GRE)

H 0-1
Van der Sar; Reiziger, Blind, De Boer F., Bogarde, Litmanen (Musampa 76), Kluivert, Davids, George, Kanu, De Boer R..

A 3-0 Litmanen (4, 77), Wooter (85)
Van der Sar; Reiziger, Blind, De Boer F., Silooy (Wooter 72), De Boer R., Litmanen, Davids (Scholten 86), George, Kanu, Bogarde.

Final JUVENTUS (ITA)

Rome
1-1 Litmanen (41)
(aet; 2-4 on pens.)
Van der Sar; Silooy, Blind, De Boer F. (Scholten 69), Bogarde, De Boer R. (Wooter 91), Litmanen, Davids, George, Kanu, Musampa (Kluivert 46).

CUP-WINNERS' CUP

● FEYENOORD

1st round DAG-LIEPAYA (LAT)

A 7-0 Larsson (2, 61), Blinker (47, 58, 62), Koeman (78), Obiku (88)
De Goey; Boateng, Koeman, Van Gobbel, Heus, Taument, Maas, Trustfull, Van Bronckhorst, Blinker (Obiku 64), Larsson (Vidmar 64).

H 6-0 Heus (37p), Trustfull (43), Obiku (57, 63, 65), Gláucio (61)
De Goey; Refos, Van Gobbel, Maas (Obiku 46), Heus, Taument, Gláucio (Jones 72), Trustfull, Van Bronckhorst, Blinker, Vidmar.

2nd round EVERTON (ENG)

A 0-0
De Goey; Boateng, Koeman, Vaan Gobbel, Zwijnenberg (Heus 61), Maas, Witschge, Van Bronckhorst, Larsson (Iwan 82), Obiku, Blinker (Trustfull 61).

H 1-0 Blinker (39)
De Goey; Boateng, Koeman, Van Gobbel, Heus, Iwan, Bosz, Trustfull (Zwijnenberg 72), Blinker (Witschge 84), Obiku, Larsson (Taument 61).

Quarter-final BORUSSIA MÖNCHENGLADBACH (GER)

A 2-2 Van Gastel (33), Koeman (45p)
De Goey; Maas, Schuiteman, Koeman, Heus (Boateng 20), Bosz, Van Gastel, Larsson, Van Bronckhorst, Taument (Iwan 83), Vos.

H 1-0 Trustfull (85)
De Goey; Boateng, Koeman, Schuiteman, Bosz, Maas, Van Gastel, Larsson (Obiku 80), Van Bronckhorst, Taument (Trustfull 75), Vos (Iwan 76).

Semi-final SK RAPID WIEN (AUT)

H 1-1 Koeman (53p)
De Goey; Boateng, Koeman, Schuiteman, Bosz, Van Bronckhorst, Van Gastel, Larsson (Trustfull 79), Taument, Vos (Obiku 76), Iwan.

A 0-3
De Goey; Boateng, Koeman, Schuiteman, Bosz, Van Bronckhorst, Van Gastel, Iwan (Obiku 46), Taument, Larsson, Vos.

UEFA CUP

● RODA JC

1st round SCT OLIMPIJA LJUBLJANA (SLO)

H 5-0 Van Galen (2), Roelofsen (23), Babangida (34), Graef (44), De Kock (88p)
Hesp R.; Senden, De Kock, Trost, Van de Luer, Doomernik, Vurens, Van Galen (Hesp D. 57), Babangida (Kasperski 71), Graef (Heeren 80), Roelofsen.

A 0-2
Hesp R.; Senden, De Kock, Trost (Hesp D. 46), Doomernik (Plum 73), Van de Luer, Roelofsen, Van Galen, Babangida (Kasperski 61), Graef, Vurens.

2nd round SL BENFICA (POR)

A 0-1
Hesp R.; Senden, De Kock, Van Hoogdalem, Trost, Van de Luer, Doomernik, Van Galen (Hesp D. 58), Babangida (Kasperski 87), Roelofsen, Vurens.

H 2-2 Hesp D. (61), Trost (74)
Hesp R.; Ooijer, De Kock, Van Hoogdalem, Trost, Van de Luer (Vurens 25), Doomernik, Hesp D., Babangida, Graef (Mores 85), Roelofsen.

EUROPEAN CUPS RESULTS 95/96 (CONTINUED)

● PSV

1st round MYPA (FIN)

A 1-1 Ronaldo (50)
Waterreus; Van der Weerden, Valckx, Faber, Numan, Pahlplatz (Linskens 68), Cocu, Jonk, Hoekstra (Van der Leegte 86), Ronaldo, Nilis.

H 7-1 Ronaldo (14, 45, 73, 83), Jonk (57, 71), Hoekstra (65)
Waterreus; Van der Weerden, Wouters, Faber, Numan (Prommayon 82), Pahlplatz (Hoekstra 46), Linskens (Vink 77), Jonk, Cocu, Ronaldo, Nilis.

2nd round LEEDS UNITED (ENG)

A 5-3 Eykelkamp (11), Vink (36), Jonk (39), Nilis (84, 89)
Waterreus; Van der Weerden, Valckx, Faber, Numan, Vink (Pahlplatz 70), Linskens, Jonk, Cocu, Nilis, Eykelkamp.

H 3-0 Cocu (12, 73), Pemberton (42og)
Waterreus; Prommayon, Valckx, Faber, Numan, Vink (Pahlplatz 74), Linskens (Hoekstra 69), Jonk, Cocu (Van der Leegte 80), Nilis, Ronaldo.

3rd round SV WERDER BREMEN (GER)

H 2-1 Ronaldo (9p), Nilis (83)
Waterreus; Van der Weerden, Valckx, Faber, Numan, Vink, Cocu, Jonk, Hoekstra (Linskens 46), Ronaldo (Eykelkamp 72), Nilis.

A 0-0
Waterreus (Menzo 62); Van der Weerden, Valckx, Faber, Numan, Vink (Hoekstra 67), Wouters, Jonk, Cocu, Ronaldo, Nilis (Eykelkamp 89).

Quarter-final FC BARCELONA (ESP)

A 2-2 Nilis (5, 50)
Waterreus; Van der Weerden, Valckx, Faber, Numan, Vink, Wouters (Zenden 72), Jonk, Cocu, Nilis (Gudjohnsen 90), Eykelkamp.

H 2-3 Zenden (44), Eykelkamp (65)
Waterreus; Van der Weerden, Klomp, Cocu, Numan, Vink, Van der Doelen (Gudjohnsen 46), Jonk (Maas 84), Zenden, Eykelkamp, Nilis.

beaten again, 2-1 by Vitesse, Ajax suddenly found themselves displaced at the top by PSV.

Slowly but surely Ajax began to recover their old poise. They had matches in hand over PSV and made them count. They also grabbed a precious 1-1 draw against their rivals in Eindhoven, with Hoekstra, of all people, scoring the vital equaliser against his old club with a deflected shot. Another deflected goal, by Michael Reiziger, provided three more important points at home to RKC, and in Ajax's next home game, a fortnight later, they were able to celebrate their title hat-trick with a thumping 5-1 revenge victory over Willem II.

That match was Ajax's last in the De Meer stadium. With the brand new, hi-tech Amsterdam Arena (complete with sliding roof) awaiting the pleasure of their company for the 1996/97 season, Ajax bade farewell to the old ground in style by completing their 26th national title triumph. In many ways that game and the Champions' Cup final marked the end of an era for Ajax. Dutch internationals Edgar Davids and Michael Reiziger reached the end of their contracts and left jointly for Milan. Finidi George, a hat-trick hero in that final league win, moved on to Spanish side Real Betis. And another Nigerian, Nwankwo Kanu, packed his bags for Inter, only to be tragically informed by the Italian club's doctors that he had a serious heart disorder and would be forced to quit the game at 20 - just weeks after inspiring Nigeria to victory in the Olympic football tournament.

Another highly gifted youngster on show in Atlanta was Brazilian striker Ronaldo. The 19-year-old had been the Eredivisie top scorer in 1994/95, but a knee injury forced him to miss all of the second half of the 95/96 season, thus diminishing PSV's hopes of a first Dutch title for four years. In fairness, Dick Advocaat's side coped well without him. A purple patch in the middle of the season enabled them to creep up on Ajax, and but for a dreadful run of results in March, they might well have taken Ajax to the wire.

In Ronaldo's absence, PSV were inspired by the magical skills of Belgian striker Luc Nilis, the league's top scorer with 21 goals and Holland's Player of the Year. One of Nilis's most memorable performances came in the quarter-final of the UEFA Cup when he scored twice in PSV's 2-2 draw against Barcelona in the Nou Camp. In the return leg PSV had no luck and lost 2-3, thus departing a competition they had seriously threatened to win after excellent earlier performances against MyPa, Leeds United and Werder Bremen.

PSV did get their hands on some long-awaited silverware when they triumphed in the KNVB Beker, the Dutch Cup.

INTERNATIONAL HONOURS

World Cup Finals appearances: 1934, 1938, 1974 (Runners-up), 1978 (Runners-up), 1990 (2nd round), 1994 (qtr-finals)

European Championship appearances (last 8): 1976 (3rd), 1980, 1988 (Winners), 1992 (semi-finals), 1996 (qtr-finals)

European Club Competitions

Champions' Cup	Feyenoord (1970)
	Ajax (1971, 1972, 1973, 1995)
	PSV (1988)
Cup-winners' Cup	Ajax (1987)
UEFA Cup	Feyenoord (1974)
	PSV (1978)
	Ajax (1992)
Super Cup	Ajax (1972, 1973, 1996)
World Club Cup	Feyenoord (1970)
	Ajax (1972, 1995)

After knocking out four other Eredivisie teams (Utrecht, De Graafschap, Twente and Roda) in handsome fashion on the way to the final in Rotterdam, they finished off their good work with the classiest performance of the lot. Inspired by Euro '96 reject Wim Jonk, they outclassed a Sparta side that had done the 'double' over them in the league and had also eliminated holders Feyenoord in the semi-finals with an extra-time 'golden goal'.

Feyenoord had a season of mixed fortunes. Arie Haan replaced Wim van Hanegem as coach early on, but the Rotterdammers never got close to the league leaders and were bumped out of the Dutch Cup by city rivals Sparta. Their best chance of success came in the European Cup-winners' Cup, especially after they edged past both Everton and Borussia Muonchengladbach. But in a very winnable semi-final against Rapid Vienna, Feyenoord went to pieces, losing calamitously 0-3 in Vienna after a tepid 1-1 draw in Rotterdam.

Runners-up in 94/95, Roda JC finished in a creditable fourth place in 95/96, winning a place in the UEFA Cup for the second season running. At the other end of the table Go Ahead Eagles finished last and were relegated, to be replaced by Eerste Divisie champions and former UEFA Cup finalists AZ. But in the play-offs both Volendam and NEC easily retained their top-flight status. Volendam won all six of their matches. That was as many victories as they had managed in the entire 34-match Eredivisie campaign.

PLAYERS OF THE SEASON

PHILIP COCU

Phlip Cocu is one of the few Dutch players who can look back on Euro '96 with satisfaction. The quarter-final against France was the first time in six appearances for Holland that he had been selected from the start, and he repaid coach Hiddink's faith with an impressive display, coming within a whisker of netting the winning goal. The former Vitesse midfielder owed his place in the European Championship squad to an outstanding first season with PSV. Eindhoven born and bred, Cocu relished the opportunity of playing for his hometown club. He did so in a variety of rôles, sometimes filling in as a defender or striker but more regularly operating on the left side of midfield, from where he struck a career-best total of 12 league goals plus the opener in the 5-2 Cup final win over Sparta.

JOHAN DE KOCK

For many years Johan de Kock has been recognised as the best traditional centre-half in Holland, a solid, highly-respected stopper whose international ambitions have been curbed only because he does not play for one of Holland's 'Big Three'. After a career spent with middle-ranking FC Groningen, FC Utrecht and Roda JC, the 32-year-old has now upped his credentials a notch by joining German side Schalke 04 on a three-year contract. He moves to the Bundesliga club after an excellent final season with Roda, in which he played all 34 Eredivisie matches, helping the club back into the UEFA Cup. De Kock also appeared in all four of Holland's matches at Euro '96, where he stood in ably for the injured Frank de Boer.

MARIANO BOMBARDA

With a name like his, Mariano Bombarda could only be a striker. And in the 1995/96 season he proved that he is also a very good one, firing 19 goals for FC Groningen to become the top Dutchman in the Eredivisie goal rankings. Only the Belgian, Luc Nilis, scored more. Whether the 24-year-old actually qualifies as Dutch is a matter for discussion. He is the son of an Italian maritime engineer, born in Cádiz, Spain and also having resided in Argentina and Venezuela before coming to Holland and studying economics at Groningen University. Just to prove that he has lost none of his *Wanderlust*, Bombarda has now left Groningen for French side FC Metz. He signed off in the Oosterpark with a brilliant hat-trick on the last day of the season. Holland will miss him.

EDWIN VAN DER SAR

For the second season running Ajax's Edwin van der Sar was the winner of the Dutch PFA's Goalkeeper of the Year award. The prize could hardly have gone to anybody else after he began the season with nine straight clean sheets. His unbeaten record lasted 845 minutes before Feyenoord defender Clemens Zwijnenberg finally put the ball past him. To say that the Ajax and Holland 'keeper is 'down to earth' when he measures 1.97m in his bare feet might seem fatuous, but that is the best way to describe Van der Sar's carefree demeanour and uncomplicated outlook on life. He is certainly a contrast to the occasionally hot-tempered Ajax coach Louis van Gaal, but his unrivalled position as the Ajax number one since the demise of the more eccentric Stanley Menzo appears to prove that opposites do indeed attract.

PROFILE
DANNY BLIND

No Dutch player received more interview requests during the 1995/96 season than the captain of Ajax and Holland, Danny Blind. A very busy season of domestic and international football saw the 35-year-old defender lift three trophies - the World Club Cup, the European Super Cup and, for the third season in a row, the Dutch championship.

Ajax just missed out on a second successive Champions' Cup triumph. And there was to be disappointment for Blind when Holland could only reach the quarter-finals of the European Championship. But overall Blind could not grumble. It was another memorable season for a player in the twilight of his career. He now ranks as one of European football's most distinguished achievers, having raked in no fewer than 12 domestic and international titles in his ten years with Ajax. Only the late Gaetano Scirea of Juventus has a comparable haul.

Born in the south-western province of Zeeland on August 1, 1961, Blind was taken as a young boy to watch Feyenoord. But it was for the other major Rotterdam club, Sparta, that he signed his first professional contract in 1979. Having made his début against AZ in Alkmaar in August of that year, Blind remained at Sparta for seven seasons. Another man who played alongside Blind for the duration of that period was present Ajax coach Louis van Gaal.

But as Van Gaal moved on to see out the remainder of his playing career (and the start of his coaching apprenticeship) with AZ, Blind was signed up by new Ajax coach Johan Cruijff on a three-year contract. At first he played in the right-back position, but when Cruijff was later succeeded by Leo Beenhakker, Blind became the team's libero. It was only after the promotion of his old pal Louis van Gaal to the Ajax hot seat, in September 1991, that Blind's career took on a new dimension.

When Jan Wouters left Ajax for Bayern Munich, Blind was handed the captaincy. He also became Van Gaal's right-hand man on the field, the man through whom all important tactical instructions were passed on to the other players. He still performs that function today.

While Blind's career with Ajax reached a crescendo as he entered his thirties, he still struggled to make any inroads into the Dutch national team. Since his international début against Scotland in April 1986, Holland have played 100 matches, but Blind has only appeared in 41 of them. At the World Cups of 1990 and 1994 and the European Championship of 1992 Blind was a member of the Dutch squad, but he did not make a single appearance in any of the three tournaments, not even one minute as a substitute. Missing out on Euro '92 was a particular blow as he had appeared in all eight of the qualifying games. But after USA '94 things changed. The international retirement of Ronald Koeman (ironically, two years younger than Blind) enabled the Ajax skipper to become the new libero and captain of the *Oranje*.

Blind nearly gave up that job after just eight matches when Holland were humbled by Belarus in the Euro '96 qualifiers, but he withdrew his decision to step down after hearing that the Czech Republic had lost in Luxembourg. A year later he finally made his big tournament bow in England (although he was suspended for the opening game against Scotland). That was to be his first and last major championship for Holland, as he announced his international retirement a couple of months later. His 11th season at Ajax is also likely to be his last. Blind's contract ends in June 1997, after which he could move to Japan or America or, more likely, join the technical staff at Ajax where he hopes one day to follow in his friend and mentor Louis van Gaal's footsteps and become the first-team coach.

AJAX

CLUB DIRECTORY

Ajax
Postbus 12522
1100 AM Amsterdam
tel - (020) 3111444
fax - (020) 3111480
Year of Formation - 1900
President - Michael van Praag
Coach - Louis van Gaal
Stadium - Amsterdam Arena (51,500)

MAJOR HONOURS
League Championship - (26)
1918, 1919, 1931, 1932, 1934, 1937, 1939, 1947, 1957, 1960, 1966, 1967, 1968, 1970, 1972, 1973, 1977, 1979, 1980, 1982, 1983, 1985, 1990, 1994, 1995, 1996.
Domestic Cup - (12)
1917, 1943, 1961, 1967, 1970, 1971, 1972, 1979, 1983, 1986, 1987, 1993.
European Champions' Cup - (4)
1971, 1972, 1973, 1995.
European Cup-winners' Cup - (1) 1987.
UEFA Cup - (1) 1992.
European Super Cup - (3) 1972, 1973, 1996.
World Club Cup - (2) 1972, 1995.

APPEARANCES 95/96

	P	Ap	(s)	Gls
Dave VAN DEN BERGH	A		(2)	
Danny BLIND	D	31		3
Frank DE BOER	D	32		4
Ronald DE BOER	M	30		7
Winston BOGARDE	D	31	(2)	2
Edgar DAVIDS	M	28		7
Andrei DEMCHENKO (RUS)	A	1	(1)	
Finidi GEORGE (NIG)	A	28	(1)	6
Fred GRIM	G	1		
Peter HOEKSTRA	A	16		5
Nwankwo KANU (NIG)	A	20	(9)	13
Patrick KLUIVERT	A	26	(2)	15
Danny LANDZAAT	D		(1)	
Jari LITMANEN (FIN)	A	22	(4)	13
MÁRCIO SANTOS (BRA)	D	4	(3)	
Kiki MUSAMPA	M	3	(14)	1
Marc OVERMARS	A	15		11
Michael REIZIGER	D	26		1
Martijn REUSER	A	5	(13)	3
Edwin VAN DER SAR	G	33		
Arnold SCHOLTEN	M	6	(10)	1
Dennis SCHULP	A		(1)	
Sonny SILOOY	D	9	(2)	
Nordin WOOTER	A	7	(18)	2

LEAGUE RESULTS 1995/96

20/08/95	FC Utrecht	H	4-0	Davids, Kluivert, Blind, Reuser
25/08/95	NEC	A	6-0	George 2, Davids, Overmars 2, Reuser
10/09/95	Sparta	H	4-0	Kanu 2, Overmars, Reuser
17/09/95	Go Ahead Eagles	A	4-0	og (Marbus), Kanu 2 (1p), Davids
20/09/95	Fortuna Sittard	H	4-0	De Boer F., Kanu, De Boer R., Overmars
24/09/95	NAC	A	1-0	Kluivert
01/10/95	SC Heerenveen	A	4-0	Davids, og (Straal), Litmanen, Kluivert
04/10/95	Vitesse	H	3-0	Kluivert, Davids, De Boer R.
15/10/95	FC Twente	A	3-0	Litmanen, Overmars 2
22/10/95	Feyenoord	A	4-2	Bogarde, Litmanen, Overmars 2
25/10/95	FC Volendam	H	4-0	De Boer F., De Boer R. 2, Wooter
28/10/95	Roda JC	H	6-1	Kluivert 2, Litmanen, Blind, Davids, Kanu
05/11/95	PSV	H	1-1	Kanu
08/11/95	RKC	A	3-0	Kluivert 2, Litmanen (p)
19/11/95	FC Groningen	H	4-1	Kluivert, Litmanen (p), Kanu, Overmars
17/12/95	FC Utrecht	A	3-0	Overmars 2, Litmanen (p)
20/12/95	De Graafschap	H	1-0	Litmanen
24/12/95	NEC	H	3-1	Litmanen, George, De Boer R. (p)
14/01/96	Willem II	A	0-1	
21/01/96	Sparta	A	3-3	Bogarde, Scholten, Hoekstra
25/02/96	SC Heerenveen	H	6-2	Kluivert 2, De Boer R., Hoekstra, Kanu, Blind
03/03/96	Vitesse	A	1-2	Kluivert
10/03/96	FC Twente	H	6-1	De Boer F., Davids, Kluivert, og (Ayupov), Musampa, Hoekstra
13/03/96	Fortuna Sittard	A	2-1	Kanu, Kluivert
17/03/96	FC Volendam	A	0-0	
24/03/96	Feyenoord	H	2-0	Litmanen, Kluivert
27/03/96	Go Ahead Eagles	H	2-1	Hoekstra, Kanu
30/03/96	Roda JC	A	0-2	
06/04/96	NAC	H	2-0	De Boer R., Kanu
08/04/96	PSV	A	1-1	Hoekstra
13/04/96	RKC	H	1-0	Reiziger
21/04/96	FC Groningen	A	4-3	Litmanen 2 (1p), Kanu, Wooter
28/04/96	Willem II	H	5-1	Litmanen, De Boer F., George 3
05/05/96	De Graafschap	A	0-0	

FEYENOORD

CLUB DIRECTORY

Feyenoord
Olympiaweg 50
3077 AL Rotterdam
tel - (010) 4929400
fax - (010) 4325819
Year of Formation - 1908
President - Jorien van den Herik
Manager - Hans Hagelstein
Coach - Wim van Hanegem; Arie Haan
Stadium - Feyenoord (52,000)

MAJOR HONOURS
League Championship - (13) 1924, 1928, 1936, 1938, 1940, 1961, 1962, 1965, 1969, 1971, 1974, 1984, 1993.
Domestic Cup - (10) 1930, 1935, 1965, 1969, 1980, 1984, 1991, 1992, 1994, 1995.
European Champions' Cup - (1) 1970.
UEFA Cup - (1) 1974.
World Club Cup - (1) 1970.

APPEARANCES 95/96

	P	Ap	(s)	Gls
Regi BLINKER	A	10	(3)	4
George BOATENG	D	21	(3)	1
Peter BOSZ	M	31		2
Giovanni VAN BRONCKHORST	A	29	(4)	9
Henk FRÄSER	D	1		
Jean-Paul VAN GASTEL	M	12	(1)	1
Ulrich VAN GOBBEL	D	17		
Ed DE GOEY	G	34		
Ruud HEUS	D	12	(7)	1
Tomasz IWAN (POL)	M	20	(11)	3
Dennis KLIUYEV (RUS)	M	6	(3)	
Ronald KOEMAN	D	31		10
Henrik LARSSON (SWE)	A	30	(2)	10
Rob MAAS	M	13	(9)	1
Mike OBIKU (NIG)	A	10	(12)	3
Errol REFOS	D		(2)	
Bernard SCHUITEMAN	D	18		
Gaston TAUMENT	A	15	(10)	3
Orlando TRUSTFULL	M	28	(1)	9
Aurelio VIDMAR (AUS)	A	1	(14)	2
Henk VOS	A	9	(2)	3
Rob WITSCHGE	D	12	(1)	
Clemens ZWIJNENBERG	D	14	(4)	1

LEAGUE RESULTS 1995/96

Date	Opponent		Score	Scorers
20/08/95	Vitesse	H	5-2	Trustfull 2, Blinker 2, Larsson
27/08/95	FC Twente	A	2-2	Van Bronckhorst, Vidmar
10/09/95	FC Volendam	H	5-1	og (Kromheer), Koeman, Van Bronckhorst, Trustfull, Vidmar (p)
17/09/95	FC Utrecht	A	0-1	
20/09/95	Roda JC	A	1-1	Van Bronckhorst
24/09/95	RKC	H	4-2	Larsson 2, Trustfull, Taument
01/10/95	PSV	A	0-3	
05/10/95	FC Groningen	H	4-1	Iwan, Obiku, Larsson, Koeman (p)
15/10/95	Willem II	A	2-2	Obiku, Van Bronckhorst
22/10/95	Ajax	H	2-4	Zwijnenberg, Larsson
26/10/95	De Graafschap	H	2-0	Van Bronckhorst, Blinker
29/10/95	NEC	A	3-1	Iwan, Trustfull, Blinker
05/11/95	Sparta	A	2-3	Koeman 2 (1p)
19/11/95	Go Ahead Eagles	H	2-2	Larsson, Koeman
24/11/95	Fortuna Sittard	A	0-1	
08/12/95	SC Heerenveen	A	1-0	Trustfull
17/12/95	Vitesse	A	2-0	Koeman, Bosz
24/12/95	FC Twente	H	1-0	Koeman (p)
13/01/96	NAC	H	2-2	Van Bronckhorst 2
21/01/96	FC Volendam	A	3-0	Vos, og (Kromheer), Larsson
04/02/96	Roda JC	H	2-0	Trustfull, Vos
11/02/96	RKC	A	1-1	Obiku
25/02/96	PSV	H	0-0	
03/03/96	FC Groningen	A	0-1	
10/03/96	FC Utrecht	H	3-0	Van Bronckhorst 2, Bosz
17/03/96	De Graafschap	A	1-1	Vos
24/03/96	Ajax	A	0-2	
27/03/96	Willem II	H	2-0	Larsson, Van Gastel
31/03/96	NEC	H	2-1	Taument, Iwan
10/04/96	Sparta	H	1-1	Koeman
14/04/96	Go Ahead Eagles	A	3-0	Taument, og (Marbus), Boateng
21/04/96	Fortuna Sittard	H	1-0	Koeman (p)
28/04/96	NAC	A	3-0	Maas, Trustfull, Koeman
05/05/96	SC Heerenveen	H	4-1	Trustfull, Heus (p), Larsson 2

FORTUNA SITTARD

CLUB DIRECTORY

Fortuna Sittard
Postbus 36
6130 AA Sittard
tel - (046) 4513947
fax - (046) 4580032
Year of Formation - 1968
President - Eric Bouwmeester
Secretary - Wil Dols
Manager - Jacques Opgenoord
Coach - Pim Verbeek
Stadium - De Baandert (14,000)

APPEARANCES 95/96

	P	Ap	(s)	Gls
Willy BOESSEN	D	26	(1)	
Mark VAN BOMMEL	A	24	(3)	
Mark BURKE (ENG)	A	31		3
Ronald DASSEN	D	1	(4)	
Jürgen DIRKX	D	12	(3)	
Ronald HAMMING	A	16	(5)	10
Michael JEFFREY (ENG)	A	15		4
Roger JUFFING	G	1	(2)	
Ruud KOOL	M	23	(2)	
Roberto LANCKOHR	M	19		1
Ervin LEE	D	32		
Robert LOONTJENS	M	6	(8)	
Rafaël LOSADA	A	10	(1)	
Martin VAN OPHUIZEN	D	13	(1)	2
Ivo PFENNINGS	D	10	(9)	
Fernando RICKSEN	D	27	(1)	1
Robert ROEST	M	33		1
Regillio SIMONS	A	23	(5)	1
Dominik VERGOOSSEN	D	8	(1)	
Roland VROOMANS	A	3	(11)	
Robert VAN DER WEERT	A	6	(4)	2
Freek DE WINTER	M		(1)	
André VAN DER ZANDER (GER)	M	2	(7)	1
Arno VAN ZWAM	G	33		

LEAGUE RESULTS 1995/96

18/08/95	PSV	H	1-3	Hamming
23/08/95	FC Groningen	A	0-2	
09/09/95	Willem II	A	0-4	
16/09/95	De Graafschap	H	1-0	Burke
20/09/95	Ajax	A	0-4	
23/09/95	NEC	H	1-1	Hamming
01/10/95	Sparta	A	1-0	Hamming
04/10/95	Go Ahead Eagles	H	2-2	Hamming 2
14/10/95	FC Utrecht	A	3-2	Hamming 2, Simons
21/10/95	SC Heerenveen	H	1-2	og (Roelofsen)
25/10/95	NAC	A	0-2	
29/10/95	Vitesse	A	1-5	Ricksen
04/11/95	FC Twente	H	1-1	Van der Zander
19/11/95	FC Volendam	A	0-2	
24/11/95	Feyenoord	H	1-0	Lanckohr
01/12/95	Roda JC	A	1-1	Burke
09/12/95	RKC	H	0-0	
16/12/95	PSV	A	0-3	
23/12/95	FC Groningen	H	0-0	
20/01/96	Willem II	H	0-0	
07/02/96	De Graafschap	A	1-1	Hamming
10/02/96	NEC	A	2-0	Van Ophuizen, Hamming
24/02/96	Sparta	H	0-1	
02/03/96	Go Ahead Eagles	A	0-2	
13/03/96	Ajax	H	1-2	Jeffrey
16/03/96	NAC	H	2-2	Van der Weert, Jeffrey
23/03/96	SC Heerenveen	A	1-5	Hamming
27/03/96	FC Utrecht	H	2-1	Roest, Jeffrey
30/03/96	Vitesse	H	0-0	
06/04/96	FC Twente	A	0-1	
12/04/96	FC Volendam	H	2-2	Burke, Van Ophuizen
21/04/96	Feyenoord	A	0-1	
28/04/96	Roda JC	H	1-1	Jeffrey
05/05/96	RKC	A	1-1	Van der Weert

GO AHEAD EAGLES

CLUB DIRECTORY

Go Ahead Eagles
Postbus 184
7400 AD Deventer
tel - (0570) 621357
fax - (0570) 637770
Year of Formation - 1902
President - Hans Horneman
Secretary - Ad van Leent
Coach - Ab Fafié; Bob Maaskant
(96/97 - Leo van Veen)
Stadium - De Adelaarshorst (11,000)

MAJOR HONOURS
League Championship - (4)
1917, 1922, 1930, 1933.

APPEARANCES 95/96

	P	Ap	(s)	Gls
Alfons ARTS	D	12	(1)	
Jan BOS	G	12		
Pieter BIJL	M	18	(1)	3
Serghei CLESCENCO (MOL)	A	25	(7)	4
Harry DECHEIVER	A	9		8
Marco HEERING	A	28		7
Arno HOFSTEDE	D	27		
Dennis HULSHOFF	D	30		1
Bas LEFERINK	M	1	(4)	
Cess MARBUS	D	33		2
Jan MICHELS	M	31	(1)	2
Oscar MOENS	G	21		
Serghei NANI (MOL)	A	16	(11)	
Kingsley OBIEKULU (NIG)	A		(4)	
Marthijn POTHOVEN	M		(5)	
Toine RORIJE	A	18	(6)	3
Mark SCHENNING	M	29	(1)	4
Viktor SIKORA	A		(14)	1
Gijs STEINMANN	D	8	(2)	
Erik TAMMER	A	15	(4)	4
Marcel VALK	M	8	(1)	
Mark VERKUYL	D	32		1
Patrick WOLBERS	G	1		

LEAGUE RESULTS 1995/96

19/08/95	FC Groningen	H	2-2	Schenning, Sikora
26/08/95	Willem II	H	0-2	
10/09/95	De Graafschap	A	2-3	Heering 2
17/09/95	Ajax	H	0-4	
20/09/95	NEC	A	2-0	Decheiver 2
23/09/95	Sparta	H	1-3	Decheiver (p)
30/09/95	FC Utrecht	H	2-3	Marbus, Decheiver
04/10/95	Fortuna Sittard	A	2-2	Schenning, Decheiver
14/10/95	NAC	H	1-1	Decheiver
20/10/95	Vitesse	H	1-3	Decheiver (p)
25/10/95	SC Heerenveen	A	1-2	Decheiver
29/10/95	FC Twente	A	1-2	Hulshoff
03/11/95	FC Volendam	H	1-2	Michels
19/11/95	Feyenoord	A	2-2	Clescenco 2
25/11/95	Roda JC	H	1-2	Heering
03/12/95	RKC	A	1-1	Michels
16/12/95	FC Groningen	A	0-0	
20/12/95	PSV	H	0-5	
23/12/95	Willem II	A	2-1	Rorije, Tammer
28/02/96	NEC	H	2-2	Tammer, Heering
02/03/96	Fortuna Sittard	H	2-0	Schenning, Bijl
09/03/96	NAC	A	0-2	
13/03/96	De Graafschap	H	4-0	Bijl 2, Clescenco, Tammer (p)
16/03/96	SC Heerenveen	H	2-3	Tammer (p), Schenning
22/03/96	Vitesse	A	3-0	Clescenco, Heering 2
27/03/96	Ajax	A	1-2	Verkuyl
30/03/96	FC Twente	H	1-3	Heering (p)
05/04/96	FC Volendam	A	1-2	Marbus
09/04/96	FC Utrecht	A	0-1	
14/04/96	Feyenoord	H	0-3	
17/04/96	Sparta	A	0-2	
20/04/96	Roda JC	A	0-5	
28/04/96	RKC	H	1-3	Rorije
05/05/96	PSV	A	1-3	Rorije

DE GRAAFSCHAP

CLUB DIRECTORY

De Graafschap
Stadion "De Vijverberg"
Lijsterbeslaan 101 A
Postbus 249
7000 AE Doetinchem
tel - (0314) 324380
fax - (0314) 362892
Year of Formation - 1954
President - Hylke Enzerink
Secretary - Cor Hunkelaar
Coach - Frans Körver; Hans van Doorneveld; Fritz Korbach
Stadium - De Vijverberg (11,000)

APPEARANCES 95/96

	P	Ap	(s)	Gls
Virgil BREETVELD	A	19	(8)	5
René VAN DE BRINK	A	28	(4)	4
Bennie DEKKER	A	1		
Robert FUCHS	M	13	(7)	1
Edwin GODEE	M	28	(2)	4
Reinder HENDRIKS	D	27	(1)	
Maarten KERKHOF	M		(2)	
Olaf LINDENBERGH	D	30		
Frank LUKASSEN	D	10	(3)	
Rob MATTHAEI	M	22	(4)	
Hennie MEIJER	A	19	(1)	5
Ron OLYSLAGER	G	34		
Jan OOSTERHUIS	D	25		1
Patrick PAAUWE	M	22	(1)	
Erik REDEKER	D	22	(4)	
Marchanno SCHULTZ	A	7	(20)	3
Raymond VICTORIA	A	18	(9)	5
Eric VISCAAL	A	18		9
Rudy VONK	M		(1)	
Richard DE VRIES	A		(2)	
Fabian WILNIS	D	31	(1)	

LEAGUE RESULTS 1995/96

20/08/95	NEC	H	2-3	Godee, Fuchs (p)
27/08/95	Sparta	A	1-4	Victoria
10/09/95	Go Ahead Eagles	H	3-2	Breetveld 3
16/09/95	Fortuna Sittard	A	0-1	
19/09/95	NAC	H	1-1	Godee
23/09/95	SC Heerenveen	A	2-2	Van de Brink, Breetveld
01/10/95	Vitesse	H	2-3	Oosterhuis, Victoria
04/10/95	FC Twente	H	0-3	
15/10/95	FC Volendam	A	1-1	Victoria
21/10/95	Roda JC	H	0-2	
26/10/95	Feyenoord	A	0-2	
28/10/95	RKC	H	1-1	Godee
07/11/95	FC Groningen	A	0-3	
18/11/95	PSV	A	0-8	
25/11/95	Willem II	H	1-2	Van de Brink
03/12/95	FC Utrecht	H	3-0	Meijer 2, Van de Brink
16/12/95	NEC	A	1-1	Meijer
20/12/95	Ajax	A	0-1	
23/12/95	Sparta	H	5-2	Schultz 2, Viscaal 2, Godee
03/02/96	NAC	A	1-2	Meijer
07/02/96	Fortuna Sittard	H	1-1	Viscaal
28/02/96	SC Heerenveen	H	2-2	Viscaal 2 (1p)
03/03/96	FC Twente	A	0-1	
09/03/96	FC Volendam	H	1-0	Viscaal
13/03/96	Go Ahead Eagles	A	0-4	
17/03/96	Feyenoord	H	1-1	Van de Brink
23/03/96	Roda JC	A	1-3	Victoria
27/03/96	Vitesse	A	1-0	Schultz
31/03/96	RKC	A	0-5	
11/04/96	PSV	H	1-2	Viscaal
14/04/96	FC Groningen	H	3-1	Breetveld, Viscaal 2
20/04/96	Willem II	A	1-1	Victoria
28/04/96	FC Utrecht	A	1-1	Meijer
05/05/96	Ajax	H	0-0	

FC GRONINGEN

CLUB DIRECTORY

FC Groningen
Postbus 1399
9701 BJ Groningen
tel - (050) 3180814
fax - (050) 3125194
Year of Formation - 1971
President - Henk van der Wal
Manager - Theo Huizinga
Coach - Hans Westerhof
Stadium - Oosterpark (18,000)

APPEARANCES 95/96

	P	Ap	(s)	Gls
Raymond BEERENS	M	29	(1)	3
Arjan BLAAUW	A	1	(9)	
Mariano BOMBARDA	A	34		19
Arnold BOS	A	1	(1)	
Marcel BOUDESTEYN	M	16	(8)	
Arjan EBBINGE	D		(2)	
Kurt ELSHOT	D	1	(1)	
Joop GALL	D	27		
Sander VAN GESSEL	M		(1)	
Dean GORRÉ	M	34		4
Jakob GREGERSEN (DEN)	D	10	(5)	
Harris HUIZINGH	A	21	(1)	5
Maarten DE JONG	D	6	(9)	1
Erwin KOEMAN	M	26	(2)	2
Edwin DE KRUIJFF	A	13	(4)	1
Roël LIEFDEN	D	31		
Patrick LODEWIJKS	G	31		
Bob MULDER	A		(3)	
Edwin PRINS	G	2		
Bas ROORDA	G	1	(1)	
Mathias RÖSÉN (SWE)	A	15	(7)	3
Romano SION	A	25	(2)	8
Bert STOKKINGREEF	A		(3)	
Jan VEENHOF	D	20		1
Zephnad WATTIMURY	D	2	(1)	
Warry VAN WATTUM	D	28		

LEAGUE RESULTS 1995/96

Date	Opponent		Score	Scorers
19/08/95	Go Ahead Eagles	A	2-2	Bombarda 2
23/08/95	Fortuna Sittard	H	2-0	Bombarda 2
29/08/95	SC Heerenveen	A	0-1	
12/09/95	NAC	H	3-1	Sion, Bombarda, Huizingh
20/09/95	Vitesse	H	2-0	Huizingh, Sion
24/09/95	FC Twente	A	2-2	Beerens, Sion
01/10/95	FC Volendam	H	2-1	Bombarda, Huizingh
05/10/95	Feyenoord	A	1-4	Gorré
14/10/95	Roda JC	H	0-1	
21/10/95	PSV	A	1-7	De Kruijff
25/10/95	RKC	A	3-1	Bombarda 2, Rösén
29/10/95	FC Utrecht	H	0-0	
04/11/95	Willem II	A	2-5	Sion, Bombarda
07/11/95	De Graafschap	H	3-0	Beerens, Bombarda, Gorré
19/11/95	Ajax	A	1-4	De Jong
03/12/95	NEC	H	0-0	
10/12/95	Sparta	A	1-1	Gorré
16/12/95	Go Ahead Eagles	H	0-0	
23/12/95	Fortuna Sittard	A	0-0	
20/01/96	NAC	A	1-1	Rösén
04/02/96	Vitesse	A	0-0	
03/03/96	Feyenoord	H	1-0	og (Koeman)
09/03/96	Roda JC	A	0-0	
12/03/96	SC Heerenveen	H	1-1	Bombarda
17/03/96	RKC	H	1-1	Huizingh
20/03/96	FC Twente	H	2-2	Bombarda, Sion
24/03/96	PSV	H	1-0	Veenhof
27/03/96	FC Volendam	A	1-2	Bombarda (p)
31/03/96	FC Utrecht	A	1-0	Bombarda (p)
06/04/96	Willem II	H	3-0	Sion, Gorré, Rösén
14/04/96	De Graafschap	A	1-3	Bombarda
21/04/96	Ajax	H	3-4	Sion 2, Bombarda
28/04/96	NEC	A	2-0	Beerens, Koeman
05/05/96	Sparta	H	5-1	Bombarda 3, Huizingh, Koeman

SC HEERENVEEN

CLUB DIRECTORY

SC Heerenveen
Postbus 513
8440 AM Heerenveen
tel - (0513) 612100
fax - (0513) 615061
Year of Formation - 1920
President - Riemer van der Velde
Manager - Tjisse Wallendal
Coach - Foppe de Haan
Stadium - Abe Lenstra (13,500)

APPEARANCES 95/96

	P	Ap	(s)	Gls
Carlo L'AMI	G	8		
Michel DOESBURG	D	20	(1)	
Leeroy ECHTELD	M	27	(3)	6
Johan HANSMA	D	31		3
Wilco HELLINGA	M		(6)	1
Igor KORNEEV (RUS)	M	8	(3)	2
Mark NYGAARD (DEN)	A		(6)	1
Arnold OOSTERVEER	D	2		
Ronnie PANDER	D	2	(3)	
Alex PASTOOR	M	25	(2)	
Erik REGTOP	A	21	(12)	7
Marco ROELOFSEN	M	27	(7)	
Melchior SCHOENMAKERS	D	16		
Tom SIER	D	31		
Roberto STRAAL	D	7	(5)	3
Aldo SWAGER	G	26		
Jeffrey TALAN	A	26		9
Erik TAMMER	A	7	(7)	6
Ole TOBIASEN (DEN)	D	12		
Jon Dahl TOMASSON (DEN)	A	30		14
André VAN TUINEN	A	2	(7)	
Ronnie VENEMA	D		(4)	
Jan DE VISSER	M	30	(1)	2
Geert-Jelle DE VRIES	D	2	(3)	
Romeo WOUDEN	A	14	(18)	11
Bert ZUURMAN	A		(1)	

LEAGUE RESULTS 1995/96

19/08/95	Roda JC	A	2-2	Wouden 2
26/08/95	RKC	H	2-1	Tammer (p), Tomasson
29/08/95	FC Groningen	H	1-0	Straal
09/09/95	PSV	A	1-5	Tammer
20/09/95	Willem II	A	1-1	Straal
23/09/95	De Graafschap	H	2-2	Hansma, Tammer (p)
01/10/95	Ajax	H	0-4	
04/10/95	NEC	A	3-1	Echteld, Talan, Tammer
14/10/95	Sparta	H	4-0	Tomasson 2, Talan, Tammer
21/10/95	Fortuna Sittard	A	2-1	Echteld, Tomasson
25/10/95	Go Ahead Eagles	H	2-1	Hansma, Tammer
28/10/95	NAC	H	1-1	Tomasson
05/11/95	FC Utrecht	A	1-1	Echteld
19/11/95	Vitesse	A	2-2	Regtop, Wouden
24/11/95	FC Twente	H	1-1	Nygaard
03/12/95	FC Volendam	A	1-1	Hansma
08/12/95	Feyenoord	H	0-1	
16/12/95	Roda JC	H	3-2	Talan, Regtop, Wouden
23/12/95	RKC	A	3-2	Wouden, Regtop (p), Talan
19/01/96	PSV	H	1-3	Regtop
25/02/96	Ajax	A	2-6	Wouden 2
28/02/96	De Graafschap	A	2-2	Regtop, Tomasson (p)
02/03/96	NEC	H	4-1	Tomasson 2, Echteld, Regtop
09/03/96	Sparta	A	2-5	Tomasson, Korneev
12/03/96	FC Groningen	A	1-1	Tomasson (p)
16/03/96	Go Ahead Eagles	A	3-2	Tomasson, Regtop, Wouden
23/03/96	Fortuna Sittard	H	5-1	Tomasson 2, Talan, Korneev, Wouden
30/03/96	NAC	A	1-5	Wouden
06/04/96	FC Utrecht	H	4-2	Talan 3, Tomasson
08/04/96	Willem II	H	2-2	Echteld, De Visser
13/04/96	Vitesse	H	1-2	Talan
21/04/96	FC Twente	A	1-0	De Visser
28/04/96	FC Volendam	H	4-3	Wouden, og (Persijn), Straal, Echteld
05/05/96	Feyenoord	A	1-4	Hellinga

NAC

CLUB DIRECTORY

NAC
Postbus 3356
4800 DJ Breda
tel - (076) 5214500
fax - (076) 5211975
Year of Formation - 1912
President - John Peek
Secretary - Cees van Haperen
Manager - Martien Vreijsen
Coach - Ron Spelbos (95/96 - Wim Rijsbergen)
Stadium - FujiFilm (16,900)

MAJOR HONOURS
League Championship - (1) 1921.
Domestic Cup - (1) 1973.

APPEARANCES 95/96

	P	Ap	(s)	Gls
Yassine ABDELLAOUI (MAR)	A	22	(5)	8
John ACHTERBERG	G	5	(1)	
Ceylan ARIKAN	M		(2)	1
Graham ARNOLD (AUS)	A	29	(1)	16
Maarten ATMODIKORO	D	32	(1)	1
Ruud BROOD	D	13	(4)	2
Geert BRUSSELERS	M	33		3
Dick VAN BURIK	D	26	(2)	1
Jan GAASBEEK	M	34		3
Francois GESTHUIZEN	M	5	(7)	
Paul JANSSEN	D	1	(1)	
John KARELSE	G	29		
Patrick LEYTENS	A		(2)	1
Edward LINSKENS	M	4	(1)	
Ton LOKHOFF	M	28		3
Sander OOSTROM	A	6	(10)	2
Yureck PERSOON	A		(1)	
Peter REMIE	M	13	(4)	5
Marco SAS	D	8	(9)	
Olaf SCHAAP	A	2	(14)	
Twan SCHEEPERS	A	22	(3)	7
Tony VIDMAR (AUS)	D	30		2
Kees VAN WONDEREN	M	32		3

LEAGUE RESULTS 1995/96

20/08/95	RKC	A	2-2	Arnold, Brusselers
27/08/95	PSV	H	3-0	Abdellaoui, Remie (p), Arnold
12/09/95	FC Groningen	A	1-3	Arnold
16/09/95	Willem II	H	0-1	
19/09/95	De Graafschap	A	1-1	Remie (p)
24/09/95	Ajax	H	0-1	
30/09/95	NEC	A	3-1	Scheepers 2, Lokhoff
04/10/95	Sparta	H	0-0	
14/10/95	Go Ahead Eagles	A	1-1	Arnold
17/10/95	FC Utrecht	H	3-0	Arnold, Remie (p), Brusselers
25/10/95	Fortuna Sittard	H	2-0	Remie 2
28/10/95	SC Heerenveen	A	1-1	Scheepers
05/11/95	Vitesse	H	2-2	Abdellaoui (p), Oostrom
19/11/95	FC Twente	A	3-0	Vidmar, Abdellaoui (p), Leytens
25/11/95	FC Volendam	H	4-0	Abdellaoui, Oostrom, Brood, Van Burik
16/12/95	RKC	H	0-1	
20/12/95	Roda JC	H	0-0	
13/01/96	Feyenoord	A	2-2	Arnold, Abdellaoui
16/01/96	PSV	A	1-4	Van Wonderen
20/01/96	FC Groningen	H	1-1	Brood
03/02/96	De Graafschap	H	2-1	Arnold 2
24/02/96	NEC	H	2-1	Gaasbeek, Scheepers
03/03/96	Sparta	A	1-3	Gaasbeek
09/03/96	Go Ahead Eagles	H	2-0	Scheepers 2
13/03/96	Willem II	A	3-1	Arnold, Abdellaoui, Scheepens
16/03/96	Fortuna Sittard	A	2-2	Lokhoff, Abdellaoui
24/03/96	FC Utrecht	A	4-0	Arnold 4
30/03/96	SC Heerenveen	H	5-1	Abdellaoui (p), Brusselers, Arnold 2, Atmodikoro
06/04/96	Ajax	A	0-2	
08/04/96	Vitesse	A	0-2	
14/04/96	FC Twente	H	4-1	Van Wonderen, Gaasbeek, Arikan, Lokhoff (p)
21/04/96	FC Volendam	A	2-1	Vidmar, Van Wonderen
28/04/96	Feyenoord	H	0-3	
05/05/96	Roda JC	A	1-5	Arnold

NEC

CLUB DIRECTORY

NEC
Stadionplein 1
Postbus 6562
6303 GB Nijmegen
tel - (024) 3590359 (ext. 3)
fax - (024) 3567475
Year of Formation - 1900
President - Lex Coenen
Secretary - Carol Boef
Manager - Ton Odenkirchen
Coach - Cees van Kooten; Leon Looyen; Wim Koevermans
Stadium - De Goffert (22,000)

APPEARANCES 95/96

	P	Ap	(s)	Gls
Carlos AALBERS	D	11		
Wilfried BROOKHUIS	G	34		
Ulrich CRÜDEN	D	27	(1)	
Patrick VAN DIEMEN	M	33		2
Emiel VAN EIJKEREN	A	16	(8)	8
Dennis GENTENAAR	D		(2)	
Danny HOEKMAN	A	6	(5)	1
Anton JANSSEN	M	34		2
Marcel KONING	M	14	(11)	2
Jeffrey KOOISTRA	A	27	(3)	2
Michel LANGERAK	M	20	(3)	3
Marcel LEBBINK	D		(1)	
Cees VAN DER LINDEN	D	8		
Luuk MAES	D	11	(2)	
Pavel MIKHALEVICH (BLS)	M		(2)	
Patrick POTHUIZEN	A	29	(1)	1
Oleg PUTILO (BLS)	A	4	(15)	2
Eric STOCK (NOR)	D	15	(4)	
Antti SUMIALA (FIN)	A	31	(2)	9
Mark VERHOEVEN	D	31		
Juan VIEDMA	M	23	(2)	1

LEAGUE RESULTS 1995/96

20/08/95	De Graafschap	A	3-2	Sumiala, Kooistra, Koning
25/08/95	Ajax	H	0-6	
09/09/95	FC Utrecht	H	2-0	Van Diemen, Kooistra
15/09/95	Sparta	A	1-3	Sumiala
20/09/95	Go Ahead Eagles	H	0-2	
23/09/95	Fortuna Sittard	A	1-1	Koning
30/09/95	NAC	H	1-3	Sumiala
04/10/95	SC Heerenveen	H	1-3	Sumiala
15/10/95	Vitesse	A	2-2	Van Diemen, Putilo
21/10/95	FC Volendam	H	2-1	Viedma, Sumiala
25/10/95	FC Twente	A	0-2	
29/10/95	Feyenoord	H	1-3	Pothuizen
04/11/95	Roda JC	H	1-4	Van Eijkeren
19/11/95	RKC	A	0-4	
26/11/95	PSV	H	0-5	
03/12/95	FC Groningen	A	0-0	
09/12/95	Willem II	H	1-1	Sumiala
16/12/95	De Graafschap	H	1-1	Janssen (p)
24/12/95	Ajax	A	1-3	Sumiala
21/01/96	FC Utrecht	A	2-1	Van Eijkeren 2
07/02/96	Sparta	H	2-2	Sumiala, Van Eijkeren
10/02/96	Fortuna Sittard	H	0-2	
24/02/96	NAC	A	1-2	Hoekman
28/02/96	Go Ahead Eagles	A	2-2	Van Eijkeren, Sumiala
02/03/96	SC Heerenveen	A	1-4	Van Eijkeren
10/03/96	Vitesse	H	0-1	
15/03/96	FC Twente	H	1-4	Putilo
24/03/96	FC Volendam	A	0-1	
31/03/96	Feyenoord	A	1-2	Van Eijkeren
06/04/96	RKC	H	2-1	Langerak 2
13/04/96	Roda JC	A	0-1	
20/04/96	PSV	A	0-1	
28/04/96	FC Groningen	H	0-2	
05/05/96	Willem II	A	3-1	Langerak, Van Eijkeren, Janssen

PSV

CLUB DIRECTORY

PSV
Frederiklaan 10 A
5616 NH Eindhoven
tel - (040) 2501501
fax - (040) 2501549
Year of Formation - 1913
President - Bill Maeyer
Manager - Frank Arnesen
Coach - Dick Advocaat
Stadium - Philips (30,000)

MAJOR HONOURS
League Championship - (13)
1929, 1935, 1951, 1963, 1975, 1976, 1978, 1986, 1987, 1988, 1989, 1991, 1992.
Domestic Cup - (7)
1950, 1974, 1976, 1988, 1989, 1990, 1996.
European Champions' Cup - (1) 1988.
UEFA Cup - (1) 1978.

APPEARANCES 95/96

	P	Ap	(s)	Gls
Wilfred BOUMA	A		(4)	
Philip COCU	M	29	(2)	12
Bjorn VAN DER DOELEN	M	5	(6)	1
René EYKELKAMP	A	20	(7)	10
Ernest FABER	D	23		2
Eidur Smári GUDJOHNSEN (ISL)	A	6	(7)	3
Peter HOEKSTRA	A	6	(9)	6
Wim JONK	D	28	(1)	6
René KLOMP	M	1	(1)	
Tom VAN DER LEEGTE	M	7	(5)	1
Edward LINSKENS	M	7	(3)	
Stanley MENZO	G	1		
Luc NILIS (BEL)	A	31		21
Arthur NUMAN	D	27		2
Boudewijn PAHLPLATZ	A	11	(9)	5
Geoffrey PROMMAYON	D	3	(3)	
RONALDO				
Luiz Nazário de Lima (BRA)	A	10	(3)	12
Jaap STAM	D	14		1
Stan VALCKX	D	30	(1)	1
Marciano VINK	M	19	(4)	2
Ronald WATERREUS	G	33		
Chris VAN DER WEERDEN	D	27		1
Jan WOUTERS	D	20		3
Boudewijn ZENDEN	A	16	(9)	7

LEAGUE RESULTS 1995/96

18/08/95	Fortuna Sittard	A	3-1	Hoekstra, Nilis, Cocu
27/08/95	NAC	A	0-3	
09/09/95	SC Heerenveen	H	5-1	Ronaldo 2, Pahlplatz, Eykelkamp, Nilis
16/09/95	Vitesse	A	1-0	Pahlplatz
20/09/95	FC Twente	H	3-0	Ronaldo 2 (1p), Faber
23/09/95	FC Volendam	A	5-0	Ronaldo, Numan, Pahlplatz, Cocu, Jonk
01/10/95	Feyenoord	H	3-0	Ronaldo, Jonk, Van der Weerden
04/10/95	Roda JC	A	1-1	Cocu
14/10/95	RKC	H	4-0	Eykelkamp 2, Cocu, Nilis (p)
21/10/95	FC Groningen	H	7-1	Eykelkamp, Zenden 3, Nilis 2, Pahlplatz
24/10/95	FC Utrecht	A	4-1	Valckx, Nilis, Jonk, Cocu
28/10/95	Willem II	H	2-0	Faber, Nilis
05/11/95	Ajax	A	1-1	Ronaldo
18/11/95	De Graafschap	H	8-0	Jonk, Ronaldo 3 (1p), Cocu 2, Eykelkamp, Hoekstra
26/11/95	NEC	A	5-0	Ronaldo 2 (1p), Hoekstra, Nilis, Cocu
02/12/95	Sparta	H	1-2	Nilis
16/12/95	Fortuna Sittard	H	3-0	Hoekstra 2, Numan
20/12/95	Go Ahead Eagles	A	5-0	Nilis 2, Eykelkamp, Wouters, Hoekstra
16/01/96	NAC	H	4-1	Pahlplatz, Nilis 2 (1p), Van der Leegte
19/01/96	SC Heerenveen	A	3-1	Zenden, Jonk, Wouters
10/02/96	FC Volendam	H	7-0	Wouters, Cocu 2, Eykelkamp, Nilis 2, Gudjohnsen
25/02/96	Feyenoord	A	0-0	
02/03/96	Roda JC	H	3-0	og (Senden), Nilis, Van der Doelen
08/03/96	RKC	A	3-1	Nilis, Stam, Vink
16/03/96	FC Utrecht	H	0-0	
24/03/96	FC Groningen	A	0-1	
27/03/96	FC Twente	A	2-3	Eykelkamp 2
30/03/96	Willem II	A	5-2	Nilis 2, Zenden 2, Gudjohnsen
06/04/96	Vitesse	H	1-0	Eykelkamp
08/04/96	Ajax	H	1-1	Nilis
11/04/96	De Graafschap	A	2-1	Jonk (p), Vink
20/04/96	NEC	H	1-0	Gudjohnsen
28/04/96	Sparta	A	1-2	Cocu
05/05/96	Go Ahead Eagles	H	3-1	Zenden, Cocu, Nilis

RKC

CLUB DIRECTORY

RKC
Postbus 4
5140 AA Waalwijk
tel - (0416) 334356
fax - (0416) 342310
Year of Formation - 1940
President - Jan Snoeren
Secretary - Jan Gerrits
Manager - Henk van Delft
Coach - Leo van Veen
(96/97 - Cees van Kooten)
Stadium - Sportpark Olympia (6,200)

APPEARANCES 95/96

	P	Ap	(s)	Gls
Romeo VAN AERDE	M	31		2
Hans VAN ARUM	A	14	(5)	1
Marcel BRANDS	D	34		1
John GARRELFS	G	1	(1)	
Ramon VAN HAAREN	D	20		
Léon HUTTEN	D	28		
Darije KALEZIC (BOS)	M	11	(3)	1
Danny MULLER	M	29	(1)	8
Dennis VAN DER PENNEN	M	1	(4)	
Zeljko PETROVIC (YUG)	M	30		9
Gregory PLAYFAIR	A	4	(2)	
René VAN RIJSWIJK	A	5	(6)	2
Bobby SCHOONENS	A		(7)	
Alfred SCHREUDER	M	28		1
Dick SCHREUDER	A	14	(10)	1
Jeffrey VAN DER STEEN	M	14	(3)	1
Jurgen STREPPEL	D	21		3
Jacky VERBEEK	D		(1)	
Hans VONK	G	33		
Regillio VREDE	D	25	(7)	3
Clyde WIJNHARD	A	31	(2)	8

LEAGUE RESULTS 1995/96

20/08/95	NAC	H	2-2	og (Brood), Petrovic (p)
26/08/95	SC Heerenveen	A	1-2	Van Aerde
08/09/95	Vitesse	H	0-2	
17/09/95	FC Twente	A	1-0	Petrovic (p)
20/09/95	FC Volendam	H	2-0	Muller, Petrovic
24/09/95	Feyenoord	A	2-4	Muller, Van Rijswijk
01/10/95	Roda JC	H	2-0	Petrovic (p), Vrede
04/10/95	FC Utrecht	H	1-0	Muller
14/10/95	PSV	A	0-4	
21/10/95	Willem II	A	2-1	Streppel, Muller
25/10/95	FC Groningen	H	1-3	Muller
28/10/95	De Graafschap	A	1-1	Wijnhard
08/11/95	Ajax	H	0-3	
19/11/95	NEC	H	4-0	Wijnhard 2, Van Rijswijk, Van der Steen
26/11/95	Sparta	A	0-1	
03/12/95	Go Ahead Eagles	H	1-1	Schreuder D.
09/12/95	Fortuna Sittard	A	0-0	
16/12/95	NAC	A	1-0	Streppel
24/12/95	SC Heerenveen	H	2-3	Streppel, Muller
21/01/96	Vitesse	A	1-2	Petrovic
07/02/96	FC Twente	H	1-0	Brands (p)
11/02/96	Feyenoord	H	1-1	Vrede
03/03/96	FC Utrecht	A	0-0	
08/03/96	PSV	H	1-3	Petrovic
13/03/96	Roda JC	A	2-2	og (Roelofsen), og (Trost)
17/03/96	FC Groningen	A	1-1	Van Arum
24/03/96	Willem II	H	3-2	Wijnhard 2, Schreuder A.
31/03/96	De Graafschap	H	5-0	Petrovic, Wijnhard, Kalezic, Van Aerde, Muller (p)
06/04/96	NEC	A	1-2	Vrede
14/04/96	Ajax	A	0-1	
17/04/96	FC Volendam	A	1-1	Petrovic (p)
21/04/96	Sparta	H	0-0	
28/04/96	Go Ahead Eagles	A	3-1	Vrede, Petrovic, Wijnhard
05/05/96	Fortuna Sittard	H	1-1	Muller

RODA JC

CLUB DIRECTORY

Roda JC
Postbus 1156
6460 BD Kerkrade
tel - (045) 5411053
fax - (045) 5426606
Year of Formation - 1962
President - Theo Pickée
Secretary - Jo Ploum
Coach - Huub Stevens
Stadium - Gemeentelijk Sportpark 'Kaalheide' (25,000)

APPEARANCES 95/96

	P	Ap	(s)	Gls
Tijjani BABANGIDA (NIG)	A	22	(7)	10
Giuseppe "Pino" CANALE (BEL)	A		(2)	
Arno DOOMERNIK	M	33		3
Barry VAN GALEN	A	19	(1)	3
Maurice GRAEF	A	21	(7)	6
Henry HEEREN	M	1	(10)	
Danny HESP	D	10	(7)	1
Ruud HESP	G	34		
Marco VAN HOOGDALEM	D	28	(1)	3
Piotr KASPERSKI (POL)	A	6	(8)	1
Johan DE KOCK	D	34		5
Eric VAN DE LUER	M	24	(5)	2
Rastislav MORES (SVK)	M	7	(10)	1
André OOIJER	D	23		1
Rick PLUM	M		(3)	
Richard ROELOFSEN	A	19	(6)	7
Anton SCHEUTJENS	G		(1)	
Gerry SENDEN	D	32		1
René TROST	D	30	(1)	1
Erwin VANDERBROECK	M		(1)	
Edwin VURENS	A	31		6
Davy ZAFARIN	A		(2)	

LEAGUE RESULTS 1995/96

19/08/95	SC Heerenveen	H	2-2	Roelofsen, De Kock
27/08/95	Vitesse	A	0-0	
09/09/95	FC Twente	H	0-0	
17/09/95	FC Volendam	A	0-1	
20/09/95	Feyenoord	H	1-1	Van Galen
23/09/95	FC Utrecht	A	1-0	Roelofsen
01/10/95	RKC	A	0-2	
04/10/95	PSV	H	1-1	Roelofsen
14/10/95	FC Groningen	A	1-0	Trost
21/10/95	De Graafschap	A	2-0	Roelofsen, De Kock
25/10/95	Willem II	H	1-1	Doomernik
28/10/95	Ajax	A	1-6	Roelofsen
04/11/95	NEC	A	4-1	Graef 3, Van Hoogdalem
18/11/95	Sparta	H	1-0	Vurens
25/11/95	Go Ahead Eagles	A	2-1	Graef, Hesp D.
01/12/95	Fortuna Sittard	H	1-1	Dooomernik
16/12/95	SC Heerenveen	A	2-3	Babangida, Van Hoogdalem
20/12/95	NAC	A	0-0	
23/12/95	Vitesse	H	0-1	
21/01/96	FC Twente	A	3-0	Vurens, Graef, Van de Luer
04/02/96	Feyenoord	A	0-2	
02/03/96	PSV	A	0-3	
09/03/96	FC Groningen	H	0-0	
12/03/96	RKC	H	2-2	Babangida, Van de Luer
16/03/96	Willem II	A	2-1	Van Galen, Roelofsen
20/03/96	FC Utrecht	H	3-1	De Kock, Senden, Vurens
23/03/96	De Graafschap	H	3-1	Roelofsen, Vurens, Mores
27/03/96	Sparta	A	2-2	Babangida 2
30/03/96	Ajax	H	2-0	Babangida, Doomernik
09/04/96	NEC	H	1-0	Van Hoogdalem
13/04/96	FC Volendam	H	2-0	Vurens, Babangida
20/04/96	Go Ahead Eagles	H	5-0	Babangida, Ooijer, Van Galen, Graef, Kasperski
28/04/96	Fortuna Sittard	A	1-1	De Kock (p)
05/05/96	NAC	H	5-1	De Kock (p), Babangida 3, Vurens

SPARTA

CLUB DIRECTORY

Sparta
Postbus 1802
3000 BV Rotterdam
tel - (010) 4151087
fax - (010) 4154960
Year of Formation - 1888
President - Peter van der Burg
Secretary - Dick Happel
Coach - Henk ten Cate
Stadium - Spangen (13,000)

MAJOR HONOURS
League Championship - (6)
1909, 1911, 1912, 1913, 1915, 1959.
Domestic Cup - (3) 1958, 1962, 1966.

APPEARANCES 95/96

	P	Ap	(s)	Gls
Lofti AMHAOUCH (MAR)	M	1	(8)	
Dennis DE BRUIN	D	5	(5)	
John DEN DUNNEN	A		(2)	
Ali EL KATTABI (MAR)	A		(9)	1
Carloss FORTES	A	33		5
Alfons GROENENDIJK	M	31		5
Jochem VAN DER HOEVEN	D	6	(7)	1
Nico JALINK	M	32		4
Frank KOOIMAN	G	1		
Dennis KRIJGSMAN	A	32	(1)	5
Arjan VAN DER LAAN	A	34		8
Dave VAN DER MEER	D	31	(1)	
Edward METGOD	G	33		
Mark NOORLANDER	D	5	(4)	
Dennis DE NOOIJER	A	32		16
Gérard DE NOOIJER	D	33		4
Milko PIEREN	M	1	(5)	
Michel RENFURM	A	3	(24)	3
Edgar VAN DER ROER	A	1	(5)	
Jerry SMITH	D	31		
John VELDMAN	D	29		

LEAGUE RESULTS 1995/96

Date	Opponent		Score	Scorers
19/08/95	Willem II	A	0-6	
27/08/95	De Graafschap	H	4-1	De Nooijer D. 2, Van der Laan, Jalink
10/09/95	Ajax	A	0-4	
15/09/95	NEC	H	3-1	og (Koning), Fortes, De Nooijer D.
20/09/95	FC Utrecht	H	0-0	
23/09/95	Go Ahead Eagles	A	3-1	Fortes, De Nooijer D. 2
01/10/95	Fortuna Sittard	H	0-1	
04/10/95	NAC	A	0-0	
14/10/95	SC Heerenveen	A	0-4	
20/10/95	FC Twente	H	4-2	Groenendijk, De Nooijer D. 2, Fortes
25/10/95	Vitesse	H	3-0	De Nooijer D., Krijgsman, Fortes
29/10/95	FC Volendam	A	1-1	Van der Laan
05/11/95	Feyenoord	H	3-2	Fortes, De Nooijer D., Renfurm
18/11/95	Roda JC	A	0-1	
26/11/95	RKC	H	1-0	Renfurm
02/12/95	PSV	A	2-1	Van der Laan, De Nooijer D.
10/12/95	FC Groningen	H	1-1	De Nooijer D. (p)
15/12/95	Willem II	H	1-1	De Nooijer D.
23/12/95	De Graafschap	A	2-5	De Nooijer G., Groenendijk
21/01/96	Ajax	H	3-3	Jalink, Krijgsman, De Nooijer D.
04/02/96	FC Utrecht	A	0-0	
07/02/96	NEC	A	2-2	Krijgsman, De Nooijer G.
24/02/96	Fortuna Sittard	A	1-0	De Nooijer D.
03/03/96	NAC	H	3-1	De Nooijer D., Groenendijk, Van der Laan
09/03/96	SC Heerenveen	H	5-2	Jalink, De Nooijer G., Van der Laan, Krijgsman, Van der Hoeven
17/03/96	Vitesse	A	2-3	Van der Laan, Groenendijk
24/03/96	FC Twente	A	0-1	
27/03/96	Roda JC	H	2-2	De Nooijer D. (p), El Kattabi
30/03/96	FC Volendam	H	1-0	De Nooijer G.
10/04/96	Feyenoord	A	1-1	Van der Laan
17/04/96	Go Ahead Eagles	H	2-0	Krijgsman, Van der Laan
21/04/96	RKC	A	0-0	
28/04/96	PSV	H	2-1	Jalink, Groenendijk
05/05/96	FC Groningen	A	1-5	Renfurm

FC TWENTE

CLUB DIRECTORY

FC Twente
JJ van Deinselaan 30
7541 PE Enschede
tel - (053) 4310080
fax - (053) 4324639
Year of Formation - 1965
President - Cees Anker
Secretary - Rob van Holten
Coach - Issy ten Donkelaar; Fred Rutten; Hans Meyer
Stadium - Het Diekman (13,500)

MAJOR HONOURS

Domestic Cup - (1) 1977.

APPEARANCES 95/96

	P	Ap	(s)	Gls
Ansar AYUPOV (RUS)	M	29	(1)	
Andreas AUGUSTSSON (SWE)	D		(1)	
Bertil TER AVEST	M	24	(4)	1
Kare BECKER	A		(1)	
Michel BOEREBACH	D	25	(2)	4
Sander BOSCHKER	G	23		
Paul BOSVELT	M	32		7
Arnold BRUGGINK	A	32		12
Theo TEN CAAT	M	21	(2)	3
Juul ELLERMAN	A	15	(6)	7
Wilfried ELZINGA	D	12	(1)	1
Jan VAN HALST	M	3	(1)	
Jeroen HEUBACH	D	6	(2)	
Nico-Jan HOOGMA	D	31		2
André KARNEBEEK	D	14	(2)	1
Michael MOLS	A	22	(9)	2
Daniël NIJHOF	D	17	(2)	
Niels OUDE KAMPHUIS	M	26	(2)	
Cees PAAUWE	G	1		
Yuri PETROV (RUS)	A	24	(4)	3
Rik PLATVOET	A	6	(11)	2
Haci SEN	D		(1)	
Joost VOLMER	D	1	(3)	1
Pascal DE VRIES	M		(2)	
Sander WESTERVELD	G	10	(1)	

LEAGUE RESULTS 1995/96

20/08/95	FC Volendam	A	3-1	Boerebach, Bruggink 2
27/08/95	Feyenoord	H	2-2	Bruggink, Boerebach (p)
09/09/95	Roda JC	A	0-0	
17/09/95	RKC	H	0-1	
20/09/95	PSV	A	0-3	
24/09/95	FC Groningen	H	2-2	Hoogma, Bruggink
29/09/95	Willem II	A	2-5	Ter Avest, Petrov
04/10/95	De Graafschap	A	3-0	Boerebach, Bruggink, Platvoet
15/10/95	Ajax	H	0-3	
20/10/95	Sparta	A	2-4	Bosvelt 2
25/10/95	NEC	H	2-0	Ellerman, Platvoet
29/10/95	Go Ahead Eagles	H	2-1	Boerebach, Mols
04/11/95	Fortuna Sittard	A	1-1	Bruggink
19/11/95	NAC	H	0-3	
24/11/95	SC Heerenveen	A	1-1	Elzinga
03/12/95	Vitesse	H	1-0	Ellerman
10/12/95	FC Utrecht	A	3-0	Hoogma, Bosvelt 2
17/12/95	FC Volendam	H	2-1	Bruggink, Ellerman
24/12/95	Feyenoord	A	0-1	
21/01/96	Roda JC	H	0-3	
07/02/96	RKC	A	0-1	
03/03/96	De Graafschap	H	1-0	Ellerman
10/03/96	Ajax	A	1-6	Ten Caat
15/03/96	NEC	A	4-1	Bosvelt, Petrov, Ten Caat (p), Ellerman
20/03/96	FC Groningen	A	2-2	Ellerman, Petrov
24/03/96	Sparta	H	1-0	Bruggink
27/03/96	PSV	H	3-2	Bosvelt, Bruggink 2
30/03/96	Go Ahead Eagles	A	3-1	Ten Caat, Ellerman, Bosvelt
02/04/96	Willem II	H	2-1	Bruggink 2
06/04/96	Fortuna Sittard	H	1-0	Karnebeek
14/04/96	NAC	A	1-4	Mols
21/04/96	SC Heerenveen	H	0-1	
28/04/96	Vitesse	A	0-2	
05/05/96	FC Utrecht	H	1-2	Volmer (p)

FC UTRECHT

CLUB DIRECTORY

FC Utrecht
Herculesplein 331
3584 AA Utrecht
tel - (030) 2512521
fax - (030) 2540374
Year of Formation - 1970
President - Jan van de Kant
Manager - Nol de Ruiter
Coach - Simon Kistemaker; Ronald Spelbos
Stadium - Nieuw Galgewaard (14,000)

MAJOR HONOURS
Domestic Cup - (1) 1985.

APPEARANCES 95/96

	P	Ap	(s)	Gls
Elroy ASMUS	D	13	(6)	
Foeke BOOY	A		(1)	
Dries BOUSSATTA	M	19	(6)	
Niels CREUTZBURG	D		(1)	
Jan-Willem VAN EDE	G	29		
Raymond GRAANOOGST	A	7	(23)	6
Erik TEN HAG	M	29	(1)	2
Ferdino HERNANDEZ	A	9	(12)	1
Peter HOFSTEDE	A	21	(2)	3
Jean-Paul DE JONG	M	24		
Eric VAN KESSEL	M	29	(1)	
John VAN LOEN	A	14		1
David Sousa NASCIMENTO (POR)	D	26	(4)	1
Marcel VAN DER NET	D	30		3
Marcus PHILLIPS (ENG)	M	5	(2)	
Ab PLUGBOER	M	13	(2)	2
Stefan POSTMA	G	5		
Errol REFOS	D	17		
Jörg SMEETS	M	11	(4)	1
Eric SMIT	M	4	(3)	
Wlodzimierz SMOLAREK (POL)	A		(2)	
Ferdy VIERKLAU	D	30		
Hans VISSER	A	34		6
Robert WIJNANDS	D	5	(6)	

LEAGUE RESULTS 1995/96

20/08/95	Ajax	A	0-4	
27/08/95	FC Volendam	H	2-2	Hernandez, Graanoogst
09/09/95	NEC	A	0-2	
17/09/95	Feyenoord	H	1-0	Visser
20/09/95	Sparta	A	0-0	
23/09/95	Roda JC	H	0-1	
30/09/95	Go Ahead Eagles	A	3-2	Hofstede, Ten Hag, Graanoogst
04/10/95	RKC	A	0-1	
14/10/95	Fortuna Sittard	H	2-3	Van der Net, og (Roest)
17/10/95	NAC	A	0-3	
24/10/95	PSV	H	1-4	Graanoogst
29/10/95	FC Groningen	A	0-0	
05/11/95	SC Heerenveen	H	1-1	Visser
19/11/95	Willem II	H	3-3	Plugboer, Graanoogst, Visser
26/11/95	Vitesse	A	1-2	Plugboer
03/12/95	De Graafschap	A	0-3	
10/12/95	FC Twente	H	0-3	
17/12/95	Ajax	H	0-3	
14/01/96	FC Volendam	A	1-0	Visser
21/01/96	NEC	H	1-2	Van Loen
04/02/96	Sparta	H	0-0	
03/03/96	RKC	H	0-0	
10/03/96	Feyenoord	A	0-3	
16/03/96	PSV	A	0-0	
20/03/96	Roda JC	A	1-3	Graanoogst
24/03/96	NAC	H	0-4	
27/03/96	Fortuna Sittard	A	1-2	Van der Net
31/03/96	FC Groningen	H	0-1	
06/04/96	SC Heerenveen	A	2-4	Nascimento, Smeets
09/04/96	Go Ahead Eagles	H	1-0	Visser
12/04/96	Willem II	A	1-1	Ten Hag
21/04/96	Vitesse	H	2-0	Hofstede 2
28/04/96	De Graafschap	H	1-1	Van der Net
05/05/96	FC Twente	A	2-1	Graanoogst, Visser

VITESSE

CLUB DIRECTORY

Vitesse
Postbus 366
6800 AJ Arnhem
tel - (026) 4427427
fax - (026) 4459088
Year of Formation - 1892
President - Karel Aalbers
Secretary - Henk Brouwer
Manager - Rein Papenburg
Coach - Ronald Spelbos; Frans Thijssen
(96/97 - Leo Beenhakker)
Stadium - Monnikenhuize (12,000)

APPEARANCES 95/96

	P	Ap	(s)	Gls
Rob ALFLEN	M	4	(3)	
Raymond ATTEVELD	D	27	(3)	3
Theo BOS	D	21	(1)	
Dejan CUROVIC (YUG)	A	20	(8)	8
Edwin GORTER	M	18		5
Raimond VAN DER GOUW	G	21		
Ben IROHA (NIG)	M	7	(2)	
Arco JOCHEMSEN	M	26	(2)	5
Abe KNOOP	G	13		
Willem KORSTEN	A		(1)	1
Leo KOSWAL	A		(7)	
Martin LAAMERS	M	21	(2)	1
Louis LAROS	A	34		4
Bart LATUHERU	A	9	(2)	1
Huub LOEFFEN	A	12	(7)	1
Erwin VAN DE LOOI	D	24	(2)	1
Roy MAKAAY	A	30	(1)	11
Ante MISE (CRO)	M	3	(6)	
Dmitri SHUKOV (RUS)	M	14		4
Jerry SIMONS	A	2	(4)	
John STEGEMAN	A	1	(6)	
Edward STURING	D	25	(1)	
Arjan VERMEULEN	D	21	(4)	
Carlos VAN WANROOY	D	21	(3)	2

LEAGUE RESULTS 1995/96

Date	Opponent		Score	Scorers
20/08/95	Feyenoord	A	2-5	Gorter, Atteveld (p)
27/08/95	Roda JC	H	0-0	
08/09/95	RKC	A	2-0	Van Wanrooy, Makaay
16/09/95	PSV	H	0-1	
20/09/95	FC Groningen	A	0-2	
24/09/95	Willem II	H	2-2	Jochemsen, Laamers
01/10/95	De Graafschap	A	3-2	Van Wanrooy, Makaay, Curovic
04/10/95	Ajax	A	0-3	
15/10/95	NEC	H	2-2	Gorter, Korsten
21/10/95	Go Ahead Eagles	A	3-1	Makaay, Gorter 2
25/10/95	Sparta	A	0-3	
29/10/95	Fortuna Sittard	H	5-1	Curovic, Jochemsen, Van de Looi, Laros, Makaay
05/11/95	NAC	A	2-2	Makaay, Latuheru
19/11/95	SC Heerenveen	H	2-2	Atteveld 2 (1p)
26/11/95	FC Utrecht	H	2-1	Jochemsen, Curovic
03/12/95	FC Twente	A	0-1	
10/12/95	FC Volendam	H	2-1	Gorter (p), Makaay
17/12/95	Feyenoord	H	0-2	
23/12/95	Roda JC	A	1-0	Curovic
21/01/96	RKC	H	2-1	og (Brands), Makaay
04/02/96	FC Groningen	H	0-0	
09/02/96	Willem II	A	5-0	Loeffen, Makaay 2, Curovic 2
03/03/96	Ajax	H	2-1	Laros 2
10/03/96	NEC	A	1-0	Shukov
17/03/96	Sparta	H	3-2	Makaay, Shukov, Curovic
22/03/96	Go Ahead Eagles	H	0-3	
27/03/96	De Graafschap	H	0-1	
30/03/96	Fortuna Sittard	A	0-0	
06/04/96	PSV	A	0-1	
08/04/96	NAC	H	2-0	Shukov, Laros
13/04/96	SC Heerenveen	A	2-1	Jochemsen, Curovic
21/04/96	FC Utrecht	A	0-2	
28/04/96	FC Twente	H	2-0	Makaay, Shukov
05/05/96	FC Volendam	A	1-1	Jochemsen

FC VOLENDAM

CLUB DIRECTORY

FC Volendam
Postbus 82
1130 AB Volendam
tel - (0299) 363303
fax - (0299) 365578
Year of Formation - 1920
President - Willem Westendorp
Manager - Cor Veerman
Coach - Bert Jacobs; Jan Brouwer
(96/97 - Hans van der Zee)
Stadium - Veronica (7,500)

APPEARANCES 95/96

	P	Ap	(s)	Gls
René BINKEN	D	34		
Krzysztof BOCIEK (POL)	A	12		2
Michael FERRIER	D	10	(3)	2
Dejan GOVEDARICA (YUG)	M	12		2
Pascal JONGSMA	D	8	(3)	
Elroy KROMHEER	D	22	(6)	2
Björn LINDENBERGH	M	1	(3)	
Robert MOLENAAR	D	21		
Jacintho MORMON	M	2	(3)	
Luc NIJHOLT	M	17		
Arie OBDAM	A	13	(4)	
Ab PERSIJN	D	32		2
Ab PLUGBOER	M	14		
Radoslav SAMARDZIC (YUG)	A	22	(5)	6
Jerry SIMONS	A	13		3
Jörg SMEETS	A	15		4
Miroslav STEFANOVIC (YUG)	A	5	(11)	1
Johan STEUR	M	30	(2)	3
Marcel VALK	M	13		
Eric VAN VELDHUIZEN	A	14	(13)	1
Mark DE VRIES	A		(2)	
Ivica VUKOV (YUG)	A	7		
Ulrich WILSON	D	23		
Edwin ZOETEBIER	G	34		

LEAGUE RESULTS 1995/96

Date	Opponent	H/A	Score	Scorers
20/08/95	FC Twente	H	1-3	Samardzic
27/08/95	FC Utrecht	A	2-2	Smeets, og (Vierklau)
10/09/95	Feyenoord	A	1-5	Kromheer
17/09/95	Roda JC	H	1-0	Samardzic
20/09/95	RKC	A	0-2	
23/09/95	PSV	H	0-5	
01/10/95	FC Groningen	A	1-2	Kromheer
04/10/95	Willem II	H	0-0	
15/10/95	De Graafschap	H	1-1	Samardzic
21/10/95	NEC	A	1-2	Smeets
25/10/95	Ajax	A	0-4	
29/10/95	Sparta	H	1-1	Smeets
03/11/95	Go Ahead Eagles	A	2-1	Ferrier, Persijn
19/11/95	Fortuna Sittard	H	2-0	Smeets, Samardzic
25/11/95	NAC	A	0-4	
03/12/95	SC Heerenveen	H	1-1	Ferrier
10/12/95	Vitesse	A	1-2	Bociek
17/12/95	FC Twente	A	1-2	Bociek
14/01/96	FC Utrecht	H	0-1	
21/01/96	Feyenoord	H	0-3	
10/02/96	PSV	A	0-7	
02/03/96	Willem II	A	0-1	
09/03/96	De Graafschap	A	0-1	
17/03/96	Ajax	H	0-0	
24/03/96	NEC	H	1-0	Steur (p)
27/03/96	FC Groningen	H	2-1	Steur, Simons
30/03/96	Sparta	A	0-1	
05/04/96	Go Ahead Eagles	H	2-1	Samardzic, Steur
09/04/96	Roda JC	A	0-2	
12/04/96	Fortuna Sittard	A	2-2	Govedarica, Van Veldhuizen
17/04/96	RKC	H	1-1	Govedarica
21/04/96	NAC	H	1-2	Stefanovic
28/04/96	SC Heerenveen	A	3-4	Samardzic, Simons 2
05/05/96	Vitesse	H	1-1	Persijn

WILLEM II

CLUB DIRECTORY

Willem II
Postbus 235
5000 AE Tilburg
tel - (013) 5490590
fax - (013) 5490500
Year of Formation - 1896
President - Wim Groels
Secretary - Jam Smarius
Manager - Martin van Geel
Coach - Theo de Jong; Jimmy Calderwood
Stadium - Willem II (14,700)

MAJOR HONOURS

League Championship - (3) 1916, 1952, 1955.
Domestic Cup - (2) 1944, 1963.

APPEARANCES 95/96

	P	Ap	(s)	Gls
Toufik AMEZIANE	D		(3)	
Arne VAN DE BERG	M	25	(4)	4
Adri BOGERS	D	28		
Nabil BOUCHLAL (MAR)	A	4	(4)	
Jattoo CEESAY (GAM)	M	8	(15)	1
Fernando DERVELD	D	4	(2)	
John FESKENS	D	32		2
Jimmy VAN FESSEM	G	27		
Jean-Paul VAN GASTEL	M	18		7
Jack DE GIER	A	29	(4)	11
Marc VAN HINTUM	M	3	(1)	1
Sami HYYPIÄ (FIN)	D	13	(1)	
Roland JANSEN	G	7		
Joonas KOLKKA (FIN)	A	5	(2)	
Bert KONTERMAN	M	13		2
John LAMMERS	A	15	(11)	9
Marc LATUPEIRISSA	M	15		
Geoffrey PROMMAYON	D	11		
Ronald ROMBOUTS	A	5	(5)	
Marc SANTEGOEDS	A		(8)	
Dave SMITS	D	23	(3)	
Jaap STAM	D	19		1
Earnest STEWART (USA)	A	17	(1)	3
Henry VAN DER VEGT	M	33		9
Ron VOS	M	6	(2)	
Robin WIJNGAARDE	D	9	(2)	
Patrick VAN ZUNDERT	A	5	(8)	1

LEAGUE RESULTS 1995/96

19/08/95	Sparta	H	6-0	Van Gastel (p), Van der Vegt 2, Stewart, og (De Bruin), De Gier
26/08/95	Go Ahead Eagles	A	2-0	Van der Vegt, Van Gastel
09/09/95	Fortuna Sittard	H	4-0	Van Gastel 2 (1p), Lammers, Stam
16/09/95	NAC	A	1-0	Van der Vegt
20/09/95	SC Heerenveen	H	1-1	De Gier
24/09/95	Vitesse	A	2-2	Van den Berg, Van Zundert
29/09/95	FC Twente	H	5-2	og (Hoogma), Van Gastel (p), De Gier, Lammers 2
04/10/95	FC Volendam	A	0-0	
15/10/95	Feyenoord	H	2-2	Van der Vegt, Feskens
21/10/95	RKC	H	1-2	Lammers
25/10/95	Roda JC	A	1-1	Van Gastel
28/10/95	PSV	A	0-2	
04/11/95	FC Groningen	H	5-2	Stewart, De Gier, Lammers 3
19/11/95	FC Utrecht	A	3-3	Van de Berg, Van der Vegt, Lammers
25/11/95	De Graafschap	A	2-1	Van Gastel, Van den Berg
09/12/95	NEC	A	1-1	Van der Vegt
15/12/95	Sparta	A	1-1	Van de Berg
23/12/95	Go Ahead Eagles	H	1-2	Stewart
14/01/96	Ajax	H	1-0	Van der Vegt
20/01/96	Fortuna Sittard	A	0-0	
09/02/96	Vitesse	H	0-5	
02/03/96	FC Volendam	H	1-0	Van Hintum (p)
13/03/96	NAC	H	1-3	Feskens
16/03/96	Roda JC	H	1-2	Lammers
24/03/96	RKC	A	2-3	De Gier, Van der Vegt (p)
27/03/96	Feyenoord	A	0-2	
30/03/96	PSV	H	2-5	De Gier 2
02/04/96	FC Twente	A	1-2	De Gier
06/04/96	FC Groningen	A	0-3	
08/04/96	SC Heerenveen	A	2-2	Ceesay, Konterman
12/04/96	FC Utrecht	H	1-1	De Gier
20/04/96	De Graafschap	H	1-1	Konterman
28/04/96	Ajax	A	1-5	De Gier
05/05/96	NEC	H	1-3	De Gier

PROMOTED CLUB

SECOND DIVISION FINAL TABLE 95/96

		Pd	W	D	L	F	A	Pt	GD
1	**AZ (*4)**	**34**	**21**	**10**	**3**	**64**	**26**	**73**	**+38**
2	Emmen (*3)	34	18	13	3	71	39	67	+32
3	FC Den Bosch	34	15	13	6	51	36	58	+15
4	SC Veendam	34	16	10	8	48	35	58	+13
5	VVV	34	15	12	7	55	33	57	+22
6	SC Cambuur Leeuwarden (*1)	34	15	12	7	49	32	57	+17
7	Dordrecht '90	34	14	12	8	62	45	54	+17
8	SC Heracles (*2)	34	14	8	12	56	50	50	+6
9	SC Telstar	34	13	11	10	42	38	50	+4
10	Haarlem	34	14	3	17	47	53	45	-6
11	MVV	34	10	12	12	41	46	42	-5
12	TOP Oss	34	8	15	11	46	50	39	-4
13	RBC	34	11	6	17	35	51	39	-16
14	FC Zwolle	34	7	12	15	37	43	33	-6
15	FC Den Haag	34	8	7	19	39	60	31	-21
16	Excelsior	34	8	5	21	42	72	29	-30
17	Eindhoven	34	5	11	18	41	75	26	-34
18	Helmond Sport	34	6	4	24	35	77	22	-42

N.B. (*) = period champion.

PROMOTION/RELEGATION PLAY-OFFS

GROUP A FINAL TABLE

		Pd	W	D	L	F	A	Pt	GD
1	FC Volendam	6	6	0	0	10	2	18	+8
2	SC Heracles	6	3	1	2	13	7	10	+6
3	VVV	6	1	1	4	3	9	4	-6
4	FC Den Bosch	6	0	2	4	2	10	2	-8

GROUP B FINAL TABLE

		Pd	W	D	L	F	A	Pt	GD
1	NEC	6	5	0	1	12	4	15	+8
2	SC Veendam	6	3	1	2	8	7	10	+1
3	Emmen	6	3	0	3	10	8	9	+2
4	SC Cambuur Leeuwarden	6	0	1	5	2	13	1	-11

CLUB DIRECTORY

AZ
Postbus 3010
1801 GA Alkmaar
tel - (072) 5154744
fax - (072) 5158388
Year of Formation - 1967
President - Dirk Scheringa
Secretary - Frits Leenart
Manager - Henk van Rijnsoever
Coach - Theo Vonk
Stadium - Alkmaarderhout (10,537)

MAJOR HONOURS
League Championship - (1) 1981.
Domestic Cup - (3) 1978, 1981, 1982.

HUNGARY

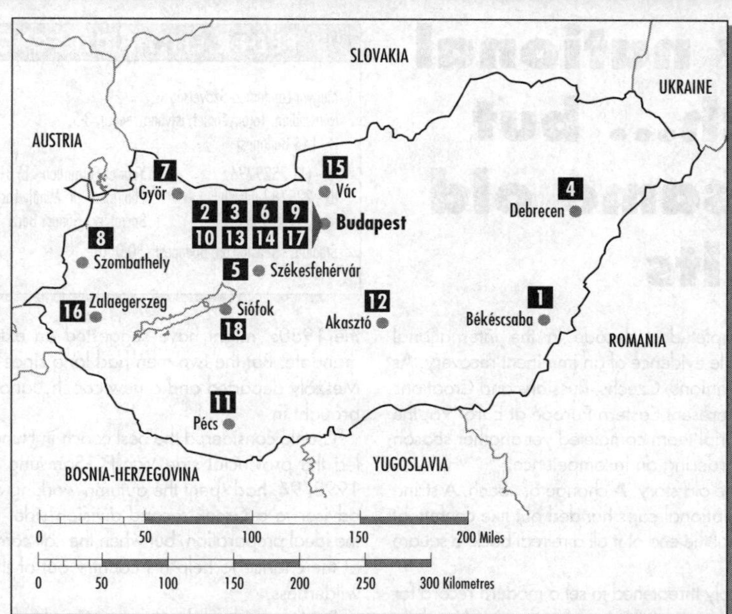

1	BÉKÉSCSABA	528	10	MTK	537
2	BVSC-DREHER	529	11	PÉCSI MFC	538
3	CSEPEL SC	530	12	INNSTADT STADLER FC	539
4	DVSC-EPONA	531	13	ÚJPESTI TE	540
5	FEHÉRVÁR 96 PARMALAT FC	532	14	VASAS CV	541
6	FERENCVÁROS	533	15	VÁC FC-SAMSUNG	542
7	GYÖRI ETO FC	534	16	ZALAEGERSZEGI TE	543
8	HALADÁS VFC	535	17	III. KERÜLETI TVE	544
9	KISPEST-HONVÉD FC	536	18	SIÓFOK	544

26TH TITLE FOR FERENCVÁROS

New national coach... but the same old results

FEDERATION DIRECTORY

Magyar Labdarúgó Szövetség
Népstadion, Toronyépület, Istvánmezéi ut. 3-5,
H-1146 Budapest

tel - (1) 2529296
tlx - 225782 mlsz h
fax - (1) 2529986
Stadium - Népstadion, Budapest (80,000)

Year of Formation - 1901
Chairman - dr. Mihály Laczkó
Secretary - Sándor Berzi

Hungary completed a decade in the international doldrums with little evidence of an imminent recovery. As Bulgarians, Romanians, Czechs, Russians and Croatians headed off to represent Eastern Europe at Euro '96, the Hungarian national team completed yet another season of mediocrity bordering on incompetence.

It was the same old story. A change of coach. A string of defeats. International caps handed out like confetti at a wedding. And at the end of it all a retreat back to square one.

Kálmán Mészöly threatened to set a modern record for a Hungarian national coach when he remained in place for 18 months and then expressed a desire to carry on for the World Cup qualifying campaign. But his fate was sealed by a change of personnel within the Hungarian FA. The return to the presidency of Mihály Laczkó, a man Mészöly had himself helped up the ladder of power in the 1980s, might have suggested an extension of his mandate. But the two men had long since fallen out, so Mészöly departed and a new coach, János Csank, was brought in.

Csank, considered the best coach in Hungary when he led the provincial side Vác FC-Samsung to the title in 1993/94, had spent the autumn working as a technical adviser to a Greek second division side. It was hardly the ideal preparation, but when the call came, he jumped at the chance to help his country out of the footballing wilderness.

But the results did not come. Csank's first four games all ended in defeat. No matter that three of the opponents were Euro '96 finalists. Hungary's glaring deficiencies were still as clear as daylight. Poor individual skill, lack of understanding, and, most significantly of all, a massive crisis of confidence.

LEAGUE CHAMPIONSHIP RESULTS 95/96

		1	2	3	4	5	6	7	8	9	10	11	12	13	14	15	16
1	Békéscsaba		0-1	2-2	2-2	1-3	3-1	2-1	1-0	3-1	3-1	1-2	0-0	2-3	2-3	1-1	1-1
2	BVSC-Dreher	1-1		0-2	2-0	0-1	2-0	2-1	2-0	0-2	2-1	2-0	2-2	1-0	2-0	1-0	3-2
3	Csepel SC	1-1	2-3		1-2	1-2	3-2	0-3	2-1	5-0	2-2	2-0	1-0	1-1	4-1	1-0	0-0
4	DVSC-Epona	1-0	1-1	5-0		2-1	4-1	3-0	2-1	0-0	2-1	1-0	4-1	2-0	2-3	2-1	2-2
5	Ferencváros	3-0	1-3	2-1	1-0		2-0	0-0	3-1	3-1	2-1	3-1	3-0	2-0	0-2	2-0	1-1
6	Györi ETO FC	0-0	1-1	3-2	1-3	2-5		3-0	1-2	1-0	0-0	1-0	2-2	4-0	1-3	2-4	2-2
7	Haladás VFC	3-1	1-5	1-2	2-1	0-3	1-0		1-0	2-2	1-2	0-1	1-0	1-1	1-1	2-5	2-1
8	Kispest-Honvéd FC	1-1	1-1	1-1	0-0	1-0	0-0	4-0		2-1	5-0	2-2	2-1	1-1	3-2	2-0	3-0
9	MTK FC	1-0	2-2	1-2	3-1	2-1	8-2	3-1	0-1		5-2	2-1	3-3	1-2	0-0	5-0	3-0
10	Fehérvár '96 Parmalat FC	0-0	1-2	1-3	4-1	1-2	0-2	1-1	3-2	3-1		3-1	0-0	2-2	0-1	2-1	1-2
11	Pécsi MFC	3-1	0-2	3-2	1-0	1-0	2-2	0-1	2-4	0-3	1-2		3-1	0-2	1-3	0-0	3-3
12	Innstadt Stadler FC	3-1	3-1	0-0	3-2	0-3	1-0	2-1	1-1	0-1	2-0	3-1		0-0	1-0	1-2	1-1
13	Újpesti TE	2-0	0-0	5-1	4-0	1-1	1-0	2-1	2-1	0-0	4-0	1-0	1-1		1-1	2-2	3-2
14	Vasas CV	1-1	1-0	1-1	1-0	0-1	0-0	1-1	2-4	1-3	2-0	2-1	2-2	2-2		2-2	2-0
15	Vác FC-Samsung	1-2	2-3	0-0	1-1	1-2	0-0	0-0	3-3	2-1	2-2	1-1	1-1	1-0	3-2		2-1
16	Zalaegerszegi TE	3-0	1-3	2-1	2-3	1-3	3-0	0-0	0-0	3-3	0-2	3-1	2-0	1-0	1-2	2-1	

LEAGUE CHAMPIONSHIP FINAL TABLE 95/96

			Home					Away					Total						
		Pd	W	D	L	F	A	W	D	L	F	A	W	D	L	F	A	Pt	GD
1	Ferencváros	30	11	2	2	28	11	10	1	4	28	14	21	3	6	56	25	66	+31
2	BVSC-Dreher	30	10	2	3	22	12	8	5	2	28	17	18	7	5	50	29	61	+21
3	Újpesti TE	30	9	6	0	29	10	3	6	6	14	21	12	12	6	43	31	48	+12
4	DVSC-Epona	30	11	3	1	33	12	3	3	9	16	28	14	6	10	49	40	48	+9
5	MTK FC	30	9	3	3	39	18	4	4	7	19	25	13	7	10	58	43	46	+15
6	Kispest-Honvéd FC	30	8	7	0	28	10	4	3	8	21	25	12	10	8	49	35	46	+14
7	Vasas CV	30	5	7	3	20	18	7	3	5	24	22	12	10	8	44	40	46	+4
8	Csepel SC	30	7	4	4	26	18	4	5	6	20	27	11	9	10	46	45	42	+1
9	Innstadt Stadler FC	30	8	4	3	21	14	0	8	7	14	27	8	12	10	35	41	36	-6
10	Zalaegerszegi TE	30	7	3	5	24	19	1	7	7	18	29	8	10	12	42	48	34	-6
11	Vác FC-Samsung	30	4	8	3	20	19	3	4	8	19	27	7	12	11	39	46	33	-7
12	Haladás VFC	30	6	3	6	19	25	2	5	8	11	23	8	8	14	30	48	32	-18
13	Fehérvar '96 Parmalat FC	30	5	4	6	22	21	3	3	9	16	33	8	7	15	38	54	31	-16
14	Békéscsaba	30	5	5	5	24	22	1	6	8	9	24	6	11	13	33	46	29	-13
15	Györi ETO FC	30	5	5	5	24	24	1	4	10	10	30	6	9	15	34	54	27	-20
16	Pécsi MFC	30	5	3	7	20	26	2	2	11	12	27	7	5	18	32	53	23	-21

N.B. Pécsi MFC deducted 3 pts.

The picture is not entirely bleak. Hungary have been drawn in a kind World Cup qualifying group. And the Hungarian U-21 team were good enough to qualify for the Atlanta Olympics (though not to earn any points when they got there), which should mean even more new players graduating to full senior level. In 1995/96 Hungary played just eight matches, but used 51 different players. Only one, midfielder Béla Illés, appeared in all eight games. Csank himself handed out ten new caps.

If reaching the Olympics was an achievement worth savouring, so too was Ferencváros's qualification for the UEFA Champions' League. The green-and-whites provided the shock of the preliminary round by knocking out Anderlecht. Then, in their first match, they really set Hungarian pulses racing by winning 3-0 away to Grasshoppers. Reality returned with a vengeance, however, in the first home game, when Cup holders Ajax resisted the racist taunts of the Ferencváros fans to cruise home 4-1. 'Fradi' managed draws in their next two home games, but big defeats in Madrid and Amsterdam eradicated any thought of further progress.

Still, Hungary's most popular club were delighted with the pots of gold they brought back from their European campaign. The money enabled them to make strong reinforcements during the Hungarian league's mid-season break. And that proved crucial in taking Ferencváros to their second successive championship triumph.

In the first half of the season, and for a sizeable chunk of the second, Ferencváros found themselves playing a chasing game, with another Budapest club, BVSC (pronounced "Bay-way-ash-tsay"), surprisingly leading the way. In the autumn Ferencváros were distracted both by their European involvement and a rash of injuries and trailed BVSC by eight points at the winter break with a match in hand.

It was time to get the chequebook out. Ferencváros immediately snapped up two internationals, Norbert Nagy from Stadler FC and Zoltán Jagodics from Györ, and later added two other major purchases, László Arany from Debrecen and Ukrainian striker Igor Nichenko from Stadler. All four newcomers were to prove their worth in the spring, none more so than Nichenko. József Stadler, the wealthy, ambitious owner of Stadler FC, tried desperately to hang on to his star striker (eight goals in the

INTERNATIONAL HONOURS

World Cup Finals appearances: 1934 (2nd round), 1938 (Runners-up), 1954 (Runners-up), 1958, 1962 (qtr-finals), 1966 (qtr-finals), 1978, 1982, 1986

European Championship appearances (last 8): 1964 (3rd), 1968, 1972 (4th)

European Club Competitions

Fairs' Cup	Ferencváros (1965)

NATIONAL TEAM RESULTS 95/96

16/08/95	Israel	H	Siófok	0-2	
06/09/95	Turkey (ECQ)	A	Istanbul	0-2	
11/10/95	Switzerland (ECQ)	A	Zürich	0-3	
11/11/95	Iceland (ECQ)	H	Budapest	1-0	Illés (11)
10/04/96	Croatia	A	Osijek	1-4	Nagy N. (39)
24/04/96	Austria	H	Budapest	0-2	
18/05/96	England	A	Wembley	0-3	
01/06/96	Italy	H	Budapest	0-2	

TOP SCORERS

18	Igor NICHENKO (Stadler FC/ Ferencváros)
15	Ferenc OROSZ (BVSC-Dreher)
14	Tamás SÁNDOR (DVSC-Epona)
12	Ferenc HORVÁTH (Fehervár '96 Parmalat FC)
11	István VINCZE (BVSC-Dreher)
	Miklós BARANYI (Csepel SC)
	Nicolae ILEA (DVSC-Epona)
	Béla ILLÉS (MTK)

DOMESTIC CUP RESULTS

1/32 FINALS
(Played in Groups)

Qualifiers
1. Haladás VSE, EMDSZ-Soproni LC
2. Vác FC-Samsung, Budafoki LC
3. Debreceni VSC, Salgótarján
4. Stadler FC, Baktalórántháza
5. Kispest-Honvéd FC, Paks
6. Kaba, Békéscsaba
7. MTK, Csákvár
8. Parmalat FC, MOTIM TE
9. Zalaegerszegi TE, Kamond
10. BVSC-Dreher, BKV Elöre
11. Ferencváros, Veszprém
12. Szigetszentmiklós, Pécsi MFC
13. Újpesti TE, Százhalombatta
14. Csepel SC, MATÁV SC Sopron
15. Kazincbarcika, Vasas CV
16. Nagykanizsa, Balatonlelle

1/16 FINALS
BKV Elöre v Újpesti TE 0-4; 0-0
(Újpesti TE 4-0)
MOTIM TE v Zalaegerszegi TE 0-0; 0-9
(Zalaegerszegi TE 9-0)
Csákvár v DVSC-Epona 2-2; 0-6
(DVSC-Epona 8-2)
Kaba v Kamond 6-0; 4-1
(Kaba 10-1)
Stadler FC v MATÁV SC Sopron 2-0; 1-0
(Stadler FC 3-0)
Százhalombatta v BVSC-Dreher 0-4; 1-2
(BVSC-Dreher 6-1)
Salgótarján v Nagykanizsa 2-1; 0-0
(Salgótarján 2-1)
Baktalórántháza v Csepel SC 2-2; 0-5
(Csepel SC 7-2)
Kazincbarcika v Haladás VSE 0-0; 3-1
(Kazincbarcika 3-1)
Ferencváros v EMDSZ-Soproni LC 2-1; 3-4
(5-5; Ferencváros on away goals)
Vasas CV v Pécsi MFC 2-0; 2-0
(Vasas CV 4-0)
MTK v Békéscsaba 0-1; 1-2
(Békéscsaba 3-1)
Parmalat FC v Budafoki LC 5-1; 1-0
(Parmalat FC 6-1)
Szigetszentmiklós v Kispest-Honvéd FC 1-8; 0-6
(Kispest-Honvéd 14-1)
Balatonlelle v Paks 3-1; 0-5
(Paks 6-3)
Vác FC-Samsung v Veszprém 2-1; 5-0
(Vác FC-Samsung 7-1)

1/8 FINALS
BVSC-Dreher v Vasas CV 4-1; 3-3
(BVSC-Dreher 7-4)
Kispest-Honvéd FC v Békéscsaba 1-0; 1-1
(Kispest-Honvéd FC 2-1)
Újpesti TE v Kazincbarcika 3-0; 0-0
(Újpesti TE 3-0)
Ferencváros v Salgótarján 2-0; 3-1
(Ferencváros 5-1)
Vác FC-Samsung v Csepel SC 1-0; 2-2
(Vác FC-Samsung 3-2)
Stadler FC v DVSC-Epona 0-1; 1-3
(DVSC-Epona 4-1)
Kaba v Paks 0-3; 2-1
(Paks 4-2)
Zalaegreszegi TE v Parmalat FC 1-2; 2-0
(Zalaegerszegi TE 3-2)

QUARTER-FINALS
BVSC-Dreher v DVSC-Epona 0-0; 2-2
(2-2; BVSC-Dreher on away goals)
Vác FC-Samsung v Zalaegerszegi TE 2-1; 1-1
(Vác FC-Samsung 3-2)
Kispest-Honvéd FC v Ferencváros 2-2; 4-1
(Kispest-Honvéd 6-3)
Újpesti TE v Paks 2-2; 2-1
(Újpesti TE 4-3)

SEMI-FINALS
BVSC-Dreher v Újpesti TE 1-0; 2-0
(BVSC-Dreher 3-0)
Kispest-Honvéd FC v Vác FC-Samsung 2-0; 3-0
(Kispest-Honvéd FC 5-0)

FINAL
08/06/96, Budapest (Szönyi út)
BVSC-DREHER 1 Csábi (35p)
KISPEST-HONVÉD FC 0
referee - Molnár
BVSC-DREHER - Koszta; Csábi; Molnár, Bondarenko, Szalma; Komódi, Zováth, Dárdai (Csordás 46), Aranyos (Farkas 25); Bükszegi, Vincze.
KISPEST-HONVÉD FC - Vezér; Hahn; Tarlue, Mátyus; Árgyelán (Dubecz 71), Kovács (Kabát 75), Urbányi, Piroska, Gabala (Jovanovic 59); Bárányos, Tóth.

20/06/96, Budapest (Bozsik stadion)
KISPEST-HONVÉD FC 2 Piroska (87), Árgyelán (88)
BVSC-DREHER 0
referee - Puhl
KISPEST-HONVÉD FC - Vezér; Hahn; Plókai, Mátyus; Forrai (Árgyelán 71), Urbányi, Bárányos, Piroska (Kovács 90), Gabala; Jovanovic (Ghinda 65), Tóth.
BVSC-DREHER - Koszta; Csábi; Molnár, Bondarenko (Csordás 89), Szalma (Potemkin 89); Komódi, Bognár, Zováth, Aranyos; Orosz (Farkas 76), Vincze.

(KISPEST-HONVÉD FC 2-1)

NATIONAL TEAM APPEARANCES 95/96

Coach - Kálmán MÉSZÖLY; János CSANK	ISR	TUR	SUI	ISL	CRO	AUT	ENG	ITA	Cps	Gls
Zsolt PETRY (23/09/66) - Gençlerbirligi (TUR)	G46	G				G	G		38	-
Gábor MÁRTON (15/10/66) - unattached	D								21	1
Péter LIPCSEI (28/03/72) - FC Porto (POR)	D	D	D						32	-
Tamás MÓNOS (03/01/68) - Vasas CV	M		s64	D					21	-
András KERESZTÚRI (02/11/67) - Parmalat FC	M								10	2
István KOZMA (03/12/64) - Újpesti TE	M	M							40	1
Gábor HALMAI (07/01/72) - KFC Germinal Ekeren (BEL)	M55	M	D			M74			19	2
István SALLÓI (26/09/66) - Beitar Jerusalem (ISR)	M75	s46							13	1
Béla ILLÉS (27/04/68) - MTK	M55	M46	M64	M89	M	M46	s62	s75	25	4
József KIPRICH (06/09/63) - APOEL Nicosia (CYP)	A	A							70	28
Kálmán KOVÁCS (11/09/65) - APOEL Nicosia (CYP)	A46								56	19
Zoltán VÉGH (07/04/71) - Hapoel Haifa (ISR)	s46								13	-
István HAMAR (06/10/70) - MTK	s46								7	4
János BÁNFI (09/11/69) - Kispest-Honvéd FC/KSC Eendracht Aalst (BEL)	s55			D		D79	D	D	18	-
László FARKASHÁZY (27/01/68) - MTK	s55	M		s75					3	-
Zoltán BÜKSZEGI (16/12/75) - BVSC-Dreher	s75			M					2	-
András TELEK (10/12/70) - Ferencváros		D	D		D	D46	s82	s85	22	-
Géza MÉSZÖLY (06/02/67) - Lille OSC (FRA)		D							18	-
László ARANY (09/03/71) - DVSC-Epona/Ferencváros		M	s64		M46				3	-
Norbert NAGY (28/06/69) - Stadler FC/Ferencváros		M46			M	M	M82	M39	5	1
László KLAUSZ (24/06/71) - FC Admira Wacker (AUT)		s46							15	2
Attila HAJDU (13/04/71) - Ferencváros			G	G	G			G	6	-
Mihály MRACSKÓ (13/06/68) - Békéscsaba			M				M82	M	12	-
Flórián URBAN (29/09/68) - KSV Waregem (BEL)/Györi ETO FC			M				M	M85	18	1
Tibor SIMON (01/09/65) - Ferencváros			M24						16	-
Elek NYILAS (03/05/69) - Ferencváros			M64	M					2	-
Robert JOVÁN (04/11/67) - Vasas CV			A						5	1
István VINCZE (22/01/67) - BVSC-Dreher			A	A88		A	A80	A69	44	8
Zoltán JAGODICS (29/07/69) - Györi ETO FC			s24		D				7	1
József CSÁBI (14/02/67) - BVSC-Dreher				D					10	-
Zoltán SZLEZÁK (26/12/67) - Újpesti TE				D					4	-
József DURÓ (26/07/66) - Kispest-Honvéd FC				M					21	-
Ferenc OROSZ (11/10/69) - BVSC-Dreher				A75	A				8	-
Tamás NAGY (06/06/76) - Csepel SC				s88					1	-
Zalán ZOMBORI (25/05/75) - Csepel SC				s89					1	-
Vilmos SEBÖK (13/06/73) - Újpesti TE					D	s74	D	D80	4	-
Miklós LENDVAI (07/04/75) - Zalaegerszegi TE					M46				1	-
Attila HORVÁTH (23/01/71) - Zalaegerszegi TE					M80	M46			2	-
Gábor EGRESSY (11/02/74) - Újpesti TE					A	s46	s80	s69	4	-
Csaba MADAR (07/10/76) - DVSC-Epona					s46	s46			2	-
Krisztián LISZTES (02/06/76) - Ferencváros					s46		s82	M75	4	-
Tamás SZEKERES (18/09/72) - MTK					s80				2	-
Attila PLÓKAI (17/07/69) - Kispest-Honvéd FC						D	D	D	3	-
Tibor BALOG (01/03/66) - RSC Charleroi (BEL)						M66	M62	M	33	2
Ferenc HORVÁTH (06/05/73) - Fehérvár '96 Parmalat FC						A	A82		2	-
Dénes VÁCZI (23/12/64) - Csepel SC						s46			7	-
Flórián ALBERT (12/12/67) - Ferencváros						s66			6	-
Miklós BARANYI (06/09/69) - Csepel SC						s79			1	-
Árpád HAHN (12/03/65) - Kispest-Honvéd FC							M	s80	4	-
Imre ARANYOS (13/06/66) - BVSC-Dreher							s82	s39	2	-
Gábor TORMA (01/08/76) - KSV Cercle Brugge (BEL)								A	1	-

EUROPEAN CUPS RESULTS 95/96

CHAMPIONS' CUP

● FERENCVÁROS

Preliminary round RSC ANDERLECHT (BEL)

A 1-0 Kuntic (58)
Hajdu; Telek; Kuznetsov; Páling, Nyilas, Simon, Lisztes, Kecskés; Albert (Vincze 82); Kopunovic (Zavadszky 90), Kuntic (Nagy Z. 78).

H 1-1 Kopunovic (50)
Hajdu; Telek; Simon, Kuznetsov; Páling, Vincze (Zavadszky 73), Nyilas, Lisztes, Kecskés; Kopunovic (Nagy Z. 59), Kuntic.

Champions' League

1st match GRASSHOPPER-CLUB ZÜRICH (SUI)

A 3-0 Lisztes (61), Vincze (82, 90)
Hajdu; Telek; Szücs; Nyilas, Lisztes, Milovanovic, Simon, Vincze; Kopunovic; Zavadszky (Nagy Z. 77), Fatusi.

2nd match AJAX (HOL)

H 1-4 Nyilas (59p)
Hajdu; Telek; Simon, Kuznetsov (Keller 80), Kecskés; Nyilas, Lisztes, Kuntic, Vincze; Zavadszky, Kopunovic.

3rd match REAL MADRID (ESP)

A 1-6 Kopunovic (63)
Hajdu; Telek; Milovanovic (Hrutka 56), Keller; Nyilas; Szücs, Vincze (Albert 46), Lisztes, Kecskés; Kuntic (Nagy Z. 68), Kopunovic.

4th match REAL MADRID (ESP)

H 1-1 Albert (36)
Hajdu; Telek; Kuznetsov, Hrutka; Páling, Nyilas, Albert (Nagy Z. 46), Lisztes, Keller; Kuntic (Vincze 89), Kopunovic (Zavadszky 80).

5th match GRASSHOPPER-CLUB ZÜRICH (SUI)

H 3-3 Albert (20), Lisztes (24), Nyilas (85p)
Hajdu; Hrutka; Szücs, Keller; Nyilas, Albert (Nagy Z. 66), Kuznetsov, Lisztes, Kecskés (Vincze 66); Kuntic, Kopunovic (Zavadszky 82).

6th match AJAX (HOL)

A 0-4
Hajdu; Hrutka; Páling (Nagy Z. 90), Kuznetsov, Keller; Nyilas, Albert, Szücs, Lisztes, Vincze; Kuntic (Kopunovic 67).

CUP-WINNERS' CUP

● VÁC FC-SAMSUNG

Preliminary round SILEKS KRATOVO (MAC)

H 1-1 Romanek (90)
Hámori; Nagy; Kasza, Puglits; Nyikos (Austin 34), Vojtekovski, Víg (Sándor 64), Schwarcz, Romanek; Andrássy, Borgulya (Hanyecz 62).

A 1-3 Borgulya (21)
Hámori; Nagy; Puglits (Siago 49), Kasza; Vojtekovszki, Schwarcz, Víg, Romanek (Sándor 70), Nyikos; Borgulya, Austin (Andrássy 46).

UEFA CUP

● ÚJPESTI TE

Preliminary round 1.FC KOSICE (SVK)

A 1-0 Tiefenbach (40)
Szücs; Füzesi; Tomka, N'Doumbe (Sebök 11); Jenei, Bérczy, Túri, Szanyó, Szlezák; Tiefenbach (Belvon 83), Egressy (Wukovics 90).

H 2-1 Bérczy (56), Szanyó (81p)
Szücs; Füzesi; Tomka, Sebök; Jenei, Bérczy, Túri, Szanyó, Szlezák; Tiefenbach, Egressy (Wukovics 85; Szili 88).

1st round RC STRASBOURG (FRA)

A 0-3
Szücs; Füzesi; Braun, Sebök, N'Dounbe; Jenei, Bérczy, Szanyó, Szlezák; Belvon (Wukovics 85), Tiefenbach (Tóth P.G. 63).

H 0-2
Szücs; Füzesi; Tomka, Tóth G., N'Doumbe; Tóth P.G. (Braun 73), Szanyó, Szlezák, Somogyi (Szili 82); Wukovics (Kun 82), Egressy.

autumn), but with the taxman beating a path to his door amidst rumours of financial collapse, his hand was forced.

Although never capped by his country or by the USSR, Nichenko was undoubtedly the goalscoring star of the 95/96 season in Hungary. He pepped up the Fradi attack in the spring, scoring ten goals to become not only Ferencváros's top marksman, but also the leading goalscorer in the whole league.

Thanks to Nichenko's goals and to outstanding contributions from goalkeeper Attila Hajdu, young midfielder Krisztián Lisztes and the other mid-season buys, Ferencváros were able to catch up with BVSC and overtake them in the run-in. The club's 26th title was confirmed with a 1-0 victory over their direct rivals at the Nép stadium on June 12. Yugoslav striker Zoran Kuntic scored the all-important goal after BVSC had earlier missed a penalty.

BVSC's season thus ended in grave disappointment. The small-time club from the capital had never won anything in their 85-year history. With such a big lead early on, they looked odds on to take the title. But in the end their nerves failed them. Four defeats in their last eight matches, including the one against Ferencváros, told the grim tale. Their only consolation was that second place was the highest they had ever reached.

BVSC's most prominent players were the ex-Kispest-Honvéd trio of Orosz, Vincze and Csábi. In the final of the Hungarian Cup - BVSC's second chance of a first major honour - they were up against their old club. Played over two legs, the final had a dramatic conclusion, and once again it was BVSC who ended up with nothing. 1-0 up from the first leg, BVSC were just three minutes away from a Cup victory when Kispest-Honvéd, down to ten men after the sending-off of Krisztián

Gabala, equalised. Another minute later the home side, sensationally, were ahead, through substitute János Árgyelan, and that was that.

Kispest had lost six internationals the previous summer, forcing coach Péter Török to build a completely new team. Sixth place in the league was just about on a par with pre-season expectations, but the Cup win was a real bonus, especially as they had destroyed the holders Ferencváros in the quarter-finals. Kispest's was a very young side, but arguably their best player was Polish veteran Robert Warzycha, who sadly missed both legs of the Cup final.

Filling the three places above Kispest in the final league table were Újpesti TE, Debrecen and MTK. None of these teams ever threatened to win the title, and for the two Budapest clubs that was a poor show. Newly-promoted, big-spending MTK, in particular, looked hungry early on, winning their first four matches. But after that they faded away and coach Bertalan Bicskei was sacked. Former Hungarian international defender Imre Garaba successfully steered the club back on course in the spring, but then he too got the boot at the end of the season.

Debrecen (later DVSC-Epona) had the best home record in the league and formed the basis of the Hungarian Olympic side, with Petö, Dombi, Sándor, Madar and Szátmari all travelling to Atlanta. Indeed, all of Hungary's three goals at the Games were scored by Debrecen players.

At the bottom of the table two First Division institutions Györ and Pécs were saved from relegation by the intervention of the Hungarian FA, who, in their wisdom, suddenly decided - in June! - that the First Division would be increased from 16 to 18 teams in 1996/97. This meant that the bottom four teams would all play off for their places against Second Division teams, and that the only two sides certain of switching divisions were the two Second Division group winners, III. Ker. TVE and Siófok.

In the event, all four top-flight teams won their ties, including the team formerly and now once again known as Videoton, which changed its name three times during the season (Parmalat FC, Fehérvár '96, Fehérvár '96 Parmalat), thereby successfully exploiting legal loopholes to clear the club's debts.

PLAYERS OF THE SEASON

KRISZTIÁN LISZTES

His first season was excellent. The second was even better. With Péter Lipcsei having left for FC Porto, teenager Krisztián Lisztes became the outstanding player in the Ferencváros midfield, guiding the team to another championship triumph with a succession of top-class performances and timely goals. The young curly-haired playmaker is the Great White Hope of Hungarian football. As well as starring for Ferencváros in domestic competition and the UEFA Champions' League, Lisztes was one of the leading figures in the Hungarian Olympic team which qualified for Atlanta. It was anticipated that he would leave 'Fradi' for German club VfB Stuttgart after the Olympics, but with the Bulgarian Balakov still in place at the Neckarstadion, Stuttgart decided to loan Lisztes back to Ferencváros for another season.

GÁBOR TORMA

Like Lisztes, Gábor Torma was born in 1976 and has a bright future in the game. But his is a name unfamiliar to most fans in Hungary. When he was given his first international cap against Italy at the beginning of June, he made history by being the first Hungarian full international never to have played in the Hungarian First Division. At the age of 17 Torma left Second Division club Dunaferr for Belgian side Cercle Bruges. And in the 95/96 season, at the age of 19, he was already being hailed as one of the best young foreigners in Belgium. He helped Cercle into the Belgian Cup final, where he opened the scoring in his team's 2-1 defeat by city rivals Club Bruges.

JÓZSEF KIPRICH

The old soldier of Hungarian football proved in 1995/96 that there is still plenty of life left in him. Some Hungarian critics felt that József Kiprich was settling down for a pleasant retirement in the sun when he left Dutch giants Feyenoord for APOEL Nicosia. But, aided and abetted by his fellow Hungarian internationals Kálmán Kovács and István Kozma, Kiprich enjoyed one of the most memorable seasons of his career. He helped APOEL to the Cypriot league and Cup 'double', scoring abundantly in both competitions to earn himself celebrity status on the Mediterranean island. As well as his two winner's medals, Kiprich won two individual prizes - the league's top scorer crown (25 goals) and the Player of the Year award.

BÉKÉSCSABA

CLUB DIRECTORY

Békéscsabai Elöre Football Club
Kórház u. 6
5601 Békéscsaba
tel - (66) 323656
fax - (66) 323656
Year of Formation - 1912
Chairman - László Papp
Coach - József Pásztor (96/97 - Silviu Iorgulescu)
Stadium - Elöre (16,000)

MAJOR HONOURS
Domestic Cup - (1) 1988.

APPEARANCES 95/96

	P	Ap	(s)	Gls
András BABÓCSY	G	8		
Tamás BAJI	G	9	(1)	
Zoltán BALOGH	M	24	(1)	
László BALÁZS	A		(7)	
János CSATÓ	M	1	(6)	
Sándor CSATÓ	M	27	(1)	6
György CSEPREGI	M		(1)	
Zoltán CZIPÓ	D		(3)	
Vladan FILIPOVIC (BOS)	M	10	(2)	1
Tibor FODOR	M	26	(3)	2
Zsolt KASIK	A	19	(6)	1
Tibor KOVÁCS	M	20		
Sándor KULCSÁR (ROM)	A	26	(3)	4
László MAJOR	A	18	(8)	2
Mihály MRACSKÓ	D	23	(1)	1
László NAGY	M	3	(8)	
Dragan PUSKAS (YUG)	A	14		3
Mátyás SÁNDOR	M	6	(2)	
Viorel STANCU (ROM)	D	2	(10)	
Attila SZABADOS	M	8	(10)	
János SZARVAS	A	23	(4)	10
Zoltán SZENTI	D	19	(2)	1
Milán UDVARÁCZ	G	13	(1)	
Yuri USHMAYEV (UKR)	D	9	(1)	
Mihály VARGA	M		(1)	
Sorin VLAICU (ROM)	M	9		1
Zoltán ZAHORÁN	D	13	(2)	1

LEAGUE RESULTS 1995/96

05/08/95	Csepel SC	H	2-2	Kulcsár, Szarvas
12/08/95	Innstadt Stadler FC	A	1-3	Szarvas (p)
19/08/95	Ferencváros	H	1-3	Szarvas
25/08/95	Zalaegerszegi TE	A	0-3	
30/08/95	BVSC-Dreher	H	0-1	
09/09/95	Pécsi MFC	A	1-3	Major
16/09/95	MTK FC	H	3-1	Kasik, Csató S., Szarvas
24/09/95	DVSC-Epona	A	0-1	
01/10/95	Újpesti TE	H	2-3	Szarvas, Kulcsár
14/10/95	Parmalat FC	H	3-1	Szarvas (p), Fodor, Major
21/10/95	Kispest-Honvéd FC	A	1-1	Csató S.
28/10/95	Haladás VFC	H	2-1	Csató S., Szarvas
04/11/95	Vasas CV	A	1-1	Kulcsár
18/11/95	Vác FC-Samsung	H	1-1	Fodor
25/11/95	Györi ETO FC	A	0-0	
16/03/96	Csepel SC	A	1-1	Puskas
20/03/96	Innstadt Stadler FC	H	0-0	
30/03/96	Ferencváros	A	0-3	
06/04/96	Zalaegerszegi TE	H	1-1	Csató S.
14/04/96	BVSC-Dreher	A	1-1	Csató S.
20/04/96	Pécsi MFC	H	1-2	Szarvas
27/04/96	MTK FC	A	0-1	
05/05/96	DVSC-Epona	H	2-2	Szarvas, Vlaicu
12/05/96	Újpesti TE	A	0-2	
20/05/96	Fehérvar '96 Parmalat FC	A	0-0	
25/05/96	Kispest-Honvéd FC	H	1-0	Puskas
05/06/96	Haladás VFC	A	1-3	Puskas (p)
12/06/96	Vasas CV	H	2-3	Mracskó, Csató S.
17/06/96	Vác FC-Samsung	A	2-1	Szenti, Szarvas
24/06/96	Györi ETO FC	H	3-1	Zahorán, Filipovic, Kulcsár

BVSC-DREHER

CLUB DIRECTORY

BVSC-Dreher (now - BVSC)
Szönyi ut 2
1142 Budapest
tel - (1) 2513698/2513888
fax - (1) 2513698
Year of Formation - 1911
Director - dr. György Mezey
Coach - Sándor Egervári (96/97 - László Dajka)
Stadium - BVSC (12,000)

APPEARANCES 95/96

	P	Ap	(s)	Gls
Imre ARANYOS	M	27		2
György BOGNÁR	M	21	(6)	3
Aleksandr BONDARENKO (UKR)	D	27	(1)	2
Zoltán BÜKSZEGI	M	27	(1)	7
József CSÁBI	D	24		
Csaba CSORDÁS	M	2	(17)	1
Pál DARDAI	M	7		
József FARKAS	M	20	(6)	
Ádám KOMLÓSI	D	9	(2)	
László KOMÓDI	M	28	(1)	6
János KOSZTA	G	30		
Zoltán KOVÁCS	A		(6)	
János MAROZSÁN	M	3	(6)	
Zoltán MOLNÁR	D	24		1
Ferenc OROSZ	A	27		15
Tibor POMPER	M		(1)	
Károly POTEMKIN	M	2	(5)	1
József SZALMA	D	14	(2)	
István VINCZE	A	28		11
Szabolcs WERNER	D	1	(2)	
János ZOVÁTH	M	9	(10)	

LEAGUE RESULTS 1995/96

05/08/95	Pécsi MFC	A	2-0	og, Bognár (p)
12/08/95	MTK FC	H	0-2	
19/08/95	DVSC-Epona	A	1-1	Bükszegi
27/08/95	Újpesti TE	H	1-0	Bondarenko
30/08/95	Békéscsaba	A	1-0	Vincze
10/09/95	Kispest-Honvéd FC	H	2-0	Orosz, Vincze
15/09/95	Haladás VFC	A	5-1	Vincze 2, Orosz 2, Bükszegi
24/09/95	Vasas CV	H	2-0	Komódi, Orosz
01/10/95	Vác FC-Samsung	A	3-2	Bükszegi, Bondarenko, Vincze
15/10/95	Györi ETO FC	H	2-0	Komódi 2
23/10/95	Csepel SC	A	3-2	Vincze 2, Bükszegi
29/10/95	Innstadt Stadler FC	H	2-2	Bükszegi, Bognár (p)
06/11/95	Ferencváros	A	3-1	Orosz, Bükszegi, Aranyos
19/11/95	Zalaegerszegi TE	H	3-2	Orosz, Komódi, Vincze
25/11/95	Parmalat FC	A	2-1	Vincze, Komódi
16/03/96	Pécsi MFC	H	2-0	Orosz, Potemkin
20/03/96	MTK FC	A	2-2	Orosz, Vincze
31/03/96	DVSC-Epona	H	2-0	Orosz, Csordás
06/04/96	Újpesti TE	A	0-0	
14/04/96	Békéscsaba	H	1-1	Orosz (p)
20/04/96	Kispest-Honvéd FC	A	1-1	Orosz (p)
28/04/96	Haladás VFC	H	2-1	Bükszegi, Aranyos
04/05/96	Vasas CV	A	0-1	
12/05/96	Vác FC-Samsung	H	1-0	Molnár
22/05/96	Györi ETO FC	A	1-1	Bognár (p)
26/05/96	Csepel SC	H	0-2	
05/06/96	Innstadt Stadler FC	A	1-3	Komódi
12/06/96	Ferencváros	H	0-1	
17/06/96	Zalaegerszegi TE	A	3-1	Orosz 3
24/06/96	Fehérvar '96 Parmalat FC	H	2-1	Vincze, Orosz

CSEPEL-SC

CLUB DIRECTORY

Csepel Sport Club
Béké tér 1
1212 Budapest
tel - (1) 4203812
fax - (1) 2764501
Year of Formation - 1912
Chairman - Imre Kiss
Coach - István Varga
Stadium - Béke téri (14,000)

MAJOR HONOURS
League Championship - (4)
1942, 1943, 1948, 1959.

APPEARANCES 95/96

	P	Ap	(s)	Gls
Krisztián ASZÓDI	M		(1)	
Gusztáv ÁCS	D	23	(2)	
Miklós BARANYI	A	30		11
Péter BERECZKI (ROM)	D	16	(8)	
Imre BIRÓ	G	30		
Norbert BUBCSÓ	D	6	(12)	1
Mihály BURILLÁK	M		(5)	
Csaba JAKAB	A	20	(1)	7
Attila KÁMÁN	A		(5)	
András KERESZTÚRI	D	6	(2)	1
Peter MEDGYES (SVK)	M	28		
Tamás NAGY	A	13	(10)	4
Tamás PETRÓK	M	7	(14)	
Dragan PUSKAS (YUG)	M	12		1
Henrik RÓSA	M	13		1
József SOMOGYI	M	1	(1)	
József SZEKERES	A	15	(8)	4
Gyula TIKOSI (ROM)	M	3	(4)	1
Zoltán TYUKODI	D	25	(2)	2
Miklós VANCSA	M	28		2
Dénes VÁCZI	M	27		3
Tamás VEIMOLA	M		(1)	
Zalán ZOMBORI	M	27	(2)	7

LEAGUE RESULTS 1995/96

05/08/95	Békéscsaba	A	2-2	Váczi, Baranyi
12/08/95	Kispest-Honvéd FC	H	2-1	Baranyi 2
18/08/95	Haladás VFC	A	2-1	Váczi (p), Nagy
26/08/95	Vasas CV	H	4-1	Zombori, Puskas, Vancsa, Bubcsó
30/08/95	Vác FC-Samsung	A	0-0	
09/09/95	Györi ETO FC	H	3-2	Zombori, Baranyi 2
16/09/95	Parmalat FC	A	3-1	Jakab 2, Szekeres
23/09/95	Innstadt Stadler FC	A	0-0	
02/10/95	Ferencváros	H	1-2	Nagy
14/10/95	Zalaegerszegi TE	A	1-2	Tyukodi
23/10/95	BVSC-Dreher	H	2-3	Jakab 2
28/10/95	Pécsi MFC	A	2-3	Nagy, og
04/11/95	MTK FC	H	5-0	Vancsa, Jakab 2, Baranyi 2
18/11/95	DVSC-Epona	A	0-5	
27/11/95	Újpesti TE	H	1-1	Váczi (p)
16/03/96	Békéscsaba	H	1-1	Tikosi
20/03/96	Kispest-Honvéd FC	A	1-1	Zombori
30/03/96	Haladás VFC	H	0-3	
06/04/96	Vasas CV	A	1-1	Szekeres
13/04/96	Vác FC-Samsung	H	1-0	Baranyi
20/04/96	Györi ETO FC	A	2-3	Szekeres, Zombori
27/04/96	Fehérvar '96 Parmalat FC	H	2-2	Nagy, Szekeres
04/05/96	Innstadt Stadler FC	H	1-0	Zombori
11/05/96	Ferencváros	A	1-2	Baranyi
22/05/96	Zalaegerszegi TE	H	0-0	
26/05/96	BVSC-Dreher	A	2-0	Zombori, Jakab
03/06/96	Pécsi MFC	H	2-0	Zombori, Baranyi
12/06/96	MTK FC	A	2-1	Tyukodi, Keresztúri
17/06/96	DVSC-Epona	H	1-2	Rósa
24/06/96	Újpesti TE	A	1-5	Baranyi

DVSC-EPONA

CLUB DIRECTORY

DVSC-Epona
Oláh Gábor u. 5
4028 Debrecen
tel - (52) 417655
fax - (52) 417595
Year of Formation - 1902
Chairman - Zoltán Erdei
Coach - Lajos Garamvölgyi
Stadium - Nagyerdei (10,000)

APPEARANCES 95/96

	P	Ap	(s)	Gls
László ARANY	M	14		7
Miklós B. SZABÓ	D	5	(2)	
Gábor BAGOLY	M	11	(1)	3
Zoltán BOOR	M		(2)	
János CSATÓ	M		(2)	
Attila DOBOS	A		(4)	
Tibor DOMBI	A	28		2
Ferenc FRIDA	M	3	(3)	
Liviu GOJAN (ROM)	D	27		
Béla HORVÁTH	G	25		
Dezsö HORVÁTH	G	3	(2)	
Nicolae ILEA (ROM)	A	29		11
Norbert KOVÁCS	M	2	(6)	
Csaba MADAR	M	29		2
Tamás MADAR	M		(2)	
Csaba MAGYARI	M		(2)	
Vyacheslav MEDVID (UKR)	A	10	(9)	
Zsolt NAGY	D		(4)	
Zsolt NAGYKAPOSI	M		(7)	
Zoltán PETÖ	D	23	(4)	1
Mihály PLÓKAI	M	7		4
Zsolt RUSKÓ	M	1	(1)	
Csaba SÁNDOR	M	29		
Tamás SÁNDOR	M	30		14
Dan STUPAR (ROM)	M	6	(3)	
János SZABÓ	M		(1)	
Csaba SZATMÁRI	M	18	(3)	2
Gábor TÉGLÁSI	G	2	(1)	
Zsolt VADICSKA	M	28		

LEAGUE RESULTS 1995/96

Date	Opponent	H/A	Score	Scorers
05/08/95	Ferencváros	H	2-1	Ilea, Sándor T. (p)
11/08/95	Zalaegerszegi TE	A	3-2	Arany 2, og
19/08/95	BVSC-Dreher	H	1-1	og
26/08/95	Pécsi MFC	A	0-1	
30/08/95	MTK FC	H	0-0	
10/09/95	Parmalat FC	H	2-1	Arany, Sándor T.
16/09/95	Újpesti TE	A	0-4	
24/09/95	Békéscsaba	H	1-0	Ilea
30/09/95	Kispest-Honvéd FC	A	0-0	
15/10/95	Haladás VFC	H	3-0	Ilea, Arany, Petö
21/10/95	Vasas CV	A	0-1	
28/10/95	Vác FC-Samsung	H	2-1	Sándor T. 2
04/11/95	Györi ETO FC	A	3-1	Arany 2, Sándor T.
18/11/95	Csepel SC	H	5-0	Dombi, Sándor T. 2, Szatmári, Madar C.
25/11/95	Innstadt Stadler FC	A	2-3	Ilea, Sándor T.
16/03/96	Ferencváros	A	0-1	
20/03/96	Zalaegerszegi TE	H	2-2	Arany, Sándor T.
31/03/96	BVSC-Dreher	A	0-2	
06/04/96	Pécsi MFC	H	1-0	Sándor T.
13/04/96	MTK FC	A	1-3	Madar C.
20/04/96	Fehérvar '96 Parmalat FC	A	1-4	Dombi
27/04/96	Újpesti TE	H	2-0	Ilea, Sándor T.
05/05/96	Békéscsaba	A	2-2	Bagoly, Plókai
11/05/96	Kispest-Honvéd FC	H	2-1	Sándor T. 2
22/05/96	Haladás VFC	A	1-2	Plókai
26/05/96	Vasas CV	H	2-3	Bagoly, Plókai
05/06/96	Vác FC-Samsung	A	1-1	Ilea
12/06/96	Györi ETO FC	H	4-1	Sándor T., Ilea, Szatmári, Bagoly
17/06/96	Csepel SC	A	2-1	Ilea 2
24/06/96	Innstadt Stadler FC	H	4-1	og, Ilea 2, Plókai

FEHÉRVÁR 96 PARMALAT FC

CLUB DIRECTORY

Fehérvár '96 Parmalat Futball Club
(now - Videoton FC Fehérvár)
Csikvári u.10
8002 Székesfehérvár
tel - (22) 319025
fax - (22) 319057
Year of Formation - 1941
Chairman - József Szuna
Coach - Károly Szabó; Ferenc Csongrádi
(96/97 - Slobodan Kustudic)
Stadium - Sóstói (23,000)

APPEARANCES 95/96

	P	Ap	(s)	Gls
Carlos ALVES (BRA)	M	1	(2)	
Balázs BEKÖ	D	27	(2)	
György BOGNÁR	M		(1)	
Péter DISZTL	G	12		
Rajmund DONÁTH	M	2	(3)	1
János DUBECZ	M	10	(2)	
Josip DULIC (YUG)	M	12	(1)	1
Zsolt DVÉRI	M	20	(3)	2
Ferenc HORVÁTH	A	29		12
Zoltán JAGODICS	D	3		1
András JÁVORKA	D	11	(1)	
András KERESZTÚRI	D	12		
Attila KORSÓS	A		(6)	
Zoltán KUJUNDZIC (YUG)	G	5	(1)	
Csaba LÁSZLÓ	D	5	(1)	
Antal LÖRINCZ	D	23	(1)	
Vasile MIRIUTA (ROM)	M	14		5
István MITRING	G	13	(1)	
Onyeabor MONYE (NIG)	M	20	(3)	1
Lajos NAGY	M	1	(9)	
László PÁLFI	A	8	(4)	1
Tamás PETÖ	M	14		3
Viktor REHAK	M		(1)	
Henrik RÓSA	M	13		1
Attila SZALAI	D	4	(4)	
Lajos TAKÁCS	A	15		1
Gábor TOLDI	A	4	(1)	
Norbert TÓTH	M	25	(2)	4
Ernö VARGA	M	3	(3)	
Sándor VARSÁNYI	A		(10)	
Tamás ZIMMERMANN	M	24	(1)	2

LEAGUE RESULTS 1995/96

Date	Opponent	H/A	Score	Scorers
05/08/95	Vasas CV	A	0-2	
12/08/95	Pécsi MFC	H	3-1	Dvéri, og, Horváth
19/08/95	Vác FC-Samsung	H	2-1	Pálfi, Horváth
26/08/95	MTK FC	A	2-5	Monye, og
30/08/95	Györi ETO FC	H	0-2	
10/09/95	DVSC-Epona	A	1-2	Tóth
16/09/95	Csepel SC	H	1-3	Rósa
23/09/95	Újpesti TE	A	0-4	
30/09/95	Innstadt Stadler FC	H	0-0	
14/10/95	Békéscsaba	A	1-3	Horváth
24/10/95	Ferencváros	H	1-2	Horváth
28/10/95	Kispest-Honvéd FC	A	0-5	
04/11/95	Zalaegerszegi TE	H	1-2	Jagodics
17/11/95	Haladás VFC	A	2-1	Horváth 2
25/11/95	BVSC-Dreher	H	1-2	Horváth
16/03/96	Vasas CV	H	0-1	
20/03/96	Pécsi MFC	A	2-1	Tóth, Horváth
30/03/96	Vác FC-Samsung	A	2-2	Petö, Dulic
06/04/96	MTK FC	H	3-1	Horváth, Miriuta (p), Zimmermann
13/04/96	Györi ETO FC	A	0-0	
20/04/96	DVSC-Epona	H	4-1	Horváth 2, Miriuta (p), Tóth
27/04/96	Csepel SC	A	2-2	Donáth, Petö
04/05/96	Újpesti TE	H	2-2	Takács, Zimmermann
11/05/96	Innstadt Stadler FC	A	0-2	
20/05/96	Békéscsaba	H	0-0	
25/05/96	Ferencváros	A	1-2	Miriuta (p)
05/06/96	Kispest-Honvéd FC	H	3-2	Tóth, og, Petö
12/06/96	Zalaegerszegi TE	A	2-0	Miriuta 2 (1p)
17/06/96	Haladás VFC	H	1-1	Dvéri
24/06/96	BVSC-Dreher	A	1-2	Horváth

FERENCVÁROS

CLUB DIRECTORY

Ferencvárosi Torna Club
Üllöi út 129
1091 Budapest
tel - (1) 2156025/2153856/2153698
fax - (1) 2153698
Year of Formation - 1899
Chairman - István Szivós
Coach - Dezsö Novák
Stadium - Üllöi út (17,743)

MAJOR HONOURS

League Championship - (26) 1903, 1905, 1907, 1909, 1910, 1911, 1912, 1913, 1926, 1927, 1928, 1932, 1934, 1938, 1940, 1941, 1949, 1963, 1964, 1967, 1968, 1976, 1981, 1992, 1995, 1996.
Domestic Cup - (18) 1913, 1922, 1927, 1928, 1933, 1935, 1942, 1943, 1944, 1958, 1972, 1974, 1976, 1978, 1991, 1993, 1994, 1995.
Fairs' Cup - (1) 1965.

APPEARANCES 95/96

	P	Ap	(s)	Gls
Flórián ALBERT	M	21		5
László ARANY	M	9	(4)	3
Babatunde FATUSI (NIG)	A	5	(6)	
Attila HAJDU	G	30		
János HRUTKA	D	11	(3)	
Zoltán JAGODICS	D	12		3
Zoltán KECSKÉS	M	15	(2)	2
József KELLER	D	10		1
Goran KOPUNOVIC (YUG)	A	15	(7)	3
Zoran KUNTIC (YUG)	A	26	(1)	6
Sergiy KUZNETSOV (UKR)	D	12		2
Krisztián LISZTES	M	28		9
Dejan MILOVANOVIC (YUG)	M	10	(8)	2
Norbert NAGY	M	10		
Zsolt NAGY	A	3	(9)	
Igor NICHENKO (UKR)	A	12	(2)	10
Elek NYILAS	M	20	(1)	3
Zsolt PÁLING	M	13	(2)	1
Levente SCHULTZ	M		(3)	
Tibor SIMON	M	12		
József SZEILER	G		(1)	
Mihály SZÜCS	D	14	(3)	
András TELEK	D	27		
Gábor VINCZE	M		(1)	
Ottó VINCZE	M	11	(6)	2
Gábor ZAVADSZKY	A	4	(17)	3

LEAGUE RESULTS 1995/96

05/08/95	DVSC-Epona	A	1-2	Nyilas (p)
14/08/95	Újpesti TE	H	2-0	Nyilas (p), Kuntic
19/08/95	Békéscsaba	A	3-1	Kuntic, Lisztes, Kopunovic
30/08/95	Haladás VFC	A	3-0	Zavadszky 2, Kecskés
09/09/95	Vasas CV	H	0-2	
17/09/95	Vác FC-Samsung	A	2-1	og, Kuznetsov
23/09/95	Györi ETO FC	H	2-0	Kopunovic, Kuntic
02/10/95	Csepel SC	A	2-1	Milovanovic, Vincze O.
14/10/95	Innstadt Stadler FC	H	3-0	Vincze O., Lisztes, Zavadszky
24/10/95	Parmalat FC	A	2-1	Kuntic, Kuznetsov
28/10/95	Zalaegerszegi TE	A	3-1	Albert, Nyilas, Lisztes
06/11/95	BVSC-Dreher	H	1-3	Kecskés
18/11/95	Pécsi MFC	A	0-1	
30/11/95	Kispest-Honvéd FC	H	3-1	Milovanovic, Keller, Albert
16/03/96	DVSC-Epona	H	1-0	Jagodics
20/03/96	Újpesti TE	A	1-1	Kopunovic
23/03/96	MTK FC	H	3-1	Lisztes, Albert 2
30/03/96	Békéscsaba	H	3-0	Nichenko 2, Jagodics
14/04/96	Haladás VFC	H	0-0	
20/04/96	Vasas CV	A	1-0	Lisztes
27/04/96	Vác FC-Samsung	H	2-0	Kuntic, Nichenko
04/05/96	Györi ETO FC	A	5-2	Páling, Nichenko 2, Lisztes, Albert
06/05/96	Kispest-Honvéd FC	A	0-1	
11/05/96	Csepel SC	H	2-1	Nichenko, Jagodics
22/05/96	Innstadt Stadler FC	A	3-0	Arany, Lisztes, Nichenko
25/05/96	Fehérvar '96 Parmalat FC	H	2-1	Arany, Lisztes
05/06/96	Zalaegerszegi TE	H	1-1	Nichenko
12/06/96	BVSC-Dreher	A	1-0	Kuntic
17/06/96	Pécsi MFC	H	3-1	Lisztes, Nichenko 2 (1p)
24/06/96	MTK FC	A	1-2	Arany

GYÖRI ETO FC

CLUB DIRECTORY

Györi ETO FC
Nagysándor József u. 31, 9027 Györ
tel - (96) 312433/312424
fax - (96) 312498
Year of Formation - 1904
Chairman - János Borbényi
Coach - László Györfi; József Póczik; Sándor Haász
Stadium - Györi (26,000)

MAJOR HONOURS
League Championship - (3) 1963, 1982, 1983.
Domestic Cup - (4) 1965, 1966, 1967, 1979.

APPEARANCES 95/96

	P	Ap	(s)	Gls
Sabahudin AGIC (BOS)	M	14	(2)	1
Catalin AZOITEI (ROM)	M	16	(1)	4
Béla BÍRÓ	G	2	(1)	
Csaba BORDÁS	D	11	(1)	1
Attila BÖJTE	D	3		
István BROCKHAUSER	G	11		
Sergiy CHABAN (UKR)	G	8		
István CSEKE	M	10		2
Sulejman DEMOLLARI (ALB)	A	3	(2)	1
Gheorghe DUMITRESCU (ROM)	M	8	(3)	
Miklós FEHÉR	A		(8)	2
István FERENCZI	A		(8)	
Ákos FÜZI	M	14	(6)	1
Gyula HAJSZÁN	M	16	(2)	
Ferenc HÁMORI	A	15		5
Vendel HORNYÁK	M	1		
Gábor HUNGLER	D	6	(1)	
Daniel IFTODI (ROM)	M	8		
László IVANICS	M	1	(3)	
Zoltán JAGODICS	D	10		1
Csaba JAKAB	G	9	(1)	
György KORSÓS	M	18	(5)	
János LAJKOVICS	D	3	(1)	
Pál LAKOS	D	14	(3)	
Lantai BALÁZS	D	21		
Ilea LAZAR (ROM)	A	8		5
Krisztián MIKÓCZI	A	4	(8)	
Vasile MIRIUTA (ROM)	M	15		3
Adede Moto MOKE (ZAI)	M	10	(6)	1
Danut OPREA (ROM)	M	3		
József ÖRDÖGH	M	5	(1)	
Tamás PETÖ	M	4	(6)	1
Gábor PUGLITS	D	5		
Zsolt RADICS	D	16	(2)	
Béla SZABÓ	D	5		
Flórián URBÁN	M	14		6
György VÉBER	M	5		
Attila VIRÁG	M	14	(4)	

LEAGUE RESULTS 1995/96

07/08/95	Kispest-Honvéd FC	A	0-0	
12/08/95	Haladás VFC	H	3-0	Hámori, Azoitei, Petö
21/08/95	Vasas CV	A	0-0	
27/08/95	Vác FC-Samsung	H	2-4	Miriuta, Jagodics
30/08/95	Parmalat FC	A	2-0	Miriuta, Azoitei
09/09/95	Csepel SC	A	2-3	Hámori, Füzi
16/09/95	Innstadt Stadler FC	H	2-2	Azoitei, Hámori
23/03/96	Ferencváros	A	0-2	
30/09/95	Zalaegerszegi TE	H	2-2	Hámori 2 (1p)
15/10/95	BVSC-Dreher	A	0-2	
21/10/95	Pécsi MFC	H	1-0	Azoitei
28/10/95	MTK FC	A	2-8	Agic, Bordás
04/11/95	DVSC-Epona	H	1-3	Miriuta
18/11/95	Újpesti TE	A	0-1	
25/11/95	Békéscsaba	H	0-0	
16/03/96	Kispest-Honvéd FC	H	1-2	Urbán
20/03/96	Haladás VFC	A	0-1	
30/03/96	Vasas CV	H	1-3	Moke
06/04/96	Vác FC-Samsung	A	0-0	
13/04/96	Parmalat FC	H	0-0	
20/04/96	Csepel SC	H	3-2	Urbán 2, Demollari
28/04/96	Innstadt Stadler FC	A	0-1	
04/05/96	Ferencváros	H	2-5	Lazar, Urbán
11/05/96	Zalaegerszegi TE	A	0-3	
22/05/96	BVSC-Dreher	H	1-1	Lazar
25/05/96	Pécsi MFC	A	2-2	Lazar, Cseke
05/06/96	MTK FC	H	1-0	Fehér
12/06/96	DVSC-Epona	A	1-4	Urbán
17/06/96	Újpesti TE	H	4-0	Cseke, Lazar 2, Urbán
24/06/96	Békéscsaba	A	1-3	Fehér

HALADÁS VFC

CLUB DIRECTORY

Haladás VFC
Rohonczi út. 3
9700 Szombathely
tel - (94) 314966/311494
fax - (94) 314966
Year of Formation - 1919
Chairman - dr. László Szabó
Coach - Sándor Fedor; István Mihalecz
Stadium - Haladás (18,000)

APPEARANCES 95/96

	P	Ap	(s)	Gls
Benito BELLIOT (HOL)	A	1	(3)	1
Zoltán BOGNÁR	D	19	(7)	1
Zsolt DÁVID	M	8	(1)	
Csaba FEHÉR (ROM)	A	24	(3)	3
László GAÁL	D	5	(4)	
András HORVÁTH	M		(3)	
István HORVÁTH	M		(1)	
László HORVÁTH	D		(1)	
Richárd HORVÁTH	A		(2)	
Gábor KIRÁLY	G	19		
Péter KISS	A	3	(10)	1
Sándor KOVÁCS	M	28		4
Kornél KURUCSAI	G	11		
Sándor LAHOS	M	2	(3)	
Miklós LENGYEL	M	2	(1)	
Zoltán MAJOROS	M	14	(4)	2
Peter MIKOCZI (SVK)	M	14	(1)	1
Adrian NEGRAU (ROM)	A	25	(1)	7
Gábor NEUDL	M	13	(3)	
Richárd NÉMETH	A		(1)	
Antal PERCZEL (SVK)	A		(2)	1
András PÉK	M		(1)	
László SÁNTA	M	13	(5)	
Gábor SCHNEIDER	A	8	(3)	1
Csaba SOMFALVI	M	10	(6)	1
István SZEKÉR	D	22	(1)	2
Vyacheslav SKUNTS (UKR)	M		(1)	
Gyula TÓTH	D	15	(3)	
László TÓTH	M	1	(1)	
Miklós TÓTH	D	23	(1)	
Krisztián VARGA	D	24		2
Sándor VARSÁNYI	M	14		1
Péter ZUGOR	D	12	(4)	

LEAGUE RESULTS 1995/96

Date	Opponent	H/A	Score	Scorers
05/08/95	Vác FC-Samsung	H	2-5	Varga, Kovács
12/08/95	Györi ETO FC	A	0-3	
18/08/95	Csepel SC	H	1-2	Majoros
26/08/95	Innstadt Stadler FC	A	1-2	Varga
30/08/95	Ferencváros	H	0-3	
06/09/95	Zalaegerszegi TE	A	0-0	
15/09/95	BVSC-Dreher	H	1-5	Somfalvi
23/09/95	Pécsi MFC	A	1-0	Majoros
29/09/95	MTK FC	H	2-2	og, Schneider
15/10/95	DVSC-Epona	A	0-3	
20/10/95	Újpesti TE	H	1-1	Negrau
28/10/95	Békéscsaba	A	1-2	Negrau
03/11/95	Kispest-Honvéd FC	H	1-0	Perczel
17/11/95	Parmalat FC	H	1-2	Szekér
25/11/95	Vasas CV	A	1-1	Fehér
16/03/96	Vác FC-Samsung	A	0-0	
20/03/96	Györi ETO FC	H	1-0	Belliot
30/03/96	Csepel SC	A	3-0	Mikóczi, og, Negrau
05/04/96	Innstadt Stadler FC	H	1-0	Negrau
14/04/96	Ferencváros	A	0-0	
20/04/96	Zalaegerszegi TE	H	2-1	Kovács (p), Fehér
28/04/96	BVSC-Dreher	A	1-2	Szekér
04/05/96	Pécsi MFC	H	0-1	
11/05/96	MTK FC	A	1-3	Negrau
22/05/96	DVSC-Epona	H	2-1	Varsányi, Negrau
25/05/96	Újpesti TE	A	1-2	Kovács
05/06/96	Békéscsaba	H	3-1	Bognár, Fehér, Negrau
12/06/96	Kispest-Honvéd FC	A	0-4	
17/06/96	Fehérvar '96 Parmalat FC	A	1-1	Kiss
24/06/96	Vasas CV	H	1-1	Kovács

KISPEST-HONVÉD FC

CLUB DIRECTORY

Kispest-Honvéd Futball Club
Újtemetö u. 1-3
1194 Budapest
tel - (1) 2829789/2807240
fax - (1) 2829791
Year of Formation - 1909
Chairman - Gábor Rácz
Director - Imre Komora
Coach - Péter Török
Stadium - József Bozsik (15,000)

MAJOR HONOURS

League Championship - (13) 1950, 1950 (autumn), 1952, 1954, 1955, 1980, 1984, 1985, 1986, 1988, 1989, 1991, 1993.
Domestic Cup - (5)
1926, 1964, 1985, 1989, 1996.

APPEARANCES 95/96

	P	Ap	(s)	Gls
János ÁRGYELÁN	M	12		1
János BÁNFI	D	13		2
Zsolt BÁRÁNYOS	M	19	(5)	5
István BROCKHAUSER	G	6		
István CSEKE	M	8	(1)	1
János DUBECZ	M	4	(6)	
József DURÓ	M	7	(2)	
Dénes ESZENYI	A	5		1
István FARAGÓ	M	2	(3)	1
Attila FORRAI	M	7	(2)	
Krisztián GABALA	D	14	(1)	
Attila GHINDA (ROM)	A	10	(7)	4
Árpád HAHN	D	27		1
Szabolcs HERCZKU	D		(2)	
Gábor HUNGLER	D	2		
Mirko JOVANOVIC (YUG)	A	10	(7)	5
Péter KABÁT	M	2	(6)	
Béla KOVÁCS	M	18	(7)	3
Róbert LÓCZI	D	1	(2)	
János MÁTYUS	D	21	(1)	4
John MOSES (LIB)	A	5	(2)	1
Gheorghe PENA (ROM)	M	4	(1)	
Zoltán PINTÉR	M	2	(3)	
Attila PIROSKA (ROM)	M	20		3
István PISONT	M	5	(1)	
Attila PLÓKAI	D	24	(3)	3
Ferenc ROTT	G	5		
Mihály TÓTH	A	19	(4)	7
István URBÁNYI	M	18	(1)	
Ádám VEZÉR	G	19		
Robert WARZYCHA (POL)	M	21		6

LEAGUE RESULTS 1995/96

07/08/95	Györi ETO FC	H	0-0	
12/08/95	Csepel SC	A	1-2	Warzycha
30/08/95	Zalaegerszegi TE	H	3-0	Cseke, Ghinda, Warzycha
10/09/95	BVSC-Dreher	A	0-2	
16/09/95	Pécsi MFC	H	2-2	Eszenyi, Hahn
23/09/95	MTK FC	A	1-0	Bárányos
27/09/95	Innstadt Stadler FC	H	2-1	Kovács, Bánfi
30/09/95	DVSC-Epona	H	0-0	
16/10/95	Újpesti TE	A	1-2	Piroska
21/10/95	Békéscsaba	H	1-1	Bárányos
28/10/95	Parmalat FC	H	5-0	Ghinda 3 (1p), Faragó, Tóth
03/11/95	Haladás VFC	A	0-1	
20/11/95	Vasas CV	H	3-2	Piroska, Bánfi, Warzycha
25/11/95	Vác FC-Samsung	A	3-3	Bárányos, Tóth, Warzycha
30/11/95	Ferencváros	A	1-3	Mátyus
16/03/96	Györi ETO FC	A	2-1	Tóth, Mátyus
20/03/96	Csepel SC	H	1-1	Tóth
30/03/96	Innstadt Stadler FC	A	1-1	Moses
06/04/96	Ferencváros	H	1-0	Warzycha
13/04/96	Zalaegerszegi TE	A	0-0	
20/04/96	BVSC-Dreher	H	1-1	Bárányos
27/04/96	Pécsi MFC	A	4-2	Kovács, Jovanovic, Árgyelán, Tóth
05/05/96	MTK FC	H	2-1	Plókai, Warzycha (p)
11/05/96	DVSC-Epona	A	1-2	Kovács
22/05/96	Újpesti TE	H	1-1	Jovanovic
25/05/96	Békéscsaba	A	0-1	
05/06/96	Fehérvar '96 Parmalat FC	A	2-3	Plókai, Jovanovic
12/06/96	Haladás VFC	H	4-0	Jovanovic, Mátyus, Piroska, Bárányos
17/06/96	Vasas CV	A	4-2	Mátyus, og, Jovanovic, Tóth
24/06/96	Vác FC-Samsung	H	2-0	Plókai, Tóth

MTK

CLUB DIRECTORY

MTK FC
Salgótarjáni út. 12-14
1087 Budapest
tel - (1) 1338368
fax - (1) 1421134
Year of Formation - 1888
Chairman - Gábor Várszegi
Director - Ferenc Fülöp
Coach - Bertalan Bicskei; István Kisteleki; Imre Garaba (96/97 - József Garami)
Stadium - Hungária úti (24,000)

MAJOR HONOURS

League Championship - (19)
1904, 1908, 1914, 1917, 1918, 1919, 1920, 1921, 1922, 1923, 1924, 1925, 1929, 1936, 1937, 1951, 1953, 1958, 1987.
Domestic Cup - (9) 1910, 1911, 1912, 1914, 1923, 1925, 1932, 1952, 1968.

APPEARANCES 95/96

	P	Ap	(s)	Gls
Gábor BABOS	G	17	(1)	
Ádám BABOS	D	15		
András BABÓCSY	G	13		
Aurél CSERTÖI	A	24	(1)	8
Krisztián CSILLAG	M	16	(1)	
László FARKASHÁZY	M	22	(2)	4
Antal FÜLE	A	9	(8)	4
István HAMAR	A	19	(7)	8
Csaba HORVÁTH	M	24	(2)	1
Béla ILLÉS	M	29		11
András JÁVORKA	D	9		
Krisztián KENESEI	A	12	(14)	4
Attila KUTTOR	D	23	(3)	2
Emil LÖRINCZ	D	12		1
Bálint LUKÁCS	M	4		
Aleksandr NIKIFOROV (UKR)	D	14	(1)	1
Adrian OPRISAN (SWE)	D	8	(4)	
László STRASSZER	M		(5)	1
Attila SZABADOS	M	2	(4)	2
Zoltán SZABÓ	A		(3)	
Tamás SZEKERES	D	19	(1)	2
Attila TAKÁCS	M		(1)	
János TALAPA	D	4	(9)	
Zoltán TAMÁSI	D	17	(2)	
Gyula ZSIVÓTZKY	A	18	(1)	6

LEAGUE RESULTS 1995/96

05/08/95	Zalaegerszegi TE	H	3-0	Hamar 2, Füle
12/08/95	BVSC-Dreher	A	2-0	Hamar, Csertöi
19/08/95	Pécsi MFC	H	2-1	Hamar, Szekeres
26/08/95	Parmalat FC	H	5-2	og, Farkasházy 2, Illés 2
30/08/95	DVSC-Epona	A	0-0	
16/09/95	Békéscsaba	A	1-3	Illés
23/09/95	Kispest-Honvéd FC	H	0-1	
29/09/95	Haladás VFC	A	2-2	Kuttor, Füle
14/10/95	Vasas CV	H	0-0	
21/10/95	Vác FC-Samsung	A	1-2	Kenesei
25/10/95	Újpesti TE	H	1-2	Horváth
28/10/95	Györi ETO FC	H	8-2	Csertöi 2, Füle 2, Nikiforov, Illés, Zsivótzky 2
04/11/95	Csepel SC	A	0-5	
18/11/95	Innstadt Stadler FC	H	3-3	og, Farkasházy, Illés
16/03/96	Zalaegerszegi TE	A	3-3	Zsivótzky, Csertöi, Illés
20/03/96	BVSC-Dreher	H	2-2	Strasser, Kuttor
23/03/96	Ferencváros	A	1-3	Illés
30/03/96	Pécsi MFC	A	3-0	Illés, Csertöi, Hamar
06/04/96	Fehérvar '96 Parmalat FC	A	1-3	Szekeres
13/04/96	DVSC-Epona	H	3-1	Illés, Lörincz, Csertöi
20/04/96	Újpesti TE	A	0-0	
27/04/96	Békéscsaba	H	1-0	Csertöi
05/05/96	Kispest-Honvéd FC	A	1-2	Zsivótzky
11/05/96	Haladás VFC	H	3-1	Kenesei 2, og
21/05/96	Vasas CV	A	3-1	Csertöi, Illés, Hamar
25/05/96	Vác FC-Samsung	H	5-0	Farkasházy, Illés, Hamar 2, Zsivótzky
05/06/96	Györi ETO FC	A	0-1	
12/06/96	Csepel SC	H	1-2	Kenesei
17/06/96	Innstadt Stadler FC	A	1-0	Szabados
24/06/96	Ferencváros	H	2-1	Szabados, Zsivótzky

PÉCSI MFC

CLUB DIRECTORY

Pécsi Mecsek FC
Stadion u. 2
7633 Pécs
tel - (72) 252880
fax - (72) 312494
Year of Formation - 1950
Chairman - László Puch
Director - Csaba Rabi Csaba
Coach - Pál Dárdai; Imre Herke
(96/97 - József Gelei)
Stadium - PMSC (16,200)

MAJOR HONOURS
Domestic Cup - (1) 1990.

APPEARANCES 95/96

	P	Ap	(s)	Gls
Zoltán ACZÉL	D	8		1
Krisztián BALÁZS	M	3	(1)	
Tamás BALOGH	G	11		
Béla BARONEK	G	1		
Károly BRAUN	D		(10)	
Roman BUJDAK (SVK)	A	4	(14)	1
Dionisius BUMB (ROM)	M	13	(1)	
Pál DÁRDAI	M	14		5
András DIENES	D	28	(1)	
Csaba FEHÉR	M	23	(1)	1
János GYÖRY	M	9	(6)	2
Antal JÄKL	M	26		1
Zoltán KOVÁCS	A	11		5
Árpád KOVÁCSEVICS	G	18		
Tibor LAJOS	D	12		
János MAROZSÁN	M	3		
Krisztián MÜLLER	D		(5)	
Roland PEST	A	5	(9)	2
Gergely RÓZSAHEGYI	M		(4)	
Tamás SCHNEIDER	D	21	(2)	2
Frank SEATOR (LIB)	M	2	(2)	1
József SZABADOS	D	26		
Csaba SZABÓ	A	2	(6)	
Roman TOLOCHKO (UKR)	A	24		1
Attila TÖKÖLI	A	26	(1)	7
Roland ULRICH	M	13	(9)	1
Zoltán ULVECZKI	M	22	(7)	2
Szabolcs WERNER	D	5	(4)	

LEAGUE RESULTS 1995/96

05/08/95	BVSC-Dreher	H	0-2	
12/08/95	Parmalat FC	A	1-3	Dárdai (p)
19/08/95	MTK FC	A	1-2	Schneider
26/08/95	DVSC-Epona	H	1-0	Tököli
30/08/95	Újpesti TE	A	0-1	
09/09/95	Békéscsaba	H	3-1	Dárdai 2, Pest
16/09/95	Kispest-Honvéd FC	A	2-2	Fehér, Bujdak
23/09/95	Haladás VFC	H	0-1	
30/09/95	Vasas CV	A	1-2	Ulveczki
14/10/95	Vác FC-Samsung	H	0-0	
21/10/95	Györi ETO FC	A	0-1	
28/10/95	Csepel SC	H	3-2	Seator, Tolochko, Tököli
04/11/95	Innstadt Stadler FC	A	1-3	Dárdai (p)
18/11/95	Ferencváros	H	1-0	Jäkl
25/11/95	Zalaegerszegi TE	A	1-3	Dárdai
16/03/96	BVSC-Dreher	A	0-2	
20/03/96	Fehérvar '96 Parmalat FC	H	1-2	Kovács
30/03/96	MTK FC	H	0-3	
06/04/96	DVSC-Epona	A	0-1	
13/04/96	Újpesti TE	H	0-2	
20/04/96	Békéscsaba	A	2-1	Kovács, Ulveczki
27/04/96	Kispest-Honvéd FC	H	2-4	Tököli 2
04/05/96	Haladás VFC	A	1-0	Kovács
11/05/96	Vasas CV	H	1-3	Kovács
22/05/96	Vác FC-Samsung	A	1-1	Tököli
25/05/96	Györi ETO FC	H	2-2	Györy, Aczél
03/06/96	Csepel SC	A	0-2	
12/06/96	Innstadt Stadler FC	H	3-1	Kovács, Ulrich, Tököli
17/06/96	Ferencváros	A	1-3	Tököli
24/06/96	Zalaegerszegi TE	H	3-3	Schneider, Pest, Györy

INNSTADT STADLER FC

CLUB DIRECTORY

Innstadt Stadler FC (now - Stadler FC)
Vörösmarty u. 18
6221 Akasztó
tel - (78) 451390
fax - (78) 351035
Year of Formation - 1994
Chairman - József Stadler
Coach - István Sándor
Stadium - Stadler (21,000)

APPEARANCES 95/96

	P	AP	(s)	Gls
József BALOGH	D	4	(9)	
Mihály BÉKÉSI	G	12	(2)	
Rolands BOULDERS (LAT)	A	8	(4)	1
István CSEHI	M	29		1
Zoltán CSEHI	A	28	(2)	4
Norbert DEME	D		(1)	
Attila DRAGONER	D	27		3
Ferenc KÁKONYI	M		(1)	
János KERTÉSZ	D	27		
Zsolt KOVÁCS	M	12	(8)	3
Mátyás LÁZÁR	M	10	(3)	
István LEHOTA	A	16	(3)	1
László MAGYARI	A		(1)	
Viktor MAKRICKI (UKR)	M	15		
Zoltán MOLNÁR	M	26		
Attila NAGY	M		(8)	
Gábor NAGY	G	18	(1)	
Norbert NAGY	M	14	(1)	
Igor NICHENKO (UKR)	A	12	(1)	8
Miroslav RESHKO (UKR)	D	25		2
Tibor RUMÁN	A	10	(10)	2
Csaba SZENTMÁRTONI	A	1	(7)	1
Vladimir VACHILYA (UKR)	D	10	(1)	
Aleksandr YELISEYEV (LAT)	A	5	(3)	
Vyacheslav YEREMEYEV (UKR)	M	21	(1)	8

LEAGUE RESULTS 1995/96

04/08/95	Újpesti TE	A	1-1	Reshko
12/08/95	Békéscsaba	H	3-1	Csehi Z., Nichenko, Dragoner
26/08/95	Haladás VFC	H	2-1	Nichenko, og
30/08/95	Vasas CV	A	2-2	Yeremeyev, Rumán
09/09/95	Vác FC-Samsung	H	1-2	Nichenko
16/09/95	Györi ETO FC	A	2-2	Yeremeyev 2
23/09/95	Csepel SC	H	0-0	
27/09/95	Kispest-Honvéd FC	A	1-2	Csehi Z.
30/09/95	Parmalat FC	A	0-0	
14/10/95	Ferencváros	A	0-3	
21/10/95	Zalaegerszegi TE	H	1-1	Nichenko
29/10/95	BVSC-Dreher	A	2-2	Yeremeyev, Nichenko
04/11/95	Pécsi MFC	H	3-1	Reshko, Nichenko, Yeremeyev
18/11/95	MTK FC	A	3-3	Kovács, Yeremeyev 2
25/11/95	DVSC-Epona	H	3-2	Yeremeyev, Nichenko 2
16/03/96	Újpesti TE	H	0-0	
20/03/96	Békéscsaba	A	0-0	
30/03/96	Kispest-Honvéd FC	H	1-1	Lehota
05/04/96	Haladás VFC	A	0-1	
13/04/96	Vasas CV	H	1-0	Rumán
20/04/96	Vác FC-Samsung	A	1-1	Dragoner
28/04/96	Györi ETO FC	H	1-0	Boulders
04/05/96	Csepel SC	A	0-1	
11/05/96	Fehérvar '96 Parmalat FC	H	2-0	Dragoner, Kovács
22/05/96	Ferencváros	H	0-3	
25/05/96	Zalaegerszegi TE	A	0-2	
05/06/96	BVSC-Dreher	H	3-1	Csehi Z., Kovács, Szentmártoni
12/06/96	Pécsi MFC	A	1-3	Csehi Z.
17/06/96	MTK FC	H	0-1	
24/06/96	DVSC-Epona	A	1-4	Csehi I. (p)

ÚJPESTI TE

CLUB DIRECTORY

Újpesti Torna Egylet
Megyeri út 13
1043 Budapest
tel - (1) 1697333/1692579
fax - (1) 1428432
Year of Formation - 1885
Chairman - dr. Imre Gedövári
Coach - József Garami (96/97 - László Nagy)
Stadium - Megyeri úti (32,000)

MAJOR HONOURS

League Championship - (19)
1930, 1931, 1933, 1935, 1939, 1945, 1946, 1947, 1960, 1969, 1970, 1971, 1972, 1973, 1974, 1975, 1978, 1979, 1990.
Domestic Cup - (7)
1969, 1970, 1975, 1982, 1983, 1987, 1992.

APPEARANCES 95/96

	P	Ap	(s)	Gls
Attila BELVON	M	8	(12)	1
Balázs BÉRCZY	D	25	(1)	3
Károly BRAUN	D	1	(1)	
Goran DJORDJEVIC (YUG)	M	13	(5)	
Gábor EGRESSY	A	30		5
Zsolt FÜZESI	D	28		1
Péter HORVÁTH	A	3	(6)	1
Sándor JENEI	D	28		6
Péter KOVÁCS	A		(1)	
György KUN	M		(1)	
László MEDGYESI	M	2	(1)	
Michel N'DOUMBE (CMR)	D	11	(2)	
Vilmos SEBÖK	D	20		1
Krisztián SOMOGYI	M	2	(1)	
Károly SZANYÓ	M	25	(1)	9
Attila SZILI	A	2	(12)	
Zoltán SZLEZÁK	D	30		2
Lajos SZÜCS	G	30		
Tamás TIEFENBACH	A	15	(7)	3
János TOMKA	D	15	(7)	1
Gábor P. TÓTH	M		(1)	
György TÓTH	M	4	(3)	
Zsolt TÚRI	M	16	(4)	5
György VÉBER	M	9		1
László WUKOVICS	A	13	(12)	3

LEAGUE RESULTS 1995/96

04/08/95	Innstadt Stadler FC	H	1-1	Tiefenbach
14/08/95	Ferencváros	A	0-2	
18/08/95	Zalaegerszegi TE	H	3-2	og, Jenei, Egressy
27/08/95	BVSC-Dreher	A	0-1	
30/08/95	Pécsi MFC	H	1-0	Túri
16/09/95	DVSC-Epona	H	4-0	Wukovics, Szanyó, Egressy, Bérczy
23/09/95	Parmalat FC	H	4-0	Belvon, Szanyó, Jenei 2
01/10/95	Békéscsaba	A	3-2	Jenei, Tomka, Szanyó
16/10/95	Kispest-Honvéd FC	H	2-1	Egressy, Szanyó
20/10/95	Haladás VFC	A	1-1	Jenei
25/10/95	MTK FC	A	2-1	Szlezák, Jenei
30/10/95	Vasas CV	H	1-1	Tiefenbach
04/11/95	Vác FC-Samsung	A	0-1	
18/11/95	Györi ETO FC	H	1-0	Szlezák
27/11/95	Csepel SC	A	1-1	Szanyó
16/03/96	Innstadt Stadler FC	A	0-0	
20/03/96	Ferencváros	H	1-1	Szanyó
30/03/96	Zalaegerszegi TE	A	0-1	
06/04/96	BVSC-Dreher	H	0-0	
13/04/96	Pécsi MFC	A	2-0	Füzesi, Bérczy
20/04/96	MTK FC	H	0-0	
27/04/96	DVSC-Epona	A	0-2	
04/05/96	Fehérvar '96 Parmalat FC	A	2-2	Tiefenbach, Egressy
12/05/96	Békéscsaba	H	2-0	Túri 2
22/05/96	Kispest-Honvéd FC	A	1-1	Wukovics
25/05/96	Haladás VFC	H	2-1	Túri, Horváth P.
05/06/96	Vasas CV	A	2-2	Bérczy, Véber
12/06/96	Vác FC-Samsung	H	2-2	Egressy, Szanyó
17/06/96	Györi ETO FC	A	0-4	
24/06/96	Csepel SC	H	5-1	Szanyó 2, Sebök, Wukovics, Turi

VASAS CV

CLUB DIRECTORY

Vasas Casino Vigadó
Fáy u. 58
1139 Budapest XIII.
tel - (1) 1296073/1294074
fax - (1) 1296073
Year of Formation - 1911
Chairman - András Gyalog
Director - Rudolf Illovszky
Coach - Imre Gellei
Stadium - Fáy utcai (18,000)

MAJOR HONOURS
League Championship - (6)
1957, 1961, 1962, 1965, 1966, 1977.
Domestic Cup - (4) 1955, 1973, 1981, 1986.

APPEARANCES 95/96

	P	Ap	(s)	Gls
Szabolcs BÍRÓ	G	1		
Géza BUKVA	D	1	(4)	
Jean-Claude Mbembe 'CLAUDE' (CON)	M	2	(5)	1
Pál FISCHER	A	20	(2)	9
Péter GALASCHEK	M	28		2
Zoltán GERESS	D	28		
Anatoly GRITSAYUK (UKR)	M	13	(5)	2
Csaba HERCZEG	D	4	(13)	2
Justice Edem 'JESSY' (CMR)	D	23		1
Róbert JOVÁN	A	21		8
Tamás JUHÁR	D	29		
Tamás KOLTAI	A		(1)	
Miklós MACZÓ	D	10	(4)	1
Zsolt MÁRIÁSI	M	25		4
Róbert MORVAI	M		(1)	
Tamás MÓNOS	M	30		1
Zoltán PÁL	A	7	(8)	1
Szabolcs SÁFÁR	G	29		
Antal SIMON	M	21	(3)	1
Ferenc SZILVESZTER	M	25	(1)	7
András TÓTH	M	6	(2)	
Zoltán VÁCZI	M	7	(15)	2

LEAGUE RESULTS 1995/96

Date	Opponent		Score	Scorers
05/08/95	Parmalat FC	H	2-0	Gritsayuk, Maczó
13/08/95	Vác FC-Samsung	A	2-3	Simon, Herczeg
21/08/95	Györi ETO FC	H	0-0	
26/08/95	Csepel SC	A	1-4	Váczi
30/08/95	Innstadt Stadler FC	H	2-2	Jován, Claude
09/09/95	Ferencváros	A	2-0	Gritsayuk, Máriási
17/09/95	Zalaegerszegi TE	H	2-0	Jován, Váczi
24/09/95	BVSC-Dreher	A	0-2	
30/09/95	Pécsi MFC	H	2-1	Jován, Galaschek
14/10/95	MTK FC	A	0-0	
21/10/95	DVSC-Epona	H	1-0	Jován
30/10/95	Újpesti TE	A	1-1	Máriási
04/11/95	Békéscsaba	H	1-1	Jessy
20/11/95	Kispest-Honvéd FC	A	2-3	Szilveszter, Pál
25/11/95	Haladás VFC	H	1-1	Fischer
16/03/96	Fehérvar '96 Parmalat FC	A	1-0	Szilveszter
20/03/96	Vác FC-Samsung	H	2-2	Jován, Fischer
30/03/96	Györi ETO FC	A	3-1	Szilveszter 2, Jován
06/04/96	Csepel SC	H	1-1	Szilveszter
13/04/96	Innstadt Stadler FC	A	0-1	
20/04/96	Ferencváros	H	0-1	
27/04/96	Zalaegerszegi TE	A	2-1	Fischer 2
04/05/96	BVSC-Dreher	H	1-0	Fischer (p)
11/05/96	Pécsi MFC	A	3-1	Fischer, Szilveszter, Mónos
21/05/96	MTK FC	H	1-3	Jován
26/05/96	DVSC-Epona	A	3-2	Szilveszter, Máriási,Fischer
05/06/96	Újpesti TE	H	2-2	Fischer, Galasek
12/06/96	Békéscsaba	A	3-2	Fischer, Máriási, Herczeg
17/06/96	Kispest-Honvéd FC	H	2-4	og, Jován
24/06/96	Haladás VFC	A	1-1	og

VÁC FC-SAMSUNG

CLUB DIRECTORY

Vác FC-Samsung
Pf. 16
Stadion u. 2
2600 Vác
tel - (27) 314324/314795
fax - (27) 314324
Year of Formation - 1889
Chairman - Károly Iványi
Coach - Dénes Tóth
Stadium - Városi (12,000)

MAJOR HONOURS
League Chamionship - (1) 1994.

APPEARANCES 95/96

	P	Ap	(s)	Gls
Csaba ANDRÁSSY (ROM)	A	22	(3)	4
Izedunor AUSTIN (NIG)	A	2	(12)	4
Zoltán BORGULYA	M	24	(5)	7
Antal FÜLE	A	4		2
Béla HANYECZ	A	5	(10)	1
István HÁMORI	G	30		
István KASZA	D	23	(3)	2
Gábor KRISKA	D	1	(6)	
János LAJKOVICS	D	4		
András LÉVAI	D	24		1
Bryce MACKAYA (GAB)	M	2	(7)	1
Tibor NAGY	D	30		2
József NYIKOS	M	17	(7)	
Gábor PUGLITS	D	21		
János ROMANEK	M	22	(1)	1
Tamás SÁNDOR	M	11	(10)	4
Zoltán SCHWARCZ	M	25		3
Vladimir SIAGO (SVK)	M	5		
István SZEDLACSEK	A	1	(1)	
Imre SZOBOSZLAI	M	9	(8)	1
Gábor VÉN	M	3	(1)	
Péter VÍG	M	17	(8)	2
Csaba VOJTEKOVSZKI	M	27		1
József ZVARA	A	1	(3)	1

LEAGUE RESULTS 1995/96

05/08/95	Haladás VFC	A	5-2	Romanek, Borgulya, Andrássy, Austin, Víg
13/08/95	Vasas CV	H	3-2	Borgulya 2, Zvara
19/08/95	Parmalat FC	A	1-2	Austin
27/08/95	Györi ETO FC	A	4-2	Nagy, Víg, Schwarcz, og
30/08/95	Csepel SC	H	0-0	
09/09/95	Innstadt Stadler FC	A	2-1	Borgulya, Sándor
17/09/95	Ferencváros	H	1-2	Hanyecz
22/09/95	Zalaegerszegi TE	A	1-2	Szoboszlai
01/10/95	BVSC-Dreher	H	2-3	Sándor, Austin
14/10/95	Pécsi MFC	A	0-0	
21/10/95	MTK FC	H	2-1	Lévai, Borgulya
28/10/95	DVSC-Epona	A	1-2	Sándor
04/11/95	Újpesti TE	H	1-0	Vojtekovszki
18/11/95	Békéscsaba	A	1-1	Borgulya
25/11/95	Kispest-Honvéd FC	H	3-3	Schwarcz 2, Austin
16/03/96	Haladás VFC	H	0-0	
20/03/96	Vasas CV	A	2-2	Andrássy, Mackaya
30/03/96	Fehérvar '96 Parmalat FC	H	2-2	Borgulya, Andrássy
06/04/96	Györi ETO FC	H	0-0	
13/04/96	Csepel SC	A	0-1	
20/04/96	Innstadt Stadler FC	H	1-1	Nagy
27/04/96	Ferencváros	A	0-2	
04/05/96	Zalaegerszegi TE	H	2-0	Kasza 2
12/05/96	BVSC-Dreher	A	0-1	
22/05/96	Pécsi MFC	H	1-1	Füle
25/05/96	MTK FC	A	0-5	
05/06/96	DVSC-Epona	H	1-1	Füle
12/06/96	Újpesti TE	A	2-2	og, Sándor
17/06/96	Békéscsaba	H	1-2	Andrássy
24/06/96	Kispest-Honvéd FC	A	0-2	

ZALAEGERSZEGI TE

CLUB DIRECTORY

Zalaegerszegi TE
Október 6. tér 16
8900 Zalaegerszeg
tel - (92) 314090
fax - (92) 314093
Year of Formation - 1920
Chairman - Gyula Gergály
Coach - Gábor Madár; János Szöcs
(96/97 - László Pusztai)
Stadium - Zalaegerszeg (20,000)

APPEARANCES 95/96

	P	Ap	(s)	Gls
Zoltán BALOG	D	26		1
Zsolt CSÓKA	D	11		1
Ferenc FUJSZ	M	14		1
Attila HORVÁTH	M	21	(1)	
Gyula HORVÁTH	A	1	(5)	1
József HORVÁTH	D	20	(6)	2
László IVANICS	M	5	(4)	1
Gergely KOCSÁRDI	D	9	(13)	
Zsolt KOVÁCS	D	16	(8)	
Gábor KUTASI	D	3	(1)	
Miklós LENDVAI	M	26		1
Tamás NÉMETH	M	30	(2)	10
Sándor PREISINGER	A	24	(2)	7
József SEBÖK	A	25	(3)	5
Zsolt SZABÓ I	D	24		
Zsolt SZABÓ II	A	21	(6)	7
Roland SZABÓ	M	3	(8)	
Zoltán SZABÓ	M	4	(13)	1
Barnabás SZTIPANOVICS	A	17	(8)	2
József TÓTH	G	25		
Zoltán TÓTH	M		(2)	
Géza VLASZÁK	G	5		

LEAGUE RESULTS 1995/96

Date	Opponent		Score	Scorers
05/08/95	MTK FC	A	0-3	
11/08/95	DVSC-Epona	H	2-3	Preisinger 2
18/08/95	Újpesti TE	A	2-3	Szabó II, Preisinger
25/08/95	Békéscsaba	H	3-0	Szabó II, Sztipánovics, Németh
30/08/95	Kispest-Honvéd FC	A	0-3	
09/09/95	Haladás VFC	H	0-0	
17/09/95	Vasas CV	A	0-2	
22/09/95	Vác FC-Samsung	H	2-1	Németh J., Horváth
30/09/95	Györi ETO FC	A	2-2	Sebök, Szabó II
14/10/95	Csepel SC	H	2-1	Németh 2
21/10/95	Innstadt Stadler FC	A	1-1	og
28/10/95	Ferencváros	H	1-3	Szabó Zo.
04/11/95	Fehérvar '96 Parmalat FC	A	2-1	Fujsz, Horváth J.
19/11/95	BVSC-Dreher	A	2-3	Sztipánovics, Preisinger
25/11/95	Pécsi MFC	H	3-1	Németh 2, Lendvai
16/03/96	MTK FC	H	3-3	Preisinger, Németh 2
20/03/96	DVSC-Epona	H	2-2	Szabó II, Sebök
30/03/96	Újpesti TE	H	1-0	Sebök
06/04/96	Békéscsaba	A	1-1	Horváth
13/04/96	Kispest-Honvéd FC	H	0-0	
20/04/96	Haladás VFC	A	1-2	Szabó II (p)
27/04/96	Vasas CV	H	1-2	Szabó II
04/05/96	Vác FC-Samsung	A	1-2	Németh
11/05/96	Györi ETO FC	H	3-0	Balog, Sebök, og
22/05/96	Csepel SC	A	0-0	
25/05/96	Innstadt Stadler FC	H	2-0	Csóka, Szabó II
05/06/96	Ferencváros	A	1-1	Preisinger
12/06/96	Fehérvar '96 Parmalat FC	H	0-2	
17/06/96	BVSC-Dreher	H	1-3	Németh
24/06/96	Pécsi MFC	A	3-3	Ivanics, Preisinger, Sebök

PROMOTED CLUBS

SECOND DIVISION FINAL TABLES 95/96

EAST

		Pd	W	D	L	F	A	Pt	GD
1	**III. Kerületi TVE**	**30**	**20**	**6**	**4**	**66**	**21**	**63**	**+45**
2	Tiszakécskei FC	30	18	6	6	53	28	60	+25
3	Diósgyöri FC	30	16	10	4	60	25	58	+35
4	KCFC-Hajdúsz.	30	17	6	7	56	33	57	+23
5	Kecskeméti TE	30	17	5	8	44	35	56	+9
6	Tiszavasvári	30	14	8	8	44	31	50	+13
7	Salgótarján	30	12	10	8	41	27	46	+14
8	Nyíregyháza	30	13	4	13	47	42	43	+5
9	Hajdúnánás	30	11	9	10	36	29	42	+7
10	Hatvan	30	9	7	14	34	43	34	-9
11	Eger	30	7	11	12	38	41	32	-3
12	Sényö	30	7	8	15	33	61	29	-28
13	Kazincbarcika	30	6	10	14	33	39	28	-6
14	KSC-RSC	30	7	6	17	30	43	27	-13
15	Gödöllö	30	6	8	16	24	52	26	-28
16	Hödmezövásárhely	30	2	2	26	13	102	5	-89

N.B. III. Kerületi TVE and Hódmezövásárhely deducted 3 pts.

WEST

		Pd	W	D	L	F	A	Pt	GD
1	**Siófok**	**30**	**19**	**8**	**3**	**63**	**25**	**65**	**+38**
2	Matáv SC Sopron	30	17	8	5	46	25	59	+21
3	Rákóczi KFC	30	17	7	6	44	19	58	+25
4	Nagykanizsa	30	15	9	6	56	40	54	+16
5	Dunaferr	30	13	12	5	52	36	51	+16
6	BKV Elöre	30	13	9	8	60	42	48	+18
7	Paks	30	14	6	10	47	33	48	+14
8	EMDSZ-Soproni LC	30	13	9	8	44	33	48	+11
9	Százhalombatta	30	10	9	11	42	44	39	-2
10	Balatonfüred	30	9	7	14	35	47	34	-12
11	Érd	30	9	6	15	35	43	33	-8
12	Budafok	30	9	5	16	43	54	32	-11
13	Veszprém	30	7	7	16	32	59	28	-27
14	Tatabánya	30	4	10	16	26	55	22	-29
15	Mohács	30	4	8	18	28	68	20	-40
16	Keszthely	30	5	4	21	32	62	16	-30

N.B. Keszthely deducted 3 pts.

PROMOTION/RELEGATION PLAY-OFFS

Pécsi MFC 0, Tiszakécskei FC 0
Tiszakécskei FC 0, Pécsi MFC 0
(0-0; Pécsi MFC 5-3 on pens.)

Matáv SC Sopron 0, Györi ETO FC 2
Györi ETO FC 1, Matáv SC Sopron 2 (aet)
(Györi ETO FC 3-2)

Diósgyöri FC 1, Fehérvár '96 Parmalat FC 2
Fehérvár '96 Parmalat FC 2, Diósgyöri FC 2 (aet)
(Fehérvár '96 Parmalat FC 4-3)

Békéscsaba 0 Rákóczi KFC 0
Rákóczi KFC 0, Békéscsaba 5
(Békéscsaba 5-0)

CLUB DIRECTORY

III. Kerületi TVE
Hévízi út
1037 Budapest
tel - (1) 1887662
fax - (1) 1887662
Year of Formation - 1887
Chairman - Péter Vigh
Coach - Károly Gergely
Stadium - Hévízi út (5,000)

CLUB DIRECTORY

Siófoki Bányász
Révész G.u. 11
8600 Siófok
tel - (84) 312443
fax - (84) 312443
Year of Formation - 1921
Chairman - János Illés
Coach - Ferenc Keszei
Stadium - Bányász (12,000)

MAJOR HONOURS
Domestic Cup - (1) 1984.

ICELAND

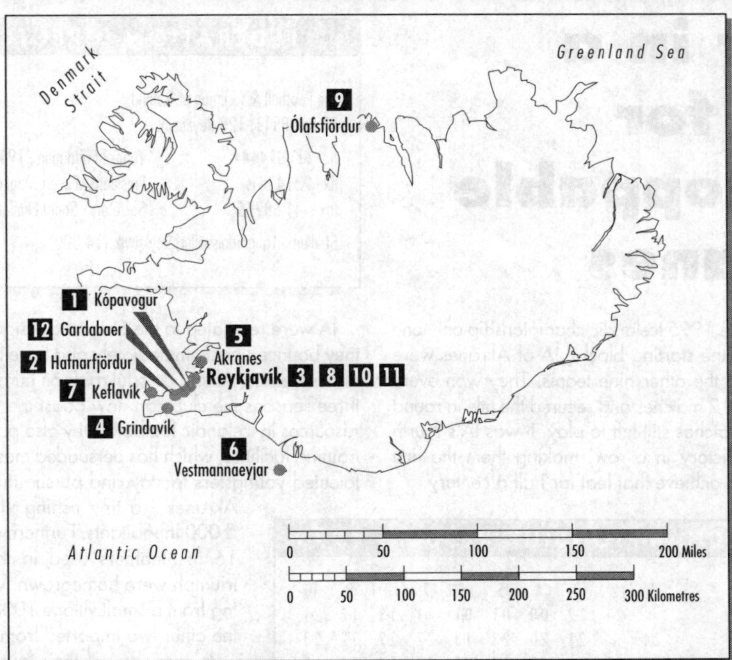

1	BREIDABLIK	550
2	FH	551
3	FRAM	552
4	GRINDAVÍK	553
5	ÍA	554
6	ÍBV	555
7	KEFLAVÍK	556
8	KR	557
9	LEIFTUR	558
10	VALUR	559
11	FYLKIR	560
12	STJARNAN	560

FATHER AND SON MAKE WORLD NEWS

Four in a row for unstoppable Akranes

FEDERATION DIRECTORY

The Football Association of Iceland
PO Box 8511, 128 Reykjavík

tel - (1) 814444
tlx - 2314 isi is
fax - (1) 689766

Year of Formation - 1947
President - Eggert Magnússon
Secretary - Snorri Finnlaugsson

Stadium - Laugardalsvöllur, Reykjavík (14,800)

In the race for the 1995 Icelandic championship only one team got out of the starting-blocks. ÍA of Akranes were streets ahead of the other nine teams. They won every one of their first 12 matches and secured the title in round 15 with three matches still left to play. It was ÍA's fourth championship victory in a row, making them the first Icelandic club to achieve that feat for half a century.

ÍA were relegated to the Second Division in 1990 but they bounced back immediately and have been champions ever since. After successful raids on Europe for the last three seasons the club can now boast the best financial resources in Icelandic football. They also possess the best training facilities, which has persuaded most of the club's talented youngsters to stay and pursue their careers in Akranes - a tiny fishing village of only 5,000 inhabitants. Furthermore, 13 of the 16 first-teamers used in the 1995 title triumph were homegrown, with one hailing from a small village 100km away and the other two imported from Yugoslavia.

In every one of their four straight title-winning seasons ÍA have also possessed the league's top scorer, only to lose him at the end of the campaign. In 1992 Arnar Gunnlaugsson went to Feyenoord, in 1993 Thórdur Gudjónsson left for Bochum, and in 1994 Mihajlo Bibercic joined arch-rivals KR. Gunnlaugsson returned home on loan in the middle of the 1995 season

LEAGUE CHAMPIONSHIP RESULTS 1995

		1	2	3	4	5	6	7	8	9	10
1	Breidablik		2-1	1-2	0-0	0-1	0-1	1-1	1-3	1-2	2-1
2	FH	2-4		2-1	2-0	2-3	1-3	2-2	2-2	2-2	2-3
3	Fram	1-0	3-0		0-2	1-2	0-0	2-4	1-4	0-4	1-3
4	Grindavík	6-3	2-1	2-2		1-2	1-0	1-2	1-0	3-2	1-2
5	ÍA	2-0	3-1	3-0	4-0		5-1	8-2	2-0	2-2	1-0
6	ÍBV	2-3	6-3	2-1	3-1	1-3		3-2	1-0	4-0	8-1
7	Keflavík	1-1	2-0	1-1	1-0	0-1	1-0		0-1	3-2	1-1
8	KR	2-1	0-1	3-1	2-1	3-2	4-2	3-3		2-0	1-0
9	Leiftur	3-1	1-2	3-1	3-1	0-2	2-1	2-2	1-2		1-4
10	Valur	0-3	3-0	3-0	0-3	1-4	1-3	0-0	2-1	1-2	

LEAGUE CHAMPIONSHIP FINAL TABLE 1995

			Home					Away					Total						
		Pd	W	D	L	F	A	W	D	L	F	A	W	D	L	F	A	Pt	GD
1	ÍA	18	8	1	0	30	6	8	0	1	20	9	16	1	1	50	15	49	+35
2	KR	18	7	1	1	20	11	4	1	4	13	11	11	2	5	33	22	35	+11
3	ÍBV	18	7	0	2	30	14	3	1	5	11	15	10	1	7	41	29	31	+12
4	Keflavík	18	4	3	2	10	7	2	5	2	18	22	6	8	4	28	29	26	-1
5	Leiftur	18	4	1	4	16	16	3	2	4	16	18	7	3	8	32	34	24	-2
6	Grindavík	18	5	1	3	18	14	2	1	6	8	15	7	2	9	26	29	23	-3
7	Valur	18	3	1	5	11	16	4	1	4	15	18	7	2	9	26	34	23	-8
8	Breidablik	18	2	2	5	8	12	3	1	5	16	19	5	3	10	24	31	18	-7
9	FH	18	2	3	4	17	20	2	0	7	9	22	4	3	11	26	42	15	-16
10	Fram	18	2	1	6	9	19	1	2	6	9	20	3	3	12	18	39	12	-21

DOMESTIC CUP RESULTS

THIRD ROUND
Breidablik u-23 0, Keflavík 5
GG 2, Thróttur R. 9
ÍA u-23 2, Víkingur R. 1
ÍBV u-23 1, Fram 5
KBS 1, Valur 3
Keflavík u-23 1, ÍA 8
KR u-23 1, Leiftur 2
KVA 1, ÍBV 6
Leiknir R. 1, Thór 1 (aet; 2-3 on pens.)
Magni 1, Grindavík 4
Selfoss 1, Fylkir 9
Sindri 0, Stjarnan 5
Valur u-23 4, Breidablik 0
Vídir 0, KR 5
Völsungur 0, FH 2
Thór u-23 3, HK 2

FOURTH ROUND
Fram 1, ÍA 0
Keflavík 4, Valur u-23 0
FH 0, Grindavík 2
Valur 3, Thróttur R. 2
Stjarnan 1, KR 2
Leiftur 3, Fylkir 6
ÍBV 2, Thór 3 (aet)
ÍA u-23 1, Thór u-23 2

QUARTER-FINALS
KR 0, Thór 0 (aet; 3-1 on pens.)
Valur 0, Grindavík 2 (aet)
Keflavík 2, Fylkir 1
Fram 1, Thór u-23 0

SEMI-FINALS
Keflavík 0, KR 1
Fram 0, Grindavík 0 (aet; 5-4 on pens.)

FINAL
27/08/95, Reykjavík
KR 2 Björnsson (39), Bibercic (84)
FRAM 1 Dadason (68)
referee - Maríasson
KR - Finnbogason; Jónsson S.Ö., Adolfsson, Egilsson, Dervic; Björnsson, Gudjónsson, Porca, Daníelsson; Benediktsson (Gunnarsson 86), Bibercic.
FRAM - Kristinsson; Ólafsson, Jónsson, Marteinsson; Gíslason, Sveinsson N. (Helgason 53), Víkingsson, Gudgeirsson, Laxdal (Haflidason 46), Einarsson (Sveinsson T. 55), Dadason.

together with twin brother Bjarki, and, incredibly, he became top scorer again with 15 goals in just seven games. Sure enough, he left the club once more at the end of the season to join French club Sochaux.

KR were regarded pre-season as the only club capable of stopping ÍA. But after a poor start they lost their chance. They did have a very good second half of the season, however, and crowned it by beating ÍA 3-2 with a hat-trick from ex-ÍA striker Bibercic. It was the champions' only league defeat of the season. KR gave their loyal supporters even more to sing and shout about when they won the Icelandic Cup for the second year on the trot, defeating Fram 2-1 in the final despite playing the second half with ten men.

The surprise team of the season were ÍBV from the volcanic Vestmann islands, coached by former German Bundesliga professional Atli Edvaldsson. Six straight wins from the end of July to early September gave ÍBV an unexpected UEFA Cup place. They played open, entertaining football and scored 41 goals. Part of their popularity with the neutrals came from their variety of elaborate goal-celebration routines, which became something of a cult trend.

The InterToto place went to fourth-placed Keflavík, who just squeezed out newcomers Leiftur. The other promoted side, Grindavík, did well to finish sixth in their first season of top-flight football. Valur, the only Icelandic team which has never played outside the top division, looked doomed for the drop before pulling off a great escape act with five wins in their last six games. But Valur's traditional rivals Fram were not so fortunate. They had a disastrous season and finished bottom of the table, joining the 1993 and 1994 runners-up FH in relegation. Their places were taken by Fylkir and Stjarnan, two clubs which had each tasted First Division football for only two short spells before.

In Europe, ÍA and KR did Iceland proud. Both teams made it through the preliminary round, with KR sampling their first ever European victory, 4-3 on aggregate against

TOP SCORERS

15	Arnar GUNNLAUGSSON (ÍA)
14	Tryggvi GUDMUNDSSON (ÍBV)
13	Mihajlo BIBERCIC (KR)
11	Rastislav LAZORIK (Breidablik)
10	Ólafur THÓRDARSON (ÍA)
8	Hördur MAGNÚSSON (FH)
7	Tómas Ingi TÓMASSON (Grindavík)
	Thorbjörn SVEINSSON (Fram)
6	Jón Thór ANDRÉSSON (Leiftur)
	Stewart BEARDS (Valur)
	Róbert SIGURDSSON (Keflavík)
	Ólafur INGÓLFSSON (Grindavík)
	Páll GUDMUNDSSON (Leiftur)
	Haraldur INGÓLFSSON (ÍA)

NATIONAL TEAM RESULTS 95/96

02/07/95	Faroe Islands	H	Neskaupstadur	2-0	Thórdarson Ó. (8), Oddsson (47)
16/08/95	Switzerland (ECQ)	H	Reykjavík	0-2	
11/10/95	Turkey (ECQ)	H	Reykjavík	0-0	
11/11/95	Hungary (ECQ)	A	Budapest	0-1	
07/02/96	Slovenia	N	Ta' Qali	1-7	Thórdarson Ó. (40)
09/02/96	Russia	N	Ta' Qali	0-3	
11/02/96	Malta	A	Ta' Qali	4-1	Thórdarson Ó. (6), Gunnlaugsson B. (27), Grétarsson (43), Gudjohnsen A. (45)
24/04/96	Estonia	A	Tallinn	3-0	Gunnlaugsson B. (6, 20, 30)
01/06/96	Macedonia (WCQ)	H	Reykjavík	1-1	Gudjohnsen A. (63)
05/06/96	Cyprus	H	Akranes	2-1	Högnason (38), Benediktsson (40)

NATIONAL TEAM APPEARANCES 95/96

Coach - Ásgeir ELÍASSON; Logi ÓLAFSSON	FAR	SUI	TUR	HUN	SLO	RUS	MLT	EST	MAC	CYP	Cps	Gls
Birkir KRISTINSSON (15/08/64) - Fram/SK Brann (NOR)	G66	G	G	G	G	G	G46	G69	G		43	-
Sigursteinn GÍSLASON (25/06/68) - ÍA	D		D	M	D60	D	D	s77			18	-
Kristján JÓNSSON (29/10/63) - Fram	D	D88		D							42	-
Ólafur ADOLFSSON (18/10/67) - ÍA	D	D	D	D	D	D	D	D	D	D	15	-
Izudin Dadi DERVIC (22/02/63) - KR	D69	s88									14	-
Gunnar ODDSSON (27/03/65) - Leiftur	M64										3	1
Arnar GRÉTARSSON (20/02/72) - Breidablik	M		s43	M79	s74	M77	M	M	M	M68	32	2
Ólafur THÓRDARSON (22/08/65) - ÍA	M	M			M	M69	M77	M	M67	M	67	5
Haraldur INGÓLFSSON (01/08/70) - ÍA	M64	s67	M71		A74		s63			s77	20	2
Bjarki GUNNLAUGSSON (06/03/73) - ÍA/SV Waldhof Mannheim (GER)	A	M	s80			M69	M63	M46	M28		18	5
Eyjólfur SVERRISSON (30/08/68) - Hertha BSC Berlin (GER)	A	A67	M80	M	s60	M	M	M			30	4
Rútur SNORRASON (28/03/74) - ÍBV	s64				s74	s77					3	-
Einar Thór DANÍELSSON (19/01/70) - KR	s64			s83							3	-
Fridrik FRIDRIKSSON (06/10/64) - ÍBV	s66										26	-
Lárus Orri SIGURDSSON (04/06/73) - Stoke City (ENG)	s69				D			D	D	D	5	-
Rúnar KRISTINSSON (05/09/69) - Örgryte IS (SWE)		D	M	M83	M74			D	D		53	2
Gudni BERGSSON (21/07/65) - Bolton Wanderers (ENG)		D	D	D				D77	D	D	68	1
Thorvaldur ÖRLYGSSON (02/08/66) - Stoke City (ENG)		M	M	M							41	7
Siggi JÓNSSON (27/09/66) - ÍA/Örebro SK (SWE)		M	M43		M	M	M	M77	M		43	2
Arnar GUNNLAUGSSON (06/03/73) - ÍA		A	A	A							19	2
Arnór GUDJOHNSEN (30/07/61) - Örebro SK (SWE)			A	A	s55	A82	A81	A62	A		66	13
Hlynur STEFÁNSSON (08/10/64) - Örebro SK (SWE)/ÍBV			s71	s79				s77	s67	M65	25	1
Thorsteinn GUDJÓNSSON (05/06/69) - KR					D	D	D69				4	-
Thórdur GUDJÓNSSON (14/10/73) - VfL Bochum (GER)					A55	s69		s46	M80	A	8	1
Helgi SIGURDSSON (17/09/74) - VfB Stuttgart (GER)					A60		s69				8	1
Ágúst GYLFASON (01/08/71) - SK Brann (NOR)					s60	D	D		s28		5	-
Helgi KOLVIDSSON (13/09/71) - Pfullendorf (GER)						s69	s77				2	-
Gudmundur BENEDIKTSSON (03/09/74) - KR						s82	s81		s80	A77	7	2
Kristján FINNBOGASON (08/05/71) - KR							s46	s69		G86	9	-
Eidur Smári GUDJOHNSEN (15/09/78) - PSV (HOL)								s62			1	-
Ólafur H. KRISTJÁNSSON (20/05/68) - KR										D	14	-
Alexander HÖGNASON (07/08/68) - ÍA										M75	3	1
Sverrir SVERRISSON (31/12/69) - Leiftur										s65	1	-
Thórhallur Dan JÓHANNSSON (05/12/72) - Fylkir										s68	1	-
Hermann HREIDARSSON (11/07/74) - ÍBV										s75	1	-
Thórdur THÓRDARSON (10/04/72) - ÍA										s86	1	-

Grevenmacher of Luxembourg. In the first round KR gave English side Everton a rough ride before bowing out of the Cup-winners' Cup, while ÍA had a similar experience against Raith Rovers in the UEFA Cup.

After promising displays against Sweden and Hungary in the spring, the Icelandic national team lost their way in the closing Euro '96 qualifiers, so ending the four-year reign of national coach Ásgeir Elíasson, who was replaced by ÍA's Logi Ólafsson. The new man got off to a dreadful start with a 1-7 defeat by Slovenia in his first match. Iceland actually took the lead and were level at half-time, but they collapsed completely in the second half and went on to suffer their heaviest defeat since August 1973. The damage to morale was not permanent, however, and Ólafsson subsequently led the team to friendly victories over Malta, Estonia and Cyprus. Bjarki Gunnlaugsson scored a first-

EUROPEAN CUPS RESULTS 95/96

CUP-WINNERS' CUP

● KR

Preliminary round CS GREVENMACHER (LUX)

A 2-3 Bibercic (50), Egilsson (80)
Finnbogason; Jónsson S,Ö. (Björnsson 46), Egilsson, Thorvaldsson, Gunnarsson, Dervic; Porca (Schram 65), Gudjónsson, Daníelsson; Bibercic, Benediktsson.

H 2-0 Bibercic (45), Porca (67)
Finnbogason; Jónsson S.Ö., Adolfsson, Egilsson, Dervic; Björnsson, Porca, Gudjónsson (Gunnarsson 89), Daníelsson; Bibercic, Haraldsson (Benediktsson 68).

1st round EVERTON (ENG)

H 2-3 Bibercic (37, 68)
Finnbogason; Jónsson S, Ö., Egilsson, Adolfsson, Dervic; Björnsson, Gudjónsson, Porca, Daníelsson; Benediktsson, Bibercic.

A 1-3 Daníelsson (22)
Finnbogason; Jónsson S.Ö., Egilsson, Adolfsson, Gunnarsson, Dervic; Björnsson, Gudjónsson, Daníelsson; Benediktsson (Haraldsson 82), Bibercic (Porca 82).

UEFA CUP

● ÍA

Preliminary round SHELBOURNE (IRL)

A 3-0 Gunnlaugsson B. (19), Gunnlaugsson A. (83), Reynisson (84)
Thórdarson T.; Haraldsson P., Adolfsson, Miljkovic, Gíslason; Gunnlaugsson B. (Reynisson 52), Jónsson S., Thórdarson Ó. (Pétursson 83), Högnason, Ingólfsson; Gunnlaugsson A..

H 3-0 Jónsson S. (45), Thórdarson Ó. (59), Pétursson (90)
Thórdarson T.; Haraldsson P., Adolfsson, Miljkovic, Gíslason; Gunnlaugsson B., Jónsson S., Thórdarson Ó. (Pétursson 63), Högnason, Ingólfsson (Thórdarson S. 81); Gunnlaugsson A. (Stojic 73).

1st round RAITH ROVERS (SCO)

A 1-3 Thórdarson Ó. (45)
Thórdarson T.; Haraldsson P., Adolfsson, Miljkovic, Gíslason; Thórdarson Ó., Jónsson S., Högnason, Ingólfsson (Thórdarson S. 80); Gunnlaugsson B., Gunnlaugsson A..

H 1-0 Gunnlaugsson A. (52)
Thórdarson T.; Haraldsson P., Adolfsson, Miljkovic, Gíslason; Thórdarson Ó., Jónsson S., Högnason, Ingólfsson (Stojic 76); Gunnlaugsson B., Gunnlaugsson A..

● FH

Preliminary round GLENAVON (NIR)

A 0-0
Arnarson S.; Helgason, Sveinsson, Mrazek, Kristjánsson Ó.; Vidarsson, Arnarson H., Toth, Kristjánsson H. (Stephensen 75); Ragnarsson, Magnússon.

H 0-1
Arnarson S.; Mrazek, Kristjánsson Ó. (Halldórsson 41), Helgason; Sveinsson, Arnarson H., Toth (Eiríksson 75), Kristjánsson H., Vidarsson; Magnússon, Ragnarsson.

half hat-trick against Estonia in Tallinn, but that match made headlines all over the world for something even rarer when, in the 62nd-minute, 34-year-old Arnór Gudjohnsen was substituted by his son, 17-year-old Eidur Smári.

It was expected that father and son would line up together for the opening World Cup qualifier against Macedonia, but Gudjohnsen junior sadly broke a leg in a youth international in May, so that particular piece of history had to be shelved (or, perhaps, abandoned). Even so, Gudjohnsen senior did have something to celebrate, scoring Iceland's goal in a 1-1 draw to take his all-time total to 13, just four short of record-holder Ríkhardur Jónsson.

INTERNATIONAL HONOURS

None

PLAYERS OF THE SEASON

ÓLAFUR THÓRDARSON

Ólafur Thórdarson's 13th season in the top flight and 12th in the national team was undoubtedly his best. The powerful, muscular midfielder captained ÍA to their fourth successive title and was voted Iceland's Players' Player of the Year for 1995. For the first time in his career Thórdarson became something of a goalscoring specialist, netting ten in the league (his previous best was three), two in the UEFA Cup and three for Iceland (he had scored just twice in 59 previous appearances). After being surprisingly dropped from the national team in the autumn, new coach Ólafsson recalled him in the spring and he went on to score against Slovenia and Malta and play against an Estonian side coached by his brother Teitur.

BIRKIR KRISTINSSON

32-year-old Birkir Kristinsson may have shared in Fram's miserable domestic season in 1995, but he remains the undisputed number one goalkeeper for the Icelandic national team. Fram's relegation sent him packing for Norwegian club SK Brann at the incredibly low cost of £10,000, but he left Iceland in style, having achieved the miraculous feat of playing 198 successive league games, i.e. 11 straight seasons without missing a match! Furthermore, in that time Kristinsson did not receive a single red or yellow card, earning himself respect and admiration from all and sundry and the appropriate nickname of 'Mr. Fair Play'.

BREIDABLIK

CLUB DIRECTORY

Ungmennafélagid Breidablik (UBK)
Knattspyrnudeild
Smárinn
200 Kópavogur
tel - 564 2699
fax - 554 0050
Year of Formation - 1950
President - Gudmundur Oddsson
Secretary - Fridjón Hólmbertsson
Coach - Bjarni Jóhansson
(96- Sigurdur Halldórsson)
Stadium - Kópavogsvöllur (1,500)

APPEARANCES 95

	P	Ap	(s)	Gls
Kjartan ANTONSSON	D	16		
Hajrudin CARDAKLIJA (BOS)	G	18		
Gunnlaugur EINARSSON	M	6	(6)	2
Anthony Karl GREGORY	A	14	(2)	4
Arnar GRÉTARSSON	M	16		1
Gudmundur GUDMUNDSSON	M	11	(5)	
Ásgeir HALLDÓRSSON	D	11		
Vilhjálmur HARALDSSON	D	2	(2)	
Thórhallur HINRIKSSON	M	6	(7)	1
Rastislav LAZORIK (SVK)	A	15		11
Arnaldur LOFTSSON	D	14	(2)	
Gunnar B. ÓLAFSSON	A		(2)	
Gústaf ÓMARSSON	M	16		1
Úlfar ÓTTARSSON	D	14	(2)	
Kristófer SIGURGEIRSSON	M	5	(3)	2
Jón STEFÁNSSON	M	12	(2)	
Grétar SVEINSSON	M		(3)	1
Hákon SVERRISSON	D	9		
Willum Thór THÓRSSON	M	13		1

LEAGUE RESULTS 1995

Date	Opponent	Venue	Score	Scorers
23/05/95	ÍA	A	0-2	
27/05/95	Valur	H	2-1	Einarsson, Gregory
05/06/95	ÍBV	A	3-2	Lazorik 2 (2p), Gregory
15/06/95	Fram	A	0-1	
21/06/95	Keflavík	H	1-1	Ómarsson
25/06/95	FH	A	4-2	Lazorik 3 (1p), Gregory
06/07/95	Leiftur	H	1-2	Lazorik (p)
16/07/95	KR	A	1-2	Grétarsson
20/07/95	Grindavík	H	0-0	
26/07/95	ÍA	H	0-1	
02/08/95	Valur	A	3-0	Lazorik 2, Thórsson
12/08/95	ÍBV	H	0-1	
18/08/95	Fram	H	1-2	Sigurgeirsson
30/08/95	Keflavík	A	1-1	Gregory
02/09/95	FH	H	2-1	Lazorik 2
09/09/95	Leiftur	A	1-3	Einarsson
17/09/95	KR	H	1-3	Lazorik
23/09/95	Grindavík	A	3-6	Sigurgeirsson, Sveinsson, Hinriksson

FH

CLUB DIRECTORY

Fimleikafélag Hafnarfjardar (FH)
Knattspyrnudeild
Kaplakriki
220 Hafnarfjördur
tel - 555 3834
fax - 565 4714
Year of Formation - 1929
President - Thórir Jónsson
Secretary - Stefán Arnarson
Coach - Ólafur Jóhannesson; Ingi Björn Albertsson
Stadium - Kaplakriki (3,000)

APPEARANCES 95

	P	Ap	(s)	Gls
Hallsteinn ARNARSON	M	18		
Lúdvik ARNARSON	A	3	(1)	2
Stefan ARNARSON	G	17		
Kristján BROOKS	A	1	(2)	
Níels DUNGAL	D	7		
Hlynur EIRÍKSSON	A	2	(9)	1
Hilmar ERLENDSSON	M		(3)	
Thorsteinn HALLDÓRSSON	M	11	(5)	
Audun HELGASON	D	17		1
Jónas HJARTARSON	G	1	(1)	
Lárus HULDARSSON	M	1	(4)	
Hrafnkell KRISTJÁNSSON	M	16	(1)	4
Ólafur KRISTJÁNSSON	D	16		2
Hördur MAGNÚSSON	A	16	(1)	8
Petr MRAZEK (TCH)	D	8		
David ÓLAFSSON	A	3	(4)	1
Jón Erling RAGNARSSON	A	15	(3)	3
Ólafur STEPHENSEN	M	11	(1)	1
Jón SVEINSSON	D	17		
Stefan TOTH (SVK)	M	11		2
Arnar VIDARSSON	M	7	(2)	

LEAGUE RESULTS 1995

23/05/95	KR	A	1-0	Ragnarsson
27/05/95	Grindavík	H	2-0	Magnússon (p), o.g. (Gudjónsson)
05/06/95	ÍA	A	1-3	Kristjánsson H.
14/06/95	Valur	H	2-3	Toth 2
22/06/95	ÍBV	A	3-6	Ragnarsson, Stephensen, Kristjánsson Ó.
25/06/95	Breidablik	H	2-4	Magnússon 2 (1p)
05/07/95	Keflavík	A	0-2	
17/07/95	Fram	A	0-3	
20/07/95	Leiftur	H	2-2	Magnússon (p), Kristjánsson H.
26/07/95	KR	H	2-2	Helgason, Magnússon
02/08/95	Grindavík	A	1-2	Ragnarsson
12/08/95	ÍA	H	2-3	Kristjánsson H., Magnússon
19/08/95	Valur	A	0-3	
30/08/95	ÍBV	H	1-3	Kristjánsson H.
02/09/95	Breidablik	A	1-2	Magnússon
09/09/95	Keflavík	H	2-2	Arnarson L. 2
17/09/95	Fram	H	2-1	Kristjánsson Ó., Magnússon
23/09/95	Leiftur	A	2-1	Eiríksson, Ólafsson

FRAM

CLUB DIRECTORY

Knattspyrnufélagid Fram
Knattspyrnudeild
Safamyri 28
105 Reykjavík
tel - 568 0342
fax - 568 1292
Year of Formation - 1908
President - Ólafur Helgi Árnason
Secretary - Jóhann G. Kristinsson
Coach - Marteinn Geirsson; Magnús Jónsson (96 - Ásgeir Elíasson)
Stadium - Laugardalsvöllur (14,800)

MAJOR HONOURS
League Championship - (18)
1913, 1914, 1915, 1916, 1917, 1918, 1921, 1922, 1923, 1925, 1939, 1946, 1947, 1962, 1972, 1986, 1988, 1990.
Domestic Cup - (7)
1970, 1973, 1979, 1980, 1985, 1987, 1989.

LEAGUE RESULTS 1995

Date	Opponent	H/A	Score	Scorers
23/05/95	Leiftur	H	0-4	
27/05/95	ÍBV	H	0-0	
05/06/95	KR	A	1-3	Dadason (p)
15/06/95	Breidablik	H	1-0	Dadason
22/06/95	Grindavík	A	2-2	Sveinsson T., Dadason
06/07/95	ÍA	A	0-3	
17/07/95	FH	H	3-0	Sveinsson T., Gíslason, Gudgeirsson
20/07/95	Valur	A	0-3	
23/07/95	Keflavík	H	2-4	Sveinsson T. 2
26/07/95	Leiftur	A	1-3	Sveinsson T.
12/08/95	KR	H	1-4	Dadason (p)
18/08/95	Breidablik	A	2-1	Gudgeirsson 2
22/08/95	ÍBV	A	1-2	Sveinsson T.
31/08/95	Grindavík	H	0-2	
04/09/95	Keflavík	A	1-1	Dadason
08/09/95	ÍA	H	1-2	Dulic
17/09/95	FH	A	1-2	Gíslason
23/09/95	Valur	H	1-3	Sveinsson T.

APPEARANCES 95

	P	Ap	(s)	Gls
Rúnar ÁGÚSTSSON	D		(3)	
Ríkhardur DADASON	A	13		5
Josip DULIC (YUG)	M	10	(3)	1
Atli EINARSSON	A	12	(4)	
Valur Fannar GÍSLASON	M	14	(1)	2
Steinar GUDGEIRSSON	D	16		3
Gudmundur K. GUDMUNDSSON	M		(3)	
Kristinn HAFLIDASON	M	1	(3)	
Atli HELGASON	M	14	(2)	
Hólmsteinn JÓNASSON	M	10	(6)	
Kristján JÓNSSON	D	17		
Birkir KRISTINSSON	G	18		
Gauti LAXDAL	M	10	(5)	
Pétur MARTEINSSON	D	16		
Ágúst ÓLAFSSON	D	12	(1)	
Haukur PÁLMASON	M	1	(2)	
Nökkvi SVEINSSON	M	9	(4)	
Thorbjörn SVEINSSON	A	16	(1)	7
Thórhallur VÍKINGSSON	M	9	(3)	

GRINDAVÍK

CLUB DIRECTORY

Ungmennafélag Grindavíkur
Knattspyrnudeild
Austurvegur
240 Grindavík
tel - 426 8605
fax - 426 8605
Year of Formation - 1963
President - Svavar Sigurdsson
Secretary - Gunnar Vilbergsson
Coach - Lúkas Kostic (96 - Gudmundur Torfason)
Stadium - Grindavíkurvöllur (1,000)

APPEARANCES 95

	P	Ap	(s)	Gls
Gudjón ÁSMUNDSSON	D	17		
Ólafur Örn BJARNASON	M	13	(2)	
Haukur BRAGASON	G	5		
Júlíus B. DANÍELSSON	M		(1)	
Ragnar EDVARDSSON	M		(2)	
Grétar EINARSSON	M	17		2
Óli Stefán FLÓVENTSSON	A	2	(2)	
Sveinn Ari GUDJÓNSSON	D	7	(7)	
Thorsteinn GUDJÓNSSON	D	17	(1)	
Gunnar Már GUNNARSSON	D	12	(2)	1
Hjálmar HALLGRÍMSSON	M		(2)	
Ármann HARDARSON	G		(1)	
Vignir HELGASON	D	3	(5)	
Ólafur INGÓLFSSON	A	16	(2)	6
Milan JANKOVIC (YUG)	D	15		4
Thorsteinn JÓNSSON	M	18		1
Lúkas KOSTIC	D		(6)	
Zoran LJUBICIC (BOS)	M	17		3
Jón Freyr MAGNÚSSON	A		(8)	1
Thórarinn ÓLAFSSON	M	2	(4)	
Albert SAEVARSSON	G	13		
Björn SKÚLASON	D	11		
Tómas Ingi TÓMASSON	A	13	(2)	7

LEAGUE RESULTS 1995

Date	Opponent	H/A	Score	Scorers
23/05/95	Keflavík	H	1-2	Einarsson
27/05/95	FH	A	0-2	
05/06/95	Leiftur	H	3-2	Gunnarsson, og (Másson), Ljubicic
14/06/95	KR	A	1-2	Jankovic (p)
22/06/95	Fram	H	2-2	Einarsson, Tómasson
25/06/95	ÍA	H	1-2	Ingólfsson
06/07/95	Valur	A	3-0	Tómasson 2, Ingólfsson
16/07/95	ÍBV	H	1-0	Jankovic (p)
20/07/95	Breidablik	A	0-0	
26/07/95	Keflavík	A	0-1	
02/08/95	FH	H	2-1	Magnússon, Jónsson
12/08/95	Leiftur	A	1-3	Ingólfsson
19/08/95	KR	H	1-0	Jankovic
31/08/95	Fram	A	2-0	Jankovic, Ljubicic
03/09/95	ÍA	A	0-4	
09/09/95	Valur	H	1-2	Ingólfsson
17/09/95	ÍBV	A	1-3	Ljubicic
23/09/95	Breidablik	H	6-3	Tómasson 4, Ingólfsson 2

ÍA

CLUB DIRECTORY

Knattspyrnufélag ÍA
Jadarsbakkar
300 Akranes
tel - 431 3311
fax - 431 3012
Year of Formation - 1946
President - Gunnar Sigurdsson
Secretary - Kristinn Reimarsson
Coach - Logi Olafsson (96 - Gudjón Thórdarson)
Stadium - Akranesvöllur (3,000)

MAJOR HONOURS
League Championship - (16) 1951, 1953, 1954, 1957, 1958, 1960, 1970, 1974, 1975, 1977, 1983, 1984, 1992, 1993, 1994, 1995.
Domestic Cup - (6)
1978, 1982, 1983, 1984, 1986, 1993.

APPEARANCES 95

	P	Ap	(s)	Gls
Ólafur ADOLFSSON	A	16		1
Árni Gautur ARASON	G	2	(1)	
Sigursteinn GÍSLASON	D	18		
Bjarni GUDJÓNSSON	M		(2)	
Arnar GUNNLAUGSSON	A	7		15
Bjarki GUNNLAUGSSON	M	7		3
Pálmi HARALDSSON	D	9	(6)	
Sturlaugur HARALDSSON	D	8	(2)	
Jóhannes HARDARSON	M		(3)	
Theodór HERVARSSON	D		(5)	
Alexander HÖGNASON	M	17		1
Haraldur INGÓLFSSON	M	17		6
Gunnlaugur JÓNSSON	D	2	(1)	
Siggi JÓNSSON	M	16		2
Zoran MILJKOVIC (YUG)	D	16		
Bjarki PÉTURSSON	A	4	(11)	
Kári Steinn REYNISSON	A	11	(2)	2
Dejan STOJIC (YUG)	A	8	(4)	4
Ólafur THÓRDARSON	M	18		10
Stefán THÓRDARSON	A	6	(7)	5
Thórdur THÓRDARSON	G	16	(1)	

LEAGUE RESULTS 1995

23/05/95	Breidablik	H	2-0	Thórdarson Ó. 2
27/05/95	Keflavík	A	1-0	Adolfsson
05/06/95	FH	H	3-1	Ingólfsson, Reynisson, Stojic
14/06/95	Leiftur	A	2-0	Stojic, Thórdarson Ó.
22/06/95	KR	H	2-0	Ingólfsson (p), Thórdarson Ó.
25/06/95	Grindavík	A	2-1	Ingólfsson (p), Thórdarson Ó.
06/07/95	Fram	H	3-0	Thórdarson Ó., Stojic, Reynisson
16/07/95	Valur	H	1-0	Thórdarson S.
20/07/95	ÍBV	A	3-1	Thórdarson S. 2, Ingólfsson
26/07/95	Breidablik	A	1-0	Högnason
02/08/95	Keflavík	H	8-2	Gunnlaugsson A. 3, Ingólfsson 2, Thórdarson Ó., Thórdarson S., og (Björgvinsson)
12/08/95	FH	A	3-2	Gunnlaugsson A. 2 (1p), Jónsson S.
19/08/95	Leiftur	H	2-2	Thórdarson Ó., Gunnlaugsson A.
31/08/95	KR	A	2-3	Gunnlaugsson A., Jónsson S.
03/09/95	Grindavík	H	4-0	Gunnlaugsson A. 3 (1p), Stojic
08/09/95	Fram	A	2-1	Thórdarson Ó., Thórdarson S.
17/09/95	Valur	A	4-1	Gunnlaugsson A. 2 (1p), Gunnlaugsson B., Thórdarson Ó.
23/09/95	ÍBV	H	5-1	Gunnlaugsson A. 3, Gunnlaugsson B. 2

ÍBV

CLUB DIRECTORY

Íthróttabandalag Vestmannaeyja (ÍBV)
Knattspyrnurád
Felagsheimild Heidarvegi
900 Vestmannaeyjar
tel - 481 2689
fax - 481 3116
Year of Formation - 1946
President - Jóhannes Ólafsson
Secretary - Ingi Sigurdsson
Coach - Atli Edvaldsson
Stadium - Hásteinsvöllur (1,500)

MAJOR HONOURS
League Championship - (1) 1979.
Domestic Cup - (3) 1968, 1972, 1981.

APPEARANCES 95

	P	Ap	(s)	Gls
Jón Bragi ARNARSSON	D	17		
Sumarlidi ÁRNASON	A	1	(11)	4
Ívar BJARKLIND	M	14	(2)	3
Yngvi BORGTHÓRSSON	D		(1)	
Martin EYJÓLFSSON	A	4	(5)	2
Fridrik FRIDRIKSSON	G	18		
Kristján GEORGSSON	M		(4)	
Tryggvi GUDMUNDSSON	M	18		14
Leifur Geir HAFSTEINSSON	A	18		5
Heimir HALLGRÍMSSON	D	6	(4)	
Hermann HREIDARSSON	D	18		1
Steingrímur JÓHANNESSON	A	18		4
Bjarnólfur LÁRUSSON	M		(13)	1
Dragan MANOJLOVIC (YUG)	D	16		1
Thórir ÓLAFSSON	M		(1)	
Fridrik SAEBJÖRNSSON	D	17		
Ingi SIGURDSSON	M	18		2
Rútur SNORRASON	M	15		4

LEAGUE RESULTS 1995

Date	Opponent	Venue	Score	Scorers
23/05/95	Valur	H	8-1	Gudmundsson 4, Bjarklind 2, Snorrason, Manojlovic
27/05/95	Fram	A	0-0	
05/06/95	Breidablik	H	2-3	Árnason 2
15/06/95	Keflavík	A	0-1	
22/06/95	FH	H	6-3	Hafsteinsson 2, Snorrason 2 (2p), Árnason, Gudmundsson
25/06/95	Leiftur	A	1-2	Árnason (p)
06/07/95	KR	H	1-0	Hafsteinsson
16/07/95	Grindavík	A	0-1	
20/07/95	ÍA	H	1-3	Jóhannesson
27/07/95	Valur	A	3-1	Jóhannesson, Gudmundsson, Snorrason
12/08/95	Breidablik	A	1-0	Gudmundsson (p)
19/08/95	Keflavík	H	3-2	Hreidarsson, Eyjölfsson, Lárusson
22/08/95	Fram	H	2-1	Hafsteinsson, Gudmundsson
30/08/95	FH	A	3-1	Gudmundsson, Sigurdsson, Eyjólfsson
02/09/95	Leiftur	H	4-0	Gudmundsson 3 (1p), Bjarklind
09/09/95	KR	A	2-4	Jóhannesson, Hafsteinsson
17/09/95	Grindavík	H	3-1	Gudmundsson 2 (1p), Sigurdsson
23/09/95	ÍA	A	1-5	Jóhannesson

KEFLAVÍK

CLUB DIRECTORY

Ungmenna- og Íthróttafélagid Keflavík
Knattspyrnurád
Hringbraut 108
230 Keflavík
tel - 421 5088
fax - 421 4137
Year of Formation - 1929
President - Jóhannes Ellertsson
Secretary - Rúnar Arnarsson
Coach - Ingi Björn Albertsson; Thórir Sigfússon & Thorsteinn Bjarnason (96 - Kjartan Másson)
Stadium - Keflavíkurvöllur (2,000)

MAJOR HONOURS
League Championship - (4)
1964, 1969, 1971, 1973.
Domestic Cup - (1) 1975.

APPEARANCES 95

	P	Ap	(s)	Gls
Georg BIRGISSON	M	6	(4)	
Helgi BJÖRGVINSSON	D	16		
Kjartan EINARSSON	M	17		3
Karl FINNBOGASON	D	14	(1)	
Ólafur GOTTSKÁLKSSON	G	17		
Kristinn GUDBRANDSSON	D	18		
Jóhann GUDMUNDSSON	A	9	(5)	4
Haukur Ingi GUDNASON	A	2	(1)	1
Hjálmar HALLGRÍMSSON	M	5	(1)	
Eysteinn HAUKSSON	M	11	(4)	1
Sigurgeir KRISTJÁNSSON	M		(5)	
Jóhann B. MAGNÚSSON	D	2		
Óli Thór MAGNÚSSON	A	12	(2)	4
Ragnar MARGEIRSSON	M	12	(3)	2
Gudmundur ODDSSON	M		(1)	
Ragnar Már RAGNARSSON	G	1		
Róbert SIGURDSSON	M	16	(2)	6
Unnar SIGURDSSON	D	3	(3)	
Ragnar STEINARSSON	M	10	(2)	1
Sverrir Thór SVERRISSON	A	5	(8)	
Marko TANASIC (YUG)	M	15		5
Árni VILHJÁLMSSON	M	7	(2)	1

LEAGUE RESULTS 1995

Date	Opponent	H/A	Score	Scorers
23/05/95	Grindavík	A	2-1	Hauksson, Magnússon Ó.
27/05/95	ÍA	H	0-1	
05/06/95	Valur	A	0-0	
15/06/95	ÍBV	H	1-0	Tanasic
21/06/95	Breidablik	A	1-1	Margeirsson
05/07/95	FH	H	2-0	Tanasic, Gudmundsson
20/07/95	KR	H	0-1	
23/07/95	Fram	A	4-2	Gudmundsson 2, Sigurdsson R., Einarsson
26/07/95	Grindavík	H	1-0	Steinarsson
02/08/95	ÍA	A	2-8	Magnússon Ó. 2
09/08/95	Leiftur	A	2-2	Einarsson, Sigurdsson R.
12/08/95	Valur	H	1-1	Tanasic
19/08/95	ÍBV	A	2-3	Vilhjálmsson, Margeirsson
30/08/95	Breidablik	H	1-1	Sigurdsson R.
04/09/95	Fram	H	1-1	Einarsson
09/09/95	FH	A	2-2	Sigurdsson R. 2
17/09/95	Leiftur	H	3-2	Sigurdsson R., Gudmundsson, Gudnason
23/09/95	KR	A	3-3	Tanasic 2, Magnússon Ó.

KR

CLUB DIRECTORY

Knattspyrnufélag Reykjavíkur (KR)
Knattspyrnudeild
Frostaskjól 2
107 Reykjavík
tel - 511 5515
fax - 511 5517
Year of Formation - 1899
President - Björgúlfur Gudmundsson
Secretary - Thorlákur Björnsson
Coach - Gudjón Thórdarson (96 - Lúkas Kostic)
Stadium - KR-völlur (2,500)

MAJOR HONOURS

League Championship - (20)
1912, 1919, 1926, 1927, 1928, 1929, 1931, 1932, 1934, 1941, 1948, 1949, 1950, 1952, 1955, 1959, 1961, 1963, 1965, 1968.
Domestic Cup - (9) 1960, 1961, 1962, 1963, 1964, 1966, 1967, 1994, 1995.

LEAGUE RESULTS 1995

Date	Opponent	H/A	Score	Scorers
23/05/95	FH	H	0-1	
27/05/95	Leiftur	A	2-1	Haraldsson, Bibercic (p)
05/06/95	Fram	H	3-1	Bibercic 2 (1p), Daníelsson
14/06/95	Grindavík	H	2-1	Dervic, Daníelsson
22/06/95	ÍA	A	0-2	
25/06/95	Valur	H	1-0	Björnsson
06/07/95	ÍBV	A	0-1	
16/07/95	Breidablik	H	2-1	Bibercic, Benediktsson
20/07/95	Keflavík	A	1-0	Bibercic
26/07/95	FH	A	2-2	Benediktsson, Bibercic (p)
02/08/95	Leiftur	H	2-0	Daníelsson, Benedeiktsson
12/08/95	Fram	A	4-1	Haraldsson 2, Björnsson, Daníelsson
19/08/95	Grindavík	A	0-1	
31/08/95	ÍA	H	3-2	Bibercic 3 (1p)
04/09/95	Valur	A	1-2	Bibercic (p)
09/09/95	ÍBV	H	4-2	Björnsson 2, Daníelsson, Gunnarsson
17/09/95	Breidablik	A	3-1	Benediktsson, Dervic, Bibercic
23/09/95	Keflavík	H	3-3	Bibercic 2, Dervic

APPEARANCES 95

	P	Ap	(s)	Gls
Steinar ADOLFSSON	D	8		
Gudmundur BENEDIKTSSON	A	14		4
Mihajlo BIBERCIC (YUG)	A	17		13
Hilmar BJÖRNSSON	M	16		4
Einar Thór DANÍELSSON	M	15		5
Izudin Dadi DERVIC	D	15		3
Thormódur EGILSSON	D	16		
Kristján FINNBOGASON	G	18		
Heimir GUDJÓNSSON	M	15		
Brynjar B. GUNNARSSON	D	14	(2)	1
Ásmundur HARALDSSON	A	4	(10)	3
Edilon HREINSSON	M		(2)	
Logi JÓNSSON	A	1	(7)	
Sigurdur B. JÓNSSON	D	2	(1)	
Sigurdur Örn JÓNSSON	D	17		
Atli KNÚTSSON	G		(1)	
Atli KRISTJÁNSSON	M		(2)	
Sigurdur ÓMARSSON	M		(2)	
Salih Heimir PORCA	M	15	(1)	
Magnús Orri SCHRAM	D	1	(3)	
Óskar H. THORVALDSSON	D	10	(1)	
Vilhjálmur VILHJÁLMSSON	D		(1)	

LEIFTUR

CLUB DIRECTORY

Íthróttafélagid Leiftur
Knattspyrnudeild
AEgisgata
625 Ólafsfjördur
tel - 466 2655
fax - 466 2410
Year of Formation - 1931
President - Thorsteinn Thorvaldsson
Secretary - Óskar Ingimundarson
Coach - Óskar Ingimundarson
Stadium - Ólafsfjardarvöllur (1,000)

APPEARANCES 95

	P	Ap	(s)	Gls
Jón Thór ANDRÉSSON	A	10	(4)	6
Sindri BJARNASON	D	11	(1)	
Baldur BRAGASON	M	10	(2)	2
Nebojsa COROVIC (YUG)	D	17		
Einar EINARSSON	M		(4)	
Ragnar GÍSLASON	M	14		1
Páll GUDMUNDSSON	M	18		6
Steinn V. GUNNARSSON	A		(6)	1
Sigurbjörn JAKOBSSON	D	16	(1)	2
Pétur Björn JÓNSSON	M	12	(3)	3
Thorvaldur JÓNSSON	G	18		
Gunnar Már MÁSSON	A	13	(3)	3
Slobodan MILISIC (YUG)	D	7		
Gunnar ODDSSON	M	18		3
Matthías SIGVALDASON	M	3	(9)	1
Sverrir SVERRISSON	A	14	(1)	4
Fridrik I. THORSTEINSSON	G		(1)	
Júlíus TRYGGVASON	D	17		

LEAGUE RESULTS 1995

23/05/95	Fram	A	4-0	Andrésson 3, Gudmundsson
27/05/95	KR	H	1-2	Sverrisson
05/06/95	Grindavík	A	2-3	Jónsson P., Gudmundsson
14/06/95	ÍA	H	0-2	
22/06/95	Valur	A	2-1	Bragason, Gíslason
25/06/95	ÍBV	H	2-1	Jakobsson, Jónsson P.
06/07/95	Breidablik	A	2-1	Gudmundsson, Sverrisson
20/07/95	FH	A	2-2	Másson, Oddsson
26/07/95	Fram	H	3-1	Oddsson, Sverrisson, Jakobsson
02/08/95	KR	A	0-2	
09/08/95	Keflavík	H	2-2	Gudmundsson, Gunnarsson
12/08/95	Grindavík	H	3-1	Sverrisson, Másson, Sigvaldason
19/08/95	ÍA	A	2-2	Jónsson P. (p), Oddsson
31/08/95	Valur	H	1-4	Másson
02/09/95	ÍBV	A	0-4	
09/09/95	Breidablik	H	3-1	Andrésson 2, Gudmundsson
17/09/95	Keflavík	A	2-3	Bragason, Gudmundsson
23/09/95	FH	H	1-2	Andrésson

VALUR

CLUB DIRECTORY

Knattspyrnufélagid Valur
Knattspyrnudeild
Hlídarenda v/Laufásveg
101 Reykjavík
tel - 562 3730
fax - 562 3734
Year of Formation - 1911
President - Theodór S. Halldórsson
Secretary - Helgi Kristjánsson
Coach - Hördur Hilmarsson; Kristinn Björnsson (96 - Sigurdur Grétarsson)
Stadium - Hlídarendi (2,000)

MAJOR HONOURS
League Championship - (19)
1930, 1933, 1935, 1936, 1937, 1938, 1940, 1942, 1943, 1944, 1945, 1956, 1966, 1967, 1976, 1978, 1980, 1985, 1987.
Domestic Cup - (8) 1965, 1974, 1976, 1977, 1988, 1990, 1991, 1992.

APPEARANCES 95

	P	Ap	(s)	Gls
Stewart BEARDS (ENG)	A	16	(1)	6
Bödvar BERGSSON	A		(4)	
Gudmundur BRYNJÓLFSSON	M	6	(6)	
Ólafur BRYNJÓLFSSON	M	6	(4)	
Gunnar EINARSSON	M	3	(6)	
Davíd GARDARSSON	M	8	(4)	5
Kristján HALLDÓRSSON	D	18		
Jón S. HELGASON	D	8	(2)	
Halldór HILMISSON	M		(1)	
Sigurbjörn HREIDARSSON	A	8	(5)	1
Tómas INGASON	G	4		
Ívar INGIMARSSON	D	7	(5)	
Jón Grétar JÓNSSON	D	17	(1)	1
Sigthór JÚLÍUSSON	M	18		3
Kristinn LÁRUSSON	A	11	(2)	4
Hördur Már MAGNÚSSON	M	11	(3)	2
Anton Björn MARKÚSSON	M	2	(2)	
Petr MRAZEK (TCH)	D	6		
Hilmar SIGHVATSSON	M	8		1
Lárus SIGURDSSON	G	14		
Bjarki STEFÁNSSON	D	17		1
Valur VALSSON	M	10	(1)	2

LEAGUE RESULTS 1995

23/05/95	ÍBV	A	1-8	Lárusson
27/05/95	Breidablik	A	1-2	Júlíusson
05/06/95	Keflavík	H	0-0	
14/06/95	FH	A	3-2	Lárusson, Júlíusson, Sighvatsson
22/06/95	Leiftur	H	1-2	Gardarsson
25/06/95	KR	A	0-1	
06/07/95	Grindavík	H	0-3	
16/07/95	ÍA	A	0-1	
20/07/95	Fram	H	3-0	Beards 2 (1p), Júlíusson
27/07/95	ÍBV	H	1-3	Gardarsson
02/08/95	Breidablik	H	0-3	
12/08/95	Keflavík	A	1-1	Lárusson
19/08/95	FH	H	3-0	Magnússon 2, Lárusson
30/08/95	Leiftur	A	4-1	Gardarsson 2, Stefánsson, Beards
04/09/95	KR	H	2-1	Gardarsson (p), Beards (p)
09/09/95	Grindavík	A	2-1	Valsson, Hreidarsson
17/09/95	ÍA	H	1-4	Valsson
23/09/95	Fram	A	3-1	Beards 2, Jónsson

PROMOTED CLUBS

SECOND DIVISION FINAL TABLE 95

		Pd	W	D	L	F	A	Pt	GD
1	**Fylkir**	**18**	**14**	**2**	**2**	**49**	**21**	**44**	**+28**
2	**Stjarnan**	**18**	**11**	**4**	**3**	**41**	**21**	**37**	**+20**
3	KA	18	7	6	5	26	26	27	=
4	Thór	18	8	3	7	28	29	27	-1
5	Skallagrímur	18	6	6	6	22	22	24	=
6	Thróttur R.	18	6	4	8	31	31	22	=
7	Víkingur R.	18	4	6	8	27	37	18	-10
8	ÍR	18	5	3	10	23	35	18	-12
9	HK	18	4	5	9	33	37	17	-4
10	Vídir	18	4	3	11	14	35	15	-21

CLUB DIRECTORY

Fylkir
Íthróttafélagid Fylkir
Knattspyrnudeild
Fylkisvegur 6
109 Reykjavík
tel - (567) 6467
fax - (567) 6091
Year of Formation - 1967
President - Gudmann Hauksson
Secretary - Gudmundur Skúlason
Coach - Magnús Pálsson
Stadium - Fylkisvöllur (1,000)

CLUB DIRECTORY

Stjarnan
Ungmennafélagid Stjarnan
Knattspyrnudeild
Stjörnuheimli v/Ásgard
210 Gardabaer
tel - (565) 1940
fax - (565) 1714
Year of Formation - 1960
President - Thórdur Ingason
Secretary - Páll Grétarsson
Coach - Helgi Thórdarson & Thórdur Lárusson
(96 - Thórdur Lárusson)
Stadium - Stjörnuvöllur (1,000)

ISRAEL

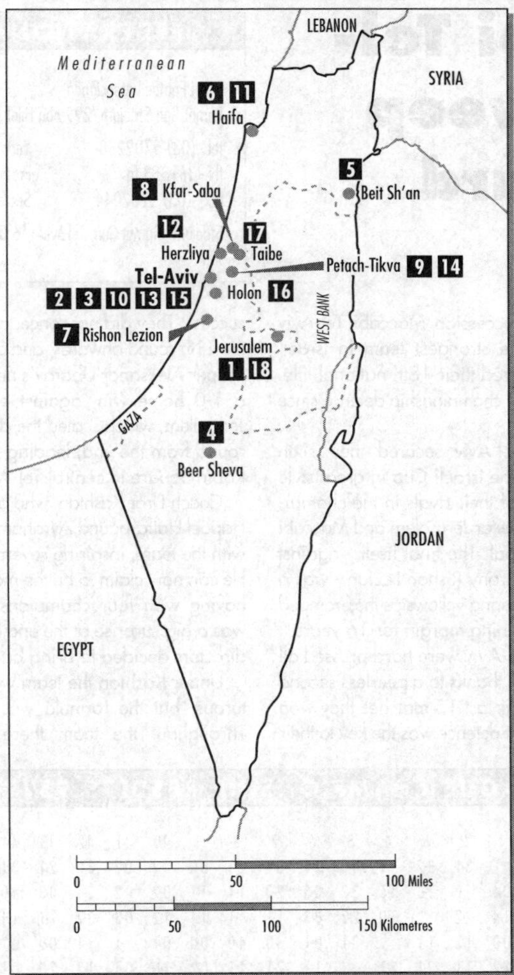

1	BEITAR JERUSALEM	567
2	BEITAR TEL-AVIV	568
3	BNEI YEHUDA	569
4	HAPOEL BEER SHEVA	570
5	HAPOEL BEIT SH'AN	571
6	HAPOEL HAIFA	572
7	HAPOEL IRONY RISHON LEZION	573
8	HAPOEL KFAR-SABA	574
9	HAPOEL PETACH-TIKVA	575
10	HAPOEL TEL-AVIV	576
11	MACCABI HAIFA	577
12	MACCABI HERZLIYA	578
13	MACCABI JAFFA	579
14	MACCABI PETACH-TIKVA	580
15	MACCABI TEL-AVIV	581
16	ZAFRIRIM HOLON	582
17	HAPOEL TAIBE	583
18	HAPOEL JERUSALEM	583

NO JOY ON INTERNATIONAL FRONT

Maccabi Tel-Aviv sweep the board

FEDERATION DIRECTORY

Israel Football Association
Ramat Gan Stadium, 299 Aba Hilell Street, Ramat Gan 52594

tel - (03) 5709238	Year of Formation - 1928
tlx - 361353 fa	President - Azrikam Milchan
fax - (03) 5702044	Secretary - Jacob Harel

Stadium - Ramat-Gan, Tel-Aviv (46,000)

For the second season in succession Maccabi Tel-Aviv proved themselves to be the strongest team in Israel. The record champions captured their 18th national title, completing their first successful championship defence since the early 1950s.

Furthermore, Maccabi Tel-Aviv secured their sixth domestic 'double', winning the Israeli Cup in great style after knocking out all three of their rivals in the championship race - Hapoel Haifa, Beitar Jerusalem and Maccabi Haifa - on the way to the final. The final itself - against relative lightweights Hapoel Irony Rishon Lezion - was a piece of cake for the all-conquering yellows as they romped to a 4-1 win, the biggest winning margin for 16 years.

In the league, Maccabi Tel-Aviv were hard pressed all season, but they won through thanks to a peerless second half of the campaign. Of their last 15 matches they won 12 and drew three. A locktight defence was the key to their success. They did not concede a single goal at home from the 11th round onwards, and only 16 goals went into goalkeeper Aleksandr Ubarov's net all season. Fittingly, it was a 1-0 home win, against early-season leaders Beitar Jerusalem, which sealed the club's championship win one round from the end, leading to extensive celebrations in Rabin Square in central Tel-Aviv.

Coach Dror Kashtan, who arrived pre-season to replace Hapoel Haifa-bound Avraham Grant, did an excellent job with the team, inspiring several players to their best form. He can now claim to be the most successful coach in Israel having won four championships and four Cups, so it was a big surprise at the end of the season when the club directors decided to bring back Grant in his place.

Under Kashtan the team were more solid than adventurous, but the formula was certainly a winning one. Throughout the team there were classy performers.

LEAGUE CHAMPIONSHIP RESULTS 95/96

		1	2	3	4	5	6	7	8	9	10	11	12	13	14	15	16
1	Beitar Jerusalem		3-1	3-2	1-1	4-0	2-1	0-1	2-1	6-0	3-2	0-2	3-0	2-1	3-1	2-0	1-0
2	Beitar Tel-Aviv	0-4		1-6	1-6	3-2	0-3	2-0	1-1	1-1	0-2	0-2	2-1	0-0	4-0	0-3	1-2
3	Bnei Yehuda	1-4	2-2		1-0	2-2	3-3	1-1	4-1	1-1	1-2	0-3	3-2	1-1	1-4	2-3	3-2
4	Hapoel Beer Sheva	0-0	1-2	1-1		3-1	0-1	3-0	4-0	0-0	0-1	1-1	1-1	0-0	0-1	1-3	0-1
5	Hapoel Beit Sh'an	2-2	1-1	2-1	2-1		1-1	2-1	1-1	0-2	1-0	0-6	1-2	2-0	0-1	0-1	1-1
6	Hapoel Haifa	3-3	2-1	4-2	3-2	3-1		1-1	2-0	1-1	2-1	2-1	1-0	4-0	2-0	3-0	4-1
7	Hapoel Irony Rishon Lezion	0-2	2-0	2-0	1-1	1-1	0-2		2-2	0-0	0-1	0-3	2-1	1-0	0-2	1-2	1-2
8	Hapoel Kfar-Saba	1-2	1-4	0-1	1-0	2-1	0-3	1-2		0-1	1-0	0-1	1-0	4-1	0-3	1-2	3-0
9	Hapoel Petach-Tikva	2-2	0-0	2-3	0-0	1-1	2-4	2-0	3-1		1-1	3-3	0-0	3-1	1-1	0-2	1-0
10	Hapoel Tel-Aviv	4-0	1-0	3-0	3-2	0-0	1-4	2-1	5-0	0-0		1-3	1-0	4-2	0-0	0-2	1-0
11	Maccabi Haifa	2-2	6-3	2-0	3-0	1-1	2-0	2-0	3-1	4-1	4-3		2-0	3-1	1-1	1-3	2-1
12	Maccabi Herzliya	2-3	3-0	1-0	1-1	3-0	2-2	1-0	1-0	2-0	0-2	1-1		3-2	1-4	1-1	0-1
13	Maccabi Jaffa	0-3	1-0	1-0	0-1	1-0	0-1	1-2	1-2	0-0	1-1	1-5	1-0		1-2	0-2	4-2
14	Maccabi Petach-Tikva	0-0	3-0	3-1	0-0	2-1	2-1	1-1	0-2	3-1	0-4	2-2	1-2	2-1		0-3	0-0
15	Maccabi Tel-Aviv	1-0	2-0	4-1	5-0	0-0	1-0	1-0	3-1	3-0	0-0	2-2	1-0	3-0	0-0		1-0
16	Zafririm Holon	0-3	2-0	5-2	1-2	2-1	3-3	1-2	0-0	0-2	0-1	1-1	0-2	0-1	4-4	0-5	

LEAGUE CHAMPIONSHIP FINAL TABLE 95/96

			Home					Away					Total						
		Pd	W	D	L	F	A	W	D	L	F	A	W	D	L	F	A	Pt	GD
1	Maccabi Tel-Aviv	30	11	4	0	27	4	12	1	2	32	12	23	5	2	59	16	74	+43
2	Maccabi Haifa	30	11	3	1	38	17	8	6	1	36	14	19	9	2	74	31	66	+43
3	Beitar Jerusalem	30	12	1	2	35	13	7	6	2	30	18	19	7	4	65	31	64	+34
4	Hapoel Haifa	30	12	3	0	37	14	7	4	4	29	19	19	7	4	66	33	64	+33
5	Hapoel Tel-Aviv	30	9	3	3	26	14	7	3	5	21	14	16	6	8	47	28	54	+19
6	Maccabi Petach-Tikva	30	6	5	4	19	19	7	5	3	24	18	13	10	7	43	37	49	+6
7	Maccabi Herzliya	30	7	4	4	22	17	3	2	10	11	20	10	6	14	33	37	36	-4
8	Hapoel Petach-Tikva	30	4	8	3	21	19	3	7	5	10	21	7	15	8	31	40	36	-9
9	Hapoel Irony Rishon Lezion	30	4	4	7	13	19	4	3	8	12	21	8	7	15	25	40	31	-15
10	Hapoel Beer Sheva	30	3	6	6	15	13	3	5	7	17	23	6	11	13	32	36	29	-4
11	Bnei Yehuda	30	4	6	5	26	31	3	1	11	20	34	7	7	16	46	65	28	-19
12	Hapoel Kfar-Saba	30	6	0	9	16	21	2	4	9	13	32	8	4	18	29	53	28	-24
13	Zafririm Holon	30	3	4	8	19	29	4	2	9	13	23	7	6	17	32	52	27	-20
14	Hapoel Beit Sh'an	30	5	5	5	16	21	0	6	9	12	28	5	11	14	28	49	26	-21
15	Beitar Tel-Aviv	30	4	3	8	16	33	2	3	10	14	30	6	6	18	30	63	24	-33
16	Maccabi Jaffa	30	5	2	8	13	21	1	3	11	11	32	6	5	19	24	53	23	-29

Goalkeeper Ubarov had a magnificent season, though his job was plainly made easier by the excellent central defensive pairing in front of him - libero Gadi Bromer and stopper Amir Shelach. In midfield, Avi Nimni, on-loan Itzhak Zohar and new Ukrainian signing Victor Moroz all had their ups and downs, but youngster Haim Hajaj, when given his chance, proved to be the discovery of the season with his buccaneering forward bursts. Up front Eli Driks had his best season yet for the club. He began the campaign on the bench but ended it as the team's leading scorer with 15 goals.

A perfect season would have been complete had Maccabi Tel-Aviv made it through to the UEFA Champions' League. They certainly had their chance. A creditable 1-1 draw in the first leg of their preliminary-round tie away to Grasshoppers Zürich (featuring an outstanding solo goal from Belarussian débutant Yevgeni Kashentsev) gave them every opportunity of making progress. But back home in Bloomfield the team were much too naïve and never looked likely to recover from the shock of conceding an early goal.

It was a bad year all round for Israeli clubs in European competition. In the Cup-winners' Cup Maccabi Haifa played suicide football against Sporting in Lisbon and crashed to a 0-4 defeat. A month earlier Hapoel Tel-Aviv had gone out of the UEFA Cup to little Zimbru Chisinau of Moldova, which left Hapoel Beer Sheva, comfortable victors against Tirana, to carry the flag in the first round

NATIONAL TEAM RESULTS 95/96

16/08/95	Hungary	A	Budapest	2-0	Revivo (18), Mizrahi O. (50)
06/09/95	Slovakia (ECQ)	A	Kosice	0-1	
20/09/95	Uruguay	H	Jerusalem	3-1	Ohana (33), Atar (57), Driks (79)
11/10/95	Azerbaijan (ECQ)	H	Tel-Aviv	2-0	Harazi R. (31, 51)
15/11/95	France (ECQ)	A	Caen	0-2	
25/01/96	Greece	A	Halkida	1-2	Harazi R. (88)
21/02/96	Lithuania	H	Haifa	4-2	Atar (23), Banin (30), Zohar (75), Turgeman (85)
26/03/96	Croatia	A	Varazdin	0-2	
30/04/96	South Korea	H	Tel-Aviv	4-5	Revivo (79, 87), Banin (80p), Zohar (90)

TOP SCORERS

26	Haim REVIVO (Maccabi Haifa)
21	Reuoven ATAR (Hapoel Haifa)
16	Alon MIZRAHI (Maccabi Haifa/Bnei Yehuda)
15	Offer SHITRIT (Maccabi Haifa)
	Eli DRIKS (Maccabi Tel-Aviv)
	Roman PILIPCHUK (Maccabi Petach-Tikva)
14	István SALLÓI (Beitar Jerusalem)
13	Amir TURGEMAN (Hapoel Haifa)
	Eli OHANA (Beitar Jerusalem)
	Ronen HARAZI (Beitar Jerusalem)

DOMESTIC CUP RESULTS

1/16 FINALS
Bnei Yehuda 5, Hapoel Bir Maksour 0
Maccabi Haifa 6, Seksiat Nes-Ziona 4
Tsairei Jaffa 1, Beitar Jeruslaem 6
Hapoel Beit Sh'an 2, Beitar Beer Sheva 1
Maccabi Netanya 1, Maccabi Herzliya 3
Hapoel Ashdod 0, Maccabi Petach-Tikva 2
Hapoel Haifa 2, Hapoel Bat-Yam 1
Irony Ashdod 1, Hapoel Kfar-Saba 0
Maccabi Tel-Aviv 1, Hapoel Jerusalem 0
Maccabi Yavne 0, Hapoel Irony Rishon Lezion 1
Maccabi Shearaym 0, Hapoel Petach-Tikva 0
(aet; 5-4 on pens.)
Hapoel Beer Sheva 1, Hapoel Kiriat Shmone 2
Hapoel Tel-Aviv 3, Maccabi Ako 4 (aet)
Maccabi Jaffa 0, Hapoel Ramat-Gan 1
Shimshon Tel-Aviv 0, Zafririm Holon 3 (aet)
Hapoel Kfar-Shalem 1, Beitar Tel-Aviv 2

1/8 FINALS
Hapoel Ramat-Gan 1, Bnei Yehuda 2
Maccabi Shearaym 1, Irony Ashdod 1
(aet; 5-4 on pens.)
Maccabi Herzliya 1, Beitar Jerusalem 2
Hapoel Haifa 0, Maccabi Tel-Aviv 1
Maccabi Haifa 2, Maccabi Ako 0
Hapoel Kiriat Shmone 0, Maccabi Petach-Tikva 1
Hapoel Irony Rishon Lezion 3, Hapoel Beit Sh'an 0
Zafririm Holon 0, Beitar Tel-Aviv 0 (aet; 4-5 on pens.)

QUARTER-FINALS
Beitar Jerusalem 0, Maccabi Tel-Aviv 1
Beitar Tel-Aviv 1, Hapoel Irony Rishon Lezion 2
Bnei Yehuda 3, Maccabi Petach-Tikva 1
Maccabi Shearaym 0, Maccabi Haifa 4

SEMI-FINALS
Maccabi Tel-Aviv 2, Maccabi Haifa 1
Hapoel Irony Rishon Lezion 4, Bnei Yehuda 1

FINAL
28/05/96, Tel-Aviv
MACCABI TEL-AVIV 4
Nimni (4), Driks (24), Bromer A. (29), Melika (59)
HAPOEL IRONY RISHON LEZION 1 Kapeta (87)
referee - Ben-Itzhak
MACCABI TEL-AVIV - Ubarov; Levi, Bromer G., Shelach, Hilel; Bromer A. (Dzilowsky 80), Klinger, Shoam (Melika 36), Nimni (Ben Luz 87), Hajaj; Driks.
HAPOEL IRONY RISHON LEZION - Elimelech; Sabag, Malukov, Ben Dov, Albert; Marziano, Tassa (Grechniev 46), Dagai (Elkaslasy 61), Azran, Koshelyuk; Shikva (Kapeta 80).

INTERNATIONAL HONOURS

World Cup Finals appearances: 1970

Maccabi Tel-Aviv's leading scorer, Eli Driks

proper against Barcelona. The Israeli media latched onto this tie in a big way, hyping it up into a major national sporting occasion. Which made it all the harder to swallow when Beer Sheva were annihilated 7-0 at home in the first leg by a rampant Catalan side. There was almost relief a fortnight later when the team from the Israeli desert only conceded a further five goals in the Nou Camp.

After suffering that hammer-blow to morale, Beer Sheva never looked likely to mount a challenge in the league and reach the UEFA Cup for the third year running. In fact, the title race was restricted to four teams - Maccabi Tel-Aviv, Maccabi Haifa, Hapoel Haifa and Beitar Jerusalem.

Jerusalem, led by young coach Eli Cohen, were the surprise package of the championship. They played very attractive football, especially at home in front of their fanatical supporters. At the midway-point of the season they led the table and looked a strong bet to regain the title won three years earlier. Several players were in good form - international strikers Eli Ohana and Ronen Harazi, Hungarian duo István Sallói and István Pisont, and new signings David Amsalem and Yossi Abuksis. But two defeats on the trot in March rocked the team on their heels and they were left with too much to do, especially with star striker Harazi out once again with injury problems.

Beitar eventually finished in third place, with just enough points and goals to secure a UEFA Cup place ahead of Hapoel Haifa. The acquisition of Avraham Grant plus several big new signings had made Hapoel Haifa one of the pre-season favourites. They did not quite justify the optimism, but their home form was the best in the league and in Reuoven Atar they had one of the most entertaining players in the entire championship. Atar scored a career-best 21 goals and provided six assists, earning himself the nickname of "Ruben" for his fluid Latin American style.

Hapoel's city rivals Maccabi finished the season empty-handed for the first time in four years. Haim Revivo was once again a roaring success, finishing as the league's top scorer for the second year in a row. And the team as a whole scored more goals than any other, with a total of 74 and at least one in every match. But in the two crunch games against Maccabi Tel-Aviv in the spring they were clearly second best. They lost 1-3 at home in the league in April and were then beaten 2-1 a month later in the semi-final of the Cup.

A number of Maccabi Haifa players disappointed. Uruguayan Edgardo Edinolfi, bought for $400,000 (a record fee in Israel for a foreigner), was a major flop. Jaded sweeper Roman Pets was loaned out to Zafririm Holon, and his replacement, the Slovakian Jaroslav Kentos, proved little better. Prolific striker Alon Mizrahi quit the team again after just ten games and went on to score his usual quantity of goals for another of his former clubs, Bnei Yehuda. Goalkeeper Rafi Cohen also suffered a confidence crisis and was frequently replaced by Israeli U-21 'keeper Nir Davidovitch. At the end of the season the team decided that a permanent replacement was needed and signed up veteran national team 'keeper Boni Ginzburg.

NATIONAL TEAM APPEARANCES 95/96

Coach - Shlomo SHARF	HUN	SVK	URU	AZB	FRA	GRE	LIT	CRO	KOR	Cps	Gls
Rafi COHEN (28/11/70) - Maccabi Haifa	G46	G	s46		G	G46	s46		s46	20	-
Felix HALFON (07/04/72) - Hapoel Haifa	D		D46	D	D		D46	D	D46	25	-
Amir SHELACH (11/07/70) - Maccabi Tel-Aviv	D	D	s61	D	D	D	D	D	D	36	-
Alon HARAZI (11/09/67) - Maccabi Haifa	D	D	s46			s46	s65			34	-
Moshe GLAM (28/12/68) - Maccabi Haifa	D	D			D	D46	D65	D57	D	26	-
Alon HAZAN (11/09/67) - Maccabi Haifa	M82	M	M61	M	M	M	M	M	M46	50	3
Nir KLINGER (25/05/65) - Maccabi Tel-Aviv	M	M46	M46	s87	M78	D46	M63	M46	M	77	2
Tal BANIN (07/03/71) - Hapoel Haifa	M	M	M	M	M	M	M	M	M	39	8
Eyal BERKOVITCH (02/04/72) - Maccabi Haifa	M85	M66		M71	M69	M	M46	M60	M60	36	4
Haim REVIVO (22/02/72) - Maccabi Haifa	M46	M		M87		M	A	A	A	23	4
Eli DRIKS (13/10/64) - Maccabi Tel-Aviv	A46	s66	s76							24	4
Boni GINZBURG (02/12/64) - Bnei Yehuda	s46		G46	G		s46	G46		G46	67	-
Avi NIMNI (26/04/72) - Maccabi Tel-Aviv	s46									24	-
Offer MIZRAHI (03/03/67) - Maccabi Herzliya	s46	A	s37		s84				A46	13	1
Roni LEVI (14/11/66) - Maccabi Haifa	s82									16	-
Avishai JANO (19/07/70) - Maccabi Haifa	s85					D	s46		s46	7	-
Gadi BROMER (05/11/73) - Maccabi Tel-Aviv		D	D	D	D		D	D	D	11	1
Ronny ROSENTHAL (04/10/63) - Tottenham Hotspur (ENG)		s46		M	M					53	11
David AMSALEM (04/09/71) - Beitar Jerusalem			D	D				s57		9	-
Arik BENADO (05/12/73) - Beitar Jerusalem			D46			s46		M	s46	5	-
Itzhak ZOHAR (30/10/70) - Maccabi Tel-Aviv			M76	s71	s78	s55	s46	s46	s46	21	6
Reuoven ATAR (03/01/69) - Hapoel Haifa			M	s79	s69	M55	M63	s60	s60	30	3
Eli OHANA (01/02/64) - Beitar Jerusalem			A37							41	14
Gadi HAZOUT (20/07/69) - Hapoel Beer Sheva			s46							1	-
Alon BROMER (05/11/73) - Maccabi Tel-Aviv			s46							1	-
Ronen HARAZI (30/03/70) - Beitar Jerusalem				A79	A84	A				32	17
Ran BEN SHIMON (08/11/70) - Hapoel Haifa							s63			9	-
Amir TURGEMAN (05/10/72) - Hapoel Haifa							s63			6	2
Golan MALUL (17/10/69) - Maccabi Petach-Tikva								G		1	-

EUROPEAN CUPS RESULTS 95/96

CHAMPIONS' CUP

● MACCABI TEL-AVIV

Preliminary round GRASSHOPPER-CLUB ZÜRICH (SUI)

A 1-1 Kashentsev (55)
Ubarov; Brumer A., Brumer G., Shelach, Hilel; Shoam, Klinger, Nimni, Zohar, Moroz (Nachman R. 86); Kashentsev (Driks 73).

H 0-1
Ubarov; Levi, Brumer G., Shelach, Hilel (Driks 17); Shoam (Melika 67), Klinger, Brumer A., Zohar (Moroz 55), Nimni; Kashentsev.

CUP-WINNERS' CUP

● MACCABI HAIFA

Preliminary round KÍ (FAR)

H 4-0 Mizrahi (9, 36, 84p), Shitrit (66)
Cohen; Zano, Harazi, Pets, Glam; Hazan, Kandaurov (Silvas 76), Levi, Revivo (Shitrit 61), Berkovitch; Mizrahi.

A 2-3 Revivo (32), Shitrit (82)
Cohen; Zano, Pets, Harazi, Glam (Balbul 46); Berkovitch (Shitrit 75), Revivo, Levi R., Hazan, Kandaurov; Mizrahi.

1st round SPORTING CP (POR)

A 0-4
Cohen; Zano, Pets, Harazi, Balbul; Levi (Adinolfi 50), Kandaurov, Hazan, Berkovitch, Revivo;Mizrahi (Shitrit 60).

H 0-0
Cohen; Zano, Pets, Harazi (Balbul 44), Glam; Levi (Mizrahi 70), Hazan (Adinolfi 59), Kandaurov, Revivo, Berkovitch; Shitrit.

UEFA CUP

● HAPOEL BEER SHEVA

Preliminary round TIRANA (ALB)

A 1-0 Zeiberlinsh (1)
Smadga; Hazout, Telesnenko, Iluoz, Biton, Elimelech, Rif (Vaknin 55), Pitussi (Haion 68), Zeiberlinsh, Avigdor, Gusev (Sagron 81).

H 2-0 Gusev (19), Avigdor (22)
Smadga; Hazout, Telesnenko, Iluoz, Biton, Elimelech (Ankri 81), Vaknin, Zeiberlinsh (Avitan S. 83), Sagron (Eliaho 74), Avigdor, Gusev.

1st round FC BARCELONA (ESP)

H 0-7
Smadga; Hazout, Telesnenko, Iluoz, Biton; Elimelech, Vaknin (Rif 32), Zeiberlinsh, Sagron, Avigdor (Eliaho 61); Avitan S. (Ankri 80).

A 0-5
Smadga; Vaknin (David 69), Telesnenko, Iluoz, Biton, Elimelech, Ankri, Zeiberlinsh, Avigdor, Sagron, Gusev (Avitan 80).

● HAPOEL TEL-AVIV

Preliminary round ZIMBRU CHISINAU (MOL)

A 0-2
Bako; Azuolay, Shraby, Lukasik, Mimer, Moskal, Shwarts (Gabay 42), Offir (Eliaho T. 87), Madar, Cohen, Eliaho S. (Avitan 70).

H 0-0
Bako; Azuolay, Shraby, Lukasik, Ben-Ami (Hadadi 30), Moskal, Offir, Shwarts (Dabah 73), Madar, Gabay (Cohen S. 67), Avitan.

Cohen and Ginzburg shared national team duties during the 95/96 season as Israel bowed out of the European Championship and set about making plans for the World Cup qualifying campaign and two big home games against Bulgaria and Russia. Shlomo Sharf became Istarel's longest-serving national coach in the Euro '96 qualifying victory at home to Azerbaijan, but the highlight of Israel's international season came a few weeks earlier when they beat South American champions Uruguay 3-1 in Jerusalem. The match was intended as a farewell for local hero Eli Ohana. He marked his international retirement in style, scoring a spectacular opening goal before leaving the field a few minutes later to deafening acclaim. Many Israelis believe that the 32-year-old is still worthy of a place in the team.

PLAYERS OF THE SEASON

HAIM REVIVO

With a total of 26 goals in 29 games Haim Revivo not only retained the Israeli First Division top scorer crown. He also netted more league goals than the entire teams of Cup finalists Hapoel Irony Rishon Lezion and relegated Maccabi Jaffa. Nominally a midfielder, Revivo was given a striker's rôle by Maccabi Haifa coach Giora Shpigel, and he more than delivered the goods with an average of a goal every 97 minutes. The 24-year-old was voted Players' Player of the Year and celebrated at the end of the season with a lucrative move to Spanish First Division side Celta Vigo.

ALEKSANDR UBAROV

He kept goal for the Soviet Union at the 1990 World Cup, but veteran Aleksandr Ubarov is now qualified as a 'football Israeli' having completed five seasons with Maccabi Tel-Aviv in the Israeli league. 1995/96 was undoubtedly his finest season yet. He won his third championship by conceding just 16 goals in 30 games and keeping no fewer than 18 clean sheets. His prowess between the sticks earned him the official Israeli Footballer of the Year award. Now aged 36 years, Ubarov intends to remain in Israel when he hangs up his gloves. He speaks fluent Hebrew and is likely to stay on with Maccabi Tel-Aviv as a goalkeeping coach.

BEITAR JERUSALEM

CLUB DIRECTORY

Beitar Jerusalem
Even Shmoel St. 13/3
Jerusalem 93715
tel - (02) 867771/385444
fax - (02) 323117
Year of Formation - 1939
Chairman - Moshe Dadash
Secretary - Avraham Levi
Coach - Eli Cohen
Stadium - "Teddi", Malcha (13,000)

MAJOR HONOURS

League Championship - (2) 1987, 1993.
Domestic Cup - (5)
1976, 1979, 1985, 1986, 1989.

APPEARANCES 95/96

Yossi ABUKSIS	M	26		2
Noam ALBUIM	M		(3)	
David AMSALEM	D	28		3
Arik BENADO	D	29		2
Ehod CAHILA	D	28		2
László CZÉH (HUN)	M	11	(1)	2
Golan DEREE	M	8	(13)	
Yaron DRORY	M	1	(6)	
Ilan ELHARAR	M	4	(18)	
Ronen HARAZI	A	18	(2)	13
Itzhak KORENFAIN	G	29		
Shmuel LEVI	D	28		2
Soni LEVI	M	2	(4)	
Shlomi MAMAN	G	1	(1)	
Eitan MIZRAHI	M	17	(10)	1
Eli OHANA	A	27		13
Roee OHANA	M		(1)	
István PISONT (HUN)	M	18		6
Nir RAYHMAN	M		(5)	
Sahar SAADO	M	1	(8)	2
Roee SAGIE	M		(1)	
István SALLÓI (HUN)	M	25	(1)	14
Sergei TRETYAK (UKR)	D	29		

LEAGUE RESULTS 1995/96

26/08/95	Hapoel Haifa	H	2-1	Sallói, Saado
10/09/95	Hapoel Kfar-Saba	A	2-1	Ohana E., Sallói
17/09/95	Maccabi Petach-Tikva	H	3-1	Saado, Cahila, Harazi
30/09/95	Maccabi Jaffa	A	0-3	
14/10/95	Hapoel Beer Sheva	H	1-1	Harazi
21/10/95	Maccabi Herzliya	A	3-2	Sallói 2, Harazi
28/10/95	Hapoel Tel-Aviv	H	3-2	Ohana E. 2, og (Mimer)
04/11/95	Maccabi Haifa	A	2-2	Ohana E., Harazi
11/11/95	Zafririm Holon	H	1-0	Amsalem
25/11/95	Hapoel Petach-Tikva	A	2-2	Czéh, Benado
02/12/95	Hapoel Irony Rishon Lezion	H	0-1	
10/12/95	Hapoel Beit Sh'an	H	4-0	Czéh, Harazi, Ohana E., og (Assor)
17/12/95	Beitar Tel-Aviv	A	4-0	Amsalem, Sallói, Ohana E. 2
24/12/95	Maccabi Tel-Aviv	H	2-0	Amsalem, Harazi
30/12/95	Bnei Yehuda	A	4-1	Levi Sh., Sallói, Harazi, Mizrahi
27/01/96	Hapoel Haifa	A	3-3	Pisont, Ohana E., Harazi
03/02/96	Hapoel Kfar-Saba	H	2-1	Harazi 2
10/02/96	Maccabi Petach-Tikva	A	0-0	
17/02/96	Maccabi Jaffa	H	2-1	Ohana E. 2
02/03/96	Hapoel Beer Sheva	A	0-0	
09/03/96	Maccabi Herzliya	H	3-0	Sallói 2, Harazi
16/03/96	Hapoel Tel-Aviv	A	0-4	
23/03/96	Maccabi Haifa	H	0-2	
30/03/96	Zafririm Holon	A	3-0	Sallói 2, Abuksis
13/04/96	Hapoel Petach-Tikva	H	6-0	Sallói 2, Pisont, Levi Sh., Cahila, Ohana E.
20/04/96	Hapoel Irony Rishon Lezion	A	2-0	Ohana E., Pisont
27/04/96	Hapoel Beit Sh'an	A	2-2	Ohana E., Abuksis
04/05/96	Beitar Tel-Aviv	H	3-1	Sallói, Pisont, Harazi
11/05/96	Maccabi Tel-Aviv	A	0-1	
18/05/96	Bnei Yehuda	H	3-2	Pisont 2, og (Levi I.)

BEITAR TEL-AVIV

CLUB DIRECTORY

Beitar Tel-Aviv
Eser Tachanot St. 2
Ramat H'chayal
P.O. Box 13248
Tel-Aviv 61140
tel - (03) 495787
fax - (03) 5218138
Year of Formation - 1940
Chairman - Bentzi Moradov
Secretary - Meir Yechzkel
Coach - Lopa Kadosh; Dov Remler
Stadium - Bloomfield (20,800)

MAJOR HONOURS
Domestic Cup - (2) 1940, 1942.

APPEARANCES 95/96

	P	Ap	(s)	Gls
Shai ABAIOV	D	6	(4)	
Yaniv ABERGIL	A	18	(8)	8
Moshe AIZENBERG	A	26		5
Doron AMAR	D	27		
Shlomi AMAR	M	12	(8)	3
Nir ARBIV	M	9	(6)	
Shmuel AVRAHAMI	M	9	(4)	
Gonen BOTEL	D	27		1
Dudi CABUDI	M	4	(4)	
Sahin DINIYEV (AZB)	M	10	(1)	
Dror EDRI	M		(1)	
Shlomi ELBAZ	M	1	(2)	
David HERSHLIKOVICH	D	26		
Itzhak IZMIRLY	M	3	(5)	
Csaba JAKAB (HUN)	M	6	(3)	1
Sasson KATAV	M	2	(8)	1
Menachem KORTZKI	G	5		
Yaron MELIKA	G		(1)	
Victor MUNDI (HUN)	M	21	(2)	1
Lubomir PAUK (SVK)	D	27		
Uddi SHNORMAN	M	7	(5)	
Yaniv SHRABY	D	17	(3)	
Arik SHRIKY	M	21	(5)	3
Sagie SHTRAUS	G	25		
Ronen SHWAIG	M	21	(4)	5

LEAGUE RESULTS 1995/96

26/08/95	Maccabi Tel-Aviv	H	0-3	
10/09/95	Bnei Yehuda	A	2-2	Amar S., Shwaig
17/09/95	Hapoel Haifa	H	0-3	
30/09/95	Hapoel Kfar-Saba	A	4-1	Aizenberg, Abergil 2, Shwaig
14/10/95	Maccabi Petach-Tikva	H	4-0	Abergil 2, Shwaig, Shriky
21/10/95	Maccabi Jaffa	A	0-1	
28/10/95	Hapoel Beer Sheva	H	1-6	Amar S.
04/11/95	Maccabi Herzliya	A	0-3	
11/11/95	Hapoel Tel-Aviv	H	0-2	
25/11/95	Maccabi Haifa	A	3-6	Shriky, Abergil, Shwaig
02/12/95	Zafririm Holon	H	1-2	Amar S.
10/12/95	Hapoel Petach-Tikva	A	0-0	
17/12/95	Beitar Jerusalem	H	0-4	
24/12/95	Hapoel Beit Sh'an	A	1-1	og (Malkin)
30/12/95	Hapoel Irony Rishon Lezion	H	2-0	Abergil 2
27/01/96	Maccabi Tel-Aviv	A	0-2	
03/02/96	Bnei Yehuda	H	1-6	Jakab
10/02/96	Hapoel Haifa	A	1-2	Aizenberg
17/02/96	Hapoel Kfar-Saba	H	1-1	og (Prizant)
02/03/96	Maccabi Petach-Tikva	A	0-3	
09/03/96	Maccabi Jaffa	H	0-0	
16/03/96	Hapoel Beer Sheva	A	2-1	Aizenberg 2
23/03/96	Maccabi Herzliya	H	2-1	Shriky, Botel
30/03/96	Hapoel Tel-Aviv	A	0-1	
13/04/96	Maccabi Haifa	H	0-2	
20/04/96	Zafririm Holon	A	0-2	
27/04/96	Hapoel Petach-Tikva	H	1-1	Abergil
04/05/96	Beitar Jerusalem	A	1-3	Mundi
11/05/96	Hapoel Beit Sh'an	H	3-2	Shwaig, Katav, Aizenberg
18/05/96	Hapoel Irony Rishon Lezion	A	0-2	

BNEI YEHUDA

CLUB DIRECTORY

Bnei Yehuda
P.O. Box 19069
Tel-Aviv 61190
tel - (03) 395444
fax - (03) 5377877
Year of Formation - 1935
Chairman - Gad Solami
Secretary - David Tassa
Manager - Ya'acov Grondman
Coach - Rami Levi
Stadium - Shchonat Htikva (8,000)

MAJOR HONOURS
League Championship - (1) 1990.
Domestic Cup - (2) 1968, 1981.

APPEARANCES 95/96

	P	Ap	(s)	Gls
Shay ADANI	M	2	(8)	
Ronen ADLAN	M	8	(2)	
Moshe AMSALEM	A	18	(2)	
József DURÓ (HUN)	M	17		
Roee FINK	M	11	(2)	
Sergei GERASIMETS (BLS)	A	5	(1)	
Boni GINZBURG	G	27		
Dmitri GURMAN	D	4		
Roee HADAD	D	1		
Itzhak LEVI	D	12	(1)	1
Offer LEVI	D	25	(1)	3
Dudu LIBERMAN	D	4	(6)	
Netsach MASUBY	A	2	(4)	
Zohar MEIR	M		(1)	
Hanoch MERARO	M	16	(6)	1
Alon MIZRAHI	A	16		13
Sahar MIZRAHI	M	18	(4)	6
Vasily MUKAN (UKR)	M	22	(2)	3
Guy NACHSHON	G	3	(2)	
Shuky NAGAR	D	9	(3)	
Bentzi ROZENFELD	M	5	(11)	2
Motti SASSON	D	23	(2)	
Igor SHKVYRIN (UZB)	A	11	(7)	5
Nir SHITRIT	D	24	(2)	1
Aharon SITON	D	16	(2)	
Nir SIVILIA	A	25	(4)	8
Y'ido SKURCHARO	M	2		
Kobi UZANA	M	2	(5)	
Igor ZHABCHENKO (UKR)	M	2	(1)	

LEAGUE RESULTS 1995/96

Date	Opponent	H/A	Score	Scorers
26/08/95	Hapoel Beit Sh'an	A	1-2	Mizrahi S.
06/09/95	Beitar Tel-Aviv	H	2-2	Sivilia, Levi O.
17/09/95	Maccabi Tel-Aviv	A	1-4	Mizrahi S.
30/09/95	Hapoel Irony Rishon Lezion	A	0-2	
14/10/95	Hapoel Haifa	H	3-3	og (Ben Shimon), Rozenfeld, Mizrahi S.
21/10/95	Hapoel Kfar-Saba	A	1-0	Mizrahi S.
28/10/95	Maccabi Petach-Tikva	H	1-4	og (Tzufin)
04/11/95	Maccabi Jaffa	A	0-1	
11/11/95	Hapoel Beer Sheva	H	1-0	Mizrahi S.
25/11/95	Maccabi Herzliya	A	0-1	
02/12/95	Hapoel Tel-Aviv	H	1-2	Sivilia
10/12/95	Maccabi Haifa	A	0-2	
17/12/95	Zafririm Holon	H	3-2	Shitrit, Sivilia, Mukan
24/12/95	Hapoel Petach-Tikva	A	3-2	Mizrahi A., Shkvyrin, Sivilia
30/12/95	Beitar Jerusalem	H	1-4	Mizrahi A.
27/01/96	Hapoel Beit Sh'an	H	2-2	Sivilia, Mizrahi A.
03/02/96	Beitar Tel-Aviv	A	6-1	Mizrahi A. 4, Sivilia, og (Hershlikovich)
10/02/96	Maccabi Tel-Aviv	H	2-3	Sivilia, Mizrahi A.
17/02/96	Hapoel Irony Rishon Lezion	H	1-1	Levi I.
02/03/96	Hapoel Haifa	A	2-4	Meraro, Mizrahi A.
09/03/96	Hapoel Kfar-Saba	H	4-1	Mizrahi A. 3, Mukan
16/03/96	Maccabi Petach-Tikva	A	1-3	Shkvyrin
23/03/96	Maccabi Jaffa	H	1-1	Mizrahi S.
30/03/96	Hapoel Beer Sheva	A	1-1	Levi O.
13/04/96	Maccabi Herzliya	H	3-2	Shkvyrin 2, Sivilia
20/04/96	Hapoel Tel-Aviv	A	0-3	
27/04/96	Maccabi Haifa	H	0-3	
04/05/96	Zafririm Holon	A	2-5	Shkvyrin, Mukan
11/05/96	Hapoel Petach-Tikva	H	1-1	Mizrahi A.
18/05/96	Beitar Jerusalem	A	2-3	Levi O., Rozenfeld

HAPOEL BEER SHEVA

CLUB DIRECTORY

Hapoel Beer Sheva
P.O. Box 4243
Beer Sheva
tel - (07) 422986
fax - (07) 422987
Year of Formation - 1949
Chairman - Eli Lahav
Secretary - Yosi Ora
Coach - Victor Hadad; Vitali Savchenko; Eli Gutman
Stadium - Municipal (17,000)

MAJOR HONOURS

League Championship (2) 1975, 1976.

APPEARANCES 95/96

	P	Ap	(s)	Gls
Eitan ANKRI	M	13	(4)	
Amir AVIGDOR	M	12		2
Sharon AVITAN	A	10	(15)	2
Shimon BITON	D	26		
Baruch DAVID	D	20	(4)	2
Idu EDMOND	M	3	(1)	
Rami ELIAHO	M	10	(6)	1
Stav ELIMELECH	M	26	(1)	2
Yussi GABAY	M		(1)	
Sergei GUSEV (UKR)	A	8	(1)	6
Gadi HAZOUT	D	26		1
Shlomo ILUOZ	D	26	(1)	
Zeljko LEKOVIC (YUG)	M	14		2
Avi PERETS	G	1	(4)	
Alon RIF	M	10	(5)	1
Oren SAGRON	M	11	(5)	2
Sharon SAGRON	M	2	(10)	1
Jacob SHWARTS	M	6		
Shaul SMADGA	G	29		
Tommer TADESSA	M	10	(1)	
Andriy TELESNENKO (UKR)	D	20	(1)	
Ilan VAKNIN	D	11	(5)	
Sharon VAKNIN	M	1	(2)	
Eli YI'SHA	M	5	(2)	
Armands ZEIBERLINSH (LAT)	M	10	(2)	2
Hisham ZOABI	A	20		5

LEAGUE RESULTS 1995/96

Date	Opponent	H/A	Score	Scorers
26/08/95	Hapoel Tel-Aviv	A	2-3	Gusev, Sagron S.
10/09/95	Maccabi Haifa	H	1-1	Gusev
17/09/95	Zafririm Holon	A	2-1	Zeiberlinsh, David
30/09/95	Hapoel Petach-Tikva	H	0-0	
14/10/95	Beitar Jerusalem	A	1-1	Avitan
21/10/95	Hapoel Beit Sh'an	H	3-1	Gusev 2, og (Krimos)
28/10/95	Beitar Tel-Aviv	A	6-1	Zeiberlinsh, Hazout, og (Amar), Gusev, Elimelech, Avitan
04/11/95	Maccabi Tel-Aviv	H	1-3	Gusev
11/11/95	Bnei Yehuda	A	0-1	
25/11/95	Hapoel Haifa	H	0-1	
02/12/95	Hapoel Kfar-Saba	A	0-1	
10/12/95	Maccabi Petach-Tikva	H	0-1	
17/12/95	Maccabi Jaffa	A	1-0	Zoabi
24/12/95	Hapoel Irony Rishon Lezion	A	1-1	Eliahu
30/12/95	Maccabi Herzliya	H	1-1	Sagron O.
27/01/96	Hapoel Tel-Aviv	H	0-1	
03/02/96	Maccabi Haifa	A	0-3	
10/02/96	Zafririm Holon	H	0-1	
17/02/96	Hapoel Petach-Tikva	A	0-0	
02/03/96	Beitar Jerusalem	H	0-0	
09/03/96	Hapoel Beit Sh'an	A	1-2	Zoabi
16/03/96	Beitar Tel-Aviv	H	1-2	Elimelech
23/03/96	Maccabi Tel-Aviv	A	0-5	
30/03/96	Bnei Yehuda	H	1-1	Avigdor
13/04/96	Hapoel Haifa	A	2-3	Zoabi, David
20/04/96	Hapoel Kfar-Saba	H	4-0	og (Aziz), Lekovic, Avigdor, Sagron O.
27/04/96	Maccabi Petach-Tikva	A	0-0	
04/05/96	Maccabi Jaffa	H	0-0	
11/05/96	Hapoel Irony Rishon Lezion	H	3-0	Lekovic, Zoabi 2
17/05/96	Maccabi Herzliya	A	1-1	Rif

HAPOEL BEIT SH'AN

CLUB DIRECTORY

Hapoel Beit Sh'an
PO Box 60
Beit Sh'an 10900
tel - (06) 581782
fax - (06) 581780
Year of Formation - 1958
Chairman - David Eliaho
Coach - Eli Gutman; Lupa Kadosh
(96/97 - Guy Levi)
Stadium - Municipal (7,000)

APPEARANCES 95/96

	P	Ap	(s)	Gls
Nissim AGABRIA	A	15	(12)	7
Yossi ALFIA	M	1	(9)	1
Yehuda AMAR	D	28		
Nini ASSOR	D	27		
Yehoram BEN GOZZI	M		(2)	
Meir COHEN	G	30		
Donat CSERVENKAI (HUN)	A	2		
Avi DANAN	M	16	(7)	
Shimon DANAN	M	23	(1)	2
Nimrod ELBAZ	M	3	(4)	
Yossi ELHARAR	A	1	(5)	
Gerka FAKUNDO (ARG)	A	5	(2)	1
Hana FARHUD	A	9	(16)	5
Jamil HADER	D	20	(3)	
Zoltán KENESEI (HUN)	M	12		
Boris KRIMOS	D	11	(6)	
Dani MALKIN	D	24		
Vyacheslav MELNIKOV (RUS)	A	10	(2)	5
David PERETS	D	14	(1)	2
Tibor SALLAI (HUN)	M	29		3
Jeki SARGUN	M	8	(12)	
Eitan TAYEB	D	23	(1)	1
Morris UZAN	M		(3)	1
Alexander YELISEYEV (LAT)	A	4	(1)	
Armands ZEIBERLINSH (LAT)	M	15	(1)	

LEAGUE RESULTS 1995/96

26/08/95	Bnei Yehuda	H	2-1	Agabria 2
10/09/95	Hapoel Haifa	A	1-3	Farhud
17/09/95	Hapoel Kfar-Saba	H	1-1	Fakundo
30/09/95	Maccabi Petach-Tikva	A	1-2	Farhud
14/10/95	Maccabi Jaffa	H	2-0	Sallai 2
21/10/95	Hapoel Beer Sheva	A	1-3	Agabria
28/10/95	Maccabi Herzliya	H	1-2	Danan S.
04/11/95	Hapoel Tel-Aviv	A	0-0	
11/11/95	Maccabi Haifa	H	0-6	
25/11/95	Zafririm Holon	A	1-2	Uzan
02/12/95	Hapoel Petach-Tikva	H	0-2	
10/12/95	Beitar Jerusalem	A	0-4	
17/12/95	Hapoel Irony Rishon Lezion	H	2-1	Agabria, Danan S.
24/12/95	Beitar Tel-Aviv	H	1-1	Perets
30/12/95	Maccabi Tel-Aviv	A	0-0	
27/01/96	Bnei Yehuda	A	2-2	Farhud, Perets
03/02/96	Hapoel Haifa	H	1-1	Agabria
10/02/96	Hapoel Kfar-Saba	A	1-2	Melnikov
17/02/96	Maccabi Petach-Tikva	H	0-1	
02/03/96	Maccabi Jaffa	A	0-1	
09/03/96	Hapoel Beer Sheva	H	2-1	Melnikov, Agabria
16/03/96	Maccabi Herzliya	A	0-3	
23/03/96	Hapoel Tel-Aviv	H	1-0	Agabria
30/03/96	Maccabi Haifa	A	1-1	Melnikov
13/04/96	Zafririm Holon	H	1-1	Farhud
20/04/96	Hapoel Petach-Tikva	A	1-1	Sallai
27/04/96	Beitar Jerusalem	H	2-2	Melnikov, Tayeb
04/05/96	Hapoel Irony Rishon Lezion	A	1-1	Farhud
11/05/96	Beitar Tel-Aviv	A	2-3	Melnikov, Alfia
18/05/96	Maccabi Tel-Aviv	H	0-0	

HAPOEL HAIFA

CLUB DIRECTORY

Hapoel Haifa
Hatzvi Blvd. 29
Haifa 32713
tel - (04) 361177/383408
fax - (04) 373881
Year of Formation - 1930
Chairman - Robi Shapira
Secretary - Avi Kaufman
Coach - Avraham Grant (96/97 - Ivan Katalinic)
Stadium - Kiriat Eliezer (17,000)

MAJOR HONOURS
Domestic Cup - (3) 1963, 1966, 1974.

APPEARANCES 95/96

	P	Ap	(s)	Gls
Eial AMAR	M	7	(7)	1
Micha ASSOLIN	M	2	(2)	
Reuoven ATAR	M	28		21
Tal BANIN	M	26		7
Liron BASIS	A	2	(17)	1
Ran BEN SHIMON	M	26		6
Assif BEN YISHAI	M	11	(3)	
Alon HALFON	D	27		2
Felix HALFON	D	29		2
Damir LESJAK (CRO)	D	28		4
Dani NIRON	A	6	(18)	2
Marian PANA (ROM)	D	6	(2)	
Nimrod ROZALES	M	8	(4)	
Nir SOHER	D	23	(1)	1
Viaceslavas SUKRISTOVAS (LIT)	M	9	(6)	2
Offer TALKER	M	24	(3)	4
Amir TURGEMAN	A	26	(2)	13
György VÉBER (HUN)	M	12	(1)	
Zoltán VÉGH (HUN)	G	30		
Hisham ZOABI	A		(7)	

LEAGUE RESULTS 1995/96

26/08/95	Beitar Jerusalem	A	1-2	Turgeman
10/09/95	Hapoel Beit Sh'an	H	3-1	Atar 2, Turgeman
17/09/95	Beitar Tel-Aviv	A	3-0	Atar 2, Turgeman
30/09/95	Maccabi Tel-Aviv	H	3-0	Soher, Turgeman, Atar
14/10/95	Bnei Yehuda	A	3-3	Atar 3
21/10/95	Hapoel Irony Rishon Lezion	A	2-0	Halfon A., Talker
28/10/95	Hapoel Kfar-Saba	H	2-0	Turgeman 2
04/11/95	Maccabi Petach-Tikva	A	1-2	Ben Shimon
11/11/95	Maccabi Jaffa	H	4-0	Ben Shimon, Lesjak, Atar, Turgeman
25/11/95	Hapoel Beer Sheva	A	1-0	Banin
02/12/95	Maccabi Herzliya	H	1-0	Niron
10/12/95	Hapoel Tel-Aviv	A	4-1	Ben Shimon 2, Turgeman 2
17/12/95	Maccabi Haifa	H	2-1	Atar, Turgeman
24/12/95	Zafririm Holon	A	3-3	Turgeman, Atar, Ben Shimon
30/12/95	Hapoel Petach-Tikva	H	1-1	Sukristovas
27/01/96	Beitar Jerusalem	H	3-3	Atar 2, Lesjak
03/02/96	Hapoel Beit Sh'an	A	1-1	Banin
10/02/96	Beitar Tel-Aviv	H	2-1	Atar, Niron
17/02/96	Maccabi Tel-Aviv	A	0-1	
02/03/96	Bnei Yehuda	H	4-2	Atar 2, Halfon F., Banin
09/03/96	Hapoel Irony Rishon Lezion	H	1-1	Lesjak
16/03/96	Hapoel Kfar-Saba	A	3-0	Banin, Turgeman, Sukristovas
23/03/96	Maccabi Petach-Tikva	H	2-0	Ben Shimon, Atar
30/03/96	Maccabi Jaffa	A	1-0	Halfon F.
12/04/96	Hapoel Beer Sheva	H	3-2	Atar 2, Talker
20/04/96	Maccabi Herzliya	A	2-2	Atar, Talker
27/04/96	Hapoel Tel-Aviv	H	2-1	Talker, Banin
04/05/96	Maccabi Haifa	A	0-2	
11/05/96	Zafririm Holon	H	4-1	Turgeman, Atar, Banin 2
18/05/96	Hapoel Petach-Tikva	A	4-2	Halfon A., Amar, Basis, Lesjak

HAPOEL IRONY RISHON LEZION

CLUB DIRECTORY

Hapoel Irony Rishon Lezion
Hapardes H'rishon St.
Rishon-Lezion
tel - (03) 9641919
fax - (03) 9666760
Year of Formation - 1940
Chairman - Uri Izersky
Coach - Vitaly Sabchenko; Victor Hadad
Stadium - New Municipal (7,000)

APPEARANCES 95/96

	P	Ap	(s)	Gls
Kobi ABRAHMOV	A		(1)	
Dan ALBERT	D	30		1
Rubi AVISAR	G	1		
Meir AZRAN	M	28	(1)	4
Mani BASSON	A		(6)	
Yaron BEN DOV	D	21	(1)	
Itamar CASSPI	M	1	(2)	
Assaf DAGAI	M	18	(4)	1
Eliezer DEKEL	D	5	(5)	
Shavit ELIMELECH	G	29		1
David ELKASLASY	A	5	(8)	1
Victor GENISH	M	9	(2)	
Yossi GORDANA	A	7	(5)	3
Vladimir GRECHNIEV (RUS)	M	10	(4)	2
Dimitri GURMAN	D	4	(1)	
Dudu HEFER	M	10	(1)	1
Nissan KAPETA	M	5	(21)	1
Oleg KOSHELYUK (UKR)	M	29		3
Oleg MALUKOV (UKR)	D	26		
Sharon MARZIANO	D	27		
Vyacheslav MELNIKOV (RUS)	A	8		1
Moshe SABAG	D	15	(10)	1
Assaf SHEMESH	M		(1)	
Nir SHIKVA	A	15	(8)	5
Oren TASSA	M	11	(1)	
Oded TZHI	M	16	(1)	

LEAGUE RESULTS 1995/96

Date	Opponent	H/A	Score	Scorers
26/08/95	Maccabi Herzliya	A	0-1	
10/09/95	Maccabi Tel-Aviv	H	1-2	Melnikov
17/09/95	Hapoel Tel-Aviv	A	1-2	Shikva
30/09/95	Bnei Yehuda	H	2-0	Azran, Hefer
14/10/95	Maccabi Haifa	A	0-2	
21/10/95	Hapoel Haifa	H	0-2	
28/10/95	Zafririm Holon	A	2-1	Gordana, Shikva
04/11/95	Hapoel Kfar-Saba	H	2-2	Gordana, Azran
11/11/95	Hapoel Petach-Tikva	A	0-2	
25/11/95	Maccabi Petach-Tikva	H	0-2	
02/12/95	Beitar Jerusalem	A	1-0	Koshelyuk
10/12/95	Maccabi Jaffa	H	1-0	Azran
17/12/95	Hapoel Beit Sh'an	A	1-2	Dagai
24/12/95	Hapoel Beer Sheva	H	1-1	Gordana
30/12/95	Beitar Tel-Aviv	A	0-2	
27/01/96	Maccabi Herzliya	H	2-1	Koshelyuk, Shikva
03/02/96	Maccabi Tel-Aviv	A	0-1	
10/02/96	Hapoel Tel-Aviv	H	0-1	
17/02/96	Bnei Yehuda	A	1-1	Albert
02/03/96	Maccabi Haifa	H	0-3	
09/03/96	Hapoel Haifa	A	1-1	Koshelyuk
16/03/96	Zafririm Holon	H	1-2	Azran
23/03/96	Hapoel Kfar-Saba	A	2-1	Grechniev 2
30/03/96	Hapoel Petach-Tikva	H	0-0	
13/04/96	Maccabi Petach-Tikva	A	1-1	Shikva
20/04/96	Beitar Jerusalem	H	0-2	
27/04/96	Maccabi Jaffa	A	2-1	Elkaslasy, Sabag
04/05/96	Hapoel Beit Sh'an	H	1-1	Elimelech
11/05/96	Hapoel Beer Sheva	A	0-3	
18/05/96	Beitar Tel-Aviv	H	2-0	Shikva, Kapeta

HAPOEL KFAR-SABA

CLUB DIRECTORY

Hapoel Kfar-Saba
P.O. Box 13
Kfar-Saba
tel - (09) 950588
fax - (09) 958116
Year of Formation - 1928
Chairman - Israel Neon
Manager - Eli Yani; Avi Cohen
Coach - Noach Aiynshtien
Stadium - Kfar-Saba (7,500)

MAJOR HONOURS
League Championship - (1) 1982.
Domestic Cup - (3) 1975, 1980, 1990.

APPEARANCES 95/96

	P	Ap	(s)	Gls
Eran AZAR	D	20	(4)	
Rami AZIZ	M	5	(1)	
Tamir BEN-HAIM	M	19		
Yariv BLOMBERG	D	6	(4)	
Dariusz DZWIGALA (POL)	M	7		
Oren FLASH	M	8	(3)	2
Oren HAJAJ	D	2	(8)	
Nir IONAY	M	12	(2)	1
Abdel KADAR-RADA	D	3		
Shmuel KORATZKY	D	8		
Valery KORLENCHUK (UKR)	A	9	(1)	
Andriy LAZOVSKY (UKR)	D	29		1
Gábor MÁRTON (HUN)	M	25		3
Guy MESSIKA	D	10	(2)	2
Eran PRIZANT	M	6	(4)	1
Kobi REFUA	A	24	(2)	11
Gaby SAPIR	D	25	(1)	
Ishay SASSON	G	5		
Ya'akov SAYMON	D	5	(10)	
Eran SHAIZINGER	G	25		
Natan SHAKURY	D	7	(3)	
Tomer SHEM-TOV	D	17	(4)	
Idan SHUM	M	3	(1)	
Dudi STOLPER	M	14	(8)	
Ahmed TAHA	M		(8)	
Eli TZOREF	A	14	(13)	2
Motti YEBERBAUM	M	22	(7)	6

LEAGUE RESULTS 1995/96

26/08/95	Hapoel Petach-Tikva	A	1-3	Yeberbaum
10/09/95	Beitar Jerusalem	H	1-2	Lozovsky
17/09/95	Hapoel Beit Sh'an	A	1-1	Messika
30/09/95	Beitar Tel-Aviv	H	1-4	Márton
14/10/95	Maccabi Tel-Aviv	A	1-3	Yeberbaum
21/10/95	Bnei Yehuda	H	0-1	
28/10/95	Hapoel Haifa	A	0-2	
04/11/95	Hapoel Irony Rishon Lezion	A	2-2	Refua 2
11/11/95	Maccabi Petach-Tikva	A	0-3	
25/11/95	Maccabi Jaffa	A	2-1	Yeberbaum, Márton
02/12/95	Hapoel Beer Sheva	H	1-0	Refua
10/12/95	Maccabi Herzliya	A	0-1	
17/12/95	Hapoel Tel-Aviv	H	1-0	Tzoref
24/12/95	Maccabi Haifa	A	1-3	Refua
30/12/95	Zafririm Holon	H	3-0	Tzoref, Refua, Yeberbaum
27/01/96	Hapoel Petach-Tikva	H	0-1	
03/02/96	Beitar Jerusalem	A	1-2	Messika
10/02/96	Hapoel Beit Sh'an	H	2-1	Ionay, Yeberbaum
17/02/96	Beitar Tel-Aviv	A	1-1	Refua
02/03/96	Maccabi Tel-Aviv	H	1-2	Yeberbaum
09/03/96	Bnei Yehuda	A	1-4	Refua
16/03/96	Hapoel Haifa	H	0-3	
23/03/96	Hapoel Irony Rishon Lezion	H	1-2	Refua
30/03/96	Maccabi Petach-Tikva	A	2-0	Flash, Prizant
13/04/96	Maccabi Jaffa	H	4-1	Refua 2, Flash, Márton
20/04/96	Hapoel Beer Sheva	A	0-4	
27/04/96	Maccabi Herzliya	H	1-0	Refua
04/05/96	Hapoel Tel-Aviv	A	0-5	
11/05/96	Maccabi Haifa	H	0-1	
18/05/96	Zafririm Holon	A	0-0	

HAPOEL PETACH-TIKVA

CLUB DIRECTORY

Hapoel Petach-Tikva
P.O. Box 2108
Volfson St. 39
Petach-Tikva
tel - (03) 9218352
fax - (03) 7522906
Year of Formation - 1930
Chairman - Lior Shahar
Manager - Gay Levi
Coach - Eli Machpud (96/97 - Nir Levin)
Stadium - Hapoel Petach-Tikva (7,500)

MAJOR HONOURS
League Championship - (6)
1955, 1959, 1960, 1961, 1962, 1963.
Domestic Cup - (2) 1957, 1992.

APPEARANCES 95/96

	P	Ap	(s)	Gls
Eli ABARBNEL	M	20	(7)	3
Daniel ABAS	M	1	(2)	
Mark ADOSSY (GHA)	M	9	(5)	
Walid BADIR	D	28		
Gabriel BALLOMI (ARG)	M		(1)	
Effi BASSON	M		(10)	
Meni BASSON	A	2	(8)	
Ilan BUARON	D	22	(1)	
Tomasz CEBULA (POL)	A	18	(9)	3
Israel COHEN	D	25	(1)	
Avi FLETCHER	D	28		3
Oren GABAY	M		(1)	1
Manor HASSAN	A	22	(7)	4
Yaniv HERMRSH	M		(2)	
Yuaab HERSHKO	M	10	(2)	
Shay HESS	G	30		
Motti KAKUN	A	24	(4)	10
Adoram KEISSY	D	13	(1)	3
Offir KOPEL	A	27		
Beni KOZOSHVILI	D	27		
Alon MAYA	A	17	(9)	3
Carmelo MICCICHE (FRA)	M	4	(7)	
Ooni RIAN	M	3	(2)	
Guy SHAMIR	M		(1)	

LEAGUE RESULTS 1995/96

Date	Opponent	H/A	Score	Scorers
26/08/95	Hapoel Kfar-Saba	H	3-1	Hassan 2, Kakun
10/09/95	Maccabi Petach-Tikva	A	1-3	Cebula
17/09/95	Maccabi Jaffa	H	3-1	Kakun 2, Hassan
30/09/95	Hapoel Beer Sheva	A	0-0	
14/10/95	Maccabi Herzliya	H	0-0	
21/10/95	Hapoel Tel-Aviv	A	0-0	
28/10/95	Maccabi Haifa	H	3-3	Kakun 2, Abarbnel
04/11/95	Zafririm Holon	A	2-0	Maya, Kakun
11/11/95	Hapoel Irony Rishon Lezion	H	2-0	Maya, Kakun
25/11/95	Beitar Jerusalem	H	2-2	Keissy, og (Benado)
02/12/95	Hapoel Beit Sh'an	A	2-0	Kakun, Keissy
10/12/95	Beitar Tel-Aviv	H	0-0	
17/12/95	Maccabi Tel-Aviv	A	0-3	
24/12/95	Bnei Yehuda	H	2-3	Fletcher, Abarbnel
30/12/95	Hapoel Haifa	A	1-1	Keissy
27/01/96	Hapoel Kfar-Saba	A	1-0	Kakun
03/02/96	Maccabi Petach-Tikva	H	1-1	Cebula
09/02/96	Maccabi Jaffa	A	0-0	
17/02/96	Hapoel Beer Sheva	H	0-0	
02/03/96	Maccabi Herzliya	A	0-2	
09/03/96	Hapoel Tel-Aviv	H	1-1	Kakun
16/03/96	Maccabi Haifa	A	1-4	Abarbnel
23/03/96	Zafririm Holon	H	1-0	Maya
30/03/96	Hapoel Irony Rishon Lezion	A	0-0	
13/04/96	Beitar Jerusalem	A	0-6	
20/04/96	Hapoel Beit Sh'an	H	1-1	Fletcher
27/04/96	Beitar Tel-Aviv	A	1-1	Hassan
04/05/96	Maccabi Tel-Aviv	H	0-2	
11/05/96	Bnei Yehuda	A	1-1	Cebula
18/05/96	Hapoel Haifa	H	2-4	Fletcher, Gabay

HAPOEL TEL-AVIV

CLUB DIRECTORY

Hapoel Tel-Aviv
P.O. Box 8402
Tel-Aviv
tel - (03) 6827711
fax - (03) 6827722
Year of Formation - 1927
Chairman - Yuval Ron
Secretary - Anye Hershkovits
Manager - Moshe Sinai
Coach - Ya'acob Cohen-Tsedek
Stadium - Bloomfield (20,800)

MAJOR HONOURS
League Championship - (12)
1934, 1935, 1936, 1938, 1940, 1943, 1957, 1966, 1969, 1981, 1986, 1988.
Domestic Cup - (7)
1928, 1934, 1937, 1938, 1940, 1960, 1972.

APPEARANCES 95/96

	P	Ap	(s)	Gls
Nissim AVITAN	A	18	(12)	12
Avi AZUOLAY	D	26		
Jaroslaw BAKO (POL)	G	30		
Yossi BALAS	M	14		
Eyal BEN AMI	D	5	(8)	1
Eyal COHEN	D	7	(6)	
Shahar COHEN	M	4	(12)	
Avi DABAH	M	2	(4)	
Sagiv ELIAHO	A	11	(8)	6
Tommer ELIAHO	M	11	(6)	1
Motti FLITER	D	6	(1)	
Ronen GABAY	M	1	(5)	
Shimon GERSHON	D	3		
Kobi HADADI	D	25	(2)	1
Yossi LEVI	M	6	(1)	
Yaron LICHTERMAN	G		(2)	
Hagay LUK	M	9		
Damian LUKASIK (POL)	D	13		
Yossi MADAR	M	17	(8)	9
Sharon MIMER	M	25		1
Kazimierz MOSKAL (POL)	M	26		5
Alon OFFIR	M	24	(1)	4
Sergei POGODIN (UKR)	M	13		3
Guy SHRABY	D	23	(5)	
Jacob SHWARTS	M	1	(1)	
Shalom TIKVA	M	10	(1)	3

LEAGUE RESULTS 1995/96

26/08/95	Hapoel Beer Sheva	H	3-2	Madar, Avitan 2
10/09/95	Maccabi Herzliya	A	2-0	Avitan, Madar
17/09/95	Hapoel Irony Rishon Lezion	H	2-1	Offir, Ben Ami
30/09/95	Maccabi Haifa	H	1-3	Avitan
14/10/95	Zafririm Holon	A	1-0	Avitan
21/10/95	Hapoel Petach-Tikva	H	0-0	
28/10/95	Beitar Jerusalem	A	2-3	Mimer, Eliaho T.
04/11/95	Hapoel Beit Sh'an	H	0-0	
11/11/95	Beitar Tel-Aviv	A	2-0	Eliaho S. 2
25/11/95	Maccabi Tel-Aviv	H	0-2	
02/12/95	Bnei Yehuda	A	2-1	Moskal, og (Amsalem)
10/12/95	Hapoel Haifa	H	1-4	Offir
17/12/95	Hapoel Kfar-Saba	A	0-1	
24/12/95	Maccabi Petach-Tikva	H	0-0	
30/12/95	Maccabi Jaffa	A	1-1	Avitan
27/01/96	Hapoel Beer Sheva	A	1-0	Pogodin
03/02/96	Maccabi Herzliya	H	1-0	Moskal
10/02/96	Hapoel Irony Rishon Lezion	A	1-0	Moskal
17/02/96	Maccabi Haifa	A	3-4	Eliaho S., Offir, Pogodin
02/03/96	Zafririm Holon	H	1-0	Eliaho S.
09/03/96	Hapoel Petach-Tikva	A	1-1	Moskal
16/03/96	Beitar Jerusalem	H	4-0	Tikva 2, Eliaho S. 2, Moskal
23/03/96	Hapoel Beit Sh'an	A	0-1	
30/03/96	Beitar Tel-Aviv	H	1-0	Avitan
13/04/96	Maccabi Tel-Aviv	A	0-0	
20/04/96	Bnei Yehuda	H	3-0	Avitan, Madar, Eliaho S.
27/04/96	Hapoel Haifa	A	1-2	Avitan
04/05/96	Hapoel Kfar-Saba	H	5-0	Madar 4, Offir
11/05/96	Maccabi Petach-Tikva	A	4-0	Avitan 2, Madar 2
18/05/96	Maccabi Jaffa	H	4-2	Hadadi, Pogodin, Tikva, Avitan

SPL
HNS
·ASSOCIATION·
URBSF
KBV

COLOUR INDEX

Plate No.

Federations & National Teams

3 ALBANIA - AZERBAIJAN
4 BELARUS - CROATIA
5 CYPRUS - ENGLAND
6 ESTONIA - FRANCE
7 GEORGIA - HOLLAND
8 HUNGARY - ITALY
9 LATVIA - LUXEMBOURG
10 MACEDONIA - N. IRELAND
11 NORWAY - REP. OF IRELAND
12 ROMANIA - SCOTLAND
13 SLOVAKIA - SWEDEN
14 SWITZERLAND - WALES

Clubs

16 ALBANIA
18 AUSTRIA
20 BELGIUM
22 BULGARIA
24 CROATIA
26 CYPRUS
28 CZECH REPUBLIC
30 DENMARK
32 ENGLAND
34 FAROE ISLANDS
36 FINLAND
38 FRANCE
40 GERMANY
42 GREECE
44 HOLLAND
46 HUNGARY
48 ICELAND
50 ISRAEL
52 ITALY
54 LUXEMBOURG
56 MALTA
58 NORTHERN IRELAND
60 NORWAY
62 POLAND
64 PORTUGAL
66 REPUBLIC OF IRELAND
68 ROMANIA
70 RUSSIA
72 SAN MARINO
74 SCOTLAND
76 SLOVAKIA
78 SLOVENIA
80 SPAIN
82 SWEDEN
84 SWITZERLAND
86 TURKEY
88 UKRAINE
90 WALES
92 YUGOSLAVIA
94 MISCELLANEOUS
96 CUP WINNERS 1995/96

NATIONAL FEDERATIONS

NATIONAL FEDERATIONS

FIRST KIT **BELARUS** SECOND KIT

FIRST KIT **BELGIUM** SECOND KIT

FIRST KIT **BULGARIA** SECOND KIT

FIRST KIT **CROATIA** SECOND KIT

NATIONAL FEDERATIONS

FIRST KIT | **CYPRUS** | SECOND KIT

FIRST KIT | **CZECH REPUBLIC** | SECOND KIT

FIRST KIT | **DENMARK** | SECOND KIT

FIRST KIT | **ENGLAND** | SECOND KIT

NATIONAL FEDERATIONS

FIRST KIT
ESTONIA
SECOND KIT

FIRST KIT
FAROE ISLANDS
SECOND KIT

FIRST KIT
FINLAND
SECOND KIT

FIRST KIT
FRANCE
SECOND KIT

NATIONAL FEDERATIONS

NATIONAL FEDERATIONS

FIRST KIT | **HUNGARY** | SECOND KIT

FIRST KIT | **ICELAND** | SECOND KIT

FIRST KIT | **ISRAEL** | SECOND KIT

FIRST KIT | **ITALY** | SECOND KIT

NATIONAL FEDERATIONS

FIRST KIT | **LATVIA** | SECOND KIT

FIRST KIT | **LIECHTENSTEIN** | SECOND KIT

FIRST KIT | **LITHUANIA** | SECOND KIT

FIRST KIT | **LUXEMBOURG** | SECOND KIT

NATIONAL FEDERATIONS

FIRST KIT **MACEDONIA** SECOND KIT

FIRST KIT **MALTA** SECOND KIT

FIRST KIT **MOLDOVA** SECOND KIT

FIRST KIT **NORTHERN IRELAND** SECOND KIT

NATIONAL FEDERATIONS

FIRST KIT NORWAY SECOND KIT

FIRST KIT POLAND SECOND KIT

FIRST KIT PORTUGAL SECOND KIT

FIRST KIT REPUBLIC OF IRELAND SECOND KIT

NATIONAL FEDERATIONS

FIRST KIT | ROMANIA | SECOND KIT

FIRST KIT | RUSSIA | SECOND KIT

FIRST KIT | SAN MARINO | SECOND KIT

FIRST KIT | SCOTLAND | SECOND KIT

NATIONAL FEDERATIONS

FIRST KIT

SLOVAKIA

SECOND KIT

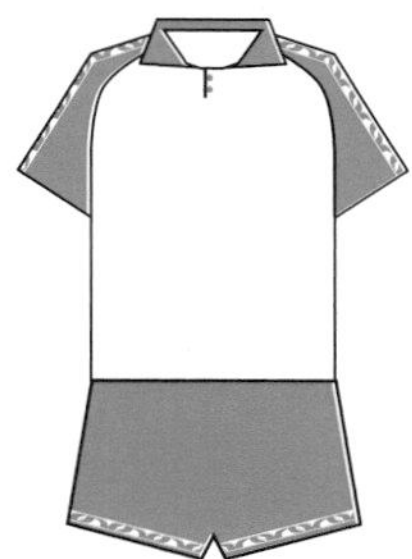

FIRST KIT

NOGOMETNA ZVEZA SLOVENIJE
NZS

SLOVENIA

SECOND KIT

FIRST KIT

SPAIN

SECOND KIT

FIRST KIT

SWEDEN

SECOND KIT

NATIONAL FEDERATIONS

THAMPTON FC
HJK
MKS "ODRA"
WODZISŁAW ŚLĄSKI
ÖSK
ÖREBRO SPORTKLUBB
PARIS S
-GERMAIN
B.F.
BARR

ALBANIA

ALBPETROL PATOS
APOLONIA FIER
BESA KAVAJË
BESËLIDHJA LEZHË
ELBASANI
FLAMURTARI VLORË
KASTRIOTI KRUJË
LAÇI
OLIMPIK TIRANË
PARTIZANI TIRANË
SHKUMBINI PEQIN
SHQIPONJA GJIROKASTËR
SKËNDERBEU KORÇË
SOPOTI LIBRAZHD
TEUTA DURRËS
TIRANA
TOMORI BERAT
VLLAZNIA SHKODËR
LUSHNË
BYLIS BALLSHI

ALBANIA

ALBPETROL PATOS

APOLONIA FIER

BESA KAVAJË

BESËLIDHJA LEZHË

ELBASANI

FLAMURTARI VLORË

KASTRIOTI KRUJË

LAÇI

OLIMPIK TIRANË

PARTIZANI TIRANË

SHKUMBINI PEQIN

SHQIPONJA GJIROKASTËR

SKËNDERBEU KORÇË

SOPOTI LIBRAZHD

TEUTA DURRËS

TIRANA

TOMORI BERAT

VLLAZNIA SHKODËR

LUSHNË

BYLIS BALLSHI

AUSTRIA

FC ADMIRA WACKER
FK AUSTRIA WIEN
GRAZER AK
LASK LINZ
SK RAPID WIEN
SV RIED
SV CASINO SALZBURG
SK VORWÄRTS STEYR
SK STURM GRAZ
FC TIROL INNSBRUCK
FC LINZ

AUSTRIA

FC ADMIRA WACKER

FK AUSTRIA WIEN

GRAZER AK

LASK LINZ

SK RAPID WIEN

SV RIED

SV CASINO SALZBURG

SK VORWÄRTS STEYR

SK STURM GRAZ

FC TIROL INNSBRUCK

FC LINZ

BELGIUM

RSC ANDERLECHT
ROYAL ANTWERP FC
KSK BEVEREN
KSV CERCLE BRUGGE
CLUB BRUGGE KV
RSC CHARLEROI
KSC EENDRACHT AALST
KAA GENT
KFC GERMINAL EKEREN
KRC HARELBEKE
K LIERSE SK
KFC LOMMELSE SK
KV MECHELEN
RWD MOLENBEEK
RFC SERAING
K ST.-TRUIDENSE VV
R STANDARD LIEGE
KSV WAREGEM
KSC LOKEREN
KRC GENK
R EXCELSIOR MOUSCRON

BELGIUM

RSC ANDERLECHT

ROYAL ANTWERP FC

KSK BEVEREN

KSV CERCLE BRUGGE

CLUB BRUGGE KV

RSC CHARLEROI

KSC EENDRACHT AALST

KAA GENT

KFC GERMINAL EKEREN

KRC HARELBEKE

K LIERSE SK

KFC LOMMELSE SK

KV MECHELEN

RWD MOLENBEEK

RFC SERAING

K ST.-TRUIDENSE VV

R STANDARD LIEGE

KSV WAREGEM

KSC LOKEREN

KRC GENK

R EXCELSIOR MOUSCRON

BULGARIA

BOTEV PLOVDIV

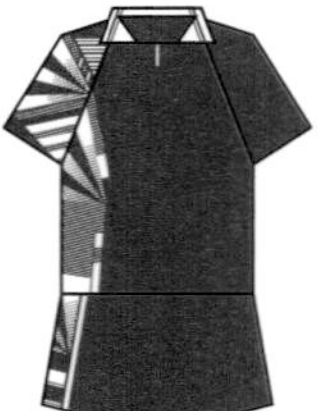
CSKA SOFIA

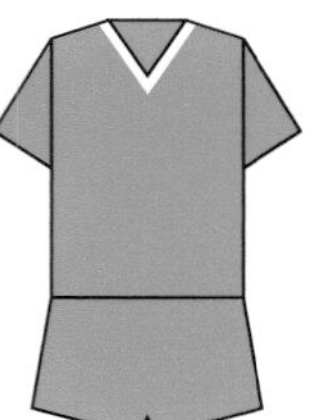
DOBRUDZHA DOBRICH

ETAR VELIKO TARNOVO

LEVSKI KIUSTENDIL

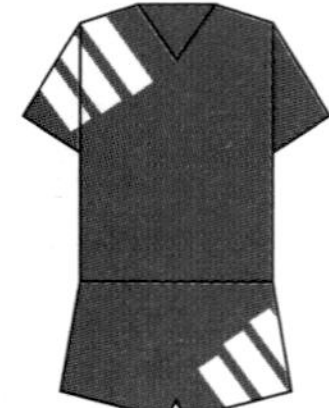
LEVSKI SOFIA

LOKOMOTIV PLOVDIV

LOKOMOTIV SOFIA

LOVECH

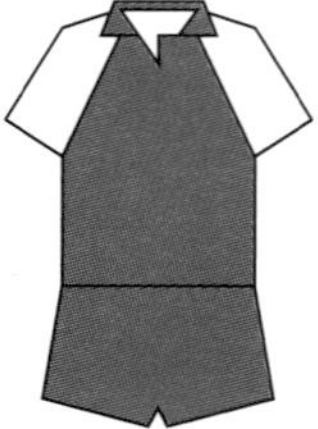
MONTANA

NEFTOCHIMIK BOURGAS

RAKOVSKI RUSE

SHUMEN

SLAVIA SOFIA

SPARTAK PLOVDIV

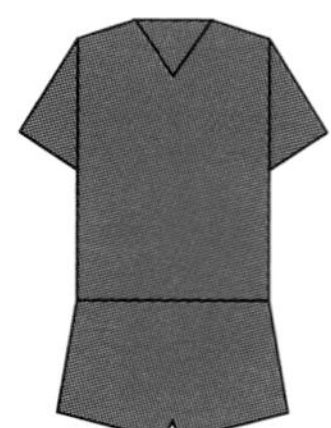
SPARTAK VARNA

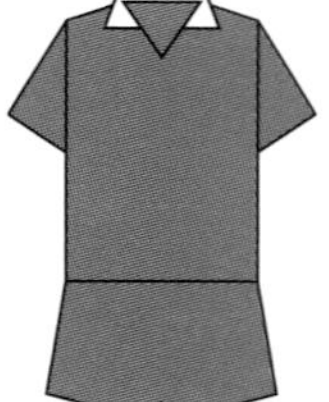
SPARTAK PLEVEN

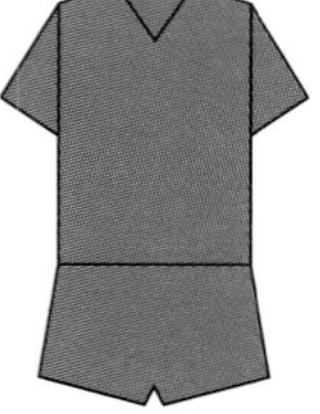
MINIOR PERNIK

MARITSA PLOVDIV

BULGARIA

BOTEV PLOVDIV

CSKA SOFIA

DOBRUDZHA DOBRICH

ETAR VELIKO TARNOVO

LEVSKI KIUSTENDIL

LEVSKI SOFIA

LOKOMOTIV PLOVDIV

LOKOMOTIV SOFIA

LOVECH

MONTANA

NEFTOCHIMIK BOURGAS

RAKOVSKI RUSE

SHUMEN

SLAVIA SOFIA

SPARTAK PLOVDIV

SPARTAK VARNA

SPARTAK PLEVEN

MINIOR PERNIK

MARITSA PLOVDIV

CROATIA

CIBALIA VINKOVCI
CROATIA ZAGREB
HAJDUK SPLIT
HRVATSKI DRAGOVOLJAC ZAGREB
INKER ZAPRESIC
ISTRA PULA
MARSONIA SLAVONSKI BROD
MLADOST 127 SUHOPOLJE
OSIJEK
RIJEKA
SEGESTA SISAK
SIBENIK
VARTEKS VARAZDIN
ZAGREB
ZADAR
ORIJENT RIJEKA

CROATIA

CIBALIA VINKOVCI

CROATIA ZAGREB

HAJDUK SPLIT

HRVATSKI DRAGOVOLJAC ZAGREB

INKER ZAPRESIC

ISTRA PULA

MARSONIA SLAVONSKI BROD

MLADOST 127 SUHOPOLJE

OSIJEK

RIJEKA

SEGESTA SISAK

SIBENIK

VARTEKS VARAZDIN

ZAGREB

ZADAR

ORIJENT RIJEKA

CYPRUS

AEK LARNACA
AEL LIMASSOL
ALKI LARNACA
ANORTHOSIS FAMAGUSTA
APOEL NICOSIA
APOLLON LIMASSOL
ARIS LIMASSOL
ETHNIKOS AKHNAS
EVAGHORAS PAPHOS
NEA SALAMINA FAMAGUSTA
OLYMPIAKOS NICOSIA
OMONIA ARADIPPOU
OMONIA NICOSIA
PARALIMNI
APOP PAPHOS
APEP PITSILIAS
ANAGENNISIS DHERYNIA

CYPRUS

AEK LARNACA

AEL LIMASSOL

ALKI LARNACA

ANORTHOSIS FAMAGUSTA

APOEL NICOSIA

APOLLON LIMASSOL

ARIS LIMASSOL

ETHNIKOS AKHNAS

EVAGHORAS PAPHOS

NEA SALAMINA FAMAGUSTA

OLYMPIAKOS NICOSIA

OMONIA ARADIPPOU

OMONIA NICOSIA

PARALIMNI

APOP PAPHOS

APEP PITSILIAS

ANAGENNISIS DHERYNIA

CZECH REPUBLIC

CZECH REPUBLIC

BANIK OSTRAVA

BOBY BRNO

SK CESKE BUDEJOVICE

SK HRADEC KRALOVE

JABLONEC NAD NISOU

KAUCUK OPAVA

PETRA DRNOVICE

SIGMA OLOMOUC

SLAVIA PRAHA

SLOVACKA SLAVIA UHERSKE HRADISTE

SLOVAN LIBEREC

SPARTA PRAHA

UNION CHEB

VIKTORIA PLZEN

VIKTORIA ZIZKOV

FC ZLIN

KARVINA VITKOVICE

FK TEPLICE

DENMARK

AAB
AGF
BRØNDBY IF
HERFØLGE BK
IKAST FS
FC KØBENHAVN
LYNGBY FC
NAESTVED BK
OB
SILKEBORG IF
VEJLE BK
VIBORG FF
HVIDOVRE IF
AB

DENMARK

AAB

AGF

BRØNDBY IF

HERFØLGE BK

IKAST FS

FC KØBENHAVN

LYNGBY FC

NAESTVED BK

OB

SILKEBORG IF

VEJLE BK

VIBORG FF

HVIDOVRE IF

AB

ENGLAND

ARSENAL

ASTON VILLA

BLACKBURN ROVERS

BOLTON WANDERERS

CHELSEA

COVENTRY CITY

EVERTON

LEEDS UNITED

LIVERPOOL

MANCHESTER CITY

MANCHESTER UNITED

MIDDLESBROUGH

NEWCASTLE UNITED

NOTTINGHAM FOREST

QUEENS PARK RANGERS

SHEFFIELD WEDNESDAY

SOUTHAMPTON

TOTTENHAM HOTSPUR

WEST HAM UNITED

WIMBLEDON

SUNDERLAND

DERBY COUNTY

LEICESTER CITY

ENGLAND

ARSENAL

ASTON VILLA

BLACKBURN ROVERS

BOLTON WANDERERS

CHELSEA

COVENTRY CITY

EVERTON

LEEDS UNITED

LIVERPOOL

MANCHESTER CITY

MANCHESTER UNITED

MIDDLESBROUGH

NEWCASTLE UNITED

NOTTINGHAM FOREST

QUEENS PARK RANGERS

SHEFFIELD WEDNESDAY

SOUTHAMPTON

TOTTENHAM HOTSPUR

WEST HAM UNITED

WIMBLEDON

SUNDERLAND

DERBY COUNTY

LEICESTER CITY

FAROE ISLANDS

FAROE ISLANDS

B 36 B 68 B 71

GÍ HB KÍ

NSÍ SUMBA/ VB TB

FS VÁGAR ÍF

FINLAND

FINNPA
FC HAKA
HJK
FC ILVES
FF JARO
FC JAZZ
FC KUUSYSI
MP
MYPA
PONNISTUS
ROPS
TPS
TPV
VPS
FC INTER TURKU

FINLAND

FINNPA

FC HAKA

HJK

FC ILVES

FF JARO

FC JAZZ

FC KUUSYSI

MP

MYPA

PONNISTUS

ROPS

TPS

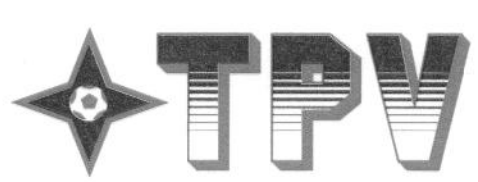

TPV

VPS

FC INTER TURKU

FRANCE

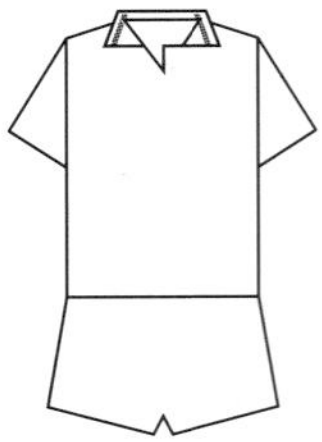

AJ AUXERRE

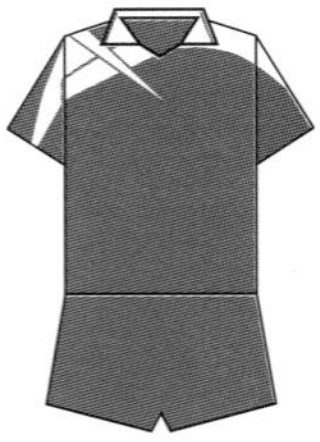

SC BASTIA

GIRONDINS DE BORDEAUX

AS CANNES

FC GUEUGNON

EN AVANT GUINGAMP

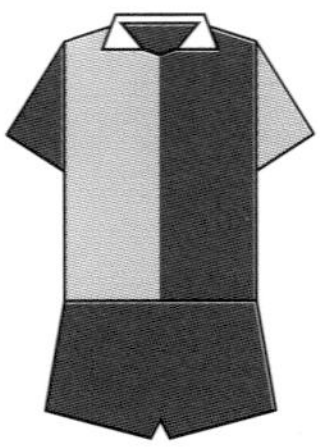

LE HAVRE AC

RC LENS

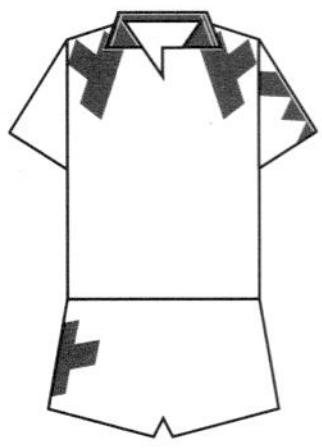

LILLE OSC

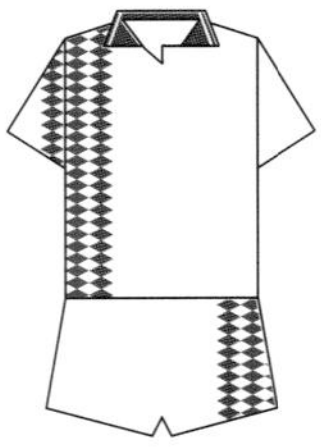

OLYMPIQUE LYONNAIS

FC MARTIGUES

FC METZ

AS MONACO

MONTPELLIER HSC

FC NANTES

OGC NICE

PARIS SAINT-GERMAIN FC

STADE RENNAIS FC

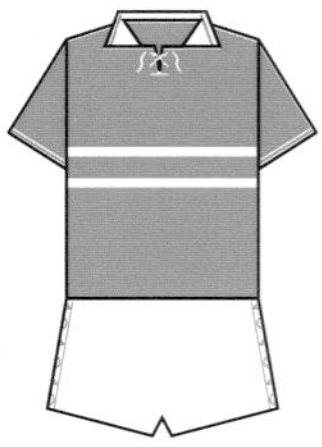

AS SAINT-ETIENNE

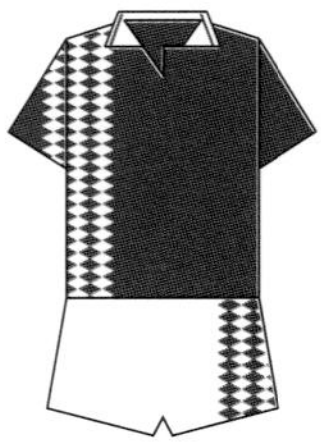

RC STRASBOURG

SM CAEN

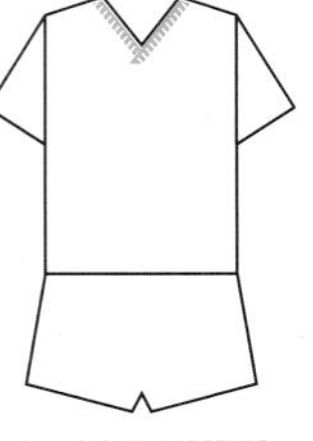

OLYMPIQUE MARSEILLE

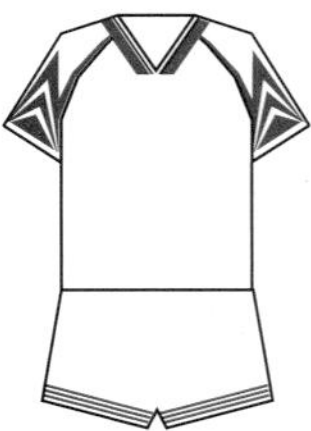

AS NANCY LORRAINE

FRANCE

AJ AUXERRE

SC BASTIA

GIRONDINS DE BORDEAUX

AS CANNES

FC GUEUGNON

EN AVANT GUINGAMP

LE HAVRE AC

RC LENS

LILLE OSC

OLYMPIQUE LYONNAIS

FC MARTIGUES

FC METZ

AS MONACO

MONTPELLIER HSC

FC NANTES

OGC NICE

PARIS SAINT-GERMAIN FC

STADE RENNAIS FC

AS SAINT-ETIENNE

RC STRASBOURG

SM CAEN

OLYMPIQUE MARSEILLE

AS NANCY-LORRAINE

GERMANY

BAYER 04 LEVERKUSEN

FC BAYERN MÜNCHEN

BORUSSIA DORTMUND

BORUSSIA MÖNCHENGLADBACH

EINTRACHT FRANKFURT

FORTUNA DÜSSELDORF

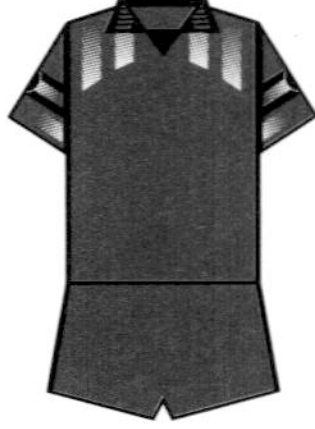
SC FREIBURG

HAMBURGER SV

FC HANSA ROSTOCK

1.FC KAISERSLAUTERN

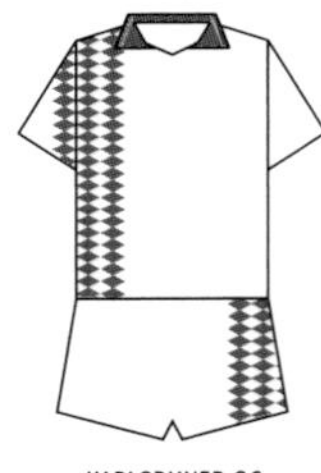
KARLSRUHER SC

1.FC KÖLN

TSV 1860 MÜNCHEN

FC ST. PAULI

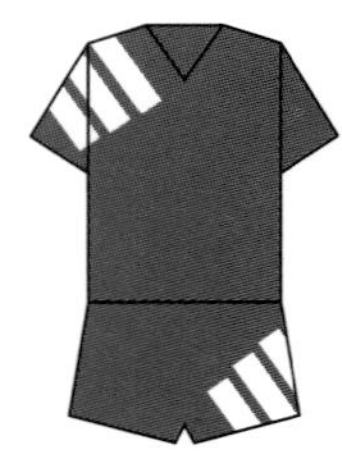
FC SCHALKE 04

VFB STUTTGART

KFC UERDINGEN 05

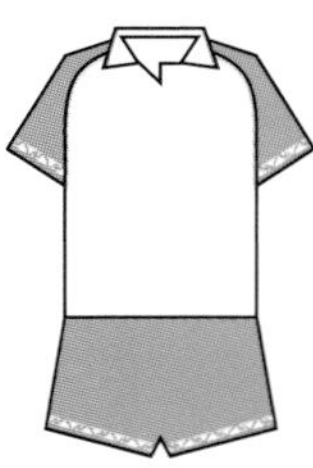
SV WERDER BREMEN

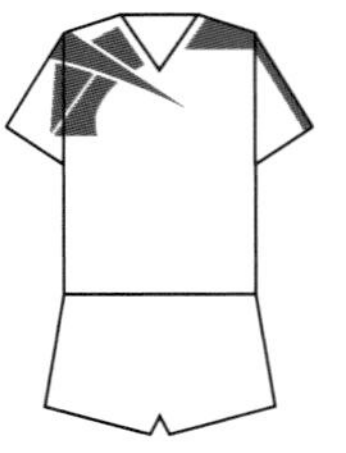
VFL BOCHUM

ARMINIA BIELEFELD

MSV DUISBURG

GERMANY

BAYER 04 LEVERKUSEN

FC BAYERN MÜNCHEN

BORUSSIA DORTMUND

BORUSSIA MÖNCHENGLADBACH

EINTRACHT FRANKFURT

FORTUNA DÜSSELDORF

SC FREIBURG

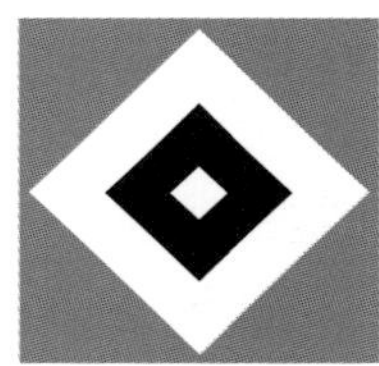

HAMBURGER SV

FC HANSA ROSTOCK

1.FC KAISERSLAUTERN

KARLSRUHER SC

1.FC KÖLN

TSV 1860 MÜNCHEN

FC ST. PAULI

FC SCHALKE 04

VFB STUTTGART

KFC UERDINGEN 05

SV WERDER BREMEN

VFL BOCHUM

ARMINIA BIELEFELD

MSV DUISBURG

GREECE

AEK
APOLLON
ARIS
ATHINAIKOS
EDESSAIKOS
ETHNIKOS
IONIKOS
IRAKLIS
KALAMATA
LARISSA
OFI
OLYMPIAKOS
PANAHAIKI
PANATHINAIKOS
PANILIAKOS
PANIONIOS
PAOK
XANTHI
KAVALA
VERIA
KASTORIA

GREECE

AEK APOLLON ARIS ATHINAIKOS

EDESSAIKOS ETHNIKOS IONIKOS IRAKLIS

KALAMATA LARISSA OFI OLYMPIAKOS

PANAHAIKI PANATHINAIKOS PANILIAKOS

PANIONIOS PAOK XANTHI

KAVALA VERIA KASTORIA

HOLLAND

AJAX
FEYENOORD
FORTUNA SITTARD
GO AHEAD EAGLES
DE GRAAFSCHAP
FC GRONINGEN
SC HEERENVEEN
NAC
NEC
PSV
RKC
RODA JC
SPARTA
FC TWENTE
FC UTRECHT
VITESSE
FC VOLENDAM
WILLEM II
AZ

HOLLAND

AJAX

FEYENOORD

FORTUNA SITTARD

GO AHEAD EAGLES

DE GRAAFSCHAP

FC GRONINGEN

SC HEERENVEEN

NAC

NEC

PSV

RKC

RODA JC

SPARTA

FC TWENTE

FC UTRECHT

VITESSE

FC VOLENDAM

WILLEM II

AZ

HUNGARY

BÉKÉSCSABA
BVSC-DREHER
CSEPEL SC
DVSC-EPONA
FEHÉRVÁR 96 PARMALAT FC
FERENCVÁROS
GYÖRI ETO FC
HALADÁS VFC
KISPEST-HONVÉD FC
MTK
PÉSCI MFC
STADLER FC
ÚPESTI TE
VASAS CV
VÁC FC-SAMSUNG
ZALAEGERSZEGI TE
III. KERÜLETI TVE
SIÓFOK

HUNGARY

BÉKÉSCSABA

BVSC-DREHER

CSEPEL SC

DVSC-EPONA

FEHÉRVÁR 96 PARMALAT FC

FERENCVÁROS

GYÖRI ETO FC

HALADÁS VFC

KISPEST-HONVÉD FC

MTK

PÉCSI MFC

STADLER FC

ÚPESTI TE

VASAS CV

VÁC FC-SAMSUNG

ZALAEGERSZEGI TE

III. KERÜLETI TVE

SIÓFOK

ICELAND

BREIDABLIK
FH
FRAM
GRINDAVÍK
ÍA
ÍBV
KEFLAVÍK
KR
LEIFTUR
VALUR
FYLKIR
STJARNAN

ICELAND

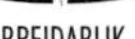
BREIDABLIK

FH

FRAM

GRINDAVÍK

ÍA

ÍBV

KEFLAVÍK

KR

LEIFTUR

VALUR

FYLKIR

STJARNAN

ISRAEL

BEITAR JERUSALEM
BEITAR TEL-AVIV
BNEI YEHUDA
HAPOEL BEER SHEVA
HAPOEL BEIT SH'AN
HAPOEL HAIFA
HAPOEL IRONY RISHON LEZION
HAPOEL KFAR-SABA
HAPOEL PETACH-TIKVA
HAPOEL TEL-AVIV
MACCABI HAIFA
MACCABI HERZLIYA
MACCABI JAFFA
MACCABI PETACH-TIKVA
MACCABI TEL-AVIV
ZAFRIRIM HOLON
HAPOEL TAIBE
HAPOEL JERUSALEM

ISRAEL

BEITAR JERUSALEM

BEITAR TEL-AVIV

BNEI YEHUDA

HAPOEL BEER SHEVA

HAPOEL BEIT SH'AN

HAPOEL HAIFA

HAPOEL IRONY RISHON LEZION

HAPOEL KFAR-SABA

HAPOEL PETACH-TIKVA

HAPOEL TEL-AVIV

MACCABI HAIFA

MACCABI HERZLIYA

MACCABI JAFFA

MACCABI PETACH-TIKVA

MACCABI TEL-AVIV

ZAFRIRIM HOLON

HAPOEL TAIBE

HAPOEL JERUSALEM

ITALY

ATALANTA
BARI
CAGLIARI
CREMONESE
FIORENTINA
INTER
JUVENTUS
LAZIO
MILAN
NAPOLI
PADOVA
PARMA
PIACENZA
ROMA
SAMPDORIA
TORINO
UDINESE
VICENZA
BOLOGNA
VERONA
PERUGIA
REGGIANA

ITALY

ATALANTA

BARI

CAGLIARI

CREMONESE

FIORENTINA

INTER

JUVENTUS

LAZIO

MILAN

NAPOLI

PADOVA

PARMA

PIACENZA

ROMA

SAMPDORIA

TORINO

UDINESE

VICENZA

BOLOGNA

VERONA

PERUGIA

REGGIANA

LUXEMBOURG

ARIS BONNEVOIE
AVENIR BEGGEN
F91 DUDELANGE
CS GREVENMACHER
JEUNESSE ESCH
CS PETANGE
RED BOYS DIFFERDANGE
FC RODANGE 91
SPORA LUXEMBOURG
SPORTING MERTZIG
UNION LUXEMBOURG
FC WILTZ 71
CS HOBSCHEID
US RUMELANGE

LUXEMBOURG

ARIS BONNEVOIE

AVENIR BEGGEN

F91 DUDELANGE

CS GREVENMACHER

JEUNESSE ESCH

CS PETANGE

RED BOYS DIFFERDANGE

FC RODANGE 91

SPORA LUXEMBOURG

SPORTING MERTZIG

UNION LUXEMBOURG

FC WILTZ 71

CS HOBSCHEID

US RUMELANGE

MALTA

BIRKIRKARA LUXOL
FLORIANA
HAMRUN SPARTANS
HIBERNIANS
NAXXAR LIONS
RABAT AJAX
ST. PATRICK
SLIEMA WANDERERS
VALLETTA
ZURRIEQ
PIETA HOTSPURS
LIJA ATHLETICS

MALTA

BIRKIRKARA LUXOL

FLORIANA

HAMRUN SPARTANS

HIBERNIANS

NAXXAR LIONS

RABAT AJAX

ST. PATRICK

SLIEMA WANDERERS

VALLETTA

ZURRIEQ

PIETA HOTSPURS

LIJA ATHLETICS

NORTHERN IRELAND

NORTHERN IRELAND

ARDS

BANGOR

CLIFTONVILLE

CRUSADERS

GLENAVON

GLENTORAN

LINFIELD

PORTADOWN

COLERAINE

NORWAY

FK BODØ/GLIMT
SK BRANN
HAMARKAMERATENE
IL HØDD
KONGSVINGER IL
LILLESTRØM SK
MOLDE FK
ROSENBORG BK
STABAEK IF
IK START
STRINDHEIM IL
TROMSØ IL
VIF FOTBALL
VIKING FK
MOSS FK
SKEID
STRØMSGODSET IF

NORWAY

FK BODØ/GLIMT

SK BRANN

HAMARKAMERATENE

IL HØDD

KONGSVINGER IL

LILLESTRØM SK

MOLDE FK

ROSENBORG BK

STABAEK IF

IK START

STRINDHEIM IL

TROMSØ IL

VIF FOTBALL

VIKING FK

MOSS FK

SKEID

STRØMSGODSET IF

POLAND

AMICA WRONKI
GKS BELCHATOW
GKS KATOWICE
GORNIK ZABRZE
HUTNIK KRAKOW
LECH POZNAN
LEGIA WARSZAWA
LKS LODZ
OLIMPIA/LECHIA GDANSK
POGON SZCZECIN
RAKOW CZESTOCHOWA
SIARKA TARNOBRZEG
SLASK WROCLAW
SOKOL TYCHY
STAL MIELEC
STOMIL OLSZTYN
WIDZEW LODZ
ZAGLEBIE LUBIN
ODRA WODZISLAW
RUCH CHORZOW
POLONIA WARSZAWA
WISLA KRAKOW

POLAND

AMICA WRONKI

GKS BELCHATOW

GKS KATOWICE

GORNIK ZABRZE

HUTNIK KRAKOW

LECH POZNAN

LEGIA WARSZAWA

LKS LODZ

OLIMPIA/LECHIA GDANSK

POGON SZCZECIN

RAKOW CZESTOCHOWA

SIARKA TARNOBRZEG

SLASK WROCLAW

SOKOL TYCHY

STAL MIELEC

STOMIL OLSZTYN

WIDZEW LODZ

ZAGLEBIE LUBIN

ODRA WODZISLAW

RUCH CHORZOW

POLONIA WARSZAWA

WISLA KRAKOW

PORTUGAL

CF OS BELENENSES
SL BENFICA
BOAVISTA FC
SC BRAGA
SC CAMPOMAIORENSE
GD CHAVES
CF ESTRELA AMADORA
SC FARENSE
FC FELGUEIRAS
GIL VICENTE FC
LEÇA FC
CS MARÍTIMO
FC PORTO
SC SALGUEIROS
SPORTING CP
FC TIRSENSE
UNIÃO LEIRIA
VITÓRIA GUIMARÃES
RIO AVE FC
VITÓRIA SETÚBAL
SC ESPINHO

PORTUGAL

CF OS BELENENSES

SL BENFICA

BOAVISTA FC

SC BRAGA

SC CAMPOMAIORENSE

GD CHAVES

CF ESTRELA AMADORA

SC FARENSE

FC FELGUEIRAS

GIL VICENTE FC

LEÇA FC

CS MARÍTIMO

FC PORTO

SC SALGUEIROS

SPORTING CP

FC TIRSENSE

UNIÃO LEIRIA

VITÓRIA GUIMARÃES

RIO AVE FC

VITÓRIA SETÚBAL

SC ESPINHO

REPUBLIC OF IRELAND

REPUBLIC OF IRELAND

ATHLONE TOWN

BOHEMIANS

CORK CITY

DERRY CITY

DROGHEDA UNITED

DUNDALK

GALWAY UNITED

ST. PATRICK'S ATHLETIC

SHAMROCK ROVERS

SHELBOURNE

SLIGO ROVERS

UCD

BRAY WANDERERS

FINN HARPS

HOME FARM EVERTON

ROMANIA

FC ARGES DACIA PITESTI
AS BACAU
FC BRASOV
CEAHLAUL PIATRA NEAMT
DINAMO BUCURESTI
FC FARUL CONSTANTA
GLORIA BISTRITA
FC INTER SIBIU
FC NATIONAL BUCURESTI
OTELUL GALATI
PETROLUL PLOIESTI
POLITEHNICA IASI
POLITEHNICA TIMISOARA
RAPID BUCURESTI
SPORTUL STUDENTESC BUCURESTI
STEAUA BUCURESTI
UNIVERSITATEA CLUJ
UNIVERSITATEA CRAIOVA
OTELUL TIRGOVISTE
JIUL PETROSANI

ROMANIA

FC ARGES DACIA PITESTI

AS BACAU

FC BRASOV

CEAHLAUL PIATRA NEAMT

DINAMO BUCURESTI

FC FARUL CONSTANTA

GLORIA BISTRITA

FC INTER SIBIU

FC NATIONAL BUCURESTI

OTELUL GALATI

PETROLUL PLOIESTI

POLITEHNICA IASI

POLITEHNICA TIMISOARA

RAPID BUCURESTI

SPORTUL STUDENTESC BUCURESTI

STEAUA BUCURESTI

UNIVERSITATEA CLUJ

UNIVERSITATEA CRAIOVA

OTELUL TIRGOVISTE

JIUL PETROSANI

RUSSIA

CHERNOMORETS NOVOROSSIISK
CSKA MOSKVA
DINAMO-GAZOVIK TYUMEN
DINAMO MOSKVA
KAMAZ-CHALLY NABEREZHNYE CHELNY
KRYLYA SOVETOV SAMARA
LOKOMOTIV MOSKVA
LOKOMOTIV NIZHNI NOVGOROD
ROSTSELMASH ROSTOV
ROTOR VOLGOGRAD
SPARTAK MOSKVA
SPARTAK-ALANIA VLADIKAVKAZ
TEKSTILSCHIK KAMYSHIN
TORPEDO MOSKVA
URALMASH YEKATERINBURG
ZHEMCHUZHINA SOCHI
BALTIKA KALNINGRAD
LADA TOGLIATTI
ZENIT SANKT-PETERBURG

RUSSIA

CHERNOMORETS NOVOROSSIISK

CSKA MOSKVA

DINAMO-GAZOVIK TYUMEN

DINAMO MOSKVA

KAMAZ-CHALLY NABEREZHNYE CHELNY

KRYLYA SOVETOV SAMARA

LOKOMOTIV MOSKVA

LOKOMOTIV NIZHNI NOVGOROD

ROSTSELMASH ROSTOV

ROTOR VOLGOGRAD

SPARTAK MOSKVA

SPARTAK-ALANIA VLADIKAVKAZ

TEKSTILSCHIK KAMYSHIN

TORPEDO MOSKVA

URALMASH YEKATERINBURG

ZHEMCHUZHINA SOCHI

BALTIKA KALININGRAD

LADA TOGLIATTI

ZENIT SANKT-PETERBURG

SAN MARINO

CAILUNGO
COSMOS
DOMAGNANO
FAETANO
FIORITA
FOLGORE
MURATA
SAN GIOVANNI
TRE FIORI
VIRTUS
LIBERTAS
JUVENES

SAN MARINO

CAILUNGO COSMOS DOMAGNANO FAETANO

FIORITA FOLGORE MURATA

SAN GIOVANNI TRE FIORI VIRTUS

LIBERTAS JUVENES

SCOTLAND

ABERDEEN
CELTIC
FALKIRK
HEART OF MIDLOTHIAN
HIBERNIAN
KILMARNOCK
MOTHERWELL
PARTICK THISTLE
RAITH ROVERS
RANGERS
DUNFERMLINE ATHLETIC
DUNDEE UNITED

SCOTLAND

ABERDEEN

CELTIC

FALKIRK

HEART OF MIDLOTHIAN

HIBERNIAN

KILMARNOCK

MOTHERWELL

PARTICK THISTLE

RAITH ROVERS

RANGERS

DUNFERMLINE ATHLETIC

DUNDEE UNITED

SLOVAKIA

BSC JAS BARDEJOV

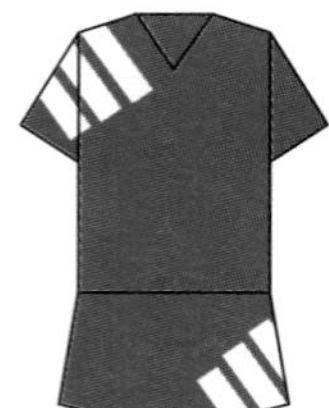
CHEMLON HUMENNE

DAC DUNAJSKA STREDA

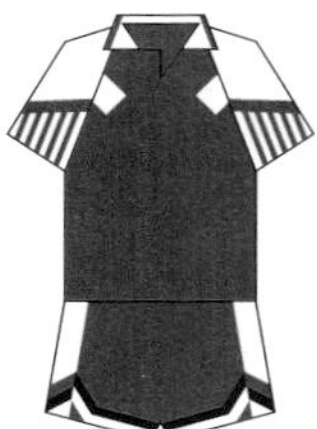
DUKLA BANSKA BYSTRICA

INTER BRATISLAVA

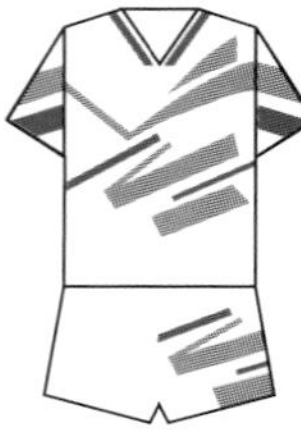
1.FC KOSICE

LOKOMOTIVA KOSICE

FC NITRA

PETRIMEX PRIEVIDZA

SLOVAN BRATISLAVA

SPARTAK TRNAVA

TATRAN PRESOV

ARTMEDIA PETRZALKA

MSK ZILINA

RIMAVSKA SOBOTA

SPARTAK DUBNICA NAD VAHOM

SLOVAKIA

BSC JAS BARDEJOV

CHEMLON HUMENNE

DAC DUNAJSKA STREDA

DUKLA BANSKA BYSTRICA

INTER BRATISLAVA

1.FC KOSICE

LOKOMOTIVA KOSICE

FC NITRA

PETRIMEX PRIEVIDZA

SLOVAN BRATISLAVA

SPARTAK TRNAVA

TATRAN PRESOV

ARTMEDIA PETRZALKA

MSK ZILINA

RIMAVSKA SOBOTA

SPARTAK DUBNICA NAD VAHOM

SLOVENIA

NK BELTINCI
HIT GORICA
NK IZOLA
MAG KOROTAN PREVALJE
MARIBOR BRANIK
MURA MURSKA SOBOTA
PRIMORJE AJDOVSCINA
PUBLIKUM CELJE
RUDAR VELENJE
SCT OLIMPIJA LJUBLJANA
ZELEZNICAR LJUBLJANA

SLOVENIA

NK BELTINCI

HIT GORICA

NK IZOLA

MAG KOROTAN PREVALJE

MARIBOR BRANIK

MURA MURSKA SOBOTA

PRIMORJE AJDOVSCINA

PUBLIKUM CELJE

RUDAR VELENJE

SCT OLIMPIJA LJUBLJANA

ZELEZNICAR LJUBLJANA

SPAIN

ALBACETE BALOMPIE
ATHLETIC BILBAO
ATLETICO MADRID
FC BARCELONA
REAL BETIS
RC CELTA
SD COMPOSTELA
RC DEPORTIVO
RCD ESPANYOL
CP MERIDA
REAL OVIEDO
RACING SANTANDER
RAYO VALLECANO
REAL MADRID
REAL SOCIEDAD
UD SALAMANCA
SEVILLA FC
SPORTING GIJON
CD TENERIFE
VALENCIA CF
REAL VALLADOLID
REAL ZARAGOZA
HERCULES CF
CD LOGROÑES
CF EXTREMADURA

SPAIN

ALBACETE BALOMPIE

ATHLETIC BILBAO

ATLETICO MADRID

FC BARCELONA

REAL BETIS

RC CELTA

SD COMPOSTELA

RC DEPORTIVO

RCD ESPANYOL

CP MERIDA

REAL OVIEDO

RACING SANTANDER

RAYO VALLECANO

REAL MADRID

REAL SOCIEDAD

UD SALAMANCA

SEVILLA FC

SPORTING GIJON

CD TENERIFE

VALENCIA CF

REAL VALLADOLID

REAL ZARAGOZA

HERCULES CF

CD LOGROÑES

CF EXTREMADURA

SWEDEN

AIK
DEGERFORS IF
DJURGÅRDENS IF
IFK GÖTEBORG
HALMSTADS BK
HAMMARBY IF
HELSINGBORGS IF
MALMÖ FF
IFK NORRKÖPING
TRELLEBORGS FF
VÄSTRA FRÖLUNDA IF
ÖREBRO SK
ÖRGRYTE IS
ÖSTERS IF
UMEÅ FC
IK ODDEVOLD

SWEDEN

AIK

DEGERFORS IF

DJURGÅRDENS IF

IFK GÖTEBORG

HALMSTADS BK

HAMMARBY IF

HELSINGBORGS IF

MALMÖ FF

IFK NORRKÖPING

TRELLEBORGS FF

VÄSTRA FRÖLUNDA IF

ÖREBRO SK

ÖRGRYTE IS

ÖSTERS IF

UMEÅ FC

IK ODDEVOLD

SWITZERLAND

FC AARAU

FC BASEL

GRASSHOPPER-CLUB ZÜRICH

LAUSANNE-SPORTS

FC LUGANO

FC LUZERN

NEUCHATEL XAMAX FC

FC ST. GALLEN

SERVETTE FC GENEVE

FC SION

BSC YOUNG BOYS

FC ZÜRICH

SWITZERLAND

FC AARAU

FC BASEL

GRASSHOPPER-CLUB ZÜRICH

LAUSANNE-SPORTS

FC LUGANO

FC LUZERN

NEUCHATEL XAMAX FC

FC ST. GALLEN

SERVETTE FC GENEVE

FC SION

BSC YOUNG BOYS

FC ZÜRICH

TURKEY

ALTAY
ANKARAGÜCÜ
ANTALYASPOR
BESIKTAS
BURSASPOR
DENIZILISPOR
ESKISEHIRSPOR
FENERBAHÇE
GALATASARAY
GAZIANTEPSPOR
GENÇLERBIRLIGI
ISTANBULSPOR
KARSIYAKA
KAYSERISPOR
KOCAELISPOR
SAMSUNSPOR
TRABZONSPOR
VANSPOR
ÇANAKKALE DARDANELSPOR
SARIYER
ZEYTINBURNU

TURKEY

ALTAY

ANKARAGÜCÜ

ANTALYASPOR

BESIKTAS

BURSASPOR

DENIZLISPOR

ESKISEHIRSPOR

FENERBAHÇE

GALATASARAY

GAZIANTEPSPOR

GENÇLERBIRLIGI

ISTANBULSPOR

KARSIYAKA

KAYSERISPOR

KOCAELISPOR

SAMSUNSPOR

TRABZONSPOR

VANSPOR

ÇANAKKALE DARDANELSPOR

SARIYER

ZEYTINBURNU

UKRAINE

CHORNOMORETS ODESA

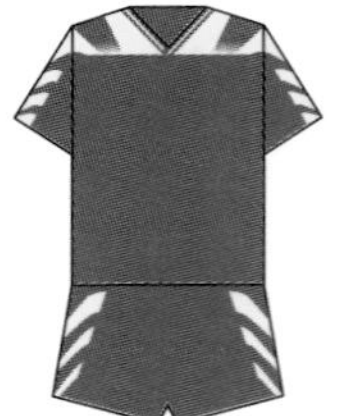
CSKA-BORYSFEN KYIV

DNIPRO DNIPROPETROVSK

DYNAMO KYIV

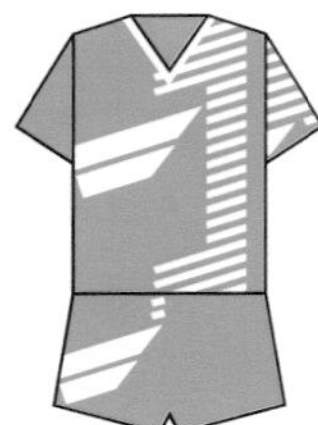
KARPATY LVIV

KREMIN KREMENCHUK

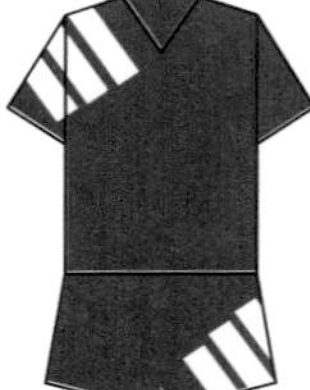
KRYVBAS KRYVYI RIH

METALLURG ZAPORIZHZHYA

SK MYKOLAIV

NYVA TERNOPIL

NYVA VYNNYTSYA

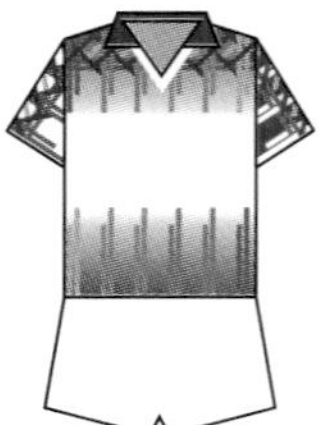
PRYKARPATTYA IVANO-FRANKIVSK

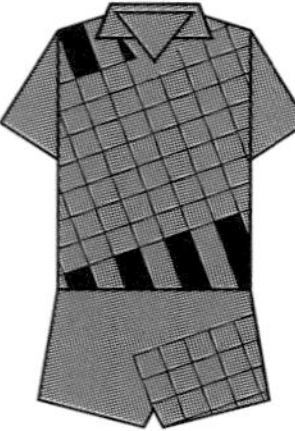
SHAKHTAR DONETSK

TAVRIYA SIMFEROPOL

TORPEDO ZAPORIZHZHYA

VOLYN LUTSK

ZIRKA NIBAS KIROVOHRAD

ZORYA MALS LUGANSK

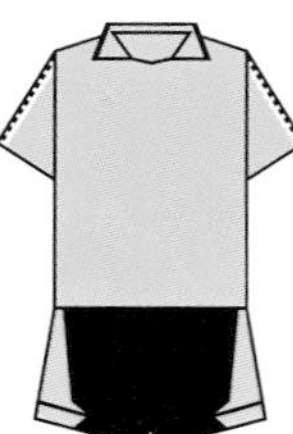
VORSKLA POLTAVA

UKRAINE

CHORNOMORETS ODESA

CSKA-BORYSFEN KYIV

DNIPRO DNIPROPETROVSK

DYNAMO KYIV

KARPATY LYIV

KREMIN KREMENCHUK

KRYVBAS KRYVYI RIH

METALLURG ZAPORIZHZHYA

SK MYKOLAIV

NYVA TERNOPIL

NYVA VYNNYTSYA

PRYKARPATTYA IVANO-FRANKIVSK

SHAKHTAR DONETSK

TAVRIYA SIMFEROPOL

TORPEDO ZAPORIZHZHYA

VOLYN LUTSK

ZIRKA NIBAS KIROVOHRAD

ZORYA MALS LUGANSK

VORSKLA POLTAVA

WALES

ABERYSTWYTH TOWN
AFAN LIDO
BANGOR CITY
BARRY TOWN
BRITON FERRY ATHLETIC
CAERNARFON TOWN
CAERSWS
CEMAES BAY
CONNAH'S QUAY NOMADS
CONWY UNITED
CWMBRAN TOWN
EBBW VALE
FFLINT TOWN UNITED
HOLYWELL TOWN
INTER CARDIFF
LLANELLI
LLANSANTFFRAID
NEWTOWN
CPD PORTHMADOG
RHYL
TON PENTRE
WELSHPOOL
CARMARTHEN TOWN

WALES

ABERYSTWYTH TOWN

AFAN LIDO

BANGOR CITY

BARRY TOWN

BRITON FERRY ATHLETIC

CAERNARFON TOWN

CAERSWS

CEMAES BAY

CONNAH'S QUAY NOMADS

CONWY UNITED

CWMBRAN TOWN

EBBW VALE

FFLINT TOWN UNITED

HOLYWELL TOWN

INTER CARDIFF

LLANELLI

LLANSANTFFRAID

NEWTOWN

CPD PORTHMADOG

RHYL

TON PENTRE

WELSHPOOL

CARMARTHEN TOWN

YUGOSLAVIA

FK BECEJ — BUDUCNOST PODGORICA — CRVENA ZVEZDA BEOGRAD — CUKARICKI BEOGRAD

MLADOST LUCANI — NAPREDAK KRUSEVAC — OFK BEOGRAD — PARTIZAN BEOGRAD

PROLETER ZRENJANIN — RAD BEOGRAD — RADNICKI NIS — SLOBODA UZICE

VOJVODINA NOVI SAD — FK ZEMUN — BORAC CACAK — HAJDUK KULA

FIRST KIT **NATIONAL TEAM** SECOND KIT

YUGOSLAVIA

FK BECEJ

BUDUCNOST PODGORICA

CRVENA ZVEZDA BEOGRAD

CUKARICKI BEOGRAD

MLADOST LUCANI

NAPREDAK KRUSEVAC

OFK BEOGRAD

PARTIZAN BEOGRAD

PROLETER ZRENJANIN

RAD BEOGRAD

RADNICKI NIS

SLOBODA UZICE

VOJVODINA NOVI SAD

FK ZEMUN

BORAC CACAK

HAJDUK KULA

NATIONAL TEAM

MISCELLANEOUS

BELARUS - FC BOBRUISK

BELARUS - DINAMO BREST

BELARUS - DINAMO MINSK

BELARUS - DINAMO-93 MINSK

BELARUS - DNEPR MOGILEV

BELARUS - DVINA VITEBSK

BELARUS - MPKC MOZYR

BELARUS - NEMAN GRODNO

BELARUS - OBUVSHCHIK LIDA

BELARUS - TORPEDO MINSK

BELARUS - VEDRICH RECHITSA

BELARUS - NAFTAN-DEVON NOVOPLOTSK

JALPALLIKLUBI
EESTI PÕLEVKIVI

ESTONIA - EP JÕHVI

ESTONIA - FC FLORA TALLINN

ESTONIA - JK/KALEV PARNU

ESTONIA - FC LaNTANA TALLINN

ESTONIA - FC TALLINNA SADAM

ESTONIA - TERVIS PÄRNU

ESTONIA - FC TEVALTE-MARLEKOR TALLINN

ESTONIA - TRANS NARVA

MISCELLANEOUS

GEORGIA - BATUMI

GEORGIA - DINAMO TBLISI

GEORGIA - DINAMO ZUGDIDI

GEORGIA - GURIA LANCHKHUTI

GEORGIA - KAKHETI TELAVI

GEORGIA - KOLKHETI-1913 POTI

GEORGIA - MARGVETI ZESTAFONI

GEORGIA - METALURGI RUSTAVI

GEORGIA - SAMTREDIA

GEORGIA - SHEVARDENI-1906 TBLISI

GEORGIA - SAMGURALI TSKALTUBO

GEORGIA - TORPEDO KUTAISI

LATVIA - DAG LIEPAYA

LATVIA - RAF YELGAVA

LATVIA - SKONTO/METALS RIGA

LATVIA - SKONTO RIGA

LIECHTENSTEIN - FC VADUZ

LITHUANIA - BANGA GARGZDAI

LITHUANIA - PANERYS VILNIUS

LITHUANIA - ZALGIRIS VILNIUS

CUP WINNERS 1995-96

EUROPEAN CHAMPIONSHIP 1996:
GERMANY

EUROPEAN CHAMPIONS' CUP 1996:
JUVENTUS

EUROPEAN CUP-WINNERS' CUP 1996:
PARIS SAINT-GERMAIN FC

UEFA CUP 1996:
FC BAYERN MÜNCHEN

WORLD CLUB CUP 1995 & EUROPEAN SUPER CUP 1996:
AJAX

MACCABI HAIFA

CLUB DIRECTORY

Maccabi Haifa
Heinrich Heine st. 14
Haifa
tel - (04) 380620
fax - (04) 371540
Year of Formation - 1919
Chairman - Jacob Shahar
Manager - Giora Shpigel
Coach - Avraham Aboukarat & Andrey Bal
Stadium - Kiriat Eliezer (18,000)

MAJOR HONOURS
League Championship - (5)
1984, 1985, 1989, 1991, 1994.
Domestic Cup - (4) 1962, 1991, 1993, 1995.

APPEARANCES 95/96

	P	Ap	(s)	Gls
Edgardo ADINOLFI (URU)	D	14	(8)	1
Marco BALBUL	D	15	(3)	
Eyal BERKOVITCH	M	29		3
Rafi COHEN	G	23	(1)	
Nir DAVIDOVITCH	G	7		
Tzabar DNIEL	D	7	(7)	
Eliran ELKAIM	M		(1)	
Kobi GANON	D		(6)	
Moshe GLAM	D	24	(2)	3
Alon HARAZI	M	19	(2)	1
Alon HAZAN	M	26	(1)	6
Avishai JANO	D	30		
Sergei KANDAUROV (RUS)	M	23		11
Jaroslav KENTOS (SVK)	D	10		1
Roni LEVI	M	28		3
Alon MIZRAHI	A	9	(2)	3
Roman PETS (UKR)	D	14		
Haim REVIVO	A	29		26
Offer SHITRIT	A	18	(12)	15
Haim SILVAS	M	5	(20)	1

LEAGUE RESULTS 1995/96

28/08/95	Maccabi Jaffa	H	3-1	Hazan, Revivo, Adinolfi
10/09/95	Hapoel Beer Sheva	A	1-1	Kandaurov
18/09/95	Maccabi Herzliya	H	2-0	Shitrit 2
02/10/95	Hapoel Tel-Aviv	A	3-1	Kandaurov 2, Mizrahi
14/10/95	Hapoel Irony Rishon Lezion	H	2-0	Revivo, Hazan
21/10/95	Zafririm Holon	H	2-1	Shitrit 2
28/10/95	Hapoel Petach-Tikva	A	3-3	Berkovitch, Kandaurov, Revivo
04/11/95	Beitar Jerusalem	H	2-2	Kandaurov, Revivo
11/11/95	Hapoel Beit Sh'an	A	6-0	Revivo 2, Mizrahi, Kandaurov 2, Shitrit
25/11/95	Beitar Tel-Aviv	H	6-3	Revivo 3, Hazan, Mizrahi, Glam
02/12/95	Maccabi Tel-Aviv	A	2-2	Berkovitch, Revivo
10/12/95	Bnei Yehuda	H	2-0	Shitrit, Glam
17/12/95	Hapoel Haifa	A	1-2	Kandaurov
24/12/95	Hapoel Kfar-Saba	H	3-1	Revivo 2, Hazan
30/12/95	Maccabi Petach-Tikva	A	2-2	Revivo 2
27/01/96	Maccabi Jaffa	A	5-1	Shitrit 2, Revivo 3
03/02/96	Hapoel Beer Sheva	H	3-0	Revivo, Shitrit, Kandaurov
10/02/96	Maccabi Herzliya	A	1-1	Revivo
17/02/96	Hapoel Tel-Aviv	H	4-3	Kandaurov, Revivo 2, Shitrit
02/03/96	Hapoel Irony Rishon Lezion	A	3-0	Kentos, Revivo, Silvas
08/03/96	Zafririm Holon	A	1-1	Levi
16/03/96	Hapoel Petach-Tikva	H	4-1	Shitrit 2, Berkovitch, Revivo
23/03/96	Beitar Jerusalem	A	2-0	Kandaurov, Hazan
30/03/96	Hapoel Beit Sh'an	H	1-1	Glam
13/04/96	Beitar Tel-Aviv	A	2-0	Revivo, Shitrit
20/04/96	Maccabi Tel-Aviv	H	1-3	Levi
27/04/96	Bnei Yehuda	A	3-0	Levi, Shitrit, Revivo
04/05/96	Hapoel Haifa	H	2-0	Harazi, Hazan
10/05/96	Hapoel Kfar-Saba	A	1-0	Shitrit
17/05/96	Maccabi Petach-Tikva	H	1-1	Revivo

MACCABI HERZLIYA

CLUB DIRECTORY

Maccabi Herzliya
Porzai Hadereech st. 2/10
Herzliya
tel - (09) 574774
fax - (09) 509865
Year of Formation - 1926
Chairman - Ronny Kliman
Coach - Elisha Levi; Gil Landau
Stadium - Irony Herzliya (10,000)

APPEARANCES 95/96

	P	Ap	(s)	Gls
Avi ALTON	D	3	(6)	
Tomer AZUOLAY	M	20	(1)	
Ilan BACHAR	A	4	(16)	2
Shlomi BEN HAMO	M	10		1
Alex BREMCHER	D	19		2
Yehuda BUARON	G	1	(1)	
Eran COHEN	D	5	(2)	
Israel COHEN	D	28		1
Nissim COHEN	M	26	(2)	2
Yaniv COHEN	M	29		3
Guy GAT	D	13	(5)	1
Shuli GILARDI	G	29		
Benni ITZHAKOV	M		(1)	
Vasili IVANOV (RUS)	M	25		1
Claudio KAHIMI (ARG)	A	10	(1)	
Ya'akov KORATZKY	M	7	(6)	
Elad KOREN	D	25	(2)	
Offer MIZRAHI	A	26		10
Gill MUA'ALEM	D	1	(4)	
Oleg NADUDA (UKR)	A	15		5
Yuval OHANA	A	2	(7)	
Yair SIMHON	A	4	(17)	3
Alexander TAIKOV (BLS)	D	28		1

LEAGUE RESULTS 1995/96

26/08/95	Hapoel Irony Rishon Lezion	H	1-0	Mizrahi
10/09/95	Hapoel Tel-Aviv	H	0-2	
17/09/95	Maccabi Haifa	A	0-2	
30/09/95	Zafririm Holon	H	0-1	
14/10/95	Hapoel Petach-Tikva	A	0-0	
21/10/95	Beitar Jerusalem	H	2-3	Simhon 2
28/10/95	Hapoel Beit Sh'an	A	2-1	Cohen Y., Cohen I.
04/11/95	Beitar Tel-Aviv	H	3-0	Mizrahi 2, Cohen Y.
11/11/95	Maccabi Tel-Aviv	A	0-1	
25/11/95	Bnei Yehuda	H	1-0	Mizrahi
02/12/95	Hapoel Haifa	A	0-1	
10/12/95	Hapoel Kfar-Saba	H	1-0	Cohen Y.
17/12/95	Maccabi Petach-Tikva	A	2-1	Mizrahi, Bachar
24/12/95	Maccabi Jaffa	H	3-2	og (Moroz), Naduda, Mizrahi
30/12/95	Hapoel Beer Sheva	A	1-1	Mizrahi
27/01/96	Hapoel Irony Rishon Lezion	A	1-2	Cohen N.
03/02/96	Hapoel Tel-Aviv	A	0-1	
10/02/96	Maccabi Haifa	H	1-1	Naduda
17/02/96	Zafririm Holon	A	2-0	Naduda, Bachar
02/03/96	Hapoel Petach-Tikva	H	2-0	Bremcher, Simhon
09/03/96	Beitar Jerusalem	A	0-3	
16/03/96	Hapoel Beit Sh'an	H	3-0	Cohen N., Mizrahi, Ivanov
23/03/96	Beitar Tel-Aviv	A	1-2	Gat
30/03/96	Maccabi Tel-Aviv	H	1-1	Taikov
13/04/96	Bnei Yehuda	A	2-3	Mizrahi 2
20/04/96	Hapoel Haifa	H	2-2	Bremcher, Naduda
27/04/96	Hapoel Kfar-Saba	A	0-1	
04/05/96	Maccabi Petach-Tikva	H	1-4	Ben Hamo
11/05/96	Maccabi Jaffa	A	0-1	
17/05/96	Hapoel Beer Sheva	H	1-1	Naduda

MACCABI JAFFA

CLUB DIRECTORY

Maccabi Jaffa
Levi eshkol st. 64
Tel-Aviv-Jaffa
tel - (03) 6991246
fax - (03) 6822885
Year of Formation - 1949
Chairman - Itzhak Assa
Secretary - Eli Birenboim
Manager - Nissim Bachar
Coaches - Shlomo Alkolombra & Eli Cohen
Stadium - R.I. Gaon (5,000)

APPEARANCES 95/96

	P	Ap	(s)	Gls
Moshe BEN HAIM	D	3	(1)	
Yossi BILU	D	23	(1)	
Boris BLOSHPKA (UKR)	G	29		
Avi COHEN	D		(1)	
Haim COHEN	M		(1)	
Yaron DRORI	M	13	(2)	3
David FARHI	G	1		
Haim GAZIT	D		(1)	
Gal HERSHLIKOVISH	M	17	(1)	
Elias HURRI	D	2	(1)	
Eduard KHMEL (UKR)	A	5	(7)	2
Mariusz KURAS (POL)	M	11		
Dan LEVI	D	2	(5)	1
Itzhak LEVI	D		(1)	
Ilan MADAR	D	16	(9)	
Kobi MASHIAH	M		(3)	
Israel MAYA	M	12	(3)	
Yury MOROZ (UKR)	D	22		2
Tamir NETZER	D	25	(1)	1
Mahmid NIDAL	M	26		1
Yuval OHANA	M	13		1
Avi PITUSI	M	23	(2)	1
Offer REHUVEN	M	19	(8)	2
Oren SAPIR	D	15	(6)	
Jacob SHWARTS	M	8	(2)	
Itzhak SWISSA	A	21	(5)	3
Avivi ZOHAR	M	24	(6)	5

LEAGUE RESULTS 1995/96

28/08/95	Maccabi Haifa	A	1-3	og (Harazi)
09/09/95	Zafririm Holon	H	4-2	Zohar 2, Rehuven, Swissa
17/09/95	Hapoel Petach-Tikva	A	1-3	Nidal
30/09/95	Beitar Jerusalem	H	0-3	
14/10/95	Hapoel Beit Sh'an	A	0-2	
21/10/95	Beitar Tel-Aviv	H	1-0	Rehuven
28/10/95	Maccabi Tel-Aviv	A	0-3	
04/11/95	Bnei Yehuda	H	1-0	Zohar
11/11/95	Hapoel Haifa	A	0-4	
25/11/95	Hapoel Kfar-Saba	H	1-2	Swissa
02/12/95	Maccabi Petach-Tikva	A	1-2	Moroz
10/12/95	Hapoel Irony Rishon Lezion	A	0-1	
17/12/95	Hapoel Beer Sheva	H	0-1	
24/12/95	Maccabi Herzliya	A	2-3	Khmel 2
30/12/95	Hapoel Tel-Aviv	H	1-1	Swissa
27/01/96	Maccabi Haifa	H	1-5	Zohar
02/02/96	Zafririm Holon	A	1-0	Drori
09/02/96	Hapoel Petach-Tikva	H	0-0	
17/02/96	Beitar Jerusalem	A	1-2	Zohar
02/03/96	Hapoel Beit Sh'an	H	1-0	Pitusi
09/03/96	Beitar Tel-Aviv	A	0-0	
16/03/96	Maccabi Tel-Aviv	H	0-2	
23/03/96	Bnei Yehuda	A	1-1	Drori
30/03/96	Hapoel Haifa	H	0-1	
13/04/96	Hapoel Kfar-Saba	A	1-4	Drori
20/04/96	Maccabi Petach-Tikva	H	1-2	Ohana
27/04/96	Hapoel Irony Rishon Lezion	H	1-2	Moroz
04/05/96	Hapoel Beer Sheva	A	0-0	
11/05/96	Maccabi Herzliya	H	1-0	Levi D.
18/05/96	Hapoel Tel-Aviv	A	2-4	og (Fliter), Netzer

MACCABI PETACH-TIKVA

CLUB DIRECTORY

Maccabi Petach-Tikva
P.O. Box 67
Petach-Tikva
tel - (03) 9224484
fax - (09) 851383
Year of Formation - 1912
Chairman - Avraham Luzon
Secretary - Nahom Besser
Coach - Menache Nuriel; Avraham Marchinsk
Stadium - Hapoel Petach-Tikva (7,500)

MAJOR HONOURS

Domestic Cup - (2) 1935, 1952.

APPEARANCES 95/96

	P	Ap	(s)	Gls
Morad ABU KISHEK	D	24	(2)	
Issmael AMAR	M	8	(6)	
Eyal BEGLAIBTER	M	12	(1)	2
Tal BENAYA	D	10	(9)	3
Nissim BEN DAVID	A	9	(6)	2
Ohad COHEN	G	1		
Tamir DANIEL	D	5	(8)	
Alexander GAYDUK (UKR)	A	5	(3)	2
Najwan GHRAYIV	A	26	(1)	10
Guy ITZHAK	M	26	(3)	4
Noam KEISSY	M	25		1
Leionid LIBERMAN	M	5	(2)	1
Guy LUZON	D	4		
Murat MAGOMEDOV (RUS)	D	24		
Golan MALUL	G	29		
Uzzi OHAION	M	9	(6)	
David PERETS	D	5	(3)	
Roman PILIPCHUK (BLS)	A	27		15
Raz RABINOVITCH	D	19	(1)	
Haim SHABO	M	11	(3)	
SHMARIAHO	M		(1)	
Yossi SHOSHANI	M	17	(4)	1
Moshe SURAMELO	A	2	(3)	1
Sharon TZOFIN	D	27		1

LEAGUE RESULTS 1995/96

Date	Opponent		Score	Scorers
26/08/95	Zafririm Holon	A	4-4	Ghrayiv, Gayduk 2, Itzhak
10/09/95	Hapoel Petach-Tikva	H	3-1	Pilipchuk 2, Itzhak
17/09/95	Beitar Jerusalem	A	1-3	Itzhak
30/09/95	Hapoel Beit Sh'an	H	2-1	Pilipchuk, Ghrayiv
14/10/95	Beitar Tel-Aviv	A	0-4	
21/10/95	Maccabi Tel-Aviv	H	0-3	
28/10/95	Bnei Yehuda	A	4-1	Ghrayiv, Pilipchuk 2, Beglaibter
04/11/95	Hapoel Haifa	H	2-1	Ghrayiv 2
11/11/95	Hapoel Kfar-Saba	A	3-0	Pilipchuk 3
25/11/95	Hapoel Irony Rishon Lezion	A	2-0	Benaya 2
02/12/95	Maccabi Jaffa	H	2-1	Keissy, Itzhak
10/12/95	Hapoel Beer Sheva	A	1-0	Ghrayiv
17/12/95	Maccabi Herzliya	H	1-2	Ghrayiv
24/12/95	Hapoel Tel-Aviv	A	0-0	
30/12/95	Maccabi Haifa	H	2-2	Pilipchuk, Benaya
27/01/96	Zafririm Holon	H	0-0	
03/02/96	Hapoel Petach-Tikva	A	1-1	Ghrayiv
10/02/96	Beitar Jerusalem	H	0-0	
17/02/96	Hapoel Beit Sh'an	A	1-0	Ghrayiv
02/03/96	Beitar Tel-Aviv	H	3-0	Liberman, Pilipchuk, Tzofin
09/03/96	Maccabi Tel-Aviv	A	0-0	
16/03/96	Bnei Yehuda	H	3-1	Ghrayiv, Beglaibter, Pilipchuk
23/03/96	Hapoel Haifa	A	0-2	
30/03/96	Hapoel Kfar-Saba	H	0-2	
13/04/96	Hapoel Irony Rishon Lezion	H	1-1	Ben David
20/04/96	Maccabi Jaffa	A	2-1	Pilipchuk 2
27/04/96	Hapoel Beer Sheva	H	0-0	
04/05/96	Maccabi Herzliya	A	4-1	Pilipchuk, Soramelo, Shoshani, Ben David
11/05/96	Hapoel Tel-Aviv	H	0-4	
18/05/96	Maccabi Haifa	A	1-1	Pilipchuk

MACCABI TEL-AVIV

CLUB DIRECTORY

Maccabi Tel-Aviv
Maccabi St. 4
Tel-Aviv 63293
tel - (03) 5250712
fax - (03) 5288503
Year of Formation - 1906
Chairman - Tamir Gilat
Secretary - Shimon Korek
Coach - Dror Kashtan (96/97 - Avraham Grant)
Stadium - Bloomfield (28,000)

MAJOR HONOURS
League Championship - (18)
1937, 1939, 1941, 1947, 1949, 1950, 1951, 1952, 1954, 1956, 1968, 1970, 1972, 1977, 1979, 1992, 1995, 1996.
Domestic Cup - (19)
1929, 1930, 1933, 1941, 1946, 1947, 1954, 1955, 1958, 1959, 1964, 1965, 1967, 1970, 1977, 1987, 1988, 1994, 1996.

APPEARANCES 95/96

	P	Ap	(s)	Gls
Kobi ABRAHMOV	A		(1)	
Alon BRUMER	M	6	(3)	
Gadi BRUMER	D	28		
Eli DRIKS	A	23	(6)	15
Ran DZILOWSKY	M		(2)	
Gal FIBACH	D	2	(10)	
Offir HAIM	D		(1)	
Haim HAJAJ	M	13	(6)	
Yehiel HIYAWI	M		(1)	
Jacob HILEL	D	23	(4)	1
Yevgeni KASHENTSEV (BLS)	A	18	(10)	8
Nir KLINGER	D	28		10
Amit LEVI	D	10	(3)	
Meir MELIKA	A	2	(10)	1
Victor MOROZ (UKR)	M	17	(8)	2
Guy NACHMAN	D	6	(9)	
Ron NACHMAN	D	22	(2)	
Avi NIMNI	M	23		10
Amir SHELACH	D	29		1
Noam SHOAM	M	29		1
Aleksander UBAROV (RUS)	G	30		
Itzhak ZOHAR	M	21		9

LEAGUE RESULTS 1995/96

Date	Opponent	H/A	Score	Scorers
26/08/95	Beitar Tel-Aviv	A	3-0	Moroz, Nimni, Kashentsev
10/09/95	Hapoel Irony Rishon Lezion	A	2-1	Zohar, Nimni
17/09/95	Bnei Yehuda	H	4-1	Zohar, Kashentsev, Klinger 2
30/09/95	Hapoel Haifa	A	0-3	
14/10/95	Hapoel Kfar-Saba	H	3-1	Klinger, Driks, Kashentsev
21/10/95	Maccabi Petach-Tikva	A	3-0	Klinger, Shelach, Driks
28/10/95	Maccabi Jaffa	H	3-0	Driks, Klinger, Nimni
04/11/95	Hapoel Beer Sheva	A	3-1	Klinger, Zohar, Driks
11/11/95	Maccabi Herzliya	H	1-0	Zohar
25/11/95	Hapoel Tel-Aviv	A	2-0	Kashentsev, Zohar
02/12/95	Maccabi Haifa	H	2-2	Klinger, Driks
10/12/95	Zafririm Holon	A	5-0	Nimni, Driks 3, Melika
17/12/95	Hapoel Petach-Tikva	H	3-0	Driks, Nimni, Klinger
24/12/95	Beitar Jerusalem	A	0-2	
31/12/95	Hapoel Beit Sh'an	H	0-0	
27/01/96	Beitar Tel-Aviv	H	2-0	Shoam, Zohar
03/02/96	Hapoel Irony Rishon Lezion	H	1-0	Driks
10/02/96	Bnei Yehuda	A	3-2	og (Amsalem), Klinger, Zohar
17/02/96	Hapoel Haifa	H	1-0	Moroz
02/03/96	Hapoel Kfar-Saba	A	2-1	Driks 2
09/03/96	Maccabi Petach-Tikva	H	0-0	
16/03/96	Maccabi Jaffa	A	2-0	Nimni, Kashentsev
23/03/96	Hapoel Beer Sheva	H	5-0	Kashentsev 3, Driks, Nimni
30/03/96	Maccabi Herzliya	A	1-1	Driks
13/04/96	Hapoel Tel-Aviv	H	0-0	
20/04/96	Maccabi Haifa	A	3-1	Driks, Klinger, Nimni
27/04/96	Zafririm Holon	H	1-0	Zohar
04/05/96	Hapoel Petach-Tikva	A	2-0	Hilel, Zohar
11/05/96	Beitar Jerusalem	H	1-0	Nimni
17/05/96	Hapoel Beit Sh'an	A	1-0	Nimni

ZAFRIRIM HOLON

CLUB DIRECTORY

Zafririm Holon
Halochamim St. 1
P.O. Box 146
Holon 58101
tel - (03) 5059926
fax - (03) 5038666
Year of Formation - 1972
Chairman - Shtern Haluba
Secretary - Toby Malach
Coach - Murdechy Shpiegler; Elisha Levi
Stadium - Zafririm (3,500)

APPEARANCES 95/96

	P	Ap	(s)	Gls
Dror AHARONOV	D	2	(1)	
Dénes ESZENYI (HUN)	A	19	(2)	7
Avi FASS	M	6		3
Ronen FAYGENBAUM	D	25	(1)	
Haim GOLDBERG	D	21	(6)	
Ran HAFIF	M	11	(2)	4
Shay HOLTZMAN	A	21	(3)	6
Shimon ISRAEL	G	2		
Motti IWANIR	M	4	(3)	
Aleksander JIDKOV (AZB)	G	28		
David KAVEDA	A	1	(2)	
Ziv KAVEDA	M	5	(7)	
Ma'ayn MASHICH	G		(1)	
Fabrice MEGE (FRA)	D	2	(3)	1
Guy MISHAL	D	26	(1)	
Oren NISSIM	M	5	(14)	
Avi PERETS	D	3	(3)	
Roman PETS (UKR)	D	15		
David PIZANTI	D	23	(4)	
Ya'akov PUSTACHI	M	4	(2)	
Amit SEGAL	D	11	(1)	
Dudu SHAAR	M	18	(7)	1
Hezi SHIRAZI	A	23		7
Idan SHUM	M	11	(8)	
Eliezer SPAYER	D	15	(2)	
Assi TUBI	A	7	(4)	1
Oren ZEITUNI	D	22	(1)	

LEAGUE RESULTS 1995/96

Date	Opponent		Score	Scorers
26/08/95	Maccabi Petach-Tikva	H	4-4	Holtzman, Mège, Tubi, Shirazi
10/09/95	Maccabi Jaffa	A	2-4	Holtzman, Shirazi
17/09/95	Hapoel Beer Sheva	H	1-2	Holtzman
30/09/95	Maccabi Herzliya	A	1-0	Shirazi
14/10/95	Hapoel Tel-Aviv	H	0-1	
21/10/95	Maccabi Haifa	A	1-2	Fass
28/10/95	Hapoel Irony Rishon Lezion	H	1-2	Fass
04/11/95	Hapoel Petach-Tikva	H	0-2	
15/11/95	Beitar Jerusalem	A	0-1	
24/11/95	Hapoel Beit Sh'an	H	2-1	Eszenyi 2
02/12/95	Beitar Tel-Aviv	A	2-1	Fass, Holtzman
10/12/95	Maccabi Tel-Aviv	H	0-5	
17/12/95	Bnei Yehuda	A	2-3	Shirazi 2
24/12/95	Hapoel Haifa	H	3-3	Holtzman, Shirazi, Eszenyi
31/12/95	Hapoel Kfar-Saba	A	0-3	
27/01/96	Maccabi Petach-Tikva	A	0-0	
02/02/96	Maccabi Jaffa	H	0-1	
09/02/96	Hapoel Beer Sheva	A	1-0	Eszenyi
17/02/96	Maccabi Herzliya	H	0-2	
02/03/96	Hapoel Tel-Aviv	A	0-1	
09/03/96	Maccabi Haifa	H	1-1	Shirazi
16/03/96	Hapoel Irony Rishon Lezion	A	2-1	Hafif, og (Ben Dov)
22/03/96	Hapoel Petach-Tikva	A	0-1	
30/03/96	Beitar Jerusalem	H	0-3	
13/04/96	Hapoel Beit Sh'an	A	1-1	Holtzman
20/04/96	Beitar Tel-Aviv	H	2-0	Hafif, Eszenyi
27/04/96	Maccabi Tel-Aviv	A	0-1	
04/05/96	Bnei Yehuda	H	5-2	og (Sivilia), Hafif 2, Shaar, Eszenyi
11/05/96	Hapoel Haifa	A	1-4	Eszenyi
18/05/96	Hapoel Kfar-Saba	H	0-0	

PROMOTED CLUBS

SECOND DIVISION FINAL TABLE 95/96

		Pd	W	D	L	F	A	Pt	GD
1	**Hapoel Taibe**	**30**	**18**	**4**	**8**	**40**	**31**	**58**	**+9**
2	**Hapoel Jerusalem**	**30**	**15**	**9**	**6**	**43**	**24**	**54**	**+19**
3	Hapoel Bat-Yam	30	10	13	7	38	31	43	+7
4	Maccabi Kiriat-Gat	30	12	6	12	33	34	42	-1
5	Irony Ashdod	30	10	10	10	43	34	40	+9
6	Hapoel Ramat-Gan	30	10	10	10	34	32	40	+2
7	Hakoah Ramat-Gan	30	11	7	12	36	36	40	=
8	Maccabi Ako	30	9	13	8	36	37	40	-1
9	Maccabi Netanya	30	9	12	9	38	28	39	+10
10	Hapoel Ashdod	30	10	9	11	42	41	39	+1
11	Maccabi Yavne	30	9	12	9	26	28	39	-2
12	Hapoel Hadera	30	10	8	12	30	38	38	-8
13	Seksiat Nes-Ziona	30	10	8	12	35	44	38	-9
14	Hapoel Kiriat Shmona	30	8	13	9	32	38	37	-6
15	Shimshon Tel-Aviv	30	9	9	12	39	44	36	-5
16	Hapoel Kfar-Shalem	30	4	9	17	19	44	21	-25

CLUB DIRECTORY

Hapoel Taibe
P.O. Box 2254
Taibe 40400
tel - (09) 993519
fax - (09) 993399
Year of Formation - 1964
Chairman - Abdel Kaader Haj Yiayee
Secretary - Halil Daher
Coach - Amy Elhadad (96/97 - Wojciech Lazarek)
Stadium - Municipal "Taibe" (3,000)

CLUB DIRECTORY

Hapoel Jerusalem
Stadium "Teddi"
Jerusalem
tel - (02) 611881
Year of Formation - 1953
President - Yaussi Sassi
Manager - Uri Malmilian
Coach - Yossi Mizrahi
Stadium - "Tedd", Malcha (13,000)

MAJOR HONOURS
Domestic Cup - (1) 1973.

ITALY

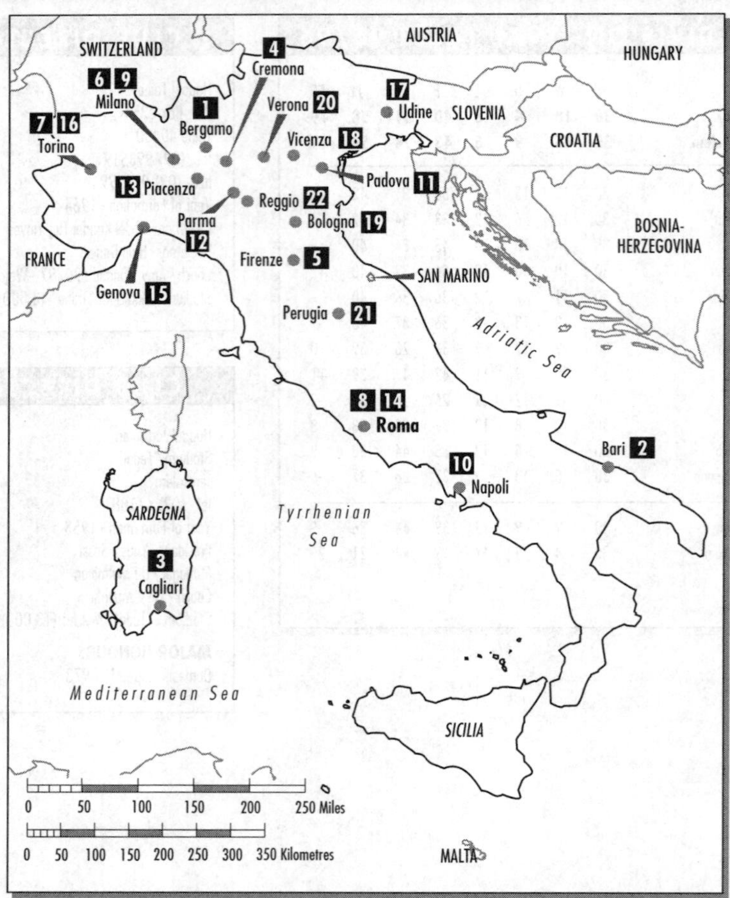

1	ATALANTA	595
2	BARI	596
3	CAGLIARI	597
4	CREMONESE	598
5	FIORENTINA	599
6	INTER	600
7	JUVENTUS	601
8	LAZIO	602
9	MILAN	603
10	NAPOLI	604
11	PADOVA	605
12	PARMA	606
13	PIACENZA	607
14	ROMA	608
15	SAMPDORIA	609
16	TORINO	610
17	UDINESE	611
18	VICENZA	612
19	BOLOGNA	613
20	VERONA	613
21	PERUGIA	613
22	REGGIANA	613

JUVENTUS LIFT CHAMPIONS' CUP

Arrogance proves fatal to 'Azzurri' bid

FEDERATION DIRECTORY

Federazione Italiana Giuoco Calcio
Via Gregorio Allegri 14, CP 2450, 00198 Roma
tel - (06) 84911
tlx - 611483 calcio i
fax - (06) 8491239

Year of Formation - 1898
President - Antonio Matarrese
Secretary - Dr. Giorgio Zappacosta

Arrigo Sacchi somehow managed to hold onto his position as national coach after Italy's flop at Euro '96. But the Italian public are unlikely to forgive and forget. In the view of many, Sacchi alone was responsible for Italy's first-round failure. Had he not committed the cardinal sin of tampering unnecessarily with a winning team, the *Azzurri* would surely not have lost their all-important second match against the Czech Republic at Anfield.

It was a foolish mistake, an arrogant and complacent reaction to the general euphoria that had greeted Italy's opening 2-1 victory over Russia. Sacchi believed he could get away with resting five of his first-choice midfielders and forwards against the Czech Republic. He was wrong. Defender Luigi Apolloni certainly didn't do his team any favours by getting himself stupidly sent off in the first half, but it was Sacchi's rash selection that had first handed the initiative to the Czechs, and he had to bear the responsibility for that.

Against Germany at Old Trafford, Italy had ample opportunity to extract themselves from their precarious position. They dominated the match from start to finish, but Gianfranco Zola's early penalty miss (and the referee's failure to show German 'keeper Andy Köpke the red card) ultimately condemned them to a goalless draw. The Czech Republic's late equaliser against Russia was the final nail in Italy's coffin. The *Azzurri* had begun the tournament as one of the favourites, but they were on their way back to Italy after just three games.

The only factor in Sacchi's defence as he returned home to frenzied calls for his dismissal was that Italy were

LEAGUE CHAMPIONSHIP RESULTS 95/96

		1	2	3	4	5	6	7	8	9	10	11	12	13	14	15	16	17	18
1	Atalanta		1-2	3-0	1-1	1-3	1-1	0-1	1-3	0-1	1-3	3-0	1-1	2-0	2-1	3-2	1-0	0-0	3-1
2	Bari	1-3		3-0	2-1	1-1	4-1	2-2	3-3	1-0	1-1	2-1	1-1	0-0	1-2	1-3	2-2	4-2	0-2
3	Cagliari	2-0	4-2		1-0	0-0	0-0	0-0	0-1	1-2	2-0	0-1	2-0	0-0	0-2	3-0	1-0	4-1	2-0
4	Cremonese	1-1	7-1	3-1		0-0	2-4	3-3	2-1	0-0	1-1	2-1	0-2	0-0	0-1	0-0	1-1	2-2	1-1
5	Fiorentina	1-0	3-2	3-1	3-2		1-1	0-1	2-0	2-2	3-0	6-4	1-0	2-1	1-4	2-2	2-0	3-0	1-1
6	Inter	1-0	3-0	4-0	2-0	1-2		1-2	0-0	1-1	4-0	8-2	1-1	0-0	2-0	0-2	4-0	2-1	1-0
7	Juventus	1-0	1-1	4-1	4-1	1-0	1-0		4-2	1-1	1-1	3-1	1-0	2-0	0-2	0-3	5-0	2-1	1-0
8	Lazio	5-1	4-3	4-0	2-1	4-0	0-1	4-0		0-1	1-0	2-0	2-1	4-1	1-0	6-3	1-1	2-2	3-0
9	Milan	3-0	3-2	3-2	7-1	3-1	0-1	2-1	0-0		0-0	1-0	3-0	3-0	3-1	3-0	1-1	2-1	4-0
10	Napoli	2-0	1-0	0-0	0-0	0-2	2-1	0-1	1-0	0-1		2-0	1-1	0-0	0-2	1-0	1-0	2-1	1-1
11	Padova	3-2	3-0	2-1	1-2	0-1	2-1	0-5	1-3	1-2	4-2		1-3	1-1	1-2	1-1	1-1	2-3	3-2
12	Parma	2-0	3-1	4-0	2-0	3-0	2-1	1-1	2-1	0-0	1-0	2-1		3-2	1-1	1-0	1-0	1-0	0-1
13	Piacenza	2-2	3-2	1-1	2-1	0-1	1-0	0-4	2-1	0-2	0-1	4-0	2-1		1-0	3-2	1-0	0-2	0-1
14	Roma	0-1	2-1	1-1	3-0	2-2	1-0	2-2	0-0	1-2	4-1	2-0	1-1	2-1		3-1	1-0	2-1	1-1
15	Sampdoria	2-3	2-0	1-2	2-0	2-1	0-0	2-0	3-3	3-0	2-2	3-1	3-0	3-0	1-1		1-0	1-0	2-2
16	Torino	0-1	3-1	1-1	1-0	0-3	0-1	1-2	0-2	1-1	0-0	2-0	2-2	4-2	2-2	1-1		2-0	1-0
17	Udinese	3-0	1-2	1-0	3-2	1-0	1-2	1-0	1-1	0-2	3-2	3-1	0-0	0-0	1-1	2-4	1-0		1-1
18	Vicenza	1-0	2-0	0-1	1-0	1-0	1-1	2-1	1-0	1-1	3-0	2-1	0-1	1-1	2-1	2-2	2-1	0-1	

LEAGUE CHAMPIONSHIP FINAL TABLE 95/96

			Home					Away					Total						
		Pd	W	D	L	F	A	W	D	L	F	A	W	D	L	F	A	Pt	GD
1	Milan	34	13	3	1	41	11	8	7	2	19	13	21	10	3	60	24	73	+36
2	Juventus	34	12	3	2	32	14	7	5	5	26	21	19	8	7	58	35	65	+23
3	Lazio	34	13	2	2	45	15	4	6	7	21	23	17	8	9	66	38	59	+28
4	Fiorentina	34	11	4	2	36	21	6	4	7	17	20	17	8	9	53	41	59	+12
5	Parma	34	13	3	1	29	9	3	7	7	15	22	16	10	8	44	31	58	+13
6	Roma	34	9	6	2	28	15	7	4	6	23	19	16	10	8	51	34	58	+17
7	Inter	34	10	4	3	35	11	5	5	7	16	19	15	9	10	51	30	54	+21
8	Sampdoria	34	10	5	2	33	15	4	5	8	26	32	14	10	10	59	47	52	+12
9	Vicenza	34	10	4	3	22	12	3	6	8	14	25	13	10	11	36	37	49	-1
10	Cagliari	34	9	4	4	22	9	2	4	11	12	38	11	8	15	34	47	41	-13
11	Udinese	34	8	5	4	23	18	3	3	11	18	31	11	8	15	41	49	41	-8
12	Napoli	34	8	5	4	14	10	2	6	9	14	31	10	11	13	28	41	41	-13
13	Atalanta	34	7	4	6	24	20	4	2	11	14	30	11	6	17	38	50	39	-12
14	Piacenza	34	9	2	6	22	21	0	8	9	9	27	9	10	15	31	48	37	-17
15	Bari	34	6	7	4	29	25	2	1	14	20	46	8	8	18	49	71	32	-22
16	Torino	34	6	6	5	21	19	0	5	12	7	27	6	11	17	28	46	29	-18
17	Cremonese	34	4	10	3	25	20	1	2	14	12	37	5	12	17	37	57	27	-20
18	Padova	34	6	3	8	27	32	1	0	16	14	47	7	3	24	41	79	24	-38

actually one of the more attractive and entertaining teams on show at Euro '96. There was excitement in every game they played, and had the Czechs not sneaked that late goal against Russia, or had Pierluigi Casiraghi put away a great injury-time chance against the Czechs, they could have gone on to win the competition. In a way, the high performance level of Italy's play made Sacchi's erroneous selection policy even harder to bear.

With Group C rivals Germany and the Czech Republic eventually going on to contest the final, Italian public and press knew that Euro '96 was a tournament they could, maybe should, have won. But the luck they had ridden on their journey to the World Cup final two years earlier was conspicuous by its absence in England. No Italian player stood out at Euro '96. There were the odd classy performances, by Casiraghi and Demetrio Albertini against Russia, by Angelo Peruzzi and Enrico Chiesa against the Czechs, and by Roberto Donadoni against Germany, but nothing which came remotely close to the sustained brilliance of Roberto Baggio in America.

Baggio was one of a number of star names missing from the Italian squad. Gianluca Vialli had joined Franco

TOP SCORERS

24	Igor PROTTI (Bari)
	Giuseppe SIGNORI (Lazio)
22	Enrico CHIESA (Sampdoria)
19	Gabriel BATISTUTA (Fiorentina)
	Marco BRANCA (Roma/Inter)
17	Oliver BIERHOFF (Udinese)
15	Luis OLIVEIRA (Cagliari)
14	Pierluigi CASIRAGHI (Lazio)
	Nicola AMORUSO (Padova)
	Nicola CACCIA (Piacenza)

NATIONAL TEAM RESULTS 95/96

06/09/95	Slovenia (ECQ)	H	Udine	1-0	Ravanelli (13)
08/10/95	Croatia (ECQ)	A	Split	1-1	Albertini (29)
11/11/95	Ukraine (ECQ)	H	Bari	3-1	Ravanelli (21, 49), Maldini (54)
15/11/95	Lithuania (ECQ)	H	Reggio Emilia	4-0	Suika (52og), Zola (65, 81), Vainoras (82og)
24/01/96	Wales	H	Terni	3-0	Del Piero (2), Ravanelli (50), Casiraghi (77)
29/05/96	Belgium	H	Cremona	2-2	Del Piero (25), Chiesa (55)
01/06/96	Hungary	A	Budapest	2-0	Casiraghi (6), Bánfi (47og)
11/06/96	Russia (ECF)	N	Liverpool	2-1	Casiraghi (5, 52)
14/06/96	Czech Republic (ECF)	N	Liverpool	1-2	Chiesa (18)
19/06/96	Germany (ECF)	N	Manchester	0-0	

NATIONAL TEAM APPEARANCES 95/96

Coach - Arrigo SACCHI	SLO	CRO	UKR	LIT	WAL	BEL	HUN	RUS	TCH	GER	Cps	Gls
Angelo PERUZZI (16/02/70) - Juventus	G		G	G	G46	G	G46	G	G	G	11	-
Ciro FERRARA (11/02/67) - Juventus	D	D84	D	D	D46	D46					33	-
Alessandro COSTACURTA (24/04/66) - Milan	D	D	D	D	D		D	D	D	D	39	2
Alessio TACCHINARDI (23/07/75) - Juventus	D										1	-
Amedeo CARBONI (06/04/65) - Roma	D		s87	s72	D	D	D46		s39	D78	14	-
Angelo DI LIVIO (26/07/66) - Juventus	M	M			M79	M46	M	M62	s81		7	-
Roberto DI MATTEO (29/05/70) - Lazio	M	M	M	M	M23	M	M	M		M68	15	-
Demetrio ALBERTINI (23/08/71) - Milan	M	M	M	M	M	M	M70	M	M	M	39	-
Alessandro DEL PIERO (09/11/74) - Juventus	M46	M86	M87	M	M73	M65	M62	M46			11	2
Gianfranco ZOLA (05/07/66) - Parma	A61	A9	A67	s46	A	A		A	s78	A	23	6
Fabrizio RAVANELLI (11/12/68) - Juventus	A81	A	A	s46	A	A46	A	s80	A58		11	5
Giuseppe SIGNORI (17/02/68) - Lazio	s46										28	7
Roberto BAGGIO (18/02/67) - Milan	s61										45	24
Dino BAGGIO (24/07/71) - Parma	s81		M46			s65			M39		31	7
Luca BUCCI (13/03/69) - Parma		G									3	-
Luigi APOLLONI (02/05/67) - Parma		D			D	D	s46	D	D		14	1
Paolo MALDINI (26/06/68) - Milan		D	D	D72			D46	D	D	D	71	3
Francesco TOLDO (02/12/71) - Fiorentina		s9			s46		s46				3	-
Antonio BENARRIVO (21/08/68) - Parma		s84	D								20	-
Massimo CRIPPA (17/05/65) - Parma		s86	s46		s79						17	1
Marco SIMONE (07/01/69) - Milan			s67	A							3	-
Roberto MUSSI (25/08/63) - Parma				D		D		D	D	D	11	-
Francesco STATUTO (13/07/71) - Roma				M46							3	-
Pierluigi CASIRAGHI (04/03/69) - Lazio				A46	s73	s46	A	A80	s58	A	34	10
Antonio CONTE (31/07/69) - Juventus					s23						6	-
Moreno TORRICELLI (23/01/70) - Juventus					s46	s46	D			s78	4	-
Enrico CHIESA (29/12/70) - Sampdoria						s46			A78	s68	3	2
Diego FUSER (11/11/68) - Lazio							s46	s62	M	M81	8	-
Roberto DONADONI (09/09/63) - NY/NJ Metrostars (USA)							s62	s46	M	M	63	5
Fabio ROSSITTO (21/09/71) - Udinese							s70				1	-

Baresi in self-enforced international retirement earlier in the season after a major fall-out with Sacchi. And Lazio striker Giuseppe Signori was bizarrely omitted from the 22 despite finishing the season as Serie A's joint-top goalscorer. With the Juventus pair of Ciro Ferrara and Antonio Conte also dropping out at the last minute due to injury problems, there was a strong feeling that Sacchi's squad lacked big-tournament experience.

Further disappointment for Italian fans came later in the summer when Italy's U-21 team, fresh from winning the European Championship in Spain, were bundled out in the first round of the Olympics in Atlanta. Defeats in their opening two games by Mexico and Ghana brought an early exit, which served to scotch the widely held notion that the U-21 coach, Cesare Maldini (father of Paolo), would be taking over from Sacchi in the senior team hot seat in time for the World Cup qualifying tournament.

It will not be an easy ride to France for Italy. They are marginal favourites to top a difficult group that includes England, Poland, Georgia and Moldova. But any major slip-up - and the trip to Wembley in February 1997 is most definitely a potential banana-skin - could see the Italian FA's patience with Sacchi finally run out.

Italian national selections may not have delivered the goods in the summer of 1996, but Italian club sides still have plenty to boast about. The 1995/96 season did not provide the across-the-board European success of recent campaigns, but there was a victory in the one competition that really carries weight in Italy - the European Champions' Cup.

Rome's Stadio Olimpico was the venue in May for Juventus's second Champions' Cup triumph. For many associated with the famous Turin club, it was their first genuine victory in Europe's premier club competition, the 1985 win over Liverpool in Brussels having taken place on a black night that every football fan would gladly see erased from the history-books.

A penalty shoot-out was required to separate Juventus from defending champions Ajax in the final, but the Italians undoubtedly deserved to lift the trophy. They were the more purposeful and ambitious team throughout the two hours, creating enough chances to have settled the outcome long before the enforced charade of the penalty competition.

Juventus reached the final having lost three matches en route. That might suggest that they struggled their way through, but the reality is that their presence in the final was only in doubt for one brief moment, when Real Madrid came tantalisingly close to a decisive away goal at the end of their quarter-final. Other than that, Juve were in complete control of their destiny. In the Champions' League during the autumn they belied their modest domestic form with a series of exceptional displays. Big wins in Dortmund and Glasgow proved that they were a class above the other tams in their section, and in young Alessandro Del Piero they possessed the star of the tournament. He scored in each of his first five Champions' League matches, and every goal bore a mark of premier quality.

Had Del Piero been able to reproduce his Wednesday night form on Sunday afternoons, Juventus might have made a better fist of their Serie A title defence. But it was clear from the outset that the club's priority was success in Europe. Everything else took a back seat.

Juventus were knocked out early in the Italian Cup by Atalanta, and they never really forced themselves into contention for a second successive *scudetto*. Early away defeats against Milan (1-2) and Lazio (0-4) distanced

DOMESTIC CUP RESULTS

FIRST ROUND
Avellino 1, Fidelis Andria 0
Varese 0, Cremonese 1
Pistoiese 0, Perugia 1
Lucchese 4, Ancona 0
Trapani 1, Reggiana 1 (aet; 5-6 on pens.)
Bologna 2, Verona 0
Forlì 1, Foggia 0
Como 0, Pescara 1
Reggina 1, Chievo 2
Gualdo 0, Genoa 4
Cosenza 0, Venezia 0 (aet; 5-6 on pens.)
Fiorenzuola 2, Brescia 1 (aet)
Ascoli 0, Salernitana 0 (aet; 3-1 on pens.)
Lecce 2, Cesena 1
Monza 0, Padova 2
Acireale 0, Palermo 2

SECOND ROUND
Avellino 1, Juventus 4
Atalanta 2, Cremonese 2 (aet; 4-2 on pens.)
Perugia 0, Sampdoria 1
Lucchese 3, Cagliari 4 (aet)
Reggiana 2, Bari 0
Bologna 1, Roma 0
Forlì 1, Piacenza 1 (aet; 4-3 on pens.)
Pescara 1, Milan 4
Chievo 1, Lazio 1 (aet; 3-4 on pens.)
Udinese 3, Genoa 0
Venezia 0, Inter 1
Fiorenzuola 2, Torino 1
Ascoli 1, Fiorentina 2
Lecce 1, Napoli 0
Vicenza 4, Padova 2
Palermo 3, Parma 0

THIRD ROUND
Atalanta 1, Juventus 0 (aet)
Cagliari 2, Sampdoria 1
Bologna 3, Reggiana 0
Forlì 0, Milan 2
Udinese 0, Lazio 1
Fiorenzuola 1, Inter 2
Lecce 0, Fiorentina 5
Palermo 1, Vicenza 0

QUARTER-FINALS
Cagliari v Atalanta 1-0; 2-4
(Atalanta 4-3)
Bologna v Milan 1-1; 1-1 (aet)
(2-2; Bologna 7-6 on pens.)
Inter v Lazio 1-1; 1-0
(Inter 2-1)
Fiorentina v Palermo 1-0; 2-1
(Fiorentina 3-1)

SEMI-FINALS
Bologna v Atalanta 1-1; 0-2 (Atalanta 3-1)
Fiorentina v Inter 3-1; 1-0 (Fiorentina 4-1)

FINAL
01/05/96, Florence
FIORENTINA 1 Batistuta (52)
ATALANTA 0
referee - Boggi
FIORENTINA - Toldo; Carnasciali, Amoruso, Piacentini, Padalino, Sottil (Bigica 85), Schwarz, Orlando M. (Banchelli 46), Batistuta, Rui Costa, Robbiati.
ATALANTA - Ferron; Pavone (Salvatori 79), Paganin, Valentini, Herrera, Montero, Gallo (Sgrò 79), Fortunato, Tovalieri (Pisani 84), Bonacina, Morfeo.

18/05/96, Bergamo
ATALANTA 0
FIORENTINA 2 Amoruso (48), Batistuta (61)
referee - Pairetto
ATALANTA - Ferron; Herrera, Pavone (Temelin 59), Valentini, Paganin (Rotella 49), Montero, Gallo (Salvatori 67), Bonacina, Tovalieri, Fortunato, Morfeo.
FIORENTINA - Toldo (Mareggini 89); Carnasciali, Cois, Amoruso, Padalino, Malusci, Piacentini, Bigica, Batistuta, Rui Costa, Flachi (Robbiati 63; Orlando M. 88).

(FIORENTINA 3-0)

Juve's Gianluca Vialli in action against Real Madrid during their Champions' Cup quarter-final encounter

them from the leading pack, and it was not until the early spring that they at last put together a prolonged run of positive results. With just one defeat in their last 14 games, assisted by an extraordinary number of own-goals, Juventus managed to climb up to a comfortable second place. But the big prize all along was waiting for the *Bianconeri* in Rome.

For captain Gianluca Vialli and other Juve stalwarts such as Pietro Vierchowod, Fabrizio Ravanelli and Paulo Sousa, the Champions' Cup triumph was the ultimate parting gift. All of those players sought pastures new in the summer as Juventus maintained the policy of austerity which had led to Roberto Baggio's departure a year earlier. One man staying put, however, was coach Marcello Lippi. In just two years at Juventus, he had won the Italian championship, the Italian Cup and now the European Champions' Cup. Whatever the financial climate, some people have no price. For Juventus, Lippi surely belongs in that category.

One big-name Italian coach who *was* on his way out at the end of the season was none other than Milan's Fabio Capello. There were tears in Capello's eyes as he strode around the San Siro pitch following the 3-1 victory over Fiorentina which gave Milan their 15th *scudetto,* and the fourth in the five years of his reign.

Initially destined to join Parma, Capello finally agreed to leave Italian football completely and join Real Madrid. It certainly would have been difficult to imagine Capello leading another Italian club into battle against his beloved *Rossoneri.* But it is likely that Milan will miss Capello as much as he will miss them. His record at the club speaks for itself.

The club's 15th Italian title was never in much doubt right from the early weeks of the season. The arrival of big Liberian forward George Weah revitalised the Milan attack, and he was to provide many important and spectacular goals, such as the winner at home to Juventus in October and a brilliant late solo effort away to Lazio in early December. The club's other major new signing, Roberto Baggio, was less effective. He seemed less at ease in his new environment. Perhaps it was the sight of his rival, Dejan Savicevic, wearing the number ten shirt that gave Baggio an inferiority complex, but his first season in Milan was not a successful one - despite his second championship medal in as many seasons.

Weah and Baggio apart, Milan were their usual consistent, resilient selves. They led from the front all season, and whenever another challenger came close to knocking them off their perch, Capello's men were able to dig out the right result and retain their leadership. An unbeaten 19-match run through the autumn and winter was the foundation for their triumph.

Their only troubled spell came in March when they were beaten 1-0 by stadium-sharers Inter and then, after a weekend off due to an unprecedented players' strike, travelled to Bordeaux and were sensationally knocked out of the UEFA Cup, losing 0-3 after they had looked certain to progress following a 2-0 win in the San Siro.

Christophe Dugarry, the Frenchman who did most to end Milan's bid for the one European trophy they had never won, was duly signed up by the *Rossoneri* a few months later. With the Ajax pair of Reiziger and Davids also arriving, and no major departures planned (not even Franco Baresi, who celebrated his 500th Serie A match by extending his contract for another season), Milan will be favourites to retain their *scudetto* and reach another

EUROPEAN CUPS RESULTS 95/96

CHAMPIONS' CUP

● JUVENTUS

Champions' League

1st match BORUSSIA DORTMUND (GER)

A 3-1 Padovano (12), Del Piero (36), Conte (68)
Peruzzi; Ferrara, Pessotto, Torricelli, Porrini, Paulo Sousa, Di Livio, Conte (Marocchi 86), Padovano, Del Piero (Deschamps 89), Jugovic.

2nd match STEAUA BUCURESTI (ROM)

H 3-0 Di Livio (34), Del Piero (39), Ravanelli (49)
Peruzzi; Ferrara, Pessotto, Tacchinardi (Vierchowod 82), Torricelli, Paulo Sousa, Di Livio, Deschamps, Vialli, Del Piero (Padovano 72), Ravanelli (Conte 66).

3rd match RANGERS (SCO)

H 4-1 Moore (15og), Conte (23), Del Piero (30), Ravanelli (75)
Peruzzi; Ferrara, Torricelli, Vierchowod, Porrini (Carrera 77), Paulo Sousa, Di Livio (Marocchi 65), Deschamps, Ravanelli, Del Piero, Conte (Tacchinardi 82).

4th match RANGERS (SCO)

A 4-0 Del Piero (11), Torricelli (65), Ravanelli (88), Marocchi (90)
Peruzzi; Torricelli, Pessotto, Carrera, Porrini (Ferrara 79), Paulo Sousa, Di Livio, Tacchinardi (Marocchi 73), Vialli (Ravanelli 70), Del Piero, Conte.

5th match BORUSSIA DORTMUND (GER)

H 1-2 Del Piero (90)
Peruzzi; Porrini, Pessotto, Carrera, Vierchowod, Tacchinardi (Fusi 82), Di Livio, Marocchi, Vialli (Del Piero 65), Jugovic (Sorin 46), Padovano.

6th match STEAUA BUCURESTI (ROM)

A 0-0
Rampulla; Ferrara, Pessotto, Torricelli, Porrini, Carrera, Deschamps, Conte, Marocchi (Lombardo 67), Jugovic, Ravanelli (Del Piero 46).

Quarter-final REAL MADRID (ESP)

A 0-1
Peruzzi; Ferrara, Torricelli, Carrera (Pessotto 77), Vierchowod, Paulo Sousa (Jugovic 65), Lombardo (Padovano 46), Conte, Ravanelli, Del Piero, Deschamps.

H 2-0 Del Piero (16), Padovano (53)
Peruzzi; Torricelli, Pessotto, Vierchowod, Porrini, Jugovic (Di Livio 46), Deschamps, Conte, Vialli, Del Piero (Marocchi 89), Padovano (Lombardo 73).

Semi-final FC NANTES (FRA)

H 2-0 Vialli (49), Jugovic (65)
Peruzzi; Ferrara, Pessotto, Vierchowod (Marocchi 62), Porrini, Paulo Sousa (Carrera 82), Di Livio (Lombardo 75), Jugovic, Vialli, Del Piero, Padovano.

A 2-3 Vialli (17), Paulo Sousa (50)
Peruzzi; Ferrara, Pessotto, Conte, Vierchowod, Carrera, Di Livio, Deschamps, Vialli (Jugovic 79), Del Piero (Paulo Sousa 46), Ravanelli (Padovano 46).

Final AJAX (HOL)

Rome

1-1 Ravanelli (12)

(aet; 4-2 on pens.)
Peruzzi; Ferrara, Pessotto, Torricelli, Vierchowod, Paulo Sousa (Di Livio 57), Deschamps, Conte (Jugovic 43), Vialli, Del Piero, Ravanelli (Padovano 77).

CUP-WINNERS' CUP

● PARMA

1st round TEUTA DURRËS (ALB)

A 2-0 Zola (82, 85)
Bucci; Cannavaro, Benarrivo, Sensini, Apolloni, Mussi (Di Chiara 83), Brolin, Stoichkov, Pin, Zola, Melli (Inzaghi 90).

H 2-0 Melli (8), Inzaghi (90)
Bucci; Benarrivo, Di Chiara, Sensini, Apolloni, Fernando Couto (Cannavaro 42), Melli (Zola 46), Brolin, Crippa (Catanese 72), Brambilla, Inzaghi.

2nd round HALMSTADS BK (SWE)

A 0-3
Bucci; Benarrivo (Mussi 76), Di Chiara, Sensini, Cannavaro, Apolloni, Brolin (Inzaghi 58), Baggio, Stoichkov, Crippa, Zola (Melli 46).

H 4-0 Inzaghi (1), Baggio (28), Stoichkov (53), Andersson T. (59og)
Bucci; Benarrivo, Di Chiara (Mussi 70), Baggio, Cannavaro, Fernando Couto, Sensini, Stoichkov, Inzaghi (Crippa 74), Zola (Brambilla 89), Pin.

Quarter-final PARIS SAINT-GERMAIN FC (FRA)

H 1-0 Stoichkov (58)
Bucci; Benarrivo, Mussi, Sensini, Cannavaro, Apolloni, Pin (Minotti 88), Stoichkov, Baggio (Crippa 75), Zola (Inzaghi 26), Brambilla.

A 1-3 Melli (26)
Bucci; Mussi (Di Chiara 82), Benarrivo, Sensini, Cannavaro, Apolloni, Melli, Stoichkov (Inzaghi 64), Baggio, Brambilla, Pin (Crippa 76).

UEFA CUP

● LAZIO

1st round OMONIA NICOSIA (CYP)

H 5-0 Casiraghi (11, 16, 88), Rambaudi (52), Signori (55p)
Marchegiani (Orsi 89); Romano, Favalli, Di Matteo, Negro, Bergodi, Rambaudi (Di Vaio 66), Fuser (Piovanelli 46), Casiraghi, Winter, Signori.

A 2-1 Casiraghi (15), Di Vaio (75)
Marchegiani; Romano, Nesta, Di Matteo (Marcolin 65), Negro, Bergodi, Rambaudi (Winter 51), Fuser, Casiraghi, Piovanelli, Signori (Di Vaio 31).

2nd round OLYMPIQUE LYONNAIS (FRA)

A 1-2 Winter (23)
Marchegiani; Nesta, Favalli, Di Matteo, Negro, Chamot, Esposito (Bergodi 46), Fuser, Boksic, Winter (Piovanelli 64), Casiraghi.

H 0-2
Orsi; Gottardi (Boksic 27), Favalli, Di Matteo, Negro, Nesta, Rambaudi (Romano 80), Piovanelli, Casiraghi, Winter (Marcolin 68), Signori.

EUROPEAN CUPS RESULTS 95/96 (CONTINUED)

● MILAN

1st round ZAGLEBIE LUBIN (POL)

H 4-0 Savicevic (11), Machaj (47og), Weah (67), Boban (71)
Ielpo; Panucci, Maldini, Albertini (Ambrosini 79), Galli, Baresi, Donadoni, Boban, Weah (Baggio 68), Savicevic (Di Canio 75), Simone.

A 4-1 Eranio (53), Simone (63), Boban (86, 90)
Ielpo; Tassotti, Maldini, Eranio, Galli, Costacurta (Coco 60), Donadoni, Desailly, Weah (Di Canio 52), Boban, Simone (Baggio 73).

2nd round RC STRASBOURG (FRA)

A 1-0 Simone (80)
Ielpo; Panucci, Maldini, Albertini, Costacurta, Baresi, Eranio, Desailly, Weah, Boban (Tassotti 83), Simone (Di Canio 81).

H 2-1 Baggio (29, 44p)
Ielpo; Panucci, Maldini, Albertini, Costacurta, Baresi, Di Canio, Desailly, Boban (Lentini 76), Baggio (Ambrosini 83), Eranio (Tassotti 86).

3rd round SPARTA PRAHA (TCH)

H 2-0 Weah (33, 77)
Ielpo; Panucci, Maldini, Albertini, Costacurta, Baresi, Donadoni (Di Canio 73), Desailly, Weah, Savicevic (Eranio 62), Simone.

A 0-0
Ielpo; Panucci, Maldini, Ambrosini, Costacurta, Baresi, Di Canio (Donadoni 62), Desailly, Weah, Boban (Locatelli 80), Eranio.

Quarter-final GIRONDINS DE BORDEAUX (FRA)

H 2-0 Eranio (29), Baggio (74)
Ielpo; Panucci, Maldini, Vieira, Costacurta, Baresi, Eranio, Desailly, Baggio, Savicevic (Donadoni 88), Simone (Di Canio 73).

A 0-3
Ielpo; Panucci, Maldini, Vieira (Locatelli 71), Costacurta, Baresi, Eranio (Albertini 25), Desailly, Weah, Baggio (Di Canio 46), Donadoni.

● ROMA

1st round NEUCHATEL XAMAX FC (SUI)

A 1-1 Moriero (19)
Cervone; Aldair, Lanna, Statuto, Petruzzi, Carboni, Moriero (Berretta 73), Cappioli, Balbo (Totti 84), Di Biagio, Fonseca (Branca 46).

H 4-0 Balbo (25, 35), Fonseca (32), Rueda (58og)
Cervone; Aldair, Lanna, Statuto, Petruzzi, Carboni (Annoni 46), Moriero (Di Biagio 63), Cappioli, Balbo, Giannini, Fonseca (Totti 75).

2nd round KSC EENDRACHT AALST (BEL)

H 4-0 Vanderhaeghe (60g), Van der Hoorn (51og), Balbo (70), Totti (77)
Cervone; Aldair, Lanna (Cherubini 76), Cappioli, Petruzzi, Statuto, Moriero, Scarchilli (Annoni 46), Balbo, Giannini, Branca (Totti 60).

A 0-0
Cervone; Annoni, Aldair, Statuto, Petruzzi, Lanna, Cappioli, Scarchilli (Moriero 63), Branca (Fonseca 33), Di Biagio (Cherubini 79), Totti.

3rd round BRØNDBY IF (DEN)

A 1-2 Fonseca (17)
Cervone; Annoni, Aldair, Lanna, Petruzzi, Carboni, Moriero, Cappioli, Balbo, Scarchilli (Cherubini 46), Fonseca.

H 3-1 Totti (23), Balbo (72), Carboni (89)
Cervone; Annoni, Lanna, Statuto, Aldair, Carboni, Moriero (Di Biagio 89), Cappioli, Balbo, Thern, Totti.

Quarter-final SLAVIA PRAHA (TCH)

A 0-2
Cervone; Annoni, Lanna, Statuto, Petruzzi, Carboni, Cappioli (Totti 53), Di Biagio, Balbo, Thern, Fonseca.

H 3-1 Moriero (60, 99), Giannini (82)
(aet) Cervone; Annoni, Lanna, Di Biagio (Statuto 65), Aldair, Carboni, Moriero, Totti, Balbo, Giannini, Fonseca (Cappioli 46).

● INTER

1st round FC LUGANO (SUI)

A 1-1 Roberto Carlos (13)
Pagliuca; Bergomi, Festa, Manicone, Fresi (Paganin 46), Roberto Carlos, Zanetti, Berti (Bianchi 85), Delvecchio (Ganz 60), Carbone, Orlandini.

H 0-1
Pagliuca; Paganin, Centofanti, Fresi, Festa, Roberto Carlos, Zanetti, Seno (Manicone 77), Ganz, Carbone (Orlandini 54), Rambert (Fontolan 54).

Champions' Cup final... assuming that new coach Oscar Washington Tabarez is able to follow successfully in the footsteps of a legend.

Milan's closest pursuers for much of the season were Fiorentina. At the turn of the year, with skipper Gabriel Batistuta in sensational goalscoring form, the *Viola* were just one point behind. But as winter became spring, Fiorentina's challenge diminished, and Claudio Ranieri's team eventually had to settle for fourth place, a full 14 points behind the champions. But Fiorentina did gain reward for their best season in years by capturing the Coppa Italia, the Italian Cup. It was some performance. They won every one of their eight matches, and in Batistuta had the runaway top scorer of the competition with eight goals, including one in each of the two legs of the final against Atalanta.

Fiorentina thus returned to Europe for the first time since losing the UEFA Cup final to Juventus in 1990. Their Cup triumph was also good news for the European aspirations of three other Serie A teams - Parma, Roma and Inter - each of whom benefitted by securing a berth in the UEFA Cup.

Inter, in fact, had to wait until Juventus's Champions' Cup final victory before their place was confirmed. It had been another turbulent season for the *Nerazzurri*, but one which finished a lot better than it started. Coach Ottavio Bianchi was sacked after just four Serie A games, and while Inter were waiting for the arrival of his successor,

PLAYERS OF THE SEASON

ENRICO CHIESA

No player had a better goals-per-game record in the 95/96 Serie A campaign than Sampdoria's Enrico Chiesa. The club's new signing from Cremonese missed several games at the start of the season with injury, but once fit he rattled in the goals like there was no tomorrow. He began with a hat-trick against Bari, followed that up with a brilliant brace against Juventus, and completed his 22-goal haul five months later with another double blast against newly-crowned champions Milan. Fast, oportunistic and an impulsive striker of the ball with both feet, Chiesa could not fail to get himself noticed by Arrigo Sacchi, who gave the 25-year-old his first cap in a friendly against Belgium and was rewarded, typically, with an equalising goal. Chiesa also found the net against the Czech Republic at Euro '96, where, albeit briefly, he gave some credence to the 'new Paolo Rossi' tag that the Italian press had tried to pin on him.

IGOR PROTTI

Bari's Igor Protti began the season by scoring the first goal in Serie A and earning himself 1,000 bottles of wine. Another 23 goals were to follow over the course of the next eight months as the 29-year-old frontman did everything in his power to assist his club in their battle to avoid relegation. His efforts were ultimately in vain, but Protti did make history by becoming the first player in a relegated side to be crowned as Serie A's top goalscorer. He also earned a summer transfer across the peninsula to Lazio, where he joined forces with the man who had shared the *capocannoniere* prize with him, Giuseppe Signori.

GEORGE WEAH

There was sorrow at the San Siro on the eve of the 1995/96 season as Marco van Basten officially announced his retirement from the game after a four-year struggle with his injured ankle. But before long it appeared that Milan had found the perfect replacement for the brilliant Dutchman. George Weah, signed for £5 million from Paris Saint-Germain, could not have made a better start to his new career in the red and black stripes of Milan. He gained rave notices from the Italian media from day one. His goals did not come in droves, but they invariably came at crucial times. When the Liberian was absent at the African Nations' Cup in January, Milan badly missed him. On his return he scored in four successive games. At the time his confidence was booming. After all, he had just been voted both European and World Footballer of the Year for 1995.

ALESSANDRO DEL PIERO

Euro '96 did not come at the right time for Alessandro Del Piero. The new golden boy of Italian football was dead on his feet when he arrived in England. The previous ten months had taken its toll on a player obliged to play for four different teams - his club Juventus, plus the senior Italian national side, the U-21 team and also the Italian military XI. As well as all the football, Del Piero was travelling back and forth every week from Turin to Naples, where he was undergoing his national service. But before his motor inevitably burned out, Del Piero was sensational. In the autumn the 21-year-old lit up the Champions' League with his breathtaking skills and goals. Juventus's decision to sell Baggio seemed totally justified as the youngster inspired the *Bianconeri* to their ultimate glory in Rome.

DEMETRIO ALBERTINI

His first Serie A goal of the season did not arrive until the final game, when Milan gave coach Fabio Capello the perfect send-off with their biggest win of the campaign, 7-1 against relegated Cremonese. But Demetrio Albertini is not in the Milan team for his goals, He is there for his regularity and consistency as the team's driving force in midfield. Once again Albertini belied his 24 years with a series of outstanding displays for both Milan and Italy. He was the only player to be selected in all ten of the Italian national team's fixtures during the season. The highlights for him were a netbusting free-kick which earned the *Azzurri* a 1-1 draw against Croatia in Split and three strong, authoritative performances at Euro '96, where he was generally considered to be Italy's outstanding player.

Demetrio Albertini

Englishman Roy Hodgson, they crashed out of the UEFA Cup under the temporary stewardship of Spaniard Luis Suárez, losing at home to a late goal against Swiss side Lugano.

Hodgson gradually turned things around, bringing the best out of expensive new English midfielder Paul Ince and making a shrewd acquisition in November when he brought in striker Marco Branca on loan from Roma. Branca went on to score 17 goals in just 24 games, and he also shone for Italy at the Olympics, where he appeared as one of three over-aged players. One of the others was his club colleague Gianluca Pagliuca, who many Italians would like to have seen keeping goal for the *Azzurri* at Euro '96. With a major new recruitment drive launched in the summer, Inter will be aiming high in 1996/97. Eight years without a domestic trophy is too long for a club of their standing.

Unlike Inter, Parma have been busily stocking up their trophy cabinet during the 1990s. But there was nothing new on display in 1996. For the first time in five seasons, the rich provincials finished the season empty-handed. A place in the UEFA Cup was a very small return considering the club's heavy investment at the start of the season. Bulgarian superstar Hristo Stoichkov was a huge flop, and the mid-season sale to England of the club's other foreign strikers, Tomas Brolin and Faustino Asprilla, left the squad looking thin on the ground in key areas. Gianfranco Zola did his best to keep Parma on an even keel, but when he was absent, as in the Cup-winners' Cup quarter-final defeat in Paris, Parma looked no more than an ordinary mid-table side.

The arrival of striking sensation Enrico Chiesa from Sampdoria in the summer should help the club out of their malaise, although they will now have to make do without the knowledge and expertise of coach Nevio Scala, who was removed from office to make way for... not Fabio Capello, as it turned out, but former Milan and Italy midfielder Carlo Ancelotti.

For the second season running both Roman clubs, Lazio and Roma, qualified for the UEFA Cup. Lazio had a wildly inconsistent Serie A campaign, symbolised by star striker Giuseppe Signori, who finished up as the league's joint-top scorer (half of his 24 goals were penalties) despite the most erratic of his four seasons with the club. Both Lazio and Roma finished very strongly. Roma had seven wins in their last nine matches, but that still could not save coach Carlo Mazzone from the chop. His place was given to Argentinian Carlos Bianchi, one of a plethora of new coaching appointments during the summer.

Giovanni Trapattoni did not even see out the season to its conclusion in Cagliari. Although his departure was officially "by mutual consent", it looked like a sacking to most people - the first time the great man had ever been dismissed in his long and successful career.

One prime candidate for Serie A's Coach of the Season award was Francesco Guidolin of Vicenza. He guided the north-eastern team into the top half of the table in their first Serie A season for 20 years. Remarkably, all four of the newly-promoted clubs - Vicenza, Udinese, Atalanta and Piacenza - survived. That was bad news for Padova, Cremonese, Torino and Bari, the latter being relegated despite the 24 goals of joint *capocannoniere* Igor Protti and the promising first season in Italy of Swedish striker Kennet Andersson.

Like Lazio-bound Protti, Andersson retained his own personal Serie A status by moving in the summer to Serie B champions Bologna, who returned to the top flight for the first time in six seasons, accompanied by Verona, Perugia and yo-yo specialists Reggiana.

INTERNATIONAL HONOURS

World Cup Finals appearances: 1934 (Winners), 1938 (Winners), 1950, 1954, 1962, 1966, 1970 (Runners-up), 1974, 1978 (4th), 1982 (Winners), 1986 (2nd round), 1990 (3rd), 1994 (Runners-up)

European Championship appearances: 1968 (Winners), 1972, 1980 (4th), 1988 (semi-finals), 1996

European Club Competitions

Champions' Cup	Milan (1963, 1969, 1989, 1990, 1994)
	Internazionale (1964, 1965)
	Juventus (1985, 1996)
Cup-winners' Cup	Fiorentina (1961)
	Milan (1968, 1973)
	Juventus (1984)
	Sampdoria (1990)
	Parma (1993)
Fairs' Cup	Roma (1961)
UEFA Cup	Juventus (1977, 1990, 1993)
	Napoli (1989)
	Internazionale (1991, 1994)
	Parma (1995)
Super Cup	Juventus (1985)
	Milan (1989, 1990, 1995)
	Parma (1994)
World Club Cup	Internazionale (1964, 1965)
	Milan (1969, 1989, 1990)
	Juventus (1985)

PROFILE
GABRIEL BATISTUTA

In Italy they call him 'BatiGol'. And for good reason. Some might argue a case for Romário or Klinsmann, or even, in the wake of Euro '96, Alan Shearer. But if a vote were cast today for the greatest goalscorer in the world, the name of Gabriel Omar Batistuta would surely come out on top.

The 27-year-old Argentinian ranks right up there with the likes of Gullit, Van Basten and Maradona as one of the few genuine world-class foreigners to have graced Italy's Serie A over the past decade. His right foot is pure dynamite. In five seasons at Fiorentina, Batistuta has already passed the 100-goal mark for the club. And he is now the all-time record goalscorer for the Argentinian national team, having reached a total of 35 goals during the early stages of the France '98 qualifying campaign.

Rumours spread during the summer that a couple of middle-ranked English clubs were interested in signing Batistuta from Fiorentina. If Shearer is worth £15 million, then the Argentinian would certainly command a similar fee. But it is all academic anyway. Batistuta has a contract with the *Viola* that will keep him where he is until the end of the millenium, and he is determined to see it out. He loves Florence as much as the people of that fine Tuscan city love him. He is the captain of the team and the man around whom all of their hopes and ambitions are built. When Batistuta made his 100th Serie A appearance for Fiorentina, against Lazio in November 1995, the local fans marked the occasion by unveiling a statue of their hero. Batistuta responded to this tribute in typical fashion by scoring both goals in a 2-0 victory.

Batistuta did not retain his Serie A top scorer crown in the 95/96 season, but he made a brave try, scoring 19 goals, just seven fewer than his record 94/95 haul, to lift Fiorentina to fourth place in the Serie A table - the club's best position for 12 seasons. More significantly, 'BatiGol' struck eight times in the Italian Cup, scoring all four goals against Inter in the semi-final and two in the final against Atalanta, to give Fiorentina their first major trophy for 21 years.

From being a Serie B side three years ago, Fiorentina are now back in Europe for the first time since 1990 and set to challenge on three fronts in 1996/97. A fully fit Batistuta will give Fiorentina every chance of continuing their progress, although their skipper's monthly visits to South America for the World Cup qualifiers could prove to be a major handicap.

Young Argentinian centre-forward Hernán Crespo, now with Parma, might have looked the business for Argentina at the Olympics, but he will have to go some to oust Batistuta. Ever since making his mark in international football with a top-scoring six goals in six games in Argentina's victorious 1991 Copa América campaign, Batistuta has been the unanimous choice to wear his country's number nine shirt. He was a big success at the 1994 World Cup, scoring four goals, including a hat-trick in the opening match against Greece. And even when new national coach Daniel Passarella insisted, bizarrely, that all of his players have their hair cut to a respectable length, 'BatiGol' agreed to pop down to the local barber's and subject his flowing locks to a quick trim.

Batistuta played for three famous Argentinian clubs - Newell's Old Boys, River Plate and Boca Juniors - before his 1991 move to Italy. But although he plans to return to his homeland when his career is over, he is happy for now to alternate between the all purple of his Italian club and the light blue and white stripes of his country.

The 1998 World Cup in France is the tournament that Batistuta hopes will bring him the global recognition he deserves. Those who worship his every kick in Florence and Buenos Aires no doubt believe that the Argentinian goalscoring maestro has already done enough to enter the realms of footballing immortality.

ATALANTA

CLUB DIRECTORY

Atalanta Bergamasca Calcio
Via Pitentino 14/A
24124 Bergamo
tel - (035) 242555
fax - (035) 239677
Year of Formation - 1907
President - Ivan Ruggeri
General Manager - Giacomo Rondazzo
Secretary - Carlo Valenti
Coach - Emiliano Mondonico
Stadium - Azzurri d'Italia (26,724)

MAJOR HONOURS
Domestic Cup - (1) 1963.

APPEARANCES 95/96

	P	Ap	(s)	Gls
Walter BONACINA	M	28	(1)	
Nicola BOSELLI	D	8	(7)	
Kewullay CONTEH (SRL)	D	1	(1)	
Fabrizio FERRON	G	29		
Daniele FORTUNATO	M	32		2
Fabio GALLO	M	25	(6)	
José HERRERA (URU)	D	28	(1)	2
Gianluca LUPPI	D	14	(3)	
Giuseppe MINAUDO	M	1	(1)	
Paulo MONTERO (URU)	D	23		
Domenico MORFEO	M	23	(7)	11
Massimo MUTARELLI	M		(1)	
Antonio PAGANIN	D	25	(2)	
Cristiano PAVONE	D	10	(4)	
Davide PINATO	G	5	(2)	
Federico PISANI	A	11	(14)	4
Franco ROTELLA	M	10	(7)	
Stefano SALVATORI	M	9	(13)	
Marco SGRÒ	M	21	(9)	1
Gianluca TEMELIN	A		(1)	
Sandro TOVALIERI	A	21	(9)	6
Mauro VALENTINI	D	26	(1)	
Christian VIERI	A	18	(1)	7
Marco ZANCHI	D	6	(4)	
Filippo ZANI	G		(1)	

LEAGUE RESULTS 1995/96

27/08/95	Parma	H	1-1	Vieri
10/09/95	Roma	A	1-0	Vieri (p)
17/09/95	Napoli	H	1-3	Vieri
24/09/95	Milan	A	0-3	
01/10/95	Piacenza	H	2-0	og (Piovani), og (Rossini)
15/10/95	Inter	H	1-1	Morfeo
22/10/95	Cremonese	A	1-1	Morfeo
29/10/95	Udinese	H	0-0	
05/11/95	Bari	A	3-1	Pisani, Tovalieri 2
19/11/95	Sampdoria	H	3-2	Herrera, og (Evani), Tovalieri
26/11/95	Torino	A	1-0	Fortunato
03/12/95	Vicenza	H	3-1	Tovalieri 2, Morfeo
10/12/95	Cagliari	A	0-2	
17/12/95	Fiorentina	H	1-3	Morfeo
23/12/95	Lazio	A	1-5	Tovalieri
07/01/96	Juventus	H	0-1	
14/01/96	Padova	A	2-3	Morfeo 2
21/01/96	Parma	A	0-2	
28/01/96	Roma	H	2-1	Pisani, Morfeo (p)
04/02/96	Napoli	A	0-2	
11/02/96	Milan	H	0-1	
18/02/96	Piacenza	A	2-2	Vieri, Pisani
25/02/96	Inter	A	0-1	
03/03/96	Cremonese	H	1-1	Pisani
10/03/96	Udinese	A	0-3	
24/03/96	Sampdoria	A	3-2	og (Balleri), Morfeo, Fortunato
31/03/96	Torino	H	1-0	Morfeo (p)
06/04/96	Vicenza	A	0-1	
10/04/96	Bari	H	1-2	Vieri (p)
14/04/96	Cagliari	H	3-0	Vieri 2, Morfeo
20/04/96	Fiorentina	A	0-1	
28/04/96	Lazio	H	1-3	Morfeo
05/05/96	Juventus	A	0-1	
12/05/96	Padova	H	3-0	og (Serao), Sgrò, Herrera

BARI

CLUB DIRECTORY

Bari Associazione Sportiva
Strada Torrebella
70124 Bari
tel - (080) 5055099
fax - (080) 5055164
Year of Formation - 1928
President - Vincenzo Mattarese
General Manager - Carlo Regalia
Secretary - Filippo Nitti
Coach - Giuseppe Materazzi; Eugenio Fascetti
Stadium - San Nicola (58,270)

APPEARANCES 95/96

	P	Ap	(s)	Gls
ABEL XAVIER (POR)	M	8		
Giuseppe ALBERGA	G	2		
Kennet ANDERSSON (SWE)	A	31	(2)	12
Michele ANDRISANI	M		(1)	
Paolo ANNONI	D	9	(14)	1
Emanuele BRIOSCHI	D	3	(8)	
Fabrizio FICINI	M	8	(13)	
Alberto FONTANA	G	32		
Carmine GAUTIERI	M	26	(3)	1
Luca GENTILI	G		(1)	
GÉRSON Candido (BRA)	M	22	(3)	
Miguel GUERRERO (COL)	A	1	(7)	1
Klas INGESSON (SWE)	M	23	(1)	1
Amedeo MANGONE	D	25	(5)	
Gian Paolo MANIGHETTI	M	23	(3)	
Marcello MONTANARI	D	23	(4)	
Pietro PARENTE	M	17	(9)	3
Francesco PEDONE	M	31	(1)	3
Igor PROTTI	A	33		24
Gianluca RICCI	D	19	(3)	
Roberto RIPA	D	12	(3)	1
Luigi SALA	D	25	(1)	2
Nicola VENTOLA	A	1	(6)	

LEAGUE RESULTS 1995/96

Date	Opponent		Score	Scorers
27/08/95	Napoli	H	1-1	Protti
10/09/95	Torino	A	1-3	Protti
17/09/95	Lazio	H	3-3	Protti 3
24/09/95	Piacenza	A	2-3	Protti, Pedone
01/10/95	Milan	H	1-0	Gautieri
15/10/95	Vicenza	A	0-2	
22/10/95	Cagliari	H	3-0	Andersson, Protti, Guerrero
29/10/95	Fiorentina	A	2-3	Annoni, Protti
05/11/95	Atalanta	H	1-3	Andersson
19/11/95	Padova	A	0-3	
26/11/95	Roma	A	1-2	Pedone
03/12/95	Sampdoria	H	1-3	Protti (p)
10/12/95	Cremonese	A	1-7	Andersson
17/12/95	Parma	H	1-1	Protti (p)
23/12/95	Udinese	A	2-1	Andersson 2
07/01/96	Inter	H	4-1	Sala, Protti 2, Ingesson
14/01/96	Juventus	A	1-1	Protti
21/01/96	Napoli	A	0-1	
28/01/96	Torino	H	2-2	Andersson, Protti
04/02/96	Lazio	A	3-4	Protti 2 (2p), Andersson
11/02/96	Piacenza	H	0-0	
18/02/96	Milan	A	2-3	Pedone, Sala
25/02/96	Vicenza	H	0-2	
03/03/96	Cagliari	A	2-4	Andersson, Protti (p)
10/03/96	Fiorentina	H	1-1	Andersson
24/03/96	Padova	H	2-1	Ripa, Protti
31/03/96	Roma	H	1-2	Parente
06/04/96	Sampdoria	A	0-2	
10/04/96	Atalanta	A	2-1	Protti 2
14/04/96	Cremonese	H	2-1	Protti 2
20/04/96	Parma	A	1-3	Andersson
28/04/96	Udinese	H	4-2	Andersson 2, Parente 2
05/05/96	Inter	A	0-3	
12/05/96	Juventus	H	2-2	Protti 2

CAGLIARI

CLUB DIRECTORY

Cagliari Calcio
Viale Bonaria 66
09125 Cagliari
tel - (070) 666013
fax - (070) 654059
Year of Formation - 1920
President - Massimo Cellino
General Manager - Roberto Pappalardo
Secretary - Sergio Loviselli
Coach - Giovanni Trapattoni; Bruno Giorgi
(96/97 - Gregorio Pérez)
Stadium - Sant' Elia (40,320)

MAJOR HONOURS
League Championship - (1) 1970.

APPEARANCES 95/96

	P	Ap	(s)	Gls
Beniamino ABATE	G	15		
Massimiliano ALLEGRI	M	1	(1)	
Pierpaolo BISOLI	M	34		1
Antonio BITETTI	M		(3)	
Mauro BONOMI	D	8	(4)	
Mauro BRESSAN	M	10	(19)	
Valerio FIORI	G	19		
Aldo FIRICANO	D	33		2
Christian LANTIGNOTTI	M	10	(13)	2
Roberto MUZZI	A	11	(12)	3
Nicolò NAPOLI	D	27	(2)	1
Fabian O'NEILL (URU)	A	11	(4)	1
Luis OLIVEIRA (BEL)	A	33		15
Giuseppe PANCARO	D	31	(1)	1
Vittorio PUSCEDDU	D	26	(2)	
Marco SANNA	M	21	(8)	
Dario SILVA (URU)	A	26	(7)	3
Francesco TRIBUNA	A		(1)	
Giorgio VENTURIN	M	24	(7)	
Matteo VILLA	D	34		2

LEAGUE RESULTS 1995/96

27/08/95	Udinese	A	0-1	
10/09/95	Lazio	H	0-1	
17/09/95	Fiorentina	A	1-3	og (Amoruso)
24/09/95	Juventus	H	0-0	
01/10/95	Sampdoria	A	2-1	Silva, Oliveira
15/10/95	Cremonese	H	1-0	Oliveira (p)
22/10/95	Bari	A	0-3	
29/10/95	Roma	H	0-2	
05/11/95	Milan	A	2-3	Oliveira 2 (1p)
19/11/95	Torino	H	1-0	Silva
26/11/95	Napoli	H	2-0	Firicano 2
03/12/95	Piacenza	A	1-1	Oliveira
10/12/95	Atalanta	H	2-0	og (Boselli), Muzzi
17/12/95	Vicenza	A	1-0	Oliveira
23/12/95	Inter	A	0-4	
07/01/96	Padova	H	0-1	
14/01/96	Parma	A	0-4	
21/01/96	Udinese	H	4-1	Muzzi, Oliveira, Silva, Villa
28/01/96	Lazio	A	0-4	
04/02/96	Fiorentina	H	0-0	
11/02/96	Juventus	A	1-4	Oliveira
18/02/96	Sampdoria	H	3-0	Napoli, Oliveira, Bisoli
25/02/96	Cremonese	A	1-3	Muzzi
03/03/96	Bari	H	4-2	Oliveira 3 (1p), Lantignotti
10/03/96	Roma	A	1-1	Oliveira (p)
24/03/96	Torino	A	1-1	Oliveira (p)
31/03/96	Napoli	A	0-0	
06/04/96	Piacenza	H	0-0	
10/04/96	Milan	H	1-2	Villa
14/04/96	Atalanta	A	0-3	
20/04/96	Vicenza	H	2-0	Pancaro, O'Neill
28/04/96	Inter	H	0-0	
05/05/96	Padova	A	1-2	Lantignotti
12/05/96	Parma	H	2-0	og (Sensini), Oliveira (p)

CREMONESE

CLUB DIRECTORY

Cremonese Unione Sportiva
Via Persico 19
26100 Cremona
tel - (0372) 434016
fax - (0372) 454593
Year of Formation - 1903
President - Domenico Luzzara
General Manager - Erminio Favalli
Secretaries - Lalla Bacchetta & Nedo Bettoli
Coach - Luigi Simoni (96/97 - Fausto Silipo)
Stadium - Giovanni Zini (20,500)

APPEARANCES 95/96

	P	Ap	(s)	Gls
John ALOISI (AUS)	A	7	(15)	2
Alfredo BASSANI	D	3	(3)	
Gianni CRISTIANI	M	7	(22)	
Giovanni DALL'IGNA	D	23		1
Stefano DE AGOSTINI	M	23		
Enrico FANTINI	A	6	(14)	1
Ettore FERRARONI	M	6	(10)	
Matjaz FLORJANCIC (SLO)	A	30	(3)	6
Luigi GARZYA	D	25	(1)	
Marco GIANDEBIAGGI	M	31	(1)	1
Luigi GUALCO	D	18	(4)	1
Simone GUARNERI	M		(1)	
Riccardo MASPERO	M	33	(1)	8
Eligio NICOLINI	M		(1)	
Angelo ORLANDO	M	24	(1)	
Marko PEROVIC (YUG)	M	24	(1)	5
Gianluca PETRACHI	M	23	(3)	
Stefano RAZZETTI	G	5	(1)	
Marco STEFFANI	M	1	(1)	
Andrea TENTONI	A	25	(7)	9
Luigi TURCI	G	29		
Corrado VERDELLI	D	31		

LEAGUE RESULTS 1995/96

27/08/95	Juventus	A	1-4	Maspero
10/09/95	Sampdoria	H	0-0	
17/09/95	Udinese	A	2-3	Maspero (p), Florjancic
24/09/95	Roma	H	0-1	
01/10/95	Fiorentina	A	2-3	Maspero, Fantini
15/10/95	Cagliari	A	0-1	
22/10/95	Atalanta	H	1-1	Perovic
29/10/95	Napoli	A	0-0	
05/11/95	Parma	H	0-2	
19/11/95	Lazio	A	1-2	Maspero (p)
26/11/95	Padova	H	2-1	Aloisi, Maspero
03/12/95	Inter	A	0-2	
10/12/95	Bari	H	7-1	og (Brioschi), Gualco, Florjancic, Perovic 2, Aloisi, Tentoni
17/12/95	Piacenza	A	1-2	Tentoni
23/12/95	Torino	H	1-1	Giandebiaggi
07/01/96	Vicenza	A	0-1	
14/01/96	Milan	H	0-0	
21/01/96	Juventus	H	3-3	og (Peruzzi), Maspero (p), Tentoni
28/01/96	Sampdoria	A	0-2	
04/02/96	Udinese	H	2-2	Tentoni, Florjancic
11/02/96	Roma	A	0-3	
18/02/96	Fiorentina	H	0-0	
25/02/96	Cagliari	H	3-1	Maspero, Dall'Igna, Perovic
03/03/96	Atalanta	A	1-1	Maspero
10/03/96	Napoli	H	1-1	Tentoni
24/03/96	Lazio	H	2-1	Tentoni 2
31/03/96	Padova	A	2-1	Florjancic 2
06/04/96	Inter	H	2-4	Tentoni 2
10/04/96	Parma	A	0-2	
14/04/96	Bari	A	1-2	Perovic
20/04/96	Piacenza	H	0-0	
28/04/96	Torino	A	0-1	
05/05/96	Vicenza	H	1-1	og (Sartor)
12/05/96	Milan	A	1-7	Florjancic

FIORENTINA

CLUB DIRECTORY

Associazione Calcio Fiorentina
Piazza Savonarola 6
50132 Firenze
tel - (055) 572625/6/7/8
fax - (055) 579556
Year of Formation - 1926
President - Vittorio Cecchi Gori
General Manager - Giancarlo Antognoni
Secretary - Raffaele Righetti
Coach - Claudio Ranieri
Stadium - Artemio Franchi (47,350)

MAJOR HONOURS
League Championship - (2) 1959, 1969.
Domestic Cup - (5)
1940, 1961, 1966, 1975, 1996.
European Cup-winners' Cup - (1) 1961.

APPEARANCES 95/96

	P	Ap	(s)	Gls
Lorenzo AMORUSO	D	31		2
Francesco BAIANO	A	27	(1)	11
Giacomo BANCHELLI	A	5	(11)	4
Gabriel BATISTUTA (ARG)	A	31		19
Federico BETTONI	M	1	(10)	
Emiliano BIGICA	M	22	(5)	
Daniele CARNASCIALI	D	31		1
Sandro COIS	M	16	(8)	1
Francesco FLACHI	A	1	(2)	
Alberto MALUSCI	D	5	(5)	
Alessandro ORLANDO	D	4	(2)	
Massimo ORLANDO	M	2	(8)	1
Pasquale PADALINO	D	30		2
Giovanni PIACENTINI	M	27	(2)	1
Anselmo ROBBIATI	M	11	(21)	6
RUI COSTA (POR)	M	33	(1)	4
Stefan SCHWARZ (SWE)	M	32		
Michele SERENA	D	24		
Andrea SOTTIL	D	7	(9)	
Francesco TOLDO	G	34		
Cristiano ZANETTI	M		(2)	

LEAGUE RESULTS 1995/96

Date	Opponent	H/A	Score	Scorers
27/08/95	Torino	H	2-0	Banchelli 2
10/09/95	Vicenza	A	0-1	
17/09/95	Cagliari	H	3-1	Baiano 2, Amoruso
24/09/95	Parma	A	0-3	
01/10/95	Cremonese	H	3-2	Padalino, Baiano, Batistuta
15/10/95	Napoli	A	2-0	Carnasciali, Orlando M.
22/10/95	Sampdoria	A	1-2	Rui Costa (p)
29/10/95	Bari	H	3-2	Robbiati, Rui Costa, Batistuta
05/11/95	Lazio	H	2-0	Batistuta 2
19/11/95	Juventus	A	0-1	
26/11/95	Inter	H	1-1	Batistuta
03/12/95	Padova	A	1-0	Batistuta
10/12/95	Udinese	H	3-0	Baiano, Batistuta 2 (1p)
17/12/95	Atalanta	A	3-1	Baiano, Batistuta 2
23/12/95	Milan	H	2-2	Robbiati, Baiano
07/01/96	Roma	A	2-2	Robbiati, Batistuta
14/01/96	Piacenza	H	2-1	Robbiati, Baiano
21/01/96	Torino	A	3-0	Batistuta 2, Baiano
28/01/96	Vicenza	H	1-1	Batistuta
04/02/96	Cagliari	A	0-0	
11/02/96	Parma	H	1-0	Amoruso
18/02/96	Cremonese	A	0-0	
25/02/96	Napoli	H	3-0	Batistuta 2, Baiano
03/03/96	Sampdoria	H	2-2	Rui Costa, Robbiati
10/03/96	Bari	A	1-1	Baiano (p)
24/03/96	Juventus	H	0-1	
31/03/96	Inter	A	2-1	Cois, Padalino
06/04/96	Padova	H	6-4	Baiano, Robbiati, Batistuta 2 (1p), Banchelli, og (Rosa)
10/04/96	Lazio	A	0-4	
14/04/96	Udinese	A	0-1	
20/04/96	Atalanta	H	1-0	Banchelli
28/04/96	Milan	A	1-3	Rui Costa
05/05/96	Roma	H	1-4	Batistuta
12/05/96	Piacenza	A	1-0	Piacentini

INTER

CLUB DIRECTORY

Internazionale Milano Football Club
Piazza Duse 1
20122 Milano
tel - (02) 77151
fax - (02) 781514
Year of Formation - 1908
President - Massimo Moratti
General Manager - Alessandro Mazzola
Secretary - Paolo Taveggia
Coach - Ottavio Bianchi; Luis Suárez; Roy Hodgson
Stadium - Giuseppe Meazza (85,443)

MAJOR HONOURS
League Championship - (13)
1910, 1920, 1930, 1938, 1940, 1953, 1954, 1963, 1965, 1966, 1971, 1980, 1989.
Domestic Cup - (3) 1939, 1978, 1982.
European Champions' Cup - (2) 1964, 1965.
UEFA Cup - (2) 1991, 1994.
World Club Cup - (2) 1964, 1965.

APPEARANCES 95/96

	P	Ap	(s)	Gls
Giuseppe BERGOMI	D	23	(4)	
Nicola BERTI	M	7	(3)	
Alessandro BIANCHI	M	7	(7)	
Marco BRANCA	A	24		17
CAIO Ribeiro (BRA)	A	1	(5)	
Benito CARBONE	M	25	(6)	2
Felice CENTOFANTI	D	4	(5)	1
Fabio CINETTI	M	1	(4)	
Francesco DELL'ANNO	M	6	(10)	
Marco DELVECCHIO	A	3	(1)	1
Gianluca FESTA	D	30	(1)	1
Davide FONTOLAN	M	13	(12)	2
Salvatore FRESI	M	28	(2)	
Maurizio GANZ	A	25	(7)	13
Paul INCE (ENG)	M	30		3
Antonio MANICONE	M	4	(3)	
Pierluigi ORLANDINI	M		(7)	
Massimo PAGANIN	D	32		1
Gianluca PAGLIUCA	G	34		
Alessandro PEDRONI	D		(3)	
Alessandro PISTONE	D	14	(5)	1
ROBERTO CARLOS Da Silva (BRA)	M	29	(1)	5
Andrea SENO	M	2		
Javier ZANETTI (ARG)	M	32		2

LEAGUE RESULTS 1995/96

27/08/95	Vicenza	H	1-0	Roberto Carlos
10/09/95	Parma	A	1-2	Roberto Carlos
17/09/95	Piacenza	H	0-0	
24/09/95	Napoli	A	1-2	Fontolan
01/10/95	Torino	H	4-0	Roberto Carlos, Ganz 2 (2p), Delvecchio
15/10/95	Atalanta	A	1-1	og (Herrera)
22/10/95	Lazio	H	0-0	
29/10/95	Milan	H	1-1	Paganin
05/11/95	Sampdoria	A	0-0	
19/11/95	Udinese	H	2-1	Branca, Carbone
26/11/95	Fiorentina	A	1-1	Ganz
03/12/95	Cremonese	H	2-0	Zanetti, Ganz
10/12/95	Padova	A	1-2	Ganz
17/12/95	Juventus	A	0-1	
23/12/95	Cagliari	H	4-0	Ganz, Branca 3
07/01/96	Bari	A	1-4	Roberto Carlos
14/01/96	Roma	H	2-0	Branca 2
21/01/96	Vicenza	A	1-1	Ganz
28/01/96	Parma	H	1-1	Branca
04/02/96	Piacenza	A	0-1	
11/02/96	Napoli	H	4-0	Ganz 2 (1p), Branca 2
18/02/96	Torino	A	1-0	Branca
25/02/96	Atalanta	H	1-0	Branca
03/03/96	Lazio	A	1-0	og (Nesta)
10/03/96	Milan	A	1-0	Branca
24/03/96	Udinese	A	2-1	Fontolan, Roberto Carlos
31/03/96	Fiorentina	H	1-2	Centofanti
06/04/96	Cremonese	A	4-2	Ince, Zanetti, Pistone, Branca
10/04/96	Sampdoria	H	0-2	
14/04/96	Padova	H	8-2	Branca 3, Carbone, Ince, Festa, Ganz 2
20/04/96	Juventus	H	1-2	Ganz
28/04/96	Cagliari	A	0-0	
05/05/96	Bari	H	3-0	Ince, Branca, Ganz
12/05/96	Roma	A	0-1	

JUVENTUS

CLUB DIRECTORY

Juventus Football Club
Piazza Crimea 7
10131 Torino
tel - (011) 65631
fax - (011) 6604134
Year of Formation - 1897
President - Vittorio Chiusano
General Manager - Luciano Moggi
Secretaries - E. Cravero & L. Guillaume
Coach - Marcello Lippi
Stadium - Delle Alpi (71,012)

MAJOR HONOURS

League Championship - (23) 1905, 1926, 1931, 1932, 1933, 1934, 1935, 1950, 1952, 1958, 1960, 1961, 1967, 1972, 1973, 1975, 1977, 1978, 1981, 1982, 1984, 1986, 1995.
Domestic Cup - (9) 1938, 1942, 1959, 1960, 1965, 1979, 1983, 1990, 1995.
European Champions' Cup - (2) 1985, 1996.
European Cup-winners' Cup - (1) 1984.
UEFA Cup - (3) 1977, 1990, 1993.
European Super Cup - (1) 1984.
World Club Cup - (1) 1985.

APPEARANCES 95/96

	P	Ap	(s)	Gls
Massimo CARRERA	D	16	(4)	
Antonio CONTE	M	22	(7)	5
Alessandro DEL PIERO	A	25	(4)	6
Didier DESCHAMPS (FRA)	M	27	(3)	2
Angelo DI LIVIO	M	22	(10)	
Ciro FERRARA	D	31		3
Vladimir JUGOVIC (YUG)	M	14	(12)	2
Attilio LOMBARDO	M	8	(5)	2
Giancarlo MAROCCHI	M	1	(7)	
Michele PADOVANO	A	5	(16)	4
PAULO SOUSA (POR)	M	27	(1)	
Angelo PERUZZI	G	29	(1)	
Gianluca PESSOTTO	D	22	(6)	
Sergio PORRINI	D	9	(6)	
Michelangelo RAMPULLA	G	5	(4)	
Fabrizio RAVANELLI	A	23	(3)	12
Juan Pablo SORIN (ARG)	D		(2)	
Alessio TACCHINARDI	M	14	(2)	
Moreno TORRICELLI	D	27	(1)	1
Gianluca VIALLI	A	29	(1)	11
Pietro VIERCHOWOD	D	18	(3)	2

LEAGUE RESULTS 1995/96

27/08/95	Cremonese	H	4-1	Jugovic, Ravanelli 2 (1p), og (Tentoni)
10/09/95	Piacenza	A	4-0	Vialli 2, Torricelli, Ravanelli
17/09/95	Vicenza	H	1-0	Vialli
24/09/95	Cagliari	A	0-0	
01/10/95	Napoli	H	1-1	Vialli
15/10/95	Milan	A	1-2	Del Piero
22/10/95	Padova	H	3-1	Del Piero, Ravanelli, Conte
29/10/95	Lazio	A	0-4	
05/11/95	Udinese	A	0-0	
19/11/95	Fiorentina	H	1-0	Del Piero
26/11/95	Parma	A	1-1	Ferrara
03/12/95	Torino	H	5-0	Vialli 3, Ferrara, Ravanelli (p)
10/12/95	Sampdoria	A	0-2	
17/12/95	Inter	H	1-0	Vialli
23/12/95	Roma	H	0-2	
07/01/96	Atalanta	A	1-0	Ravanelli (p)
14/01/96	Bari	H	1-1	Ravanelli (p)
21/01/96	Cremonese	A	3-3	Vialli, Ravanelli (p), Vierchowod
28/01/96	Piacenza	H	2-0	Conte, Ferrara
04/02/96	Vicenza	A	1-2	Ravanelli
11/02/96	Cagliari	H	4-1	og (Bonomi), Ravanelli, Del Piero, Jugovic
18/02/96	Napoli	A	1-0	Ravanelli
25/02/96	Milan	H	1-1	Conte
02/03/96	Padova	A	5-0	Del Piero 2, Lombardo, Padovano 2
10/03/96	Lazio	H	4-2	Deschamps, og (Chamot), Conte, Padovano
24/03/96	Fiorentina	A	1-0	og (Amoruso)
30/03/96	Parma	H	1-0	og (Bucci)
06/04/96	Torino	A	2-1	og (Sogliano), Vialli
10/04/96	Udinese	H	2-1	Ravanelli, Vierchowod
13/04/96	Sampdoria	H	0-3	
20/04/96	Inter	A	2-1	Lombardo, Conte
28/04/96	Roma	A	2-2	og (Cappioli), Padovano
05/05/96	Atalanta	H	1-0	Deschamps
12/05/96	Bari	A	2-2	og (Montanari), Vialli

LAZIO

CLUB DIRECTORY

Società Sportiva Lazio
Via U. Novaro 32
00195 Roma
tel - (06) 37497200
fax - (06) 37497224
Year of Formation - 1900
President - Dino Zoff
General Manager - Nello Governato
Secretary - Gabriella Grassi
Coach - Zdenek Zeman
Stadium - Olimpico (82,922)

MAJOR HONOURS
League Championship - (1) 1974.
Domestic Cup - (1) 1958.

APPEARANCES 95/96

	P	Ap	(s)	Gls
Cristiano BERGODI	D	8	(7)	
Alen BOKSIC (CRO)	A	20	(3)	4
Pierluigi CASIRAGHI	A	25	(3)	14
José Antonio CHAMOT (ARG)	D	32		
Roberto DI MATTEO	M	30	(1)	2
Massimiliano ESPOSITO	M	8	(9)	3
Giuseppe FAVALLI	D	26		1
Daniele FRANCESCHINI	M	1	(1)	
Diego FUSER	M	32		6
Guerino GOTTARDI	D	12	(8)	
Alessandro GRANDONI	D	3	(1)	
Alessandro IANNUZZI	M		(4)	1
Francesco MANCINI	G	6		
Luca MARCHEGIANI	G	26		
Dario MARCOLIN	M	8	(12)	
Paolo NEGRO	D	31		1
Alessandro NESTA	D	20	(3)	
Fernando ORSI	G	2	(3)	
Marco PIOVANELLI	M	1	(15)	
Roberto RAMBAUDI	A	18	(10)	1
Alessandro ROMANO	M	5	(2)	
Giuseppe SIGNORI	A	31		24
Aron WINTER (HOL)	M	29	(1)	6

LEAGUE RESULTS 1995/96

Date	Opponent	H/A	Score	Scorers
27/08/95	Piacenza	H	4-1	Signori, Esposito 2, Casiraghi (p)
10/09/95	Cagliari	A	1-0	Signori
17/09/95	Bari	A	3-3	Winter, Casiraghi, Signori (p)
24/09/95	Udinese	H	2-2	Signori (p), Fuser
01/10/95	Roma	A	0-0	
15/10/95	Padova	H	2-0	og (Rosa), Fuser
22/10/95	Inter	A	0-0	
29/10/95	Juventus	H	4-0	Signori, Casiraghi 2, Rambaudi
05/11/95	Fiorentina	A	0-2	
19/11/95	Cremonese	H	2-1	Winter, Casiraghi
26/11/95	Vicenza	A	0-1	
03/12/95	Milan	H	0-1	
10/12/95	Parma	A	1-2	Di Matteo
17/12/95	Sampdoria	H	6-3	Signori 2 (1p), og (Mihajlovic), Winter, Casiraghi, Fuser
23/12/95	Atalanta	H	5-1	Winter 2, Signori 2 (2p), Boksic
07/01/96	Napoli	A	0-1	
14/01/96	Torino	H	1-1	Iannuzzi
21/01/96	Piacenza	A	1-2	Boksic
28/01/96	Cagliari	H	4-0	Signori (p), Casiraghi 3
04/02/96	Bari	H	4-3	Signori 3 (2p), Boksic
11/02/96	Udinese	A	1-1	Fuser
18/02/96	Roma	H	1-0	Signori (p)
25/02/96	Padova	A	3-1	Signori, Casiraghi, Fuser
03/03/96	Inter	H	0-1	
10/03/96	Juventus	A	2-4	Favalli, Casiraghi
24/03/96	Cremonese	A	1-2	Negro
31/03/96	Vicenza	H	3-0	Signori 3 (2p)
06/04/96	Milan	A	0-0	
10/04/96	Fiorentina	H	4-0	Winter, Signori 2, Casiraghi
14/04/96	Parma	H	2-1	Fuser, Casiraghi
20/04/96	Sampdoria	A	3-3	Casiraghi, Signori 2
28/04/96	Atalanta	A	3-1	og (Valentini), Signori (p), Esposito
05/05/96	Napoli	H	1-0	Di Matteo
12/05/96	Torino	A	2-0	Boksic, Signori

MILAN

CLUB DIRECTORY

Milan Associazione Calcio
Via Turati 3
20121 Milano
tel - (02) 62281
fax - (02) 6598876
Year of Formation - 1899
President - Silvio Berlusconi
General Manager - Ariedo Braida
Secretary - Rina Barbara Ercoli
Coach - Fabio Capello (96/97 - Oscar Washington Tabarez)
Stadium - Giuseppe Meazza (85,443)

MAJOR HONURS
League Championship - (15) 1901, 1906, 1907, 1951, 1955, 1957, 1959, 1962, 1968, 1979, 1988, 1992, 1993, 1994, 1996.
Domestic Cup - (4)
1967, 1972, 1973, 1977.
European Champions' Cup - (5)
1963, 1969, 1989, 1990, 1994.
European Cup-winners' Cup - (2) 1968, 1973.
European Super Cup - (3) 1989, 1990, 1995.
World Club Cup - (3) 1969, 1989, 1990.

APPEARANCES 95/96

	P	Ap	(s)	Gls
Demetrio ALBERTINI	M	29	(1)	1
Massimo AMBROSINI	M	1	(6)	
Roberto BAGGIO	A	26	(2)	7
Franco BARESI	D	30		1
Zvonimir BOBAN (CRO)	M	13		3
Francesco COCO	D	3	(2)	
Alessandro COSTACURTA	D	30		
Marcel DESAILLY (FRA)	M	32		2
Paolo DI CANIO	M	4	(18)	5
Roberto DONADONI	M	14	(9)	1
Stefano ERANIO	M	17	(7)	1
Paulo FUTRE (POR)	A	1		
Filippo GALLI	D	3	(3)	
Gianluigi LENTINI	M	5	(4)	1
Tomas LOCATELLI	M		(5)	
Paolo MALDINI	D	30		3
Christian PANUCCI	D	29		5
Sebastiano ROSSI	G	34		
Dejan SAVICEVIC (YUG)	M	23		6
Marco SIMONE	A	16	(11)	8
Gianluca SORDO	M		(5)	
Mauro TASSOTTI	D	7	(8)	
Patrick VIEIRA (FRA)	M	1	(1)	
George WEAH (LIB)	A	26		11

LEAGUE RESULTS 1995/96

Date	Opponent		Score	Scorers
27/08/95	Padova	A	2-1	Weah, Baresi
10/09/95	Udinese	H	2-1	og (Sergio), Baggio
17/09/95	Roma	A	2-1	Weah 2
24/09/95	Atalanta	H	3-0	Desailly, Baggio, Di Canio
01/10/95	Bari	A	0-1	
15/10/95	Juventus	H	2-1	Simone, Weah
22/10/95	Vicenza	A	1-1	Eranio
29/10/95	Inter	A	1-1	Savicevic
05/11/95	Cagliari	H	3-2	Di Canio, Lentini, Simone
19/11/95	Parma	A	0-0	
26/11/95	Piacenza	H	3-0	Savicevic, Panucci, Maldini
03/12/95	Lazio	A	1-0	Weah
10/12/95	Napoli	H	0-0	
17/12/95	Torino	H	1-1	Boban
23/12/95	Fiorentina	A	2-2	Weah, Baggio (p)
07/01/96	Sampdoria	H	3-0	Panucci, Savicevic, Baggio
14/01/96	Cremonese	A	0-0	
21/01/96	Padova	H	1-0	Baggio (p)
28/01/96	Udinese	A	2-0	Maldini, Boban
04/02/96	Roma	H	3-1	Weah, og (Aldair), Panucci
11/02/96	Atalanta	A	1-0	Weah
18/02/96	Bari	H	3-2	Simone 2 (1p), Weah
25/02/96	Juventus	A	1-1	Weah
02/03/96	Vicenza	H	4-0	Savicevic, Simone 2 (1p), Di Canio
10/03/96	Inter	H	0-1	
24/03/96	Parma	H	3-0	Baggio, Donadoni, Savicevic
31/03/96	Piacenza	A	2-0	Desailly, Simone
06/04/96	Lazio	H	0-0	
10/04/96	Cagliari	A	2-1	og (Napoli), og (Oliveira)
14/04/96	Napoli	A	1-0	Panucci
20/04/96	Torino	A	1-1	Maldini
28/04/96	Fiorentina	H	3-1	Savicevic, Baggio (p), Simone
05/05/96	Sampdoria	A	0-3	
12/05/96	Cremonese	H	7-1	og (Gualco), Weah, Albertini, Panucci, Di Canio 2, Boban

NAPOLI

CLUB DIRECTORY

Società Sportiva Calcio Napoli
Via Vicinale Paradiso 70
80126 Napoli
tel - (081) 7661701
fax - (081) 7662763
Year of Formation - 1926
President - Gian Marco Innocenti
General Manager/Secretary - Luigi Pavarese
Coach - Vujadin Boskov (96/97 - Luigi Simoni)
Stadium - San Paolo (72,810)

MAJOR HONOURS
League Championship - (2) 1987, 1990.
Domestic Cup - (3) 1962, 1976, 1987.
UEFA Cup - (1) 1989.

APPEARANCES 95/96

	P	Ap	(s)	Gls
Massimo AGOSTINI	A	30		4
Luca ALTOMARE	M		(2)	
Roberto AYALA (ARG)	D	28	(1)	
Francesco BALDINI	D	20	(7)	
Alain BOGHOSSIAN (FRA)	M	15	(8)	2
Roberto BORDIN	M	29		
Renato BUSO	M	32		4
Ciro CARUSO	D		(1)	
Francesco COLONNESE	D	7	(9)	
André CRUZ (BRA)	D	29		1
Arturo DI NAPOLI	A	8	(19)	5
Carmelo IMBRIANI	A	17	(8)	3
Raffaele LONGO	M	4	(8)	
Salvatore MATRECANO	D		(1)	
Fausto PARI	D	31		
Fabio PECCHIA	M	27	(1)	4
Fausto PIZZI	M	32		3
Roberto POLICANO	M	2	(15)	1
Mirko TACCOLA	D	3	(2)	
Giuseppe TAGLIALATELA	G	34		
Massimo TARANTINO	D	26		

LEAGUE RESULTS 1995/96

27/08/95	Bari	A	1-1	Cruz (p)
10/09/95	Padova	H	2-0	Pecchia, Agostini
17/09/95	Atalanta	A	3-1	Buso, Imbriani, Agostini
24/09/95	Inter	H	2-1	Imbriani, Buso
01/10/95	Juventus	A	1-1	Pecchia
15/10/95	Fiorentina	H	0-2	
22/10/95	Piacenza	A	1-0	og (Taibi)
29/10/95	Cremonese	H	0-0	
05/11/95	Torino	A	0-0	
19/11/95	Vicenza	H	1-1	Agostini
26/11/95	Cagliari	A	0-2	
03/12/95	Parma	H	1-1	Pizzi
10/12/95	Milan	A	0-0	
17/12/95	Roma	H	0-2	
23/12/95	Sampdoria	A	2-2	Di Napoli, Buso
07/01/96	Lazio	H	1-0	Di Napoli
14/01/96	Udinese	A	2-3	Agostini, Pecchia
21/01/96	Bari	H	1-0	Di Napoli
28/01/96	Padova	A	2-4	Pizzi, Di Napoli
04/02/96	Atalanta	H	2-0	Boghossian, Imbriani
11/02/96	Inter	A	0-4	
18/02/96	Juventus	H	0-1	
25/02/96	Fiorentina	A	0-3	
03/03/96	Piacenza	H	0-0	
10/03/96	Cremonese	A	1-1	Buso
24/03/96	Vicenza	A	0-3	
31/03/96	Cagliari	H	0-0	
06/04/96	Parma	A	0-1	
10/04/96	Torino	H	1-0	Boghossian
14/04/96	Milan	H	0-1	
20/04/96	Roma	A	1-4	Pecchia
28/04/96	Sampdoria	H	1-0	Di Napoli (p)
05/05/96	Lazio	A	0-1	
12/05/96	Udinese	H	2-1	Pizzi (p), Policano

PADOVA

CLUB DIRECTORY

Padova Calcio
Via Sorio 43
35141 Padova
tel - (049) 8723555
fax - (049) 8723522
Year of Formation - 1910
President - Sergio Giordani
General Manager - Piero Aggradi
Secretary - Giovanni Gardini
Coach - Mauro Sandreani
(96/97 - Giuseppe Materazzi)
Stadium - Euganeo (27,900)

APPEARANCES 95/96

	P	Ap	(s)	Gls
Nicola AMORUSO	A	31	(2)	14
Adriano BONAIUTI	G	31		
Massimo CIOCCI	A	8	(5)	2
Maurizio COPPOLA	M	16	(8)	
Andrea CUICCHI	D	21	(7)	2
Ennio DAL BIANCO	G	1	(1)	
Stefano FIORE	M	6	(18)	1
Franco GABRIELI	D	30		2
Giuseppe GALDERISI	A	3	(4)	
Alberto GALLO	A		(1)	
Silvio GIAMPIETRO	D	29		1
Michel KREEK (HOL)	M	28	(1)	3
Alexi LALAS (USA)	D	11		
Damiano LONGHI	M	32		
Federico MOLINARI	D		(2)	
Mauro MORELLO	G	2	(1)	
Stefano NAVA	D	15	(2)	
Carmine NUNZIATA	M	30		
Massimiliano OSSARI	D		(2)	
Alessandro PIOVESAN	M		(1)	
Stefano PIOLI	D		(1)	
Massimiliano ROSA	D	27	(1)	
Antonio SCONZIANO	D	20	(5)	
Giovanni SERAO	D	5		1
Leonard VAN UTRECHT (HOL)	A	5	(15)	1
Goran VLAOVIC (CRO)	A	23		13

LEAGUE RESULTS 1995/96

Date	Opponent	H/A	Score	Scorers
27/08/95	Milan	H	1-2	Amoruso
10/09/95	Napoli	A	0-2	
17/09/95	Torino	H	1-1	Kreek
24/09/95	Vicenza	A	1-2	Amoruso
01/10/95	Parma	H	1-3	Amoruso (p)
15/10/95	Lazio	A	0-2	
22/10/95	Juventus	A	1-3	Amoruso
29/10/95	Sampdoria	H	1-1	Ciocci
05/11/95	Roma	A	0-2	
19/11/95	Bari	H	3-0	Amoruso 2, Ciocci
26/11/95	Cremonese	A	1-2	Giampietro
03/12/95	Fiorentina	H	0-1	
10/12/95	Inter	H	2-1	Vlaovic 2
17/12/95	Udinese	A	1-3	Vlaovic
23/12/95	Piacenza	H	1-1	Gabrieli
07/01/96	Cagliari	A	1-0	Kreek
14/01/96	Atalanta	H	3-2	Van Utrecht, Vlaovic 2
21/01/96	Milan	A	0-1	
28/01/96	Napoli	H	4-2	Vlaovic 2, Amoruso, Fiore
04/02/96	Torino	A	0-2	
11/02/96	Vicenza	H	3-2	Cuicchi, Vlaovic, og (Lopez)
18/02/96	Parma	A	1-2	Kreek
25/02/96	Lazio	H	1-3	Amoruso (p)
02/03/96	Juventus	H	0-5	
10/03/96	Sampdoria	A	1-3	Vlaovic
24/03/96	Bari	A	1-2	Gabrieli
31/03/96	Cremonese	H	1-2	Amoruso
06/04/96	Fiorentina	A	4-6	Amoruso 2, Vlaovic 2
10/04/96	Roma	H	1-2	Vlaovic
14/04/96	Inter	A	2-8	Amoruso 2
20/04/96	Udinese	H	2-3	Cuicchi, Amoruso
28/04/96	Piacenza	A	0-4	
05/05/96	Cagliari	H	2-1	Vlaovic, Serao
12/05/96	Atalanta	A	0-3	

PARMA

CLUB DIRECTORY

Parma Associazione Calcio
Via Partigiani d'Italia 1
43100 Parma
tel - (0521) 200419
fax - (0521) 289924
Year of Formation - 1913
President - Giorgio Pedraneschi
General Manager - Giambattista Pastorello
Secretary - Renzo Ongaro
Coach - Nevio Scala (96/97 - Carlo Ancelotti)
Stadium - Ennio Tardini (29,048)

MAJOR HONOURS
Domestic Cup - (1) 1992.
European Cup-winners' Cup - (1) 1993.
UEFA Cup - (1) 1995.
European Super Cup - (1) 1994.

APPEARANCES 95/96

	P	Ap	(s)	Gls
Luigi APOLLONI	D	26		1
Giovanni ARIOLI	M		(1)	1
Faustino ASPRILLA (COL)	A	4	(2)	2
Dino BAGGIO	M	28		4
Antonio BENARRIVO	D	22	(5)	3
Massimo BRAMBILLA	M	20	(6)	
Tomas BROLIN (SWE)	A		(4)	
Luca BUCCI	G	26		
Gian Luigi BUFFON	G	7	(2)	
Fabio CANNAVARO	D	29		1
Marcello CASTELLINI	D	5	(4)	
Tarcisio CATANESE	M	1	(4)	
Massimo CRIPPA	M	24	(7)	1
Alberto DI CHIARA	D	14	(8)	2
FERNANDO COUTO (POR)	D	10	(2)	
Filippo INZAGHI	A	7	(8)	2
Alessandro MELLI	A	12	(12)	4
Lorenzo MINOTTI	D	16	(2)	
Roberto MUSSI	D	31	(1)	2
Alessandro NISTA	G	1		
Gabriele PIN	M	14	(6)	1
Ferdinando PIRO	A	1	(5)	1
Néstor SENSINI (ARG)	M	30	(1)	2
Hristo STOICHKOV (BUL)	A	18	(5)	5
Gianfranco ZOLA	A	28	(1)	10

LEAGUE RESULTS 1995/96

27/08/95	Atalanta	A	1-1	Stoichkov
10/09/95	Inter	H	2-1	Zola, Baggio
17/09/95	Sampdoria	A	0-3	
24/09/95	Fiorentina	H	3-0	Stoichkov, Crippa, Benarrivo
01/10/95	Padova	A	3-1	Stoichkov 2, Zola
15/10/95	Udinese	H	1-0	Melli
22/10/95	Roma	A	1-1	Baggio
29/10/95	Piacenza	H	3-2	Zola 2, Inzaghi
05/11/95	Cremonese	A	2-0	Cannavaro, Zola
19/11/95	Milan	H	0-0	
26/11/95	Juventus	H	1-1	Asprilla
03/12/95	Napoli	A	1-1	Zola (p)
10/12/95	Lazio	H	2-1	Asprilla, Zola
17/12/95	Bari	A	1-1	Melli
23/12/95	Vicenza	H	0-1	
07/01/96	Torino	A	2-2	Sensini, Baggio
14/01/96	Cagliari	H	4-0	Mussi, Di Chiara 2, og (Firicano)
21/01/96	Atalanta	H	2-0	Pin, Melli
28/01/96	Inter	A	1-1	Stoichkov
04/02/96	Sampdoria	H	1-0	og (Lamonica)
11/02/96	Fiorentina	A	0-1	
18/02/96	Padova	H	2-1	Melli, Benarrivo
25/02/96	Udinese	A	0-0	
02/03/96	Roma	H	1-1	Sensini
10/03/96	Piacenza	A	1-2	Arioli
24/03/96	Milan	A	0-3	
30/03/96	Juventus	A	0-1	
06/04/96	Napoli	H	1-0	Apolloni
10/04/96	Cremonese	H	2-0	Mussi, Zola
14/04/96	Lazio	A	1-2	Zola
20/04/96	Bari	H	3-1	Baggio, Inzaghi, Piro
28/04/96	Vicenza	A	1-0	Benarrivo
05/05/96	Torino	H	1-0	Zola
12/05/96	Cagliari	A	0-2	

PIACENZA

CLUB DIRECTORY

Piacenza Football Club
Via Gorra 25
29100 Piacenza
tel - (0523) 757010/757015
fax - (0523) 453405
Year of Formation - 1919
President - Leonardo Garilli
General Manager - Gian Pietro Marchetti
Secretary - Giovanni Rubini
Coach - Luigi Cagni (96/97 - Bortolo Mutti)
Stadium - Galleana (21,800)

APPEARANCES 95/96

	P	Ap	(s)	Gls
Gabriele BALLOTTA	A		(1)	
Massimo BRIOSCHI	D		(1)	
Nicola CACCIA	A	30	(3)	14
Massimiliano CAPPELINI	A	7	(21)	2
Angelo CARBONE	M	29	(1)	2
Mirko CONTE	D	14	(9)	
Eugenio CORINI	M	32		1
Eusebio DI FRANCESCO	M	33		2
Roberto LORENZINI	D	11	(5)	
Settimio LUCCI	D	32		
Stefano MACCOPPI	D	23	(6)	
Daniele MORETTI	M	10	(16)	1
Gian Pietro PIOVANI	A	32		8
Cleto POLONIA	D	32		
Stefano ROSSINI	D	26	(2)	
Luigi SIMONI	G	1	(2)	
Massimo TAIBI	G	33		
Cristian TRAPELLA	M	1	(6)	
Francesco TURRINI	M	28	(2)	1

LEAGUE RESULTS 1995/96

27/08/95	Lazio	A	1-4	Caccia (p)
10/09/95	Juventus	H	0-4	
17/09/95	Inter	A	0-0	
24/09/95	Bari	H	3-2	Caccia 2, Piovani
01/10/95	Atalanta	A	0-2	
15/10/95	Sampdoria	H	3-2	Corini, Piovani, Caccia
22/10/95	Napoli	H	0-1	
29/10/95	Parma	A	2-3	Carbone, Caccia (p)
05/11/95	Vicenza	A	1-1	Piovani
19/11/95	Roma	H	1-0	Di Francesco
26/11/95	Milan	A	0-3	
03/12/95	Cagliari	H	1-1	Caccia
10/12/95	Torino	A	2-4	Caccia 2
17/12/95	Cremonese	H	2-1	Caccia, Piovani
23/12/95	Padova	A	1-1	Piovani
07/01/96	Udinese	H	0-2	
14/01/96	Fiorentina	A	1-2	Turrini
21/01/96	Lazio	H	2-1	Piovani, Caccia
28/01/96	Juventus	A	0-2	
04/02/96	Inter	H	1-0	Carbone
11/02/96	Bari	A	0-0	
18/02/96	Atalanta	H	2-2	Caccia, Piovani
25/02/96	Sampdoria	A	0-3	
03/03/96	Napoli	A	0-0	
10/03/96	Parma	H	2-1	Caccia 2 (1p)
24/03/96	Roma	A	1-2	Cappellini
31/03/96	Milan	H	0-2	
06/04/96	Cagliari	A	0-0	
10/04/96	Vicenza	H	0-1	
14/04/96	Torino	H	1-0	Piovani
20/04/96	Cremonese	A	0-0	
28/04/96	Padova	H	4-0	Caccia, Cappellini, Di Francesco, Moretti
05/05/96	Udinese	A	0-0	
12/05/96	Fiorentina	H	0-1	

ROMA

CLUB DIRECTORY

Associazione Sportiva Roma
Via di Trigoria km. 3.600
00128 Roma
tel - (06) 5060200
fax - (06) 5061736
Year of Formation - 1927
President - Francesco Sensi
General Manager - Emiliano Mascetti
Secretary - Giorgio Catalano
Coach - Carlo Mazzone (96/97 - Carlos Bianchi)
Stadium - Olimpico (82,922)

MAJOR HONOURS
League Championship - (2) 1942, 1983.
Domestic Cup - (7)
1964, 1969, 1980, 1981, 1984, 1986, 1991.
Fairs' Cup - (1) 1961.

APPEARANCES 95/96

	P	Ap	(s)	Gls
ALDAIR dos Santos (BRA)	D	30		
Enrico ANNONI	D	12	(11)	
Abel BALBO (ARG)	A	23	(3)	13
Daniele BERRETTA	M	1	(2)	
Marco BRANCA	A	3	(4)	2
Massimiliano CAPPIOLI	M	24	(7)	4
Amedeo CARBONI	D	29		
Giovanni CERVONE	G	33		
Gianluca CHERUBINI	D	1	(4)	
Lampros CHOUTOS	A		(1)	
Marco DELVECCHIO	A	18	(6)	10
Luigi DI BIAGIO	M	19	(11)	2
Daniel FONSECA (URU)	A	17	(6)	8
Giuseppe GIANNINI	M	13	(7)	
Marco LANNA	D	32		
Francesco MORIERO	M	19	(8)	3
Fabio PETRUZZI	D	28		
Alessio SCARCHILLI	M	2	(5)	
Francesco STATUTO	M	29	(2)	2
Giorgio STERCHELE	G	1		
Jonas THERN (SWE)	M	20	(2)	1
Francesco TOTTI	A	20	(8)	2

LEAGUE RESULTS 1995/96

Date	Opponent	H/A	Score	Scorers
27/08/95	Sampdoria	A	1-1	Branca
10/09/95	Atalanta	H	0-1	
17/09/95	Milan	H	1-2	Balbo
24/09/95	Cremonese	A	1-0	og (Tentoni)
01/10/95	Lazio	H	0-0	
15/10/95	Torino	A	2-2	Branca, Cappioli
22/10/95	Parma	H	1-1	Fonseca
29/10/95	Cagliari	A	2-0	Fonseca 2
05/11/95	Padova	H	2-0	Balbo, Fonseca
19/11/95	Piacenza	A	0-1	
26/11/95	Bari	H	2-1	Fonseca, Totti
03/12/95	Udinese	A	1-1	Balbo
10/12/95	Vicenza	H	1-1	og (Lopez)
17/12/95	Napoli	A	2-0	Thern, Delvecchio
23/12/95	Juventus	A	2-0	Balbo, og (Ferrara)
07/01/96	Fiorentina	H	2-2	Balbo 2
14/01/96	Inter	A	0-2	
21/01/96	Sampdoria	H	3-1	Balbo 3 (1p)
28/01/96	Atalanta	A	1-2	Delvecchio
04/02/96	Milan	A	1-3	Moriero
11/02/96	Cremonese	H	3-0	Di Biagio, Balbo, Cappioli
18/02/96	Lazio	A	0-1	
25/02/96	Torino	H	1-0	Statuto
02/03/96	Parma	A	1-1	Fonseca
10/03/96	Cagliari	H	1-1	Balbo (p)
24/03/96	Piacenza	H	2-1	Delvecchio, Cappioli
31/03/96	Bari	A	2-1	Totti, Statuto
06/04/96	Udinese	H	2-1	Delvecchio, Moriero
10/04/96	Padova	A	2-1	Fonseca, Cappioli
14/04/96	Vicenza	A	1-2	Fonseca (p)
20/04/96	Napoli	H	4-1	Delvecchio 3, og (Cruz)
28/04/96	Juventus	H	2-2	Delvecchio, Moriero
05/05/96	Fiorentina	A	4-1	Balbo 2 (2p), Delvecchio 2
12/05/96	Inter	H	1-0	Di Biagio (p)

SAMPDORIA

CLUB DIRECTORY

Sampdoria Unione Calcio
Via XX Settembre 33/1
16121 Genova
tel - (010) 585343
fax - (010) 591712
Year of Formation - 1946
President - Enrico Mantovani
General Manager - Emiliano Salvarezza
Secretary - Lorenzo Traverso
Coach - Sven Göran Eriksson
Stadium - Luigi Ferraris (41,917)

MAJOR HONOURS

League Championship - (1) 1991.
Domestic Cup - (4)
1985, 1988, 1989, 1994.
European Cup-winners' Cup - (1) 1990.

APPEARANCES 95/96

	P	Ap	(s)	Gls
Giovanni ABATE	M	1		
David BALLERI	D	32		4
Claudio BELLUCCI	A	7	(9)	1
Mauro BERTARELLI	A		(8)	
Enrico CHIESA	A	27		22
Davide DI TERLIZZI	M		(2)	
Alberigo EVANI	M	24	(5)	
Riccardo FERRI	D	11	(5)	
Marco FRANCESCHETTI	D	10	(5)	
Giovanni INVERNIZZI	M	25	(5)	
Vincenzo JACOPINO	A		(4)	
Christian KAREMBEU (FRA)	M	32		5
Alessandro LAMONICA	D	4	(6)	
Roberto MANCINI	M	25	(1)	11
Filippo MANIERO	A	12	(13)	6
Moreno MANNINI	D	27		1
Sinisa MIHAJLOVIC (YUG)	D	29	(1)	4
Angelo PAGOTTO	G	23	(1)	
Emanuele PESARESI	D	10		
Stefano SACCHETTI	D	16	(8)	
Fausto SALSANO	M	20	(7)	1
Clarence SEEDORF (HOL)	M	28	(4)	3
Matteo SERENI	G	4		
Walter ZENGA	G	7		

LEAGUE RESULTS 1995/96

27/08/95	Roma	H	1-1	Karembeu
10/09/95	Cremonese	A	0-0	
17/09/95	Parma	H	3-0	Karembeu 2, Bellucci
24/09/95	Torino	A	1-1	Maniero
01/10/95	Cagliari	H	1-2	Maniero
15/10/95	Piacenza	A	2-3	Maniero, Mancini
22/10/95	Fiorentina	H	2-1	Maniero, Salsano
29/10/95	Padova	A	1-1	Mancini
05/11/95	Inter	H	0-0	
19/11/95	Atalanta	A	2-3	Maniero, Seedorf
26/11/95	Udinese	H	1-0	Mihajlovic
03/12/95	Bari	A	3-1	Chiesa 3
10/12/95	Juventus	H	2-0	Chiesa 2
17/12/95	Lazio	A	3-6	Mihajlovic, Chiesa 2 (1p)
23/12/95	Napoli	H	2-2	og (Cruz), Chiesa
07/01/96	Milan	A	0-3	
14/01/96	Vicenza	H	2-2	Chiesa, Karembeu
21/01/96	Roma	A	1-3	Mannini
28/01/96	Cremonese	H	2-0	Balleri, Chiesa
04/02/96	Parma	A	0-1	
11/02/96	Torino	H	1-0	Mancini
18/02/96	Cagliari	A	0-3	
25/02/96	Piacenza	H	3-0	Mihajlovic, Chiesa, Mancini
03/03/96	Fiorentina	A	2-2	Mancini, Karembeu
10/03/96	Padova	H	3-1	Chiesa 3
24/03/96	Atalanta	H	2-3	Balleri, Chiesa
31/03/96	Udinese	A	4-2	Mancini 2, Chiesa, Mihajlovic
06/04/96	Bari	H	2-0	Maniero, Mancini
10/04/96	Inter	A	2-0	Chiesa 2 (1p)
13/04/96	Juventus	A	3-0	Chiesa, Balleri, Seedorf
20/04/96	Lazio	H	3-3	Balleri, Mancini, Chiesa (p)
28/04/96	Napoli	A	0-1	
05/05/96	Milan	H	3-0	Chiesa 2, Mancini
12/05/96	Vicenza	A	2-2	Seedorf, Mancini

TORINO

CLUB DIRECTORY

Torino Calcio
Via Maria Vittoria 1
10123 Torino
tel - (011) 5623941
fax - (011) 5622018
Year of Formation - 1906
President - Gian Marco Calleri
General Manager - Giorgio Vitali
Secretary - Federico Bonetto
Coach - Nedo Sonetti; Francesco Scoglio; Lido Vieri
(96/97 - Mauro Sandreani)
Stadium - Delle Alpi (71,012)

MAJOR HONOURS
League Championship - (7)
1928, 1943, 1946, 1947, 1948, 1949, 1976.
Domestic Cup - (5)
1936, 1943, 1968, 1971, 1993.

APPEARANCES 95/96

	P	Ap	(s)	Gls
Jocelyn ANGLOMA (FRA)	D	31		3
Roberto BACCI	D	27	(1)	
Alberto BERNARDI	A		(4)	
Antonio BERNARDINI	M	17	(6)	2
Enzo BIATO	G	13	(1)	
Massimiliano CANIATO	G	15		
Roberto CRAVERO	D	18	(2)	
Paolo CRISTALLINI	M	25		1
Alessandro DAL CANTO	D	12	(4)	
Davide DIONIGI	A	6	(16)	1
Domenico DOARDO	G	6	(2)	
Giulio FALCONE	D	27	(4)	
Valeriano FIORIN	M		(1)	
Felice FOGLIA	A	2		
HAKAN Sükür (TUR)	A	5		1
Veldin KARIC (CRO)	A	22	(1)	1
Moreno LONGO	D	6	(5)	
Roberto MALTAGLIATI	D	34		
Luca MEZZANO	D	10	(1)	2
Mauro MILANESE	D	31		
Giuseppe MINAUDO	M	4	(9)	
Fabio MORO	D	6	(2)	
Abedi PELE (GHA)	M	17		3
Ruggiero RIZZITELLI	A	28		11
Augustin SIMO	M	4	(2)	
Sean SOGLIANO	D	6	(7)	
Vincenzo SOMMESE	M	2	(3)	

LEAGUE RESULTS 1995/96

Date	Opponent	H/A	Score	Scorers
27/08/95	Fiorentina	A	0-2	
10/09/95	Bari	H	3-1	og (Ricci), Hakan, Rizzitelli (p)
17/09/95	Padova	A	1-1	Bernardini
24/09/95	Sampdoria	H	1-1	Rizzitelli
01/10/95	Inter	A	0-4	
15/10/95	Roma	H	2-2	Pelé, og (Cervone)
22/10/95	Udinese	A	0-1	
29/10/95	Vicenza	H	1-0	og (Lopez)
05/11/95	Napoli	H	0-0	
19/11/95	Cagliari	A	0-1	
26/11/95	Atalanta	H	0-1	
03/12/95	Juventus	A	0-5	
10/12/95	Piacenza	H	4-2	Rizzitelli 2 (1p), Pelé, Bernardini
17/12/95	Milan	A	1-1	Rizzitelli (p)
23/12/95	Cremonese	A	1-1	Pelé
07/01/96	Parma	H	2-2	Dionigi, Angloma
14/01/96	Lazio	A	1-1	Rizzitelli
21/01/96	Fiorentina	H	0-3	
28/01/96	Bari	A	2-2	Rizzitelli, Karic
04/02/96	Padova	H	2-0	Rizzitelli, Angloma
11/02/96	Sampdoria	A	0-1	
18/02/96	Inter	H	0-1	
25/02/96	Roma	A	0-1	
03/03/96	Udinese	H	2-0	Rizzitelli (p), Mezzano
10/03/96	Vicenza	A	1-2	Angloma
24/03/96	Cagliari	H	1-1	Rizzitelli (p)
31/03/96	Atalanta	A	0-1	
06/04/96	Juventus	H	1-2	Rizzitelli
10/04/96	Napoli	A	0-1	
14/04/96	Piacenza	A	0-1	
20/04/96	Milan	H	1-1	Cristallini (p)
28/04/96	Cremonese	H	1-0	Mezzano
05/05/96	Parma	A	0-1	
12/05/96	Lazio	H	0-2	

UDINESE

CLUB DIRECTORY

Udinese Calcio
Via Cotonificio 94
33100 Udine
tel - (0432) 477141
fax - (0432) 482193
Year of Formation - 1896
President - Giovanni Caratozzolo
General Manager - Carlo Piazzolla
Secretary - Sigfrido Marcatti
Coach - Alberto Zaccheroni
Stadium - Friuli (41,825)

APPEARANCES 95/96

	P	Ap	(s)	Gls
Raffaele AMETRANO	M	31	(1)	1
Graziano BATTISTINI	G	26	(1)	
Valerio BERTOTTO	D	18	(10)	1
Giovanni BIA	D	31		4
Oliver BIERHOFF (GER)	A	31		17
Stefano BORGONOVO	A	3	(4)	
Alessandro CALORI	D	28	(2)	
Stefano DESIDERI	M	31	(1)	
Giuliano GIANNICHEDDA	M	5	(3)	
Attilio GREGORI	G	8	(2)	
Thomas HELVEG (DEN)	D	30	(1)	2
Marek KOZMINSKI (POL)	M	7	(5)	
Alessandro MANNI	M		(1)	
Francesco MARINO	A	6	(11)	3
Salvatore MATRECANO	D	7	(12)	1
Cristian MAURO	M		(3)	
Vincenzo MONTALBANO	D	1	(1)	
Stefano PELLEGRINI	D	3	(5)	
Paolo POGGI	A	26	(4)	9
Roberto RIPA	D	3	(5)	
Fabio ROSSITTO	M	30	(1)	
Raffaele SERGIO	D	13	(2)	
Igor SHALIMOV (RUS)	M	10	(10)	
David STEFANI	M		(1)	
Giovanni STROPPA	M	26	(6)	1
Alessandro TESTAFERRATA	G		(1)	

LEAGUE RESULTS 1995/96

27/08/95	Cagliari	H	1-0	Bierhoff
10/09/95	Milan	A	1-2	Poggi
17/09/95	Cremonese	H	3-2	Bierhoff 2, Poggi
24/09/95	Lazio	A	2-2	Helveg, Bierhoff
01/10/95	Vicenza	H	1-1	Bierhoff
15/10/95	Parma	A	0-1	
22/10/95	Torino	H	1-0	Bierhoff (p)
29/10/95	Atalanta	A	0-0	
05/11/95	Juventus	H	1-0	Bierhoff
19/11/95	Inter	A	1-2	Bia (p)
26/11/95	Sampdoria	A	0-1	
03/12/95	Roma	H	1-1	Bierhoff
10/12/95	Fiorentina	A	0-3	
17/12/95	Padova	H	3-1	Bierhoff, Ametrano, Poggi
23/12/95	Bari	H	1-2	Bia (p)
07/01/96	Piacenza	A	2-0	Bierhoff, Matrecano
14/01/96	Napoli	H	3-2	Bertotto, Poggi, Bia
21/01/96	Cagliari	A	1-4	Bierhoff
28/01/96	Milan	H	0-2	
04/02/96	Cremonese	A	2-2	Poggi, Bia (p)
11/02/96	Lazio	H	1-1	og (Negro)
18/02/96	Vicenza	A	1-0	Helveg
25/02/96	Parma	H	0-0	
03/03/96	Torino	A	0-2	
10/03/96	Atalanta	H	3-0	Poggi 2, Bierhoff
24/03/96	Inter	H	1-2	Bierhoff
31/03/96	Sampdoria	H	2-4	Bierhoff, Marino
06/04/96	Roma	A	1-2	Marino
10/04/96	Juventus	A	1-2	Stroppa
14/04/96	Fiorentina	H	1-0	Poggi
20/04/96	Padova	A	3-2	Bierhoff 2 (1p), Poggi
28/04/96	Bari	A	2-4	Marino, Bierhoff
05/05/96	Piacenza	H	0-0	
12/05/96	Napoli	A	1-2	og (Pecchia)

VICENZA

CLUB DIRECTORY

Vicenza Calcio
Via Schio 21
36100 Vicenza
tel - (0444) 505044
fax - (0444) 544764
Year of Formation - 1902
President - Pieraldo Dalle Carbonare
General Manager - Sergio Gasparin
Secretary - Fabio Rizzitelli
Coach - Francesco Guidolin
Stadium - Romeo Menti (20,920)

APPEARANCES 95/96

	P	Ap	(s)	Gls
Gabriele AMBROSETTI	A	16	(8)	3
Daniele AMERINI	M	4	(20)	
Davide BELOTTI	D	7	(9)	
Joachim BJÖRKLUND (SWE)	D	33		
Alberto BRIASCHI	A	3	(4)	
Pierluigi BRIVIO	G	2		
Riccardo CASTAGNA	D		(4)	
Domenico DI CARLO	M	27		2
Gilberto D'IGNAZIO	D	8	(4)	
Ferdinando GASPARINI	A	1	(5)	
Gabriele GROSSI	D	16		
Massimo LOMBARDINI	M	20	(10)	
Giovanni LOPEZ	D	26		1
Giampiero MAINI	M	32		2
Gustavo MENDEZ (URU)	M	18	(7)	
Luca MONDINI	G	32		
Roberto MURGITA	A	32	(2)	10
Marcelo OTERO (URU)	A	28	(2)	12
Alessandro PISTONE	D	5	(1)	
Willi PITTANA	M		(6)	
Maurizio ROSSI	M	26	(5)	4
Luigi SARTOR	D	15		
Fabio VIVIANI	M	23	(5)	1

LEAGUE RESULTS 1995/96

27/08/95	Inter	A	0-1	
10/09/95	Fiorentina	H	1-0	Rossi
17/09/95	Juventus	A	0-1	
24/09/95	Padova	H	2-1	Murgita, Otero
01/10/95	Udinese	A	1-1	Otero
15/10/95	Bari	H	2-0	Otero 2
22/10/95	Milan	H	1-1	Murgita
29/10/95	Torino	A	0-1	
05/11/95	Piacenza	H	1-1	Maini
19/11/95	Napoli	A	1-1	Otero
26/11/95	Lazio	H	1-0	Maini
03/12/95	Atalanta	A	1-3	Murgita
10/12/95	Roma	A	1-1	Viviani
17/12/95	Cagliari	H	0-1	
23/12/95	Parma	A	1-0	Murgita
07/01/96	Cremonese	H	1-0	Otero
14/01/96	Sampdoria	A	2-2	Rossi, Ambrosetti
21/01/96	Inter	H	1-1	Otero (p)
28/01/96	Fiorentina	A	1-1	Di Carlo
04/02/96	Juventus	H	2-1	Otero (p), Murgita
11/02/96	Padova	A	2-3	Murgita, Ambrosetti
18/02/96	Udinese	H	0-1	
25/02/96	Bari	A	2-0	Otero, Lopez
02/03/96	Milan	A	0-4	
10/03/96	Torino	H	2-1	Otero 2
24/03/96	Napoli	H	3-0	Di Carlo, Murgita, Ambrosetti
31/03/96	Lazio	A	0-3	
06/04/96	Atalanta	H	1-0	Rossi
10/04/96	Piacenza	A	1-0	Rossi
14/04/96	Roma	H	2-1	Otero, Murgita
20/04/96	Cagliari	A	0-2	
28/04/96	Parma	H	0-1	
05/05/96	Cremonese	A	1-1	Murgita
12/05/96	Sampdoria	H	2-2	og (Mannini), Murgita

PROMOTED CLUBS

SECOND DIVISION FINAL TABLE 95/96

		Pd	W	D	L	F	A	Pt	GD
1	**Bologna**	**38**	**16**	**17**	**5**	**42**	**23**	**65**	**+19**
2	**Verona**	**38**	**17**	**12**	**9**	**50**	**33**	**63**	**+17**
3	**Perugia**	**38**	**16**	**13**	**9**	**52**	**42**	**61**	**+10**
4	**Reggiana**	**38**	**16**	**13**	**9**	**42**	**32**	**61**	**+10**
5	Salernitana	38	15	13	10	46	32	58	+14
6	Lucchese	38	13	15	10	45	43	54	+2
7	Genoa	38	14	10	14	56	52	52	+4
8	Palermo	38	12	16	10	36	35	52	+1
9	Pescara	38	13	11	14	47	50	50	-3
10	Cesena	38	13	10	15	50	49	49	+1
11	Foggia	38	13	9	16	31	50	48	-19
12	Cosenza	38	11	15	12	47	51	48	-4
13	Venezia	38	11	15	12	34	39	48	-5
14	Reggina	38	11	14	13	38	46	47	-8
15	Chievo	38	9	20	9	37	30	47	+7
16	Brescia	38	12	10	16	48	49	46	-1
17	Fidelis Andria	38	10	15	13	42	45	45	-3
18	Avellino	38	11	10	17	39	54	43	-15
19	Ancona	38	11	9	18	42	51	42	-9
20	Pistoiese	38	7	11	20	35	53	32	-18

CLUB DIRECTORY

Bologna 1909 Football Club
Via Casteldebole 10
40132 Bologna
tel - (051) 577451
fax - (051) 591442
Year of Formation - 1909
President - Giuseppe Gazzoni Frascara
General Manager - Gabriele Oriali
Secretary - Stefano Pedrelli
Coach - Renzo Ulivieri
Stadium - Renato Dall'Ara (39,603)

MAJOR HONOURS
League Championship - (7)
1925, 1929, 1936, 1937, 1939, 1941, 1964.
Domestic Cup - (2) 1970, 1974.

CLUB DIRECTORY

Hellas Verona Football Club
Piazzale Olimpia
37121 Verona
tel - (045) 577555
fax - (045) 568665
Year of Formation - 1903
President - Alberto Mazzi
General Manager - Nardino Previdi
Secretary - Enzo Bertolini
Coach - Attilio Perotti (96/97 - Luigi Cagni)
Stadium - Marc'Antonio Bentegodi (44,500)

MAJOR HONOURS
League Championship - (1) 1985.

CLUB DIRECTORY

Reggiana Associazione Calcio
Via Mogadiscio 1
42100 Reggio Emilia
tel - (0522) 921130
fax - (0522) 921825
Year of Formation - 1919
President - Loris Fantinel
General Manager - Daniela Gozzi
Secretary - Roberto Fontanili
Coach - Carlo Ancelotti (96/97 - Mircea Lucescu)
Stadium - Giglio (29,650)

CLUB DIRECTORY

Perugia Associazione Calcio
Località Pian di Massiano
06125 Perugia
tel - (075) 5006641
fax - (075) 5051616
Year of Formation - 1905
President - Silvio Alfredo Salerni
General Manager - Francesco Ghirelli
Secretary - Ilvano Ercoli
Coach - Walter Novellino; Diego Giannattasio;
Giovanni Galeone
Stadium - Renato Curi (37,000)

LATVIA

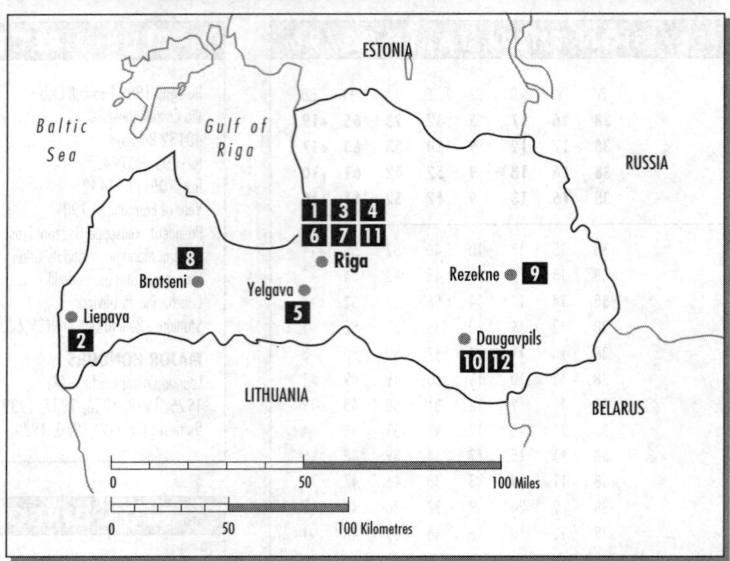

1	AMSTRIG RIGA	619	7	SKONTO RIGA	625
2	DAG LIEPAYA	620	8	STARTS BROTSENI	626
3	KVADRATS RIGA	621	9	VAIROGS REZEKNE	627
4	OLYMPIA RIGA	622	10	VILAN-D DAUGAVPILS	628
5	RAF YELGAVA	623	11	YURNIEKS RIGA	629
6	SKONTO/METALS RIGA	624	12	LOKOMOTIVE DAUGAVPILS	629

ALL TOO EASY FOR SKONTO RIGA

Encouraging end to Euro '96 qualifying campaign

Just five years after the country gained national independence, Latvian football is beginning to make its mark on the international scene.

The European Championship qualifying campaign brought some formidable results. Latvia may have finished up fifth in a six-team group, but they ruffled more than a few feathers along the way, including those of group winners Portugal. Four wins and 12 points was a very satisfactory return from Yanis Gilis's team. And the manner in which they ended the campaign suggested that even better times could be around the corner.

When Latvia beat Liechtenstein 1-0 in Riga in September, it meant that the team had won three European Championship matches in a row. The second of the three, in mid-August at home to Austria, was arguably the most gratifying of all. The Austrians had put themselves back into contention for a qualifying place with a 3-1 win in Dublin, but in Riga the Latvians kept on coming at them. Two goals from the team's leading scorer, Vitas Rimkus, plus a glorious winner from Israeli-based Armands Zeiberlinsh two minutes before the end, completed a truly memorable win. The Austrians will not have been too happy to find themselves

FEDERATION DIRECTORY

Latvijas Futbola Federacija
1 Augsiela, LV-1009 Riga

tel - (2) 292988
tlx - 161183 ritm su
fax - 8828331

Year of Formation - 1921
President - Guntis Indricksons
Secretary - Yanis Mezhetsky

Stadium - Daugava, Riga (15,000)

LEAGUE CHAMPIONSHIP RESULTS 1995

FIRST PHASE

		1	2	3	4	5	6	7	8	9	10
1	Amstrig Riga		0-1	1-1	2-3	1-2	2-0	0-3	0-1	0-1	2-2
2	DAG-Liepaya	1-1		3-2	2-0	1-2	0-1	2-2	1-1	3-1	0-2
3	Kvadrats Riga	0-2	3-1		1-4	0-3	0-6	0-7	0-3	1-5	0-2
4	Olympia Riga	0-7	2-2	3-0		0-1	1-1	0-1	0-2	1-0	1-0
5	RAF Yelgava	1-1	0-0	5-0	2-0		2-0	0-1	3-0	2-0	3-2
6	Skonto/Metals Riga	2-2	3-1	2-0	4-3	1-1		0-4	2-3	0-8	1-5
7	Skonto Riga	3-2	4-0	6-1	7-1	5-0	2-1		0-0	1-0	3-0
8	Starts Brotseni	3-0	1-0	1-0	2-0	0-4	3-0	0-3		0-0	0-1
9	Vairogs Rezekne	1-2	1-1	2-0	3-3	1-0	1-1	0-3	1-1		1-1
10	Vilan-D Daugavpils	0-1	2-0	2-1	3-1	0-2	4-0	1-4	3-0	1-2	

SECOND PHASE

GROUP A

		1	2	3	4	5	6
1	Amstrig Riga		1-1	2-2	5-1	3-0	1-2
2	RAF Yelgava	1-1		1-2	1-0	0-1	0-1
3	Skonto Riga	2-1	5-1		8-1	8-0	4-0
4	Starts Brotseni	0-1	3-0	1-4		1-1	0-1
5	Vairogs Rezekne	2-6	1-2	0-3	1-3		1-3
6	Vilan-D Daugavpils	2-0	0-0	0-2	3-0	2-0	

GROUP B

		1	2	3	4
1	DAG-Liepaya		0-2	3-1	1-0
2	Kvadrats Riga	1-0		2-1	0-1
3	Olympia Riga	1-1	2-2		0-2
4	Skonto/Metals Riga	1-2	1-5	7-1	

TOP SCORERS

19 Vitaly ASTAFYEV (Skonto Riga)
16 Oleg DULUB (Vairogs Rezekne)
14 Vladimir BABICHEV (Skonto Riga)
12 Marian PAKHAR (Skonto/Metals Riga/Skonto Riga)
11 Mikhail MIKHOLAP (Amstrig Riga)
Alexander YELISEYEV (Skonto Riga)
10 Vladlen BAUSHEV (Skonto Riga)
Valery IVANOV (Skonto Riga)
Renars VUTSANS (Skonto/Metals Riga)
8 Vitas RIMKUS (Amstrig Riga)
Boris MONYAK (Skonto Riga)
Eduard KUDRYASHOV (Starts Brotseni)
Sergey TARASOV (Vilan-D Daugavpils)
Vyacheslav ZHEVNEROVICH (Vilan-D Daugavpils)

LEAGUE CHAMPIONSHIP FINAL TABLE 1995

FIRST PHASE

			Home					Away					Total						
		Pd	W	D	L	F	A	W	D	L	F	A	W	D	L	F	A	Pt	GD
1	Skonto Riga	18	8	1	0	31	5	8	1	0	28	3	16	2	0	59	8	50	+51
2	RAF Yelgava	18	6	2	1	18	4	6	1	2	15	9	12	3	3	33	13	39	+20
3	Starts Brotseni	18	5	1	3	10	8	4	3	2	11	10	9	4	5	21	18	31	+3
4	Vilan-D Daugavpils	18	5	0	4	16	11	4	2	3	15	11	9	2	7	31	22	29	+9
5	Vairogs Rezekne	18	2	5	2	11	12	4	1	4	17	9	6	6	6	28	21	24	+7
6	Amstrig Riga	18	1	2	6	8	14	4	3	2	18	11	5	5	8	26	25	20	+1
7	Skonto/Metals Riga	18	3	2	4	15	27	2	2	5	10	15	5	4	9	25	42	19	-17
8	DAG-Liepaya	18	3	3	3	13	12	1	3	5	6	16	4	6	8	19	28	18	-9
9	Olympia Riga	18	3	2	4	8	14	2	1	6	15	26	5	3	10	23	40	18	-17
10	Kvadrats Riga	18	1	0	8	5	33	0	1	8	5	25	1	1	16	10	58	4	-48

SECOND PHASE

GROUP A

			Home					Away					Total						
		Pd	W	D	L	F	A	W	D	L	F	A	W	D	L	F	A	Pt	GD
1	Skonto Riga	28	13	1	0	58	8	12	2	0	41	7	25	3	0	99	15	78	+84
2	Vilan-D Daugavpils	28	8	1	5	23	13	8	2	4	22	17	16	3	9	45	30	51	+15
3	RAF Yelgava	28	7	3	4	21	9	7	3	4	19	19	14	6	8	40	28	48	+12
4	Starts Brotseni	28	6	2	6	15	15	5	3	6	16	28	11	5	12	31	43	38	-12
5	Amstrig Riga	28	3	4	7	20	20	6	4	4	27	18	9	8	11	47	38	35	+9
6	Vairogs Rezekne	28	2	5	7	16	29	5	2	7	19	23	7	7	14	35	52	28	-17

GROUP B

			Home					Away					Total						
		Pd	W	D	L	F	A	W	D	L	F	A	W	D	L	F	A	Pt	GD
7	Skonto/Metals Riga	24	4	2	6	24	35	4	2	6	13	16	8	4	12	37	51	28	-14
8	DAG-Liepaya	24	5	3	4	17	15	2	4	6	9	19	7	7	10	26	34	28	-8
9	Olympia Riga	24	3	4	5	11	19	2	1	9	18	38	5	5	14	29	57	20	-28
10	Kvadrats Riga	24	3	0	9	8	35	2	2	8	14	28	5	2	17	22	63	17	-41

N.B. After 18 matches the top six play off for the title and the bottom four play off to avoid relegation. When two or more teams are level on points, classification is determined by the results of the matches between them.

DOMESTIC CUP RESULTS

FIRST ROUND

Vetsriga Riga 3, Lokomotive Daugavpils 1
Yekabpils-Vide 0, Yurnieks Riga 1
Venta Ventspils 2, Vairogs Rezekne 1
FK Smiltene 1, OFRISS-Yuniors Riga 4
FK Valmiera 1, Skonto/Metals Riga 2 (aet)
Dardedze Aizkraukle 2, Lignums Riga 2 (aet; 4-5 on pens.)
Gauya Valmiera 1, AVV Riga 3
Nafta Ventspils 7, Tseriba Preili 1
ASK/Flaminko Riga 5, FK Balvi 0

SECOND ROUND

Vetsriga Riga 1, Daugava Riga 1 (aet; 5-6 pens.)
FK Valka 0, Skonto Riga 14
Yurnieks Riga 1, Venta Ventspils 1 (aet; 4-3 on pens.)
OFRISS-Yuniors Riga 1, FK Liepaya 7
Skonto/Metals Riga 0, Starts Brotseni 1
Lignums Riga 0, Dinaburg Daugavpils 4
AVV Riga 0, Nafta Ventspils 1
ASK/Flaminko Riga 0, RAF Yelgava 4

QUARTER-FINALS

Daugava Riga 0, Skonto Riga 2
FK Liepaya 1, Yurnieks Riga 1 (aet; 1-3 on pens.)
Dinaburg Daugavpils 6, Starts Brotseni 1
Nafta Ventspils 1, RAF Yelgava 3 (aet)

SEMI-FINALS

Skonto Riga 8, Yurnieks Riga 0
RAF Yelgava 0, Dinaburg Daugavpils 0 (aet; 4-3 on pens.)

FINAL

18/06/96, Riga
RAF YELGAVA 2 Korotkevich (54), Dragun (115)
SKONTO RIGA 1 Zemlinsky (57p)
(aet)
referee - Direktorenko
RAF YELGAVA - Oleinik; Ivanov, Dragun, Mastyanitsa, Dolgopolov, Murin (Shkele 98), Dubina, Korotkevich (Torgashov 120), Sergeyev, Bogdan, Zarinsh (Kachanov 118).
SKONTO RIGA - Laizans; Troitsky, Astafyev, Zemlinsky, Shevlyakov, Stepanov, Ivanov, Blagonadezhdin, Shtolcers (Lobanyov 75), Babichev (Pakhar 61), Pindeyev (Baushev 116).

grouped once again with Latvia for the 1998 World Cup qualifying competition.

At club level also Latvia experienced a degree of success in 1995/96, with both DAG-Liepaya (albeit by default) and RAF Yelgava reaching the first round proper of European competition. Surprisingly, the one team from Latvia that did not make it past the preliminary round was Skonto Riga, who had won each of their opening ties in Europe during the previous three seasons. But after beating Maribor Branik 1-0 at home in the first leg, they were knocked out by a 0-2 defeat in Slovenia.

That was to be Skonto's only defeat in 1995. Once again the country's top club annihilated the opposition in the domestic championship to take their fifth national title in a row. As in 1994, Skonto were undefeated throughout the campaign. A new league format had been set up to try and make it more difficult for Skonto to continue their championship monopoly. But it failed miserably. Skonto, packed full of Latvian internationals and with the only bona fide youth development policy in the country, were never going to be stopped. They won 26 of their 28 matches, drawing the other two. The title was theirs with half a dozen matches still to play. Nowhere else in Europe was one team quite so dominant.

The only objective Skonto failed to reach was a century of goals for the season. They managed 99, thanks to eight in their final match of the season, which included a hat-trick from the league's leading scorer - and Skonto's best player - Vitaly Astafyev. Skonto did actually score 103 goals in the championship, but a 4-0 victory in their second game of the season was annulled when their opponents, Pardaugava Riga, later withdrew from the league.

Pardaugava's departure left ten teams in the First Division. In the new format four teams dropped out of the leading group after 18 matches, with the top six - theoretically, at least - playing off for the title. The only significant contest was the battle for second place, eventually won, surprisingly, by Vilan-D Daugavpils, who celebrated their qualification for the UEFA Cup by promptly renaming themselves 'Dinaburg'.

The third-placed team, RAF Yelgava, had to wait until the following spring before they could book their European place. That came their way when champions Skonto Riga

NATIONAL TEAM RESULTS 95/96

Date	Opponent		Venue	Score	Scorers
16/08/95	Austria (ECQ)	H	Riga	3-2	Rimkus (11, 59), Zeiberlinsh (88)
06/09/95	Liechtenstein (ECQ)	H	Riga	1-0	Zeiberlinsh (83)
11/10/95	Republic of Ireland (ECQ)	A	Dublin	1-2	Rimkus (78)
12/03/96	Cyprus	A	Larnaca	0-1	

NATIONAL TEAM APPEARANCES 95/96

Coach - Yanis GILIS	AUT	LIE	IRL	CYP	Cps	Gls
Raimonds LAIZANS (05/08/64) - Skonto Riga	G				17	-
Igor TROITSKY (11/01/69) - Skonto Riga	D	D	D	D	24	-
Mikhail ZEMLINSKY (21/12/69) - Skonto Riga	D	D	D	D	25	2
Yury SHEVLYAKOV (24/01/59) - Skonto Riga	D	D	D	D46	27	-
Artur ZAKRESHEVSKY (07/08/71) - RAF Yelgava/Daugava Riga	D82		D	s46	6	-
Imants BLEIDELIS (16/08/75) - Skonto Riga	M	D28		M46	7	-
Vitaly ASTAFYEV (03/04/71) - Skonto Riga	M	M	M	M	33	6
Valery IVANOV (23/02/70) - Skonto Riga	M	M	M		31	1
Armands ZEIBERLINSH (13/08/65) - Hapoel Beer Sheva (ISR)	M	M	M		14	4
Vladimir BABICHEV (22/04/68) - Skonto Riga	A75	A75	A73		20	1
Vitas RIMKUS (21/06/73) - Amstrig Riga/FC Winterthur (SUI)	A	A	A	A	8	5
Alexander YELISEYEV (11/08/71) - Skonto Riga	s75		s73		21	-
Boris MONYAK (04/11/70) - Skonto Riga	s82	D			15	-
Oleg KARAVAYEV (13/02/61) - FSV Zwickau (GER)		G	G		19	-
Rolands BOULDERS (12/03/65) - IK Brage (SWE)		s28			17	2
Yury KARASHAUSKAS (18/01/70) - RAF Yelgava		s75		s82	2	-
Igor N. STEPANOV (21/01/76) - Skonto Riga			D	D	3	-
Erik GRIGYAN (25/12/64) - Lokomotive Daugavpils				G	3	-
Oleg BLAGONADEZHDIN (16/05/73) - Skonto Riga				M	12	-
Andrey SHTOLCERS (07/07/74) - Skonto Riga				M	5	-
Maryan PAKHAR (05/08/76) - Skonto Riga				A	1	-
Rikhards BUTKUS (25/08/72) - Daugava Riga				s46 /82	3	-

EUROPEAN CUPS RESULTS 95/96

CUP-WINNERS' CUP

● DAG-LIEPAYA

Preliminary round FC LANTANA TALLINN (EST)

H 1-2 Dobretsov (5) (later awarded 3-0)
Grigyan; Osichenko, Kibartas, Rinkus (Kalyuzhny 30; Bukovsky 56), Movko, Kragliks, Dobretsov, Baskakov, Intenbergs, Linards, Fasakhov (Kasyan 50).

A 0-0
Grigyan; Osichenko (Stepanov 84), Kibartas, Rinkus (Kalyuzhny 66), Movko, Kragliks, Kasyan, Baskakov, Bukovsky (Dobretsov 72), Linards, Zile.

1st round FEYENOORD (HOL)

H 0-7
Grigyan; Osichenko, Kibartas, Rinkus, Movko (Osipov 73), Kragliks, Kasyan, Baskakov (Kalyzhny 55), Zile, Linards, Fasakhov (Dobretsov 46).

A 0-6
Grigyan; Kalyuzhny, Kibartas, Rinkus, Bukovsky, Kragliks, Kasyan, Baskakov (Dobretsov 12; Intenbergs 82), Zile, Linards, Fasakhov (Osipov 46).

UEFA CUP

● SKONTO RIGA

Preliminary round MARIBOR BRANIK (SLO)

H 1-0 Babichev (11)
Laizans; Troitsky, Astafyev, Zemlinsky, Shevlyakov, Monyak, Ivanov, Bleidelis (Blagonadezhdin 56), Baushev (Yeliseyev 61), Babichev, Pindeyev.

A 0-2
Laizans; Troitsky, Astafyev, Zemlinsky, Shevlyakov, Monyak, Ivanov, Bleidelis (Yeliseyev 78), Baushev (Semyonov 55), Babichev, Pindeyev (Blagonadezhdin 61).

● RAF YELGAVA

Preliminary round AFAN LIDO (WAL)

A 2-1 Karashauskas (20), Bogdan (68)
Oleinik; Ivanov, Erglis, Zakreshevsky, Dolgopolov, Gilis (Aizazars 68), Zuyev, Karashauskas, Sergeyev (Mikhalchouk 70), Savalnieks, Bogdan.

H 0-0
Oleinik; Aizazars (Mikhalchouk 88), Erglis, Zakreshevsky, Dolgopolov, Gilis, Zuyev, Karashauskas, Sergeyev (Shvans 64), Savalnieks, Bogdan.

1st round ZIMBRU CHISINAU (MOL)

A 0-1
Oleinik; Shvans, Erglis, Zakreshevsky, Dolgopolov, Mikhalchouk (Sergeyev 70), Zuyev (Gilis 90), Karashauskas, Aizazars, Savalnieks, Bogdan.

H 1-2 Zuyev (77)
Oleinik; Ivanov, Erglis, Zakresehevsky, Dolgopolov, Gilis (Aizazars 78), Zuyev (Mikhalchouk 82), Karashauskas, Shvans (Sergeyev 40), Savalnieks, Bogdan.

INTERNATIONAL HONOURS

None

hammered newly-promoted Yurnieks Riga 8-0 in the semi-final of the Cup. RAF also made it to the final, with much greater difficulty, beating Dinaburg on penalties after a goalless draw. That secured a place in the Cup-winners' Cup (rather than the UEFA Cup), but RAF's ambition did not stop there. The 1993 Cup winners made it to the top of the podium again, inflicting on Skonto their first Cup defeat since the quarter-finals of the 1994 competition. RAF won an exciting game 2-1 after extra-time, with new signing Vladimir Dragun netting the winner in the 115th minute.

PLAYERS OF THE SEASON

YURY SHEVLYAKOV

The oldest player in the Latvian national side is 37-year-old captain Yury Shevlyakov. Born in Moscow on January 24, 1959, Shevlyakov is now seeing out the end of his career at Skonto Riga after playing in both the Soviet and the Finnish premier divisions. He is an uncompromising centre-back of the old school, a player who gives 100 per cent and is not afraid to pick up the odd yellow card now and then. An authoritative and imposing figure, his experience has served both Skonto and Latvia well. At the end of the 1995 season he was voted by Latvian journalists as the best defender in the league.

RAIMONDS LAIZANS

German-based veteran Oleg Karavayev is still Latvia's first-choice goalkeeper, but Raimonds Laizans, three and a half years younger at 32, is challenging him more and more every year. In 1995 the Riga-born 'keeper earned his fifth successive championship-winner's medal with Skonto, playing to a high standard all season even if in some games he was given very little to do. Laizans played for two Ukrainian clubs, Volyn Lutsk and Karpaty Lviv, earlier in his career, but he is now dedicated to Skonto, where he has been the unrivalled number one 'keeper since joining the club in 1991.

AMSTRIG RIGA

CLUB DIRECTORY

Amstrig Riga (now - Daugava Riga)
Tallinas str. 40-2
1001 Riga
tel - (2) 276375
fax - (2) 272833
President - Igor Rogozin
Secretary - Igor Klyosov
Coach - Anatoly Kondratenko; Yury Popkov
Stadium - LU (6,000)

APPEARANCES 95

	P	Ap	(s)	Gls
Alexander ATAMAN	M	2	(5)	1
Georgs ATVARS	G	2	(2)	1
Sergey BORISOV	D	13	(5)	
Rikhards BUTKUS	M	24		6
Alexander DANILOV	D	20	(2)	
Vladimir DRAGUN	M	16	(10)	3
Gints GILIS	M	6	(1)	1
Sergey IVANOV	M	25		
Alexander KONDRATENKO	D	19	(1)	
Mikhail KURILYAK (RUS)	A	10	(1)	2
Victor LAZARENKO	D	14	(3)	2
Mikhail MIKHOLAP (RUS)	A	15		11
Denis MURIN	A	4	(14)	
Vladislav NESTERENKO	D	25	(1)	1
Andrey PIEDELS	G	26		5
Vladimir POLYANSKY (RUS)	D	11	(1)	
Yury POPKOV	M	16		5
Vitas RIMKUS	A	26		8
Oleg RUDENKO	M	15	(5)	2
Roman SIDOROV	M	19	(3)	2

LEAGUE RESULTS 1995

Date	Opponent	H/A	Score	Scorers
16/04/95	Starts Brotseni	A	3-2	Gilis, Butkus (p), Ataman (later awarded 0-3)
19/04/95	Vairogs Rezekne	H	0-1	
29/04/95	DAG-Liepaya	A	1-1	Rimkus
10/05/95	Kvadrats Riga	H	1-1	Kurilyak
14/05/95	Vilan-D Daugavpils	A	1-0	Rimkus
28/05/95	Skonto Riga	H	0-3	
10/06/95	RAF Yelgava	A	1-1	Kurilyak
18/06/95	Olympia Riga	H	2-3	Butkus, Rudenko
01/07/95	Skonto/Metals Riga	H	2-0	Dragun (p), Nesterenko
08/07/95	Starts Brotseni	H	0-1	
12/07/95	Vairogs Rezekne	A	2-1	Sidorov, Butkus
16/07/95	DAG-Liepaya	H	0-1	
22/07/95	Kvadrats Riga	A	2-0	Butkus, Popkov
29/07/95	Vilan-D Daugavpils	H	2-2	Dragun 2
02/08/95	Skonto Riga	A	2-3	Rudenko, Lazarenko
05/08/95	RAF Yelgava	H	1-2	Mikholap
19/08/95	Olympia Riga	A	7-0	Mikholap 3, Popkov 2, Rimkus 2
30/08/95	Skonto/Metals Riga	A	2-2	Lazarenko, Popkov
07/09/95	RAF Yelgava	H	1-1	Piedels (p)
17/09/95	Skonto Riga	A	1-2	Mikholap
20/09/95	Starts Brotseni	H	5-1	Rimkus, Mikholap 3, Popkov
24/09/95	Vilan-D Daugavpils	A	0-2	
30/09/95	Vairogs Rezekne	A	6-2	Sidorov, Mikholap 2, Piedels 2 (2p), Rimkus
04/10/95	RAF Yelgava	A	1-1	Mikholap
15/10/95	Skonto Riga	H	2-2	Butkus, Rimkus
22/10/95	Starts Brotseni	A	1-0	Butkus
25/10/95	Vilan-D Daugavpils	H	1-2	Piedels (p)
29/10/95	Vairogs Rezekne	H	3-0	Piedels (p), Rimkus, Atvars

DAG-LIEPAYA

CLUB DIRECTORY

DAG-Liepaya (now - FK Liepaya)
Yurmalas parks
Stadions
3400 Liepaya
tel - 36976
fax - (2) 297672
President - Sergey Nasonov
Secretary - Yury Romanenkov
Coach - Victor Nesterenko
Stadium - Daugava Liepaya (8,000)

APPEARANCES 95

	P	Ap	(s)	Gls
Victor BASKAKOV	M	18	(2)	1
Alexander BEREZIN	D		(1)	
Mikola BILIK (UKR)	D	1	(2)	
Ainars BUKOVSKIS	D	17	(1)	
Victor DOBRETSOV	A	13	(4)	5
Tagir FASAKHOV (UKR)	A	4		
Erik GRIGYAN	G	6	(1)	
Janis INTENBERGS	A	12		6
Roman KALYUZHNY	M	8		1
Igor KARAVAYEV	D		(1)	
Maxim KASYAN	M	16	(2)	1
Yonas KIBARTAS	D	18	(1)	2
Yonas KIBARTAS (same player)	G	1		
Igor KORSHAKOV	G	17	(2)	
Mikhail KOVALYOV	D	1	(1)	
Feliks KOTOV	M	4	(7)	1
Rolands KRAGLIKS	M	21		3
Ainars LINARDS	A	19	(1)	5
Valery MOVKO	M	17	(1)	
Andrey OSICHENKO	M	15	(1)	
Vladlen OSIPOV	M	8	(10)	
Janis RINKUS	D	16	(1)	
Alexander SCHEGLOV	M	2	(2)	
Andrey STEPANOV	M	3	(1)	
Denis VASILYEV	A	1		
Ilmars VERPAKOVSKY	M	3	(1)	
Vasily VLASIK	M	3	(7)	
Maxim YAKOVLEV	M	3		
Normunds ZILE	D	15	(2)	1
Janis ZUYEV	M	2	(4)	

LEAGUE RESULTS 1995

Date	Opponent	H/A	Score	Scorers
16/04/95	Vairogs Rezekne	A	1-1	Intenbergs
29/04/95	Amstrig Riga	H	1-1	Intenbergs
03/05/95	Kvadrats Riga	A	1-3	Intenbergs
10/05/95	Vilan-D Daugavpils	H	0-2	
14/05/95	Skonto Riga	A	0-4	
28/05/95	RAF Yelgava	H	1-2	Kragliks
09/06/95	Olympia Riga	A	2-2	Linards, Kotov
28/06/95	Skonto/Metals Riga	A	1-3	Intenbergs
01/07/95	Starts Brotseni	H	1-1	Intenbergs
08/07/95	Vairogs Rezekne	H	3-1	Kragliks, Intenbergs, Dobretsov
16/07/95	Amstrig Riga	A	1-0	Dobretsov
19/07/95	Kvadrats Riga	H	3-2	Baskakov, Kasyan, Kibartas (p)
22/07/95	Vilan-D Daugavpils	A	0-2	
29/07/95	Skonto Riga	H	2-2	Linards 2
02/08/95	RAF Yelgava	A	0-0	
06/08/95	Olympia Riga	H	2-0	Kalyuzhny, Kibartas (p)
27/08/95	Skonto/Metals Riga	H	0-1	
30/08/95	Starts Brotseni	A	0-1	
09/09/95	Olympia Riga	H	3-1	Linards 2 (2p), Kragliks
17/09/95	Kvadrats Riga	A	0-1	
23/09/95	Skonto/Metals Riga	H	1-0	Dobretsov
01/10/95	Olympia Riga	A	1-1	Zile
14/10/95	Kvadrats Riga	H	0-2	
22/10/95	Skonto/Metals Riga	A	2-1	Dobretsov 2

KVADRATS RIGA

CLUB DIRECTORY

Kvadrats Riga
Maskavas str. 322
LV 1063 Riga
tel - (2) 254669
fax - (2) 252008 "Avots"
President - Iosif Polischouk
Secretary - Viktor Vitsekhovsky
Coach - Alexander Koulakov; Vladimir Zhuk; Victor Vitsekhovsky
Stadium - LU (6,000)

APPEARANCES 95

	P	Ap	(s)	Gls
Maris BABKEVICH	M	3	(3)	
Alexander BARANOVSKY	D	21		1
Mikhail CHEBOTARYOV	D	17	(1)	
Yury IDIONOV	A	15	(1)	3
Sergey ILYIN	A	7	(3)	1
Yevgeny KAPUSTA	M		(2)	
Andrey KATKEVICH	G	6	(1)	
Boris KOROTKEVICH	M	18		6
Dmitry KORYAYEVS	M	12		
Sergey KOZLOVTSEV	D		(1)	
Norman LITTE	M		(3)	
Igor MAZURINOV	M	17	(2)	1
Raitis MILLERS	M		(1)	
Yury NAGAITSEV	A	10	(3)	
Vadim NAUMOV	M	8	(3)	1
Sergey NIKIFOROV	M	9		
Girts PAULIS	D	21		
Dmitry PONOMARCHOUK	M	4	(4)	
Boris SHAPPO	M	11	(4)	2
Sergey VITSEKHOVSKY	M	19	(2)	1
Victor VITSEKHOVSKY	D	20	(1)	2
Andrey VOLOKHO	M	2	(6)	
Andrey YAKIMOV	A	6	(6)	1
Andrey YAKOVLEV	M	14	(2)	3
Vladislav ZABLOTSKY	G	18		
Andris ZVEINIEKS	M		(2)	
Normunds ZVEINIEKS	A	5	(2)	

LEAGUE RESULTS 1995

Date	Opponent	H/A	Score	Scorers
16/04/95	Skonto/Metals Riga	A	0-2	
19/04/95	Starts Brotseni	H	0-3	
29/04/95	Vairogs Rezekne	A	0-2	
03/05/95	DAG-Liepaya	H	3-1	Korotkevich 2, Idionov
10/05/95	Amstrig Riga	A	1-1	Ilyin
28/05/95	Vilan-D Daugavpils	H	0-2	
11/06/95	Skonto Riga	A	1-6	Yakimov
18/06/95	RAF Yelgava	H	0-3	
27/06/95	Olympia Riga	A	0-3	
08/07/95	Skonto/Metals Riga	H	0-6	
12/07/95	Starts Brotseni	A	0-1	
15/07/95	Vairogs Rezekne	H	1-5	Vitsekhovsky V. (p)
19/07/95	DAG-Liepaya	A	2-3	Yakovlev 2
22/07/95	Amstrig Riga	H	0-2	
05/08/95	Skonto Riga	H	0-7	
19/08/95	RAF Yelgava	A	0-5	
26/08/95	Olympia Riga	H	1-4	Korotkevich
02/09/95	Vilan-D Daugavpils	A	1-2	Korotkevich
10/09/95	Skonto/Metals Riga	H	0-1	
17/09/95	DAG-Liepaya	H	1-0	Vitsekhovsky V. (p)
24/09/95	Olympia Riga	A	2-2	Idionov, Naumov
30/09/95	Skonto/Metals Riga	A	5-1	Shappo 2, Vitsekhovsky S., Korotkevich 2
14/10/95	DAG-Liepaya	A	2-0	Yakovlev, Mazurinov
21/10/95	Olympia Riga	H	2-1	Baranovsky, Idionov

OLYMPIA RIGA

CLUB DIRECTORY

Olympia Riga
Zhagatu 2a-116
1014 Riga
tel - (2) 569060
President - Janis Skredelis
Secretary - Stanislav Androsov
Coach - Genady Shitik
Stadium - LU (6,000)

MAJOR HONOURS
Domestic Cup - (1) 1994.

APPEARANCES 95

	P	Ap	(s)	Gls
Andrey ABZHINOV	D	8	(6)	
Guntis ANDREYEV	M		(2)	
Andris BAUMANIS	D	13	(4)	
Dmitry BORISOV	D	15	(3)	
Edijs DANILOV	A	17	(4)	6
Alexander DIBRIVNY	M	23	(2)	5
Boris DOLINSKY	D	9		
Leonid DVORKIN	G	12	(2)	1
Igor KORABLYOV	D	22		1
Boris KOROTKEVICH	M	1		
Genady LEVCHENKO	M	3	(7)	2
Mikhail LISYAKOV	D	22	(2)	
Eriks PELTSIS	M	2		
Roman PETUSHKOV	D		(1)	
Roman PLATONOV	M		(1)	
Nikolay POLYAKOV	A	20	(3)	5
Andrey PROKHORENKOV	M	5	(3)	
Andrey PUMPA	M	15	(2)	
Vitaly RYABININ	A	10	(12)	4
Sergey SEMYONOV	D	17		
Vladislaav SKORODIKHIN	M	23	(1)	4
Alexey SOSNIN	M	7	(2)	1
Vladimir VERBITSKY	A	2		
Valery VOICHENKO	G	13		
Alexander ZVERUGO	D	16	(9)	1

LEAGUE RESULTS 1995

Date	Opponent	H/A	Score	Scorers
16/04/95	Skonto Riga	H	0-1	
20/04/95	RAF Yelgava	A	0-2	
03/05/95	Pardaugava Riga	H	1-0	Sosnin (later declared void)
10/05/95	Skonto/Metals Riga	A	3-4	Dvorkin (p), Polyakov, Levchenko
14/05/95	Starts Brotseni	H	0-2	
28/05/95	Vairogs Rezekne	A	3-3	Danilov, Zverugo, Polyakov
09/06/95	DAG-Liepaya	H	2-2	Ryabinin, Dibrivny (p)
18/06/95	Amstrig Riga	A	3-2	Dibrivny, Korablyov, Levchenko
27/06/95	Kvadrats Riga	H	3-0	Skorodikhin, Danilov, Polyakov
02/07/95	Vilan-D Daugavpils	A	1-3	Dibrivny (p)
08/07/95	Skonto Riga	A	1-7	Ryabinin
12/07/95	RAF Yelgava	H	0-1	
23/07/95	Skonto/Metals Riga	H	1-1	Danilov
28/07/95	Starts Brotseni	A	0-2	
02/08/95	Vairogs Rezekne	H	1-0	Dibrivny (p)
06/08/95	DAG-Liepaya	A	0-2	
19/08/95	Amstrig Riga	H	0-7	
26/08/95	Kvadrats Riga	A	4-1	Danilov 2, Polyakov 2
30/08/95	Vilan-D Daugavpils	H	1-0	Ryabinin
09/09/95	DAG-Liepaya	A	1-3	Skorodikhin
16/09/95	Skonto/Metals Riga	A	1-7	Skorodikhin
24/09/95	Kvadrats Riga	H	2-2	Ryabinin, Dibrivny (p)
01/10/95	DAG-Liepaya	H	1-1	Danilov
14/10/95	Skonto/Metals Riga	H	0-2	
21/10/95	Kvadrats Riga	A	1-2	Skorodikhin

RAF YELGAVA

CLUB DIRECTORY

RAF Yelgava
Kr. Barona 116a
1012 Riga
tel - 7292703
fax - 7291818
President - Maris Shmid
Secretary - Gdalijs Yerukhimovich
Coach - Sergey Zaikin
Stadium - Daugava Yelgava (3,000)

MAJOR HONOURS

Domestic Cup - (2) 1993, 1996.

APPEARANCES 95

	P	Ap	(s)	Gls
Andrey AIZAZARS	M	18	(5)	5
Valery BOGDAN	M	23	(5)	1
Alexander CHUMAKOV	G	2	(1)	
Vitaly DOLGOPOLOV	D	20	(2)	
Gatis ERGLIS	D	24		7
Gints GILIS	M	10	(3)	
Vasily IVANOV	D	25	(2)	
Yury KARASHAUSKAS	A	22	(2)	7
Victor MASTYANITSA	D	15	(2)	
Ruslan MIKHALCHOUK	M	4	(8)	1
Andrey OLEINIK	G	27		
Yevgeny PRIEDESLAIPA	M		(4)	
Janis SAMSONOV	M	1	(8)	
Dzintars SAVALNIEKS	A	28		4
Mikhail SERGEYEV	M	22	(2)	2
Dzintars SPROGIS	D	10		
Alberts SHVANS	A	9	(10)	
Vitaly TEPLOV	A	10	(1)	1
Artur ZAKRESHEVSKY	D	22		1
Armands ZEIBERLINSH	M	10		4
Alexey ZUBOV	D		(1)	
Modris ZUYEV	A	17	(5)	7

LEAGUE RESULTS 1995

20/04/95	Olympia Riga	H	2-0	og (Baumanis), Aizazars
29/04/95	Pardaugava Riga	A	1-0	Zeiberlinsh (later declared void)
03/05/95	Skonto/Metals Riga	H	2-0	Zuyev 2
10/05/95	Starts Brotseni	A	4-0	Zuyev, Erglis 2, Zeiberlinsh
14/05/95	Vairogs Rezekne	H	2-0	Karashauskas, Savalnieks
28/05/95	DAG-Liepaya	A	2-1	Aizazars, Zakreshevsky
10/06/95	Amstrig Riga	H	1-1	Erglis (p)
18/06/95	Kvadrats Riga	A	3-0	Sergeyev, Zeiberlinsh 2
28/06/95	Vilan-D Daugavpils	H	3-2	Aizazars, Karashauskas 2
02/07/95	Skonto Riga	H	0-1	
12/07/95	Olympia Riga	A	1-0	Erglis
19/07/95	Skonto/Metals Riga	A	1-1	Aizazars
23/07/95	Starts Brotseni	H	3-0	Erglis 2 (1p), Zuyev
28/07/95	Vairogs Rezekne	A	0-1	
02/08/95	DAG-Liepaya	H	0-0	
05/08/95	Amstrig Riga	A	2-1	Karashauskas 2
19/08/95	Kvadrats Riga	H	5-0	Zuyev, Savalnieks, Erglis (p), Aizazars, Karashauskas
26/08/95	Vilan-D Daugavpils	A	2-0	Sergeyev, Zuyev
30/08/95	Skonto Riga	A	0-5	
07/09/95	Amstrig Riga	A	1-1	Savalnieks (p)
16/09/95	Vairogs Rezekne	A	2-1	Teplov, Karashauskas
20/09/95	Skonto Riga	H	1-2	Mikhalchouk
24/09/95	Starts Brotseni	A	0-3	
30/09/95	Vilan-D Daugavpils	H	0-1	
04/10/95	Amstrig Riga	H	1-1	Zuyev
14/10/95	Vairogs Rezekne	H	0-1	
21/10/95	Skonto Riga	A	1-5	Savalnieks
25/10/95	Starts Brotseni	H	1-0	Bogdan
29/10/95	Vilan-D Daugavpils	A	0-0	

SKONTO/METALS RIGA

CLUB DIRECTORY

Skonto/Metals Riga
Elizabetes str. 75
1050 Riga
tel - 7282669
fax - 7284390
President - Guntis Indricksons
Secretary - Yury Simonenkov
Coach - Andrey Karpov
Stadium - Tsarnikava (2,000)

APPEARANCES 95

	P	Ap	(s)	Gls
Yury AZAROV	D	5	(9)	
Andrey DMITRYAK	M	17	(4)	1
Konstantin GORBACH	D	16	(3)	
Vyacheslav IZMAILOV	M	2	(6)	
Ruslan KLIMCHENKO	A	6	(2)	
Alexey KLISHIN (KAZ)	M	7		4
Alexey KOLESNICHENKO	M	6	(5)	
Alexander KOLINKO	G	24		
Genady LEVCHENKO	M	7		
Vsevolod LIDAKS	D	18	(1)	
Ruslan MIKHALCHOUK	M	7		1
Vadim MIKUTSKY	M	4	(1)	
Marian PAKHAR	A	15	(1)	4
Nickolay PEREDISTY	M	18	(1)	3
Denis ROMANOV	G		(1)	
Sergey RUBLYOV	G	1		
Alexander SAKHNOVICH	D	18	(1)	2
Yury SIMONENKOV	A		(1)	1
Vadim SINITSIN	M	2	(1)	
Genady SKLYAR	M	7	(1)	1
Janis SKRIBIS	D	9	(7)	
Igor SLESARCHOUK	A	7	(1)	5
Alexander SOLOMKA	M	16	(1)	1
Igor SVINTOZELSKY	A	17	(2)	4
Victor TERENTYEV	D	23		1
Roman VORONOV	M		(3)	
Renars VUTSANS	A	23		10

LEAGUE RESULTS 1995

16/04/95	Kvadrats Riga	H	2-0	Sklyar, Simonenkov
20/04/95	Vilan-D Daugavpils	H	1-5	Solomka (p)
30/04/95	Skonto Riga	H	0-4	
03/05/95	RAF Yelgava	A	0-2	
10/05/95	Olympia Riga	H	4-3	Pakhar 2, Klishin 2
14/05/95	Pardaugava Riga	A	1-1	Peredisty (later declared void)
10/06/95	Starts Brotseni	H	2-3	Sakhnovich 2
18/06/95	Vairogs Rezekne	A	1-1	Vutsans
28/06/95	DAG-Liepaya	H	3-1	Peredisty, Klishin, Vutsans
01/07/95	Amstrig Riga	A	0-2	
08/07/95	Kvadrats Riga	A	6-0	Dmitryak, Klishin, Vutsans 3, Svintozelsky
12/07/95	Vilan-D Daugavpils	A	0-4	
16/07/95	Skonto Riga	A	1-2	Vutsans (p)
19/07/95	RAF Yelgava	H	1-1	Mikhalchouk
23/07/95	Olympia Riga	A	1-1	Pakhar
05/08/95	Starts Brotseni	A	0-3	
20/08/95	Vairogs Rezekne	H	0-8	
27/08/95	DAG-Liepaya	A	1-0	Pakhar
30/08/95	Amstrig Riga	H	2-2	Vutsans, Slesarchouk
10/09/95	Kvadrats Riga	A	1-0	Svintozelsky
16/09/95	Olympia Riga	H	7-1	Svintozelsky 2 (1p), Slesarchouk 4, Terentyev
23/09/95	DAG-Liepaya	A	0-1	
30/09/95	Kvadrats Riga	H	1-5	Vutsans
14/10/95	Olympia Riga	A	2-0	Vutsans, Peredisty
22/10/95	DAG-Liepaya	H	1-2	Vutsans (p)

SKONTO RIGA

CLUB DIRECTORY

Skonto Riga
Elizabetes str. 75
1050 Riga
tel - 7282669
fax - 7284390
President - Guntis Indricksons
Secretary - Genady Karavayev
Coach - Alexander Starkov
Stadium - Daugava (15,000)

MAJOR HONOURS
League Championship - (4)
1992, 1993, 1994, 1995.
Domestic Cup - (2) 1992, 1995.

APPEARANCES 95

	P	Ap	(s)	Gls
Vitaly ASTAFYEV	M	27	(1)	19
Vladimir BABICHEV	A	26	(1)	14
Vladlen BAUSHEV (RUS)	A	14	(3)	10
Oleg BLAGONADEZHDIN	M	9	(11)	3
Imants BLEIDELIS	M	22	(2)	1
Oleg GRISHIN	G	3	(1)	
Valery IVANOV	M	23	(1)	10
Raimonds LAIZANS	G	26		
Valentin LOBANYOV	D	4	(15)	1
Vadim MIKUTSKY	M		(2)	1
Boris MONYAK	D	26	(2)	8
Marian PAKHAR	A	7	(2)	8
Alexander PINDEYEV (UKR)	A	5	(4)	3
Alexey SEMYONOV	A	8	(12)	1
Igor SLESARCHOUK	A	1	(5)	1
Igor N. STEPANOV	D	16	(7)	1
Igor V. STEPANOV	M	8	(12)	
Yury SHEVLYAKOV	D	23		3
Igor TROITSKY	D	27		1
Alexander YELISEYEV	A	16	(12)	11
Mikhail ZEMLINSKY	D	28	(1)	6

LEAGUE RESULTS 1995

16/04/95	Olympia Riga	A	1-0	Baushev
19/04/95	Pardaugava Riga	H	4-0	Baushev, Mikutsky, Monyak, Shevlyakov (later declared void)
30/04/95	Skonto/Metals Riga	A	4-0	Astafyev 2, Baushev, Monyak
03/05/95	Starts Brotseni	H	0-0	
10/05/95	Vairogs Rezekne	A	3-0	Blagonadezhdin, Babichev, Slesarchouk
14/05/95	DAG-Liepaya	H	4-0	Shevlyakov, Zemlinsky (p), Astafyev, Ivanov
28/05/95	Amstrig Riga	A	3-0	Yeliseyev 2, Ivanov
11/06/95	Kvadrats Riga	H	6-1	Yeliseyev 4, Lobanyov, Babichev
18/06/95	Vilan-D Daugavpils	A	4-1	Yeliseyev, Babichev 2, Astafyev
02/07/95	RAF Yelgava	A	1-0	Baushev
08/07/95	Olympia Riga	H	7-1	Astafyev 3 (1p), Zemlinsky (p), Baushev, Yeliseyev, Blagonadezhdin
16/07/95	Skonto/Metals Riga	H	2-1	Baushev 2
19/07/95	Starts Brotseni	A	3-0	Babichev, Semyonov, Ivanov
22/07/95	Vairogs Rezekne	H	1-0	Monyak
26/07/95	Vilan-D Daugavpils	H	3-0	Zemlinsky (p), Babichev, Ivanov
29/07/95	DAG-Liepaya	A	2-2	Astafyev, Monyak
02/08/95	Amstrig Riga	H	3-2	Ivanov, Baushev, Yeliseyev
05/08/95	Kvadrats Riga	A	7-0	Babichev, Pindeyev 3, Stepanov I.N., Yeliseyev, Zemlinsky (p)
30/08/95	RAF Yelgava	H	5-0	Babichev, Monyak, Ivanov, Bleidelis, Baushev
10/09/95	Vilan-D Daugavpils	A	2-0	Ivanov, Monyak
17/09/95	Amstrig Riga	H	2-1	Astafyev, Baushev
20/09/95	RAF Yelgava	A	2-1	Troitsky, Babichev
24/09/95	Vairogs Rezekne	H	8-0	Zemlinsky 2 (1p), Pakhar, Yeliseyev, Ivanov, Astafyev 2, Blagonadezhdin
30/09/95	Starts Brotseni	A	4-1	Astafyev 2, Babichev, Ivanov
04/10/95	Vilan-D Daugavpils	H	4-0	Pakhar 2, Babichev, Shevlyakov
15/10/95	Amstrig Riga	A	2-2	og (Polyansky), Pakhar
21/10/95	RAF Yelgava	H	5-1	Pakhar 3, Astafyev 2
25/10/95	Vairogs Rezekne	A	3-0	Monyak, Ivanov, Astafyev (p)
29/10/95	Starts Brotseni	H	8-1	Astafyev 3 (2p), Monyak, Pakhar, Babichev 3

STARTS BROTSENI

CLUB DIRECTORY

Starts Brotseni
Sporta Kompleks
Brotseni
Saldus rajons
tel - 65725
Coach - Agris Bandolis
Secretary - Gunars Dobkevichins

APPEARANCES 95

	P	Ap	(s)	Gls
Oleg ALYOKHIN	D	28		
Raimonds ALEXANDROV	M		(5)	
Rolandas BANIS (LIT)	D	20	(4)	3
Yuris BARANCHANS	M	8	(11)	
Vitaly DENISOV	A	1	(2)	
Aivars DONINSH	G	1		
Einars GNEDOY	D	13		1
Alexander KHABAROV	M	1	(7)	
Sergey KOTOV	A	27	(1)	7
Eduard KUDRYASHOV	A	24		8
Vadim MIKHAILOV	G	21	(1)	
Sergey NIKIFOROV	M	5	(2)	
Yulius NOREIKA (LIT)	D	26		
Vitaly SHANDOV	G	7		
Ivars SHKELE	M	5	(3)	
Rimantas SHTUOPIS	A	22	(6)	2
Dmitry SIDOROV	M		(3)	
Eduard SIDOROV	A	7	(17)	1
Sergey SOLOMONOV	M	8		1
Haralds SPROGIS	D	5		
Karlis SVARENS	D	20	(5)	3
Valery TIMASHKOV	D	2	(3)	
Andrey TROITSKY	M	26		3
Vidmanis VERTELIS (LIT)	M	29		1
Denis ZHELTOV	M		(1)	
Dmitry ZHELTOV	M	13	(14)	2

LEAGUE RESULTS 1995

Date	Opponent	H/A	Score	Scorers
16/04/95	Amstrig Riga	H	2-3	Kotov (p), Kudryashov (later awarded 3-0)
19/04/95	Kvadrats Riga	A	3-0	Kudryashov, og (Chebotaryov), Kotov
29/04/95	Vilan-D Daugavpils	H	0-1	
03/05/95	Skonto Riga	A	0-0	
10/05/95	RAF Yelgava	H	0-4	
14/05/95	Olympia Riga	A	2-0	Kotov, Kudryashov
28/05/95	Pardaugava Riga	H	3-1	Banis 2, Kotov (later declared void)
10/06/95	Skonto/Metals Riga	A	3-2	Troitsky, Shtuopis, Kotov (p)
27/06/95	Vairogs Rezekne	H	0-0	
01/07/95	DAG-Liepaya	A	1-1	Kudryashov
08/07/95	Amstrig Riga	A	1-0	Gnedoy (p)
12/07/95	Kvadrats Riga	H	1-0	Svarens
15/07/95	Vilan-D Daugavpils	A	0-3	
19/07/95	Skonto Riga	H	0-3	
23/07/95	RAF Yelgava	A	0-3	
28/07/95	Olympia Riga	H	2-0	Kotov, Shtuopis
05/08/95	Skonto/Metals Riga	H	3-0	Zheltov Dm., Kotov, Banis
26/08/95	Vairogs Rezekne	A	1-1	Troitsky
30/08/95	DAG-Liepaya	H	1-0	Svarens
09/09/95	Vairogs Rezekne	H	1-1	Svarens
16/09/95	Vilan-D Daugavpils	H	0-1	
20/09/95	Amstrig Riga	A	1-5	Vertelis
24/09/95	RAF Yelgava	H	3-0	Kudryashov 2, Sidorov E.
30/09/95	Skonto Riga	H	1-4	Kudryashov
04/10/95	Vairogs Rezekne	A	3-1	Kudryashov, Zheltov Dm., Solomonov
14/10/95	Vilan-D Daugavpils	A	0-3	
21/10/95	Amstrig Riga	H	0-1	
25/10/95	RAF Yelgava	A	0-1	
29/10/95	Skonto Riga	A	1-8	Troitsky

VAIROGS REZEKNE

CLUB DIRECTORY

Vairogs Rezekne
Kr. Valdemara 21
4600 Rezekne
President - Vladimir Kloss
Coach - Alexander Dorofeyev
Stadium - Town Stadium (3,000)

APPEARANCES 95

	P	Ap	(s)	Gls
Valery ARAKCHEYEV	A	6	(16)	
Zhanis ARMANIS	D	22	(5)	
Vadim BEKERIS		16	(7)	1
Vladislav BELOV	D	21	(4)	
Andrey CHERNISHOV	M	4	(5)	
Oleg DULUB (BLS)	A	27		16
Andris GRUZDE	G	11	(1)	
Alexander IVANOV	M	7	(4)	
Valery KIRILOV	M		(5)	
Sergey KRIKUNOV	M	14	(1)	
Alexey KROUTS	G	17	(1)	
Oleg KUBAREV (BLS)	M	26	(1)	
Ilmars LOGINS	D	24		
Aivars POZNYAK	A	19	(7)	7
Igor SALOV	A	13	(8)	3
Andris SHMAUKSTELIS	A	27		
Alexey VOLOSANOV	M	16	(9)	6
Vitaly VOSKANS	M	19	(8)	1
Alexey YEGOROV	M	19	(3)	1
Sergey YEVSEYEV	D		(8)	

LEAGUE RESULTS 1995

Date	Opponent	H/A	Score	Scorers
16/04/95	DAG-Liepaya	H	1-1	Poznyak
19/04/95	Amstrig Riga	A	1-0	Dulub
29/04/95	Kvadrats Riga	H	2-0	Voskans, Poznyak
03/05/95	Vilan-D Daugavpils	A	2-1	Dulub, Volosanov
10/05/95	Skonto Riga	H	0-3	
14/05/95	RAF Yelgava	A	0-2	
28/05/95	Olympia Riga	H	3-3	Dulub 2, Yegorov
18/06/95	Skonto/Metals Riga	H	1-1	Poznyak (p)
27/06/95	Starts Brotseni	A	0-0	
08/07/95	DAG-Liepaya	A	1-3	Poznyak
12/07/95	Amstrig Riga	H	1-2	Volosanov
15/07/95	Kvadrats Riga	A	5-1	Dulub 3, Poznyak (p), Volosanov
19/07/95	Vilan-D Daugavpils	H	1-1	Dulub
22/07/95	Skonto Riga	A	0-1	
28/07/95	RAF Yelgava	H	1-0	Poznyak
02/08/95	Olympia Riga	A	0-1	
20/08/95	Skonto/Metals Riga	A	8-0	Salov 2, Volosanov, Dulub 5
26/08/95	Starts Brotseni	H	1-1	Bekeris
09/09/95	Starts Brotseni	A	1-1	Volosanov
16/09/95	RAF Yelgava	H	1-2	Salov
20/09/95	Vilan-D Daugavpils	A	0-2	
24/09/95	Skonto Riga	A	0-8	
30/09/95	Amstrig Riga	H	2-6	Dulub 2
04/10/95	Starts Brotseni	H	1-3	Poznyak
14/10/95	RAF Yelgava	A	1-0	Volosanov
21/10/95	Vilan-D Daugavpils	H	1-3	Dulub
25/10/95	Skonto Riga	H	0-3	
29/10/95	Amstrig Riga	A	0-3	

VILAN-D DAUGAVPILS

CLUB DIRECTORY

Vilan-D Daugavpils (now - Dinaburg Daugavpils)
Yelgavas 7
5400 Daugavpils
tel - (54) 51209
fax - (54) 35611
President - Victor Daletsky
Secretary - Alexandr Kohan
Coach - Vladimir Serbin; Vladimir Pachko
Stadium - Tseltnieks (3,000)

APPEARANCES 95

	P	Ap	(s)	Gls
Mikhail BORONENKO	D	1	(2)	
Edgar BURLAKOV	M	28		4
Yury DEMENTYEV	M	26	(2)	4
Sergey DIGULYOV	G	1	(6)	
Alexander FEDOTOV	M	24	(1)	3
Alexander GLAZOV	D	22		
Alexey ILYIN	D	2	(4)	
Alexander ISAKOV	D	26		2
Dmitry KHOROLSKY	M	3	(7)	
Albert MARTYANOV	D	4	(10)	
Sergey POGODIN	M	25		2
Alexander SAVELYEEV (BLS)	M	7	(4)	1
Nikita SHMIKOV (RUS)	D	12		1
Maris SMIRNOV	M		(16)	
Victor SPOLE	G	8		
Alexander STRADINSH	M	27		1
Sergey TARASOV	A	28		8
Andris TSATLAKSH	G	20		
Andris TSIRSHS	D	10	(7)	1
Vladimir ZHAVORONKOV	A		(20)	6
Vyacheslav ZHEVNEROVICH	A	29		8
Mikhail ZIZILEV	M	16	(11)	3

LEAGUE RESULTS 1995

Date	Opponent	H/A	Score	Scorers
16/04/95	Pardaugava Riga	A	0-0	(later decalred void)
20/04/95	Skonto/Metals Riga	A	5-1	Dementyev, Pogodin, Tarasov 2, Ziziliev
29/04/95	Starts Brotseni	A	1-0	Tarasov
03/05/95	Vairogs Rezekne	H	1-2	Dementyev
10/05/95	DAG-Liepaya	A	2-0	Savelyev, Fedotov
14/05/95	Amstrig Riga	H	0-1	
28/05/95	Kvadrats Riga	A	2-0	Tarasov, Zhevnerovich
18/06/95	Skonto Riga	H	1-4	Pogodin
28/06/95	RAF Yelgava	A	2-3	Tarasov, Zhavoronkov
02/07/95	Olympia Riga	H	3-1	Zizilev, Zhevnerovich, Tarasov
12/07/95	Skonto/Metals Riga	H	4-0	Zizilev, Tsirshs (p), Zhavoronkov, Burlakov
15/07/95	Starts Brotseni	H	3-0	Zhavoronkov, Dementyev, og (Baranchans)
19/07/95	Vairogs Rezekne	A	1-1	Burlakov
22/07/95	DAG-Liepaya	H	2-0	Stradinsh, Zhevnerovich
26/07/95	Skonto Riga	A	0-3	
29/07/95	Amstrig Riga	A	2-2	Tarasov, Zhavoronkov
26/08/95	RAF Yelgava	H	0-2	
30/08/95	Olympia Riga	A	0-1	
02/09/95	Kvadrats Riga	H	2-1	Burlakov, Fedotov
10/09/95	Skonto Riga	H	0-2	
16/09/95	Starts Brotseni	A	1-0	Zhevnerovich
20/09/95	Vairogs Rezekne	H	2-0	Dementyev, Zhavoronkov
24/09/95	Amstrig Riga	H	2-0	Shimkov, Burlakov
30/09/95	RAF Yelgava	A	1-0	Zhevnerovich
04/10/95	Skonto Riga	A	0-4	
14/10/95	Starts Brotseni	H	3-0	Zhevnerovich, Isakov, Zhavoronkov
21/10/95	Vairogs Rezekne	A	3-1	Tarasov, Zhevnerovich, Fedotov
25/10/95	Amstrig Riga	A	2-1	Isakov (p), Zhevnerovich
29/10/95	RAF Yelgava	H	0-0	

PROMOTED CLUBS

SECOND DIVISION FINAL TABLE 95

		Pd	W	D	L	F	A	Pt	GD
1	**Yurnieks Riga**	**22**	**18**	**3**	**1**	**59**	**16**	**57**	**+43**
2	**Lokomotive Daugavpils**	**22**	**14**	**5**	**3**	**57**	**22**	**47**	**+35**
3	Yauniba Daugavpils	22	14	1	7	56	30	43	+26
4	Latgale Daugavpils	22	12	3	7	56	45	39	+11
5	AVV-LSPA Riga	22	9	5	8	30	29	32	+1
6	Venta Ventspils	22	8	4	10	25	29	28	-4
7	FK Valmiera	22	8	3	11	40	65	27	-25
8	Z/S Beikas Riga	22	7	3	12	20	42	24	-22
9	FK Liepaya	22	7	3	12	33	45	24	-12
10	Sardzes Pulks Riga	22	5	5	12	22	37	20	-15
11	Yekabpils-Vide	22	5	3	14	33	53	18	-20
12	Dialogs Yelgava	22	5	2	15	25	43	17	-18

CLUB DIRECTORY

Yurnieks Riga
Visby Str. 37-1
1014 Riga
tel - (2) 518431
Secretary - Grigory Rozhkov
Coach - Astraty Rozhkov
Stadium - Yurnieks (2,000)

CLUB DIRECTORY

Lokomotive Daugavpils
Marijas 1
5400 Daugavpils
tel - (54) 38124
fax - (54) 36051
President - Cheslav Lizbouskis
Coach - Mikhail Ilyashov
Stadium - Vishky (1,000)

LIECHTENSTEIN

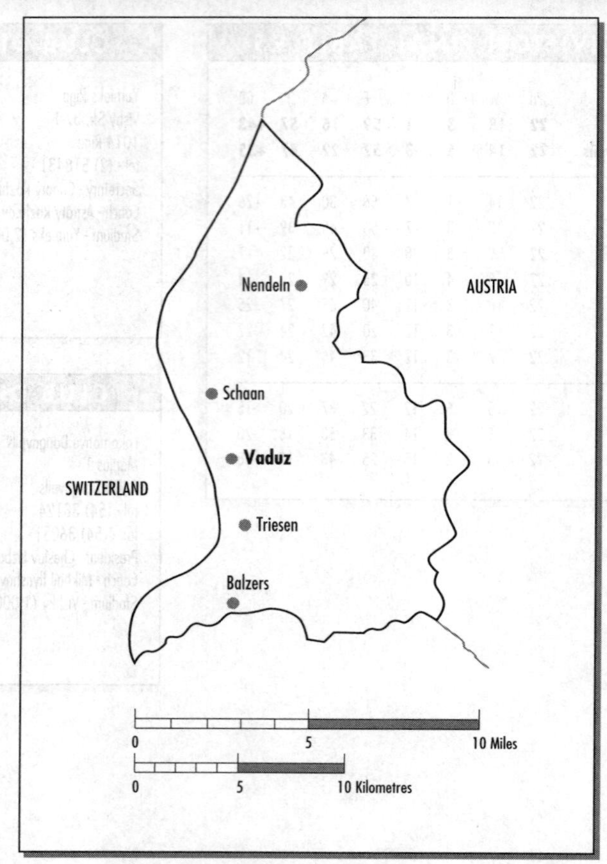

CUP RETURNS TO FC VADUZ

National team make their World Cup début

Liechtenstein's national football team made history in Skopje, Macedonia on April 24, 1996 as they played the country's first match ever in the World Cup. Predictably, it took only six minutes for Dietrich Weise's team to concede a goal. And the final result was a clear 3-0 win for their opponents. But for Liechtenstein - if for few others - the Olympian maxim that taking part is just as important as winning still holds true.

With such meagre resources to call from, it will ever be thus - although the footballers from this tiny principality would no doubt relish the opportunity to actually put it to the test.

The sensational 0-0 draw against the Republic of Ireland apart, Liechtenstein had little to savour from their inaugural European Championship appearance. The campaign ended with three straight defeats and no more goals to add to the one they had managed in their opening match, away to Northern Ireland. But the overall performance was felt to be good enough to earn coach Weise a two-year extension to his contract.

FEDERATION DIRECTORY

Liechtensteiner Fussball-Verband
Am Schrägen Weg 17,
Postfach 165, 9490 Vaduz

tel - (075) 2332428
fax - (075) 2332430

Year of Formation - 1933
President - Ernst Nigg
Secretary - Manfred Ohri

The first international of the season, against Portugal in August, drew a near-capacity crowd of 3,500 to the Sportpark Eschen/Mauren. The locals, perhaps anticipating a similar result to the Ireland game, gave their team rousing support, but once Portugal got one goal, the floodgates opened and the decibel level subsided from all but the Portuguese 'end' of the ground.

Late on, however, Liechtenstein staged a tremendous rally and were desperately unlucky not to score. First of all, star striker Mario Frick pushed a golden chance just wide, then Roland Hilti struck the bar, and, just to prove that bad luck comes in threes, Frick fired home a free-kick, only for the referee to disallow it as he was not ready!

Liechtenstein played five matches during the season and it was not until their last one, away to Germany in Mannheim, that they finally scored a goal. The fixture was clearly set up to provide the Germans with shooting-practice before they flew off to England for Euro '96, and although Berti Vogts' men scored nine goals, the biggest cheer of the evening was raised when the visitors grabbed a consolation goal, through 18-year-old débutant Marco Perez.

Perez had earned his first call-up by scoring an even more important goal a few weeks earlier - the winner in the Liechtenstein Cup final. The 1996 final was a repeat of the previous season, with FC Vaduz taking on USV Eschen/Mauren in neutral Triesen. 650 fans attanded the

EUROPEAN CUPS RESULTS 95/96

CUP-WINNERS' CUP

● FC VADUZ

Preliminary round SK HRADEC KRALOVE (TCH)

H 0-5
Heeb; Ritter, Hasler H., Hasler D., Moser; Kindle (Ospelt J. 62), Beeli, Zech, Perez, Nikolic (Hanselmann 46); Polverino (Fremuth 75).

A 1-9 Ritter (28)
Gassner; Moser, Hasler D., Hasler H., Birchler; Ritter (Foser 85), Hanselmann (Hemmerle 46), Beeli, Zech, Ospelt J. (Frick 76); Polverino.

INTERNATIONAL HONOURS

None

NATIONAL TEAM RESULTS 95/96

15/08/95	Portugal (ECQ)	H	Eschen	0-7	
06/09/95	Latvia (ECQ)	A	Riga	0-1	
11/10/95	Northern Ireland (ECQ)	H	Eschen	0-4	
24/04/96	Macedonia (WCQ)	A	Skopje	0-3	
04/06/96	Germany	A	Mannheim	1-9	Perez (70)

NATIONAL TEAM APPEARANCES 95/96

Coach - Dietrich WEISE	POR	LAT	NIR	MAC	GER	Cps	Gls
Martin HEEB (05/11/69) - FC Vaduz	G	G		G	G	10	-
Heini STOCKER (26/08/73) - FC Balzers	D46	D85	D46	D46		7	-
Jürgen ZECH (20/11/65) - USV Eschen/Mauren	D	D		D	D	5	-
Daniel TELSER (24/01/70) - FC Balzers	D67	D	D	M60		13	-
Roland MOSER (19/09/62) - USV Eschen/Mauren	D					11	-
Thomas HANSELMANN (21/04/76) - FC Vaduz	D		s78	D		8	-
Roland HILTI (02/10/63) - USV Eschen/Mauren	M	M	M66	M	M	9	-
Peter KLAUNZER (09/12/67) - USV Eschen/Mauren	M46	s85	M		M50	11	-
Daniel HASLER (18/05/74) - FC Vaduz	M	M	M	D	D	13	1
Harry ZECH (25/02/69) - FC Vaduz	M		M		M	13	-
Mario FRICK (07/09/74) - FC St. Gallen (SUI)	A	A		A	A76	12	-
Christoph FRICK (28/08/74) - FC Balzers	s46	D	D78	M		7	-
Patrik MARXER (10/12/76) - USV Eschen/Mauren	s46	A73			s83	6	-
Ralf OEHRI (26/10/76) - FC Balzers	s67	M63	M	M		7	-
Harry SCHÄDLER (17/04/67) - FC Triesenberg		M			M	2	-
Herbert BICKER (01/11/75) - FC Schaan		s63				1	-
Daniel FRICK (19/06/78) - FC Balzers		s73		M	M61	3	-
Martin OEHRY (11/10/64) - SV Franstanz			G			4	-
Patrik HEFTI (19/11/69) - FC Vaduz			D			7	-
Franz SCHÄDLER (03/02/68) - FC Triesenberg			A		M	2	-
Rolf SELE (12/04/67) - FC Triesen			s46	s60	s76	3	-
Jürgen OSPELT (16/01/74) - FC Vaduz			s66		s50	7	-
Alex QUADERER (13/02/71) - FC Schaan				s46		4	-
Marco PEREZ (21/03/78) - FC Vaduz					M83	1	1
Martin TELSER (16/10/78) - FC Balzers					s61	1	-

game and there was little to cheer other than Perez's right-foot shot in the 25th minute that decided the game in Vaduz's favour. Eschen/Mauren created nothing at all in a very poor game and they certainly missed their top two players - midfielder Roland Hilti, who was injured, and defender Jürgen Zech, who was getting married!

It was the 26th Cup triumph for FC Vaduz and allowed the team from the capital another crack at the European Cup-winners' Cup, the competition from which they had departed somewhat shamefaced some nine months earlier, beaten 14-1 on aggregate by Czech Republic side SK Hradec Kralove. That was even worse than the 12-1 beating Vaduz had suffered from Chornomorets Odesa three years earlier on their only other previous outing in Europe.

DOMESTIC CUP RESULTS

FIRST ROUND

FC Triesenberg II 0, FC Schaan 5
FC Vaduz II 1, FC Triesen 0
FC Ruggell II 0, FC Triesen II 3 (w/o)
USV Eschen/Mauren II 0, FC Balzers 9
FC Balzers II 0, FC Triesenberg 2
FC Schaan II 3, FC Ruggell 0 (w/o)

QUARTER-FINALS

FC Schaan II 0, FC Balzers 8
FC Vaduz II 1, FC Schaan 4
FC Triesenberg 0, FC Vaduz 6
FC Triesen II 0, USV Eschen/Mauren 4

SEMI-FINALS

USV Eschen/Mauren 3, FC Schaan 2
FC Vaduz 3, FC Balzers 2

FINAL

15/05/96, Triesen
FC VADUZ 1 Perez (25)
USV ESCHEN/MAUREN 0
referee - Stadler
FC VADUZ - Heeb; Zech; Erdogan, Hasler, Hefti (Hassler 67; Frick J. 92); Heidegger, Hanselmann, Perez, Cimino; Milosavljevic, Polverino (Kindle 82).
USV ESCHEN/MAUREN - Walser; Kamaryt; Marxer (Batliner 70), Stocklasa, Blumenthal; Kaiser (Matt 58), Klaunzer, Ferrati, Ospelt (Ender 79); Jovic, Schädler.

LITHUANIA

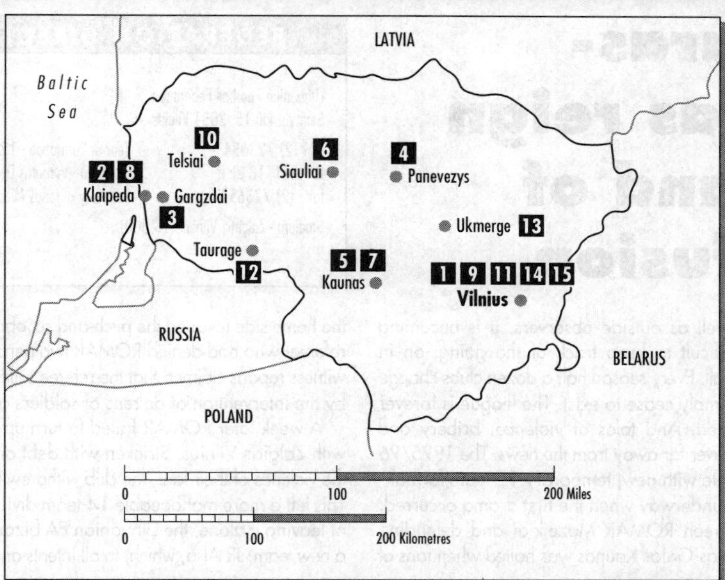

1	JR ALSA	638
2	ATLANTAS KLAIPEDA	639
3	BANGA GARGZDAI	640
4	EKRANAS PANEVEZYS	641
5	INKARAS-GRIFAS KAUNAS	642
6	KAREDA SIAULIAI	643
7	FBK KAUNAS	644
8	FK KLAIPEDA	645
9	LOKOMOTYVAS VILNIUS	646
10	MASTIS TELSIAI	647
11	PANERYS VILNIUS	648
12	TAURAS TAURAGE	649
13	UKMERGE	650
14	ZALGIRIS VILNIUS	651
15	ZALGIRIS II VILNIUS	652

ZALGIRIS LEFT EMPTY-HANDED AGAIN

Inkaras-Grifas reign in land of confusion

FEDERATION DIRECTORY

Lithuanian Football Federation
Seimyniskiu 15, 2051 Vilnius

tel - (2) 723654
tlx - 261118 isk lt
fax - (2) 723651

Year of Formation - 1922
President - Vytautas Dirmeikis
Secretary - Pranas Miezelis

Stadium - Zalgiris, Vilnius (15,000)

For inside as well as outside observers, it is becoming increasingly difficult to keep track of the goings-on in Lithuanian football. Every season half a dozen clubs change their name or simply cease to exist. The league is forever being restructured. And tales of violence, bribery and corruption are never far away from the news. The 1995/96 season - complete with new, temporary 15-team format - had barely got underway when the first drama occurred. The match between ROMAR Mazeikiai and defending champions Inkaras-Grifas Kaunas was halted when fans of the home side invaded the pitch and set about attacking the referee, who had denied ROMAR two penalty claims. Eye-witness reports claimed that the referee's life was saved only by the intervention of dozens of soldiers and policemen.

A week later ROMAR failed to turn up for their fixture with Zalgiris Vilnius. Stricken with debt and tarnished by the violence of their fans, the club withdrew from the league. This left a more manageable 14-team division, but instead of leaving it alone, the Lithuanian FA bizarrely introduced a new team, JR Alsa, which, to all intents and purposes, was

LEAGUE CHAMPIONSHIP RESULTS 95/96

FIRST PHASE		1	2	3	4	5	6	7	8	9	10	11	12	13	14	15
1	JR Alsa			2-1		0-1	1-3				0-6	0-2		0-2		0-3
2	Aras Klaipeda	1-0				1-2		2-0		0-0			5-0	4-0		1-0
3	Banga Gargzdai		0-3			2-4	0-5				1-1		1-1	2-1		2-1
4	Ekranas Panevezys	3-0	2-1	3-2						3-2	2-0		7-0			2-2
5	Inkaras-Grifas Kaunas				2-1		3-1	0-0	2-0		5-1	3-0			0-0	
6	Kareda-Sakalas Siauliai		0-2		2-1			3-2	3-0			2-0		2-0	0-1	
7	FBK Kaunas	2-0		3-0	3-1				1-2	3-0		2-1			1-2	
8	FK Klaipeda	2-0	0-5	1-1	2-1					1-2		0-3	2-0			
9	Lokomotyvas Vilnius	2-1		1-2		1-3	0-1					0-2		0-0		1-1
10	Mastis Telsiai		1-3				0-4	1-4	0-1	1-2				0-0	1-14	
11	Panerys Vilnius		0-2	3-0	2-1						2-0		6-0		2-3	1-3
12	Tauras Taurage	1-0				0-4	0-6	2-4		2-0	0-1			2-0		
13	Ukmerge				2-2	0-6		0-2	2-1			0-4			0-4	0-5
14	Zalgiris-EBSW Vilnius	9-0	5-1	4-0	5-0				3-0	5-2			7-0			
15	Zalgiris-EBSW II Vilnius					0-2	0-3	1-6	2-0		2-2		2-0		0-1	

SECOND PHASE

CHAMPIONSHIP GROUP		1	2	3	4	5	6	7	8
1	Atlantas Klaipeda		1-1	0-2	0-1	1-3	1-2	3-4	2-0
2	Ekranas Panevezys	0-1		0-2	0-1	2-2	1-0	1-1	1-1
3	Inkaras-Grifas Kaunas	1-0	2-0		0-0	2-0	4-0	2-0	5-0
4	Kareda Siauliai	3-0	3-1	1-0		5-2	4-1	1-1	3-0
5	FBK Kaunas	1-0	1-1	0-1	0-1		1-0	0-1	2-0
6	Panerys Vilnius	1-1	1-0	0-3	0-7	2-1		2-2	1-0
7	Zalgiris Vilnius	5-1	3-0	1-3	2-1	3-0	5-0		9-1
8	Zalgiris II Vilnius	0-0	2-2	0-3	0-1	1-2	1-2	0-6	

LEAGUE CHAMPIONSHIP FINAL TABLE 95/96

FIRST PHASE			Home					Away					Total							
		Pd	W	D	L	F	A	W	D	L	F	A	W	D	L	F	A	Pt	GD	
1	Zalgiris-EBSW Vilnius	14	7	0	0	38	3	6	1	0	25	4	13	1	0	63	7	40	+56	(20)
2	Inkaras-Grifas Kaunas	14	5	2	0	15	3	7	0	0	22	4	12	2	0	37	7	38	+30	(19)
3	Kareda-Sakalas Siauliai	14	5	0	2	12	6	6	0	1	23	4	11	0	3	35	10	33	+25	(17)
4	Aras Klaipeda	14	5	1	1	14	2	5	0	2	17	8	10	1	3	31	10	31	+21	(16)
5	FBK Kaunas	14	5	0	2	15	6	4	1	2	18	9	9	1	4	33	15	28	+18	(14)
6	Panerys Vilnius	14	4	0	3	16	9	4	0	3	12	7	8	0	6	28	16	24	+12	(12)
7	Ekranas Panevezys	14	6	1	0	22	7	0	1	6	7	18	6	2	6	29	25	20	+4	(10)
8	Zalgiris-EBSW II Vilnius	14	2	1	4	7	14	3	2	2	15	7	5	3	6	22	21	18	+1	(9)
9	FK Klaipeda	14	3	1	3	8	12	2	0	5	4	13	5	1	8	12	25	16	-13	(8)
10	Banga Gargzdai	14	2	2	3	8	16	1	1	5	6	17	3	3	8	14	33	12	-19	(6)
11	Lokomotyvas Vilnius	14	1	2	4	5	10	2	1	4	8	15	3	3	8	13	25	12	-12	(6)
12	Tauras Taurage	14	3	0	4	7	15	0	1	6	1	30	3	1	10	8	45	10	-37	(5)
13	Mastis Telsiai	14	0	1	6	4	28	2	2	3	11	12	2	3	9	15	40	9	-25	(5)
14	Ukmerge	14	1	1	5	4	24	1	2	4	3	10	2	3	9	7	34	9	-27	(5)
15	JR Alsa	14	1	0	6	3	18	0	0	7	1	20	1	0	13	4	38	3	-34	(2)

SECOND PHASE Championship Grouop			Home					Away					Total						
		Pd	W	D	L	F	A	W	D	L	F	A	W	D	L	F	A	Pt	GD
1	Inkaras-Grifas Kaunas	14	6	1	0	16	0	6	0	1	14	2	12	1	1	30	2	56	+28
2	Kareda Siauliai	14	6	1	0	20	5	5	1	1	12	2	11	2	1	32	7	52	+25
3	Zalgiris Vilnius	14	6	0	1	28	6	3	3	1	15	9	9	3	2	43	15	50	+28
4	FBK Kaunas	14	3	1	3	5	4	2	1	4	10	16	5	2	7	15	20	31	-5
5	Panerys Vilnius	14	3	2	2	7	14	2	0	5	5	17	5	2	7	12	31	29	-19
6	Atlantas Klaipeda	14	1	1	5	8	13	1	2	4	3	11	2	3	9	11	24	25	-13
7	Ekranas Panevezys	14	1	3	3	5	8	0	3	4	5	13	1	6	7	10	21	19	-11
8	Zalgiris II Vilnius	14	0	2	5	4	16	0	1	6	2	23	0	3	11	6	39	12	-33

N.B. After 14 matches the top eight play off for the title, taking half their points total (figures in brackets above). The bottom seven teams enter a promotion/relegation play-off group (Division 1 B). Mid-season name changes- Zalgiris-EBSW Vilnius to Zalgiris Vilnius; Kareda-Sakalas Siauliai to Kareda Siauliai; Aras Klaipeda to Atlantas Klaipeda; Zalgiris-EBSW II Vilnius to Zalgiris II Vilnius.

nothing more than a national youth selection, in which young players of other clubs could occasionally parade their talents should they fail to make the grade in their own team.

Another anomaly was the presence of Zalgiris Vilnius's reserve side in the same division as the club's first team. The two teams met in the opening game of the season, and not surprisingly, big brother prevailed, though only by one goal to nil. By the end of the first phase of the season, in which every team played the others just once, Zalgiris I had run up another 12 wins to lead the table by two points ahead

TOP SCORERS

25 Edgardas JANKAUSKAS (Zalgiris Vilnius)
18 Remigijus POCIUS (Kareda Siauliai)
15 Tomas RAZANAUSKAS (Panerys Vilnius/ Zalgiris Vilnius)
14 Eimantas PODERIS (Inkaras-Grifas Kaunas)
Aidas PREIKSAITIS (Zalgiris Vilnius)
Audrius ZUTA (Atlantas Klaipeda)
13 Darius MACIULEVICIUS (Inkaras-Grifas Kaunas)
Igoris MORINAS (Panerys Vilnius)

NATIONAL TEAM RESULTS 95/96

29/07/95	Belarus	H	Vilnius	1-1	Skarbalius (10)
16/08/95	Estonia (ECQ)	A	Tallinn	1-0	Maciulevicius (48)
06/09/95	Ukraine (ECQ)	H	Vilnius	1-3	Maciulevicius (17)
11/10/95	Estonia (ECQ)	H	Vilnius	5-0	Maciulevicius (8), Suika (13, 39), Slekys (44), Ivanauskas (62)
15/11/95	Italy (ECQ)	A	Reggio Emilia	0-4	
21/02/96	Israel	A	Haifa	2-4	Maciulevicius (32), Rimkus (89)

NATIONAL TEAM APPEARANCES 95/96

Coach - Benjaminas ZELKEVICIUS	BLS	EST	UKR	EST	ITA	ISR	Cps	Gls
Marius POSKUS (07/08/70) - Inkaras-Grifas Kaunas	G79						10	-
Tomas KANCELSKIS (19/08/75) - Kareda Siauliai	D	s75		D			3	-
Raimondas VAINORAS (16/07/65) - Inkaras-Grifas Kaunas	D	D	D	D	D	D	29	-
Tomas ZIUKAS (02/12/70) - Romar Mazeikiai/Kareda Siauliai	D	D	D		D		32	-
Andrius TERESKINAS (10/07/70) - Zalgiris Vilnius	D60	D	D68		D	D	34	2
Ramunas STONKUS (31/12/70) - Zalgiris Vilnius	M	M	M	D	D	D	17	1
Virginijus BALTUSNIKAS (22/10/68) - Zalgiris Vilnius	M			D			29	8
Darius MACIULEVICIUS (06/11/73) - Inkaras-Grifas Kaunas	M76	M	M	M	M46	M	10	5
Igoris STUKALINAS (19/06/72) - Kareda Siauliai	M46						2	-
Aurelijus SKARBALIUS (12/05/73) - Inkaras-Grifas Kaunas/Brøndby IF (DEN)	A	M75	M77		M		25	5
Rimas ZVINGILAS (03/09/73) - Kareda Siauliai	A71		s77	s74	s46		7	1
Irmantas STUMBRYS (30/05/72) - Kareda Siauliai	s46						20	1
Igoris KIRILOVAS (19/08/71) - Kareda Siauliai	s60						15	-
Audrius ZUTA (05/01/69) - Atlantas Klaipeda	s71	s65					26	2
Donatas VENCEVICIUS (28/11/73) - Zalgiris Vilnius	s76			M	s79		6	-
Arturas RAMOSKA (09/08/63) - FBK Kaunas	s79						1	-
Gintaras STAUCE (24/12/69) - Galatasaray (TUR)/Karsiyaka (TUR)		G	G	G46	G		24	-
Viaceslavas SUKRISTOVAS (01/01/60) - Hapoel Haifa (ISR)		M	M			M	22	2
Arunas SUIKA (16/05/70) - Lyngby FC (DEN)		M	M	M74	M79		15	3
Valdas IVANAUSKAS (31/07/66) - Hamburger SV (GER)		A	A	A	A59		16	4
Vaidotas SLEKYS (02/11/72) - FC Wil (SUI)		A65	A	A46			23	2
Aidas PREIKSAITIS (15/07/70) - Zalgiris Vilnius			s68		M	M	8	2
Gintaras RIMKUS (30/11/68) - Zalgiris Vilnius				M	M	M	3	1
Valdemaras MARTINKENAS (10/03/65) - FC Wil (SUI)				s46			14	-
Edgaras JANKAUSKAS (12/03/75) - Zalgiris Vilnius				s46		A	2	-
Raimondas ZUTAUTAS (04/09/72) - Atlantas Klaipeda/Inkaras-Grifas Kaunas					s59	s55	4	-
Darius SPETYLA (14/10/69) - Zalgiris Vilnius						G	1	-
Sergejus NOVIKOVAS (05/05/72) - Zalgiris Vilnius						D	1	-
Tomas RAZANAUSKAS (07/01/76) - Panerys Vilnius						M55	2	1

of Inkaras-Grifas Kaunas, the only team to deny them victory. Zalgiris went into the winter break on a high, annihilating Mastis Telisiai 14-1 to record the biggest victory in Lithuanian First Division history. But if the first half of the campaign belonged to Zalgiris, the second, in which the 15 teams were split into two groups, was marked with the stamp of the defending champions. Inkaras-Grifas made their big push for the title with a 3-1 away win over Zalgiris at the beginning of May. Remarkably, the goal against was the first they had conceded in seven matches of the spring campaign. And that locktight defence was to remain unbreached for the next four games as well as the team from Kaunas closed in on the title.

But three games from the end, Inkaras-Grifas's surge was brought to an abrupt halt when they lost 0-1 away to in-form Kareda Siauliai. It was their first defeat in 39 games, and it meant that with two games to go they held a two-point lead over Kareda and a three-point lead over Zalgiris.

In the next match Zalgiris inflicted on Kareda their only defeat of a spectacular spring revival, and with Inkaras-Grifas easily disposing of Zalgiris reserves, it meant that the defending champions needed only a draw at home to Zalgiris to make sure of their second successive title. They did better than that, winning the match 2-0 and thereby sending Zalgiris down into third place.

Ten days after sealing the championship, Inkaras-Grifas travelled to Vilnius to defend their other domestic title in the final of the Lithuanian Cup. Their opponents were Kareda Siauliai, who had shown their worth in the semi-finals, beating Zalgiris 2-1 in both games. And in the final Kareda were to prove that their league win over Inkaras-Grifas was no fluke. A brace of second-half goals from Vidas Dancenka and Remigijus Pocius gave Kareda their first major trophy, shattering the champions' 'double double' dreams.

EUROPEAN CUPS RESULTS 95/96

CUP-WINNERS' CUP

● ZALGIRIS VILNIUS

Preliminary round MURA MURSKA SOBOTA (SLO)

H 2-0 Baltusnikas (53), Tereskinas (67)
Koncevicius; Skirmantas (Zvirgzdauskas 51), Rimkus, Suliauskas, Stonkus, Vencevicius, Karvelis (Mikulenas 44), Tereskinas, Preiksaitis, Baltusnikas, Jankauskas.

A 1-2 Vencevicius (73)
Koncevicius; Tereskinas, Baltusnikas, Zvirgzdauskas, Suliauskas, Stonkus (Pukelevicius 85), Preiksaitis, Vencevicius, Rimkus, Mikulenas, Jankauskas.

1st round TRABZONSPOR (TUR)

H 2-2 Tereskinas (7), Mikulenas (67)
Spetyla; Suliauskas, Baltusnikas, Zvirgzdauskas (Mikulenas 46), Novikovas, Vencevicius, Tereskinas (Pukelevicius 71), Preiksaitis, Stonkus, Rimkus, Jankauskas.

A 0-1
Spetyla; Suliauskas, Baltusnikas, Zvirgzdauskas, Novikovas, Stonkus (Pukelevicius 78), Tereskinas (Mikulenas 28), Preiksaitis, Vencevicius, Rimkus, Jankauskas.

UEFA CUP

● INKARAS-GRIFAS KAUNAS

Preliminary round BRØNDBY IF (DEN)

A 0-3
Poskus; Matlasaitis (Rudzionis 34), Vainoras, Kazlauskas, Mika, Vaskunas, Upstas (Sanajevas 83), Markevicius, Skarbalius, Maciulevicius, Poderis (Slekys 68).

H 0-3
Poskus; Mika, Vainoras, Kazlauskas (Slekys 27), Markevicius, Vaskunas, Upstas (Butkus 72), Rudzionis, Skarbalius, Maciulevicius, Poderis (Sanajevas 58).

PLAYER OF THE SEASON

DARIUS MACIULEVICIUS

There were raised eyebrows when Lithuanian national team goalkeeper Gintaras Stauce won the country's 1995 Footballer of the Year award. Most people expected the prize to go to the eventual runner-up, 22-year-old Inkaras-Grifas Kaunas midfielder Darius Maciulevicius. He had struck four goals for the national team during the course of the year and had been the play-off hero in his club's 94/95 title success. As if to prove the voters wrong, Maciulevicius played even better in the first half of 1996, scoring another goal for Lithuania, against Israel, and starring in Inkaras-Grifas's drive to a second successive national title.

With Zalgiris missing out once again on both domestic prizes, the club's president/coach Benjaminas Zelkevicius quit to concentrate full-time on his other job, that of coach to the Lithuanian national team. Drawn in the easiest of the World Cup qualifying groups, Lithuania might feel they have a realistic outside chance of qualifying for France '98. Although the team finished their Euro '96 campaign poorly, third place in the group was a positive performance, providing Zelkevicius with something to build on for the future.

INTERNATIONAL HONOURS

None

DOMESTIC CUP RESULTS

FIRST ROUND

Andas Vilnius 0, FK Klaipeda 4
Volmeta-KKI Kaunas 0, Atlantas Klaipeda 3
Klevas-Sakalas Siauliai 0, Zalgiris Vilnius 6
Intermetas Vilkaviskis 0, Kareda Siauliai 11
JR Alsa w/o Romar Mazeikiai
Daisotra Alytus 0, Panerys Vilnius 3
Zerutis Radviliskis 0, Inkaras-Grifas Kaunas 4
Grigiskes 1, Tauras Taurage 2 (aet)
FK Klaipeda II 0, Banga Gargzdai 2
Lietava Jonava 0, Interas Visaginas 2
Zalgiris II Vilnius w/o Cementininkas Naujoji Akmene
Anyksciu FK 0, Lokomotyvas Vilnius 4
Savinge Kaisiadorys 0, Mastis Telsiai 2
Ranga-Politechnika Kaunas 0, FBK Kaunas 4
Sandoris Vilnius 3, Ukmerge 2 (aet)
Inkaras-Grifas II Kaunas 0, Ekranas Panevezys 3

SECOND ROUND

FK Klaipeda v Zalgiris Vilnius 1-1; 0-2
(Zalgiris Vilnius 3-1)
Interas Visaginas v FBK Kaunas 1-2; 0-2
(FBK Kaunas 4-1)
JR Alsa v Lokomotyvas Vilnius 0-1; 0-1
(Lokomotyvas Vilnius 2-0)
Banga Gargzdai v Panerys Vilnius 4-2; 1-7
(Panerys Vilnius 9-5)
Atlantas Klaipeda v Ekranas Panevezys 1-1; 3-1
(Atlantas Klaipeda 4-2)
Tauras Taurage v Inkaras-Grifas Kaunas 0-3; 1-10
(Inkaras-Grifas Kaunas 13-1)
Sandoris Vilnius v Kareda Siauliai 0-6; 0-3
(Kareda Siauliai 9-0)
Mastis Telsiai v Zalgiris II Vilnius 0-4; 0-2
(Zalgiris II Vilnius 6-0)

QUARTER-FINALS

Kareda Siauliai v Panerys Vilnius 2-0; 2-1
(Kareda Siauliai 4-1)
Zalgiris II Vilnius v Zalgiris Vilnius 1-3; 1-1
(Zalgiris Vilnius 4-2)
Lokomotyvas Vilnius v Inkaras-Grifas Kaunas 1-3; 0-4
(Inkaras-Grifas Kaunas 7-1)
FBK Kaunas v Atlantas Klaipeda 2-3; 0-1
(Atlantas Klaipeda 4-2)

SEMI-FINALS

Kareda Siauliai v Zalgiris Vilnius 2-1; 2-1
(Kareda Siauliai 4-2)
Atlantas Klaipeda v Inkaras-Grifas Kaunas 2-4; 0-6
(Inkaras-Grifas Kaunas 10-2)

FINAL

17/06/96, Vilnius
KAREDA SIAULIAI 2 Dancenka (69), Pocius (90)
INKARAS-GRIFAS KAUNAS 0
referee - Dubinskas
KAREDA SIAULIAI - Zutautas; Ziukas, Dancenka, Korsakovas, Zudys; Baranauskas, Stumbrys, Mikalajunas, Stukalinas (Vaineikis 83); Zvingilas (Bicka 61), Pocius.
INKARAS-GRIFAS KAUNAS - Poskus; Mika, Kazlauskas, Matlasaitis, Vainoras (Zevzikovas 87); Poderis, Maciulevicius, Vaskunas (Upstas 46), Zutautas; Rudzionis (Sanajevas 72), Slekys.

JR ALSA

CLUB DIRECTORY

JR Alsa (now - Alsa-Panerys Vilnius)
Siltnnamiu 38, 2043 Vilnius
tel - (2) 448043/440908/445773
fax - (2) 445888
President - Stanislovas Danisevicius
Secretary - Rimantas Radzevicius
Coach - Vincas Kateiva
Stadium - Panerys (5,000)

APPEARANCES 95/96

	P	Ap	(s)	Gls
Andrius BALAIKA	M	2	(1)	
Tomas BEDALIUS	M		(3)	
Darius CELESINSKAS	M	5	(2)	
Mindaugas CEPAS	A	4	(1)	1
Tomas CEPULIS	G		(2)	
Evaldas CERBAUSKAS	A	2		
Nerijus CIULADA	M	1		
Tomas DANILEVICIUS	M	1		
Rolandas DZIAUKSTAS	D	13		
Mantas GALINIS	A	1		
Tadas GRAZIUNAS	D	13		
Andrejus JAKOVENKA	M		(1)	
Ramunas JANULAITIS	M	1		
Rolandas JERENKEVICIUS	M		(1)	1
Andrius JUODEIKIS	D	2	(1)	
Gintaras JUODIS	M		(1)	
Tadas KARINAUSKAS	M	1		
Hermis KLIMAITIS	A	1	(1)	
Marijusas KRIUKOVSKIS	M	12		
Vytautas LENKUTIS	G	3		
Pavelas LEUSAS	G	11		
Sarunas LITVINAS	A	1		
Povilas LUKSYS	M	12		1
Andrius MANGEVICIUS	D	13		
Gintaras NARKEVICIUS	D	9	(3)	
Marius PRASCEVICIUS	A	10		
Marius RIMAS	M	1	(7)	
Arturas SABUOLIS	M		(2)	
Kestutis SAMAJAUSKAS	M	3	(5)	
Mantas SAMUSIOVAS	M	4		
Dainius SAULENAS	A	2	(1)	1
Deividas SEMBERAS	M	13		
Andrejus SEMOROVAS	M	10		
Darius SIRVINSKAS	M		(1)	
Janas SIVICKIS	M		(1)	
Valdas TRAKYS	M	2		
Benjaminas ZELKEVICIUS	A		(1)	

LEAGUE RESULTS 1995/96

Date	Opponent	H/A	Score	Scorers
04/09/95	Tauras Taurage	A	0-1	
10/09/95	FK Klaipeda	A	0-2	
17/09/95	Atlantas Klaipeda	A	0-1	
23/09/95	FBK Kaunas	A	0-2	
26/09/95	Panerys Vilnius	H	0-2	
01/10/95	Kareda Siauliai	H	1-3	Saulenas
06/10/95	Ekranas Panevezys	A	0-3	
11/10/95	Mastis Telsiai	H	0-6	
14/10/95	Banga Gargzdai	H	2-1	Cepas, Luksys (p)
22/10/95	Ukmerge	H	0-2	
26/10/95	Inkaras-Grifas Kaunas	H	0-1	
03/11/95	Zalgiris Vilnius	A	0-9	
07/11/95	Zalgiris II Vilnius	H	0-3	
11/11/95	Lokomotyvas Vilnius	H	1-2	Jerenkevicius

ATLANTAS KLAIPEDA

CLUB DIRECTORY

Atlantas Klaipeda
Taikos pr. 42
5800 Klaipeda
tel - (6) 255046/214683
fax - (6) 238403
President - Vytautas Gedgaudas
Secretary - Vacys Lekevicius
Coach - Algimantas Mitigaila
Stadium - Zalgiris (10,000)

APPEARANCES 95/96

	P	Ap	(s)	Gls
Vytis AMBRIZAS	A	3		
Zenonas ATUTIS	D	14	(1)	2
Rolandas BUBLIAUSKAS	A	27		12
Denisas BUDAJEVAS	M		(1)	
Robertas BUTKEVICIUS	M	23	(1)	1
Maksimas DAVYDOVAS	D	7	(4)	
Edmundas GAIGALAS	D	16	(1)	1
Mantas GALINIS	A		(2)	
Andrius GEDGAUDAS	M	5		
Vitalijus JOSCIONIS	M		(1)	
Gintaras JUODEIKIS	M	14	(8)	1
Tadas KARINAUSKAS	M	1	(1)	
Gintaras KNIUKSTA	M	5	(12)	2
Gediminas KONTAUTAS	D	19	(1)	1
Vaclovas LEKEVICIUS	G	14		
Sarunas LITVINAS	A		(1)	
Edvinas LUKOSEVICIUS	D	1		
Romas MACIULEVICIUS	D	11	(5)	
Kastytis MACIULIS	G	9		
Marius MAJAUSKAS	M	5	(4)	
Zydrunas MISIUNAS	M		(4)	
Vadimas PETRENKA	A	27		3
Dainius PETRUTIS	M		(6)	
Linas POCIUS	M		(1)	
Robertas POSKUS	A	1	(2)	
Robertas RINGYS	M		(1)	
Arturas SAFONOVAS	A	2	(4)	1
Rimas STECKIS	D	23		1
Raimondas VENSKUS	G	5	(3)	
Saulius VILCIAUSKAS	M	1		
Romas VOLUNGEVICIUS	D	28		
Egidijus ZUKAUSKAS	D	19		1
Audrius ZUTA	M	21		14
Raimondas ZUTAUTAS	M	7		2

LEAGUE RESULTS 1995/96

16/07/95	Banga Gargzdai	A	3-0	Safonovas, Bubliauskas, Zuta
20/07/95	Zalgiris II Vilnius	H	1-0	Zuta
25/07/95	Lokomotyvas Vilnius	H	0-0	
04/08/95	Mastis Telsiai	A	3-1	Zuta 3
12/08/95	Tauras Taurage	H	5-0	Bubliauskas 2, Zuta, Petrenka, Kniuksta
29/08/95	Inkaras-Grifas Kaunas	H	1-2	Bubliauskas
10/09/95	Zalgiris Vilnius	A	1-5	Kniuksta
17/09/95	JR Alsa	H	1-0	Kontautas
23/09/95	Panerys Vilnius	A	2-0	Zutautas, Juodeikis
06/10/95	FBK Kaunas	H	2-0	Bubliauskas, Zutautas (p)
14/10/95	Kareda Siauliai	A	2-0	Bubliauskas, Zuta
22/10/95	Ekranas Panevezys	A	1-2	Zuta
05/11/95	Ukmerge	H	4-0	Atutis 2 (1p), Bubliauskas 2
11/11/95	FK Klaipeda	A	5-0	Bubliauskas, Zuta 2, Butkevicius, Petrenka
31/03/96	FBK Kaunas	A	0-1	
06/04/96	Zalgiris II Vilnius	H	2-0	Gaigalas, Zuta
14/04/96	Kareda Siauliai	H	0-1	
19/04/96	Inkaras-Grifas Kaunas	A	0-1	
28/04/96	Zalgiris Vilnius	A	1-5	Zuta
01/05/96	Ekranas Panevezys	H	1-1	Zuta
05/05/96	Panerys Vilnius	H	1-2	Zuta
11/05/96	FBK Kaunas	H	1-3	Bubliauskas
19/05/96	Zalgiris II Vilnius	A	0-0	
25/05/96	Kareda Siauliai	A	0-3	
30/05/96	Inkaras-Grifas Kaunas	H	0-2	
04/06/96	Zalgiris Vilnius	H	3-4	Steckis, Petrenka, Bubliauskas
09/06/96	Ekranas Panevezys	A	1-0	Zukauskas
13/06/96	Panerys Vilnius	A	1-1	Bubliauskas

BANGA GARGZDAI

CLUB DIRECTORY

Banga Gargzdai
Kranto 5
5840 Gargzdai
tel - (40) 52505
President - Antanas Blinstrubas
Coach - Leonas Lukavicius
Stadium - Gargzdai (2,000)

LEAGUE RESULTS 1995/96

Date	Opponent	H/A	Score	Scorers
16/07/95	Atlantas Klaipeda	H	0-3	
20/07/95	Ekranas Panevezys	A	2-3	Rauktys, Lubinas
04/08/95	Ukmerge	H	2-1	Lubinas 2
11/08/95	FK Klaipeda	A	1-1	Drasutis
19/08/95	Zalgiris II Vilnius	H	2-1	Samsonikas 2
09/09/95	Lokomotyvas Vilnius	A	2-1	Samsonikas, Lubinas
17/09/95	Mastis Telsiai	H	1-1	Drasutis
23/09/95	Tauras Taurage	H	1-1	Rauktys
01/10/95	Inkaras-Grifas Kaunas	H	2-4	Petkevicius, Sileika
06/10/95	Zalgiris Vilnius	A	0-4	
14/10/95	JR Alsa	A	1-2	Drasutis
24/10/95	Panerys Vilnius	A	0-3	
04/11/95	FBK Kaunas	A	0-3	
11/11/95	Kareda Siauliai	H	0-5	

APPEARANCES 95/96

	P	Ap	(s)	Gls
Remigijus DAUGELA	A	4	(1)	
Saulius DRASUTIS	M	13		3
Arunas GEDMINAS	G	3	(2)	
Saulius JAKUMAITIS	D	13		
Andrius JOKSAS	M	1	(7)	
Audrius KANCLERIS	M	11		
Jonas LUBINAS	A	12		4
Rimvydas MARTINAITIS	D	6	(1)	
Vitas MINEIKIS	M		(3)	
Kestutis NAZAROVAS	M	5	(7)	
Romas PETKEVICIUS	M	13		1
Gintas POCIUNAS	D	9	(2)	
Petras RAUKTYS	M	14		2
Robertas REPSYS	M	1	(2)	
Rimas RUDYS	D	14		
Genadijus SAMSONIKAS	A	14		3
Rimantas SARUNAS	M		(1)	
Romas SILEIKA	M	4	(10)	1
Algis URMONAS	G	11	(2)	
Darius ZUTAUTAS	D	6	(4)	

EKRANAS PANEVEZYS

CLUB DIRECTORY

Ekranas Panevezys
Elektronikos 1
5319 Panevezys
tel - (54) 35515/69687
fax - (54) 23873
President - Robertas Gobulas
Secretary - Valdemaras Steinas
Coach - Virginijus Liubsys; Albertas Klimavicius; Virginijus Liubsys
Stadium - Aukstaitija (10,000)

MAJOR HONOURS
League Championship - (1) 1993.

APPEARANCES 95/96

	P	Ap	(s)	Gls
Tomas ABROMAVICIUS	M	1	(6)	
Kestutis ALEKSANDRAVICIUS	D	17	(2)	
Mindaugas BALVOCIUS	M	2	(4)	
Audrius BANEVICIUS	A	27	(1)	8
Marius BARANAUSKAS	A	2		1
Stasys BARANAUSKAS	M	5		
Darius BUTKUS	D	17	(3)	
Zilvinas CENYS	M	14	(4)	4
Mindaugas CEPAS	A		(8)	1
Arturas FOMENKA	M	11	(12)	7
Dainius GLEVECKAS	M	9		3
Tomas GRAZIUNAS	D	9		2
Arturas JAKELIUNAS	D	11		
Albertas KLIMAVICIUS	D	11		
Egidijus LIUBAUSKAS	G	4	(4)	
Dainius LUKSYS	M	23	(1)	
Povilas LUKSYS	M	6	(5)	1
Audrius MARCINKEVICIUS	M	21	(1)	2
Tomas NEMANIS	M	2	(5)	
Linas NIURKA	M	25	(2)	2
Virginijus NUTAUTAS	A	18	(5)	5
Raimundas PETRUKAITIS	D	26	(1)	1
Zilvinas RIMSA	D	1		
Arvydas SKRUPSKIS	G	24		1
Audrius STALIUNAS	M	9	(3)	
Aurelijus VEKEROTAS	M		(1)	
Arunas ZELVYS	M	10	(1)	
Kestutis ZENIAUSKAS	M	3	(8)	1

LEAGUE RESULTS 1995/96

16/07/95	FBK Kaunas	A	1-3	Banevicius
20/07/95	Banga Gargzdai	H	3-2	Cenys, Banevicius, Nutautas
25/07/95	Ukmerge	A	2-2	Zeniauskas, Cenys
06/08/95	FK Klaipeda	A	1-2	Petrukaitis
12/08/95	Zalgiris II Vilnius	H	2-2	Baranauskas M., Marclksevicius
18/08/95	Lokomotyvas Vilnius	H	3-2	Banevicius, Fomenka, Nutautas
10/09/95	Mastis Telsiai	H	2-0	Graziunas, Nutautas
16/09/95	Tauras Taurage	H	7-0	Banevicius 3, Nutautas, Cenys 2 (2p), Fomenka
22/09/95	Inkaras-Grifas Kaunas	H	1-2	Graziunas
02/10/95	Zalgiris Vilnius	A	0-5	
06/10/95	JR Alsa	H	3-0	Fomenka 2, Niurka
14/10/95	Panerys Vilnius	A	1-2	Banevicius
22/10/95	Atlantas Klaipeda	H	2-1	Nutautas, Cepas
04/11/95	Kareda Siauliai	A	1-2	Niurka
31/03/96	Inkaras-Grifas Kaunas	H	0-2	
06/04/96	Zalgiris Vilnius	H	1-1	Luksys P.
13/04/96	Zalgiris II Vilnius	A	2-2	Marclnkevicius (p), Skrupskis
20/04/96	Panerys Vilnius	A	0-1	
28/04/96	FBK Kaunas	H	2-2	Fomenka 2
01/05/96	Atlantas Klaipeda	A	1-1	Fomenka
05/05/96	Kareda Siauliai	A	1-3	Gleveckas
11/05/96	Inkaras-Grifas Kaunas	A	0-2	
19/05/96	Zalgiris Vilnius	A	0-3	
25/05/96	Zalgiris II Vilnius	H	1-1	Banevicius
30/05/96	Panerys Vilnius	H	1-0	Gleveckas
04/06/96	FBK Kaunas	A	1-1	Gleveckas
09/06/96	Atlantas Klaipeda	H	0-1	
13/06/96	Kareda Siauliai	H	0-1	

INKARAS-GRIFAS KAUNAS

CLUB DIRECTORY

Inkaras-Grifas Kaunas
Vandziogalos 110
4302 Domeikava, Kauno rajonas
tel - (7) 258690
fax - (7) 258094
President - Arvydas Raizys
Secretary - Vytautas Klimasauskas
Coach - Julius Kvedaras
Stadium - Inkaras (2,000) or Darius ir Girenas (15,000)

MAJOR HONOURS
League Championship - (2) 1995, 1996.
Domestic Cup - (1) 1995.

APPEARANCES 95/96

	P	Ap	(s)	Gls
Rimvydas BAKUS	M	2	(7)	1
Deivis BUCINSKAS	G		(1)	
Saulius BUTKUS	M	1	(13)	
Rimas KAZLAUSKAS	D	26	(1)	3
Darius MACIULEVICIUS	M	28		13
Paulius MALZINSKAS	M		(2)	
Audrius MARKEVICIUS	D	20	(2)	3
Minvydas MATLASAITIS	D	11	(9)	
Arunas MIKA	D	24	(2)	1
Eimantas PODERIS	A	20	(2)	14
Marius POSKUS	G	28		
Kestutis RUDZIONIS	M	21	(7)	7
Darius SANAJEVAS	A	7	(15)	2
Arunas SIRKA	A		(3)	
Aurelijus SKARBALIUS	M	9		1
Audrius SLEKYS	A	26	(2)	11
Andrius UPSTAS	M	25	(1)	3
Raimondas VAINORAS	D	24		
Vytas VASKUNAS	M	22	(1)	4
Genadijus ZEVZIKOVAS	M		(4)	
Raimundas ZUTAUTAS	M	14		4

LEAGUE RESULTS 1995/96

15/07/95	Lokomotyvas Vilnius	A	3-1	Kazlauskas, Markevicius, Poderis
25/07/95	Zalgiris Vilnius	H	0-0	
12/08/95	Panerys Vilnius	H	3-0	Poderis 2, Maciulevicius
29/08/95	Atlantas Klaipeda	A	2-1	Rudzionis, Slekys
09/09/95	FBK Kaunas	H	0-0	
16/09/95	Kareda Siauliai	H	3-1	Slekys 2, Rudzionis
22/09/95	Ekranas Panevezys	H	2-1	Poderis 2
30/09/95	Banga Gargzdai	A	4-2	Skarbalius, Markevicius, Slekys, Maciulevicius
06/10/95	Ukmerge	A	6-0	Poderis 3, Slekys, Kazlauskas, Maciulevicius
14/10/95	FK Klaipeda	H	2-0	Kazlauskas, Poderis
22/10/95	Zalgiris II Vilnius	A	2-0	Maciulevicius, Upstas
26/10/95	JR Alsa	A	1-0	Sanajevas
05/11/95	Mastis Telsiai	H	5-1	Upstas, Markevicius, Rudzionis, Vaskunas, Bakus
11/11/95	Tauras Taurage	A	4-0	Vaskunas, Rudzionis 2, Slekys
31/03/96	Ekranas Panevezys	A	2-0	Vaskunas, Rudzionis
06/04/96	Panerys Vilnius	H	4-0	Slekys 2, Zutautas, Poderis
14/04/96	FBK Kaunas	H	2-0	Maciulevicius 2
19/04/96	Atlantas Klaipeda	H	1-0	Slekys
28/04/96	Kareda Siauliai	H	0-0	
01/05/96	Zalgiris II Vilnius	A	3-0	Mika, Poderis 2
05/05/96	Zalgiris Vilnius	A	3-1	Slekys 2, Maciulevicius (p)
11/05/96	Ekranas Panevezys	H	2-0	Vaskunas, Upstas
19/05/96	Panerys Vilnius	A	3-0	Zutautas, Maciulevicius (p), Rudzionis
26/05/96	FBK Kaunas	A	1-0	Maciulevicius
30/05/96	Atlantas Klaipeda	A	2-0	Maciulevicius (p), Sanajevas
04/06/96	Kareda Siauliai	A	0-1	
09/06/96	Zalgiris II Vilnius	H	5-0	Poderis 2, Zutautas, Maciulevicius 2
13/06/96	Zalgiris Vilnius	H	2-0	Maciulevicius (p), Zutautas

KAREDA SIAULIAI

CLUB DIRECTORY

Kareda Siauliai
Bielskio 36a
5419 Siauliai
tel - (1) 441279
fax - (1) 441982
President - Egidijus Simkus
Secretary - Sigitas Griksas
Coach - Fiodoras Finkelis
(96/97 - Algimantas Liubinskas)
Stadium - Zalgiris (8,000)

MAJOR HONOURS

Domestic Cup - (1) 1996.

APPEARANCES 95/96

	P	Ap	(s)	Gls
Stasys BARANAUSKAS	M	13		2
Deimantas BICKA	M	6	(19)	4
Vidas DANCENKA	A	9	(5)	7
Vitalijus DANILICEVAS	M	10	(12)	2
Mindaugas DELKUS	M	3	(2)	
Darius DILDA	G	22		
Arturas JAKELIUNAS	D	11		
Egidijus JUSKA	M	10	(3)	
Tomas KANCELSKIS	D	20		
Igoris KIRILOVAS	M	2	(8)	1
Arvydas KORSAKOVAS	D	14		
Kastytis MACIULIS	G		(2)	
Saulius MIKALAJUNAS	M	20	(3)	5
Remigijus POCIUS	A	22	(3)	18
Vaidotas SARKIS	D	1		
Marius SKINDERIS	D	19		
Igoris STUKALINAS	M	22	(1)	7
Irmantas STUMBRYS	M	27	(1)	5
Rolandas VAINEIKIS	M	9		2
Raimondas VILENISKIS	D	3	(3)	
Tomas ZIUKAS	D	19	(1)	3
Zilvinas ZUDYS	D	14	(7)	2
Audrius ZUTA	M	1	(6)	
Vaidotas ZUTAUTAS	G	6	(1)	
Rimas ZVINGILAS	A	25	(1)	9

LEAGUE RESULTS 1995/96

20/07/95	Ukmerge	H	2-0	Bicka, Pocius
25/07/95	FK Klaipeda	H	3-0	Stumbrys, Stukalinas (p), Kirilovas
05/08/95	Zalgiris II Vilnius	A	3-0	Pocius 2, Stukalinas (p)
12/08/95	Lokomotyvas Vilnius	A	1-0	Stukalinas (p)
18/08/95	Mastis Telsiai	A	4-0	Stumbrys 2, Pocius 2
10/09/95	Tauras Taurage	A	6-0	Stukalinas (p), Mikalajunas, Zvingilas 2, Pocius 2
16/09/95	Inkaras-Grifas Kaunas	A	1-3	Danilicevas
23/09/95	Zalgiris Vilnius	H	0-1	
01/10/95	JR Alsa	A	3-1	Ziukas, Stukalinas, Zudys
06/10/95	Panerys Vilnius	H	2-0	Zvingilas, Pocius
14/10/95	Atlantas Klaipeda	H	0-2	
22/10/95	FBK Kaunas	H	3-2	Bicka 2, Ziukas
04/11/95	Ekranas Panevezys	H	2-1	Pocius, Stukalinas (p)
11/11/95	Banga Gargzdai	A	5-0	Zvingilas, Pocius 3, Ziukas
31/03/96	Panerys Vilnius	A	7-0	Zvingilas, Vaineikis 2, Stumbrys, Dancenka 2, Zudys
06/04/96	FBK Kaunas	H	5-2	Zvingilas, Stukalinas, Dancenka 2, Pocius (p)
14/04/96	Atlantas Klaipeda	A	1-0	Zvingilas
19/04/96	Zalgiris II Vilnius	H	3-0	Stumbrys, Zvingilas, Pocius (p)
28/04/96	Inkaras-Grifas Kaunas	A	0-0	
01/05/96	Zalgiris Vilnius	H	1-1	Baranauskas (p)
05/05/96	Ekranas Panevezys	H	3-1	Dancenka, Mikalajunas, Zvingilas
11/05/96	Panerys Vilnius	H	4-1	Danilicevas, Dancenka, Mikalajunas, Pocius
19/05/96	FBK Kaunas	A	1-0	Dancenka
25/05/96	Atlantas Klaipeda	H	3-0	Pocius 3
30/05/96	Zalgiris II Vilnius	A	1-0	Mikalajunas
04/06/96	Inkaras-Grifas Kaunas	H	1-0	Mikalajunas
09/06/96	Zalgiris Vilnius	A	1-2	Baranauskas
13/06/96	Ekranas Panevezys	A	1-0	Bicka

FBK KAUNAS

CLUB DIRECTORY

FBK Kaunas
Donelaicio 60
3000 Kaunas
tel - (7) 221408/261500
fax - (7) 202888
President - Vidas Damalakas
Secretary - Romualdas Kontrimas
Coach - Raimundas Kotovas
(96/97 - Senderis Girsovicius)
Stadium - Darius ir Girenas (15,000)

APPEARANCES 95/96

	P	Ap	(s)	Gls
Vytautas APANAVICIUS	M	20	(2)	2
Saulius ATMANAVICIUS	D	12		
Marius BEZYKORNOVAS	M	15	(7)	3
Orestas BUITKUS	M	24		7
Svajunas CERNIAUSKAS	M	9	(13)	4
Martynas CIKAS	M	1	(4)	
Ignas DEDURA	M		(1)	
Eduardas DOROFEJEVAS	M		(1)	
Darius GVILDYS	M	22	(6)	4
Gintaras JASILIONIS	M		(3)	
Igoris KIRILOVAS	M	6		
Arvydas KORSAKOVAS	D	14		
Andrius KSANAVICIUS	A	20	(8)	3
Aivaras LAURISAS	A	16	(10)	7
Zydrunas MERKELIS	D	4	(2)	
Naglis MIKNEVICIUS	M	25		6
Gytis PADIMANSKAS	G	1	(5)	
Saulius RAMANAUSKAS	M	12	(2)	1
Arturas RAMOSKA	G	27		
Darius REGELSKIS	D	25		1
Vilmantas RUKAVICIUS	D	9	(1)	1
Mantas SAMUSIOVAS	M	7	(13)	
Raimondas VILENISKIS	D		(2)	1
Robertas ZALYS	A	27		8
Giedrius ZUTAUTAS	D	12		

LEAGUE RESULTS 1995/96

Date	Opponent		Score	Scorers
16/07/95	Ekranas Panevezys	H	3-1	Buitkus, Ramanauskas, Bezykornovas
20/07/95	FK Klaipeda	H	1-2	Bezykornovas
25/07/95	Zalgiris II Vilnius	A	6-1	Buitkus 2, Zalys 2, Gvildys, Laurisas
12/08/95	Mastis Telsiai	A	4-1	Cerniauskas, Miknevicius, Laurisas, Ksanavicius
20/08/95	Tauras Taurage	A	4-2	Miknevicius, Regelskis, Apanavicius 2
29/08/95	Lokomotyvas Vilnius	H	3-0	Zalys, Bezykornovas, Gvildys
09/09/95	Inkaras-Grifas Kaunas	A	0-0	
17/09/95	Zalgiris Vilnius	H	1-2	Buitkus
23/09/95	JR Alsa	H	2-0	Laurisas, Gvildys
01/10/95	Panerys Vilnius	H	2-1	Laurisas, Zalys
06/10/95	Atlantas Klaipeda	A	0-2	
22/10/95	Kareda Siauliai	A	2-3	Laurisas, Miknevicius
04/11/95	Banga Gargzdai	H	3-0	Cerniauskas, Laurisas, Ksanavicius
11/11/95	Ukmerge	A	2-0	Buitkus, Gvildys
31/03/96	Atlantas Klaipeda	H	1-0	Zalys
06/04/96	Kareda Siauliai	A	2-5	Rukavicius, Zalys
14/04/96	Inkaras-Grifas Kaunas	A	0-2	
19/04/96	Zalgiris Vilnius	A	0-3	
28/04/96	Ekranas Panevezys	A	2-2	Miknevicius, Zalys
01/05/96	Panerys Vilnius	H	1-0	Cerniauskas
05/05/96	Zalgiris II Vilnius	H	2-0	Ksanavicius, Buitkus
11/05/96	Atlantas Klaipeda	A	3-1	Laurisas, Miknevicius (p), Cerniauskas
19/05/96	Kareda Siauliai	H	0-1	
26/05/96	Inkaras-Grifas Kaunas	H	0-1	
30/05/96	Zalgiris Vilnius	H	0-1	
04/06/96	Ekranas Panevezys	H	1-1	Miknevicius
09/06/96	Panerys Vilnius	A	1-2	Buitkus
13/06/96	Zalgiris II Vilnius	A	2-1	Zalys, Vileniskis

FK KLAIPEDA

CLUB DIRECTORY

FK Klaipeda
Salomejos Neries 6-14
5800 Klaipeda
tel - (6) 256218
fax - (6) 216833
President - Petras Kravtas
Secretary - Algis Bukartas
Coach - Senderis Girsovicius
Stadium - Zalgiris (10,000)

MAJOR HONOURS
Domestic Cup - (1) 1990.

LEAGUE RESULTS 1995/96

20/07/95	FBK Kaunas	A	2-1	Sirins (p), Cikas
25/08/95	Kareda Siauliai	A	0-3	
06/08/95	Ekranas Panevezys	H	2-1	Kiseliovas, Sirins (p)
11/08/95	Banga Gargzdai	H	1-1	Cesna
20/08/95	Ukmerge	A	1-2	Bubliauskas
10/09/95	JR Alsa	H	2-0	Kiseliovas, Bubliauskas
16/09/95	Zalgiris II Vilnius	A	0-2	
23/09/95	Lokomotyvas Vilnius	H	1-2	Kokanauskas
01/10/95	Mastis Telsiai	A	1-0	Gurjanov
07/10/95	Tauras Taurage	H	2-0	Bubliauskas 2
14/10/95	Inkaras-Grifas Kaunas	A	0-2	
23/10/95	Zalgiris Vilnius	A	0-3	
04/11/95	Panerys Vilnius	H	0-3	
11/11/95	Atlantas Klaipeda	H	0-5	

APPEARANCES 95/96

	P	Ap	(s)	Gls
Saulius ADOMAUSKAS	G	5	(1)	
Saulius ATMANAVICIUS	D	13		
Nerijus BARASA	A	1		
Jonas BITARIS	D		(1)	
Remigijus BUBLIAUSKAS	M	7	(5)	4
Saulius CESNA	M	11		1
Stasys CESNAUSKAS	D	12		
Martynas CIKAS	M	14		1
Eduardas DOROFEJEVAS	M	5		
Ruslanas FIODOROVAS	M	2	(4)	
Igor GURJANOV (RUS)	A	7	(1)	1
Linas JAKOVLEVAS	M	4		
Viaceslavas JAKUSENKOVAS	A	3		
Mindaugas KAIRYS	M	1	(1)	
Valerijus KISELIOVAS	A	11	(2)	2
Vaidas KOKANAUSKAS	M	11	(3)	1
Vitalijus KUTYRINAS	M	2		
Dainius LEIPUS	A		(1)	
Marius MAJAUSKAS	M		(1)	
Igoris METELICA	D	2	(3)	
Rolandas NAVIKAS	D	6	(2)	
Genadijs SIRINS (LAT)	A	7		2
Evaldas SIUSA	M	3	(3)	
Edgaras STANIKAS	M		(3)	
Aleksandr TKACUK (RUS)	M	1	(2)	
Erikas ZABURAS	G	9	(1)	
Dainius ZERNYS	M	3		
Giedrius ZUTAUTAS	D	14		

LOKOMOTYVAS VILNIUS

CLUB DIRECTORY

Lokomotyvas Vilnius
Liepkalnio 5
2006 Vilnius
tel - (2) 695402
President - Kamil Manatov
Secretary - Ivan Shvabovich
Coach - Kamil Manatov; Kestutis Latoza
Stadium - Lokomotyvas (2,000)

APPEARANCES 95/96

	P	Ap	(s)	Gls
Ricardas ALISAUSKAS	M	11	(3)	2
Miroslavas AVIZENIS	M	12	(2)	2
Vitalijus BAJUS	G	12		
Arturas CICENAS	D	13		
Zydrius GRUDZINSKAS	D	13		1
Dainius GUDAITIS	D	1	(3)	
Dmitrijus GUSCINAS	M	8	(3)	1
Viaceslavas JEVDOKIMOVAS	A	6	(6)	3
Petras LINGE	M	3	(2)	
Zigmuntas MARKOVSKIS	G	2	(1)	
Virginijus MIKNEVICIUS	M	12		
Richardas NIKANDRINAS	M	2	(5)	
Aleksandras NOVIKOVAS	A	10	(3)	2
Julius ROLIUKONIS	D	11		
Andzejus RUDZIANECAS	M	9	(2)	
Albert SARKISJAN (ARM)	D	4	(1)	
Eduardas SKURATOVICIUS	D	14		
Igoris VERBOVIKAS	A	11	(3)	2

LEAGUE RESULTS 1995/96

Date	Opponent		Score	Scorers
15/07/95	Inkaras-Grifas Kaunas	H	1-3	Avizenis
19/07/95	Panerys Vilnius	H	0-2	
25/07/95	Atlantas Klaipeda	A	0-0	
04/08/95	Zalgiris Vilnius	A	2-5	Novikovas, Jevdokimovas
12/08/95	Kareda Siauliai	H	0-1	
18/08/95	Ekranas Panevezys	A	2-3	Guscinas, Jevdokimovas
29/08/95	FBK Kaunas	A	0-3	
09/09/95	Banga Gargzdai	H	1-2	Jevdokimovas
17/09/95	Ukmerge	H	0-0	
23/09/95	FK Klaipeda	A	2-1	Novikovas, Avizenis
30/09/95	Zalgiris II Vilnius	H	1-1	Verbovikas
13/10/95	Mastis Telsiai	A	2-1	Alisauskas, Verbovikas
22/10/95	Tauras Taurage	A	0-2	
11/11/95	JR Alsa	H	2-1	Alisauskas (p), Grudzinskas

MASTIS TELSIAI

CLUB DIRECTORY

Mastis Telsiai
Birutes 5
2610 Telsiai
tel - (94) 53130
President - Vygantas Garbaliauskas
Coach - Leonas Dunauskas
Stadium - Telsiai (5,000)

LEAGUE RESULTS 1995/96

16/07/95	Tauras Taurage	A	1-0	Mickevicius
28/07/95	Panerys Vilnius	A	0-2	
04/08/95	Atlantas Klaipeda	H	1-3	Vasiliauskas (p)
12/08/95	FBK Kaunas	H	1-4	Vasiliauskas (p)
18/08/95	Kareda Siauliai	H	0-4	
10/09/95	Ekranas Panevezys	A	0-2	
17/09/95	Banga Gargzdai	A	1-1	Miseikis
23/09/95	Ukmerge	H	0-0	
01/10/95	FK Klaipeda	H	0-1	
07/10/95	Zalgiris II Vilnius	A	2-2	Skodminas, Kvedaras
11/10/95	JR Alsa	H	6-0	Mickevicius, Savickis, Vasiliauskas (p), Norvaisas V. 2, Dunauskas
13/10/95	Lokomotyvas Vilnius	H	1-2	Norvaisas V.
05/11/95	Inkaras-Grifas Kaunas	A	1-5	Skodminas
10/11/95	Zalgiris Vilnius	H	1-14	Vasiliauskas

APPEARANCES 95/96

	P	Ap	(s)	Gls
Audrius BAGUZIS	D	6	(4)	
Arturas BUDGINAS	D	1	(2)	
Alvydas BUDRYS	M	3	(4)	
Giedrius BULASAS	M	2	(11)	
Nerijus DUNAUSKAS	M	1	(7)	1
Ernestas INDRIUSKA	M	1		
Raimundas KENSTAVICIUS	G		(3)	
Kastytis KVEDARAS	M	14		1
Algis KVEINYS	D	10	(1)	
Algis LUNGYS	G	3		
Alvydas MICKEVICIUS	A	14		2
Anupras MISEIKIS	M	6		1
Alvydas NORVAISAS	M	1	(2)	
Vidas NORVAISAS	A	13		3
Ernestas REGELSKIS	G	11	(1)	
Edvinas SAKALYS	D	14		
Zilvinas SAVICKIS	D	14		1
Saulius SKODMINAS	M	13	(1)	2
Vijunas VASILIAUSKAS	M	14		4
Rimvaldas ZALYS	D	13		

PANERYS VILNIUS

CLUB DIRECTORY

Panerys Vilnius
Siltnamiu 38
2043 Vilnius
tel - (2) 448043/440908/445773
fax - (2) 445888
President - Stanislovas Danisevicius
Secretary - Rimantas Radzevicius
Coach - Saulius Sirmelis
Stadium - Panerys (5,000)

APPEARANCES 95/96

	P	Ap	(s)	Gls
Virginijus ANUSAUSKAS	M	6	(3)	
Giedrius BAREVICIUS	A	26	(2)	2
Virmantas CERNIAUSKAS	M	12		1
Aleksandras DARINCEVAS	A	20	(8)	2
Audrius DILYS	G	6	(1)	
Gytis GELGOTA	M	6	(4)	1
Tadas GRAZIUNAS	D	11	(2)	
Tomas GRAZIUNAS	D	10		1
Aidas GRIGALIUNAS	D	16	(1)	
Aleksandr IGNATJEV (RUS)	G	3	(1)	
Jonas JAKIMAVICIUS	D	23	(2)	
Andrius JUODEIKIS	D		(1)	
Juozas LATANAUSKAS	M	5	(6)	
Pavelas LEUSAS	G	14		
Paulius MALZINSKAS	M	4	(6)	4
Andrius MAZALIAUSKAS	M	1	(3)	1
Virginijus MIKNEVICIUS	M	11		1
Aleksandr MOISEEV (RUS)	D	4	(1)	
Igoris MORINAS	M	28		13
Juozas PURONAS	M		(9)	1
Tomas RAZANAUSKAS	M	13	(1)	7
Remigijus SAKALAS	D	18		2
Kestutis SAMAJAUSKAS	M		(2)	
Irmantas SATAS	G	5	(1)	
Dainius SAULENAS	A	2	(3)	
Vidas SAVICKAS	M	7	(1)	1
Andrejus SEMOROVAS	M	4	(8)	
Vytautas SKIRMANTAS	A	20	(5)	1
Andrejus SOROKINAS	D	25		
Valdas TRAKYS	M		(6)	1
Deimantas ZIUPKA	D	8		

LEAGUE RESULTS 1995/96

19/07/95	Lokomotyvas Vilnius	A	2-0	Morinas 2
28/07/95	Mastis Telsiai	H	2-0	Malzinskas, Barevicius
03/08/95	Tauras Taurage	H	6-0	Sakalas, Morinas 2, Darincevas, Malzinskas 2
12/08/95	Inkaras-Grifas Kaunas	A	0-3	
20/08/95	Zalgiris Vilnius	H	2-3	Cerniauskas, Razanauskas
29/08/95	Ukmerge	A	4-0	Razanauskas 4
23/09/95	Atlantas Klaipeda	H	0-2	
26/09/95	JR Alsa	A	2-0	Morinas, Savickas
01/10/95	FBK Kaunas	A	1-2	Malzinskas
06/10/95	Kareda Siauliai	A	0-2	
14/10/95	Ekranas Panevezys	H	2-1	Morinas, Puronas
24/10/95	Banga Gargzdai	H	3-0	Darincevas, Morinas, Razanauskas
04/11/95	FK Klaipeda	A	3-0	Razanauskas, Morinas 2
11/11/95	Zalgiris II Vilnius	H	1-3	Morinas
31/03/96	Kareda Siauliai	H	0-7	
06/04/96	Inkaras-Grifas Kaunas	A	0-4	
14/04/96	Zalgiris Vilnius	A	0-5	
20/04/96	Ekranas Panevezys	H	1-0	Sakalas
27/04/96	Zalgiris II Vilnius	H	1-0	og (Klisys)
01/05/96	FBK Kaunas	A	0-1	
05/05/96	Atlantas Klaipeda	A	2-1	Skirmantas, Graziunas To.
11/05/96	Kareda Siauliai	A	1-4	Trakys
19/05/96	Inkaras-Grifas Kaunas	H	0-3	
26/05/96	Zalgiris Vilnius	H	2-2	Morinas, Barevicius
30/05/96	Ekranas Panevezys	A	0-1	
04/06/96	Zalgiris II Vilnius	A	2-1	Morinas 2
09/06/96	FBK Kaunas	H	2-1	Gelgota, Mazaliauskas (p)
13/06/96	Atlantas Klaipeda	H	1-1	Miknevicius

TAURAS TAURAGE

CLUB DIRECTORY

Tauras Taurage
Progreso 13
5900 Taurage
tel - 53142/51661
President - Ramunas Samoska
Coach - Jonas Staizys
Stadium - Taurage (5,000)

APPEARANCES 95/96

	P	Ap	(s)	Gls
Kestutis BARANAUSKAS	M		(2)	
Kestutis CERAUSKAS	A		(1)	
Virginijus DAPKUS	M	13		3
Darius JOKUBAITIS	M	2	(9)	2
Vytas JONCA	M	3	(2)	
Robertas JURKSAITIS	M		(1)	
Remigijus KASTRICKAS	M	6	(3)	
Egidijus KATAUSKAS	G	8		
Virginijus KAZLAUSKAS	M		(1)	
Ivan KOGAN (RUS)	M	2		
Gediminas KRENCIUS	D	14		
Eduardas KURSKIS	G	5	(1)	
Vitalijus KUTYRINAS	M	4		
Vidas LAURINAITIS	D	12		1
Dainius LEIPUS	A	8	(1)	2
Mindaugas MATULA	D	14		
Ovidijus MOZURAITIS	D	4		
Egidijus PAULIKAITIS	G	1	(2)	
Eugenijus POSKA	D	8	(2)	
Virginijus RASOVAS	M	14		
Raimondas SAULEVICIUS	D	13		
Oleg SERSTNEV (RUS)	M	12		
Vladimir SMIRNOV (RUS)	A	2		
Darius STAZYS	A	1	(10)	
Arvydas TOLIUSIS	D	8	(1)	

LEAGUE RESULTS 1995/96

16/07/95	Mastis Telsiai	H	0-1	
19/07/95	Zalgiris Vilnius	A	0-7	
04/08/95	Panerys Vilnius	A	0-6	
12/08/95	Atlantas Klaipeda	A	0-5	
20/08/95	FBK Kaunas	H	2-4	Leipus 2 (1p)
04/09/95	JR Alsa	H	1-0	Dapkus
10/09/95	Kareda Siauliai	H	0-6	
16/09/95	Ekranas Panevezys	A	0-7	
23/09/95	Banga Gargzdai	A	1-1	Jokubaitis
01/10/95	Ukmerge	H	2-0	Laurinaitis, Dapkus
07/10/95	FK Klaipeda	A	0-2	
14/10/95	Zalgiris II Vilnius	A	0-2	
22/10/95	Lokomotyvas Vilnius	H	2-0	Dapkus, Jokubaitis
11/11/95	Inkaras-Grifas Kaunas	H	0-4	

UKMERGE

CLUB DIRECTORY

Ukmerge
Deltuvos 33
4120 Ukmerge
tel - (11) 59542/54997
fax - (11) 52751
President - Raimondas Staniulis
Coach - Vytautas Starkus
Stadium - Ukmerge (5,000)

LEAGUE RESULTS 1995/96

20/07/95	Kareda Siauliai	A	0-2	
25/07/95	Ekranas Panevezys	H	2-2	Bankauskas 2
04/08/95	Banga Gargzdai	A	1-2	Verbickas
20/08/95	FK Klaipeda	H	2-1	Juodis, Strumeckas (p)
29/08/95	Panerys Vilnius	H	0-4	
09/09/95	Zalgiris II Vilnius	H	0-5	
17/09/95	Lokomotyvas Vilnius	A	0-0	
23/09/95	Mastis Telsiai	A	0-0	
01/10/95	Tauras Taurage	A	0-2	
06/10/95	Inkaras-Grifas Kaunas	H	0-6	
14/10/95	Zalgiris Vilnius	H	0-4	
22/10/95	JR Alsa	A	2-0	Kuzmickas, Bankauskas
05/11/95	Atlantas Klaipeda	A	0-4	
11/11/95	FBK Kaunas	H	0-2	

APPEARANCES 95/96

	P	Ap	(s)	Gls
Virginijus ANUSAUSKAS	M	3	(3)	
Rolandas BANKAUSKAS	M	7	(5)	3
Pranas BRAZDEIKIS	D	13		
Mindaugas GARDZIJAUSKAS	M		(2)	
Gytis GELGOTA	M	13		
Dainius JUODIS	M	7	(6)	1
Romas KIULKIS	G	13		
Nerijus KUZMICKAS	A	4	(2)	1
Andrius MAZALIAUSKAS	M	6		
Jevgenijus MEDVEDEVAS	A	10		
Vitalis PURONAS	D	5	(4)	
Arunas SADAUSKAS	D	11	(1)	
Gintaras SARKA	D	9		
Irmantas SATAS	G	1	(1)	
Gintas SIRMELIS	M		(1)	
Andrius SPIECIUS	M	4		
Dalius STALELIUNAS	D	5		
Valdas STRUMECKAS	D	13		1
Egidijus VARNAS	A	7		
Vitalis VARNAS	M	1		
Raimundas VERBICKAS	M	8	(2)	1
Dainius ZIGMANTAVICIUS	M	14		

ZALGIRIS VILNIUS

CLUB DIRECTORY

Zalgiris Vilnius
Zolyno 29
2040 Vilnius
tel - (2) 741494/742360
fax - (2) 744187
Year of Formation - 1947
President - Benjaminas Zelkevicius
Secretary - Stasys Paberzis
Coach - Benjaminas Zelkevicius (96/97 - Eugenijus Riabovas)
Stadium - Zalgiris (15,000)

MAJOR HONOURS

League Championship - (2) 1991, 1992.
Domestic Cup - (3) 1991, 1993, 1994.

APPEARANCES 95/96

	P	Ap	(s)	Gls
Virginijus BALTUSNIKAS	D	11	(1)	3
Edgaras JANKAUSKAS	A	27		25
Vytautas KARVELIS	A	17	(6)	11
Alvydas KONCEVICIUS	G	8		
Vytautas LENKUTIS	G		(1)	
Grazvydas MIKULENAS	M	9	(11)	7
Sergejus NOVIKOVAS	D	15	(2)	
Aidas PREIKSAITIS	M	24	(1)	14
Arunas PUKELEVICIUS	M	11	(15)	9
Tomas RAZANAUSKAS	M	13		8
Gintaras RIMKUS	D	25		7
Andrius SKERLA	D	10	(3)	
Rimas SKIRMANTAS	D	4	(2)	
Darius SPETYLA	G	20		
Andrius SRIUBAS	D	5	(1)	
Ramunas STONKUS	D	25		8
Dainius SULIAUSKAS	D	21	(4)	
Andrius TERESKINAS	D	19		2
Valdas URBONAS	M	7	(8)	
Donatas VENCEVICIUS	M	23	(3)	10
Tomas ZVIRGZDAUSKAS	D	14	(1)	

LEAGUE RESULTS 1995/96

16/07/95	Zalgiris II Vilnius	A	1-0	Mikulenas
20/07/95	Tauras Taurage	H	7-0	Jankauskas, Pukelevicius 2, Mikulenas 2, Vencevicius 2
25/07/95	Inkaras-Grifas Kaunas	H	0-0	
04/08/95	Lokomotyvas Vilnius	H	5-2	Karvelis 2, Tereskinas 2 (1p), Rimkus
20/08/95	Panerys Vilnius	A	3-2	Jankauskas, Stonkus, Vencevicius
10/09/95	Atlantas Klaipeda	H	5-1	Rimkus 2, Jankauskas, Preiksaitis, Stonkus
17/09/95	FBK Kaunas	A	2-1	Vencevicius, Stonkus
23/09/95	Kareda Siauliai	A	1-0	Jankauskas
02/10/95	Ekranas Panevezys	H	5-0	Stonkus 2, Baltusnikas, Preiksaitis, Vencevicius
06/10/95	Banga Gargzdai	H	4-0	Jankauskas, Preiksaitis, Baltusnikas, Karvelis
14/10/95	Ukmerge	A	4-0	Vencevicius, Stonkus (p), Pukelevicius, Jankauskas
23/10/95	FK Klaipeda	H	3-0	Mikulenas, Preiksaitis, Karvelis
03/11/95	JR Alsa	H	9-0	Rimkus, Karvelis, Preiksaitis 2, Vencevicius 2, Baltusnikas, Stonkus, Pukelevicius
10/11/95	Mastis Telsiai	A	14-1	Rimkus, Karvelis 2, Jankauskas 5, Preiksaitis 2, Pukelevicius 2, og (Kveinys), Vencevicius
30/03/96	Zalgiris II Vilnius	A	6-0	Mikulenas 2, Jankauskas 3, og (Klisys)
06/04/96	Ekranas Panevezys	A	1-1	Jankauskas
14/04/96	Panerys Vilnius	H	5-0	Preiksaitis, Razanauskas 2, Jankauskas 2
19/04/96	FBK Kaunas	H	3-0	Preiksaitis, Razanauskas, Karvelis
28/04/96	Atlantas Klaipeda	H	5-1	Karvelis, Preiksaitis, Jankauskas, Rimkus, Pukelevicius
01/05/96	Kareda Siauliai	A	1-1	Vencevicius
05/05/96	Inkaras-Grifas Kaunas	H	1-3	Preiksaitis
11/05/96	Zalgiris II Vilnius	H	9-1	Jankauskas 4, Razanauskas, Pukelevicius, Rimkus, Mikulenas, Karvelis
19/05/96	Ekranas Panevezys	H	3-0	Stonkus, Razanauskas, Preiksaitis
26/05/96	Panerys Vilnius	A	2-2	Jankauskas 2 (1p)
20/05/96	FBK Kaunas	A	1-0	Razanauskas
04/06/96	Atlantas Klaipeda	A	4-3	Razanauskas 2, Pukelevicius, Preiksaitis
09/06/96	Kareda Siauliai	H	2-1	Jankauskas, Karvelis
13/06/96	Inkaras-Grifas Kaunas	A	0-2	

ZALGIRIS II VILNIUS

CLUB DIRECTORY

Zalgiris II Vilnius
Zolyno 29
2040 Vilnius
tel - (2) 741494/742360
fax - (2) 744187
President - Benjaminas Zelkevicius
Secretary - Audrius Dilys
Coach - Gintas Kaledinskas
Stadium - Vingis (3,000)

APPEARANCES 95/96

	P	Ap	(s)	Gls
Laimonas BYTAUTAS	A	21	(6)	4
Mindaugas CEPAS	A	5	(2)	1
Nerijus CIULADA	M	12	(8)	1
Rolandas DZIUAKSTAS	D	4	(2)	
Tomas JAKUTIS	G	7		
Arturas JANUSKEVICIUS	D	20	(1)	2
Girius KALVAITIS	D	5		
Vidas KAUSPADAS	M	24	(2)	3
Saulius KIJANSKAS	M	3	(15)	
Rimas KLISYS	D	25		2
Marijusas KRIUKOVSKIS	M		(7)	
Dainius KRUMINAS	M	2	(5)	
Vytautas LENKUTIS	G	1	(1)	
Nerijus MERKELIS	G	1		
Ramunas MERKELIS	G	19	(1)	
Nerijus RADZIUS	M	22		
Deividas SEMBERAS	M	1	(4)	
Virginijus SINKEVICIUS	D	13	(2)	1
Andrius SKERLA	D	14		1
Andrius SRIUBAS	D	13		
Arturas STESKO	M	26		4
Igoris STESKO	M	28		2
Nerijus VASILIAUSKAS	M	20	(6)	5
Benjaminas ZELKEVICIUS	A	22	(3)	2

LEAGUE RESULTS 1995/96

16/07/95	Zalgiris Vilnius	H	0-1	
20/07/95	Atlantas Klaipeda	A	0-1	
25/07/95	FBK Kaunas	H	1-6	Klisys
05/08/95	Kareda Siauliai	H	0-3	
12/08/95	Ekranas Panevezys	A	2-2	Kauspadas 2
19/08/95	Banga Gargzdai	A	1-2	Ciulada
09/09/95	Ukmerge	A	5-0	Vasiliauskas 3, Bytautas 2
16/09/95	FK Klaipeda	H	2-0	Stesko A. 2
30/09/95	Lokomotyvas Vilnius	A	1-1	Bytautas
07/10/95	Mastis Telsiai	H	2-2	Zelkevicius, Vasiliauskas
14/10/95	Tauras Taurage	H	2-0	Skerla, Stesko I.
22/10/95	Inkaras-Grifas Kaunas	H	0-2	
07/11/95	JR Alsa	A	3-0	Januskevicius, Klisys, Bytautas
11/11/95	Panerys Vilnius	A	3-1	Slksevicius, Zelkevicius, Stesko A.
30/03/96	Zalgiris Vilnius	H	0-6	
06/04/96	Atlantas Klaipeda	A	0-2	
13/04/96	Ekranas Panevezys	H	2-2	Vasiliauskas, Januskevicius
19/04/96	Kareda Siauliai	A	0-3	
27/04/96	Panerys Vilnius	A	0-1	
01/05/96	Inkaras-Grifas Kaunas	H	0-3	
05/05/96	FBK Kaunas	A	0-2	
11/05/96	Zalgiris Vilnius	A	1-9	Stesko I.
19/05/96	Atlantas Klaipeda	H	0-0	
25/05/96	Ekranas Panevezys	A	1-1	Stesko A.
30/05/96	Kareda Siauliai	H	0-1	
04/06/96	Panerys Vilnius	H	1-2	Kauspadas
09/06/96	Inkaras-Grifas Kaunas	A	0-5	
13/06/96	FBK Kaunas	H	1-2	Cepas

PROMOTED CLUBS

SECOND DIVISION FINAL TABLE 95/96

		Pd	W	D	L	F	A	Pt	GD
1	Ranga-Politechnika Kaunas	24	17	4	3	62	19	55	+43
2	Interas Visaginas	24	16	5	3	36	6	53	+30
3	Nevezis-Fostra Kedainiai	24	15	3	6	38	21	48	+17
4	Laisve Silute	24	14	4	6	35	30	46	+5
5	Daisotra Alytus	24	12	6	6	39	20	42	+19
6	Klevas-Sakalas Siauliai	24	10	8	6	24	14	38	+10
7	Volmeta-KKI Kaunas	24	10	8	6	38	16	38	+22
8	Suduva Marijampole	24	9	4	11	35	37	31	-2
9	Andas Vilnius	24	8	4	12	24	43	28	-19
10	Lietava Jonava	24	8	1	15	21	41	25	-20
11	Kauno Jegeriai	24	4	4	16	13	37	16	-24
12	Savinge Kaisiadorys	24	4	3	17	18	48	15	-30
13	Minija Kretinga	24	1	4	19	10	61	7	-51

DIVISION 1 B RELEGATION GROUP

		Pd	W	D	L	F	A	Pt	GD
1	Banga Gargzdai	12	8	2	2	17	11	32	+6
2	Lokomotyvas Vilnius	12	8	0	4	24	11	30	+13
3	Tauras Taurage	12	5	6	1	9	3	26	+6
4	Ukmerge	12	6	2	4	19	13	25	+6
5	Mastis Telsiai	12	3	4	5	16	14	18	+2
6	Alsa-Panerys Vilnius	12	1	5	6	7	14	14	-7
7	JR Klaipeda	12	0	3	9	3	29	11	-26

PROMOTION/RELEGATION PLAY-OFFS

(Division 1)
Banga Gargzdai 1, Zalgiris II Vilnius 1
Zalgiris II Vilnius 2, Banga Gargzdai 1
(Zalgiris II Vilnius 3-2)

(Division 1 B)
Alsa-Panerys Vilnius 0, Nevezis-Fostra Kedainai 0 (aet; 4-3 on pens.)

LUXEMBOURG

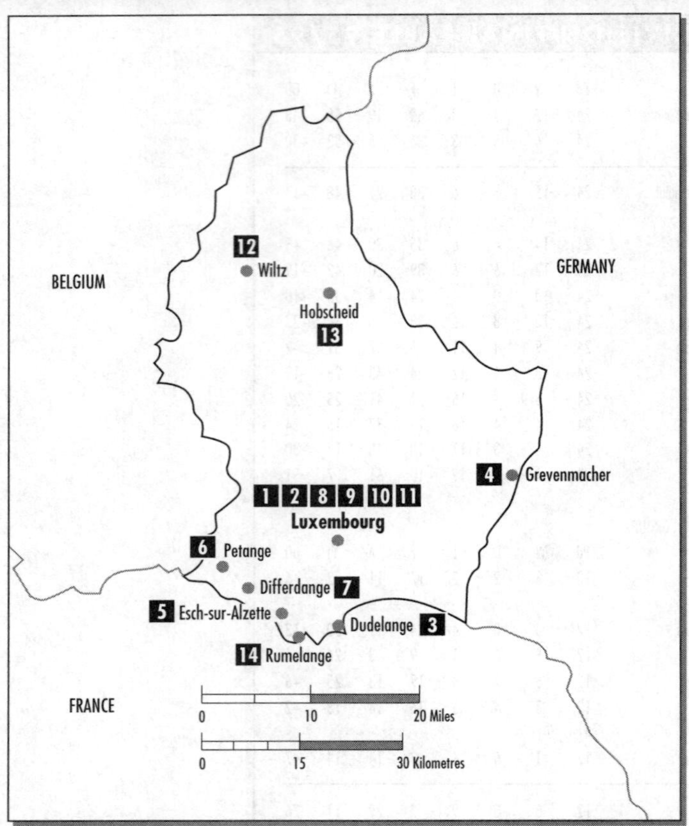

1	ARIS BONNEVOIE	659
2	AVENIR BEGGEN	660
3	F91 DUDELANGE	661
4	CS GREVENMACHER	662
5	JEUNESSE ESCH	663
6	CS PETANGE	664
7	RED BOYS DIFFERDANGE	665
8	FC RODANGE 91	666
9	SPORA LUXEMBOURG	667
10	SPORTING MERTZIG	668
11	UNION LUXEMBOURG	669
12	FC WILTZ 71	670
13	CS HOBSCHEID	671
14	US RUMELANGE	671

PHILIPP EXTENDS CONTRACT TO 2002

Jeunesse Esch win gripping title struggle

FEDERATION DIRECTORY

Fédération Luxembourgeoise de Football
50 rue de Strasbourg, 2560 Luxembourg

tel - 488665/488666 | Year of Formation - 1908
tlx - 2426 flf lu | President - Norbert Konter
fax - 400201 | Secretary - Joël Wolff

Stadium - Municipal, Luxembourg (9,200)

It was a case of *déjà vu* in Luxembourg's First Division as Jeunesse Esch and Grevenmacher repeated their head-to-head championship battle of the season before. Sadly for Grevenmacher, the outcome was frustratingly similar. They had been denied their first ever national title on goal difference in 1994/95. Now they finished runners-up again, just one point below Jeunesse, whose victory was the 23rd in their history.

Throughout the season it had been nip and tuck between the best two teams in the country. But in the final straight Jeunesse, led by ex-Union Luxembourg coach Alex Pecqueur, held their nerve the better and just edged home. The all-important match came one round before the end when the two challengers met face to face on Grevenmacher's home ground. A victory would have all but guaranteed a first title for the home side. Before a record crowd of 3,824 they got off to the perfect start with a goal from German Achim Wilbois, whose only other goal of the campaign, strangely enough, had decided the previous meeting between the two clubs in Esch. But on this occasion Jeunesse equalised - with a Dany Theis penalty just before half-time - and as Grevenmacher's mental strength dwindled in the second half, the defending champions were able to keep the score at 1-1 through to the final whistle - a result good enough to maintain their one-point lead over Grevenmacher at the top of the table.

A week later Jeunesse were the champions again, treating a crowd of 4,000 to a thoroughly convincing 3-0 victory over old adversaries Avenir Beggen. There were euphoric scenes in the border town as the locals bade farewell to Germany-bound Manuel Cardoni amidst the joy of yet another hardfought championship success.

On the same day, Grevenmacher thrashed CS Pétange 5-1, but the result served only to relegate their opponents, who were plunged beyond the point of no return as Aris Bonnevoie simultaneously beat third-placed Union Luxembourg 1-0 to leapfrog over Pétange into the safety zone. The minds of the Union players were evidently elsewhere. They had a much more important engagement the following week - against champions Jeunesse in the Luxembourg Cup final. Union had reached the final courtesy of two outstanding 1-0 away wins against Avenir Beggen and Cup holders Grevenmacher, and they deservedly took the trophy for the tenth time (in 20 finals) with a professionally crafted 3-1 victory over a weary-looking Jeunesse, whose 'double' dream thus died,

INTERNATIONAL HONOURS

European Championship: 1964

LEAGUE CHAMPIONSHIP RESULTS 95/96

		1	2	3	4	5	6	7	8	9	10	11	12
1	Aris Bonnevoie		0-5	0-1	3-3	1-2	1-1	5-1	0-1	0-4	1-3	1-0	2-4
2	Avenir Beggen	1-1		3-2	1-0	2-6	2-0	1-1	3-0	3-2	0-1	0-1	3-1
3	F91 Dudelange	0-0	2-0		0-3	5-0	4-1	2-2	5-0	1-0	3-4	1-1	3-0
4	CS Grevenmacher	3-1	6-4	2-0		1-1	2-1	1-2	1-0	1-1	2-1	0-0	1-0
5	Jeunesse Esch	7-1	3-0	1-0	0-1		3-0	3-0	3-2	5-0	3-0	0-1	2-0
6	CS Pétange	0-2	2-1	0-1	1-5	1-3		1-0	3-1	0-1	1-0	0-8	1-0
7	Red Boys Differdange	4-4	0-4	0-4	1-6	1-0	7-1		0-3	2-7	0-4	0-7	1-3
8	FC Rodange 91	0-2	2-0	2-2	0-0	0-4	1-0	3-0		1-3	2-2	0-3	1-0
9	Spora Luxembourg	6-1	1-1	2-2	0-2	1-6	1-0	1-1	0-1		3-1	0-1	1-3
10	Sporting Mertzig	2-1	0-3	2-1	0-2	0-0	2-1	3-2	1-0	1-0		0-2	0-0
11	Union Luxembourg	3-3	2-1	0-2	1-2	1-1	1-0	5-2	1-0	0-0	2-2		1-2
12	FC Wiltz 71	1-2	0-0	0-2	1-0	1-6	0-5	4-2	3-2	1-1	0-3	1-2	

LEAGUE CHAMPIONSHIP FINAL TABLE 95/96

			Home					Away					Total						
		Pd	W	D	L	F	A	W	D	L	F	A	W	D	L	F	A	Pt	GD
1	Jeunesse Esch	22	9	0	2	30	5	6	3	2	29	14	15	3	4	59	19	48	+40
2	CS Grevenmacher	22	7	3	1	20	11	7	2	2	24	8	14	5	3	44	19	47	+25
3	Union Luxembourg	22	4	4	3	17	15	8	2	1	26	3	12	6	4	43	18	42	+25
4	F91 Dudelange	22	6	3	2	26	11	5	2	4	17	12	11	5	6	43	23	38	+20
5	Sporting Mertzig	22	6	2	3	11	12	5	2	4	21	17	11	4	7	32	29	37	+3
6	Avenir Beggen	22	6	2	3	19	15	3	2	6	19	18	9	4	9	38	33	31	+5
7	Spora Luxembourg	22	3	3	5	16	19	4	3	4	19	15	7	6	9	35	34	27	+1
8	FC Rodange 91	22	4	3	4	12	16	3	0	8	10	20	7	3	12	22	36	24	-14
9	FC Wiltz 71	22	3	2	6	12	25	4	1	6	13	16	7	3	12	25	41	24	-16
10	Aris Bonnevoie	22	2	2	7	14	25	3	4	4	18	27	5	6	11	32	52	21	-20
11	CS Pétange	22	5	0	6	10	22	1	1	9	10	24	6	1	15	20	46	19	-26
12	Red Boys Differdange	22	2	1	8	16	43	1	3	7	13	29	3	4	15	29	72	13	-43

as it had done a year earlier, in the last match of the season. Union's matchwinner was half-fit striker Serge Makoumbou, who came off the substitutes' bench with half an hour to go and struck home the two decisive late goals for Gilbert Neumann's team.

Only one Union player, defender Marc Birsens, was called up to the Luxembourg national team during the season. And only goalkeeper Paul Koch from league runners-up Grevenmacher featured in Paul Philipp's team. But there was plenty of representation from Jeunesse Esch

DOMESTIC CUP RESULTS

1/32 FINALS
Beckerich 0, Aris Bonnevoie 6
Canach 0, Union Luxembourg 6
Remich 0, CS Grevenmacher 1
Sanem 1, Red Boys Differdange 8
Aspelt 0, FC Rodange 91 3
Schifflange 0, F91 Dudelange 5
Hosingen 0, FC Wiltz 71 4
Ell 0, Spora Luxembourg 10
Walferdange 0, Jeunesse Esch 9
Consdorf 0, Sporting Mertzig 7
Perlé 1, CS Pétange 4
Kopstal 0, Hautcharage 8
Beyren 1, Victoria Rosport 8
RM Luxembourg 0, Young Boys Diekirch 1
Strassen 0, Swift Hesperange 6
Echternach 3, Progrès Niedercorn 5 (aet)
Weiler 2, FC Mondercange 4
Beles 0, Etzella Ettelbrück 7
Schieren 2, Tricolore Gasperich 2 (aet; 1-4 on pens.)
Harlingen/Tarchamps 0, Fola Esch 5
Fels 2, Koeppchen Wormeldange 6 (aet)
Kehlen 1, CS Hollerich 6
Red Black 1, FC Hamm 37 4
Rambrouch 3, Bertrange 1
Steinfort 0, Mertert/Wasserbillig 4
CS Oberkorn 2, US Esch 0
Weiswampach 1, Itzig 3
Sandweiler 4, Brouch 2
Moutfort 0, Eischen 2
Koerich 1, AS Differdange 6
Redange 0, CS Hobscheid 2
Vianden 0, Avenir Beggen 5 (aet)

1/16 FINALS
Rambrouch 0, Mertert/Wasserbillig 3
AS Differdange 1, Red Boys Differdange 7
Swift Hesperange 1, CS Grevenmacher 4 (aet)
FC Mondercange 0, Spora Luxembourg 4
Tricolore Gasperich 0, FC Rodange 91 2
Hautcharage 0, Victoria Rosport 1
Sandweiler 1, Etzella Ettelbrück 3
Progrès Niedercorn 2, CS Hollerich 0
Fola Esch 0, Union Luxembourg 4
CS Oberkorn 0, Koeppchen Wormeldange 3
FC Hamm 37 3, FC Wiltz 71 1
Itzig 0, Jeunesse Esch 4
CS Hobscheid 1, Young Boys Diekirch 0
Aris Bonnevoie 3, CS Pétange 4
Eischen 0, Avenir Beggen 5
Sporting Mertzig 2, F91 Dudelange 1

1/8 FINALS
Etzella Ettelbrück 1, Progrès Niedercorn 2
Avenir Beggen 0, Union Luxembourg 1
Spora Luxembourg 0, CS Grevenmacher 3
CS Pétange 1, Red Boys Differdange 3
FC Rodange 91 0, Victoria Rosport 0 (5-4 on pens.)
Jeunesse Esch 3, Sporting Mertzig 1
Koeppchen Wormeldange 2, CS Hobscheid 1
Mertert/Wasserbillig 0, FC Hamm 37 0 (3-4 on pens.)

QUARTER-FINALS
FC Rodange 91 2, Jeunesse Esch 4
CS Grevenmacher 0, Union Luxembourg 1
FC Hamm 37 0, Koeppchen Wormeldange 2
Red Boys Differdange 2, Progrès Niedercorn 0

SEMI-FINALS
Red Boys Differdange 1, Jeunesse Esch 6
Koeppchen Wormeldange 1, Union Luxembourg 5

FINAL
25/05/96, Luxembourg
UNION LUXEMBOURG 3
Mangen (19), Makoumbou (72, 90)
JEUNESSE ESCH 1 Theis (40p)
referee - Wiltgen
UNION LUXEMBOURG - Van Rijswijck; Birsens, Feyder, Schammel (Makoumbou 61; Carème 90), Afrika, Feiereisen, Mangen, Deville, Kunen, Kharoubi, Lahéry.
JEUNESSE ESCH - Felgen; Lamborelle, Schaack (Thill 38), Wagner, Ganser, Scuto, Theis, Cardoni, Meylender, Marchione (Amodio 75), Morocutti.

PLAYERS OF THE SEASON

MANUEL CARDONI

For the second season in a row Manuel Cardoni was voted as Luxembourg's Player of the Year. It was the icing on the cake of a magnificent campaign, which saw the gifted 24-year-old play-maker attain the dream of every Luxembourg player - to play full-time with a major foreign club. Cardoni's move to Germany's Bayer Leverkusen, on a two-year contract, makes him only the third Luxembourg footballer - after Nico Braun (Schalke) and Roby Langers (Borussia Mönchengladbach) - to play in the Bundesliga. He earned his move with a series of strong performances for both Jeunesse Esch and the Luxembourg national team. Jeunesse's successful title defence, to which he contributed 13 goals and numerous assists, enabled him to leave for Germany on a real high.

Marc Birsens

MARC BIRSENS

Shy and unassuming off the field, Union Luxembourg defender Marc Birsens has for years been one of the most commanding and influential players in Paul Philipp's national team. He was in particularly outstanding form during the 1995/96 season. With Birsens marshalling the defence, Luxembourg conceded just three goals in four games. And there was much to be proud of at club level too as he led Union to third place in the league, victory in the Cup and a return to Europe after a two-year absence. It was to be Birsens' last season with Union. CS Grevenmacher have turned to the 30-year-old libero as the man who will finally turn their burning championship ambitions into reality.

NATIONAL TEAM APPEARANCES 95/96

Coach - Paul PHILIPP	MLT	BLS	TCH	MAR	SUI	Cps	Gls
Paul KOCH (07/06/68) - CS Grevenmacher	G	G	G	G	G	20	-
Jean VANEK (19/01/69) - Avenir Beggen	D	D	D	D	D	18	-
Carlo WEIS (04/12/58) - Sporting Mertzig	D	D	D	D	D	80	1
Frank DEVILLE (12/08/70) - Avenir Beggen/1.FC Union Berlin (GER)	D	D	M59	M73		9	-
Marc BIRSENS (17/09/66) - Union Luxembourg	D	D		D	D	35	-
Jeff STRASSER (05/10/74) - FC Metz (FRA)	D	D	D	D	D	14	-
Jeff SAIBENE (13/09/68) - FC Aarau (SUI)	M	M	M90		M	30	-
Guy HELLERS (10/10/64) - R Standard Liège (BEL)	M	M	M			49	2
Luc HOLTZ (14/04/69) - Avenir Beggen	M84	M90	M76	M46		19	1
Joël GROFF (11/09/68) - F91 Dudelange	M68		M	M88	M	30	-
Roby LANGERS (01/08/60) - Eintracht Trier (GER)	A	A81	A	A	A87	64	8
Dany THEIS (11/09/67) - Jeunesse Esch	s68	s81	s59	s88	s41	12	-
Manuel CARDONI (22/09/72) - Jeunesse Esch	s84	s72	s90	M	M	17	2
Patrick MOROCUTTI (19/02/68) - Jeunesse Esch		A72		s46		18	-
Marc LAMBORELLE (13/10/71) - Jeunesse Esch		s90		M	M	4	-
Ralph FERRON (13/05/72) - Avenir Beggen			D			9	-
Claude GANSER (07/09/67) - Jeunesse Esch			s76	s73	M41	5	-
Stefano FANELLI (20/10/69) - F91 Dudelange					s87	5	1

and Avenir Beggen. Beggen had endured a miserable season in the league, but they did achieve the rare distinction of winning a European tie, albeit by default, when they stole through to the first round of the UEFA Cup after Swedish team Örebro had been found guilty of fielding too many foreigners.

But while Luxembourg's clubs continue to live off scraps, the national team have made considerable strides up the European pecking order. Following the sensational 1-0 triumph over the Czech Republic the previous spring, Paul Philipp's men consolidated their new-found status by taking four more points in their European Championship group with a 1-0 victory over Malta and a 0-0 draw with Belarus.

Luc Holtz's début international goal gave his team a deserved 'double' over Malta, and the draw against Belarus took Luxembourg's points tally into double figures - quite an achievement for a country of such limited footballing resources. The Euro '96 trail ended with a 0-3 'revenge' defeat by the Czechs, but there was no shame in that. Indeed, the FLF, favouring continuity, decided to reward coach Philipp by extending his contract for another six years. Further proof of the team's progress arrived in March with a 1-1 draw at home to a Switzerland side gearing up for the European Championship finals. Luxembourg led for most of the game through Manuel Cardoni's early goal, and it was only an unfortunate late equaliser that spared Swiss blushes and prevented the home side from registering yet another sensational victory.

Nevertheless, that 1-1 draw extended Luxembourg's unbeaten home record to beyond a year. No wonder, then, that Luxembourg's sports journalists voted Paul Philipp's side as the country's Team of the Year, with Belgian-based midfielder Guy Hellers taking the Sportsman of the Year crown, one place ahead of world-class skier Marc Girardelli.

EUROPEAN CUPS RESULTS 95/96

CUP-WINNERS' CUP

● CS GREVENMACHER

Preliminary round KR (ISL)

H 3-2 Jungblut (8, 52), Alves Silva (58)
Koch; Giesser, Wolf, Petry, Lauer, Funck, Jungblut (Dias 80), Thomé, Schneider, Wilbois, Alves Silva.

A 0-2
Koch; Klodt, Wolf, Giesser (Dias 46), Petry, Funck, Thomé, Wilbois, Alves Silva, Jungblut, Schneider.

UEFA CUP

● JEUNESSE ESCH

Preliminary round FC LUGANO (SUI)

H 0-0
Felgen; Nigra, Schaack, Lamborelle, Wagner, Ganser (Meyers 52), Scuto, Cardoni, Theis, Marchione, Morocutti.

A 0-4
Felgen; Wagner (Thill 74), Nigra, Lamborelle, Meylender, Cardoni, Scuto, Theis (Braun 80), Amodio, Morocutti (De Sousa 80), Marchione.

● AVENIR BEGGEN

Preliminary round ÖREBRO SK (SWE)

A 0-0
Konsbrück; Delangre, Moreira, Posing, Deville, Wilhelm, Heiles (Peters 89), Picard, Scholten, Holtz, Krahen.

H 1-1 Holtz (21) (later awarded as 3-0)
Konsbrück; Delangre, Vanek, Wilhelm, Posing, Deville, Heiles, Scholten, Holtz, Krahen, Muratovic (Biver 87).

1st round RC LENS (FRA)

H 0-7
Konsbrück; Ferron, Delangre, Deville, Posing, Heiles (Libar 78), Krahen, Scholten, Vanek, Holtz (Gomes 75), Muratovic (Biver 64).

A 0-6
Konsbrück; De Pina (Heiles 74), Delangre, Ferron, Deville, Posing, Peters (Wilhelm 58), Scholten, Vanek, Holtz, Muratovic.

NATIONAL TEAM RESULTS 95/96

Date	Opponent		Venue	Score	Scorers
06/09/95	Malta (ECQ)	H	Luxembourg	1-0	Holtz (45)
11/10/95	Belarus (ECQ)	H	Luxembourg	0-0	
15/11/95	Czech Republic (ECQ)	A	Prague	0-3	
08/02/96	Morocco	A	Rabat	0-2	
13/03/96	Switzerland	H	Luxembourg	1-1	Cardoni (8)

TOP SCORERS

18 Mikhail ZARITSKI (Avenir Beggen)
17 Patrick MOROCUTTI (Jeunesse Esch)
13 Manuel CARDONI (Jeunesse Esch)
12 Laurent CAREME (Union Luxembourg)
11 Marco MORGANTE (F91 Dudelange)
10 Lidio ALVES SILVA (CS Grevenmacher)
9 Gordon BRAUN (Union Luxembourg)
Didier CHAILLOU (Spora Luxembourg)
Cosimo BARNABO (CS Pétange)
Dany THEIS (Jeunesse Esch)
Franco IOVINO (FC Wiltz 71)

ARIS BONNEVOIE

CLUB DIRECTORY

FC Aris Bonnevoie
14 rue des Prés
2349 Luxembourg
tel - 485998
fax - 408922
Year of Formation - 1922
President - Laurent Mosar
Secretary - André Friedrich
Coach - Jean Noël; Norbert Hoor (96/97 - Jean-Claude Wagener)
Stadium - Camille-Polfer (3,000)

MAJOR HONOURS
League Championship - (3) 1964, 1966, 1972.
Domestic Cup - (1) 1967.

APPEARANCES 95/96

	P	Ap	(s)	Gls
Adriano ABBRUZZESE (ITA)	M		(2)	
Michel BECHET	D	19		
François BRANDAO	A	10	(1)	6
Dragoljub BRNOVIC (YUG)	M	18		2
Adnan DERVISEVIC (YUG)	M	14	(1)	6
Pedro DOS SANTOS (POR)	A	8	(4)	4
Patrick GRETTNICH	A	15	(2)	7
Norbert HOOR (GER)	D	7	(1)	
Wolf-Peter KLOHE (GER)	M	10	(1)	
Patrick LEOGRANDE	M	21		2
Frank LESSURE	D	21		
Frank LUCHETTI	M	1	(3)	
Thierry PETITJEAN	M	1	(2)	
Samir RASTODER (YUG)	A	2	(7)	1
Marc REUTER	G	22		
Frédéric RIOT (FRA)	D	19		2
Marc SCHODER	D	14	(2)	
Luís SOARES (POR)	A		(1)	
Nene Carlos SOARES (POR)	A	11	(4)	
Christophe SOUMANN	A	5		
Steve THULL	D	3	(3)	
Laurent WARCKEN	M		(1)	
Michel ZACCARIA	M	21	(1)	2

LEAGUE RESULTS 1995/96

16/09/95	CS Grevenmacher	H	3-3	Dervisevic 2 (1p), Brandao
20/09/95	Avenir Beggen	A	1-1	Grettnich
24/09/95	Jeunesse Esch	H	1-2	Zaccaria
01/10/95	CS Pétange	A	2-0	Dervisevic (p), Zaccaria
15/10/95	Spora Luxembourg	H	0-4	
22/10/95	FC Wiltz 71	H	2-4	Dos Santos 2
05/11/95	F91 Dudelange	A	0-0	
26/11/95	Red Boys Differdange	H	5-1	Grettnich 2, Riot, Dos Santos, Brnovic
03/12/95	Sporting Mertzig	A	1-2	Grettnich
10/12/95	FC Rodange 91	H	0-1	
17/12/95	Union Luxembourg	A	3-3	Riot, Dos Santos, Grettnich
03/03/96	Avenir Beggen	H	0-5	
09/03/96	Jeunesse Esch	A	1-7	Dervisevic (p)
17/03/96	CS Pétange	H	1-1	Brnovic
24/03/96	Spora Luxembourg	A	1-6	Brandao
31/03/96	CS Grevenmacher	A	1-3	Grettnich
14/04/96	FC Wiltz 71	A	2-1	Grettnich, Brandao
21/04/96	F91 Dudelange	H	0-1	
28/04/96	Red Boys Differdange	A	4-4	Dervisevic 2 (1p), Leogrande, Rastoder
05/05/96	Sporting Mertzig	H	1-3	Brandao
12/05/96	FC Rodange 91	A	2-0	Brandao 2
19/05/96	Union Luxembourg	H	1-0	Leogrande

AVENIR BEGGEN

CLUB DIRECTORY

FC Avenir Beggen
BP 382
2013 Luxembourg
tel - 338243
fax - 422009
Year of Formation - 1915
President - Théo Mersch
Secretary - Albert Adams
Coach - Jacky Perignon; Théo Scholten & Etienne Delangre (96/97 - Michel Clément)
Stadium - Beggen (5,500)

MAJOR HONOURS

League Championship - (6)
1969, 1982, 1984, 1986, 1993, 1994.
Domestic Cup - (6)
1983, 1984, 1987, 1992, 1993, 1994.

APPEARANCES 95/96

	P	Ap	(s)	Gls
Luc BIVER	M	6	(6)	1
Lionel DA SILVA (POR)	D	5	(5)	
Carlos DE PINA LOPES (POR)	D	4	(1)	
Etienne DELANGRE (BEL)	D	9		
Frank DEVILLE	D	8	(1)	1
Georges EIDEN	G	1	(1)	
Ralph FERRON	D	10		1
Patrick GOMES	M	3		
John HEILES	A	4	(4)	
Steve HEWITT	M	1	(2)	
Luc HOLTZ	M	15		2
Nico KONSBRÜCK	G	21		
Markus KRAHEN (GER)	A	12	(1)	8
Claude LIBAR	M	7		2
Gabriel LOPES (POR)	M	11		1
Steve MEYER	A	8	(3)	2
Jaba MOREIRA (POR)	M	7	(6)	
Esmir MURATOVIC (YUG)	M	11	(6)	1
Roby PETERS	M	3	(5)	
Patrick POSING	D	21		
Théo SCHOLTEN	M	21		
Jean VANEK	D	21		1
Alex WILHELM	D	16	(1)	
Mikhail ZARITSKI (RUS)	A	17	(5)	18

LEAGUE RESULTS 1995/96

20/09/95	Aris Bonnevoie	H	1-1	Ferron
23/09/95	FC Wiltz 71	A	0-0	
01/10/95	F91 Dudelange	H	3-2	Muratovic, Deville, Zaritski
15/10/95	Red Boys Differdange	A	4-0	Krahen 3, Holtz
21/10/95	Sporting Mertzig	H	0-1	
25/10/95	CS Pétange	A	1-2	Vanek
05/11/95	FC Rodange 91	A	0-2	
26/11/95	Union Luxembourg	H	0-1	
03/12/95	CS Grevenmacher	A	4-6	Zaritski 2, Biver, Krahen
10/12/95	Spora Luxembourg	H	3-2	Krahen 3
17/12/95	Jeunesse Esch	H	2-6	Zaritski 2
03/03/96	Aris Bonnevoie	A	5-0	Zaritski 3, Krahen, Meyer
09/03/96	FC Wiltz 71	H	3-1	Zaritski 2, Libar
17/03/96	F91 Dudelange	A	0-2	
24/03/96	Red Boys Differdange	H	1-1	Meyer
31/03/96	CS Pétange	H	2-0	Zaritski 2
14/04/96	Sporting Mertzig	A	3-0	Zaritski 2, Libar
21/04/96	FC Rodange 91	H	3-0	Zaritski 2, Lopes
27/04/96	Union Luxembourg	A	1-2	Zaritski
05/05/96	CS Grevenmacher	H	1-0	Zaritski
10/05/96	Spora Luxembourg	A	1-1	Holtz
19/05/96	Jeunesse Esch	A	0-3	

F91 DUDELANGE

CLUB DIRECTORY

F91 Dudelange
14 rue Eugène Conrad
3445 Dudelange
tel - 514267
fax - 512583
Year of Formation - 1991
President - Tony Manderscheid
Secretary - Mil Manderschied
Coach - Philippe Guérard; Claude Hausknecht
(96/97 - Benny Reiter)
Stadium - Jos Nosbaum (5,000)

APPEARANCES 95/96

	P	Ap	(s)	Gls
Thorvic AMARI (FRA)	A	10	(2)	4
Roger BAMBI (FRA)	D		(1)	
Pedro BORREGA	A	8	(6)	1
Rico CARDONI	M	10	(9)	2
Serge CARDONI	D	3	(8)	
Philippe COHY (BEL)	D	2	(3)	
Stefano FANELLI	A	19	(2)	8
Miguel FERRAZ	M		(2)	
Angelo FIORUCCI	M	12	(8)	
Marco GALLI (FRA)	D	22		2
Frank GOERGEN	M	11	(3)	
Stephan GOFFINET (BEL)	G		(1)	
Manuel GOMES (FRA)	M	19		1
Joël GROFF	M	17	(1)	
Gerry HUTMACHER	D	6		1
Evariste KABONGO (BEL)	A	20	(2)	7
Marco MORGANTE (FRA)	M	22		11
José NORA FAVITA (POR)	D	22		
Franck PETITFRERE (FRA)	M	17	(2)	6
Carlos PINTO (POR)	M		(1)	
Serge ROHMANN	G	22		

LEAGUE RESULTS 1995/96

17/09/95	FC Rodange 91	H	5-0	Amari 2, Fanelli (p), Galli, Morgante
20/09/95	Union Luxembourg	A	2-0	Amari, Morgante
24/09/95	CS Grevenmacher	H	0-3	
01/10/95	Avenir Beggen	A	2-3	Morgante, Amari
15/10/95	Jeunesse Esch	H	5-0	Fanelli 2 (1p), Kabongo, Petitfrère, Morgante
22/10/95	CS Pétange	A	1-0	Fanelli (p)
05/11/95	Aris Bonnevoie	H	0-0	
26/11/95	FC Wiltz 71	A	2-0	Kabongo, Gomes
03/12/95	Spora Luxembourg	A	2-2	Kabongo, Fanelli
10/12/95	Red Boys Differdange	H	2-2	Petitfrère, Fanelli
03/03/96	Union Luxembourg	H	1-1	Morgante
09/03/96	CS Grevenmacher	A	0-2	
17/03/96	Avenir Beggen	H	2-0	Borrega, Morgante
20/03/96	Sporting Mertzig	A	1-2	Morgante
24/03/96	Jeunesse Esch	A	0-1	
31/03/96	FC Rodange 91	A	2-2	Morgante, Petitfrère
14/04/96	CS Pétange	H	4-1	Fanelli 2, Kabongo, Petitfrère
21/04/96	Aris Bonnevoie	A	1-0	Petitfrère
28/04/96	FC Wiltz 71	H	3-0	Hutmacher, Morgante, Galli
05/05/96	Spora Luxembourg	H	1-0	Kabongo
12/05/96	Red Boys Differdange	A	4-0	Petitfrère, Kabongo, Morgante, Cardoni R.
19/05/96	Sporting Mertzig	H	3-4	Kabongo, Cardoni R., Morgante

CS GREVENMACHER

CLUB DIRECTORY

Club Sportif Grevenmacher
3 rue de la Congrégation
1352 Luxembourg
tel - 4782635/6
fax - 475241
Year of Formation - 1909
President - Jos Theysen
Secretary - Norry Stoltz
Coach - Alfons Jochem
Stadium - Op Flohr (4,500)

MAJOR HONOURS
Domestic Cup - (1) 1995.

APPEARANCES 95/96

	P	Ap	(s)	Gls
Lidio ALVES SILVA (POR)	A	21		10
Peter BEHR (GER)	A	11	(10)	6
Adelino DIAS	A	13	(9)	2
Nico FUNCK	D	21		2
Laurent GIESSER	D	12	(9)	
Karl-Heinz GRÜN (GER)	D	6	(3)	
Jerry JUNGBLUT	A	9	(9)	3
Krzysztof KEMPNY (POL)	M	11	(5)	2
Elmar KLODT (GER)	D	13	(1)	
Paul KOCH	G	22		
Jörg LAUER (GER)	M	22		5
Pierre PETRY	D	9	(1)	
Marco REULAND	D	2	(4)	
Sacha SCHNEIDER	A	14	(6)	7
Marc THOME	M	21		2
Achim WILBOIS (GER)	M	15	(1)	2
Thomas WOLF	D	20		3

LEAGUE RESULTS 1995/96

16/09/95	Aris Bonnevoie	A	3-3	Jungblut, Dias, Behr
20/09/95	FC Wiltz 71	H	1-0	Schneider
24/09/95	F91 Dudelange	A	3-0	Thomé, Lauer, Wolf
01/10/95	Red Boys Differdange	H	1-2	Alves Silva
14/10/95	Sporting Mertzig	A	2-0	Behr, Lauer
22/10/95	FC Rodange 91	H	1-0	Jungblut
05/11/95	Union Luxembourg	A	2-1	Alves Silva, Behr
25/11/95	Spora Luxembourg	H	1-1	Wolf (p)
03/12/95	Avenir Beggen	H	6-4	Alves Silva 3, Lauer 2, Dias
10/12/95	Jeunesse Esch	A	1-0	Wilbois
16/12/95	CS Pétange	H	2-1	Schneider, Kempny
03/03/96	FC Wiltz 71	A	0-1	
09/03/96	F91 Dudelange	H	2-0	Alves Silva, Schneider
17/03/96	Red Boys Differdange	A	6-1	Schneider 2, Wolf (p), Kempny, Alves Silva, Behr
24/03/96	Sporting Mertzig	H	2-1	Schneider, Behr
31/03/96	Aris Bonnevoie	H	3-1	Alves Silva, Funck, Schneider
13/04/96	FC Rodange 91	A	0-0	
20/04/96	Union Luxembourg	H	0-0	
28/04/96	Spora Luxembourg	A	2-0	Funck, Behr
05/05/96	Avenir Beggen	A	0-1	
12/05/96	Jeunesse Esch	H	1-1	Wilbois
19/05/96	CS Pétange	A	5-1	Alves Silva 2, Lauer, Jungblut, Thomé

JEUNESSE ESCH

CLUB DIRECTORY

AS La Jeunesse d'Esch
BP 45
4001 Esch-sur-Alzette
tel - 547383-260
fax - 543297
Year of Formation - 1907
President - Dr. Carel Achen
Secretary - John Fries
Coach - Alex Pecqueur
Stadium - De la Frontière (7,000)

MAJOR HONOURS
League Championship - (23) 1921, 1937, 1951, 1954, 1958, 1959, 1960, 1963, 1967, 1968, 1970, 1973, 1974, 1975, 1976, 1977, 1980, 1983, 1985, 1987, 1988, 1995, 1996.
Domestic Cup - (9) 1935, 1937, 1946, 1954, 1973, 1974, 1976, 1981, 1988.

APPEARANCES 95/96

	P	Ap	(s)	Gls
Paolo AMODIO	A	11	(7)	3
Eric BRAUN	A	2	(4)	
Manuel CARDONI	M	22		13
Dinis DE SOUSA (POR)	M	1		
Laurent DOBRAS (FRA)	M	2	(3)	1
Philippe FELGEN	G	22		
Enrico FRANCINELLA	G		(1)	
Claude GANSER	D	18	(1)	2
Marc LAMBORELLE	D	18		5
Vito MARCHIONE	A	12	(4)	3
Patrick MEYERS	M	2	(7)	
Claude MEYLENDER	M	16	(3)	2
Patrick MOROCUTTI	A	22		17
Laurent NIGRA	D	5	(8)	
Roland SCHAACK	D	8	(4)	
Ralph SCHILTZ	D		(3)	
Denis SCUTO	M	20		2
Dany THEIS	A	22		9
Johny THILL	D	18	(1)	
Jean WAGNER	D	21		1

LEAGUE RESULTS 1995/96

17/09/95	Spora Luxembourg	H	5-0	Cardoni 3, Morocutti, Marchione
20/09/95	CS Pétange	H	3-0	Theis 2, Morocutti
24/09/95	Aris Bonnevoie	A	2-1	Morocutti 2
01/10/95	FC Wiltz 71	H	2-0	Morocutti 2
15/10/95	F91 Dudelange	A	0-5	
22/10/95	Red Boys Differdange	H	3-0	Theis 2, Ganser
05/11/95	Sporting Mertzig	A	0-0	
26/11/95	FC Rodange 91	H	3-2	Theis, Cardoni, Morocutti
03/12/95	Union Luxembourg	A	1-1	Theis
10/12/95	CS Grevenmacher	H	0-1	
17/12/95	Avenir Beggen	A	6-2	Cardoni 2, Amodio, Morocutti, Lamborelle, Marchione
03/03/96	CS Pétange	A	3-1	Theis, Cardoni, Lamborelle
09/03/96	Aris Bonnevoie	H	7-1	Meylender, Theis, Lamborelle, Ganser, Scuto, Morocutti, og (Bechet)
17/03/96	FC Wiltz 71	A	6-1	Morocutti 4, Amodio, Cardoni
24/03/96	F91 Dudelange	H	1-0	Amodio
31/03/96	Spora Luxembourg	A	6-1	Morocutti 2, Cardoni 2, Dobras, Wagner
14/04/96	Red Boys Differdange	A	0-1	
21/04/96	Sporting Mertzig	H	3-0	Lamborelle 2, Cardoni
28/04/96	FC Rodange 91	A	4-0	Cardoni 2, Scuto, Meylender
05/05/96	Union Luxembourg	H	0-1	
12/05/96	CS Grevenmacher	A	1-1	Theis (p)
19/05/96	Avenir Beggen	H	3-0	Morocutti 2, Marchione

CS PETANGE

CLUB DIRECTORY

CS Pétange
18 rue Charlotte
4719 Pétange
tel - 500375
fax - 500375
Year of Formation - 1909
President - Norbert Pierre
Secretary - Johny Majerus
Coach - Joé Hansen; Dominique Gardeur; Joé Hansen
Stadium - Municipal (3,500)

APPEARANCES 95/96

	P	Ap	(s)	Gls
Cosimo BARNABO	A	19	(2)	9
Steve BERTERNES	D	21		
Kamel BOUKELLAL (MAR)	A	10	(3)	
Omar BOUKHAROUBA (MAR)	M	16	(3)	
Paolo CARDOSO	D	16	(1)	
Steve D'ANZICO	D	5	(3)	
Jasmin DERVISEVIC (YUG)	M	20		
Steve GLODY	G	5		
Luc HILGER	M	14	(2)	
Christian HOFFMANN	G	17		
Romain JUNGERS	M	8	(2)	
Jean-Jacques KAYL	M	8	(7)	
Alain KLEIN	A	13	(3)	3
Sylvain LAMBERT (BEL)	M	17	(3)	5
Laurent MARINONI (FRA)	D	4	(4)	
Fabrice MENNUNI	M		(10)	
Alberto RODRIGUES (POR)	M	12	(2)	
Fabio TADDEI	D		(1)	
Frank TOFFART (FRA)	A	15	(2)	3
Dany WABLE (BEL)	D	22		

LEAGUE RESULTS 1995/96

Date	Opponent		Score	Scorers
20/09/95	Jeunesse Esch	A	0-3	
24/09/95	Spora Luxembourg	H	0-1	
01/10/95	Aris Bonnevoie	H	0-2	
15/10/95	FC Wiltz 71	A	5-0	Barnabo 2, Lambert 2, Klein
22/10/95	F91 Dudelange	H	0-1	
25/10/95	Avenir Beggen	H	2-1	Klein, Lambert
05/11/95	Red Boys Differdange	A	1-7	Barnabo
26/11/95	Sporting Mertzig	H	1-0	Klein
03/12/95	FC Rodange 91	A	0-1	
10/12/95	Union Luxembourg	H	0-8	
16/12/95	CS Grevenmacher	A	1-2	Barnabo
03/03/96	Jeunesse Esch	H	1-3	Barnabo (p)
10/03/96	Spora Luxembourg	A	0-1	
17/03/96	Aris Bonnevoie	A	1-1	Barnabo
24/03/96	FC Wiltz 71	H	1-0	Barnabo
31/03/96	Avenir Beggen	A	0-2	
14/04/96	F91 Dudelange	A	1-4	Lambert
21/04/96	Red Boys Differdange	H	1-0	Toffart
28/04/96	Sporting Mertzig	A	1-2	Toffart
07/05/96	FC Rodange 91	H	3-1	Barnabo 2, Lambert
12/05/96	Union Luxembourg	A	0-1	
19/05/96	CS Grevenmacher	H	1-5	Toffart

RED BOYS DIFFERDANGE

CLUB DIRECTORY

FA Red Boys Differdange
BP 38
4501 Differdange
tel - 544646/588792
fax - 587750
Year of Formation - 1907
President - Erny Muller
Secretary - Jacques Pollarini
Coach - Giulio Nezi; Jean-Philippe Guérard
Stadium - Thillenberg (6,500)

MAJOR HONOURS
League Championship - (6)
1923, 1926, 1931, 1932, 1933, 1979.
Domestic Cup - (15) 1925, 1926, 1927, 1929, 1930, 1931, 1934, 1936, 1952, 1953, 1958, 1972, 1979, 1982, 1985.

APPEARANCES 95/96

	P	Ap	(s)	Gls
Miguel ALVES DOS SANTOS	D	14	(4)	
Suad BERBERI (BEL)	A	10	(1)	6
Abdel BERRIH (FRA)	M	16	(1)	2
Ralf BUNK (GER)	M	17	(1)	1
Vincent CARNEVALE (FRA)	M	8	(2)	
Mauro CASTELLANI	G	20		
Mike DEL BON	D	18		1
Abdé ENNASSOUH (FRA)	A	20		
Jean-Philippe FACQUES (FRA)	D	21		2
Claudio FECCHI	M	1	(3)	
Marc FRISCH	G	2	(1)	
Alain GOBLET	M	5	(3)	
Yves HEINEN	A	11		4
Alain KIRSCH	D	4		
Pascal MAY	D	11		
Raphael MENDES DA SILVA (BEL)	M	7	(8)	2
Luc MEYER	M		(1)	
Paulo PACE (ITA)	M	17	(5)	5
Emidio SEVIVAS	D	9		
Christian SINNER	A	10	(9)	1
Luc SPELLER	D	11	(2)	1
Ange TOUBOUIBI (FRA)	A	10	(3)	3
Laurent ZAHLES	M		(2)	

LEAGUE RESULTS 1995/96

Date	Opponent	H/A	Score	Scorers
16/09/95	Sporting Mertzig	H	0-4	
20/09/95	FC Rodange 91	A	0-3	
24/09/95	Union Luxembourg	H	0-7	
01/10/95	CS Grevenmacher	A	2-1	Pace, Heinen
15/10/95	Avenir Beggen	H	0-4	
22/10/95	Jeunesse Esch	A	0-3	
05/11/95	CS Pétange	H	7-1	Heinen 2, Facques 2, Berberi 2, Berrih
25/11/95	Aris Bonnevoie	A	1-5	Pace
03/12/95	FC Wiltz 71	H	1-3	Berberi
10/12/95	F91 Dudelange	A	2-2	Heinen, Toubouibi
17/12/95	Spora Luxembourg	A	1-1	Berberi
09/03/96	Union Luxembourg	A	2-5	Pace, og (Borbiconi)
17/03/96	CS Grevenmacher	H	1-6	Toubouibi
20/03/96	FC Rodange 91	H	0-3	
24/03/96	Avenir Beggen	A	1-1	Toubouibi
31/03/96	Sporting Mertzig	A	2-3	Pace, Mendes
14/04/96	Jeunesse Esch	H	1-0	Berberi
21/04/96	CS Pétange	A	0-1	
28/04/96	Aris Bonnevoie	H	4-4	Berberi, Pace, Berrih, Del Bon
05/05/96	FC Wiltz 71	A	2-4	Sinner, Speller
12/05/96	F91 Dudelange	H	0-4	
19/05/96	Spora Luxembourg	H	2-7	Bunk, Mendes

FC RODANGE 91

CLUB DIRECTORY

FC Rodange 91
177 rue Klopp
4810 Rodange
tel - 500427
fax - 505190
Year of Formation - 1991
President - Romain Rosenfeld
Secretary - Jean Hoffmann
Coach - Daniel Alverdi
(96/97 - Francis Angonese)
Stadium - Jos Philippart (3,500)

APPEARANCES 95/96

	P	Ap	(s)	Gls
Christian ALVERDI	M	20		3
Johan ANDREUX (FRA)	A	8	(4)	5
Reynald BOURGEOIS (FRA)	G	18		
Joachim CONTANT (BEL)	D	13	(6)	1
Jacek CZECH (POL)	A	21		3
Pietro DARESTA	A	13	(3)	1
Antonio DE MATTEIS	D		(3)	
Álvaro DINIS MACHADO (POR)	D	1	(1)	
Marco DRIULINI	D	21		
Antonio DUARTE	M		(2)	
Pascal DUPONT (FRA)	D	4	(1)	1
Nico GILBERTZ	G	4	(1)	
Gilles INGLEBERT	M	6		
Ricky LEBRUN (BEL)	D	5		
Daniel MULLER	D	16		
Sébastien MULLER	M		(1)	
Kalambay MUTOMBO (ZAI)	D	20		
Arthur NEVES (FRA)	A	15	(1)	4
Marcel NKOLE (FRA)	A	13	(4)	1
Christian NOESEN	M	1	(2)	
Franky SCHANK	D	20		
Laurent SCHMIT	M	18	(1)	2
Gilbert TINANT (BEL)	A	1	(8)	1
Jean-Luc WELTER	D	4	(3)	
Joël WINTERSDORF	D		(3)	

LEAGUE RESULTS 1995/96

Date	Opponent		Score	Scorers
17/09/95	F91 Dudelange	A	0-5	
20/09/95	Red Boys Differdange	H	3-0	Czech, Schmit, Contant
24/09/95	Sporting Mertzig	A	0-1	
01/10/95	Spora Luxembourg	A	1-1	Andreux
15/10/95	Union Luxembourg	H	0-3	
21/10/95	CS Grevenmacher	A	0-1	
05/11/95	Avenir Beggen	H	2-0	Daresta, Andreux
26/11/95	Jeunesse Esch	A	2-3	Nkole, Neves
03/12/95	CS Pétange	H	1-0	Czech
10/12/95	Aris Bonnevoie	A	1-0	Andreux
17/12/95	FC Wiltz 71	H	1-0	Neves
09/03/96	Sporting Mertzig	H	2-2	Andreux 2
17/03/96	Spora Luxembourg	H	1-3	Alverdi
20/03/96	Red Boys Differdange	A	3-0	Alverdi, Czech, Neves
24/03/96	Union Luxembourg	A	0-1	
31/03/96	F91 Dudelange	H	2-2	Neves (p), Schmit
13/04/96	CS Grevenmacher	H	0-0	
21/04/96	Avenir Beggen	A	0-3	
28/04/96	Jeunesse Esch	H	0-4	
07/05/96	CS Pétange	A	1-3	Alverdi
12/05/96	Aris Bonnevoie	H	0-2	
19/05/96	FC Wiltz 71	A	2-3	Dupont, Tinant

SPORA LUXEMBOURG

CLUB DIRECTORY

CA Spora Luxembourg
15 rue du St. Esprit
1475 Luxembourg
tel - 332371
fax - 465569/332371
Year of Formation - 1923
President - Roland Michel
Secretary - Roger Lorang
Coach - Jean-François Zdun; Joé Hansen
Stadium - Municipal (9,200)

MAJOR HONOURS
League Championship - (11)
1925, 1928, 1929, 1934, 1935, 1936, 1938, 1949, 1956, 1961, 1989.
Domestic Cup - (8) 1928, 1932, 1940, 1950, 1957, 1965, 1966, 1980.

APPEARANCES 95/96

	P	Ap	(s)	Gls
Jean-Pierre ALMEIDA	M	7	(11)	
Patrick BEI	D	15	(3)	
Christophe BOULARD (FRA)	D	18		
Tom BURQUEL	G	1		
Didier CHAILLOU (FRA)	A	21		9
Marc CHAUSSY	D	21		1
Pawel CHODAKOWSKI (POL)	A	8	(2)	3
Vicky DA ROCHA	M		(1)	
Eric DELOBEL (FRA)	M	22		2
Yvo DOS SANTOS PINTO (POR)	M	7	(4)	4
Olivier DURAND (FRA)	D	16		2
Christian FELTEN	M	6		
Cosimo LENTINI	M	3	(6)	
Luc MISCHO	A	12	(7)	7
Philippe PLASKACZ (POL)	M		(2)	
Albert POLO (FRA)	G	21		
Paulo RODRIGO	M	8	(8)	1
Claude SCHUMACHER	D	17	(1)	
Christian STRAUS	D	3	(2)	
Laurent THILL (FRA)	D	22		1
Pascal WAMPACH	A	14	(3)	5

LEAGUE RESULTS 1995/96

16/09/95	Jeunesse Esch	A	0-5	
20/09/95	Sporting Mertzig	H	3-1	Mischo 2, Chaillou
24/09/95	CS Pétange	A	1-0	Chaillou
01/10/95	FC Rodange 91	H	0-1	
15/10/95	Aris Bonnevoie	A	4-0	Delobel, Chodakowski, Durand, Wampach
22/10/95	Union Luxembourg	A	0-0	
05/11/95	FC Wiltz 71	H	1-3	Chaillou
25/11/95	CS Grevenmacher	A	1-1	Mischo
03/12/95	F91 Dudelange	H	2-2	Chaillou, Mischo
10/12/95	Avenir Beggen	A	2-3	Chaillou 2
17/12/95	Red Boys Differdange	H	1-1	Durand
03/03/96	Sporting Mertzig	A	0-1	
10/03/96	CS Pétange	H	1-0	Wampach
17/03/96	FC Rodange 91	A	3-1	Chaillou, Chodakowski, Wampach
24/03/96	Aris Bonnevoie	H	6-1	Mischo 2, Chaillou, Wampach, Rodrigo, Chaussy
31/03/96	Jeunesse Esch	H	1-6	Delobel
14/04/96	Union Luxembourg	H	0-1	
20/04/96	FC Wiltz 71	A	1-1	Mischo
28/04/96	CS Grevenmacher	H	0-2	
05/05/96	F91 Dudelange	A	0-1	
11/05/96	Avenir Beggen	H	1-1	Chaillou
19/05/96	Red Boys Differdange	A	7-2	Dos Santos Pinto 4, Wampach, Thill, Chodakowski

SPORTING MERTZIG

CLUB DIRECTORY

FC Sporting Mertzig
2 rue du Lavoir
9189 Vichten
tel - 889039
fax - 889176
Year of Formation - 1908
President - Jeannot Stadtfeld
Secretary - Claude Decker
Coach - Carlo Weis
Stadium - An de Burwiessen (2,500)

APPEARANCES 95/96

	P	Ap	(s)	Gls
Florim ALIJAJ (YUG)	A	19	(3)	8
Walter ANTUNEZ	M	16	(4)	
Robert BESCH	D	5	(2)	
Enzo BONGIOVANNI (BEL)	A	18	(3)	4
Sérgio DA SILVA (POR)	A	9	(10)	2
Michel DEZA (FRA)	M	8	(2)	4
Eduardo DINIS OLIVEIRA (POR)	M	17	(4)	2
Armand GOLDSCHMIT	G	19		
Kamel MEFTOUH (ALG)	M	15	(1)	1
André MERGEN	M	19	(2)	7
Victor MESTRE	D	21		1
Claude OTTELE	A	18	(1)	1
Ronny OTTELE	M	2	(2)	
Marc SCHEECK	D	4	(5)	
Carlo SCHMITZ	G	3		
Bernard SIEBERT (FRA)	M	6	(5)	1
Ralph STANGE (POR)	D	18		
Carlo WEIS	D	19		1
Fernand WOSKO	M	6	(8)	

LEAGUE RESULTS 1995/96

16/09/95	Red Boys Differdange	A	4-0	Deza, Da Silva, Meftouh, Bongiovanni
20/09/95	Spora Luxembourg	A	1-3	Mergen
24/09/95	FC Rodange 91	H	1-0	Da Silva
30/09/95	Union Luxembourg	A	2-2	Mergen, Alijaj
14/10/95	CS Grevenmacher	H	0-2	
21/10/95	Avenir Beggen	A	1-0	Mergen
05/11/95	Jeunesse Esch	H	0-0	
26/11/95	CS Pétange	A	0-1	
03/12/95	Aris Bonnevoie	H	2-1	Bongiovanni, Alijaj
10/12/95	FC Wiltz 71	A	3-0	Siebert, Alijaj, Bongiovanni
03/03/96	Spora Luxembourg	H	1-0	Mergen
09/03/96	FC Rodange 91	A	2-2	Ottelé C., Alijaj
17/03/96	Union Luxembourg	H	0-2	
20/03/96	F91 Dudelange	H	2-1	Alijaj, Dinis Oliveira
24/03/96	CS Grevenmacher	A	1-2	Alijaj
31/03/96	Red Boys Differdange	H	3-2	Bongiovanni, Alijaj, Mergen
14/04/96	Avenir Beggen	H	0-3	
21/04/96	Jeunesse Esch	A	0-3	
28/04/96	CS Pétange	H	2-1	Mergen, Deza
04/05/96	Aris Bonnevoie	A	3-1	Deza, Mergen, Alijaj
11/05/96	FC Wiltz 71	H	0-0	
19/05/96	F91 Dudelange	A	4-3	Weis (p), Dinis Oliveira, Mestre, Deza

UNION LUXEMBOURG

CLUB DIRECTORY

FC Union Sportive Luxembourg
BP 1614
1016 Luxembourg
tel - 475981301/472472
fax - 404747
Year of Formation - 1908
President - Georges Pierret
Secretary - Marcel Eicher
Coach - Gilbert Neumann
Stadium - Achille-Hammerel (6,000)

MAJOR HONOURS
League Championship - (11)
1912, 1914, 1915, 1916, 1917, 1927, 1962, 1971, 1990, 1991, 1992.
Domestic Cup - (10) 1947, 1959, 1963, 1964, 1969, 1970, 1986, 1989, 1991, 1996.

APPEARANCES 95/96

	P	Ap	(s)	Gls
Eugène AFRIKA	M	11	(8)	
Anibal ALVES SILVA (POR)	A	1	(7)	1
Marc BIRSENS	D	22		1
David BORBICONI (FRA)	M	15		1
Gordon BRAUN	A	15	(3)	9
Laurent CAREME (FRA)	A	11	(7)	12
Laurent DEVILLE	M	20		1
Luc FEIEREISEN	D	2	(6)	
Patrick FEYDER	D	18		
Mustapha KHAROUBI (ALG)	A	15	(5)	2
Steve KOENIG	M		(1)	
Marc KUNEN	M	11	(8)	2
Benoît LAHERY (FRA)	M	22		8
Serge MAKOUMBOU (FRA)	M	21		6
Claude MANGEN	M	4	(3)	
Laurent PELLEGRINO (FRA)	M	20		
Dany SCHAMMEL	D	12	(2)	
John VAN RIJSWIJCK	G	22		
Claude WOLTER	M		(4)	

LEAGUE RESULTS 1995/96

16/09/95	FC Wiltz 71	A	2-1	Braun, Borbiconi
20/09/95	F91 Dudelange	H	0-2	
24/09/95	Red Boys Differdange	A	7-0	Braun 3, Lahéry 2, Alves Silva, Makoumbou
30/09/95	Sporting Mertzig	H	2-2	Kharoubi, Lahéry
15/10/95	FC Rodange 91	A	3-0	Braun, Makoumbou, Carème
22/10/95	Spora Luxembourg	H	0-0	
05/11/95	CS Grevenmacher	H	1-2	Deville
26/11/95	Avenir Beggen	A	1-0	Lahéry
03/12/95	Jeunesse Esch	H	1-1	Makoumbou
10/12/95	CS Pétange	A	8-0	Carème 4, Braun 3, Makoumbou
17/12/95	Aris Bonnevoie	H	3-3	Carème 2, Makoumbou
03/03/96	F91 Dudelange	A	1-1	Kunen
09/03/96	Red Boys Differdange	H	5-2	Carème 3, Lahéry 2
17/03/96	Sporting Mertzig	A	2-0	Carème, Kharoubi
24/03/96	FC Rodange 91	H	1-0	Braun
31/03/96	FC Wiltz 71	H	1-2	Carème
14/04/96	Spora Luxembourg	A	1-0	Lahéry
20/04/96	CS Grevenmacher	A	0-0	
27/04/96	Avenir Beggen	H	2-1	Birsens, Kunen
05/05/96	Jeunesse Esch	A	1-0	Makoumbou
12/05/96	CS Pétange	H	1-0	Lahéry
19/05/96	Aris Bonnevoie	A	0-1	

FC WILTZ 71

CLUB DIRECTORY

FC Wiltz 71
BP 47
9501 Wiltz
tel - 957061/957391
fax - 957391
Year of Formation - 1971
President - John Shinn
Secretary - Raymond Shinn
Coach - Marc Grosjean & Marc Glod
Stadium - Niederwiltz (3,000)

APPEARANCES 95/96

	P	Ap	(s)	Gls
Marco BAUS	D	16		
Diego CASTELLO (ARG)	D	20		
Mike CZEKANOWICZ	D	6		
Rob DELAHAYE (HOL)	M	17		
Marc GIRA	A	14	(2)	5
Pierre GRISIUS	D	17	(2)	2
Marc GROSJEAN (BEL)	D	2		
Boris HENRY (BEL)	D	4		
Franco IOVINO (BEL)	A	20	(1)	9
Claude KANDELS	A	17	(4)	1
David MALANNEE (BEL)	G	22		
Joe MATGEN	A	5	(6)	
Luc MELCHIOR	D	14	(3)	
Dany MUNIKEN (BEL)	M	19		3
Pascal PANTUSA (BEL)	M	14		
João PEREIRA	D	8	(11)	
Steve SCHAACK	M	3		
Françoiss TOEX	D	20	(1)	5
Frank WELTER	A	4	(13)	

LEAGUE RESULTS 1995/96

Date	Opponent		Score	Scorers
16/09/95	Union Luxembourg	H	1-2	Iovino
20/09/95	CS Grevenmacher	A	0-1	
23/09/95	Avenir Beggen	H	0-0	
01/10/95	Jeunesse Esch	A	0-2	
15/10/95	CS Pétange	H	0-5	
22/10/95	Aris Bonnevoie	A	4-2	Iovino 2, Kandels, Toex
05/11/95	Spora Luxembourg	A	3-1	Iovino, Toex, Grisius
26/11/95	F91 Dudelange	H	0-2	
03/12/95	Red Boys Differdange	A	3-1	Toex 2, Iovino
10/12/95	Sporting Mertzig	H	0-3	
16/12/95	FC Rodange 91	A	0-1	
03/03/96	CS Grevenmacher	H	1-0	Gira
10/03/96	Avenir Beggen	A	1-3	Iovino
17/03/96	Jeunesse Esch	H	1-6	Gira
24/03/96	CS Pétange	A	0-1	
31/03/96	Union Luxembourg	A	2-1	Gira, Grisius
14/04/96	Aris Bonnevoie	H	1-2	Toex
21/04/96	Spora Luxembourg	H	1-1	Iovino
28/04/96	F91 Dudelange	A	0-3	
05/05/96	Red Boys Differdange	H	4-2	Muniken 2 (2p), Iovino, Gira
11/05/96	Sporting Mertzig	A	0-0	
19/05/96	FC Rodange 91	H	3-2	Muniken (p), Gira, Iovino

PROMOTED CLUBS

SECOND DIVISION FINAL TABLE 95/96

		Pd	W	D	L	F	A	Pt	GD
1	**CS Hobscheid**	**26**	**18**	**3**	**5**	**71**	**31**	**57**	**+40**
2	**US Rumelange**	**26**	**13**	**7**	**6**	**46**	**26**	**46**	**+20**
3	Etzella Ettelbrück	26	12	9	5	39	23	45	+16
4	FC Mondercange	26	11	10	5	48	32	43	+16
5	Victoria Rosport	26	9	12	5	35	31	39	+4
6	FC Hamm 37	26	11	5	10	45	39	38	+6
7	AS Differdange	26	11	4	11	52	49	37	+3
8	Progrès Niedercorn	26	8	11	7	45	48	35	-3
9	Young Boys Diekirch	26	10	3	13	29	39	33	-10
10	Fola Esch	26	9	5	12	42	49	32	-7
11	CS Hollerich	26	8	7	11	34	43	31	-9
12	Koeppchen Wormeldange	26	6	11	9	34	35	29	-1
13	Swift Hesperange	26	5	6	15	29	48	21	-19
14	Tricolore Gasperich	26	3	3	20	28	84	12	-56

CLUB DIRECTORY

CS Hobscheid
8 Stee Kaul
8370 Hobscheid
tel - 399735
fax - 399735
Year of Formation - 1932
President - Camille Stockreiser
Secretary - Charles Hutmacher
Coach - Benny Reiter (96/97 - Aly Thill)
Stadium - Koericherberg (2,000)

CLUB DIRECTORY

US Rumelange
BP 3
3701 Rumelange
tel - 562333
fax - 562333
Year of Formation - 1908
President - René Minelli
Secretary - Alain Ostrowski
Coach - Gérard Jeitz
Stadium - Municipal (3,500)

MAJOR HONOURS

Domestic Cup - (2) 1968, 1974.

MACEDONIA

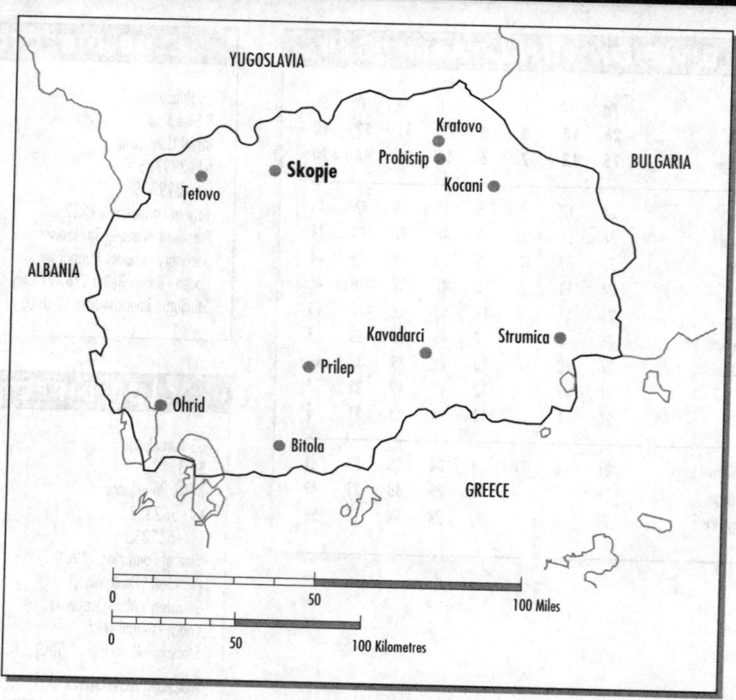
YUGOSLAVIA
BULGARIA
ALBANIA
GREECE
Kratovo
Probistip
Skopje
Tetovo
Kocani
Kavadarci
Strumica
Prilep
Ohrid
Bitola
0
50
100 Miles
0
50
100 Kilometres

UNBEATEN SILEKS END VARDAR REIGN

New coach off to good World Cup start

FEDERATION DIRECTORY

Football Union of Macedonia
Osma Udarna Brigada 31-a, PO Box 84, 91000 Skopje
tel - (91) 229042
fax - (91) 235448

Year of Formation - 1992
President - Ljubisav Ivanov
Secretary - Ilija Atanasovski

Stadium - Gradski, Skopje (25,000)

LEAGUE CHAMPIONSHIP RESULTS 95/96

		1	2	3	4	5	6	7	8	9	10	11	12	13	14	15
1	Balkan Bisi Skopje		1-0	3-0	2-1	1-1	1-1	3-0	1-1	2-5	2-0	0-2	0-2	1-3	3-0	0-0
2	Belasica Strumica	2-2		2-0	2-0	3-0	2-0	4-1	0-0	1-3	2-0	4-3	0-1	0-1	0-0	2-1
3	FCU-55 Skopje	1-0	4-2		4-0	3-1	1-1	3-0	1-3	1-1	1-0	1-0	2-2	1-2	2-0	1-2
4	Ljuboten Tetovo	0-1	1-0	1-3		2-3	2-1	4-3	4-3	1-3	3-2	1-2	0-3	0-4	2-1	0-2
5	Makedonja Skopje	0-1	2-0	3-1	2-0		2-0	1-1	4-0	2-1	2-1	3-0	0-0	1-0	2-3	1-2
6	FK Ohrid	0-0	1-1	3-1	2-1	0-0		1-0	0-1	1-1	2-1	2-0	1-2	1-0	6-2	1-0
7	Osogovo Kocani	0-1	1-1	1-1	6-2	1-0	1-1		2-0	2-2	0-1	0-2	1-2	1-0	3-0	1-0
8	Pelister Bitola	3-1	2-1	6-0	7-0	3-0	1-0	1-1		2-3	4-0	2-0	0-1	3-0	5-1	2-1
9.	Pobeda Prilep	3-0	0-1	6-1	3-0	3-1	2-0	2-2	2-0		1-0	2-0	1-2	1-1	1-1	1-1
10	Rudar Probistip	2-1	2-1	1-0	2-2	1-1	3-0	1-0	2-1	4-3		0-1	2-2	0-3	3-2	0-5
11	Sasa Makedonska Kamenica	3-1	1-0	1-1	7-0	3-1	2-1	1-1	1-0	1-1	0-0		0-2	1-2	2-2	1-1
12	Sileks Kratovo	4-2	3-0	3-1	10-0	2-0	7-1	5-0	3-0	2-1	3-1	5-1		2-0	1-0	2-2
13	Sloga Jugomagnat Skopje	1-0	5-2	3-0	3-0	1-1	1-0	4-0	1-1	1-0	3-0	1-0	0-0		5-1	1-0
14	Tikves Kavadarci	1-1	0-0	3-0	4-0	1-0	2-1	4-0	3-0	3-2	0-0	0-0	1-1	1-2		0-1
15	Vardar Skopje	3-0	3-1	2-1	2-0	1-1	2-1	6-0	7-0	1-0	3-1	4-1	2-2	1-0	5-1	

LEAGUE CHAMPIONSHIP FINAL TABLE 95/96

		Pd	W	D	L	F	A	Pt	GD
1	Sileks Kratovo	28	21	7	0	74	19	70	+55
2	Sloga Jugomagnat Skopje	28	18	4	6	48	19	58	+29
3	Vardar Skopje	28	17	6	5	60	22	57	+38
4	Pobeda Prilep	28	12	8	8	54	34	44	+20
5	Pelister Bitola	28	13	4	11	51	40	43	+11
6	Makedonja Skopje	28	10	7	11	35	35	37	=
7	Sasa Makedonska Kamenica	28	10	7	11	36	38	37	-2
8	Balkan Bisi Skopje	28	9	7	12	31	39	34	-8
9	Belasica Strumica	28	9	6	13	34	38	33	-4
10	Tikves Kavadarci	28	8	8	12	37	48	32	-11
11	FCU-55 Skopje	28	9	5	14	36	52	32	-16
12	Rudar Probistip	28	9	5	14	30	48	32	-18
13	FK Ohrid	28	8	7	13	29	39	31	-10
14	Osogovo Kocani	28	6	8	14	29	53	26	-24
15	Ljuboten Tetovo	28	6	1	21	27	87	19	-60

NATIONAL TEAM RESULTS 95/96

Date	Opponent		Venue	Score	Scorers
06/09/95	Armenia (ECQ)	H	Skopje	1-2	Micevski (10)
11/10/95	Cyprus (ECQ)	A	Limassol	1-1	Jovanovski (31)
15/11/95	Spain (ECQ)	A	Elche	0-3	
27/03/96	Malta	H	Prilep	1-0	Ciric (73)
24/04/96	Liechtenstein (WCQ)	H	Skopje	3-0	Milosevski (8), Babunski (49p), Zaharievski (90)
28/05/96	Bulgaria	A	Sofia	0-3	
01/06/96	Iceland (WCQ()	A	Reykjavik	1-1	Memed (58)

DOMESTIC CUP FINAL

SLOGA JUGOMAGNAT SKOPJE 0 VARDAR SKOPJE 0 (aet; 4-2 on pens.)

The Former Yugoslav Republic of Macedonia's first European Championship campaign did not end as they would have wished. The team's final home game in Skopje was played in an empty stadium - courtesy of UEFA's two-match spectator ban - and it resulted in a 1-2 home defeat by Armenia. A disappointing 1-1 draw in Cyprus and a predictable 0-3 defeat in Spain left Andon Doncevski's team fourth in the group but with only seven points to their credit.

A new national team coach, ex-Vardar Skopje and CSKA Sofia boss Djoko Hadjilevski, was in place for the start of the World Cup qualifiers the following spring, when Macedonia made a bright start, beating Liectenstein 3-0 at home and drawing 1-1 in Iceland.

In the domestic championship, Vardar were denied a fourth successive title by the previous season's runners-up, Sileks Kratovo. Sileks went through the 28-match season undefeated, winning the title a clear 12 points ahead of second-placed Slogo Jugomagnat, who confirmed Vardar's decline by beating their city rivals on penalties in the final of the Cup.

NATIONAL TEAM APPEARANCES 95/96

Coach - Andon DONCEVSKI; Djoko HADJILEVSKI	ARM	CYP	ESP	MLT	LIE	BUL	ISL	Cps	Gls
Danco CELESKI (09/09/67) - FK Ohrid	G	G	G	G	G	G75	G	14	-
Saso NIKOLOVSKI (16/07/73) - Vardar Skopje	D	D	s72		s60	D	D	6	-
Mitko STOJKOVSKI (18/12/72) - Real Oviedo (ESP)	D		D		D	s75	D	17	1
Ljupco MARKOVSKI (24/02/67) - Vardar Skopje	D	D			D60	D	D	16	1
Zoran JOVANOVSKI (21/08/72) - Vardar Skopje	D	D	D72	D	D	s68		17	1
Boban BABUNSKI (05/05/68) - UE Lleida (ESP)	M		M	M46	M			10	1
Zarko SERAFIMOVSKI (13/02/71) - Vardar Skopje	M46	M77	M52					15	1
Nedzmedin MEMED (20/03/66) - Sileks Kratovo	M65	M	M			M	M	14	1
Toni SAVEVSKI (14/06/63) - AEK (GRE)	M	M		M46				4	-
Georgi HRISTOV (30/01/76) - Partizan Beograd (YUG)	A	s84	s78		A71	A74	A84	8	1
Toni MICEVSKI (20/01/70) - Sileks Kratovo	A		A					15	1
Saso KARADZOV (11/12/70) - Vardar Skopje	s46	D	D					3	-
Dragan VESELINOSKI (11/08/68)	s65	M84	s52/78					3	-
Borce JOVANOVSKI (30/10/61)		D	D					2	-
Sasa CIRIC (11/01/68) - FC Aargu (SUI)		A	A	A	A	A	A36	7	1
Rade KARANFILOVSKI - Sileks Kratovo		s77						1	-
Zoran BOSKOVSKI (11/12/67) - Sileks Kratovo			M	M	M	M46		16	5
Goce SEDLOSKI (10/04/74) - Pobeda Prilep				D		D	D	3	-
Vlado GOSEV (10/09/74) - Sasa Makedonska Kamenica				D	M75	M57	M	4	-
Ilija NAJDOSKI (26/03/64) - CSKA Sofia (BUL)				D				10	-
Risto MILOSAVOV - CSKA Sofia (BUL)				M70	M	M68	M	4	-
Sasa MILOSEVSKI (06/12/73) - Vojvodina Novi Sad (YUG)				M80	M	M46	M	5	1
Ljupco NAUMOVSKI (15/02/65)				s46	s71	s74		3	-
Srdjan ZAHARIEVSKI (12/09/73) - Sileks Kratovo				s46	s75	s46		3	1
Goran PETREVSKI (23/05/72) - Vardar Skopje				s70				3	-
Artim SACIRI (23/09/73) - Vardar Skopje				s80		s46	s36	3	-
Ilco BOROV (25/07/66) - Sileks Kratovo						s57/75	s84	3	-
Zoran MICEVSKI (06/05/68) - Pobeda Prilep						s75		3	-

EUROPEAN CUPS RESULTS 95/96

CUP-WINNERS' CUP

● **SILEKS KRATOVO**

Preliminary round VÁC FC-SAMSUNG (HUN)

A 1-1 Micevski (58)
Trajcev; Nikolovski, Andovski (Duzelov 81), Ljusev, Bizimoski, Milosevic, Memed, Karanfilovski (Senev 89), Micevski (Angelovic 80), Borov, Zaharievski.

H 3-1 Memed (15), Borov (36, 67)
Trajcev; Nikolov, Andovski, Ljusev, Bizimoski (Duzelov 69), Milosevic, Memed, Karanfilovski, Micevski (Milosovski 68), Borov, Zaharievski (Angelovic 87).

1st round BORUSSIA MÖNCHENGLADBACH (GER)

A 0-3
Trajcev; Nikolov, Andovski (Nacev 71), Duzelov, Bizimoski, Milosevic, Memed, Karanfilovski, Boskovski (Micevski 54), Borov, Zaharievski (Ljusev 76).

H 2-3 Memed (51), Boskovski (62)
Trajcev; Nikolov, Andovski (Nacev 61), Ljusev, Duzelov, Milosevic, Memed, Karanfilovski, Boskovski, Zaharievski, Micevski (Angelovic 63; Nacevski 66).

UEFA CUP

● **VARDAR SKOPJE**

Preliminary round SAMTREDIA (GEO)

H 1-0 Nikolovski (9)
Zekir; Savov (Stankovski 89), Karadzov, Markovski, Nikolovski, Jovanovski, Vujovic (Angelov 67), Sainovski, Petreski, Serafimovski, Saciri.

A 2-0 Serafimovski (19), Petreski (39)
Zekir; Stankovski, Karadzov, Markovski, Nikolovski, Jovanovski, Vujovic (Trajcov 65), Sainovski, Petreski, Serafimovski, Saciri (Dordievski 80; Angelov 85).

1st round GIRONDINS DE BORDEAUX (FRA)

H 0-2
Zekir; Stankovski (Stojkovski 78), Karadzov, Markovski, Nikolovski, Jovanovski, Bojcevski (Vujovic 54), Sainovski, Petreski, Serafimovski, Saciri (Trajcov 68).

A 1-1 Serafimovski (58)
Zekir; Bojcevski, Karadzov, Markovski (Stojkovski 46), Nikolovski, Jovanovski, Vujovic, Dordievski, Petreski, Serafimovski, Saciri.

MALTA

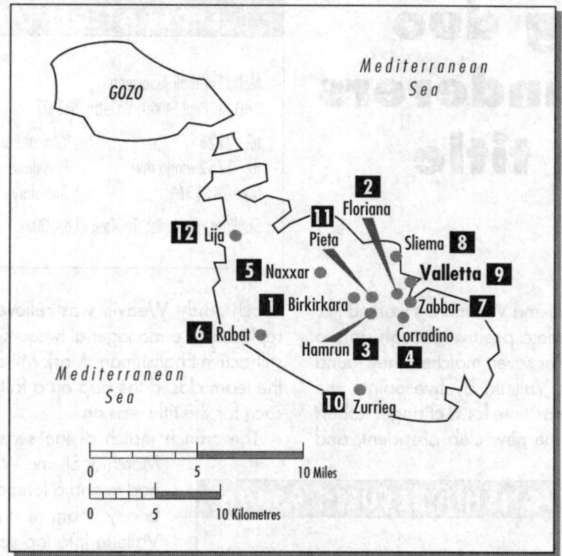

1	BIRKIRKARA LUXOL	680	7	ST. PATRICK	686
2	FLORIANA	681	8	SLIEMA WANDERERS	687
3	HAMRUN SPARTANS	682	9	VALLETTA	688
4	HIBERNIANS	683	10	ZURRIEQ	689
5	NAXXAR LIONS	684	11	PIETA HOTSPURS	690
6	RABAT AJAX	685	12	LIJA ATHLETICS	690

BAD START FOR NEW NATIONAL COACH

Coaching duo lead Wanderers back on title course

FEDERATION DIRECTORY

Malta Football Association
280 St. Paul Street, Valletta, VLT 07

tel - 222697	Year of Formation - 1900
tlx - 1752 malfa mw	President - Joseph Mifsud
fax - 245136	Secretary - Joseph A. Sacco

Stadium - National, Ta' Qali (18,000)

A mid-season shake-up at Sliema Wanderers worked like a dream. The club had made a positive enough start to the campaign, but when, after seven matches, they found themselves trailing leaders Valletta by five points, the club's directors decided it was time for a change. Robert Arrigo was appointed as the new club president, and coach Andy Weavill was relieved of his duties, to be replaced by a managerial twosome - John Calleja and the still-active Englishman, Mark Miller. Almost immediately, the team closed the gap on a faltering Valletta, and the race for the title was on.

The crunch match of the season was scheduled for March 3. Sliema Wanderers knew that they had to end a long dismal run against their bogey team if they were to leapfrog Valletta into top spot. They had not beaten the team from the capital in 16 meetings - a run stretching back to December 1990. And another defeat looked on the cards when they went in at the break one goal and one man down. But a spirited second-half revival brought an equaliser when Valletta defender Darren Debono headed into his own net from a cross by New Zealander Kim Wright. And late on Sliema got their long-awaited victory with a winning goal from leading scorer Aldrin Muscat, who had surprisingly started the match on the substitutes' bench.

Now two points in front, Sliema had the bit between their teeth, and, with just five games left, the finishing post was already in sight. It came into even sharper focus when Valletta could only draw their next game, against Floriana. Sliema responded by hammering Naxxar Lions 7-1. They were on their way. Crucial victories then followed against Hibernians and Hamrun Spartans, and the championship was secured in the penultimate match with a straightforward 3-0 victory over relegated St. Patrick.

The Wanderers' seven-match winning run was particularly impressive, because

LEAGUE CHAMPIONSHIP RESULTS 95/96

		1	2	3	4	5	6	7	8	9	10
1	Birkirkara Luxol		0-0	2-1	1-3	1-2	0-2	5-0	1-4	0-1	2-0
2	Floriana	1-0		1-1	1-1	3-1	2-1	2-0	1-0	0-0	5-0
3	Hamrun Spartans	1-0	0-3		1-1	3-0	3-0	1-2	1-1	2-1	3-2
4	Hibernians	1-1	2-1	0-0		1-0	4-1	2-0	0-2	1-1	6-0
5	Naxxar Lions	0-1	0-2	1-1	1-1		3-2	2-3	1-2	0-3	2-1
6	Rabat Ajax	2-2	1-2	2-4	1-4	0-2		4-2	1-5	1-3	2-2
7	St. Patrick	0-1	2-3	0-2	0-4	1-2	1-4		0-3	1-3	1-2
8	Sliema Wanderers	3-1	1-0	2-1	4-2	7-1	7-2	3-0		1-2	1-0
9	Valletta	4-0	2-1	1-0	3-0	1-1	4-0	8-0	1-2		7-0
10	Zurrieq	1-5	0-4	2-4	0-2	0-3	0-2	1-2	1-7	1-4	

LEAGUE CHAMPIONSHIP FINAL TABLE 95/96

		Pd	W	D	L	F	A	Pt	GD
1	Sliema Wanderers	18	15	1	2	55	16	46	+39
2	Valletta	18	13	3	2	49	11	42	+38
3	Floriana	18	11	4	3	32	12	37	+20
4	Hibernians	18	9	6	3	35	18	33	+17
5	Hamrun Spartans	18	8	5	5	29	21	29	+8
6	Birkirkara Luxol	18	6	3	9	23	26	21	-3
7	Naxxar Lions	18	6	3	9	22	33	21	-11
8	Rabat Ajax	18	4	2	12	28	50	14	-22
9	St. Patrick	18	3	0	15	15	52	9	-37
10	Zurrieq	18	1	1	16	13	62	4	-49

DOMESTIC CUP RESULTS

FIRST ROUND
Mellieha 2, Birkira Luxol 4
Naxxar Lions 3, St. Lucia 0
Lija Athletics 2, St. George's 1
Marsa 7, Dingli Swallows 2
St. Patrick 1, Mosta 0
Hamrun Spartans 1, Tarxien Rainbows 0
Gzira United 0, Zurrieq 2
Rabat Ajax 1, Pieta Hotspurs 2 (aet)

SECOND ROUND
Birkirkara Luxol 1, Naxxar Lions 0
St. Patrick 2, Marsa 0
Zurrieq 2, Lija Athletics 4
Pieta Hotspurs 1, Hamrun Spartans 1
(aet; 6-5 on pens.)

QUARTER-FINALS
Sliema Wanderers 3, Lija Athletics 1
St. Patrick 0, Valletta 3
Hibernians 3, Pieta Hotspurs 1
Floriana 4, Birkirkara Luxol 2

SEMI-FINALS
Sliema Wanderers 2, Floriana 0 (aet)
Valletta 3, Hibernians 0

FINAL
19/05/96, Ta' Qali
VALLETTA 0
SLIEMA WANDERERS 0
(aet)
referee - Zerafa
VALLETTA - Cini; Camilleri, Chetcuti, Laferla, Debono, Zammit, Agius G., Saliba, Doncic, Zarb, Galea (Woods 91).
SLIEMA WANDERERS - Barry; Bonnici, Zammit Fava, Sant Fournier J. (Bonello 111), Ciantar, Navarro, Turner, Dimech, Wright (Busuttil 73), Suda, Muscat (Mallia 97).

(replay)
23/05/96, Ta' Qali
VALLETTA 1 Agius G. (51)
SLIEMA WANDERERS 0
referee - Mintoff
VALLETTA - Cini; Camilleri, Chetcuti, Laferla, Debono, Zammit, Agius G. (Woods 84), Saliba, Doncic (Agius J. 87), Zarb, Galea.
SLIEMA WANDERERS - Barry; Ciantar, Bonnici (Muscat 74), Zammit Fava, Navarro, Sant Fournier J., Turner, Dimech, Wright, Suda (Bonello 74), Mallia (Busuttil 39).

during that sequence the team had been without the services of three key players - defender Sandro Zammit Fava, national team veteran Carmel Busuttil and player-coach Miller.

The younger players in the squad came to the fore, especially striker Muscat, who, with 18 goals, finished as the league's top scorer, and 21-year-old midfielder Noel "Guy" Turner, who was voted as the Player of the Year. Only two squad members remained from the 1988/89 title-winning side, and they both played a substantial part in taking the team back to the top. James Navarro was the man of experience in a youthful defence, and sureshot striker Hubert Suda contributed 11 goals.

Having begun the season in such style, Valletta were disappointed to end up in second place. But they rounded off the league season with four big victories, scoring 17 goals and conceding none in the process. Although that was not enough to catch Sliema Wanderers, it restored confidence for the post-season FA Trophy competition.

Valletta's defence, the best in the league, continued to hold firm, remaining unbreached in the quarter-final (3-0 v St. Patrick), the semi-final (3-0 v Hibernians), and again in the final, where they once more came face to face with Sliema Wanderers.

The first match ended goalless after 120 minutes, but four days later, in the replay, Valletta successfully retained the trophy, with young star striker Gilbert Agius netting the winning goal. They only needed one goal, of course, because their brilliant defence of Cini, Camilleri, Debono, Zammit and Chetcuti recorded yet another clean sheet.

Floriana, with an unbeaten run in the second half of the league campaign, finished third to seize Malta's second UEFA Cup spot and push defending champions Hibernians into the InterToto. There was another mass departure of Maltese clubs in the preliminary round of the European club competitions at the start of the season, with Valletta's goalless draw at home to Slovakian side Inter Bratislava rating as the only respectable result in six matches.

NATIONAL TEAM RESULTS 95/96

Date	Opponent	H/A	Venue	Score	Scorers
16/08/95	Albania	H	Ta' Qali	2-1	Saliba (21), Sant Fournier (83)
06/09/95	Luxembourg (ECQ)	A	Luxembourg	0-1	
11/10/95	Holland (ECQ)	H	Ta' Qali	0-4	
12/11/95	Belarus (ECQ)	H	Ta' Qali	0-2	
07/02/96	Russia	H	Ta' Qali	0-2	
09/02/96	Slovenia	H	Ta' Qali	0-0	
11/02/96	Iceland	H	Ta' Qali	1-4	Zahra (69)
27/03/96	Macedonia	A	Prilep	0-1	
02/06/96	Yugoslavia (WCQ)	A	Belgrade	0-6	

TOP SCORERS

Goals	Player
18	Aldrin MUSCAT (Sliema Wanderers)
17	Danilo DONCIC (Valletta)
11	Hubert SUDA (Sliema Wanderers)
10	Stefan SULTANA (Hamrun Spartans)
	Henry PULLICINO (Naxxar Lions)
9	John STIVALA (Birkirkara Luxol)
	Antoine ZAHRA (Birkirkara Luxol)
	Paul ZAMMIT (Rabat Ajax)
8	Brian CRAWLEY (Hibernians)
	Gilbert AGIUS (Valletta)

NATIONAL TEAM APPEARANCES 95/96

Coach - Pietro GHEDIN; Robert GATT; Milorad KOSANOVIC	ALB	LUX	HOL	BLS	RUS	SLO	ISL	MAC	YUG	Cps	Gls
Reggie CINI (22/10/70) - Valletta	G				G	G	G66			20	-
Silvio VELLA (08/02/67) - Hibernians	D			D	D	D	D	D	D	68	1
David CARABOTT (18/06/68) - Hibernians	D	A46	A	s63	s79	s48	s8/84	A46		57	3
Joe GALEA (09/02/65) - Birkirkara Luxol	D80	D	s70							57	-
Michael WOODS (23/07/62) - Hibernians	D	D	D	D	D	D67			s46	20	-
John BUTTIGIEG (05/10/63) - Floriana	M	M			M	M	M			77	-
Carmel BUSUTTIL (29/02/64) - Sliema Wanderers	M46	M	M	M					M	79	20
Nicky SALIBA (26/08/66) - Valletta	M	M	M	M	M51	s85		s58		44	3
Gilbert AGIUS (21/02/74) - Valletta	A86	s27/89	A6	A63	M87	A87	A	A46	A	15	-
Christian LAFERLA (23/03/67) - Valletta	A64	A	A	A						62	6
Joe SANT FOURNIER (27/01/71) - Sliema Wanderers	A	A	s6	s50	s51		s46			12	1
Ivan ZAMMIT (17/03/72) - Valletta	s46		D	D		M	M	M	M	7	-
Richard BUHAGIAR (17/03/72) - Floriana	s64	D	D	D	D	D	D	D	D	38	-
Lawrence ATTARD (06/06/66) - Hibernians	s80	s46	D70	D				D	D46	8	-
Nigel ZERAFA (13/06/68) - Birkirkara Luxol	s86									1	-
David CLUETT (02/08/65) - Floriana		G	G	G				G	G	68	-
Jesmond DELIA (20/03/70) - Floriana		D27								11	-
Martin GREGORY (10/02/65) - Floriana		s89								63	1
Joe BRINCAT (05/08/70) - Floriana			M	M50	A		A46	M62	M	51	3
Darren DEBONO (09/01/74) - Valletta					D	D	D	D	D	5	-
Jeffrey CHETCUTI (22/04/74) - Valletta					D79	D48		s62	M	5	-
Stefan SULTANA (18/07/68) - Hamrun Spartans					A	s87	A58	s82		13	2
Hubert SUDA (29/09/69) - Sliema Wanderers					s87	M	s84	A58		43	5
Noel TURNER (09/12/74) - Sliema Wanderers						M85	M	M82	M	4	-
Joe CAMILLERI (23/12/66) - Valletta						s67	D8			34	1
Antoine ZAHRA (05/03/77) - Birkirkara Luxol							s58	s46		2	1
Sean SULLIVAN (16/09/71) - Hamrun Spartans							s66			3	-
Aldrin MUSCAT (11/09/71) - Sliema Wanderers								s46		1	-

The Malta national team also endured a fruitless season. The European Championship qualifying campaign finished with three more defeats and no further points or goals being added to the meagre tally of two acquired earlier in the campaign. The team were whistled and booed off the Ta' Qali pitch after their final 0-2 defeat against Belarus (with whom they had shared a draw in Minsk). Italian coach Pietro Ghedin was offered a new two-year contract, but he declined it.

Another man bidding farewell to the national team was Carmel Busuttil. Malta's record goalscorer also became the country's most-capped international when he made his 78th appearance against Belarus, but he decided that enough was enough... only to change his mind a few weeks later and return to the fold for the World Cup opener against Yugoslavia.

By that time the new coach, a Yugoslav himself, Milorad Kosanovic, had taken over the reins of the team. He had sat on the sidelines as Malta, coached by Under-21 boss Robert Gatt, struggled against Russia, Slovenia and - most

PLAYERS OF THE SEASON

ALDRIN MUSCAT

Sliema Wanderers knew they were buying a good striker when they signed Aldrin Muscat from Zurrieq in the summer of 1995. But they could hardly have expected that he would hit it off quite so quickly with his new team-mates. The 24-year-old bagged a hat-trick in his league début for Sliema and went on to become the dominant figure in the team's exciting three-man strikeforce alongside internationals Carmel Busuttil and Hubert Suda. By the end of the season Muscat was an international himself, having won his first cap in a friendly against Macedonia. He was also the league's top scorer, pipping Valletta''s Yugoslav striker Danilo Doncic to the prize when he scored his 18th goal in the very last minute of the final game of the season.

IVAN ZAMMIT

Valletta failed to win the Maltese title, but they could not blame their defence, who conceded just 11 goals in 18 games. The man at the heart of the backline was 24-year-old libero Ivan Zammit. He was in brilliant form all season and was rewarded with a regular place in the Maltese national team. His full début, against Holland, won high praise from the local media. But although he impressed in that game as the spare man at the back, Malta's new national coach Milorad Kosanovic preferred to deploy Zammit in midfield, where he felt the long-haired youngster's passing skills would be more beneficial to the team. The heavy World Cup defeat in Belgrade suggested that Malta could also have done with him in defence.

EUROPEAN CUPS RESULTS 95/96

CUP-WINNERS' CUP

● VALLETTA

Preliminary round INTER BRATISLAVA (SVK)

H 0-0
Cini; Spiteri, Chetcuti, Camilleri, Debono, Zammit, Agius G., Ragab, Doncic (Woods 85), Zarb, Agius J. (Giglio 66).

A 2-5 Doncic (60), Zarb (85)
Cini; Camilleri, Chetcuti, Laferla, Debono, Zammit, Agius G., Saliba, Doncic, Zarb, Giglio (Spiteri 55).

UEFA CUP

● HIBERNIANS

Preliminary round CHORNOMORETS ODESA (UKR)

H 2-5 Lawrence (28), Sultana (87)
Muscat; Attard L., Farrugia J., Vella S., Woods, Attard D. (Cassar 31), Scerri (Sultana 74), Lawrence (Busuttil 80), Carabott, Saunders, Docherty.

A 0-2
Vella C.; Attard L., Farruhia J. (Cassar 72), Vella S., Woods, Zerafa, Scerri (Attard D. 66), Farrugia S., Carabott, Sultana, Docherty.

● SLIEMA WANDERERS

Preliminary round OMONIA NICOSIA (CYP)

A 0-3
Barry; Sant Fournier D. (Muscat 63), Ciantar, Zammit Fava, Navarro, Sant Fournier J. (Dimech 53), Turner, Busuttil, Miller, Suda, Wright.

H 1-2 Suda (44)
Barry; Ciantar, Wright, Dimech, Navarro, Sant Fournier J., Turner, Busuttil, Miller, Suda, Muscat (Mamo 70).

INTERNATIONAL HONOURS

None

depressingly - Iceland in the annual Rothmans tournament in February. Kosanovic's first game was a 0-1 defeat in Macedonia. His second, back in his homeland, was a 6-0 mauling by Yugoslavia. Not the best of starts in a World Cup group where any goal or point will be very difficult to come by for Kosanovic and his team. Perhaps there will be something to be had from the two games against the Faroe Islands in the spring of 1997. Judged on Malta's 95/96 form, anything else will be a major bonus.

BIRKIRKARA LUXOL

CLUB DIRECTORY

Birkirkara Luxol FC
220 Valley Road
Birkirkara
tel - 488910/443422
fax - 442245
Year of Formation - 1994
Presidents - Joseph Gauci & Paul Falzon
Secretary - Joe Brincat
Coach - Lawrence Borg
Stadium - National, Ta' Qali (18,000)

APPEARANCES 95/96

	P	Ap	(s)	Gls
Marco BALLESTRINO (ITA)	M	16		
CARUANA	M		(3)	
Andy EMINYAN	M	7	(3)	2
Joe GALEA	D	15		
Giles LANZON	D	5	(6)	
Anthony MALLIA	G	4		
Christian MICALLEF	D	14		1
Chucks NWOKO (NIG)	A	17		6
Simon SAMMUT	M	12	(5)	
Ian SCHEMBRI	D	16	(2)	
Charles SCIBERRAS	G	14	(1)	
Brandon SCICLUNA	G		(1)	
Gordon SPITERI	M	9	(2)	
Godwin STIVALA	D	18		
John STIVALA	A	11	(3)	9
Justin TELLUS	A	13	(3)	
Raymond VELLA	D	4		
Ranier XUEREB	D		(2)	
Antoine ZAHRA	M	18		9
Jesmond ZERAFA	A	4	(1)	
Nigel ZERAFA	A	1	(7)	

LEAGUE RESULTS 1995/96

26/08/95	Floriana	0-1	
10/09/95	Zurrieq	2-0	Zahra (p), Nwoko
17/09/95	Valletta	0-4	
24/09/95	Naxxar Lions	1-2	Nwoko
01/10/95	Hibernians	1-1	Zahra (p)
15/10/95	Hamrun Spartans	2-1	Stivala J., Zahra
25/11/95	St. Patrick	1-0	Stivala J.
08/12/95	Rabat Ajax	4-0	Stivala J. 2, Zahra, Nwoko (later awarded as 0-2)
23/12/95	Sliema Wanderers	1-4	Stivala J.
13/01/96	Floriana	0-0	
27/01/96	Zurrieq	5-1	Zahra 2, Stivala J. 3
25/02/96	Valletta	0-1	
16/03/96	Naxxar Lions	1-0	Nwoko
24/03/96	Hibernians	1-3	Zahra
31/03/96	Hamrun Spartans	0-1	
13/04/96	St. Patrick	5-0	Micallef, Eminyan 2, Zahra 2 (2p)
19/04/96	Rabat Ajax	2-2	Nwoko 2
27/04/96	Sliema Wanderers	1-3	Stivala J.

FLORIANA

CLUB DIRECTORY

Floriana FC
28 St. Anne Street
Floriana VLT 15
tel - 238664/236059
fax - 233498
Year of Formation - 1900
President - Anthony Grech Sant
Secretary - Mario Gauci
Coach - Ron Fenton
Stadium - National, Ta' Qali (18,000)

MAJOR HONOURS
League Championship - (25)
1910, 1912, 1913, 1921, 1922, 1925, 1927, 1928, 1929, 1931, 1935, 1937, 1950, 1951, 1952, 1953, 1955, 1958, 1962, 1968, 1970, 1973, 1975, 1977, 1993.
Domestic Cup - (18) 1938, 1945, 1947, 1949, 1950, 1953, 1954, 1955, 1957, 1958, 1961, 1966, 1967, 1972, 1976, 1981, 1993, 1994.

APPEARANCES 95/96

	P	Ap	(s)	Gls
David BRINCAT	G	1	(1)	
Joe BRINCAT	M	14	(1)	4
Pierre BRINCAT	D	10	(2)	
Richard BUHAGIAR	D	16	(1)	7
Albert BUSUTTIL	M	14	(3)	
John BUTTIGIEG	D	15	(1)	
CAMENZULI	M	1		
Mario CARUANA	M	6	(8)	1
Dennis CAUCHI	D	2	(4)	
Fabio CAUCHI	D	2		
J. CAUCHI	M		(2)	
David CLUETT	G	17		
Jesmond DELIA	M	5	(1)	
David GALEA	D	15	(2)	1
Mark GALEA	A	14	(3)	6
Martin GREGORY	M	14	(1)	2
Jonathon HOLLAND	M	8	(3)	1
Christophe OKOH (NIG)	A	5		2
Brian SAID	D	16		2
Charles SCIBERRAS	A	10	(5)	2
Igor STEFANOVIC (YUG)	A	11	(6)	4
Nenad VESLJI (YUG)	A	2		

LEAGUE RESULTS 1995/96

Date	Opponent	Score	Scorers
26/08/95	Birkirkara Luxol	1-0	Galea D.
09/09/95	Sliema Wanderers	0-1	
15/09/95	Rabat Ajax	2-1	Said, Galea M.
22/09/95	Zurrieq	5-0	Brincat J., Sciberras, Stefanovic 3
30/09/95	Valletta	1-2	Stefanovic
15/10/95	Naxxar Lions	3-1	Brincat J. 2, Galea M.
02/12/95	Hibernians	1-2	Said
17/12/95	Hamrun Spartans	1-1	Gregory
30/12/95	St. Patrick	3-2	Brincat J., Buhagiar 2 (1p)
13/01/96	Birkirkara Luxol	0-0	
27/01/96	Sliema Wanderers	1-0	Caruana
17/02/96	Rabat Ajax	2-1	Galea M., Okoh
02/03/96	Zurrieq	4-0	Holland (p), Galea M., Sciberras, Okoh
17/03/96	Valletta	0-0	
30/03/96	Naxxar Lions	2-0	Buhagiar (p), Gregory
14/04/96	Hibernians	1-1	Galea M.
20/04/96	Hamrun Spartans	3-0	Buhagiar 3
28/04/96	St. Patrick	2-0	Buhagiar, Galea M

HAMRUN SPARTANS

CLUB DIRECTORY

Hamrun Spartans FC
42 Triq Dun Nerik Cordina Perez
Hamrun
tel - 241682/221489
Year of Formation - 1907
President - Gaetano Debattista
Secretary - Anselm Sciberras
Coach - Lolly Aquilina
Stadium - National, Ta' Qali (18,000)

MAJOR HONOURS
League Championship - (7)
1914, 1918, 1947, 1983, 1987, 1988, 1991.
Domestic Cup - (6)
1983, 1984, 1987, 1988, 1989, 1992.

APPEARANCES 95/96

	P	Ap	(s)	Gls
Bin Krema ABUBAKER (LBY)	A	6		2
Simon AQUILINA	M	1	(1)	
Darren ATTARD	A	8	(1)	2
Emanuel BRINCAT	M	8	(5)	
David CAMILLERI	M	14		1
Ivan CASHA	G	1		
James CUTAJAR	D	2		
Carmel FORMOSA	A	5	(6)	2
Marco GRECH	D	18		
Edmund LUFI (ALB)	D	17		1
Charlo MAGRO	D	17		
Rupert MANGION	M	17		4
Mark MARLOW	M	14	(3)	
Duncan MICALLEF	M	1		
John MICALLEF	D	12	(1)	
Dennis MIZZI	M	7	(3)	1
Antvin MONSIGNEUR	A		(2)	
Kevin SAMMUT	M	10	(8)	5
Sean SULLIVAN	G	17		
Stefan SULTANA	A	16		10
Michael ZAMMIT	M	7	(3)	

LEAGUE RESULTS 1995/96

28/08/95	Valletta	0-1	
10/09/95	Naxxar Lions	3-0	Mangion, Abubaker, Sultana
16/09/95	Hibernians	0-0	
23/09/95	Rabat Ajax	3-0	Lufi, Abubaker, og (Braunovic)
30/09/95	St. Patrick	1-2	Sultana
15/10/95	Birkirkara Luxol	1-2	Camilleri
02/12/95	Sliema Wanderers	1-1	Sultana
17/12/95	Floriana	1-1	Sammut
30/12/95	Zurrieq	3-2	Sammut, Mangion, Sultana
20/01/96	Valletta	2-1	Sammut, Sultana
03/02/96	Naxxar Lions	1-1	Sultana
25/02/96	Hibernians	1-1	Mangion
03/03/96	Rabat Ajax	4-2	Mangion, Sultana, Mizzi (p), Formosa
23/03/96	St. Patrick	2-0	Attard, Sultana
31/03/96	Birkirkara Luxol	1-0	Formosa
14/04/96	Sliema Wanderers	1-2	Sultana
20/04/96	Floriana	0-3	
28/04/96	Zurrieq	4-2	Sammut 2, Sultana, Attard

HIBERNIANS

CLUB DIRECTORY

Hibernians FC
Hibernians Football Ground
Corradino
tel - 677764
fax - 240887
Year of Formation - 1932
President - Anthony Bezzina
Secretary - Joe Cini
Coach - Brian Talbot
Stadium - National, Ta' Qali (18,000)

MAJOR HONOURS
League Championship - (8) 1961, 1967, 1969, 1979, 1981, 1982, 1994, 1995.
Domestic Cup - (5)
1962, 1970, 1971, 1980, 1982.

APPEARANCES 95/96

	P	Ap	(s)	Gls
Darren ATTARD	A	5	(2)	
Lawrence ATTARD	D	16		
Alex BUSUTTIL	A	5	(9)	
Edwin CAMILLEERI	D	13		
Silvio CAMILLERI	D		(4)	
David CARABOTT	A	17		6
Andre CASSAR	M	5	(4)	
Brian CRAWLEY (IRL)	A	9		8
Jesmond DELIA	D	8		
Robert DOCHERTY (SCO)	A	8		
Jeffrey FARRUGIA	D	16	(1)	2
Stefan FARRUGIA	D	1	(1)	1
Alan FRENDO	M		(1)	
George LAWRENCE (ENG)	A	13	(1)	4
Alan MIFSUD	M	3	(3)	1
Mario MUSCAT	G	12	(1)	
Charles SCERRI	M	15	(1)	3
Michael SPITERI	D	1	(1)	
Konrad SULTANA	A	4	(3)	4
Malcolm THIRCHETT	A	5	(9)	3
Clyde VELLA	G	6		
Silvio VELLA	D	13		1
Michael WOODS	D	16		1
Simon ZERAFA	M	7	(3)	1

LEAGUE RESULTS 1995/96

27/08/95	Naxxar Lions	1-1	Carabott
09/09/95	Rabat Ajax	4-1	Scerri, Sultana, Carabott (p), Farrugia S.
16/09/95	Hamrun Spartans	0-0	
24/09/95	St. Patrick	4-0	Carabott, Sultana 2, Lawrence
01/10/95	Birkirkara Luxol	1-1	Sultana
18/11/95	Sliema Wanderers	2-4	Thirchett, Carabott (p)
02/12/95	Floriana	2-1	Lawrence 2
20/12/95	Zurrieq	2-0	Carabott (p), Lawrence
23/12/95	Valletta	1-1	Crawley (p)
06/01/96	Naxxar Lions	1-0	Vella S.
20/01/96	Rabat Ajax	4-1	Crawley, Thirchett 2, Zerafa
25/02/96	Hamrun Spartans	1-1	Crawley
16/03/96	St. Patrick	2-0	Crawley 2
24/03/96	Birkirkara Luxol	3-1	Scerri, Farrugia J., Crawley
31/03/96	Sliema Wanderers	0-2	
14/04/96	Floriana	1-1	Crawley
19/04/96	Zurrieq	6-0	Farrugia J., Scerri, Crawley, Woods, Carabott, Mifsud
27/04/96	Valletta	0-3	

NAXXAR LIONS

CLUB DIRECTORY

Naxxar Lions FC
29/30 Victory Square
Naxxar
tel - 411974
fax - 332004
Year of Formation - 1946
President - Michael Zammit Tabona
Secretary - Dennis Borg
Coach - Ray Farrugia
Stadium - National, Ta' Qali (18,000)

APPEARANCES 95/96

	P	Ap	(s)	Gls
Ludvic BARTOLO	A	5	(7)	1
BELLIA	A		(1)	
Gordon CAMENZULI	M	12	(2)	1
Victor CARUANA	A	3	(5)	
Kevin CASSAR	D		(2)	
David CHIRCOP	G		(1)	
Carlos CLUETT	D	17		
Rueben DEBONO	G	18		
Michael DEGIORGIO	M	17		1
Patrick DEGUARA	M		(1)	
Etienne FARRUGIA	D	4	(3)	
Ray FARRUGIA	D	18		1
Jason GALEA	D	18		
Sandro GAMBIN	M	14		
Ivan GAUCI	D	4	(3)	
Charles MAGRI	D		(1)	
MUSCAT	A		(1)	
Robert PELLEGRINI PETIT	D	15	(1)	1
Henry PULLICINO	M	18		10
Sinisi RADAK (YUG)	A	18		2
Paul SIXSMITH	M	17		4
Carmel SPITERI	D		(2)	

LEAGUE RESULTS 1995/96

27/08/95	Hibernians	1-1	Degiorgio
10/09/95	Hamrun Spartans	0-3	
17/09/95	St. Patrick	2-3	Sixsmith, Pullicino
24/09/95	Birkirkara Luxol	2-1	Pullicino 2
01/10/95	Sliema Wanderers	1-2	Sixsmith
15/10/95	Floriana	1-3	Sixsmith (p)
25/11/95	Zurrieq	2-1	Pullicino, Farrugia R.
08/12/95	Valletta	1-1	Radak
17/12/95	Rabat Ajax	2-0	Pullicino, Sixsmith
06/01/96	Hibernians	0-1	
03/02/96	Hamrun Spartans	1-1	Pellegrini Petit
02/03/96	St. Patrick	2-1	og (Daja), Pullicino
16/03/96	Birkirkara Luxol	0-1	
23/03/96	Sliema Wanderers	1-7	Camenzuli
30/03/96	Floriana	0-2	
13/04/96	Zurrieq	3-0	Pullicino, Bartolo, Radak
18/04/96	Valletta	0-3	
26/04/96	Rabat Ajax	3-2	Pullicino 3

RABAT AJAX

CLUB DIRECTORY

Rabat Ajax FC
2nd Floor
Civic Centre
Parish Square
Rabat
tel - 454244/455847
Year of Formation - 1930
President - Paul Abela
Secretary - Mario Grima
Coach - Ziya Yildiz
Stadium - National, Ta' Qali (18,000)

MAJOR HONOURS

League Championship - (2) 1985, 1986.
Domestic Cup - (1) 1986.

APPEARANCES 95/96

	P	Ap	(s)	Gls
Roderick ASCIAK	M	18		2
Edward AZZOPARDI	D	9	(4)	
Nicholas BILOCCA	M	5		
Charles BORG	D	5	(2)	
Drasko BRAUNOVIC (YUG)	D	12	(1)	1
Ivan CALLEJA	D	2		
Patrick CAMILLERI	D	4	(1)	
Rodney CAMILLERI	M	5		
John CASSAR	A	1	(4)	
Neville CIANTAR	G	8		
Michael CUTAJAR	M	7	(1)	
Franco DEGABRIELE	M	1	(1)	
Joseph FARRUGIA	M	7	(2)	
Charlie GALEA	G	4	(1)	
Joe GALEA	D	15		
MICALLEF	A		(5)	
Adrian MIFSUD	M	9	(4)	5
Clive MIZZI	M	16	(2)	3
MUSCAT	M	6	(1)	
Ronald SCERRI	D	15	(1)	2
Herbert VASSALLO	D	9	(6)	1
Kevin VELLA	A		(1)	
Zija YILDIZ (YUG)	M	17		2
Alan ZAMMIT	G	6		
Paul ZAMMIT	A	17		9

LEAGUE RESULTS 1995/96

26/08/95	Sliema Wanderers	1-5	Zammit P.
09/09/95	Hibernians	1-4	Zammit P.
15/09/95	Floriana	1-2	Zammit P.
23/09/95	Hamrun Spartans	0-3	
29/09/95	Zurrieq	2-2	og (Spiteri), Zammit P.
14/10/95	St. Patrick	4-1	Mizzi (p), Zammit P. 2, Yildiz (p)
18/11/95	Valletta	1-3	Asciak
08/12/95	Birkirkara Luxol	0-4	(later awarded as 2-0)
17/12/95	Naxxar Lions	0-2	
06/01/96	Sliema Wanderers	2-7	Braunovic, Scerri
20/01/96	Hibernians	1-4	Zammit P.
17/02/96	Floriana	1-2	Zammit P.
03/03/96	Hamrun Spartans	2-4	Mizzi (p), Yildiz
17/03/96	Zurrieq	2-0	Mizzi, Vassallo
30/03/96	St. Patrick	4-2	Asciak, Mifsud 2, Zammit P.
12/04/96	Valletta	0-4	
19/04/96	Birkirkara Luxol	2-2	Mifsud 2
26/04/96	Naxxar Lions	2-3	Mifsud, Scerri (p)

ST. PATRICK

CLUB DIRECTORY

St. Patrick FC
217 Main Street
Zabbar
tel - 804035
Year of Formation - 1912
President - Frans Catania
Secretary - Manuel Gauci
Coach - Edward Darmanin
Stadium - National, Ta' Qali (18,000)

APPEARANCES 95/96

	P	Ap	(s)	Gls
Kevin BONNICI	D	9	(5)	
Johnathan BUHAGIAR	D	12		1
Alex CAMILLERI	G	3	(1)	
Robert CASSAR	D	9	(3)	
Gotthard CONTI	A	9	(2)	1
Fatos DAJA (ALB)	M	18		
Stefan FARRUGIA	M	6		3
GALEA	M		(1)	
Peter GATT	D	11		1
Simon GRECH	G	4	(3)	
Ferenc LOVASU (HUN)	M	17		1
Kevin MAMO	A	12		
Jimmy MICALLEF	G	10	(1)	
Julian MICALLEF	M	6	(3)	1
Chris MUSCAT	A	18		3
Joseph SCHEMBRI	D	5	(4)	
Massimo SCHEMBRI	D	17		
Ray SCIBERRAS	D	15		1
Konrad SULTANA	A	8		2
Johann TONNA	M		(1)	
Kevin TONNA	A	1	(4)	
Charles VELLA	A	1	(3)	
Jonathan VELLA	D	1	(4)	1
Reuben VELLA	D	4	(1)	
ZERAFA	D	2		

LEAGUE RESULTS 1995/96

27/08/95	Zurrieq	2-1	Micallef Ju., Buhagiar
11/09/95	Valletta	1-3	Lovasu
17/09/95	Naxxar Lions	3-2	Conti, Muscat, Vella J.
24/09/95	Hibernians	0-4	
30/09/95	Hamrun Spartans	2-1	Gatt, Muscat
14/10/95	Rabat Ajax	1-4	Sciberras (p)
25/11/95	Birkirkara Luxol	0-1	
20/12/95	Sliema Wanderers	0-3	
30/12/95	Floriana	2-3	Farrugia (p), Sultana
13/01/96	Zurrieq	1-2	Farrugia
03/02/96	Valletta	0-8	
02/03/96	Naxxar Lions	1-2	Farrugia
16/03/96	Hibernians	0-2	
23/03/96	Hamrun Spartans	0-2	
30/03/96	Rabat Ajax	2-4	Sultana, Muscat
13/04/96	Birkirkara Luxol	0-5	
20/04/96	Sliema Wanderers	0-3	
28/04/96	Floriana	0-2	

SLIEMA WANDERERS

CLUB DIRECTORY

Sliema Wanderers FC
21 Tower Road
Sliema
tel - 332033/318314
fax - 320219
Year of Formation - 1909
President - Robert Arrigo
Secretary - Alex Mafrè
Coach - Andrew Weavill; Mark Miller/John Calleja
Stadium - National, Ta' Qali (18,000)

MAJOR HONOURS

League Championship - (23) 1920, 1923, 1924, 1926, 1930, 1933, 1934, 1936, 1938, 1939, 1940, 1949, 1954, 1956, 1957, 1964, 1965, 1966, 1971, 1972, 1976, 1989, 1996.
Domestic Cup - (17) 1935, 1936, 1937, 1940, 1946, 1948, 1951, 1952, 1956, 1959, 1963, 1965, 1968, 1969, 1974, 1979, 1990.

APPEARANCES 95/96

	P	Ap	(s)	Gls
Roderick AGIUS	G		(4)	
Ernest BARRY	G	18		
Graham BENCINI	A		(1)	
Andrew BONELLO	A	5	(1)	2
Karl BONNICI	D	7	(2)	
Carmel BUSUTTIL	M	12	(2)	7
Cedric CARUANA	D		(3)	
Ian CIANTAR	D	18		1
Luke DIMECH	D	10	(6)	
Anthony GALEA	M	1	(2)	1
George MALLIA	M	2	(4)	1
Kevin MAMO	A		(3)	
Mark MILLER (ENG)	M	10		2
Aldrin MUSCAT	A	16	(2)	18
James NAVARRO	D	17	(1)	1
Damian SANT FOURNIER	D		(3)	
Joe SANT FOURNIER	M	16	(1)	2
Hubert SUDA	A	17		11
Noel TURNER	M	18		4
Kim WRIGHT (NZL)	M	18		4
Sandro ZAMMIT FAVA	M	13	(2)	

LEAGUE RESULTS 1995/96

Date	Opponent	Score	Scorers
26/08/95	Rabat Ajax	5-1	Muscat 3, Turner, Busuttil
09/09/95	Floriana	1-0	Muscat
16/09/95	Zurrieq	7-1	Suda 3, Muscat, Busuttil, Turner, Navarro
23/09/95	Valletta	1-2	Muscat (p)
01/10/95	Naxxar Lions	2-1	Miller, Wright
18/11/95	Hibernians	4-2	Suda 2 (2p), Muscat, Busuttil
02/12/95	Hamrun Spartans	1-1	Wright
20/12/95	St. Patrick	3-0	Sant Fournier J., Ciantar, Suda
23/12/95	Birkirkara Luxol	4-1	Busuttil 3, Suda
06/01/96	Rabat Ajax	7-2	Suda 2, Muscat 2, Miller, Busuttil, Turner
27/01/96	Floriana	0-1	
17/02/96	Zurrieq	1-0	Wright
03/03/96	Valletta	2-1	og (Debono), Muscat
23/03/96	Naxxar Lions	7-1	Muscat 3 (1p), Suda 2, Turner, Wright
31/03/96	Hibernians	2-0	Bonello, Sant Fournier J.
14/04/96	Hamrun Spartans	2-1	Muscat (p), Bonello
20/04/96	St. Patrick	3-0	Muscat 2, Galea
27/04/96	Birkirkara Luxol	3-1	Muscat 2, Mallia

VALLETTA

CLUB DIRECTORY

Valletta FC
126 St. Lucia Street
Valletta
tel - 224939/238083
fax - 240709
Year of Formation - 1904
President - Joe Caruana Curran
Secretary - Benny Pace
Coach - Edward Aquilina
Stadium - National, Ta' Qali (18,000)

MAJOR HONOURS
League Championship - (14)
1915, 1932, 1945, 1946, 1948, 1959, 1960, 1963, 1974, 1978, 1980, 1984, 1990, 1992.
Domestic Cup - (8) 1960, 1964, 1975, 1977, 1978, 1991, 1995, 1996.

APPEARANCES 95/96

	P	Ap	(s)	Gls
Bin Krema ABUBAKER (LBY)	A	3	(3)	1
Gilbert AGIUS	M	17		8
Jeremy AGIUS	A	4	(8)	3
Joe CAMILLERI	D	16		2
Jeffrey CHETCUTI	D	18		
Reggie CINI	G	17		
Darren DEBONO	D	17		2
Danilo DONCIC (YUG)	A	18		17
Lino GALEA	D	8	(5)	
Stefan GIGLIO	D		(11)	
Christian LAFERLA	M	16		5
Anjan METARAKU (ALB)	A	1		
Adrian MIFSUD	G	1	(1)	
Nicky SALIBA	M	18		3
Ragab SAZENTATI (LBY)	A	1	(1)	
Robert SPITERI	D	8	(1)	
Ivan WOODS	M	2	(9)	2
Ivan ZAMMIT	D	16		2
Joe ZARB	M	17		4

LEAGUE RESULTS 1995/96

28/08/95	Hamrun Spartans	1-0	Laferla
11/09/95	St. Patrick	3-1	Camilleri, Laferla, Agius J.
17/09/95	Birkirkara Luxol	4-0	Saliba 2, Debono, Doncic
23/09/95	Sliema Wanderers	2-1	Doncic, Zarb
30/09/95	Floriana	2-1	Laferla, Agius J.
14/10/95	Zurrieq	4-1	Doncic 3, Laferla
18/11/95	Rabat Ajax	3-1	Laferla, Agius G., Woods
08/12/95	Naxxar Lions	1-1	Doncic (p)
23/12/95	Hibernians	1-1	Zammit
20/01/96	Hamrun Spartans	1-2	Zarb (p)
03/02/96	St. Patrick	8-0	Agius G. 4 (1p), Doncic 3, Abubaker
25/02/96	Birkirkara Luxol	1-0	Debono
03/03/96	Sliema Wanderers	1-2	Zarb
17/03/96	Floriana	0-0	
24/03/96	Zurrieq	7-0	Saliba, Doncic 4 (1p), Agius G., Woods
12/04/96	Rabat Ajax	4-0	Doncic 2 (2p), Agius G., Zarb
18/04/96	Naxxar Lions	3-0	Doncic, Agius G., Camilleri
27/04/96	Hibernians	3-0	Doncic (p), Zammit, Agius J.

ZURRIEQ

CLUB DIRECTORY

Zurrieq FC
30 Main Street
Zurrieq
tel - 820642/827853
Year of Formation - 1949
President - Carmel Mangion
Secretary - Charles Gauci
Coach - Jimmy Briffa; George Busuttil
Stadium - National, Ta' Qali (18,000)

MAJOR HONOURS
Domestic Cup - (1) 1985.

APPEARANCES 95/96

	P	Ap	(s)	Gls
Jean-Pierre ABDILLA	M	8	(1)	1
Ian ATTARD	D		(4)	
Roderick BALDACCHINO	A	18		
BELLIZZI	A		(3)	
Petar BOIKOV (BUL)	M	3		1
Tony BRIFFA	D	6	(9)	
Frans CASSAR	A		(4)	
Joe FALZON	M	13	(1)	
C. FARRUGIA	A		(1)	
J.P. FARRUGIA	M		(2)	
Mark FARRUGIA	G	7	(1)	
S. FARRUGIA	M		(2)	
Jason GRECH	D	15		1
Simon GRECH	A	14	(2)	6
Oscar MAGRI	M	2		
Jonathan MAGRI OVERAND	D	11		1
Paul MASSA	M	1	(1)	
Joe MUSCAT	G	2		
Slavicho NIKLENOV (BUL)	G	9	(2)	
A. SALIBA	A	5	(1)	
Jason SALIBA	M	8	(2)	
Joe SALIBA	D	12	(2)	
Rageb SAZENTATI (LBY)	A	3		
Aldo SCARDINO	D	14		
Mark SPITERI	M	6		
Mark SULTANA	M	13	(2)	1
Angel TERZYSKI (BUL)	A	1		1
Michael WATERS (ENG)	A	4		
Valentin ZAHARILJEV (SWE)	A	7		1
Edmond ZAMMIT	D	16		

LEAGUE RESULTS 1995/96

27/08/95	St. Patrick	1-2	Terzyski (p)
10/09/95	Birkirkara Luxol	0-2	
16/09/95	Sliema Wanderers	1-7	Boikov (p)
22/09/95	Floriana	0-5	
29/09/95	Rabat Ajax	2-2	Grech S. 2
14/10/95	Valletta	1-4	Magri Overand (p)
25/11/95	Naxxar Lions	1-2	Grech S.
20/12/95	Hibernians	0-2	
30/12/95	Hamrun Spartans	2-3	Grech S., Zahariljev
13/01/96	St. Patrick	2-1	Grech S., Abdilla
27/01/96	Birkirkara Luxol	1-5	Grech J.
17/02/96	Sliema Wanderers	0-1	
02/03/96	Floriana	0-4	
17/03/96	Rabat Ajax	0-2	
24/03/96	Valletta	0-7	
13/04/96	Naxxar Lions	0-3	
19/04/96	Hibernians	0-6	
28/04/96	Hamrun Spartans	2-4	Sultana, Grech S.

PROMOTED CLUBS

SECOND DIVISION FINAL TABLE 95/96

		Pd	W	D	L	F	A	Pt	GD
1	**Pieta Hotspurs**	**18**	**14**	**4**	**0**	**48**	**15**	**46**	**+33**
2	**Lija Athletics**	**18**	**13**	**1**	**4**	**42**	**19**	**40**	**+23**
3	Mellieha	18	6	5	7	29	26	23	+3
4	Tarxien Rainbows	18	5	8	5	18	19	23	-1
5	Mosta	18	7	2	9	21	28	23	-7
6	Marsa	18	6	5	7	18	26	23	-8
7	Dingli Swallows	18	6	4	8	26	29	22	-3
8	St. Lucia	18	4	8	6	21	23	20	-2
9	St. George's	18	5	5	8	18	27	20	-9
10	Gzira United	18	2	2	14	18	47	8	-29

CLUB DIRECTORY

Pieta Hotspurs FC
Our Lady of Sorrows Street
Pieta
tel - 231336
Year of Formation - 1932
President - Edward Schembri
Secretary - Mario Mollia
Coach - Georgi Deanov
Stadium - National, Ta' Qali (18,000)

CLUB DIRECTORY

Lija Athletics FC
38 Bakery Street
Lija
tel - 435868
Year of Formation - 1932
President - Joe Azzopardi
Secretary - Carmelu Bonnici
Coach - Joe Bugeja
Stadium - National, Ta' Qali (18,000)

MOLDOVA

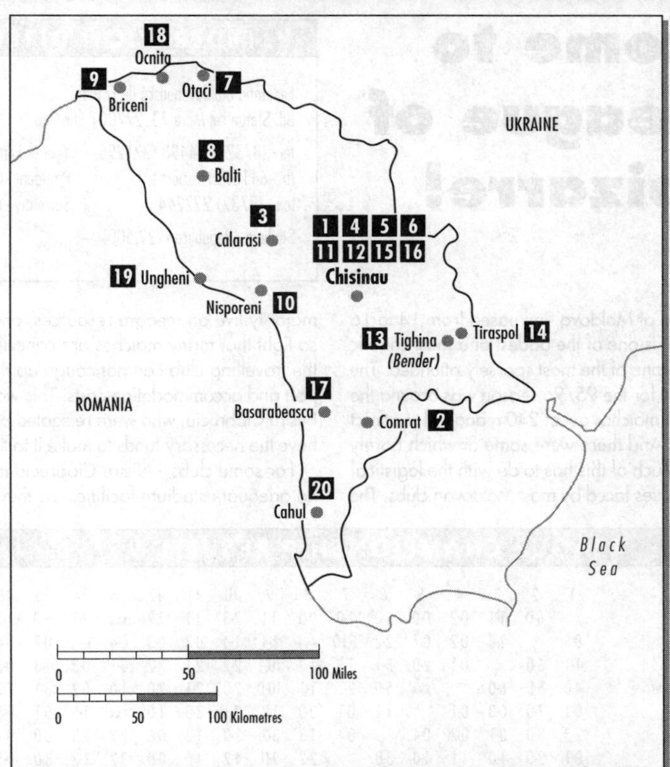

1	FC AGRO CHISINAU	695	11	SPORTUL STUDENTESC CHISINAU	705
2	BUGEAC COMRAT	696	12	SPUMANTE CRICOVA	706
3	CODRU CALARASI	697	13	TIGHINA BENDER	707
4	CONSTRUCTORUL CHISINAU	698	14	TILIGUL TIRASPOL	708
5	MHM-93 CHISINAU	699	15	TORENTUL CHISINAU	709
6	NISTRU CIOBRUCIU	700	16	ZIMBRU CHISINAU	710
7	NISTRU OTACI	701	17	LOKOMOTIVA BASARABEASCA	711
8	OLIMPIA BALTI	702	18	CIUHUR OCNITA	711
9	PROGRESUL BRICENI	703	19	ATTILA UNGHENI	711
10	SPERANTA NISPORENI	704	20	VICTORIA CAHUL	711

FIVE OUT OF FIVE FOR ZIMBRU

Welcome to the league of the bizarre!

FEDERATION DIRECTORY

Federatia Moldoveneasca de Fotbal
Bd. Stefan cel Mare 73, 277001 Chisinau

tel - (3732) 224498/221295
tlx - 64163218 sport
fax - (3732) 222244

Stadium - Republican (22,500)

Year of Formation - 1990
President - Constantin Tampiza
Secretary - Anatol Teslev

The national league of Moldova, increased from 14 to 16 teams in 1995/96, is one of the oddest and most chaotic in Europe. It is also one of the most sparsely attended. The average attendance for the 95/96 season was around the 200 mark. Only ten matches out of 240 managed to attract a four-figure gate. And there were some at which barely 50 were present. Much of this has to do with the logistical and financial difficulties faced by most Moldovan clubs. The majority live on meagre resources, and purse-strings are so tight that many matches are cancelled simply because the travelling club can not cough up the necessary transport and accommodation costs. This was even the case for Nistru Ciobruciu, who were relegated because they did not have the necessary funds to make it to their play-off match.

For some clubs - Nistru Ciobruciu included - there are no adequate stadium facilities, so they have to play their

LEAGUE CHAMPIONSHIP RESULTS 95/96

		1	2	3	4	5	6	7	8	9	10	11	12	13	14	15	16
1	FC Agro Chisinau		6-0	1-1	0-2	0-0	5-0	1-0	0-0	3-1	2-3	2-1	2-2	xxx	2-1	5-0	1-3
2	Bugeac Comrat	0-5		1-8	0-2	0-7	2-2	1-10	+++	1-4	1-4	0-3	0-3	0-4	+++	0-7	0-4
3	Codru Calarasi	1-1	6-0		0-1	2-0	3-1	1-3	1-2	10-1	2-2	2-1	3-2	0-1	0-3	1-3	0-8
4	Constructorul Chisinau	4-0	5-0	6-0		xxx	5-0	2-1	1-1	10-0	2-0	2-1	2-0	1-0	0-2	3-1	1-2
5	MHM-93 Chisinau	0-1	7-0	0-0	0-1		1-1	0-1	0-0	1-0	2-1	3-0	1-0	xxx	1-5	5-1	0-3
6	Nistru Ciobruciu	2-3	3-0	0-1	0-2	0-4		0-4	1-3	3-2	1-0	1-2	0-6	2-2	2-5	0-0	0-1
7	Nistru Otaci	0-1	3-0	1-0	1-1	1-0	3-0		2-2	9-0	4-2	4-0	0-0	3-2	1-2	3-0	0-1
8	Olimpia Balti	0-1	xxx	3-0	1-0	1-0	4-0	1-0		3-0	6-1	2-1	3-3	4-0	0-4	7-1	0-3
9	Progresul Briceni	0-3	xxx	1-0	1-2	1-4	2-2	1-1	0-1		1-2	1-0	0-3	0-0	+++	0-5	0-2
10	Speranta Nisporeni	1-2	7-0	1-2	0-1	2-2	5-1	0-0	0-5	xxx		1-1	0-1	1-0	0-1	2-2	0-2
11	Sportul Studentesc Chisinau	1-2	4-0	2-0	1-2	1-2	4-0	1-1	0-2	13-0	0-0		1-4	5-0	1-1	1-0	1-7
12	Spumante Cricova	0-4	9-0	1-1	1-2	0-1	xxx	0-2	1-1	2-1	0-0	1-0		7-0	2-1	6-0	1-1
13	Tighina Bender	0-2	6-0	1-4	0-3	0-1	1-1	1-1	1-0	12-0	1-4	1-2	0-0		0-2	3-0	0-1
14	Tiligul Tiraspol	2-1	7-0	8-0	1-2	1-0	5-1	3-1	3-0	7-0	2-1	3-0	2-0	3-1		13-1	0-2
15	Torentul Chisinau	1-3	5-0	0-1	0-6	1-1	0-0	0-3	0-1	2-2	3-1	1-2	0-1	2-3	0-6		0-7
16	Zimbru Chisinau	1-1	8-0	3-1	2-0	2-0	9-0	5-0	1-2	4-0	4-0	8-0	3-0	3-1	2-2	8-0	

+++ - match void; awarded as away win   xxx - match void; awarded as home win

NATIONAL TEAM RESULTS 95/96

06/09/95	Wales (ECQ)	A	Cardiff	0-1	
08/10/95	Germany (ECQ)	A	Leverkusen	1-6	Rebeja (80)
15/11/95	Georgia (ECQ)	H	Chisinau	3-2	Testimitanu (5p), Miterev (17, 68)
09/04/96	Ukraine	H	Chisinau	2-2	Testimitanu (72), Popovici (84)
01/06/96	Romania	A	Bucharest	1-3	Testimitanu (78)

TOP SCORERS

34 Vladimir GAVRILIUC (Zimbru Chisinau)
32 Vladimir KOSSE (Tiligul Tiraspol)
25 Serghei ROGACIOV (Olimpia Balti)
20 Iurie MITEREV (Zimbru Chisinau)
18 Ruslan BARBAROS (FC Agro Chisinau)
Igor RAICEV (Tighina Bender)

LEAGUE CHAMPIONSHIP FINAL TABLE 95/96

			Home					Away					Total						
		Pd	W	D	L	F	A	W	D	L	F	A	W	D	L	F	A	Pt	GD
1	Zimbru Chisinau	30	12	2	1	63	7	14	1	0	47	4	26	3	1	110	11	81	+99
2	Tiligul Tiraspol	30	13	0	2	60	10	11	2	2	35	11	24	2	4	95	21	74	+74
3	Constructorul Chisinau	30	12	1	2	44	8	12	1	2	27	8	24	2	4	71	16	74	+55
4	FC Agro Chisinau	30	8	4	3	30	14	11	2	2	30	13	19	6	5	60	27	63	+33
5	Olimpia Balti	30	11	1	3	35	14	8	5	2	20	11	19	6	5	55	25	63	+30
6	Nistru Otaci	30	9	3	3	35	11	6	4	5	28	17	15	7	8	63	28	52	+35
7	Spumante Cricova	30	7	4	4	31	14	6	4	5	25	17	13	8	9	56	31	47	+25
8	MHM-93 Chisinau	30	7	3	5	21	14	6	3	6	22	12	13	6	11	43	26	45	+17
9	Codru Calarasi	30	6	2	7	32	29	5	3	7	19	29	11	5	14	51	58	38	-7
10	Sportul Studentesc Chisinau	30	6	3	6	36	21	4	1	10	14	32	10	4	16	50	53	34	-3
11	Speranta Nisporeni	30	4	4	7	20	20	4	3	8	21	31	8	7	15	41	51	31	-10
12	Tighina Bender	30	4	3	8	27	21	3	2	10	14	31	7	5	18	41	52	26	-11
13	Torentul Chisinau	30	2	3	10	15	37	3	2	10	21	57	5	5	20	36	94	20	-58
14	Nistru Ciobruciu	30	3	2	10	15	35	0	5	10	9	49	3	7	20	24	84	16	-60
15	Progresul Briceni	30	3	3	9	8	25	1	1	13	11	80	4	4	22	19	105	16	-86
16	Bugeac Comrat	30	0	1	14	6	63	0	0	15	0	76	0	1	29	6	139	1	-133

DOMESTIC CUP RESULTS

1/16 FINALS
Lims Vital Anenii Noi 1, Progresul Briceni 0 (aet)
Ciuhur Ocnita 2, MHM-93 Chisinau 1
Prut Cantemir 0, FC Agro Chisinau 4
Dumbrava Cojusna 1, Speranta Nisporeni 1 (aet; 3-5 on pens.)
Spicul Falesti 0, Tighina Bender 1
Flacara Nemireuca 1, Nistru Ciobruciu 0 (aet)
Locomotiva Balti 4, Codru Calarasi 0
Tiras Criuleni 1, Constructorul Chisinau 3
Maiak Chirsova 0, Spumante Cricova 4
Vierul Sângerei 3, Bugeac Comrat 0
Zarea Hlinaia 0, Torentul Chisinau 1
Raut Orhei 0, Sportul Studentesc Chisinau 2
Locomotiva Basarabeasca 4, Olimpia Balti 1
Attila Ungheni 1, Nistru Otaci 1 (aet; 3-5 on pens.)
Victoria Cahul 0, Tiligul Tiraspol 1
Zimbru Chisinau w/o Izvoras Draslicieni

1/8 FINALS
Tiligul Tiraspol v Sportul Studentesc Chisinau 4-0; 3-0 (Tiligul Tiraspol 7-0)
Vierul Sângerei v Zimbru Chisinau 0-4; 0-16 (Zimbru Chisinau 20-0)
Constructorul Chisinau v Speranta Nisporeni 1-0; 2-1 (Constructorul Chisinau 3-1)
Spumante Cricova v Limas Vital Anenii Noi 2-0; 2-1 (Spumante Cricova 4-1)
Ciugur Ocnita v Locomotiva Basarabeasca 0-2; 0-3 (Locomotiva Basarabeasca 5-0)
Flacara Nemireuca v Locomotiva Balti 1-4; 0-3 (Locomotiva Balti 7-1)
FC Agro Chisinau v Nistru Otaci 1-1; 1-3 (Nistru Otaci 4-2)
Tighina Bender v Torentul Chisinau 1-1; 5-0 (Tighina Bender 6-1)

QUARTER-FINALS
Zimbru Chisinau v Tiligul Tiraspol 1-1; 0-1 (Tiligul Tiraspol 2-1)
Nistru Otaci v Constructorul Chisinau 0-1; 1-0 (1-1; Constructorol Chisinau 3-2 on pens.)
Locomotiva Basarabeasca v Tighina Bender 0-0; 2-0 (Locomotiva Basarabeasca 2-0)
Locomotiva Balti v Spumante Cricova 1-2; 0-6 (Spumante Cricova 8-1)

SEMI-FINALS
Spumante Cricova v Tiligul Tiraspol 0-2; 1-3 (Tiligul Tiraspol 5-1)
Constructorul Chisinau v Locomotiva Basarabeasca 4-1; 1-2 (Constructorul Chisinau 5-3)

FINAL
12/05/96, Chisinau
CONSTRUCTORUL CHISINAU 2 Tverdohlebov (24), Cuciuc (65)
TILIGUL TIRASPOL 1 Melnicov (87)
referee - Cepoi
CONSTRUCTORUL CHISINAU - Dinov; Filip, Tabanov, Platon I., Tverdohlebov, Cuciuc, Sischin (Zubarev 77), Tiron, Bursuc, Scrupski (Pavlov 46), Martâniuc (Pusca 70).
TILIGUL TIRASPOL - Ivanov; Secu (Priganiuc 78), Tâtâc (Melnicov 56), Pogorelov, Gaidamasciuc, Stroenco S., Stroenco A. (Mincev 74), Parhomenco, Belous, Kosse, Popovici.

home games in other towns. Many of the matches cancelled during the 95/96 season were down to players refusing to play because of unpaid wages. On more than one occasion, with kick-off imminent, a team would find themselves short of their full 11-man complement. There were plenty of weird and wonderful scorelines, too. Sportul Studentesc Chisnau recorded the biggest win, 13-0 against Progresul Chisinau. But there were several more double-figure results. And Bugeac Comrat must have set some kind of European record by losing 29 and drawing one of their 30 matches. At the other end of the table the title went, as it had for the previous four years, to Zimbru Chisinau. Distracted by a very good run in Europe, they were challenged early on by Constructorul, but in the spring, inspired

EUROPEAN CUPS RESULTS 95/96

CUP-WINNERS' CUP

● TILIGUL TIRASPOL

Preliminary round FC SION (SUI)

H 0-0
Ivanov; Secu, Luchiancikov (Kotliar 69), Gaidamasciuc (Dovghii 76), Pogorelov, Stroenco S., Stroenco A. (Mincev 46), Parhomenko, Belous, Kosse, Oprea.

A 2-3 Oprea (79), Popovici (90)
Ivanov; Secu, Luchiancikov, Pogorelov, Gaidamasciuc (Tîrîk 76), Stroenco S., Stroenco A. (Popovici 70), Minchev, Belous, Kosse, Oprea.

UEFA CUP

● ZIMBRU CHISINAU

Preliminary round HAPOEL TEL-AVIV (ISR)

H 2-0 Gavriliuc (27), Rebeja (71)
Coselev; Fistican, Tolokonikov, Testimitanu, Rebeja (Spînu 77), Nani, Curtianu (Caras E. 86), Cebotar, Miterev (Suharev 56), Gavriliuc, Clescenco.

A 0-0
Coselev; Fistican, Caras, Testimitanu, Rebeja, Tolokonikov, Curtianu, Cebotar, Suharev (Miterev 72), Gavriliuc (Caras E. 85), Boret (Spînu 66).

1st round RAF YELGAVA (LAT)

H 1-0 Testimitanu (40)
Coselev; Fistican, Tolokonikov, Testimitanu, Rebeja, Boret, Spînu (Caras E. 75), Cebotar, Suharev (Miterev 46), Gavriliuc, Culibaba

A 2-1 Gavriliuc (5, 25)
Coselev; Fistican, Tolokonikov, Testimitanu, Rebeja (Boret 88), Spînu, Curtianu (Caras E. 67), Culibaba, Miterev, Gavriliuc, Suharev (Caras D. 61).

2nd round SPARTA PRAHA (TCH)

A 3-4 Suharev (56), Testimitanu (62, 90p)
Coselev; Fistican, Tolokonikov, Testimitanu, Rebeja, Spînu, Curtianu, Caras E. (Boret 58), Miterev, Gavriliuc (Tîmbur 81), Suharev.

H 0-2
Coselev; Culibaba, Tolokonikov, Testimitanu, Rebeja (Cebotar 53), Spînu, Boret, Caras E., Miterev, Gavriliuc, Suharev (Caras D. 77).

NATIONAL TEAM APPEARANCES 95/96

Coach - Ion CARAS	WAL	GER	GEO	UKR	ROM	Cps	Gls
Evgheni IVANOV (21/06/66) - Tiligul Tiraspol	G	G				4	-
Oleg FISTICAN (01/02/75) - Zimbru Chisinau	D					3	-
Serghei BELOUS (21/11/71) - Tiligul Tiraspol	D	D	D	D46	M46	15	1
Serghei STROENCO (20/08/67) - Tiligul Tiraspol	D	D				17	-
Ion TESTIMITANU (27/04/74) - Zimbru Chisinau	D	D	D	D	D	8	3
Vitali CULIBABA (26/01/71) - Zimbru Chisinau	M	M	M	D	s46	5	-
Radu REBEJA (08/06/73) - Zimbru Chisinau	M84	M		M46	M	13	1
Igor OPREA (05/10/69) - Tiligul Tiraspol	M	M86	M52			19	2
Serghei NANI (10/08/70) - Go Ahead Eagles (HOL)	M76	M60	M		D46	17	-
Boris CEBOTAR (03/02/75) - Zimbru Chisinau	M		s72			5	-
Serghei CLESCENCO (25/05/72) - Go Ahead Eagles (HOL)	A	A	A		A53	15	5
Alexandru SUHAREV (23/07/70) - Zimbru Chisinau	s76		s52			2	-
Vadim GAVRILIUC (07/03/72) - Zimbru Chisinau	s84	s86	s74		s72	4	-
Serghiu SECU (03/09/72) - Tiligul Tiraspol		D	D	D	D	21	1
Alexandru CURTIANU (11/02/74) - Zimbru Chisinau		M	M72	A	A	14	1
Iurie MITEREV (28/11/75) - Zimbru Chisinau		s60	M	A61	M46	10	5
Vasile COSELEV (12/02/72) - Zimbru Chisinau			G		s50	17	-
Serghei KIRILOV (05/06/73) - Sportul Studentesc Bucuresti (ROM)			M74	s61	s53	4	-
Denis ROMANENCO (18/11/74) - Zimbru Chisinau				G	G50	2	-
Oleg SISCIN (07/01/75) - Constructorul Chisinau				M46	s46	2	-
Vladimir GAIDAMASCIUC (30/06/71) - Tiligul Tiraspol				M	M	12	-
Sergiu EPUREANU (19/09/76) - FC Agro Chisinau				A87		1	-
Alexandr POPOVICI (09/04/77) - Tiligul Tiraspol				s46	s46	2	1
Serghei PARHOMENCO (1973) - Tiligul Tiraspol				s46	D72	3	-
Igor CUCIUC (1974) - Constructorul Chisinau				s46		7	-
Marin SPÎNU (18/11/73) - Zimbru Chisinau				s87		1	-

by their young national team triumvirate of defender Ion Testimitanu, playmaker Alexandru Curtianu and top scorer Vadim Gavriliuc, Zimbru were uncatchable, and they finished seven points clear of perennial runners-up Tiligul Tiraspol. Tiligul did not have their usual Cup triumph as consolation. They were surprisingly beaten 2-1 in the final by Constructorul.

Constructorul's ascent was recognised by national team coach Ion Caras, who called up a couple of the team's players to his squad to join the big contingent from Zimbru and Tiligul and the two foreign-based players, Nani and Clescenco, both of Dutch club Go Ahead Eagles.

Moldova finished their Euro '96 qualifying campaign on a high, doing the 'double' over Georgia with a 3-2 win in Chisinau. This was an excellent recovery from their 6-1 mauling by Germany in Leverkusen and enabled the team to finish ahead of both Wales and Albania in the Group Seven final table.

INTERNATIONAL HONOURS

None

FC AGRO CHISINAU

CLUB DIRECTORY

FC Agro Chisinau
str. Miron Costin 7
camera 801
277001 Chisinau
President - Petru Efros
Coach - S. Caramanov; Iuri Gavrilov

APPEARANCES 95/96

	P	Ap	Gls
Ruslan BARBAROS	A	29	18
Oleg BELAN	M	30	2
Valeriu CATANSUS	M	29	5
P. CEBOTARI	A	11	2
Ruslan CMIT	D	18	1
Mihai COJUSEA	A	6	
Vladimir COLBASIUC	D	27	1
Sergiu EPUREANU	M	26	4
Oleg FLENTEA	M	26	7
A. GARIUC	D	6	1
Iuri GAVRILOV	A	13	
Eugen GÂLCA	D	28	
A. GOREACEV		3	1
Veaceslav JIGAILOV	G	10	
Aleksandr KIRILOV	G	20	
Iuri MAZARATI	D	3	
S. MOCANU	M	6	1
MUNTEANU	A	9	2
F. ONU		1	
Victor PLATON	M	4	1
Lilian POPESCU	M	23	6
Viaceslav SISIANU	M	8	2
Oleg SOIMU	M	23	4
Anatoli TCACIUC	D	29	1
Serghei VACARIUC	D	18	

LEAGUE RESULTS 1995/96

02/08/95	Bugeac Comrat	A	5-0	Catansus, Platon., Sisianu, Barbaros 2
05/08/95	Olimpia Balti	H	0-0	
12/08/95	Zimbru Chisinau	H	1-3	Mocanu
19/08/95	Codru Calarasi	A	1-1	Epureanu (p)
26/08/95	Sportul Studentesc Chisinau	H	2-1	Popescu, Barbaros
09/09/95	Speranta Nisporeni	A	2-1	Flentea, Catansus
16/09/95	Progresul Briceni	H	3-1	Sisianu, Belan, Epureanu
23/09/95	Spumante Cricova	H	2-2	Barbaros, Catansus
11/10/95	Nistru Otaci	A	1-0	Popescu
14/10/95	Torentul Chisinau	A	3-1	Catansus, Popescu, Flentea
21/10/95	Nistru Ciobruciu	H	5-0	Cmit, Barbaros, Belan, Goreacev, Flentea
28/10/95	Tiligul Tiraspol	A	1-2	Epureanu (p)
08/11/95	MHM-93 Chisnau	H	0-0	
11/11/95	Tighina Bender	H	0-0	(awarded as home win)
18/11/95	Constructorul Chisinau	A	0-4	
16/03/96	Olimpia Balti	A	1-0	Barbaros
24/03/96	Zimbru Chisinau	A	1-1	Barbaros
30/03/96	Codru Calarasi	H	1-1	og (Osipenco)
13/04/96	Speranta Nisporeni	H	2-3	Barbaros, Munteanu
17/04/96	Sportul Studentesc Chisinau	A	2-1	Barbaros 2 (1p)
20/04/96	Progresul Briceni	A	3-0	Tcaciuc, Munteanu, Barbaros
24/04/96	Bugeac Comrat	H	6-0	Popescu, Cebotari, Barbaros 2, Colbasiuc, Flentea
28/04/96	Spumante Cricova	A	4-0	Soimu, Barbaros 2, Epureanu
04/05/96	Nistru Otaci	H	1-0	Popescu
11/05/96	Torentul Chisinau	H	5-0	Catansus, Barbaros 2, Soimu 2
18/05/96	Nistru Ciobruciu	A	3-2	Gariuc, Cebotari, Flentea
26/05/96	Tiligul Tiraspol	H	2-1	Soimu, Flentea (p)
08/06/96	Tighina Bender	A	2-0	Popescu, Barbaros
12/06/96	MHM-93 Chisnau	A	1-0	Flentea (p)
16/06/96	Constructorul Chisinau	H	0-2	

BUGEAC COMRAT

CLUB DIRECTORY

Bugeac Comrat
str. Lenin 15
278710 Comrat
President - none
Coach - V. Sukman; C. Gheorghiev; Stefan Ceban
Stadium - Bugeac

MAJOR HONOURS
Domestic Cup - (1) 1992

APPEARANCES 95/96

	P	Ap	Gls
V. ALADOV		2	
Nikolai ARNAUT	M	22	
Constantin BASARAB	A	11	
Vladimir BASARAB	D	2	
CARA	A	12	
CÂLICIC	D	1	
CEBANICA	M	10	
Victor CURSUNJI	D	13	1
CUTER	D	9	
Stefan DOBRIOGLO	D	17	1
Igor EFREMOV	M	12	1
A. GAFONIC	M	2	
GAVRILITA	M	9	
A. GRIGORCIUC	M	16	1
Serghei MIHAILOV	A	8	
G. MOLDOVAN	M	18	2
Andrei NEDIALCOV	G	6	
Vladimir PETRENKO	M	12	
Vitali PETROV	A	25	
V. POPOV	M	12	
Arkadi RAHMANIUC	D	5	
RADUCAN	M	4	
ROMANENCO	M	1	
S. SAPUNJI	G	21	
SIRCHILI	D	6	
Georgi SOMPOL	A	9	
A. UZUN	D	16	
VELICOV	G	7	
V. VETLUGHIN	M	17	
Constantin ZLATOVCEN	M	6	
G. ZLATOVCEN		3	

LEAGUE RESULTS 1995/96

Date	Opponent	H/A	Score	Scorers
02/08/95	FC Agro Chisinau	H	0-5	
05/08/95	MHM-93 Chisnau	A	0-7	
12/08/95	Nistru Otaci	A	0-3	
19/08/95	Nistru Ciobruciu	H	2-2	Cursunji, Moldovan
26/08/95	Torentul Chisinau	A	0-5	
09/09/95	Constructorul Chisinau	H	0-2	
16/09/95	Sportul Studentesc Chisinau	A	0-4	
23/09/95	Tiligul Tiraspol	H	0-3	
30/09/95	Tighina Bender	A	0-6	
14/10/95	Speranta Nisporeni	H	1-4	Dobrioglo
21/10/95	Zimbru Chisinau	A	0-8	
28/10/95	Spumante Cricova	A	0-9	
04/11/95	Progresul Briceni	H	1-4	Moldovan
08/11/95	Olimpia Balti	A	0-0	(awarded as home win)
18/11/95	Codru Calarasi	H	1-8	Efremov
24/03/96	Nistru Otaci	H	1-10	Grigorciuc
30/03/96	Nistru Ciobruciu	A	0-3	
07/04/96	Torentul Chisinau	H	0-7	
13/04/96	Constructorul Chisinau	A	0-5	
17/04/96	MHM-93 Chisnau	H	0-7	
20/04/96	Sportul Studentesc Chisinau	H	0-3	
24/04/96	FC Agro Chisinau	A	0-6	
27/04/96	Tiligul Tiraspol	A	0-7	
04/05/96	Tighina Bender	H	0-4	
11/05/96	Speranta Nisporeni	A	0-7	
18/05/96	Zimbru Chisinau	H	0-4	
25/05/96	Spumante Cricova	H	0-3	
31/05/96	Codru Calarasi	A	0-6	
08/06/96	Progresul Briceni	A	0-0	(awarded as home win)
12/06/96	Olimpia Balti	H	0-0	(awarded as away win)

CODRU CALARASI

CLUB DIRECTORY

Codru Calarasi
str. Uzinelor nr.1
279000 Calarasi
President - George Olaru
Coach - Iuri Gamart; Evgheni Piunovski
Stadium - Codru

APPEARANCES 95/96

	P	Ap	Gls
Iurie ARCAN	D	26	4
S. BARVINENCO		5	
G. BORTNICOV	G	3	
Valeriu CATANA	D	29	5
Nicolae CHIRIAC	A	8	
CIUDAC		13	7
O. DEICUNOV		4	
DIACENCO	D	1	
EMELIANOV	D	6	
1. FILIP		8	
GOLUBTOV	D	14	
Pavel GORBULEAC	D	19	
Sergiu HAREA	G	9	
Valentin IVAHNENCO	D	4	
Iuri LÂSENCO	A	22	1
Iuri MAISTRENCO	A	15	1
Ghenadi MALINOVSCHI	M	29	1
Sakro MARCAREAN	A	30	11
S. MUNTEAN	D	6	1
Iuri NAZAROV	M	14	2
Iuri OSIPENCO		20	5
PRONEVOI		15	
Anatol PRUTEANU	D	20	1
V. SOFRONENCO		16	5
A. SOSNOVSCHI		9	
Vladimir STAROSTENKO	G	21	
N. TROFAILA		12	6
Aleksandr VÎBLOV	M	9	1
ZELENCO	D	1	

LEAGUE RESULTS 1995/96

02/08/95	Spumante Cricova	H	3-2	Sofronenco (p), Marcarean, Trofaila
05/08/95	Torentul Chisinau	A	1-0	Sofronenco
12/08/95	Constructorul Chisinau	H	0-1	
19/08/95	FC Agro Chisinau	H	1-1	Maistrenco
27/08/95	Tiligul Tiraspol	A	0-8	
09/09/95	Progresul Briceni	A	0-1	
16/09/95	Nistru Otaci	H	1-3	Sofronenco
23/09/95	MHM-93 Chisnau	H	2-0	Marcarean, Sofronenco (p)
30/09/95	Olimpia Balti	A	0-3	
14/10/95	Tighina Bender	H	0-1	
21/10/95	Sportul Studentesc Chisinau	A	0-2	
28/10/95	Zimbru Chisinau	H	0-8	
04/11/95	Nistru Ciobruciu	A	1-0	Lasenco
08/11/95	Speranta Nisporeni	H	2-2	Arcan, Trofaila
18/11/95	Bugeac Comrat	A	8-1	Catana (p), Marcarean, Arcan 2, Trofaila 4
09/03/96	Spumante Cricova	A	1-1	Osipenco
16/03/96	Torentul Chisinau	H	1-3	Marcarean
24/03/96	Constructorul Chisinau	A	0-6	
30/03/96	FC Agro Chisinau	A	1-1	Malinovschi
13/04/96	Progresul Briceni	H	10-1	Pruteanu, Ciudac 4, Marcarean 4, Sofronenco
20/04/96	Nistru Otaci	A	0-1	
27/04/96	MHM-93 Chisnau	A	0-0	
04/05/96	Olimpia Balti	H	1-2	Marcarean
11/05/96	Tighina Bender	A	4-1	Ciudac 2, Osipenco, Muntean
18/05/96	Sportul Studentesc Chisinau	H	2-1	Arcan, Marcarean
22/05/96	Tiligul Tiraspol	H	0-3	
25/05/96	Zimbru Chisinau	A	1-3	Catana (p)
31/05/96	Bugeac Comrat	H	6-0	Vîblov, Osipenco 2, Nazarov, Catana 2
08/06/96	Nistru Ciobruciu	H	3-1	Catana, Osipenco, Marcarean
12/06/96	Speranta Nisporeni	A	2-1	Ciudac, Nazarov

CONSTRUCTORUL CHISINAU

CLUB DIRECTORY

Constructorul Chisinau
Chisinau
President - Valeriu Rotaru
Coach - F. Veronean; Alexandru Matiura
Stadium - Constructorul

MAJOR HONOURS
Domestic Cup - (1) 1996.

APPEARANCES 95/96

	P	Ap	Gls
I. BAZALEI	G	1	
Iulian BURSUC	M	29	1
Vladimir CEBAN	G	16	
Vlad CIORICI	A	1	
Igor CUCIUC	M	29	7
O. DEICUNOV	A	5	1
Serghei DINOV	G	13	
Igor FILIP	D	20	1
Vitali KOMLENOK	M	8	2
Viktor KUZNETOV	M	1	
Iuri MARTÂNIUC	A	14	12
E. MUNTEANU	M	6	
Erik OKOKO	M	7	
I. PASECINIC	M	9	
Mihail PAVLOV	A	25	10
Iurie PLATON	D	24	1
POCATILO	M	2	
PUSCA	D	12	
Vlad ROBU	M	11	
Ghenadie SÂRBU	M	5	
Aleksandr SCRUPSKI	A	26	14
Alexei SKALA	D	8	
Iurie SKALA	M	9	
SOFRONENKO	M	5	
STARODULET	A	6	
Oleg SISKIN	M	14	2
Ivan TABANOV	D	27	1
V. TABACIUC	D	4	
Costel TIRON (ROM)	A	18	11
TRICOLICI	D	4	
Oleg TVERDOHLEBOV	D	27	6
N. VASILIEV	M	9	
Aleksandr ZUBAREV	D	14	

LEAGUE RESULTS 1995/96

02/08/95	Nistru Ciobruciu	A	2-0	Pavlov, og (Veriovchin)
05/08/95	Sportul Studentesc Chisinau	H	2-1	Deicunov, Tverdohlebov
12/08/95	Codru Calarasi	A	1-0	Pavlov
19/08/95	Progresul Briceni	A	2-1	Tverdohlebov, Pavlov
26/08/95	Spumante Cricova	H	2-0	Scrupski 2
09/09/95	Bugeac Comrat	A	2-0	Pavlov., Tverdohlebov
17/09/95	Zimbru Chisinau	H	1-2	Scrupski
23/09/95	Tighina Bender	H	1-0	Scrupski
29/09/95	Tiligul Tiraspol	A	2-1	Pavlov 2
14/10/95	MHM-93 Chisnau	H	0-1	
21/10/95	Speranta Nisporeni	A	1-0	Cuciuc
28/10/95	Torentul Chisinau	H	3-1	Cuciuc (p), Tverdohlebov, Tiron
04/11/95	Olimpia Balti	H	1-1	Tiron
08/11/95	Nistru Otaci	A	1-1	Pavlov
18/11/95	FC Agro Chisinau	H	4-0	Tiron, Sischin, Cuciuc, Scrupski
09/03/96	Nistru Ciobruciu	H	5-0	Tiron, Cuciuc 2, Pavlov (p), Martâniuc
16/03/96	Sportul Studentesc Chisinau	A	2-1	Tiron (p), Scrupski
24/03/96	Codru Calarasi	H	6-0	Pavlov, Martâniuc 4, Tiron
30/03/96	Progresul Briceni	H	10-0	Martâniuc 2, Cuciuc, Pavlov, Platon, Tabanov, Tiron 3 (1p), Sischin
13/04/96	Bugeac Comrat	H	5-0	og (Arnaut), Tiron 2 (1p), Martâniuc 2
20/04/96	Zimbru Chisinau	A	0-2	
27/04/96	Tighina Bender	A	3-0	Scrupski 3
04/05/96	Tiligul Tiraspol	H	0-2	
18/05/96	Speranta Nisporeni	H	2-0	Cuciuc (p), Martâniuc
22/05/96	Spumante Cricova	A	2-1	Scrupski, Tverdohlebov
25/05/96	Torentul Chisinau	H	6-0	Tverdohlebov, Scrupski 3, Komlenok 2
05/06/96	MHM-93 Chisnau	A	1-0	Filip
08/06/96	Olimpia Balti	A	0-1	
12/06/96	Nistru Otaci	H	2-1	Martâniuc 2
16/06/96	FC Agro Chisinau	A	2-0	Bursuc, Scrupski

MHM-93 CHISINAU

CLUB DIRECTORY

MHM-93 Chisinau
str. Mesterul Manole 7
Chisinau
President - Valeri Beregoi
Coach - N. Esin; Vladimir Gosperski

APPEARANCES 95/96

	P	Ap	Gls
Vinitu ANGHEL	D	23	
Valeri BOGDANET	M	7	
V. BOTEZATU		1	
Adrian BULARDA	M	4	
Serghei BUTELSCHI	M	3	1
Aleksandr CIUMAC	M	8	
Ghenadie COSTIUC	D	16	
Vladislav GOIAN	M	27	
Dumitru GUSILA	A	16	4
Serghei KRASILEVSKI	G	3	
Vadim KVARTENKO	D	3	
Veaceslav MAXIM	M	24	4
Ion MUNTEANU	D	7	
Iurie MUNTEANU	M	23	
L. OLEKSICI		1	
Iuri OSIPENCO		4	
Nicolae PANU	D	24	
Oleg PETROV	A	19	2
Victor RUSSU	M	9	
Serghei SAVCENCO	M	9	1
Igor SPELNICOV	D	23	1
Georgi STRATULAT	M	4	
SARAPOV	D	10	3
Vladimir SOHIREV	A	26	7
Dorin STEFANESCU	A	1	
TEACA		1	
Alexandru TOPALA	M	14	1
Gabrile TUDORACHE	G	28	1
Veaceslav UNTILA	M	26	4
Igor URSACHI	A	25	13

LEAGUE RESULTS 1995/96

02/08/95	Nistru Otaci	A	0-1	
05/08/95	Bugeac Comrat	H	7-0	Ursachi 3, Untila, Sohirev, Tudorache, og (Basarab V.)
12/08/95	Tighina Bender	H	0-0	(awarded as home win)
17/08/95	Zimbru Chisinau	A	0-2	
27/08/95	Progresul Briceni	H	1-0	Ursachi
09/09/95	Olimpia Balti	H	0-0	
16/09/95	Spumante Cricova	A	1-0	Ursachi
23/09/95	Codru Calarasi	A	0-2	
30/09/95	Nistru Ciobruciu	H	1-1	Ursachi
14/10/95	Constructorul Chisinau	A	1-0	Ursachi
21/10/95	Torentul Chisinau	H	5-1	Maxim 2, Ursachi, Gusila, Butelschi
28/10/95	Speranta Nisporeni	A	2-2	Gusila, Ursachi
04/11/95	Sportul Studentesc Chisinau	H	3-0	Spelnicov, Sohirev, Petrov
08/11/95	FC Agro Chisinau	A	0-0	
18/11/95	Tiligul Tiraspol	H	1-5	Ursachi (p)
09/03/96	Nistru Otaci	H	0-1	
24/03/96	Tighina Bender	A	1-0	Untila
30/03/96	Zimbru Chisinau	H	0-3	
07/04/96	Progresul Briceni	A	4-1	Sarapov 2, Sohirev, Ursachi
13/04/96	Olimpia Balti	A	0-1	
17/04/96	Bugeac Comrat	A	7-0	Maxim 2, Topala, Sohirev 3, og (Moldovan)
20/04/96	Spumante Cricova	H	1-0	Sohirev
27/04/96	Codru Calarasi	H	0-0	
04/05/96	Nistru Ciobruciu	A	4-0	Sarapov, Ursachi, Petrov, Savcenco
18/05/96	Torentul Chisinau	A	1-1	Untila
25/05/96	Speranta Nisporeni	H	2-1	Ursachi, Gusila
05/06/96	Constructorul Chisinau	H	0-1	
08/06/96	Sportul Studentesc Chisinau	A	2-1	Untila, Gusila
12/06/96	FC Agro Chisinau	H	0-1	
16/06/96	Tiligul Tiraspol	A	0-1	

NISTRU CIOBRUCIU

CLUB DIRECTORY

Nistru Ciobruciu
str. Matrasov 16
Ciobruciu
President - none
Coach - Petru Caraman
Stadium - Tineretea

APPEARANCES 95/96

	P	Ap	Gls
Denis BARANOV	M	22	1
Oleg BARANOV	A	9	
Victor BARÂSEV	A	1	
BEJENARI	A	1	
Aleksandr BOGACI	M	7	1
D. CARAMAN		1	
Eduard CARAMAN	M	22	
Valeri CHILIENCO	A	4	3
COJUHARI	G	1	
COTLEAR	A	11	6
Andrei CRIVOI	M	10	1
DEJINARI	M	3	
Sergiu DODUL	M	15	
Ghenadi EFREMOV	D	5	
ERMURACHI	A	1	
Vitali GLUHENCI	M	22	2
Andrei GOIAN	G	1	
Serghei GOLOVCENCO	D	26	1
Serghei GRJIBOVSCHI	A	25	1
Evgheni HMARUC	G	3	
HODOS	A	11	2
Aleksei IAROVÂH	M	19	1
Vladimir IAROVÂH	M	21	2
Oleg IORDACHESCU	D	25	
Oleg MASLOV	M	6	
Viktor MATIUNIN	D	3	
Aleksandr MELNIK	D	17	
V. MORCOV	G	7	
Iuri PRIGANIUC	M	10	
Pavel SAULENCO	D	7	
Egor SAVIN	A	4	
Igor SEREDA	M	9	2
I. STAJILA		2	
Mihail TCACIUC	A	2	1
Serghei VENEDIKTOV	G	17	
Aleksandr VERIOVCHIN	D	5	
Serghei VÂHODET	D	19	

LEAGUE RESULTS 1995/96

02/08/95	Constructorul Chisinau	H	0-2	
05/08/95	Speranta Nisporeni	A	1-5	Tcaciuc
13/08/95	Tiligul Tiraspol	H	2-5	Chilienco 2
19/08/95	Bugeac Comrat	A	2-2	Crivoi, Sereda
26/08/95	Olimpia Balti	H	1-3	Chilienco
09/09/95	Spumante Cricova	H	0-6	
16/09/95	Torentul Chisinau	A	0-0	
23/09/95	Nistru Otaci	H	0-4	
30/09/95	MHM-93 Chisnau	A	1-1	Bogaci
14/10/95	Progresul Briceni	H	3-2	Iarovâh A., Gluhenci, Sereda
21/10/95	FC Agro Chisinau	A	0-5	
28/10/95	Sportul Studentesc Chisinau	A	0-4	
04/11/95	Codru Calarasi	H	0-1	
08/11/95	Tighina Bender	A	1-1	Grjibovschi
18/11/95	Zimbru Chisinau	H	0-1	
09/03/96	Constructorul Chisinau	A	0-5	
16/03/96	Speranta Nisporeni	H	1-0	Cotlear
24/03/96	Tiligul Tiraspol	A	1-5	Cotlear
30/03/96	Bugeac Comrat	H	3-0	Cotlear 2, Golovcenco
13/04/96	Spumante Cricova	A	0-0	(awarded as home win)
17/04/96	Olimpia Balti	A	0-4	
20/04/96	Torentul Chisinau	H	0-0	
27/04/96	Nistru Otaci	A	0-3	
04/05/96	MHM-93 Chisnau	H	0-4	
11/05/96	Progresul Briceni	A	2-2	Gluhenci, Cotlear
15/05/96	Zimbru Chisinau	A	0-9	
18/05/96	FC Agro Chisinau	H	2-3	Baranov D., Iarovâh V.
25/05/96	Sportul Studentesc Chisinau	H	1-2	Cotlear
08/06/96	Codru Calarasi	A	1-3	Hodos
12/06/96	Tighina Bender	H	2-2	Hodos, Iarovâh V.

NISTRU OTACI

CLUB DIRECTORY

Nistru Otaci
str. Lazo 14
Otaci
President - Vasile Traghira
Coach - Nicolae Cebotaru; I. Rontea
Stadium - Calaraseuca

APPEARANCES 95/96

	P	Ap	Gls
Gocha BREGVADZE	A	10	
Vitali CARMAC	G	13	
CAPATÂNA	D	1	
Aurel COLUN	M	24	
Vlad COPOT	M	18	5
Nikolai CUCERUC	D	15	1
Serghei DINOV	G	2	
Serghei FILIPCENKO	M	22	2
Iuri GHII	D	13	1
Vlad GOIAN	M	1	
GUDZICHIEVICI	D	4	1
Alexandru GUZUN	D	26	4
Gheorghe HAREA	A	23	9
LANOVOI	G	1	
Vitali MAEVICI	D	23	1
MALITCHI		2	
Vasili MALIUTA	A	26	9
Mamuca MANAGADZE	A	13	4
Ivan MANDRICENKO	D	28	
MIHAILISIN	M	1	
MIHAESCU	A	8	
Oleg OBOROC	D	4	1
V. OLEINIC		10	5
PASIHOV	M	1	
Anatoli PODGAETCHI	D	28	2
Lilian POPESCU	M	2	
PRIT	M	2	2
Iuri REABKO	D	19	
Dmitri RIPCA	G	15	
RÂBCO	A	1	
Gheorghe STRATULAT	M	13	2
Anatoli SABLEVSCHI	A	21	3
Dorin STEFANESCU	A	16	10

LEAGUE RESULTS 1995/96

02/08/95	MHM-93 Chisnau	H	1-0	Copot
04/08/95	Spumante Cricova	A	2-0	Guzun, Oboroc
12/08/95	Bugeac Comrat	H	3-0	Guzun, Stefanescu 2
19/08/95	Tiligul Tiraspol	A	1-3	Stefanescu
26/08/95	Tighina Bender	H	3-2	Stefanescu, Guzun, Oleinic
16/09/95	Codru Calarasi	A	3-1	Sablevschi, Managadze, Harea
23/09/95	Nistru Ciobruciu	A	4-0	Stratulat, Oleinic 3
11/10/95	FC Agro Chisinau	H	0-1	
14/10/95	Sportul Studentesc Chisinau	H	4-0	Managadze 2, Maliuta 2
21/10/95	Progresul Briceni	A	1-1	Sablevschi
28/10/95	Olimpia Balti	A	0-1	
04/11/95	Speranta Nisporeni	H	4-2	Stefanescu 2, Managadze, Oleinic (p)
08/11/95	Constructorul Chisinau	H	1-1	Cuceruc
18/11/95	Torentul Chisinau	A	3-0	Guzun, Maliuta 2
29/11/95	Zimbru Chisinau	H	0-1	
09/03/96	MHM-93 Chisnau	A	1-0	Filipcenko
16/03/96	Spumante Cricova	H	0-0	
24/03/96	Bugeac Comrat	A	10-1	Maliuta 3, Podgaetchi, Harea, Stratulat, Stefanescu 2 (1p), og (Dobrioglo), Filipcenko
30/03/96	Tiligul Tiraspol	H	1-2	Harea (p)
07/04/96	Tighina Bender	A	1-1	Maevici
13/04/96	Zimbru Chisinau	A	0-5	
20/04/96	Codru Calarasi	H	1-0	Harea
27/04/96	Nistru Ciobruciu	H	3-0	Prit, Ghii, Sablevschi
04/05/96	FC Agro Chisinau	A	0-1	
11/05/96	Sportul Studentesc Chisinau	A	1-1	Copot
18/05/96	Progresul Briceni	H	9-0	Stefanescu 2, Copot 3, Harea 3 (1p), Prit
25/05/96	Olimpia Balti	H	2-2	Harea 2 (1p)
08/06/96	Speranta Nisporeni	A	0-0	
12/06/96	Constructorul Chisinau	A	1-2	Maliuta
16/06/96	Torentul Chisinau	H	3-0	Maliuta, Gudzichievici, Podgaetchi

OLIMPIA BALTI

CLUB DIRECTORY

Olimpia Balti
str. Kiev 155
279200 Balti
President - Gennadi Grigorishin
Coach - Vladimir Oleanski
Stadium - Olimpia

APPEARANCES 95/96

	P	Ap	Gls
Andrei ALBU	G	15	
Dmitri ARALCHIN	A	13	
Anatol BALICA	M	23	
Nicolae BABALAU	M	14	1
A. BELEAI		9	1
V. BERCO	A	12	3
Oleg BOBU	M	10	
Nicolae BUNEA	G	14	
Valeriu CIRES	M	26	2
Vladimir DIJOVSCHI	A	28	6
Ivan DOLINTA	M	28	2
GRAB	M	4	
IVAHNIUC	A	12	3
KUROV	D	2	
V. LEBEDEV		14	1
Eduard LEBEDINSKI	D	26	
LOHMAI	M	13	1
PATROMAN	M	4	2
Serghei ROGACIOV	A	26	25
RUCODAINÂI	D	3	
Veaceslav RUSNAC	D	27	1
Oleg SARAPOV	M	5	
Leonid TKACI	D	18	
Valeriu TOFAN	M	21	4
ZAMA	A	11	3

LEAGUE RESULTS 1995/96

02/08/95	Torentul Chisinau	H	7-1	Rogaciov 4 (1p), Dijovschi 2, Dolinta
05/08/95	FC Agro Chisinau	A	0-0	
12/08/95	Progresul Briceni	A	1-0	Rogaciov
19/08/95	Sportul Studentesc Chisinau	H	2-1	Rogaciov 2
26/08/95	Nistru Ciobruciu	A	3-1	Rogaciov 2, Cires
09/09/95	MHM-93 Chisnau	A	0-0	
16/09/95	Tighina Bender	H	4-0	Tofan, Rogaciov, Rusnac, Berco
21/09/95	Zimbru Chisinau	A	2-1	Dijovschi, Rogaciov
30/09/95	Codru Calarasi	H	3-0	Rogaciov 2, Dijovschi
14/10/95	Spumante Cricova	A	1-1	Lebedev
21/10/95	Tiligul Tiraspol	H	0-4	
28/10/95	Nistru Otaci	H	1-0	Tofan
04/11/95	Constructorul Chisinau	A	1-1	Babalau
08/11/95	Bugeac Comrat	H	0-0	(awarded as home win)
18/11/95	Speranta Nisporeni	A	5-0	Cires, Dijovschi, Rogaciov 2, Beleai
09/03/96	Torentul Chisinau	A	1-0	Dolinta
16/03/96	FC Agro Chisinau	H	0-1	
24/03/96	Progresul Briceni	H	3-0	Rogaciov 2, Ivahniuc
30/03/96	Sportul Studentesc Chisinau	A	2-0	Rogaciov, Zama
13/04/96	MHM-93 Chisnau	H	1-0	Ivahniuc
17/04/96	Nistru Ciobruciu	H	4-0	Lohmai, Patroman, Tofan, Ivahniuc
20/04/96	Tighina Bender	A	0-1	
27/04/96	Zimbru Chisinau	H	0-3	
04/05/96	Codru Calarasi	A	2-1	Dijovschi, Berco
11/05/96	Spumante Cricova	H	3-3	Rogaciov 2, Berco
18/05/96	Tiligul Tiraspol	A	0-3	
25/05/96	Nistru Otaci	A	2-2	Patroman, Zama
08/06/96	Constructorul Chisinau	H	1-0	Rogaciov
12/06/96	Bugeac Comrat	A	0-0	(awarded as away win)
15/06/96	Speranta Nisporeni	H	6-1	Rogaciov 4, Zama, Tofan

PROGRESUL BRICENI

CLUB DIRECTORY

Progresul Briceni
str. Independentei 28
279620 Briceni
President - none
Coach - Valentin Goian; V. Antochi
Stadium - Moldova

APPEARANCES 95/96

	P	Ap	Gls
BOTNARI	A	9	
Nicolae BUDZAN	D	1	
CIORNÂI	D	4	
V. COROLIOV		1	
Oleg COZELCO	A	16	4
Pavel CUDREAVTEV	A	8	3
I. DMITRENCO		2	1
DRAGAN	M	2	
Oleg DRONIC	M	27	1
DUDU		1	
R. EROHIN	G	1	
Vitali GALANCIUC	M	21	2
Anatoli GAMALI	M	2	
HMELI	G	8	
Vladimir IATIUK	D	16	
JMURCOV	M	9	2
JUCOV	M	1	
Vitali KUNITA	G	17	
Serghei LAVRIK	A	17	
Nicolai LESIC	M	4	
V. LUNGU		1	
MARUSIC	D	4	
C. MORARU	A	3	
Eugeniu MORARI	D	23	
Veacaslav MORARU	D	4	
Andrei NOVAC	D	10	1
Vitalie PASCARU	A	12	
Vladimir PAVLOV	M	10	2
V. PAVLOV II		1	
PISTRUGA	D	10	
PLACINTA	M	5	
Andrei ROMANOV	D	16	
RUSU	A	7	1
Aleksei SOTSCOV	M	4	
STÂNCA	M	4	
Aleksandr SEVCIUK	M	17	
TÂNCA	M	1	
Iuri TOLOV		9	2
VACARCIUC	G	5	
A. VACARITA		9	
VORNOVITCHI	D	8	

LEAGUE RESULTS 1995/96

Date	Opponent	H/A	Score	Scorers
02/08/95	Zimbru Chisinau	A	0-4	
05/08/95	Tiligul Tiraspol	A	0-7	
12/08/95	Olimpia Balti	H	0-1	
19/08/95	Constructorul Chisinau	H	1-2	Cozelco
27/08/95	MHM-93 Chisnau	A	0-1	
09/09/95	Codru Calarasi	H	1-0	Pavlov Vl.
16/09/95	FC Agro Chisinau	A	1-3	Novac
23/09/95	Torentul Chisinau	A	2-2	Pavlov Vl., Cozelco
30/09/95	Speranta Nisporeni	H	1-2	Dmitrenco
14/10/95	Nistru Ciobruciu	A	2-3	Cudreavtev, Tolov (p)
21/10/95	Nistru Otaci	H	1-1	Cudreavtev
28/10/95	Tighina Bender	H	0-0	
04/11/95	Bugeac Comrat	A	4-1	Galanciuc, Tolov (p), Cudreavtev, Cozelco
08/11/95	Sportul Studentesc Chisinau	H	1-0	Galanciuc
18/11/95	Spumante Cricova	A	1-2	Cozelco
09/03/96	Zimbru Chisinau	H	0-2	
16/03/96	Tiligul Tiraspol	H	0-0	(awarded as away win)
24/03/96	Olimpia Balti	A	0-3	
30/03/96	Constructorul Chisinau	A	0-10	
07/04/96	MHM-93 Chisnau	H	1-4	Dronic
13/04/96	Codru Calarasi	A	1-10	Jmurcov
20/04/96	FC Agro Chisinau	H	0-3	
27/04/96	Torentul Chisinau	H	0-5	
04/05/96	Speranta Nisporeni	A	0-0	(awarded as home win)
11/05/96	Nistru Ciobruciu	H	2-2	Rusu, Jmurcov
18/05/96	Nistru Otaci	A	0-9	
25/05/96	Tighina Bender	A	0-12	
08/06/96	Bugeac Comrat	H	0-0	(awarded as home win)
12/06/96	Sportul Studentesc Chisinau	A	0-13	
15/06/96	Spumante Cricova	H	0-3	

SPERANTA NISPORENI

CLUB DIRECTORY

Speranta Nisporeni
Nisporeni
President - Nicolae Bogat
Coach - Pavel Ciobanu; Alexandru Shicov

APPEARANCES 95/96

	P	Ap	Gls
Vasile ARLET	D	25	2
Mihail ARTENI	M	19	2
V. ARTENI	M	5	
Igor BALAUR	M	14	4
A. BARANENCOV		2	
Ghenadie BOLDURESCU	D	28	1
Vitalie BOLDURESCU	M	12	
Ghenadie BORTNIKOV	G	9	
Vladimir BUCUR	M	20	1
Iurie CIORICI	D	24	
Vlad CIORICI	A	19	2
Victor CÂRLIG	A	28	10
CRIVOI	M	11	2
Sergiu DOBZEU	G	2	
DOVGHII	A	10	5
V. EMELIANOV		4	
Dumitru GHETMAN	M	17	
Ioan GRIGORAS	G	23	
Toma IONITA	M	24	4
Boris PRONEVOI	M	13	1
Vlad ROBU	M	15	4
Serghei SAVCENCO	M	7	1
Serghei SÂRBU	D	3	
Vitali SPATARU	A	3	
Radu TALPA	D	28	
Toni TABARANU	A	4	
Pavel ZLOBIN	M	9	

LEAGUE RESULTS 1995/96

02/08/95	Tighina Bender	A	4-1	Cârlig, Robu, Balaur, Arteni
05/08/95	Nistru Ciobruciu	H	5-1	Balaur 2, Arteni, Robu, og (Iarovâh)
12/08/95	Torentul Chisinau	H	2-2	Cârlig 2 (1p)
19/08/95	Spumante Cricova	A	0-0	
26/08/95	Zimbru Chisinau	A	0-4	
09/09/95	FC Agro Chisinau	H	1-2	Cârlig (p)
16/09/95	Tiligul Tiraspol	A	1-2	Robu
23/09/95	Sportul Studentesc Chisinau	H	1-1	Cârlig (p)
30/09/95	Progresul Briceni	A	2-1	Cârlig, Bucur
14/10/95	Bugeac Comrat	A	4-1	Pronevoi, Ionita, Cârlig, Ciorici V.
21/10/95	Constructorul Chisinau	H	0-1	
28/10/95	MHM-93 Chisnau	H	2-2	Ionita, Balaur
04/11/95	Nistru Otaci	A	2-4	Ionita 2
08/11/95	Codru Calarasi	A	2-2	Robu, Savcenco
18/11/95	Olimpia Balti	H	0-5	
09/03/96	Tighina Bender	H	1-0	Cârlig
16/03/96	Nistru Ciobruciu	A	0-1	
24/03/96	Torentul Chisinau	A	1-3	og (Ilarionov)
30/03/96	Spumante Cricova	H	0-1	
13/04/96	FC Agro Chisinau	A	3-2	Dovghii, Cârlig (p), Crivoi
17/04/96	Zimbru Chisinau	H	0-2	
20/04/96	Tiligul Tiraspol	H	0-1	
04/05/96	Progresul Briceni	H	0-0	(awarded as home win)
11/05/96	Bugeac Comrat	H	7-0	Ciorici V., Arlet, Crivoi, Boldurescu G., Dovghii 3
18/05/96	Constructorul Chisinau	A	0-2	
22/05/96	Sportul Studentesc Chisinau	A	0-0	
25/05/96	MHM-93 Chisnau	A	1-2	Arlet
08/06/96	Nistru Otaci	H	0-0	
12/06/96	Codru Calarasi	H	1-2	Dovghii
15/06/96	Olimpia Balti	A	1-6	Cârlig

SPORTUL STUDENTESC CHISINAU

CLUB DIRECTORY

Sportul Studentesc Chisinau
str. Dacia nr.7 ap.60
Chisinau
President - Pavel Tolmachev
Coach - Viaceslav Chiricenco

APPEARANCES 95/96

	P	Ap	Gls
Ghenadie ANGHEL	A	19	3
Sergiu BERCO	M	24	1
Anatoli BOROVIKOV	G	7	
Ghenadie CIBOTARI	D	16	
Oleg CIUPAC	M	28	7
Mihail COJUSEA	A	10	2
Igor CORJAN	A	29	10
COROLCOV	M	9	3
Igor CRISTINOI	M	26	1
Andrei DROZDOV	D	16	
Vladimir GENUNCHI	M	5	2
Vladimir GUDEV	M	27	2
Vladimir KRIVENKO	D	26	
Vitalie LUNGU	D	6	
Iurie MÂRZA	M	22	3
Aleksandr MELNICOV	A	9	2
Ruslan MIHAILE	M	5	
Andrei MIRON	A	22	9
Sergiu MUNTEANU	M	5	1
Vladimir MURA	G	26	
Aurel NELIPOVSCHI	A	11	1
Vitali PASCARI	A	3	
Anatol TÂMBUR	D	14	
Vladimir TONURCOV	M	19	2
Aleksei TÂTIURA	D	23	

LEAGUE RESULTS 1995/96

02/08/95	Tiligul Tiraspol	H	1-1	Munteanu
05/08/95	Constructorul Chisinau	A	1-2	Mârza
13/08/95	Spumante Cricova	H	1-4	Melnicov
19/08/95	Olimpia Balti	A	1-2	Miron
26/08/95	FC Agro Chisinau	A	1-2	og (Gâlca)
09/09/95	Torentul Chisinau	H	1-0	Ciupac
16/09/95	Bugeac Comrat	H	4-0	Ciupac, Nelipovschi, Corjan, Melnicov
23/09/95	Speranta Nisporeni	A	1-1	Berco
01/09/95	Zimbru Chisinau	H	1-7	Miron
14/10/95	Nistru Otaci	A	0-4	
21/10/95	Codru Calarasi	H	2-0	Anghel, Tonurcov
28/10/95	Nistru Ciobruciu	H	4-0	Ciupac, Corjan (p), Anghel, Mârza
04/11/95	MHM-93 Chisnau	A	0-3	
08/11/95	Progresul Briceni	A	0-1	
18/11/95	Tighina Bender	H	5-0	Gudev, Ciupac, Miron 3
09/03/96	Tiligul Tiraspol	A	0-3	
16/03/96	Constructorul Chisinau	H	1-2	Mârza
24/03/96	Spumante Cricova	A	0-1	
30/03/96	Olimpia Balti	H	0-2	
13/04/96	Torentul Chisinau	A	2-1	Ciupac, Cojusea
17/04/96	FC Agro Chisinau	H	1-2	Genunchi
20/04/96	Bugeac Comrat	A	3-0	Corjan, Miron 2
04/05/96	Zimbru Chisinau	A	0-8	
11/05/96	Nistru Otaci	H	1-1	Cristinoi (p)
18/05/96	Codru Calarasi	A	1-2	Corjan
22/05/96	Speranta Nisporeni	H	0-0	
25/05/96	Nistru Ciobruciu	A	2-1	Corjan, Tonurcov
08/06/96	MHM-93 Chisnau	H	1-2	Miron
12/06/96	Progresul Briceni	H	13-0	Corjan 5, Anghel, Corolcov 3, Genunchi, Miron, Ciupac, Gudev
16/06/96	Tighina Bender	A	2-1	Cojusea, Ciupac

SPUMANTE CRICOVA

CLUB DIRECTORY

Spumante Cricova
Cricova
President - Vasile Turcanu
Coach - Sergiu Sârbu; Corneliu Costachescu; Ilie Carp

APPEARANCES 95/96

	P	Ap	Gls
Cristian BADALUTA	A	14	4
Adrian BOGDAN	G	24	
Daniel CANTEA	M	23	1
Emil CARAS	D	12	
Igor CARAUS	D	8	
Marin CHIRTOACA	M	4	
Paul CODRU	M	12	3
Igor GHEORGHIES	A	27	9
Oleg IVANOV	D	14	1
Valentin LUPASCU	M	27	2
Serghei MACARI	D	8	
Andrei MARTIN	M	27	5
Ruslan MOLDOVAN	D	25	
Roman ONICA	M	23	2
Florin ONOFREI	A	14	13
Mihail PASNICU	G	1	
Vadim POCATILO	M	22	7
Gheorghe RUSU	D	20	
Daniel SUCIUC	D	22	3
Oleg SISCHIN	D	10	2
SISIANU		6	1
Alexadru TATARU	G	7	
Serghei TVERDOHLER	D	17	
Nicolae VOZIAN	A	9	2

LEAGUE RESULTS 1995/96

Date	Opponent	H/A	Score	Scorers
02/08/95	Codru Calarasi	A	2-3	Gheorghies 2
04/08/95	Nistru Otaci	H	0-2	
13/08/95	Sportul Studentesc Chisinau	A	4-1	Onofrei 3, Sischin
19/08/95	Speranta Nisporeni	A	0-0	
26/08/95	Constructorul Chisinau	A	0-2	
09/09/95	Nistru Ciobruciu	A	6-0	Codru, Lupascu (p), Onofrei 3, Cantea
16/09/95	MHM-93 Chisnau	H	0-1	
23/09/95	FC Agro Chisinau	A	2-2	Gheorghies, Onofrei
30/09/95	Torentul Chisinau	H	6-0	Lupascu (p), Martin, Pocatilo 2, Onofrei (p), Gheorghies
14/10/95	Olimpia Balti	H	1-1	Pocatilo
21/10/95	Tighina Bender	A	0-0	
28/10/95	Bugeac Comrat	H	9-0	Gheorghies, Onofrei 5, Sischin, Codru, Ivanov
04/11/95	Zimbru Chisinau	A	0-3	
08/11/95	Tiligul Tiraspol	A	0-2	
18/11/95	Progresul Briceni	H	2-1	Codru, Suciuc
09/03/96	Codru Calarasi	H	1-1	Onica
16/03/96	Nistru Otaci	A	0-0	
24/03/96	Sportul Studentesc Chisinau	H	1-0	Suciuc
30/03/96	Speranta Nisporeni	A	1-0	og (Ciorici I.)
13/04/96	Nistru Ciobruciu	H	0-0	(awarded as home win)
20/04/96	MHM-93 Chisnau	A	0-1	
28/04/96	FC Agro Chisinau	H	0-4	
04/05/96	Torentul Chisinau	A	1-0	Badaluta
11/05/96	Olimpia Balti	A	3-3	Badaluta, Gheorghies 2
17/05/96	Tighina Bender	H	7-0	Martin 3, Gheorghies 2, Vozian, Sisianu
22/05/96	Constructorul Chisinau	H	1-2	Martin
25/05/96	Bugeac Comrat	A	3-0	Pocatilo 2, Vozian
08/06/96	Zimbru Chisinau	H	1-1	Suciuc (p)
12/06/96	Tiligul Tiraspol	H	2-1	Badaluta, Onica
15/06/96	Progresul Briceni	A	3-0	Pocatilo 2, Badaluta

TIGHINA BENDER

CLUB DIRECTORY

Tighina Bender
str. Tkachenko 10
278100 Bender
President - Ion Rata
Coach - Evgheni Piunovschi; Vladimir Belâi
Stadium - Selkovic

APPEARANCES 95/96

	P	Ap	Gls
Oleg ARTIUKOV	A	1	
Iuri BODIU	D	12	
Serghei CALISTRU	M	12	1
Aleksandr CIUDAC	A	4	1
CRETU	M	4	
Deins DIDE	M	3	
Igor GOLUBTOV	D	13	
Iuri HODÂKIN	G	1	
Igor ILIUSIN	D	29	
JDANOV	M	3	
Serghei KUZNETOV	M	21	2
Denis LOZINSCHI	D	1	
MARTÂNIUC	D	1	
Miroslav MARTÂNOVICI	M	20	
V. MATIUNIN		3	
Anatoli MIGULI	G	29	
Sergiu MIHAI	A	16	1
Aleksandr MURAHOVSCHI	M	11	4
Serghei PROHOROV	A	16	2
Igor RAICEV	A	22	18
Vladimir REAZANOV	M	5	
Andrei RÂBALCO	A	16	2
Ruslan ROIC	D	9	2
Aleksandr RUBAHA	M	22	
Viaceslav SEMIONOV	D	14	
Iuri TOLOV	D	15	
Vladimir TRUBACIOV	M	28	3
Aleksandr ZAITEV	M	16	2
Aleksandr ZELENIUC	D	27	3

LEAGUE RESULTS 1995/96

Date	Opponent	H/A	Score	Scorers
02/08/95	Speranta Nisporeni	H	1-4	Raicev
12/08/95	MHM-93 Chisnau	A	0-0	(awarded as home win)
19/08/95	Torentul Chisinau	H	3-0	Raicev 3 (1p)
26/08/95	Nistru Otaci	A	2-3	Roic 2
10/09/95	Tiligul Tiraspol	H	0-2	
16/09/95	Olimpia Balti	A	0-4	
23/09/95	Constructorul Chisinau	A	0-1	
30/09/95	Bugeac Comrat	H	6-0	Raicev 4, Râbalco, Prohorov
14/10/95	Codru Calarasi	A	1-0	Calistru
21/10/95	Spumante Cricova	H	0-0	
28/10/95	Progresul Briceni	A	0-0	
08/11/95	Nistru Ciobruciu	H	1-1	Ciudac
11/11/95	FC Agro Chisinau	A	0-3	
18/11/95	Sportul Studentesc Chisinau	A	0-5	
25/11/95	Zimbru Chisinau	A	1-3	Raicev
09/03/96	Speranta Nisporeni	A	0-1	
16/03/96	Zimbru Chisinau	H	0-1	
24/03/96	MHM-93 Chisnau	H	0-1	
30/03/96	Torentul Chisinau	A	3-2	Raicev, Zeleniuc, Râbalco
07/04/96	Nistru Otaci	H	1-1	Kuznetov
13/04/96	Tiligul Tiraspol	A	1-3	Trubaciov
20/04/96	Olimpia Balti	H	1-0	Raicev
27/04/96	Constructorul Chisinau	H	0-3	
04/05/96	Bugeac Comrat	A	4-0	Zeleniuc, Kuznetov, Murahovschi 2
11/05/96	Codru Calarasi	H	1-4	Mihai
17/05/96	Spumante Cricova	A	0-7	
25/05/96	Progresul Briceni	H	12-0	Zeleniuc, Raicev 6, Zaitev, Trubaciov 2, Murahovschi 2
08/06/96	FC Agro Chisinau	H	0-2	
12/06/96	Nistru Ciobruciu	A	2-2	Raicev, Prohorov
16/06/96	Sportul Studentesc Chisinau	H	1-2	Zaitev

TILIGUL TIRASPOL

CLUB DIRECTORY

Tiligul Tiraspol
str. Mira 21
278000 Tiraspol
President - Grigori Korzun
Coach - Alexandru Matiura; Alexandr Shtelin
Stadium - Municipal (12,000)

MAJOR HONOURS
Domestic Cup - (3) 1993, 1994, 1995.

APPEARANCES 95/96

	P	Ap	Gls
Viktor BARÂSEV	A	11	
Serghei BELOUS	M	26	3
COTLEAR	M	3	
CUCEREAVTEV	M	1	
Vladimir DOVGHII	M	11	1
Vladimir GAIDAMASCIUC	M	28	5
Evgheni HMARUK	G	3	
Evgheni IVANOV	G	28	
Valeri KILIENKO	A	14	
Vladimir KOSSE	A	28	32
Aleksei KRIVOI	M	2	
Anatoli LUCHIANCICOV	A	10	9
V. MARKOV	G	1	
Aleksandr MELNIKOV	A	16	9
Nicolai MINCEV	D	23	
Igor OPREA	M	8	3
Serghei PARHOMENCO	M	21	1
Valeri POGORELOV	D	23	4
Aleksandr POPOVICI	M	28	14
Iuri PRIGANIUK	D	8	
Sergiu SECU	D	24	3
Vadim SEREDA	M	2	1
Andrei STROENCO	D	19	3
Serghei STROENCO	D	29	2
Igor TÂTÂC	D	19	2
Veaceslav TRUHANOV	M	9	1

LEAGUE RESULTS 1995/96

Date	Opponent	H/A	Score	Scorers
02/08/95	Sportul Studentesc Chisinau	A	1-1	Kosse
05/08/95	Progresul Briceni	H	7-0	og (Pavlov), Kosse (p), Dovghii, Luchiancicov 2, Stroenco A., Popovici
13/08/95	Nistru Ciobruciu	A	5-2	Popovici, Kosse 2, Luchiancicov, Oprea
19/08/95	Nistru Otaci	H	3-1	Kosse, Luchiancicov, Stroenco A.
27/08/95	Codru Calarasi	H	8-0	Oprea, Luchiancicov 2, Kosse 3, Popovici, Tâtâc
10/09/95	Tighina Bender	A	2-0	Luchiancicov, Kosse
16/09/95	Speranta Nisporeni	H	2-1	Luchiancicov, Oprea
23/09/95	Bugeac Comrat	A	0-0	(awarded as away win)
29/09/95	Constructorul Chisinau	H	1-2	Kosse
12/10/95	Zimbru Chisinau	A	2-2	Kosse (p), Gaidamasciuc
21/10/95	Olimpia Balti	A	4-0	og (Tcaci), Sereda, Pogorelov, Popovici
28/10/95	FC Agro Chisinau	H	2-1	Popovici, Kosse (p)
04/11/95	Torentul Chisinau	A	6-0	Belous, Popovici 2, Stroenco A., Parhomenco, Pogorelov
08/11/95	Spumante Cricova	H	2-0	Gaidamasciuc, Popovici
18/11/95	MHM-93 Chisnau	A	5-1	Kosse 3 (1p), Luchiancicov, Melnicov
09/03/96	Sportul Studentesc Chisinau	H	3-0	Kosse (p), Secu, Melnicov
16/03/96	Progresul Briceni	A	0-0	(awarded as away win)
24/03/96	Nistru Ciobruciu	H	5-1	Gaidamasciuc, Stroenco S. 2, Kosse, Popovici
30/03/96	Nistru Otaci	A	2-1	Kosse (p), Secu
13/04/96	Tighina Bender	H	3-1	Kosse (p), Popovici, Melnicov
20/04/96	Speranta Nisporeni	A	1-0	Pogorelov
27/04/96	Bugeac Comrat	H	7-0	Gaidamasciuc, Kosse 2 (1p), Popovici 2, Melnicov 2
04/05/96	Constructorul Chisinau	A	2-0	Kosse 2
18/05/96	Olimpia Balti	H	3-0	Kosse, Gaidamasciuc, Melnicov
22/05/96	Codru Calarasi	A	3-0	Secu, Belous, Kosse (p)
26/05/96	FC Agro Chisinau	A	1-2	Kosse (p)
05/06/96	Zimbru Chisinau	H	0-2	
08/06/96	Torentul Chisinau	H	13-1	Kosse 4, Popovici 2, Belous, Pogorelov, Truhanov, Tâtâc, Melnicov 3
12/06/96	Spumante Cricova	A	1-2	Kosse
16/06/96	MHM-93 Chisnau	H	1-0	Kosse

TORENTUL CHISINAU

CLUB DIRECTORY

Torentul Chisinau
str. Gagarin 2
277009 Chisinau
President - Ion Martia
Coach - V. Doibani; Viaceslav Katkov

APPEARANCES 95/96

	P	Ap	Gls
Vitali ANTONOV	A	15	5
Oleg COLEADIN	D	28	1
Iuri COROLCOV	M	6	2
Igor DENISENCO	D	12	
V. GENUNCHI		6	
Maksim GOPTARI	M	26	8
Igor GORE	A	3	
Victor GRAUR	M	24	5
Mihail GRIGORIEV	M	12	
HORVIN	M	1	
Constantin ILARIONOV	A	14	
Oleg IVANOV	M	6	
Vitali LINCAUTEANU	A	2	
Victor MAIMESCU	M	8	
Viaceslav MAXIMCIUC	M	5	1
Ruslan MIRON	M	10	
Anatol MOCANOV	D	29	
S. MONZOLEVSCHI		6	
C. MORARU		2	
Victor PETREA	M	27	
Gheorghe PÂRCIU	M	4	1
Evgheni PORUBIN	M	16	
Vadim REUZARI	G	20	
Valeri ROMANCIUC	M	4	
Petru SILIVESTRU	M	19	1
Sergiu SILI	D	27	
Aleksandr SOROCHIN	A	3	
Vadim TABACIUC	M	24	5
Aleksei TATARU	G	12	
Aleksandr TOLSTICOV	D	14	6
Valeriu ZGARDAN	M	8	

LEAGUE RESULTS 1995/96

Date	Opponent	H/A	Score	Scorers
02/08/95	Olimpia Balti	A	1-7	Silivestru
05/08/95	Codru Calarasi	H	0-1	
12/08/95	Speranta Nisporeni	A	2-2	Maximciuc, Tolsticov
19/08/95	Tighina Bender	A	0-3	
26/08/95	Bugeac Comrat	H	5-0	Goptari 2, Coroicov 2, Tolsticov
09/09/95	Sportul Studentesc Chisinau	A	0-1	
16/09/95	Nistru Ciobruciu	H	0-0	
23/09/95	Progresul Briceni	H	2-2	Tolsticov 2 (2p)
30/09/95	Spumante Cricova	A	0-6	
14/10/95	FC Agro Chisinau	H	1-3	Goptari (p)
21/10/95	MHM-93 Chisnau	A	1-5	Goptari (p)
28/10/95	Constructorul Chisinau	A	1-3	Tabaciuc
04/11/95	Tiligul Tiraspol	H	0-6	
08/11/95	Zimbru Chisinau	A	0-8	
18/11/95	Nistru Otaci	H	0-3	
09/03/96	Olimpia Balti	H	0-1	
16/03/96	Codru Calarasi	A	3-1	og (Arcan), Pârciu, Graur
24/03/96	Speranta Nisporeni	H	3-1	Graur, Antonov 2
30/03/96	Tighina Bender	H	2-3	Goptari, Graur
07/04/96	Bugeac Comrat	A	7-0	Coleadin, Goptari, Tabaciuc 2, Antonov 2, Graur
13/04/96	Sportul Studentesc Chisinau	H	1-2	Tabaciuc
20/04/96	Nistru Ciobruciu	A	0-0	
27/04/96	Progresul Briceni	A	5-0	Graur, Tolsticov 2, Goptari 2 (1p)
04/05/96	Spumante Cricova	H	0-1	
08/05/96	Zimbru Chisinau	H	0-7	
11/05/96	FC Agro Chisinau	A	0-5	
18/05/96	MHM-93 Chisnau	H	1-1	Tabaciuc
25/05/96	Constructorul Chisinau	H	0-6	
08/06/96	Tiligul Tiraspol	A	1-13	Antonov
16/06/96	Nistru Otaci	A	0-3	

ZIMBRU CHISINAU

CLUB DIRECTORY

Zimbru Chisinau
str. Butuclui 1
277060 Chisinau
tel - (02) 566481
fax - (02) 222244
President - Nicolae Ciornîi
Coach - Alexandru Spiridon
Stadium - Republican (22,500)

MAJOR HONOURS
League Championship - (5)
1992, 1993, 1994, 1995, 1996.

APPEARANCES 95/96

	P	Ap	Gls
Vadim BORET	A	24	4
Dinu CARAS	M	17	2
Emil CARAS	D	12	
Boris CIBOTARU	M	20	4
Sergiu CLESCENCO	A	2	1
Vitali CULIBABA	D	27	
Alexandru CURTIANU	M	26	4
Oleg FISTICAN	D	8	
Vladimir GAVRILIUC	A	25	34
Vasili KOSELEV	G	10	
Valeri LEBEDEV	M	14	1
LUNGU	M	3	1
Iurie MITEREV	A	26	20
Serghei NANI	D	2	3
Igor OPREA	M	10	1
Radu REBEJA	M	25	7
Ruslan ROIC	D	9	1
Denis ROMANENCO	G	22	
SCRELEA	D	2	
SOSNOVSCHI	D	5	1
Alexandru SPIRIDON	A	3	2
Marin SPÂNU	M	29	5
Aleksandr SUHAREV	M	28	8
Ion TESTIMITANU	D	28	11
Anatoli TÂMBUR	M	2	
Vasili TOLOKONNIKOV	D	30	

LEAGUE RESULTS 1995/96

02/08/95	Progresul Briceni	H	4-0	Nani, Gavriliuc, Clescenco (p), Miterev
12/08/95	FC Agro Chisinau	A	3-1	Nani 2, Gavriliuc
17/08/95	MHM-93 Chisnau	H	2-0	Gavriliuc, Cibotaru
26/08/95	Speranta Nisporeni	H	4-0	Cibotaru, Gavriliuc 3
17/09/95	Constructorul Chisinau	A	2-1	Rebeja, Gavriliuc
21/09/95	Olimpia Balti	H	1-2	Gavriliuc
01/10/95	Sportul Studentesc Chisinau	A	7-1	Testimitanu 2, Rebeja, Gavriliuc 3, Spânu
12/10/95	Tiligul Tiraspol	H	2-2	Gavriliuc, Miterev
21/10/95	Bugeac Comrat	H	8-0	Spiridon, Gavriliuc 2 (1p), Miterev 3, Lungu, Testimitanu
28/10/95	Codru Calarasi	A	8-0	Gavriliuc, Testimitanu 2 (1p), Rebeja 2, Miterev, Suharev, Spiridon
04/11/95	Spumante Cricova	H	3-0	Miterev, Spânu 2
08/11/95	Torentul Chisinau	H	8-0	Testimitanu 2 (2p), Miterev 2, Gavriliuc 3, Caras D.
18/11/95	Nistru Ciobruciu	A	1-0	Miterev
25/11/95	Tighina Bender	H	3-1	Suharev, Testimitanu (p), Miterev
29/11/95	Nistru Otaci	A	1-0	Gavriliuc
09/03/96	Progresul Briceni	A	2-0	Gavriliuc 2
16/03/96	Tighina Bender	A	1-0	Roic
24/03/96	FC Agro Chisinau	H	1-1	Rebeja
30/03/96	MHM-93 Chisnau	A	3-0	Boret, Curtianu, Oprea
13/04/96	Nistru Otaci	H	5-0	Miterev 2, Rebeja, Suharev 2
17/04/96	Speranta Nisporeni	A	2-0	Cibotaru, Suharev
20/04/96	Constructorul Chisinau	H	2-0	Cibotaru, Curtianu
27/04/96	Olimpia Balti	A	3-0	Curtianu, Gavriliuc, Rebeja
04/05/96	Sportul Studentesc Chisinau	H	8-0	Suharev 2, Boret, Gavriliuc, Curtianu, Caras D., Testimitanu, Miterev
08/05/96	Torentul Chisinau	A	7-0	Spânu, Gavriliuc, Miterev 2, Boret 2, Testimitanu
15/05/96	Nistru Ciobruciu	H	9-0	Gavriliuc 6, Miterev 3
18/05/96	Bugeac Comrat	A	4-0	Suharev, Gavriliuc, Lebedev, Sosnovschi
25/05/96	Codru Calarasi	H	3-1	Spânu, Gavriliuc 2
05/06/96	Tiligul Tiraspol	A	2-0	Gavriliuc, Miterev
08/06/96	Spumante Cricova	A	1-1	Testimitanu (p)

PROMOTED CLUBS

SECOND DIVISION FINAL TABLE 95/96

		Pd	W	D	L	F	A	Pt	GD
1	**Locomotiva Basarabeasca**	**42**	**27**	**8**	**7**	**81**	**39**	**89**	**+42**
2	**Ciuhur Ocnita**	**42**	**27**	**8**	**7**	**64**	**31**	**89**	**+33**
3	**Attila Ungheni**	**42**	**25**	**10**	**7**	**78**	**41**	**85**	**+37**
4	**Victoria Cahul**	**42**	**25**	**7**	**10**	**66**	**35**	**82**	**+31**
5	Cimentul Ribnita	42	20	7	15	68	64	67	+4
6	MIF Malaesti	42	19	9	14	70	52	66	+18
7	Dumbrava Cojusna	42	15	19	8	53	43	64	+10
8	Bucuria Truseni	42	18	9	15	62	53	63	+9
9	Raut Orhei	42	16	13	13	36	39	61	-3
10	Gloria Edinet	42	15	13	14	62	51	58	+11
11	Spicul Sarata Galbena	42	17	7	18	56	58	58	-2
12	Olimpia II Balti	42	16	9	17	62	57	57	+5
13	Zimbru II Chisinau	42	14	14	14	43	42	56	+1
14	Moldova Slobozia Mare	42	16	8	18	54	54	56	=
15	Migdal Carahasani	42	16	8	18	65	71	56	-6
16	Spicul Falesti	42	15	9	18	54	74	54	-20
17	Vierul Singerei	42	12	14	16	48	60	50	-12
18	Tiras Soroca	42	13	10	19	49	57	49	-8
19	Lims Anenii Noi	42	12	11	19	50	73	47	-23
20	Izvoras Drasliceni	42	9	5	28	43	81	32	-38
21	Agro-Sind Chauseni	42	6	8	28	46	90	26	-44
22	Prut Cantemir	42	3	4	35	21	66	13	-45

PROMOTION/RELEGATION PLAY-OFFS

Torentul Chisinau 2, Victoria Cahul 3

Attila Ungheni w/o Nistru Ciobruciu

NORTHERN IRELAND

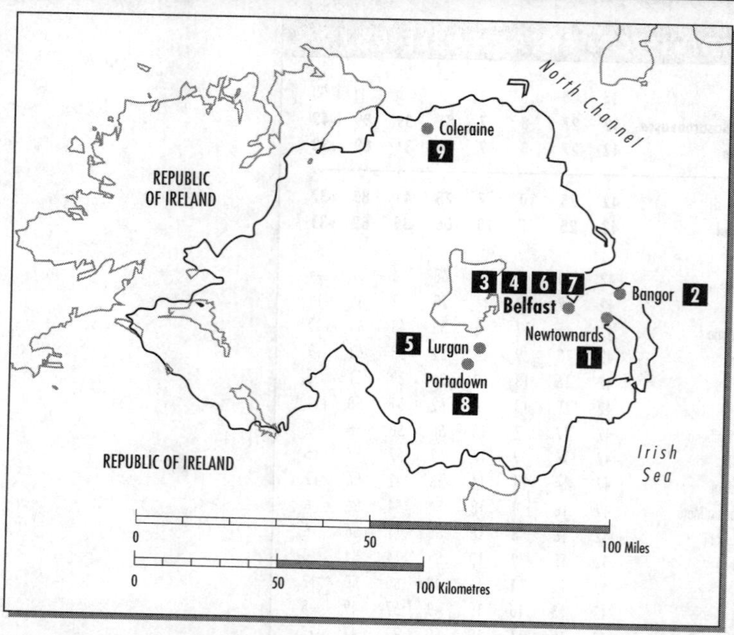

1	ARDS	717
2	BANGOR	718
3	CLIFTONVILLE	719
4	CRUSADERS	720
5	GLENAVON	721
6	GLENTORAN	722
7	LINFIELD	723
8	PORTADOWN	724
9	COLERAINE	725

ENCOURAGING END TO EURO '96 BID

Party time again for Portadown

FEDERATION DIRECTORY

The Irish Football Association
20 Windsor Avenue, Belfast BT9 6EE

tel - (01232) 669458/9
tlx - 747317 ifa ni g
fax - (01232) 667620

Year of Formation - 1880
President - Jim Boyce
Secretary - David I. Bowen

Stadium - Windsor Park, Belfast (28,500)

The 1995/96 season was the beginning of a new era for Northern Irish football. Previously the Irish League had consisted of one division containing 16 teams, with no promotion or relegation. But in 95/96 those 16 teams were split into two eight-team leagues - the new Premier Division and First Division - in which each club played the others four times. Who would become the inaugural Premier Division champions? The usual candidates were there at the starting line - Belfast's traditional giants Linfield and Glentoran, the mid-Ulster 'Big Two' of Glenavon and Portadown, and defending champions Crusaders.

One event which had an important bearing on the destination of the championship trophy occurred before any of these teams had kicked a ball. In the 94/95 campaign Englishman Garry Haylock had been a prolific scorer for Linfield. But, much to the chagrin of the team and their supporters, Portadown managed to sign him in the close season for nothing, due to an administrative error which allowed Haylock to become a free agent.

On signing, Haylock promised that he would deliver the championship to Portadown, and he turned out to be as good as his word, scoring 19 goals in 25 league games (and 41 in all competitions), a total which enabled him to retain his top scorer crown and bring Portadown the title. The "Ports" wrapped up their triumph in the penultimate game of the season, winning 2-1 at home to local rivals Glenavon, the team which a few days earlier had knocked Portadown out of the Irish Cup and which, earlier in the

LEAGUE CHAMPIONSHIP RESULTS 95/96

		1	2	3	4	5	6	7	8
1	Ards		3-0	3-0	0-0	1-1	1-4	2-3	1-1
			2-1	2-2	0-1	1-2	0-2	1-2	0-2
2	Bangor	2-1		3-2	1-2	0-1	1-6	1-2	0-3
		0-1		2-3	0-2	1-2	1-1	0-2	0-0
3	Cliftonville	0-0	2-1		1-4	2-2	0-0	1-1	0-3
		1-0	1-1		2-1	0-1	1-0	0-0	0-4
4	Crusaders	1-2	2-0	1-0		1-2	2-1	3-0	3-1
		2-0	1-0	1-1		1-0	1-3	4-2	3-3
5	Glenavon	3-0	1-0	1-2	4-0		2-3	0-3	0-1
		3-1	0-1	1-1	1-1		1-3	2-2	7-0
6	Glentoran	3-2	1-1	1-1	3-1	0-2		0-3	1-1
		3-1	3-0	2-1	2-2	1-2		3-0	3-3
7	Linfield	0-0	0-0	0-0	1-2	0-3	0-4		1-0
		0-0	2-1	3-1	0-1	2-1	2-0		0-1
8	Portadown	3-1	4-2	6-1	1-1	2-1	3-1	3-2	
		1-3	4-3	4-1	1-1	2-1	3-2	1-1	

LEAGUE CHAMPIONSHIP FINAL TABLE 95/96

			Home					Away					Total						
		Pd	W	D	L	F	A	W	D	L	F	A	W	D	L	F	A	Pt	GD
1	Portadown	28	10	3	1	38	21	6	5	3	23	19	16	8	4	61	40	56	+21
2	Crusaders	28	9	2	3	26	15	6	5	3	19	17	15	7	6	45	32	52	+13
3	Glentoran	28	6	5	3	26	20	7	2	5	30	18	13	7	8	56	38	46	+18
4	Glenavon	28	5	3	6	26	18	8	2	4	21	14	13	5	10	47	32	44	+15
5	Linfield	28	5	4	5	11	14	6	4	4	23	21	11	8	9	34	35	41	-1
6	Cliftonville	28	4	6	4	11	18	2	5	7	16	30	6	11	11	27	48	29	-21
7	Ards	28	3	4	7	17	21	3	3	8	12	22	6	7	15	29	43	25	-14
8	Bangor	28	2	2	10	12	28	1	3	10	11	26	3	5	20	23	54	14	-31

NATIONAL TEAM APPEARANCES 95/96

Manager - Bryan HAMILTON	POR	LIE	AUT	NOR	SWE	GER	Cps	Gls
Alan FETTIS (01/02/71) - Hull City (ENG)/Nottingham Forest (ENG)	G	G75	G	G		G	15	
Steve MORROW (02/07/70) - Arsenal (ENG)	D				M		19	1
Colin HILL (12/11/63) - Leicester City (ENG)	D	D	D	D	D	D	14	1
Barry HUNTER (18/11/68) - Wrexham (WAL)	D	D	D		D	D	6	1
Nigel WORTHINGTON (04/11/61) - Leeds United (ENG)	D	D	D	D56	D77	D46	64	-
Keith GILLESPIE (18/02/75) - Newcastle United (ENG)	M		M	M		M66	12	1
Steve LOMAS (18/01/74) - Manchester City (ENG)	M	D	D	D	M	M	12	1
Jim MAGILTON (06/05/69) - Southampton (ENG)	M79			M46		M	32	4
Neil LENNON (25/06/71) - Crewe Alexandra (ENG)/Leicester City (ENG)	M	M	M	M			6	-
Michael HUGHES (02/08/71) - West Ham United (ENG)	M	M90	M	M		M	31	2
Iain DOWIE (09/01/65) - Crystal Palace (ENG)/West Ham United (ENG)	A76		A81	A		A	36	8
Philip GRAY (02/10/68) - Sunderland (ENG)	s76	A	A78				17	5
Keith ROWLAND (01/09/71) - West Ham United (ENG)	s79	s90		s56	M	s46	9	-
Gerry McMAHON (29/12/73) - Tottenham Hotspur (ENG)		M80		s61	A	A	7	2
Michael O'NEILL (05/07/69) - Hibernian (SCO)		M	M	M61	M65		29	4
Jimmy QUINN (18/11/59) - Reading (ENG)		A	s81				46	12
Trevor WOOD (03/11/68) - Walsall (ENG)		s75					1	-
Pat McGIBBON (06/09/73) - Manchester United (ENG)		s80					4	-
Alan McDONALD (12/10/63) - Queens Park Rangers (ENG)			s78	D			52	3
Darren PATTERSON (15/10/69) - Luton Town (ENG)				s46	D		10	-
Aidan DAVISON (11/05/68) - Bolton Wanderers (ENG)					G		1	-
Jon McCARTHY (18/08/70) - Port Vale (ENG)					M		1	-
George O'BOYLE (14/12/67) - St. Johnstone (SCO)					s65	s66	8	1
James QUINN (15/12/74) - Blackpool (ENG)					s77		1	-
Danny GRIFFIN (10/08/77) - St. Johnstone (SCO)						D	1	-

campaign, had sensationally thrashed the champions-to-be 7-0.

While Portadown had occupied top place in the Premier Division for the majority of the season, Glenavon, Glentoran and Crusaders all put together good runs of form which suggested that the title might go elsewhere. But Portadown got the right results when it mattered most to bring the Irish League title to Shamrock Park for the third time in seven seasons - an excellent achievement by manager Ronnie McFall in his ten years in charge. Not surprisingly, McFall was honoured with the Coaches Association Manager of the Year award. The Northern Ireland Football Writers' Player of the Season vote went not to Garry Haylock but to his midfield accomplice, and scorer of ten league goals himself, 23-year-old Peter Kennedy. Portadown also had success in the various Cup competitions which help to fill out the domestic football calendar, lifting both the League Cup (2-1 against Crusaders in the final) and the Ulster Cup (a penalty shoot-out victory after a 2-2 draw with Linfield).

In the Cup that really counts, the Irish Cup, Portadown were defeated in the semi-finals by Glenavon, but a mid-Ulster 'double' was destroyed in the final by Glentoran, who made a victorious stand for the Belfast clubs by defeating Glenavon 1-0, the winning goal coming from 20-year-old Englishman Glen Little, who fired home a shot from 25 yards 15 minutes from time. Little's decisive strike helped him to pick up the Football Writers' Young Player of the Year award.

INTERNATIONAL HONOURS

World Cup Finals appearances: 1958 (qtr-finals), 1982 (2nd round), 1986

That Cup final defeat left Glenavon with only the County Antrim Shield to show for their season's work, although they did make quite a splash in Europe at the beginning of the campaign, beating Icelandic team FH to book themselves a high-profile UEFA Cup first-round tie with German club Werder Bremen.

At the end of the 94/95 season, due to the controversial rules governing how teams were to be split into the two divisions, many had thought Coleraine unlucky to be placed in the First Division while Bangor gained entry to the Premier Division. But a year later Coleraine had the last laugh, practically walking away with the First Division title. They went on a goal spree and were already assured of promotion with seven games left. In contrast, Bangor struggled all season to match their more powerful Premier Division rivals and were relegated. What goes around, comes around, as they say.

The Northern Ireland national team would not be averse to a change in their fortunes. As expected, they failed to reach the European Championship finals in England, thus completing a full decade of qualifying failures. Bryan Hamilton's young team certainly gave it their best shot, and they finished the campaign with three excellent results - a 1-1 draw in Portugal, a 4-0 victory in Liechtenstein and a 5-3 home win against Austria. One more point from somewhere and they would have taken second place in the group. On reflection, it was the 1-2 defeat at home to Latvia which cost them a place at least in the play-off match. That was one of three home defeats which they suffered during the competition - compared to a highly impressive unbeaten record of three wins and two draws on their travels.

The last qualifier against Austria finally ended that gruesome run of results at Windsor Park. Indeed, it was the first time that the team had scored five goals at home for 24 years. But in the spring the Belfast bogey returned to haunt the team as they played three friendlies against European opposition and failed to win any of them. An extremely lack-lustre display against Norway at the end of March

EUROPEAN CUPS RESULTS 95/96

CUP-WINNERS' CUP

● **LINFIELD**

Preliminary round SHAKHTAR DONETSK (UKR)

A 1-4 Ewing (47)
Lamont; Crothers, Easton, Ewing, McLean, Beatty, Campbell Ray, McGee, Erskine, Spiers, Bailie.

H 0-1
Lamont; Dornan, Easton, Ewing (McCoosh 77), Spiers, Beatty (McLaughlin 58), Campbell Ray, Gorman, Erskine, Fenlon, Bailie.

UEFA CUP

● **CRUSADERS**

Preliminary round SILKEBORG IF (DEN)

H 1-2 Hunter G. (67)
McKeown; McMullan, McCartney, Dunlop, Callaghan, Hunter K. (Morgan 87), Livingstone, Dunne, Baxter, Hunter G., Burrows.

A 0-4
McKeown; McMullan, McCartney, Dunlop, Callaghan, Hunter K. (Dwyer 69), Baxter (Morgan 83), Livingstone, Dunne, Gardiner, Burrows.

● **GLENAVON**

Preliminary round FH (ISL)

H 0-0
O'Neill; Byrne, Glendinning, Doherty, Brown, Smyth G., McCoy, Johnston (Collins 74), Ferguson, McBride, Smyth J..

A 1-0 Johnston (65)
O'Neill; Byrne, Glendinning, Doherty, Brown, Smyth G., McCoy, Johnston, Ferguson, McBride, Smyth J..

1st round SV WERDER BREMEN (GER)

H 0-2
O'Neill; Birney (Byrne 76), Glendinning, Doherty, Brown (McCoy 79), Smyth G., Murphy A., Johnston, Ferguson, McBride, Smyth J. (Collins 84).

A 0-5
O'Neill; Byrne, Glendinning, Kenny (McCoy 73), Brown (Murphy A. 78), Smyth G., Collins, Johnston, Ferguson, McBride, Murphy D..

NATIONAL TEAM RESULTS 95/96

Date	Opponent		Venue	Score	Scorers
03/09/95	Portugal (ECQ)	A	Oporto	1-1	Hughes (67)
11/10/95	Liechtenstein (ECQ)	A	Eschen	4-0	O'Neill (36), McMahon (49), Quinn Ji. (55), Gray (72)
15/11/95	Austria (ECQ)	H	Belfast	5-3	O'Neill (27, 78), Dowie (32p), Hunter (53), Gray (64)
27/03/96	Norway	H	Belfast	0-2	
24/04/96	Sweden	H	Belfast	1-2	McMahon (84)
29/05/96	Germany	H	Belfast	1-1	O'Boyle (79)

TOP SCORERS

Goals	Player
19	Garry HAYLOCK (Portadown)
10	Stephen BAXTER (Crusaders)
	Peter KENNEDY (Portadown)
9	Glenn FERGUSON (Glenavon)
	Glen LITTLE (Glentoran)
	Stephen McBRIDE (Glenavon)
	Glenn HUNTER (Crusaders)
8	Raymond McCOY (Glenavon)
	Justin McBRIDE (Glentoran)

PLAYERS OF THE SEASON

NEIL LENNON

One of the most important players in Bryan Hamilton's new, young Northern Ireland team is undoubtedly 25-year-old Neil Lennon. The diminutive red-head made giant strides during the 1995/96 season, both at club and international level. For his country, the Lurgan-born midfielder looked every inch an international-quality player as he tackled and passed with confidence and authority in the middle of the park. And for his new club Leicester City, who signed him from Crewe Alexandra during the course of the season, Lennon proved to be an inspirational buy. His was the dominant performance in a classy Leicester victory over Crystal Palace in the First Division play-off final at Wembley. Two days after that match, Northern Ireland faced Germany at Windsor Park, but Lennon did not play. He was still celebrating Leicester's promotion to the Premiership.

KEITH GILLESPIE

Had Newcastle United manager Kevin Keegan not made unnecessary changes to his team in the Premiership title run-in, the general belief is that the Magpies would have been crowned English champions. The man displaced by expensive new signing Faustino Asprilla was 21-year-old Northern Irish winger Keith Gillespie, and his absence denied Newcastle the width they needed on the right-hand side. During the first part of the season Gillespie was in exceptional form, his pace and trickery giving Premiership full-backs countless problems to solve. It was a travesty that he should lose his place. There is not much chance of Bryan Hamilton making the same mistake at international level. Gillespie is an essential part of Northern Ireland's future, his flair on the right counterbalancing that of another gifted winger, Michael Hughes, on the left.

resulted in a 0-2 defeat. It also brought the first sending-off of a Northern Ireland international for 14 years when Iain Dowie was red carded four minutes from the end. A month later, Northern Ireland lost again, 1-2 against Sweden, although there were some signs of encouragement from a side missing several first-choice players. One was the headed goal from youngster Gerard McMahon, who had been selected in an unaccustomed forward rôle.

The last visitors of the season to Windsor Park were Germany, and, ironically, it was against the soon-to-be-crowned European champions that Bryan Hamilton's team gave their best display. Admittedly, they were helped when the Germans missed two penalties in the first half. But the team playing in the novel green and navy quartered shirts defended solidly, tackled tenaciously and looked lively up front. Their reward for a committed display came in the 79th minute when substitute George O'Boyle stabbed in a close-range shot from a McMahon corner. But, true to tradition, the Germans came straight back to equalise within a minute.

It was a high note on which to finish the season, especially with the Germans being in Northern Ireland's World Cup qualifying group. But with Portugal also involved in their section, it will be a major feat for Bryan Hamilton's team to end their sorry sequence of major championship failures. One thing is certain. With such tough opposition to face on the road to France, Northern Ireland will have to make better use of home advantage than they did in their European Championship qualifying campaign.

DOMESTIC CUP RESULTS

FIFTH ROUND

Ards 10, Cookstown United 0
Armagh City 2, Dundela 1
Bangor 0, Portadown 4
Chimney Corner 0, Ballymena United 1
Crumlin 0, Linfield 8
Crusaders 4, Dungiven Celtic 0
Distillery 4, Larne Tech. Old Boys 2
Dungannon Swifts 2, Omagh Town 4
East Belfast 4, Malachians 1
Glenavon 12, First Liverpool RR 0
Glentoran 4, Limavady United 1
Kilmore Recreation 0, Cliftonville 3
Larne 3, Banbridge Town 0
Newry Town 2, Coleraine 1
RUC 2, Carrick Rangers 3
Tobermore United 2, Ballyclare Comrades 3

SIXTH ROUND

Ards 1, Larne 0
Ballyclare Comrades 0, Crusaders 1
Ballymena United 4, Armagh City 0
Carrick Rangers 1, Newry Town 0
Glenavon 3, Cliftonville 1
Glentoran 2, Distillery 0
Linfield 1, East Belfast 0
Portadown 3, Omagh Town 1

QUARTER-FINALS

Crusaders 2, Linfield 0
Glenavon 3, Carrick Rangers 1
Glentoran 0, Balymena United 0
(replay) Ballymena United 2, Glentoran 4
Portadown 2, Ards 1

SEMI-FINALS

Glentoran 2, Crusaders 2
(replay) Glentoran 2, Crusaders 1
Glenavon 1, Portadown 1
(replay) Glenavon 4, Portadown 1

FINAL

04/05/96, Belfast
GLENTORAN 1 Little (75)
GLENAVON 0
referee - Snoddy
GLENTORAN - Devine D.; Nixon, Finlay, Walker, Devine J., Parker, Smith T., Little, Coyle, Batey, McBride.
GLENAVON - Straney; Smyth J., Glendinning, Murphy D., Gauld, Smyth G., Johnston, Shepherd, Ferguson, McBride (McCoy 77), Shipp.

ARDS

CLUB DIRECTORY

Ards FC
Castlereagh Park
Newtownards
Co. Down
tel - (01247) 813370
Year of Formation - 1902
Chairman - Hugh Owens
Secretary - Kenneth Lowry
Manager - Roy Coyle
Stadium - Castlereagh Park (10,000)

MAJOR HONOURS
League Championshp - (1) 1958.
Domestic Cup - (4) 1927, 1952, 1969, 1974.

APPEARANCES 95/96

	P	Ap	(s)	Gls
Ritchie BARKER (ENG)	A	7		3
Andy BEATTIE	A		(3)	
Salvatore BIBBO (ENG)	G	4		
Barney BOWERS	D	23	(1)	1
Michael BOYLE	A	22	(2)	5
Brian CAMPBELL	D	1		
Chris CULLEN	M	14	(2)	
Paul CULLEN (IRL)	A	25	(1)	5
Paul DUNNION	M		(2)	
Patrick FLANNERY (SCO)	A	11	(1)	2
Con GETTY	A		(1)	
Paul GRAY	A		(2)	
Andrew HAWKINS (SCO)	M	2		
Paul KEE	G	23		
Michael KELLY	D	15		
Paul McBRIDE	D	18	(3)	
Martin McCANN (IRL)	M	18	(1)	3
Declan McGREEVY	D	7	(2)	1
Paul McLAUGHLIN (SCO)	D	16		3
Kyle MALONEY	D	4		1
Paul MOONEY	D	25		2
Raymond MORRISON	M	25	(1)	2
William MURPHY	D	10	(5)	
Gary O'SULLIVAN (IRL)	M	9	(11)	
Dwaine SHANLEY (IRL)	M	20	(4)	1
Mark SIMPSON (SCO)	M	1	(2)	
Dean SMYTH	G	1		
Gary WALKER	D		(4)	
John WILLS (ENG)	D	6	(1)	

LEAGUE RESULTS 1995/96

Date	Opponent	H/A	Score	Scorers
30/09/95	Cliftonville	A	0-0	
07/10/95	Glenavon	H	1-1	Flannery
14/10/95	Portadown	A	1-3	Shanley
21/10/95	Crusaders	H	0-0	
28/10/95	Glentoran	A	2-3	Boyle 2
04/11/95	Bangor	A	1-2	Maloney
11/11/95	Linfield	H	2-3	Boyle, Flannery (p)
18/11/95	Cliftonville	H	3-0	Cullen P. 2, McLaughlin
25/11/95	Glenavon	A	0-3	
02/12/95	Portadown	H	1-1	Mooney (p)
09/12/95	Crusaders	A	2-1	McGreevy, Cullen P.
16/12/95	Glentoran	H	1-4	McCann
01/01/96	Linfield	A	0-0	
06/01/96	Cliftonville	A	0-1	
13/01/96	Glenavon	H	1-2	Boyle
27/01/96	Portadown	A	3-1	Boyle, Barker 2
30/01/96	Bangor	H	3-0	McLaughlin, Bowers, Morrison
03/02/96	Crusaders	H	0-1	
10/02/96	Glentoran	A	1-3	Barker
17/02/96	Bangor	A	1-0	Cullen P.
02/03/96	Linfield	H	1-2	Morrison
16/03/96	Cliftonville	H	2-2	McLaughlin, McCann
23/03/96	Glenavon	A	1-3	McCann
30/03/96	Portadown	H	0-2	
06/04/96	Crusaders	A	0-2	
08/04/96	Glentoran	H	0-2	
20/04/96	Bangor	H	2-1	Mooney (p), Cullen P.
27/04/96	Linfield	A	0-0	

BANGOR

CLUB DIRECTORY

Bangor FC
Clandeboye Park, Clandeboye Road
Bangor, Co. Down BT20 3JT
tel - (01247) 457712/469826
Year of Formation - 1918
Chairman - vacant
Secretary - Fred Anderson
Manager - Paul Malone; Andy Dougan
Stadium - Clandeboye Park (5,000)

MAJOR HONOURS
Domestic Cup - (1) 1993.

APPEARANCES 95/96

	P	Ap	(s)	Gls
John BAILIE	D	20	(1)	1
Dominic BARCLAY (ENG)	A	2		
Colin BELL	A		(1)	
John BYRNE (IRL)	M	8	(1)	1
Michael CASH	D	13	(1)	
Jackie COULTER	D	10	(1)	1
Niall CURRIE	G	10		
Will DAVIES (ENG)	M	11		3
Michael DAVIS (ENG)	A	5		2
Reg DORNAN	D	16		
David EDDIS	M	3	(2)	
Marc FALCONER (SCO)	A	1		
Gary FERGUSON	D	3		
Andrew FOX	G	1		
Matt GREEN (ENG)	M	11		1
Raymond HILL	M	13	(1)	
Stephen HILL	D	1		
Darren HOLMES (ENG)	M	8		1
Allen HUXLEY	G	6		
Brian IRWIN (IRL)	A	8	(8)	3
John JOHNSTON	D	1		
Brian KENNEDY	D	3		
Alaistair McCOMBE	D	15		2
Ricky McEVOY (IRL)	M	7		1
Ray McGUINNESS	D	7	(2)	
Michael McKEOWN	D	23		
Gary McKINSTRY	A	3	(1)	
Jeff McNAMARA	M	5	(2)	
Stuart McPHERSON	A	2		
Paul MISKELLY	G	11		
Hillyard MENDES (ENG)	A	4		
Keith MORROW	A	7	(20)	1
Jason MURTAGH	M	5	(2)	
Dean NELSON	M	3	(2)	
Patrick O'CONNELL (IRL)	A	13	(9)	2
Keith PERCY	D	14		1
Derek SIMPSON (ENG)	M	3		
Eddie SPIERS	D	25		1
Lee THORPE (ENG)	A	3		1
Gary WILKINSON	M		(5)	
Martin WILLIAMS (ENG)	A	3		1

LEAGUE RESULTS 1995/96

30/09/95	Portadown	H	0-3	
07/10/95	Glentoran	A	1-1	Thorpe
14/10/95	Linfield	H	1-2	Percy
21/10/95	Glenavon	A	0-1	
28/10/95	Crusaders	H	1-2	Byrne (p)
04/11/95	Ards	H	2-1	Morrow, Irwin (p)
11/11/95	Cliftonville	A	1-2	Irwin
18/11/95	Portadown	A	2-4	Bailie, Irwin
25/11/95	Glentoran	H	1-6	Davis
02/12/95	Linfield	A	0-0	
09/12/95	Glenavon	H	0-1	
16/12/95	Crusaders	A	0-2	
01/01/96	Cliftonville	H	3-2	Coulter (p), Davis, Williams
06/01/96	Portadown	H	0-0	
13/01/96	Glentoran	A	0-3	
27/01/96	Linfield	H	0-2	
30/01/96	Ards	A	0-3	
03/02/96	Glenavon	A	1-0	Davies
10/02/96	Crusaders	H	0-2	
17/02/96	Ards	H	0-1	
02/03/96	Cliftonville	A	1-1	Green (p)
16/03/96	Portadown	A	3-4	Davies 2, McCombe
23/03/96	Glentoran	H	1-1	Holmes
30/03/96	Linfield	A	1-2	McEvoy
06/04/96	Glenavon	H	1-2	O'Connell
09/04/96	Crusaders	A	0-1	
20/04/96	Ards	A	1-2	Spiers
27/04/96	Cliftonville	H	2-3	McCombe, O'Connell

CLIFTONVILLE

CLUB DIRECTORY

Cliftonville FC
Solitude
Cliftonville Street
Belfast BT14
tel - (01232) 754628
Year of Formation - 1879
Chairman - Jim Boyce
Secretary - John Duffy
Manager - Marty Quinn
Stadium - Solitude (17,000)

MAJOR HONOURS
League Championship - (2) 1906, 1910.
Domestic Cup - (8) 1883, 1888, 1897, 1900, 1901, 1907, 1909, 1979.

APPEARANCES 95/96

	P	Ap	(s)	Gls
Pat CAVANAGH	A	2	(4)	1
Rod COLLINS (IRL)	A	6		1
Jonathan CROSS (ENG)	A	8		
Damien DAVEY	D	1		
Michael DONNELLY	M	25		5
Ciaran FEEHAN	A	9	(11)	2
Gerry FLYNN	D	27		1
Mark GRUGEL (ENG)	M	2		
Martin HAYES (ENG)	M	3		
Seamus HEATH	M	6	(6)	
Ian HILL (IRL)	D	25		
Joe KERR	D	24		1
Kieran LOUGHRAN	D		(2)	
Tim McCANN	M	25	(2)	1
Tommy McDONALD	M	21	(2)	
Jim McFADDEN	M	1		
David McGLINCHEY	A		(1)	
Ian McPARLAND (SCO)	A	3	(3)	1
Ron MANLEY	A	7	(8)	
Mark O'NEILL (IRL)	A	17	(7)	1
Joe QUINN	D		(1)	
Paul RICE	G	24		1
Gary SLINEY (IRL)	M	21		1
Dean SMITH	G	4		
Paul STOKES	A	14		7
Sean STRANG (SCO)	M	11	(3)	3
Martin TABB	D	22	(1)	1

LEAGUE RESULTS 1995/96

30/09/95	Ards	H	0-0	
07/10/95	Portadown	A	1-6	Sliney
14/10/95	Glentoran	H	0-0	
21/10/95	Linfield	A	0-0	
28/10/95	Glenavon	H	2-2	Collins, Feehan
04/11/95	Crusaders	A	0-1	
11/11/95	Bangor	H	2-1	Strang 2
18/11/95	Ards	A	0-3	
25/11/95	Portadown	H	0-3	
02/12/95	Glentoran	A	1-1	Donnelly
09/12/95	Linfield	H	1-1	Strang
16/12/95	Glenavon	A	2-1	McParland, O'Neill
26/12/95	Crusaders	H	1-4	Tabb
01/01/96	Bangor	A	2-3	Donnelly, Stokes
06/01/96	Ards	H	1-0	Donnelly
13/01/96	Portadown	A	1-4	Flynn
27/01/96	Glentoran	H	1-0	Stokes
03/02/96	Linfield	A	1-3	Rice (p)
10/02/96	Glenavon	H	0-1	
17/02/96	Crusaders	A	1-1	Cavanagh
02/03/96	Bangor	H	1-1	Kerr
16/03/96	Ards	A	2-2	Donnelly, McCann
23/03/96	Portadown	H	0-4	
30/03/96	Glentoran	A	1-2	Stokes
06/04/96	Linfield	H	0-0	
09/04/96	Glenavon	A	1-1	Stokes
20/04/96	Crusaders	H	2-1	Stokes 2
27/04/96	Bangor	A	3-2	Donnelly (p), Feehan, Stokes

CRUSADERS

CLUB DIRECTORY

Crusaders FC
Seaview
Shore Road
Belfast BT15 3PL
tel - (01232) 370777
Year of Formation - 1898
Chairman - Jim Semple
Secretary - Harry Davison
Manager - Roy Walker
Stadium - Seaview (9,000)

MAJOR HONOURS
League Championship - (3) 1973, 1976, 1995.
Domestic Cup - (2) 1967, 1968.

APPEARANCES 95/96

	P	Ap	(s)	Gls
Stephen BAXTER	A	26		10
Sid BURROWS	M	24	(1)	4
Aaron CALLAGHAN (IRL)	D	14		2
Derek CARROLL (IRL)	D	23		
Frank DARBY (IRL)	D	2		1
Michael DEEGAN (IRL)	D	13	(3)	
Glenn DUNLOP	D	24		2
Liam DUNNE (IRL)	M	24		2
Paul DWYER	A		(1)	
Glenn HUNTER	A	19	(5)	9
Kirk HUNTER	M	6	(10)	4
Martin LAWLOR (IRL)	D		(1)	
Robert LAWLOR (IRL)	D	24		
Stephen LIVINGSTONE	M	8	(3)	1
Gary McCARTNEY	D	7	(5)	
Kevin McKEOWN (SCO)	G	28		
Trevor McMULLAN	D	24	(1)	2
Stewart MELLON	A	1	(1)	
Chris MORGAN	A	1	(4)	1
Martin MURRAY (IRL)	M	20	(3)	4
Donal O'BRIEN (IRL)	M	20	(2)	2

LEAGUE RESULTS 1995/96

Date	Opponent	H/A	Score	Scorers
30/09/95	Glentoran	H	2-1	Dunlop, Baxter
07/10/95	Linfield	A	2-1	Callaghan, og (Bailie)
14/10/95	Glenavon	H	1-2	Hunter G.
21/10/95	Ards	A	0-0	
28/10/95	Bangor	A	2-1	McMullan, Burrows
04/11/95	Cliftonville	H	1-0	Hunter K.
11/11/95	Portadown	A	1-1	Hunter G.
18/11/95	Glentoran	A	1-3	Baxter
25/11/95	Linfield	H	3-0	Hunter K. 2, Baxter
02/12/95	Glenavon	A	0-4	
09/12/95	Ards	H	1-2	Hunter K.
16/12/95	Bangor	H	2-0	Morgan, Dunlop
26/12/95	Cliftonville	A	4-1	Baxter, Burrows 2, Hunter G.
01/01/96	Portadown	H	3-1	Hunter G. 2, Baxter
06/01/96	Glentoran	H	1-3	Murray
13/01/96	Linfield	A	1-0	Murray
27/01/96	Glenavon	H	1-0	Dunne
03/02/96	Ards	A	1-0	Baxter
10/02/96	Bangor	A	2-0	Callaghan, Murray
17/02/96	Cliftonville	H	1-1	O'Brien
02/03/96	Portadown	A	1-1	Murray
16/03/96	Glentoran	A	2-2	Baxter 2
23/03/96	Linfield	H	4-2	Dunne, Burrows, Baxter 2
30/03/96	Glenavon	A	1-1	Hunter G.
06/04/96	Ards	H	2-0	O'Brien, Hunter G.
09/04/96	Bangor	H	1-0	Darby
20/04/96	Cliftonville	A	1-2	Hunter G.
27/04/96	Portadown	H	3-3	Hunter G., McMullan, Livingstone

GLENAVON

CLUB DIRECTORY

Glenavon FC
Mourneview Park
Lurgan
tel - (01762) 322472
fax - (01762) 327694
Year of Formation - 1889
Chairman - Adrian Teer
Secretary - T.R. Kerr
Manager - Nigel Best
Stadium - Mourneview Park (15,000)

MAJOR HONOURS
League Championship - (3) 1952, 1957, 1960.
Domestic Cup - (4) 1957, 1959, 1961, 1992.

APPEARANCES 95/96

	P	Ap	(s)	Gls
Nigel BIRNEY	D	1		
Stephen BROWN	D	7	(1)	
Sean BURNS	A	2	(1)	
Paul BYRNE	M	16	(3)	
Sean COLLINS	M	5	(9)	
Lee DOHERTY	M	23		
Glenn FERGUSON	A	23	(1)	9
Darren FREEMAN (ENG)	A	2		1
Stuart GAULD (SCO)	D	16		
Mark GLENDINNING	D	25		2
Damian GRANT	G	1		
Donal GRAY	D	2		
Sammy JOHNSTON (SCO)	M	18	(6)	7
Marc KENNY (IRL)	M	5	(1)	
Stephen McBRIDE	A	28		9
John McCARTAN	A	2		
Raymond McCOY	M	14	(7)	8
Shane MULHOLLAND	M	1	(4)	
Alan MURPHY	M	4	(1)	
Darren MURPHY	D	18	(8)	3
Dermot O'NEILL (IRL)	G	25		
Alex RUSSELL (ENG)	D	4		
Tony SHEPHERD (SCO)	M	11		
Danny SHIPP (ENG)	A	9		6
Gary SMYTH	D	24		
John SMYTH (IRL)	D	20		2
Paul STRANEY	G	2		

LEAGUE RESULTS 1995/96

Date	Opponent	H/A	Score	Scorers
30/09/95	Linfield	H	0-3	
07/10/95	Ards	A	1-1	McBride
14/10/95	Crusaders	A	2-1	McCoy, Ferguson
21/10/95	Bangor	H	1-0	McCoy
28/10/95	Cliftonville	A	2-2	McBride 2
04/11/95	Portadown	H	0-1	
11/11/95	Glentoran	A	2-0	McCoy, McBride
18/11/95	Linfield	A	3-0	McCoy, McBride, Ferguson (p)
25/11/95	Ards	H	3-0	McBride (p), Ferguson, McCoy
02/12/95	Crusaders	H	4-0	Glendinning, Smyth J. 2, Johnston
09/12/95	Bangor	A	1-0	McBride
16/12/95	Cliftonville	H	1-2	McCoy
01/01/96	Glentoran	H	2-3	Murphy D., McCoy
06/01/96	Linfield	H	2-2	Glendinning, Freeman
13/01/96	Ards	A	2-1	Ferguson, Johnston
27/01/96	Crusaders	A	0-1	
03/02/96	Bangor	H	0-1	
10/02/96	Cliftonville	A	1-0	Johnston
13/02/96	Portadown	A	1-2	Ferguson
17/02/96	Portadown	H	7-0	Johnston, Shipp 2, McBride 2, Murphy D., McCoy
02/03/96	Glentoran	A	2-1	Ferguson 2
16/03/96	Linfield	A	1-2	Shipp
23/03/96	Ards	H	3-1	Johnston, Shipp 2
30/03/96	Crusaders	H	1-1	Shipp
06/04/96	Bangor	A	2-1	Johnston, Murphy D.
09/04/96	Cliftonville	H	1-1	Johnston
20/04/96	Portadown	A	1-2	Ferguson
27/04/96	Glentoran	H	1-3	Ferguson

GLENTORAN

CLUB DIRECTORY

Glentoran FC
The Oval, Mersey Street
Belfast BT4 1FG
tel - (01232) 456137
fax - (01232) 732956
Year of Formation - 1882
Chairman - David Chick
Secretary - Jackie Warren
Manager - Tommy Cassidy
Stadium - The Oval (30,000)

MAJOR HONOURS

League Championship - (19)
1894, 1897, 1905, 1912, 1913, 1921, 1925, 1931, 1951, 1953, 1964, 1967, 1968, 1970, 1972, 1977, 1981, 1988, 1992.
Domestic Cup - (16) 1914, 1917, 1921, 1932, 1933, 1935, 1951, 1966, 1973, 1983, 1985, 1986, 1987, 1988, 1990, 1996.

APPEARANCES 95/96

	P	Ap	(s)	Gls
Neil ARMSTRONG	G	22		
Peter BATEY (ENG)	M	23		6
Derek COOK (SCO)	A	12	(9)	6
Liam COYLE	A	9	(3)	4
Eddie CUNNINGTON (SCO)	M	13		3
Declan DEVINE	G	4		
John DEVINE	D	24		2
Stuart ELLIOTT	A		(1)	
Darren FINLAY	M	8	(6)	2
Jonathan HOUSTON	D		(1)	
Brian HUTCHINSON	G	2		
Damien KELLY	M	1	(5)	
John KENNEDY	M	20	(3)	1
Andrew KIRK	A		(1)	1
Paul LEEMAN	D		(1)	
Glen LITTLE (ENG)	M	22		9
Justin McBRIDE	A	23	(1)	8
Conor McCAFFREY	D	2		
Dugald McCARRISON	M	7	(4)	1
Roddy McDOWELL	A		(1)	
Richard McEVOY (IRL)	M	1	(2)	
Andy MATHIESON	M	10	(5)	1
George NEILL	D	4		
Colin NIXON	D	24		2
Darren PARKER	D	16	(4)	1
James QUIGLEY (IRL)	M	15	(3)	
Trevor SMITH (SCO)	A	11	(5)	7
Michael SMYTH	D	24		2
Chris WALKER	D	11	(1)	

LEAGUE RESULTS 1995/96

Date	Opponent		Score	Scorers
30/09/95	Crusaders	A	1-2	Little
07/10/95	Bangor	H	1-1	Devine J.
14/10/95	Cliftonville	A	0-0	
21/10/95	Portadown	H	1-1	Batey
28/10/95	Ards	H	3-2	Smith, Nixon, Cunnington
04/11/95	Linfield	A	4-0	Cunnington, McBride, McCarrison, Little
11/11/95	Glenavon	H	0-2	
18/11/95	Crusaders	H	3-1	McBride 2, Smith
25/11/95	Bangor	A	6-1	Batey, Kennedy, Cunnington, Cook 2, McBride
02/12/95	Cliftonville	H	1-1	Coyle
09/12/95	Portadown	A	1-3	Batey
16/12/95	Ards	A	4-1	Finlay, Batey, Smith, McBride
26/12/95	Linfield	H	0-3	
01/01/96	Glenavon	A	3-2	Smyth, Little 2
06/01/96	Crusaders	A	3-1	Cook, Mathieson, Little
13/01/96	Bangor	H	3-0	Cook, Batey, Little
27/01/96	Cliftonville	A	0-1	
03/02/96	Portadown	H	3-3	Nixon, Little, Smith
10/02/96	Ards	H	3-1	Coyle, Finlay, Smith
17/02/96	Linfield	A	0-2	
02/03/96	Glenavon	H	1-2	Coyle
16/03/96	Crusaders	H	2-2	McBride, Devine J. (p)
23/03/96	Bangor	A	1-1	Parker
30/03/96	Cliftonville	H	2-1	Coyle, McBride
06/04/96	Portadown	A	2-3	Little, McBride
08/04/96	Ards	A	2-0	Smith 2
20/04/96	Linfield	H	3-0	Little, Smyth, Batey
27/04/96	Glenavon	A	3-1	Cook 2, Kirk

LINFIELD

CLUB DIRECTORY

Linfield FC
Windsor Park, Donegal Ave, Belfast BT12 6LW
tel - (01232) 244198
fax - (01232) 244691
Year of Formation - 1886
Chairman - Billy McCoubrey
Secretary - Derek Brooks
Manager - Trevor Anderson
Stadium - Windsor Park (28,500)

MAJOR HONOURS
League Championship - (42)
1891, 1892, 1893, 1895, 1898, 1902, 1904, 1907, 1908, 1909, 1911, 1914, 1922, 1923, 1930, 1932, 1934, 1935, 1949, 1950, 1954, 1955, 1956, 1959, 1961, 1962, 1966, 1969, 1971, 1975, 1978, 1979, 1980, 1982, 1983, 1984, 1985, 1986, 1987, 1989, 1993, 1994.
Domestic Cup - (35)
1891, 1892, 1893, 1895, 1898, 1899, 1902, 1904, 1912, 1913, 1915, 1916, 1919, 1922, 1923, 1930, 1931, 1934, 1936, 1939, 1942, 1945, 1946, 1948, 1950, 1953, 1960, 1962, 1963, 1970, 1978, 1980, 1982, 1994, 1995.

APPEARANCES 95/96

	P	Ap	(s)	Gls
Noel BAILLIE	M	28		
Stephen BEATTY	M	17	(3)	1
Alan BYRNE (IRL)	M	4	(1)	1
Andrew CAMPBELL	G		(1)	
Raymond CAMPBELL	M	21	(1)	6
Robert CAMPBELL	M	5		
Darren CRAWFORD	G	13		
Peter CROTHERS	D	7		
Alan DORNAN	D	22		
John EASTON	D	10	(1)	
Darren ERSKINE	A	15	(9)	5
Alan EWING (SCO)	M	14	(6)	3
Pat FENLON (IRL)	M	22		6
Maurice GAMBLE	D	1		
Dessie GORMAN (IRL)	M	13	(2)	1
Jonathan HILL	D	3		
Jack HOSICK	A	4	(3)	
Richard JOHNSTON	A	12		2
Philip KNELL	M	5	(3)	
Wesley LAMONT	G	15		
Ian McCOOSH	M	19		1
Paul McGEE (IRL)	A	7	(3)	
Tommy McILROY	M	1	(5)	
Ryan McLAUGHLIN	M	1	(1)	
Stuart McLEAN (SCO)	D	3		
Pat McSHANE	D	5	(1)	
Jamie MARKS	D	1	(3)	
Paul MILLAR	A	15	(2)	7
Mike NORBURY (ENG)	A	1		
Jeff SPIERS	D	24		

LEAGUE RESULTS 1995/96

30/09/95	Glenavon	A	3-0	og (Brown), Fenlon, Erskine
07/10/95	Crusaders	H	1-2	Fenlon
14/10/95	Bangor	A	2-1	Campbell Ra. 2
21/10/95	Cliftonville	H	0-0	
28/10/95	Portadown	A	2-3	Erskine, Byrne
04/11/95	Glentoran	H	0-4	
11/11/95	Ards	A	3-2	Fenlon 2 (1p), Campbell Ra.
18/11/95	Glenavon	H	0-3	
25/11/95	Crusaders	A	0-3	
02/12/95	Bangor	H	0-0	
09/12/95	Cliftonville	A	1-1	Gorman
16/12/95	Portadown	H	1-0	Erskine
26/12/95	Glentoran	A	3-0	Ewing 2, McCoosh
01/01/96	Ards	H	0-0	
06/01/96	Glenavon	A	2-2	Johnston, Erskine
13/01/96	Crusaders	H	0-1	
27/01/96	Bangor	A	2-0	Millar 2
03/02/96	Cliftonville	H	3-1	Campbell Ra., Erskine, Millar
10/02/96	Portadown	A	1-1	Fenlon
17/02/96	Glentoran	H	2-0	Millar 2
02/03/96	Ards	A	2-1	Johnston, Millar
16/03/96	Glenavon	H	2-1	Beatty, Millar
23/03/96	Crusaders	A	2-4	Campbell Ra., Ewing
30/03/96	Bangor	H	2-1	Campbell Ra., Fenlon
06/04/96	Cliftonville	A	0-0	
09/04/96	Portadown	H	0-1	
20/04/96	Glentoran	A	0-3	
27/04/96	Ards	H	0-0	

PORTADOWN

CLUB DIRECTORY

Portadown FC
Shamrock Park
Brownstown Road
Portadown
tel - (01762) 332726
fax - (01762) 334907
Year of Formation - 1924
Chairman - Paul Hunniford
Secretary - L. Singleton
Manager - Ronnie McFall
Stadium - Shamrock Park (15,000)

MAJOR HONOURS
League Championship - (3) 1990, 1991, 1996.
Domestic Cup - (1) 1991.

APPEARANCES 95/96

	P	Ap	(s)	Gls
Kevin BAIN (SCO)	M	6		
Wesley BOYLE	A	1	(1)	1
Raymond BYRNE	D	17		
Neil CANDLISH (SCO)	A	19	(6)	5
Paul CARLYLE	M	8	(4)	1
Robert CASEY	M	26		4
Tim DALTON (IRL)	G	22		
Greg DAVIDSON	D	22		1
Paul EVANS	A	3	(4)	1
Iain FERGUSON (SCO)	A	12	(3)	3
Ian FERGUSON (SCO)	A	3		1
Gareth FULTON	D	13	(1)	
Rory GALLAGHER	D		(2)	
Garry HAYLOCK (ENG)	A	25		19
Michael KEENAN	G	6	(1)	
Peter KENNEDY	M	23		10
Scott LEITCH (SCO)	M	3		
Conor McKEEVER	D	1		
Jonathon MAGEE	A	1	(1)	
Philip MAJOR	D	20		2
Peter MURRAY	M		(1)	
Gary PEEBLES (SCO)	M	22	(1)	1
Derek RAE (SCO)	M	2		
Martin RUSSELL (IRL)	M	7	(2)	1
Alfie STEWART	D	16	(2)	
Brian STRAIN	D	24		3
Jamie WOODSFORD (ENG)	A	6		6

LEAGUE RESULTS 1995/96

30/09/95	Bangor	A	3-0	Major, Kennedy, Haylock
07/10/95	Cliftonville	H	6-1	Candlish 3, Haylock 2, Kennedy
14/10/95	Ards	H	3-1	Russell, Haylock (p), Candlish
21/10/95	Glentoran	A	1-1	Kennedy
28/10/95	Linfield	H	3-2	Kennedy 2, Peebles
04/11/95	Glenavon	A	1-0	og (Byrne)
11/11/95	Crusaders	H	1-1	Haylock
18/11/95	Bangor	H	4-2	Ferguson Iain, og (McKeown), Haylock 2
25/11/95	Cliftonville	A	3-0	Candlish, Strain 2
02/12/95	Ards	A	1-1	Haylock
09/12/95	Glentoran	H	3-1	Ferguson Iain, Boyle, Haylock
16/12/95	Linfield	A	0-1	
01/01/96	Crusaders	A	1-3	Carlyle
06/01/96	Bangor	A	0-0	
13/01/96	Cliftonville	H	4-1	Haylock 3, Casey
27/01/96	Ards	H	1-3	Evans
03/02/96	Glentoran	A	3-3	Haylock, Kennedy, Casey
10/02/96	Linfield	H	1-1	Casey
13/02/96	Glenavon	H	2-1	Ferguson Ian, Strain
17/02/96	Glenavon	A	0-7	
02/03/96	Crusaders	H	1-1	Woodsford
16/03/96	Bangor	H	4-3	Woodsford 2, Kennedy 2
23/03/96	Cliftonville	A	4-0	Major, Woodsford 3
30/03/96	Ards	A	2-0	Kennedy, Haylock
06/04/96	Glentoran	H	3-2	Haylock, Davidson, Kennedy
09/04/96	Linfield	A	1-0	Haylock
20/04/96	Glenavon	H	2-1	Ferguson Iain, Haylock (p)
27/04/96	Crusaders	A	3-3	Casey, Haylock 2

PROMOTED CLUB

SECOND DIVISION FINAL TABLE 95/96

		Pd	W	D	L	F	A	Pt	GD
1	**Coleraine**	**28**	**21**	**4**	**3**	**82**	**28**	**67**	**+54**
2	Ballymena United	28	13	10	5	38	25	49	+13
3	Omagh Town	28	12	7	9	50	43	43	+7
4	Distillery	28	10	7	11	35	34	37	+1
5	Ballyclare Comrades	28	10	3	15	29	48	33	-19
6	Carrick Rangers	28	9	3	16	32	56	30	-24
7	Larne	28	7	7	14	31	36	28	-5
8	Newry Town	28	7	5	16	31	58	26	-27

CLUB DIRECTORY

Coleraine FC
The Showgrounds
Ballycastle Road
Coleraine
tel - (01265) 53655/43724
Year of Formation - 1927
Chairman - Hugh Wade
Secretary - Freddie Monahan
Manager - Kenny Shiels
Stadium - The Showgrounds (8,000)

MAJOR HONOURS

League Championship - (1) 1974.
Domestic Cup - (4) 1965, 1972, 1975, 1977.

NORWAY

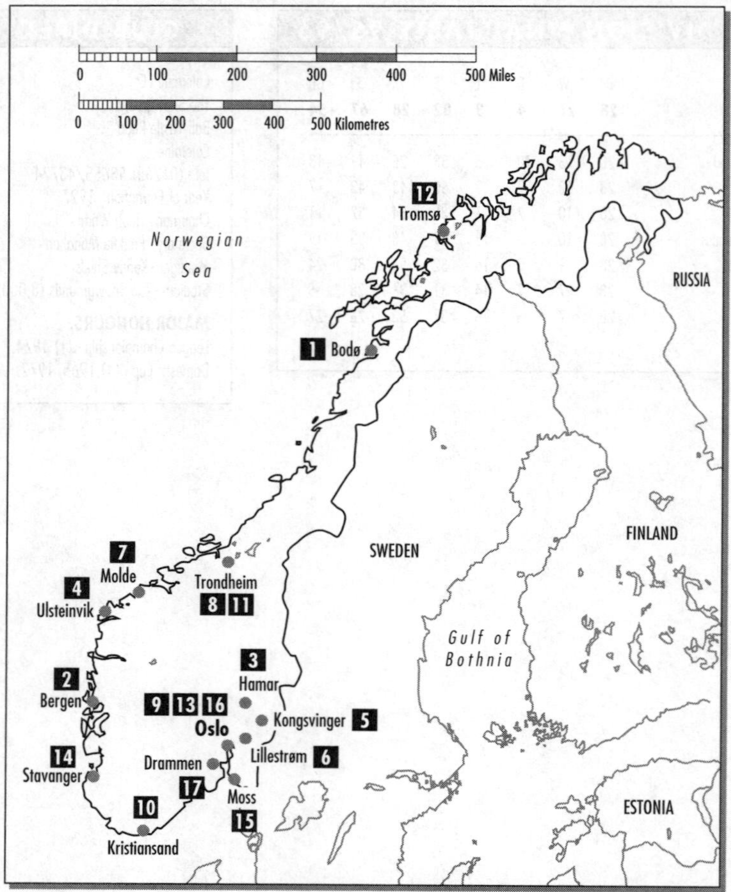

1	FK BODØ/GLIMT	732
2	SK BRANN	733
3	HAMARKAMERATENE	734
4	IL HØDD	735
5	KONGSVINGER IL	736
6	LILLESTRØM SK	737
7	MOLDE FK	738
8	ROSENBORG BK	739
9	STABAEK IF	740
10	IK START	741
11	STRINDHEIM IL	742
12	TROMSØ IL	743
13	VIF FOTBALL	744
14	VIKING FK	745
15	MOSS FK	746
16	SKEID	746
17	STRØMSGODSET IF	746

ROSENBORG REIGN SUPREME

"Drillo" still motoring despite Euro burn-out

FEDERATION DIRECTORY

Norges Fotballforbund
Boks 3823, Ullevaal Hageby, 0805 Oslo 8

tel - (22) 951000
tlx - 71722 nff n
fax - (22) 951010

Year of Formation - 1902
President - Per Ravn Omdal
Secretary - Ivar Egeberg

Stadium - Ullevaal stadion, Oslo (28,000)

Like the long-distance runner who commits himself too early, Norway ran out of steam and stamina in the European Championship qualifying run-in. With three games left, Egil Olsen's team were a hair's breadth away from reaching the finals in England.. Victory in their first match - the mid-August encounter with the Czech Republic in Oslo - would have confirmed the Norwegians as the very first of the 15 qualifiers. With just six minutes remaining, the fans in the Ullevaal stadium were already celebrating that remarkable achievement. But then the Czechs equalised. And from that moment on, everything that could go wrong did go wrong.

Qualification was still in Norway's hands, but they were well beaten 2-0 by a strong Czech side in the Prague rematch three weeks later, and then, in the do-or-die final qualifier away to Holland in Rotterdam, they defended well for 45 minutes before the balance swung in Holland's favour with a lucky goal from Clarence Seedorf. Ultimately the Dutch ran out comfortable 3-0 winners to leapfrog over their opponents and eliminate Norway on goal-difference.

Disappointment was immense, but there was no clamour for the head of coach Olsen. The man they call "Drillo" (for his dribbling skills as a player) was not about to lose his national hero status overnight. Like Jack Charlton with the Republic of Ireland, he had single-handedly transformed the fortunes of Norwegian football, at last giving the nation a team they could be proud of, a team fit to do battle with the best that Europe and the rest of the world had to offer.

Now Olsen's task is to rebuild a new side capable of holding its place in the global hierarchy. A strong performance from the U-21/Olympic team in their European Championship group gives him a fertile selection base. Indeed, by the time Norway's opening World Cup qualifier had come around at the beginning of June, several new faces had already been introduced to the senior team. And against Azerbaijan there were competitive débuts for two of the new crop - midfielder Petter Rudi and striker Ole Gunnar Solskjaer. Solskjaer, in particular, commanded immediate attention by scoring two goals in the comfortable 5-0 win, one of them a brilliant volley.

Rudi and Solskjaer both made the international grade after a highly impressive domestic season with their club, Molde. The newly-promoted side finished runners-up in the 1995 Tippeligaen, earning themselves a second successive season of European competition with a place in the UEFA Cup. But, well though they played, Molde were never remotely in with a chance of winning their first Norwegian title. Once again, they and the rest of the Tippeligaen teams had to take a back seat to all-conquering Rosenborg BK.

The team from Trondheim were everybody's pre-season favourites to take a fourth successive domestic title. They warmed up for the 1995 campaign by winning the

LEAGUE CHAMPIONSHIP RESULTS 1995

		1	2	3	4	5	6	7	8	9	10	11	12	13	14
1	FK Bodø/Glimt		3-1	5-0	4-0	2-2	3-3	3-2	1-2	0-1	1-2	3-2	1-2	2-2	6-2
2	SK Brann	4-2		4-1	1-2	1-1	1-1	0-6	1-1	1-0	0-4	4-1	4-2	2-1	2-1
3	Hamarkameratene	0-6	1-3		2-1	2-1	0-2	1-2	1-3	5-0	0-0	0-0	0-1	1-0	0-5
4	IL Hødd	0-0	1-0	4-1		3-0	0-1	2-2	1-4	1-1	2-1	1-1	2-3	3-0	0-1
5	Kongsvinger IL	1-2	1-0	4-1	2-1		1-3	0-2	1-1	0-0	2-0	5-1	1-1	2-2	3-4
6	Lillestrøm SK	1-1	1-3	2-2	6-0	3-1		0-1	1-3	2-2	3-1	3-0	5-4	1-3	4-1
7	Molde FK	0-3	4-2	3-2	7-2	3-1	1-2		2-2	1-0	2-1	4-1	0-7	0-1	5-4
8	Rosenborg BK	3-3	3-1	9-1	6-1	6-0	2-1	2-0		5-2	4-1	2-1	2-0	3-2	1-0
9	Stabaek IF	4-0	3-0	3-1	3-1	0-0	0-2	3-1	2-1		1-3	3-0	0-2	0-2	2-0
10	IK Start	2-5	1-0	1-2	0-2	6-2	2-1	1-3	1-3	4-1		4-6	2-1	0-1	0-2
11	Strindheim IL	1-1	2-2	2-4	1-5	1-3	1-1	1-3	0-5	2-1	2-6		1-0	1-2	5-3
12	Tromsø IL	0-4	2-2	4-1	4-1	8-0	0-0	2-2	1-2	2-2	1-4	1-0		2-1	1-0
13	VIF Fotball	0-4	3-1	1-2	3-2	1-3	0-0	2-2	2-1	2-2	4-1	9-2	2-1		1-1
14	Viking FK	6-0	2-0	0-2	3-0	0-0	3-1	2-2	2-2	2-0	1-3	2-1	3-1	5-0	

LEAGUE CHAMPIONSHIP FINAL TABLE 1995

		Home						Away					Total						
		Pd	W	D	L	F	A	W	D	L	F	A	W	D	L	F	A	Pt	GD
1	Rosenborg BK	26	12	1	0	48	13	7	4	2	30	16	19	5	2	78	29	62	+49
2	Molde FK	26	8	1	4	32	28	6	4	3	28	19	14	5	7	60	47	47	+13
3	FK Bodø/Glimt	26	6	3	4	34	21	6	4	3	31	22	12	7	7	65	43	43	+22
4	Lillestrøm SK	26	6	3	4	32	22	5	5	3	18	14	11	8	7	50	36	41	+14
5	Viking FK	26	8	3	2	31	12	4	1	8	24	30	12	4	10	55	42	40	+13
6	Tromsø IL	26	6	4	3	28	19	5	1	7	25	23	11	5	10	53	42	38	+11
7	VIF Fotball	26	6	4	3	30	22	5	2	6	17	22	11	6	9	47	44	37	+3
8	IK Start	26	5	0	8	24	29	6	1	6	27	23	11	1	14	51	52	34	-1
9	Stabaek IF	26	8	1	4	24	13	1	5	7	12	27	9	6	11	36	40	33	-4
10	SK Brann	26	7	3	3	25	23	2	2	9	15	27	9	5	12	40	50	32	-10
11	Kongsvinger IL	26	5	4	4	23	18	2	4	7	14	36	7	8	11	37	54	29	-17
12	IL Hødd	26	5	4	4	20	15	3	0	10	18	42	8	4	14	38	57	28	-19
13	Hamarkameratene	26	4	2	7	13	24	4	1	8	20	42	8	3	15	33	66	27	-33
14	Strindheim IL	26	3	3	7	20	36	1	2	10	16	41	4	5	17	36	77	17	-41

N.B. Viking FK deducted 2 pts.

national indoor championship (played undercover on full-size pitches) and then proceeded to fulfil all predictions by romping into an early lead in the race for the 'real thing', winning 10 of their first 11 games and remaining undefeated until match16. Rosenborg were simply in a class of their own, and they wrapped up the title with a 2-0 victory at home to Molde (in front of their second biggest crowd of the season, 13,932) with three matches remaining.

For the second season running, Rosenborg adorned their triumph by scoring in every game (though it was only an 89th-minute effort from new signing Trond Egil Soltvedt in the final match which preserved that record). As in 1994, the league's top scorer crown went to prolific young forward Harald Brattbakk, who struck at the rate of a goal a game to notch 26, nine better than his previous year's tally. Other significant contributors to Rosenborg's title stroll were national team players "Mini" Jakobsen and Karl-Petter Løken, while the most consistently impressive player was undoubtedly 29-year-old Bent Skammelsrud. A dynamic grafter with fine technique and a powerful left-foot shot, he has never done himself justice when given his opportunity in the national team, but for RBK he has always been an outstanding team player and 1995 was his best season yet.

Not content to lord it over all and sundry in the expanded 14-team Tippeligaen, Rosenborg also grabbed further

INTERNATIONAL HONOURS

World Cup Finals appearances: 1938, 1994

TOP SCORERS

26	Harald BRATTBAKK (Rosenborg BK)
22	Petter BELSVIK (IK Start)
20	Ole Gunnar SOLSKJAER (Molde FK)
19	Stig JOHANSEN (FK Bodø/Glimt)
18	Tore André FLO (Tromsø IL)
16	Arild STAVRUM (Molde FK)
13	Ståle SOLBAKKEN (Lillestrøm SK)
	Ole Bjørn SUNDGOT (Molde FK)
	Geir TELEVIK (IL Hødd)

NATIONAL TEAM RESULTS 95/96

22/07/95	France	H	Oslo	0-0	
16/08/95	Czech Republic (ECQ)	H	Oslo	1-1	Berg H. (27)
06/09/95	Czech Republic (ECQ)	A	Prague	0-2	
11/10/95	England	H	Oslo	0-0	
15/11/95	Holland (ECQ)	A	Rotterdam	0-3	
26/11/95	Jamaica	A	Kingston	1-1	Solskjaer (80)
29/11/95	Trinidad & Tobago	A	Port of Spain	2-3	Flo T-A. (11), Levernes (20)
07/02/96	Spain	A	Las Palmas	0-1	
27/03/96	Northern Ireland	A	Belfast	2-0	Solskjaer (51), Østenstad (83)
24/04/96	Spain	H	Oslo	0-0	
02/06/96	Azerbaijan (WCQ)	H	Oslo	5-0	Solbakken (8, 46), Solskjaer (37, 90), Strandli (60)

NATIONAL TEAM APPEARANCES 95/96

Coach - Egil OLSEN	FRA	TCH	TCH	ENG	HOL	JAM	TRI	ESP	NIR	ESP	AZB	Cps	Gls
Erik THORSTVEDT (28/10/62) - Tottenham Hotspur (ENG)	G	G	G	G					s46			97	-
Gunnar HALLE (11/08/65) - Oldham Athletic (ENG)	D46											52	5
Erland JOHNSEN (05/04/67) - Chelsea (ENG)	D		D		D							24	2
Henning BERG (01/09/69) - Blackburn Rovers (ENG)	D	D	D	D	D			D	D	D	D	37	4
Roger NILSEN (08/08/69) - Sheffield United (ENG)	D64							D		s77		28	3
Jostein FLO (03/10/64) - Sheffield United (ENG)	M	D	M									37	9
Ståle SOLBAKKEN (27/02/68) - Lillestrøm SK	M	M	M	s63	s81	M	M	s72	M86	M	M80	19	2
Øyvind LEONHARDSEN (17/08/70) - Wimbledon (ENG)	M	M	M	M63	s59			M	M24		M46	46	11
Kjetil REKDAL (06/11/68) - K Lierse SK (BEL)	M87		s75	M	M			M	M	M	M	51	10
Jan Åge FJØRTOFT (10/01/67) - Middlesbrough (ENG)	A	A80	A71	A80	A			A	A75	A77		70	20
Mons Ivar MJELDE (17/11/67) - FK Austria Wien (AUT)	A											3	2
Alf-Inge HÅLAND (23/11/72) - Nottingham Forest (ENG)	s46	D			s62			D	D	D	D	17	-
Ronny JOHNSEN (10/06/69) - Lillestrøm SK/Besiktas (TUR)	s64	D	D	D					D		D	23	1
Kåre INGEBRIGTSEN (11/11/65) - Lillestrøm SK	s87											23	1
Karl-Petter LØKEN (14/08/66) - Rosenborg BK		D	D	D	D62							36	1
Lars BOHINEN (08/09/69) - Nottingham Forest (ENG)/Blackburn Rovers (ENG)		M	M75	M	M81			M72				46	10
Jahn Ivar JAKOBSEN (08/11/65) - Rosenborg BK		M64	M	M	M			s65	s24	M46		63	10
Geirmund BRENDESAETHER (22/03/70) - SK Brann		s64				D	D					6	-
Harald BRATTBAKK (01/02/71) - Rosenborg BK		s80	s71	s80								8	3
Stig Inge BJØRNEBYE (11/12/69) - Liverpool (ENG)				D	D			D	D	D77	D	48	1
Tore André FLO (15/06/73) - Tromsø IL/SK Brann				M	M	A	A	A65			s46	6	1
Frode GRODÅS (24/10/69) - Lillestrøm SK					G	G	G46	G	G46	G	G	24	-
Erik MYKLAND (21/07/71) - IK Start					M59	M28	M74					37	2
Egil ULFSTEIN (01/10/71) - Viking FK						D	D46					2	-
Claus LUNDEKVAM (22/02/73) - SK Brann						D	s46		s86	s85		4	-
Claus EFTEVAAG (20/12/69) - IK Start						D	D					3	-
Arild STAVRUM (16/04/72) - Molde FK						M46	M76					2	-
Petter RUDI (17/09/73) - Molde FK						M	M	M	M	M	M	6	-
Ole Gunnar SOLSKJAER (26/02/73) - Molde FK						A	s74		A	A	A	5	4
Bjørn Arild LEVERNES (27/04/72) - VIF Fotball						s28	A					2	1
Gunnar AASE (29/09/71) - Viking FK						s46	s76					4	1
Christer BASMA (01/08/72) - Stabaek IF							D					1	-
Frode OLSEN (12/10/67) - IK Start							s46					2	-
Egil ØSTENSTAD (02/01/72) - Viking FK									s75	s77		3	3
Tore PEDERSEN (29/09/69) - FC St. Pauli (GER)										D85		38	-
Tommy Svindal LARSEN (11/08/73) - Stabaek IF										s46	s80	2	-
Frank STRANDLI (16/05/72) - Lillestrøm SK											A	9	2

glory in the Norwegian Cup and the Champions' League.

The club's fifth domestic 'double' was completed with a 3-1 victory over SK Brann in the Cup final replay - after a 1-1 draw in the first match, played, as usual, before a full house at the Ullevaal in Oslo. In 1995 it was estimated that the old stadium could have been sold out three times over such was the demand for tickets from the country's two best-supported teams. The first encounter was particularly notable for an incident in the 35th minute when referee Skjervold sent off Brann striker Eivind Karlsbakk for feigning a dive in the penalty area. TV evidence proved the official wrong, and, following discussions between the NFF and the referee, Karlsbakk was reinstated to play in the replay. It didn't help Brann's cause, though. They took an early lead, but the champions bounced back to run out convincing 3-1 winners. Brann's consolation was a place in the 96/97 Cup-winners'

Cup, which they had achieved thanks to a remarkable come-back in the semi-final against Lillestrøm, scoring four goals in the last half-hour of the second leg to take the tie 5-4. This made up for a difficult season in the league for the Bergen club, whose coach, ex-national team skipper Hallvar Thoresen, had been sacked midway through the campaign, his major crime in the eyes of the fans having been to offload star player Soltvedt to Rosenborg as a disciplinary measure following a pre-season 'booze-up' in Cyprus.

Brann avoided relegation by just four points. The three

EUROPEAN CUPS RESULTS 95/96

CHAMPIONS' CUP

● ROSENBORG BK

Preliminary round BESIKTAS (TUR)

H 3-0 Hoftun (21), Strand (26), Brattbakk (75)
Jamtfall; Kvarme, Hoftun, Bragstad (Staurvik 81), Stensaas; Strand, Skammelsrud, Soltvedt; Løken, Brattbakk, Jakobsen.

A 1-3 Brattbakk (68)
Jamtfall; Kvarme, Hoftun, Bragstad, Stensaas; Strand (Staurvik 90), Skammelsrud, Soltvedt (Iversen 53); Løken, Brattbakk, Jakobsen.

Champions' League

1st match LEGIA WARSZAWA (POL)

A 1-3 Jakobsen (63)
Jamtfall; Kvarme, Hoftun, Bragstad, Stensaas; Strand, Skammelsrud, Løken, Soltvedt (Heggem 78); Iversen (Staurvik 88), Jakobsen.

2nd match BLACKBURN ROVERS (ENG)

H 2-1 Løken (30), Stensaas (86)
By Rise; Kvarme, Hoftun, Bragstad, Stensaas; Strand (Staurvik 82), Skammelsrud, Soltvedt; Løken (Iversen 73), Brattbakk (Heggem 89), Jakobsen.

3rd match SPARTAK MOSKVA (RUS)

H 2-4 Løken (2), Brattbakk (45)
Jamtfall; Kvarme (Heggem 46), Hoftun, Bragstad, Stensaas; Strand (Staurvik 75), Skammelsrud, Soltvedt (Iversen 67); Løken, Brattbakk, Jakobsen.

4th match SPARTAK MOSKVA (RUS)

A 1-4 Løken (90)
By Rise; Løken, Hoftun, Bragstad, Stensaas; Strand (Heggem 63), Skammelsrud, Brattbakk, Jakobsen, Iversen; Staurvik.

5th match LEGIA WARSZAWA (POL)

H 4-0 Strand (17), Brattbakk (44), Jakobsen (65), Heggem (89)
By Rise; Kvarme, Staurvik, Hoftun, Stensaas; Strand (Heggem 88), Skammelsrud, Soltvedt; Iversen, Brattbakk, Jakobsen.

6th match BLACKBURN ROVERS (ENG)

A 1-4 Iversen (30)
By Rise; Kvarme, Hoftun, Bragstad (Staurvik 46), Stensaas; Strand (Heggem 46), Skammelsrud, Soltvedt, Iversen; Brattbakk, Jakobsen.

CUP-WINNERS' CUP

● MOLDE FK

Preliminary round DINAMO-93 MINSK (BLS)

A 1-1 Solskjaer (85)
Bakke; Andersen, Flaco, Singsaas, Fostervold (Skuseth 6); Berg Hestad, Rudi, Nordstrand Jacobsen; Stavrum A., Solskjaer, Sundgot.

H 2-1 Solskjaer (4), Stavrum A. (67)
Bakke; Andersen, Rekdal, Flaco, Fostervold; Berg Hestad, Rudi, Nordstrand Jacobsen (Skuseth 60); Stavrum A., Solskjaer, Sundgot.

1st round PARIS SAINT-GERMAIN FC (FRA)

H 2-3 Solskjaer (55), Stavrum A. (81)
Bakke; Lyngstad, Rekdal, Stavrum O.E. (Wenaas 82), Fostervold; Berg Hestad, Rudi, Andersen (Saetre 54); Stavrum A., Solskjaer, Sundgot.

A 0-3
Bakke; Lyngstad, Rekdal, Stavrum O.E. (Singsaas 46), Fostervold; Berg Hestad, Rudi, Wenaas (Johnsen 75; Flaco 86); Stavrum A., Solskjaer, Sundgot.

UEFA CUP

● LILLESTRØM SK

Preliminary round FC FLORA TALLINN (EST)

H 4-0 Ingelstad (43), Ingebrigtsen (60), Gulbrandsen (68, 87)
Grodås; Bergdølmo, Berntsen, Bjarmann, Sognnaes; Solbakken, Ingebrigtsen, Gulbrandsen; Sandstø (Frigård 85), Ingelstad, Pedersen.

A 0-1
Grodås; Bergdølmo, Berntsen, Bjarmann (Werni 76), Sognnaes (Schiller 46); Solbakken, Ingebrigtsen, Gulbrandsen, Ingelstad, Pedersen; Sandstø (Frigård 69).

1st round BRØNDBY IF (DEN)

A 0-3
Grodås; Schiller, Berntsen, Bjarmann, Bergdølmo; Pedersen, Ingebrigtsen, Solbakken, Sandstø, Hedman (Gulbrandsen 56); Frigård.

H 0-0
Grodås; Schiller (Sognnaes 43), Berntsen, Bjarmann, Bergdølmo; Pedersen (Hedman 78), Ingebrigtsen, Solbakken, Kristiansen; Ingelstad, Frigård.

● VIKING FK

Preliminary round TPV (FIN)

A 4-0 Gawara (48og), Østenstad (58), Medalen (73), Sørloth (87)
Myhre; Meinseth, Solberg T., Ulfstein, Bøe (Sørloth 67); Solberg S., Pedersen, Fugelstad; Aase (Medalen 42), Østenstad (Bergersen 86), Storvik.

H 3-1 Bergersen (4, 41), Sørloth (64)
Myhre; Bøe, Solberg T., Ulfstein (Karlsen 46), Fuglestad; Solberg S., Pedersen, Bergersen (Medalen 77); Aase, Østenstad (Sørloth 63), Storvik.

1st round AJ AUXERRE (FRA)

H 1-1 Ulfstein (56)
Myhre; Solberg T., Karlsen (Meinseth 27), Ulfstein, Fuglestad; Pedersen, Lunde Aarsheim, Storvik; Aase (Medalen 76), Sørloth, Bergersen.

A 0-1
Myhre; Meinseth, Solberg T., Ulfstein, Fuglestad; Pedersen (Østenstad 69), Solberg S. (Medalen 82), Lunde Aarsheim; Aase (Bergersen 46), Sørloth, Storvik.

DOMESTIC CUP RESULTS

THIRD ROUND
Fyllingen IL 1, SK Brann 3
Bryne FK 2, Viking FK 0
Gevir Bodø 0, FK Bodø/Glimt 4
Kongsvinger IL 4, Kjelsås IL 2
FK Mjølner-Narvik 0, Tromsø IL 3
Strindheim IL 4, Os 2
Alta IF 2, Rosenborg BK 6
Molde FK 2, Aalesund FK 1
Lillestrøm SK 7, Strømmen IF 0
Strømsgodset IF 1, Moss FK 0
Hamarkameratene 2, Sogndal IL 0 (aet)
Drøbak/Frogn IL 0, Lyn 1 (aet)
Sarpsborg FK 0, Eik-Tønsberg IF 0 (aet; 6-7 on pens.)
Odd BK 2, IK Start 2 (aet; 4-5 on pens.)
Nardo 2, IL Hødd 4 (aet)
Stabaek IF 2, Åsane 2 (aet; 4-2 on pens.)

FOURTH ROUND
SK Brann 3, Bryne FK 1
Eik-Tønsberg IF 1, Rosenborg BK (aet)
(replay) Rosenborg BK 4, Eik-Tønsberg IF 1
Hamarkameratene 3, Strømsgodset IF 2 (aet)
IL Hødd 2, Molde FK 0
Lyn 1, Stabaek IF 1 (aet)
(replay) Stabaek IF 2, Lyn 2 (aet; 2-4 on pens.)
IK Start 7, FK Bodø/Glimt 1
Strindheim IL 0, Lillestrøm SK 1
Tromsø IL 3, Kongsvinger IL 1

QUARTER-FINALS
SK Brann 4, Lyn 1
IL Hødd 3, Hamarkameratene 2
Lillestrøm SK 3, Tromsø IL 1
Rosenborg BK 2, IK Start 0

SEMI-FINALS
Lillestrøm SK v SK Brann 3-1; 1-4 (SK Brann 5-4)
IL Hødd v Rosenborg BK 0-5; 1-2 (Rosenborg BK 7-1)

FINAL
29/10/95, Oslo
SK BRANN 1 Strandli (72)
ROSENBORG BK 1 Strand (61) (aet)
referee - Skjervold
SK BRANN - Bahus; Brendesaether (Skjaelaaen 112), Helland, Ludvigsen I., Lundekvam; Gylfason, Johansson, Ludvigsen P.O., Hasund; Karlsbakk, Strandli.
ROSENBORG BK - By Rise; Løken, Hoftun, Bragstad, Stensaas; Strand (Heggeem 110), Skammelsrud, Soltvedt (Staurvik 67); Iversen, Brattbakk, Jacobsen.

(replay)
05/11/95, Oslo
ROSENBORG BK 3
Staurvik (23p), Hoftun (36), Iversen (49)
SK BRANN 1 Ludvigsen I. (21)
referee - Pedersen
ROSENBORG BK - Jamtfall; Løken, Staurvik, Hoftun, Stensaas; Strand (Winsnes 90), Skammelsrud, Heggem (Hjelde 90); Iversen, Brattbakk, Jacobsen (Solheim 90).
SK BRANN - Bahus; Brendesaether, Helland, Ludvigsen I., Lundekvam; Gylfason, Bakkerud, Ludvigsen P.O., Skjaelaaen (Nordstrand 67); Karlsbakk (Johannessen 57), Strandli.

teams to go down were Hødd, HamKam and bottom club Strindheim, who ground-shared with Rosenborg but had the poorest average attendance (1,933) in the whole of the league. Up in their place came divisional champions Moss and Skeid plus perennial yo-yo club Strømsgodset, who defeated the other runners-up Sogndal in a play-off.

In Europe, interest focussed firmly on Rosenborg's progress in the Champions' League. Lillestrøm, Viking and Molde all won their preliminary round ties before succumbing to superior opponents in the first round proper. Rosenborg, however, made history by eliminating Turkish champions Besiktas (including recently-acquired Norwegian record signing Ronny Johnsen) to qualify for the Champions' League and then beating both Blackburn Rovers and Legia Warsaw at home in the Lerkendal to keep their hopes of quarter-final qualification alive until the very last game. Sadly, they failed to make the last eight, submitting meekly to Blackburn in the first 45 minutes at Ewood Park and going down 4-1 when a draw would have sealed their progress. But at least they finished 1995 by holding onto one remarkable record. Youngster Steffen Iversen's brilliant 30th-minute equaliser meant that Rosenborg had scored at least one goal in each of their last 77 successive competitive matches. An incredible achievement by any standards.

PLAYERS OF THE SEASON

OLE GUNNAR SOLSKJAER
A novice to top-flight football at the beginning of the 1995 Tippeligaen , Ole Gunnar Solskjaer made massive strides during the course of the season, scoring 10 goals in his first six games and doubling that tally by the end of the campaign to help newly-promoted Molde into the UEFA Cup. A prolific scorer in the Norwegian U-21 team (nine goals in the European Championship qualifiers), the 23-year-old red-head scored on his senior début against Jamaica and made it four goals in five internationals with his double strike in the World Cup opener against Azerbaijan. Suitably impressed, English 'double' winners Manchester United promptly signed him up for the 96/97 season in a joint swoop involving fellow Norwegian international Ronny Johnsen.

PETTER RUDI
A poll conducted by the daily newspaper *Verdens Gang* voted Molde midfielder Petter Rudi as the best player during the 1995 Tippeligaen. National team coach Egil Olsen was in firm agreement with the paper's choice, selecting him from the start in all six of Norway's post-European Championship matches. A gutsy, forceful midfield schemer, Rudi was responsible for setting up a large proportion of the 49 league goals shared by Molde's 'triple-S' strike-force of Solskjaer, Stavrum and Sundgot.

FK BODØ/GLIMT

CLUB DIRECTORY

Fotballklubben Bodø/Glimt
Boks 179
8001 Bodø
tel - (75) 524330
Year of Formation - 1916
President - Bjørn Tore Hansen
Coach - Trond Sollied
Stadium - Aspmyra stadion (13,000)

MAJOR HONOURS
Domestic Cup - (2) 1975, 1993.

APPEARANCES 95

	P	Ap	(s)	Gls
Arild BERG	M	16	(6)	3
Runar BERG	M	24		2
Ørjan BERG	M	14	(1)	2
Aasmund BJØRKAN	A	20	(4)	8
Jan Egil BREKKE	D	2	(8)	
Andreas EVJEN	D	19	(5)	
Ola HALDORSEN	D	14	(4)	
Cato HANSEN	D	4	(2)	
Tommy HANSEN	M	16		5
Raymond HARDY	D	6	(4)	
Stig JOHANSEN	A	24	(2)	19
Bent Inge JOHNSEN	A	24		8
Thor MIKALSEN	M	26		1
Håvard SAKARIASSEN	A		(1)	
Petter SOLLI	D	25	(1)	1
Per Ivar STEINBAKK	A		(12)	3
Jan Derek SØRENSEN	A	26		12
Rohnny WESTAD	G	26		

LEAGUE RESULTS 1995

Date	Opponent		Score	Scorers
22/04/95	Viking FK	A	0-6	
30/04/95	Lillestrøm SK	H	3-3	Hansen T. (p), Johnsen, Johansen
03/05/95	Stabaek IF	A	0-4	
06/05/95	Hamarkameratene	H	5-0	Hansen T. 2, Johansen 2, Johnsen
14/05/95	IL Hødd	A	0-0	
16/05/95	Tromsø IL	H	1-2	Johansen
21/05/95	VIF Fotball	A	4-0	Johnsen 2, Bjørkan, Sørensen
28/05/95	IK Start	H	1-2	Johnsen
02/06/95	Strindheim IL	A	1-1	Sørensen
11/06/95	Molde FK	A	3-0	Hansen T. (p), Sørensen, Berg A.
18/06/95	Kongsvinger IL	H	2-2	Hansen T., Johansen
25/06/95	Rosenborg BK	A	3-3	Sørensen 2, Johansen
02/07/95	SK Brann	H	3-1	Johansen, Bjørkan, Sørensen
16/07/95	SK Brann	A	2-4	Sørensen 2
23/07/95	Rosenborg BK	H	1-2	Johansen
30/07/95	Kongsvinger IL	A	2-1	Johansen, Sørensen (p)
06/08/95	Molde FK	H	3-2	Solli, Mikalsen, Steinbakk
20/08/95	Strindheim IL	H	3-2	Steinbakk, Johansen, Johnsen
26/08/95	IK Start	A	5-2	Berg R. 2, Bjørkan, Sørensen, Johnsen (p)
02/09/95	VIF Fotball	H	2-2	Johansen 2
09/09/95	Tromsø IL	A	4-0	Johansen 2, Berg Ø., Berg A.
24/09/95	IL Hødd	H	4-0	Johansen 2, Bjørkan, Berg Ø.
01/10/95	Hamarkameratene	A	6-0	Bjørkan 2, og (Folland), Johnsen, Berg A., Steinbakk
08/10/95	Stabaek IF	H	0-1	
15/10/95	Lillestrøm SK	A	1-1	Sørensen
22/10/95	Viking FK	H	6-2	Johansen 3, Bjørkan 2, Sørensen

SK BRANN

CLUB DIRECTORY

Sportsklubben Brann
Boks 161
5032 Minde
tel - (55) 297617/299825
fax - (55) 293280
Year of Formation - 1908
President - Lars Henrik Berge
Secretary - Kari Larsen
Coach - Hallvar Thoresen; Kjell Tennfjord
Stadium - Brann stadion (24,000)

MAJOR HONOURS
League Championship - (2) 1962, 1963
Domestic Cup - (5)
1923, 1925, 1972, 1976, 1982.

APPEARANCES 95

	P	Ap	(s)	Gls
Vidar BAHUS	G	11		
Lars BAKKERUD	M	24		
Geirmund BRENDESAETHER	D	21		1
Cato GUNTVEIT	D	9	(2)	
Ágúst GYLFASON (ISL)	D	10	(4)	
Geor HASUND	A	22	(2)	6
Roger HELLAND	D	26		2
Martin HOLLUND	G	15		
Erik JOHANNESSEN	D	6	(4)	
Magnus JOHANSSON (SWE)	M	22	(1)	4
Christian KALVENES	A		(1)	
Eivind KARLSBAKK	A	23	(2)	8
Inge LUDVIGSEN	D	13	(4)	
Per-Ove LUDVIGSEN	M	8	(3)	1
Claus LUNDEKVAM	D	13	(1)	
Trevor MORLEY (ENG)	A	7		4
Roger NORDSTRAND (SWE)	M	3	(4)	1
Gunnar NOREBØ	M	1	(2)	
Tore PEDERSEN	D	12		
Eirik SKJAELAAEN	M	17	(6)	4
Frank STRANDLI	A	23		7
Asbjørn TENDEN	A		(9)	1

LEAGUE RESULTS 1995

22/04/95	Molde FK	H	0-6	
30/04/95	Kongsvinger IL	A	0-1	
03/05/95	Rosenborg BK	H	1-1	Strandli
07/05/95	Strindheim IL	H	4-1	Karlsbakk 2, Strandli (p), Brendesaether
14/05/95	Viking FK	A	0-2	
16/05/95	Lillestrøm SK	H	1-1	Strandli
21/05/95	Stabaek IF	A	0-3	
28/05/95	Hamarkameratene	H	4-1	Karlsbakk, Strandli, Skjaelaaen, Johansson
02/06/95	IL Hødd	A	0-1	
11/06/95	Tromsø IL	H	4-2	Morley 2 (1p), Karlsbakk, Skjaelaaen
18/06/95	VIF Fotball	A	1-3	Morley
25/06/95	IK Start	H	0-4	
02/07/95	FK Bodø/Glimt	A	1-3	Johansson
16/07/95	FK Bodø/Glimt	H	4-2	Skjaelaaen, Morley, og (Mikalsen), Karlsbakk
23/07/95	IK Start	A	0-1	
30/07/95	VIF Fotball	H	2-1	Hasund, Karlsbakk
06/08/95	Tromsø IL	A	2-2	Hasund, Strandli (p)
20/08/95	IL Hødd	H	1-2	Hasund
27/08/95	Hamarkameratene	A	3-1	Skjaelaaen, Hasund, Tenden
02/09/95	Stabaek IF	H	1-0	Strandli (p)
09/09/95	Lillestrøm SK	A	3-1	Hasund, Strandli (p), Karlsbakk
01/10/95	Strindheim IL	A	2-2	Helland, Ludvigsen P.O.
04/10/95	Viking FK	H	2-1	Karlsbakk, Helland
08/10/95	Rosenborg BK	A	1-3	Johansson
15/10/95	Kongsvinger IL	H	1-1	Nordstrand
22/10/95	Molde FK	A	2-4	Hasund, Johansson

HAMARKAMERATENE

CLUB DIRECTORY

Hamarkameratene
Bakkegt. 2
2300 Hamar
tel - (62) 522124/530003
fax - (62) 527498
Year of Formation - 1918
President - Odd Røste
Coach - Peter Engelbrektsson
(96 - Knut Hagen)
Stadium - Briskeby Gressbane (11,500)

APPEARANCES 95

	P	Ap	(s)	Gls
Frode AURMO	M	14	(4)	
Knut Erik FOLLAND	D	14	(1)	
Clas André GUTTULSRØD	G	12		
Stian HAGELUND	D	7	(15)	
Thorstein HELSTAD	A	13	(4)	4
Kjetil HODDØ	A		(1)	
Jørn HOLMEN	A	6	(5)	4
Tom Henning HOVI	D	25		
Heine JENSSEN	D	23		
Kent KARLSEN	D	21		
Frode LUND	G	14	(1)	
Atle MAURUD	A	18	(3)	4
Darko NESTOROVIC (YUG)	A	9	(1)	4
Leif NORDLI	D	16		4
Ronny PEDERSEN	D	13	(1)	1
Arild REBNE	M	14	(1)	
Stein Jøran SANDEN	A	4	(9)	2
Vegard SKOGHEIM	M	21	(2)	2
Iver SLETTEN	A	3	(7)	2
Svein Erik SAETRE	M	17	(1)	2
Rune SØRUM	M	1	(1)	
Jon Eirik ØDEGAARD	M	12	(7)	2
Thomas ØVERBY	A	9	(7)	2

LEAGUE RESULTS 1995

Date	Opponent	H/A	Score	Scorers
22/04/95	Tromsø IL	H	0-1	
30/04/95	VIF Fotball	A	2-1	Maurud, Saetre
03/05/95	IK Start	H	0-0	
06/06/95	FK Bodø/Glimt	A	0-5	
14/05/95	Molde FK	H	1-2	Øverby
16/05/95	Kongsvinger IL	A	1-4	Sletten
21/05/95	Rosenborg BK	H	1-3	Øverby
28/05/95	SK Brann	A	1-4	Maurud
02/06/95	Viking FK	H	0-5	
11/06/95	Lillestrøm SK	A	2-2	Pedersen, Nordli
18/06/95	Stabaek IF	H	5-0	Helstad 2, Skogheim 2, Maurud
25/06/95	Strindheim IL	H	0-0	
02/07/95	IL Hødd	A	1-4	Helstad
16/07/95	IL Hødd	H	2-1	Nestorovic, Holmen
23/07/95	Strindheim IL	A	4-2	Saetre, Holmen, Sanden, Nordli
30/07/95	Stabaek IF	A	1-3	Holmen
06/08/95	Lillestrøm SK	H	0-2	
18/08/95	Viking FK	A	2-0	Holmen, Nestorovic (p)
27/08/95	SK Brann	H	1-3	Helstad
02/09/95	Rosenborg BK	A	1-9	Nestorovic
10/09/95	Kongsvinger IL	H	2-1	Ødegaard 2
24/09/95	Molde FK	A	2-3	Nordli 2
01/10/95	FK Bodø/Glimt	H	0-6	
08/10/95	IK Start	A	2-1	Nestorovic, Maurud
15/10/95	VIF Fotball	H	1-0	Sletten
22/10/95	Tromsø IL	A	1-4	Sanden

IL HØDD

CLUB DIRECTORY

Idrottslaget Hødd
Boks 248
6065 Ulsteinvik
tel - (70) 010492
Year of Formation - 1919
President - Eldor Skeide
Secretary - Steinar Hauge
Coach - Erik Brakstad
Stadium - Høddvoll stadion (5,000)

APPEARANCES 95

	P	Ap	(s)	Gls
Even BLAKSTAD	D	25		2
Hans Jørgen BRANDAL	M	3	(6)	
Sindre EID	M	22	(1)	
Stig ENGEN	G	9		
Karl Oskar FJØRTOFT	M	25		3
Kenneth GISKE	M	20		3
Tor Arild HADDAL	M	11	(8)	2
Petter HAGEN	D	14	(4)	
Trond HELGESEN	D	23		1
Trond HJELLE	G	17		
Stein HOLSVIK	A	15	(6)	
André NEVSTAD	M	25		3
Per Ivar ROALD	D		(6)	1
André SKOTHEIM	A	2	(14)	1
Geir SUNDAL	D	2		
Arild SUNDGOT	A	6	(4)	2
Tommy SYLTE	A	18		7
Geir TELEVIK	A	23		13
Kenneth TRONES	D	21	(5)	
Harald ÅSLAND RIISE	M	5	(13)	

LEAGUE RESULTS 1995

Date	Opponent	H/A	Score	Scorers
22/04/95	Strindheim IL	H	1-1	Televik
30/04/95	Tromsø IL	A	1-4	Skotheim
03/05/95	VIF Fotball	H	3-0	Televik, Blakstad, Haddal
07/05/95	IK Start	A	2-0	Televik (p), Roald
14/05/95	FK Bodø/Glimt	H	0-0	
16/05/95	Molde FK	A	2-7	Sylte, Nevstad
21/05/95	Kongsvinger IL	H	3-0	Fjørtoft, Sylte, Televik
28/05/95	Rosenborg BK	A	1-6	Televik
02/06/95	SK Brann	H	1-0	Sylte
11/06/95	Viking FK	A	0-3	
18/06/95	Lillestrøm SK	H	0-1	
25/06/95	Stabaek IF	A	1-3	Sylte
02/07/95	Hamarkameratene	H	4-1	Televik 2 (1p), Sylte, Fjørtoft
16/07/95	Hamarkameratene	A	1-2	Giske
23/07/95	Stabaek IF	H	1-1	Televik
30/07/95	Lillestrøm SK	A	0-6	
05/08/95	Viking FK	H	0-1	
20/08/95	SK Brann	A	2-1	Sylte, Televik (p)
27/08/95	Rosenborg BK	H	1-4	Sylte
02/09/95	Kongsvinger IL	A	1-2	Televik
10/09/95	Molde FK	H	2-2	Sundgot, Televik
24/09/95	FK Bodø/Glimt	A	0-4	
01/10/95	IK Start	H	2-1	Sundgot, Giske
08/10/95	VIF Fotball	A	2-3	Haddal, Televik
15/10/95	Tromsø IL	H	2-3	Nevstad (p), Giske
22/10/95	Strindheim IL	A	5-1	Televik, Nevstad, Blakstad, Helgesen, Fjørtoft

KONGSVINGER IL

CLUB DIRECTORY

Kongsvinger Idrettslag
Boks 682
2201 Kongsvinger
tel - (62) 816266/816882
fax - (62) 816803
Year of Formation - 1892
Chairman - Hans Petter Adolfsen
Coach - Per Brogeland (96 - Åge Steen)
Stadium - Gjemselund stadion (6,500)

APPEARANCES 95

	P	Ap	(s)	Gls
Bjørn BERG	A	4	(5)	
Trym BERGMANN	D	20		1
Charles BERSTAD	D	23		1
Per Gunnar DALLØKEN	M	26		
Arnfinn ENGERBAKK	M	23		5
Caleb FRANCIS	A	23	(2)	5
Tommy GRØNVOLD	D	5	(15)	
Svein Inge HAAGENRUD	G	7	(1)	
Espen HAGH	M	4	(10)	
Pål HÅPNES	A	11	(10)	3
Jørn KARLSRUD	M	25		7
Jørn KOPPERUD	M	3	(3)	
Ole Einar MARTINSEN	M	23		2
Jørgen NEUMANN	D	22		
Kenneth RINGSRØD	G	19	(1)	
Vidar RISETH	A	24		12
Hai Ngoe TRAN	D	24		

LEAGUE RESULTS 1995

21/04/95	Rosenborg BK	A	0-6	
30/04/95	SK Brann	H	1-0	Martinsen
03/05/95	Viking FK	A	0-0	
07/05/95	Lillestrøm SK	H	1-3	Karlsrud
14/05/95	Stabaek IF	A	0-0	
16/05/95	Hamarkameratene	H	4-1	Martinsen, Riseth (p), Engerbakk, Karlsrud
21/05/95	IL Hødd	A	0-3	
28/05/95	Tromsø IL	H	1-1	Riseth
02/06/95	VIF Fotball	A	3-1	Riseth, Engerbakk, Francis
11/06/95	IK Start	H	2-0	Berstad, Riseth
18/06/95	FK Bodø/Glimt	A	2-2	Francis, Håpnes
25/06/95	Molde FK	H	0-2	
02/07/95	Strindheim IL	A	3-1	Riseth 2, Karlsrud
16/07/95	Strindheim IL	H	5-1	Riseth 2, Bergmann, Engerbakk, Francis
23/07/95	Molde FK	A	1-3	Riseth
30/07/95	FK Bodø/Glimt	H	1-2	Francis
06/08/95	IK Start	A	2-6	Francis, og (Belsvik)
20/08/95	VIF Fotball	H	2-2	Karlsrud, Engerbakk
27/08/95	Tromsø IL	A	0-8	
02/09/95	IL Hødd	H	2-1	Karlsrud, Engerbakk
10/09/95	Hamarkameratene	A	1-2	Karlsrud
24/09/95	Stabaek IF	H	0-0	
01/10/95	Lillestrøm SK	A	1-3	Riseth (p)
08/10/95	Viking FK	H	3-4	Riseth (p), Karlsrud, Håpnes
15/10/95	SK Brann	A	1-1	Riseth
22/10/95	Rosenborg BK	H	1-1	Håpnes

LILLESTRØM SK

CLUB DIRECTORY

Lillestrøm Sportsklubb
Boks 196
2001 Lillestrøm
tel - (63) 812341/812342
fax - (63) 818561
Year of Formation - 1917
President - Einar Krokan
Secretary - Frank Grønlund
Coach - Teitur Thórdarson; Kjetil Osvold (96 - Per Brogeland)
Stadium - Åråsen stadion (15,000)

MJAOR HONOURS

League Championship (5)
1959, 1976, 1977, 1986, 1989.
Domestic Cup - (4) 1977, 1978, 1981, 1985.

APPEARANCES 95

	P	Ap	(s)	Gls
André BERGDØLMO	D	23	(2)	3
Thomas BERNTSEN	D	15	(2)	
Torgeir BJARMANN	D	23		
Geir FRIGÅRD	A	15	(8)	7
Frode GRODÅS	G	25		
Tom GULBRANDSEN	M	15	(6)	5
Peter HEDMAN (SWE)	A	9	(6)	2
Kåre INGEBRIGTSEN	M	24		7
Stein Arne INGELSTAD	A	7	(7)	1
Ronny JOHNSEN	D	13		1
Jon KNUDSEN	G	1	(1)	
Gard KRISTIANSEN	M	5	(2)	
Jan Ove PEDERSEN	M	25	(1)	1
Erik RUDI	M		(1)	
Arne SANDSTØ	A	22	(4)	7
Dennis SCHILLER (SWE)	D	19	(1)	1
Bjarne SOGNNAES	D	16	(5)	1
Ståle SOLBAKKEN	M	26		13
Peter WERNI	D	3	(2)	

LEAGUE RESULTS 1995

22/04/95	IK Start	H	3-1	Solbakken (p), Gulbrandsen, og (Bjønsaas)
30/04/95	FK Bodø/Glimt	A	3-3	Ingebrigtsen, Solbakken, Bergdølmo
03/05/95	Molde FK	H	0-1	
07/05/95	Kongsvinger IL	A	3-1	Bergdølmo 2, Sandstø
13/05/95	Rosenborg BK	H	1-3	Solbakken
16/05/95	SK Brann	A	1-1	Sandstø
21/05/95	Viking FK	H	4-1	Frigård, Sandstø, Solbakken, Johnsen
28/05/95	Strindheim IL	H	3-0	Sandstø 2, Solbakken (p)
02/06/95	Stabaek IF	A	2-0	Frigård, Gulbrandsen
11/06/95	Hamarkameratene	H	2-2	Ingebrigtsen, Sognnaes
14/06/95	Tromsø IL	H	5-4	Solbakken 2 (1p), Ingebrigtsen, Gulbrandsen, Sandstø
18/06/95	IL Hødd	A	1-0	Ingebrigtsen
02/07/95	VIF Fotball	A	0-0	
16/07/95	VIF Fotball	H	1-3	Solbakken (p)
19/07/95	Tromsø IL	A	0-0	
30/07/95	IL Hødd	H	6-0	Solbakken 3, Ingelstad, Gulbrandsen, Frigård
06/08/95	Hamarkameratene	A	2-0	Solbakken (p), Gulbrandsen
20/08/95	Stabaek IF	H	2-2	Ingebrigtsen 2
27/08/95	Strindheim IL	A	1-1	Hedman
02/09/95	Viking FK	A	1-3	Frigård
09/09/95	SK Brann	H	1-3	Hedman
23/09/95	Rosenborg BK	A	1-2	Frigård
01/10/95	Kongsvinger IL	H	3-1	Pedersen, Solbakken, Frigård
07/10/95	Molde FK	A	2-1	Schiller, Sandstø
15/10/95	FK Bodø/Glimt	H	1-1	Frigård
22/10/95	IK Start	A	1-2	Ingebrigtsen (p)

MOLDE FK

CLUB DIRECTORY

Molde Fotballklubb
Boks 316
6401 Molde
tel - (71) 256922/254323
fax - (71) 254323
Year of Formation - 1911
President - Sondre Kåfjord
Coach - Åge Hareide
Stadium - Molde stadion (13,000)

MAJOR HONOURS
Domestic Cup - (1) 1994.

APPEARANCES 95

	P	Ap	(s)	Gls
Trond ANDERSEN	D	11	(7)	1
Morten BAKKE	G	26		
Jan BERG	M		(2)	1
Daniel BERG HESTAD	M	26		4
José Glaria "FLACO" (ESP)	D	10	(7)	1
Knut Anders FOSTERVOLD	D	22		
Anders HASSELGÅRD	A		(1)	
Tor Gunnar JOHNSEN	A		(4)	
Terje LERVIK	M		(1)	
Odd Petter LYNGSTAD	D	6		
Tarje NORDSTRAND JACOBSEN	D	14	(6)	
Sindre REKDAL	D	22	(1)	3
Petter RUDI	M	25		1
Petter Christian SINGSAAS	D	14		
Bjarte SKUSETH	M	2	(10)	
Ole Gunnar SOLSKJAER	A	26		20
Arild STAVRUM	A	26		16
Ole Erik STAVRUM	D	8	(4)	
Trond STRANDE	D	16	(1)	
Ole Bjørn SUNDGOT	A	26		13
Per Olav SAETRE	D		(2)	
Berdon SØNDERLAND	D	2	(1)	
Ronald WENAAS	M	4	(2)	

LEAGUE RESULTS 1995

Date	Opponent		Score	Scorers
22/04/95	SK Brann	A	6-0	Solskjaer 2, Sundgot 2, Rekdal, Stavrum A. (p)
29/04/95	Viking FK	H	5-4	Solskjaer 3, Sundgot 2
03/05/95	Lillestrøm SK	A	1-0	Stavrum A.
07/05/95	Stabaek IF	H	1-0	Berg Hestad
14/05/95	Hamarkameratene	A	2-1	Solskjaer 2
16/05/95	IL Hødd	H	7-2	Stavrum A. 3, Solskjaer 3, Sundgot
21/05/95	Tromsø IL	A	2-2	Berg Hestad, Flaco
28/05/95	VIF Fotball	H	0-1	
02/06/95	IK Start	A	3-1	Sundgot, Stavrum A., Solskjaer
11/06/95	FK Bodø/Glimt	H	0-3	
18/06/95	Strindheim IL	A	3-1	Stavrum A. (p), Solskjaer, Sundgot
25/06/95	Kongsvinger IL	A	2-0	Andersen, Solskjaer
02/07/95	Rosenborg BK	H	2-2	Stavrum A., Rekdal
23/07/95	Kongsvinger IL	H	3-1	Stavrum A., Solskjaer, Sundgot
30/07/95	Strindheim IL	H	4-1	Stavrum A., Sundgot, Solskjaer (p), Berg
06/08/95	FK Bodø/Glimt	A	2-3	Stavrum A., Sundgot
20/08/95	IK Start	H	2-1	Stavrum A. 2
27/08/95	VIF Fotball	A	2-2	Sundgot, Solskjaer
02/09/95	Tromsø IL	H	0-7	
10/09/95	IL Hødd	A	2-2	Stavrum A. 2
24/09/95	Hamarkameratene	H	3-2	Sundgot, Stavrum A. (p), Berg Hestad
01/10/95	Stabaek IF	A	1-3	Solskjaer
04/10/95	Rosenborg BK	A	0-2	
07/10/95	Lillestrøm SK	H	1-2	Berg Hestad
15/10/95	Viking FK	A	2-2	Sundgot, Solskjaer
22/10/95	SK Brann	H	4-2	Solskjaer 2, Rekdal, Rudi

ROSENBORG BK

CLUB DIRECTORY

Rosenborg Ballklubb
Boks 4126
7002 Trondheim
tel - (73) 940240
fax - (73) 944070
Year of Formation - 1917
President - Nils Skutle
Coach - Nils Arne Eggen
Stadium - Lerkendal stadion (30,000)

MAJOR HONOURS
League Championship - (10) 1967, 1969, 1971, 1985, 1988, 1990, 1992, 1993, 1994, 1995.
Domestic Cup - (7)
1960, 1964, 1971, 1988, 1990, 1992, 1995.

APPEARANCES 95

	P	Ap	(s)	Gls
Bjørn Otto BRAGSTAD	D	25		6
Harald BRATTBAKK	A	26		26
Ola BY RISE	G	18		
Vegard HEGGEM	A	1	(14)	1
Jon Olav HJELDE	A	3	(4)	
Erik HOFTUN	D	24	(2)	
Steffen IVERSEN	A	8	(17)	8
Jahn Ivar "Mini" JAKOBSEN	A	25		10
Jørn JAMTFALL	G	8	(1)	
Bjørn Tore KVARME	D	19	(4)	
Karl-Petter LØKEN	M	24		6
Bent SKAMMELSRUD	M	25		7
Espen SOLHEIM	D		(3)	
Trond Egil SOLTVEDT	A	19	(6)	4
Tom Kåre STAURVIK	M	18	(6)	4
Ståle STENSAAS	D	20	(4)	1
Roar STRAND	A	23		4
Arne WINSNES	A		(1)	

LEAGUE RESULTS 1995

Date	Opponent	H/A	Score	Scorers
21/04/95	Kongsvinger IL	H	6-0	Jakobsen 2, Skammelsrud 2, Brattbakk, Strand
30/04/95	Strindheim IL	A	5-0	Brattbakk, og (Grevskott), Jakobsen (p), Strand, Stensaas
03/05/95	SK Brann	A	1-1	Soltvedt
07/05/95	Viking FK	H	1-0	Jakobsen
13/05/95	Lillestrøm SK	A	3-1	Brattbakk 2, Staurvik
16/05/95	Stabaek IF	H	5-2	Brattbakk 2, Løken, Bragstad, Iversen
21/05/95	Hamarkameratene	A	3-1	Brattbakk 2, Iversen
28/05/95	IL Hødd	H	6-1	Brattbakk 2, Skammelsrud, Strand, Soltvedt, Jakobsen
02/06/95	Tromsø IL	A	2-1	Jakobsen, Bragstad
11/06/95	VIF Fotball	H	3-2	Bragstad 2, Iversen
18/06/95	IK Start	A	3-1	Staurvik, Strand, Brattbakk
25/06/95	FK Bodø/Glimt	H	3-3	Staurvik, Skammelsrud 2
02/07/95	Molde FK	A	2-2	Soltvedt, Bragstad
23/07/95	FK Bodø/Glimt	A	2-1	Brattbakk 2
30/07/95	IK Start	H	4-1	Brattbakk 2, Skammelsrud, Bragstad
06/08/95	VIF Fotball	A	1-2	Skammelsrud
20/08/95	Tromsø IL	H	2-0	Jakobsen, Løken
27/08/95	IL Hødd	A	4-1	Iversen 2, Jakobsen, Brattbakk
02/09/95	Hamarkameratene	H	9-1	Brattbakk 3, Iversen 3, Løken 2, Jakobsen
10/09/95	Stabaek IF	A	1-2	Brattbakk
23/09/95	Lillestrøm SK	H	2-1	Brattbakk 2
30/09/95	Viking FK	A	2-2	Jakobsen, Heggem
04/10/95	Molde FK	H	2-0	Løken 2 (1p)
08/10/95	SK Brann	H	3-1	Brattbakk 2, Staurvik
15/10/95	Strindheim IL	H	2-1	Brattbakk 2
22/10/95	Kongsvinger IL	A	1-1	Soltvedt

STABAEK IF

CLUB DIRECTORY

Stabaek Idrettsforening
Boks 308
1341 Bekkestua
tel - (67) 121212
fax - (67) 582610
Year of Formation - 1912
President - Erik Loe
Secretary - Jan Dybsjord
Coach - Lars Tjernås (96 - Hans Backe)
Stadium - Nadderud stadion (10,000)

APPEARANCES 95

	P	Ap	(s)	Gls
Geir BAKKE	M	23	(1)	3
Christer BASMA	D	26		
Philip BORGEN	M	2	(9)	
Dag Petter BREIVIK	A	3	(12)	
Paul DAVIES (ENG)	M		(1)	
André FLEM	D	18		2
Thomas FRIGÅRD	A	11	(12)	1
Henning FRIISE	G	25		
Fredrik GÄRDEMAN (SWE)	A	20	(4)	4
Espen GRANLI	G	1		
Lars Joakim GRIMSTAD	M	14	(6)	2
Bjørn Tore HANSEN	A		(1)	
Knut HOLTE	D	16		1
Christian HOLTER	D	23	(1)	
Kjell Roar KAASA	A	20	(4)	8
Kim LØKKE	D		(4)	
Andreas MAYER (GER)	M	7		1
Anders NORSTAD	M	2	(5)	
John Arvid SKISTAD	D	21	(3)	1
Ståle SLETTEBØ	D	13	(3)	1
Tommy STENERSEN	A		(2)	
Tommy SVINDAL LARSEN	M	20	(1)	5
Bjørn VILJUGREIN	M	21	(3)	4

LEAGUE RESULTS 1995

Date	Opponent	H/A	Score	Scorers
22/04/95	VIF Fotball	H	0-2	
30/04/95	IK Start	A	1-4	Gärdeman
03/05/95	FK Bodø/Glimt	H	4-0	Kaasa 2, Svindal Larsen (p), Flem
07/05/95	Molde FK	A	0-1	
14/05/95	Kongsvinger IL	H	0-0	
16/05/95	Rosenborg BK	A	2-5	og (Staurvik), Viljugrein
21/05/95	SK Brann	H	3-0	Gärdeman, Holte, Svindal Larsen (p)
28/05/95	Viking FK	A	0-2	
02/06/95	Lillestrøm SK	H	0-2	
11/06/95	Strindheim IL	H	3-0	Kaasa 2, Flem
18/06/95	Hamarkameratene	A	0-5	
25/06/95	IL Hødd	H	3-1	Grimstad 2, Bakke
28/06/95	Tromsø IL	A	2-2	og (Larsen), og (Hafstad)
05/07/95	Tromsø IL	H	0-2	
23/07/95	IL Hødd	A	1-1	Bakke
30/07/95	Hamarkameratene	H	3-1	Frigård, Viljugrein, Svindal Larsen
06/08/95	Strindheim IL	A	1-2	Slettebø
20/08/95	Lillestrøm SK	A	2-2	Gärdeman, Kaasa
27/08/95	Viking FK	H	2-0	Viljugrein, Gärdeman
02/09/95	SK Brann	A	0-1	
10/09/95	Rosenborg BK	H	2-1	Mayer, Kaasa
24/09/95	Kongsvinger IL	A	0-0	
01/10/95	Molde FK	H	3-1	Kaasa, Svindal Larsen, Bakke
08/10/95	FK Bodø/Glimt	A	1-0	Viljugrein
15/10/95	IK Start	H	1-3	Skistad
22/10/95	VIF Fotball	A	2-2	Kaasa, Svindal Larsen (p)

IK START

CLUB DIRECTORY

Idrettsklubben Start
Postboks 1533
Valhalla
4602 Kristiansand
tel - (38) 096091
fax - (38) 097535
Year of Formation - 1905
President - Erik Geelmuyden
Coach - Erik Ruthford Pedersen; Brede Skistad; Steve Perryman
Stadium - Kristiansand stadion (75,000)

MAJOR HONOURS

League Championship - (2) 1978, 1980.

APPEARANCES 95

	P	Ap	(s)	Gls
Vetle ANDERSEN	D	12	(4)	
Petter BELSVIK	A	25		22
Tom BERHUS	M	4	(5)	
Bernt Christian BIRKELAND	M	8	(5)	
Helge BJØNSAAS	D	22		2
Tore André DAHLUM	A	24	(2)	4
Claus EFTEVAAG	D	25		1
Sindre GUNDERSEN	G	1		
Andreas LUND	A	15	(7)	9
Pål LYDERSEN	D	23		
Tore LØVLAND	D	19	(3)	5
Slobodan MILETIC (YUG)	M	6	(9)	3
Erik MYKLAND	M	25		
Frode OLSEN	G	25		
Steinar PEDERSEN	D	13	(9)	1
Morten PETTERSEN	M	25	(1)	3
Frank TØNNESEN	D	14	(5)	

LEAGUE RESULTS 1995

Date	Opponent		Score	Scorers
22/04/95	Lillestrøm SK	A	1-3	Belsvik
30/04/95	Stabaek IF	H	4-1	Bjønsaas, Dahlum, Miletic, Løvland
03/05/95	Hamarkameratene	A	0-0	
07/05/95	IL Hødd	H	0-2	
14/05/95	Tromsø IL	A	4-1	Belsvik 2 (1p), Pettersen, Eftevaag
16/05/95	VIF Fotball	H	0-1	
21/05/95	Strindheim IL	A	6-2	Belsvik 4 (2p), Dahlum, Løvland
28/05/95	FK Bodø/Glimt	A	2-1	Belsvik 2 (1p)
02/06/95	Molde FK	H	1-3	Løvland
11/06/95	Kongsvinger IL	A	0-2	
18/06/95	Rosenborg BK	H	1-3	Løvland
25/06/95	SK Brann	A	4-0	Belsvik 2 (1p), Lund, Dahlum
02/07/95	Viking FK	H	0-2	
16/07/95	Viking FK	A	3-1	Lund, Pettersen, og (Karlsen)
23/07/95	SK Brann	H	1-0	Belsvik
30/07/95	Rosenborg BK	A	1-4	Lund
06/08/95	Kongsvinger IL	H	6-2	Lund 4, Belsvik 2
20/08/95	Molde FK	A	1-2	Belsvik
26/08/95	FK Bodø/Glimt	H	2-5	Pedersen, Belsvik (p)
02/09/95	Strindheim IL	H	4-6	Miletic, Bjønsaas, Pettersen, Belsvik
10/09/95	VIF Fotball	A	1-4	Lund
24/09/95	Tromsø IL	H	2-1	Belsvik 2 (1p)
01/10/95	IL Hødd	A	1-2	Belsvik
08/10/95	Hamarkameratene	H	1-2	Miletic
15/10/95	Stabaek IF	A	3-1	Belsvik, Dahlum, Lund
22/10/95	Lillestrøm SK	H	2-1	Belsvik, Løvland

STRINDHEIM IL

CLUB DIRECTORY

Strindheim Idrettslag
Boks 1406
7002 Trondheim
tel - (73) 916880
fax - (73) 916991
Year of Formation - 1926
President - Svein O. Berg
Secretary - Atle Darell
Coach - Trond Hansen; Per Joar Hansen
(96 - Ivar Selnaes)
Stadium - Lerkendal stadion (30,000)

APPEARANCES 95

	P	Ap	(s)	Gls
Arne BONDE	G	10	(2)	
Stian EDVARDSEN	D	17	(2)	2
Vidar EVENSEN	D	24		5
Rune FEIRUD	G	16		
Per Arne GJELTEN	D	13	(10)	
Lars GREVSKOTT	D	17	(1)	1
Per Joar HANSEN	A	24	(2)	2
Per Morten HAUGEN	M	13		2
Terje HØSØIEN	M	20	(3)	6
Ole Gunnar IVERSEN	M	25		1
Jørgen JOHANNESSEN	M	9	(6)	1
John MADUKA (MLW)	A	5		
Thomas MEHLUM	D		(3)	
Frank Roger MYRENGET	A		(2)	
Arild NORDFJAERN	A	21	(5)	2
Jon Kristian OLSEN	A		(2)	
Roy RINNAN	D	4	(6)	
Torgeir RUGTVEDT	D	14	(1)	1
Jan Magne SCHANKE	A		(2)	1
Francis SONGO (MLW)	D		(1)	
Ronny STØBAKK	M	15	(6)	1
Kristian SØRLI	A	16	(3)	6
Joachim WALLTIN	M	23		5

LEAGUE RESULTS 1995

Date	Opponent	H/A	Score	Scorers
22/04/95	IL Hødd	A	1-1	Walltin
30/04/95	Rosenborg BK	H	0-5	
03/05/95	Tromsø IL	H	1-0	Haugen
07/05/95	SK Brann	A	1-4	Iversen
14/05/95	VIF Fotball	H	1-2	Hansen
16/05/95	Viking FK	A	1-2	Grevskott
21/05/95	IK Start	H	2-6	Hansen, Walltin
28/05/95	Lillestrøm SK	A	0-3	
02/06/95	FK Bodø/Glimt	H	1-1	Evensen
11/06/95	Stabaek IF	A	0-3	
18/06/95	Molde FK	H	1-3	Evensen
25/06/95	Hamarkameratene	A	0-0	
02/07/95	Kongsvinger IL	H	1-3	Høsøien
16/07/95	Kongsvinger IL	A	1-5	Sørli
23/07/95	Hamarkameratene	H	2-4	Evensen, Haugen
30/07/95	Molde FK	A	1-4	Høsøien (p)
06/08/95	Stabaek IF	H	2-1	Edvardsen, Sørli
20/08/95	FK Bodø/Glimt	A	2-3	Nordfjaern, Høsøien (p)
27/08/95	Lillestrøm SK	H	1-1	Nordfjaern
02/09/95	IK Start	A	6-4	Sørli 3, Høsøien, Johannessen, Evensen
08/09/95	Viking FK	H	5-3	Walltin 2, Høsøien (p), Sørli, Rugtvedt
24/09/95	VIF Fotball	A	2-9	Høsøien (p), Støbakk
01/10/95	SK Brann	H	2-2	Evensen, Edvardsen
08/10/95	Tromsø IL	A	0-1	
15/10/95	Rosenborg BK	A	1-2	Walltin
22/10/95	IL Hødd	H	1-5	Schanke

TROMSØ IL

CLUB DIRECTORY

Tromsø Idrettslag
Postboks 5
9001 Tromsø
tel - (77) 684430
fax - (77) 682013
Year of Formation - 1920
President - Kjell N. Olsen
Secretary - Odd Viggo Wilhelmsen
Coach - Harald Aabrekk (96 - Terje Skarsfjord)
Stadium - Alfheim stadion (11,000)

MAJOR HONOURS
Domestic Cup - (1) 1986.

APPEARANCES 95

	P	Ap	(s)	Gls
Svein Are ANDREASSEN	A	3	(8)	
Tobias APPELBOM	D		(1)	
Stein BERG-JOHANSEN	A	6	(12)	2
Tore André FLO	A	26		18
Tore André GRENERSEN	G	14		
Thomas HAFSTAD	M	14	(1)	3
Johnny HANSSEN	D	13	(10)	3
Bjørn JOHANSEN	M	24		7
Svein Morten JOHANSEN	M	15	(5)	1
Morten KRAEMER	D	21	(1)	1
Stian LARSEN	D	22	(2)	
Bjørn LUDVIKSEN	D	20	(5)	
Arne Vidar MOEN	D	23	(1)	
Ole Andreas NILSEN	M	5		
Steinar NILSEN	D	9	(1)	
Morten PEDERSEN	M	17	(5)	4
Sigurd RUSHFELDT	A	15	(1)	8
Per Egil SWIFT	D	23	(1)	4
Thomas TØLLEFSEN	G	12	(1)	
Ole Martin ÅRST	A	4	(3)	1

LEAGUE RESULTS 1995

22/04/95	Hamarkameratene	A	1-0	Flo
30/04/95	IL Hødd	H	4-1	Rushfeldt, Flo, Swift (p), Johansen B.
03/05/95	Strindheim IL	A	0-1	
07/05/95	VIF Fotball	A	1-2	Flo
14/05/95	IK Start	H	1-4	Pedersen (p)
16/05/95	FK Bodø/Glimt	A	2-1	Rushfeldt, Hafstad
21/05/95	Molde FK	H	2-2	Hafstad, Flo
28/05/95	Kongsvinger IL	A	1-1	Pedersen
02/06/95	Rosenborg BK	H	1-2	Flo
11/06/95	SK Brann	A	2-4	Hafstad, Årst
14/06/95	Lillestrøm SK	A	4-5	Johansen B. 2, Swift, Flo
18/06/95	Viking FK	H	1-0	Pedersen (p)
28/06/95	Stabaek IF	H	2-2	Swift (p), Hanssen
05/07/95	Stabaek IF	A	2-0	Flo, Hanssen
19/07/95	Lillestrøm SK	H	0-0	
30/07/95	Viking FK	A	1-3	Rushfeldt
06/08/95	SK Brann	H	2-2	Flo, Swift
20/08/95	Rosenborg BK	A	0-2	
27/08/95	Kongsvinger IL	H	8-0	Rushfeldt 3, Johansen B. 2, Flo, Moen, Hanssen
02/09/95	Molde FK	A	7-0	Flo 3, Johansen B. 2, Rushfeldt, Pedersen
09/09/95	FK Bodø/Glimt	H	0-4	
24/09/95	IK Start	A	1-2	Flo
01/10/95	VIF Fotball	H	2-1	Flo, Berg-Johansen
08/10/95	Strindheim IL	H	1-0	Kraemer
15/10/95	IL Hødd	A	3-2	Rushfeldt, Flo (p), Johansen S.M.
22/10/95	Hamarkameratene	H	4-1	Flo 3 (1p), Berg-Johansen

VIF FOTBALL

CLUB DIRECTORY

Vålerengen IF Fotball
PB 6064
Etterstad
0601 Oslo
tel - (22) 657932
fax - (22) 657944
Year of Formation - 1913
President - Knut Aga
Coach - Vidar Davidsen
Stadium - Ullevaal stadion (28,000)

MAJOR HONOURS
League Championship - (4)
1965, 1981, 1983, 1984.
Domestic Cup - (1) 1980.

APPEARANCES 95

	P	Ap	(s)	Gls
Knut AGA	A	25	(1)	7
Alexander AKERJORDET	M	1	(6)	
Ståle ANDERSEN	D	14	(5)	1
Kent BERGERSEN	A	23	(1)	6
Lorenzo CAROPRESE	D		(1)	
Espen HAUG	M	23	(1)	9
Terje JOELSEN	A		(2)	
Morten KIHLE	D	10	(3)	1
Fredrik KJØLNER	D	24		1
Tore KROGSTAD	G	26		
Jan Erlend KRUSE	D	17	(3)	1
Bjørn Arild LEVERNES	M	26		4
Håvard LUNDE	D	12	(6)	
Espen MUSAEUS	A	6	(8)	2
Kenneth NYSAETHER	A	20	(2)	10
Terje OLSEN	D	3	(5)	
Svein Erik PETTERSEN	D	14	(2)	
Dag RIISNAES	M	25		5
Viggo STRØMME	D	17		
Stian ÅSEN	A		(1)	

LEAGUE RESULTS 1995

22/04/95	Stabaek IF	A	2-0	Bergersen, Aga
30/04/95	Hamarkameratene	H	1-2	Musaeus
03/05/95	IL Hødd	A	0-3	
07/05/95	Tromsø IL	H	2-1	Aga 2
14/05/95	Strindheim IL	A	2-1	Levernes 2
16/05/95	IK Start	A	1-0	Haug
21/05/95	FK Bodø/Glimt	H	0-4	
28/05/95	Molde FK	A	1-0	Kihle
02/06/95	Kongsvinger IL	H	1-3	Haug
11/06/95	Rosenborg BK	A	2-3	Haug, Nysaether
18/06/95	SK Brann	H	3-1	Aga, Bergersen, Riisnaes
25/06/95	Viking FK	A	0-5	
02/07/95	Lillestrøm SK	H	0-0	
16/07/95	Lillestrøm SK	A	3-1	Aga, Levernes, Haug
23/07/95	Viking FK	H	1-1	Nysaether
30/07/95	SK Brann	A	1-2	Nysaether
06/08/95	Rosenborg BK	H	2-1	Nysaether, Haug
20/08/95	Kongsvinger IL	A	2-2	Haug, Musaeus
27/08/95	Molde FK	H	2-2	Aga, Nysaether
02/09/95	FK Bodø/Glimt	A	2-2	Haug (p), Riisnaes
10/09/95	IK Start	H	4-1	Levernes, Haug, Riisnaes, Bergersen
24/09/95	Strindheim IL	H	9-2	Nysaether 5, Aga, Bergersen, Kruse, Haug (p)
01/10/95	Tromsø IL	A	1-2	Riisnaes
08/10/95	IL Hødd	H	3-2	Bergersen 2, Riisnaes
15/10/95	Hamarkameratene	A	0-1	
22/10/95	Stabaek IF	H	2-2	Kjølner, Andersen

VIKING FK

CLUB DIRECTORY

Viking Fotballklubb
Boks 4516
Stokka
4004 Stavanger
tel - (51) 528117
fax - (51) 532974
Year of Formation - 1899
President - Jan Olav Pedersen
Coach - Bjarne Berntsen (96 - Poul Erik Andreassen)
Stadium - Stavanger stadion (17,000)

MAJOR HONOURS

League Championship - (8) 1958, 1972, 1973, 1974, 1975, 1979, 1982, 1991.
Domestic Cup - (4) 1953, 1959, 1979, 1989.

APPEARANCES 95

	P	Ap	(s)	Gls
Gunnar AASE	A	19	(2)	7
Tommy BERGERSEN	A	6	(10)	5
Trond BJØRNSEN	M		(2)	
Ingve BØE	D	16		1
Odd Arne ESPEVOLL	D		(1)	
Erik FUGLESTAD	D	23	(2)	2
Vidar GEITLE	G	2		
Steffen HORPESTAD	M		(1)	
Ulf KARLSEN	D	12	(6)	
Bjarte LUNDE AARSHEIM	M	16	(7)	2
Rune MEDALEN	A	5	(12)	3
Børre MEINSETH	A	17	(8)	2
Thomas MYHRE	G	24		
Erik PEDERSEN	M	23		2
Børge RANNESTAD	A		(3)	
Sander SOLBERG	M	23		7
Thomas SOLBERG	D	18	(2)	
Kenneth STORVIK	M	20	(3)	5
Gøran SØRLOTH	A	17	(6)	5
Egil ULFSTEIN	D	25		1
Egil ØSTENSTAD	A	20	(1)	12

LEAGUE RESULTS 1995

Date	Opponent	H/A	Score	Scorers
22/04/95	FK Bodø/Glimt	H	6-0	Aase 2, Solberg S. 2, Østenstad, Bøe (p)
29/04/95	Molde FK	A	4-5	Østenstad 2, Medalen 2
03/05/95	Kongsvinger IL	H	0-0	
07/05/95	Rosenborg BK	A	0-1	
14/05/95	SK Brann	H	2-0	Østenstad, Sørloth
16/05/95	Strindheim IL	H	2-1	Solberg S., Østenstad
21/05/95	Lillestrøm SK	A	1-4	Østenstad
28/05/95	Stabaek IF	H	2-0	Storvik, Bergersen
02/06/95	Hamarkameratene	A	5-0	Solberg S. 2, Østenstad, Bergersen, Lunde Aarsheim
11/06/95	IL Hødd	H	3-0	Storvik, Sørloth, Solberg S.
18/06/95	Tromsø IL	A	0-1	
25/06/95	VIF Fotball	H	5-0	og (Kjølner), Solberg S., Aase, Ulfstein, Meinseth
02/07/95	IK Start	A	2-0	Fuglestad, Storvik
16/07/95	IK Start	H	1-3	Fuglestad
23/07/95	VIF Fotball	A	1-1	Meinseth
30/07/95	Tromsø IL	H	3-1	Aase, Storvik, Østenstad
05/08/95	IL Hødd	A	1-0	Medalen
18/08/95	Hamarkameratene	H	0-2	
27/08/95	Stabaek IF	A	0-2	
02/09/95	Lillestrøm SK	H	3-1	Bergersen, Aase, Sørloth
08/09/95	Strindheim IL	A	3-5	Storvik, Bergersen, Aase
30/09/95	Rosenborg BK	H	2-2	Bergersen, Pedersen (p)
04/10/95	SK Brann	A	1-2	Sørloth
08/10/95	Kongsvinger IL	A	4-3	Aase, Lunde Aarsheim, Østenstad, Pedersen (p)
15/10/95	Molde FK	H	2-2	Østenstad 2
22/10/95	FK Bodø/Glimt	A	2-6	Sørloth, Østenstad

PROMOTED CLUBS

SECOND DIVISION FINAL TABLE 95

		Pd	W	D	L	F	A	Pt	GD
1	**Moss FK**	**22**	**13**	**7**	**2**	**40**	**22**	**46**	**+18**
2	**Sogndal IL**	**22**	**13**	**5**	**4**	**42**	**21**	**44**	**+21**
3	Drøbak/Frogn IL	22	13	4	5	60	35	43	+25
4	FK Haugesund	22	12	2	8	41	33	38	+8
5	Åsane IL	22	10	4	8	38	31	34	+7
6	Aalesund FK	22	8	8	6	43	33	32	+10
7	Bryne FK	22	7	9	6	28	31	30	-3
8	Fana	22	8	4	10	31	42	28	-11
9	Fyllingen IL	22	4	8	10	33	45	20	-12
10	Åndalsnes IF	22	4	6	12	22	38	18	-16
11	Sarpsborg FK	22	3	8	11	17	38	17	-21
12	Vard-Haugesund	22	4	1	17	17	43	13	-26

SECTION 2

		Pd	W	D	L	F	A	Pt	GD
1	**Skeid**	**22**	**19**	**1**	**2**	**59**	**21**	**58**	**+38**
2	**Strømsgodset IF**	**22**	**16**	**3**	**3**	**51**	**15**	**51**	**+36**
3	Eik-Tønsberg IF	22	14	4	4	57	24	46	+33
4	Odd BK	22	12	2	8	54	25	38	+29
5	Tromsdalen UIL	22	10	5	7	37	25	35	+12
6	Lyn Fotball	22	11	1	10	31	29	34	+2
7	Nardo	22	7	1	14	31	45	22	-14
8	Stålkameratene IL	22	6	4	12	24	53	22	-29
9	Jevnaker IF	22	6	3	13	30	44	21	-14
10	Alta IF	22	6	3	13	30	53	21	-23
11	Sandefjord BK	22	4	7	11	17	38	19	-21
12	FK Mjølner-Narvik	22	3	2	17	20	69	11	-49

PROMOTION PLAY-OFF

Strømsgodset IF 3, Sogndal IL 1
Sogndal IL 0, Strømsgodset IF 0
(Strømsgodset IF 3-1)

CLUB DIRECTORY

Moss Fotballklubb
Boks 47
tel - (69) 252277
fax - (69) 256650
Year of Formation - 1906
President - Arve Bergan
Coach - Per Høgmo
Stadium - Melløs (9,000)

MAJOR HONOURS

League Championship - (1) 1987.
Domestic Cup - (1) 1983.

CLUB DIRECTORY

Skeid
Postboks 5
Grefsen
0409 Oslo
tel - (22) 222882
fax - (22) 222963
Year of Formation - 1915
President - Terje Martinsen
Coach - Bjarne Rønning
Stadium - Ullevaal (28,000)

MAJOR HONOURS

League Championship - (1) 1966.
Domestic Cup - (8) 1947, 1954, 1955, 1956, 1958, 1963, 1965, 1974.

CLUB DIRECTORY

Strømsgodset Idrettsforening
Fotballgruppa
Postboks 4140
3002 Drammen
tel - (32) 831503
fax - (32) 830175
President - Jan Reidar Bergwitz-Larsen
Secretary - Inger K. Johansen
Coach - Dag Vidar Kristoffersen
Stadium - Marienlyst (10,000)

MAJOR HONOURS

League Championship - (1) 1970.
Domestic Cup - (4) 1969, 1970, 1973, 1991.

POLAND

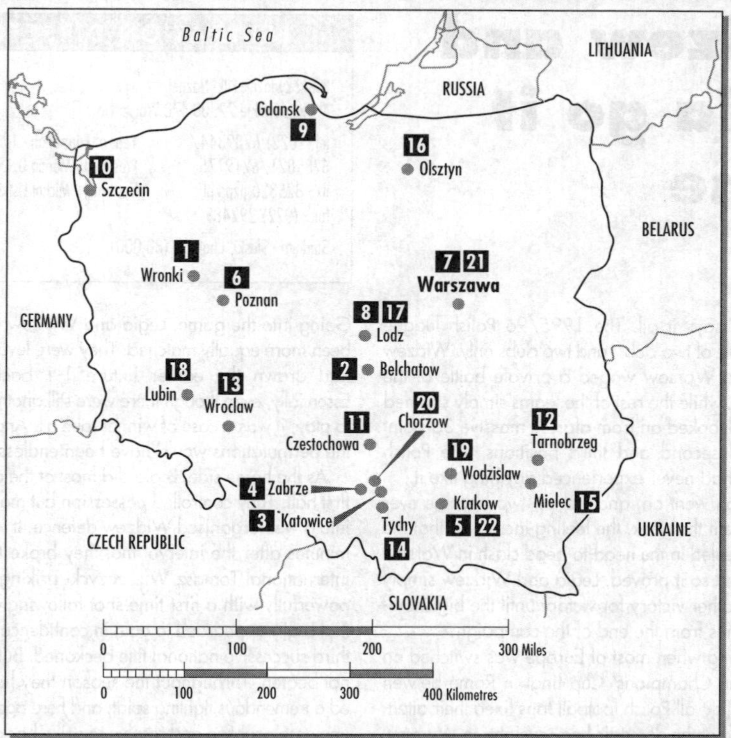

1	AMICA WRONKI	754
2	GKS BELCHATOW	755
3	GKS KATOWICE	756
4	GORNIK ZABRZE	757
5	HUTNIK KRAKOW	758
6	LECH POZNAN	759
7	LEGIA WARSZAWA	760
8	LKS LODZ	761
9	OLIMPIA/LECHIA GDANSK	762
10	POGON SZCZECIN	763
11	RAKOW CZESTOCHOWA	764
12	SIARKA TARNOBRZEG	765
13	SLASK WROCLAW	766
14	SOKOL TYCHY	767
15	STAL MIELEC	768
16	STOMIL OLSZTYN	769
17	WIDZEW LODZ	770
18	ZAGLEBIE LUBIN	771
19	ODRA WODZISLAW	772
20	RUCH CHORZOW	772
21	POLONIA WARSZAWA	772
22	WISLA KRAKOW	772

CHANGES GALORE IN NATIONAL TEAM

Widzew and Legia go it alone

FEDERATION DIRECTORY

Polski Zwiazek Pilki Noznej
Al Ujazdowskie 22, 00-478 Warszawa

tel - (022) 6289344/
6285821/6219175
tlx - 825320 pzpn pl
fax - (022) 292489

Year of Formation - 1919
President - Marian Dziurowicz
Secretary - Michal Listkiewicz

Stadium - Slaski, Chorzow (80,000)

The final table says it all. The 1995/96 Polish league season was a tale of two clubs, and two clubs only. Widzew Lodz and Legia Warsaw waged a private battle at the top of the table, while the rest of the teams simply strained their necks and looked on from afar. A massive 33-point gap separated second and third positions. The Polish championship had never experienced anything like it.

As the season went on, and the top two became ever more distant from the pack, the feeling increased that the title would be settled in the head-to-head clash in Warsaw on May 22. And so it proved. Legia and Widzew simply matched each other victory for victory until the big show-down four games from the end of the campaign.

On an evening when most of Europe was switched on to the European Champions' Cup final in Rome betwen Juventus and Ajax, all Polish football fans fixed their attention on the battle of the domestic heavyweights in Warsaw. Going into the game, Legia and Widzew could not have been more equally matched. They were level on points and had drawn the earlier fixture 1-1 back in October. Essentially, even though there were still another three rounds to play, it was a case of winner take all. Another draw and the permutations would have been endless.

As the home side, Legia did most of the attacking in the first half. They controlled possession but made few inroads into a well-organised Widzew defence. It was not until six minutes after the interval that they broke through, Polish international Tomasz Wieszczycki striking the ball home powerfully with a first-time shot following a corner. After that Legia appearaed to gain in confidence, and the club's third successive national title beckoned. But Widzew were not beaten. Throughout the season they had demonstrated a tremendous fighting spirit, and here again they showed immense courage and resolve to strike back - not once, but

LEAGUE CHAMPIONSHIP RESULTS 95/96

		1	2	3	4	5	6	7	8	9	10	11	12	13	14	15	16	17	18
1	Amica Wronki		1-2	0-0	2-0	2-1	0-1	1-6	1-0	2-0	1-1	3-1	1-0	2-0	1-1	0-0	1-2	0-2	2-0
2	GKS Belchatow	1-2		2-1	3-4	0-2	2-1	0-1	3-0	1-4	2-1	1-0	4-0	0-0	0-0	1-2	2-1	1-4	1-1
3	GKS Katowice	2-1	3-1		2-0	1-2	1-1	0-5	1-2	3-0	1-1	1-0	3-1	0-0	0-1	0-1	2-0	1-4	1-0
4	Gornik Zabrze	2-1	3-3	0-4		2-2	2-2	3-2	3-2	2-0	1-1	1-2	0-0	2-2	0-0	3-1	3-2	1-1	1-2
5	Hutnik Krakow	0-0	0-1	0-0	0-0		3-0	0-3	2-1	3-1	2-0	0-0	3-1	1-2	2-0	3-0	2-0	1-4	3-2
6	Lech Poznan	2-1	2-0	4-1	4-1	3-0		1-1	0-0	0-0	1-0	1-2	2-0	0-1	1-2	2-0	0-1	1-1	0-0
7	Legia Warszawa	2-0	2-0	1-0	1-0	6-1	5-1		2-0	4-0	5-0	4-2	3-0	3-1	2-0	5-1	3-0	1-2	1-0
8	LKS Lodz	0-0	1-0	1-1	1-0	0-0	1-1	2-1		2-3	3-1	2-1	2-0	4-0	2-0	1-1	4-0	1-1	1-1
9	Olimpia/Lechia Gdansk	2-0	2-0	0-3	1-1	1-3	0-3	1-3	4-2		2-0	4-1	1-0	2-1	0-0	1-1	1-2	1-7	0-0
10	Pogon Szczecin	1-1	1-1	1-0	0-0	0-3	3-1	1-2	1-1	0-1		2-1	3-0	2-0	3-1	2-0	1-0	0-1	1-1
11	Rakow Czestochowa	0-1	1-0	3-0	2-2	1-0	0-0	0-1	1-3	4-0	2-1		1-1	0-0	1-1	2-0	1-0	0-1	1-0
12	Siarka Tarnobrzeg	2-3	1-2	0-0	0-2	0-2	1-0	2-7	1-1	3-3	0-1	0-1		0-0	0-4	2-0	0-1	1-3	2-3
13	Slask Wroclaw	2-2	1-1	2-2	2-1	2-0	0-1	0-0	3-0	1-1	1-0	0-0	3-0		1-1	4-1	1-1	1-2	1-1
14	Sokol Tychy	0-0	2-0	0-0	1-2	4-3	3-2	1-3	0-2	1-0	0-0	0-1	4-1	1-1		2-1	3-1	0-1	2-0
15	Stal Mielec	0-2	3-4	0-1	0-1	1-2	3-2	0-5	0-1	2-1	3-1	0-0	0-2	1-3	2-0		1-0	1-2	1-2
16	Stomil Olsztyn	2-0	2-0	1-1	0-0	2-1	0-0	1-1	1-0	0-2	0-1	1-0	2-0	3-2	2-1	1-4		0-1	1-0
17	Widzew Lodz	2-0	5-0	1-0	4-1	2-0	3-3	1-1	3-1	1-0	3-0	4-1	2-1	4-0	5-0	4-1	2-2		1-0
18	Zaglebie Lubin	0-1	0-1	1-0	2-1	1-1	2-2	0-3	1-0	3-0	0-2	1-0	3-2	2-1	0-0	5-1	0-0	0-0	

LEAGUE CHAMPIONSHIP FINAL TABLE 95/96

			Home					Away					Total						
		Pd	W	D	L	F	A	W	D	L	F	A	W	D	L	F	A	Pt	GD
1	Widzew Lodz	34	14	3	0	47	11	13	4	0	37	11	27	7	0	84	22	88	+62
2	Legia Warszawa	34	16	0	1	50	8	11	4	2	45	14	27	4	3	95	22	85	+73
3	Hutnik Krakow	34	9	4	4	25	15	6	3	8	23	28	15	7	12	48	43	52	+5
4	LKS Lodz	34	9	7	1	28	11	4	3	10	16	27	13	10	11	44	38	49	+6
5	Amica Wronki	34	8	4	5	20	17	5	5	7	15	20	13	9	12	35	37	48	-2
6	Stomil Olsztyn	34	9	4	4	19	14	4	3	10	13	27	13	7	14	32	41	46	-9
7	Lech Poznan	34	8	5	4	24	11	3	7	7	21	29	11	12	11	45	40	45	+5
8	Rakow Czestochowa	34	8	5	4	20	11	4	3	10	13	25	12	8	14	33	36	44	-3
9	Sokol Tychy	34	8	4	5	24	18	3	7	7	12	22	11	11	12	36	40	44	-4
10	Zaglebie Lubin	34	8	5	4	21	15	3	6	8	13	20	11	11	12	34	35	44	-1
11	GKS Katowice	34	8	3	6	22	20	3	7	7	14	17	11	10	13	36	37	43	-1
12	Gornik Zabrze	34	6	8	3	29	27	4	5	8	16	25	10	13	11	45	52	43	-7
13	GKS Belchatow	34	7	3	7	24	24	5	3	9	16	30	12	6	16	40	54	42	-14
14	Slask Wroclaw	34	6	9	2	25	14	3	6	8	14	27	9	15	10	39	41	42	-2
15	Pogon Szczecin	34	8	5	4	22	14	3	4	10	11	27	11	9	14	33	41	42	-8
16	Olimpia/Lechia Gdansk	34	7	4	6	23	27	4	3	10	16	32	11	7	16	39	59	40	-20
17	Stal Mielec	34	5	1	11	18	29	3	3	11	15	38	8	4	22	33	67	28	-34
18	Siarka Tarnobrzeg	34	2	4	11	15	33	1	2	14	9	37	3	6	25	24	70	15	-46

N.B. When two or more teams are level on points, classification is determined by the results of the matches between them.

twice - and steal the match 2-1. Both goals came from counter-attacks, the first finished off by veteran striker Marek Koniarek, the second by midfielder Piotr Szarpak. The tactical battle had been won by Widzew coach Franciszek Smuda, and the title was all but in the bag. It was too much for the Legia fans to take. Their dreams in tatters, they decided to try and demolish everything they could get their hands on. The ensuing riot resulted in a three-match home ban.

Widzew duly negotiated their last three games to confirm themselves as Polish champions for the first time since 1982, when such legendary names as Boniek, Smolarek, Mlynarczyk and Wojcicki were in the team. They maintained their three-point advantage despite being held away to a 1-1 draw at Lech Poznan (Legia had already dropped two points of their own, at Slask Wroclaw). Coach Smuda, a former defender with Legia, Ruch Chorzow and Stal Mielec whose coaching experience took in spells with German and Turkish clubs, received a huge amount of praise for his efforts. It was his first full season with the club, and he transformed Widzew into a team of real character, always highly motivated and with strong self-belief. They were unbeaten all season and only failed to score in one match.

Widzew did not have any great creative players in their ranks, and their football was not always appealing to the eye, but they did have their strengths, and one of them was 34-year-old striker Koniarek. He won the league's top scorer crown with a mammoth 29 goals - the biggest winning total for 48 years. It was the crowning moment of a career that has seen Koniarek play for nine different clubs. Inevitably there were calls for his return to the Polish national team (he had only appeared twice before, scoring once), but his age counted against him.

Koniarek aside, Widzew counted heavily on goalkeeper Andrzej Wozniak, defenders Tomasz Lapinski and Waldemar Jaskulski, and midfielders Marek Citko and Ryszard Czerwiec. There were national team call-ups for all of these Widzew players (and more, besides) in what proved to be a memorable season all round for the club.

Despite the excesses of their fans, Legia deserved some sympathy for their narrow failure to complete a championship hat-trick. In any other season their record of 27 victories and four draws in 34 games would have been enough to take first place. They outgunned Widzew by 95 goals to 84 and were generally more entertaining than the team that usurped them. The squad was full of internationals - Maciej Szczesny in goal, Jacek Zielinski, Krzysztof Ratajczyk and Marek Jozwiak at the back, Radoslaw

INTERNATIONAL HONOURS

World Cup Finals appearances: 1938, 1974 (3rd), 1978 (2nd phase), 1982 (3rd), 1986 (2nd round)

NATIONAL TEAM APPEARANCES 95/96

Coach - Henryk APOSTEL; Wladyslaw STACHURSKI; Antoni PIECHNICZEK	FRA	ROM	SVK	AZB	JPN	CRO	SLO	BLS	RUS	Cps	Gls
Andrzej WOZNIAK (23/10/65) - Widzew Lodz	G	G	G	G	G	G	G			15	-
Tomasz LAPINSKI (01/08/69) - Widzew Lodz	D		D		D46	s80				19	-
Jacek ZIELINSKI (10/10/67) - Legia Warszawa	D	D	D				D	D	D	8	-
Tomasz WALDOCH (10/05/71) - VfL Bochum	D	D	D	D		D80				33	2
Marek KOZMINSKI (07/02/71) - Udinese (ITA)	D	D	D59							18	1
Tomasz IWAN (12/06/71) - Feyenoord (HOL)	M	M76	M					M	M46	5	-
Piotr SWIERCZEWSKI (08/04/72) - SC Bastia (FRA)	M	M	M							23	1
Roman KOSECKI (15/02/66) - FC Nantes (FRA)	M72	A	M							69	19
Piotr NOWAK (05/07/64) - TSV 1860 München (GER)	M57					M	M			13	3
Andrzej JUSKOWIAK (03/11/70) - Olympiakos (GRE)	A	A	A				A	A68	A46	20	9
Wojciech KOWALCZYK (14/04/72) - Real Betis (ESP)	A61							A	A39	26	6
Ryszard CZERWIEC (28/02/68) - Widzew Lodz	s57	s76		M	M	M				21	-
Krzysztof BUKALSKI (22/09/70) - Hutnik Krakow	s61	s63	M	M71					s46	9	-
Pawel WOJTALA (27/10/72) - Lech Poznan	s72			M	D	D				6	-
Waldemar JASKULSKI (23/04/67) - Pogon Szczecin/Widzew Lodz		D		D	D	D			s46	13	1
Tomasz WIESZCZYCKI (21/12/71) - Legia Warszawa		M70						M		10	3
Jacek BEDNARZ (05/06/67) - Legia Warszawa		M63	s59				M	s68		5	-
Jerzy PODBROZNY (17/12/66) - Legia Warszawa		s70								6	-
Henryk BALUSZYNSKI (15/07/72) - VfL Bochum (GER)			A80	A65		A63		M68		11	3
Sylwester CZERESZEWSKI (04/10/71) - Stomil Olsztyn			s80	M	A		s78			11	1
Marek SWIERCZEWSKI (02/03/67) - GKS Katowice				D						6	-
Tomasz SOKOLOWSKI (21/09/70) - Stomil Olsztyn				M						3	-
Slawomir MAJAK (12/01/69) - Zaglebie Lubin				A46						1	-
Rafal SIADACZKA (21/02/72) - Widzew Lodz				s46						1	-
Marcin KUZBA (15/04/77) - Gornik Zabrze				s65						1	-
Tomasz LENART (11/04/69) - LKS Lodz				s71	s85					2	-
Kazimierz WEGRZYN (13/04/67) - GKS Katowice					D	D	D			16	-
Pawel SKRZYPEK (23/08/71) - Rakow Czestochowa					M85					1	-
Zbigniew WYCISZKIEWICZ (16/09/69) - Widzew Lodz					M	M	s63			3	-
Marek CITKO (27/03/74) - Widzew Lodz					M	M	M63			3	-
Grzegorz KALICIAK (10/03/75) - Wisla Krakow					A60					1	-
Dariusz GESIOR (09/10/69) - Ruch Chorzow					s46	M	M	M	M	18	1
Mariusz SRUTWA (15/07/71) - Ruch Chorzow					s60	s63	A78			3	-
Marek JOZWIAK (21/08/67) - Legia Warszawa							D	D	D	4	-
Radoslaw MICHALSKI (21/09/69) - Legia Warszawa							M	M46	M	5	-
Maciej SZCZESNY (28/06/65) - Legia Warszawa								G	G	6	-
Krzysztof RATAJCZYK (09/11/73) - Legia Warszawa								D	D	3	-
Ryszard STANIEK (13/03/71) - Legia Warszawa								s46		10	-
Marek SAGANOWSKI (31/10/78) - LKS Lodz								s68	s39	2	-
Grzegorz LEWANDOWSKI (01/09/69) - Legia Warszawa									M	4	-
Leszek PISZ (18/12/66) - Legia Warszawa									M	14	1

NATIONAL TEAM RESULTS 95/96

16/08/95	France (ECQ)	A	Paris	1-1	Juskowiak (35)
06/09/95	Romania (ECQ)	H	Zabrze	0-0	
11/10/95	Slovakia (ECQ)	A	Bratislava	1-4	Juskowiak (19)
15/11/95	Azerbaijan (ECQ)	A	Trabzon	0-0	
19/02/96	Japan	N	Hong Kong	0-5	
28/02/96	Croatia	A	Rijeka	1-2	Baluszynski (18)
27/03/96	Slovenia	H	Lodz	0-0	
01/05/96	Belarus	H	Mielec	1-1	Kowalczyk (7)
02/06/96	Russia	A	Moscow	0-2	

TOP SCORERS

29 Marek KONIAREK (Widzew Lodz)
19 Jerzy PODBROZNY (Legia Warszawa)
18 Tomasz WIESZCZYCKI (Legia Warszawa)
17 Robert DYMKOWSKI (Pogon Szczecin)
14 Piotr PRABUCKI (Lech Poznan)
13 Boguslaw CYGAN (Stal Mielec)
Cezary KUCHARSKI (Legia Warszawa)
12 Ryszard CZERWIEC (Widzew Lodz)
11 Krzysztof BUKALSKI (Hutnik Krakow)
Leszek PISZ (Legia Warszawa)
Marcin MIECIEL (LKS Lodz/Legia Warszawa)
Marek SAGANOWSKI (LKS Lodz)

Michalski, Grzegorz Lewandowski, Tomasz Wieszczycki and Jacek Bednarz in midfield, Jerzy Podbrozny and Cezary Kucharski in attack. Another who surprisingly did not make the national team in 95/96 was midfielder Tomasz Sokolowski, signed from Stomil Olsztyn during the winter break for a record Polish domestic fee.

Just after Sokolwoski's signing, there was a major disruption at Legia when the club's sponsors decided to withdraw their support having been denied unlimited control after a tug of war with Legia's one-time exclusive patrons, the Polish military. This power struggle appeared to have an adverse effect on the team as they succumbed meekly to Panathinaikos in the quarter-finals of the Champions' Cup, drawing 0-0 at home and losing 0-3 in Athens.

Still, Legia did extremely well to make it that far in Europe's premier competition. They became Poland's first ever Champions' League participants when they confidently dismissed the previous season's quarter-finalists IFK Gothenburg in the preliminary round. And although Pawel Janas's side never really matched that form again in their group, they profitted sufficiently from the poor performances of others to squeeze through to the last eight.

Poland's other European representatives paled into insignificance compared with Legia's high-profile exploits. Zaglebie Lubin played sacrificial lambs to mighty Milan in the UEFA Cup, while both Widzew Lodz (UEFA Cup) and GKS Katowice (Cup-winners' Cup) were eliminated by clubs from the former Soviet Union after a penalty shoot-out.

Katowice's defeat by Ararat Yerevan ended the club's tenth successive season in European competition. And that was where the sequence stopped. The Upper Silesians had a wretched season in the league, finishing a solitary point above the relegation zone, and in the Cup they exited early at the hands of a Third Division side.

The Cup was full of upsets and giant-killing feats and resulted in a final between lowly First Division side GKS

DOMESTIC CUP RESULTS

FOURTH ROUND
Bug Wyszkow 0, Rakow Czestochowa 7
Petrochemia Plock 0, GKS Belchatow 2
Miedz Legnica 2, Sokol Tychy 3
Wisla Krakow 1, Widzew Lodz 3
Szombierki Bytom 1, Pogon Szczecin 0
Okocimski Brzesko 2, LKS Lodz 1
Pogon Olesnica 2, Olimpia Poznan 1
Amica Wronki 4, Stomil Olsztyn 0
Zawisza Bydgoszcz 0, Stal Stalowa Wola 1
Siarka Tarnobrzeg 3, Hutnik Krakow 2 (aet)
Avia Swidnik 1, Stal Mielec 4
Polonia Warszawa 2, Lech Poznan 6
Arka Gdynia 3, GKS Katowice 1
Motor Lublin 1, Gornik Zabrze 3
Ruch Chorzow 2, Legia Warszawa 1
Wartaa Poznan 2, Zaglebie Lubin 1

FIFTH ROUND
Ruch Chorzow 5, Warta Poznan 2
Okocimski Brzesko 0, Szombierki Bytom 2
Arka Gdynia 2, Gornik Zabrze 4 (aet)
Pogon Olesnica 1, Lech Poznan 0
Rakow Czestochowa 1, Amica Wronki 0
Siarka Tarnobrzeg 2, GKS Belchatow 5
Stal Mielec 1, Sokol Tychy 1 (aet; 3-4 on pens.)
Stal Stalowa Wola 0, Widzew Lodz 1

QUARTER-FINALS
Sokol Tychy 1, Widzew Lodz 2 (aet)
Pogon Olesnica 1, Gornik Zabrze 0 (aet)
Ruch Chorzow 2, Rakow Czestochowa 1
GKS Belchatow 3, Szombierki Bytom 1

SEMI-FINALS
GKS Belchatow 2, Widzew Lodz 1
Ruch Chorzow 3, Pogon Olesnica 0

FINAL
16/06/96, Warsaw
RUCH CHORZOW 1 Gesior (86)
GKS BELCHATOW 0
referee - Listkiewicz
RUCH CHORZOW - Lech; Fornalak, Grzesik (Pieniazek 85), Baszczynski, Rowicki, Jaworski, Gesior, Wawrzyczek (Katolik 71), Mosor, Srutwa, Bak.
GKS BELCHATOW - Miller; Szkudlarek, Rogovskoi, Lamch, Cheda (Nowicki 88), Rogan, Berensztajn, Pruchenski, Rzezniczek, Kukulski, Gorski (Trzebny 62).

EUROPEAN CUPS RESULTS 95/96

CHAMPIONS' CUP

● LEGIA WARSZAWA

Preliminary round IFK GÖTEBORG (SWE)

H 1-0 Podbrozny (49p)
Szczesny; Jozwiak, Zielinski, Mandziejewicz, Lewandowski, Michalski, Pisz, Wieszczycki, Bednarz, Kucharski (Kubica 78), Podbrozny (Staniek 88).

A 2-1 Pisz (73), Bednarz (90)
Szczesny; Jozwiak, Zielinski, Mandziejewicz, Bednarz, Lewandowski (Fedoruk 87), Michalski, Wieszczycki, Ratajczyk (Pisz 38), Podbrozny, Kucharski (Staniek 56).

Champions' League

1st match ROSENBORG BK (NOR)

H 3-1 Pisz (65, 74), Staniek (69)
Szczesny; Jozwiak, Zielinski, Mandziejewicz, Ratajczyk, Lewandowski, Pisz, Wieszczycki (Michalski 81), Bednarz (Fedoruk 84), Staniek, Kubica (Kucharski 46).

2nd match SPARTAK MOSKVA (RUS)

A 1-2 Jozwiak (82)
Szczesny; Jozwiak, Zielinski, Mandziejewicz, Lewandowski (Ratajczyk 34), Michalski (Fedoruk 71), Pisz, Wieszczycki, Bednarz, Staniek (Kubica 83), Kucharski.

3rd match BLACKBURN ROVERS (ENG)

H 1-0 Podbrozny (26)
Szczesny; Jozwiak, Zielinski, Mandziejewicz, Lewandowski, Staniek, Pisz, Michalski, Bednarz, Podbrozny, Kucharski.

4th match BLACKBURN ROVERS (ENG)

A 0-0
Szczesny; Jozwiak, Mandziejewicz, Michalski, Lewandowski, Jalocha (Mosor 66), Pisz, Wieszczycki, Bednarz, Podbrozny (Kucharski 46), Staniek.

5th match ROSENBORG BK (NOR)

A 0-4
Szczesny; Jalocha, Zielinski, Jozwiak, Mandziejewicz, Lewandowski, Pisz (Kucharski 17), Wieszczycki (Bednarz 62), Michalski, Staniek, Podbrozny.

6th match SPARTAK MOSKVA (RUS)

H 0-1
Szczesny; Jozwiak, Zielinski, Mandziejewicz, Lewandowski, Staniek (Wieszczycki 82), Michalski, Pisz, Bednarz, Podbrozny, Kucharski.

Quarter-final PANATHINAIKOS (GRE)

H 0-0
Szczesny; Jozwiak, Zielinski, Mandziejewicz, Lewandowski (Wieszczycki 77), Staniek, Michalski, Pisz, Bednarz, Podbrozny, Kucharski (Sokolowski 65).

A 0-3
Szczesny; Mandziejewicz, Zielinski, Michalski, Lewandowski, Jalocha, Pisz, Sokolowski (Kacprzak 82), Wieszczycki, Staniek (Kucharski 76), Podbrozny.

CUP-WINNERS' CUP

● GKS KATOWICE

Preliminary round ARARAT YEREVAN (ARM)

H 2-0 Bilski (27), Karwan (29)
Jojko; Ledwon, Swierczewski, Wegrzyn, Borawski, Widuch, Marzec, Wojciechowski, Kucz (Szala 63), Karwan (Pawluszek 46), Bilski (Walczak 79).

A 0-2 (aet; 4-5 on pens.)
Jojko; Ledwon, Swierczewski, Wegrzyn, Borawski (Karwan 46), Widuch, Marzec (Szala 46), Wojciechowski, Kucz, Strojek, Bilski (Pawluszek 115).

UEFA CUP

● WIDZEW LODZ

Preliminary round BANGOR CITY (WAL)

A 4-0 Czerwiec (25, 42), Koniarek (51, 90)
Wozniak; Bajor (Bogus 61), Lapinski, Bogusz, Szymkowiak, Wyciszkiewicz (Podolski 64), Czerwiec (Mikhalchuk 58), Miaszkiewicz, Szarpak, Siadaczka, Koniarek.

H 1-0 Pikuta (83)
Muchinski; Bajor, Lapinski (Bogus 29), Bogusz, Szymkowiak, Wyciszkiewicz, Czerwiec (Mikhalchuk 70), Miaszkiewicz, Szarpak (Pikuta 80), Koniarek, Siadaczka.

1st round CHORNOMORETS ODESA (UKR)

A 0-1
Wozniak; Bajor, Lapinski, Bogusz, Mikhalchuk, Wyciszkiewicz, Czerwiec, Podolski, Szarpak, Koniarek (Pikuta 88), Siadaczka (Miaszkiewicz 89).

H 1-0 Mikhalchuk (81)
(aet; 5-6 on pens.)
Wozniak; Bajor, Lapinski, Bogusz (Podolski 60), Mikhalchuk, Wyciszkiewicz, Czerwiec, Miaszkiewicz (Pikuta 70), Szarpak (Bogus 36), Koniarek, Siadaczka.

● ZAGLEBIE LUBIN

Preliminary round SHIRAK GYUMRI (ARM)

H 0-0
Dreszer; Lewandowski (Rogovskoi 46), Machaj, Kaluzny, Krzyzanowski, Nalepka, Gorski, Czajkowski (Jasinski 57), Przerywacz, Szeliga (Szczypkowski 70), Majak.

A 1-0 Machaj (23)
Dreszer; Bubnowicz, Rogovskoi, Kaluzny, Krzyzanowski, Machaj (Lewandowski 76), Nalepka, Gorski, Przerywacz, Majak (Jasinski 79), Szczypkowski (Czajkowski 85).

1st round MILAN (ITA)

A 0-4
Dreszer; Machaj, Rogovskoi, Kaluzny, Przerywacz, Najewski (Jasinski 70), Nalepka, Gorski, Krzyzanowski (Hebda 83), Szczypkowski (Szeliga 88), Majak.

H 1-4 Krzyzanowski (72)
Dreszer; Rogovskoi, Machaj, Kaluzny, Gorski, Bubnowicz (Szeliga 66), Dziarmaga, Nalepka, Przerywacz (Krzyzanowski 46), Majak, Szczypkowski (Najewski 60).

Belchatow and once-great Ruch Chorzow of Division Two. Ruch, who had eliminated holders Legia Warsaw in an earlier round, won an unspectacular match 1-0 with a late goal from international midfielder Dariusz Gesior to complete a formidable season. They also achieved promotion back to the top flight after just a season away, finishing second in their group behind Odra Wodzislaw. In the other group Polonia Warsaw and Wisla Krakow both made it back to the First Division after just two seasons in the wilderness.

The bottom of the First Division was in many ways just as fascinating as the top-of-the-table battle. As many as a dozen teams were sucked into the relegation struggle. Siarka Tarnobrzeg and Stal Mielec lost their fight relatively early, but the other two places were not decided until the closing moments of the season. Olimpia/Lechia, one of the two newly merged clubs in the league (Sokol Tychy was the other), were eventually relegated on a technical formality. Early in the season they had been instructed by the Polish FA to play their home matches in Olimpia's home town of Poznan. But, with ten times as many fans likely to show up in Gdansk, the new club moved their headquarters to the famous port city. It was a costly show of bravado. When GKS Katowice and Lech Poznan both turned up at Olimpia's stadium on the day of their appointed fixture, their hosts were waiting up in Gdansk. The FA responded by handing the two visiting sides statutory 3-0 victories.

The final relegation place was decided late on in a tense final game between GKS Belchatow and Pogon Szczecin. Eventually Belchatow saved themselves with a 2-1 win, and that result, because of the league's new rules over teams finishing level on points, also sent Pogon down.

The Polish national team endured another season of ill fortune. Nine matches were played, no victories were recorded. The best result was the 1-1 draw in Paris which kept European Championship hopes alive. But that counted for nothing when the Poles could not beat Romania at home in their next match. The team sank to new depths with a 1-4 defeat in Slovakia, the team's disgraceful performance being characterised by the sending-off of both Roman Kosecki and Piotr Swierczewski. Both players received lengthy bans from the Polish FA for taking off their shirts and making gestures to the crowd.

After the disaster in Bratislava, coach Henryk Apostel resigned. He was replaced by Wladyslaw Stachurski, but after starting his reign with a 0-5 defeat by Japan, his days were always numbered from the outset. Five months after his appointment Stachurski was sacked, enabling one of Poland's most successful national team coaches of all time, Antoni Piechniczek (the man in charge at the1982 and 1986 World Cups) to return from a long spell abroad and seize the reins once again in time for the arduous challenge of qualifying for France '98.

PLAYERS OF THE SEASON

MARCIN MIECIEL

One of the most promising players in Poland, lanky 20-year-old Marcin Mieciel impressed all observers in 95/96 with his light, almost balletic forward play. Legia Warsaw loaned him out to LKS Lodz at the start of the season and were made to pay heavily when Mieciel played out of his skin and scored twice against them in LKS's 2-1 win. That prompted Legia to re-recruit him in the winter break, but, well though the youngster performed when given his chance, his earlier 'misdeed' was to have a major bearing on Legia's title bid. A key member of the U-21 team, Mieciel looks set for senior recognition - perhaps in the World Cup qualifying campaign.

ANDRZEJ WOZNIAK

Balding and moustachioed, 31-year-old goalkeeper Andrzej Wozniak looked every inch the journeyman Polish pro until his big moment arrived in the European Championship qualifying match against France in Paris. The French threw everything they could at the Widzew Lodz 'keeper, but he held firm with a series of incredible saves, including one from the penalty spot. A late Djorkaeff free-kick eventually beat him, but Wozniak's name was already made. In the 12 months that followed he not only confirmed himself as Poland's undisputed no.1 goalkeeper. He also played a starring rôle in Widzew's Polish title success and then, to complete his joy, landed a lucrative contract at FC Porto where none other than his idol, Jozef Mlynarczyk, is the goalkeeping coach.

MAREK CITKO

Poland have not had an outstanding left-winger for many a year. 22-year-old Marek Citko looks ready to fill the gap. Without doubt he was the outstanding individual in the 95/96 Polish league season. Widzew Lodz coach Franciszek Smuda felt he was taking a gamble when he signed up Citko from Second Division Jagiellonia Bialystok. His reputation was one of inconsistency, producing his best only once every five games. But at Widzew he was a revelation, his penetrative running and appreciative eye for an opening adding real quality to the team's play. His national team début, against Japan, was not a success, but Citko will almost certainly come again.

AMICA WRONKI

CLUB DIRECTORY

Klub Sportowy Amica Wronki
ul. Lesna 15a
64-510 Wronki
tel - (067) 540724
fax - (067) 540320
Year of Formation - 1992
President - Stanislaw Grynhoff
Secretary - Ryszard Forbich
Coach - Grzegorz Lato; Marian Kurowski
Stadium - Amica (4,000)

APPEARANCES 95/96

	P	Ap	(s)	Gls
Arkadiusz BAK	M	16		4
Radoslaw BILINSKI	M	34		
Artur BUGAJ	A	20	(7)	8
Piotr DUBIELA	M	9	(19)	
Adam FEDORUK	M	16		2
Slawomir KOSMELA	D	14	(4)	
Pawel KRYSZALOWICZ	A	28	(3)	6
Zbigniew MALACHOWSKI	D	33		4
Mariusz MIZGALA	M	3	(6)	
Wieslaw OSIECKI	M	6	(3)	
Czeslaw OWCZAREK	M	13	(12)	1
Zbigniew PLESNIEROWICZ	G	23	(1)	
Wojciech POLAKOWSKI	M	1	(7)	
Miroslaw RZEPA	D	17		1
Miroslaw SIARA	D	31		
Fode SOUMAH (GUI)	A	3	(8)	1
Miroslaw STROZYNSKI	G	11		
Tomasz SUWARY	A	13	(14)	3
Marek SZAFER	M	6	(4)	
Yury SHATALOV (UKR)	M	19	(5)	1
Mariusz TOMZINSKI	M	25	(2)	3
Grzegorz WODKIEWICZ	D	33		1
Slawomir ZGRAJEWSKI	A		(2)	

LEAGUE RESULTS 1995/96

29/07/95	Rakow Czestochowa	H	3-1	Tomzinski, Bugaj, Malachowski (p)
05/08/95	Olimpia/Lechia Gdansk	A	0-2	
20/08/95	Stomil Olsztyn	H	1-2	Bugaj
26/08/95	GKS Belchatow	A	2-1	Rzepa, Kryszalowicz
30/08/95	Siarka Tarnobrzeg	H	1-0	Kryszalowicz
09/09/95	GKS Katowice	A	1-2	Bugaj
16/09/95	Widzew Lodz	H	0-2	
20/09/95	Slask Wroclaw	H	2-0	Kryszalowicz, Owczarek
23/09/95	Legia Warszawa	A	0-2	
30/09/95	Stal Mielec	H	0-0	
04/10/95	Lech Poznan	A	1-2	Shatalov
14/10/95	Zaglebie Lubin	H	2-0	Malachowski, Bugaj
21/10/95	Sokol Tychy	A	0-0	
28/10/95	Hutnik Krakow	H	2-1	Suwary, Malachowski (p)
04/11/95	Pogon Szczecin	A	1-1	Tomzinski
08/11/95	Gornik Zabrze	H	2-0	Wodkiewicz, Kryszalowicz
18/11/95	LKS Lodz	A	0-0	
24/03/96	Slask Wroclaw	A	2-2	Malachowski, Soumah
31/03/96	Stomil Olsztyn	A	0-2	
06/04/96	GKS Belchatow	H	1-2	Bak
13/04/96	Siarka Tarnobrzeg	A	3-2	Bugaj 2, Bak
17/04/96	Rakow Czestochowa	A	1-0	Bugaj
20/04/96	GKS Katowice	H	0-0	
24/04/96	Widzew Lodz	A	0-2	
27/04/96	Legia Warszawa	H	1-6	Kryszalowicz
04/05/96	Stal Mielec	A	2-0	Suwary, Fedoruk
08/05/96	Olimpia/Lechia Gdansk	H	2-0	Bak, Bugaj
11/05/96	Lech Poznan	H	0-1	
15/05/96	Zaglebie Lubin	A	1-0	Tomzinski
18/05/96	Sokol Tychy	H	1-1	Kryszalowicz
22/05/96	Hutnik Krakow	A	0-0	
25/05/96	Pogon Szczecin	H	1-1	Bak
05/06/96	Gornik Zabrze	A	1-2	Fedoruk
12/06/96	LKS Lodz	H	1-0	Suwary

GKS BELCHATOW

CLUB DIRECTORY

Klub Sportowy GKS Belchatow
ul. Sportowa 3
97-400 Belchatow
tel - (044) 322078/325569
Year of Formation - 1977
President - Zdzislaw Drobniewski
Secretary - Dariusz Marzec
Coach - Wladyslaw Lach; Krzysztof Pawlak
(96/97 - Janusz Bialek)
Stadium - GKS (10,000)

APPEARANCES 95/96

	P	Ap	(s)	Gls
Jacek BERENSZTAJN	M	34		9
Grzegorz CHEDA	M		(6)	
Jaroslaw CHWIALKOWSKI	M	5	(8)	2
Dariusz DURDA	M	25	(4)	
Mariusz GAWLICA	D	1		
Robert GORSKI	A	29	(1)	8
Zbigniew GRZESIAK	A	8	(4)	1
Slawomir GULA	D	1	(3)	
Robert HIRSCH	M	4	(3)	
Juliusz KRUSZANKIN	D	15		
Krzysztof KUKULSKI	A	17	(3)	4
Artur LAMCH	D	22	(7)	2
Marcin LESZCZAK	G	1		
Dariusz MARCINIAK	A	6	(2)	2
Zbigniew MILLER	G	20	(2)	
Marek NOWICKI	M	7	(4)	
Boris OLEYNIK (UKR)	D	1		
Konrad PACIORKOWSKI	G	13		
Marek PIEGSA	D	2		
Jacek PIENIAZEK	D	10	(2)	
Janusz PRUCHENSKI	A	16	(11)	7
Aleksander PTAK	G		(1)	
Robert ROGAN	M	30	(3)	3
Vadim ROGOVSKOI (RUS)	D	13		
Dariusz RZEZNICZEK	M	31		1
Krzysztof STOCKI	D	12	(4)	
Sylwester SZKUDLAREK	D	31		1
Waldemar TESIOROWSKI	M	19		
Marek TRZEBNY	A	1	(9)	

LEAGUE RESULTS 1995/96

Date	Opponent	H/A	Score	Scorers
29/07/95	Gornik Zabrze	H	3-4	Gorski 2, Chwialkowski
06/08/95	LKS Lodz	A	0-1	
19/08/95	Olimpia/Lechia Gdansk	A	0-2	
26/08/95	Amica Wronki	H	1-2	Grzesiak
30/08/95	Stomil Olsztyn	A	0-2	
10/09/95	Slask Wroclaw	H	0-0	
16/09/95	Siarka Tarnobrzeg	H	4-0	Marciniak, Gorski, Berensztajn 2 (1p)
20/09/95	Rakow Czestochowa	H	1-0	Rogan
24/09/95	GKS Katowice	A	1-3	Marciniak
30/09/95	Widzew Lodz	H	1-4	Gorski
04/10/95	Legia Warszawa	A	0-2	
14/10/95	Stal Mielec	H	1-2	Chwialkowski
21/10/95	Lech Poznan	A	0-2	
28/10/95	Zaglebie Lubin	H	1-1	Rogan
04/11/95	Sokol Tychy	A	0-2	
08/11/95	Hutnik Krakow	H	0-2	
18/11/95	Pogon Szczecin	A	1-1	Pruchenski
16/03/96	LKS Lodz	H	3-0	Szkudlarek, Rogan, Pruchenski
23/03/96	Rakow Czestochowa	A	0-1	
30/03/96	Olimpia/Lechia Gdansk	H	1-4	Kukulski
03/04/96	Gornik Zabrze	A	3-3	Berensztajn (p), Gorski 2
06/04/96	Amica Wronki	A	2-1	Gorski, Lamch
14/04/96	Stomil Olsztyn	H	2-1	Kukulski, Rzezniczek
20/04/96	Slask Wroclaw	A	1-1	Berensztajn
24/04/96	Siarka Tarnobrzeg	A	2-1	Kukulski, Pruchenski
27/04/96	GKS Katowice	H	2-1	Pruchenski, Berensztajn
04/05/96	Widzew Lodz	A	0-5	
11/05/96	Legia Warszawa	H	0-1	
15/05/96	Stal Mielec	A	4-3	Kukulski, Gorski, Pruchenski 2
18/05/96	Lech Poznan	H	2-1	Berensztajn, Pruchenski
22/05/96	Zaglebie Lubin	A	1-0	Berensztajn (p)
25/05/96	Sokol Tychy	H	0-0	
05/06/96	Hutnik Krakow	A	1-0	Berensztajn
12/06/96	Pogon Szczecin	H	2-1	Lamch, Berensztajn

GKS KATOWICE

CLUB DIRECTORY

Gorniczy Klub Sportowy Katowice
ul. Bukowa 1
40-157 Katowice
tel - (03) 1546321/1548618
fax - (03) 1501825
Year of Formation - 1964
President - Jerzy Gesikowski
Secretary - Romuald Laszczyk
Coach - Orest Lenczyk; Adam Musial; Henryk Gornik; Piotr Piekarczyk
Stadium - GKS (14,000)

MAJOR HONOURS
Domestic Cup - (3) 1986, 1991, 1993.

APPEARANCES 95/96

	P	Ap	(s)	Gls
Adam BALA	M	11	(8)	2
Arkadiusz BILSKI	A	9	(15)	2
Grzegorz BORAWSKI	M	31		
Jan FURTOK	A	17		4
Janusz JOJKO	G	31		
Bartosz KARWAN	A	15	(8)	1
Adam KUCZ	M	18	(10)	2
Adam LEDWON	D	29		
Mariusz LUNCIK	G	2		
Krzysztof MACIEJEWSKI	D	8	(2)	
Tomasz MALCHAREK	A		(2)	
Dariusz MARZEC	M	6	(4)	
Andrzej NIKODEM	D	10	(2)	
Grzegorz PAWLUSZEK	A	13	(1)	2
Bogdan PIKUTA	A	12	(4)	3
Zdzislaw STROJEK	M	23	(3)	2
Wojciech SZALA	D	26		
Arkadiusz SZCZYGIEL	A	4	(12)	1
Marek SWIERCZEWSKI	D	14		
Krzysztof WALCZAK	A	1	(4)	
Kazimierz WEGRZYN	D	30		6
Miroslaw WIDUCH	M	30		1
Slawomir WOJCIECHOWSKI	M	23	(3)	4

LEAGUE RESULTS 1995/96

29/07/95	Hutnik Krakow	H	1-2	Wojciechowski
05/08/95	Pogon Szczecin	A	0-1	
19/08/95	LKS Lodz	A	1-1	Bilski
27/08/95	Rakow Czestochowa	H	1-0	Strojek
30/08/95	Olimpia/Lechia Gdansk	A	3-0	(w/o)
09/09/95	Amica Wronki	H	2-1	Strojek, Pawluszek
16/09/95	Stomil Olsztyn	A	1-1	Wegrzyn
20/09/95	Gornik Zabrze	H	2-0	Pawluszek, Karwan
24/09/95	GKS Belchatow	H	3-1	Kucz, Wegrzyn, Bilski
30/09/95	Siarka Tarnobrzeg	A	0-0	
04/10/95	Slask Wroclaw	H	0-0	
14/10/95	Widzew Lodz	H	1-4	Wegrzyn
22/10/95	Legia Warszawa	A	0-1	
29/10/95	Stal Mielec	H	0-1	
04/11/95	Lech Poznan	A	1-4	Wegrzyn
08/11/95	Zaglebie Lubin	H	1-0	Wegrzyn
18/11/95	Sokol Tychy	A	0-0	
16/03/96	Pogon Szczecin	H	1-1	Pikuta
23/03/96	Gornik Zabrze	A	4-0	og, Furtok, Widuch, Bala
30/03/96	LKS Lodz	H	1-2	Pikuta
06/04/96	Rakow Czestochowa	A	0-3	
10/04/96	Hutnik Krakow	A	0-0	
13/04/96	Olimpia/Lechia Gdansk	H	3-0	Furtok, Wojciechowski, Kucz
20/04/96	Amica Wronki	A	0-0	
24/04/96	Stomil Olsztyn	H	2-0	Pikuta, Szczygiel
27/04/96	GKS Belchatow	A	1-2	Wegrzyn
04/05/96	Siarka Tarnobrzeg	H	3-1	Furtok, og 2
11/05/96	Slask Wroclaw	A	2-2	Bala, Wojciechowski
15/05/96	Widzew Lodz	A	0-1	
19/05/96	Legia Warszawa	H	0-5	
22/05/96	Stal Mielec	A	1-0	Furtok
25/05/96	Lech Poznan	H	1-1	Wojciechowski
05/06/96	Zaglebie Lubin	A	0-1	
12/06/96	Sokol Tychy	H	0-1	

GORNIK ZABRZE

CLUB DIRECTORY

Klub Sportowy Gornik Zabrze
ul. Roosevelta 81
41-800 Zabrze
tel - (03) 1714926/1712942
fax - (03) 1710530
Year of Formation - 1948
President - Wolfgang Paschek
Secretary - Stanislaw Ploskon
Coach - Stanislaw Oslizlo (96/97 - Jan Zurek)
Stadium - Gornik (23,000)

MAJOR HONOURS
League Championship - (14)
1957, 1959, 1961, 1963, 1964, 1965, 1966, 1967, 1971, 1972, 1985, 1986, 1987, 1988.
Domestic Cup - (6)
1965, 1968, 1969, 1970, 1971, 1972.

APPEARANCES 95/96

	P	Ap	(s)	Gls
Mieczyslaw AGAFON	M	31		6
Grzegorz BONK	M	15	(6)	1
Piotr BRZOZA	M	8	(2)	2
Grzegorz DZIUK	D	21	(4)	
Piotr GRUSZKA	M	13	(11)	1
Tomasz HAJTO	D	21	(4)	1
Rafal JAROSZ	A		(15)	1
Piotr JEGOR	D	6		
Arkadiusz KAMPKA	A	27	(2)	5
Boris KARASIEV (BLS)	D		(3)	
Dariusz KLYTTA	G	16		
Rafal KOCYBA	D	20	(4)	
Dariusz KOSELA	D	29		3
Leszek KRACZKIEWICZ	M	32	(1)	1
Maciej KRZETOWSKI	D	20	(5)	
Arkadiusz KUBIK	M	14		1
Marcin KUZBA	A	18	(8)	8
Vladimir LOMAKO (BLS)	D	1	(2)	
Mariusz NOSAL	A	12	(6)	6
Andrzej ORZESZEK	D	24	(4)	1
Rafal ROGALSKI	D		(1)	
Marek SZEMONSKI	A	20	(9)	8
Slawomir SZYMASZEK	G	1	(1)	
Miroslaw WARZECHA	G	17	(1)	
Jaroslaw ZADYLAK	D	8		

LEAGUE RESULTS 1995/96

29/07/95	GKS Belchatow	A	4-3	Kosela (p), Kampka, Agafon, Kubik
05/08/95	Siarka Tarnobrzeg	H	0-0	
19/08/95	Widzew Lodz	H	1-1	Kuzba
27/08/95	Legia Warszawa	A	0-1	
30/08/95	Stal Mielec	H	3-1	Kraczkiewicz, Szemonski 2
08/09/95	Lech Poznan	A	1-4	Kampka
17/09/95	Zaglebie Lubin	H	1-2	Kampka
20/09/95	GKS Katowice	A	0-2	
23/09/95	Sokol Tychy	A	2-1	Kosela (p), Agafon
30/09/95	Hutnik Krakow	H	2-2	Kampka, Kuzba
04/10/95	Pogon Szczecin	A	0-0	
15/10/95	Slask Wroclaw	A	1-2	Kuzba
21/10/95	LKS Lodz	H	3-2	Kuzba 3
28/10/95	Rakow Czestochowa	A	2-2	Kuzba, Gruszka
04/11/95	Olimpia/Lechia Gdansk	H	2-0	Kampka, Kuzba
08/11/95	Amica Wronki	A	0-2	
18/11/95	Stomil Olsztyn	H	3-2	Szemonski, Brzoza 2
23/03/96	GKS Katowice	H	0-4	
30/03/96	Widzew Lodz	A	1-4	Szemonski
03/04/96	GKS Belchatow	H	3-3	Nosal, Agafon, Szemonski
06/04/96	Legia Warszawa	H	3-2	Szemonski, Nosal, Kosela (p)
13/04/96	Stal Mielec	A	1-0	Bonk
20/04/96	Lech Poznan	H	2-2	Nosal, Jarosz
24/04/96	Zaglebie Lubin	A	1-2	Orzeszek
28/04/96	Sokol Tychy	H	0-0	
04/05/96	Hutnik Krakow	A	0-0	
08/05/96	Siarka Tarnobrzeg	A	2-0	Szemonski, Agafon
11/05/96	Pogon Szczecin	H	1-1	Agafon
15/05/96	Slask Wroclaw	H	2-2	Nosal, Agafon
18/05/96	LKS Lodz	A	0-1	
22/05/96	Rakow Czestochowa	H	1-2	Nosal
25/05/96	Olimpia/Lechia Gdansk	A	1-1	Hajto
05/06/96	Amica Wronki	H	2-1	Nosal, Szemonski
12/06/96	Stomil Olsztyn	A	0-0	

HUTNIK KRAKOW

CLUB DIRECTORY

Klub Sportowy Hutnik Krakow
ul. Ptaszyckiego 4
31-969 Krakow
tel - (012) 441200/444305
Year of Formation - 1950
President - Jan Figut
Secretary - Jan Tyrka
Coach - Jerzy Kasalik
Stadium - Hutnik (14,000)

APPEARANCES 95/96

	P	Ap	(s)	Gls
Waldemar ADAMCZYK	A	27	(4)	9
Jacek BOBROWICZ	G	8	(1)	
Krzysztof BUKALSKI	M	32		11
Ryszard FUDALI	M	32	(1)	
Bartlomiej JAMROZ	A	18	(5)	2
Andrzej JASKOT	A	20	(8)	3
Arkadiusz KALISZAN	D	12		1
Jerzy KOWALIK	M	21	(4)	
Grzegorz KRUPA	M		(6)	
Mariusz KRZYWDA	A	4	(9)	2
Zakari LAMBO (NIG)	A	13	(3)	7
Jerzy LAPCZYNSKI	M		(3)	
Wojciech OZIMEK	M	14	(2)	
Krzysztof POPCZYNSKI	M	6	(4)	
Dariusz ROMUZGA	M	31		5
Michal STOLARZ	M		(12)	
Sergiy SHIPOVSKY (UKR)	G	26		
Leszek WALANKIEWICZ	D	34		
Jerzy WOJNECKI	D	27	(2)	3
Marek ZAJAC	D	30	(1)	4
Andrzej ZIEBA	M	15	(12)	
Robert ZIOLOWSKI	D	4	(13)	

LEAGUE RESULTS 1995/96

29/07/95	GKS Katowice	A	2-1	Lambo, Wojnecki
05/08/95	Widzew Lodz	H	1-4	Lambo
19/08/95	Stal Mielec	H	3-0	Romuzga, Zajac, Adamczyk
26/08/95	Lech Poznan	A	0-3	
30/08/95	Zaglebie Lubin	H	3-2	Lambo, Jaskot, Bukalski
09/09/95	Sokol Tychy	A	3-4	Lambo, Bukalski, Zajac
16/09/95	Slask Wroclaw	A	0-2	
20/09/95	Legia Warszawa	A	1-6	Adamczyk
23/09/95	Pogon Szczecin	H	2-0	Adamczyk 2
30/09/95	Gornik Zabrze	A	2-2	Zajac, Romuzga
04/10/95	LKS Lodz	H	2-1	Jamroz, Bukalski (p)
14/10/95	Rakow Czestochowa	A	0-1	
22/10/95	Olimpia/Lechia Gdansk	H	3-1	Romuzga, Bukalski, Lambo
28/10/95	Amica Wronki	A	1-2	Zajac
04/11/95	Stomil Olsztyn	H	2-0	Romuzga, Bukalski
08/11/95	GKS Belchatow	A	2-0	Jamroz, Adamczyk
19/11/95	Siarka Tarnobrzeg	H	3-1	Adamczyk, og, Bukalski
24/03/96	Legia Warszawa	H	0-3	
30/03/96	Stal Mielec	A	2-1	Wojnecki 2
06/04/96	Lech Poznan	H	3-0	Kaliszan, Adamczyk 2
10/04/96	GKS Katowice	H	0-0	
14/04/96	Zaglebie Lubin	A	1-1	Bukalski (p)
20/04/96	Sokol Tychy	H	2-0	Jaskot, Adamczyk (p)
24/04/96	Slask Wroclaw	H	1-2	Krzywda
27/04/96	Pogon Szczecin	A	3-0	Romuzga, Jaskot, Bukalski
04/05/96	Gornik Zabrze	H	0-0	
08/05/96	Widzew Lodz	A	0-2	
11/05/96	LKS Lodz	A	0-0	
14/05/96	Rakow Czestochowa	H	0-0	
19/05/96	Olimpia/Lechia Gdansk	A	3-1	Krzywda, Bukalski 2
22/05/96	Amica Wronki	H	0-0	
25/05/96	Stomil Olsztyn	A	1-2	Bukalski (p)
05/06/96	GKS Belchatow	H	0-1	
12/06/96	Siarka Tarnobrzeg	A	2-0	Lambo 2

LECH POZNAN

CLUB DIRECTORY

Kolejowy Klub Sportowy Lech Poznan
ul. Bulgarska 5/7
61-875 Poznan
tel - (061) 693886/673061/676512
fax - (061) 672661
Year of Formation - 1922
President - Ryszard Dolata
Secretary - Roman Jakobczak
Coach - Zbigniew Franiak; Remigiusz Marchlewicz (96/97 - Ryszard Polak)
Stadium - Lech (23,734)

MAJOR HONOURS
League Championship - (5)
1983, 1984, 1990, 1992, 1993.
Domestic Cup - (3) 1982, 1984, 1988.

APPEARANCES 95/96

	P	Ap	(s)	Gls
Tomasz AUGUSTYNIAK	D	5	(5)	
Mariusz BEKAS	G	1		
Tomasz BEKAS	A	1	(7)	1
Przemyslaw BERESZYNSKI	D	3	(2)	
Pawel BOCIAN	D	28		2
Bartosz BOSACKI	D	25	(1)	
Jacek DEMBINSKI	A	15		4
Marcin DRAJER	D	7	(3)	
Sekou DRAME (GUI)	D	14	(3)	1
Marcin GODLEWSKI	M		(1)	
Waldemar KRYGER	D	29	(1)	
Adam MAJEWSKI	M	29		
Robert MIODUSZEWSKI	G	6		
Gift MUZADZI (ZIM)	G	19	(1)	
Jakub OSTROWSKI	M	12	(15)	
Krzysztof PISKULA	M	23	(2)	3
Piotr PRABUCKI	A	21	(5)	14
Piotr REISS	A	24	(6)	6
Ryszard REMIEN	M	12	(1)	
Jacek RUCINSKI	G	7		
Miroslaw TRZECIAK	A	27	(1)	6
Slawomir TWARDYGROSZ	M	6	(2)	
Przemyslaw URBANIAK	M	10	(10)	
Artur WICHNIAREK	A	4	(4)	
Dariusz WOJCIECHOWSKI	A	5	(8)	
Pawel WOJTALA	D	27		4
Adam WROBLEWSKI	M		(1)	
Leszek ZAWADZKI	D	3	(3)	

LEAGUE RESULTS 1995/96

30/07/95	Stal Mielec	A	2-3	Piskula, Wojtala
05/08/95	Slask Wroclaw	A	1-0	Reiss
19/08/95	Sokol Tychy	A	2-3	Prabucki 2
26/08/95	Hutnik Krakow	H	3-0	Piskula, Prabucki, Wojtala
30/08/95	Pogon Szczecin	A	1-3	og
08/09/95	Gornik Zabrze	H	4-1	Trzeciak, Reiss 2, Prabucki
16/09/95	LKS Lodz	A	1-1	Reiss
20/09/95	Zaglebie Lubin	H	0-0	
23/09/95	Rakow Czestochowa	H	1-2	Wojtala
01/10/95	Olimpia/Lechia Gdansk	A	3-0	(w/o)
04/10/95	Amica Wronki	H	2-1	Prabucki (p), Bocian
14/10/95	Stomil Olsztyn	A	0-0	
21/10/95	GKS Belchatow	H	2-0	Prabucki 2 (1p)
28/10/95	Siarka Tarnobrzeg	A	0-1	
04/11/95	GKS Katowice	H	4-1	Reiss, Prabucki 2, Bocian
08/11/95	Widzew Lodz	A	3-3	Trzeciak, Prabucki, Drame
17/11/95	Legia Warszawa	H	1-1	Prabucki
24/03/96	Zaglebie Lubin	A	2-2	Trzeciak, Prabucki
31/03/96	Sokol Tychy	H	1-2	Piskula
03/04/96	Stal Mielec	H	2-0	Trzeciak, Dembinski
06/04/96	Hutnik Krakow	A	0-3	
13/04/96	Pogon Szczecin	H	1-0	Prabucki
20/04/96	Gornik Zabrze	A	2-2	Dembinski 2
24/04/96	LKS Lodz	H	0-0	
27/04/96	Rakow Czestochowa	A	0-0	
05/05/96	Olimpia/Lechia Gdansk	H	0-0	
08/05/96	Slask Wroclaw	H	0-1	
11/05/96	Amica Wronki	A	1-0	Trzeciak
15/05/96	Stomil Olsztyn	H	0-1	
18/05/96	GKS Belchatow	A	1-2	Prabucki
22/05/96	Siarka Tarnobrzeg	H	2-0	Dembinski, Bekas T.
25/05/96	GKS Katowice	A	1-1	Trzeciak
05/06/96	Widzew Lodz	H	1-1	Reiss (p)
12/06/96	Legia Warszawa	A	1-5	Wojtala

LEGIA WARSZAWA

CLUB DIRECTORY

ASPN Legia Warszawa
ul. Lazienkowska 3
00-950 Warszawa
tel - (02) 6210896/6281360
fax - (02) 6218261
Year of Formation - 1916
President - Zygmunt Skuza
Secretary - Artur Mazurek
Coach - Pawel Janas
(96/97 - Wladyslaw Stachurski)
Stadium - Wojska Polskiego (21,940)

MAJOR HONOURS

League Championship - (6)
1955, 1956, 1969, 1970, 1994, 1995.
Domestic Cup - (11) 1955, 1956, 1964, 1966, 1973, 1980, 1981, 1989, 1990, 1994, 1995.

APPEARANCES 95/96

	P	Ap	(s)	Gls
Annor AZIZ (GHA)	A		(3)	
Jacek BEDNARZ	M	24	(4)	2
Adam FEDORUK	M	3	(12)	5
Marcin JALOCHA	D	10	(8)	1
Marek JOZWIAK	D	29		1
Jacek KACPRZAK	M	2	(2)	1
Andrzej KUBICA	A	4	(6)	4
Cezary KUCHARSKI	A	21	(9)	13
Grzegorz LEWANDOWSKI	M	25	(1)	1
Zbigniew MANDZIEJEWICZ	D	18	(3)	1
Radoslaw MICHALSKI	M	27	(1)	2
Marcin MIECIEL	A	8	(5)	5
Piotr MOSOR	D	3	(4)	
Roman ORESHCHUK (RUS)	A		(1)	
Leszek PISZ	M	32		11
Jerzy PODBROZNY	A	24	(4)	19
Krzysztof RATAJCZYK	D	24	(3)	1
Tomasz SOKOLOWSKI	M	11	(5)	1
Ryszard STANIEK	M	18	(15)	7
Maciej SZCZESNY	G	34		
Tomasz UNTON	M	1		
Tomasz WIESZCZYCKI	M	27	(4)	18
Jacek ZIELINSKI	D	29		

LEAGUE RESULTS 1995/96

Date	Opponent			Scorers
29/07/95	Zaglebie Lubin	H	1-0	Mandziejewicz
05/08/95	Sokol Tychy	A	3-1	Podbrozny 2, Kubica
19/08/95	Pogon Szczecin	A	2-1	Fedoruk, Podbrozny
27/08/95	Gornik Zabrze	H	1-0	Podbrozny
30/08/95	LKS Lodz	A	1-2	Kucharski
09/09/95	Rakow Czestochowa	H	4-2	Kubica, Wieszczycki, Staniek, Fedoruk (p)
17/09/95	Olimpia/Lechia Gdansk	A	3-1	Wieszczycki, Staniek, Fedoruk (p)
20/09/95	Hutnik Krakow	H	6-1	Kucharski, Staniek 2, Pisz 2 (1p), Fedoruk
23/09/95	Amica Wronki	H	2-0	Kucharski 2
01/10/95	Stomil Olsztyn	A	1-1	Bednarz
04/10/95	GKS Belchatow	H	2-0	Fedoruk (p), Kubica
14/10/95	Siarka Tarnobrzeg	A	7-2	Podbrozny 2, Staniek, Kucharski 2, Pisz, Kubica
22/10/95	GKS Katowice	H	1-0	Podbrozny
28/10/95	Widzew Lodz	A	1-1	Wieszczycki
05/11/95	Slask Wroclaw	H	3-1	Michalski, Kucharski 2
08/11/95	Stal Mielec	H	5-1	Jalocha, Pisz 2, Staniek, Kacprzak
17/11/95	Lech Poznan	A	1-1	Podbrozny
16/03/96	Sokol Tychy	H	2-0	Sokolowski, Wieszczycki
24/03/96	Hutnik Krakow	A	3-0	Podbrozny, Bednarz, Staniek
30/03/96	Pogon Szczecin	H	5-0	Pisz, Ratajczyk, Lewandowski, Podbrozny, Wieszczycki
03/04/96	Zaglebie Lubin	A	3-0	og, Podbrozny, Wieszczycki
06/04/96	Gornik Zabrze	A	2-3	Pisz 2
13/04/96	LKS Lodz	H	2-0	Wieszczycki 2
21/04/96	Rakow Czestochowa	A	1-0	Podbrozny
24/04/96	Olimpia/Lechia Gdansk	H	4-0	Wieszczycki, Mieciel 3
27/04/96	Amica Wronki	A	6-1	Mieciel, Podbrozny, Wieszczycki 2, Pisz, Kucharski
04/05/96	Stomil Olsztyn	H	3-0	Pisz, Wieszczycki, Michalski
11/05/96	GKS Belchatow	A	1-0	Jozwiak
15/05/96	Siarka Tarnobrzeg	H	3-0	Podbrozny (p), Mieciel, Kucharski
19/05/96	GKS Katowice	A	5-0	Wieszczycki 3, Podbrozny 2 (1p)
22/05/96	Widzew Lodz	H	1-2	Wieszczycki
26/05/96	Slask Wroclaw	A	0-0	
05/06/96	Stal Mielec	A	5-0	Wieszczycki, og, Kucharski 3
12/06/96	Lech Poznan	H	5-1	Pisz, Wieszczycki, Podbrozny 3 (1p)

LKS LODZ

CLUB DIRECTORY

Lodzki Klub Sportowy
Al. Unii 2
94-020 Lodz
tel - (042) 860236/863778/863745
fax - (042) 884236/873497
Year of Formation - 1908
President - Antoni Ptak
Secretary - Marek Lopinski
Coach - Zbigniew Lepczyk; Leszek Jezierski
(96/97 - Marek Dziuba)
Stadium - LKS (35,000)

MAJOR HONOURS
League Championship - (1) 1958.
Domestic Cup - (1) 1957.

APPEARANCES 95/96

	P	Ap	(s)	Gls
Witold BENDKOWSKI	D	27		1
Michal BIALAS	A		(4)	
Tomasz CEBULA	A	4		1
Marek CHOJNACKI	D	24	(1)	
Piotr CZACHOWSKI	M	29	(2)	2
Daniel DUBICKI	A	33		4
Dariusz JANCZAK	A	1	(2)	
Tomasz KLOS	D	30	(1)	4
Artur KOSCIUK	D	9	(20)	
Grzegorz KRYSIAK	M	29	(2)	3
Rafal KUPIDURA	A		(7)	
Tomasz LENART	M	31		
Piotr LESZCZYK	D		(2)	
Marcin MIECIEL	A	16		6
Miroslaw MYSLINSKI	M	11	(1)	
Rafal NIZNIK	M	18	(15)	2
Zbigniew ROBAKIEWICZ	G	34		
Marek SAGANOWSKI	A	22	(7)	11
Michal SLAWUTA	G		(1)	
Maciej SZPAK	M		(3)	
Maciej TERLECKI	M	26		3
Grzegorz WEDZYNSKI	M	30		6

LEAGUE RESULTS 1995/96

29/07/95	Stomil Olsztyn	A	0-1	
06/08/95	GKS Belchatow	H	1-0	Krysiak
19/08/95	GKS Katowice	H	1-1	Mieciel
26/08/95	Widzew Lodz	A	1-3	Mieciel
30/08/95	Legia Warszawa	H	2-1	Mieciel 2
09/09/95	Stal Mielec	A	1-0	Terlecki
16/09/95	Lech Poznan	H	1-1	Dubicki
20/09/95	Siarka Tarnobrzeg	A	1-1	Mieciel
23/09/95	Zaglebie Lubin	A	0-1	
30/09/95	Sokol Tychy	H	2-0	Czachowski, og
04/10/95	Hutnik Krakow	A	1-2	Terlecki
14/10/95	Pogon Szczecin	H	3-1	Terlecki, Saganowski 2
21/10/95	Gornik Zabrze	A	2-3	Wedzynski, Mieciel
29/10/95	Slask Wroclaw	A	0-3	
04/11/95	Rakow Czestochowa	H	2-1	Klos, Wedzynski
08/11/95	Olimpia/Lechia Gdansk	A	2-4	Czachowski, Saganowski
18/11/95	Amica Wronki	H	0-0	
16/03/96	GKS Belchatow	A	0-3	
23/03/96	Siarka Tarnobrzeg	H	2-0	Klos, Wedzynski
30/03/96	GKS Katowice	A	2-1	Saganowski, Dubicki
06/04/96	Widzew Lodz	H	1-1	Saganowski
10/04/96	Stomil Olsztyn	H	4-0	Bendkowski, Saganowski, Dubicki, Wedzynski (p)
13/04/96	Legia Warszawa	A	0-2	
20/04/96	Stal Mielec	H	1-1	Saganowski
24/04/96	Lech Poznan	A	0-0	
27/04/96	Zaglebie Lubin	H	1-1	Saganowski
05/05/96	Sokol Tychy	A	2-0	Niznik, Krysiak
11/05/96	Hutnik Krakow	H	0-0	
15/05/96	Pogon Szczecin	A	1-1	Saganowski
18/05/96	Gornik Zabrze	H	1-0	Klos
22/05/96	Slask Wroclaw	H	4-0	Krysiak, Niznik, Wedzynski 2
25/05/96	Rakow Czestochowa	A	3-1	Saganowski, Klos, Dubicki
05/06/96	Olimpia/Lechia Gdansk	H	2-3	Saganowski, Cebula
12/06/96	Amica Wronki	A	0-1	

OLIMPIA/LECHIA GDANSK

CLUB DIRECTORY

Klub Sportowy Olimpia/Lechia Gdansk
ul. Traugutta 29
80-221 Gdansk
tel - (058) 451088
Year of Formation - 1945
President - Henryk Wozniak
Coach - Hubert Kostka; Stanislaw Stachura
Stadium - Lechia (15,000)

APPEARANCES 95/96

	P	Ap	(s)	Gls
Annor AZIZ (GHA)	A	1	(1)	
Arkadiusz BAK	M	13	(1)	2
Piotr BURLIKOWSKI	A	3	(1)	
Marcin CILINSKI	M	22	(4)	3
Tomasz DAWIDOWSKI	M	9	(5)	
Jacek DABROWSKI	A	5	(7)	1
Dariusz GLADYS	G	10	(2)	
Adam GRAD	A	6	(15)	2
Jacek GREMBOCKI	D	3		
Marcin JANUS	D	15		1
Kamil KOWALCZYK	M	2	(7)	
Igor KOZIOL	D	10	(10)	
Grzegorz KROL	A	15	(15)	2
Juliusz KRUSZANKIN	D	4		
Marcin KUPSIK	M	4	(4)	
Andrzej MAGOWSKI	M		(1)	
Slawomir MATUK	D	7	(4)	
Piotr MOSOR	D	16		1
Grzegorz MOTYKA	D	18	(2)	1
Sebastian NOWAK	D	7	(6)	2
Mariusz PAWLAK	D	25		1
Piotr RAJKIEWICZ	M	15	(1)	1
Rafal RUTA	M	12	(2)	1
Krzysztof SADZAWICKI	D	31		1
Slawomir SUCHOMSKI	A	28	(1)	6
Emmanuel TETTEH (GHA)	A	29	(1)	9
Tomasz UNTON	M	20	(1)	5
Piotr WOJDYGA	G	22		

LEAGUE RESULTS 1995/96

Date	Opponent	H/A	Score	Scorers
29/07/95	Slask Wroclaw	H	2-1	Cilinski, Krol
05/08/95	Amica Wronki	H	2-0	Suchomski, Krol
19/08/95	GKS Belchatow	H	2-0	Janus, Grad
26/08/95	Siarka Tarnobrzeg	A	3-3	Dabrowski, Nowak, Suchomski
30/08/95	GKS Katowice	H	0-3	(w/o)
09/09/95	Widzew Lodz	A	0-1	
17/09/95	Legia Warszawa	H	1-3	Tetteh
20/09/95	Stomil Olsztyn	A	2-0	Motyka, Bak
24/09/95	Stal Mielec	A	1-2	Unton
01/10/95	Lech Poznan	H	0-3	(w/o)
04/10/95	Zaglebie Lubin	A	0-3	
15/10/95	Sokol Tychy	H	0-0	
22/10/95	Hutnik Krakow	A	1-3	Bak
28/10/95	Pogon Szczecin	A	1-0	Suchomski
04/11/95	Gornik Zabrze	A	0-2	
08/11/95	LKS Lodz	H	4-2	Unton, Suchomski, Grad, Tetteh
19/11/95	Rakow Czestochowa	A	0-4	
24/03/96	Stomil Olsztyn	H	1-2	Cilinski
30/03/96	GKS Belchatow	A	4-1	Unton, Tetteh 2, Cilinski
03/04/96	Slask Wroclaw	A	1-1	Mosor
06/04/96	Siarka Tarnobrzeg	H	1-0	Rajkiewicz
13/04/96	GKS Katowice	A	0-3	
20/04/96	Widzew Lodz	H	1-7	Tetteh
24/04/96	Legia Warszawa	A	0-4	
28/04/96	Stal Mielec	H	1-1	Unton
05/05/96	Lech Poznan	A	0-0	
08/05/96	Amica Wronki	A	0-2	
12/05/96	Zaglebie Lubin	H	0-0	
15/05/96	Sokol Tychy	A	0-1	
19/05/96	Hutnik Krakow	H	1-3	Unton
22/05/96	Pogon Szczecin	H	2-0	Tetteh 2
25/05/96	Gornik Zabrze	H	1-1	Suchomski
05/06/96	LKS Lodz	A	3-2	Tetteh 2, Ruta
12/06/96	Rakow Czestochowa	H	4-1	Pawlak, Sadzawicki, Suchomski, Nowak

POGON SZCZECIN

CLUB DIRECTORY

Morski Klub Sportowy Pogon Szczecin
ul. Karlowicza 28
71-102 Szczecin
tel - (091) 878031/878056
fax - (091) 878680
Year of Formation - 1948
President - Roman Wilczek
Secretary - Andrzej Rynkiewicz
Coach - Janusz Pekowski
(96/97 - Romuald Szukielowicz)
Stadium - Pogon (17,000)

APPEARANCES 95/96

	P	Ap	(s)	Gls
Dariusz ADAMCZUK	M	4	(2)	
Jacek CYZIO	M	28		
Robert DYMKOWSKI	A	33		17
Maciej FALTYNSKI	M	19	(11)	
Marcin GUTOWSKI	M		(3)	
Waldemar JASKULSKI	D	15		1
Marcin KACZMAREK	M	21	(5)	
Andrzej KAMINSKI	M	6	(9)	
Robert KRUSIEWICZ	M	2	(6)	
Wojciech KSENIAK	M		(6)	
Mariusz KURAS	D	3		1
Radoslaw MAJDAN	G	28		
Piotr MANDRYSZ	M	16		2
Andrzej MIAZEK	D	34		
Olgierd MOSKALEWICZ	A	21	(2)	3
Grzegorz NICINSKI	M	22	(1)	1
Tomasz OLESZEK	D	15	(7)	
Leszek POKLADOWSKI	M	16	(3)	
Slawomir RAFALOWICZ	M	20	(7)	3
Jacek RATAJCZYK	A		(2)	
Andrzej RYCAK	A	17	(12)	4
Maciej STOLARCZYK	D	16	(1)	1
Janusz STUDZINSKI	D	32		
Wojciech TOMASIEWICZ	G	6	(1)	
Marek WALBURG	D		(1)	

LEAGUE RESULTS 1995/96

Date	Opponent	H/A	Score	Scorers
29/07/95	Siarka Tarnobrzeg	A	1-0	Kuras
05/08/95	GKS Katowice	H	1-0	Dymkowski
19/08/95	Legia Warszawa	H	1-2	Dymkowski
26/08/95	Stal Mielec	A	1-3	Dymkowski
30/08/95	Lech Poznan	H	3-1	Moskalewicz, Dymkowski, Jaskulski
09/09/95	Zaglebie Lubin	A	2-0	Moskalewicz, Dymkowski (p)
16/09/95	Sokol Tychy	H	3-1	Dymkowski, Rafalowicz, Moskalewicz
20/09/95	Widzew Lodz	A	0-3	
23/09/95	Hutnik Krakow	A	0-2	
30/09/95	Slask Wroclaw	A	0-1	
04/10/95	Gornik Zabrze	H	0-0	
14/10/95	LKS Lodz	A	1-3	Rafalowicz
21/10/95	Rakow Czestochowa	H	2-1	Rycak, Stolarczyk
28/10/95	Olimpia/Lechia Gdansk	H	0-1	
04/11/95	Amica Wronki	H	1-1	Dymkowski
08/11/95	Stomil Olsztyn	A	1-0	Rafalowicz
18/11/95	GKS Belchatow	H	1-1	Dymkowski
16/03/96	GKS Katowice	A	1-1	Dymkowski
23/03/96	Widzew Lodz	H	0-1	
30/03/96	Legia Warszawa	A	0-5	
03/04/96	Siarka Tarnobrzeg	H	3-0	Dymkowski, Rycak 2
06/04/96	Stal Mielec	H	2-0	Rycak, Dymkowski
13/04/96	Lech Poznan	A	0-1	
20/04/96	Zaglebie Lubin	H	1-1	Dymkowski
24/04/96	Sokol Tychy	A	0-0	
27/04/96	Hutnik Krakow	H	0-3	
03/05/96	Slask Wroclaw	H	2-0	Dymkowski 2
11/05/96	Gornik Zabrze	A	1-1	Nicinski
15/05/96	LKS Lodz	H	1-1	Mandrysz
18/05/96	Rakow Czestochowa	A	1-2	Dymkowski
22/05/96	Olimpia/Lechia Gdansk	A	0-2	
25/05/96	Amica Wronki	A	1-1	Mandrysz
05/06/96	Stomil Olsztyn	H	1-0	Dymkowski
12/06/96	GKS Belchatow	A	1-2	Dymkowski

RAKOW CZESTOCHOWA

CLUB DIRECTORY

Klub Sportowy Rakow Czestochowa
ul. Limanowskiego 83
42-200 Czestochowa
tel - (034) 231517
Year of Formation - 1921
President - Waclaw Korczak
Coach - Gothard Kokott
Stadium - Rakow (10,000)

APPEARANCES 95/96

	P	Ap	(s)	Gls
Piotr BANSKI	A	15	(12)	3
Janusz BODZIOCH	D	31		3
Marcin BOJARSKI	A		(2)	
Robert CIESLEWICZ	A	1	(1)	
Andrzej DZIEDZIC	M	13	(5)	2
Witold GWIZDZIEL	D	29	(1)	
Marek KOLTKO	D	13	(2)	1
Pawel KONIECZKO	M		(2)	
Andrzej KRETEK	G	12		
Jacek MAGIERA	D	14	(2)	2
Piotr MANDRYSZ	M	14		5
Marek MATUSZEK	G	22	(1)	
Robert MROZ	D	1		
Rafal POPKO	A	1	(1)	
Mariusz PURZYCKI	M		(1)	
Zbigniew SIEJA	D	16	(6)	
Pawel SKRZYPEK	M	33		5
Grzegorz SKWARA	A	17	(8)	5
Jan SPYCHALSKI	M	33		1
Krzysztof STEPIEN	A	22	(12)	3
Sebastian SYNORADZKI	M	7	(11)	
Robert SZOPA	A	11	(3)	2
Wojciech SZYMCZYK	M	3	(3)	
Tomasz WIECKOWSKI	A		(1)	
Bartlomiej WILK	M	9	(15)	1
Andrzej WROBLEWSKI	D	31		
Robert ZALESKI	M	26	(6)	

LEAGUE RESULTS 1995/96

29/07/95	Amica Wronki	A	1-3	Mandrysz
05/08/95	Stomil Olsztyn	H	1-0	Skrzypek
19/08/95	Siarka Tarnobrzeg	H	1-1	Mandrysz (p)
27/08/95	GKS Katowice	A	0-1	
30/08/95	Widzew Lodz	H	0-1	
09/09/95	Legia Warszawa	A	2-4	Banski 2
16/09/95	Stal Mielec	H	2-0	Magiera, Bodzioch
20/09/95	GKS Belchatow	A	0-1	
23/09/95	Lech Poznan	A	2-1	Mandrysz 2
30/09/95	Zaglebie Lubin	H	1-0	Koltko
04/10/95	Sokol Tychy	A	1-0	Szopa
14/10/95	Hutnik Krakow	H	1-0	Stepien
21/10/95	Pogon Szczecin	A	1-2	Banski
28/10/95	Gornik Zabrze	H	2-2	Stepien 2
04/11/95	LKS Lodz	A	1-2	Spychalski
11/11/95	Slask Wroclaw	A	0-0	
19/11/95	Olimpia/Lechia Gdansk	H	4-0	Mandrysz, Dziedzic 2, Skwara
17/03/96	Stomil Olsztyn	A	0-1	
23/03/96	GKS Belchatow	H	1-0	Skrzypek
30/03/96	Siarka Tarnobrzeg	A	1-0	Skwara
06/04/96	GKS Katowice	H	3-0	Bodzioch, Skrzypek 2
14/04/96	Widzew Lodz	A	1-4	Wilk
17/04/96	Amica Wronki	H	0-1	
21/04/96	Legia Warszawa	H	0-1	
24/04/96	Stal Mielec	A	0-0	
27/04/96	Lech Poznan	H	0-0	
04/05/96	Zaglebie Lubin	A	0-1	
11/05/96	Sokol Tychy	H	1-1	Szopa
14/05/96	Hutnik Krakow	A	0-0	
18/05/96	Pogon Szczecin	H	2-1	Bodzioch, Skwara
22/05/96	Gornik Zabrze	A	2-1	Magiera, Skwara
25/05/96	LKS Lodz	H	1-3	Skrzypek
05/06/96	Slask Wroclaw	H	0-0	
12/06/96	Olimpia/Lechia Gdansk	A	1-4	Skwara

SIARKA TARNOBRZEG

CLUB DIRECTORY

Klub Sportowy Siarka Tarnobrzeg
ul. Niepodleglosci 2
39-400 Tarnobrzeg
tel - (015) 224151
Year of Formation - 1957
President - Antoni Jakubowicz
Secretary - Wojciech Jugo
Coach - Wlodzimierz Gasior; Stanislaw Gielarek
(96/97 - Jan Zlomanczuk)
Stadium - Siarka (5,000)

APPEARANCES 95/96

	P	Ap	(s)	Gls
Artur ADAMUS	D	32		3
Andrzej BIALEK	A	25	(2)	4
Dariusz DRAGOWSKI	M	20	(1)	
Piotr GOLCZYNSKI	A	1	(8)	1
Sylwester JANOWSKI	G	11		
Leszek JEDRASZCZYK	M	11	(6)	
Tomasz KIELBOWICZ	M	33	(1)	
Tomasz KOMADA	D		(3)	
Mariusz KUKIELKA	M	31		1
Jacek KURANTY	M	13	(3)	2
Rafal OLENIACZ	A	2	(1)	
Adam OZIMEK	D		(5)	
Mieczyslaw OZOG	M	16		2
Marek PAWLAK	G	16		
Krzysztof PRZYPKOWSKI	M	9	(9)	
Jacek RACZKOWSKI	M		(6)	
Artur ROZMUS	A	11	(15)	
Grzegorz ROZMUS	M	6	(13)	1
Mariusz SLOMKA	A	5	(1)	1
Jozef STEFANIK	M	6	(5)	
Edward TYBURSKI	D	13	(2)	3
Grzegorz WILCZOK	D	33		1
Grzegorz WITON	G	7		
Krzysztof ZAGORSKI	A	29	(5)	5
Krzysztof ZLOTEK	D	27	(1)	
Roman ZUCHNIK	D	17	(2)	

LEAGUE RESULTS 1995/96

Date	Opponent		Score	Scorers
29/07/95	Pogon Szczecin	H	0-1	
05/08/95	Gornik Zabrze	A	0-0	
19/08/95	Rakow Czestochowa	A	1-1	Bialek
26/08/95	Olimpia/Lechia Gdansk	H	3-3	Ozog 2, Tyburski (p)
30/08/95	Amica Wronki	A	0-1	
09/09/95	Stomil Olsztyn	H	0-1	
16/09/95	GKS Belchatow	A	0-4	
20/09/95	LKS Lodz	H	1-1	Rozmus G.
23/09/95	Slask Wroclaw	H	0-0	
30/09/95	GKS Katowice	H	0-0	
04/10/95	Widzew Lodz	A	1-2	Bialek
14/10/95	Legia Warszawa	H	2-7	Bialek, Tyburski (p)
21/10/95	Stal Mielec	A	2-0	Adamus, Zagorski
28/10/95	Lech Poznan	H	1-0	Zagorski (p)
05/11/95	Zaglebie Lubin	A	2-3	Kukielka, Adamus
08/11/95	Sokol Tychy	H	0-4	
19/11/95	Hutnik Krakow	A	1-3	Tyburski (p)
23/03/96	LKS Lodz	A	0-2	
30/03/96	Rakow Czestochowa	H	0-1	
03/04/96	Pogon Szczecin	A	0-3	
06/04/96	Olimpia/Lechia Gdansk	A	0-1	
13/04/96	Amica Wronki	H	2-3	Golczynski, Wilczok
20/04/96	Stomil Olsztyn	A	0-2	
24/04/96	GKS Belchatow	H	1-2	Zagorski
28/04/96	Slask Wroclaw	A	0-3	
04/05/96	GKS Katowice	A	1-3	Bialek
08/05/96	Gornik Zabrze	H	0-2	
11/05/96	Widzew Lodz	H	1-3	Adamus
15/05/96	Legia Warszawa	A	0-3	
18/05/96	Stal Mielec	H	2-0	Zagorski, Kuranty
22/05/96	Lech Poznan	A	0-2	
25/05/96	Zaglebie Lubin	H	2-3	Zagorski, Slomka
05/06/96	Sokol Tychy	A	1-4	Kuranty
12/06/96	Hutnik Krakow	H	0-2	

SLASK WROCLAW

CLUB DIRECTORY

Klub Sportowy Slask Wroclaw
ul. Oporowska 62
54-434 Wroclaw
tel - (071) 613342/612211
fax - (071) 612211
Year of Formation - 1947
President - Aleksander Topczak
Secretary - Waldemar Prusik
Coach - Boguslaw Wilk; Romuald Szukielowicz; Jan Calinski (96/97 - Wieslaw Wajno)
Stadium - Slask (14,000)

MAJOR HONOURS
League Championship - (1) 1977.
Domestic Cup - (1) 1987.

APPEARANCES 95/96

	P	Ap	(s)	Gls
Pawel ADAMCZYK	M	14	(1)	1
Ireneusz ADAMSKI	D	1		
Tomasz BOBEL	G	27		
Robert CIESLEWICZ	A	7	(7)	
Tadeusz GAJDZIS	M	7	(2)	
Jaroslaw GORA	M	32		6
Leslaw GRECH	M	19	(2)	3
Zbigniew ILSKI	M	21	(3)	1
Tomasz JAWOREK	A	12	(4)	1
Janusz JEDYNAK	G	7		
Dariusz KASPEREK	M	14	(2)	4
Robert KILDANOWICZ	M	6	(3)	
Rafal KLAJNSZMIT	D	8	(2)	
Jozef KOSTEK	A	28		10
Tomasz KOSZTOWNIAK	A		(1)	
Marek KOWALCZYK	M	4	(13)	2
Janusz KUDYBA	A	3	(9)	2
Romuald KUJAWA	D	34		8
Mariusz KURZEJA	M	1	(8)	
Zdzislaw LESZCZYNSKI	M	23		
Rafal LIS	D		(1)	
Marek MAZUR	M	2	(6)	
Rafal MOLEWSKI	M	20	(1)	
Tomasz MOSKAL	M	15	(9)	
Rafal PAWLAK	D	13	(1)	
Jacek SORBIAN	M	1	(3)	
Bogdan SZCZESNY	D	18	(2)	
Marcin SZYMANSKI	D	33		
Waldemar ZELASKO	M	4	(6)	

LEAGUE RESULTS 1995/96

Date	Opponent	Venue	Score	Scorers
29/07/95	Olimpia/Lechia Gdansk	A	1-2	Grech
05/08/95	Lech Poznan	H	0-1	
19/08/95	Zaglebie Lubin	H	1-1	Kujawa
26/08/95	Stomil Olsztyn	A	2-3	Kostek, Adamczyk
30/08/95	Sokol Tychy	H	1-1	Gora
10/09/95	GKS Belchatow	A	0-0	
16/09/95	Hutnik Krakow	H	2-0	Kostek, Kujawa
20/09/95	Amica Wronki	A	0-2	
23/09/95	Siarka Tarnobrzeg	A	0-0	
30/09/95	Pogon Szczecin	H	1-0	Kostek
04/10/95	GKS Katowice	A	0-0	
15/10/95	Gornik Zabrze	H	2-1	Kostek, Gora
21/10/95	Widzew Lodz	A	0-4	
29/10/95	LKS Lodz	H	3-0	Gora, Kujawa 2
05/11/95	Legia Warszawa	A	1-3	Kostek
11/11/95	Rakow Czestochowa	H	0-0	
18/11/95	Stal Mielec	A	3-1	Grech, og, Gora
24/03/96	Amica Wronki	H	2-2	Kostek, Kujawa (p)
31/03/96	Zaglebie Lubin	A	1-2	Kasperek
03/04/96	Olimpia/Lechia Gdansk	H	1-1	Kostek
06/04/96	Stomil Olsztyn	H	1-1	Kostek
14/04/96	Sokol Tychy	A	1-1	Kowalczyk
20/04/96	GKS Belchatow	H	1-1	Grech
24/04/96	Hutnik Krakow	A	2-1	Gora, Ilski
28/04/96	Siarka Tarnobrzeg	H	3-0	Kujawa 2 (1p), Kostek
03/05/96	Pogon Szczecin	A	0-2	
08/05/96	Lech Poznan	A	1-0	Kasperek
11/05/96	GKS Katowice	H	2-2	Kostek, Kujawa (p)
15/05/96	Gornik Zabrze	A	2-2	Kasperek, Kowalczyk
19/05/96	Widzew Lodz	H	1-2	Kasperek
22/05/96	LKS Lodz	A	0-4	
26/05/96	Legia Warszawa	H	0-0	
05/06/96	Rakow Czestochowa	A	0-0	
12/06/96	Stal Mielec	H	4-1	Jaworek, Kudyba 2, Gora

SOKOL TYCHY

CLUB DIRECTORY

Klub Sportowy Sokol Tychy
ul. Edukacji 9
43-100 Tychy
tel - (032) 1274770/1274720
fax - (032) 1274770
Year of Formation - 1966
President - Piotr Buller
Secretary - Ryszard Mofina
Coach - Janusz Bialek
(96/97 - Boguslaw Kaczmarek)
Stadium - Sokol (14,000)

APPEARANCES 95/96

	P	Ap	(s)	Gls
Przemyslaw BERESZYNSKI	D	17		
Krzysztof BIZACKI	A	30	(3)	6
Piotr BURLIKOWSKI	A	7	(2)	2
Maciej BYKOWSKI	A	2	(10)	
Edeberth DINHA (ZIM)	M	1	(2)	
Jerzy DUDEK	G	15		
Lukasz GORSZKOW	D	28	(3)	1
Andrzej JARKIEWICZ	G	3	(1)	
Dariusz JASKULSKI	M	15	(2)	1
Jerzy KAZIOW	A		(1)	
Zbigniew KONIECZKO	M	20	(6)	
Krzysztof KONON	A	10	(15)	1
Tomasz KOS	D	24	(6)	4
Maciej LUDWICZAK	D	3	(9)	
Elasto LUNGU (ZIM)	M		(2)	
Prince MATORE (ZIM)	D	20		
Mariusz MAZUR	M		(1)	
Janusz NAWROCKI	M	29	(2)	
Krzysztof NOWAK	D	15		
Marek PIOTROWICZ	D	24		
Dariusz PLACZKIEWICZ	G	16		
Bogdan PRUSEK	A	23	(7)	10
Miroslaw ROZKOSZNY	D		(1)	
Marek RZEPKA	D	16	(1)	1
Tomasz SZCZEPANEK	D	3		
Alexander SHEMYETYEV (UKR)	M		(4)	
Rafal SZWED	M	6	(8)	
Robert WILK	M	34		5
Moussa YAHAYA (NIG)	A	13		5

LEAGUE RESULTS 1995/96

30/07/95	Widzew Lodz	A	0-5	
05/08/95	Legia Warszawa	H	1-3	Bizacki
19/08/95	Lech Poznan	H	3-2	Prusek 2, Konon
27/08/95	Zaglebie Lubin	A	0-0	
30/08/95	Slask Wroclaw	A	1-1	Prusek
09/09/95	Hutnik Krakow	H	4-3	Wilk, Rzepka, Prusek, Bizacki
16/09/95	Pogon Szczecin	A	1-3	Prusek
20/09/95	Stal Mielec	A	0-2	
23/09/95	Gornik Zabrze	H	1-2	Kos
30/09/95	LKS Lodz	A	0-2	
04/10/95	Rakow Czestochowa	H	0-1	
15/10/95	Olimpia/Lechia Gdansk	A	0-0	
21/10/95	Amica Wronki	H	0-0	
29/10/95	Stomil Olsztyn	A	1-2	Bizacki
04/11/95	GKS Belchatow	H	2-0	Burlikowski, Bizacki
08/11/95	Siarka Tarnobrzeg	A	4-0	Prusek 2, Wilk, Burlikowski
18/11/95	GKS Katowice	H	0-0	
16/03/96	Legia Warszawa	A	0-2	
23/03/96	Stal Mielec	H	2-1	Wilk, Yahaya
31/03/96	Lech Poznan	A	2-1	Yahaya 2
06/04/96	Zaglebie Lubin	H	2-0	Kos 2
14/04/96	Slask Wroclaw	H	1-1	Kos
20/04/96	Hutnik Krakow	A	0-2	
24/04/96	Pogon Szczecin	H	0-0	
28/04/96	Gornik Zabrze	A	0-0	
01/05/96	Widzew Lodz	H	0-1	
05/05/96	LKS Lodz	H	0-2	
11/05/96	Rakow Czestochowa	A	1-1	Jaskulski (p)
15/05/96	Olimpia/Lechia Gdansk	H	1-0	Wilk
18/05/96	Amica Wronki	A	1-1	Gorszkow
22/05/96	Stomil Olsztyn	H	3-1	Bizacki, Yahaya 2
25/05/96	GKS Belchatow	A	0-0	
05/06/96	Siarka Tarnobrzeg	H	4-1	Wilk, Prusek 2, Bizacki
12/06/96	GKS Katowice	A	1-0	Prusek

STAL MIELEC

CLUB DIRECTORY

Klub Sportowy Stal Mielec
ul. Solskiego 1
39-300 Mielec
tel - (0196) 2426/3905
Year of Formation - 1939
President - Thomas Mertel
Secretary - Edward Socha
Coach - Jan Zlomanczuk; Leszek Brzezinski
(96/97 - Grzegorz Lato)
Stadium - Stal (30,000)

MAJOR HONOURS
League Championship - (2) 1973, 1976.

APPEARANCES 95/96

	P	Ap	(s)	Gls
Tomasz ABRAMOWICZ	A	2	(5)	1
Wieslaw BARTKOWSKI	D	22	(7)	
Krzysztof BOCIEK	A	9		1
Boguslaw CYGAN	A	33		13
Janusz CZYREK	M	14	(1)	5
Rafal DOMARSKI	A	26	(1)	3
Ryszard FEDERKIEWICZ	D	14		
Janusz GALICA	M	1	(1)	
Wojciech JARZYNKA	D	14		
Piotr JEGOR	D	8		1
Janusz KACZOWKA	M	14	(2)	
Pawel KLOC	M	28	(2)	3
Grzegorz KOLISZ	M		(7)	
Daniel KONOPELSKI	M	6	(13)	1
Tomasz KUKOWSKI	M	26	(3)	1
Krzysztof LETOCHA	D	14	(1)	
Rafal OPRZONDEK	D	17	(2)	
Damian PANCERZ	A		(4)	
Krzysztof PETRYKOWSKI	G	1		
Sebastian PIECHOTA	M	15	(8)	
Rafal PIOTROWSKI	M	10	(15)	1
Wojciech PSZENICZNY	A		(1)	
Rafal RUTA	M	13	(1)	2
Wojciech RYCAK	D	13		
Krzysztof TOMANEK	D	21		
Tomasz WROTON	M	20	(9)	1
Boguslaw WYPARLO	G	33		

LEAGUE RESULTS 1995/96

30/07/95	Lech Poznan	H	3-2	Cygan, Czyrek, Kloc
05/08/95	Zaglebie Lubin	A	1-5	Cygan (p)
19/08/95	Hutnik Krakow	A	0-3	
26/08/95	Pogon Szczecin	H	3-1	Cygan 2, Bociek
30/08/95	Gornik Zabrze	A	1-3	Cygan
09/09/95	LKS Lodz	H	0-1	
16/09/95	Rakow Czestochowa	A	0-2	
20/09/95	Sokol Tychy	H	2-0	Czyrek 2
24/09/95	Olimpia/Lechia Gdansk	H	2-1	Ruta, Cygan
30/09/95	Amica Wronki	A	0-0	
04/10/95	Stomil Olsztyn	H	1-0	Czyrek
14/10/95	GKS Belchatow	A	2-1	Kloc, Czyrek
21/10/95	Siarka Tarnobrzeg	H	0-2	
29/10/95	GKS Katowice	A	1-0	Ruta
04/11/95	Widzew Lodz	H	1-2	Wroton
08/11/95	Legia Warszawa	A	1-5	Cygan (p)
18/11/95	Slask Wroclaw	H	1-3	Cygan
23/03/96	Sokol Tychy	A	1-2	Cygan
30/03/96	Hutnik Krakow	H	1-2	Cygan
03/04/96	Lech Poznan	A	0-2	
06/04/96	Pogon Szczecin	A	0-2	
13/04/96	Gornik Zabrze	H	0-1	
20/04/96	LKS Lodz	A	1-1	Domarski
24/04/96	Rakow Czestochowa	H	0-0	
28/04/96	Olimpia/Lechia Gdansk	A	1-1	Kloc
04/05/96	Amica Wronki	H	0-2	
08/05/96	Zaglebie Lubin	H	1-2	Kukowski
11/05/96	Stomil Olsztyn	A	4-1	Domarski 2, Cygan 2
15/05/96	GKS Belchatow	H	3-4	Piotrowski, Jegor, Abramowicz
18/05/96	Siarka Tarnobrzeg	A	0-2	
22/05/96	GKS Katowice	H	0-1	
26/05/96	Widzew Lodz	A	1-4	Cygan
05/06/96	Legia Warszawa	H	0-5	
12/06/96	Slask Wroclaw	A	1-4	Konopelski

STOMIL OLSZTYN

CLUB DIRECTORY

Klub Sportowy Stomil Olsztyn
ul. Pilsudskiego 69a
10-596 Olsztyn
tel - (089) 333160
Year of Formation - 1945
President - Jozef Grzegorczyk
Coach - Ryszard Polak; Mieczyslaw Korzeniowski (96/97 - Jerzy Masztaler)
Stadium - Stomil (30,000)

APPEARANCES 95/96

	P	Ap	(s)	Gls
Andrzej BIEDRZYCKI	D	31	(1)	1
Jacek CHANKO	M	16		4
Pawel CHARBICKI	G	1		
Sylwester CZERESZEWSKI	M	32		7
Pawel GADZIALA	M	17	(5)	2
Andrzej JANKOWSKI	D	31		3
Rafal KACZMARCZYK	M	27	(1)	1
Maciej KASICA	D	2	(6)	
Robert KILDANOWICZ	M		(2)	
Arkadiusz KLIMEK	A	17	(9)	
Mariusz MACHNIAK	M	1		
Bogdan MICHALEWSKI	M	1	(5)	
Andrzej NAKIELSKI	D	12	(1)	
Boguslaw OBLEWSKI	D	7	(1)	
Slawomir OPALINSKI	D	9	(18)	
Jacek PLUCIENNIK	A	31		2
Janusz PRUCHENSKI	A		(2)	
Bogdan PUDLIS	A		(2)	
Kiril RYBAKOV (RUS)	A	4	(5)	
Kazimierz SIDORCZUK	G	33		
Andrei SINITSYN (BLS)	M	17		2
Tomasz SOKOLOWSKI	M	15		5
Alhaly SOUMAH (GUI)	A	6		
Mariusz STEFANOWICZ	A		(1)	
Grzegorz WAGNER	D	27		
Tomasz WLODARCZYK	M		(7)	
Waldemar ZABECKI	D	10	(1)	
Adam ZEJER	M	23	(6)	4
Czeslaw ZUKOWSKI	M	4	(20)	

LEAGUE RESULTS 1995/96

Date	Opponent	H/A	Score	Scorers
29/07/95	LKS Lodz	H	1-0	Zejer
05/08/95	Rakow Czestochowa	A	0-1	
20/08/95	Amica Wronki	A	2-1	Sokolowski 2
26/08/95	Slask Wroclaw	H	3-2	Czereszewski, og, Sokolowski
30/08/95	GKS Belchatow	H	2-0	Sokolowski, Zejer
09/09/95	Siarka Tarnobrzeg	A	1-0	Gadziala
16/09/95	GKS Katowice	H	1-1	Kaczmarczyk
20/09/95	Olimpia/Lechia Gdansk	H	0-2	
01/10/95	Legia Warszawa	H	1-1	Sokolowski (p)
04/10/95	Stal Mielec	A	0-1	
14/10/95	Lech Poznan	H	0-0	
22/10/95	Zaglebie Lubin	A	0-0	
29/10/95	Sokol Tychy	H	2-1	Czereszewski, Zejer
04/11/95	Hutnik Krakow	A	0-2	
08/11/95	Pogon Szczecin	H	0-1	
11/11/95	Widzew Lodz	A	2-2	Gadziala, Czereszewski
18/11/95	Gornik Zabrze	A	2-3	Biedrzycki, Czereszewski
17/03/96	Rakow Czestochowa	H	1-0	Chanko
24/03/96	Olimpia/Lechia Gdansk	A	2-1	Pluciennik, Czereszewski
31/03/96	Amica Wronki	H	2-0	Jankowski, Sinitsyn
06/04/96	Slask Wroclaw	A	1-1	Sinitsyn
10/04/96	LKS Lodz	A	0-4	
14/04/96	GKS Belchatow	A	1-2	Jankowski
20/04/96	Siarka Tarnobrzeg	H	2-0	Czereszewski, Chanko
24/04/96	GKS Katowice	A	0-2	
28/04/96	Widzew Lodz	H	0-1	
04/05/96	Legia Warszawa	A	0-3	
11/05/96	Stal Mielec	H	1-4	Chanko
15/05/96	Lech Poznan	A	1-0	Chanko
18/05/96	Zaglebie Lubin	H	1-0	Zejer
22/05/96	Sokol Tychy	A	1-3	Jankowski
25/05/96	Hutnik Krakow	H	2-1	Czereszewski, Pluciennik
05/06/96	Pogon Szczecin	A	0-1	
12/06/96	Gornik Zabrze	H	0-0	

WIDZEW LODZ

CLUB DIRECTORY

Sekcja Pilki Noznej Widzew Lodz
ul. Pilsudskiego 138
92-300 Lodz
tel - (042) 747218/745133/743224
Year of Formation - 1910
President - Andrzej Pawelec
Coach - Franciszek Smuda
Stadium - Widzew (22,000)

MAJOR HONOURS
League Championship - (3) 1981, 1982, 1996.
Domestic Cup - (1) 1985.

APPEARANCES 95/96

	P	Ap	(s)	Gls
Marek BAJOR	D	20	(7)	
Maciej BIELECKI	M		(1)	
Marcin BOGUS	D	7	(5)	
Daniel BOGUSZ	D	28	(2)	1
Marek CITKO	M	26	(1)	5
Ryszard CZERWIEC	M	31		12
Slawomir GULA	D	5	(5)	1
Waldemar JASKULSKI	D	16		
Marek KONIAREK	A	34		29
Rafal KUBIAK	A		(12)	1
Tomasz LAPINSKI	D	28		2
Pawel MIASZKIEWICZ	M	16	(17)	5
Andriy MIKHALCHUK (UKR)	M	29	(4)	6
Tomasz MUCHINSKI	G	2		
Bogdan PIKUTA	A		(8)	
Dariusz PODOLSKI	D	1	(13)	
Rafal SIADACZKA	A	33		9
Piotr SZARPAK	M	28	(2)	2
Miroslaw SZYMKOWIAK	M	4	(1)	1
Andrzej WOZNIAK	G	32		
Zbigniew WYCISZKIEWICZ	M	34		10

LEAGUE RESULTS 1995/96

Date	Opponent		Score	Scorers
30/07/95	Sokol Tychy	H	5-0	Siadaczka, Czerwiec, Szymkowiak, Lapinski 2
05/08/95	Hutnik Krakow	A	4-1	Czerwiec, Wyciszkiewicz, Siadaczka, Szarpak
19/08/95	Gornik Zabrze	A	1-1	Koniarek (p)
26/08/95	LKS Lodz	H	3-1	Koniarek 2, Czerwiec
30/08/95	Rakow Czestochowa	A	1-0	Koniarek
09/09/95	Olimpia/Lechia Gdansk	H	1-0	Siadaczka
16/09/95	Amica Wronki	A	2-0	Koniarek, Mikhalchuk
20/09/95	Pogon Szczecin	H	3-0	Koniarek 3
30/09/95	GKS Belchatow	A	4-1	Koniarek 2, Czerwiec, Wyciszkiewicz
04/10/95	Siarka Tarnobrzeg	H	2-1	Miaszkiewicz (p), Koniarek
14/10/95	GKS Katowice	A	4-1	Mikhalchuk, Wyciszkiewicz 2, Koniarek
21/10/95	Slask Wroclaw	H	4-0	Czerwiec, Siadaczka, Koniarek 2
28/10/95	Legia Warszawa	H	1-1	Siadaczka
04/11/95	Stal Mielec	A	2-1	Citko, Miaszkiewicz
08/11/95	Lech Poznan	H	3-3	Siadaczka, Czerwiec, Wyciszkiewicz
11/11/95	Stomil Olsztyn	H	2-2	Koniarek 2
19/11/95	Zaglebie Lubin	A	0-0	
23/03/96	Pogon Szczecin	A	1-0	Koniarek
30/03/96	Gornik Zabrze	H	4-1	Mikhalchuk, Citko, Wyciszkiewicz, Kubiak
06/04/96	LKS Lodz	A	1-1	Siadaczka
14/04/96	Rakow Czestochowa	H	4-1	Czerwiec, Miaszkiewicz, Koniarek 2
20/04/96	Olimpia/Lechia Gdansk	A	7-1	Wyciszkiewicz, Czerwiec, Miaszkiewicz 2, Siadaczka, Koniarek, Citko
24/04/96	Amica Wronki	H	2-0	Mikhalchuk, Gula
28/04/96	Stomil Olsztyn	A	1-0	Mikhalchuk
01/05/96	Sokol Tychy	A	1-0	Koniarek
04/05/96	GKS Belchatow	H	5-0	Wyciszkiewicz, Koniarek 2, Citko 2
08/05/96	Hutnik Krakow	H	2-0	Bogusz, Mikhalchuk
11/05/96	Siarka Tarnobrzeg	A	3-1	Wyciszkiewicz, Czerwiec 2
15/05/96	GKS Katowice	H	1-0	Czerwiec
19/05/96	Slask Wroclaw	A	2-1	Wyciszkiewicz, Czerwiec
22/05/96	Legia Warszawa	A	2-1	Koniarek, Szarpak
26/05/96	Stal Mielec	H	4-1	Koniarek 4 (2p)
05/06/96	Lech Poznan	A	1-1	Koniarek
12/06/96	Zaglebie Lubin	H	1-0	Siadaczka

ZAGLEBIE LUBIN

CLUB DIRECTORY

Klub Sportowy Zaglebie Lubin
ul. Marii Sklodowskiej-Curie 58
59-300 Lubin
tel - (070) 478500/478520
fax - (070) 478509
Year of Formation - 1946
President - Tadeusz Szelag
Secretary - Michal Lulek
Coach - Wieslaw Wojno; Janusz Stanczyk; Andrzej Strejlau (96/97 - Miroslaw Dragan)
Stadium - Zaglebie (34,000)

MAJOR HONOURS
League Championship - (1) 1991.

APPEARANCES 95/96

	P	Ap	(s)	Gls
Marcin BOGUS	D	4	(6)	
Robert BUBNOWICZ	D	12	(10)	
Edward CECOT	D	2	(3)	
Zbigniew CZAJKOWSKI	M	26	(6)	1
Miroslaw DRESZER	G	34		
Dariusz DZIARMAGA	M	12	(1)	
Wojciech GORSKI	A	28		6
Andrzej HEBDA	D		(3)	
Radoslaw JASINSKI	A	1	(8)	
Radoslaw KALUZNY	D	31		8
Jaroslaw KRZYZANOWSKI	M	17	(6)	4
Dariusz LEWANDOWSKI	D	26	(2)	1
Stefan MACHAJ	D	29	(1)	
Slawomir MAJAK	A	17		2
Piotr NAJEWSKI	M	2	(7)	1
Krzysztof NALEPKA	M	23	(3)	
Mariusz PIEKARSKI	M	15		1
Piotr PRZERYWACZ	D	26	(4)	
Vadim ROGOVSKOI (RUS)	D	15		2
Andrzej SZCZYPKOWSKI	M	30	(4)	2
Grzegorz SZELIGA	A	22	(5)	6
Mariusz UJEK	A		(2)	
Jaroslaw WOJEWODKA	M	2	(10)	

LEAGUE RESULTS 1995/96

29/07/95	Legia Warszawa	A	0-1	
05/08/95	Stal Mielec	H	5-1	Gorski 2, Szeliga, Krzyzanowski 2
19/08/95	Slask Wroclaw	A	1-1	Gorski
27/08/95	Sokol Tychy	H	0-0	
30/08/95	Hutnik Krakow	A	2-3	Kaluzny, Najewski
09/09/95	Pogon Szczecin	H	0-2	
17/09/95	Gornik Zabrze	A	2-1	Szeliga, Gorski
20/09/95	Lech Poznan	A	0-0	
23/09/95	LKS Lodz	H	1-0	Rogovskoi (p)
30/09/95	Rakow Czestochowa	A	0-1	
04/10/95	Olimpia/Lechia Gdansk	H	3-0	Szeliga, Kaluzny, Majak
14/10/95	Amica Wronki	A	0-2	
22/10/95	Stomil Olsztyn	H	0-0	
28/10/95	GKS Belchatow	A	1-1	Szczypkowski
05/11/95	Siarka Tarnobrzeg	H	3-2	Rogovskoi (p), Majak, Szczypkowski
08/11/95	GKS Katowice	A	0-1	
19/11/95	Widzew Lodz	H	0-0	
24/03/96	Lech Poznan	H	2-2	Piekarski, Kaluzny
31/03/96	Slask Wroclaw	H	2-1	Szeliga, Kaluzny
03/04/96	Legia Warszawa	H	0-3	
06/04/96	Sokol Tychy	A	0-2	
14/04/96	Hutnik Krakow	H	1-1	Czajkowski
20/04/96	Pogon Szczecin	A	1-1	Gorski
24/04/96	Gornik Zabrze	H	2-1	Lewandowski, Szeliga
27/04/96	LKS Lodz	A	1-1	Kaluzny
04/05/96	Rakow Czestochowa	H	1-0	Gorski
08/05/96	Stal Mielec	A	2-1	Krzyzanowski, Kaluzny
12/05/96	Olimpia/Lechia Gdansk	A	0-0	
15/05/96	Amica Wronki	H	0-1	
18/05/96	Stomil Olsztyn	A	0-1	
22/05/96	GKS Belchatow	H	0-1	
25/05/96	Siarka Tarnobrzeg	A	3-2	Szeliga, Kaluzny 2
05/06/96	GKS Katowice	H	1-0	Krzyzanowski
12/06/96	Widzew Lodz	A	0-1	

PROMOTED CLUBS

SECOND DIVISION FINAL TABLES 95/96

GROUP ONE

		Pd	W	D	L	F	A	Pt	GD
1	**Odra Wodzislaw**	**34**	**21**	**7**	**6**	**86**	**37**	**70**	**+49**
2	**Ruch Chorzow**	**34**	**20**	**8**	**6**	**65**	**24**	**68**	**+41**
3	Zawisza Bydgoszcz	34	17	8	9	47	35	59	+12
4	Krisbut Myszkow	34	14	14	6	45	31	56	+14
5	Polonia Bytom	34	14	7	13	46	40	49	+6
6	Szombierki Bytom	34	13	10	11	44	39	49	+5
7	Gornik Konin	34	13	9	12	40	42	48	-2
8	Varta Namyslow	34	11	14	9	38	29	47	+9
9	Stilon Gorzow	34	11	10	13	46	41	43	+5
10	Naprzod Rydultowy	34	11	9	14	41	50	42	-9
11	Miedz Legnica	34	10	12	12	38	42	42	-4
12	Chrobry Glogow	34	11	8	15	31	43	41	-12
13	Chemik Police	34	9	13	12	36	50	40	-14
14	Lechia Zielona Gora	34	11	7	16	38	65	40	-27
15	Warta Poznan	34	9	12	13	32	47	39	-15
16	Sleza Wroclaw	34	10	8	16	41	51	38	-10
17	Polonia Gdansk	34	8	8	18	40	63	32	-23
18	Baltyk Gdynia	34	7	8	19	39	64	29	-25

GROUP TWO

		Pd	W	D	L	F	A	Pt	GD
1	**Polonia Warszawa**	**34**	**21**	**9**	**4**	**77**	**37**	**72**	**+40**
2	**Wisla Krakow**	**34**	**22**	**6**	**6**	**69**	**29**	**72**	**+40**
3	Petrochemia Plock	34	19	10	5	56	24	67	+32
4	Jeziorak Ilawa	34	17	9	8	50	32	60	+18
5	Unia Tarnow	34	13	11	10	49	37	50	+12
6	Swit Nowy Dwor	34	14	7	13	37	37	49	=
7	Cracovia Krakow	34	13	10	11	43	36	49	+7
8	Stal Stalowa Wola	34	11	14	9	58	37	47	+21
9	TED Radomsko	34	13	7	14	49	51	46	-2
10	Okocimski Brzesko	34	12	10	12	33	36	46	-3
11	Avia Swidnik	34	12	9	13	31	35	45	-4
12	Pomezania Malbork	34	13	4	17	38	53	43	-15
13	KSZO Ostrowiec	34	12	7	15	37	52	43	-15
14	Hetman Zamosc	34	11	8	15	35	45	41	-10
15	Jagiellonia Bialystok	34	12	4	18	35	54	40	-19
16	Hutnik Warszawa	34	11	6	17	38	53	39	-15
17	Lublinianka Lublin	34	3	11	20	20	57	20	-37
18	Motor Lublin	34	2	8	24	26	76	14	-50

CLUB DIRECTORY

Miejski Klub Sportowy Odra Wodzislaw
ul. Boguminska 8, 44-300 Wodzislaw
tel - (036) 551394
Year of Formation - 1922
President - Ireneusz Serwotka
Secretary - Jerzy Knopek
Coach - Marcin Bochynek
Stadium - Odra (12,000)

CLUB DIRECTORY

Klub Sportowy Ruch Chorzow
ul. Cicha 6, 41-506 Chorzow
tel - (032) 462012/461040
Year of Formation - 1920
President - Krystian Rogala
Secretary - Ksawery Bibrzycki
Coach - Jerzy Wyrobek
Stadium - Ruch (30,000)

MAJOR HONOURS
League Championship - (14)
1933, 1934, 1935, 1936, 1938, 1951, 1952, 1953, 1960, 1968, 1974, 1975, 1979, 1989.
Domestic Cup - (3) 1951, 1974, 1996.

CLUB DIRECTORY

Kolejowy Klub Sportowy Polonia Warszawa
ul. Konwiktorska 6, 00-206 Warszawa
tel - (022) 6351256/6351684/6351893
Year of Formation - 1911
President - Janusz Dorosiewicz
Secretary - Krzysztof Dmoszynski
Coach - Grzegorz Bakalarczyk; Stefan Majewski
Stadium - Polonia (15,000)

MAJOR HONOURS
League Championship - (1) 1946.

CLUB DIRECTORY

Towarzystwo Sportowe Wisla Krakow
ul. Reymonta 22, 30-039 Krakow
tel - (012) 377120/101532/101509
Year of Formation - 1906
President - Piotr Skrobowski
Coach - Lucjan Franczak; Henryk Apostel
Stadium - Wisla (12,000)

MAJOR HONOURS
League Championship - (5)
1927, 1928, 1949, 1950, 1978.
Domestic Cup - (2) 1926, 1967.

PORTUGAL

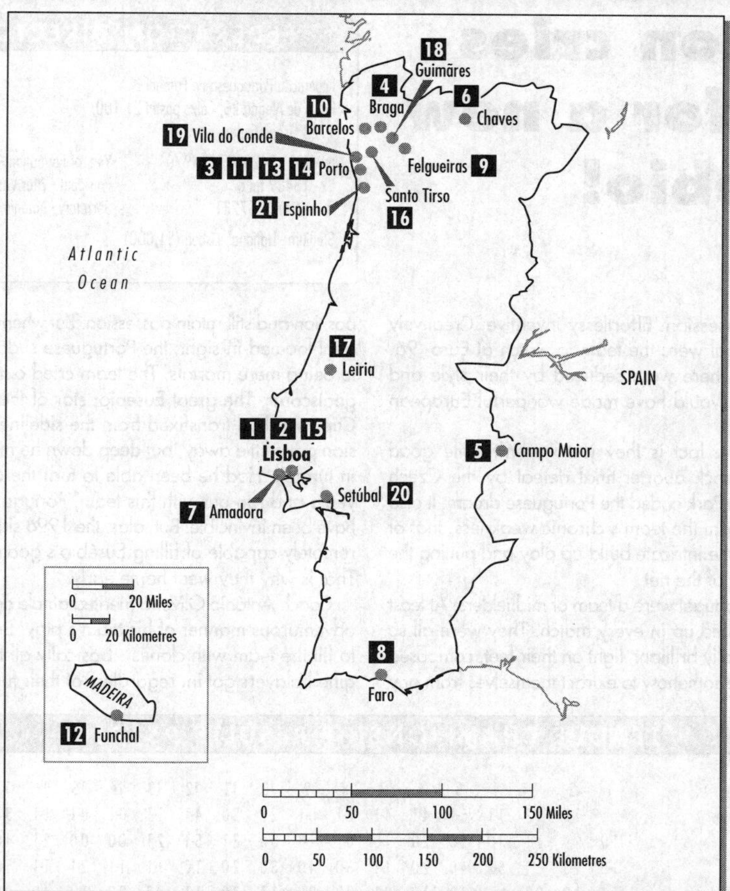

1	CF OS BELENENSES	783	12	CS MARÍTIMO	794
2	SL BENFICA	784	13	FC PORTO	795
3	BOAVISTA FC	785	14	SC SALGUEIROS	796
4	SC BRAGA	786	15	SPORTING CP	797
5	SC CAMPOMAIORENSE	787	16	FC TIRSENSE	798
6	GD CHAVES	788	17	UNIÃO LEIRIA	799
7	CF ESTRELA AMADORA	789	18	VITÓRIA GUIMARÃES	800
8	SC FARENSE	790	19	RIO AVE FC	801
9	FC FELGUEIRAS	791	20	VITÓRIA SETÚBAL	801
10	GIL VICENTE FC	792	21	SC ESPINHO	801
11	LEÇA FC	793			

PEERLESS PORTO TRIUMPH AGAIN

Nation cries out for a new Eusébio!

FEDERATION DIRECTORY

Federação Portuguesa de Futebol
Praça de Alegria 25, Caixa postal 21 100,
1128 Lisboa Codex

tel - (01) 3428207/8/9/0
tlx - 13489 fpf p
fax - (01) 3467231

Year of Formation - 1914
President - Vítor Vasques
Secretary - António Sequeira

Stadium - National, Lisboa (51,000)

Dazzling in possession. Effortlessy inventive. Creatively inspired. Portugal were the team to watch at Euro '96. Neutrals everywhere were seduced by their style and elegance. They would have made wonderful European champions.

And yet... the fact is they just weren't quite good enough. The shock quarter-final defeat by the Czech Republic at Villa Park ended the Portuguese dream. It also served to highlight the team's chronic weakness, that of finishing off all the intricate build-up play and putting the ball in the back of the net.

Essentially, Portugal were a team of midfielders. At least eight of them lined up in every match. They were all so similar. Technically brilliant, light on their feet, composed on the ball, able somehow to extract themselves from any position and still retain possession. But when the opposition goal loomed in sight, the Portuguese suddenly returned to being mere mortals. The team cried out for a ruthless goalscorer. The great Eusébio, star of the 1966 World Cup, watched transfixed from the sidelines. His expression gave little away, but deep down he must have been in turmoil. Had he been able to turn the clock back 30 years and run out with this team, Portugal would surely have been invincible. But, alas, the 1996 side had nobody remotely capable of filling Eusébio's goalscoring boots. That is why they went home early.

Coach António Oliveira merited ample applause for the adventurous manner of his team's play. But his decision to fill the team with clones - basically all the technically gifted players got in, regardless of their function - was a

LEAGUE CHAMPIONSHIP RESULTS 95/96

		1	2	3	4	5	6	7	8	9	10	11	12	13	14	15	16	17	18
1	CF Os Belenenses		1-0	1-2	1-1	3-1	4-1	4-1	2-1	0-1	2-2	5-0	4-1	1-1	0-1	0-1	1-1	3-1	1-0
2	SL Benfica	1-0		1-1	3-0	2-0	2-0	1-0	0-1	1-0	3-0	3-1	5-1	2-1	0-0	0-0	2-1	4-0	1-1
3	Boavista FC	1-0	1-3		5-2	4-0	2-0	1-1	3-0	4-0	3-0	2-0	1-0	1-1	1-1	2-1	1-1	5-0	2-1
4	SC Braga	1-1	1-2	2-0		1-0	1-0	2-1	3-2	2-0	1-1	3-0	1-1	0-3	2-2	1-3	4-0	0-0	4-0
5	SC Campomaiorense	2-3	0-0	0-2	2-0		2-1	2-1	1-0	2-0	2-0	1-1	3-1	0-1	0-0	0-1	3-1	4-2	0-1
6	GD Chaves	1-0	1-2	2-3	1-0	4-1		0-0	2-1	1-0	1-0	2-2	0-2	2-3	1-1	1-1	2-0	0-1	1-2
7	CF Estrela Amadora	2-2	0-1	0-0	4-2	2-0	2-3		1-1	2-1	3-1	1-0	1-1	1-1	1-1	1-1	0-0	2-4	0-0
8	SC Farense	1-3	1-3	2-0	1-0	3-1	0-0	1-0		0-0	5-0	2-0	2-0	0-2	4-1	0-1	2-1	1-1	0-1
9	FC Felgueiras	0-0	1-2	2-0	1-1	3-0	2-2	2-1	3-1		2-2	1-2	0-3	1-1	2-0	0-1	0-1	3-0	0-3
10	Gil Vicente FC	0-0	1-2	1-1	1-2	3-1	2-0	0-1	2-2	2-0		0-0	1-0	0-1	1-1	0-2	1-0	1-0	2-0
11	Leça FC	0-5	0-0	0-3	0-1	4-1	4-1	0-2	2-1	1-0	0-2		0-0	0-2	1-1	1-1	3-1	0-1	1-0
12	CS Marítimo	1-2	2-2	2-0	2-1	3-0	0-2	1-1	0-0	0-2	1-0	2-0		1-1	3-1	0-5	1-0	1-0	4-0
13	FC Porto	1-0	3-0	1-0	6-3	5-0	2-0	6-0	2-0	6-2	2-0	2-0	6-0		2-0	2-1	5-0	1-0	2-3
14	SC Salgueiros	1-3	4-2	0-2	0-0	0-2	2-2	0-0	1-0	0-0	2-3	3-0	2-0	0-4		2-2	1-1	4-0	1-2
15	Sporting CP	3-1	2-0	0-0	0-1	7-1	4-1	6-2	5-0	4-0	4-1	2-0	2-0	0-2	2-2		1-0	0-0	2-3
16	FC Tirsense	0-0	0-1	1-3	2-0	2-0	2-1	0-0	2-1	0-0	1-1	1-3	2-1	2-4	2-0	1-1		0-1	2-2
17	União Leiria	1-0	0-2	1-0	1-0	4-0	4-1	2-1	1-0	0-0	2-0	1-3	0-4	0-0	3-2	1-2	5-1		1-2
18	Vitória Guimarães	1-0	2-4	1-3	1-1	4-0	2-1	3-0	1-0	2-0	2-0	2-0	6-0	0-2	1-2	1-1	2-1	3-0	

LEAGUE CHAMPIONSHIP FINAL TABLE 95/96

			Home					Away					Total					
		Pd	W	D	L	F	A	W	D	L	F	A	W	D	L	F	A	Pt	GD
1	FC Porto	34	16	0	1	54	9	10	6	1	30	11	26	6	2	84	20	84	+64
2	SL Benfica	34	12	4	1	31	7	10	3	4	26	20	22	7	5	57	27	73	+30
3	Sporting CP	34	11	3	3	44	14	8	7	2	25	13	19	10	5	69	27	67	+42
4	Boavista FC	34	12	4	1	39	11	7	4	6	20	17	19	8	7	59	28	65	+31
5	Vitória Guimarães	34	11	2	4	34	15	8	3	6	21	24	19	5	10	55	39	62	+16
6	CF Os Belenenses	34	9	4	4	33	16	5	5	7	20	17	14	9	11	53	33	51	+20
7	União Leiria	34	10	2	5	27	18	4	3	10	11	32	14	5	15	38	50	47	-12
8	SC Braga	34	9	5	3	29	16	3	4	10	15	31	12	9	13	44	47	45	-3
9	CS Marítimo	34	9	4	4	24	17	3	3	11	15	36	12	7	15	39	53	43	-14
10	SC Farense	34	9	3	5	25	14	1	3	13	11	31	10	6	18	36	45	36	-9
11	Gil Vicente FC	34	7	5	5	18	13	2	4	11	13	36	9	9	16	31	49	36	-18
12	SC Salgueiros	34	5	6	6	23	23	2	9	6	16	26	7	15	12	39	49	36	-10
13	CF Estrela Amadora	34	5	9	3	23	19	2	5	10	12	31	7	14	13	35	50	35	-15
14	Leça FC	34	6	4	7	17	22	3	3	11	12	33	9	7	18	29	55	34	-26
15	GD Chaves	34	7	4	6	22	19	2	3	12	16	37	9	7	18	38	56	34	-18
16	FC Felgueiras	34	6	5	6	23	20	2	4	11	6	27	8	9	17	29	47	33	-18
17	SC Campomaiorense	34	9	3	5	24	15	1	0	16	8	54	10	3	21	32	69	33	-37
18	FC Tirsense	34	6	6	5	20	19	1	4	12	10	34	7	10	17	30	53	31	-23

N.B. When two or more teams are level on points, classification is determined by the results of the matches between them.

risky one, to say the least. Sá Pinto was his first-choice central striker, but he did not fit the bill as João Pinto's partner. Domingos, a prolific striker in the Portuguese league, was strangely only ever used as a substitute, while Paulo Alves, a more direct forward with a fine scoring record for the national team, oddly failed to make even the squad.

Portugal scored five goals in their four games. On the number of chances created from midfield, they could and should have doubled that tally. There were three neat finishes - from Figo, João Pinto and Domingos - in the 3-0 victory over Croatia that enabled Portugal to qualify for the quarter-finals as Group D winners. But against Denmark, Turkey and the Czech Republic similar opportunities were squandered. When substitute Cadete (another underused striker) missed a simple header late on against the Czechs, that was the end of Portugal's tournament. A real chance of glory had gone.

Nevertheless, the men in red and green left behind them many pleasant memories. Ther opening performance against Denmark in Sheffield was mesmeric. The Hillsborough crowd could have been forgiven for believing that they were watching one of the great Brazilian sides of the past such was the arrogant, flowing quality of their touch and movement. And there were snippets of genius on display in all of their other games (except in that abject second half against the Czechs). Rui Costa had a magnificent tournament, bestriding the Portuguese midfield with poise and panache. The other three big names - Figo, João Pinto and Paulo Sousa - never reached Rui Costa's level of consistency, but their talent was there for all to see, albeit in fits and starts. At the back Fernando Couto looked very solid and accomplished, while goalkeeper Vítor Baía recovered well from his early aberration against the Danes. On the flanks, too, there were some fine exhibitions from Secretário, Dimas and Folha.

INTERNATIONAL HONOURS

World Cup Finals appearances: 1966 (3rd), 1986

European Championship appearances: 1960, 1984 (semi-finals), 1996 (qtr-finals)

European Club Competitions

Champions' Cup	SL Benfica (1961, 1962) FC Porto (1987)
Cup-winners' Cup	Sporting CP (1964)
Super Cup	FC Porto (1987)
World Club Cup	FC Porto (1987)

One thing is certain. This Portugal side will be around for a long while yet. Only the veteran Oceano is past it. The rest are still primed and hungry and sure to benefit from the experience of Euro '96, which, lest it be forgotten, was Portugal's first major tournament for a decade. Plus, the likes of Nuno Gomes, Dani and Dominguez from the team which reached the Olympic semi-finals in Atlanta will soon be knocking on the door of the senior side. António Oliveira will not be around to coach them, however. Euro '96 proved to be his one and only tournament in charge when it was announced in the summer that he was off to take over at FC Porto. In a country where the top clubs still assume a higher profile than the national team, Oliveira will consider the move as a step upwards. How his successor in the national team hot seat, Artur Jorge, will feel about his new job remains to be seen. He has been in charge of Portugal before, but his major achievements have come at club sides, notably FC Porto and Paris Saint-Germain.

It is safe to assume that had Artur Jorge been in charge of Portugal (rather than a much inferior Switzerland) at Euro '96 they would have played in a different style. Less attractive, probably. More efficient, definitely. The new coach is not a man who looks favourably upon self-indulgence and showmanship. His cavaliers have always been cautious ones. Perhaps Artur Jorge will be able to harness all the great talent in the team and make them into a more effective unit. The challenge of the World Cup qualifiers, in which Portugal will be up against, among others, Germany, will test his credentials to the full. If he can unearth a decent goalscorer, then he will be half way to completing his task.

Portuguese journalists seeking to explain the lack of a 'Eusébio-type forward' in the present national team often point to the fact that there are too many foreign strikers in the Portuguese league. But in the 95/96 season the top two names in the goalscoring lists were current Portuguese internationals - Domingos, of FC Porto, and João Pinto, of Benfica.

Domingos finished comfortably on top of the pile with 25 goals and played a major rôle in helping Porto to retain the Portuguese title. It was a comfortable ride for

DOMESTIC CUP RESULTS

FOURTH ROUND
FC Tirsense 0, SL Benfica 2
GD Chaves 1, Sporting CP 3
CF Os Belenenses 2, SC Braga 1
CF Estrela Amadora 2, CS Marítimo 3
União Leiria 3, SC Salgueiros 1
SC Campomaiorense 1, CD Nacional 0
Gil Vicente FC 0, GD Estoril-Praia 2
FC Paços Ferreira 1, Vitória Guimarães 4
FC Porto 6, Amora FC 0
SC Farense 3, Varzim SC 2
Leça FC 3, ASS Naval 1 de Maio 2
Lusitânia Lourosa 1, FC Felgueiras 1 (aet)
(replay) FC Felgueiras 1, Lusitânia Lourosa 0
Anadia FC 2, Boavista FC 8
Académica Coimbra 1, SC Espinho 0
FC Alverca 0, Rio Ave FC 2
FC Penafiel 4, Silves FC 0
União Madeira 0, SC Vila Real 1
Portimonense SC 2, Moreirense FC 1
CD Torres Novas 1, União Lamas 3
AD Camacha 3, SC Beira Mar 0
Louletano DC 0, Vitória Setúbal 2
CD Feirense 4, Pescadores C. Caparica 0
CD Arrifanense 0, Desportivo Aves 2 (aet)
SC Olhanense 2, UD Oliveirense 1
Casa Pia AC 3, FC Infesta 2
FC Lixa 4, AC Cucujães 1
SC Lamego 0, CD Alcaíns 0 (aet)
(replay) CD Alcaíns 0, SC Lamego 1
FC Marco 4, Caldas SC 3 (aet)
FC Barreirense 2, O Elvas 3

FIFTH ROUND
Sporting CP 2, Boavista FC 1
Académica Coimbra 2, CS Marítimo 2 (aet)
(replay) CS Marítimo 2, Académica Coimbra 1
O Elvas 0, Vitória Guimarães 1 (aet)
SC Farense 2, CD Feirense 2 (aet)
(replay) CD Feirense 2, SC Farense 2
(aet; 3-4 on pens.)
GD Estoril-Praia 1, União Leiria 1 (aet)
(replay) União Leiria 0, GD Estoril-Praia 0
(aet; 4-3 on pens.)
Vitória Setúbal 1, SC Olhanense 2
SC Lamego 2, Casa Pia AC 1
FC Penafiel 6, FC Lixa 0
Rio Ave FC 0, SC Campomaiorense 1
SC Portimonense 2, Leça FC 1
FC Porto 0, União Lamas 0 (aet)
(replay) União Lamas 1, FC Porto 3
Desportivo Aves 1, SC Vila Real 2
AD Camacha 1, FC Felgueiras 2
CF Os Belenenses 2, FC Marco 0

SIXTH ROUND
Sporting CP 4, SC Campomairense 1
SC Farense 1, SL Benfica 1 (aet)
(replay) SL Benfica 3 SC Farense 0
SC Lamego 1, FC Porto 1 (aet)
(replay) FC Porto 1, SC Lamego 0
Vitória Guimarães 1, CF Os Belenenses 0
FC Felgueiras 1, FC Penafiel 2
CS Marítimo 2, SC Vila Real 0
Portimonense SC 0, União Leiria 1

QUARTER-FINALS
SL Benfica 1, Vitória Guimarães 0 (aet)
União Leiria 2, CS Marítimo 1
SC Olhanense 1, Sporting CP 2
FC Porto 2, FC Penafiel 0

SEMI-FINALS
SL Benfica 2, União Leiria 0
FC Porto 1, Sporting CP 1 (aet)
(replay) Sporting CP 1, FC Porto 0 (aet)

FINAL
18/05/96, Lisbon
SL BENFICA 3 Mauro Airez (8), João Pinto (40, 67)
SPORTING CP 1 Carlos Xavier (84p)
referee - Vítor Pereira
SL BENFICA - Preud'homme; Calado, Ricardo, Hélder, Dimas, Kenedy (Iliev 86), Paulo Bento, Valdo, Bruno Caires (Marcelo 88), João Pinto, Mauro Airez (Paredão 83).
SPORTING CP - Costinha; Luís Miguel, Naybet, Marco Aurélio, Nélson, Vidigal, Peixe (Paulo Alves 34), Pedro Martins, Afonso Martins, Sá Pinto, Yordanov (Dominguez 46).

the defending champions, more straightforward even than the previous season's triumph, with their final winning margin up to 11 points compared with a nine-point gap in 1994/95.

FC Porto may not have the historical prestige of their two Lisbon rivals Benfica and Sporting, but they are undoubtedly Portugal's Team of the Nineties. The 95/96 title was their fifth in the present decade, taking the club's all-time total to 15 wins, just one behind Sporting.

All the qualities which Bobby Robson's team manifested

NATIONAL TEAM APPEARANCES 95/96

Coach - ANTÓNIO OLIVEIRA	LIE	NIR	AUT	IRL	ENG	FRA	GER	GRE	IRL	DEN	TUR	CRO	TCH	Cps	Gls
ALFREDO (05/10/62) - Boavista FC	G82													3	-
OCEANO (29/07/62) - Sporting CP	D46	M	M	M			M84	s46	M68	M37		M	M65	43	8
FERNANDO COUTO (02/08/69) - Parma (ITA)	D	D		D	D	D	D		D	D	D	D	D	36	4
JORGE COSTA (04/10/71) - FC Porto	D	D74	D		D	D	D							16	-
DIMAS (16/02/69) - SL Benfica	D55				D	D	D75	s57	D	D	D	D	D	10	-
SECRETÁRIO (12/05/70) - FC Porto	M	D	M59	D	D	M	D84		s73			D	D	15	1
RUI COSTA (29/03/72) - Fiorentina (ITA)	M	M82	M	M		M	M64			M	M	M61	M	25	7
PAULINHO SANTOS (21/11/70) - FC Porto	M	D	D	D		M60			D	D	D			14	2
RUI BARROS (24/11/65) - FC Porto	A	s74												34	4
DOMINGOS (02/01/69) - FC Porto	A	A	A72	A68				A73		s63		s46	s46	30	8
FOLHA (21/05/71) - FC Porto	A	A	s46	s72	M69	A75	A62	M57	A	s37	M46		s65	22	5
SÁ PINTO (10/10/72) - Sporting CP	s46		s59		A		A	A46	s46	A	A65	A46	A46	14	1
PAULO ALVES (10/12/69) - Sporting CP	s55	s82			s46	A	s62	s57						11	7
RUI CORREIA (22/10/67) - SC Braga	s82													1	-
VÍTOR BAÍA (15/10/69) - FC Porto		G	G	G85			G	G	G	G	G	G	G	45	-
PAULO SOUSA (30/08/70) - Juventus (ITA)		M	M	M	M46		M			M79	M	M70	M	28	-
FIGO (04/11/72) - FC Barcelona (ESP)		M		M	M46		M46			M63	M	M	M83	31	5
NÉLSON (05/11/71) - Sporting CP			D			D62	s84	D46						5	-
HÉLDER (21/03/71) - SL Benfica			D	D	D	D79	s84	D	D	D	D	D	D	23	2
JOÃO PINTO (19/08/71) - SL Benfica			A46	A72	A63			M	M	A	A77	A	A	28	7
DOMINGUEZ (16/02/74) - Sporting CP			s72		s46	s62								3	-
CADETE (27/08/68) - Sporting CP/Celtic (SCO)				s68					A73		s65		s83	25	5
NENO (27/01/62) - Vitória Guimarães				s85	G	G								9	-
DANI (02/11/76) - Sporting CP					s63	s75								2	-
PEDRO BARBOSA (06/08/70) - Sporting CP					s69	s60						s61		10	1
NUNO GOMES (05/07/76) - Boavista FC						s79								1	-
VÍTOR PANEIRA (16/02/66) - Vitória Guimarães							s46		M46					44	4
CAPUCHO (21/02/72) - Vitória Guimarães							s64	s46						2	-
FERNANDO MENDES (05/11/66) - CF Os Belenenses							s75	D						11	-
PAULO MADEIRA (06/09/70) - CF Os Belenenses								D57						12	-
TAVARES (25/04/65) - Boavista FC								M	M	s79	s46	s70		8	-
PAULO BENTO (20/06/69) - SL Benfica								M46						4	-
NEVES (24/12/70) - CF Os Belenenses								s46						1	-
TULIPA (16/10/72) - CF Os Belenenses								s73						1	-
PORFÍRIO (28/09/73) - União Leiria									s68		s77			2	-

EUROPEAN CUPS RESULTS 95/96

CHAMPIONS' CUP

● FC PORTO

Champions' League

1st match FC NANTES (FRA)

A 0-0
Vítor Baía; João Pinto, Paulinho Santos, Aloísio, José Carlos, Emerson (Bino 89), Latapy, Secretário, Rui Barros, Domingos (Folha 77), Mielcarski.

2nd match AAB (DEN)

H 2-0 Rui Barros (40, 63)
Vítor Baía; João Pinto (Bino 73), José Carlos, Jorge Costa, Paulinho Santos, Emerson, Secretário, Latapy, Drulovic (Folha 80), Domingos, Mielcarski (Rui Barros 35).

3rd match PANATHINAIKOS (GRE)

H 0-1
Vítor Baía; João Pinto (Folha 56), Paulinho Santos, Aloísio, José Carlos, Emerson, Secretário (Bino 84), Rui Barros (Jorge Couto 76), Domingos, Latapy, Drulovic.

4th match PANATHINAIKOS (GRE)

A 0-0
Vítor Baía; Secretário, Rui Jorge, Aloísio, Jorge Costa, Emerson, Edmilson, Rui Barros (Bino 78), Domingos, Paulinho Santos, Drulovic (Folha 85).

5th match FC NANTES (FRA)

H 2-2 Drulovic (10), José Carlos (55)
Vítor Baía; Secretário, José Carlos, Jorge Costa, Paulinho Santos, Lipcsei, Emerson, Edmilson (Folha 81), Rui Barros (Jorge Couto 59), Drulovic (Bino 81), Domingos.

6th match AAB (DEN)

A 2-2 Emerson (63, 75)
Vítor Baía; João Pinto (Rui Barros 52), Rui Jorge (Folha 67), Aloísio, José Carlos (João M. Pinto 74), Emerson, Drulovic, Secretário, Domingos, Paulinho Santos, Edmilson.

CUP-WINNERS' CUP

● SPORTING CP

1st round MACCABI HAIFA (ISR)

H 4-0 Pedro Barbosa (7, 10, 47), Sá Pinto (88)
Costinha; Nélson, Naybet, Marco Aurélio, Nuno Valente, Oceano, Pedro Martins (Vidigal 85), Pedro Barbosa (Paulo Alves 75), Sá Pinto, Amunike, Ouattara (Dominguez 63).

A 0-0
Costinha; Nélson, Naybet, Marco Aurélio, Nuno Valente, Oceano, Pedro Martins (Vidigal 75), Pedro Barbosa (Dominguez 46), Sá Pinto, Amunike, Ouattara (Paulo Alves 62).

2nd round SK RAPID WIEN (AUT)

H 2-0 Sá Pinto (12), Paulo Alves (23)
Costinha; Nélson, Naybet, Marco Aurélio, Vujacic, Sá Pinto (Afonso Martins 84), Pedro Martins, Oceano, Paulo Alves (Pedro Barbosa 86), Assis (Dani 71), Dominguez.

A 0-4 (aet)
Costinha; Nélson, Naybet, Oceano, Vujacic, Marco Aurélio, Sá Pinto, Pedro Martins, Paulo Alves (Carlos Xavier 87), Dominguez (Pedro Barbosa 85), Amunike (Dani 66).

UEFA CUP

● SL BENFICA

1st round K LIERSE SK (BEL)

A 3-1 Valdo (25p), Marcelo (51), Paulo Bento (62)
Preud'homme; King (Calado 46), Paulo Perreira, Hélder, Dimas, Paulo Bento, Kenedy, Valdo, João Pinto, Marcelo (Edgar 72), Panduru (Maniche 83).

H 2-1 João Pinto (25), Kenedy (60)
Preud'homme; Calado, Ricardo, Hélder, Dimas, Paulo Bento, Maniche (Bruno Caires 55), João Pinto, Marcelo, Edgar (Kenedy 55), Panduru (Paulo Pereira 89).

2nd round RODA JC (HOL)

H 1-0 Panduru (79)
Preud'homme; Marinho, Paredão, Hélder, Dimas, Paulo Bento, Kenedy (Bruno Caires 88), João Pinto, Marcelo (Edgar 30), Ailton, Panduru.

A 2-2 Hassan (86, 90)
Preud'homme; Paulo Pereira, Ricardo, Hélder, Dimas, Paredão, Bruno Caires (Edgar 77), Kenedy, Calado (Marcelo 71), João Pinto, Hassan.

3rd round FC BAYERN MÜNCHEN (GER)

A 1-4 Dimas (30)
Preud'homme; Marinho (Edgar 56), Paulo Pereira, Hélder, Dimas, Paulo Bento, Calado, João Pinto, Hassan, Valdo, Kenedy (Marcelo 75).

H 1-3 Valdo (14)
Brassard; Marinho, Ricardo, Hélder, Pedro Henriques, Paulo Bento, Calado, Edgar, Hassan, Valdo, Marcelo.

● VITÓRIA GUIMARÃES

1st round R STANDARD LIEGE (BEL)

H 3-1 Gilmar (22, 89), Edinho (69)
Neno; José Carlos, Arley, Tanta (Basílio 62), Quim Berto, Soeiro, Vítor Paneira, N'Dinga, Gilmar, Capucho (Kupresanin 59), Ricardo (Edinho 41).

A 0-0
Neno; José Carlos, Vítor Silva, Tanta, Basílio, Soeiro, Vítor Paneira (Kupresanin 60), N'Dinga, Edinho (Gilmar 67), Capucho, Quim Berto.

2nd round FC BARCELONA (ESP)

A 0-3
Neno; José Carlos, Vítor Silva, Tanta, Quim Berto, Soeiro, Vítor Paneira (Kupresanin 74), N'Dinga, Edinho, Zahovic (Gilmar 69), Capucho.

H 0-4
Neno; José Carlos, Vítor Silva, Tanta, Quim Berto, Soeiro (Vítor Paneira 46), N'Dinga, Capucho, Edinho, Kupresanin (Marco Freitas 65), Zahovic (Gilmar 65).

● SC FARENSE

1st round OLYMPIQUE LYONNAIS (FRA)

H 0-1
Rufai; Paiva, Idalécio, Jorge Soares, Eugénio, Barrigana (Christian 13), Tozé (Marco Nuno 56), Carlos Costa, Helcinho (Camilo 78), Hajri, Djukic.

A 0-1
Rufai; Paiva, Idalécio (Tozé 68), Jorge Soares, Eugénio, Pedro Miguel (Romicha 84), Carlos Costa, Punisic, Helcinho, Hajri, Barrigana (Christian 49).

in 94/95 were repeated in their title defence - consistency, stability, resilience, hard work and an unerring self-belief. These were all characteristics absent from the two Lisbon giants, whose trials and tribulations both on and off the field during the campaign undoubtedly made life easier for their northern rivals.

Porto could have been excused for making a slow start to the season. Coach Robson was back in England recuperating from facial cancer surgery and did not return until mid-October. But the 'Dragoons' began brilliantly, beating Sporting 2-1 at home (after being a goal behind) in the opening match of the season and dropping just two points (away to newly-promoted Felgueiras) before Robson returned to work.

All of the team's big home matches were scheduled for the first half of the season, and Porto won them all. Having seen off Sporting on the opening day, they overcame local rivals and joint league leaders Boavista 1-0 in early October. Then, a month later, they completed an important hat-trick with the best victory of the lot - 3-0 against Benfica. It was a masterful performance by Porto, and one that had Robson himself cooing in unrestrained admiration of his team. Two goals from the ever-reliable Domingos plus a glorious effort from Hungarian import Péter Lipcsei decided the outcome of an extremely high-quality encounter, and the result left Porto six points clear at the top. Even with three points being awarded for a win for the first time in Portugal, the gap already looked unbridgeable.

But success at home was not matched by Porto's performances in the UEFA Champions' League. Drawn in a relatively modest group, the Portuguese champions anticipated a hazard-free passage into the quarter-finals. They started brightly enough, with a 0-0 draw in France and a 2-0 win at home to latecomers AaB of Denmark. But on the day that the club welcomed back Bobby Robson to the Das Antas stadium, it all went wrong. Despite dominating a Panathinaikos side which managed just two shots all game, Porto lost the match 0-1. The wound, though deep, was not fatal. After drawing the return match 0-0 in Athens, Porto knew that they could still reach the quarter-finals if they won their last home game, against Nantes. Twice they were forced to come from behind after falling victim to two more sucker punches on the counter-attack, but, true to their tradition, Porto did not give up, and late in the game they were awarded a penalty and with it the chance to win the match 3-2. But Domingos missed the kick and Porto's European dream was over.

In the league, however, there were no such hard-luck stories. Relentlessy Porto pushed on into the new year, increasing their lead to an uncatchable advantage when another Domingos double secured a 2-0 victory away to Sporting. With the title securely packaged, focus switched

Porto coach Bobby Robson

to the team's long unbeaten run which threatened to surpass the record 56-match sequence set by Benfica 20 years earlier. Away to Boavista, Robson's men came within seconds of defeat until Lipcsei rescued them with a last-ditch equaliser. But the following month, with the run standing at 53 games, it did come to an end. And, fittingly, it was Benfica who brought it to a halt with a 2-1 victory in the Stadium of Light.

For that match, and several others in the run-in, Porto had to make do without their goalkeeper Vítor Baía, who had been suspended for two months by the Portuguese FA after physically assaulting an official of Campomaiorense in the riotous aftermath of a league encounter which Porto had won with another last-minute goal. Vítor Baía returned for the final match of the season, and that was to be his last for the club as he agreed to follow Bobby Robson to Barcelona at the season's end. With two other key players, Secretário and Emerson, also quitting the club in the summer, for Real Madrid and Middlesbrough respectively, Porto, and their new coach António Oliveira, will certainly have their work cut out as they seek a hat-trick of Portuguese titles - something the club has never previously achieved in its 103-year history.

Benfica will be desperate to bring the championship trophy back to Lisbon in 1997. They had another disturbingly inept season in 95/96. Only a late flourish, engendered by that confidence-boosting 2-1 win at home to Porto, brought them up into the runners-up spot. But to finish 11 points adrift was unacceptable. Benfica's season was saved by victory in the Portuguese Cup final, where, inspired by an in-form João Pinto, they easily defeated Sporting 3-1. But even that triumph was tainted by calamity. Just after Benfica scored their opening goal a firework was hurled into the Sporting end of the ground, and a spectator was killed. News of the tragedy spread around the ground, and as a mark of respect for the dead fan the Cup was not presented to Benfica at the end of the game.

Benfica's woes were chiefly in the first half of the campaign. Two depressing draws in the opening two home games ended Artur Jorge's brief reign at the club. He was replaced for the remainder of the season by caretaker coach Mário Wilson, pending the arrival in the summer of 1996 of Paulo Autuori from Brazilian champions Botafogo. Defeats away to both Sporting and Porto compounded Benfica's misery, but they were as nothing compared to the inferiority complex induced by the double thrashing the team received from Bayern Munich in the third round of the UEFA Cup.

Benfica's European downfall meant that no Portuguese sides made it past Christmas in the three UEFA club competitions. Farense and Vitória Guimarães were eliminated in earlier rounds of the UEFA Cup, while Sporting, going strongly in the Cup-winners' Cup after three matches without conceding a goal, suddenly crashed out after extra-time to Rapid Vienna having come within seconds of quarter-final qualification.

That defeat in Austria summed up yet another frustrating, disappointing year for Sporting and their fans. The previous season's long-awaited Portuguese Cup triumph was supposed to be a new beginning for the club, but it had quite the opposite effect. Figo, Balakov and Juskowiak left for pastures new. A welter of new players arrived, but none of them commanded the popularity of their predecessors. The season began with Pedro Santana Lopes as president and Carlos Queiros as coach, but neither was in place by the end of it. The writing was on the wall for Queiroz after the 0-2 home defeat by Porto in January. He lasted another month before being jettisoned at a cost to the club of roughly £500,000.

Sporting gave their supporters something to cheer when, with Fernando Mendes now installed as coach, they defeated Porto after a replay in the Cup semi-final. But they were outclassed in the final by their great rivals Benfica, so another season ended with nothing more to show for their efforts and expenditure than a *de rigueur* place in the UEFA Cup.

Predictably, Boavista and Vitória Guimarães joined Sporting in the UEFA Cup zone, the former sacrificing a possible second place with a wretched run of form in the early spring. As is customary, the bottom half of the table produced a real scrap for survival, with half of the teams in the division involved until the axe finally fell on Tirsense, Campomaiorense and Felgueiras. Rio Ave won the Second Division, bringing Vitória Setúbal and Espinho up with them. It was a good year to get promoted, for in 1997/98 the top division is to be reduced to 16 teams, with plans to trim it still further in 1998/99.

NATIONAL TEAM RESULTS 95/96

Date	Opponent	Venue	City	Score	Scorers
15/08/95	Liechtenstein (ECQ)	A	Eschen	7-0	Domingos (25), Paulinho Santos (33), Rui Costa (41, 71p), Paulo Alves (67, 73, 90)
03/09/95	Northern Ireland (ECQ)	H	Oporto	1-1	Domingos (47)
11/10/95	Austria (ECQ)	A	Vienna	1-1	Paulinho Santos (49)
15/11/95	Rep. Ireland (ECQ)	H	Lisbon	3-0	Rui Costa (59), Hélder (74), Cadete (89)
12/12/95	England	A	Wembley	1-1	Paulo Alves (58)
24/01/96	France	A	Paris	2-3	Fernando Couto (23), Rui Costa (31)
21/02/96	Germany	H	Oporto	1-2	Folha (51)
27/03/96	Greece	H	Lisbon	1-0	Oceano (87p)
29/05/96	Republic of Ireland	A	Dublin	1-0	Folha (90)
09/06/96	Denmark (ECF)	N	Sheffield	1-1	Sá Pinto (53)
14/06/96	Turkey (ECF)	N	Nottingham	1-0	Fernando Couto (66)
19/06/96	Croatia (ECF)	N	Nottingham	3-0	Figo (4), João Pinto (33), Domingos (83)
23/06/96	Czech Republic (ECF)	N	Birmingham	0-1	

TOP SCORERS

Goals	Player
25	DOMINGOS (FC Porto)
18	JOÃO PINTO (SL Benfica)
15	EDINHO (Vitória Guimarães)
	Leo LEWIS (FC Felgueiras)
14	ARTUR (Boavista FC)
	CONSTANTINO (Leça FC)
13	MAURÍCIO (União Leiria)
	EDMILSON (FC Porto)
12	JIMMY (SC Campomaiorense)
10	ALEX (CS Marítimo)
	RENATO (CF Estrela Amadora)
	PAULO ALVES (Sporting CP)
	CÉSAR BRITO (CF Os Belenenses)

PLAYERS OF THE SEASON

DOMINGOS

Quite why Portuguese coach António Oliveira failed to include FC Porto striker Domingos in any of his starting line-ups at Euro '96 remains a mystery. The 27-year-old lost his place to the more aggressive but less potent Sá Pinto and failed to win it back despite an excellent goal against Croatia. Domingos also had his best season yet in domestic football, winning the Portuguese league top scorer title for the first time and spearheading Porto's title triumph. Six of his 25 goals came against arch-rivals Sporting and Benfica, proving that Domingos is clearly a man who relishes the spotlight.

Domingos celebrates his goal against Croatia during Euro '96

JOÃO PINTO

As a team Benfica may have struggled in 95/96, but for their outstanding player, João Pinto, it was a season to remember. He struck a career-best total of 18 goals in the league and almost single-handedly dragged the team back into runners-up spot after a glittering second half of the campaign. He struck a hat-trick in Benfica's final league game then carried his exceptional form into the Portuguese Cup final a week later, where his brace gave Benfica a 3-1 win over Sporting. At Euro '96 João Pinto confirmed his reputation as a high-quality support striker, but the expected avalanche of transfer requests did not materialise, so he decided to stay with Benfica for another year.

SECRETÁRIO

One of the unsung heroes of FC Porto's recent successes is Carlos Alberto Oliveira Secretário. A favourite of Bobby Robson, he epitomises the classic FC Porto virtues of industry, verve and 100% application. His ability as a raiding right-back was put on show in Portugal's final two matches at Euro '96, and he performed excellently in both games. His efforts did not go unnoticed, as Real Madrid - no less - promptly offered him a contract to become the latest foreign member of the Fabio Capello 'Dream Team'. In 1996/97 Secretário will stand comparison with Brazilian left back Roberto Carlos as the pair carry out a double shuffle up the touchlines.

DIMAS

27-year-old Benfica left-back proved his coming of age in international football by appearing from first minute to last in all four of Portugal's matches in England. Faced with stiff competition from FC Porto's Paulinho Santos, Dimas held his place with a series of fine performances, notably against the Czech Republic, when he was one of the few Portuguese players who seemed capable of maintaining the tempo as the dream faded in the second half. Dimas was uncapped before the season started, but after a strong campaign with Benfica he thoroughly earned his national team place. Now he will take some shifting.

PORFÍRIO

When António Oliveira announced his European Championship squad on May 21, one name was greeted with general astonishment. Hugo Cardoso Porfírio had been a leading member of the Under-21 Portuguese team that had reached the Olympics, but he had never played a full international. Furthermore, his club was unfashionable União Leiria. But Porfírio was in, and he went on to make his senior début against the Irish Republic just before Euro '96. Following a trip to Atlanta, the pacy 23-year-old returned from Leiria to his erstwhile club Sporting.

PROFILE
RUI COSTA

The Euro '96 finals were big news in Portugal. The country had been absent from the last two European Championships and World Cups, and 1996 was expected to be the year when the national team's rehabilitation proved to be complete. Much was made in the build-up to the tournament of the exciting individuals in the Portuguese side. Five of them stood out from the pack. There was Figo from Barcelona, Paulo Sousa from Juventus, Fernando Couto from Parma, João Pinto from Benfica, and Rui Costa from Fiorentina.

All of the famous five did enough to uphold or confirm their lofty reputations in England. But only one of them proved himself to be truly world-class.

Rui Manuel César Costa was without doubt one of the stars of Euro '96. His lithe, languid frame glided elegantly through the Portuguese midfield, always on the lookout for the killer pass or the slightest breachable opening in the opposition defence. No other player at Euro '96 showed such masterful control of the ball. In an age when the playmaker, the classic 'number ten', appears to be a dying breed, Rui Costa showed that there is at least one survivor potentially worthy of mention in the same breath as the Hoddles, Platinis and Zicos of the past.

It is hardly a coincidence that Rui Costa earns his living at Italian club Fiorentina. The *Viola* have long had a passionate affinity for the *numero dieci*, with Giancarlo Antognoni and Roberto Baggio having both filled the shirt in the not too distant past. Nowadays the big local hero in Tuscany is Argentine striker Gabriel Batistuta. But Rui Costa is fast closing the gap. Not that there is any particular popularity competition at stake. The two players are the perfect complement for one another. What Rui Costa would give for a goalscorer of Batistuta's quality alongside him in the Portuguese national team!

Success for Rui Costa has come at some speed. A native of Lisbon, he joined Benfica in his teens, but before he could don the famous red shirt he was loaned out to Third Division Fafe. At the time the player felt rejected, but the experience proved positive. He was voted the best player in Division Three and subsequently earned himself a winner's medal in Portugal's 1991 World Youth Cup victory.

The following season Rui Costa returned to Benfica and gradually began to forge a place for himself in the team. One of his most memorable early games was in the European Champions' Cup against Arsenal. He was given the number ten shirt by coach Sven Göran Eriksson and he played a blinder to help Benfica to a brilliant 3-1 win.

Over the course of the next two seasons Rui Costa's appearances in the Benfica first team became more and more frequent, and by the 93/94 campaign he was a regular not only in the Benfica side but also in the Portuguese national team, having made his senior début two days after his 21st birthday in a World Cup qualifier against Switzerland. One of the player's finest performances in a Benfica shirt came on the occasion of his 22nd birthday in a European Cup-winners' Cup tie at home to Parma, when he rounded off a brilliant all-round display with the deciding goal in a 2-1 victory.

Suddenly Serie A clubs were alerted to the young midfielder's exquisite talents. In the summer of 1994 Fiorentina made cash-strapped Benfica an offer they dare not refuse, splashing out £5 million to take the player to Italy. It made Rui Costa the most expensive foreign import of that post-World Cup close season. And with the price tag, of course, came the pressure to succeed.

Rui Costa's first season in Florence was excellent. His second, despite the team's victory in the Italian Cup and strong showing in the league, was comparatively disappointing. But Euro '96 quickly revived his stature, and at only 24, the best of Rui Costa is surely yet to come. Fiorentina could do with some of that immediately as they chase European Cup-winners' Cup glory in 96/97. Portugal will be happy to wait until the 1998 World Cup in France.

CF OS BELENENSES

CLUB DIRECTORY

Clube de Futebol "Os Belenenses"
Avenida do Restelo
1400 Lisboa
tel - (01) 3010461/3011143
fax - (01) 3016525
Year of Formation - 1919
President - José António Matias
Coach - João Alves (96/97 - Quinito)
Stadium - Restelo (42,000)

MAJOR HONOURS
League Championship - (1) 1946.
Domestic Cup - (6)
1927, 1929, 1933, 1942, 1960, 1989.

APPEARANCES 95/96

	P	Ap	(s)	Gls
CALILA	M	1	(19)	5
CATANHA	A	10	(4)	5
CÉSAR BRITO	A	16	(9)	10
CHIPENDA	M	3	(3)	
CHIQUINHO CONDE	A	2	(2)	
DARCI	A		(1)	
FERNANDO MENDES	D	31		2
Youssef FERTOUT (MAR)	A	21	(8)	8
GIOVANELLA	M	17	(2)	3
Tomislav IVKOVIC (CRO)	G	32		
LITO	M	7	(2)	
LULA (BRA)	D	28		
MAURO AIREZ (ARG)	A	6	(3)	
MAURO SOARES	M	4		2
MIGUEL MOTA	M	2		
Abdel M'JID (MAR)	M	16	(4)	2
NEVES	D	23	(2)	1
NITO	M	2		
PACHECO	A	1	(5)	
PAULO GOMES	A	1	(5)	1
PAULO MADEIRA	D	33		2
PEDRO BARNY	D	26	(1)	3
QUIM	A		(2)	
RAUL	D	6	(3)	
ROGÉRIO	D	19	(7)	2
RUI ESTEVES	M	11	(12)	
TAIRA	M	26	(3)	2
TONANHA	A	2	(3)	
TULIPA	M	26	(1)	5
VALENTE	G	2		

LEAGUE RESULTS 1995/96

20/08/95	Boavista FC	A	0-1	
27/08/95	SC Braga	H	1-1	Calila
08/09/95	SC Campomaiorense	A	3-2	M'Jid, Fernando Mendes, Mauro Soares
17/09/95	SC Farense	H	2-1	Mauro Soares, César Brito
22/09/95	SL Benfica	A	0-1	
30/09/95	União Leiria	H	3-1	Fertout, Calila, César Brito
14/10/95	CS Marítimo	A	2-1	Fertout 2
21/10/95	SC Salgueiros	H	0-1	
28/10/95	FC Tirsense	A	0-0	
05/11/95	Vitória Guimarães	H	1-0	Calila
19/11/95	CF Estrela Amadora	A	2-2	César Brito, M'Jid
26/11/95	FC Felgueiras	H	0-1	
08/12/95	Sporting CP	H	0-1	
17/12/95	Gil Vicente FC	A	0-0	
23/12/95	GD Chaves	H	4-1	Tulipa 2, Pedro Barny, Calila
30/12/95	Leça FC	A	5-0	Paulo Madeira, Fertout 2, Tulipa, César Brito (p)
07/01/96	FC Porto	H	1-1	Giovanella
13/01/96	Boavista FC	H	1-2	Fernando Mendes
20/01/96	SC Braga	A	1-1	Rogério
27/01/96	SC Campomaiorense	H	3-1	César Brito, Calila, Fertout
04/02/96	SC Farense	A	3-1	César Brito, Paulo Madeira, Giovanella
11/02/96	SL Benfica	H	1-0	Giovanella
18/02/96	União Leiria	A	0-1	
03/03/96	CS Marítimo	H	4-1	Fertout, Tulipa, og (Robson), Pedro Barny
10/03/96	SC Salgueiros	A	3-1	César Brito 2, Taira
17/03/96	FC Tirsense	H	1-1	Catanha
24/03/96	Vitória Guimarães	A	0-1	
30/03/96	CF Estrela Amadora	H	4-1	Taira, Catanha, Neves (p), Fertout
07/04/96	FC Felgueiras	A	0-0	
14/04/96	Sporting CP	A	1-3	Rogério
21/04/96	Gil Vicente FC	H	2-2	Catanha, Pedro Barny
28/04/96	GD Chaves	A	0-1	
05/05/96	Leça FC	H	5-0	Catanha, Tulipa, César Brito 2, Paulo Gomes
12/05/96	FC Porto	A	0-1	

SL BENFICA

CLUB DIRECTORY

Sport Lisboa e Benfica
Avenida General Norton de Matos
1500 Lisboa
tel - (01) 7266129
fax - (01) 7264761
Year of Formation - 1904
President - Manuel Damásio
Coach - Artur Jorge; Mário Wilson
(96/97 - Paulo Autuori)
Stadium - Sport Lisboa e Benfica (92,385)

MAJOR HONOURS

League Championship - (30) 1936, 1937, 1938, 1942, 1943, 1945, 1950, 1955, 1957, 1960, 1961, 1963, 1964, 1965, 1967, 1968, 1969, 1971, 1972, 1973, 1975, 1976, 1977, 1981, 1983, 1984, 1987, 1989, 1991, 1994.
Domestic Cup - (26)
1930, 1931, 1935, 1940, 1943, 1944, 1949, 1951, 1952, 1953, 1955, 1957, 1959, 1962, 1964, 1969, 1970, 1972, 1980, 1981, 1983, 1985, 1986, 1987, 1993, 1996.
European Champions' Cup - (2) 1961, 1962.

APPEARANCES 95/96

	P	Ap	(s)	Gls
AILTON (BRA)	A	4		
BRASSARD	G	1	(1)	
BRUNO CAIRES	D	12	(4)	
CALADO	M	11	(3)	
DIMAS	D	30		2
EDGAR	A	7	(14)	2
HASSAN Nader (MAR)	A	5	(4)	6
HÉLDER	D	32		1
Ilian ILIEV (BUL)	M	13	(6)	1
JOÃO PINTO	A	31		18
KENEDY	M	11	(11)	1
LUIZ GUSTAVO	A	2	(12)	
MARCELO	A	17	(10)	7
MARINHO	D	18		1
MAURO AIREZ (ARG)	A	10	(5)	
Basarab Nica PANDURU (ROM)	M	11	(4)	3
PAREDÃO	D	6	(2)	1
PAULÃO	A	7	(11)	3
PAULO BENTO	M	29		2
PAULO PEREIRA	D	7		
PEDRO HENRIQUES	D	16		
Michel PREUD'HOMME (BEL)	G	33		
RICARDO (BRA)	D	29		5
VALDO (BRA)	M	30		4
VERISSIMO	D	2	(1)	

LEAGUE RESULTS 1995/96

Date	Opponent	H/A	Score	Scorers
27/08/95	FC Tirsense	A	1-0	Panduru
06/09/95	SC Salgueiros	H	0-0	
09/09/95	Vitória Guimarães	H	1-1	Hassan
17/09/95	CF Estrela Amadora	A	1-0	João Pinto
22/09/95	CF Os Belenenses	H	1-0	Marcelo
03/10/95	Sporting CP	A	0-2	
14/10/95	Gil Vicente FC	H	3-0	Panduru, Hélder, Hassan (p)
22/10/95	GD Chaves	A	2-1	Valdo, Hassan
27/10/95	Leça FC	H	3-1	Paulão, Iliev, Hassan
05/11/95	FC Porto	A	0-3	
18/11/95	Boavista FC	H	1-1	Hassan
26/11/95	SC Braga	A	2-1	João Pinto, Hassan (p)
09/12/95	SC Campomaiorense	H	2-0	Edgar, Marcelo
16/12/95	SC Farense	A	3-1	Ricardo, Paulo Bento, João Pinto
23/12/95	FC Felgueiras	A	2-1	Edgar, Ricardo
30/12/95	União Leiria	H	4-0	Marinho, João Pinto, Ricardo, Panduru
06/01/96	CS Marítimo	A	2-2	Marcelo, João Pinto
13/01/96	SC Salgueiros	A	2-4	Valdo (p), Marcelo
20/01/96	FC Tirsense	H	2-1	João Pinto, Dimas
27/01/96	Vitória Guimarães	A	4-2	João Pinto 2, Marcelo, Ricardo
04/02/96	CF Estrela Amadora	H	1-0	Paulão
11/02/96	CF Os Belenenses	A	0-1	
18/02/96	Sporting CP	H	0-0	
02/03/96	Gil Vicente FC	A	2-1	João Pinto, Marcelo
09/03/96	GD Chaves	H	2-0	João Pinto, Marcelo
17/03/96	Leça FC	A	0-0	
24/03/96	FC Porto	H	2-1	Valdo (p), João Pinto
31/03/96	Boavista FC	A	3-1	Ricardo, João Pinto 2
07/04/96	SC Braga	H	3-0	Kenedy, João Pinto 2 (2p)
14/04/96	SC Campomaiorense	A	0-0	
21/04/96	SC Farense	H	0-1	
28/04/96	FC Felgueiras	H	1-0	Paulão
04/05/96	União Leiria	A	2-0	Paulo Bento, Valdo
11/05/96	CS Marítimo	H	5-1	João Pinto 3, Dimas, Paredão

BOAVISTA FC

CLUB DIRECTORY

Boavista Futebol Clube
Rua O Primeiro de Janeiro
4100 Porto
tel - (02) 698159/668506
fax - (02) 6003743
Year of Formation - 1903
President - Valentim Loureiro
Coach - Manuel José (96/97 - Zoran Filipovic)
Stadium - Bessa (26,000)

MAJOR HONOURS
Domestic Cup - (4) 1975, 1976, 1979, 1992.

APPEARANCES 95/96

	P	Ap	(s)	Gls
ALFREDO	G	9		
ARTUR (BRA)	A	31	(1)	14
Zoran BAN (CRO)	A	10	(6)	4
BOBÓ	M	3	(7)	
CAETANO	D	6	(2)	1
CALITA	M		(4)	
DELFIM	M	1	(1)	
HÉLDER	M	31		1
JAIME ALVES	M	21	(5)	5
Samir LAGNAOUI (MAR)	A	2	(1)	
LITOS	D	26		4
MÁRIO SILVA	M	2	(3)	
MIGUEL SERODIO	D	13	(4)	
NELO	M	29		
NÉLSON BERTOLAZZI (BRA)	A	10	(8)	3
NUNO GOMES	A	6	(22)	7
PAULO SOUSA	D	20	(7)	
RAUL	D	4	(8)	
RUI BENTO	D	22	(3)	1
RUI BORGES	M	3	(7)	1
Erwin SANCHEZ (BOL)	M	19	(3)	5
SÉRGIO DUARTE (BRA)	M	31		4
TAVARES	D	30		
TAVARES II	A	1	(1)	
Ion TIMOFTE (ROM)	M	19	(5)	7
TÓ LUÍS	G	25		

LEAGUE RESULTS 1995/96

20/08/95	CF Os Belenenses	H	1-0	Timofte
28/08/95	Sporting CP	A	0-0	
08/09/95	Gil Vicente FC	H	3-0	Timofte 2, Nélson Bertolazzi
17/09/95	GD Chaves	A	3-2	Artur (p), Sánchez, Nuno Gomes
24/09/95	Leça FC	H	2-0	Artur, Nuno Gomes
01/10/95	FC Porto	A	0-1	
15/10/95	FC Felgueiras	A	0-2	
22/10/95	SC Braga	H	5-2	Jaime Alves 2, Nuno Gomes 2, Timofte
29/10/95	SC Campomaiorense	A	2-0	Timofte, Artur
05/11/95	SC Farense	H	3-0	Litos, Nélson Bertolazzi, Sánchez
18/11/95	SL Benfica	A	1-1	Artur
25/11/95	União Leiria	H	5-0	Sérgio Duarte, Nélson Bertolazzi, Sánchez, Caetano, Artur
09/12/95	CS Marítimo	A	0-2	
17/12/95	SC Salgueiros	H	1-1	Jaime Alves
23/12/95	FC Tirsense	A	3-1	Artur 2, Sánchez
30/12/95	Vitória Guimarães	H	2-1	Nuno Gomes, Litos
07/01/96	CF Estrela Amadora	A	0-0	
13/01/96	CF Os Belenenses	A	2-1	Artur, Timofte
20/01/96	Sporting CP	H	2-1	og (Vidigal), Artur
27/01/96	Gil Vicente FC	A	1-1	Ban
04/02/96	GD Chaves	H	2-0	Timofte, Ban
11/02/96	Leça FC	A	2-0	Sérgio Duarte, Artur (p)
18/02/96	FC Porto	H	1-1	Sánchez
03/03/96	FC Felgueiras	H	4-0	Ban 2, Rui Bento, Sérgio Duarte
10/03/96	SC Braga	A	0-2	
17/03/96	SC Campomaiorense	H	4-0	Litos, Artur, Hélder, Nuno Gomes
24/03/96	SC Farense	A	0-2	
31/03/96	SL Benfica	H	1-3	Artur
07/04/96	União Leiria	A	0-1	
14/04/96	CS Marítimo	H	1-0	Rui Borges
21/04/96	SC Salgueiros	A	2-0	Artur, Litos
28/04/96	FC Tirsense	H	1-1	Jaime Alves
05/05/96	Vitória Guimarães	A	3-1	Sérgio Duarte, Artur (p), Jaime Alves
12/05/96	CF Estrela Amadora	H	1-1	Nuno Gomes

SC BRAGA

CLUB DIRECTORY

Sporting Clube de Braga
Estádio 1. de Maio
Parque da Ponte
4700 Braga
tel - (053) 616593/610591
fax - (053) 611686
Year of Formation - 1921
President - Joaquim Nuno Cunha
Coach - Manuel Cajuda
Stadium - Primeiro de Maio (40,000)

MAJOR HONOURS
Domestic Cup - (2) 1966, 1992.

APPEARANCES 95/96

	P	Ap	(s)	Gls
Bo ANDERSSON (SWE)	A	11	(5)	4
ARTUR JORGE	D	30		1
BALTASAR	M	16	(13)	1
BARROSO	M	30		7
BRUNO	M	25	(7)	5
CHICO SILVA	D	18		1
EDUARDO	M		(1)	
EVANDRO (BRA)	M	23	(6)	
FLORIS	M	4	(1)	
GANGA	A	3	(6)	
HUGO	M	1	(1)	
JONI	A		(1)	
JORGE FERREIRA	D	15	(5)	
JOSÉ NUNO AZEVEDO	D	31		2
Mladen KAROGLAN (CRO)	A	28		8
LINO	D	10		1
LUIZINHO (ANG)	A	2	(6)	
Srdjan OBRADOVIC (YUG)	D	7	(4)	
PAULO MONTEIRO	M	2	(7)	
PEDRO ESTRELA	A	27	(2)	4
PEDRO MIGUEL	A	15	(8)	3
QUIM	G		(1)	
Jonny RÖDLUND (SWE)	M	9		2
RUI CORREIA	G	34		
SÉRGIO	D	23	(2)	3
TONI	A	2	(13)	2
VADO	M	8	(11)	

LEAGUE RESULTS 1995/96

20/08/95	CF Estrela Amadora	H	2-1	Karoglan, Pedro Miguel
27/08/95	CF Os Belenenses	A	1-1	Pedro Miguel
08/09/95	Sporting CP	H	1-3	Karoglan
17/09/95	Gil Vicente FC	A	2-1	Sérgio, Karoglan
24/09/95	GD Chaves	H	1-0	Chico Silva
30/09/95	Leça FC	A	1-0	Bruno
14/10/95	FC Porto	H	0-3	
22/10/95	Boavista FC	A	2-5	José Nuno Azevedo, Bruno
29/10/95	FC Felgueiras	A	1-1	Karoglan
05/11/95	SC Campomaiorense	H	1-0	Pedro Estrela
19/11/95	SC Farense	A	0-1	
26/11/95	SL Benfica	H	1-2	Andersson
09/12/95	União Leiria	A	0-1	
17/12/95	CS Marítimo	H	1-1	Pedro Miguel
23/12/95	SC Salgueiros	A	0-0	
30/12/95	FC Tirsense	H	4-0	Karoglan 2, Sérgio, Rödlund
07/01/96	Vitória Guimarães	A	1-1	Andersson
13/01/96	CF Estrela Amadora	A	2-4	Rödlund, Barroso
20/01/96	CF Os Belenenses	H	1-1	Bruno
27/01/96	Sporting CP	A	1-0	Pedro Estrela
04/02/96	Gil Vicente FC	H	1-1	Barroso
11/02/96	GD Chaves	A	0-1	
18/02/96	Leça FC	H	3-0	Karoglan, Andersson, Bruno
03/03/96	FC Porto	A	3-6	Barroso 2 (2p), José Nuno Azevedo
10/03/96	Boavista FC	H	2-0	Pedro Estrela, Lino
17/03/96	FC Felgueiras	H	2-0	Baltasar, Karoglan
24/03/96	SC Campomaiorense	A	0-2	
30/03/96	SC Farense	H	3-2	Andersson, Artur Jorge, Barroso (p)
07/04/96	SL Benfica	A	0-3	
14/04/96	União Leiria	H	0-0	
21/04/96	CS Marítimo	A	1-2	Pedro Estrela
28/04/96	SC Salgueiros	H	2-2	Sérgio, Barroso
04/05/96	FC Tirsense	A	0-2	
11/05/96	Vitória Guimarães	H	4-0	Toni 2, Bruno, Barroso (p)

SC CAMPOMAIORENSE

CLUB DIRECTORY

Sporting Clube Campomaiorense
Rua Vasco Sardinha n.10
7370 Campo Maior
tel - (068) 686274
Year of Formation - 1926
President - José António Nabeiro
Coach - Manuel Fernandes; Diamantino Miranda
Stadium - Capitão César Correia (5,000)

APPEARANCES 95/96

	P	Ap	(s)	Gls
ÁLVARO	G	23	(1)	
ARRIAGA	M	16	(4)	2
AZINHAIS	D	9	(1)	
BETO	M	13	(5)	1
Mikael BRUNDIN (SWE)	D	11	(1)	
BRUNO SILVA	M	1	(2)	
EURICO	D	28		
GILA	M	8	(2)	
JIMMY (SUR)	A	30	(1)	12
JOEL (BRA)	M	17		
JORGE SILVÉRIO	A	15	(7)	2
JOSÉ ALBANO	A		(9)	1
JOSÉ ARMINDO	A		(6)	
JOVO	A		(4)	
NUNO AFONSO	D	23		
NUNO LUÍS	D	26	(1)	2
PAULO RENATO	G	3		
PAULO SÉRGIO	G	8	(2)	
PAULO TORRES	D	23		
PITEIRA	D	2	(2)	
PORTELA	D	21	(5)	
QUIM	A	3	(7)	
SÉRGIO	M	9	(11)	
SOUSA	A	20	(2)	
STEFAN	A	1	(9)	
Goran STEVANOVIC (YUG)	A	17	(1)	3
Stanimir STOILOV (BUL)	M	28	(3)	7
TARCÍSIO (BRA)	A	2	(1)	
VÍTOR MANUEL	M	17	(8)	1

LEAGUE RESULTS 1995/96

Date	Opponent	H/A	Score	Scorers
20/08/95	Vitória Guimarães	H	0-1	
27/08/95	CF Estrela Amadora	A	0-2	
08/09/95	CF Os Belenenses	H	2-3	Jorge Silvério 2
18/09/95	Sporting CP	A	1-7	Stoilov
24/09/95	Gil Vicente FC	H	2-0	Jimmy 2
30/09/95	GD Chaves	A	1-4	Beto
15/10/95	Leça FC	H	1-1	José Albano
22/10/95	FC Porto	A	0-5	
29/10/95	Boavista FC	H	0-2	
05/11/95	SC Braga	A	0-1	
19/11/95	FC Felgueiras	A	0-3	
26/11/95	SC Farense	H	1-0	Stoilov
09/12/95	SL Benfica	A	0-2	
17/12/95	União Leiria	H	4-2	Nuno Luís, Jimmy, Stoilov 2
23/12/95	CS Marítimo	A	0-3	
30/12/95	SC Salgueiros	H	0-0	
07/01/96	FC Tirsense	A	0-2	
13/01/96	Vitória Guimarães	A	0-4	
20/01/96	CF Estrela Amadora	H	2-1	Stoilov, Jimmy
27/01/96	CF Os Belenenses	A	1-3	Vítor Manuel
04/02/96	Sporting CP	H	0-1	
11/02/96	Gil Vicente FC	A	1-3	Stevanovic
18/02/96	GD Chaves	H	2-1	Arriaga, Jimmy
03/03/96	Leça FC	A	1-4	Jimmy
10/03/96	FC Porto	H	0-1	
17/03/96	Boavista FC	A	0-4	
24/03/96	SC Braga	H	2-0	Stevanovic, og (Floris)
30/03/96	FC Felgueiras	H	2-0	Jimmy 2
07/04/96	SC Farense	A	1-3	Jimmy
14/04/96	SL Benfica	H	0-0	
21/04/96	União Leiria	A	0-4	
28/04/96	CS Marítimo	H	3-1	Stevanovic, Stoilov, Arriaga
04/05/96	SC Salgueiros	A	2-0	Jimmy, Nuno Luís
11/05/96	FC Tirsense	H	3-1	Stoilov, Jimmy 2

GD CHAVES

CLUB DIRECTORY

Grupo Desportivo de Chaves
Rua de Santo António 24, 1.F
5400 Chaves
tel - (039) 341846/333269
fax - (039) 341846
Year of Formation - 1949
President - António Castanheira
Coach - Vítor Urbano; Joaquim Teixeira; José Romão
Stadium - Municipal (25,000)

APPEARANCES 95/96

	P	Ap	(s)	Gls
AGOSTINHO	A	6	(7)	
AMARILDO	D	21	(2)	3
CHICO OLIVEIRA	D	24	(2)	
DACROCE	M	12	(3)	
DIAZ	M	23	(1)	2
DINO (BRA)	A	6		2
EDGAR	D	5	(1)	
FABINHO	M	2		
JOÃO PEDRO	M		(3)	
JOSÉ MARIA	M	1	(7)	
JOSÉ NUNO AMARO	G	26	(1)	
LEONEL	D	12	(1)	
MANU	A		(12)	1
MANUEL CORREIA	D	22	(2)	2
MINER	M	26		6
ORLANDO	G	8	(1)	
Ulf OTTOSSON (SWE)	A	11		
PAULO ALEXANDRE	D	32		3
QUIM MACHADO	D	31		
RIVA (BRA)	M	28		2
RUI ALBERTO	M	16	(11)	5
RUI LOJA	A	11	(14)	2
SERRINHA	M	9	(6)	
TONANHA	M	5	(10)	1
TONIÑO (ESP)	M	25		7
VINAGRE	M	12	(7)	

LEAGUE RESULTS 1995/96

20/08/95	FC Felgueiras	A	2-2	Dino, Paulo Alexandre
27/08/95	Leça FC	H	2-2	Dino, Toniño
08/09/95	FC Porto	A	0-2	
17/09/95	Boavista FC	H	2-3	Rui Alberto, Diaz
24/09/95	SC Braga	A	0-1	
30/09/95	SC Campomaiorense	H	4-1	Toniño, Manuel Correia, Amarildo, Manu
15/10/95	SC Farense	A	0-0	
22/10/95	SL Benfica	H	1-2	Rui Loja
29/10/95	União Leiria	A	1-4	Manuel Correia
05/11/95	CS Marítimo	H	0-2	
19/11/95	SC Salgueiros	A	2-2	Miner 2 (1p)
26/11/95	FC Tirsense	H	2-0	Paulo Alexandre, Miner (p)
09/12/95	Vitória Guimarães	A	1-2	Paulo Alexandre
17/12/95	CF Estrela Amadora	H	0-0	
23/12/95	CF Os Belenenses	A	1-4	Rui Alberto
30/12/95	Sporting CP	H	1-1	Diaz (p)
07/01/96	Gil Vicente FC	A	0-2	
13/01/96	FC Felgueiras	H	1-0	Toniño
20/01/96	Leça FC	A	1-4	Rui Loja
27/01/96	FC Porto	H	2-3	og (Aloísio), og (Secretário)
04/02/96	Boavista FC	A	0-2	
11/02/96	SC Braga	H	1-0	Miner (p)
18/02/96	SC Campomaiorense	A	1-2	Rui Alberto
03/03/96	SC Farense	H	2-1	Miner, Rui Alberto
09/03/96	SL Benfica	A	0-2	
17/03/96	União Leiria	H	0-1	
24/03/96	CS Marítimo	A	2-0	Amarildo 2
31/03/96	SC Salgueiros	H	1-1	Toniño
04/04/96	FC Tirsense	A	1-2	Miner
11/04/96	Vitória Guimarães	H	1-2	Riva (p)
21/04/96	CF Estrela Amadora	A	3-2	Riva, Toniño 2
28/04/96	CF Os Belenenses	H	1-0	Toniño
04/05/96	Sporting CP	A	1-4	Tonanha
11/05/96	Gil Vicente FC	H	1-0	Rui Alberto

CF ESTRELA AMADORA

CLUB DIRECTORY

Clube de Futebol Estrela da Amadora
Rua Gomes Freire 27
2700 Amadora
tel - (01) 4951309/4952395
fax - (01) 4951309
Year of Formation - 1932
President - Jaime Salvado
Coach - Fernando Santos
Stadium - José Gomes (25,000)

MAJOR HONOURS
Domestic Cup - (1) 1990.

APPEARANCES 95/96

	P	Ap	(s)	Gls
ANDRADE	D	23	(3)	
BAMBO	A	12	(11)	3
Mame BIRAME (SEN)	A	4	(9)	2
CARLOS	G	8	(1)	
CHAINHO	M	24		1
ELISEU (BRA)	M	8	(10)	
FONSECA	D	24	(1)	
GONÇALVES	A	5	(8)	1
HUGO COSTA	D	9	(1)	
JORDÃO	M	25	(5)	1
JOSÉ CARLOS	D	32		5
MARQUINHOS	A	12	(6)	7
ORLANDO	M	3	(6)	
PAULINHO	D	19		
PAULO FERREIRA	A	6	(4)	2
PAULO SANTOS	G	26		
PAULO SÉRGIO	M	6	(6)	
POEJO	M	13	(8)	
REBELO	D	32	(1)	
RENATO	A	24	(6)	10
RODOLFO	M	19	(1)	
RUI NEVES	D	26	(2)	
Ilia VOINOV (BUL)	A	14	(7)	3

LEAGUE RESULTS 1995/96

20/08/95	SC Braga	A	1-2	Renato
27/08/95	SC Campomaiorense	H	2-0	José Carlos, Voinov (p)
08/09/95	SC Farense	A	0-1	
17/09/95	SL Benfica	H	0-1	
24/09/95	União Leiria	A	1-2	José Carlos
30/09/95	CS Marítimo	H	1-1	Voinov (p)
15/10/95	SC Salgueiros	A	0-0	
21/10/95	FC Tirsense	H	0-0	
28/10/95	Vitória Guimarães	A	0-3	
05/11/95	FC Felgueiras	H	2-1	Renato, Voinov (p)
19/11/95	CF Os Belenenses	H	2-2	Bambó, Renato
26/11/95	Sporting CP	A	2-6	Marquinhos 2
09/12/95	Gil Vicente FC	H	3-1	Birame, José Carlos, Marquinhos
17/12/95	GD Chaves	A	0-0	
23/12/95	Leça FC	H	1-0	Renato
30/12/95	FC Porto	A	0-6	
07/01/96	Boavista FC	H	0-0	
13/01/96	SC Braga	H	4-2	Bambó, Paulo Ferreira, Marquinhos, José Carlos
20/01/96	SC Campomaiorense	A	1-2	Gonçalves
27/01/96	SC Farense	H	1-1	Marquinhos
04/02/96	SL Benfica	A	0-1	
11/02/96	União Leiria	H	2-4	Marquinhos, Renato
18/02/96	CS Marítimo	A	1-1	Paulo Ferreira
02/03/96	SC Salgueiros	H	1-1	Renato
06/03/96	FC Tirsense	A	0-0	
17/03/96	Vitória Guimarães	H	0-0	
24/03/96	FC Felgueiras	A	1-2	Renato
30/03/96	CF Os Belenenses	A	1-4	Birame
05/04/96	Sporting CP	H	1-1	Jordão
14/04/96	Gil Vicente FC	A	1-0	Renato
21/04/96	GD Chaves	H	2-3	Bambó, Marquinhos
28/04/96	Leça FC	A	2-0	José Carlos, Renato
04/05/96	FC Porto	H	1-1	Renato
11/05/96	Boavista FC	A	1-1	Chainho

SC FARENSE

CLUB DIRECTORY

Sporting Clube Farense
Estádio de São Luís
Praça de Tânger
8000 Faro
tel - (089) 804859/803666
fax - (089) 804859/802754
Year of Formation - 1910
President - Rui Fernandes
Coach - Paco Fortes
Stadium - São Luís (15,000)

APPEARANCES 95/96

	P	Ap	(s)	Gls
BARRIGANA	M	4	(5)	
CACIOLI (BRA)	M	26	(5)	5
CAMILO	M	5	(2)	
CANDEIAS	G	3		
CARLOS COSTA	M	18	(8)	2
CHRISTIAN	A	12	(18)	4
Milonja DJUKIC (YUG)	A	19	(2)	6
DRASKOVIC (YUG)	D	5	(2)	
EDVALDO	M	1	(3)	
EUGÉNIO	D	27	(3)	1
Radouane HAJRI (MAR)	M	29		4
HELCINHO	A	29		1
IDALÉCIO	D	22		3
IVO	G	8	(1)	
JORGE SOARES	D	32		1
LUÍS MIGUEL	D	22	(3)	
MARCO NUNO	M	2	(16)	3
MAURO	A		(2)	
PAIVA	D	30		
PAIXÃO	D	15	(2)	
PEDRO MIGUEL	D	19	(1)	1
Dragan PUNISIC (YUG)	M	13	(6)	3
RAMOS	M		(1)	
ROGÉRIO MARTINS	A		(2)	
Peter RUFAI (NIG)	G	23		
TOZÉ	A	10	(14)	2

LEAGUE RESULTS 1995/96

Date	Opponent		Score	Scorers
20/08/95	FC Tirsense	H	2-1	Djukic, Tozé
27/08/95	Vitória Guimarães	A	0-1	
08/09/95	CF Estrela Amadora	H	1-0	Hajri
17/09/95	CF Os Belenenses	A	1-2	Cacioli
23/09/95	Sporting CP	H	0-1	
30/09/95	Gil Vicente FC	A	2-2	Punisic, Djukic
15/10/95	GD Chaves	H	0-0	
22/10/95	Leça FC	A	1-2	Christian
28/10/95	FC Porto	H	0-2	
05/11/95	Boavista FC	A	0-3	
19/11/95	SC Braga	H	1-0	Cacioli
26/11/95	SC Campomaiorense	A	0-1	
09/12/95	FC Felgueiras	A	1-3	Carlos Costa
16/12/95	SL Benfica	H	1-3	Hajri
23/12/95	União Leiria	A	0-1	
30/12/95	CS Marítimo	H	2-0	Idalécio, Hajri
07/01/96	SC Salgueiros	A	0-1	
13/01/96	FC Tirsense	A	1-2	Christian
20/01/96	Vitória Guimarães	H	0-1	
27/01/96	CF Estrela Amadora	A	1-1	Idalécio
04/02/96	CF Os Belenenses	H	1-3	Marco Nuno
11/02/96	Sporting CP	A	0-5	
18/02/96	Gil Vicente FC	H	5-0	Helcinho, Cacioli 2, Christian, Marco Nuno
03/03/96	GD Chaves	A	1-2	Djukic
10/03/96	Leça FC	H	2-0	Djukic 2 (2p)
17/03/96	FC Porto	A	0-2	
24/03/96	Boavista FC	H	2-0	Pedro Miguel, Punisic
30/03/96	SC Braga	A	2-3	Tozé, Eugénio
07/04/96	SC Campomaiorense	H	3-1	Punisic, Djukic, Christian
14/04/96	FC Felgueiras	H	0-0	
21/04/96	SL Benfica	A	1-0	Jorge Soares
28/04/96	União Leiria	H	1-1	Carlos Costa
04/05/96	CS Marítimo	A	0-0	
11/05/96	SC Salgueiros	H	4-1	Cacioli, Idalécio, Hajri (p), Marco Nuno

FC FELGUEIRAS

CLUB DIRECTORY

Futebol Clube Felgueiras
Av. Dr. Leonardo Coimbra
Centro Comercial Orson
2., Sala 7-Margaride
4610 Felgueiras
tel - (055)923191/923900
Year of Formation - 1934
President - Álvaro Costa
Coach - Jorge Jesus
Stadium - Dr. Machado de Matos (20,000)

APPEARANCES 95/96

	P	Ap	(s)	Gls
ABEL SILVA	D	17	(6)	
ACÁCIO	D	33		
AMARAL	A	15	(8)	4
AVELINO	G		(1)	
Ronald BARONI (PER)	A	12	(5)	1
Vlado BOZINOSKI (AUS)	M	16	(4)	
COELHO	A		(1)	
COSTA	M	26	(1)	
EARL	A	8	(13)	2
ERINOVALDO	M	11	(1)	
FERNANDO GOMES	A		(2)	
FILIPE AZEVEDO	M	3	(8)	
JOÃO	M	6	(1)	
JOSÉ CARLOS	G	26		
JOSÉ JOAQUIM	M	20	(2)	1
Aleksandar KRSTIC (YUG)	A	5	(10)	2
LEAL	D	32		
Leo LEWIS (TRI)	A	31	(2)	15
LOPES	G	8	(1)	
LOPES DA SILVA	M	10	(2)	
ROSÁRIO	A	1	(10)	
RUI GREGÓRIO	D	29		
SÉRGIO CONCEIÇÃO	D	30		4
Clint TARCELLE (TRI)	A	8	(13)	
TEIXEIRA	D	3	(4)	
VICENTE	M	24	(3)	

LEAGUE RESULTS 1995/96

20/08/95	GD Chaves	H	2-2	Earl, Sérgio Conceicão
27/08/95	CS Marítimo	A	2-0	Earl, Krstic
08/09/95	Leça FC	H	1-2	Lewis
17/09/95	SC Salgueiros	A	0-0	
23/09/95	FC Porto	H	1-1	Lewis
30/09/95	FC Tirsense	A	0-0	
15/10/95	Boavista FC	H	2-0	Amaral, Lewis
22/10/95	Vitória Guimarães	A	0-2	
29/10/95	SC Braga	H	1-1	Amaral
05/11/95	CF Estrela Amadora	A	1-2	Lewis
19/11/95	SC Campomaiorense	H	3-0	José Joaquim, Lewis 2
26/11/95	CF Os Belenenses	A	1-0	Baroni
09/12/95	SC Farense	H	3-1	Amaral, Lewis, Sérgio Conceição
16/12/95	Sporting CP	A	0-4	
23/12/95	SL Benfica	H	1-2	Lewis
30/12/95	Gil Vicente FC	H	2-2	Amaral, Lewis
07/01/96	União Leiria	A	0-0	
13/01/96	GD Chaves	A	0-1	
21/01/96	CS Marítimo	H	0-3	
27/01/96	Leça FC	A	0-1	
04/02/96	SC Salgueiros	H	2-0	Lewis 2
11/02/96	FC Porto	A	2-6	Lewis 2
18/02/96	FC Tirsense	H	0-1	
03/03/96	Boavista FC	A	0-4	
10/03/96	Vitória Guimarães	H	0-3	
17/03/96	SC Braga	A	0-2	
24/03/96	CF Estrela Amadora	H	2-1	Sérgio Conceição, Lewis (p)
30/03/96	SC Campomaiorense	A	0-2	
07/04/96	CF Os Belenenses	H	0-0	
14/04/96	SC Farense	A	0-0	
21/04/96	Sporting CP	H	0-1	
28/04/96	SL Benfica	A	0-1	
04/05/96	Gil Vicente FC	A	0-2	
11/05/96	União Leiria	H	3-0	Sérgio Conceição, Lewis, Krstic

GIL VICENTE FC

CLUB DIRECTORY

Gil Vicente Futebol Clube
Rua D. Diogo Pinheiro 25
4750 Barcelos
tel - (053) 811523
fax - (053) 823102
Year of Formation - 1924
President - Francisco Silva
Coach - Bernardino Pedroto
Stadium - Adelino Ribeiro Novo (15,000)

APPEARANCES 95/96

	P	Ap	(s)	Gls
BETO	A	17	(5)	2
CARLITOS	M	18	(15)	5
JAIME CERQUEIRA	M	16	(7)	1
Zeljko JANOVIC (YUG)	A	19	(9)	4
JOÃO PINTO	M	11	(9)	
JOÃO PAULO	A	1	(1)	
JOÃO PEDRO	G	1		
JOAQUIM JORGE	D	15		
JOSÉ CARLOS	D	7		
LEMOS	D	29		2
LILA	M	32		1
LIM	M	7	(9)	3
LUCIANO (BRA)	A	13	(3)	1
MADUREIRA	D	1	(7)	
MIGUEL	D	24	(2)	
Vatroslav MIHACIC (CRO)	G	16	(1)	
NENE SANTAREM (BRA)	A	4	(8)	
PEDRO	M		(1)	
PEDROSA	D	22		1
ROBERTO CARLOS (BRA)	A	9	(7)	3
SÉRGIO CRUZ	D	28		1
SIDÓNIO	A		(2)	
TUCK	M	32		4
VASCO	D	4	(4)	1
VITAL	G	17		
WILSON	D	28		1
Christopher ZWANE (SAF)	A	3	(2)	

LEAGUE RESULTS 1995/96

20/08/95	Leça FC	A	2-0	Carlitos 2
27/08/95	FC Porto	H	0-1	
08/09/95	Boavista FC	A	0-3	
17/09/95	SC Braga	H	1-2	Roberto Carlos
24/09/95	SC Campomaiorense	A	0-2	
30/09/95	SC Farense	H	2-2	Roberto Carlos, Vasco
14/10/95	SL Benfica	A	0-3	
22/10/95	União Leiria	H	1-0	Lila
29/10/95	CS Marítimo	A	0-1	
05/11/95	SC Salgueiros	H	1-1	Lemos
19/11/95	FC Tirsense	A	1-1	Wilson
26/11/95	Vitória Guimarães	H	2-0	Beto, Janovic
09/12/95	CF Estrela Amadora	A	1-3	Beto
17/12/95	CF Os Belenenses	H	0-0	
23/12/95	Sporting CP	A	1-4	og (Marco Aurélio)
30/12/95	FC Felgueiras	A	2-2	Pedrosa, Lemos
07/01/96	GD Chaves	H	2-0	Tuck, Luciano
13/01/96	Leça FC	H	0-0	
20/01/96	FC Porto	A	0-2	
27/01/96	Boavista FC	H	1-1	Janovic
04/02/96	SC Braga	A	1-1	Tuck
11/02/96	SC Campomaiorense	H	3-1	Sérgio Cruz, Janovic, Tuck
18/02/96	SC Farense	A	0-5	
02/03/96	SL Benfica	H	1-2	Jaime Cerqueira
10/03/96	União Leiria	A	0-2	
17/03/96	CS Marítimo	H	1-0	Lim
24/03/96	SC Salgueiros	A	3-2	Roberto Carlos, Carlitos, Lim
30/03/96	FC Tirsense	H	1-0	Tuck
07/04/96	Vitória Guimarães	A	0-2	
14/04/96	CF Estrela Amadora	H	0-1	
21/04/96	CF Os Belenenses	A	2-2	Janovic, Carlitos
28/04/96	Sporting CP	H	0-2	
04/05/96	FC Felgueiras	H	2-0	Carlitos, Lim
11/05/96	GD Chaves	A	0-1	

LEÇA FC

CLUB DIRECTORY

Leça Futebol Clube
Rua Moninho de Vento 336
4450 Leça da Palmeira
tel - (02) 9952631
Year of Formation - 1923
President - Manuel Rodrigues
Coach - Fernando Festas; Pinto & Manuel Bento
(96/97 - Rodolfo Reis)
Stadium - Leça (18,000)

APPEARANCES 95/96

	P	Ap	(s)	Gls
ALFAÍA	D	17	(2)	
ARMANDO	D	23	(4)	
BEST	G	4		
BRUNO XAVIER	D	4	(2)	
CÃO	D	24	(2)	2
CHICO NELO	A	5	(4)	1
CONSTANTINO	A	22	(5)	14
CRISTOVÃO	M	30	(3)	
Milan DJURDJEVIC (YUG)	A	1		
FERNANDO LOPES	M	5	(16)	
FONSECA	D	21	(1)	
ISAÍAS (BRA)	D	30		1
JAIME MAGALHÃES	M	2	(2)	
JOSÉ ARMINDO	A	4	(3)	
JOSÉ LOPES	M	7	(5)	1
JOSÉ ROCHA	A	22	(1)	2
MATIAS	D	13		1
MIGUEL BARROS	A	2	(16)	2
NANDO	M	32	(1)	
PAULINHO	A	2	(11)	2
PEDRO INÁCIO	D	1		
REISINHO	M	1	(3)	
RICARDO	A	20	(9)	2
RUI OSCAR	D	27		
SERIFO (GUI)	M	18	(5)	
Vladan STOJKOVIC (YUG)	G	30		
TOZÉ	D	7	(1)	

LEAGUE RESULTS 1995/96

Date	Opponent	H/A	Score	Scorers
20/08/95	Gil Vicente FC	H	0-2	
27/08/95	GD Chaves	A	2-2	Constantino, Miguel Barros
08/09/95	FC Felgueiras	A	2-1	Isaías, Chico Nelo
18/09/95	FC Porto	H	0-2	
24/09/95	Boavista FC	A	0-2	
30/09/95	SC Braga	H	0-1	
15/10/95	SC Campomaiorense	A	1-1	Cão
22/10/95	SC Farense	H	2-1	Matias, Constantino
27/10/95	SL Benfica	A	1-3	og (Paredão)
05/11/95	União Leiria	H	0-1	
18/11/95	CS Marítimo	A	0-2	
26/11/95	SC Salgueiros	H	1-1	Constantino
10/12/95	FC Tirsense	A	3-1	Paulinho, Constantino, Miguel Barros
17/12/95	Vitória Guimarães	H	1-0	Constantino
23/12/95	CF Estrela Amadora	A	0-1	
30/12/95	CF Os Belenenses	H	0-5	
07/01/96	Sporting CP	A	0-2	
13/01/96	Gil Vicente FC	A	0-0	
20/01/96	GD Chaves	H	4-1	Constantino 2, Ricardo, José Lopes
27/01/96	FC Felgueiras	H	1-0	Constantino
04/02/96	FC Porto	A	0-2	
11/02/96	Boavista FC	H	0-2	
18/02/96	SC Braga	A	0-3	
03/03/96	SC Campomaiorense	H	4-1	José Rocha 2, Ricardo, Constantino
10/03/96	SC Farense	A	0-2	
17/03/96	SL Benfica	H	0-0	
24/03/96	União Leiria	A	3-1	Constantino 2, Paulinho
30/03/96	CS Marítimo	H	0-0	
07/04/96	SC Salgueiros	A	0-3	
14/04/96	FC Tirsense	H	3-1	Constantino 3 (2p)
21/04/96	Vitória Guimarães	A	0-2	
28/04/96	CF Estrela Amadora	H	0-2	
05/05/96	CF Os Belenenses	A	0-5	
12/05/96	Sporting CP	H	1-1	Cão

CS MARÍTIMO

CLUB DIRECTORY

Clube Sport Marítimo
Rua D. Carlos I 17
9000 Funchal
tel - (091) 233063/223679
fax - (091) 222939/763776
Year of Formation - 1910
President - Rui Fontes
Coach - Raul Águas; Rui Vieira
(96/97 - Marinho Peres)
Stadium - Barreiros (16,000)

MAJOR HONOURS
Domestic Cup - (1) 1926.

APPEARANCES 95/96

	P	Ap	(s)	Gls
"ALEX" BUNBURY (CAN)	A	25	(1)	10
BIZARRO	G	4		
BRAGANÇA	M		(1)	
CABRAL	M	31		
CARLOS JORGE	D	21		3
CUCA	G	1		
EDMILSON (BRA)	A	28	(1)	9
EUSÉBIO	M	1	(1)	
EVERTON	G	2		
FERNANDO PIRES	M	10	(10)	3
FILGUEIRA	D	26		1
GUIDO	M		(1)	
GUSTAVO (BRA)	M	33		4
Ferenc HÁMORI (HUN)	M	3	(1)	
HERIVELTO	M	2	(14)	1
HUMBERTO	D	29	(1)	2
JOÃO LUÍS	D	6		
Predrag JOKANOVIC (YUG)	M	12	(8)	2
JOSÉ PEDRO	D	22		
LADEIRA	M	4	(2)	
Zoran LEMAJIC (YUG)	G	27		
MARCO	M		(1)	
MARGARIDO	M	7	(2)	1
MÁRIO JORGE	M	14	(4)	
ROBSON (BRA)	D	19	(5)	1
SILVEIRA	M	1		
TIAGO	M	18	(2)	
VÍTOR VIEIRA	M	13	(12)	1
ZECA	D	15	(10)	

LEAGUE RESULTS 1995/96

Date	Opponent	H/A	Score	Scorers
20/08/95	União Leiria	A	4-0	Jokanovic, Edmilson, Alex, Margarido
27/08/95	FC Felgueiras	H	0-2	
08/09/95	SC Salgueiros	H	3-1	Alex 2 (1p), Fernando Pires
17/09/95	FC Tirsense	A	1-2	Alex
23/09/95	Vitória Guimarães	H	4-0	Fernando Pires, Gustavo, og (Quim Berto), Alex
30/09/95	CF Estrela Amadora	A	1-1	Filgueira
14/10/95	CF Os Belenenses	H	1-2	Robson
22/10/95	Sporting CP	A	0-2	
29/10/95	Gil Vicente FC	H	1-0	Jokanovic (p)
05/11/95	GD Chaves	A	2-0	Gustavo 2
18/11/95	Leça FC	H	2-0	Edmilson 2
26/11/95	FC Porto	A	0-6	
09/12/95	Boavista FC	H	2-0	Carlos Jorge, Alex
17/12/95	SC Braga	A	1-1	Edmilson
23/12/95	SC Campomaiorense	H	3-0	Edmilson 2, Alex
30/12/95	SC Farense	A	0-2	
07/01/96	SL Benfica	H	2-2	Alex, Carlos Jorge
13/01/96	União Leiria	H	1-0	Humberto
20/01/96	FC Felgueiras	A	3-0	Vitor Vieira, Gustavo, Fernando Pires
27/01/96	SC Salgueiros	A	0-2	
04/02/96	FC Tirsense	H	1-0	Carlos Jorge
11/02/96	Vitória Guimarães	A	0-6	
18/02/96	CF Estrela Amadora	H	1-1	Edmilson (p)
03/03/96	CF Os Belenenses	A	1-4	Humberto
10/03/96	Sporting CP	H	0-5	
17/03/96	Gil Vicente FC	A	0-1	
24/03/96	GD Chaves	H	0-2	
30/03/96	Leça FC	A	0-0	
07/04/96	FC Porto	H	1-1	Herivelto
14/04/96	Boavista FC	A	0-1	
21/04/96	SC Braga	H	2-1	Edmilson 2
28/04/96	SC Campomaiorense	A	1-3	Alex
04/05/96	SC Farense	H	0-0	
11/05/96	SL Benfica	A	1-5	Alex

FC PORTO

CLUB DIRECTORY

Futebol Clube do Porto
Estádio das Antas
Avenida Fernão de Magalhães
4300 Porto
tel - (02) 5505844/5/6/7
fax - (02) 5505859
Year of Formation - 1893
President - Jorge Nuno Pinto da Costa
Coach - Bobby Robson (96/97 - António Oliveira)
Stadium - Das Antas (76,000)

MAJOR HONOURS

League Championship - (15) 1935, 1939, 1940, 1956, 1959, 1978, 1979, 1985, 1986, 1988, 1990, 1992, 1993, 1995, 1996.
Domestic Cup - (12)
1922, 1925, 1932, 1937, 1956, 1958, 1968, 1977, 1984, 1988, 1991, 1994.
European Champions' Cup - (1) 1987.
European Super Cup - (1) 1987.
World Club Cup - (1) 1987.

APPEARANCES 95/96

	P	Ap	(s)	Gls
ALOÍSIO (BRA)	D	29		
BANDEIRINHA	D		(1)	
BINO	M	4	(9)	2
DOMINGOS	A	28	(1)	25
Ljubinko DRULOVIC (YUG)	A	26	(5)	8
EDMILSON (BRA)	A	27	(4)	13
EMERSON (BRA)	M	29		4
Lars ERIKSSON (SWE)	G	4		
FOLHA	A	14	(17)	4
JOÃO M. PINTO	D	9	(7)	3
JOÃO PINTO	D	11	(2)	
JORGE COSTA	D	19	(2)	1
JORGE COUTO	A	4	(6)	3
JORGE SILVA	G		(1)	
JOSÉ CARLOS (BRA)	D	8		
Russel LATAPY (TRI)	M	16	(10)	5
Péter LIPCSEI (HUN)	M	21	(2)	6
MATIAS	D	3	(1)	
Grzegorz MIELCARSKI (POL)	A	2	(3)	2
PAULINHO SANTOS	M	23	(2)	
QUINZINHO	A	3	(6)	2
RUI BARROS	A	18	(9)	4
RUI JORGE	D	20	(2)	2
SECRETÁRIO	M	26	(1)	
SEMEDO	M		(1)	
SILVINO	G	3	(2)	
VÍTOR BAÍA	G	26		
VÍTOR NOVOA	G	1	(1)	

LEAGUE RESULTS 1995/96

Date	Opponent	H/A	Score	Scorers
20/08/95	Sporting CP	H	2-1	Domingos 2
27/08/95	Gil Vicente FC	A	1-0	Domingos
08/09/95	GD Chaves	H	2-0	Mielcarski, Latapy
18/09/95	Leça FC	A	2-0	Mielcarski, Domingos
23/09/95	FC Felgueiras	A	1-1	Latapy
01/10/95	Boavista FC	H	1-0	Folha
14/10/95	SC Braga	A	3-0	Domingos 2, Drulovic
22/10/95	SC Campomaiorense	H	5-0	Edmilson 2, Domingos 2, Drulovic
28/10/95	SC Farense	A	2-0	Domingos 2 (1p)
05/11/95	SL Benfica	H	3-0	Domingos 2 (1p), Lipcsei
18/11/95	União Leiria	A	0-0	
26/11/95	CS Marítimo	H	6-0	Rui Jorge 2, Jorge Couto, Emerson, Bino, Domingos
09/12/95	SC Salgueiros	A	4-0	Domingos, Lipcsei, Edmilson 2
17/12/95	FC Tirsense	H	5-0	Emerson, Rui Barros, Latapy 2, Folha
23/12/95	Vitória Guimarães	A	2-0	Edmilson, Domingos
30/12/95	CF Estrela Amadora	H	6-0	Domingos, Latapy, Lipcsei 2, Jorge Costa, Edmilson
07/01/96	CF Os Belenenses	A	1-1	Domingos
13/01/96	Sporting CP	A	2-0	Domingos 2
20/01/96	Gil Vicente FC	H	2-0	Edmilson, Domingos
27/01/96	GD Chaves	A	3-2	Drulovic 2, Domingos
04/02/96	Leça FC	H	2-0	Lipcsei, Domingos
11/02/96	FC Felgueiras	H	6-2	João M. Pinto, Rui Barros, Drulovic 2, Quinzinho, Jorge Couto
18/02/96	Boavista FC	A	1-1	Lipcsei
03/03/96	SC Braga	H	6-3	Edmilson 3, Drulovic 2, Folha
10/03/96	SC Campomaiorense	A	1-0	Edmilson
17/03/96	SC Farense	H	2-0	João M. Pinto, Domingos
23/03/96	SL Benfica	A	1-2	Emerson
30/03/96	União Leiria	H	1-0	Domingos
07/04/96	CS Marítimo	A	1-1	Jorge Couto
14/04/96	SC Salgueiros	H	2-0	Domingos, Emerson
21/04/96	FC Tirsense	A	4-2	João M. Pinto, Rui Barros, Folha, Bino
28/04/96	Vitória Guimarães	H	2-3	Edmilson (p), Quinzinho
04/05/96	CF Estrela Amadora	A	1-1	Rui Barros
11/05/96	CF Os Belenenses	H	1-0	Edmilson

SC SALGUEIROS

CLUB DIRECTORY

Sport Comércio e Salgueiros
Rua Álvares Cabral 366
4000 Porto
tel - (02) 2000004
fax - (02) 2008397
Year of Formation - 1911
President - José António Linhares
Coach - Mário Reis (96/97 - Carlos Manuel)
Stadium - Vidal Pinheiro (11,000)

APPEARANCES 95/96

	P	Ap	(s)	Gls
ABÍLIO	M	32	(1)	6
BASÍLIO	M	22	(5)	8
CHICO FONSECA	D	14		
FERNANDO ALMEIDA (BRA)	A	23	(3)	3
Zoran HAJDIC (YUG)	D	6	(2)	
JONI	M	2	(7)	
LEÃO	M	16	(6)	
LUÍS CARLOS (BRA)	M	26	(2)	2
LUÍS MANUEL	D	29		
MARIANO	M	27		
MIGUEL	D	3	(6)	1
MIGUEL BRUNO	A	6	(10)	1
Stevan MILOVAC (YUG)	D	30		1
NANDINHO	M	20	(9)	3
NILTON	M	3	(18)	3
PAULINHO	M		(3)	
PEDRO ESPINHA	G	34		
PEDRO SILVA	D	32		
RENATO	D	27	(2)	1
TONI	A	6	(16)	7
VINHA	A	16	(10)	2

LEAGUE RESULTS 1995/96

27/08/95	União Leiria	H	4-0	Abílio, Miguel Bruno, Fernando Almeida, Toni
07/09/95	SL Benfica	A	0-0	
09/09/95	CS Marítimo	A	1-3	og (Humberto)
17/09/95	FC Felgueiras	H	0-0	
24/09/95	FC Tirsense	H	1-1	Fernando Almeida
30/09/95	Vitória Guimarães	A	2-1	Basílio 2
15/10/95	CF Estrela Amadora	H	0-0	
22/10/95	CF Os Belenenses	A	1-0	Vinha
29/10/95	Sporting CP	H	2-2	Vinha, Renato
05/11/95	Gil Vicente FC	A	1-1	Basílio
19/11/95	GD Chaves	H	2-2	Basílio, Nilton
26/11/95	Leça FC	A	1-1	Fernando Almeida
09/12/95	FC Porto	H	0-4	
17/12/95	Boavista FC	A	1-1	Nandinho
23/12/95	SC Braga	H	0-0	
30/12/95	SC Campomaiorense	A	0-0	
07/01/96	SC Farense	H	1-0	Nandinho
13/01/96	SL Benfica	H	4-2	Nandinho, Abílio (p), Nilton, Basílio
20/01/96	União Leiria	A	2-3	Basílio, Abílio (p)
27/01/96	CS Marítimo	H	2-0	Milovac, Toni
04/02/96	FC Felgueiras	A	0-2	
11/02/96	FC Tirsense	A	0-2	
18/02/96	Vitória Guimarães	H	1-2	Toni
02/03/96	CF Estrela Amadora	A	1-1	Basílio
10/03/96	CF Os Belenenses	H	1-3	Nilton
17/03/96	Sporting CP	A	2-2	Abílio, Luís Carlos
24/03/96	Gil Vicente FC	H	2-3	Toni 2
31/03/96	GD Chaves	A	1-1	Luís Carlos
07/04/96	Leça FC	H	3-0	Abílio (p), Toni 2
14/04/96	FC Porto	A	0-2	
21/04/96	Boavista FC	H	0-2	
28/04/96	SC Braga	A	2-2	Basílio, Miguel
05/05/96	SC Campomaiorense	H	0-2	
12/05/96	SC Farense	A	1-4	Abílio (p)

SPORTING CP

CLUB DIRECTORY

Sporting Clube de Portugal
Estádio José Alvalade
R. Francisco Stromp
1600 Lisboa
tel - (01) 7589021
fax - (01) 7599391
Year of Formation - 1906
President - José Roquete
Coach - Carlos Queiroz; Fernando Mendes; Octávio (96/97 - Robert Waseige)
Stadium - José Alvalade (52,411)

MAJOR HONOURS
League Championship - (16) 1941, 1944, 1947, 1948, 1949, 1951, 1952, 1953, 1954, 1958, 1962, 1966, 1970, 1974, 1980, 1982.
Domestic Cup - (16) 1923, 1934, 1936, 1938, 1941, 1945, 1946, 1948, 1954, 1963, 1971, 1973, 1974, 1978, 1982, 1995.
European Cup-winners' Cup - (1) 1964.

APPEARANCES 95/96

	P	Ap	(s)	Gls
AFONSO MARTINS	M	16	(5)	2
Emanuel AMUNIKE (NIG)	A	23		7
Roberto ASSIS (BRA)	A	3	(2)	
CADETE	A		(3)	
CARLOS FERNANDES	D	1		
CARLOS XAVIER	M	9	(10)	6
CHIQUINHO CONDE	A	1	(3)	
COSTINHA	G	29		
DANI	A	1	(6)	
DOMINGUEZ	A	21	(9)	1
FILIPE	M		(2)	
LUÍS MIGUEL	A	4	(2)	
LUÍS VASCO	G	4		
MARCO AURÉLIO	D	31		1
MARCO CANEIRA	D		(1)	
MAURO SOARES	M	3	(2)	
Noureddine NAYBET (MAR)	D	28		3
NÉLSON	D	32		1
NUNO VALENTE	D	8	(1)	
OCEANO	M	22	(1)	6
Ahmed OUATTARA (CIV)	A	6	(7)	3
PAULO ALVES	A	21	(11)	10
PEDRO BARBOSA	M	20	(2)	8
PEDRO MARTINS	M	14	(12)	1
PEIXE	M	9	(1)	1
SÁ PINTO	A	26		9
Tomas SKUHRAVY (TCH)	A	1	(3)	
TIAGO	G	1		
VIDIGAL	D	8	(9)	
Budimir VUJACIC (YUG)	D	17		3
Ivailo YORDANOV (BUL)	A	15	(4)	5

LEAGUE RESULTS 1995/96

Date	Opponent		Score	Scorers
20/08/95	FC Porto	A	1-2	Ouattara
28/08/95	Boavista FC	H	0-0	
08/09/95	SC Braga	A	3-1	Ouattara, Vujacic, Sá Pinto
18/09/95	SC Campomaiorense	H	7-1	Amunike 2, Oceano 2 (1p), Pedro Barbosa, Sá Pinto, Paulo Alves
23/09/95	SC Farense	A	1-0	Vujacic
03/10/95	SL Benfica	H	2-0	Pedro Barbosa, Amunike
15/10/95	União Leiria	A	2-1	Naybet, Oceano
22/10/95	CS Marítimo	H	2-0	Paulo Alves, Vujacic
29/10/95	SC Salgueiros	A	2-2	Paulo Alves 2
01/11/95	CS Marítimo	H	2-0	Paulo Alves, Vujacic
08/11/95	FC Tirsense	H	1-0	Paulo Alves
19/11/95	Vitória Guimarães	A	1-1	Ouattara
26/11/95	CF Estrela Amadora	H	6-2	Oceano (p), Pedro Barbosa, Amunike, Sá Pinto 2, Pedro Martins (p)
08/12/95	CF Os Belenenses	A	1-0	Sá Pinto
16/12/95	FC Felgueiras	H	4-0	Paulo Alves, Sá Pinto, Pedro Barbosa, Marco Aurélio
23/12/95	Gil Vicente FC	H	4-1	Naybet, og (Beto), Carlos Xavier, Oceano (p)
30/12/95	GD Chaves	A	1-1	Carlos Xavier
06/01/96	Leça FC	H	2-0	Paulo Alves, og (Nando)
13/01/96	FC Porto	H	0-2	
20/01/96	Boavista FC	A	1-2	Pedro Barbosa
27/01/96	SC Braga	H	0-1	
04/02/96	SC Campomaiorense	A	1-0	Yordanov
11/02/96	SC Farense	H	5-0	Amunike 2, Afonso Martins, Paulo Alves, Yordanov
18/02/96	SL Benfica	A	0-0	
03/03/96	União Leiria	H	0-0	
10/03/96	CS Marítimo	A	5-0	Oceano, Paulo Alves, Nélson, Yordanov 2
17/03/96	SC Salgueiros	H	2-2	Pedro Barbosa, Yordanov
24/03/96	FC Tirsense	A	1-1	Naybet
31/03/96	Vitória Guimarães	H	2-3	Pedro Barbosa, Sá Pinto
06/04/96	CF Estrela Amadora	A	1-1	Sá Pinto
14/04/96	CF Os Belenenses	H	3-1	Pedro Barbosa, Amunike, Carlos Xavier
21/04/96	FC Felgueiras	A	1-0	Peixe
28/04/96	Gil Vicente FC	A	2-0	Paulo Alves, Carlos Xavier (p)
04/05/96	GD Chaves	H	4-1	Afonso Martins, Dominguez, Sá Pinto, Carlos Xavier
12/05/96	Leça FC	A	1-1	Carlos Xavier

FC TIRSENSE

CLUB DIRECTORY

Futebol Clube Tirsense
Rua D. Maria do Carmo Azevedo
Apartado 50
4780 Santo Tirso
tel - (052) 52714/52253
fax - (052) 56309
Year of Formation - 1938
President - José Lopes
Coach - José Romão; Eurico Gomes
Stadium - Abel Alves de Figueiredo (15,000)

APPEARANCES 95/96

	P	Ap	(s)	Gls
BASAULA Lemba (ZAI)	M	1	(4)	
BATISTA (BRA)	D	30		4
CAETANO	A	29		2
Goran CUMIC (YUG)	G	23		
Rashid DAOUDI (MAR)	A	20	(1)	2
EUSÉBIO	M	30		2
FOLHA	D	2	(6)	
GASPAR	D	23	(2)	2
JOÃO MÁRIO	M		(2)	
JORGE	D	1	(2)	
JOSÉ CARLOS	G	1		
LUISÃO	D	5		1
Makopoloka MANGONGA (ZAI)	A	10	(7)	2
MIGUEL ANGELO	G	10		
MONTEIRO	M	24	(3)	1
MOREIRA DE SÁ	A	7	(16)	3
MOTA	D	19	(3)	
NITO	M	14		
NOVERÇA	A	6	(12)	1
REBELO	A	10	(19)	4
REDONDO	D	3	(3)	
RISTIC (YUG)	A	5	(6)	4
RUI MANUEL	M	32		2
SAMUEL	D	8		
Samson SIASIA (NIG)	A	14	(1)	
TONINHO CRUZ	M	7	(1)	
TOZÉ	M	28	(4)	
VALIDO	D	12	(3)	

LEAGUE RESULTS 1995/96

Date	Opponent	H/A	Score	Scorers
20/08/95	SC Farense	A	1-2	Eusébio
27/08/95	SL Benfica	H	0-1	
08/09/95	União Leiria	A	1-5	Mangonga
17/09/95	CS Marítimo	H	2-1	Luisão, Batista
24/09/95	SC Salgueiros	A	1-1	Moreira de Sá
30/09/95	FC Felgueiras	H	0-0	
14/10/95	Vitória Guimarães	H	2-2	Daoudi (p), Rebelo
21/10/95	CF Estrela Amadora	A	0-0	
28/10/95	CF Os Belenenses	H	0-0	
08/11/95	Sporting CP	A	0-1	
19/11/95	Gil Vicente FC	H	1-1	Caetano
26/11/95	GD Chaves	A	0-2	
09/12/95	Leça FC	H	1-3	Daoudi (p)
17/12/95	FC Porto	A	0-5	
23/12/95	Boavista FC	H	1-3	Mangonga
30/12/95	SC Braga	A	0-4	
07/01/96	SC Campomaiorense	H	2-0	Gaspar, Moreira de Sá
13/01/96	SC Farense	H	2-1	Batista, Moreira de Sá
20/01/96	SL Benfica	A	1-2	Rui Manuel
27/01/96	União Leiria	H	0-1	
04/02/96	CS Marítimo	A	0-1	
11/02/96	SC Salgueiros	H	2-0	Caetano, Noverça
18/02/96	FC Felgueiras	A	1-0	Eusébio
03/03/96	Vitória Guimarães	A	1-2	Rebelo
06/03/96	CF Estrela Amadora	H	0-0	
17/03/96	CF Os Belenenses	A	1-1	Batista
23/03/96	Sporting CP	H	1-1	Batista
30/03/96	Gil Vicente FC	A	0-1	
04/04/96	GD Chaves	H	2-1	Ristic 2
14/04/96	Leça FC	A	1-3	Rebelo
21/04/96	FC Porto	H	2-4	Gaspar, Rebelo
28/04/96	Boavista FC	A	1-1	Monteiro
05/05/96	SC Braga	H	2-0	Rui Manuel, Ristic (p)
12/05/96	SC Campomaiorense	A	1-3	Ristic

UNIÃO LEIRIA

CLUB DIRECTORY

União Desportiva de Leiria
Rua Mouzinho de Albuquerque
Edifício do Bingo
2400 Leiria
tel - (044) 823532
Year of Formation - 1966
President - João Bartolomeu
Coach - Vítor Manuel
Stadium - Municipal (25,000)

APPEARANCES 95/96

	P	Ap	(s)	Gls
ABEL	M	3	(13)	
ADRIANO PAZ	A		(1)	
ÁLVARO GREGÓRIO	D	11	(1)	1
AYEW Pelé (GHA)	A	8	(5)	1
BILRO	D	22	(1)	
CABRAL	D	5	(16)	
CRESPO	D	19	(3)	
Tahar EL KHALEJ (MAR)	M	21	(1)	3
FERREIRA	G	9		
FUA	A	14	(8)	
Gabriel GERVINO (ARG)	M	25	(2)	1
HUGO	M	24	(2)	4
JOÃO ARMANDO	M	7	(8)	
JOÃO MANUEL	A	26		1
Michael KIMMEL (GER)	M	8	(9)	
LAVOS	G		(1)	
MÁRIO ARTUR	M	26	(4)	
MAURÍCIO	A	21	(4)	13
MIGUEL	M		(1)	
NUNO NETO	G	2		
PAULITO	D	24	(4)	
PAULO DUARTE	D	27	(1)	1
PINTO	A		(1)	
PORFÍRIO	A	24	(4)	8
REINALDO	A	24	(5)	2
RUI PEREIRA	A		(1)	
SÉRGIO COUTO	A		(3)	
SÉRGIO SANTOS	D	1	(1)	
Miroslav ZITNJAK (CRO)	G	23		

LEAGUE RESULTS 1995/96

Date	Opponent	H/A	Score	Scorers
20/08/95	CS Marítimo	H	0-4	
27/08/95	SC Salgueiros	A	0-4	
08/09/95	FC Tirsense	H	5-1	Maurício, João Manuel, Paulo Duarte, Reinaldo, Porfírio
17/09/95	Vitória Guimarães	A	0-3	
24/09/95	CF Estrela Amadora	H	2-1	Gervino, Maurício (p)
30/09/95	CF Os Belenenses	A	1-3	Álvaro Gregório
15/10/95	Sporting CP	H	1-2	og (Marco Aurélio)
22/10/95	Gil Vicente FC	A	0-1	
29/10/95	GD Chaves	H	4-1	Porfírio, El Khalej (p), Hugo, Maurício
05/11/95	Leça FC	A	1-0	Porfírio
18/11/95	FC Porto	H	0-0	
25/11/95	Boavista FC	A	0-5	
09/12/95	SC Braga	H	1-0	Maurício
17/12/95	SC Campomaiorense	A	2-4	Maurício 2
23/12/95	SC Farense	H	1-0	Hugo
30/12/95	SL Benfica	A	0-4	
07/01/96	FC Felgueiras	H	0-0	
13/01/96	CS Marítimo	A	0-1	
20/01/96	SC Salgueiros	H	3-2	Reinaldo 2, Porfírio
27/01/96	FC Tirsense	A	1-0	Maurício
04/02/96	Vitória Guimarães	H	1-2	Gervino
11/02/96	CF Estrela Amadora	A	4-2	Maurício 2, El Khalej 2
18/02/96	CF Os Belenenses	H	1-0	og (Raul)
03/03/96	Sporting CP	A	0-0	
10/03/96	Gil Vicente FC	H	2-0	Ayew, Maurício
17/03/96	GD Chaves	A	1-0	Porfírio
24/03/96	Leça FC	H	1-3	Maurício
30/03/96	FC Porto	A	0-1	
07/04/96	Boavista FC	H	1-0	Porfírio
14/04/96	SC Braga	A	0-0	
21/04/96	SC Campomaiorense	H	4-0	Hugo 2, Porfírio, Maurício
28/04/96	SC Farense	A	1-1	Porfírio
04/05/96	SL Benfica	H	0-2	
11/05/96	FC Felgueiras	A	0-3	

VITÓRIA GUIMARÃES

CLUB DIRECTORY

Vitória Sport Clube
Complexo Desportivo-Margaride
4800 Guimarães
tel - (053) 512570/1/2/3
fax - (053) 512573
Year of Formation - 1922
President - António Pimenta Machado
Coach - Vítor Oliveira; Jaime Pacheco
Stadium - Vitória Sport Clube (33,000)

APPEARANCES 95/96

	P	Ap	(s)	Gls
ARLEY (BRA)	D	23	(2)	
ARMANDO	M		(7)	1
BASÍLIO	D	8	(2)	
CAPUCHO	A	32	(1)	8
EDINHO (BRA)	A	19	(13)	15
EMERSON (BRA)	A	4	(16)	2
FERNANDO MEIRA	D		(1)	
GILMAR	A	20	(10)	4
JOSÉ CARLOS	D	29		
Dane KUPRESANIN (BOS)	A	8	(6)	3
MADUREIRA	G		(1)	
MARCO FREITAS	M	12	(6)	
N'DINGA Mbote (ZAI)	M	20	(4)	
NENO	G	21		
NUNO	G	13		
NUNO MARTINHO	D	1		
QUIM BERTO	D	30		2
RAMIREZ	M		(2)	
RICARDO	A	12	(5)	5
SOEIRO	M	22	(8)	
TANTA	D	21		2
VÍTOR PANEIRA	M	27	(3)	5
VÍTOR SILVA	D	22	(1)	
VORKAPIC (YUG)	M		(4)	
WALTER	D	3		
Zlatko ZAHOVIC (SLO)	M	27	(2)	8

LEAGUE RESULTS 1995/96

20/08/95	SC Campomaiorense	A	1-0	Emerson
27/08/95	SC Farense	H	1-0	Zahovic (p)
08/09/95	SL Benfica	A	1-1	Ricardo
17/09/95	União Leiria	H	3-0	Gilmar, Zahovic, Edinho
23/09/95	CS Marítimo	A	0-4	
30/09/95	SC Salgueiros	H	1-2	Vítor Paneira (p)
14/10/95	FC Tirsense	A	2-2	Capucho, Edinho
22/10/95	FC Felgueiras	H	2-0	Tanta, Capucho
28/10/95	CF Estrela Amadora	H	3-0	Zahovic, Vítor Paneira, Gilmar
05/11/95	Bts	A	0-1	
19/11/95	Sporting CP	H	1-1	Capucho
26/11/95	Gil Vicente FC	A	0-2	
09/12/95	GD Chaves	H	2-1	Vítor Paneira, Edinho
17/12/95	Leça FC	A	0-1	
23/12/95	FC Porto	H	0-2	
30/12/95	Boavista FC	A	1-2	Kupresanin
07/01/96	SC Braga	H	1-1	Zahovic
13/01/96	SC Campomaiorense	H	4-0	Quim Berto 2, Tanta, Edinho
20/01/96	SC Farense	A	1-0	Kupresanin
27/01/96	SL Benfica	H	2-4	Zahovic, Ricardo
04/02/96	União Leiria	A	2-1	Edinho, Kupresanin
11/02/96	CS Marítimo	H	6-0	Ricardo, Edinho 3, Vítor Paneira, Capucho
18/02/96	SC Salgueiros	A	2-1	Capucho, Edinho
03/03/96	FC Tirsense	H	2-1	Capucho, Emerson
10/03/96	FC Felgueiras	A	3-0	Ricardo, Gilmar 2
17/03/96	CF Estrela Amadora	A	0-0	
24/03/96	CF Os Belenenses	H	1-0	Edinho
30/03/96	Sporting CP	A	3-2	Edinho, Capucho, Armando
07/04/96	Gil Vicente FC	H	2-0	Edinho 2
11/04/96	GD Chaves	A	2-1	Zahovic, Vítor Paneira
21/04/96	Leça FC	H	2-0	Capucho, Edinho (p)
28/04/96	FC Porto	A	3-2	Edinho (p), Ricardo, Zahovic
04/05/96	Boavista FC	H	1-3	Zahovic
11/05/96	SC Braga	A	0-4	

PROMOTED CLUBS

SECOND DIVISION FINAL TABLE 95/96

		Pd	W	D	L	F	A	Pt	GD
1	**Rio Ave FC**	**34**	**21**	**5**	**8**	**58**	**42**	**68**	**+16**
2	**Vitória Setúbal**	**34**	**18**	**8**	**8**	**55**	**22**	**62**	**+33**
3	**SC Espinho**	**34**	**19**	**5**	**10**	**49**	**27**	**62**	**+22**
4	Desportivo Aves	34	17	7	10	53	41	58	+12
5	FC Paços Ferreira	34	16	9	9	44	38	57	+6
6	FC Penafiel	34	15	7	12	57	44	52	+13
7	União Madeira	34	14	9	11	43	37	51	+6
8	CD Feirense	34	15	5	14	52	48	50	+4
9	Académico Viseu	34	13	10	11	29	28	49	+1
10	SC Beira Mar	34	13	8	13	39	37	47	+2
11	Moreirense FC	34	12	9	13	39	41	45	-2
12	GD Estoril Praia	34	12	8	14	52	42	44	+10
13	FC Alverca	34	12	8	14	28	38	44	-10
14	União Lamas	34	11	8	15	36	42	41	-6
15	Académica Coimbra	34	11	8	15	38	48	41	-10
16	CD Nacional	34	11	6	17	39	43	39	-4
17	FC Famalicão	34	8	4	22	27	57	28	-30
18	AD Ovarense	34	3	6	25	25	88	15	-63

CLUB DIRECTORY

Rio Ave Futebol Clube
Praça da República No 35, Apartado 42
4480 Vila do Conde
tel - (052) 632999
Year of Formation - 1939
President - Paulo Carvalho
Coach - Henrique Calisto
Stadium - Rio Ave (43,627)

CLUB DIRECTORY

Vitória Futebol Clube
Rua do Bocage 4
2900 Setúbal
tel - (065) 526959
Year of Formation - 1910
President - Justo Tomás
Coach - Quinito (96/97 - Mário Reis)
Stadium - Bonfim (30,676)

MAJOR HONOURS

Domestic Cup - (2) 1965, 1967.

CLUB DIRECTORY

Sporting Clube de Espinho
Rua Oito no. 737
4500 Espinho
tel - (02) 721532/723462/723112
Year of Formation - 1914
President - Ilídio Oliveira e Silva
Coach - Adelino Teixeira (96/97 - Zinho)
Stadium - Comendador Manuel de Oliveira Violas (20,000)

REPUBLIC OF IRELAND

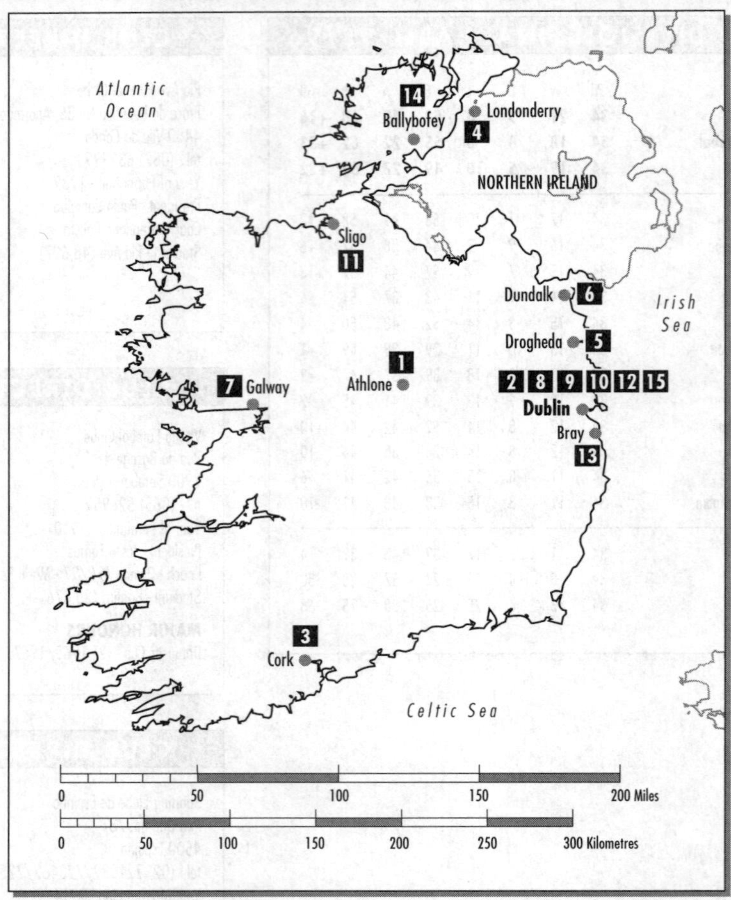

1	ATHLONE TOWN	808
2	BOHEMIANS	809
3	CORK CITY	810
4	DERRY CITY	811
5	DROGHEDA UNITED	812
6	DUNDALK	813
7	GALWAY UNITED	814
8	ST. PATRICK'S ATHLETIC	815
9	SHAMROCK ROVERS	816
10	SHELBOURNE	817
11	SLIGO ROVERS	818
12	UCD	819
13	BRAY WANDERERS	820
14	FINN HARPS	820
15	HOME FARM EVERTON	820

ST. PATRICK'S HAVE THEIR DAY

End of an era as Charlton departs

FEDERATION DIRECTORY

The Football Association of Ireland
80 Merrion Square, Dublin 2
tel - (01) 6766864/6761354/661481/6761178
tlx - 91397 fai ei
fax - (01) 6614264
Stadium - Lansdowne Road, Dublin (48,000)

Year of Formation - 1921
Chairman - Michael Hyland
Secretary - Brendan Menton

In the end it was all a bit of a mess. The Republic of Ireland's Euro '96 play-off defeat by Holland at Anfield brought the Jack Charlton era to a sad but inevitable conclusion. And yet the great man would not come forward and make the announcement everybody expected. Summoned by FAI officials back to Dublin, Charlton was eventually forced into a corner, announcing his resignation in reluctant, unceremonious fashion to a nation that for the best part of a decade had idolised and worshipped him.

Charlton's time as national team manager had brought unprecedented success to Irish football. Before the Englishman took charge, the Republic were habitual underachievers. Charlton led the 'Boys in Green' to two World Cups and one European Championship. He would dearly have loved to bow out with a second appearance at the European finals, in his native land, but it was not to be.

Charlton's team were a declining force long before the axe finally fell in Liverpool. Even the manager appeared to have 'lost it' towards the end of the qualifying campaign. His long-ball methods no longer worked. Opponents knew exactly what they would be up against when they took on the Irish, and the 'Giraffe' was unable to change his spots. A bevy of strange selections and substitutions also hinted that Charlton was not quite as tuned in to his task as he had once been.

Two 1-3 defeats against Austria preceded a last-match mauling by Portugal in Lisbon. Had the Irish won that game, they would have been through to England as group winners, but they were never in with a shout once Rui Costa had put the home side ahead with a sublime chip after an hour's play. Ultimately the Republic owed their place in the play-off to Northern Ireland, who beat Austria 5-3 in Belfast.

With Liverpool being the venue for the play-off against Holland, the Irish were guaranteed huge

LEAGUE CHAMPIONSHIP RESULTS 95/96

		1	2	3	4	5	6	7	8	9	10	11	12
1	Athlone Town		2-5	2-4	1-1	0-2	0-0	0-2	0-1	2-0	1-2	1-2	1-0
			0-3				0-0	1-0	2-2		4-3		
2	Bohemians	3-1		1-1	1-0	6-0	3-2	3-0	0-1	1-1	1-0	2-0	0-0
				1-0	1-1				0-0	1-0		1-2	3-1
3	Cork City	2-0	1-0		0-1	1-2	0-2	1-1	1-0	2-0	1-1	2-1	2-1
		0-2				2-1		3-0	0-0		2-1		
4	Derry City	5-3	1-1	2-0		1-0	1-1	2-0	5-1	1-1	1-2	1-2	3-1
		1-1		2-1		1-1	0-1					4-0	1-1
5	Drogheda United	0-1	2-5	2-2	2-2		3-2	3-0	1-3	1-2	1-1	0-0	0-1
		0-1	0-1				2-1	6-1			1-3	0-1	
6	Dundalk	2-1	1-2	0-0	2-1	2-2		2-0	3-2	1-0	1-1	0-1	2-0
			2-4	0-1					1-2	0-0		0-1	
7	Galway United	2-2	1-5	3-1	1-1	0-3	0-1		0-1	1-1	1-1	2-3	1-1
			0-2		0-3		2-1			0-2	1-3		0-2
8	St. Patrick's Athletic	3-2	3-3	2-1	3-3	1-0	2-1	1-2		1-0	2-1	1-0	2-1
					1-1	3-2		3-0		2-2	3-0		2-0
9	Shamrock Rovers	1-1	1-0	1-1	2-0	1-1	1-0	2-1	0-1		0-1	0-2	0-2
		2-1		2-0	2-1	1-0							2-0
10	Shelbourne	1-0	1-0	1-1	1-2	0-0	3-1	2-0	1-1	3-0		0-0	1-1
			1-0		1-0		0-1			1-2		2-1	
11	Sligo Rovers	4-2	0-0	3-1	1-1	1-0	3-3	3-2	0-0	0-1	0-1		2-0
		2-1		4-1				0-2	1-1	3-1			
12	UCD	3-0	3-1	0-1	2-0	0-0	1-2	2-0	0-2	0-1	0-3	2-1	
		1-2		2-1		4-1	0-0				3-2	3-1	

LEAGUE CHAMPIONSHIP FINAL TABLE 95/96

			Home					Away					Total						
		Pd	W	D	L	F	A	W	D	L	F	A	W	D	L	F	A	Pt	GD
1	St. Patrick's Athletic	33	12	4	1	35	19	7	6	3	18	15	19	10	4	53	34	67	+19
2	Bohemians	33	10	5	2	28	10	8	3	5	32	19	18	8	7	60	29	62	+31
3	Sligo Rovers	33	8	5	3	27	17	8	2	7	18	21	16	7	10	45	38	55	+7
4	Shelbourne	33	8	5	3	19	10	7	4	6	26	23	15	9	9	45	33	54	+12
5	Shamrock Rovers	33	9	3	4	18	12	5	5	7	14	20	14	8	11	32	32	50	=
6	Derry City	33	8	6	3	32	17	3	7	6	18	21	11	13	9	50	38	46	+12
7	Dundalk	33	6	4	6	19	18	5	5	7	19	21	11	9	13	38	39	42	-1
8	UCD	33	9	2	6	26	18	3	4	9	12	22	12	6	15	38	40	42	-2
9	Cork City	33	9	3	4	20	13	3	5	9	17	28	12	8	13	37	41	41	-4
10	Athlone Town	33	4	4	8	17	27	4	3	10	21	32	8	7	18	38	59	31	-21
11	Drogheda United	33	4	4	9	24	27	3	5	8	15	24	7	9	17	39	51	30	-12
12	Galway United	33	2	5	10	15	33	3	1	12	11	34	5	6	22	26	67	21	-41

N.B. Cork City deducted 3 pts.

support. But on the night, the encouragement of their fans counted for little. Ireland were totally outplayed from first minute to last. Holland had knocked Ireland out of the 1994 World Cup with a 2-0 win, and they were to repeat that scoreline at Anfield, with youngster Patrick Kluivert netting the two all-important goals.

So, Charlton and his ageing team were denied a final fling. It was indeed the end of an era.

Once Big Jack had officially stepped down, the race was on to find a worthy successor. Several names were put forward as likely candidates, with Kenny Dalglish the most prominent of a group that included Liam Brady, Dave Bassett, Mike Walker, Joe Kinnear and Ronnie Whelan. The favourite all along, however, was Charlton's own choice, Mick McCarthy, the manager of English First Division club Millwall and a one-time captain of the Republic in the early period of Charlton's reign. After several weeks of interviewing and speculation, the FAI duly gave McCarthy the job, offering him a two-year contract to lead Ireland through to their third successive World Cup finals.

The appointment of the new manager came at a time of huge internal unrest at the FAI, with several top officials, led by secretary Sean Connolly, all resigning from their

TOP SCORERS

20	Stephen GEOGHEGAN (Shelbourne)
16	Mick O'BYRNE (UCD)
14	Ricky O'FLAHERTY (St. Patrick's Athletic)
	Padraig MORAN (Sligo Rovers)
12	Tommy GAYNOR (Athlone Town)
	Ian GILZEAN (Sligo Rovers)
11	Derek SWAN (Bohemians)
	Warren PARKES (Athlone Town)
	John CAULFIELD (Cork City)
10	Mark REID (Shamrock Rovers)
	John RYAN (Drogheda United)

NATIONAL TEAM RESULTS 95/96

06/09/95	Austria (ECQ)	A	Vienna	1-3	McGrath (74)
11/10/95	Latvia (ECQ)	H	Dublin	2-1	Aldridge (61p, 64)
15/11/95	Portugal (ECQ)	A	Lisbon	0-3	
13/12/95	Holland (ECQ)	N	Liverpool	0-2	
27/03/96	Russia	H	Dublin	0-2	
24/04/96	Czech Republic	A	Prague	0-3	
29/05/96	Portugal	H	Dublin	0-1	
02/06/96	Croatia	H	Dublin	2-2	O'Neill (24), Quinn (87)
04/06/96	Holland	A	Rotterdam	1-3	Breen (13)
09/06/96	United States	A	Massachussetts	1-2	Connolly (57)
12/06/96	Mexico	N	East Rutherford	2-2	Connolly (44), Davino (49og)
15/06/96	Bolivia	N	East Rutherford	3-0	O'Neill (12, 33), Harte (45)

NATIONAL TEAM APPEARANCES 95/96

Manager - Jack CHARLTON; Mick McCARTHY	AUT	LAT	POR	HOL	RUS	TCH	POR	CRO	HOL	USA	MEX	BOL	Cps	Gls
Alan KELLY (11/08/68) - Sheffield United (ENG)	G	G	G	G									14	-
Gary KELLY (09/07/74) - Leeds United (ENG)	D	D	D	D									18	1
Denis IRWIN (31/10/65) - Manchester United (ENG)	D		D	D		D46							40	1
Alan KERNAGHAN (25/04/67) - Manchester City (ENG)	D		s79	s72	D		D	s64	D	D		D35	22	1
Paul McGRATH (04/12/59) - Aston Villa (ENG)	D	D	D	D	D	D							82	8
Roy KEANE (10/08/71) - Manchester United (ENG)	M				M								30	1
Andy TOWNSEND (23/07/63) - Aston Villa (ENG)	M	M		M50	M46	M	M						60	6
Ray HOUGHTON (09/01/62) - Crystal Palace (ENG)	M68					M							66	5
John SHERIDAN (01/10/64) - Sheffield Wednesday (ENG)	M			M									34	5
Mark KENNEDY (15/05/76) - Liverpool (ENG)	M	s84	M73		M	M		M	s46	s61	M72	s65	10	-
Niall QUINN (06/10/66) - Manchester City (ENG)	A	A	A		A86	A	s75	A	s64	A87			60	14
Tony CASCARINO (01/09/62) - Olympique Marseille (FRA)	s68		s73	A	s63		A75	s74	A46				63	12
Phil BABB (30/11/70) - Liverpool (ENG)		D	D	D		D77							20	-
Terry PHELAN (16/03/67) - Manchester City (ENG)/Chelsea (ENG)		D		M	D		D88	M46	D	D	s72	M	35	-
Jason McATEER (18/06/71) - Liverpool (ENG)		M	M	s50	M								18	-
Jeff KENNA (27/08/70) - Blackburn Rovers (ENG)		M	M	M	s46	D	M	D64	D78	D40			12	-
Steve STAUNTON (19/01/69) - Aston Villa (ENG)		M	M79		D								62	5
John ALDRIDGE (18/09/58) - Tranmere Rovers (ENG)		A79	A	A72	A63								68	19
David KELLY (25/11/65) - Sunderland (ENG)		s79 /84											20	8
Shay GIVEN (20/04/76) - Blackburn Rovers (ENG)					G	G	G	G	G	G		G85	7	-
Tommy COYNE (14/11/62) - Motherwell (SCO)					s86								21	6
Ken CUNNINGHAM (28/06/71) - Wimbledon (ENG)					D		D	D90	s70	D		D	6	-
Alan MOORE (21/11/74) - Middlesbrough (ENG)					A			s46	A46		A	A	5	-
Curtis FLEMING (08/10/68) - Middlesbrough (ENG)						s46	D	s90	s78	s40	D	D	7	-
Liam DAISH (23/09/68) - Coventry City (ENG)						s77		D			D		4	-
Alan McLOUGHLIN (20/04/67) - Portsmouth (ENG)							M	M71	M	M	M	s46	23	1
Gareth FARRELLY (28/08/75) - Aston Villa (ENG)							M60			M61		M65	3	-
David CONNOLLY (06/06/77) - Watford (ENG)							M63		M64	M	M		4	2
Dave SAVAGE (30/07/73) - Millwall (ENG)							s60	s71		s87	M	M	5	-
Keith O'NEILL (16/02/76) - Norwich City (ENG)							s63	A46	s46	s87	A	A	6	3
Gary BREEN (12/12/73) - Birmingham City (ENG)							s88	D74	D	M	D	s35	6	1
Liam O'BRIEN (05/09/64) - Tranmere Rovers (ENG)								M	M70	M87		M46	15	-
Ian HARTE (31/08/77) - Leeds United (ENG)								s46	M		D	D	4	1
Pat BONNER (25/05/60) - Celtic (SCO)											G	s85	80	-

posts after a series of corruption scandals were unearthed. The final chapter in what became known as the 'Merriongate' saga was written when FAI president Louis Kilcoyne found himself voted out of office. Among other disgressions, Kilcoyne had publicly acknowledged that McCarthy was not his first choice as the new Ireland manager. Following in the footsteps of a living legend was never going to be easy for McCarthy. His task was made more difficult by the fact that many of Charlton's regulars were approaching the end of their international careers.

McCarthy took the bold step of changing not only the team's formation, but of bringing in a whole batch of fresh faces. Fortunately, there was a whole spate of friendlies already lined up for him in the spring, and he used these to experiment with his own ideas and blood several untried youngsters.

The first few results were far from encouraging - three defeats and no goals in the first three matches - but an end-of-season tour to the United States heralded a sudden improvement, and after seven matches in charge, McCarthy got his first win when the Republic beat Bolivia 3-0. The most impressive of the newcomers were Shay Given, Gary Breen, Ian Harte and Keith O'Neill. Whether they will prove to be capable replacements for the veterans of the Charlton era remains open to doubt. But at least Ireland have landed themselves in an easy World Cup qualifying group. The team may have lost their lustre, but they surely won't lose too many games against Lithuania, Macedonia, Iceland and Liechtenstein.

McCarthy may be looking to youth, but as yet he has not dipped into the League of Ireland to bolster his squad. Granted, the standard of the League is uniformly low, but one or two gifted individuals are perhaps deserving of a call-up to the national colours. It would certainly give the League a huge boost.

The 95/96 Premier Division champions were St. Patrick's Athletic from Dublin. They took the title for the second time in seven years, with the same manager, Brian Kerr, who had overseen the club's previous triumph in 1989/90. A St. Pat's man through and through, Kerr displayed his managerial ability by signing Rick O'Flaherty from Galway United at the start of the season. 30-year-old O'Flaherty was one of a number of ex-Galway players in the team and he was St. Patrick's' key player in the title-winning campaign, scoring 14 league goals, the last of which, a header from the edge of the penalty-area, gave his team the lead against Dundalk in the penultimate game of the season. St. Patrick's won that match against the defending champions 2-1, thereby confirming themselves as the League of Ireland champions after a season-long battle to fend off the challenge of another Dublin side, Bohemians.

St. Patrick's suffered a major setback in mid-December when they were walloped 5-1 by Derry City at the Brandywell. But thereafter they remained unbeaten for 18 matches. That was too much for Bohemians, who, with the strongest squad of players in the country, were the pre-season favourites. The Bohs gave it their best shot, but defeats against each of their Dublin rivals proved costly. It was little consolation to them that they finished with the best attack and the best defence in the Premier Division.

DOMESTIC CUP RESULTS

FIRST ROUND
Dundalk 1, Drogheda United 1
(replay) Drogheda United 2, Dundalk 1
Athlone Town 2, Monaghan United 1
Bohemians 2, Moyle Park College 0
St. Patrick's Athletic 3, Workman's/Dunleary 1
Finn Harps 5, Longford Town 2
Avondale United 3, CYM Terenure 1
Bray Wanderers 0, Fanad United 4
UCD 1, Kilkenny City 2
TEK United 0, Cork City 1
Derry City 0, St. James's Gate 0
(replay) St. James's Gate 0, Derry City 1
Shamrock Rovers 0, Shelbourne 0
(replay) Shelbourne 1, Shamrock Rovers 0
Temple United 2, Home Farm Everton 3
UCC 0, Limerick 1
Waterford United 3, Galway United 2
Wayside Celtic 2, Cherry Orchard 1
Cobh Ramblers 1, Sligo Rovers 2

SECOND ROUND
Bohemians 4, Kilkenny 0
Drogheda United 0, Shelbourne 2
St. Patrick's Athletic 3, Fanad United 0
Finn Harps 1, Athlone Town 1
(replay) Athlone Town 1, Finn Harps 4
Derry City 2, Avondale United 0
Home Farm Everton 1, Cork City 1
(replay) Cork City 1, Home Farm Everton 0
Waterford United 0, Wayside Celtic 0
(replay) Wayside Celtic 1, Waterford United 1
(2nd replay) Wayside Celtic 2, Waterford United 1
Limerick 1, Sligo Rovers 3

QUARTER-FINALS
Finn Harps 0, Bohemians 0
(replay) Bohemians 2, Finn Harps 0
Cork City 1, Sligo Rovers 2
Derry City 0, Shelbourne 3
Wayside Celtic 0, St. Patrick's Athletic 3

SEMI-FINALS
Bohemians 0, St. Patrick's Athletic 0
(replay) St. Patrick's Athletic 0, Bohemians 0 (aet)
(2nd replay) Bohemians 1, St. Patrick's Athletic 2
Sligo Rovers 0, Shelbourne 1

FINAL
06/05/96, Dublin
ST. PATRICK'S ATHLETIC 1 Campbell D. (76)
SHELBOURNE 1 Sheridan (86)
referee - Kelly
ST. PATRICK'S ATHLETIC - Byrne; Burke, McDonnell, Campbell D., Carpenter, Campbell P., Mernagh, Gormley, Osam, O'Flaherty (Glynn 79), Burkley (Reilly 69).
SHELBOURNE - Gough; Costello, Neville, Duffy (Rutherford 82), Geoghegan D., Sheridan, Kelly (McKop 66), Flood, O'Rourke, Tilson, Geoghegan S..

(replay)
12/05/96, Dublin
SHELBOURNE 2 Sheridan (71), Geoghegan S. (82)
ST. PATRICK'S ATHLETIC 1 Campbell D. (63)
referee - Wallace
SHELBOURNE - Gough; Costello, Neville, Duffy, Geoghegan D., Sheridan, Kelly (Rutherford 64), Flood, O'Rourke, Tilson, Geoghegan S..
ST. PATRICK'S ATHLETIC - Byrne; Burke, McDonnell (Campbell P. 30), Campbell D., Carpenter, Osam (Reilly 45), Mernagh (Glynn 82), Gormley, Buckley, Morris-Roe, O'Flaherty.

PLAYERS OF THE SEASON

ANDY TOWNSEND
Like most of the old guard in Jack Charlton's team, Irish skipper Andy Townsend was excused from duty at the end of the season as new boss Mick McCarthy sought to experiment with new players and new tactics. But, despite his 33 years, the Aston Villa midfielder seems sure to add to his 60 caps as Ireland strive to qualify for the 1998 World Cup. While the likes of McGrath, Aldridge and Bonner wave farewell to the international scene, the 1995 FAI Player of the Year still has plenty to offer. He showed that right through the 1995/96 season when he shone in an Aston Villa team that challenged strongly in all three English domestic competitions and won the Coca-Cola (League) Cup.

STEPHEN GEOGHEGAN
26-year-old Shelbourne striker Stephen Geoghegan was undoubtedly the man of the Irish domestic season in 1995/96. He won the League of Ireland top scorer prize for the second time in three seasons, having also scooped the award in 93/94 when playing for Dublin rivals Shamrock Rovers. And Geoghegan was also the matchwinner for Shelbourne in the final of the FAI Cup, denying St. Patrick's a first ever 'double' with his late strike in the final replay. His fans in Dublin would like to see him called up to the Irish national team. There is little more Geoghegan can do to impress Mick McCarthy within his present confines.

Sligo Rovers, on the other hand, surpassed all expectations to finish third. Having lost manager Lawrie Sanchez and a clutch of top players, they rode the storm brilliantly under new boss Steve Cotterill - a one-time colleague of Sanchez at Wimbledon. Sligo also finished runners-up in the League Cup (on penalties) and reached the semi-finals of the FAI Cup. They were beaten on both occasions by the 95/96 Cup specialists, Shelbourne.

The Shels added the FAI Cup to the League Cup by overcoming 'double'-chasing St. Patrick's after two exciting finals - the first between two Dublin clubs for 12 years. The first match, at Lansdowne Road, looked to be heading St. Pat's' way when Shelbourne goalkeeper Alan Gough was sent off for handling outside the area. But a late equaliser by Shelbourne forced a replay at Dalymount Park. Gough, not suspended for the second game, redeemed himself by saving a penalty with the scores level at 1-1. Shortly afterwards, the league's top scorer, Stephen Geoghegan, scored the winning goal for Shelbourne.

The number of Dublin clubs in the top flight rose to six - fifty per cent of the division - with the promotion of Home Farm Everton (sponsored by the English club), who went up after defeating Athlone Town on penalties in the promotion/relegation play-off. The two automatically-promoted teams were First Division champions Bray Wanderers and runners-up Finn Harps, the team from Donegal who had missed out on penalties in the play-off against Athlone a year earlier.

EUROPEAN CUPS RESULTS 95/96

CUP-WINNERS' CUP

● DERRY CITY

Preliminary round LOKOMOTIV SOFIA (BUL)

H 1-0 McCourt (44)
O'Dowd; Vaudequin, Curran, Gauld, McLoughlin, McCourt, Carlyle, Doolin, Mohan (Heaney 61), Fraser, Coyle.

A 0-2
O'Dowd; Vaudequin, Curran, Gauld, McLoughlin, McCourt (Tohill 65), Carlyle, Doolin, Hutton, Mohan, Coyle.

UEFA CUP

● DUNDALK

Preliminary round MALMÖ FF (SWE)

H 0-2
Van Boxtel; Futcher, Whelan, Doohan, Coady, Britton, McNulty, Kelly, Byrne, Withnell, Hanrahan.

A 0-2
Van Boxtel; Britton (Byrne M. 65), Coady, Doohan, Whelan, Futcher, Hanrahan (Long 46), McNulty, Kelly, Byrne B., Withnell (Lopez 85).

● SHELBOURNE

Preliminary round ÍA (ISL)

H 0-3
Gough; Flood, Duffy, Neville, Dunne, Byrne (Devereaux 85), Howlett, O'Rourke, Geoghegan D. (Smith 58), Arkins, Geoghegan S..

A 0-3
Gough; Costello, Flood, Neville, Dunne, Devereaux, Howlett, Byrne, O'Rourke, Arkins, Geoghegan S..

INTERNATIONAL HONOURS

World Cup Finals appearances: 1990 (qtr-finals), 1994 (2nd round)
European Championship appearances: 1964, 1988

ATHLONE TOWN

CLUB DIRECTORY

Athlone Town FC
St. Mel's Park
Athlone
Co. Westmeath
tel - (0902) 78377/74132/75840
fax - (0902) 72583
Year of Formation - 1887
Chairman - Paddy McCaul
Secretary - Jack McKervey
Manager - Michael O'Connor
Stadium - St. Mel's Park (10,200)

MAJOR HONOURS
League Championship - (2) 1981, 1983.
Domestic Cup - (1) 1924.

APPEARANCES 95/96

	P	Ap	(s)	Gls
Paul BRADY	M	7		
Mark BURKE	M		(1)	
Adrian CARBERRY	D	14	(3)	1
Dave COLLINS	M	26		1
Michael COLLINS	A	30		3
Shane CURRAN	G	28		
Frank DARBY	D	17	(1)	
David DOWLING	A	18	(8)	3
Colin FORTUNE	A	1	(4)	1
Brian FRAWLEY	M	1	(4)	
Conor FRAWLEY	M	28	(3)	2
Tommy GAYNOR	A	27		12
Donal GOLDEN	A	19	(11)	2
Keith HOGAN	M	1	(4)	
Tommy KEANE	A		(1)	
Anthony KEENAN	G	5		
Val KEENAN	D	22		
Rod DE KHORS	M	13		1
Ian KIERNAN	D	2		
Alan KINSELLA	D	20		
Ray McLOUGHLIN	D	11	(1)	
Chris MALONE	D	10	(2)	
John MORRIS-BURKE	A	7	(11)	
Colm MULDOON	D	1		
Barry MURPHY	D	22		
Michael O'CONNOR	A	6	(7)	
Warren PARKES	M	27	(4)	11
Keith REYNOLDS	D		(1)	

LEAGUE RESULTS 1995/96

Date	Opponent		Score	Scorers
26/08/95	Sligo Rovers	A	2-4	Parkes 2
02/09/95	Galway United	H	0-2	
08/09/95	Dundalk	H	0-0	
15/09/95	Drogheda United	A	1-0	Parkes
22/09/95	St. Patrick's Athletic	H	0-1	
29/09/95	Cork City	A	0-2	
06/10/95	Bohemians	H	2-5	Gaynor 2
15/10/95	Shamrock Rovers	A	1-1	Fortune
20/10/95	Shelbourne	H	1-2	Gaynor
29/10/95	UCD	A	0-3	
05/11/95	Derry City	A	3-5	De Khors, Gaynor, Frawley C.
10/11/95	Derry City	H	1-1	Gaynor
17/11/95	Sligo Rovers	H	1-2	Golden
25/11/95	Galway United	A	2-2	Dowling, Collins D.
30/11/95	Dundalk	A	1-2	Gaynor (p)
08/12/95	Drogheda United	H	0-2	
15/12/95	St. Patrick's Athletic	A	2-3	Gaynor (p), Parkes
22/12/95	Cork City	H	2-4	Parkes, Dowling
31/12/95	Bohemians	A	1-3	Parkes
05/01/96	Shamrock Rovers	H	2-0	Gaynor, Parkes
19/01/96	Shelbourne	A	0-1	
26/01/96	UCD	H	1-0	Gaynor
03/02/96	Sligo Rovers	A	1-2	Frawley C.
16/02/96	Galway United	H	1-0	Parkes
23/02/96	Dundalk	H	0-0	
01/03/96	Drogheda United	A	1-0	Gaynor
16/03/96	St. Patrick's Athletic	H	2-2	Parkes 2
24/03/96	Cork City	A	2-0	og (Shaw), Collins M.
29/03/96	Bohemians	H	0-3	
07/04/96	Shamrock Rovers	A	1-2	Carberry
12/04/96	Shelbourne	H	4-3	Collins M. 2, Golden, Gaynor
21/04/96	UCD	A	2-1	Dowling, Gaynor
27/04/96	Derry City	A	1-1	Parkes

BOHEMIANS

CLUB DIRECTORY

Bohemian FC
Dalymount Park
Phibsborough
Dublin 7
tel - (01) 8680923/8681022/8682880
fax - (01) 8681022
Year of Formation - 1890
Chairman - Anthony O'Connell
Secretary - Donal Crowther
Manager - Turlough O'Connor
Stadium - Dalymount Park (20,000)

MAJOR HONOURS
League Championship - (7)
1924, 1928, 1930, 1934, 1936, 1975, 1978.
Domestic Cup - (5)
1928, 1935, 1970, 1976, 1992.

APPEARANCES 95/96

	P	Ap	(s)	Gls
Robbie BEST	D	30		
Kevin BRADY	D	30		1
Donal BROUGHAN	D	22		3
John BYRNE	M	1		
Tommy BYRNE	D	30	(2)	4
James COLL	D	24	(1)	1
Tony COUSINS	A	24	(5)	5
Jason COYLE	M	1		
Michael DEMPSEY	G	2	(1)	
Ian DOUGLAS	A	4	(1)	
Padraig DULLY	A	9	(2)	4
DUNNE	M		(1)	
Peter HANRAHAN	A	12	(7)	
Dave HENDERSON	G	31		
Tommy LAWLESS	D		(2)	
Paul McGEE	M	7		
Brendan MARKEY	A	5	(4)	6
Mick MOODY	D	12	(4)	
Brian MOONEY	A	25		6
Tony O'CONNOR	M	29		5
Maurice O'DRISCOLL	D	30		8
Jonathan PRIZEMAN	M	6	(15)	3
Derek SWAN	M	28	(1)	11
Dave TILSON	A	1	(1)	

LEAGUE RESULTS 1995/96

Date	Opponent		Score	Scorers
27/08/95	Dundalk	A	2-1	Mooney, og (Purdy)
01/09/95	Cork City	H	1-1	Swan
08/09/95	Shelbourne	A	0-1	
15/09/95	Sligo Rovers	H	2-0	O'Driscoll 2
22/09/95	Drogheda United	A	5-2	Mooney, Cousins 2, Byrne T. (p), O'Connor
29/09/95	Derry City	H	1-0	O'Connor
06/10/95	Athlone Town	A	5-2	Cousins, Byrne T., O'Driscoll, og (Keenan), Mooney
13/10/95	St. Patrick's Athletic	H	0-1	
20/10/95	UCD	H	0-0	
28/10/95	Galway United	A	5-1	O'Driscoll, Swan, O'Connor, Coll, Prizeman
03/11/95	Shamrock Rovers	H	1-1	Swan
12/11/95	Shamrock Rovers	A	0-1	
17/11/95	Dundalk	H	3-2	Markey 2, Cousins
24/11/95	Cork City	A	0-1	
01/12/95	Shelbourne	H	1-0	Markey
09/12/95	Sligo Rovers	A	0-0	
15/12/95	Drogheda United	H	6-0	Markey 3, Mooney, Prizeman, Cousins
31/12/95	Athlone Town	H	3-1	O'Driscoll, O'Connor, Swan
05/01/96	St. Patrick's Athletic	A	3-3	Swan 3
21/01/96	UCD	A	1-3	og (Palmer)
26/01/96	Galway United	H	3-0	O'Driscoll 2, Prizeman
04/02/96	Dundalk	A	4-2	Dully, Broughan, Mooney, O'Connor
16/02/96	Cork City	H	1-0	Broughan
23/02/96	Shelbourne	A	0-1	
01/03/96	Sligo Rovers	H	1-2	Swan
03/03/96	Derry City	A	1-1	O'Driscoll
15/03/96	Drogheda United	A	1-0	Swan
22/03/96	Derry City	H	1-1	Broughan (p)
29/03/96	Athlone Town	A	3-0	Dully 2, Swan
08/04/96	St. Patrick's Athletic	H	0-0	
12/04/96	UCD	H	3-1	Brady, Swan, Byrne T. (p)
20/04/96	Galway United	A	2-0	Byrne T. (p), Dully
27/04/96	Shamrock Rovers	H	1-0	Mooney

CORK CITY

CLUB DIRECTORY

Cork City FC
Curaheen Road
Bishopstown
Cork
tel - (021) 344613
fax - (021) 543692
Year of Formation - 1984
Chairman - Pat O'Donovan
Secretary - Richard O'Brien
Manager - Rob Hindmarch
Stadium - Bishopstown (12,800)

MAJOR HONOURS

League Championship - (1) 1993.

APPEARANCES 95/96

	P	Ap	(s)	Gls
Brian BARRY-MURPHY	A	7	(6)	
Anthony BUCKLEY	M	1		
Jody BYRNE	G	29		
Melvin CAPLETON	G	4		
Gary CASTLEDINE	A	2		
John CAULFIELD	A	33		11
Tony CONNOLLY	M	11	(1)	1
Cormac COTTER	M	3	(1)	
Danny CRAINIE	A	3		1
Brian CROFT	A	1		
Gareth CRONIN	D	33		1
Owen DALY	M	1	(1)	
Pat DUGGAN	M	5	(2)	
Kelvin FLANAGAN	M	28		3
Fergal GILTENAN	M	15	(8)	1
David HILL	D	30		2
Rob HINDMARCH	M	20		1
Mike KERLEY	D	17	(1)	
Alex LUDZIC	G		(1)	
David LUDZIC	A		(2)	
Paul MATTISON	M	8		1
Pat MORLEY	A	30		9
Liam MURPHY	A	1		
Kieran NAGLE	M	1	(1)	
Colin O'BRIEN	D	20		
Trevor O'BRIEN	M	8	(4)	
Willie O'KEEFE	M	1	(1)	
Declan ROCHE	M	2	(2)	
Barry RYAN	A	10	(1)	1
Darren SHAW	D	21	(3)	
SHORT	D	1		
WELDRON	M	1		
WIMBLETON	A	6		1

LEAGUE RESULTS 1995/96

25/08/95	St. Patrick's Athletic	H	1-0	Morley
01/09/95	Bohemians	A	1-1	Caulfield
08/09/95	Galway United	H	1-1	Flanagan
16/09/95	Dundalk	A	0-0	
24/09/95	Shamrock Rovers	A	1-1	Caulfield
29/09/95	Athlone Town	H	2-0	Giltenan, Morley
07/10/95	Sligo Rovers	A	1-3	Flanagan
13/10/95	Shelbourne	H	1-1	Crainie
22/10/95	Derry City	A	0-2	
26/10/95	Drogheda United	H	1-2	Hindmarch
05/11/95	UCD	A	1-0	Caulfield
10/11/95	UCD	H	2-1	Flanagan, og (Kelly)
17/11/95	St. Patrick's Athletic	A	1-2	Mattison
24/11/95	Bohemians	H	1-0	Hill
02/12/95	Galway United	A	1-3	Caulfield
09/12/95	Dundalk	H	0-2	
15/12/95	Shamrock Rovers	H	2-0	Morley, Caulfield
22/12/95	Athlone Town	A	4-2	Morley, Caulfield, Cronin, Wimbleton
07/01/96	Shelbourne	A	1-1	Caulfield
17/01/96	Sligo Rovers	H	2-1	og (McLean), Morley
21/01/96	Derry City	H	0-1	
04/02/96	St. Patrick's Athletic	H	0-0	
16/02/96	Bohemians	A	0-1	
25/02/96	Galway United	H	3-0	Morley 2, Hill
03/03/96	Dundalk	A	1-0	Caulfield
05/03/96	Drogheda United	A	2-2	og (Treason), Morley
18/03/96	Shamrock Rovers	A	0-2	
24/03/96	Athlone Town	H	0-2	
30/03/96	Sligo Rovers	A	1-4	Ryan
14/04/96	Derry City	A	1-2	Connolly
21/04/96	Drogheda United	H	2-1	Caulfield 2
23/04/96	Shelbourne	H	2-1	Morley, og (Smith)
27/04/96	UCD	A	1-2	Caulfield

DERRY CITY

CLUB DIRECTORY

Derry City FC
12 Queen Street
Londonderry BT48 7EF
Northern Ireland
tel - (01504) 374542
fax - (01504) 383755
Year of Formation - 1928
Chairman - Paul Diamond
Secretary - Kevin Friel
Manager - Felix Healy
Stadium - Brandywell (10,000)

MAJOR HONOURS
League Championship - (1) 1989.
Domestic Cup - (2) 1989, 1995.

APPEARANCES 95/96

	P	Ap	(s)	Gls
Gary BECKETT	M	12		1
Paul CARLYLE	M	14	(2)	3
Ryan COYLE	M		(3)	
Liam COYLE	A	13		2
Adrian CREANE	D	10	(3)	
Paul CURRAN	D	33		3
Paul DOOLIN	M	30		5
Tommy DUNNE	D	15		
Mark FEENEY	A	5	(4)	2
Sandy FRASER	A	20	(7)	7
Shaun GALLAGHER	M		(1)	
Stuart GAULD	D	13		
Gareth GORMAN	M	1	(2)	1
Sean HARGAN	M	5		5
Gary HEANEY	A		(3)	1
Paul HEGARTY	M	14		1
Peter HUTTON	M	33		2
Darren KELLY	D	7	(1)	
Thomas McCALLION	M	7	(4)	3
Harry McCOURT	A	26	(2)	6
Kevin McKEEVER	D	9	(6)	3
Paul McLAUGHLIN	D	5		1
Tom MOHAN	A	26		1
Tony O'DOWD	G	33		
Ryan SEMPLE	D	3	(3)	
Anthony TOHILL	D	5	(2)	
Pascal VAUDEQUIN (FRA)	D	24		

LEAGUE RESULTS 1995/96

27/08/95	Shelbourne	A	2-1	Carlyle, Coyle L.
03/09/95	Sligo Rovers	H	1-2	Doolin
10/09/95	Drogheda United	H	1-0	Fraser
15/09/95	St. Patrick's Athletic	A	3-3	Fraser, McKeever, McCourt
24/09/95	UCD	H	3-1	McLaughlin, Doolin, Mohan
29/09/95	Bohemians	A	0-1	
08/10/95	Dundalk	H	1-1	Fraser
14/10/95	Galway United	A	1-1	Heaney
22/10/95	Cork City	H	2-0	Fraser, Doolin
29/10/95	Shamrock Rovers	A	0-2	
05/11/95	Athlone Town	H	5-3	Fraser, Coyle L., Hutton, og (Malone), Carlyle
10/11/95	Athlone Town	A	1-1	Doolin
19/11/95	Shelbourne	H	1-2	Hutton
25/11/95	Sligo Rovers	A	1-1	Carlyle
01/12/95	Drogheda United	A	2-2	Doolin, McCourt
10/12/95	St. Patrick's Athletic	H	5-1	Feeney 2, Gorman, Fraser 2
16/12/95	UCD	A	0-2	
31/12/95	Dundalk	A	1-2	McCourt
07/01/96	Galway United	H	2-0	McCourt 2
21/01/96	Cork City	A	1-0	og (Duggan)
02/02/96	Shelbourne	A	0-1	
18/02/96	Sligo Rovers	H	4-0	McCallion 3, og (Brunton)
21/02/96	Shamrock Rovers	H	1-1	McKeever
25/02/96	Drogheda United	H	1-1	Beckett
01/03/96	St. Patrick's Athletic	A	1-1	McCourt
03/03/96	Bohemians	H	1-1	Curran (p)
18/03/96	UCD	H	1-1	Curran (p)
22/03/96	Bohemians	A	1-1	Hegarty
31/03/96	Dundalk	H	0-1	
06/04/96	Galway United	A	3-0	Hargan 3
14/04/96	Cork City	H	2-1	Hargan 2
21/04/96	Shamrock Rovers	A	1-2	McKeever
27/04/96	Athlone Town	H	1-1	Curran (p)

DROGHEDA UNITED

CLUB DIRECTORY

Drogheda United FC
United Park
Windmill Road
Drogheda
Co. Louth
tel - (041) 30190
Fax - (041) 30190
Year of Formation - 1919
Chairman - Vincent Hoey
Secretary - Charlie Hurley
Manager - Jim McLaughlin
Stadium - United Park (6,396)

APPEARANCES 95/96

	P	Ap	(s)	Gls
Martin BEGGS	D		(1)	
Bobby BROWNE	M	33		3
John CARROLL	D	26	(2)	
Stephen COONEY	M		(1)	
Trevor CROLLY	A	30		8
David FAIRCLOUGH	A	2	(2)	
John FLANAGAN	M		(1)	
John GRACE	G	33		
Michael HARTE	M	8	(14)	1
Barry KEHOE	M	7		
Martin LAWLOR	D	15		1
Paul McLAUGHLIN	D	31	(1)	1
David NUGENT	M		(3)	
Barry O'CONNOR	A	26	(2)	6
Noel REID	M	33		1
John RYAN	A	33		10
Mick SHELLEY	A	11	(2)	
David STAUNTON	M		(1)	
Tom SULLIVAN	M	27	(3)	3
Colm TRESSON	D	33		2
Trevor VAUGHAN	A	15		3

LEAGUE RESULTS 1995/96

27/08/95	Shamrock Rovers	A	1-1	O'Connor
01/09/95	Shelbourne	H	1-1	O'Connor
10/09/95	Derry City	A	0-1	
15/09/95	Athlone Town	H	0-1	
22/09/95	Bohemians	H	2-5	Reid, Ryan
29/09/95	St. Patrick's Athletic	A	0-1	
06/10/95	Galway United	H	3-0	Crolly (p), Lawlor, Browne
15/10/95	UCD	A	0-0	
20/10/95	Dundalk	H	3-2	Crolly (p), Browne, Ryan
26/10/95	Cork City	A	2-1	Crolly, Browne
03/11/95	Sligo Rovers	H	0-0	
11/11/95	Sligo Rovers	A	0-1	
17/11/95	Shamrock Rovers	H	1-2	Harte
24/11/95	Shelbourne	A	0-0	
01/12/95	Derry City	H	2-2	Ryan, Crolly (p)
08/12/95	Athlone Town	A	2-0	Crolly, Ryan
15/12/95	Bohemians	A	0-6	
22/12/95	St. Patrick's Athletic	H	1-3	Ryan
01/01/96	Galway United	A	3-0	Sullivan 2, Tresson
05/01/96	UCD	H	0-1	
21/01/96	Dundalk	A	2-2	Ryan, Tresson
04/02/96	Shamrock Rovers	A	0-1	
16/02/96	Shelbourne	H	1-3	Crolly (p)
25/02/96	Derry City	A	1-1	Ryan
01/03/96	Athlone Town	H	0-1	
05/03/96	Cork City	H	2-2	Ryan, Vaughan
15/03/96	Bohemians	H	0-1	
22/03/96	St. Patrick's Athletic	A	2-3	Vaughan, O'Connor
29/03/96	Galway United	H	6-1	O'Connor 2, Crolly, Ryan, Sullivan, Vaughan
07/04/96	UCD	A	1-4	Ryan
14/04/96	Dundalk	H	2-1	O'Connor, Crolly
21/04/96	Cork City	A	1-2	McLoughlin
27/04/96	Sligo Rovers	H	0-1	

DUNDALK

CLUB DIRECTORY

Dundalk FC
Oriel Park
Dundalk
Co. Louth
tel - (042) 35894/35398
fax - (042) 30003
Year of Formation - 1926
Chairman - Enda McGuill
Secretary - Ms. Elizabeth Duffy
Manager - Dermot Keely
Stadium - Oriel Park (13,600)

MAJOR HONOURS

League Championship - (9) 1933, 1963, 1967, 1976, 1979, 1982, 1988, 1991, 1995.
Domestic Cup - (8) 1942, 1949, 1952, 1958, 1977, 1979, 1981, 1988.

APPEARANCES 95/96

	P	Ap	(s)	Gls
Joe BAGNELL	G	1		
Matt BRITTON	M	16	(8)	
Brian BYRNE	A	31	(1)	4
Mick BYRNE	A	9	(7)	3
John COADY	D	29		1
John CONNOLLY	G	10		
David CRAWLEY	M	4	(2)	
Marcus DALY	M		(3)	
Mick DOOHAN	D	31		2
Joe GALLEN	A	15	(4)	8
Joe HANRAHAN	A	24	(1)	3
David HOEY	M		(1)	
Stephen KELLY	M	21		5
Keith LONG	D	28	(3)	1
Cesar LOPEZ (HOL)	M		(4)	
Tom McNULTY	M	24	(4)	
Stehen NAPIER	D	30		2
Richie PURDY	D	26	(1)	
Declan ROCHE	M	4	(5)	
Eddie VAN BOXTEL	G	22		
Anto WHELAN	D	17	(3)	
Peter WITHNELL	A	21	(6)	6

LEAGUE RESULTS 1995/96

27/08/95	Bohemians	H	1-2	og
03/09/95	UCD	A	2-1	Kelly, Hanrahan
08/09/95	Athlone Town	A	0-0	
16/09/95	Cork City	H	0-0	
22/09/95	Shelbourne	A	1-3	Withnell
28/09/95	Shamrock Rovers	H	1-0	Coady
08/10/95	Derry City	A	1-1	Withnell
12/10/95	Sligo Rovers	H	0-1	
20/10/95	Drogheda United	A	2-3	Hanrahan, Byrne M.
26/10/95	St. Patrick's Athletic	H	3-2	Hanrahan, Kelly, Gallen
04/11/95	Galway United	A	1-0	Long
09/11/95	Galway United	H	2-0	Withnell, og
17/11/95	Bohemians	A	2-3	Napier, Kelly (p)
23/11/95	UCD	H	2-0	Byrne B., Kelly (p)
30/11/95	Athlone Town	H	2-1	Gallen, Byrne B.
09/12/95	Cork City	A	2-0	Byrne M., Withnell
17/12/95	Shelbourne	H	1-1	Withnell
31/12/95	Derry City	H	2-1	Byrne M., Byrne B.
06/01/96	Sligo Rovers	A	3-3	Gallen 2, Doohan
21/01/96	Drogheda United	H	2-2	og (Carroll), Kelly
24/01/96	Shamrock Rovers	A	0-1	
28/01/96	St. Patrick's Athletic	A	1-2	Byrne B.
04/02/96	Bohemians	H	2-4	Gallen, Withnell
16/02/96	UCD	A	0-0	
23/02/96	Athlone Town	A	0-0	
03/03/96	Cork City	H	0-1	
09/03/96	Galway United	A	1-2	Gallen
15/03/96	Shelbourne	A	1-0	Doohan
21/03/96	Shamrock Rovers	H	0-0	
31/03/96	Derry City	A	1-0	Gallen
08/04/96	Sligo Rovers	H	0-1	
14/04/96	Drogheda United	A	1-2	Gallen
19/04/96	St. Patrick's Athletic	H	1-2	Napier

GALWAY UNITED

CLUB DIRECTORY

Galway United FC
Terryland Park
Dyke Road
Galway
tel - (091) 561000
fax - (091) 561000
Year of Formation - 1937
Chairman - Gerry Gray
Secretary - Séan Hynes
Manager - Tony Mannion; Denis Clarke
Stadium - Terryland Park (6,580)

MAJOR HONOURS
Domestic Cup - (1) 1991.

APPEARANCES 95/96

	P	Ap	(s)	Gls
Ricky BREZZA	A	1		
Damien BRENNAN	D	9		
John BRENNAN	A	26		7
Gordon BRETT	M	7		
John CARR	M		(2)	
Fran CARTER	D	15	(3)	
Denis CLARKE	M		(3)	
Billy CLEARY	M	21	(4)	3
Norman COSTELLO	G	1		
Donnie FARRAGHER	A	13	(3)	5
Donal FLYNN	D	8	(1)	
Robert FORDE	G	12		
GLYNN	D	2		
Rodney GRANT	M		(2)	
Mark HERRICK	M	32		4
Mark KEANE	M	4	(5)	
Ronan KILLEEN	M	19	(1)	1
Stephen LALLY	D	15	(1)	
Keith LAMBERT	D	26	(1)	1
Gerry MULLEN	M	30	(1)	1
Donal MURRAY	M	16	(7)	
Ollie NEARY	M	21	(9)	2
Gary O'CONNOR	M	2	(2)	
Ray O'HALLORAN	D	17		
Alan OLIVER	M	2	(7)	
Joey POWER	G	20		
Michael QUIRKE	A	13	(7)	1
Derek RODGERS	D	27		
Eamonn SHERLOCK	A	4	(7)	

LEAGUE RESULTS 1995/96

Date	Opponent	H/A	Score	Scorers
26/08/95	UCD	H	1-1	Brennan J.
02/09/95	Athlone Town	A	2-0	Herrick, Brennan J.
08/09/95	Cork City	A	1-1	Brennan J.
16/09/95	Shamrock Rovers	H	1-1	Neary
23/09/95	Sligo Rovers	A	2-3	Herrick, Quirke
30/09/95	Shelbourne	H	1-1	Cleary
05/10/95	Drogheda United	A	0-3	
14/10/95	Derry City	H	1-1	Brennan J.
20/10/95	St. Patrick's Athletic	A	2-1	Farragher 2
28/10/95	Bohemians	H	1-5	Brennan J.
04/11/95	Dundalk	H	0-1	
09/11/95	Dundalk	A	0-2	
19/11/95	UCD	A	0-2	
25/11/95	Athlone Town	H	2-2	Farragher 2
02/12/95	Cork City	H	3-1	Farragher, Lambert, Mullen
10/12/95	Shamrock Rovers	A	1-2	Herrick
16/12/95	Sligo Rovers	H	2-3	og (Dykes), Killean
22/12/95	Shelbourne	A	0-2	
01/01/96	Drogheda United	H	0-3	
07/01/96	Derry City	A	0-2	
20/01/96	St. Patrick's Athletic	H	0-1	
26/01/96	Bohemians	A	0-3	
03/02/96	UCD	H	0-2	
16/02/96	Athlone Town	A	0-1	
25/02/96	Cork City	A	0-3	
02/03/96	Shamrock Rovers	H	0-2	
09/03/96	Dundalk	H	2-1	Cleary 2
16/03/96	Sligo Rovers	A	2-0	Herrick, Brennan J.
23/03/96	Shelbourne	H	1-3	Neary
29/03/96	Drogheda United	A	1-6	Brennan J.
06/04/96	Derry City	H	0-3	
12/04/96	St. Patrick's Athletic	A	0-3	
20/04/96	Bohemians	H	0-2	

ST. PATRICK'S ATHLETIC

CLUB DIRECTORY

St. Patrick's Athletic FC
Richmond Park
125 Emmet Road
Inchicore
Dublin 8
tel - (01) 4546332/4546211
fax - (01) 4546211
Year of Formation - 1929
Chairman - Tim O'Flaherty
Secretary - Frank Boylan
Manager - Brian Kerr
Stadium - Richmond Park (7,000)

MAJOR HONOURS
League Championship - (5)
1952, 1955, 1956, 1990, 1996.
Domestic Cup - (2) 1959, 1961.

APPEARANCES 95/96

	P	Ap	(s)	Gls
Liam BUCKLEY	A	20	(2)	3
Willie BURKE	D	32		
Gareth BYRNE	G	32		
Jason BYRNE	A	6	(8)	
John BYRNE	D	10	(3)	
Dave CAMPBELL	D	32		4
Paul CAMPBELL	D	22	(7)	5
Peter CARPENTER	D	26		
Johnny GLYNN	A	13	(15)	4
Eddie GORMLEY	M	25		7
Alan KANE	G	1		
Alan KELLY	M		(1)	
John McDONNELL	D	31	(1)	2
Christy McELLIGOTT	D	3	(5)	
Eddie MEIR	M		(1)	
Noel MERNAGH	M	23	(2)	
Brian MORRIS-ROE	A	23	(6)	3
Mark MULRANEY	D	3	(3)	
Ricky O'FLAHERTY	A	30	(1)	14
Paul OSAM	A	16		4
Martin REILLY	A	15	(7)	7

LEAGUE RESULTS 1995/96

Date	Opponent		Score	Scorers
25/08/95	Cork City	A	0-1	
01/09/95	Shamrock Rovers	H	1-0	O'Flaherty
09/09/95	Sligo Rovers	A	0-0	
15/09/95	Derry City	H	3-3	O'Flaherty, Gormley 2
22/09/95	Athlone Town	A	1-0	Buckley
29/09/95	Drogheda United	H	1-0	Buckley
06/10/95	UCD	H	2-1	Morris-Roe, Gormley
13/10/95	Bohemians	A	1-0	Osam
20/10/95	Galway United	H	1-2	Gormley (p)
26/10/95	Dundalk	A	2-3	Glynn 2
03/11/95	Shelbourne	H	2-1	Campbell D., Osam
10/11/95	Shelbourne	A	1-1	Gormley (p)
17/11/95	Cork City	H	2-1	Reilly, Glynn
01/12/95	Sligo Rovers	H	1-0	O'Flaherty
10/12/95	Derry City	A	1-5	McDonnell
15/12/95	Athlone Town	H	3-2	O'Flaherty 2, Gormley (p)
17/12/95	Shamrock Rovers	A	1-0	Campbell D.
22/12/95	Drogheda United	A	3-1	O'Flaherty, Reilly 2
31/12/95	UCD	A	2-0	O'Flaherty, Reilly
05/01/96	Bohemians	H	3-3	Campbell P., O'Flaherty, Morris-Roe
20/01/96	Galway United	A	1-0	Campbell D.
28/01/96	Dundalk	H	2-1	Reilly, Campbell P.
04/02/96	Cork City	A	0-0	
16/02/96	Shamrock Rovers	H	2-2	Campbell P., O'Flaherty
25/02/96	Sligo Rovers	A	1-1	Campbell D.
01/03/96	Derry City	H	1-1	Osam
16/03/96	Athlone Town	A	2-2	Osam, Gormley
22/03/96	Drogheda United	H	3-2	Buckley, O'Flaherty 2
29/03/96	UCD	H	2-0	McDonnell, O'Flaherty
08/04/96	Bohemians	A	0-0	
12/04/96	Galway United	H	3-0	Morris-Roe, O'Flaherty, Campbell P.
19/04/96	Dundalk	A	2-1	O'Flaherty, Campbell P.
27/04/96	Shelbourne	H	3-0	Reilly 2, Glynn

SHAMROCK ROVERS

CLUB DIRECTORY

Shamrock Rovers FC
RDS, Ballsbridge, Dublin 4
tel - (01) 6685433
fax - (01) 6606950
Year of Formation - 1901
Chairman - John McNamara
Secretary - Brian Murphy
Manager - Ray Treacy; Alan O'Neill & Terry Eviston
Stadium - Royal Dublin Society Showgrounds (20,500)

MAJOR HONOURS

League Championship - (15) 1923, 1925, 1927, 1932, 1938, 1939, 1954, 1957, 1959, 1964, 1984, 1985, 1986, 1987, 1994.

Domestic Cup - (24) 1925, 1929, 1930, 1931, 1932, 1933, 1936, 1940, 1944, 1945, 1948, 1955, 1956, 1962, 1964, 1965, 1966, 1967, 1968, 1969, 1978, 1985, 1986, 1987.

APPEARANCES 95/96

	P	Ap	(s)	Gls
Gino BRAZIL	D	28	(1)	
Martin BUCKLEY	M	1	(2)	
Ray CAROLAN	D	22		
Leonard CURTIS	D	14	(1)	
Alan DODD	M	2	(1)	
Padraig DULLY	A	11		3
Terry EVISTON	A	7	(9)	
Sean FRANCIS	A	18	(3)	2
Karl GANNON	A	29	(1)	7
Brian HONAN	M	1	(1)	
Stephen HORAN	A		(2)	
Robbie HORGAN	G	1	(1)	
Gareth KELLY	D	24	(2)	
Rod DE KHORS	M	4	(4)	
Brian LEAVY	A	1		
Aaron LYNCH	M	2	(1)	
Mark McCORMACK	D		(1)	
Derek McGRATH	M	24	(1)	2
Trevor MOLLOY	M		(4)	
Eoin MULLEN	D	22	(3)	
Greg O'DOWD	M	1		
Michael O'KEEFE	D	1	(2)	
Alan O'NEILL	G	32		
Kenny O'ROURKE	M	13	(8)	1
Mark REID	A	22	(4)	10
John TOAL	M	29		5
Derek TREACY	A	29	(1)	2
Paul WHELAN	D	25		

LEAGUE RESULTS 1995/96

27/08/95	Drogheda United	H	1-1	Gannon
01/09/95	St. Patrick's Athletic	A	0-1	
10/09/95	UCD	H	0-2	
16/09/95	Galway United	A	1-1	Reid
24/09/95	Cork City	H	1-1	Toal (p)
28/09/95	Dundalk	A	0-1	
06/10/95	Shelbourne	A	0-3	
15/10/95	Athlone Town	H	1-1	Toal
21/10/95	Sligo Rovers	A	1-0	Reid
29/10/95	Derry City	H	2-0	Reid, McGrath
03/11/95	Bohemians	A	1-1	Gannon
12/11/95	Bohemians	H	1-0	Reid
17/11/95	Drogheda United	A	2-1	Dully 2
03/12/95	UCD	A	1-0	Treacy
10/12/95	Galway United	H	2-1	Gannon, Dully
15/12/95	Cork City	A	0-2	
17/12/95	St. Patrick's Athletic	H	0-1	
01/01/96	Shelbourne	H	0-1	
05/01/96	Athlone Town	A	0-2	
21/01/96	Sligo Rovers	H	0-2	
24/01/96	Dundalk	H	1-0	Treacy
04/02/96	Drogheda United	H	1-0	Reid
16/02/96	St. Patrick's Athletic	A	2-2	Reid, Toal
21/02/96	Derry City	A	1-1	Gannon
25/02/96	UCD	H	2-0	Reid, Francis
02/03/96	Galway United	A	2-0	McGrath, Francis
18/03/96	Cork City	H	2-0	O'Rourke, Gannon
21/03/96	Dundalk	A	0-0	
29/03/96	Shelbourne	A	2-1	Reid, Toal (p)
07/04/96	Athlone Town	H	2-1	Gannon 2
13/04/96	Sligo Rovers	A	1-3	Toal
21/04/96	Derry City	H	2-1	Reid 2
27/04/96	Bohemians	A	0-1	

SHELBOURNE

CLUB DIRECTORY

Shelbourne FC
Tolka Park
Richmond Road
Dublin 3
tel - (01) 8375536/8375754/8368781
fax - (01) 8375588
Year of Formation - 1895
Chairman - Finbarr Flood
Secretary - Ollie Byrne
Manager - Damien Richardson
Stadium - Tolka Park (9,500)

MAJOR HONOURS
League Championship - (8) 1926, 1929, 1931, 1944, 1947, 1953, 1962, 1992.
Domestic Cup - (5)
1939, 1960, 1963, 1993, 1996.

APPEARANCES 95/96

	P	Ap	(s)	Gls
Vinny ARKINS	A	2		1
Anto BRENNAN	M	1	(1)	
Alan BYRNE	M	2		
Mick BYRNE	A	1	(6)	2
Dave COLLINS	D	3		
Greg COSTELLO	D	31		5
Robbie DEVEREAUX	M	2	(6)	
Ray DUFFY	D	21	(1)	
Padraig DULLY	A		(1)	
Tommy DUNNE	D	7		
Brian FLOOD	D	28		1
Declan GEOGHEGAN	D	29	(1)	2
Stephen GEOGHEGAN	A	32		20
Alan GOUGH	G	33		
Gary HOWLETT	M	31		1
Darren KELLY	M	5	(8)	
Henry McKOP	D	16	(1)	
Mick NEVILLE	D	29		
John O'ROURKE	M	28	(2)	8
Mark RUTHERFORD	A	9	(2)	
Tony SHERIDAN	M	27	(2)	5
David SMITH	D	14	(6)	
Mark SMITH	M		(1)	
Dave TILSON	A	12	(6)	
Trevor VAUGHAN	A		(3)	

LEAGUE RESULTS 1995/96

Date	Opponent		Score	Scorers
27/08/95	Derry City	H	1-2	Geoghegan S.
01/09/95	Drogheda United	A	1-1	Arkins
08/09/95	Bohemians	H	1-0	Geoghegan S.
16/09/95	UCD	A	3-0	Geoghegan S. 3 (1p)
22/09/95	Dundalk	H	3-1	O'Rourke, Geoghegan S., Costello (p)
30/09/95	Galway United	A	1-1	Costello (p)
06/10/95	Shamrock Rovers	H	3-0	Geoghegan D. 2, Geoghegan S.
13/10/95	Cork City	A	1-1	O'Rourke
20/10/95	Athlone Town	A	2-1	O'Rourke, Sheridan
27/10/95	Sligo Rovers	H	0-0	
03/11/95	St. Patrick's Athletic	A	1-2	Geoghegan S.
10/11/95	St. Patrick's Athletic	H	1-1	O'Rourke
19/11/95	Derry City	A	2-1	Howlett, Sheridan
24/11/95	Drogheda United	H	0-0	
01/12/95	Bohemians	A	0-1	
08/12/95	UCD	H	1-1	Geoghegan S.
17/12/95	Dundalk	A	1-1	O'Rourke
22/12/95	Galway United	H	2-0	O'Rourke, Geoghegan S.
01/01/96	Shamrock Rovers	A	1-0	Costello
07/01/96	Cork City	H	1-1	Costello (p)
19/01/96	Athlone Town	H	1-0	Geoghegan S.
27/01/96	Sligo Rovers	A	1-0	Geoghegan S.
02/02/96	Derry City	H	1-0	Geoghegan S.
16/02/96	Drogheda United	A	3-1	Sheridan 2, Geoghegan S.
23/02/96	Bohemians	H	1-0	Flood
03/03/96	UCD	A	2-3	Geoghegan S., Byrne M.
15/03/96	Dundalk	H	0-1	
23/03/96	Galway United	A	3-1	Sheridan, Costello (p), Geoghegan S.
29/03/96	Shamrock Rovers	H	1-2	Geoghegan S.
12/04/96	Athlone Town	A	3-4	Geoghegan S., O'Rourke, Byrne M.
19/04/96	Sligo Rovers	H	2-1	Geoghegan S., O'Rourke
23/04/96	Cork City	A	1-2	Geoghegan S. (p)
27/04/96	St. Patrick's Athletic	A	0-3	

SLIGO ROVERS

CLUB DIRECTORY

Sligo Rovers FC
P.O. Box 275
Showgrounds
Sligo
tel - (071) 71212
fax - (071) 71331
Year of Formation - 1928
Chairman - Ray Gallagher
Secretary - Ms. Yvonne Byrne
Manager - Steve Cotterill
Stadium - Showgrounds (7,650)

MAJOR HONOURS
League Championship - (2) 1937, 1977
Domestic Cup - (2) 1983, 1994.

APPEARANCES 95/96

	P	Ap	(s)	Gls
Brendan ASPINALL	D	31		4
Steve BERKS	M	13	(5)	
Nick BRUJOS	G		(1)	
Robert BRUNTON	D	32		1
Gavin DYKES	D	31		2
Ian GILZEAN	A	30		12
Darren GROGAN	M	16		
John KELLY	A	1		
Mark KELLY	D	14	(8)	1
John KENNY	A	27	(1)	3
Ian LYNCH	D	23	(4)	
Martin McDONNELL	M	9	(9)	
Mark McLEAN	G	33		
Padraig MORAN	A	30	(3)	14
James MULLIGAN	M	12	(3)	3
Andy RAMAGE	M	27		1
Matthew RAWLINS	M		(3)	
David REID	D	21	(2)	
Tony RICHARDS	A	3	(1)	1
Aidan ROONEY	M	3	(10)	1
Ray ROONEY	D	4	(4)	
Paul TOVEY	M	3		

LEAGUE RESULTS 1995/96

Date	Opponent		Score	Scorers
26/08/95	Athlone Town	H	4-2	Gilzean, Dykes, Ramage, Kenny
03/09/95	Derry City	A	2-1	Moran, Rooney A.
09/09/95	St. Patrick's Athletic	H	0-0	
15/09/95	Bohemians	A	0-2	
23/09/95	Galway United	H	3-2	Gilzean, Moran 2
01/10/95	UCD	A	1-2	Gilzean
07/10/95	Cork City	H	3-1	Moran, Kenny, Gilzean
12/10/95	Dundalk	A	1-0	Gilzean
21/10/95	Shamrock Rovers	H	0-1	
27/10/95	Shelbourne	A	0-0	
03/11/95	Drogheda United	A	0-0	
11/11/95	Drogheda United	H	1-0	Richards
17/11/95	Athlone Town	A	2-1	Moran, Aspinall
25/11/95	Derry City	H	1-1	Aspinall
01/12/95	St. Patrick's Athletic	A	0-1	
09/12/95	Bohemians	H	0-0	
16/12/95	Galway United	A	3-2	Kenny, Kelly M., Moran
23/12/95	UCD	H	2-0	Gilzean, Moran
06/01/96	Dundalk	H	3-3	Brunton (p), Gilzean 2
17/01/96	Cork City	A	1-2	Gilzean
21/01/96	Shamrock Rovers	A	2-0	Aspinall, Gilzean
27/01/96	Shelbourne	H	0-1	
03/02/96	Athlone Town	H	2-1	Moran 2
18/02/96	Derry City	A	0-4	
25/02/96	St. Patrick's Athletic	H	1-1	Moran
01/03/96	Bohemians	A	2-1	Moran, og (Mooney)
16/03/96	Galway United	A	0-2	
24/03/96	UCD	A	1-3	Moran
30/03/96	Cork City	H	4-1	Moran, Mulligan 2, og (Kerley)
08/04/96	Dundalk	A	1-0	Dykes
13/04/96	Shamrock Rovers	H	3-1	Mulligan, Gilzean, Aspinall
19/04/96	Shelbourne	A	1-2	Gilzean
27/04/96	Drogheda United	A	1-0	Moran (p)

UCD

CLUB DIRECTORY

University College Dublin AFC
Belfield Park
Stillorgan
Co. Dublin
tel - (01) 7062183
fax - (01) 2968099
Year of Formation - 1895
Chairman - Gerry Horkan
Secretary - Brendan Dillon
Managers - Theo Dunne
Stadium - Belfield Park (4,500)

MAJOR HONOURS
Domestic Cup - (1) 1984.

APPEARANCES 95/96

		P	Ap	(s)	Gls
Stefan BACKES	G	1			
Jason COLWELL	M	33			3
Stephen COSTELLO	M		(4)		
Declan FITZGERALD	M	4	(4)		
Robbie GRIFFIN	A	21	(3)		
Ciaran KAVANAGH	M	32			2
James KEDDY	M	20	(1)		4
Seamus KELLY	G	32			
Aidan LYNCH	M	3	(1)		
Jody LYNCH	D	11	(3)		
Packie LYNCH	D	29			
Tony McDONNELL	D	13	(2)		2
Eamonn McLAUGHLIN	D	25	(2)		1
Andy MYLER	M	10	(5)		2
Darren O'BRIEN	A	8	(6)		
Mick O'BYRNE	A	31			16
Terry PALMER	D	31			3
Lasse PALTONEN	M		(1)		
Jason SHERLOCK	A	21	(2)		4
Willie SMITH	M		(1)		
Conor TIMMONS	D	5			
Jonathan TRACEY	D	33			

LEAGUE RESULTS 1995/96

26/08/95	Galway United	A	1-1	og (Rodgers)
03/09/95	Dundalk	H	1-2	McLaughlin
10/09/95	Shamrock Rovers	A	2-0	O'Byrne 2
16/09/95	Shelbourne	H	0-3	
24/09/95	Derry City	A	1-3	O'Byrne
01/10/95	Sligo Rovers	H	2-1	O'Byrne 2
06/10/95	St. Patrick's Athletic	A	1-2	O'Byrne
15/10/95	Drogheda United	H	0-0	
20/10/95	Bohemians	A	0-0	
29/10/95	Athlone Town	H	3-0	Myler, Palmer, Colwell
05/11/95	Cork City	H	0-1	
10/11/95	Cork City	A	1-2	Sherlock
19/11/95	Galway United	H	2-0	O'Byrne, Keddy
23/11/95	Dundalk	A	0-2	
03/12/95	Shamrock Rovers	H	0-1	
08/12/95	Shelbourne	A	1-1	Myler
16/12/95	Derry City	H	2-0	Palmer, O'Byrne
23/12/95	Sligo Rovers	A	0-2	
31/12/95	St. Patrick's Athletic	H	0-2	
05/01/96	Drogheda United	A	1-0	O'Byrne
21/01/96	Bohemians	H	3-1	O'Byrne, Keddy 2
26/01/96	Athlone Town	A	0-1	
03/02/96	Galway United	A	2-0	McDonnell, O'Byrne
16/02/96	Dundalk	H	0-0	
25/02/96	Shamrock Rovers	A	0-2	
03/03/96	Shelbourne	H	3-2	Sherlock, O'Byrne, Colwell
18/03/96	Derry City	A	1-1	O'Byrne
24/03/96	Sligo Rovers	H	3-1	O'Byrne 2 (1p), Kavanagh
29/03/96	St. Patrick's Athletic	A	0-2	
07/04/96	Drogheda United	H	4-1	Keddy, Kavanagh, Sherlock, O'Byrne
12/04/96	Bohemians	A	1-3	Palmer
21/04/96	Athlone Town	H	1-2	Sherlock
27/04/96	Cork City	H	2-1	Colwell, McDonnell

PROMOTED CLUBS

SECOND DIVISION FINAL TABLE 95/96

		Pd	W	D	L	F	A	Pt	GD
1	**Bray Wanderers**	**27**	**16**	**7**	**4**	**53**	**21**	**55**	**+32**
2	**Finn Harps**	**27**	**14**	**7**	**6**	**50**	**25**	**49**	**+25**
3	**Home Farm Everton**	**27**	**15**	**4**	**8**	**44**	**33**	**46**	**+11**
4	Cobh Ramblers	27	10	13	4	30	18	43	+12
5	St. James's Gate	27	10	11	6	35	30	38	+5
6	Limerick	27	10	6	11	38	34	36	+4
7	Kilkenny City	27	9	8	10	32	35	35	-3
8	Waterford United	27	9	7	11	37	39	34	-2
9	Longford Town	27	5	6	16	25	49	21	-24
10	Monaghan United	27	2	5	20	11	71	11	-60

PROMOTION/RELEGATION PLAY-OFF
Home Farm Everton 2, Athlone Town 0
Atholne Town 2, Home Farm Everton 0
(2-2; Home Farm Everton 4-3 on pens.)

CLUB DIRECTORY

Bray Wanderers FC
Carlisle Grounds
Bray
Co. Wicklow
tel - (01) 2828214
Year of Formation - 1942
Chairman - Edmond J. Cox
Secretary - John O'Brien
Manager - Pat Devlin
Stadium - Carlisle Grounds (7,000)

MAJOR HONOURS
Domestic Cup - (1) 1990.

CLUB DIRECTORY

Finn Harps FC
Finn Park
Ballybofey
Co. Donegal
tel - (074) 32635
Year of Formation - 1954
Chairman - Jimmy Harte
Secretary - Pat Gallen
Manager - Patsy McGowan
Stadium - Finn Park (7,000)

MAJOR HONOURS
Domestic Cup - (1) 1974.

CLUB DIRECTORY

Home Farm Everton FC
97A Swords Road
Whitehall
Dublin 9
tel - (01) 8371001
fax - (01) 8367821
Year of Formation - 1928
Chairman - Brendan Menton
Secretary - Brendan Menton
Manager - Martin Bayly
Stadium - Whitehall (3,000)

MAJOR HONOURS
Domestic Cup - (1) 1975.

ROMANIA

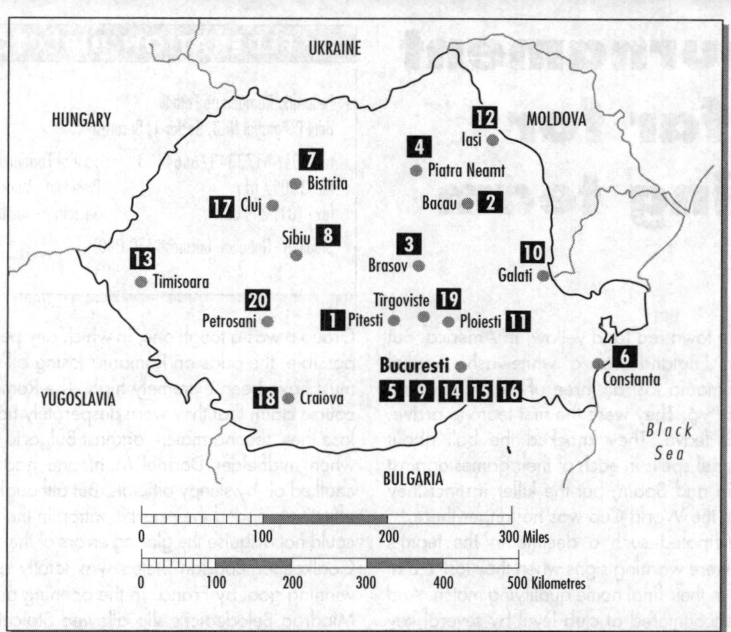

1	FC ARGES DACIA PITESTI	828	11	PETROLUL PLOIESTI	838
2	AS BACAU	829	12	POLITEHNICA IASI	839
3	FC BRASOV	830	13	POLITEHNICA TIMISOARA	840
4	CEAHLAUL PIATRA NEAMT	831	14	RAPID BUCURESTI	841
5	DINAMO BUCURESTI	832	15	SPORTUL STUDENTESC BUCURESTI	842
6	FC FARUL CONSTANTA	833	16	STEAUA BUCURESTI	843
7	GLORIA BISTRITA	834	17	UNIVERSITATEA CLUJ	844
8	FC INTER SIBIU	835	18	UNIVERSITATEA CRAIOVA	845
9	FC NATIONAL BUCURESTI	836	19	OTELUL TÎRGOVISTE	846
10	OTELUL GALATI	837	20	JIUL PETROSANI	846

UNCHALLENGED STEAUA STEAM AHEAD

A tournament too far for ageing team

FEDERATION DIRECTORY

Federatia Romāna de Fotbal
Bdul Poligrafiei Nr.3, Sector 1, Bucuresti

tel - (01) 6173343/6664400
tlx - 10097 frf r
fax - (01) 3128324

Year of Formation - 1909
President - Mircea Sandu
Secretary - Adalbert Kassai

Stadium - National, Bucuresti (70,000)

They painted the town red (and yellow) in America. But all they got in England was a whitewash. Anghel Iordanescu's Romania lost all three of their first-round matches at Euro '96. They were the first team to arrive, and the first to leave. They knocked the ball about attractively for brief spells in each of their games against France, Bulgaria and Spain, but the killer instinct they demonstrated at the World Cup was no longer there.

Nobody anticipated such a decline in the team's fortunes. There were warning signs when they lost 1-3 at home to France in their final home qualifying match. And the difficulties encountered at club level by several key members of the squad - Hagi, Raducioiu, Belodedici, Dumitrescu - also raised doubts about the team's readiness for the big challenge ahead. But even though Group B was a tough one, in which any permutation was possible, the odds on Romania losing all three matches must have been extremely high. The Romanians can of course claim that they were desperately hard done by to lose their second match, against Bulgaria in Newcastle, when midfielder Dorinel Munteanu had a valid goal chalked off by sleepy officials. But although that decision effectively ended their participation in the tournament, it could not disguise the glaring errors of their own making. Goalkeeper Bogdan Stelea was totally at fault for the winning goal by France in the opening game. Sweeper Miodrag Belodedici's slip allowed Stoichkov to fire his early goal in the Bulgaria match. And against Spain, it was more defensive complacency and indiscipline that allowed their opponents to sneak a late winner.

LEAGUE CHAMPIONSHIP RESULTS 95/96

		1	2	3	4	5	6	7	8	9	10	11	12	13	14	15	16	17	18
1	FC Arges Dacia Pitesti		2-0	1-1	1-1	1-0	2-1	2-1	2-1	4-0	2-2	2-1	6-0	0-0	3-2	1-0	1-2	0-2	2-0
2	AS Bacau	3-1		1-2	2-0	2-0	3-0	3-1	2-1	2-1	3-0	1-0	3-1	4-1	1-0	0-1	1-2	1-0	1-0
3	FC Brasov	1-1	2-1		0-0	2-1	3-1	1-0	2-1	0-0	1-0	1-0	2-0	1-1	1-0	4-3	1-0	1-0	1-1
4	Ceahlaul Piatra Neamt	1-0	3-1	2-1		2-0	0-0	1-0	2-0	1-2	3-1	1-2	1-0	1-0	0-1	1-0	2-1	2-0	0-2
5	Dinamo Bucuresti	3-1	3-0	3-1	0-0		2-1	2-1	2-1	0-3	2-0	1-0	2-0	3-0	1-1	0-1	1-1	1-0	2-1
6	FC Farul Constanta	3-0	1-0	4-0	2-0	1-2		1-0	4-0	0-2	1-0	3-3	7-0	1-4	4-2	1-0	1-1	1-0	2-1
7	Gloria Bistrita	4-0	2-0	3-2	1-0	2-0	0-2		2-0	3-1	2-0	1-0	3-0	0-0	1-2	3-1	0-2	1-0	3-0
8	FC Inter Sibiu	0-0	0-2	3-0	2-0	0-0	3-2	0-0		1-0	1-1	2-1	0-1	1-1	2-1	2-0	0-0	1-0	2-0
9	FC National Bucuresti	4-1	4-1	5-1	3-1	1-1	2-1	1-3	5-0		3-1	3-0	2-3	2-1	0-4	0-0	1-0	3-1	4-3
10	Otelul Galati	2-0	3-1	4-0	2-0	0-2	1-0	1-0	2-0	3-1		2-0	3-1	1-0	0-3	3-1	1-2	2-0	2-0
11	Petrolul Ploiesti	1-0	3-0	4-2	3-2	1-0	2-0	2-0	1-0	0-0	2-0		5-0	2-0	2-1	1-0	2-2	2-0	1-0
12	Politehnica Iasi	1-2	3-0	2-1	0-1	0-0	1-2	2-1	2-1	0-1	2-1	2-1		0-0	0-1	0-1	1-2	0-0	2-0
13	Politehnica Timisoara	2-0	2-0	4-1	4-3	2-2	3-1	3-0	5-1	0-1	3-1	2-0	9-1		1-3	3-1	2-1	2-0	0-0
14	Rapid Bucuresti	3-0	3-0	3-0	2-1	2-0	3-4	2-0	2-0	1-1	2-0	1-0	3-0	4-1		1-1	1-1	5-0	0-1
15	Sportul Studentesc Bucuresti	3-0	3-0	2-0	1-0	0-1	2-1	2-1	0-1	0-0	1-1	2-1	3-1	1-0	0-0		0-2	2-3	0-0
16	Steaua Bucuresti	4-0	5-0	5-0	6-2	4-2	2-2	3-1	3-1	5-1	1-0	2-1	4-0	5-1	3-0	1-1		4-0	1-0
17	Universitatea Cluj	1-0	7-1	1-1	2-0	2-0	3-0	1-1	1-1	1-3	3-2	2-0	3-1	2-0	2-0	1-0	2-1		1-1
18	Universitatea Craiova	2-1	1-0	3-1	4-0	3-1	2-1	1-0	2-0	1-0	3-0	3-0	3-0	3-1	2-0	1-0	1-1	0-0	

LEAGUE CHAMPIONSHIP FINAL TABLE 95/96

			Home					Away					Total						
		Pd	W	D	L	F	A	W	D	L	F	A	W	D	L	F	A	Pt	GD
1	Steaua Bucuresti	34	15	2	0	58	12	6	6	5	21	18	21	8	5	79	30	71	+49
2	FC National Bucuresti	34	12	2	3	43	22	6	4	7	17	22	18	6	10	60	44	60	+16
3	Rapid Bucuresti	34	12	3	2	38	10	6	2	9	21	23	18	5	11	59	33	59	+26
4	Universitatea Craiova	34	15	2	0	35	6	2	4	11	10	24	17	6	11	45	30	57	+15
5	Dinamo Bucuresti	34	12	3	2	28	12	3	4	10	12	25	15	7	12	40	37	52	+3
6	Petrolul Ploiesti	34	15	2	0	34	7	1	1	15	10	31	16	3	15	44	38	51	+6
7	Politehnica Timisoara	34	13	2	2	47	16	1	5	11	11	31	14	7	13	58	47	49	+11
8	FC Farul Constanta	34	12	2	3	37	15	3	2	12	19	34	15	4	15	56	49	49	+7
9	Universitatea Cluj	34	12	4	1	35	12	2	2	13	6	28	14	6	14	41	40	48	+1
10	FC Brasov	34	12	5	0	24	10	1	2	14	14	50	13	7	14	38	60	46	-22
11	Gloria Bistrita	34	13	1	3	31	10	1	2	14	10	28	14	3	17	41	38	45	+3
12	Otelul Galati	34	14	0	3	32	11	0	3	14	10	35	14	3	17	42	46	45	-4
13	AS Bacau	34	14	0	3	33	11	1	0	16	7	47	15	0	19	40	58	45	-18
14	Sportul Studentesc Bucuresti	34	9	4	4	22	12	3	3	11	11	21	12	7	15	33	35	43	-2
15	Ceahlaul Piatra Neamt	34	12	1	4	23	11	1	3	13	11	35	13	4	17	34	46	43	-12
16	FC Arges Dacia Pitesti	34	11	4	2	32	14	1	2	14	7	38	12	6	16	39	52	42	-13
17	FC Inter Sibiu	34	9	6	2	20	9	1	1	15	9	39	10	7	17	29	48	37	-19
18	Politehnica Iasi	34	7	3	7	18	15	2	0	15	9	59	9	3	22	27	74	30	-47

Too many Romanian players were off form. Mihali, Stelea and Belodedici all had a wretched tournament. Strikers Lacatus, Raducioiu and Moldovan were not much better. Only the evergreen Gheorghe Hagi, who won his 100th cap against Spain, appeared to be spurred by the occasion. He may be well past his best now, but Hagi's left foot remains one of the most lethal weapons in the armoury of international football.

Whether the classy centurion has one more major tournament in him is open to doubt. But Romania without Hagi somehow seems inconceivable. One thing is certain, however. Coach Iordanescu will have to reassemble his troops if Romania are to revive themselves in time for France '98. Luckily, the team have been gifted an easy qualifying group, and there seems every chance that they will reach their third successive World Cup finals. But new blood is needed. In England, Iordanescu remained totally loyal to his USA '94 heroes. The only newcomer in the starting XI for the opening match against France was in fact an 'oldie', recalled veteran Marius Lacatus. Of the

TOP SCORERS

26	Ion VLADOIU (Steaua Bucuresti)
17	Marin DUNA (FC National Bucuresti)
15	Marcel BABAN (Politehnica Timisoara)
14	Ionel DANCIULESCU (Dinamo Bucuresti)
	Bucurel Adrian ILIE (Steaua Bucuresti)
12	Horia Radu NICULESCU (FC National Bucuresti)
	Dumitru TÂRTAU (Rapid Bucuresti)
	Daniel SCÎNTEIE (AS Bacau)
	Gheorghe BUTOIU (FC Farul Constanta)
11	Viorel ION (Otelul Galati)
	Radu SABO (Universitatea Cluj)
	Constantin BARBU (FC Arges Dacia Pitesti)

NATIONAL TEAM RESULTS 95/96

06/09/95	Poland (ECQ)	A	Zabrze	0-0	
11/10/95	France (ECQ)	H	Bucharest	1-3	Lacatus (51)
15/11/95	Slovakia (ECQ)	A	Kosice	2-0	Hagi (68), Munteanu (82)
27/03/96	Yugoslavia	A	Belgrade	0-1	
24/04/96	Georgia	H	Bucharest	5-0	Moldovan (25, 29, 37), Lacatus (50), Gâlca (88)
01/06/96	Moldova	H	Bucharest	3-1	Petrescu (28), Popescu (37, 40)
10/06/96	France (ECF)	N	Newcastle	0-1	
13/06/96	Bulgaria (ECF)	N	Newcastle	0-1	
18/06/96	Spain (ECF)	N	Leeds	1-2	Raducioiu (29)

genuine rookies in the squad, Adrian Ilie was the only one to be given a decent run-out. He should soon become a fixture in the side, but will there be places for other colts such as Filipescu, Radulescu, Contra, Serban and Danciulescu on the road to France? Iordanescu is the man with the answers.

With seven of the 16 Euro '96 coaches leaving their jobs within two months of the event, it was perhaps a surprise to some outsiders to note that Iordanescu was not one of them. After all, three defeats in as many matches is hardly a glowing reference. But in Romania, the 'General', as he is called, remains fireproof to criticism. Iordanescu knows that. Because in March, three months before Euro '96, he put his popularity to the test, announcing his resignation as a protest against widespread corruption in the Romanian domestic game. The reaction was a national outcry. Everybody from former tennis champion Ilie Nastase to President Iliescu urged him to reconsider. It took Iordanescu three days before he decided to return.

Subsequently rumours spread that the national coach had stage-managed his own personal referendum, perhaps because he knew that his team would not be able to recreate their World Cup heroics in England. Nevertheless, Iordanescu's stand against corruption was taken seriously, and for good reason. It is an open secret in Romania that football matches are rigged, officials are bribed and thick brown envelopes exchange hands on a regular basis. Iordanescu simply wanted this to be acknowledged at official level and for someone to start doing something to stop it. The FRF reacted by setting up a committee to investigate the problem. Whether any firm action will be taken remains to be seen. The wheels of Romanian officialdom are notoriously slow and squeaky.

In the really bad old days, when the Ceaucescu clan ran the rule over every aspect of Romanian life, football in particular, Steaua Bucharest were given every assistance to maximise their haul of domestic and international trophies. Nowadays they are still Romania's number one club, but, rather than relying on greased palms and subterfuge for their success, they count on lucrative foreign sponsorship and a quality infrastructure that makes them virtually invincible in their own land.

For the fourth year running Steaua waltzed to the national title, dominating the season from first kick to last and even adding the national Cup for good measure. They looked for rivals but found none. One-time arch-enemy Dinamo finished 19 points behind Steaua in the final league table, missing out on a place in one of the three European club competitions for the first time in 16 years. Universitatea Craiova, five points above Dinamo in fourth place, also missed out on a UEFA Cup spot. The two places available went to FC National and Rapid.

INTERNATIONAL HONOURS

World Cup Finals appearances: 1930, 1934, 1938, 1970, 1990 (2nd round), 1994 (qtr-finals)

European Championship appearances: 1960, 1972, 1984, 1996

European Club Competitions

Champions' Cup	Steaua Bucuresti (1986)
Super Cup	Steaua Bucuresti (1986)

DOMESTIC CUP RESULTS

1/16 FINALS

Petrolistul Boldesti 0, Steaua Bucuresti 3
Tractorul Brasov 1, FC Inter Sibiu 2
Danubiana Bucuresti 5, Politehnica Timisoara 1
Dunarea Calarasi 1, FC National Bucuresti 3
ASA Tîrgu Mures 2, Politehnica Iasi 0
CFR Timisoara 2, Sportul Studentesc Bucuresti 3
Gloria Iris Cornesti 0, Gloria Bistrita 1
Sportul Municipal Vaslui 1, FC Arges Dacia Pitesti 3
Petrolul Dragasani 1, Otelul Galati 3
CSM Resita 0, Dinamo Bucuresti 1
FC Brasov 0, FC Farul Constanta 1
Petrolul Ploiesti 4, Universitatea Cluj 1
Gaz Metan Medias 4, Ceahlaul Piatra Neamt 3
Armatura Zalau 0, Universitatea Craiova 0 (5-3 on pens.)
Foresta Falticeni 1, Rapid Bucuresti 1 (5-3 on pens.)
Petrolul Stoina 1, AS Bacau 1 (6-5 on pens.)

1/8 FINALS

FC Farul Constanta 1, Otelul Galati 0
Sportul Studentesc Bucuresti 0, FC Inter Sibiu 2
FC Arges Dacia Pitesti 1, Danubiana Bucuresti 0
Dinamo Bucuresti 1, Gaz Metan Medias 0
Steaua Bucuresti 3, Petrolul Stoiana 0
FC National Bucuresti 2, ASA Tîrgu Mures 0
Gloria Bistrita 3, Armatura Zalau 1
Petrolul Ploiesti 2, Foresta Falticeni 1

QUARTER-FINALS

Dinamo Bucuresti 0, Steaua Bucuresti 1
Gloria Bistrita 2, FC Farul Constanta 1
FC National Bucuresti 1, Petrolul Ploiesti 1 (3-1 on pens.)
FC Arges Dacia Pitesti 1, FC Inter Sibiu 1 (3-4 on pens.)

SEMI-FINALS

Steaua Bucuresti 4, FC Inter Sibiu 1
FC National Bucuresti 0, Gloria Bistrita 2

FINAL

28/04/96, Bucharest
STEAUA BUCURESTI 3 Ilie S. (59), Bucur (77), Gâlca (89)
GLORIA BISTRITA 1 Miszti (44)
referee - Porumboiu
STEAUA BUCURESTI - Stelea; Csik (Ilie S. 52), Prodan, Dobos, Pîrvu; Filipescu, Gâlca, Raducan (Bucur 70), Rosu (Nagy 56); Lacatus, Vladoiu.
GLORIA BISTRITA - Cîmpeanu; Miszti, Cristea, Mironas, Sasarman (Halosta 79); Dancus, Voica (Nastase 59), Purdea, Iftodi (Raduta 81), Lazar, Matei.

National recovered from a dreadful start (five defeats in their first seven games) and stormed up the table in the spring - despite miserable home attendances which occasionally forced them to let spectators in for free. The man who guided them all the way up to the runners-up spot was Florin Halagian, without question the best Romanian coach never to have taken charge of the national team or been offered a top job abroad.

Rapid stalked Steaua in fits and starts but they never genuinely threatened to pull up alongside them. A poor finish cost them second place and almost allowed Craiova to deprive them of their UEFA Cup ticket.

It was not a memorable championship for the neutrals. Even the issue of relegation was cut and dried once the league officials decided mid-season to scrap their original plans to reduce the First Division to 16 teams in 1996/97. The four relegation places suddenly became two, and while a number of teams breathed a sigh of relief, FC Inter Sibiu and Politehnica Iasi were already doomed to drop down a division.

The national team aside, the only significant focus of attention for Romanian football-watchers in 1995/96 was the involvement of Steaua in the UEFA Champions' League. While Universitatea Craiova and Dinamo Bucharest were both enduring a UEFA Cup preliminary-round exit for the second year running - Craiova losing

NATIONAL TEAM APPEARANCES 95/96

Coach - Anghel IORDANESCU	POL	FRA	SVK	YUG	GEO	MOL	FRA	BUL	ESP	Cps	Gls
Bogdan STELEA (05/12/67) - Steaua Bucuresti	G	G	G		G65	G53	G	G		35	-
Dan PETRESCU (22/12/67) - Sheffield Wednesday (ENG)/Chelsea (ENG)	D	D	D	D60		D66	D77	D	D	54	6
Gheorghe MIHALI (09/12/65) - En Avant Guingamp (FRA)	D	D46		s60	s68	D	D			32	-
Gheorghe POPESCU (09/10/67) - FC Barcelona (ESP)	D	D	M		M60	M66	M	M78	M	65	5
Daniel PRODAN (23/03/72) - Steaua Bucuresti	D	D	D	D	D78	s62		D	D86	34	1
Tibor SELYMES (14/05/70) - KSV Cercle Brugge (BEL)	D	D	D	D	s51	D62	D	D	D	31	-
Ioan Ovidiu SABAU (12/02/68) - Brescia (ITA)	M			M	M51					47	8
Ioan LUPESCU (09/12/68) - Bayer 04 Leverkusen (GER)	M	M	M	M46	M	M53	M	M46	s86	51	5
Dorinel MUNTEANU (25/06/68) - 1.FC Köln (GER)	M75	M	M	M82	D	M53	M	M	s66	49	4
Marius LACATUS (05/04/64) - Steaua Bucuresti	A84	A	A72	A64	A51	A53	A56	A29		78	13
Ion VLADOIU (05/11/68) - Steaua Bucuresti	A64	s46		s76	s60	s66			s78	19	-
Basarab PANDURU (11/07/70) - SL Benfica (POR)	s64	s63	s84							21	1
Constantin GÂLCA (08/03/72) - Steaua Bucuresti	s75			s46	s60	s53		s46	M	19	1
Ion TIMOFTE (16/12/67) - Boavista FC (POR)	s84		s87							10	1
Gheorghe HAGI (05/02/65) - FC Barcelona (ESP)		M63	M84	A60	M65	M62	M	M	A	100	27
Ilie DUMITRESCU (06/01/69) - Tottenham Hotspur (ENG)		A46	s72							54	19
Danut LUPU (27/02/67) - Dinamo Bucuresti		s46								13	-
Anton DOBOS (13/10/65) - Steaua Bucuresti			D	D	s78	s62			D	8	-
Dinu Viorel MOLDOVAN (08/08/72) - Neuchâtel Xamax FC (SUI)			A87	A76	A60	s53	s46	s29		10	3
Florian PRUNEA (08/08/68) - Dinamo Bucuresti				G76	s65	s53 /73			G	32	-
Adrian ILIE (20/04/74) - Steaua Bucuresti				s60		s53	s56	s78	M66	6	-
Gheorghe CRAIOVEANU (14/02/68) - Real Sociedad (ESP)				s64	s51					8	-
Florin Alexandru TENE (10/11/68) - Rapid Bucuresti				s76		s73				5	-
Iulian FILIPESCU (29/03/74) - Steaua Bucuresti				s82	D	s66	s77			4	-
Miodrag BELODEDICI (20/05/64) - Villarreal CF (ESP)					D68	D62	D	D		49	5
Cosmin Marius CONTRA (15/12/75) - Dinamo Bucuresti					s65					1	-
Florin RADUCIOIU (17/03/70) - RCD Espanyol (ESP)						A	A46	A	A78	40	21
Ovidiu STÎNGA (05/12/72) - UD Salamanca (ESP)						s62			M	13	-

EUROPEAN CUPS RESULTS 95/96

CHAMPIONS' CUP

● STEUA BUCURESTI

Preliminary round SV CASINO SALZBURG (AUT)

A 0-0
Stelea; Csik, Prodan, Dobos, Panait; Militaru, Bucur, Gâlca, Ilie A. (Filipescu 70); Lacatus, Vladoiu (Rosu 82).

H 1-0 Ilie A. (32)
Stelea; Panait, Prodan, Dobos, Pârvu; Militaru (Csik 89), Gâlca, Ilie A. (Filipescu 62), Bucur; Lacatus (Rosu 60), Vladoiu.

Champions' League

1st match RANGERS (SCO)

H 1-0 Prodan (85)
Stelea; Csik, Prodan, Dobos, Pârvu; Militaru, Gâlca, Bucur (Filipescu 46), Raducan; Ilie A. (Rosu 60), Vladoiu (Ilie S. 77).

2nd match JUVENTUS (ITA)

A 0-3
Stelea; Dobos, Prodan, Csik, Pârvu; Raducan, Gâlca, Ilie A. (Panait 77), Filipescu (Nagy 83); Vladoiu, Lacatus (Rosu 54).

3rd match BORUSSIA DORTMUND (GER)

A 0-1
Stelea; Panait (Rosu 85), Csik, Prodan, Dobos, Pârvu; Filipescu (Nagy 71), Gâlca, Ilie A. (Raducan 63); Lacatus, Vladoiu.

4th match BORUSSIA DORTMUND (GER)

H 0-0
Stelea; Csik, Prodan, Dobos, Pârvu; Panait, Bucur, Ilie A. (Nagy 79), Filipescu (Raducan 66); Lacatus (Rosu 59), Vladoiu.

5th match RANGERS (SCO)

A 1-1 Ilie A. (55)
Stelea; Csik, Prodan, Dobos, Pârvu; Filipescu, Militaru (Rosu 90), Bucur, Ilie A. (Nagy 75); Lacatus (Raducan 87), Vladoiu.

6th match JUVENTUS (ITA)

H 0-0
Stelea; Panait, Csik, Dobos, Prodan, Pârvu (Rosu 46); Militaru (Ilie S. 83), Gâlca, Nagy; Filipescu (Raducan 63), Vladoiu.

CUP-WINNERS' CUP

● PETROLUL PLOIESTI

Preliminary round WREXHAM (WAL)

A 0-0
Preda; Chirita, Balaceanu, Rachita, Leahu; Grigore, Pîrlog (Bastina 81), Abaluta, Zmoleanu; Toader (Mihai M. 87), Zafiris (Andreicut 71).

H 1-0 Pîrlog (59)
Preda; Chirita, Balaceanu, Rachita, Leahu; Grigore, Pîrlog, Abaluta, Zmoleanu (Bastina 88); Zafiris (Toader 65; Balaban 86), Andreicut.

1st round SK RAPID WIEN (AUT)

A 1-3 Toader (65)
Preda; Chirita, Grigore, Rachita, Pîrlog, Leahu; Bastina, Abaluta, Zmoleanu; Zafiris (Toader 62), Andreicut (Grama 81).

H 0-0
Preda; Bastina, Balaceanu, Rachita, Leahu; Grama (Mihai M. 66), Grigore, Abaluta, Zmoleanu; Andreicut (Zafiris 46), Toader (Pîrlog 75).

UEFA CUP

● UNIVERSITATEA CRAIOVA

Preliminary round DINAMO MINSK (BLS)

H 0-0
Arcanu; Cristescu (Popescu A. 17), Curt, Papura, Olaroiu, Mitrita; Calin (Trica 79), Popescu G., Badea; Ungur (Gane 61), Cârstea.

A 0-0
(aet; 1-3 on pens.)
Arcanu; Cristescu, Naicu, Papura, Curt, Mitrita; Stoican (Popescu A. 46; Ungur 117), Popescu G., Olaroiu, Badea (Calin 84); Gane.

● DINAMO BUCURESTI

Preliminary round LEVSKI SOFIA (BUL)

H 0-1
Tene; Kadar, Sburlea, Mironas, Varga; Cheregi (Petre 65), Fulga, Mateut, Lupu; Ivan, Danciulescu (Zotinca 31).

A 1-1 Lupu (70)
(aet) Tene; Grozavu, Kadar, Sburlea, Cheregi, Varga; Zotinca (Danciulescu 75), Fulga, Mateut, Lupu; Ivan (Savu M. 100).

on penalties, Dinamo after extra-time - Steaua overcame Austrian side Casino Salzburg to reach the Champions' League group phase, also for the second year in a row.

With things going smoothly at home, Dumitru Dumitriu's side could afford to throw all their energy into a competition they desperately wanted to succeed in. They could not have been placed in a tougher group, but optimism was permitted after a 1-0 victory at home to Scottish champions Rangers in their first match. It was misplaced. Steaua predictably lost their next two fixtures, away to Juventus and Borussia Dortmund, and their hopes of reaching the quarter-finals disappeared when they could only draw 0-0 in the return against the German champions. Two further draws completed their campaign, thereby matching precisely the club's 1994/95 record of one win, three draws and two defeats.

The target of a quarter-final place had been missed, but Steaua had plenty to console themselves with in the domestic competitions. They continued to increase their lead at the top of the league table and by Easter they had become one of the first national champions to be crowned in Europe, with skipper Lacatus setting a post-war record by winning his eighth championship winner's medal for the club. A first Romanian Cup victory in four years was the club's next target, and after eliminating Dinamo with a 1-0 away win in the quarter-finals, Steaua duly took the trophy for the 19th time by coming back from a goal behind to defeat Gloria Bistrita in the final.

There were many individual heroes in Steaua's first 'double' triumph for seven years, and just about all of them were rewarded with a place in Anghel Iordanescu's European Championship 22. In all, eight Steaua players travelled to England - goalkeeper Bogdan Stelea, defenders Daniel Prodan and Anton Dobos, midfielders Iulian Filipescu, Constantin Gâlca and Adrian Ilie, and strikers Ion Vladoiu and Marius Lacatus. And to prove just how big a gulf there is between Steaua and the rest of the Romanian clubs, Iordanescu selected only two other home-based players for his squad, both of them goalkeepers - Prunea from Dinamo and Tene from Rapid.

PLAYERS OF THE SEASON

ION VLADOIU

After a year and a half with Bucharest rivals Rapid, Ion Vladoiu returned to champions Steaua and immediately added sting and subtlety to their attack. His decision to shave off his moustache appeared to work wonders. Goals flowed from his left boot like never before, and at the end of the season he was the league's top scorer, his 25-goal tally putting him well clear of the rest of the field. A return to the national team also boosted Vladoiu's season, although coach Iordanescu barely used him at all in the Euro '96 finals, mindful no doubt that, for all his goals in domestic competition, Vladoiu had yet to get off the mark for Romania.

ADRIAN ILIE

Romanian football's great hope for the future is 22 -year-old Bucurel Adrian Ilie. The Craiova-born midfielder joined Steaua in 1993 and he has now won three straight Romanian titles with them. He is a skilful schemer who can also play in attack. He scored 13 league goals for Steaua in 1995/96 and another two in the Champions' League, including the crucial winner in the preliminary tie against Salzburg. He also grabbed a hat-trick for the national team against Thailand in the King's Cup in February. But as official caps were not awarded for that tournament - which Romania won, beating Denmark in the final - the youngster's international goal tally remained on zero after his three appearances, two as a substitute, at Euro '96.

GHEORGHE POPESCU

He did not have the influential European Championship he had longed for on his return to England, but Gheorghe "Gica" Popescu remains far and away the most successful of Romania's many footballing exports. After a modest interlude at Tottenham, the big versatility man came roaring back to his best form in an outstanding first season at Barcelona. He arrived as the replacement for Ronald Koeman - just as he had at PSV Eindhoven several years earlier - and his impact was similarly profound. At the end of 1995 Popescu was once again voted as Romania's Player of the Year. It is becoming something of a habit for the brawny 29-year-old. He has now won the award on five occasions.

Adrian Ilie (above) and Gheorghe Popescu (left)

FC ARGES DACIA PITESTI

CLUB DIRECTORY

FC Arges Dacia Pitesti
str. Armand Calinescu 15
0300 Pitesti
tel - (048) 632842
Year of Formation - 1953
President - Gabriel Sicoe
Coach - Constantin Stancu; Constantin Cârstea (96/97 - Ion Moldovan)
Stadium - Trivale (18,000)

MAJOR HONOURS
League Championship - (2) 1972, 1979.

APPEARANCES 95/96

	P	Ap	(s)	Gls
Mihai BAICU	A	1	(1)	
Constantin BARBU	A	27	(1)	11
Nicolae Radu BRATU	G	2	(3)	
Ion Romica CEAUSU	M	20	(4)	
Viorel Mihail CIOBANU	D	1	(3)	
Cornel CRISTESCU	D	28	(1)	1
Iulian CRIVAC	M	15	(9)	1
Gabriel DUMITRU	M	18	(6)	3
Ion Cristian GALES	M		(5)	
Marcel GHERGU	D	24	(5)	1
Catalin GÎRLESTEANU	D	15		1
Marian GRAMA	M	5	(4)	2
Ion Cristinel IVAN	A		(3)	
Florian Dan LACUSTA	D	14	(7)	
Virgil Alexandru LUP	D	10	(1)	
Florin Dan MOCANU	D	27		1
Ovidiu Traian MORDONU	D	2	(1)	
Vasile Valentin NASTASE	M	13	(7)	
Cristian Eugen NEGRU	A	25	(6)	5
Constantin PANA	A	2	(1)	
Marian PANA	D	14	(3)	4
Vasile Nicolae POPA	D	32		1
Marius Nicolae PRISECEANU	M	9	(13)	
Daniel PROCORODIE	M		(6)	
Constantin SCHUMACHER	M	31		8
George TIMIS	A	6	(3)	
Ion UNGURIANU	G	32	(1)	
Iulian VILAU	D	1		

LEAGUE RESULTS 1995/96

12/08/95	AS Bacau	A	1-3	Pana M. (p)
19/08/95	FC National Bucuresti	H	4-0	Barbu 3, Schumacher
27/08/95	Petrolul Ploiesti	A	0-1	
30/08/95	Universitatea Craiova	H	2-0	Pana M. (p), Barbu (p)
09/09/95	Dinamo Bucuresti	A	1-3	Barbu
16/09/95	Rapid Bucuresti	H	3-2	Ghergu, Negru, Crivac
23/09/95	Otelul Galati	A	0-2	
01/10/95	Ceahlaul Piatra Neamt	H	1-1	Barbu
04/10/95	FC Brasov	A	1-1	Pana M.
14/10/95	Gloria Bistrita	H	2-1	Dumitru, Negru
21/10/95	Universitatea Cluj	H	0-2	
25/10/95	FC Farul Constanta	A	0-3	
28/10/95	Steaua Bucuresti	H	1-2	Pana M. (p)
04/11/95	Sportul Studentesc Bucuresti	A	0-3	
08/11/95	FC Inter Sibiu	H	2-1	Negru, Popa
18/11/95	Politehnica Iasi	A	2-1	Dumitru, Schumacher
25/11/95	Politehnica Timisoara	H	0-0	
29/11/95	AS Bacau	H	2-0	Mocanu, Schumacher
02/12/95	FC National Bucuresti	A	1-4	Dumitru
08/12/95	Petrolul Ploiesti	H	2-1	Schumacher, Cristescu
13/12/95	Universitatea Craiova	A	1-2	Gîrlesteanu
27/02/96	Dinamo Bucuresti	H	1-0	Grama
02/03/96	Rapid Bucuresti	A	0-3	
06/03/96	Otelul Galati	H	2-2	Schumacher, Negru
09/03/96	Ceahlaul Piatra Neamt	A	0-1	
16/03/96	FC Brasov	H	1-1	Grama
20/03/96	Gloria Bistrita	A	0-4	
23/03/96	Universitatea Cluj	A	0-1	
30/03/96	FC Farul Constanta	H	2-1	Schumacher, Barbu
06/04/96	Steaua Bucuresti	A	0-4	
10/04/96	Sportul Studentesc Bucuresti	H	1-0	Barbu
13/04/96	FC Inter Sibiu	A	0-0	
17/04/96	Politehnica Iasi	H	6-0	Schumacher 2 (1p), Barbu 3, Negru
20/04/96	Politehnica Timisoara	A	0-2	

AS BACAU

CLUB DIRECTORY

AS Bacau
str. Pictor Aman 94
5500 Bacau
tel (034) 141922
Year of Formation - 1950
President - Nicolae Paduraru
Coach - Costel Orac; Mircea Nedelcu
Stadium - Municipal (18,000)

APPEARANCES 95/96

	P	Ap	(s)	Gls
Vasile Maricel ARDELEANU	D	13	(3)	
Jean Daniel BOGDAN	G	17	(2)	
Marius BRATU	G	17	(2)	
Ionel Giani CAPUSA	M	17	(11)	1
Radu Eduard CIOBANU	D	13	(9)	
Cristian CIOCOIU	A	31		5
Sorin CONDURACHE	D	4	(3)	
Petru FIRICI	A	4	(3)	1
Marius GIREADA	D	17	(3)	
Florin Paul IONESCU	D	27		3
Vasile JERCALAU	M	32		9
Claudiu Adamec MANTA	M	27	(1)	4
Danut MUNTEANU	D	23		
Vasile Valentin PAVALUTA	M	2	(7)	
Florin PAVEL	M	17	(9)	
Cristian Daniel POPOVICI	D	26	(1)	
Vasile Ovidiu ROTARIU	M	26	(3)	1
Daniel SCÎNTEIE	A	29		12
Ionica SEREA	M	17	(13)	4
Aurelian Ionel ZLATI	M	15	(4)	

LEAGUE RESULTS 1995/96

Date	Opponent	H/A	Score	Scorers
12/08/95	FC Arges Dacia Pitesti	H	3-1	Scînteie, Manta (p), Ciocoiu
19/08/95	FC Farul Constanta	A	0-1	
27/08/95	Steaua Bucuresti	H	1-2	Ciocoiu
30/08/95	Sportul Studentesc Bucuresti	A	0-3	
09/09/95	FC Inter Sibiu	H	2-1	Ionescu, Manta (p)
16/09/95	Politehnica Iasi	A	0-3	
23/09/95	Politehnica Timisoara	H	4-1	Jercalau (p), Firici, Ciocoiu 2
01/10/95	Universitatea Cluj	A	1-7	Scînteie
04/10/95	FC National Bucuresti	A	1-4	Manta
14/10/95	Petrolul Ploiesti	H	1-0	Scînteie
21/10/95	Universitatea Craiova	A	0-1	
25/10/95	Dinamo Bucuresti	H	2-0	Jercalau, Scînteie
28/10/95	Rapid Bucuresti	A	0-3	
03/11/95	Otelul Galati	H	3-0	Jercalau (p), Scînteie, Capusa
08/11/95	Ceahlaul Piatra Neamt	A	1-3	Jercalau (p)
18/11/95	FC Brasov	H	1-2	Scînteie
25/11/95	Gloria Bistrita	A	0-2	
29/11/95	FC Arges Dacia Pitesti	A	0-2	
02/12/95	FC Farul Constanta	H	3-0	Serea 2, Scînteie
09/12/95	Steaua Bucuresti	A	0-5	
13/12/95	Sportul Studentesc Bucuresti	H	0-1	
28/02/96	FC Inter Sibiu	A	2-0	Scînteie, Rotariu
02/03/96	Politehnica Iasi	H	3-1	Scînteie 3
06/03/96	Politehnica Timisoara	A	0-2	
09/03/96	Universitatea Cluj	H	1-0	Jercalau (p)
16/03/96	FC National Bucuresti	H	2-1	Manta, Ionescu
20/03/96	Petrolul Ploiesti	A	0-3	
23/03/96	Universitatea Craiova	H	1-0	Serea
30/03/96	Dinamo Bucuresti	A	0-3	
06/04/96	Rapid Bucuresti	H	1-0	Jercalau (p)
10/04/96	Otelul Galati	A	1-3	Serea
13/04/96	Ceahlaul Piatra Neamt	H	2-0	Jercalau (p), Ionescu
17/04/96	FC Brasov	A	1-2	Ciocoiu
20/04/96	Gloria Bistrita	H	3-1	Jercalau 2 (2p), Scînteie

FC BRASOV

CLUB DIRECTORY

FC Brasov
str. Titan 1
2200 Brasov
tel - (068) 116033
Year of Formation - 1937
President - Romeo Pascu
Coach - Gabriel Stan; Csaba Györfi; Viorel Hizo
Stadium - Tineretului (15,000)

APPEARANCES 95/96

	P	Ap	(s)	Gls
Florin Adrian ANGHEL	M		(1)	
Iuliu Paris ANDRASI	D	16	(4)	
Marin Dorel BALINT	D	26	(1)	3
Valentin Florin BERARU	M	13	(6)	1
Cosmin BODEA	D	21	(1)	1
Aurel Cosmin BRÎNDAS	M	4	(1)	
Costin CARAMAN	A		(8)	
Ionel CAZANGIU	D	31	(1)	
Valentin Ion DAVID	G	14		
Ioan DRAGAN	D	22	(3)	
Adrian DRAGANOIU	D	11	(2)	
John Adrian ENE	G	18		
Iosif ERDEI	D	11	(1)	
Ion Viorel GANEA	M	19	(1)	4
Vasile GHINDARU	A	2	(6)	
Adrian Ioan GONGOLEA	D	1	(1)	
Ion Lavi HRIB	A	20	(4)	7
Marian JILAVEANU	A	6	(7)	
Ovidiu Traian LAZAR	A	2	(3)	
Bebe Radu MANOLE	M	17	(8)	3
Ion Calin MOLDOVAN	D	10	(2)	
Cristian MUCENICA	M	3	(7)	
Istvan NAGY	M	11	(6)	
Fanel Daniel NIIA	M	23	(7)	3
Karuso Altafino PALACIAN	M	1	(1)	
Nicolae Sorin PETRE	G	1	(1)	
Marian POPA	A	13		4
Dorel PURDEA	D	11		
Gabi Marian RADUTA	M	13		
Andrei SANTA	G	1		
Leonard Mario STRIZU	A	8	(2)	5
Gabriel Alin TIBICHI	M	1		
Lucian Vasile ULICI	D	3	(3)	1
Cristian Marius VASC	M	21		5

LEAGUE RESULTS 1995/96

14/08/95	Petrolul Ploiesti	A	2-4	Niia, Ganea (p)
19/08/95	Universitatea Craiova	H	1-1	Balint
26/08/95	Dinamo Bucuresti	A	1-3	Vasc
30/08/95	Rapid Bucuresti	H	1-0	Ganea
09/09/95	Otelul Galati	A	0-4	
16/09/95	Ceahlaul Piatra Neamt	H	0-0	
23/09/95	Universitatea Cluj	H	1-0	Manole
01/10/95	Gloria Bistrita	A	2-3	Vasc, Manole
04/10/95	FC Arges Dacia Pitesti	H	1-1	Vasc
14/10/95	FC Farul Constanta	A	0-4	
22/10/95	Steaua Bucuresti	H	1-0	Vasc (p)
25/10/95	Sportul Studentesc Bucuresti	A	0-2	
28/10/95	FC Inter Sibiu	H	2-1	Hrib, Balint
04/11/95	Politehnica Iasi	A	1-2	Balint
08/11/95	Politehnica Timisoara	H	1-1	Hrib
18/11/95	AS Bacau	A	2-1	Hrib, Ganea
25/11/95	FC National Bucuresti	H	0-0	
29/11/95	Petrolul Ploiesti	H	1-0	Ganea
02/12/95	Universitatea Craiova	A	1-3	og (Curt)
09/12/95	Dinamo Bucuresti	H	2-1	Vasc, Beraru
13/12/95	Rapid Bucuresti	A	0-3	
28/02/96	Otelul Galati	H	1-0	Strizu
02/03/96	Ceahlaul Piatra Neamt	A	1-2	Hrib
06/03/96	Universitatea Cluj	A	1-1	Popa
09/03/96	Gloria Bistrita	H	1-0	Popa
16/03/96	FC Arges Dacia Pitesti	A	1-1	Hrib
20/03/96	FC Farul Constanta	H	3-1	Popa 2, Manole
23/03/96	Steaua Bucuresti	A	0-5	
30/03/96	Sportul Studentesc Bucuresti	H	4-3	Hrib (p), Bodea, Strizu, Niia
06/04/96	FC Inter Sibiu	A	0-3	
10/04/96	Politehnica Iasi	H	2-0	Niia, Strizu
13/04/96	Politehnica Timisoara	A	1-4	Hrib
17/04/96	AS Bacau	H	2-1	Strizu 2
20/04/96	FC National Bucuresti	A	1-5	Ulici

CEAHLAUL PIATRA NEAMT

CLUB DIRECTORY

Ceahlaul Piatra Neamt
Str. Eroilor 18
5600 Piatra Neamt
tel - (033) 612702/616613
Year of Formation - 1919
President - Gheorghe Stefan
Coach - Mircea Nedelcu; Silviu Stanescu
(96/97 - Florin Marin)
Stadium - Ceahlaul (15,000)

APPEARANCES 95/96

	P	Ap	(s)	Gls
Cristinel ATOMULESEI	M	29		
Niculai ALEXA	G	11		
Florin Vasile AXINIA	A	24	(2)	4
Gheorghe Iulian AXINIA	D	9	(6)	
Valeriu Ionut BORDEANU	M	3	(7)	
Gheorghe BURLEANU	M	18	(1)	2
Cristinel COSERARIU	G	2	(2)	
Codrut Stefan DOMSA	D	25	(1)	1
Constantin ENACHE	A	28	(5)	9
Florin GRIGORAS	D	1		
Mihai Adrian IENCSI	D	17	(5)	1
Mihai Dan IONESCU	M	28	(4)	6
Leon IVANOV	D	28		
Radu Gabriel LEFTER	G	21	(2)	
Dan Ciprian MANEA	D	25	(2)	
Ovidiu MARC	A	19	(1)	7
Marian MIREA	A	6	(13)	
Florin MOTROC	M	12		
Ion Ovidiu MURARIU	M		(2)	
Gheorghe PANTAZI	M	33		3
Traian Claudiu SALAGEAN	M	3		
Tiberiu SERBAN	A	1	(2)	
Tudorel Cristian SOIMARU	D	20	(3)	
Adrian Constantin SOLOMON	M	1	(7)	
Florin STANCU	M	10	(2)	1

LEAGUE RESULTS 1995/96

12/08/95	Universitatea Craiova	A	0-4	
19/08/95	Dinamo Bucuresti	H	2-0	Ionescu, Marc
26/08/95	Rapid Bucuresti	A	1-2	Ionescu
30/08/95	Otelul Galati	H	3-1	Ionescu (p), Axinia F.V., Marc
09/09/95	Universitatea Cluj	H	2-0	Axinia F.V., Enache
16/09/95	FC Brasov	A	0-0	
23/09/95	Gloria Bistrita	H	1-0	Marc (p)
01/10/95	FC Arges Dacia Pitesti	A	1-1	Enache
04/10/95	FC Farul Constanta	H	0-0	
14/10/95	Steaua Bucuresti	A	2-6	Pantazi, Ionescu (p)
21/10/95	Sportul Studentesc Bucuresti	H	1-0	Marc
25/10/95	FC Inter Sibiu	A	0-2	
28/10/95	Politehnica Iasi	H	1-0	Ionescu
04/11/95	Politehnica Timisoara	A	3-4	Burleanu, Pantazi, Domsa
08/11/95	AS Bacau	H	3-1	Enache, Marc 2
18/11/95	FC National Bucuresti	A	1-3	Burleanu
25/11/95	Petrolul Ploiesti	H	1-2	Marc (p)
29/11/95	Universitatea Craiova	H	0-2	
02/12/95	Dinamo Bucuresti	A	0-0	
09/12/95	Rapid Bucuresti	H	0-1	
13/12/95	Otelul Galati	A	0-2	
28/02/96	Universitatea Cluj	A	0-2	
02/03/96	FC Brasov	H	2-1	Enache (p), Ionescu
06/03/96	Gloria Bistrita	A	0-1	
09/03/96	FC Arges Dacia Pitesti	H	1-0	Enache (p)
16/03/96	FC Farul Constanta	A	0-2	
20/03/96	Steaua Bucuresti	H	2-1	Axinia F.V. 2
23/03/96	Sportul Studentesc Bucuresti	A	0-1	
30/03/96	FC Inter Sibiu	H	2-0	Enache 2 (1p)
06/04/96	Politehnica Iasi	A	1-0	Iencsi
10/04/96	Politehnica Timisoara	H	1-0	Enache
13/04/96	AS Bacau	A	0-2	
17/04/96	FC National Bucuresti	H	1-2	Stancu
20/04/96	Petrolul Ploiesti	A	2-3	Enache, Pantazi

DINAMO BUCURESTI

CLUB DIRECTORY

FC Dinamo Bucuresti
Sos. Stefan cel Mare 9
71401 Bucuresti
tel - (01) 3129959/2103519
fax - (01) 3129959
Year of Formation - 1948
President - Petre Buduru
Coach - Remus Vlad; Florin Cheran; Marian Bondrea
Stadium - Dinamo (18,000)

MAJOR HONOURS
League Championship - (14)
1955, 1962, 1963, 1964, 1965, 1971, 1973, 1975, 1977, 1982, 1983, 1984, 1990, 1992.
Domestic Cup - (7)
1959, 1964, 1968, 1982, 1984, 1986, 1990.

APPEARANCES 95/96

	P	Ap	(s)	Gls
Lucian BALABAN	A		(2)	
Daniel Eugen BASTON	A	3	(2)	1
Florin BATRÎNU	D	26		1
Marius CHEREGI	M	14	(7)	
Cosmin Marius CONTRA	D	12		1
Marius Mihai COPORAN	M	2	(7)	
Claudiu Mircea CORNACI	M	2	(3)	
Levente Zsolt CSIK	D	18	(6)	1
Ionel DANCIULESCU	A	27	(5)	14
Cezar DINU	M	6	(4)	
Mihai DRAGUS	A	10	(7)	1
Ionel FULGA	M	6	(11)	1
Dumitru GHEORGHE	M		(1)	
Leo Florian GROZAVU	D	25	(1)	3
Catalin HÎLDAN	M	11	(2)	
Mihai Dan IOSIF	M		(2)	
Marian IVAN	M	4		
Zoltán KADAR	D	7	(4)	
Florin LAZAR	D	1		
Danut LUPU	M	29		3
Florin MACAVEI	D	9		
Dorin MATEUT	M	19		8
Mitica MERE	M		(2)	
Ioan Sebastian MOGA	M	21	(4)	1
Calin Gabriel PANTELIMON	M		(1)	
Florentin PETRE	M	27	(3)	3
Florian PRUNEA	G	29		
Marian SAVU	A	1	(5)	
Ion SBURLEA	D	4		
Mihai TARARACHE	M	22	(2)	
Alexandru Florin TENE	G	4	(1)	
Daniel Ovidiu TUDOR	G	1		
Constantin VARGA	D	30	(2)	2
Dorin Bogdan ZOTINCA	M	4	(6)	

LEAGUE RESULTS 1995/96

12/08/95	Otelul Galati	H	2-0	Lupu, Mateut
19/08/95	Ceahlaul Piatra Neamt	A	0-2	
26/08/95	FC Brasov	H	3-1	Mateut 2 (1p), Danciulescu
30/08/95	Gloria Bistrita	A	0-2	
09/09/95	FC Arges Dacia Pitesti	H	3-1	Lupu, Grozavu, Mateut (p)
16/09/95	FC Farul Constanta	A	2-1	Danciulescu, Mateut
22/09/95	Steaua Bucuresti	H	1-1	Csik
01/10/95	Sportul Studentesc Bucuresti	A	1-0	Danciulescu
04/10/95	FC Inter Sibiu	H	2-1	Petre, Varga
14/10/95	Politehnica Iasi	A	0-0	
21/10/95	Politehnica Timisoara	H	3-0	Mateut, Danciulescu, Petre
25/10/95	AS Bacau	A	0-2	
29/10/95	FC National Bucuresti	H	0-3	
04/11/95	Petrolul Ploiesti	A	0-1	
09/11/95	Universitatea Craiova	H	2-1	Danciulescu, Mateut (p)
18/11/95	Universitatea Cluj	H	1-0	Mateut
25/11/95	Rapid Bucuresti	A	0-2	
29/11/95	Otelul Galati	A	2-0	Varga, Danciulescu
02/12/95	Ceahlaul Piatra Neamt	H	0-0	
09/12/95	FC Brasov	A	1-2	Grozavu
13/12/95	Gloria Bistrita	H	2-1	Fulga, Lupu (p)
27/02/96	FC Arges Dacia Pitesti	A	0-1	
02/03/96	FC Farul Constanta	H	2-1	Baston, Danciulescu
06/03/96	Steaua Bucuresti	A	2-4	Danciulescu 2
09/03/96	Sportul Studentesc Bucuresti	H	0-1	
16/03/96	FC Inter Sibiu	A	0-0	
20/03/96	Politehnica Iasi	H	2-0	Contra, Dragus
23/03/96	Politehnica Timisoara	A	2-2	Grozavu, Batrînu
30/03/96	AS Bacau	H	3-0	Danciulescu 3
06/04/96	FC National Bucuresti	A	1-1	Moga
10/04/96	Petrolul Ploiesti	H	1-0	Danciulescu
13/04/96	Universitatea Craiova	A	1-3	Petre
17/04/96	Universitatea Cluj	A	0-2	
20/04/96	Rapid Bucuresti	H	1-1	Danciulescu

FC FARUL CONSTANTA

CLUB DIRECTORY

FC Farul Constanta
str. Primaverii 2
8700 Constanta
tel - (041) 616142
fax - (041) 644827
Year of Formation - 1949
President - Hacic Garabet
Coach - Florin Marin (96/97 - Marin Ion)
Stadium - Farul (20,000)

APPEARANCES 95/96

	P	Ap	(s)	Gls
Catalin Constantin ANGHEL	A	9	(5)	3
Marius AXINCIUC	M	24	(4)	3
Gheorghe BARBU	M	31		8
Gheorghe BUTOIU	A	19		12
Stelian CARABAS	M	25	(4)	2
Gheorghe CEAUSILA	A	6	(14)	3
Aristica CIOABA	D	2	(1)	
Gheorghe CIUREA	M	24		3
Marian DINU	D	33		1
Daniel Marian ENACHE	M	1	(3)	
Daniel Constantin GHISAN	D	30		
Zoltan Martin IASKO	G		(5)	
Mihai MATEI	D	10	(7)	1
Danut MOISESCU	M	1	(1)	
Cristian Marian MUNTEANU	G	34		
Cristian Viorel MUSTACA	M	12	(7)	1
Stefan Dumitru NANU	D	26		
Nicusor NEATA	A	1	(4)	1
Banica OPREA	M	31		10
Ionel Cristian PETCU	D	1	(2)	
Marian POPA	A	1		
Denis Georgian SERBAN	M	30	(2)	5
Gabriel TOMA	A	23	(8)	2
Lucian Vasile ULICI	D		(1)	
Daniel Nicolaie USVAT	M		(3)	
Marius Laurentiu ZADEA	M		(10)	

LEAGUE RESULTS 1995/96

Date	Opponent	H/A	Score	Scorers
12/08/95	Politehnica Timisoara	A	1-3	Matei
19/08/95	AS Bacau	H	1-0	Butoiu
26/08/95	FC National Bucuresti	A	1-2	Butoiu
30/08/95	Petrolul Ploiesti	H	3-3	Oprea, Toma, Butoiu
09/09/95	Universitatea Craiova	A	1-2	Butoiu
16/09/95	Dinamo Bucuresti	H	1-2	Butoiu
23/09/95	Rapid Bucuresti	A	4-3	Ceausila, Serban, Butoiu, Dinu
01/10/95	Otelul Galati	H	1-0	Butoiu
04/10/95	Ceahlaul Piatra Neamt	A	0-0	
14/10/95	FC Brasov	H	4-0	Barbu 2, Butoiu, Oprea
21/10/95	Gloria Bistrita	A	2-0	Ciurea, og (Cîmpeanu)
25/10/95	FC Arges Dacia Pitesti	H	3-0	Butoiu, Serban, Oprea
28/10/95	Universitatea Cluj	H	1-0	Barbu (p)
05/11/95	Steaua Bucuresti	A	2-2	Butoiu, Oprea
08/11/95	Sportul Studentesc Bucuresti	H	1-0	Oprea
18/11/95	FC Inter Sibiu	A	2-3	Mustaca, Ceausila
25/11/95	Politehnica Iasi	H	7-0	Barbu, Axinciuc, Serban, Oprea, Ciurea, Butoiu 2 (1p)
29/11/95	Politehnica Timisoara	H	1-4	Serban
02/12/95	AS Bacau	A	0-3	
09/12/95	FC National Bucuresti	H	0-2	
13/12/95	Petrolul Ploiesti	A	0-2	
28/02/96	Universitatea Craiova	H	2-1	Barbu (p), Axinciuc
02/03/96	Dinamo Bucuresti	A	1-2	Oprea
06/03/96	Rapid Bucuresti	H	4-2	Toma, Carabas, Barbu, Oprea
09/03/96	Otelul Galati	A	0-1	
16/03/96	Ceahlaul Piatra Neamt	H	2-0	Ceausila, Neata
20/03/96	FC Brasov	A	1-3	Barbu
23/03/96	Gloria Bistrita	H	1-0	Axinciuc
30/03/96	FC Arges Dacia Pitesti	A	1-2	Carabas
06/04/96	Universitatea Cluj	A	0-3	
10/04/96	Steaua Bucuresti	H	1-1	Barbu (p)
13/04/96	Sportul Studentesc Bucuresti	A	1-2	Anghel
17/04/96	FC Inter Sibiu	H	4-0	Anghel, Oprea 2, Ciurea
20/04/96	Politehnica Iasi	A	2-1	Anghel, Serban

GLORIA BISTRITA

CLUB DIRECTORY

Gloria Bistrita
str. Parcului 3
4400 Bistrita
tel - (063) 212998
fax - (063) 217437
Year of Formation - 1926
President - Ioan Horoba
Coach - Constantin Cîrstea; Ion Balaur
(96/97 - Remus Vlad)
Stadium - Municipal (12,000)

APPEARANCES 95/96

	P.	Ap	(s)	Gls
Eugen Catalin ANGHEL	G		(1)	
Ioan BACIU	D		(2)	
Ionel BALAUR	M	2	(5)	
Sabin Dutu BRICI	D	3	(2)	
Marcu CHIBULCUDEAN	D	1		
Costel CÎMPEANU	G	34		
Gabriel CRISTEA	D	26		
Emil DANCUS	M	10	(9)	
Alexandru DARHA	A		(5)	
Ciprian Virgil DIANU	D	1	(4)	1
Cristian Alexandru DULCA	D	6	(6)	
Mircea DUMITRIU	D	22	(8)	
Claudiu Robert FRUMOCA	A	1	(1)	
Dumitru HALOSTA	D	4	(5)	
Daniel IFTODI	M	31	(1)	3
Ilie LAZAR	A	24	(4)	10
Sergiu Sebastian MÂNDREAN	D	1	(1)	
Danut MATEI	A	31		7
Simion MIRONAS	D	27	(1)	6
Ioan MISZTI	M	33		2
Vasile Adrian MOLDOVAN	M		(1)	
Marian NASTASE	A	20	(12)	3
Gheorghe Bogdan NICOLAE	D	4	(8)	
Ionel Narcis PANDURU	D	1	(1)	
Horatiu Leonard PÎRTIU	M		(1)	
Dorel PURDEA	D	9	(2)	
Marius RADUTA	M	16	(5)	1
Valer SASARMAN	D	34		
Florin STANCU	M	5	(5)	2
Eugen VOICA	M	28	(5)	6
Liviu ZAHARIUC	A		(1)	

LEAGUE RESULTS 1995/96

Date	Opponent	H/A	Score	Scorers
12/08/95	FC National Bucuresti	A	3-1	Mironas, Lazar, Matei
19/08/95	Petrolul Ploiesti	H	1-0	Miszti
26/08/95	Universitatea Craiova	A	0-1	
30/08/95	Dinamo Bucuresti	H	2-0	Nastase, Miszti
09/09/95	Rapid Bucuresti	A	0-2	
16/09/95	Otelul Galati	H	2-0	Lazar, Iftodi
23/09/95	Ceahlaul Piatra Neamt	A	0-1	
01/10/95	FC Brasov	H	3-2	Stancu 2, Matei
04/10/95	Universitatea Cluj	H	1-0	Matei
14/10/95	FC Arges Dacia Pitesti	A	1-2	Dianu
21/10/95	FC Farul Constanta	H	0-2	
25/10/95	Steaua Bucuresti	A	1-3	Nastase
28/10/95	Sportul Studentesc Bucuresti	H	3-1	Mironas 2 (2p), Nastase
04/11/95	FC Inter Sibiu	A	0-0	
08/11/95	Politehnica Iasi	H	3-0	Raduta, Lazar 2
18/11/95	Politehnica Timisoara	A	0-3	
25/11/95	AS Bacau	H	2-0	Lazar 2
29/11/95	FC National Bucuresti	H	3-1	Matei 3
02/12/95	Petrolul Ploiesti	A	0-2	
09/12/95	Universitatea Craiova	H	3-0	Mironas (p), Iftodi, Lazar
13/12/95	Dinamo Bucuresti	A	1-2	Mironas (p)
28/02/96	Rapid Bucuresti	H	1-2	Mironas
02/03/96	Otelul Galati	A	0-1	
06/03/96	Ceahlaul Piatra Neamt	H	1-0	Voica
09/03/96	FC Brasov	A	0-1	
16/03/96	Universitatea Cluj	A	1-1	Voica
20/03/96	FC Arges Dacia Pitesti	H	4-0	Lazar 3, Matei
23/03/96	FC Farul Constanta	A	0-1	
30/03/96	Steaua Bucuresti	H	0-2	
06/04/96	Sportul Studentesc Bucuresti	A	1-2	Voica
10/04/96	FC Inter Sibiu	H	2-0	Voica 2
13/04/96	Politehnica Iasi	A	1-2	Voica
17/04/96	Politehnica Timisoara	H	0-0	
20/04/96	AS Bacau	A	1-3	Iftodi

FC INTER SIBIU

CLUB DIRECTORY

FC Inter Sibiu
Str. Mihai Eminescu 1-3
2400 Sibiu
tel - (069) 422144/421935
Year of Formation - 1986
President - Mircea Dancu
Coach - Cornel Talnar
Stadium - Municipal (15,000)

APPEARANCES 95/96

	P	Ap	(s)	Gls
Marius Achim BACIU	D	32		1
Constantin Adrian BLID	G	30		
Ilie Cornel CASOLTAN	A	26		3
Florin COTORA	G	3	(1)	
Lucian COTORA	D	25		1
Ioan Adrian DEMIAN	M	28	(1)	1
Daniel GALEA	M		(3)	
Victor GLAVAN	D	31		2
Adrian HOLOM	G	1	(1)	
Robert Marius KILIN	M	1	(7)	
Constantin Cristian LAZAR	M	33		
Marian MARGARIT	M	6	(17)	
Cornel MIREA	D	7	(2)	
Nicolae Claudiu MOLDOVAN	D	10	(7)	
Florin Flavius POGACEAN	M	33		8
Corneliu SZEGHEDI	M	25	(5)	2
Marius Dumitru SZEGHEDI	A	26	(7)	8
Iosif Ovidiu TÂLVAN	D	28	(1)	1
Daniel TERCHILA	D	7	(9)	
Razvan Sorin TOBOSARU	A		(5)	
Sebastian TOLCIU	D	12	(11)	
Adrian VASÎI	A	5	(3)	1
Dorin Bogdan ZOTINCA	M	5	(4)	1

LEAGUE RESULTS 1995/96

Date	Opponent	H/A	Score	Scorers
12/08/95	Sportul Studentesc Bucuresti	H	2-0	Szeghedi M.D., Pogaçean
19/08/95	Universitatea Cluj	A	1-1	Szeghedi M.D.
26/08/95	Politehnica Iasi	A	1-2	Pogacean
29/08/95	Politehnica Timisoara	H	1-1	Cotora L. (p)
09/09/95	AS Bacau	A	1-2	Pogacean
16/09/95	FC National Bucuresti	H	1-0	Szeghedi C.
23/09/95	Petrolul Ploiesti	A	0-1	
01/10/95	Universitatea Craiova	H	2-0	Glavan (p), Pogacean
04/10/95	Dinamo Bucuresti	A	1-2	Vasîi
14/10/95	Rapid Bucuresti	H	2-1	Pogacean, Szeghedi M.D.
21/10/95	Otelul Galati	A	0-2	
25/10/95	Ceahlaul Piatra Neamt	H	2-0	Casoltan, Szeghedi M.D.
28/10/95	FC Brasov	A	1-2	Tâlvan
04/11/95	Gloria Bistrita	H	0-0	
08/11/95	FC Arges Dacia Pitesti	A	1-2	Demian
18/11/95	FC Farul Constanta	H	3-2	Pogacean, Szeghedi C., Baciu
25/11/95	Steaua Bucuresti	A	1-3	Szeghedi M.D.
29/11/95	Sportul Studentesc Bucuresti	A	1-0	Szeghedi M.D.
02/12/95	Universitatea Cluj	H	1-0	Casoltan
09/12/95	Politehnica Iasi	H	0-1	
13/12/95	Politehnica Timisoara	A	1-5	Casoltan
28/02/96	AS Bacau	H	0-2	
02/03/96	FC National Bucuresti	A	0-5	
06/03/96	Petrolul Ploiesti	H	2-0	Zotinca, Szeghedi M.D.
09/03/96	Universitatea Craiova	A	0-2	
16/03/96	Dinamo Bucuresti	H	0-0	
20/03/96	Rapid Bucuresti	A	0-2	
23/03/96	Otelul Galati	H	1-1	Glavan
30/03/96	Ceahlaul Piatra Neamt	A	0-2	
06/04/96	FC Brasov	H	3-0	Pogacean 2, Szeghedi M.D.
10/04/96	Gloria Bistrita	A	0-2	
13/04/96	FC Arges Dacia Pitesti	H	0-0	
17/04/96	FC Farul Constanta	A	0-4	
20/04/96	Steaua Bucuresti	H	0-0	

FC NATIONAL BUCURESTI

CLUB DIRECTORY

FC National Bucuresti
Str. Dr. Lister 37
76202 Bucuresti
tel - (01) 4106606
Year of Formation - 1934
President - Gino Iorgulescu
Coach - Marian Bondrea; Florin Halagian
Stadium - Cotroceni (16,000)

MAJOR HONOURS
Domestic Cup - (1) 1960.

APPEARANCES 95/96

	P	Ap	(s)	Gls
Cristian ALBEANU	A	14	(12)	5
Mihai BAICU	A		(1)	
Florin Ionel Cornelas BATRÎNU	D	3	(1)	
Gheorghe CEAUSILA	A		(3)	
Liviu CIOBOTARIU	D	27		6
Sorin Dorel COLCEAG	G	4		
Razvan DRAGNEA	A		(2)	
Marin DUNA	A	30		17
Remus Traian GANEA	D	2		
Ovidiu Cornel HANGANU	A	9	(7)	2
Nicolae Catalin LITA	M	25	(5)	2
Stefan Alexandru LIVADARU	M		(2)	
Ionut LUTU	M	4	(14)	
Petre MARIN	D	31		1
Vasile MATINCA	A	7	(2)	1
Danut MOISESCU	M	26	(4)	5
Catalin Raducan NECULA	D	32	(1)	
Horia Radu NICULESCU	M	21		12
Ioan PAP DEAC	G	9	(3)	
Tanase Tinel PETRE	D	6	(3)	1
Adrian Ion PIGULEA	M	12	(8)	1
Dan Ioan POTOCIANU	D	30	(3)	3
Gabi Marian RADUTA	M	4	(10)	1
Ion SBURLEA	D	22		1
Paul STEFANESCU	G	21	(2)	
Cristian TEACA	D	1	(5)	
Paul TUDOR	M		(2)	
Cristian Marius VASC	M	10	(2)	2
Dorel Ioan ZEGREAN	D	24	(1)	

LEAGUE RESULTS 1995/96

12/08/95	Gloria Bistrita	H	1-3	Niculescu
19/08/95	FC Arges Dacia Pitesti	A	0-4	
26/08/95	FC Farul Constanta	H	2-1	Duna (p), Matinca
30/08/95	Steaua Bucuresti	A	1-5	Duna
09/09/95	Sportul Studentesc Bucuresti	H	0-0	
16/09/95	FC Inter Sibiu	A	0-1	
23/09/95	Politehnicaa Iasi	H	2-3	Hanganu, Raduta
01/10/95	Politehnica Timisoara	A	1-0	Ciobotariu
04/10/95	AS Bacau	H	4-1	Albeanu, Sburlea, Moisescu, Duna
14/10/95	Universitatea Cluj	A	3-1	Duna 3
21/10/95	Petrolul Ploiesti	A	0-0	
25/10/95	Universitatea Craiova	H	4-3	Moisescu 2, Marin, Duna
29/10/95	Dinamo Bucuresti	A	3-0	Duna 3 (1p)
04/11/95	Rapid Bucuresti	H	0-4	
08/11/95	Otelul Galati	A	1-3	Hanganu
18/11/95	Ceahlaul Piatra Neamt	H	3-1	Lita, Albeanu, Duna
25/11/95	FC Brasov	A	0-0	
29/11/95	Gloria Bistrita	A	1-3	Niculescu
02/12/95	FC Arges Dacia Pitesti	H	4-1	Ciobotariu, Albeanu, Niculescu, Potocianu
09/12/95	FC Farul Constanta	A	2-0	Duna (p), Niculescu
13/12/95	Steaua Bucuresti	H	1-0	Niculescu
28/02/96	Sportul Studentesc Bucuresti	A	0-0	
02/03/96	FC Inter Sibiu	H	5-0	Potocianu, Moisescu, Albeanu, Niculescu 2
06/03/96	Politehnica Iasi	A	1-0	Ciobotariu
09/03/96	Politehnica Timisoara	H	2-1	Potocianu, Ciobotariu
16/03/96	AS Bacau	A	1-2	Moisescu
20/03/96	Universitatea Cluj	H	3-1	Duna 2, Niculescu
23/03/96	Petrolul Ploiesti	H	3-0	Niculescu 2, Duna (p)
30/03/96	Universitatea Craiova	A	0-1	
06/04/96	Dinamo Bucuresti	H	1-1	Ciobotariu
10/04/96	Rapid Bucuresti	A	1-1	Niculescu
13/04/96	Otelul Galati	H	3-1	Duna, Albeanu, Pigulea
17/04/96	Ceahlaul Piatra Neamt	A	2-1	Lita, Petre
20/04/96	FC Brasov	H	5-1	Duna, Niculescu, Vasc 2, Ciobotariu

OTELUL GALATI

CLUB DIRECTORY

Otelul Galati
str. Smîrdan 2
6200 Galati
tel - (036) 452321
fax (036) 462150
Year of Formation - 1964
President - Marius Stan
Coach - Vasile Simionas
Stadaium - Otelul (15,000)

APPEARANCES 95/96

	P	Ap	(s)	Gls
Iulian ARHIRE	D		(16)	
Constantin BADAN	G	7		
Mihai BARBU	G		(1)	
Stelian BORDEIANU	G	13		
Constantin BOSÎNCEANU	D	14	(8)	
Ionel Panait BUDACA	D	1	(3)	
Cristian Daniel CHEBUTIU	G	14		
Gheorghe CORNEA	A	28	(4)	7
Daniel FLOREA	M	24	(4)	1
Florin Sorin HARAGA	D	18	(2)	1
Gigi ION	D	31		1
Viorel ION	A	29		11
Costin MALES	M	18	(9)	3
Catalin MIREA	D	8	(12)	
Daniel Emil MOGOSANU	D	30		2
Danut Stelian OPREA	A		(1)	
Tudorel PELIN	M	28	(1)	1
Marin PETRACHE	M	1	(3)	
Alin Cristinel PÎNZARU	A		(6)	
Nelu Daniel POPLIACA	M		(2)	
Emil SPIREA	M	27	(1)	3
Eusebio Adrian STATE	A	21	(5)	5
Viorel TANASE	M	30		6
Catalin TOFAN	D	32		1

LEAGUE RESULTS 1995/96

12/08/95	Dinamo Bucuresti	A	0-2	
19/08/95	Rapid Bucuresti	H	0-3	
26/08/95	Universitatea Cluj	H	2-0	Ion G., Tanase (p)
30/08/95	Ceahlaul Piatra Neamt	A	1-3	State
09/09/95	FC Brasov	H	4-0	Cornea, Tanase (p), State, Spirea
16/09/95	Gloria Bistrita	A	0-2	
23/09/95	FC Arges Dacia Pitesti	H	2-0	Males, Cornea
01/10/95	FC Farul Constanta	A	0-1	
04/10/95	Steaua Bucuresti	H	1-2	Cornea
14/10/95	Sportul Studentesc Bucuresti	A	1-1	Pelin
21/10/95	FC Inter Sibiu	H	2-0	State, Ion V.
25/10/95	Politehnica Iasi	A	1-2	Cornea
28/10/95	Politehnica Timisoara	H	1-0	Florea
03/11/95	AS Bacau	A	0-3	
08/11/95	FC National Bucuresti	H	3-1	State, Mogosanu, Spirea (p)
18/11/95	Petrolul Ploiesti	A	0-2	
25/11/95	Universitatea Craiova	H	2-0	Spirea, Tanase
29/11/95	Dinamo Bucuresti	H	0-2	
02/12/95	Rapid Bucuresti	A	0-2	
09/12/95	Universitatea Cluj	A	2-3	Tanase (p), Ion V.
13/12/95	Ceahlaul Piatra Neamt	H	2-0	Ion V., Cornea
28/02/96	FC Brasov	A	0-1	
02/03/96	Gloria Bistrita	H	1-0	Ion V. (p)
06/03/96	FC Arges Dacia Pitesti	A	2-2	Ion V. 2 (1p)
09/03/96	FC Farul Constanta	H	1-0	Haraga
16/03/96	Steaua Bucuresti	A	0-1	
20/03/96	Sportul Studentesc Bucuresti	H	3-1	Cornea, Ion V. 2 (1p)
23/03/96	FC Inter Sibiu	A	1-1	Tanase
30/03/96	Politehnica Iasi	H	3-1	Cornea, Tanase, Tofan
06/04/96	Politehnica Timisoara	A	1-3	Ion V. (p)
10/04/96	AS Bacau	H	3-1	Ion V. 2, Males
13/04/96	FC National Bucuresti	A	1-3	State
17/04/96	Petrolul Ploiesti	H	2-0	Mogosanu, Males
20/04/96	Universitatea Craiova	A	0-3	

PETROLUL PLOIESTI

CLUB DIRECTORY

Petrolul Ploiesti
str. Stadionului 26
2000 Ploiesti
tel - (044) 122258/146436
Year of Formation - 1924
President - Ion Radu
Coach - Marin Ion (96/97 - Marin Olteanu)
Stadium - Petrolul (16,000)

MAJOR HONOURS
League Championship - (3) 1958, 1959, 1966.
Domestic Cup - (2) 1963, 1995.

APPEARANCES 95/96

	P	Ap	(s)	Gls
Marcel Cristian ABALUTA	M	32		8
Ion Claudiu ANDREICUT	A	10	(9)	5
Lucian BALABAN	A		(9)	
Gheorghe Adrian BALACEANU	D	26		1
Daniel Eugen BASTINA	M	28	(4)	
Gheorghe Iulian CADAR	G		(1)	
Daniel CHIRITA	D	27		
Ion Orlando GHEORGHE	M		(2)	
Marian GRAMA	M	3	(9)	
Octavian GRIGORE	D	33		4
Gheorghe Aurelian LEAHU	D	31		
Gheorghe MATEI	A	16	(4)	2
Marian MIHAI	M	2	(6)	
Marius MIHALCEA	M		(2)	
Ciprian MOISE	M		(1)	
Victor Mihai OANCEA	M		(3)	
Mihai PÎRLOG	M	25	(3)	1
Florian Cristian PÎRVU	A	3	(11)	1
Costin POGONSCHI	A	5	(7)	
Stefan Gabriel PREDA	G	34		
Valeriu RACHITA	D	30		4
Adrian SANDULESCU	M	1	(6)	
Adrian Orlin TOADER	A	18	(3)	1
Claudiu TOADER	M		(1)	
Daniel ZAFIRIS	A	19	(7)	6
Cristian ZMOLEANU	M	31		9

LEAGUE RESULTS 1995/96

14/08/95	FC Brasov	H	4-2	Grigore, Andreicut 2, Abaluta
19/08/95	Gloria Bistrita	A	0-1	
27/08/95	FC Arges Dacia Pitesti	H	1-0	Zafiris
30/08/95	FC Farul Constanta	A	3-3	Andreicut 2, Zmoleanu
09/09/95	Steaua Bucuresti	H	2-2	Abaluta 2
17/09/95	Sportul Studentesc Bucuresti	A	1-2	Zafiris
23/09/95	FC Inter Sibiu	H	1-0	Rachita
01/10/95	Politehnica Iasi	A	1-2	Abaluta
04/10/95	Politehnica Timisoara	H	2-0	Abaluta 2
14/10/95	AS Bacau	A	0-1	
21/10/95	FC National Bucuresti	H	0-0	
25/10/95	Universitatea Cluj	A	0-2	
28/10/95	Universitatea Craiova	A	0-3	
04/11/95	Dinamo Bucuresti	H	1-0	Grigore
08/11/95	Rapid Bucuresti	A	0-1	
18/11/95	Otelul Galati	H	2-0	Toader A.O. (p), Zmoleanu (p)
25/11/95	Ceahlaul Piatra Neamt	A	2-1	Balaceanu, Zmoleanu (p)
29/11/95	FC Brasov	A	0-1	
02/12/95	Gloria Bistrita	H	2-0	Abaluta (p), Rachita
08/12/95	FC Arges Dacia Pitesti	A	1-2	Andreicut
13/12/95	FC Farul Constanta	H	2-0	Zmoleanu 2 (2p)
28/02/96	Steaua Bucuresti	A	1-2	Zafiris
02/03/96	Sportul Studentesc Bucuresti	H	1-0	Zafiris
06/03/96	FC Inter Sibiu	A	0-2	
09/03/96	Politehnica Iasi	H	5-0	Zafiris 2, Pîrlog, Rachita 2
16/03/96	Politehnica Timisoara	A	0-2	
20/03/96	AS Bacau	H	3-0	Zmoleanu, Abaluta, Matei
23/03/96	FC National Bucuresti	A	0-3	
30/03/96	Universitatea Cluj	H	2-0	Zmoleanu, og (Banceu)
06/04/96	Universitatea Craiova	H	1-0	Zmoleanu
10/04/96	Dinamo Bucuresti	A	0-1	
13/04/96	Rapid Bucuresti	H	2-1	Grigore 2
17/04/96	Otelul Galati	A	0-2	
20/04/96	Ceahlaul Piatra Neamt	H	3-2	Zmoleanu, Pîrvu, Matei

POLITEHNICA IASI

CLUB DIRECTORY

Politehnica Iasi
str. George Cosbuc 6
6600 Iasi
tel - (032) 146833
Year of Formation - 1945
President - Romeo Olteanu
Coach - Leonida Antohi; Narcis Ciocârlan; Dumitru Anton
Stadium - Emil Alexandru (20,000)

APPEARANCES 95/96

	P	Ap	(s)	Gls
Catalin Petronel ABALASEI	D	30	(1)	
Mihai ALEXA	D	1	(2)	
Adrian AMBROSIE	A	10	(13)	6
Vasile APACHITEI	D	25	(2)	1
Constantin ARAPASU	A	4		
Mihai BOTAN	M		(2)	
Daniel CAUNEI	M	20	(11)	1
Mihai CÎMPANU	M	5	(11)	1
Ioan CÎMPEANU	G	32		
Marian Ghiorghita COBULIANU	M	26	(2)	
Ioan Adi COTAN	M	25	(2)	7
Levente CSIFO	A	2		
Adrian DOBREA	A	29		3
Flavius Octavian FRUNZA	D		(3)	
Adrian KERESZY	M	16	(3)	2
Andras LORINCZI	A	6	(1)	
Bogdanel MANDRIC	G	2	(4)	
Nicolae MIHAI	A	14	(3)	2
Ioan Leonard NEMTANU	M	29		1
Daniel Gabriel PANCU	A	17	(11)	2
Ciprian Constantin PARASCHIV	D	29	(1)	1
Liviu PETRACHE	D	14	(4)	
Vasile Adrian RUDAC	D	1	(3)	
Dumitru STAFIE	D	2	(1)	
Dragos Constantin TANASE	D	10	(10)	
Emil TRÎMBITAS	M		(1)	
Aurelian TUTU	M		(2)	
Dragos URDARU	D	21		
Ion VINTILA	A	4	(4)	

LEAGUE RESULTS 1995/96

13/08/95	Steaua Bucuresti	H	1-2	Cotan
19/08/95	Sportul Studentesc Bucuresti	A	1-3	Dobrea
26/08/95	FC Inter Sibiu	H	2-1	Ambrosie, Pancu
30/08/95	Universitatea Cluj	A	1-3	Kereszy
09/09/95	Politehnica Timisoara	A	1-9	Ambrosie
16/09/95	AS Bacau	H	3-0	Mihai, Cotan 2
23/09/95	FC National Bucuresti	A	3-2	Caunei, Ambrosie 2
01/10/95	Petrolul Ploiesti	H	2-1	Dobrea, Ambrosie
04/10/95	Universitatea Craiova	A	0-3	
14/10/95	Dinamo Bucuresti	H	0-0	
21/10/95	Rapid Bucuresti	A	0-3	
25/10/95	Otelul Galati	H	2-1	Apachitei, Cotan
28/10/95	Ceahlaul Piatra Neamt	A	0-1	
04/11/95	FC Brasov	H	2-1	Cîmpanu, Paraschiv
08/11/95	Gloria Bistrita	A	0-3	
18/11/95	FC Arges Dacia Pitesti	H	1-2	Pancu
25/11/95	FC Farul Constanta	A	0-7	
29/11/95	Steaua Bucuresti	A	0-4	
02/12/95	Sportul Studentesc Bucuresti	H	0-1	
09/12/95	FC Inter Sibiu	A	1-0	Mihai
13/12/95	Universitatea Cluj	H	0-0	
28/02/96	Politehnica Timisoara	H	0-0	
02/03/96	AS Bacau	A	1-3	Ambrosie
06/03/96	FC National Bucuresti	H	0-1	
09/03/96	Petrolul Ploiesti	A	0-5	
16/03/96	Universitatea Craiova	H	2-0	Nemtanu, Cotan
20/03/96	Dinamo Bucuresti	A	0-2	
23/03/96	Rapid Bucuresti	H	0-1	
30/03/96	Otelul Galati	A	1-3	Dobrea
06/04/96	Ceahlaul Piatra Neamt	H	0-1	
10/04/96	FC Brasov	A	0-2	
13/04/96	Gloria Bistrita	H	2-1	Kereszy (p), Cotan
17/04/96	FC Arges Dacia Pitesti	A	0-6	
20/04/96	FC Farul Constanta	H	1-2	Cotan (p)

POLITEHNICA TIMISOARA

CLUB DIRECTORY

Politehnica Timisoara
Bulevardul Politehnicii 2
1900 Timisoara
tel - (056) 190350
fax - (056) 190350
Year of Formation - 1920
President - Viorel Boit
Coach - Constantin Radulescu; Emerich Dembrovschi
Stadium - Politehnica (40,000)

MAJOR HONOURS
Domestic Cup - (2) 1958, 1980.

APPEARANCES 95/96

	P	Ap	(s)	Gls
Ioan ALMASAN	G	22	(1)	
Marcel BABAN	A	32		15
Paul Vasile BARNA	M	1	(10)	
Calin BOTA	M		(4)	
Ovidiu BREHUI	M		(1)	
Florian Dan CALIN	M	32		4
Cristian CONTESCU	M	11	(12)	1
Cosmin Marius CONTRA	D	11		
Sandër Leon GRUNASI (ALB)	A		(1)	
Radu Mugur GUSATU	A	21	(7)	9
Roberto Iulian IVAN	D	19	(10)	
Stefan KOVACS	A	26		5
Florin MACAVEI	D	12		
Costel MIHALACHE	M	1	(5)	
Marius Vasile MUNTEANU	D	3	(1)	
Alexandru PELICI	D	31		1
Gabriel PERSA	M	1	(2)	
Iosif ROTARIU	M	17		6
Roco Rafael SANDU	D	2	(3)	
Petru Adrian SAVOIU	A	17	(16)	7
Adrian STOICOV	D	30		1
Orlando Dumitru TRANDU	D	23	(4)	
Petru TURCAS	G	12	(2)	
Valentin VELCEA	M	28	(2)	4
Sorin VLAICU	M	22		2

LEAGUE RESULTS 1995/96

12/08/95	FC Farul Constanta	H	3-1	Calin, Kovacs 2
19/08/95	Steaua Bucuresti	A	1-5	Velcea
26/08/95	Sportul Studentesc Bucuresti	H	3-1	Baban, Velcea, Gusatu (p)
29/08/95	FC Inter Sibiu	A	1-1	Velcea
09/09/95	Politehnica Iasi	H	9-1	Kovacs 3, Baban 3 (1p), Gusatu 2, Velcea
16/09/95	Universitatea Cluj	A	0-2	
23/09/95	AS Bacau	A	1-4	Gusatu
01/10/95	FC National Bucuresti	H	0-1	
04/10/95	Petrolul Ploiesti	A	0-2	
14/10/95	Universitatea Craiova	H	0-0	
21/10/95	Dinamo Bucuresti	A	0-3	
25/10/95	Rapid Bucuresti	H	1-3	Baban (p)
28/10/95	Otelul Galati	A	0-1	
04/11/95	Ceahlaul Piatra Neamt	H	4-3	Gusatu 2, og (Manea), Baban (p)
08/11/95	FC Brasov	A	1-1	Baban (p)
18/11/95	Gloria Bistrita	H	3-0	Baban, Calin, Savoiu
25/11/95	FC Arges Dacia Pitesti	A	0-0	
29/11/95	FC Farul Constanta	A	4-1	Vlaicu, Savoiu 2, Rotariu
02/12/95	Steaua Bucuresti	H	2-1	Contescu, Savoiu
09/12/95	Sportul Studentesc Bucuresti	A	0-1	
13/12/95	FC Inter Sibiu	H	5-1	Vlaicu, Baban (p), Savoiu, og (Glavan), Calin
28/02/96	Politehnica Iasi	A	0-0	
02/03/96	Universitatea Cluj	H	2-0	Baban (p), Gusatu
06/03/96	AS Bacau	H	2-0	Rotariu, Baban
09/03/96	FC National Bucuresti	A	1-2	Gusatu
16/03/96	Petrolul Ploiesti	H	2-0	Pelici, Rotariu (p)
20/03/96	Universitatea Craiova	A	1-3	og (Mohora)
23/03/96	Dinamo Bucuresti	H	2-2	Gusatu, Baban (p)
30/03/96	Rapid Bucuresti	A	1-4	Baban
06/04/96	Otelul Galati	H	3-1	Baban, Savoiu, Stoicov
10/04/96	Ceahlaul Piatra Neamt	A	0-1	
13/04/96	FC Brasov	H	4-1	Rotariu 3 (1p), Savoiu
17/04/96	Gloria Bistrita	A	0-0	
20/04/96	FC Arges Dacia Pitesti	H	2-0	Calin, Baban

RAPID BUCURESTI

CLUB DIRECTORY

Rapid Bucuresti
Calea Giulesti 18
78254 Bucuresti
tel - (01) 6170301
fax - (01) 3121356
Year of Formation - 1923
President - Jean Padureanu
Secretary - Dan Matei
Coach - Viorel Hizo; Mircea Radulescu
Stadium - Rapid (15,000)

MAJOR HONOURS
League Championship - (1) 1967.
Domestic Cup - (9) 1935, 1937, 1938, 1939, 1940, 1941, 1942, 1972, 1975.

APPEARANCES 95/96

	P	Ap	(s)	Gls
Romulus BEALCU	D	33	(1)	1
Cristian Mugur BOLOHAN	D	12	(11)	
Zeno BUNDEA	A	4	(13)	1
Ionel CHEBAC	M	16	(8)	2
Iulian CHIRITA	M	22	(1)	10
Florin CONSTANTINOVICI	M	33		6
Cristian Alexandru DULCA	D	8	(1)	
Mihai Dan IOSIF	M		(1)	
Adrian MATEI	A	27	(1)	2
Florin MOTROC	M	10	(7)	2
Dorel MUTICA	M	13	(8)	1
Vasile NICULAE	G	3		
Nicolae Catalin POPA	A	16	(7)	8
Cristian RONTEA	D	7	(2)	
Traian Claudiu SALAGEAN	M	6	(3)	1
Marian SAVU	A	7	(8)	1
Florin SIMION	A	1	(4)	
Nicolae STANCIU	D	33		
Dumitru TÂRTAU	A	32	(1)	12
Alexandru Florin TENE	G	19		
Georgica VAMESU	D	25	(2)	3
Bogdan Arges VINTILA	G	12	(1)	
Rodin VOINEA	A	7	(14)	
Iulius Cezar ZAMFIR	M	28	(3)	7

LEAGUE RESULTS 1995/96

Date	Opponent	H/A	Score	Scorers
12/08/95	Universitatea Cluj	H	5-0	Popa 2, Bealcu, Chirita, Mutica
19/08/95	Otelul Galati	A	3-0	Matei, Chirita, Târtau
26/08/95	Ceahlaul Piatra Neamt	H	2-1	Chebac, Motroc
30/08/95	FC Brasov	A	0-1	
09/09/95	Gloria Bistrita	H	2-0	Chirita, Constantinovici
16/09/95	FC Arges Dacia Pitesti	A	2-3	Popa 2
23/09/95	FC Farul Constanta	H	3-4	Târtau, Chirita, og (Dinu)
01/10/95	Steaua Bucuresti	A	0-3	
05/10/95	Sportul Studentesc Bucuresti	H	1-1	Chirita
14/10/95	FC Inter Sibiu	A	1-2	Chirita
21/10/95	Politehnica Iasi	H	3-0	Târtau 2, Zamfir (p)
25/10/95	Politehnica Timisoara	A	3-1	Târtau 2, Motroc
28/10/95	AS Bacau	H	3-0	Constantinovici, Târtau, Chebac
04/11/95	FC National Bucuresti	A	4-0	Vamesu, Constantinovici, Zamfir, Târtau
08/11/95	Petrolul Ploiesti	H	1-0	Constantinovici
19/11/95	Universitatea Craiova	A	0-2	
25/11/95	Dinamo Bucuresti	H	2-0	Popa (p), Vamesu
29/11/95	Universitatea Cluj	A	0-2	
02/12/95	Otelul Galati	H	2-0	Bundea, Matei
09/12/95	Ceahlaul Piatra Neamt	A	1-0	Zamfir (p)
13/12/95	FC Brasov	H	3-0	Zamfir, Salagean, Vamesu
28/02/96	Gloria Bistrita	A	2-1	Târtau, Savu
02/03/96	FC Arges Dacia Pitesti	H	3-0	Zamfir, Târtau, Chirita
06/03/96	FC Farul Constanta	A	2-4	Chirita 2
09/03/96	Steaua Bucuresti	H	1-1	Târtau
16/03/96	Sportul Studentesc Bucuresti	A	0-0	
20/03/96	FC Inter Sibiu	H	2-0	Popa, Constantinovici
23/03/96	Politehnica Iasi	A	1-0	Târtau
30/03/96	Politehnica Timisoara	H	4-1	Popa 2, Chirita, Constantinovici
06/04/96	AS Bacau	A	0-1	
10/04/96	FC National Bucuresti	H	1-1	Zamfir (p)
13/04/96	Petrolul Ploiesti	A	1-2	og (Grigore)
17/04/96	Universitatea Craiova	H	0-1	
20/04/96	Dinamo Bucuresti	A	1-1	Zamfir (p)

SPORTUL STUDENTESC BUCURESTI

CLUB DIRECTORY

Sportul Studentesc Bucuresti
str. Mihail Moxa 5
78109 Bucuresti
tel - (01) 3111286
Year of Formation - 1916
President - Barbu Emil Popescu
Coach - Mircea Radulescu; Ioan Andone
(96/97 - Mihail Marian)
Stadium - Sportul Studentesc (15,000)

APPEARANCES 95/96

	P	Ap	(s)	Gls
Bogdan Ion ANDONE	A	33		3
Danut BICA	M	3	(2)	
Ion BIVOLARU	D	18	(5)	1
Romulus Adrian BUIA	M	20	(1)	3
Petru BUNACIU	D	16	(4)	
Dan BURCA	A		(2)	
Horia CODOREANU	A		(10)	
Victoras Ovidiu COSTACHE	M		(1)	
Tudorel CRISTEA	D	29	(1)	4
Silvian DOBRE	M	17	(8)	1
Danut FRUNZA	M	4	(1)	
Musa KALLON (SRL)	A	2		
Serghei KIRILOV (MOL)	A	14	(6)	2
Giuliano LALCIU	M	15	(5)	4
Razvan LUCESCU	G	34		
Dorin MATEUT	M	3		
Lucian Ioan MEZEI	M	2	(10)	
Romica Iulian NEACSU	A	5	(7)	2
Cristian PETRE	D	27	(1)	
Adrian Dragos PITU	A	2	(3)	
Antonio POPA	M	5	(19)	
Florin ROMAN	D	22	(3)	
Constantin STANICI	M	6		
Marius Ninel SUMUDICA	A	27		7
Gabriel VOCHIN	D	30		2
Tudorel ZAMFIRESCU	D	31		4
Andrei Calin ZANC	M	9		

LEAGUE RESULTS 1995/96

12/08/95	FC Inter Sibiu	A	0-2	
19/08/95	Politehnica Iasi	H	3-1	Sumudica, Kirilov, Zamfirescu
26/08/95	Politehnica Timisoara	A	1-3	Andone
30/08/95	AS Bacau	H	3-0	Dobre, Andone, Sumudica
09/09/95	FC National Bucuresti	A	0-0	
17/09/95	Petrolul Ploiesti	H	2-1	Kirilov, Zamfirescu
23/09/95	Universitatea Craiova	A	0-1	
01/10/95	Dinamo Bucuresti	H	0-1	
05/10/95	Rapid Bucuresti	A	1-1	Sumudica
14/10/95	Otelul Galati	H	1-1	Vochin
21/10/95	Ceahlaul Piatra Neamt	A	0-1	
25/10/95	FC Brasov	H	2-0	Vochin, Zamfirescu
28/10/95	Gloria Bistrita	A	1-3	Buia
04/11/95	FC Arges Dacia Pitesti	H	3-0	Bivolaru, Sumudica 2 (1p)
08/11/95	FC Farul Constanta	A	0-1	
18/11/95	Steaua Bucuresti	H	0-2	
25/11/95	Universitatea Cluj	A	0-1	
29/11/95	FC Inter Sibiu	H	0-1	
02/12/95	Politehnica Iasi	A	1-0	Lalciu (p)
09/12/95	Politehnica Timisoara	H	1-0	Sumudica (p)
13/12/95	AS Bacau	A	1-0	Sumudica
28/02/96	FC National Bucuresti	H	0-0	
02/03/96	Petrolul Ploiesti	A	0-1	
06/03/96	Universitatea Craiova	H	0-0	
09/03/96	Dinamo Bucuresti	A	1-0	Neacsu
16/03/96	Rapid Bucuresti	H	0-0	
20/03/96	Otelul Galati	A	1-3	Cristea
23/03/96	Ceahlaul Piatra Neamt	H	1-0	Lalciu
30/03/96	FC Brasov	A	3-4	Buia 2 (1p), Andone
06/04/96	Gloria Bistrita	H	2-1	Cristea 2
10/04/96	FC Arges Dacia Pitesti	A	0-1	
13/04/96	FC Farul Constanta	H	2-1	Lalciu 2
17/04/96	Steaua Bucuresti	A	1-1	Zamfirescu
20/04/96	Universitatea Cluj	H	2-3	Neacsu, Cristea

STEAUA BUCURESTI

CLUB DIRECTORY

Steaua Bucuresti
bd. Ghencea 35
76803 Bucuresti
tel - (01) 4102182
fax - (01) 6310682/3120186
Year of Formation - 1947
President - Ion Alexandrescu
Coach - Dumitru Dumitriu
Stadium - Steaua (30,000)

MAJOR HONOURS
League Championship - (18)
1951, 1952, 1953, 1956, 1960, 1961, 1968, 1976, 1978, 1985, 1986, 1987, 1988, 1989, 1993, 1994, 1995, 1996.
Domestic Cup - (19)
1949, 1950, 1951, 1952, 1955, 1962, 1966, 1967, 1969, 1970, 1971, 1976, 1979, 1985, 1987, 1988, 1989, 1992, 1996.
European Champions' Cup - (1) 1986.
European Super Cup - (1) 1986.

APPEARANCES 95/96

	P	Ap	(s)	Gls
Bogdan Visan BUCUR	D	16	(5)	
Tiberiu CSIK	D	24	(2)	2
Anton DOBOS	D	31		2
Marin DUNA	A		(1)	
Iulian Sebastian FILIPESCU	M	27	(3)	3
Constantin GÂLCA	M	29		4
Daniel GHERASIM	G	9	(3)	
Bucurel Adrian ILIE	M	24		14
Sabin ILIE	A	1	(22)	2
Edward IORDANESCU	M		(1)	
Marius Mihai LACATUS	A	27		9
Damian MILITARU	M	26		3
Marius MINDILEAC	G		(1)	
Dan Marius MITU	M		(1)	
Roland NAGY	M	4	(19)	
Aurel Silviu PANAIT	D	12	(6)	
Ionel Antonel PÎRVU	D	26	(1)	2
Daniel Claudiu PRODAN	D	31		5
Narcis Claudiu RADUCAN	M	19	(11)	3
Laurentiu Dumitru ROSU	M	10	(19)	3
Bogdan STELEA	G	25		
Alin Tudor STOICA	M		(1)	
Ion VLADOIU	A	33		26

LEAGUE RESULTS 1995/96

13/08/95	Politehnica Iasi	A	2-1	Lacatus, Ilie B.A.
19/08/95	Politehnica Timisoara	H	5-1	Vladoiu, Militaru, Lacatus 2, Ilie B.A.
27/08/95	AS Bacau	A	2-1	Pîrvu, Vladoiu
30/08/95	FC National Bucuresti	H	5-1	Lacatus, Vladoiu, Csik, Ilie B.A., Gâlca
09/09/95	Petrolul Ploiesti	A	2-2	Gâlca (p), og (Leahu)
17/09/95	Universitatea Craiova	H	1-0	Filipescu
22/09/95	Dinamo Bucuresti	A	1-1	Rosu
01/10/95	Rapid Bucuresti	H	3-0	Vladoiu 2, Militaru
04/10/95	Otelul Galati	A	2-1	Dobos, Vladoiu
14/10/95	Ceahlaul Piatra Neamt	H	6-2	Ilie B.A. 2, Gâlca, Raducan, Ilie S., Vladoiu
22/10/95	FC Brasov	A	0-1	
25/10/95	Gloria Bistrita	H	3-1	Vladoiu 2 (1p), Ilie B.A.
28/10/95	FC Arges Dacia Pitesti	A	2-1	Ilie B.A. 2
05/11/95	FC Farul Constanta	H	2-2	Vladoiu 2 (2p)
08/11/95	Universitatea Cluj	A	1-2	Vladoiu
18/11/95	Sportul Studentesc Bucuresti	A	2-0	Dobos, Ilie B.A.
25/11/95	FC Inter Sibiu	H	3-1	Prodan 2, Vladoiu (p)
29/11/95	Politehnica Iasi	H	4-0	Vladoiu 2, Militaru, Ilie B.A.
02/12/95	Politehnica Timisoara	A	1-2	Vladoiu
09/12/95	AS Bacau	H	5-0	Filipescu, Rosu, Gâlca, Lacatus 2
13/12/95	FC National Bucuresti	A	0-1	
28/02/96	Petrolul Ploiesti	H	2-1	Lacatus 2 (1p)
02/03/96	Universitatea Craiova	A	1-1	Ilie B.A.
06/03/96	Dinamo Bucuresti	H	4-2	Pîrvu, Vladoiu 3 (1p)
09/03/96	Rapid Bucuresti	A	1-1	Prodan
16/03/96	Otelul Galati	H	1-0	Lacatus
20/03/96	Ceahlaul Piatra Neamt	A	1-2	Vladoiu
23/03/96	FC Brasov	H	5-0	Vladoiu 2, Raducan, Prodan, Ilie B.A.
30/03/96	Gloria Bistrita	A	2-0	Ilie B.A. 2
06/04/96	FC Arges Dacia Pitesti	H	4-0	Rosu, Vladoiu 2, Ilie S.
10/04/96	FC Farul Constanta	A	1-1	Vladoiu
13/04/96	Universitatea Cluj	H	4-0	Csik, Prodan, Vladoiu, Raducan
17/04/96	Sportul Studentesc Bucuresti	H	1-1	Filipescu
20/04/96	FC Inter Sibiu	A	0-0	

UNIVERSITATEA CLUJ

CLUB DIRECTORY

Universitatea Cluj
Pavlov 33
3400 Cluj
tel - (064) 195590
fax - (064) 191692
Year of Formation - 1919
President - Sorin Bagiu
Coach - Ioan Andone; Dan Anca
Stadium - Ion Moina (28,000)

MAJOR HONOURS

Domestic Cup - (1) 1965.

APPEARANCES 95/96

	P	Ap	(s)	Gls
Gheorghe Alin BANCEU	D	27	(4)	
Dan Ioan BORLEAN	M		(3)	
Vasile BRATIANU	D	19		2
Cristian CERNATESCU	D		(4)	
Horatiu Daniel CIOLOBOC	A	29	(2)	1
Adrian FALUB	D	33		1
Iulian FLORESCU	M	2	(4)	1
Petre GRIGORAS	A	25		5
Vasile Ilie JULA	D	28	(1)	
Zoltán KADAR	D	13		
Ovidiu MAIER	M	27		1
Alexandru MARCA	M	27	(3)	5
Vasile MARE NAGY	G	2	(1)	
Cosmin Adrian MARIS	A	15	(10)	9
Valentin NEFERIOU	D		(4)	
Vasile ORTELECAN	D	8	(2)	
Marius POPESCU	M	3	(4)	
Zoltán RITLI	G	32		
Radu SABO	M	27	(3)	11
Traian Claudiu SALAGEAN	M	10		3
Valentin SANDRU	D	23	(5)	
Claudiu Ovidiu SARMASAN	M		(1)	
Florin SIMA	A		(7)	
Valerica Mircea STAN	D	5	(11)	1
Elek SZEMELY	M	3	(3)	1
Andrei Calin ZANC	M	16	(1)	

LEAGUE RESULTS 1995/96

Date	Opponent	H/A	Score	Scorers
12/08/95	Rapid Bucuresti	A	0-5	
19/08/95	FC Inter Sibiu	H	1-1	Florescu (p)
26/08/95	Otelul Galati	A	0-2	
30/08/95	Politehnica Iasi	H	3-1	Salagean 2 (1p), Grigoras
09/09/95	Ceahlaul Piatra Neamt	A	0-2	
16/09/95	Politehnica Timisoara	H	2-0	Salagean, Marca
23/09/95	FC Brasov	A	0-1	
01/10/95	AS Bacau	H	7-1	Falub, Marca 2, Sabo 2, Maier (p), Cioloboc
04/10/95	Gloria Bistrita	A	0-1	
14/10/95	FC National Bucuresti	H	1-3	Sabo
21/10/95	FC Arges Dacia Pitesti	A	2-0	Grigoras, Sabo
25/10/95	Petrolul Ploiesti	H	2-0	Maris 2
28/10/95	FC Farul Constanta	A	0-1	
04/11/95	Universitatea Craiova	A	0-0	
08/11/95	Steaua Bucuresti	H	2-1	Sabo (p), Grigoras
18/11/95	Dinamo Bucuresti	A	0-1	
25/11/95	Sportul Studentesc Bucuresti	H	1-0	Maris
29/11/95	Rapid Bucuresti	H	2-0	Maris 2
02/12/95	FC Inter Sibiu	A	0-1	
09/12/95	Otelul Galati	H	3-2	Sabo 2, Marca
13/12/95	Politehnica Iasi	A	0-0	
28/02/96	Ceahlaul Piatra Neamt	H	2-0	Maris 2
02/03/96	Politehnica Timisoara	A	0-2	
06/03/96	FC Brasov	H	1-1	Sabo (p)
09/03/96	AS Bacau	A	0-1	
16/03/96	Gloria Bistrita	H	1-1	Marca
20/03/96	FC National Bucuresti	A	1-3	Stan
23/03/96	FC Arges Dacia Pitesti	H	1-0	Sabo
30/03/96	Petrolul Ploiesti	A	0-2	
06/04/96	FC Farul Constanta	H	3-0	Sabo (p), Grigoras, Maris
10/04/96	Universitatea Craiova	H	1-1	Maris
13/04/96	Steaua Bucuresti	A	0-4	
17/04/96	Dinamo Bucuresti	H	2-0	Bratianu, Szemely
20/04/96	Sportul Studentesc Bucuresti	A	3-2	Grigoras, Sabo (p), Bratianu

UNIVERSITATEA CRAIOVA

CLUB DIRECTORY

Universitatea Craiova
str. Gheorghe Doja 2A
1100 Craiova
tel - (051) 132480
fax - (051) 115067
Year of Formation - 1948
President - Victor Becali
Coach - Sorin Cîrtu
Stadium - Central (35,000)

MAJOR HONOURS
League Championship - (4)
1974, 1980, 1981, 1991.
Domestic Cup - (7)
1977, 1978, 1981, 1983, 1991, 1993, 1994.

APPEARANCES 95/96

	P	Ap	(s)	Gls
Dorin ARCANU	G	20		
Pavel BADEA	M	19		4
Catalin BELDEANU	M		(1)	
Aurel Augustin CALIN	M	13	(8)	4
Daniel CIOCANESCU	D	2	(6)	
Florin CÎRSTEA	A	5		
Silvian CRISTESCU	M	30		9
Tiberiu Cristian CURT	D	30		1
Valentin Ion DAVID	G	11		
Iulian FLORESCU	M	4	(13)	
Tersinio Ionel GANE	A	21	(10)	8
Ion Viorel GANEA	A	10	(1)	5
Flavius Sebastian LINGURAR	D	5	(3)	
Dumitru MITRITA	D	27		
Narcis Lucian MOHORA	M	15	(2)	
Victor NAICU	D	12	(12)	
Nicu NASTASIE	M	9	(1)	
Alin Gabriel NICOLA	M		(1)	
Aurelian Cosmin OLAROIU	M	28		1
Corneliu PAPURA	D	28		2
Gabriel POPESCU	M	30		2
Mihai Adrian POPESCU	D	2	(5)	
Marius SAVA	M		(2)	
Vladimir Flavius STOICAN	M	10	(5)	
Valentin Octavian SUCIU	M	1	(2)	1
Eugen TRICA	M	15	(9)	
Adrian UNGUR	A	23	(8)	8
Doru Antonio VARZARU	D	1	(2)	
Eugen VODA	G	3	(2)	
Bogdan Mihaita VRAJITOAREA	A		(1)	

LEAGUE RESULTS 1995/96

12/08/95	Ceahlaul Piatra Neamt	H	4-0	Badea 2, Ungur, Gane
19/08/95	FC Brasov	A	1-1	Cristescu
26/08/95	Gloria Bistrita	H	1-0	Popescu G.
30/08/95	FC Arges Dacia Pitesti	A	0-2	
09/09/95	FC Farul Constanta	H	2-1	Suciu, Cristescu
17/09/95	Steaua Bucuresti	A	0-1	
23/09/95	Sportul Studentesc Bucuresti	H	1-0	Cristescu (p)
01/10/95	FC Inter Sibiu	A	0-2	
04/10/95	Politehnica Iasi	H	3-0	Gane, Popescu G., Ungur
14/10/95	Politehnica Timisoara	A	0-0	
21/10/95	AS Bacau	H	1-0	Curt
25/10/95	FC National Bucuresti	A	3-4	Papura, Gane, Badea
28/10/95	Petrolul Ploiesti	H	3-0	Cristescu 2, Gane
04/11/95	Universitatea Cluj	H	0-0	
09/11/95	Dinamo Bucuresti	A	1-2	Gane
19/11/95	Rapid Bucuresti	H	2-0	Badea, Cristescu
25/11/95	Otelul Galati	A	0-2	
29/11/95	Ceahlaul Piatra Neamt	A	2-0	Cristescu, Ungur
02/12/95	FC Brasov	H	3-1	Gane, Ungur 2
09/12/95	Gloria Bistrita	A	0-3	
13/12/95	FC Arges Dacia Pitesti	H	2-1	Gane, Olaroiu
28/02/96	FC Farul Constanta	A	1-2	Ungur
02/03/96	Steaua Bucuresti	H	1-1	Ungur
06/03/96	Sportul Studentesc Bucuresti	A	0-0	
09/03/96	FC Inter Sibiu	H	2-0	Cristescu, Ganea
16/03/96	Politehnica Iasi	A	0-2	
20/03/96	Politehnica Timisoara	H	3-1	Calin 2, Gane
23/03/96	AS Bacau	A	0-1	
30/03/96	FC National Bucuresti	H	1-0	Ganea
06/04/96	Petrolul Ploiesti	A	0-1	
10/04/96	Universitatea Cluj	A	1-1	Papura
13/04/96	Dinamo Bucuresti	H	3-1	Ungur (p), Ganea, Calin
17/04/96	Rapid Bucuresti	A	1-0	Cristescu
20/04/96	Otelul Galati	H	3-0	Ganea 2, Calin

PROMOTED CLUBS

SECOND DIVISION FINAL TABLES 95/96

SERIA I

		Pd	W	D	L	F	A	Pt	GD
1	**Otelul Târgoviste**	**34**	**20**	**7**	**7**	**74**	**29**	**67**	**+45**
2	Dacia Unirea Braila	34	21	3	10	56	27	66	+29
3	Metrom Brasov	34	17	5	12	43	35	56	+8
4	Gloria Buzau	34	16	6	12	51	46	54	+5
5	Tractorul Brasov	34	17	3	14	39	38	54	+1
6	FC Onesti	34	15	5	14	51	43	50	+8
7	Dacia Pitesti	34	15	5	14	49	47	50	+2
8	Electroputere Craiova	34	14	5	15	45	46	47	-1
9	Rocar Bucuresti	34	14	5	15	38	50	47	-12
10	Dunarea Calarasi	34	14	4	16	52	47	46	+5
11	Aro Câmpulung-Muscel	34	12	10	12	29	40	46	-11
12	Steaua Mizil	34	14	4	16	43	56	46	-13
13	Metalul Plopeni	34	11	10	13	31	39	43	-8
14	Poiana Câmpina	34	13	4	17	42	51	43	-9
15	Cetatea Tîrgu Neamt	34	12	6	16	43	43	42	=
16	Dunarea Galati	34	12	3	19	30	39	39	-9
17	FC Caracal	34	9	10	15	42	51	37	-9
18	Portul Constanta	34	10	5	19	40	71	35	-31

SERIA II

		Pd	W	D	L	F	A	Pt	GD
1	**Jiul Petrosani**	**34**	**23**	**4**	**7**	**59**	**20**	**73**	**+39**
2	Foresta Falticeni	34	22	2	10	50	29	68	+21
3	ASA Tîrgu Mures	34	17	4	13	58	37	55	+21
4	Gaz Metan Medias	34	15	9	10	48	38	54	+10
5	UTA Arad	34	15	8	11	59	36	53	+23
6	Bucovina Suceava	34	17	2	15	51	51	53	=
7	Unirea Dej	34	16	4	14	56	42	52	+14
8	CFR Timisoara	34	17	4	13	50	44	52	+6
9	Corvinul Hunedoara	34	13	8	13	52	43	47	+9
10	CSM Resita	34	14	5	15	45	44	47	+1
11	Minerul Motru	34	13	7	14	33	40	46	-7
12	Olimpia Satu Mare	34	14	3	17	46	52	45	-6
13	FC Maramures	34	13	6	15	48	55	45	-7
14	Minaur Zlatna	34	13	5	16	48	42	44	+6
15	Unirea Alba Iulia	34	13	4	17	49	58	43	-9
16	Gloria Resita	34	12	5	17	30	58	41	-28
17	FC Bihor	34	9	4	21	33	74	31	-41
18	FC Vâlcea	34	5	6	23	26	78	21	-52

N.B. CFR Timisoara deducted 3 pts

CLUB DIRECTORY

Otelul Târgoviste (now - FC Chindia Târgoviste)
Calea Câmpulung 72
Târgoviste
Year of Formation - 1946
President - Marius Chivu
Coach - Silviu Dumitrescu
Stadium - Municipal (17,500)

CLUB DIRECTORY

Jiul Petrosani
str. Lunca 100
2675 Petrosani
tel - (093) 542183
fax - (093) 541318
Year of Formation - 1919
President - Victor Badârca
Coach - Ion Dumitru
Stadium - Jiul (20,000)

RUSSIA

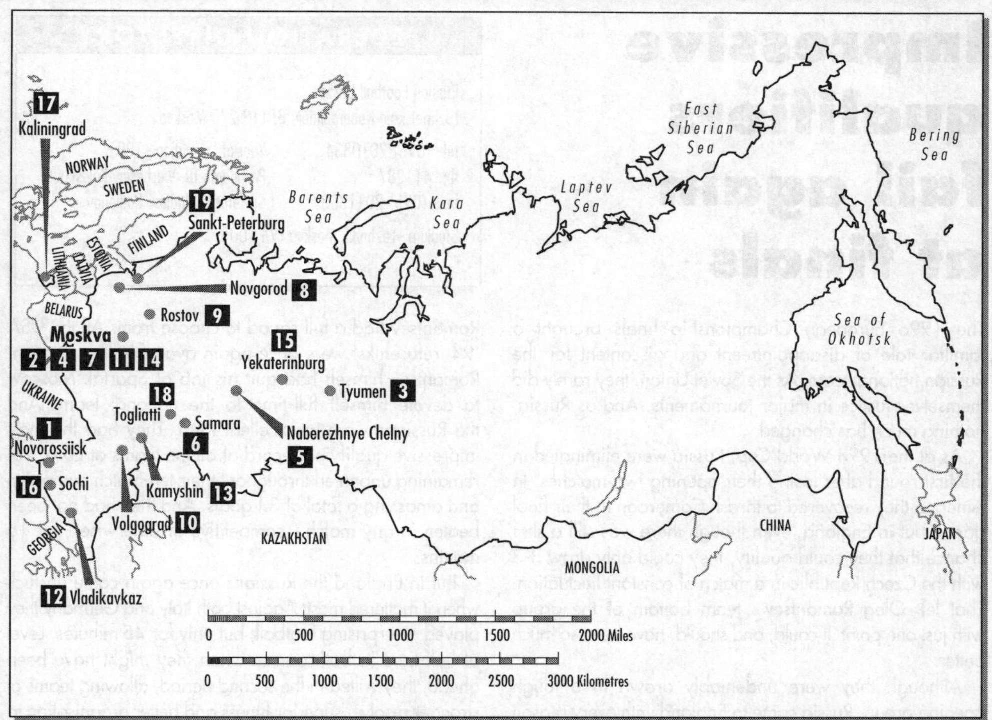

1	CHERNOMORETS NOVOROSSIISK	854
2	CSKA MOSKVA	855
3	DINAMO-GAZOVIK TYUMEN	856
4	DINAMO MOSKVA	857
5	KAMAZ-CHALLY NABEREZHNYE CHELNY	858
6	KRYLYA SOVETOV SAMARA	859
7	LOKOMOTIV MOSKVA	860
8	LOKOMOTIV NIZHNI NOVGOROD	861
9	ROSTSELMASH ROSTOV	862
10	ROTOR VOLGOGRAD	863
11	SPARTAK MOSKVA	864
12	SPARTAK-ALANIA VLADIKAVKAZ	865
13	TEKSTILSCHIK KAMYSHIN	866
14	TORPEDO MOSKVA	867
15	URALMASH YEKATERINBURG	868
16	ZHEMCHUZHINA SOCHI	869
17	BALTIKA KALININGRAD	870
18	LADA TOGLIATTI	870
19	ZENIT SANKT-PETERBURG	870

TITLE GOES SOUTH TO VLADIKAVKAZ

Impressive qualifiers fail again at finals

FEDERATION DIRECTORY

Russian Football Union
Luzhnetskaja Naberezhnaja 8, 119 270 Moskva

tel - (095) 2010834
tlx - 411287
fax - (095) 2011303

Year of Formation - 1991
President - Dr. Viacheslav Koloskov
Secretary - Vladimir Radionov

Stadium - Luzhniki, Moskva (96,000)

The 1996 European Championship finals brought a familiar tale of disappointment and discontent for the Russian national team. As the Soviet Union, they rarely did themselves justice in major tournaments. And as Russia, nothing much has changed.

As at the 1994 World Cup, Russia were eliminated in the first round after losing their opening two matches. In America they recovered to thrash Cameroon in their final game, but in England, even though there was still a slim chance that they could qualify, they could only draw 3-3 with the Czech Republic in a match of constant fluctuation. That left Oleg Romantsev's team bottom of the group with just one point. It could, and should, have been so much better.

Although they were undeniably drawn in a tough opening group, Russia came to England with every reason to feel confident. With one or two exceptions, coach Romantsev had a full squad to choose from. All the USA '94 'refuseniks' were once again available for selection. Romantsev himself had quit his job at Spartak Moscow to devote himself full-time to the national team. And the Russians were in excellent form. They had the most impressive qualifying record of all the teams at Euro '96, remaining unbeaten throughout their ten-match campaign and amassing a total of 34 goals. And they had not been beaten in any match - competitive or otherwise - for 16 months.

But in England the Russians once again came unstuck when it mattered most. Against both Italy and Germany they played enterprising football, but only for 45 minutes. Level at half-time in both games when they might have been ahead, they wilted in the second period, allowing teams of stronger resolve, superior fitness and better organisation to shrug them aside and take the three points.

LEAGUE CHAMPIONSHIP RESULTS 1995

		1	2	3	4	5	6	7	8	9	10	11	12	13	14	15	16
1	Chernomorets Novorossiisk		1-3	2-0	0-1	2-1	2-0	2-4	2-3	2-1	2-1	1-1	0-3	2-2	0-1	3-2	4-0
2	CSKA Moskva	4-0		3-1	1-3	2-2	4-1	0-1	4-0	4-0	1-4	1-2	1-2	2-2	2-1	2-0	4-0
3	Dinamo-Gazovik Tyumen	1-2	2-0		2-2	0-0	3-2	2-3	0-0	2-0	1-6	0-6	0-4	0-3	1-3	0-2	1-2
4	Dinamo Moskva	2-0	0-1	1-0		1-0	4-1	2-1	2-0	1-1	1-0	0-2	1-2	0-0	0-0	3-0	4-3
5	KamAZ Naberezhnye Chelny	2-0	0-0	1-1	5-2		1-0	0-2	1-1	0-1	2-0	2-0	1-0	2-1	3-1	4-0	3-0
6	Krylya Sovetov Samara	1-0	1-2	6-3	1-4	2-1		0-4	1-1	2-6	3-3	1-6	0-1	0-3	0-2	3-2	0-0
7	Lokomotiv Moskva	5-0	0-1	1-1	1-1	1-0	2-1		1-0	2-1	4-3	1-0	4-1	2-0	0-0	0-1	1-1
8	Lokomotiv Nizhni Novgorod	0-1	0-0	0-0	1-1	0-0	1-0	0-2		2-1	1-1	0-1	2-4	4-1	2-3	3-1	2-2
9	Rostselmash Rostov	0-2	1-3	3-0	2-2	2-0	2-2	0-2	2-1		0-4	1-1	0-1	2-1	1-2	2-0	1-4
10	Rotor Volgograd	5-1	2-2	5-4	0-2	2-0	0-0	2-1	1-1	4-1		1-1	1-1	3-1	1-2	1-2	7-0
11	Spartak Moskva	5-0	3-1	4-1	2-0	2-0	5-1	1-2	3-1	2-0	1-2		1-2	4-2	5-0	5-1	6-0
12	Spartak-Alania Vladikavkaz	3-0	2-1	4-0	2-0	0-0	1-1	0-1	3-0	4-1	3-2	1-1		2-0	0-0	4-2	5-0
13	Tekstilschik Kamyshin	2-0	1-2	3-1	1-2	1-0	1-2	1-1	1-2	2-0	1-0	2-2	0-1		1-1	0-1	2-1
14	Torpedo Moskva	1-0	1-2	2-1	0-0	2-1	0-0	1-0	2-0	1-0	3-0	1-2	1-4	0-0		3-0	3-0
15	Uralmash Yekaterinburg	6-0	1-0	5-0	0-2	0-0	0-0	1-2	1-0	2-0	5-0	0-0	0-1	2-0	1-2		4-3
16	Zhemchuzhina Sochi	2-1	0-3	2-0	0-1	4-2	1-2	0-1	0-0	1-3	2-1	1-2	0-2	0-2	3-1	4-1	

LEAGUE CHAMPIONSHIP FINAL TABLE 1995

		Home						Away					Total						
		Pd	W	D	L	F	A	W	D	L	F	A	W	D	L	F	A	Pt	GD
1	Spartak-Alania Vladikavkaz	30	10	4	1	34	9	12	1	2	29	12	22	5	3	63	21	71	+42
2	Lokomotiv Moskva	30	9	4	2	25	11	11	1	3	27	12	20	5	5	52	23	65	+29
3	Spartak Moskva	30	12	0	3	49	13	7	6	2	27	13	19	6	5	76	26	63	+50
4	Dinamo Moskva	30	9	3	3	22	11	7	5	3	23	18	16	8	6	45	29	56	+16
5	Torpedo Moskva	30	9	3	3	21	10	7	4	4	19	20	16	7	7	40	30	55	+10
6	CSKA Moskva	30	8	2	5	35	19	8	3	4	21	15	16	5	9	56	34	53	+22
7	Rotor Volgograd	30	7	5	3	35	19	4	2	9	27	30	11	7	12	62	49	40	+13
8	Uralmash Yekaterinburg	30	8	3	4	28	10	4	0	11	15	37	12	3	15	43	47	39	-4
9	KamAZ-Ch. Naberezhnye Chelny	30	10	3	2	27	9	0	5	10	7	21	10	8	12	34	30	38	+4
10	Tekstilschik Kamyshin	30	6	3	6	19	16	3	4	8	18	25	9	7	14	37	41	34	-4
11	Chernomorets Novorossiisk	30	7	2	6	25	23	3	0	12	7	39	10	2	18	32	62	32	-30
12	Lokomotiv Nizhni Novgorod	30	4	6	5	18	18	2	5	8	10	24	6	11	13	28	42	29	-14
13	Zhemchuzhina Sochi	30	6	1	8	20	22	2	3	10	16	47	8	4	18	36	69	28	-33
14	Rostselmash Rostov	30	5	3	7	19	25	3	1	11	16	31	8	4	18	35	56	28	-21
15	Krylya Sovetov Samara	30	4	3	8	21	38	2	5	8	13	27	6	8	16	34	65	26	-31
16	Dinamo-Gazovik Tyumen	30	3	3	9	15	35	0	3	12	13	42	3	6	21	28	77	15	-49

N.B. When teams are level on points, classification is determined by the number of victories, then by the results of the matches between them.

Accusations flew from every direction in the aftermath of the team's exit. The coach blamed the foreign-based players for putting money and personal welfare before national honour. The players in turn criticised the training methods and tactical errors of the coach. It was the same old story, and there was a predictable end to it all when Romantsev was relieved of his duties. Like Valery Lobanovsky, Andrei Byshovets and Pavel Sadyrin before him, Romantsev discovered that, for Russia (and the USSR), failure to go past the first round in a major tournament equates to immediate dismissal.

TOP SCORERS

25	Oleg VERETENNIKOV (Rotor Volgograd)
18	Aleksandr MASLOV (Rostselmash Rostov)
16	Valeri SHMAROV (Spartak Moskva)
14	Vladimir NIDERGAUS (Rotor Volgograd)
13	Oleg GARIN (Lokomotiv Moskva)
12	Mikheil KAVELASHVILI (Spartak-Alania Vladikavkaz)
	Yevgeni KHARLACHOV (Lokomotiv Moskva)
11	Oleg TERYOKHIN (Dinamo Moskva)
10	Dmitri KARSAKOV (CSKA Moskva)
	Garnik AVALYAN (Krylya Sovetov Samara)
	Mirdzhalol KASYMOV (Spartak-Alania Vladikavkaz)
	Bakhva TEDEYEV (Spartak-Alania Vladikavkaz)
	Sergei NATALUSHKO (Tekstilschik Kamyshin)
	Timur BOGATYRYOV (Zhemchuzhina Sochi)

NATIONAL TEAM RESULTS 95/96

16/08/95	Finland (ECQ)	A	Helsinki	6-0	Kulkov (32, 49), Karpin (39), Radchenko (42), Kolyvanov (67, 69)
06/09/95	Faroe Islands (ECQ)	A	Toftir	5-2	Mostovoi (10p), Kiryakov (60), Kolyvanov (65), Tsymbalar (83), Shalimov (88)
11/10/95	Greece (ECQ)	H	Moscow	2-1	Ouzounidis (38og), Onopko (72)
15/11/95	Finland (ECQ)	H	Moscow	3-1	Radchenko (40), Kulkov (55), Kiryakov (71)
07/02/96	Malta	A	Ta' Qali	2-0	Karpin (26), Kiryakov (61)
09/02/96	Iceland	N	Ta' Qali	3-0	Kanchelskis (10), Karpin (64, 67)
11/02/96	Slovenia	N	Ta' Qali	3-1	Simutenkov (14, 73), Alenichev (19)
27/03/96	Republic of Ireland	A	Dublin	2-0	Mostovoi (34), Kolyvanov (53)
24/04/96	Belgium	A	Brussels	0-0	
25/05/96	Qatar	A	Doha	5-2	Kiryakov (1, 57), Kanchelskis (8), Kolyvanov (26), Mostovoi (77)
29/05/96	United Arab Emirates	H	Moscow	1-0	Simutenkov (84)
02/06/96	Poland	H	Moscow	2-0	Kovtun (21), Beschastnykh (72)
11/06/96	Italy (ECF)	N	Liverpool	1-2	Tsymbalar (20)
16/06/96	Germany (ECF)	N	Manchester	0-3	
19/06/96	Czech Republic (ECF)	N	Liverpool	3-3	Mostovoi (49), Tetradze (54), Beschastnykh (85)

Romantsev may have made mistakes behind the scenes, but it is difficult to find fault with his choice of personnel. The fact is that most of the best Russian players, such as Kanchelskis, Nikiforov, Onopko, Karpin and Kolyvanov, simply failed to perform. The atmosphere within the camp was clearly not right, as demonstrated by the early eviction of Sergei Kiryakov. The most impressive Russian players were the home-based duo of Tsymbalar and Tetradze, while the three youngsters, Yanovski, Radimov and Khokhlov, all benefitted from the experience and provided encouragement for new coach Boris Ignatiev (Romantsev's assistant at Euro '96) in his quest to qualify for the 1998 World Cup.

Russian teams have always been impressive qualifiers. Take Spartak Moscow in the 1995/96 Champions' League. The team played phenomenally well in the group phase, winning all six of their matches in considerable style. But once the knock-out phase was reached, their ambition and resolve vanished. So, too, did half the team's best players.

It is a sad comment on the state of Russian football that a team going for glory in Europe's foremost club competition should self-destruct midway through the competition simply because the players feel their careers will be better served elsewhere. The prospect of playing in a European Cup quarter-final - and possibly winning the competition - obviously held less appeal for Sergei Yuran and Vasili Kulkov than the challenge of assisting Millwall's relegation plight in the English First Division. Theirs was not the only significant departure. Viktor Onopko left to join Spanish side Real Oviedo, and goalkeeper Stanislav Cherchesov, who like Yuran and Kulkov had only returned to Spartak from abroad a few months earlier, packed his bags again and quit for Austrian club FC Tirol Innsbruck. Just to add to Spartak's woes, coach Romantsev decided to jump ship as well. Then international defender Dmitri Khlestov broke his leg in a winter indoor tournament, thus weakening the team still further. After crushing Blackburn Rovers, Rosenborg and Legia Warsaw in the Champions' League, Spartak suddenly found themselves cast as the underdogs in their quarter-final clash with Nantes. The team that took the field for the first leg in the Stade de la Beaujoire was barely recognisable, and the result - a 0-2 defeat - was hardly a surprise. Inspired by Yuri Nikiforov, one of the team's few remaining stars, Spartak almost staged a brilliant comeback in Moscow, but two second-half goals by Frenchman Nicolas Ouédec - the scourge of two Russian teams in the previous season's UEFA Cup - finished off Spartak's dreams for good.

It was to be a season of under-achievement for Spartak right across the board. Two months after their European exit the team now coached by Georgi Yartsev lost the final of the Russian Cup 2-3 to Lokomotiv Moscow. Lokomotiv had been the bogey team of Spartak in the 1995 league campaign, beating them home and away, and they grabbed their first major trophy for 39 years by coming back from 1-2 down to win an enthralling game with a rare late goal from defender Yuri Drozdov.

Lokomotiv's victory gave them a place in the 96/97 European Cup-winners' Cup. They had already qualified for the UEFA Cup by virtue of finishing second in the championship, two points above Spartak, who thus finished empty-handed for the first time since the formation of an independent Russian league. Having been automatic qualifiers for the 95/96 Champions' League, they now found themselves forced to do battle in the preliminary round of the 96/97 UEFA Cup. How the mighty had fallen!

DOMESTIC CUP RESULTS

1/16 FINALS

FK Orekhovo Orekhovo-Zuyevo 0, Rotor Volgograd 3
Irtysh Omsk 3, Krylya Sovetov Samara 1
Lada Dimitrovgrad 0, Lokomotiv Nizhni Novgorod 1
Baltika Kaliningrad 1, CSKA Moskva 2 (aet)
Angusht Malgobek 1, Rostselmash Rostov 0
Nosta Novotroitsk 1, KamAZ-Chally Naberezhnye Chelny 2 (aet)
Amur Blagoveschensk w/o Dinamo-Gazovik Tyumen
Tekstilschik Ivanovo 0, Dinamo Moskva 1
Zarya Leninsk-Kuznetski 1, Chernomorets Novorossiisk 3
Anzhi Makhachkala 2, Spartak-Alania Vladikavkaz 1 (aet)
Kuban Krasnodar 2, Zhemchuzhina Sochi 3
Zenit Sankt-Peterburg 0, Lokomotiv Moskva 4
Metallurg Krasnoyarsk 0, Uralmash Yekaterinburg 3
Neftekhimik Nizhnekamsk 1, Tekstilschik Kamyshin 1 (aet; 4-5 on pens.)
Metallurg Lipetsk 1, Torpedo Moskva 0 (aet)
Spartak Moskva w/o Asmaral Moskva

1/8 FINALS

Zhemchuzhina Sochi 0, Anzhi Makhachkala 3
Rotor Volgograd 4, Irtysh Omsk 0
CSKA Moskva 3, Lokomotiv Nizhni Novgorod 0
Lokomotiv Moskva 4, Uralmash Yekaterinburg 0
Tekstilschik Kamyshin 1, Metallurg Lipetsk 0 (aet)
Chernomorets Novorossiisk 0, Dinamo Moskva 2
Spartak Moskva 2, Angusht Nazran 0
KamAZ-Chally Naberezhnye Chelny w/o Amur Blagoveschensk

QUARTER-FINALS

Lokomotiv Moskva 1, Tekstilschik Kamyshin 0
KamAZ-Chally Naberezhnye Chelny 0, Spartak Moskva 1
Dinamo Moskva 2, Anzhi Makhachkala 1
Rotor Volgograd 2, CSKA Moskva 0

SEMI-FINALS

Dinamo Moskva 0, Lokomotiv Moskva 1
Spartak Moskva 3, Rotor Volgograd 1

FINAL

11/05/96, Moscow
LOKOMOTIV MOSKVA 3 Kosolapov (9, 43p), Drozdov (84)
SPARTAK MOSKVA 2 Lipko (22), Nikiforov (30p)
referee - Levnikov
LOKOMOTIV MOSKVA - Ovchinnikov; Cherevchenko, Drozdov, Kharlachov, Oganesyan, Chugainov, Kosolapov, Gurenko, Snigiryov (Dzhanashia 84), Yelyshev, Solomatin.
SPARTAK MOSKVA - Filimonov; Ananko, Nikiforov, Tsymbalar, Gorlukovich, Lipko (Titov 68), Pyatnitski (Kechinov 60), Meleshin, Shirko, Yevseyev (Dzhubanov 87), Tikhonov.

NATIONAL TEAM APPEARANCES 95/96

Coach - Oleg ROMANTSEV	FIN	FAR	GRE	FIN	MLT	ISL	SLO	IRL	BEL	QTR	UAE	POL	ITA	GER	TCH	Cps	Gls
Dmitri KARPIN (16/08/68) - Chelsea (ENG)	G82		G			G	s46		s46	G85		G		G		21	-
Dmitri KHLESTOV (21/01/71) - Spartak Moskva	D		D	D												20	-
Yuri KOVTUN (05/01/70) - Dinamo Moskva	D	D	D		D	D8		D	D		D	D	D	D		18	1
Yuri NIKIFOROV (16/09/70) - Spartak Moskva	D	D	D	D	D	D75	D	D	D	D		s46		D	D	28	3
Viktor ONOPKO (14/10/69) - Spartak Moskva/Real Oviedo (ESP)	D	D	D	M	D	D46		D	D	D64	D	D46	D	D		41	2
Vasili KULKOV (11/06/66) - Spartak Moskva	D	D65	D	D												21	4
Ilya TSYMBALAR (17/06/69) - Spartak Moskva	M	M	M61	M				M46		M46	M69	M58	M71	M	M67	19	3
Valeri KARPIN (02/02/69) - Real Sociedad (ESP)	M61		M76	D75	M	M		M	M	M60	M	M	M63	s46	M	33	8
Aleksandr MOSTOVOI (22/08/68) - RC Strasbourg (FRA)	M	M	M	M	M	M46		M	M	M			M	M	s46	20	6
Dmitri RADCHENKO (02/12/70) - RC Deportivo (ESP)	A68	A46	s61	A62		A	A	s46	s69							30	9
Igor KOLYVANOV (06/03/68) - Foggia (ITA)	A	A	A					A70	A79	A46	A	A46	A	A	A46	21	8
Andrei KANCHELSKIS (23/01/69) - Everton (ENG)	s61	M58		s75		s8	M	M	D	M	M46	M	M	M		23	3
Sergei KIRYAKOV (01/01/70) - Karlsruher SC (GER)	s68	s46	s46	s62	A			A66	A69	A	A	A46	s63			26	10
Stanislav CHERCHESOV (02/09/63) - Spartak Moskva/FC Tirol Innsbruck (AUT)	s82	G		G	G		G46	G	G46		G		G		G	28	-
Igor SHALIMOV (02/02/69) - FC Lugano (SUI)/Udinese (ITA)		M	s76		M			s70	M	s60		s86			s67	22	3
Vladimir BESCHASTNYKH (01/04/74) - SV Werder Bremen (GER)		s58			s46	A	A78					s46			s46	18	6
Ramiz MAMEDOV (21/08/72) - Spartak Moskva		s65		D46	D		s71									7	-
Sergei YURAN (11/06/69) - Spartak Moskva/Millwall (ENG)			A46	A	A					s46						16	3
Igor DOBROVOLSKI (27/08/67) - unattached				s46		M75				s46	s46	s58	s71			17	2
Andrei TIKHONOV (16/10/70) - Spartak Moskva					A46		s78									2	-
Omari TETRADZE (13/10/69) - Alania Vladikavkaz						D	D	s46		D	D	D	D	M	D	23	1
Vladislav RADIMOV (26/11/75) - CSKA Moskva						M	M71	D46	M		M	M86	M	M46	M	12	-
Yevgeni BUSHMANOV (02/11/71) - CSKA Moskva						s46	D78			s64			D46			4	-
Igor SIMUTENKOV (04/03/73) - Reggiana (ITA)						s46	A	s66	s79		s69	s46		s66	A46	9	4
Igor CHUGAINOV (06/04/70) - Lokomotiv Moskva						s75	s78									2	-
Dmitri ALENICHEV (20/10/72) - Spartak Moskva						s75	M									2	1
Valeri KECHINOV (05/08/74) - Spartak Moskva							A									2	1
Sergei GORLUKOVICH (18/11/61) - Spartak Moskva										D					D	17	-
Sergei OVCHINNIKOV (10/11/70) - Lokomotiv Moskva										s85						3	-
Igor YANOVSKI (03/08/74) - Alania Vladikavkaz											M	M	s46		M	4	-
Dmitri KHOKHLOV (22/12/75) - CSKA Moskva														M66	M	2	-

The lowering of Russia's UEFA co-efficient rating was due to the poor overall performances of the country's European participants (Spartak Moscow excepted) in recent seasons. In 1995/96 Dinamo Moscow made it through to the Cup-winners' Cup quarter-finals, but once again there were a glut of early eliminations in the UEFA Cup. In fairness, the Russian sides all had immensely difficult opening ties, and it was a credit to Rotor Volgograd that they managed to overcome Manchester United on away goals, their two decisive early strikes at Old Trafford coming from the team's impressive attacking twosome of Vladimir Nidergaus and Oleg Veretennikov. Veretennikov was to become the Russian Premier Division's top scorer with a record total of 25 goals.

Spartak Vladikavkaz's tussle with another famous club from England's north-east, Liverpool, ended with an honourable defeat. Beaten 2-1 at home, they drew 0-0 at Anfield and could not be too disenchanted with their overall display. In any case, Vladikavkaz had another, more important issue to consider - maintaining their challenge for a first ever domestic championship title.

EUROPEAN CUPS RESULTS 95/96

CHAMPIONS' CUP

● SPARTAK MOSKVA

Champions' League

1st match BLACKBURN ROVERS (ENG)

A 1-0 Yuran (41)
Cherchesov; Khlestov, Nikiforov, Tsymbalar, Mamedov, Yuran, Onopko, Kulkov, Shmarov (Kechinov 90), Pyatnitski, Tikhonov.

2nd match LEGIA WARSZAWA (POL)

H 2-1 Nikiforov (13p), Yuran (52)
Cherchesov; Khlestov, Nikiforov, Tsymbalar, Mamedov, Yuran, Onopko, Kulkov, Shmarov, Pyatnitski, Tikhonov.

3rd match ROSENBORG BK (NOR)

A 4-2 Alenichev (59), Nikiforov (66), Kechinov (75, 82)
Cherchesov; Khlestov, Nikiforov, Tsymbalar, Mamedov, Yuran, Onopko, Kulkov, Shmarov (Kechinov 58), Pyatnitski (Alenichev 46), Tikhonov.

4th match ROSENBORG BK (NOR)

H 4-1 Shmarov (1), Yuran (9), Tsymbalar (19), Tikhonov (80)
Cherchesov; Khlestov, Nikiforov, Tsymbalar (Kechinov 58), Ananko, Yuran, Onopko, Kulkov, Shmarov, Alenichev (Titov 85), Tikhonov.

5th match BLACKBURN ROVERS (ENG)

H 3-0 Alenichev (28), Nikiforov (47), Mamedov (54)
Cherchesov; Khlestov, Nikiforov, Tsymbalar, Mamedov, Yuran (Pyatnitski 73), Onopko, Kulkov, Shmarov (Kechinov 64), Alenichev, Tikhonov (Mukhamadiev 87).

6th match LEGIA WARSZAWA (POL)

A 1-0 Mamedov (41)
Cherchesov; Khlestov, Nikiforov, Tsymbalar, Mamedov, Kechinov, Onopko (Ananko 82), Kulkov, Shmarov, Alenichev, Tikhonov.

Quarter-final FC NANTES (FRA)

A 0-2
Nigmatullin; Lipko, Nikiforov, Tsymbalar (Shmarov 46), Mamedov (Chudin 35), Ananko, Pyatnitski, Alenichev (Bezrodnyi 72), Yevseyev, Kechinov, Tikhonov.

H 2-2 Nikiforov (32, 38)
Nigmatullin; Ananko, Nikiforov, Tsymbalar, Yevseyev, Lipko, Nagornyak (Bezrodnyi 74), Alenichev, Shmarov (Pyatnitski 59), Kechinov, Tikhonov.

CUP-WINNERS' CUP

● DINAMO MOSKVA

1st round ARARAT YEREVAN (ARM)

H 3-1 Teryokhin (45, 90), Safronov (73)
Smetanin; Yakhimovich, Shulgin, Kolotovkin, Sabitov (Tishkov 80), Kobelev (Grishin 55), Samatov, Cheryshev (Safronov 62), Nekrasov, Kuznetsov, Teryokhin.

A 1-0 Teryokhin (65)
Kleimenov; Grishin (Kobelev 85), Kovtun, Kolotovkin, Shulgin, Kuznetsov, Samatov, Cheryshev, Nekrasov (Safronov 85), Podpalyi, Teryokhin.

2nd round SK HRADEC KRALOVE (TCH)

H 1-0 Kuznetsov (58)
Kleimenov; Kuznetsov, Kovtun, Nekrasov, Shulgin, Kobelev (Grishin 46), Samatov, Cheryshev, Safronov, Podpalyi, Tishkov (Kutsenko 78).

A 0-1 (aet; 3-0 on pens)
Smetanin; Kuznetsov, Kolotovkin, Kovtun, Yakhimovich, Grishin, Samatov, Cheryshev (Kobelev 120), Safronov (Tishkov 70), Podpalyi, Teryokhin.

Quarter-final SK RAPID WIEN (AUT)

H 0-1
Smetanin; Yakhimovich, Kovtun, Shulgin (Kutsenko 63), Nekrasov, Kobelev, Samatov, Cheryshev (Tishkov 40), Safronov (Grishin 39), Kuznetsov, Teryokhin.

A 0-3
Smetanin; Yakhimovich, Kovtun, Shulgin (Safronov 59), Nekrasov, Kobelev, Samatov (Lemeshko 65), Cheryshev, Grishin (Tishkov 56), Podpalyi, Teryokhin.

UEFA CUP

● LOKOMOTIV MOSKVA

1st round FC BAYERN MÜNCHEN (GER)

A 1-0 Kharlachov (71)
Ovchinnikov; Arifullin, Drozdov, Kharlachov, Oganesyan, Chugainov, Kosolapov, Gurenko, Yelyshev, Solomatin, Garin (Maminov 82).

H 0-5
Ovchinnikov; Arifullin, Drozdov, Kharlachov, Solomatin, Chugainov, Kosolapov, Gurenko (Pashinin 9; Maminov 46), Yelyshev, Kuznetsov, Garin.

● SPARTAK-ALANIA VLADIKAVKAZ

1st round LIVERPOOL (ENG)

H 1-2 Kasymov (21)
Khapov; Pagayev (Derkach 46), Gorlukovich (Kornienko 81), Shelia, Dzhioyev, Tetradze, Yanovski, Tedeyev, Kasymov (Timofeyev 46), Kanischev, Kavelashvili.

A 0-0
Khapov; Pagayev, Kornienko (Derkach 46), Shelia, Dzhioyev, Tetradze, Yanovski, Tedeyev, Kasymov, Suleimanov, Kanischev (Timofeyev 46).

● ROTOR VOLGOGRAD

1st round MANCHESTER UNITED (ENG)

H 0-0
Samorukov; Shmarko, Burlachenko, Geraschenko, Yeschenko, Zhunenko, Korniets, Nidergaus, Veretennikov, Yesipov, Zernov (Krivov 80).

A 2-2 Nidergaus (18), Veretennikov (25)
Samorukov; Shmarko, Burlachenko, Berketov, Yeschenko (Tsarenko 70), Zhunenko, Korniets, Nidergaus (Krivov 79), Veretennikov, Yesipov, Zernov (Ilyushin 74).

2nd round GIRONDINS DE BORDEAUX (FRA)

A 1-2 Nidergaus (40)
Samorukov; Shmarko, Berketov, Geraschenko, Yeschenko, Zhunenko, Korniets, Nidergaus (Ilyushin 87), Veretennikov, Yesipov, Zernov (Krivov 84).

H 0-1
Samorukov; Shmarko, Burlachenko, Geraschenko, Yeschenko, Berketov, Korniets, Nidergaus, Veretennikov, Yesipov, Zernov (Ilyushin 67).

Vladikavkaz had begun the 1995 league season with a fierce determination to rival the traditional Muscovite giants. Backed with considerable local government funds, the club recruited a number of high-quality players to bolster the squad, including two Georgians, Mikheil Kavelashvili and Murtaz Shelia, and Russian international Omari Tetradze. The Vladikavkaz squad, moulded into shape by ex-Dinamo Moscow coach Valeri Gazzaev, contained internationals from three former Soviet republics - Azerbaijan, Uzbekistan and Georgia - as well as several players knocking on the door of the Russian national team.

Although the club had only ever competed twice in the Soviet Supreme League (1970 and 1991), they had shown considerable progress in the three seasons of Russian league football, finishing second, sixth and fifth. The arrival of Gazzaev and the new players heightened ambitions for the 1995 season, and despite a couple of early defeats the team were quickly into their stride. A tremendous 2-1 win away to champions Spartak Moscow set them up for a rousing run of nine consecutive victories, which gave Vladikavkaz a huge 11-point advantage over the rest of the field.

A second defeat by Lokomotiv Moscow - 4-1 in the capital - halted that run, but backed by huge home support - an average attendance of around 30,000 compared with the overall Premier Division average of 9,280 - Gazzaev's team continued to pick up points from all of their remaining matches, sealing the title in their penultimate fixture away to CSKA Moscow. It was fitting that Vladikavkaz should complete their triumph in Moscow. The 2-1 win against CSKA was their fourth of the season in the capital.

With Spartak Moscow unable to recover from a bad start, Vladikavkaz were the dominant force throughout the championship and thoroughly deserved their title. Gazzaev fielded what generally amounted to a 3-6-1 formation, with the switching of Tetradze from midfield to libero proving to be a master stroke. In a packed midfield the tall blond Igor Yanovski stood out as the dominant creative force, with Mirdzhalol Kasymov and Bakhva Tedeyev breaking forward to support top-scoring striker Kavelashvili.

In 1996 Spartak Vladikavkaz became Alania Vladikavkaz, and the club set about retaining their title in a Premier Division restored to its original 18-team complement. Relegated Dinamo-Gazovik Tyumen, stranded all season at the foot of the table, made room for three newcomers - Baltika Kaliningrad, Lada Togliatti and the top team from Russia's second city, Zenit Sankt-Peterburg, coached by former national team boss Pavel Sadyrin.

INTERNATIONAL HONOURS

World Cup Finals Appearances: 1994.

European Championship Appearances: 1996.

PLAYERS OF THE SEASON

ILYA TSYMBALAR

It was one thing for Ilya Tsymbalar to be voted Russia's Player of the Year for 1995. But when Norwegian national team coach Egil Olsen selected him as the world's best player in the annual FIFA poll, the foreign scouts really began to prick up their ears. But unlike several of his Spartak Moscow colleagues, Tsymbalar decided to remain at the club and see their Champions' League campaign through to its conclusion. Despite an ankle injury which threatened his presence at Euro '96, Tsymbalar was one of Russia's better players in England. He roamed the left flank with skill and purpose, and scored his team's equalising goal in the opening game against Italy.

YURI NIKIFOROV

Like Tsymbalar, Yuri Nikiforov hails originally from Ukraine. A native of Odessa, he too preferred to select Russia as the team in which to pursue his international career. His Euro '96 was a grave disappointment, encompassed by a shabby display against Germany, when he was twice embarrassed by Jürgen Klinsmann. But, for Spartak Moscow, both at home and in Europe, Nikiforov was a giant. His brilliant performances in the Champions' League, in which he scored five goals, marked him out as one of Europe's top sweepers. Outstanding going forward and an expert at finding the target from free-kicks, Nikiforov looked set to quit Spartak for one of Europe's top clubs. That he ended up 'only' at modest Spanish side Sporting Gijón was something of a let-down for his many Russian (and Ukrainian) fans.

MIRDZHALOL KASYMOV

He is by no means a household name around Europe, but Mirdzhalol Kasymov is certainly big in Asia after helping Uzbekistan to a surprise victory in the 1995 Asian Nations' championship. The 26-year-old attacking midfielder completed a highly satisfactory year by playing a major part in Spartak Vladikavkaz's Russian championship success. As well as scoring ten goals, he helped to set up many others with his incisive through-balls from midfield and his accurate delivery from set-pieces. Although he was voted third in Russia's 1995 Player of the Year poll, Kasymov remains one of the most underrated players in the country.

CHERNOMORETS NOVOROSSIISK

CLUB DIRECTORY

Chernomorets Novorossiisk
Trud Stadium
Novorossiisk
tel - (86134) 54329/52191
Year of Formation - 1960
President - Boris Pupko
Secretary - Avalu Shamkhanov
Coach - Oleg Dolmatov; Sergei Butenko
Stadium - Trud (8,100)

APPEARANCES 95

	P	Ap	(s)	Gls
Igor ABDRAZAKOV	M	1	(5)	
Armen ADAMYAN (ARM)	A		(1)	
Sergei BURDIN	A	28		8
Vitali BUT	M	9	(7)	1
Albert DOGUZOV	M	30		9
Khazret DYSHEKOV	A	26	(4)	8
Albert FEDOSOV	M	7	(7)	
Aleksei FILIPPOV	M	8	(10)	
Vyacheslav GERASCHENKO	D	12		
Khas-Magomed GILAGAYEV	A	8	(9)	1
Nikolai KARPENKO	D	4	(3)	
Yegor KIRYAKOV	D	3	(4)	
Arkadi KRASAVIN	D		(1)	
Ruslan LYASCHUK	G	3	(1)	
Lev MAYOROV (AZB)	M	28	(1)	2
Andrei MULIKOV	D	19	(3)	
Arsen PAPIKYAN	D	8		
Sergei PAVLOV	G	25		
Vitali PINYASKIN	M	4	(2)	
Gisa PSHUKOV	G	1		
Eduard SARKISOV	M	16	(7)	1
Aleksandr SEDIEV	D	4	(1)	
Andrei SHKURIN	D	24	(3)	
Igor VARLAMOV	D	5	(1)	
Vyacheslav VOLKOV	D	11	(1)	
Sergei VOLOBUYEV	D	2		
Sergei YARMOLICH	D	2		
Aramais YEPISKOPOSYAN	M	21	(5)	1
Timur ZAKIROV	A		(5)	
Gennadi ZHILKIN	G	1		
Andrei ZHIROV	D	20	(5)	

LEAGUE RESULTS 1995

Date	Opponent		Score	Scorers
01/04/95	CSKA Moskva	H	1-3	Dyshekov
08/04/95	Lokomotiv Nizhni Novgorod	A	1-0	Mayorov
15/04/95	Dinamo Moskva	H	0-1	
29/04/95	Krylya Sovetov Samara	A	0-1	
09/05/95	Lokomotiv Moskva	H	2-4	Burdin 2 (1p)
13/05/95	Rotor Volgograd	H	2-1	Burdin, Dyshekov
20/05/95	Zhemchuzhina Sochi	A	1-2	Doguzov
24/05/95	Rostselmash Rostov	A	2-0	Dyshekov 2
27/05/95	Spartak Moskva	H	1-1	Burdin
10/06/95	Torpedo Moskva	A	0-1	
17/06/95	Spartak-Alania Vladikavkaz	H	0-3	
24/06/95	KamAZ-Chally Neberezhnye Chelny	A	0-2	
28/06/95	Uralmash Yekaterinburg	H	3-2	Burdin, Dyshekov, Zhirov
01/07/95	Dinamo-Gazovik Tyumen	A	2-1	Burdin 2
08/07/95	Tekstilschik Kamyshin	H	2-2	Gilagayev (p), Doguzov
15/07/95	Spartak Moskva	A	0-5	
22/07/95	Rostselmash Rostov	H	2-1	Doguzov 2 (1p)
26/07/95	Spartak-Alania Vladikavkaz	A	0-3	
05/08/95	Torpedo Moskva	H	0-1	
09/08/95	CSKA Moskva	A	0-4	
15/08/95	KamAZ-Chally Neberezhnye Chelny	H	2-1	Dyshekov, Yepiskoposyan
19/08/95	Dinamo-Gazovik Tyumen	H	2-0	Doguzov (p), Dyshekov
26/08/95	Tekstilschik Kamyshin	A	0-2	
07/09/95	Lokomotiv Moskva	A	0-5	
16/09/95	Rotor Volgograd	A	1-5	Sarkisov
23/09/95	Zhemchuzhina Sochi	H	4-0	Doguzov 2, Burdin, Mayorov
01/10/95	Dinamo Moskva	A	0-2	
14/10/95	Krylya Sovetov Samara	H	2-0	But, Doguzov (p)
21/10/95	Uralmash Yekaterinburg	A	0-6	
26/10/95	Lokomotiv Nizhni Novgorod	H	2-3	Doguzov (p), Dyshekov

CSKA MOSKVA

CLUB DIRECTORY

Centralnyi Sportivnyi Klub Armyi (CSKA) Moskva
Leningradski prospekt 39
125 167 Moskva
tel - (095) 2131898/2132809
fax - (095) 2132809
Year of Formation - 1923
President - Tengiz Verdzadze
Secretary - Viktor Kardivar
Coach - Aleksandr Tarkhanov
Stadium - CSKA (7,000) or Dinamo (50,000)

MAJOR HONOURS
League Championship (USSR) - (7)
1946, 1947, 1948, 1950, 1951, 1970, 1991.
Domestic Cup (USSR) - (5)
1945, 1948, 1951, 1955, 1991.

APPEARANCES 95

	P	Ap	(s)	Gls
Yuri ANTONOVICH (BLS)	M	13	(9)	
Yevgeni BUSHMANOV	M	29		1
Ilshat FAIZULIN	A	16		6
Deni GAISUMOV (AZB)	D	6	(4)	2
Aleksei GERASIMOV	M	12	(5)	6
Valeri GLUSHAKOV	D	11	(3)	
Dmitri GRADILENKO	D	16	(4)	
Aleksei GUSCHIN	D	1	(2)	
Dmitri KARSAKOV	M	19	(9)	10
Dmitri KHOKHLOV	M	25	(5)	5
Vladimir LEBED	A	12	(5)	8
Sergei MAMCHUR	D	25		2
Denis MASHKARIN	D	14	(6)	2
Valeri MINKO	D	24		
Andrei NOVOSADOV	G	11	(1)	
Roman ORESCHUK	A		(2)	
Tigran PETROSYAN (ARM)	M	2	(8)	
Yevgeni PLOTNIKOV	G	19		
Vladislav RADIMOV	M	27		5
Sergei SEMAK	M	22		4
Dmitri SHIRSHAKOV	D	3	(1)	
Dmitri SHUKOV	M	6	(3)	
Dmitri ULYANOV	M	17	(4)	4

LEAGUE RESULTS 1995

01/04/95	Chernomorets Novorossiisk	A	3-1	Lebed, Radimov, Khokhlov
08/04/95	Torpedo Moskva	H	2-1	Gerasimov, Karsakov
01/05/95	Rostselmash Rostov	H	4-0	Lebed 3 (2p), Faizulin
09/05/95	Tekstilschik Kamyshin	H	2-2	Lebed, Faizulin
13/05/95	Dinamo-Gazovik Tyumen	A	0-2	
20/05/95	KamAZ-Chally Neberezhnye Chelny	H	2-2	Gaisumov 2
24/05/95	Dinamo Moskva	H	1-3	Lebed (p)
27/05/95	Uralmash Yekaterinburg	A	0-1	
10/06/95	Krylya Sovetov Samara	H	4-1	Bushmanov, Karsakov, Lebed, Khokhlov
17/06/95	Lokomotiv Nizhni Novgorod	A	0-0	
24/06/95	Rotor Volgograd	H	1-4	Mamchur (p)
28/06/95	Spartak Moskva	A	1-3	Radimov
01/07/95	Zhemchuzhina Sochi	H	4-0	Semak 2, Faizulin 2
04/07/95	Spartak-Alania Vladikavkaz	A	1-2	Faizulin
08/07/95	Lokomotiv Moskva	A	1-0	Karsakov
15/07/95	Uralmash Yekaterinburg	H	2-0	Karsakov, Faizulin
22/07/95	Dinamo Moskva	A	1-0	Semak
29/07/95	Lokomotiv Nizhni Novgorod	H	4-0	Karsakov, Ulyanov 2 (2p), Khokhlov
05/08/95	Krylya Sovetov Samara	A	2-1	Karsakov, Khokhlov
09/08/95	Chernomorets Novorossiisk	H	4-0	Karsakov 2, Mashkarin, Radimov
19/08/95	Zhemchuzhina Sochi	A	3-0	Gerasimov, Ulyanov, Khokhlov
26/08/95	Lokomotiv Moskva	H	0-1	
30/08/95	Rotor Volgograd	A	2-2	Gerasimov 2
09/09/95	Tekstilschik Kamyshin	A	2-1	Gerasimov, Karsakov
16/09/95	Dinamo-Gazovik Tyumen	H	3-1	Lebed, Ulyanov, og (Burdinski)
23/09/95	KamAZ-Chally Neberezhnye Chelny	A	0-0	
30/09/95	Rostselmash Rostov	A	3-1	Gerasimov, Mamchur (p), Mashkarin
14/10/95	Spartak Moskva	H	1-2	Radimov
21/10/95	Spartak-Alania Vladikavkaz	H	1-2	Radimov
26/10/95	Torpedo Moskva	A	2-1	Karsakov, Semak

DINAMO-GAZOVIK TYUMEN

CLUB DIRECTORY

Dinamo-Gazovik Tyumen
Kommuny Str. 22
625 003 Tyumen
tel - (3452) 291534/292653
Year of Formation - 1961
President - Vladimir Dolbonosov
Secretary - Aleksandr Tarasov
Coach - Sergei Rozhkov; Aleksandr Irkhin; Eduard Malofeyev
Stadium - Dinamo-Gazovik (12,500)

APPEARANCES 95

	P	Ap	(s)	Gls
Vyacheslav AFONIN	A		(3)	
Anatoli BESSMERTNYI (UKR)	M	26	(1)	2
Yevgeni BURDINSKI	D	12	(3)	2
Ruslan DANILYUK	M	9	(2)	
Vladimir DOLBONOSOV	M	24	(2)	2
Konstantin FISHMAN	M	2	(7)	
Aleksandr GERASIMOV	M	27	(3)	1
Igor GORELOV	D	5		
Yuri GRITSYNA (UKR)	M	22	(2)	
Vyacheslav KAMOLTSEV	A	16	(1)	2
Sabir KHAMZIN	A	2	(6)	
Vyacheslav KHRUSLOV (UKR)	D	18		
Yevgeni KNYAZHEV	M	11	(2)	1
Igor KOVALEVICH	D	5	(4)	
Nikolai KOVARDAYEV	A	26	(2)	7
Sergei KRUTOV	M	9	(3)	1
Igor KUTEPOV (UKR)	G	14		
Maksim LAYUSHKIN	D	9	(4)	
Oleg MASLENNIKOV	G	16	(1)	
Yevgeni MASLOV	D	17	(3)	1
Maksim NAUMOV	D	3	(3)	
Vitali PONOMARENKO (UKR)	D	12	(2)	1
Aleksandr PRIZETKO (UKR)	A	23		5
Aleksei SAVCHENKO	M	8	(7)	2
Dmitri SHIRSHAKOV	D	12		
Aleksandr SIDORYUK	M	2	(3)	1

LEAGUE RESULTS 1995

Date	Opponent		Score	Scorers
01/04/95	Torpedo Moskva	A	1-2	Bessmertnyi
08/04/95	Rostselmash Rostov	H	2-0	Gerasimov, Maslov (p)
15/04/95	Spartak Moskva	A	1-4	Prizetko (p)
29/04/95	Spartak-Alania Vladikavkaz	H	0-4	
09/05/95	KamAZ-Chally Neberezhnye Chelny	A	1-1	Kovardayev
13/05/95	CSKA Moskva	H	2-0	Kamoltsev, Kovardayev
20/05/95	Tekstilschik Kamyshin	H	0-3	
24/05/95	Uralmash Yekaterinburg	H	0-2	
27/05/95	Krylya Sovetov Samara	A	3-6	Dolbonosov, Kovardayev, Savchenko
10/06/95	Lokomotiv Nizhni Novgorod	H	0-0	
17/06/95	Dinamo Moskva	A	0-1	
24/06/95	Zhemchuzhina Sochi	H	1-2	Kovardayev
28/06/95	Lokomotiv Moskva	A	1-1	Bessmetnyi
01/07/95	Chernomorets Novorossiisk	H	1-2	Prizetko (p)
08/07/95	Rotor Volgograd	A	4-5	Dolbonosov, Kovardayev, Prizetko, Savchenko
15/07/95	Krylya Sovetov Samara	H	3-2	Burdinski, Kovardayev 2
22/07/95	Uralmash Yekaterinburg	A	0-5	
29/07/95	Dinamo Moskva	H	2-2	Knyazhev, Krutov
05/08/95	Lokomotiv Nizhni Novgorod	A	0-0	
09/08/95	Lokomotiv Moskva	H	2-3	Ponomarenko, Prizetko (p)
19/08/95	Chernomorets Novorossiisk	A	0-2	
26/08/95	Rotor Volgograd	H	1-6	Kamoltsev
30/08/95	Zhemchuzhina Sochi	A	0-2	
09/09/95	KamAZ-Chally Neberezhnye Chelny	H	0-0	
16/09/95	CSKA Moskva	A	1-3	Prizetko (p)
23/09/95	Tekstilschik Kamyshin	A	1-3	Burdinski
30/09/95	Torpedo Moskva	H	1-3	Sidoryuk
14/10/95	Spartak-Alania Vladikavkaz	A	0-4	
21/10/95	Spartak Moskva	H	0-6	
26/10/95	Rostselmash Rostov	A	0-3	

DINAMO MOSKVA

CLUB DIRECTORY

Dinamo Moskva
Leningradski prospekt 36
125 167 Moskva
tel - (095) 2125463/2128432/2128582
fax - (095) 2138305
Year of Formation - 1923
President - Nikolai Tolstykh
Secretary - Sergei Nikulin
Coach - Konstantin Beskov; Adamas Golodets
Stadium - Dinamo (50,000)

MAJOR HONOURS
League Championship (USSR) - (11)
1936, 1937, 1940, 1945, 1949, 1954, 1955, 1957, 1959, 1963, 1976.
Domestic Cup - (1) 1995.
Domestic Cup (USSR) - (6)
1937, 1953, 1967, 1970, 1977, 1984.

APPEARANCES 95

	P	Ap	(s)	Gls
Dmitri CHERYSHEV	A	25	(2)	5
Eduard DYOMIN	D	1		
Andrei DYOMKIN	A		(4)	
Aleksandr GRISHIN	M	10	(4)	1
Ruslan ISHKININ	M		(1)	
Valeri KLEIMENOV	G	9	(1)	
Andrei KOBELEV	M	12	(5)	2
Sergei KOLOTOVKIN	D	27		
Yuri KOVTUN	D	25		
Aleksei KUTSENKO	A		(10)	
Yuri KUZNETSOV	A	14	(1)	8
Sergei LEMESHKO	M		(4)	
Igor NEKRASOV	A	1		
Sergei NEKRASOV	A	22	(3)	3
Sergei PODPALYI	D	25	(1)	1
Ravil SABITOV	D	19		2
Vitali SAFRONOV	A	23	(5)	4
Oleg SAMATOV	D	29		5
Vladimir SEMYONOV	M	2	(7)	
Sergei SHULGIN	D	9	(3)	
Andrei SMETANIN	G	21	(1)	
Oleg TERYOKHIN	A	26		11
Yuri TISHKOV	A	2	(7)	1
Aleksandr TOCHILIN	D	5	(1)	
Erik YAKHIMOVICH (BLS)	D	22		

LEAGUE RESULTS 1995

Date	Opponent		Score	Scorers
01/04/95	Zhemchuzhina Sochi	A	1-0	Cheryshev
08/04/95	Lokomotiv Moskva	H	2-1	Safronov, Teryokhin
15/04/95	Chernomorets Novorossiisk	A	1-0	og (Mulikov)
29/04/95	Rotor Volgograd	H	1-0	Teryokhin (p)
09/05/95	Krylya Sovetov Samara	A	4-1	Teryokhin, Cheryshev 3
13/05/95	Uralmash Yekaterinburg	H	3-0	Nekrasov, Teryokhin 2
20/05/95	Lokomotiv Nizhni Novgorod	A	1-1	Samatov
24/05/95	CSKA Moskva	A	3-1	Grishin, Sabitov, Teryokhin (p)
27/05/95	Tekstilschik Kamyshin	H	0-0	
10/06/95	KamAZ-Chally Neberezhnye Chelny	A	2-5	Nekrasov, Safronov
17/06/95	Dinamo-Gazovik Tyumen	H	1-0	Nekrasov
24/06/95	Spartak Moskva	H	0-2	
28/06/95	Torpedo Moskva	A	0-0	
01/07/95	Rostselmash Rostov	A	2-2	Safronov, Teryokhin
08/07/95	Spartak-Alania Vladikavkaz	H	1-2	Sabitov
15/07/95	Tekstilschik Kamyshin	A	2-1	Kobelev, Kuznetsov
22/07/95	CSKA Moskva	H	0-1	
29/07/95	Dinamo-Gazovik Tyumen	A	2-2	Kuznetsov, Podpalyi
05/08/95	KamAZ-Chally Neberezhnye Chelny	H	1-0	Kobelev (p)
09/08/95	Spartak-Alania Vladikavkaz	A	0-2	
19/08/95	Torpedo Moskva	H	0-0	
26/08/95	Rostselmash Rostov	H	1-1	Kuznetsov
30/08/95	Spartak Moskva	A	0-2	
09/09/95	Lokomotiv Nizhni Novgorod	H	2-0	Kuznetsov, og (Oskolkov)
18/09/95	Uralmash Yekaterinburg	A	2-0	Teryokhin 2
23/09/95	Krylya Sovetov Samara	H	4-1	Samatov, Teryokhin, Tishkov, Cheryshev
01/10/95	Chernomorets Novorossiisk	H	2-0	Samatov, Safronov
14/10/95	Rotor Volgograd	A	2-0	Kuznetsov 2
22/10/95	Zhemchuzhina Sochi	H	4-3	Kuznetsov 2 (1p), Samatov, Teryokhin
26/10/95	Lokomotiv Moskva	A	1-1	Samatov

KAMAZ-CHALLY NABEREZHNYE CHELNY

CLUB DIRECTORY

KamAZ-Chally Naberezhnye Chelny
Moskovski prospekt
Grenada Park
Stadium KamAZ
Naberezhnye Chelny
tel - (8439) 539221/533594
fax - (8439) 533594
Year of Formation - 1981
President - Vadim Paslov
Secretary - Nikolai Salov
Coach - Valeri Chetverik
Stadium - KamAZ (15,000)

APPEARANCES 95

	P	Ap	(s)	Gls
Andrei ALEKSANENKOV (UKR)	M	9	(1)	
Adnan AL-SHABAT (JOR)	M	2		
Badran AL-SHADRAN (JOR)	M	5	(2)	
Aleksei BABENKO	M	14	(2)	
Dmitri BUTALYI	D		(1)	
Aleksei DUDIN	D	1		
Yevgeni DURNEV	A	27		9
Aleksandr GORBACHOV	D	25		1
Dmitri GORBATENKO	M	1	(10)	
Ruslan IDIGOV	M	2		
Aleksei ILATOVSKI	M		(1)	
Mikheil JISHKARIANI (GEO)	A	8		2
Oleg KAPUSTNIKOV	A	1	(4)	
Aleksandr KARATAYEV	M	15	(1)	
Vladimir KLONTSAK	D	30		1
Andrei KNYAZEV	M		(7)	1
Pavel KURAKIN	M		(2)	
Lev MATVEYEV	M	8	(6)	
Vitali MILENIN	M	24	(1)	
Viktor PANCHENKO	A		(1)	
Pavel PRYGUNOV	A		(1)	
Alimzhan RAFIKOV	D	1	(6)	
Vladimir SHUTOV	M		(5)	
Arnold SLOBODICH	A	2	(14)	1
Boris TROPANETS	M	29		5
Yevgeni VARLAMOV	D	30		1
Ivan VINNIKOV	M	1	(11)	
Yevgeni YEFREMOV	D	25	(2)	
Robert YEVDOKIMOV	M	28	(1)	9
Platon ZAKHARCHUK	G	30		
Andrei ZAVYALOV	M	3		
Vladislav ZUBKOV	D	9	(1)	4

LEAGUE RESULTS 1995

01/04/95	Rostselmash Rostov	A	0-2	
08/04/95	Spartak-Alania Vladikavkaz	H	1-0	Yevdokimov
15/04/95	Torpedo Moskva	A	1-2	Yevdokimov
29/04/95	Spartak Moskva	H	2-0	Durnev 2
09/05/95	Dinamo-Gazovik Tyumen	H	1-1	Yevdokimov
13/05/95	Tekstilschik Kamyshin	A	0-1	
20/05/95	CSKA Moskva	A	2-2	Durnev 2
24/05/95	Krylya Sovetov Samara	H	1-0	Yevdokimov
27/05/95	Lokomotiv Nizhni Novgorod	A	0-0	
10/06/95	Dinamo Moskva	H	5-2	Durnev, Yevdokimov 2, Tropanets 2 (2p)
17/06/95	Uralmash Yekaterinburg	A	0-0	
24/06/95	Chernomorets Novorossiisk	H	2-0	Yevdokimov (p), Tropanets
28/06/95	Rotor Volgograd	A	0-2	
01/07/95	Lokomotiv Moskva	H	0-2	
08/07/95	Zhemchuzhina Sochi	A	2-4	Yevdokimov (p), Slobodich
15/07/95	Lokomotiv Nizhni Novgorod	H	1-1	Durnev
22/07/95	Krylya Sovetov Samara	A	1-2	Klontsak
29/07/95	Uralmash Yekaterinburg	H	4-0	Gorbachov, Yevdokimov, Durnev, Tropanets
05/08/95	Dinamo Moskva	A	0-1	
09/08/95	Rotor Volgograd	H	2-0	Jishkariani, Zubkov
12/08/95	Zhemchuzhina Sochi	H	3-0	Varlamov, Zubkov, Knyazev
15/08/95	Chernomorets Novorossiisk	A	1-2	Durnev
19/08/95	Lokomotiv Moskva	A	0-1	
09/09/95	Dinamo-Gazovik Tyumen	A	0-0	
16/09/95	Tekstilschik Kamyshin	H	2-1	Jishkariani, Zubkov
23/09/95	CSKA Moskva	H	0-0	
01/10/95	Spartak Moskva	A	0-2	
14/10/95	Rostselmash Rostov	H	0-1	
21/10/95	Torpedo Moskva	H	3-1	Durnev, Zubkov, Tropanets (p)
26/10/95	Spartak-Alania Vladikavkaz	A	0-0	

KRYLYA SOVETOV SAMARA

CLUB DIRECTORY

Krylya Sovetov Samara
Shushenskaya Str. 50A
443 011 Samara
tel - (8462) 351440/351635
fax - (8462) 351635
Year of Formation - 1943
President - Mikhail Balagezyan
Secretary - Boris Valkov
Coach - Aleksandr Averyanov
Stadium - Metallurg (38,800)

APPEARANCES 95

	P	Ap	(s)	Gls
Andrei ANISCHENKO	D	6		
Garnik AVALYAN	A	30		10
Aleksandr AVERYANOV	M	28	(1)	2
Viktor BULATOV	M	24	(3)	3
Vyacheslav DAYEV	D	29		
Oleg DELOV	M	15		
Rustem FAKHRUTDINOV	A		(1)	
Fyodor GAGLOYEV	M	8		2
Sergei GRIBOV	D	16	(2)	
Aleksandr GRYAZIN	M	13	(11)	2
Andrei KHLEBOSOLOV (BLS)	A	5	(6)	
Sergei KORCHAGIN	M	1	(2)	
Aleksandr MARTYOSHKIN (BLS)	G	23	(1)	
Vladislav MATVIENKO	M	25		2
Igor MEDA	D	7	(4)	1
Mamuka MINASHVILI (GEO)	M	12	(13)	3
Aleksandr ORESHNIKOV (BLS)	M	3		
Gennadi REMEZOV	M	1	(2)	
Andrei REZANTSEV	D	20	(3)	
Sergei SHISHKIN	D	23	(2)	
Vasili SLOBODKO (UKR)	G	7	(2)	
Yevgeni SONIN	M		(3)	1
Zurab TSIKLAURI	A	10	(18)	7
Aleksandr TSILYURIK	A	4	(1)	
Mikhail YEVSTIGNEYEV	D	3		
Pavel YUMATOV	M		(5)	
Igor ZAKHAROV	D	4	(1)	
Aleksandr ZHIDKOV	M	13		1

LEAGUE RESULTS 1995

01/04/95	Lokomotiv Moskva	A	1-2	Minashvili
08/04/95	Zhemchuzhina Sochi	H	0-0	
15/04/95	Rotor Volgograd	A	0-0	
29/04/95	Chernomorets Novorossiisk	H	1-0	Matvienko
09/05/95	Dinamo Moskva	H	1-4	Avalyan
13/05/95	Lokomotiv Nizhni Novgorod	H	1-1	Meda
20/05/95	Uralmash Yekaterinburg	A	0-0	
24/05/95	KamAZ-Chally Neberezhnye Chelny	A	0-1	
27/05/95	Dinamo-Gazovik Tyumen	H	6-3	Avalyan, Gryazin, Sonin, Tsiklauri 3
10/06/95	CSKA Moskva	A	1-4	Bulatov
17/06/95	Tekstilschik Kamyshin	H	0-3	
24/06/95	Rostselmash Rostov	A	2-2	Bulatov, Gryazin
28/06/95	Spartak-Alania Vladikavkaz	H	0-1	
01/07/95	Torpedo Moskva	A	0-0	
08/07/95	Spartak Moskva	H	1-6	Averyanov
15/07/95	Dinamo-Gazovik Tyumen	A	2-3	Matvienko, Minashvili
22/07/95	KamAZ-Chally Neberezhnye Chelny	H	2-1	Avalyan 2
29/07/95	Tekstilschik Kamyshin	A	2-1	Avalyan, Gagloyev
05/08/95	CSKA Moskva	H	1-2	Tsiklauri
09/08/95	Spartak Moskva	A	1-5	Tsiklauri
19/08/95	Rostselmash Rostov	H	2-6	Avalyan, Gagloyev (p)
26/08/95	Torpedo Moskva	H	0-2	
30/08/95	Spartak-Alania Vladikavkaz	A	1-1	Minashvili
09/09/95	Uralmash Yekaterinburg	H	3-2	Avalyan 2, Averyanov
16/09/95	Lokomotiv Nizhni Novgorod	A	0-1	
23/09/95	Dinamo Moskva	A	1-4	Avalyan
30/09/95	Rotor Volgograd	H	3-3	Zhidkov (p), Tsiklauri 2
14/10/95	Chernomorets Novorossiisk	A	0-2	
21/10/95	Lokomotiv Moskva	H	0-4	
26/10/95	Zhemchuzhina Sochi	A	2-1	Avalyan, Bulatov

LOKOMOTIV MOSKVA

CLUB DIRECTORY

Lokomotiv Moskva
B. Cherkizovskaja Str. 125A
107 553 Moskva
tel - (095) 1619704
fax - (095) 1619977
Year of Formation - 1923
President - Valeri Filatov
Secretary - Vladimir Korotkov
Coach - Yury Syomin
Stadium - Lokomotiv (30,000)

MAJOR HONOURS
Domestic Cup (USSR) - (2) 1936, 1957.

APPEARANCES 95

	P	Ap	(s)	Gls
Aleksei ARIFULLIN	D	20	(1)	
Ansar AYUPOV	M	6	(8)	1
Yuri BATURENKO (TAD)	M	3		
Khasambi BIDZHIEV	G	3		
Igor CHUGAINOV	D	30		1
Yuri DROZDOV	D	30		
Oleg GARIN	A	28		13
Sergei GURENKO (BLS)	D	12	(1)	
Aleksandr KATASONOV	A	3	(10)	1
Yevgeni KHARLACHOV	M	26		12
Aleksei KOSOLAPOV	M	29		9
Yevgeni KUZNETSOV	M	5	(5)	1
Vladimir MAMINOV	M	2	(9)	1
Sarkis OGANESYAN (ARM)	D	22	(1)	2
Sergei OVCHINNIKOV	G	27		
Vitali PARAKHNEVICH (UKR)	A	5	(5)	
Oleg PASHININ	D	12	(2)	
Sergei PEREPADENKO	M	1	(3)	
Aleksandr SMIRNOV	M	12	(4)	2
Aleksei SNIGIRYOV	A	6	(3)	3
Andrei SOLOMATIN	M	22	(5)	4
Aleksandr TATARKIN	A	1	(5)	
Vyacheslav TSARYOV	D	2	(2)	
Oleg YELYSHEV	M	23	(3)	2
Sergei ZHUKOV	M		(1)	

LEAGUE RESULTS 1995

01/04/95	Krylya Sovetov Samara	H	2-1	Kosolapov (p), Kharlachov
08/04/95	Dinamo Moskva	A	1-2	Kharlachov
15/04/95	Lokomotiv Nizhni Novgorod	H	1-0	Kosolapov
29/04/95	Uralmash Yekaterinburg	A	2-1	Garin, Smirnov
09/05/95	Chernomorets Novorossiisk	A	4-2	Ayupov, Smirnov, Kharlachov, og (Shkurin)
13/05/95	Zhemchuzhina Sochi	H	1-1	Kharlachov
20/05/95	Rotor Volgograd	A	1-2	Kharlachov
24/05/95	Spartak-Alania Vladikavkaz	A	1-0	Garin
27/05/95	Torpedo Moskva	H	0-0	
10/06/95	Spartak Moskva	A	2-1	Yelyshev, Oganesyan
17/06/95	Rostselmash Rostov	H	2-1	Kosolapov (p), Kharlachov
24/06/95	Tekstilschik Kamyshin	A	1-1	Garin
28/06/95	Dinamo-Gazovik Tyumen	H	1-1	Chugainov
01/07/95	KamAZ-Chally Neberezhnye Chelny	A	2-0	Kosolapov, Solomatin
08/07/95	CSKA Moskva	H	0-1	
15/07/95	Torpedo Moskva	A	0-1	
22/07/95	Spartak-Alania Vladikavkaz	H	4-1	Garin 3 (1p), Kosolapov
29/07/95	Rostselmash Rostov	A	2-0	Garin, Kosolapov
05/08/95	Spartak Moskva	H	1-0	Solomatin
09/08/95	Dinamo-Gazovik Tyumen	A	3-2	Kharlachov 2 (2p), Snigiryov
19/08/95	KamAZ-Chally Neberezhnye Chelny	H	1-0	Garin
26/08/95	CSKA Moskva	A	1-0	Kharlachov
30/08/95	Tekstilschik Kamyshin	H	2-0	Garin, Kharlachov
07/09/95	Chernomorets Novorossiisk	H	5-0	Garin, Yelyshev, Snigiryov, Solomatin 2
16/09/95	Zhemchuzhina Sochi	A	1-0	Kharlachov
21/09/95	Rotor Volgograd	H	4-3	Garin 2, Kosolapov, Oganesyan
30/09/95	Lokomotiv Nizhni Novgorod	A	2-0	Maminov, Kharlachov
14/10/95	Uralmash Yekaterinburg	H	0-1	
21/10/95	Krylya Sovetov Samara	A	4-0	Garin, Kosolapov 2, Kuznetsov
26/10/95	Dinamo Moskva	H	1-1	Snigiryov

LOKOMOTIV NIZHNI NOVGOROD

CLUB DIRECTORY

Lokomotiv Nizhni Novgorod
Balaklavski per. 1
603 010 Nizhni Novgorod
tel - (8312) 422929
fax - (8312) 429345
Year of Formation - 1987
President - Valeri Ovchinnikov
Secretary - Igor Bachurko
Coach - Valeri Ovchinnikov
Stadium - Lokomotiv (20,400)

APPEARANCES 95

	P	Ap	(s)	Gls
Nazim ADZHIEV	M		(1)	
Aleksei AREFYEV	M	13	(1)	
Mikhail BESCHASTNYKH	A	7	(2)	3
Sergei BOZHKO	M	16	(5)	1
Marat DZOBLAYEV	M	10	(3)	
Eduard DORONIN	D		(1)	
Stanislav FEOKTISTOV	M	23	(4)	
Fyodor GAGLOYEV	M	9	(1)	4
Ivan GETSKO (UKR)	A	15		8
Mário dos Santos JÚNIOR (BRA)	A	5	(2)	1
Vladimir KAZAKOV	M	25	(2)	3
Yuri KONOVALOV	M	10	(8)	2
Aleksandr KUZMICHOV	A	9	(3)	2
Andrei LEBEDEV	M	12	(7)	
Vladimir NAIDANOV	M	14	(9)	1
Sergei NIKOLAYEV	A		(1)	
Vitali NIKULKIN	A	3	(1)	
Albert OSKOLKOV	D	26	(1)	
Maksim PUTILIN	D	15	(1)	1
Viktor PYATANOV	M	3	(2)	
Sergei RAGULIN	D	21	(3)	
Andrei SATSUNKEVICH (BLS)	G	8		
Valeri SHANTALOSOV (BLS)	G	22		
Yevgeni SHURKO	D	25		
Luís André da SILVA (BRA)	M	4	(3)	1
Yevgeni SMERTIN	M	7	(2)	
Oleg STOGOV	M	5	(1)	
Aleksei SUDARIKOV	A	4	(8)	
Pavel SUDARIKOV	A	1		
Viktor VASCHENKO	D	4	(4)	
Konstantin VESELOVSKI	M	8	(2)	
Dmitri VLASOV	D	6		

LEAGUE RESULTS 1995

01/04/95	Rotor Volgograd	A	1-1	Kuzmichov
08/04/95	Chernomorets Novorossiisk	H	0-1	
15/04/95	Lokomotiv Moskva	A	0-1	
29/04/95	Zhemchuzhina Sochi	H	2-2	Kuzmichov, Putilin
09/05/95	Uralmash Yekaterinburg	A	0-1	
13/05/95	Krylya Sovetov Samara	A	1-1	Gagloyev (p)
20/05/95	Dinamo Moskva	H	1-1	Gagloyev (p)
24/05/95	Tekstilschik Kamyshin	A	2-1	Bozhko, Gagloyev
27/05/95	KamAZ-Chally Neberezhnye Chelny	H	0-0	
10/06/95	Dinamo-Gazovik Tyumen	A	0-0	
17/06/95	CSKA Moskva	H	0-0	
24/06/95	Spartak-Alania Vladikavkaz	A	0-3	
28/06/95	Rostselmash Rostov	H	2-1	Gagloyev, Kazakov
01/07/95	Spartak Moskva	A	1-3	Kazakov
08/07/95	Torpedo Moskva	H	2-3	Silva, Naidanov
15/07/95	KamAZ-Chally Neberezhnye Chelny	A	1-1	Konovalov
22/07/95	Tekstilschik Kamyshin	H	4-1	Júnior, Kazakov, Konovalov, og (Volgin)
29/07/95	CSKA Moskva	A	0-4	
05/08/95	Dinamo-Gazovik Tyumen	H	0-0	
09/08/95	Torpedo Moskva	A	0-2	
19/08/95	Spartak Moskva	H	0-1	
26/08/95	Spartak-Alania Vladikavkaz	H	2-4	Beschastnykh, Getsko
30/08/95	Rostselmash Rostov	A	1-2	Getsko
09/09/95	Dinamo Moskva	A	0-2	
16/09/95	Krylya Sovetov Samara	H	1-0	Getsko
23/09/95	Uralmash Yekaterinburg	H	3-1	Getsko 3 (1p)
30/09/95	Lokomotiv Moskva	H	0-1	
14/10/95	Zhemchuzhina Sochi	A	0-0	
22/10/95	Rotor Volgograd	H	1-1	Beschastnykh
27/10/95	Chernomorets Novorossiisk	A	3-2	Getsko 2, Beschastnykh

ROSTSELMASH ROSTOV

CLUB DIRECTORY

Rostselmash Rostov
Pervaya Konnaya Str. 6 A
344 077 Rostov
tel - (8632) 527947
Year of Formation - 1930
President - Viktor Usachov
Secretary - Vasili Maznev
Coach - Enver Yulgushov; Sergei Andreyev
Stadium - Rostselmash (15,600)

APPEARANCES 95

	P	Ap	(s)	Gls
Dmitri ANANKO	D	12		
Sergei ANDREYEV	A	4	(2)	1
Sergei BALAKHNIN	D	11	(6)	2
Yuri BOROVSKOI	D	8	(4)	
Sergei DEMENTYEV	D	1	(4)	
Akaki DEVADZE (GEO)	G	22		
Yuri DYADYUK	M	30		2
Nikolai GOLUBKIN	D	7	(7)	
Gocha GUDZHABIDZE (GEO)	D	13		
Grigori IVANOV	A		(4)	
Yuri KLYUCHNIKOV	D	6		
Sergei LEMESHKO	M	11	(2)	
Dmitri LOSKOV	M	27		5
Vyacheslav LUGOVKIN	M	22	(2)	1
Aleksandr MASLOV	A	28	(2)	18
Sergei NECHAI	D	11		
Roman ORESCHUK	A	9	(1)	4
Vitali PAPADOPULO	M	4	(14)	
Gennadi PAROVIN	D	25		
Andrei REDKIN	D	11		
Oleg SANKO	M	1	(3)	
Aleksandr SHUTOV	M	16	(7)	
Badri SPANDERASHVILI	M	14	(10)	
Edgar STRELTSOV	A	1	(2)	
Andrei TIMOSHENKO	M	3	(3)	
Ramil VALEYEV	G	3	(1)	
Aleksandr VLADIMIROV	G	5	(1)	
Aleksandr VOROBYOV	A	11	(9)	2
Aleksandr YESCHENKO	D	14	(1)	

LEAGUE RESULTS 1995

Date	Opponent		Score	Scorers
01/04/95	KamAZ-Chally Neberezhnye Chelny	H	2-0	Loskov, Maslov
08/04/95	Dinamo-Gazovik Tyumen	A	0-2	
15/04/95	Tekstilschik Kamyshin	A	2-1	Balakhnin, Maslov
01/05/95	CSKA Moskva	A	0-4	
09/05/95	Spartak-Alania Vladikavkaz	A	1-4	Maslov
13/05/95	Torpedo Moskva	H	1-2	Balakhnin
20/05/95	Spartak Moskva	H	1-1	Maslov
24/05/95	Chernomorets Novorossiisk	H	0-2	
27/05/95	Rotor Volgograd	A	1-4	Maslov
10/06/95	Zhemchuzhina Sochi	H	1-4	Vorobyov
17/06/95	Lokomotiv Moskva	A	1-2	Maslov
24/06/95	Krylya Sovetov Samara	H	2-2	Maslov 2
28/06/95	Lokomotiv Nizhni Novgorod	A	1-2	Maslov
01/07/95	Dinamo Moskva	H	2-2	Maslov 2
08/07/95	Uralmash Yekaterinburg	A	0-2	
15/07/95	Rotor Volgograd	H	0-4	
22/07/95	Chernomorets Novorossiisk	A	1-2	Maslov
29/07/95	Lokomotiv Moskva	H	0-2	
05/08/95	Zhemchuzhina Sochi	A	3-1	Loskov, Maslov, Oreschuk
09/08/95	Uralmash Yekaterinburg	H	2-0	Maslov, Oreschuk
19/08/95	Krylya Sovetov Samara	A	6-2	Dyadyuk, Loskov (p), Lugovkin, Maslov, Oreschuk 2
26/08/95	Dinamo Moskva	A	1-1	Loskov
30/08/95	Lokomotiv Nizhni Novgorod	H	2-1	Maslov 2
09/09/95	Spartak Moskva	A	0-2	
16/09/95	Spartak-Alania Vladikavkaz	H	0-1	
23/09/95	Torpedo Moskva	A	0-1	
30/09/95	CSKA Moskva	H	1-3	Andreyev
14/10/95	KamAZ-Chally Neberezhnye Chelny	A	1-0	Loskov
21/10/95	Tekstilschik Kamyshin	A	0-2	
26/10/95	Dinamo-Gazovik Tyumen	H	3-0	Vorobyov, Dyadyuk, Maslov

ROTOR VOLGOGRAD

CLUB DIRECTORY

Rotor Volgograd
Prospekt Lenina 76
400 005 Volgograd
tel - (8442) 341179
fax - (8442) 346804
Year of Formation - 1929
President - Vladimir Goryunov
Secretary - Rokhus Shokh
Coach - Viktor Prokopenko
Stadium - Central (30,000)

APPEARANCES 95

	P	Ap	(s)	Gls
Aleksandr BERKETOV	M	20	(5)	3
Aleksandr BONDAR	D	15	(3)	1
Ilya BORODIN	A		(1)	
Valeri BURLACHENKO	D	24	(1)	
Yevgeni CHUMACHENKO	D	7	(5)	
Vladimir GERASCHENKO	D	14		3
Sergei ILYUSHIN	A	10	(8)	4
Igor KORNIETS	M	29		
Andrei KRIVOV	M	15	(10)	3
Konstantin KULIK	M	3	(7)	
Igor MENSCHIKOV	M	1	(10)	1
Sergei NECHAI	D	11		
Oleg NECHAYEV	A	12	(10)	4
Vladimir NIDERGAUS (KAZ)	A	27	(1)	14
Andrei SAMORUKOV	G	30		
Aleksandr SHMARKO	D	6		
Aleksandr TROININ	M	1	(4)	1
Aleksandr TSARENKO	M	16	(6)	1
Oleg VERETENNIKOV	M	29		25
Aleksandr YESCHENKO	D	10		
Valeri YESIPOV	A	25		2
Sergei ZHUNENKO	M	25		

LEAGUE RESULTS 1995

Date	Opponent		Score	Scorers
01/04/95	Lokomotiv Nizhni Novgorod	H	1-1	Veretennikov
08/04/95	Uralmash Yekaterinburg	A	0-5	
15/04/95	Krylya Sovetov Samara	H	0-0	
29/04/95	Dinamo Moskva	A	0-1	
09/05/95	Zhemchuzhina Sochi	A	7-0	Veretennikov 3 (1p), Menschikov, Nidergaus 3
13/05/95	Chernomorets Novorossiisk	A	1-2	Nidergaus
20/05/95	Lokomotiv Moskva	H	2-1	Bondar, Nechayev
24/05/95	Spartak Moskva	A	2-1	Berketov, Veretennikov
27/05/95	Rostselmash Rostov	H	4-1	Veretennikov, Nidergaus, Troinin, Tsarenko
10/06/95	Spartak-Alania Vladikavkaz	A	2-3	Veretennikov, Nidergaus
17/06/95	Torpedo Moskva	H	1-2	Veretennikov
24/06/95	CSKA Moskva	A	4-1	Veretennikov (p), Krivov 2, Nidergaus
28/06/95	KamAZ-Chally Neberezhnye Chelny	H	2-0	Veretennikov, Nidergaus
01/07/95	Tekstilschik Kamyshin	A	0-1	
08/07/95	Dinamo-Gazovik Tyumen	H	5-4	Veretennikov (p), Geraschenko, Nechayev 2, Nidergaus
15/07/95	Rostselmash Rostov	A	4-0	Berketov, Veretennikov 2 (1p), Ilyushin
22/07/95	Spartak Moskva	H	1-1	Ilyushin
29/07/95	Torpedo Moskva	A	0-3	
05/08/95	Spartak-Alania Vladikavkaz	H	1-1	Veretennikov
09/08/95	KamAZ-Chally Neberezhnye Chelny	A	0-2	
19/08/95	Tekstilschik Kamyshin	H	3-1	Veretennikov 2, Yesipov
26/08/95	Dinamo-Gazovik Tyumen	A	6-1	Berketov, Veretennikov 2, Geraschenko 2, Yesipov
30/08/95	CSKA Moskva	H	2-2	Veretennikov, Nechayev
07/09/95	Zhemchuzhina Sochi	H	1-2	Veretennikov
16/09/95	Chernomorets Novorossiisk	H	5-1	Veretennikov 3 (1p), Ilyushin, Nidergaus
21/09/95	Lokomotiv Moskva	A	3-4	Veretennikov 2 (1p), Nidergaus
30/09/95	Krylya Sovetov Samara	A	3-3	Krivov, Nidergaus 2
14/10/95	Dinamo Moskva	H	0-2	
22/10/95	Lokomotiv Nizhni Novgorod	A	1-1	Nidergaus
26/10/95	Uralmash Yekaterinburg	H	1-2	Ilyushin

SPARTAK MOSKVA

CLUB DIRECTORY

Spartak Moskva
1st Koptelski per. 18/2
129 010 Moskva
tel - (095) 2088736
fax - (095) 9752385
Year of Formation - 1922
President - Oleg Romantsev
Secretary - Salikh Khadzhi
Coach - Oleg Romantsev (96 - Georgi Yartsev)
Stadium - Luzhniki (96,000)

MAJOR HONOURS
League Championship - (3) 1992, 1993, 1994.
League Championship (USSR) - (12) 1936, 1938, 1939, 1952, 1953, 1956, 1958, 1962, 1969, 1979, 1987, 1989.
Domestic Cup - (1) 1994.
Domestic Cup (USSR) - (10) 1938, 1939, 1946, 1947, 1950, 1958, 1963, 1965, 1971, 1992.

APPEARANCES 95

	P	Ap	(s)	Gls
Andrei AFANASYEV	D	11	(8)	1
Dmitri ALENICHEV	M	25	(2)	4
Dmitri ANANKO	D	3		
Stanislav CHERCHESOV	G	8		
Sergei CHUDIN	M	2	(3)	
Andrei IVANOV	D	6	(3)	
Valeri KECHINOV	A	14	(7)	4
Dmitri KHLESTOV	D	26		1
Andrei KONOVALOV	A	3	(8)	2
Vasili KULKOV	M	11	(1)	
Ramiz MAMEDOV	D	30		3
Valeri MASALITIN	A		(1)	
Mukhsin MUKHAMADIEV (TAD)	A	11	(4)	7
Sergei NAGORNYAK (UKR)	A	5	(5)	
Ruslan NIGMATULLIN	G	14	(1)	
Yuri NIKIFOROV	D	22		8
Viktor ONOPKO	D	29		7
Nikolai PISAREV	A	14		2
Andrei PYATNITSKI	M	10		
Sergei RODIONOV	A	4	(5)	3
Aleksandr SHIRKO	A		(1)	
Valeri SHMAROV	A	20		16
Andrei TIKHONOV	A	19	(1)	7
Yegor TITOV	M	9	(3)	1
Ilya TSYMBALAR	M	21		8
Dmitri TYAPUSHKIN (UKR)	G	8		
Valeri VELICHKO (BLS)	A		(2)	
Sergei YURAN	A	5	(3)	2

LEAGUE RESULTS 1995

Date	Opponent	H/A	Score	Scorers
01/04/95	Uralmash Yekaterinburg	H	5-1	Kechinov, Mukhamadiev 3, Tsymbalar
08/04/95	Tekstilschik Kamyshin	A	2-2	Konovalov, Onopko (p)
15/04/95	Dinamo-Gazovik Tyumen	H	4-1	Alenichev, Afanasyev, Mukhamadiev, Tsymbalar
29/04/95	KamAZ-Chally Neberezhnye Chelny	A	0-2	
09/05/95	Torpedo Moskva	A	2-1	Nikiforov (p), Khlestov
13/05/95	Spartak-Alania Vladikavkaz	H	1-2	Mamedov
20/05/95	Rostselmash Rostov	A	1-1	Mukhamadiev
24/05/95	Rotor Volgograd	H	1-2	Mukhamadiev
27/05/95	Chernomorets Novorossiisk	A	1-1	Onopko
10/06/95	Lokomotiv Moskva	H	1-2	Konovalov
17/06/95	Zhemchuzhina Sochi	A	2-1	Nikiforov (p), Shmarov
24/06/95	Dinamo Moskva	A	2-0	Mamedov, Shmarov
28/06/95	CSKA Moskva	H	3-1	Onopko, Shmarov 2
01/07/95	Lokomotiv Nizhni Novgorod	H	3-1	Onopko (p), Pisarev 2
08/07/95	Krylya Sovetov Samara	A	6-1	Nikiforov 2, Tikhonov 2, Tsymbalar, Shmarov
15/07/95	Chernomorets Novorossiisk	H	5-0	Onopko, Tikhonov 2, Shmarov 2
22/07/95	Rotor Volgograd	A	1-1	Tsymbalar
29/07/95	Zhemchuzhina Sochi	H	6-0	Alenichev, Rodionov, Tikhonov, Tsymbalar 2, Shmarov
05/08/95	Lokomotiv Moskva	A	0-1	
09/08/95	Krylya Sovetov Samara	H	5-1	Alenichev, Nikiforov (p), Rodionov 2, Tsymbalar
19/08/95	Lokomotiv Nizhni Novgorod	A	1-0	Mukhamadiev
26/08/95	Uralmash Yekaterinburg	A	0-0	
30/08/95	Dinamo Moskva	H	2-0	Tikhonov, Shmarov
09/09/95	Rostselmash Rostov	H	2-0	Nikiforov (p), Tsymbalar
17/09/95	Torpedo Moskva	H	5-0	Nikiforov 2 (1p), Shmarov 2, Yuran
21/09/95	Spartak-Alania Vladikavkaz	A	1-1	Onopko (p)
01/10/95	KamAZ-Chally Neberezhnye Chelny	H	2-0	Shmarov 2
14/10/95	CSKA Moskva	H	2-1	Alenichev, Shmarov
22/10/95	Dinamo-Gazovik Tyumen	A	6-0	Kechinov, Mamedov, Onopko (p), Titov, Tikhonov, Yuran (p)
26/10/95	Tekstilschik Kamyshin	H	4-2	Kechinov 2, Shmarov 2

SPARTAK-ALANIA VLADIKAVKAZ

CLUB DIRECTORY

Spartak-Alania Vladikavkaz (now - Alania Vladikavkaz)
Shmulevicha Str. 6
362 007 Vladikavkaz
tel - (86722) 38548/30340/35225
fax - (86722) 48806
Year of Formation - 1921
President - Batraz Bitarov
Secretary - Aleksandr Stelmakh
Coach - Valeri Gazzayev
Stadium - Spartak (30,000)

MAJOR HONOURS
League Championship - (1) 1995.

APPEARANCES 95

	P	Ap	(s)	Gls
Alan AGAYEV	D	3	(4)	1
Ali ALCHAGIROV	D	5	(2)	
Georgi BOTSIEV	M		(9)	
Aslan DATDEYEV	D	5	(13)	1
Sergei DERKACH	M	19	(7)	5
Inal DZHIOYEV	D	16	(6)	2
Aslan GOPLACHOV	A	2		
Igor GORELOV	D	4	(5)	
Sergei GORLUKOVICH	D	4	(1)	
Iosif GRISHIKASHVILI (GEO)	G	1	(2)	
Shamil ISAYEV	M		(1)	
Anatoli KANISCHEV	M	24	(2)	7
Mirdzhalol KASYMOV (UZB)	M	20	(2)	10
Mikheil KAVELASHVILI (GEO)	A	24		12
Zaur KHAPOV	G	29		
Oleg KORNIENKO	D	13	(6)	
Artur PAGAYEV	D	28		2
Zaza REVISHVILI (GEO)	M	1		
Murtaz SHELIA (GEO)	D	21	(1)	4
Tamerlan SIKOYEV	A		(3)	
Nazim SULEIMANOV (AZB)	M	8	(5)	4
Bakhva TEDEYEV	M	26	(2)	10
Omari TETRADZE	D	30		
Sergei TIMOFEYEV	D	18	(6)	2
Igor YANOVSKI	M	29		2

LEAGUE RESULTS 1995

01/04/95	Tekstilschik Kamyshin	H	2-0	Tedeyev, Yanovski
08/04/95	KamAZ-Chally Neberezhnye Chelny	A	0-1	
29/04/95	Dinamo-Gazovik Tyumen	A	4-0	Dzhioyev 2, Derkach, Pagayev
09/05/95	Rostselmash Rostov	H	4-1	Kasymov 2, Kanischev, Shelia
13/05/95	Spartak Moskva	A	2-1	Derkach, Kanischev
20/05/95	Torpedo Moskva	A	4-1	Tedeyev 2, Kavelashvili, Kanischev
24/05/95	Lokomotiv Moskva	H	0-1	
27/05/95	Zhemchuzhina Sochi	A	2-0	Timofeyev, og (Bondar)
10/06/95	Rotor Volgograd	H	3-2	Kavelashvili, Pagayev, Tedeyev
17/06/95	Chernomorets Novorossiisk	A	3-0	Derkach, Kavelashvili, Kanischev
24/06/95	Lokomotiv Nizhni Novgorod	H	3-0	Kasymov 3 (1p)
28/06/95	Krylya Sovetov Samara	A	1-0	Kavelashvili
01/07/95	Uralmash Yekaterinburg	H	4-2	Kasymov 2, Datdeyev, Kavelashvili
04/07/95	CSKA Moskva	H	2-1	Kanischev, Tedeyev
08/07/95	Dinamo Moskva	A	2-1	Kasymov, Tedeyev
15/07/95	Zhemchuzhina Sochi	H	5-0	Kavelashvili 2, Tedeyev, Shelia, Yanovski
22/07/95	Lokomotiv Moskva	A	1-4	Kavelashvili
26/07/95	Chernomorets Novorossiisk	H	3-0	Kavelashvili 2, Shelia
05/08/95	Rotor Volgograd	A	1-1	Kanischev
09/08/95	Dinamo Moskva	H	2-0	Kasymov, Timofeyev
19/08/95	Uralmash Yekaterinburg	A	1-0	Tedeyev
26/08/95	Lokomotiv Nizhni Novgorod	A	4-2	Suleimanov 2, Tedeyev, Shelia
30/08/95	Krylya Sovetov Samara	H	1-1	Suleimanov
09/09/95	Torpedo Moskva	H	0-0	
16/09/95	Rostselmash Rostov	A	1-0	Suleimanov
21/09/95	Spartak Moskva	H	1-1	Kasymov (p)
30/09/95	Tekstilschik Kamyshin	A	1-0	Kavelashvili
14/10/95	Dinamo-Gazovik Tyumen	H	4-0	Agayev, Derkach, Kavelashvili, Kanischev
21/10/95	CSKA Moskva	A	2-1	Derkach, Tedeyev
26/10/95	KamAZ-Chally Neberezhnye Chelny	H	0-0	

TEKSTILSCHIK KAMYSHIN

CLUB DIRECTORY

Tekstilschik Kamyshin
Titova Str. 9
403 850 Kamyshin
tel - (84457) 49595
fax - (84457) 46252
Year of Formation - 1958
Secretary - Yuri Shishlov
Coach - Sergei Pavlov
Stadium - Tekstilschik (17,000)

APPEARANCES 95

	P	Ap	(s)	Gls
Vitali ABRAMOV	A	19	(9)	3
Aleksandr FILIMONOV	G	30		
Yevgeni GERASIMOV	M	9	(11)	1
Yuri GUSAKOV	A		(6)	
Vladimir KURAYEV	D	19	(1)	1
Aleksandr MINAYEV	D	11	(6)	
Aleksei MOROZOV	D	26	(1)	
Oleg MOROZOV	M	29		2
Sergei NATALUSHKO	A	26	(4)	10
Viktor NAVOCHENKO	M	30		6
Konstantin PAVLYUCHENKO	M	9	(1)	1
Sergei PIMENOV	A	10	(6)	1
Sergei POLSTYANOV	A	14	(3)	5
Vyacheslav SHIRYAYEV	M		(4)	
Oleg SIZOV	D		(1)	
Oleg SOLOVYOV	A	26	(3)	
Mikhail TRUKHLOV	A	5	(11)	2
Sergei VOLGIN	M	29		5
Yevgeni YARKOV	M	13	(12)	
Valeri ZHABKO	D	25	(1)	

LEAGUE RESULTS 1995

Date	Opponent	H/A	Score	Scorers
01/04/95	Spartak-Alania Vladikavkaz	A	0-2	
08/04/95	Spartak Moskva	H	2-2	Navochenko, Trukhlov
15/04/95	Rostselmash Rostov	A	1-2	Pimenov
29/04/95	Torpedo Moskva	H	1-1	Volgin
09/05/95	CSKA Moskva	A	2-2	Abramov, Morozov O.
13/05/95	KamAZ-Chally Neberezhnye Chelny	H	1-0	Gerasimov
20/05/95	Dinamo-Gazovik Tyumen	A	3-0	Abramov, Navochenko 2
24/05/95	Lokomotiv Nizhni Novgorod	H	1-2	Volgin
27/05/95	Dinamo Moskva	A	0-0	
10/06/95	Uralmash Yekaterinburg	H	0-1	
17/06/95	Krylya Sovetov Samara	A	3-0	Navochenko, Natalushko, Polstyanov
24/06/95	Lokomotiv Moskva	H	1-1	Natalushko
28/06/95	Zhemchuzhina Sochi	A	2-0	Natalushko, Polstyanov
01/07/95	Rotor Volgograd	H	1-0	Natalushko (p)
08/07/95	Chernomorets Novorossiisk	A	2-2	Abramov, Navochenko
15/07/95	Dinamo Moskva	H	1-2	Volgin
22/07/95	Lokomotiv Nizhni Novgorod	A	1-4	Natalushko
29/07/95	Krylya Sovetov Samara	H	1-2	Polstyanov
05/08/95	Uralmash Yekaterinburg	A	0-2	
09/08/95	Zhemchuzhina Sochi	H	2-1	Morozov O., Polstyanov
19/08/95	Rotor Volgograd	A	1-3	Natalushko
26/08/95	Chernomorets Novorossiisk	H	2-0	Volgin, Kurayev
30/08/95	Lokomotiv Moskva	A	0-2	
09/09/95	CSKA Moskva	H	1-2	Polstyanov
16/09/95	KamAZ-Chally Neberezhnye Chelny	A	1-2	Natalushko (p)
23/09/95	Dinamo-Gazovik Tyumen	H	3-1	Navochenko, Natalushko, Pavlyuchenko
30/09/95	Spartak-Alania Vladikavkaz	H	0-1	
14/10/95	Torpedo Moskva	A	0-0	
21/10/95	Rostselmash Rostov	H	2-0	Natalushko, Trukhlov
26/10/95	Spartak Moskva	A	2-4	Volgin, Natalushko (p)

TORPEDO MOSKVA

CLUB DIRECTORY

Torpedo Moskva
Avtozavodskaya Str. 23
109 280 Moskva
tel - (095) 2773212/2779674
fax - (095) 2746141
Year of Formation - 1924
President - Vladimir Nosov
Secretary - Yuri Mishin
Coach - Valentin Ivanov
Stadium - Torpedo (16,500)

MAJOR HONOURS
League Championship (USSR) - (3)
1960, 1965, 1976.
Domestic Cup - (1) 1993.
Domestic Cup (USSR) - (6)
1949, 1952, 1960, 1968, 1972, 1986.

APPEARANCES 95

	P	Ap	(s)	Gls
Sergei AGASHKOV	M	30		6
Nikolai BARKALOV	M	2		
Sergei BORISOV	M		(5)	
Aleksandr BORODKIN	D	2	(5)	1
Maksim CHELTSOV	D	9	(3)	
Sergei CHUMACHENKO	M	6		2
Vladimir GRECHNEV	A		(3)	
Gennadi GRISHIN	M	14	(8)	3
Valeri KLIMOV	A	9	(5)	2
Oleg KORNAUKHOV	D	26		
Dmitri KRAMARENKO	G	2	(2)	
Vladimir LEONCHENKO	D	20	(6)	2
Marat MAKHMUTOV	D	8		
Mikhail MARKHEL (BLS)	A	9	(6)	
Mikhail MURASHOV	D	10		2
Gleb PANFYOROV	M	17	(9)	5
Vladimir PCHELNIKOV	G	28	(1)	
Dmitri PROKOPENKO	A	25	(4)	6
Aleksei SAVELYEV	A	2	(1)	
Oleg SHIRINBEKOV (TAD)	D	28		3
Sergei SHUSTIKOV	M	29		1
Yevgeni SMERTIN	M	14		3
Andrei TALALAYEV	A	2	(6)	1
Igor VOLKOV	D	9	(13)	2
Boris VOSTROSABLIN	D	24	(1)	1
Oleg ZHIVOTNIKOV	D	5	(6)	

LEAGUE RESULTS 1995

01/04/95	Dinamo-Gazovik Tyumen	H	2-1	Vostrosablin, Shirinbekov
08/04/95	CSKA Moskva	A	1-2	Chumachenko
15/04/95	KamAZ-Chally Neberezhnye Chelny	H	2-1	Panfyorov, Chumachenko
29/04/95	Tekstilschik Kamyshin	A	1-1	Agashkov
09/05/95	Spartak Moskva	H	1-2	Agashkov
13/05/95	Rostselmash Rostov	A	2-1	Prokopenko, Talalayev
20/05/95	Spartak-Alania Vladikavkaz	H	1-4	Volkov
24/05/95	Zhemchuzhina Sochi	H	3-0	Agashkov, Volkov, Shirinbekov
27/05/95	Lokomotiv Moskva	A	0-0	
10/06/95	Chernomorets Novorossiisk	H	1-0	Agashkov (p)
17/06/95	Rotor Volgograd	A	2-1	Grishin, Panfyorov
24/06/95	Uralmash Yekaterinburg	A	2-1	Panfyorov, Prokopenko
28/06/95	Dinamo Moskva	H	0-0	
01/07/95	Krylya Sovetov Samara	H	0-0	
08/07/95	Lokomotiv Nizhni Novgorod	A	3-2	Murashov, Prokopenko 2
15/07/95	Lokomotiv Moskva	H	1-0	Shirinbekov
22/07/95	Zhemchuzhina Sochi	A	1-3	Panfyorov
29/07/95	Rotor Volgograd	H	3-0	Grishin, Prokopenko, Smertin
05/08/95	Chernomorets Novorossiisk	A	1-0	Leonchenko
09/08/95	Lokomotiv Nizhni Novgorod	H	2-0	Murashov, Panfyorov
19/08/95	Dinamo Moskva	A	0-0	
26/08/95	Krylya Sovetov Samara	A	2-0	Borodkin, Prokopenko
30/08/95	Uralmash Yekaterinburg	H	3-0	Agashkov 2 (1p), Klimov
09/09/95	Spartak-Alania Vladikavkaz	A	0-0	
17/09/95	Spartak Moskva	A	0-5	
23/09/95	Rostselmash Rostov	H	1-0	Leonchenko
30/09/95	Dinamo-Gazovik Tyumen	A	3-1	Grishin, Klimov, Smertin
14/10/95	Tekstilschik Kamyshin	H	0-0	
21/10/95	KamAZ-Chally Neberezhnye Chelny	A	1-3	Smertin
26/10/95	CSKA Moskva	H	1-2	Shustikov

URALMASH YEKATERINBURG

CLUB DIRECTORY

Uralmash Yekaterinburg
Festivalnaya Str. 8
620 088 Yekaterinburg
tel - (3432) 372208
fax - (3432) 322568
Year of Formation - 1928
Secretary - Boris Yarkin
Coach - Vladimir Kalashnikov
Stadium - Central (30,000)

APPEARANCES 95

	P	Ap	(s)	Gls
Sergei ALYAPKIN	G	3	(3)	
Vyacheslav BAKHAREV	D	8	(10)	
Igor BAKHTIN	M	28		6
Aleksei BAKUNIN	D	6	(6)	
Vladimir BLUZHIN	M	27	(1)	2
Vladimir FEDOTOV	D	23		
Marat GALIMOV	D	20		
Valeri GORODOV	G	27		
Igor KHANKEYEV	M	27		8
Oleg KOKAREV	A	30		8
Konstantin LYZHIN	M	1		
Yuri MATVEYEV	A	21		9
Asan MUSTAFAYEV	D		(1)	
Aleksandr NEFEDOV	M	1		
Sergei PEREDNYA	A	16	(5)	3
Ilya RATNICHKIN	D	11	(6)	
Miroslav ROMASCHENKO (BLS)	M	17	(4)	6
Andrei SOSNITSKI (BLS)	D	1	(6)	
Vyacheslav VISHNEVSKI	M	2	(8)	
Radik YAMLIKHANOV	M	24		1
Aleksei YUSHKOV	D	22	(2)	
Sergei ZAYETS (UKR)	D	15		

LEAGUE RESULTS 1995

01/04/95	Spartak Moskva	A	1-5	Bluzhin
08/04/95	Rotor Volgograd	H	5-0	Bakhtin, Kokarev 2 (1p), Matveyev, Perednya
15/04/95	Zhemchuzhina Sochi	A	1-4	Bluzhin
29/04/95	Lokomotiv Moskva	H	1-2	Perednya
09/05/95	Lokomotiv Nizhni Novgorod	H	1-0	Kokarev (p)
13/05/95	Dinamo Moskva	A	0-3	
20/05/95	Krylya Sovetov Samara	H	0-0	
24/05/95	Dinamo-Gazovik Tyumen	A	2-0	Kokarev, Khankeyev
27/05/95	CSKA Moskva	H	1-0	Khankeyev
10/06/95	Tekstilschik Kamyshin	A	1-0	Matveyev
17/06/95	KamAZ-Chally Neberezhnye Chelny	H	0-0	
24/06/95	Torpedo Moskva	H	1-2	Kokarev
28/06/95	Chernomorets Novorossiisk	A	2-3	Bakhtin, Matveyev
01/07/95	Spartak-Alania Vladikavkaz	A	2-4	Romaschenko, Khankeyev
08/07/95	Rostselmash Rostov	H	2-0	Romaschenko, Khankeyev
15/07/95	CSKA Moskva	A	0-2	
22/07/95	Dinamo-Gazovik Tyumen	H	5-0	Kokarev (p), Matveyev, Romaschenko, Khankeyev 2
29/07/95	KamAZ-Chally Neberezhnye Chelny	A	0-4	
05/08/95	Tekstilschik Kamyshin	H	2-0	Bakhtin, Kokarev
09/08/95	Rostselmash Rostov	A	0-2	
19/08/95	Spartak-Alania Vladikavkaz	H	0-1	
26/08/95	Spartak Moskva	H	0-0	
30/08/95	Torpedo Moskva	A	0-3	
09/09/95	Krylya Sovetov Samara	A	2-3	Matveyev, Perednya
18/09/95	Dinamo Moskva	H	0-2	
23/09/95	Lokomotiv Nizhni Novgorod	A	1-3	Kokarev
30/09/95	Zhemchuzhina Sochi	H	4-3	Matveyev 2, Romaschenko, Yamlikhanov
14/10/95	Lokomotiv Moskva	A	1-0	Bakhtin
21/10/95	Chernomorets Novorossiisk	H	6-0	Bakhtin 2, Matveyev, Romaschenko 2, Khankeyev (p)
26/10/95	Rotor Volgograd	A	2-1	Matveyev, Khankeyev

ZHEMCHUZHINA SOCHI

CLUB DIRECTORY

Zhemchuzhina Sochi
Chernomorskaya Str. 3
354 076 Sochi
tel - (8622) 933650
fax - (8622) 992141
Year of Formation - 1990
Secretary - Irakli Tserekidze
Coach - Arsen Naidenov
Stadium - Central (12,500)

APPEARANCES 95

	P	Ap	(s)	Gls
Oleg AKULOV	M	2	(5)	
Timur BOGATYRYOV	A	29		10
Stanislav BONDAREV	M	23		
Gennadi BONDARUK	D	28		1
Yevgeni BURDINSKI	D	2	(2)	
Andrei CHEKUNOV	D	15	(3)	
Andrei CHUPRINA	D	9		
Stanislav DUBROVIN	A		(11)	3
Vladimir FILIMONOV	A	14	(9)	2
Aleksandr IGNATYEV	M	28		1
Yevgeni KNYAZHEV	M	7	(2)	
Yevgeni KRYUKOV	G	30		
Artur KUZNETSOV	M	6	(1)	
Sergei LEDOVSKIKH	M	9	(5)	1
Igor MAKAROV	D	22	(1)	4
Andrei NOVGORODOV	M	24	(1)	5
Sergei NOZIKOV	M	20		
Ruslan OKHTOV	M	1	(2)	
Viktor OPARENYUK	M		(1)	
Tigran PETROSYAN (ARM)	M	1	(15)	
Vyacheslav PROTSENKO	M	9	(4)	1
Aleksandr SHTYN	M		(4)	1
Ruslan SUANOV	A	12	(17)	5
Said TARBA	D	20		
Murad ZEKOKH	M	19	(3)	1

LEAGUE RESULTS 1995

Date	Opponent	H/A	Score	Scorers
01/04/95	Dinamo Moskva	H	0-1	
08/04/95	Krylya Sovetov Samara	A	0-0	
15/04/95	Uralmash Yekaterinburg	H	4-1	Bogatyryov 2, Zekokh, Makarov
29/04/95	Lokomotiv Nizhni Novgorod	A	2-2	Makarov (p), Filimonov
09/05/95	Rotor Volgograd	H	0-7	
13/05/95	Lokomotiv Moskva	A	1-1	Bogatyryov
20/05/95	Chernomorets Novorossiisk	H	2-1	Makarov (p), Suanov
24/05/95	Torpedo Moskva	A	0-3	
27/05/95	Spartak-Alania Vladikavkaz	H	0-2	
10/06/95	Rostselmash Rostov	A	4-1	Bogatyryov, Novgorodov, Suanov, Filimonov
17/06/95	Spartak Moskva	H	1-2	Protsenko
24/06/95	Dinamo-Gazovik Tyumen	A	2-1	Bogatyryov, Dubrovin
28/06/95	Tekstilschik Kamyshin	H	0-2	
01/07/95	CSKA Moskva	A	0-4	
08/07/95	KamAZ-Chally Neberezhnye Chelny	H	4-2	Bogatyryov, Novgorodov, Suanov, og (Durnev)
15/07/95	Spartak-Alania Vladikavkaz	A	0-5	
22/07/95	Torpedo Moskva	H	3-1	Bogatyryov, Dubrovin, Suanov (p)
29/07/95	Spartak Moskva	A	0-6	
05/08/95	Rostselmash Rostov	H	1-3	Dubrovin
09/08/95	Tekstilschik Kamyshin	A	1-2	Novgorodov (p)
12/08/95	KamAZ-Chally Neberezhnye Chelny	A	0-3	
19/08/95	CSKA Moskva	H	0-3	
30/08/95	Dinamo-Gazovik Tyumen	H	2-0	Bondaruk, Novgorodov (p)
07/09/95	Rotor Volgograd	A	2-1	Bogatyryov 2
16/09/95	Lokomotiv Moskva	H	0-1	
23/09/95	Chernomorets Novorossiisk	A	0-4	
30/09/95	Uralmash Yekaterinburg	A	3-4	Bogatyryov, Novgorodov (p), Shtyn
14/10/95	Lokomotiv Nizhni Novgorod	H	0-0	
22/10/95	Dinamo Moskva	A	3-4	Ignatyev, Makarov, Suanov
26/10/95	Krylya Sovetov Samara	H	1-2	Ledovskikh

PROMOTED CLUBS

SECOND DIVISION FINAL TABLE 95

		Pd	W	D	L	F	A	Pt	GD
1	**Baltika Kaliningrad**	**42**	**29**	**5**	**8**	**83**	**30**	**92**	**+53**
2	**Lada Togliatti**	**42**	**25**	**4**	**13**	**67**	**39**	**79**	**+28**
3	**Zenit Sankt-Peterburg**	**42**	**24**	**5**	**13**	**65**	**42**	**77**	**+23**
4	Zvezda Irkutsk	42	23	4	15	61	50	73	+11
5	Shinnik Yaroslavl	42	21	9	12	56	39	72	+17
6	Luch Vladivostok	42	20	6	16	51	48	66	+3
7	Neftekhimik Nizhnekamsk	42	20	5	17	55	50	65	+5
8	Lokomotiv Chita	42	20	5	17	66	67	65	-1
9	Dinamo Stavropol	42	20	3	19	66	51	63	+15
10	Sokol-PZD Saratov	42	19	4	19	62	56	61	+6
11	Chkalovets Novosibirsk	42	19	4	19	58	65	61	-7
12	Zarya Leninsk-Kuznetski	42	17	7	18	69	53	58	+16
13	Fakel Voronezh	42	17	6	19	54	48	57	+6
14	Torpedo Arzamas	42	17	6	19	60	67	57	-7
15	Uralan Elista	42	16	8	18	56	61	56	-5
16	Torpedo Volzhyki	42	16	7	19	75	74	55	+1
17	Okean Nakhodka	42	15	5	22	43	56	50	-13
18	Druzhba Maikop	42	14	8	20	51	65	50	-14
19	Saturn-1991 Sankt-Peterburg	42	14	7	21	45	62	49	-17
20	Irtysh Omsk	42	13	6	23	47	82	45	-35
21	Kolos Krasnodar	42	13	6	23	44	66	45	-22
22	Asmaral Moskva	42	8	4	30	35	98	28	-63

CLUB DIRECTORY

Baltika Kaliningrad
D. Donskogo Str. 2
235 000 Kaliningrad
tel - (0112) 216501/211920
Year of Formation - 1955
President - Kornei Shperling
Coach - Leonid Tkachenko
Stadium - Baltika (18,000)

CLUB DIRECTORY

Lada Togliatti
Revolyutsionnaya Str. 80
445 028 Togliatti
tel - (08469) 363625/352947
Year of Formation - 1969
President - Viktor Ens
Coach - Viktor Antikhovich (1996 - Viktor Tischenko)
Stadium - Torpedo (15,000)

CLUB DIRECTORY

Zenit Sankt-Peterburg
Krasnogvardeiski Blvd 4-23
190 000 Sankt Peterburg
tel - (0812) 3127934
fax - (0812) 3117798
Year of Formation - 1931
President - Stepan Krisevich
Coach - Pavel Sadyrin
Stadium - Petrovski (23,258)

MAJOR HONOURS
League Championship (USSR) - (1) 1984.
Domestic Cup (USSR) - (1) 1944.

SAN MARINO

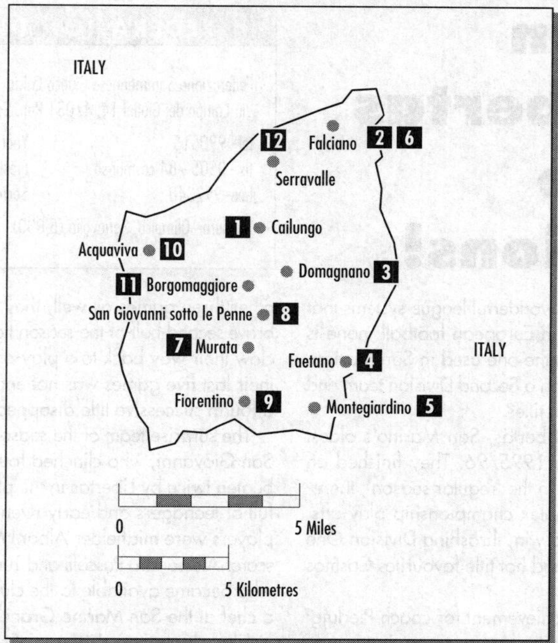

1	CAILUNGO	875	7	MURATA	878
2	COSMOS	875	8	SAN GIOVANNI	878
3	DOMAGNANO	876	9	TRE FIORI	879
4	FAETANO	876	10	VIRTUS	879
5	FIORITA	877	11	LIBERTAS	880
6	FOLGORE	877	12	JUVENES	880

BONINI TAKES NATIONAL TEAM JOB

Division Two Libertas are the champions!

FEDERATION DIRECTORY

Federazione Sammarinese Giuoco Calcio
Via Campo dei Giudei 14, 47031 Rep. San Marino

tel - 990515
tlx - 0505 284 cosmar so
fax - 992348

Year of Formation - 1931
President - Giorgio Crescentini
Secretary - Luciano Casadei

Stadium - Olimpico, Serravalle (5,000)

Of all the many weird and wonderful league systems that are employed these days in European football, none is quite so mind-boggling as the one used in San Marino. Where else, for instance, can a Second Division team end up by winning the national title?

That is precisely what Libertas, San Marino's oldest sporting institution, did in 1995/96. They finished on top of the Second Division in the 'regular season', thereby qualifying for the complex championship play-offs, which they then went on to win, thrashing Division One 'regular season' winners and hot title favourites Cosmos 4-1 in the final.

It was a phenomenal achievement for coach Pierluigi Parenti and his players. Libertas had never previously won the national title, and without their confidence-boosting spell in the Second Division, who is to say that they would have achieved their goal? But, led by star striker Teodoro Bernardini and midfield grafter Franco Agarici, they came through to triumph against all odds.

Certainly, Libertas's task was made easier by the non-appearance in the play-offs of Tre Fiori, champions in each of the previous three seasons. Their season was effectively over at an early stage when the San Marino FA punished them for breaking the rules over the engagement of an Italian player. The penalty was four matches 'gifted' to their opponents as a statutory 3-0 victory. As Tre Fiori had lost their other three games as well, they were in real trouble. A brave second-half-of-the-season fightback almost saw them claw their way back to a play-off place, but five wins in their last five games was not enough, and the dream of a fourth successive title disappeared.

The surprise team of the season were newly-promoted San Giovanni, who clinched fourth place but were then beaten twice by Libertas in the play-offs. A team packed full of teenagers and early-twentysomethings, their best players were midfielder Albani Matteo, the league's top scorer Alessandro Pascotti and Turkish striker Yasar Yazici, who became available to the club after landing a job as a chef at the San Marino Grand Hotel.

Like champions Libertas, San Giovanni could not

LEAGUE CHAMPIONSHIP RESULTS 95/96

		1	2	3	4	5	6	7	8	9	10
1	Cailungo		1-0	1-3	1-2	1-1	0-1	1-3	0-2	1-0	1-1
2	Cosmos	1-1		1-0	4-1	3-1	0-3	2-1	1-1	3-0	2-1
3	Domagnano	2-2	1-0		2-0	1-0	1-2	1-1	2-2	3-0	0-1
4	Faetano	2-1	0-1	0-4		0-1	0-1	0-3	2-5	0-1	8-1
5	Fiorita	1-1	0-2	3-1	1-0		2-2	2-1	4-1	1-1	1-0
6	Folgore	2-4	1-3	0-0	1-0	1-1		1-1	0-0	0-1	3-1
7	Murata	0-0	4-1	0-0	4-0	1-0	1-1		0-0	4-2	1-1
8	San Giovanni	2-1	1-4	0-1	2-0	1-0	1-0	3-2		1-3	2-2
9	Tre Fiori	4-1	2-0	1-0	5-0	0-2	0-3	0-1	2-2		0-3
10	Virtus	5-2	1-1	2-0	1-1	0-2	2-0	0-1	0-0	0-1	

NATIONAL TEAM RESULTS 95/96

06/09/95	Greece (ECQ)	H	Serravalle	0-4	
11/10/95	Faroe Islands (ECQ)	H	Serravalle	1-3	Valentini M. (52)
15/11/95	Scotland (ECQ)	A	Glasgow	0-5	
02/06/96	Wales (WCQ)	H	Serravalle	0-5	

TOP SCORERS

(excluding Play-offs)

11	Alessandro PANCOTTI (San Giovanni)
10	Andrea BERNARDI (Virtus)
	Yasar YAZICI (San Giovanni)

LEAGUE CHAMPIONSHIP FINAL TABLE 95/96

			Home					Away					Total						
		Pd	W	D	L	F	A	W	D	L	F	A	W	D	L	F	A	Pt	GD
1	Cosmos	18	6	2	1	17	9	4	1	4	12	11	10	3	5	29	20	33	+9
2	Murata	18	4	5	0	15	5	4	2	3	14	10	8	7	3	29	15	31	+14
3	Fiorita	18	5	3	1	15	9	3	2	4	8	8	8	5	5	23	17	29	+6
4	San Giovanni	18	5	1	3	13	13	2	6	1	13	11	7	7	4	26	24	28	+2
5	Folgore	18	2	4	3	9	11	5	2	2	13	7	7	6	5	22	18	27	+4
6	Domagnano	18	4	3	2	13	8	3	2	4	9	8	7	5	6	22	16	26	+6
7	Tre Fiori	18	4	1	4	14	12	4	1	4	9	13	8	2	8	23	25	26	-2
8	Virtus	18	3	3	3	11	8	2	3	4	11	18	5	6	7	22	26	21	-4
9	Cailungo	18	2	2	5	7	13	1	4	4	13	19	3	6	9	20	32	15	-12
10	Faetano	18	2	0	7	12	18	1	1	7	4	21	3	1	14	16	39	10	-23

N.B. The top four teams play off for the title together with the champions of the Second Division

CHAMPIONSHIP PLAY-OFFS

FIRST ROUND
Libertas 1, San Giovanni 0
Murata 0, Fiorita 2
San Giovanni 2, Murata 0
(Murata eliminated)

SECOND ROUND
Libertas 2, Fiorita 2
(aet; 6-7 on pens.)
Libertas 3, San Giovanni 0
(San Giovanni eliminated)

SEMI-FINALS
Cosmos 1, Fiorita 0
Libertas 4, Fiorita 3 (aet)
(Fiorita eliminated)

FINAL
LIBERTAS 4 Agarici (22), Sensolo (73og), Bernardini (76), Betti (84)
COSMOS 1 Marani (52)

sustain their form in the end-of-season Coppa Titano, failing even to reach the quarter-finals. Cosmos made it through to another final, but again their luck was out as Domagnano, placed just sixth in the league, won the Cup for the fifth time with a 2-0 victory.

There was a more conventional look to the knock-out stages of the Cup in 1995/96 (no second chances for beaten teams), and this more rational outlook has been carried forward to the league in 96/97. Libertas's exploit will not be repeated, as there are now, instead of a First and Second Division, two eight-team groups of equal standing. The play-offs remain, however, with the top three teams from each group earning the right to battle it out for the title.

DOMESTIC CUP RESULTS

FIRST ROUND

Group A
Folgore 2, Tre Fiori 1
Murata 4, Dogana 1
Dogana 1, Folgore 3
Tre Fiori 1, Murata 2
Dogana 3, Tre Fiori 0
Folgore 2, Murata 2
(Murata and Folgore qualify for quarter-finals)

Group B
Juvenes 0, Tre Penne 1
Faetano 2, Pennarossa 0
Pennarossa 1, Juvenes 1
Tre Penne 2, Faetano 1
Tre Penne 1, Pennarossa 0
Faetano 6, Juvenes 0
(Tre Penne and Faetano qualify for quarter-finals)

Group C
Cosmos 4, Montevito 1
San Giovanni 0, Fiorita 2
Fiorita 1, Cosmos 1
Montevito 2, San Giovanni 0
Fiorita 4, Montevito 2
Cosmos 1, San Giovanni 1
(Fiorita and Cosmos qualify for quarter-finals)

Group D
Domagnano 2, Libertas 2
Cailungo 0, Virtus 2
Libertas 1, Cailungo 2
Virtus 1, Domagnano 1
Libertas 0, Virtus 6
Cailungo 0, Domagnano 5
(Virtus and Domagnano qualify for quarter-finals)

QUARTER-FINALS
Fiorita 4, Faetano 2
Murata 2, Domagnana 7
Virtus 0, Cosmos 3
Tre Penne 1, Folgore 3

SEMI-FINALS
Fiorita 2, Domagnana 7
Cosmos 1, Folgore 0

FINAL
DOMAGNANO 2 Zucchi (36), Mularoni (73)
COSMOS 0

The strange domestic goings-on are of only marginal concern to new San Marino national team coach Massimo Bonini. He will continue to select players belonging to lowly-ranked clubs in the Italian league pyramid rather than fish out players from the San Marino league. He will, however, continue to organise the regular weekly training sessions which he instigated soon after taking over the job in January.

The appointment of San Marino's most illustrious footballer was on the cards following the whitewash suffered by Giorgio Leoni's side in the European Championship qualifiers. Even the home encounter with fellow small fry the Faroe Isles ended in defeat. The final count was ten matches, ten defeats, two goals for, 36 against.

Despite the arrival of Bonini, a similar stream of heavy defeats beckons in the World Cup qualifiers. The 0-5 home defeat to Wales in June - Bonini's first match in charge - showed that nothing much had changed.

NATIONAL TEAM APPEARANCES 95/96

Coach - Giorgio LEONI; Massimo BONINI	GRE	FAR	SCO	WAL	Cps	Gls
Stefano MUCCIOLI (19/01/68) - Valconca (ITA)	G	G	G	G	6	-
Luca GOBBI (12/06/71) - Juvenes (ITA)	D			D	23	-
William GUERRA (24/02/68) - Juvenes (ITA)	D	D	D71	D	28	-
Mirco GENNARI (29/03/66) - Juvenes (ITA)	D	D	D		21	-
Ivan MATTEONI (21/08/70) - Juvenes (ITA)	D	D75	M		20	-
Marco MAZZA (01/07/63) - unattached	M	M	M82	M	26	-
Pier Angelo MANZAROLI (25/03/69) - San Marino (ITA)	M89	M57	M	M	23	-
Pier Domenico DELLA VALLE (04/05/70) - Juvenes (ITA)	M		s82		12	1
Fabio FRANCINI (06/03/69) - Bellaria Igea Marina (ITA)	M76	M	M		25	-
Marco MULARONI (30/11/67) - Juvenes (ITA)	A79	s57	A52	A46	14	-
Nicola BACCIOCCHI (16/12/71) - Santarcangiolese (ITA)	A	A	A		22	1
Paolo MONTAGNA (28/05/76) - Juvenes (ITA)	s79	A81	s71	A	6	-
Claudio CANTI (24/01/59) - Juvenes (ITA)	s76		s52		21	-
Claudio PEVERANI (07/05/64) - Juvenes (ITA)	s89	s75		s75	4	-
Vittorio VALENTINI (09/10/73) - Ponte Verucchio (ITA)		D		s46	2	-
Mauro VALENTINI (27/07/73) - Rimini (ITA)		D	D	D	16	1
Bryan GASPERONI (26/09/74) - San Marino (ITA)		s81			4	-
Federico MORONI (08/09/76) - Juvenes (ITA)			D		1	-
Leone GASPERONI (03/09/74) - CBR Pietracuta (ITA)				D	1	-
Waldes PASOLINI (03/06/62) - Ponte Verucchio (ITA)				M71	14	1
Alessandro CASADEI (23/12/72) - Secchiaro (ITA)				M75	1	-
Riccardo MUCCIOLI (27/08/74) - Bagnacavallo (ITA)				s71	1	-

INTERNATIONAL HONOURS

None

PLAYERS OF THE SEASON

TEODORO BERNARDINI

A 20-year attachment to his local club Libertas finally ended in glory for 30-year-old striker Teodoro Bernardini. Although he had helped the club to three domestic Cup successes, plus two Super Cup wins, he had never won the championship... until Libertas's bizarre rags-to-riches adventure in 1995/96. Bernardini more than played his part, scoring 15 goals in the Second Division and then firing another in the play-off final with Cosmos. He is the top scorer of all-time in the San Marino First Division with over 100 goals to his credit, and he also holds the record goals tally for a single season with 23 in 1987/88. Work and family commitments have always prevented him from finding time to play and train with the San Marino national team.

FEDERICO GASPERONI

With veteran San Marino goalkeeper Pierluigi Benedettini having decided to hang up his gloves and devote himself to his public transport business, a vacancy has arisen for one of the busiest jobs in football. BenedeTtini's long-time understudy, 28-year-old Stefano Muccioli, took over during the 1995/96 season, but a more long-term replacement is 20-year-old Federico Gasperoni, who plays alongside national team striker Nicola Bacciocchi for Italian Sixth Division club Santarcangiolese and has already represented San Marino at every level bar the senior team. Massimo Bonini has voiced his appreciation of the agile young 'keeper, and Gasperoni's full international début can only be a matter of time.

CAILUNGO

CLUB DIRECTORY

Società Polisportiva Cailungo
Via cà del Lunghi 11
47031 Cailungo
tel - 902413
Year of Formation - 1974
President - Flavio Gasperoni
Secretary - Luigi Forcellini
Coach - Gilberto Rossi
Stadium - Fonte dell' Ovo (500)

SQUAD 95/96

	P
Danilo ALBANI	D
Guerrino ALBANI	M
Omar BENEDETTINI	M
Marco BERARDI	G
Paolo BERARDI	M
Roberto CASADEI	A
Roberto CEVOLI	D
Emilio DI STASIO	D
Daniele FORCELLINI	D
Fabrizio FRANCIONI	M
Domenico GASPERONI	G
Danilo GRASSI	D
Luciano MULARONI	D
Marco MULARONI	D
Giampiero PASQUALI	M
Tomas ROMANI	A
Gianluca STEFANELLI	M
Gabriele VENTURINI	D

LEAGUE RESULTS 1995/96

30/09/95	Fiorita	A	1-1
07/10/95	Tre Fiori	H	1-0
14/10/95	Cosmos	A	1-1
21/10/95	Faetano	H	1-2
28/10/95	Murata	A	0-0
04/11/95	Virtus	H	1-1
11/11/95	Folgore	A	4-2
18/11/95	Domagnano	A	2-2
25/11/95	San Giovanni	H	0-2
02/12/95	Fiorita	H	1-1
09/12/95	Tre Fiori	A	1-4
10/02/96	Cosmos	H	1-0
17/02/96	Faetano	A	1-2
24/02/96	Murata	H	1-3
02/03/96	Virtus	A	2-5
09/03/96	Folgore	H	0-1
16/03/96	Domagnano	H	1-3
23/03/96	San Giovanni	A	1-2

COSMOS

CLUB DIRECTORY

Società Polisportiva Cosmos
Strada del Bargello 36
47031 Falciano
Year of Formation - 1979
President - Adelmiro Bartolini
Secretary - Samuele Colaa
Coach - Dante Maiani
Stadium - Dogana (500)

MAJOR HONOURS

Domestic Cup - (3) 1980, 1981, 1995.

SQUAD 95/96

	P
Simone AMICI	M
Davide BRASCHI	D
Cristian COLONNA	D
Claudio CORBELLI	M
Luca DELLA BALDA	M
Luciano FUCCHI	G
Giuliano GIANNINI	D
Franco LEARDINI	D
Massimo MACCIO	M
Pierangelo MANZAROLI	M
Mauro MARANI	D
Bruno MUCCIOLI	M
Stefano MUCCIOLI	G
Diego PEDINI	M
Angelo PINTO	A
Giovanni PODAVINI	A
Roberto RASCHI	A
Giuliano RONCI	D
Cristian SELVA	M
Angelo SENSOLO	D

LEAGUE RESULTS 1995/96

30/09/95	Virtus	H	2-1
07/10/95	Folgore	A	3-1
14/10/95	Cailungo	H	1-1
21/10/95	Domagnano	A	0-1
28/10/95	Tre Fiori (w/o)	H	3-0
04/11/95	San Giovanni	A	4-1
11/11/95	Fiorita	H	3-1
18/11/95	Faetano	A	1-0
25/11/95	Murata	H	2-1
02/12/95	Virtus	A	1-1
09/12/95	Folgore	H	0-3
10/02/96	Cailungo	A	0-1
17/02/96	Domagnano	H	1-0
24/02/96	Tre Fiori	A	0-2
02/03/96	San Giovanni	H	1-1
09/03/96	Fiorita	A	2-0
16/03/96	Faetano	H	4-1
23/03/96	Murata	A	1-4

DOMAGNANO

CLUB DIRECTORY

Società Polisportiva Domagnano
Via Cà Giannino 1
47031 Domagnano
Year of Formation - 1966
President - Marino Moretti
Secretary - Filippo Guidi
Coach - Marino Marani
Stadium - Domagnano (500)

MAJOR HONOURS
League Championship - (1) 1989.
Domestic Cup - (4) 1972, 1988, 1990, 1992.

SQUAD 95/96

	P
Davide BACCIOCCHI	A
Fabio BACCIOCCHI	A
Gabriele BARTOLETTI	M
Pierluigi BENEDETTINI	G
Carlo CASADEI	G
Maurizio CONTI	G
Daniele DONATI	D
Marino GASPERONI	G
Paolo GIACOBBI	A
Bruno MONTANUCCI	M
Ivan PALMIERI	D
Loris PALMIERI	M
Alessandro PASOLINI	M
Massimo ROSSI	D
Pier Marino SARTI	D
Mauro VALENTINI	D
Marco VOLPINARI	M
Gian Luigi ZANOTTI	D
Paolo ZONZINI	D
Silvano ZONZINI	M
Enea ZUCCHI	A

LEAGUE RESULTS 1995/96

30/09/95	Faetano	A	4-0
07/10/95	Murata	H	1-1
14/10/95	Fiorita	A	1-3
21/10/95	Cosmos	H	1-0
28/10/95	Virtus	A	0-2
04/11/95	Tre Fiori (w/o)	H	3-0
11/11/95	San Giovanni	A	1-0
18/11/95	Cailungo	H	2-2
25/11/95	Folgore	A	0-0
02/12/95	Faetano	H	2-0
09/12/95	Murata	A	0-0
10/02/96	Fiorita	H	1-0
17/02/96	Cosmos	A	0-1
24/02/96	Virtus	H	0-1
02/03/96	Tre Fiori	A	0-1
09/03/96	San Giovanni	H	2-2
16/03/96	Cailungo	A	3-1
23/03/96	Folgore	H	1-2

FAETANO

CLUB DIRECTORY

Società Calcio Faetano
Piazza del Massaro 2
47031 Faetano
tel - 996057
Year of Formation - 1962
President - Graziano Bartolini
Secretary - Riccardo Gasperoni
Coach - Fabio Gasperoni
Stadium - Faetano (500)

MAJOR HONOURS
League Championship - (2) 1986, 1991.
Domestic Cup - (2) 1993, 1994.

SQUAD 95/96

	P
Oscar BEDETTI	G
Alessandro CASADEI	A
Fulvio CASADEI	D
Pier Marino CECCOLI	G
Massimo CENCI	G
Pier Marino DELLA VALLE	M
Stefano DE LUIGI	A
Pier Paolo DONATI	M
Riccardo GASPERONI	M
Giancarlo GIANCECCHI	A
Giuliano GIANNI	M
Massimiliano GIANNI	A
Andrea GIORGETTI	A
Mirco MULARONI	D
Denis RICCARDI	A
Luca RICCARDI	M
Silvio RICCARDI	D
Angelo RIGHI	M
Luigi RINALDI	D
Vittorio VALENTINI	D
Giuseppe ZANOTTI	M

LEAGUE RESULTS 1995/96

30/09/95	Domagnano	H	0-4
07/10/95	Virtus	A	1-1
14/10/95	Folgore	H	0-1
21/10/95	Cailungo	A	2-1
28/10/95	San Giovanni	A	0-2
04/11/95	Fiorita	H	0-1
11/11/95	Murata	A	0-4
18/11/95	Cosmos	H	0-1
25/11/95	Tre Fiori	H	0-1
02/12/95	Domagnano	A	0-2
09/12/95	Virtus	H	8-1
10/02/96	Folgore	A	0-1
17/02/96	Cailungo	H	2-1
24/02/96	San Giovanni	H	2-5
02/03/96	Fiorita	A	0-1
09/03/96	Murata	H	0-3
16/03/96	Cosmos	A	1-4
23/03/96	Tre Fiori	A	0-5

FIORITA

CLUB DIRECTORY

Società Polisportiva La Fiorita
Via del Dragone 17
47031 Montegiardino
tel - 996202
Year of Formation - 1967
President - Luigi Gasperoni
Secretary - Paolo Crescentini
Coach - Bruno Albani
Stadium - Montegiardino (200)

MAJOR HONOURS
League Championship - (2) 1987, 1990.
Domestic Cup - (1) 1986.

SQUAD 95/96

	P
Fabrizio ALBANI	M
Massimo BEDETTI	M
Claudio BERTONI	G
Francesco CESARINI	A
Stefano COLOMBINI	D
Igor CRESCENTINI	A
Marco CRESCENTINI	M
Paolo CRESCENTINI	M
Orazio DELLA VALLE	D
Marcello FABBI	M
Ivan GASPERONI	G
Liviero LIDINI	D
Manuel MATTEONI	M
Massimo MECA	G
Gian Luca MENICUCCI	A
Daniele MORETTI	M
Danilo PASOLINI	M
Pier Marino PIERGIOVANNI	D
Claudio RENZETTI	A
Marco RIGHI	D
Fabrizio ZANOTTI	A
Paolo ZANOTTI	M
Stefano ZANOTTI	A

LEAGUE RESULTS 1995/96

30/09/95	Cailungo	H	1-1
07/10/95	San Giovanni	A	0-1
14/10/95	Domagnano	H	3-1
21/10/95	Tre Fiori	A	2-0
28/10/95	Folgore	H	2-2
04/11/95	Faetano	A	1-0
11/11/95	Cosmos	A	1-3
18/11/95	Murata	H	2-1
25/11/95	Virtus	H	1-0
02/12/95	Cailungo	A	1-1
09/12/95	San Giovanni	H	4-1
10/02/96	Domagnano	A	0-1
17/02/96	Tre Fiori	H	1-1
24/02/96	Folgore	A	1-1
02/03/96	Faetano	H	1-0
09/03/96	Cosmos	H	0-2
16/03/96	Murata	A	0-1
23/03/96	Virtus	A	2-0

FOLGORE

CLUB DIRECTORY

Società Sportiva Folgore Falciano
Strada La Zanetta 10
47031 Falciano
tel - 908088
Year of Formation - 1972
President - Svenio Piastra
Secretary - Francesco Prosperini
Coach - Sereno Uraldi
Stadium - Falciano (500)

SQUAD 95/96

	P
Natalino BERARDI	D
Cristian BERNARDINI	A
Augusto BIANCHI	D
Simone BIANCHI	A
Angelo BOLOGNA	A
Giacomo CASADEI	M
Alessandro DELLA VALLE	M
Francesco DONNINI	D
Ferdinando GASPERONI	M
Giuseppe GIOVANARDI	G
Matteo MAZZA	D
Stefano PALLADINI	M
Fabrizio PELLICCIONI	D
Federico PELLICCIONI	M
Mario PELLICCIONI	G
Enrico PROSPERINI	A
Gianfranco PROSPERINI	D
Elio ZAFFERANI	M
Angelo ZANOTTI	A

LEAGUE RESULTS 1995/96

30/09/95	Tre Fiori (w/o)	A	3-0
07/10/95	Cosmos	H	1-3
14/10/95	Faetano	A	1-0
21/10/95	San Giovanni	H	0-0
28/10/95	Fiorita	A	2-2
04/11/95	Murata	H	1-1
11/11/95	Cailungo	H	2-4
18/11/95	Virtus	A	0-2
25/11/95	Domagnano	H	0-0
02/12/95	Tre Fiori	H	0-1
09/12/95	Cosmos	A	3-0
10/02/96	Faetano	H	1-0
17/02/96	San Giovanni	A	0-1
24/02/96	Fiorita	H	1-1
02/03/96	Murata	A	1-1
09/03/96	Cailungo	A	1-0
16/03/96	Virtus	H	3-1
23/03/96	Domagnano	A	2-1

MURATA

CLUB DIRECTORY

Società Sportiva Murata
Via del Serrone
47031 Murata
tel - 992311
Year of Formation - 1966
President - Libero Casadei
Secretary - Giancarlo Simoncini
Coach - Domenico Pedini
Stadium - Acquaviva (500)

SQUAD 95/96

	P
Gian Luca AMICI	G
Andrea BATTISTINI	M
Pierangelo BATTISTINI	D
Manuel BERARDI	M
William BUGLI	A
Stefano CAPICCHIONI	A
Gilberto GASPERONI	A
Lorenzo GIARDI	A
Gerardo LETTONI	M
Giorgio MIGANI	A
Alan MULARONI	A
Marco PELLICCIONI	G
Michele PELLICCIONI	D
Stefano PENSERINI	M
Luigi PROTTI	M
Marco RAGINI	G
Michele SERRA	M
Serafino TERENZI	D
Jader VAGNINI	D

LEAGUE RESULTS 1995/96

30/09/95	San Giovanni	H	0-0
07/10/95	Domagnano	A	1-1
14/10/95	Tre Fiori	A	1-0
21/10/95	Virtus	H	1-1
28/10/95	Cailungo	H	0-0
04/11/95	Folgore	A	1-1
11/11/95	Faetano	H	4-0
18/11/95	Fiorita	A	1-2
25/11/95	Cosmos	A	1-2
02/12/95	San Giovanni	A	2-3
09/12/95	Domagnano	H	0-0
10/02/96	Tre Fiori	H	4-2
17/02/96	Virtus	A	1-0
24/02/96	Cailungo	A	3-1
02/03/96	Folgore	H	1-1
09/03/96	Faetano	A	3-0
16/03/96	Fiorita	H	1-0
23/03/96	Cosmos	H	4-1

SAN GIOVANNI

CLUB DIRECTORY

Società Sportiva San Giovanni
Strada di San Gianno
47031 San Giovanni sotto le Penne
tel - 906715
Year of Formation - 1948
President - Valerio Zanotti
Secretary - Walter Santi
Coach - Carlo Ricci
Stadium - Chiesanuova (500)

SQUAD 95/96

	P
Giorgio GATA	M
Matteo ALBANI	D
Pier Angelo AMATI	M
Ettore ARGENZIANO	D
Alex BACIOCCHI	D
Danilo CIACCI	D
Daniele FAETANINI	A
Giovanni GASPERONI	A
Massimiliano GERI	A
Claudio GUERRA	G
Nicola MAMI	D
Alessandro PANCOTTI	A
Riccardo PANCOTTI	M
Stefano RIDOLFI	M
Angelo ROSSI	M
Massimo TAMAGNINI	M
Nicola TIRAFERI	D
Angelo VANDI	G
Luciano VILLANI	D
Yasar YAZICI (TUR)	A

LEAGUE RESULTS 1995/96

30/09/95	Murata	A	0-0
07/10/95	Fiorita	H	1-0
14/10/95	Virtus	A	0-0
21/10/95	Folgore	A	0-0
28/10/95	Faetano	H	2-0
04/11/95	Cosmos	H	1-4
11/11/95	Domagnano	H	0-1
18/11/95	Tre Fiori	A	2-2
25/11/95	Cailungo	A	2-0
02/12/95	Murata	H	3-2
09/12/95	Fiorita	A	1-4
10/02/96	Virtus	H	2-2
17/02/96	Folgore	H	1-0
24/02/96	Faetano	H	5-2
02/03/96	Cosmos	A	1-1
09/03/96	Domagnano	A	2-2
16/03/96	Tre Fiori	H	1-3
23/03/96	Cailungo	H	2-1

TRE FIORI

CLUB DIRECTORY

Società Polisportiva Tre Fiori
Via 21 Settembre 93
47031 Fiorentino
tel - 878026
Year of Formation - 1949
President - Marino Casali
Secretary - Giuliano Moraccini
Coach - Duilio Felici
Stadium - Fiorentino (2,000)

MAJOR HONOURS
League Championship - (4)
1988, 1993, 1994, 1995.
Domestic Cup - (5)
1966, 1971, 1974, 1975, 1985.

SQUAD 95/96

	P
Diego BALDACCI	M
Loris BALDACCI	D
Gianluca BORGAGNI	D
Gabriele CAPICCHIONI	M
Giovanni CHIARUZZI	D
Massimiliano DE CARLI	M
Stefano DE LUIGI	A
Denis FABBRI	A
Michele FRANCIONI	D
Maurizio GASPERONI	D
Gianluca GUALTIERI	A
Fabio GUIDI	M
Michele LEONI	D
Andrea MARIOTTI	G
Massimo MARIOTTI	M
Ivan MATTEONI	M
Jader MATTEONI	M
Danilo MUSCIONI	M
Luigi NICOLINI	A
Matteo QUADRONI	G
Andrea UGOLINI	A
Matteo UGOLINI	M
Denis VENERUCCI	G
Matteo ZAVOLI	D

LEAGUE RESULTS 1995/96

30/09/95	Folgore (w/o)	H	0-3
07/10/95	Cailungo	A	0-1
14/10/95	Murata	H	0-1
21/10/95	Fiorita	H	0-2
28/10/95	Cosmos (w/o)	A	0-3
04/11/95	Domagnano (w/o)	A	0-3
11/11/95	Virtus (w/o)	H	0-3
18/11/95	San Giovanni	H	2-2
25/11/95	Faetano	A	1-0
02/12/95	Folgore	A	1-0
09/12/95	Cailungo	H	4-1
10/02/96	Murata	A	2-4
17/02/96	Fiorita	A	1-1
24/02/96	Cosmos	H	2-0
02/03/96	Domagnano	H	1-0
09/03/96	Virtus	A	1-0
16/03/96	San Giovanni	A	3-1
23/03/96	Faetano	H	5-0

VIRTUS

CLUB DIRECTORY

Società Sportiva Virtus
Via Il Gualdaria
47031 Acquaviva
tel - 999068
Year of Formation - 1964
President - Pietro Rossi
Secretary - Corrado Selva
Coach - Mario Muscioni
Stadium - Acquaviva (500)

SQUAD 95/96

	P
Andrea BERNARDI	A
Davide BOLLINI	D
Cristian BUCCI	M
Gabriele BUCCI	M
Alessandro CARDELLI	G
Corrado CASADEI	D
Leonardo CESARINI	M
Nevio DE ANGELIS	D
Irish DE BIAGI	A
Emanuele FRANCIONI	D
Fabrizio FRANCIONI	D
Roberto FRANCIONI	D
Nicola GIACOBBI	A
Tiziano GIACOBBI	M
Nevio GIANNOTTI	A
Marco GUIDI	D
Simone GUIDI	D
Pier Luigi LIVIDINI	D
Mauro MANCINI	D
Silvano MULARONI	G
Raffaele PIATTELLI	D
Wladimiro SERRA	A
Evert ZAVOLI	M

LEAGUE RESULTS 1995/96

30/09/95	Cosmos	A	1-2
07/10/95	Faetano	H	1-1
14/10/95	San Giovanni	H	0-0
21/10/95	Murata	A	1-1
28/10/95	Domagnano	H	2-0
04/11/95	Cailungo	A	1-1
11/11/95	Tre Fiori (w/o)	A	3-0
18/11/95	Folgore	H	2-0
25/11/95	Fiorita	A	0-1
02/12/95	Cosmos	H	1-1
09/12/95	Faetano	A	1-8
10/02/96	San Giovanni	A	2-2
17/02/96	Murata	H	0-1
24/02/96	Domagnano	A	1-0
02/03/96	Cailungo	H	5-2
09/03/96	Tre Fiori	H	0-1
16/03/96	Folgore	A	1-3
23/03/96	Fiorita	H	0-2

PROMOTED CLUBS

SECOND DIVISION FINAL TABLE 95/96

		Pd	W	D	L	F	A	Pt	GD
1	**Libertas**	**15**	**9**	**4**	**2**	**35**	**12**	**31**	**+23**
2	**Juvenes**	**15**	**7**	**5**	**3**	**31**	**19**	**26**	**+12**
3	Montevito	15	6	5	4	18	17	23	+1
4	Dogana	15	1	10	4	9	19	13	-10
5	Pennarossa	15	1	9	5	13	27	12	-14
6	Tre Penne	15	2	5	8	11	23	11	-12

CLUB DIRECTORY

Società Polisportiva Libertas
Via 28 Luglio 1/B
47031 Borgomaggiore
tel - 906472
Year of Formation - 1928
President - Paride Andreoli
Secretary - Primo Toccaceli
Coach - Pier Luigi Parenti
Stadium - Fonte dell'Ovo (500)

MAJOR HONOURS
League Championship - (1) 1996.
Domestic Cup - (9) 1937, 1950, 1954, 1958, 1959, 1961, 1987, 1989, 1991.

CLUB DIRECTORY

Società Sportiva Juvenes
Via E. Balducci
47031 Serravalle
tel - 900689/900161
Year of Formation - 1953
President - Bruno Passerini
Secretary - Luigi Zafferani
Coach - Emanuele Vannucci
Stadium - Domagnano (500)

MAJOR HONOURS
Domestic Cup - (5)
1965, 1968, 1976, 1978, 1984.

SCOTLAND

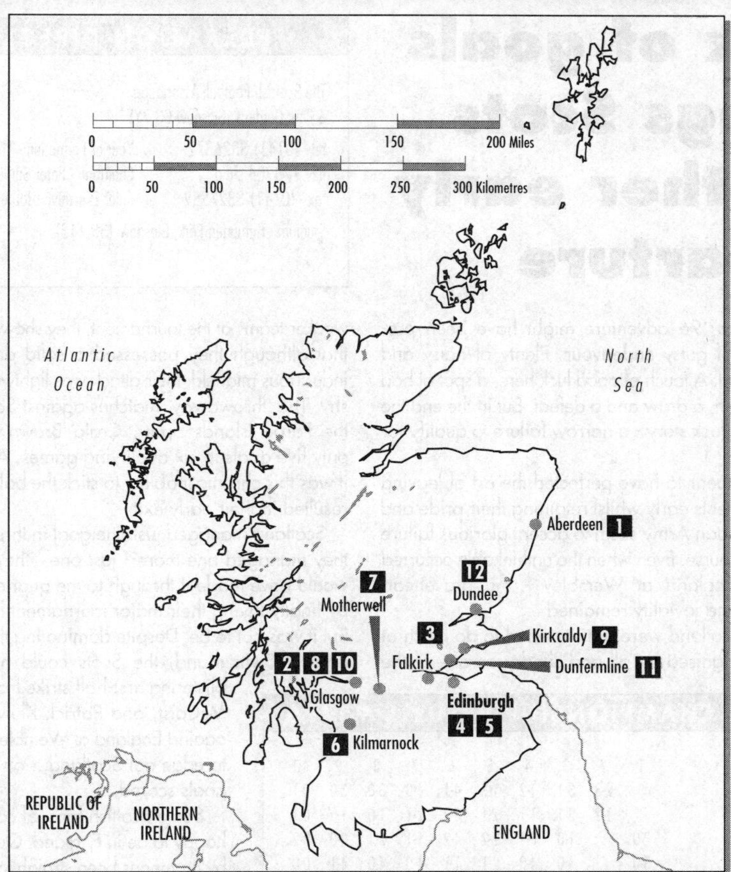

1	ABERDEEN	888	7	MOTHERWELL	894
2	CELTIC	889	8	PARTICK THISTLE	895
3	FALKIRK	890	9	RAITH ROVERS	896
4	HEART OF MIDLOTHIAN	891	10	RANGERS	897
5	HIBERNIAN	892	11	DUNFERMLINE ATHLETIC	898
6	KILMARNOCK	893	12	DUNDEE UNITED	898

GASCOIGNE INSPIRES RANGERS 'DOUBLE'

Lack of goals brings Scots another early departure

FEDERATION DIRECTORY

The Scottish Football Association
6 Park Gardens, Glasgow G3 7YF

tel - (0141) 3326372
tlx - 778904 sfa g
fax - (0141) 3327559

Year of Formation - 1873
Chairman - Peter Gardiner
Chief Executive - James Farry

Stadium - Hampden Park, Glasgow (38,113)

Scotland's Euro '96 adventure might have been pre-scripted. Lots of gutsy endeavour. Plenty of noisy and colourful support. A touch of good luck here, a spot of bad luck there. A win, a draw and a defeat. But in the end the same old hard-luck story - a narrow failure to qualify for the next round.

Scotland appear to have perfected the art of leaving major tournaments early whilst retaining their pride and dignity. The Tartan Army seem to accept glorious failure as par for the course. Even when the unthinkable occurred - defeat by England at Wembley - the braveheart camaraderie and joviality remained.

Certainly, Scotland were not expected to do much at Euro '96. Recognised by all and sundry as one of the weaker teams at the tournament, they showed in qualifying that although they possessed a solid defence and an industrious midfield, their attack was lightweight and goal-shy. The 'throwaway' matches against San Marino and the Faroe Islands apart, Craig Brown's team scored only five goals in six qualifying games. And in England it was this chronic inability to stick the ball in the net that resulted in their early exit.

Scotland managed just one goal in three games. Had they managed one more - just one - they, not Holland, would have made it through to the quarter-finals, thereby finally laying their major tournament hoodoo to rest. But it was not to be. Despite dominating their final game against Switzerland, the Scots could not add to the blistering first-half strike from veteran Ally McCoist, and Patrick Kluivert's late goal against England at Wembley was sufficient to edge out Scotland... on the number of goals scored.

Some Scottish fans, of course, were just happy to be in England. Qualification had by no means been straightforward, but two crucial 1-0 home wins against Greece and Finland ensured that the Scots did not miss out on the party 'down south' as they had 30 years earlier. It had been feared before the tournament that Scotland would put too much into the match with the Auld Enemy at Wembley, to the detriment of their other two fixtures. In the event, that was the only game they lost, Scottish dreams dying within the space of 60 seconds as skipper Gary McAllister's penalty miss was quickly followed by Paul Gascoigne's wonder goal at the other end.

That Gascoigne should be the player to sink Scotland was particularly ironic, as he had just completed an excellent first season

LEAGUE CHAMPIONSHIP RESULTS 95/96

		1	2	3	4	5	6	7	8	9	10
1	Aberdeen		2-3	3-1	1-2	1-2	4-1	1-0	3-0	3-0	0-1
			1-2	2-1	1-1	2-1	3-0	2-1	1-0	1-0	0-1
2	Celtic	2-0		1-0	3-1	2-2	4-2	1-1	2-1	0-0	0-2
		5-0		4-0	4-0	2-1	1-1	1-0	4-0	4-1	0-0
3	Falkirk	2-3	0-1		2-0	2-0	0-2	0-0	0-1	2-1	0-2
		1-1	0-0		0-2	1-1	4-2	0-1	1-2	2-3	0-4
4	Heart of Midlothian	1-2	0-4	4-1		2-1	2-1	1-1	3-0	4-2	0-2
		1-3	1-2	2-1		1-1	1-0	4-0	2-5	2-0	2-0
5	Hibernian	1-1	0-4	2-1	2-2		2-0	4-2	3-0	1-2	1-4
		1-2	1-2	2-1	2-1		1-1	0-0	1-0	1-1	0-2
6	Kilmarnock	1-2	0-0	4-0	3-1	0-3		1-1	2-1	5-1	0-2
		1-1	0-0	1-0	0-2	3-2		0-1	2-1	2-0	0-3
7	Motherwell	2-1	0-2	1-1	0-0	0-2	3-0		1-1	0-2	0-0
		1-0	0-0	1-0	1-1	3-0	0-1		0-2	1-0	1-3
8	Partick Thistle	1-0	1-2	1-1	2-0	1-1	1-1	1-0		0-2	0-4
		1-1	2-4	0-3	0-1	0-0	0-1	0-2		0-3	1-2
9	Raith Rovers	1-0	0-1	0-1	1-1	3-0	2-0	0-0	3-1		2-2
		2-2	1-3	1-0	1-3	1-0	1-1	2-0	0-2		2-4
10	Rangers	1-1	3-3	2-0	4-1	0-1	1-0	2-1	1-0	4-0	
		3-1	1-1	3-2	0-3	7-0	3-0	3-2	5-0	4-0	

LEAGUE CHAMPIONSHIP FINAL TABLE 95/96

			Home					Away					Total						
		Pd	W	D	L	F	A	W	D	L	F	A	W	D	L	F	A	Pt	GD
1	Rangers	36	13	3	2	47	16	14	3	1	38	9	27	6	3	85	25	87	+60
2	Celtic	36	12	5	1	40	12	12	6	0	34	13	24	11	1	74	25	83	+49
3	Aberdeen	36	11	1	6	31	17	5	6	7	21	28	16	7	13	52	45	55	+7
4	Heart of Midlothian	36	10	2	6	33	26	6	5	7	22	27	16	7	13	55	53	55	+2
5	Hibernian	36	7	5	6	25	26	4	5	9	18	31	11	10	15	43	57	43	-14
6	Raith Rovers	36	7	5	6	23	21	5	2	11	18	36	12	7	17	41	57	43	-16
7	Kilmarnock	36	8	4	6	25	21	3	4	11	14	33	11	8	17	39	54	41	-15
8	Motherwell	36	6	6	6	15	16	3	6	9	13	23	9	12	15	28	39	39	-11
9	Partick Thistle	36	3	5	10	12	28	5	1	12	17	34	8	6	22	29	62	30	-33
10	Falkirk	36	4	4	10	17	26	2	2	14	14	34	6	6	24	31	60	24	-29

in Scottish football, helping Rangers to the Premier Division and Scottish Cup 'double' and helping himself to both Scottish Footballer of the Year awards.

There is nothing new, of course, about Rangers winning domestic prizes. The title was their eighth in succession, leaving the club just one short of Celtic's nine-in-a-row record set between 1966 and 1974. And the 'double' was the 14th in the club's 123-year history.

Proving themselves to be kings of the castle in Scotland is somewhat *de rigueur* for Rangers and their fans these days. What really tickles their palate is the prospect of achieving something in Europe. After two successive preliminary-round failures, Rangers did at last make it into the UEFA Champions' League in 1995/96. It was a tight squeeze, with Cypriot champions Anorthosis giving Walter Smith's side two sweaty and nervy pre-season work-outs before they reached the promised land of plenty.

Rangers' previous Champions' League experience, in 1992/93, had been a notable success, with no defeats in their six matches. This time, however, there were three defeats, but no victories, leaving Rangers propping up the Group C table behind Juventus, Borussia Dortmund and Steaua Bucharest. Right from the moment that Steaua defender Daniel Prodan rifled a late winning volley into Andy Goram's net in the opening match, the Scottish champions were struggling for survival.

An eventful draw at home to Dortmund hinted that better times might be around the corner, but Juventus destroyed such optimism at a stroke. The Italians were simply in a different league to Scotland's finest, dismissing Rangers impudently both in the Stadio delle Alpi (4-1) and at Ibrox (4-0). Rangers' fate was sealed one round from the end when they could only draw at home to Steaua - despite a mesmering solo goal from Gascoigne - and Dortmund simultaneously clinched an improbable win in Turin.

It was back to the European drawing-board for Walter Smith. So, too, for the managers of the other Scottish representatives, each of whom departed their respective competitions early. Raith Rovers could be excused for going out to Bayern Munich having lasted three rounds on their European début. But, also in the UEFA Cup, Motherwell's preliminary-round demise against Finnish part-timers MyPa was pitiful. And in the Cup-winners' Cup, Celtic, like Rangers, were humiliated in front of their own fans by the team that eventually went on to win the competition, going down 0-3 to Paris Saint-Germain in the second round.

Overall, the Scottish clubs' performances in Europe were an improvement on the sorry showing of the previous season, but once again they found their technical and tactical frailties glaringly exposed by quality foreign opposition.

Year after year, Rangers are back for another stab at the Champions' League. No other team in Europe appears with such frequency on the preliminary-round starting line in August. And the Light Blues assured themselves of

INTERNATIONAL HONOURS

World Cup Finals appearances: 1954, 1958, 1974, 1978, 1982, 1986, 1990

European Championship appearances: 1992, 1996

European Club Competitions

Champions' Cup	Celtic (1967)
Cup-winners' Cup	Rangers (1972)
	Aberdeen (1983)
Super Cup	Aberdeen (1983)

DOMESTIC CUP RESULTS

THIRD ROUND
Caledonian Thistle 1, East Fife 1
(replay) East Fife 1, Caledonian Thistle 1
(aet; 1-3 on pens.)
Hibernian 0, Kilmarnock 2
Keith 1, Rangers 10
Raith Rovers 3, Queen's Park 0
Ross County 0, Forfar Athletic 3
Whitehall Welfare 0, Celtic 3
Clydebank 0, Stirling Albion 1
Dumbarton 1, Airdrieonians 3
Falkirk 0, Stenhousemuir 2
Motherwell 0, Aberdeen 2
Clyde 3, Dundee 1
Hamilton Academical 0, St. Johnstone 1
Heart of Midlothian 1, Partick Thistle 0
Dunfermline Athletic 3, St. Mirren 0
Greenock Morton 1, Montrose 1
(replay) Montrose 3, Greenock Morton 2
Berwick Rangers 1, Dundee United 2

FOURTH ROUND
Clyde 1, Rangers 4
Airdrieonians 2, Forfar Athletic 2
(replay) Forfar Athletic 0, Airdrieonians 0
(aet; 2-4 on pens.)
Celtic 2, Raith Rovers 0
Dundee United 1, Dunfermline Athletic 0
Kilmarnock 1, Heart of Midlothian 2
St. Johnstone 3, Montrose 0
Stenhousemuir 0, Caledonian Thistle 1
Stirling Albion 0, Aberdeen 2

QUARTER-FINALS
St. Johnstone 1, Heart of Midlothian 2
Aberdeen 2, Airdrieonians 1
Caledonian Thistle 0, Rangers 3
Celtic 2, Dundee United 1

SEMI-FINALS
Heart of Midlothian 2, Aberdeen 1
Rangers 2, Celtic 1

FINAL
18/05/96, Glasgow
RANGERS 5 Laudrup (37, 49), Durie (67, 79, 85)
HEART OF MIDLOTHIAN 1 Colquhoun (76)
referee - Dallas
RANGERS - Goram; Cleland, Robertson, Gough, McLaren, Brown, Durie, Gascoigne, Ferguson (Durrant 89), McCall, Laudrup.
HEART OF MIDLOTHIAN - Rousset; Locke (Lawrence 8), Ritchie, McManus, McPherson, Bruno (Robertson 58), Johnston A., Mackay, Colquhoun, Fulton, Pointon.

another appearance in 1996/97 by registering a European record 46th national title.

It was not, however, the casual victory procession of previous seasons. For once, Rangers had a serious challenger to their crown. Celtic, back at their refurbished Parkhead home and buoyed by their Scottish Cup win, pushed the perennial champions all the way. In Tommy Burns, Celtic appeared at last to have found a manager worthy of the club's tradition and ambition. In the end they had to accept second best once again - Rangers also knocked them out of both domestic Cups - but it had not been for the want of trying. After losing the first Old Firm game of the season, Celtic were not beaten again in the league all season. They clung to Rangers' coat-tails throughout, and it was only a succession of costly 0-0 draws away to teams they should have beaten - Kilmarnock, Falkirk, Motherwell - that ultimately kept them in second place.

There were no trophies for Burns and his Bhoys at the end of the season, but signs that Celtic might be closing the gap on Rangers gave encouragement to the club's long-suffering fans. Good news was also provided by Celtic's new foreign strike-force of Andreas Thom and Pierre van Hooijdonk. The latter was particularly impressive, topping the Premier Division hit list with 26 goals, a performance which ought to have been rewarded with a place in Holland's Euro '96 squad. The rapid development of youngsters Simon Donnelly and Jackie McNamara is

TOP SCORERS

26	Pierre VAN HOOIJDONK (Celtic)
17	Gordon DURIE (Rangers)
16	Ally McCOIST (Rangers)
14	Paul GASCOIGNE (Rangers)
13	Paul WRIGHT (Kilmarnock)
11	John COLLINS (Celtic)
	John ROBERTSON (Heart of Midlothian)
9	Joe MILLER (Aberdeen)
	Scott BOOTH (Aberdeen)
	Allan JOHNSTON (Heart of Midlothian)
	Darren JACKSON (Hibernian)
	Keith WRIGHT (Hibernian)
	Colin CAMERON (Raith Rovers)

NATIONAL TEAM RESULTS 95/96

16/08/95	Greece (ECQ)	H	Glasgow	1-0	McCoist (72)
06/09/95	Finland (ECQ)	H	Glasgow	1-0	Booth (10)
11/10/95	Sweden	A	Solna	0-2	
15/11/95	San Marino (ECQ)	H	Glasgow	5-0	Jess (30), Booth (45), McCoist (49), Nevin (71), Francini (90og)
27/03/96	Australia	H	Glasgow	1-0	McCoist (53)
24/04/96	Denmark	A	Copenhagen	0-2	
26/05/96	United States	A	New Britain	1-2	Durie (9)
29/05/96	Colombia	N	Miami	0-1	
10/06/96	Holland (ECF)	N	Birmingham	0-0	
15/06/96	England (ECF)	A	Wembley	0-2	
18/06/96	Switzerland (ECF)	N	Birmingham	1-0	McCoist (36)

NATIONAL TEAM APPEARANCES 95/96

Coach - Craig BROWN	GRE	FIN	SWE	SMR	AUS	DEN	USA	COL	HOL	ENG	SUI	Cps	Gls
Jim LEIGHTON (24/07/58) - Hibernian	G	G	G83	G	G	G46	G82					74	-
Stewart McKIMMIE (27/10/62) - Aberdeen	D	D88	D			D		s46	D85	D		40	1
Colin CALDERWOOD (20/01/65) - Tottenham Hotspur (ENG)	D	D	D	D			D	D	D	D	D	14	1
Tom BOYD (24/11/65) - Celtic	D	D	D	M	D	D	M	D	D	D	D	38	-
Tosh McKINLAY (03/12/64) - Celtic	D	M				D		M		M82	M60	6	-
Craig BURLEY (24/09/71) - Chelsea (ENG)	M		M46		D	M	M60	M	s85	s82	D	12	-
Stuart McCALL (10/06/64) - Rangers	M					M46	s60	M	M	M	M	37	1
Gary McALLISTER (25/12/64) - Leeds United (ENG)	M	M	M69	M48	M	M	s46	M	M	M	M	44	4
John COLLINS (31/01/68) - Celtic	M	M	M	M59	M	M	s46	M	M	M	M	36	8
Darren JACKSON (25/07/66) - Hibernian	A73	s80	s69	s66	s72	s72	M46					12	-
Duncan SHEARER (28/08/62) - Aberdeen	A71											7	2
Ally McCOIST (24/09/62) - Rangers	s71	s75		s48	A70	s72		A60		s67	A84	54	19
John ROBERTSON (02/10/64) - Heart of Midlothian	s73		A83									16	3
Alan McLAREN (04/01/71) - Rangers		D	D	D								24	-
Colin HENDRY (07/12/65) - Blackburn Rovers (ENG)		D	D	D	D	D74	D	D46	D	D	D	21	1
Scott BOOTH (16/12/71) - Aberdeen		A80		A66	s46		A		A46		s60	13	5
John SPENCER (11/09/70) - Chelsea (ENG)		A75			M	A72	s46	A69	s46	A67	s84	12	-
Billy McKINLAY (22/04/69) - Dundee United/Blackburn Rovers (ENG)		s88	s46	s59	M72	s74			s56			18	4
John McGINLAY (08/04/64) - Bolton Wanderers (ENG)			A46									9	3
Eoin JESS (13/12/70) - Aberdeen/Coventry City (ENG)			s46	A			M	s69		s87		13	1
Andy GORAM (13/04/64) - Rangers			s83			s46		G	G	G	G	39	-
Pat NEVIN (06/09/63) - Tranmere Rovers (ENG)			s83	A	s70							28	5
Scot GEMMILL (02/01/71) - Nottingham Forest (ENG)				M		s46	M46					6	-
Brian O'NEIL (06/09/72) - Celtic					D46							1	-
Paul McSTAY (22/10/64) - Celtic					M46							73	9
Kevin GALLACHER (23/11/66) - Blackburn Rovers (ENG)					s46	A72		s60	M56			23	2
Derek WHYTE (31/08/68) - Middlesbrough (ENG)							D					9	-
Gordon DURIE (06/12/65) - Rangers							A46		A	A87	A	31	5
Nicky WALKER (29/09/62) - Partick Thistle							s82					2	-

also a reason for Celtic fans to look forward to the future with a good deal more optimism than of late.

But, for now, Rangers remain the number one team in Scotland. Celtic may have pushed them hard for the championship, but Rangers will have taken immense pleasure from the three wins and three draws they registered against their Glasgow rivals. They were rarely troubled by any other team, except Hearts, who beat them twice in the second half of the season, the first time with an incredible 3-0 victory at Ibrox. When the two teams met again, in the final of the Scottish Cup at Hampden, Rangers put the Edinburgh club in their place, destroying them 5-1 with a brilliant display of counter-attacking football led by two-goal Brian Laudrup, who also laid on the other three goals for Gordon Durie.

The Danish winger had missed most of the first half of the season with injury, which left the stage clear for new signing Paul Gascoigne. After a slow beginning, the Englishman soon began to pick up the pace of the Premier Division, and by the second half of the campaign, with Laudrup at his side, he was back to the brilliant form he had shown in the early years of his career. Fittingly, it was Gascoigne who wrapped the title up for Rangers, scoring a scintillating hat-trick against Aberdeen in the penultimate match. If Gascoigne was undoubtedly the star, there were other players who made decisive contributions to Rangers' success. Another new signing, Gordan Petric, oozed class alongside Gough and McLaren at the back. Goalkeeper Andy Goram had another excellent season, especially in the Old Firm clashes. And the front two of McCoist and Durie ensured that Gascoigne was not the only provider of important goals. New Russian striker Oleg Salenko did not last the course, however. He was sold mid-season to Turkish side Istanbulspor in a swap deal involving Dutch winger Peter van Vossen. And before the season was out Rangers had added another foreign attacker to their ranks, bringing in the Dane Erik Bo Andersen, who made an immediate impact, scoring six goals in as many games during the run-in.

Rangers won the 'double', but they were denied a

EUROPEAN CUPS RESULTS 95/96

CHAMPIONS' CUP

● RANGERS

Preliminary round ANORTHOSIS FAMAGUSTA (CYP)

H 1-0 Durie (68)
Goram; Wright, Robertson, Gough, McLaren, Reid (Durie 46), McCall, Gascoigne, Laudrup, Hateley, Ferguson (Miller 67).

A 0-0
Goram; Wright, Robertson, Gough, McLaren, Petric, McCall, Gascoigne (Durrant 25; Murray 90), Durie, Hateley, Miller.

Champions' League

1st match STEAUA BUCURESTI (ROM)

A 0-1
Goram; Wright, Gough, McLaren, Cleland, Miller (Durie 78), Gascoigne, Petric, McCoist, Laudrup, Durrant (Murray 60)

2nd match BORUSSIA DORTMUND (GER)

H 2-2 Gough (62), Ferguson (72)
Goram; Wright, Petric, McCall, Gough, Cleland, Durie (Durrant 74), Gascoigne, McCoist, Laudrup (Ferguson 46), Miller.

3rd match JUVENTUS (ITA)

A 1-4 Gough (77)
Goram; Wright (Brown 46), Robertson, McCall (Murray 69), Petric, Gough, Moore, Cleland, Durie, Salenko, McCoist.

4th match JUVENTUS (ITA)

H 0-4
Goram (Thomson 46); Wright (Durrant 25), Brown, Petric, Gough, McCall, Ferguson, Gascoigne, Miller (McCoist 90), Bollan, Salenko.

5th match STEAUA BUCURESTI (ROM)

H 1-1 Gascoigne (39)
Goram; McLaren, Robertson, Brown (Bollan 75), Gough, Petric, McCall (Murray 46), Gascoigne, McCoist, Durrant (Miller 86), Laudrup.

6th match BORUSSIA DORTMUND (GER)

A 2-2 Laudrup (11), Durie (85)
Goram; Cleland (Durrant 79), Robertson, Gough, McLaren, Bollan, Miller (McCoist 62), Gascoigne, Durie, McCall, Laudrup.

CUP-WINNERS' CUP

● CELTIC

1st round DINAMO BATUMI (GEO)

A 3-2 Thom (21, 87), Donnelly (39)
Marshall; Boyd, McKinlay, Vata, Hughes, Grant, O'Donnell, Donnelly (Falconer 75), Walker (McLaughlin 89), Thom, Collins.

H 4-0 Thom (18, 20), Donnelly (46), Walker (90)
Marshall; Vata, McKinlay, McStay, Boyd, Hughes, Donnelly (Hay 56), McLaughlin, Thom (Gray 70), Van Hooijdonk (Walker 62), Grant.

2nd round PARIS SAINT-GERMAIN FC (FRA)

A 0-1
Marshall; Vata, McKinlay, McStay, Boyd, Hughes, Grant, O'Donnell (Donnelly 69), Van Hooijdonk, Thom, Collins.

H 0-3
Marshall; Vata (Donnelly 46), McKinlay, Hughes, Boyd, McStay, Grant, Thom, Walker, Van Hooijdonk (McLaughlin 63), Collins.

UEFA CUP

● RAITH ROVERS

Preliminary round GÍ (FAR)

H 4-0 Dair (40), Rougier (47), McAnespie (78), Cameron (80)
Thomson; McAnespie, Broddle, McInally, Dennis, Sinclair, Rougier (Graham 65), Cameron, Crawford (Lennon 78), Taylor, Dair.

A 2-2 Lennon (30), Crawford (81)
Thomson; Kirkwood, Broddle, Lennon, Dennis (Raeside 83), Sinclair, Rougier, Graham, Crawford, Taylor (Forrest 75), Cameron

1st round ÍA (ISL)

H 3-1 Lennon (14, 66), Wilson (79)
Thomson; McAnespie, Broddle, Kirkwood, Dennis, Sinclair, Wilson (Coyle 85), Cameron, Crawford (Graham 59), Lennon, Rougier (Dair 28).

A 0-1
Thomson; McAnespie, Broddle, Coyle, Dennis, Sinclair, Kirkwood, Cameron, Crawford (Wilson 75), Lennon, Dair (McInally 87).

2nd round FC BAYERN MÜNCHEN (GER)

H 0-2
Thomson; Coyle, Dennis, Sinclair, Kirkwood, Lennon, McInally (Rougier 75), Dair (Crawford 74), Broddle, Graham, Cameron.

A 1-2 Herzog (42og)
Thomson; Taylor (Kirkwood 90), Broddle, Coyle (McInally 85), Dennis, Sinclair, Rougier (Graham 61), Cameron, Crawford, Lennon, Dair.

● MOTHERWELL

Preliminary round MYPA (FIN)

H 1-3 McSkimming (9)
Woods; May, McKinnon, Van der Gaag, Martin, McCart, Lambert (Davies), Dolan, Coyne, Hendry (Essandoh), McSkimming.

A 2-0 Burns (28), Arnott (69)
Howie; May, McKinnon, Roddie (McCullough), Martin, McCart, Lambert, Dolan, Burns, Arnott, Davies.

PLAYERS OF THE SEASON

ALLY McCOIST

Even at the grand old age of 34, Ally McCoist is still doing what he has always done - scoring goals. The 1995/96 season saw the Rangers striker reach a number of milestones. At club level he began the season by netting his 300th competitive goal for Rangers and then went on to break Ibrox legend Bob McPhail's 56-year-old Scottish league goal-scoring record of 230. McCoist returned to play for Scotland for the first time in over two years and promptly scored the all-important winning goal in the European Championship qualifier against Greece. Later on in the season he marked his 50th international appearance by captaining the team and scoring another winning goal against Australia. And at Euro '96 he was the only Scotsman to score, his stunning drive against the Swiss begging the question as to why he had not started the previous games against Holland and England.

ALLAN JOHNSTON

Described by no less an authority than Rangers and Scotland striker Gordon Durie as "the best non-Ranger in Scotland", Allan Johnston no longer qualifies as such because he has now left Hearts for a new career in France with Rennes. But the young striker certainly lived up to the billing before he departed, scoring a remarkable hat-trick at Ibrox in January to give Hearts a sensational 3-0 win. Johnston's pace and skill earned him the nickname "Magic" from the Tynecastle fans. Capped by Scotland at U-21 level (he played in the European Championship semi-final defeat by Spain), Johnston should graduate to full international honours if he can maintain his present level of progress in France.

JOHN COLLINS

Scotland's most consistently impressive player during the Euro '96 qualifying competition was also their outstanding player at the finals. John Collins held things together with calm assurance in the Scotland midfield, making light of the injury which had forced him to miss a number of matches towards the end of the league season with Celtic. Collins has now left Celtic for French club Monaco on a free transfer having come to the end of his contract. In six years at the Parkhead club he developed into one of Scottish football's most reliable assets, but it was his misfortune to play with Celtic at a time when they were consistently second-best to Rangers. His last season in green and white was undoubtedly one of his best at the club - despite the late injury setback.

John Collins

repeat of their 1992/93 'treble' when they lost 2-1 to Aberdeen in the semi-final of the Coca-Cola (League) Cup. Roy Aitken's team went on to lift the trophy, beating First Division Dundee 2-0 in the final with goals from Billy Dodds and Duncan Shearer. Aberdeen also won an intriguing duel with Hearts to take third place in the league. It didn't count for a lot, because their UEFA Cup place was already assured with the Coca-Cola win, and Hearts earned a Cup-winners' Cup place by reaching the Scottish Cup final.

At the bottom of the Premier Division it looked for a long time that Motherwell, the previous season's runners-up, would be the team automatically relegated, but a dramtic run of seven wins in nine games lifted them to safety. Falkirk, with just two points from their last 11 games, eventually finished bottom, and Partick Thistle joined them in relegation after a nail-biting play-off with Dundee United, whose extra-time winner in the second leg took them up along with First Division champions Dunfermline Athletic.

ABERDEEN

CLUB DIRECTORY

Aberdeen FC
Pittodrie Stadium
Pittodrie Street
Aberdeen AB2 1QH
tel - (01224) 632328
fax - (01224) 644173
Year of Formation - 1903
Chairman - Ian R. Donald
Secretary - Ian J. Taggart
Manager - Roy Aitken
Stadium - Pittodrie Stadium (21,634)

MAJOR HONOURS

League Championship - (4)
1955, 1980, 1984, 1985.
Domestic Cup - (7)
1947, 1970, 1982, 1983, 1984, 1986, 1990.
European Cup-winners' Cup - (1) 1983
European Super Cup - (1) 1983.

APPEARANCES 95/96

	P	Ap	(s)	Gls
Paul BERNARD	M	27	(4)	1
Scott BOOTH	A	20	(4)	9
James BUCHAN	D	1	(3)	1
Kevin CHRISTIE	A		(2)	
Michael CRAIG	A		(1)	
Billy DODDS	A	28	(3)	7
Stephen GLASS	M	32		3
Brian GRANT	M	22	(3)	
Peter HETHERSTONE	M	9	(2)	
John INGLIS	D	24		1
Brian IRVINE	D	17	(1)	3
Eoin JESS	A	25		3
Malcolm KPEDEKPO	A	1	(4)	
Stewart McKIMMIE	D	29		
Ray McKINNON	M		(1)	
Joe MILLER	M	31		9
Hugh ROBERTSON	M	5	(6)	
David ROWSON	D	7	(2)	
Duncan SHEARER	A	15	(15)	3
Gary SMITH	D	33		
Theo SNELDERS (HOL)	G	6	(1)	
Scott THOMSON	M		(4)	
Michael WATT	G	30		
Dean WINDASS (ENG)	M	19	(1)	6
Colin WOODTHORPE (ENG)	D	15		1

LEAGUE RESULTS 1995/96

26/08/95	Falkirk	A	3-2	Inglis, Dodds, Booth
10/09/95	Celtic	H	2-3	og (Boyd), Jess
16/09/95	Hibernian	A	1-1	Shearer
23/09/95	Kilmarnock	A	2-1	Miller, Woodthorpe
30/09/95	Raith Rovers	H	3-0	Booth 2, Miller
04/10/95	Heart of Midlothian	A	2-1	Dodds, Booth
07/10/95	Rangers	H	0-1	
14/10/95	Motherwell	A	1-2	Booth
21/10/95	Partick Thistle	H	3-0	og (Craig), Jess, Bernard
28/10/95	Celtic	A	0-2	
04/11/95	Hibernian	H	1-2	Glass
08/11/95	Falkirk	H	3-1	Dodds, Miller, og (McGowan)
11/11/95	Rangers	A	1-1	Jess
18/11/95	Raith Rovers	A	0-1	
02/12/95	Partick Thistle	A	0-1	
09/12/95	Motherwell	H	1-0	Shearer
13/12/95	Kilmarnock	H	4-1	Miller 3, Windass
16/12/95	Heart of Midlothian	H	1-2	Windass
08/01/96	Hibernian	A	2-1	Miller, Dodds
14/01/96	Celtic	H	1-2	Dodds
16/01/96	Falkirk	A	1-1	Windass
20/01/96	Partick Thistle	H	1-0	Dodds (p)
23/01/96	Kilmarnock	A	1-1	Irvine
03/02/96	Raith Rovers	H	1-0	Windass
10/02/96	Heart of Midlothian	A	3-1	Windass, Shearer, Glass
13/02/96	Motherwell	A	0-1	
25/02/96	Rangers	H	0-1	
02/03/96	Kilmarnock	H	3-0	Booth 2, Miller
16/03/96	Raith Rovers	A	2-2	Miller, Buchan
23/03/96	Hibernian	H	2-1	Dodds, Booth
01/04/96	Celtic	A	0-5	
13/04/96	Motherwell	H	2-1	og (McCart), Irvine
16/04/96	Partick Thistle	A	1-1	Booth
20/04/96	Heart of Midlothian	H	1-1	Windass (p)
28/04/96	Rangers	A	1-3	Irvine
04/05/96	Falkirk	H	2-1	Glass, og (McGowan)

CELTIC

CLUB DIRECTORY

Celtic FC
95 Kerrydale Street, Glasgow G40 3RE
tel - (0141) 5562611
fax - (0141) 5518106
Year of Formation - 1888
Managing Director - Fergus McCann
Secretary - Dominic Keane
Manager - Tommy Burns
Stadium - Celtic Park (47,500)

MAJOR HONOURS
League Championship - (35) 1893, 1894, 1896, 1898, 1905, 1906, 1907, 1908, 1909, 1910, 1914, 1915, 1916, 1917, 1919, 1922, 1926, 1936, 1938, 1954, 1966, 1967, 1968, 1969, 1970, 1971, 1972, 1973, 1974, 1977, 1979, 1981, 1982, 1986, 1988.
Domestic Cup - (30) 1892, 1899, 1900, 1904, 1907, 1908, 1911, 1912, 1914, 1923, 1925, 1927, 1931, 1933, 1937, 1951, 1954, 1965, 1967, 1969, 1971, 1972, 1974, 1975, 1977, 1980, 1985, 1988, 1989, 1995.
European Champions' Cup - (1) 1967.

APPEARANCES 95/96

	P	Ap	(s)	Gls
Tom BOYD	D	34		
Jorge CADETE (POR)	A	2	(4)	5
John COLLINS	M	26	(3)	11
Simon DONNELLY	A	35		6
Willie FALCONER	A		(2)	
Peter GRANT	M	30		3
Stuart GRAY	D	3	(2)	1
Chris HAY	A	1	(3)	
John HUGHES	D	26		2
Malky MACKAY	D	9	(2)	1
Tosh McKINLAY	D	32		
Brian McLAUGHLIN	A	11	(15)	4
Jackie McNAMARA	D	26		1
James McQUILKEN	D	3	(1)	
Paul McSTAY	M	29	(1)	2
Gordon MARSHALL	G	36		
Phil O'DONNELL	M	14	(1)	3
Brian O'NEIL	D	3	(2)	
Andreas THOM (GER)	A	31	(1)	5
Pierre VAN HOOIJDONK (HOL)	A	34		26
Rudi VATA (ALB)	D	5	(1)	
Andy WALKER	A	4	(12)	3
Morten WIEGHORST (DEN)	D	2	(9)	1

LEAGUE RESULTS 1995/96

26/08/95	Raith Rovers	A	1-0	Van Hooijdonk
10/09/95	Aberdeen	A	3-2	Collins 2, Thom
16/09/95	Motherwell	H	1-1	O'Donnell
23/09/95	Heart of Midlothian	A	4-0	McLaughlin 2, Walker 2
30/09/95	Rangers	H	0-2	
04/10/95	Falkirk	A	1-0	Hughes
07/10/95	Partick Thistle	H	2-1	Van Hooijdonk, Collins
14/10/95	Hibernian	H	2-2	Collins, Van Hooijdonk
21/10/95	Kilmarnock	A	0-0	
28/10/95	Aberdeen	H	2-0	McLaughlin, Van Hooijdonk (p)
04/11/95	Motherwell	A	2-0	Donnelly, Collins
08/11/95	Raith Rovers	H	0-0	
11/11/95	Partick Thistle	A	2-1	Van Hooijdonk 2 (1p)
19/11/95	Rangers	A	3-3	Thom, Collins (p), Van Hooijdonk
25/11/95	Heart of Midlothian	H	3-1	Collins 3 (1p)
02/12/95	Kilmarnock	H	4-2	Grant, Thom, Van Hooijdonk 2
09/12/95	Hibernian	A	4-0	McNamara, O'Donnell, Van Hooijdonk, Donnelly
16/12/95	Falkirk	H	1-0	Van Hooijdonk
03/01/96	Rangers	H	0-0	
06/01/96	Motherwell	H	1-0	Van Hooijdonk
09/01/96	Raith Rovers	A	3-1	O'Donnell, Collins, Van Hooijdonk
14/01/96	Aberdeen	A	2-1	Collins, Van Hooijdonk
17/01/96	Heart of Midlothian	A	2-1	Van Hooijdonk, Walker
20/01/96	Kilmarnock	A	0-0	
03/02/96	Hibernian	H	2-1	Van Hooijdonk, McStay
10/02/96	Falkirk	A	0-0	
24/02/96	Partick Thistle	H	4-0	Grant, Van Hooijdonk 2 (1p), Wieghorst
02/03/96	Heart of Midlothian	H	4-0	McStay, Van Hooijdonk, McLaughlin, Donnelly
17/03/96	Rangers	A	1-1	Hughes
23/03/96	Motherwell	A	0-0	
01/04/96	Aberdeen	H	5-0	Donnelly 2, Van Hooijdonk 2, Cadete
10/04/96	Kilmarnock	H	1-1	Van Hooijdonk
14/04/96	Hibernian	A	2-1	Van Hooijdonk 2
20/04/96	Falkirk	H	4-0	Thom 2, Cadete, Donnelly
27/04/96	Partick Thistle	A	4-2	Van Hooijdonk 2 (1p), Cadete, Mackay
04/05/96	Raith Rovers	H	4-1	Cadete 2, Gray, Grant

FALKIRK

CLUB DIRECTORY

Falkirk FC
Brockville Park, Hope Street, Falkirk FK1 5AX
tel - (01324) 624121/632487
fax - (01324) 612418
Year of Formation - 1876
Chairman - George J. Fulston
Secretary - Alexander D. Moffat
Manager - John Lambie; Eamonn Bannon
Stadium - Brockville Park (13,401)

MAJOR HONOURS
Domestic Cup - (1) 1957.

APPEARANCES 95/96

	P	Ap	(s)	Gls
Gordon ABBOTT	M		(1)	
John CLARK	D	14	(3)	2
Albert CRAIG	M	14		3
David ELLIOTT	M	31	(1)	
Derek FERGUSON	M	26		
Tony FINNIGAN	D	8	(1)	1
Steve FULTON	M	4	(1)	
Ally GRAHAM	A	8		
Andy GRAY	M	16		
David HAGEN	A	21	(4)	
Graeme HAMILTON	D		(1)	
Nicky HENDERSON	A		(9)	
Neil INGLIS	G	1		
Dominic IORFA (NIG)	A	3	(1)	1
Kevin JAMES	D	10	(3)	2
Forbes JOHNSTON	A	3	(3)	
Maurice JOHNSTON	A	31		5
Steve KIRK	A	16	(4)	4
Billy LAMONT	G	7		
Andrew LAWRIE	D	1		
Colin McDONALD	A	4	(5)	1
Jamie McGOWAN	D	27	(2)	1
Mark McGRAW	A	2	(7)	
Paul McGRILLEN	A	24	(6)	6
Scott MacKENZIE	M	27	(3)	1
Joe McLAUGHLIN	D	15	(1)	1
Stuart MUNRO	D	13		
Craig NAPIER	D	3	(1)	
Neil OLIVER	D	3		
Tony PARKS (ENG)	G	28		
Brian RICE	M	1	(4)	
Andrew SEATON	A		(1)	
David WEIR	D	34		3
Gary WHITESIDE	A		(2)	
George WRIGHT	D	1	(1)	

LEAGUE RESULTS 1995/96

26/08/95	Aberdeen	H	2-3	McLaughlin, Kirk
09/09/95	Heart of Midlothian	A	1-4	McDonald
16/09/95	Rangers	H	0-2	
23/09/95	Motherwell	H	0-0	
30/09/95	Partick Thistle	A	1-1	Johnston M. (p)
04/10/95	Celtic	H	0-1	
07/10/95	Hibernian	A	1-2	MacKenzie
14/10/95	Kilmarnock	H	0-2	
21/10/95	Raith Rovers	A	1-0	McGrillen
28/10/95	Heart of Midlothian	H	2-0	Weir, Johnston M.
04/11/95	Rangers	A	0-2	
08/11/95	Aberdeen	A	1-3	McGrillen
11/11/95	Hibernian	H	2-0	Johnston M. 2
18/11/95	Partick Thistle	H	0-1	
25/11/95	Motherwell	A	1-1	Clark (p)
02/12/95	Raith Rovers	H	2-1	McGrillen 2
09/12/95	Kilmarnock	A	0-4	
16/12/95	Celtic	A	0-1	
06/01/96	Rangers	H	0-4	
09/01/96	Partick Thistle	A	3-0	Craig, McGowan, Weir
13/01/96	Heart of Midlothian	A	1-2	Kirk
16/01/96	Aberdeen	H	1-1	Clark
20/01/96	Raith Rovers	A	0-1	
23/01/96	Motherwell	H	0-1	
03/02/96	Kilmarnock	H	4-2	Finnigan, Craig, Iorfa, Kirk
10/02/96	Celtic	H	0-0	
24/02/96	Hibernian	A	1-2	Kirk (p)
02/03/96	Motherwell	A	0-1	
16/03/96	Partick Thistle	H	1-2	Weir
23/03/96	Rangers	A	2-3	Johnston M., James
30/03/96	Heart of Midlothian	H	0-2	
06/04/96	Raith Rovers	H	2-3	James, Craig
13/04/96	Kilmarnock	A	0-1	
20/04/96	Celtic	A	0-4	
27/04/96	Hibernian	H	1-1	McGrillen
04/05/96	Aberdeen	A	1-2	McGrillen

HEART OF MIDLOTHIAN

CLUB DIRECTORY

Heart of Midlothian FC
Tynecastle Park, Gorgie Road, Edinburgh EH11 2NL
tel - (0131) 3376132
fax - (0131) 3460699
Year of Formation - 1874
Chairman - Christopher Robinson
Secretary - Leslie W. Porteous
Manager - Jim Jefferies
Stadium - Tynecastle Park (16,613)

MAJOR HONOURS
League Championship - (4)
1895, 1897, 1958, 1960.
Domestic Cup - (5)
1891, 1896, 1901, 1906, 1956.

APPEARANCES 95/96

	P	Ap	(s)	Gls
Neil BERRY	D	16	(3)	
Pasquale BRUNO (ITA)	D	22		1
Stuart CALLAGHAN	M		(1)	
Colin CAMERON	M	4		2
John COLQUHOUN	A	20	(11)	4
Hans ESKILSSON (SWE)	A	9	(2)	2
Steve FULTON	M	26		2
David HAGEN	A	5	(2)	1
Brian HAMILTON	M	8	(4)	
Myles HOGARTH	G	1		
Willie JAMIESON	D	2	(3)	
Allan JOHNSTON	A	30	(3)	9
Alan LAWRENCE	A	17	(9)	5
Scott LEITCH	M	4	(2)	
Craig LEVEIN	D	1		
Gary LOCKE	D	29		4
Gary MACKAY	M	21	(5)	2
Alan McMANUS	D	16	(1)	2
David McPHERSON	D	22	(4)	1
John MILLAR	M	16	(4)	4
Colin MILLER	D	2	(1)	
Gary NAYSMITH	M		(1)	
Craig NELSON	G	4		
Gary O'CONNOR	G	3		
Neil POINTON (ENG)	M	21	(1)	3
Paul RITCHIE	D	28		1
John ROBERTSON	A	28	(5)	11
Gilles ROUSSET (FRA)	G	25		
Henry SMITH	G	3		
Paul SMITH	D	4	(5)	
Kevin THOMAS	A		(3)	
David WINNIE	D	6		
Fraser WISHART	D	1		
George WRIGHT	D	2		

LEAGUE RESULTS 1995/96

26/08/95	Motherwell	H	1-1	Hagen
09/09/95	Falkirk	H	4-1	Lawrence 2, Colquhou2, Robertson (p)
16/09/95	Partick Thistle	A	0-2	
23/09/95	Celtic	H	0-4	
01/10/95	Hibernian	A	2-2	McPherson, Robertson
04/10/95	Aberdeen	H	1-2	Robertson
07/10/95	Kilmarnock	A	1-3	Lawrence
14/10/95	Raith Rovers	H	4-2	Millar, Lawrence 2, Robertson
21/10/95	Rangers	A	1-4	Millar
28/10/95	Falkirk	A	0-2	
04/11/95	Partick Thistle	H	3-0	og (McWilliams), Millar, Eskilsson
07/11/95	Motherwell	A	0-0	
11/11/95	Kilmarnock	H	2-1	Locke, Robertson
19/11/95	Hibernian	H	2-1	Millar, Johnston (p)
25/11/95	Celtic	A	1-3	Bruno
02/12/95	Rangers	H	0-2	
09/12/95	Raith Rovers	A	1-1	Robertson
16/12/95	Aberdeen	A	2-1	Johnston, Colquhoun
01/01/96	Hibernian	A	1-2	Pointon
06/01/96	Partick Thistle	A	1-0	McManus
10/01/96	Motherwell	H	4-0	Fulton, Colquhoun, Johnston 2
13/01/96	Falkirk	H	2-1	Robertson, Fulton
17/01/96	Celtic	H	1-2	Robertson
20/01/96	Rangers	A	3-0	Johnston 3
03/02/96	Raith Rovers	H	2-0	Robertson, Locke
10/02/96	Aberdeen	H	1-3	Robertson
24/02/96	Kilmarnock	A	2-0	Colquhoun, Robertson
02/03/96	Celtic	A	0-4	
16/03/96	Hibernian	H	1-1	Mackay
23/03/96	Partick Thistle	H	2-5	Johnston, Eskilsson
30/03/96	Falkirk	A	2-0	Ritchie, Locke
10/04/96	Rangers	H	2-0	Pointon, Johnston
13/04/96	Raith Rovers	A	3-1	Cameron, Pointon, Mackay
20/04/96	Aberdeen	A	1-1	Locke
27/04/96	Kilmarnock	H	1-0	McManus
04/05/96	Motherwell	A	1-1	Cameron

HIBERNIAN

CLUB DIRECTORY

Hibernian FC
Easter Road Stadium
Albion Road
Edinburgh EH7 5QG
tel - (0131) 6612159
fax - (0131) 6596488
Year of Formation - 1875
Chairman - Douglas W.M. Cromb
Secretary - Cecil F. Graham
Manager - Alex Miller
Stadium - Easter Road (16,218)

MAJOR HONOURS
League Championship - (4)
1903, 1948, 1951, 1952.
Domestic Cup - (2) 1887, 1902.

APPEARANCES 95/96

	P	Ap	(s)	Gls
Graeme DONALD	M	2	(11)	1
Darren DODS	D	14	(1)	
Andy DOW	M	8		1
Gareth EVANS (ENG)	M	12	(11)	2
David FARRELL	M	7	(1)	
Kevin HARPER	A	14	(2)	3
Gordon HUNTER	D	22		
Chris JACKSON	M	19	(4)	2
Darren JACKSON	A	36		9
Jim LEIGHTON	G	36		
Graeme LOVE	M	10	(4)	
Kevin McALLISTER	A	29	(2)	4
Pat McGINLAY	M	30	(1)	5
Joe McLAUGHLIN	D	9		
Andy MILLEN	D	25		
Graeme MILLER	M	1	(3)	
Willie MILLER	D	13		
Graham MITCHELL	D	6		
Michael O'NEILL (NIR)	M	26	(2)	6
Michael RENWICK	M	1	(1)	
Joe TORTOLANO	A	15	(1)	
Stephen TWEED	D	31		
Michael WEIR	A	5	(4)	1
Keith WRIGHT	A	25	(3)	9

LEAGUE RESULTS 1995/96

26/08/95	Partick Thistle	A	1-1	O'Neill
09/09/95	Kilmarnock	A	3-0	Wright 2, Evans
16/09/95	Aberdeen	H	1-1	Jackson D.
23/09/95	Rangers	A	1-0	Jackson D. (p)
01/10/95	Heart of Midlothian	H	2-2	Donald, McGinlay
04/10/95	Raith Rovers	A	0-3	
07/10/95	Falkirk	H	2-1	Jackson D. (p), McAllister
14/10/95	Celtic	A	2-2	Harper, Jackson D. (p)
21/10/95	Motherwell	H	4-2	Jackson D. 2 (1p), Wright, O'Neill
28/10/95	Kilmarnock	H	2-0	O'Neill, Wright
04/11/95	Aberdeen	A	2-1	Wright, O'Neill
11/11/95	Falkirk	A	0-2	
19/11/95	Heart of Midlothian	A	1-2	Jackson C.
22/11/95	Partick Thistle	H	3-0	Jackson D., Weir, McAllister
25/11/95	Rangers	H	1-4	Jackson C.
02/12/95	Motherwell	A	2-0	Wright 2
09/12/95	Celtic	H	0-4	
16/12/95	Raith Rovers	H	1-2	McGinlay
30/12/95	Rangers	A	0-7	
01/01/96	Heart of Midlothian	H	2-1	O'Neill, Harper
08/01/96	Aberdeen	H	1-2	Harper
13/01/96	Kilmarnock	A	2-3	O'Neill, Wright
16/01/96	Partick Thistle	A	0-0	
20/01/96	Motherwell	H	0-0	
03/02/96	Celtic	A	1-2	Jackson D.
10/02/96	Raith Rovers	A	0-1	
24/02/96	Falkirk	H	2-1	Evans, Wright
03/03/96	Rangers	H	0-2	
16/03/96	Heart of Midlothian	A	1-1	Dow
23/03/96	Aberdeen	A	1-2	McAllister
30/03/96	Kilmarnock	H	1-1	McAllister
06/04/96	Motherwell	A	0-3	
14/04/96	Celtic	H	1-2	McGinlay
20/04/96	Raith Rovers	H	1-1	McGinlay
27/04/96	Falkirk	A	1-1	McGinlay
04/05/96	Partick Thistle	H	1-0	Jackson D.

KILMARNOCK

CLUB DIRECTORY

Kilmarnock FC
Rugby Park
Kilmarnock
KA1 2DP
tel - (01563) 525184
fax - (01563) 522181
Year of Formation - 1869
Chairman - James Moffat
Secretary - Kevin D. Collins
Manager - Alex Totten
Stadium - Rugby Park (18,128)

MAJOR HONOURS
League Championship - (1) 1965.
Domestic Cup - (2) 1920, 1929.

APPEARANCES 95/96

	P	Ap	(s)	Gls
Derek ANDERSON	D	28		
Tom BLACK	D	30		4
Tom BROWN	M	19	(5)	6
Robert CONNOR	D	22	(1)	
Willie FINDLAY	A	2	(1)	
Bobby GEDDES	G	2		
John HENRY	M	22	(6)	3
Gary HOLT	M	16	(8)	
Jim LAUCHLAN	D	5		
Dragoje LEKOVIC (YUG)	G	33		
Jim McINTYRE	A	7		2
Colin McKEE	A	19	(9)	4
Angus MacPHERSON	D	35		1
Steve MASKREY	M	14	(8)	1
Colin MELDRUM	G	1		
Ally MITCHELL	A	29		3
Ray MONTGOMERIE	D	12	(2)	
Mark REILLY	D	22	(6)	
Mark ROBERTS	A	2	(9)	
Mark SKILLING	M	13	(1)	1
Neil WHITWORTH	D	28		
Paul WRIGHT	A	35	(1)	13

LEAGUE RESULTS 1995/96

Date	Opponent	H/A	Score	Scorers
26/08/95	Rangers	A	0-1	
09/09/95	Hibernian	H	0-3	
16/09/95	Raith Rovers	A	0-2	
23/09/95	Aberdeen	H	1-2	Brown
30/09/95	Motherwell	A	0-3	
04/10/95	Partick Thistle	A	1-1	og (Watson)
07/10/95	Heart of Midlothian	H	3-1	Brown, McKee 2
14/10/95	Falkirk	A	2-0	Mitchell, Wright
21/10/95	Celtic	H	0-0	
28/10/95	Hibernian	A	0-2	
04/11/95	Raith Rovers	H	5-1	Henry 2, Wright 2, Brown
08/11/95	Rangers	H	0-2	
11/11/95	Heart of Midlothian	A	1-2	McKee
18/11/95	Motherwell	H	1-1	Mitchell
02/12/95	Celtic	A	2-4	Mitchell, Brown
09/12/95	Falkirk	H	4-0	Brown 2, Black (p), MacPherson
13/12/95	Aberdeen	A	1-4	Wright
16/12/95	Partick Thistle	H	2-1	Wright 2
26/12/95	Rangers	A	0-3	
06/01/96	Raith Rovers	A	1-1	Black (p)
13/01/96	Hibernian	H	3-2	Maskrey, Wright, Henry
16/01/96	Motherwell	A	1-0	Wright
20/01/96	Celtic	H	0-0	
23/01/96	Aberdeen	H	1-1	Wright
03/02/96	Falkirk	A	2-4	Wright 2
10/02/96	Partick Thistle	A	1-0	Black (p)
24/02/96	Heart of Midlothian	H	0-2	
02/03/96	Aberdeen	A	0-3	
16/03/96	Motherwell	H	0-1	
23/03/96	Raith Rovers	H	2-0	McKee, Wright
30/03/96	Hibernian	A	1-1	Wright
10/04/96	Celtic	A	1-1	McIntyre
13/04/96	Falkirk	H	1-0	McIntyre
20/04/96	Partick Thistle	H	2-1	Skilling, Black (p)
27/04/96	Heart of Midlothian	A	0-1	
04/05/96	Rangers	H	0-3	

MOTHERWELL

CLUB DIRECTORY

Motherwell FC
Fir Park
Motherwell ML1 2QN
tel - (01698) 333333
fax - (01698) 276333
Year of Formation - 1886
Chairman - John C. Chapman
Secretary - Alan C. Dick
Manager - Alex McLeish
Stadium - Fir Park (13,742)

MAJOR HONOURS
League Championship - (1) 1932.
Domestic Cup - (2) 1952, 1991.

APPEARANCES 95/96

	P	Ap	(s)	Gls
Dougie ARNOTT	A	23	(4)	3
Alex BURNS	A	14	(14)	3
Tommy COYNE (IRL)	A	9	(5)	4
Billy DAVIES	M	26	(7)	2
Greig DENHAM	D	11	(2)	
Jamie DOLAN	M	24	(3)	
Ray ESSANDOH	M		(4)	
Willie FALCONER	A	15		5
Paul FERGUSON	D	1		
John HENDRY	A	8	(8)	2
Scott HOWIE	G	36		
Miodrag KRIVOKAPIC (CRO)	D	13		
Paul LAMBERT	M	35		2
Chris McCART	D	20		
Lee McCULLOUGH	A		(1)	
Rab McKINNON	D	27		
Alex McLEISH	D	1		
Stephen McMILLAN	M	10	(2)	
Shaun McSKIMMING	M	13	(2)	1
Brian MARTIN	D	33		2
Eddie MAY	D	28		1
John PHILLIBEN	D	19	(5)	
Innes RITCHIE	D	5	(5)	
Andy RODDIE	M	12	(12)	
Ian ROSS	M	1		
Mitchell VAN DER GAAG (HOL)	M	12		1

LEAGUE RESULTS 1995/96

26/08/95	Heart of Midlothian	A	1-1	Arnott
09/09/95	Partick Thistle	H	1-1	og (Walker)
16/09/95	Celtic	A	1-1	Arnott
23/09/95	Falkirk	A	0-0	
30/09/95	Kilmarnock	H	3-0	Coyne 2 (1p), May
03/10/95	Rangers	A	1-2	McSkimming
07/10/95	Raith Rovers	H	0-2	
14/10/95	Aberdeen	H	2-1	Coyne, Lambert
21/10/95	Hibernian	A	2-4	Hendry 2
28/10/95	Partick Thistle	A	0-1	
04/11/95	Celtic	H	0-2	
07/11/95	Heart of Midlothian	H	0-0	
11/11/95	Raith Rovers	A	0-0	
18/11/95	Kilmarnock	A	1-1	Burns
25/11/95	Falkirk	H	1-1	Burns
02/12/95	Hibernian	H	0-2	
09/12/95	Aberdeen	A	0-1	
19/12/95	Rangers	H	0-0	
06/01/96	Celtic	A	0-1	
10/01/96	Heart of Midlothian	A	0-4	
13/01/96	Partick Thistle	H	0-2	
16/01/96	Kilmarnock	H	0-1	
20/01/96	Hibernian	A	0-0	
23/01/96	Falkirk	A	1-0	og (McLaughlin)
10/02/96	Rangers	A	2-3	Martin, Falconer
13/02/96	Aberdeen	H	1-0	Burns
24/02/96	Raith Rovers	H	1-0	Falconer
02/03/96	Falkirk	H	1-0	Falconer
16/03/96	Kilmarnock	A	1-0	Lambert (p)
23/03/96	Celtic	H	0-0	
30/03/96	Partick Thistle	A	2-0	Davies, Van der Gaag
06/04/96	Hibernian	H	3-0	Falconer, Martin, Coyne
13/04/96	Aberdeen	A	1-2	Falconer
20/04/96	Rangers	H	1-3	Arnott
27/04/96	Raith Rovers	A	0-2	
04/05/96	Heart of Midlothian	H	1-1	Davies

PARTICK THISTLE

CLUB DIRECTORY

Partick Thistle FC
Firhill Park
80 Firhill Road
Glasgow G20 7BA
tel - (0141) 9454811
fax - (0141) 9451525
Year of Formation - 1876
Chairman - James Oliver
Secretary - Lorna Bryce
Manager - Murdo MacLeod
Stadium - Firhill (21,776)

MAJOR HONOURS
Domestic Cup - (1) 1921.

APPEARANCES 95/96

	P	Ap	(s)	Gls
Charlie ADAMS	M	1	(4)	
Stuart AYTON	M	1	(4)	
Mark CAIRNS	G	3		
Ian CAMERON	M	32	(3)	1
Albert CRAIG	M	9		2
Henry CURRAN	A	3	(4)	
Alan DINNIE	D	31		
Steve DOCHERTY	A	19	(5)	3
Wayne FOSTER (ENG)	A	19		1
Andy GIBSON	A	8	(13)	1
Nicky HENDERSON	A	12	(4)	1
Andy LYONS	A	9		5
James McCUE	A	2	(1)	
Billy MACDONALD	M	11	(6)	1
Roddy McDONALD	A	12	(4)	5
Kevin McKEE	D	10	(1)	
Murdo MacLEOD	M	1		
Steven McMAHON	A		(1)	
Derek McWILLIAMS	M	25	(2)	3
Callum MILNE	M	19	(3)	
Steve PITTMAN	D	14		
Tony SHEPHERD	M		(1)	
Jim SLAVIN	D	8		
Tom SMITH	M	24	(1)	2
Jerod STIRLING	D	2		
Grant TIERNEY	D	1		
Thomas TURNER	M	20	(2)	3
Nicky WALKER	G	33		
Greg WATSON	D	32		1
Steven WELSH	D	35		

LEAGUE RESULTS 1995/96

26/08/95	Hibernian	H	1-1	Gibson
09/09/95	Motherwell	A	1-1	McDonald
16/09/95	Heart of Midlothian	H	2-0	McWilliams, Docherty
23/09/95	Raith Rovers	A	1-3	McDonald
30/09/95	Falkirk	H	1-1	Craig
04/10/95	Kilmarnock	H	1-1	Craig (p)
07/10/95	Celtic	A	1-2	Smith
14/10/95	Rangers	H	0-4	
21/10/95	Aberdeen	A	0-3	
28/10/95	Motherwell	H	1-0	Docherty
04/11/95	Heart of Midlothian	A	0-3	
11/11/95	Celtic	H	1-2	Docherty
18/11/95	Falkirk	A	1-0	Foster
22/11/95	Hibernian	A	0-3	
25/11/95	Raith Rovers	H	0-2	
02/12/95	Aberdeen	H	1-0	Smith
09/12/95	Rangers	A	0-1	
16/12/95	Kilmarnock	A	1-2	McWilliams
06/01/96	Heart of Midlothian	H	0-1	
09/01/96	Falkirk	H	0-3	
13/01/96	Motherwell	A	2-0	Turner, Watson
16/01/96	Hibernian	H	0-0	
20/01/96	Aberdeen	A	0-1	
23/01/96	Raith Rovers	A	2-0	McDonald. 2
03/02/96	Rangers	H	1-2	McDonald
10/02/96	Kilmarnock	H	0-1	
24/02/96	Celtic	A	0-1	
02/03/96	Raith Rovers	H	0-3	
16/03/96	Falkirk	A	2-1	Lyons 2
23/03/96	Heart of Midlothian	A	5-2	Lyons 2, Turner, Macdonald, Cameron
30/03/96	Motherwell	H	0-2	
13/04/96	Rangers	A	0-5	
16/04/96	Aberdeen	H	1-1	McWilliams
20/04/96	Kilmarnock	A	1-2	Turner
27/04/96	Celtic	H	2-4	Henderson, Lyons
04/05/96	Hibernian	A	0-1	

RAITH ROVERS

CLUB DIRECTORY

Raith Rovers
Stark's Park, Pratt Street, Kirkcaldy
Fife KY1 1SA
tel - (01592) 263514
fax - (01592) 642833
Year of Formation - 1883
Chairman - Alex Penman
Secretary - C. Cant
Manager - Jimmy Nicholl; Jimmy Thomson
Stadium - Stark's Park (9,300)

APPEARANCES 95/96

	P	Ap	(s)	Gls
Paul BONAR	D	4	(1)	
Julian BRODDLE	D	23	(4)	
Mark BUIST	D	2		
Colin CAMERON	M	30		9
Ronnie COYLE	D	22	(2)	
Steve CRAWFORD	A	21	(7)	3
Jason DAIR	M	18	(1)	3
Craig DARGO	D		(1)	
Shaun DENNIS	D	25		
Peter DUFFIELD	A	9		5
Gordon FORREST	M		(1)	
Les FRIDGE	G	1		
Bobby GEDDES	G	9		
Ally GRAHAM	A	18	(7)	5
Mark HUMPHRIES	D	9		
Steve KIRK	M	6	(1)	1
David KIRKWOOD	M	25	(3)	2
Miodrag KRIVOKAPIC (CRO)	D	5		
Graham LANDELLS	M		(1)	
Danny LENNON	M	31	(3)	5
Stephen McANESPIE	D	2	(1)	
Greig McCULLOUGH	D	7		1
Jim McINALLY	M	23	(2)	
Neil McKILLIGAN	D	1	(2)	
Ian McMILLAN	D	4	(4)	
John MILLAR	M	3		1
Jimmy NICHOLL (NIR)	D		(1)	
Robert RAESIDE	D	6	(2)	1
Tony ROUGIER (TRI)	A	17	(5)	1
Neil SELLARS	A		(1)	
David SINCLAIR	D	31	(1)	3
Alex TAYLOR	M	1	(9)	
Scott M. THOMSON	M	9		1
Scott Y. THOMSON	G	26		
Barry WILSON	M	8	(5)	

LEAGUE RESULTS 1995/96

Date	Opponent		Score	Scorers
26/08/95	Celtic	H	0-1	
09/09/95	Rangers	A	0-4	
16/09/95	Kilmarnock	H	2-0	Graham, Dair
23/09/95	Partick Thistle	H	3-1	Cameron 2, Dair
30/09/95	Aberdeen	A	0-3	
04/10/95	Hibernian	H	3-0	Cameron 2, Sinclair
07/10/95	Motherwell	A	2-0	Dair, Sinclair
14/10/95	Heart of Midlothian	A	2-4	Graham, Crawford
21/10/95	Falkirk	H	0-1	
28/10/95	Rangers	H	2-2	Lennon, Cameron
04/11/95	Kilmarnock	A	1-5	Cameron
08/11/95	Celtic	A	0-0	
11/11/95	Motherwell	H	0-0	
18/11/95	Aberdeen	H	1-0	Lennon (p)
25/11/95	Partick Thistle	A	2-0	Graham, Crawford
02/12/95	Falkirk	A	1-2	Graham
09/12/95	Heart of Midlothian	H	1-1	Lennon (p)
16/12/95	Hibernian	A	2-1	Crawford, Graham
06/01/96	Kilmarnock	H	1-1	Lennon
09/01/96	Celtic	H	1-3	Cameron
13/01/96	Rangers	A	0-4	
20/01/96	Falkirk	H	1-0	Sinclair
23/01/96	Partick Thistle	H	0-2	
03/02/96	Heart of Midlothian	A	0-2	
07/02/96	Aberdeen	A	0-1	
10/02/96	Hibernian	H	1-0	Kirkwood
24/02/96	Motherwell	A	0-1	
02/03/96	Partick Thistle	A	3-0	Cameron, Duffield, McCullough (p)
16/03/96	Aberdeen	H	2-2	Kirk, Cameron
23/03/96	Kilmarnock	A	0-2	
30/03/96	Rangers	H	2-4	Duffield, Kirkwood (p)
06/04/96	Falkirk	A	3-2	Rougier, Raeside, Duffield
13/04/96	Heart of Midlothian	H	1-3	Lennon (p)
20/04/96	Hibernian	A	1-1	Millar
27/04/96	Motherwell	H	2-0	Duffield, Thomson S.M.
04/05/96	Celtic	A	1-4	Duffield

RANGERS

CLUB DIRECTORY

Rangers FC
Ibrox Stadium, Edminston Drive, Glasgow G51 2XD
tel - (0141) 4278500 . fax - (0141) 4272676
Year of Formation - 1873
Chairman - David E. Murray
Secretary - R. Campbell Ogilvie
Manager - Walter Smith
Stadium - Ibrox Stadium (50,411)

MAJOR HONOURS
League Championship - (46)
1891, 1899, 1900, 1901, 1902, 1911, 1912, 1913, 1918, 1920, 1921, 1923, 1924, 1925, 1927, 1928, 1929, 1930, 1931, 1933, 1934, 1935, 1937, 1939, 1947, 1949, 1950, 1953, 1956, 1957, 1959, 1961, 1963, 1964, 1975, 1976, 1978, 1987, 1989, 1990, 1991, 1992, 1993, 1994, 1995, 1996
Domestic Cup - (27)
1894, 1897, 1898, 1903, 1928, 1930, 1932, 1934, 1935, 1936, 1948, 1949, 1950, 1953, 1960, 1962, 1963, 1964, 1966, 1973, 1976, 1978, 1979, 1981, 1992, 1993, 1996.
European Cup-winners' Cup - (1) 1972.

APPEARANCES 95/96

	P	Ap	(s)	Gls
Erik Bo ANDERSEN (DEN)	A	6		6
Gary BOLLAN	D	4		
John BROWN	D	8	(6)	
Alex CLELAND	D	21	(4)	1
Gordon DURIE	A	21	(6)	17
Ian DURRANT	M	6	(9)	
Ian FERGUSON	M	16	(2)	2
Paul GASCOIGNE (ENG)	M	27	(1)	14
Andy GORAM	G	30		
Richard GOUGH	D	29		3
Brian LAUDRUP (DEN)	A	22		2
Stuart McCALL	M	19	(2)	3
Ally McCOIST	A	18	(7)	16
Brian McGINTY	M	2		
Derek McINNES	M	5	(1)	
Alan McLAREN	D	36		3
Aleksei MIKHAILICHENKO (UKR)	M	6	(5)	
Charlie MILLER	M	17	(6)	3
Craig MOORE (AUS)	D	9	(2)	1
Neil MURRAY	D	2	(3)	
Gordan PETRIC (YUG)	D	32	(1)	1
David ROBERTSON	D	25		3
Oleg SALENKO (RUS)	A	14	(2)	7
Colin SCOTT	G	3		
Greg SHIELDS	D	1		
Theo SNELDERS (HOL)	G	2		
Trevor STEVEN (ENG)	M	5	(1)	
Billy THOMSON	G	1		
Peter VAN VOSSEN (HOL)	A	3	(4)	
Stephen WRIGHT	D	6		

LEAGUE RESULTS 1995/96

Date	Opponent		Score	Scorers
26/08/95	Kilmarnock	H	1-0	McCall
09/09/95	Raith Rovers	H	4-0	McCoist 2, Miller, Robertson
16/09/95	Falkirk	A	2-0	Salenko, Robertson
23/09/95	Hibernian	H	0-1	
30/09/95	Celtic	A	2-0	Cleland, Gascoigne
03/10/95	Motherwell	H	2-1	Gascoigne, McCoist
07/10/95	Aberdeen	A	1-0	Moore
14/10/95	Partick Thistle	A	4-0	Gough, Durie 3
21/10/95	Heart of Midlothian	H	4-1	Gascoigne, Salenko 2, Durie
28/10/95	Raith Rovers	A	2-2	Gough, Petric
04/11/95	Falkirk	H	2-0	McCoist 2
08/11/95	Kilmarnock	A	2-0	McLaren, Salenko
11/11/95	Aberdeen	H	1-1	Salenko
19/11/95	Celtic	H	3-3	Laudrup, McCoist, og (McKinlay)
25/11/95	Hibernian	A	4-1	McCoist, og (Dods), Miller, Durie
02/12/95	Heart of Midlothian	A	2-0	McCoist (p), Gascoigne
09/12/95	Partick Thistle	H	1-0	Durie
19/12/95	Motherwell	A	0-0	
26/12/95	Kilmarnock	H	3-0	Salenko, Durie (p), Gascoigne
30/12/95	Hibernian	H	7-0	Miller, Durie 4, Gascoigne, Salenko
03/01/96	Celtic	A	0-0	
06/01/96	Falkirk	A	4-0	Durie, McCoist 2 (1p), Robertson
13/01/96	Raith Rovers	H	4-0	McCoist, Durie 2, Ferguson
20/01/96	Heart of Midlothian	H	0-3	
03/02/96	Partick Thistle	A	2-1	Gascoigne 2
10/02/96	Motherwell	H	3-2	Ferguson, McLaren, McCoist (p)
25/02/96	Aberdeen	A	1-0	Gascoigne (p)
03/03/96	Hibernian	A	2-0	og (Mitchell), Laudrup (p)
17/03/96	Celtic	H	1-1	McLaren
23/03/96	Falkirk	H	3-2	Gascoigne, Andersen 2
30/03/96	Raith Rovers	A	4-2	McCoist 3 (1p), Durie (p)
10/04/96	Heart of Midlothian	A	0-2	
13/04/96	Partick Thistle	H	5-0	Andersen 3, McCall, Gough
20/04/96	Motherwell	A	3-1	McCall, Andersen, Gascoigne
28/04/96	Aberdeen	H	3-1	Gascoigne 3 (1p)
04/05/96	Kilmarnock	A	3-0	McCoist, Durie 2

PROMOTED CLUBS

SECOND DIVISION FINAL TABLE 95/96

		Pd	W	D	L	F	A	Pt	GD
1	**Dunfermline Athletic**	**36**	**21**	**8**	**7**	**73**	**41**	**71**	**+32**
2	**Dundee United**	**36**	**19**	**10**	**7**	**73**	**37**	**67**	**+36**
3	Greenock Morton	36	20	7	9	57	39	67	+18
4	St. Johnstone	36	19	8	9	60	36	65	+24
5	Dundee	36	15	12	9	53	40	57	+13
6	St. Mirren	36	13	8	15	46	51	47	-5
7	Clydebank	36	10	10	16	39	58	40	-19
8	Airdrieonians	36	9	11	16	43	54	38	-11
9	Hamilton Academical	36	10	6	20	40	57	36	-17
10	Dumbarton	36	3	2	31	23	94	11	-71

PROMOTION/RELEGATION PLAY-OFF
Partick Thistle 1, Dundee United 1
Dundee United 2, Partick Thistle 1 (aet)
(Dundee United 3-2)

CLUB DIRECTORY

Dunfermline Athletic FC
East End Park
Halbeath Road
Dunfermline
KY12 7RB
tel - (01383) 724295
fax - (01383) 723468
Year of Formation - 1885
Chairman C.R. Woodrow
Secretary - Paul A.M. D'Mello
Manager - Bert Paton
Stadium - East End Park (18,328)

MAJOR HONOURS
Domestic Cup - (2) 1961, 1968.

CLUB DIRECTORY

Dundee United FC
Tannadice Park
Tannadice Street
Dundee DD3 7JW
tel - (01382) 833166
fax - (01382) 882689
Year of Formation - 1909
Chairman - Jim McLean
Secretary - Miss Priti Trivedi
Manager - Billy Kirkwood
Stadium - Tannadice Park (12,616)

MAJOR HONOURS
League Championship - (1) 1983.
Domestic Cup - (1) 1994.

SLOVAKIA

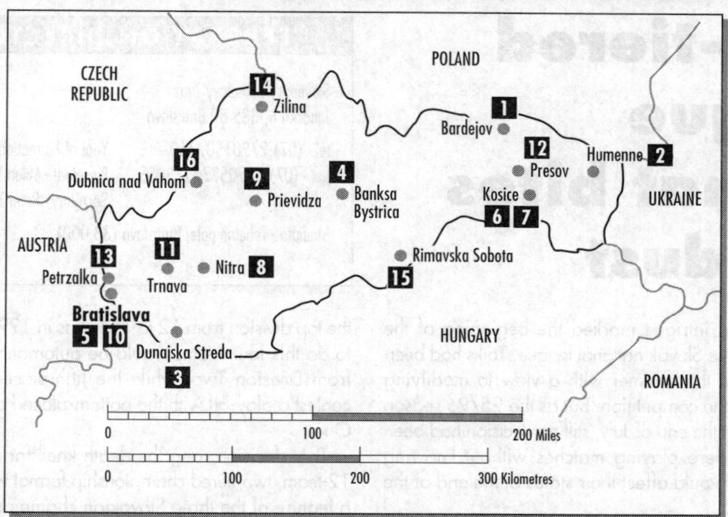

1	BSC JAS BARDEJOV	905
2	CHEMLON HUMENNE	906
3	DAC DUNAJSKA STREDA	907
4	DUKLA BANSKA BYSTRICA	908
5	INTER BRATISLAVA	909
6	1.FC KOSICE	910
7	LOKOMOTIVA KOSICE	911
8	FC NITRA	912
9	PETRIMEX PRIEVIDZA	913
10	SLOVAN BRATISLAVA	914
11	SPARTAK TRNAVA	915
12	TATRAN PRESOV	916
13	ARTMEDIA PETRZALKA	917
14	MSK ZILINA	917
15	RIMAVSKA SOBOTA	917
16	SPARTAK DUBNICA NAD VAHOM	917

TITLE HAT-TRICK FOR SLOVAN

Two-tiered league format bites the dust

FEDERATION DIRECTORY

Slovensky Futbalovy Zvaz
Junácka 6, 835 80 Bratislava

tel - (07) 2790150/160
fax - (07) 2790577/279055

Year of Formation - 1990
President - Milan Sluzanic
Secretary - Peter Zidovsky

Stadium - Tehelne pole, Bratislava (33,000)

Uncertainty and intrigue marked the beginning of the third season of the Slovak national league. Talks had been held throughout the summer with a view to modifying the structure of the competition. But as the 95/96 season got underway at the end of July, still no decision had been made. Teams were playing matches without knowing how the results would affect their status at the end of the season.

It was not until October, several weeks into the campaign, that a decision was finally made and ratified. The conference of league delegates resolved to increase the top division from 12 to 16 teams in 1996/97. In order to do this four teams would be automatically promoted from Division Two, while the fifth-placed team would contest a play-off with the bottom-placed club in Division One.

That decision rang the death knell for the rather odd 12-team, two-tiered championship format which had been a feature of the three Slovakian championships to date. Whether the increase in numbers will improve the mediocre fare dished up so far since the break with the Czech Republic is doubtful.

LEAGUE CHAMPIONSHIP RESULTS 95/96

FIRST PHASE

		1	2	3	4	5	6	7	8	9	10	11	12
1	BSC JAS Bardejov		4-0	4-0	3-1	2-1	1-2	3-0	1-0	2-0	1-2	0-0	1-0
2	Chemlon Humenne	3-1		6-0	1-1	1-2	0-1	2-0	2-2	5-0	1-1	1-2	4-1
3	DAC Dunajska Streda	2-3	4-0		4-0	3-2	0-2	1-1	2-0	2-0	2-4	0-0	1-1
4	Dukla Banska Bystrica	3-0	1-0	2-1		3-0	3-1	4-0	2-0	2-0	0-0	1-0	0-0
5	Inter Bratislava	2-0	2-3	3-1	2-2		1-1	0-3	1-0	2-2	1-3	1-2	3-2
6	1.FC Kosice	1-0	2-0	4-0	1-0	5-1		2-1	2-0	5-0	2-5	3-0	1-2
7	Lokomotiva Kosice	0-1	3-2	3-1	1-0	0-2	0-3		4-0	2-0	1-0	1-2	0-1
8	FC Nitra	3-4	2-1	4-0	2-2	0-0	1-3	1-2		1-1	0-4	0-2	2-1
9	Petrimex Prievidza	0-3	1-2	2-3	1-2	1-0	0-4	0-2	3-1		0-0	1-2	0-2
10	Slovan Bratislava	2-0	3-1	7-1	5-2	1-1	3-1	3-0	6-1	5-0		3-0	4-0
11	Spartak Trnava	1-0	0-3	5-1	2-0	1-0	5-1	3-1	3-0	3-1	1-1		5-2
12	Tatran Presov	2-0	0-0	3-0	0-1	1-0	2-0	2-1	1-0	4-0	0-0	1-1	

SECOND PHASE

CHAMPIONSHIP GROUP		1	2	3	4	5	6
1	BSC JAS Bardejov		0-0	0-3	1-2	0-1	1-0
2	Dukla Banska Bystrica	1-1		1-3	0-0	2-2	1-0
3	1.FC Kosice	3-1	3-1		0-2	1-0	2-1
4	Slovan Bratislava	3-0	0-0	1-0		5-2	3-1
5	Spartak Trnava	3-0	2-0	0-0	0-1		1-0
6	Tatran Presov	1-0	1-1	1-0	0-0	1-3	

RELEGATION GROUP		1	2	3	4	5	6
1	Chemlon Humenne		0-1	1-0	2-0	1-0	4-2
2	DAC Dunajska Streda	3-1		0-4	0-1	1-2	3-1
3	Inter Bratislava	0-0	3-2		3-0	1-0	2-1
4	Lokomotiva Kosice	0-3	5-1	1-0		3-0	0-3
5	FC Nitra	2-0	0-1	1-1	4-1		1-0
6	Petrimex Prievidza	3-0	3-0	2-1	0-0	3-0	

LEAGUE CHAMPIONSHIP FINAL TABLE 95/96

FIRST PHASE		Home						Away					Total						
		Pd	W	D	L	F	A	W	D	L	F	A	W	D	L	F	A	Pt	GD
1	Slovan Bratislava	22	10	1	0	42	7	5	5	1	20	9	15	6	1	62	16	51	+46
2	1.FC Kosice	22	9	0	2	28	9	6	1	4	19	16	15	1	6	47	25	46	+22
3	Spartak Trnava	22	9	1	1	29	10	5	3	3	11	12	14	4	4	40	22	46	+18
4	Dukla Banska Bystrica	22	9	2	0	21	2	2	3	6	11	22	11	5	6	32	24	38	+8
5	BSC JAS Bardejov	22	8	1	2	22	6	4	0	7	12	19	12	1	9	34	25	37	+9
6	Tatran Presov	22	7	3	1	16	3	3	2	6	12	21	10	5	7	28	24	35	+4
7	Chemlon Humenne	22	5	3	3	26	11	3	1	7	12	22	8	4	10	38	33	28	+5
8	Lokomotiva Kosice	22	6	0	5	15	12	3	1	7	11	21	9	1	12	26	33	28	-7
9	Inter Bratislava	22	4	3	4	18	19	2	2	7	9	18	6	5	11	27	37	23	-10
10	DAC Dunajska Streda	22	5	3	3	21	13	1	0	10	8	43	6	3	13	29	56	21	-27
11	FC Nitra	22	3	3	5	16	20	0	1	10	4	27	3	4	15	20	47	13	-27
12	Petrimex Prievidza	22	2	1	8	9	21	0	2	9	4	33	2	3	17	13	54	9	-41

SECOND PHASE

CHAMPIONSHIP GROUP		Home						Away					Total						
		Pd	W	D	L	F	A	W	D	L	F	A	W	D	L	F	A	Pt	GD
1	Slovan Bratislava	32	14	2	0	54	10	8	7	1	25	10	22	9	1	79	20	75	+59
2	1.FC Kosice	32	13	0	3	37	14	8	2	6	25	19	21	2	9	62	33	65	+29
3	Spartak Trnava	32	12	2	2	35	11	7	4	5	19	21	19	6	7	54	32	63	+22
4	Dukla Banska Bystrica	32	10	5	1	26	8	2	6	8	13	28	12	11	9	39	36	47	+3
5	Tatran Presov	32	9	5	2	20	7	3	2	11	14	29	12	7	13	34	36	43	-2
6	BSC JAS Bardejov	32	9	2	5	24	12	4	1	11	14	30	13	3	16	38	42	42	-4

RELEGATION GROUP		Home						Away					Total						
		Pd	W	D	L	F	A	W	D	L	F	A	W	D	L	F	A	Pt	GD
7	Chemlon Humenne	32	9	3	4	34	14	4	2	10	16	30	13	5	14	50	44	44	+6
8	Lokomotiva Kosice	32	9	0	7	24	19	4	2	10	13	30	13	2	17	37	49	41	-12
9	Inter Bratislava	32	8	4	4	27	22	3	3	10	15	23	11	7	14	42	45	40	-3
10	DAC Dunajska Streda	32	7	3	6	28	22	3	0	13	13	54	10	3	19	41	76	33	-35
11	FC Nitra	32	6	4	6	24	23	1	1	14	6	36	7	5	20	30	59	33	-29
12	Petrimex Prievidza	32	6	2	8	20	22	1	2	13	11	43	7	4	21	31	65	25	-34

N.B. After 22 matches the top six play off for the title and the bottom six play off to avoid relegation.

The 95/96 season was expected to provide a great deal more excitement and competitiveness than the previous edition, which had seen Slovan Bratislava blast to a second successive dometic title with 20 points to spare. Two teams - the traditionally strong Spartak Trnava and the financially strong 1.FC Kosice - paraded themselves as potential challengers to Slovan's crown.

In the autumn it was Trnava who made the running. They got off on the wrong foot with a 0-3 defeat by Kosice but steadied themselves thereafter and reached the winter break with a one-point advantage over the defending champions. Slovan began disastrously, winning just three of their opening nine matches, which was a major surprise coming as it did in tandem with three fine UEFA Cup victories (Slovan hammered Osijek, then, for the second year in a row, went out to a big German team after winning the home leg 2-1 and losing the return 0-3)

The scapegoat for this false start in the league was new coach Anton Dragun. With the team placed embarrassingly in the middle of the table, he was given the boot and replaced immediately by Dusan Galis - the man who had guided Slovan to all their triumphs in the '90s but who had voluntarily moved 'upstairs' to a technical director rôle in the summer.

Consolidated by Galis's return, Slovan set out in pursuit of the leaders and rapidly began to munch away at the deficit. Their last seven matches before the mid-season interval yielded a maximum 21 points and a remarkable tally of 29 goals.

Up the road in Trnava the locals were getting excited. The Spartak stadium was a fun place to be on match days as the club's traditionally impressive support grew in numbers and provided easily the best atmosphere at any ground in the country. As a rule, when Trnava played at home, their attendance was bigger than those at the other five grounds put together.

The team's ambitious coach Karol Pecze was not satisfied with first place at the halfway point. He had his eyes on the title itself. Aware that his squad was not sufficiently deep in quality to withstand a rash of injuries or suspensions, he made every effort to strengthen the team during the winter break. But the funds were not forthcoming, and as the campaign resumed, the inevitable happened. Trnava began to slip down the table and at the 22-match cut-off point they were down in third place behind Slovan and 1.FC Kosice.

The club's fall from grace was characterised by an unsavoury episode at the end of their home match with Chemlon Humenne when club skipper Jan Gabriel and U-21 defender Jaroslav Hrabal were involved in a scuffle with officials. The result of this fracas was a lengthy ban for each of the perpetrators and, worse still, the transformation of the 0-0 scoreline into a statury 3-0 win for Humenne. Two months later Gabriel and Hrabal would be missing as Trnava were genuinely beaten by the same opponents, 2-1 in the final of the Slovakian Cup.

With Trnava falling away, 1.FC Kosice were expected to take up the challenge to Slovan. But they had lost to Slovan twice in the first phase of the campaign, and they were to be defeated twice more by the title holders in the play-offs. As far as the championship was concerned, that was that. Slovan had again shown themselves to be on a different plane from their rivals.

INTERNATIONAL HONOURS

European Club Competitions	
Cup-winners' Cup	Slovan Bratislava (1969)

NATIONAL TEAM RESULTS 95/96

16/08/95	Azerbaijan (ECQ)	A	Trabzon	1-0	Jancula (60)
06/09/95	Israel (ECQ)	H	Kosice	1-0	Jancula (55)
11/10/95	Poland (ECQ)	H	Bratislava	4-1	Dubovsky (32p), Jancula (68), Ujlaky (77), Simon (83)
15/11/95	Romania (ECQ)	H	Kosice	0-2	
27/03/96	Belarus	H	Nitra	4-0	Simon (24), Timko (32), Ujlaky (60), Juriga (83)
24/04/96	Bulgaria	H	Trnava	0-0	
09/05/96	Sweden	A	Helsingborg	1-2	Zeman (65)
18/05/96	Mexico	N	Chicago	2-5	Maixner (34), Juriga (65)

DOMESTIC CUP RESULTS

1/8 FINALS

Spartak Dubnica 0, Spartak Trnava 3
Selce 0, Dukla Banska Bystrica 2
Matador Puchov 0, SK Zilina 0 (3-1 on pens.)
Piestany 1, Chemlon Humenne 5
Slovan Levice 2, BSC JAS Bardejov 1
SP Trebisov 1, Slovan Bratislava 1 (3-1 on pens.)
Rimavska Sobota 4, DAC Dunajska Streda 1
TJ Gabcikovo 2, Inter Bratislava 0

QUARTER-FINALS

Slovan Levice 0, Chemlon Humenne 2
Dukla Banska Bystrica 7, TJ Gabcikovo 0
Spartak Trnava 2, SP Trebisov 1
Rimavska Sobota 2, Matador Puchov 0

SEMI-FINALS

Dukla Banska Bystrica v Spartak Trnava 1-0; 1-3 (Spartak Trnava 3-2)
Chemlon Humenne v Rimavska Sobota 4-0; 1-1 (Chemlon Humenne 5-1)

FINAL

26/05/96, Vranov
CHEMLON HUMENNE 2 Lubarsky (37), Mati (61)
SPARTAK TRNAVA 1 Formanko (83)
referee - Ihring
CHEMLON HUMENNE - Bucek; Boliat; Sivy (Scviranka 61), Dzurik, Hanc; Valkucak, Sukennik, Tomovcik, Sovic; Lubarsky, Mati.
SPARTAK TRNAVA - Fisan; Tibensky; Kapko, Karhan; Balis, Kostka, Simon, Vegh; Macak (Sotak 77), Radvanyi (Formanko 60), Ujlaky.

TOP SCORERS

29	Robert SEMENIK (1.FC Kosice)
12	Szilard NEMETH (Slovan Bratislava)
10	Fabio Luis GOMES (Slovan Bratislava)
	Lubos LUHOVY (Inter Bratislava)
	Julius SIMON (Spartak Trnava)
	Marek UJLAKY (Spartak Trnava)
	Ruslan LUBARSKY (Chemlon Humenne)
9	Stefan MAIXNER (Slovan Bratislava)
	Mikulas RADVANYI (Spartak Trnava)
	Norbert HRNCAR (FC Nitra)

NATIONAL TEAM APPEARANCES 95/96

Coach - Jozef JANKECH	AZB	ISR	POL	ROM	BLS	BUL	SWE	MEX	Cps	Gls
Ladislav MOLNAR (12/09/60) - Slovan Bratislava	G	G	G	G	G72	G	G	G42	18	-
Ladislav PECKO (27/06/68) - Slovan Bratislava	D	D		D46				s46	4	-
Milos SOBONA (25/11/75) - Slovan Bratislava	D								1	-
Dusan TITTEL (27/12/66) - Slovan Bratislava	D	D	D	D	D46	D	D	D	18	2
Vladimir KINDER (04/03/69) - Slovan Bratislava	D	D	M	D		s75	D	D	21	1
Igor BALIS (05/01/70) - Spartak Trnava	M89	M89	M	M	M	M61	M81	M	9	-
Robert TOMASCHEK (25/08/72) - Slovan Bratislava	M			M	M	M	M	M	19	-
Julius SIMON (19/07/65) - Spartak Trnava	M	M80	M	M78	M72	M	M65	M	10	2
Lubomir MORAVCIK (22/06/65) - AS Saint-Etienne (FRA)	M78	M	M	M	M	M	M		17	2
Peter DUBOVSKY (07/05/72) - Real Oviedo (ESP)	A	A	A	A		M	M75		16	7
Stefan RUSNAK (07/08/71) - Slovan Bratislava	A58	s61							7	1
Tibor JANCULA (16/06/69) - SV Casino Salzburg (AUT)	s58	A61	A87	A69				s46	5	3
Lubomir FAKTOR (18/03/67) - Slovan Bratislava	s78	s80							5	1
Karol PRAZENICA (15/11/70) - OFI (GRE)	s89								5	-
Miroslav KARHAN (21/06/76) - Spartak Trnava		D	D	D	D	D	D	D	7	-
Jozef JURIGA (09/09/68) - Slovan Bratislava		M	M71	s46	s72			M	5	2
Rastislav KOSTKA (11/09/72) - Spartak Trnava		s89							1	-
Marian ZEMAN (07/07/74) - Slovan Bratislava/Istanbulspor (TUR)			D			D	D		11	1
Marek UJLAKY (26/03/74) - Spartak Trnava			s71	s69	s46	A75	s65		6	2
Marian BOCHNOVIC (03/03/70) - Dukla Banska Bystrica			s87						1	-
Robert SEMENIK (13/01/73) - 1.FC Kosice				s78	A64		s75		3	-
Milos GLONEK (26/09/68) - SM Caen (FRA)					D				12	-
Dusan TOTH (08/02/71) - Dukla Banska Bystrica					M				1	-
Jaroslav TIMKO (28/09/65) - Petra Drnovice (TCH)					A46	A	A75		13	5
Ivan KOZAK (18/06/70) - 1.FC Kosice					s46	s61	s81	D46	10	-
Szilard NEMETH (08/08/78) - Slovan Bratislava					s64				1	-
Miroslav SEMAN (14/01/73) - Tatran Presov					s72				1	-
Vladislav ZVARA (11/12/71) - 1.FC Kosice							s75	M	10	-
Stefan MAIXNER (14/04/68) - Slovan Bratislava								A46	3	1
Ivan ONDRUSKA (12/09/67) - Dukla Banska Bystrica								s42	1	-

Slovan's superiority was down to a good coach, a substantial squad of players, and phenomenal consistency in the games that mattered. As well as taking maximum points off the eventual runners-up, Slovan won three and drew one of their four encounters with Spartak Trnava. Unbeaten since August, they won the championship with a brilliant series of performances in the middle third of the campaign. As many as 50 of their 79 goals came in a 12-match sequence during that period. And they were all shared out amongst the squad, with teenager Szilard Nemeth - the "new Dubovsky" - finishing as the club's top scorer on 12 goals.

That tally was nowhere near good enough to rival the remarkable scoring feats of Kosice's goal-machine Robert Semenik. Top scorer the season before whilst with Dukla Banska Bystrica, Semenik helped himself to 29 goals, retaining the Golden Boot by a veritable landslide.

Surprisingly, the 23-year-old made just three appearances for the Slovakian national team during the season, and he did not complete 90 minutes in any of those matches against Romania, Belarus and Sweden. Slovakia's best performance of the season came a month before Semenik made his début, with a 4-1 thrashing of Poland in Bratislava. That unlikely scoreline provided new coach

EUROPEAN CUPS RESULTS 95/96

CUP-WINNERS' CUP

● INTER BRATISLAVA

Preliminary round VALLETTA (MLT)

A 0-0

Hyll; Tomko; Kitka, Sevela, Kuna (Dojcan 74); Rupec, Greguska, Obsitnik, Schulz; Vasik (Luhovy 65), Medved.

H 5-2 Rupec (10), Tomko (15, 58), Greguska (79), Landerl (85)
Hyll; Tomko; Sevela, Kuna (Schulz 10), Schulcz; Rupec, Greguska, Obsitnik; Vasik, Medved, Luhovy (Landerl 71).

1st round REAL ZARAGOZA (ESP)

H 0-2

Hyll; Tomko; Dojcan, Kuna, Schulz; Rupec, Greguska (Malatinsky 61), Obsitnik, Prokop (Kitka 75); Luhovy, Landerl (Medved 71).

A 1-3 Obsitnik (76)
Hyll; Tomko; Rupec (Schulcz 79), Kuna, Sevela; Prokop, Greguska, Obsitnik, Malatinsky (Vasik 68); Luhovy, Medved (Landerl 46).

UEFA CUP

● SLOVAN BRATISLAVA

Preliminary round OSIJEK (CRO)

H 4-0 Tittel (8), Rusnak (15, 41), Faktor (90)
Molnar; Tittel; Pecko, Zeman, Kinder; Juriga, Tomaschek, Faktor, Demo; Rusnak (Nemeth 70), Gomes (Nigro 60).

A 2-0 Rusnak (55), Gomes (86)
Molnar; Tittel; Sobona, Zeman, Kinder; Pecko (Nigro 72), Tomaschek, Demo (Gomes 62), Juriga; Faktor, Rusnak (Nemeth 60).

1st round 1.FC KAISERSLAUTERN (GER)

H 2-1 Tittel (28), Sobona (74)
Molnar; Tittel; Pecko, Sobona (Nigro 77), Kinder; Slovak, Juriga, Tomaschek, Demo; Faktor (Nemeth 58), Rusnak (Muzlay 73).

A 0-3

Molnar; Tittel; Pecko, Zeman, Kinder; Slovak, Juriga, Tomaschek, Faktor; Rusnak, Nemeth (Gomes 3).

● 1.FC KOSICE

Preliminary round ÚJPESTI TE (HUN)

H 0-1

Ondruska; Weiss; Kozak, Hipp, Hornyak; Bugar, Kral, Dina, Labant (Chytil 85); Semenik (Janocko 75), Gostic.

A 1-2 Weiss (85)
Ondruska; Weiss; Kozak, Kral, Hornyak; Labant, Danko, Dina (Gostic 70); Janocko, Semenik (Bugar 61), Pancik.

Jozef Jankech with his third successive European Championship victory and went a long way to making up for the 0-5 humiliation suffered against the same opponents a few months earlier in Zabrze.

Slovakia's Euro '96 challenge ended on a low, however, with the subsequent 0-2 home defeat by Romania. And there was worse news a month later when the World Cup qualifying draw was made in Paris, handing Slovakia a mission impossible as they found themselves grouped with Spain, Yugoslavia and...the Czech Republic.

Granted, the draw served up a tasty menu for Slovakian fans to get their teeth into, but it offered little prospect of qualification for the 1998 finals in France. Jozef Jankech's team will do blindingly well to finish third in such exalted company. A victory at home to the Czechs would no doubt ease the pain of elimination.

PLAYERS OF THE SEASON

MIROSLAV KARHAN

Real quality is not easy to find in the Slovakian league, but one player who looks set for a prolonged career at 'European level' is young Spartak Trnava defender Miroslav Karhan. Slovakian national team coach Jozef Jankech certainly believes he has a real jewel at his disposal. After making the step up from the U-21 side and representing the senior team for the first time against Israel, Karhan did not let the opportunity slip, clinging tenaciously to his place on the left side of defence for every remaining minute of Slovakia's 95/96 international season. Tall, quick and two-footed, the 20-year-old only needs to improve his technique to become a complete defender.

JULIUS SIMON

At 31, Spartak Trnava midfielder is showing no sign that he is on the wane. On the contrary, his performances have improved beyond recognition in recent years, and the 95/96 season was undoubtedly his best yet, ending as it did with his election as the Slovakian Players' Player of the Year. Simon moved to Trnava after falling out with the coach at 1.FC Kosice and he quickly became a favourite of the Spartak fans with his vision and invention in midfield. His ability to act as the team's string-pulling playmaker was soon recognised by Jozef Jankech, who handed Simon the same rôle in the Slovakian national side.

BSC JAS BARDEJOV

CLUB DIRECTORY

BSC JAS Bardejov
Druzstevná 1
085 01 Bardejov
tel - (0935) 2840
fax - (0935) 4264
Year of Formation - 1922
President - Frantisek Hvisc
Coach - Jozef Bubenko (96/97 - Karol Kisel)
Stadium - Bardejov (8,000)

APPEARANCES 95/96

	P	Ap	(s)	Gls
Jan CHRENKO	M	26		
Jozef DANKO	M	25		4
Peter FUTEJ	D	31		
Robert HARCAR	M		(5)	
Jozef HRIVNAK	A	19	(7)	8
Stanislav HVOZDA	G	12		
Stefan JACKO	M	19	(6)	1
Jan JURCAK	D	22	(5)	
Igor KASANA	M	5	(7)	1
Peter KAVKA	A	4	(9)	
Marian LALIK	A	12	(1)	
Vladimir LEITNER	D	3		
Jozef LUKAC	M	15	(2)	2
Lubos LUKAC	G	20	(1)	
Lubomir MICAK	M	9	(2)	
Jozef PAVLIK	M	16		3
Slavomir PRUCNY	D	30		5
Radoslav STOJAK	M	2	(9)	2
Marian SUCHANCOK	D	28		3
Alexander TYC	A	9	(12)	2
Jozef URBLIK	A	24	(5)	7
Frantisek VILIM	M	21	(4)	
Patrik ZAJAC	M		(2)	

LEAGUE RESULTS 1995/96

29/07/95	Inter Bratislava	A	0-2	
05/08/95	Dukla Banska Bystrica	H	3-1	Hrivnak 2, Suchancok
19/08/95	Chemlon Humenne	A	1-3	Urblik
30/08/95	Petrimex Prievidza	H	2-0	Kasana, Prucny
09/09/95	1.FC Kosice	A	0-1	
16/09/95	Spartak Trnava	H	0-0	
22/09/95	Slovan Bratislava	A	0-2	
30/09/95	FC Nitra	H	1-0	Urblik
04/10/95	DAC Dunajska Streda	A	3-2	Urblik, Lukac J., Danko
14/10/95	Lokomotiva Kosice	A	1-0	Urblik
21/10/95	Tatran Presov	H	1-0	Urblik
28/10/95	Inter Bratislava	H	2-1	Hrivnak, Prucny
04/11/95	Dukla Banska Bystrica	A	0-3	
18/11/95	Chemlon Humenne	H	4-0	Prucny (p), Hrivnak, Suchancok 2
25/11/95	Petrimex Prievidza	A	3-0	Danko, Hrivnak 2
02/12/95	1.FC Kosice	H	1-2	Hrivnak
02/03/96	Spartak Trnava	A	0-1	
09/03/96	Slovan Bratislava	H	1-2	Urblik
16/03/96	FC Nitra	A	4-3	Pavlik, Hrivnak, Prucny, Stojak
23/03/96	DAC Dunajska Streda	H	4-0	Danko, Lukac J., Pavlik, Jacko
30/03/96	Lokomotiva Kosice	H	3-0	Pavlik, Tyc 2
12/04/96	Tatran Presov	A	0-2	
PLAY-OFFS				
16/04/96	Slovan Bratislava	H	1-2	Urblik
20/04/96	Tatran Presov	A	0-1	
27/04/96	Spartak Trnava	H	0-1	
04/05/96	Dukla Banska Bystrica	A	1-1	Prucny
14/05/96	1.FC Kosice	H	0-3	
23/05/96	Tatran Presov	H	1-0	Danko
28/05/96	Slovan Bratislava	A	0-3	
01/06/96	Spartak Trnava	A	0-3	
06/06/96	Dukla Banska Bystrica	H	0-0	
12/06/96	1.FC Kosice	A	1-3	Stojak

CHEMLON HUMENNE

CLUB DIRECTORY

FC Chemlon Humenne
Chemlonska 1
066 01 Humenne
tel - (0933) 62696
fax - (0933) 64643
Year of Formation - 1903
President - Dusan Kapral
Secretary - Viktor Pcola
Coach - Ondrej Danko
Stadium - Chemlon (18,000)

MAJOR HONOURS
Domestic Cup - (1) 1996.

APPEARANCES 95/96

	P	Ap	(s)	Gls
Lubos BABJAK	G	1		
Niksa BOLJAT (CRO)	D	18	(1)	
Juraj BUCEK	G	13	(1)	
Peter DZURIK	D	26	(1)	3
Stefan GABRIA	M	1	(3)	
Frantisek HANC	D	25	(2)	1
Marcel HULAK	D	1		
Stefan KALEJA	A	5	(10)	2
Robert KEREKES	G	8		
Vojtech KISS	M	18	(5)	5
Leonid KOCURISIN	M	2		
Igor KRAPIVKIN (UKR)	G	7		
Marian KRIVJANCIN	D	16	(4)	
Jan LISIVKA	D	2		
Ruslan LUBARSKY (UKR)	A	27	(1)	10
Jozef MALINAK	D	3	(4)	
Lubomir MATI	A	16	(1)	5
Rudolf MATTA	M	2	(8)	
Marian PRUSAK	A	11	(13)	2
Ivo PILIP	G	3		
Milan SCIRANKA	D	1	(7)	
Vladimir SIVY	D	31		3
Milan SOTAK	A	3	(3)	2
Jaroslav SOVIC	M	22	(1)	2
Cyril STACHURA	D	12	(8)	
Igor SUKENNIK	M	27	(2)	4
Rastislav TOMOVCIK	A	21	(1)	4
Jozef VALKUCAK	M	29		4
Pavol VYTYKAC	A	1	(1)	

LEAGUE RESULTS 1995/96

29/07/95	FC Nitra	H	2-2	Sivy, Lubarsky
05/08/95	DAC Dunajska Streda	A	0-4	
19/08/95	BSC JAS Bardejov	H	3-1	Kiss, Sukennik, Valkucak
30/08/95	Tatran Presov	A	0-0	
09/09/95	Inter Bratislava	H	1-2	Kiss
16/09/95	Dukla Banska Bystrica	A	0-1	
22/09/95	Lokomotiva Kosice	H	2-0	Sovic, Kaleja
30/09/95	Petrimex Prievidza	H	5-0	Lubarsky, Kaleja, Sukennik, Dzurik, Sovic
04/10/95	1.FC Kosice	A	0-2	
15/10/95	Spartak Trnava	H	1-2	Dzurik
21/10/95	Slovan Bratislava	A	1-3	Kiss
28/10/95	FC Nitra	A	1-2	Sotak
04/11/95	DAC Dunajska Streda	H	6-0	Hanc, Dzurik, Lubarsky, Prusak, Tomovcik, Sotak
18/11/95	BSC JAS Bardejov	A	0-4	
25/11/95	Tatran Presov	H	4-1	Lubarsky, Kiss 2, Sivy
02/12/95	Inter Bratislava	A	3-2	Prusak, Tomovcik, Lubarsky
02/03/96	Dukla Banska Bystrica	H	1-1	Mati
09/03/96	Lokomotiva Kosice	A	2-3	Valkucak, Tomovcik
16/03/96	Petrimex Prievidza	A	2-1	Lubarsky 2 (1p)
23/03/96	1.FC Kosice	H	0-1	
30/03/96	Spartak Trnava	A	0-0	(later awarded 3-0)
12/04/96	Slovan Bratislava	H	1-1	Sukennik
PLAY-OFFS				
16/04/96	DAC Dunajska Streda	A	1-3	Mati
20/04/96	Lokomotiva Kosice	H	2-0	Sivy, Valkucak
27/04/96	Petrimex Prievidza	A	0-3	
04/05/96	FC Nitra	A	0-2	
14/05/96	Inter Bratislava	H	1-0	Lubarsky
18/05/96	DAC Dunajska Streda	H	0-1	
23/05/96	Lokomotiva Kosice	A	3-0	Mati, Tomovcik, Lubarsky
01/06/96	Petrimex Prievidza	H	4-2	Mati, Sukennik, Lubarsky, Valkucak
06/06/96	FC Nitra	H	1-0	Mati
12/06/96	Inter Bratislava	A	0-0	

DAC DUNAJSKA STREDA

CLUB DIRECTORY

FC DAC Gemer Dunajska Streda
Sportova 18
929 01 Dunajska Streda
tel - (0709) 526874
fax - (0709) 526660
Year of Formation - 1904
President - Imrich Santa
Secretary - Ladislav Molnar
Coach - Jozef Valovic; Anton Grajcar; Juraj Szikora; Jozef Adamec
Stadium - DAC (12,410)

MAJOR HONOURS

Domestic Cup (Czechoslovakia) - (1) 1987.

APPEARANCES 95/96

	P	Ap	(s)	Gls
Jozef BALASKA	M	6	(9)	
Vojtech BALLA	M		(2)	
Eugen BARI	A	28	(3)	8
Jan BLAHUSIAK	D	12	(1)	1
Roman CHUDIK	D	4		
Tibor CSEFAI	G	1	(1)	
Erik CHYTIL	A	17	(2)	4
Norbert CSOKNAI	D	6	(1)	
Peter FIEBER	M	13	(2)	1
Arpad GÖGH	D	6		
Roman GREGUSKA	M	16		1
Peter KALAVSKY	M	3	(11)	2
Zsolt KIANEK	M	29		
Szilard KLEMPA	D	2	(5)	
Milan KRAL	A	2	(13)	2
Peter LERANT	M	20	(2)	
Matej MEHES	M	7	(5)	
Miroslav ORSULA	M		(1)	
Rudolf PAVLIK	M	18	(7)	2
Attila PINTE	D	13	(1)	4
Rastislav PROKOP	D	8		2
Milan RIMANOVSKY	A	24	(7)	8
Ivan SCHULCZ	D	13		
Peter SANTA	G	31		
Richard TRUTZ	D	28	(1)	1
Jozef ÜRGE	D	4	(6)	2
Alexander VEGH	D	16		
Vladimir VESELY	D	3		
Tibor ZSAKOVICS	D	22	(3)	3
Lubos ZUZIAK	D		(1)	

LEAGUE RESULTS 1995/96

29/07/95	Dukla Banska Bystrica	A	1-2	Zsakovics
05/08/95	Chemlon Humenne	H	4-0	Pinte, Blahusiak, Zsakovics, Ürge
19/08/95	Petrimex Prievidza	A	3-2	Fieber, Zsakovics, Bari
30/08/95	1.FC Kosice	H	0-2	
09/09/95	Spartak Trnava	A	1-5	Bari
16/09/95	Slovan Bratislava	H	2-4	Bari, Ürge
23/09/95	FC Nitra	A	0-4	
30/09/95	Lokomotiva Kosice	A	1-3	Pinte
04/10/95	BSC JAS Bardejov	H	2-3	Rimanovsky, Bari (p)
14/10/95	Tatran Presov	A	0-3	
21/10/95	Inter Bratislava	H	3-2	Bari, Pavlik (p), Pinte
28/10/95	Dukla Banska Bystrica	H	4-0	Chytil 2, Pinte, Rimanovsky
04/11/95	Chemlon Humenne	A	0-6	
18/11/95	Petrimex Prievidza	H	2-0	Rimanovsky, Bari
25/11/95	1.FC Kosice	A	0-4	
02/12/95	Spartak Trnava	H	0-0	
02/03/96	Slovan Bratislava	A	1-7	Bari
09/03/96	FC Nitra	H	2-0	Rimanovsky 2
16/03/96	Lokomotiva Kosice	H	1-1	Prokop
23/03/96	BSC JAS Bardejov	A	0-4	
30/03/96	Tatran Presov	H	1-1	Bari
12/04/96	Inter Bratislava	A	1-3	Chytil
PLAY-OFFS				
16/04/96	Chemlon Humenne	H	3-1	Prokop, Trutz, Chytil (p)
20/04/96	Inter Bratislava	A	2-3	Kalavsky 2
28/04/96	FC Nitra	H	1-2	Greguska
04/05/96	Lokomotiva Kosice	H	0-1	
14/05/96	Petrimex Prievidza	A	0-3	
18/05/96	Chemlon Humenne	A	1-0	Rimanovsky
23/05/96	Inter Bratislava	H	0-4	
01/06/96	FC Nitra	A	1-0	Rimanovsky
06/06/96	Lokomotiva Kosice	A	1-5	Pavlik (p)
12/06/96	Petrimex Prievidza	H	3-1	Kral 2, Rimanovsky

DUKLA BANSKA BYSTRICA

CLUB DIRECTORY

FK Dukla Banska Bystrica
Stadion SNP na Stiavnickach
974 01 Banska Bystrica
tel - (088) 32593
fax - (088) 32593
Year of Formation - 1965
President - Ivan Korbel
Secretary - Jozef Parso
Coach - Jan Ilavsky (96/97 - Jan Kocian)
Stadium - SNP na Stiavnickach (11,500)

APPEARANCES 95/96

	P	Ap	(s)	Gls
Peter BABNIC	A	15	(13)	4
Ivan BARTOS	M	5	(2)	
Marek BAZIK	M	2	(14)	1
Miroslav BAZIK	M	10		
Marian BOCHNOVIC	M	27		7
Martin DANKO	D	13	(2)	1
Norbert DIKACZ	A	16	(8)	3
Vratislav GRESKO	A		(1)	
Peter GUNDA	D	15		
Jozef HANAK	G	1		
Vladimir HELBICH	M	1	(8)	
Miroslav JANTEK	M	2		
Stefan KARASEK	D	15		1
Milan KMET	D	1	(3)	
Ivan LAPSANSKY	A	1	(11)	1
Mario MICHALIK	G	2		
Jozef MORES	A		(1)	
Ivan ONDRUSKA	G	16		
Robert OVAD	D	26	(2)	
Martin POLJOVKA	D	24	(1)	1
Ivo SCHMUCKER	G	13		
Jozef SLOBODNIK	M	19	(6)	
Miroslav SOVIC	M	10	(3)	3
Marian STRELEC	M	27		3
Norbert TOMAN	A	31	(1)	6
Michal TOT (YUG)	D	1	(1)	
Dusan TOTH	D	27		5
Tibor ZATEK	D	32		1

LEAGUE RESULTS 1995/96

29/07/95	DAC Dunajska Streda	H	2-1	Bochnovic, Lapsansky
05/08/95	BSC JAS Bardejov	A	1-3	Toth (p)
19/08/95	Tatran Presov	H	0-0	
30/08/95	Inter Bratislava	A	2-2	Toth 2 (1p)
09/09/95	Lokomotiva Kosice	H	4-0	Poljovka, Sovic, Zatek, Bazik Ma.
16/09/95	Chemlon Humenne	H	1-0	Babnic
23/09/95	Petrimex Prievidza	A	2-1	Sovic, Karasek
30/09/95	1.FC Kosice	H	3-1	Babnic 2, Toman
06/10/95	Spartak Trnava	A	0-2	
14/10/95	Slovan Bratislava	H	0-0	
21/10/95	FC Nitra	A	2-2	Strelec, Toman
28/10/95	DAC Dunajska Streda	A	0-4	
04/11/95	BSC JAS Bardejov	H	3-0	Danko, Bochnovic, Sovic
18/11/95	Tatran Presov	A	1-0	og (Varga)
25/11/95	Inter Bratislava	H	3-0	Bochnovic 2, Toman
02/12/95	Lokomotiva Kosice	A	0-1	
02/03/96	Chemlon Humenne	A	1-1	Strelec
09/03/96	Petrimex Prievidza	H	2-0	Dikacz, Bochnovic
16/03/96	1.FC Kosice	A	0-1	
23/03/96	Spartak Trnava	H	1-0	Dikacz
30/03/96	Slovan Bratislava	A	2-5	og (Stupala), Toman
12/04/96	FC Nitra	H	2-0	Toman 2
PLAY-OFFS				
16/04/96	Tatran Presov	H	1-0	Dikacz
20/04/96	Spartak Trnava	A	0-2	
27/04/96	1.FC Kosice	H	1-3	Bochnovic
04/05/96	BSC JAS Bardejov	H	1-1	Toth
14/05/96	Slovan Bratislava	A	0-0	
23/05/96	Spartak Trnava	H	2-2	Strelec, Babnic
28/05/96	Tatran Presov	A	1-1	Toth
01/06/96	1.FC Kosice	A	1-3	Bochnovic
06/06/96	BSC JAS Bardejov	A	0-0	
12/06/96	Slovan Bratislava	H	0-0	

INTER BRATISLAVA

CLUB DIRECTORY

ASK Inter Slovnaft Bratislava
Vajnorska 100
832 84 Bratislava
tel - (07) 271007
fax - (07) 271012
Year of Formation - 1940
President - Juraj Oblozinsky
Secretary - Rudolf Jancek
Coach - Jozef Adamec; Jozef Valovic
(96/97 - Jozef Bubenko)
Stadium - Inter (15,000)

MAJOR HONOURS
League Championship (Czechoslovakia) - (1) 1959.
Domestic Cup - (1) 1995.

APPEARANCES 95/96

	P	Ap	(s)	Gls
Miroslav CHVILA	D	23	(2)	1
Juraj CZINEGE	M	10	(3)	1
Jozef DOJCAN	D	10	(3)	1
Jozef GASPAROVIC	M		(1)	
Pavol GOSTIC	A	4	(4)	
Roman GREGUSKA	M	14	(2)	
Miroslav HYLL	G	16		
Frantisek KAMANCZA	M		(3)	
Boris KITKA	D	14		
Vladimir KOZUCH	A	1	(9)	
Roman KRATOCHVIL	D	10		
Peter KRETT	A	7	(6)	3
Martin KUNA	D	27		2
Rolf LANDERL (AUT)	A	19	(6)	5
Lubos LUHOVY	A	25	(2)	10
Milan MALATINSKY	M	8	(9)	
Tomas MEDVED	A	11		5
Peter MRAZ	M	11	(8)	1
Martin OBSITNIK	M	16		5
Jozef PAVLIK	M	1	(2)	
Attila PINTE	M	14		
Vladimir PROKOP	M	17	(3)	3
Dusan RUPEC	M	13	(2)	
Karol SCHULZ	D	5	(6)	1
Jan SOLAR	M	11		2
Kamil SUSKO	G	16		
Martin SEVELA	D	26	(2)	1
Marian TIMKO	D	6		
Lubos TOMKO	D	11	(2)	
Jozef VALACHOVIC	D	4		
Radovan VASIK	A	2	(8)	1

LEAGUE RESULTS 1995/96

29/07/95	BSC JAS Bardejov	H	2-0	Vasik, Medved
05/08/95	Tatran Presov	A	0-1	
19/08/95	Lokomotiva Kosice	H	0-3	
30/08/95	Dukla Banska Bystrica	H	2-2	Obsitnik (p), Landerl
09/09/95	Chemlon Humenne	A	2-1	Dojcan, Obsitnik
18/09/95	Petrimex Prievidza	H	2-2	Medved, Obsitnik (p)
23/09/95	1.FC Kosice	A	1-5	Obsitnik (p)
02/10/95	Spartak Trnava	H	1-2	Medved
06/10/95	Slovan Bratislava	A	1-1	Medved
14/10/95	FC Nitra	H	1-0	Obsitnik (p)
21/10/95	DAC Dunajska Streda	A	2-3	Schulz, Chvila
28/10/95	BSC JAS Bardejov	A	1-2	Luhovy
04/11/95	Tatran Presov	H	3-2	Czinege, Luhovy, Landerl
18/11/95	Lokomotiva Kosice	A	2-0	Mraz, Luhovy
25/11/95	Dukla Banska Bystrica	A	0-3	
02/12/95	Chemlon Humenne	H	2-3	Medved, Kuna
02/03/96	Petrimex Prievidza	A	0-1	
09/03/96	1.FC Kosice	H	1-1	Luhovy
16/03/96	Spartak Trnava	A	0-1	
23/03/96	Slovan Bratislava	H	1-3	Luhovy
30/03/96	FC Nitra	A	0-0	
12/04/96	DAC Dunajska Streda	H	3-1	Prokop, Solar, Luhovy
PLAY-OFFS				
16/04/96	FC Nitra	H	1-0	Krett
20/04/96	DAC Dunajska Streda	H	3-2	Kuna, Landerl 2
27/04/96	Lokomotiva Kosice	A	0-1	
04/05/96	Petrimex Prievidza	H	2-1	Luhovy 2
14/05/96	Chemlon Humenne	A	0-1	
18/05/96	FC Nitra	A	1-1	Luhovy
23/05/96	DAC Dunajska Streda	A	4-0	Solar, Landerl, Luhovy, Prokop
01/06/96	Lokomotiva Kosice	H	3-0	Krett, Prokop (p), Sevela
06/06/96	Petrimex Prievidza	A	1-2	Krett
12/06/96	Chemlon Humenne	H	0-0	

1.FC KOSICE

CLUB DIRECTORY

1.FC Kosice
Alejova 2
040 11 Kosice
tel - (095) 424871
fax - (095) 436956
Year of Formation - 1992
President - Julius Rezes
Secretary - Stanislav Seman
Coach - Dusan Radolsky; Jan Bodnar; Jan Kozak
Stadium - Vsesportovy areal (30,312)

MAJOR HONOURS
Domestic Cup (Czechoslovakia) - (1) 1993.

APPEARANCES 95/96

	P	Ap	(s)	Gls
Martin BENKO	G	9	(1)	
Michal BORDAS	D	5	(1)	
Peter BUGAR	A	15	(1)	6
Erik CHYTIL	A		(1)	
Vladimir CIFRANIC	D	7	(2)	
Ondrej DANKO	M	8	(3)	4
Pavol DINA	A	3	(12)	1
Pavol GOSTIC	A	6	(3)	3
Michal HIPP	D	2		
Zsolt HORNYAK	D	29		1
Vladimir JANOCKO	M	12	(13)	2
Peter KALAVSKY	M		(1)	
Stefan KARASEK	D	15		
Ivan KOZAK	D	31		1
Radovan KRAL	D	28		3
Vladimir LABANT	M	15	(4)	
Marian LALIK	A	15	(1)	1
Ivan LAPSANSKY	A	11	(4)	4
Tomas MEDVED	A	5	(7)	1
Stefan MIHALIK	D		(1)	
Roland MODER	M	2	(16)	1
Martin OBSITNIK	M	7	(4)	2
Ivan ONDRUSKA	G	9		
Michal PANCIK	A	16		2
Ivo SCHMUCKER	G	14		
Robert SEMENIK	A	32		29
Miroslav SOVIC	M	12	(1)	
Erich VAGNER	D	7	(7)	
Vladimir WEISS	D	11		
Vladislav ZVARA	M	26		1

LEAGUE RESULTS 1995/96

29/07/95	Spartak Trnava	H	3-0	Danko 2, Semenik
04/08/95	Slovan Bratislava	A	1-3	Dina (p)
19/08/95	FC Nitra	H	2-0	Semenik, Pancik
30/08/95	DAC Dunajska Streda	A	2-0	Semenik, Danko
09/09/95	BSC JAS Bardejov	H	1-0	Hornyak
16/09/95	Tatran Presov	A	0-2	
23/09/95	Inter Bratislava	H	5-1	Semenik 3, Kral, Gostic
30/09/95	Dukla Banska Bystrica	A	1-3	Gostic
04/10/95	Chemlon Humenne	H	2-0	Kral, Semenik
14/10/95	Petrimex Prievidza	A	4-0	Gostic, Semenik 3
21/10/95	Lokomotiva Kosice	H	2-1	Semenik 2
28/10/95	Spartak Trnava	A	1-5	Bugar
04/11/95	Slovan Bratislava	H	2-5	Semenik 2 (2p)
18/11/95	FC Nitra	A	3-1	Bugar 2, Kozak
25/11/95	DAC Dunajska Streda	H	4-0	Bugar 2, Semenik (p), Danko
02/12/95	BSC JAS Bardejov	A	2-1	Pancik, Bugar
02/03/96	Tatran Presov	H	1-2	Semenik (p)
09/03/96	Inter Bratislava	A	1-1	Lapsansky
16/03/96	Dukla Banska Bystrica	H	1-0	Semenik
23/03/96	Chemlon Humenne	A	1-0	Moder
30/03/96	Petrimex Prievidza	H	5-0	Obsitnik, Semenik (p), Zvara, Lapsansky, Janocko
12/04/96	Lokomotiva Kosice	A	3-0	Semenik 2, Lapsansky
PLAY-OFFS				
16/04/96	Spartak Trnava	A	0-0	
20/04/96	Slovan Bratislava	H	0-2	
27/04/96	Dukla Banska Bystrica	A	3-1	Semenik 3 (1p)
04/05/96	Tatran Presov	H	2-1	Semenik, Kral
14/05/96	BSC JAS Bardejov	A	3-0	Semenik, Lapsansky, Janocko
22/05/96	Slovan Bratislava	A	0-1	
28/05/96	Spartak Trnava	H	1-0	Lalik
01/06/96	Dukla Banska Bystrica	H	3-1	Semenik 2, Medved
06/06/96	Tatran Presov	A	0-1	
12/06/96	BSC JAS Bardejov	H	3-1	Semenik 2 (1p), Obsitnik

LOKOMOTIVA KOSICE

CLUB DIRECTORY

FK Lokomotiva Kosice
Cermelska1
042 25 Kosice
tel - (095) 6337659
fax - (095) 6337659
Year of Formation - 1946
President - Igor Onuska
Secretary - Juraj Rimsky
Coach - Jan Kozak; Peter Fecko; Ondrej Istok; Peter Fecko
Stadium - Lokomotiva (28,000)

MAJOR HONOURS
Domestic Cup (Czechoslovakia) - (2)
1977, 1979.

APPEARANCES 95/96

	P	Ap	(s)	Gls
Slavomir BALINT	G	2	(2)	
Rastislav BELANSKY	M	5	(3)	
Michal BORDAS	D	10	(1)	1
Tomas DANKO	M	7	(3)	
Pavol DINA	M	13		4
Pavol GOSTIC	A	2		
Ondrej ISTOK	D	25	(1)	
Miroslav JANTEK	M	6	(1)	
Stefan KISS	M	16		1
Marcel KORINEK	M	4	(6)	
Frantisek KUNZO	M	1	(1)	
Radoslav KUNZO	D	6	(9)	
Jan LESNIAK	M	8	(20)	4
Miroslav MATULAJ	A	16	(3)	
Stefan MIHALIK	D	17		1
Milan ONDRIK	D	32		
Ladislav ONOFREJ	A	4	(2)	2
Robert PETRUS	M	2		
Jaroslav POLOMSKY	D	10	(3)	
Igor POPOVEC	A	24	(3)	7
Marek RODAK	G	30		
Ladislav SIMCO	M	26	(6)	8
Anton SOLTIS	A	14	(4)	3
Ladislav STECAK	M	11	(3)	
Marian STAS	D	7	(10)	1
Gabriel UNGVÖLGYI	A	25	(2)	3
Martin URBAN	D	29		

LEAGUE RESULTS 1995/96

29/07/95	Tatran Presov	A	1-2	Lesniak (p)
05/08/95	Spartak Trnava	H	1-2	Soltis
19/08/95	Inter Bratislava	A	3-0	Simco 2, Lesniak
30/08/95	Slovan Bratislava	H	1-0	Popovec
09/09/95	Dukla Banska Bystrica	A	0-4	
16/09/95	FC Nitra	H	4-0	Popovec 2, og (Hipp), Bordas
23/09/95	Chemlon Humenne	A	0-2	
30/09/95	DAC Dunajska Streda	H	3-1	Simco, Ungvölgyi, Popovec
04/10/95	Petrimex Prievidza	A	2-0	Kiss, Ungvölgyi
14/10/95	BSC JAS Bardejov	H	0-1	
21/10/95	1.FC Kosice	A	1-2	Stas
28/10/95	Tatran Presov	H	0-1	
04/11/95	Spartak Trnava	A	1-3	Simco
18/11/95	Inter Bratislava	H	0-2	
25/11/95	Slovan Bratislava	A	0-3	
02/12/95	Dukla Banska Bystrica	H	1-0	Lesniak (p)
02/03/96	FC Nitra	A	2-1	Dina, Onofrej
09/03/96	Chemlon Humenne	H	3-2	Mihalik, Ungvölgyi, Popovec
16/03/96	DAC Dunajska Streda	A	1-1	Dina
23/03/96	Petrimex Prievidza	H	2-0	Dina (p), Onofrej
30/03/96	BSC JAS Bardejov	A	0-3	
12/04/96	1.FC Kosice	H	0-3	
PLAY-OFFS				
16/04/96	Petrimex Prievidza	H	0-3	
20/04/96	Chemlon Humenne	A	0-2	
27/04/96	Inter Bratislava	H	1-0	Popovec
04/05/96	DAC Dunajska Streda	A	1-0	Simco
14/05/96	FC Nitra	H	3-0	Soltis, Simco, Lesniak
18/05/96	Petrimex Prievidza	A	0-0	
22/05/96	Chemlon Humenne	H	0-3	
01/06/96	Inter Bratislava	A	0-3	
06/06/96	DAC Dunajska Streda	H	5-1	Dina, Popovec, og (Lerant), Simco, Soltis
12/06/96	FC Nitra	A	1-4	Simco (p)

FC NITRA

CLUB DIRECTORY

FC Nitra
Jesenskeho 4
949 01 Nitra
tel - (087) 513255
fax - (087) 414958
Year of Formation - 1909
President - Jan Kovarcik
Secretary - Stefan Hunady
Coach - Ivan Horn; Rastislav Vincur; Valer Svec
(96/97 - Jozef Valovic)
Stadium - FC Nitra (11,384)

APPEARANCES 95/96

	P	Ap	(s)	Gls
Jozef ANTALOVIC	D	25		
Miroslav BAGOCKY	M	4	(2)	
Robert BARBORIK	A	24	(2)	6
Miroslav BEDI	M	15		
Peter BURAK	A	1		
Frantisek HALAS	A	12	(2)	
Michal HIPP	D	24		
HOK	M		(1)	
Miroslav HRDINA	G	21	(1)	
Erik HRNCAR	A	5	(4)	
Norbert HRNCAR	M	31		9
Roman HRNCAR	D	26	(1)	2
Juraj KANAS	A	10	(5)	
Lubos KOLLAR	A	7	(6)	
Jozef KOTULA	D	17		
LABAJ	M	1		
Miroslav LÖRINCZ	A	1		1
Frantisek LÖRINCZI	M		(1)	
Mikulas MAGDEME	M	1	(3)	
Robert MATO	M		(8)	
Juraj MOLNAR	M	21	(3)	4
Jan MUCHA	G	1		
Ondrej ONDROVIC	M	17	(3)	1
Peter OREMUS	M	10	(8)	1
Martin PESKO	G	10		
Jozef PETRANI	M	1	(1)	
Martin PROCHAZSKA	A	1	(10)	1
Milan SANDOR	M	10	(1)	1
Martin SEVCIK	A	14	(9)	2
Alojz SPAK	A	20	(4)	1
Richard SPANIK	D		(1)	
Richard VLCEK	D	12		
Juraj VRABEL	A	10	(3)	

LEAGUE RESULTS 1995/96

29/07/95	Chemlon Humenne	A	2-2	Barborik 2
05/08/95	Petrimex Prievidza	H	1-1	Ondrovic
19/08/95	1.FC Kosice	A	0-2	
30/08/95	Spartak Trnava	H	0-2	
16/09/95	Lokomotiva Kosice	A	0-4	
23/09/95	DAC Dunajska Streda	H	4-0	Oremus, Lörincz, Sevcik, Hrncar N.
30/09/95	BSC JAS Bardejov	A	0-1	
04/10/95	Tatran Presov	H	2-1	Hrncar N., Hrncar R.
14/10/95	Inter Bratislava	A	0-1	
21/10/95	Dukla Banska Bystrica	H	2-2	Barborik, Sevcik
28/10/95	Chemlon Humenne	H	2-1	Sandor, Molnar
04/11/95	Petrimex Prievidza	A	1-3	Barborik
08/11/95	Slovan Bratislava	A	1-6	Hrncar N.
18/11/95	1.FC Kosice	H	1-3	Spak
25/11/95	Spartak Trnava	A	0-3	
02/12/95	Slovan Bratislava	H	0-4	
02/03/96	Lokomotiva Kosice	H	1-2	Hrncar N. (p)
09/03/96	DAC Dunajska Streda	A	0-2	
16/03/96	BSC JAS Bardejov	H	3-4	Hrncar N. 2, Barborik
23/03/96	Tatran Presov	A	0-1	
30/03/96	Inter Bratislava	H	0-0	
12/04/96	Dukla Banska Bystrica	A	0-2	
PLAY-OFFS				
16/04/96	Inter Bratislava	A	0-1	
20/04/96	Petrimex Prievidza	H	1-0	Hrncar N.
27/04/96	DAC Dunajska Streda	A	2-1	og (Trutz), Hrncar N.
04/05/96	Chemlon Humenne	H	2-0	Hrncar R., Molnar
14/05/96	Lokomotiva Kosice	A	0-3	
18/05/96	Inter Bratislava	H	1-1	Hrncar N.
22/05/96	Petrimex Prievidza	A	0-3	
01/06/96	DAC Dunajska Streda	H	0-1	
06/06/96	Chemlon Humenne	A	0-1	
12/06/96	Lokomotiva Kosice	H	4-1	Molnar 2, Barborik, Prochazska

PETRIMEX PRIEVIDZA

CLUB DIRECTORY

MSK Petrimex Prievidza
Sportova 37
971 01 Prievidza
tel - (0862) 22858
fax - (0862) 22858
Year of Formation - 1919
President - Tibor Stacha
Secretary - Ladislav Gelacak
Coach - Jan Rosinsky; Petar Jozic; Anton Dragun
Stadium - Prievidza (6,500)

APPEARANCES 95/96

	P	Ap	(s)	Gls
Lubos BABJAK	G	6		
Ivan BALAZ	A		(1)	
Michal BALAZ	G	3		
Mohammed BENDALLA (LIB)	D	3	(3)	
Jan BLAHAC	A	2		
Marek BOSKOVIC	D	3	(2)	
Robert GALO	A	4	(8)	
Daniel Omar GAZZANIGA (ARG)	G	5		
Peter GREGOR	G	18	(1)	
Juraj HALASKA	M	28	(3)	
Jozef HEPNER	D	2	(6)	1
Norbert HOKSA	D	18		6
Marek HOLMIK	A	22	(8)	8
Stanislav HORNAK	A	14	(1)	2
Michal JAKUBIS	D	9	(15)	
Boris KITKA	D	21		1
Dmitri KRAUS (RUS)	A	26	(4)	1
Ladislav KUNA	M	16		
Rastislav LAZORIK	A	7		
Peter MAJERNIK	M	12	(3)	1
Peter MASAROVIC	A	1		
Marek MIKUS	D	5	(5)	
Daniel NEMEC	M		(2)	
Peter NEMETH	D	13	(1)	1
Fabio NIGRO (ARG)	M	6		2
Stefan ONDRAS	M	16		
Miroslav ORSULA	M	11	(4)	1
Lubos PLEVKA	A	17		5
Ivan PROCKA	G		(1)	
Peter RYBAR	M	3		
Ivan SCHULCZ	D	8		
Roman SLANY	D	13	(1)	
Jozef SLUKA	A	13	(2)	2
Jan SUSOL	A	5	(3)	
Oleg TARASOV (RUS)	M	2	(3)	
Frantisek TRUNGEL	D	16		
Robert VEBER (YUG)	M	4	(2)	

LEAGUE RESULTS 1995/96

29/07/95	Slovan Bratislava	H	0-0	
04/08/95	FC Nitra	A	1-1	Holmik
19/08/95	DAC Dunajska Streda	H	2-3	Sluka, Holmik
30/08/95	BSC JAS Bardejov	A	0-2	
09/09/95	Tatran Presov	H	0-2	
16/09/95	Inter Bratislava	A	2-2	Sluka, Hepner
22/09/95	Dukla Banska Bystrica	H	1-2	Nigro
30/09/95	Chemlon Humenne	A	0-5	
04/10/95	Lokomotiva Kosice	H	0-2	
14/10/95	1.FC Kosice	H	0-4	
21/10/95	Spartak Trnava	A	1-3	Nemeth
28/10/95	Slovan Bratislava	A	0-5	
04/11/95	FC Nitra	H	3-1	Nigro, Plevka 2 (1p)
18/11/95	DAC Dunajska Streda	A	0-2	
25/11/95	BSC JAS Bardejov	H	0-3	
02/12/95	Tatran Presov	A	0-4	
02/03/96	Inter Bratislava	H	1-0	Majernik
09/03/96	Dukla Banska Bystrica	A	0-2	
16/03/96	Chemlon Humenne	H	1-2	Plevka
23/03/96	Lokomotiva Kosice	A	0-2	
30/03/96	1.FC Kosice	A	0-5	
12/04/96	Spartak Trnava	H	1-2	Holmik
PLAY-OFFS				
16/04/96	Lokomotiva Kosice	A	3-0	Orsula, Hornak, Hoksa
20/04/96	FC Nitra	A	0-1	
27/04/96	Chemlon Humenne	H	3-0	Holmik, Hoksa 2
04/05/96	Inter Bratislava	A	1-2	Hornak
14/05/96	DAC Dunajska Streda	H	3-0	Hoksa, Plevka 2 (1p)
18/05/96	Lokomotiva Kosice	H	0-0	
23/05/96	FC Nitra	H	3-0	Kitka, Hoksa, Holmik
01/06/96	Chemlon Humenne	A	2-4	Holmik, Kraus
06/06/96	Inter Bratislava	H	2-1	Hoksa, Holmik
12/06/96	DAC Dunajska Streda	A	1-3	Holmik

SLOVAN BRATISLAVA

CLUB DIRECTORY

SK Slovan Bratislava
Junacka 2
831 04 Bratislava
tel - (07) 66576
fax - (07) 66406
Year of Formation - 1919
President - Jaroslav Caniga
Secretary - Anton Urban
Coach - Anton Dragun; Dusan Galis
Stadium - Tehelne pole (32,000)

MAJOR HONOURS
League Championship (Czechoslovakia) - (8) 1949, 1950, 1951, 1955, 1970, 1974, 1975, 1992.
Domestic Cup (Czechoslovakia) - (5) 1962, 1963, 1968, 1974, 1982.
League Championship - (3) 1994, 1995, 1996.
Domestic Cup - (1) 1994.
European Cup-winners' Cup - (1) 1969.

APPEARANCES 95/96

	P	Ap	(s)	Gls
Burim BERISHA (BUL)	M		(2)	
Marek BOSKOVIC	D		(6)	
Milos CERNANSKY	A	1		
Igor DEMO	M	21	(9)	6
Lubomir FAKTOR	M	25	(4)	6
Fabio Luís GOMES (BRA)	M	23	(3)	10
Jozef JURIGA	M	27	(2)	1
Vladimir KINDER	D	21	(2)	3
Miroslav KÖNIG	G	1	(3)	
Pavol KRAVARIK	M	1	(2)	
Miroslav LACLAVIK	D		(2)	
Stefan MAIXNER	A	12	(2)	9
Ladislav MOLNAR	G	31		1
Jozef MUZLAY	A	12	(11)	3
Szilard NEMETH	A	24	(4)	12
Fabio NIGRO (ARG)	M	9	(10)	1
Ladislav PECKO	D	30		2
Stefan RUSNAK	A	8	(3)	3
Samuel SLOVAK	M	17	(9)	6
Milos SOBONA	D	11	(5)	1
Tomas STUPALA	D	15	(4)	
Rudolf TALAJKA	M		(1)	
Dusan TITTEL	D	31		8
Robert TOMASCHEK	M	31		3
Marian ZEMAN	D	1		

LEAGUE RESULTS 1995/96

29/07/95	Petrimex Prievidza	A	0-0	
04/08/95	1.FC Kosice	H	3-1	Rusnak, Faktor, Nemeth
26/08/95	Spartak Trnava	A	1-1	Demo
30/08/95	Lokomotiva Kosice	A	0-1	
16/09/95	DAC Dunajska Streda	A	4-2	Muzlay, Sobona, Nemeth, Tittel
22/09/95	BSC JAS Bardejov	H	2-0	Pecko, Nemeth
30/09/95	Tatran Presov	A	0-0	
06/10/95	Inter Bratislava	H	1-1	Faktor (p)
14/10/95	Dukla Banska Bystrica	A	0-0	
21/10/95	Chemlon Humenne	H	3-1	Tomaschek, Faktor, Gomes
28/10/95	Petrimex Prievidza	H	5-0	Muzlay, Gomes, Nemeth 2, Molnar (p)
04/11/95	1.FC Kosice	A	5-2	Tomaschek, Tittel 3, Rusnak
08/11/95	FC Nitra	H	6-1	Rusnak, Tittel (p), Demo 2, Nemeth 2
19/11/95	Spartak Trnava	H	3-0	Tomaschek, Gomes, Nemeth
25/11/95	Lokomotiva Kosice	H	3-0	Tittel, Slovak, Kinder
02/12/95	FC Nitra	A	4-0	Kinder, Tittel, Nemeth, Slovak
02/03/96	DAC Dunajska Streda	H	7-1	Nemeth, Gomes 2, Demo 2, Faktor (p), Maixner
09/03/96	BSC JAS Bardejov	A	2-1	og (Vilim), Nemeth
16/03/96	Tatran Presov	H	4-0	Gomes 2, Maixner, Muzlay
23/03/96	Inter Bratislava	A	3-1	Maixner, Faktor, Demo
30/03/96	Dukla Banska Bystrica	H	5-2	Maixner 2, Nemeth, Gomes, og (Bazik Mi.)
12/04/96	Chemlon Humenne	A	1-1	Juriga
PLAY-OFFS				
16/04/96	BSC JAS Bardejov	A	2-1	Nigro, Gomes
20/04/96	1.FC Kosice	A	2-0	Maixner 2
27/04/96	Tatran Presov	H	3-1	Maixner 2, Gomes
04/05/96	Spartak Trnava	A	1-0	Slovak
14/05/96	Dukla Banska Bystrica	H	0-0	
22/05/96	1.FC Kosice	H	1-0	Pecko
28/05/96	BSC JAS Bardejov	H	3-0	og (Pavlik), Faktor, Slovak
01/06/96	Tatran Presov	A	0-0	
06/06/96	Spartak Trnava	H	5-2	Tittel, Slovak 2, Kinder, og (Kostka)
12/06/96	Dukla Banska Bystrica	A	0-0	

SPARTAK TRNAVA

CLUB DIRECTORY

FC Spartak Trnava
Sportova 1
917 60 Trnava
tel - (0805) 24210
fax - (0805) 25381
Year of Formation - 1923
President - Jozef Bachraty
Secretary - Stefan Batalik
Coach - Karol Pecze
Stadium - FC Spartak (24,500)

MAJOR HONOURS
League Championship (Czechoslovakia) - (5)
1968, 1969, 1971, 1972, 1973.
Domestic Cup (Czechoslovakia) - (4)
1967, 1971, 1975, 1986.

APPEARANCES 95/96

	P	Ap	(s)	Gls
Michal BALAZ	G	4	(1)	
Igor BALIS	M	32		
Petr CMILANSKY	D	28	(1)	1
Jan FILAK	D	26	(3)	1
Miroslav FILIPKO	G	2		
Stanislav FISAN	G	26		
Robert FORMANKO	A	5	(18)	2
Marcel FULIER	M		(1)	
Jan GABRIEL	M	17	(1)	1
Stanislav HLAVAC	M		(3)	
Jaroslav HRABAL	D	21		1
Jan KAPKO	D	10	(9)	
Miroslav KARHAN	D	32		6
Rastislav KOSTKA	M	31		7
Jaroslav MACAK	A	29	(2)	5
Stanislav MORAVEC	A	1	(12)	
Miroslav PAPRANEC	A		(2)	
Pavol PAVLUS	D	3	(7)	
Mikulas RADVANYI	A	18	(9)	9
Jozef RYBNIKAR	M		(1)	
Julius SIMON	M	29		10
Milan SOTAK	A		(8)	
Marian TIBENSKY	D	3	(7)	
Marek UJLAKY	A	30		10
Alexander VEGH	M	5	(6)	

LEAGUE RESULTS 1995/96

29/07/95	1.FC Kosice	A	0-3	
05/08/95	Lokomotiva Kosice	A	2-1	Simon 2
26/08/95	Slovan Bratislava	H	1-1	Ujlaky
30/08/95	FC Nitra	A	2-0	Filak, Hrabal
09/09/95	DAC Dunajska Streda	H	5-1	Simon 3 (1p), Radvanyi 2
16/09/95	BSC JAS Bardejov	A	0-0	
24/09/95	Tatran Presov	H	5-2	Karhan, Ujlaky 4
02/10/95	Inter Bratislava	A	2-1	Ujlaky, Karhan
06/10/95	Dukla Banska Bystrica	H	2-0	Simon, Radvanyi
15/10/95	Chemlon Humenne	A	2-1	Macak 2
21/10/95	Petrimex Prievidza	H	3-1	Karhan, Macak, Kostka
28/10/95	1.FC Kosice	H	5-1	Radvanyi, Gabriel, og (Weiss), Kostka 2
04/11/95	Lokomotiva Kosice	H	3-1	Radvanyi, Karhan, Formanko
19/11/95	Slovan Bratislava	A	0-3	
25/11/95	FC Nitra	H	3-0	Radvanyi, Ujlaky, Karhan
02/12/95	DAC Dunajska Streda	A	0-0	
02/03/96	BSC JAS Bardejov	H	1-0	Simon
09/03/96	Tatran Presov	A	1-1	Simon
16/03/96	Inter Bratislava	H	1-0	Macak
23/03/96	Dukla Banska Bystrica	A	0-1	
30/03/96	Chemlon Humenne	H	0-0	(later awarded 0-3)
12/04/96	Petrimex Prievidza	A	2-1	Radvanyi, Kostka
PLAY-OFFS				
16/04/96	1.FC Kosice	H	0-0	
20/04/96	Dukla Banska Bystrica	H	2-0	Simon 2
27/04/96	BSC JAS Bardejov	A	1-0	Ujlaky
04/05/96	Slovan Bratislava	H	0-1	
14/05/96	Tatran Presov	A	3-1	Macak, Karhan, Kostka
22/05/96	Dukla Banska Bystrica	A	2-2	Radvanyi 2
28/05/96	1.FC Kosice	A	0-1	
01/06/96	BSC JAS Bardejov	H	3-0	Cmilansky, Kostka, Ujlaky
06/06/96	Slovan Bratislava	A	2-5	Ujlaky (p), Formanko
12/06/96	Tatran Presov	H	1-0	Kostka

TATRAN PRESOV

CLUB DIRECTORY

FC Tatran Presov
Capajevova 47
080 92 Presov
tel - (091) 711464
fax - (091) 713005
Year of Formation - 1898
President - Vladimir Varga
Secretary - Jozef Matuscin
Coach - Anton Janos
Stadium - Tatran (14,000)

APPEARANCES 95/96

	P	Ap	(s)	Gls
Karim AL HASAN (KEN)	A	2	(3)	
Kennedy CHIHURI (ZIM)	M	23	(2)	2
Rastislav DORD	A	12	(2)	1
Miroslav DROBNAK	M	1	(1)	
Rastislav DZUBINSKY	D		(1)	
Mikulas DVOROZNAK	M	7	(6)	
Marek FABULA	A	6	(2)	
Tomas GERICH	D	29		
Miroslav HAJDUCKO	M	28		6
Peter HLUSKO	D	27		1
Richard HÖGER	M	21		1
Peter JAKUBECH	G	5		
Miroslav JANTEK	M	16		
Jaroslav KENTOS	D	16		
Radovan KOCUREK	A	15	(3)	5
Robert KOCIS	A	23	(7)	6
Igor KUREK	A	5	(6)	1
Adrian LESKO	M	1	(7)	
Marcel MISCIK	A	2	(4)	3
Vladimir NENADIC (YUG)	A	9	(5)	1
Roman ORSULA	M		(1)	
Marek PETRUS	M	3	(1)	
Lubomir PUHAK	A	3	(12)	
Miroslav SECEN	M	8	(3)	
Miroslav SEMAN	G	27		
Marek SPILAR	D	27		
Marian SKALKA	M	14		5
Marek VALENCIN	M		(2)	
Stanislav VARGA	D	21		2
Peter VASIL	M		(1)	
Vladislav ZVARA	M	1	(1)	

LEAGUE RESULTS 1995/96

Date	Opponent	H/A	Score	Scorers
29/07/95	Lokomotiva Kosice	H	2-1	Skalka, Kocis
05/08/95	Inter Bratislava	H	1-0	Skalka (p)
19/08/95	Dukla Banska Bystrica	A	0-0	
30/08/95	Chemlon Humenne	H	0-0	
09/09/95	Petrimex Prievidza	A	2-0	Höger, Skalka
16/09/95	1.FC Kosice	H	2-0	Hajducko, Kurek
24/09/95	Spartak Trnava	A	2-5	Hajducko, Kocurek
30/09/95	Slovan Bratislava	H	0-0	
04/10/95	FC Nitra	A	1-2	Kocis
14/10/95	DAC Dunajska Streda	H	3-0	Kocis, Chihuri, Hajducko
21/10/95	BSC JAS Bardejov	A	0-1	
28/10/95	Lokomotiva Kosice	A	1-0	Skalka
04/11/95	Inter Bratislava	A	2-3	Kocis, Hajducko
18/11/95	Dukla Banska Bystrica	H	0-1	
25/11/95	Chemlon Humenne	A	1-4	Skalka
02/12/95	Petrimex Prievidza	H	4-0	Kocurek 3, Chihuri
02/03/96	1.FC Kosice	A	2-1	Hajducko 2
09/03/96	Spartak Trnava	H	1-1	Nenadic
16/03/96	Slovan Bratislava	A	0-4	
23/03/96	FC Nitra	H	1-0	Hlusko (p)
30/03/96	DAC Dunajska Streda	A	1-1	Varga
12/04/96	BSC JAS Bardejov	H	2-0	Varga, Kocis
PLAY-OFFS				
16/04/96	Dukla Banska Bystrica	A	0-1	
20/04/96	BSC JAS Bardejov	H	1-0	Miscik
27/04/96	Slovan Bratislava	A	1-3	Kocis
04/05/96	1.FC Kosice	A	1-2	Miscik
14/05/96	Spartak Trnava	H	1-3	Dord
22/05/96	BSC JAS Bardejov	A	0-1	
28/05/96	Dukla Banska Bystrica	H	1-1	Miscik
01/06/96	Slovan Bratislava	H	0-0	
06/06/96	1.FC Kosice	H	1-0	Kocurek
12/06/96	Spartak Trnava	A	0-1	

PROMOTED CLUBS

SECOND DIVISION FINAL TABLE 95/96

		Pd	W	D	L	F	A	Pt	GD
1	**ARTMEDIA Petrzalka**	**30**	**19**	**6**	**5**	**54**	**29**	**63**	**+25**
2	**MSK Zilina**	**30**	**17**	**5**	**8**	**57**	**27**	**56**	**+30**
3	**Rimavska Sobota**	**30**	**15**	**9**	**6**	**41**	**17**	**54**	**+24**
4	**Spartak Dubnica nad Vahom**	**30**	**13**	**10**	**7**	**48**	**35**	**49**	**+13**
5	Slovan Levice	30	15	3	12	41	42	48	-1
6	MSK Ruzomberok	30	14	5	11	54	44	47	+10
7	Matador Puchov	30	12	9	9	44	27	45	+17
8	Tatran Devin	30	11	6	13	38	48	39	-10
9	OZETA Trencin	30	10	7	13	41	42	37	-1
10	Tesla Stropkov	30	10	7	13	33	37	37	-4
11	FC Vrable	30	10	5	15	32	56	35	-24
12	PFK Piestany	30	10	4	16	36	47	34	-11
13	SM Gabcikovo	30	8	9	13	36	42	33	-6
14	SP Trebisov	30	10	3	17	25	31	33	-6
15	Kalcit Roznava	30	8	8	14	23	56	32	-33
16	SKP Bratislava	30	7	6	17	30	53	27	-23

PROMOTION/RELEGATION PLAY-OFF
Petrimex Prievidza 6, Slovan Levice 0
Slovan Levice 1, Petrimex Prievidza 2
(Petrimex Prievidza 8-1)

CLUB DIRECTORY

FC ARTMEDIA Petrzalka
Krasovskeho 1, 851 01 Bratislava
tel - (07) 850043
fax - (07) 850043
Year of Formation - 1898
President - Juraj Vysoky
Secretary - Ondrej Kadak
Coach - Jozef Prochotsky
Stadium - Petrzalka (12,000)

CLUB DIRECTORY

MSK Zilina
Uholna 3, 010 01 Zilina
tel - (89) 623194
fax - (89) 53242
Year of Formation - 1908
President - Jan Slota
Secretary - Jozef Balazovic
Coach - Stanislav Griga
Stadium - Pod Dubnom (15,000)

CLUB DIRECTORY

FC Rimavska Sobota
Sportova 2, 979 01 Rimavska Sobota
tel - (866) 25754
fax - (866) 26087
Year of Formation - 1913
President - Stefan Szanto
Secretary - Peter Blasko
Coach - Karol Kisel
Stadium - Rimavska Sobota (8,000)

CLUB DIRECTORY

FK Spartak Dubnica nad Vahom
ul. Sportovcov, Dubnica nad Vahom
tel - (827) 21906
fax - (827) 26982
Year of Formation - 1921
President - Ivan Nemeckay
Secretary - Viliam Simko
Coach - Ivan Kralik
Stadium - Dubnica (8,000)

SLOVENIA

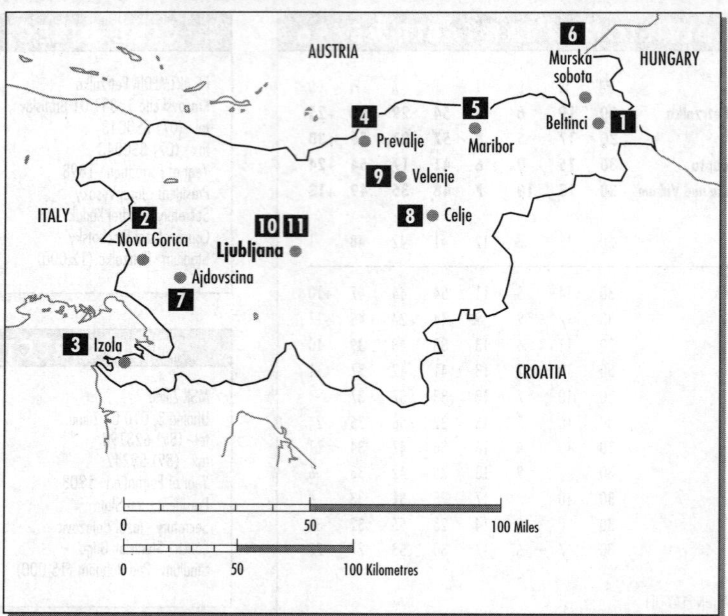

1	NK BELTINCI	924
2	HIT GORICA	925
3	NK IZOLA	926
4	MAG KOROTAN PREVALJE	927
5	MARIBOR BRANIK	928
6	MURA MURSKA SOBOTA	929
7	PRIMORJE AJDOVSCINA	930
8	PUBLIKUM CELJE	931
9	RUDAR VELENJE	932
10	SCT OLIMPIJA LJUBLJANA	933
11	ZELEZNICAR LJUBLJANA	934

TEN-TEAM LEAGUE REAPS DIVIDENDS

HIT Gorica end Olimpija's title monopoly

FEDERATION DIRECTORY

Nogometna Zveza Slovenije
Dunajska 47/V, 61 000 Ljubljana
tel - (061) 1334063
fax - (061) 302337
Year of Formation - 1920
President - Rudolf Zavrl
Secretary - Dane Jost
Stadium - Bezigrad, Ljubljana (18,000)

For the first time since Slovenia broke away from Yugoslavia and staged a fully independent national league, the country's premier club, SCT Olimpija Ljubljana, failed to win the title. Their crown was passed on to the rank outsiders of HIT Gorica, who duly celebrated a first ever championship success, the years of pre-independence included. Their previous best performance had been second place in 1975/76, when the Slovenian championship was the equivalent of a regional Third Division in the old Yugoslav league.

It had been the objective of the NZS (Slovenian FA), when setting up a new ten-strong premier league in 1995/96, to make the championship more competitive and to boost the overall quality of the football. The change was drastic - as many as six teams were axed from the previous season - but it turned out to be the right move. With the notable exception of NK Izola, stranded all season in the basement, the teams were evenly matched, all capable of taking points off one another. This provided for plenty of unpredictable results and a vast improvement in the all-round excitement. HIT Gorica's emergence as champions proved the point in spectacular fashion.

Placed third the season before, the team from Nova Gorica on the Italian border made wholesale changes to their squad, buying in as many as 16 new recruits to compensate for the loss of their two best players, Novica Nikcevic and Branislav Kojicic, to SCT Olimpija. Coach Milos Soskic also upped and left for the defending champions, enabling Milan Miklavic, a former Rapid Vienna player who had just taken the minnows of DSV Leoben to the Austrian Cup final, to be appointed in his place.

Miklavic oversaw the arrival of virtually an entire new team, the club's purchasing power having been boosted thanks to the generosity of the club's benefactors, HIT, a local hotel and travel agency. Amongst the new arrivals were former SCT Olimpija players Nenad Protega, Sandi Valentincic, Zoran Ubavic and - latterly, just after the season had started - regular Slovenian international midfielder Alfred Jermanis, who also arrived from Austria.

The team made only an average start in the first two months. But after staging one of the biggest upsets in Slovenian football history with a sensational smash-and-grab 3-0 victory away to SCT Olimpija - Valentincic scored a hat-trick - HIT Gorica exploded into a remarkable run of form

LEAGUE CHAMPIONSHIP RESULTS 95/96

		1	2	3	4	5	6	7	8	9	10
1	NK Beltinci		1-1	5-1	2-1	0-0	0-0	0-3	1-2	0-2	2-1
			0-0	3-0	4-1	2-0	2-0	0-2	2-1	1-0	1-2
2	HIT Gorica	0-0		3-0	2-0	0-0	2-1	3-1	2-1	3-1	2-1
		2-1		3-0	1-0	0-0	1-0	1-1	1-1	1-0	2-2
3	NK Izola	0-2	0-2		1-0	2-2	1-1	1-1	0-2	0-1	0-6
		0-3	0-2		1-1	0-5	0-3	1-5	1-1	0-2	0-5
4	MAG Korotan Prevalje	1-1	1-2	2-0		0-0	1-1	0-0	3-2	2-0	1-2
		0-0	0-0	8-0		2-0	0-1	4-2	0-1	0-1	1-2
5	Maribor Branik	1-2	1-0	5-1	1-2		1-2	2-0	0-0	2-0	5-1
		3-0	1-0	3-1	1-0		1-1	2-0	2-2	0-2	2-1
6	Mura Murska sobota	1-1	1-0	4-0	2-0	1-0		1-1	1-0	1-1	1-1
		1-0	1-1	7-0	2-2	1-0		2-1	0-0	1-0	0-0
7	Primorje Ajdovscina	1-0	1-4	6-0	1-1	1-0	5-1		3-1	1-1	0-3
		0-0	0-2	7-0	0-1	0-1	1-0		4-1	2-1	1-4
8	Publikum Celje	2-0	2-1	5-1	2-3	3-3	1-1	3-1		4-6	1-1
		0-1	1-0	11-0	5-0	1-1	1-0	1-1		0-0	3-1
9	Rudar Velenje	1-1	1-1	5-1	2-3	2-0	0-1	2-0	0-1		2-1
		0-0	1-1	5-0	0-1	1-1	1-0	3-1	0-0		1-3
10	SCT Olimpija Ljubljana	5-0	0-3	10-0	2-1	0-1	1-2	1-1	3-0	1-1	
		5-3	0-0	4-0	2-1	1-0	2-0	0-1	3-0	2-0	

LEAGUE CHAMPIONSHIP FINAL TABLE 95/96

			Home					Away					Total						
		Pd	W	D	L	F	A	W	D	L	F	A	W	D	L	F	A	Pt	GD
1	HIT Gorica	36	12	6	0	29	10	6	7	5	20	12	18	13	5	49	22	67	+27
2	SCT Olimpija Ljubljana	36	11	3	4	42	14	8	4	6	37	25	19	7	10	79	39	64	+40
3	Mura Murska sobota	36	10	8	0	28	8	5	5	8	15	21	15	13	8	43	29	58	+14
4	Maribor Branik	36	11	3	4	33	15	3	8	7	14	17	14	11	11	47	32	53	+15
5	Publikum Celje	36	9	6	3	46	21	4	6	8	16	26	13	12	11	62	47	51	+15
6	NK Beltinci	36	9	4	5	26	17	4	7	7	15	23	13	11	12	41	40	50	+1
7	Rudar Velenje	36	7	6	5	27	16	6	4	8	19	21	13	10	13	46	37	49	+9
8	Primorje Ajdovscina	36	9	3	6	34	21	4	6	8	22	27	13	9	14	56	48	48	+8
9	MAG Korotan Prevalje	36	6	6	6	26	15	5	3	10	18	31	11	9	16	44	46	42	-2
10	NK Izola	36	1	5	12	8	44	0	0	18	5	96	1	5	30	13	140	8	-127

that was to take them into the mid-season break with a healthy five-point advantage over second-placed Mura Murska sobota. More significantly, SCT Olimpija were nowhere to be seen, cast adrift as far back as 12 points behind.

Miklavic and his squad had three months to get used to the idea that the championship was theirs for the taking. With the pressure gauge rising, it was little surprise that they embarked on the second half of the season with extreme caution. Of the first nine matches they played after the resumption they only managed to win two... and drew the rest. They were never going to win any prizes for the aesthetic appeal of their football. HIT set great store by their defence and were more than content to soak up pressure and then strike on the counter-attack. Most of their goals came on the break or from long diagonal passes from the back.

But the one prize that mattered was to be theirs. Just when they needed to, the team squeezed out some important victories. Crucially they held ever-improving Olimpija to a 2-2 draw and were just able to keep their noses in front long enough to ward off the title holders' concerted late challenge. Ironically, it was the day after HIT's 23-match unbeaten run had come to an end with a 0-1 defeat away to Maribor Branik that the championship was officially wrapped up. Olimpija's shock 1-3 defeat at Publikum Celje ended the chase. They eventually finished three points behind the new champions - despite having scored 30 goals more than them in their 36 matches.

Evidently, it was the HIT defence, led by ever-present goalkeeper Borut Mavric and Bosnian libero Blagoje Radovanovic, which did most to bring the title to Nova Gorica. But the majority of the praise was showered on

TOP SCORERS

28 Ermin SILJAK (SCT Olimpija Ljubljana)
24 Faik KAMBEROVIC (Publikum Celje)
18 Dinko VRABAC (Primorje Ajdovscina)
16 Sandi VALENTINCIC (HIT Gorica)
14 Kliton BOZGO (SCT Olimpija Ljubljana)
Ismet EKMECIC (Rudar Velenje)
Mihael VONCINA (Primorje Ajdovscina)
13 Novica NIKCEVIC (SCT Olimpija Ljubljana/ MAG Korotan Prevalje)
Mikhail HLEBALIN (Mura Murska sobota)
10 Matjaz CVIKL (Rudar Velenje)
Roman PLESEC (MAG Korotan Prevalje)
Stefan SKAPER (NK Beltinci)

NATIONAL TEAM RESULTS 95/96

Date	Opponent		Venue	Score	Scorers
06/09/95	Italy (ECQ)	A	Udine	0-1	
11/10/95	Ukraine (ECQ)	H	Ljubljana	3-2	Udovic (53, 89), Zahovic (73)
15/11/95	Croatia (ECQ)	H	Ljubljana	1-2	Gliha (36)
06/12/95	Mexico	A	Hermosillo	2-1	Ceh (8), Siljak (20)
07/02/96	Iceland	N	Ta' Qali	7-1	Udovic (42, 48, 57, 69, 74), Florjancic (79), Siljak (83)
09/02/96	Malta	A	Ta' Qali	0-0	
11/02/96	Russia	N	Ta' Qali	1-3	Gliha (89p)
27/03/96	Poland	A	Lodz	0-0	
24/04/96	Greece (WCQ)	A	Athens	0-2	
21/05/96	United Arab Emirates	H	Ljubljana	2-2	Siljak (57), Karic (60)

NATIONAL TEAM APPEARANCES 95/96

Coach - Zdenko VERDENIK	ITA	UKR	CRO	MEX	ISL	MLT	RUS	POL	GRE	UAE	Cps	Gls
Branko ZUPAN (22/09/64) - Publikum Celje	G	G	G			G					9	
Marinko GALIC (22/04/70) - Maribor Branik	D	D	D	D	s85	D60	s46	D	D	D	26	
Darko MILANIC (18/12/67) - SK Sturm Graz (AUT)	D	D			D85	D	D46	D	D		19	
Andrej POLJSAK (24/06/68) - Mura Murska sobota/HIT Gorica	D				D79						9	-
Alfred JERMANIS (21/01/67) - HIT Gorica	M		M	M					M	M	24	1
Ales CEH (07/04/68) - Grazer AK (AUT)	M	M	M	M	M79	M	M56	M	M		22	1
Vladimir KOKOL (03/01/72) - Mura Murska sobota	M46					s84	s56	s74		s46	10	1
Matjaz CVIKL (13/01/67) - Rudar Velenje	M78	s71	s62								7	1
Zlatko ZAHOVIC (01/12/71) - Vitória Guimarães (POR)	M58	M			M			M	M	M46	17	4
Saso UDOVIC (13/12/68) - KSK Beveren (BEL)	A	A	A		A			A	A70		14	10
Primoz GLIHA (08/10/67) - Chamois Niortais (FRA)	A	A	A			A	A	A52	s70		22	6
Peter BINKOVSKI (28/06/72) - Maribor Branik	s46				s79	s60	M	M			15	1
Vilijem BECAJ (08/09/67) - HIT Gorica	s58									M46	2	-
Sandi VALENTINCIC (25/08/67) - HIT Gorica	s78			A80		s70	s63			s75	5	-
Robert ENGLARO (25/08/69) - SCT Olimpija Ljubljana		D	D		D	D	D	D	D		24	-
Mladen RUDONJA (26/07/71) - SCT Olimpija Ljubljana/ Marsonia Slavonski Brod (CRO)		M	s62		M79	M70				M	10	-
Dzoni NOVAK (04/09/69) - SCT Olimpija Ljubljana		M	M	M	M	M	M	M	M		21	2
Matjaz FLORJANCIC (18/10/67) - Cremonese (ITA)		A71	A62		A			A74	A	A	17	1
Ales KRIZAN (25/07/71) - Maribor Branik			D	D						D	15	-
Samir ZULIC (08/01/66) - SCT Olimpija Ljubljana			M62								10	1
Bosko BOSKOVIC (12/01/69) - NK Beltinci				G	G		G	G	G	G	15	-
Gregor BLATNIK (15/12/72) - MAG Korotan Prevalje				D							2	-
Gregor ZIDAN (05/10/65) - Maribor Branik				M	s79	M84	M	M37			21	-
Damjan GAJSER (08/05/70) - Mura Murska sobota				M	s85		M		s37		4	-
Ermin SILJAK (11/05/73) - SCT Olimpija Ljubljana				A	A85	A	A63	s52		A75	7	3
Mihael VONCINA (25/02/69) - Primorje Ajdovscina				s80							2	-
Franc CIFER (17/02/71) - Mura Murska sobota					s79	D	D			s46	7	-
Miran SREBRNIC (08/01/70) - HIT Gorica										D46	1	-
Igor BENEDEJCIC (28/07/69) - SCT Olimpija Ljubljana										M	7	1
Amir KARIC (31/12/73) - Maribor Branik										s46	1	1

Miklavic, significantly the only coach in the entire league who held his place for the duration of the season.

SCT Olimpija, on the other hand, were forever changing their coach. They even took on national team boss Zdenko Verdenik in an attempt to halt their early-season slide, but he left almost as soon as he had arrived, complaining about the modest size of his wage packet.

In the second half of the season Olimpija were far and away the best team on view. Every week they chipped away at HIT Gorica's lead, but ultimately the 12-point deficit at the end of the autumn campaign left them with too much to do and they never managed to catch their prey. There was a consolation, however, in the form of the Slovenian Cup, which Olimpija won for a record 17th time, defeating Primorje Ajdovscina 2-1 on aggregate in the two-legged final. The team's most impressive performance of the competition came in the quarter-final when they knocked out HIT Gorica after beating them both home and away. This result contrasted starkly with the outcome of their league meetings. Of the four matches played

DOMESTIC CUP RESULTS

FIRST ROUND
Nafta 2, Maribor Branik 6
MAG Korotan Prevalje 0, Primorje Ajdovscina 0 (aet; 3-4 on pens.)
Cankova 0, Sentjur 8
Pobrezje 0, Koper 3
Alumonij 3, Drava 1
Dravinja 0, Zeleznicar Oscar Ljubljana 2
Bakovci 3, Jadran Dekani 0 (w/o)
Crnuce 3, Zagorje 1
Vevce 1, SCT Olimpija Ljubljana 3
NK Izola 0, Mura Murska sobota 0 (aet; 3-5 on pens.)
Rudar Velenje 1, NK Beltinci 0
Transport 2, Zeleznicar Maribor 1
Adri Miren 0, HIT Gorica 3
Gaj Kocevje 0, Publikum Celje 3 (w/o)
Visoko 1, Naklo 2
Centiba Wreng 3, Sava 1

SECOND ROUND
Aluminij 0, Primorje Ajdovscina 5
Koper 0, HIT Gorica 1
Bakovci 0, SCT Olimpija Ljubljana 2
Transport 1, Mura Murska sobota 3
Zeleznicar Oscar Ljubljana 4, Crnuce 2 (aet)
Centiba Wreng 1, Publikum Celje 17
Naklo 0, Sentjur 0 (aet; 3-2 on pens.)
Rudar Velenje 0, Maribor Branik 0 (aet; 4-2 on pens.)

QUARTER-FINALS
SCT Olimpija Ljubljana v HIT Gorica 3-1; 2-0 (SCT Olimpija Ljubljana 5-1)
Publikum Celje v Mura Murska sobota 2-0; 1-2 (Publikum Celje 3-2)
Zeleznicar Oscar Ljubljana v Rudar Velenje 0-1; 1-2 (Rudar Velenje 3-1)
Primorje Ajdovscina v Naklo 2-0; 3-2 (Primorje Ajdovscina 5-2)

SEMI-FINALS
SCT Olimpija Ljubljana v Rudar Velenje 3-1; 0-0 (SCT Olimpija Ljubljana 3-1)
Primorje Ajdovscina v Publikum Celje 0-1; 2-0 (Primorje Ajdovscina 2-1)

FINAL
15/05/96, Ajdovscina
PRIMORJE AJDOVSCINA 0
SCT OLIMPIJA LJUBLJANA 1 Siljak (13)
referee - Kranjc
PRIMORJE AJDOVSCINA - Strajnar; Bozic, Ibranovic, Mulahmetovic, Ruznic, Vrabac, Voncina, Zelko, Lucic T. (Kodelja), Sabadin, Stanic (Cermelj).
SCT OLIMPIJA LJUBLJANA - Pejkovic; Bozic (Krzisnik), Hadzic, Zulic, Kosic, Knavs, Djuranovic, Pavlin, N'Toko (Velkoski), Kojicic, Siljak.

05/06/96, Ljubljana
SCT OLIMPIJA LJUBLJANA 1 Velkoski (3)
PRIMORJE AJDOVSCINA 1 Vrabac (89)
referee - Novarlic
SCT OLIMPIJA LJUBLJANA - Pejkovic; Zulic, Hadzic, Knavs, Novak, Krzisnik, Djuranovic, N'Toko, Pavlin, Velkoski (Kosic), Siljak.
PRIMORJE AJDOVSCINA - Strajnar; Ibranovic, Cermelj, Mulahmetovic, Zelko (Shala), Vrabac, Kodelja, Ruznic, Lucic B., Stanic, Sabadin.

(SCT OLIMPIJA LJUBLJANA 2-1)

EUROPEAN CUPS RESULTS 95/96

CUP-WINNERS' CUP

● MURA MURSKA SOBOTA

Preliminary round ZALGIRIS VILNIUS (LIT)

A 0-2
Cernjavic; Kokol, Baranja, Breznik, Stampfer, Alihodzic, Kardos, Gajser, Belec (Rous), Bakula, Hlebalin (Kmetec).

H 2-1 Kokol (11), Alihodzic (89)
Cernjavic; Baranja, Kokol, Cifer, Poljsak, Alihodzic, Brezic (Kmetec), Gajser, Breznik, Bakula, Stampfer (Bloudek).

UEFA CUP

● SCT OLIMPIJA LJUBLJANA

Preliminary round APOLLON (GRE)

A 0-1
Simeunovic; Englaro, Krzisnik, Kosic (Hadzic), Hadjialagic, Knaus, Novak, Kojicic, Benedejcic (Rudonja), Siljak, Bozgo.

H 3-1 Bozgo (11, 66), Zulic (81)
Simeunovic; Englaro, Krzisnik, Benedejcic (Bozic), Hadjialagic, Knaus, Novak, Kojicic (Zulic), Siljak (Nikcevic), Bozgo, Cimerotic.

1st round RODA JC (HOL)

A 0-5
Simeunovic; Krzisnik, Bozic (Rudonja), Zulic, Hadjialagic, Knaus (Hadzic), Novak (Pavlin), Kojicic, Nikcevic, Benedejcic, N'Toko.

H 2-0 Bozgo (38), Zulic (78)
Simeunovic; Hadjialagic, Englaro, Knaus, Krzisnik, Rudonja, Zulic, N'Toko, Benedejcic (Kosic), Siljak (Djuranovic), Bozgo (Cimerotic).

● MARIBOR BRANIK

Preliminary round SKONTO RIGA (LAT)

A 0-1
Dabanovic; Lukic, Galic, Milinovic, Kek, Karic, Binkovski (Makragic), Zirojevic, Simundza (Sterbal), Fricelj, Pejovic (Zidan).

H 2-0 Sterbal (17), Fricelj (20)
Lalic; Galic (Binkovski), Sterbal, Milinovic, Makragic (Poznic), Krizan, Zirojevic, Zidan, Simundza (Fridl), Fricelj, Karic.

1st round OLYMPIAKOS (GRE)

A 0-2
Lalic; Galic, Karic, Milinovic, Kek, Krizan, Zirojevic, Zidan, Simundza (Binkovski), Fricelj, Pejovic.

H 1-3 Karic (70)
Lalic; Sterbal, Karic, Milinovic, Kek, Krizan, Galic, Zidan, Simundza, Fricelj (Poznic), Pejovic.

PLAYERS OF THE SEASON

SEBASTIJAN CIMEROTIC

The discovery of the 95/96 season in Slovenia was undoubtedly 22-year-old Sebastijan Cimerotic of SCT Olimpija. Four years earlier the youngster had made big headlines by scoring a goal from the halfway line on his First Division début. Having finally won himself a regular place in both the Olimpia and Slovenian U-21 teams, he began to demonstrate his prowess on a regular basis. An outstanding dribbler with a very powerful shot, Cimerotic really impressed in the toughest of the U-21 qualifiers against Italy and Croatia. His natural skill allied to a fine overall tactical appreciation of the game should take him far.

ERMIN SILJAK

The captain of the Slovenian Under-21 team had a brilliant season in 95/96, winning the First Division top scorer prize with 28 goals for his club, SCT Olimpija, and adding another eight in the Slovenian Cup, another competition in which he finished as leading marksman following his decisive goal in the first leg of the final. On the back of his excellent domestic performances Ermin Siljak achieved graduation to the senior national team and made an instant impact with a flawless performance and a goal in Slovenia's shock 2-1 victory away to Mexico. Strong with both feet and an outstanding jumper in the penalty area, the 23-year-old caused a major stir in the summer when he was found guilty of signing contracts for two different clubs - Bastia in France and Reggiana in Italy. The Corsicans eventually won the fight to keep him.

Ermin Siljak

between the two clubs, HIT Gorica won two and the other two were drawn. HIT may have gone down 0-2 on their own ground to Olimpija in the Cup, but in the league they maintained an unbeaten record at home. So, too, did third-placed Mura, who thus made it into European competition for the third year in succession. That left Maribor Branik in a very disappointing fourth place, with just the InterToto competition to look forward to.

Maribor lasted a round longer than Mura in 95/96 European competition, eliminating Latvian champions Skonto Riga in the UEFA Cup preliminary round before meeting their match against Olympiakos of Greece. Mura fell at the first hurdle of the Cup-winners' Cup to their Baltic opponents, Zalgiris Vilnius. Champions SCT Olimpija came back from a first-leg deficit to eliminate Apollon of Athens in their preliminary-round tie, but a 0-5 pounding by Roda in the next round was far too much to make up back in Ljubljana, so they too went out.

At national team level, Slovenia again began the season with a good performance against World Cup runners-up Italy, going down only 0-1 in nearby Udine. They followed that with one of their best performances of the European Championship qualifying campaign, beating Ukraine 3-2 in Ljubljana with a late winning goal - his second of the game - from Belgian-based striker Saso Udovic. Udovic enjoyed an even better personal triumph later on in the season. Following a startling 2-1 victory away to Mexico in December, Slovenia were invited to the annual four-team Rothmans tournament in Malta, and in the first match, against Iceland, they hammered in seven goals, with five of them going to Udovic. The 27-year-old marksman completed his hat-trick in 15 minutes and took his personal haul to five just 17 minutes later. He even dared to claim a sixth goal five minutes later, but that was later officially credited to his Italian-based strike partner Matjaz Florjancic, who, unlike Udovic, had never previously found the net for his country.

After that romp in the mid-winter sun things turned a little sour for Zdenko Verdenik and his team. A goalless draw away to Poland sent the team into their opening World Cup tie in reasonable spirits. But against Greece in Athens the Slovenians were well beaten and could feel relieved at getting away with only a 0-2 defeat.

INTERNATIONAL HONOURS

None

NK BELTINCI

CLUB DIRECTORY

NK Beltinci
Stefana Kovaca 19
69 231 Beltinci
tel - (069) 42853
fax - (069) 77108
Year of Formation - 1970
President - Viktor Ketler
Secretary - Slavko Horvat
Coach - Petar Nadoveza; Zoran Cirkvencic;
Vojislav Simeunovic (96/97 - Ivica Frkic)
Stadium - Beltinci (4,000)

APPEARANCES 95/96

	P	Ap	(s)	Gls
Dean BARANJA	M	33	(1)	2
Bosko BOSKOVIC	G	17		
Kristijan CENER	M	15	(8)	2
Erik CIRKVENCIC	M	9	(1)	1
Bogdan CRNKO	M	21	(7)	3
Emir DZAFIC	A	9	(21)	4
Tomislav GODINA	D	21	(2)	
Mirsad GRANOV	D	10	(4)	
Goran GUTALJ (BOS)	A	9	(5)	3
Zlatko HERCEG	A	12	(8)	1
Srecko ILIC (BOS)	D	29		2
Martin JERAJ	M	20	(4)	1
Stanko KUZMA	G	1	(1)	
Rade MOJOVIC (YUG)	G	5		
Sergei NEIMAN (RUS)	M	27	(1)	4
Milan OSTERC	A	18	(5)	5
Ivica PESIC	M	3		
Robert PIRC	A	1	(2)	
Robert SABJAN	M	16	(6)	
Marinko SARKEZI	D	33		1
Boris SIRK	D	32		1
Stefan SKAPER	A	26	(1)	10
Dzemo SMJECANIN (BOS)	A	1		
Bostjan TRATNJAK	D	14	(5)	1
Kristijan ZVER	G	13		
Mario ZVER	A	1	(3)	

LEAGUE RESULTS 1995/96

Date	Opponent	H/A	Score	Scorers
30/07/95	Mura Murska sobota	A	1-1	Crnko
06/08/95	Primorje Ajdovscina	H	0-3	
13/08/95	SCT Olimpija Ljubljana	A	0-5	
20/08/95	Rudar Velenje	H	0-2	
27/08/95	HIT Gorica	A	0-0	
02/09/95	NK Izola	A	2-0	Skaper, Sirk
10/09/95	Maribor Branik	H	0-0	
17/09/95	MAG Korotan Prevalje	A	1-1	Baranja
24/09/95	Publikum Celje	H	1-2	Herceg
01/10/95	Publikum Celje	A	0-2	
07/10/95	Mura Murska sobota	H	0-0	
15/10/95	Primorje Ajdovscina	A	0-1	
22/10/95	SCT Olimpija Ljubljana	H	2-1	Skaper 2
29/10/95	Rudar Velenje	A	1-1	Neiman
05/11/95	HIT Gorica	H	1-1	Osterc
12/11/95	NK Izola	H	5-1	Dzafic, Osterc, Neiman, Cirkvencic, Ilic
19/11/95	Maribor Branik	A	2-1	Dzafic
26/11/95	MAG Korotan Prevalje	H	2-1	Baranja, Crnko
25/02/96	Mura Murska sobota	H	2-0	Sarkezi, Ilic
03/03/96	Primorje Ajdovscina	A	0-0	
10/03/96	SCT Olimpija Ljubljana	H	1-2	Cener
17/03/96	Rudar Velenje	A	0-0	
24/03/96	HIT Gorica	H	0-0	
31/03/96	NK Izola	H	3-0	Skaper 2, Cener
06/04/96	Maribor Branik	A	0-3	
09/04/96	MAG Korotan Prevalje	H	4-1	Skaper 2, Neiman, Osterc
14/04/96	Publikum Celje	A	1-0	Tratnjak
19/04/96	Publikum Celje	H	2-1	Gutalj 2
28/04/96	Mura Murska sobota	A	0-1	
01/05/96	Primorje Ajdovscina	H	0-2	
05/05/96	SCT Olimpija Ljubljana	A	3-5	Osterc, Jeraj, Skaper
13/05/96	Rudar Velenje	H	1-0	Osterc
19/05/96	HIT Gorica	A	1-2	Crnko
26/05/96	NK Izola	A	3-0	Skaper 2, Dzafic
02/06/96	Maribor Branik	H	2-0	Neiman, Gutalj
08/06/96	MAG Korotan Prevalje	A	0-0	

HIT GORICA

CLUB DIRECTORY

NK HIT Gorica
Bidovceva 4
65 000 Nova Gorica
tel - (065) 22458
fax - (065) 22458
Year of Formation - 1938
President - Danilo Likar
Secretary - Josip Koradin
Coach - Milan Miklavic
Stadium - Nova Gorica (5,000)

MAJOR HONOURS
League Championship - (1) 1996.

APPEARANCES 95/96

	P	Ap	(s)	Gls
Vili BECAJ	M	28		7
Milos BREZNIKAR	A	16	(13)	3
Radislav CURCIC (YUG)	M	1		
Florijan DEBENJAK	A	9	(6)	1
Enes DEMIROVIC (BOS)	M	32		1
Uros DOVZAK	D	16	(4)	1
Aleksander GRUDEN	M	4	(6)	
Mehmet HADZIC (BOS)	D	1		
Alfred JERMANIS	M	22	(6)	7
Miha KEBE	M		(6)	
Milos KOSTIC	D	4	(2)	
Marko MADON	D	21		
Robert MARUSIC	A		(6)	1
Damir MATANIC	D	4	(6)	
Borut MAVRIC	G	36		
Andrej POLJSAK	D	14	(1)	1
Nenad PROTEGA	D	29	(1)	1
Blagoje RADOVANOVIC (BOS)	M	32		
Elvis RIBARIC	M	10	(5)	
Miran SREBRNIC	M	34		2
Dzevad TURKOVIC (CRO)	A	1	(1)	
Zoran UBAVIC	A	9	(11)	6
Sandi VALENTINCIC	A	31		16
Marko VOGRIC	M	1	(2)	
Aleksandr VOROBYOV (RUS)	D	31		2
Ivica VULIC	A	10	(13)	

LEAGUE RESULTS 1995/96

30/07/95	Primorje Ajdovscina	A	4-1	Valentincic 2, Debenjak, Marusic
06/08/95	SCT Olimpija Ljubljana	H	2-1	Valentincic 2
13/08/95	Rudar Velenje	A	1-1	Becaj
20/08/95	NK Izola	A	2-0	Becaj, Jermanis
27/08/95	NK Beltinci	H	0-0	
02/09/95	Maribor Branik	A	0-1	
10/09/95	MAG Korotan Prevalje	H	2-0	Vorobjov, Breznikar
17/09/95	Publikum Celje	A	1-2	Dovzak
24/09/95	Mura Murska sobota	H	2-1	Vorobjov, Becaj
01/10/95	Mura Murska sobota	A	0-1	
07/10/95	Primorje Ajdovscina	H	3-1	Valentincic, Becaj, Srebrnic
15/10/95	SCT Olimpija Ljubljana	A	3-0	Valentincic 3
22/10/95	Rudar Velenje	H	3-1	Jermanis, Srebrnic, Becaj
29/10/95	NK Izola	H	3-0	Valentincic 3
05/11/95	NK Beltinci	A	1-1	Protega
12/11/95	Maribor Branik	H	0-0	
19/11/95	MAG Korotan Prevalje	A	2-1	Breznikar, Jermanis
26/11/95	Publikum Celje	H	2-1	Ubavic 2
25/02/96	Primorje Ajdovscina	H	1-1	Becaj
03/03/96	SCT Olimpija Ljubljana	A	0-0	
10/03/96	Rudar Velenje	H	1-0	Ubavic
17/03/96	NK Izola	H	3-0	Ubavic, Valentincic, Poljsak
24/03/96	NK Beltinci	A	0-0	
31/03/96	Maribor Branik	H	0-0	
06/04/96	MAG Korotan Prevalje	A	0-0	
09/04/96	Publikum Celje	H	1-1	Valentincic
13/04/96	Mura Murska sobota	A	1-1	Valentincic
19/04/96	Mura Murska sobota	H	1-0	Ubavic
28/04/96	Primorje Ajdovscina	A	2-0	Jermanis, Valentincic
01/05/96	SCT Olimpija Ljubljana	H	2-2	Demirovic, Becaj
05/05/96	Rudar Velenje	A	1-1	Breznikar
13/05/96	NK Izola	A	2-0	Jermanis, Valentincic
19/05/96	NK Beltinci	H	2-1	Jermanis, Ubavic
25/05/96	Maribor Branik	A	0-1	
02/06/96	MAG Korotan Prevalje	H	1-0	Jermanis
08/06/96	Publikum Celje	A	0-1	

NK IZOLA

CLUB DIRECTORY

NK Izola
p.p. 13
66 310 Izola
tel - (066) 65330
fax - (066) 65482
Year of Formation - 1946
President - Drago Mikulin
Secretary - Miran Zlogar
Coach - Salih Softic; Danilo Sergas; Ivan Pataric
Stadium - Izola (6,000)

MAJOR HONOURS

League Championship - (1) 1990.

APPEARANCES 95/96

	P	Ap	(s)	Gls
Velimir BABIC	M	5	(7)	
Borut BAUER	D		(2)	
Milenko BOJANIC	G	20	(1)	
Bosko BOSKOVIC	G	5		
Igor BOZIC	M	24	(4)	
Zoran BOZICIC	D		(8)	
Musli BULJUKBASHI (YUG)	A	8		1
Marjan CENDAK	M	33		2
Aljosa COTAR	D	13	(2)	
Muamer DALIPAGIC (BOS)	M	5		
Nenad DONCIC	M	15		
Damjan GREGORIC	M	16	(3)	1
Danijel GREGORIC	A	22	(3)	
Simon GREGORIC	D	17	(3)	
Behrija HADZIC	D	13	(1)	
Miodrag JANJIC	D	14		
Florent KARAHODA (ALB)	G	8		
Edin KENDIC	D	5		
Denis KOVAC	M	5	(2)	
Suarez KRAJA	D	11	(1)	
Vedran MACOLIC	A	16	(5)	1
Dejan MAKIVIC	M	5	(7)	
Damjan MALETIC	A		(3)	
Dejan MAMILOVIC	D	16	(2)	1
Gino MAZZOLENIS	A	4	(1)	
Dusan NOVAK	M	7	(1)	
Nedzet OKCIC	M	8		
Dejan PATARIC	M	8	(3)	
Davor PERKAT	D	15		2
Simon PIRC	A	7		3
Zoran SANTIN	M		(2)	
Alen SCULAC	M	6		
Elvis SIROTIC	G	3	(2)	
Miroslav STAMPFER	M	14		1
Damjan TONEJC	A	9	(4)	
Tomi TRESKAVICA	D		(1)	
Miljan UBIPARIPOVIC	M	8	(5)	1
Damir VRABAC (BOS)	D	6		
Anton ZLOGAR	M	25	(4)	

LEAGUE RESULTS 1995/96

30/07/95	MAG Korotan Prevalje	A	0-2	
06/08/95	Rudar Velenje	H	0-1	
13/08/95	Publikum Celje	A	1-5	Perkat
20/08/95	HIT Gorica	H	0-2	
27/08/95	Mura Murska sobota	A	0-4	
02/09/95	NK Beltinci	H	0-2	
10/09/95	Primorje Ajdovscina	A	0-6	
17/09/95	Maribor Branik	H	2-2	Buljukbashi, Perkat
24/09/95	SCT Olimpija Ljubljana	A	0-10	
01/10/95	SCT Olimpija Ljubljana	H	0-6	
07/10/95	MAG Korotan Prevalje	H	1-0	Cendak
15/10/95	Rudar Velenje	A	1-5	Pirc
22/10/95	Publikum Celje	H	0-2	
29/10/95	HIT Gorica	A	0-3	
05/11/95	Mura Murska sobota	H	1-1	Pirc
12/11/95	NK Beltinci	A	1-5	Pirc
19/11/95	Primorje Ajdovscina	H	1-1	Cendak
26/11/95	Maribor Branik	A	1-5	Gregoric Dam.
25/02/96	MAG Korotan Prevalje	H	1-1	Mamilovic
03/03/96	Rudar Velenje	A	0-5	
10/03/96	Publikum Celje	H	1-1	Macolic
17/03/96	HIT Gorica	A	0-3	
24/03/96	Mura Murska sobota	H	0-3	
31/03/96	NK Beltinci	A	0-3	
06/04/96	Primorje Ajdovscina	H	1-5	Ubiparipovic
09/04/96	Maribor Branik	A	1-3	Stampfer
14/04/96	SCT Olimpija Ljubljana	H	0-5	
19/04/96	SCT Olimpija Ljubljana	A	0-4	
28/04/96	MAG Korotan Prevalje	A	0-8	
01/05/96	Rudar Velenje	H	0-2	
05/05/96	Publikum Celje	A	0-11	
13/05/96	HIT Gorica	H	0-2	
19/05/96	Mura Murska sobota	A	0-7	
26/05/96	NK Beltinci	H	0-3	
02/06/96	Primorje Ajdovscina	A	0-7	
08/06/96	Maribor Branik	H	0-5	

MAG KOROTAN PREVALJE

CLUB DIRECTORY

NK MAG Korotan
Ugasle peci 1
62 391 Prevalje
tel - (0602) 33558
fax - (0602) 31239
Year of Formation - 1933
President - Vlado Petric
Secretary - Franjo Klaric
Coach - Drago Kostanjsek; Milan Zezelj; Rastslav Matic (96/97 - Marjan Pusnik)
Stadium - Korotan (5,000)

APPEARANCES 95/96

	P	Ap	(s)	Gls
Marko AZMAN	G		(1)	
Gregor BLATNIK	D	31		
Ilir CAUSHLLARI (ALB)	M	21	(7)	2
Zlatko CERIMOVIC	D	27		
Sami DOBREVA (ALB)	M	13	(2)	3
Simon DVORSAK	M	30	(2)	5
Bostjan GRIZOLD	M	1	(14)	
Mitja JUDEZ	D	5	(4)	
Renato KOTNIK	M	14		
Peter KOZELJ	G	34		
Erion MEHILLI (ALB)	M	2	(2)	
Novica NIKCEVIC	A	17	(1)	5
Dejan OBREZ	A		(1)	
Vukasin PETRANOVIC (BOS)	G	2		
Roman PLESEC	M	25	(9)	10
Samo PLIMEN	M		(1)	
Niko PODVINSKI	D	26	(4)	5
Dzemo SMJECANIN (BOS)	A	17	(4)	3
Peter SMREKAR	M		(2)	
Alen SULEJMANI	M		(3)	
Peter SUMNIK	A	20	(10)	2
Kristijan SVAB	M	13	(4)	1
Matej VIDOVIC	A	25	(4)	1
Samo VIDOVIC	A	33		7
Andrej VRSIC	D	16	(7)	
Tomaz VRSIC	D	24	(2)	
Robi ZEC	M		(4)	

LEAGUE RESULTS 1995/96

Date	Opponent		Score	Scorers
30/07/95	NK Izola	H	2-0	Plesec 2
06/08/95	Publikum Celje	H	3-2	Sumnik, Vidovic S., Dobreva
13/08/95	Mura Murska sobota	A	0-2	
20/08/95	Primorje Ajdovscina	H	0-0	
27/08/95	SCT Olimpija Ljubljana	A	1-2	Sumnik
02/09/95	Rudar Velenje	H	2-0	Vidovic S., Plesec
10/09/95	HIT Gorica	A	0-2	
17/09/95	NK Beltinci	H	1-1	Dvorsak
24/09/95	Maribor Branik	A	2-1	Dobreva 2
01/10/95	Maribor Branik	H	0-0	
07/10/95	NK Izola	A	0-1	
15/10/95	Publikum Celje	A	3-2	Vidovic S., Smjecanin, Podvinski
22/10/95	Mura Murska sobota	H	1-1	Caushllari
29/10/95	Primorje Ajdovscina	A	1-1	Vidovic S.
05/11/95	SCT Olimpija Ljubljana	H	1-2	Vidovic M.
12/11/95	Rudar Velenje	A	3-2	Plesec 2, Podvinski
19/11/95	HIT Gorica	H	1-2	Dvorsak
26/11/95	NK Beltinci	A	1-2	Plesec
25/02/96	NK Izola	A	1-1	Nikcevic
03/03/96	Publikum Celje	A	0-5	
10/03/96	Mura Murska sobota	H	0-1	
17/03/96	Primorje Ajdovscina	A	1-0	Plesec
24/03/96	SCT Olimpija Ljubljana	H	1-2	Smjecanin
31/03/96	Rudar Velenje	A	1-0	Vidovic S.
06/04/96	HIT Gorica	H	0-0	
09/04/96	NK Beltinci	A	1-4	Svab
14/04/96	Maribor Branik	H	2-0	Nikcevic, Smjecanin
19/04/96	Maribor Branik	A	0-1	
28/04/96	NK Izola	H	8-0	Nikcevic 3, Plesec, Caushllari, Vidovic S., Dvorsak, Podvinski
01/05/96	Publikum Celje	H	0-1	
05/05/96	Mura Murska sobota	A	2-2	Podvinski 2
13/05/96	Primorje Ajdovscina	H	4-2	Plesec 2, Vidovic S., Dvorsak
19/05/96	SCT Olimpija Ljubljana	A	1-2	Dvorsak
26/05/96	Rudar Velenje	H	0-1	
02/06/96	HIT Gorica	A	0-1	
08/06/96	NK Beltinci	H	0-0	

MARIBOR BRANIK

CLUB DIRECTORY

NK Maribor Branik
Mladinska 29
62 000 Maribor
tel - (062) 28534/224645
fax - (062) 28534
Year of Formation - 1958
President - Dr. Rudi Turk
Secretary - Zeljko Fundak
Coach - Branko Horjak; Janez Zavrl; Zvonko Breber
Stadium - Ljudski vrt (15,000)

MAJOR HONOURS
League Championship - (5)
1961, 1976, 1982, 1984, 1986.
Domestic Cup - (15) 1965, 1966, 1968, 1973, 1974, 1978, 1980, 1982, 1984, 1986, 1987, 1989, 1990, 1992, 1994.

APPEARANCES 95/96

	P	Ap	(s)	Gls
Marko BARUN	D		(1)	
Peter BINKOVSKI	M	25	(4)	
Mladen DABANOVIC	G	4		
Alojz FRICELJ	M	31	(1)	3
Franc FRIDL	M	1	(10)	
Marinko GALIC	D	27		6
Amir KARIC	M	19	(2)	4
Matjaz KEK	D	27	(1)	4
Ales KRIZAN	D	33		
Dino LALIC	G	17	(1)	
Zvjezdan LJUBOBRATOVIC (CRO)	A	12	(3)	6
Saso LUKIC	D	19	(7)	
Dejan MAKRAGIC	A	5	(7)	
Zeljko MILINOVIC	D	33		1
Sinisa NIKOLIC (YUG)	A	5	(5)	1
Ratko PEJOVIC (YUG)	A	10	(6)	4
Igor POZNIC	A	11	(13)	3
Ante SIMUNDZA	A	28	(2)	7
Matej SNOFL	M		(3)	
Robert SRAGA	G	15	(10)	
Milan STERBAL	D	21	(5)	
Gregor ZIDAN	M	33		7
Ranko ZIROJEVIC (YUG)	M	20	(7)	1

LEAGUE RESULTS 1995/96

Date	Opponent		Score	Scorers
30/07/95	Publikum Celje	A	3-3	Karic, Pejovic, Zidan
06/08/95	Mura Murska sobota	H	1-2	Simundza
13/08/95	Primorje Ajdovscina	A	0-1	
20/08/95	SCT Olimpija Ljubljana	H	5-1	Fricelj, Zidan, Pejovic, Karic, Galic
27/08/95	Rudar Velenje	A	0-2	
02/09/95	HIT Gorica	H	1-0	Pejovic
10/09/95	NK Beltinci	A	0-0	
17/09/95	NK Izola	A	2-2	Galic, Simundza
24/09/95	MAG Korotan Prevalje	H	1-2	Zirojevic
01/10/95	MAG Korotan Prevalje	A	0-0	
07/10/95	Publikum Celje	H	0-0	
15/10/95	Mura Murska sobota	A	0-1	
22/10/95	Primorje Ajdovscina	H	2-0	Zidan 2
29/10/95	SCT Olimpija Ljubljana	A	1-0	Milinovic
05/11/95	Rudar Velenje	H	2-0	Pejovic, Kek
12/11/95	HIT Gorica	A	0-0	
19/11/95	NK Beltinci	H	1-2	Galic
26/11/95	NK Izola	H	5-1	Poznic 2, Galic, Kek, Simundza
25/02/96	Publikum Celje	H	2-2	Galic 2
03/03/96	Mura Murska sobota	A	0-1	
10/03/96	Primorje Ajdovscina	H	2-0	Ljubobratovic 2
17/03/96	SCT Olimpija Ljubljana	A	0-1	
24/03/96	Rudar Velenje	H	0-2	
31/03/96	HIT Gorica	A	0-0	
06/04/96	NK Beltinci	H	3-0	Karic, Zidan, Simundza
09/04/96	NK Izola	H	3-1	Poznic, Kek, Simundza
14/04/96	MAG Korotan Prevalje	A	0-2	
19/04/96	MAG Korotan Prevalje	H	1-0	Ljubobratovic
28/04/96	Publikum Celje	A	1-1	Ljubobratovic
01/05/96	Mura Murska sobota	H	1-1	Karic
05/05/96	Primorje Ajdovscina	A	1-0	Fricelj
12/05/96	SCT Olimpija Ljubljana	H	2-1	Fricelj, Nikolic
19/05/96	Rudar Velenje	A	1-1	Ljubobratovic
25/05/96	HIT Gorica	H	1-0	Simundza
02/06/96	NK Beltinci	A	0-2	
08/06/96	NK Izola	A	5-0	Ljubobratovic, Kek, Zidan 2, Simundza

MURA MURSKA SOBOTA

CLUB DIRECTORY

NK Mura
Miklosiceva 89
69 000 Murska sobota
tel - (069) 32701
fax - (069) 32701
Year of Formation - 1946
President - Milan Moerec
Secretary - Vlado Banko
Coach - Marin Kovacic; Miran Skalic; Zoran Cirkvencic
Stadium - Fazanerija (5,000)

MAJOR HONOURS
League Championship - (1) 1970.
Domestic Cup - (1) 1995.

APPEARANCES 95/96

	P	Ap	(s)	Gls
Haris ALIHODZIC (BOS)	D	35		5
Marijan BAKULA (CRO)	M	29		2
Adamo BARANJA	M	33	(2)	2
Simon BARANJA	D	4	(1)	
Robert BELEC	A	6	(3)	1
Ingmar BLOUDEK	D	19	(2)	
Danijel BREZIC	M	20	(11)	
Peter BREZNIK	D	32		6
Stefan CERNJAVIC	G	32		
Franc CIFER	D	29	(1)	2
Erik CIRKVENCIC	M	15	(2)	2
Damjan GAJSER	M	26	(2)	2
Mikhail HLEBALIN (RUS)	A	30	(1)	13
Janez KARDOS	M	12	(8)	
Marko KMETEC	A	3	(17)	4
Vladimir KOKOL	A	32	(1)	2
Franc KRANCIC	M		(3)	
Dejan NEMEC	G	4	(1)	
Damjan OSLAJ	D	1	(1)	
Andrej POLJSAK	D	17		
Bojan ROUS	A	15	(14)	2
Miroslav STAMPFER	M	2	(5)	

LEAGUE RESULTS 1995/96

30/07/95	NK Beltinci	H	1-1	Bakula
06/08/95	Maribor Branik	A	2-1	Hlebalin, Kokol
13/08/95	MAG Korotan Prevalje	H	2-0	Breznik, Baranja A.
20/08/95	Publikum Celje	A	1-1	Kmetec
27/08/95	NK Izola	H	4-0	Alihodzic 2, Hlebalin 2
02/09/95	Primorje Ajdovscina	H	1-1	Hlebalin
10/09/95	SCT Olimpija Ljubljana	A	2-1	Hlebalin, Gajser
17/09/95	Rudar Velenje	H	1-1	Kmetec
24/09/95	HIT Gorica	A	1-2	Breznik
01/10/95	HIT Gorica	H	1-0	Hlebalin
07/10/95	NK Beltinci	A	0-0	
15/10/95	Maribor Branik	H	1-0	Hlebalin
22/10/95	MAG Korotan Prevalje	A	1-1	Breznik
29/10/95	Publikum Celje	H	1-0	Rous
05/11/95	NK Izola	A	1-1	Gajser
12/11/95	Primorje Ajdovscina	A	1-5	Bakula
19/11/95	SCT Olimpija Ljubljana	H	1-1	Alihodzic
26/11/95	Rudar Velenje	A	1-0	Breznik
25/02/96	NK Beltinci	A	0-2	
03/03/96	Maribor Branik	H	1-0	Hlebalin
10/03/96	MAG Korotan Prevalje	A	1-0	Hlebalin
17/03/96	Publikum Celje	H	0-0	
24/03/96	NK Izola	A	3-0	Hlebalin 2, Cirkvencic
31/03/96	Primorje Ajdovscina	A	0-1	
06/04/96	SCT Olimpija Ljubljana	H	0-0	
09/04/96	Rudar Velenje	A	0-1	
13/04/96	HIT Gorica	H	1-1	Rous
19/04/96	HIT Gorica	A	0-1	
28/04/96	NK Beltinci	H	1-0	Cifer
01/05/96	Maribor Branik	A	1-1	Cirkvencic
05/05/96	MAG Korotan Prevalje	H	2-2	Breznik, Belec
13/05/96	Publikum Celje	A	0-1	
19/05/96	NK Izola	H	7-0	Hlebalin 2, Cifer, Kokol, Alihodzic, Baranja A., Kmetec
26/05/96	Primorje Ajdovscina	H	2-1	Breznik, Alihodzic
02/06/96	SCT Olimpija Ljubljana	A	0-2	
08/06/96	Rudar Velenje	H	1-0	Kmetec

PRIMORJE AJDOVSCINA

CLUB DIRECTORY

NK Primorje
p.p. 3
65 270 Ajdovscina
tel - (065) 61042
fax - (065) 61698
Year of Formation - 1924
President - Dusan Cernigoj
Secretary - Savo Slokar
Coach - Vladan Mladenovic; Marin Kovacic
Stadium - Primorje (5,000)

APPEARANCES 95/96

	P	Ap	(s)	Gls
Bojan ADZIC	D		(7)	
Miodrag BOZIC	D	25	(4)	
Iztok CERMELJ	D	22	(7)	1
Dejan DONCIC	D	15	(3)	1
Andi ERGAVER	M		(2)	
Adriano FEGIC	M	16		
Edmond GUNJAC	M	22	(1)	1
Kadrija IBRANOVIC	D	33		1
Ales KODELJA	M	5	(10)	
Borivoje LUCIC (BOS)	A	31		4
Trivko LUCIC (BOS)	M	7	(4)	3
Kristijan MARKOVIC	M		(1)	
Iztok MERMOLJA	D	1	(7)	2
Sefik MULAHMETOVIC (YUG)	M	23	(2)	
Amir RUZNIC	D	28		1
Valter SABADIN	M	13	(1)	1
Agron SHALA	M	1	(4)	
Uros STANIC	A	19	(11)	4
Janez STRAJNAR	G	35		
Mihael VONCINA	A	29	(1)	14
Dinko VRABAC (BOS)	M	35		18
Andrej ZELKO	A	35		5
Bostjan ZIBERNA	G	1	(1)	

LEAGUE RESULTS 1995/96

Date	Opponent	H/A	Score	Scorers
30/07/95	HIT Gorica	H	1-4	Voncina
06/08/95	NK Beltinci	A	3-0	Voncina 2, Lucic B.
13/08/95	Maribor Branik	H	1-0	Lucic T.
20/08/95	MAG Korotan Prevalje	A	0-0	
27/08/95	Publikum Celje	H	3-1	Vrabac 3
02/09/95	Mura Murska sobota	A	1-1	Voncina
10/09/95	NK Izola	H	6-0	Vrabac 3, Stanic, Voncina, Mermolja
17/09/95	SCT Olimpija Ljubljana	H	0-3	
24/09/95	Rudar Velenje	A	0-2	
01/10/95	Rudar Velenje	H	1-1	Vrabac
07/10/95	HIT Gorica	A	1-3	Lucic T.
15/10/95	NK Beltinci	H	1-0	Zelko
22/10/95	Maribor Branik	A	0-2	
29/10/95	MAG Korotan Prevalje	H	1-1	Lucic B.
05/11/95	Publikum Celje	A	1-3	Doncic
12/11/95	Mura Murska sobota	H	5-1	Vrabac 2, Voncina 2, Gunjac
19/11/95	NK Izola	A	1-1	Voncina
26/11/95	SCT Olimpija Ljubljana	A	1-1	Zelko
25/02/96	HIT Gorica	A	1-1	Cermelj
03/03/96	NK Beltinci	H	0-0	
10/03/96	Maribor Branik	A	0-2	
17/03/96	MAG Korotan Prevalje	H	0-1	
24/03/96	Publikum Celje	A	1-1	Sabadin
31/03/96	Mura Murska sobota	H	1-0	Lucic B.
06/04/96	NK Izola	A	5-1	Voncina 3, Lucic T., Ruznic
09/04/96	SCT Olimpija Ljubljana	A	1-0	Mermolja
14/04/96	Rudar Velenje	H	2-1	Vrabac, Stanic
19/04/96	Rudar Velenje	A	1-3	Stanic
28/04/96	HIT Gorica	H	0-2	
01/05/96	NK Beltinci	A	2-0	Vrabac 2
05/05/96	Maribor Branik	H	0-1	
13/05/96	MAG Korotan Prevalje	A	2-4	Voncina 2
19/05/96	Publikum Celje	H	4-1	Voncina, Zelko 2, Stanic
26/05/96	Mura Murska sobota	A	1-2	Vrabac
02/06/96	NK Izola	H	7-0	Vrabac 4, Zelko, Ibranovic, Lucic B.
08/06/96	SCT Olimpija Ljubljana	H	1-4	Vrabac

PUBLIKUM CELJE

CLUB DIRECTORY

NK Publikum
Cesta na grad 12
63 000 Celje
tel - (063) 25022
fax - (063) 27606
Year of Formation - 1946
President - Darko Klaric
Secretary - Tomaz Ambrozic
Coach - Borut Jarc; Kasim Kokot; Milovan Tarbuk
Stadium - Skalna klet (5,000)

MAJOR HONOURS
League Championship - (1) 1964.
Domestic Cup - (1) 1964.

APPEARANCES 95/96

	P	Ap	(s)	Gls
Nihzad ADEMOVIC (BOS)	M	2	(2)	
Edo BAJRAKTAREVIC	M	28		4
Ante BASIC (CRO)	D	29	(1)	
Dean BAUMAN	M	28	(2)	6
Spasoje BULAJIC	D	29		2
Dragutin CELIC (CRO)	M	7		1
Robert CUGMAS	M	12	(7)	
Andrej GORSEK	A	14	(1)	7
Faik KAMBEROVIC (BOS)	A	29	(1)	24
Denis KOCJANCIC	M		(3)	
Savo KOMAR (YUG)	A	5	(3)	
Ales KOS	D		(1)	
Andrej KRACMAN	G	2		
Simon PIRC	A		(1)	
Ermin RAKOVIC	M	14	(9)	5
Bojan ROMIH	A	3	(6)	
Damjan ROMIH	M	19	(3)	
Simon SESLAR	M	28	(1)	3
Aljosa SIVKO	A	1	(11)	1
Matjaz STANCAR	M	30	(2)	3
Slavisa STOJANOVIC	M	3	(6)	
Peter TOSIC	D	12	(2)	1
Ales TURK	D	34		1
Nenad ULAGA	D	9	(11)	3
Anton USNIK	M	11	(11)	
Adnan ZILDZEVIC (BOS)	A	13	(4)	1
Branko ZUPAN	G	34		

LEAGUE RESULTS 1995/96

Date	Opponent	H/A	Score	Scorers
30/07/95	Maribor Branik	H	3-3	Gorsek 2, Bauman
06/08/95	MAG Korotan Prevalje	A	2-3	Gorsek, Rakovic
13/08/95	NK Izola	H	5-1	Kamberovic 2, Stancar, Bauman, Celic
20/08/95	Mura Murska sobota	H	1-1	Bajraktarevic
27/08/95	Primorje Ajdovscina	A	1-3	Kamberovic
02/09/95	SCT Olimpija Ljubljana	H	1-1	Bauman
10/09/95	Rudar Velenje	A	1-0	Gorsek
17/09/95	HIT Gorica	H	2-1	Seslar, Gorsek
24/09/95	NK Beltinci	A	2-1	Kamberovic, Gorsek
01/10/95	NK Beltinci	H	2-0	Kamberovic, Turk
07/10/95	Maribor Branik	A	0-0	
15/10/95	MAG Korotan Prevalje	H	2-3	Kamberovic, Bulajic
22/10/95	NK Izola	A	2-0	Kamberovic, Bulajic
29/10/95	Mura Murska sobota	A	0-1	
05/11/95	Primorje Ajdovscina	H	3-1	Seslar, Kamberovic, Gorsek
12/11/95	SCT Olimpija Ljubljana	A	0-3	
19/11/95	Rudar Velenje	H	4-6	Rakovic 2, Kamberovic 2
26/11/95	HIT Gorica	A	1-2	Ulaga
25/02/96	Maribor Branik	A	2-2	Kamberovic 2
03/03/96	MAG Korotan Prevalje	H	5-0	Kamberovic 2, Tosic, Seslar, Sivko
10/03/96	NK Izola	A	1-1	Kamberovic
17/03/96	Mura Murska sobota	A	0-0	
24/03/96	Primorje Ajdovscina	H	1-1	Stancar
31/03/96	SCT Olimpija Ljubljana	A	0-3	
06/04/96	Rudar Velenje	H	0-0	
09/04/96	HIT Gorica	A	1-1	Rakovic
14/04/96	NK Beltinci	H	0-1	
19/04/96	NK Beltinci	A	1-2	Ulaga
28/04/96	Maribor Branik	H	1-1	Kamberovic
01/05/96	MAG Korotan Prevalje	A	1-0	Kamberovic
05/05/96	NK Izola	H	11-0	Kamberovic 4, Bauman 3, Bajraktarevic 3, Stancar
13/05/96	Mura Murska sobota	H	1-0	Rakovic
19/05/96	Primorje Ajdovscina	A	1-4	Kamberovic
26/05/96	SCT Olimpija Ljubljana	H	3-1	Kamberovic 2, Zildzevic
02/06/96	Rudar Velenje	A	0-0	
08/06/96	HIT Gorica	H	1-0	Ulaga

RUDAR VELENJE

CLUB DIRECTORY

NK Rudar
Cesta ob jezeru 7
63 320 Velenje
tel - (063) 856656
fax - (063) 854986
Year of Formation - 1948
President - Janko Lukner
Secretary - Boris Ograjensek
Coach - Bojan Prasnikar; Josip Vugrinec; Borut Jarc
Stadium - Ob jezeru (7,000)

MAJOR HONOURS
League Championship - (2) 1977, 1991.

APPEARANCES 95/96

	P	Ap	(s)	Gls
Samir BALAGIC	D	32	(1)	1
Matjaz CVIKL	A	29	(2)	10
Mladen DABANOVIC	G	13		
Gjergji DEMA (ALB)	M	15	(1)	2
Robert DOLER	D	13	(11)	1
Ismet EKMECIC (BOS)	A	29	(4)	14
Sabahudin GOLAC	D	1		
Borce HRISTOV	A	3	(4)	
Milos HUDARIN	D	23	(3)	
Jernej JAVORNIK	M	7	(1)	
Slavko JAVORNIK	M	21	(5)	1
Bojan JOVANOVIC	G	1	(1)	
Slavko KOMAR (YUG)	A	9	(6)	3
Peter MERNIK	D		(1)	
Alen MUJANOVIC	M	5	(6)	
Simon OBLAK	D	15	(13)	
Branko PAVIC	A		(2)	
Zoran PAVLOVIC	M	24	(3)	2
Ivica PESIC	A	1	(3)	
Robert PEVNIK	M		(6)	
Ervin POLOVSAK	D	8	(6)	
Stjepan PRANJIC	M	27	(1)	5
Bostjan RATKOVIC	D	32		
Ilir SILLO (ALB)	D	27		
Sergej SOSTAR	M	4	(8)	
Goran STANKOVIC	G	22		
Almir SULEJMANOVIC	M		(1)	
Janez ZILNIK	D	14		
Milan ZURMAN	D	21	(1)	7

LEAGUE RESULTS 1995/96

Date	Opponent		Score	Scorers
30/07/95	SCT Olimpija Ljubljana	A	1-1	Cvikl
06/08/95	NK Izola	A	1-0	Zurman
13/08/95	HIT Gorica	H	1-1	Ekmecic
20/08/95	NK Beltinci	A	2-0	Zurman, Ekmecic
27/08/95	Maribor Branik	H	2-0	Pranjic, Zurman
02/09/95	MAG Korotan Prevalje	A	0-2	
10/09/95	Publikum Celje	H	0-1	
17/09/95	Mura Murska sobota	A	1-1	Javornik S.
24/09/95	Primorje Ajdovscina	H	2-0	Zurman, Komar
01/10/95	Primorje Ajdovscina	A	1-1	Cvikl
07/10/95	SCT Olimpija Ljubljana	H	2-1	Pavlovic 2
15/10/95	NK Izola	H	5-1	Komar 2, Cvikl, Zurman, Ekmecic
22/10/95	HIT Gorica	A	1-3	Ekmecic
29/10/95	NK Beltinci	H	1-1	Ekmecic
05/11/95	Maribor Branik	A	0-2	
12/11/95	MAG Korotan Prevalje	H	2-3	Doler, Ekmecic
19/11/95	Publikum Celje	A	6-4	Ekmecic 3, Cvikl, Balagic, Zurman
26/11/95	Mura Murska sobota	H	0-1	
25/02/96	SCT Olimpija Ljubljana	H	1-3	Ekmecic
03/03/96	NK Izola	H	5-0	Pranjic 2, Cvikl, Ekmecic, Zurman
10/03/96	HIT Gorica	A	0-1	
17/03/96	NK Beltinci	H	0-0	
24/03/96	Maribor Branik	A	2-0	Ekmecic, Pranjic
31/03/96	MAG Korotan Prevalje	H	0-1	
06/04/96	Publikum Celje	A	0-0	
09/04/96	Mura Murska sobota	H	1-0	Cvikl
14/04/96	Primorje Ajdovscina	A	1-2	Ekmecic
19/04/96	Primorje Ajdovscina	H	3-1	Cvikl 2, Dema
28/04/96	SCT Olimpija Ljubljana	A	0-2	
01/05/96	NK Izola	A	2-0	Ekmecic, Pranjic
05/05/96	HIT Gorica	H	1-1	Cvikl
13/05/96	NK Beltinci	A	0-1	
19/05/96	Maribor Branik	H	1-1	Cvikl
26/05/96	MAG Korotan Prevalje	A	1-0	Dema
02/06/96	Publikum Celje	H	0-0	
08/06/96	Mura Murska sobota	A	0-1	

SCT OLIMPIJA LJUBLJANA

CLUB DIRECTORY

NK SCT Olimpija
Vodovodna 20
61 009 Ljubljana
tel - (061) 348397
fax - (061) 341847
Year of Formation - 1911
President - Ivan Zidar
Manager - Peter Amersek
Secretary - Janez Tusar
Coach - Branko Oblak; Milos Soskic; Zdenko Verdenik; Petar Nadoveza
Stadium - Bezigrad (18,000)

MAJOR HONOURS

League Championship - (8) 1947, 1952, 1962, 1987, 1992, 1993, 1994, 1995.
Domestic Cup - (17) 1953, 1954, 1955, 1956, 1958, 1962, 1963, 1969, 1970, 1971, 1972, 1976, 1977, 1981, 1988, 1993, 1996.

APPEARANCES 95/96

	P	Ap	(s)	Gls
Igor BENEDEJCIC	M	20	(2)	
Kliton BOZGO (ALB)	M	27		14
Branko BOZIC	D	22	(4)	2
Sebastijan CIMEROTIC	A	20	(4)	4
Dejan DJURANOVIC	M	14	(10)	2
Robert ENGLARO	D	24		
Edin HADJIALAGIC (BOS)	D	13		1
Safet HADZIC	D	23		2
Aleksander KNAVS	M	20	(2)	1
Branislav KOJICIC (YUG)	M	18	(9)	3
Dusan KOSIC	M	6	(15)	3
Erik KRZISNIK	D	15	(4)	
Novica NIKCEVIC	A	9	(7)	8
Dzoni NOVAK	M	27	(1)	3
Roland N'TOKO (CMR)	M	10	(7)	1
Miran PAVLIN	M	18	(5)	2
Nihad PEJKOVIC	G	22		
Mladen RUDONJA	A	12	(3)	1
Ermin SILJAK	A	32	(3)	28
Marko SIMEUNOVIC	G	14		
Virginio VELKOSKI	A	2	(9)	2
Samir ZULIC	M	28		2

LEAGUE RESULTS 1995/96

30/07/95	Rudar Velenje	H	1-1	Bozgo
06/08/95	HIT Gorica	A	1-2	Hadjialagic
13/08/95	NK Beltinci	H	5-0	Novak 2, Kojicic, Rudonja, Bozgo
20/08/95	Maribor Branik	A	1-5	Kojicic
27/08/95	MAG Korotan Prevalje	H	2-1	Zulic, Siljak
02/09/95	Publikum Celje	A	1-1	Siljak
10/09/95	Mura Murska sobota	H	1-2	Nikcevic
17/09/95	Primorje Ajdovscina	A	3-0	Siljak, Nikcevic, Bozgo
24/09/95	NK Izola	H	10-0	Bozgo 4, Siljak 3, Bozic, Kosic, Nikcevic
01/10/95	NK Izola	A	6-0	Nikcevic 3, Siljak 2, Djuranovic
07/10/95	Rudar Velenje	A	1-2	Nikcevic
15/10/95	HIT Gorica	H	0-3	
22/10/95	NK Beltinci	A	1-2	Knavs
29/10/95	Maribor Branik	H	0-1	
05/11/95	MAG Korotan Prevalje	A	2-1	Bozgo, Nikcevic
12/11/95	Publikum Celje	H	3-0	Bozic, Siljak, Djuranovic
19/11/95	Mura Murska sobota	A	1-1	Siljak
26/11/95	Primorje Ajdovscina	H	1-1	Siljak
25/02/96	Rudar Velenje	A	3-1	Siljak 2, Cimerotic
03/03/96	HIT Gorica	H	0-0	
10/03/96	NK Beltinci	A	2-1	Cimerotic, Pavlin
17/03/96	Maribor Branik	H	1-0	Siljak
24/03/96	MAG Korotan Prevalje	A	2-1	Velkoski, Siljak
31/03/96	Publikum Celje	H	3-0	Zulic, Hadzic, Siljak
06/04/96	Mura Murska sobota	A	0-0	
09/04/96	Primorje Ajdovscina	H	0-1	
14/04/96	NK Izola	A	5-0	Siljak 3, Bozgo 2
19/04/96	NK Izola	H	4-0	Siljak 2, Bozgo 2
28/04/96	Rudar Velenje	H	2-0	Cimerotic, Bozgo
01/05/96	HIT Gorica	A	2-2	Bozgo, Siljak
05/05/96	NK Beltinci	H	5-3	Siljak 3, Cimerotic, Kosic
12/05/96	Maribor Branik	A	1-2	Kojicic
19/05/96	MAG Korotan Prevalje	H	2-1	Siljak, Kosic
26/05/96	Publikum Celje	A	1-3	Velkoski
02/06/96	Mura Murska sobota	H	2-0	Hadzic, Novak
08/06/96	Primorje Ajdovscina	A	4-1	Siljak 2, Pavlin, N'Toko

PROMOTED CLUB

SECOND DIVISION FINAL TABLE 95/96

		Pd	W	D	L	F	A	Pt	GD
1	**Zeleznicar Ljubljana**	**29**	**20**	**7**	**2**	**62**	**20**	**67**	**+42**
2	Nafta Lendava	29	18	5	6	51	19	59	+32
3	Crnuce	29	15	6	8	60	41	51	+19
4	Sentjur	29	13	5	11	45	36	44	+9
5	Zeleznicar Maribor	29	13	5	11	51	47	44	+4
6	Koper	29	11	8	10	33	30	41	+3
7	Family Shop	29	12	5	12	35	54	41	+1
8	Napredak	29	10	9	10	32	34	39	-2
9	ERA Smartno	29	10	7	12	35	34	37	+1
10	Zagorje	29	11	3	15	30	54	36	-24
11	Vevce	29	9	6	14	43	40	33	+3
12	Rudar Trbovlje	29	9	6	14	24	39	33	-15
13	Naklo	29	7	10	12	33	38	31	-5
14	Drava	29	8	7	14	32	53	-31	-21
15	Filc Menges	29	7	9	13	24	42	30	-18
16	Radece Papir	15	2	2	11	12	41	8	-29

N.B. Radece Papir withdrew after first half of the season.

PROMOTION/RELEGATION PLAY-OFF
MAG Korotan Prevalje 1, Nafta Lendava 0
Nafta Lendava 1, MAG Korotan Prevalje 2
(MAG Korotan Prevalje 3-1)

CLUB DIRECTORY

NK Zeleznicar Ljubljana
Milcinskega 2
61 000 Ljubljana
tel - (061) 1313144
fax - (061) 1325050
Year of Formation - 1910
President - Janez Potocnik
Secretary - Karel Kokec
Coach - Milos Soskic
Stadium - ZSD Ljubljana (10,000)

MAJOR HONOURS
League Championship - (5)
1949, 1963, 1967, 1968, 1969.

SPAIN

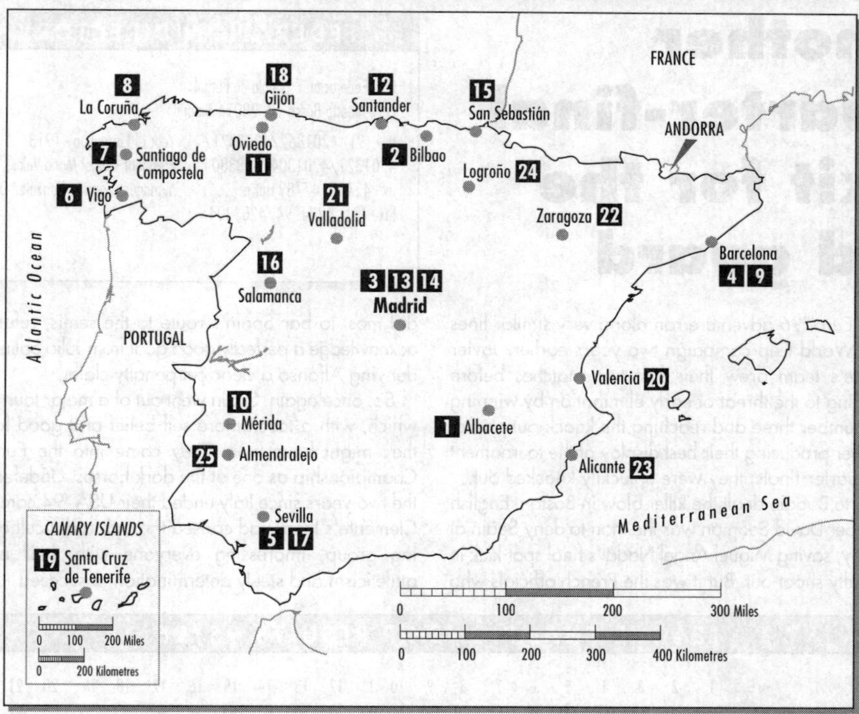

1	ALBACETE BALOMPIE	946
2	ATHLETIC BILBAO	947
3	ATLETICO MADRID	948
4	FC BARCELONA	949
5	REAL BETIS	950
6	RC CELTA	951
7	SD COMPOSTELA	952
8	RC DEPORTIVO	953
9	RCD ESPANYOL	954
10	CP MERIDA	955
11	REAL OVIEDO	956
12	RACING SANTANDER	957
13	RAYO VALLECANO	958
14	REAL MADRID	959
15	REAL SOCIEDAD	960
16	UD SALAMANCA	961
17	SEVILLA FC	962
18	SPORTING GIJON	963
19	CD TENERIFE	964
20	VALENCIA CF	965
21	REAL VALLADOLID	966
22	REAL ZARAGOZA	967
23	HERCULES CF	968
24	CD LOGROÑES	968
25	CF EXTREMADURA	968

ATLETICO JOY, REAL DESPAIR

Another quarter-final exit for the old guard

FEDERATION DIRECTORY

Real Federación Española de Fútbol
Calle Alberto Bosch 13, 28014 Madrid

tel - (91) 4201362/4203321/ 4201321/4201304/4203304
tlx - 42420/47789 rfef e
fax - (91) 4204294/4203304

Year of Formation - 1913
President - Angel María Villar
Manager - Gerardo González Otero

Spain's Euro '96 adventure ran along very similar lines to their World Cup campaign two years earlier. Javier Clemente's team drew their first two matches before responding to the threat of early elimination by winning match number three and reaching the knock-out phase. Then, after producing their best display of the tournament in the quarter-finals, they were unluckily knocked out.

Roberto Baggio dealt the killer blow in Boston. English goalkeeper David Seaman was the man to deny Spain at Wembley, saving Miguel Angel Nadal's final spot-kick in the penalty shoot-out. But it was the French officials who did most to bar Spain's route to the semis, refusing to acknowledge a perfectly good goal from Julio Salinas and denying Alfonso a clear-cut penalty claim.

So, once again, Spain went out of a major tournament which, with a touch more self-belief and good fortune, they might have won. They came into the European Championship as one of the dark horses. Undefeated in the two years since Italy ended their USA '94 campaign, Clemente's team had cruised through a difficult qualifying group, impressing everyone with their energy, athleticism and steely determination to succeed.

LEAGUE CHAMPIONSHIP RESULTS 95/96

		1	2	3	4	5	6	7	8	9	10	11	12	13	14	15	16	17	18	19	20	21	22
1	Albacete Balompié		2-0	1-1	0-1	0-0	4-0	2-1	1-0	0-0	2-0	0-1	2-2	1-2	1-1	3-5	3-3	3-2	1-3	0-0	1-3	4-2	0-1
2	Athletic Bilbao	2-2		0-2	0-0	0-1	3-0	0-0	1-0	0-0	1-1	0-1	4-0	3-1	0-5	0-0	3-1	1-1	2-1	2-0	0-1	2-1	1-0
3	Atlético Madrid	2-0	4-1		3-1	1-1	3-2	3-0	1-0	2-1	1-1	3-0	2-0	0-0	1-2	4-1	2-1	0-1	2-0	3-1	2-3	0-2	1-1
4	FC Barcelona	3-0	4-1	1-3		1-0	3-2	1-0	1-1	2-1	2-2	4-1	1-1	2-0	3-0	1-0	4-1	1-1	1-0	2-2	1-0	1-0	3-1
5	Real Betis	2-3	0-0	2-1	1-5		0-3	5-0	1-0	2-3	0-1	2-1	2-2	0-0	0-0	3-1	4-0	1-1	2-5	3-3	3-0	3-0	3-1
6	RC Celta	2-2	3-1	0-3	1-0	2-0		0-1	0-0	4-2	2-0	1-0	0-0	2-0	1-1	1-1	2-1	4-0	0-0	2-2	1-1	1-1	1-1
7	SD Compostela	3-1	2-1	1-3	2-1	1-2	1-1		4-0	2-1	1-0	4-1	2-0	1-0	3-3	2-0	0-0	0-0	1-0	0-2	0-4	1-3	3-2
8	RC Deportivo	5-0	0-0	2-2	2-2	0-0	2-1	2-0		0-1	2-1	0-4	2-3	1-0	3-0	1-1	2-0	3-2	1-0	1-1	3-0	3-1	2-3
9	RCD Espanyol	1-0	3-0	0-2	1-1	1-1	2-2	0-0	0-0		3-0	5-0	1-0	4-2	3-1	0-0	3-1	0-1	0-0	2-1	2-0	2-0	1-1
10	CP Mérida	1-1	1-0	0-1	0-0	1-1	2-0	0-2	0-2	0-1		3-1	3-1	0-1	2-2	1-2	0-0	3-2	1-0	2-0	0-2	1-0	1-1
11	Real Oviedo	1-0	0-0	1-1	1-2	0-1	1-1	3-1	0-2	1-2	0-0		2-1	2-0	1-2	0-0	2-2	2-3	1-0	1-3	0-1	3-8	1-1
12	Racing Santander	5-5	1-1	0-4	1-1	0-0	2-1	1-0	2-1	1-1	2-0	0-0		1-2	2-0	2-3	2-1	1-1	1-1	1-2	0-3	0-0	0-0
13	Rayo Vallecano	2-0	2-2	0-3	1-1	1-2	1-3	0-1	0-6	1-0	4-1	1-2	1-2		1-5	2-0	1-4	0-0	2-0	2-4	3-2	0-2	4-3
14	Real Madrid	2-0	1-2	1-0	1-1	4-2	1-0	2-1	1-0	1-2	4-0	2-3	1-2	1-2		3-2	5-0	4-1	0-1	2-0	0-0	4-1	2-2
15	Real Sociedad	8-1	2-2	1-0	1-1	1-1	3-1	0-1	2-1	0-1	1-2	1-1	2-1	2-1	1-1		1-0	1-0	2-0	0-1	5-2	1-0	3-1
16	UD Salamanca	2-4	2-1	1-3	1-3	2-1	0-1	1-0	0-5	2-2	2-2	0-1	5-0	1-2	0-2	3-3		4-1	3-0	1-2	4-0	0-0	0-1
17	Sevilla FC	1-1	1-1	0-0	1-0	1-0	0-0	0-1	0-0	0-3	3-0	1-1	0-1	1-0	0-1	2-1	3-1		2-0	0-1	1-2	1-1	1-1
18	Sporting Gijón	3-0	1-2	1-2	0-3	2-3	1-0	2-1	1-1	2-3	3-1	0-1	4-2	3-1	0-0	1-1	3-2	3-1		0-2	1-3	4-2	4-1
19	CD Tenerife	1-3	3-2	1-1	1-1	1-2	1-0	1-1	1-1	1-4	1-0	3-3	2-0	2-2	3-0	1-0	4-0	4-2	3-0		2-1	1-0	1-2
20	Valencia CF	1-0	3-1	0-1	4-1	1-1	3-0	5-2	2-1	1-0	4-1	3-1	2-1	3-0	4-3	0-1	2-0	1-0	1-0	2-2		1-0	0-0
21	Real Valladolid	3-0	1-1	0-1	0-2	3-1	1-1	0-0	2-2	0-0	1-1	2-2	3-1	1-1	0-3	3-0	1-0	3-3	1-0	3-0	2-5		0-0
22	Real Zaragoza	3-1	1-0	0-1	0-3	1-2	0-0	1-0	2-3	1-1	3-1	1-0	1-2	1-1	0-1	1-2	1-1	0-1	1-1	0-2	4-1	5-3	

LEAGUE CHAMPIONSHIP FINAL TABLE 95/96

			Home					Away					Total						
		Pd	W	D	L	F	A	W	D	L	F	A	W	D	L	F	A	Pt	GD
1	Atlético Madrid	42	13	4	4	40	19	13	5	3	35	13	26	9	7	75	32	87	+43
2	Valencia CF	42	16	3	2	43	16	10	2	9	34	35	26	5	11	77	51	83	+26
3	FC Barcelona	42	15	5	1	42	17	7	9	5	30	22	22	14	6	72	39	80	+33
4	RCD Espanyol	42	11	8	2	34	13	9	6	6	29	23	20	14	8	63	36	74	+27
5	CD Tenerife	42	11	6	4	38	25	9	6	6	31	29	20	12	10	69	54	72	+15
6	Real Madrid	42	12	3	6	42	22	8	7	6	33	29	20	10	12	75	51	70	+24
7	Real Sociedad	42	12	5	4	38	19	5	7	9	24	34	17	12	13	62	53	63	+9
8	Real Betis	42	9	6	6	39	30	7	8	6	22	24	16	14	12	61	54	62	+7
9	RC Deportivo	42	11	6	4	37	22	5	7	9	26	22	16	13	13	63	44	61	+19
10	SD Compostela	42	12	4	5	34	25	5	4	12	13	29	17	8	17	47	54	59	-7
11	RC Celta	42	9	10	2	30	17	3	6	12	19	34	12	16	14	49	51	52	-2
12	Sevilla FC	42	7	8	6	19	16	4	7	10	24	39	11	15	16	43	55	48	-12
13	Real Zaragoza	42	7	5	9	27	27	4	10	7	24	32	11	15	16	51	59	48	-8
14	Real Oviedo	42	5	7	9	23	31	7	5	9	25	36	12	12	18	48	67	48	-19
15	Athletic Bilbao	42	9	7	5	25	18	2	8	11	19	37	11	15	16	44	55	48	-11
16	Real Valladolid	42	7	10	4	30	24	4	4	13	27	38	11	14	17	57	62	47	-5
17	Racing Santander	42	6	10	5	25	27	5	4	12	22	42	11	14	17	47	69	47	-22
18	Sporting Gijón	42	10	3	8	39	32	3	4	14	12	28	13	7	22	51	60	46	-9
19	Rayo Vallecano	42	7	3	11	29	43	5	5	11	18	32	12	8	22	47	75	44	-28
20	Albacete Balompié	42	7	7	7	31	28	3	5	13	24	53	10	12	20	37	62	42	-25
21	CP Mérida	42	8	6	7	22	20	2	6	13	15	42	10	12	20	55	81	42	-26
22	UD Salamanca	42	7	4	10	34	34	1	5	15	19	48	8	9	25	53	82	33	-29

An immensely difficult team to play against, Spain fancied their chances of doing well in England. Optimism might have been even greater had Clemente not made his Euro '96 squad a closed shop for players who had lent their assistance in the qualifying round. The national petition to have young guns Raúl and De la Peña included in the 22 was completely ignored by the coach, who, in keeping with his reputation, stuck rigidly to the experienced players he knew and trusted. In any case, with just two preparation matches, both against Norway, in the build-up to the tournament, he scarcely had time to experiment.

In the first round Spain did little to impress, but they proved their resilience, scoring late goals in all three games. In the first two, against Bulgaria and France, they came back to equalise. Against Romania, they poached a late winner to seal their passage into the last eight.

Throughout the tournament Clemente seemed happy enough with his defence - goalkeeper Zubizarreta was every bit as good as in World Cups gone by, and Sergi was a dynamic presence on the left - but he continually chopped and changed the midfield and attack. When Pizzi, his first-choice centre-forward, was harshly sent off in the first match, the coach seemed unsure what to do. None of his subsequent forward combinations were wholly convincing, and no striker played consistently well enough to warrant automatic inclusion. Against England, Clemente even resorted to bringing back the old warhorse Julio Salinas, who had not started an international for 15 months. Had Salinas's first-half strike not been erroneously chalked off, Clemente's choice might have been hailed as inspirational, but the veteran striker lasted only 45 minutes, and his replacement Alfonso, unconvincing in his earlier games, suddenly looked sharper than ever, which in turn brought Clemente unjustified criticism from the Spanish media for not having started with him.

At 24, Alfonso is certainly one to watch for the future. Apart from Julen Guerrero, whose early miss against Bulgaria shrivelled his confidence for the remainder of the tournament, the Real Betis forward was the youngest of the Spanish squad in England. Whether Clemente feels the need to bring in even younger players from the Spanish U-21 team that finished runners-up to Italy in the European Championship (and which he himself led to the Atlanta Olympics) will probably depend on early results in the World Cup qualifiers. Spain have once again been drawn in the trickiest group. Yugoslavia and the Czech Republic will make life extremely tough for them, and it will be a major achievement if Spain can get through another qualifying competition without defeat.

Life is made no easier for Clemente by the marathon 22-team Primera Division, which, bizarrely, has been retained for the 1996/97 season despite the furore which greeted its farcical introduction in the summer of 1995.

In the event, fears that the performances of Spanish clubs in Europe would be jeopardised by the increase in the number of domestic games were largely unfounded, with all six Spanish clubs surviving at least until the third round of their respective competitions. However, it was surely no coincidence that the winners of this inaugural 22-team league were a team without any international commitments at all in 1995/96 - Atlético Madrid.

A lowly 14th the previous season, Atlético were not expected to make any impression on the championship race. Yet they led from the front all season and were thoroughly deserved winners of their first Liga title for 19 years. Atlético were consistently the most attractive and efficient team in the country. They responded well to adversity, and even though the final weeks of the campaign brought fear that the prize would ultimately elude them, the team held their nerve sufficiently to cross the line first, thereby fulfilling the long-cherished dream of the club's power-broker president Jesús Gil y Gil.

Ironically, after nine years of constant upheaval during the Gil régime, it was Atlético's stability that saw them through to their ninth championship crown. At last the president found a coach who could do the job the way

DOMESTIC CUP RESULTS

SECOND ROUND
CD Alaves v Athletic Bilbao 0-1; 1-4
(Athletic Bilbao 5-1)
CD Numancia v Real Sociedad 2-0; 0-2
(2-2; CD Numancia on pens.)
CD Logroñés v Racing Santander 1-2; 1-3
(Racing Santander 5-2)
SDC Durango v UD Salamanca 0-2; 0-4
(UD Salamanca 6-0)
CD Endesa As Pontes v RC Celta 0-0; 1-2
(RC Celta 2-1)
CA Osasuna v Real Oviedo 3-3; 1-2
(Real Oviedo 5-4)
CD Leonesa v Real Valladolid 1-1; 1-3
(Real Valladolid 4-2)
RC Ferrol v Sporting Gijón 1-1; 0-4
(Sporting Gijón 5-1)
SD Eibar v SD Compostela 1-0; 0-2
(SD Compostela 2-1)
CF Extremadura v RCD Espanyol 1-1; 1-3
(RCD Espanyol 4-2)
Atlético Marbella v Rayo Vallecano 0-0; 1-3
(Rayo Vallecano 3-1)
RCD Mallorca v Valencia CF 0-0; 0-0
(0-0; Valencia CF on pens.)
Vélez CF v CD Tenerife 1-2; 0-8
(CD Tenerife 10-1)
Córdoba CF v Mérida CP 1-3; 0-2
(Mérida CP 5-1)
Almería CF v Atlético Madrid 1-4; 1-2
(Atlético Madrid 6-2)
UD Las Palmas v CD Leganés 1-1; 0-0
(1-1; CD Leganés on away goal)
Andorra FC v Getafe CF 3-0; 1-2
(Andorra FC 4-2)
Club Endesa Andorra v Levante UD 1-1; 1-4
(Levante UD 5-2)
Novelda CF v Hércules CF 0-0; 0-2
(Hércules CF 2-0)
UE Lleida v Ecija Balompié 0-2; 1-0
(Ecija Balompié 2-1)

THIRD ROUND
Ecija Balompié v Sporting Gijón 2-0; 0-5
(Sporting Gijón 5-2)
CD Leganés v RCD Espanyol 0-1; 1-5
(RCD Espanyol 6-1)
Andorra FC v RC Celta 0-5; 0-2
(RC Celta 7-0)
CD Numancia v Racing Santander 0-0; 1-0
(CD Numancia 1-0)
Levante UD v CD Tenerife 1-0; 1-6
(CD Tenerife 6-2)
Hércules CF v Rayo Vallecano 1-1; 1-0
(Hércules CF 2-1)
Atlético Madrid v Mérida CP 4-1; 4-4
(Atlético Madrid 8-5)
SD Compostela v Real Valladolid 1-0; 1-1
(SD Compostela 2-1)
UD Salamanca v Athletic Bilbao 0-0; 1-3
(Athletic Bilbao 3-1)
Real Oviedo v Valencia CF 1-1; 0-1
(Valencia CF 2-1)

FOURTH ROUND
Hércules CF v FC Barcelona 0-0; 1-4
(FC Barcelona 4-1)
CD Numancia v Sporting Gijón 2-1; 0-0
(CD Numancia 2-1)
RCD Espanyol v Real Madrid 4-1; 1-2
(RCD Espanyol 5-3)
Atlético Madrid v Real Betis 1-1; 2-1
(Atlético Madrid 3-2)
Sevilla FC v SD Compostela 2-1; 1-0
(Sevilla FC 3-1)
RC Deportivo v CD Tenerife 1-1; 1-2
(CD Tenerife 3-2)
Athletic Bilbao v Real Zaragoza 2-3; 1-0
(3-3; Real Zaragoza on away goals)
RC Celta v Valencia CF 1-1; 0-3
(Valencia CF 4-1)

QUARTER-FINALS
CD Numancia v FC Barcelona 2-2; 1-3
(FC Barcelona 5-3)
CD Tenerife v Atlético Madrid 0-0; 0-3
(Atlético Madrid 3-0)
Sevilla FC v Valencia CF 1-1; 0-2
(Valencia CF 3-1)
RCD Espanyol v Real Zaragoza 0-0; 1-1
(1-1; RCD Espanyol on away goal)

SEMI-FINALS
FC Barcelona v RCD Espanyol 1-0; 3-2
(FC Barcelona 4-2)
Valencia CF v Atlético Madrid 3-5; 2-1
(Atlético Madrid 6-5)

FINAL
10/04/96, Zaragoza
ATLETICO MADRID 1 Pantic (102)
FC BARCELONA 0
(aet)
referee - Díaz Vega
ATLETICO MADRID - Molina; Geli, Solozábal, Santi, Toni; Caminero, Vizcaíno (Biagini 81), Simeone, Pantic; Penev (López 61), Kiko (Roberto 84).
FC BARCELONA - Busquets; Celades (Ferrer 17), Nadal, Sergi; Guardiola, Popescu, Amor, Bakero (Roger 61), Hagi; Cruijff, Figo (Prosinecki 75).

NATIONAL TEAM APPEARANCES 95/96

Coach - Javier CLEMENTE	CYP	ARG	DEN	MAC	NOR	NOR	BUL	FRA	ROM	ENG	Cps	Gls
Andoni ZUBIZARRETA (23/10/61) - Valencia CF	G	G	G	G		G	G	G	G	G	110	-
Alberto BELSUE (02/03/68) - Real Zaragoza	D		D	D		D	D			D	14	-
Rafael ALKORTA (16/09/68) - Real Madrid	D	D	D	D	D80		D	D	D	D74	39	-
Miguel Angel NADAL (28/07/66) - FC Barcelona	D	D	D	D	s46	D			M	D	32	2
Agustín ARANZABAL (15/03/73) - Real Sociedad	D										2	-
LUIS ENRIQUE Martínez (08/05/70) - Real Madrid	M	s76	M		M	M53	M	M55			24	3
Fernando Ruiz HIERRO (23/03/68) - Real Madrid	M	s46	M		M46	M53	M	M	M	M	45	11
Julen GUERRERO (07/01/74) - Athletic Bilbao	M77	s54			A18	A53	M52		s72		24	7
José Luis Pérez CAMINERO (08/11/67) - Atlético Madrid	M	M46	M29	M	s46		M82	M		s46	21	8
José Emilio AMAVISCA (19/06/71) - Real Madrid	A53			M46			s52	M	M72		13	1
ALFONSO Pérez (26/09/72) - Real Betis	A61	s46	s46	s46		s53	s73	A83	s57	s46	15	3
Francisco Javier González "FRAN" (14/07/69) - RC Deportivo	s53	M54	s29		s46						8	-
Juan Antonio PIZZI (07/06/68) - CD Tenerife	s61	A46	A46	A46	A	A	A		A57		13	4
Javier MANJARIN (31/12/69) - RC Deportivo	s77	A	M61	M	M46	M		s55	M	M46	9	2
Albert FERRER (06/06/70) - FC Barcelona		D		s46	D46	D					28	-
ABELARDO Fernández (19/03/70) - FC Barcelona		D	D		D	D	D	D	D64	D	29	2
SERGI Barjuán (28/12/71) - FC Barcelona		D	D	D	D		D	D	D	D	22	1
DONATO Gama da Silva (30/12/62) - RC Deportivo		M76	s61	M	M	s53	s82				12	3
Francisco Narváez "KIKO" (26/04/72) - Atlético Madrid				A74	s18	s53		s59	A	A	11	2
Jon Andoni GOIKOETXEA (21/10/65) - Athletic Bilbao				s74	s80						36	4
Santiago CAÑIZARES (18/12/69) - Real Madrid					G						9	-
Guillermo AMOR (04/12/69) - FC Barcelona						M53	M73		s64	M	21	2
Juan Manuel LOPEZ (03/09/69) - Atlético Madrid						s53		D	D	s74	10	-
						/76						
José Francisco MOLINA (08/08/70) - Atlético Madrid						s76					1	-
Jorge OTERO (08/01/69) - Valencia CF								D59			9	-
Julio SALINAS (11/09/62) - Sporting Gijón								s83		A46	56	21

he wanted and still get the desired results. Radomir Antic, once in charge of arch-rivals Real Madrid, arrived in the summer from Real Oviedo, and his impact was immediate. Fortified with a nucleus of new players, Atlético won all the summer tournaments they entered and carried that form into the league campaign, winning each of their first four matches and nine of their first 11.

The Spanish press had predicted that Antic would go the way of his many predecessors. The average life of an Atlético coach under Gil's presidency was less than six months. But Antic had clearly done his homework. His biggest coup was to bring in unknown Yugoslav midfielder Milinko Pantic from Greek side Panionios. Pantic was given the number ten shirt and he showed all the attributes of the classic playmaker, setting up chances for the strikers with astute through-balls and flighted crosses and curling in free-kicks from any range and angle.

Antic had the knack of getting the best out of new and old players alike. Pantic was the final piece in the jigsaw, and, once assembled, the coach saw no reason to break it up. Throughout the campaign he relied on a core of just 14 players. The first-choice team consisted of goalkeeper Molina, full-backs Geli and Toni, centre-backs Santi and Solozábal, midfielders Caminero, Vizcaíno and Simeone, playmaker Pantic and strikers Kiko and Penev, with López, Roberto and Biagini in reserve. Every one of these players, without exception, enjoyed the best season of their careers. They all put in 100 per cent effort and

EUROPEAN CUPS RESULTS 95/96

CHAMPIONS' CUP

● REAL MADRID

Champions' League

1st match AJAX (HOL)

A 0-1

Buyo; Chendo, Hierro, Sanchis, Lasa; Redondo, Raúl, Luis Enrique, Sandro (Rincón 54), Amavisca (Míchel 69); Zamorano.

2nd match GRASSHOPPER-CLUB ZÜRICH (SUI)

H 2-0 Zamorano (69, 89)

Buyo; Quique, Hierro, Sanchis, Lasa; Milla, Raúl, Rincón (Míchel 46), Laudrup (Luis Enrique 74); Zamorano, Amavisca (Soler 59).

3rd match FERENCVÁROS (HUN)

H 6-1 Raúl (23, 25, 84), Zamorano (33, 46), Hierro (54)

Buyo; Quique, Hierro (Nando 63), Sanchis, Soler; Milla, Míchel, Laudrup (Esnáider 58); Raúl, Zamorano, Amavisca (Luis Enrique 58).

4th match FERENCVÁROS (HUN)

A 1-1 Raúl (74)

Buyo; Quique, Alkorta, Sanchis, Soler; Redondo, Míchel (Luis Enrique 60), Laudrup; Raúl, Zamorano, Amavisca.

5th match AJAX (HOL)

H 0-2

Buyo; Chendo (Míchel 74), Alkorta, Sanchis, Quique; Redondo, Raúl, Luis Enrique, Laudrup (Milla 72); Zamorano, Amavisca.

6th match GRASSHOPPER-CLUB ZÜRICH (SUI)

A 2-0 Raúl (55), Míchel (66)

Buyo; Quique, Hierro (Alkorta 62), Sanchis, Lasa; Milla, Raúl, Luis Enrique, Laudrup (Rincón 69); Esnáider, Amavisca (Míchel 60).

Quarter-final JUVENTUS (ITA)

H 1-0 Raúl (21)

Buyo; Chendo, García Calvo, Alkorta; Redondo, Laudrup (Míchel 64), Hierro, Raúl, Soler (Quique 26); Zamorano, Luis Enrique.

A 0-2

Cañizares; Chendo, García Calvo, Alkorta, Lasa; Milla, Raúl, Míchel (Esnáider 63), Laudrup, Quique (Rincón 55); Luis Enrique.

CUP-WINNERS' CUP

● REAL ZARAGOZA

1st round INTER BRATISLAVA (SVK)

A 2-0 Morientes (43), Oscar (61)

Juanmi; Belsúe, Paqui, Cáceres, Oscar, Aguado; Nayim (Gay 64), Berti (Pardeza 69), Poyet; Dani, Morientes (García Sanjuán 75).

H 3-1 Poyet (12), Nayim (64), Dani (72)

Juanmi; Belsúe (Solana 74), Paqui, Cáceres, Oscar, Aguado; Nayim, Berti (Aragón 46), Poyet (Dani 61); Pardeza, Higuera.

2nd round CLUB BRUGGE KV (BEL)

H 2-1 Aragón (28p), Dani (34)

Juanmi; Belsúe, Cáceres, Nayim, Cuartero, Solana; Dani, Aragón, Poyet; Morientes (Pardeza 46; Oscar 88), Higuera (Berti 60).

A 1-0 Dani (90)

Juanmi; Belsúe, Cáceres, Berti (García Sanjuán 74), Aguado, Solana (Paqui 46); Oscar, Aragón, Poyet; Morientes, Higuera (Dani 58).

Quarter-final RC DEPORTIVO (ESP)

A 0-1

Belman; Belsúe, García Sanjuán, Cáceres; Nayim (López 76), Aguado, Aragón, Higuera (Gay 52), Poyet; Dani (Pardeza 81), Morientes.

H 1-1 Morientes (37)

Belman; Belsúe, Cuartero, García Sanjuán, Solana; Aragón, Higuera, Poyet, Nayim (Pardeza 67); Dani (Oscar 62), Morientes.

● RC DEPORTIVO

1st round APOEL NICOSIA (CYP)

A 0-0

Canales; Voro, Cascallar, Djukic, Nando; Mauro Silva, Paco, Aldana; Manjarín (Riesco 84), Radchenko (Viqueira 46), Beguiristáin (David 78).

H 8-0 Bebeto (17, 22, 45), Radchenko (28, 67), Beguiristáin (43), Donato (60), Aldana (79)

Canales; Voro, Djukic, Nando; Donato, Paco, Manjarín (Aldana 58), Fran; Beguiristáin, Radchenko, Bebeto (Alfredo 46).

2nd round TRABZONSPOR (TUR)

A 1-0 Donato (61)

Liaño; Voro, Ribera, Djukic, Nando; Donato, Alfredo, Aldana (Manjarín 85), Fran (Beguiristáin 74), Villarrota (Viqueira 90); Radchenko.

H 3-0 Donato (22), Bebeto (39, 80)

Liaño; Voro, Paco, Djukic, Villarroya (Nando 69); Donato (Aldana 79), Alfredo (López Recarte 46), Manjarín, Fran; Beguiristáin, Bebeto.

Quarter-final REAL ZARAGOZA (ESP)

H 1-0 David (70)

Liaño; Voro, Paco, Djukic, Villarroya; Donato, Manjarín (David 58), Viqueira, Fran; Radchenko (Milovanovic 72), Beguiristáin (Aldana 66).

A 1-1 Bebeto (63)

Liaño; Voro, Djukic, Paco, Villarroya; López Recarte, Mauro Silva (Donato 5), Aldana, Fran, Manjarín (Alfredo 77); Bebeto.

Semi-final PARIS SAINT-GERMAIN FC (FRA)

H 0-1

Liaño; Voro, Djukic, Paco (David 63), Alfredo; Donato, López Recarte, Aldana (Viqueira 69), Fran; Manjarín (Beguiristáin 80), Bebeto.

A 0-1

Liaño; Voro, Paco, Ribera, Alfredo (Aldana 50); Viqueira (Beguiristáin 58), Donato, Villarroya, Manjarín; Bebeto, Radchenko (Martín Vázquez 62).

UEFA CUP

● REAL BETIS

1st round FENERBAHÇE (TUR)

A 2-1 Pier (27), Sabas (80)

Jaro; Jaime, Ureña, Vidakovic, Josete; Alexis, Merino, Cañas, Stosic (Sabas 64), Jarni (Menéndez 90); Pier.

H 2-0 Alexis (21p), Cañas (38)

Jaro; Jaime, Olías, Merino, Josete; José Mari (Márquez 83), Alexis, Cañas, Sabas; Alfonso (Arpón 74), Jarni (Menéndez 28).

EUROPEAN CUPS RESULTS 95/96 (CONTINUED)

2nd round 1.FC KAISERSLAUTERN (GER)
A 3-1 Alfonso (45, 73), Alexis (54)
Jaro; Jaime, Olías, Merino, Josete; Alexis, Stosic (Quico 88), Cañas, Jarni (Menéndez 79); Pier, Alfonso (Sánchez Jara 82).
H 1-0 Jarni (55)
Jaro; Jaime, Merino, Vidakovic, Josete; Alexis, Stosic, Cañas, Jarni (Menéndez 84); Pier (Arpón 71), Alfonso (Sabas 88).

3rd round GIRONDINS DE BORDEAUX (FRA)
A 0-2
Jaro; Jaime, Olías, Vidakovic, Josete, Sánchez Jara (Menéndez 74); Alexis, Cañas, Stosic, Arpón (Sabas 67); Pier.
H 2-1 Alexis (30), Stosic (45)
Jaro; Jaime (Arpón 51), Vidakovic, Merino, Josete (Menéndez 84); Alexis, Cañas (Márquez 85), Jarni, Stosic; Sabas, Pier.

● FC BARCELONA

1st round HAPOEL BEER SHEVA (ISR)
A 7-0 De la Peña (5), Roger (45, 68, 78), Oscar (63), Figo (66, 82)
Busquets; Celades, Nadal, Carreras; Popescu, Bakero (Oscar 54), De la Peña (Ferrer 69), Roger; Figo, Kodro, Cruijff (Moreno 54).
H 5-0 Guardiola (12), Hagi (27), Toni (52), Carreras (62), Amor (66)
Angoy; Celades, Abelardo, Guardiola (Figo 72), Alvarez; Bakero (De la Peña 46), Amor (Cruijff 72), Carreras, Hagi; Moreno, Toni.

2nd round VITÓRIA GUIMARÃES (POR)
H 3-0 Kodro (45, 67), Celades (76)
Busquets; Ferrer, Guardiola (Nadal 46), Popescu (Abelardo 68), Sergi; Bakero, Celades, Roger, De la Peña (Carreras 61), Figo, Kodro.
A 4-0 Kodro (19), Oscar (62), Celades (67), Sergi (77)
Busquets; Ferrer, Nadal, Guardiola, Popescu (Bakero 76), Sergi; Celades, Amor, Roger (Abelardo 40); Figo, Kodro (Oscar 50).

3rd round SEVILLA FC (ESP)
A 1-1 Hagi (65)
Busquets; Ferrer, Carreras, Nadal, Sergi; Bakero, Celades, Roger (Guardiola 70), Hagi (De la Peña 87); Figo, Kodro (Toni 70).
H 3-1 Bakero (61), Popescu (79), Roger (81)
Lopetegui; Ferrer, Nadal, Guardiola, Popescu, Sergi; Bakero, Roger, Oscar (Celades 84), Hagi; Figo (Toni 85).

Quarter-final PSV (HOL)
H 2-2 Bakero (20), Abelardo (70)
Busquets; Abelardo, Popescu, Sergi; Guardiola, Amor, Bakero (De la Peña 78), Roger (Moreno 83); Kodro, Cuéllar (Oscar 64), Figo.
A 3-2 Bakero (3), Figo (22), Sergi (78)
Busquets; Ferrer, Abelardo, Guardiola, Popescu, Sergi; Bakero (Roger 52), Amor, Nadal, Hagi (Cuéllar 64); Figo (Celades 71).

Semi-final FC BAYERN MÜNCHEN (GER)
A 2-2 Oscar (14), Hagi (76)
Busquets; Ferrer, Celades, Guardiola, Popescu; Bakero (De la Peña 74), Amor, Oscar (Cruijff 52), Hagi (Carreras 78), Roger; Figo.
H 1-2 De la Peña (88)
Busquets; Ferrer (Abelardo 81), Nadal, Sergi; Popescu, Bakero, Amor, Roger (De la Peña 75); Figo, Kodro (Cuéllar 59), Cruijff.

● SEVILLA FC

1st round BOTEV PLOVDIV (BUL)
H 2-0 Suker (29, 34)
Unzúe; Diego, Jiménez, Prieto, Marcos; Moacir, Paz, Moya (Carlos 82), Peixe (Martagón 53); Suker, Estebaranz (Monchu 77).
A 1-1 Monchu (57)
Unzúe; Martagón, Jiménez, Prieto, Diego; Moacir, Paz, Marcos (Ferreras 81), Peixe; Suker (Moya 83), Carlos (Monchu 46).

2nd round OLYMPIAKOS (GRE)
H 1-0 Juanito (90)
Unzúe; Martagón, Pedro, Prieto, Diego; Moacir, Ferreras, Moya (Marcos 70), Peixe (Juanito 35); Suker, Carlos (Monchu 62).
A 1-2 Suker (110)
Unzúe; Martagón, Jiménez, Juanito, Diego; Moacir (Moya 91), Paz, Pepelu, Marcos; Suker, Tevenet (Carlos 66).

3rd round FC BARCELONA (ESP)
H 1-1 Suker (45)
Unzúe; Pedro, Jiménez, Prieto, Diego; Juanito, Paz, Marcos, Moya; Suker, Carlos (Tevenet 73).
A 1-3 Moya (80)
Unzúe; Martagón, Jiménez, Prieto, Diego; Juanito (Tevenet 87), Pepelu, Moya, Marcos; Suker, Carlos (Estebaranz 71).

revealed or revived hidden talents that had Atlético's long-suffering fans cooing in rapturous appreciation.

Inevitably, in such an arduously long season, Atlético began to show signs of tiredness in the closing weeks. At the halfway point in the season they had held a seven-point lead, but a run of five home games without a win in March and April, including a 1-2 defeat by Real Madrid, threatened to undo all of the team's previous good work. Fortunately, Atlético held things together on their travels. No fixture was more important than the visit to Barcelona's Nou Camp stadium on April 20.

Ten days earlier Atlético had outfoxed the Catalans to win the final of the Copa del Rey, the Spanish Cup, in Zaragoza, taking the game 1-0 after extra-time thanks to an unlikely headed goal by Pantic. Revenge was in the air at a packed-out Nou Camp, especially as Barcelona were still heavily involved in the championship race, just three points behind the leaders. But the visitors from Madrid left the 115,000 crowd breathless as they ran out 3-1 winners, apeing their victory over Johan Cruijff's team earlier in the season at the Vicente Calderón. At that moment, the title race looked over, but a week later Atlético lost 2-3 at home to an in-form Valencia, and suddenly, with just four games left, Antic and his players had it all to do again.

But there were to be no more major slip-ups. A draw away to Tenerife prolonged the agony into the final

PLAYERS OF THE SEASON

IVAN DE LA PEÑA

No player was more frequently in the media spotlight during the 95/96 Spanish season than Barcelona's "little Buddha", 20-year-old midfielder Ivan De la Peña. The diminutive, crop-haired youngster was the revelation of the season, his energetic and skilful midfield promptings adding an extra dimension to the Catalans' attacking potential. It was De la Peña's début season in the Barcelona first team, but he was soon regarded as an indispensable asset by most Barça-watchers. Not, however, by the man who mattered - Johan Cruijff. The Dutchman's reluctance to include De la Peña on a permanent basis provoked much ill feeling and was a factor in his eventual departure. Several observers claimed that if the youngster had been given the opportunity he merited, Barcelona would have won the championship. A similar reaction was sparked nationwide when Javier Clemente refused to incorporate De la Peña in his Euro '96 squad.

RAUL

Another Spanish youngster tipped for a future at the very top is Real Madrid's 19-year-old striker Raúl González. Like De la Peña, he had to make do with the consolation of a trip to the Atlanta Olympics after controversially missing out on Euro '96. The potential he had shown in his first season for Real was confirmed in his second. In a season of constant change at the Bernabéu, Raúl's development was the one steady factor. He played more league matches (40) than any other Real player, and also scored more goals (19). In the Champions' League he was an even bigger hit, taking the team to the brink of the semi-finals with half a dozen goals, including the winner at home to Juventus. A couple of years ago Raúl would wait at the bus-stop with his mates before heading off for training. Now he drives to the Bernabéu in a Mercedes.

KIKO

Spain's Olympic Games hero of 1992 moved from Cádiz to Atlético Madrid in 1993, but he never really got to grips with life in the capital and seemed set for a move back to his native south. That was until new Atlético coach Radomir Antic arrived and completely transformed Kiko from a lethargic want-away into a dynamic and hungry striker who was prepared to sweat blood for the Atlético cause. Kiko did not become a prolific goalscorer overnight, but the goals he did score were invariably decisive ones, such as the winner in Mérida, the brace against Salamanca and the title-clinching strike against Albacete. When Atlético were struggling to impose themselves against lesser opposition, Kiko would come to rescue them. National coach Javier Clemente admired Kiko's fighting qualities and called him up for Euro '96, where he was arguably Spain's most consistent forward.

JUAN ANTONIO PIZZI

In a championship where the best strikers are usually foreign imports, it was a pleasant change for the locals to see a Spanish international top the Pichichi goal charts. Not that Juan Antonio Pizzi is entirely homegrown. He is in fact Argentinian-born and only qualified to play for Spain in 1994. Since then he has made a bold claim for permanent possession of the Spanish number nine shirt. He even proved his loyalty to the Spanish cause by scoring a goal in a friendly against Argentina. At Euro '96 his hopes were crushed by a red card in the opening game against Bulgaria and he failed to add to his four international goals. At club level Pizzi had a brilliant season for Tenerife, scoring 31 times, including four in one game against Sevilla, to lead his team into the UEFA Cup and earn himself a lucrative mainland move to Barcelona.

ANDONI ZUBIZARRETA

When Andoni Zubizarreta pulled a thigh muscle in the warm-up of Valencia's Spanish league match at Valladolid, it meant that the veteran goalkeeper was forced to miss a game through injury for the first time in his career. He even had to pull out of Spain's friendly international against Norway. But at Euro '96 the 34-year-old Basque was back for his fifth major tournament and back to his very best form. Great saves from Lechkov, Guérin and Shearer proved coach Javier Clemente's claims that 'Zubi' is still far and away the best goalkeeper in Spain. With 110 caps already to his name, the international milestones set by Ravelli and Shilton seem certain to be overhauled. Barcelona's decision to let Zubizarreta go on a free transfer two years ago looks even crazier now than it did then.

TOP SCORERS

31 Juan Antonio PIZZI (CD Tenerife)
28 Predrag MIJATOVIC (Valencia CF)
25 BEBETO (RC Deportivo)
23 Alen PETERNAC (Real Valladolid)
19 RAUL González (Real Madrid)
18 Julio SALINAS (Sporting Gijón)
17 Jordi LARDIN (RCD Espanyol)
16 Liuboslav PENEV (Atlético Madrid)
Davor SUKER (Sevilla FC)
15 Vladimir GUDELJ (RC Celta)
Juan Manuel PRIETO (CP Mérida)

NATIONAL TEAM RESULTS 95/96

06/09/95	Cyprus (ECQ)	H	Granada	6-0	Guerrero (45), Alfonso (60), Pizzi (74, 79), Hierro (78), Caminero (83)
20/09/95	Argentina	H	Madrid	2-1	Pizzi (35), Guerrero (68)
11/10/95	Denmark (ECQ)	A	Copenhagen	1-1	Hierro (17p)
15/11/95	Macedonia (ECQ)	H	Elche	3-0	Kiko (17), Manjarín (72), Caminero (79)
07/02/96	Norway	H	Las Palmas	1-0	Kiko (44)
24/04/96	Norway	A	Oslo	0-0	
09/06/96	Bulgaria (ECF)	N	Leeds	1-1	Alfonso (74)
15/06/96	France (ECF)	N	Leeds	1-1	Caminero (85)
18/06/96	Romania (ECF)	N	Leeds	2-1	Manjarín (11), Amor (84)
22/06/96	England (ECF)	A	Wembley	0-0	

match of the season, but Atlético were sufficiently composed to see off struggling Albacete without any undue alarm. Goals from Simeone and Kiko were greeted with uncontrolled glee by president Gil up in the VIP box. The 2-0 win was enough. Atlético had won the title. What's more, for the first time in the club's history, they had achieved the Spanish 'double'. The post-match revelries were predictably euphoric, with Gil embracing Antic as if he were his long-lost son.

Alongside the surprise champions there were unexpected runners-up in Valencia, the only other club still in contention on the final day. They too had a new coach, ex-Atlético boss Luis Aragonés, and he manufactured an excellent team out of few outstanding players. Yugoslav import Predrag Mijatovic was the team's one big star, but while his haul of 28 goals was evenly spread across the season, Valencia picked up 47 of their 83 points in the second half of the campaign, highlights of which were a 4-1 victory over Barcelona and that championship-reviving 3-2 win over Atlético in Madrid. Significantly, Valencia were not involved in European competition either. They did reach the semi-finals of the Spanish Cup, but Atlético were their conquerors in that competition as well, eliminating them 6-5 on aggregate after a dramatic 5-3 first-leg victory in Valencia's Luis Casanova stadium.

Barcelona had to settle for third place and a second successive season without a trophy - unprecedented during Johan Cruijff's eight-year reign. All season long the Barça coach struggled to carry out his work in peace. If it wasn't journalists trying to tie him in knots, it was his own players, many of whom were displeased at having to keep the bench warm every other match. One moment Cruijff was being accused of giving favourable treatment to his son Jordi. The next he was being lambasted for his tactics and erratic team selections. The crux of the matter was that Cruijff was spoilt for choice. There were no fewer than 25 first-teamers on Barcelona's books, most of whom considered themselves worthy of a regular place in the

Celebration time for Spanish league champions Atlético Madrid

side. An additional problem was posed by the arrival of a highly talented bunch of youngsters known collectively as the *Quinta del Tordo* (Group of the Baldie), so named after the leading figure, the shaven-headed midfielder Iván De la Peña. Cruijff wanted to give these youngsters only sporadic exposure to the first team, but many fans and critics regarded the likes of Oscar, Roger, Toni and De la Peña himself as the best players in the team.

Everything came to the boil in April, when in "ten horrible days", as Cruijff put it, Barcelona crashed out of contention in all three of the competitions they were vying to win. The Spanish Cup was the first trophy to slip through their fingers after the 1-0 defeat by Atlético Madrid in Zaragoza. Six days later Barcelona were dumped out of the UEFA Cup after losing 1-2 at home to Bayern Munich. And finally, four days after that, Barça were forced to wave bye-bye to the championship after crashing 1-3 at home to Atlético.

Relations between Cruijff and club president Nuñez had been strained all season, but after this triple setback Nuñez's patience finally ran out, and before the season had even run its course, Cruijff was out of a job. His assistant Carlos Rexach saw the team through to the end of the league campiagn before Nuñez announced that the new coach for 1996/97 would be ex-England manager Bobby Robson. An era had ended, and it had ended in bitterness, with Cruijff vowing to take Barcelona to court over unlawful dismissal and breach of contract.

Events over at Barcelona's great rivals Real Madrid were even more fraught during a season which saw the 94/95 champions slip down the table to sixth position and finish without a place in Europe for only the second time in 40 years. Changes abounded, with Ramón Mendoza, Real's president for the past decade, being forced out of office after being held responsible for the club's massive financial crisis. He was replaced by Lorenzo Sanz, who wasted no time in getting rid of Jorge Valdano, the coach who had guided the team to championship victory the previous season but who had followed it up by overseeing Real's worst start to a league campaign for 65 years.

Real also struggled in the Champions' League. They were completely outclassed by Ajax in the group phase and could not defend a 1-0 lead from the first leg of the quarter-final against Juventus. By that time a new man was in charge of the team, the recently-retired veteran Deportivo coach Arsenio Iglesias. His arrival sparked a run of three successive victories, but a 0-3 defeat in Barcelona quickly brought Real back down to earth. Back-to-back home defeats, against Santander, Sporting Gijón and Cup conquerors Espanyol, finished off Real's last realistic hopes of a European place. Victories in each of their final four matches came too late, leaving José Camacho's Espanyol and Jupp Heynckes' Tenerife to finish above them and join Valencia in the UEFA Cup.

Other prominent losers in the battle for European places were Deportivo La Coruña and Real Zaragoza. These two sides were paired together in the quarter-finals of the Cup-winners' Cup, with Deportivo coming through to win thanks to a priceless away goal from their top-scoring Brazilian Bebeto. In the semi-final, however, Deportivo were beaten home and away by Paris Saint-Germain, thus ending Spain's last hope of a European trophy.

Bebto decided to quit Deportivo and return to Brazil at the end of the campaign, but his departure was more than offset by a whole host of impressive new arrivals to Spain, including his Brazilian team-mates Ronaldo (Barcelona), Roberto Carlos (Real Madrid) and Romário (Valencia). With big sums of money new flowing into Spanish football through vastly increased television and sponsorship revenue, the Liga is beginning to compete more and more with Italy's Serie A as Europe's most glamorous national championship.

But how Real Madrid, allegedly £60 million in debt, can find the funds to tempt Fabio Capello away from Italian champions Milan and secure players such as Davor Suker, Predrag Mijatovic and Clarence Seedorf for big fees on lucrative long-term contracts is a mystery that continues to provide more questions than answers.

INTERNATIONAL HONOURS

World Cup Finals appearances: 1934, 1950 (4th), 1962, 1966, 1978, 1982 (2nd phase), 1986 (qtr-finals), 1990 (2nd round), 1994 (qtr-finals)

European Championship appearances: 1964 (Winners), 1968, 1976, 1980, 1984 (runners-up), 1988, 1996 (qtr-finals)

European Club Competitions

Champions' Cup	Real Madrid (1956, 1957, 1958, 1959, 1960, 1966) FC Barcelona (1992)
Cup-winners' Cup	Atlético Madrid (1962) FC Barcelona (1979, 1982, 1989) Valencia CF (1980) Real Zaragoza (1995)
Fairs' Cup	FC Barcelona (1958, 1960, 1966) Valencia CF (1962, 1963) Real Zaragoza (1964)
UEFA Cup	Real Madrid (1985, 1986)
Super Cup	Valencia CF (1981) FC Barcelona (1992)
World Club Cup	Real Madrid (1960) Atlético Madrid (1974)

PROFILE

JOSE LUIS PEREZ CAMINERO

José Luis Pérez Caminero's career has been one long tale of ups and downs. Great goals, injuries and red cards have been stamped on his CV in equal profusion. A typical 90 minutes would see Caminero smash in a volley from 30 yards, tweak a hamstring and then get sent off for dissent.

The 1995/96 season was largely a chapter of positives for the 28-year-old midfielder. After two seasons spent helping Atlético Madrid to avoid relegation, it was a relief and a joy for him to be in a winning team challenging for honours. Like most of the Atlético players, Caminero responded positively to the arrival of new coach Radomir Antic. He fitted perfectly into the new midfield. With Vizcaíno and Simeone predominantly assigned to defensive duties and Milinko Pantic making the play, Caminero was free to float from wing to wing, providing danger to opposition defences with his skilful footwork and his strong runs from deep.

Caminero was not Atlético's most consistent performer, but on his day he was the most influential. When the team needed him most, he responded with a match-winning performance. The 5-3 victory over Valencia in the first leg of the Cup semi-final was arguably the match of his life, and he was Atlético's star man once again in the final against Barcelona. Equally impressive was his performance in the crucial 3-1 league win against Barça at the Nou Camp. But along with the great displays and his nine goals, there were also red cards, which threatened to disrupt Atlético in their all-conquering stride. With Caminero, you take the rough with the smooth. It is doubtful that he will ever change.

Atlético's 'double' triumph was the ultimate revenge for Caminero. As a youngster in his native Madrid he had been snubbed by the city's other big club, Real, who felt that they could not find a place in the team for him. From Castilla, Real's nursery club, Caminero moved to Real Valladolid, where he spent four seasons, the last of which, 1992/93, saw the team promoted to the Primera Division.

It was then that Caminero returned to Madrid to play for Atlético. So impressive was his start that within no time he had received a first call-up for the Spanish national team, making his début as a half-time substitute in a friendly against Chile in Alicante. In his first full appearance - a World Cup qualifier against Albania in Tirana - Caminero scored in a 5-1 win. He was also on target again in Spain's next game, scoring early before leaving the field injured after half an hour of his team's memorable 3-1 victory over the Republic of Ireland in Dublin.

After that, with injury problems hampering his progress, Caminero did not play again for Spain for another eight months. But his return coincided with the World Cup finals in America, where he was to be widely appreciated as Spain's most popular and consistent performer. He scored twice against Bolivia in the first round, but picked up a silly yellow card in injury-time which barred him from the next game against Switzerland. He returned with another goal in the quarter-final against Italy to become Spain's top scorer in the competition.

Caminero was in and out of the Spanish team for the Euro '96 qualifiers, but when he did play, he almost always delivered. Coach Javier Clemente certainly appreciated Caminero's qualities and saw him as a key component in his 4-5-1 system. Back on the big stage at Euro '96, Caminero netted Spain's vital equalising goal against France, but then found himself dropped for the next match against Romania, only to return, as an influential substitute, against England.

Before Caminero left for England, he caused a major heart-flutter at Atlético by announcing that he wanted to leave for a "bigger and better club", possibly in Italy. It took everybody by surprise, but eventually, by offering him an improved contract, the Atlético board of directors persuaded him to stay. With the Champions' League to come, it was a crucial piece of negotiation.

ALBACETE BALOMPIE

CLUB DIRECTORY

Albacete Balompié
Avenida de la Estación 5
02080 Albacete
tel - (967) 521100
fax - (967) 522123
Year of Formation - 1940
President - José Ramón Remiro Brotons
Manager - Juan Ignacio Rodríguez
Coach - Benito Floro; Ignacio Sáez
Stadium - Carlos Belmonte (19,000)

APPEARANCES 95/96

	P	Ap	(s)	Gls
ALBERTO Jiménez Monteagudo	M	2	(2)	
ALEJANDRO Sánchez Gómez	D	31		1
Juan Carlos BALAGUER Zamora	G	17		
Nenad BJELICA (CRO)	M	39	(1)	13
Miguel Angel BRAU Puente	M	4		
Rafael Collado García 'COCO'	D	30	(4)	2
Juan Antonio CHESA	D	1	(11)	
EMILIO Gutiérrez González	M		(1)	
Xavier ESCAICH Ferrer	A	12	(20)	4
FERNANDO Cebrián	A		(4)	
José Luis GARZON Muñoz	A		(1)	
Alejandro GONZALEZ Nappi (URU)	D	1		
JESUS Muñoz Calonge	M	26	(9)	
JOSE ANGEL Moreno Castro	D		(7)	
José Joaquín Moreno Verdú 'JOSICO'	M	28		2
Julián Romero Cañego 'JULI'	D	5	(10)	
Velli KASUMOV (AZB)	M	16	(6)	4
Francisco Javier Aguilera Blanco 'LUNA'	A	24	(1)	10
Francisco LUQUE Bermúdez	A	4	(10)	
Manuel Salvador Serra 'MANOLO'	M	34	(3)	
Juan José Sánchez MAQUEDA	M	17	(3)	1
Fernando MARCOS Santiago	G	24	(1)	
MARIO Romero Cañego	D	10	(5)	1
Francisco Rodrigo ORTEGA	M	13	(5)	1
Yevgeni PLOTNIKOV (RUS)	G	1		
Pedro RIESCO	M	21	(4)	4
José Carlos SORIA Gil	D	3		
SOTERO López Clemente	D	14	(7)	
Alberto TOMAS Sobrepera	D	27		
Petar VASILJEVIC (YUG)	D	21	(1)	
José Luis ZALAZAR Rodríguez (URU)	A	37	(1)	11

LEAGUE RESULTS 1995/96

Date	Opponent		Score	Scorers
02/09/95	Sporting Gijón	A	0-3	
09/09/95	Sevilla FC	H	3-2	Kasumov, Bjelica 2
17/09/95	RCD Espanyol	A	0-1	
24/09/95	RC Celta	H	4-0	Zalazar 2 (1p), Alejandro, Coco
01/10/95	RC Deportivo	A	0-5	
04/10/95	Real Valladolid	H	4-2	Kasumov 2, Bjelica, Zalazar (p)
08/10/95	CP Mérida	A	1-1	Escaich
15/10/95	Real Zaragoza	H	0-1	
22/10/95	Rayo Vallecano	A	0-2	
28/10/95	Real Madrid	H	1-1	Maqueda
05/11/95	Real Oviedo	A	0-1	
12/11/95	Real Betis	H	0-0	
18/11/95	FC Barcelona	A	0-3	
26/11/95	Valencia CF	H	1-3	Escaich
03/12/95	SD Compostela	A	1-3	Kasumov
10/12/95	UD Salamanca	H	3-3	Bjelica, Zalazar, Escaich
17/12/95	CD Tenerife	A	3-1	Bjelica 2, Mario
20/12/95	Athletic Bilbao	H	2-0	Zalazar, Luna
03/01/96	Real Sociedad	H	3-5	Luna, Josico, Bjelica
07/01/96	Racing Santander	A	5-5	Bjelica 2 (1p), Josico, Coco, Luna
13/01/96	Atlético Madrid	H	1-1	og (Solozábal)
21/01/96	Sporting Gijón	H	1-3	Luna
24/01/96	Sevilla FC	A	1-1	Luna
28/01/96	RCD Espanyol	H	0-0	
04/02/96	RC Celta	A	2-2	Zalazar 2 (1p)
11/02/96	RC Deportivo	H	1-0	Zalazar (p)
18/02/96	Real Valladolid	A	0-3	
25/02/96	CP Mérida	H	2-0	Riesco, Zalazar (p)
03/03/96	Real Zaragoza	A	1-3	Luna
10/03/96	Rayo Vallecano	H	1-2	Bjelica (p)
16/03/96	Real Madrid	A	0-2	
24/03/96	Real Oviedo	H	0-1	
27/03/96	Real Betis	A	3-2	Luna, Bjelica 2 (1p)
31/03/96	FC Barcelona	H	0-1	
07/04/96	Valencia CF	A	0-1	
14/04/96	SD Compostela	H	2-1	Riesco, Escaich
21/04/96	UD Salamanca	A	4-2	Luna, Riesco, Zalazar, Bjelica (p)
28/04/96	CD Tenerife	H	0-0	
05/05/96	Athletic Bilbao	A	2-2	Riesco, Ortega
12/05/96	Real Sociedad	A	1-8	Zalazar (p)
19/05/96	Racing Santander	H	2-2	Luna 2
25/05/96	Atlético Madrid	A	0-2	

ATHLETIC BILBAO

CLUB DIRECTORY

Athletic Club de Bilbao
Avenida Alameda Mazarredo 23
48009 Bilbao
tel - (94) 4240877/8
fax - (94) 4233324
Year of Formation - 1898
President - José María Arrate Llosa
Manager - Fernando Lamikiz
Coach - Dragoslav Stepanovic;
José María Amorrortu (96/97 - Luis Fernandez)
Stadium - San Mamés (46,223)

MAJOR HONOURS
League Championship - (8) 1930, 1931, 1934, 1936, 1943, 1956, 1983, 1984.
Domestic Cup - (23) 1903, 1904, 1910, 1911, 1914, 1915, 1916, 1921, 1923, 1930, 1931, 1932, 1933, 1943, 1944, 1945, 1950, 1955, 1956, 1958, 1969, 1973, 1984.

APPEARANCES 95/96

	P	Ap	(s)	Gls
Jorge AIZCORRETA Jurado	G	7	(1)	
Bittor ALKIZA Fernández	M	13	(14)	
Genaro ANDRINUA Cortabarría	D	15	(1)	2
Gorka BIDAURRAZAGA Rebolleda	A		(1)	
Juan Antonio Pérez Alonso 'BOLO'	A	14	(6)	3
Aitor CARANCA de la Hoz	D	31		
Eduardo ESTIVARIZ Ruiz de Equiluz	D	10	(11)	
Joseba ETXEBERRIA Lizardi	A	28	(5)	7
FELIPE Gurendez	A	6	(2)	
José Manuel GALDAMES Ibáñez	D	14	(2)	
Carlos GARCIA García	M	26	(12)	5
Ander GARITANO Urquizu	M	23	(2)	2
Jon Andoni GOIKOETXEA Lasa	M	28	(5)	
Julen GUERRERO López	M	33		9
Andoni LACABEG Fraile	D		(2)	
Juan Andrés LAMBEA	D	4		
Iñigo LARRAINZAR Santamaría	D	39		
Aitor LARRAZABAL Bilbao	D	35		2
Ricardo MENDIGUREN Egaña	M		(2)	
Oscar Javier TABUENKA Berges	D	13	(10)	1
Jesús Emilio Diez de Mier 'TXUTXI'	D	9	(1)	
Josu URRUTIA Telleria	M	22	(3)	
Juan José VALENCIA de la Serna	G	35		
Oscar VALES Varela	D	34	(3)	1
Ernesto VALVERDE Tejedor	A	5	(8)	1
José Angel ZIGANDA Lacunza	A	18	(15)	9

LEAGUE RESULTS 1995/96

Date	Opponent		Score	Scorers
03/09/95	Racing Santander	H	4-0	Ziganda 2, Etxeberria, Guerrero
09/09/95	Real Madrid	A	2-1	Etxeberria, Ziganda
16/09/95	Atlético Madrid	H	0-2	
24/09/95	Real Oviedo	A	0-0	
30/09/95	Sporting Gijón	H	2-1	Guerrero 2
04/10/95	Real Betis	A	0-0	
08/10/95	Sevilla FC	H	1-1	García
14/10/95	FC Barcelona	A	1-4	García
22/10/95	RCD Espanyol	H	0-0	
29/10/95	Valencia CF	A	1-3	Guerrero
05/11/95	RC Celta	H	3-0	og (Alejo), Andrinúa, García
12/11/95	SD Compostela	A	1-2	Guerrero
19/11/95	RC Deportivo	H	1-0	Tabuenka
26/11/95	UD Salamanca	A	1-2	Guerrero
03/12/95	Real Valladolid	H	2-1	Etxeberria, Andrinúa
10/12/95	CD Tenerife	A	2-3	Larrazábal, Vales
17/12/95	CP Mérida	H	1-1	Larrazábal
20/12/95	Albacete Balompié	A	0-2	
03/01/96	Real Zaragoza	H	1-0	García
06/01/96	Real Sociedad	H	0-0	
14/01/96	Rayo Vallecano	A	2-2	Etxeberria, Garitano
21/01/96	Racing Santander	A	1-1	og (Esteban Torres)
24/01/96	Real Madrid	H	0-5	
28/01/96	Atlético Madrid	A	1-4	Etxeberria
04/02/96	Real Oviedo	H	0-1	
11/02/96	Sporting Gijón	A	2-1	Etxeberria, Bolo
18/02/96	Real Betis	H	0-1	
25/02/96	Sevilla FC	A	1-1	Bolo
02/03/96	FC Barcelona	H	0-0	
10/03/96	RCD Espanyol	A	0-3	
17/03/96	Valencia CF	H	0-1	
24/03/96	RC Celta	A	1-3	Bolo
27/03/96	SD Compostela	H	0-0	
31/03/96	RC Deportivo	A	0-0	
07/04/96	UD Salamanca	H	3-1	García, Ziganda 2
14/04/96	Real Valladolid	A	1-1	Guerrero
21/04/96	CD Tenerife	H	2-0	Valverde, Ziganda
28/04/96	CP Mérida	A	0-1	
05/05/96	Albacete Balompié	H	2-2	Guerrero, Etxeberria
12/05/96	Real Zaragoza	A	0-1	
19/05/96	Real Sociedad	A	2-2	Guerrero, Garitano (p)
25/05/96	Rayo Vallecano	H	3-1	Ziganda 3

ATLETICO MADRID

CLUB DIRECTORY

Club Atlético de Madrid
Estádio Vicente Calderón
Paseo Virgen del Puerto 67
28026 Madrid
tel - (91) 3664707
fax - (91) 3669811
Year of Formation - 1903
President - Jesús Gil y Gil
Manager - Clemente Villaverde
Coach - Radomir Antic
Stadium - Vicente Calderón (62,000)

MAJOR HONOURS

League Championship - (9) 1940, 1941, 1950, 1951, 1966, 1970, 1973, 1977, 1996.
Domestic Cup - (9) 1960, 1961, 1965, 1972, 1976, 1985, 1991, 1992, 1996.
European Cup-winners' Cup - (1) 1962.
World Club Cup - (1) 1974.

APPEARANCES 95/96

	P	Ap	(s)	Gls
Leonardo Angel BIAGINI (ARG)	A	5	(22)	4
José Luis Pérez CAMINERO	M	35	(2)	9
Fernando CORREA Ayala (URU)	A	1	(9)	
Daniel González Sanz 'DANI'	M	1		
José Antonio DE LA SAGRA Fermin	M		(1)	
Quinton FORTUNE (SAF)	M		(3)	
Delfi GELI Roura	D	39		1
JUAN CARLOS Gómez Díaz	A	3	(10)	2
Francisco Narváez Machón 'KIKO'	A	33		11
Juan Manuel LOPEZ Martínez	D	11	(21)	2
José Francisco MOLINA Giménez	G	42		
Milinko PANTIC (YUG)	M	41		10
Liuboslav PENEV (BUL)	A	36	(1)	16
Francisco Javier Mori Cuesta 'PIRRI'	M	5	(14)	1
ROBERTO Fresnedoso Prieto	M	20	(12)	3
Santiago Denia Sánchez 'SANTI'	D	37		
Diego Pablo SIMEONE (ARG)	M	37		12
Roberto SOLOZABAL Villanueva	D	40		
TOMAS Reñones Crespo	D	2	(10)	
Antonio Muñoz Gómez 'TONI'	D	40		
Juan VIZCAINO Morcillo	M	34	(7)	3

LEAGUE RESULTS 1995/96

03/09/95	Real Sociedad	H	4-1	Pantic, Penev 2 (1p), Simeone
10/09/95	Racing Santander	A	4-0	Penev 2 (1p), Caminero, Simeone
16/09/95	Athletic Bilbao	A	2-0	Kiko, Penev
24/09/95	Sporting Gijón	H	2-0	Vizcaíno, Penev (p)
01/10/95	Sevilla FC	A	0-0	
05/10/95	RCD Espanyol	H	2-1	Kiko, Pantic
08/10/95	RC Celta	A	3-0	Simeone, Kiko 2
14/10/95	RC Deportivo	H	1-0	Simeone
21/10/95	Real Valladolid	A	1-0	Simeone
29/10/95	CP Mérida	H	1-1	og (Angel Luis)
05/11/95	Real Zaragoza	A	1-0	Simeone
12/11/95	Rayo Vallecano	H	0-0	
18/11/95	Real Madrid	A	0-1	
26/11/95	Real Oviedo	H	3-0	Vizcaíno, Simeone, López
03/12/95	Real Betis	A	1-2	Penev (p)
09/12/95	FC Barcelona	H	3-1	Penev 2 (1p), Caminero
17/12/95	Valencia CF	A	1-0	Caminero
20/12/95	SD Compostela	H	3-0	Penev, Simeone, Roberto
03/01/96	UD Salamanca	A	3-1	Caminero, Penev (p), Roberto
06/01/96	CD Tenerife	H	3-1	Juan Carlos, López, Penev
13/01/96	Albacete Balompié	A	1-1	Simeone
21/01/96	Real Sociedad	A	0-1	
24/01/96	Racing Santander	H	2-0	Penev, Kiko
28/01/96	Athletic Bilbao	H	4-1	Kiko, Pantic, Penev (p), Biagini
03/02/96	Sporting Gijón	A	2-1	Pantic, Caminero
10/02/96	Sevilla FC	H	0-1	
18/02/96	RCD Espanyol	A	2-0	Kiko, Penev
25/02/96	RC Celta	H	3-2	Juan Carlos, Simeone, Caminero
03/03/96	RC Deportivo	A	2-2	Penev, Pantic (p)
10/03/96	Real Valladolid	H	0-2	
17/03/96	CP Mérida	A	1-0	Kiko
24/03/96	Real Zaragoza	H	1-1	Pantic (p)
27/03/96	Rayo Vallecano	A	3-0	Biagini, Pantic 2 (1p)
30/03/96	Real Madrid	H	1-2	Pantic (p)
06/04/96	Real Oviedo	A	1-1	Caminero
14/04/96	Real Betis	H	1-1	Pirri
20/04/96	FC Barcelona	A	3-1	Roberto, Vizcaíno, Biagini
27/04/96	Valencia CF	H	2-3	Pantic, Geli
04/05/96	SD Compostela	A	3-1	Caminero 2, Simeone
12/05/96	UD Salamanca	H	2-1	Kiko 2
18/05/96	CD Tenerife	A	1-1	Biagini
25/05/96	Albacete Balompié	H	2-0	Simeone, Kiko

FC BARCELONA

CLUB DIRECTORY

Fútbol Club Barcelona
Av. Arístides Maillol s/n
08028 Barcelona
tel - (93) 3309411
fax - (93) 4112219
Year of Formation - 1899
President - Josep Lluís Núñez Clemente
Manager - Antón Parera
Coach - Johan Cruijff; Carlos Rexach (96/97 - Bobby Robson)
Stadium - Camp Nou (115,000)

MAJOR HONOURS
League Championship - (14) 1929, 1945, 1948, 1949, 1952, 1953, 1959, 1960, 1974, 1985, 1991, 1992, 1993, 1994.
Domestic Cup - (22) 1910, 1912, 1913, 1920, 1922, 1925, 1926, 1928, 1942, 1951, 1952, 1953, 1957, 1959, 1963, 1968, 1971, 1978, 1981, 1983, 1988, 1990.
European Champions' Cup - (1) 1992.
European Cup-winners' Cup - (3) 1979, 1982, 1989.
Fairs' Cup - (3) 1958, 1960, 1966.
European Super Cup - (1) 1992.

APPEARANCES 95/96

	P	Ap	(s)	Gls
ABELARDO Fernández Artuña	D	25	(6)	1
Enrique ALVAREZ Sanjuán	D	1		
Guillermo AMOR Martínez	M	16	(11)	6
Jesús Maríano ANGOY Gil	G	3	(1)	
José María BAKERO Escudero	M	26	(4)	6
Carlos BUSQUETS Barroso	G	37		
Luis CARRERAS Ferrer	D	8	(10)	
Albert CELADES López	M	11	(5)	2
Johan Jordi CRUIJFF (HOL)	A	11	(2)	2
Angel Manuel CUELLAR Llanos	A	3	(9)	2
Iván DE LA PEÑA López	M	24	(6)	7
Albert FERRER Llopis	D	28		
Luis Filipe Madeira Caeiro 'FIGO' (POR)	M	33	(2)	5
Francisco Javier GARCIA Pimienta	A	1		
José GUARDIOLA Sala	M	28	(4)	1
Gheorghe HAGI (ROM)	M	12	(7)	3
Juan José 'JUANJO'	M		(1)	
Meho KODRO (BOS)	A	26	(6)	9
Julen LOPETEGUI Agote	G	2		
Juan Carlos MORENO Rodríguez	A	2	(4)	
Miguel Angel NADAL Homar	D	32	(4)	2
OSCAR García Junyent	M	11	(17)	10
Gheorghe POPESCU (ROM)	D	35	(4)	5
Robert PROSINECKI (CRO)	M	12	(7)	2
Javier ROCA Mateu	D	1		
ROGER García Junyent	M	27	(6)	5
Francisco Javier Pérez RUFETE	A		(1)	
Sergio Barjuán Esclusa 'SERGI'	D	40	(1)	
Josep SETVALLS Morera	M		(1)	
Antonio Velamazán Tejedor 'TONI'	M	7	(4)	

LEAGUE RESULTS 1995/96

03/09/95	Real Valladolid	A	2-0	Popescu, De la Peña
09/09/95	CP Mérida	H	2-2	Kodro 2 (1p)
17/09/95	Real Zaragoza	A	3-0	Cruijff, Kodro, Figo
23/09/95	Rayo Vallecano	H	2-0	Nadal, Figo
30/09/95	Real Madrid	A	1-1	Roger
04/10/95	Real Oviedo	H	4-1	Bakero 3, Hagi
07/10/95	Real Betis	A	5-1	Roger, Figo, Celades, Toni, De la Peña
14/10/95	Athletic Bilbao	H	4-1	Toni, De la Peña, Oscar, og (Tabuenka)
22/10/95	Valencia CF	H	1-0	Prosinecki (p)
28/10/95	SD Compostela	A	1-2	Kodro
05/11/95	UD Salamanca	H	4-1	Popescu 2 (1p), Kodro, Oscar
12/11/95	CD Tenerife	A	1-1	Roger
18/11/95	Albacete Balompié	H	3-0	Hagi, Popescu, Prosinecki
25/11/95	Real Sociedad	A	1-1	Oscar
02/12/95	Racing Santander	H	1-1	Kodro
09/12/95	Atlético Madrid	A	1-3	Toni
16/12/95	Sporting Gijón	H	1-0	Popescu
20/12/95	Sevilla FC	A	0-1	
04/01/96	RCD Espanyol	H	2-1	Nadal, Oscar
07/01/96	RC Celta	A	0-1	
14/01/96	RC Deportivo	H	1-1	Abelardo
21/01/96	Real Valladolid	H	1-0	Bakero
25/01/96	CP Mérida	A	0-0	
28/01/96	Real Zaragoza	H	3-1	Oscar, De la Peña 2
04/02/96	Rayo Vallecano	A	1-1	De la Peña
10/02/96	Real Madrid	H	3-0	Kodro 2, Figo
18/02/96	Real Oviedo	A	2-1	Bakero, Amor
25/02/96	Real Betis	H	1-0	Kodro
02/03/96	Athletic Bilbao	A	0-0	
09/03/96	Valencia CF	A	1-4	Amor
16/03/96	SD Compostela	H	1-0	Roger
24/03/96	UD Salamanca	A	3-1	Amor, Roger, Oscar
27/03/96	CD Tenerife	H	2-2	Amor, Celades
31/03/96	Albacete Balompié	A	1-0	Oscar
06/04/96	Real Sociedad	H	1-0	Amor
13/04/96	Racing Santander	A	1-1	Cuéllar
20/04/96	Atlético Madrid	H	1-3	Cruijff
28/04/96	Sporting Gijón	A	3-0	De la Peña, Hagi, Oscar
05/05/96	Sevilla FC	H	1-1	Bakero
15/05/96	RCD Espanyol	A	1-1	Figo
19/05/96	RC Celta	H	3-2	Cuéllar, Oscar 2
26/05/96	RC Deportivo	A	2-2	Guardiola, Amor

REAL BETIS

CLUB DIRECTORY

Real Betis Balompié
Avenida de Heliópolis s/n
41012 Sevilla
tel - (954) 610340
fax - (954) 614774
Year of Formation - 1907
President - José León Gómez
Secretary - Antonio Picchi Castro
Coach - Lorenzo Serra Ferrer
Stadium - Benito Villamarín (47,500)

MAJOR HONOURS
League Championship - (1) 1935.
Domestic Cup - (1) 1977.

APPEARANCES 95/96

	P	Ap	(s)	Gls
Humberto ALEXIS Trujillo Oramas	M	39		4
ALFONSO Pérez Muñoz	A	35		12
Oscar ARPON Ochoa	M	5	(13)	1
Juan José CAÑAS Gutiérrez	M	34	(3)	2
José Luis DIEZMA Izquierdo	G	2		
JAIME Quesada Chevarria	D	27	(2)	
Robert JARNI (CRO)	M	34		8
Pedro Luis JARO Reguero	G	40		
José María García Lfuente 'JOSE MARI'	M	15	(7)	
José Tomás Valdovinos 'JOSETE'	D	33	(2)	
Wojciech KOWALCZYK (POL)	A	9	(7)	4
Luis MARQUEZ Martín	M	9	(7)	
José María Cabrera MENENDEZ	M	6	(9)	1
Juan MERINO Ruiz	D	37	(1)	1
Tomás OLIAS Gutiérrez	D	25	(4)	
PIER Luigi Cherubino Lolli	A	27	(12)	14
Francisco J. Gómez García 'QUICO'	D	1		
Roberto RIOS Patus	M	6	(5)	
Juan SABAS Huertas-Lorente	A	8	(23)	7
Francisco Javier SANCHEZ JARA	M	8	(4)	1
Vlada STOSIC (YUG)	M	30	(7)	4
Juan Antonio González UREÑA	D	5		
Hristo VIDAKOVIC (YUG)	D	27	(1)	1

LEAGUE RESULTS 1995/96

Date	Opponent		Score	Scorers
03/09/95	CP Mérida	A	1-1	Stosic
09/09/95	Real Zaragoza	H	3-1	Alfonso 2, Pier
17/09/95	Rayo Vallecano	A	2-1	Merino, Jarni
23/09/95	Real Madrid	H	0-0	
01/10/95	Real Oviedo	A	1-0	Menéndez
04/10/95	Athletic Bilbao	H	0-0	
07/10/95	FC Barcelona	H	1-5	Pier
14/10/95	Valencia CF	A	1-1	Pier
22/10/95	SD Compostela	H	5-0	Jarni, Cañas, Pier 2, Arpón
29/10/95	UD Salamanca	A	1-2	Pier
05/11/95	CD Tenerife	H	3-3	Alfonso, Alexis 2 (1p)
12/11/95	Albacete Balompié	A	0-0	
18/11/95	Real Sociedad	H	3-1	Stosic, Sabas 2
26/11/95	Racing Santander	A	0-0	
03/12/95	Atlético Madrid	H	2-1	Jarni, Pier
10/12/95	Sporting Gijón	A	3-2	Jarni 2 (1p), Cañas
16/12/95	Sevilla FC	H	1-1	Pier
20/12/95	RCD Espanyol	A	1-1	Pier
03/01/96	RC Celta	H	0-3	
07/01/96	RC Deportivo	A	0-0	
13/01/96	Real Valladolid	H	3-0	Pier 2, Kowalczyk
21/01/96	CP Mérida	H	0-1	
24/01/96	Real Zaragoza	A	2-1	Jarni, Alfonso
28/01/96	Rayo Vallecano	H	0-0	
04/02/96	Real Madrid	A	2-4	Stosic, Alfonso
11/02/96	Real Oviedo	H	2-1	Pier, Alexis (p)
18/02/96	Athletic Bilbao	A	1-0	Jarni
25/02/96	FC Barcelona	A	0-1	
03/03/96	Valencia CF	H	3-0	Sabas 3
10/03/96	SD Compostela	A	2-1	Alfonso 2
17/03/96	UD Salamanca	H	4-0	Alfonso 2, Pier, Sabas
23/03/96	CD Tenerife	A	2-1	Sabas, Kowalczyk
27/03/96	Albacete Balompié	H	2-3	Jarni, Alfonso
31/03/96	Real Sociedad	A	1-1	Kowalczyk
07/04/96	Racing Santander	H	2-2	Alfonso, Alexis (p)
14/04/96	Atlético Madrid	A	1-1	Alfonso
21/04/96	Sporting Gijón	H	2-5	Kowalczyk, Vidakovic (p)
28/04/96	Sevilla FC	A	0-1	
05/05/96	RCD Espanyol	H	2-3	og (Urzaiz), Pier
12/05/96	RC Celta	A	0-2	
19/05/96	RC Deportivo	H	1-0	Stosic
25/05/96	Real Valladolid	A	1-3	Sánchez Jara

RC CELTA

CLUB DIRECTORY

Real Club Celta de Vigo
Avenida de Balaídos s/n
11739 Vigo (Pontevedra)
tel - (986) 292850
fax - (986) 292040
Year of Formation - 1923
President - Horacio Gómez
Manager - Angeles Santos Pérez
Coach - Carlos Aimar; Fernando Santos
Stadium - Balaídos (33,000)

APPEARANCES 95/96

	P	Ap	(s)	Gls
Francisco Borja AGUIRRETXU Barreiro	D	24	(3)	
ALEJO Indias Alvarez	D	39	(1)	2
Srdjan BAJCETIC (YUG)	M	11	(4)	2
Rafael BERGES Martín	D	29	(1)	
CARLOS Pérez Alvarez	M	4	(8)	2
Hermes Aldo DESIO (ARG)	M	24	(4)	
EUSEBIO Sacristán Mena	M	31	(4)	1
Angel de Juana García 'GELI'	M	7	(15)	1
José GIL Gordillo	M	22	(7)	1
Vladimir GUDELJ (BOS)	A	32	(5)	15
Andoni LACABEG Fraile	D	4	(5)	
MARIANO Hoyas de la Cruz	D	24	(3)	
Angel Miguel MERINO Torres	M	32	(1)	4
Miguel Salgado Fernández 'MICHEL'	M	2	(16)	
Goran MILOJEVIC (YUG)	A	10	(15)	6
Antonio PRATS Servera	G	41		
Milorad RATKOVIC (YUG)	M	31	(5)	5
Francisco SALINAS Fernández	D	40		
Juan Ginés SANCHEZ Romero	A	31	(6)	10
José Manuel TARREGA Valero	D	17	(5)	
VICENTE Alvarez Núñez	M	6	(14)	
Francisco Javier VILLANUEVA Medina	G	1		

LEAGUE RESULTS 1995/96

03/09/95	SD Compostela	H	0-1	
10/09/95	UD Salamanca	A	1-0	Milojevic
17/09/95	CD Tenerife	H	2-2	Sánchez, Bajcetic
24/09/95	Albacete Balompié	A	0-4	
01/10/95	Real Sociedad	H	1-1	Gil
04/10/95	Racing Santander	A	1-2	Sánchez
08/10/95	Atlético Madrid	H	0-3	
15/10/95	Sporting Gijón	A	0-1	
22/10/95	Sevilla FC	H	4-0	Gudelj 3, Carlos
29/10/95	RCD Espanyol	A	2-2	Gudelj (p), Sánchez
05/11/95	Athletic Bilbao	A	0-3	
11/11/95	RC Deportivo	H	0-0	
19/11/95	Real Valladolid	A	1-1	Gudelj (p)
26/11/95	CP Mérida	H	2-0	Ratkovic, Bajcetic
03/12/95	Real Zaragoza	A	0-0	
10/12/95	Rayo Vallecano	H	2-0	Sánchez, Milojevic
17/12/95	Real Madrid	A	0-1	
20/12/95	Real Oviedo	H	1-0	Gudelj
03/01/96	Real Betis	A	3-0	Merino, Gudelj, Geli
07/01/96	FC Barcelona	H	1-0	Sánchez
14/01/96	Valencia CF	A	0-3	
21/01/96	SD Compostela	A	1-1	Sánchez
24/01/96	UD Salamanca	H	2-1	Eusebio, Ratkovic
28/01/96	CD Tenerife	A	0-1	
04/02/96	Albacete Balompié	H	2-2	Gudelj, Milojevic
11/02/96	Real Sociedad	A	1-3	Milojevic
18/02/96	Racing Santander	H	0-0	
25/02/96	Atlético Madrid	A	2-3	Gudelj 2
03/03/96	Sporting Gijón	H	0-0	
10/03/96	Sevilla FC	A	0-0	
17/03/96	RCD Espanyol	H	4-2	Gudelj 2 (1p), Ratkovic, Merino
24/03/96	Athletic Bilbao	H	3-1	Ratkovic, Sánchez, Merino
27/03/96	RC Deportivo	A	1-2	Sánchez
31/03/96	Real Valladolid	H	1-1	Merino
07/04/96	CP Mérida	A	0-2	
14/04/96	Real Zaragoza	H	1-1	Ratkovic
21/04/96	Rayo Vallecano	A	3-1	Sánchez, Milojevic, Alejo
28/04/96	Real Madrid	H	1-1	Sánchez
05/05/96	Real Oviedo	A	1-1	Gudelj
12/05/96	Real Betis	H	2-0	Gudelj, Carlos
19/05/96	FC Barcelona	A	2-3	Alejo, Gudelj
25/05/96	Valencia CF	H	1-1	Milojevic

SD COMPOSTELA

CLUB DIRECTORY

Sociedad Deportiva Compostela
San Lázaro s/n
15703 Santiago de Compostela
tel - (981) 580671
fax - (981) 580671
Year of Formation - 1962
President - José María Caneda
Secretary - José González Fidalgo
Coach - Fernando Vázquez
Stadium - San Lazaro (12,000)

APPEARANCES 95/96

	P	Ap	(s)	Gls
Agustín ABADIA Plana	M	3	(11)	
Festus AGU (NIG)	M		(8)	
Javier BELLIDO Plaza	D	36	(1)	2
Antonio CASTRO Fernández	D	4	(4)	1
Bent CHRISTENSEN (DEN)	A	27	(11)	12
Jesús DULCE Prado	D	5	(5)	
Ignacio ERAÑA Cassi	M	24	(14)	
FABIANO Soares Pessoa (BRA)	M	35		5
Francisco Javier FALAGAN Hernández	G	42		
JOSE RAMON González Pérez	M	39	(1)	6
Angel LECUMBERRI García	M	37		3
Francisco LLORENTE Gento	M	4	(7)	
MAURO García Juncal	M	28	(10)	1
José Ignacio Fernández Pacios 'NACHO'	D	39		
Christopher OHEN (NIG)	A	34		11
Juan Carlos PANIAGUA Prieto	A	1	(14)	2
Franck PASSI (FRA)	M	35		
Dragan SKOCIC (CRO)	M		(1)	
Fernando TOCORNAL Linares	D	27	(5)	
José Antonio Rodríguez Saavedra 'TONI'	M	1	(3)	
Francisco Javier Mulero VILLENA	D	38	(1)	3
VIRGILIO Hernández Paesa	D	3	(14)	1

LEAGUE RESULTS 1995/96

Date	Opponent		Score	Scorers
03/09/95	RC Celta	A	1-0	Bellido
10/09/95	RC Deportivo	H	4-0	Fabiano 2, José Ramón, Ohen
16/09/95	Real Valladolid	A	0-0	
24/09/95	CP Mérida	H	1-0	Christensen
01/10/95	Real Zaragoza	A	0-1	
04/10/95	Rayo Vallecano	H	1-0	Christensen
08/10/95	Real Madrid	A	1-2	José Ramón
15/10/95	Real Oviedo	H	4-1	Christensen 2, José Ramón 2
22/10/95	Real Betis	A	0-5	
28/10/95	FC Barcelona	H	2-1	Christensen (p), Ohen
05/11/95	Valencia CF	A	2-5	José Ramón, Christensen
12/11/95	Athletic Bilbao	H	2-1	Ohen, Mauro
19/11/95	UD Salamanca	H	0-0	
26/11/95	CD Tenerife	A	1-1	Ohen
03/12/95	Albacete Balompié	H	3-1	Christensen, Ohen 2
10/12/95	Real Sociedad	A	1-0	Ohen
17/12/95	Racing Santander	H	2-0	Villena, Ohen
20/12/95	Atlético Madrid	A	0-3	
03/01/96	Sporting Gijón	H	1-0	Lecumberri
07/01/96	Sevilla FC	A	1-0	Ohen
14/01/96	RCD Espanyol	H	2-1	Lecumberri, José Ramón
21/01/96	RC Celta	H	1-1	Christensen
24/01/96	RC Deportivo	A	0-2	
28/01/96	Real Valladolid	H	1-3	Villena (p)
04/02/96	CP Mérida	A	2-0	Christensen, Paniagua
11/02/96	Real Zaragoza	H	3-2	Villena, Fabiano, Ohen
18/02/96	Rayo Vallecano	A	1-0	Fabiano
25/02/96	Real Madrid	H	3-3	Fabiano, Christensen, Virgilio
03/03/96	Real Oviedo	A	1-3	Ohen
10/03/96	Real Betis	H	1-2	Bellido
16/03/96	FC Barcelona	A	0-1	
24/03/96	Valencia CF	H	0-4	
27/03/96	Athletic Bilbao	A	0-0	
31/03/96	UD Salamanca	A	0-1	
07/04/96	CD Tenerife	H	0-2	
14/04/96	Albacete Balompié	A	1-2	Paniagua
21/04/96	Real Sociedad	H	2-0	Lecumberri, Castro
28/04/96	Racing Santander	A	0-1	
04/05/96	Atlético Madrid	H	1-3	Christensen
12/05/96	Sporting Gijón	A	1-2	Christensen (p)
19/05/96	Sevilla FC	H	0-0	
26/05/96	RCD Espanyol	A	0-0	

RC DEPORTIVO

CLUB DIRECTORY

Real Club Deportivo
Plaza de Pontevedra 19-1.
15003 La Coruña
tel - (981) 259500
fax - (981) 265919
Year of Formation - 1904
President - Augusto César Lendoiro
Manager - Manuel Montiel Duque
Coach - John Toshack
Stadium - Riazor (28,956)

MAJOR HONOURS

Domestic Cup - (1) 1995.

APPEARANCES 95/96

	P	Ap	(s)	Gls
José Manuel AIRA Lindoso	D	1		
Adolfo ALDANA Torres	M	21	(13)	6
ALFREDO Santaelena Aguado	M	24	(4)	1
Roberto Gama de Oliveira 'BEBETO' (BRA)	A	34		25
Aitor BEGUIRISTAIN Múgica	M	20	(13)	2
BRAULIO Vázquez Benítez	A		(2)	
Juan Garrido CANALES	G	7		
DAVID Fernández Miramontes	A	4	(18)	3
Miroslav DJUKIC (YUG)	D	35		
DONATO Gama da Silva	M	33	(6)	5
Francisco Javier González Pérez 'FRAN'	M	29	(4)	3
Francisco LIAÑO Fernández	G	35		
Luis María LOPEZ RECARTE	D	21	(6)	2
MAIKEL H. Naujoks García	A		(1)	
Javier MANJARIN Pereda	A	33	(4)	8
Rafael MARTIN VAZQUEZ	M	2	(3)	
MAURO da SILVA Gomes (BRA)	M	18	(4)	
Branko MILOVANOVIC (YUG)	M	4	(8)	
Fernando Martínez Perales 'NANDO'	D	18	(6)	
Francisco Jémez Martín 'PACO'	D	34	(2)	1
Dmitri RADCHENKO (RUS)	A	13	(15)	5
José Luis RIBERA Uranga	D	14	(1)	
Francisco Javier Pérez VILLARROYA	M	21	(4)	
Emilio José VIQUEIRA Moure	M	12	(7)	
Salvador González Marco 'VORO'	D	29	(1)	

LEAGUE RESULTS 1995/96

02/09/95	Valencia CF	H	3-0	Manjarín, Bebeto 2
10/09/95	SD Compostela	A	0-4	
17/09/95	UD Salamanca	H	2-0	Donato, Fran
24/09/95	CD Tenerife	A	1-1	Bebeto
01/10/95	Albacete Balompié	H	5-0	Bebeto 5
04/10/95	Real Sociedad	A	1-2	Radchenko
08/10/95	Racing Santander	H	2-3	Bebeto, og (Merino)
14/10/95	Atlético Madrid	A	0-1	
22/10/95	Sporting Gijón	H	1-0	Radchenko
28/10/95	Sevilla FC	A	0-0	
05/11/95	RCD Espanyol	H	0-1	
11/11/95	RC Celta	A	0-0	
19/11/95	Athletic Bilbao	A	0-1	
26/11/95	Real Valladolid	H	3-1	og (Antía), Bebeto 2
03/12/95	CP Mérida	A	2-0	Aldana, Manjarín
10/12/95	Real Zaragoza	H	2-3	Bebeto (p), Manjarín
17/12/95	Rayo Vallecano	A	6-0	Donato, Aldana, Alfredo, Bebeto, Manjarín, López Recarte
21/12/95	Real Madrid	H	3-0	Bebeto 3
03/01/96	Real Oviedo	A	2-0	Beguiristáin, Fran
07/01/96	Real Betis	H	0-0	
14/01/96	FC Barcelona	A	1-1	Radchenko
20/01/96	Valencia CF	A	1-2	Aldana
24/01/96	SD Compostela	H	2-0	Aldana, Bebeto
27/01/96	UD Salamanca	A	5-0	Aldana 2, Bebeto 2, Manjarín
04/02/96	CD Tenerife	H	1-1	Manjarín
11/02/96	Albacete Balompié	A	0-1	
18/02/96	Real Sociedad	H	1-1	David
24/02/96	Racing Santander	A	1-2	Beguiristáin (p)
03/03/96	Atlético Madrid	H	2-2	David, Radchenko
10/03/96	Sporting Gijón	A	1-1	López Recarte
17/03/96	Sevilla FC	H	3-2	Fran, Paco, Bebeto
24/03/96	RCD Espanyol	A	0-0	
27/03/96	RC Celta	H	2-1	Manjarín, Bebeto
31/03/96	Athletic Bilbao	H	0-0	
07/04/96	Real Valladolid	A	2-2	Donato 2 (2p)
14/04/96	CP Mérida	H	2-1	Bebeto 2 (1p)
21/04/96	Real Zaragoza	A	3-2	Donato (p), David, Manjarín
28/04/96	Rayo Vallecano	H	1-0	Radchenko
05/05/96	Real Madrid	A	0-1	
12/05/96	Real Oviedo	H	0-4	
19/05/96	Real Betis	A	0-1	
26/05/96	FC Barcelona	H	2-2	Bebeto 2

RCD ESPANYOL

CLUB DIRECTORY

Reial Club Deportiu Espanyol de Barcelona
Ricardo Villa s/n
08017 Barcelona
tel - (93) 2034800
fax - (93) 2053452
Year of Formation - 1900
President - Francesc Perelló
Secretary - Alfredo Torras
Coach - José Antonio Camacho
96/97 - José Ródenas Carcelén
Stadium - Sarriá (41,000)

MAJOR HONOURS
Domestic Cup - (2) 1929, 1940.

APPEARANCES 95/96

	P	Ap	(s)	Gls
Alejandro Fernández Sánchez 'ALEX'	M	6	(8)	2
Moisés García Fernández 'ARTEAGA'	M	37		3
Miguel Angel BENITEZ Pavón (PAR)	A	35	(1)	6
Goran BOGDANOVIC (YUG)	M	8	(16)	5
Branko BRNOVIC (YUG)	M	41		1
CRISTOBAL Parralo Aguilera	D	40		
FRANCISCO Javier López Alfaro	M	34		3
Sebastián HERRERA Zamora	D	36		
Javier García Almendro 'JAVI'	A	3	(32)	2
Jordi LARDIN Cruz	A	38		17
LUIS Cembranos Martínez	M	3	(8)	
MIGUEL Hernández Sánchez	D	1		
Fernando Muñoz García 'NANDO'	D	8	(2)	
José Rojo Martín 'PACHETA'	M	10	(24)	2
José Antonio PERAILE Tinaut	G		(1)	
Mauricio POCHETTINO Trossero (ARG)	D	38	(1)	3
Florin RADUCIOIU (ROM)	A	8	(8)	5
RAUL Arribas Torre	G	2		
Antonio Jiménez Sistachs 'TONI'	G	40		
José Alberto TORIL Rodríguez	M	2	(15)	
Víctor Manuel TORRES MESTRE	D	40		1
Ismael URZAIZ Aranda	A	32	(9)	13

LEAGUE RESULTS 1995/96

03/09/95	UD Salamanca	H	3-1	Raducioiu 2, Urzaiz
10/09/95	CD Tenerife	A	4-1	Arteaga, Raducioiu, Lardín, Benítez
17/09/95	Albacete Balompié	H	1-0	Pochettino
24/09/95	Real Sociedad	A	1-0	Raducioiu
01/10/95	Racing Santander	H	1-0	Javi
05/10/95	Atlético Madrid	A	1-2	Lardín
08/10/95	Sporting Gijón	H	0-0	
14/10/95	Sevilla FC	A	3-0	Lardín, Urzaiz 2
22/10/95	Athletic Bilbao	A	0-0	
29/10/95	RC Celta	H	2-2	Lardín 2
05/11/95	RC Deportivo	A	1-0	Brnovic
12/11/95	Real Valladolid	H	2-0	Urzaiz, Benítez
19/11/95	CP Mérida	A	1-0	Benítez
26/11/95	Real Zaragoza	H	1-1	Benítez
02/12/95	Rayo Vallecano	A	0-1	
10/12/95	Real Madrid	H	3-1	Francisco, Benítez, Lardín
17/12/95	Real Oviedo	A	2-1	Raducioiu, Bogdanovic
20/12/95	Real Betis	H	1-1	Francisco
04/01/96	FC Barcelona	A	1-2	Bogdanovic
07/01/96	Valencia CF	H	2-0	Lardín 2
14/01/96	SD Compostela	A	1-2	Urzaiz
21/01/96	UD Salamanca	A	2-2	Arteaga, Pacheta
24/01/96	CD Tenerife	H	2-1	Lardín, Pochettino
28/01/96	Albacete Balompié	A	0-0	
04/02/96	Real Sociedad	H	0-0	
11/02/96	Racing Santander	A	1-1	Pacheta
18/02/96	Atlético Madrid	H	0-2	
25/02/96	Sporting Gijón	A	3-2	Bogdanovic, Javi, Alex (p)
02/03/96	Sevilla FC	H	0-1	
10/03/96	Athletic Bilbao	H	3-0	Pochettino, Francisco, Benítez
17/03/96	RC Celta	A	2-4	Lardín 2
24/03/96	RC Deportivo	H	0-0	
27/03/96	Real Valladolid	A	0-0	
31/03/96	CP Mérida	H	3-0	Urzaiz 2, Bogdanovic
06/04/96	Real Zaragoza	A	1-1	Urzaiz
14/04/96	Rayo Vallecano	H	4-2	Arteaga, Urzaiz 3
21/04/96	Real Madrid	A	2-1	Lardín 2
05/05/96	Real Betis	A	3-2	Alex, Lardín 2
08/05/96	Real Oviedo	H	5-0	Urzaiz, Lardín 2, Bogdanovic, Torres Mestre
15/05/96	FC Barcelona	H	1-1	Urzaiz
19/05/96	Valencia CF	A	0-1	
25/05/96	SD Compostela	H	0-0	

CP MERIDA

CLUB DIRECTORY

Club Polideportivo Mérida
Rambla de Santa Eulalia 41
06800 Mérida (Badajoz)
tel - (924) 300402
fax - (924) 300401
Year of Formation - 1912
President - José Fouto Carvajal
Secretary - Manuel Molina Domínguez
Coach - Sergei Kresic
Stadium - Estadio Municipal (7,000)

APPEARANCES 95/96

	P	Ap	(s)	Gls
ANGEL LUIS Fernández Serrano	M	21	(6)	1
Manuel CANABAL Fiestras	M		(1)	
Sergio CORINO Ramón	D	16		3
Carlos Gabriel CORREA Viana (URU)	M	29	(4)	3
Crescencio CUELLAR Tainta	A	3	(1)	
Alfonso A. DULANTO Corzo (PER)	D	8	(3)	
Miguel Angel GUERRERO (COL)	A	9	(12)	
JOSE MARIA López Duque	D	27	(1)	
Francisco LEAL Rodríguez	G	42		
Lorenzo Morrón Vizcaíno 'LOREN'	D	22		
LLUIS González Pujol	A	3	(12)	1
Enrique 'QUIQUE' MARTIN Sánchez	A	26	(11)	4
César González López 'MENDIONDO'	D		(1)	
Manuel Ortega MOMPARLET	D	32	(1)	
Antonio MONREAL Rodríguez	D	30	(2)	
David Almazán Abril 'PIRRI'	M	23	(5)	
Nikolai PISAREV (RUS)	A	3	(17)	
Sergei POGODIN (RUS)	M	3		1
Juan Manuel PRIETO Velasco	A	34	(5)	15
Antonio REYES González	M	26	(6)	3
José Luis SIERRA Mediavilla	D	31	(1)	
José SINVAL de Campos (BRA)	A	37	(1)	5
Juan Antonio López TORIBIO	D	22	(4)	
URBANO Ortega Cuadros	M	9	(20)	
Goran VUCEVIC (CRO)	M	6	(4)	

LEAGUE RESULTS 1995/96

Date	Opponent		Score	Scorers
03/09/95	Real Betis	H	1-1	Quique Martín
09/09/95	FC Barcelona	A	2-2	Reyes (p), Correa
17/09/95	Valencia CF	H	0-2	
24/09/95	SD Compostela	A	0-1	
01/10/95	UD Salamanca	H	0-0	
04/10/95	CD Tenerife	A	0-1	
08/10/95	Albacete Balompié	H	1-1	Prieto
15/10/95	Real Sociedad	A	2-1	Pogodin, Prieto
22/10/95	Racing Santander	H	3-1	Sinval 2, Reyes
29/10/95	Atlético Madrid	A	1-1	Prieto
05/11/95	Sporting Gijón	H	1-0	Prieto
12/11/95	Sevilla FC	A	0-3	
19/11/95	RCD Espanyol	H	0-1	
26/11/95	RC Celta	A	0-2	
03/12/95	RC Deportivo	H	0-2	
10/12/95	Real Valladolid	A	1-1	Prieto
17/12/95	Athletic Bilbao	A	1-1	Sinval
20/12/95	Real Zaragoza	H	1-1	Prieto
03/01/96	Rayo Vallecano	A	1-4	Correa
07/01/96	Real Madrid	H	2-2	Prieto, Angel Luis
14/01/96	Real Oviedo	A	0-0	
21/01/96	Real Betis	A	1-0	Reyes
25/01/96	FC Barcelona	H	0-0	
28/01/96	Valencia CF	A	1-4	Corino
04/02/96	SD Compostela	H	0-2	
11/02/96	UD Salamanca	A	2-2	Corino, Prieto
18/02/96	CD Tenerife	H	2-0	Prieto 2
25/02/96	Albacete Balompié	A	0-2	
03/03/96	Real Sociedad	H	1-2	Prieto
10/03/96	Racing Santander	A	0-2	
17/03/96	Atlético Madrid	H	0-1	
23/03/96	Sporting Gijón	A	1-3	Prieto
27/03/96	Sevilla FC	H	3-2	og (Prieto), Quique Martín (p), Prieto
31/03/96	RCD Espanyol	A	0-3	
07/04/96	RC Celta	H	2-0	Prieto 2
14/04/96	RC Deportivo	A	1-2	Sinval
21/04/96	Real Valladolid	H	1-0	Corino
28/04/96	Athletic Bilbao	H	1-0	Lluís
05/05/96	Real Zaragoza	A	1-3	Sinval
12/05/96	Rayo Vallecano	H	0-1	
19/05/96	Real Madrid	A	0-4	
26/05/96	Real Oviedo	H	3-1	Quique Martin 2, Correa

REAL OVIEDO

CLUB DIRECTORY

Real Oviedo Club de Fútbol
Marqués de Santa Cruz 9-1.
33007 Oviedo (Asturias)
tel - (985) 212897/215300
fax - (985) 224058
Year of Formation - 1926
President - Eugenio Prieto Alvarez
Manager - Pedro Luis Fernández
Coach - Ivan Brzic (96/97 - Juan Manuel Lillo)
Stadium - Carlos Tartiere (22,284)

APPEARANCES 95/96

	P	Ap	(s)	Gls
Daniel AMIEVA Villa	M		(2)	
Juan Antonio ANDRADES Gutiérrez	M	1	(2)	
ANDRES de la Rosa Bolaños	D	23	(7)	
Iván ANIA Cadavieco	M	4	(19)	1
ARMANDO Alvarez Alvarez	M	38		1
Alberto Martínez Díaz 'BERTO'	M	37		1
Carlos David CANO Marín	G	3		
CARLOS Muñoz Cobo	A	26	(10)	10
CESAR Martín Villar	D	14	(6)	1
José Tomé Martínez 'CHECHU'	M		(1)	1
Tomás CHRISTIANSEN Tarin	A	12	(4)	5
DAVID Fernández Rodríguez	A	1		
Peter DUBOVSKY (SVK)	A	27	(4)	7
EMILIO Fernández Pertierra	A	1	(1)	
Heliodoro Alvarez Barrera 'HELIO'	D		(1)	
IVAN Casquero Cosio	M		(1)	
Nikola JERKAN (CRO)	D	35		1
JORGE Ordóñez García	M	2	(3)	
Roberto LOSADA Rodríguez	A	2	(14)	3
José Manuel Menéndez Erimia 'MANEL'	M	36	(2)	1
Juan Luis MORA Palacios	G	38		
Oliveira Jesús Alvarez González 'OLI'	A	38		11
Viktor ONOPKO (RUS)	M	18	(1)	1
PEDRO ALBERTO Cano Arenas	M	20	(12)	1
Rafael González Robles 'RAFA'	G	1		
Antonio RIVAS Martínez	D	8		1
Francisco SANZ Durán	M	3	(4)	
Nebojsa SCEPANOVIC (YUG)	M	4	(3)	
Manuel Cuervo SIMON	M		(1)	
Mitko STOJKOVSKI (MAC)	D	35	(3)	
Roberto SUAREZ Alvarez	M	35	(3)	1

LEAGUE RESULTS 1995/96

03/09/95	Real Zaragoza	A	0-1	
10/09/95	Rayo Vallecano	H	2-0	Pedro Alberto, Oli
17/09/95	Real Madrid	A	3-2	Oli 2, Rivas
24/09/95	Athletic Bilbao	H	0-0	
01/10/95	Real Betis	H	0-1	
04/10/95	FC Barcelona	A	1-4	Oli
08/10/95	Valencia CF	H	0-1	
15/10/95	SD Compostela	A	1-4	Dubovsky
22/10/95	UD Salamanca	H	2-2	Carlos, Dubovsky (p)
29/10/95	CD Tenerife	A	3-3	Manel, Oli, Dubovsky (p)
05/11/95	Albacete Balompié	H	1-0	Dubovsky
12/11/95	Real Sociedad	A	1-1	Oli
19/11/95	Racing Santander	H	2-1	Dubovsky (p), Oli
26/11/95	Atlético Madrid	A	0-3	
03/12/95	Sporting Gijón	H	1-0	og (Bango)
10/12/95	Sevilla FC	A	1-1	Oli
17/12/95	RCD Espanyol	H	1-2	Carlos
20/12/95	RC Celta	A	0-1	
03/01/96	RC Deportivo	H	0-2	
07/01/96	Real Valladolid	A	2-2	Losada 2
14/01/96	CP Mérida	H	0-0	
21/01/96	Real Zaragoza	H	1-1	Berto
24/01/96	Rayo Vallecano	A	2-1	Armando, Oli
28/01/96	Real Madrid	H	1-2	Carlos
04/02/96	Athletic Bilbao	A	1-0	Suárez
11/02/96	Real Betis	A	1-2	Losada
18/02/96	FC Barcelona	H	1-2	Oli
25/02/96	Valencia CF	A	1-3	César
03/03/96	SD Compostela	H	3-1	Christiansen 2, Carlos
10/03/96	UD Salamanca	A	1-0	Carlos
17/03/96	CD Tenerife	H	1-3	Oli (p)
24/03/96	Albacete Balompié	A	1-0	Dubovsky
28/03/96	Real Sociedad	H	0-0	
31/03/96	Racing Santander	A	0-0	
06/04/96	Atlético Madrid	H	1-1	Carlos
14/04/96	Sporting Gijón	A	1-0	Carlos
21/04/96	Sevilla FC	H	2-3	Onopko, Dubovsky
05/05/96	RC Celta	H	1-1	Christiansen (p)
08/05/96	RCD Espanyol	A	0-5	
12/05/96	RC Deportivo	A	4-0	Carlos 2, Jerkan, Ania
19/05/96	Real Valladolid	H	3-8	Christiansen 2 (2p), Carlos
26/05/96	CP Mérida	A	1-3	Chechu

RACING SANTANDER

CLUB DIRECTORY

Real Club Racing de Santander
Paseo de Pereda 28
39004 Santander
tel - (942) 214000
fax - (942) 364200
Year of Formation - 1913
President - Francisco de la Mora
Manager - Luis Anselmo Sáinz
Coach - Vicente Miera; Fernando Trío 'Yosu'
(96/97 - Marcos Alonso)
Stadium - El Sardinero (25,000)

APPEARANCES 95/96

	P	Ap	(s)	Gls
ALBERTO López Moreno	A	28	(12)	6
ALVARO Cervera Díaz	M	10	(12)	1
José María CEBALLOS Vega	G	41		
José María Alonso Fernández 'CHEMA'	M	29	(2)	1
Ilshat FAIZULIN (RUS)	A	16	(17)	6
Jesús HERRERA López	D	2	(1)	
José Ignacio Bollain Ochoa 'IÑAQUI'	D	19	(13)	2
ISMAEL Ruiz Salmón	M		(7)	
LUIS Fernández Gutiérrez	D	37	(2)	2
MARIO Bermejo Castanedo	D		(1)	
Jesús María MERINO Landaluce	D	39		4
Pedro MUNITIS Alvarez	A		(4)	
MUTIU Adepoju (NIG)	A	34	(3)	7
José A. Rodríguez de la Peña 'NENE'	A	2	(3)	
José Manuel OCHOTORENA Santacruz	G	1		
PABLO Alfaro Armengot	D	38		
Dmitri POPOV (RUS)	M	30	(2)	8
Francisco Javier RONCAL Puertas	D	17	(4)	
Enrique SETIEN Solar	M	9	(3)	
Gonzalo SUANZES Begueria	A	4	(11)	3
TOMAS González Rivera	D	26	(6)	1
ESTEBAN TORRE Ontañón	M	25	(8)	
José Antonio Montes TORRECILLA	D	15	(1)	
David VILLABONA Echalecu	M	33		5
Andrei ZYGMANTOVICH (BLS)	D	7	(6)	

LEAGUE RESULTS 1995/96

03/09/95	Athletic Bilbao	A	0-4	
10/09/95	Atlético Madrid	H	0-4	
17/09/95	Sporting Gijón	A	2-4	Alberto, Merino
23/09/95	Sevilla FC	H	1-1	Suanzes
01/10/95	RCD Espanyol	A	0-1	
04/10/95	RC Celta	H	2-1	Popov, Mutiu
08/10/95	RC Deportivo	A	3-2	Mutiu, Faizulin, Luis
15/10/95	Real Valladolid	H	0-0	
22/10/95	CP Mérida	A	1-3	Alberto
29/10/95	Real Zaragoza	H	0-0	
05/11/95	Rayo Vallecano	A	2-1	Alberto, Popov
12/11/95	Real Madrid	H	2-0	Alberto, Mutiu
19/11/95	Real Oviedo	A	1-2	Popov
26/11/95	Real Betis	H	0-0	
02/12/95	FC Barcelona	A	1-1	Chema
09/12/95	Valencia CF	H	0-3	
17/12/95	SD Compostela	A	0-2	
20/12/95	UD Salamanca	H	2-1	Mutiu, Suanzes
03/01/96	CD Tenerife	A	0-2	
07/01/96	Albacete Balompié	H	5-5	Villabona, Faizulin, Popov, Alberto 2
14/01/96	Real Sociedad	A	1-2	Iñaqui
21/01/96	Athletic Bilbao	H	1-1	og (Larraínzar)
24/01/96	Atlético Madrid	A	0-2	
28/01/96	Sporting Gijón	H	1-1	Mutiu
04/02/96	Sevilla FC	A	1-0	Mutiu
11/02/96	RCD Espanyol	H	1-1	Villabona
18/02/96	RC Celta	A	0-0	
24/02/96	RC Deportivo	H	2-1	Popov, Merino
02/03/96	Real Valladolid	A	1-3	Popov
10/03/96	CP Mérida	H	2-0	Faizulin, Villabona
16/03/96	Real Zaragoza	A	2-1	Popov 2
24/03/96	Rayo Vallecano	H	1-2	Luis
27/03/96	Real Madrid	A	2-1	Alvaro, Merino
31/03/96	Real Oviedo	H	0-0	
07/04/96	Real Betis	A	2-2	Villabona, Faizulin
13/04/96	FC Barcelona	H	1-1	Suanzes
20/04/96	Valencia CF	A	1-2	Villabona
28/04/96	SD Compostela	H	1-0	Faizulin
05/05/96	UD Salamanca	A	0-5	
12/05/96	CD Tenerife	H	1-2	Faizulin
19/05/96	Albacete Balompié	A	2-2	Mutiu, Tomás
25/05/96	Real Sociedad	H	2-3	Iñaqui, Merino

RAYO VALLECANO

CLUB DIRECTORY

Rayo Vallecano de Madrid
Payaso Fofó s/n
28018 Madrid
tel - (91) 4782253
fax - (91) 4771754
Year of Formation - 1924
President - Maria Teresa Rivero
Secretary - Adolfo Rivero
Coach - Pedro María Zabalza; Marcos Alonso; Fernando Zambrano
(96/97 - Francisco García 'Paquito')
Stadium - Vallecas (19,500)

APPEARANCES 95/96

	P	Ap	(s)	Gls
ABEL Resino Gómez	G	21		
Angel Luis ALCAZAR Gutiérrez	D	29	(7)	
Stjepan ANDRIJASEVIC (CRO)	M	11	(4)	4
Toribio Daniel AQUINO (ARG)	A	33	(7)	14
José Manuel BARLA García	M	33	(4)	2
José Luis BAROJA Galán	D	29	(3)	2
Antonio CALDERON Burgos	M	24	(13)	2
Ezequiel CASTILLO Monte (ARG)	M	35		1
Alfonso CORTIJO Cabrera	D	31	(2)	2
Jesús Diego COTA	D	32		1
Ramón DE QUINTANA Dalmau	D	37	(1)	
Eduardo Rodríguez Marín 'EDU'	D		(9)	1
Miguel Angel ESPAÑA Rosado	G	5	(1)	
FERNANDO Moreno López	M	1	(3)	
José Luis GALLEGO García	M	6	(7)	
GUILHERME Cassio Alves (BRA)	A	27	(7)	10
José Miguel López 'JOSEMI'	A	4	(10)	
Benigno LEMA Mejuto	D	12		
Angel MARTIN GONZALEZ	M	17	(8)	
Miguel Angel Sánchez Muñoz 'MICHEL'	M	2	(8)	
Jesús MORILLAS Fernández	D		(1)	
ONESIMO Sánchez González	A	28	(11)	6
Julián PALACIOS San Milán	D	24	(6)	
Francisco M. RUANO Bausán	A	5	(4)	1
WILFRED Agbonavbare (NIG)	G	16		

LEAGUE RESULTS 1995/96

03/09/95	Real Madrid	H	1-5	Guilherme
10/09/95	Real Oviedo	A	0-2	
17/09/95	Real Betis	H	1-2	Guilherme
23/09/95	FC Barcelona	A	0-2	
01/10/95	Valencia CF	H	3-2	Aquino, Onésimo, Calderón
04/10/95	SD Compostela	A	0-1	
08/10/95	UD Salamanca	H	1-4	Guilherme
15/10/95	CD Tenerife	A	2-2	Andrijasevic, Aquino
22/10/95	Albacete Balompié	H	2-0	Guilherme, Onésimo
29/10/95	Real Sociedad	A	1-2	Andrijasevic (p)
05/11/95	Racing Santander	H	1-2	Andrijasevic
12/11/95	Atlético Madrid	A	0-0	
19/11/95	Sporting Gijón	H	2-0	Baroja (p), Aquino
26/11/95	Sevilla FC	A	0-1	
02/12/95	RCD Espanyol	H	1-0	Aquino
10/12/95	RC Celta	A	0-2	
17/12/95	RC Deportivo	H	0-6	
20/12/95	Real Valladolid	A	1-1	Onésimo
03/01/96	CP Mérida	H	4-1	Cortijo, Andrijasevic, Onésimo, Edu
07/01/96	Real Zaragoza	A	1-1	Baroja
14/01/96	Athletic Bilbao	H	2-2	Onésimo, Aquino
21/01/96	Real Madrid	A	2-1	Guilherme 2
24/01/96	Real Oviedo	H	1-2	Guilherme
28/01/96	Real Betis	A	0-0	
04/02/96	FC Barcelona	H	1-1	Aquino
10/02/96	Valencia CF	A	0-3	
18/02/96	SD Compostela	H	0-1	
25/02/96	UD Salamanca	A	2-1	Guilherme, Onésimo
03/03/96	CD Tenerife	H	2-4	Guilherme 2
10/03/96	Albacete Balompié	A	2-1	Aquino, Cortijo
17/03/96	Real Sociedad	H	2-0	Castillo, Aquino
24/03/96	Racing Santander	A	2-1	Aquino, og (Villabona)
27/03/96	Atlético Madrid	H	0-3	
31/03/96	Sporting Gijón	A	1-3	Cota
07/04/96	Sevilla FC	H	0-0	
14/04/96	RCD Espanyol	A	2-4	Ruano, Aquino
21/04/96	RC Celta	H	1-3	Aquino (p)
28/04/96	RC Deportivo	A	0-1	
05/05/96	Real Valladolid	H	0-2	
12/05/96	CP Mérida	A	1-0	Barla
19/05/96	Real Zaragoza	H	4-3	Aquino 3 (1p), Calderón (p)
25/05/96	Athletic Bilbao	A	1-3	Barla

REAL MADRID

CLUB DIRECTORY

Real Madrid Club de Fútbol
Avda. Concha Espina 1
28036 Madrid
tel - (91) 3440052
fax - (91) 3440695
Year of Formation - 1902
President - Lorenzo Sanz Mancebo
Manager - José María Stampa Casas
Coach - Jorge Valdano; Arsenio Iglesias (96/97 - Fabio Capello)
Stadium - Santiago Bernabéu (95,000)

MAJOR HONOURS
League Championship - (26)
1932, 1933, 1954, 1955, 1957, 1958, 1961, 1962, 1963, 1964, 1965, 1967, 1968, 1969, 1972, 1975, 1976, 1978, 1979, 1980, 1986, 1987, 1988, 1989, 1990, 1995.
Domestic Cup - (17) 1905, 1906, 1907, 1908, 1917, 1934, 1936, 1946, 1947, 1962, 1970, 1974, 1975, 1980, 1982, 1989, 1993.
European Champions' Cup - (6)
1956, 1957, 1958, 1959, 1960, 1966.
UEFA Cup - (2) 1985, 1986.
World Club Cup - (1) 1960.

APPEARANCES 95/96

	P	Ap	(s)	Gls
Rafael ALKORTA Martínez	D	21	(4)	2
ALVARO Benito Villar	A	9	(5)	2
José Emilio AMAVISCA Gárate	M	21	(5)	3
Francisco BUYO Sánchez	G	31		
José Santiago CAÑIZARES Ruiz	G	11	(1)	
Miguel Porlan Noguera 'CHENDO'	D	20	(3)	
Juan Eduardo ESNAIDER (ARG)	A	8	(12)	1
José Antonio GARCIA CALVO	D	9		
Antonio GOMEZ Pérez	M	3	(3)	2
José M. Gutiérrez Hernández 'GUTI'	M	4	(5)	1
Fernando Ruiz HIERRO	D	30		7
IVAN PEREZ Muñoz	A	1	(2)	1
Mikel LASA Goicoechea	D	19	(3)	1
Michael LAUDRUP (DEN)	M	26	(3)	8
LUIS ENRIQUE Martínez García	M	29	(2)	2
José Miguel González Martínez 'MICHEL'	M	8	(25)	6
Luis MILLA Aspas	M	24	(8)	
Fernando Muñoz García 'NANDO'	D	2		
Dejan PETKOVIC (YUG)	M		(3)	
Enrique Sánchez Flores 'QUIQUE'	D	26	(7)	1
RAUL González Blanco	A	40		19
Fernando Carlos REDONDO Neri (ARG)	M	21	(2)	2
Fredy Eusebio RINCON Valencia (COL)	M	9	(5)	
Manuel SANCHIS Hontiyuelo	D	32		1
Carlos Alejandro Sierra Fumero 'SANDRO'	M	5	(4)	2
Fernando SANZ Durán	D	12	(2)	
Miguel SOLER Sarasols	D	14		1
VICTOR Sánchez del Amo	M		(1)	
Iván Luis ZAMORANO Zamora (CHI)	A	27	(2)	

LEAGUE RESULTS 1995/96

03/09/95	Rayo Vallecano	A	5-1	Amavisca, Sandro, Hierro 2, Quique
09/09/95	Athletic Bilbao	H	1-2	Raúl
17/09/95	Real Oviedo	H	2-3	Zamorano 2
23/09/95	Real Betis	A	0-0	
30/09/95	FC Barcelona	H	1-1	Raúl
04/10/95	Valencia CF	A	3-4	Laudrup (p), Alkorta, Míchel
08/10/95	SD Compostela	H	2-1	Hierro, Zamorano
15/10/95	UD Salamanca	A	2-0	Zamorano, Amavisca
22/10/95	CD Tenerife	H	2-0	Esnáider, Sandro
28/10/95	Albacete Balompié	A	1-1	Raúl
04/11/95	Real Sociedad	H	3-2	Raúl, Laudrup, Míchel (p)
12/11/95	Racing Santander	A	0-2	
18/11/95	Atlético Madrid	H	1-0	Raúl
26/11/95	Sporting Gijón	A	0-0	
02/12/95	Sevilla FC	H	4-1	Alkorta, Alvaro, Raúl 2
10/12/95	RCD Espanyol	A	1-3	Laudrup
17/12/95	RC Celta	H	1-0	Alvaro
21/12/95	RC Deportivo	A	0-3	
03/01/96	Real Valladolid	H	4-1	Gómez, Hierro 2 (2p), Zamorano
07/01/96	CP Mérida	A	2-2	Gómez, Redondo
14/01/96	Real Zaragoza	H	2-2	Zamorano, Amavisca
21/01/96	Rayo Vallecano	H	1-2	Raúl
24/01/96	Athletic Bilbao	A	5-0	Zamorano, Laudrup 2, Raúl, Míchel
28/01/96	Real Oviedo	A	2-1	Raúl 2
04/02/96	Real Betis	H	4-2	Sanchis, Raúl, Zamorano, Redondo
10/02/96	FC Barcelona	A	0-3	
17/02/96	Valencia CF	H	0-0	
25/02/96	SD Compostela	A	3-3	Zamorano, Raúl, Hierro
02/03/96	UD Salamanca	H	5-0	Raúl, Zamorano 2, Laudrup, Luis Enrique
10/03/96	CD Tenerife	A	0-3	
16/03/96	Albacete Balompié	H	2-0	Luis Enrique, Raúl
24/03/96	Real Sociedad	A	1-1	Raúl
27/03/96	Racing Santander	H	1-2	Míchel (p)
30/03/96	Atlético Madrid	A	2-1	Soler, Laudrup
07/04/96	Sporting Gijón	H	0-1	
13/04/96	Sevilla FC	A	1-0	Laudrup
21/04/96	RCD Espanyol	H	1-2	Raúl
28/04/96	RC Celta	A	1-1	Zamorano
05/05/96	RC Deportivo	H	1-0	og (Donato)
12/05/96	Real Valladolid	A	3-0	Lasa, Raúl, Guti
19/05/96	CP Mérida	H	4-0	Míchel 2 (1p), Raúl, Iván Pérez
25/05/96	Real Zaragoza	A	1-0	Hierro (p)

REAL SOCIEDAD

CLUB DIRECTORY

Real Sociedad de Fútbol
Paseo del Arbol de Guernica s/n
20006 San Sebastián
tel - (943) 451109
fax - (943) 458941
Year of Formation - 1909
President - Luis Uranga
Manager - Iñaki Otegui
Coach - Salvador Iriarte; Javier Iruretagoyena
Stadium - Anoeta (30,000)

MAJOR HONOURS
League Championship - (2) 1981, 1982.
Domestic Cup - (2) 1909, 1987.

APPEARANCES 95/96

	P	Ap	(s)	Gls
José Luis AGUIRRE Oliden	A	1		
ALBERTO López Fernández	G	41		
Alberto ALBISTEGI Zamacola	D	25	(4)	3
Agustín ARANZABAL Alkorta	D	38		
Gheorghe CRAIOVEANU (ROM)	A	23	(6)	11
Oscar DE PAULA Gamero	A	15	(10)	6
Francisco Javier DE PEDRO Falque	M	34	(4)	5
Unai EMERY Etxegoien	M		(5)	1
Juan Manuel FUENTES Aizpiroz	D	40		
Javier GRACIA Carlos	M	29	(3)	2
Iñigo IDIAKEZ Barcaiztegui	A	11	(22)	4
José Manuel Alguacil Barrenechea 'IMANOL'	D	9	(5)	1
Andoni IMAZ Garmendia	M	19	(10)	
Valeri KARPIN (RUS)	M	36	(1)	13
Lorenzo Juarros García 'LOREN'	D	39		2
José María LUMBRERAS Paños	D	1	(6)	
Roberto OLABE Aranzábal	G	1		
Luis PEREZ Pascual	A	20	(9)	8
José Antonio PICABEA Larrarte	D	36		
Markus PÜRK (AUT)	A	17	(13)	5
Miguel Mauricio RAMIREZ (CHI)	M	7	(3)	
Joaquín URIA Lecuona	D	11	(8)	
Joachim YAW Acheampong (GHA)	M	9	(4)	

LEAGUE RESULTS 1995/96

03/09/95	Atlético Madrid	A	1-4	Karpin
10/09/95	Sporting Gijón	H	2-0	Karpin 2
17/09/95	Sevilla FC	A	1-2	Karpin
24/09/95	RCD Espanyol	H	0-1	
01/10/95	RC Celta	A	1-1	Pürk
04/10/95	RC Deportivo	H	2-1	De Pedro, Pürk
08/10/95	Real Valladolid	A	0-3	
15/10/95	CP Mérida	H	1-2	Karpin
22/10/95	Real Zaragoza	A	2-1	Albístegi, De Paula
29/10/95	Rayo Vallecano	H	2-1	De Paula, Imanol
04/11/95	Real Madrid	A	2-3	De Pedro, Idiakez
12/11/95	Real Oviedo	H	1-1	Pürk
18/11/95	Real Betis	A	1-3	Craioveanu
25/11/95	FC Barcelona	H	1-1	Idiakez
03/12/95	Valencia CF	A	1-0	Idiakez
10/12/95	SD Compostela	H	0-1	
17/12/95	UD Salamanca	A	3-3	Karpin 2, De Paula
20/12/95	CD Tenerife	H	0-1	
03/01/96	Albacete Balompié	A	5-3	Albístegi, Karpin 2, De Pedro, De Paula
06/01/96	Athletic Bilbao	A	0-0	
14/01/96	Racing Santander	H	2-1	De Paula, Craioveanu
21/01/96	Atlético Madrid	H	1-0	De Paula
24/01/96	Sporting Gijón	A	1-1	Craioveanu
28/01/96	Sevilla FC	H	1-0	Craioveanu
04/02/96	RCD Espanyol	A	0-0	
11/02/96	RC Celta	H	3-1	Craioveanu 2, og (Alejo)
18/02/96	RC Deportivo	A	1-1	Pérez
25/02/96	Real Valladolid	H	1-0	Loren
03/03/96	CP Mérida	A	2-1	Karpin 2
10/03/96	Real Zaragoza	H	3-1	Karpin, Pérez, Gracia
17/03/96	Rayo Vallecano	A	0-2	
24/03/96	Real Madrid	H	1-1	Loren
28/03/96	Real Oviedo	A	0-0	
31/03/96	Real Betis	H	1-1	De Pedro
06/04/96	FC Barcelona	A	0-1	
14/04/96	Valencia CF	H	5-2	Pérez 3, Craioveanu, Karpin
21/04/96	SD Compostela	A	0-2	
28/04/96	UD Salamanca	H	1-0	Gracia
05/05/96	CD Tenerife	A	0-1	
12/05/96	Albacete Balompié	H	8-1	Pürk 2, Craioveanu 3, Pérez 2, Emery
19/05/96	Athletic Bilbao	H	2-2	Craioveanu, Albístegi
25/05/96	Racing Santander	A	3-2	Pérez, De Pedro, Idiakez

UD SALAMANCA

CLUB DIRECTORY

Union Deportiva Salamanca
Carretera de Zamora s/n
37184 Villares de la Reina (Salamanca)
tel - (923) 222090
fax - (923) 247658
Year of Formation - 1923
President - Juan José Hidalgo Acera
Secretary - Clemente Tomás Sánchez
Coach - Juan Manuel Lillo; Jorge D'Alessandro
Stadium - El Helmántico (25,000)

APPEARANCES 95/96

	P	Ap	(s)	Gls
José Ignacio AIZPURUA Alzaga	G	40		
Enrique AYUCAR Alberdi	M		(5)	1
Joan BARBARA Mata	A	36	(6)	12
CLAUDIO Barragán Escobar	A	36	(2)	11
José Guillermo DEL SOLAR Alvarez (PER)	M	35	(1)	6
Luciano ITURRINO Cenecorta	M	30	(9)	1
Alejandro Arenales Marchena 'JANDRI'	D	12	(1)	
José María López Echevarria 'JOSEMA'	M	28	(1)	
Jesús Anuzita Alegria 'JOSU'	G	2		
Diego Fernando LATORRE (ARG)	M	5	(18)	1
Raúl LOZANO Marcos	D		(2)	
LUIS MANUEL Arias Vega	D	13	(1)	
Angel Pedro MEDINA Ruiz	M	37		3
Francisco Javier Rey García 'QUICO'	A	5	(20)	1
José Antonio QUIROGA Fernández	M	14	(13)	
RODOLFO Condado Rodríguez	D	21	(1)	
José Agustín Cenzual Coca 'SITO'	D	31		1
Ovidiu STÎNGA (ROM)	M	28	(11)	11
Juan Luis SUCUNZA Suárez	M	10	(12)	
Miguel Montes TORRECILLA	D	39		1
Martín VELLISCA González	A	40		1
César VILLAFAÑE Blanco	M		(7)	1

LEAGUE RESULTS 1995/96

03/09/95	RCD Espanyol	A	1-3	Del Solar
10/09/95	RC Celta	H	0-1	
17/09/95	RC Deportivo	A	0-2	
24/09/95	Real Valladolid	H	0-0	
01/10/95	CP Mérida	A	0-0	
04/10/95	Real Zaragoza	H	0-1	
08/10/95	Rayo Vallecano	A	4-1	Claudio 3, Ayúcar
15/10/95	Real Madrid	H	0-2	
22/10/95	Real Oviedo	A	2-2	Barbará, Del Solar
29/10/95	Real Betis	H	2-1	og (Stosic), Barbará
05/11/95	FC Barcelona	A	1-4	Stînga
12/11/95	Valencia CF	H	4-0	Barbará 2, Claudio, Stînga
19/11/95	SD Compostela	A	0-0	
26/11/95	Athletic Bilbao	H	2-1	Stînga, Barbará
03/12/95	CD Tenerife	H	1-2	Del Solar
10/12/95	Albacete Balompié	A	3-3	Stînga, Del Solar, Claudio
17/12/95	Real Sociedad	H	3-3	Barbará, Torrecilla, Stînga
20/12/95	Racing Santander	A	1-2	Claudio
03/01/96	Atlético Madrid	H	1-3	Vellisca
07/01/96	Sporting Gijón	A	2-3	Medina, Barbará (p)
14/01/96	Sevilla FC	H	4-1	Barbará 2, Iturrino, Del Solar
21/01/96	RCD Espanyol	H	2-2	Medina, Del Solar
24/01/96	RC Celta	A	1-2	Claudio
27/01/96	RC Deportivo	H	0-5	
04/02/96	Real Valladolid	A	0-1	
11/02/96	CP Mérida	H	2-2	Barbará 2
17/02/96	Real Zaragoza	A	1-1	Stînga
25/02/96	Rayo Vallecano	H	1-2	Claudio
02/03/96	Real Madrid	A	0-5	
10/03/96	Real Oviedo	H	0-1	
17/03/96	Real Betis	A	0-4	
24/03/96	FC Barcelona	H	1-3	Medina
27/03/96	Valencia CF	A	0-2	
31/03/96	SD Compostela	H	1-0	Quico
07/04/96	Athletic Bilbao	A	1-3	Barbará
14/04/96	CD Tenerife	A	0-4	
21/04/96	Albacete Balompié	H	2-4	og (Tomás), Stînga
28/04/96	Real Sociedad	A	0-1	
05/05/96	Racing Santander	H	5-0	Latorre, Stînga 3 (1p), Claudio
12/05/96	Atlético Madrid	A	1-2	Stînga
19/05/96	Sporting Gijón	H	3-0	Claudio 2, Sito
25/05/96	Sevilla FC	A	1-3	Villafañe

SEVILLA FC

CLUB DIRECTORY

Sevilla Fútbol Club
Avda. Eduardo Dato s/n, 41005 Sevilla
tel - (954) 535353
fax - (954) 536061
Year of Formation - 1905
President - José María González de Caldas
Manager - José Ramón Cisneros
Coach - António Oliveira "Toni"; Víctor Espárrago (96/97 - José Antonio Camacho)
Stadium - Sánchez Pizjuán (70,000)

MAJOR HONOURS
League Championship - (1) 1946.
Domestic Cup - (3) 1935, 1939, 1948.

APPEARANCES 95/96

	P	Ap	(s)	Gls
ARTURO Pavón Jiménez	D	2		
CARLOS Domínguez Domínguez	A	14	(15)	4
DIEGO Rodríguez Fernández	D	28	(1)	
Enrique ESTEBARANZ López	A	4	(7)	
Víctor Javier FERRERAS Quintanilla	D	19	(5)	
Jesús GALVAN Carrillo	D	6		
Josko JELICIC (CRO)	M	10	(4)	1
Manuel JIMENEZ Jiménez	D	32		
Juan F. Rodríguez Herrera 'JUANITO'	D	25	(4)	2
MARCOS Martín de la Fuente	M	35	(1)	1
Juan MARTAGON Romero	D	30	(2)	
José Miguel Zafra Sánchez 'MICHEL'	M	2		
MOACIR Rodrigues dos Santos (BRA)	M	10	(3)	1
Ramón Rodríguez Verdejo 'MONCHI'	G	18		
Ramón Suárez del Valle 'MONCHU'	A	15	(15)	5
Gabriel MOYA Sanz	M	36		8
Tarik OULIDA (HOL)	M	3	(2)	
PEDRO González Martínez	D	16	(3)	
Emilio Delgado PEIXE (POR)	M	4	(1)	
José Luis Raimundo Romero 'PEPELU'	D	14	(4)	1
Dejan PETKOVIC (YUG)	M	7	(1)	1
Francisco Javier Carpio PINEDA	M	3	(9)	
José Miguel PRIETO Castillo	D	39		
RAFAel PAZ Marín	M	29	(3)	2
Salvador Ballesta Vialcho 'SALVA'	A		(1)	
Juan Antonio SANTAELLA Rando	M	1	(7)	
Davor SUKER (CRO)	A	31	(1)	16
Luis Garcia TEVENET	A	4	(14)	
Juan Carlos UNZUE Labiana	G	24		
Jorge González Díaz 'YORDI'	A	1	(5)	

LEAGUE RESULTS 1995/96

Date	Opponent	H/A	Score	Scorers
03/09/95	CD Tenerife	H	0-1	
09/09/95	Albacete Balompié	A	2-3	Moacir, Suker (p)
17/09/95	Real Sociedad	H	2-1	Suker, Carlos
23/09/95	Racing Santander	A	1-1	Carlos
01/10/95	Atlético Madrid	H	0-0	
04/10/95	Sporting Gijón	A	1-3	Carlos
08/10/95	Athletic Bilbao	A	1-1	Carlos
14/10/95	RCD Espanyol	H	0-3	
22/10/95	RC Celta	A	0-4	
28/10/95	RC Deportivo	H	0-0	
05/11/95	Real Valladolid	A	3-3	Moya 2, Juanito
12/11/95	CP Mérida	H	3-0	Juanito, Suker 2 (1p)
18/11/95	Real Zaragoza	A	1-0	Suker
26/11/95	Rayo Vallecano	H	1-0	Suker
02/12/95	Real Madrid	A	1-4	Moya
10/12/95	Real Oviedo	H	1-1	Jelicic
16/12/95	Real Betis	A	1-1	Monchu
20/12/95	FC Barcelona	H	1-0	Monchu
03/01/96	Valencia CF	A	0-1	
07/01/96	SD Compostela	H	0-1	
14/01/96	UD Salamanca	A	1-4	Monchu
21/01/96	CD Tenerife	A	2-4	Moya 2
24/01/96	Albacete Balompié	H	1-1	Suker
28/01/96	Real Sociedad	A	0-1	
04/02/96	Racing Santander	H	0-1	
10/02/96	Atlético Madrid	A	1-0	Moya
18/02/96	Sporting Gijón	H	2-0	Moya, Marcos
25/02/96	Athletic Bilbao	H	1-1	Petkovic
02/03/96	RCD Espanyol	A	1-0	Pepelu
10/03/96	RC Celta	H	0-0	
16/03/96	RC Deportivo	A	2-3	Suker, Monchu
24/03/96	Real Valladolid	H	1-1	Suker
27/03/96	CP Mérida	A	2-3	Suker, Yordi
31/03/96	Real Zaragoza	H	1-1	Suker
07/04/96	Rayo Vallecano	A	0-0	
13/04/96	Real Madrid	H	0-1	
21/04/96	Real Oviedo	A	3-2	Rafa Paz 2, Monchu
28/04/96	Real Betis	H	1-0	Suker
05/05/96	FC Barcelona	A	1-1	Moya
12/05/96	Valencia CF	H	1-2	Suker
19/05/96	SD Compostela	A	0-0	
25/05/96	UD Salamanca	H	3-1	Suker 3

SPORTING GIJON

CLUB DIRECTORY

Real Sporting de Gijón
Plaza del Monte de Piedad 2
33201 Gijón
tel - (985) 341457/344104
fax - (985) 340478
Year of Formation - 1905
President - José Fernández Alvarez
Manager - Herminio Menéndez
Coach - Ricardo Rezza; José Manuel Díaz Novoa (96/97 - Benito Floro)
Stadium - El Molinón (38,500)

APPEARANCES 95/96

	P	Ap	(s)	Gls
Juan Carlos Iglesias ABLANEDO	G	36		
Rubén Dario ACEBAL Vázquez	D	13		
AITOR Tornavaca Fernández	M	1		1
Alejandro Fernández Sam 'ALEX'	M		(1)	
AVELINO Riopedre Muiña	M	22	(7)	1
Ricardo González BANGO	M	37	(1)	1
Daniel BOUZAS Pan	A	13	(18)	1
David Sánchez CANO	M	25	(6)	2
ELOY José Olaya Prendes	A	21	(12)	3
Fernando GINER Gil	D	24		
IVAN Iglesias Corteguera	M	14	(3)	
JOSE MANUEL Colmenero Crespo	M	4	(1)	
Igor LEDYAKHOV (RUS)	M	29	(1)	8
MARCELINO Elena Sierra	D	3	(1)	
MARIO Gutiérrez Cotelo	M	14	(9)	2
José Luis MORALES Martín	A		(4)	
Juan Ramón López MUÑIZ	D	25	(1)	
PABLO José Díaz Stalla	D	37		
Hugo Leonardo PEREZ (ARG)	M	26	(11)	4
RAMON Ruiz Fernández	G	6	(2)	
ROGELIO Lamar Heredia	D	1		
Marcel SABOU (ROM)	M	8	(7)	2
Julio SALINAS Fernández	A	36	(1)	18
SERGIO Fernández González	D	2		
Valentín Aller García 'TINO'	D	9		
TOMAS Alberto Hervás Girón	M	21	(14)	2
Marcos VALES Illanes	A	2	(8)	
Jesús Enrique VELASCO Muñoz	D	29	(4)	1
Rashid YEKINI (NIG)	A	4	(6)	3

03/09/95	Albacete Balompié	H	3-0	og (Maqueda), Salinas, Tomás
10/09/95	Real Sociedad	A	0-2	
17/09/95	Racing Santander	H	4-2	Ledyakhov 2, Salinas 2
24/09/95	Atlético Madrid	A	0-2	
30/09/95	Athletic Bilbao	A	1-2	Salinas
04/10/95	Sevilla FC	H	3-1	Tomás, Salinas, Pérez
08/10/95	RCD Espanyol	A	0-0	
15/10/95	RC Celta	H	1-0	Sabou
22/10/95	RC Deportivo	A	0-1	
29/10/95	Real Valladolid	H	4-2	Pérez, Aitor, Eloy, Salinas
05/11/95	CP Mérida	A	0-1	
12/11/95	Real Zaragoza	H	4-1	Salinas 2, Sabou, Cano
19/11/95	Rayo Vallecano	A	0-2	
26/11/95	Real Madrid	H	0-0	
03/12/95	Real Oviedo	A	0-1	
10/12/95	Real Betis	H	2-3	Pérez, Bango
16/12/95	FC Barcelona	A	0-1	
20/12/95	Valencia CF	H	1-3	Yekini
03/01/96	SD Compostela	A	0-1	
07/01/96	UD Salamanca	H	3-2	Salinas 2, Ledyakhov
14/01/96	CD Tenerife	A	0-3	
21/01/96	Albacete Balompié	A	3-1	Yekini, Avelino, Salinas
24/01/96	Real Sociedad	H	1-1	og (Loren)
28/01/96	Racing Santander	A	1-1	Pérez
03/02/96	Atlético Madrid	H	1-2	Ledyakhov (p)
11/02/96	Athletic Bilbao	H	1-2	Yekini
18/02/96	Sevilla FC	A	0-2	
25/02/96	RCD Espanyol	H	2-3	Eloy, Salinas
03/03/96	RC Celta	A	0-0	
10/03/96	RC Deportivo	H	1-1	Eloy
17/03/96	Real Valladolid	A	0-1	
23/03/96	CP Mérida	H	3-1	Salinas, Bouzas, Mario
27/03/96	Real Zaragoza	A	1-1	Ledyakhov (p)
31/03/96	Rayo Vallecano	H	3-1	Salinas 3
07/04/96	Real Madrid	A	1-0	Velasco
14/04/96	Real Oviedo	H	0-1	
21/04/96	Real Betis	A	5-2	Mario, Ledyakhov, Salinas 2, Cano
28/04/96	FC Barcelona	H	0-3	
04/05/96	Valencia CF	A	0-1	
12/05/96	SD Compostela	H	2-1	Ledyakhov 2 (1p)
19/05/96	UD Salamanca	A	0-3	
25/05/96	CD Tenerife	H	0-2	

CD TENERIFE

CLUB DIRECTORY

Club Deportivo Tenerife
Callejón del Combate 1-1.
38002 Santa Cruz de Tenerife
tel - (922) 291699
fax - (922) 240613
Year of Formation - 1910
President - José Javier Pérez
Manager - Enrique Roca
Coach - Jupp Heynckes
Stadium - Heliodoro Rodríguez (24,000)

APPEARANCES 95/96

	P	Ap	(s)	Gls
Carlos AGUILERA Martín	D	29	(10)	5
ALEXIS Suearez Martín	D	23	(2)	
José María BULJUBASICH (ARG)	G	1		
CESAR GOMEZ del Rey	D	36		
Sebastián Cruzado Fernández 'CHANO'	M	34	(4)	2
Ignacio CONTE Crespo	M	4	(12)	
FELIPE Miñambres Fernández	M	31	(4)	2
Pavel HAPAL (TCH)	M	26	(5)	1
Slavisa JOKANOVIC (YUG)	M	31	(3)	2
Juan Castaõ Quirós 'JUANELE'	A	20	(5)	7
Diego Fernando LATORRE (ARG)	A	1	(1)	
Julio LLORENTE Gento	D	39		4
Antonio MATA Olivera	D	20	(4)	2
Marcelo Leonardo OJEDA Ojeda (ARG)	G	41		
Antonio PINILLA Miranda	A	23	(13)	7
Juan Antonio PIZZI Torroja	A	39	(2)	31
Luis Miguel RAMIS Monfort	D	18	(7)	1
Antonio Segura ROBAINA	A	25	(14)	1
SERGIO Ballesteros	M	3	(3)	
VICTOR Manuel Fernández Gutiérrez	A	3	(6)	1
Angel Manuel VIVAR DORADO	M	15	(14)	1

LEAGUE RESULTS 1995/96

03/09/95	Sevilla FC	A	1-0	og (Jiménez)
10/09/95	RCD Espanyol	H	1-4	Víctor
17/09/95	RC Celta	A	2-2	Pizzi, og (Berges)
24/09/95	RC Deportivo	H	1-1	Pizzi
01/10/95	Real Valladolid	A	0-3	
04/10/95	CP Mérida	H	1-0	Pizzi (p)
08/10/95	Real Zaragoza	A	2-0	Pizzi, Pinilla
15/10/95	Rayo Vallecano	H	2-2	Jokanovic, Felipe
22/10/95	Real Madrid	A	0-2	
29/10/95	Real Oviedo	H	3-3	Llorente 2, Felipe
05/11/95	Real Betis	A	3-3	Pizzi 2 (1p), Aguilera
12/11/95	FC Barcelona	H	1-1	Llorente
19/11/95	Valencia CF	A	2-2	Pizzi 2
26/11/95	SD Compostela	H	1-1	Vivar Dorado
03/12/95	UD Salamanca	A	2-1	Pizzi 2 (1p)
10/12/95	Athletic Bilbao	H	3-2	Juanele, Pizzi (p), Pinilla
17/12/95	Albacete Balompié	H	1-3	Pinilla
20/12/95	Real Sociedad	A	1-0	Aguilera
03/01/96	Racing Santander	H	2-0	Juanele, Pizzi
06/01/96	Atlético Madrid	A	1-3	Juanele
14/01/96	Sporting Gijón	H	3-0	Chano, Ramis, Pizzi
21/01/96	Sevilla FC	H	4-2	Pizzi 4 (1p)
24/01/96	RCD Espanyol	A	1-2	Mata
28/01/96	RC Celta	H	1-0	Mata
04/02/96	RC Deportivo	A	1-1	Aguilera
11/02/96	Real Valladolid	H	1-0	Juanele
18/02/96	CP Mérida	A	0-2	
25/02/96	Real Zaragoza	H	1-2	Juanele
03/03/96	Rayo Vallecano	A	4-2	Jokanovic, Pizzi 2 (1p), Pinilla
10/03/96	Real Madrid	H	3-0	Robaina, Pizzi 2
17/03/96	Real Oviedo	A	3-1	Juanele, Pizzi, Pinilla
23/03/96	Real Betis	H	1-2	Pizzi
27/03/96	FC Barcelona	A	2-2	Pizzi, Pinilla
31/03/96	Valencia CF	H	2-1	Llorente, Pizzi
07/04/96	SD Compostela	A	2-0	Aguilera, Pizzi
14/04/96	UD Salamanca	H	4-0	Pizzi 2, Juanele, Hapal
21/04/96	Athletic Bilbao	A	0-2	
28/04/96	Albacete Balompié	A	0-0	
05/05/96	Real Sociedad	H	1-0	Pizzi
12/05/96	Racing Santander	A	2-1	Pizzi, Chano
18/05/96	Atlético Madrid	H	1-1	Pizzi
25/05/96	Sporting Gijón	A	2-0	Aguilera, Pinilla

VALENCIA CF

CLUB DIRECTORY

Valencia Club de Fútbol
Avda. Aragón 33
46010 Valencia
tel - (96) 3600550
fax - (96) 3611235
Year of Formation - 1919
President - Francisco Roig
Manager - vacant
Coach - Luis Aragonés
Stadium - Luis Casanova (49,291)

MAJOR HONOURS
League Championship - (4)
1942, 1944, 1947, 1971.
Domestic Cup - (5)
1941, 1949, 1954, 1967, 1979.
European Cup-winners' Cup - (1) 1980.
Fairs' Cup - (2) 1962, 1963.
European Super Cup - (1) 1980.

APPEARANCES 95/96

	P	Ap	(s)	Gls
Carlos ARROYO Ayala	M	6	(24)	6
Jorge BARTUAL Medina	G	3	(1)	
Francisco José CAMARASA Castellar	D	39		2
Vicente ENGONGA Maté	M	19	(6)	
Xabier ESKURZA García	M	11	(16)	1
FERNANDO Gómez Colomer	M	42		10
Francisco FERREIRA Colmenero	D	17	(6)	
José GALVEZ Estévez	A	27	(1)	11
José Ignacio Hurtado López 'IÑAQUI'	M	1	(10)	
JOSE IGNACIO Sáenz Marín	M	21	(6)	
Iomar do Nascimento 'MAZINHO' (BRA)	M	39	(1)	
Gaizka MENDIETA Zabala	M	30	(4)	
Predrag MIJATOVIC (YUG)	A	39		28
Francisco Javier NAVARRO Vicente	D	16	(4)	
Jorge OTERO Bouza	D	37		
Antonio POYATOS Medina	M	19	(13)	5
RAUL Martínez	A		(2)	
Enrique Fernández ROMERO	D	29	(1)	1
José Manuel Suárez Riva 'SIETES'	M	13	(7)	
Paulo Sergio Rosa 'VIOLA' (BRA)	A	15	(15)	11
Andoni ZUBIZARRETA Urreta	G	39		

LEAGUE RESULTS 1995/96

02/09/95	RC Deportivo	A	0-3	
10/09/95	Real Valladolid	H	1-0	Gálvez
17/09/95	CP Mérida	A	2-0	Mijatovic, Fernando
24/09/95	Real Zaragoza	H	0-0	
01/10/95	Rayo Vallecano	A	2-3	Mijatovic 2 (1p)
04/10/95	Real Madrid	H	4-3	Gálvez, Fernando, Mijatovic, Arroyo
08/10/95	Real Oviedo	A	1-0	Fernando
14/10/95	Real Betis	H	1-1	Gálvez
22/10/95	FC Barcelona	A	0-1	
29/10/95	Athletic Bilbao	H	3-1	Camarasa, Gálvez, Mijatovic
05/11/95	SD Compostela	H	5-2	Mijatovic 2 (1p), Viola, Gálvez, og (Passi)
12/11/95	UD Salamanca	A	0-4	
19/11/95	CD Tenerife	H	2-2	Gálvez, og (Gómez)
26/11/95	Albacete Balompié	A	3-1	Mijatovic 2, Viola
03/12/95	Real Sociedad	H	0-1	
09/12/95	Racing Santander	A	3-0	Mijatovic 2, Fernando
17/12/95	Atlético Madrid	H	0-1	
20/12/95	Sporting Gijón	A	3-1	Mijatovic 2, Viola
03/01/96	Sevilla FC	H	1-0	Arroyo
07/01/96	RCD Espanyol	A	0-2	
14/01/96	RC Celta	H	3-0	Romero, Arroyo, Poyatos
20/01/96	RC Deportivo	H	2-1	Mijatovic 2 (1p)
24/01/96	Real Valladolid	A	5-2	Gálvez 3, Fernando 2
28/01/96	CP Mérida	H	4-1	Poyatos, Mijatovic 2 (1p), Gálvez
03/02/96	Real Zaragoza	A	1-4	Gálvez
10/02/96	Rayo Vallecano	H	3-0	Mijatovic, Camarasa, Eskurza
17/02/96	Real Madrid	A	0-0	
25/02/96	Real Oviedo	H	3-1	Poyatos, Mijatovic, Arroyo
03/03/96	Real Betis	A	0-3	
09/03/96	FC Barcelona	H	4-1	Fernando, Viola, Mijatovic 2
17/03/96	Athletic Bilbao	A	1-0	Viola
24/03/96	SD Compostela	A	4-0	Viola 2, Arroyo, Mijatovic
27/03/96	UD Salamanca	H	2-0	Poyatos, Viola
31/03/96	CD Tenerife	A	1-2	Fernando
07/04/96	Albacete Balompié	H	1-0	Fernando
14/04/96	Real Sociedad	A	2-5	Fernando, Mijatovic
20/04/96	Racing Santander	H	2-1	Viola 2
27/04/96	Atlético Madrid	A	3-2	Mijatovic 2 (1p), Poyatos
04/05/96	Sporting Gijón	H	1-0	Viola
12/05/96	Sevilla FC	A	2-1	Mijatovic 2 (1p)
19/05/96	RCD Espanyol	H	1-0	Arroyo
25/05/96	RC Celta	A	1-1	Mijatovic

REAL VALLADOLID

CLUB DIRECTORY

Real Valladolid Deportivo
Avda. del Mundial 82, s/n
47014 Valladolid
tel - (983) 370875
fax - (983) 372164
Year of Formation - 1928
President - Marcos Fernández
Manager - Carlos Antonio Palacios
Coach - Rafael Benítez; Vicente Cantatore
Stadium - Nuevo José Zorrilla (37,500)

APPEARANCES 95/96

	P	Ap	(s)	Gls
Iván ALONSO	G	2		
Mikel ANTIA Mendiaraz	D	39		
Aljosa ASANOVIC (CRO)	M	6	(3)	1
Rubén BARAJA Vegas	M	12	(15)	1
BENJAMIN Zarandona Esono	D	11	(5)	3
Iván CAMPO Ramos	D	24		2
CESAR Sánchez Domínguez	G	40		
FERNANDO Sánchez Cipitria	M	40		7
Gregorio FONSECA Recio	A	7	(4)	1
Amado GUEVARA (HON)	M	3	(5)	
Alvaro GUTIERREZ Felscher (URU)	M	16	(5)	1
Sead HALILOVIC (BOS)	M	12	(5)	
JUAN CARLOS Rodríguez Moreno	D	23	(5)	
Alberto MARCOS Rey	D	25	(1)	1
José Luis MOSQUERA Losada	M	4	(5)	
Carlos Alberto PAVON (HON)	M	2	(7)	
Juan Manuel PEÑA (BOL)	A	17		
Alen PETERNAC (CRO)	A	36	(3)	23
José María QUEVEDO García	M	38		13
RAMON González Expósito	D	6	(4)	
RAUL Ibáñez Galdón	A	13	(15)	1
Francisco Manuel RUANO Bausan	M		(1)	
Oscar SALAMANCA	M		(1)	
Marco Antonio SANDY (BOL)	M	3	(1)	
José Luis SANTAMARIA Buitrago	D	13	(2)	
José SOTO María	A	14	(13)	
Javier TORRES GOMEZ	M	26	(5)	1
Jesús A. TURIEL de la Cruz	M	7	(1)	1
Agustín VARA Sánchez	D	23	(4)	

LEAGUE RESULTS 1995/96

03/09/95	FC Barcelona	H	0-2	
10/09/95	Valencia CF	A	0-1	
16/09/95	SD Compostela	H	0-0	
24/09/95	UD Salamanca	A	0-0	
01/10/95	CD Tenerife	H	3-0	Peternac, Quevedo, Asanovic
04/10/95	Albacete Balompié	A	2-4	og (Sotero), Quevedo
08/10/95	Real Sociedad	H	3-0	Fonseca, Baraja, Fernando
15/10/95	Racing Santander	A	0-0	
21/10/95	Atlético Madrid	H	0-1	
29/10/95	Sporting Gijón	A	2-4	Fernando, Torres Gómez
05/11/95	Sevilla FC	H	3-3	Quevedo, Peternac 2
12/11/95	RCD Espanyol	A	0-2	
19/11/95	RC Celta	H	1-1	Peternac
26/11/95	RC Deportivo	A	1-3	Turiel
03/12/95	Athletic Bilbao	A	1-2	Peternac
10/12/95	CP Mérida	H	1-1	Quevedo
17/12/95	Real Zaragoza	A	3-5	Peternac, Quevedo, Benjamín
20/12/95	Rayo Vallecano	H	1-1	Fernando
03/01/96	Real Madrid	A	1-4	Fernando
07/01/96	Real Oviedo	H	2-2	Fernando, Campo
13/01/96	Real Betis	A	0-3	
21/01/96	FC Barcelona	A	0-1	
24/01/96	Valencia CF	H	2-5	Quevedo, Benjamín
28/01/96	SD Compostela	A	3-1	Peternac, Quevedo, Fernando
04/02/96	UD Salamanca	H	1-0	Benjamín
11/02/96	CD Tenerife	A	0-1	
18/02/96	Albacete Balompié	H	3-0	Raúl, Peternac, Fernando
25/02/96	Real Sociedad	A	0-1	
02/03/96	Racing Santander	H	3-1	Peternac 3 (1p)
10/03/96	Atlético Madrid	A	2-0	Peternac 2
17/03/96	Sporting Gijón	H	1-0	Marcos
24/03/96	Sevilla FC	A	1-1	Campo
27/03/96	RCD Espanyol	H	0-0	
31/03/96	RC Celta	A	1-1	Gutiérrez
07/04/96	RC Deportivo	H	2-2	Quevedo, Peternac
14/04/96	Athletic Bilbao	H	1-1	Peternac
21/04/96	CP Mérida	A	0-1	
28/04/96	Real Zaragoza	H	0-0	
05/05/96	Rayo Vallecano	A	2-0	Peternac (p), Quevedo (p)
12/05/96	Real Madrid	H	0-3	
19/05/96	Real Oviedo	A	8-3	Peternac 5 (4p), Quevedo 3
25/05/96	Real Betis	H	3-1	Peternac 2, Quevedo

REAL ZARAGOZA

CLUB DIRECTORY

Real Zaragoza Club Deportivo
c/Luis Bermejo 1-3
50009 Zaragoza
tel - (976) 567777
fax - (976) 568863
Year of Formation - 1932
President - Alfonso Solans Serrano
Manager - Javier Paricio Agueras
Coach - Víctor Fernández
Stadium - La Romareda (43,554)

MAJOR HONOURS
Domestic Cup - (4)
1964, 1966, 1986, 1994.
European Cup-winners' Cup - (1) 1995.
Fairs' Cup - (1) 1964.

APPEARANCES 95/96

	P	Ap	(s)	Gls
Xavier AGUADO Companys	D	36		2
Santiago ARAGON Martínez	M	37	(1)	4
José Francisco BELMAN González	G	11		
Alberto BELSUE Arias	D	37		
Sergio Angel BERTI (ARG)	M	12	(4)	
Fernando Gabriel CACERES (ARG)	D	30		2
Luis Carlos CUARTERO Laforga	D	13	(5)	
Daniel García Lara 'DANI'	A	26	(12)	3
Jesús GARCIA SANJUAN	M	16	(11)	
José Aurelio GAY López	M		(14)	
Francisco HIGUERA Fernández	A	16	(13)	2
IÑIGO Rodríguez Martínez	A		(1)	
Juan Miguel García Inglés 'JUANMI'	G	31		
Gustavo LOPEZ (ARG)	A	9	(9)	2
Fernando MORIENTES Sánchez	A	28	(2)	13
Mohamed Ali Hamar 'NAYIM'	M	22	(10)	2
OSCAR Luis Celada	M	26	(6)	1
Francisco Veza Fragoso 'PAQUI'	D	20	(6)	
Miguel PARDEZA Pichardo	A	15	(11)	2
Gustavo POYET Domínguez (URU)	M	34	(2)	11
Sebastián RAMBERT (ARG)	M	17	(3)	5
Jesús Angel SOLANA Bermejo	D	26	(1)	

LEAGUE RESULTS 1995/96

03/09/95	Real Oviedo	H	1-0	Aguado
09/09/95	Real Betis	A	1-3	Morientes
17/09/95	FC Barcelona	H	0-3	
24/09/95	Valencia CF	A	0-0	
01/10/95	SD Compostela	H	1-0	Morientes
04/10/95	UD Salamanca	A	1-0	Aragón
08/10/95	CD Tenerife	H	0-2	
15/10/95	Albacete Balompié	A	1-0	Poyet
22/10/95	Real Sociedad	H	1-2	Poyet
29/10/95	Racing Santander	A	0-0	
05/11/95	Atlético Madrid	H	0-0	
12/11/95	Sporting Gijón	A	1-4	Nayim
18/11/95	Sevilla FC	H	0-1	
26/11/95	RCD Espanyol	A	1-1	Dani
03/12/95	RC Celta	H	0-0	
10/12/95	RC Deportivo	A	3-2	Pardeza, Morientes, Dani
17/12/95	Real Valladolid	H	5-3	og (Campo), Rambert (p), og (Torres Gómez), Poyet 2
20/12/95	CP Mérida	A	1-1	Oscar
03/01/96	Athletic Bilbao	A	0-1	
07/01/96	Rayo Vallecano	H	1-1	Rambert
14/01/96	Real Madrid	A	2-2	Morientes, Rambert
21/01/96	Real Oviedo	A	1-1	Aragón
24/01/96	Real Betis	H	1-2	Poyet
28/01/96	FC Barcelona	A	1-3	Higuera
03/02/96	Valencia CF	H	4-1	Poyet, Morientes 3
11/02/96	SD Compostela	A	2-3	Morientes, Rambert
17/02/96	UD Salamanca	H	1-1	Aguado
25/02/96	CD Tenerife	A	2-1	Poyet, Cáceres
03/03/96	Albacete Balompié	H	3-1	Morientes 2, Higuera
10/03/96	Real Sociedad	A	1-3	Nayim
16/03/96	Racing Santander	H	1-2	Cáceres
24/03/96	Atlético Madrid	A	1-1	Morientes
27/03/96	Sporting Gijón	H	1-1	Rambert
31/03/96	Sevilla FC	A	1-1	Morientes
06/04/96	RCD Espanyol	H	1-1	Poyet
14/04/96	RC Celta	A	1-1	Aragón (p)
21/04/96	RC Deportivo	H	2-3	Morientes, Aragón (p)
28/04/96	Real Valladolid	A	0-0	
05/05/96	CP Mérida	H	3-1	Pardeza, Poyet, López
12/05/96	Athletic Bilbao	H	1-0	Poyet
19/05/96	Rayo Vallecano	A	3-4	Dani, Poyet, López (p)
25/05/96	Real Madrid	H	0-1	

PROMOTED CLUBS

SECOND DIVISION FINAL TABLE 95/96

		Pd	W	D	L	F	A	Pt	GD
1	**Hércules CF**	**38**	**21**	**10**	**7**	**61**	**30**	**73**	**+31**
2	**CD Logroñés**	**38**	**20**	**9**	**9**	**69**	**49**	**69**	**+20**
3	RCD Mallorca	38	20	9	9	59	35	69	+24
4	Real Madrid B	38	18	10	10	50	41	64	+9
5	**CF Extremadura**	**38**	**17**	**11**	**10**	**48**	**33**	**62**	**+15**
6	CD Badajoz	38	18	8	12	48	31	62	+17
7	CD Alavés	38	17	10	11	52	42	61	+10
8	CD Leganés	38	17	10	11	42	40	61	+2
9	CD Toledo	38	16	11	11	38	30	59	+8
10	CA Osasuna	38	15	7	16	49	43	52	+6
11	UE Lleida	38	12	12	14	40	49	48	-9
12	SD Eibar	38	10	16	12	24	31	46	-7
13	Ecija Balompié	38	12	9	17	34	60	45	-26
14	FC Barcelona B	38	13	5	20	55	63	44	-8
15	Villarreal CF	38	11	11	16	32	39	44	-7
16	Almería CF	38	10	14	14	42	47	44	-5
17	Sestao SC	38	10	12	16	36	45	42	-9
18	Athletic Bilbao B	38	10	10	18	49	63	40	-14
19	Getafe CF	38	7	11	20	30	52	32	-22
20	Atlético Marbella	38	4	9	25	28	63	21	-35

N.B. Real Madrid B ineligible for promotion.

PROMOTION/RELEGATION PLAY-OFFS

RCD Mallorca 1, Rayo Vallecano 0
Rayo Vallecano 2, RCD Mallorca 0
(Rayo Vallecano 2-1)

CF Extremadura 1, Albacete Balompié 0
Albacete Balompié 0, CF Extremadura 1
(CF Extremadura 2-0)

CLUB DIRECTORY

Hércules Club de Fútbol
Foguerer Romeu Zarandieta s/n
03005 Alicante
tel - (96) 5243212
fax - (96) 5245783
Year of Formation - 1922
President - Aniceto Benito Núñez
Manager - Vicente Compañ Cerver
Coach - Manuel Jiménez González
(96/97 - Ivan Brzic)
Stadium - José Rico Pérez (32,700)

CLUB DIRECTORY

Club Deportivo Logroñés
Cabo Noval 2
26006 Logroño (La Rioja)
tel - (941) 261690
fax - (941) 261700
Year of Formation - 1940
President - Emilio Ganuza Bacaicoa
Manager - Juan Manuel Fernández García
Coach - Juan de la Cruz Ramos
(96/97 - Angel Lotina)
Stadium - Las Gaunas (15,000)

CLUB DIRECTORY

Club de Fútbol Extremadura
Ctra de Badajoz s/n
06200 Almendralejo (Badajoz)
tel - (924) 662025
fax - (924) 670530
Year of Formation - 1923
President - Pedro Nieto Cortés
Coach - José Ortuondo
Stadium - Francisco de la Hera (6,000)

SWEDEN

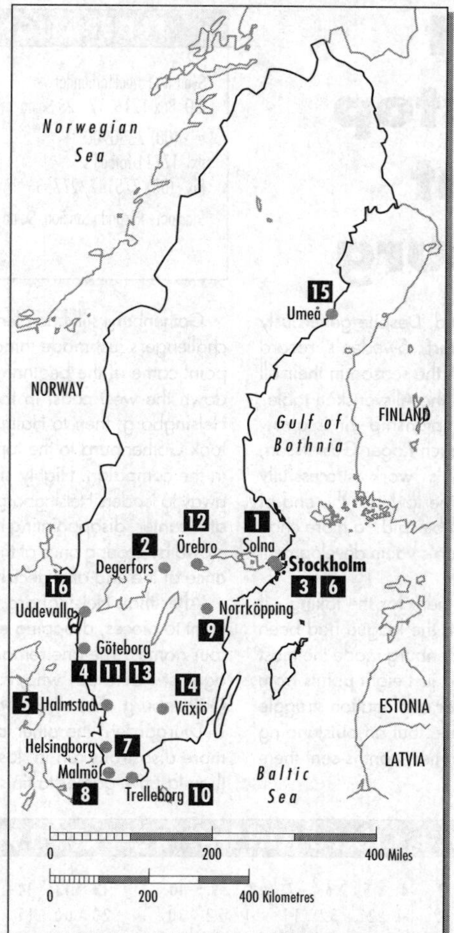

1	AIK	976	9	IFK NORRKÖPING	984
2	DEGERFORS IF	977	10	TRELLEBORGS FF	985
3	DJURGÅRDENS IF	978	11	VÄSTRA FRÖLUNDA IF	986
4	IFK GÖTEBORG	979	12	ÖREBRO SK	987
5	HALMSTADS BK	980	13	ÖRGRYTE IS	988
6	HAMMARBY IF	981	14	ÖSTERS IF	989
7	HELSINGBORGS IF	982	15	UMEÅ FC	990
8	MALMÖ FF	983	16	IK ODDEVOLD	990

SVENSSON STAYS ON FOR WORLD CUP

Bad start fails to stop resurgent Gothenburg

FEDERATION DIRECTORY

Svenska Fotbollförbundet
P.O. Box 1216, 171 23 Solna

tel - (08) 7350900
tlx - 17711 fotboll s
fax - (08) 275147/277536

Year of Formation - 1904
President - Lars-Åke Lagrell
Secretary - Lars-Christer Olsson

Stadium - Råsunda Stadion, Solna (36,000)

IFK Gothenburg will not be moved. Despite generously offering their rivals a head start, Sweden's record champions still managed to finish the season in their all too familiar position at the top of the Allsvenskan table.

It was Gothenburg's third championship win in a row and the fifth in six seasons for coach Roger Gustafsson, who, with yet another season's work successfully completed, decided to throw in the towel at the end of the campaign, preferring - dare it be said - a more challenging position as head of the club's youth development programme.

The 1995 championship was there for the taking - if only one of the other 13 teams in the league had been able to rise to the challenge. Gothenburg made the most catastrophic of starts. After taking just eight points from as many games, they looked set for a relegation struggle rather than another bid for the title. But an outstanding six-match winning run in the summer months sent them surging back up the table.

Gothenburg still had plenty of work to do, but the other challengers just made things easy for them. The turning point came at the beginning of October when two trips down the west coast in the space of five days, first to Helsingborg, then to Halmstad, yielded four points and took Gothenburg to the top of the table for the first time in the campaign. Highly significant was the first match, away to leaders Helsingborg, which Gustafsson's men won at a canter, disappointing most of the 16,015 fans in the crowd by scoring once at the start, once in the middle and once at the end of a decisive 3-0 victory.

After that, Helsingborg, gunning for a first ever title, went to pieces, dropping eight more points in their final four games. The one remaining match they did win was against Halmstad, who, following their 0-0 draw with Gothenburg, thus slipped out of the title picture as well.

Djurgården, the other challengers, suffered an even more disastrous run-in, losing four and drawing one of their last five games to finish up way off the pace in sixth

LEAGUE CHAMPIONSHIP RESULTS 1995

		1	2	3	4	5	6	7	8	9	10	11	12	13	14
1	AIK		1-2	1-2	3-1	2-2	3-2	1-1	1-1	2-2	3-0	1-1	2-0	0-0	1-1
2	Degerfors IF	2-1		1-1	0-3	3-3	0-0	2-2	0-3	0-3	1-0	2-0	2-1	0-0	3-2
3	Djurgårdens IF	1-2	2-0		1-1	0-3	2-0	1-3	0-2	2-0	1-1	4-2	2-0	1-3	1-1
4	IFK Göteborg	0-0	3-0	2-0		0-1	2-0	1-1	2-1	2-0	2-0	1-1	3-1	3-0	3-1
5	Halmstads BK	3-0	5-1	1-2	0-0		1-0	2-1	2-2	2-0	1-2	1-1	2-1	2-0	2-2
6	Hammarby IF	1-2	2-1	0-1	2-2	0-3		2-1	1-1	0-2	1-3	3-1	2-2	0-1	2-2
7	Helsingborgs IF	2-1	3-3	2-3	0-3	3-0	3-5		2-1	0-0	2-1	1-0	3-0	0-1	0-2
8	Malmö FF	2-2	3-1	0-0	1-1	2-1	1-0	0-1		1-3	2-1	3-1	0-0	1-1	2-1
9	IFK Norrköping	1-1	1-1	2-0	0-5	1-1	1-1	0-3	0-1		2-2	0-3	1-0	0-2	4-1
10	Trelleborgs FF	1-0	2-2	1-1	2-2	4-0	0-0	0-2	0-0	4-0		2-0	0-0	4-1	1-1
11	Västra Frölunda IF	1-1	0-0	2-2	3-0	1-1	2-6	2-3	0-0	5-1	1-0		1-2	0-1	1-0
12	Örebro SK	3-0	2-2	0-0	1-0	1-0	2-1	4-1	5-0	1-0	2-0	4-4		0-1	1-0
13	Örgryte IS	2-1	0-1	0-2	1-1	0-2	0-1	0-1	0-0	2-1	0-0	1-2	0-0		4-2
14	Östers IF	0-2	2-2	3-1	0-0	3-0	1-1	1-1	2-2	2-3	3-1	4-0	2-2	1-1	

LEAGUE CHAMPIONSHIP FINAL TABLE 1995

			Home					Away					Total						
		Pd	W	D	L	F	A	W	D	L	F	A	W	D	L	F	A	Pt	GD
1	IFK Göteborg	26	9	3	1	24	6	3	7	3	19	14	12	10	4	43	20	46	+23
2	Helsingborgs IF	26	6	2	5	21	20	6	4	3	21	16	12	6	8	42	36	42	+6
3	Halmstads BK	26	7	4	2	24	12	4	4	5	17	20	11	8	7	41	32	41	+9
4	Malmö FF	26	6	5	2	18	13	3	7	3	14	15	9	12	5	32	28	39	+4
5	Örebro SK	26	9	3	1	26	9	1	5	7	9	20	10	8	8	35	29	38	+6
6	Djurgårdens IF	26	5	3	5	18	18	5	5	3	15	15	10	8	8	33	33	38	=
7	Örgryte IS	26	3	4	6	10	14	6	4	3	12	12	9	8	9	22	26	35	-4
8	AIK	26	4	7	2	21	15	3	4	6	13	19	7	11	8	34	34	32	=
9	Degerfors IF	26	5	5	3	16	19	2	6	5	16	26	7	11	8	32	45	32	-13
10	Trelleborgs FF	26	5	7	1	21	9	2	3	8	11	21	7	10	9	32	30	31	+2
11	Östers IF	26	4	7	2	24	16	1	6	6	17	25	5	13	8	41	41	28	=
12	IFK Norrköping	26	3	5	5	13	21	4	2	7	15	23	7	7	12	28	44	28	-16
13	Hammarby IF	26	3	4	6	16	22	3	4	6	17	18	6	8	12	33	40	26	-7
14	Västra Frölunda IF	26	3	6	4	19	18	2	4	7	16	27	5	10	11	35	45	25	-10

position. Their final match, at home to Halmstad, did not even reach its conclusion. After 67 minutes the game was stopped following a serious outbreak of rioting by the home fans. At first it seemed as if the Stockholm club would be punished by enforced relegation, but they eventually escaped with a heavy fine and a two-match spectator ban.

On the same day that Djurgården's fans disgraced themselves, another Stockholm club, Hammarby, were making life easier for IFK Gothenburg by walloping their only remaining title challengers Helsingborg 5-3. That shock scoreline meant that Gothenburg could afford to lose their final match, at home to Trelleborg, and still lift the championship. But the Gothenburg players were eager for their coach to go out on a high, and they won 2-0 with second-half goals from Magnus Erlingmark and Mikael Martinsson. The second-biggest Allsvenskan crowd of the season - 17, 356 - congregated in the Gamla Ullevi stadium to celebrate the Blåvitt's triumph.

Once again Gothenburg had seen off all pretenders to their throne simply by remaining unflustered by bad results and maintaining their stamina through to the end of the 26-match campaign. It helped, of course, that they had by far the strongest squad in the country and were able to withstand injuries and suspensions without any adverse reaction to the overall team performance.

The title win was very much a triumph of the collective. Remarkably, although Gothenburg as a team were the highest scorers in the league with 43 goals, not one of their players contributed more than half a dozen. There was no dominant personality in the team, although an honourable mention is due to defender Mikael Nilsson, the team's joint top scorer and the only player to appear from the start in every match.

Gothenburg could perhaps have done with a stronger individual profile in the UEFA Champions' League. Seeking to reach the lucrative group phase for the second season running, they came fearfully unstuck in their preliminary tie against Legia Warsaw, losing both home and away.

There was, however, to be one more big European night in Gothenburg before the year was out. Halmstad hired out the Gamla Ullevi for the first leg of their second-round Cup-winners' Cup tie against Italian giants Parma, and - lo and behold - conjured up one of the most dramatic scorelines in Europe for many a season, winning 3-0. But that was only half the story. Back in Parma, the Italians staged an equally remarkable fightback to take the tie 4-3 on aggregate and book their place in the quarter-finals.

That defeat in Parma was to be the last match for Halmstad coach Mats Jingblad. He had already signed a

INTERNATIONAL HONOURS

World Cup Finals appearances: 1934 (2nd round), 1938 (4th), 1950 (3rd), 1958 (runners-up), 1970, 1974 (2nd phase), 1978, 1990, 1994 (3rd)

European Championship appearances: 1964, 1992 (semi-finals)

European Club Competitions

UEFA Cup	IFK Göteborg (1982, 1987)

NATIONAL TEAM APPEARANCES 95/96

Coach - Tommy SVENSSON	USA	SUI	SCO	TUR	JPN	AUS	AUS	NIR	SVK	KOR	BLS	Cps	Gls
Bengt ANDERSSON (11/08/66) - Örgryte IS	G	G	G			G		G	G	G46	G	9	-
Roland NILSSON (27/11/63) - Helsingborgs IF	D77				D	D	D	D	D	D73	D	83	1
Patrik ANDERSSON (18/08/71) - Borussia Mönchengladbach (GER)	D	D	D	D				D	D	D	D	43	2
Joachim BJÖRKLUND (15/03/71) - Vicenza (ITA)	D	D	D	D				D	D	D	D	44	-
Pontus KÅMARK (05/04/69) - IFK Göteborg	D	D	s90									28	-
Tomas BROLIN (29/11/69) - Parma (ITA)	M	M78	M	M70								47	26
Jonas THERN (20/03/67) - Roma (ITA)	M	M						M	M46	M	M	64	6
Stefan SCHWARZ (18/04/69) - Fiorentina (ITA)	M	M90	M	M				M				45	6
Stefan LANDBERG (05/05/70) - IFK Göteborg	M74				s104	s68	M					14	1
Kennet ANDERSSON (06/10/67) - Bari (ITA)	A59	A	A81					A59	A	A76	A	49	24
Martin DAHLIN (16/04/68) - Borussia Mönchengladbach (GER)	A	A		A				A80	A	A	A77	47	26
Jörgen PETTERSSON (29/09/75) - Malmö FF/ Borussia Mönchengladbach (GER)	s59		A	A83				s59		s76		5	2
Niklas GUDMUNDSSON (29/02/72) - Halmstads BK	s74		M66									7	-
Mikael NILSSON (28/09/68) - IFK Göteborg	s77	D	M		D	D	D					22	-
Niclas ALEXANDERSSON (29/12/71) - Halmstads BK/IFK Göteborg		M	M	M	M	M	M		s56	s63		16	2
Henrik LARSSON (20/09/71) - Feyenoord (HOL)		s78						s80	s72		s77	25	7
Magnus ERLINGMARK (08/07/68) - IFK Göteborg		s90	s81		M	A	A					34	1
Teddy LUCIC (15/04/73) - Västra Frölunda IF/IFK Göteborg			D90	D	D	D	D			s73		9	-
Martin PRINGLE (18/11/70) - Helsingborgs IF			s66		s45/104							2	-
Thomas RAVELLI (13/08/59) - IFK Göteborg				G	G		G					130	-
Håkan MILD (14/06/71) - IFK Göteborg				M	M	M	M59			M63	s85	31	5
Christer FURSTH (06/07/70) - Helsingborgs IF				M								4	-
Pär ZETTERBERG (14/10/70) - RSC Anderlecht (BEL)				s70				s46	s46	M	M	13	1
Dan SAHLIN (18/04/67) - Hammarby IF/Örebro SK				s83	A46							2	-
Christian KARLSSON (20/09/69) - Malmö FF					D	D						2	-
Magnus SVENSSON (10/03/69) - Halmstads BK					M	M68						2	-
Mattias JONSSON (16/01/74) - Helsingborgs IF					A80		s68					2	-
Sebastian HENRIKSSON (21/10/74) - Örgryte IS					s80	M56						2	-
Andreas ANDERSSON (10/04/74) - IFK Göteborg						A	A68					2	2
Peter WIBRÅN (23/03/69) - Helsingborgs IF						s56	M	M46	M56			5	-
Andreas JACOBSSON (06/10/72) - Helsingborgs IF							D					1	-
Anders ANDERSSON (15/03/74) - Malmö FF							s59					2	-
Gary SUNDGREN (25/10/67) - AIK								D	D	D	D	8	-
Klas INGESSON (20/08/68) - Bari (ITA)								M	M		M85	56	13
Anders LIMPAR (24/09/65) - Everton (ENG)									M72	M	M	56	6
Jonnie FEDEL (22/11/66) - Malmö FF										s46		2	-

contract to replace Roger Gustafsson at champions IFK Gothenburg. He certainly earned his 'promotion', having taken Halmstad to victory in the Swedish Cup and into Europe two years on the trot. Jingblad also took with him Halmstad's young midfielder Niclas Alexandersson, who joined fellow Swedish internationals Andreas Andersson (Degerfors) and Teddy Lucic (Västra Frölunda) as IFK Gothenburg's chief recruits for the 1996 season.

Lucic ended the 1995 campaign with a relegated team. Västra Frölunda were able to beat champions Gothenburg 3-0 and supply the league's leading scorer in Swedish U-21 striker Niklas Skoog. But their inconsistency condemned them. Hammarby, like Västra Frölunda, were relegated a year after surviving in the end-of-season play-offs. The Stockholm club also had their own scoring sensation in Dan Sahlin, but not even his 12 goals - six in the last three matches - could save them.

One major turn-up at the foot of the table was Norrköping's appearance in the play-off zone. The Allsvenskan regulars were just one game away from relegation, but clawed their way to a 1-0 victory over GAIS and thus managed to preserve their long-held top-flight status. Östers IF also won their play-off, 4-0 against Gefle, so that left just two teams promoted, divisional champions Umeå FC and IK Oddevold, neither of whom had experienced life at the top before.

A season of surprises from the little clubs continued in the Swedish Cup where, sensationally, IFK Gothenburg fell at the hands of tiny IF Sylvia. The final, in May 1996, was a north-south derby between AIK, the 1995 beaten finalists, and Malmö FF, attempting to win their first trophy of the 1990s. The match was decided in extra-time by a golden goal from AIK striker Pascal Simpson, giving the black-and-yellows a place in the 96/97 Cup-winners' Cup. Normally Malmö's defeat would have seen their hopes of a place in Europe dashed. But the granting of an extra 'Fair Play' place to Sweden enabled Lars Zetterlund's team to return to the UEFA Cup, where they had unluckily lost out to Nottingham Forest on the away-goals rule in the 95/96 competition.

Had Malmö won the Cup, that 'Fair Play' bonus ball would have bounced the way of fifth-placed Örebro, whose 95/96 UEFA Cup campaign began and ended in

DOMESTIC CUP RESULTS

1/8 FINALS
AIK 2, GIF Sundsvall 1 (asd)
Malmö FF 0, Halmstads BK 0 (aet; 4-3 on pens.)
Örgryte IS 4, IF Elfsborg 0
Östers IF 4, IK Sirius FK 3 (asd)
Hammarby IF 2, Västra Frölunda IF 1
IF Brommapojkarna 1, Degerfors IF 0
IF Sylvia 2, IFK Göteborg 1
IFK Malmö FK 4, IS Halmia 3

QUARTER-FINALS
AIK 2, Örgryte IS 1
Malmö FF 2, Östers IF 1 (asd)
Hammarby IF 3, IF Sylvia 0
IF Brommapojkarna 1, IFK Malmö FK 0 (asd)

SEMI-FINALS
AIK 1, Hammarby IF 0
Malmö FF 3, IF Brommapojkarna 1

FINAL
23/05/96, Gothenburg
AIK 1 Simpson (102)
MALMÖ FF 0
(asd)
referee - Fällström
AIK - Hedman; Millqvist, Englund, Mjällby, Sundgren; Nordin, Lagerlöf (Johansson M. 80), Andersson O., Ciardi; Lidman (Fredholm 84), Simpson.
MALMÖ FF - Fedel; Olsson J., Karlsson C., Wirmola; Nylén, Andersson D., Andersson A., Persson J., Fjellström; Kindvall (Olsson P. 73), Andrijevski (Osmanovski 73).

TOP SCORERS

17	Niklas SKOOG (Västra Frölunda IF)
15	Jörgen PETTERSSON (Malmö FF)
13	Andreas ANDERSSON (Degerfors IF)
12	Patrik KARLSSON (IFK Norrköping)
	Miroslaw KUBISZTAL (Örebro SK)
	Dan SAHLIN (Hammarby IF)
11	Niklas GUDMUNDSSON (Halmstads BK)
	Bo ANDERSSON (Djurgårdens IF)
	Robert ANDERSSON (Halmstads BK)
	Hans EKLUND (Östers IF)

NATIONAL TEAM RESULTS 95/96

16/08/95	United States	H	Norrköping	1-0	Brolin (86p)
06/09/95	Switzerland (ECQ)	H	Gothenburg	0-0	
11/10/95	Scotland	H	Solna	2-0	Pettersson (31), Schwarz (36)
15/11/95	Turkey (ECQ)	H	Solna	2-2	Alexandersson (25), Pettersson (64)
22/02/96	Japan	N	Hong Kong	1-1	Pringle (52)
25/02/96	Australia	A	Brisbane	2-0	Andersson Andreas (86, 88)
28/02/96	Australia	A	Sydney	0-0	
24/04/96	Northern Ireland	A	Belfast	2-1	Dahlin (22), Ingesson (58)
09/05/96	Slovakia	H	Helsingborg	2-1	Dahlin (51), Zeman (85og)
16/05/96	South Korea	A	Seoul	2-0	Dahlin (13), Limpar (59)
01/06/96	Belarus (WCQ)	H	Solna	5-1	Andersson K. (20p, 62), Dahlin (30), Andersson P. (77), Larsson (87)

the preliminary round. On the field Örebro just scraped through with a late away goal against Luxembourg's Avenir Beggen, but the man who scored what he believed to be the decisive goal, Iceland's Hlynur Birgisson, should not have been on the pitch. Although he came on as a substitute for Polish striker Miroslaw Kubisztal, he was the fourth foreigner Örebro fielded during the match. That was against the rules. A statutory 3-0 victory was awarded to Beggen, and Örebro, victims of their own silly mistake, were out.

Early misery for Swedish clubs in Europe coincided with the national team's predictable failure to reach the European Championship finals in England. Even if Sweden had won their last two matches, at home to the Group Three front-runners Switzerland and Turkey, they would still have collected insufficient points to oust their rivals from the two qualifying places.

The damage had been done much earlier on, with three successive away defeats. In the event, the Swedes could only manage two draws from their final two matches, leaving themselves with an unenviable record of just two wins from eight games.

For a couple of weeks after the team's elimination, there were doubts about whether Tommy Svensson would continue in his rôle as national coach. But eventually he signed a new contract lasting through to the World Cup finals in 1998.

Despite the magnitude of their European Championship failure, Sweden should not be overstretched in their quest to reach France. They have been drawn in a relatively straightforward group. The only teams who might trouble them are Austria and Scotland, and their recent record against both of those countries is good. Sweden helped to eliminate Austria en route to the 1994 World Cup finals, and Svensson's team easily defeated the Scots 2-0 in a friendly in October 1995.

Svensson actually used that match to experiment with a new 3-5-2 sweeper system. He tried it again in the final Euro '96 qualifier against Turkey, but by the end of the season he had reverted back to his tried-and-trusted

EUROPEAN CUPS RESULTS 95/96

CHAMPIONS' CUP

● IFK GÖTEBORG

Preliminary round LEGIA WARSZAWA (POL)

A 0-1
Ravelli (Last 43); Kåmark, Johansson, Ohlsson, Nilsson, Martinsson, Landberg, Erlingmark, Blomqvist (Eriksson 57), Lilienberg (Wahlstedt 81), Pettersson.

H 1-2 Blomqvist (25)
Last; Kåmark, Johansson, Ohlsson, Nilsson, Landberg (Eriksson 69), Erlingmark, Lindqvist, Blomqvist, Lilienberg (Wahlstedt 50), Pettersson.

CUP-WINNERS' CUP

● HALMSTADS BK

1st round LOKOMOTIV SOFIA (BUL)

A 1-3 Svensson M. (33)
Svensson H.; Borgstrand, Mattsson, Andersson T., Andersson F., Alexandersson (Ljungberg), Johansson-Smith, Arvidsson (Vougt), Svensson M., Andersson R., Gudmundsson.

H 2-0 Andersson R. (22), Andersson T. (75)
Svensson H.; Borgstrand, Mattsson, Andersson T., Andersson F., Alexandersson (Ljungberg), Johansson-Smith, Arvidsson, Svensson M., Andersson R. (Vougt), Gudmundsson.

2nd round PARMA (ITA)

H 3-0 Gudmundsson (7, 31), Andersson R. (75)
Svensson H.; Borgstrand, Mattsson, Andersson T., Arvidsson, Alexandersson, Johansson-Smith, Ljungberg, Svensson M., Andersson R., Gudmundsson.

A 0-4
Svensson H.; Borgstrand, Mattsson, Andersson T., Andersson F., Ljungberg, Johansson-Smith, Alexandersson, Svensson M., Andersson R., Vougt (Stierna 85).

UEFA CUP

● ÖREBRO SK

Preliminary round AVENIR BEGGEN (LUX)

H 0-0
Karlsson A.; Sköldmark, Karlsson M., Andersson T., Ståhl, Andersson M. (Karlsson P.), Stefánsson, Kubisztal, Rasck (Birgisson), Jonsson, Wowoah (Pelgander).

A 1-1 Birgisson (88) (later awarded as 0-3)
Karlsson A.; Karlsson M., Andersson T., Ståhl, Gudjohnsen, Peglander (Wahlqvist), Stefánsson, Zetterlund, Rasck (Andersson H.), Jonsson, Kubisztal (Birgisson).

● MALMÖ FF

Preliminary round DUNDALK (IRL)

A 2-0 Pettersson (1), Andersson A. (11)
Fedel; Nylén, Olsson J., Wirmola, Persson P., Persson J. (Nilsson 62), Prytz, Andersson D., Fjellström, Andersson A., Pettersson (Olsson P. 48)

H 2-0 Andersson A. (22), Fjellström (50)
Fedel; Nylén, Olsson J., Wirmola, Persson T., Persson J., Prytz, Thylander (Andersson D.), Fjellström, Andersson A., Pettersson.

1st round NOTTINGHAM FOREST (ENG)

H 2-1 Persson J. (59), Andersson A. (72)
Fedel; Nylén, Olsson J., Wirmola, Persson T., Persson J., Prytz, Andersson D., Fjellström (Thylander 75), Andersson A., Pettersson.

A 0-1
Fedel; Nylén, Olsson J., Wirmola, Persson T., Andersson D. (Dahlström 75), Persson J., Prytz, Fjellström (Olsson P. 61), Andersson A., Pettersson.

4-4-2, the logic being that Sweden had reached third place in America playing that way and, in any case, it was a system which his main central defenders, Patrik Andersson and Joachim Björklund, were accustomed to playing in at their respective clubs.

After a winter tour to Australia and the Far East, during which Svensson was able to size up a number of untried international hopefuls from the Allsvenskan such as striker Andreas Andersson and defender Christian Karlsson, Sweden warmed up for the World Cup with three friendly internationals, for which the regular 'exiles' were recalled and which all resulted in victory. Despite the successful restoration of his old formation and the return to goalscoring form of Martin Dahlin, there was nothing else in those three games which suggested that Sweden would begin their World Cup qualifying campaign with quite so much brio and confidence as they did.

The 5-1 destruction of Belarus in Solna turned out to be one of the team's finest performances in years. Kennet Andersson, fresh from a fine first season in Italy, opened the scoring from the penalty spot, and thereafter Sweden were irresistible, running up a further five goals. It was a great way to start the journey to France and an opportune reminder to those teams waiting to compete at Euro '96 that Sweden are still a force to be reckoned with in international football.

PLAYERS OF THE SEASON

JÖRGEN PETTERSSON

Although Malmö FF remained without a trophy for the sixth season in a row, they did provide the outstanding individual of the 1995 season in fresh-faced young striker Jörgen Pettersson. The 20-year-old redhead was a consistent goalscorer throughout the campaign, finishing up with a total of 15 goals, one better than his 1994 total but two short of the 17-goal tally with which Västra Frölunda's Niklas Skoog topped the scoring charts. Pettersson is not just a goalscorer. He also has tremendous natural skill. Malmö were always going to struggle to hold on to him, and it was no surprise when he joined the Swedish clan at German club Borussia Mönchengladbach in November 1995, three months after making his senior international début for Sweden.

MARTIN DAHLIN

Awaiting Pettersson at Mönchengladbach was another ex-Malmö FF striker, Martin Dahlin, midway through his fifth and most successful season at the German club. Dahlin has always been a major star for Sweden, but until 1995/96 he had always found it difficult to impose himself in the Bundesliga. Perseverance paid off, however, for the 28-year-old as he rattled in the goals like never before - 15 in just 23 appearances - to help Gladbach into a respectable fourth place in the Bundesliga. His early injury in the European Cup-winners' Cup quarter-final against Feyenoord was a major blow, but Dahlin recovered in time to make his mark once more on the international stage with goals in four successive games for Sweden, taking his all-time international total to a remarkable 26 goals in 47 games, a record identical to that of his national team colleague Tomas Brolin.

NICLAS ALEXANDERSSON

The rise to prominence of Halmstads BK in the last couple of years owes a great deal to the work of coach Mats Jingblad and his handling of the team's many young up-and-coming stars. One of those players is Niclas Alexandersson (pictured above), who has now joined Jingblad at IFK Gothenburg for a Swedish domestic record fee, having helped Halmstad to Swedish Cup success and third place in the Allsvenskan in his final season. At 24, Alexandersson is one of the few newcomers to have earned himself a regular berth in the Swedish national team since the 1994 World Cup. A right-sided midfielder with a strong engine and a good mental attitude, he seems certain to move to a top foreign club when his Gothenburg contract expires at the end of 1997.

AIK

CLUB DIRECTORY

Allmänna Idrottsklubben
Box 1408
171 27 Solna
tel - (08) 7359600
fax - (08) 7359696
Year of Formation - 1891
President - Sune Hellströmer
Director - Stefan Söderberg
Coach - Hans Backe & Erik Hamrén
(96 - Erik Hamrén)
Stadium - Råsunda Stadion (36.000)

MAJOR HONOURS

League Championship - (9) 1900, 1901, 1911, 1914, 1916, 1923, 1932, 1937, 1992.
Domestic Cup - (5)
1949, 1950, 1976, 1985, 1996.

APPEARANCES 95

	P	Ap	(s)	Gls
Matts ANDERSSON	G	1		
Ola ANDERSSON	M	26		
Michael BORGQVIST	M	6	(5)	
Marco CIARDI	M	22		2
Patrick ENGLUND	D	13		3
Jan ERIKSSON	D	7		
Fredrik ESPMARK	D	21		
Pierre GALLO	M	3	(5)	
Magnus HEDMAN	G	25		
Jesper JANSSON	M	9		2
Mattias JOHANSSON	M	19	(4)	4
Robert JOHANSSON	A	4	(7)	3
Thomas LAGERLÖF	D	11	(7)	
Dick LIDMAN	A	22	(1)	7
Johan MJÄLLBY	D	19		
Krister NORDIN	M	23	(1)	3
Per OLSSON	M		(2)	
Jarmo SAASTAMOINEN	D	8		
Pascal SIMPSON	A	21	(3)	6
Gary SUNDGREN	D	25		2
Alexander ÖSTLUND	A	1	(2)	1

LEAGUE RESULTS 1995

Date	Opponent		Score	Scorers
09/04/95	Östers IF	A	2-0	Lidman, Jansson
17/04/95	Örgryte IS	H	0-0	
01/05/95	Trelleborgs FF	A	0-1	
08/05/95	Hammarby IF	H	3-2	Jansson, og (Lefvert), Johansson R.
15/05/95	Degerfors IF	H	1-2	Johansson R.
18/05/95	Djurgårdens IF	A	2-1	Nordin, Johansson R.
21/05/95	IFK Göteborg	H	3-1	Lidman 2, Nordin (p)
28/05/95	Malmö FF	A	2-2	Nordin, Johansson M.
14/06/95	Örebro SK	A	0-3	
20/06/95	IFK Norrköping	H	2-2	Lidman, Ciardi
28/06/95	Västra Frölunda IF	H	1-1	Ciardi
03/07/95	Helsingborgs IF	A	1-2	Simpson
29/07/95	Halmstads BK	A	0-3	
03/08/95	Halmstads BK	H	2-2	Johansson M., Englund
13/08/95	Helsingborgs IF	H	1-1	Simpson
21/08/95	Västra Frölunda IF	A	1-1	Simpson
28/08/95	Trelleborgs FF	H	3-0	Englund, Simpson 2
31/08/95	Hammarby IF	A	2-1	Johansson M., Lidman
10/09/95	Degerfors IF	A	1-2	Sundgren
19/09/95	Djurgårdens IF	H	1-2	Lidman
25/09/95	IFK Göteborg	A	0-0	
01/10/95	Malmö FF	H	1-1	Englund
08/10/95	Örgryte IS	A	1-2	Johansson M.
16/10/95	Östers IF	H	1-1	Sundgren
23/10/95	IFK Norrköping	A	1-1	Lidman
28/10/95	Örebro SK	H	2-0	Simpson, Östlund

DEGERFORS IF

CLUB DIRECTORY

Degerfors Idrottsförening
Box 17
693 21 Degerfors
tel - (0586) 40140/40540
fax - (0586) 41084
Year of Formation - 1907
President - Yngve Hjärpe
Secretary - Gunnar Walldén
Coach - Sören Cratz
Stadium - Stora Valla (15,800)

MAJOR HONOURS
Domestic Cup - (1) 1993.

APPEARANCES 95

	P	Ap	(s)	Gls
Andreas ANDERSSON	A	25	(1)	13
Henrik BERGER	M	11	(8)	1
Ivan DJURIC	D	13	(1)	
Jonas GRANATH	D	23		2
Ulf KARLSSON	G	20		
Aleksandar KRISTIC (YUG)	M	7		
Dan LARSSON	G	6		
Mikael MÅRTENSSON	D	26		2
Leif OLSSON	M	8	(3)	1
Tomas OLSSON	M	8	(9)	1
Ulf OTTOSSON	A	24	(1)	9
Dusko RADINOVIC (YUG)	D	26		
Jonny RÖDLUND	M	13	(3)	1
Vujadin STANOJKOVIC (MAC)	D	7		
Ola SVENSSON	M	13	(7)	
Daniel TJERNSTRÖM	M	10	(11)	
Milenko VUKCEVIC (YUG)	M	25		1
Patrik WERNER	A		(3)	1
Mikael ÖHRMAN	D	21	(3)	

LEAGUE RESULTS 1995

Date	Opponent	H/A	Score	Scorers
09/04/95	Malmö FF	H	0-3	
17/04/95	Västra Frölunda IF	A	0-0	
01/05/95	Djurgårdens IF	A	0-2	
08/05/95	Halmstads BK	H	3-3	Andersson 3
15/05/95	AIK	A	2-1	Andersson, Ottosson
18/05/95	Helsingborgs IF	H	2-2	Granath, Andersson
22/05/95	Örebro SK	A	2-2	Olsson T., Olsson L.
28/05/95	IFK Norrköping	H	0-3	
14/06/95	Östers IF	A	2-2	Ottosson 2
19/06/95	Örgryte IS	H	0-0	
25/06/95	Trelleborgs FF	A	2-2	Ottosson 2
02/07/95	Hammarby IF	H	0-0	
30/07/95	IFK Göteborg	A	0-3	
05/08/95	IFK Göteborg	H	0-3	
14/08/95	Hammarby IF	A	1-2	Ottosson
20/08/95	Trelleborgs FF	H	1-0	Granath
27/08/95	Djurgårdens IF	H	1-1	Mårtensson
31/08/95	Halmstads BK	A	1-5	Rödlund
10/09/95	AIK	H	2-1	Vukcevic, Andersson
17/09/95	Helsingborgs IF	A	3-3	Ottosson, Mårtensson, Andersson
23/09/95	Örebro SK	H	2-1	Andersson, Berger
07/10/95	Västra Frölunda IF	H	2-0	Ottosson, Andersson
15/10/95	Malmö FF	A	1-3	Werner
19/10/95	IFK Norrköping	A	1-1	Andersson
23/10/95	Örgryte IS	A	1-0	Andersson
28/10/95	Östers IF	H	3-2	Andersson 2, Ottosson

DJURGÅRDENS IF

CLUB DIRECTORY

Djurgårdens Idrottsförening
Klocktornet
Olympiastadion
114 33 Stockholm
tel - (08) 4115711
fax - (08) 211583
Year of Formation - 1891
President - Mats Olsson
Secretary - Dan Svanell
Coach - Anders Grönhagen
Stadium - Stockholm Stadion (12,500)

MAJOR HONOURS

League Championship - (8) 1912, 1915, 1917, 1920, 1955, 1959, 1964, 1966.
Domestic Cup - (1) 1990.

APPEARANCES 95

	P	Ap	(s)	Gls
Stefan ALVÉN	D	24		
Bo ANDERSSON	A	23		11
Johan ANDERSSON	D	20		2
Kenneth BERGQVIST	D	25		
Kaj ESKELINEN	M	25		8
Stefan JANSSON	M	1	(1)	
Peter LANGEMAR	D	5		
Kenneth MARON	D	5		
Daniel MARTINEZ	M	5	(6)	1
Darko MAVRAK	M	18	(4)	1
Mikael NILSSON	D	11	(7)	
Nebojsa NOVAKOVIC	A	23		6
Thor-André OLSEN (NOR)	G	26		
Magnus PEHRSSON	M	25		2
Fred PERSSON	M	19	(1)	1
Kleber SAARENPÄÄ	D	14	(1)	1
Ferdinand SIPÖCZ	A	2		
Zoran STOJCEVSKI	M	15	(4)	
Martin ÅSLUND	M		(8)	

LEAGUE RESULTS 1995

10/04/95	IFK Göteborg	H	1-1	Eskelinen
17/04/95	Malmö FF	A	0-0	
01/05/95	Degerfors IF	H	2-0	Novakovic 2
09/05/95	Västra Frölunda IF	A	2-2	Andersson B., Martinez
15/05/95	IFK Norrköping	A	0-2	
18/05/95	AIK	H	1-2	Andersson B.
22/05/95	Hammarby IF	A	1-0	Eskelinen
28/05/95	Örebro SK	H	2-0	Andersson B., Persson F.
14/06/95	Halmstads BK	A	2-1	Andersson J., Eskelinen
19/06/95	Östers IF	H	1-1	Andersson B.
26/06/95	Örgryte IS	A	2-0	Persson M., Eskelinen (p)
03/07/95	Trelleborgs FF	H	1-1	Persson M.
30/07/95	Helsingborgs IF	A	3-2	Andersson B. 2, Novakovic
07/08/95	Helsingborgs IF	H	1-3	Andersson B.
13/08/95	Trelleborgs FF	A	1-1	Novakovic
21/08/95	Örgryte IS	H	1-3	Andersson J.
27/08/95	Degerfors IF	A	1-1	Andersson B.
01/09/95	Västra Frölunda IF	H	4-2	Novakovic 2, Andersson B., Eskelinen (p)
10/09/95	IFK Norrköping	H	2-0	Eskelinen 2
19/09/95	AIK	A	2-1	Andersson B., Mavrak
25/09/95	Hammarby IF	H	2-0	Saarenpää, Eskelinen
08/10/95	Malmö FF	H	0-2	
16/10/95	IFK Göteborg	A	0-2	
19/10/95	Örebro SK	A	0-0	
23/10/95	Östers IF	A	1-3	Andersson B.
28/10/95	Halmstads BK	H	0-2	(later awarded as 0-3)

IFK GÖTEBORG

CLUB DIRECTORY

Idrottsföreningen Kamraterna Göteborg
Alfreds Gärdes Väg
416 55 Göteborg
tel - (031) 408600
fax - (031) 404121
Year of Formation - 1904
President - Gunnar Larsson
Secretary - Ronny Sjölund
Coach - Roger Gustafsson (96 - Mats Jingbladh)
Stadium - Gamla Ullevi (18,000)

MAJOR HONOURS
League Championship - (16) 1908, 1910, 1918, 1935, 1942, 1958, 1969, 1982, 1983, 1984, 1987, 1990, 1991, 1993, 1994, 1995.
Domestic Cup - (4) 1979, 1982, 1983, 1991.
UEFA Cup - (2) 1982, 1987.

APPEARANCES 95

		P	Ap	(s)	Gls
Joachim BJÖRKLUND	D	12		
Jesper BLOMQVIST	M	15	(3)	3
Peter ERIKSSON	M	1	(2)	
Magnus ERLINGMARK	M	24	(2)	5
Magnus JOHANSSON	D	18	(2)	1
Pontus KÅMARK	D	18	(2)	1
Stefan LANDBERG	M	21	(2)	4
Dick LAST	G	6		
Mats LILIENBERG	A	15	(8)	6
Stefan LINDQVIST	M	23	(2)	4
Olof MAGNUSSON	D	1	(1)	
Mikael MARTINSSON	M	20	(1)	4
Håkan MILD	M	7	(2)	2
Mikael NILSSON	D	26		6
Jonas OLSSON	D	25		1
Stefan PETTERSSON	A	17	(3)	4
Thomas RAVELLI	G	20		
Stefan REHN	M	10	(1)	2
Erik WAHLSTEDT	A	7	(6)	

LEAGUE RESULTS 1995

10/04/95	Djurgårdens IF	A	1-1	Rehn
15/04/95	Halmstads BK	H	0-1	
01/05/95	Östers IF	A	0-0	
08/05/95	Örgryte IS	H	3-0	Nilsson, Martinsson, Erlingmark
13/05/95	Västra Frölunda IF	H	1-1	Erlingmark
18/05/95	Malmö FF	A	1-1	Lilienberg
21/05/95	AIK	A	1-3	Erlingmark
28/05/95	Helsingborgs IF	H	1-1	Rehn
20/06/95	Hammarby IF	H	2-0	Olsson, Lindqvist
26/06/95	Örebro SK	A	0-1	
29/06/95	Trelleborgs FF	A	2-2	Nilsson, Lilienberg
05/07/95	IFK Norrköping	H	2-0	Martinsson, Landberg
30/07/95	Degerfors IF	H	3-0	Pettersson, Lilienberg 2
05/08/95	Degerfors IF	A	3-0	Lilienberg 2, Pettersson
13/08/95	IFK Norrköping	A	5-0	Nilsson 2, Landberg 2, Kåmark
19/08/95	Örebro SK	H	3-1	Johansson, Lindqvist 2
28/08/95	Östers IF	H	3-1	Erlingmark, Blomqvist, Pettersson
31/08/95	Örgryte IS	A	1-1	Pettersson (p)
09/09/95	Västra Frölunda IF	A	0-3	
17/09/95	Malmö FF	H	2-1	Blomqvist, Nilsson
25/09/95	AIK	H	0-0	
02/10/95	Helsingborgs IF	A	3-0	Landberg, Martinsson, Blomqvist
07/10/95	Halmstads BK	A	0-0	
16/10/95	Djurgårdens IF	H	2-0	Lindqvist, Martinsson
23/10/95	Hammarby IF	A	2-2	Mild 2
28/10/95	Trelleborgs FF	H	2-0	Erlingmark, Nilsson

HALMSTADS BK

CLUB DIRECTORY

Halmstads Bollklubb
Box 223
301 06 Halmstad
tel - (035) 103285
fax - (035) 103436
Year of Formation - 1914
President - Stig Nilsson
Director - Mikael Kaller
Coach - Mats Jingbladh (96 - Tom Prahl)
Stadium - Örjans Vall (15,000)

MAJOR HONOURS
League Championship - (2) 1976, 1979.
Domestic Cup - (1) 1995.

APPEARANCES 95

	P	Ap	(s)	Gls
Niclas ALEXANDERSSON	M	26		5
Fredrik ANDERSSON	D	26		2
Robert ANDERSSON	A	26		11
Tommy ANDERSSON	D	26		3
Torbjörn ARVIDSSON	M	20	(2)	2
Joel BORGSTRAND	D	20	(2)	
Niklas GUDMUNDSSON	A	25	(1)	11
Andreas HEDSTRÖM	M		(1)	
Marcus JÖNSSON	D		(2)	
Mattias KARLSSON	M		(1)	
Peter LENNARTSSON	M	10	(1)	
Fredrik LJUNGBERG	M	7	(9)	1
Jesper MATTSSON	D	25		
Anders SMITH	M	21	(1)	1
Tomas STIERNA	A	1	(7)	
Håkan SVENSSON	G	26		
Magnus SVENSSON	M	15	(6)	2
Peter VOUGT	A	12	(8)	2

LEAGUE RESULTS 1995

09/04/95	Helsingborgs IF	H	2-1	Vougt, Andersson R.
15/04/95	IFK Göteborg	A	1-0	Gudmundsson
01/05/95	Malmö FF	H	2-2	Andersson R., Arvidsson
08/05/95	Degerfors IF	A	3-3	Andersson R., Svensson M., Andersson T.
14/05/95	Örebro SK	A	0-1	
18/05/95	IFK Norrköping	H	2-0	Smith, Andersson F.
21/05/95	Trelleborgs FF	A	0-4	
28/05/95	Hammarby IF	H	1-0	Gudmundsson
14/06/95	Djurgårdens IF	H	1-2	Vougt
19/06/95	Västra Frölunda IF	A	1-1	Andersson R.
28/06/95	Östers IF	A	0-3	
02/07/95	Örgryte IS	H	2-0	Svensson M., Gudmundsson
29/07/95	AIK	H	3-0	Alexandersson, Andersson R., Gudmundsson
03/08/95	AIK	A	2-2	Gudmundsson 2
10/08/95	Örgryte IS	A	2-0	Andersson R. 2
20/08/95	Östers IF	H	2-2	Andersson T. (p), Gudmundsson
28/08/95	Malmö FF	A	1-2	Andersson R.
31/08/95	Degerfors IF	H	5-1	Alexandersson 3, Gudmundsson, Andersson F.
09/09/95	Örebro SK	H	2-1	Arvidsson, Ljungberg
18/09/95	IFK Norrköping	A	1-1	Andersson R.
24/09/95	Trelleborgs FF	H	1-2	Gudmundsson
02/10/95	Hammarby IF	A	3-0	Andersson R., Alexandersson, Gudmundsson
07/10/95	IFK Göteborg	H	0-0	
15/10/95	Helsingborgs IF	A	0-3	
23/10/95	Västra Frölunda IF	H	1-1	Gudmundsson
28/10/95	Djurgårdens IF	A	2-0	Andersson R., Andersson T. (later awarded as 3-0)

HAMMARBY IF

CLUB DIRECTORY

Hammarby Idtrottsförening
Box 200 56
104 60 Stockholm
tel - (08) 6413592
fax - (08) 6431113
Year of Formation - 1897
President - Ulf Edstedt
Secretary - Tomas Eriksson
Coach - Tommy Davidsson (96 - Göran Göransson)
Stadium - Söderstadion (10,200)

APPEARANCES 95

	P	Ap	(s)	Gls
Andreas ALM	D	11		1
Lasse ASP	M		(2)	
Peter BERGGREN	D	24	(2)	2
Hans BERGH	M	20	(4)	2
Niclas BERGH	D	15		
Kim BERGSTRAND	A	24		8
Johan BLOMGREN	M	2	(3)	
Hans ESKILSSON	A	2	(8)	
Per FAHLSTRÖM	G	26		
Jens GUSTAFSON	M	20	(5)	2
Johan HAMMARSTRÖM	D	26		1
Mikael HELLSTRÖM	M	24		
Magnus LEFVERT	D	5	(6)	1
Cebrail MERMER	A		(1)	
Michael MÖLLER	D	16		
Anders PREZENT	M	1	(2)	1
Dan SAHLIN	A	24		12
Leif STRANDH	M	14	(9)	1
Peter THÖRNQVIST	D	16	(4)	
Jean-Paul VON DER BURG	D	16		1

LEAGUE RESULTS 1995

09/04/95	Västra Frölunda IF	H	3-1	Sahlin, Bergstrand 2
17/04/95	Örebro SK	A	1-2	Gustafson
01/05/95	IFK Norrköping	H	0-2	
08/05/95	AIK	A	2-3	Sahlin 2
13/05/95	Östers IF	H	2-2	Gustafson, Bergstrand
17/05/95	Örgryte IS	A	1-0	Bergh H. (p)
22/05/95	Djurgårdens IF	H	0-1	
28/05/95	Halmstads BK	A	0-1	
14/06/95	Helsingborgs IF	H	2-1	Hammarström, Sahlin
20/06/95	IFK Göteborg	A	0-2	
26/06/95	Malmö FF	H	1-1	Sahlin
02/07/95	Degerfors IF	A	0-0	
31/07/95	Trelleborgs FF	H	1-3	og (Blixt)
07/08/95	Trelleborgs FF	A	0-0	
14/08/95	Degerfors IF	H	2-1	Bergstrand (p), Berggren
20/08/95	Malmö FF	A	0-1	
28/08/95	IFK Norrköping	A	1-1	Bergstrand
31/08/95	AIK	H	1-2	Berggren
11/09/95	Östers IF	A	1-1	Sahlin
18/09/95	Örgryte IS	H	0-1	
25/09/95	Djurgårdens IF	A	0-2	
02/10/95	Halmstads BK	H	0-3	
07/10/95	Örebro SK	H	2-2	Von der Burg, Bergstrand
15/10/95	Västra Frölunda IF	A	6-2	Bergstrand 2, Sahlin 3, Strandh
23/10/95	IFK Göteborg	H	2-2	Sahlin, Lefvert
28/10/95	Helsingborgs IF	A	5-3	Sahlin 2, Bergh H., Prezent, Alm

HELSINGBORGS IF

CLUB DIRECTORY

Helsingborgs Idrottsförening
Box 2074
250 02 Helsingborg
tel - (042) 199400
fax - (042) 180606
Year of Formation - 1907
President - Ingvar Wenehed
Secretary - Claes Johansson
Coach - Reine Almqvist
Stadium - Olympia (16,000)

MAJOR HONOURS
League Championship - (5)
1929, 1930, 1933, 1934, 1941.
Domestic Cup - (1) 1941.

APPEARANCES 95

	P	Ap	(s)	Gls
Patrick ANDERSSON	A	9	(9)	1
Sven ANDERSSON	G	26		
Jonas DAHLGREN	M	22	(4)	6
Christer FURSTH	M	26		4
Andreas JACOBSSON	D	25		2
Ulrik JANSSON	M	16	(5)	2
Anders JÖNSSON	D	24		
Peter HILLGREN	A	8		2
Marcus LANTZ	M	7	(3)	2
Jesper LJUNG	M	20	(5)	6
Per-Ola LJUNG	D	8	(10)	
Ola NILSSON	D	25		
Roland NILSSON	D	15	(1)	1
Magnus POWELL	A	10	(13)	5
Martin PRINGLE	A	19	(3)	7
Christoffer SKOOG	M		(1)	
Urban STOLTZ	D	4	(2)	1
Patrik SUNDSTRÖM	M	22	(1)	3

LEAGUE RESULTS 1995

Date	Opponent		Score	Scorers
09/04/95	Halmstads BK	A	1-2	Lantz
17/04/95	Östers IF	H	0-2	
01/05/95	Örgryte IS	A	1-0	Lantz
08/05/95	Trelleborgs FF	H	2-1	Ljung J., Hillgren
15/05/95	Malmö FF	H	2-1	Hillgren, Jansson
18/05/95	Degerfors IF	A	2-2	Andersson P., Ljung J.
21/05/95	Västra Frölunda IF	H	1-0	Sundström
28/05/95	IFK Göteborg	A	1-1	Pringle
14/06/95	Hammarby IF	A	1-2	Pringle
19/06/95	Örebro SK	H	3-0	Powell, Pringle, Sundström
28/06/95	IFK Norrköping	A	3-0	Ljung J., Powell, Stoltz
03/07/95	AIK	H	2-1	Pringle, Ljung J.
30/07/95	Djurgårdens IF	H	2-3	Powell, Pringle
07/08/95	Djurgårdens IF	A	3-1	Powell, Nilsson, Dahlgren
13/08/95	AIK	A	1-1	Fursth
20/08/95	IFK Norrköping	H	0-0	
27/08/95	Örgryte IS	H	0-1	
31/08/95	Trelleborgs FF	A	2-0	Jacobsson (p), Powell
10/09/95	Malmö FF	A	1-0	Ljung J.
17/09/95	Degerfors IF	H	3-3	Pringle, Sundström, Dahlgren
24/09/95	Västra Frölunda IF	A	3-2	Ljung J., Dahlgren, Pringle
02/10/95	IFK Göteborg	H	0-3	
08/10/95	Östers IF	A	1-1	Jacobsson
15/10/95	Halmstads BK	H	3-0	Fursth (p), Dahlgren 2
23/10/95	Örebro SK	A	1-4	Dahlgren
28/10/95	Hammarby IF	H	3-5	Fursth 2 (1p), Jansson

MALMÖ FF

CLUB DIRECTORY

Malmö Fotbollförening
Box 19067
200 73 Malmö
tel - (040) 194245
fax - (040) 191707
Year of Formation - 1910
President - Hans Cavalli-Björkman
Secretary - Einar Malmborg
Coach - Rolf Zetterlund
Stadium - Malmö Stadion (32,000)

MAJOR HONOURS
League Championship - (14)
1944, 1949, 1950, 1951, 1953, 1965, 1967, 1970, 1971, 1974, 1975, 1977, 1986, 1988.
Domestic Cup - (14)
1944, 1946, 1947, 1951, 1953, 1967, 1973, 1974, 1975, 1977, 1980, 1984, 1986, 1989.

APPEARANCES 95

	P	Ap	(s)	Gls
Anders ANDERSSON	M	23		3
Daniel ANDERSSON	D	18	(3)	2
Greger ANDRIJEVSKI	A	5		
Fredrik DAHLSTRÖM	A	2	(13)	3
Jonnie FEDEL	G	26		
Jens FJELLSTRÖM	M	26		1
Tommy JÖNSSON	D	4	(1)	
Henrik NILSSON	D	7	(3)	
Mika NURMELA (FIN)	M	2	(8)	
Niclas NYLÉN	D	22	(2)	
Jörgen OHLSSON	M	26		1
Patrik OLSSON	A	6	(7)	1
Yksel OSMANOVSKI	A		(1)	
Joakim PERSSON	M	17	(3)	3
Torbjörn PERSSON	D	25		
Jörgen PETTERSSON	A	26		15
Robert PRYTZ	M	17		1
Mattias THYLANDER	M	10	(5)	2
Jonas WIRMOLA	D	24		

LEAGUE RESULTS 1995

09/04/95	Degerfors IF	A	3-0	Thylander 2, Pettersson
17/04/95	Djurgårdens IF	H	0-0	
01/05/95	Halmstads BK	A	2-2	Pettersson, Andersson A.
08/05/95	Östers IF	H	2-1	Prytz (p), Olsson J.
15/05/95	Helsingborgs IF	A	1-2	Pettersson
18/05/95	IFK Göteborg	H	1-1	Andersson D.
21/05/95	IFK Norrköping	A	1-0	Olsson P.
28/05/95	AIK	H	2-2	Pettersson 2
14/06/95	Örgryte IS	A	0-0	
19/06/95	Trelleborgs FF	H	2-1	Pettersson 2
26/06/95	Hammarby IF	A	1-1	Andersson A.
02/07/95	Örebro SK	H	0-0	
31/07/95	Västra Frölunda IF	H	3-1	Pettersson 3
05/08/95	Västra Frölunda IF	A	0-0	
13/08/95	Örebro SK	A	0-5	
20/08/95	Hammarby IF	H	1-0	Persson J.
28/08/95	Halmstads BK	H	2-1	Pettersson, Dahlström
31/08/95	Östers IF	A	2-2	Persson J., Dahlström
10/09/95	Helsingborgs IF	H	0-1	
17/09/95	IFK Göteborg	A	1-2	Andersson D.
23/09/95	IFK Norrköping	H	1-3	Pettersson
01/10/95	AIK	A	1-1	Fjellström
08/10/95	Djurgårdens IF	A	2-0	Pettersson, Dahlström
15/10/95	Degerfors IF	H	3-1	Pettersson 2, Andersson A.
23/10/95	Trelleborgs FF	A	0-0	
28/10/95	Örgryte IS	H	1-1	Persson J.

IFK NORRKÖPING

CLUB DIRECTORY

Idrottsföreningen Kamraterna Norrköping
Box 12067
600 12 Norrköping
tel - (011) 132225
fax - (011) 101490
Year of Formation - 1897
President - Björn Ahlberg
Secretary - Roland Tillberg
Coach - Kent Karlsson; Thomas Nordahl
(96 - Colin Toal)
Stadium - Norrköpings Idrottsparken (21,000)

MAJOR HONOURS
League Championship - (12)
1943, 1945, 1946, 1947, 1948, 1952, 1956, 1957, 1960, 1962, 1963, 1989.
Domestic Cup - (6)
1943, 1945, 1960, 1988, 1992, 1994.

APPEARANCES 95

	P	Ap	(s)	Gls
Joachim ACHEAMPONG (GHA)	M	9	(2)	
Søren ANDERSEN (DEN)	A	10		4
Patrik ANDERSSON	A	11	(2)	
Göran BERGORT	D	26		
Per BLOHM	M	20	(2)	1
Mikael BLOMBERG	D	6	(9)	
Hasan CETINKAYA	M	4	(1)	1
Lars ERIKSSON	G	26		
Daniel HAMZU	D		(1)	
Mikael HANSSON	D	26		2
Jan JANSSON	M	24	(1)	
Patrik KARLSSON	A	22	(4)	12
Jonas LIND	D	21	(4)	
Erik NORRBY	D	2	(10)	
George PARRIS (ENG)	M	4		
Magnus SAMUELSSON	M	9	(2)	3
Patrik SANDSTRÖM	M	20	(6)	3
Robert STEINER	A	6	(10)	2
Mikael STRÖM	D	14	(1)	
Donny SUNDELL	M		(1)	
Sulo VAATTOVAARA	D	26		
Jonas WALLERSTEDT	M		(3)	

LEAGUE RESULTS 1995

10/04/95	Örgryte IS	A	1-2	Karlsson
17/04/95	Trelleborgs FF	H	2-2	Sandström, Karlsson
01/05/95	Hammarby IF	A	2-0	Karlsson, Hansson
08/05/95	Örebro SK	H	1-0	Karlsson
15/05/95	Djurgårdens IF	H	2-0	Sandström, Karlsson
18/05/95	Halmstads BK	A	0-2	
21/05/95	Malmö FF	H	0-1	
28/05/95	Degerfors IF	A	3-0	Hansson, Karlsson, Blohm
14/06/95	Västra Frölunda IF	H	0-3	
20/06/95	AIK	A	2-2	Steiner, Karlsson
28/06/95	Helsingborgs IF	H	0-3	
05/07/95	IFK Göteborg	A	0-2	
30/07/95	Östers IF	H	4-1	Karlsson 2, Sandström, Andersen
05/08/95	Östers IF	A	3-2	Cetinkaya, Karlsson 2
13/08/95	IFK Göteborg	H	0-5	
20/08/95	Helsingborgs IF	A	0-0	
28/08/95	Hammarby IF	H	1-1	Steiner
31/08/95	Örebro SK	A	0-1	
10/09/95	Djurgårdens IF	A	0-1	
18/09/95	Halmstads BK	H	1-1	Samuelsson
23/09/95	Malmö FF	A	3-1	Samuelsson 2, Andersen
08/10/95	Trelleborgs FF	A	0-4	
15/10/95	Örgryte IS	H	0-2	
19/10/95	Degerfors IF	H	1-1	Andersen
23/10/95	AIK	H	1-1	Karlsson
28/10/95	Västra Frölunda IF	A	1-5	Andersen

TRELLEBORGS FF

CLUB DIRECTORY

Trelleborgs Fotbollsförening
Hejderidaregatan 2
231 44 Trelleborg
tel - (0410) 13190
fax - (0410) 13125
Year of Formation - 1926
President - Gunnar Persson
Secretary - Bengt Cederberg
Coach - Tom Prahl (96 - Magnus Andersson)
Stadium - Vångavallen (10,000)

APPEARANCES 95

	P	Ap	(s)	Gls
Magnus ANDERSSON	D	24		
Peter ANDERSSON	M	4	(3)	
Lars BLIXT	M	11	(5)	1
Jonas BRORSSON	D	21	(3)	
Frederick ENAHOLO	G	1		
Jörgen ERIKSSON	D	14	(3)	
Anders FRIBERG	D	3		
Michael HANSSON	M	19	(1)	6
Andreas HERMANSSON	A	16	(3)	4
Ryszard JANKOWSKI (POL)	G	25		
Christian KARLSSON	D	25		2
Joachim KARLSSON	A	18	(3)	5
Patrik LARSSON	D	12		1
Issa MANGLIND	A	5	(9)	
Niklas MATTSSON	D	5		
Fredrik PERSSON	M	3	(7)	
Rami RANTANEN (FIN)	M	22	(1)	5
Mikael RASMUSSON	M	23		2
Fredrik SANDELL	A	13		2
Ola SEVERIN	M	22	(2)	3

LEAGUE RESULTS 1995

09/04/95	Örebro SK	H	0-0	
17/04/95	IFK Norrköping	A	2-2	Severin, Karlsson J.
01/05/95	AIK	H	1-0	Rantanen
08/05/95	Helsingborgs IF	A	1-2	Blixt
14/05/95	Örgryte IS	H	4-1	Hermansson 2, Rantanen 2
18/05/95	Västra Frölunda IF	A	0-1	
21/05/95	Halmstads BK	H	4-0	Rasmusson, Rantanen, Hermansson, Karlsson C. (p)
28/05/95	Östers IF	A	1-3	Hermansson
19/06/95	Malmö FF	A	1-2	Hansson
25/06/95	Degerfors IF	H	2-2	Severin, Hansson
29/06/95	IFK Göteborg	H	2-2	Rantanen, Hansson
03/07/95	Djurgårdens IF	A	1-1	Karlsson C.
31/07/95	Hammarby IF	A	3-1	og (Vonderburg), Hansson, Karlsson J.
07/08/95	Hammarby IF	H	0-0	
13/08/95	Djurgårdens IF	A	1-1	Hansson
20/08/95	Degerfors IF	A	0-1	
28/08/95	AIK	A	0-3	
31/08/95	Helsingborgs IF	H	0-2	
11/09/95	Örgryte IS	A	0-0	
18/09/95	Västra Frölunda IF	H	2-0	Sandell, Karlsson J.
24/09/95	Halmstads BK	A	2-1	Rasmusson, Karlsson J.
08/10/95	IFK Norrköping	H	4-0	Karlsson J., Sandell, Larsson, Hansson
14/10/95	Örebro SK	A	0-2	
19/10/95	Östers IF	H	1-1	Severin
23/10/95	Malmö FF	H	0-0	
28/10/95	IFK Göteborg	A	0-2	

VÄSTRA FRÖLUNDA IF

CLUB DIRECTORY

Västra Frölunda Idrottsförening
Box 213
421 43 Västra Frölunda
tel - (031) 452660
fax - (031) 492080
Year of Formation - 1930
President - Mats Persson
Secretary - Rolf Nilsson
Coach - Glenn Holm
Stadium - Ruddalen (5,500)

APPEARANCES 95

	P	Ap	(s)	Gls
Jan AHLBOM	D	17	(2)	
Thomas ANDERSSON	D	8		
Filip APELSTAV	D	22		
Patrik BENGTSSON	M	14		4
Robert BENGTSSON	D	25		
Lars-Gunnar CARLSTRAND	A	6	(7)	5
Peter GRANQVIST	M	3	(3)	
Mikael GÖRANSSON	M	23		1
Dane IVARSSON	M	5	(4)	
Kjell JOHANSSON	G	15		
Nicklas JOHANSSON	M	9	(4)	
Magnus KÄLLANDER	M	25		5
Joakim LJUNGBERG	M	2		
Teddy LUCIC	D	26		
Bosko OROVIC	A	5	(2)	
Tomas ROSENQVIST	A	10	(1)	2
Kristófer SIGURGEIRSSON (ISL)	M		(1)	
Niklas SKOOG	A	24		17
Rikard TEBERIO	A	13	(6)	1
Christer THOR	D	23		
Robert TRANBERG	G	11	(1)	

LEAGUE RESULTS 1995

Date	Opponent		Score	Scorers
09/04/95	Hammarby IF	A	1-3	Skoog
17/04/95	Degerfors IF	H	0-0	
01/05/95	Örebro SK	A	4-4	Rosenqvist 2, Källander, Skoog
08/05/95	Djurgårdens IF	H	2-2	Skoog 2
13/05/95	IFK Göteborg	A	1-1	Skoog
18/05/95	Trelleborgs FF	H	1-0	Skoog
21/05/95	Helsingborgs IF	A	0-1	
27/05/95	Örgryte IS	H	0-1	
14/06/95	IFK Norrköping	A	3-0	Skoog 3
19/06/95	Halmstads BK	H	1-1	Källander
28/06/95	AIK	A	1-1	Skoog
06/07/95	Östers IF	H	1-1	Skoog
31/07/95	Malmö FF	A	1-3	Teberio
05/08/95	Malmö FF	H	0-0	
13/08/95	Östers IF	A	0-4	
21/08/95	AIK	H	1-1	Skoog
27/08/95	Örebro SK	H	1-2	Bengtsson P.
01/09/95	Djurgårdens IF	A	2-4	Carlstrand 2
09/09/95	IFK Göteborg	H	3-0	Källander 2, Skoog
18/09/95	Trelleborgs FF	A	0-2	
24/09/95	Helsingborgs IF	H	2-3	Skoog, Bengtsson P.
02/10/95	Örgryte IS	A	2-1	Bengtsson P., Göransson (p)
07/10/95	Degerfors IF	A	0-2	
15/10/95	Hammarby IF	H	2-6	Skoog, Carlstrand
23/10/95	Halmstads BK	A	1-1	Bengtsson P.
28/10/95	IFK Norrköping	H	5-1	Skoog 2, Källander, Carlstrand 2

ÖREBRO SK

CLUB DIRECTORY

Örebro Sportklubb
Eyragatan 1
702 25 Örebro
tel - (019) 167300
fax - (019) 167319
Year of Formation - 1908
President - Kenneth Karlsson
Secretary - Anders Rutqvist
Coach - Sven Dahlkvist
Stadium - Eyravallen (13,000)

APPEARANCES 95

	P	Ap	(s)	Gls
Henrik ANDERSSON	A	5	(2)	
Mikael ANDERSSON	M	15	(3)	4
Thomas ANDERSSON	D	24		
Hlynur BIRGISSON (ISL)	D	6	(3)	
Arnor GUDJOHNSEN (ISL)	M	24		3
Mattias JONSSON	M	20		9
Anders KARLSSON	G	25		
Magnus KARLSSON	D	26		1
Miroslaw KUBISZTAL (POL)	A	26		12
Jonas MÅHLBERG	G	1	(1)	
Janne OINAS	A	3	(1)	1
Jonas PELGANDER	M	4	(6)	
Niklas RASCK	M	4	(11)	
Magnus SKÖLDMARK	D	24		
Hlynur STEFÁNSSON (ISL)	M	23	(1)	
Tommy STÅHL	D	25		
Mattias WAHLQVIST	D	7	(7)	2
Samuel WOWOAH	M		(1)	
Salar YASIN	A		(1)	
Lars ZETTERLUND	D	24		2

LEAGUE RESULTS 1995

Date	Opponent	Venue	Score	Scorers
09/04/95	Trelleborgs FF	A	0-0	
17/04/95	Hammarby IF	H	2-1	Zetterlund, Jonsson
01/05/95	Västra Frölunda IF	H	4-4	og (Thor), Jonsson, Kubisztal 2 (1p)
08/05/95	IFK Norrköping	A	0-1	
14/05/95	Halmstads BK	H	1-0	Kubisztal
18/05/95	Östers IF	A	2-2	Gudjohnsen, Andersson M.
22/05/95	Degerfors IF	H	2-2	Zetterlund, Kubisztal
28/05/95	Djurgårdens IF	A	0-2	
14/06/95	AIK	H	3-0	Kubisztal, Andersson M. 2
19/06/95	Helsingborgs IF	A	0-3	
26/06/95	IFK Göteborg	H	1-0	Karlsson
02/07/95	Malmö FF	A	0-0	
30/07/95	Örgryte IS	H	0-1	
03/08/95	Örgryte IS	A	0-0	
13/08/95	Malmö FF	H	5-0	Jonsson 2, Kubisztal 3
19/08/95	IFK Göteborg	A	1-3	Wahlqvist
27/08/95	Västra Frölunda IF	A	2-1	Jonsson 2
31/08/95	IFK Norrköping	H	1-0	Kubisztal
09/09/95	Halmstads BK	A	1-2	Jonsson
18/09/95	Östers IF	H	1-0	Oinas
23/09/95	Degerfors IF	A	1-2	Kubisztal
07/10/95	Hammarby IF	A	2-2	Jonsson, Kubisztal (p)
14/10/95	Trelleborgs FF	H	2-0	Gudjohnsen, Kubisztal
19/10/95	Djurgårdens IF	H	0-0	
23/10/95	Helsingborgs IF	H	4-1	Gudjohnsen, Wahlqvist, Jonsson, Andersson M.
28/10/95	AIK	A	0-2	

ÖRGRYTE IS

CLUB DIRECTORY

Örgryte Idrottssällskap
Box 52025
400 25 Göteborg
tel - (031) 879310
fax - (031) 879547
Year of Formation - 1887
President - Denny Rosén
Secretary - Jan Björklund
Coach - Karl-Gunnar Björklund
Stadium - Gamla Ullevi (18,000)

MAJOR HONOURS

League Championship - (14)
1896, 1897, 1898, 1899, 1902, 1904, 1905, 1906, 1907, 1909, 1913, 1926, 1928, 1985.

APPEARANCES 95

	P	Ap	(s)	Gls
Marcus ALLBÄCK	A	15	(7)	4
Bengt ANDERSSON	G	26		
Jonas BARTHOLDSSON	A	1	(1)	
Henrik BERTILSSON	A	10		2
Pontus EKBLOM	M		(1)	
Joakim GRANDELIUS	M	12	(9)	2
Henrik HANSSON	M	9	(5)	1
Sebastian HENRIKSSON	D	26		3
Erik JOHANSSON	M	3	(8)	
Ola KARLSSON	M	6	(4)	
Magnus KIHLBERG	M	26		1
Runar KRISTINSSON (ISL)	M	25		3
Jozo MATOVAC	D	26		
Jonas NILSSON	M	19	(2)	
Morgan NILSSON	M	25		3
Roger NORDSTRAND	A	5	(1)	2
Percy OLSSON	A	6	(5)	
Svante SAMUELSSON	D	15	(1)	1
Niclas SJÖSTEDT	D	24		
Jens WÅLEMARK	D	7	(1)	

LEAGUE RESULTS 1995

10/04/95	IFK Norrköping	H	2-1	Allbäck, Kristinsson
17/04/95	AIK	A	0-0	
01/05/95	Helsingborgs IF	H	0-1	
08/05/95	IFK Göteborg	A	0-3	
14/05/95	Trelleborgs FF	A	1-4	Allbäck
17/05/95	Hammarby IF	H	0-1	
21/05/95	Östers IF	H	4-1	Nordstrand, Hansson, Allbäck 2
27/05/95	Västra Frölunda IF	A	1-0	Nordstrand
14/06/95	Malmö FF	H	0-0	
19/06/95	Degerfors IF	A	0-0	
26/06/95	Djurgårdens IF	H	0-2	
02/07/95	Halmstads BK	A	0-2	
30/07/95	Örebro SK	A	1-0	Nilsson M.
03/08/95	Örebro SK	H	0-0	
10/08/95	Halmstads BK	H	0-2	
21/08/95	Djurgårdens IF	A	3-1	Samuelsson, Kristinsson, Bertilsson
27/08/95	Helsingborgs IF	A	1-0	Grandelius
31/08/95	IFK Göteborg	H	1-1	Henriksson
11/09/95	Trelleborgs FF	H	0-0	
18/09/95	Hammarby IF	A	1-0	Grandelius
25/09/95	Östers IF	A	1-1	Kristinsson
02/10/95	Västra Frölunda IF	H	1-2	Henriksson
08/10/95	AIK	H	2-1	Bertilsson, Nilsson M.
15/10/95	IFK Norrköping	A	2-0	Kihlberg, Nilsson M.
23/10/95	Degerfors IF	H	0-1	
28/10/95	Malmö FF	A	1-1	Henriksson

ÖSTERS IF

CLUB DIRECTORY

Östers Idrottsförening
Tipshallen
Värendsvallen
Hejaregatan
352 46 Växjö
tel - (0470) 19020/19021
fax - (0470) 16845
Year of Formation - 1930
President - Carl-Gunnar Rönn
Secretary - Sture Andersson
Coach - Nanne Bergstrand
Stadium - Värendsvallen (17,000)

MAJOR HONOURS
League Championship - (4)
1968, 1978, 1980, 1981.
Domestic Cup - (1) 1977.

APPEARANCES 95

	P	Ap	(s)	Gls
Erik ANDERSSON	A		(1)	
Jonas AXELDAHL	A	17	(5)	3
Andreas BILD	M	20	(2)	4
Fredrik BILD	D	16	(5)	
Hans EKLUND	A	26		11
Ludwig ERNSTSSON	A	15	(8)	6
Christer FRISK	D	21	(1)	1
Fredrik GUSTAVSSON	M	2	(1)	
Lasse JOHANSSON	M	13	(8)	
Björn LILIUS	D	16	(1)	
Pål LUNDIN	G	26		
Mark NEWSON (ENG)	D	11		1
Andreas OTTOSSON	M	10	(6)	4
Stefan PALDAN	M	25		2
Stavros PAPADOPOULOS	D	15		
Nicklas PERSSON	D	25		
Jens SVENSSON	M	3	(9)	
Peter WIBRÅN	M	25		8

LEAGUE RESULTS 1995

09/04/95	AIK	H	0-2	
17/04/95	Helsingborgs IF	A	2-0	Wibrån, Ernstsson
01/05/95	IFK Göteborg	H	0-0	
08/05/95	Malmö FF	A	1-2	Bild A.
13/05/95	Hammarby IF	A	2-2	Wibrån, Bild A.
18/05/95	Örebro SK	H	2-2	Eklund 2 (2p)
21/05/95	Örgryte IS	A	2-4	Axeldahl, Ernstsson
28/05/95	Trelleborgs FF	H	3-1	Wibrån 2, Paldan
14/06/95	Degerfors IF	H	2-2	Axeldahl, Ernstsson
19/06/95	Djurgårdens IF	A	1-1	Paldan
28/06/95	Halmstads BK	H	3-0	Eklund 3 (2p)
06/07/95	Västra Frölunda IF	A	1-1	Wibrån
30/07/95	IFK Norrköping	A	1-4	Eklund
05/08/95	IFK Norrköping	H	2-3	Eklund, Ottosson
13/08/95	Västra Frölunda IF	H	4-0	Eklund 2, Wibrån, Ernstsson
20/08/95	Halmstads BK	A	2-2	Eklund, Wibrån
28/08/95	IFK Göteborg	A	1-3	Newson
31/08/95	Malmö FF	H	2-2	Bild A., Ernstsson
11/09/95	Hammarby IF	H	1-1	Ottosson
18/09/95	Örebro SK	A	0-1	
25/09/95	Örgryte IS	H	1-1	Ottosson
08/10/95	Helsingborgs IF	H	1-1	Ottosson
16/10/95	AIK	A	1-1	Ernstsson
19/10/95	Trelleborgs FF	A	1-1	Bild A.
23/10/95	Djurgårdens IF	H	3-1	Frisk, Ernstsson, Axeldahl
28/10/95	Degerfors IF	A	2-3	Eklund, og (Granath)

PROMOTED CLUBS

SECOND DIVISION FINAL TABLES 95

NORTH

		Pd	W	D	L	F	A	Pt	GD
1	**Umeå FC**	**26**	**13**	**9**	**4**	**41**	**22**	**48**	**+19**
2	Gefle IF	26	12	9	5	49	26	45	+23
3	Vasalunds IF	26	11	11	4	46	28	44	+18
4	Visby IF Gute	26	11	7	8	45	52	40	-7
5	IK Brage	26	11	6	9	50	44	39	+6
6	IFK Luleå	26	9	9	8	45	38	36	+7
7	GIF Sundsvall	26	8	10	8	31	23	34	+8
8	IF Brommapojkarna	26	9	7	10	39	32	34	+7
9	Västerås SK FK	26	9	7	10	35	36	34	-1
10	BK Forward	26	8	10	8	28	34	34	-6
11	IK Sirius FK	26	7	8	11	29	41	29	-12
12	Assyriska Föreningen	26	6	7	13	24	41	25	-17
13	Väsby IK FK	26	4	12	10	23	40	24	-17
14	Lira Luleå BK	26	4	8	14	25	53	20	-28

SOUTH

		Pd	W	D	L	F	A	Pt	GD
1	**IK Oddevold**	**26**	**17**	**3**	**6**	**59**	**29**	**54**	**+30**
2	GAIS	26	13	9	4	55	35	48	+20
3	IF Elfsborg	26	14	5	7	55	40	47	+15
4	Kalmar FF	26	12	6	8	60	45	42	+15
5	Ljungskile SK	26	10	9	7	42	35	39	+7
6	Gunnilse IS	26	9	7	10	40	36	34	+4
7	BK Häcken	26	8	10	8	42	47	34	-5
8	IFK Hässleholm	26	10	4	12	48	65	34	-17
9	Falkenbergs FF	26	9	6	11	35	36	33	-1
10	Stenungsunds IF	26	7	11	8	31	33	32	-2
11	Norrby IF	26	9	4	13	37	40	31	-3
12	Myresjö IF	26	8	6	12	37	50	30	-13
13	Skövde AIK	26	6	5	15	43	58	23	-15
14	Landskrona BoIS	26	7	1	18	31	66	22	-35

PROMOTION/RELEGATION PLAY-OFFS

Gefle IF 0, Östers IF 1
Östers IF 3, Gefle IF 0
(Östers IF 4-0)

GAIS 1, IFK Norrköping 1
IFK Norrköping 1, GAIS 0
(IFK Norrköping 2-1)

CLUB DIRECTORY

Umeå Fotbollclub
Gammliavägen 5
903 42 Umeå
tel - (090) 139001
fax - (090) 136430
Year of Formation - 1987
President - Mats Lindberg
Secretary - Ulf Bergström
Coach - Jan Westerlund
Stadium - Gammliavallen (8,000)

CLUB DIRECTORY

Idrottsklubben Oddevold
Box 85
451 15 Uddevalla
tel - (0522) 16038
fax - (0522) 33720
Year of Formation - 1932
President - Stig Larsson
Secretary - Magnus Söderhjelm
Coach - Torbjörn Nilsson (96 - Olof Engelbrektsson)
Stadium - Rimnersvallen (15,000)

SWITZERLAND

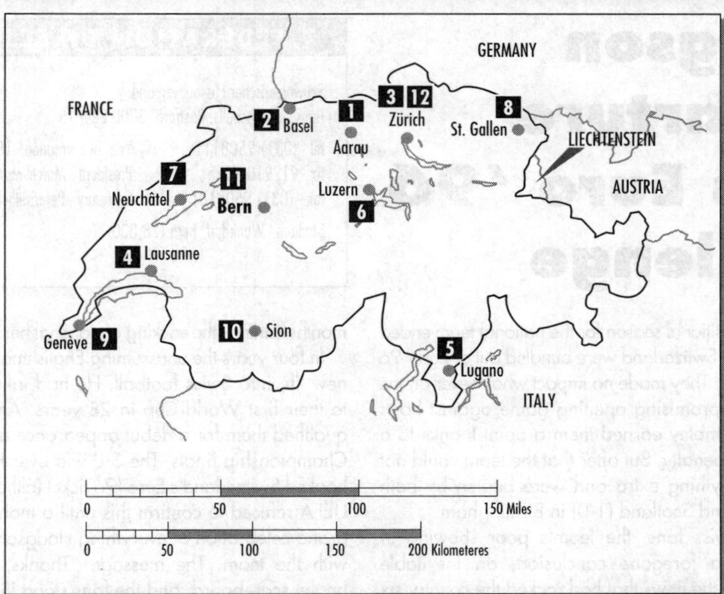

1	FC AARAU	999	7	NEUCHATEL XAMAX FC	1005
2	FC BASEL	1000	8	FC ST. GALLEN	1006
3	GRASSHOPPER-CLUB ZÜRICH	1001	9	SERVETTE FC GENEVE	1007
4	LAUSANNE-SPORTS	1002	10	FC SION	1008
5	FC LUGANO	1003	11	BSC YOUNG BOYS	1009
6	FC LUZERN	1004	12	FC ZÜRICH	1010

LEAGUE AND CUP BOTH RETAINED

Hodgson departure kills Euro '96 challenge

FEDERATION DIRECTORY

Schweizerischer Fussballverband
Haus des Fussballs, Postfach, 3000 Bern 15

tel - (031) 9508111
tlx - 912910 sfv ch
fax - (031) 9508181

Year of Formation - 1895
President - Marcel Mathier
Secretary - Peter Gilliéron

Stadium - Wankdorf, Bern (28,000)

A turbulent, transitional season for the national team ended unhappily when Switzerland were bundled out of Euro '96 in the first round. They made no impact whatsoever on the tournament. A promising opening game against hosts England at Wembley earned them a point thanks to a debatable late penalty. But after that the team could not summon up anything extra and were beaten by both Holland (2-0) and Scotland (1-0) in Birmingham.

To many Swiss fans, the team's poor showing in England was a foregone conclusion, an inevitable consequence of the news that had rocked the country six months earlier - the sacking of national hero Roy Hodgson.

In four years the unassuming Englishman had breathed new life into Swiss football. He had taken Switzerland to their first World Cup in 28 years. And he had also qualified them for a début appearance at the European Championship finals. The 3-0 win over Hungary which booked Switzerland's Euro '96 ticket (although, bizarrely, UEFA refused to confirm this until a month later) was a grand celebration of everything Hodgson had achieved with the team. The message "Thanks, Roy!" flashed on the scoreboard, and the fans stood in tribute to their adopted saviour.

At the time Hodgson had already agreed to take over as the new coach at Italian club Inter. But an agreement had been made with the Swiss FA that Hodgson would continue to work part-time with the national team until after Euro '96. After all, the least he deserved for services rendered was a triumphant return to his homeland - a country where, until his presence with Switzerland at the 1994 World Cup, he had been a complete unknown.

But then, just before Christmas, came the bombshell. Hodgson's non-appearance at the Euro '96 draw in Birmingham was a hint that something was amiss. A few days later an announcement was made that Hodgson's 'gentleman's agreement' had been terminated, and that the new Swiss coach would be the Portuguese, Artur Jorge. The immediate resentment at Hodgson's dismissal was intense.

LEAGUE CHAMPIONSHIP RESULTS 95/96

AUTUMN (FIRST PHASE)

		1	2	3	4	5	6	7	8	9	10	11	12
1	FC Aarau		2-0	1-1	3-0	5-0	1-1	2-2	5-1	2-4	0-1	0-0	2-0
2	FC Basel	2-1		1-3	0-1	0-2	2-0	0-2	0-0	2-2	2-1	1-0	0-3
3	Grasshopper-Club Zürich	2-1	1-3		1-1	1-0	4-0	2-1	3-1	1-1	2-0	3-0	2-0
4	Lausanne-Sports	0-2	1-0	1-2		3-0	3-1	1-1	0-0	0-0	1-1	2-0	3-0
5	FC Lugano	2-0	0-1	1-1	1-1		1-1	0-3	1-1	0-2	1-3	2-0	1-1
6	FC Luzern	3-0	3-1	2-0	1-1	1-1		3-2	1-1	2-1	3-2	3-1	1-0
7	Neuchâtel Xamax FC	3-2	1-0	2-1	4-2	4-0	1-1		3-0	1-0	3-0	0-1	0-2
8	FC St. Gallen	0-0	0-1	1-2	2-1	3-0	1-1	1-1		4-0	3-0	0-0	1-0
9	Servette FC Genève	2-1	1-2	2-0	1-1	2-3	1-0	3-0	2-2		0-1	0-0	0-0
10	FC Sion	2-1	4-1	2-1	1-0	5-2	1-3	1-1	1-0	3-1		1-0	2-2
11	BSC Young Boys	0-4	1-4	0-1	1-1	3-1	0-4	1-2	2-0	1-2	1-4		2-0
12	FC Zürich	1-1	0-0	1-4	3-1	1-2	0-1	1-3	0-4	2-1	0-1	0-0	

SPRING (FINAL ROUND)

		1	2	3	4	5	6	7	8
1	FC Aarau		1-0	0-0	2-2	3-2	4-0	3-0	1-0
2	FC Basel	1-3		0-2	1-0	1-2	1-1	2-0	2-0
3	Grasshopper-Club Zürich	0-0	3-0		2-1	3-3	3-0	2-0	3-0
4	FC Luzern	4-0	1-1	1-2		0-1	5-0	2-1	2-3
5	Neuchâtel Xamax FC	3-1	1-1	0-0	1-1		3-0	1-1	2-0
6	FC St. Gallen	3-4	3-0	0-4	1-0	0-0		0-0	0-4
7	Servette FC Genève	1-1	1-1	2-2	3-4	4-1	3-2		0-1
8	FC Sion	2-0	2-0	0-0	1-0	1-1	3-1	3-2	

LEAGUE CHAMPIONSHIP FINAL TABLE 95/96

AUTUMN (FIRST PHASE)

			Home					Away					Total						
		Pd	W	D	L	F	A	W	D	L	F	A	W	D	L	F	A	Pt	GD
1	Grasshopper-Club Zürich	22	8	2	1	22	8	5	2	4	16	14	13	4	5	38	22	43	+16
2	FC Sion	22	8	2	1	23	12	5	1	5	14	16	13	3	6	37	28	42	+9
3	Neuchâtel Xamax FC	22	8	1	2	22	9	4	4	3	18	15	12	5	5	40	24	41	+16
4	FC Luzern	22	8	3	0	23	10	3	4	4	13	15	11	7	4	36	25	40	+11
5	FC Basel	22	4	2	5	10	15	5	1	5	13	14	9	3	10	23	29	30	-6
6	Servette FC Genève	22	4	4	3	14	10	3	3	5	14	18	7	7	8	28	28	28	=
7	FC Aarau	22	5	4	2	23	10	2	2	7	13	17	7	6	9	36	27	27	+9
8	FC St. Gallen	22	5	4	2	16	6	1	5	5	10	18	6	9	7	26	24	27	+2
9	Lausanne-Sports	22	5	4	2	15	7	1	5	5	10	18	6	9	7	25	25	27	=
10	FC Lugano	22	2	5	4	10	14	3	1	7	11	28	5	6	11	21	42	21	-21
11	FC Zürich	22	2	3	6	9	18	2	3	6	8	14	4	6	12	17	32	18	-15
12	BSC Young Boys	22	3	1	7	12	23	1	4	6	2	12	4	5	13	14	35	17	-21

SPRING (FINAL ROUND)

			Home					Away					Total						
		Pd	W	D	L	F	A	W	D	L	F	A	W	D	L	F	A	Pt	GD
1	Grasshopper-Club Zürich	14	5	2	0	16	4	3	4	0	10	3	8	6	0	26	7	52	+19
2	FC Sion	14	5	2	0	12	4	3	0	4	8	10	8	2	4	20	14	47	+6
3	Neuchâtel Xamax FC	14	3	4	0	11	4	2	3	2	10	12	5	7	2	21	16	43	+5
4	FC Aarau	14	5	2	0	14	4	2	2	3	9	14	7	4	3	23	18	39	+5
5	FC Luzern	14	3	1	3	15	8	1	2	4	8	11	4	3	7	23	19	35	+4
6	FC Basel	14	3	1	3	8	8	0	3	4	3	12	3	4	7	11	20	28	-9
7	Servette FC Genève	14	2	3	2	14	12	0	2	5	4	13	2	5	7	18	25	25	-7
8	FC St. Gallen	14	2	2	3	7	12	0	1	6	4	22	2	3	9	11	34	23	-23

N.B. After 22 matches the top eight play off for the title, taking half their points total. The bottom four enter a promotion/relegation play-off group with the top two from the Second Division. In the Final Round, when teams are level on points, classification is determined by the position of the teams at the end of the First Phase.

It was a difficult rôle for Artur Jorge to step into, but he hardly endeared himself to the Swiss fans when he could only guide them to a 1-1 draw against Luxembourg in his first game. Further European Championship warm-up games brought similarly disappointing results, and the general feeling was that Euro '96 would be a very short-lived adventure for the Swiss.

The final straw for many of the Swiss faithful came when Artur Jorge sensationally dropped national team monuments Alain Sutter and Adrian Knup from the 22-man squad. The move came totally without warning, both for the players and the fans. And in the first match of the tournament, against England, further friction ensued when the coach omitted from his starting line-up another big crowd favourite, Stéphane Chapuisat.

Throughout his long and generally successful career, Artur Jorge had always done things his way - regardless of what supporters or anybody else thought. When his intransigence brought the desired results, he got away with it. But at Euro '96, Artur Jorge failed to pull the rabbit out of the hat. Consequently, his reign ended after less than six months. And few people in Switzerland mourned his passing.

His legacy was not entirely negative, however. Some players - notably the Grasshoppers pair of Ramon Vega and Johann Vogel - emerged as top-class internationals under his guidance. And striker Kubilay Türkyilmaz seemed hungrier and more dynamic than he ever had under the Hodgson régime. New coach Rolf Fringer - recruited in August from German club VfB Stuttgart - will have the task of getting all the Swiss players fired up for the World Cup campaign. Drawn in a far from difficult group, the Swiss are a reasonable bet to reach their third

INTERNATIONAL HONOURS

World Cup Finals appearances: 1934, 1938 (2nd round), 1950, 1954 (qtr-finals), 1962, 1966, 1994 (2nd round)

European Championship appearances: 1996

DOMESTIC CUP RESULTS

1/16 FINALS
FC Aarau 1, FC Lugano 0
Lausanne-Sports 2, Neuchâtel Xamax FC 5
FC Baden 1, Grasshopper-Club Zürich 1
(aet; 3-5 on pens.)
Meyrin 1, BSC Young Boys 2 (aet)
Renens 0, Servette FC Genève 1
Tuggen 0, FC Zürich 2
Gossau 0, FC Basel 2
Concordia Basel 0, FC Luzern 2
FC Sion 3, Bulle 0
Ascona 1, FC St. Gallen 4
FC Locarno 0, FC Wil 1
Serrières Neuchâtel 0, SR Delémont 2
Bümpliz 1, FC Naters 1 (aet; 9-8 on pens.)
Gunzwil 0, FC Schaffhausen 2
Raron 1, Biel-Bienne 2
Schötz 2, Seefeld 0

1/8 FINALS
FC Aarau 2, FC Zürich 0
Neuchâtel Xamax FC 2, Bümpliz 0
FC Wil 1, FC Luzern 2 (aet)
Schötz 2, FC Schaffhausen 0 (aet)
Biel-Bienne 1, FC Basel 4
SR Delémont 1, FC Sion 2
Servette FC Genève 3, BSC Young Boys 1
FC St. Gallen 2, Grasshopper-Club Zürich 1

QUARTER-FINALS
FC Aarau 1, Servette FC Genève 4
Schötz 0, FC St. Gallen 0 (aet; 1-4 on pens.)
FC Sion 2, FC Luzern 0
Neuchâtel Xamax FC 2, FC Basel 1 (aet)

SEMI-FINALS
FC Sion 2, FC St. Gallen 1
Neuchâtel Xamax FC 0, Servette FC Genève 1

FINAL
19/05/96, Berne
FC SION 3 Bonvin (63), Wicky (67), Vidmar (73)
SERVETTE FC GENEVE 2 Karlen (30), Neuville (62)
referee - Meier
FC SION - Lehmann; Gaspoz, Wicky, Herr (Moser 59), Quentin; Sylvestre (Zambaz 90), Lonfat, Colombo (Mirandinha 46), Fournier; Vidmar, Bonvin.
SERVETTE FC GENEVE - Pascolo; Aeby; Barea, Karlen; Ippoliti (Baumann 81), Pizzinat (Fernandez 85), Nemecek, Barberis; Sesa (Weiler 69), Sogbie, Neuville.

major competition in a row - assuming Fringer can quickly restore the harmony and spirit of the Hodgson years.

One of the problems Fringer faces is keeping tabs on all the Swiss players who are now earning their living in foreign leagues. The number of exiled stars has grown considerably in recent seasons and it now amounts to the vast bulk of his first-choice team.

One man who returned from abroad during the 1995/96 season was Türkyilmaz. He came back from Turkish side Galatasaray in the early spring, and his arrival at injury-hit Grasshoppers was to turn the course of the Swiss championship in the Zürich side's favour.

For much of the season, in both domestic competition and a rather forgettable début Champions' League campaign, Grasshoppers resembled a cast of the walking wounded. It was virtually impossible for coach Christian Gross to field the same team from one match to the next. Key players such as Yakin, Thüler, Zuberbühler, Geiger and Vogel were among the serious casualties. And when chief goalgetter Nestor Subiat broke down again in March, the call for Türkyilmaz proved to be perfect timing.

Until that point Grasshoppers had been involved in a three-way tussle for the title with francophone rivals Sion and Neuchâtel Xamax. But after hammering Sion 3-0 at the Hardturm, the 'Hoppers went on to win all of their next six matches, with Türkyilmaz scoring at roughly a goal-a-game strikerate.

NATIONAL TEAM RESULTS 95/96

16/08/95	Iceland (ECQ)	A	Reykjavík	2-0	Knup (4), Türkyilmaz (18)
06/09/95	Sweden (ECQ)	A	Gothenburg	0-0	
11/10/95	Hungary (ECQ)	H	Zürich	3-0	Türkyilmaz (23), Sforza (56), Ohrel (89)
15/11/95	England	A	Wembley	1-3	Knup (40)
13/03/96	Luxembourg	A	Luxembourg	1-1	Vega (75)
27/03/96	Austria	A	Vienna	0-1	
24/04/96	Wales	H	Lugano	2-0	Coleman (32og), Türkyilmaz (42p)
01/06/96	Czech Republic	H	Basle	1-2	Grassi (33)
08/06/96	England (ECF)	A	Wembley	1-1	Türkyilmaz (82p)
13/06/96	Holland (ECF)	N	Birmingham	0-2	
18/06/96	Scotland (ECF)	N	Birmingham	0-1	

TOP SCORERS

19	Petar ALEKSANDROV (FC Luzern)
	Dinu Viorel MOLDOVAN (Neuchâtel Xamax FC)
16	Adrian KUNZ (Neuchâtel Xamax FC)
15	Oliver NEUVILLE (Servette FC Genève)
12	Tomislav ERCEG (FC Lugano/ Grasshopper-Club Zürich)
10	Alexandre REY (FC Basel)
	Agent SAWU (FC Luzern)
	Patrick ISABELLA (Neuchâtel Xamax FC)
9	Adrian ALLENSPACH (FC Aarau)
	Everson RATINHO (FC Aarau)
	Martin FINK (FC Luzern)

It was the surge that won the championship. Sion and Xamax were unable to match Grasshoppers' powerplay, and with two matches remaining the club's record 24th national title was confirmed in a 2-0 victory at home to traditional rivals Servette. Grasshoppers went on to complete the spring final round unbeaten. In their 14 games they conceded just seven goals and kept ten clean sheets. Much of the credit for that belonged to the excellent central defensive pairing of Swedish veteran Mats Gren and young buck Ramon Vega. In all coach Gross was forced to use 30 players during the championship campaign (more than any other club), and of those Gren and Vega were the most consistent along with the two international newcomers in midfield, Alexandre Comisetti and Massimo Lombardo.

One-time front-runners Xamax finished the season with five draws in a row, and that was only good enough to earn them third place in the final table. As well as a second successive qualification for the UEFA Cup, Gilbert Gress's side also boasted the joint-top goalscorer in the NLA, Romanian striker Dinu Viorel Moldovan, who hit an impressive tally of 19 in his first season to share the prize with his predecessor at Xamax, Lucerne's Petar Aleksandrov. Despite his goals Moldovan was the object of some harsh criticism from his coach at the end of the campaign, and that signalled his summer departure to

NATIONAL TEAM APPEARANCES 95/96

Coach - Roy HODGSON; ARTUR JORGE	ISL	SWE	HUN	ENG	LUX	AUT	WAL	TCH	ENG	HOL	SCO	Cps	Gls
Marco PASCOLO (09/05/66) - Servette FC Genève	G	G	G	G	G	G	G84	G	G	G	G	40	-
Marc HOTTIGER (07/11/67) - Newcastle United (ENG)/Everton (ENG)	D	D	D	D	D	D	s46	s46		M	D	63	5
Alain GEIGER (05/11/60) - Grasshopper-Club Zürich	D	D	D	D				D	M67			112	2
Stéphane HENCHOZ (07/09/74) - Hamburger SV (GER)	D	D	D	D	D	D	D		D	D	D	19	-
Yvan QUENTIN (02/05/70) - FC Sion	D	D	D	D82	D	D	D	D	D	D	D80	30	-
Christophe OHREL (07/04/68) - AS Saint-Etienne (FRA)	M	M	M	M	M69	M61	M64	M46				48	6
Ciriaco SFORZA (02/03/70) - FC Bayern München (GER)	M	M	M	M	M		M	M	M	M	M	44	6
Sébastien FOURNIER (27/06/71) - FC Sion	M	M	M81	M70	s61			M46			s46	13	1
Alain SUTTER (22/01/68) - FC Bayern München (GER)/SC Freiburg (GER)	M79	M46	s85	M80	M61		s64					62	5
Adrian KNUP (02/07/68) - Karlsruher SC (GER)	A	A	A89	A	A	A	s76					46	26
Kubilay TÜRKYILMAZ (04/03/67) - Galatasaray (TUR)/Grasshopper-Club Zürich	A85	A90	A85	A			A85	A	A	A	A	52	20
Thomas BICKEL (06/10/63) - Vissel Kobe (JPN)	s79		s81									52	5
Christophe BONVIN (14/04/65) - FC Sion	s85		s89						M69		A	43	8
Dominique HERR (25/10/65) - FC Sion		s46			D61							52	4
Marco GRASSI (08/08/68) - Stade Rennais FC (FRA)		s90		s80	s46	A	A76	A78	A	A		25	3
Murat YAKIN (15/09/74) - Grasshopper-Club Zürich			M									3	-
Stefan WOLF (31/01/71) - FC Luzern				s70								1	-
Ramon VEGA (14/06/71) - Grasshopper-Club Zürich				s82	s61		D	D	D	D	D	12	1
Christian COLOMBO (24/04/68) - FC Sion					M46	M						6	-
Stéphane CHAPUISAT (28/06/69) - Borussia Dortmund (GER)					A61		A64	s78	s69	A	A46	50	12
Alexandre COMISETTI (21/07/73) - Grasshopper-Club Zürich					s61	M	s85	s46		s68	s80	6	-
Marcel KOLLER (11/11/60) - Grasshopper-Club Zürich					s69	M61	s84	s78	s67		M46	55	3
Sébastien JEANNERET (12/12/73) - Neuchâtel Xamax FC						D			D	D68		3	-
Johann VOGEL (08/03/77) - Grasshopper-Club Zürich						s61	D46	M	M	M	M	8	-
David SESA (10/07/73) - Servette FC Genève						s61						1	-
Raphaël WICKY (26/04/77) - FC Sion							M84	D78			s46	3	-
Massimo LOMBARDO (09/01/73) - Grasshopper-Club Zürich							s64					1	-
Stephan LEHMANN (15/08/63) - FC Sion							s84					7	-

champions Grasshoppers. The runners-up spot went to Michel Decastel's Sion, the best supported club in the league with an average home gate of 11,457. The Valaisans had begun the campaign as championship favourites but only when the veteran Christophe Bonvin became influential did they look like title-winning material. The French pair of Vercruysse and Kombouaré slotted in well, but perhaps the best performances from a foreigner in the entire Swiss season came from Australian striker Aurelio Vidmar, who made an immediate impact in the final round after his winter transfer from Feyenoord.

Vidmar's big moment came in the Swiss Cup final against Servette when he struck the winning goal to complete an amazing Sion comeback from 0-2 down. Three goals in a ten-minute period midway through a dramatic second half completely transformed the match, enabling Sion to keep up their incredible 100 per cent success rate in Swiss Cup finals. This was their eighth final and their eighth win.

For Servette, defeat spelt another wasted season. The Geneva club had high hopes at the start of the campaign, but they were far too inconsistent in the league and could only finish seventh in the final round, winning just two of their 14 matches. The arrival of Umberto Barberis to replace Bernard Challandes did little to improve their fate, and he too was ousted in the summer...by a very big name in European football, 65-year-old Serie A veteran Vujadin Boskov.

Even more disappointing than Servette were Lugano. The club from the Italian-speaking region of Ticino brought great delight to Swiss football when they eliminated Italian giants Inter from the first round of the UEFA Cup, winning 1-0 in the San Siro. But things went steeply downhill from that moment on, and by the end of the season Lugano were holding onto their NLA status by their fingertips, having dropped into the promotion/relegation group at the mid-season cut-off point.

For the second season running all four NLA teams survived the play-offs and returned to the top flight. Young Boys' revival was remarkable. Rock bottom and without funds or a sponsor at the end of the first phase, they decided to launch their own anti-drugs campaign on their shirts. The crowds suddenly returned, and the Berne side proceeded to win the play-off group by five clear points.

PLAYERS OF THE SEASON

KUBILAY TÜRKYILMAZ

Switzerland's premier striker at Euro '96 was not Adrian Knup, nor Stéphane Chapuisat, but 29-year-old speed merchant Kubilay Türkyilmaz. He had a splendid first match against England and fully deserved to put his name on the scoresheet, albeit from a dodgy penalty. Alas for him and his team, that was to be Switzerland's only goal of the tournament. But at least Türkyilmaz had put himself in the international shop window. Having missed out on Switzerland's USA '94 adventure through injury, Euro '96 was a big event for the Grasshoppers striker. He certainly came to England in vibrant form, having almost single-handedly directed an injury-hit team in the direction of the Swiss title with eight goals and six assists in 12 matches following his mid-season move from Galatasaray.

RAMON VEGA

A son of Spanish immigrants, Ramon Vega only took out Swiss nationality at the age of 21. A national team fringe player during Roy Hodgson's reign, he was one of the few Swiss players to benefit from the Englishman's departure. Artur Jorge liked the look of the Grasshoppers centre-back and made him a first choice at Euro '96, where he played every minute of Switzerland's three matches. A jovial, happy-go-lucky individual, popular with everyone he meets, Vega can communicate in five different languages. He will be using his Italian more frequently now after agreeing to join Serie A side Cagliari. A return to his native Spain looked imminent until the Sardinians stepped up with an offer the 25-year-old could not refuse.

YVAN QUENTIN

He is not the most conspicuous or demonstrative player in the Swiss national team, but Yvan Quentin is undoubtedly one of his country's more consistent and reliable performers. In 1995/96 he played from the start in all 11 of the national team's fixtures, and there appears no imminent challenger to his place at left-back. A fan of heavy metal music and a restaurant waiter in his spare time, Quentin has remained loyal to his long-time club FC Sion while other internationals (Geiger, Hottiger etc.) have chosen to fly the nest. With one championship and three Swiss Cup wins already under his belt, he sees no urgent necessity to leave.

EUROPEAN CUPS RESULTS 95/96

CHAMPIONS' CUP

● GRASSHOPPER-CLUB ZÜRICH

Preliminary round MACCABI TEL-AVIV (ISR)

H 1-1 Yakin (50)
Zuberbühler; Gämperle, Vega, Gren, Vogel; Lombardo, Geiger, Yakin, Comisetti (Sermeter 72); Ibrahim (Magnin 61), Viscaal.

A 1-0 Comisetti (4)
Zuberbühler; Gämperle, Vega, Gren, Thüler; Lombardo, Geiger, Yakin, Comisetti (Vogel 63); Magnin (De Napoli 74), Viscaal (Ibrahim 46).

Champions' League

1st match FERENCVÁROS (HUN)

H 0-3
Zuberbühler; Vogel, Vega, Gren, Thüler (Viscaal 67); Lombardo, Koller, Geiger, Yakin, Comisetti (Ibrahim 58); Magnin (De Napoli 67).

2nd match REAL MADRID (ESP)

A 0-2
Zuberbühler; Nemtsoudis, Vega, Geiger, Thüler; Lombardo, Koller, Yakin, Vogel (Viscaal 76), Comisetti (Magnin 65); Udi (De Napoli 55).

3rd match AJAX (HOL)

A 0-3
Zuberbühler; Gämperle, Gren, Vega, Vogel; Lombardo, Geiger, Koller, Rzasa (Sermeter 73); Magnin, Viscaal.

4th match AJAX (HOL)

H 0-0
Foletti; Haas, Gren, Vega, Thüler; Lombardo, Geiger, Koller, Comisetti (Sermeter 81); Ibrahim (Viscaal 87), Magnin (De Napoli 68).

5th match FERENCVÁROS (HUN)

A 3-3 Subiat (22), Comisetti (48), Ibrahim (64)
Foletti; Haas, Vega, Gren, Gämperle; Lombardo, Geiger, Koller, Comisetti; Subiat, Ibrahim (Magnin 88).

6th match REAL MADRID (ESP)

H 0-2
Foletti; Haas, Vega, Gren, Gämperle; Lombardo, Geiger, Koller, Comisetti (Sermeter 76); Subiat (Magnin 66), Ibrahim (De Napoli 82).

CUP-WINNERS' CUP

● FC SION

Preliminary round TILIGUL TIRASPOL (MOL)

A 0-0
Lehmann; Sylvestre, Herr, Kombouaré, Quentin; Wicky, Vercruysse, Fournier, Bonvin (Moser 80); La Placa (Mirandinha 61), Chassot.

H 3-2 Moser (23), Herr (29), Bonvin (45)
Lehmann; Sylvestre, Kombouaré, Herr, Quentin (Bühlmann 72); Moser, Wicky, Vercruysse, Fournier (Giallanza 64); Chassot (Mirandinha 67), Bonvin.

1st round AEK (GRE)

A 0-2
Lehmann; Wicky; Sylvestre, Herr, Kombouaré, Quentin; Moser, Vercruysse, Fournier, La Placa (Bonvin 77); Mirandinha (Giallanza 83).

H 2-2 Bonvin (20), Giallanza (85)
Lehmann; Sylvestre, Herr, Kombouaré, Quentin; La Placa (Moser 63), Wicky, Fournier, Bühlmann (Giallanza 78); Chassot (Yenay 83), Bonvin.

UEFA CUP

● FC LUGANO

Preliminary round JEUNESSE ESCH (LUX)

A 0-0
Walker; Morf, Penzavalli, Fiechter, Fornera; Flindt (Gentizon 46), Esposito, Colombo, Shalimov (Manfreda 72), Carrasco; Sinval.

H 4-0 Erceg (18, 46, 54), Esposito (35)
Walker; Morf, Penzavalli, Fiechter, Fornera; Gentizon (Belloni 72), Shalimov (Bugnard 84), Colombo, Esposito; Erceg (Carrasco 57), Sinval.

1st round INTER (ITA)

H 1-1 Carrasco (67)
Walker; Morf, Penzavalli, Mauro Galvão, Fornera; Shalimov, Esposito (Manfreda 72), Colombo, Carrasco; Gentizon (Belloni 77), Erceg (Bugnard 90).

A 1-0 Carrasco (86)
Walker; Morf, Mauro Galvão, Penzavalli, Fornera; Gentizon (Belloni 81), Colombo, Shalimov, Esposito (Manfreda 9; Bugnard 71), Carrasco; Erceg.

2nd round SLAVIA PRAHA (TCH)

H 1-2 Shalimov (84)
Walker; Belloni (Bugnard 46), Morf, Penzavalli, Fornera; Gentizon (Fiechter 74), Shalimov, Colombo, Carrasco; Erceg, Sinval.

A 0-1
Walker; Morf, Penzavalli, Fiechter, Bugnard; Sinval, Colombo, Shalimov, Carrasco; Manfreda, Erceg.

● NEUCHATEL XAMAX FC

Preliminary round CRVENA ZVEZDA BEOGRAD (YUG)

A 1-0 Wittl (86)
Corminboeuf; Rueda; Jeanneret, Martin, Bonalair; Wittl, Rothenbühler, Détári, Gigon (Moret 75), Isabella (Dal Santo 86), Kunz (Tropiano 82).

H 0-0
Corminboeuf; Jeanneret (Moret 86), Rueda, Martin, Bonalair; Gigon, Perret, Rothenbühler; Isabella, Moldovan (Tropiano 77), Wittl.

1st round ROMA (ITA)

H 1-1 Jeanneret (14)
Corminboeuf; Jeanneret (Vernier 91), Rueda, Martin, Rothenbühler; Perret, Pana (Kunz 62), Bonalair; Isabella (Kägi 84), Moldovan, Wittl.

A 0-4
Corminboeuf; Jeanneret, Rueda, Martin, Bonalair; Rothenbühler, Perret (Vernier 46), Pana (Gigon 76); Isabella, Moldovan, Kunz (Wittl 46).

PROFILE

MARCO PASCOLO

Euro '96 was a forgettable experience for most people connected with the Switzerland team. But, for Marco Pascolo, the Swiss goalkeeper, the tournament is one he will remember with personal fondness.

Granted, his team were knocked out in the first round with just one point and one goal to their credit. But Pascolo kept the Swiss goal difference down to a minimum with three excellent displays. He started well against England at Wembley, thereby erasing from memory a far less distinguished display on the same ground against the same opposition some seven months earlier. And against Holland and Scotland he again looked a 'keeper of true international class. The Scots, especially, were frustrated time and again by Pascolo's interventions as they desperately strove to boost their goal tally and reach the next round.

In England, Pascolo got his revenge. On those Swiss fans who had doubted his ability. And partcularly on the media, who had never been kind to him. The biggest daily newspaper in Switzerland publicly apologised to Pascolo after Euro '96 for frequently referring to him as "Flopolo" in the past. Now, all over Switzerland, they refer to him once more as "Topolo".

The earlier criticism had not entirely been unjust. Pascolo had been known for suffering the odd goal-keeping nightmare on more than one big occasion. Once, in his early days with Sion, he was so bad in an important European Cup match that he was ousted from the team, to be replaced by Stephan Lehmann. Then, at Neuchâtel Xamax, his next club, he often had to play second fiddle to Joël Corminboeuf. Now this "half-Swiss, half-Italian" (his own term) is unquestionably Switzerland's number one, and his deputies in the national team go by the names of... Lehmann and Corminboeuf.

Pascolo's performances in England opened up a whole new career path. Before Euro '96 it was quite conceivable that the 30-year-old would go on to see out his career with Servette, happily living the quiet life on the banks of Lake Geneva with his wife and two daughters, Megan and Mélanie, and ocasionally popping down to his native Valais region to sample the wines from his brother-in-law's vineyard. But three big games later Pascolo was on the move. A lifetime's dream had been fulfilled. He was to quit Servette for Italy's Serie A and a lucrative contract with Sardinian club Cagliari.

Only one foreign goalkeeper has ever previously played in Italy's top league - the Brazilian World Cup winner Claudio Taffarel (ex-Parma and Reggiana). Now Pascolo has the chance to follow in his footsteps and perhaps, in this post-Bosman era, pave the way for many others. The pressure in Italy is sure to be something new, but Cagliari is not Inter, where Pascolo would surely have loved to rejoin his former mentor in the Swiss national team, Roy Hodgson.

Hodgson remains arguably the biggest single influence on Pascolo's career. The Englishman gave the goalkeeper his first big break when he was coach at Neuchâtel Xamax. He also handed Pascolo his international début in his own first match in charge of the Swiss national team - a 2-0 victory away to the United Arab Emirates in January 1992. And throughout his successful spell in the Switzerland hot seat Hodgson consistently maintained his confidence in the player despite a frequently hostile press. Artur Jorge, too, was not slow to appreciate the goalkeeper's many qualities.

At 30, Pascolo is not yet at his peak. Cagliari's gain will undoubtedly be Servette's loss. Pascolo was a key man in the club's surprise Swiss championship triumph of 1993/94 and in his five seasons at Les Charmilles, most of them as team captain, he brought much-needed stability and solidity to one of the country's more turbulent footballing institutions.

FC AARAU

CLUB DIRECTORY

FC Aarau
Postfach 2738
5001 Aarau
tel - (062) 8232922
fax - (062) 8232924
Year of Formation - 1902
President - Ernst Lämmli
Secretaries - Rolf Suter & Fredy Strasser
Coach - Martin Trümpler
Stadium - Brügglifeld (13,200)

MAJOR HONOURS

League Championship - (3) 1912, 1914, 1993.
Domestic Cup - (1) 1985.

APPEARANCES 95/96

	P	Ap	(s)	Gls
Adrian ALLENSPACH	A	12	(14)	9
Philipp ANDRIS	A		(1)	
David BADER	D	21	(8)	
Renato BRUGNOLI	D	3		
Sven CHRIST	D	31		1
Sasa CIRIC (MAC)	A	23	(8)	8
Moritz GNEHM	A		(1)	
Marcel HELDMANN	M	14		2
Andreas HILFIKER	G	32		
Bernd KILIAN	D	24	(3)	3
Daniel KRENN	A		(1)	
Dejan MARKOVIC	M	14	(12)	3
Walter MÜLLER	G	4		
Mirko PAVLICEVIC (CRO)	D	34	(1)	2
Everson RATINHO (BRA)	A	32		9
Jeff SAIBENE (LUX)	A	24	(8)	
Remo SENN	M	11	(15)	2
Dariusz SKRZYPCZAK (POL)	M	33	(1)	6
Beat STUDER	D	33		2
André WIEDERKEHR	A	18	(11)	4
Daniel WYSS	M	33	(1)	5
Davide ZITOLA (ITA)	A		(5)	

LEAGUE RESULTS 1995/96

19/07/95	FC Zürich	H	2-0	Wiederkehr 2
26/07/95	FC Luzern	A	0-3	
02/08/95	BSC Young Boys	H	0-0	
05/08/95	FC Sion	A	1-2	Wyss
19/08/95	Servette FC Genève	H	2-4	Markovic, Ciric
26/08/95	FC Lugano	A	0-2	
29/08/95	FC Basel	H	2-0	Markovic, Allenspach
09/09/95	Neuchâtel Xamax FC	A	2-3	Senn, Ratinho
16/09/95	Lausanne-Sports	A	2-0	Skrzypczak, Allenspach
19/09/95	FC St. Gallen	H	5-1	Ciric, Senn, Skrzypczak 2 (1p), Kilian
23/09/95	Grasshopper-Club Zürich	A	1-2	Ciric
30/09/95	FC Zürich	A	1-1	Allenspach
04/10/95	FC Luzern	H	1-1	Ratinho
15/10/95	Grasshopper-Club Zürich	H	1-1	Skrzypczak
21/10/95	BSC Young Boys	A	4-0	Ratinho 2 (1p), Christ, Skrzypczak
29/10/95	FC Sion	H	0-1	
05/11/95	Servette FC Genève	A	1-2	Wyss (p)
12/11/95	FC Lugano	H	5-0	Kilian, Allenspach 2, Pavlicevic, Ratinho
19/11/95	FC Basel	A	1-2	Ratinho
26/11/95	Neuchâtel Xamax FC	H	2-2	Wiederkehr, Ciric
03/12/95	Lausanne-Sports	H	3-0	Allenspach, Ratinho, Pavlicevic
10/12/95	FC St. Gallen	A	0-0	
PLAY-OFFS				
25/02/96	FC St. Gallen	H	4-0	Ciric 2 (1p), Allenspach, Wiederkehr
03/03/96	Grasshopper-Club Zürich	A	0-0	
17/03/96	FC Luzern	H	2-2	Heldmann 2
24/03/96	FC Basel	A	3-1	Studer 2, Markovic
31/03/96	Servette FC Genève	A	1-1	Ciric
04/04/96	Neuchâtel Xamax FC	H	3-2	og 2 (Rueda 2), Kilian
14/04/96	FC Sion	H	1-0	Wyss
18/04/96	FC Sion	A	0-2	
21/04/96	Neuchâtel Xamax FC	A	1-3	Wyss (p)
27/04/96	Servette FC Genève	H	3-0	Skrzypczak, Ciric, Ratinho
30/04/96	FC Basel	H	1-0	Ratinho
04/05/96	FC Luzern	A	0-4	
11/05/96	Grasshopper-Club Zürich	H	0-0	
14/05/96	FC St. Gallen	A	4-3	Allenspach 2, og (Tejeda), Wyss

FC BASEL

CLUB DIRECTORY

FC Basel
Postfach 260
4028 Basel
tel - (061) 3133666
fax - (061) 3133633
Year of Formation - 1893
President - Peter Epting
Secretary - Dr. Heinz Moser
Coach - Claude "Didi" Andrey; Karl Engel
Stadium - St. Jakob (42,000)

MAJOR HONOURS
League Championship - (8) 1953, 1967, 1969, 1970, 1972, 1973, 1977, 1980.
Domestic Cup - (5)
1933, 1947, 1963, 1967, 1975.

APPEARANCES 95/96

	P	Ap	(s)	Gls
Mario CANTALUPPI	M	25	(1)	
Masimo CECCARONI	A	31	(2)	
Theodoros DISSERIS (GRE)	M	1	(9)	
Yassine DOUIMI	A		(2)	
Yannick HASLER	D	2	(1)	
Stefan HUBER	G	36		
Oumar KONDE	D		(7)	
André MEIER	D	16	(5)	
Dominic MOSER	M	9	(15)	1
Daniele MORO	M	11	(3)	1
Alex NYARKO (GHA)	A	25	(1)	3
Gabriel OKOLOSI (NIG)	A	14	(11)	2
Lars OLSEN (DEN)	D	14		
Davide ORLANDO	A	20	(2)	
Alexandre REY	A	27	(3)	10
Roger SCHREIBER	M		(2)	
Admir SMAJIC (BOS)	M	33		2
Bruno SUTTER	A	26	(9)	3
Samir TABAKOVIC (BOS)	D	23		
Marco TSCHOPP	A		(1)	
Barbosa VILMAR	D	7	(1)	
Marco WALKER	D	30		2
Hakan YAKIN	A	18	(15)	6
Dario ZUFFI	A	28		3

LEAGUE RESULTS 1995/96

19/07/95	FC Sion	H	2-1	Rey 2
22/07/95	BSC Young Boys	A	4-1	Walker, Rey, Zuffi 2
29/07/95	Neuchâtel Xamax FC	A	0-1	
02/08/95	FC Luzern	H	2-0	Okolosi 2
05/08/95	FC Zürich	A	0-0	
19/08/95	FC Lugano	H	0-2	
26/08/95	Servette FC Genève	A	2-1	Smajic, Rey
29/08/95	FC Aarau	A	0-2	
09/09/95	Lausanne-Sports	H	0-1	
16/09/95	FC St. Gallen	A	1-0	Rey
19/09/95	Grasshopper-Club Zürich	H	1-3	Moro
30/09/95	FC Sion	A	1-4	Smajic (p)
04/10/95	BSC Young Boys	H	1-0	Yakin
14/10/95	Neuchâtel Xamax FC	H	0-2	
21/10/95	FC Luzern	A	1-3	Zuffi (p)
28/10/95	FC Zürich	H	0-3	
05/11/95	FC Lugano	A	1-0	Nyarko
12/11/95	Servette FC Genève	H	2-2	Rey 2
19/11/95	FC Aarau	H	2-1	Sutter, Moser
26/11/95	Lausanne-Sports	A	0-1	
03/12/95	FC St. Gallen	H	0-0	
10/12/95	Grasshopper-Club Zürich	A	3-1	Rey 2, og (Vega)
PLAY-OFFS				
25/02/96	Servette FC Genève	A	1-1	Yakin
03/03/96	Neuchâtel Xamax FC	H	1-2	Sutter
17/03/96	FC Sion	A	0-2	
24/03/96	FC Aarau	H	1-3	Nyarko
31/03/96	FC St. Gallen	H	1-1	Walker
14/04/96	Grasshopper-Club Zürich	A	0-3	
18/04/96	Grasshopper-Club Zürich	H	0-2	
21/04/96	FC Luzern	H	1-0	Yakin
27/04/96	FC St. Gallen	A	0-3	
30/04/96	FC Aarau	A	0-1	
04/05/96	FC Sion	H	2-0	Yakin, Rey
07/05/96	FC Luzern	A	1-1	Yakin
11/05/96	Neuchâtel Xamax FC	A	1-1	Yakin
14/05/96	Servette FC Genève	H	2-0	Nyarko, Sutter

GRASSHOPPER-CLUB ZÜRICH

CLUB DIRECTORY

Grasshopper-Club Zürich
Fussball-Sektion
Postfach 217
8037 Zürich
tel - (01) 2723388
fax - (01) 2719790
Year of Formation - 1886
President - Romano Spadaro
Secretary - Erich Vogel
Coach - Christian Gross
Stadium - Hardturm (20,079)

MAJOR HONOURS

League Championship - (24) 1898, 1900, 1901, 1905, 1921, 1927, 1928, 1931, 1937, 1939, 1942, 1943, 1945, 1952, 1956, 1971, 1978, 1982, 1983, 1984, 1990, 1991, 1995, 1996.
Domestic Cup - (18) 1926, 1927, 1932, 1934, 1937, 1938, 1940, 1941, 1942, 1943, 1946, 1952, 1956, 1983, 1988, 1989. 1990, 1994.

APPEARANCES 95/96

	P	Ap	(s)	Gls
Heyman ABDULLAHI (NIG)	A	10	(13)	2
Stefan BALMER	D	1		
Jan BERGER	M	2		
Rainer BIELI	A		(1)	
Alexandre COMISETTI	M	32		8
Patrick DE NAPOLI	A	8	(12)	3
Tomislav ERCEG (CRO)	A	4	(5)	3
Patrick FOLETTI	G	10		
Harald GÄMPERLE	D	27		
Alain GEIGER	M	23	(2)	1
Mats GREN (SWE)	D	33		2
Bernt HAAS	D	19	(1)	
Ali IBRAHIM (GHA)	A	17	(7)	6
Luca JODICE	D		(8)	
Marcel KOLLER	M	28		1
Massimo LOMBARDO	M	32	(1)	5
Joël MAGNIN	A	17	(9)	4
Giorgios NEMTSOUDIS	A	3	(1)	
Dusan PAVLOVIC	A		(1)	
Tomasz RZASA (POL)	M	3	(4)	
Boris SMILJANIC	D	3	(3)	
Nestor SUBIAT	A	4	(2)	3
Patrick THÜLER	D	15		1
Kubilay TÜRKYILMAZ	A	12		8
Duke UDI	A		(7)	
Ramon VEGA	D	30		4
Eric VISCAAL (HOL)	A	9	(4)	7
Johann VOGEL	M	22	(2)	
Murat YAKIN	M	6	(2)	3
Patrick ZUBERBÜHLER	G	26		

LEAGUE RESULTS 1995/96

19/07/95	Servette FC Genève	H	1-1	Thüler
22/07/95	FC Sion	A	1-2	Comisetti
02/08/95	FC Zürich	A	4-1	Viscaal 2, Ibrahim, Comisetti
05/08/95	FC Lugano	A	1-1	Lombardo
19/08/95	FC Luzern	H	4-0	Comisetti, og (Van Eck), Yakin, Magnin
26/08/95	BSC Young Boys	A	1-0	Magnin
30/08/95	Lausanne-Sports	A	2-1	De Napoli, Lombardo
09/09/95	FC St. Gallen	H	3-1	Yakin, Viscaal 2
16/09/95	Neuchâtel Xamax FC	H	2-1	Viscaal 2 (1p)
19/09/95	FC Basel	A	3-1	Comisetti 2, De Napoli
23/09/95	FC Aarau	H	2-1	Viscaal, De Napoli
30/09/95	Servette FC Genève	A	0-2	
04/10/95	FC Sion	H	2-0	Subiat, Keller
15/10/95	FC Aarau	A	1-1	Comisetti
22/10/95	FC Zürich	H	2-0	Geiger, Ibrahim
27/10/95	FC Lugano	H	1-0	Ibrahim
05/11/95	FC Luzern	A	0-2	
12/11/95	BSC Young Boys	H	3-0	Magnin, Ibrahim, Comisetti
18/11/95	Lausanne-Sports	H	1-1	Lombardo
26/11/95	FC St. Gallen	A	2-1	Lombardo, Subiat (p)
03/12/95	Neuchâtel Xamax FC	A	1-2	Subiat
10/12/95	FC Basel	H	1-3	Yakin
PLAY-OFFS				
25/02/96	Neuchâtel Xamax FC	A	0-0	
03/03/96	FC Aarau	H	0-0	
17/03/96	Servette FC Genève	A	2-2	Türkyilmaz, Vega
24/03/96	FC Sion	H	3-0	Comisetti, Türkyilmaz, Abdullahi
31/03/96	FC Luzern	H	2-1	Ibrahim, Magnin
08/04/96	FC St. Gallen	A	4-0	Lombardo, Türkyilmaz 2, og (Brunner)
14/04/96	FC Basel	H	3-0	Vega, Türkyilmaz 2
17/04/96	FC Basel	A	2-0	Erceg, Türkyilmaz
21/04/96	FC St. Gallen	H	3-0	Gren, Ibrahim, og (Koch)
27/04/96	FC Luzern	A	2-1	Abdullah, Gren
30/04/96	FC Sion	A	0-0	
04/05/96	Servette FC Genève	H	2-0	Vega, Erceg
11/05/96	FC Aarau	A	0-0	
14/05/96	Neuchâtel Xamax FC	H	3-3	Vega, Erceg, Türkyilmaz

LAUSANNE-SPORTS

CLUB DIRECTORY

Lausanne-Sports
Case postale 175
1018 Lausanne 18
tel - (021) 6461341
fax - (021) 6461359
Year of Formation - 1896
President - Jean-François Kurz
Secretary - Blaise Richard
Coach - Georges Bregy
Stadium - Stade Olympique La Pontaise (16,000)

MAJOR HONOURS
League Championship - (7)
1913, 1932, 1935, 1936, 1944, 1951, 1965.
Domestic Cup - (7)
1935, 1939, 1944, 1950, 1962, 1964, 1981.

APPEARANCES 95/96

	P	Ap	(s)	Gls
Philippe BATEZA	M	1	(5)	
Olivier BIAGGI	D	22		4
Benny BITARELLI	A		(1)	
Martin BRUNNER	G	22		
Fabio CELESTINI	M		(4)	
Raphaël COMISETTI	M	9	(10)	
Jacek DEMBINSKI (POL)	A	19		3
Paolo DIOGO	M	3	(10)	
Martin FRYAND	A	20	(2)	5
Erich HÄNZI	D	21		
Ricardo IGLESIAS	D		(1)	
Thomas KÄSLIN	M	19	(2)	2
Roger KÜFFER	D	16	(4)	1
Badile LUBANBA	A		(2)	
Manfred OGGIER	D	22		
Blaise PIFFARETTI	M	21		
Thierry PISTER (BEL)	D	20		
Stefan REHN (SWE)	M	22		6
Salvatore ROMANO (ITA)	A	5	(4)	2
Stéphane SAVOVIC	M		(5)	
Léonard THURRE	A		(10)	1

LEAGUE RESULTS 1995/96

19/07/95	FC Luzern	H	3-1	Käslin, Romano, og (Aleksandrov)
22/07/95	FC Lugano	A	1-1	Romano
29/07/95	FC St. Gallen	A	1-2	Dembinski
02/08/95	Servette FC Genève	H	0-0	
05/08/95	BSC Young Boys	A	1-1	Käslin
19/08/95	FC Zürich	H	3-0	Biaggi 2, Dembinski
26/08/95	FC Sion	A	0-1	
30/08/95	Grasshopper-Club Zürich	H	1-2	Fryand
09/09/95	FC Basel	A	1-0	Küffer
16/09/95	FC Aarau	H	0-2	
19/09/95	Neuchâtel Xamax FC	A	2-4	Fryand 2
30/09/95	FC Luzern	A	1-1	Rehn
04/10/95	FC Lugano	H	3-0	Rehn 2 (1p), Thurre
15/10/95	FC St. Gallen	H	0-0	
21/10/95	Servette FC Genève	A	1-1	Biaggi
28/10/95	BSC Young Boys	H	2-0	Fryand, Rehn
05/11/95	FC Zürich	A	1-3	Biaggi
12/11/95	FC Sion	H	1-1	Rehn
18/11/95	Grasshopper-Club Zürich	A	1-1	Rehn
26/11/95	FC Basel	H	1-0	Dembinski
03/12/95	FC Aarau	A	0-3	
10/12/95	Neuchâtel Xamax FC	H	1-1	Fryand

FC LUGANO

CLUB DIRECTORY

FC Lugano
CP 4136
6904 Lugano
tel - (091) 9409040
fax - (091) 9409055
Year of Formation - 1908
President - Helios Jermini
Secretary - Angelo Maina
Coach - Roberto Morinini (96/97 - Michel Pont)
Stadium - Cornaredo (15,000)

MAJOR HONOURS
League Championship - (3) 1938, 1941, 1949.
Domestic Cup - (3) 1931, 1968, 1993.

APPEARANCES 95/96

	P	Ap	(s)	Gls
Sebastiano BELLONI	M	1	(8)	
Jane BUGNARD	D	12	(7)	
José CARRASCO	M	17	(5)	1
Christian COLOMBO	M	20		1
Patrick ENGLUND (SWE)	D	6		
Tomislav ERCEG (CRO)	A	17	(1)	9
Antonio ESPOSITO	M	7	(2)	1
Mark FIECHTER	M	9	(5)	
Christian FLINDT (DEN)	M	14	(1)	
William FORNERA	D	15	(1)	
Ivan GENTIZON	D	20	(2)	
Massimo GHEZZI	M		(2)	
Mohammed KALLON	A	1		
Giuseppe MANFREDA	A	8	(9)	1
MAURO GALVÃO (BRA)	D	12		
Antonio MODICA	D		(1)	
René MORF	D	22		1
Daniele PENZAVALLI	M	18	(1)	
Igor SHALIMOV (RUS)	M	5	(1)	3
SINVAL Ferreira (BRA)	A	16	(2)	4
Philipp WALKER	G	22		

LEAGUE RESULTS 1995/96

19/07/95	FC St. Gallen	A	0-3	
22/07/95	Lausanne-Sports	H	1-1	Erceg
29/07/95	BSC Young Boys	A	1-3	Esposito
02/08/95	Neuchâtel Xamax FC	H	0-3	
05/08/95	Grasshopper-Club Zürich	H	1-1	Sinval
19/08/95	FC Basel	A	2-0	Erceg, Shalimov
26/08/95	FC Aarau	H	2-0	Carrasco, Erceg
30/08/95	FC Sion	H	1-3	Morf
09/09/95	FC Luzern	A	1-1	Erceg
16/09/95	FC Zürich	H	1-1	Manfreda
19/09/95	Servette FC Genève	A	3-2	Sinval, Shalimov 2
30/09/95	FC St. Gallen	H	1-1	Sinval
04/10/95	Lausanne-Sports	A	0-3	
13/10/95	BSC Young Boys	H	2-0	Erceg, Sinval
21/10/95	Neuchâtel Xamax FC	A	0-4	
27/10/95	Grasshopper-Club Zürich	A	0-1	
05/11/95	FC Basel	H	0-1	
12/11/95	FC Aarau	A	0-5	
19/11/95	FC Sion	A	2-5	Erceg 2
26/11/95	FC Luzern	H	1-1	Erceg
03/12/95	FC Zürich	A	2-1	Erceg, Colombo
10/12/95	Servette FC Genève	H	0-2	

FC LUZERN

CLUB DIRECTORY

FC Luzern
Kauffmannweg 7
Postfach 2918
6002 Luzern
tel - (041) 2102041
fax - (041) 2102141
Year of Formation - 1901
President - Romano Simioni
Secretary - Raymond Lütenegger
Coach - Jean-Paul Brigger
Stadium - Allmend (25,300)

MAJOR HONOURS
League Championship - (1) 1989.
Domestic Cup - (2) 1960, 1992.

APPEARANCES 95/96

	P	Ap	(s)	Gls
Petar ALEKSANDROV (BUL)	A	29	(1)	19
Manuel BACHMANN	A	6	(10)	
Herbert BAUMANN	D	36		
Eric BOUDOUMA	A		(1)	
Johnson BWALYA (ZAM)	A	12	(10)	
Oliver CAMENZIND	A	24	(2)	
Martin FINK	A	32	(1)	9
Peter GMÜR	D	34		2
Manfred JOLLER	D	22	(6)	
Ivan KNEZ	D	11	(14)	
Pavel KARPF	G	2	(1)	
Ludwig KÖGL (GER)	A	7	(1)	2
Yulianto KURNIAWAN (INA)	A	4	(9)	2
Maurizio MELINA	M	2	(3)	1
Moreno MERENDA	A		(7)	1
Sascha MÜLLER	A	5	(4)	
Beat MUTTER	G	34		
Stefan RENGGLI	A	4	(10)	
Agent SAWU (ZIM)	A	28	(3)	10
Gerardo SEOANE	M	22	(4)	2
René VAN ECK (HOL)	D	34		
Stefan WOLF	D	22		5
Thomas WYSS	M	26	(1)	5

LEAGUE RESULTS 1995/96

19/07/95	Lausanne-Sports	A	1-3	Gmür
26/07/95	FC Aarau	H	3-0	Aleksandrov 2, Fink
29/07/95	FC Zürich	H	1-0	Aleksandrov
02/08/95	FC Basel	A	0-2	
12/08/95	Neuchâtel Xamax FC	H	3-2	Wyss, Melina, Aleksandrov
19/08/95	Grasshopper-Club Zürich	A	0-4	
26/08/95	FC St. Gallen	H	1-1	Fink
30/08/95	BSC Young Boys	A	4-0	Fink 3, Merenda
09/09/95	FC Lugano	H	1-1	Wyss
16/09/95	Servette FC Genève	H	2-1	Wolf 2
20/09/95	FC Sion	A	3-1	Kurniawan, Sawu, Wyss
30/09/95	Lausanne-Sports	H	1-1	Wolf
03/10/95	FC Aarau	A	1-1	Aleksandrov
14/10/95	FC Zürich	A	1-0	Wolf
21/10/95	FC Basel	H	3-1	Aleksandrov, Fink, Kurniawan
28/10/95	Neuchâtel Xamax FC	A	1-1	Fink
05/11/95	Grasshopper-Club Zürich	H	2-0	Sawu 2
12/11/95	FC St. Gallen	A	1-1	Aleksandrov
19/11/95	BSC Young Boys	H	3-1	Wyss, Sawu, Aleksandrov
26/11/95	FC Lugano	A	1-1	Wolf (p)
03/12/95	Servette FC Genève	A	0-1	
10/12/95	FC Sion	H	3-2	Aleksandrov 2, Wyss (p)
PLAY-OFFS				
25/02/96	FC Sion	A	0-1	
03/03/96	Servette FC Genève	H	2-1	Sawu, Aleksandrov
17/03/96	FC Aarau	A	2-2	Aleksandrov 2
24/03/96	Neuchâtel Xamax FC	H	0-1	
31/03/96	Grasshopper-Club Zürich	A	1-2	Seoane
14/04/96	FC St. Gallen	H	5-0	Fink, Aleksandrov, Sawu, Seoane, Kögl
18/04/96	FC St. Gallen	A	0-1	
21/04/96	FC Basel	A	0-1	
27/04/96	Grasshopper-Club Zürich	H	1-2	Aleksandrov
01/05/96	Neuchâtel Xamax FC	A	1-1	Gmür
04/05/96	FC Aarau	H	4-0	Aleksandrov, Sawu 2, Fink
07/05/96	FC Basel	H	1-1	Sawu
11/05/96	Servette FC Genève	A	4-3	Sawu, Aleksandrov, Kögl, og (Baumann)
14/05/96	FC Sion	H	2-3	Aleksandrov 2 (1p)

NEUCHATEL XAMAX FC

CLUB DIRECTORY

Neuchâtel Xamax FC
Boîte postale 78
2000 Neuchâtel 8 Monruz
tel - (038) 254428
fax - (038) 242128
Year of Formation - 1970
President - Gilbert Facchinetti
Secretary - Michel Favre
Coach - Gilbert Gress
Stadium - La Maladière (20,000)

MAJOR HONOURS
League Championship - (2) 1987, 1988.

APPEARANCES 95/96

	P	Ap	(s)	Gls
Thierry BONALAIR (FRA)	D	34		3
Joël CORMINBOEUF	G	34		
Ivan DAL SANTO	M		(1)	
Florent DELAY	G	2		
Lajos DÉTÁRI (HUN)	M	3		
Samuele DRAKOPOULOS	A		(16)	2
Zdravko DRNCIC	M		(1)	
Didier GIGON	M	20	(9)	1
Patrick ISABELLA	A	35		10
Sébastien JEANNERET	D	33	(2)	1
Mario KÄGI	M	4	(6)	1
Adrian KUNZ	A	29	(5)	16
Lionel MARTIN	D	19	(7)	
Dinu Viorel MOLDOVAN (ROM)	A	32		19
Lionel MORET	D	2	(7)	
Christophe MOULIN	M		(1)	
Constantin PANA (ROM)	M	9	(9)	1
Basarab Nica PANDURU (ROM)	M	2	(5)	
Philippe PERRET	M	32		
Régis ROTHENBÜHLER	M	35		
Martin RUEDA	D	35		1
Roberto TROPIANO (ITA)	A		(8)	
Alain VERNIER	D	14	(8)	2
Charles WITTL (GHA)	M	22	(7)	3

LEAGUE RESULTS 1995/96

19/07/95	BSC Young Boys	H	0-1	
22/07/95	Servette FC Genève	A	0-3	
29/07/95	FC Basel	H	1-0	Kunz
02/08/95	FC Lugano	A	3-0	Kunz, Moldovan 2
12/08/95	FC Luzern	A	2-3	Wittl, Bonalair
19/08/95	FC Sion	H	3-0	Isabella, Kunz, Moldovan
26/08/95	FC Zürich	A	3-1	Wittl, Moldovan, Bonalair
30/08/95	FC St. Gallen	A	1-1	Moldovan
09/09/95	FC Aarau	H	3-2	Isabella, Moldovan 2
16/09/95	Grasshopper-Club Zürich	A	1-2	Kägi
19/09/95	Lausanne-Sports	H	4-2	Rueda, Kunz 2, Vernier
30/09/95	BSC Young Boys	A	2-1	Drakopoulos, Kunz
04/10/95	Servette FC Genève	H	1-0	Kunz
14/10/95	FC Basel	A	2-0	Moldovan, Drakopoulos
21/10/95	FC Lugano	H	4-0	Moldovan 2, Kunz 2
28/10/95	FC Luzern	H	1-1	Jeanneret
05/11/95	FC Sion	A	1-1	Moldovan
12/11/95	FC Zürich	H	0-2	
19/11/95	FC St. Gallen	H	3-0	Moldovan 2, Vernier
26/11/95	FC Aarau	A	2-2	Gigon, Bonalair
03/12/95	Grasshopper-Club Zürich	H	2-1	Isabella 2
10/12/95	Lausanne-Sports	A	1-1	Kunz
PLAY-OFFS				
25/02/96	Grasshopper-Club Zürich	H	0-0	
03/03/96	FC Basel	A	2-1	Moldovan, Kunz
17/03/96	FC St. Gallen	H	3-0	Kunz, Isabella 2
24/03/96	FC Luzern	A	1-0	Pana
31/03/96	FC Sion	H	2-0	Isabella, Kunz
04/04/96	FC Aarau	A	2-3	Moldovan, og (Christ)
14/04/96	Servette FC Genève	A	1-4	Moldovan
18/04/96	Servette FC Genève	H	1-1	Isabella
21/04/96	FC Aarau	H	3-1	Isabella 2, Moldovan
27/04/96	FC Sion	A	1-1	Moldovan
01/05/96	FC Luzern	H	1-1	Kunz
04/05/96	FC St. Gallen	A	0-0	
11/05/96	FC Basel	H	1-1	Moldovan
14/05/96	Grasshopper-Club Zürich	A	3-3	Wittl, Kunz 2

FC ST. GALLEN

CLUB DIRECTORY

FC St. Gallen
Postfach 14
9009 St. Gallen
tel - (071) 2456765
fax - (071) 2454671
Year of Formation - 1879
President - Dr. Hans Hurni
Secretary - Philippe Lutz
Coach - Uwe Rapolder; Roger Hegi
Stadium - Espenmoos (13,700)

MAJOR HONOURS
League Championship - (1) 1904.
Domestic Cup - (1) 1969.

APPEARANCES 95/96

	P	Ap	(s)	Gls
Paulo ANDRIOLI (BRA)	M	11		
Markus BRUNNER	D	31		3
Patrick BÜHLMANN	M	8	(3)	1
Stéphane DE SIEBENTHAL	D	14	(1)	
Mamadou DIALLO (SEN)	A	19	(3)	7
Adrian EUGSTER	D		(3)	
Leandro FONSECA (BRA)	A	11	(21)	4
Mario FRICK (LIE)	A	28	(1)	6
Marco GIANNINI	M	15	(4)	
Heribert KOCH	D	36		1
Reto LOEPFE	G	1		
Luíz MILTON (BRA)	M	32		3
Marzio MOROCUTTI	A	1	(9)	1
Mohammed MOUIDI (MAR)	D	34	(2)	2
Eric PEDAT	G	35		
Georgi SLAVCHEV (BUL)	M	6	(3)	
Ralph STEINGRUBER	M	5	(16)	1
Beat SUTTER	A	16	(13)	2
Julio TEJEDA	M	27	(2)	1
Dorjee TSAWA	D	4	(6)	
Markus WANNER	D	13	(3)	
Patrick WINKLER	M	20	(6)	
Marc ZELLWEGER	A	29	(5)	4

LEAGUE RESULTS 1995/96

19/07/95	FC Lugano	H	3-0	Brunner, Frick 2
22/07/95	FC Zürich	A	4-0	Tejeda, Milton, Frick, Zellweger
29/07/95	Lausanne-Sports	H	2-1	Zellweger, Steingruber
02/08/95	FC Sion	A	0-1	
05/08/95	Servette FC Genève	A	2-2	Frick, Sutter
19/08/95	BSC Young Boys	H	0-0	
26/08/95	FC Luzern	A	1-1	Zellweger
30/08/95	Neuchâtel Xamax FC	H	1-1	Sutter
09/09/95	Grasshopper-Club Zürich	A	1-3	og (Thüler)
16/09/95	FC Basel	H	0-1	
19/09/95	FC Aarau	A	1-5	Fonseca
30/09/95	FC Lugano	A	1-1	Mouidi
04/10/95	FC Zürich	H	1-0	Brunner
15/10/95	Lausanne-Sports	A	0-0	
21/10/95	FC Sion	H	3-0	Milton, Fonseca, Morocutti
28/10/95	Servette FC Genève	H	4-0	Frick, Brunner, Diallo 2
05/11/95	BSC Young Boys	A	0-2	
12/11/95	FC Luzern	H	1-1	Diallo
19/11/95	Neuchâtel Xamax FC	A	0-3	
26/11/95	Grasshopper-Club Zürich	H	1-2	Koch
03/12/95	FC Basel	A	0-0	
10/12/95	FC Aarau	H	0-0	
PLAY-OFFS				
25/02/96	FC Aarau	A	0-4	
17/03/96	Neuchâtel Xamax FC	A	0-3	
24/03/96	Servette FC Genève	H	0-0	
31/03/96	FC Basel	A	1-1	Frick (p)
04/04/96	FC Sion	H	0-4	
08/04/96	Grasshopper-Club Zürich	H	0-4	
14/04/96	FC Luzern	A	0-5	
18/04/96	FC Luzern	H	1-0	Zellweger
21/04/96	Grasshopper-Club Zürich	A	0-3	
27/04/96	FC Basel	H	3-0	Bühlmann, Diallo 2 (1p)
30/04/96	Servette FC Genève	A	2-3	Diallo, Mouidi
04/05/96	Neuchâtel Xamax FC	H	0-0	
11/05/96	FC Sion	A	1-3	Fonseca
14/05/96	FC Aarau	H	3-4	Diallo, Fonseca, Milton

SERVETTE FC GENEVE

CLUB DIRECTORY

Servette FC Genève
Case postale 431
1219 Châtelaine (Genève)
tel - (022) 3450666
fax - (022) 3450608
Year of Formation - 1890
President - Paul-Annick Weiller
Coach - Bernard Challandes; Umberto Barberis
(96/97 - Vujadin Boskov)
Stadium - Les Charmilles (11,078)

MAJOR HONOURS
League Championship - (16) 1907, 1918, 1922, 1925, 1926, 1930, 1933, 1934, 1940, 1946, 1950, 1961, 1962, 1979, 1985, 1994.
Domestic Cup - (6)
1928, 1949, 1971, 1978, 1979, 1984.

APPEARANCES 95/96

	P	Ap	(s)	Gls
Jean-Michel AEBY	D	25	(3)	
Sébastien BARBERIS	M	33	(2)	4
Eddy BAREA	D	19	(6)	
Julien BAUMANN	A	2	(12)	1
Denis DUCHOSAL	D		(7)	1
Jan ERIKSSON (SWE)	D	6		
Walter FERNANDEZ	D	18	(2)	3
Luca IPPOLITI (ITA)	A	23	(5)	6
JUAREZ de Sousa (BRA)	D	19		
Jean-Philippe KARLEN	D	32		
Samuel MARGARINI	D	13	(14)	2
Pascal MARGUERAT	G	1		
Patrick MÜLLER	A	10	(18)	
Vaclav NEMECEK (TCH)	M	30		1
Oliver NEUVILLE	A	34		15
Marco PASCOLO	G	35		
Alberto PALAZZONI	M		(1)	
Lionel PIZZINAT	M	4	(2)	
RENATO Canil (BRA)	M	18	(2)	1
David SESA	A	31	(2)	8
Jonathan SOGBIE (LIB)	A	22	(3)	4
Eddy VARELA	M		(1)	
René WEILER	A	21	(4)	

LEAGUE RESULTS 1995/96

19/07/95	Grasshopper-Club Zürich	A	1-1	Neuville
22/07/95	Neuchâtel Xamax FC	H	3-0	Sesa, Fernandez (p), Neuville
29/07/95	FC Sion	H	0-1	
02/08/95	Lausanne-Sports	A	0-0	
05/08/95	FC St. Gallen	H	2-2	Neuville, Sesa
19/08/95	FC Aarau	A	4-2	Neuville 2, Sesa 2
26/08/95	FC Basel	H	1-2	Duchosal
30/08/95	FC Zürich	A	1-2	Sesa
09/09/95	BSC Young Boys	H	0-0	
16/09/95	FC Luzern	A	1-2	Barberis
19/09/95	FC Lugano	H	2-3	Fernandez, Neuville
30/09/95	Grasshopper-Club Zürich	H	2-0	Neuville, Nemecek
04/10/95	Neuchâtel Xamax FC	A	0-1	
14/10/95	FC Sion	A	1-3	Neuville
21/10/95	Lausanne-Sports	H	1-1	Neuville
28/10/95	FC St. Gallen	A	0-4	
05/11/95	FC Aarau	H	2-1	Fernandez, Neuville
12/11/95	FC Basel	A	2-2	Margarini, Neuville
19/11/95	FC Zürich	H	0-0	
26/11/95	BSC Young Boys	A	2-1	Renato, Sogbie
03/12/95	FC Luzern	H	1-0	Neuville
10/12/95	FC Lugano	A	2-0	Barberis, Sogbie
PLAY-OFFS				
25/02/96	FC Basel	H	1-1	Ippoliti
03/03/96	FC Luzern	A	1-2	Barberis
17/03/96	Grasshopper-Club Zürich	H	2-2	Sesa, Ippoliti
24/03/96	FC St. Gallen	A	0-0	
31/03/96	FC Aarau	H	1-1	Ippoliti
08/04/96	FC Sion	A	2-3	Sesa, Neuville
14/04/96	Neuchâtel Xamax FC	H	4-1	Neuville, Ippoliti, Sogbie 2
18/04/96	Neuchâtel Xamax FC	A	1-1	Neuville
21/04/96	FC Sion	H	0-1	
27/04/96	FC Aarau	A	0-3	
30/04/96	FC St. Gallen	H	3-2	Ippoliti 2, Margarini
04/05/96	Grasshopper-Club Zürich	A	0-2	
11/05/96	FC Luzern	H	3-4	Sesa (p), Baumann, Barberis
14/05/96	FC Basel	A	0-2	

FC SION

CLUB DIRECTORY

FC Sion
Rue des Echutes
1950 Sion
tel - (027) 317172
fax - (027) 317173
Year of Formation - 1909
President - Christian Constantin
Secretary - Paul-André Dubosson
Coach - Michel Decastel
Stadium - Tourbillon (19,526)

MAJOR HONOURS
League Championship - (1) 1992.
Domestic Cup - (8) 1965, 1974, 1980, 1982, 1986, 1991, 1995, 1996.

APPEARANCES 95/96

	P	Ap	(s)	Gls
Christophe BONVIN	M	22	(7)	5
Fabrice BORER	G	2	(4)	
Patrick BÜHLMANN	M	10	(6)	2
Frédéric CHASSOT	A	7	(10)	2
Christian COLOMBO	M	10	(2)	2
Grégory DURUZ	D		(1)	
Sébastien FOURNIER	D	31		1
Alain GASPOZ	D	14	(6)	2
Gaetano GIALLANZA	A	9	(14)	3
Dominique HERR	D	26	(1)	1
Antoine KOMBOUARE (FRA)	D	25		7
Jean-Pierre LA PLACA	A	7	(14)	4
Stephan LEHMANN	G	34		
Johan LONFAT	M	14	(3)	
MIRANDINHA Isailton (BRA)	A	23	(6)	4
Heinz MOSER	M	19	(8)	1
Antonio PASCALE	A		(3)	
Yvan QUENTIN	D	27		4
Patrick SYLVESTRE	M	32		1
Philippe VERCRUYSSE (FRA)	M	26		6
Aurelio VIDMAR (AUS)	A	13		7
Raphaël WICKY	D	32		1
Josephus YENAY (LIB)	A	5	(2)	1
Sébastien ZAMBAZ	D	8	(5)	1

LEAGUE RESULTS 1995/96

19/07/95	FC Basel	A	1-2	Vercruysse
22/07/95	Grasshopper-Club Zürich	H	2-1	Vercruysse 2
29/07/95	Servette FC Genève	A	1-0	Kombouaré
02/08/95	FC St. Gallen	H	1-0	La Placa
05/08/95	FC Aarau	H	2-1	Kombouaré 2 (1p)
19/08/95	Neuchâtel Xamax FC	A	0-3	
26/08/95	Lausanne-Sports	H	1-0	Quentin
30/08/95	FC Lugano	A	3-1	Vercruysse, Giallanza, La Placa
09/09/95	FC Zürich	H	2-2	Giallanza, Vercruysse
19/09/95	FC Luzern	H	1-3	Kombouaré (p)
23/09/95	BSC Young Boys	A	4-1	Bühlmann 2 (1p), Chassot, La Placa
01/10/95	FC Basel	H	4-1	Quentin, Kombouaré 2 (2p), Mirandinha
04/10/95	Grasshopper-Club Zürich	A	0-2	
14/10/95	Servette FC Genève	H	3-1	Quentin, Chassot, og (Nemecek)
21/10/95	FC St. Gallen	A	0-3	
29/10/95	FC Aarau	A	1-0	Mirandinha
05/11/95	Neuchâtel Xamax FC	H	1-1	Yenay
12/11/95	Lausanne-Sports	A	1-1	Fournier
19/11/95	FC Lugano	H	5-2	Vercruysse, Wicky, Bonvin, Mirandinha, Zambaz
26/11/95	FC Zürich	A	1-0	La Placa
03/12/95	BSC Young Boys	H	1-0	Bonvin
10/12/95	FC Luzern	A	2-3	Herr, Vercruysse
PLAY-OFFS				
25/02/96	FC Luzern	H	1-0	Vidmar
17/03/96	FC Basel	H	2-0	Vidmar (p), Colombo
24/03/96	Grasshopper-Club Zürich	A	0-3	
31/03/96	Neuchâtel Xamax FC	A	0-2	
04/04/96	FC St. Gallen	A	4-0	Vidmar 2, Kombuaré, Bonvin
08/04/96	Servette FC Genève	H	3-2	Vidmar, Bonvin 2
14/04/96	FC Aarau	A	0-1	
17/04/96	FC Aarau	H	2-0	Quentin, Giallanza
21/04/96	Servette FC Genève	A	1-0	Vidmar
27/04/96	Neuchâtel Xamax FC	H	1-1	Vidmar
30/04/96	Grasshopper-Club Zürich	H	0-0	
04/05/96	FC Basel	A	0-2	
11/05/96	FC St. Gallen	H	3-1	Gaspoz 2, Moser
14/05/96	FC Luzern	A	3-2	Colombo, Sylvestre, Mirandinha

BSC YOUNG BOYS

CLUB DIRECTORY

BSC Young Boys
Postfach 61
3000 Bern 22
tel - (031) 3318484
fax - (031) 3330555
Year of Formation - 1898
President - Roland Schönenberger
Secretary - Jürg Wittwer
Coach - Jean-Marie Conz
Stadium - Wankdorf (37,551)

MAJOR HONOURS
League Championship - (11)
1903, 1909, 1910, 1911, 1920, 1929, 1957, 1958, 1959, 1960, 1986.
Domestic Cup - (6)
1930, 1945, 1953, 1958, 1977, 1987.

APPEARANCES 95/96

	P	Ap	(s)	Gls
Gottfried ADUOBE (GHA)	M	8	(2)	1
Adrian AEBI	D	17	(1)	
Alain BAUMANN	D	18		
Marc BRECHBUHL	A	2	(1)	
Bent CHRISTENSEN (DEN)	M	18		2
Marco DITTGEN (GER)	A	21		5
Philipp EICH	D	5	(3)	
Andres GERBER	M	13	(8)	1
Reto GERTSCHEN	M	14	(2)	
Luca GIANINAZZI	A	1	(4)	1
Bahram HATTES	D		(1)	
Rafael KEHRLI	M	2		
Martin LENGEN	D	12	(1)	
Michel MAIANO	A	7	(5)	
Dominik NEFF	M	5	(6)	
Rachid NEQROUZ (MAR)	D	19		2
Antonio PAGANO	M	6	(4)	
Lubos PLEVKA (SVK)	A	6	(2)	
Robert PRYTZ (SWE)	M	5		
Bernard PULVER	G	22		
Rolf ROTZETTER	D	1	(1)	
Markus RUEF	A	4	(8)	
Hugo STREUN	D	19		
René SUTTER	M	17	(1)	2
Jann TADORIAN	D		(1)	

LEAGUE RESULTS 1995/96

19/07/95	Neuchâtel Xamax FC	A	1-0	Dittgen
22/07/95	FC Basel	H	1-4	Dittgen
29/07/95	FC Lugano	H	3-1	Neqrouz, Christensen, Dittgen
02/08/95	FC Aarau	A	0-0	
05/08/95	Lausanne-Sports	H	1-1	Gerber
19/08/95	FC St. Gallen	A	0-0	
26/08/95	Grasshopper-Club Zürich	H	0-1	
30/08/95	FC Luzern	H	0-4	
09/09/95	Servette FC Genève	A	0-0	
19/09/95	FC Zürich	A	0-0	
23/09/95	FC Sion	H	1-4	Aduobe
30/09/95	Neuchâtel Xamax FC	H	1-2	Christensen
04/10/95	FC Basel	A	0-1	
13/10/95	FC Lugano	A	0-2	
21/10/95	FC Aarau	H	0-4	
29/10/95	Lausanne-Sports	A	0-2	
05/11/95	FC St. Gallen	H	2-0	Sutter, Dittgen
12/11/95	Grasshopper-Club Zürich	A	0-3	
19/11/95	FC Luzern	A	1-3	Sutter
26/11/95	Servette FC Genève	H	1-2	Dittgen
03/12/95	FC Sion	A	0-1	
10/12/95	FC Zürich	H	2-0	Gianinazzi, Neqrouz

FC ZÜRICH

CLUB DIRECTORY

FC Zürich
Postfach 413
8021 Zürich
tel - (01) 4927474
fax - (01) 4910759
Year of Formation - 1896
President - Sven Hotz
Secretary - Erich Schmid
Coach - Raimondo Ponte
Stadium - Letzigrund (23,500)

MAJOR HONOURS

League Championship - (9) 1902, 1924, 1963, 1966, 1968, 1974, 1975, 1976, 1981.
Domestic Cup - (5)
1966, 1970, 1972, 1973, 1976.

APPEARANCES 95/96

	P	Ap	(s)	Gls
Aljosa ALEKSANDRIC	D		(1)	
Jørn ANDERSEN (NOR)	D	14		1
Roberto BALDASSARRI (ITA)	M	17	(3)	1
Pascal CASTILLO (ITA)	A	9	(6)	2
Franco DI JORIO	M	11	(7)	1
Mark DISLER	D	6	(4)	
Urs FISCHER	D	21		
Giuseppe GAMBINO	D	19		2
Urs GÜNTENSPERGER	A	19		7
Marc HODEL	D	7		
John HOEKS	A	3	(2)	
Robert HUBER	D	13	(3)	
Nicolo KOSIK	D		(1)	
August MAKALAKALANE (SAF)	M	11	(7)	1
Giuseppe MAZZARELLI	M	20	(1)	
Jerry NIXON (TRI)	M	17	(2)	2
Pino NOCITA	M		(1)	
Andreas SCHMID	A		(1)	
Jörg STIEL	G	22		
Jürg STUDER	D	13	(6)	
Daniel TARONE	M	12	(6)	
Carmelo TRANDE	A		(1)	
Roger WALKER	M	2	(4)	
Roland WIDMER	D	6	(3)	

LEAGUE RESULTS 1995/96

19/07/95	FC Aarau	A	0-2	
22/07/95	FC St. Gallen	H	0-4	
29/07/95	FC Luzern	A	0-1	
02/08/95	Grasshopper-Club Zürich	H	1-4	Güntensperger
05/08/95	FC Basel	H	0-0	
19/08/95	Lausanne-Sports	A	0-3	
26/08/95	Neuchâtel Xamax FC	H	1-3	Baldassarri
30/08/95	Servette FC Genève	H	2-1	Di Jorio, Gambino
09/09/95	FC Sion	A	2-2	Güntensperger 2
16/09/95	FC Lugano	A	1-1	Andersen
19/09/95	BSC Young Boys	H	0-0	
30/09/95	FC Aarau	H	1-1	Nixon
04/10/95	FC St. Gallen	A	0-1	
14/10/95	FC Luzern	H	0-1	
22/10/95	Grasshopper-Club Zürich	A	0-2	
28/10/95	FC Basel	A	3-0	Güntensperger, Gambino, Castillo
05/11/95	Lausanne-Sports	H	3-1	Makalakalane, Güntensperger, Nixon
12/11/95	Neuchâtel Xamax FC	A	2-0	Güntensperger 2
19/11/95	Servette FC Genève	A	0-0	
26/11/95	FC Sion	H	0-1	
03/12/95	FC Lugano	H	1-2	Castillo
10/12/95	BSC Young Boys	A	0-2	

PROMOTED CLUBS

SECOND DIVISION FINAL TABLE 95/96

		Pd	W	D	L	F	A	Pt	GD
1	SC Kriens	22	14	2	6	43	23	44	+20
2	Yverdon-Sports	22	11	5	6	41	23	38	+18
3	SR Delémont	22	11	5	6	40	33	38	+7
4	Etoile-Carouge FC	22	9	8	5	26	24	35	+2
5	FC Winterthur	22	9	5	8	26	21	32	+5
6	FC Baden	22	9	5	8	31	27	32	+4
7	FC Schaffhausen	22	7	7	8	33	31	28	+2
8	FC Wil	22	7	7	8	34	36	28	-2
9	FC Chiasso	22	6	7	9	19	25	25	-6
10	FC Solothurn	22	6	5	11	26	37	23	-11
11	FC Locarno	22	5	6	11	20	33	21	-13
12	FC Naters	22	4	6	12	16	42	18	-26

PROMOTION/RELEGATION PLAY-OFFS FINAL TABLE 94/95

		Pd	W	D	L	F	A	Pt	GD
1	BSC Young Boys	14	10	3	1	28	13	33	+15
2	FC Zürich	14	8	4	2	21	12	28	+9
3	Lausanne-Sports	14	7	6	1	24	10	27	+14
4	FC Lugano	14	4	5	5	13	17	17	-4
5	Yverdon-Sports	14	3	4	7	16	22	13	-6
6	SR Delémont	14	3	4	7	17	26	13	-9
7	SC Kriens	14	2	5	7	14	22	11	-8
8	Etoile Carouge FC	14	1	5	8	9	20	8	-11

TURKEY

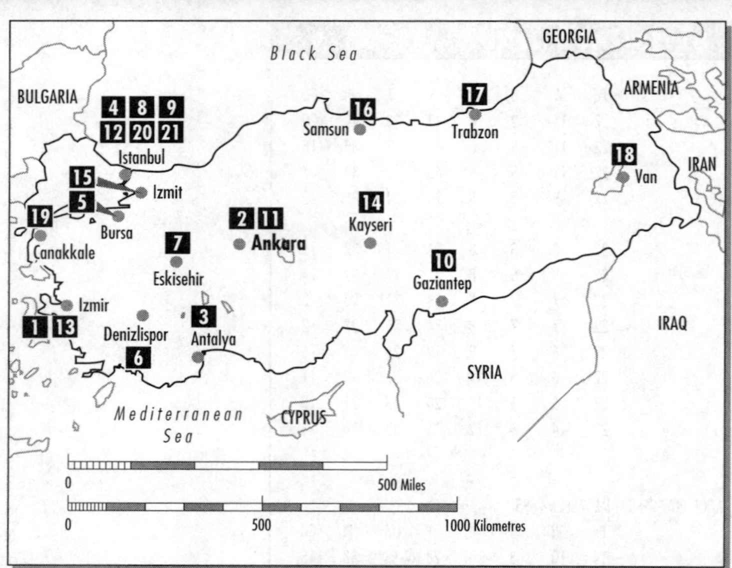

1	ALTAY	1018
2	ANKARAGÜCÜ	1019
3	ANTALYASPOR	1020
4	BESIKTAS	1021
5	BURSASPOR	1022
6	DENIZLISPOR	1023
7	ESKISEHIRSPOR	1024
8	FENERBAHÇE	1025
9	GALATASARAY	1026
10	GAZIANTEPSPOR	1027
11	GENÇLERBIRLIGI	1028
12	ISTANBULSPOR	1029
13	KARSIYAKA	1030
14	KAYSERISPOR	1031
15	KOCAELISPOR	1032
16	SAMSUNSPOR	1033
17	TRABZONSPOR	1034
18	VANSPOR	1035
19	ÇANAKKALE DARDANELSPOR	1037
20	SARIYER	1037
21	ZEYTINBURNU	1037

TRABZONSPOR THROW TITLE AWAY

No points, no goals... but a lesson learned

FEDERATION DIRECTORY

Türkiye Futbol Federasyonu
Konaklar Mahallesi Ihlamurlu Sokak 9, 80620, 4.Levent, Istanbul
tel - (212) 2827020 | Year of Formation - 1923
tlx - 46308 btff tr | President - Senes Erzik
fax - (212) 2827008 | Secretary - Abdullah Kigili
Stadium - Inönu, Istanbul (45,000)

Turkey fulfilled their dream of reaching the European Championship finals for the first time. But, like Greece at the 1994 World Cup, the ecstasy of earning their qualifying ticket soon turned to agony when they arrived at their destination. Fatih Terim and his players had done the country proud by reaching their first major tournament in 32 years. The celebrations that greeted Turkey's qualification after the team's gritty 2-2 draw in Sweden were typically wild and elaborate. But seven months later in England, despite the comforting presence of around 20,000 of their fellow countrymen, the team were unable to lift themselves to greater heights.

Turkey's Euro '96 figures do not make pleasant reading. Three games, three defeats, no goals scored, five conceded. Not quite as bad as the Greeks in America, but a comprehensive failure all the same. And yet the Turks did not play all that poorly. They certainly deserved a draw in their opening match with Croatia. For the first half-hour they appeared full of confidence as they stroked the ball about smartly and sharply in midfield. But what they lacked, both against Croatia and the Portuguese and Danes, was a potent attacking thrust to fix onto their bright midfield interplay.

The man everybody expected to shine in England was central striker Hakan Sükür, the so-called 'Bull of the Bosphorous'. But if there were any red rags around, he was blind to them. He scored seven goals in the qualifiers, but in England he barely got a sniff. True, the service to him was poor, but he generally loitered without intent and his reputation shrivelled as a result. Abdullah Ercan, the buzzing blond on the left side of midfield, was far and away Turkey's most enterprising player. The rest were much of a muchness, though young central defender Vedat Inceefe, from the Turkish Second Division, looked a very fine prospect and, despite his inexperience, was one of only five Turkish players rewarded with a full 90 minutes in each of the team's three games.

LEAGUE CHAMPIONSHIP RESULTS 95/96

		1	2	3	4	5	6	7	8	9	10	11	12	13	14	15	16	17	18
1	Altay		1-0	1-2	3-0	1-3	1-2	1-0	0-1	2-5	2-1	1-3	0-0	0-0	2-0	3-2	0-0	2-5	1-1
2	Ankaragücü	4-0		2-1	0-1	1-0	1-1	1-2	0-3	2-2	0-0	2-0	3-1	1-0	1-1	4-0	1-0	1-3	0-0
3	Antalyaspor	2-1	2-1		0-3	4-2	1-0	1-0	0-1	0-2	0-1	1-0	0-0	4-0	3-3	1-1	2-1	0-2	4-1
4	Besiktas	3-0	2-1	3-0		4-1	0-4	2-0	1-2	1-2	5-3	2-2	5-2	4-0	4-1	3-5	4-2	2-0	3-1
5	Bursaspor	0-1	8-0	2-1	1-2		2-2	2-2	0-0	2-0	3-0	1-1	2-1	3-1	1-2	2-2	2-4	1-2	5-0
6	Denizlispor	1-0	2-3	3-1	0-3	0-0		1-2	0-2	1-3	0-1	3-0	1-2	1-0	2-2	0-0	1-2	0-3	0-0
7	Eskisehirspor	1-2	2-1	0-2	2-3	1-3	1-1		1-2	1-2	2-0	2-0	1-2	0-2	4-0	0-3	3-0	0-2	2-1
8	Fenerbahçe	2-2	2-0	3-1	2-0	1-1	0-0	6-0		3-1	1-0	0-0	2-0	4-0	2-1	4-0	1-0	3-1	3-0
9	Galatasaray	3-1	5-0	1-2	1-3	3-1	1-0	3-0	2-0		2-0	0-1	4-2	3-0	5-0	0-4	1-0	0-0	2-0
10	Gaziantepspor	2-1	1-0	2-0	1-1	3-0	3-2	3-0	2-2	1-1		2-0	1-6	3-0	1-0	2-4	3-0	0-0	1-0
11	Gençlerbirligi	1-2	1-2	6-3	1-2	2-1	1-1	3-2	3-1	1-2	1-0		2-0	2-0	1-1	1-1	0-0	1-3	1-1
12	Istanbulspor	1-1	0-0	1-0	2-3	1-1	2-3	1-3	1-2	1-1	2-0	1-1		0-4	5-2	1-2	0-2	1-4	1-1
13	Karsiyaka	1-1	0-0	1-2	0-2	0-3	2-0	3-2	0-1	0-3	2-1	1-1	0-3		1-3	1-2	1-0	1-4	2-1
14	Kayserispor	1-1	4-1	4-0	1-1	0-0	0-0	0-1	1-3	1-2	1-2	2-2	0-1	1-1		1-0	3-2	1-2	3-1
15	Kocaelispor	1-1	2-0	2-2	1-0	4-2	4-2	2-1	0-1	1-1	2-2	2-0	0-0	2-0	5-0		3-1	1-3	1-0
16	Samsunspor	4-0	2-1	2-2	0-1	1-0	1-3	3-1	0-3	3-2	1-0	3-0	4-4	4-1	0-0	0-0		0-1	4-1
17	Trabzonspor	2-0	3-1	2-0	3-1	0-0	3-0	7-1	1-2	4-1	0-0	3-1	2-1	3-0	3-1	2-0	1-0		0-1
18	Vanspor	2-0	4-1	1-1	2-0	1-1	3-1	3-0	0-3	0-1	2-0	0-1	0-0	1-1	1-0	2-2	0-0	0-5	

LEAGUE CHAMPIONSHIP FINAL TABLE 95/96

			Home					Away					Total						
		Pd	W	D	L	F	A	W	D	L	F	A	W	D	L	F	A	Pt	GD
1	Fenerbahçe	34	13	4	0	39	7	13	2	2	29	12	26	6	2	68	19	84	+49
2	Trabzonspor	34	13	2	2	39	10	13	2	2	40	14	26	4	4	79	24	82	+55
3	Besiktas	34	12	1	4	48	26	10	2	5	26	20	22	3	9	74	46	69	+28
4	Galatasaray	34	12	1	4	36	14	9	4	4	31	24	21	5	8	67	38	68	+29
5	Kocaelispor	34	10	5	2	33	16	6	6	5	28	27	16	11	7	61	43	59	+18
6	Gaziantepspor	34	11	4	2	31	17	3	3	11	11	26	14	7	13	42	43	49	-1
7	Antalyaspor	34	9	3	5	25	19	4	3	10	20	36	13	6	15	45	55	45	-10
8	Samsunspor	34	9	4	4	32	20	3	3	11	14	26	12	7	15	46	46	43	=
9	Bursaspor	34	7	5	5	37	21	3	6	8	19	27	10	11	13	56	48	41	+8
10	Gençlerbirligi	34	7	5	5	28	22	3	6	8	13	26	10	11	13	41	48	41	-7
11	Ankaragücü	34	8	5	4	24	15	1	2	13	12	41	10	7	17	36	56	37	-20
12	Altay	34	6	4	7	21	25	3	5	9	14	31	9	9	16	35	56	36	-21
13	Istanbulspor	34	3	6	8	21	30	5	5	7	25	27	8	11	15	46	57	35	-11
14	Vanspor	34	7	6	4	22	17	1	5	11	10	33	8	11	15	32	50	35	-18
15	Denizlispor	34	4	4	9	16	24	4	6	7	22	26	8	10	16	38	50	34	-12
16	Kayserispor	34	5	6	6	24	20	2	5	10	17	41	7	11	16	41	61	32	-20
17	Eskisehirspor	34	6	1	10	23	26	4	1	12	17	42	10	2	22	40	68	32	-28
18	Karsiyaka	34	5	3	9	16	29	2	3	12	10	36	7	6	21	26	65	27	-39

The general reaction to Turkey's poor showing was one of shame and anger. But beneath the disappointment lay an acknowledgement of Fatih Terim's achievement in taking the team to the finals and of the invaluable experience gained for the future. The coach probably committed a faux pas when he announced just prior to Euro '96 that he would be quitting the national team to join Galatasaray. But he still left with his head held high. In less than three years he and his assistant Rasim Kara had transformed Turkey from complete no-hopers into one of the top 16 sides in Europe, taking them on an unparalleled 16-match unbeaten run along the way. Only the happy ending was missing.

With Fatih Terim being offered a king's ransom to take over at Galatasaray, and Rasim Kara becoming the first non-foreign coach for 15 years at Besiktas, Turkish club football is no doubt about the pair's credentials. In fact, 96/97 sees all three big Istanbul clubs changing their coach. Fenerbahçe have appointed Brazil's 1990 World Cup boss Sebastião Lazaroni to take over from the 1994 incumbent Carlos Alberto Parreira.

INTERNATIONAL HONOURS

World Cup Finals appearances: 1954

European Championship appearances: 1996

TOP SCORERS

25	Shota ARVELADZE (Trabzonspor)
22	Elvir BOLIC (Fenerbahçe)
21	SAFFET Sancakli (Galatasaray/Kocaelispor)
18	ERTUGRUL Saglam (Besiktas)
16	HAKAN Sükür (Galatasaray)
15	Majed MUSISI (Bursaspor)
	Dean SAUNDERS (Galatasaray)
14	SERKAN Aykut (Samsunspor)

NATIONAL TEAM RESULTS 95/96

30/08/95	Macedonia	H	Istanbul	2-1	Ogün (7), Hami (49)
06/09/95	Hungary (ECQ)	H	Istanbul	2-0	Hakan (9, 32)
04/10/95	Finland	A	Helsinki	0-0	
11/10/95	Iceland (ECQ)	A	Reykjavík	0-0	
15/11/95	Sweden (ECQ)	A	Solna	2-2	Hakan (63), Andersson P. (72og)
14/02/96	Belarus	H	Izmir	3-2	Ertugrul (26p, 34p), Kemalettin (75)
26/03/96	Czech Republic	A	Ostrava	0-3	
09/04/96	Azerbaijan	A	Baku	1-0	Rahim (47)
01/05/96	Ukraine	H	Samsun	3-2	Hakan (8), Faruk (13), Tugay (32)
29/05/96	Estonia	A	Tallinn	0-0	
02/06/96	Finland	A	Helsinki	2-1	Tugay (35), Saffet (54)
11/06/96	Croatia (ECF)	N	Nottingham	0-1	
14/06/96	Portugal (ECF)	N	Nottingham	0-1	
19/06/96	Denmark (ECF)	N	Sheffield	0-3	

NATIONAL TEAM APPEARANCES 95/96

Coach - FATIH Terim	MAC	HUN	FIN	ISL	SWE	BLS	TCH	AZB	UKR	EST	FIN	CRO	POR	DEN	Cps	Gls
RÜSTÜ Reçber (10/05/73) - Fenerbahçe	G	G	G	G	G	G				G	G	G	G	G	19	-
RECEP Çetin (01/10/65) - Besiktas	D	D	D	D		D	D46		D46	D	D46		D	D68	50	1
ALPAY Özalan (29/05/73) -Besiktas	D	D	D	D	D	D	D		D	D	D	D	D	D	23	1
OSMAN Özköylü (26/08/71) - Trabzonspor	D46	D	D	D	D										11	-
TUGAY Kerimoglu (24/08/70) - Galatasaray	D	M	M	M	M	M	M75		M		M	M	M	M	41	2
OGÜN Temizkanoglu (06/10/69) - Trabzonspor	M82	D		D	M	D	D			M46	D	M	D46	D	40	4
OGUZ Çetin (15/02/63) - Fenerbahçe	M46	M	M58	M	M68	M46	M46			M46	s46		M69		60	2
SERGEN Yalçin (05/10/72) - Besiktas	M46	M46	s58	M74					M88		M46	M	M		16	3
ABDULLAH Ercan (08/12/71) - Trabzonspor	M72	M	M	M		M	M				M	M	M	M	28	-
HAKAN Sükür (01/09/71) - Torino (ITA)/Galatasaray	A	A89			A	A46	A64		A46	A46	A	A	A	A46	31	14
HAMI Mandirali (20/07/68) - Trabzonspor	A	A86	A	A			s75			s71		s82		A	40	7
TOLUNAY Kafkas (31/03/68) - Trabzonspor	s46	s46	M	s74	M	M46	M			M70	M	M88	s62		21	2
BÜLENT Uygun (01/08/71) - Fenerbahçe	s46	s89				s46				s70					11	1
EMRE Asik (24/10/73) - Fenerbahçe	s46														9	1
ORHAN Çikrikçi (15/04/67) - Trabzonspor	s72									s46			M68		27	2
KEMALETTIN Sentürk (09/02/70) - Fenerbahçe	s82				s46	s46	s75								4	1
BÜLENT Korkmaz (24/11/68) - Galatasaray		s86	D			s78	D		s85	D46	D			s68	48	1
ERTUGRUL Saglam (19/11/69) - Besiktas			A	A	s68	A78	s46		s46	s46					23	9
TAYFUN Korkut (02/04/74) - Fenerbahçe					M		s46		s46	s46				M	5	-
HALIL IBRAHIM Kara (26/09/72) - Fenerbahçe					M46										2	-
OKTAY Derelioglu (17/12/75) - Besiktas					A46										1	-
ARIF Erdem (02/01/72) - Galatasaray					s46	M	A75			s46	A46	A82	s69	s46	14	1
SAFFET Sancakli (27/02/66) - Kocaelispor						s46	s64		s46	A71	s46	s88	A62	s68	16	4
ENGIN Ipekoglu (07/06/61) - Fenerbahçe							G								28	-
SANVER Göymen (22/01/67) - Altay								G46	G						5	-
RAHIM Zafer (25/01/71) - Gençlerbirligi								D	D	D		D	s46		5	1
VEDAT Inceefe (01/04/74) - Karabükspor								D	D85			D	D	D	5	-
CÜNEYT Aksu (1969) - Denizlispor								D46							1	-
ERKAN Avseren (01/07/71) - Vanspor								M	M	M46					3	-
SELAHETTIN Özbir (22/07/74) - Yeni Afyonspor								M46	s88						2	-
ENGIN Özdemir (01/10/68) - Gençlerbirligi								M88	M46						2	-
IBRAHIM Köseoglu (18/01/68) - Bursaspor								M46							1	-
ÜMIT Davala (30/07/73) - Diyarbakirspor								M							1	-
FARUK Yigit (15/04/66) - Kocaelispor								A83	A67	s46					7	1
SAFFET Akyüz (11/03/70) - Istanbulspor								A							2	-
ADNAN Erkan (15/01/68) - Ankaragücü								s46							1	-
ÜMIT Hatipoglu (1973) - Elazigspor								s46	s67						2	-
OSMAN Akyol (01/09/69) - Antalyaspor								s46							2	-
ILHAN Sancaktar (1973) - Kayserispor								s46							1	-
ERBIL Uzel (1974) - Karsiyaka								s83							1	-
MEHMET ALI Honca (1971) - Gaziantepspor								s88							1	-
SINAN Yesil (19/02/72) - Samsunspor									s46						1	-

EUROPEAN CUPS RESULTS 95/96

CHAMPIONS' CUP

● BESIKTAS

Preliminary round ROSENBORG BK (NOR)

A 0-3
Aumann; Ali, Mutlu, Johnsen, Alpay, Ertugrul, Orhan, Serdar (Mehmet), Riza, Sergen (Oktay), Kuntz.

H 3-1 Kuntz (9, 85p), Mehmet (88)
Aumann; Recep, Johnsen, Alpay, Riza, Sergen, Mehmet, Mutlu, Sertan (Oktay), Orhan, Kuntz.

CUP-WINNERS' CUP

● TRABZONSPOR

1st round ZALGIRIS VILNIUS (LIT)

A 2-2 Arveladze S. (25), Abdullah (54)
Metin; Ogün, Cengiz, Iskender, Lemi, Tolunay, Ünal (Arveladze A.), Fatih, Abdullah, Hami (Orhan), Arveladze S..

H 1-0 Hami (37)
Nihat; Ogün, Cengiz, Osman, Lemi (Hamdi), Tolunay, Ünal, Arveladze A. (Soner), Abdullah, Hami, Arveladze S. (Fatih).

2nd round RC DEPORTIVO (ESP)

H 0-1
Nihat; Ogün, Osman, Cengiz, Lemi, Tolunay (Soner), Ünal (Fatih), Hami, Abdullah (Orhan), Arveladze S., Arveladze A..

A 0-3
Nihat; Lemi, Okan, Osman, Cengiz, Abdullah, Arveladze S. (Soner), Ünal, Fatih, Hami (Hasan), Orhan (Hami).

UEFA CUP

● GALATASARAY

Preliminary round SPARTA PRAHA (TCH)

A 1-3 Saunders (57)
Nezihi; Bekir, Venison, Bülent, Tugay, Suat (Okan), Hakan Ünsal, Yusuf, Saffet (Türkyilmaz), Arif (Feti), Saunders.

H 1-1 Saunders (3)
Nezihi; Bekir, Venison, Bülent, Tugay, Suat, Hakan Ünsal, Feti (Ugur), Saffet (Arif), Türkyilmaz, Saunders.

● FENERBAHÇE

Preliminary round PARTIZANI TIRANË (ALB)

H 2-0 Bolic (71), Bülent (87)
Rüstü; Saffet (Bülent), Okechukwu, Høgh, Erol (Halil Ibrahim), Tarik, Oguz, Kemalettin, Tayfun, Bolic, Feyyaz (Aykut).

A 4-0 Bülent (15), Kemalettin (23), Bolic (59), Aygün (86)
Rüstü; Ilker, Emre, Høgh, Erol (Halil Ibrahim), Kemalettin, Oguz (Aygün), Ali Nail, Tayfun, Bülent, Bolic (Aykut).

1st round REAL BETIS (ESP)

H 1-2 Aykut (73)
Rüstü; Ilker (Mustafa), Høgh, Okechukwu, Erol, Kemalettin, Oguz, Aygün (Ali Nail), Tayfun, Bülent (Aykut), Bolic.

A 0-2
Rüstü; Emre, Saffet, Okechukwu, Halil Ibrahim, Aygün (Feyyaz), Tayfun, Høgh, Oguz, Aykut, Bülent (Tarik).

The man who guided the *selecção* to USA '94 glory came up trumps again for Turkey's most popular club in 95/96, giving 'Fener' their first Turkish championship win for seven years. Controversial, charismatic club president Ali Sen dearly wanted to keep Carlos Alberto on, but the Brazilian opted to return home to coach FC São Paulo.

Faithful to his reputation, Carlos Alberto created a Fenerbahçe team with the emphasis on security and solidity in defence and midfield. The team's three outstanding players were all defenders. Young national team goalkeeper Rüstü was consistently excellent, and the central defensive pairing of Danish sweeper Jes Høgh and Nigerian stopper Uche Okechukwu revived the marvellous understanding built when paired together a couple of years earlier at Brøndby.

Not that Fenerbahçe were a boring, defensive team. They also scored goals - at an average of two per game - and in Bosnian Elvir Bolic and Englishman Dalian Atkinson they possessed a mobile and versatile strikeforce. Frontman Aykut Kocaman also chipped in with his usual supply of vital goals, none more crucial than the one he netted in the 83rd minute of the team's penultimate away game of the season, against title rivals Trabzonspor, which gave Fenerbahçe a 2-1 win and effectively sealed the championship.

For Trabzonspor, without a national title since 1984, that 1-2 defeat (coming after they had taken an early lead) was excruciatingly hard to take. Indeed, two of the club's supporters were so depressed by the outcome of the match that they took their own lives. It was the match Trabzonspor could not afford to lose. They had been the front-runners for most of the season. An 11-match winning run in the autumn had sounded the alarm to the Istanbul giants, and as they entered the home run, the team from the Black Sea still held sway at the top of the table.

The first major dent to their ambitions came with an unthinkable 0-1 home defeat by Vanspor. It was remarkable for many reasons. Trabzonspor had not lost a league match at home for 18 months, Vanspor had not won away all season, and in the first meeting between the two clubs back in November Trabzonspor had knocked in five goals.

Trabzonspor's next home game, a fortnight later, was against Fenerbahçe. A draw would have maintained their one-point lead with two matches remaining, but Aykut's late winner completely transformed the championship picture. Trabzonspor predictably thrashed relegation candidates Karsiyaka and Eskisehirspor in their last two games, with Georgian striker Shota Arveladze raising his goals total to a league-best 25, but it was not enough. Fenerbahçe also took six points from their final two games, the latter, curiously enough, at Vanspor, where two penalties and an own-goal sealed their triumph.

Fenerbahçe had been denied a possible 'double' a month earlier when arch-rivals Galatasaray beat them in the two-legged Cup final 2-1 thanks to an extra-time winner from Welshman Dean Saunders. Galatasaray coach Graeme Souness caused an outrage when he marked his team's win by planting a Galatasaray flag in the middle of the pitch at Fenerbahçe's stadium. The Scotsman won few friends in Turkey, and it was no surprise that his first season at Galatasaray was also his last. The team never had a settled look about it. Marsh, Venison, Türkyilmaz and Saffet all left at various intervals, while Hakan and goalkeeper Friedel arrived after the season was already underway.

Besiktas's season was one of similar woe. It started badly with a Champions' League preliminary-round exit at the hands of Rosenborg and ended in disaster with five heavy league defeats on the trot. German coach Christoph Daum, a title-winning hero the previous season, was sent packing before the season was complete, though he lasted a lot longer than another high-profile foreign coach, Dutchman Leo Beenhakker. He was sacked after just eight games (seven of them defeats) of Istanbulspor's league campaign.

The ambitious newly-promoted side just managed to avoid relegation thanks to the goals of mid-season signing Oleg Salenko from Rangers. With Sariyer and Zeytinburnu achieving promotion (along with Division Two champions Çanakkale Dardanelspor), the number of Istanbul clubs in the top flight has now risen to six - a third of the total in the entire division.

DOMESTIC CUP RESULTS

FIFTH ROUND

Kocaelispor 2, Yeni Afyonspor 1
Kartalspor 1, Denizlispor 2
Trabzon Beldespor 0, Eskisehirspor 2
Karsiyaka 1, Altay 2 (aet)
Antalyaspor 1, Sariyer 0
Malatyaspor 3, Çanakkale Dardanelspor 2
Mersinspor 1, Ankaragücü 2
Vanspor 1, Kayserispor 0

SIXTH ROUND

Altay 1, Gaziantepspor 2
Samsunspor 2, Vanspor 0
Bursaspor 0, Ankaragücü 0 (aet; 3-4 on pens.)
Eskisehirspor 1, Gençlerbirligi 4
Malatyaspor 1, Trabzonspor 3
Besiktas 2, Antalyaspor 0
Fenerbahçe 1, Kocaelispor 1 (aet; 6-5 on pens.)
Galatasaray 4, Denizlispor 0

QUARTER-FINALS

Galatasaray v Besiktas 0-0; 2-1
(Galatasaray 2-1)
Samsunspor v Trabzonspor 0-1; 2-1
(2-2; Samsunspor on away goals)
Gaziantepspor v Ankaragücü 1-0; 1-2
(2-2; Gaziantepspor on away goal)
Gençlerbirligi v Fenerbahçe 1-1; 1-2
(Fenerbahçe 3-2)

SEMI-FINALS

Gaziantepspor v Fenerbahçe 1-2; 2-2
(Fenerbahçe 4-3)
Galatasaray v Samsunspor 3-1; 0-1
(Galatasaray 3-2)

FINAL

11/04/96, Istanbul
GALATASARAY 1 Saunders (5p)
FENERBAHÇE 0
referee - Ahmet Çakar
GALATASARAY - Friedel; Feti, Bülent, Van Gobbel, Arif, Ufuk (Hakan Ünsal 60), Tugay, Evren, Ergün (Ilyas 79), Hakan Sükür, Saunders (Mert 72).
FENERBAHÇE - Rüstü; Ilker, Okechukwu, Høgh, Erol (Halil Ibrahim 68), Tayfun, Kemalettin (Aygün 68), Oguz, Bülent, Atkinson, Bolic.

24/04/96, Istanbul
FENERBAHÇE 1 Aykut (35)
GALATASARAY 1 Saunders (116) (aet)
referee - Ayhan Yücebilgiç
FENERBAHÇE - Rüstü; Ilker, Okechukwu, Høgh, Erol, Tayfun, Kemalettin (Saffet 38), Oguz (Tarik 113), Bülent, Bolic, Aykut (Atkinson 75).
GALATASARAY - Friedel; Feti, Bülent, Van Gobbel, Ergün (Ilyas 85), Arif (Okan 63), Tugay, Hakan Ünsal, Suat (Ufuk 114), Hakan Sükür, Saunders.

(GALATASARAY 2-1)

PLAYERS OF THE SEASON

RÜSTÜ REÇBER

One of the most valuable pieces of Fatih Terim's legacy to the Turkish national team is 23-year-old goalkeeper Rüstü Reçber. The former national coach discovered him when he was in charge of the U-21 team and Rüstü was playing Second Division football with his hometown club Anatlayaspor. Now Rüstü is unquestionably the best 'keeper in Turkey. He enjoyed an extraordinary season in 95/96, helping Fenerbahçe to their 13th national title with a string of brilliant performances and keeping goal for Turkey at Euro '96. Quick to come for high balls and confident in one-on-one situations, Rüstü is the long-term solution to what has always been a problem position in the national team.

OGÜN TEMIZKANOGLU

Nobody felt the pain of Trabzonspor's championship collapse more intensely than the team's versatility man Ogün Temizkanoglu. The 27-year-old German-born Turkish international was an ever-present for the Claret and Blues throughout the season, encouraging and inspiring his colleagues from whatever position he was asked to fill. Sweeper, stopper, wing-back, midfield anchorman - Ogün was used all over the place by Trabzonspor coach Senol Günes, and his adaptability was also recognised by national team coach Fatih Terim, who fielded him as both right-back and libero at Euro '96.

ALTAY

CLUB DIRECTORY

Altay Spor Kulübü
Sehitlar Caddesi
Alsancak Stadi C Blok
Alsancak
Izmir
tel - (232) 4210626
fax - (232) 4215666
Year of Formation - 1914
President - Erdinç Altinyeleklioglu
Secretary - Iskender Odabasoglu
Coach - Rasit Çetiner; Milorad Mitrovic
(96/97 - Ivan Kiuchukov)
Stadium - Alsancak (20,000)

MAJOR HONOURS
Domestic Cup - (2) 1967, 1980.

APPEARANCES 95/96

	P	Ap	(s)	Gls
AHMET Akuygur	M	19	(9)	5
FARUK Korkmaz	A	28		5
Edema FULUDU (NIG)	M	30		3
HAKAN Demir	M	22	(12)	4
HAKAN Kayalar	M	32	(1)	2
HAYATI Sen	A		(1)	
MEHMET Yilmaz	M	5	(3)	
MURAT Deniz	A	11	(16)	4
MÜFIT Ikizoglu	D	15	(4)	1
ORHAN Üstündag	D	27	(2)	1
ÖZGÜR Kaymaz	M	2	(5)	
RAMAZAN Torunoglu	A	25	(3)	4
Yury SHELEPNITSKY (UKR)	D	27	(3)	
SERKAN Dökme	A		(2)	
SERKAN Gültang	M	14	(5)	1
SERKAN Karababa	D	19	(7)	
SANVER Göymen	G	29		
Vladko SHALAMANOV (BUL)	M	8	(2)	3
TAHIR Karapinar	M	28	(2)	
ÜNSAL Aka	D	28	(2)	2
VAROL Özhan	G	5	(2)	

LEAGUE RESULTS 1995/96

Date	Opponent	H/A	Score	Scorers
13/08/95	Denizlispor	H	1-2	Murat
19/08/95	Galatasaray	A	1-3	Fuludu
27/08/95	Vanspor	A	0-2	
10/09/95	Kayserispor	H	2-0	Ahmet, Faruk
17/09/95	Gençlerbirligi	A	2-1	Müfit, Hakan Demir
24/09/95	Antalyaspor	H	1-2	Hakan Demir
01/10/95	Samsunspor	A	0-4	
15/10/95	Trabzonspor	H	2-5	Ahmet 2 (1p)
21/10/95	Istanbulspor	A	1-1	Hakan Kayalar
27/10/95	Fenerbahçe	H	0-1	
12/11/95	Karsiyaka	A	1-1	Murat
19/11/95	Eskisehirspor	H	1-0	Ramazan
26/11/95	Ankaragücü	A	0-4	
03/12/95	Gaziantepspor	H	2-1	Faruk, Hakan Kayalar
10/12/95	Bursaspor	A	1-0	Ünsal
17/12/95	Kocaelispor	H	3-2	Ünsal, Ahmet, Faruk
22/12/95	Besiktas	A	0-3	
28/01/96	Denizlispor	A	0-1	
03/02/96	Galatasaray	H	2-5	Orhan, Fuludu
11/02/96	Vanspor	H	1-1	Hakan Demir
18/02/96	Kayserispor	A	1-1	Ahmet
25/02/96	Gençlerbirligi	H	1-3	Ramazan (p)
03/03/96	Antalyaspor	A	1-2	Faruk
10/03/96	Samsunspor	H	0-0	
16/03/96	Trabzonspor	A	0-2	
24/03/96	Istanbulspor	H	0-0	
30/03/96	Fenerbahçe	A	2-2	Faruk, Hakan Demir
07/04/96	Karsiyaka	H	0-0	
14/04/96	Eskisehirspor	A	2-1	Murat, Shalamanov
21/04/96	Ankaragücü	H	1-0	Ramazan
28/04/96	Gaziantepspor	A	1-2	Serkan Gültang
03/05/96	Bursaspor	H	1-3	Murat
12/05/96	Kocaelispor	A	1-1	Shalamanov
19/05/96	Besiktas	H	3-0	Shalamanov, Ramazan (p), Fuludu

ANKARAGÜCÜ

CLUB DIRECTORY

Makina Kimya Endüstrisi Ankaragücü Kulübü
Sosyal Tesisleri
GMK Bulvari
Tandogan
Ankara
tel - (312) 2220175
fax - (312) 2312772
Year of Formation - 1910
President - Nevzat Karatas
Secretary - Zülküf Aker
Coach - Ali Osman Renklibay; Tinaz Tirpan (96/97 - Jozef Jarabinsky)
Stadium - 19 Mayis (24,000)

MAJOR HONOURS
Domestic Cup - (2) 1972, 1981.

APPEARANCES 95/96

	P	Ap	(s)	Gls
ADNAN Erkan	G	30	(1)	
AHMET Vildirim	M	26		1
BATUR Altiparmak	A	4	(4)	
BUNENE Ngudane (ZAI)	A	24	(3)	6
BÜLENT Ostuner	M	11	(4)	
CAFER Aydin	A	27	(3)	8
ERGUN Yücel	M	6	(8)	1
GÖKHAN Sakar	M		(1)	
GÖKMEN Baris	D	30	(2)	1
GÖKMEN Yildiran	M	1	(1)	
GÖKSEL Demirel	M		(1)	1
HAKAN Kutlu	D	30	(1)	1
HASAN Sas	M	15	(4)	1
HAYATI Soydas	D	30	(1)	
HÜSEYIN Demirbay	A	5	(7)	
Ndayi KALENGA (ZAI)	M	30		7
KAZIM Nas	M	26	(6)	
Norman MAPEZA (ZIM)	D	30	(1)	2
MURAT Türksoy	G	4		
RAMAZAN Tunç	D	16	(6)	4
TARIK Özdemir	A		(1)	
TARIK Üstün	M	8	(11)	
YILDIRAY Arslan	A	3	(16)	1
YUSUF Tokuç	M	18	(6)	1

LEAGUE RESULTS 1995/96

13/08/95	Trabzonspor	A	1-3	Kalenga
18/08/95	Istanbulspor	H	3-1	Cafer 2, Bunene
27/08/95	Fenerbahçe	A	0-2	
08/09/95	Karsiyaka	H	1-0	Cafer
17/09/95	Eskisehirspor	A	1-2	Gökmen Baris
24/09/95	Vanspor	H	0-0	
29/09/95	Gaziantepspor	H	0-0	
13/10/95	Bursaspor	A	0-8	
22/10/95	Kocaelispor	H	4-0	Mapeza (p), Cafer, Ahmet, Kalenga
29/10/95	Besiktas	A	1-2	Cafer
05/11/95	Denizlispor	H	1-1	Mapeza
19/11/95	Galatasaray	A	0-5	
26/11/95	Altay	H	4-0	og (Hakan Kayalar), Bunene, Kalenga, Cafer
03/12/95	Kayserispor	A	1-4	Hakan
10/12/95	Gençlerbirligi	H	2-0	Bunene, Kalenga
17/12/95	Antalyaspor	A	1-2	Bunene
23/12/95	Samsunspor	H	1-0	Yusuf
28/01/96	Trabzonspor	H	1-3	Yildiray
04/02/96	Istanbulspor	A	0-0	
10/02/96	Fenerbahçe	H	0-3	
18/02/96	Karsiyaka	A	0-0	
25/02/96	Eskisehirspor	H	1-2	Bunene
03/03/96	Vanspor	A	1-4	Ergun
10/03/96	Gaziantepspor	A	0-1	
17/03/96	Bursaspor	H	1-0	Kalenga (p)
24/03/96	Kocaelispor	A	0-2	
31/03/96	Besiktas	H	0-1	
07/04/96	Denizlispor	A	3-2	Ramazan, Kalenga (p), Hasan
14/04/96	Galatasaray	H	2-2	Ramazan 2
21/04/96	Altay	A	0-1	
28/04/96	Kayserispor	H	1-1	Ramazan
05/05/96	Gençlerbirligi	A	2-1	Bunene, Cafer
12/05/96	Antalyaspor	H	2-1	Cafer, Kalenga
19/05/96	Samsunspor	A	1-2	Göksel

ANTALYASPOR

CLUB DIRECTORY

Antalyaspor Kulübü
Kilinçarslan Mahallesi Park Sok. No:12
Antalya
tel - (242) 2478062
fax - (242) 2474760
Year of Formation - 1966
President - Hasan Subasi
Secretary - Gültekin Çeki
Coach - Metin Türel (96/97 - Ümit Kayihan)
Stadium - Atatürk (12,000)

APPEARANCES 95/96

	P	Ap	(s)	Gls
ABDÜLKERIM Koç	M	26	(2)	
ADNAN Karahan	G	4	(3)	
AHMET Sönmez	D	1	(3)	
ALI RIZA Yilmaz	M	13	(5)	5
BURHAN Saatçioglu	D	33		
BÜLENT Selvü	A	25	(6)	4
CANER Yilmaz	M		(4)	
ENGIN Sentürk	M	5	(10)	
FEYYAZ Uçar	A	23		8
GÖKSEL Kirikoglu	M	7	(13)	
IHSAN Okay	M	34		3
KADIR Durum	M	11	(8)	3
KÖKSAL Kir	M		(1)	
Fani MADIDA (SAF)	M	32		12
MEHMET Gümrükçü	A		(1)	
MEHMET Mutlu	D	2	(3)	
MURAT Özduran	A	21	(10)	3
NURI Kanburoglu	D	34		1
Thompson OLIHA (NIG)	M	10	(10)	4
ORHAN Atik	D	34		
OSMAN Akyol	M	29	(1)	1
RAMAZAN Silin	G	30		

LEAGUE RESULTS 1995/96

Date	Opponent	H/A	Score	Scorers
13/08/95	Bursaspor	H	4-2	Ali Riza, Bülent 3
20/08/95	Kocaelispor	A	2-2	Bülent, Ali Riza (p)
27/08/95	Besiktas	H	0-3	
10/09/95	Denizlispor	H	1-0	Madida
17/09/95	Galatasaray	H	0-2	
24/09/95	Altay	A	2-1	Madida, Kadir
01/10/95	Kayserispor	H	3-3	Madida 2, Ihsan
15/10/95	Gençlerbirligi	A	3-6	Kadir, Madida, Ali Riza
22/10/95	Vanspor	A	1-1	Murat
29/10/95	Samsunspor	H	2-1	Ali Riza, Madida
05/11/95	Trabzonspor	A	0-2	
19/11/95	Istanbulspor	H	0-0	
25/11/95	Fenerbahçe	A	1-3	Feyyaz (p)
03/12/95	Karsiyaka	H	4-0	Madida, Feyyaz 2, Ali Riza (p)
10/12/95	Eskisehirspor	A	2-0	Madida, Feyyaz
17/12/95	Ankaragücü	H	2-1	Feyyaz (p), Madida
23/12/95	Gaziantepspor	A	0-2	
26/01/96	Bursaspor	A	1-2	Madida
04/02/96	Kocaelispor	H	1-1	Oliha
10/02/96	Besiktas	A	0-3	
18/02/96	Denizlispor	A	1-3	Ihsan
25/02/96	Galatasaray	A	2-1	Madida, Oliha
03/03/96	Altay	H	2-1	Oliha, Nuri
10/03/96	Kayserispor	A	0-4	
17/03/96	Gençlerbirligi	H	1-0	Murat
24/03/96	Vanspor	H	4-1	Feyyaz 2, og (Aykut), Murat
31/03/96	Samsunspor	A	2-2	Ihsan, Madida
06/04/96	Trabzonspor	H	0-2	
12/04/96	Istanbulspor	A	0-1	
21/04/96	Fenerbahçe	H	0-1	
28/04/96	Karsiyaka	A	2-1	Feyyaz, Kadir
05/05/96	Eskisehirspor	H	1-0	Osman
12/05/96	Ankaragücü	A	1-2	Oliha
19/05/96	Gaziantepspor	H	0-1	

BESIKTAS

CLUB DIRECTORY

Besiktas Jimnastik Kulübü
Spor Caddesi No: 92 Akaretler
Besiktas
Istanbul
tel - (212) 2618804
fax - (212) 2588194
Year of Formation - 1903
President - Süleyman Seba
Secretary - Sardar Bilgili
Coach - Christoph Daum (96/97 - Rasim Kara)
Stadium - Inönü (45,000)

MAJOR HONOURS

League Championship - (9) 1960, 1966, 1967, 1982, 1986, 1990, 1991, 1992, 1995.
Domestic Cup - (4) 1975, 1989, 1990, 1994.

APPEARANCES 95/96

	P	Ap	(s)	Gls
ALI Günçar	D	22	(3)	1
ALPAY Özalan	D	31		2
Raimond AUMANN (GER)	G	8		
BARBAROS Yavasoglu	D		(1)	
ERTUGRUL Saglam	A	30		18
FEVZI Tuncay	G	17	(1)	
FUAT Usta	M	1	(5)	
GÖKHAN Keskin	D	16	(3)	
Ronny JOHNSEN (NOR)	D	22		1
Stefan KUNTZ (GER)	A	30		9
MEHMET Özdilek	M	31	(2)	11
METIN Tekin	M	7	(6)	1
METIN Uzun	D	4	(3)	
MUSTAFA Özkan	A	14	(8)	7
MUTLU Topçu	D	14	(1)	
OKTAY Derelioglu	A	17	(10)	9
ORHAN Kaynak	A	10	(9)	4
OZAN	M		(1)	
RECEP Çetin	D	29		
RIZA Çalimbay	M	17	(10)	
SERDAR Topraktepe	D	12	(4)	
SERGEN Yalçin	M	20	(4)	10
SERTAN Eser	M	4	(13)	
SINAN Demircioglu	D	9	(4)	
SENER Kurtulmus	G	9		

LEAGUE RESULTS 1995/96

Date	Opponent	H/A	Score	Scorers
13/08/95	Kayserispor	A	1-1	Ertugrul (p)
20/08/95	Gençlerbirligi	H	2-2	Ertugrul, Sergen
27/08/95	Antalyaspor	A	3-0	Mehmet 2, Oktay
10/09/95	Samsunspor	H	4-2	Ertugrul 2, Oktay, Orhan
17/09/95	Trabzonspor	A	1-3	Oktay
24/09/95	Istanbulspor	H	5-2	Oktay 2, Orhan, Mehmet, Kuntz
30/09/95	Fenerbahçe	A	0-2	
15/10/95	Karsiyaka	H	4-0	Ertugrul 3, Orhan
22/10/95	Eskisehirspor	A	3-2	Oktay, Kuntz, og (Metin)
29/10/95	Ankaragücü	H	2-1	Alpay, Orhan
05/11/95	Gaziantepspor	A	1-1	Kuntz
18/11/95	Bursaspor	H	4-1	Mehmet 2, Ertugrul 2
26/11/95	Kocaelispor	A	0-1	
03/12/95	Vanspor	H	3-1	Sergen, Kuntz, Mehmet
09/12/95	Denizlispor	A	3-0	Sergen, Metin Tekin, Ertugrul
17/12/95	Galatasaray	A	3-1	Ertugrul (p), Mehmet, Sergen
22/12/95	Altay	H	3-0	Oktay 2, Mehmet
27/01/96	Kayserispor	H	4-1	Sergen, Mehmet, Mustafa 2
02/02/96	Gençlerbirligi	A	2-1	Ertugrul 2
10/02/96	Antalyaspor	H	3-0	Ertugrul, Mustafa, Kuntz
18/02/96	Samsunspor	A	1-0	Mustafa
24/02/96	Trabzonspor	H	2-0	Ertugrul 2
02/03/96	Istanbulspor	A	3-2	Sergen, Mehmet 2
10/03/96	Fenerbahçe	H	1-2	Johnsen
17/03/96	Karsiyaka	A	2-0	Mustafa 2
23/03/96	Eskisehirspor	H	2-0	Sergen 2
31/03/96	Ankaragücü	A	1-0	Ertugrul
05/04/96	Gaziantepspor	H	5-3	Kuntz (p), Ali, Sergen 2, Oktay
14/04/96	Bursaspor	A	2-1	Mustafa, Ertugrul
21/04/96	Kocaelispor	H	3-5	Kuntz 2, Alpay
28/04/96	Vanspor	A	0-2	
05/05/96	Denizlispor	H	0-4	
12/05/96	Galatasaray	H	1-2	Kuntz
19/05/96	Altay	A	0-3	

BURSASPOR

CLUB DIRECTORY

Bursaspor Kulübü
Vakifköy Tesisleri
Vakifköy
Bursa
tel - (224) 3664883
fax - (224) 3664995
Year of Formation - 1963
President - Hüseyin Silahçi
Secretary - Osman Yilmaz
Coach - Nejat Biyediç (96/97 - Gordon Milne)
Stadium - Atatürk (24,000)

MAJOR HONOURS
Domestic Cup - (1) 1986.

APPEARANCES 95/96

	P	Ap	(s)	Gls
ABDULLAH Kiliç	G	9		
ADNAN Örnek	D	20		
Elvir BALJIC (BOS)	A	25	(2)	9
DENIZ Kolgu	M	10	(4)	
ERCÜMENT Sahin	A	28	(4)	12
ERSEL Uzgur	D	5	(2)	
Ivko GANCHEV (BUL)	G	21		
HAKAN Keles	A	1	(24)	2
HAYRETTIN Yildiz	D	28	(1)	1
İBRAHIM Köseoglu	M	24		5
LEVENT Devrim	M	19	(9)	2
MESUT Ünal	D	13	(3)	1
Majed MUSISI (UGA)	A	28	(2)	15
MUSTAFA Gönden	M	1	(7)	
NEVZAT Dinçbudak	G	4	(1)	
ÖMER Kiliç	D	22	(1)	
SELIM Özer	D	31	(1)	2
SABAN Yildirim	M	14	(1)	2
TUNAHAN Akdogan	M	23	(7)	2
TUNCAY Akgün	M	17	(7)	2
TURAN Sen	D	10	(5)	
ÜMIT Sengül	D	15		1
VOLKAN Velioglu	M	1	(3)	
ZAFER Bastan	M	5	(4)	

LEAGUE RESULTS 1995/96

Date	Opponent		Score	Scorers
13/08/95	Antalyaspor	A	2-4	Musisi, Baljic
19/08/95	Samsunspor	H	2-4	Ercüment, Ümit
26/08/95	Trabzonspor	A	0-0	
09/09/95	Istanbulspor	H	2-1	Baljic, Ibrahim
16/09/95	Fenerbahçe	A	1-1	Musisi
24/09/95	Karsiyaka	H	3-1	Musisi 2, Ercüment (p)
01/10/95	Eskisehirspor	A	3-1	Baljic, Musisi 2
13/10/95	Ankaragücü	H	8-0	Hayrettin, Ercüment 3 (1p), Selim, Ibrahim, Hakan, Levent
22/10/95	Gaziantepspor	A	0-3	
29/10/95	Vanspor	H	5-0	Baljic 2, Musisi, Ercüment 2
05/11/95	Kocaelispor	H	2-2	Musisi, Saban
18/11/95	Besiktas	A	1-4	Baljic
26/11/95	Denizlispor	H	2-2	Musisi, Baljic
02/12/95	Galatasaray	A	1-3	Hakan
10/12/95	Altay	H	0-1	
17/12/95	Kayserispor	A	0-0	
22/12/95	Gençlerbirligi	H	1-1	Ibrahim
26/01/96	Antalyaspor	H	2-1	Baljic 2
04/02/96	Samsunspor	A	0-1	
11/02/96	Trabzonspor	H	1-2	Musisi
16/02/96	Istanbulspor	A	1-1	Musisi
23/02/96	Fenerbahçe	H	0-0	
03/03/96	Karsiyaka	A	3-0	Levent, Ercüment, Tunahan
10/03/96	Eskisehirspor	H	2-2	Tunahan, Selim
17/03/96	Ankaragücü	A	0-1	
24/03/96	Gaziantepspor	H	3-0	Musisi 2, Ibrahim
31/03/96	Vanspor	A	1-1	Tuncay
06/04/96	Kocaelispor	A	2-4	Ibrahim, Ercüment
14/04/96	Besiktas	H	1-2	Ercüment
21/04/96	Denizlispor	A	0-0	
27/04/96	Galatasaray	H	2-0	Saban, Musisi
03/05/96	Altay	A	3-1	Mesut, Musisi, Ercüment
12/05/96	Kayserispor	H	1-2	Tuncay
19/05/96	Gençlerbirligi	A	1-2	Ercüment

DENIZLISPOR

CLUB DIRECTORY

Denizlispor Kulübü
Kenan Evren Bulvari No:9
Denizli
tel - (258) 2620721
fax - (258) 2651466
Year of Formation - 1966
President - Ali Marim
Secretary - Mustafa Baysal
Coach - Ümit Kayihan; Ersun Yenal
(96/97 - Milorad Mitrovic)
Stadium - Denizli Sehir (15,000)

APPEARANCES 95/96

	P	Ap	(s)	Gls
ALI Yalçin	M	10	(24)	5
AMIR Alibaz	A	10	(16)	4
CÜNEYT Aksu	D	21	(6)	3
Gosho GINCHEV (BUL)	D	32		
HASAN Sermet	M	12	(5)	2
KADRI Sancak	D	30		5
KASIM Vedsaya (NIG)	A	1	(3)	
David KASSIAN (FRA)	A	15	(7)	2
Richard KASSIAN (FRA)	A	11		1
MECNUN Çolak	M	18	(6)	3
MEHMET Altiparmak	M	30		5
MURAT Dogansay	D	29		
MUSTAFA Ceviz	M		(2)	
MUSTAFA Karakaya	A		(4)	
MUSTAFA Kocakaya	G	3	(2)	
MUTLU Sozer	M	3	(4)	
NECMETTIN Inan	M		(14)	
SEMAVI Uzun	M	34		1
SEYFETTIN Kurtulmus	M	12		3
SEVKET Çandar	M	29	(1)	
TAMER Tuna	M	33		2
ZAFER Öger	G	31		
ZAFER Tüzün	A	10		2

LEAGUE RESULTS 1995/96

Date	Opponent	H/A	Score	Scorers
13/08/95	Altay	A	2-1	Mehmet, Cüneyt
20/08/95	Kayserispor	A	0-0	
27/08/95	Gençlerbirligi	A	1-1	Kadri
10/09/95	Antalyaspor	A	0-1	
16/09/95	Samsunspor	A	3-1	Kadri, Seyfettin 2
23/09/95	Trabzonspor	A	0-3	
01/10/95	Istanbulspor	A	3-2	Mecnun, Kassian D., Seyfettin
14/10/95	Fenerbahçe	A	0-0	
22/10/95	Karsiyaka	A	0-2	
29/10/95	Eskisehirspor	A	1-1	Ali (p)
05/11/95	Ankaragücü	A	1-1	Kassian D.
19/11/95	Gaziantepspor	A	2-3	Kassian R., Amir
26/11/95	Bursaspor	A	2-2	Tamer, Ali (p)
03/12/95	Kocaelispor	H	0-0	
09/12/95	Besiktas	H	0-3	
17/12/95	Vanspor	A	1-3	Semavi
23/12/95	Galatasaray	H	1-3	Mehmet
28/01/96	Altay	H	1-0	Ali
04/02/96	Kayserispor	H	2-2	Cüneyt, Ali (p)
11/02/96	Gençlerbirligi	H	3-0	Zafer Tüzün, Ali, Tamer
18/02/96	Antalyaspor	H	3-1	Mecnun, Mehmet, Zafer Tüzün
25/02/96	Samsunspor	H	1-2	Kadri
03/03/96	Trabzonspor	H	0-3	
10/03/96	Istanbulspor	H	1-2	Amir
17/03/96	Fenerbahçe	H	0-2	
24/03/96	Karsiyaka	H	1-0	Cüneyt
31/03/96	Eskisehirspor	H	1-2	Mecnun
07/04/96	Ankaragücü	H	2-3	Hasan, Mehmet (p)
14/04/96	Gaziantepspor	H	0-1	
21/04/96	Bursaspor	H	0-0	
28/04/96	Kocaelispor	A	2-4	Mehmet, Hasan
05/05/96	Besiktas	A	4-0	Amir 2, Kadri 2
12/05/96	Vanspor	H	0-0	
19/05/96	Galatasaray	A	0-1	

ESKISEHIRSPOR

CLUB DIRECTORY

Eskisehirspor Kulübü
Arifiye Mahallesi
Bakim Sokak 4/2
26010 Eskisehir
tel (222) 2313360
fax - (222) 2212576
Year of Formation - 1965
President - Aydin Arat
Secretary - Oguz Türkmen
Coach - Yilmaz Vural; Güvenç Kurtar
Stadium - Atatürk (15,000)

MAJOR HONOURS
Domestic Cup - (1) 1971.

APPEARANCES 95/96

	P	Ap	(s)	Gls
ALI Akdemir	D	27	(1)	
ALI RIZA Haper	A	7	(18)	3
ALPARSLAN Kartal	M	1	(2)	
ARIF Bacaci	A	7	(12)	2
BAYRAM Çolak	A	4		2
BENHUR Özden	A	9	(4)	6
CIHAT Arslan	D	25	(2)	1
Emmanuel DUAH (GHA)	M	16	(2)	
ENGIN Çalasir	D	1	(4)	
ERDOGAN Özalp	D	7	(4)	
EROL Usta	D	16		
HAKAN Simsek	A	18	(3)	8
Slavisa KUZMANOVSKI (MAC)	D	26		
MELIH Gürbüztürk	M	6		
METIN Arvas	M	4	(4)	
MURAT Erdeger	G	5		
Isaac NANA (GHA)	M	10	(1)	1
NEZIHI Bologlu	G	5		
ÖMER Çatkiç	G	24	(4)	
RECEP Seçkin	M	9	(5)	1
SEDAT Balkanli	D	18	(1)	
SEFER Yilmaz	M	1	(8)	
ÜLKEN Durak	D	19	(4)	1
ÜMIT Birol	M	13		
VEYSEL Kupan	M	17	(14)	1
VOLKAN Sabinkol	M	29	(2)	2
YAHYA Ünal	M	31	(2)	5
ZAFER Tüzün	A	19		6

LEAGUE RESULTS 1995/96

11/08/95	Istanbulspor	A	3-1	Ulken, Zafer (p), Bayram
19/08/95	Fenerbahçe	H	1-2	Volkan
27/08/95	Karsiyaka	A	2-3	Veysel, Zafer (p)
10/09/95	Vanspor	H	2-1	Bayram, Recep
17/09/95	Ankaragücü	H	2-1	Zafer 2
24/09/95	Gaziantepspor	A	0-3	
01/10/95	Bursaspor	H	1-3	Cihat
15/10/95	Kocaelispor	A	1-2	Yahya
22/10/95	Besiktas	H	2-3	Zafer, Yahya
29/10/95	Denizlispor	H	1-1	Zafer (p)
04/11/95	Galatasaray	H	1-2	Ali Riza
19/11/95	Altay	A	0-1	
26/11/95	Kayserispor	H	4-0	Hakan 3, Ali Riza
03/12/95	Gençlerbirligi	A	2-3	Arif, Ali Riza
10/12/95	Antalyaspor	H	0-2	
17/12/95	Samsunspor	A	1-3	Yahya
23/12/95	Trabzonspor	H	0-2	
28/01/96	Istanbulspor	H	1-2	Arif
04/02/96	Fenerbahçe	A	0-6	
11/02/96	Karsiyaka	H	0-2	
18/02/96	Vanspor	A	0-3	
25/02/96	Ankaragücü	A	2-1	Yahya, Benhur
03/03/96	Gaziantepspor	H	2-0	Benhur, Hakan
10/03/96	Bursaspor	A	2-2	Yahya, Hakan
17/03/96	Kocaelispor	H	0-3	
23/03/96	Besiktas	A	0-2	
31/03/96	Denizlispor	A	2-1	og (Murat), Hakan
07/04/96	Galatasaray	A	0-3	
14/04/96	Altay	H	1-2	Benhur
21/04/96	Kayserispor	A	1-0	Hakan
28/04/96	Gençlerbirligi	H	2-0	Benhur 2
05/05/96	Antalyaspor	A	0-1	
12/05/96	Samsunspor	H	3-0	Volkan, Hakan, Nana
19/05/96	Trabzonspor	A	1-7	Benhur

FENERBAHÇE

CLUB DIRECTORY

Fenerbahçe Spor Kulübü
Derosgan Tesisleri
Kadiköy
Istanbul
tel - (216) 3450940
fax - (216) 3483060
Year of Formation - 1907
President - Ali Sen
Secretary - Orhan Koçeli
Coach - Carlos Alberto Parreira (96/97 - Sebastião Lazaroni)
Stadium - Fenerbahçe (30,000)

MAJOR HONOURS

League Championship - (13)
1959, 1961, 1964, 1965, 1968, 1970, 1974, 1975, 1978, 1983, 1985, 1989, 1996.
Domestic Cup - (4) 1968, 1974, 1979, 1983.

APPEARANCES 95/96

	P	Ap	(s)	Gls
AHMET Habiboglu	M		(1)	
ALI NAIL Durmus	M		(2)	
Dalian ATKINSON (ENG)	A	20	(4)	10
AYGÜN Taskiran	A	2	(13)	
AYKUT Kocaman	A	19	(13)	8
Elvir BOLIC (BOS)	A	31		22
BÜLENT Uygun	M	27	(6)	8
EMRE Asik	D	2	(2)	
ENGIN Ipekoglu	G	5	(1)	
EROL Bulut	D	22	(3)	1
FEYYAZ Uçar	A	2	(3)	
HALIL IBRAHIM Kara	D	12	(13)	
Jes HØGH (DEN)	D	34		2
ILKER Yagcioglu	D	28		
KEMALETTIN Sentürk	M	27	(3)	3
MUSTAFA Katip	D		(3)	
MUSTAFA Özer	D	2		
OGUZ Çetin	M	31		4
Ushe OKECHUKWU (NIG)	D	28		1
RÜSTÜ Reçber	G	29		
SAFFET Akbas	D	9	(2)	
SERKAN Rençber	M	9	(5)	
TARIK Dasgün	M	6	(13)	1
TAYFUN Korkut	M	29	(1)	5

LEAGUE RESULTS 1995/96

12/08/95	Karsiyaka	H	4-0	Bolic 2 (1p), Bülent, Oguz
19/08/95	Eskisehirspor	A	2-1	Bolic (p), Høgh
27/08/95	Ankaragücü	H	2-0	Bülent, Bolic
09/09/95	Gaziantepspor	A	2-2	Bolic, Tayfun
16/09/95	Bursaspor	H	1-1	Tayfun
23/09/95	Kocaelispor	A	1-0	Bolic
30/09/95	Besiktas	H	2-0	Høgh, Atkinson
14/10/95	Denizlispor	H	0-0	
22/10/95	Galatasaray	H	3-1	Atkinson 3
27/10/95	Altay	A	1-0	og (Orhan)
04/11/95	Kayserispor	H	2-1	Kemalettin, Aykut
13/11/95	Gençlerbirligi	A	1-3	Atkinson
25/11/95	Antalyaspor	H	3-1	Bülent, Bolic 2
03/12/95	Samsunspor	A	3-0	Bolic 3
09/12/95	Trabzonspor	H	3-1	Tayfun, Atkinson, Kemalettin
16/12/95	Istanbulspor	A	2-1	Erol, Aykut
23/12/95	Vanspor	H	3-0	Atkinson, Bolic (p), Aykut
27/01/96	Karsiyaka	A	1-0	Atkinson
04/02/96	Eskisehirspor	H	6-0	Bülent 2, og (Volkan), Bolic 2 (1p), Kemalettin
10/02/96	Ankaragücü	A	3-0	Bolic 2 (1p), Bülent
17/02/96	Gaziantepspor	H	1-0	Aykut
23/02/96	Bursaspor	A	0-0	
03/03/96	Kocaelispor	H	4-0	Aykut 2, Oguz, Tarik
10/03/96	Besiktas	A	2-1	Bolic, Oguz
17/03/96	Denizlispor	A	2-0	Bolic, Atkinson (p)
22/03/96	Galatasaray	A	0-2	
30/03/96	Altay	H	2-2	Atkinson, Tayfun
07/04/96	Kayserispor	A	3-1	Tayfun, Bolic, Bülent (p)
14/04/96	Gençlerbirligi	H	0-0	
21/04/96	Antalyaspor	A	1-0	Aykut
28/04/96	Samsunspor	H	1-0	Bülent
05/05/96	Trabzonspor	A	2-1	Oguz, Aykut
12/05/96	Istanbulspor	H	2-0	Okechukwu, Bolic
19/05/96	Vanspor	A	3-0	Bolic 2 (2p), og (Abdülkadir)

GALATASARAY

CLUB DIRECTORY

Galatasaray Spor Kulübü
Hasnun Galip Sokak 7-11
Beyoglu
Istanbul
tel - (212) 5738888
fax - (212) 5740424
Year of Formation - 1905
President - Faruk Süren
Secretary - Ales Ünal Erzen
Coach - Graeme Souness (96/97 - Fatih Terim)
Stadium - Ali Sami Yen (40,000)

MAJOR HONOURS
League Championship - (10) 1962, 1963, 1969, 1971, 1972, 1973, 1987, 1988, 1993, 1994.
Domestic Cup - (11) 1963, 1964, 1965, 1966, 1973, 1976, 1982, 1985, 1991, 1993, 1996.

APPEARANCES 95/96

	P	Ap	(s)	Gls
ARIF Erdem	A	24	(8)	8
BEKIR Gür	D	11		1
BÜLENT Korkmaz	D	28	(1)	
CEYHUN Eris	M	1	(2)	
ERGÜN Penbe	M	9	(9)	
EVREN Turhan	M	14	(1)	1
FETI Okuroglu	D	29	(1)	2
Brad FRIEDEL (USA)	G	30		
HAKAN Sükür	A	25		16
HAKAN Ünsal	M	23	(5)	1
HAYRETTIN Demirbas	G	1	(1)	
ILYAS Kahraman	M	8	(13)	
ISMAIL	M		(2)	
Mike MARSH (ENG)	M	3		
MERT Korkmaz	D	16	(3)	
NEZIHI Bologlu	G	3		
OKAN Buruk	M	17	(11)	1
SAFFET Sancakli	A	9	(2)	7
Dean SAUNDERS (WAL)	A	21	(6)	15
SUAT Kaya	M	26	(2)	5
TUGAY Kerimoglu	M	30		3
Kubilay TÜRKYILMAZ (SUI)	A	7	(3)	3
UFUK Talay (AUS)	M	15	(4)	1
UGUR Tütüneker	M		(7)	
Ulrich VAN GOBBEL (HOL)	D	16		2
Barry VENISON (ENG)	D	8		
YUSUF Tepekule	M		(3)	

LEAGUE RESULTS 1995/96

13/08/95	Vanspor	A	1-0	Tugay
19/08/95	Altay	H	3-1	Saunders 2 (1p), Saffet
26/08/95	Kayserispor	A	2-1	Suat, Arif
09/09/95	Gençlerbirligi	H	0-1	
17/09/95	Antalyaspor	A	2-0	Saunders, Türkyilmaz (p)
22/09/95	Samsunspor	H	1-0	Arif
01/10/95	Trabzonspor	A	1-4	Türkyilmaz
14/10/95	Istanbulspor	H	4-2	Saunders 2 (1p), Arif, Türkyilmaz
22/10/95	Fenerbahçe	A	1-3	Saffet
28/10/95	Karsiyaka	H	3-0	og (Serhat), Suat, Saunders (p)
04/11/95	Eskisehirspor	A	2-1	Saunders, Hakan Sükür
19/11/95	Ankaragücü	H	5-0	Saffet 2, Tugay, Hakan Sükür 2 (1p)
25/11/95	Gaziantepspor	A	1-1	Saffet
02/12/95	Bursaspor	H	3-1	Saffet 2 (1p), Hakan Sükür
10/12/95	Kocaelispor	A	1-1	Arif
17/12/95	Besiktas	H	1-3	Ufuk
23/12/95	Denizlispor	A	3-1	Hakan Ünsal, Hakan Sükür, Arif
28/01/96	Vanspor	H	2-0	Hakan Sükür (p), Van Gobbel (p)
03/02/96	Altay	A	5-2	Van Gobbel, Feti 2, Hakan Sükür 2 (1p)
11/02/96	Kayserispor	H	5-0	Suat 2, Hakan Sükür 2, Arif
17/02/96	Gençlerbirligi	A	2-1	Saunders 2
25/02/96	Antalyaspor	H	1-2	Suat
02/03/96	Samsunspor	A	2-3	Bekir, Hakan Sükür
09/03/96	Trabzonspor	H	0-0	
16/03/96	Istanbulspor	A	1-1	Hakan Sükür
22/03/96	Fenerbahçe	H	2-0	Hakan Sükür, Arif
30/03/96	Karsiyaka	A	3-0	Hakan Sükür, Okan, Saunders
07/04/96	Eskisehirspor	H	3-0	Saunders 2, Hakan Sükür
14/04/96	Ankaragücü	A	2-2	Arif, Saunders
20/04/96	Gaziantepspor	H	2-0	Saunders, Tugay
27/04/96	Bursaspor	A	0-2	
04/05/96	Kocaelispor	H	0-4	
11/05/96	Besiktas	A	2-1	Evren, Hakan Sükür
19/05/96	Denizlispor	H	1-0	Saunders

GAZIANTEPSPOR

CLUB DIRECTORY

Gaziantepspor Kulübü
Subarcu Caddesi No:2
Gaziantep
tel - (342) 2311259
fax - (342) 2308420
Year of Formation - 1969
President - Celal Dogan
Secretary - Naci Topcuoglu
Coach - Sakip Özberk
Stadium - Kamil Ocak (20,000)

APPEARANCES 95/96

	P	Ap	(s)	Gls
ALI Ravci	M		(1)	
ALI KEMAL Alatas	M	24	(4)	
AYHAN Akman	M	31		8
BÜNYAMIN Kubat	A	5	(8)	3
CAVIT Ögrüce	M	1		
CEM Beceren	D	33		
Fernand COULIBALY (MLI)	A	13	(10)	7
ÇETIN Nalbantoglu	M	4	(7)	1
ERDAL Tarhan	A		(1)	
EROL Gündogdu	M	30		
HACI Ikizer	M	11	(4)	2
HACI HASAN Yasar	M		(3)	
HASAN Çelik	A	3	(1)	
HASAN Yigit	D	28	(2)	
HAYATI Köse	M	7	(11)	
HÜSEYIN Sari	D	26	(3)	1
ISA Dündat	D	11	(5)	1
Stephen KOMPHELA (SAF)	D	25	(2)	
KUBILAY Toptas	M	7	(8)	2
MARCELLO Monteiro (BRA)	M	16	(5)	3
MEHMET Gönülaçar	A	22	(3)	6
MEHMET Tezcan	G	4	(1)	
MEHMET ALI Honca	D	27	(2)	
METIN Akçevre	G	30		3
SERKAN Özen	A	16	(9)	5

LEAGUE RESULTS 1995/96

Date	Opponent		Score	Scorers
13/08/95	Samsunspor	A	0-1	
20/08/95	Trabzonspor	H	0-0	
26/08/95	Istanbulspor	A	0-2	
09/09/95	Fenerbahçe	H	2-2	Marcello, Hüseyin
17/09/95	Karsiyaka	A	1-2	Marcello
24/09/95	Eskisehirspor	H	3-0	Bünyamin 2, Coulibaly
29/09/95	Ankaragücü	A	0-0	
15/10/95	Vanspor	H	1-0	Metin (p)
22/10/95	Bursaspor	H	3-0	Mehmet Gönülaçar, Serkan 2
29/10/95	Kocaelispor	A	2-2	Kubilay, Coulibaly
05/11/95	Besiktas	H	1-1	Mehmet Gönülaçar
19/11/95	Denizlispor	H	3-2	Mehmet Gönülaçar, Serkan, Metin (p)
25/11/95	Galatasaray	H	1-1	Serkan
03/12/95	Altay	A	1-2	Bünyamin
10/12/95	Kayserispor	H	1-0	Ayhan
17/12/95	Gençlerbirligi	A	0-1	
23/12/95	Antalyaspor	H	2-0	Ayhan, Kubilay
28/01/96	Samsunspor	H	3-0	Coulibaly 3
03/02/96	Trabzonspor	A	0-0	
11/02/96	Istanbulspor	H	1-6	Serkan
17/02/96	Fenerbahçe	A	0-1	
25/02/96	Karsiyaka	H	3-0	Ayhan, Haci, Çetin
03/03/96	Eskisehirspor	A	0-2	
10/03/96	Ankaragücü	H	1-0	Coulibaly
17/03/96	Vanspor	A	0-2	
24/03/96	Bursaspor	A	0-3	
31/03/96	Kocaelispor	H	2-4	Ayhan, Haci
05/04/96	Besiktas	A	3-5	Isa, Mehmet Gönülaçar, Ayhan
14/04/96	Denizlispor	A	1-0	Mehmet Gönülaçar
20/04/96	Galatasaray	A	0-2	
28/04/96	Altay	H	2-1	Mehmet Gönülaçar, Ayhan
05/05/96	Kayserispor	A	2-1	Ayhan 2
12/05/96	Gençlerbirligi	H	2-0	Metin (p), Coulibaly
19/05/96	Antalyaspor	A	1-0	Marcello

GENÇLERBIRLIGI

CLUB DIRECTORY

Gençlerbirligi Spor Kulübü
Gazi Mustafa Kemal Bulvari 75/B
06570 Maltepe
Ankara
tel - (312) 2295852
fax - (312) 2321946
Year of Formation - 1923
President - Ilhan Cavcav
Secretary - Gültekin Aktan
Coach - Georges Heylens (96/97 - Muhsin Ertugral)
Stadium - 19 Mayis (25,000)

MAJOR HONOURS
Domestic Cup - (1) 1987.

APPEARANCES 95/96

	P	Ap	(s)	Gls
AHMET Ersoy	G	1		
ALI Isik	A	14	(12)	4
ALI EREN Beserler	D	20	(1)	1
ENGIN Özdemir	M	31		9
ERKAN Sözeri	M	30	(1)	5
HAKAN Kaygusuz	D	4	(1)	
HASAN Sönmez	G	3		
IDRIS Gümüsdere	A	4	(4)	1
ILHAN Mansiz	M		(2)	
ILKER Dalçiçek	M	13	(15)	
Donald KHUSE (SAF)	M	30		
André KONA-NGOLE (ZAI)	A	24		11
MEHMET Ömur	A		(4)	
MEHMET Simsek	M	30	(1)	1
METIN Diyadin	M	31		1
NIHAT Bastürk	M	7	(13)	
OSMAN Coskun	M	18	(9)	3
Zsolt PETRY (HUN)	G	30		
RAHIM Zafer	D	33		2
SEVIT Ünsal	A	1	(10)	1
SINAN Ertan	A	8	(1)	2
TANER Taskin	D	33		
TARIK Sariskal	A	2	(4)	
ÜMIT Özat	D	7	(10)	

LEAGUE RESULTS 1995/96

Date	Opponent	H/A	Score	Scorers
12/08/95	Kocaelispor	H	1-1	Engin
20/08/95	Besiktas	A	2-2	Engin, Ali Isik
27/08/95	Denizlispor	H	1-1	Engin (p)
09/09/95	Galatasaray	A	1-0	Ali Isik
17/09/95	Altay	H	1-2	Seyit
24/09/95	Kayserispor	A	2-2	Erkan, Rahim
01/10/95	Vanspor	A	1-0	Osman
15/10/95	Antalyaspor	H	6-3	Engin, Erkan 2, Ali Isik 2, Kona-Ngole
21/10/95	Samsunspor	A	0-3	
29/10/95	Trabzonspor	H	1-3	Kona-Ngole
03/11/95	Istanbulspor	A	1-1	Kona-Ngole
18/11/95	Fenerbahçe	H	3-1	Engin (p), Ali Eren, Kona-Ngole
26/11/95	Karsiyaka	A	1-1	Osman
03/12/95	Eskisehirspor	H	3-2	Sinan 2, Osman
10/12/95	Ankaragücü	A	0-2	
17/12/95	Gaziantepspor	H	1-0	Engin
22/12/95	Bursaspor	A	1-1	Kona-Ngole
28/01/96	Kocaelispor	A	0-2	
02/02/96	Besiktas	H	1-2	Kona-Ngole
11/02/96	Denizlispor	A	0-3	
17/02/96	Galatasaray	H	1-2	Kona-Ngole
25/02/96	Altay	A	3-1	Idris, Erkan, Engin (p)
03/03/96	Kayserispor	H	1-1	Erkan
10/03/96	Vanspor	H	1-1	Kona-Ngole
17/03/96	Antalyaspor	A	0-1	
24/03/96	Samsunspor	H	0-0	
31/03/96	Trabzonspor	A	1-3	Kona-Ngole
07/04/96	Istanbulspor	H	2-0	Engin, Kona-Ngole
14/04/96	Fenerbahçe	A	0-0	
20/04/96	Karsiyaka	H	2-0	Engin, Mehmet
28/04/96	Eskisehirspor	A	0-2	
05/05/96	Ankaragücü	H	1-2	Rahim
12/05/96	Gaziantepspor	A	0-2	
19/05/96	Bursaspor	H	2-1	Metin, Kona-Ngole (p)

ISTANBULSPOR

CLUB DIRECTORY

Istanbulspor Kulübü
Basin Ekspres Yolu Star Sokak No:2
Günesli
Istanbul
tel - (212) 6979840
fax - (212) 6984970
Year of Formation - 1926
President - Cem Uzan
Secretary - Adnan Sezgin
Coach - Leo Beenhakker; Herbert Neumann
Stadium - Bayrampasa (15,000)

APPEARANCES 95/96

	P	Ap	(s)	Gls
ALI Aydogan	D	6	(2)	
ALTAN Aksoy	M	7	(2)	
ATAKAN Sancarbarlaz	M	31	(1)	5
DOGAN Pek	M		(4)	
ENDER Iras	M	3	(8)	
ERKUT Cagdas	D	4	(1)	
FUAT Buruk	M	23	(1)	1
HALUK Güngör	G	8	(1)	
HAMDI Demirtas	A	9	(9)	2
HAMZA Hamzaoglu	M	34		5
HASAN Gültang	G	9		
ILKAN Aksoy	M	16	(7)	1
ISMET Tasdemir	M	5	(1)	
Cedomir JANEVSKI (MAC)	D	2		
KAMIL Ustaömer	D	26	(1)	
KENAN Arayici	M	2	(4)	
MITHAT Yavas	M		(3)	
NEJAT Barut	D	1		
NESIM Özgur	D	32		
Fahrettin OMEROVIC (BOS)	G	17		
SAFFET Akyüz	A	25	(2)	8
Oleg SALENKO (RUS)	A	15		11
SUAT Türker	M	2	(6)	
SENOL Yavas	D	25	(3)	2
TIMUR Yanyah	D	5	(4)	
ÜMIT Davala	M	3	(2)	1
John VAN DEN BROM (HOL)	M	22		3
Peter VAN VOSSEN (HOL)	A	16		5
Marian ZEMAN (SVK)	D	26		1

LEAGUE RESULTS 1995/96

11/08/95	Eskisehirspor	H	1-3	Van den Brom
18/08/95	Ankaragücü	A	1-3	Fuat
26/08/95	Gaziantepspor	H	2-0	Saffet, Hamza
09/09/95	Bursaspor	A	1-2	Van Vossen (p)
15/09/95	Kocaelispor	H	1-2	Van den Brom
24/09/95	Besiktas	A	2-5	Zeman, Van Vossen
01/10/95	Denizlispor	H	2-3	Hamza, Saffet
14/10/95	Galatasaray	A	2-4	og (Bülent), Saffet
21/10/95	Altay	H	1-1	Van Vossen (p)
29/10/95	Kayserispor	A	1-0	Ümit
03/11/95	Gençlerbirligi	H	1-1	Atakan
19/11/95	Antalyaspor	A	0-0	
26/11/95	Samsunspor	H	0-2	
01/12/95	Trabzonspor	A	1-2	Van Vossen (p)
10/12/95	Vanspor	H	1-1	Atakan
16/12/95	Fenerbahçe	H	1-2	Hamza
23/12/95	Karsiyaka	A	3-0	Van Vossen, Ilkan, Saffet
28/01/96	Eskisehirspor	A	2-1	Hamdi, Atakan
04/02/96	Ankaragücü	H	0-0	
11/02/96	Gaziantepspor	A	6-1	Salenko 3, Hamza, Atakan, Saffet
16/02/96	Bursaspor	H	1-1	Saffet
25/02/96	Kocaelispor	A	0-0	
02/03/96	Besiktas	H	2-3	Senol, Salenko
10/03/96	Denizlispor	A	2-1	Salenko 2
16/03/96	Galatasaray	H	1-1	Salenko
24/03/96	Altay	A	0-0	
29/03/96	Kayserispor	H	5-2	Van den Brom, Salenko 2 (1p), Hamza, Hamdi
07/04/96	Gençlerbirligi	A	0-2	
12/04/96	Antalyaspor	H	1-0	Atakan
21/04/96	Samsunspor	A	4-4	Senol, Salenko 2 (1p), Saffet
27/04/96	Trabzonspor	H	1-4	Saffet
05/05/96	Vanspor	A	0-0	
12/05/96	Fenerbahçe	A	0-2	
19/05/96	Karsiyaka	H	0-4	

KARSIYAKA

CLUB DIRECTORY

Karsiyaka Kulübü
Yali Caddesi No:396
Karsiyaka
Izmir
tel - (232) 3815711
fax - (232) 3235900
Year of Formation - 1912
President - Iskender Mesudiyeli
Secretary - Müfit Yararbas
Coach - Hüseyin Hamamci; Allan Harris; Erol Togay; Ilyas Sazalan; Zeynel Soyuer
Stadium - Alsancak (20,000)

APPEARANCES 95/96

	P	Ap	(s)	Gls
ARAP Öztürk	M	24	(5)	
ATILLA Günes	M	22	(4)	1
BAHADIR Tamsan	D	2	(6)	
BIRKAN Tural	M		(2)	
CENK Gürgenç	A	3	(10)	1
ERBIL Uzel	D	17	(5)	
Youssouf FOFANA (CIV)	A	6		3
HAYRETTIN Aksoy	A	1		
ILHAN Akgül	M	21	(2)	
KASIM Çikla	D	32		3
LEVENT Kurt	A	16	(4)	3
MAHIR Nergiz	M	4	(4)	
MEHMET Yildirim	A	24	(5)	4
MURAT Sir	M	19	(5)	
MUSTAFA Özer	D	12	(1)	
MUTLU Karakas	A	1	(9)	1
NAIL Dinçer	M	17	(9)	6
SERHAT Güller	D	31		1
Gintaras STAUCE (LIT)	G	34		
TANER Alpak	D	29		1
TURGUT Uçar	M	15	(6)	
Kancho YORDANOV (BUL)	A	8	(2)	
Ben YUSUEF Haraoui (ALG)	M	22	(4)	2
YUSUF Küçük	M		(1)	
YUSUF Tepekule	M	14	(1)	

LEAGUE RESULTS 1995/96

12/08/95	Fenerbahçe	A	0-4	
20/08/95	Vanspor	H	2-1	Mehmet, Nail
27/08/95	Eskisehirspor	H	3-2	Mehmet 2, Yusuef
08/09/95	Ankaragücü	A	0-1	
17/09/95	Gaziantepspor	H	2-1	Fofana, Kasim
24/09/95	Bursaspor	A	1-3	Fofana
01/10/95	Kocaelispor	H	1-2	Fofana
15/10/95	Besiktas	A	0-4	
22/10/95	Denizlispor	H	2-0	Nail 2
28/10/95	Galatasaray	A	0-3	
12/11/95	Altay	H	1-1	Levent
19/11/95	Kayserispor	A	1-1	Levent
26/11/95	Gençlerbirligi	H	1-1	Levent
03/12/95	Antalyaspor	A	0-4	
10/12/95	Samsunspor	H	1-0	Serhat
16/12/95	Trabzonspor	A	0-3	
23/12/95	Istanbulspor	H	0-3	
27/01/96	Fenerbahçe	H	0-1	
04/02/96	Vanspor	A	1-1	Yusuef
11/02/96	Eskisehirspor	A	2-0	Atilla, Mehmet
18/02/96	Ankaragücü	H	0-0	
25/02/96	Gaziantepspor	A	0-3	
03/03/96	Bursaspor	H	0-3	
08/03/96	Kocaelispor	A	0-2	
17/03/96	Besiktas	H	0-2	
24/03/96	Denizlispor	A	0-1	
30/03/96	Galatasaray	H	0-3	
07/04/96	Altay	A	0-0	
14/04/96	Kayserispor	H	1-3	Taner
20/04/96	Gençlerbirligi	A	0-2	
28/04/96	Antalyaspor	H	1-2	Kasim
05/05/96	Samsunspor	A	1-4	Nail
12/05/96	Trabzonspor	H	1-4	Mutlu
19/05/96	Istanbulspor	A	4-0	Nail 2, Cenk, Kasim

KAYSERISPOR

CLUB DIRECTORY

Kayserispor Kulübü
Erkilet Bulvari
Karpuzatan Mokvii
38080 Kocasinan
Kayseri
tel - (352) 3384952
fax - (352) 3384092
Year of Formation - 1966
President - Mehmet Özhaseki
Secretary - Bekir Yildiz
Coach - Nevzat Güzelirmak; Rasit Cetiner; Samet Aybabs
Stadium - Atatürk (15,000)

APPEARANCES 95/96

	P	Ap	(s)	Gls
ABDULLAH Duran	M	15	(8)	
Alloy AGU (NIG)	G	31		
ALI Gültiken	A	2	(2)	
AYKAN Atik	M		(2)	
BAHATTIN Yildirim	G	2	(1)	
BARIS Karabiyik	D	14	(4)	
BIROL Demirhan	D	23	(2)	3
CENGIZ Alp	A	21	(6)	1
CENGIZHAN Hincal	M	11	(1)	
Valentin DARTILOV (BUL)	D	3		
HAKAN Azman	M	28	(6)	
HAKAN Polat	G	1	(1)	
HASAN Çelik	A	22	(1)	9
HASAN HÜSEYIN Köse	M	9	(7)	
HAYRETTIN Kiliç	M	21	(5)	
HÜSEYIN Topkaya	M	3	(4)	
ILHAN Sancaktar	D	28		4
ISMAIL Müderrisoglu	A	9	(14)	2
ISMET Tasdemir	M	17	(2)	1
MUSTAFA Ugur	D	25	(3)	
Musa N'DAW (SEN)	A	4		1
Slavcho PAVLOV (BUL)	M	21	(2)	5
RECEP Umut	A	21	(7)	7
SALIH Bozoglu	D	2	(1)	
SALIH Eken	M	27	(3)	5
SERKAN Bonsol	M	13	(9)	1
ZAFER Türkman	A	1		

LEAGUE RESULTS 1995/96

Date	Opponent	H/A	Score	Scorers
13/08/95	Besiktas	H	1-1	Salih Eken
20/08/95	Denizlispor	H	0-0	
26/08/95	Galatasaray	H	1-2	N'Daw
10/09/95	Altay	A	0-2	
17/09/95	Vanspor	A	0-1	
24/09/95	Gençlerbirligi	H	2-2	Recep, Hasan
01/10/95	Antalyaspor	A	3-3	Recep 2, Pavlov
15/10/95	Samsunspor	H	3-2	Recep 2, Salih Eken
22/10/95	Trabzonspor	A	1-3	Hasan
29/10/95	Istanbulspor	H	0-1	
04/11/95	Fenerbahçe	A	1-2	Pavlov
19/11/95	Karsiyaka	H	1-1	Birol (p)
26/11/95	Eskisehirspor	A	0-4	
03/12/95	Ankaragücü	H	4-1	Ismet, Hasan, Birol (p), Pavlov
10/12/95	Gaziantepspor	A	0-1	
17/12/95	Bursaspor	H	0-0	
23/12/95	Kocaelispor	A	0-5	
27/01/96	Besiktas	A	1-4	Ismail
04/02/96	Denizlispor	A	2-2	Hasan, Birol (p)
11/02/96	Galatasaray	A	0-5	
18/02/96	Altay	H	1-1	Recep
25/02/96	Vanspor	H	3-1	Ilhan, og (Abdülkadir), Serkan
03/03/96	Gençlerbirligi	A	1-1	Ilhan
10/03/96	Antalyaspor	H	4-0	Ilhan, Ismail, Salih Eken, og (Orhan)
17/03/96	Samsunspor	A	0-0	
23/03/96	Trabzonspor	H	1-2	Cengiz
29/03/96	Istanbulspor	A	2-5	Pavlov (p), Hasan
07/04/96	Fenerbahçe	H	1-3	Pavlov (p)
14/04/96	Karsiyaka	A	3-1	Hasan 2, Salih Eken
21/04/96	Eskisehirspor	H	0-1	
28/04/96	Ankaragücü	A	1-1	Hasan
05/05/96	Gaziantepspor	H	1-2	Hasan
12/05/96	Bursaspor	A	2-1	Salih Eken, Ilhan
19/05/96	Kocaelispor	H	1-0	Recep (p)

KOCAELISPOR

CLUB DIRECTORY

Kocaelispor Kulübü
Ankara Caddesi 396
Dostluk Ishani No:55
Izmit
tel - (262) 2294498
fax - (262) 3247124
Year of Formation - 1966
President - Sefa Sirmen
Secretary - Suat Temaçin
Coach - Mustafa Denizli
Stadium - Ismetpasa (20,000)

APPEARANCES 95/96

	P	Ap	(s)	Gls
ALPER Boguslu	G	22		
Roman DABROWSKI (POL)	A	19	(7)	10
ENGIN Öztenga	M		(1)	
ERGUN Kula	A	3	(6)	3
EVREN Turhan	M	12	(3)	2
FARUK Yigit	A	28	(2)	9
GÖKMEN Özcan	M	2	(16)	
ILHAMI Arslan	M	2	(1)	
ILHAN Özer	M	9	(6)	
Misko MIRKOVIC (YUG)	D	34		1
John MOSHOEU (SAF)	M	31		13
MURAT Barut	M		(2)	
MÜCAHIT	M	1		
NURI Çolak	M	11	(3)	1
OSMAN Çakir	D	28	(1)	
Fahrettin OMEROVIC (BOS)	G	2		
SAFFET Sancakli	A	16		14
TAYFUR Havutçu	M	34		3
TOPRAK Kirtoglu	D	23	(8)	
TURAN Uzun	D	32		1
ÜMIT Inal	A	13	(14)	2
VOLKAN Gökdemir	M	6	(3)	
VOLKAN Kilimci	G	10		
YALÇIN Kildiran	M	26	(3)	1
ZEKI Önatli	M	10	(9)	

LEAGUE RESULTS 1995/96

12/08/95	Gençlerbirligi	A	1-1	Ümit
20/08/95	Antalyaspor	H	2-2	Turan, Evren
25/08/95	Samsunspor	A	0-0	
10/09/95	Trabzonspor	H	1-3	Dabrowski
15/09/95	Istanbulspor	A	2-1	Moshoeu, Faruk
23/09/95	Fenerbahçe	H	0-1	
01/10/95	Karsiyaka	A	2-1	Nuri, Moshoeu
15/10/95	Eskisehirspor	H	2-1	Ergun 2
22/10/95	Ankaragücü	A	0-4	
29/10/95	Gaziantepspor	H	2-2	Moshoeu, Tayfur
05/11/95	Bursaspor	A	2-2	Faruk, Moshoeu (p)
19/11/95	Vanspor	H	1-0	Dabrowski
26/11/95	Besiktas	H	1-0	Moshoeu
03/12/95	Denizlispor	A	0-0	
10/12/95	Galatasaray	H	1-1	Faruk
17/12/95	Altay	A	2-3	Dabrowski, og (Fuludu)
23/12/95	Kayserispor	H	5-0	Ümit, Mirkovic, Tayfur, Evren, Ergun
28/01/96	Gençlerbirligi	H	2-0	Yalçin, Saffet
04/02/96	Antalyaspor	A	1-1	Saffet
11/02/96	Samsunspor	H	3-1	Dabrowski, Faruk, Tayfur
18/02/96	Trabzonspor	A	0-2	
25/02/96	Istanbulspor	H	0-0	
03/03/96	Fenerbahçe	A	0-4	
08/03/96	Karsiyaka	H	2-0	Saffet, Faruk
17/03/96	Eskisehirspor	A	3-0	Saffet 2, Dabrowski
24/03/96	Ankaragücü	H	2-0	Saffet, Faruk
31/03/96	Gaziantepspor	A	4-2	Moshoeu 2, Saffet, Dabrowski
06/04/96	Bursaspor	H	4-2	Dabrowski, Moshoeu, Faruk, Saffet
14/04/96	Vanspor	A	2-2	Dabrowski, Faruk
21/04/96	Besiktas	A	5-3	Dabrowski, Faruk, Moshoeu 2, Saffet
28/04/96	Denizlispor	H	4-2	Moshoeu 3, Saffet
04/05/96	Galatasaray	A	4-0	Saffet 3 (1p), Dabrowski
12/05/96	Altay	H	1-1	Saffet
19/05/96	Kayserispor	A	0-1	

SAMSUNSPOR

CLUB DIRECTORY

Samsunspor Kulübü
Tesisleri
Samsun
tel - (362) 2383696
fax - (362) 2383788
Year of Formation - 1965
President - Ismail Uyanik
Secretary - Tarik Kaptan
Coach - Gheorghe Multescu
Stadium - 19 Mayis (20,000)

APPEARANCES 95/96

	P	Ap	(s)	Gls
Alex AGBO (NIG)	A	2	(11)	1
Aliouin BOUKAR (CMR)	G	28	(1)	
BÜLENT Dasdan	M		(1)	
CELIL Sagir	M	19	(1)	2
CENK Isler	A	12	(10)	5
ERCAN Kologlu	D	28	(1)	1
ERKUT Cagdas	D	9	(2)	
FARUK Sarman	D	25	(2)	3
FATIH Sezer	M	6	(5)	1
GÖKSEL Gencer	G	6		
GÜRHAN Yürük	M	3	(7)	
IMDAT Arslan	D	29		
ISA Turan	M	31	(2)	1
MEVLÜT Kahraman	M	1	(3)	
MUSTAFA Caskun	M		(2)	
ORHAN Eren	D	2	(4)	
SABRI Sirinsoylu	D	13	(2)	
SERDAR Samin	A	3	(5)	3
SERKAN Aykut	A	26	(2)	14
SINAN Yesil	M	20	(6)	5
Daniel TIMOFTE (ROM)	M	20		1
UGUR Dagdelen	A	25	(2)	7
VEDAT Vatansever	A	10	(12)	1
VURAL Korkmaz	M	27	(1)	1
YASIN Averoglu	M	3	(14)	
YASAR Isik	D	26	(4)	

LEAGUE RESULTS 1995/96

Date	Opponent	H/A	Score	Scorers
13/08/95	Gaziantepspor	H	1-0	Sinan (p)
20/08/95	Bursaspor	A	4-2	Serkan 3, Sinan (p)
25/08/95	Kocaelispor	H	0-0	
10/09/95	Besiktas	A	2-4	Sinan 2
16/09/95	Denizlispor	H	1-3	Cenk
22/09/95	Galatasaray	A	0-1	
01/10/95	Altay	H	4-0	Faruk, Serkan, Cenk, Celil
15/10/95	Kayserispor	A	2-3	Vural, Serkan
21/10/95	Gençlerbirligi	H	3-0	Serdar 2, Serkan
29/10/95	Antalyaspor	A	1-2	Faruk
05/11/95	Vanspor	A	0-0	
19/11/95	Trabzonspor	H	0-1	
26/11/95	Istanbulspor	A	2-0	Fatih, Serdar
03/12/95	Fenerbahçe	H	0-3	
10/12/95	Karsiyaka	A	0-1	
17/12/95	Eskisehirspor	H	3-1	Ugur 3
23/12/95	Ankaragücü	A	0-1	
28/01/96	Gaziantepspor	A	0-3	
04/02/96	Bursaspor	H	1-0	Serkan
11/02/96	Kocaelispor	A	1-3	Celil
18/02/96	Besiktas	H	0-1	
25/02/96	Denizlispor	A	2-1	Agbo, Vedat
02/03/96	Galatasaray	H	3-2	Ugur, Cenk, Serkan
10/03/96	Altay	A	0-0	
17/03/96	Kayserispor	H	0-0	
24/03/96	Gençlerbirligi	A	0-0	
31/03/96	Antalyaspor	H	2-2	Sinan, Serkan
07/04/96	Vanspor	H	4-1	Ugur 2, Cenk 2
13/04/96	Trabzonspor	A	0-1	
21/04/96	Istanbulspor	H	4-4	Serkan 3 (1p), Ercan
28/04/96	Fenerbahçe	A	0-1	
05/05/96	Karsiyaka	H	4-1	Ugur, Timofte, Serkan 2
12/05/96	Eskisehirspor	A	0-3	
19/05/96	Ankaragücü	H	2-1	Faruk, Isa

TRABZONSPOR

CLUB DIRECTORY

Trabzonspor Kulübü
Mehmet Ali Yilmaz Tesisleri
Trabzon
tel - (462) 3250967
fax - (462) 3265767
Year of Formation - 1967
President - Faruk Özak
Secretary - Kenan Iskender
Coach - Senol Günes
Stadium - Avni Aker (30,000)

MAJOR HONOURS
League Championship - (6)
1976, 1977, 1979, 1980, 1981, 1984.
Domestic Cup - (5)
1977, 1978, 1984, 1992, 1995.

APPEARANCES 95/96

	P	Ap	(s)	Gls
ABDULLAH Ercan	M	33		2
Archil ARVELADZE (GEO)	A	12	(2)	6
Shota ARVELADZE (GEO)	A	34		25
CENGIZ Atilla	D	33		2
ERHAN Koç	A		(2)	
FATIH Tekke	M	7	(13)	3
HAMDI Aslan	M		(15)	1
HAMI Mandirali	A	30		13
HASAN Özer	A		(20)	2
ISKENDER Iroglu	D	1	(3)	
LEMI Çelik	M	33		3
MEHMET Ipek	M		(2)	
METIN Mert	G	19		
NIHAT Tümkaya	G	15		
OGÜN Temizkanoglu	D	34		4
OKAN Özke	D	13	(7)	
ORHAN Çikrikçi	A	20	(11)	2
OSMAN Özköylü	D	25	(3)	1
SONER Boz	M	10	(17)	1
TOLUNAY Kafkas	M	33		7
ÜNAL Karaman	M	22		5

LEAGUE RESULTS 1995/96

Date	Opponent		Score	Scorers
13/08/95	Ankaragücü	H	3-1	Tolunay, Hami, Hasan
20/08/95	Gaziantepspor	A	0-0	
26/08/95	Bursaspor	H	0-0	
10/09/95	Kocaelispor	A	3-1	Tolunay, Arveladze S.., Hami
17/09/95	Besiktas	H	3-1	Arveladze A. 2, Lemi
23/09/95	Denizlispor	H	3-0	Arveladze A., Hami (p), Hamdi
01/10/95	Galatasaray	H	4-1	Hami 2 (1p), Arveladze S. 2
15/10/95	Altay	A	5-2	Arveladze A., Arveladze S., Hami, Osman, Ogün
22/10/95	Kayserispor	H	3-1	Hami, Arveladze S. 2
29/10/95	Gençlerbirligi	A	3-1	Arveladze S. 2, Arveladze A.
05/11/95	Antalyaspor	H	2-0	Arveladze S., Ünal
12/11/95	Samsunspor	A	1-0	Tolunay
26/11/95	Vanspor	A	5-0	Hami (p), Arveladze S. 3, Fatih
01/12/95	Istanbulspor	H	2-1	Arveladze A., Abdullah
09/12/95	Fenerbahçe	A	1-3	Lemi
16/12/95	Karsiyaka	H	3-0	Ogün, Tolunay 2
23/12/95	Eskisehirspor	A	2-0	Ogün, Hasan
28/01/96	Ankaragücü	A	3-1	Abdullah, Tolunay, og (Gökmen)
03/02/96	Gaziantepspor	H	0-0	
11/02/96	Bursaspor	A	2-1	Orhan, Hami
18/02/96	Kocaelispor	H	2-0	Hami, Arveladze S.
24/02/96	Besiktas	A	0-2	
03/03/96	Denizlispor	A	3-0	Tolunay, Arveladze S. 2
09/03/96	Galatasaray	A	0-0	
16/03/96	Altay	H	2-0	Arveladze S., Ogün
23/03/96	Kayserispor	A	2-1	Arveladze S., Ünal
31/03/96	Gençlerbirligi	H	3-1	Ünal, Hami, Lemi
06/04/96	Antalyaspor	A	2-0	Orhan, Ünal
13/04/96	Samsunspor	H	1-0	Hami (p)
19/04/96	Vanspor	H	0-1	
27/04/96	Istanbulspor	A	4-1	Arveladze S. 3, Hami
05/05/96	Fenerbahçe	H	1-2	Abdullah
12/05/96	Karsiyaka	A	4-1	Cengiz, Fatih 2, Soner
19/05/96	Eskisehirspor	H	7-1	Cengiz, Ünal, Arveladze S. 5

VANSPOR

CLUB DIRECTORY

Vanspor Kulübü
Iskele Caddesi
Çevik Kuvvet Arkasi
Van
tel - (432) 2231490
fax - (432) 2233495
Year of Formation - 1974
President - Pasa Kursunluoglu
Secretary - Abdurrahman Çamas
Coach - Petar Gavrila; Ali Osman Renklibay
(96/97 - Mehmet Basaygün)
Stadium - Vali Mahmut Yilbas (10,000)

APPEARANCES 95/96

	P	Ap	(s)	Gls
ABDÜLKADIR Demirci	D	31		2
ADNAN Baytar	A	32		8
ALI NAIL Durmus	M	21		5
ALPARSLAN Tice	A		(6)	
ALTAY Dagdalen	G	2		
Kiril ANDONOV (BUL)	D	16		
AYKUT Canik	D	32		1
Samuel BERNARD (CMR)	M	23	(5)	4
BÜNYAMIN Kubat	A	1		
CENGIZ Büyüksanalan	D	10	(3)	
ERCAN Yildiz	M		(3)	
ERHAN Namli	M	21	(8)	2
ERKAN Avseren	D	30		4
ERKAN Tabak	A		(1)	
ESREF Kestano	D	5	(9)	1
FADIL Kurt	M	32		1
HAYATI Köse	M	6		
HAYRETTIN Aksoy	A	3	(2)	
IBRAHIM Kutlug	M	10	(10)	
ISMAIL Öztürkçü	A		(1)	
KURTHAN Yilmaz	A	24	(6)	1
METIN Halaç	M		(12)	1
MEVLÜT Can	M	21	(5)	1
MURAT Vigiter	G	9	(1)	
SERHAN Hacihüseyinoglu	M	2	(4)	
SINAN Aydin	M	12	(12)	
Piotr SOCZYNSKI (POL)	D	4	(1)	
Dumitru STÎNGACIU (ROM)	G	23		
Adrian VASAI (ROM)	A	4	(2)	

LEAGUE RESULTS 1995/96

Date	Opponent	H/A	Score	Scorers
13/08/95	Galatasaray	H	0-1	
20/08/95	Karsiyaka	A	1-2	Bernard
27/08/95	Altay	H	2-0	Abdülkadir, Erhan
10/09/95	Eskisehirspor	A	1-2	Adnan
17/09/95	Kayserispor	H	1-0	Adnan
24/09/95	Ankaragücü	A	0-0	
01/10/95	Gençlerbirligi	H	0-1	
15/10/95	Gaziantepspor	A	0-1	
22/10/95	Antalyaspor	H	1-1	Bernard
29/10/95	Bursaspor	A	0-5	
05/11/95	Samsunspor	H	0-0	
19/11/95	Kocaelispor	A	0-1	
26/11/95	Trabzonspor	H	0-5	
03/12/95	Besiktas	A	1-3	Ali Nail
10/12/95	Istanbulspor	A	1-1	Adnan (p)
17/12/95	Denizlispor	H	3-1	Ali Nail, Adnan, Metin
23/12/95	Fenerbahçe	A	0-3	
28/01/96	Galatasaray	A	0-2	
04/02/96	Karsiyaka	H	1-1	Abdülkadir
11/02/96	Altay	A	1-1	Adnan
18/02/96	Eskisehirspor	H	3-0	Erkan Avseren, Ali Nail, Adnan
25/02/96	Kayserispor	A	1-3	Mevlüt
03/03/96	Ankaragücü	H	4-1	Ali Nail, og (Ramazan), Adnan, Kurthan
10/03/96	Gençlerbirligi	A	1-1	Erkan Avseren
17/03/96	Gaziantepspor	H	2-0	Aykut, Ali Nail
24/03/96	Antalyaspor	A	1-4	Bernard
31/03/96	Bursaspor	H	1-1	Erkan Avseren
07/04/96	Samsunspor	A	1-4	Fadil
14/04/96	Kocaelispor	H	2-2	Bernard, Esref
19/04/96	Trabzonspor	A	1-0	Erkan Avseren
28/04/96	Besiktas	H	2-0	Adnan, Erhan
05/05/96	Istanbulspor	H	0-0	
12/05/96	Denizlispor	A	0-0	
19/05/96	Fenerbahçe	H	0-3	

PROMOTED CLUBS

SECOND DIVISION FINAL TABLES 95/96

FIRST PHASE

GROUP ONE

		Pd	W	D	L	F	A	Pt	GD
1	Çanakkale Dardanelspor	18	12	4	2	37	16	40	+21
2	Sariyer	18	10	4	4	31	9	34	+22
3	Anadoluhisamspor	18	8	4	6	20	15	28	+5
4	Gaziosmanpasa	18	8	4	6	27	29	28	-2
5	Zeytinburnu	18	7	5	6	28	23	26	+5
6	Çorluspor	18	7	4	7	23	25	25	-2
7	Edirnespor	18	6	4	8	19	27	22	-8
8	Kartalspor	18	6	3	9	26	29	21	-3
9	Bakirköyspor	18	4	5	9	25	27	17	-2
10	Lüleburgazspor	18	3	1	14	18	54	10	-36

GROUP TWO

		Pd	W	D	L	F	A	Pt	GD
1	Balikesirspor	18	9	6	3	29	18	33	+11
2	Göztepe	18	8	7	3	25	14	31	+11
3	Aydinspor	18	8	3	7	24	21	27	+3
4	Yeni Salihlispor	18	8	3	7	29	27	27	+2
5	Yeni Turgutluspor	18	7	5	6	21	22	26	-1
6	Soma Linyitspor	18	8	2	8	22	25	26	-3
7	Bucaspor	18	7	4	7	27	25	25	+2
8	Yeni Afyonspor	18	6	4	8	20	17	22	+3
9	Fethiyespor	18	6	2	10	21	35	20	-14
10	Bergamaspor	18	4	2	12	23	37	14	-14

GROUP THREE

		Pd	W	D	L	F	A	Pt	GD
1	Mersin Idmanyurdu	18	12	4	2	31	17	40	+14
2	Konyaspor	18	11	1	6	28	17	34	+11
3	Adanaspor	18	9	2	7	30	23	29	+7
4	Kemerspor	18	8	4	6	28	21	28	+7
5	Yeni Yozgatspor	18	7	5	6	20	22	26	-2
6	Alanyaspor	18	6	4	8	21	25	22	-4
7	Sekerspor	18	6	3	9	18	20	21	-2
8	Adana Demirspor	18	4	6	8	23	23	18	=
9	Beypazarispor	18	3	8	7	12	20	17	-8
10	Mersinspor	18	2	7	9	12	35	13	-23

PROMOTED CLUBS

SECOND DIVISION FINAL TABLES 95/96

GROUP FOUR

		Pd	W	D	L	F	A	Pt	GD
1	Sakaryaspor	18	11	5	2	35	16	38	+19
2	Karabükspor	18	11	5	2	32	14	38	+18
3	Zonguldakspor	18	6	7	5	20	22	25	-2
4	Çorumspor	18	6	4	8	25	26	22	-1
5	Çaykur Rizespor	18	5	7	6	19	28	22	-9
6	Boluspor	18	5	5	8	27	24	20	+3
7	Erzurumspor	18	4	8	6	23	23	20	=
8	Orduspor	18	5	5	8	22	30	20	-8
9	Erzincanspor	18	4	7	7	21	31	19	-10
10	Düzcespor	18	3	7	8	20	30	16	-10

GROUP FIVE

		Pd	W	D	L	F	A	Pt	GD
1	Diyarbakirspor	18	12	3	2	30	13	39	+17
2	Siirt Köyhizmetleri	18	11	4	3	34	18	37	+16
3	Elazigspor	18	11	3	4	28	17	36	+11
4	Malatyaspor	18	10	3	5	28	17	33	+11
5	Sanliurfaspor	18	10	2	6	31	26	32	+5
6	PTT	18	7	1	10	36	34	22	+2
7	Hatayspor	18	6	4	8	21	27	22	-6
8	Adiyamanspor	18	5	3	10	18	23	18	-5
9	Kahramanmarasspor	18	1	5	12	14	39	8	-25
10	Petrolofisi	18	1	4	13	14	40	7	-26

PROMOTION GROUP

		Pd	W	D	L	F	A	Pt	GD
1	**Çanakkale Dardanelspor**	**18**	**10**	**4**	**4**	**23**	**13**	**34**	**+10**
2	**Sariyer**	**18**	**8**	**9**	**1**	**29**	**17**	**33**	**+12**
3	Karabükspor	18	9	5	4	29	15	32	+14
4	**Balikesirspor**	**18**	**8**	4	**6**	**26**	**23**	**28**	**+3**
5	Diyarbakirspor	18	7	5	6	24	26	26	-2
6	Sakaryaspor	18	6	5	7	22	21	23	+1
7	Göztepe	18	7	1	10	20	26	22	-6
8	Mersin Idmanyurdu	18	5	3	10	15	23	18	-8
9	Siirt Köyhizmetleri	18	3	7	8	15	22	16	-7
10	Konyaspor	18	4	3	11	14	31	15	-17

PROMOTION PLAY-OFFS

N.B. Teams 3-5 in Promotion Group join the five Second Division group winners after the second phase.

QUARTER-FINALS

Karabükspor 2, Balikesirspor 1
Çaykur Rizespor 2, Diyarbakirspor 2
(Çaykur Rizespor on pens.)
Elazigspor 2, Yeni Salihlispor 1
Zeytinburnu 2, Kemerspor 1

SEMI-FINALS

Diyarbakirspor 1, Karabükspor 1 (Diyarbakirspor on pens.)
Zeytinburnu 1, Elazigspor 1 (Zeytinburnu on pens.)

FINAL

Zeytinburnu 1, Diyarbakirspor 0

CLUB DIRECTORY

Çanakkale Dardanelspor Kulübü
Çanakkale
tel - (286) 2175699
fax - (286) 2171555
Year of Formation - 1966
President - Niyazi Önen
Secretary - Ismet Güneshan
Coach - Kamuran Yavuz; Rasit Çetiner
Stadium - 18 Mart (15,000)

CLUB DIRECTORY

Sariyer Spor Kulübü
Eski Sular Yolu No:42
Istanbul
tel - (212) 2429498
fax - (212) 2427079
Year of Formation - 1940
President - Yetkin Gürsel
Secretary - Atalay Kazan
Coach - Adnan Dinçer; Yilmaz Vural
Stadium - Yusuf Ziya Önis (10,000)

CLUB DIRECTORY

Zeytinburnu
Zübeyde Hanim Caddesi No.1
Istanbul
tel - (212) 5828383
Year of Formation - 1953
President - Adil Emecan
Coach - Bahri Kaya
Stadium - Zeytinburnu (15,000)

UKRAINE

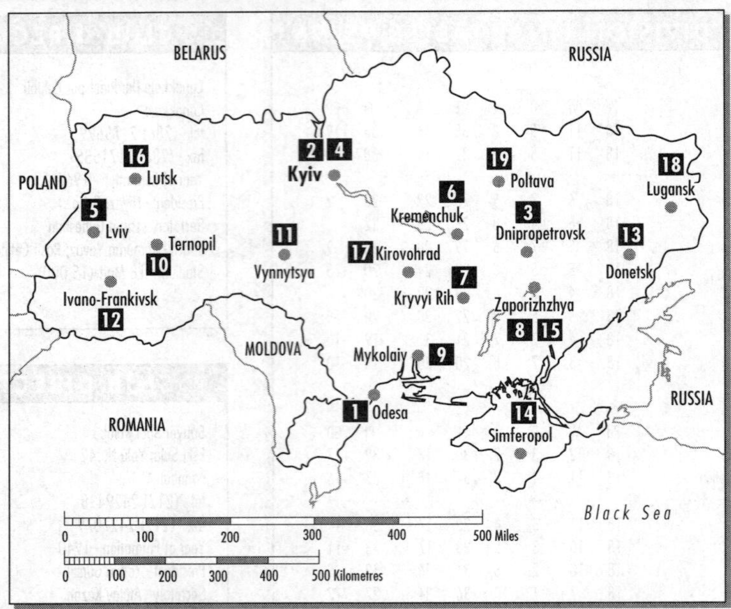

1	CHORNOMORETS ODESA	1044
2	CSKA BORYSFEN KYIV	1045
3	DNIPRO DNIPROPETROVSK	1046
4	DYNAMO KYIV	1047
5	KARPATY LVIV	1048
6	KREMIN KREMENCHUK	1049
7	KRYVBAS KRYVYI RIH	1050
8	METALLURG ZAPORIZHZHYA	1051
9	SK MYKOLAIV	1052
10	NYVA TERNOPIL	1053
11	NYVA VYNNYTSYA	1054
12	PRIKARPATTYA IVANO-FRANKIVSK	1055
13	SHAKHTAR DONETSK	1056
14	TAVRIYA SIMFEROPOL	1057
15	TORPEDO ZAPORIZHZHYA	1058
16	VOLYN LUTSK	1059
17	ZIRKA NIBAS KIROVOHRAD	1060
18	ZORYA MALS LUGANSK	1061
19	VORSKLA POLTAVA	1062

SHAKHTAR PRESIDENT ASSASSINATED

Bribes scandal masks Dynamo 'double'

FEDERATION DIRECTORY

Football Federation of Ukraine
vul. Ulyanovykh 1, 252 023 Kyiv

tel - (044) 2649430
tlx - 161866
fax - (044) 2647564

Year of Formation - 1991
President - Viktor Bannikov
Secretary - Mykola Chernysh

Stadium - National Sport Komplex Olimpiyskyi, Kiev (100,169)

The chaos and disruption prevalent in Ukrainian everyday life manifested itself on a grand scale in football during the 1995/96 season. It was a season dominated by scandal. Dynamo Kiev's fourth successive championship win and second Ukrainian 'double' almost passed unnoticed as the nation's football followers were sidetracked from the action by a series of dark, doom-filled incidents off the field.

The murkiest episode - and the one which made the biggest international headlines - was the bribery scandal surrounding Dynamo Kiev's opening Champions' League match against Panathinaikos.

Kiev had been fortunate to make it through to Europe's premier competition in the first place. UEFA's surprising decision to 'demote' Yugoslav champions Red Star Belgrade to the UEFA Cup gave Dynamo a late back-door entry to the preliminary round, and they negotiated that hurdle with ease, beating AaB of Denmark 4-1 over the two legs. A crowd approaching 100,000 (inconceivably vast, by Ukrainian standards) filled the Republican Stadium for the opening Champions' League encounter against Panathinaikos and the fans all left happy after a goal from midfielder Vitaliy Kosovskyi gave Kiev a 1-0 win. But then came the awful news...

Spanish referee López Nieto reported to UEFA that he had been approached by leading Dynamo officials the day before the game and offered money and valuables if he would swing the game in the Ukrainian champions'

LEAGUE CHAMPIONSHIP RESULTS 95/96

		1	2	3	4	5	6	7	8	9	10	11	12	13	14	15	16	17	18
1	Chornomorets Odesa		1-0	2-1	1-0	1-0	6-1	2-0	4-3	1-0	2-0	2-0	0-0	2-1	4-3	3-1	4-1	1-1	2-0
2	CSKA-Borysfen Kyiv	1-0		0-0	1-2	2-1	1-1	2-0	0-2	0-0	1-1	1-0	3-0	4-0	2-0	2-0	3-1	0-1	4-0
3	Dnipro Dnipropetrovsk	0-2	2-0		0-0	3-0	2-0	4-2	5-0	5-0	2-1	1-2	1-0	2-2	2-0	2-0	2-1	3-1	3-1
4	Dynamo Kyiv	3-0	0-0	5-1		2-0	2-0	3-0	2-0	3-0	2-0	1-0	1-1	3-1	2-0	2-0	4-0	5-1	1-0
5	Karpaty Lviv	3-2	1-1	2-1	1-1		2-0	2-2	1-0	3-0	3-0	3-0	0-0	1-0	1-1	1-2	2-1	2-0	2-1
6	Kremin Kremenchuk	0-1	1-1	0-3	0-1	6-1		1-1	1-0	3-2	3-0	0-1	4-2	3-2	1-0	3-2	3-1	2-1	1-0
7	Kryvbas Kryvyi Rih	0-0	2-0	1-0	2-2	1-3	2-1		2-1	1-1	1-0	1-1	2-1	1-0	2-0	2-3	5-1	5-4	2-0
8	Metalurg Zaporizhzhya	0-0	0-1	2-1	0-2	1-1	1-0	2-1		3-2	1-0	3-0	2-1	2-0	3-0	2-0	2-0	1-1	5-0
9	SK Mykolaiv	1-2	0-2	0-2	0-2	0-0	2-0	2-1	1-0		2-0	2-0	3-0	0-0	1-2	2-1	0-3	0-0	4-1
10	Nyva Ternopil	0-1	1-0	0-1	1-0	1-0	0-0	3-1	2-1	4-1		2-0	3-1	1-3	1-0	2-0	1-2	0-0	3-1
11	Nyva Vynnytsya	0-0	1-1	2-0	0-2	0-0	0-2	1-1	0-1	2-1	3-2		1-0	0-0	1-3	2-0	2-0	0-1	5-0
12	Prykarpattya Ivano-Frankivsk	1-1	3-2	1-1	2-3	1-0	5-2	1-0	4-1	2-2	3-1	2-1		2-0	4-3	4-0	3-0	0-0	4-0
13	Shakhtar Donetsk	2-0	2-3	1-0	2-3	2-0	4-1	4-0	1-2	0-1	2-4	1-2	1-0		0-0	2-1	1-1	1-0	3-0
14	Tavriya Simferopol	0-0	2-2	3-3	0-2	2-0	1-2	1-1	1-1	5-2	0-2	1-0	3-0	1-3		2-0	xxx	0-0	3-0
15	Torpedo Zaporizhzhya	2-1	0-1	1-3	1-1	1-1	3-1	3-1	1-0	2-1	1-0	1-0	2-0	3-0	2-3		1-1	1-0	3-0
16	Volyn Lutsk	0-3	1-1	1-5	0-2	1-0	2-0	0-0	2-1	3-3	3-1	0-0	2-0	0-0	0-3	0-1		1-0	3-1
17	Zirka-NIBAS Kirovohrad	0-2	0-0	1-1	2-1	2-1	3-0	2-0	4-1	0-1	1-0	1-0	3-0	0-1	2-1	1-0	1-0		2-0
18	Zorya-MALS Lugansk	0-3	1-5	0-3	0-0	1-1	1-3	1-0	1-5	0-0	xxx	0-1	1-1	0-2	0-2	0-1	3-2	2-1	

xxx- match void; awarded as home win.

LEAGUE CHAMPIONSHIP FINAL TABLE 95/96

			Home					Away					Total						
		Pd	W	D	L	F	A	W	D	L	F	A	W	D	L	F	A	Pt	GD
1	Dynamo Kyiv	34	15	2	0	41	4	9	5	3	24	13	24	7	3	65	17	79	+48
2	Chornomorets Odesa	34	15	2	0	38	12	7	5	5	18	13	22	7	5	56	25	73	+31
3	Dnipro Dnipropetrovsk	34	13	2	2	39	12	6	4	7	26	22	19	6	9	65	34	63	+31
4	CSKA-Borysfen Kyiv	34	10	4	3	27	9	5	7	5	20	18	15	11	8	47	27	56	+20
5	Metalurg Zaporizhzhya	34	12	3	2	30	10	4	1	12	19	32	16	4	14	49	42	52	+7
6	Zirka-NIBAS Kirovohrad	34	12	2	3	25	9	2	6	9	12	24	14	8	12	37	33	50	+4
7	Torpedo Zaporizhzhya	34	11	3	3	28	14	4	0	13	12	32	15	3	16	40	46	48	-6
8	Karpaty Lviv	34	11	5	1	30	12	1	5	11	9	27	12	10	12	39	39	46	=
9	Kremin Kremenchuk	34	11	2	4	32	19	3	2	12	14	37	14	4	16	46	56	46	-10
10	Shakhtar Donetsk	34	9	2	6	29	18	4	4	9	15	25	13	6	15	44	43	45	+1
11	Prykarpattya Ivano-Frankivsk	34	12	4	1	42	17	0	4	13	7	32	12	8	14	49	49	44	=
12	Tavriya Simferopol	34	7	6	4	25	18	5	2	10	21	28	12	8	14	46	46	44	=
13	Nyva Ternopil	34	11	2	4	25	12	2	1	14	12	30	13	3	18	37	42	42	-5
14	Kryvbas Kryvyi Rih	34	11	4	2	32	18	0	5	12	11	34	11	9	14	43	52	42	-9
15	Nyva Vynnytsya	34	7	5	5	20	14	4	2	11	8	22	11	7	16	28	36	40	-8
16	SK Mykolaiv	34	8	3	6	20	16	2	5	10	17	37	10	8	16	37	53	38	-16
17	Volyn Lutsk	34	7	5	5	19	21	2	2	13	15	37	9	7	18	34	58	34	-24
18	Zorya-MALS Lugansk	34	4	4	9	11	30	0	0	17	5	50	4	4	26	16	80	16	-64

favour. UEFA sought confirmation, but, inevitably, Dynamo denied all knowledge of involvement. A UEFA disciplinary commission was immediately assembled, and the outcome was severe. Dynamo Kiev were to be thrown out of the Champions' League and banned from competing in Europe for a further two years.

The Ukrainian people were numbed with shock. The affair soon assumed national significance, with the president and ex-preseident of the Ukrainian state lobbying UEFA for a full investigation and a reduction in the severity of the punishment. It was as if Dynamo Kiev's alleged misdeeds threatened the good name of the whole

DOMESTIC CUP RESULTS

1/16 FINALS

CSKA Borysfen Kyiv 0, Shakhtar Donetsk 1
Halychyna Drohobych 0, Kryvbas Kryvyi Rih 0
(aet; 6-5 on pens.)
Metalurg Nikopol 2, Prykarpattya Ivano-Fraankivsk 0
Yavir Krasnopillya 2, Zorya-MALS Lugansk 0
Nyva Myronivka 3, Karpaty Lviv 4
Haraj Zhovka 0, Volyn Lutsk 1
Metalurg Novomoskovsk 0, Dynamo Kyiv 3
Zirka NIBAS Kirovohrad 1, Chornomorets Odesa 0
Stal Alchevsk 1, Kremin Kremenchuk 3
Naftokhimik Kremenchuk 1, Tavriya Simferopol 2
Dynamo-2 Kyiv 2, SK Mykolaiv 2 (aet; 5-4 on pens.)
Chaika Sevastopol 0, Torpedo Zaporizhzhya 1
Podillya Khmelnytskyi 2, Dnipro Dnipropetrovsk 5
Gazovyk Komarne 0, Nyva Vynnytsya 0
(aet; 6-7 on pens.)
Khutrovyk Tysmenytsya 0, Nyva Ternopil 1
Shakhtar-2 Donetsk 0, Metalurg Zaporizhzhya 1

1/8 FINALS

Nyva Ternopil 3, Volyn Lutsk 1
Nyva Vynnytsya 2, Halychyna Drohobych 0
Dnipro Dnipropetrovsk 4, Karpaty Lviv 1
Shakhtar Donetsk 2, Dynamo-2 Kyiv 0 (aet)
Tavriya Simferopol 2, Yavir Krasnopillya 0
Dynamo Kyiv 2, Zirka NIBAS Kirovohrad 0
Kremin Kremenchuk 1, Metalurg Nikopol 0
Metalurg Zaporizhzhya 2, Torpedo Zaporizhzhya 0
(aet)

QUARTER-FINALS

Tavriya Simferopol 0, Dynamo Kyiv 1
Shakhtar Donetsk 2, Dnipro Dnipropetrovsk 2
(aet; 4-2 on pens.)
Nyva Vynnytsya 1, Nyva Ternopil 0
Kremin Kremenchuk 2, Metalurg Zaporizhzhya 1

SEMI-FINALS

Dynamo Kyiv 2, Kremin Kremenchuk 0
Nyva Nynnytsya 0, Shakhtar Donetsk 0
(aet; 3-0 on pens.)

FINAL

26/05/95, Kiev
DYNAMO KYIV 2 Rebrov (29), Maximov (59)
NYVA VYNNYTSYA 0
referee - Ardysh
DYNAMO KYIV - Shovkovskyi, Luzhnyi, Bezhenar, Holovko, Shmatovalenko, Mykhailenko, Rebrov (Shkapenko 84), Maximov (Kalitvintsev 69), Kosovskyi, Leonenko (Pokhlebayev 60), Shevchenko.
NYVA VYNNYTSYA - Tsytkin (Nemodruk 67); Gaidarzhi, Sosenko, Zaporozhchenko, Solovienko, Lelyuk, Balatskyi, Ryabtsev, Romanchuk, Chervonyi, Lyubynskyi .

NATIONAL TEAM APPEARANCES 95/96

Coach - Anatoliy KONKOV; Jozsef SZABO	LIT	SLO	ITA	MOL	TUR	Cps	Gls
Oleg SUSLOV (02/01/69) - Chornomorets Odesa	G	G	G	G	G	8	-
Oleg LUZHNYI (06/08/68) - Dynamo Kyiv	D	D	D	D66	D	14	-
Viktor SKRYPNYK (19/11/69) - Dnipro Dnipropetrovsk	D	D	D		s46	6	1
Alexander HOLOVKO (06/01/72) - Dynamo Kyiv	D	D		D66	D	6	-
Volodymyr HORILYI (11/10/65) - Dnipro Dnipropetrovsk	D		D15			3	-
Sergiy BEZHENAR (09/08/70) - Dynamo Kyiv	D	D	D	s66		14	1
Igor ZHABCHENKO (01/07/68) - Bnei Yehuda (ISR)/ Chornomorets Odesa	D68	D		D66	D46	11	-
Gennadiy ORBU (23/07/70) - Shakhtar Donetsk	M	M	M	M	M46	10	-
Yuriy KALITVINTSEV (05/05/68) - Dynamo Kyiv	M	M71	M			6	1
Andriy GUSIN (11/12/72) - CSKA-Borysfen Kyiv	A	A46				3	2
Timerlan GUSEINOV (24/01/68) - Chornomorets Odesa	A86	A	A	A74	A	11	8
Yevhen POKHLEBAYEV (25/11/71) - Dynamo Kyiv	s68		s70	s66	s46	12	-
Alexander YEVTUSHOK (11/01/70) - Dnipro Dnipropetrovsk	s86	s71	s15			6	-
Sergiy SHMATOVALENKO (29/01/67) - Dynamo Kyiv		D89		D	D	8	-
Sergiy NAHORNYAK (05/09/71) - Dnipro Dnipropetrovsk		s46	A70			5	-
Andriy POLUNIN (05/03/71) - Dnipro Dnipropetrovsk		s89	M			7	1
Volodymyr SHARAN (18/09/71) - Dnipro Dnipropetrovsk			M51			1	-
Sergiy POPOV (22/04/71) - Shakhtar Donetsk			s51			13	1
Dmytro PARFENOV (11/09/74) - Chornomorets Odesa				D	D46	2	-
Vasyl KARDASH (14/01/73) - Chornomorets Odesa				A	A61	2	-
Valeriy KRIVENTSOV (30/07/72) - Shakhtar Donetsk				A		1	-
Alexei ANTYUKHIN (05/11/71) - Tavriya Simferopol				A66		1	-
Vladyslav VASHCHUK (02/01/75) - Dynamo Kyiv				s66		1	-
Dmytro MYKHAILENKO (13/07/73) - Dynamo Kyiv				s66	s35	10	2
Andriy SHEVCHENKO (29/09/76) - Dynamo Kyiv				s74	A	4	1
Alexander ZOTOV (23/02/75) - Chornomorets Odesa					M35	1	-
Sergiy REBROV (03/06/74) - Dynamo Kyiv					s61	5	-
Vitaliy KOSOVSKYI (11/08/73) - Dynamo Kyiv					s46	1	

immediately afterwards, winning eight of their next nine matches and surging into a commanding lead at the top of the table. At the winter break they led second-placed Chornomorets by four points, and in the spring they more or less held onto that advantage, winning every one of their matches in Kiev and rolling home with six points to spare at the finish.

A 2-0 home win over Niva Ternopil, with goals from star player Vitaliy Kosovskyi and top scorer Andriy Shevchenko, confirmed Dynamo's title. It also completed the second stage of their 'double', the first having come the previous month against the other Nyva, from Vynnytsya, in the Ukrainian Cup final. With 47,000 fans in attendance, Kiev annihilated the modest provincials, the 2-0 scoreline not accurately reflecting their dominance over opponents who could not muster a single shot at Alexander Shovkovskyi's goal during the entire 90 minutes.

Nyva Vynnytsya's lethargy was perhaps understandable as they knew that with Kiev on the verge of championship success their mere presence in the final would guarantee qualification for the European Cup-winners' Cup. That ticket

country. For months the diplomatic activity continued, and ultimately the fight was won when UEFA backed down and annulled the additional two-year penalty, which allowed Kiev back into the Champions' League in 1996/97.

Given all that was going on around them, the Dynamo players did miraculously well to concentrate on their football and win yet another championship. Their triumph was predominantly down to three factors - consistency of performance, invincibility at home and a strong defence. The team had made a good enough start before the scandal erupted, but, ironically, they got even better

had been booked with a penalty shoot-out victory over Shakhtar Donetsk in the semi-final, a match which invoked further scandal after six Shakhtar players had mysteriously gone down with food poisoning on the eve of the game.

That incident was minor, however, in comparison to what Shakhtar's players and supporters had endured some six months earlier. On October 16, with the league match between Shakhtar and Tavriya Simferopol just a few minutes old, a bomb exploded in the directors' box, killing Shakhtar's young reformist president Alexander Bragin and five others. The players fled the pitch and the match

INTERNATIONAL HONOURS

European Club Competitions

Cup-winners' Cup	Dynamo Kyiv (1975, 1986)
Super Cup	Dynamo Kyiv (1975)

NATIONAL TEAM RESULTS 95/96

06/09/95	Lithuania (ECQ)	A	Vilnius	3-1	Guseinov (62, 72), Gusin (83)
11/10/95	Slovenia (ECQ)	A	Ljubljana	2-3	Skrypnyk (24), Guseinov (45)
11/11/95	Italy (ECQ)	A	Bari	1-3	Polunin (19)
09/04/96	Moldova	A	Chisinau	2-2	Guseinov (49, 66)
01/05/96	Turkey	A	Samsun	2-3	Shevchenko (11), Guseinov (35)

was abandoned. Nobody doubted that Bragin had been assassinated by rivals in the criminal underworld, but by the following summer nobody had been charged with the murder and it appeared increasingly unlikely that the killers would ever be brought to justice.

Not surprisingly, Shakhtar went on to have their worst season since Ukrainian football became independent, finishing way down the table in tenth place, just seven points above the relegation zone. One of Alexander Bragin's proposed reforms before his death was to reduce the size of the top division, and this duly occurred at the end of the season, with three teams - SK Mykolaiv, Volyn Lutsk and Zorya-MALS Lugansk - going down, to be replaced only by the

EUROPEAN CUPS RESULTS 95/96

CHAMPIONS' CUP

● DYNAMO KYIV

Preliminary round AAB (DEN)

H 1-0 Pokhlebayev (82p)
Shovkovskyi; Khomyn, Bezhenar, Holovko, Maximov, Dmitrulin, Pokhlebayev, Kalitvintsev (Shkapenko 84), Kosovskyi, Skachenko (Rebrov 46), Shevchenko.

A 3-1 Kalitvintsev (37), Shevchenko (50, 77)
Shovkovskyi; Luzhny (Khomyn 81), Bezhenar, Holovko, Maximov (Mykhailenko 78), Dmitrulin, Pokhlebayev, Kalitvintsev, Kosovskyi, Skachenko (Rebrov 73), Shevchenko.

Champions' League

1st match PANATHINAIKOS (GRE)

H 1-0 Kosovskyi (60)
Shovkovskyi; Luzhny (Shmatovalenko 71), Bezhenar, Holovko, Maximov (Mizin 84), Dmitrulin, Pokhlebayev, Kalitvintsev, Kosovskyi, Rebrov (Skachenko 74), Shevchenko.

(disqualified)

CUP-WINNERS' CUP

● SHAKHTAR DONETSK

Preliminary round LINFIELD (NIR)

H 4-1 Atelkin (9), Matveyev (18), Orbu (28, 90)
Shutov; Pyatenko, Koval, Chikhradze, Kochvar, Spivak, Orbu, Atelkin (Fedkov 14; Voskoboinik 75), Petrov, Kriventsov, Matveyev (Onopko 81).

A 1-0 Voskoboinik (87)
Nikitin; Pyatenko, Koval, Chikhradze, Popov, Kochvar, Orbu, Voskoboinik, Petrov (Shutkov 46), Kriventsov (Leonov 78), Matveyev (Fedkov 86).

1st round CLUB BRUGGE KV (BEL)

A 0-1
Shutkov; Martyuk, Koval, Chikhradze, Popov, Kochvar, Orbu, Petrov, Voskoboinik (Onopko 67), Spivak, Fedkov.

H 1-1 Voskoboinik (61)
Shutkov; Leonov (Pyatenko 74), Koval, Chikhradze, Starostyak, Orbu, Kochvar, Voskoboinik (Zubov 68), Petrov, Spivak, Fedkov.

UEFA CUP

● CHORNOMORETS ODESA

Preliminary round HIBERNIANS (MLT)

A 5-2 Guseinov (13), Gashkin (22), Musolitin (39, 53), Kardash (48)
Suslov; Kardash, Musolitin, Kolchin (Gorshkov 66), Ternavskyi, Parfenov, Gashkin, Guseinov, Zotov, Sak, Kolesnychenko (Vasylkiv 28).

H 2-0 Kozakevych (34), Musolitin (76)
Suslov (Dolhansky 79); Kardash, Musolitin, Bukel, Ternavskyi, Parfenov, Gashkin, Vasylkiv (Gorshkov 72), Zotov, Sak, Kozakevych (Mocchulyak 63).

1st round WIDZEW LODZ (POL)

H 1-0 Kozakevych (84)
Suslov; Kardash (Vasylkiv 72), Musolitin (Kozakevych 71), Bukel, Ternavskyi, Parfenov, Gashkin, Guseinov, Zotov, Sak, Gorshkov (Seleznov 46).

A 0-1
Suslov; Kardash, Musolitin, Bukel, Ternavskyi, Parfenov, Kolesnychenko (Vasylkiv 22), Guseinov (Kozakevych 53), Zotov, Sak, Gorshkov (Kolchin 46).

2nd round RC LENS (FRA)

H 0-0
Suslov; Kolchin (Kolesnychenko 46; Mochulyak 79), Bukel, Ternavskyi, Vasylkiv, Gashkin, Zotov, Gorshkov (Kozakevych 54), Parfenov, Guseinov, Seleznev.

A 0-4
Suslov; Kardash, Musolitin, Bukel, Ternavskyi, Parfenov (Kolchin 59), Gashkin, Guseinov, Zotov, Vasylkiv (Kolesnychenko 69), Seleznev (Kozachevych 52).

PLAYERS OF THE SEASON

OLEG SUSLOV

Strikers are judged by their goal output, midfielders by their work-rate and creativity. The best goal-keepers provide reliability and stability, and Oleg Suslov, of Chornomorets Odesa and Ulkraine, is undoubtedly one of those. He rarely has a bad game, and in 1995/96, the best season of his career so far, he added several brilliant one-off performances to his all-round consistency. His most memorable match was against Widzew Lodz in Poland when his tireless heroics, both during regular play and the penalty shoot-out, took Chornomorets through to the next round. Penalties are something of a speciality for the 27-year-old 'keeper. He not only saves them, but takes them as well, scoring twice from the spot for his club in successive league games in April.

VITALIY KOSOVSKYI

In just two years of top-grade football for Dynamo Kiev, young left-sided midfielder Vitaliy Kosovskyi (pictured right) has developed into one of the finest footballing prospects in Ukraine. He had an intense 95/96 season, with activity on all fronts for Kiev supplemented by regular appearances in the national U-21 team and a first senior call-up for the friendly against Turkey. He starred in Kiev's brief European campaign and was the most influential player in their league and Cup 'double' triumph, providing industry and flair in equal measure. Ukrainian pundits believe that the whole of Europe will soon be talking about this precocious 23-year-old all-rounder.

Second Division's runaway leaders Volska Potava in the new 16-team top flight.

With Dynamo Kiev's enforced departure from the Champions' League, there was little else of interest to Ukrainian fans on the international front during 1995/96. Chornomorets Odesa, the eventual league runners-up for the second year in a row, could only reach the second round of the UEFA Cup before crashing out to Lens. And the Ukrainian national team did not play a single fixture at home all season - the only country in Europe (Bosnia-Herzegovina included) which did not host an international match in 1995/96.

The five away trips brought one win, one draw and three defeats. The opening victory - 3-1 in Lithuania - revitalised European Championship hopes, but subsequent defeats in Slovenia and Italy soon buried them again. This led to the resignation of coach Anatoly Konkov, who was replaced by his predecessor, Dynamo Kiev boss Jozsef Szabo, with progressive Chornomorets coach Leonid Buryak acting as his assistant. Two friendlies in Moldova and Turkey provided little fresh optimism for the forthcoming début World Cup campaign, but Chornomorets striker Timerlan Guseinov, the top scorer in the domestic league with 20 goals, did plenty to enhance his own reputation, scoring three goals in the two games to take his international total for the season to six.

TOP SCORERS

20	Timerlan GUSEINOV (Chornomorets Odesa)
16	Andriy SHEVCHENKO (Dynamo Kyiv)
13	Alexander PALYANYTSYA (Dnipro Dnipropetrovsk)
	Andriy POKLADOK (Karpaty Lviv)
	Oleg MATVEYEV (Shakhtar Donetsk/ Kremin Kremenchuk)
12	Volodymyr MOZOLYUK (Volyn Lutsk)
11	Ivan KORPONAY (Kremin Kremenchuk)
	Volodymyr SHARAN (Dnipro Dnipropetrovsk)
10	Sergiy BORYSENKO (Zirka-NIBAS Kirovohrad)
	Roman HRYHORCHUK (Kryvbas Krvyi Rih)
	Mikhail POTSKHVERIYA (Metalurg Zaporizhzhya/Shakhtar Donetsk)
	Yuriy VERNYDUB (Torpedo Zaporizhzhya)
	Oleg YASHCHUK (Nyva Ternopil)

CHORNOMORETS ODESA

CLUB DIRECTORY

Chornomorets Odesa
Central Stadium
Shevchenko Park
270 014 Odesa
tel - (0482) 250411/259250/251479
fax - (0482) 223367
Year of Formation - 1958
President - Grigoriy Bibergal
Secretary - Oleg Taraday
Coach - Leonid Buryak
Stadium - Central (43,000)

MAJOR HONOURS
Domestic Cup - (2) 1992, 1994.

APPEARANCES 95/96

	P	Ap	(s)	Gls
Igor BELANOV	A	3		1
Yuriy BUKEL	D	28	(2)	
Sergiy DOLHANSKYI	G		(3)	
Andriy GASHKIN	M	31		8
Alexander GORSHKOV	M	8	(7)	
Timerlan GUSEINOV	A	33		20
Vasyl KARDASH	A	32		7
Denis KOLCHIN	D	2	(17)	
Vitaliy KOLESNYCHENKO	M	6	(15)	1
Alexander KOZAKEVYCH	A	2	(20)	2
Sergiy LEZHENTSEV	D	6		
Gennadiy LYTOVCHENKO	M	10		1
Oleg MOCHULYAK	A	2	(5)	
Volodymyr MUSOLITIN	A	32		1
Matviy NYKOLAICHUK	M	7		2
Dmytro PARFENOV	D	34		
Yuriy SAK	M	17		2
Yuriy SELEZNEV	A	7	(11)	1
Vitaliy SKYSH	D	9		1
Oleg SUSLOV	G	34		2
Vladyslav TERNAVSKYI	D	16		3
Ruslan VASYLKIV	M	2	(11)	2
Igor ZHABCHENKO	M	20		
Alexander ZOTOV	M	33		2

LEAGUE RESULTS 1995/96

25/07/95	Kryvbas Kryvyi Rih	H	2-0	Belanov, Guseinov
29/07/95	Zirka-NIBAS Kirovohrad	H	1-1	Guseinov
02/08/95	Kremin Kremenchuk	A	1-0	Kardash
17/08/95	Zorya-MALS Lugansk	H	2-0	Kardash, Gashkin
27/08/95	Volyn Lutsk	A	3-0	Zotov, Kardash 2
31/08/95	Dynamo Kyiv	H	1-0	Guseinov
17/09/95	Tavriya Simferopol	H	4-3	Gashkin 2, Kardash, Kozakevych
22/09/95	Karpaty Lviv	A	2-3	Sak, Vasylkiv
01/10/95	Dnipro Dnipropetrovsk	H	2-1	Guseinov, Vasylkiv
05/10/95	Torpedo Zaporizhzhya	A	1-2	Guseinov
23/10/95	SK Mykolaiv	A	2-1	Guseinov, Kardash
27/10/95	Nyva Vynnytsya	H	2-0	Guseinov, Sak
05/11/95	CSKA-Borysfen Kyiv	A	0-1	
16/11/95	Shakhtar Donetsk	A	0-2	
20/11/95	Metalurg Zaporizhzhya	H	4-3	Guseinov 2, Ternavskyi (p), Gashkin
24/11/95	Prykarpattya Ivano-Frankivsk	A	1-1	Ternavskyi (p)
28/11/95	Nyva Ternopil	H	2-0	Ternovskyi (p), Musolitin
13/03/96	CSKA-Borysfen Kyiv	H	1-0	Kozakevych
18/03/96	Nyva Vynnytsya	A	0-0	
23/03/96	SK Mykolaiv	H	1-0	Guseinov
28/03/96	Nyva Ternopil	A	1-0	Guseinov
06/04/96	Torpedo Zaporizhzhya	H	3-1	Suslov (p), Lytovchenko, Guseinov
13/04/96	Dnipro Dnipropetrovsk	A	2-0	Skysh, Suslov (p)
17/04/96	Karpaty Lviv	H	1-0	Guseinov
22/04/96	Tavriya Simferopol	A	0-0	
27/04/96	Prykarpattya Ivano-Frankivsk	H	0-0	
06/05/96	Dynamo Kyiv	A	0-3	
11/05/96	Volyn Lutsk	H	4-1	Kolesnychenko, Guseinov 2, Gashkin
16/05/96	Zorya-MALS Lugansk	A	3-0	Gashkin, Nykolaichuk, Guseinov
21/05/96	Shakhtar Donetsk	H	2-1	Gashkin, Guseinov (p)
25/05/96	Metalurg Zaporizhzhya	A	0-0	
31/05/96	Kremin Kremenchuk	H	6-1	Guseinov 2, Gashkin, Seleznev, Zotov, Nykolaichuk
09/06/96	Zirka-NIBAS Kirovohrad	A	2-0	Guseinov, Kardash
17/06/96	Kryvbas Kryvyi Rih	A	0-0	

CSKA-BORYSFEN KYIV

CLUB DIRECTORY

CSKA-Borysfen Kyiv
vul. Hospitalna 4
Hotel Rus ap. 511
252091 Kyiv
tel - (044)
2942225/2942211/2948211/2942222
fax - (044) 2942217
Year of Formation - 1993
President - Dmytro Zlobenko
Secretary - Yuriy Karman
Coach - Mykhailo Fomenko; Viktor Chanov
Stadium - CSK ZSU (25,000)

APPEARANCES 95/96

	P	Ap	(s)	Gls
Andriy ANNENKOV	M	28		
Konstantyn BABYCH	A	14	(2)	3
Viktor BELKIN	M	2	(12)	1
Volodymyr BOGACH	M	1		
Sergiy DIRYAVKA	D	22	(3)	2
Sergiy FEDOROV	D	26		3
Alexander GORYAINOV	G	1	(2)	
Andriy GUSIN	A	22	(4)	9
Dmytro KORENEV	M		(2)	
Oleg KUZNETSOV	D	10	(1)	1
Vitaliy LEVCHENKO (TAD)	M	13	(5)	1
Volodymyr LOBAS	A		(4)	
Volodymyr MATSIGURA	D	11	(5)	
Stepan MATVYIV	M		(1)	
Mafumba MFILIU (ZAI)	A	2		
Oleg PESTRYAKOV	A	13	(12)	3
Vladyslav PRUDIUS	M	2	(6)	1
Vitaily PUSHKUTSA	A	27	(2)	5
Vitaliy REVA	G	31		
Sergiy REVUT	D	23	(5)	3
Volodymyr SAVCHENKO	G	2		
Sergiy SELEZNEV	D		(1)	
Alexander SVISTUNOV	M	28	(3)	3
Eduard TSYKHMEISTRUK	A	32	(2)	2
Viktor ULANYTSKYI	D	6	(7)	1
Mykola VOLOSYANKO	D	33		6
Mykola ZAKOTYUK	D	25	(1)	1

LEAGUE RESULTS 1995/96

Date	Opponent	H/A	Score	Scorers
25/07/95	Zirka-NIBAS Kirovohrad	A	0-0	
29/07/95	Kremin Kremenchuk	H	1-1	Diryavka (p)
02/08/95	Metalurg Zaporizhzhya	A	1-0	Pushkutsa
06/08/95	Shakhtar Donetsk	H	4-0	Tsykhmeistruk, Volosyanko 2, Diryavka
12/08/95	Zorya-MALS Lugansk	A	5-1	Svistunov, Gusin 3, Belkin
27/08/95	Dynamo Kyiv	A	0-0	
31/08/95	Prykarpattya Ivano-Frankivsk	H	3-0	Gusin, Pushkutsa, Prudius
10/09/95	Tavriya Simferopol	A	2-2	Revut, Volosyanko
17/09/95	Karpaty Lviv	H	2-1	Svistunov, Gusin
22/09/95	Dnipro Dnipropetrovsk	A	0-2	
27/09/95	Torpedo Zaporizhzhya	H	2-0	Pestryakov, Gusin
01/10/95	Volyn Lutsk	H	3-1	Svistunov, Pushkutsa, Gusin
05/10/95	Nyva Ternopil	A	0-1	
15/10/95	SK Mykolaiv	H	0-0	
23/10/95	Nyva Vynnytsya	A	1-1	Kuznetsov
27/10/95	Kryvbas Kryvyi Rih	A	0-2	
05/11/95	Chornomorets Odesa	H	1-0	Volosyanko
13/03/96	Chornomorets Odesa	A	0-1	
18/03/96	Kryvbas Kryvyi Rih	H	2-0	Revut, og (Portnov)
23/03/96	Nyva Vynnytsya	H	1-0	Ulyanytskyi
28/03/96	SK Mykolaiv	A	2-0	Pushkutsa, Babych
06/04/96	Nyva Ternopil	H	1-1	Volosyanko
13/04/96	Torpedo Zaporizhzhya	A	1-0	Gusin
17/04/96	Dnipro Dnipropetrovsk	H	0-0	
22/04/96	Karpaty Lviv	A	1-1	Fedorov
27/04/96	Tavriya Simferopol	H	2-0	Revut, og (Smigunov)
06/05/96	Prykarpattya Ivano-Frankivsk	A	2-3	Pushkutsa, Pestryakov
11/05/96	Dynamo Kyiv	H	1-2	Volosyanko
16/05/96	Volyn Lutsk	A	1-1	Levchenko
21/05/96	Zorya-MALS Lugansk	H	4-0	Fedorov 2, Tsykhmeistruk, Gusin (p)
25/05/96	Shakhtar Donetsk	A	3-2	Zakotyuk, Babych, Pestryakov
31/05/96	Metalurg Zaporizhzhya	H	0-2	
09/06/96	Kremin Kremenchuk	A	1-1	Babych
17/06/96	Zirka-NIBAS Kirovohrad	H	0-1	

DNIPRO DNIPROPETROVSK

CLUB DIRECTORY

Dnipro Dnipropetrovsk
vul. Bilshovytska 1
320 070 Dnipropetrovsk
tel - (0562) 421908/929565/929542
fax - (0562) 929492
Year of Formation - 1962
President - Fedir Petrenko
Coach - Bernd Stange
Stadium - Meteor (34,000)

MAJOR HONOURS
League Championship (USSR) - (2) 1983, 1988.
Domestic Cup (USSR) - (1) 1989.

APPEARANCES 95/96

	P	Ap	(s)	Gls
Konstantyn BABYCH	A		(2)	1
Volodymyr BAGMUT	D	33		3
Luís Firminho EMERSON (BRA)	A	14		7
Volodymyr HORILYI	D	18	(1)	
Sergiy KOVALETS	M	6	(9)	
Volodymyr KOVALYUK	M	9	(3)	2
Gennadiy KOZAR	D	14		
Alexei KUPTSOV	M		(2)	
Alexei KURYLENKO	D	3	(9)	
Mykola MEDIN	G	17		
Sergiy MIZIN	M	17		4
Valentyn MOSKVIN	A	7	(14)	2
Sergiy NAHORNYAK	A	18	(2)	6
Alexander PALYANYTSYA	A	30	(2)	13
Sergiy PERKHUN	G	5	(1)	
Valentyn PLATONOV	D		(1)	
Andriy POLUNIN	M	34		4
Andreas SASSEN (GER)	M	3	(3)	
Volodymyr SHARAN	M	27		11
Viktor SKRYPNYK	D	31		6
Svyatoslav SYROTA	G	12	(2)	
Artur TEODOROVYCH	A	1	(1)	
Dmytro TOPCHIYEV	M	12	(7)	
Dmytro YAKOVENKO	D	12	(6)	1
Alexander YEVTUSHOK	D	29		2
Andriy YUDIN	M	6	(7)	1
Sergiy ZADOROZHNYI	A		(1)	
Alexander ZAKHAROV	M	16	(14)	2

LEAGUE RESULTS 1995/96

Date	Opponent		Score	Scorers
25/07/95	Volyn Lutsk	A	5-1	Skrypnyk, Yevtushok, Palyanytsya, Sharan, Zakharov
29/07/95	Dynamo Kyiv	H	0-0	
02/08/95	Prykarpattya Ivano-Frankivsk	A	1-1	Skrypnyk
06/08/95	Tavriya Simferopol	H	2-0	Polunin, Palyanytsya
13/08/95	Karpaty Lviv	A	1-2	Palyanytsya
17/08/95	Kryvbas Kryvyi Rih	A	0-1	
27/08/95	Torpedo Zaporizhzhya	H	2-0	Palyanytsya, Moskvin
31/08/95	Nyva Ternopil	A	1-0	Kovalyuk
10/09/95	SK Mykolaiv	H	5-0	Sharan 3, Nahornyak 2
17/09/95	Nyva Vynnytsya	A	0-2	
22/09/95	CSKA-Borysfen Kyiv	H	2-0	Bagmut (p), Sharan
01/10/95	Chornomorets Odesa	A	1-2	Nahornyak
05/10/95	Zirka-NIBAS Kirovohrad	H	3-1	Skrypnyk, Nahornyak, Sharan
16/10/95	Kremin Kremenchuk	A	3-0	Yevtushok, Nahornyak, Babych
23/10/95	Metalurg Zaporizhzhya	H	5-0	Palyanytsya, Yudin, Kovalyuk, Sharan, Polunin
27/10/95	Shakhtar Donetsk	A	0-1	
04/11/95	Zorya-MALS Lugansk	H	3-1	Yakovenko, Bagmut 2
13/03/96	Zorya-MALS Lugansk	A	3-0	Mizin 2, Palyanytsya
18/03/96	Shakhtar Donetsk	H	2-2	Sharan 2
23/03/96	Metalurg Zaporizhzhya	A	1-2	Palyanytsya
28/03/96	Kremin Kremenchuk	H	2-0	Moskvin, Emerson
06/04/96	Zirka-NIBAS Kirovohrad	A	1-1	Palyanytsya
13/04/96	Chornomorets Odesa	H	0-2	
17/04/96	CSKA-Borysfen Kyiv	A	0-0	
22/04/96	Nyva Vynnytsya	H	1-2	Nahornyak
27/04/96	SK Mykolaiv	A	2-0	Palyanytsya, Emerson
06/05/96	Nyva Ternopil	H	2-1	Sharan, Emerson
11/05/96	Torpedo Zaporizhzhya	A	3-1	Polunin 2, Palyanytsya
16/05/96	Kryvbas Kryvyi Rih	H	4-2	Skrypnyk, Palyanytsya, Mizin, Sharan
21/05/96	Karpaty Lviv	H	3-0	Emerson 2, Palyanytsya
25/05/96	Tavriya Simferopol	A	3-3	Palyanytsya, Skrypnyk, Emerson (p)
31/05/96	Prykarpattya Ivano-Frankivsk	H	1-0	Emerson
09/06/96	Dynamo Kyiv	A	1-5	Mizin
17/06/96	Volyn Lutsk	H	2-1	Skrypnyk (p), Zakharov

DYNAMO KYIV

CLUB DIRECTORY

Dynamo Kyiv
vul. Hrushevskoho 3
252 001 Kyiv
tel - (044) 2296270/2292135/2287088/2280851/2244307
fax - (044) 2281435
Year of Formation - 1927
President - Grigory Surkis
Secretary - Alexei Semenenko
Coach - Jozsef Szabo
Stadium - Republican (100,169)

MAJOR HONOURS

League Championship (USSR) - (13) 1961, 1966, 1967, 1968, 1971, 1974, 1975, 1977, 1980, 1981, 1985, 1986, 1990.
Domestic Cup (USSR) - (9) 1954, 1964, 1966, 1974, 1978, 1982, 1985, 1987, 1990.
League Championship - (4) 1993, 1994, 1995, 1996.
Domestic Cup - (2) 1993, 1996.
European Cup-winners' Cup - (2) 1975, 1986.
European Super Cup - (1) 1975.

APPEARANCES 95/96

	P	Ap	(s)	Gls
Sergiy BALANCHUK	D	1	(4)	
Sergiy BEZHENAR	D	28		5
Yuriy DMITRULIN	D	16	(4)	
Alexander HOLOVKO	D	31		
Yuriy KALITVINTSEV	M	13	(2)	2
Andriy KHOMYN	D	4	(5)	
Sergiy KONOVALOV	A	7	(13)	2
Vitaliy KOSOVSKYI	M	29		6
Igor KOSTYUK	M	6	(4)	1
Andriy KOVTUN	G	9		
Viktor LEONENKO	A	8	(5)	5
Sergiy LEZHENTSEV	D	2	(2)	
Oleg LUZHNYI	D	24		1
Yuriy MAXIMOV	M	19	(3)	7
Sergiy MIZIN	M	4	(5)	
Dmytro MYKHAILENKO	M	27	(5)	1
Matviy NYKOLAICHUK	M		(1)	
Yevhen POKHLEBAYEV	M	23	(10)	6
Sergiy REBROV	A	21	(10)	9
Andriy SHEVCHENKO	A	26	(5)	16
Pavlo SHKAPENKO	M	11	(8)	2
Sergiy SHMATOVALENKO	D	26	(2)	
Alexander SHOVKOVSKYI	G	25		
Sergiy SKACHENKO	A	7	(3)	2
Vladyslav VASHCHUK	D	7	(1)	

LEAGUE RESULTS 1995/96

25/07/95	Karpaty Lviv	H	2-0	Pokhlebayev, Bezhenar
29/07/95	Dnipro Dnipropetrovsk	A	0-0	
02/08/95	Torpedo Zaporizhzhya	H	2-0	Maximov, Bezhenar
13/08/95	SK Mykolaiv	H	3-0	Skachenko, Konovalov, Rebrov
17/08/95	Nyva Vynnytsya	A	2-0	Kalitvintsev, Maximov
27/08/95	CSKA-Borysfen Kyiv	H	0-0	
31/08/95	Chornomorets Odesa	A	0-1	
17/09/95	Kremin Kremenchuk	a	1-0	Skachenko
22/09/95	Metalurg Zaporizhzhya	H	2-0	Rebrov 2
27/09/95	Shakhtar Donetsk	A	3-2	Luzhnyi, Kosovskyi, Bezhenar
05/10/95	Zorya-MALS Lugansk	H	1-0	Shevchenko
16/10/95	Volyn Lutsk	A	2-0	Kosovskyi, Mykhailenko
23/10/95	Kryvbas Kryvyi Rih	H	3-0	Kalitvintsev, Rebrov, Pokhlebayev (p)
27/10/95	Prykarpattya Ivano-Frankivsk	H	1-1	Shevchenko
01/11/95	Zirka-NIBAS Kirovohrad	H	5-1	Bezhenar 2 (1p), Shevchenko, Kosovskyi, Rebrov
05/11/95	Tavriya Simferopol	A	2-0	Shevchenko, Rebrov
16/11/95	Nyva Ternopil	A	0-1	
13/03/96	Tavriya Simferopol	H	2-0	Kosovskyi, Shkapenko
18/03/96	Prykarpattya Ivano-Frankivsk	A	3-2	Shevchenko, Pokhlebayev (p), Leonenko
23/03/96	Kryvbas Kryvyi Rih	A	2-2	Shevchenko, Pokhlebayev (p)
28/03/96	Volyn Lutsk	H	4-0	Shevchenko, Shkapenko, Konovalov, Leonenko
06/04/96	Zorya-MALS Lugansk	A	0-0	
13/04/96	Shakhtar Donetsk	H	3-1	Shevchenko 2, Maximov
17/04/96	Metalurg Zaporizhzhya	A	2-0	Leonenko, Shevchenko
22/04/96	Kremin Kremenchuk	H	2-0	Rebrov, Shevchenko
06/05/96	Chornomorets Odesa	H	3-0	Kostyuk, Maximov, Shevchenko
11/05/96	CSKA-Borysfen Kyiv	A	2-1	Shevchenko, Rebrov
16/05/96	Nyva Vynnytsya	H	1-0	Maximov
21/05/96	SK Mykolaiv	A	2-0	Pokhlebayev (p), Leonenko
31/05/96	Torpedo Zaporizhzhya	A	1-1	Maximov
05/06/96	Zirka-NIBAS Kirovohrad	A	1-2	Kosovskyi
09/06/96	Dnipro Dnipropetrovsk	H	5-1	Rebrov, Maximov, Pokhlebayev (p), Shevchenko 2
13/06/96	Nyva Ternopil	H	2-0	Kosovskyi, Shevchenko
17/06/96	Karpaty Lviv	A	1-1	Leonenko

KARPATY LVIV

CLUB DIRECTORY

Karpaty Lviv
Av. Adam Mickewicz 6/7
290 005 Lviv
tel - (0322)
724972/724827/726641/746641
fax - (0322) 743827
Year of Formation - 1963
President - Roman Hirnyk
Secretary - Yuriy Nazarkevych
Coach - Volodymyr Zhuravchak
Stadium - Ukraina (40,600)

MAJOR HONOURS
Domestic Cup (USSR) - (1) 1969.

APPEARANCES 95/96

	P	Ap	(s)	Gls
Vasyl BONDARCHUK	A	3	(2)	
Anatoliy BORYSENKO	A	3		
Alexander CHYZHEVSKYI	D	32		1
Roman HNATIV	M	21	(6)	3
Petro HOLUBKO	D		(2)	
Andriy HRINER	D	3		
Mykhailo HURKA	A		(1)	
Vadym KOLESNYK	A	26	(3)	7
Igor MAKOVEI	A	12	(11)	4
Yuriy MOKRYTSKYI	D	30		1
Yevhen NAZAROV	M	1	(3)	
Ivan PANCHYSHYN	D	31		1
Ivan PAVLYUKH	D	32		
Anatoliy PETRYK	M	23	(6)	
Andriy POKLADOK	A	22	(2)	13
Sergiy PRONIN	D	2	(3)	
Elkhan RASULOV (AZB)	G	23		
Andriy SAPUHA	M	22	(7)	2
Andriy SHULYATYTSKYI	M	4	(8)	1
Vitaliy SHUMSKYI	M	17	(10)	
Bohdan STRONTSYTSKYI	G	11	(1)	
Andriy VASYLYTCHUK	D	3		
Lyubomyr VOVCHUK	M	33		4
Vyacheslav YEFIMENKO	A	3	(8)	1
Roman ZUB	M	17	(2)	1

LEAGUE RESULTS 1995/96

Date	Opponent	H/A	Score	Scorers
25/07/95	Dynamo Kyiv	A	0-2	
29/07/95	Prykarpattya Ivano-Frankivsk	H	0-0	
02/08/95	Tavriya Simferopol	A	0-2	
06/08/95	Kryvbas Kryvyi Rih	A	3-1	Hnativ, Zub (p), Vovchuk
13/08/95	Dnipro Dnipropetrovsk	H	2-1	Pokladok, Hnativ
17/08/95	Torpedo Zaporizhzhya	A	1-1	Kolesnyk
27/08/95	Nyva Ternopil	H	3-0	Vovchuk, Pokladok 2
31/08/95	SK Mykolaiv	A	0-0	
10/09/95	Nyva Vynnytsya	H	3-0	Kolesnyk 2, Shulyatytskyi
17/09/95	CSKA-Borysfen Kyiv	A	1-2	Panchyshyn
22/09/95	Chornomorets Odesa	H	3-2	Pokladok, Kolesnyk 2
19/09/95	Zirka-NIBAS Kirovohrad	A	1-2	Hnativ
05/10/95	Kremin Kremenchuk	H	2-0	Sapuha, Kolesnyk
15/10/95	Metalurg Zaporizhzhya	A	1-1	Makovei
23/10/95	Shakhtar Donetsk	H	1-0	Sapuha
27/10/95	Zorya-MALS Lugansk	A	1-1	Chyzhevskyi
05/11/95	Volyn Lutsk	H	2-1	Pokladok 2
13/03/96	Volyn Lutsk	A	0-1	
18/03/96	Zorya-MALS Lugansk	H	2-1	Vovchuk, Pokladok (p)
23/03/96	Shakhtar Donetsk	A	0-2	
28/03/96	Metalurg Zaporizhzhya	H	1-0	Makovei
06/04/96	Kremin Kremenchuk	A	1-6	Pokladok
13/04/96	Zirka-NIBAS Kirovohrad	H	2-0	Makovei, Pokladok
17/04/96	Chornomorets Odesa	A	0-1	
22/04/96	CSKA-Borysfen Kyiv	H	1-1	Mokrytskyi
06/05/96	SK Mykolaiv	H	3-0	Makovei, Pokladok 2 (1p)
11/05/96	Nyva Ternopil	A	0-1	
16/05/96	Torpedo Zaporizhzhya	H	1-2	Yefimenko
21/05/96	Dnipro Dnipropetrovsk	A	0-3	
25/05/96	Kryvbas Kryvyi Rih	H	2-2	Pokladok 2
31/05/96	Tavriya Simferopol	H	1-1	Vovchuk
05/06/96	Nyva Vynnytsya	A	0-0	
09/06/96	Prykarpattya Ivano-Frankivsk	A	0-1	
17/06/96	Dynamo Kyiv	H	1-1	Kolesnyk

KREMIN KREMENCHUK

CLUB DIRECTORY

Kremin Kremenchuk
vul. rokiv 56
315 302 Kremenchuk
tel - (05366) 53817/34026
fax - (05366) 30011
Year of Formation - 1985
President - Vitaliy Dmytrenko
Coach - Anatoliy Skurskyi; Tiberiy Korponay; Valeriy Yaremchenko
Stadium - Dnipro (14,000)

APPEARANCES 95/96

	P	Ap	(s)	Gls
Roman ANDREIKO	A	9	(3)	
Sergiy ATELKIN	A	14		5
Yevhen BARANOV	M	3	(1)	
Sergiy BARKALOV	G	1		
Ruslan BOYAR	M	1	(1)	
Andriy CHERNOV	M	9	(6)	1
Yuriy CHUMAK	G	25		
Valeriy DUDKA	G	8	(1)	
Alexander GUSHCHIN	A	6	(3)	
Volodymyr KARETNYK	M	2	(2)	
Anzor KAVTELADZE (GEO)	M	8	(9)	3
Oleg KAZMIN	D		(2)	
Oleg KAZMYRCHUK	M	11	(4)	1
Adalbert KORPONAI	M	26	(1)	5
Ivan KORPONAI	A	27	(3)	11
Konstantyn KOVALENKO	A	9	(1)	1
Valeriy KOVALENKO	D	6	(2)	
Sergiy KOVALEV	M	6	(3)	
Oleg KRYVENKO	D	15		
Andriy KUPTSOV	D	13	(2)	
Andriy KYRLYK	M	30	(2)	1
Igor LEONOV	D	13		1
Sergiy LUKASH	D	20	(3)	1
Oleg MATVEYEV	A	16		12
Vyacheslav NOVIKOV	M	15	(2)	1
Konstantyn POLISHCHUK	D	7	(3)	
Oleg RATIY	D	5	(1)	
Sergiy ROMANYSHYN	D	14		1
Igor SALO	D	1	(7)	
Tolyat SHEIKHAMETOV	A	3	(12)	1
Sergiy TROITSKYI	D	22	(4)	
Igor YEFREMOV	A	9	(3)	1
Sergiy ZAHORULKO	D		(1)	
Vyacheslav ZHENYLENKO	D	20	(5)	

LEAGUE RESULTS 1995/96

25/07/95	Nyva Vynnytsya	H	0-1	
29/07/95	CSKA-Borysfen Kyiv	A	1-1	Kavteladze
02/08/95	Chornomorets Odesa	H	0-1	
06/08/95	Zirka-NIBAS Kirovohrad	A	0-3	
13/08/95	Kryvbas Kryvyi Rih	H	1-1	Korponai I.
17/08/95	Metalurg Zaporizhzhya	H	1-0	Kazmyrchuk
28/08/95	Shakhtar Donetsk	A	1-4	Korponai A.
31/08/95	Zorya-MALS Lugansk	H	1-0	Romanyshyn
10/09/95	Volyn Lutsk	A	0-2	
17/09/95	Dynamo Kyiv	H	0-1	
22/09/95	Prykarpattya Ivano-Frankivsk	A	2-5	Yefremov, Korponai A.
27/09/95	Tavriya Simferopol	H	1-0	Lukash
05/10/95	Karpaty Lviv	A	0-2	
16/10/95	Dnipro Dnipropetrovsk	H	0-3	
23/10/95	Torpedo Zaporizhzhya	A	1-3	Kavteladze
27/10/95	Nyva Ternopil	H	3-0	Korponai A. 2, Kavteladze
05/11/95	SK Mykolaiv	A	0-2	
13/03/96	SK Mykolaiv	H	3-2	Matveyev 2 (1p), Atelkin
18/03/96	Nyva Ternopil	A	0-0	
23/03/96	Torpedo Zaporizhzhya	H	3-2	Novikov, Leonov, Korponai A. (p)
28/03/96	Dnipro Dnipropetrovsk	A	0-2	
06/04/96	Karpaty Lviv	H	6-1	Matveyev 2 (1p), Atelkin, Korponai I. 2, Kovalenko K.
13/04/96	Tavriya Simferopol	A	2-1	Atelkin, Korponai I.
17/04/96	Prykarpattya Ivano-Frankivsk	H	4-2	Matveyev 3 (1p), Korponai I. 2
22/04/96	Dynamo Kyiv	A	0-2	
06/05/96	Zorya-MALS Lugansk	A	3-1	Matveyev 2, Chernov
11/05/96	Shakhtar Donetsk	H	3-2	Atelkin, Korponai I. 2
16/05/96	Metalurg Zaporizhzhya	A	0-1	
21/05/96	Kryvbas Kryvyi Rih	A	1-2	Sheikhametov
25/05/96	Zirka-NIBAS Kirovohrad	H	2-1	Atelkin, Matveyev (p)
31/05/96	Chornomorets Odesa	A	1-6	Matveyev (p)
05/06/96	Volyn Lutsk	H	3-1	Matveyev, Korponai I. 2
09/06/96	CSKA-Borysfen Kyiv	H	1-1	Kyrlyk
17/06/96	Nyva Vynnytsya	A	2-0	Korponai I. 2

KRYVBAS KRYVYI RIH

CLUB DIRECTORY

Kryvbas Kryvyi Rih
vul. F. Engels 14
324 006 Kryvyi Rih
tel - (0564) 236139/236161
Year of Formation - 1966
President - Viktor Fomin
Secretary - Yuriy Rasputin
Coach - Yuriy Koval; Yuriy Gruznov; Myron Markevych
Stadium - Metalurg (38,000)

APPEARANCES 95/96

	P	Ap	(s)	Gls
Ivan AZOVSKYI (KAZ)	D	1		
Andriy BELOUSOV	D		(2)	
Dmytro BIDULKO	A	5	(2)	
Sergiy BILOKIN	M	14	(1)	1
Alexander BILOZERSKYI	D	13	(1)	1
Viktor BOGATYR	M	12		1
Alexei CHEREDNYK	D	4	(1)	
Sergiy DERENOV	G	1		
Yuriy DUDNYK	M	8		2
Yuriy GABISKIRIYA	M	5	(1)	
Viktor GROMOV	A	33		3
Sergiy HONCHARENKO	A	3		
Stepan HREDIL	D	14	(1)	
Roman HRYHORCHUK	A	18	(8)	10
Volodymyr HRYN	M	4	(7)	1
Gennediy KOZAR	D	8		
Andriy KUPTSOV	M	14		
Alexei KUPTSOV	D	8		
Alexei KURYLENKO	D	7		
Vladyslav MALTSEV	A	13	(10)	5
Sergiy MAZUR	D	7	(6)	
Vasyl MAZUR	M	17	(1)	
Yuriy MYKOLAYENKO	M	2	(1)	
Alexander NEFEDOV	D	4	(2)	
Vladyslav NOSENKO	D	16	(1)	
Igor PORTNOV	M	15	(8)	
Gennadiy POPOVYCH	A	7	(3)	
Gennadiy PRYKHODKO	M	27	(4)	5
Alexander SEVIDOV	A	13		3
Pavlo SKORYK	D	1		
Gennadiy SKYDAN	D	20	(5)	3
Yevhen SYSOYEV	D	5	(1)	
Andriy TARAKHTIY	G	1	(1)	
Valeriy VOROBIOV	G	32		
Yuriy YAKOVENKO	A	15	(16)	5
Yevhen YAROVENKO	D	7		2

LEAGUE RESULTS 1995/96

Date	Opponent	H/A	Score	Scorers
25/07/95	Chornomorets Odesa	A	0-2	
29/07/95	Tavriya Simferopol	H	2-0	Skydan, Yakovenko
02/08/95	Zirka-NIBAS Kirovohrad	A	0-2	
06/08/95	Karpaty Lviv	H	1-3	Yarovenko (p)
13/08/95	Kremin Kremenchuk	A	1-1	Bogatyr
17/08/95	Dnipro Dnipropetrovsk	H	1-0	Prykhodko
27/08/95	Metalurg Zaporizhzhya	A	1-2	Yarovenko
31/08/95	Torpedo Zaporizhzhya	H	2-3	Hryhorchuk 2 (1p)
10/09/95	Shakhtar Donetsk	A	0-4	
17/09/95	Nyva Ternopil	H	1-0	Hryhorchuk (p)
22/09/95	Zorya-MALS Lugansk	A	0-1	
27/09/95	SK Mykolaiv	H	1-1	Hryhorchuk (p)
05/10/95	Volyn Lutsk	A	0-0	
15/10/95	Nyva Vynnytsya	H	1-1	Hryhorchuk
23/10/95	Dynamo Kyiv	A	0-3	
27/10/95	CSKA-Borysfen Kyiv	H	2-0	Hryhorchuk (p), Yakovenko
05/11/95	Prykarpattya Ivano-Frankivsk	A	0-1	
13/03/96	Prykarpattya Ivano-Frankivsk	H	2-1	Hryhorchuk, Maltsev
18/03/96	CSKA-Borysfen Kyiv	A	0-2	
23/03/96	Dynamo Kyiv	H	2-2	Maltsev 2
28/03/96	Nyva Vynnytsya	A	1-1	Bilozerskyi
06/04/96	Volyn Lutsk	H	5-1	Gromov 2, Sevidov, Maltsev, og (Tarasenko)
13/04/96	SK Mykolaiv	A	1-2	Bilokin
17/04/96	Zorya-MALS Lugansk	H	2-0	Prykhodko (p), Gromov
22/04/96	Nyva Ternopil	A	1-3	Maltsev
06/05/96	Torpedo Zaporizhzhya	A	1-3	Yakovenko
11/05/96	Metalurg Zaporizhzhya	H	2-1	Hryhorchuk (p), Skydan
16/05/96	Dnipro Dnipropetrovsk	A	2-4	Yakovenko, Prykhodko
21/05/96	Kremin Kremenchuk	H	2-1	Hryhorchuk 2 (1p)
25/05/96	Karpaty Lviv	A	2-2	Hryn, Dudnyk
31/05/96	Zirka-NIBAS Kirovohrad	H	5-4	Dudnyk (p), Prykhodko, Sevidov 2, Skydan
05/06/96	Shakhtar Donetsk	H	1-0	Prykhodko (p)
09/06/96	Tavriya Simferopol	A	1-1	Yakovenko
17/06/96	Chornomorets Odesa	H	0-0	

METALURG ZAPORIZHZHYA

CLUB DIRECTORY

Metalurg Zaporizhzhya
vul. 12 April 2
330 037 Zaporizhzhya
tel - (0612) 326672/26281/25218
fax - (0612) 607408
Year of Formation - 1949
President - Viktor Mezheiko
Coach - Alexander Tomakh
Stadium - Metallurg (23,500)

APPEARANCES 95/96

	P	Ap	(s)	Gls
Alexander BABIY	D	14		1
Ivan BOGATYR	M	19	(8)	3
Alexander CHERNYAVSKYI	D	16		1
Oleg DEREVYNSKYI	M	15	(7)	1
Yuriy DUDNYK	M	16	(3)	1
Igor FOKIN	D	22	(3)	1
Alexander GUIGANOV	D	12		
Taras HREBENYUK	G	34		
Sergiy ILCHENKO	D	15		
Alexander KABACHENKO	D		(3)	
Andriy KARYAKA	M	2	(7)	
Dmytro KOLODIN	M	2	(5)	
Ruslan KOLOKOLOV	D	31		
Sergiy KLYUCHYK	M	13	(14)	4
Yakiv KRIPAK	A	16		7
Igor LUCHKEVYCH	M	33		7
Oleg LUTKOV	G		(1)	
Oleg LYPSKYI	A	5	(2)	
Vladyslav LYUTYI	A	9	(9)	1
Yuriy MARKIN	D	33		7
Alexei OLIYNYK	M	8	(2)	
Mikhail POTSKHVERIYA (GEO)	A	22	(1)	9
Valentyn POLTAVETS	M	29	(3)	5
Volodymyr VANIN	A		(6)	1
Yevhen YAROVENKO	D	7	(1)	
Sergiy ZABLODSKYI	D	1	(3)	

LEAGUE RESULTS 1995/96

Date	Opponent	H/A	Score	Scorers
25/07/95	SK Mykolaiv	H	3-2	Potskhveriya, Luchkevych, Vanin
29/07/95	Nyva Vynnytsya	A	1-0	Luchkevych
02/08/95	CSKA-Borysfen Kyiv	H	0-1	
13/08/95	Zirka-NIBAS Kirovohrad	H	1-1	Lyutyi
17/08/95	Kremin Kremenchuk	A	0-1	
27/08/95	Kryvbas Kryvyi Rih	H	2-1	Markin (p), Luchkevych
31/08/95	Shakhtar Donetsk	H	2-0	Poltavets, Chernyavskyi
10/09/95	Zorya-MALS Lugansk	A	5-1	Potskhveriya, Markin (p), Poltavets, Dudnyk, Bogatyr
17/09/95	Volyn Lutsk	H	2-0	Potskhveriya, Markin (p)
22/09/95	Dynamo Kyiv	A	0-2	
27/09/95	Prykarpattya Ivano-Frankivsk	H	2-1	Fokin, Bogatyr
05/10/95	Tavriya Simferopol	A	1-1	Luchkevych
15/10/95	Karpaty Lviv	H	1-1	Markin (p)
23/10/95	Dnipro Dnipropetrovsk	A	0-5	
27/10/95	Torpedo Zaporizhzhya	H	2-0	Potskhveriya 2
05/11/95	Nyva Ternopil	A	1-2	Luchkevych
20/11/95	Chornomorets Odesa	A	3-4	Potskhveriya, Klyuchyk 2
13/03/96	Nyva Ternopil	H	1-0	Luchkevych
18/03/96	Torpedo Zaporizhzhya	A	0-1	
23/03/96	Dnipro Dnipropetrovsk	H	2-1	Kripak, Bogatyr
28/03/96	Karpaty Lviv	A	0-1	
06/04/96	Tavriya Simferopol	H	3-0	Poltavets 2, Markin
13/04/96	Prykarpattya Ivano-Frankivsk	A	1-4	Kripak
17/04/96	Dynamo Kyiv	H	0-2	
22/04/96	Volyn Lutsk	A	1-2	Kripak
27/04/96	Zorya-MALS Lugansk	H	5-0	Kripak 2, Potskhveriya 2, Klyuchyk
06/05/96	Shakhtar Donetsk	A	2-1	Klyuchyk, Derevynskyi
11/05/96	Kryvbas Kryvyi Rih	A	1-2	Kripak
16/05/96	Kremin Kremenchuk	H	1-0	Potskhveriya
21/05/96	Zirka-NIBAS Kirovohrad	A	1-4	Markin (p)
25/05/96	Chornomorets Odesa	H	0-0	
31/05/96	CSKA-Borysfen Kyiv	A	2-0	Poltavets, Luchkevych
09/06/96	Nyva Vynnytsya	H	3-0	Babiy (p), Markin, Kripak
17/06/96	SK Mykolaiv	A	0-1	

SK MYKOLAIV

CLUB DIRECTORY

SK Mykolaiv
vul. Sportyvna 1
327 015 Mykolaiv
tel - (0512) 377837/340156/377869/342072/377243
fax - (0512) 375380
Year of Formation - 1936
President - Viktor Vovchenko
Secretary - Volodymyr Stoyanov
Coach - Yevhen Kucherevskyi
Stadium - EVIS (25,000)

APPEARANCES 95/96

	P	Ap	(s)	Gls
Andriy ANDROSOV	A	17		3
Sergiy BUGAI	D	32		5
Sergiy CHORNYI	D	1		
Sergiy CHMERUK	D		(3)	
Sergiy DUMENKO	A	15	(5)	1
Ovik GALSTYAN (ARM)	A	2	(8)	2
Alexander GURALSKYI	M	29	(1)	2
Dmytro HOROBETS	A	6	(3)	
Viktor HRYSHKO	G	3		
Andriy HUZENKO	M	21	(1)	4
Adalbert KORPONAI	M	3		
Alexander KOVALENKO	G	2		
Valeriy KUDLYUK	A	1	(5)	1
Yuriy KULISH	M	2	(5)	
Oleg LYASHENKO	D	7	(4)	
Sergiy MAIBORODA	D	14		4
Alexander MATROSOV	D	19	(7)	
Yuriy MYKOLAYENKO	M	11	(2)	1
Volodymyr PONOMARENKO	M	31		2
Sergiy PUCHKOV	D	14		4
Fanas SALIMOV (KAZ)	M	9	(1)	
Oleg SANDUL	D	6	(4)	
Valeriy SHAPOVALOV	D	2	(5)	2
Sergiy SOBESHCHAKOV	G	18		
Yevhen SONIN	A	6	(4)	
Oleg SYCH	D	5		
Sergiy SYLETSKYI	M	31		
Ruslan VASYLKIV	M	14		1
Vadym VINOKUROV	G	11		
Alexei YAKYMENKO	M	19	(7)	1
Ruslan ZABRANSKYI	A	17	(6)	2
Yuriy ZAICHENKO	A		(1)	
Spartak ZHIGULIN	D	6	(4)	1

LEAGUE RESULTS 1995/96

25/07/95	Metalurg Zaporizhzhya	A	2-3	Bugai, Puchkov (p)
29/07/95	Shakhtar Donetsk	H	0-0	
02/08/95	Zorya-MALS Lugansk	A	0-0	
06/08/95	Volyn Lutsk	H	0-3	
13/08/95	Dynamo Kyiv	A	0-3	
17/08/95	Prykarpattya Ivano-Frankivsk	H	3-0	Androsov, Zabranskyi, Puchkov
27/08/95	Tavriya Simferopol	A	2-5	Androsov, Zhigulin
31/08/95	Karpaty Lviv	H	0-0	
10/09/95	Dnipro Dnipropetrovsk	A	0-5	
17/09/95	Torpedo Zaporizhzhya	H	2-1	Guralskyi, Androsov
22/09/95	Nyva Ternopil	A	1-4	Dumenko
27/09/95	Kryvbas Kryvyi Rih	A	1-1	Huzenko
05/10/95	Nyva Vynnytsya	H	2-0	og (Balatskyi), Huzenko
15/10/95	CSKA-Borysfen Kyiv	A	0-0	
23/10/95	Chornomorets Odesa	H	1-1	Puchkov (p)
27/10/95	Zirka-NIBAS Kirovohrad	A	1-0	Huzenko
05/11/95	Kremin Kremenchuk	H	2-0	Puchkov, Guralskyi
13/03/96	Kremin Kremenchuk	A	2-3	Bugai 2
18/03/96	Zirka-NIBAS Kirovohrad	H	0-0	
23/03/96	Chornomorets Odesa	A	0-1	
28/03/96	CSKA-Borysfen Kyiv	H	0-2	
06/04/96	Nyva Vynnytsya	A	1-2	Huzenko
13/04/96	Kryvbas Kryvyi Rih	H	2-1	Mykolayenko (p), Zabranskyi
17/04/96	Nyva Ternopil	H	2-0	Maiboroda, Kudlyuk
22/04/96	Torpedo Zaporizhzhya	A	1-2	Ponomarenko
27/04/96	Dnipro Dnipropetrovsk	H	0-2	
06/05/96	Karpaty Lviv	A	0-3	
11/05/96	Tavriya Simferopol	H	1-2	Bugai
16/05/96	Prykarpattya Ivano-Frankivsk	A	2-2	Maiboroda 2
21/05/96	Dynamo Kyiv	H	0-2	
25/05/96	Volyn Lutsk	A	3-3	Galstyan, Vasylkiv, Shapovalov
31/05/96	Zorya-MALS Lugansk	H	4-1	Maiboroda, Bugai, Galstyan, Shapovalov
09/06/96	Shakhtar Donetsk	A	1-0	Yakymenko
17/06/96	Metalurg Zaporizhzhya	H	1-0	Ponomarenko

NYVA TERNOPIL

CLUB DIRECTORY

Nyva Ternopil
vul. Stepan Bandera 5
282 000 Ternopil
tel - (03522) 54742/51837/50550/52763
fax - (03522) 24572
Year of Formation - 1983
President - Volodymyr Koval
Coach - Igor Yavorskyi
Stadium - Central (17,500)

APPEARANCES 95/96

	P	Ap	(s)	Gls
Yevhen BEZUBKO	M		(3)	
Igor BISKUP	D	32		
Viktor CHERVONYI	M	17	(5)	
Mykhailo DEMYANCHUK	A	17	(15)	2
Vasyl DEMYDYAK	A	7	(2)	
Viktor DOTSENKO	D	20	(2)	
Valentyn GREGUL	D	17	(1)	
Avtandil KAPANADZE (GEO)	M	10	(3)	5
Tariel KAPANADZE (GEO)	M	12	(2)	
Sergei KOCHVAR	D	1		
Igor KOROL	M	6	(5)	1
Yuriy KULISH	D	6	(6)	
Andriy KURAYEV	G	29	(1)	
Matviy NYKOLAICHUK	M	9	(3)	2
Yuriy NYKYTENKO	G	4	(1)	
Andriy PARKHOMENKO	M	25	(4)	
Alexei PROKHORENKOV	A	5	(7)	1
Vitaliy RUDNYTSKYI	M	19	(6)	3
Sergiy SHYSHCHENKO	A	26	(2)	3
Igor SUSHKO	D	29	(1)	2
Sergei TANASYUK	D	29		
Dmytro TUTICHENKO	M	12	(3)	
Oleg YASHCHUK	A	18	(1)	10
Igor YAVORSKYI	M	13	(2)	6

LEAGUE RESULTS 1995/96

25/07/95	Shakhtar Donetsk	A	4-2	Yashchuk 3, Rudnytskyi (p)
29/07/95	Zorya-MALS Lugansk	H	3-1	Yavorskyi 2, og (Kondratenko)
02/08/95	Volyn Lutsk	A	1-3	Shyshchenko
13/08/95	Prykarpattya Ivano-Frankivsk	A	1-3	Sushko (p)
17/08/95	Tavriya Simferopol	H	1-0	Yavorskyi
27/08/95	Karpaty Lviv	A	0-3	
31/08/95	Dnipro Dnipropetrovsk	H	0-1	
10/09/95	Torpedo Zaporizhzhya	A	0-1	
17/09/95	Kryvbas Kryvyi Rih	A	0-1	
22/09/95	SK Mykolaiv	H	4-1	Sushko, Nykolaichuk 2, Yashchuk
27/09/95	Nyva Vynnytsya	A	2-3	Korol, Rudnytskyi
05/10/95	CSKA-Borysfen Kyiv	H	1-0	Yavorskyi
23/10/95	Zirka-NIBAS Kirovohrad	H	0-0	
27/10/95	Kremin Kremenchuk	A	0-3	
05/11/95	Metalurg Zaporizhzhya	H	2-1	Yashchuk, Demyanchuk
16/11/95	Dynamo Kyiv	H	1-0	Yashchuk
28/11/95	Chornomorets Odesa	A	0-2	
13/03/96	Metalurg Zaporizhzhya	A	0-1	
18/03/96	Kremin Kremenchuk	H	0-0	
23/03/96	Zirka-NIBAS Kirovohrad	A	0-1	
28/03/96	Chornomorets Odesa	H	0-1	
06/04/96	CSKA-Borysfen Kyiv	A	1-1	Kapanadze A.
13/04/96	Nyva Vynnytsya	H	2-0	Yavorskyi, Prokhorenkov
17/04/96	SK Mykolaiv	A	0-2	
22/04/96	Kryvbas Kryvyi Rih	H	3-1	Yavorskyi (p), Shyshchenko (p), Kapanadze A.
27/04/96	Torpedo Zaporizhzhya	H	2-0	Yashchuk, Kapanadze A.
06/05/96	Dnipro Dnipropetrovsk	A	1-2	Rudnytskyi
11/05/96	Karpaty Lviv	H	1-0	Kapanadze A.
16/05/96	Tavriya Simferopol	A	2-0	Yashchuk 2
21/05/96	Prykarpattya Ivano-Frankivsk	H	3-1	Kapanadze A., og (Savka), Yashchuk
31/05/96	Volyn Lutsk	H	1-2	Demyanchuk
09/06/96	Zorya-MALS Lugansk	A	0-0	(awarded as home win)
13/06/96	Dynamo Kyiv	A	0-2	
17/06/96	Shakhtar Donetsk	H	1-3	Shyshchenko

NYVA VYNNYTSYA

CLUB DIRECTORY

Nyva Vynnytsya
vul. Pirogova 7
286 000 Vynnytsya
tel - (0432) 272820/271628
fax - (0432) 324687
Year of Formation - 1980
President - Sergiy Tatusyak
Secretary - Alexander Kolyada
Coach - Sergiy Morozov
Stadium - Central (25,000)

LEAGUE RESULTS 1995/96

25/07/95	Kremin Kremenchuk	A	1-0	Parshin
29/07/95	Metalurg Zaporizhzhya	H	0-1	
02/08/95	Shakhtar Donetsk	A	2-1	Lyubynskyi, Laktionov
06/08/95	Zorya-MALS Lugansk	H	5-0	Gaidarzhi, Laktionov, Lyubynskyi 2, Balatskyi
13/08/95	Volyn Lutsk	A	0-0	
17/08/95	Dynamo Kyiv	H	0-2	
27/08/95	Prykarpattya Ivano-Frankivsk	A	1-2	Brovchenko
31/08/95	Tavriya Simferopol	H	1-3	Golokolosov
10/09/95	Karpaty Lviv	A	0-3	
17/09/95	Dnipro Dnipropetrovsk	H	2-0	Romanchuk, Laktionov
22/09/95	Torpedo Zaporizhzhya	A	0-1	
27/09/95	Nyva Ternopil	H	3-2	Romanchuk, Golokolosov 2
05/10/95	SK Mykolaiv	A	0-2	
15/10/95	Kryvbas Kryvyi Rih	A	1-1	Romanchuk
23/10/95	CSKA-Borysfen Kyiv	H	1-1	Laktionov
27/10/95	Chornomorets Odesa	A	0-2	
05/11/95	Zirka-NIBAS Kirovohrad	H	0-1	
13/03/96	Zirka-NIBAS Kirovohrad	A	0-1	
18/03/96	Chornomorets Odesa	H	0-0	
23/03/96	CSKA-Borysfen Kyiv	A	0-1	
28/03/96	Kryvbas Kryvyi Rih	H	1-1	Balatskyi
06/04/96	SK Mykolaiv	H	2-1	Romanchuk (p), Holovko
13/04/96	Nyva Ternopil	A	0-2	
17/04/96	Torpedo Zaporizhzhya	H	2-0	Gaidarzhi, Holovko
22/04/96	Dnipro Dnipropetrovsk	A	2-1	Holovko 2
06/05/96	Tavriya Simferopol	A	0-1	
11/05/96	Prykarpattya Ivano-Frankivsk	H	1-0	Gaidarzhi
16/05/96	Dynamo Kyiv	A	0-1	
21/05/96	Volyn Lutsk	H	2-0	Romanchuk, Matviychenko
31/05/96	Shakhtar Donetsk	H	0-0	
05/06/96	Karpaty Lviv	H	0-0	
09/06/96	Metalurg Zaporizhzhya	A	0-3	
13/06/96	Zorya-MALS Lugansk	A	1-0	Gaidarzhi
17/06/96	Kremin Kremenchuk	H	0-2	

APPEARANCES 95/96

	P	Ap	(s)	Gls
Anatoliy BALATSKYI	D	24	(1)	2
Alexander BESARAB	A		(3)	
Andriy BORYSYUK	M	5	(13)	
Viktor BROVCHENKO	M	10	(11)	1
Alexander CHERVONYI	M	30		
Alexander DERIK	D	5	(4)	
Leonid GARDARZHI	D	33		4
Alexander GOLOKOLOSOV	A	7	(7)	3
Andriy HOLOVKO	A	9	(6)	4
Dmytro KOPETSKYI	D	1	(1)	
Alexander LAKTIONOV	M	21	(6)	4
Dmytro LELYUK	D	9		
Alexander LYUBYNSKYI	M	31	(2)	3
Pavlo MATVIYCHENKO	M	8	(9)	1
Yevhen NEMODRUK	G	12	(3)	
Yuriy OVCHARENKO	A	2	(2)	
Pavlo PARSHIN	A	16	(7)	1
Ruslan ROMANCHUK	A	31	(2)	5
Alexei RYABTSEV	M	16	(4)	
Yuriy SOLOVIENKO	D	19	(2)	
Konstantyn SOSENKO	D	33		
Vitaliy TARASENKO	D	1	(1)	
Volodymyr TSYTKIN	G	22		
Oleg VERETYNSKYI	M		(2)	
Mykola ZUYENKO	D	16	(1)	
Vyacheslav ZAPOROZHCHENKO	D	13		

PRYKARPATTYA IVANO-FRANKIVSK

CLUB DIRECTORY

Prykarpattya Ivano-Frankivsk
vul. Taras Shevchenko 47
284 001 Ivano-Frankivsk
tel - (03422) 25222/22009/38800/32240
fax - (03422) 22195
Year of Formation - 1981
President - Anatoliy Revutskyi
Secretary - Orest Babiy
Coach - Igor Yurchenko
Stadium - Rukh (15,000)

APPEARANCES 95/96

	P	Ap	(s)	Gls
Sergiy AMILEKHIN	M	20	(3)	4
Artur APIYAN	A		(1)	
Sergiy BARANOVSKYI	A	1		
Gennadiy CHERNIKOV	G		(1)	
Roman DANYLKO	M	1		
Bohdan HUSAK	M	6	(1)	
Pavlo IRYCHUK	A	15	(3)	9
Volodymyr KARETNYK	M	4	(1)	
Andriy KHOMYN	D	14		4
Volodymyr LARIN	M		(1)	
Stepan MATVYIV	M	11	(1)	1
Roman MAXYMYUK	A	11	(14)	
Dmytro MAZUR	D	30	(2)	4
Alexander MYKULYAK	A		(12)	
Mykola NESTERUK	A		(3)	
Anatoliy REDUSHKO	A	17	(11)	2
Petro RUSAK	A	21	(3)	9
Roman RUSANOVSKYI	D	31	(2)	
Oleg RYPAN	G	30		
Volodymyr SALIY	D	2		
Mykhailo SAVKA	M	26		1
Vitaliy SKYSH	D	12	(1)	
Yuriy SMOTRYCH	D	7		
Igor STAKHIV	M	4	(1)	
Mykhailo STAROSTYAK	D		(1)	
Sergei STASHKO	G	1		
Vasyl TOFAN	M	2	(8)	
Sergiy TURYANSKYI	A	16		6
Yaroslav VATAMANYUK	D	32		
Vadym VINOKUROV	G	3		
Sergiy YEVHLEVSKYI	M	32	(1)	4
Igor YURCHENKO	M	17		4
Mykola ZUYENKO	D	8	(5)	

LEAGUE RESULTS 1995/96

25/07/95	Tavriya Simferopol	H	4-3	Mazur, Rusak 2, Irychuk
29/07/95	Karpaty Lviv	A	0-0	
02/08/95	Dnipro Dnipropetrovsk	H	1-1	Redushko
06/08/95	Torpedo Zaporizhzhya	A	0-2	
13/08/95	Nyva Ternopil	H	3-1	Redushko, Irychuk 2
17/08/95	SK Mykolaiv	A	0-3	
27/08/95	Nyva Vynnytsya	H	2-1	Irychuk, Rusak
31/08/95	CSKA-Borysfen Kyiv	A	0-3	
17/09/95	Zirka-NIBAS Kirovohrad	A	0-3	
22/09/95	Kremin Kremenchuk	H	5-2	Irychuk, Yurchenko, Mazur, Rusak, Amilekhin
27/09/95	Metalurg Zaporizhzhya	A	1-2	Rusak
05/10/95	Shakhtar Donetsk	H	2-0	Rusak 2
15/10/95	Zorya-MALS Lugansk	A	1-1	Matvyiv
23/10/95	Volyn Lutsk	H	3-0	Irychuk 2, Yevhlevskyi
27/10/95	Dynamo Kyiv	A	1-1	Irychuk
05/11/95	Kryvbas Kryvyi Rih	H	1-0	Irychuk
24/11/95	Chornomorets Odesa	H	1-1	Rusak (p)
13/03/96	Kryvbas Kryvyi Rih	A	1-2	Savka
18/03/96	Dynamo Kyiv	H	2-3	Yurchenko, Mazur
23/03/96	Volyn Lutsk	A	0-2	
28/03/96	Zorya-MALS Lugansk	H	4-0	Turyanskyi, Khomyn 2, Yevhlevskyi
06/04/96	Shakhtar Donetsk	A	0-1	
13/04/96	Metalurg Zaporizhzhya	H	4-1	Turyanskyi, Yevhlevskyi, Amilekhin 2
17/04/96	Kremin Kremenchuk	A	2-4	Amilekhin, Yevhlevskyi
22/04/96	Zirka-NIBAS Kirovohrad	H	0-0	
27/04/96	Chornomorets Odesa	A	0-0	
06/05/96	CSKA-Borysfen Kyiv	H	3-2	og (Revut), Turyanskyi 2
11/05/96	Nyva Vynnytsya	A	0-1	
16/05/96	SK Mykolaiv	H	2-2	Khomyn 2
21/05/96	Nyva Ternopil	A	1-3	Yurchenko
25/05/96	Torpedo Zaporizhzhya	H	4-0	Rusak, Yurchenko, Turyanskyi 2
31/05/96	Dnipro Dnipropetrovsk	A	0-1	
09/06/96	Karpaty Lviv	H	1-0	Mazur
17/06/96	Tavriya Simferopol	A	0-3	

SHAKHTAR DONETSK

CLUB DIRECTORY

Shakhtar Donetsk
vul. Artema 86a
340 050 Donetsk
tel - (0622) 904126/911675/927315
Year of Formation - 1946
President - Ravil Safiullin
Secretary - Vyacheslav Sharafutdinov
Coach - Volodymyr Salkov; Valeriy Rudakov
Stadium - Lokomotyv (40,485)

MAJOR HONOURS
Domestic Cup (USSR) - (4)
1961, 1962, 1980, 1983.
Domestic Cup - (1) 1995.

APPEARANCES 95/96

	P	Ap	(s)	Gls
Sergiy ATELKIN	A	3	(4)	
Sergiy CHAPLYGIN	D		(1)	
Giorgi CHIKHRADZE (GEO)	D	20	(2)	1
Sergiy DRANOV	A	1	(4)	1
Andriy FEDKOV	A	11	(5)	4
Yuriy GABISKIRIYA (GEO)	M		(1)	
Oleg KASTORNYI	M		(2)	
Sergiy KOCHVAR	D	29	(1)	
Alexander KOVAL	D	27	(1)	
Sergiy KOVALEV	M	17		2
Valeriy KRIVENTSOV	A	18		3
Igor LEONOV	D	2	(5)	
Alexander MARTYUK	D	1	(1)	
Oleg MATVEYEV	A	7	(2)	1
Andriy NIKITIN	G	5		
Sergiy ONOPKO	M	10	(10)	
Gennadiy ORBU	M	27		7
Alexander OSTASHOV	A	12	(5)	3
Igor PETROV	M	16	(9)	4
Sergiy POPOV	D	16		2
Gennadiy POPOVYCH	A	1	(2)	
Mikhail POTSKHVERIYA (GEO)	A	1		1
Volodymyr PYATENKO	D	23	(5)	1
Dmytro SHUTKOV	G	29		
Alexander SPIVAK	M	29	(4)	6
Mykhailo STAROSTYAK	D	25	(2)	
Alexander VOSKOBOINIK	A	17	(5)	1
Volodymyr YAXMANYTSKYI	M	9	(4)	
Gennadiy ZUBOV	A	18	(7)	6

LEAGUE RESULTS 1995/96

25/07/95	Nyva Ternopil	H	2-4	Popov, Kriventsov
29/07/95	SK Mykolaiv	A	0-0	
02/08/95	Nyva Vynnytsya	H	1-2	Popov
06/08/95	CSKA-Borysfen Kyiv	A	0-4	
28/08/95	Kremin Kremenchuk	H	4-1	Fedkov, Petrov, Matveyev, Orbu (p)
31/08/95	Metalurg Zaporizhzhya	A	0-2	
10/09/95	Kryvbas Kryvyi Rih	H	4-0	Orbu 2, og (Sysoyev), Fedkov
18/09/95	Zorya-MALS Lugansk	H	3-0	Petrov 2, Chikhradze
23/09/95	Volyn Lutsk	A	0-0	
02/10/95	Dynamo Kyiv	H	2-3	Fedkov, Orbu
05/10/95	Prykarpattya Ivano-Frankivsk	A	0-2	
19/10/95	Zirka-NIBAS Kirovohrad	A	1-0	Spivak
23/10/95	Karpaty Lviv	A	0-1	
27/10/95	Dnipro Dnipropetrovsk	H	1-0	Zubov
31/10/95	Tavriya Simferopol	H	0-0	
05/11/95	Torpedo Zaporizhzhya	A	0-3	
16/11/95	Chornomorets Odesa	H	2-0	Dranov, Fedkov
13/03/96	Torpedo Zaporizhzhya	H	2-1	Kovalev, Kriventsov
18/03/96	Dnipro Dnipropetrovsk	A	2-2	Ostashov, Orbu (p)
23/03/96	Karpaty Lviv	H	2-0	Zubov, Spivak
28/03/96	Tavriya Simferopol	A	3-1	Spivak, Kriventsov, Petrov
06/04/96	Prykarpattya Ivano-Frankivsk	H	1-0	Spivak
13/04/96	Dynamo Kyiv	A	1-3	Ostashov
17/04/96	Volyn Lutsk	H	1-1	Spivak
22/04/96	Zorya-MALS Lugansk	A	2-0	Kovalev, Orbu
06/05/96	Metalurg Zaporizhzhya	H	1-2	Pyatenko
11/05/96	Kremin Kremenchuk	A	2-3	Orbu, Zubov
16/05/96	Zirka-NIBAS Kirovohrad	H	1-0	Zubov
21/05/96	Chornomorets Odesa	A	1-2	Zubov
25/05/96	CSKA-Borysfen Kyiv	H	2-3	Zubov (p), Ostashov
31/05/96	Nyva Vynnytsya	A	0-0	
05/06/96	Kryvbas Kryvyi Rih	A	0-1	
09/06/96	SK Mykolaiv	H	0-1	
17/06/96	Nyva Ternopil	A	3-1	Spivak, Potskhveriya, Voskoboinik

TAVRIYA SIMFEROPOL

CLUB DIRECTORY

Tavriya Simferopol
vul. A. Pushkin 46
333 000 Simferopol
tel - (0652) 270147/276083/279402
fax - (0652) 270147
Year of Formation - 1963
President - Viktor Karasev
Secretary - Gerinald Nemirovskyi
Coach - Anatoliy Zayayev; Yuriy Kerman
Stadium - Lokomotiv (23,612)

MAJOR HONOURS
League Championship - (1) 1992.

APPEARANCES 95/96

	P	Ap	(s)	Gls
Alexei ANTYUKHIN	A	27		9
Alexander BURDIN	M	19	(12)	3
Dmytro DEMYANENKO	D	12		
Yuriy DONYUSHKIN	D	9	(5)	
Yuriy FENIN	M		(5)	
Yuriy FOKIN	M	7	(5)	
Volodymyr FURSOV	A	17	(10)	5
Alexander GAYDASH	A	14		2
Sergiy KALYAN	D	6	(1)	
Alexander KUNDENOK	M	33		7
Gennadiy KUNDENOK	M	15	(8)	4
Alexei KUZNETSOV	D	1		
Maxym LEVYTSKYI	G	29		
Volodymyr MARTINOV	A	4	(3)	
Oleg MURAVIOV	D	27		
Dmytro NAZAROV	D	2		
Andriy OPARIN	M	33		5
Andriy ROSLYAKOV	M	3	(2)	
Andriy SOKOLENKO	D		(1)	
Viktor SMIGUNOV	D	30		
Alexander TARABRIN	D	1	(5)	1
Sergei VETRENNIKOV	M	15	(3)	
Igor VOLKOV	D	30		6
Sergiy YESIN	M	20	(2)	2
Oleg ZARUTSKYI	A	5	(11)	1
Mykola ZBARAKH	G	4		

LEAGUE RESULTS 1995/96

Date	Opponent	H/A	Score	Scorers
25/07/95	Prykarpattya Ivano-Frankivsk	A	3-4	og (Saliy), Burdin, Oparin
29/07/95	Kryvbas Kryvyi Rih	A	0-2	
02/08/95	Karpaty Lviv	H	2-0	Gaydash, Antyukhin
06/08/95	Dnipro Dnipropetrovsk	A	0-2	
13/08/95	Torpedo Zaporizhzhya	H	2-0	Volkov (p), Kundenok A.
17/08/95	Nyva Ternopil	A	0-1	
27/08/95	SK Mykolaiv	H	5-2	Volkov (p), Gaydash, Burdin, Kundenok A., Kundenok H.
31/08/95	Nyva Vynnytsya	A	3-1	Antyukhin 2, Volkov
10/09/95	CSKA-Borysfen Kyiv	H	2-2	Oparin, Volkov (p)
17/09/95	Chornomorets Odesa	A	3-4	Yesin, Fursov 2
22/09/95	Zirka-NIBAS Kirovohrad	H	0-0	
27/09/95	Kremin Kremenchuk	A	0-1	
05/10/95	Metalurg Zaporizhzhya	H	1-1	Volkov (p)
23/10/95	Zorya-MALS Lugansk	H	3-0	Antyukhin 3
27/10/95	Volyn Lutsk	A	3-0	Kundenok H., Fursov, Zarutskyi
31/10/95	Shakhtar Donetsk	A	0-0	
05/11/95	Dynamo Kyiv	H	0-2	
13/03/96	Dynamo Kyiv	A	0-2	
18/03/96	Volyn Lutsk	H	0-0	(awarded as home win)
23/03/96	Zorya-MALS Lugansk	A	2-0	Kundenok H., Antyukhin
28/03/96	Shakhtar Donetsk	H	1-3	Oparin (p)
06/04/96	Metalurg Zaporizhzhya	A	0-3	
13/04/96	Kremin Kremenchuk	H	1-2	Antyukhin
17/04/96	Zirka-NIBAS Kirovohrad	A	1-2	Burdin
22/04/96	Chornomorets Odesa	H	0-0	
27/04/96	CSKA-Borysfen Kyiv	A	0-2	
06/05/96	Nyva Vynnytsya	H	1-0	Kundenok A.
11/05/96	SK Mykolaiv	A	2-1	Oparin, Antyukhin
16/05/96	Nyva Ternopil	H	0-2	
21/05/96	Torpedo Zaporizhzhya	A	3-2	Fursov 2, Oparin
25/05/96	Dnipro Dnipropetrovsk	H	3-3	Yesin, Volkov (p), Kundenok A.
31/05/96	Karpaty Lviv	A	1-1	Kundenok A.
09/06/96	Kryvbas Kryvyi Rih	H	1-1	Kundenok A.
17/06/96	Prykarpattya Ivano-Frankivsk	H	3-0	Tarabrin S., Kundenok H., Kundenok A.

TORPEDO ZAPORIZHZHYA

CLUB DIRECTORY

Torpedo Zaporizhzhya
vul. KIM 2
330 027 Zaporizhzhya
tel - (0612)
955563/963745/960081/956381
Year of Formation - 1982
President - Alexei Baburin
Secretary - Volodymyr Stepanov
Coach - Igor Nedein
Stadium - ZAZ (12,500)

APPEARANCES 95/96

	P	Ap	(s)	Gls
Arsen AVAKOV	A	15		4
Alexander BABIY	D	3	(1)	
Alexander BAZYLYAK	M	8	(6)	1
Roman BONDARENKO	A	33	(1)	9
Yuriy BONDARENKO	M	19	(11)	3
Kyrylo BURKHAN	D	12	(2)	
Igor CHERKUN	D	22		
Andriy HLUSHCHENKO	G	4	(1)	
Oleg KOLESOV	G	21		
Alexei KOSENKO	A	10	(18)	3
Alexander KOSYRIN	A	3	(6)	
Andriy MAXYMENKO	D	17	(1)	
Alexander NEFEDOV	D	14		
Alexander NOGIN	G	9		
Vadym PANIN	A		(3)	
Igor PAVLYK	M	13	(2)	
Igor PLOTKO	M	22	(1)	1
Andriy POLYVODA	M	1	(1)	
Yuriy ROMANOV	D	2	(2)	
Alexei SHUBIN	D	11	(7)	1
Denis SMIRNOV	M	32	(1)	6
Igor STOLOVYTSKYI	M	10	(6)	
Yuriy VERNYDUB	D	33		10
Oleg VETROV	D	21	(9)	
Alexander VOLKOV	D	26	(2)	1
Andriy ZUBCHENKO	M	13	(4)	1

LEAGUE RESULTS 1995/96

Date	Opponent		Score	Scorers
25/07/95	Zorya-MALS Lugansk	A	1-0	Avakov
29/07/95	Volyn Lutsk	H	1-1	Kosenko
02/08/95	Dynamo Kyiv	A	0-2	
06/08/95	Prykarpattya Ivano-Frankivsk	H	2-0	Verydub (p), Bondarenko R.
13/08/95	Tavriya Simferopol	A	0-2	
17/08/95	Karpaty Lviv	H	1-1	Vernydub (p)
27/08/95	Dnipro Dnipropetrovsk	A	0-2	
31/08/95	Kryvbas Kryvyi Rih	A	3-2	Avakov, Plotko, Bondarenko R.
10/09/95	Nyva Ternopil	H	1-0	Bondarenko Y.
17/09/95	SK Mykolaiv	A	1-2	Vernydub (p)
22/09/95	Nyva Vynnytsya	H	1-0	Bondarenko R.
27/09/95	CSKA-Borysfen Kyiv	A	0-2	
05/10/95	Chornomorets Odesa	H	2-1	Smirnov, Vernydub
15/10/95	Zirka-NIBAS Kirovohrad	A	0-1	
23/10/95	Kremin Kremenchuk	H	3-1	Vernydub (p), Avakov, Bondarenko Y.
27/10/95	Metalurg Zaporizhzhya	A	0-2	
05/11/95	Shakhtar Donetsk	H	3-0	Bondarenko R., Avakov, Kosenko
13/03/96	Shakhtar Donetsk	A	1-2	Vernydub (p)
18/03/96	Metalurg Zaporizhzhya	H	1-0	Zubchenko
23/03/96	Kremin Kremenchuk	A	2-3	Bondarenko R., Vernydub (p)
28/03/96	Zirka-NIBAS Kirovohrad	H	1-0	Smirnov
06/04/96	Chornomorets Odesa	A	1-3	Smirnov
13/04/96	CSKA-Borysfen Kyiv	H	0-1	
17/04/96	Nyva Vynnytsya	A	0-2	
22/04/96	SK Mykolaiv	H	2-1	Vernydub, Volkov
27/04/96	Nyva Ternopil	A	0-2	
06/05/96	Kryvbas Kryvyi Rih	H	3-1	Bondarenko R. 2, Bazylak
11/05/96	Dnipro Dnipropetrovsk	H	1-3	Vernydub (p)
16/05/96	Karpaty Lviv	A	2-1	Vernydub, Bondarenko Y.
21/05/96	Tavriya Simferopol	H	2-3	Smirnov, Kosenko
25/05/96	Prykarpattya Ivano-Frankivsk	A	0-4	
31/05/96	Dynamo Kyiv	H	1-1	Shubin
09/06/96	Volyn Lutsk	A	1-0	Smirnov
17/06/96	Zorya-MALS Lugansk	H	3-0	Bondarenko R. 2, Smirnov

VOLYN LUTSK

CLUB DIRECTORY

Volyn Lutsk
Av. Peremohy 7
263 007 Lutsk
tel - (03322) 47031/40137/40128/40557
fax - (03322) 47031
Year of Formation - 1960
President - Anatoliy Barabasevych
Coach - Vitaliy Kvartsyanyi; Alexei Yeshchenko; Yuriy Dyachuk-Stavytskyi
Stadium - Metalurg (15,000)

APPEARANCES 95/96

	P	Ap	(s)	Gls
Roman BAYRASHEVSKYI	G	2		
Pavlo BLAZHAYEV	G	5		
Sergiy BOGUNOV	M	13	(12)	1
Dmytro BOHORADA	D	11	(2)	
Mykhailo BURCH	G	10		
Sergiy DRANYTSKYI	M	1		
Volosymyr DYKYI	A	6	(20)	4
Andriy FEDETSKYI	M	1	(4)	
Oleg FEDYUKOV	D	32		3
Volodymyr GASHCHIN	M	15	(1)	
Volodymyr HAPON	M		(1)	
Alexander IVANOV	M	23	(3)	6
Roman KHMIL	M	2		
Yaroslav KHOMA	M	2	(5)	
Alexander KOTYK	M	3	(5)	
Sergiy KRUKOVETS	D	16		2
Viktor KURYLENKO	D	1	(5)	
Alexander MALEVANOV	D	24	(2)	
Volodymyr MARCHUK	G	16	(1)	
Volodymyr MOZOLYUK	A	33		12
Yevhen MYKHAILIV	D	31	(1)	
Ruslan NIKITIN	M	13	(12)	
Vitaliy SHEVCHUK	M	9	(3)	
Vadym SOLODKYI	A	23		3
Sergiy SUKHARIEV	D	17		1
Mykola SYCH	D	16	(3)	
Vadym TARAN	D	2	(3)	
Vitaliy TARASENKO	D	15		
Igor TYMOSHCHUK	D	1	(9)	1
Volodymyr USHTAN	M	5	(4)	
Vasyl YATSURAK	M	7		1
Alexander YESHCHENKO (RUS)	D	8		

LEAGUE RESULTS 1995/96

25/07/95	Dnipro Dnipropetrovsk	H	1-5	Mozolyuk
29/07/95	Torpedo Zaporizhzhya	A	1-1	Ivanov
02/08/95	Nyva Ternopil	H	3-1	Krukovets 2 (2p), Dykyi
06/08/95	SK Mykolaiv	A	3-0	Mozolyuk 2, Solodkyi
13/08/95	Nyva Vynnytsya	H	0-0	
27/08/95	Chornomorets Odesa	H	0-3	
31/08/95	Zirka-NIBAS Kirovohrad	A	0-1	
10/09/95	Kremin Kremenchuk	H	2-0	Sukhariev, Mozolyuk
17/09/95	Metalurg Zaporizhzhya	A	0-2	
23/09/95	Shakhtar Donetsk	H	0-0	
27/09/95	Zorya-MALS Lugansk	A	2-3	Ivanov 2
01/10/95	CSKA-Borysfen Kyiv	A	1-3	Ivanov
05/10/95	Kryvbas Kryvyi Rih	H	0-0	
16/10/95	Dynamo Kyiv	H	0-2	
23/10/95	Prykarpattya Ivano-Frankivsk	A	0-3	
27/10/95	Tavriya Simferopol	H	0-3	
05/11/95	Karpaty Lviv	A	1-2	Dykyi
13/03/96	Karpaty Lviv	H	1-0	Mozolyuk (p)
18/03/96	Tavriya Simferopol	A	0-0	(awarded as home win)
23/03/96	Prykarpattya Ivano-Frankivsk	H	2-0	Mozolyuk 2 (1p)
28/03/96	Dynamo Kyiv	A	0-4	
06/04/96	Kryvbas Kryvyi Rih	A	1-5	Yatsurak
13/04/96	Zorya-MALS Lugansk	H	3-1	Ivanov 2, Dykyi
17/04/96	Shakhtar Donetsk	A	1-1	Dykyi
22/04/96	Metalurg Zaporizhzhya	H	2-1	Mozolyuk 2
06/05/96	Zirka-NIBAS Kirovohrad	H	1-0	Mozolyuk
11/05/96	Chornomorets Odesa	A	1-4	Solodkyi
16/05/96	CSKA-Borysfen Kyiv	H	1-1	Fedyukov
21/05/96	Nyva Vynnytsya	A	0-2	
25/05/96	SK Mykolaiv	H	3-3	Fedyukhov 2, Mozolyuk
31/05/96	Nyva Ternopil	A	2-1	Tymoshchuk, Solodkyi
05/06/96	Kremin Kremenchuk	A	1-3	Bogunov
09/06/96	Torpedo Zaporizhzhya	H	0-1	
17/06/96	Dnipro Dnipropetrovsk	A	1-2	Mozolyuk

ZIRKA-NIBAS KIROVOHRAD

CLUB DIRECTORY

FC Zirka-NIBAS Kirovohrad
vul. Yuriy Gagarin 1A
P.O. Box 342
316050 Kirovohrad
tel - (0522) 224720/223430/222457
fax - (0522) 222457
Year of Formation - 1922
President - Vasyl Kovalskyi
Secretary - Mykola Kovalev
Coach - Alexander Ischchenko
Stadium - Zirka NIBAS (22,000)

APPEARANCES 95/96

	P	Ap	(s)	Gls
Yuriy BELICHENKO	M	23	(1)	6
Illya BLYZNYUK	G	33		
Vasyl BONDARCHUK	D	7	(4)	
Yuriy BOGDANOV	A	1	(17)	1
Sergiy BORYSENKO	A	23	(8)	10
Stanislav BOROVSKYI	D	28		
Yevhen BURKHAN	A	21	(11)	4
Igor DUKHNOVSKYI	M	8		
Leonid FEDOROV	M	25	(2)	1
Alexei GRACHOV	A	19	(9)	4
Stanislav KAZAKOV	M	16	(12)	2
Sergiy LAVRYNENKO	D	22	(3)	
Igor MAKOHON	D	11	(1)	
Yuriy MARTINOV	M	1	(14)	1
Igor MOSHEVYCH	D	25	(5)	
Alexander MYKHAILENKO	D	4	(4)	1
Alexander MYZENKO	M	26	(2)	7
Viktor OLIYNYK	A		(1)	
Eduard PISKUN	M	20	(4)	
Ivan RUSNAK	D	30		
Alexander SOBOL	D	30		
Sergiy ZOLOTNYTSKYI	G	1		

LEAGUE RESULTS 1995/96

25/07/95	CSKA-Borysfen Kyiv	H	0-0	
29/07/95	Chornomorets Odesa	A	1-1	Belichenko (p)
02/08/95	Kryvbas Kryvyi Rih	H	2-0	Belichenko 2 (1p)
06/08/95	Kremin Kremenchuk	H	3-0	Grachov, Belichenko (p), Burkhan
13/08/95	Metalurg Zaporizhzhya	A	1-1	Borysenko
27/08/95	Zorya-MALS Lugansk	A	1-2	Myzenko
31/08/95	Volyn Lutsk	H	1-0	Myzenko (p)
17/09/95	Prykarpattya Ivano-Frankivsk	H	3-0	Belichenko 2 (2p), Borysenko
22/09/95	Tavriya Simferopol	A	0-0	
27/09/95	Karpaty Lviv	H	2-1	Borysenko 2
05/10/95	Dnipro Dnipropetrovsk	A	1-3	Kazakov
15/10/95	Torpedo Zaporizhzhya	H	1-0	Myzenko (p)
19/10/95	Shakhtar Donetsk	H	0-1	
23/10/95	Nyva Ternopil	A	0-0	
27/10/95	SK Mykolaiv	H	0-1	
01/11/95	Dynamo Kyiv	A	1-5	Bogdanov
05/11/95	Nyva Vynnytsya	A	1-0	Kazakov
13/03/96	Nyva Vynnytsya	H	1-0	Borysenko
18/03/96	SK Mykolaiv	A	0-0	
23/03/96	Nyva Ternopil	H	1-0	Grachov
28/03/96	Torpedo Zaporizhzhya	A	0-1	
06/04/96	Dnipro Dnipropetrovsk	H	1-1	Burkhan
13/04/96	Karpaty Lviv	A	0-2	
17/04/96	Tavriya Simferopol	H	2-1	Burkhan, Borysenko
22/04/96	Prykarpattya Ivano-Frankivsk	A	0-0	
06/05/96	Volyn Lutsk	A	0-1	
11/05/96	Zorya-MALS Lugansk	H	2-0	Grachov 2
16/05/96	Shakhtar Donetsk	A	0-1	
21/05/96	Metalurg Zaporizhzhya	H	4-1	Fedorov, Burkhan, Myzenko (p), Mykhailenko
25/05/96	Kremin Kremenchuk	A	1-2	Myzenko
31/05/96	Kryvbas Kryvyi Rih	A	4-5	Borysenko 2, Myzenko 2
05/06/96	Dynamo Kyiv	H	2-1	Borysenko, Martinov
09/06/96	Chornomorets Odesa	H	0-2	
17/06/96	CSKA-Borysfen Kyiv	A	1-0	Borysenko

ZORYA-MALS LUGANSK

CLUB DIRECTORY

Zorya-MALS Lugansk
vul. 50r. utvorennya SU (CPCP) 33
348 016 Lugansk
tel - (0642) 536508/573148/547355/547372
fax - (0642) 551181
Year of Formation - 1964
President - Volodymyr Tarasenko
Secretary - Yulian Tkachev
Coach - Anatoliy Korshikov; Alexander Zhuravlev; Viktor Aristov
Stadium - Avangard (31,243)

MAJOR HONOURS
League Championship (USSR) - (1) 1972.

APPEARANCES 95/96

	P	Ap	(s)	Gls
Anatoliy ANDRYUSHCHENKO	D	10		
Vasyl BARANOV	A	1	(4)	
Alexander BATSMANOV	D		(1)	
Vitaliy CHAIKA	D	4		
Temur DIMITRISHVILI (GEO)	D	22	(1)	
Vitaliy DUNAI	A	5	(1)	1
Mamuka DZHUGELI (GEO)	M	15	(2)	3
Illya GALYUZA	M		(3)	
Alexander GUSHCHIN	A	2	(1)	
Alexander KIRYUKHIN	M	1		
Stanislav KITTO (EST)	M	1	(3)	
Samir KHAIROV (AZB)	D	9	(1)	
Andriy KONDRATENKO	M	7	(1)	
Alexei KOROBCHENKO	M	19		5
Andriy KRAVCHENKO	M	14	(14)	3
Vagif KULIYEV (TAD)	M	6	(1)	
Gela KVITATIANI (GEO)	D	7	(1)	2
Volodymyr KYYAN	M	22	(1)	
Alexander MALYGIN	M	5	(4)	
Yuriy MALYGIN	G	26	(2)	
Alexander MARASHOV (EST)	M	5		
Dmytro MASHCHENKO	M		(1)	
Sergiy MAXYMYCH	M	13	(3)	
Roman MELESHKO (BLS)	A	2		
Asan MUSTAFAYEV	D	25	(2)	
Volodymyr MYKYTYN	D	20	(1)	
Roman MYROSHNYCHENKO	A	6	(2)	
Yevhen NAZAROV	M	4		
Dmytro PERIGRIM	D		(5)	
Mykola RIZUN	D	18	(3)	
Valeriy RUBANCHUK	A	1	(2)	
Valeriy SERCHENKO	G	7	(2)	
Sergiy SHAKUN	M		(6)	
Oleg SHELAYEV	M	31	(1)	1
Igor SHOPIN	M	13	(8)	
Vitaliy STAROVYK	D	14	(5)	
Vyacheslav SUVOROV	A	16		1
Sergiy YARMOLYCH	D	9		
Yuriy ZENIN (BLS)	M	3		

LEAGUE RESULTS 1995/96

25/07/95	Torpedo Zaporizhzhya	H	0-1	
29/07/95	Nyva Ternopil	A	1-3	Kravchenko
02/08/95	SK Mykolaiv	H	0-0	
06/08/95	Nyva Vynnytsya	A	0-5	
12/08/95	CSKA-Borysfen Kyiv	H	1-5	Kravchenko
17/08/95	Chornomorets Odesa	A	0-2	
27/08/95	Zirka-NIBAS Kirovohrad	H	2-1	Korobchenko 2
31/08/95	Kremin Kremenchuk	A	0-1	
10/09/95	Metalurg Zaporizhzhya	H	1-5	Kvitatiani (p)
18/09/95	Shakhtar Donetsk	A	0-3	
22/09/95	Kryvbas Kryvyi Rih	H	1-0	Dunai
27/09/95	Volyn Lutsk	H	3-2	Dzhugeli, Kvitatiani, Korobchenko
05/10/95	Dynamo Kyiv	A	0-1	
15/10/95	Prykarpattya Ivano-Frankivsk	H	1-1	Korobchenko
23/10/95	Tavriya Simferopol	A	0-3	
27/10/95	Karpaty Lviv	H	1-1	Dzhugeli
04/11/95	Dnipro Dnipropetrovsk	A	1-3	Dzhugeli
13/03/96	Dnipro Dnipropetrovsk	H	0-3	
18/03/96	Karpaty Lviv	A	1-2	Korobchenko
23/03/96	Tavriya Simferopol	H	0-2	
28/03/96	Prykarpattya Ivano-Frankivsk	A	0-4	
06/04/96	Dynamo Kyiv	H	0-0	
13/04/96	Volyn Lutsk	A	1-3	Suvorov
17/04/96	Kryvbas Kryvyi Rih	A	0-2	
22/04/96	Shakhtar Donetsk	H	0-2	
27/04/96	Metalurg Zaporizhzhya	A	0-5	
06/05/96	Kremin Kremenchuk	H	1-3	Shelayev
11/05/96	Zirka-NIBAS Kirovohrad	A	0-2	
16/05/96	Chornomorets Odesa	H	0-3	
21/05/96	CSKA-Borysfen Kyiv	A	0-4	
31/05/96	SK Mykolaiv	A	1-4	Kravchenko
09/06/96	Nyva Ternopil	H	0-0	(awarded as home win)
13/06/96	Nyva Vynnytsya	H	0-1	
17/06/96	Torpedo Zaporizhzhya	A	0-3	

PROMOTED CLUB

SECOND DIVISION FINAL TABLE 95/96

		Pd	W	D	L	F	A	Pt	GD
1	**Vorslka Poltava**	**42**	**32**	**7**	**3**	**92**	**37**	**103**	**+55**
2	Bukovyna Chernivtsi	42	30	5	7	83	34	95	+49
3	Stal Alchevsk	42	26	5	11	73	40	83	+33
4	Poligraftekhnika Alexandriya	42	23	7	12	69	37	76	+32
5	Metalurg Nikopol	42	23	5	14	59	40	74	+19
6	Dynamo-2 Kyiv	42	20	12	10	64	42	72	+22
7	Khimik Severodonetsk	42	20	11	11	68	32	71	+36
8	Naftovyk Okhtyrka	42	18	12	12	52	37	66	+15
9	Shakhtar Makyivka	42	19	7	16	63	55	64	+8
10	Krystal Chortkiv	42	19	6	17	70	54	63	+16
11	FC Lviv	42	18	8	16	55	42	62	+13
12	Podillya Khmelnytskyi	42	17	11	14	57	50	62	+7
13	Yavir Krasnopillya	42	17	9	16	53	43	60	+10
14	Khimik Zhytomyr	42	16	10	16	55	57	58	-2
15	Naftokhimik Kremenchuk	42	16	7	19	43	45	55	-2
16	Veres Rivne	42	15	9	18	39	49	54	-10
17	Zakarpattya Uzhgorod	42	14	8	20	49	67	50	-18
18	SK Odesa	42	11	11	20	35	63	44	-28
19	Metalist Kharkiv	42	10	9	23	40	54	39	-14
20	Dnipro Cherkasy	42	6	4	32	26	91	22	-65
21	Ratusha Kamyanets-Podilskyi	42	6	2	34	14	103	20	-89
22	Skala Stryi	42	2	3	37	21	108	9	-87

CLUB DIRECTORY

FC Vorskla Poltava
Nezalezhnosti square 16
314000 Poltava
tel - (05322) 21670/21903/29598
fax - (05322) 21670
Year of Formation - 1987
President - Volodymyr Artemov
Coach - Viktor Pozhychevskyi
Secretary - Stanislav Mejzus
Stadium - Vorskla (32,500)

WALES

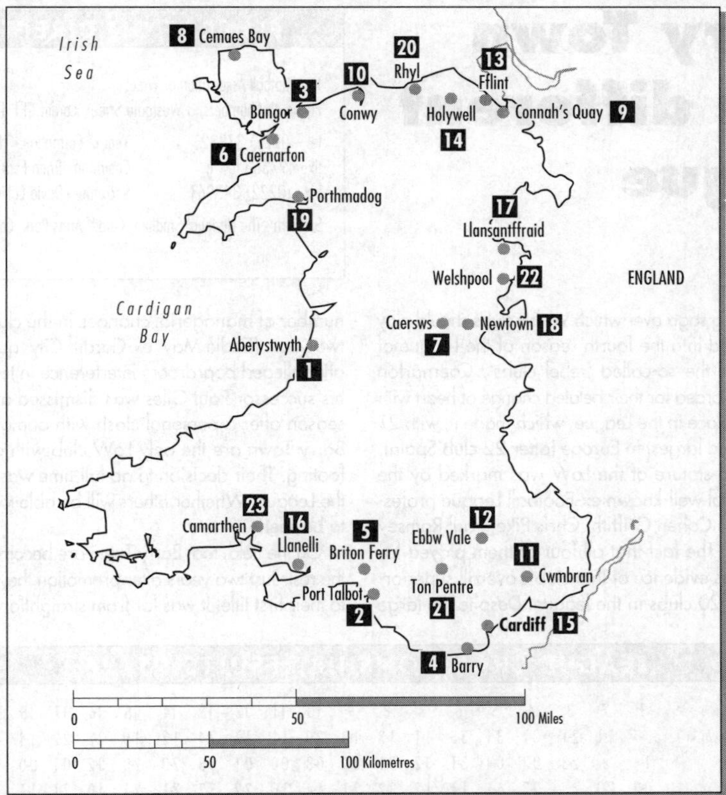

1	ABERYSTWYTH TOWN	1069	13	FFLINT TOWN UNITED	1081
2	AFAN LIDO	1070	14	HOLYWELL TOWN	1082
3	BANGOR CITY	1071	15	INTER CARDIFF	1083
4	BARRY TOWN	1072	16	LLANELLI	1084
5	BRITON FERRY ATHLETIC	1073	17	LLANSANTFFRAID	1085
6	CAERNARFON TOWN	1074	18	NEWTOWN	1086
7	CAERSWS	1075	19	CPD PORTHMADOG	1087
8	CEMAES BAY	1076	20	RHYL	1088
9	CONNAH'S QUAY NOMADS	1077	21	TON PENTRE	1089
10	CONWY UNITED	1078	22	WELSHPOOL	1090
11	CWMBRAN TOWN	1079	23	CARMARTHEN TOWN	1090
12	EBBW VALE	1080			

LITTLE LLANSANTFFRAID INTO EUROPE

Barry Town in a different league

FEDERATION DIRECTORY

The Football Association of Wales
Plymouth Chambers, 3 Westgate Street, Cardiff CF1 1DD

tel - (0222) 372325
tlx - 497363 faw g
fax - (0222) 343961

Year of Formation - 1876
Chairman - Brian Fear
Secretary - David Collins

Stadium - The National Stadium, Cardiff Arms Park, Cardiff (40,240)

The long-running saga over which Welsh clubs should play where continued into the fourth season of the League of Wales. One of the so-called 'rebel clubs', Caernarfon Town, were rewarded for their belated change of heart with an immediate place in the League, which made it, with 21 clubs, the second largest in Europe (after 22-club Spain).

The growing stature of the LoW was marked by the arrival of several well-known ex-Football League professionals, such as Cohen Griffith, Chris Pike, Paul Ramsey and Tony Bird. The fact that all four of them played for Barry Town was evidence of that club's overall superiority to the other 20 clubs in the league. Despite the large number of managerial changes in the club over the past two years (Eddie May, ex-Cardiff City, quit in November after alleged boardroom interference in team affairs, and his successor Paul Giles was dismissed at the end of the season after a personal clash with one of the directors), Barry Town are the only LoW club with a firm financial footing. Their decision to go full-time was a real boost to the League. Whether others will be able to follow remains to be seen.

On the field, too, Barry Town are becoming a cut above the rest. Just two years after promotion they cantered home to their first title. It was far from straightforward in the first

LEAGUE CHAMPIONSHIP RESULTS 95/96

		1	2	3	4	5	6	7	8	9	10	11	12	13	14	15	16	17	18	19	20	21
1	Aberystwyth Town		1-1	2-1	0-1	3-1	3-3	1-1	1-3	1-0	2-0	1-1	1-1	2-4	1-2	1-0	2-2	2-2	1-4	4-1	1-2	2-0
2	Afan Lido	1-4		2-3	0-3	0-4	3-1	3-2	0-1	2-0	0-3	0-0	0-1	0-3	2-0	2-0	3-2	0-1	0-0	1-0	2-3	0-2
3	Bangor City	0-3	2-0		0-3	4-1	1-1	1-2	3-2	2-1	4-4	1-0	2-2	3-2	2-1	2-1	4-0	2-1	1-1	1-1	3-1	2-0
4	Barry Town	2-1	6-0	0-1		4-0	1-0	1-1	2-0	2-0	3-1	2-2	1-0	3-1	4-0	2-1	3-0	2-1	2-0	4-1	4-0	2-0
5	Briton Ferry Athletic	3-1	1-1	4-1	1-6		3-1	2-3	1-1	1-1	2-5	0-5	3-1	0-2	2-0	1-1	5-0	2-1	0-1	5-1	1-1	1-2
6	Caernarfon Town	2-1	1-0	1-2	0-2	1-1		2-0	1-0	1-4	2-2	3-1	0-0	1-1	1-1	3-1	4-0	3-3	0-1	2-2	8-1	2-0
7	Caersws	1-3	0-0	3-1	0-4	3-0	3-2		4-3	3-2	1-3	2-1	3-4	2-4	5-3	2-2	4-0	0-7	0-2	4-1	4-2	2-2
8	Cemaes Bay	2-2	2-2	3-2	2-1	5-1	0-4	2-2		7-1	0-2	1-1	2-1	3-0	4-1	1-2	2-0	0-0	2-4	2-1	2-1	3-0
9	Connah's Quay Nomads	1-0	4-0	1-2	0-0	8-3	4-1	6-3	3-3		2-4	5-1	1-1	0-3	1-4	3-1	3-1	0-0	0-2	1-1	2-1	1-1
10	Conwy United	5-2	5-0	4-0	0-2	1-1	1-1	7-3	3-0	2-2		2-3	4-0	2-1	1-1	1-0	2-0	2-2	1-1	1-0	7-2	2-2
11	Cwmbran Town	1-0	0-0	0-0	0-0	2-1	1-2	2-1	3-1	1-1	2-2		1-3	4-2	1-0	3-0	2-3	3-1	1-2	0-1	1-2	2-2
12	Ebbw Vale	1-2	2-2	1-2	0-1	4-1	3-2	3-3	3-0	1-1	3-3	0-1		1-0	4-1	1-1	0-1	0-1	1-3	1-2	3-1	3-0
13	Fflint Town United	4-0	0-3	3-2	5-1	4-0	3-2	1-1	2-1	0-0	2-2	1-3	1-1		1-2	1-1	2-1	0-5	2-1	2-0	0-1	1-1
14	Holywell Town	2-1	2-0	0-1	0-2	2-2	1-2	3-4	2-1	1-3	1-1	2-0	3-1	3-5		2-3	4-2	2-1	0-3	1-0	0-1	1-1
15	Inter Cardiff	2-0	2-0	4-2	0-0	2-1	2-2	3-1	5-2	2-1	2-1	0-2	0-0	0-5	0-3		3-3	1-1	2-2	3-0	4-1	4-0
16	Llanelli	4-2	4-0	1-3	0-5	2-3	2-2	3-1	2-0	2-0	2-4	1-1	0-2	0-1	1-1	0-1		0-1	3-3	1-4	2-2	1-2
17	Llansantffraid	3-1	1-2	0-2	1-1	3-1	1-3	4-1	5-0	1-2	2-5	1-1	0-1	1-0	3-0	3-2	0-2		1-0	0-3	5-1	1-1
18	Newtown	1-1	1-0	2-1	0-0	3-0	0-0	4-0	3-0	0-0	3-0	0-0	1-2	0-2	2-0	2-0	2-0	3-0		0-1	2-0	3-0
19	CPD Porthmadog	1-0	3-1	4-1	2-3	1-2	1-2	1-1	4-0	1-1	1-2	0-2	3-1	1-1	2-0	1-1	4-1	1-1	0-5		0-0	3-3
20	Rhyl	1-2	1-0	0-3	1-5	2-1	1-5	1-2	3-0	1-1	0-1	2-2	1-0	1-1	1-1	3-2	1-1	3-0	0-1	0-1		0-2
21	Ton Pentre	1-2	0-0	3-2	1-2	2-2	2-3	1-3	2-0	0-1	1-3	1-1	1-2	2-3	2-0	1-1	0-0	2-1	1-1	1-1	1-1	

LEAGUE CHAMPIONSHIP FINAL TABLE 95/96

			Home					Away					Total						
		Pd	W	D	L	F	A	W	D	L	F	A	W	D	L	F	A	Pt	GD
1	Barry Town	40	17	2	1	50	10	13	5	2	42	13	30	7	3	92	23	97	+69
2	Newtown	40	12	5	3	32	7	11	6	3	37	18	23	11	6	69	25	80	+44
3	Conwy United	40	11	7	2	53	23	10	6	4	48	35	21	13	6	101	58	76	+43
4	Bangor City	40	12	5	3	40	27	9	1	10	32	38	21	6	13	72	65	69	+7
5	Fflint Town United	40	9	6	5	35	28	10	3	7	41	29	19	9	12	76	57	66	+19
6	Caernarfon Town	40	9	7	4	38	23	7	6	7	39	36	16	13	11	77	59	61	+18
7	Cwmbran Town	40	8	6	6	30	24	6	9	5	28	25	14	15	11	58	49	57	+9
8	Inter Cardiff	40	11	6	3	41	27	3	6	11	21	35	14	12	14	62	62	54	=
9	Caersws	40	10	3	7	46	46	5	6	9	35	51	15	9	16	81	97	54	-16
10	Connah's Quay Nomads	40	9	6	5	46	32	4	8	8	22	31	13	14	13	68	63	53	+5
11	Ebbw Vale	40	7	5	8	35	28	7	6	7	24	28	14	11	15	59	56	53	+3
12	Llansantffraid	40	9	3	8	36	29	5	7	8	30	28	14	10	16	66	57	52	+9
13	CPD Porthmadog	40	7	7	6	34	28	6	4	10	22	34	13	11	16	56	62	50	-6
14	Aberystwyth Town	40	7	7	6	32	30	6	2	12	28	38	13	9	18	60	68	48	-8
15	Cemaes Bay	40	11	5	4	45	28	2	2	16	18	52	13	7	20	63	80	46	-17
16	Holywell Town	40	8	3	9	32	34	4	4	12	21	40	12	7	21	53	74	43	-21
17	Briton Ferry Athletic	40	8	5	7	38	35	3	4	13	26	56	11	9	20	64	91	42	-27
18	Rhyl	40	6	5	9	23	31	5	4	11	24	52	11	9	20	47	83	42	-36
19	Ton Pentre	40	4	8	8	25	29	4	8	8	21	36	8	16	16	46	65	40	-19
20	Afan Lido	40	7	2	11	21	33	2	7	11	12	38	9	9	22	33	71	36	-38
21	Llanelli	40	5	5	10	31	38	3	4	13	19	50	8	9	23	50	88	33	-38

half of the season, when there appeared to be new leaders every week. But once Barry got into their stride, they were unstoppable. From the end of September through to Boxing Day they won 12 matches in succession, and they carried that dominant form into an invincible run that lasted all of 34 matches - a new LoW record, smashing the previous 20-game mark set in the League's inaugural season by Cwmbran Town.

A couple of late slip-ups prevented Barry from reaching the 100-point mark, but by then they already had the title safely under wraps, confirming their triumph with five matches still left to play. Dropping a few insignificant points after the championship race was over mattered little, but there was extreme consternation at the club when they failed to complete the 'double', falling in the final of the Welsh Cup to tiny mid-Wales outfit Llansantffraid.

Llansantffraid, from a village with a population of just 952, completed a competition full of shocks by lifting the old trophy after a thrilling final at the National Stadium. The 'Saints' had reached the final very impressively, beating Inter Cardiff 4-1 on aggregate in the semis. But nobody gave them much of a hope in the final against the newly-crowned League of Wales champions - especially as the minnows had already secured their place in the European Cup-winners' Cup. But Llansantffraid did not travel to Cardiff simply to make up the numbers. They took the lead on three occasions - in the first half, in the second half, and again in extra-time - before Barry striker Tony Bird struck the cruellest of blows with a spectacular volleyed equaliser in the 118th minute. Fate appeared to be against the outsiders, but in the penalty competition Llansantffraid kept their nerve - just - while Barry lost theirs to transform fantasy into reality and win the shoot-out 3-2.

Llansantffraid and Barry Town were joined in the 96/97 European competitions by Newtown, who saw their excellent youth policy pay off with a late sprint into second place, forcing Conwy United to seek refuge in the InterToto Cup.

The three League of Wales teams who tasted European football in 1995/96 (or, more precisely, in the summer of 1995) all had undistinguished league campaigns. Bangor City, beaten handsomely but gallantly in the UEFA

INTERNATIONAL HONOURS

World Cup Finals appearances: 1958 (qtr-finals)

European Championship appearances: 1976

NATIONAL TEAM RESULTS 95/96

06/09/95	Moldova (ECQ)	H	Cardiff	1-0	Speed (55)
11/10/95	Germany (ECQ)	H	Cardiff	1-2	Helmer (78og)
15/11/95	Albania (ECQ)	A	Tirana	1-1	Pembridge (43)
24/01/96	Italy	A	Terni	0-3	
24/04/96	Switzerland	A	Lugano	0-2	
02/06/96	San Marino (WCQ)	A	Serravalle	5-0	Melville (20), Hughes (32, 43), Giggs (50), Pembridge (85)

TOP SCORERS

38	Ken McKENNA (Conwy United)
29	Eifion WILLIAMS (Caernarfon Town)
25	Frank MOTTRAM (Bangor City)
22	Stuart AUBURY (Caersws)
21	Steven JONES (Fflint Town United)
19	Christopher CAMDEN (Conwy United)
18	Darren EMMITT (Fflint Town United)
	Paul HUNTER (Barry Town)
	Paul BURROWS (Briton Ferry Athletic)
	Antony SMOLKA (Llanelli)

Cup by Polish champions-to-be Widzew Lodz, never pressed for their third consecutive title. Afan Lido, who earned the League of Wales' first ever European 'point' with a 0-0 draw in Latvia, sank to the bottom of the table and were relegated. And InterToto entrants (and four-time losers) Ton Pentre only just survived the drop themselves.

Up from the feeder leagues came Carmarthen Town (from the south) and Welshpool (from the north). Welshpool finished two points behind champions Oswestry Town, but Oswestry's facilities were not considered to be up to standard for the League of Wales so they remained in the Cymru Alliance.

The three Welsh clubs performing in the Endsleigh League in England all had an uninspiring season. As a result of FIFA's decision, they were no longer permitted to enter the Welsh Cup (which, of course, had much to do with Llansantffraid's fairy-tale win). So league fare was all that kept them going. Wrexham, knocked out of the Cup-winners' Cup preliminary round by Petrolul Ploiesti of Romania, missed out narrowly on the Second Division

DOMESTIC CUP RESULTS

SECOND ROUND
Ebbw Vale 3, BP Landarcy 1
Aberaman Athletic 1, Llandrindod Wells 1
(replay) Llandridnod Wells 4, Aberaman Athletic 1
AFC Porth 3, Grange Harlequins 3
(replay) Grange Harlequins 3, AFC Porth 2
Ammanford 1, Cardiff Corinthians 4
Briton Ferry Athletic 3, Pontardawe Athletic 1
Brymbo 1, Conwy United 3
Connah's Quay Nomads 5, Welshpool 1
Goytre United 4, Penrhiwceiber Rangers 2
Llandudno 3, Mostyn 2
Llandyrnog United 2, Buckley Town 1
Llanrwst United 2, Cemaes Bay 6
Maesteg Park 2, Morriston Town 1
Nantlle Vale Penygroes 1, Caersws 3
Newport YMCA 2, Pontypridd Town 4
Oswestry Town 1, Chirk AAA 0
CPD Porthmadog 2, Mold Alexandra 1
Porth Tywyn Suburbs 0, Taffs Well 0
(replay) Taffs Well 3, Porth Tywyn Suburbs 1
Port Talbot Athletic 2, Aberystwyth Town 7
Rhayader Town 1, Abergavenny Thursdays 2
Ruthin Town 0, Lex XI Wrexham 3
Penparcau 0, Rhyl 2
Treowen Stars 1, Llanelli 3

THIRD ROUND
Ebbw Vale 1, Briton Ferry Athletic 0
Abergavenny Thursdays 3, Caersws 2
Aberystwyth Town 1, Newtown 1
(replay) Newtown 0, Aberystwyth Town 1 (aet)
Bangor City 2, Cwmbran Town 3
Cemaes Bay 3, Maesteg Park 0
Connah's Quay Nomads 1, Llandudno 3
Conwy United 0, Barry Town 2
Goytre United 8, Llanelli 2
Llandrindod Wells 1, Afan Lido 0
Holywell Town 0, Grange Harlequins 2
Lex XI Wrexham 0, Ton Pentre 0
(replay) Ton Pentre 3, Lex XI Wrexham 2
Llansantffraid 2, Landyrnog United 1
Oswestry Town 2, Fflint Town United 1
CPD Porthmadog 1, Cardiff Corinthians 0
Rhyl 1, Inter Cardiff 0 (Rhyl later disqualified)
Taffs Well 0, Pontypridd Town 1
Ton Pentre 0, Barry Town 1
Pontypridd Town 1, Cemaes Bay 0

FOURTH ROUND
Grange Harlequins 1, Ebbw Vale 2
Cwmbran Town 3, Goytre United 0
Llansantffraid 4, Abergavenny Thursdays 0
Aberystwyth Town 0, Oswestry Town 0
(replay) Oswestry Town 3, Aberystwyth Town 2
CPD Porthmadog 2, Llandridnod Wells 1
Inter Cardiff 2, Llandudno 0

QUARTER-FINALS
Ebbw Vale 0, Inter Cardiff 1
Cwmbran Town 2, CPD Porthmadog 0
Oswestry Town 0, Barry Town 2
Pontypridd Town 1, Llansantffraid 2

SEMI-FINALS
Barry Town v Cwmbran Town 1-0; 2-3
(3-3; Barry Town on away goals)
Inter Cardiff v Llansantffraid 0-1; 1-3
(Llansantffraid 4-1)

FINAL
19/05/96, Cardiff
LLANSANTFFRAID 3 Morgan (29), Evans G. (54), Whelan C. (95)
BARRY TOWN 3 Lloyd (35), Mulliner (61og), Bird (118)
(aet; 3-2 on pens.)
LLANSANTFFRAID - Mulliner; Whelan J., Curtiss, Brown, Jones Ar., O'Brien (Watt 112), Evans I. (Nunnerly 112), Evans G., Morgan, Whelan C., Abercrombie.
BARRY TOWN - Ovendale; Evans, Lloyd, Mayer, Batchelor, Barnett (Griffith 105), Giles (Withers 96), Bird, Hunter (Pike 58), Jones, O'Gorman.

NATIONAL TEAM APPEARANCES 95/96

Manager - Bobby GOULD	MOL	GER	ALB	ITA	SUI	SMR	Cps	Gls
Neville SOUTHALL (16/09/58) - Everton (ENG)	G	G	G	G		G	86	-
Mark BOWEN (07/12/62) - Norwich City (ENG)	D	D	D		D	D	37	3
Chris COLEMAN (10/06/70) - Crystal Palace (ENG)/Blackburn Rovers (ENG)	D			D	D88	D	14	3
Adrian WILLIAMS (16/08/71) - Reading (ENG)	D			D			7	-
Kit SYMONS (08/03/71) - Manchester City (ENG)	D	D		D	D		22	-
Mark PEMBRIDGE (29/11/70) - Sheffield Wednesday (ENG)	M	M82	M		M	D	16	3
Barry HORNE (18/05/62) - Everton (ENG)	M	M		M	M74	M81	54	2
Gary SPEED (08/09/69) - Leeds United (ENG)	M	M		M77	s30		35	2
Lee NOGAN (21/05/69) - Reading (ENG)	M46						2	-
Mark HUGHES (01/11/63) - Chelsea (ENG)	M			M		M	60	14
Ian RUSH (20/10/61) - Liverpool (ENG)	A69			A64			73	28
David PHILLIPS (29/07/63) - Nottingham Forest (ENG)	s46		D	D			62	2
John HARTSON (05/04/75) - Arsenal (ENG)	s69				A		5	-
Stephen JENKINS (16/07/72) - Huddersfield Town (ENG)		D71	D	D			3	-
Andy MELVILLE (29/11/68) - Sunderland (ENG)		D	D			D	27	1
Nathan BLAKE (27/01/72) - Sheffield United (ENG)/Bolton Wanderers (ENG)		M82		s77			6	1
Dean SAUNDERS (21/06/64) - Galatasaray (TUR)		A	A			A	52	16
Ryan GIGGS (29/11/73) - Manchester United (ENG)		A	A			A	16	4
Paul MARDON (14/09/69) - West Bromwich Albion (ENG)		s71					1	-
Geraint WILLIAMS (05/01/62) - Ipswich Town (ENG)		s82					13	-
Glyn HODGES (30/04/63) - Sheffield United (ENG)		s82		M57			18	2
Eric YOUNG (25/03/60) - Wolverhampton Wanderers (ENG)			D				21	1
Ceri HUGHES (26/02/71) - Luton Town (ENG)			M63				5	-
Gareth TAYLOR (25/02/73) - Crystal Palace (ENG)/Sheffield United (ENG)			M84	s64	A46		3	-
Robbie SAVAGE (18/10/74) - Crewe Alexandra (ENG)			s63		s65	s81	3	-
John ROBINSON (29/08/71) - Charlton Athletic (ENG)			s84		D	M79	3	-
Marcus BROWNING (22/04/71) - Bristol Rovers (ENG)				s57		D70	2	-
Danny COYNE (27/08/73) - Tranmere Rovers (ENG)					G46		1	-
Vinnie JONES (05/01/65) - Wimbledon (ENG)					M65		5	-
Andy LEGG (28/07/66) - Birmingham City (ENG)					M30	s79	2	-
Andy MARRIOTT (11/10/70) - Wrexham					s46		1	-
Simon DAVIES (23/04/74) - Manchester United (ENG)					s46		1	-
Jeremy GOSS (11/05/65) - Norwich City (ENG)					s74	s70	9	-
Christian EDWARDS (23/11/75) - Swansea City					s88		1	-

play-offs. At the other end of the table Swansea City dropped into Division Three despite the appointment of ex-Liverpool midfielder Jan Mølby as player-manager. Another ex-Anfield stalwart, Phil Neal, took over the managerial reins at Cardiff City, but problems behind the scenes at Ninian Park put paid to any plans the ex-England full-back had of ending the season on a high note. They finished a lowly 22nd in Division Three, prompting further calls for the club to take the plunge and join the League of Wales sooner rather than later.

One man who has made the move from England to Wales is new national team boss Bobby Gould. The

EUROPEAN CUPS RESULTS 95/96

CUP-WINNERS' CUP

● WREXHAM

Preliminary round PETROLUL PLOIESTI (ROM)

H 0-0

Marriott; Brace, Hardy, Hunter, Jones B., Phillips, Owen, Durkin, Connolly, Watkin, Futcher.

A 0-1

Marriott; Hardy, Hunter, Jones, Phillips, Owen, Cross, Connolly, Watkin, Thomas, Futcher (Barnes).

UEFA CUP

● BANGOR CITY

Preliminary round WIDZEW LODZ (POL)

H 0-4

Deegan; Jones K., Carberry (Jones A.), Langley, Rutter, Humphreys (Parry D.), Wiggins, Parry J. (Barry), Mottram, Colville, Evans.

A 0-1

Innes; Jones K., Jones A., Langley, Rutter, Parry D., Wiggins, Barnett, Mottram, Parry J. (Evans), Noble.

● AFAN LIDO

Preliminary round RAF YELGAVA (LAT)

H 1-2 Moore (30)

Thomas; Duggan (Jones D.), Preece, Moore, Cook, Rickard, Patton (Jones N.), Glover, Bartley, Radford, Evans D..

A 0-0

Thomas; Duggan, Evans D. (Preece), Moore, Webber (Jones D.), Rickard, Patton, Glover, Bartley, Radford, Jones N. (Evans P.).

former Coventry and Wimbledon manager brought tremendous enthusiasm to his new job but little in the way of results. Gould's first season saw the team play just half a dozen matches. The sequqnce began with a 1-0 victory against Moldova - Wales's first win for a year - and ended with a 5-0 romp away to San Marino in the opening World Cup qualifier. In between there were three defeats and a draw - nothing too terrible but, equally, nothing to offer any likelihood of the team finally ending their long barren run and reaching the 1998 World Cup finals.

Gould gave first caps to a whole range of players whose names and faces were unfamiliar to the Welsh supporters. But the more newcomers the manager introduced, the more the fans longed for the return of the big names. Southall, Hughes, Saunders and Giggs all came back for the San Marino game, and, irrespective of the level of opposition, the result spoke for itself.

Gould's experimentation did not stretch to including any League of Wales players, but his determined quest to introduce a 'B' team could change all that, allowing the country's part-timers a more ongoing diet of international football than the crumbs they are currently restricted to feeding on in the middle of the summer.

PLAYERS OF THE SEASON

KEN McKENNA

Given the size of the League of Wales and the modest quality of its teams, impressive individual goalscoring exploits are always a possibility. In 93/94 Dave Taylor of CPD Porthmadog struck 43 goals to become Europe's top league goalscorer, and in 95/96 Conwy United's Ken McKenna came close to emulating him with 38 goals, a tally which included no fewer than five hat-tricks. The 35-year-old striker did more than anyone else to secure his club's InterToto spot. He also acted as assistant to manager John Hulse throughout the season, preparing himself for a managerial career of his own when he hangs up his boots in a couple of years' time.

TOMMY MORGAN

A veteran of Welsh football, 38-year-old Tommy Morgan achieved the undoubted highlight of his long career when he he helped his club Llansantffraid to their sensational victory in the Welsh Cup. His opening goal in the final against Barry Town was his 26th of the season, and so impressive was his overall performance that a South Korean club were actually prepared to offer him a contract...until they discovered his age! Formerly with Newtown, Telford United (England) and Aberystwyth Town, Morgan is assistant manager to Graham Breeze at Llansantffraid, where his wealth of experience is of great benefit to a young side.

DEAN SAUNDERS

At 32, Dean Saunders is no spring chicken himself, but such is his fitness and overall enthusiasm for the game that 'Deano' looks a good bet to extend his career at the top for a good few years yet, the Welsh national team included. In the summer he joined Nottingham Forest for £1 million having spent a successful season in Turkey with Galatasaray. He left for Turkey alongside his former Aston Villa strike partner Dalian Atkinson. And although Atkinson won the title with Fenerbahçe, Saunders scored more goals in the league (15 to 10) and had the last laugh when Galatasaray beat Fenerbahçe in the Cup final thanks to his excellent winning goal in extra-time.

ABERYSTWYTH TOWN

CLUB DIRECTORY

Aberystwyth Town FC
The Lodge
Nat. Library of Wales, Aberystwyth
tel - (01970) 623520
fax - (01970) 617939
Year of Formation - 1884
Chairman - Derrick Dawson
Secretary - Rhun Owens
Manager - Meirion Appleton
Stadium - Park Avenue (5,500)

MAJOR HONOURS
Domestic Cup - (1) 1900.

APPEARANCES 95/96

	P	Ap	(s)	Gls
Gari APPLETON	D		(3)	
Paul BENNETT (ENG)	A	29	(4)	4
David BLAIR	M	10	(14)	2
Ian BLAIR	D		(1)	
Damian BURKE	A	23	(10)	4
John DAVIES	G	8		
Martin DAVIES	A	5	(5)	1
Michael DAVIES	A		(1)	
Mark DEVEREUX	D	37	(2)	
Ceri EVANS	M		(2)	
William EVANS	G	1		
Martyn GRIFFITHS	M	30	(4)	5
Peter GRIFFITHS	M		(3)	
Gary HAMAN	G		(2)	
Matthew HARRISON	M	17	(5)	2
Richard HOCKIN (ENG)	D	1		
Glyndwr HUGHES	A		(1)	
Marc HUGHES	M	36	(1)	5
Gareth JAMES	A	4	(3)	1
Peter JAMES	D	7	(2)	
Kevin JONES	A	4	(7)	
Matthew JONES	D	19	(6)	
Donald KANE (SCO)	M	31	(5)	4
Stuart KINNINMONTH	G	31		
Gari LEWIS	M	1	(3)	
Patrick LEWIS-BROWN (ENG)	M		(5)	
Dylan MORRIS	M	1		1
Kevin MORRISON (SCO)	A	31	(1)	13
Nigel NICHOLAS	D	11		
Sean PARRY	D	2		
Mark POUND (ENG)	A	22	(3)	11
Christopher ROBERTS	M	4	(2)	
Aneurin THOMAS	D	7	(1)	2
Anthony THOMAS	M	4	(2)	
Rhodri THOMAS	D	25	(1)	2
Paul WARRINGTON	A	1		
Jason WILLIAMS	D	6	(5)	
Jonathan WILLIAMS	D	26	(4)	3
Stephen WILLIAMS	A	6	(2)	

LEAGUE RESULTS 1995/96

19/08/95	Fflint Town United	H	2-4	Bennett, Morrison (p)
26/08/95	Bangor City	A	3-0	Morrison, Blair D., Bennett
30/08/95	Cwmbran Town	A	0-1	
02/09/95	CPD Porthmadog	H	4-1	Kane 2, Thomas A., Burke
09/09/95	Briton Ferry Athletic	A	1-3	Hughes M.
16/09/95	Inter Cardiff	H	1-0	Pound (p)
23/09/95	Llansantffraid	A	1-3	Kane
30/09/95	Llanelli	A	2-4	Bennett, Hughes M. (p)
07/10/95	Caernarfon Town	H	3-3	Morrison (p), Bennett, Thomas A.
21/10/95	Rhyl	H	1-2	Griffiths M.
28/10/95	Cemaes Bay	A	2-2	Davies Ma., Blair D.
01/11/95	Cwmbran Town	H	1-1	Griffiths M.
11/11/95	Barry Town	H	0-1	
18/11/95	Newtown	A	1-1	Morrison
25/11/95	Holywell Town	A	1-2	Morrison
02/12/95	Conwy United	H	2-0	Harrison, Morrison
09/12/95	Afan Lido	A	4-1	Pound 3, Williams Ja.
23/12/95	Fflint Town United	A	0-4	
06/01/96	Connah's Quay Nomads	A	0-1	
13/01/96	Llansantffraid	H	2-2	Hughes M., Griffiths M.
20/01/96	Briton Ferry Athletic	H	3-1	Griffiths M., Burke, Pound
24/01/96	Ebbw Vale	H	1-1	Burke
03/02/96	Barry Town	A	1-2	Morrison
10/02/96	Newtown	H	1-4	Morrison
17/02/96	Llanelli	H	2-2	Pound 2
24/02/96	Caernarfon Town	A	1-2	Hughes M.
02/03/96	Rhyl	A	2-1	Morrison 2
06/03/96	CPD Porthmadog	A	0-1	
09/03/96	Cemaes Bay	H	1-3	Morrison
13/03/96	Caersws	H	1-1	Pound
23/03/96	Connah's Quay Nomads	H	1-0	Pound
26/03/96	Inter Cardiff	A	0-2	
30/03/96	Bangor City	H	2-1	Morrison, Pound
03/04/96	Ton Pentre	A	2-1	Morrison, Williams Ja.
06/04/96	Holywell Town	H	1-2	Williams Ja.
08/04/96	Caersws	A	3-1	Burke, James G., Pound
20/04/96	Afan Lido	H	1-1	Griffiths M.
27/04/96	Ebbw Vale	A	2-1	Harrison, Thomas R.
04/05/96	Ton Pentre	H	2-0	Thomas R., Hughes M.
06/05/96	Conwy United	A	2-5	Morris, Kane

AFAN LIDO

CLUB DIRECTORY

Afan Lido FC
56 Abbeyville Avenue
Sandfields Estate, Port Talbot SA12 6PY
tel - (01639) 885638
fax - (01639) 872068
Year of Formation - 1967
Chairman - vacant
Secretary - Phil Robinson
Manager - Nigel Rees
Stadium - Afan Lido Sports Ground (5,000)

APPEARANCES 95/96

	P	Ap	(s)	Gls
Kevin BARTLEY	A	10	(3)	4
David BLACKMORE	D	8		
Steven COOK	D	12	(12)	
David CUSACK (ENG)	D	4		
Craig DUGGAN	D	8		
Andrew EDWARDS	G		(2)	
David EVANS	D	9	(9)	
Paul EVANS	M	25	(9)	
Carl GLOVER	M	26	(3)	1
Martin GOLDSMITH	A	7	(1)	1
Carl HARRIS	M	39	(1)	1
Neil HENDRA	A		(4)	
Gregory HURLEY	M	7	(15)	1
Darryl JOHN	A	4	(2)	
Dean JOHNSTONE	M	10	(2)	1
David JONES	M	14	(6)	1
Leighton JONES	D		(3)	1
Neil JONES	A	1		
Phillip LYONS	A	1	(1)	
Karl MILLER	D		(2)	
Adam MOORE	M	20		3
David MORGAN	G	8		
James MULLAN	D	6	(3)	
Shaun O'LEARY	M	2	(5)	
Mitchell PATTON	A	11	(3)	7
Ryan PREECE	D	18	(7)	
Andrew RADFORD	M	25		1
Andrew RICKARD	D	40		2
James RICKARD	M	13	(4)	
Alan ROBERTS	A	3	(5)	
Gavin ROBINSON	D		(1)	
Mark ROBINSON	D	7	(3)	
Kevin ROGERS	D	26	(1)	2
Morys SCOTT	A	24		5
Lee STEPHENS	M	16	(1)	2
Paul STEPHENS	M		(3)	
Brian THOMAS	G	32	(1)	
Andrew WEBBER	D	4	(2)	
Gavin WELLINGTON	D		(2)	

LEAGUE RESULTS 1995/96

26/08/95	Ebbw Vale	H	0-1	
02/09/95	Inter Cardiff	H	2-0	Scott, Moore
09/09/95	Llansantffraid	A	2-1	Moore, Scott
12/09/95	Caersws	H	3-2	Patton, Harris, Scott
15/09/95	Cwmbran Town	H	0-0	
23/09/95	Bangor City	A	0-2	
30/09/95	CPD Porthmadog	A	1-3	Patton
07/10/95	Cemaes Bay	A	2-2	Jones D., Scott
17/10/95	Ton Pentre	H	0-2	
21/10/95	Holywell Town	H	2-0	Patton, Scott
01/11/95	Barry Town	A	0-6	
10/11/95	Llanelli	H	3-2	Bartley 3
18/11/95	Conwy United	A	0-5	
25/11/95	Newtown	H	0-0	
09/12/95	Aberystwyth Town	H	1-4	Moore
13/12/95	Briton Ferry Athletic	A	1-1	Rogers
16/12/95	Fflint Town United	H	0-3	
06/01/96	Rhyl	H	2-3	Bartley, Rogers
13/01/96	Cwmbran Town	A	0-0	
20/01/96	Llansantffraid	H	0-1	
03/02/96	Llanelli	A	0-4	
10/02/96	Conwy United	H	0-3	
13/02/96	Inter Cardiff	A	0-2	
17/02/96	Newtown	A	0-1	
24/02/96	Cemaes Bay	H	0-1	
28/02/96	Ton Pentre	A	0-0	
02/03/96	Holywell Town	A	0-2	
09/03/96	Caernarfon Town	A	0-1	
12/03/96	Barry Town	H	0-3	
16/03/96	Bangor City	H	2-3	Glover, Patton
23/03/96	Rhyl	A	0-1	
30/03/96	Caernarfon Town	H	3-1	Patton 2, Goldsmith
06/04/96	Connah's Quay Nomads	H	2-0	Patton, Stephens L.
08/04/96	Briton Ferry Athletic	H	0-4	
10/04/96	Ebbw Vale	A	2-2	Radford, Rickard A.
13/04/96	CPD Porthmadog	H	1-0	Hurley
20/04/96	Aberystwyth Town	A	1-1	Rickard A.
27/04/96	Caersws	A	0-0	
04/05/96	Fflint Town United	A	3-0	Stephens L., Jones L., Johnstone
06/05/96	Connah's Quay Nomads	A	0-4	

BANGOR CITY

CLUB DIRECTORY

Bangor City FC
12 Lon y Bryn
Menai Bridge, Ynys Mon LL57 5NM
tel - (01248) 712820
fax - (01248) 372132
Year of Formation - 1875
Chairman - Gwyn Pierce Owen
Secretary - Alun Griffiths
Manager - Nigel Atkins; Bryan Griffiths
Stadium - Farrar Road (10,000)

MAJOR HONOURS

League Championship - (2) 1994, 1995.
Domestic Cup - (3) 1889, 1896, 1962.

APPEARANCES 95/96

	P	Ap	(s)	Gls
Nigel ADKINS (ENG)	G	22		
David BARNETT (ENG)	M	15		
Nigel BARRY	M		(1)	
Anthony BISHOP (ENG)	A	8		1
Stephen BUXTON (ENG)	A	11	(4)	4
James CARBERRY (ENG)	D	28	(7)	1
Ricky COMBER (ENG)	D		(1)	
Neil DAVIES	A	18	(4)	5
Timothy EDWARDS	D	30	(2)	4
Alun EVANS	A	29	(7)	5
Robert GRIFFITHS (ENG)	D	5	(1)	
Ian HAIGH (ENG)	G	7		
Steven HUMPHRIES	M	1	(4)	
Michael INNES	G		(4)	
Arwel JONES	D	10	(8)	1
Kevin JONES	D	38	(1)	
Steven JONES (ENG)	M	9	(4)	2
Kevin LANGLEY (ENG)	M	39	(1)	6
Michael LEWIS	D	3	(5)	
Anthony LIVENS (ENG)	A		(8)	
Barrie LOVE	D		(2)	
Phillip LUNN	D	1		
Michael McCANN (ENG)	D		(1)	
Richard McNEILL (ENG)	A	1	(5)	
Paul MOORE (ENG)	G	8		
Frank MOTTRAM (ENG)	A	40		25
Lee NOBLE (ENG)	M	24	(6)	5
Dewi PARRY	D	4	(5)	
Jonathan PARRY	M	19	(13)	3
Stuart PICKTHALL	D	13	(3)	
Dylan PRITCHARD	G	3	(2)	
Stephen PUGH	A	4	(1)	1
Richard ROBINSON (ENG)	A		(1)	
Damien RODEN	M	3	(5)	1
Mark RUTTER (ENG)	D	21	(2)	3
Steven SMITH	D		(2)	
Jason THOMAS	D	4	(3)	
Karl THOMAS	M	7	(5)	4
Harold WIGGINS (ENG)	D	15		

LEAGUE RESULTS 1995/96

Date	Opponent	H/A	Score	Scorers
19/08/95	Rhyl	A	3-0	Mottram, Langley 2
26/08/95	Aberystwyth Town	H	0-3	
29/08/95	Caernarfon Town	H	1-1	Parry J.
02/09/95	Barry Town	A	1-0	Mottram
09/09/95	Newtown	H	1-1	Langley
13/09/95	Cemaes Bay	A	2-3	Noble, Rutter
16/09/95	Ton Pentre	A	2-3	Jones A., Langley
23/09/95	Afan Lido	H	2-0	Langley, Mottram
30/09/95	Conwy United	H	4-4	Langley, Mottram 3
07/10/95	Llansantffraid	A	2-0	Parry J., Pugh
14/10/95	Ton Pentre	H	2-0	Mottram 2
28/10/95	Cwmbran Town	A	0-0	
01/11/95	Caernarfon Town	A	2-1	Mottram, Edwards
11/11/95	Briton Ferry Athletic	H	4-1	Roden, Noble, Evans, Mottram
18/11/95	Fflint Town United	A	2-3	Noble, Mottram
25/11/95	Ebbw Vale	H	2-2	Noble, Mottram
02/12/95	Inter Cardiff	H	2-1	Mottram, Davies
09/12/95	Caersws	A	1-3	Thomas K.
12/12/95	Connah's Quay Nomads	H	2-1	Evans, Edwards
16/12/95	Llanelli	A	3-1	Thomas K. (p), Davies, og (Arthur)
23/12/95	Rhyl	H	3-1	Buxton, Parry J., Davies
01/01/96	Cemaes Bay	H	3-2	Mottram 2, Davies
06/01/96	CPD Porthmadog	A	1-4	Mottram
16/01/96	Holywell Town	H	2-1	Noble, Buxton
20/01/96	Newtown	A	1-2	Edwards
03/02/96	Briton Ferry Athletic	A	1-4	Mottram
10/02/96	Fflint Town United	H	3-2	Mottram 2, Jones S.
17/02/96	Conwy United	A	0-4	
24/02/96	Llansantffraid	H	2-1	Rutter (p), Jones S.
09/03/96	Cwmbran Town	H	1-0	Davies
16/03/96	Afan Lido	A	3-2	Thomas K. 2, Evans
19/03/96	CPD Porthmadog	H	1-1	Carberry
30/03/96	Aberystwyth Town	A	1-2	Bishop
06/04/96	Ebbw Vale	A	2-1	Mottram 2
08/04/96	Holywell Town	A	1-0	Buxton
16/04/96	Connah's Quay Nomads	A	2-1	Mottram, Buxton (p)
20/04/96	Caersws	H	1-2	Rutter (p)
27/04/96	Inter Cardiff	A	2-4	Mottram, Evans
04/05/96	Llanelli	H	4-0	Mottram 2, Evans, Edwards
06/05/96	Barry Town	H	0-3	

BARRY TOWN

CLUB DIRECTORY

Barry Town FC
166 Jenner Road
Barry
South Glamorgan CF6 8HR
tel - (01446) 737188
Year of Formation - 1912
Chairman - Paula O'Halloran
Secretary - Alan Whelan
Manager - Paul Giles (96/97 - Gary Barnett)
Stadium - Jenner Park (8,000)

MAJOR HONOURS
League Championship - (1) 1996.
Domestic Cup - (2) 1955, 1994.

APPEARANCES 95/96

	P	Ap	(s)	Gls
Gary BARNETT (ENG)	A	31	(1)	4
William BATCHELOR (ENG)	D	37		8
Anthony BIRD	A	15	(1)	9
Terence EVANS	D	23	(2)	
Ian FRENCH	D	32		6
David GILES	M		(1)	
Paul GILES	M	27	(7)	5
Cohen GRIFFITH (GUY)	A	12	(10)	4
Ashley GRIFFITHS	D	3	(1)	
Adrian HARDING	M	1	(2)	
Matthew HOLTHAM	M	20	(4)	1
Paul HUNTER (ENG)	A	25	(13)	18
Richard JONES	M	33	(1)	3
Ross KNIGHT (ENG)	M	14	(3)	1
Gary LLOYD	D	37		
Michael MAYER	D	16	(13)	
Mark OVENDALE (ENG)	G	40		
David O'GORMAN	A	28	(9)	7
Steven O'SHAUGHNESSY	M	6	(1)	1
Christopher PIKE (ENG)	A	18	(11)	16
Lee PRICE	M		(2)	
Paul RAMSEY (NIR)	M	3		
Steven RUTTER (ENG)	A		(3)	
Phillip WILLIAMS	M	7	(15)	1
David WITHERS	A	12	(16)	8

LEAGUE RESULTS 1995/96

19/08/95	Briton Ferry Athletic	H	4-0	Jones, Hunter, Withers, O'Shaughnessy
26/08/95	Caersws	A	4-0	Hunter 2, French, Knight
02/09/95	Bangor City	H	0-1	
09/09/95	Fflint Town United	A	1-5	Griffith
12/09/95	Cwmbran Town	H	2-2	French, Pike
16/09/95	CPD Porthmadog	H	4-1	Griffith, Pike, O'Gorman, French
23/09/95	Connah's Quay Nomads	A	0-0	
30/09/95	Cemaes Bay	H	2-0	French 2
07/10/95	Conwy United	A	2-0	Griffith 2
21/10/95	Caernarfon Town	A	2-0	Withers, O'Gorman
28/10/95	Newtown	H	2-0	Pike, Hunter
01/11/95	Afan Lido	H	6-0	Batchelor, Hunter 3, Withers, O'Gorman
11/11/95	Aberystwyth Town	A	1-0	Holtham
18/11/95	Rhyl	H	4-0	Giles P., Pike, Hunter, O'Gorman
25/11/95	Llanelli	A	5-0	Pike 3, Giles P., Hunter
09/12/95	Holywell Town	A	2-0	Hunter, Pike
12/12/95	Ton Pentre	H	2-0	Pike. O'Gorman
23/12/95	Briton Ferry Athletic	A	6-1	Batchelor, Hunter 4, Jones
26/12/95	Ebbw Vale	H	1-0	French
05/01/96	Inter Cardiff	A	0-0	
13/01/96	Connah's Quay Nomads	H	2-0	Withers 2
20/01/96	Fflint Town United	H	3-1	Bird 2, Batchelor
03/02/96	Aberystwyth Town	H	2-1	Bird, Williams
24/02/96	Conwy United	H	3-1	Giles P., Batchelor, Pike
27/02/96	Llansantffraid	A	1-1	Barnett (p)
02/03/96	Caernarfon Town	H	1-0	Pike
09/03/96	Newtown	A	0-0	
12/03/96	Afan Lido	A	3-0	Pike 2, Barnett
19/03/96	Inter Cardiff	H	2-1	Giles P., Hunter
23/03/96	CPD Porthmadog	A	3-2	Jones, Barnett, Hunter
30/03/96	Caersws	H	1-1	Bird (p)
06/04/96	Llanelli	H	3-0	Pike, Withers, Giles P.
08/04/96	Ton Pentre	A	2-1	Withers, Batchelor
16/04/96	Ebbw Vale	A	1-0	Batchelor
20/04/96	Holywell Town	H	4-0	Hunter 2, Barnett, Withers
27/04/96	Rhyl	A	5-1	Pike 2, Bird 2, O'Gorman
30/04/96	Llansantffraid	H	2-1	Bird 2
02/05/96	Cwmbran Town	A	0-0	
04/05/96	Cemaes Bay	A	1-2	Batchelor
06/05/96	Bangor City	A	3-0	Batchelor, O'Gorman, Bird

BRITON FERRY ATHLETIC

CLUB DIRECTORY

Briton Ferry Athletic FC
314 Old Road
Briton Ferry, Neath
tel - (01639) 820459
fax - (01639) 644755
Year of Formation - 1926
Chairman - Graham Jenkins
Secretary - Jeff Watkins
Manager - Paul Burrows
Stadium - Old Road Ground (2,000)

APPEARANCES 95/96

	P	Ap	(s)	Gls
Martin ARMSTRONG	M	19		4
Darren BLACK	D		(1)	
Paul BURKE (ENG)	D	6	(5)	
David BURROWS	M	2		
Paul BURROWS	A	24	(11)	18
Michael COOK	D	11	(4)	
Kevin CREEDEN	G	1		
Mark DAVIES	D	14	(1)	1
Paul DAVIES	D	11		
Steven DICKERSON	M	12	(8)	
Andrew DYER	M		(1)	
Francis FORD	A	4		2
Ian FRASER	D	5	(14)	
Nigel FRENCH	M	19	(3)	5
Richard GAY	A	29		6
Michael GEORGE	A	1		
Wayne GOODRIDGE	M	21	(2)	3
Ashley HOPKINS	D	11	(15)	
Michael JOHNSTON (ENG)	D	10	(8)	
Andrew JONES	A		(1)	
Ian JONES	M		(1)	
John JONES	M	40		2
John Kenneth JONES	D	1		
Huw KNIGHT	D	2		
Michael LENEHAN	M		(2)	
Nigel LEWIS	D	3	(5)	
Wayne MEYRICK	M	19	(7)	3
Carl MILLER	D		(5)	
David MORGAN	G	8		
Ryland MORGAN (ENG)	M	1	(10)	
Simon MORSE	D	19		1
Anthony MYERSCOUGH	M	2	(1)	
Mark OTTEN	D	35		4
Patrick O'HAGAN	G	13		
Martin REES	G	1		
Lee STEPHENS	M	6		1
Robert THOMAS	A	26	(3)	6
Steven THOMAS	D	8		
Paul WALKER	D	39		5
Lee WILLIAMS	G		(1)	
Nigel WILLIAMS	G	17		

LEAGUE RESULTS 1995/96

Date	Opponent	H/A	Score	Scorers
19/08/95	Barry Town	A	0-4	
26/08/95	Caernarfon Town	H	3-1	Otten, Walker, Jones J.
28/08/95	Newtown	H	0-1	
02/09/95	Cemaes Bay	A	1-5	og (Turner)
09/09/95	Aberystwyth Town	H	3-1	Armstrong, Gay, Thomas R.
16/09/95	Conwy United	A	1-1	French
23/09/95	Ton Pentre	H	1-2	Gay
30/09/95	Connah's Quay Nomads	A	3-8	Gay 2, Armstrong
07/10/95	Cwmbran Town	H	0-5	
21/10/95	Llanelli	A	3-2	Thomas R., Armstrong, Gay
28/10/95	Fflint Town United	H	0-2	
11/11/95	Bangor City	A	1-4	Thomas R.
25/11/95	CPD Porthmadog	A	2-1	Walker, Gay
02/12/95	Llansantffraid	H	2-1	Stephens, Burrows P.
13/12/95	Afan Lido	H	1-1	Burrows P.
16/12/95	Holywell Town	A	2-2	Burrows P. og (Williams)
23/12/95	Barry Town	H	1-6	Burrows P.
06/01/96	Caersws	A	0-3	
13/01/96	Conwy United	H	2-5	Burrows P., French
20/01/96	Aberystwyth Town	A	1-3	Burrows P.
03/02/96	Bangor City	H	4-1	French 3, Meyrick
07/02/96	Inter Cardiff	H	1-1	Burrows P.
10/02/96	Caersws	H	2-3	Walker, Morse
17/02/96	Connah's Quay Nomads	H	1-1	Goodridge
24/02/96	Rhyl	H	1-1	Jones J.
01/03/96	Llanelli	H	5-0	Burrows P. 2, og (Davies G.), Armstrong, Meyrick
06/03/96	Cwmbran Town	A	1-2	Walker
09/03/96	Fflint Town United	A	0-4	
16/03/96	Cemaes Bay	H	1-1	Goodridge
19/03/96	Llansantffraid	A	1-3	Burrows P.
23/03/96	Ton Pentre	A	2-2	Meyrick, Burrows P.
30/03/96	Rhyl	A	1-2	Burrows P.
06/04/96	CPD Porthmadog	H	5-1	Otten, Davies, Burrows P. 2, Ford
08/04/96	Afan Lido	A	4-0	Burrows P. 3, Otten
10/04/96	Inter Cardiff	A	1-2	Thomas R.
14/04/96	Ebbw Vale	A	1-4	Ford
20/04/96	Ebbw Vale	H	3-1	Goodridge, Thomas R., Burrows P.
23/04/96	Newtown	A	0-3	
27/04/96	Caernarfon Town	A	1-1	Walker
04/05/96	Holywell Town	H	2-0	Otten, Thomas R.

CAERNARFON TOWN

CLUB DIRECTORY

Caernarfon Town FC
20 South Penrallt
Caernarfon
Gwynedd
LL55 1NS
tel - (01286) 674045
Year of Formation - 1876
Chairman - G. Lloyd Owen
Secretary - John Watkins
Manager - John Aspinall
Stadium - The Oval (3,000)

APPEARANCES 95/96

	P	Ap	(s)	Gls
John ASPINALL (ENG)	D	26	(7)	1
Stephen ASPINALL (ENG)	M	36	(1)	5
Trevor BALL (ENG)	G	2		
Paul BENNETT (ENG)	M	26	(2)	
Craig CAMPBELL (ENG)	M	1	(3)	1
Andrew DIGGLE (ENG)	D	21	(2)	
Anthony DRAPER (ENG)	M	31	(2)	2
Jason GALLAGHER (ENG)	A	4		
Nicholas HARLAND (ENG)	M	7	(4)	2
Derek HIGHDALE (ENG)	A	19	(5)	5
Paul HOWARD (ENG)	A	29	(10)	6
Jason JOYCE (ENG)	D	2		
Phillip MYDDLETON	D	6	(6)	
Phillip OWEN	G	38		
Brendan REDMOND (ENG)	D	2	(4)	
Damien RODEN	M	2	(5)	
Alan SCHUMAKER (ENG)	D	26	(3)	1
Timothy STEEL	M	9	(6)	4
Elliott SUTTON (ENG)	A	9	(5)	6
Andrew TAYLOR (ENG)	D	35	(1)	5
Christopher WARING (ENG)	M	28		7
David WILLIAMS	D		(4)	
Eifion WILLIAMS	A	34	(2)	29
Emrys WILLIAMS	D	35	(2)	1
Robert WILLIAMS	A	2	(7)	1
Alan WOAN (ENG)	M	10	(24)	

LEAGUE RESULTS 1995/96

Date	Opponent	H/A	Score	Scorers
19/08/95	Connah's Quay Nomads	A	1-4	Schumaker
26/08/95	Briton Ferry Athletic	A	1-3	Williams R.
29/08/95	Bangor City	A	1-1	Sutton
02/09/95	Fflint Town United	H	1-1	Taylor
09/09/95	Cwmbran Town	A	2-1	Aspinall S., Sutton
13/09/95	Llansantffraid	H	3-3	Campbell, Williams Ei., Sutton
16/09/95	Caersws	H	2-0	Sutton, Draper (p)
23/09/95	CPD Porthmadog	A	2-1	Aspinall S., Waring
30/09/95	Holywell Town	H	1-1	Williams Ei.
07/10/95	Aberystwyth Town	A	3-3	Aspinall S., Waring (p), Williams Ei.
18/10/95	Conwy United	H	2-2	Sutton 2
21/10/95	Barry Town	H	0-2	
28/10/95	Rhyl	A	5-1	Williams Ei. 4, Taylor
01/11/95	Bangor City	H	1-2	Taylor
04/11/95	Ebbw Vale	H	0-0	
11/11/95	Newtown	H	0-1	
18/11/95	Cemaes Bay	A	4-0	Williams Ei. 2, Taylor, Waring
02/12/95	Ton Pentre	H	2-0	Howard, Waring
09/12/95	Inter Cardiff	H	3-1	Howard, Waring, Williams Ei.
16/12/95	Ebbw Vale	A	2-3	Williams Em., Highdale
06/01/96	Llanelli	A	2-2	Highdale, Steel
13/01/96	CPD Porthmadog	H	2-2	og (Jones R.), Aspinall S.
20/01/96	Cwmbran Town	H	3-1	Highdale, Steel, Williams Ei.
03/02/96	Newtown	A	0-0	
10/02/96	Cemaes Bay	H	1-0	Williams Ei.
17/02/96	Rhyl	H	8-1	Waring 2, Williams Ei. 4, Howard, Highdale
24/02/96	Aberystwyth Town	H	2-1	Williams Ei. 2
02/03/96	Barry Town	A	0-1	
05/03/96	Llansantffraid	A	3-1	Williams Ei. 3
09/03/96	Afan Lido	H	1-0	Howard
16/03/96	Caersws	A	2-3	Howard, Williams Ei.
20/03/96	Conwy United	A	1-1	Williams Ei.
23/03/96	Llanelli	H	4-0	Williams Ei. 2, Steel 2
30/03/96	Afan Lido	A	1-3	Highdale
10/04/96	Holywell Town	A	2-1	Harland, Williams Ei.
13/04/96	Ton Pentre	A	3-2	Taylor, Aspinall S., Williams Ei.
16/04/96	Fflint Town United	A	2-3	Aspinall J., Draper
21/04/96	Inter Cardiff	A	2-2	Howard, Williams Ei.
27/04/96	Briton Ferry Athletic	H	1-1	Williams Ei.
04/05/96	Connah's Quay Nomads	H	1-4	Harland

CAERSWS

CLUB DIRECTORY

Caersws FC
3 Hafren Terrace
Caersws
Powys
tel - (01686) 688103
fax - (01686) 688103
Year of Formation - 1887
Chairman - Garth Williams
Secretary - Mike Jones
Manager - Mickey Evans
Stadium - Recreation Ground (3,500)

APPEARANCES 95/96

	P	Ap	(s)	Gls
Michael ANDREWS (ENG)	D	2	(2)	
Stuart AUBURY (ENG)	A	31		22
Russell CADWALLADER	G	39		
Marcus CANNING (ENG)	D	4	(4)	
Paul CANNING (ENG)	D	3	(5)	
Ian CLARKE (ENG)	M	15	(3)	3
Michael CLARKE (ENG)	D	12		4
Simon COOK (ENG)	A	2	(3)	
Craig EDWARDS	M	13	(1)	1
Andrew EVANS (ENG)	D	32	(5)	3
Graham EVANS	M	1	(5)	1
Mark EVANS (ENG)	A	31		7
Anthony GRIFFITHS	D	33		3
David GRIFFITHS	D	34		2
Daniel GURNEY (ENG)	A	8		1
Robert HAMER	M	28		7
Lee HARDING	D	6	(6)	
Sean JEHU	M	13	(7)	5
Gary JONES	A	8	(13)	
Paul JONES	D	28		1
Robert JONES	G		(19)	
Mark LEWIS	M		(3)	
Neil LEWIS	M	2	(2)	
Steven NICHOLS	D	4		
Lyn OWEN	D	5	(15)	
John SILLITOE (ENG)	G	1	(1)	
Andrew THOMAS	D	26	(13)	
Andrew WHITTICASE	A	36		17
David WILLIAMS	D	19		3
Gwyn WILLIAMS	D	4	(5)	

LEAGUE RESULTS 1995/96

Date	Opponent	H/A	Score	Scorers
19/08/95	Ton Pentre	A	3-1	Evans M. 2, Jones P.
26/08/95	Barry Town	H	0-4	
29/08/95	Holywell Town	H	5-3	Griffiths A., Hamer, Evans M., Williams D. 2
02/09/95	Conwy United	A	3-7	Hamer 2, Griffiths D. (p)
09/09/95	Llanelli	H	4-0	Griffiths D., Whitticase 2, Gurney
12/09/95	Afan Lido	A	2-3	Whitticase 2
16/09/95	Caernarfon Town	A	0-2	
23/09/95	Newtown	H	0-2	
29/09/95	Llansantffraid	H	0-7	
07/10/95	Rhyl	A	2-1	Griffiths A., Whitticase
21/10/95	Connah's Quay Nomads	A	3-6	og (Smyth), Aubury, Griffiths A.
28/10/95	CPD Porthmadog	H	4-1	Whitticase, Jehu, Evans M., Aubury
31/10/95	Holywell Town	A	4-3	Evans A., Hamer, Aubury, Whitticase
11/11/95	Inter Cardiff	A	1-3	Evans M.
18/11/95	Ebbw Vale	A	3-3	Aubury, Evans A., Jehu
25/11/95	Cwmbran Town	H	2-1	Aubury 2
02/12/95	Fflint Town United	A	1-1	Clarke M.
09/12/95	Bangor City	H	3-1	Clarke M. (p), Williams D., Whitticase
16/12/95	Rhyl	H	4-2	Whitticase, Evans A., Hamer, Aubury
06/01/96	Briton Ferry Athletic	H	3-0	Aubury, Evans M., Clarke M.
13/01/96	Newtown	A	0-4	
20/01/96	Llanelli	A	1-3	Aubury
10/02/96	Briton Ferry Athletic	A	3-2	Clarke M. (p), Whitticase, Aubury
17/02/96	Ton Pentre	H	2-2	Aubury, Clarke I.
02/03/96	Connah's Quay Nomads	H	3-2	Aubury 2, Whitticase
09/03/96	CPD Porthmadog	A	1-1	Aubury
13/03/96	Aberystwyth Town	A	1-1	Aubury
16/03/96	Caernarfon Town	H	3-2	Evans M., Jehu, Whitticase
28/03/96	Cemaes Bay	H	4-3	Jehu 2, Aubury 2
30/03/96	Barry Town	A	1-1	Whitticase
06/04/96	Cwmbran Town	A	1-2	Hamer
08/04/96	Aberystwyth Town	H	1-3	Hamer
13/04/96	Fflint Town United	H	2-4	Aubury (p), Whitticase
16/04/96	Llansantffraid	A	1-4	Clarke I.
20/04/96	Bangor City	A	2-1	Aubury, Whitticase
23/04/96	Conwy United	H	1-3	Edwards
27/04/96	Afan Lido	H	0-0	
30/04/96	Inter Cardiff	H	2-2	Aubury, Evans G.
04/05/96	Ebbw Vale	H	3-4	Aubury (p), Whitticase 2
06/05/96	Cemaes Bay	A	2-2	Clarke I., Aubury

CEMAES BAY

CLUB DIRECTORY

Cemaes Bay FC
12 Maes Garnedd
Tregele, Cemaes Bay, Anglesey
tel - (01407) 710297
Year of Formation - 1946
Chairman - Ivan Clews
Secretary - Nel Hugehs
Manager - Bryn Howes
Stadium - School Lane (4,500)

APPEARANCES 95/96

	P	Ap	(s)	Gls
Darren BAKER	A	7	(8)	5
Mark BOWEN (ENG)	M	5		
Stephen BUTLER (ENG)	D		(1)	
Stephen CARBERRY (ENG)	D	2		
Anthony CLARKE (ENG)	D	12		
David COCKRAM (ENG)	M	6	(1)	
Peter DALEY (ENG)	A	14		8
Joseph DONNELY (ENG)	D	23	(1)	
Ian DUNROE (ENG)	A	16		4
Steven EDWARDS (ENG)	D	3	(9)	
John EVANS (ENG)	M	8	(7)	2
Kevin FEENEY (ENG)	A	17	(9)	5
Kevin FITZPATRICK (ENG)	M	1		
John GRAY	D	19	(2)	
Kevin HAGAN (ENG)	A	28		12
Oliver HALL (ENG)	M	1	(2)	
Campbell HARRISON (ENG)	D	13	(4)	2
Steven HUMPHREYS	M	29	(3)	8
Derek JACKSON (ENG)	D	15	(1)	
Benjamin JONES	D	1	(1)	
Martin JONES	A	14	(5)	
Richard JONES	M	1		
Robert JONES	G		(1)	
Warren JONES (ENG)	M	4	(2)	
Joseph KEARNS (ENG)	M	2	(9)	
Wayne KINNEAR (ENG)	G	4		
Richard LAUGHTON (ENG)	M	7	(5)	1
Anthony LIVENS (ENG)	A	10	(3)	4
Geoffrey LIVENS (ENG)	G	5	(1)	
Stuart MANDERS (ENG)	A	4	(4)	
Gregory MOFFATT (ENG)	D	18		1
Michael MOLONEY (ENG)	D	5	(11)	
Ian MURPHY (ENG)	D	6		
Barry NORRIS (ENG)	M	18	(1)	1
David OWENS (ENG)	D	1	(3)	
Mark PARKINSON (ENG)	D	12	(8)	
Joseph RICE (ENG)	A	4	(1)	
Christopher ROBERTS (ENG)	M	14	(1)	
Paul RUDKIN (ENG)	A	1		
Alan SHIRLEY (ENG)	M	12	(5)	
Barry SMITH (ENG)	A	4	(5)	
Neil THOMAS (ENG)	D	4	(1)	
David TURNER (ENG)	G	31		
Mark TURNER (ENG)	M	31	(4)	8
Stuart WALKER (ENG)	D		(1)	
Geoffrey WOODS (ENG)	D	8	(1)	1

LEAGUE RESULTS 1995/96

19/08/95	Cwmbran Town	H	1-1	Livens A.
26/08/95	Fflint Town United	A	1-2	Turner M.
30/08/95	Connah's Quay Nomads	A	3-3	Harrison, Turner M., Laughton
02/09/95	Briton Ferry Athletic	H	5-1	Baker 3, Livens A., Turner M.
13/09/95	Bangor City	H	3-2	Evans 2, Baker
16/09/95	Ebbw Vale	A	0-3	
23/09/95	Inter Cardiff	A	2-5	Baker, Turner M.
30/09/95	Barry Town	A	0-2	
07/10/95	Afan Lido	H	2-2	Turner M., og (Moore)
21/10/95	Newtown	A	0-3	
28/10/95	Aberystwyth Town	H	2-2	Turner M., Livens A. (p)
01/11/95	CPD Porthmadog	H	2-1	Livens A., Humphreys
11/11/95	Rhyl	A	0-3	
18/11/95	Caernarfon Town	H	0-4	
25/11/95	Ton Pentre	A	0-2	
02/12/95	Holywell Town	H	4-1	Hagan, Turner M., Feeney, Harrison
09/12/95	Llansantffraid	A	0-5	
01/01/96	Bangor City	A	2-3	Feeney 2
06/01/96	Conwy United	A	0-3	
13/01/96	Inter Cardiff	H	1-2	Hagan
20/01/96	Ebbw Vale	H	2-1	Feeney, Humphreys
03/02/96	Rhyl	H	2-1	Hagan, Moffatt
10/02/96	Caernarfon Town	A	0-1	
24/02/96	Afan Lido	A	1-0	Feeney
02/03/96	Newtown	H	2-4	Hagan, Humphreys
09/03/96	Aberystwyth Town	A	3-1	Hagan, Turner M., Woods
16/03/96	Briton Ferry Athletic	A	1-1	Dunroe
20/03/96	Fflint Town United	H	3-0	Daley 2 (1p), Hagan
23/03/96	Conwy United	H	0-2	
28/03/96	Caersws	A	3-4	Humphreys 2, Dunroe
30/03/96	Llanelli	H	2-0	Humphreys, Dunroe
06/04/96	Ton Pentre	H	3-0	Daley 2, Hagan
08/04/96	CPD Porthmadog	A	0-4	
13/04/96	Holywell Town	A	1-2	Daley (p)
20/04/96	Llansantffraid	H	0-0	
24/04/96	Connah's Quay Nomads	H	7-1	Humphreys 2, Hagan 2, Daley 2 (1p), Dunroe (p)
27/04/96	Llanelli	A	0-2	
28/04/96	Cwmbran Town	A	1-3	Daley
04/05/96	Barry Town	H	2-1	Hagan 2
06/05/96	Caersws	H	2-2	Hagan, Norris

CONNAH'S QUAY NOMADS

CLUB DIRECTORY

Connah's Quay Nomads FC
40 Brookdale Avenue
Connah's Quay
Clwyd CH5 4LU
tel - (01244) 831212
fax - (01244) 836784
Year of Formation - 1946
Chairman - T.R. Morris
Secretary - Rob Hunter
Manager - Nev Powell
Stadium - Halfway Ground (3,000)

APPEARANCES 95/96

	P	Ap	(s)	Gls
Michael CARROLL (ENG)	M	35		1
Phillip COLLISTER (ENG)	G	36		
Chris DAVIES	A	29	(4)	6
Nathan DAVIES	M		(12)	
Darren FAWCETT (ENG)	M		(2)	
Dale HARLEY	G		(4)	
Geoffrey HINCHCLIFFE	D	7	(7)	
Phillip HINCHCLIFFE	M		(1)	
Peter HUGHES	A	34	(2)	13
Vernon KEEP (ENG)	M	33	(2)	8
Shaun KINNAIR	M		(1)	
Malcolm LATTER	M		(2)	
Marc LIMBERT	A	33	(1)	4
Martin LITTLEWOOD (ENG)	M	13		
Daniel McGOONA	M	21	(7)	8
Damon OLDFIELD	M		(3)	
Darren PETERS	M	1	(13)	
Christopher POWELL	D		(2)	
David POWELL	M	3	(8)	
Neville POWELL	M	11	(22)	1
Stuart RAIN (CYP)	A	28	(1)	15
Graham RANDLES	A	5	(7)	3
Carl ROBERTS	M		(4)	
Phillip SHELBOURNE	M	2	(1)	
Mark SIMPSON (ENG)	G	4		
Carl SMYTH (ENG)	D	36		3
Barry THOMAS	D	37		2
Neil WHITLEY (ENG)	M	1		
Darren WYNNE	D	33	(2)	3
Garry WYNNE	D	38	(1)	

LEAGUE RESULTS 1995/96

19/08/95	Caernarfon Town	H	4-1	Hughes 2, Wynne D., McGoona
26/08/95	Llanelli	H	3-1	Hughes, McGoona, Keep
30/08/95	Cemaes Bay	H	3-3	Smyth, Randles, Hughes
02/09/95	Ton Pentre	A	1-0	Rain
08/09/95	Holywell Town	H	1-4	Randles
16/09/95	Rhyl	A	1-1	Randles
23/09/95	Barry Town	H	0-0	
30/09/95	Briton Ferry Athletic	H	8-3	McGoona, Rain 5, Keep 2
07/10/95	Ebbw Vale	A	1-1	Davies C.
21/10/95	Caersws	H	6-3	Rain 3, Smyth, Davies C. 2
28/10/95	Llansantffraid	A	2-1	McGoona, og (Jones)
11/11/95	CPD Porthmadog	A	1-1	Limbert (p)
18/11/95	Inter Cardiff	H	3-1	Hughes, Wynne D., Davies C.
02/12/95	Cwmbran Town	A	1-1	Limbert (p)
06/12/95	Conwy United	A	2-2	Rain, Keep
09/12/95	Fflint Town United	H	0-3	
12/12/95	Bangor City	A	1-2	Keep
16/12/95	Conwy United	H	2-4	Hughes 2
06/01/96	Aberystwyth Town	H	1-0	Davies C.
13/01/96	Barry Town	A	0-2	
19/01/96	Holywell Town	A	3-1	Smyth, Limbert, Rain
03/02/96	CPD Porthmadog	H	1-1	Thomas
17/02/96	Briton Ferry Athletic	A	1-1	Carroll
24/02/96	Ebbw Vale	H	1-1	Powell N.
02/03/96	Caersws	A	2-3	Rain 2
05/03/96	Newtown	A	0-0	
09/03/96	Llansantffraid	H	0-0	
16/03/96	Llanelli	A	0-2	
19/03/96	Rhyl	H	2-1	Hughes, Keep
23/03/96	Aberystwyth Town	A	0-1	
30/03/96	Ton Pentre	H	1-1	Davies C.
06/04/96	Afan Lido	A	0-2	
08/04/96	Cwmbran Town	H	5-1	McGoona, Hughes 3, Rain
13/04/96	Newtown	H	0-2	
16/04/96	Bangor City	H	1-2	Keep (p)
20/04/96	Inter Cardiff	A	1-2	Limbert
24/04/96	Cemaes Bay	A	1-7	Thomas
01/05/96	Fflint Town United	A	0-0	
04/05/96	Caernarfon Town	A	4-1	Hughes, McGoona 3
06/05/96	Afan Lido	H	4-0	Wynne D., Hughes, Keep, Rain

CONWY UNITED

CLUB DIRECTORY

Conwy United FC
Iolyn, Iolyn Park
Conwy LL32 8UX
tel - (01492) 593496
fax - (01492) 573243
Year of Formation - 1977
Chairman - Graham Rees
Secretary - Cecil Jones
Manager - John Hulse
Stadium - Morfa Conwy (4,000)

APPEARANCES 95/96

	P	Ap	(s)	Gls
Gary ANDERSON (ENG)	D	2		
Dafydd APOLLONI	A		(1)	
Michael BAILEY	M		(2)	
Ian BAMFORD (ENG)	G	32	(7)	
David BARNETT (ENG)	M	9	(3)	1
Nicholas BROOKMAN (ENG)	M	15	(17)	
Christopher CAMDEN (ENG)	A	26		19
Neil CLARKE (ENG)	D	14		3
Matthew CORCORAN	M	1		
Phillip DAVIES	M		(2)	
Phillip Peter DAVIES	M	1	(7)	
Ian DORAN (ENG)	M	33		2
Mark EDWARDS (ENG)	D	37		4
David EVANS (ENG)	D	9	(2)	1
Paul EVANS	M	1	(5)	
Neil GRIFFITHS (ENG)	G	7		
John HAMMOND (ENG)	M	3	(1)	
Martin Albert JONES	M	12	(6)	1
Martin Richard JONES	G	1	(2)	
Scott JONES	D		(1)	
Seth JONES	D		(2)	
Steven JONES (ENG)	M	15		3
Stuart JONES (ENG)	D	3		
Paul LACEY (ENG)	D	11	(3)	2
Anthony LIVENS (ENG)	A	1	(10)	
Dave MARTINDALE (ENG)	M	1	(1)	
Hugh McAULEY (ENG)	M	16		4
James McILVOGUE	A	9	(5)	3
Ken McKENNA (ENG)	A	35		38
William MORRIS (IRL)	A	2	(1)	
Paul MULLEN (ENG)	M	26	(2)	4
Steven ROBERTS	A	3	(12)	2
Michael SMITH	A	1		
Timothy STEEL	M	6		2
Christopher TAYLOR (ENG)	M	37		2
Scott TAYLOR (ENG)	M	16	(12)	3
Harold WIGGINS (ENG)	M	14		
Geraint WILLIAMS	A		(1)	
Mark WILLIAMS	D	8	(3)	
Peter WOOLLAND (ENG)	D	1	(3)	
Neil YOUNG (ENG)	D	32	(2)	5

LEAGUE RESULTS 1995/96

Date	Opponent	H/A	Score	Scorers
19/08/95	Inter Cardiff	H	1-0	Roberts
26/08/95	CPD Porthmadog	A	2-1	McKenna, Taylor S.
29/08/95	Llansantffraid	A	5-2	Clarke, McKenna 3, Roberts
02/09/95	Caersws	H	7-3	Clarke 2, McKenna 3, McIlvogue, Young
09/09/95	Ebbw Vale	H	4-0	Jones Ste., Lacey 2, Evans D.
16/09/95	Briton Ferry Athletic	H	1-1	McKenna
30/09/95	Bangor City	A	4-4	McKenna 2, Taylor S., Jones Ste.
07/10/95	Barry Town	H	0-2	
18/10/95	Caernarfon Town	A	2-2	Mullen, Edwards
21/10/95	Ton Pentre	A	3-1	McKenna, McIlvogue, Jones Ste.
28/10/95	Llanelli	H	2-0	Steel, McKenna
01/11/95	Llansantffraid	H	2-2	Doran, Young
11/11/95	Holywell Town	A	1-1	McKenna (p)
18/11/95	Afan Lido	H	5-0	Edwards, Mullen 2, Steel, McIlvogue
25/11/95	Rhyl	H	7-2	Camden 3, McKenna 3, Young
02/12/95	Aberystwyth Town	A	0-2	
06/12/95	Connah's Quay Nomads	H	2-2	McKenna 2
16/12/95	Connah's Quay Nomads	A	4-2	Camden 2 (1p), McKenna 2
23/12/95	Inter Cardiff	A	1-2	og (Wigley)
06/01/96	Cemaes Bay	H	3-0	Taylor S., Camden 2
13/01/96	Briton Ferry Athletic	A	5-2	McKenna 2, Camden 2, Young
24/01/96	CPD Porthmadog	H	1-0	Young
03/02/96	Holywell Town	H	1-1	McKenna
10/02/96	Afan Lido	A	3-0	Mullen, McKenna 2
17/02/96	Bangor City	H	4-0	og (Rutter), McKenna 3
24/02/96	Barry Town	A	1-3	McAuley
27/02/96	Fflint Town United	A	2-2	Camden, McKenna
02/03/96	Ton Pentre	H	2-2	Camden, Doran
09/03/96	Llanelli	A	4-2	Camden 2, McKenna (p), McAuley
20/03/96	Caernarfon Town	H	1-1	McAuley
23/03/96	Cemaes Bay	A	2-0	Taylor C., Camden
30/03/96	Cwmbran Town	H	2-3	Barnett, Camden
02/04/96	Newtown	A	0-3	
06/04/96	Rhyl	A	1-0	Edwards
08/04/96	Fflint Town United	H	2-1	McKenna 2
13/04/96	Ebbw Vale	A	3-3	Taylor C., McKenna 2
23/04/96	Caersws	A	3-1	Camden 2, Jones M.A.
27/04/96	Newtown	H	1-1	McAuley
04/05/96	Cwmbran Town	A	2-2	Camden, McKenna
06/05/96	Aberystwyth Town	H	5-2	McKenna 3, Camden, Edwards

CWMBRAN TOWN

CLUB DIRECTORY

Cwbran Town AFC
36 Gregory Close
Pencoed
Bridgend CF3 56RF
tel - (01656) 861274
fax - (01656) 861274
Year of Formation - 1955
Chairman - George Thorneycroft
Secretary - Phil Dauncey
Manager - Tony Wilcox
Stadium - Cwmbran (13,200)

MAJOR HONOURS
League Championship - (1) 1993.

APPEARANCES 95/96

	P	Ap	(s)	Gls
Andrew BATTLE	M	7	(3)	1
Richard CARTER	D	23	(4)	
Michael COPEMAN	D	30	(1)	1
Simon DYER	A	30		11
Aneurin EVANS	A	4		
Mark EVANS	A	3	(1)	1
Craig FILER	D	4	(1)	
Roger GIBBINS (ENG)	M	21	(14)	2
Craig HEWINGS	D	28	(2)	
Wayne HEWITT	D	31	(2)	8
Daniel JENKINS	D	6	(3)	1
Christopher LILYGREEN	A	2	(4)	
Andrew MAINWARING (ENG)	A	28		17
Stephen MARDENBOROUGH (ENG)	A	1		
Dennis McCOY (ENG)	D	29	(3)	
John MILNE (SCO)	D	6		2
Mark PARFITT	M	27	(9)	
Norman PARSELLE	M	37		1
Kevin PAYNE	M	22	(10)	
Raymond PENNOCK	A	1	(1)	
Darreen PERRETT	A	9	(2)	2
John POWELL	M	17	(8)	1
Mark SMITH	A	3	(8)	1
Jason THOMAS	M	2	(15)	
Neil THOMAS	G	40		
Dean THRELFALL	A		(6)	
Christopher WATKINS	M		(12)	
Sean WHARTON	M	29	(2)	8

LEAGUE RESULTS 1995/96

19/08/95	Cemaes Bay	A	1-1	Smith
30/08/95	Aberystwyth Town	H	1-0	Milne
02/09/95	Rhyl	A	2-2	Evans M., Parselle
09/09/95	Caernarfon Town	H	1-2	Hewitt
12/09/95	Barry Town	A	2-2	Hewitt, Milne
15/09/95	Afan Lido	A	0-0	
23/09/95	Llanelli	H	2-3	Dyer 2
30/09/95	Inter Cardiff	H	3-0	Mainwaring, Gibbins, Dyer
07/10/95	Briton Ferry Athletic	A	5-0	Wharton, Dyer, Mainwaring 3
14/10/95	Newtown	H	1-2	Mainwaring
21/10/95	Fflint Town United	A	3-1	Gibbins, Wharton, Mainwaring
28/10/95	Bangor City	H	0-0	
01/11/95	Aberystwyth Town	A	1-1	Hewitt
18/11/95	Holywell Town	H	1-0	Hewitt
25/11/95	Caersws	A	1-2	Mainwaring
02/12/95	Connah's Quay Nomads	H	1-1	Mainwaring
09/12/95	CPD Porthmadog	A	2-0	Wharton, Hewitt
06/01/96	Llansantffraid	H	3-1	Mainwaring, Dyer, Hewitt
10/01/96	Ebbw Vale	A	1-0	Hewitt
13/01/96	Afan Lido	H	0-0	
20/01/96	Caernarfon Town	A	1-3	og (Taylor)
14/02/96	Ton Pentre	A	1-1	Dyer
02/03/96	Fflint Town United	H	4-2	Mainwaring 2 (1p), Hewitt, Wharton
06/03/96	Briton Ferry Athletic	H	2-1	Mainwaring, Dyer
09/03/96	Bangor City	A	0-1	
13/03/96	Llanelli	A	1-1	Mainwaring
20/03/96	Ebbw Vale	H	1-3	Dyer
23/03/96	Holywell Town	A	0-2	
26/03/96	Newtown	A	0-0	
30/03/96	Conwy United	A	3-2	Perrett, Dyer, Mainwaring
06/04/96	Caersws	H	2-1	Mainwaring 2 (1p)
08/04/96	Connah's Quay Nomads	A	1-5	Powell
16/04/96	Inter Cardiff	A	2-0	Copeman, Perrett
20/04/96	CPD Porthmadog	H	0-1	
24/04/96	Ton Pentre	H	2-2	Dyer, Mainwaring
27/04/96	Llansantffraid	A	1-1	Jenkins
28/04/96	Cemaes Bay	H	3-1	Battle, Wharton, Dyer
02/05/96	Barry Town	H	0-0	
04/05/96	Conwy United	H	2-2	Wharton 2
06/05/96	Rhyl	H	1-2	Wharton

EBBW VALE

CLUB DIRECTORY

Ebbw Vale AFC
8 Furnace Street, Ebbw Vale, Gwent NP3 5NP
tel - (01495) 350364
Year of Formation - 1906
Chairman - John Hopkins
Secretary - Nicky Pepper
Manager - John Lewis
Stadium - Eugene Cross Park (18,000)

MAJOR HONOURS
Domestic Cup - (1) 1926.

APPEARANCES 95/96

	P	Ap	(s)	Gls
Gareth ASTLEY	M	12	(7)	
Stephen BAKER	D	4	(5)	
Gary BARRELL	D		(1)	
Andrew BATTLE	M	10	(6)	
George BROWN	D	15	(1)	1
Matthew CABLE	D	34	(1)	1
Jan CEGIELSKI	A	4		1
Ryan CONWAY	M		(1)	
Matthew COOPER	A	3	(4)	1
Neil COOPER	D	12	(4)	
Kevin CREEDEN	G	4		
Mark CROSS	A	16	(9)	3
Lloyd DAVIES	G	1		
Lloyd DAVIES	M	1	(7)	2
Richard DAVIES	M	4		
Michael DICKS	M	28	(1)	1
Andrew DILLON	G	9		
Shane DRAPER	D		(3)	
Gareth EDWARDS	M	2	(10)	1
Craig EVANS	A	11		7
Simon EVANS	D	7	(10)	
Ben GRAHAM	D	23		
Jason GUMMER	M	6	(5)	1
Kyle HOLMES	D	2	(1)	
Andrew JAMES	A	6	(1)	2
John LEWIS	D		(7)	
Kristian LEWIS	D	6	(2)	
Ian MITCHELL	A	1	(1)	1
Steven MORRIS	G	25		
Adrian NEEDS	M	35	(2)	2
Michael PENGELLY	M	31	(4)	4
Nicholas PEPPER	G	1		
Geoffrey POOLE	M	5	(1)	
Lee POWELL	D	18		1
Jason PRICE	M	2	(2)	
Paul SANDERSON (ENG)	A	10	(4)	2
Mark SPENCER	D	3	(2)	
Simon TYLER	A	29	(1)	8
Lee WALKER	D	23	(2)	3
David WEBB	A	8	(1)	4
Ceri WILLIAMS	M	6	(1)	3
Steven WILLIAMS	D	5		2
Sean WOODS	A	1	(3)	
Steven WOODS	A	17	(8)	6

LEAGUE RESULTS 1995/96

19/08/95	Newtown	A	2-1	Webb, og (Hanmer)
26/08/95	Afan Lido	A	1-0	Tyler
30/08/95	Ton Pentre	A	2-1	Sanderson, Tyler
02/09/95	Holywell Town	H	4-1	Sanderson, Webb 2, Tyler
09/09/95	Conwy United	A	0-4	
13/09/95	Llanelli	A	2-0	Webb, Pengelly
16/09/95	Cemaes Bay	H	3-0	Tyler, Pengelly, Needs
23/09/95	Rhyl	A	0-1	
30/09/95	Fflint Town United	A	1-1	Pengelly
07/10/95	Connah's Quay Nomads	H	1-1	Tyler
14/10/95	Holywell Town	A	1-3	Cross
21/10/95	CPD Porthmadog	A	1-3	Cegielski
27/10/95	Inter Cardiff	H	1-1	Dicks
04/11/95	Caernarfon Town	A	0-0	
11/11/95	Llansantffraid	H	0-1	
18/11/95	Caersws	H	3-3	Cross 2, Pengelly
25/11/95	Bangor City	A	2-2	Tyler, James
16/12/95	Caernarfon Town	H	3-2	James, Cable, Woods St.
26/12/95	Barry Town	A	0-1	
10/01/96	Cwmbran Town	H	0-1	
17/01/96	Ton Pentre	H	3-0	Walker, Powell, Woods St.
20/01/96	Cemaes Bay	A	1-2	Williams S.
24/01/96	Aberystwyth Town	A	1-1	Williams S.
03/02/96	Llansantffraid	A	1-0	Evans C.
17/02/96	Fflint Town United	H	1-0	Woods St.
24/02/96	Connah's Quay Nomads	A	1-1	Brown
02/03/96	CPD Porthmadog	H	1-2	Mitchell
05/03/96	Llanelli	H	0-1	
08/03/96	Inter Cardiff	A	0-0	
20/03/96	Cwmbran Town	A	3-1	Evans C., Tyler, Walker
06/04/96	Bangor City	H	1-2	Evans C.
08/04/96	Rhyl	H	3-1	Evans C. 2, Woods St.
10/04/96	Afan Lido	H	2-2	Evans C., Davies L.
13/04/96	Conwy United	H	3-3	Edwards, Walker, Cooper M.
14/04/96	Briton Ferry Athletic	H	4-1	Evans C., Gummer, Davies L., Woods St.
16/04/96	Barry Town	H	0-1	
20/04/96	Briton Ferry Athletic	A	1-3	Tyler
27/04/96	Aberystwyth Town	H	1-2	Williams C.
30/04/96	Newtown	H	1-3	og (Evans J.)
04/05/96	Caersws	A	4-3	Williams C. 2, Woods St., Needs

FFLINT TOWN UNITED

CLUB DIRECTORY

Fflint Town United
45 Bron-y-Wern
Bagillt, Clwyd
tel - (01352) 763571
fax - (01532) 763571
Year of Formation - 1880
Chairman - Alan Baines
Secretary - Glyn Davies
Manager - Steff Rush
Stadium - Cae y Castell (9,000)

MAJOR HONOURS
Domestic Cup - (1) 1954.

APPEARANCES 95/96

	P	Ap	(s)	Gls
James BEVAN	A		(1)	
Andrew DAVIES	M	35	(1)	4
Andrew EDWARDS	A	3		
Darren EMMITT (ENG)	M	22		18
David EVANS (ENG)	D	19	(1)	1
Phillip EVANS	D	2	(10)	
Glen GRAHAM	D	40		4
Neil GRIFFITHS (ENG)	G	22	(1)	
Stephen HARLEY (ENG)	M	2	(2)	
Andrew HIGGINS	M		(1)	
Paul HIGGINS	D		(1)	
Geoffrey HINCHCLIFFE (ENG)	D	6	(7)	1
Phillip HINCHCLIFFE	M	4	(4)	
Darren HORNE	M	32	(4)	7
Gary JONES	D	9		
Simon JONES	D	12	(5)	
Steven JONES (ENG)	A	38	(1)	21
Richard LAUGHTON (ENG)	A	3	(9)	1
Darren MARTIN	M	13	(12)	
Tam McKEE (SCO)	G	7	(6)	
Damien McKEOWN	D	36	(4)	1
Peter McKERTH	M		(1)	
Richard McNEIL (ENG)	A	7	(7)	1
Anthony MEROLA (ENG)	A	1	(4)	3
Gregory MOFFATT	M	5	(3)	
Paul NELSON (ENG)	D		(1)	
Dewi PARRY	D	27	(1)	2
James PIERCE	A		(1)	
Gary POWELL	A	15		6
Andrew RENSHAW	G	1		
Neil SALATHIEL	D	23	(1)	
Christian SMART	D	5	(5)	
Timothy STEEL	M	7	(1)	1
Andrew STRATULIS (ENG)	M		(22)	
Lee WILLIAMS	G	10		
Timothy WILLIAMS	D	10	(1)	3
Kenneth WOODS (ENG)	A	24		

LEAGUE RESULTS 1995/96

19/08/95	Aberystwyth Town	A	4-2	Merola 3, Horne
26/08/95	Cemaes Bay	H	2-1	McKeown, Jones S.
29/08/95	Rhyl	H	0-1	
02/09/95	Caernarfon Town	A	1-1	Graham
09/09/95	Barry Town	H	5-1	Williams T. 2, Jones S., Graham, Steel
12/09/95	Newtown	A	2-0	Graham, Hinchcliffe
16/09/95	Llanelli	A	1-0	Emmitt
23/09/95	Holywell Town	H	1-2	Williams T.
30/09/95	Ebbw Vale	H	1-1	Jones S.
14/10/95	Llansantffraid	A	0-1	
21/10/95	Cwmbran Town	H	1-3	Emmitt
28/10/95	Briton Ferry Athletic	A	2-0	Emmitt, Jones S.
01/11/95	Rhyl	A	1-1	Emmitt
11/11/95	Ton Pentre	A	3-2	Jones S. 2, Horne
18/11/95	Bangor City	H	3-2	Emmitt 3
25/11/95	Inter Cardiff	A	5-0	Jones S., Emmitt 3, McNeil
02/12/95	Caersws	H	1-1	Emmitt
09/12/95	Connah's Quay Nomads	A	3-0	Emmitt 3 (1p)
12/12/95	CPD Porthmadog	H	2-0	Jones S., Horne
16/12/95	Afan Lido	A	3-0	Emmitt 2, Jones S.
23/12/95	Aberystwyth Town	H	4-0	Jones S. 3, Emmitt
02/01/96	Newtown	H	2-1	Emmitt, Graham
06/01/96	Ton Pentre	H	1-1	Jones S.
13/01/96	Llanelli	H	2-1	Jones S. 2
20/01/96	Barry Town	A	1-3	Jones S.
10/02/96	Bangor City	A	2-3	Davies 2 (1p)
17/02/96	Ebbw Vale	A	0-1	
27/02/96	Conwy United	H	2-2	Horne, Parry
02/03/96	Cwmbran Town	A	2-4	Powell 2
09/03/96	Briton Ferry Athletic	H	4-0	Jones S. 3, Evans D.
16/03/96	Holywell Town	A	5-3	og (Spellman), Laughton, Davies 2 (1p), Horne
20/03/96	Cemaes Bay	A	0-3	
23/03/96	Llansantffraid	H	0-5	
06/04/96	Inter Cardiff	H	1-1	Horne
08/04/96	Conwy United	A	1-2	Powell
13/04/96	Caersws	A	4-2	Powell, Jones S. 2, Parry
16/04/96	Caernarfon Town	H	3-2	Powell 2, Horne
27/04/96	CPD Porthmadog	A	1-1	og (Jones G.)
01/05/96	Connah's Quay Nomads	H	0-0	
04/05/96	Afan Lido	H	0-3	

HOLYWELL TOWN

CLUB DIRECTORY

Holywell Town FC
Bryn Awel, Holway Road, Holywell CH8 7NH
tel - (01352) 714216
fax - (01352) 714216
Year of Formation - 1906
Chairman - Emile Moore
Secretary - Carol Hughes
Manager - Mark Jones
Stadium - Halkyn Road (4,000)

APPEARANCES 95/96

	P	Ap	(s)	Gls
Paul ALLEN	D	33	(1)	3
Paul BARKER	A	2	(8)	
Simon BRAMMER	D	5	(3)	1
Simon CARTER (ENG)	D	5		1
Matthew CORCORAN	M	5	(4)	2
Neil DAVIES	A	14		7
Paul DAVIES	D	6		
Darren DONNELLY (ENG)	A	20	(5)	5
Daniel EMBLETON (ENG)	G	20	(1)	
James GRIFFITHS	D	22		3
Andrew HARPER	M	23	(3)	1
Anthony HOGAN	M	4	(2)	
Richard HORNER (ENG)	D	17		1
Stephen HUGHES	M		(1)	
Craig HUTCHINSON (ENG)	M		(1)	
Mark JONES	D	28	(1)	4
Nathan JONES	A	1	(9)	1
Simon JONES	D	3	(5)	
Stuart JONES (ENG)	M	34		1
Thomas JONES	A	16	(3)	6
Craig KNIGHT	D	5		
Edward LANGTON (ENG)	D	31	(1)	1
Martin LITTLEWOOD (ENG)	M	15	(1)	
Edward McCULLAGH (ENG)	A	15	(9)	2
Christopher MILROY	A	26	(5)	5
Andrew NOBLE	A	1	(3)	
Gareth OWEN	A	1	(6)	
Dyfed PARRY	A		(1)	
John PARRY	D	2	(2)	
Richard POWELL	A		(1)	
Andrew PRITCHARD	D	20	(7)	
David RICHARDSON (ENG)	M	17	(1)	1
Richard SIM	G	17	(8)	
Richard SIM	D	1	(1)	
Peter SPELLMAN (ENG)	D	10	(4)	
David TAYLOR	A	6	(4)	5
Malcolm TIDSWELL	D	6	(3)	
Jason TURNER	G	3	(4)	
Andrew WAGSTAFFE (ENG)	M		(1)	
Mark WILLIAMS (ENG)	D	6		

LEAGUE RESULTS 1995/96

19/08/95	Llansantffraid	H	2-1	Davies N., Allen
26/08/95	Inter Cardiff	H	2-3	Taylor, Jones S.
29/08/95	Caersws	A	3-5	Taylor 2, og (Griffiths A.)
02/09/95	Ebbw Vale	A	1-4	Davies N.
08/09/95	Connah's Quay Nomads	A	4-1	Davies N., Griffiths, Carter, Donnelly
12/09/95	CPD Porthmadog	H	1-0	Brammer
23/09/95	Fflint Town United	A	2-1	Langton, Griffiths
30/09/95	Caernarfon Town	A	1-1	Harper
07/10/95	Llanelli	H	4-2	Corcoran, Davies N. 2, Griffiths
14/10/95	Ebbw Vale	H	3-1	Milroy 3 (1p)
21/10/95	Afan Lido	A	0-2	
28/10/95	Ton Pentre	H	1-1	Jones M.
31/10/95	Caersws	H	3-4	Corcoran, Davies N., Jones M.
11/11/95	Conwy United	H	1-1	og (Jones Ste.)
18/11/95	Cwmbran Town	A	0-1	
25/11/95	Aberystwyth Town	H	2-1	Davies N., Donnelly
02/12/95	Cemaes Bay	A	1-4	Jones N.
09/12/95	Barry Town	H	0-2	
12/12/95	Rhyl	A	1-1	Richardson
16/12/95	Briton Ferry Athletic	H	2-2	Taylor 2
06/01/96	Newtown	H	0-3	
10/01/96	CPD Porthmadog	A	0-2	
16/01/96	Bangor City	A	1-2	Allen
19/01/96	Connah's Quay Nomads	H	1-3	og (Carroll)
27/01/96	Newtown	A	0-2	
03/02/96	Conwy United	A	1-1	McCullagh
17/02/96	Inter Cardiff	A	3-0	Jones T. 3
02/03/96	Afan Lido	H	2-0	Milroy (p), Jones T.
09/03/96	Ton Pentre	A	0-2	
16/03/96	Fflint Town United	H	3-5	Milroy, Jones T., Donnelly
23/03/96	Cwmbran Town	H	2-0	Jones M., Jones T.
30/03/96	Llansantffraid	A	0-3	
06/04/96	Aberystwyth Town	A	2-1	Donnelly, Horner
08/04/96	Bangor City	H	0-1	
10/04/96	Caernarfon Town	H	1-2	Allen
13/04/96	Cemaes Bay	H	2-1	Donnelly, McCullagh
20/04/96	Barry Town	A	0-4	
30/04/96	Rhyl	H	0-1	
04/05/96	Briton Ferry Athletic	A	0-2	
06/05/96	Llanelli	A	1-1	Jones M.

INTER CARDIFF

CLUB DIRECTORY

Inter Cardiff FC (now - Inter Cabletel AFC)
48 Radyr Court Close
Llandaff, Cardiff CF5 2QG
tel - (01222) 552679
fax - (01222) 552679
Year of Formation - 1990
Chairman - Max James
Secretary - Colin Hicks
Manager - George Wood
Stadium - Leckwith (4,000)

APPEARANCES 95/96

	P	Ap	(s)	Gls
Paul BIDDESCOMBE (ENG)	D	5	(1)	1
Darren BODENHAM	D	5	(3)	
Terrence BOYLE	D	37		1
Robert CALDWELL	D	19	(12)	3
Peter CHEESEMAN	A	9	(7)	1
Neil COOPER	D	18	(2)	2
James DIBBLE	M	1	(2)	
Mark EVANS	D	5	(3)	
Francis FORD	A	6	(2)	2
Ashley GRIFFITHS	D	29		
Nathan JOHNSON	A	26	(8)	13
Ian JONES	A	4	(12)	3
Shane JONES	D	3	(4)	1
Paul KRAZIZKY	M	1	(4)	
Wayne MORGAN	M	3	(5)	
Jamie MURRAY	M	27	(8)	2
Frank NUTTALL (SCO)	D	12		
Patrick O'HAGAN	G	19	(1)	
David PAGE	D		(2)	
Robert PAINTER	A	10	(4)	1
Raymond PENNOCK	A	17	(4)	12
Dean PHILPOTT	D	11	(3)	
Lee PRICE	M	19		2
Jason ROBERTS	M	12	(1)	
Paul STEPHENS	M	4		
Paul SUGRUE (ENG)	A		(6)	
Kenneth SYMONDS	D	4	(4)	
Jason THOMAS	M	12	(1)	1
Dean THRELFALL	A	17	(3)	12
Adrian TUCKER	G	14	(2)	
David WARE	D	28	(5)	1
Russell WIGLEY	D	31		1
Richard WILLIAMS	M	19	(4)	2
Paul WIMBLETON (ENG)	M	6		
George WOOD (SCO)	G	7	(5)	

LEAGUE RESULTS 1995/96

19/08/95	Conwy United	A	0-1	
26/08/95	Holywell Town	A	3-2	Pennock 2, Painter
29/08/95	Llanelli	H	3-3	Jones I., Pennock, Jones S.
02/09/95	Afan Lido	A	0-2	
09/09/95	Rhyl	H	4-1	Ford 2, Pennock 2
13/09/95	Ton Pentre	A	1-1	Pennock
16/09/95	Aberystwyth Town	A	0-1	
23/09/95	Cemaes Bay	H	5-2	Pennock 2, Caldwell, Johnson 2
30/09/95	Cwmbran Town	A	0-3	
07/10/95	CPD Porthmadog	H	3-0	Johnson 2, Caldwell
21/10/95	Llansantffraid	H	1-1	Pennock
27/10/95	Ebbw Vale	A	1-1	Pennock (p)
01/11/95	Llanelli	A	1-0	Pennock
11/11/95	Caersws	H	3-1	Johnson, Williams, Pennock
18/11/95	Connah's Quay Nomads	A	1-3	Murray
25/11/95	Fflint Town United	H	0-5	
02/12/95	Bangor City	A	1-2	Jones I.
09/12/95	Caernarfon Town	A	1-3	Jones I.
23/12/95	Conwy United	H	2-1	Boyle, Biddescombe
01/01/96	Ton Pentre	H	4-0	Johnson, Threlfall 2, Murray
05/01/96	Barry Town	H	0-0	
13/01/96	Cemaes Bay	A	2-1	Threlfall 2
20/01/96	Rhyl	A	2-3	Threlfall, Johnson
07/02/96	Briton Ferry Athletic	A	1-1	Johnson
13/02/96	Afan Lido	H	2-0	Cooper, Johnson
17/02/96	Holywell Town	H	0-3	
24/02/96	CPD Porthmadog	A	1-1	Ware
02/03/96	Llansantffraid	A	2-3	Caldwell, Price
08/03/96	Ebbw Vale	H	0-0	
19/03/96	Barry Town	A	1-2	Johnson
26/03/96	Aberystwyth Town	H	2-0	Cheeseman, Williams
30/03/96	Newtown	H	2-2	og (Brown), Wigley
06/04/96	Fflint Town United	A	1-1	Threlfall
10/04/96	Briton Ferry Athletic	H	2-1	Threlfall 2
16/04/96	Cwmbran Town	H	0-2	
20/04/96	Connah's Quay Nomads	H	2-1	Threlfall 2
21/04/96	Caernarfon Town	H	2-2	Johnson 2
27/04/96	Bangor City	H	4-2	Price, Threlfall, Cooper, Johnson
30/04/96	Caersws	A	2-2	Threlfall, Thomas
04/05/96	Newtown	A	0-2	

LLANELLI

CLUB DIRECTORY

Llanelli AFC
29 Pemberton Park
Llanelli
Dyfed SA14 8NN
tel - (01554) 756176
fax - (01554) 751958
Year of Formation - 1896
Chairman - John James
Secretary - Roger Davies
Manager - Gilbert Lloyd
Stadium - Stebonheath Park (3,700)

APPEARANCES 95/96

	P	Ap	(s)	Gls
Marvin ARTHUR	D	23	(13)	
Darren BLACK	M	3	(2)	
Jason CHAPMAN	G		(1)	
Philip DAVIDSON	M	39	(1)	10
Gregory DAVIES	D	33	(6)	1
Mark DAVIES	D	14	(1)	1
Nathan DAVIES	D	13	(16)	
Simon DAVIES	M	10	(6)	
Darren DICKESON	D	2	(2)	
Mark DICKESON	A	8		1
Andrew EVANS	D	25	(4)	
Aneurin EVANS	A	16	(1)	4
Mark EVANS	A	27		3
Stephen EVANS	D	35	(2)	1
Paul FOWLER	A	8	(1)	1
Robert JAMES	M	34	(1)	1
Matthew JENKINS	M	4	(3)	
Jamie MANSEL	A		(10)	
Gareth MORGAN	M		(7)	
Steven MYERS	M	36		4
Leigh RANDALL	M	24	(2)	2
Alan ROBERTS	A	4	(12)	1
Antony SMOLKA	A	39	(1)	18
Richard THOMAS	G	40		
Stephen THOMAS	M		(4)	
Ian WALDIE (SCO)	A		(1)	
Neil WILLIAMS	A		(4)	
Stephen WILLIAMS	D	3	(3)	

LEAGUE RESULTS 1995/96

19/08/95	CPD Porthmadog	H	1-4	Smolka
26/08/95	Connah's Quay Nomads	A	1-3	Fowler
29/08/95	Inter Cardiff	A	3-3	Randall, Myers, Smolka
02/09/95	Llansantffraid	H	0-1	
09/09/95	Caersws	A	0-4	
13/09/95	Ebbw Vale	H	0-2	
16/09/95	Fflint Town United	H	0-1	
23/09/95	Cwmbran Town	A	3-2	Davidson 2, Smolka
30/09/95	Aberystwyth Town	H	4-2	Davidson, Smolka 2, Evans Ane.
07/10/95	Holywell Town	A	2-4	Smolka, Roberts
21/10/95	Briton Ferry Athletic	H	2-3	Evans Ane., Smolka
28/10/95	Conwy United	A	0-2	
01/11/95	Inter Cardiff	H	0-1	
10/11/95	Afan Lido	A	2-3	Davidson, Dickeson M.
18/11/95	Ton Pentre	H	1-2	Smolka
25/11/95	Barry Town	H	0-5	
02/12/95	Rhyl	A	1-1	Smolka
09/12/95	Newtown	H	3-3	Smolka, Myers, Davidson (p)
16/12/95	Bangor City	H	1-3	og (Lewis)
23/12/95	CPD Porthmadog	A	1-4	Evans M.
06/01/96	Caernarfon Town	H	2-2	Evans M., Smolka
13/01/96	Fflint Town United	A	1-2	Evans S.
20/01/96	Caersws	H	3-1	og (Andrews), Davidson 2
03/02/96	Afan Lido	H	4-0	James, Evans Ane. 2, Smolka
17/02/96	Aberystwyth Town	A	2-2	Davidson (p), Evans M.
01/03/96	Briton Ferry Athletic	A	0-5	
05/03/96	Ebbw Vale	A	1-0	Davies G.
09/03/96	Conwy United	H	2-4	Myers, Davidson
13/03/96	Cwmbran Town	H	1-1	Davies M.
16/03/96	Connah's Quay Nomads	H	2-0	Randall, Smolka
20/03/96	Ton Pentre	A	0-0	
23/03/96	Caernarfon Town	A	0-4	
30/03/96	Cemaes Bay	A	0-2	
06/04/96	Barry Town	A	0-3	
08/04/96	Llansantffraid	A	2-0	Smolka, Myers
13/04/96	Rhyl	H	2-2	Davidson, Smolka
20/04/96	Newtown	A	0-2	
27/04/96	Cemaes Bay	H	2-0	Smolka 2
04/05/96	Bangor City	A	0-4	
06/05/96	Holywell Town	H	1-1	Smolka

LLANSANTFFRAID

CLUB DIRECTORY

Llansantffraid FC
5 Maes-y-Garreg
Llansantffraid
Powys SY22 6BD
tel - (01691) 828535
fax - (01691) 828441
Year of Formation - 1959
Chairman - Edgar Jones
Secretary - Tony Williams
Manager - Graham Breeze
Stadium - Recreation Field (2,000)

MAJOR HONOURS
Domestic Cup - (1) 1996.

APPEARANCES 95/96

	P	Ap	(s)	Gls
Simon ABERCROMBIE (ENG)	A	29		6
Mark BAKER	D	3	(4)	
Darren BARRETT (ENG)	M	7	(18)	3
Michael BROWN	D	19	(12)	
Alan CLARKE (ENG)	D		(5)	
Ian CLARKE (ENG)	M	11	(7)	
Gary CURTISS (ENG)	D	39		2
James DAVIES	A	1	(2)	
Gary EVANS	M	35		2
Ian EVANS	M	31	(2)	6
Keith FAIRHURST (ENG)	G		(3)	
Vaughan HARDING	M		(1)	
Anthony HENRY (ENG)	D	19	(1)	6
Craig HUTCHINSON (ENG)	D	3	(4)	
Adrian JONES	M	17		8
Arwel JONES	D	15		1
Gary JONES	D	36	(1)	1
Griffith JONES	M		(1)	
Stephen JONES (ENG)	D	1		
Carlton LEONARD (ENG)	D	2	(4)	
Gary LEWIS	M		(1)	
Thomas MORGAN	A	37	(2)	17
Andrew MULLINER	G	40		
David NORMAN	D	4		
Timothy NUNNERLEY (ENG)	A	9	(7)	6
Neil O'BRIEN	M	2		
Kevin O'NEILL (ENG)	A	1	(3)	
Sean RYDER	D	10	(7)	1
Andrew TAYLOR (ENG)	D	2		
Andrew WATKINS	A		(1)	
Michael WATT (ENG)	D	18	(7)	1
Christopher WHELAN (ENG)	A	13	(20)	1
John WHELAN (ENG)	D	36	(2)	3

LEAGUE RESULTS 1995/96

Date	Opponent	H/A	Score	Scorers
19/08/95	Holywell Town	A	1-2	Evans I.
26/08/95	Ton Pentre	H	1-1	Morgan
29/08/95	Conwy United	H	2-5	Morgan 2
02/09/95	Llanelli	A	1-0	Morgan
09/09/95	Afan Lido	H	1-2	Jones G.
13/09/95	Caernarfon Town	A	3-3	Morgan 2, Nunnerley
16/09/95	Newtown	A	0-3	
23/09/95	Aberystwyth Town	H	3-1	Nunnerley 2, Abercrombie
29/09/95	Caersws	A	7-0	Henry 3 (2p), Nunnerley, Abercrombie, Morgan, Ryder
07/10/95	Bangor City	H	0-2	
14/10/95	Fflint Town United	H	1-0	Abercrombie
21/10/95	Inter Cardiff	A	1-1	Morgan
28/10/95	Connah's Quay Nomads	H	1-2	Henry (p)
01/11/95	Conwy United	A	2-2	Morgan, Evans G.
11/11/95	Ebbw Vale	A	1-0	og (Cable)
18/11/95	CPD Porthmadog	H	0-3	
02/12/95	Briton Ferry Athletic	A	1-2	Morgan
09/12/95	Cemaes Bay	H	5-0	Henry (p), Abercrombie, Whelan C., Morgan, Whelan J.
06/01/96	Cwmbran Town	A	1-3	Morgan
13/01/96	Aberystwyth Town	A	2-2	Barrett, Henry
20/01/96	Afan Lido	A	1-0	Evans I.
03/02/96	Ebbw Vale	H	0-1	
20/02/96	Rhyl	A	0-3	
24/02/96	Bangor City	A	1-2	Morgan
27/02/96	Barry Town	H	1-1	Jones Ad.
02/03/96	Inter Cardiff	H	3-2	Evans I., Jones Ad. 2
05/03/96	Caernarfon Town	H	1-3	Jones Ad.
09/03/96	Connah's Quay Nomads	A	0-0	
19/03/96	Briton Ferry Athletic	H	3-1	Abercrombie, Jones Ad., Morgan
23/03/96	Fflint Town United	A	5-0	Abercrombie, Evans I. 2, Whelan J. 2
27/03/96	CPD Porthmadog	A	1-1	Jones Ad. (p)
30/03/96	Holywell Town	H	3-0	Watt, Morgan, Barrett
06/04/96	Newtown	H	1-0	Curtiss
08/04/96	Llanelli	H	0-2	
16/04/96	Caersws	H	4-1	Evans G., Jones Ad., Curtiss, Nunnerley
20/04/96	Cemaes Bay	A	0-0	
27/04/96	Cwmbran Town	H	1-1	Jones Ad.
30/04/96	Barry Town	A	1-2	Barrett
04/05/96	Rhyl	H	5-1	og (Smith), Evans I., Morgan 2, Nunnerley
06/05/96	Ton Pentre	A	1-2	Jones Ar.

NEWTOWN

CLUB DIRECTORY

Newtown AFC
13 Brynwood Drive
Newtown
Powys SY16
tel - (01686) 628089
fax - (01686) 623813
Year of Formation - 1875
Chairman - Keith Harding
Secretary - Shirley Reynolds
Manager - Brian Coyne & J. King
Stadium - Latham Park (5,000)

MAJOR HONOURS
Domestic Cup - (2) 1879, 1895.

APPEARANCES 95/96

	P	Ap	(s)	Gls
Michael BARTON	G	26		
Matthew BOSWELL (ENG)	G	6	(6)	
Romilly BROWN	A	38	(1)	1
Hugh CLARKE	A	4		
Brian COYNE (SCO)	M		(1)	
Michael DURBRIDGE	A		(2)	
Jason EVANS (ENG)	D	16	(7)	
Martin EVANS	D	20	(5)	1
Gary HAMAN	G	3		
Gareth HANMER (ENG)	D	40		1
Stephen HANMER (ENG)	M	2	(14)	
Keith HOLMANS (ENG)	M	28	(1)	13
Gareth JONES	A	3	(1)	
Richard JONES	A	6	(14)	
John MORRIS	D		(4)	
Richard PIKE (ENG)	M	37	(2)	4
Nigel PRYCE	M	38	(1)	15
Colin REYNOLDS	M	39		12
Christopher ROBERTS	A		(5)	
Marc ROBERTS	M	35	(3)	2
Lee ROBINSON	M		(7)	
David TAYLOR (ENG)	A	3	(13)	3
Mark THOMAS	D	13	(19)	
Anthony TOLLEY (ENG)	G	5		
Justin WICKHAM (ENG)	A	5	(5)	
Peter WILDING (ENG)	D	38		1
Mark WILLIAMS	A	35	(1)	16

LEAGUE RESULTS 1995/96

Date	Opponent		Score	Scorers
19/08/95	Ebbw Vale	H	1-2	Pryce
26/08/95	Rhyl	A	1-0	Pryce
28/08/95	Briton Ferry Athletic	A	1-0	Reynolds
09/09/95	Bangor City	A	1-1	Hanmer G.
12/09/95	Fflint Town United	H	0-2	
16/09/95	Llansantffraid	H	3-0	Pryce 2, Reynolds
23/09/95	Caersws	A	2-0	Pryce, Pike (p)
30/09/95	Rhyl	H	2-0	Holmans 2
14/10/95	Cwmbran Town	A	2-1	Williams, Reynolds
21/10/95	Cemaes Bay	H	3-0	Reynolds 2, Williams
28/10/95	Barry Town	A	0-2	
11/11/95	Caernarfon Town	A	1-0	Brown
18/11/95	Aberystwyth Town	H	1-1	Pryce
25/11/95	Afan Lido	A	0-0	
02/12/95	CPD Porthmadog	H	0-1	
09/12/95	Llanelli	A	3-3	Holmans 2, Pryce
02/01/96	Fflint Town United	A	1-2	Taylor (p)
06/01/96	Holywell Town	A	3-0	Reynolds, Holmans, Pryce
13/01/96	Caersws	H	4-0	Williams 3, Holmans
20/01/96	Bangor City	H	2-1	Williams, Pryce
27/01/96	Holywell Town	H	2-0	Taylor, Pryce
03/02/96	Caernarfon Town	H	0-0	
10/02/96	Aberystwyth Town	A	4-1	Williams, Holmans, Wilding, Reynolds
17/02/96	Afan Lido	H	1-0	Williams
24/02/96	Ton Pentre	H	3-0	Williams, Holmans, Reynolds (p)
02/03/96	Cemaes Bay	A	4-2	Reynolds 2, Holmans, Roberts M.
05/03/96	Connah's Quay Nomads	H	0-0	
09/03/96	Barry Town	H	0-0	
16/03/96	Ton Pentre	A	1-1	Williams
26/03/96	Cwmbran Town	H	0-0	
30/03/96	Inter Cardiff	A	2-2	Reynolds (p), Pike
02/04/96	Conwy United	H	3-0	Pryce 2, Pike
06/04/96	Llansantffraid	A	0-1	
13/04/96	Connah's Quay Nomads	A	2-0	Pryce, Holmans
20/04/96	Llanelli	H	2-0	Williams, Taylor
23/04/96	Briton Ferry Athletic	H	3-0	Williams, Roberts M., Evans M.
27/04/96	Conwy United	A	1-1	Holmans
30/04/96	Ebbw Vale	A	3-1	Holmans 2, Pike
04/05/96	Inter Cardiff	H	2-0	Pryce, Reynolds
06/05/96	CPD Porthmadog	A	5-0	Williams 4, Pryce

CPD PORTHMADOG

CLUB DIRECTORY

CPD Porthmadog
Llwyn yr Eryr
Ynys, Criccieth
tel - (01766) 810349
fax - (01766) 514687
Year of Formation - 1884
Chairman - Bob Havelock
Secretary - R.I. Griffiths
Manager - Colin Hawkins
Stadium - Y Traeth (4,000)

APPEARANCES 95/96

	P	Ap	(s)	Gls
Adrian ADAMS	M	5	(18)	2
Chris BANKS	M	40		3
Nigel BARRY	M	29	(1)	2
Michael DAVIES	A	36		11
David EVANS	M	32	(5)	1
Simon FLOWER	D	20	(3)	1
Michael FOSTER	D	36	(1)	
Dylan HARRISON	A	1	(3)	
Lee HAWKINS (ENG)	A		(2)	
David HUGHES	M		(2)	
Gareth HUGHES	G	34		
Richard HUGHES	D	17		1
Martin JOLLEY	D		(5)	
Adrian JONES	M	2	(14)	
Geraint JONES	D	35		3
John JONES	A		(1)	
Kevin JONES	M		(10)	1
Richard JONES	D	8		
Cai LLOYD-WILLIAMS	A	3	(2)	1
Paul MAGUIRE (ENG)	M	13	(1)	4
Peter McCANN (ENG)	D	1	(2)	
Adrian OWEN	A	1	(3)	
Aled OWEN	M		(1)	
Anthony OWEN	M	17	(16)	
Stephen OWEN	M	11	(2)	1
Paul ROBERTS	A		(9)	1
Gethyn ROBYNS	G	2	(2)	
Colin SAYNOR	D	36	(1)	5
Nigel SMITH	A		(1)	
Jackie WELSH	M	5		
Paul WHELAN	M	34	(3)	15
Merfyn WILLIAMS	G	4		
Robert WILLIAMS	A	18	(10)	4

LEAGUE RESULTS 1995/96

19/08/95	Llanelli	A	4-1	Whelan, Evans, Jones K., Jones G.
26/08/95	Conwy United	H	1-2	Maguire
02/09/95	Aberystwyth Town	A	1-4	Whelan
09/09/95	Ton Pentre	H	3-3	Maguire 2, Owen S.
12/09/95	Holywell Town	A	0-1	
16/09/95	Barry Town	A	1-4	Maguire
23/09/95	Caernarfon Town	H	1-2	Saynor
30/09/95	Afan Lido	H	3-1	Lloyd-Williams, Davies, Jones G. (p)
07/10/95	Inter Cardiff	A	0-3	
21/10/95	Ebbw Vale	H	3-1	Banks, Davies, Adams
28/10/95	Caersws	A	1-4	Adams
01/11/95	Cemaes Bay	A	1-2	Davies
11/11/95	Connah's Quay Nomads	H	1-1	Davies
18/11/95	Llansantffraid	A	3-0	Barry, Jones G. (p), Whelan
25/11/95	Briton Ferry Athletic	H	1-2	Whelan
02/12/95	Newtown	A	1-0	Davies
09/12/95	Cwmbran Town	H	0-2	
12/12/95	Fflint Town United	A	0-2	
23/12/95	Llanelli	H	4-1	Davies 3, Barry
06/01/96	Bangor City	H	4-1	Saynor 2, Whelan, Hughes R.
10/01/96	Holywell Town	H	2-0	Whelan 2
13/01/96	Caernarfon Town	A	2-2	Whelan, Davies
17/01/96	Rhyl	H	0-0	
20/01/96	Ton Pentre	A	1-1	Whelan
24/01/96	Conwy United	A	0-1	
03/02/96	Connah's Quay Nomads	A	1-1	Whelan
24/02/96	Inter Cardiff	H	1-1	Banks
02/03/96	Ebbw Vale	A	2-1	Davies, Whelan
06/03/96	Aberystwyth Town	H	1-0	Saynor
09/03/96	Caersws	H	1-1	Williams R.
16/03/96	Rhyl	A	1-0	Flower
19/03/96	Bangor City	A	1-1	Whelan
23/03/96	Barry Town	H	2-3	Whelan, Roberts
27/03/96	Llansantffraid	H	1-1	Williams R.
06/04/96	Briton Ferry Athletic	A	1-5	Saynor
08/04/96	Cemaes Bay	H	4-0	Whelan 2, Williams R., Davies
13/04/96	Afan Lido	A	0-1	
20/04/96	Cwmbran Town	A	1-0	Williams R.
27/04/96	Fflint Town United	H	1-1	Banks
06/05/96	Newtown	H	0-5	

RHYL

CLUB DIRECTORY

Rhyl FC
Shalom, Rhes-y-cau, Holywell, Clwyd CH8 8JQ
tel - (01352) 780049
Year of Formation - 1883
Chairman - J. Tinson
Secretary - D. Johnson
Manager - Mark Ferguson
Stadium - Belle Vue (4,000)

MAJOR HONOURS

Domestic Cup - (2) 1952, 1953.

APPEARANCES 95/96

	P	Ap	(s)	Gls
David BARBOUR (ENG)	D	10	(6)	1
Allan BICKERSTAFF	D	17		1
Steven BOWEN	M	1	(1)	
David BRETT (ENG)	M	2		
Richard CUNNINGHAM	M	6		1
Timothy EDWARDS	D	7		
Christopher ESPLEY	D	5	(2)	
Neil FOSTER	M	37	(1)	5
Ian GRIMES	D	14		
Jonathan GURNEY	D		(3)	
Ian HAIGH (ENG)	G	21	(1)	
Phillip HINCHCLIFFE	M	12		
James HOLYWELL (ENG)	D	1	(2)	
Adrian JONES	A	21		3
Justin JONES	A	11	(7)	4
Lee JONES	A	7	(6)	3
Simon JONES	D	2	(1)	
Tony LEE (ENG)	A	16	(2)	2
Paul LEECE	M	1	(9)	
Ian McMULLEN (ENG)	M	12	(1)	4
Mathew McQUILLAN (ENG)	D	2		
Anthony MEROLA (ENG)	A	12	(5)	1
Scott MILLINGTON (ENG)	M	33	(2)	6
Scott MILLINGTON (ENG)	G	1		
Stephen MORGAN (ENG)	D	2		1
Paul MULLEN (ENG)	M	2	(2)	
Thomas MURPHY (ENG)	A	5	(7)	2
Simon NEVITT	D	21	(4)	1
Matthew OWEN (ENG)	A	2	(2)	1
Steven OWEN (ENG)	A	2		
Phillip OWENS	M	9	(3)	
Jason O'NEILL (ENG)	M	4	(5)	
Carl PICKTHALL	D	11	(3)	
Stuart PICKTHALL	D	16	(2)	
Gary POWELL	A	23	(1)	5
Barry ROBERTS	D	4	(5)	
David ROBERTS	D	14	(1)	
Steven ROBERTS	A	12	(1)	5
Paul SALISBURY	A		(2)	
Christian SMART	D	26		
James SMITH	D	8	(7)	
Leighton SUMNER	M	7	(8)	
Elliott SUTTON (ENG)	A	2		1
Andrew THOMAS	A		(1)	
Jason TURNER	G	2	(1)	
Anthony WALSH	G	16		
Stephen WARING	D	1	(2)	
John WATSON (ENG)	M		(1)	

LEAGUE RESULTS 1995/96

19/08/95	Bangor City	H	0-3	
26/08/95	Newtown	H	0-1	
29/08/95	Fflint Town United	A	1-0	Owen M.
02/09/95	Cwmbran Town	H	2-2	Lee, McMullen
09/09/95	Inter Cardiff	A	1-4	Powell
16/09/95	Connah's Quay Nomads	H	1-1	McMullen
23/09/95	Ebbw Vale	H	1-0	McMullen (p)
30/09/95	Newtown	A	0-2	
07/10/95	Caersws	H	1-2	Barbour
21/10/95	Aberystwyth Town	A	2-1	Millington, Powell
28/10/95	Caernarfon Town	H	1-5	Lee
01/11/95	Fflint Town United	H	1-1	Millington
11/11/95	Cemaes Bay	H	3-0	Millington, Powell, Murphy
18/11/95	Barry Town	A	0-4	
25/11/95	Conwy United	A	2-7	Foster 2
02/12/95	Llanelli	H	1-1	McMullen (p)
12/12/95	Holywell Town	H	1-1	Foster
16/12/95	Caersws	A	2-4	Merola, Powell
23/12/95	Bangor City	A	1-3	Jones A.
06/01/96	Afan Lido	A	3-2	Powell, Murphy, Jones A.
13/01/96	Ton Pentre	H	0-2	
17/01/96	CPD Porthmadog	A	0-0	
20/01/96	Inter Cardiff	H	3-2	Foster, Jones A., Jones J.
03/02/96	Cemaes Bay	A	1-2	Roberts S.
17/02/96	Caernarfon Town	A	1-8	Roberts S.
20/02/96	Llansantffraid	H	3-0	Morgan, Sutton, Roberts S.
24/02/96	Briton Ferry Athletic	A	1-1	Cunningham
02/03/96	Aberystwyth Town	H	1-2	Millington
16/03/96	CPD Porthmadog	H	0-1	
19/03/96	Connah's Quay Nomads	A	1-2	Roberts S.
23/03/96	Afan Lido	H	1-0	Millington
30/03/96	Briton Ferry Athletic	H	2-1	Foster, Jones J.
06/04/96	Conwy United	H	0-1	
08/04/96	Ebbw Vale	A	1-3	Nevitt
13/04/96	Llanelli	A	2-2	Bickerstaff, Roberts S.
20/04/96	Ton Pentre	A	1-1	Jones J.
27/04/96	Barry Town	H	1-5	Jones L.
30/04/96	Holywell Town	A	1-0	Jones L.
04/05/96	Llansantffraid	A	1-5	Millington
06/05/96	Cwmbran Town	A	2-1	Jones L., Jones J

TON PENTRE

CLUB DIRECTORY

Ton Pentre AFC
37 Bailey Street
Ton Pentre
Rhondda CF41 7EN
tel - (01443) 438281
Year of Formation - 1935
Chairman - Jeff Orrells
Secretary - Paul Willoughby
Manager - John Emanuel
Stadium - Ynys Park (2,700)

APPEARANCES 95/96

	P	Ap	(s)	Gls
Graham BASSETT	M		(7)	
James BLACKIE	D	40		
Kevin BOUNDS	A	2		
Phillip BOWDEN	D	18	(5)	
Paul CLEMENTS	D	33		2
Brett DAVEY	A	2	(1)	
Mark DAVIES	M	16		2
Martin ELLACOTT (ENG)	G	20		
Mark EVANS	D	7	(1)	1
Brian GIBSON	M	17	(5)	2
Paul GODDARD	A	1	(1)	
David GRIFFITHS	D	6	(12)	
Brian GULLETT	D	8	(2)	
Richard HAIG	A	27	(2)	10
Andrew HEDDITCH	D	17	(11)	1
Andrew JAMES	A		(2)	
David JONES	A	9	(3)	
Ian JONES	A	4	(2)	1
Phillip JONES	A		(2)	
Phillip McNEILL	M	16	(5)	
Ricky MORRIS	M	10	(8)	
Mark PARRY	A	12		2
Christopher RICHARDS	G	16	(2)	
Kevin RICHARDS	M	36		1
Jason ROBERTS	M	24	(1)	3
Wayne SAVAGE	A	3	(4)	
Gary SHEPPARD	A	19	(7)	4
Christopher SIER	D	4		
Christopher SUMMERS	A	6	(2)	1
Lee TAPPER	M		(12)	
Adrian TUCKER	G	4		
Brandon WALTERS	M	1	(2)	
Jason WATKINS	M	33	(6)	1
John WILE	M	29	(9)	13

LEAGUE RESULTS 1995/96

19/08/95	Caersws	H	1-3	Davies M.
26/08/95	Llansantffraid	A	1-1	Haig
30/08/95	Ebbw Vale	H	1-2	Wile
02/09/95	Connah's Quay Nomads	H	0-1	
09/09/95	CPD Porthmadog	A	3-3	Summers, Evans, Wile
13/09/95	Inter Cardiff	H	1-1	og (Roberts)
16/09/95	Bangor City	H	3-2	Richards K., Gibson (p), Wile
23/09/95	Briton Ferry Athletic	A	2-1	Clements, Wile
14/10/95	Bangor City	A	0-2	
17/10/95	Afan Lido	A	2-0	Haig, Wile
21/10/95	Conwy United	H	1-3	Wile (p)
28/10/95	Holywell Town	A	1-1	Davies M.
11/11/95	Fflint Town United	H	2-3	Wile, Haig
18/11/95	Llanelli	A	2-1	Haig, Wile
25/11/95	Cemaes Bay	H	2-0	Wile, Sheppard
02/12/95	Caernarfon Town	A	0-2	
12/12/95	Barry Town	A	0-2	
01/01/96	Inter Cardiff	A	0-4	
06/01/96	Fflint Town United	A	1-1	Jones I.
13/01/96	Rhyl	A	2-0	Gibson (p), Haig
17/01/96	Ebbw Vale	A	0-3	
20/01/96	CPD Porthmadog	H	1-1	Clements
14/02/96	Cwmbran Town	H	1-1	Haig
17/02/96	Caersws	A	2-2	og (Griffiths D.), Sheppard
24/02/96	Newtown	A	0-3	
28/02/96	Afan Lido	H	0-0	
02/03/96	Conwy United	A	2-2	Haig, Wile
09/03/96	Holywell Town	H	2-0	Parry, Haig
16/03/96	Newtown	H	1-1	Parry
20/03/96	Llanelli	H	0-0	
23/03/96	Briton Ferry Athletic	H	2-2	Wile, Sheppard
30/03/96	Connah's Quay Nomads	A	1-1	Roberts
03/04/96	Aberystwyth Town	H	1-2	Roberts
06/04/96	Cemaes Bay	A	0-3	
08/04/96	Barry Town	H	1-2	Wile (p)
13/04/96	Caernarfon Town	H	2-3	Wile, Roberts
20/04/96	Rhyl	H	1-1	Watkins
24/04/96	Cwmbran Town	A	2-2	Sheppard, Hedditch
04/05/96	Aberystwyth Town	A	0-2	
06/05/96	Llansantffraid	H	2-1	Haig 2

PROMOTED CLUBS

SECOND DIVISION FINAL TABLES 95/96

NORTH (P.A. ROWLANDS CYMRU ALLIANCE)

		Pd	W	D	L	F	A	Pt	GD
1	Oswestry Town	36	25	3	8	84	41	78	+43
2	**Welshpool**	**36**	**23**	**7**	**6**	**83**	**40**	**76**	**+43**
3	Brymbo	36	23	4	9	81	57	73	+24
4	Llandudno	36	21	9	6	94	42	72	+52
5	Rhydymwyn	36	21	8	7	73	40	71	+33
6	Rhayader Town	36	20	5	11	66	44	65	+22
7	Penryncoch	35	18	10	7	74	45	64	+29
8	Cefn Druids	36	19	4	13	82	57	61	+25
9	Lex XI Wrexham	36	18	4	14	67	49	58	+18
10	Penycae	36	13	8	15	58	71	47	-13
11	Llandrinod Wells	36	11	11	14	50	58	44	-8
12	Mostyn	36	13	4	19	78	78	43	=
13	Knighton Town	36	11	2	23	52	83	35	-31
14	Mold Alexandra	36	10	6	20	61	90	33	-29
15	Ruthin Town	36	9	6	21	42	71	33	-29
16	Rhos Aelwyd	35	10	5	20	47	74	32	-27
17	Llanidloes Town	36	8	5	23	34	70	29	-36
18	Buckley Town	36	7	6	23	38	107	27	-69
19	Carno	36	6	3	27	42	89	21	-47

N.B. Oswestry Town ineligible for promotion. Penrhyncoch v Rhos Aelwyd match not played. Mold Alexandra and Rhos Aelwyd deducted 3 pts.

SOUTH (OFFICE VISIONS LEAGUE DIVISION ONE)

		Pd	W	D	L	F	A	Pt	GD
1	**Carmarthen Town**	**34**	**25**	**7**	**2**	**101**	**37**	**82**	**+64**
2	Haverfordwest County	34	23	7	4	116	34	76	+82
3	Maesteg Park	34	20	8	6	73	47	68	+26
4	Cardiff Civil Service	34	19	6	9	82	47	63	+35
5	Treowen Stars	34	18	6	10	67	46	60	+21
6	Llanwern	34	15	7	12	57	56	52	+1
7	Penrhiwceiber Rangers	34	14	9	11	69	58	51	+11
8	Taffs Well	34	14	9	11	66	63	51	+3
9	Caldicot Town	34	14	4	16	60	68	46	-8
10	AFC Porth	34	11	10	13	57	67	43	-10
11	Pontypridd Town	34	12	7	15	58	73	43	-15
12	Risca United	34	12	6	16	50	67	42	-17
13	Cardiff Corinthians	34	11	7	16	46	56	40	-10
14	Aberaman Athletic	34	11	7	16	64	79	40	-15
15	Abergavenny Thursdays	34	10	8	16	50	62	38	-12
16	Brecon Corinthians	34	8	3	23	48	90	27	-42
17	Ammanford	34	6	5	23	43	105	23	-62
18	Caerleon	34	2	6	26	30	82	12	-52

CLUB DIRECTORY

Welshpool AFC (now Welshpool Town AFC)
36 Dolyfelen
Welshpool
Powys SY21 7NB
tel - (01938) 552989
fax - (01939) 554567
Year of Formation - 1878
Chairman - Mike Edwards
Secretary - Andrew Jones
Manager - Gareth Cadwallader
Stadium - Maesydre (3,000)

CLUB DIRECTORY

Carmarthen Town AFC
3 Maesdolau
Idole
Carmarthen SA32 8DQ
tel - (01267) 232432
fax - (01267) 2201116
Year of Formation - 1948
Chairman - Malcolm Williams
Secretary - Alan Latham
Manager - Wyndham Evans
Stadium - Richmond Park (3,000)

YUGOSLAVIA

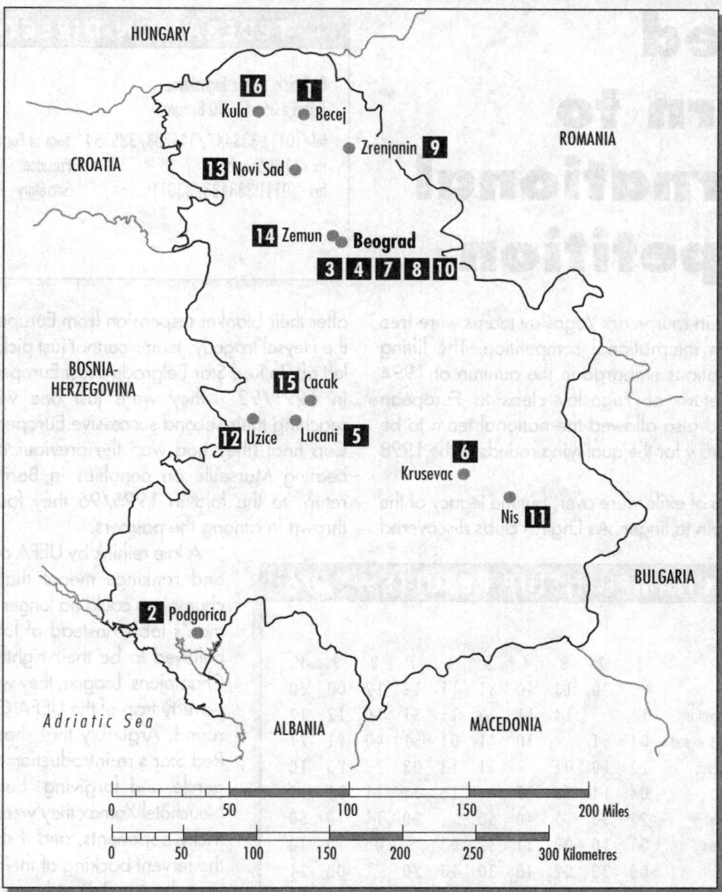

1	FK BECEJ	1098	9	PROLETER ZRENJANIN	1106
2	BUDUCNOST PODGORICA	1099	10	RAD BEOGRAD	1107
3	CRVENA ZVEZDA BEOGRAD	1100	11	RADNICKI NIS	1108
4	CUKARICKI BEOGRAD	1101	12	SLOBODA UZICE	1109
5	MLADOST LUCANI	1102	13	VOJVODINA NOVI SAD	1110
6	NAPREDAK KRUSEVAC	1103	14	FK ZEMUN	1111
7	OFK BEOGRAD	1104	15	BORAC CACAK	1112
8	PARTIZAN BEOGRAD	1105	16	HAJDUK KULA	1112

PARTIZAN'S TURN TO TAKE TITLE

Mixed return to international competition

FEDERATION DIRECTORY

Fudbalski Savez Jugoslavije
Terazije 35, 11000 Beograd

tel - (011) 333447/346208/335354
tlx - 11666 yu fsj
fax - (011) 333433/330110

Year of Formation - 1919
President - Miljan Miljanic
Secretary - Branko Bulatovic

For the first time in four years Yugoslav teams were free to participate in international competition. The lifting of the United Nations embargo in the autumn of 1994 heralded the return of Yugoslav clubs to European Cup football and also allowed the national team to be included in the draw for the qualifying rounds of the 1998 World Cup.

The dark days of exile were over, but the legacy of the long ban is certain to linger. As English clubs discovered after their blanket suspension from Europe in the wake of the Heysel tragedy, teams cannot just pick up where they left off. In Red Star Belgrade's last European campaign - in 1991/92 - they were just one win away from reaching their second successive European Champions' Cup final (they had won the previous one, of course, beating Marseille on penalties in Bari). But on their return to the fold in 1995/96 they found themselves thrown in among the paupers.

A late rethink by UEFA over co-efficients and rankings meant that the Yugoslav champions could no longer dine at the rich man's table. Instead of taking what they believed to be their rightful place in the Champions' League, they were cast into the poverty trap of the UEFA Cup preliminary round. Arguably that should have made Red Star's re-introduction to Europe more gentle and forgiving, but in Swiss side Neuchâtel Xamax they were drawn against tricky opponents, and it showed. Despite the fervent backing of their fans, Red Star were beaten 1-0 at home in the first leg, and were unable to recover in the return, drawing 0-0 in Switzerland.

Such an unforeseen early departure for the champions was a bitter blow to Yugoslav football. The only other Yugoslav club UEFA had deigned to offer a European place to were Second Division side Oblic Belgrade, the Cup runners-up, and they too went out at the first time of asking after losing their opening match 0-1 (to Dinamo Batumi of Georgia) in Belgrade. So, before the European competitions began in earnest, Yugoslav interest had already been wiped out. Clearly, the lack of international experience

LEAGUE CHAMPIONSHIP RESULTS 95/96

FIRST PHASE

		1	2	3	4	5	6	7	8	9	10
1	FK Becej		2-0	1-3	6-0	3-1	1-1	1-1	1-2	0-0	3-0
2	Buducnost Podgorica	1-1		1-4	1-1	2-3	1-5	3-1	1-0	1-2	1-2
3	Crvena zvezda Beograd	0-1	5-1		3-0	4-1	0-1	5-1	4-0	2-1	2-1
4	Napredak Krusevac	2-2	1-0	0-1		1-1	1-3	0-3	2-3	2-3	1-0
5	OFK Beograd	0-4	1-1	2-6	2-2		1-8	3-1	1-1	0-1	1-1
6	Partizan Beograd	2-1	3-0	1-1	4-0	6-0		2-0	1-1	1-0	5-0
7	Proleter Zrenjanin	0-1	1-0	0-3	3-1	3-2	0-3		0-0	1-0	1-0
8	Radnicki Nis	0-0	2-0	0-2	4-0	3-0	1-3	2-0		0-0	2-1
9	Vojvodina Novi Sad	2-0	3-0	3-2	6-0	3-0	1-1	4-2	2-1		2-0
10	FK Zemun	1-0	3-0	1-2	1-0	6-1	0-2	1-1	1-1	1-1	

FINAL ROUND

		1	2	3	4	5	6	7	8	9	10
1	FK Becej		1-0	1-0	1-0	0-0	1-0	1-0	2-1	1-0	1-0
2	Crvena zvezda Beograd	1-1		1-0	2-0	2-3	3-1	3-1	1-1	1-0	1-0
3	Cukaricki Beograd	1-1	0-0		1-1	1-2	0-1	3-1	4-1	3-0	0-1
4	Mladost Lucani	2-0	3-2	2-1		1-0	0-1	3-1	4-1	5-1	1-2
5	Partizan Beograd	4-1	0-0	4-2	5-0		4-1	2-1	4-0	5-0	6-3
6	Proleter Zrenjanin	2-2	3-1	5-3	0-2	0-1		4-3	0-1	3-0	0-2
7	Rad Beograd	0-1	0-1	1-1	0-0	2-1	1-0		3-1	4-0	2-2
8	Radnicki Nis	2-2	1-3	0-2	2-0	1-4	1-1	0-0		2-1	3-1
9	Sloboda Uzice	1-1	0-4	0-0	2-0	1-5	2-1	0-1	1-1		1-2
10	Vojvodina Novi Sad	5-0	1-1	1-1	5-0	1-1	1-1	0-0	4-0	2-0	

LEAGUE CHAMPIONSHIP FINAL TABLE 95/96

FIRST PHASE (AUTUMN)

			Home					Away					Total						
		Pd	W	D	L	F	A	W	D	L	F	A	W	D	L	F	A	Pt	GD
1	Partizan Beograd	18	7	2	0	25	3	7	2	0	27	6	14	4	0	52	9	46	+43
2	Crvena zvezda Beograd	18	7	0	2	25	7	7	1	1	24	9	14	1	3	49	16	43	+33
3	Vojvodina Novi Sad	18	8	1	0	26	6	3	3	3	8	8	11	4	3	34	14	37	+20
4	Radnicki Nis	18	5	2	2	14	6	2	4	3	9	13	7	6	5	23	19	27	+4
5	FK Becej	18	4	3	2	18	8	3	3	3	10	8	7	6	5	28	16	27	+12
6	Proleter Zrenjanin	18	5	1	3	9	10	1	2	6	10	21	6	3	9	19	31	21	-12
7	FK Zemun	18	4	3	2	15	8	1	1	7	5	18	5	4	9	20	26	19	-6
8	OFK Beograd	18	1	4	4	11	25	1	1	7	9	31	2	5	11	20	56	11	-36
9	Napredak Krusevac	18	2	2	5	10	16	0	2	7	4	30	2	4	12	14	46	10	-32
10	Buducnost Podgorica	18	2	2	5	12	19	0	1	8	2	21	2	3	13	14	40	9	-26

FINAL ROUND (SPRING)

			Home					Away					Total						
		Pd	W	D	L	F	A	W	D	L	F	A	W	D	L	F	A	Pt	GD
1	Partizan Beograd	18	8	1	0	34	8	5	2	2	17	9	13	3	2	51	17	60	+34 (18)
2	Crvena zvezda Beograd	18	6	2	1	15	7	3	3	3	12	9	9	5	4	27	16	48	+11 (16)
3	Vojvodina Novi Sad	18	4	5	0	20	4	4	1	4	13	15	8	6	4	33	19	43	+14 (13)
4	FK Becej	18	8	1	0	9	1	1	5	3	9	18	9	6	3	18	19	41	-1 (8)
5	Mladost Lucani	18	7	0	2	21	9	1	2	6	3	18	8	2	8	24	27	32	-3 (6)
6	Cukaricki Beograd	18	3	3	3	13	8	1	3	5	10	15	4	6	8	23	23	29	= (11)
7	Rad Beograd	18	4	3	2	13	7	1	2	6	8	16	5	5	8	21	23	28	-2 (8)
8	Proleter Zrenjanin	18	4	1	4	17	15	2	2	5	7	13	6	3	9	24	28	27	-4 (6)
9	Radnicki Nis	18	3	3	3	12	14	1	2	6	7	23	4	5	9	19	37	26	-18 (9)
10	Sloboda Uzice	18	2	3	4	8	15	0	0	9	2	26	2	3	13	10	41	14	-31 (5)

N.B. After 18 matches the bottom four are relegated to Group B (Second Divison) and replaced by the top four in Group B.
Figures in brackets indicate bonus points accumulated from first phase.

BONUS POINTS SYSTEM

Position (1st phase)	Bonus Pts
1	7
2	6
3	5
4	5
5	4
6	4

Points (1st phase)	Bonus Pts
52-54	13
49-51	12
46-48	11
43-45	10
40-42	9
37-39	8
34-36	7
31-33	6
28-30	5
25-27	4
22-24	3
19-21	2
16-18	1
0-15	0

INTERNATIONAL HONOURS

World Cup Finals appearances: 1930 (semi-finals), 1950, 1954 (qtr-finals), 1958 (qtr-finals), 1962 (4th), 1974 (2nd phase), 1982, 1990 (qtr-finals)

European Championship appearances: 1960 (runners-up), 1968 (runners-up), 1972, 1976 (4th), 1984

European Club Competitions

Champions' Cup	FK Crvena zvezda Beograd (1991)

was a damaging factor. Only one Yugoslav player - Red Star goalkeeper Zvonko Milojevic - had sampled European club competition before. And the added pressure of re-establishing the country on the footballing map simply exacerbated an already daunting task.

With the Yugoslav national team, however, the reintegration is made much easier by the presence in the side of numerous foreign-based stars, whose big-match experience is unrivalled after several seasons spent learning the ropes in top European clubs like Milan,

DOMESTIC CUP RESULTS

1/16 FINALS
Crvena stjena Tolosi 1, Napredak Krusevac 8
Rudar Pljevlja 2, Rad Beograd 3
FK Indjija 0, Partizan Beograd 5
Crvena zvezda Beograd 6, FK Novi Pazar 1
Cukaricki Beograd 2, FK Zemun 1
Buducnost Podgorica 3, Dinamo Pancevo 3 (5-4 on pens.)
Radnicki Novi Beograd 4, Buducnost Valjevo 1
Mladost Lucani 2, Hajduk Kula 0
Sutjeska Niksic 1, FK Becej 0
FK Novi Sad 4, Obilic Beograd 2
OFK Beograd 1, FK Pristina 2
Spartak Subotica 1, Proleter Zrenjanin 2
OFK Kikinda 3, FK Loznica 5
Sloboda Uzice 0, Radnicki Nis 2
Borac Cacak 4, Mornar Bar 0
FK Badnjevac 2, Vojvodina Novi Sad 1

1/8 FINALS
Rad Beograd v Buducnost Podgorica 4-0; 0-1 (Rad Beograd 4-1)
Radnicki Novi Beograd v Crvena zvezda Beograd 0-1; 0-3 (Crvena zvezda Beograd 4-0)
FK Novi Sad v Sutjeska Niksic 1-0; 1-1 (FK Novi Sad 2-1)
FK Pristina v Napredak Krusevac 1-0; 1-4 (Napredak Krusevac 4-2)
Mladost Lucani v Partizan Beograd 1-2; 0-5 (Partizan Beograd 7-1)
Radnicki Nis v FK Badnjevac 1-1; 0-1 (FK Badnjevac 2-1)
Cukaricki Beograd v Proleter Zrenjanin 3-0; 2-3 (Cukaricki Beograd 5-3)
FK Loznica v Borac Cacak 1-0; 1-2 (2-2; FK Loznica on away goal)

QUARTER-FINALS
Rad Beograd v Partizan Beograd 0-0; 1-2 ((Partizan Beograd 2-1)
FK Loznica v Crvena zvezda Beograd 2-2; 1-6 (Crvena zvezda Beograd 8-3)
FK Badnjevac v Cukaricki Beograd 1-1; 1-0 (FK Badnjevac 2-1)
FK Novi Sad v Napredak Krusevac 2-0; 1-2 (FK Novi Sad 3-2)

SEMI-FINALS
FK Novi Sad v Crvena zvezda Beograd 0-4; 0-3 (Crvena zvezda Beograd 7-0)
FK Badnjevac v Partizan Beograd 1-1; 1-2 (Partizan Beograd 3-2)

FINAL
08/05/96, Belgrade
CRVENA ZVEZDA BEOGRAD 3
Jovicic (8), Krupnikovic (37), Zivkovic (51)
PARTIZAN BEOGRAD 0
referee - Babarogic
CRVENA ZVEZDA BEOGRAD - Milojevic Z.; Zivkovic (Ognjenovic 79), Djorovic G., Radmilovic, Stankovic P., Marinovic, Adzic (Puaca 89), Stankovic D., Jovicic (Milivojev 80), Krupnikovic, Njegus.
PARTIZAN BEOGRAD - Kralj; Mirkovic, Saveljic, Tesovic (Tomic 66), Mijalkovic, Djuric (Tasevski 46), Vukicevic, Nadj, Trenevski (Hristov 46), Ciric, Cakar.

15/05/96, Belgrade
PARTIZAN BEOGRAD 1 Vukicevic (62)
CRVENA ZVEZDA BEOGRAD 3
Stankovic P. (45), Krupnikovic (65), Stankovic D. (79)
referee - Vidic
PARTIZAN BEOGRAD - Kralj; Mirkovic, Saveljic (Vukicevic 46), Tesovic, Mijalkovic, Tasevski, Svetlicic, Tomic (Krstajic 62), Hristov, Ciric, Jovic (Besirovic 46).
CRVENA ZVEZDA BEOGRAD - Milojevic Z.; Zivkovic (Ognjenovic 85), Djorovic G., Radmanovic (Milivojev 27), Stankovic P., Marinovic, Adzic, Stankovic D., Sakic, Krupnikovic, Njegus.

(CRVENA ZVEZDA BEOGRAD 6-1)

Juventus, Valencia and Sampdoria. But, like the clubs, the Yugoslav national team's residual punishment from the four-year ban is a sharp drop in the rankings. So, although the country was delighted to be included once more in the World Cup draw (Yugoslavia were quarter-finalists on their last participation, in 1990), jubilation was tempered by the knowledge that the team would be placed in only the fourth-ranked 'pot'. A tough qualifying draw was inevitable, and that was exactly what Yugoslavia got, joining Spain, the Czech Republic and Slovakia in by far the most difficult of the nine European groups.

Qualification for France will be hard, but not impossible. Yugoslavia's opponents have as much to fear from them as vice versa. The team put together an impressive run of results during the 1995/96 season. Friendly victories away to both Greece and Mexico, plus a morale-boosting 1-0 success in Belgrade against Euro '96 finalists Romania, paved the way for two convincing home wins in the opening two World Cup qualifiers, against the Faroe Islands and Malta.

EUROPEAN CUPS RESULTS 95/96

CUP-WINNERS' CUP

● **OBILIC BEOGRAD**

Preliminary round DINAMO BATUMI (GEO)

H 0-1
Saric; Zoric, Aranitovic, Novic, Vukcevic, Vilotijevic (Markovic), Tasic, Pasic, Puaca (Spasic), Sarac, Popovic.

A 2-2 Sarac (8), Popovic (35)
Saric; Zoric, Markovic, Novic (Stekovic 67), Vukcevic, Vilotijevic, Spasic, Rasic (Kostic 56), Sarac, Popovic, Tasic (Aranitovic 80).

UEFA CUP

● **CRVENA ZVEZDA BEOGRAD**

Preliminary round NEUCHATEL XAMAX FC (SUI)

H 0-1
Milojevic Z.; Stefanovic, Djorovic G., Njegus, Sakic, Podunavac, Adzic, Krupnikovic (Dragas 60), Kovacevic, Petkovic, Zivkovic (Stankovic D. 72).

A 0-0
Milojevic Z.; Stefanovic, Djorovic G., Njegus (Stankovic D. 31), Stankovic P., Podunavac, Adzic, Krupnikovic (Masic 67), Kovacevic, Petkovic, Ognjenovic (Zivkovic 67).

NATIONAL TEAM APPEARANCES 95/96

Coach - Slobodan SANTRAC	GRE	SAL	MEX	ROM	FAR	MEX	JPN	MLT	Cps	Gls
Zvonko MILOJEVIC (30/08/71) - Crvena zvezda Beograd	G	G46	s46	s89					7	-
Zoran MIRKOVIC (21/09/71) - Partizan Beograd	D	D68			s61	D	D	D	10	-
Goran DJOROVIC (11/11/71) - Crvena zvezda Beograd	D	D	D	s65	D	D	D	D86	13	-
Miroslav DJUKIC (19/02/66) - RC Deportivo (ESP)	D			D89				D	7	-
Dejan STEFANOVIC (28/10/74) - Crvena zvezda/Sheffield Wednesday (ENG)	D	D	D	s75			s83		7	-
Slavisa JOKANOVIC (16/08/68) - CD Tenerife (ESP)	M			M	D			M	13	-
Sasa CURCIC (14/02/72) - Partizan Beograd/Bolton Wanderers (ENG)	M78			M75	M61	M	s73		10	1
Dejan SAVICEVIC (15/09/66) - Milan (ITA)	M64	A65	M77		M	A	A	M	36	16
Albert NADJ (29/10/74) - Partizan Beograd	M56	M	M		s86	s46	M83	s50	12	1
Predrag MIJATOVIC (19/01/69) - Valencia CF (ESP)	A			A	A			A	15	1
Savo MILOSEVIC (02/09/73) - Aston Villa (ENG)	A	A	A85	A	A86	A82	A73	A79	13	6
Dejan PETKOVIC (10/09/72) - Crvena zvezda Beograd	s56	M60	s77						5	1
Miodrag PANTELIC (04/09/73) - Vojvodina Novi Sad	s64		s76						5	-
Drazen BOLIC (12/09/71) - Partizan Beograd	s78								1	-
Goran SAULA (01/09/70) - Vojvodina Novi Sad		D	D	s89		D	D24		9	-
Dejan GOVEDARICA (02/10/69) - Vojvodina Novi Sad		M63	M						7	-
Sinisa MIHAJLOVIC (20/02/69) - Sampdoria (ITA)		M	M77	M	D40	M	M	D	14	2
Aleksandar KOCIC (18/03/69) - Vojvodina Novi Sad		s46	G46	G89	G	G	G	G	9	-
Dragan CIRIC (15/09/74) - Partizan Beograd		s60	s77						2	-
Nisa SAVELJIC (23/03/70) - Partizan Beograd		s63	D			D	D	s86	8	1
Darko KOVACEVIC (18/11/73) - Crvena zvezda/Sheffield Wednesday (ENG)		s65	A76	s87		s82	s24	s79	11	3
Perica OGNJENOVIC (24/02/77) - Crvena zvezda Beograd		s68	s85						2	-
Branko BRNOVIC (08/08/67) - RCD Espanyol (ESP)				D	D				11	-
Budimir VUJACIC (04/01/64) - Sporting CP (POR)				D65					11	-
Vladimir JUGOVIC (30/08/69) - Juventus (ITA)				M	M		M	M50	10	1
Dragan STOJKOVIC (03/03/65) - Nagoya Grampus 8 (JPN)				M87	M	M	M	M	51	11
Milinko PANTIC (05/06/65) - Atlético Madrid (ESP)					s40				1	-
Bratislav ZIVKOVIC (28/11/70) - Crvena zvezda Beograd						M46			1	-

By choosing to stage the team's two easiest fixtures before their chief group rivals had even got round to thinking about the World Cup, Yugoslavia cunningly threw down an early gauntlet to the Spaniards and the Czechs. The two games also allowed the Yugoslavs to test the water and reaquaint themselves with international competition rather than being plunged straight into the deep end. The 3-1 win against the Faroe Islands was a shade disappointing after Yugoslavia went in 3-0 up at half-time. But the 6-0 hammering of Malta had the look of a job well done.

There would be much tougher nuts to crack in the future, but Yugoslav coach Slobodan Santrac, confirmed in the job at the start of the season, could be pleased with his team's progress. Not surprisingly, his selections for the two World Cup games were dominated by expatriates, with only Vojvodina goalkeeper Aleksandar Kocic and Red Star defender Goran Djorovic, of the home-based players, appearing from the start in both games.

Two men who remain central to Santrac's plans are the two veterans of the 1990 World Cup, skipper Dragan Stojkovic, of Japanese side Grampus 8, and skill merchant Dejan Savicevic, of Italian champions Milan. These are the only two players in the squad with more than 15 international caps to their name (Stojkovic made his 50th appearance in his adopted country in May) and although both are now in their thirties, they still remain highly ambitious and determined to make up for lost time. Predrag Mijatovic is another highly gifted player burning to make a name for himself in international football. In Spain he is as big a star as they come. So too, after an amazing début season for Atlético Madrid, is late developer Milinko Pantic. And in Italy, Vladimir Jugovic and Sinisa Mihajlovic have long been known for their elaborate, if inconsistent, talent. Of the younger breed, Savo Milosevic and Sasa Curcic, now playing together in England at Aston Villa, are developing nicely. Add a few precocious home-based stars such as Partizan Belgrade pair Albert Nadj and Dragan Ciric to the equation, and the end product is a team which could go far.

But while the outlook for the national team is bright, the domestic game in Yugoslavia continues to live from hand to mouth. The lifting of the ban is an obvious source of encouragement, but it is unlikely that Yugoslav clubs will ever return to the days when they were opponents to be feared in Europe. The watering-down of the national league through the withdrawal of Croatians, Slovenians and Macedonians, and especially the continuous selling-off of the country's best players, has left a domestic competition short on quality and excitement.

But, come what may, the two big Belgrade clubs continue to dominate. Partizan and Red Star have shared the Yugoslav title between them in every season of the present decade. In 1995/96 it was Partizan's turn to wrest the trophy back from their eternal rivals, and they did so without much opposition, from Red Star or anybody else.

Victories in each of Partizan's first seven matches set the scene for an uncomplicated triumph. The most important of those wins was match number six, away to Red Star, where Partizan conquered enemy soil for the first time in 18 years, sending most of the 55,000 spectators into deep depression.

Red Star recovered brilliantly from that setback to win their next eight matches, but a 1-1 draw in the return fixture, in which the team's three best players - Darko Kovacevic, Dejan Stefanovic and Dejan Petkovic - were all making their farewell appearance before moves abroad, served as a watershed in the defending champions' title ambitions. They were sensationally beaten at home the following week by Becej and ended the first half of the season three points behind unbeaten leaders Partizan.

Thanks to the idiosyncratic league system in Yugoslavia, that lead was cut to two at the start of the spring campaign. But it mattered not. Red Star were beaten at home yet again by Partizan (2-3) in March, and this time they were unable to bounce back, losing once more to Becej and then dropping out of the championship race completely.

Partizan, on the other hand, went from strength to strength, and by the end of the season they were able to breeze home with a mammoth 12 points to spare. It was the third title for Ljubisa Tumbakovic, Partizan's wily, authoritarian coach, who was duly rewarded with a further two-year extension to his contract. He had overcome the loss of star players Milosevic and Curcic to England by building an entertaining young team which combined individual star quality with effective and efficient team play. The team's real strength lay in midfield, where captain and fans' favourite Albert Nadj linked brilliantly with revelation of the season Dragan Ciric and dead-ball expert Damir Cakar. Full-backs Zoran Mirkovic and Nisa Saveljic also impressed and they were both honoured with regular call-ups to the Yugoslav national team.

TOP SCORERS

19	Nebojsa KRUPNIKOVIC (Crvena zvezda Beograd)
16	Damir CAKAR (Partizan Beograd)
15	Dragan CIRIC (Partizan Beograd)
13	Darko KOVACEVIC (Crvena zvezda Beograd)
	Milan STOJANOVSKI (Proleter Zrenjanin)
	Darko TESOVIC (Partizan Beograd)
12	Petar PUACA OFK Beograd/ Crvena zvezda Beograd)
11	Rahim BESIROVIC (Partizan Beograd)
9	Vojislav BUDIMIROVIC (Cukaricki Beograd)
	Georgi HRISTOV (Partizan Beograd)
	Goran SAULA (Vojvodina Novi Sad)
	Zoran CIRIC (FK Becej)

NATIONAL TEAM RESULTS 95/96

20/09/95	Greece	A	Salonika	2-0	Curcic (35), Milosevic (85)
12/11/95	El Salvador	A	San Salvador	4-1	Mihajlovic (12), Savicevic (23p, 38), Martínez (60og)
16/11/95	Mexico	A	Monterrey	4-1	Kovacevic (5, 16), Mihajlovic (39), Saveljic (48)
27/03/96	Romania	H	Belgrade	1-0	Stojkovic (52)
24/04/96	Faroe Islands (WCQ)	H	Belgrade	3-1	Savicevic (3, 29), Milosevic (38)
23/05/96	Mexico	N	Shizuoka	0-0	
26/05/96	Japan	A	Tokyo	0-1	
02/06/96	Malta (WCQ)	H	Belgrade	6-0	Zammit (2og), Mijatovic (38), Stojkovic (45), Milosevic (68), Savicevic (70p, 71)

PLAYERS OF THE SEASON

PREDRAG MIJATOVIC

At 27, Predrag Mijatovic is still something of an untapped talent. Had Yugoslavia been permitted to take part in the 1994 World Cup and the 1996 European Championship, he would now be as big a name internationally as, say, Davor Suker - the Croatian striker he now partners at Real Madrid. "Pedje", as the Spaniards call him, had a spectacularly fine season in 1995/96, scoring 28 goals, many of them works of art, to take Valencia into the runners-up spot (above both Barcelona and Real Madrid) in the Spanish First Division. Once a playmaker in the mould of his fellow Montenegrin Dejan Savicevic, he was turned into a striker by Valencia coach Luis Aragonés...with devastating results. When Valencia sold Mijativic to Real for roughly £7 million, they brought in Brazilian World Cup hero Romário instead. But still the Valencia fans wept. To them "Pedje" is, and always will be, that extra bit special.

MILINKO PANTIC

If Spain knew all about Mijatovic before the 95/96 began, very few people in the country had ever heard of Milinko Pantic. One who had was new Atlético Madrid coach Radomir Antic, and when he bought him from Greek club Panionios, most pundits said that it was a case once again of Atlético demonstrating their limited ambition. How the 31-year-old midfielder made them eat their words! Pantic adapted with extraordinary speed to the Spanish game and was soon being heralded as the finest player in the entire league. He was the player who made Atlético tick, his free-kicks and corner-kicks bringing a plethora of important goals as Atlético went on to capture the Spanish 'double'. Two particular highlights for the player were his winning goal in the Cup final against Barcelona (with a rare header) and his first cap for Yugoslavia, as a sub in the World Cup qualifier against the Faroe Islands.

DRAGAN CIRIC

Yugoslavia has long been regarded as the 'Brazil of Europe' in terms of the naturally skilful footballers it produces. One youngster who plays in tune with the samba beat is 22-year-old Dragan Ciric of Partizan Belgrade. He was voted the number one player in the Yugoslav First Division at the end of 1995, and that is still the case now. His was the most influential contribution towards Partizan's 1995/96 championship triumph. Burdened with the tag of the "new Savicevic", the young playmaker simply concentrated on his own game and drew constant admiration from the crowd with his skill and spectacular goalscoring.

Partizan's stamp of authority came in the big games. They took eight points from both Red Star and Vojvodina and were undefeated by either of them. In fact, the only teams to beat Partizan were Mladost Lucani and Rad, who had both come up from the Second Division in mid-season.

In the final of the Yugoslav Cup, however, things were different. For the third time in five seasons Partizan and Red Star met in the final (in the other two years they had also been drawn together, at an earlier stage). Red Star had lost face with their poor performances in the UEFA Cup and the league and replaced coach Ljupko Petrovic with another Petrovic, Vladimir. His appointment appeared to be a master stroke as Red Star, looking more confident and buoyant than they had all season, thrashed Partizan 3-0 in the first leg and then completed the job with a 3-1 away win in the return. Partizan's 'double' dreams were in tatters. Nebojsa Krupnikovic, the league's top marksman, scored in both games to round off a fine season before leaving for a new career in Belgium with Standard Liège.

Krupnikovic thus became the eighth Red Star player in as many months to quit the club for foreign fields, joining fellow 'mercenaries' Petkovic, Kovacevic, Stefanovic, Stankovic, Masic, Podunavac and Adzic. It was a similar story at Partizan (Curcic, Mirkovic, Djuric, Besirovic and Nadj) and Vojvodina (Govedarica, Kocic, Saula and Jezdimirovic).

Yugoslavian football is simply caught in a financial web, from which the only means of disentanglement is to sell off its best players to wealthy foreign buyers. Each year the situation is the same. The top three clubs sell in bulk to the West, then fill the gaps by buying in young replacements from the smaller Yugoslav clubs. This maintains the domestic status quo and, as a result, the chain of command continues. It's painful and it's predictable, but, barring an intervention of revolutionary dimensions (and the change to a more conventional 12-team top division in 96/97 hardly amounts to that), it seems set to remain that way for the foreseeable future.

FK BECEJ

CLUB DIRECTORY

FK Becej
Gradski stadion
21220 Becej
tel - (021) 815949/813544
Year of Formation - 1919
President - Momcilo Radmilac
Secretary - Milorad Tatalovic
Coach - Dragan Okuka
(96/97 - Zvonko Ivezic)
Stadium - Gradski (10,000)

APPEARANCES 95/96

	P	Ap	(s)	Gls
Ergin AJDINOVIC	M	25	(9)	2
Ljubisa ALEKSIC	D	31		1
Budimir BASIC	D	3	(2)	
Zoran CILINSEK	M	10		2
Zoran CIRIC	A	34		9
Nebojsa COROVIC	D	1	(2)	
Vladimir GACINOVIC	M	26		3
Milorad KORAC	G	36		
Dragan KRSMANOVIC	A	1	(7)	
Djordje KUNOVAC	A	12	(18)	4
Ivica MILIVOJEV	M	17		3
Sinisa MULINA	M	32		4
Dalibor NOVCIC	M	26	(7)	8
Zivko PAVICEVIC	D		(5)	
Miroslav PEKEZ	M	28	(2)	4
Sinisa RADISIC	D	32		2
Milentje STEVANOVIC	M	15	(14)	
Damir STOJAK	A	4	(6)	1
Vladan VICEVIC	D	32		1
Boro ZAGORAC	M	31	(3)	1

LEAGUE RESULTS 1995/96

Date	Opponent	H/A	Score	Scorers
12/08/95	Radnicki Nis	A	0-0	
19/08/95	OFK Beograd	H	3-1	Kunovac 2, Ciric
27/08/95	Partizan Beograd	A	1-2	Kunovac
02/09/95	FK Zemun	A	0-1	
09/09/95	Napredak Krusevac	H	6-0	Ciric 2, Mulina, Cilinsek, Milivojev, Vicevic
16/09/95	Proleter Zrenjanin	A	1-0	Gacinovic
23/09/95	Crvena zvezda Beograd	H	1-3	Cilinsek
30/09/95	Buducnost Podgorica	A	1-1	Stojak
07/10/95	Vojvodina Novi Sad	H	0-0	
14/10/95	Radnicki Nis	H	1-2	Gacinovic
21/10/95	OFK Beograd	A	4-0	Milivojev 2, Pekez, Ciric
28/10/95	Partizan Beograd	H	1-1	Aleksic
04/11/95	FK Zemun	H	3-0	Ajdinovic, Gacinovic, Radisic
18/11/95	Napredak Krusevac	A	2-2	Novcic, Kunovac
25/11/95	Proleter Zrenjanin	H	1-1	Novcic
02/12/95	Crvena zvezda Beograd	A	1-0	Novcic
09/12/95	Buducnost Podgorica	H	2-0	Novcic, Ciric
16/12/95	Vojvodina Novi Sad	A	0-2	
17/02/96	Rad Beograd	H	1-0	Pekez
24/02/96	Partizan Beograd	A	1-4	og (Mijalkovic)
28/02/96	Cukaricki Beograd	A	1-1	Mulina
02/03/96	Mladost Lucani	H	1-0	Ajdinovic
06/03/96	Radnicki Nis	A	2-2	Ciric 2
09/03/96	Proleter Zrenjanin	A	2-2	Mulina, Zagorac
15/03/96	Crvena zvezda Beograd	H	1-0	Novcic
20/03/96	Sloboda Uzice	A	1-1	Radisic
23/03/96	Vojvodina Novi Sad	H	1-0	Pekez
30/03/96	Radnicki Nis	H	2-1	Ciric, Novcic
03/04/96	Rad Beograd	A	1-0	Novcic
06/04/96	Partizan Beograd	A	0-0	
12/04/96	Cukaricki Beograd	H	1-0	Pekez
17/04/96	Mladost Lucani	A	0-2	
27/04/96	Proleter Zrenjanin	H	1-0	Novcic
03/05/96	Crvena zvezda Beograd	A	1-1	Ciric
11/05/96	Sloboda Uzice	H	1-0	Mulina
18/05/96	Vojvodina Novi Sad	A	0-5	

BUDUCNOST PODGORICA

CLUB DIRECTORY

FK Buducnost
Vaka Djurovica bb
81000 Podgorica
tel - (081) 44955/41560
fax - (081) 51651
Year of Formation - 1925
President - Dragan Milic
Secreatary - Danilo Karadzic
Coach - Dragan Sakovic; Momcilo Vujacic
Stadium - FK Buducnost (15,230)

APPEARANCES 95/96

	P	Ap	(s)	Gls
Nikola BABOVIC	M		(1)	
Aleksandar BOJANIC	D	2		
Milan BOSKOVIC	M	2	(2)	
Oleg BULATOVIC	D	12		1
Dalibor COVIC	M	1	(1)	
Srdjan DMITROVIC	M	6		2
Igor DRAGICEVIC	M	6	(3)	
Sahmir GARCEVIC	A	11		3
Milinko ILIC	D	1		
Borisa JANKOVIC	D		(1)	
Nebojsa JOVOVIC	A	9	(3)	1
Dejan KAPLANOVIC	D	6	(2)	3
Zarko KNEZEVIC	M		(1)	
Darko LUBARDA	G	4		
Dragan MARAS	M	15		1
Jovan MILOJEVIC	M		(1)	
Mladen MIROCEVIC	M	6	(3)	
Sasa MITIC	A	9	(6)	1
Nusret MURATBASIC	M	1	(1)	
Aleksandar NEDOVIC	M	4	(4)	1
Goran PERISIC	D	12	(1)	
Zoran PEROVIC	G	14	(1)	
Vladimir POPOVIC	M	8	(1)	
Dejan RABRENOVIC	D	12		
Miodrag RADULOVIC	D	1	(1)	
Obren SARIC	M	1	(4)	
Danko STANISIC	M		(3)	
Dragan STANKOVIC	D	14	(1)	
Goran TROBOK	M	17	(1)	1
Srdjan VELIMIROVIC	D	5		
Dusan VLAISAVLJEVIC	D	12		
Nenad VUKCEVIC	A	7		

LEAGUE RESULTS 1995/96

Date	Opponent	H/A	Score	Scorers
12/08/95	Proleter Zrenjanin	H	3-1	Dmitrovic (p), Garcevic, Kaplanovic
18/08/95	Crvena zvezda Beograd	A	1-5	Kaplanovic
26/08/95	FK Zemun	H	1-2	Kaplanovic
03/09/95	Vojvodina Novi Sad	H	1-2	Bulatovic
09/09/95	Radnicki Nis	A	0-2	
16/09/95	OFK Beograd	H	2-3	Maras, Dmitrovic
24/09/95	Partizan Beograd	A	0-3	
30/09/95	FK Becej	H	1-1	Mitic
07/10/95	Napredak Krusevac	A	0-1	
14/10/95	Proleter Zrenjanin	A	0-1	
21/10/95	Crvena zvezda Beograd	H	1-4	Garcevic
28/10/95	FK Zemun	A	0-3	
04/11/95	Vojvodina Novi Sad	A	0-3	
18/11/95	Radnicki Nis	H	1-0	Trobok
25/11/95	OFK Beograd	A	1-1	Garcevic
02/12/95	Partizan Beograd	H	1-5	Jovovic (p)
09/12/95	FK Becej	A	0-2	
16/12/95	Napredak Krusevac	H	1-1	Nedovic

CRVENA ZVEZDA BEOGRAD

CLUB DIRECTORY

FK Crvena zvezda
Ljutice Bogdana 1a, 11000 Beograd
tel - (011) 668213/660216
fax - (011) 661753
Year of Formation - 1945
President - Cedomir Petrovic
Secretary - Vladimir Cvetkovic
Coach - Ljubomir Petrovic; Vladimir Petrovic
Stadium - Crvena zvezda (97,422)

MAJOR HONOURS

League Championship - (20)
1951, 1953, 1956, 1957, 1959, 1960, 1964, 1968, 1969, 1970, 1973, 1977, 1980, 1981, 1984, 1988, 1990, 1991, 1992, 1995.
Domestic Cup - (15) 1948, 1949, 1950, 1958, 1959, 1964, 1968, 1970, 1971, 1982, 1985, 1990, 1993, 1995, 1996.
European Champions' Cup - (1) 1991.
World Club Cup - (1) 1991.

APPEARANCES 95/96

	P	Ap	(s)	Gls
Ivan ADZIC	M	23	(4)	
Goran DJOROVIC	D	23		1
Zoran DJOROVIC	D	1	(1)	
Zarko DRAGAS	A	2	(5)	2
Goran DRULIC	A	2	(2)	1
Ivan DUDIC	D	1		
Dragoslav JEVRIC	G	2		
Zoran JOVICIC	A	6	(10)	3
Darko KOVACEVIC	A	16		13
Nebojsa KRUPNIKOVIC	M	32		19
Nikola LAZETIC	M	2	(2)	
Vinko MARINOVIC	D	16	(5)	1
Zoran MASIC	A	3	(3)	1
Ivica MILIVOJEV	M	14	(1)	3
Vladan MILOJEVIC	D	11	(2)	
Zvonko MILOJEVIC	G	34		
Marko MITROVIC	M		(1)	
Zoran NJEGUS	M	9	(6)	
Konstantin OGNJANOVIC	A		(1)	
Perica OGNJENOVIC	A	26	(7)	8
Miodrag PANTELIC	A	12		2
Srdjan PECELJ	D	6	(7)	1
Dejan PETKOVIC	M	14		5
Drazen PODUNAVAC	M	17	(3)	1
Petar PUACA	A	5	(6)	2
Nikola RADMANOVIC	M	26	(1)	
Nenad SAKIC	D	25	(1)	2
Dejan STANKOVIC	M	14	(10)	4
Jovan STANKOVIC	A		(1)	
Predrag STANKOVIC	D	20	(4)	4
Dejan STEFANOVIC	D	15		1
Zoran URUMOV	D		(2)	
Bratislav ZIVKOVIC	D	19	(8)	1

LEAGUE RESULTS 1995/96

13/08/95	FK Zemun	H	2-1	Krupnikovic, Petkovic
18/08/95	Buducnost Podgorica	H	5-1	Stankovic D. 2, Ognjenovic 2, Stankovic P.
26/08/95	Vojvodina Novi Sad	A	2-3	Krupnikovic, Petkovic
02/09/95	Radnicki Nis	H	4-0	Sakic, Masic, Stankovic D., Kovacevic (p)
09/09/95	OFK Beograd	A	6-2	Kovacevic 2, Krupnikovic, Podunavac, Sakic, og (Terzic)
16/09/95	Partizan Beograd	H	0-1	
23/09/95	FK Becej	A	3-1	Krupnikovic (p), Marinovic, Dragas
30/09/95	Napredak Krusevac	H	3-0	Krupnikovic 2, Zivkovic
07/10/95	Proleter Zrenjanin	A	3-0	Kovacevic 2, Krupnikovic
14/10/95	FK Zemun	A	2-1	Kovacevic 2
21/10/95	Buducnost Podgorica	A	4-1	Petkovic 2, Stankovic P., Kovacevic
28/10/95	Vojvodina Novi Sad	H	2-1	Krupnikovic (p), Ognjenovic
04/11/95	Radnicki Nis	A	2-0	Kovacevic 2 (1p)
20/11/95	OFK Beograd	H	4-1	Kovacevic 2, Petkovic, Djorovic G.
25/11/95	Partizan Beograd	A	1-1	Stefanovic
02/12/95	FK Becej	H	0-1	
09/12/95	Napredak Krusevac	A	1-0	Kovacevic
16/12/95	Proleter Zrenjanin	H	5-1	Krupnikovic 2, Jovicic, Ognjenovic, Pecelj
17/02/96	Sloboda Uzice	H	1-0	Krupnikovic (p)
24/02/96	Vojvodina Novi Sad	A	1-1	Pantelic
28/02/96	Radnicki Nis	H	1-1	Puaca (p)
02/03/96	Rad Beograd	A	1-0	Stankovic P.
06/03/96	Cukaricki Beograd	H	1-0	Ognjenovic
10/03/96	Partizan Beograd	H	2-3	Krupnikovic (p), Pantelic
15/03/96	FK Becej	A	0-1	
20/03/96	Mladost Lucani	H	2-0	Ognjenovic, Drulic
23/03/96	Proleter Zrenjanin	A	1-3	Milivojev
30/03/96	Cukaricki Beograd	A	0-0	
02/04/96	Sloboda Uzice	A	4-0	Jovicic 2, Milivojev, Krupnikovic
06/04/96	Vojvodina Novi Sad	H	1-0	Krupnikovic (p)
13/04/96	Radnicki Nis	A	3-1	Krupnikovic 2 (1p), Stankovic P.
17/04/96	Rad Beograd	H	3-1	Stankovic D., Krupnikovic, Ognjenovic
27/04/96	Partizan Beograd	A	0-0	
03/05/96	FK Becej	H	1-1	Krupnikovic
11/05/96	Mladost Lucani	A	2-3	Ognjenovic, Puaca
18/05/96	Proleter Zrenjanin	H	3-1	Milivojev, Krupnikovic, Dragas

CUKARICKI BEOGRAD

CLUB DIRECTORY

FK Cukaricki Beograd
Beogradskog bataljona 25
11030 Beograd
tel - (011) 551302/558627
fax - (011) 545646/544091
Year of Formation - 1926
President - Aleksandar Mihajlovic
Secretary - Miodrag Jankovic
Coach - Timotije Davidovic
(96/97 - Dragan Okuka)
Stadium - Cukaricki (8,000)

APPEARANCES 95/96

	P	Ap	(s)	Gls
Predrag BRZAKOVIC	G	18		
Vojislav BUDIMIROVIC	A	15		9
Srdjan CEROVIC	M	4	(2)	
Nemanja DANCETOVIC	M		(2)	
Srbo DIMITRIJEVIC	D	3	(1)	
Aleksandar DJORDJEVIC	D	17		
Nenad DJUKANOVIC	D	15		
Dejan DJURDJEVIC	M	7	(4)	1
Dejan FEMIC	M	1	(9)	1
Srdjan GOLOVIC	M	7	(2)	1
Rudi GUSNIC	D	14		
Aleksandar JOVIC	A	8	(3)	1
Sasa MARKOVIC	M	14	(2)	7
Dragan MIJANOVIC	M	8	(1)	1
Miodrag NIKOLIC	D	6	(5)	
Dragan PAUNOVIC	M	17		
Darko PIVALJEVIC	A	8	(1)	1
Slobodan SCEPANOVIC	A	6	(8)	
Mladen STANISIC	D	1		
Zoran STOJANOVIC	G		(1)	
Stevo VORKAPIC	D	13		
Miloje VUKIC	M	16		1

LEAGUE RESULTS 1995/96

17/02/96	Partizan Beograd	H	1-2	Budimirovic (p)
23/02/96	Sloboda Uzice	A	0-0	
28/02/96	FK Becej	H	1-1	Budimirovic (p)
01/03/96	Vojvodina Novi Sad	A	1-1	Markovic
06/03/96	Crvena zvezda Beograd	A	0-1	
08/03/96	Mladost Lucani	H	1-1	Markovic
16/03/96	Radnicki Nis	A	2-0	Pivaljevic, Budimirovic
20/03/96	Proleter Zrenjanin	H	0-1	
23/03/96	Rad Beograd	A	1-1	Markovic
30/03/96	Crvena zvezda Beograd	H	0-0	
03/04/96	Partizan Beograd	A	2-4	Budimirovic, Markovic
05/04/96	Sloboda Uzice	H	3-0	Budimirovic, Golovic, Markovic
12/04/96	FK Becej	A	0-1	
17/04/96	Vojvodina Novi Sad	H	0-1	
27/04/96	Mladost Lucani	A	1-2	Mijanovic
04/05/96	Radnicki Nis	H	4-1	Budimirovic 2, Djurdjevic, Markovic
11/05/96	Proleter Zrenjanin	A	3-5	Markovic, Femic, Budimirovic
18/05/96	Rad Beograd	H	3-1	Vukic, Budimirovic (p), Jovic

MLADOST LUCANI

CLUB DIRECTORY

FK Mladost Lucani
Radnicka b.b.
32240 Lucani
tel - (032) 818671
fax - (032) 818058
Year of Formation - 1952
President - Rados Milovanovic
Secretary - Dragan Djurovljevic
Coach - Jusuf Cizmic
(96/97 - Dusan Radonjic)
Stadium - Mladost (10,000)

APPEARANCES 95/96

	P	Ap	(s)	Gls
Veljko ALEKSIC	M		(4)	
Predrag ALIMPIJEVIC	D	1	(3)	
Zeljko ANDJELIC	M		(1)	
Goran BOSKOVIC	D	16		
Igor DIMITRIJEVIC	G	1	(1)	
Dusan JEVRIC	D	16		
Sinisa LUCIC	M	16		1
Zoran MARICIC	M	10	(2)	2
Vladimir MATIJASEVIC	D	8	(5)	
Nenad MILOVANOVIC	M	12		1
Dejan NIKOLIC	M	16		1
Predrag PLAZINIC	A	15		8
Radisa RADOJICIC	D	10	(7)	
Vladan RISTOVIC	M		(10)	
Milorad SLAVKOVIC	G	17		
Vasilije STANISIC	D		(3)	
Branko STOJANOVIC	A	10	(4)	2
Nenad VANIC	D	18		1
Radojica VASIC	D	7	(3)	
Nikola VUKOSLAVCEVIC	D	9	(5)	
Dragan VULEVIC	A	16		8

LEAGUE RESULTS 1995/96

Date	Opponent	H/A	Score	Scorers
17/02/96	Radnicki Nis	H	4-1	Vulevic, Plazinic, Milovanovic, Maricic
24/02/96	Rad Beograd	A	0-0	
27/02/96	Partizan Beograd	H	1-0	Plazinic
02/03/96	FK Becej	A	0-1	
06/03/96	Vojvodina Novi Sad	A	0-5	
08/03/96	Cukaricki Beograd	A	1-1	Vanic
16/03/96	Proleter Zrenjanin	H	0-1	
20/03/96	Crvena zvezda Beograd	A	0-2	
22/03/96	Sloboda Uzice	H	5-1	Vulevic 4, Plazinic
30/03/96	Vojvodina Novi Sad	H	1-2	Vulevic
03/04/96	Radnicki Nis	A	0-2	
06/04/96	Rad Beograd	H	3-1	Plazinic (p), Stojanovic, Nikolic
13/04/96	Partizan Beograd	A	0-5	
17/04/96	FK Becej	H	2-0	Plazinic, Lucic
27/04/96	Cukaricki Beograd	H	2-1	Plazinic (p), Maricic
04/05/96	Proleter Zrenjanin	A	2-0	Vulevic, Plazinic
11/05/96	Crvena zvezda Beograd	H	3-2	Vulevic, Stojanovic, Plazinic
18/05/96	Sloboda Uzice	A	0-2	

NAPREDAK KRUSEVAC

CLUB DIRECTORY

FK Napredak
Stadion Mladost
37000 Krusevac
tel - (037) 27455/29432
fax - (037) 27455
Year of Formation - 1946
President - Branislav Karajovic
Secretary - Milan Vidojevic
Coach - Vladimir Milosavljevic; Bosko Prodanovic
Stadium - Mladost (25,000)

APPEARANCES 95/96

	P	Ap	(s)	Gls
Goran ATANASKOVIC	D	14	(1)	
Olivio DAUTOVSKI	A	10	(3)	1
Dejan DJURIC	D	15		
Mladen DODIC	A	12		2
Bojan FILIPOVIC	M	4	(2)	
Slobodan FILIPOVIC	D	6	(4)	
Goran GASIC	A	6	(6)	
Predrag GVOZDENOVIC	D	3		
Predrag JOVANOVIC	M	17		5
Sasa JOVANOVIC	D		(4)	
Sinisa JOVANOVIC	D	13		
Dragisa KRSTIC	M	14	(2)	
Bojan LAZIC	D	13	(2)	
Nenad LUKIC	G	5		
Miroslav MIJATOVIC	M	2	(4)	
Miroslav MILOSEVIC	M		(1)	
Slobo NOVAKOVIC	M	9	(3)	
Ivica PAVLOVIC	M	12		1
Dragan PETROVIC	A	7	(6)	
Milan RATKOVIC	A	13	(2)	2
Dusan STARINAC	M		(1)	
Milomir STEFANOVIC	M		(2)	
Predrag STEFANOVIC	G	13	(1)	
Darko VOJVODIC	A	10		2

LEAGUE RESULTS 1995/96

12/08/95	Vojvodina Novi Sad	A	0-6	
18/08/95	Radnicki Nis	H	2-3	Jovanovic P., Pavlovic
27/08/95	OFK Beograd	A	2-2	Dodic, Ratkovic
02/09/95	Partizan Beograd	H	1-3	Jovanovic P.
09/09/95	FK Becej	A	0-6	
16/09/95	FK Zemun	A	0-1	
23/09/95	Proleter Zrenjanin	H	0-3	
30/09/95	Crvena zvezda Beograd	A	0-3	
07/10/95	Buducnost Podgorica	H	1-0	Dodic
14/10/95	Vojvodina Novi Sad	H	2-3	Ratkovic, Vojvodic
21/10/95	Radnicki Nis	A	0-4	
28/10/95	OFK Beograd	H	1-1	Dautovski
04/11/95	Partizan Beograd	A	0-4	
18/11/95	FK Becej	H	2-2	Jovanovic P., og (Zagorac)
25/11/95	FK Zemun	H	1-0	Jovanovic P.
02/12/95	Proleter Zrenjanin	A	1-3	Jovanovic P.
09/12/95	Crvena zvezda Beograd	H	0-1	
16/12/95	Buducnost Podgorica	A	1-1	Vojvodic

OFK BEOGRAD

CLUB DIRECTORY

OFK Beograd
Mije Kovacevica 10
11000 Beograd
tel - (011) 765425/767045
fax - (011) 762364
Year of Formation - 1945
President - Dragutin Jocic
Secretary - Djordje Hadzikostic
Coach - Blagomir Krivokuca; Krsta Mitrovic; Bozidar Milenkovic
Stadium - Omladinski (25,000)

MAJOR HONOURS
Domestic Cup - (4) 1953, 1958, 1962, 1966.

APPEARANCES 95/96

	P	Ap	(s)	Gls
Miodrag ANDJELKOVIC	M	2	(5)	1
Goran ARNAUT	M	1		
Branko BANJAC	M	14		
Novo CUJOVIC	M		(5)	
Radovan CURCIC	A	4	(1)	1
Velibor DJEKIC	G	1		
Dusko DJURISIC	D	4	(2)	
Aleksandar ILIC	M		(1)	
Rade IVLJANIN	M	16		1
Zeljko JOKSIMOVIC	D	3		
Srdjan KARANOVIC	D		(1)	
Zlatko KOSTIC	A	12	(3)	4
Aleksandar MALINOVIC	D	3	(1)	
Slavko MATIC	D	9	(3)	
Sladjan MILOJEVIC	D	12		
Milos MIRKOVIC	D	1	(1)	
Svetislav NIKOLICIC	A	13		
Branimir OBRADOVIC	D	1	(2)	
Milorad PEKOVIC	D	5		1
Dusan PETKOVIC	M	11		
Sasa PETROVIC	G	16		
Mihajlo PJANOVIC	M	3	(6)	
Petar PUACA	A	15	(1)	10
Vanja RADINOVIC	D	5		
Darko RAMOVS	D	7	(1)	1
Branko RANKOVIC	G	1		
Slobodan SCEPANOVIC	A	4	(3)	
Milorad SLJIVIC	M	3	(2)	
Zvezdan TERZIC	D	15		1
Rade TODOROVIC	D	4	(2)	
Zarko TODOROVIC	M	7	(1)	
Dejan ZERADJANIN	M	6		

LEAGUE RESULTS 1995/96

19/08/95	FK Becej	A	1-3	Kostic
23/08/95	Partizan Beograd	H	1-8	Curcic
26/08/95	Napredak Krusevac	H	2-2	Puaca, Ivljanin
02/09/95	Proleter Zrenjanin	A	2-3	Puaca 2
09/09/95	Crvena zvezda Beograd	H	2-6	Puaca 2 (1p)
16/09/95	Buducnost Podgorica	A	3-2	Kostic, Pekovic, Ramovs
23/09/95	Vojvodina Novi Sad	H	0-1	
30/09/95	Radnicki Nis	A	0-3	
07/10/95	FK Zemun	H	1-1	Kostic
14/10/95	Partizan Beograd	A	0-6	
21/10/95	FK Becej	H	0-4	
28/10/95	Napredak Krusevac	A	1-1	Puaca
04/11/95	Proleter Zrenjanin	H	3-1	Puaca 2, Andjelkovic
20/11/95	Crvena zvezda Beograd	A	1-4	Kostic
25/11/95	Buducnost Podgorica	H	1-1	Terzic
02/12/95	Vojvodina Novi Sad	A	0-3	
09/12/95	Radnicki Nis	H	1-1	Puaca
16/12/95	FK Zemun	A	1-6	Puaca (p)

PARTIZAN BEOGRAD

CLUB DIRECTORY

FK Partizan
Humska 1
11000 Beograd
tel - (011) 647777/648158
fax - (011) 648158
Year of Formation - 1945
President - Bozidar Martinovic
Secretary - Zarko Zecevic
Coach - Ljubisa Tumbakovic
Stadium - Partizan (50,819)

MAJOR HONOURS

League Championship - (14)
1947, 1949, 1961, 1962, 1963, 1965, 1976, 1978, 1983, 1986, 1987, 1993, 1994, 1996.
Domestic Cup - (7)
1947, 1952, 1954, 1957, 1989, 1992, 1994.

APPEARANCES 95/96

	P	Ap	(s)	Gls
Rahim BESIROVIC	A	23	(6)	11
Drazen BOLIC	D	22		6
Damir CAKAR	A	31	(1)	16
Dragan CIRIC	M	32		15
Sasa CURCIC	M	10		2
Nikola DAMJANAC	G	25		
Milenko DJEDOVIC	M	1		
Zoran DJURIC	D	33		3
Georgi HRISTOV (MAC)	A	13	(12)	9
Ivica KRALJ	G	11	(2)	
Mladen KRSTAJIC	D	4	(2)	1
Marko MARKOVIC	M		(1)	
Bratislav MIJALKOVIC	D	11		
Zoran MIRKOVIC	D	26	(1)	1
Albert NADJ	M	26		2
Predrag PAZIN	D	6	(6)	1
Dejan PEKOVIC	M	1	(9)	1
Vladimir PETKOVIC	M	1		
Nisa SAVELJIC	D	23	(1)	1
Djordje SVETLICIC	M	10	(15)	
Stanko SVITLICA	A		(1)	
Igor TASEVSKI	D	25	(6)	
Darko TESOVIC	M	27	(3)	13
Ivan TOMIC	M	5	(21)	8
Viktor TRENEVSKI	M	15	(9)	6
Dejan VUKICEVIC	M	15	(2)	5

LEAGUE RESULTS 1995/96

19/08/95	FK Zemun	A	2-0	Besirovic, Cakar
24/08/95	OFK Beograd	A	8-1	Cakar 2, Hristov 2, Tesovic, Curcic, Besirovic, Ciric (p)
26/08/95	FK Becej	H	2-1	Bolic, Tesovic
02/09/95	Napredak Krusevac	A	3-1	Bolic, Ciric, Hristov
09/09/95	Proleter Zrenjanin	H	2-0	Curcic, Besirovic
16/09/95	Crvena zvezda Beograd	A	1-0	Tesovic
24/09/95	Buducnost Podgorica	H	3-0	Besirovic, Djuric, Ciric
30/09/95	Vojvodina Novi Sad	A	1-1	Ciric
07/10/95	Radnicki Nis	H	1-1	Bolic
14/10/95	OFK Beograd	H	6-0	Ciric 2 (1p), Cakar 2, Djuric, Hristov
21/10/95	FK Zemun	H	5-0	Ciric 2 (1p), Hristov 2, Bolic
28/10/95	FK Becej	A	1-1	og (Zagorac)
04/11/95	Napredak Krusevac	H	4-0	Besirovic, Bolic, Saveljic, Pekovic
19/11/95	Proleter Zrenjanin	A	3-0	Tesovic 2, Ciric
25/11/95	Crvena zvezda Beograd	H	1-1	Besirovic
02/12/95	Buducnost Podgorica	A	5-1	Ciric 2 (1p), Tomic 2, Trenevski
09/12/95	Vojvodina Novi Sad	H	1-0	Tesovic
16/12/95	Radnicki Nis	A	3-1	Ciric, Tesovic, Tomic
17/02/96	Cukaricki Beograd	A	2-1	Bolic, Vukicevic
24/02/96	FK Becej	H	4-1	Tomic 2, Besirovic, Vukicevic
27/02/96	Mladost Lucani	A	0-1	
02/03/96	Proleter Zrenjanin	H	4-1	Cakar 3 (2p), Vukicevic
05/03/96	Rad Beograd	A	1-2	Cakar (p)
10/03/96	Crvena zvezda Beograd	A	3-2	Pazin, Nadj, Cakar
16/03/96	Sloboda Uzice	H	5-0	Cakar 2 (1p), Vukicevic, Tomic, Ciric
20/03/96	Vojvodina Novi Sad	A	1-1	Djuric
23/03/96	Radnicki Nis	H	4-0	Trenevski, Tesovic, Krstajic, Besirovic
29/03/96	Rad Beograd	H	2-1	Besirovic, og (Raosavljevic)
03/04/96	Cukaricki Beograd	H	4-2	Tesovic, Vukicevic, Trenevski, Cakar (p)
06/04/96	FK Becej	A	0-0	
13/04/96	Mladost Lucani	H	5-0	Ciric 2, Trenevski, Cakar (p), Tesovic
16/04/96	Proleter Zrenjanin	A	1-0	Trenevski
27/04/96	Crvena zvezda Beograd	H	0-0	
04/05/96	Sloboda Uzice	A	5-1	Tomic 2, Hristov 2, Besirovic
11/05/96	Vojvodina Novi Sad	H	6-3	Cakar 2, Trenevski (p), Hristov, Tesovic (p), Mirkovic (p)
18/05/96	Radnicki Nis	A	4-1	Tesovic 2, Nadj, Besirovic

PROLETER ZRENJANIN

CLUB DIRECTORY

FK Proleter
Karadjordjev trg 100
23000 Zrenjanin
tel - (023) 64856/66550
fax - (023) 66550
Year of Formation - 1947
President - Bosko Kovac
Secretary - Dragisa Radovancev
Coach - Tomislav Manojlovic
(96/97 - Radivoje Draskovic)
Stadium - Gradski (20,000)

APPEARANCES 95/96

	P	Ap	(s)	Gls
Goran GAVRILOVIC	G	27		
Vladimir IVIC	M	3	(13)	1
Dragan JANJATOVIC	M		(3)	
Slavoljub JANKOVIC	M	13	(2)	
Dragan JOVIC	A	28	(4)	4
Nikola KOBERSKI	D	5	(6)	
Sinisa KUJUNDZIC	M	27	(7)	2
Zoran LISICA	M	9	(13)	
Nenad LJUBENOVIC	M	15	(2)	
Predrag LUBURIC	D	29		2
Dejan LUKIC	M	13	(9)	1
Bosko MIHAJLOVIC	M	34	(1)	7
Goran MILOSEVIC	A	7	(17)	2
Stevan NEDELJKOV	D	22	(8)	4
Danijel PANKARICANIN	M		(1)	
Petar RAJLIC	D	1	(4)	
Branko SAVIC	D	32	(1)	
Zoran SRDIC	M	30		
Milan STOJANOVSKI	A	32	(1)	13
Sasa TODIC	G	9	(1)	
Sreten VASIC	M	33		3
Srdjan ZAKIC	D	10	(8)	
Aleksandar ZELENOVIC	A	17		4

LEAGUE RESULTS 1995/96

Date	Opponent	H/A	Score	Scorers
12/08/95	Buducnost Podgorica	A	1-3	Stojanovski
18/08/95	Vojvodina Novi Sad	H	1-0	Jovic
26/08/95	Radnicki Nis	A	0-2	
02/09/95	OFK Beograd	H	3-2	Nedeljkov, Mihajlovic, Stojanovski
09/09/95	Partizan Beograd	A	0-2	
16/09/95	FK Becej	H	0-1	
23/09/95	Napredak Krusevac	A	3-0	Vasic, Milosevic, Jovic
30/09/95	FK Zemun	A	1-1	Vasic
07/10/95	Crvena zvezda Beograd	H	0-3	
14/10/95	Buducnost Podgorica	H	1-0	Stojanovski
21/10/95	Vojvodina Novi Sad	A	2-4	Luburic, Stojanovski
28/10/95	Radnicki Nis	H	0-0	
04/11/95	OFK Beograd	A	1-3	Stojanovski
19/11/95	Partizan Beograd	H	0-3	
25/11/95	FK Becej	A	1-1	Nedeljkov
02/12/95	Napredak Krusevac	H	3-1	Mihajlovic, Stojanovski (p), Lukic
09/12/95	FK Zemun	H	1-0	Stojanovski
16/12/95	Crvena zvezda Beograd	A	1-5	Ivic
17/02/96	Vojvodina Novi Sad	H	0-2	
24/02/96	Radnicki Nis	A	1-1	Stojanovski
28/02/96	Rad Beograd	H	4-3	Mihajlovic, Zelenovic, Luburic (p), Milosevic
02/03/96	Partizan Beograd	A	1-4	Mihajlovic
06/03/96	Sloboda Uzice	A	1-2	Nedeljkov
09/03/96	FK Becej	H	2-2	Nedeljkov, Kujundzic
16/03/96	Mladost Lucani	A	1-0	Stojanovski
20/03/96	Cukaricki Beograd	A	1-0	Stojanovski
23/03/96	Crvena zvezda Beograd	H	3-1	Mihajlovic 2, Zelenovic
30/03/96	Sloboda Uzice	H	3-0	Stojanovski, Kujundzic, Zelenovic
03/04/96	Vojvodina Novi Sad	A	1-1	Mihajlovic
06/04/96	Radnicki Nis	H	0-1	
13/04/96	Rad Beograd	A	0-1	
16/04/96	Partizan Beograd	H	0-1	
27/04/96	FK Becej	A	0-1	
04/05/96	Mladost Lucani	H	0-2	
11/05/96	Cukaricki Beograd	H	5-3	Jovic 2, Zelenovic, Stojanovski, Vasic
18/05/96	Crvena zvezda Beograd	A	1-3	Stojanovski

RAD BEOGRAD

CLUB DIRECTORY

FK Rad
Crnotravska bb
11000 Beograd
tel - (011) 663039/666884/664194
fax - (011) 663631
Year of Formation - 1958
President - Milos Rajkovic
Secretary - Branko Rosic
Coach - Milenko Kikovic
Stadium - Rad (13,000)

APPEARANCES 95/96

	P	Ap	(s)	Gls
Aleksandar BRATIC	D	16		
Goran BUNJEVCEVIC	M	13		2
Zeljko CICOVIC	G	8		
Boban DMITROVIC	M	13	(2)	3
Miodrag GARDASEVIC	M		(1)	
Dragutin IVKOVIC	A	1	(15)	1
Aleksandar JANJIC	A	17	(1)	4
Goran JERINIC	D	4	(3)	
Mile KNEZEVIC	D	15		3
Ivica MOMCILOVIC	M	14		1
Sladjan NIKOLIC	A	6	(3)	1
Vladimir PASIC	D	7	(1)	1
Resid PEPIC	M	17		
Blazo RAOSAVLJEVIC	D	16		
Vuk RASOVIC	D	14		
Milan SEVO	G	7		
Dalibor SKORIC	M	15		4
Dragan STEVANOVIC	A	6	(3)	1
Milovan TODOROVIC	M		(1)	
Rade TODOROVIC	D		(1)	
Nebojsa TOPALOV	M	2	(10)	
Agbo UCE (NIG)	M	4	(6)	
Slavko VUJIC	G	3		

LEAGUE RESULTS 1995/96

17/02/96	FK Becej	A	0-1	
24/02/96	Mladost Lucani	H	0-0	
28/02/96	Proleter Zrenjanin	A	3-4	Skoric, Janjic, Dmitrovic
02/03/96	Crvena zvezda Beograd	H	0-1	
05/03/96	Partizan Beograd	H	2-1	Pasic, Bunjevcevic
09/03/96	Sloboda Uzice	A	1-0	Knezevic (p)
16/03/96	Vojvodina Novi Sad	H	2-0	Skoric 2 (1p)
19/03/96	Radnicki Nis	A	0-0	
23/03/96	Cukaricki Beograd	H	1-1	Stevanovic
29/03/96	Partizan Beograd	A	1-2	Knezevic
03/04/96	FK Becej	H	0-1	
06/04/96	Mladost Lucani	A	1-3	Skoric
13/04/96	Proleter Zrenjanin	H	1-0	Nikolic
17/04/96	Crvena zvezda Beograd	A	1-3	Momcilovic
27/04/96	Sloboda Uzice	H	4-0	Janjic 2, Knezevic, Ivkovic
04/05/96	Vojvodina Novi Sad	A	0-0	
11/05/96	Radnicki Nis	H	3-1	Dmitrovic 2, Bunjevcevic
18/05/96	Cukaricki Beograd	A	1-3	Janjic

RADNICKI NIS

CLUB DIRECTORY

FK Radnicki
Sportska hala "Cair"
18000 Nis
tel - (018) 22016/25030
fax - (018) 21336
Year of Formation - 1923
President - Stojan Randjelovic
Secretary - Miodrag Knezevic
Coach - Milorad Jankovic; Nenad Cvetkovic
Stadium - Cair (25,000)

APPEARANCES 95/96

	P	Ap	(s)	Gls
Dejan DIMITRIJEVIC	D	31		4
Goran DJORDJEVIC	M	9		
Dejan DJORDJEVIC	D	8		
Dragan GAVRILOVIC	D	28	(2)	
Vladislav GROZDANOVIC	A	1	(2)	
Dragan ILIC	M	33		3
Ivan ILIC	D	11	(1)	
Zoran ILIJEVIC	M	26	(3)	4
Goran JOVANOVIC	M	26		
Sasa JOVANOVIC	M	28	(2)	8
Uros KALINIC	A	5	(7)	1
Aleksandar KOMADINA	D	6	(1)	
Srdjan KOSTIC	M		(4)	
Radivoje MANIC	A	12		8
Dejan MICIC	A	1	(1)	
Bojan MILENKOVIC	D	25	(1)	3
Dusan MILUTINOVIC	M	19	(10)	1
Srdjan MLADENOVIC	M	13	(1)	1
Dejan NINKOVIC	M	1	(3)	
Ninoslav PAVLOVIC	A	1	(3)	1
Dejan PESIC	G	8	(3)	
Dragan PETROVIC	M		(3)	
Ivan RANDJELOVIC	G	28	(1)	
Slobodan RANGELOV	D	3	(2)	
Borisav STEVANOVIC	A	23	(7)	6
Sasa STOJILJKOVIC	M		(4)	
Dejan TRICKOVIC	M	4	(6)	
Aleksandar VESELLINOVIC	M	30		
Dragoljub ZIVADINOVIC	M	4	(11)	1
Aleksandar ZIVKOVIC	M	12	(8)	1

LEAGUE RESULTS 1995/96

12/08/95	FK Becej	H	0-0	
18/08/95	Napredak Krusevac	A	3-2	Ilic D., Dimitrijevic, Manic
26/08/95	Proleter Zrenjanin	H	2-0	Manic 2
02/09/95	Crvena zvezda Beograd	A	0-4	
09/09/95	Buducnost Podgorica	H	2-0	Manic (p), Milenkovic
16/09/95	Vojvodina Novi Sad	A	1-2	Ilijevic
23/09/95	FK Zemun	H	2-1	Dimitrijevic, Jovanovic S.
30/09/95	OFK Beograd	H	3-0	Zivkovic, Manic, Ilijevic
07/10/95	Partizan Beograd	A	1-1	Ilijevic
14/10/95	FK Becej	A	2-1	Jovanovic S., Manic
21/10/95	Napredak Krusevac	H	4-0	Manic 2, Ilijevic, Stevanovic
28/10/95	Proleter Zrenjanin	A	0-0	
04/11/95	Crvena zvezda Beograd	H	0-2	
18/11/95	Buducnost Podgorica	A	0-1	
25/11/95	Vojvodina Novi Sad	H	0-0	
02/12/95	FK Zemun	A	1-1	Milutinovic
09/12/95	OFK Beograd	A	1-1	Zivadinovic
16/12/95	Partizan Beograd	H	1-3	Stevanovic (p)
17/02/96	Mladost Lucani	A	1-4	Kalinic
24/02/96	Proleter Zrenjanin	H	1-1	Dimitrijevic
28/02/96	Crvena zvezda Beograd	A	1-1	Stevanovic
02/03/96	Sloboda Uzice	H	2-1	Jovanovic S. 2
06/03/96	FK Becej	H	2-2	Ilic D., Milenkovic
09/03/96	Vojvodina Novi Sad	A	0-4	
16/03/96	Cukaricki Beograd	H	0-2	
19/03/96	Rad Beograd	H	0-0	
23/03/96	Partizan Beograd	A	0-4	
30/03/96	FK Becej	A	1-2	Ilic D.
03/04/96	Mladost Lucani	H	2-0	Mladenovic, Pavlovic
06/04/96	Proleter Zrenjanin	A	1-0	Jovanovic S.
13/04/96	Crvena zvezda Beograd	H	1-3	Milenkovic (p)
17/04/96	Sloboda Uzice	A	1-1	Jovanovic S.
26/04/96	Vojvodina Novi Sad	H	3-1	Stevanovic 2, Jovanovic S.
04/05/96	Cukaricki Beograd	A	1-4	Dimitrijevic (p)
11/05/96	Rad Beograd	A	1-3	Stevanovic
18/05/96	Partizan Beograd	H	1-4	Jovanovic S.

SLOBODA UZICE

CLUB DIRECTORY

FK Sloboda Uzice
Omladinska b.b.
31000 Uzice
tel - (031) 24385
Year of Formation - 1925
President - Ratomir Golubovic
Secretary - Vladimir Acimovic
Coach - Slobodan Dogandzic; Milovan Rajevac; Jesetrije Jovanovic
Stadium - Sloboda (12,000)

APPEARANCES 95/96

	P	Ap	(s)	Gls
Nikola ANDJELIC	M		(1)	
Nenad CIRKOVIC	M		(2)	
Dragan CULUM	G	13		
Ivica CVETANOVSKI	D	6		
Vujica DRAGUTINOVIC	M	12		1
Djoko ILIC	D	8	(2)	
Radisa ILIC	G		(1)	
Predrag KOPRIVICA	D	10		
Dusan LEKOVIC	G	5		
Vladimir MATIJASEVIC	M	6	(6)	1
Slobodan MILANOVIC	A	7	(4)	
Dejan MILICEVIC	M	7	(2)	
Goran MILOVANOVIC	A	11	(4)	3
Sladjan NIKOLIC	M	8	(3)	1
Dusko PANTELIC	M	7	(2)	
Dragan PEJIC	M	1	(3)	
Predrag POPOVIC	M	14	(1)	1
Aleksandar RADOVIC	A	15	(1)	1
Predrag RISTANOVIC	D	9	(1)	
Uros STAMATOVIC	M	4	(2)	1
Dragan STOJANOVIC	M	3	(3)	
Dragan TOMIC	D	14		1
Vladan VASIC	D		(1)	
Zivojin VIDOJEVIC	M	7	(7)	
Milorad VRANJES	M	16		
Ivan VUKOMANOVIC	M	1	(5)	
Goran ZDRAVKOVIC	D	14		

LEAGUE RESULTS 1995/96

Date	Opponent	H/A	Score	Scorers
17/02/96	Crvena zvezda Beograd	A	0-1	
23/02/96	Cukaricki Beograd	H	0-0	
28/02/96	Vojvodina Novi Sad	H	1-2	Popovic
02/03/96	Radnicki Nis	A	1-2	Matijasevic
06/03/96	Proleter Zrenjanin	H	2-1	Tomic, Dragutinovic
09/03/96	Rad Beograd	H	0-1	
16/03/96	Partizan Beograd	A	0-5	
20/03/96	FK Becej	H	1-1	Milovanovic (p)
22/03/96	Mladost Lucani	A	1-5	Milovanovic
30/03/96	Proleter Zrenjanin	A	0-3	
02/04/96	Crvena zvezda Beograd	H	0-4	
05/04/96	Cukaricki Beograd	A	0-3	
13/04/96	Vojvodina Novi Sad	A	0-2	
17/04/96	Radnicki Nis	H	1-1	Nikolic (p)
27/04/96	Rad Beograd	A	0-4	
04/05/96	Partizan Beograd	H	1-5	Stamatovic
11/05/96	FK Becej	A	0-1	
18/05/96	Mladost Lucani	H	2-0	Milovanovic, Radovic (p)

VOJVODINA NOVI SAD

CLUB DIRECTORY

FK Vojvodina
Zarka Zrenjanina 8, 21000 Novi Sad
tel - (021) 25481/25288
fax - (021) 20270
Year of Formation - 1914
President - Nenad Knezevic
Secretary - Nestor Sremcev
Coach - Djoko Hadzijevski
(96/97 - Dragoljub Bekvalac)
Stadium - Gradski (22,000)

MAJOR HONOURS
League Championship - (2) 1968, 1989.

APPEARANCES 95/96

	P	Ap	(s)	Gls
Darko ANIC	A	27	(2)	4
Savo BARAC	M		(3)	
Nikoslav BJEGOVIC	D	24		1
Branko BOZOVIC	D		(3)	
Zoran CILINSEK	M	20		2
Bozo DJURKOVIC	M	16	(8)	5
Zdravko DRINCIC	A	10	(2)	2
Ljubisa DUNDJERSKI	D	26	(4)	
Igor GLUSCEVIC	M	8	(21)	5
Dejan GOVEDARICA	M	14		7
Dusan GRUJIC	M		(3)	
Sead HALILAGIC	M		(1)	
Ivan ILIC	D	8	(2)	1
Goran JEZDIMIROVIC	M	23		2
Aleksandar KOCIC	G	35		
Leo LERINC	A	2	(2)	
Zoran MIJANOVIC	G	1		
Sasa MILOSEVSKI (MAC)	M	32		8
Damir OZEGOVIC	M	8	(13)	1
Miodrag PANTELIC	A	15		5
Dragan RADOJICIC	A	12	(9)	5
Zoltan SABO	D	27	(1)	
Zoran SARABA	D	11	(4)	2
Goran SAULA	D	32		9
Nebojsa SCEPANOVIC	M	3		2
Damir STOJAK	A	7	(6)	4
Mico VRANJES	M	10	(16)	1
Miodrag VUKOTIC	D	25	(1)	

LEAGUE RESULTS 1995/96

12/08/95	Napredak Krusevac	H	6-0	Govedarica 2, Jezdimirovic, Gluscevic, Scepanovic, Djurkovic
18/08/95	Proleter Zrenjanin	A	0-1	
27/08/95	Crvena zvezda Beograd	H	3-2	Scepanovic, Djurkovic, Pantelic (p)
03/09/95	Buducnost Podgorica	A	2-1	Pantelic, Milosevski
09/09/95	FK Zemun	H	2-0	Milosevski, Saraba
16/09/95	Radnicki Nis	H	2-1	Saraba, Saula
23/09/95	OFK Beograd	A	1-0	Anic (p)
30/09/95	Partizan Beograd	H	1-1	Govedarica
07/10/95	FK Becej	A	0-0	
14/10/95	Napredak Krusevac	A	3-2	Pantelic (p), Milosevski, Anic
21/10/95	Proleter Zrenjanin	H	4-2	Saula, Pantelic (p), Govedarica, Milosevski
28/10/95	Crvena zvezda Beograd	A	1-2	Pantelic
04/11/95	Buducnost Podgorica	H	3-0	Govedarica, Gluscevic, Milosevski
19/11/95	FK Zemun	A	1-1	Gluscevic
25/11/95	Radnicki Nis	A	0-0	
02/12/95	OFK Beograd	H	3-0	Saula, Govedarica, og (Ramovs)
09/12/95	Partizan Beograd	A	0-1	
16/12/95	FK Becej	H	2-0	Govedarica, Jezdimirovic
16/02/96	Proleter Zrenjanin	A	2-0	Saula, Vranjes
24/02/96	Crvena zvezda Beograd	H	1-1	Saula (p)
28/02/96	Sloboda Uzice	A	2-1	Djurkovic, Milosevski
01/03/96	Cukaricki Beograd	H	1-1	Gluscevic
06/03/96	Mladost Lucani	H	5-0	Stojak 2, Milosevski, Cilinsek, Anic
09/03/96	Radnicki Nis	H	4-0	Stojak, Drincic, Bjegovic, Radojicic
16/03/96	Rad Beograd	A	2-2	Saula (p), Radojicic
20/03/96	Partizan Beograd	H	1-1	Saula
23/03/96	FK Becej	A	0-1	
30/03/96	Mladost Lucani	A	2-1	Saula, Anic
03/04/96	Proleter Zrenjanin	H	1-1	Ilic
06/04/96	Crvena zvezda Beograd	A	0-1	
13/04/96	Sloboda Uzice	H	2-0	Drincic, Stojak
17/04/96	Cukaricki Beograd	A	0-1	
26/04/96	Radnicki Nis	A	1-3	Gluscevic
04/05/96	Rad Beograd	H	0-0	
11/05/96	Partizan Beograd	A	3-6	Saula (p), Radojicic, Cilinsek
18/05/96	FK Becej	H	5-0	Djurkovic 2, Radojicic, Milosevski, Ozegovic

FK ZEMUN

CLUB DIRECTORY

FK Zemun
Ugrinovacka 80
11080 Zemun
tel - (011) 612949/618889/615944
fax - (011) 193879
Year of Formation - 1946
President - Dusan Celar
Secretary - Slobodan Pejovic
Coach - Jovan Kovrlija
Stadium - Gradski (15,000)

APPEARANCES 95/96

	P	Ap	(s)	Gls
Bojan BANJAC	A	14		
Igor BOGDANOVIC	A	12	(1)	2
Milan BOSANAC	M	3		
Goran CELAR	D		(1)	
Nenad DZODIC	M	6	(3)	
Gavrilo GAJIC	M	1	(1)	
Dejan ILIC	M	11	(1)	
Sasaa ILIC	A	3	(1)	5
Djordje INDJIC	M		(2)	
Ivan LITERA	D	2	(7)	
Dusko LJUBICIC	M	12	(4)	1
Srdjan MAKSIMOVIC	G	3	(1)	
Aleksandar MARKOVIC	G	10		
Predrag MARKOVIC	D	10		1
Vladimir MARTINOVIC	M	8	(1)	
Velibor MATANOVIC	D	13	(2)	1
Dragoslav MILENKOVIC	D	11		
Milan MILIJAS	D	7	(2)	
Goran MILOSEVIC	M	16		4
Dragan POPOV	D	7		
Slavko RADOVIC	G	5		
Radoslav RADULOVIC	M	12	(1)	2
Zoran SMILJANIC	M	1	(5)	
Vladimir SUBERT	M	12	(1)	1
Dusan SVEDIC	D		(3)	
Nenad TOMIC	M	1	(4)	
Zoran TOMIC	M	3	(7)	
Radovan TURUDIJA	D	15	(1)	

LEAGUE RESULTS 1995/96

13/08/95	Crvena zvezda Beograd	A	1-2	Milosevic
19/08/95	Partizan Beograd	H	0-2	
26/08/95	Buducnost Podgorica	A	2-1	og 2 (Vlaisavljevic 2)
02/09/95	FK Becej	H	1-0	Ljubicic
09/09/95	Vojvodina Novi Sad	A	0-2	
16/09/95	Napredak Krusevac	H	1-0	Radulovic
23/09/95	Radnicki Nis	A	1-2	Radulovic
30/09/95	Proleter Zrenjanin	H	1-1	Subert
07/10/95	OFK Beograd	A	1-1	Milosevic
14/10/95	Crvena zvezda Beograd	H	1-2	og (Stefanovic)
21/10/95	Partizan Beograd	A	0-5	
28/10/95	Buducnost Podgorica	H	3-0	Bogdanovic, Markovic P., Milosevic
04/11/95	FK Becej	A	0-3	
19/11/95	Vojvodina Novi Sad	H	1-1	Bogdanovic
25/11/95	Napredak Krusevac	A	0-1	
02/12/95	Radnicki Nis	H	1-1	Matanovic
09/12/95	Proleter Zrenjanin	A	0-1	
16/12/95	OFK Beograd	H	6-1	Ilic S. 5, Milosevic

PROMOTED CLUBS

SECOND DIVISION FINAL TABLES 95/96

FIRST PHASE

		Pd	W	D	L	F	A	Pt	GD
1	Cukaricki Beograd	18	10	8	0	34	6	38	+28
2	Rad Beograd	18	9	5	4	32	12	32	+20
3	Mladost Lucani	18	8	4	6	25	20	28	+5
4	Sloboda Uzice	18	8	3	7	19	24	27	-5
5	Radnicki Novi Beograd	18	7	3	8	30	32	24	-2
6	Hajduk Kula	18	5	7	6	16	19	22	-3
7	Obilic Beograd	18	6	4	8	28	34	22	-6
8	Mladost Backi Jarak	18	5	5	8	23	37	20	-14
9	FK Loznica	18	4	5	9	24	37	17	-13
10	Borac Cacak	18	4	4	10	15	25	16	-10

FINAL ROUND

		Pd	W	D	L	F	A	Pt	GD	
1	FK Zemun	18	10	3	5	29	14	40	+15	(7)
2	**Borac Cacak**	**18**	**10**	**2**	**6**	**24**	**13**	**34**	**+11**	**(2)**
3	**Hajduk Kula**	**18**	**8**	**4**	**6**	**20**	**20**	**34**	**=**	**(6)**
4	Buducnost Podgorica	18	8	5	5	15	14	32	+1	(3)
5	Obilic Beograd	18	8	2	8	20	18	31	+2	(5)
6	OFK Beograd	18	8	3	7	23	22	31	+1	(4)
7	FK Loznica	18	7	4	7	23	22	27	+1	(2)
8	Mladost Backi Jarak	18	7	2	9	18	25	27	-7	(4)
9	Napredak Krusevac	18	6	3	9	22	27	24	-5	(3)
10	Radnicki Novi Beograd	18	2	4	12	13	32	17	-19	(7)

N.B. Figures in brackets indicate points carried through from First Phase.

PROMOTION PLAY-OFFS
Buducnost Valjevo 1, Buducnost Podgorica 0
Buducnost Podgorica 3, Buducnost Valjevo 0
(Buducnost Podgorica 3-1)

RELEGATION PLAY-OFFS
Rudar Plevlja 2, Napredak Krusevac 0
Napredak Krusevac 2, Rudar Plevlja 2
(Rudar Plevlja 4-2)

CLUB DIRECTORY

FK Borac
Gradski Bedem 6
32000 Cacak
tel - (032) 22481/22700
Year of Formation - 1926
President - Dragovan Krivokuca
Secretary - Marko Radocaj
Coach - Slavko Vojcic; Milorad Kosanovic; Dusan Maric; Dimitrije Mitrovic
Stadium - Gradski (12,000)

CLUB DIRECTORY

FK Hajduk
Svetozara Markovica 8
25230 Kula
tel - (025) 723569
fax - (025) 722812
Year of Formation - 1925
President - Radoman Vasovic
Secretary - Aleksandar Vlaskalic
Coach - Dragoljub Bekvalac
Stadium - Hajduk (10,000)

MAJOR SUMMER TRANSFERS 1996

AUSTRIA

PLAYER	OLD CLUB	NEW CLUB
Reinhold BREU (GER)	1.FC Köln (GER)	FK Austria Wien
Ronald BRUNMAYR	FC Linz	FK Austria Wien
Herbert GAGER	SC Niederösterreich FC Admira	FK Austria Wien
Franz GRUBER	SC Niederösterreich FC Admira	FK Austria Wien
Attila HORVÁTH (HUN)	Zalaegerszegi TE (HUN)	FK Austria Wien
Patrick KASUBA	VfB Mödling	FK Austria Wien
Günter KREISSL	Himberg	FK Austria Wien
Michael ZECHNER	VfB Mödling	FK Austria Wien
Michael ANICIC (YUG)	Eintracht Frankfurt (GER)	Grazer AK
Erwin DAMPFHOFER	SV Ried	Grazer AK
Boban DMITROVIC (YUG)	Rad Beograd (YUG)	Grazer AK
Bruno FRIESENBICHLER	Flavia Solva	Grazer AK
Enrico KULOVITS	SV Oberwart	Grazer AK
Alexander MANNINGER	SV Casino Salzburg	Grazer AK
Thomas SILBERBERGER	FC Tirol Innsbruck	Grazer AK
Manfred ZSAK	unattached	Grazer AK
Dietmar BERCHTOLD	SK Vorwärts Steyr	LASK Linz
Christian HAUSER	Telfs	LASK Linz
Johann KOGLER	SC Niederösterreich FC Admira	LASK Linz
Vidar RISETH (NOR)	Kongsvinger IL (NOR)	LASK Linz
Markus SCHARRER	SC Niederösterreich FC Admira	LASK Linz
Alain BETTAGNO (BEL)	R Standard Liège (BEL)	FC Linz
Matthias BLEYER	SV Braunau	FC Linz
Erik MYKLAND (NOR)	IK Start (NOR)	FC Linz
Zeljko PAVLOVIC (CRO)	Zagreb (CRO)	FC Linz
Josko POPOVIC (CRO)	Zagreb (CRO)	FC Linz
Ernst AIGNER	VSE St. Pölten	SC Niederösterreich FC Admira
Dragan BODUL (YUG)	Favoritner AC	SC Niederösterreich FC Admira
Rainer HOFFMANN	SV Gerasdorf	SC Niederösterreich FC Admira
Christian KRAIGNER	SV Braunau	SC Niederösterreich FC Admira
Peter MRAZ (SVK)	Inter Bratislava (SVK)	SC Niederösterreich FC Admira
Arminas NARBEKOVAS (LIT)	FK Austria Wien	SC Niederösterreich FC Admira
Gerald OBRECHT	VfB Mödling	SC Niederösterreich FC Admira
Christian SALABA	VSE St. Pölten	SC Niederösterreich FC Admira
Andrzej LESIAK (POL)	SV Ried	SK Rapid Wien
Marek PENKSA (SVK)	Grazer AK	SK Rapid Wien
Christian PROSENIK	SV Casino Salzburg	SK Rapid Wien
Krzysztof RATAJCZYK (POL)	Legia Warszawa (POL)	SK Rapid Wien
Thomas ZINGLER	SC Niederösterreich FC Admira	SK Rapid Wien
Rene WAGNER (TCH)	Slavia Praha (TCH)	SK Rapid Wien
Zoltán ACZÉL (HUN)	Pécsi MFC (HUN)	SV Ried
Dirk KLINGE (GER)	SG Wattenscheid 09 (GER)	SV Ried
Marcel OERLEMANS (HOL)	VfB Mödling	SV Ried
Rainer SCHÜTTERLE (GER)	MSV Duisburg (GER)	SV Ried
Martin AMERHAUSER	Grazer AK	SV Casino Salzburg
Eduard GLIEDER	Grazer AK	SV Casino Salzburg
Walter KOGLER	FK Austria Wien	SV Casino Salzburg
Heiko LAESSIG (GER)	KFC Uerdingen (GER)	SV Casino Salzburg
Roman SZEWCZYK (POL)	FC Sochaux (FRA)	SV Casino Salzburg
Enzo GAMBARO (ITA)	Grimsby Town (ENG)	SK Sturm Graz
Giuseppe GIANNINI (ITA)	Roma (ITA)	SK Sturm Graz
Martin HIDEN	SV Casino Salzburg	SK Sturm Graz
Pål LYDERSEN (NOR)	IK Start (NOR)	SK Sturm Graz
Marcus PÜRK	Real Sociedad (ESP)	SK Sturm Graz
Christian FLINDT (DEN)	FC Lugano (SUI)	FC Tirol Innsbruck
Simon HENZLER (GER)	VfB Stuttgart (GER)	FC Tirol Innsbruck
Christian MAYRLEB	SC Niederösterreich FC Admira	FC Tirol Innsbruck
Maciej SLIWOWSKI (POL)	SK Rapid Wien	FC Tirol Innsbruck

BELGIUM

PLAYER	OLD CLUB	NEW CLUB
Oleg YASHCHUK (UKR)	Nyva Ternopil (UKR)	RSC Anderlecht
Samuel JOHNSON (GHA)	Kalamata (GRE)	RSC Anderlecht
Chidi NWANU (NIG)	K St.-Truidense VV	RSC Anderlecht
Tibor SELYMES (ROM)	KSV Cercle Brugge	RSC Anderlecht
Alin STOICA (ROM)	Steaua Bucuresti (ROM)	RSC Anderlecht
Igor NIKOLOVSKI (MAC)	Vardar Skopje (MAC)	Royal Antwerp FC
Gouran MAKAEV (KAZ)	KFC Lommelse SK	Royal Antwerp FC
Gerry POPPE	KV Oostende	Royal Antwerp FC
Anthony ANNICAERT	KRC Genk	KSV Cercle Brugge
Frode FERMANN (NOR)	Tromsø IL (NOR)	KSV Cercle Brugge
Christophe LYCKE	KV Oostende	KSV Cercle Brugge
Dominique VANMAELE	KSK Beveren	KSV Cercle Brugge
Eric DEFLANDRE	KFC Germinal Ekeren	Club Brugge KV
Anders NIELSEN (DEN)	K St.-Truidense VV	Club Brugge KV
Oliver SURAY	RSC Anderlecht	RSC Charleroi
Zsolt PETRY (HUN)	Gençlerbirligi (TUR)	RSC Charleroi
Dirk DAELMANS	K St.-Truidense VV	KSC Eendracht Aalst
Dimitri DELIERE	La Louvière	KSC Eendracht Aalst
Dany D'HONDT	KSV Waregem	KSC Eendracht Aalst
Christophe LAUWERS	KSV Cercle Brugge	KSC Eendracht Aalst
Krist PORTE	Royal Antwerp FC	KSC Eendracht Aalst
Vincas JONAITIS	La Louvière	R Excelsior Mouscron
Lokondo MPENZA	KV Kortrijk	R Excelsior Mouscron
Mbo MPENZA	KV Kortrijk	R Excelsior Mouscron
Alex CZERNIATYNSKI	KV Mechelen	KFC Germinal Ekeren
Nick DESCAMPS	KSV Waregem	KFC Germinal Ekeren
Cvijan MILOSEVIC (BOS)	Royal Antwerp FC	KFC Germinal Ekeren
Eddy SNELDERS	K Lierse SK	KFC Germinal Ekeren
Flórián URBAN (HUN)	Györi ETO FC (HUN)	KFC Germinal Ekeren
Edwin VAN ANKEREN (HOL)	KSC Eendracht Aalst	KFC Germinal Ekeren
István BROCKHAUSER (HUN)	Györi ETO FC (HUN)	KRC Genk
Didier GAENS	Tongeren	KRC Genk
Bart GOOR	Verbroedering Geel	KRC Genk
Stijn HAELDERMANS	MVV (HOL)	KRC Genk
Souleymane OULARE (GUI)	KSV Waregem	KRC Genk
Serge SWINNEN	Overpelt VV	KRC Genk
Bart VANMARSENILLE	K St.-Truidense VV	KRC Genk
Sretko VUKSANOVIC (BOS)	KAA Gent	KRC Genk
Vujica DRAGUTINOVIC (YUG)	Barac Cacak (YUG)	KAA Gent
Ronald FOGUENNE	R Standard Liège	KAA Gent
Nordin JBARI	RSC Anderlecht	KAA Gent
Tomas VASOV (YUG)	Borac Cacak (YUG)	KAA Gent
Olivier BAUDRY (FRA)	FC Mulhouse (FRA)	KRC Harelbeke
Danny DEVUYST	KV Oostende	KRC Harelbeke
Ronald GASPERCIC	KRC Genk	KRC Harelbeke
Martin LAAMERS (HOL)	Vitesse (HOL)	KRC Harelbeke
Daniel MAES	KV Oostende	KRC Harelbeke
Mike ORIGI (KEN)	KV Oostende	KRC Harelbeke
Piet VERSCHELDE	R Excelsior Mouscron	KRC Harelbeke
Filip HAAGDOREN	KSK Beveren	K Lierse SK
Stanley MENZO (HOL)	PSV (HOL)	K Lierse SK
Eric VAN MEIR	RSC Charleroi	K Lierse SK
Vaclav BUDKA (TCH)	Sparta Praha (TCH)	KSC Lokeren
Christiaan JANSSENS	St.-Niklaas	KSC Lokeren
Jan KOLLER (TCH)	Sparta Praha (TCH)	KSC Lokeren
Edward LINSKENS (HOL)	NAC (HOL)	KSC Lokeren
Hervé VAN OVERTVELT	KSK Beveren	KSC Lokeren
Roman VONASEK (TCH)	Sparta Praha (TCH)	KSC Lokeren
René KLOMP (HOL)	PSV (HOL)	KFC Lommelse SK
Benny LUNENBURG	Overpelt VV	KFC Lommelse SK
Michel NOBEN	Patro Eisden	KFC Lommelse SK
Revaz ARVELADZE (GEO)	FC Homburg (GER)	KV Mechelen
Ralph HASENHÜTTL (AUT)	SV Casino Salzburg (AUT)	KV Mechelen
Dirk LEHMANN (GER)	K Lierse SK	RWD Molenbeek
Aleksandar VESELINOVIC (YUG)	Radnicki Nis (YUG)	RWD Molenbeek

MAJOR SUMMER TRANSFERS 1996

PLAYER	OLD CLUB	NEW CLUB
Patrick GOOTS	KSK Beveren	K St.-Truidense VV
Philippe LENGLOIS	KSV Waregem	K St.-Truidense VV
Mircea REDNIC (ROM)	R Standard Liège	K St.-Truidense VV
Patrick TEPPERS	RFC Seraing	K St.-Truidense VV
Marc WUYTS	RWD Molenbeek	K St.-Truidense VV
Zouir EL KAHAJJAJ (MAR)	WAC Casablanca (MAR)	R Standard Liège
Waldemar JASKULSKI (POL)	Widzew Lodz (POL)	R Standard Liège
Nebojsa KRUPNIKOVIC (YUG)	Crvena zvezda Beograd (YUG)	R Standard Liège
Andrzej KUBICA (POL)	KSV Waregem	R Standard Liège
Peter MAES	KSK Beveren	R Standard Liège

DENMARK

PLAYER	OLD CLUB	NEW CLUB
Steffen HØJER	Viborg FF	AaB
John SIVEBAEK	Vejle BK	AGF
Kern LYHNE	Ikast FS	AGF
Michael NONBO	Naestved BK	AGF
Johnny VILSTRUP	Luton Town (ENG)	AGF
Kenny THORUP	FC København	Hvidovre IF
Martin NIELSEN	AGF	FC København
Nicolai WAEL	Naestved BK	FC København
Henrik LARSEN	Lyngby FC	FC København
Jacob SVINGGAARD	Fortuna Köln (GER)	FC København
Bjarne GOLDBAEK	1.FC Köln (GER)	FC København
Carsten HEMMINGSEN	OB	FC København
Miklos MOLNAR	Herfølge BK	Lyngby FC
Michael HANSEN	Silkeborg IF	OB
Johnny HANSEN	OB	Silkeborg IF
Jan SØNKSEN	Ikast FS	Silkeborg IF
Nocko JOKOVIC	AGF	Silkeborg IF
Bo HARDER	Ikast FS	Vejle BK
Dan SØRENSEN	Ikast FS	Vejle BK
Henrik KASTBJERG	Silkeborg IF	Viborg FF
Kenni SOMMER	Silkeborg IF	Viborg FF

ENGLAND

PLAYER	OLD CLUB	NEW CLUB
John LUKIC	Leeds United	Arsenal
Patrick VIEIRA (FRA)	Milan (ITA)	Arsenal
Rémi GARDE (FRA)	RC Strasbourg (FRA)	Arsenal
NÉLSON (POR)	Sporting CP (POR)	Aston Villa
Sasa CURCIC (YUG)	Bolton Wanderers	Aston Villa
Yorgos DONIS (GRE)	Panathinaikos (GRE)	Blackburn Rovers
Gianluca VIALLI (ITA)	Juventus (ITA)	Chelsea
Roberto DI MATTEO (ITA)	Lazio (ITA)	Chelsea
Franck LEBOEUF (FRA)	RC Strasbourg (FRA)	Chelsea
Gary McALLISTER (SCO)	Leeds United	Coventry City
Michael O'NEILL (NIR)	Hibernian (SCO)	Coventry City
Régis GENAUX (BEL)	R Standard Liège (BEL)	Coventry City
Aljosa ASANOVIC (CRO)	Hajduk Split (CRO)	Derby County
Christian DAILLY (SCO)	Dundee United (SCO)	Derby County
Jacob LAURSEN (DEN)	Silkeborg IF (DEN)	Derby County
Gary SPEED (WAL)	Leeds United	Everton
Paul GERRARD	Oldham Athletic	Everton
Lee BOWYER	Charlton Athletic	Leeds United
Nigel MARTYN	Crystal Palace	Leeds United
Ian RUSH (WAL)	Liverpool	Leeds United
Lee SHARPE	Manchester United	Leeds United
Mustafa IZZET	Chelsea	Leicester City
Kasey KELLER (USA)	Millwall	Leicester City
Spencer PRIOR	Norwich City	Leicester City
Ian MARSHALL	Ipswich Town	Leicester City
Patrik BERGER (TCH)	Borussia Dortmund (GER)	Liverpool
Karel POBORSKY (TCH)	Slavia Praha (TCH)	Manchester United
Jordi CRUIJFF (HOL)	FC Barcelona (ESP)	Manchester United
Ronny JOHNSEN (NOR)	Besiktas (TUR)	Manchester United
Ole Gunnar SOLSKJAER (NOR)	Molde FK (NOR)	Manchester United
Raimond VAN DER GOUW (HOL)	Vitesse (HOL)	Manchester United
Fabrizio RAVANELLI (ITA)	Juventus (ITA)	Middlesbrough
EMERSON (BRA)	FC Porto (POR)	Middlesbrough
Mikkel BECK (DEN)	Fortuna Köln (GER)	Middlesbrough
Alan SHEARER	Blackburn Rovers	Newcastle United
Dean SAUNDERS (WAL)	Galatasaray (TUR)	Nottingham Forest
Nikola JERKAN (CRO)	Real Oviedo (ESP)	Nottingham Forest
Andy BOOTH	Huddersfield Town	Sheffield Wednesday
Scott OAKES	Luton Town	Sheffield Wednesday
Matthew CLARKE	Rotherham	Sheffield Wednesday
Orlando TRUSTFULL (HOL)	Feyenoord (HOL)	Sheffield Wednesday
Wayne COLLINS	Crewe Alexandra	Sheffield Wednesday
Richard DRYDEN	Bristol City	Southampton
Alex RAE (SCO)	Millwall	Sunderland
Paul STEWART	Liverpool	Sunderland
Tony COTON	Manchester United	Sunderland
Niall QUINN (IRL)	Manchester City	Sunderland
Allan NIELSEN (DEN)	Brøndby IF (DEN)	Tottenham Hotspur
Florin RADUCIOIU (ROM)	RCD Espanyol (ESP)	West Ham United
Paulo FUTRE (POR)	Milan (ITA)	West Ham United
Richard HALL	Southampton	West Ham United
Mark BOWEN (WAL)	Norwich City	West Ham United
Ben THATCHER	Millwall	Wimbledon
Duncan JUPP	Fulham	Wimbledon

FRANCE

PLAYER	OLD CLUB	NEW CLUB
Steve MARLET	Red Star 93	AJ Auxerre
Thomas DENIAUD	SCO Angers	AJ Auxerre
Antoine SIBIERSKI	Lille OSC	AJ Auxerre
Ned ZELIC (AUS)	Eintracht Frankfurt (GER)	AJ Auxerre
Laurent CIECHELSKI	FC Gueugnon	AJ Auxerre
Patrick MOREAUS	AS Saint-Etienne	SC Bastia
Sébastien PEREZ	AS Saint-Etienne	SC Bastia
Lubomir MORAVCIK (SVK)	AS Saint-Etienne	SC Bastia
Fabien PIVETEAU	AS Monaco	SC Bastia
Wilfried GOHEL	RC Strasbourg	SC Bastia
Laurent WEBER	RC Strasbourg	SC Bastia
Pascal CAMADINI	Perpignan FC	SC Bastia
Ermin SILJAK (SLO)	SCT Olimpija Ljubljana (SLO)	SC Bastia
Patrick VALERY	AS Monaco	SC Bastia
Jamie FULLARTON (SCO)	St. Mirren (SCO)	SC Bastia
Cyril DOMORAUD	Red Star 93	Girondins de Bordeaux
Lionel PEREZ	Stade Lavallois	Girondins de Bordeaux
Johan MICOUD	AS Cannes	Girondins de Bordeaux
Bernard LAMBOURDE	AS Cannes	Girondins de Bordeaux
Ibrahima BA	Le Havre AC	Girondins de Bordeaux
Michel PAVON	Montpellier HSC	Girondins de Bordeaux
Miklós LENDVAI (HUN)	Újpesti TE (HUN)	Girondins de Bordeaux
Gilbert BODART (BEL)	R Standard Liège (BEL)	Girondins de Bordeaux
Marc ZANOTTI	SC Toulon	Girondins de Bordeaux
Patrick COLLETER	Paris Saint-Germain FC	Girondins de Bordeaux
Stéphane ZIANI	Stade Rennais FC	Girondins de Bordeaux
PAULO SÉRGIO Gralak (BRA)	Coritiba (BRA)	Girondins de Bordeaux
Claudio BIAGGIO (ARG)	San Lorenzo (ARG)	Girondins de Bordeaux
Jean-Pierre PAPIN (FRA)	FC Bayern München (GER)	Girondins de Bordeaux
Marc DELAROCHE	AS Monaco	SM Caen
Etienne MENDY	FC Sochaux	SM Caen
Stéphane ROCHE	Olympique Lyonnais	SM Caen
Jimmy HEBERT	US Dunkerque	SM Caen

MAJOR SUMMER TRANSFERS 1996

PLAYER	OLD CLUB	NEW CLUB
Grzegorz LEWANDOWSKI (POL)	Legia Warszawa (POL)	SM Caen
Stéphane MOREAU	FC Nantes	SM Caen
Jean-Yves DE BLASIIS	Girondins de Bordeaux	SM Caen
Anthony BANCAREL	Girondins de Bordeaux	SM Caen
Joachim FERNANDEZ	Girondins de Bordeaux	SM Caen
Samassi ABOU	Olympique Lyonnais	AS Cannes
Victor KONWLO (LIB)	AS Nancy-Lorraine	AS Cannes
Cédric DAURY	Le Havre AC	AS Cannes
Yannick FISCHER	Girondins de Bordeaux	AS Cannes
Christophe HORLAVILLE	AS Cannes	En Avant Guingamp
Marek JOZWIAK (POL)	Legia Warszawa (POL)	En Avant Guingamp
Eric ASSADOURIAN	Olympique Lyonnais	En Avant Guingamp
Jean-Marc MOULIN	Olympique Lyonnais	En Avant Guingamp
Jean-Luc VANNUCHI	OGC Nice	En Avant Guingamp
Yannick BARET	AS Monaco	En Avant Guingamp
Christopher WREH (LIB)	AS Monaco	En Avant Guingamp
Ardijan KOZNIKU (CRO)	AS Cannes	Le Havre AC
Roger BOLI	RC Lens	Le Havre AC
Dzoni NOVAK (SLO)	SCT Olimpija Ljubljana (SLO)	Le Havre AC
David MAZZONCINI	FC Martigues	Le Havre AC
Tomasz WIESZCZYCKI (POL)	Legia Warszawa (POL)	Le Havre AC
Abder RAMDANE	Nîmes-Olympique	Le Havre AC
David REGIS	RC Strasbourg	RC Lens
Vladimir SMICER (TCH)	Slavia Praha (TCH)	RC Lens
Philippe BRUNEL	FC Gueugnon	RC Lens
Sébastien DALLET	En Avant Guingamp	RC Lens
Sasha RYCHKOV (RUS)	R Standard Liège (BEL)	RC Lens
Jean-Claude NADON	Lille OSC	RC Lens
Bojan BANJAC (YUG)	FK Zemun (YUG)	Lille OSC
David GARCION	FC Nantes	Lille OSC
Gilles HAMPARTZOUMIAN	AS Cannes	Lille OSC
Pegguy ARPHEXAD	RC Lens	Lille OSC
Alain CAVEGLIA	Le Havre AC	Olympique Lyonnais
Christophe COCARD	AJ Auxerre	Olympique Lyonnais
Eric ROY	Olympique Lyonnais	Olympique Marseille
Reynald PEDROS	FC Nantes	Olympique Marseille
Xavier GRAVELAINE	Paris Saint-Germain FC	Olympique Marseille
Yordan LECHKOV (BUL)	Hamburger SV (GER)	Olympique Marseille
Mehdi BEN SLIMANE (TUN)	AS Marsa (TUN)	Olympique Marseille
Chris MAKIN (ENG)	Oldham Athletic (ENG)	Olympique Marseille
Andreas KÖPKE (GER)	Eintracht Frankfurt (GER)	Olympique Marseille
Alberto MALUSCI (ITA)	Parma (ITA)	Olympique Marseille
Ivan FRANCESCHINI (ITA)	Parma (ITA)	Olympique Marseille
Lionel LETIZI	OGC Nice	FC Metz
Hassan KACHLOUL	US Dunkerque	FC Metz
Amara TRAORE (SEN)	FC Gueugnon	FC Metz
André BIANCARELLI	SC Bastia	FC Metz
Mariano BOMBARDA (HOL)	FC Groningen (HOL)	FC Metz
Philippe LEONARD (BEL)	R Standard Liège (BEL)	AS Monaco
Martin DJETOU	RC Strasbourg	AS Monaco
Lilian MARTIN	US Dunkerque	AS Monaco
Marco GRASSI (SUI)	Stade Rennais FC	AS Monaco
John COLLINS (SCO)	Celtic (SCO)	AS Monaco
Franck SAUZEE	RC Strasbourg	Montpellier HSC
Fabrice DIVERT	En Avant Guingamp	Montpellier HSC
Kader FERHAOUI (ALG)	AS Cannes	Montpellier HSC
William PRUNIER	FC København (DEN)	Montpellier HSC
Pascal FUGIER	Stade Rennais FC	Montpellier HSC
Frédéric MARTIN	OGC Nice	Montpellier HSC
Roman KOSECKI (POL)	FC Nantes	Montpellier HSC
Christophe ROBERT	Louhans-Cuiseaux 71	AS Nancy-Lorraine
Jean-Philippe SECHET	AS Saint-Etienne	AS Nancy-Lorraine

PLAYER	OLD CLUB	NEW CLUB
David FANZEL	FC Gueugnon	AS Nancy-Lorraine
Philip GRAY (NIR)	Sunderland (ENG)	AS Nancy-Lorraine
Wilson ORUMA (NIG)	RC Lens	AS Nancy-Lorraine
Wagneau ELOI	RC Lens	AS Nancy-Lorraine
Adel SELLIMI (TUN)	CA Tunis (TUN)	FC Nantes
Nenad BJEKOVIC (YUG)	Olympique Marseille	FC Nantes
Bruno VALENCONY	SC Bastia	OGC Nice
RUBENILSON Monteiro Ferreira (BEL)	Royal Antwerp FC (BEL)	OGC Nice
Zoran MILINKOVIC (YUG)	KSV Waregem (BEL)	OGC Nice
Frédéric TATARIAN	Olympique Marseille	OGC Nice
Roberto ONORATI (ITA)	Genoa (ITA)	OGC Nice
Arjan VERMEULEN (HOL)	Vitesse (HOL)	OGC Nice
Patrick MBOMA	FC Metz	Paris Saint-Germain FC
Benoît CAUET	FC Nantes	Paris Saint-Germain FC
Jérôme LEROY	Stade Lavallois	Paris Saint-Germain FC
LEONARDO Nascimento (BRA)	Kashima Antlers (JPN)	Paris Saint-Germain FC
KENEDY (POR)	SL Benfica (POR)	Paris Saint-Germain FC
Jimmy ALGERINO	LB Châteauroux	Paris Saint-Germain FC
Farid DIAF	Olympique Alès	Paris Saint-Germain FC
Stéphane MAHE	Stade Rennais FC	Stade Rennais FC
Corneliu PAPURA (ROM)	Universiatea Craiova (ROM)	Stade Rennais FC
Gary SMITH (SCO)	Aberdeen (SCO)	Stade Rennais FC
Alan JOHNSTON (SCO)	Heart of Midlothian (SCO)	Stade Rennais FC
Fabien DEBEC	Olympique Lyonnais	Stade Rennais FC
Stéphane GUIVARC'H	AJ Auxerre	Stade Rennais FC
Kjetil REKDAL (NOR)	K Lierse SK (BEL)	Stade Rennais FC
Jean-Luc DOGON	Girondins de Bordeaux	RC Strasbourg
Vincent PETIT	Montpellier HSC	RC Strasbourg
Godwin OKPARA (NIG)	KSC Eendracht Aalst (BEL)	RC Strasbourg
Jan SUCHOPAREK (TCH)	Slavia Praha (TCH)	RC Strasbourg
Stéphane COLLET	OGC Nice	RC Strasbourg
Francis LLACER	Paris Saint-Germain FC	RC Strasbourg
Bruno RODRIGUEZ	SC Bastia	RC Strasbourg
Karim M'GHOGHI (BEL)	KFC Germinal Ekeren (BEL)	RC Strasbourg
Pascal NOUMA	Paris Saint-Germain FC	RC Strasbourg
GERMANY		
Sonny SILOOY (HOL)	Ajax (HOL)	Arminia Bielefeld
Rob MAAS (HOL)	Feyenoord (HOL)	Arminia Bielefeld
Heiko GERBER	Chemnitzer FC	Arminia Bielefeld
Silvio MEISSNER	Chemnitzer FC	Arminia Bielefeld
Giuseppe REINA	SG Wattenscheid 09	Arminia Bielefeld
Rainer RAUFFMANN	Eintracht Frankfurt	Arminia Bielefeld
Stefan KUNTZ	Besiktas (TUR)	Arminia Bielefeld
Erik MEIJER (HOL)	KFC Uerdingen 05	Bayer 04 Leverkusen
Jan HEINTZE (DEN)	KFC Uerdingen 05	Bayer 04 Leverkusen
Manuel CARDONI (LUX)	Jeunesse Esch (LUX)	Bayer 04 Leverkusen
Jens NOWOTNY	Karlsruher SC	Bayer 04 Leverkusen
Rene RYDLEWICZ	TSV 1860 München	Bayer 04 Leverkusen
Robert KOVAC	1.FC Nürnberg	Bayer 04 Leverkusen
Nico KOVAC	Hertha BSC Berlin	Bayer 04 Leverkusen
Mario BASLER	SV Werder Bremen	FC Bayern München
Bernd DREHER	KFC Uerdingen 05	FC Bayern München
Ruggiero RIZZITELLI (ITA)	Torino (ITA)	FC Bayern München
Markus MÜNCH	Bayer 04 Leverkusen	FC Bayern München
Markus OBERLEITNER	SpVgg Unterhaching	FC Bayern München
Samuel KUFFOUR (GHA)	1.FC Nürnberg	FC Bayern München
Carsten JANCKER	SK Rapid Wien (AUT)	FC Bayern München
Olaf SCHREIBER	FSV Zwickau	VfL Bochum
Danny WINKLER	TSG Pfeddersheim	VfL Bochum
Georgi DONKOV (BUL)	CSKA Sofia (BUL)	VfL Bochum
Engibar ENGIBAROV (BUL)	CSKA Sofia (BUL)	VfL Bochum

MAJOR SUMMER TRANSFERS 1996

PLAYER	OLD CLUB	NEW CLUB
Zoran MAMIC (CRO)	Croatia Zagreb (CRO)	VfL Bochum
Rene SCHNEIDER	FC Hansa Rostock	Borussia Dortmund
PAULO SOUSA (POR)	Juventus (ITA)	Borussia Dortmund
Wolfgang FEIERSINGER (AUT)	SV Casino Salzburg (AUT)	Borussia Dortmund
Andrzej JUSKOWIAK (POL)	Olympiakos (GRE)	Borussia Mönchengladbach
Stefan PASSLACK	KFC Uerdingen 05	Borussia Mönchengladbach
Ioan LUPESCU (ROM)	Bayer 04 Leverkusen	Borussia Mönchengladbach
Robert ENKE	FC Carl Zeiss Jena	Borussia Mönchengladbach
Hubert FOURNIER (FRA)	En Avant Guingamp (FRA)	Borussia Mönchengladbach
Horst STEFFEN	KFC Uerdingen 05	MSV Duisburg
Michael ZEYER	SV Waldhof Mannheim	MSV Duisburg
Miroslav BICANIC (CRO)	Osijek (CRO)	MSV Duisburg
Dirk ANDERS	1.FC Kaiserslautern	MSV Duisburg
Thomas GILL (NOR)	SK Sturm Graz (AUT)	MSV Duisburg
Marino SABBADINI (BEL)	RWD Molenbeek (BEL)	MSV Duisburg
David NIELSEN (DEN)	Lyngby FC (DEN)	Fortuna Düsseldorf
Rene TENGSTEDT (DEN)	FC København (DEN)	Fortuna Düsseldorf
Andreas GOLOMBEK	SG Wattenscheid 09	Fortuna Düsseldorf
Macchambes YOUNGA-MOUHANI (CON)	Borussia Mönchengladbach	Fortuna Düsseldorf
Vladimir PASIC (YUG)	Rad Beograd (YUG)	Fortuna Düsseldorf
Robert KOCIS (SVK)	Tatran Presov (SVK)	Fortuna Düsseldorf
Dieter FREY	FC Bayern München	SC Freiburg
Stefan MARASEK (AUT)	SK Rapid Wien (AUT)	SC Freiburg
Michael WAGNER (AUT)	FK Austria Wien (AUT)	SC Freiburg
Marouene GUEZMIR (TUN)	Espérance Tunis (TUN)	SC Freiburg
Jens DOWE	TSV 1860 München	Hamburger SV
Jakob FRIIS-HANSEN (DEN)	Girondins de Bordeaux (FRA)	Hamburger SV
Markus SCHOPP (AUT)	SK Sturm Graz (AUT)	Hamburger SV
Markus SCHUPP	Eintracht Frankfurt	Hamburger SV
Martin PIECKENHAGEN	MSV Duisburg	FC Hansa Rostock
Sergej BARBAREZ	1.FC Union Berlin	FC Hansa Rostock
Thomas ZIEMER	FSV Mainz 05	FC Hansa Rostock
Steffen BENTHIN	Hannover 96	FC Hansa Rostock
Thomas HENGEN	1.FC Kaiserslautern	Karlsruher SC
Timur EROGLU	SV Waldhof Mannheim	Karlsruher SC
Marc KELLER (FRA)	RC Strasbourg (FRA)	Karlsruher SC
Michael KOSTNER	FC Homburg	1.FC Köln
Ion VLADOIU (ROM)	Steaua Bucuresti (ROM)	1.FC Köln
Bodo SCHMIDT	Borussia Dortmund	1.FC Köln
Marco WALKER (SUI)	FC Basel (SUI)	TSV 1860 München
Ronny ERNST	Dynamo Dresden	TSV 1860 München
Rayk SCHRÖDER	1.FC Union Berlin	TSV 1860 München
Jörg BÖHME	Eintracht Frankfurt	TSV 1860 München
Demir DURIC	FSV Frankfurt	FC St. Pauli
Luís Firminho EMERSON (BRA)	Dnipro Dnipropetrovsk (UKR)	FC St. Pauli
Johan DE KOCK (HOL)	Roda JC (HOL)	FC Schalke 04
Marco KURZ	Borussia Dortmund	FC Schalke 04
Marc WILMOTS (BEL)	R Standard Liège (BEL)	FC Schalke 04
Matthias HAGNER	Eintracht Frankfurt	VfB Stuttgart
Franz WOHLFAHRT (AUT)	FK Austria Wien (AUT)	VfB Stuttgart
Sébastien FOURNIER (SUI)	FC Sion (SUI)	VfB Stuttgart
Zvonimir SOLDO (CRO)	Croatia Zagreb (CRO)	VfB Stuttgart
Andreas HERZOG (AUT)	FC Bayern München	SV Werder Bremen
Jens TODT	SC Freiburg	SV Werder Bremen
Heimo PFEIFENBERGER (AUT)	SV Casino Salzburg (AUT)	SV Werder Bremen
HOLLAND		
John VELDMAN	Sparta	Ajax
Mariano JUAN (ARG)	River Plate (ARG)	Ajax
Richard WITSCHGE	Girondins de Bordeaux (FRA)	Ajax
Tijani BABANGIDA (NIG)	Roda JC	Ajax
DANI (POR)	Sporting CP (POR)	Ajax
Oscar MOENS	Go Ahead Eagles	AZ

PLAYER	OLD CLUB	NEW CLUB
Ruud HEUS	Feyenoord	AZ
Barry OBDAM	FC Volendam	AZ
Kees VAN WONDEREN	NAC	Feyenoord
Patricio GRAFF (ARG)	Rosario Central (ARG)	Feyenoord
Pablo SANCHEZ (ARG)	Rosario Central (ARG)	Feyenoord
Geoffrey CLAEYS (BEL)	KSV Cercle Brugge (BEL)	Feyenoord
Jerzy DUDEK (POL)	Sokol Tychy (POL)	Feyenoord
Marek SAGANOWSKI (POL)	LKS Lodz (POL)	Feyenoord
Patrick PAAUWE	De Graafschap	Fortuna Sittard
Ali IBRAHIM (GHA)	Grasshopper-Club Zürich (SUI)	De Graafschap
Jeffrey KOOISTRA	NEC	FC Groningen
Peter SØRENSEN (DEN)	Silkeborg IF (DEN)	FC Groningen
Marco BOOGERS	West Ham United (ENG)	FC Groningen
Hans VONK	RKC	SC Heerenveen
Ole TOBIASEN (DEN)	FC København (DEN)	SC Heerenveen
Børre MEINSETH (NOR)	Viking FK (NOR)	SC Heerenveen
Earnest STEWART (USA)	Willem II	NAC
Barry VAN GALEN	Roda JC	NAC
Edwin GORTER	Vitesse	NAC
Nico JALINK	Sparta	NAC
Jeffrey VAN AS	MVV	NAC
Jean-Claude MUKANYA (ZAI)	KFC Lommelse SK (BEL)	NAC
Pascal BEEKEN (BEL)	RFC Seraing (BEL)	NAC
Bas ROORDA	FC Groningen	NEC
Maurice GRAEF	Roda JC	NEC
Jörg SOBIECH (GER)	SG Wattenscheid 09 (GER)	NEC
VAMPETA (BRA)	Fluminense (BRA)	PSV
Mark DEGRYSE (BEL)	Sheffield Wednesday (ENG)	PSV
Zeljko PETROVIC (YUG)	RKC	PSV
Jan-Willem VAN EDE	FC Utrecht	PSV
MARCELO (BRA)	Cruzeiro (BRA)	PSV
John LAMMERS	Willem II	RKC
Adri BOGERS	Willem II	RKC
Patrick VAN DIEMEN	NEC	RKC
Regillio VREDE	RKC	Roda JC
Stéphane VAN DER HEYDEN (BEL)	Club Brugge KV (BEL)	Roda JC
Martin SCHOPS (BEL)	KFC Lommelse SK (BEL)	Roda JC
Jan-Pieter MARTENS (BEL)	KV Mechelen (BEL)	Roda JC
Rob ALFLEN	Vitesse	Sparta
John BOSMAN	RSC Anderlecht (BEL)	FC Twente
Aldo SWAGER	SC Heerenveen	FC Twente
Rob McKINNON (SCO)	Motherwell (SCO)	FC Twente
Rob WITSCHGE	Feyenoord	FC Utrecht
René VAN DE BRINK	De Graafschap	FC Utrecht
Michael MOLS	FC Twente	FC Utrecht
Dick VAN BURIK	NAC	FC Utrecht
René STAM	FC Den Haag	FC Utrecht
Richard NASS	NEC	Vitesse
Sander WESTERVELD	FC Twente	Vitesse
Ferdy VIERKLAU	FC Utrecht	Vitesse
John VAN DEN BROM	Istanbulspor (TUR)	Vitesse
Yevgeni LEVCHENKO (RUS)	CSKA Moskva (RUS)	Vitesse
Nikos MAHLAS (GRE)	OFI (GRE)	Vitesse
Marc HEERING	Go Ahead Eagles	Willem II
Mark SCHENNING	Go Ahead Eagles	Willem II
Huub LOEFFEN	Vitesse	Willem II
Tomas GALASEK (TCH)	Banik Ostrava (TCH)	Willem II
ITALY		
Davide MICILLO	Cesena	Atalanta
Massimo CARRERA	Juventus	Atalanta
Zoran MIRKOVIC (YUG)	Partizan Beograd (YUG)	Atalanta
Stefano ROSSINI	Piacenza	Atalanta

MAJOR SUMMER TRANSFERS 1996

PLAYER	OLD CLUB	NEW CLUB
Andrea SOTTIL	Fiorentina	Atalanta
Emanuele TRESOLDI	Pistoiese	Atalanta
Joakim PERSSON (SWE)	Malmö FF (SWE)	Atalanta
Federico MAGALLANES (URU)	Peñarol (URU)	Atalanta
Gianluigi LENTINI	Milan	Atalanta
Alex BRUNNER	Foggia	Bologna
Cristiano PAVONE	Atalanta	Bologna
Giuseppe CARDONE	Lucchese	Bologna
Davide FONTOLAN	Inter	Bologna
Giancarlo MAROCCHI	Juventus	Bologna
Oscar MAGONI	Genoa	Bologna
Kennet ANDERSSON (SWE)	Bari	Bologna
Pierpaolo BRESCIANIA	Foggia	Bologna
Igor KOLYVANOV (RUS)	Foggia	Bologna
Marco PASCOLO (SUI)	Servette FC Genève (SUI)	Cagliari
Stefano BETTARINI	Lucchese	Cagliari
Gianluca GRASSADONIA	Salernitana	Cagliari
Ramon VEGA (SUI)	Grasshopper-Club Zürich (SUI)	Cagliari
Francesco COZZA	Lucchese	Cagliari
Christian LØNSTRUP (DEN)	FC København (DEN)	Cagliari
Eric TINKLER (SAF)	Vitória Setúbal (POR)	Cagliari
Giacomo BANCHELLI	Fiorentina	Cagliari
Luis ROMERO (URU)	Peñarol (URU)	Cagliari
Giulio FALCONE	Torino	Fiorentina
Aldo FIRICANO	Cagliari	Fiorentina
Vittorio PUSCEDDU	Cagliari	Fiorentina
Luis OLIVEIRA (BEL)	Cagliari	Fiorentina
Andrea MAZZANTINI	Venezia	Inter
Jocelyn ANGLOMA (FRA)	Torino	Inter
Gianmarco FREZZA	Salernitana	Inter
Fabio GALANTE	Genoa	Inter
Salvatore TARANTINO	Napoli	Inter
Youri DJORKAEFF (FRA)	Paris Saint-Germain FC (FRA)	Inter
Ciriaco SFORZA (SUI)	FC Bayern München (GER)	Inter
Aron WINTER (HOL)	Lazio	Inter
Iván ZAMORANO (CHI)	Real Madrid (ESP)	Inter
Nwankwo KANU (NIG)	Ajax (HOL)	Inter
Mark IULIANO	Salernitana	Juventus
Paulo MONTERO (URU)	Atalanta	Juventus
Raffaele AMETRANO	Udinese	Juventus
Zinedine ZIDANE (FRA)	Girondins de Bordeaux (FRA)	Juventus
Nicola AMORUSO	Padova	Juventus
Alen BOKSIC (CRO)	Lazio	Juventus
Christian VIERI	Atalanta	Juventus
Mark FISH (SAF)	Orlando Pirates (SAF)	Lazio
Paul OKON (AUS)	Club Brugge KV (BEL)	Lazio
Roberto BARONIO	Brescia	Lazio
Pavel NEDVED (TCH)	Sparta Praha (TCH)	Lazio
Giorgio VENTURIN	Cagliari	Lazio
Renato BUSO	Napoli	Lazio
Igor PROTTI	Bari	Lazio
Angelo PAGOTTO	Sampdoria	Milan
Michael REIZIGER (HOL)	Ajax (HOL)	Milan
Edgar DAVIDS (HOL)	Ajax (HOL)	Milan
Christophe DUGARRY (FRA)	Girondins de Bordeaux (FRA)	Milan
Pietro VIERCHOWOD	Juventus	Milan
Bertrand CRASSON (BEL)	RSC Anderlecht (BEL)	Napoli
Mauro MILANESE	Torino	Napoli
Joubert BETO (BRA)	Botafogo (BRA)	Napoli
Francesco TURRINI	Piacenza	Napoli
Alfredo AGLIETTI	Reggina	Napoli
Nicola CACCIA	Piacenza	Napoli
Ribeiro CAIO (BRA)	Inter	Napoli

PLAYER	OLD CLUB	NEW CLUB
Massimiliano ESPOSITO	Lazio	Napoli
Lilian THURAM (FRA)	AS Monaco (FRA)	Parma
ZÉ MARIA (BRA)	Palmeiras (BRA)	Parma
Alexandre AMARAL (BRA)	Palmeiras (BRA)	Parma
Daniel BRAVO (FRA)	Paris Saint-Germain FC (FRA)	Parma
Pietro STRADA	Reggiana	Parma
Enrico CHIESA	Sampdoria	Parma
Hernán CRESPO (ARG)	River Plate (ARG)	Parma
Aleksandar KOCIC (YUG)	Vojvodina Novi Sad (YUG)	Perugia
Giampaolo SPAGNULO	Genoa	Perugia
Marcello CASTELLINI	Parma	Perugia
Alberto DI CHIARA	Parma	Perugia
Salvatore MATRECANO	Napoli	Perugia
Martino TRAVERSA	Pescara	Perugia
Michel KREEK (HOL)	Padova	Perugia
Antonio MANICONE	Inter	Perugia
Edoardo ARTISTICO	Ancona	Perugia
Carmine GAUTIERI	Bari	Perugia
Milan RAPAJIC (CRO)	Hajduk Split (CRO)	Perugia
Paolo TRAMEZZANI	Cesena	Piacenza
Fausto PARI	Napoli	Piacenza
Gabriele PIN	Parma	Piacenza
Giuseppe SCIENZA	Venezia	Piacenza
Aladino VALOTTI	Verona	Piacenza
Pasquale LUISO	Avellino	Piacenza
Andrea TENTONI	Cremonese	Piacenza
Fabian VALTOLINA	Bologna	Piacenza
Dietmar BEIERSDORFER (GER)	1.FC Köln (GER)	Reggiana
Gianluca CHERUBINI	Roma	Reggiana
Georges GRÜN (BEL)	RSC Anderlecht (BEL)	Reggiana
Michael HATZ (AUT)	SK Rapid Wien (AUT)	Reggiana
Gianluca SORDO	Milan	Reggiana
Angelo CARBONE	Piacenza	Reggiana
Francesco PEDONE	Bari	Reggiana
Ioan Ovidiu SABAU (ROM)	Brescia	Reggiana
Nicolo SCIACCA	Foggia	Reggiana
Sandro TOVALIERI	Atalanta	Reggiana
Adolfo VALENCIA (COL)	Independiente Santa Fé (ARG)	Reggiana
Gabriele GROSSI	Vicenza	Roma
Roberto TROTTA (ARG)	Velez Sarsfield (ARG)	Roma
Antonio BERNARDINI	Torino	Roma
Damiano TOMMASI	Verona	Roma
Martin DAHLIN (SWE)	Borussia Mönchengladbach (GER)	Roma
Fabrizio FERRON	Atalanta	Sampdoria
Oumar DIENG (FRA)	Paris Saint-Germain FC (FRA)	Sampdoria
Pierre LAIGLE (FRA)	RC Lens (FRA)	Sampdoria
Juan VERON (ARG)	Boca Juniors (ARG)	Sampdoria
Nicola ZANINI	Verona	Sampdoria
Vincenzo MONTELLA	Genoa	Sampdoria
Massimiliano CANIATO	Torino	Udinese
Alessandro TURCI	Cremonese	Udinese
Alessandro PIERINI	Fidelis Andria	Udinese
Márcio AMORUSO (BRA)	Guarani (BRA)	Udinese
Hazem EMAM (EGY)	Zamalek (EGY)	Udinese
Davide STEFANI	Avellino	Udinese
Alessandro ORLANDO	Fiorentina	Udinese
Claudio CLEMENTI	Fiorenzuola	Udinese
Attilio GREGORI	Udinese	Verona
Antonio PAGANIN	Atalanta	Verona
Roberto BACCI	Torino	Verona
Jonathan BINOTTO	Cesena	Verona
Leonardo COLUCCI	Reggiana	Verona
Eugenio CORINI	Piacenza	Verona

MAJOR SUMMER TRANSFERS 1996

PLAYER	OLD CLUB	NEW CLUB
Pierluigi ORLANDINI	Inter	Verona
Fabrizio CAMMARATA	Juventus	Verona
REINALDO (BRA)	Palmeiras (BRA)	Verona
Filippo MANIERO	Sampdoria	Verona
Massimo BEGHETTO	Perugia	Vicenza
Alessandro DAL CANTO	Torino	Vicenza
Pierre WOME (CMR)	Canon Yaoundé (CMR)	Vicenza
Giovanni CORNACCHINI	Bologna	Vicenza
Ferdinando GASPARINI	Fidelis Andria	Vicenza
Alessandro IANNUZZI	Lazio	Vicenza
PORTUGAL		
SILVINO	Vitória Setúbal	CF Os Belenenses
AMARILDO	GD Chaves	CF Os Belenenses
CAETANO	Boavista FC	CF Os Belenenses
FILGUEIRA (BRA)	CS Marítimo	CF Os Belenenses
FONSECA (MOZ)	Leça FC	CF Os Belenenses
Rashid DAOUDI (MAR)	FC Tirsense	CF Os Belenenses
EMERSON (BRA)	Vitória Guimarães	CF Os Belenenses
TONANHA	GD Chaves	CF Os Belenenses
ZITO	Vitória Guimarães	CF Os Belenenses
PEDRO MIGUEL	SC Braga	CF Os Belenenses
QUINZINHO (ANG)	FC Porto	CF Os Belenenses
Jorge BERMUDEZ (COL)	America Cali (COL)	SL Benfica
JAMIR (BRA)	Botafogo (BRA)	SL Benfica
JORGE SOARES	SC Farense	SL Benfica
Tahar EL KHALEJ (MAR)	União Leiria	SL Benfica
LUÍS GUSTAVO (BRA)	CS Marítimo	SL Benfica
DONIZETE (BRA)	Verdy Kawasaki (JPN)	SL Benfica
ISAÍAS (BRA)	Leça FC	Boavista FC
JORGE COUTO	FC Porto	Boavista FC
Russel LATAPY (TRI)	FC Porto	Boavista FC
RICARDO	Leça FC	Boavista FC
JIMMY (SUR)	SC Campomaiorense	Boavista FC
Sasa SIMIC (YUG)	União Madeira	Boavista FC
IDALÉCIO	SC Farense	SC Braga
LEONEL	GD Chaves	SC Braga
JOÃO PINTO	Gil Vicente FC	SC Braga
Dragoslav POLEKSIC (YUG)	Hajduk Kula (YUG)	GD Chaves
Denis PUTNIK (CRO)	Sibenik (CRO)	GD Chaves
RAUL (ESP)	Sporting Gijón (ESP)	GD Chaves
Etienne N'TSUNDA (ZAI)	Académica Coimbra	GD Chaves
Marcel SABOU (ROM)	Sporting Gijón (ESP)	GD Chaves
TONINHO CRUZ	FC Tirsense	GD Chaves
Mario VOJKOVIC (CRO)	SAK Klagenfurt (AUT)	GD Chaves
LEAL	FC Felgueiras	CF Estrela Amadora
MÁRIO JORGE (ANG)	CS Marítimo	CF Estrela Amadora
Alberto BODELON (ESP)	SD Compostela (ESP)	CF Estrela Amadora
Erik ANDERSSON (SWE)	Östers IF (SWE)	CF Estrela Amadora
LINO (ANG)	SC Braga	SC Espinho
LUÍS MIGUEL (ESP)	SC Farense	SC Espinho
CAETANO	FC Tirsense	SC Espinho
MONTEIRO	FC Tirsense	SC Farense
MARGARIDO	CS Marítimo	Gil Vicente FC
CARLOS COELHO	SC Braga	Gil Vicente FC
NILDO (BRA)	Inter Porto Alegre (BRA)	Gil Vicente FC
POSSI (BRA)	Fluminense (BRA)	Gil Vicente FC
TARCÍSIO (BRA)	Desportivo Aves	Gil Vicente FC
WALTER	Vitória Guimarães	Leça FC
TOZÉ	FC Tirsense	Leça FC
REBELO	FC Tirsense	Leça FC
Thor-André OLSEN (NOR)	Djurgårdens IF (SWE)	CS Marítimo
JOSÉ CARLOS (BRA)	Vasco da Gama (BRA)	CS Marítimo
MÁRCIO TEODORO (BRA)	Botafogo (BRA)	CS Marítimo
MARVILLA (BRA)	Botafogo (BRA)	CS Marítimo
NUNO VALENTE	Sporting CP	CS Marítimo
DAURI (BRA)	Botafogo (BRA)	CS Marítimo
FILIPE	Sporting CP	CS Marítimo
EDMILSON (BRA)	Botafogo (BRA)	CS Marítimo
Andrzej WOZNIAK (POL)	Widzew Lodz (POL)	FC Porto
Alejandro DIAZ (URU)	Liverpool Montevideo (URU)	FC Porto
FERNANDO MENDES	CF Os Belenenses	FC Porto
LULA (BRA)	CF Os Belenenses	FC Porto
NEVES	CF Os Belenenses	FC Porto
RUI OSCAR	Leça FC	FC Porto
BARROSO	SC Braga	FC Porto
COSTA	FC Felgueiras	FC Porto
SÉRGIO CONCEIÇÃO	FC Felgueiras	FC Porto
TULIPA	CF Os Belenenses	FC Porto
Zlatko ZAHOVIC (SLO)	Vitória Guimarães	FC Porto
ARTUR (BRA)	Boavista FC	FC Porto
JARDEL (BRA)	Grêmio (BRA)	FC Porto
Arnold WETL (AUT)	SK Sturm Graz (AUT)	FC Porto
NITO	FC Tirsense	Rio Ave FC
Filip DE WILDE (BEL)	RSC Anderlecht (BEL)	Sporting CP
ANDRADE	CF Estrela Amadora	Sporting CP
Andrija BALAJIC (CRO)	Varteks Varazdin (CRO)	Sporting CP
BETO	SC Campomaiorense	Sporting CP
PEDROSA	Gil Vicente FC	Sporting CP
Mustapha HADJI (MAR)	AS Nancy-Lorraine (FRA)	Sporting CP
PORFÍRIO	União Leiria	Sporting CP
Jran-Jacques MISSE-MISSE (CMR)	RSC Charleroi (BEL)	Sporting CP
Stojan BELAIC (CRO)	FK Austria Wien (AUT)	União Leiria
POEJO	CF Estrela Amadora	União Leiria
ALEXANDRE (BRA)	Atletico Mineiro (BRA)	Vitória Guimarães
BASÍLIO	SC Salgueiros	Vitória Guimarães
RIVA (BRA)	GD Chaves	Vitória Guimarães
TONIÑO (ESP)	GD Chaves	Vitória Guimarães
Sylvain SANSONE (FRA)	FC Felgueiras	Vitória Setúbal
GASPAR	FC Tirsense	Vitória Setúbal
MATIAS	FC Porto	Vitória Setúbal
FERNANDO PIRES	CS Marítimo	Vitória Setúbal
Kwame AYEW (GHA)	União Leiria	Vitória Setúbal
CHIQUINHO CONDE (MOZ)	CF Os Belenenses	Vitória Setúbal
SCOTLAND		
Ilian KIRIAKOV (BUL)	Anorthosis Famagusta (CYP)	Aberdeen
Antoine KOMBOUARE (FRA)	FC Sion (SUI)	Aberdeen
Paolo DI CANIO (ITA)	Milan (ITA)	Celtic
Alan STUBBS (ENG)	Bolton Wanderers (ENG)	Celtic
Lance KEY (NIR)	Sheffield Wednesday (ENG)	Dundee United
Gerry BRITTON	Dundee	Dunfermline Athletic
Brian HAMILTON	Heart of Midlothian	Falkirk
Craig NELSON	Heart of Midlothian	Falkirk
David WEIR	Falkirk	Heart of Midlothian
Jeremy GOSS (WAL)	Norwich City (ENG)	Heart of Midlothian
Neil McCANN	Dundee	Heart of Midlothian
Paul HARVEY	Airdrieonians	Raith Rovers
Kevin TWADDLE	St, Johnstone	Raith Rovers
Joachim BJÖRKLUND (SWE)	Vicenza (ITA)	Rangers
Jörg ALBERTZ (GER)	Hamburger SV (GER)	Rangers

MAJOR SUMMER TRANSFERS 1996

PLAYER	OLD CLUB	NEW CLUB
SPAIN		
Bixente LIZARAZU (FRA)	Girondins de Bordeaux (FRA)	Athletic Bilbao
Ismael URZAIZ	RCD Espanyol	Athletic Bilbao
Sergio CORINO	CP Mérida	Athletic Bilbao
JOSE MARI García	Real Betis	Athletic Bilbao
Santiago EZQUERRO	CA Osasuna	Atlético Madrid
Carlos AGUILERA	CD Tenerife	Atlético Madrid
IVAN ROCHA	Real Valladolid	Atlético Madrid
Juan Eduardo ESNAIDER (ARG)	Real Madrid	Atlético Madrid
Pablo ALFARO	Racing Santander	Atlético Madrid
Radek BEJBL (TCH)	Slavia Praha (TCH)	Atlético Madrid
VÍTOR BAÍA (POR)	FC Porto (POR)	FC Barcelona
RONALDO (BRA)	PSV (HOL)	FC Barcelona
Hristo STOICHKOV (BUL)	Parma (ITA)	FC Barcelona
Juan Antonio PIZZI	CD Tenerife	FC Barcelona
Laurent BLANC (FRA)	AJ Auxerre (FRA)	FC Barcelona
LUIS ENRIQUE Martínez	Real Madrid	FC Barcelona
GIOVANNI Silva (BRA)	Santos (BRA)	FC Barcelona
FERNANDO COUTO (POR)	Parma (ITA)	FC Barcelona
Albert NADJ (YUG)	Partizan Beograd (YUG)	Real Betis
Antonio PRATS	RC Celta	Real Betis
Finidi GEORGE (NIG)	Ajax (HOL)	Real Betis
LUIS Fernández	Racing Santander	Real Betis
Nenad BJELICA (CRO)	Albacete Balompié	Real Betis
Virgilio FERREIRA (PAR)	Cerro Porteño (PAR)	Real Betis
Daniel DUTUEL (FRA)	Girondins de Bordeaux (FRA)	RC Celta
David BELENGUER	CD Leganés	RC Celta
Guillermo DEL SOLAR (PER)	UD Salamanca	RC Celta
Haim REVIVO (ISR)	Maccabi Haifa (ISR)	RC Celta
Iomar MAZINHO (BRA)	Valencia CF	RC Celta
JAVI GONZALEZ Cruces	Sestao SC	RC Celta
José Luis DIEZMA	Real Betis	RC Celta
JOSEMA López	UD Salamanca	RC Celta
Juan Manuel PRIETO	CP Mérida	RC Celta
ADRIANO (BRA)	Sport Recife (BRA)	RC Celta
Carlos SASTRE	CF Extremadura	SD Compostela
Dmitri POPOV (RUS)	Racing Santander	SD Compostela
Goran SAULA (YUG)	Vojvodina Novi Sad (YUG)	SD Compostela
José M. GALDAMES	Athletic Bilbao	SD Compostela
Manuel MOSQUERO	CF Extremadura	SD Compostela
Saib CHIBA (SAU)	Al-Ihla (SAU)	SD Compostela
WILLIAM (POR)	SC Bastia (FRA)	SD Compostela
ARMANDO Alvarez	Real Oviedo	RC Deportivo
Corentin MARTINS (FRA)	AJ Auxerre (FRA)	RC Deportivo
Jacques SONGO'O (CMR)	FC Metz (FRA)	RC Deportivo
Jérôme BONNISSEL (FRA)	Montpellier HSC (FRA)	RC Deportivo
Michaël MADAR (FRA)	AS Monaco (FRA)	RC Deportivo
Noureddine NAYBET (MAR)	Sporting CP (POR)	RC Deportivo
Petr KOUBA (TCH)	Sparta Praha (TCH)	RC Deportivo
RIVALDO (BRA)	Palmeiras (BRA)	RC Deportivo
Adolfo ALDANA	RC Deportivo	RCD Espanyol
Nenad PRALIJA (CRO)	Hajduk Split (CRO)	RCD Espanyol
Nicolas OUEDEC	FC Nantes (FRA)	RCD Espanyol
Carlos TORRES	CD Badajoz	CF Extremadura
José Ignacio SOLER	Atlético Marbella	CF Extremadura
Carlos Alejandro DURE (ARG)	Ferro Carril Oeste (ARG)	CF Extremadura
Igor GLUSCEVIC (YUG)	Vojvodina Novi Sad (YUG)	CF Extremadura
Francisco Javier GARCIA	FC Barcelona	CF Extremadura
Enrique ESTEBARANZ	Sevilla FC	CF Extremadura
IVAN Pérez	Real Betis	CF Extremadura
Virgilio FERREIRA (PAR)	Real Betis	CF Extremadura
Francisco Javier PINEDA	Sevilla FC	CF Extremadura

PLAYER	OLD CLUB	NEW CLUB
Flavio MAESTRI (PER)	Sporting Cristal (PER)	Hércules CF
Andrei MOKH (UKR)	CD Toledo	Hércules CF
Francisco Vela "PAQUI"	Real Zaragoza	Hércules CF
Gaétan HUARD (FRA)	Girondins de Bordeaux (FRA)	Hércules CF
Peter ARTNER (AUT)	SV Casino Salzburg (AUT)	Hércules CF
Víctor Javier FERRERAS	Sevilla FC	Hércules CF
Gabriel AMATO (ARG)	River Plate (ARG)	Hércules CF
Pablo MORANT (ARG)	Gimnasia y Esgrima (ARG)	Hércules CF
Andoni CEDRUN	Real Zaragoza	CD Logroñés
Ivan ADZIC (YUG)	Crvena zvezda Beograd (YUG)	CD Logroñés
JESUS Dulce	SD Compostela	CD Logroñés
Jochem KIENTZ	RCD Mallorca	CD Logroñés
José Luis MORALES	RCD Mallorca	CD Logroñés
Kazuyoshi MIURA (JPN)	Verdy Kawasaki (JPN)	CD Logroñés
Ricardo CANALS (URU)	Nacional (URU)	CD Logroñés
Rubén SOSA (URU)	Borussia Dortmund (GER)	CD Logroñés
Marcelo TEJERA (URU)	Defensor Sporting (URU)	CD Logroñés
Danilo BALTIERRA (URU)	Peñarol (URU)	CD Logroñés
TONI Velamazán	FC Barcelona	Real Oviedo
IVAN IGLESIAS	Sporting Gijón	Real Oviedo
José Aurelio GAY	Real Zaragoza	Real Oviedo
Juan José BORELLI (ARG)	Panathinaikos (GRE)	Real Oviedo
Francisco Javier SANCHEZ JARA	Real Betis	Racing Santander
Francisco PINILLOS	CD Logroñés	Racing Santander
Francisco SANZ	Real Oviedo	Racing Santander
Jaime SANCHEZ	Real Madrid	Racing Santander
Javi López AGUILAR	Real Madrid	Racing Santander
José Luis ZALAZAR (URU)	Albacete Balompié	Racing Santander
Oscar ARPON	Real Betis	Racing Santander
Sergei SHUSTIKOV (RUS)	Torpedo Moskva (RUS)	Racing Santander
Vladimir BESCHASTNYKH (GER)	SV Werder Bremen (GER)	Racing Santander
Fernando MARCOS	Albacete Balompié	Racing Santander
José María LOPEZ	CP Mérida	Rayo Vallecano
José R. López MUÑIZ	Sporting Gijón	Rayo Vallecano
Pedro CONTRERAS	Real Madrid	Rayo Vallecano
Horacio AMELLI (ARG)	Colon (ARG)	Rayo Vallecano
SECRETÁRIO (POR)	FC Porto (POR)	Real Madrid
Clarence SEEDORF (HOL)	Sampdoria (ITA)	Real Madrid
Davor SUKER (CRO)	Sevilla FC	Real Madrid
Dejan PETKOVIC (YUG)	Sevilla FC	Real Madrid
Predrag MIJATOVIC (YUG)	Valencia CF	Real Madrid
ROBERTO CARLOS (BRA)	Inter (ITA)	Real Madrid
Bodo ILLGNER (GER)	1.FC Köln (GER)	Real Madrid
Darko KOVACEVIC (YUG)	Sheffield Wednesday (ENG)	Real Sociedad
Håkan MILD (SWE)	IFK Göteborg (SWE)	Real Sociedad
Juan Andres GOMEZ (ARG)	River Plate (ARG)	Real Sociedad
MUTIU Adepoju (NIG)	Racing Santander	Real Sociedad
Zigor ARANALDE	Atlético Marbella	Sevilla FC
Antonio GOMEZ	Real Madrid	Sevilla FC
Ivica MORNAR (CRO)	Eintracht Frankfurt (GER)	Sevilla FC
Luis Miguel RAMIS	CD Tenerife	Sevilla FC
Mirsad HIBIC (BOS)	Hajduk Split (CRO)	Sevilla FC
ONESIMO Sánchez	Rayo Vallecano	Sevilla FC
Vassilis TSARTAS (GRE)	AEK (GRE)	Sevilla FC
Petros MARINAKIS (GRE)	Olympiakos (GRE)	Sevilla FC
Matias ALMEYDA (ARG)	River Plate (ARG)	Sevilla FC
FREDI Lobeiras	UE Lleida	Sporting Gijón
Francisco OLIETE	Villarreal CF	Sporting Gijón
Francisco LIAÑO	RC Deportivo	Sporting Gijón
Francisco ROJAS (CHI)	Colo Colo (CHI)	CD Tenerife
DANI González	Atlético Madrid	CD Tenerife
Oliver NEUVILLE (SUI)	Servette FC Genève (SUI)	CD Tenerife

MAJOR SUMMER TRANSFERS 1996

PLAYER	OLD CLUB	NEW CLUB
Pablo Ariel PAZ (ARG)	Banfield (ARG)	CD Tenerife
Meho KODRO (BOS)	FC Barcelona	CD Tenerife
Claudio Javier LOPEZ (ARG)	Racing (ARG)	Valencia CF
Gabriel MOYA	Sevilla FC	Valencia CF
Goran VLAOVIC (CRO)	Padova (ITA)	Valencia CF
IVAN CAMPO	Real Valladolid	Valencia CF
ROMÁRIO (BRA)	Flamengo (BRA)	Valencia CF
Valeri KARPIN (RUS)	Real Sociedad	Valencia CF
Harold LOZANO (COL)	América Cali (COL)	Real Valladolid
JÚLIO CÉSAR Campos (BRA)	America (MEX)	Real Valladolid
EDU (BRA)	Atletico Parana (BRA)	Real Valladolid
Vladislav RADIMOV (RUS)	CSKA Moskva (RUS)	Real Zaragoza
Enrique Sánchez "QUIQUE"	Real Madrid	Real Zaragoza
"KILY" GONZALEZ (ARG)	Boca Juniors (ARG)	Real Zaragoza

SWITZERLAND

PLAYER	OLD CLUB	NEW CLUB
Ivo GEORGIEV (BUL)	Spartak Varna (BUL)	FC Aarau
Marc HODEL	FC Zürich	FC Aarau
Patrick DE NAPOLI	FC Winterthur	FC Aarau
Gaetano GIALLANZA	FC Sion	FC Basel
Jean-Pierre LA PLACA	FC Sion	FC Basel
Mario FLICK (LIE)	FC St. Gallen	FC Basel
Yann POULARD	SR Delémont	FC Basel
Andreas ARMENTANO (ARG)	Racing Club (ARG)	FC Basel
Dinu Viorel MOLDOVAN (ROM)	Neuchâtel Xamax FC	Grasshopper-Club Zürich
Antonio ESPOSITO	FC Lugano	Grasshopper-Club Zürich
Joël MAGNIN	FC Lugano	Grasshopper-Club Zürich
Tomasz RZASA (POL)	FC Lugano	Grasshopper-Club Zürich
Alessandro GUALCO (ITA)	Cremonese (ITA)	Lausanne-Sports
Ismaël Smahi TRIKI (MAR)	LB Châteauroux (FRA)	Lausanne-Sports
Christophe OHREL	AS Saint-Etienne (FRA)	Lausanne-Sports
Philippe DOUGLAS	Yverdon-Sports	Lausanne-Sports
Saso UDOVIC (SLO)	KSK Beveren (BEL)	Lausanne-Sports
Veldin KARIC (CRO)	Torino (ITA)	FC Lugano
Augustin SIMO (CMR)	Torino (ITA)	FC Lugano
Vaidotas SLEKYS (LIT)	FC Wil	FC Lugano
Mauro GIANNINI	FC St. Gallen	FC Lugano
Christopher KANU (NIG)	Eagle Cement (NIG)	FC Lugano
Gürkan SERMETER	BSC Young Boys	FC Luzern
Daniel WYSS	FC Aarau	FC Luzern
Heinz MOSER	FC Sion	FC Luzern
Marek LESNIAK (POL)	KFC Uerdingen 05 (GER)	Neuchâtel Xamax FC
Liazid SANDJAK (FRA)	AS Saint-Etienne (FRA)	Neuchâtel Xamax FC
Phil MASINGA (SAF)	Leeds United (ENG)	FC St. Gallen
David NYATHI (SAF)	Kaizer Chiefs (SAF)	FC St. Gallen
Sizwe MOTAUNG (SAF)	Mamelodie Sundowns (SAF)	FC St. Gallen
Jörg STIEL	FC Zürich	FC St. Gallen
Adrian ALLENSPACH	FC Aarau	FC St. Gallen
Tamás TIEFENBACH (HUN)	Újpesti TE (HUN)	FC St. Gallen
Eric PEDAT	FC St. Gallen	Servette FC Genève
Cyrille POUGET (FRA)	FC Metz (FRA)	Servette FC Genève
Olivier BIAGGI	Lausanne-Sports	Servette FC Genève
Babatunde FATUSI (NIG)	Ferencváros (HUN)	Servette FC Genève
Mario CANTALUPPI	FC Basel	Servette FC Genève
Stefano NAVA (ITA)	Milan (ITA)	Servette FC Genève
Patrick BÜHLMANN	FC St. Gallen	FC Sion
Luíz MILTON (BRA)	FC St. Gallen	FC Sion
Frédéric CHASSOT	Lausanne-Sports	FC Sion
Alexandre REY	FC Basel	FC Sion
Darko PANCEV (MAC)	Fortuna Düsseldorf (GER)	FC Sion
Ilija NAJDOSKI (MAC)	CSKA Sofia (BUL)	FC Sion
Ottó VINCZE (HUN)	Ferencváros (HUN)	FC Sion
Vladan LUKIC (YUG)	Atlético Marbella (ESP)	FC Sion
Josephus YENAY (LIB)	Yverdon-Sports	FC Sion
Gabriel OKOLOSI (NIG)	FC Basel	BSC Young Boys
Roger KÜFFER	Lausanne-Sports	BSC Young Boys
Mohamed KONJIC (BOS)	Zagreb (CRO)	FC Zürich
Patrick MÄDER	FC Baden	FC Zürich
Ueli BRUNNER	SC Kriens	FC Zürich
Julio TEJEDA	FC St. Gallen	FC Zürich
Giuseppe MAZZARELLI	Manchester City (ENG)	FC Zürich
Tomas BROLIN (SWE)	Leeds United (ENG)	FC Zürich

TURKEY

PLAYER	OLD CLUB	NEW CLUB
Ronald BARONI (PER)	FC Porto (POR)	Ankaragücü
ÜMIT Hatipoglu	Elazigspor	Ankaragücü
Andre KONA-NGOLE (ZAI)	Gençlerbirligi	Antalyaspor
Donald KHUSE (SAF)	Gençlerbirligi	Antalyaspor
Filip FILIPOV (BUL)	CSKA Sofia (BUL)	Antalyaspor
Gosho GINCHEV (BUL)	Denizlispor	Antalyaspor
Marijan MRMIC (CRO)	Varteks Varazdin (CRO)	Besiktas
RAHIM Zafer	Gençlerbirligi	Besiktas
ERKAN Avseren	Vanspor	Besiktas
Daniel AMOKACHI (NIG)	Everton (ENG)	Besiktas
Zlatko YANKOV (BUL)	KFC Uerdingen 05 (GER)	Besiktas
Fani MADIDA (SAF)	Antalyaspor	Bursaspor
MURAT Salar	Galatasaray	Bursaspor
Ergin AJDINOVIC (YUG)	FK Becej (YUG)	Çanakkale Dardanelspor
Vladimir SUBERT (YUG)	FK Zemun (YUG)	Çanakkale Dardanelspor
Dragan POPOV (YUG)	FK Zemun (YUG)	Çanakkale Dardanelspor
Stephan KOMPHELA (SAF)	Gaziantepspor	Çanakkale Dardanelspor
KUBILAY Toptas	Gaziantepspor	Çanakkale Dardanelspor
ENGIN Ipekoglu	Fenerbahçe	Çanakkale Dardanelspor
Emil KOSTADINOV (BUL)	FC Bayern München (GER)	Fenerbahçe
Agustine OKOCHA (NIG)	Eintracht Frankfurt (GER)	Fenerbahçe
SEDAT Balkanli	Galatasaray	Fenerbahçe
BENHUR Özden	Galatasaray	Fenerbahçe
MUSTAFA Dogan	KFC Uerdingen 05 (GER)	Fenerbahçe
TUNCAY Akgün	Bursaspor	Fenerbahçe
Adrian KNUP (SUI)	Karlsruher SC (GER)	Galatasaray
BURHANETTIN Kaymak	Eintracht Frankfurt (GER)	Galatasaray
VEDAT Inceefe	Karabükspor	Galatasaray
RASIN Süksür	Fortuna Düsseldorf (GER)	Galatasaray
ÜMIT Davala	Diyarbakirspor	Galatasaray
Gheorghe HAGI (ROM)	FC Barcelona (ESP)	Galatasaray
LIMA (BRA)	FC São Paulo (BRA)	Gaziantepspor
KADRI Sancak	Denizlispor	Gaziantepspor
SEMAVI Uzun	Denizlispor	Gaziantepspor
OGUZ Çetin	Fenerbahçe	Istanbulspor
AYKUT Kocaman	Fenerbahçe	Istanbulspor
EMRE Asik	Fenerbahçe	Istanbulspor
GÖKHAN Keskin	Besiktas	Istanbulspor
Candido GÉRSON (BRA)	Bari (ITA)	Istanbulspor
Dumitru STÎNGACIU (ROM)	Vanspor	Kocaelispor
SONER Boz	Trabzonspor	Kocaelispor
Gintaras STAUCE (LIT)	Galatasaray	Sariyer
ERBIL Uzel	Karsiyaka	Sariyer
Vyacheslav LICHKIN (AZB)	Neftchi Baku (AZB)	Trabzonspor
MEHMET Yildirim	Karsiyaka	Trabzonspor
Slobodan DUBAJIC (YUG)	VfB Stuttgart	Zeytinburnu
Mamadou DIALLO (SEN)	FC St. Gallen (SUI)	Zeytinburnu
Matjaz CVIKL (SLO)	Rudar Velenje (SLO)	Zeytinburnu